LONDON
M25 Master

CONTENTS

Published by Collins
An imprint of HarperCollins*Publishers*
77-85 Fulham Palace Road, Hammersmith, London W6 8JB
www.collins.co.uk

Copyright © HarperCollins*Publishers* Ltd 2003
Collins ® is a registered trademark of HarperCollins*Publishers* Limited
Mapping generated from Collins/Bartholomew digital databases

London Underground Map by permission of Transport Trading Limited
Registered User No. 02/3682

ISBN 0 00 715535 2 Spiral   imp 001   QM11430   Printed in Italy   UDM

e-mail: roadcheck@harpercollins.co.uk

KEY TO MAIN MAP SYMBOLS

M4 Motorway

A4 Primary route

A40 'A' road

B504 'B' road

Other road/
One way street

Toll

Street market

Restricted access road

Pedestrian street

Cycle path

Track/Footpath

Long distance footpath

LC Level crossing

P Pedestrian ferry

V Vehicle ferry

County/Borough boundary

Postal district boundary

Main railway station

Other railway station

London Underground station

DLR Docklands Light Railway station

Tramlink station

P Car park

Bus/Coach station

Leisure & tourism

Shopping

Administration & law

Health & welfare

Education

Industry & commerce

Cemetery

Golf course

Public open space/
Allotments

Park/Garden/Sports ground

Wood/Forest

Orchard

USA Embassy

Pol Police station

Fire Sta Fire station

PO Post Office

Lib Library

i Tourist information centre

▲ Youth hostel

□ Tower block

⊞ Heliport

+ Church

☾ Mosque

✡ Synagogue

Extent of London Congestion Charging Zone

The reference grid on this atlas coincides with the Ordnance Survey National Grid System. The grid interval is 500 metres.

🏠 Page Continuation Number **AT** Grid Reference **03** OS National Grid Kilometre Square

SCALE

| 0 | ¼ | ½ | ¾ | 1 mile |

| 0 | 0.25 | 0.5 | 0.75 | 1 | 1.25 | 1.5 kilometres |

1:20,000 3.2 inches to 1 mile/5 cms to 1 km

● London's congestion charging zone operates inside the 'Inner Ring Road' linking Marylebone Road, Euston Road, Pentonville Road, Tower Bridge, Elephant and Castle, Vauxhall Bridge and Park Lane (see map below). The 'Inner Ring Road' provides a route around the charging zone and charges do not apply to vehicles travelling on it. The daily operating time is from 7.00 am to 6.30 pm, Monday to Friday, excluding public holidays.

● Payment of a £5 congestion charge allows you to enter, drive around and leave the charging zone as many times as you like that day. Payments can be made online at www.cclondon.com where you can get a receipt if required, or by phone on 0845 900 1234 charged at the local rate. The web site or phone number may also be used to register for payment by mobile phone text message. Once registered, you will be able to pay the £5 daily charge on the day you travel up until 10pm by sending a simple text message from your mobile phone. Please remember you should never text while driving. Other methods of payment are at most self service machines in major public car parks within the charging zone or selected petrol stations, newsagents and convenience stores, displaying the PayPoint logo, throughout the Greater London area. To pay by post, write to: Congestion charging, P O Box 2985, Coventry CV7 8ZR and request the application form 'Paying the congestion charge'. Regular drivers in central London can pay the charge on a weekly, monthly or annual basis. Residents in the charging zone, by paying a £10 annual registration fee to Transport for London, may obtain a 90% reduction, for one private vehicle only, in the weekly, monthly and annual charges. When paying you will be required to know your vehicle registration number, the dates you want to pay for and details of how you intend to pay.

● There are no tollbooths or barriers around the zone. On payment of the charge your vehicle number plate is registered on a database and on entering or driving within the zone cameras read your number plate and check it against the database. You can pay the charge, without penalty, until 10.00 pm on the day of travel. Between 10.00 pm and midnight a £5 surcharge will be made, making a total of £10; after midnight the registered owner of the vehicle will be sent a penalty charge notice for £80, payment within 14 days will reduce this to £40. Failure to pay within 28 days will result in the penalty being increased to £120.

● To avoid paying the congestion charge you can find your easiest route by public transport by visiting www.journeyplanner.org or calling London Travel Information on 020 7918 4300.

For any further information, including a list of vehicles eligible for exemption or a discount, please visit www.cclondon.com or call 0845 900 1234.

KEY TO MAP SYMBOLS

A4 Primary route	Main railway station	Fire Sta — Fire station		Leisure and tourism
A40 'A' road	Other railway station	PO — Post office		Shopping
B504 'B' road	London Underground station	Lib — Library		Administration and law
Other road / One way street	DLR Docklands Light Railway station	▲ Monument / Statue		Health and welfare
Street market	Bus / Coach station	Cinema		Education
Pedestrian street	P Car park	+ Church		Industry and commerce
Access restriction	i Tourist information centre	☾ Mosque		Public open space
Track / Footpath	Theatre	✡ Synagogue		Park / Garden / Sports ground
Ferry	Major hotel	Mormon ■ Other place of worship		Cemetery
CITY Borough boundary	USA Embassy	WC Public toilet		
EC2 Postal district boundary	POL Police station	Tower block		

Extent of London Congestion Charging Zone

The reference grid on this atlas coincides with the Ordnance Survey National Grid System. The grid interval is 250 metres.

10 Grid reference   **200** Page continuation number

Scale
1: 10,000 6.3 inches to 1 mile/10cm to 1 km

0	¼	½ mile
0	0.25	0.5	0.75 kilometre

Notes on how to use the index

The index starting on page 208 combines entries for street names, place names, places of interest, stations and hospitals.

Place names are shown in capital letters,
e.g.**ACTON**, W3 ......**80**   CN74
These include towns, villages and other localities within the area covered by this atlas.

Places of interest are shown with a star symbol,
e.g. ★**British Mus**, WC1 . . .**195**   P7
These include parks, museums, galleries, other important buildings and tourist attractions.

Hospitals and types of station are shown by symbols as listed :-
H   Hospital
≹   Railway station
⊖   London Underground station
DLR   Docklands Light Railway station
⬦   Tramlink station

All other entries are for street names. When there is more than one street with exactly the same name then that name is shown only once in the index. It is then followed by a list of entries for each postal district that contains a street with that same name. For example, there are three streets called **Ardley Close** in this atlas and the index entry shows that one of these is in London postal district NW10, one is in London postal district SE6 and one is in Ruislip HA4.
e.g.**Ardley Cl**, NW10 . . .**62**   CS62
SE6 . . . .**123**   DY90
Ruislip HA4 . . . . . .**59**   BQ59
All entries are followed by the page number and grid reference on which the name will be found. So, in the example above, **Ardley Close**, NW10 will be found on page **62** in square CS62.
All entries are indexed to the largest scale map on which they are shown.

The index also contains some streets which are not actually named on the maps because there is not enough space. In these cases the adjoining or nearest named thoroughfare to such a street is shown in *italic*. The reference indicates where the unnamed street is located *off* the named thoroughfare.
e.g.**Bacton St**, E2
off Roman Rd **84**   DW69
This means that **Bacton Street** is not named on the map, but it is located *off Roman Road* on page **84** in square DW69.

A strict letter-by-letter alphabetical order is followed in this index. All non-alphabetic characters such as spaces, hyphens or apostrophes have not been included in the index order. For example **Belle Vue Road** and **Bellevue Road** will be found listed together.

Standard terms such as **Avenue, Close, Rise** and **Road** are abbreviated in the index but are ordered alphabetically as if given in full. So, for example, **Abbots Ri** comes before **Abbots Rd**.

Names beginning with a definite article (i.e. **The**) are indexed from their second word onwards with the definite article being placed at the end of the name.
e.g. **Avenue, The**, E4 . . .**47** ED51
The alphabetical order extends to include postal information so that where two or more streets have exactly the same name, London postal district references are given first in alpha-numeric order and are followed by non-London post town references in alphabetical order, e.g. **Ardley Close**, NW10 is followed by **Ardley Close**, SE6 and then **Ardley Close**, Ruislip HA4.

In cases where there are two or more streets of the same name in the same postal area, extra information is given in brackets to aid location. For example, **High St**, Orpington BR6 (Farnborough), and **High St**, Orpington BR6 (Green St Grn), distinguishes between two streets called **High Street** which are both in the post town of Orpington and within the same postal district of BR6.

Extra locational information is also given for some localities within large post towns. This is also to aid location.
e.g.**Adrian Cl**, Uxb. (Hare.) UB9. . .**38** BK53
This street is within the locality of Harefield which is part of the post town of Uxbridge, and it is within postal district UB9.

A full list of locality and post town abbreviations used in this atlas is given on the following page.

General abbreviations

All	Alley	Ct	Court	Hosp	Hospital	Rd	Road
Allot	Allotments	Cts	Courts	Hts	Heights	Rds	Roads
Amb	Ambulance	Ctyd	Courtyard	Ind	Industrial	Rec	Recreation
App	Approach	Dep	Depot	Int	International	Res	Reservoir
Arc	Arcade	Dev	Development	Junct	Junction	Ri	Rise
Av	Avenue	Dr	Drive	La	Lane	S	South
Bdy	Broadway	Dws	Dwellings	Las	Lanes	Sch	School
Bk	Bank	E	East	Lib	Library	Sec	Secondary
Bldgs	Buildings	Ed	Education	Lo	Lodge	Shop	Shopping
Boul	Boulevard	Elec	Electricity	Lwr	Lower	Sq	Square
Bowl	Bowling	Embk	Embankment	Mag	Magistrates	St.	Saint
Br	Bridge	Est	Estate	Mans	Mansions	St	Street
C of E	Church of	Ex	Exchange	Mem	Memorial	Sta	Station
England		Exhib	Exhibition	Mkt	Market	Sts	Streets
Cath	Cathedral	FB	Footbridge	Mkts	Markets	Sub	Subway
Cem	Cemetery	FC	Football Club	Ms	Mews	Swim	Swimming
Cen	Central, Centre	Fld	Field	Mt	Mount	TA	Territorial Army
Cft	Croft	Flds	Fields	Mus	Museum	TH	Town Hall
Cfts	Crofts	Fm	Farm	N	North	Tenn	Tennis
Ch	Church	Gall	Gallery	NT	National Trust	Ter	Terrace
Chyd	Churchyard	Gar	Garage	Nat	National	Thea	Theatre
Cin	Cinema	Gdn	Garden	PH	Public House	Trd	Trading
Circ	Circus	Gdns	Gardens	PO	Post Office	Twr	Tower
Cl	Close	Gen	General	Par	Parade	Twrs	Towers
Co	County	Govt	Government	Pas	Passage	Uni	University
Coll	College	Gra	Grange	Pav	Pavilion	Vil	Villas
Comm	Community	Grd	Ground	Pk	Park	Vil	Villa
Conv	Convent	Grds	Grounds	Pl	Place	Vw	View
Cor	Corner	Grn	Green	Pol	Police	W	West
Coron	Coroners	Grns	Greens	Prec	Precinct	Wd	Wood
Cors	Corners	Gro	Grove	Prim	Primary	Wds	Woods
Cotts	Cottages	Gros	Groves	Prom	Promenade	Wf	Wharf
Cov	Covered	Gt	Great	Pt	Point	Wk	Walk
Crem	Crematorium	Ho	House	Quad	Quadrant	Wks	Works
Cres	Crescent	Hos	Houses	RC	Roman Catholic	Yd	Yard

Locality & post town abbreviations

Note: In the list of abbreviations shown below Post Towns are in bold type.

Abbr.	Full name
Abb.L.	**Abbots Langley**
Add.	**Addlestone**
Ald.	Aldenham
Amer.	**Amersham**
Ashf.	**Ashford**
Ashtd.	**Ashtead**
Bad.Dene	Badgers Dene
Bad.Mt.	Badgers Mount
Bans.	**Banstead**
Bark.	**Barking**
Barn.	**Barnet**
Barne.	Barnehurst
Beac.	**Beaconsfield**
Beck.	**Beckenham**
Bedd.	Beddington
Bedd.Cor.	Beddington Corner
Belv.	**Belvedere**
Berry's Grn.	Berry's Green
Bet.	**Betchworth**
Bex.	**Bexley**
Bexh.	**Bexleyheath**
Bigg.H.	Biggin Hill
Bkhm.	Bookham
Bletch.	Bletchingley
Borwd.	**Borehamwood**
Bov.	Bovingdon
Brent.	**Brentford**
Brick.Wd.	Bricket Wood
Brock.	Brockham
Brom.	**Bromley**
Brook.Pk.	Brookmans Park
Brox.	**Broxbourne**
Brwd.	**Brentwood**
Buck.H.	**Buckhurst Hill**
Burgh Hth.	Burgh Heath
Bushey Hth.	Bushey Heath
Carp.Pk.	Carpenders Park
Cars.	**Carshalton**
Cat.	**Caterham**
Ch.End	Church End
Ch.St.G.	**Chalfont St. Giles**
Chad.Hth.	Chadwell Heath
Chad.St.M	Chadwell St. Mary
Chaff.Hun.	Chafford Hundred
Chal.St.P.	Chalfont St. Peter
Chel.	Chelsham
Chels.	Chelsfield
Cher.	**Chertsey**
Chesh.	**Chesham**
Chess.	**Chessington**
Chev.	Chevening
Chig.	**Chigwell**
Chipper.	Chipperfield
Chis.	**Chislehurst**
Chob.Com.	Chobham Common
Chorl.	Chorleywood
Chsht.	Cheshunt
Clay.	Claygate
Cob.	**Cobham**
Cockfos.	Cockfosters
Coll.Row	Collier Row
Coln.Hth.	Colney Heath
Coln.St.	Colney Street
Colnbr.	Colnbrook
Cooper.	Coopersale
Couls.	**Coulsdon**
Cran.	Cranford
Cray.	Crayford
Crock.	Crockenhill
Crock.H.	Crockham Hill
Crox.Grn.	Croxley Green
Croy.	**Croydon**
Dag.	**Dagenham**
Dance.H.	Dancers Hill
Dart.	**Dartford**
Denh.	Denham
Dor.	**Dorking**
Down.	Downside
Dunt.Grn.	Dunton Green
E.Bed.	East Bedfont
E.Croy.	East Croydon
E.Ewell	East Ewell
E.Hors.	East Horsley
E.Mol.	**East Molesey**
E.Til.	East Tilbury
Eastcote Vill.	Eastcote Village

Abbr.	Full name
Eden.	**Edenbridge**
Edg.	**Edgware**
Eff.	Effingham
Eff.Junct.	Effingham Junction
Egh.	**Egham**
Egh. & Wind.	**Egham & Windsor**
Egh.H.	Egham Hythe
Elm Pk.	Elm Park
Elm.Wds.	Elmstead Woods
Enf.	**Enfield**
Eng.Grn.	Englefield Green
Epp.	**Epping**
Epp. & Loug.	**Epping & Loughton**
Epp.Grn.	Epping Green
Ewell E.	Ewell East
Ewell W.	Ewell West
Eyns.	Eynsford
Farnboro.	Farnborough
Fawk.	Fawkham
Fawk.Grn.	Fawkham Green
Felt.	**Feltham**
Fetch.	Fetcham
Flam.	Flamstead
Flaun.	Flaunden
Fnghm.	Farningham
Frog.	Frogmore
Gdse.	**Godstone**
Geo.Grn.	George Green
Ger.Cr.	**Gerrards Cross**
Gidea Pk.	Gidea Park
Godden Grn.	Godden Green
Grav.	**Gravesend**
Green.	**Greenhithe**
Grn.St.Grn.	Green Street Green
Grnf.	**Greenford**
Gt.Warley	Great Warley
Guil.	**Guildford**
Hackbr.	Hackbridge
Had.Wd.	Hadley Wood
Halst.	Halstead
Han.	Hanworth
Har.	**Harrow**
Har.Hill	Harrow on the Hill
Har.Wld.	Harrow Weald
Hare.	Harefield
Harm.	Harmondsworth
Harold Wd.	Harold Wood
Hat.	**Hatfield**
Hatt.Cr.	Hatton Cross
Hav.at.Bow.	Havering-atte-Bower
Hedg.	Hedgerley
Hem.H.	**Hemel Hempstead**
Herons.	Heronsgate
Hert.	**Hertford**
Hext.	Hextable
High Barn.	High Barnet
Highams Pk.	Highams Park
Hinch.Wd.	Hinchley Wood
Hlgdn.	Hillingdon
Hmptn.	**Hampton**
Hmptn.H.	Hampton Hill
Hmptn.W.	Hampton Wick
Hook Grn.	Hook Green
Horn.	**Hornchurch**
Hort.Kir.	Horton Kirby
Houns.	**Hounslow**
Houns.W.	Hounslow West
Hthrw.Air.	Heathrow Airport
Hthrw.Air.N.	Heathrow Airport North
Ickhm.	Ickenham
Ilf.	**Ilford**
Islw.	**Isleworth**
Ken.	**Kenley**
Kes.	**Keston**
Kgfld.	Kingfield
Kgswd.	Kingswood
Kings L.	**Kings Langley**
Kings.T.	**Kingston upon Thames**
Knap.	Knaphill
Knock.	Knockholt
Knock.P.	Knockholt Pound
Lamb.End	Lambourne End
Let.Hth.	Letchmore Heath

Lmpfld.	Limpsfield
Lmpfld.Ch.	Limpsfield Chart
Lon.Col.	London Colney
Long Dit.	Long Ditton
Long.	**Longfield**
Longcr.	Longcross
Loud.	Loudwater
Loug.	**Loughton**
Lt.Chal.	Little Chalfont
Lt.Hth.	Little Heath
Lt.Warley	Little Warley
Lthd.	**Leatherhead**
Lwr.Kgswd.	Lower Kingswood
Lwr.Sydenham	Lower Sydenham
Lyon Pk Av	Lyon Park Avenue
Map.Cr.	Maple Cross
Mdgrn.	Middlegreen
Merst.	Merstham
Mick.	Mickleham
Mimbr.	Mimbridge
Mitch.	**Mitcham**
Mord.	**Morden**
Mots.Pk.	Motspur Park
Mtnsg.	Mountnessing
N.Finchley	North Finchley
N.Har.	North Harrow
N.Mal.	**New Malden**
N.Mymms	North Mymms
N.Ock.	North Ockendon
N.Stfd.	North Stifford
N.Wld.	North Weald
N.Wld.Bas.	North Weald Bassett
Nave.	Navestock
Nave.S.	Navestock Side
New Adgtn.	New Addington
New Barn.	New Barnet
Newgate St.	Newgate Street
Northumb.Hth.	Northumberland Heath
Norwood Junct.	Norwood Junction
Nthflt.	Northfleet
Nthlt.	**Northolt**
Nthwd.	**Northwood**
Nutfld.	Nutfield
Old Wind.	Old Windsor
Old Wok.	Old Woking
Ong.	**Ongar**
Orch.L.	Orchard Leigh
Orp.	**Orpington**
Ott.	Ottershaw
Oxt.	**Oxted**
Park St.	Park Street
Perry St.	Perry Street
Petts Wd	Petts Wood
Pilg.Hat.	Pilgrim's Hatch
Pnr.	**Pinner**
Pond.End	Ponders End
Pot.B.	**Potters Bar**
Pr.Bot.	Pratt's Bottom
Pur.	**Purley**
Purf.	**Purfleet**
Rad.	**Radlett**
Rain.	**Rainham**
Red.	**Redhill**
Reig.	**Reigate**
Rich.	**Richmond**
Rick.	**Rickmansworth**
Rod.Val.	Roding Valley
Rom.	**Romford**
Rosh.	Rosherville
Ruis.	**Ruislip**
Runny.	Runnymede
Rush Grn.	Rush Green
Russ.Hill	Russell Hill
Rvrhd.	Riverhead
S.Croy.	**South Croydon**
S.Darenth	South Darenth
S.Har.	South Harrow
S.Merst.	South Merstham
S.Mimms	South Mimms
S.Norwood	South Norwood
S.Nutfld.	South Nutfield
S.Ock.	**South Ockendon**
S.Oxhey	South Oxhey
S.Ruis.	South Ruislip

Abbr.	Full name
S.Stfd.	South Stifford
S.le H.	**Stanford-le-Hope**
Scad.Pk.	Scadbury Park
Send M.	Send Marsh
Sev.	**Sevenoaks**
Sev.Wld.	Sevenoaks Weald
Sheer.	Sheerwater
Shenf.	Shenfield
Shep.	**Shepperton**
Shore.	Shoreham
Short.	Shortlands
Sid.	**Sidcup**
Slade Grn.	Slade Green
Slou.	**Slough**
St.Alb.	**St. Albans**
St.Geo.H.	St. George's Hill
St.M.Cray	St. Mary Cray
St.P.Cray	St. Paul's Cray
Stai.	**Staines**
Stan.	**Stanmore**
Stanw.	Stanwell
Stap.Abb.	Stapleford Abbotts
Stap.Taw.	Stapleford Tawney
Sthflt.	Southfleet
Sthl.	**Southall**
Sthl.Grn.	Southall Green
Stoke D'Ab.	Stoke D'Abernon
Stoke P.	Stoke Poges
Sun.	**Sunbury-on-Thames**
Sund.	Sundridge
Surb.	**Surbiton**
Sutt.	**Sutton**
Sutt.Grn.	Sutton Green
Sutt.H.	Sutton at Hone
Swan.	**Swanley**
Swans.	**Swanscombe**
T.Ditt.	**Thames Ditton**
Tad.	**Tadworth**
Tand.	Tandridge
Tats.	Tatsfield
Tedd.	**Teddington**
Th.Hth.	**Thornton Heath**
They.B.	Theydon Bois
Thnwd.	Thornwood
Til.	**Tilbury**
Tkgtn.	Tokyngton
Turnf.	Turnford
Twick.	**Twickenham**
Tyr.Wd.	Tyrrell's Wood
Undrvr.	Underriver
Upmin.	**Upminster**
Uxb.	**Uxbridge**
Vir.W.	**Virginia Water**
W.Byf.	**West Byfleet**
W.Croy.	West Croydon
W.Ewell	West Ewell
W.Hors.	West Horsley
W.Mol.	**West Molesey**
W.Thur.	West Thurrock
W.Til.	West Tilbury
W.Wick.	**West Wickham**
Wal.Abb.	**Waltham Abbey**
Wal.Cr.	**Waltham Cross**
Wall.	**Wallington**
Walt.	**Walton-on-Thames**
Warl.	**Warlingham**
Wat.	**Watford**
Wdf.Grn.	**Woodford Green**
Well.	**Welling**
Wem.	**Wembley**
Wenn.	Wennington
West Dr.	**West Drayton**
West.	**Westerham**
Wey.	**Weybridge**
Whel.Hill	Whelpley Hill
Whyt.	**Whyteleafe**
Wilm.	Wilmington
Wind.	**Windsor**
Wldste.	Wealdstone
Wok.	**Woking**
Wold.	Woldingham
Woodside Pk.	Woodside Park
Wor.Pk.	**Worcester Park**
Wrays.	Wraysbury
Yiew.	Yiewsley

02 - Adn

02 Shop Cen, NW3
  off Finchley Rd 82 DC65

A

Aaron Hill Rd, E6 ....87 EN71
Abberley Ms, SW4
  off Cedars Rd 101 DH83
Abberton Wk, Rain. RM13
  off Ongar Way 89 FE66
Abbess Cl, E6 *off Oliver Gdns* .
  SW2 ....121 DP88
Abbeville Rd, N8
  off Barrington Rd 65 DK56
  SW4 ....121 DJ86
Abbey Av, Wem. HA0 ......80 CL68
Abbey Business Cen, SW8
  off Ingate Pl 101 DH81
Abbey Cl, Hayes UB3 ......77 BV74
  Northolt UB5
  off Invicta Gro 78 BZ69
  Pinner HA5 ....59 BV55
  Romford RM1 ....71 FG58
  Woking GU22 ....167 BA116
Abbey Ct, Wal.Abb. EN9 ...15 EB34
Abbey Cres, Belv. DA17 ...106 FA77
Abbeydale Rd, Wem. HA0 ..80 CN67
Abbey Dr, SW17
  off Church La 120 DG92
  Abbots Langley WD5 .....7 BU32
  Staines TW18 ....134 BJ98
Abbeyfield Rd, SE16 ....202 F8
Abbeyfields Cl, NW10 .....80 CN68
Abbeyfields Mobile Home Pk,
  Cher. KT16 ....134 BK101
Abbey Gdns, NW8 ....82 DC68
  SE16 ....202 C8
  W6 ....99 CY79
  Chertsey KT16 ....134 BG100
  Chislehurst BR7 ....145 EN95
  Waltham Abbey EN9 .....15 EC33
Abbey Grn, Cher. KT16 ....134 BG100
Abbey Gro, SE2 ....106 EV77
Abbeyhill Rd, Sid. DA15 ...126 EW89
Abbey Ind Est, Mitch. CR4 .140 DF99
  Wembley HA0 ....80 CM67
Abbey La, E15 ....85 EC68
  Beckenham BR3 ....123 EA94
Abbey Mead Ind Pk, Wal.Abb.
  EN9 ....15 EC34
Abbey Ms, E17
  off Leamington Av 67 EA57
Abbey Orchard St, SW1 ....199 N6
Abbey Par, SW19
  off Merton High St 120 DC94
  W5 *off Hanger La* 80 CM69
Abbey Pk, Beck. BR3 ......123 EA94
Abbey Pl, Dart. DA1
  off Priory Rd N 128 FK85
Abbey Retail Pk, Bark. IG11 .87 EP67
Abbey Rd, E15 ....86 EE68
  NW6 ....82 DB66
  NW8 ....82 DC68
  NW10 ....80 CQ68
  SE2 ....106 EX77
  SW19 ....120 DC94
  Barking IG11 ....87 EP66
  Belvedere DA17 ....106 EX77
  Bexleyheath DA7 ....106 EY84
  Chertsey KT16 ....134 BH101
  Croydon CR0 ....141 DP104
  Enfield EN1 ....30 DS43
  Gravesend DA12 ....131 GL88
  Greenhithe DA9 ....129 FW85
  Ilford IG2 ....69 ER57
  Shepperton TW17 ......134 BN102
  South Croydon CR2 ....161 DX110
  Virginia Water GU25 ...132 AX99
  Waltham Cross EN8 ....15 DY34
  Woking GU21 ....166 AW117
Abbey Rd Est, NW8 ....82 DB66
Abbey St, E13 ....86 EG70
  SE1 ....201 N6
Abbey Ter, SE2 ....106 EW77
Abbey Vw, NW7 ....43 CT48
  Radlett WD7 ....25 CF35
  Waltham Abbey EN9 ....15 EB33
  Watford WD25 ....24 BX36
Abbey Vw Roundabout, Wal.Abb.
  EN9 ....15 EC33
Abbey Wk, W.Mol. KT8 ....136 CB97
Abbey Way, SE2 ....106 EX76
Abbey Wf Ind Est, Bark. IG11 .87 ER68
ABBEY WOOD, SE2 ....106 EV76
  ⇌ Abbey Wood 106 EV76
Abbey Wd La, Rain. RM13 ..90 FK68
Abbey Wd Rd, SE2 ....106 EV77
Abbot Cl, Stai. TW18 ......114 BK94
  West Byfleet (Byfleet)
  KT14 ....152 BK110
Abbots Av, Epsom KT19 ...156 CN111
Abbotsbury Cl, E15 ....85 EC68
  W14 *off Abbotsbury Rd* ..99 CZ75
Abbotsbury Gdns, Pnr. HA5 .60 BW58
Abbotsbury Ms, SE15 .....102 DW83
Abbotsbury Rd, W14 ......99 CY75
  Bromley BR2 ....144 EF103
  Morden SM4 ....140 DB99
Abbots Cl, N1
  off Alwyne Rd 84 DQ65
  Brentwood CM15 ....55 GA46
  Orpington BR5 ....145 EQ102
  Rainham RM13 ....90 FJ68
  Ruislip HA4 ....60 BX62
Abbots Dr, Har. HA2 ......60 CA61
  Virginia Water GU25 ...132 AW98
Abbots Fld, Grav. DA12
  off Ruffets Wd 131 GJ93
Abbotsford Av, N15 ....66 DQ56
Abbotsford Cl, Wok. GU22
  off Onslow Cres 167 BA117

Abbotsford Gdns, Wdf.Grn.
  IG8 ....48 EG52
Abbotsford Lo, Nthwd. HA6 .39 BS50
Abbotsford Rd, Ilf. IG3 ....70 EU61
Abbots Gdns, N2 ....64 DD56
  W8 *off St. Mary's Pl* 100 DB76
Abbots Grn, Croy. CR0 ....161 DX107
Abbotshade Rd, SE16 .....203 J3
Abbotshall Av, N14 ....45 DJ48
Abbotshall Rd, SE6 ....123 ED88
Abbots La, SE1 ....201 N3
  Kenley CR8 ....176 DQ116
ABBOTS LANGLEY 7 BR31
Abbotsleigh Cl, Sutt. SM2 .158 DB108
Abbotsleigh Rd, SW16 ....121 DJ91
Abbots Manor Est, SW1 ...199 H9
Abbotsmede Cl, Twick. TW1 .117 CF89
Abbots Pk, SW2 ....121 DN88
Abbot's Pl, NW6 ....82 DB67
Abbots Ri, Kings L. WD4 ...6 BM26
  Redhill RH1 ....184 DG132
Abbot's Rd, E6 ....86 EK67
Abbots Rd, Abb.L WD5 ....7 BS30
  Edgware HA8 ....42 CQ52
Abbots Ter, N8 ....65 DL58
Abbotstone Rd, SW15 ....99 CW83
Abbot St, E8 ....84 DT65
Abbots Vw, Kings L. WD4 ..6 BM27
Abbots Wk, W8
  off St. Mary's Pl 100 DB76
  Caterham CR3
  off Tillingdown Hill 176 DU122
Abbots Way, Beck. BR3 ...143 DY99
  Chertsey KT16 ....133 BF101
Abbotswell Rd, SE4 ......123 DZ85
Abbotswood Cl, Belv. DA17
  off Coptefield Dr 106 EY76
Abbotswood Dr, Wey. KT13 .153 BR110
Abbotswood Gdns, Ilf. IG5 ..69 EM55
Abbotswood Rd, SE22 ....102 DS84
  SW16 ....121 DK90
Abbotswood Way, Hayes UB3 .77 BV74
Abbott Av, SW20 ....139 CX96
Abbott Cl, Hmptn. TW12 ..116 BY93
  Northolt UB5 ....78 BZ65
Abbott Rd, E14 ....85 EC71
Abbotts Cl, SE28 ....88 EW73
  Romford RM7 ....71 FB55
  Swanley BR8 ....147 FG98
  Uxbridge UB8 ....58 BK71
Abbotts Cres, E4 ....47 ED49
  Enfield EN2 ....29 DP40
Abbotts Dr, Wal.Abb. EN9 ..16 EG34
  Wembley HA0 ....61 CH61
Abbotts Pk Rd, E10 ....67 EC59
Abbotts Rd, Barn. EN5 ....28 DB42
  Mitcham CR4 ....141 DJ98
  Southall UB1 ....78 BY74
  Sutton SM3 ....139 CZ104
Abbott's Tilt, Walt. KT12 ..136 BY104
Abbotts Wk, Bexh. DA7 ...106 EX80
Abbs Cross Gdns, Horn.
  RM12 ....72 FJ60
Abbs Cross La, Horn. RM12 .72 FJ63
Abchurch La, EC4 ....197 L10
Abchurch Yd, EC4 ....197 K10
Abdale Rd, W12 ....81 CV74
Abenberg Way, Brwd. (Hutton)
  CM13 ....55 GB47
Aberavon Rd, E3 ....85 DY69
Abercairn Rd, SW16 ......121 DJ94
Aberconway Rd, Mord. SM4 .140 DB97
Abercorn Cl, NW7 ....43 CY52
  NW8 ....82 DC69
  South Croydon CR2 ....161 DX112
Abercorn Cres, Har. HA2 ..60 CB60
Abercorn Gdns, Har. HA3 ..61 CK59
  Romford RM6 ....70 EV58
Abercorn Gro, Ruis. HA4 ..59 BR56
Abercorn Pl, NW8 ....82 DC69
Abercorn Rd, NW7 ....43 CY52
  Stanmore HA7 ....41 CJ52
Abercorn Way, SE1 ......202 B10
  Woking GU21 ....166 AU118
Abercrombie Dr, Enf. EN1
  off Linwood Cres 30 DU39
Abercrombie St, SW11 ...100 DE82
Aberdale Ct, SE16
  off Poolmans St 103 DX75
Aberdale Gdns, Pot.B. EN6 .11 CZ33
Aberdare Cl, W.Wick. BR4 .143 EC103
Aberdare Gdns, NW6 .....82 DB66
  NW7 ....43 CX52
Aberdare Rd, Enf. EN3 ...30 DW42
Aberdeen La, N5 ....66 DQ64
Aberdeen Par, N18
  off Angel Rd 46 DV50
Aberdeen Pk, N5 ....65 DP64
Aberdeen Pk Ms, N5 .....66 DQ63
Aberdeen Pl, NW8 ....82 DD70
Aberdeen Rd, N5 ....66 DQ63
  N18 ....46 DV50
  NW10 ....63 CT64
  Croydon CR0 ....160 DQ105
  Harrow HA3 ....41 CF54
Aberdeen Sq, E14 ....203 P2
Aberdeen Ter, SE3 ....103 ED82
Aberdour Rd, Ilf. IG3 .....70 EV62
Aberdour St, SE1 ....201 M8
Aberfeldy St, E14 ....85 EC72
Aberford Gdns, SE18 .....104 EL81
Aberford Rd, Borwd. WD6 .26 CN40
Aberfoyle Rd, SW16 .....121 DK93
Abergeldie Rd, SE12 .....124 EH86
Aberglen Ind Est, Hayes UB3 .95 BR75
Abernethy Rd, SE13 .....104 EE84
Abersham Rd, E8 ....84 DT64
Abery St, SE18 ....105 ES77
Abigail Ms, Rom. RM3
  off King Alfred Rd 52 FM54
Abingdon Cl, NW1
  off Camden Sq 83 DK65
  SE1 ....202 A10
  SW19 ....120 DC93
  Uxbridge UB10 ....76 BM67
  Woking GU21 ....166 AV118
Abingdon Pl, Pot.B. EN6 ..12 DB32

Abingdon Rd, N3 ....44 DC54
  SW16 ....141 DL96
  W8 ....100 DA76
Abingdon St, SW1 ....199 P6
Abingdon Vil, W8 ....100 DA76
Abingdon Way, Orp. BR6 ..164 EV105
Abinger Av, Sutt. SM2 ....157 CW109
Abinger Cl, Bark. IG11 ....70 EU63
  Bromley BR1 ....144 EL97
  Croydon CR0 ....161 EC107
  Wallington SM6 ....159 DL106
Abinger Gdns, Islw. TW7 ..97 CE83
Abinger Gro, SE8 ....103 DZ79
Abinger Ms, W9
  off Warlock Rd 82 DA70
Abinger Rd, W4 ....98 CS76
Abney Gdns, N16 *off Stoke*
  Newington High St 66 DT61
Aboyne Dr, SW20 ....139 CU96
Aboyne Est, SW17 ....120 DD90
Aboyne Rd, NW10 ....62 CS62
  SW17 ....120 DD90
Abraham Cl, Wat. WD19
  off Muirfield Rd 39 BV49
ABRIDGE, Rom. 34 EV41
Abridge Cl, Wal.Cr. EN8 ..31 DX35
Abridge Gdns, Rom. RM5 ..50 FA51
Abridge Pk, Rom. (Abridge)
  RM4 ....34 EU42
Abridge Rd, Chig. IG7 ....33 ER44
  Epping (They.B.) CM16 ..33 ES36
  Romford (Abridge) RM4 ..34 EU39
Abridge Way, Bark. IG11 ..88 EV68
Abyssinia Cl, SW11
  off Cairns Rd 100 DE84
Abyssinia Rd, SW11
  off Auckland Rd 100 DE84
Acacia Av, N17 ....46 DR52
  Brentford TW8 ....97 CH80
  Hayes UB3 ....77 BT72
  Hornchurch RM12 .....71 FF61
  Mitcham CR4
  off Acacia Rd 141 DH96
  Ruislip HA4 ....59 BU60
  Shepperton TW17 .....134 BN99
  Staines (Wrays.) TW19 ..92 AY84
  Wembley HA9 ....62 CL64
  West Drayton UB7 .....76 BM73
  Woking GU22 ....166 AX120
Acacia Cl, SE8 ....203 K9
  SE20 *off Selby Rd* 142 DU96
  Addlestone (Woodham)
  KT15 ....151 BF110
  Orpington BR5 ....145 ER99
  Stanmore HA7 ....41 CE51
  Waltham Cross EN7 ....14 DS27
Acacia Ct, Wal.Abb. EN9
  off Farthingale La 16 EG34
Acacia Dr, Add. (Woodham)
  KT15 ....151 BF110
  Banstead SM7 ....157 CX114
  Sutton SM3 ....139 CZ102
  Upminster RM14 ....72 FN63
Acacia Gdns, NW8
  off Acacia Rd 82 DD68
  Upminster RM14 ....73 FT59
  West Wickham BR4 ....143 EC103
Acacia Gro, SE21 ....122 DR89
  New Malden KT3 ....138 CR97
Acacia Ms, West Dr. UB7 ..94 BK79
Acacia Pl, NW8 ....82 DD68
Acacia Rd, E11 ....68 EE61
  E17 ....67 DY58
  N22 ....45 DN53
  NW8 ....82 DD68
  SW16 ....141 DL95
  W3 ....80 CQ73
  Beckenham BR3 ....143 DZ97
  Dartford DA1 ....128 FK88
  Enfield EN2 ....30 DR39
  Greenhithe DA9 ....129 FS86
  Hampton TW12 ....116 CA93
  Mitcham CR4 ....141 DH96
  Staines TW18 ....114 BH92
Acacia Wk, Swan. BR8 ...147 FD96
Acacia Way, Sid. DA15 ...125 ET88
Academy Gdns, Croy. CR0 .142 DT102
  Northolt UB5 ....78 BX68
Academy Pl, SE18 ....105 EM81
Academy Rd, SE18 ......105 EM81
Acanthus Dr, SE1 ....202 C10
Acanthus Rd, SW11 .....100 DG83
Accommodation La, West Dr.
  UB7 ....94 BJ79
Accommodation Rd, NW11 .63 CZ59
  Chertsey (Longcr.) KT16 .132 AX104
A.C. Ct, T.Ditt. KT7
  off Harvest La 137 CG100
Acer Av, Hayes UB4 ......78 BY71
  Rainham RM13 ....90 FK69
Acer Rd, West. (Bigg.H.)
  TN16 ....178 EK116
Acers, St.Alb. (Park St.) AL2 ..8 CC28
Acfold Rd, SW6 ....100 DB81
Achilles Cl, SE1 ....202 C10
Achilles Pl, Wok. GU21 ...166 AW117
Achilles Rd, NW6 ....64 DA64
Achilles St, SE14 ....103 DY80
Achilles Way, W1 ....198 G3
Acklam Rd, W10 ....81 CZ71
Acklington Dr, NW9 .....42 CS53
Ackmar Rd, SW6 ....100 DA81
Ackroyd Dr, E3 ....85 DZ71
Ackroyd Rd, SE23 ....123 DX87
Acland Cl, SE18
  off Clothworkers Rd ...105 ER80
Acland Cres, SE5 ....102 DR84
Acland Rd, NW2 ....81 CV65
Acme Rd, Wat. WD24 ....23 BU38
Acock Gro, Nthlt. UB5 ...60 CB63
Acol Cres, Ruis. HA4 ....59 BV64
Acol Rd, NW6 ....82 DA66
Aconbury Rd, Dag. RM9 ..88 EV67
Acorn Cl, E4 ....47 EA50
  Chislehurst BR7 ....125 EQ92
  Enfield EN2 ....29 DP39

Acorn Cl, Hmptn. TW12 ...116 CB93
  Stanmore HA7 ....41 CH52
Acorn Ct, Ilf. IG2 ....69 ES58
Acorn Gdns, SE19 ....142 DT95
  W3 ....80 CR71
Acorn Gro, Hayes UB3 ...95 BT80
  Ruislip HA4 ....59 BT63
  Tadworth KT20 ....173 CY124
  Woking GU22
  off Old Sch Pl 166 AY121
Acorn Ind Pk, Dart. DA1 ..127 FG85
Acorn La, Pot.B. (Cuffley)
  EN6 ....13 DL29
Acorn Par, SE15
  off Carlton Gro 102 DV80
Acorn Pl, Wat. WD24 ....23 BU37
Acorns, The, Chig. IG7 ...49 ES49
Acorns Way, Esher KT10 ..154 CC106
Acorn Wk, SE16 ....203 L2
Acorn Way, SE23 ....123 DX90
  Beckenham BR3 ....143 EC99
  Orpington BR6 ....163 EP105
Acre Dr, SE22 ....102 DU84
Acrefield Rd, Ger.Cr. (Chal.St.P.)
  SL9 ....56 AX55
Acre La, SW2 ....101 DL84
  Carshalton SM5 ....158 DG105
  Wallington SM6 ....158 DG105
Acre Path, Nthlt. UB5
  off Arnold Rd 78 BY65
Acre Rd, SW19 ....120 DD93
  Dagenham RM10 ......89 FB66
  Kingston upon Thames
  KT2 ....138 CL95
Acris St, SW18 ....120 DC85
ACTON, W3 ....80 CN74
Acton Cl, N9 ....46 DU47
  Waltham Cross (Chsht.)
  EN8 ....15 DY31
⇌ Acton Central 80 CP74
Acton Hill Ms, W3
  off Uxbridge Rd 80 CP74
[H] Acton Hosp, W3 ....98 CN75
Acton La, NW10 ....80 CS68
  W3 ....98 CQ75
  W4 ....98 CR76
⇌ Acton Main Line 80 CQ72
Acton Ms, E8 ....84 DT67
Acton Pk Ind Est, W3 ....98 CR75
Acton St, WC1 ....196 B3
⊖ Acton Town 98 CN75
Acuba Rd, SW18 ....120 DB89
Acworth Cl, N9 *off Turin Rd* .46 DW45
Ada Gdns, E14 ....86 ED72
  E15 ....86 EF67
Adair Cl, SE25 ....142 DV99
Adair Rd, W10 ....81 CY70
Adair Twr, W10
  off Appleford Rd 81 CY70
Adam & Eve Ct, W1 ......195 L8
Adam & Eve Ms, W8 ....100 DA76
Adam Cl, SE6 ....123 DZ91
  SE7 ....
Adam Ct, SW7
  off Gloucester Rd 100 DC77
Adam Pl, N16 *off Stoke*
  Newington High St 66 DT61
Adam Rd, E4 ....47 DZ51
Adams Cl, N3 *off Falkland Av* .44 DA52
  NW9 ....62 CP61
  Surbiton KT5 ....138 CM100
Adams Ct, EC2 ....197 L8
Adamsfield, Wal.Cr. EN7 ..14 DU72
Adams Gdns Est, SE16 ...202 F4
Adams Ms, SW17
  off King's Av 121 DK88
  N22 ....45 DN53
Adams Pl, N7 *off George's Rd* .65 DM64
Adamsrill Cl, Enf. EN1 ...30 DR44
Adamsrill Rd, SE26 ......123 DY91
Adams Rd, N17 ....46 DS54
  Beckenham BR3 ....143 DY99
Adams Row, W1 ....198 G1
  off Regency Way 106 EY83
Adam St, WC2 ....200 A1
Adams Wk, Kings.T. KT1 ..138 CL96
Adams Way, Croy. CR0 ...142 DT100
Adastral Est, NW9 ....42 CS53
Ada St, E8 ....84 DV67
Adcock Wk, Orp. BR6
  off Borkwood Pk 163 ET105
Adderley Gdns, SE9 .....125 EN91
Adderley Gro, SW11
  off Culmstock Rd 120 DG85
Adderley Rd, Har. HA3 ...41 CF53
Adderley St, E14 ....85 EC72
ADDINGTON, Croy. 161 DZ106
Addington Border, Croy.
  CR0 ....161 DY110
Addington Ct, SW14 .....98 CR83
Addington Dr, N12 ....44 DC51
Addington Gro, SE26 ....123 DY91
Addington Rd, E3 ....85 EA69
  E16 ....86 EE70
  N4 ....65 DN58
  Croydon CR0 ....141 DN102
  South Croydon CR2 ....160 DU111
  West Wickham BR4 ....144 EE103
Addington Sq, SE5 ......102 DQ80
Addington St, SE1 ......200 C5
⬥ Addington Village 161 EA107
Addington Village Rd, Croy.
  CR0 ....161 EA106
Addis Cl, Enf. EN3 ......31 DX39
ADDISCOMBE, Croy. 142 DT102
  ⬥ Addiscombe 142 DU102
Addiscombe Av, Croy. CR0 .142 DU101
Addiscombe Cl, Har. HA3 .61 CJ57

Addiscombe Ct Rd, Croy.
  CR0 ....142 DS102
Addiscombe Gro, Croy. CR0 .142 DR103
Addiscombe Rd, Croy. CR0 .142 DS103
  Watford WD18 ....23 BV42
Addison Av, N14 ....29 DH44
  W11 ....81 CY74
  Hounslow TW3 ....96 CC81
Addison Br Pl, W14 ......99 CZ77
Addison Cl, Cat. CR3 .....176 DR122
  Northwood HA6 ....39 BU53
  Orpington BR5 ....145 EQ100
Addison Ct, Epp. CM16
  off Centre Dr 18 EU31
Addison Cres, W14 ......99 CY76
Addison Dr, SE12
  off Eltham Rd 124 EH85
Addison Gdns, W14 ......99 CX76
  Grays RM17
  off Palmers Dr 110 GC77
  Surbiton KT5 ....138 CM98
Addison Gro, W4 ....98 CS76
Addison Pl, W11 ....81 CY74
  Southall UB1
  off Longford Av 78 CA73
Addison Rd, E11 ....68 EG58
  E17 ....67 EB57
  SE25 ....142 DU98
  W14 ....99 CZ76
  Bromley BR2 ....144 EJ99
  Caterham CR3 ....176 DR121
  Enfield EN3 ....30 DW39
  Ilford IG6 ....49 EQ53
  Teddington TW11 ......117 CH93
  Woking GU21
  off Chertsey Rd 167 AZ117
Addison's Cl, Croy. CR0 ..143 DZ103
Addison Way, NW11 .....63 CZ56
  Hayes UB3 ....77 BU72
  Northwood HA6 ....39 BT53
ADDLESTONE 152 BJ106
  ⇌ Addlestone 152 BK105
ADDLESTONE MOOR, Add. .134 BG103
Addlestone Moor, Add.
  KT15 ....134 BJ103
Addlestone Pk, Add. KT15 .152 BH106
Addlestone Rd, Add. KT15 .152 BL105
Addle St, EC2 ....197 J7
Adecroft Way, W.Mol. KT8 .136 CC97
Adela Av, N.Mal. KT3 ....139 CV99
Adelaide Av, SE4 ....103 DZ84
Adelaide Cl, Enf. EN1 ...30 DT38
  Stanmore HA7 ....41 CG49
Adelaide Cotts, W7 .....97 CF75
Adelaide Gdns, Rom. RM6 .70 EY57
Adelaide Gro, W12 ......81 CU74
Adelaide Pl, Wey. KT13 ..153 BR105
Adelaide Rd, E10 ....67 EB62
  NW3 ....82 DD66
  SW18 *off Putney Br Rd* .120 DA85
  W13 ....79 CG74
  Ashford TW15 ....114 BK92
  Chislehurst BR7 ....125 EP92
  Hounslow TW5 ....96 BY81
  Ilford IG1 ....69 EP61
  Richmond TW9 ....98 CM84
  Southall UB2 ....96 BY77
  Surbiton KT6 ....138 CL99
  Teddington TW11 ......117 CF93
  Tilbury RM18 ....111 GF81
  Walton-on-Thames KT12 .135 BU104
Adelaide St, WC2 ....199 P1
Adelaide Ter, Brent. TW8 .97 CK78
Adelaide Wk, SW9
  off Sussex Wk 101 DN84
Adela St, W10 *off Kensal Rd* .81 CY70
Adelina Gro, E1 ....84 DW71
Adelina Ms, SW12
  off King's Av 121 DK88
Adeline Pl, WC1 ....195 N7
Adeliza Cl, Bark. IG11
  off North St 87 EP66
Adelphi Ct, SE16
  off Poolmans St 103 DX75
Adelphi Cres, Hayes UB4 .77 BT69
  Hornchurch RM12 .....71 FG61
Adelphi Gdns, Slou. SL1 ..92 AS75
Adelphi Rd, Epsom KT17 .156 CR113
Adelphi Ter, WC2 ....200 A1
Adelphi Way, Hayes UB4 ..77 BT69
Adeney Cl, W6 ....99 CX79
Aden Gro, N16 ....66 DR63
Adenmore Rd, SE6 ......123 EA87
Aden Rd, Enf. EN3 ......31 DY42
  Ilford IG1 ....69 EP59
Aden Ter, N16 ....66 DR63
Adie Rd, W6 ....99 CW76
Adine Rd, E13 ....86 EH70
Adler Ind Est, Hayes UB3 .95 BR75
Adler St, E1 ....84 DU72
Adley St, E5 ....67 DY64
Adlington Cl, N18 ....46 DR50
Admaston Rd, SE18 .....105 EQ80
Admiral Cl, Orp. BR5 ....146 EX98
Admiral Ct, NW4
  off Barton Cl 63 CU57
Admiral Ho, Tedd. TW11
  off Twickenham Rd 117 CG91
Admiral Pl, SE16 ....203 L2
Admirals Cl, E18 ....68 EH56
Admiral Seymour Rd, SE9 .105 EM84
Admiral St, SW10 ....100 DD81
Admiral Stirling Ct, Wey. KT13 .152 BM105
Admiral St, SE8 ....103 EA82
Admirals Wk, NW3 ......64 DC62
  Coulsdon CR5 ....175 DM120
  Greenhithe DA9 ....129 FV85
Admirals Way, E14 ......204 A4
★ Admiralty Arch, SW1 ...199 N2
Admiralty Cl, SE8
  off Reginald Sq 103 EA80
Admiralty Rd, Tedd. TW11 .117 CF93
Admiral Wk, W9 ....82 DA71
Adnams Wk, Rain. RM13
  off Lovell Wk 89 FF65

Adolf St, SE6 . . . . .123 EB91
Adolphus Rd, N4 . . . . .65 DP61
Adolphus St, SE8 . . . . .103 DZ80
Adomar Rd, Dag. RM8 . . . . . .70 EX62
Adpar St, W2 . . . . .82 DD70
off North Circular Rd 63 CV60
Adrian Av, NW2
Adrian Cl, Uxb. (Hare.) UB9 . .38 BK53
Adrian Ms, SW10 . . . . .100 DB79
Adrian Rd, Abb.L. WD5 . . . . . .7 BS31
Adrians Wk, Slou. SL2 . . . . . .74 AT74
Adrienne Av, Sthl. UB1 . . . . . .78 BZ70
Adstock Ms, Ger.Cr. (Chal.St.P.)
SL9 *off Church La* AX53
Adstock Way, Grays (Bad.Dene)
RM17 . . . . .110 FZ77
Advance Rd, SE27 . . . . .122 DQ91
Advent Ct, Wdf.Grn. IG8
off Wood La 48 EF50
Advent Way, N18 . . . . .47 DX50
Advice Av, Grays RM16 . . . . .110 GA75
Adys Rd, SE15 . . . . .102 DT83
Aerodrome Rd, NW4 . . . . .63 CT55
NW9 . . . . .43 CT54
Aerodrome Way, Houns. TW5 .96 BW79
Aeroville, NW9 . . . . .42 CS54
Affleck St, N1 . . . . .196 C1
Afghan Rd, SW11 . . . . .100 DE82
Africa Cen, WC2
off King St 195 P10
Africa Ho, SE16 . . . . .202 E6
Afton Dr, S.Ock. RM15 . . . . . .91 FV72
Agamemnon Rd, NW6 . . . . . . .63 CZ64
Agar Cl, Surb. KT6 . . . . .138 CM103
Agar Gro, NW1 . . . . .83 DJ66
Agar Gro Est, NW1 . . . . .83 DK66
Agar Pl, NW1 . . . . .83 DJ66
Agars Plough, Slou. (Datchet)
SL3 . . . . .92 AU79
Agar St, WC2 . . . . .199 P1
Agate Cl, E16 . . . . .86 EK72
Agate Rd, W6 . . . . .99 CW76
Agates La, Ashtd. KT21 . . . . .171 CK118
Agatha Cl, E1 . . . . .202 E2
Agaton Rd, SE9 . . . . .125 EQ89
Agave Rd, NW2 . . . . .63 CW63
Agdon St, EC1 . . . . .196 F4
Agincourt Rd, NW3 . . . . .64 DF63
Agister Rd, Chig. IG7 . . . . . . .50 EU50
Agnes Av, Ilf. IG1 . . . . .69 EP63
Agnes Cl, E6 . . . . .87 EN73
Agnesfield Cl, N12 . . . . .44 DE51
Agnes Gdns, Dag. RM8 . . . . . .70 EX63
Agnes Rd, W3 . . . . .81 CT74
Agnes Scott Ct, Wey. KT13
off Palace Dr 135 BP104
Agnes St, E14 . . . . .85 DZ72
Agnew Rd, SE23 . . . . .123 DX87
Agricola Cl, SE13 *off Parnell Rd* .85 DZ67
Agricola Pl, Enf. EN1 . . . . .30 DT43
Aidan Cl, Dag. RM8 . . . . .70 EY63
Aileen Wk, E15 . . . . .86 EF66
Ailsa Av, Twick. TW1 . . . . . . .117 CG85
Ailsa Rd, Twick. TW1 . . . . . . .117 CH85
Ailsa St, E14 . . . . .85 EC71
AIMES GREEN, Wal.Abb. 16 EF28
Ainger Ms, NW3
off Ainger Rd 82 DF66
Ainger Rd, NW3 . . . . .82 DF66
Ainsdale Cl, Orp. BR6 . . . . . .145 ER102
Ainsdale Cres, Pnr. HA5 . . . . .60 CA55
Ainsdale Dr, SE1 . . . . .102 DU78
Ainsdale Rd, W5 . . . . .79 CK70
Watford WD19 . . . . .40 BW48
Ainsdale Way, Wok. GU21 . . .166 AU118
Ainsley Av, Rom. RM7 . . . . . .71 FB58
Ainsley Cl, N9 . . . . .46 DS46
Ainsley St, E2 . . . . .84 DV69
Ainslie Wk, SW12 . . . . .121 DH87
Ainslie Wd Cres, E4 . . . . .47 EB50
Ainslie Wd Gdns, E4 . . . . . . .47 EB49
Ainslie Wd Rd, E4 . . . . .47 EA50
Ainsty Est, SE16 . . . . .203 H5
Ainsworth Cl, NW2 . . . . .63 CU62
SE15 *off Lyndhurst Gro* . .102 DS82
Ainsworth Rd, E9 . . . . .84 DW66
Croydon CR0 . . . . .141 DP103
Ainsworth Way, NW8 . . . . . . .82 DC67
Aintree Av, E6 . . . . .86 EL67
Aintree Cl, Grav. DA12 . . . . .131 GH90
Slough (Colnbr.) SL3 . . . . . .93 BE81
Uxbridge UB8
off Craig Dr 77 BP72
Aintree Cres, Ilf. IG6 . . . . .49 EQ54
Aintree Est, SW6
off Dawes Rd 99 CY80
Aintree Gro, Upmin. RM14 . . .72 FM62
Aintree Rd, Grnf. UB6 . . . . . . .79 CH68
Aintree St, SW6 . . . . .99 CY80
Aird Ct, Hmptn. TW12
off Oldfield Rd 136 BZ95
Airdrie Cl, N1 . . . . .83 DM66
Hayes UB4 *off Glencoe Rd* .78 BY71
Airedale Av, W4 . . . . .99 CT77
Airedale Av S, W4
off Netheravon Rd S 99 CT78
Airedale Cl, Dart. DA2 . . . . . .128 FQ88
Airedale Rd, SW12 . . . . .120 DF87
W5 .97 CJ76
Aire Dr, S.Ock. RM15 . . . . . . .91 FV70
Airey Neave Ct, Grays RM17 .110 GA75
Airfield Way, Horn. RM12 . . . .89 FH63
Watford WD25 *off Ashfields* .7 BU32
★ Air Forces Mem, Egh. (Runny.)
TW20 . . . . .112 AX91
Airlie Gdns, W8 . . . . .100 DA76
Ilford IG1 . . . . .69 EP60
Air Links Ind Est, Houns. TW5 .96 BW78
Air Pk Way, Felt. TW13 . . . . .115 BV89
Airport Ind Est, West. TN16 . .162 EK114
Airport Roundabout, E16
off Connaught Br 86 EK74
Airport Way, Stai. TW19 . . . . .93 BF84
Air St, W1 . . . . .199 L1
Airthrie Rd, Ilf. IG3 . . . . .70 EV61
Aisgill Av, W14 . . . . .99 CZ78
Aisher Rd, SE28 . . . . .88 EW73

Aisher Way, Sev. (Rvrhd.)
TN13 . . . . .190 FE121
Aislibie Rd, SE12 . . . . .104 EE84
Aiten Pl, W6 *off Standish Rd* .99 CU77
Aitken Cl, E8 *off Pownall Rd* .84 DU67
Mitcham CR4 . . . . .140 DF101
Aitken Rd, SE6 . . . . .123 EB89
Barnet EN5 . . . . .27 CW43
Ajax Av, NW9 . . . . .62 CS55
Ajax Rd, NW6 . . . . .64 DA64
Akabusi Cl, Croy. CR0 . . . . . .142 DU100
Akehurst La, Sev. TN13 . . . . .191 FJ125
Akehurst St, SW15 . . . . .119 CU86
Akenside Rd, NW3 . . . . .64 DD64
Akerman Rd, SW9 . . . . .101 DP82
Surbiton KT6 . . . . .137 CJ100
Akers Way, Rick. (Chorl.) WD3 .21 BD40
Alabama St, SE18 . . . . .105 ER80
Alacross Rd, W5 . . . . .97 CJ75
Alamein Gdns, Dart. DA2 . . . .129 FR87
Alamein Rd, Swans. DA10 . . .129 FX86
Alanbrooke, Grav. DA12 . . . .131 GJ87
Alan Cl, Dart. DA1 . . . . .108 FJ84
Alandale Dr, Pnr. HA5 . . . . . . .59 BV54
Aland Ct, SE16 . . . . .203 L6
Alander Ms, E17 . . . . .67 EC56
Alan Dr, Barn. EN5 . . . . .27 CY44
Alan Gdns, Rom. RM7 . . . . . . .70 FA59
Alan Hocken Way, E15 . . . . . .86 EE68
Alan Rd, SW19 . . . . .119 CY92
Alanthus Cl, SE12 . . . . .124 EF86
Alan Way, Slou. (Geo.Grn.)
SL3 . . . . .74 AY72
Alaska St, SE1 . . . . .200 D3
Alba Cl, Hayes UB4
off Ramulis Dr 78 BX70
Albacore Cres, SE13 . . . . . . .123 EB86
Alba Gdns, NW11 . . . . .63 CY58
Albain Cres, Ashf. TW15 . . . .114 BL89
Alban Cres, Borwd. WD6 . . . . .26 CP39
Dartford (Fngthm.) DA4 . . .148 FN102
Alban Highwalk, EC2
off London Wall 84 DQ71
Albans Vw, Wat. WD25 . . . . . .7 BV33
Albany, W11 . . . . .199 K1
Albany, The, Wdf.Grn. IG8 . . . .48 EF49
Albany Cl, N15 . . . . .65 DP56
SW14 . . . . .98 CP84
Bexley DA5 . . . . .126 EW87
Bushey WD23 . . . . .25 CD44
Esher KT10 . . . . .154 CA109
Reigate RH2 . . . . .184 DA132
Uxbridge UB10 . . . . .58 BN64
Albany Ct, E4
off Chelwood Cl 31 EB44
Epping CM16 . . . . .17 ET30
Albany Ctyd, W1 . . . . .199 L1
Albany Cres, Edg. HA8 . . . . . .42 CN52
Esher (Clay.) KT10 . . . . . . .155 CE107
Albany Mans, SW11 . . . . . . .100 DE80
Albany Ms, N1
off Barnsbury Pk 83 DN66
SE5 *off Albany Rd* 102 DQ79
Bromley BR1 . . . . .124 EG93
Kingston upon Thames KT2
off Albany Pk Rd 117 CK93
St. Albans AL2
off North Orbital Rd 8 CA27
Sutton SM1
off Camden Rd 158 DB106
⇌ Albany Park 126 EX89
Albany Pk, Slou. (Colnbr.)
SL3 . . . . .93 BD81
Albany Pk Av, Enf. EN3 . . . . . .30 DW39
Albany Pk Rd, Kings.T. KT2 . .118 CL93
Leatherhead KT22 . . . . . . .171 CG119
Albany Pas, Rich. TW10 . . . . .118 CM85
Albany Pl, N7 *off Benwell Rd* .65 DN63
Brentford TW8
off Albany Rd 98 CL79
Egham TW20 . . . . .113 BA91
Albany Rd, E10 . . . . .67 EA59
E12 . . . . .68 EK63
E17 . . . . .67 DY58
N4 .65 DM58
N18 . . . . .46 DV50
SE5 . . . . .102 DR79
SW19 . . . . .120 DB92
W13 . . . . .79 CH73
Belvedere DA17 . . . . .106 EZ79
Bexley DA5 . . . . .126 EW87
Brentford TW8 . . . . .97 CK79
Chislehurst BR7 . . . . .125 EP92
Enfield EN3 . . . . .31 DX37
Hornchurch RM12 . . . . .71 FG60
New Malden KT3 . . . . .138 CR98
Richmond TW10
off Albert Rd 118 CM85
Romford RM6 . . . . .70 EZ58
Walton-on-Thames KT12 . .154 BX105
Windsor (Old Wind.) SL4 . .112 AU85
Albanys, The, Reig. RH2 . . . .184 DA131
Albany St, NW1 . . . . .83 DH68
Albany Ter, NW1
off Marylebone Rd 83 DH70
Albatross Gdns, S.Croy. CR2 .161 DX111
Albatross St, SE18 . . . . .105 ES80
Albatross Way, SE16 . . . . . . .103 DX75
Albemarle, SW19 . . . . .119 CX89
Albemarle App, Ilf. IG2 . . . . . .69 EP58
Albemarle Av, Pot.B. EN6 . . . .12 DB33
Twickenham TW2 . . . . .116 CB88
Waltham Cross (Chsht.)
EN8 . . . . .14 DW28
Albemarle Gdns, Grays RM17 .110 GA75
Ilford IG2 . . . . .69 EP58
New Malden KT3 . . . . .138 CR98
Albemarle Pk, Stan. HA7
off Marsh La 41 CJ50
Albemarle Rd, Barn. EN4 . . . . .44 DE45
Beckenham BR3 . . . . .143 EB95
Albemarle St, W1 . . . . .199 J1
Albemarle Way, EC1 . . . . . . .196 F5
Alberon Gdns, NW11 . . . . .63 CZ56

Alberta Av, Sutt. SM1 . . . . . .157 CY105
Alberta Est, SE17 . . . . .200 G10
Alberta Rd, Enf. EN1 . . . . .30 DT44
Erith DA8 . . . . .107 FC81
Alberta St, SE17 . . . . .200 F10
Albert Av, E4 . . . . .47 EA49
SW8 . . . . .101 DM80
Chertsey KT16 . . . . .134 BG97
Albert Br, SW3 . . . . .100 DE79
SW11 . . . . .100 DE79
Albert Br Rd, SW11 . . . . .100 DE80
Albert Carr Gdns, SW16 . . . .121 DL92
Albert Cl, E9 *off Northiam St* .84 DV67
N22 . . . . .45 DK53
Grays RM16 . . . . .110 GC76
Slough SL1 *off Albert St* . .92 AT76
Albert Ct, SW7 . . . . .100 DD75
off Prince Consort Rd . . .100 DD75
Albert Cres, E4 . . . . .47 EA49
Albert Dr, SW19 . . . . .119 CY89
Woking GU21 . . . . .151 BD111
Albert Embk, SE1 . . . . .101 DL78
Albert Gdns, E1 . . . . .85 DX72
Albert Gate, SW1 . . . . .198 E4
Albert Gro, SW20 . . . . .139 CX95
★ Albert Hall Mans, SW7
off Kensington Gore 100 DD75
Albertine Cl, Epsom KT17 . . .173 CV116
Albert Mans, SW11
off Albert Br Rd 100 DF81
★ Albert Mem, SW7 . . . . . . .100 DD75
Albert Ms, E14 *off Narrow St* .85 DY73
W8 *off Victoria Gro* 100 DC76
Albert Murray Cl, Grav. DA12
off Armoury Dr 131 GJ87
Albert Pl, N3 . . . . .44 DA53
N17 *off High Rd* 66 DT55
W8 . . . . .100 DB75
Albert Rd, E10 . . . . .67 EC65
E16 . . . . .86 EL74
E17 . . . . .67 EA57
E18 . . . . .68 EH55
N4 .65 DM60
N15 . . . . .66 DS58
N22 . . . . .45 DJ53
NW4 . . . . .63 CX56
NW6 . . . . .81 CZ68
NW7 . . . . .43 CT50
SE9 . . . . .124 EL90
SE20 . . . . .123 DX94
SE25 . . . . .142 DU98
W5 .79 CH70
Addlestone KT15 . . . . .134 BK104
Ashford TW15 . . . . .114 BM92
Ashtead KT21 . . . . .172 CM118
Barnet EN4 . . . . .28 DC42
Belvedere DA17 . . . . .106 EZ78
Bexley DA5 . . . . .126 FA86
Bromley BR2 . . . . .144 EK99
Buckhurst Hill IG9 . . . . .48 EK47
Dagenham RM8 . . . . .70 FA60
Dartford DA2 . . . . .128 FJ90
Egham (Eng.Grn.) TW20 . . .112 AX93
Epsom KT17 . . . . .157 CT113
Hampton (Hmptn.H.)
TW12 . . . . .116 CC92
Harrow HA2 . . . . .60 CC55
Hayes UB3 . . . . .95 BS76
Hounslow TW3 . . . . .96 CA84
Ilford IG1 . . . . .69 EP62
Kingston upon Thames
KT1 . . . . .138 CM96
Mitcham CR4 . . . . .140 DF97
New Malden KT3 . . . . .139 CT98
Orpington (Chels.) BR6 . . .164 EU106
Orpington (St.M.Cray)
BR5 . . . . .146 EV100
Redhill RH1 . . . . .185 DJ129
Richmond TW10 . . . . .118 CL85
Romford RM1 . . . . .71 FF57
Southall UB2 . . . . .96 BX76
Sutton SM1 . . . . .158 DD106
Swanscombe DA10 . . . . . .130 FZ86
Teddington TW11 . . . . .117 CF93
Twickenham TW1 . . . . .117 CF88
Warlingham CR6 . . . . .177 DZ117
West Drayton UB7 . . . . .76 BL74
Albert Rd Est, Belv. DA17 . . .106 EZ78
Albert Rd N, Reig. RH2 . . . . .183 CZ133
Watford WD17 . . . . .23 BV41
Albert Rd S, Wat. WD17 . . . . .23 BV41
Albert Sq, E15 . . . . .68 EE64
SW8 . . . . .101 DM80
Albert St, N12 . . . . .44 DC50
NW1 . . . . .83 DH67
Brentwood CM14 . . . . .54 FW50
Slough SL1 . . . . .92 AT76
Albert Ter, NW1 . . . . .82 DG67
NW10 . . . . .80 CR67
Buckhurst Hill IG9 . . . . .48 EK47
Albert Ter Ms, NW1
off Regents Pk Rd 82 DG67
Albert Way, SE15 . . . . .102 DV80
Albion Av, N10 . . . . .44 DG53
SW8 . . . . .101 DK82
Albion Bldgs, EC1
off Bartholomew Cl 84 DQ71
Albion Cl, W2 . . . . .194 C10
Romford RM7 . . . . .71 FD58
Slough SL2 . . . . .74 AU74
Albion Cres, Ch.St.G. HP8 . . . .36 AV48
Albion Dr, E8 . . . . .84 DT66
Albion Est, SE16 . . . . .203 H5
Albion Gdns, W6 . . . . .99 CV77
Albion Gro, N16 . . . . .66 DS63
Albion Hill, SE13 . . . . .183 EB82
Loughton IG10 . . . . .32 EJ43
Albion Ho, Slou. SL3 . . . . .93 BB78
Albion Ms, N1 . . . . .83 DN67
NW6 *off Kilburn High Rd* . .81 CZ66
W2 . . . . .194 C9
W6 *off Galena Rd* 99 CV77
Albion Par, N16 *off Albion Rd* .66 DR63
Gravesend DA12 . . . . .131 GK86
Albion Pl, EC1 . . . . .196 F6
off Lower Sta Rd 127 FE86

Albion Pl, SE25 *off High St* ..142 DU97
W6 .99 CV77
Albion Rd, E17 . . . . .67 EC55
N16 . . . . .66 DR63
N17 . . . . .46 DT54
Bexleyheath DA6 . . . . .106 EZ84
Chalfont St. Giles HP8 . . . . .36 AV47
Gravesend DA12 . . . . .131 GJ87
Hayes UB3 . . . . .77 BS72
Hounslow TW3 . . . . .96 CA84
Kingston upon Thames
KT2 . . . . .138 CQ95
Sutton SM2 . . . . .158 DD107
Twickenham TW2 . . . . .117 CE88
Albion Sq, E8 . . . . .84 DT66
Albion St, SE16 . . . . .202 G5
W2 . . . . .194 C9
Croydon CR0 . . . . .141 DP102
Albion Ter, E8 . . . . .84 DT66
Gravesend DA12 . . . . .131 GJ86
Albion Vil Rd, SE26 . . . . .122 DW90
Albion Wk, EC1 . . . . .197 H7
SE13 . . . . .103 EC84
Wembley HA9
off North End Rd 62 CP62
Albright Ind Est, Rain. RM13 . .89 FF71
Albrighton Rd, SE22 . . . . . . .102 DS83
Albuhera Cl, Enf. EN2 . . . . . . .29 DN39
Albury Av, Bexh. DA7 . . . . . . .106 EY82
Isleworth TW7 . . . . .97 CF80
Sutton SM2 . . . . .157 CW109
Albury Cl, Cher. (Longcr.)
KT16 . . . . .132 AU104
Hampton TW12 . . . . .116 CA93
Albury Ct, Sutt. SM1
off Ripley Gdns 158 DC105
Albury Dr, Pnr. HA5 . . . . .40 BX52
Albury Gro Rd, Wal.Cr. (Chsht.)
EN8 . . . . .15 DX30
Albury Ms, E12 . . . . .68 EJ60
Albury Ride, Wal.Cr. (Chsht.)
EN8 . . . . .15 DX31
Albury Rd, Chess. KT9 . . . . . .156 CL106
Redhill RH1 . . . . .185 DJ129
Walton-on-Thames KT12 . .153 BS107
Albury St, SE8 . . . . .103 EA79
Albury Wk, Wal.Cr. (Chsht.)
EN8 . . . . .15 DX32
Albyfield, Brom. BR1 . . . . . . .145 EM97
Albyn Rd, SE8 . . . . .103 EA81
Albyns Cl, Rain. RM13 . . . . . . .89 FG66
Albyns La, Rom. RM4 . . . . . . .35 FC40
Alcester Cres, E5 . . . . .66 DV61
Alcester Rd, Wall. SM6 . . . . . .159 DH105
Alcock Cl, Wall. SM6 . . . . . . .159 DK108
Alcock Rd, Houns. TW5 . . . . . .96 BX80
Alcocks Cl, Tad. KT20 . . . . . .173 CY120
Alcocks La, Tad. (Kgswd.)
KT20 . . . . .173 CY120
Alconbury Rd, E5 . . . . .66 DU61
Alcorn Cl, Sutt. SM3 . . . . . . .140 DA103
Alcott Cl, W7
off Westcott Cres 79 CF71
Alcuin Ct, Stan. HA7
off Old Ch La 41 CJ52
ALDBOROUGH HATCH, Ilf. . .69 ES55
Aldborough Rd, Dag. RM10 . .89 FC65
Upminster RM14 . . . . .72 FM61
Aldborough Rd N, Ilf. IG2 . . . .69 ET57
Aldborough Rd S, Ilf. IG3 . . . .69 ES60
Aldborough Spur, Slou. SL1 . .74 AS72
Aldbourne Rd, W12 . . . . .81 CT74
Aldbridge St, SE17 . . . . .201 N10
Aldburgh Ms, W1 . . . . .194 G8
Aldbury Av, Wem. HA9 . . . . . .80 CP66
Aldbury Cl, Wat. WD25 . . . . . .24 BX36
Aldbury Ms, N9 . . . . .46 DR45
Aldbury Rd, Rick. (Mill End)
WD3 . . . . .37 BF45
Aldebert Ter, SW8 . . . . .101 DL80
Aldeburgh Cl, E5
off Southwold Rd 66 DV61
Aldeburgh Pl, SE10 . . . . .205 M9
Woodford Green IG8 . . . . . . .48 EG49
Aldeburgh St, SE10 . . . . .205 M10
Alden Av, E15 . . . . .86 EF69
ALDENHAM, Wat. 24 CB38
Aldenham Av, Rad. WD7 . . . . .25 CG36
★ Aldenham Country Pk, Borwd.
(Elstree) WD6 . . . . .25 CH43
Aldenham Dr, Uxb. UB8 . . . . . .77 BP70
Aldenham Gro, Rad. WD7 . . . . .9 CH34
Aldenham Rd, Borwd. (Elstree)
WD6 . . . . .25 CH44
Bushey WD23 . . . . .24 BZ42
Radlett WD7 . . . . .25 CG35
Watford WD19 . . . . .24 BX44
Watford (Let.Hth.) WD25 . . .25 CE39
Aldenham St, NW1 . . . . .195 L1
Aldenholme, Wey. KT13 . . . . .153 BS107
Aldensley Rd, W6 . . . . .99 CV76
Alder Av, Upmin. RM14 . . . . . .72 FM63
Alderbourne La, Iver SL0 . . . . .57 BA64
Slough (Fulmer) SL3 . . . . . .56 AX63
Alderbrook Rd, SW12 . . . . . . .121 DH86
Alderbury Rd, SW13 . . . . .99 CU79
Slough SL3 . . . . .93 AZ75
Alderbury Rd W, Slou. SL3 . . .93 AZ75
Alder Cl, SE15 . . . . .102 DT79
Egham (Eng.Grn.) TW20 . . .112 AY92
St. Albans (Park St.) AL2 . . .8 CB28
Alder Gro, NW2 . . . . .63 CV61
off Bath Rd 96 BY82
Aldergrove Gdns, Houns. TW3
off Airfield Way 90 FJ65
Alderholt Way, SE15
off Daniel Gdns 102 DT80
Alderman Av, Bark. IG11 . . . . .88 EU69
Aldermanbury, EC2 . . . . .197 J8
Aldermanbury Sq, EC2 . . . . .197 J7
Alderman Cl, Dart. DA1

Column 5 (Ado - Ald section)

Alderman Judge Mall, Kings.T.
KT1 *off Eden St* 138 CL96
Aldermans Hill, N13 . . . . .45 DL49
Alderman's Wk, EC2 . . . . . . .197 M7
Aldermary Rd, Brom. BR1 . . .144 EG95
Alder Ms, N19 *off Bredgar Rd* .65 DJ61
Aldermoor Rd, SE6 . . . . .123 DZ90
Alderney Av, Houns. TW5 . . . .96 CB80
Alderney Gdns, Nthlt. UB5 . . .78 BZ66
Alderney Ms, SE1 . . . . .201 K6
Alderney Rd, E1 . . . . .85 DX70
Erith DA8 . . . . .107 FG80
Alderney St, SW1 . . . . .199 J10
Alder Rd, SW14 . . . . .98 CR83
Iver SL0 . . . . .75 BC68
Sidcup DA14 . . . . .125 ET90
Uxbridge (Denh.) UB9 . . . . .76 BJ65
Alders, The, N21 . . . . .29 DN44
Feltham TW13 . . . . .116 BY91
Hounslow TW5 . . . . .96 BZ79
West Byfleet KT14 . . . . . . .152 BJ112
West Wickham BR4 . . . . . .143 EB102
Alders Av, Wdf.Grn. IG8 . . . . .48 EE51
ALDERSBROOK, E12 . . . . . . .68 EH61
Aldersbrook Av, Enf. EN1 . . . .30 DS40
Aldersbrook Dr, Kings.T. KT2 .118 CM93
Aldersbrook La, E12 . . . . .69 EM62
Aldersbrook Rd, E11 . . . . .68 EH61
E12 . . . . .68 EK62
Alders Cl, E11
off Aldersbrook Rd 68 EH61
W5 .97 CK76
Edgware HA8 . . . . .42 CQ50
Aldersey Gdns, Bark. IG11 . . .87 ER65
Aldersford Cl, SE4 . . . . .123 DX85
Aldersgate St, EC1 . . . . .197 H8
Alders Gro, E.Mol. KT8
off Esher Rd 137 CD99
Aldersgrove, Wal.Abb. EN9
off Roundhills 16 EE34
Aldersgrove Av, SE9 . . . . . . .124 EJ90
Aldershot Rd, NW6 . . . . .81 CZ67
Alderside Wk, Egh. (Eng.Grn.)
TW20 . . . . .112 AY92
Aldersmead Av, Croy. CR0 . .143 DX100
Aldersmead Rd, Beck. BR3 . .123 DY94
Alderson Pl, Sthl. UB2 . . . . . .78 CC74
Alderson St, W10
off Kensal Rd 81 CY70
Alders Rd, Edg. HA8 . . . . .42 CQ50
Reigate RH2 . . . . .184 DB132
Alderstead Heath, Red. RH1 .175 DK124
Alderstead Heath Caravan Club,
Red. RH1 . . . . .175 DK123
Alderstead La, Red. RH1 . . . .185 DK126
Alderton Cl, NW10 . . . . .62 CR62
Brentwood CM15 . . . . .54 FV43
Loughton IG10 . . . . .33 EN42
Alderton Cres, NW4 . . . . .63 CV57
Alderton Hall La, Loug. IG10 . .33 EN42
Alderton Hill, Loug. IG10 . . . . .32 EL43
Alderton Ms, Loug. IG10
off Alderton Hall La 33 EN42
Alderton Ri, Loug. IG10 . . . . . .33 EN42
Alderton Rd, SE24 . . . . .102 DQ83
Croydon CR0 . . . . .142 DT101
Alderton Way, NW4 . . . . .63 CV57
Loughton IG10 . . . . .33 EM43
Alderville Rd, SW6 . . . . .99 CZ82
Alder Wk, Ilf. IG1 . . . . .69 EQ64
Watford WD25
off Aspen Pk Dr 23 BV35
Alder Way, Swan. BR8 . . . . . .147 FD96
Alderwick Dr, Houns. TW3 . . .97 CD83
Alderwood Cl, Cat. CR3 . . . .186 DS125
Romford (Abridge) RM4 . . . .34 EV41
Alderwood Dr, Rom. (Abridge)
RM4 . . . . .34 EV41
Alderwood Rd, SE9 . . . . .125 ER86
Aldford St, W1 . . . . .198 F2
⊖ Aldgate 197 P8
Aldgate, EC3 . . . . .197 P9
Aldgate Av, E1 . . . . .197 P8
Aldgate Barrs Shop Cen, E1
off Whitechapel High St . . .84 DT72
⊖ Aldgate East 84 DT72
Aldgate High St, EC3 . . . . . . .197 P9
Aldham Dr, S.Ock. RM15 . . . . .91 FW71
Aldin Av N, Slou. SL1 . . . . . . .92 AV75
Aldin Av S, Slou. SL1 . . . . . . .92 AU75
Aldine Ct, W12 *off Aldine St* .81 CW74
Aldine Pl, W12
off Uxbridge Rd 81 CW74
Aldine St, W12 . . . . .99 CW75
Aldingham Ct, Horn. RM12
off Easedale Dr 71 FG64
Aldingham Gdns, Horn. RM12 .71 FG64
Aldington Cl, Dag. RM8 . . . . . .70 EW59
Aldington Rd, SE18 . . . . .104 EK76
Aldis Ms, SW17 *off Aldis St* .120 DE92
Enfield EN3
off Government Row 31 EA37
Aldis St, SW17 . . . . .120 DE92
Aldred Rd, NW6 . . . . .64 DA64
Aldren Rd, SW17 . . . . .120 DC90
Aldrich Cres, Croy. (New Adgtn.)
CR0 . . . . .161 EC109
Aldriche Way, E4 . . . . .47 EC51
Aldrich Gdns, Sutt. SM3 . . . .139 CZ104
Aldrich Ter, SW18
off Lidiard Rd 120 DC88
Aldridge Av, Edg. HA8 . . . . . . .42 CP48
Enfield EN3 . . . . .31 EA38
Ruislip HA4 . . . . .60 BX61
Stanmore HA7 . . . . .42 CL53
Aldridge Ri, N.Mal. KT3 . . . . .138 CS101
Aldridge Rd Vil, W11 . . . . .81 CZ71
Aldrington Rd, SW16 . . . . . . .121 DJ92
Aldsworth Cl, W9 . . . . .82 DB70
Aldwick Cl, SE9 . . . . .125 ER90
Aldwick Rd, Croy. CR0 . . . . . .141 DM104
Aldworth Gro, SE13 . . . . .123 EC86
Aldworth Rd, E15 . . . . .86 EE66

Ald - Amb

Aldwych, WC2 . . . . . .196 B10
Aldwych Av, Ilf. IG6 . . . . .69 EQ56
Aldwych Cl, Horn. RM12 . . .71 FG61
Aldwych Underpass, WC2
  off Kingsway 83 DM72
Alers Rd, Bexh. DA6 . . . . .126 EX85
Alesia Cl, N22
  off Nightingale Rd 45 DL52
Alexa Ct, W8
  off Lexham Gdns 100 DA77
Sutton SM2
  off Mulgrave Rd 158 DA107
Alexander Av, NW10 . . . . . . .81 CV66
Alexander Cl, Barn. EN4 . . . . .28 DD42
Bromley BR2 . . . . .144 EG102
Sidcup DA15 . . . . .125 ES85
Southall UB2 . . . . .78 CC74
Twickenham TW2 . . . . . . .117 CF89
Alexander Ct, Wal.Cr. (Chsht.)
EN8 . . . . .15 DX30
Alexander Cres, Cat. CR3
  off Coulsdon Rd 176 DQ122
Alexander Evans Ms, SE23
  off Sunderland Rd 123 DX88
★ Alexander Fleming Laboratory
  Mus, W2 off Praed St . .194 A8
Alexander Godley Cl, Ashtd.
KT21 . . . . .172 CM119
Alexander La, Brwd. CM13,
CM15 . . . . .55 GB44
Alexander Ms, W2
  off Alexander St 82 DB72
Alexander Pl, SW7 . . . . .198 B8
Alexander Rd, N19 . . . . .65 DL62
Bexleyheath DA7 . . . . . . .106 EX82
Chislehurst BR7 . . . . .125 EP92
Coulsdon CR5 . . . . .175 DH115
Egham TW20 . . . . .113 BB92
Greenhithe DA9 . . . . .129 FW85
St. Albans (Lon.Col.) AL2 . .9 CJ25
Alexander Sq, SW3 . . . . .198 B8
Alexander St, W2 . . . . .82 DA72
Alexanders Wk, Cat. CR3 . . . .186 DT126
Alexandra Av, N22 . . . . .45 DK53
SW11 . . . . .100 DG81
W4 . . . . .98 CR80
Harrow HA2 . . . . .60 BZ60
Southall UB1 . . . . .78 BZ73
Sutton SM1 . . . . .140 DA104
Warlingham CR6 . . . . . . .177 DZ117
Alexandra Cl, SE8 . . . . .103 DZ79
Ashford TW15
  off Alexandra Rd 115 BR94
Grays RM16 . . . . .111 GH75
Harrow HA2
  off Alexandra Av 60 CA62
Staines TW18 . . . . .114 BK93
Swanley BR8 . . . . .147 FE96
Walton-on-Thames KT12 . .135 BU103
Alexandra Cotts, SE14 . . . . . .103 DZ81
Alexandra Ct, N14 . . . . .29 DJ43
N16 off Belgrade Rd 66 DT63
Ashford TW15
  off Alexandra Rd 115 BR93
Wembley HA9 . . . . .62 CM63
Alexandra Cres, Brom. BR1 . .124 EF93
Alexandra Dr, SE19 . . . . .122 DS92
Surbiton KT5 . . . . .138 CN101
Alexandra Gdns, N10 . . . . . . .65 DH56
W4 . . . . .98 CR80
Carshalton SM5 . . . . .158 DG109
Hounslow TW3 . . . . .96 CB82
Alexandra Gro, N4 . . . . .65 DP60
N12 . . . . .44 DB50
Alexandra Ms, N2
  off Fortis Grn 64 DF55
SW19 off Alexandra Rd . . .120 DA93
★ Alexandra Palace, N22 . . . .45 DK54
⇌ Alexandra Palace 45 DL54
Alexandra Palace, N22 . . . . . .45 DK54
Alexandra Palace Way, N22 . .65 DJ55
Alexandra Pk Rd, N10 . . . . . .45 DH54
N22 . . . . .45 DK54
Alexandra Pl, NW8 . . . . .82 DC67
SE25 . . . . .142 DR99
Croydon CR0
  off Alexandra Rd 142 DS102
Alexandra Rd, E6 . . . . .87 EN69
E10 . . . . .67 EC62
E17 . . . . .67 DZ58
E18 . . . . .68 EH55
N8 . . . . .65 DN55
N9 . . . . .46 DV45
N10 . . . . .45 DH51
N15 . . . . .66 DR57
NW4 . . . . .63 CX56
NW8 . . . . .82 DC66
SE26 . . . . .123 DX93
SW14 . . . . .98 CR83
SW19 . . . . .119 CZ93
W4 . . . . .98 CR78
Addlestone KT15 . . . . . . .152 BK105
Ashford TW15 . . . . .115 BR94
Borehamwood WD6 . . . . . .26 CR38
Brentford TW8 . . . . .97 CK79
Brentwood CM14 . . . . .54 FW48
Croydon CR0 . . . . .142 DS102
Egham (Eng.Grn.) TW20 . .112 AW93
Enfield EN3 . . . . .31 DX42
Epsom KT17 . . . . .157 CT113
Erith DA8 . . . . .107 FF79
Gravesend DA12 . . . . .131 GL87
Hounslow TW3 . . . . .96 CB82
Kings Langley WD4 . . . . . . .6 BN29
Kings Langley (Chipper.)
WD4 . . . . .6 BG30
Kingston upon Thames
KT2 . . . . .118 CN94
Mitcham CR4 . . . . .120 DE94
Rainham RM13 . . . . .89 FF67
Richmond TW9 . . . . .98 CM82
Rickmansworth (Sarratt)
WD3 . . . . .22 BG36

Alexandra Rd, Rom. RM1 . . . .71 FF58
Romford (Chad.Hth.) RM6 . .70 EX58
Thames Ditton KT7 . . . . . .137 CF99
Tilbury RM18 . . . . .111 GF82
Twickenham TW1 . . . . . . .117 CJ86
Uxbridge UB8 . . . . .76 BK68
Warlingham CR6 . . . . . . .177 DY117
Watford WD17 . . . . .23 BU40
Westerham (Bigg.H.) TN16 .178 EH119
Alexandra Sq, Mord. SM4 . . .140 DA99
Alexandra St, E16 . . . . .86 EG71
SE14 . . . . .103 DY80
Alexandra Wk, SE19 . . . . . . .122 DS92
Alexandra Way, Epsom KT19 .156 CN112
Waltham Cross EN8 . . . . . .15 DZ34
Alexandria Rd, W13 . . . . .79 CG73
Alexis St, SE16 . . . . .202 B8
Alfan La, Dart. DA2 . . . . .127 FD92
Alfearn Rd, E5 . . . . .66 DW63
Alford Grn, Croy. (New Adgtn.)
CR0 . . . . .161 ED107
Alford Pl, N1 . . . . .197 J1
Alford Rd, SW8 . . . . .101 DK81
Erith DA8 . . . . .107 FD78
Alfoxton Av, N15 . . . . .65 DP56
Alfreda St, SW11 . . . . .101 DH81
Alfred Cl, W4 off Belmont Rd .98 CR77
Alfred Gdns, Sthl. UB1 . . . . . .78 BY73
Alfred Ms, W1 . . . . .195 M6
Alfred Pl, WC1 . . . . .195 M6
Alfred Prior Ho, E12 . . . . .69 EN63
Alfred Rd, E15 . . . . .68 EF64
Gravesend (Nthflt.) DA11 . .131 GF88
W2 . . . . .82 DA71
W3 . . . . .80 CQ74
Belvedere DA17 . . . . .106 EZ78
Brentwood CM14 . . . . .54 FX47
Buckhurst Hill IG9 . . . . . . .48 EK47
Dartford (Hawley) DA2 . . .128 FL91
Feltham TW13 . . . . .116 BW89
Gravesend DA11 . . . . .131 GH89
Kingston upon Thames
KT1 . . . . .138 CL97
South Ockendon (Aveley)
RM15 . . . . .90 FQ74
Sutton SM1 . . . . .158 DC106
Alfred's Gdns, Bark. IG11 . . . .87 ES68
Alfred St, E3 . . . . .85 DZ69
Grays RM17 . . . . .110 GC79
Alfreds Way, Bark. IG11 . . . . .87 EQ69
Alfreds Way Ind Est, Bark.
IG11 . . . . .88 EU67
Alfreton Cl, SW19 . . . . .119 CX90
Alfriston Av, Croy. CR0 . . . . .141 DL101
Harrow HA2 . . . . .60 CA58
Alfriston Cl, Dart. DA1
  off Lower Sta Rd 127 FE86
Surbiton KT5 . . . . .138 CM99
Alfriston Rd, SW11 . . . . .120 DF85
Algar Cl, Islw. TW7
  off Algar Rd 97 CG83
Stanmore HA7 . . . . .41 CF50
Algar Rd, Islw. TW7 . . . . .97 CG83
Algarve Rd, SW18 . . . . .120 DB88
Algernon Rd, NW4 . . . . .63 CU58
NW6 . . . . .82 DA67
SE13 . . . . .103 EB84
Algers Cl, Loug. IG10 . . . . . . .32 EK43
Algers Mead, Loug. IG10 . . . .32 EK43
Algers Rd, Loug. IG10 . . . . . .32 EK43
Algiers Rd, SE13 . . . . .103 EA84
Alibon Gdns, Dag. RM10 . . . .70 FA64
Alibon Rd, Dag. RM9, RM10 . .70 FA64
Alice Cl, Barn. EN5 . . . . .28 DC42
Alice Ct, SW15 off Deodar Rd .99 CZ84
Alice Gilliatt Ct, W14 . . . . . . .99 CZ79
Alice La, E3 . . . . .85 DZ67
Alice Ms, Tedd. TW11
  off Luther Rd 117 CF92
Alice Ruston Pl, Wok. GU22 . .166 AW119
Alice St, SE1 . . . . .201 M7
Alice Thompson Cl, SE12 . . . .124 EJ89
Alice Walker Cl, SE24
  off Shakespeare Rd 101 DP84
Alice Way, Houns. TW3 . . . . .96 CB84
Alicia Av, Har. HA3 . . . . .61 CH56
Alicia Cl, Har. HA3 . . . . .61 CJ56
Alicia Gdns, Har. HA3 . . . . . . .61 CH56
Alie St, E1 . . . . .84 DT72
Alington Cres, NW9 . . . . .62 CQ60
Alington Gro, Wall. SM6 . . . . .159 DJ109
Alison Cl, E6 . . . . .87 EN72
Croydon CR0
  off Shirley Oaks Rd 143 DX102
Woking GU21 . . . . .166 AY115
Aliwal Rd, SW11 . . . . .100 DE84
Alkerden La, Green. DA9 . . . .129 FW86
Swanscombe DA10 . . . . . .129 FW86
Alkerden Rd, W4 . . . . .98 CS78
Alkham Rd, N16 . . . . .66 DT61
Allan Barclay Cl, N15
  off High Rd 66 DT58
Allan Cl, N.Mal. KT3 . . . . . . .138 CR99
Allandale Av, N3 . . . . .63 CY55
Allandale Cres, Pot.B. EN6 . . .11 CY32
Allandale Pl, Orp. BR6 . . . . . .146 EX104
Allandale Rd, Enf. EN3 . . . . . .31 DX36
Hornchurch RM11 . . . . . . .71 FF59
Allan Way, W3 . . . . .80 CQ71
Allard Cl, Orp. BR5 . . . . .146 EW101
Waltham Cross (Chsht.)
EN7 . . . . .14 DT27
Allard Cres, Bushey (Bushey Hth.)
WD23 . . . . .40 CC46
Allard Gdns, SW4 . . . . .121 DK85
Allardyce St, SW4 . . . . .101 DM84
Allbrook Cl, Tedd. TW11 . . . . .117 CE92
Allcot Cl, Felt. TW14 . . . . . . .115 BT88
Allcroft Rd, NW5 . . . . .64 DG64
Allenby Av, S.Croy. CR2 . . . .160 DQ109
Allenby Cl, Grnf. UB6 . . . . . . .78 CA69
Allenby Cres, Grays RM17 . . .110 GB78
Allenby Dr, Horn. RM11 . . . . .72 FL60
Allenby Rd, SE23 . . . . .123 DY90
Southall UB1 . . . . .78 CA72
Westerham (Bigg.H.) TN16 .178 EL117

Allen Cl, Mitch. CR4 . . . . . . .141 DH95
Radlett (Shenley) WD7
  off Russet Dr 10 CL32
Sunbury-on-Thames
TW16 . . . . .135 BV95
Allen Ct, Grnf. UB6 . . . . .61 CF64
Allendale Av, Sthl. UB1 . . . . . .78 CA72
Allendale Cl, SE5
  off Daneville Rd 102 DR81
SE26 . . . . .123 DX92
Dartford DA2
  off Princes Rd 129 FR88
Allendale Rd, Grnf. UB6 . . . . .79 CH65
Allen Edwards Dr, SW8 . . . . .101 DL81
Allenford Ho, SW15
  off Tunworth Cres 119 CT86
Allen Ho Pk, Wok. GU22 . . . .166 AW120
Allen Pl, Twick. TW1
  off Church St 117 CG88
Allen Rd, E3 . . . . .85 DZ68
N16 . . . . .66 DS63
Beckenham BR3 . . . . .143 DX96
Croydon CR0 . . . . .141 DM101
Rainham RM13 . . . . .90 FJ69
Sunbury-on-Thames
TW16 . . . . .135 BV95
Allensbury Pl, NW1 . . . . .83 DK66
Allens Rd, Enf. EN3 . . . . .30 DW43
Allen St, W8 . . . . .100 DA76
Allenswood Rd, SE9 . . . . . . .104 EL83
Allerford Ct, Har. HA2 . . . . . . .60 CB57
Allerford Rd, SE6 . . . . .123 EB91
Allerton Cl, Borwd. WD6 . . . .26 CM38
Allerton Ct, NW4
  off Holders Hill Rd 43 CX54
Allerton Rd, N16 . . . . .66 DQ61
Borehamwood WD6 . . . . . .26 CL38
Allerton Wk, N7
  off Durham Rd 65 DM61
Allestree Rd, SW6 . . . . .99 CY80
Alleyn Cres, SE21 . . . . .122 DR89
Alleyndale Rd, Dag. RM8 . . . .70 EW61
Alleyn Pk, SE21 . . . . .122 DR89
Southall UB2 . . . . .96 BZ77
Alleyn Rd, SE21 . . . . .122 DR90
Allfarthing La, SW18 . . . . . . .120 DB86
Allgood Cl, Mord. SM4 . . . . . .139 CX100
Allgood St, E2
  off Hackney Rd 84 DT68
Allhallows La, EC4 . . . . .201 K1
★ All Hallows-on-the-Wall C of E
Church, EC2
  off London Wall 197 L7
Allhallows Rd, E6 . . . . .86 EL71
All Hallows Rd, N17 . . . . .46 DS53
Allhusen Gdns, Slou. (Fulmer)
SL3 off Alderbourne La . .56 AY63
Alliance Cl, Wem. HA0 . . . . . .61 CK63
Alliance Ct, W3
  off Alliance Rd 80 CP70
Alliance Rd, E13 . . . . .86 EJ70
SE18 . . . . .106 EU79
W3 . . . . .80 CP70
Allied Way, W3 off Larden Rd .98 CS75
Allingham Cl, W7 . . . . .79 CF73
Allingham Ms, N1
  off Allingham St 84 DQ68
Allingham St, N1 . . . . .84 DQ68
Allington Av, N17 . . . . .46 DS51
Allington Cl, SW19
  off High St Wimbledon . . .119 CX92
Gravesend DA12 . . . . .131 GM88
  off Farley Rd
Greenford UB6 . . . . .78 CC66
Allington Ct, Enf. EN3 . . . . . . .31 DX43
Slough SL2 off Myrtle Cres .74 AT73
Allington Rd, NW4 . . . . .63 CV57
W10 . . . . .81 CY68
Harrow HA2 . . . . .60 CC57
Orpington BR6 . . . . .145 ER103
Allington St, SW1 . . . . .199 K7
Allison Cl, SE10
  off Dartmouth Hill 103 EC81
Waltham Abbey EN9 . . . . . .16 EG33
Allison Gro, SE21 . . . . .122 DS88
Allison Rd, N8 . . . . .65 DN57
W3 . . . . .80 CQ72
Allitsen Rd, NW8 . . . . .194 B1
Allmains Cl, Wal.Abb. EN9 . . .16 EH25
Alloa Rd, SE8 . . . . .203 J10
Ilford IG3 . . . . .70 EU61
Allonby Dr, Ruis. HA4 . . . . . . .59 BP59
Allonby Gdns, Wem. HA9 . . . .61 CJ60
Allotment Way, NW2
  off Midland Ter 63 CX62
Alloway Cl, Wok. GU21
  off Inglewood 166 AV118
Alloway Rd, E3 . . . . .85 DY69
Allports Ms, E1
  off Stepney Grn 84 DW70
All Saints Cl, N9 . . . . .46 DT47
SW8 off Lansdowne Way . .101 DL81
Chigwell IG7 . . . . .50 EU48
Swanscombe DA10
  off High St 130 FZ85
All Saints Ms, Har. HA3 . . . . .41 CE51
All Saints Pas, SW18
  off Wandsworth High St . .120 DB85
All Saints Rd, SW19 . . . . . . .120 DC94
W3 . . . . .98 CQ76
W11 . . . . .81 CZ71
Gravesend (Nthflt.) DA11 . .131 GF88
Sutton SM1 . . . . .140 DB104
All Saints St, N1 . . . . .83 DM68
All Saints Twr, E10 . . . . .67 EB59
Allsop Pl, NW1 . . . . .194 E5
All Souls Av, NW10 . . . . .81 CV68
All Souls Pl, W1 . . . . .195 J7

Allum Cl, Borwd. (Elstree)
WD6 . . . . .26 CL42
Allum Gro, Tad. KT20
  off Preston La 173 CV121
Allum La, Borwd. (Elstree)
WD6 . . . . .26 CM42
Allum Way, N20 . . . . .44 DC46
Allwood Cl, SE26 . . . . .123 DX91
Allwood Rd, Wal.Cr. EN7 . . . .14 DT27
Allyn Cl, Stai. TW18
  off Penton Rd 113 BF93
Alma Cl, N10 . . . . .47 EC52
Hornchurch RM12 . . . . . . .72 FL63
Almack Rd, E5 . . . . .66 DW63
Alma Cl, Wok. (Knap.) GU21 . .166 AS118
Alma Cres, Sutt. SM1 . . . . . .157 CY106
Alma Gro, SE1 . . . . .202 A9
Alma Pl, NW10 off Harrow Rd .81 CV69
SE19 . . . . .122 DT94
Thornton Heath CR7 . . . . .141 DN99
Alma Rd, N10 . . . . .44 DG52
Carshalton SM5 . . . . .158 DE106
Enfield EN3 . . . . .31 DY43
Esher KT10 . . . . .137 CE102
Orpington BR5 . . . . .146 EX103
Reigate RH2 . . . . .184 DB133
Sidcup DA14 . . . . .126 EU90
Southall UB1 . . . . .78 BY73
Swanscombe DA10 . . . . . .130 FZ85
Alma Row, Har. HA3 . . . . .41 CD53
Alma Sq, NW8 . . . . .82 DC69
Alma St, E15 . . . . .85 ED65
NW5 . . . . .83 DH65
Alma Ter, SW18 . . . . .120 DD87
W8 off Allen St 100 DA76
Almeida St, N1 . . . . .83 DP66
Almer Rd, SW20 . . . . .119 CU94
Almington St, N4 . . . . .65 DM60
Almners Rd, Cher. (Lyne)
KT16 . . . . .133 BC100
Almond Av, W5 . . . . .98 CL76
Carshalton SM5 . . . . .140 DF103
Uxbridge UB10 . . . . .59 BP62
West Drayton UB7 . . . . . . .94 BN76
Woking GU22 . . . . .166 AX121
Almond Cl, SE15 . . . . .102 DU82
Bromley BR2 . . . . .145 EN101
Egham (Eng.Grn.) TW20 . .112 AV93
Feltham TW13
  off Highfield Rd 115 BU88
Grays RM16 . . . . .111 GG76
Hayes UB3 . . . . .78 BS73
Ruislip HA4 off Roundways .59 BT62
Shepperton TW17 . . . . . . .135 BQ96
Almond Dr, Swan. BR8 . . . . . .147 FD96
Almond Gro, Brent. TW8 . . . .97 CH80
Almond Rd, N17 . . . . .46 DU52
SE16 . . . . .202 E8
Dartford DA2 . . . . .128 FQ87
Epsom KT19 . . . . .156 CR111
Almonds Av, Buck.H. IG9 . . . .48 EG47
Almond Way, Borwd. WD6 . . .26 CP42
Bromley BR2 . . . . .145 EN101
Harrow HA2 . . . . .40 CB54
Mitcham CR4 . . . . .141 DK99
Almons Way, Slou. SL2 . . . . .74 AV71
Almorah Rd, N1 . . . . .84 DR66
Hounslow TW5 . . . . .96 BX81
Alms Heath, Wok. (Ockham)
GU23 . . . . .169 BP121
Almshouse La, Chess. KT9 . . .155 CJ109
Enfield EN1 . . . . .30 DV37
Alnwick Gro, Mord. SM4
  off Bordesley Rd 140 DB98
Alnwick Rd, E16 . . . . .86 EJ72
SE12 . . . . .124 EH87
ALPERTON, Wem. 80 CM67
❷ Alperton 80 CL67
Alperton La, Grnf. UB6 . . . . . .79 CK69
Wembley HA0 . . . . .79 CK69
Alperton St, W10 . . . . .81 CY70
Alphabet Gdns, Cars. SM5 . . .140 DD100
Alphabet Sq, E3
  off Hawgood St 85 EA71
Alpha Cl, NW1 . . . . .194 C3
Alpha Gro, E14 . . . . .204 A5
Alpha Ms, Rom. RM7 . . . . . . .71 FC57
Alpha Pl, NW6 . . . . .82 DA68
SW3 . . . . .100 DE79
Alpha Rd, E4 . . . . .47 EB48
N18 . . . . .46 DU51
SE14 . . . . .103 DZ81
Brentwood CM13 . . . . .55 GD44
Croydon CR0 . . . . .142 DS102
Enfield EN3 . . . . .31 DY42
Surbiton KT5 . . . . .138 CM100
Teddington TW11 . . . . . . .117 CD92
Uxbridge UB10 . . . . .77 BP70
Woking GU22 . . . . .167 BB116
Woking (Chobham) GU24 . .150 AT110
Alpha St, SE15 . . . . .102 DU82
Alpha St N, Slou. SL1 . . . . . . .92 AU75
Alpha St S, Slou. SL1 . . . . . . .92 AT76
Alphea Cl, SW19
  off Courtney Rd 120 DE94
Alpine Av, Surb. KT5 . . . . . . .138 CQ103
Alpine Business Cen, E6 . . . . .87 EN71
Alpine Cl, Croy. CR0 . . . . . . .142 DS104
Alpine Copse, Brom. BR1 . . . .145 EN96
Alpine Gro, E9 . . . . .84 DW66
Alpine Rd, E10 . . . . .67 EB61
SE16 . . . . .203 H10
Redhill RH1 . . . . .184 DG133
Walton-on-Thames KT12 . .135 BU101
Alpine Vw, Cars. SM5 . . . . . .158 DE106
Alpine Wk, Stan. HA7 . . . . . . .41 CE47
Alpine Way, E6 . . . . .87 EN71
Alric Av, NW10 . . . . .80 CR66
New Malden KT3 . . . . .138 CS97
Alroy Rd, N4 . . . . .65 DN59
Alsace Rd, SE17 . . . . .201 M10
Alscot Rd, SE1 . . . . .202 A8
Alscot Way, SE1 . . . . .201 P8
Alsike Rd, SE2 . . . . .106 EX76

Alsike Rd, Erith DA18 . . . . . . .106 EY76
Alsom Av, Wor.Pk. KT4 . . . . .157 CU105
Alsop Cl, St.Alb. (Lon.Col.)
AL2 . . . . .10 CL27
Alston Cl, Surb. KT6 . . . . . . .137 CH101
Alston Rd, N18 . . . . .46 DV50
SW17 . . . . .120 DD91
Barnet EN5 . . . . .27 CY41
Altair Cl, N17 . . . . .46 DT51
Altair Way, Nthwd. HA6 . . . . .39 BT49
Altash Way, SE9 . . . . .125 EM89
Altenburg Av, W13 . . . . .97 CH76
Altenburg Gdns, SW11 . . . . .100 DF84
Alterton Cl, Wok. GU21 . . . . .166 AU117
Alt Gro, SW19
  off St. George's Rd 119 CZ94
Altham Rd, Pnr. HA5 . . . . . . .40 BY52
Althea St, SW6 . . . . .100 DB83
Althorne Gdns, E18 . . . . .68 EF56
Althorne Way, Dag. RM10 . . .70 FA61
Althorp Cl, Barn. EN5 . . . . . . .43 CU45
Althorpe Av, E6 . . . . .88 EM66
Althorpe Gro, SW11
  off Westbridge Rd 100 DD81
Althorpe Ms, SW11
  off Westbridge Rd 100 DD81
Althorpe Rd, Har. HA1 . . . . . .60 CC57
Althorp Rd, SW17 . . . . .120 DF88
Altmore Av, E6 . . . . .87 EM66
Alton Cl, Bex. DA5 . . . . .126 EY88
Isleworth TW7 . . . . .97 CF82
Alton Ct, Stai. TW18 . . . . . . .133 BE95
Alton Gdns, Beck. BR3 . . . . . .123 EA94
Twickenham TW2 . . . . . . .117 CD87
Alton Rd, N17 . . . . .66 DR55
SW15 . . . . .119 CU88
Croydon CR0 . . . . .141 DN104
Richmond TW9 . . . . .98 CL84
Alton St, E14 . . . . .85 EB71
Altyre Cl, Beck. BR3 . . . . . . .143 DZ99
Altyre Rd, Croy. CR0 . . . . . . .142 DR103
Altyre Way, Beck. BR3 . . . . . .143 DZ99
Aluric Cl, Grays RM16 . . . . . .111 GH77
Alvanley Gdns, NW6 . . . . .64 DB64
Alva Way, Wat. WD19 . . . . . . .40 BX47
Alverstoke Rd, Rom. RM3 . . . .52 FL52
Alverstone Av, SW19 . . . . . . .120 DA89
Barnet EN4 . . . . .44 DE45
Alverstone Gdns, SE9 . . . . . .125 EQ88
Alverstone Rd, E12 . . . . .69 EN63
NW2 . . . . .81 CW66
New Malden KT3 . . . . .139 CT98
Wembley HA9 . . . . .62 CM60
Alverston Gdns, SE25 . . . . . .142 DS99
Alverton St, SE8 . . . . .103 DZ78
Alveston Av, Har. HA3 . . . . . .61 CH55
Alvey Est, SE17 . . . . .201 M9
Alvey St, SE17 . . . . .201 M10
Alvia Gdns, Sutt. SM1 . . . . . .158 DC105
Alvington Cres, E8 . . . . .66 DT64
Alway Av, Epsom KT19 . . . . .156 CQ106
Alwen Gro, S.Ock. RM15 . . . .91 FV71
Alwold Cres, SE12 . . . . .124 EH86
Alwyn Av, W4 . . . . .98 CR78
Alwyn Cl, Borwd. (Elstree)
WD6 . . . . .26 CM44
Croydon (New Adgtn.)
CR0 . . . . .161 EB108
Alwyne Av, Brwd. CM15 . . . . .55 GA44
Alwyne Cl, Wok. GU21 . . . . . .166 AY116
Alwyne La, N1
  off Alwyne Vil 83 DP66
Alwyne Pl, N1 . . . . .84 DQ65
Alwyne Rd, N1 . . . . .84 DQ66
SW19 . . . . .119 CZ93
W7 . . . . .79 CE73
Alwyne Sq, N1 . . . . .84 DQ65
Alwyne Vil, N1 . . . . .83 DP66
Alwyn Gdns, NW4 . . . . .63 CU56
W3 . . . . .80 CP72
Alwyns Cl, Cher. KT16
  off Alwyns La 134 BG100
Alwyns La, Cher. KT16 . . . . .133 BF100
Alyth Gdns, NW11 . . . . .64 DA58
Alzette Ho, E2 . . . . .85 DX69
Amalgamated Dr, Brent. TW8 .97 CG79
Amanda Cl, Chig. IG7 . . . . . . .49 ER51
Amanda Ct, Slou. SL3 . . . . . .92 AX76
Amanda Ms, Rom. RM7 . . . . .71 FC57
Amazon St, E1 off Hessel St . .84 DV72
Ambassador Cl, Houns. TW3 .96 BY82
Ambassador Gdns, E6 . . . . . .87 EM71
Ambassador's Ct, SW1 . . . . .199 L3
Ambassador Sq, E14 . . . . . . .204 B9
Amber Av, E17 . . . . .47 DY53
Amber Ct, SW17
  off Brudenell Rd 120 DG91
Staines TW18
  off Laleham Rd 113 BF92
Ambercroft Way, Couls. CR5 .175 DP119
Amberden Av, N3 . . . . .64 DA55
Ambergate St, SE17 . . . . .200 G10
Amber Gro, NW2
  off Prayle Gro 63 CX60
Amberley Cl, Orp. BR6
  off Warnford Rd 163 ET106
Pinner HA5 . . . . .60 BZ55
Amberley Ct, Sid. DA14 . . . . .126 EW92
Amberley Dr, Add. (Woodham)
KT15 . . . . .151 BF110
Amberley Gdns, Enf. EN1 . . . .46 DS45
Epsom KT19 . . . . .157 CT105
Amberley Gro, SE26 . . . . . . .122 DV91
Croydon CR0 . . . . .142 DT101
Amberley Rd, E10 . . . . .67 EB59
N13 . . . . .45 DM47
SE2 . . . . .106 EX79
W9 . . . . .82 DA71
Buckhurst Hill IG9 . . . . . . .48 EJ46
Enfield EN1 . . . . .46 DT45
Amberley Way, Houns. TW4 . .116 BW85
Morden SM4 . . . . .139 CZ101
Romford RM7 . . . . .71 FB56
Uxbridge UB10 . . . . .76 BL69
Amber Ms, N22
  off Brampton Pk Rd 65 DN55

Amber St, E15
  off Great Eastern Rd 85 ED65
Amberwood Cl, Wall. SM6
  off The Chase 159 DL106
Amberwood Ri, N.Mal. KT3 .138 CS100
Amblecote, Cob. KT11 ....154 BY111
Amblecote Cl, SE12 .....124 EH90
Amblecote Meadows, SE12 .124 EH90
Amblecote Rd, SE12 .....124 EH90
Ambler Rd, N4 ....65 DP62
Ambleside, Brom. BR1 ....123 ED93
  Epping CM16 ....18 EU31
Ambleside Av, SW16 .....121 DK91
  Beckenham BR3 ....143 DY99
  Hornchurch RM12 ....71 FH64
  Walton-on-Thames KT12 .136 BW102
Ambleside Cl, E9
  off Churchill Wk 66 DW64
  E10 ....67 EB60
Ambleside Cres, Enf. EN3 ..31 DX41
Ambleside Dr, Felt. TW14 ..115 BT88
Ambleside Gdns, SW16 ....121 DK92
  Ilford IG4 ....68 EL56
  South Croydon CR2 .....161 DX109
  Sutton SM2 ....158 DC107
  Wembley HA9 ....61 CK60
Ambleside Pt, SE15
  off Ilderton Rd 102 DW80
Ambleside Rd, NW10 .....81 CT66
  Bexleyheath DA7 ....106 FA82
Ambleside Wk, Uxb. UB8
  off High St 76 BK67
Ambleside Way, Egh. TW20 .113 BB94
Ambrey Way, Wall. SM6 ...159 DK109
Ambrooke Rd, Belv. DA17 ..106 FA76
Ambrosden Av, SW1 ......199 L7
Ambrose Av, NW11 ....63 CY59
Ambrose Cl, E6
  off Lovage App 86 EL71
  Dartford (Cray.) DA1 ....107 FF84
  Orpington BR6
  off Stapleton Rd 145 ET104
Ambrose Ms, SW11 ......100 DE82
Ambrose St, SE16 ....202 D8
Ambrose Wk, E3
  off Malmesbury Rd 85 EA68
Amelia Cl, W3 ....80 CP74
Amelia St, SE17 ....200 G10
Amen Cor, EC4 ....196 G9
  SW17 ....120 DF93
Amen Ct, EC4 ....196 G8
Amenity Way, Mord. SM4 ..139 CW101
America Sq, EC3 ....197 P10
America St, SE1 ....201 H3
Amerland Rd, SW18 .....119 CZ86
Amersham Av, N18 ......46 DR49
Amersham Cl, Rom. RM3 ..52 FM51
Amersham Dr, Rom. RM3 ..52 FL51
Amersham Gro, SE14 .....103 DZ80
Amersham Pl, Amer. HP7 ..20 AW39
Amersham Rd, SE14 .....103 DZ80
  Amersham (Lt.Chal.) HP6 ..20 AX39
  Chalfont St. Giles HP8 ....20 AU43
  Croydon CR0 ....142 DQ100
  Gerrards Cross SL9 ......57 BB59
  Gerrards Cross (Chal.St.P.)
  SL9 ....56 AY55
  Rickmansworth WD3 .....21 BB39
  Romford RM3 ....52 FM51
Amersham Vale, SE14 ....103 DZ80
Amersham Wk, Rom. RM3
  off Amersham Rd 52 FM51
Amersham Way, Amer. HP6 .20 AX39
Amery Gdns, NW10 ......81 CV67
  Romford RM2 ....72 FK55
Amery Rd, Har. HA1 ......61 CG61
Amesbury, Wal.Abb. EN9 ..16 EG32
Amesbury Av, SW2 ......121 DL89
Amesbury Cl, Epp. CM16
  off Amesbury Rd 17 ET31
  Worcester Park KT4 .....139 CW102
Amesbury Dr, E4 ....31 EB44
Amesbury Rd, Brom. BR1 ..144 EK67
  Dagenham RM9 ....88 EX66
  Epping CM16 ....17 ET31
  Feltham TW13 ....116 BX89
Amesbury Twr, SW8
  off Westbury Rd 101 DJ82
Ames Rd, Swans. DA10 ...130 FY86
Amethyst Rd, E15 ....67 ED63
Amey Dr, Lthd. (Bkhm.)
  KT23 ....170 CC124
Amherst Av, W13 ....79 CJ72
Amherst Cl, Orp. BR5 ....146 EU98
Amherst Dr, Orp. BR5 ....145 ET98
Amherst Hill, Sev. TN13 ...190 FE122
Amherst Rd, W13 ....79 CJ72
  Sevenoaks TN13 ....191 FH122
Amhurst Gdns, Islw. TW7 ..97 CF81
Amhurst Par, N16
  off Amhurst Pk 66 DT59
Amhurst Pk, N16 ....66 DR59
Amhurst Pas, E8 ....66 DU64
Amhurst Rd, E8 ....66 DV64
  N16 ....66 DT63
Amhurst Ter, E8 ....66 DU63
Amhurst Wk, SE28
  off Pitfield Cres 88 EU74
Amidas Gdns, Dag. RM8 ...70 EV63
Amiel St, E1 ....84 DW70
Amies St, SW11 ....100 DF83
Amina Way, SE16 ....202 B7
Amis Av, Add. (New Haw)
  KT15 ....152 BG111
  Epsom KT19 ....156 CP107
Amis Rd, Wok. GU21 .....166 AS119
Amity Gro, SW20 ....139 CW95
Amity Rd, E15 ....86 EF67
Ammanford Grn, NW9
  off Ruthin Cl 62 CS58

Ampthill Sq Est, NW1 .....195 L1
Ampton Pl, WC1 ....196 B3
Ampton St, WC1 ....196 B3
Amroth Cl, SE23 ....122 DV88
Amroth Grn, NW9
  off Fryent Gro 62 CS58
Amstel Way, Wok. GU21 ..166 AT118
Amsterdam Rd, E14 .....204 E7
Amundsen Ct, E14
  off Napier Av 103 EA78
Amwell Cl, Enf. EN2 ......30 DR43
  Watford WD25
  off Phillipers 24 BY35
Amwell Ct, Wal.Abb. EN9 ..16 EF33
Amwell Ct Est, N4 ....66 DQ60
Amwell St, EC1 ....196 D2
Amyand Cotts, Twick. TW1
  off Amyand Pk Rd 117 CH86
Amyand La, Twick. TW1
  off Marble Hill Gdns ...117 CH87
Amyand Pk Gdns, Twick. TW1
  off Amyand Pk Rd 117 CH87
Amyand Pk Rd, Twick. TW1 .117 CG87
Amy Cl, Wall. SM6
  off Mollison Dr 159 DL108
Amy Rd, Oxt. RH8 ....188 EE129
Amyruth Rd, SE4 ....123 EA85
Amy Warne Cl, E6
  off Evelyn Denington Rd .86 EL70
Anatola Rd, N19
  off Dartmouth Pk Hill ...65 DH61
Ancaster Cres, N.Mal. KT3 .139 CU100
Ancaster Ms, Beck. BR3 ...143 DX97
Ancaster Rd, Beck. BR3 ...143 DX97
Ancaster St, SE18 ....105 ES80
Anchorage Cl, SW19 .....120 DA93
Anchorage Pt, E14 ....203 P4
Anchorage Pt Ind Est, SE7 .104 EJ76
Anchor & Hope La, SE7 ...104 EH76
Anchor Bay Ind Est, Erith
  DA8 ....107 FG79
Anchor Cl, Bark. IG11 ....88 EV69
  Waltham Cross (Chsht.)
  EN8 ....15 DX28
Anchor Dr, Rain. RM13 ...89 FH69
Anchor Ms, SW12
  off Hazelbourne Rd 121 DH86
Anchor Retail Pk, E1 .....84 DW70
Anchor St, SE16 ....202 D8
Anchor Ter, E1 *off Cephas Av* .84 DW70
Anchor Wf, E3 *off Watts Gro* .85 EB71
Ancill Cl, W6 ....99 CY79
Ancona Rd, NW10 ....81 CU68
  SE18 ....105 ER80
Andace Pk Gdns, Brom. BR1 .144 EJ95
Andalus Rd, SW9 ....101 DL83
Ander Cl, Wem. HA0 ......61 CK63
Anderson Cl, N21 ....29 DM43
  W3 ....80 CR72
  Epsom KT19 ....156 CP112
  Sutton SM3 ....140 DA102
  Uxbridge (Hare.) UB9 ....38 BG53
Anderson Dr, Ashf. TW15 ..115 BQ91
Anderson Ho, Bark. IG11
  off The Coverdales 87 ER68
Anderson Pl, Houns. TW3 ..96 CB84
Anderson Rd, E9 ....85 DX65
  Radlett (Shenley) WD7 ...10 CN33
  Weybridge KT13 ....135 BR104
  Woodford Green IG8 .....68 EK55
Andersons Sq, N1
  off Gaskin St 83 DP67
Anderson St, SW3 ....198 D10
Anderson Way, Belv. DA17 ..107 FB75
Anderton Cl, SE5 ....102 DR83
Andmark Ct, Sthl. UB1
  off Herbert Rd 78 BZ74
Andover Av, E16
  off King George Av 86 EK72
Andover Cl, Epsom KT19 ..156 CR111
  Feltham TW14 ....115 BT88
  Greenford UB6
  off Ruislip Rd 78 CB67
  Uxbridge UB8 ....76 BH68
Andover Pl, NW6 ....82 DB68
Andover Rd, N7 ....65 DM61
  Orpington BR6 ....145 ER102
  Twickenham TW2 ......117 CD88
Andre St, E8 ....66 DU64
Andrea Av, Grays RM16 ...110 GA75
Andre St, E8 ....66 DU64
Andrew Borde St, WC2 ...195 N8
Andrew Cl, Dart. DA1 ....127 FD85
  Ilford IG6 ....49 ER51
  Radlett (Shenley) WD7 ...10 CM33
Andrewes Gdns, E6 ......86 EL72
Andrewes Ho, EC2 ......197 J7
Andrew Pl, SW8
  off Cowthorpe Rd 101 DK81
Andrew Reed Ho, SW18
  off Linstead Way 119 CY87
Andrews Cl, E6
  off Linton Gdns 86 EL72
  Buckhurst Hill IG9 ......48 EJ47
  Epsom KT17 ....157 CT114
  Harrow HA1
  off Bessborough Rd 61 CD59
  Orpington BR5 ....146 EX96
  Worcester Park KT4 ....139 CX103
Andrews Crosse, WC2 ...196 D9
Andrews La, Wal.Cr. (Chsht.)
  EN7 ....14 DU28
Andrews Pl, SE9 ....125 EP86
Andrew's Rd, E8 ....84 DV67
Andrew St, E14 ....85 EC72
Andrews Wk, SE17
  off Dale Rd 101 DP79
Andwell Cl, SE2 ....106 EV75
⊖ Anerley 122 DV94
ANERLEY 122 DV94
Anerley Gro, SE19 ......122 DT94
Anerley Hill, SE19 ......122 DT93
Anerley Pk, SE20 ....122 DU94
Anerley Pk Rd, SE20 ....122 DU94
Anerley Rd, SE19 ....122 DU94
  SE20 ....122 DU94

Anerley Sta Rd, SE20 ....142 DV95
Anerley St, SW11 ....100 DF82
Anerley Vale, SE19 ......122 DT94
Anfield Cl, SW12
  off Belthorn Cres 121 DJ87
Angas Ct, Wey. KT13 ....153 BQ106
⊖ Angel 83 DN68
Angel All, E1
  off Whitechapel Rd 84 DU72
Angel Cl, N18 ....46 DT49
Angel Cor Par, N18
  off Fore St 46 DU50
Angel Ct, EC2 ....197 L8
  SW1 ....199 L3
  SW17 ....120 DF91
Angelfield, Houns. TW3 ...96 CB84
Angel Gate, EC1 ....196 G2
Angel Hill, Sutt. SM1 ....140 DB105
  off Sutton Common Rd .140 DB104
Angel Hill Dr, Sutt. SM1 ..140 DB104
Angelica Cl, West Dr. UB7
  off Lovibonds Av 76 BL72
Angelica Dr, E6 ....87 EN71
Angelica Gdns, Croy. CR0 .143 DX102
Angel La, E15 ....85 ED65
  Hayes UB3 ....77 BR71
Angell Pk Gdns, SW9 ....101 DN83
Angell Rd, SW9 ....101 DN83
Angell Town Est, SW9 ...101 DN82
Angel Ms, E1 *off Cable St* .84 DU73
  N1 ....196 E1
  SW15
  off Roehampton High St .119 CU87
Angel Pas, EC4 ....201 K1
Angel Pl, N18 ....46 DU50
  SE1 ....201 K4
⇌ Angel Road 46 DW50
Angel Rd, N18 ....46 DV50
  Harrow HA1 ....61 CE58
  Thames Ditton KT7 .....137 CG101
Angel Rd Wks, N18 .....46 DW50
Angel Sq, EC1 ....196 E1
Angel St, EC1 ....197 H8
Angel Wk, W6 ....99 CW77
Angel Way, Rom. RM1 ...71 FE57
Angerstein La, SE3 ......104 EF80
Angle Cl, Uxb. UB10 .....76 BN67
Angle Grn, Dag. RM8 ....70 EW60
Angle Rd, Grays RM20 ...109 FX79
Anglers Cl, Rich. TW10
  off Locksmeade Rd 117 CJ91
Angler's La, NW5 ....83 DH65
Anglers Reach, Surb. KT6 .137 CK99
Anglesea Av, SE18 ......105 EP77
Anglesea Cen, Grav. DA11
  off New Rd 131 GH86
Anglesea Ms, SE18
  off Anglesea Av 105 EP77
Anglesea Pl, Grav. DA11
  off Clive Rd 131 GH86
Anglesea Rd, SE18 .....105 EP77
  Kingston upon Thames
  KT1 ....137 CK98
  Orpington BR5 ....146 EW100
Anglesea Ter, W6
  off Wellesley Av 99 CV76
Anglesey Cl, Ashf. TW15 ..114 BN90
Anglesey Ct Rd, Cars. SM5 .158 DG107
Anglesey Dr, Rain. RM13 ..89 FG71
Anglesey Gdns, Cars. SM5 .158 DG107
Anglesey Rd, Enf. EN3 ....30 DV42
  Watford WD19 ....40 BW50
Anglesmede Cres, Pnr. HA5 .60 CA55
Anglesmede Way, Pnr. HA5 .60 BZ55
Angles Rd, SW16 ....121 DL91
Anglia Cl, N17 *off Park La* .46 DV52
Anglia Ct, Dag. RM8
  off Spring Cl 70 EX60
Anglia Ho, E14 ....85 DY72
Anglian Cl, Wat. WD24 ...24 BW40
Anglian Rd, E11 ....67 ED62
Anglia Wk, E6 ....87 EM67
Anglo Rd, E3 ....85 DZ68
Anglo Way, Red. RH1 ....184 DG132
Angrave Ct, E8 ....84 DT67
Angrave Pas, E8
  off Haggerston Rd 84 DT67
Angus Cl, Chess. KT9 ....156 CN106
Angus Dr, Ruis. HA4 .....60 BW63
Angus Gdns, NW9 ......42 CR53
Angus Rd, E13 ....86 EJ69
Angus St, SE14 ....103 DY80
Anhalt Rd, SW11 ....100 DE80
Ankerdine Cres, SE18 ...105 EN80
Ankerwycke Priory, Stai. (Wrays.)
  TW19 ....113 AZ89
Anlaby Rd, Tedd. TW11 ..117 CE92
Anley Rd, W14 ....99 CX75
Anmersh Gro, Stan. HA7 ..41 CK53
Annabel Cl, E14 ....85 EB72
Anna Cl, E8 ....84 DT67
Annalee Gdns, S.Ock. RM15 .91 FV71
Annalee Rd, S.Ock. RM15 ..91 FV71
Annandale Gro, Uxb. UB10
  off Thorpland Av 59 BQ62
Annandale Rd, SE10 ....104 EF79
  W4 ....98 CS78
  Croydon CR0 ....142 DU103
  Sidcup DA15 ....125 ES87
Annan Dr, Cars. SM5
  off Kenny Dr 158 DG109
Anna Neagle Cl, E7
  off Dames Rd 68 EG63
Annan Way, Rom. RM1 ...51 FD53
Anne Boleyn's Wk, Kings.T.
  KT2 ....117 CK92
  Sutton SM3 ....157 CX108
Anne Case Ms, N.Mal. KT3
  off Sycamore Gro 138 CR97
Anne Compton Ms, SE12 ..124 EF87
Anne of Cleves Rd, Dart.
  DA1 ....128 FK85
Anners Cl, Egh. TW20 ....133 BC97
Annesley Av, NW9 ....42 CR55
Annesley Cl, NW10 ......62 CS62
Annesley Dr, Croy. CR0 ..143 DZ104
Annesley Rd, SE3 ....104 EH81

Annesley Wk, N19 ......65 DJ61
Anne St, E13 ....86 EG70
Anne's Wk, Cat. CR3 ....176 DS120
Anne Taylor Ho, E12
  off Walton Rd 69 EN63
Annett Cl, Shep. TW17 ...135 BS98
Annette Cl, Har. HA3
  off Spencer Rd 41 CE54
Annette Cres, N1
  off Essex Rd 84 DQ66
Annette Rd, N7 ....65 DM63
Annett Rd, Walt. KT12 ...135 BU101
Anne Way, Ilf. IG6 ......49 EQ51
  West Molesey KT8 .....136 CB98
Annie Besant Cl, E3 .....85 DZ67
Annie Brooks Cl, Stai. TW18 .113 BD90
Annifer Way, S.Ock. RM15 .91 FV71
Anning St, EC2 ....197 N4
Annington Rd, N2 ....64 DF57
Annis Rd, E9 ....85 DY65
Ann La, SW10 ....100 DD80
Ann Moss Way, SE16 ...202 F6
Ann's Cl, SW1 ....198 E5
Ann's Pl, E1 ....197 P7
Ann St, SE18 ....105 ER77
Annsworthy Av, Th.Hth. CR7
  off Grange Pk Rd 142 DR97
Annsworthy Cres, SE25
  off Grange Rd 142 DR96
Ansdell Rd, SE15 ....102 DW82
Ansdell St, W8 ....100 DB76
Ansdell Ter, W8
  off Ansdell St 100 DB76
Ansell Gro, Cars. SM5 ...140 DG102
Ansell Rd, SW17 ....120 DE90
Anselm Cl, Croy. CR0
  off Park Hill Ri 142 DT104
Anselm Rd, SW6 ....100 DA79
  Pinner HA5 ....40 BZ52
Ansford Rd, Brom. BR1 ..123 EC92
Ansleigh Pl, W11 ....81 CX73
Ansley Cl, S.Croy. CR2 ...160 DV114
Anslow Gdns, Iver SL0 ...133 BD68
Anson Cl, Hem.H. (Bov.) HP3 .5 AZ27
  Kenley CR8 ....176 DR120
  Romford RM7 ....51 FB54
Anson Pl, SE28 ....105 ER75
Anson Rd, N7 ....65 DJ63
  NW2 ....63 CX64
Anson Ter, Nthlt. UB5 ....78 CB65
Anson Wk, Nthwd. HA6 ...39 BQ49
Anstead Dr, Rain. RM13 ..89 FG68
Anstey Rd, SE15 ....102 DU83
Anstey Wk, N15 ....65 DP56
Anstice Cl, W4 ....98 CS80
Anstridge Path, SE9 ....125 ER86
Anstridge Rd, SE9 ......125 ER86
Antelope Av, Grays RM16
  off Hogg La 110 GA76
Antelope Rd, SE18 .....105 EM76
Anthony Cl, NW7 ....42 CS49
  Sevenoaks (Dunt.Grn.)
  TN13 ....181 FE120
  Watford WD19 ....40 BW46
★ Anthony d'Offay Gall, W1 .195 J9
Anthony La, Swan. BR8 ..147 FG95
Anthony Rd, SE25 ......142 DU100
  Borehamwood WD6 .....26 CM40
  Greenford UB6 ....79 CE68
  Welling DA16 ....106 EU81
Anthonys, Wok. GU21 ...151 BB112
Anthony St, E1
  off Commercial Rd 84 DV72
Anthorne Cl, Pot.B. EN6 ..12 DB31
Anthus Ms, Nthwd. HA6 ..39 BS52
Antigua Cl, SE19
  off Salters Hill 122 DR92
Antigua Wk, SE19 ......122 DR92
Antill Rd, E3 ....85 DY69
  N15 ....66 DT56
Antill Ter, E1 ....85 DX72
Antlers Hill, E4 ....31 EB43
Antoinette Ct, Abb.L. WD5
  off Dairy Way 7 BT29
Anton Cres, Sutt. SM1 ...140 DA104
Antoneys Cl, Pnr. HA5 ...40 BX54
Anton Pl, Wem. HA9 .....62 CP62
Anton Rd, S.Ock. RM15 ..91 FV70
Anton St, E8 ....66 DU64
Antrim Gro, NW3 ....82 DF65
Antrim Mans, NW3 .....82 DE65
Antrim Rd, NW3 ....82 DF65
Antrobus Cl, Sutt. SM1 ..157 CZ106
Antrobus Rd, W4 ....98 CQ77
Anvil Cl, SW16 ....121 DJ94
  Hemel Hempstead (Bov.) HP3
  off Yew Tree Dr 5 BB28
Anvil Ct, Slou. (Langley) SL3
  off Blacksmith Row 93 BA77
Anvil La, Cob. KT11 .....153 BU114
Anvil Pl, St.Alb. AL2 ......8 CA24
Anvil Rd, Sun. TW16 ....135 BU97
Anworth Cl, Wdf.Grn. IG8 ..48 EH51
Anyards Rd, Cob. KT11 ..153 BV113
Apeldoorn Dr, Wall. SM6 ..159 DL109
Aperdele Rd, Lthd. KT22 ..171 CG118
APERFIELD, West. 179 EM117
Aperfield Rd, Erith DA8 ...107 FF79
  Westerham (Bigg.H.) TN16 .178 EL117
Apers Av, Wok. GU22 ....167 AZ121
Apex Cl, Beck. BR3 ......143 EB95
  Weybridge KT13 ....135 BR104
Apex Cor, NW7 ....42 CR49
Apex Ind Est, NW10
  off Hythe Rd 81 CU69
Apex Retail Pk, Felt. TW13 ..116 BZ90
Apex Twr, N.Mal. KT3 ...138 CS97
Aplin Way, Islw. TW7 ....97 CE81
Apollo Av, Brom. BR1
  off Rodway Rd 144 EH95
  Northwood HA6 ....39 BU50
Apollo Cl, Horn. RM12 ...71 FH61
★ Apollo Hammersmith, W6 .99 CW78
Apollo Pl, E11 ....68 EE62
  SW10 ....100 DD80
  Woking (St. John's) GU21
  off Church Rd 166 AU119

★ Apollo Thea, W1
  off Shaftesbury Av 195 M10
★ Apollo Victoria Thea,
  SW1 ....199 K7
Apollo Way, SE28
  off Broadwater Rd 105 ER76
Apostle Way, Th.Hth. CR7 .141 DP96
Apothecary St, EC4 ....196 F9
Appach Rd, SW2 ....121 DN86
Apple Blossom Ct, SW8
  off Pascal St 101 DK80
Appleby Cl, E4 ....47 EC51
  N15 ....66 DR57
  Twickenham TW2 ......117 CD89
Appleby Dr, Rom. RM3 ...52 FJ50
Appleby Gdns, Felt. TW14 .115 BT88
Appleby Grn, Rom. RM3
  off Appleby Dr 52 FJ50
Appleby Rd, E8 ....84 DU66
  E16 ....86 EF72
Appleby St, E2 ....84 DT68
  Waltham Cross (Chsht.)
  EN7 ....14 DT26
Apple Cotts, Hem.H. (Bov.)
  HP3 ....5 BA27
Applecroft, St.Alb. (Park St.)
  AL2 ....8 CB28
Appledore Av, Bexh. DA7 ..107 FC81
  Ruislip HA4 ....59 BV62
Appledore Cl, SW17 ....120 DF89
  Bromley BR2 ....144 EF99
  Edgware HA8 ....42 CN53
  Romford RM3 ....52 FJ53
Appledore Cres, Sid. DA14 .125 ES90
Appledore Way, NW7
  off Bittacy Hill 43 CY52
Appledown Ri, Couls. CR5 .175 DJ115
Applefield, Amer. HP7 ....20 AW39
Appleford Rd, W10 ......81 CY70
Apple Garth, Brent. TW8 ..97 CK77
Applegarth, Croy. (New Adgtn.)
  CR0 ....161 EB108
  Esher (Clay.) KT10 .....155 CF106
Applegarth Dr, Dart. DA1 ..128 FL89
  Ilford IG2 ....69 ET56
Applegarth Ho, Erith DA8 .107 FF82
  W14 ....99 CX76
Applegarth Rd, SE28 ....88 EV74
  W14 ....99 CX76
Applegate, Brwd. CM14 ..54 FT43
Apple Gro, Chess. KT9 ...156 CL105
  Enfield EN1 ....30 DS41
Apple Mkt, Kings.T. KT1
  off Eden St 137 CK96
Apple Orchard, Swan. BR8 .147 FD98
Apple Rd, E11 ....68 EE62
Appleshaw Cl, Grav. DA11 .131 GG92
Appleton Cl, Amer. HP7 ...20 AV40
Appleton Dr, Dart. DA2 ...127 FH90
Appleton Gdns, N.Mal. KT3 .139 CU100
Appleton Rd, SE9 ......104 EL83
  Loughton IG10 ....33 EP41
Appleton Sq, Mitch. CR4
  off Silbury Av 140 DE95
Appleton Way, Horn. RM12 .72 FK60
Appletree Av, Uxb. UB8 ..76 BM71
  West Drayton UB7 .....76 BM71
Appletree Cl, SE20
  off Jasmine Gro 142 DV95
  Leatherhead KT22 .....170 CC124
Appletree Gdns, Barn. EN4 .28 DE42
Appletree La, Slou. SL3 ..92 AW76
Apple Tree Roundabout, West Dr.
  UB7 ....76 BM73
Appletree Wk, Wat. WD25 ..7 BV34
Apple Tree Yd, SW1 .....199 L2
Applewood Cl, N20 ......44 DE46
  NW2 ....63 CV62
Applewood Dr, E13 ......86 EH70
  Erith DA8 ....107 FF79
Apprentice Way, E5
  off Clarence Rd 66 DV63
Approach, The, NW4 .....63 CX57
  W3 ....80 CR72
  Enfield EN1 ....30 DV40
  Orpington BR6 ....145 ET103
  Potters Bar EN6 ....11 CZ32
  Upminster RM14 ......72 FP62
Approach Cl, N16
  off Cowper Rd 66 DS64
Approach Rd, E2 ....84 DW68
  SW20 ....139 CW96
  Ashford TW15 ....115 BQ93
  Barnet EN4 ....28 DD42
  Purley CR8 ....159 DP112
  West Molesey KT8 .....136 CA99
Aprey Gdns, NW4 ......63 CW56
April Cl, W7 ....79 CE73
  Ashtead KT21 ....172 CM117
  Feltham TW13 ....115 BU90
  Orpington BR6
  off Briarswood Way ...163 ET106
April Glen, SE23 ....123 DX90
April St, E8 ....66 DT63
Aprilwood Cl, Add. (Woodham)
  KT15 ....151 BF111
Apsledene, Grav. DA12
  off Miskin Way 131 GK93
APSLEY, Hem.H. 6 BL25
⇌ Apsley 6 BL25
Apsley Cl, Har. HA2 .....60 CC57
★ Apsley Ho, Wellington Mus,
  W1 ....198 F4
Apsley Rd, SE25 ....142 DV98
  New Malden KT3 ......138 CQ97
Apsley Way, NW2 ......63 CU61
  W1 ....198 G4
Aquarius Business Pk, NW2 .63 CU60
Aquarius Way, Nthwd. HA6 .39 BU50
★ Aquatic Experience, Brent.
  TW8 ....97 CH81
Aquila Cl, Lthd. KT22 ...172 CL121
Aquila St, NW8 ....82 DD68
Aquinas St, SE1 ....200 E3

A B C D E F G H I J K L M N O P Q R S T U V W X Y Z

Ara - Ash

A

Arabella Dr, SW15 . . . . .98 CS84
Arabia Cl, E4 . . . . .47 ED45
Arabin Rd, SE4 . . . . .103 DY84
Araglen Av, S.Ock. RM15 . . . . . .91 FV71
Aragon Av, Epsom KT17 . . . . .157 CV109
  Thames Ditton KT7 . . . . .137 CF99
Aragon Cl, Brom. BR2 . . . .145 EM102
  Croydon (New Adgtn.)
  CR0 . . . . .162 EE110
  Enfield EN2 . . . . .29 DM38
  Loughton IG10 . . . . .32 EL44
  Romford RM5 . . . . .51 FB51
  Sunbury-on-Thames TW16 . .115 BT94
Aragon Dr, Ilf. IG6 . . . . .49 EQ52
  Ruislip HA4 . . . . .60 BX60
Aragon Rd, Kings.T. KT2 . . . . .118 CL92
  Morden SM4 . . . . .139 CX100
Aragon Twr, SE8 . . . . .103 DZ77
Aragon Wk, W.Byf. (Byfleet)
  KT14 . . . . .152 BM113
Aran Ct, Wey. KT13
  off Mallards Reach 135 BR103
Arandora Cres, Rom. RM6 . . . .70 EV59
Aran Dr, Stan. HA7 . . . . .41 CJ49
Aran Hts, Ch.St.G. HP8 . . . . . .36 AV49
Arbery Rd, E3 . . . . .85 DY69
Arbor Cl, Beck. BR3 . . . . .143 EB96
Arbor Ct, N16 off Lordship Rd .66 DR61
Arborfield Cl, SW2 . . . . .121 DM88
  Slough SL1 . . . . .92 AS76
Arbor Rd, E4 . . . . .47 ED48
Arbour Cl, Brwd. CM14 . . . . . .54 FW50
  Leatherhead (Fetch.) KT22 .171 CF123
Arbour Rd, Enf. EN3 . . . . .31 DX42
Arbour Sq, E1 . . . . .85 DX72
Arbour Vw, Amer. HP7 . . . . . . .20 AV39
Arbour Way, Horn. RM12 . . . . .71 FH64
Arbroath Grn, Wat. WD19 . . . .39 BU48
Arbroath Rd, SE9 . . . . .104 EL83
Arbrook Chase, Esher KT10 . .154 CC107
Arbrook Cl, Orp. BR5 . . . . . . .146 EU97
Arbrook La, Esher KT10 . . . . .154 CC107
Arbury Ter, SE26
  off Oaksford Av 122 DV90
Arbuthnot La, Bex. DA5 . . . . . .126 EY86
Arbuthnot Rd, SE14 . . . . .103 DX82
Arbutus St, E8 . . . . .84 DS67
Arcade, The, EC2 . . . . .197 M7
  Croydon CR0 off High St . . .142 DQ104
Arcade Pl, Rom. RM1 . . . . .71 FE57
Arcadia Av, N3 . . . . .44 DA53
Arcadia Caravans, Stai.
  TW18 . . . . .134 BH95
Arcadia Cl, Cars. SM5 . . . . . . .158 DG105
Arcadian Av, Bex. DA5 . . . . . .126 EY86
Arcadian Cl, Bex. DA5 . . . . . . .126 EY86
Arcadian Gdns, N22 . . . . .45 DM52
Arcadian Rd, Bex. DA5 . . . . . .126 EY86
Arcadia Shop Cen, W5 . . . . . . .79 CK73
Arcadia St, E14 . . . . .85 EA72
Arcany Rd, S.Ock. RM15 . . . . .91 FV70
Archangel St, SE16 . . . . .203 J5
Archates Av, Grays RM16 . . . .110 GA76
Archbishops Pl, SW2 . . . . .121 DM86
Archdale Pl, N.Mal. KT3 . . . . .138 CP97
Archdale Rd, SE22 . . . . .122 DT85
Archel Rd, W14 . . . . .99 CZ79
Archer Cl, Kings L. WD4 . . . . . .6 BM29
  Kingston upon Thames
  KT2 . . . . .118 CL94
Archer Ho, SW11
  off Vicarage Cres 100 DD81
Archer Ms, Hmptn. (Hmptn.H.)
  TW12 off Windmill Rd 116 CC93
Archer Rd, SE25 . . . . .142 DV98
  Orpington BR5 . . . . .146 EU99
Archers Ct, S.Ock. RM15 . . . . .91 FV71
Archers Dr, Enf. EN3 . . . . .30 DW40
Archer Sq, SE14
  off Chubworthy St 103 DY79
Archer St, W1 . . . . .195 M10
Archer Ter, West Dr. UB7
  off Yew Av 76 BL73
Archer Way, Swan. BR8 . . . . . .147 FF96
Archery Cl, W2 . . . . .194 C9
  Harrow HA3 . . . . .61 CF55
Archery Rd, SE9 . . . . .125 EM85
Arches, The, SW6
  off Munster Rd 99 CZ82
  WC2 . . . . .200 A2
  Harrow HA2 . . . . .60 CB61
Archibald Ms, W1 . . . . .198 G2
Archibald Rd, N7 . . . . .65 DK63
  Romford RM3 . . . . .52 FN53
Archibald St, E3 . . . . .85 EA69
Archie Cl, West Dr. UB7 . . . . . .94 BN75
Archie St, SE1 . . . . .201 N5
Arch Rd, Walt. KT12 . . . . .136 BX104
Arch St, SE1 . . . . .201 H7
Archway, Rom. RM3 . . . . .51 FH51
Archway Cl, N19 . . . . .65 DJ61
  off St. Johns Way 65 DJ61
  SW19 . . . . .120 DB91
  W10 . . . . .81 CX71
  Wallington SM6 . . . . .141 DK104
Archway Mall, N19
  off Magdala Av 65 DJ61
Archway Ms, SW15
  off Putney Br Rd 99 CY84
Archway Rd, N6 . . . . .64 DG58
  N19 . . . . .65 DJ60
Archway St, SW13 . . . . .98 CS83
Arcola St, E8 . . . . .66 DT64
Arctic St, NW5 off Gillies St . .64 DG64
Arcus Rd, Brom. BR1 . . . . . . .124 EE93
Ardbeg Rd, SE24 . . . . .122 DR86
Arden Cl, Bushey (Bushey Hth.)
  WD23 . . . . .41 CF45
  Harrow HA1 . . . . .61 CD62
  Hemel Hempstead (Bov.)
  HP3 . . . . .5 BA28
Arden Ct Gdns, N2 . . . . .64 DD58
Arden Cres, E14 . . . . .204 A8

Arden Cres, Dag. RM9 . . . . . . .88 EW66
Arden Est, N1 . . . . .197 M1
Arden Gro, Orp. BR6 . . . . .163 EP105
Arden Ho, SW9
  off Grantham Rd 101 DL82
Arden Ms, E17 . . . . .67 EB57
Arden Mhor, Pnr. HA5 . . . . . . .59 BV56
Arden Rd, N3 . . . . .63 CY55
  W13 . . . . .79 CJ73
Ardent Cl, SE25 . . . . .142 DS97
Ardesley Wd, Wey. KT13 . . . .153 BS105
Ardfern Av, SW16 . . . . .141 DN97
Ardfillan Rd, SE6 . . . . .123 ED88
Ardgowan Rd, SE6 . . . . .124 EE87
Ardilaun Rd, N5 . . . . .66 DQ63
Ardingly Cl, Croy. CR0 . . . . . . .143 DX104
Ardleigh Cl, Horn. RM11 . . . . .72 FK55
Ardleigh Ct, Brwd. CM15 . . . . .55 FZ45
Ardleigh Gdns, Brwd. CM13
  off Fairview Av 55 GE44
  Sutton SM3 . . . . .140 DA101
ARDLEIGH GREEN, Horn. 72 FJ56
Ardleigh Grn Rd, Horn. RM11 .72 FK57
Ardleigh Ho, Bark. IG11
  off St. Ann's 87 EQ67
Ardleigh Ms, Ilf. IG1
  off Bengal Rd 69 EP62
  N1 .84 DR65
Ardleigh Rd, E17 . . . . .47 DZ53
  N1 .84 DR65
Ardleigh Ter, E17 . . . . .47 DZ53
Ardley Cl, NW10 . . . . .62 CS62
  SE6 . . . . .123 DY90
  Ruislip HA4 . . . . .59 BQ59
Ardlui Rd, SE27 . . . . .122 DQ89
Ardmay Gdns, Surb. KT6 . . . .138 CL99
Ardmere La, Buck.H. IG9 . . . . .48 EH45
Ardmere Pl, Buck.H. IG9 . . . . .48 EH45
Ardmere Rd, S.Ock. RM15 . . . .91 FV70
Ardoch Rd, SE6 . . . . .123 ED89
Ardra Rd, N9 . . . . .47 DX48
Ardrossan Gdns, Wor.Pk.
  KT4 . . . . .139 CU104
Ardross Av, Nthwd. HA6 . . . . .39 BS50
Ardshiel Cl, SW15
  off Bemish Rd 99 CX83
Ardwell Av, Ilf. IG6 . . . . .69 EQ57
Ardwell Rd, SW2 . . . . .121 DL89
Ardwick Rd, NW2 . . . . .64 DA63
Arena .142 DW99
Arena, The, Enf. EN3 . . . . .31 DZ38
Arewater Grn, Loug. IG10 . . . .33 EM39
Argali Ho, Erith DA18
  off Kale Rd 106 EY76
Argall Av, E10 . . . . .67 DX59
Argall Way, E10 . . . . .67 DX60
Argenta Way, NW10 . . . . .80 CP66
Argent Cl, Egh. TW20
  off Holbrook Meadow 113 BC93
Argent St, SE1 . . . . .200 G4
  Grays RM17 . . . . .110 FY79
Argent Way, Wal.Cr. (Chsht.)
  EN7 . . . . .14 DR26
Argles Cl, Green. DA9
  off Cowley Av 129 FU85
Argon Ms, SW6 . . . . .100 DA80
Argon Rd, N18 . . . . .46 DW50
Argosy Gdns, Stai. TW18 . . . .113 BF93
Argosy La, Stai. (Stanw.)
  TW19 . . . . .114 BK87
Argus Cl, Rom. RM7 . . . . .51 FB53
Argus Way, W3 . . . . .98 CP76
  Northolt UB5 . . . . .78 BY69
Argyle Av, Houns. TW3 . . . . . .116 CA86
Argyle Cl, W13 . . . . .79 CG70
Argyle Gdns, Upmin. RM14 . . .73 FR61
Argyle Pas, N17 . . . . .46 DT53
Argyle Pl, W6 . . . . .99 CV77
Argyle Rd, E1 . . . . .85 DX70
  E15 . . . . .68 EE63
  E16 . . . . .86 EJ72
  N12 . . . . .44 DA50
  N17 . . . . .46 DU53
  N18 . . . . .46 DU49
  W13 . . . . .79 CG71
  Barnet EN5 . . . . .27 CW42
  Greenford UB6 . . . . .79 CF69
  Harrow HA2 . . . . .60 CB58
  Hounslow TW3 . . . . .116 CB85
  Ilford IG1 . . . . .69 EN61
  Sevenoaks TN13 . . . . .191 FH125
  Teddington TW11 . . . . .117 CE92
Argyle Sq, WC1 . . . . .196 A2
Argyle St, WC1 . . . . .195 P2
Argyle Wk, WC1 . . . . .196 A3
Argyle Way, SE16 . . . . .102 DU78
Argyll Av, Sthl. UB1 . . . . .78 CB74
Argyll Cl, SW9 off Dalyell Rd .101 DM83
Argyll Gdns, Edg. HA8 . . . . . . .42 CP54
Argyll Rd, W8 . . . . .100 DA75
  Grays RM17 . . . . .110 GA78
Argyll St, W1 . . . . .195 K9
Arica Rd, SE4 . . . . .103 DY84
Ariel Cl, Grav. DA12 . . . . .131 GM91
Ariel Rd, NW6 . . . . .82 DA65
Ariel Way, W12 . . . . .81 CW74
  Hounslow TW4 . . . . .95 BV83
Arisdale Av, S.Ock. RM15 . . . .91 FV71
Aristotle Rd, SW4 . . . . .101 DK83
Ark Av, Grays RM16 . . . . .110 GA76
Arkell Gro, SE19 . . . . .121 DP94
Arkindale Rd, SE6 . . . . .123 EC90
ARKLEY, Barn. 27 CU43
Arkley Cres, E17 . . . . .67 DZ57
Arkley Dr, Barn. EN5 . . . . .27 CU42
Arkley La, Barn. EN5 . . . . .27 CU41
Arkley Pk, Barn. EN5 . . . . .26 CR44
Arkley Rd, E17 . . . . .67 DZ57
Arkley Vw, Barn. EN5 . . . . . . .27 CV42
Arklow Ct, Rick. (Chorl.) WD3
  off Station App 21 BC42
Arklow Ms, Surb. KT6
  off Vale Rd S 138 CL103
Arklow Rd, SE14 . . . . .103 DZ79
Arkwright Rd, NW3 . . . . .64 DC64
  Slough (Colnbr.) SL3 . . . . . .93 BE82
  South Croydon CR2 . . . . . .160 DT110

Arkwright Rd, Til. RM18 . . . . .111 GG82
Arlesey Cl, SW15 . . . . .119 CY86
  off Lytton Gro
Arlesford Rd, SW9 . . . . .101 DL83
Arlingford Rd, SW2 . . . . .121 DN85
Arlingham Ms, Wal.Abb. EN9
  off Sun St 15 EC33
Arlington, N12 . . . . .44 DA48
Arlington Av, N1 . . . . .84 DQ68
Arlington Cl, SE13 . . . . .123 ED86
  Sidcup DA15 . . . . .125 ES87
  Sutton SM1 . . . . .140 DA103
  Twickenham TW1 . . . . .117 CJ86
Arlington Ct, Hayes UB3
  off Shepiston La 95 BR78
  Reigate RH2
  off Oakfield Dr 184 DB132
Arlington Cres, Wal.Cr. EN8 . .15 DY34
Arlington Dr, Cars. SM5 . . . . .140 DF103
  Ruislip HA4 . . . . .59 BR58
Arlington Gdns, W4 . . . . .98 CQ78
  Ilford IG1 . . . . .69 EN60
  Romford RM3 . . . . .52 FL53
Arlington Grn, NW7
  off Bittacy Hill 43 CY52
Arlington Lo, SW2 . . . . .101 DM84
  Weybridge KT13 . . . . .153 BP105
Arlington Ms, Twick. TW1
  off Arlington Rd 117 CJ86
Arlington Pl, SE10
  off Greenwich S St 103 EC80
Arlington Rd, N14 . . . . .45 DH47
  NW1 . . . . .83 DH67
  W13 . . . . .79 CH70
  Ashford TW15 . . . . .114 BM92
  Richmond TW10 . . . . .117 CK89
  Surbiton KT6 . . . . .137 CK100
  Teddington TW11 . . . . .117 CF91
  Twickenham TW1 . . . . .117 CJ86
  Woodford Green IG8 . . . . . .48 EG53
Arlington Sq, N1 . . . . .84 DQ67
Arlington St, SW1 . . . . .199 K2
Arlington Way, EC1 . . . . .196 E2
Arliss Way, Nthlt. UB5 . . . . . . .78 BW67
Arlow Rd, N21 . . . . .45 DN46
Armada Ct, SE8
  off Watergate St 103 EA79
  Grays RM16 off Hogg La . .110 GA76
Armadale Cl, N17 . . . . .66 DV56
Armadale Rd, SW6 . . . . .100 DA80
  Feltham TW14 . . . . .115 BU85
  Woking GU21 . . . . .166 AU117
Armada St, SE8 . . . . .103 EA79
Armada Way, E6 . . . . .87 EQ73
Armagh Rd, E3 . . . . .85 DZ67
Armand Cl, Wat. WD17 . . . . . .23 BT38
Armfield Cl, W.Mol. KT8 . . . . .136 BZ99
Armfield Cres, Mitch. CR4 . . .140 DF96
Armfield Rd, Enf. EN2 . . . . . . .30 DR39
Arminger Rd, W12 . . . . .81 CV74
Armistice Gdns, SE25
  off Penge Rd 142 DU97
Armitage Cl, Rick. (Loud.)
  WD3 . . . . .22 BK42
Armitage Rd, NW11 . . . . .63 CZ60
  SE10 . . . . .205 K10
Armour Cl, N7
  off Roman Way 83 DM65
Armoury Dr, Grav. DA12 . . . . .131 GJ87
Armoury Rd, SE8 . . . . .103 EB82
Armoury Way, SW18 . . . . .120 DA85
Armstead Wk, Dag. RM10 . . . .88 FA66
Armstrong Av, Wdf.Grn. IG8 . .48 EE51
Armstrong Cl, E6
  off Porter Rd 87 EM72
  Borehamwood WD6
  off Manor Way 26 CQ41
  Dagenham RM8
  off Palmer Rd 70 EX60
  Pinner HA5 . . . . .59 BU58
  St. Albans (Lon.Col.) AL2
  off Willowside 10 CL27
  Sevenoaks (Halst.) TN14 . .181 FB115
  Walton-on-Thames KT12
  off Sunbury La 135 BU100
Armstrong Cres, Barn. EN4 . . .28 DD41
Armstrong Gdns, Rad. (Shenley)
  WD7 . . . . .10 CL32
Armstrong Rd, SW7 . . . . .100 DD76
  W3 .81 CT74
  Egham (Eng.Grn.) TW20 . .112 AW93
  Feltham TW13 . . . . .116 BY92
Armstrong Way, Sthl. UB2 . . . .96 CB75
Armytage Rd, Houns. TW5 . . .96 BX80
Arnal Cres, SW18 . . . . .119 CY87
Arncliffe Cl, N11
  off Kettlewell Cl 44 DG51
Arncroft Ct, Bark. IG11
  off Renwick Rd 88 EV69
Arndale Wk, SW18
  off Garratt La 120 DB85
Arndale Way, Egh. TW20
  off Church Rd 113 BA92
Arne Gro, Orp. BR6 . . . . .145 ET104
Arne St, WC2 . . . . .196 A9
Arnett Cl, Rick. WD3 . . . . .22 BG44
Arne Wk, SE3 . . . . .104 EF84
Arneways Av, Rom. RM6 . . . . .70 EX55
Arneway St, SW1 . . . . .199 N7
Arnewood Cl, SW15 . . . . .119 CU88
  Leatherhead (Oxshott)
  KT22 . . . . .154 CB113
Arney's La, Mitch. CR4 . . . . . .140 DG100
Arngask Rd, SE6 . . . . .123 ED87
Arnhem Av, S.Ock. (Aveley)
  RM15 . . . . .90 FQ74
Arnhem Dr, Croy. (New Adgtn.)
  CR0 . . . . .161 ED111
Arnhem Pl, E14 . . . . .203 P7
Arnhem Way, SE22
  off East Dulwich Gro 122 DS85
Arnhem Wf, E14
  off Arnhem Pl 103 EA76

Amison Rd, E.Mol. KT8 . . . . . .137 CD98
Arnold Av E, Enf. EN3 . . . . . . .31 EA38
Arnold Av W, Enf. EN3 . . . . . . .31 DZ38
Arnold Circ, E2 . . . . .197 P3
Arnold Cl, Har. HA3 . . . . .62 CM59
Arnold Dr, Chess. KT9 . . . . . .155 CK107
Arnold Est, SE1 . . . . .202 A5
Arnold Gdns, N13 . . . . .45 DP50
Arnold Pl, Til. RM18
  off Kipling Av 111 GJ81
Arnold Rd, E3 . . . . .85 EA69
  N15 . . . . .66 DT55
  SW17 . . . . .120 DF94
  Dagenham RM9, RM10 . . . .88 EZ66
  Gravesend DA12 . . . . .131 GJ89
  Northolt UB5 . . . . .78 BX65
  Staines TW18 . . . . .114 BJ94
  Waltham Abbey EN9 . . . . . .31 EC35
  Woking GU21 . . . . .167 BB116
Arnolds Av, Brwd. CM15 . . . . .55 GC43
Arnolds Cl, Brwd. CM15 . . . . .55 GC43
Arnolds Fm La, Brwd. CM13 . .55 GE41
Arnolds La, Dart. (Sutt.H.)
  DA4 . . . . .128 FM93
Arnos Grove, N14 . . . . .45 DJ49
Arnos Gro, N14 . . . . .45 DK49
Arnos Rd, N11 . . . . .45 DJ50
Arnott Cl, SE28
  off Applegarth Rd 88 EW73
  W4 off Fishers La 98 CR77
Arnould Av, SE5 . . . . .102 DR84
Arnsberg Way, Bexh. DA7 . . . .106 FA84
Arnside Gdns, Wem. HA9 . . . .61 CK60
Arnside Rd, Bexh. DA7 . . . . . .106 FA81
Arnside St, SE17 . . . . .102 DQ79
Arnulf St, SE6 . . . . .123 EB91
Arnulls Rd, SW16 . . . . .121 DN93
Arodene Rd, SW2 . . . . .121 DM86
Arosa Rd, Twick. TW1 . . . . . . .117 CK86
Arpley Sq, SE20 off High St . .122 DW94
Arragon Gdns, SW16 . . . . . . .121 DL94
  West Wickham BR4 . . . . . .143 EB104
Arragon Rd, E6 . . . . .86 EK67
  SW18 . . . . .120 DB88
  Twickenham TW1 . . . . .117 CG87
Arran Cl, Erith DA8 . . . . .107 FD79
  Wallington SM6 . . . . .159 DH105
  Arran Dr, E12 . . . . .68 EK60
Arran Grn, Wat. WD19
  off Prestwick Rd 40 BW46
Arran Ms, W5 . . . . .80 CM74
Arranmore Ct, Bushey WD23
  off Bushey Hall Rd 24 BY42
Arran Rd, SE6 . . . . .123 EB89
Arran Wk, N1 . . . . .84 DQ66
Arran Way, Esher KT10 . . . . . .136 CB103
Arras Av, Mord. SM4 . . . . .140 DC99
Arreton Mead, Wok. (Horsell)
  GU21 . . . . .150 AY114
Arrol Rd, Beck. BR3 . . . . .142 DW97
Arrow Rd, E3 . . . . .85 EB69
Arrowscout Wk, Nthlt. UB5
  off Argus Way 78 BY69
Arrowsmith Cl, Chig. IG7 . . . .49 ET50
Arrowsmith Path, Chig. IG7 . .49 ET50
Arrowsmith Rd, Chig. IG7 . . . .49 ES50
  Loughton IG10 . . . . .32 EL41
Arsenal 65 DN62
Arsenal FC, N5 . . . . .65 DP62
Arsenal Rd, SE9 . . . . .105 EM82
Arterberry Rd, SW20 . . . . .119 CW94
Arterial Av, Rain. RM13 . . . . . .89 FH70
Arterial Rd N Stifford, Grays
  RM17 . . . . .110 FY75
Arterial Rd Purfleet, Purf.
  RM19 . . . . .108 FN76
Arterial Rd W Thurrock, Grays
  RM16, RM20 . . . . .109 FU76
Artesian Cl, NW10 . . . . .80 CR66
  Hornchurch RM11 . . . . .71 FF58
Artesian Gro, Barn. EN5 . . . . .28 DC42
Artesian Rd, W2 . . . . .82 DA72
Artesian Wk, E11 . . . . .68 EE62
Arthingworth St, E15 . . . . .86 EE67
Arthur Ct, W2 off Queensway .82 DB72
Arthurdon Rd, SE4 . . . . .123 EA85
Arthur Gro, SE18 . . . . .105 EQ77
Arthur Henderson Ho, SW6 . .99 CZ82
  off Magpie Cl
Arthur Horsley Wk, E7
  off Magpie Cl 68 EF64
Arthur Jacob Nature Reserve,
  Slou. SL3 . . . . .93 BC83
Arthur Rd, E6 . . . . .87 EM68
  N7 .65 DM63
  N9 .46 DT47
  SW19 . . . . .120 DA90
  Kingston upon Thames
  KT2 . . . . .118 CN94
  New Malden KT3 . . . . .139 CV99
  Romford RM6 . . . . .70 EW59
  Westerham (Bigg.H.) TN16 .178 EJ115
Arthur's Br Rd, Wok. GU21 . .166 AW117
Arthur St, EC4 . . . . .201 L1
  Bushey WD23 . . . . .24 BX42
  Erith DA8 . . . . .107 FF80
  Gravesend DA11 . . . . .131 GG87
  Grays RM17 . . . . .110 GC79
Arthur St W, Grav. DA11 . . . . .131 GG87
Arthur Toft Ho, Grays RM17
  off New Rd 110 GB79
Artichoke Dell, Rick. (Chorl.)
  WD3 . . . . .21 BE43
Artichoke Hill, E1 . . . . .202 D1
Artichoke Pl, SE5
  off Camberwell Ch St 102 DR81
Artillery Cl, Ilf. IG2
  off Horns Rd 69 EQ58
Artillery La, E1 . . . . .197 N7
  W12 . . . . .81 CU72
Artillery Pas, E1 . . . . .197 N7
Artillery Pl, SE18 . . . . .105 EM77
  SW1 . . . . .199 M7
  Harrow HA3
  off Chicheley Rd 40 CC52
Artillery Row, SW1 . . . . .199 M7

Artillery Row, Grav. DA12 . . . .131 GJ87
Artington Cl, Orp. BR6 . . . . . .163 EQ105
Artisan Cl, E6 off Ferndale St .87 EP72
Artizan St, E1 . . . . .197 N8
Arundel Av, Epsom KT17 . . . .157 CV110
  Morden SM4 . . . . .139 CZ98
  South Croydon CR2 . . . . . .160 DU110
Arundel Cl, E15 . . . . .68 EE63
  SW11 off Chivalry Rd 120 DE85
  Bexley DA5 . . . . .126 EZ86
  Croydon CR0 . . . . .141 DP104
  Hampton (Hmptn.H.)
  TW12 . . . . .116 CB92
  Waltham Cross (Chsht.)
  EN8 . . . . .14 DW29
Arundel Ct, N12 . . . . .44 DE51
  Harrow HA2 . . . . .60 CA63
  Slough SL3 . . . . .92 AX77
Arundel Dr, Borwd. WD6 . . . . .26 CQ43
  Harrow HA2 . . . . .60 BZ63
  Orpington BR6 . . . . .164 EV106
  Woodford Green IG8 . . . . . .48 EG52
Arundel Gdns, N21 . . . . .45 DN46
  W11 . . . . .81 CZ73
  Edgware HA8 . . . . .42 CR52
  Ilford IG3 . . . . .70 EU61
Arundel Gt Ct, WC2 . . . . .196 C10
Arundel Gro, N16 . . . . .66 DS64
Arundel Pl, N1 . . . . .83 DN65
Arundel Rd, Abb.L. WD5 . . . . . .7 BU32
  Barnet EN4 . . . . .28 DE41
  Croydon CR0 . . . . .142 DR100
  Dartford DA1 . . . . .108 FJ84
  Hounslow TW4 . . . . .96 BW83
  Kingston upon Thames
  KT1 . . . . .138 CP96
  Romford RM3 . . . . .52 FM53
  Sutton SM2 . . . . .157 CZ108
  Uxbridge UB8 . . . . .76 BH68
Arundel Sq, N7 . . . . .83 DN65
Arundel St, WC2 . . . . .196 C10
Arundel Ter, SW13 . . . . .99 CV79
Arvon Rd, N5 . . . . .65 DN64
Asbaston Ter, Ilf. IG1
  off Buttsbury Rd 69 EQ64
Ascalon St, SW8 . . . . .101 DJ80
Ascension Rd, Rom. RM5 . . . .51 FC51
Ascham Dr, E4
  off Rushcroft Rd 47 EB52
Ascham End, E17 . . . . .47 DY53
Ascham St, NW5 . . . . .65 DJ64
Aschurch Rd, Croy. CR0 . . . . .142 DT101
Ascot Cl, Borwd. (Elstree)
  WD6 . . . . .26 CN43
  Ilford IG6 . . . . .49 ES51
  Northolt UB5 . . . . .60 CA64
Ascot Gdns, Enf. EN3 . . . . . . .30 DW37
  Hornchurch RM12 . . . . .72 FL63
  Southall UB1 . . . . .78 BZ71
Ascot Ms, Wall. SM6 . . . . .159 DJ109
Ascot Rd, E6 . . . . .87 EM69
  N15 . . . . .66 DR57
  N18 . . . . .46 DU49
  SW17 . . . . .120 DG93
  Feltham TW14 . . . . .114 BN88
  Gravesend DA12 . . . . .131 GH90
  Orpington BR5 . . . . .145 ET98
  Watford WD18 . . . . .23 BS43
Ascott Av, W5 . . . . .98 CL75
Ashbeam Cl, Brwd. CM13
  off Canterbury Way 53 FW51
Ashbourne Av, E18 . . . . .68 EH56
  N20 . . . . .44 DF47
  NW11 . . . . .63 CZ57
  Bexleyheath DA7 . . . . .106 EY80
  Harrow HA2 . . . . .61 CD61
Ashbourne Cl, N12 . . . . .44 DB49
  W5 .80 CN71
  Coulsdon CR5 . . . . .175 DJ118
Ashbourne Ct, E5
  off Daubeney Rd 67 DY63
Ashbourne Gro, NW7 . . . . .42 CR50
  SE22 . . . . .122 DT85
  W4 .98 CS78
Ashbourne Par, W5
  off Ashbourne Rd 80 CM70
Ashbourne Ri, Orp. BR6 . . . . .163 ER105
Ashbourne Rd, W5 . . . . .80 CM71
  Mitcham CR4 . . . . .120 DG93
  Romford RM3 . . . . .52 FJ49
Ashbourne Sq, Nthwd. HA6 . . .39 BS51
Ashbourne Ter, SW19 . . . . . . .120 DA94
Ashbourne Way, NW11
  off Ashbourne Av 63 CZ57
Ashbridge Rd, E11 . . . . .68 EF59
Ashbridge St, NW8 . . . . .194 B5
Ashbrook Rd, N19 . . . . .65 DK60
  Dagenham RM10 . . . . .71 FB62
  Windsor (Old Wind.) SL4 . .112 AV87
Ashburn Gdns, SW7 . . . . .100 DC77
Ashburnham Av, Har. HA1 . . . .61 CF58
Ashburnham Cl, N2 . . . . .64 DD55
  Sevenoaks TN13
  off Fiennes Way 191 FJ127
  Watford WD19
  off Ashburnham Dr 39 BU48
Ashburnham Dr, Wat. WD19 . .39 BU48
Ashburnham Gdns, Har.
  HA1 . . . . .61 CF58
  Upminster RM14 . . . . .72 FP60
Ashburnham Gro, SE10 . . . . . .103 EB80
Ashburnham Pk, Esher KT10 .154 CC105
Ashburnham Retreat, SE10 . .103 EB80
Ashburnham Rd, NW10 . . . . . .81 CW69
  SW10 . . . . .100 DC80
  Belvedere DA17 . . . . .107 FC77
  Richmond TW10 . . . . .117 CH90
Ashburn Pl, SW7 . . . . .100 DC77
Ashburton Av, Croy. CR0 . . . .142 DV102
  Ilford IG3 . . . . .69 ES63
Ashburton Cl, Croy. CR0 . . . .142 DU102
Ashburton Ct, Pnr. HA5 . . . . . .60 BX56
Ashburton Gdns, Croy. CR0 . .142 DU103
Ashburton Gro, N7 . . . . .65 DN63
Ashburton Rd, E16 . . . . .86 EG72
  Croydon CR0 . . . . .142 DU102

A

Ashburton Rd, Ruis. HA4 . . . .59 BU61
Ashburton Ter, E13
 off Grasmere Rd 86 EG68
Ashbury Dr, Uxb. UB10 . . . .59 BP61
Ashbury Pl, SW11 . . . . . . .120 DC93
Ashbury Rd, SW11 . . . . . . .100 DF83
Ashby Av, Chess. KT9 . . . . .156 CN107
Ashby Cl, Horn. RM11
 off Holme Rd 72 FN60
Ashby Gro, N1 . . . . .84 DQ66
Ashby Ms, SE4 . . . . .103 DZ82
Ashby Rd, N15 . . . . .66 DU57
 SE4 . . . . .103 DZ82
 Watford WD24 . . . . .23 BU38
Ashby St, EC1 . . . . .196 G3
Ashby Wk, Croy. CR0 . . . . .142 DQ100
Ashby Way, West Dr. UB7 . . .94 BN80
Aschchurch Gro, W12 . . . . . .99 CU75
Aschchurch Pk Vil, W12 . . . . .99 CU76
Aschchurch Ter, W12 . . . . . .99 CU76
Ash Cl, SE20 . . . . .142 DW96
 Abbots Langley WD5 . . . . . .7 BR32
 Brentwood CM15 . . . . .54 FT43
 Carshalton SM5 . . . . . . .140 DF103
 Edgware HA8 . . . . .42 CQ49
 Hatfield AL9 . . . . .12 DA25
 New Malden KT3 . . . . . . .138 CR96
 Orpington BR5 . . . . .145 ER99
 Redhill RH1 . . . . .185 DJ130
 Romford RM5 . . . . .51 FB52
 Sidcup DA14 . . . . .126 EV90
 Slough SL3 . . . . .93 BB76
 Stanmore HA7 . . . . .41 CG51
 Swanley BR8 . . . . .147 FC96
 Uxbridge (Hare.) UB9 . . . . .38 BK53
 Watford WD25 . . . . .23 BV35
 Woking GU22 . . . . .166 AY120
 Woking (Pyrford) GU22 . . .168 BG115
Ashcombe Av, Surb. KT6 . . .137 CK101
Ashcombe Gdns, Edg. HA8 . . .42 CN49
Ashcombe Ho, Enf. EN3 . . . .31 DX41
Ashcombe Pk, NW2 . . . . . . .62 CS62
Ashcombe Rd, SW19 . . . . .120 DA92
 Carshalton SM5 . . . . . . .158 DG107
 Redhill RH1 . . . . .185 DJ127
Ashcombe Sq, N.Mal. KT3 . .138 CQ97
Ashcombe St, SW6 . . . . . .100 DB82
Ashcombe Ter, Tad. KT20 . . .173 CV120
Ash Copse, St.Alb. (Brick.Wd.)
 AL2 . . . . .8 BZ31
Ash Ct, Epsom KT19 . . . . .156 CQ105
Ashcroft, Pnr. HA5 . . . . . . .40 CA51
Ashcroft Av, Sid. DA15 . . . .126 EU86
Ashcroft Ct, N20
 off Oakleigh Rd N 44 DD47
Ashcroft Cres, Sid. DA15 . . .126 EU86
Ashcroft Dr, Uxb. (Denh.)
 UB9 . . . . .57 BF58
Ashcroft Pk, Cob. KT11 . . . .154 BY112
Ashcroft Ri, Couls. CR5 . . . .175 DL116
Ashcroft Rd, E3 . . . . .85 DY69
 Chessington KT9 . . . . . . .138 CM104
Ashcroft Sq, W6 off King St . . .99 CW77
Ashdale, Stai. TW19 . . . . . .114 BL89
 Twickenham TW2 . . . . . . .116 CC87
Ashdale Cl, Stan. HA7 . . . . . .41 CF51
Ashdale Rd, SE12 . . . . . . .124 EH88
Ashdale Way, Twick. TW2
 off Ashdale Cl 116 CC87
Ashdene, SE15 . . . . .102 DV81
 Pinner HA5 . . . . .60 BW55
Ashdene Cl, Ashf. TW15 . . . .115 BQ94
Ashdon Cl, Brwd. CM13
 off Poplar Dr 55 GC44
 South Ockendon RM15
 off Afton Dr 91 FV72
 Woodford Green IG8 . . . . . .48 EH51
Ashdon Rd, NW10 . . . . .80 CS67
 Bushey WD23 . . . . .24 BX41
Ashdown Cl, Beck. BR3 . . . .143 EB96
 Bexley DA5 . . . . .127 FC87
Ashdown Cres, NW5
 off Queen's Cres 64 DG64
 Waltham Cross (Chsht.)
 EN8 . . . . .15 DY28
Ashdown Dr, Borwd. WD6 . . .26 CM40
Ashdown Est, E11
 off High Rd Leytonstone . . .68 EE63
Ashdown Gdns, S.Croy. CR2 .176 DV115
Ashdown Rd, Enf. EN3 . . . . .30 DW41
 Epsom KT17 . . . . .157 CT113
 Kingston upon Thames
 KT1 . . . . .138 CL96
 Uxbridge UB10 . . . . .76 BN68
Ashdown Wk, E14 . . . . . . .204 A8
 Romford RM7 . . . . .51 FB54
Ashdown Way, SW17 . . . . .120 DG89
Ashen, E6 off Downings 87 EN72
Ashen Cross, Slou. SL3 . . . . .75 BB71
Ashen Gro, SW19 . . . . . . .120 DA90
Ashentree Ct, EC4 . . . . . . .196 E9
Ashen Vale, S.Croy. CR2 . . .161 DX109
Asher Loftus Way, N11 . . . . .44 DF51
Asher Way, E1 . . . . .202 C2
Ashfield Av, Bushey WD23 . . .24 CB44
 Feltham TW13 . . . . .115 BV88
Ashfield Cl, Beck. BR3 . . . . .123 EA94
 Richmond TW10 . . . . . . .118 CL88
Ashfield La, Chis. BR7 . . . . .125 EQ93
Ashfield Par, N14 . . . . .45 DK46
Ashfield Rd, N4 . . . . .66 DQ58
 N14 . . . . .45 DJ48
 W3 . . . . .81 CT74
Ashfields, Loug. IG10 . . . . . .33 EM40
 Reigate RH2 . . . . .184 DB132
 Watford WD25 . . . . .23 BT35
Ashfield St, E1 . . . . .84 DU71
Ashfield Yd, E1 off Ashfield St .84 DV71
ASHFORD 114 BM92
≈ Ashford 114 BL91
Ashford Av, N8 . . . . .65 DL56
 Ashford TW15 . . . . .115 BP93
 Brentwood CM14 . . . . .54 FV48
 Hayes UB4 . . . . .78 BX72

Ashford Cl, E17 . . . . .67 DZ58
Ashford Cl, Ashf. TW15 . . . .114 BL91
Ashford Cres, Ashf. TW15 . . .114 BL90
 Enfield EN3 . . . . .30 DW40
Ashford Gdns, Cob. KT11 . . .170 BX116
Ashford Ind Est, Wat. WD19 . .40 BX50
H Ashford Hosp, Ashf.
 TW15 . . . . .114 BL89
Ashford Ind Est, Ashf. TW15 .115 BQ91
Ashford Ms, N17
 off Vicarage Rd 46 DU53
Ashford Rd, E6 . . . . .87 EN65
 E18 . . . . .48 EH54
 NW2 . . . . .63 CX63
 Ashford TW15 . . . . .115 BQ94
 Feltham TW13 . . . . .115 BT90
 Iver SL0 . . . . .75 BC66
 Staines TW18 . . . . .134 BK95
Ashford St, N1 . . . . .197 M2
Ash Grn, Uxb. (Denh.) UB9 . . .76 BH65
Ash Gro, E8 . . . . .84 DV67
 N13 . . . . .46 DQ48
 NW2 . . . . .63 CX63
 SE20 . . . . .142 DW96
 W5 . . . . .98 CL75
 Enfield EN1 . . . . .46 DS45
 Feltham TW14 . . . . .115 BS88
 Hayes UB3 . . . . .77 BR73
 Hounslow TW5 . . . . .96 BX81
 Slough (Stoke P.) SL2 . . . . .74 AT66
 Southall UB1 . . . . .78 CA71
 Staines TW18 . . . . .114 BJ93
 Uxbridge (Hare.) UB9 . . . . .38 BK53
 Wembley HA0 . . . . .61 CG63
 West Drayton UB7 . . . . . . .76 BM73
 West Wickham BR4 . . . . . .143 EC103
Ashgrove Rd, Ashf. TW15 . . .115 BQ92
 Bromley BR1 . . . . .123 ED93
 Ilford IG3 . . . . .69 ET60
 Sevenoaks TN13 . . . . . . .190 FG127
Ash Hill Cl, Bushey WD23 . . . .40 CB46
Ash Hill Dr, Pnr. HA5 . . . . . .60 BW55
Ashingdon Cl, E4 . . . . .47 EC48
Ashington Rd, SW6 . . . . . . .99 CZ82
Ash Island, E.Mol. KT8 . . . .137 CD97
Ashlake Rd, SW16 . . . . . . .121 DL91
Ashland Pl, W1 . . . . .194 F6
Ash La, Rom. RM11
 off Southend Arterial Rd . . .72 FN56
 Romford RM1 . . . . .51 FG51
Ashlar Pl, SE18 . . . . .105 EP77
Ashlea Rd, Ger.Cr. (Chal.St.P.)
 SL9 . . . . .36 AX54
Ashleigh Av, Egh. TW20 . . . .113 BC94
Ashleigh Cl, Amer. HP7 . . . . .20 AS39
Ashleigh Ct, Wal.Abb. EN9
 off Lamplighters Cl 16 EG34
Ashleigh Gdns, Sutt. SM1 . . .140 DB103
 Upminster RM14 . . . . .73 FR62
Ashleigh Pt, SE23
 off Dacres Rd 123 DX90
Ashleigh Rd, SE20 . . . . . . .142 DV97
 SW14 . . . . .98 CS83
Ashley Av, Epsom KT18 . . . .156 CR113
 Ilford IG6 . . . . .49 EP54
 Morden SM4
 off Chalgrove Av 140 DA99
Ashley Cen, Epsom KT18 . . .156 CR113
 Walton-on-Thames KT12 . . .153 BV107
Ashley Cl, NW4 . . . . .43 CW54
 Pinner HA5 . . . . .39 BV54
 Sevenoaks TN13 . . . . . . .191 FH124
 Walton-on-Thames KT12 . . .135 BT102
Ashley Ct, Epsom KT18 . . . .156 CR113
 Woking GU21 . . . . .166 AT118
Ashley Cres, N22 . . . . .45 DN54
 SW11 . . . . .100 DG83
Ashley Dr, Bans. SM7 . . . . .158 DA114
 Borehamwood WD6 . . . . . .26 CQ43
 Isleworth TW7 . . . . .97 CE79
 Twickenham TW2 . . . . . . .116 CB87
 Walton-on-Thames KT12 . . .135 BU104
Ashley Gdns, N13 . . . . .46 DQ49
 Orpington BR6 . . . . .163 ES106
 Richmond TW10 . . . . . . .117 CK90
 Wembley HA9 . . . . .62 CL61
Ashley Gro, Loug. IG10
 off Staples Rd 32 EL41
Ashley La, NW4 . . . . .43 CW54
 Croydon CR0 . . . . .159 DP105
ASHLEY PARK, Walt. 135 BT104
Ashley Pk Av, Walt. KT12 . . .135 BT103
Ashley Pk Cres, Walt. KT12 . .135 BT102
Ashley Pk Rd, Walt. KT12 . . .135 BU103
Ashley Pl, SW1 . . . . .199 K7
Ashley Ri, Walt. KT12 . . . . .153 BU105
Ashley Rd, E4 . . . . .47 EA50
 E7 . . . . .86 EJ66
 N17 . . . . .66 DU55
 N19 . . . . .65 DL60
 SW19 . . . . .120 DB93
 Enfield EN3 . . . . .30 DW40
 Epsom KT18 . . . . .156 CR114
 Hampton TW12 . . . . .136 CA95
 Richmond TW9
 off Jocelyn Rd 98 CL83
 Sevenoaks TN13 . . . . . . .191 FH123
 Thames Ditton KT7 . . . . . .137 CF100
 Thornton Heath CR7 . . . . .141 DM98
 Uxbridge UB8 . . . . .76 BH68
 Walton-on-Thames KT12 . . .135 BU102
 Woking GU21 . . . . .166 AT118
Ashleys, Rick. WD3 . . . . . . .37 BF45
Ashley Sq, Epsom KT18 . . . .156 CR113
Ashling Rd, Croy. CR0 . . . . .142 DU102
Ashlin Rd, E15 . . . . .67 ED63
Ashlone Rd, SW15 . . . . .99 CW83
Ashlyn Cl, Bushey WD23 . . . .24 BY42
Ashlyns Gro, Rom. RM11 . . . .72 FK55
Ashlyns Pk, Cob. KT11 . . . . .154 BY113
Ashlyns Rd, Epp. CM16 . . . . .17 ET30
Ashlyns Way, Chess. KT9 . . .155 CK107
Ashmead, N14 . . . . .29 DJ43
Ashmead Dr, Uxb. (Denh.)
 UB9 . . . . .58 BG61

Ashmead Gate, Brom. BR1 . .144 EJ95
Ashmead La, Uxb. (Denh.) UB9 .58 BG61
Ashmead Rd, SE8 . . . . .103 EA82
 Feltham TW14 . . . . .115 BU88
Ashmeads Ct, Rad. (Shenley)
 WD7 off Porters Pk Dr 9 CK33
Ashmere Av, Beck. BR3 . . . .143 ED96
Ashmere Cl, Sutt. SM3 . . . .157 CW106
Ashmere Gro, SW2 . . . . . . .101 DL84
Ash Ms, Epsom KT18 . . . . .156 CS113
Ashmill St, NW1 . . . . .194 B6
Ashmole Pl, SW8 . . . . .101 DM79
Ashmole St, SW8 . . . . .101 DM79
Ashmore Ct, Houns. TW5
 off Wheatlands 96 CA79
Ashmore Gdns, Grav. (Nthflt.)
 DA11 . . . . .130 GD91
Ashmore Gro, Well. DA16 . . .105 ER83
Ashmore La, Kes. BR2 . . . . .162 EH115
Ashmore Rd, W9 . . . . .81 CZ70
Ashmount Est, N19
 off Ashmount Rd 65 DK59
Ashmount Rd, N15 . . . . .66 DT57
 N19 . . . . .65 DJ59
Ashmount Ter, W5
 off Murray Rd 97 CK77
Ashmour Gdns, Rom. RM1 . . .51 FD54
Ashneal Gdns, Har. HA1 . . . .61 CD62
Ashness Gdns, Grnf. UB6 . . . .79 CH65
Ashness Rd, SW11 . . . . . . .120 DF85
Ash Platt, The, Sev. (Seal)
 TN14 . . . . .191 FL121
Ash Platt Rd, Sev. (Seal)
 TN15 . . . . .191 FL121
Ash Ride, Enf. EN2 . . . . .29 DN35
Ashridge Cl, Har. HA3 . . . . . .61 CJ58
 Hemel Hempstead (Bov.)
 HP3 . . . . .5 BA28
Ashridge Cres, SE18 . . . . . .105 EQ80
Ashridge Dr, St.Alb. (Brick.Wd.)
 AL2 . . . . .8 BY30
 Watford WD19 . . . . .40 BW50
Ashridge Gdns, N13 . . . . . . .45 DK50
 Pinner HA5 . . . . .60 BY56
Ashridge Rd, Chesh. HP5 . . . . .4 AW31
Ashridge Way, Mord. SM4 . . .139 CZ97
 Sunbury-on-Thames TW16 . .115 BU93
Ash Rd, E15 . . . . .68 EE64
 Croydon CR0 . . . . .143 EA103
 Dartford DA1 . . . . .128 FK88
 Dartford (Hawley) DA2 . . . .128 FM91
 Gravesend DA12 . . . . . . .131 GJ91
 Orpington BR6 . . . . .163 ET108
 Shepperton TW17 . . . . . .134 BN98
 Sutton SM3 . . . . .139 CY101
 Westerham TN16 . . . . . . .189 ER125
 Woking GU22 . . . . .166 AX120
Ash Row, Brom. BR2 . . . . . .145 EN101
ASHTEAD 172 CL118
≈ Ashtead 171 CK117
Ashtead Gap, Lthd. KT22 . . .171 CH116
H Ashtead Hosp, Ashtd.
 KT21 . . . . .171 CL119
ASHTEAD PARK, Ashtd. 172 CN118
Ashtead Rd, E5 . . . . .66 DU59
Ashtead Wds Rd, Ashtd.
 KT21 . . . . .171 CJ117
Ashton Cl, Sutt. SM1 . . . . . .158 DA105
 Walton-on-Thames KT12 . . .153 BV107
Ashton Gdns, Houns. TW4 . . .96 BZ84
 Romford RM6 . . . . .70 EY58
Ashton Rd, E15 . . . . .67 ED64
 Enfield EN3 . . . . .31 DY36
 Romford RM3 . . . . .52 FK52
 Woking GU21 . . . . .166 AT117
Ashton St, E14 . . . . .85 EC73
Ashtree Av, Mitch. CR4 . . . .140 DE96
Ash Tree Cl, Croy. CR0 . . . .143 DY100
Ashtree Cl, Orp. BR6
 off Broadwater Gdns 163 EP105
Ash Tree Cl, Surb. KT6 . . . .138 CL102
Ashtree Ct, Wal.Abb. EN9
 off Farthingale La 16 EG34
Ash Tree Dell, NW9 . . . . . . .62 CQ57
Ash Tree Rd, Wat. WD24 . . . .23 BV36
Ash Tree Way, Croy. CR0 . . .143 DY99
Ashurst Cl, SE20 . . . . .142 DV95
 Dartford DA1 . . . . .107 FF83
 Kenley CR8 . . . . .176 DR115
 Northwood HA6 . . . . .39 BS52
Ashurst Dr, Ilf. IG2, IG6 . . . .69 EP58
 Shepperton TW17 . . . . . .134 BL99
 Tadworth KT20 . . . . .182 CP130
Ashurst Rd, N12 . . . . .44 DE50
 Barnet EN4 . . . . .28 DF43
 Tadworth KT20 . . . . .173 CV121
Ashurst Wk, Croy. CR0 . . . .142 DV103
Ash Vale, Rick. (Map.Cr.) WD3 .37 BD50
Ashvale Dr, Upmin. RM14 . . . .73 FS61
Ashvale Gdns, Rom. RM5 . . . .51 FD50
 Upminster RM14 . . . . .73 FS61
Ashvale Rd, SW17 . . . . .120 DF92
Ashview Cl, Ashf. TW15 . . . .114 BL93
Ashview Gdns, Ashf. TW15 . .114 BL92
Ashville Rd, E11 . . . . .67 ED61
Ash Wk, SW2 . . . . .121 DM88
 South Ockendon RM15 . . . .91 FX69
 Wembley HA0 . . . . .61 CJ63
Ashwater Rd, SE12 . . . . . . .124 EG88
Ashwell Cl, E6
 off Northumberland Rd 86 EL72
Ashwells Rd, Brwd. CM15 . . . .53 FS41
Ashwells Way, Ch.St.G. HP8 . .36 AW47
Ashwick Cl, Cat. CR3 . . . . . .186 DU125
Ashwin St, E8 . . . . .84 DT65
Ashwindham Ct, Wok. GU21 .166 AS118
Ashwood, Warl. CR6 . . . . . .176 DW120
Ashwood Av, Rain. RM13 . . . .89 FH70
 Uxbridge UB8 . . . . .76 BN72
Ashwood Gdns, Croy.
 (New Adgtn.) CR0 . . . . . .161 EB107
 Hayes UB3 off Cranford Dr . .95 BT77
Ashwood Pl, Dart. (Bean) DA2
 off Bean La 129 FV90

Ashwood Rd, E4 . . . . .47 ED48
Ashwood Rd, Egh. (Eng.Grn.)
 TW20 . . . . .112 AV93
 Potters Bar EN6 . . . . .12 DB33
 Woking GU22 . . . . .167 AZ118
Ashworth Cl, SE5
 off Love Wk 102 DR82
Ashworth Rd, W9 . . . . .82 DB69
Askern Cl, Bexh. DA6 . . . . .106 EX84
Askes Ct, SW11 . . . . .120 DD87
Ask Ms, Epsom KT18 . . . . .156 CS113
Askew Cres, W12 . . . . .99 CT75
Askew Fm La, Grays RM17 . .110 FY78
Askew Rd, W12 . . . . .81 CT74
 Northwood HA6 . . . . .39 BR47
Askham Ct, W12 . . . . .81 CU74
Askham Rd, W12 . . . . .81 CU74
Askill Dr, SW15
 off Keswick Rd 119 CY85
Askwith Rd, Rain. RM13 . . . . .89 FD69
Asland Rd, E15 . . . . .86 EE67
Aslett St, SW18 . . . . .120 DB87
Asmara Rd, NW2 . . . . .63 CY64
Asmar Cl, Couls. CR5 . . . . .175 DL115
Asmuns Hill, NW11 . . . . .64 DA57
Asmuns Pl, NW11 . . . . .63 CZ57
Asolando Dr, SE17 . . . . . . .201 J9
Aspdin Rd, Grav. (Nthflt.)
 DA11 . . . . .130 GD90
Aspen Cl, N19
 off Hargrave Pk 65 DJ61
 W5 . . . . .98 CM75
 Cobham (Stoke D'Ab.)
 KT11 . . . . .170 BY116
 Orpington BR6 . . . . .164 EU106
 St. Albans (Brick.Wd.) AL2 . . .8 BY30
 Staines TW18 . . . . .113 BF90
 Swanley BR8 . . . . .147 FD96
 West Drayton UB7 . . . . . . .76 BM74
Aspen Copse, Brom. BR1 . . .145 EM96
Aspen Ct, Hayes UB3 . . . . . .95 BS77
 Virginia Water GU25 . . . . .132 AX98
Aspen Dr, Wem. HA0 . . . . . .61 CG63
Aspen Gdns, W6 . . . . .99 CV78
 Ashford TW15 . . . . .115 BQ92
 Mitcham CR4 . . . . .140 DG99
Aspen Grn, Erith DA18 . . . .106 EZ76
Aspen Gro, Upmin. RM14 . . . .72 FN63
Aspen La, Nthlt. UB5 . . . . . .78 BY69
Aspen Pk Dr, Wat. WD25 . . . .23 BV35
Aspen Sq, Wey. KT13
 off Oatlands Dr 135 BR104
Aspen Vale, Whyt. CR3
 off Whyteleafe Hill 176 DT118
Aspen Way, E14 . . . . .204 A1
 Banstead SM7 . . . . .157 CX114
 Enfield EN3 . . . . .31 DX35
 Feltham TW13 . . . . .115 BV90
 South Ockendon RM15 . . . .91 FX69
Aspern Gro, NW3 . . . . .64 DE64
Aspinall Rd, SE4 . . . . .103 DX83
Aspinden Rd, SE16 . . . . . . .202 E8
Aspley Rd, SW18 . . . . .120 DB85
Asplins Rd, N17 . . . . .46 DU53
Asprey Gro, Cat. CR3 . . . . .176 DU124
Asprey Pl, Brom. BR1
 off Chislehurst Rd 144 EK96
Asquith Cl, Dag. RM8 . . . . . .70 EW60
Assam St, E1
 off White Ch La 84 DU72
Assata Ms, N1
 off St. Paul's Rd 83 DP65
Assembly Pas, E1 . . . . .84 DW71
Assembly Wk, Cars. SM5 . . .140 DE101
Assher Rd, Walt. KT12 . . . . .136 BY104
Ass Ho La, Har. HA3 . . . . . . .40 CB49
Assurance Cotts, Belv. DA17
 off Heron Hill 106 EZ78
Astall Cl, Har. HA3 . . . . .41 CE53
Astbury Rd, SE15 . . . . .102 DW81
Astede Pl, Ashtd. KT21 . . . .172 CM118
Astell St, SW3 . . . . .198 C10
Asters, The, Wal.Cr. EN7 . . . .14 DR28
Aste St, E14 . . . . .204 D5
Asteys Row, N1 off River Pl . . .83 DP66
Asthall Gdns, Ilf. IG6 . . . . . . .69 EQ56
Astleham Rd, Shep. TW17 . . .134 BL97
Astle St, SW11 . . . . .100 DG82
Astley, Grays RM17 . . . . . . .110 FZ79
Astley Av, NW2 . . . . .63 CW64
Aston Av, Har. HA3 . . . . .61 CJ59
Aston Cl, Ashtd. KT21 . . . . .171 CJ118
 Bushey WD23 . . . . .24 CC44
 Sidcup DA14 . . . . .126 EU90
 Watford WD24 . . . . .24 BW40
Aston Grn, Houns. TW4 . . . . .96 BW82
Aston Ms, Rom. RM6 . . . . . .70 EW59
Aston Pl, SW16
 off Averil Gro 121 DP93
Aston Rd, SW20 . . . . .139 CW96
 W5 . . . . .79 CK72
 Esher (Clay.) KT10 . . . . . .155 CE106
Astons Rd, Nthwd. HA6 . . . . .39 BQ48
Aston St, E14 . . . . .85 DY72
Aston Ter, SW12
 off Cathles Rd 121 DH86
Astonville St, SW18 . . . . . .120 DA88
Aston Way, Epsom KT18 . . . .173 CT116
 Potters Bar EN6 . . . . .12 DD32
Astor Av, Rom. RM7 . . . . . . .71 FC58
Astor Cl, Add. KT15 . . . . . . .152 BK105
 Kingston upon Thames
 KT2 . . . . .118 CP93
Astoria Wk, SW9 . . . . .101 DN83
Astra Cl, Horn. RM12 . . . . . .89 FH65
Astra Dr, Grav. DA12 . . . . . .131 GL92
Astrop Ms, W6 . . . . .99 CW76
Astrop Ter, W6 . . . . .99 CW76
Astwood Ms, SW7 . . . . . . .100 DB77
Asylum Rd, SE15 . . . . .102 DV80
Atalanta Cl, Pur. CR8 . . . . . .159 DN110
Atalanta St, SW6 . . . . .99 CX81
Atbara Ct, Tedd. TW11 . . . . .117 CH93
Atbara Rd, Tedd. TW11 . . . . .117 CH93
Atcham Rd, Houns. TW3 . . . . .96 CC84
Atcost Rd, Bark. IG11 . . . . . .88 EU71
Atheldene Rd, SW18 . . . . . .120 DB88

Athelney St, SE6 . . . . .123 EA90
Athelstan Cl, Rom. RM3
 off Athelstan Rd 52 FM54
Athelstane Gro, E3 . . . . .85 DZ68
Athelstane Ms, N4
 off Stroud Grn Rd 65 DN60
Athelstan Rd, Kings.T. KT1 . .138 CM98
 Romford RM3 . . . . .52 FM53
Athelstan Way, Orp. BR5 . . .146 EU95
Athelstone Rd, Har. HA3 . . . .41 CD54
Athena Cl, Har. HA2
 off Byron Hill Rd 61 CE61
 Kingston upon Thames
 KT1 . . . . .138 CM97
Athenaeum Pl, N10
 off Fortis Grn Rd 65 DH55
Athenaeum Rd, N20 . . . . . . .44 DC46
Athena Pl, Nthwd. HA6
 off The Drive 39 BT53
Athenia Cl, Wal.Cr. EN7
 off Cuffley Hill 13 DP29
Athenlay Rd, SE15 . . . . . . .123 DX85
Athens Gdns, W9
 off Harrow Rd 82 DA70
Atherden Rd, E5 . . . . .66 DW63
Atherfold Rd, SW9 . . . . . . .101 DL83
Atherley Way, Houns. TW4 . .116 BZ87
Atherstone Ct, W2
 off Delamere Ter 82 DB71
Atherstone Ms, SW7 . . . . . .100 DC77
Atherton Cl, Stai. (Stanw.)
 TW19 . . . . .114 BK86
Atherton Dr, SW19 . . . . . . .119 CX91
Atherton Gdns, Grays RM16 .111 GJ77
Atherton Hts, Wem. HA0 . . . .79 CJ65
Atherton Ms, E7 . . . . .86 EF65
Atherton Pl, Har. HA2 . . . . . .61 CD55
 Southall UB1
 off Longford Av 78 CB73
Atherton Rd, E7 . . . . .68 EF64
 SW13 . . . . .99 CU80
 Ilford IG5 . . . . .48 EL54
Atherton St, SW11 . . . . . . .100 DE82
Athlone, Esher (Clay.) KT10 . .155 CE107
Athlone Cl, E5 off Goulton Rd . .66 DV63
 Radlett WD7 . . . . .25 CH36
H Athlone Ho, N6 . . . . .64 DF60
Athlone Rd, SW2 . . . . .121 DM87
Athlone St, NW5 . . . . .82 DG65
Athlon Rd, Wem. HA0 . . . . . .79 CK68
Atholl Cl, Pnr. HA5 . . . . .39 BV53
Athol Gdns, Pnr. HA5 . . . . . .39 BV53
Athole Gdns, Enf. EN1 . . . . .30 DS43
Athol Gdns, Ilf. IG3 . . . . .70 EL58
Athol Rd, Erith DA8 . . . . . . .107 FC78
Athol Sq, E14 . . . . .85 EC72
Athol Way, Uxb. UB10 . . . . . .76 BN69
Atkins Dr, W.Wick. BR4 . . . .143 ED103
Atkinson Cl, Orp. BR6
 off Martindale Av 164 EU106
H Atkinson Morley's Hosp,
 SW20 . . . . .119 CV94
Atkinson Rd, E16 . . . . .86 EJ71
Atkins Rd, E10 . . . . .67 EB58
 SW12 . . . . .121 DK87
Atlanta Boul, Rom. RM1 . . . .71 FE58
Atlantic Rd, SW9 . . . . .101 DN84
Atlantis Cl, Bark. IG11 . . . . . .88 EV69
Atlas Ms, E8 off Tyssen St . . .84 DT65
 N7 . . . . .83 DM65
Atlas Rd, E13 . . . . .86 EG68
 N11 . . . . .45 DH51
 NW10 . . . . .80 CS69
 Dartford DA1
 off Cornwall Rd 108 FM83
 Wembley HA9 . . . . .62 CQ63
Atley Rd, E3 . . . . .85 EA67
Atlip Rd, Wem. HA0 . . . . . . .80 CL67
Atney Rd, SW15 . . . . .99 CY84
Atria Rd, Nthwd. HA6 . . . . . .39 BU50
Attenborough Cl, Wat. WD19
 off Harrow Way 40 BY48
Atterbury Cl, West. TN16 . . .189 ER126
Atterbury Rd, N4 . . . . .65 DN58
Atterbury St, SW1 . . . . .199 N9
Attewood Av, NW10 . . . . . . .62 CS62
Attewood Rd, Nthlt. UB5 . . . .78 BY65
Attfield Cl, N20 . . . . .44 DD47
Attle Cl, Uxb. UB10 . . . . . . .76 BN68
Attlee Cl, Hayes UB4 . . . . . . .77 BV69
 Thornton Heath CR7 . . . . .142 DQ100
Attlee Ct, Grays RM17 . . . . .110 GA76
Attlee Dr, Dart. DA1 . . . . . .128 FN85
Attlee Rd, SE28 . . . . .88 EV73
 Hayes UB4 . . . . .77 BU69
Attlee Ter, E17 . . . . .67 EB56
Attneave St, WC1 . . . . .196 D3
Attwood Cl, S.Croy. CR2 . . .160 DV114
Atwater Cl, SW2 . . . . .121 DN88
Atwell Cl, E10
 off Belmont Pk Rd 67 EB58
Atwell Pl, T.Ditt. KT7 . . . . . .137 CF102
Atwell Rd, SE15
 off Rye La 102 DU82
Atwood, Lthd. (Bkhm.) KT23 .170 BY124
Atwood Av, Rich. TW9 . . . . . .98 CN82
Atwood Rd, W6 . . . . .99 CV77
Atwoods All, Rich. TW9
 off Leyborne Pk 98 CN81
Aubert Pk, N5 . . . . .65 DP63
Aubert Rd, N5 . . . . .65 DP63
Aubretia Cl, Rom. RM3 . . . . .52 FL53
Aubrey Av, St.Alb. (Lon.Col.)
 AL2 . . . . .9 CJ26
Aubrey Pl, NW8 off Violet Hill .82 DC68
Aubrey Rd, E17 . . . . .67 EA55
 N8 . . . . .65 DL57
 W8 . . . . .81 CZ74
Aubrey Wk, W8 . . . . .81 CZ74
Auburn Cl, SE14 . . . . .103 DY80
Aubyn Hill, SE27 . . . . .122 DQ91

★ Place of interest   ≈ Railway station   ⊖ London Underground station   DLR Docklands Light Railway station   ⊷ Tramlink station   H Hospital

Aub - Bad

Aubyn Sq, SW15 .....99 CU84
Auckland Av, Rain. RM13 .....89 FF69
Auckland Cl, SE19 .....142 DT95
  Enfield EN1 .....30 DT37
  Tilbury RM18 .....111 GG82
Auckland Gdns, SE19 .....142 DS95
Auckland Hill, SE27 .....122 DQ91
Auckland Ri, SE19 .....142 DS95
Auckland Rd, E10 .....67 EB62
  SE19 .....142 DT95
  SW11 .....100 DE84
  Caterham CR3 .....176 DS122
  Ilford IG1 .....69 EP60
  Kingston upon Thames
  KT1 .....138 CM98
  Potters Bar EN6 .....11 CY32
Auckland St, SE11
  off Kennington La 101 DM78
Auden Pl, NW1 .....82 DG67
  Sutton SM3
  off Wordsworth Dr 157 CW105
Audleigh Pl, Chig. IG7 .....49 EN51
Audley Cl, N10 .....45 DH52
  SW11 .....100 DG83
  Addlestone KT15 .....152 BH106
  Borehamwood WD6 .....26 CN41
Audley Ct, E18 .....68 EF56
  Pinner HA5
  off Rickmansworth Rd 40 BW54
Audley Dr, E16 .....205 P2
  Warlingham CR6 .....176 DW115
Audley Firs, Walt. KT12 .....154 BW105
Audley Gdns, Ilf. IG3 .....69 ET61
  Loughton IG10 .....33 EQ40
  Waltham Abbey EN9 .....15 EC34
Audley Pl, Sutt. SM2 .....158 DA108
Audley Rd, NW4 .....63 CV58
  W5 .....80 CM71
  Enfield EN2 .....29 DP40
  Richmond TW10 .....118 CM85
Audley Sq, W1 .....198 G2
Audley Wk, Orp. BR5 .....146 EW100
Audrey Cl, Beck. BR3 .....143 EB100
Audrey Gdns, Wem. HA0 .....61 CH61
Audrey Rd, Ilf. IG1 .....69 EP62
Audrey St, E2 .....84 DU68
Audric Cl, Kings.T. KT2 .....138 CN95
Audwick Cl, Wal.Cr. (Chsht.)
  EN8 .....15 DX28
Augur Cl, Stai. TW18 .....113 BF92
Augurs La, E13 .....86 EH69
Augusta Cl, W.Mol. KT8
  off Freeman Dr 136 BZ97
Augusta Rd, Twick. TW2 .....116 CC89
Augusta St, E14 .....85 EB72
August End, Slou. (Geo.Grn.)
  SL3 .....74 AY72
Augustine Cl, Slou. (Colnbr.)
  SL3 .....93 BE83
Augustine Rd, Wal.Abb. EN9
  off Beaulieu Dr 15 EB33
Augustine Rd, W14 .....99 CX76
  Gravesend DA12 .....131 GJ87
  Harrow HA3 .....40 CB53
  Orpington BR5 .....146 EX97
Augustus Cl, Brent. TW8 .....97 CJ80
Augustus La, Orp. BR6 .....146 EU103
Augustus Rd, SW19 .....119 CY88
Augustus St, NW1 .....195 J1
Aultone Way, Cars. SM5 .....140 DF104
  Sutton SM1 .....140 DB103
Aulton Pl, SE11 .....101 DN78
Aurelia Gdns, Croy. CR0 .....141 DM99
Aurelia Rd, Croy. CR0 .....141 DL100
Auriel Av, Dag. RM10 .....89 FD65
Auriga Ms, N16 .....66 DR64
Auriol Cl, Wor.Pk. KT4
  off Auriol Pk Rd 138 CS104
Auriol Dr, Grnf. UB6 .....79 CD66
  Uxbridge UB10 .....76 BN65
Auriol Pk Rd, Wor.Pk. KT4 .....138 CS104
Auriol Rd, W14 .....99 CY77
Austell Gdns, NW7 .....42 CS48
Austen Cl, SE28 .....88 EV74
  Greenhithe DA9 .....129 FW85
  Loughton IG10 .....33 ER41
  Tilbury RM18
  off Coleridge Rd 111 GJ82
Austen Gdns, Dart. DA1 .....108 FM84
Austen Ho, NW6 .....82 DA69
Austen Rd, Erith DA8 .....107 FB80
  Harrow HA2 .....60 CB61
Austenway, Ger.Cr. (Chal.St.P.)
  SL9 .....36 AX55
Austenwood Cl, Ger.Cr. (Chal.St.P.)
  SL9 .....36 AX54
Austenwood La, Ger.Cr. (Chal.St.P.)
  SL9 .....36 AX54
Austin Av, Brom. BR2 .....144 EL99
Austin Cl, SE23 .....123 DZ87
  Coulsdon CR5 .....175 DP118
  Twickenham TW1 .....117 CJ85
Austin Ct, E6 *off Kings Rd* 86 EJ67
Austin Friars, EC2 .....197 L8
Austin Friars Pas, EC2 .....197 L8
Austin Friars Sq, EC2 .....197 L8
Austin Rd, SW11 .....100 DG81
  Gravesend (Nthflt.) DA11 .....131 GF88
  Hayes UB3 .....95 BT75
  Orpington BR5 .....146 EU100
Austin's La, Uxb. UB10 .....59 BR63
Austins Mead, Hem.H. (Bov.)
  HP3 .....5 BB28
Austin St, E2 .....197 P3
Austin Waye, Uxb. UB8 .....76 BJ67
Austral Cl, Sid. DA15 .....125 ET90
Austral Dr, Horn. RM11 .....72 FK59
Australia Rd, W12 .....81 CV73
  Slough SL1 .....92 AV75
Austral St, SE11 .....200 F8
Austyn Gdns, Surb. KT5 .....138 CP102
Autumn Cl, SW19 .....120 DC93
  Enfield EN1 .....30 DU39
Autumn Dr, Sutt. SM2 .....158 DB109

Autumn St, E3 .....85 EA67
Auxiliaries Way, Uxb. UB9 .....57 BF57
Avalon Cl, SW20 .....139 CY96
  W13 .....79 CG71
  Enfield EN2 .....29 DN40
  Orpington BR6 .....146 EX104
  Watford WD25 .....8 BY32
Avalon Rd, SW6 .....100 DB81
  W13 .....79 CG70
  Orpington BR6 .....146 EW103
Avard Gdns, Orp. BR6 .....163 EQ105
Avarn Rd, SW17 .....120 DF93
Avebury Ct, N1 *off Poole St* 84 DR67
Avebury Pk, Surb. KT6 .....137 CK101
Avebury Rd, E11
  off Southwest Rd 67 ED60
  SW19 .....139 CZ95
  Orpington BR6 .....145 ER104
Avebury St, N1 *off Poole St* 84 DR67
AVELEY, S.Ock. 91 FR73
Aveley Bypass, S.Ock. RM15 .....90 FQ73
Aveley Cl, Erith DA8 .....107 FF79
  South Ockendon (Aveley)
  RM15 .....91 FR74
Aveley Rd, Rom. RM1 .....71 FD56
  Upminster RM14 .....90 FP65
Aveline St, SE11 .....200 D10
Aveling Cl, Pur. CR8 .....159 DM113
  Purley HA3 .....47 EA54
Aveling Pk Rd, E17 .....47 EA54
Avelon Rd, Rain. RM13 .....89 FG67
  Romford RM5 .....51 FD51
Ave Maria La, EC4 .....196 G9
Avenell Rd, N5 .....65 DP62
Avening Rd, SW18
  off Brathway Rd 120 DA87
Avening Ter, SW18 .....120 DA86
Avenons Rd, E13 .....86 EG70
Avenue, The, E4 .....47 ED51
  E11 (Leytonstone) 68 EF61
  E11 (Wanstead) 68 EH58
  N3 .....44 DA54
  N8 .....65 DN55
  N10 .....45 DJ54
  N11 .....45 DH49
  N17 .....46 DS54
  NW6 .....81 CX67
  SE7 .....104 EJ80
  SE10 .....103 ED80
  SW4 .....120 DG85
  SW11 .....120 DE87
  SW18 .....120 DE87
  W4 .....98 CS76
  W13 .....79 CH73
  Addlestone (New Haw)
  KT15 .....152 BG110
  Barnet EN5 .....27 CY41
  Beckenham BR3 .....143 EB95
  Betchworth (Brock.) RH3 .....182 CN134
  Bexley DA5 .....126 EX87
  Brentwood CM13 .....53 FX51
  Bromley BR1 .....144 EK97
  Bushey WD23 .....24 BZ42
  Carshalton SM5 .....158 DG108
  Coulsdon CR5 .....175 DK115
  Croydon CR0 .....142 DS104
  Egham TW20 .....113 BB91
  Epsom KT17 .....157 CV108
  Esher (Clay.) KT10 .....155 CE107
  Gravesend DA11 .....131 GG88
  Greenhithe DA9 .....109 FV84
  Hampton TW12 .....116 BZ93
  Harrow HA3 .....41 CF53
  Hornchurch RM12 .....72 FJ61
  Hounslow TW3 .....116 CB85
  Hounslow (Cran.) TW5 .....95 BU81
  Isleworth TW7 .....97 CD79
  Keston BR2 .....144 EK104
  Leatherhead KT22 .....155 CF112
  Loughton IG10 .....32 EK44
  Northwood HA6 .....39 BQ51
  Orpington BR6 .....145 ET100
  Orpington (St.P.Cray) BR5 .....126 EV94
  Pinner HA5 .....60 BZ58
  Pinner (Hatch End) HA5 .....40 CA52
  Potters Bar EN6 .....11 CZ32
  Radlett WD7 .....9 CG33
  Richmond TW9 .....98 CM82
  Romford RM1 .....71 FD56
  Slough (Datchet) SL3 .....92 AV81
  Staines TW18 .....134 BH95
  Staines (Wrays.) TW19 .....92 AX83
  Sunbury-on-Thames
  TW16 .....135 BV95
  Surbiton KT5 .....138 CM100
  Sutton SM2 .....157 CZ109
  Sutton (Cheam) SM3 .....157 CW108
  Tadworth KT20 .....173 CV122
  Twickenham TW1 .....117 CJ85
  Uxbridge (Cowley) UB8 .....76 BK70
  Uxbridge (Ickhm.) UB10 .....58 BN63
  Waltham Abbey (Nazeing)
  EN9 .....16 EJ25
  Watford WD17 .....23 BU40
  Wembley HA9 .....62 CM61
  West Drayton UB7 .....94 BL76
  West Wickham BR4 .....143 EC101
  Westerham TN16 .....179 EQ123
  Whyteleafe CR3 .....176 DU119
  Windsor (Old Wind.) SL4 .....112 AV85
  Woking (Chobham) GU24 .....150 AT109
  Worcester Park KT4 .....139 CT103
Avenue App, Kings.L. WD4 .....6 BN30
Avenue Ct, N14 .....29 DJ44
  NW2 .....63 DE67
  Hounslow TW5
  off The Avenue 95 BU81
  Romford RM3 .....52 FM52
  Tadworth KT20 .....173 CV122
  West Drayton UB7 .....94 BK76
Avenue Ct, Tad. KT20
  off The Avenue 173 CV123
Avenue Cres, W3 .....98 CP75
  Hounslow TW5 .....95 BV80
Avenue Dr, Slou. SL3 .....75 AZ71
Avenue Elmers, Surb. KT6 .....138 CL99
Avenue Gdns, SE25 .....142 DU97
  SW14 .....98 CS83

Avenue Gdns, W3 .....98 CP75
  Hounslow TW5
  off The Avenue 95 BU80
  Teddington TW11 .....117 CF94
Avenue Gate, Loug. IG10 .....32 EJ44
Avenue Ind Est, E4 .....47 DZ51
  Romford RM3 .....52 FK54
Avenue Ms, N10 .....65 DH55
Avenue Pk Rd, SE27 .....121 DP89
Avenue Ri, Bushey WD23 .....24 CA43
✧ Avenue Road 143 DX96
Avenue Rd, E7 .....68 EH64
  N6 .....65 DJ59
  N12 .....44 DC49
  N14 .....45 DH45
  N15 .....66 DR57
  NW3 .....82 DD66
  NW8 .....82 DD66
  NW10 .....81 CT68
  SE20 .....142 DW95
  SE25 .....142 DU96
  SW16 .....141 DK96
  SW20 .....139 CV96
  W3 .....98 CP75
  Banstead SM7 .....174 DB115
  Beckenham BR3 .....142 DW95
  Belvedere DA17 .....107 FC77
  Bexleyheath DA7 .....106 EY83
  Brentford TW8 .....97 CJ78
  Brentwood CM14 .....54 FW49
  Caterham CR3 .....176 DR122
  Cobham KT11 .....170 BX116
  Epping (They.B.) CM16 .....33 ER36
  Epsom KT18 .....156 CR114
  Erith DA8 .....107 FC80
  Feltham TW13 .....115 BT90
  Hampton TW12 .....136 CB95
  Isleworth TW7 .....97 CF81
  Kingston upon Thames
  KT1 .....138 CL97
  New Malden KT3 .....138 CS98
  Pinner HA5 .....60 BY55
  Romford (Chad.Hth.) RM6 .....70 EV59
  Romford (Harold Wd.) RM3 .....52 FM52
  Sevenoaks TN13 .....191 FJ123
  Southall UB1 .....96 BZ75
  Staines TW18 .....113 BD92
  Sutton SM2 .....158 DA101
  Teddington TW11 .....117 CG94
  Wallington SM6 .....159 DJ108
  Westerham (Tats.) TN16 .....178 EL120
  Woodford Green IG8 .....48 EJ51
Avenue S, Surb. KT5 .....138 CM101
Avenue Ter, N.Mal. KT3
  off Kingston Rd 138 CQ97
  Watford WD19 .....24 BY44
Averil Gro, SW16 .....121 DP95
Averill St, W6 .....99 CX79
Avern Gdns, W.Mol. KT8 .....136 CB98
Avern Rd, W.Mol. KT8 .....136 CB99
Avery Fm Row, SW1 .....198 G9
Avery Gdns, Ilf. IG2 .....69 EM57
AVERY HILL, SE9 .....125 EQ86
★ Avery Hill Pk, SE9
  (Eltham) 125 EQ86
Avery Hill Rd, SE9 .....125 ER86
Avery Row, W1 .....195 H10
Avey La, Loug. IG10 .....32 EH39
  Waltham Abbey EN9 .....31 ED36
Aviary Cl, E16 .....86 EF71
Aviary Rd, Wok. GU22 .....168 BG116
Aviemore Cl, Beck. BR3 .....143 DZ99
Aviemore Way, Beck. BR3 .....143 DX83
Avignon Ct, SE1
  off Old Kent Rd 102 DS77
Avington Gro, SE20 .....122 DW94
Avington Way, SE15
  off Daniel Gdns 102 DT80
Avion Cres, NW9 .....43 CU53
Avior Dr, Nthwd. HA6 .....39 BT49
Avis Gro, Croy. CR0 .....161 DY110
Avis Sq, E1 .....85 DX72
Avoca Rd, SW17 .....120 DG91
Avocet Ms, SE28 .....105 ER76
Avon Cl, Add. KT15 .....152 BG107
  Gravesend DA12 .....131 GK89
  Hayes UB4 .....78 BW70
  Sutton SM1 .....158 DC105
  Watford WD25 .....8 BW34
  Worcester Park KT4 .....139 CU103
Avon Ct, Grnf. UB6
  off Braund Av 78 CB70
Avondale Av, N12 .....44 DB50
  NW2 .....62 CS62
  Barnet EN4 .....44 DF46
  Esher KT10 .....137 CG104
  Staines TW18 .....113 BF94
  Worcester Park KT4 .....139 CT102
Avondale Cl, Loug. IG10 .....49 EM45
  Walton-on-Thames KT12
  off Pleasant Pl 154 BW106
Avondale Ct, E11 .....68 EE60
  E16 *off Avondale Rd* 86 EE71
  E18 .....48 EH53
Avondale Cres, Enf. EN3 .....31 DY41
  Ilford IG4 .....68 EK57
Avondale Dr, Hayes UB3 .....77 BU74
  Loughton IG10 .....49 EM45
Avondale Gdns, Houns. TW4 .....116 BZ85
Avondale Ms, Brom. BR1
  off Avondale Rd 124 EG93
Avondale Pk Gdns, W11 .....81 CY73
Avondale Pk Rd, W11 .....81 CY73
Avondale Pavement, SE1
  off Avondale Sq 102 DU78
Avondale Ri, SE15 .....102 DT83
Avondale Rd, E16 .....86 EE71
  E17 .....67 EA59
  N3 .....44 DC53
  N13 .....45 DN47
  N15 .....65 DP57
  SE9 .....124 EL89
  SW14 .....98 CR83
  SW19 .....120 DB92
  Ashford TW15 .....114 BK90
  Bromley BR1 .....124 EE93

Avondale Rd, Harrow HA3 .....61 CF55
  South Croydon CR2 .....160 DQ107
  Welling DA16 .....106 EW82
Avondale Sq, SE1 .....102 DU78
Avon Gm, S.Ock. RM15 .....91 FV72
Avonley Rd, SE14 .....102 DW80
Avonmead, Wok. GU21
  off Silversmiths Way 166 AW118
Avonmore Gdns, W14
  off Avonmore Rd 99 CY77
Avonmore Pl, W14
  off Avonmore Rd 99 CY77
Avonmore Rd, W14 .....99 CZ77
Avonmouth Rd, Dart. DA1 .....128 FK85
Avonmouth St, SE1 .....201 H6
Avon Path, S.Croy. CR2 .....160 DQ107
Avon Pl, SE1 .....201 J5
Avon Rd, E17 .....67 ED55
  SE4 .....103 EA83
  Greenford UB6 .....78 CA70
  Sunbury-on-Thames
  TW16 .....115 BT94
  Upminster RM14 .....73 FR58
Avonstowe Cl, Orp. BR6 .....145 EQ104
Avontar Rd, S.Ock. RM15 .....91 FV70
Avon Way, E18 .....68 EG55
Avonwick Rd, Houns. TW3 .....96 CB82
Avril Way, E4 .....47 EC50
Avro Way, Wall. SM6 .....159 DL108
  Weybridge KT13 .....152 BL110
Awlfield Av, N17 .....46 DR53
Awliscombe Rd, Well. DA16 .....105 ET82
Axe St, Bark. IG11 .....87 EQ67
Axholme Av, Edg. HA8 .....42 CN53
Axis Pk, Slou. (Langley) SL3 .....93 BB78
Axminster Cres, Well. DA16 .....106 EW81
Axminster Rd, N7 .....65 DL62
Axtaine Rd, Orp. BR5 .....146 EX101
Axtane, Grav. (Sthflt.) DA13 .....130 FZ94
Axtane Cl, Dart. (Sutt.H.)
  DA4 .....148 FQ96
Axwood, Epsom KT18 .....172 CQ115
Aybrook St, W1 .....194 F7
Aycliffe Cl, Brom. BR1 .....145 EM98
Aycliffe Rd, W12 .....81 CT74
  Borehamwood WD6 .....26 CL39
Ayebridges Av, Egh. TW20 .....113 BC94
Aylands Cl, Wem. HA9
  off Preston Rd 62 CL61
Aylands Rd, Enf. EN3 .....30 DW36
Aylesbury Cl, E7
  off Atherton Rd 86 EF65
Aylesbury Ct, Sutt. SM1
  off Benhill Wd Rd 140 DC104
Aylesbury Est, SE17
  off Villa St 102 DR78
Aylesbury Rd, SE17 .....102 DR78
  Bromley BR2 .....144 EG97
Aylesbury St, EC1 .....196 F5
  NW10 .....62 CR62
Aylesford Av, Beck. BR3 .....143 DY99
Aylesford St, SW1 .....199 M10
Aylesham Cen, The, SE15 .....102 DU81
Aylesham Cl, NW7 .....43 CU52
Aylesham Rd, Orp. BR6 .....145 ET101
Ayles Rd, Hayes UB4 .....77 BV69
Aylestone Av, NW6 .....81 CX67
Aylesworth Spur, Wind.
  (Old Wind.) SL4 .....112 AV87
Aylett Rd, SE25 .....142 DV98
  Isleworth TW7 .....97 CE82
  Upminster RM14 .....72 FQ61
Ayley Cft, Enf. EN1 .....30 DU43
Ayliffe Cl, Kings.T. KT1
  off Cambridge Gdns 138 CN96
Aylmer Cl, Stan. HA7 .....41 CG49
Aylmer Dr, Stan. HA7 .....41 CG49
Aylmer Par, N2 .....64 DF57
Aylmer Rd, E11 .....68 EF60
  N2 .....64 DE57
  W12 .....99 CT75
  Dagenham RM8 .....70 EY62
Ayloffe Rd, Dag. RM9 .....88 EZ65
Ayloffs Cl, Horn. RM11 .....72 FL57
Ayloffs Wk, Horn. RM11 .....72 FK57
Aylsham Dr, Uxb. UB10 .....59 BR62
Aylsham La, Rom. RM3 .....52 FJ49
Aylton Est, SE16 .....202 G5
Aylward Rd, SE23 .....123 DX89
  SW20 .....139 CZ96
Aylwards Ri, Stan. HA7 .....41 CG49
Aylward St, E1 .....84 DW72
Aylwyn Est, SE1 .....201 P6
Aymer Cl, Stai. TW18 .....133 BE95
Aymer Dr, Stai. TW18 .....133 BE95
Aynhoe Rd, W14 .....99 CX77
Aynho St, Wat. WD18 .....23 BV43
Aynscombe Angle, Orp. BR6 .....146 EV101
Aynscombe La, SW14 .....98 CQ83
Aynscombe Path, SW14
  off Thames Bk 98 CQ82
Ayot Path, Borwd. WD6 .....26 CN37
Ayr Ct, W3 *off Monks Dr* 80 CN71
Ayres Cl, E13 .....86 EG69
Ayres Cres, NW10 .....80 CR66
Ayres St, SE1 .....201 J4
Ayr Grn, Rom. RM1 .....51 FE52
Ayron Rd, S.Ock. RM15 .....91 FV70
Ayrsome Rd, N16 .....66 DS62
Ayrton Rd, SW7 .....100 DD76
Ayr Way, Rom. RM1 .....51 FE52
Aysgarth Ct, Sutt. SM1
  off Sutton Common Rd 140 DB104
Aysgarth Rd, SE21 .....122 DS86
Aytoun Pl, SW9 .....101 DM82
Aytoun Rd, SW9 .....101 DM82
Azalea Cl, W7 .....79 CF74
  Ilford IG1 .....69 EP64
Azalea Cl, Wok. GU22 .....166 AX119
  Woodford Green IG8
  off The Bridle Path 48 EE52
Azalea Dr, Swan. BR8 .....147 FD98
Azalea Wk, Pnr. HA5 .....59 BV57
  Southall UB2
  off Navigator Dr 96 CC75

Azalea Way, Slou. (Geo.Grn.) SL3
  off Blinco La 74 AY72
Azania Ms, NW5
  off Cathcart St 83 DH65
Azenby Rd, SE15 .....102 DT82
Azile Everitt Ho, SE18
  off Vicarage Pk 105 EQ78
Azof St, SE10 .....205 J9

B

Baalbec Rd, N5 .....65 DP64
Babbacombe Cl, Chess. KT9 .....155 CK106
Babbacombe Gdns, Ilf. IG4 .....68 EL56
Babbacombe Rd, Brom. BR1 .....144 EG95
Baber Dr, Felt. TW14 .....116 BW86
Babington Ri, Wem. HA9 .....80 CN65
Babington Rd, NW4 .....63 CV56
  SW16 .....121 DK92
  Dagenham RM8 .....70 EW64
  Hornchurch RM12 .....71 FH60
Babmaes St, SW1 .....199 L1
Babylon La, Tad. (Lwr.Kgswd.)
  KT20 .....184 DA127
Bacchus Wk, N1 .....197 M1
Bachelor's La, Wok. GU23 .....168 BN124
Baches St, N1 .....197 L3
Back Ch La, E1 .....84 DU73
Back Grn, Walt. KT12 .....154 BW107
Back Hill, EC1 .....196 D5
Backhouse Pl, SE17 .....201 N9
Back La, N8 .....65 DL57
  NW3 *off Heath St* 64 DC63
  Bexley DA5 .....126 FA87
  Brentford TW8 .....97 CK79
  Chalfont St. Giles HP8 .....36 AU48
  Edgware HA8 .....42 CQ53
  Grays (N.Stfd.) RM16 .....91 FW74
  Purfleet RM19 .....109 FS76
  Richmond TW10 .....117 CJ90
  Rickmansworth (Chenies)
  WD3 .....21 BB38
  Romford RM6
  off St. Chad's Rd 70 EY59
  Sevenoaks (Godden Grn.)
  TN15 .....191 FN124
  Sevenoaks (Ide Hill) TN14 .....190 FC126
  Watford (Let.Hth.) WD25 .....25 CE39
Backley Gdns, SE25 .....142 DU100
Back Rd, Sid. DA14 .....126 EU91
Bacon Gro, SE1 .....201 P7
Bacon La, NW9 .....62 CP56
  Edgware HA8 .....42 CN53
Bacon Link, Rom. RM5 .....51 FB51
Bacons Dr, Pot.B. (Cuffley)
  EN6 .....13 DL29
Bacons La, N6 .....64 DG60
Bacons Mead, Uxb. (Denh.)
  UB9 .....58 BG61
Bacon St, E1 .....84 DT70
  E2 .....84 DT70
Bacon Ter, Dag. RM8
  off Fitzstephen Rd 70 EV64
Bacton, NW5 .....64 DG64
Bacton St, E2 *off Roman Rd* 84 DW69
Badburgham Ct, Wal.Abb. EN9 .....16 EF33
Baddeley Cl, Enf. EN3
  off Government Row 31 EA38
Baddow Cl, Dag. RM10 .....88 FA67
  Woodford Green IG8 .....48 EK51
Baddow Wk, N1 .....84 DQ67
Baden Cl, Stai. TW18 .....114 BG94
Baden Pl, SE1 .....201 K4
Baden Powell Cl, Dag. RM9 .....88 EY67
  Surbiton KT6 .....138 CM103
Baden Powell Rd, Sev. TN13 .....190 FE121
Baden Rd, N8 .....65 DK56
  Ilford IG1 .....69 EP64
Bader Cl, Ken. CR8 .....176 DR115
Bader Wk, Grav. (Nthflt.)
  DA11 .....130 GE90
Bader Way, Rain. RM13 .....89 FG65
Badger Cl, Felt. TW13
  off Sycamore Cl 115 BU90
  Hounslow TW4 .....96 BW83
  Ilford IG2 .....69 EQ59
Badgers Cl, Ashf. TW15
  off Fordbridge Rd 114 BM92
  Borehamwood WD6
  off Kingsley Av 26 CM40
  Enfield EN2 .....29 DP41
  Harrow HA1 .....61 CD58
  Hayes UB3 .....77 BS73
  Woking GU21 .....166 AW118
Badgers Copse, Orp. BR6 .....145 ET103
  Worcester Park KT4 .....139 CT103
Badgers Cft, N20 .....43 CY46
  SE9 .....125 EN90
Badgers Hill, Vir.W. GU25 .....132 AW99
Badgers Hole, Croy. CR0 .....161 DX105
Badgers La, Warl. CR6 .....176 DW120
BADGERS MOUNT, Sev. 165 FB110
Badgers Mt, Grays (Orsett)
  RM16 .....111 GF75
Badgers Ri, Sev. (Bad.Mt.)
  TN14 .....164 FA110
Badgers Rd, Sev. (Bad.Mt.)
  TN14 .....165 FB110
Badgers Wk, N.Mal. KT3 .....138 CS96
  Purley CR8 .....159 DK111
  Rickmansworth (Chorl.)
  WD3 .....21 BF42
  Whyteleafe CR3 .....176 DT119
Badgers Wd, Cat. CR3 .....186 DQ125
Badingham Dr, Lthd. (Fetch.)
  KT22 .....171 CE123
Badlis Rd, E17 .....47 EA54
Badlow Cl, Erith DA8 .....107 FE80
Badminton Cl, Borwd. WD6 .....26 CN40
  Harrow HA1 .....61 CE56
  Northolt UB5 .....78 CA65
Badminton Ms, E16 .....205 N2
Badminton Rd, SW12 .....120 DG86

★ Place of interest   ⇌ Railway station   ⊖ London Underground station   DLR Docklands Light Railway station   ✧ Tramlink station   H Hospital

Badric Ct, SW11
off Yelverton Rd 100 DD82
Badsworth Rd, SE5 ......102 DQ80
Baffin Way, E14
off Prestons Rd 85 EC73
Bagley Cl, West Dr. UB7 ..94 BL75
Bagley's La, SW6 ......100 DB81
Bagleys Spring, Rom. RM6 ..70 EY56
Bagot Cl, Ashtd. KT21 ..172 CM116
Bagshot Rd, SE18
off Prince Imperial Rd ..105 EN81
TW20 ......112 AW94
Enfield EN1 ......46 DT45
Bagshot St, SE17 ......102 DS78
Bahram Rd, Epsom KT19 ..156 CR110
Baildon St, SE8 ......103 DZ80
Bailey Cl, E4 ......47 EC49
N11 ......45 DK52
Purfleet RM19
off Gabion Av 109 FR77
Bailey Pl, SE26 ......123 DX93
Baillie Cl, Rain. RM13 ..89 FH70
Baillies Wk, W5
off Liverpool Rd 97 CK75
Bainbridge Cl, Rich. TW10
off Latchmere Cl 118 CL92
Bainbridge Rd, Dag. RM9 ..70 EZ63
Bainbridge St, WC1 ......195 N8
Baines Cl, S.Croy. CR2
off Brighton Rd 160 DQ106
Bainton Mead, Wok. GU21 ..166 AU117
Baird Av, Sthl. UB1 ......78 CB73
Baird Cl, E10 off Marconi Rd ..67 EA60
NW9 ......62 CQ58
Bushey WD23
off Ashfield Av 24 CB44
Baird Gdns, SE19 ......122 DS91
Baird Rd, Enf. EN1 ......30 DV42
Baird St, EC1 ......197 J4
Bairstow Cl, Borwd. WD6 ..26 CL39
Baizdon Rd, SE3 ......104 EE82
Bakeham La, Egh. (Eng.Grn.)
TW20 ......112 AW94
Baker Boy La, Croy. 161 DZ112
DA11 ......131 GF91
Baker La, Mitch. CR4 ......140 DG96
Baker Pas, NW10 off Acton La .80 CS67
Baker Rd, NW10 ......80 CS67
SE18 ......104 EL80
Bakers Av, E17 ......67 EB58
Bakers Cl, Ken. CR8
off Park Rd 160 DQ114
Bakers Ct, SE25 ......142 DS97
Bakers End, SW20 ......139 CY96
Bakers Fld, N7
off Crayford Rd 65 DK63
Bakers Gdns, Cars. SM5 ..140 DE103
Bakers Hill, E5 ......66 DW60
Barnet EN5 ......28 DB40
Bakers La, N6 ......64 DF57
Epping CM16 ......17 ET30
Bakers Mead, Gdse. RH9 ..186 DW130
Baker's Ms, W1 ......194 F8
Bakers Ms, Orp. BR6 ......163 ET107
Baker's Pas, NW3 off Heath St ..64 DC63
Baker's Rents, E2 ......197 P3
Bakers Rd, Uxb. UB8 ......76 BK66
Waltham Cross (Chsht.)
EN7 ......14 DV30
Bakers Row, E15 ......86 EE68
Baker's Row, EC1 ......196 D5
⊖ Baker Street 194 E5
Baker St, NW1 ......194 E5
W1 ......194 E6
Enfield EN1 ......30 DR41
Potters Bar EN6 ......27 CY35
Weybridge KT13 ......152 BN105
Bakers Wd, Uxb. (Denh.) UB9 ..57 BD60
Baker's Yd, EC1
off Baker's Row 83 DN70
Uxbridge UB8
off Bakers Rd 76 BK66
Bakery Cl, SW9 ......101 DM81
Bakery Path, Edg. HA8
off Station Rd 42 CP51
Bakery Pl, SW11
off Altenburg Gdns 100 DF84
Bakewell Way, N.Mal. KT3 ..138 CS96
Balaams La, N14 ......45 DK47
Balaam St, E13 ......86 EG69
Balaclava Rd, SE1 ......202 A9
Surbiton KT6 ......137 CJ101
Bala Grn, NW9
off Snowdon Dr 62 CS58
Balcaskie Rd, SE9 ......125 EM85
Balchen Rd, SE3 ......104 EK82
Balchier Rd, SE22 ......122 DV86
Balcombe Cl, Bexh. DA6 ..106 EX84
Balcombe St, NW1 ......194 D4
Balcon Ct, W5 off Boileau Rd ..80 CM72
Balcon Way, Borwd. WD6 ..26 CQ39
Balcorne St, E9 ......84 DW66
Balder Ri, SE12 ......124 EH89
Balderton St, W1 ......194 G9
Baldocks Rd, Epp. (They.B.)
CM16 ......33 ES35
Baldock St, E3 ......85 EB69
Baldock Way, Borwd. WD6 ..26 CM39
Baldry Gdns, SW16 ......121 DL93
Baldwin Cres, SE5 ......102 DQ81
Baldwin Gdns, Houns. TW3
off Chamberlain Gdns ..96 CC81
Baldwin's Gdns, EC1 ......196 D6
Baldwins Hill, Loug. IG10 ..33 EM40
Baldwins La, Rick. (Crox.Grn.)
WD3 ......22 BM43
Baldwin St, EC1 ......197 K3
Baldwin Ter, N1 ......84 DQ68
Baldwyn Gdns, W3 ......80 CR73
Baldwyns Pk, Bex. DA5 ..127 FD89
Baldwyns Rd, Bex. DA5 ..127 FD89
Bale Rd, E1 ......85 DY71
Balfern Gro, W4 ......98 CS78
Balfern St, SW11 ......100 DE81
Balfe St, N1 ......196 A1

Balfont Cl, S.Croy. CR2 .....160 DU113
Balfour Av, W7 ......79 CF74
Balfour Av, Wok. GU22 ..166 AY122
Balfour Business Cen, Sthl.
UB2 ......96 BX76
Balfour Gro, N20 ......44 DF48
Balfour Ho, W10
off St. Charles Sq 81 CX71
Balfour Ms, N9
off The Broadway 46 DU48
W1 ......198 G2
Balfour Pl, SW15 ......99 CV84
W1 ......198 G1
Balfour Rd, N5 ......66 DQ63
SE25 ......142 DU98
SW19 ......120 DB94
W3 ......80 CQ71
W13 ......97 CG75
Bromley BR2 ......144 EK99
Carshalton SM5 ......158 DF108
Grays RM17 ......110 GC77
Harrow HA1 ......61 CD57
Hounslow TW3 ......96 CB83
Ilford IG1 ......69 EP61
Southall UB2 ......96 BX76
Weybridge KT13 ......152 BN105
Balfour St, SE17 ......201 K8
Balfron Twr, E14
off St. Leonards Rd 85 EC72
Balgonie Rd, E4 ......47 ED46
Balgores Cres, Rom. RM2 ..71 FH55
Balgores La, Rom. RM2 ..71 FH55
Balgores Sq, Rom. RM2 ..71 FH56
Balgowan Cl, N.Mal. KT3 ..138 CS99
Balgowan Rd, Beck. BR3 ..143 DY97
Balgowan St, SE18 ......105 ET77
BALHAM, SW12 ......120 DF88
⇌ Balham 121 DH88
⊖ Balham 121 DH88
Balham Continental Mkt,
SW12 off Shipka Rd 121 DH88
Balham Gro, SW12 ......120 DG87
Balham High Rd, SW12 ..120 DG88
SW17 ......120 DG89
Balham Hill, SW12 ......121 DH87
Balham New Rd, SW12 ..120 DG87
Balham Pk Rd, SW12 ......120 DF88
Balham Rd, N9 ......46 DU47
Balham Sta Rd, SW12 ..121 DH88
Balkan Wk, E1 ......202 E1
Balladier Wk, E14 ......85 EB71
Ballamore Rd, Brom. BR1 ..124 EG90
Ballance Rd, E9 ......85 DX65
Ballands N, The, Lthd. KT22 ..171 CE122
Ballands S, The, Lthd. KT22 ..171 CE123
Ballantine St, SW18 ......100 DC84
Ballantyne Dr, Tad. (Kgswd.)
KT20 ......173 CZ121
Ballard Cl, Kings.T. KT2 ..118 CR94
Ballards Cl, Dag. RM10 ..89 FB67
Ballards Fm Rd, Croy. CR0 ..160 DU107
South Croydon CR2 ..160 DU107
Ballards Grn, Tad. KT20 ..173 CY119
Ballards La, N3 ......44 DA53
N12 ......44 DA53
Oxted RH8 ......188 EJ129
Ballards Ms, Edg. HA8 ......42 CN51
Ballards Ri, S.Croy. CR2 ..160 DU107
Ballards Rd, NW2 ......63 CU61
Dagenham RM10 ......89 FB67
Ballards Way, Croy. CR0 ..160 DV107
South Croydon CR2 ..160 DU107
Ballast Quay, SE10 ......204 G10
Ballater Cl, Wat. WD19 ..40 BW49
Ballater Rd, SW2 ......101 DL84
South Croydon CR2 ......160 DT106
Ballenger Ct, Wat. WD18 ..23 BV41
Ballina St, SE23 ......123 DX86
Ballingdon Rd, SW11 ......120 DG86
Ballinger Pt, E3
off Bromley High St 85 EB69
Balliol Av, E4 ......47 ED49
Balliol Rd, N17 ......46 DS53
W10 ......81 CW72
Welling DA16 ......106 EV82
Balloch Rd, SE6 ......123 ED88
Ballogie Av, NW10 ......62 CS63
Ballow Cl, SE5 off Harris Rd ..102 DS80
Balls Bridge Pt, N1
off Balls Pond Rd 84 DR65
Balls Pond Rd, N1 ......84 DR65
Balmain Cl, W5 ......79 CK74
Balmer Rd, E3 ......85 DZ68
Balmes Rd, N1 ......84 DR67
Balmoral Av, N11 ......44 DG50
Beckenham BR3 ......143 DY98
Balmoral Cl, SW15
off Westleigh Av 119 CX86
St. Albans (Park St.) AL2 ..8 CC28
Balmoral Cres, W.Mol. KT8 ..136 CA97
Balmoral Dr, Borwd. WD6 ..26 CR43
Hayes UB4 ......77 BT71
Southall UB1 ......78 BZ70
Woking GU22 ......167 BC116
Balmoral Gdns, W13 ......97 CG76
Bexley DA5 ......126 EZ87
Ilford IG3 ......69 ET60
South Croydon CR2 ......160 DR110
Balmoral Gro, N7 ......83 DM65
Balmoral Ms, W12 ......99 CT75
Balmoral Rd, E7 ......68 EJ63
E10 ......67 EB61
NW2 ......81 CV65
Abbots Langley WD5 ......7 BU32
Brentwood CM15 ......54 FV44
Dartford (Sutt.H.) DA4 ..128 FP94
Enfield EN3 ......31 DX36
Harrow HA2 ......60 CA63
Hornchurch RM12 ......72 FK62
Kingston upon Thames
KT1 ......138 CM98
Romford RM2 ......71 FH56
Watford WD24 ......24 BW38
Worcester Park KT4 ......139 CV104
Balmoral Way, Sutt. SM2 ..158 DA110
Balmore Cl, E14 ......85 EC72

Balmore Cres, Barn. EN4 ..28 DG43
Balmore St, N19 ......65 DH61
Balmuir Gdns, SW15 ......99 CW84
Balnacraig Av, NW10 ......62 CS63
Balniel Gate, SW1 ......199 N10
Balquhain Cl, Ashtd. KT21 ..171 CK117
Baltic Cl, SW19 ......120 DD94
Baltic Ct, SE16 ......203 J4
Baltic Pl, N1
off Kingsland Rd 84 DS67
Baltic St E, EC1 ......197 H5
Baltic St W, EC1 ......197 H5
Baltimore Pl, Well. DA16 ..105 ET82
Balvaird Pl, SW1 ......101 DK78
Balvernie Gro, SW18 ......119 CZ87
Bamber Ho, Bark. IG11
off St. Margarets 87 EQ67
Bamborough Gdns, W12 ..99 CW75
Bamford Av, Wem. HA0 ..80 CM67
Bamford Ct, E15 off Clays La ..67 EB64
Bamford Rd, Bark. IG11 ..87 EQ65
Bromley BR1 ......123 EC92
Bamford Way, Rom. RM5 ..51 FB50
Bampfylde Cl, Wall. SM6 ..141 DJ104
Bampton Dr, NW7 ......43 CU52
Bampton Rd, SE23 ......123 DX90
Romford RM3 ......52 FL53
Bampton Way, Wok. GU21 ..166 AU118
Banavie Gdns, Beck. BR3 ..143 EC95
Banbury Cl, Enf. EN1
off Holtwhites Hill 29 DP39
Banbury Ct, WC2 ......195 P10
Sutton SM2 ......158 DA108
Banbury Enterprise Cen, Croy.
CR0 off Factory La 141 DP103
Banbury Rd, E9 ......85 DX66
E17 ......47 DX52
Banbury St, SW11 ......100 DE82
Watford WD18 ......23 BU42
Banbury Vil, Grav. DA13 ..130 FZ94
Banbury Wk, Nthlt. UB5
off Brabazon Rd 78 CA68
Banchory Rd, SE3 ......104 EH80
Bancroft Av, N2 ......64 DE57
Buckhurst Hill IG9 ......48 EG47
Bancroft Cl, Ashf. TW15
off Feltham Hill Rd 114 BN92
Bancroft Ct, Nthlt. UB5 ......78 BW67
Reigate RH2 ......184 DB134
Bancroft Gdns, Har. HA3 ..40 CC53
Orpington BR6 ......145 ET102
Bancroft Rd, E1 ......84 DW69
Harrow HA3 ......40 CC54
Reigate RH2 ......184 DA134
Band La, Egh. TW20 ......113 AZ92
Bandon Cl, Uxb. UB10 ......76 BM67
Bandon Ri, Wall. SM6 ......159 DK106
Banfield Rd, SE15 ......102 DV84
Bangalore St, SW15 ......99 CW83
Bangor Cl, Nthlt. UB5 ......60 CB64
Bangors Cl, Iver SL0 ......75 BE72
Bangors Rd N, Iver SL0 ..75 BD67
Bangors Rd S, Iver SL0 ..75 BE71
Banim St, W6 ......99 CV76
Banister Rd, W10 ......81 CX69
⊖ Bank 197 K9
DLR Bank 197 K9
Bank, The, N6
off Cholmeley Pk 65 DH60
Bank Av, Mitch. CR4 ......140 DD96
Bank Ct, Dart. DA1
off High St 128 FL86
Bank End, SE1 ......201 J2
Bankfoot, Grays (Bad.Dene)
RM17 ......110 FZ77
Bankfoot Rd, Brom. BR1 ..124 EE91
Bankhurst Rd, SE6 ......123 DZ87
Bank La, SW15 ......118 CS85
Kingston upon Thames
KT2 ......118 CL94
Bank Ms, Sutt. SM1
off Sutton Ct Rd 158 DC107
★ Bank of England, EC2 ..197 K9
★ Bank of England Mus,
EC2 ......197 L9
Bank Pl, Brwd. CM14
off High St 54 FW47
Banksian Wk, Islw. TW7 ..97 CE81
Banksia Rd, N18 ......46 DW50
Bankside, SE1 ......201 H1
Enfield EN2 ......29 DP39
Gravesend (Nthflt.) DA11 ..130 GC86
Sevenoaks (Dunt.Grn.)
TN13 ......190 FE121
South Croydon CR2 ......160 DT107
Southall UB1 ......78 BX74
Woking GU21
off Wyndham Rd 166 AV118
Bankside Av, Nthlt. UB5
off Townson Av 77 BU68
Bankside Cl, Bex. DA5 ......127 FD91
Carshalton SM5 ......158 DE107
Isleworth TW7 ......97 CF84
Westerham (Bigg.H.) TN16 ..178 EJ118
Dartford (S.Dart.) KT7 ..137 CH102
★ Bankside Gall, SE1
off Hopton St 200 G1
Bankside Rd, Ilf. IG1 ......69 EQ64
Bankside Way, SE19
off Lunham Rd 122 DS93
Banks La, Bexh. DA6 ......106 EZ84
Epping CM16 ......17 ET78
Bank's La, Lthd. KT24 ......169 BV122
Banks Rd, Borwd. WD6 ..26 CQ40
Bank St, E14 ......204 A3
Gravesend DA12 ......131 GH86
Sevenoaks TN13 ......191 FH125
Banks Way, E12
off Grantham Rd 69 EN63
Bankton Rd, SW2 ......101 DN84
Bankwell Rd, SE13 ......104 EE84
Bann Cl, S.Ock. RM15 ......91 FV73
Banner Cl, Purf. RM19
off Brimfield Rd 109 FR77
Bannerman Ho, SW8 ......101 DM79
Banner St, EC1 ......197 J5
Banning St, SE10 ......104 EE78

Bannister Cl, SW2
off Ewen Cres 121 DN88
Bannister Cl, Grnf. UB6 ..61 CD64
Slough SL3 ......92 AY75
Bannister Dr, Brwd. CM13 ..55 GC44
Bannister Gdns, Orp. BR5
off Main Rd 146 EW97
Bannister Ho, E9
off Homerton High St ..67 DX64
Bannockburn Rd, SE18 ..105 ES77
★ Banqueting Ho, SW1 ..199 P3
BANSTEAD 174 DB115
⇌ Banstead 157 CY116
Banstead Gdns, N9 ......46 DS48
Banstead Pl, Bans. SM7 ..174 DC116
Banstead Rd, Bans. SM7 ..157 CX112
Carshalton SM5 ......158 DE107
Caterham CR3 ......176 DR121
Epsom KT17 ......157 CV110
Purley CR8 ......159 DN111
Banstead Rd S, Sutt. SM2 ..158 DD110
Banstead St, SE15 ......102 DW83
Banstead Way, Wall. SM6 ..159 DL106
Banstock Rd, Edg. HA8 ..42 CP51
Banting Dr, N21 ......29 DM43
Banton Cl, Enf. EN1
off Central Av 30 DV40
Bantry St, SE5 ......102 DR80
Banwell Rd, Bex. DA5
off Woodside La 126 EX86
Banyard Rd, SE16 ......202 E7
Banyards, Horn. RM11 ......72 FL56
Bapchild Pl, Orp. BR5 ......146 EW98
Baptist Gdns, NW5
off Queen's Cres 82 DG65
Barandon Wk, W11 ......81 CX73
Barbara Brosnan Ct, NW8
off Grove End Rd 82 DD68
Barbara Hucklesby Cl, N22
off The Sandlings 45 DP54
Barbauld Rd, N16 ......66 DS62
Barbel Cl, Wal.Cr. EN8 ......15 EA34
Barber Cl, N21 ......45 DN45
Barberry Cl, Rom. RM3 ..52 FJ52
Barber's All, E13 ......86 EH69
Barbers Rd, E15 ......85 EB68
BARBICAN, EC2 ......197 H7
⇌ Barbican 196 G6
⊖ Barbican 196 G6
Barbican, The, EC2 ......197 H6
★ Barbican Arts & Conf Cen,
EC2 ......197 J6
Barbican Rd, Grnf. UB6 ..78 CB72
Barb Ms, W6 ......99 CW76
Barbon Cl, WC1 ......196 B6
Barbot Cl, N9 ......46 DU48
Barchard St, SW18 ......120 DB85
Barchester Cl, W7 ......79 CF74
Uxbridge UB8 ......76 BJ70
Barchester Rd, Har. HA3 ..41 CD54
Slough SL3 ......93 AZ75
Barchester St, E14 ......85 EB71
Barclay Cl, SW6 ......100 DA80
Leatherhead (Fetch.) KT22 ..170 CB123
Watford WD18 ......23 BU44
Barclay Oval, Wdf.Grn. IG8 ..48 EG49
Barclay Path, E17 ......67 EC57
Barclay Rd, E11 ......68 EE60
E13 ......86 EJ70
E17 ......67 EC57
N18 ......46 DR51
SW6 ......100 DA80
Croydon CR0 ......142 DR104
Barclay Way, SE22
off Lordship La 122 DU87
Grays (W.Thur.) RM20 ..109 FT78
Barcombe Av, SW2 ......121 DL89
Barcombe Cl, Orp. BR5 ..145 ET98
Barden Cl, Uxb. (Hare.) UB9 ..38 BJ52
Barden St, SE18 ......105 ES80
Bardeswell Cl, Brwd. CM14 ..54 FW47
Bardfield Av, Rom. RM6 ..70 EX55
Bardney Rd, Mord. SM4 ..140 DB98
Bardolph Av, Croy. CR0 ..161 DZ109
Bardolph Rd, N7 ......65 DL63
Richmond TW9
off St. Georges Rd 98 CM83
Bardsey Pl, E1
off Mile End Rd 84 DW71
Bardsley Cl, Croy. CR0 ..142 DT104
Bardsley La, SE10 ......103 EC79
Barfett St, W10 ......81 CZ70
Barfield, Dart. (Sutt.H.) DA4 ..148 FP95
Barfield Av, N20 ......44 DF48
Barfield Rd, E11 ......68 EF60
Bromley BR1 ......145 EN97
Barfields, Loug. IG10 ......33 EN42
Redhill (Bletch.) RH1 ..185 DP133
Barfields Path, Loug. IG10 ..33 EN42
Barford Cl, NW4 ......43 CU53
Barford St, N1 ......83 DN67
Barforth Rd, SE15 ......102 DV83
Barfreston Way, SE20 ..142 DV95
Bargate Cl, SE18 ......105 ET78
New Malden KT3 ......139 CU100
Barge Ho Rd, E16 ......87 EP74
Barge Ho St, SE1 ......200 E2
Bargery Rd, SE6 ......123 EB88
Barge Wk, E.Mol. KT8 ..137 CK96
Kingston upon Thames
KT1 ......137 CK95
Walton-on-Thames KT12 ..136 CC96
Bargrove Cl, SE20 ......122 DU94
Bargrove Cres, SE6
off Elm La 123 DZ89
Barham Av, Borwd. (Elstree)
WD6 ......26 CM41
Barham Cl, Brom. BR2 ..144 EL102
Chislehurst BR7 ......125 EP92

Bad - Bar

Barham Cl, Grav. DA12 ..131 GM88
Romford RM7 ......51 FB54
Wembley HA0 ......79 CH65
Weybridge KT13 ......153 BQ105
Barham Rd, SW20 ......119 CU94
Chislehurst BR7 ......125 EP92
Dartford DA1 ......128 FN87
South Croydon CR2 ......160 DQ106
Baring Cl, SE12 ......124 EG89
Baring Rd, SE12 ......124 EG87
Barnet EN4 ......28 DD41
Croydon CR0 ......142 DU102
Baring St, N1 ......84 DR67
Barkantine Shop Par, E14
off The Quarterdeck 103 EA75
Bark Burr Rd, Grays RM16 ..110 FZ75
Barker Cl, N.Mal. KT3 ......138 CP98
Northwood HA6 ......39 BT52
Barker Dr, NW1 ......83 DJ66
Barker Ms, SW4 ......101 DH84
Barker Rd, Cher. KT16 ..133 BE101
Barker St, SW10 ......100 DC79
Barker Wk, SW16 ......121 DK90
Barker Way, SE22
off Dulwich Common ..122 DU88
Barkham Rd, N17 ......46 DR52
Barkham Ter, SE1 ......200 E6
Bark Hart Rd, Orp. BR6 ..146 EV102
BARKING 87 EP67
⇌ Barking 87 EQ66
⊖ Barking 87 EQ66
Barking Ind Pk, Bark. IG11 ..87 ET67
Barking Rd, E6 ......86 EK68
E13 ......86 EH70
E16 ......86 EF71
BARKINGSIDE, Ilf. 69 EP55
⊖ Barkingside 69 ER56
Bark Pl, W2 ......82 DB73
Barkston Gdns, SW5 ......100 DB77
Barkston Path, Borwd. WD6 ..26 CN37
Barkwood Cl, Rom. RM7 ..71 FC57
Barkworth Rd, SE16 ......102 DV78
Barlborough St, SE14 ......102 DW80
Barlby Gdns, W10 ......81 CX70
Barlby Rd, W10 ......81 CX71
Barlee Cres, Uxb. UB8 ......76 BJ71
Barle Gdns, S.Ock. RM15 ..91 FV72
Barley Brow, Wat. WD25
off High Elms La 8 BW31
Bushey WD23 ......24 CB43
Barleycorn Way, E14 ......85 DZ73
Hornchurch RM11 ......72 FM58
Barleyfields Cl, Rom. RM6 ..70 EV59
Barley La, Ilf. IG3 ......70 EU60
Romford RM6 ......70 EV58
Barley Mow Ct, Bet. RH3 ..182 CQ134
Barley Mow Pas, EC1 ......196 G7
W4 ......98 CR78
Barley Mow Rd, Egh. (Eng.Grn.)
TW20 ......112 AW92
Barley Mow Way, Shep.
TW17 ......134 BN98
Barley Shotts Business Pk, W10
off St. Ervans Rd 81 CZ71
Barlow Dr, SE18 ......104 EL81
Barlow Pl, W1 ......199 J1
Barlow Rd, NW6 ......81 CZ65
W3 ......80 CP74
Hampton TW12 ......116 CA94
Barlow St, SE17 ......201 L9
Barlow Way, Rain. RM13 ..89 FD71
Barmeston Rd, SE6 ......123 EB89
Barmor Cl, Har. HA2 ......40 CB54
Barmouth Av, Grnf. UB6 ..79 CF68
Barmouth Rd, SW18 ......120 DC86
Croydon CR0 ......143 DX103
Barnabas Ct, N21
off Cheyne Wk 29 DN43
Barnabas Rd, E9 ......67 DX64
Barnaby Cl, Har. HA2 ......60 CC61
Barnaby Pl, SW7 ......100 DD77
Barnaby Way, Chig. IG7 ..49 EP48
Barnacre Cl, Uxb. UB8
off New Peachey La 76 BK72
Barnacres Rd, Hem.H. HP3 ..6 BM25
Barnard Cl, SE18 ......105 EN77
Chislehurst BR7 ......145 ER95
Sunbury-on-Thames TW16
off Oak Gro 115 BV94
Wallington SM6 ......159 DK108
Barnard Ct, Wok. GU21
off Raglan Rd 166 AS118
Barnard Gdns, Hayes UB4 ..77 BV70
New Malden KT3 ......139 CU98
Barnard Gro, E15
off Vicarage La 86 EF66
Barnard Hill, N10 ......44 DG54
Barnard Ms, SW11 ......100 DE84
Barnardo Dr, Ilf. IG6 ......69 EQ56
Barnardo Gdns, E1
off Devonport St 85 DX73
Barnardo St, E1
off Devonport St 85 DX72
Barnardos Village, Ilf. IG6 ..69 EQ55
Barnard Rd, SW11 ......100 DE84
Enfield EN1 ......30 DV40
Mitcham CR4 ......140 DG97
Warlingham CR6 ......177 EB119
Barnard's Inn, EC1 ......196 E8
Barnato Cl, W.Byf. KT14
off Viscount Gdns 152 BL112
Barnby Sq, E15 off Barnby St ..86 EE67
Barnby St, E15 ......86 EE67
NW1 ......195 L1
Barn Cl, Ashf. TW15 ......115 BP92
Banstead SM7 ......174 DD115
Epsom KT18 ......172 CQ115
Northolt UB5 ......78 BW68
Radlett WD7 ......25 CG35
Barn Cres, Pur. CR8 ......160 DR113
Stanmore HA7 ......41 CJ51
Barncroft Cl, Loug. IG10 ..33 EN43

Bar - Bay

Barncroft Cl, Uxb. UB8 . . . . . .77 BP71
Barncroft Grn, Loug. IG10 . . .33 EN43
Barncroft Rd, Loug. IG10 . . . .33 EN43
BARNEHURST, Bexh. 107 FD83
⇌ Barnehurst 107 FC81
Barnehurst Av, Bexh. DA7 . . .107 FC81
  Erith DA8 . . . . .107 FC81
Barnehurst Cl, Erith DA8 . . .107 FC81
Barnehurst Rd, Bexh. DA7 . . .107 FC82
Barn Elms Pk, SW15 . . . . .99 CW82
Barn End Dr, Dart. DA2 . . . . .128 FJ90
Barn End La, Dart. DA2 . . . . .128 FJ90
BARNES, SW13 . . . . .99 CU82
⇌ Barnes 99 CU83
Barnes All, Hmptn. TW12
  off Hampton Ct Rd 136 CC96
Barnes Av, SW13 . . . . .99 CU82
  Southall UB2 . . . . .96 BZ77
⇌ Barnes Bridge 98 CS82
Barnes Br, SW13 . . . . .98 CS82
  W4 .98 CS82
Barnesbury Ho, SW4 . . . . . . .121 DK85
Barnes Cl, E12 . . . . .68 EK63
★ Barnes Common, SW13 . . .99 CU83
Barnes Ct, E16
  off Ridgwell Rd 86 EJ71
  Woodford Green IG8 . . . . . . .48 EK50
BARNES CRAY, Dart. 107 FH84
Barnes Cray Cotts, Dart. DA1
  off Maiden La 127 FG85
Barnes Cray Rd, Dart. DA1 . .107 FG84
Barnesdale Cres, Orp. BR5 . .146 EU100
Barnes End, N.Mal. KT3 . . . .139 CU99
Barnes High St, SW13 . . . . . . .99 CT82
Ⓗ Barnes Hosp, SW14 . . . . . .98 CS83
Barnes Ho, Bark. IG11
  off St. Marys 87 ER67
Barnes La, Kings L. WD4 . . . . .6 BH27
Barnes Pikle, W5 . . . . .79 CK73
Barnes Ri, Kings L. WD4 . . . . .6 BM27
Barnes Rd, N18 . . . . .46 DW49
  Ilford IG1 . . . . .69 EQ64
Barnes St, E14 . . . . .85 DY72
Barnes Ter, SE8 . . . . .103 DZ78
Barnes Wallis Dr, Wey.
Barnes Way, Iver SL0 . . . . . . .75 BZ73
BARNET 27 CZ41
Barnet Bypass, Barn. EN5 . . .26 CS41
Barnet Dr, Brom. BR2 . . . . . .144 EL103
BARNET GATE, Barn. 27 CT44
Barnet Gate La, Barn. 27 CT44
Ⓗ Barnet Gen Hosp, Barn.
  EN5 . . . . .27 CX42
Barnet Gro, E2 . . . . .84 DU69
Barnet Hill, Barn. EN5 . . . . . .28 DA42
Barnet Ho, N20 . . . . .44 DC47
Barnet La, N20 . . . . .43 CZ46
  Barnet EN5 . . . . .27 CZ44
  Borehamwood WD6 . . . . . . .25 CK44
★ Barnet Mus, Barn. EN5
  off Wood St 27 CY42
Barnet Rd, Barn. EN5 . . . . . . .27 CV43
  Potters Bar EN6 . . . . .28 DA35
  St. Albans (Lon.Col.) AL2 . . .10 CL27
Barnett Cl, Erith DA8 . . . . . .107 FF82
  Leatherhead KT22 . . . . . . .171 CH119
Barnett Trd Est, Barn. EN5 . . .27 CZ41
Barnetts Shaw, Oxt. RH8 . . .187 ED127
Barnett St, E1
  off Cannon St Rd 84 DV72
Barnett Wd La, Ashtd. KT21 .171 CJ119
  Leatherhead KT22 . . . . . . .171 CH120
Barney Rd, NW7 . . . . .42 CR45
Barnet Wd Rd, Brom. BR2 . .144 EJ103
Barney Cl, SE7 . . . . .104 EJ78
Barnfield, Bans. SM7 . . . . . . .158 DB114
  Epping CM16 . . . . .18 EU28
  Gravesend DA11 . . . . .131 GG89
  Iver SL0 . . . . .75 BE72
  New Malden KT3 . . . . .138 CS100
Barnfield, Croy. CR0 . . . . . . .142 DW103
  Kingston upon Thames
  KT2 . . . . .118 CL92
  Mitcham CR4 . . . . .141 DH98
Barnfield Cl, N4
  off Crouch Hill 65 DL59
  SW17 . . . . .120 DC90
  Coulsdon CR5 . . . . .176 DQ119
  Greenhithe DA9 . . . . .129 FT86
  Swanley BR8 . . . . .147 FC101
Barnfield Gdns, SE18 off Plumstead
  Common Rd 105 EP79
  Kingston upon Thames
  KT2 . . . . .118 CL91
Barnfield Pl, E14 . . . . .204 A9
Barnfield Rd, SE18 . . . . .105 EP79
  W5 .79 CJ70
  Belvedere DA17 . . . . .106 EZ79
  Edgware HA8 . . . . .42 CQ53
  Orpington BR5 . . . . .146 EX97
  Sevenoaks TN13 . . . . .190 FD123
  South Croydon CR2 . . . . . .160 DS109
  Westerham (Tats.) TN16 . . .178 EJ121
Barnfield Way, Oxt. RH8 . . . .188 EG133
Barnfield Wd Cl, Beck. BR3 . .143 ED100
Barnfield Wd Rd, Beck. BR3 .143 ED100
Barnham Dr, SE28 . . . . .87 ET74
Barnham Rd, Grnf. UB6 . . . . . .78 CC69
Barnham St, SE1 . . . . .201 N4
Barnhill, Pnr. HA5 . . . . .60 BW57
Barn Hill, Wem. HA9 . . . . .62 CP61
Barnhill Av, Brom. BR2 . . . . .144 EF99
Barnhill La, Hayes UB4 . . . . . .77 BV69
Barnhill Rd, Hayes UB4 . . . . . .77 BV70
  Wembley HA9 . . . . .62 CQ62
Barnhurst Path, Wat. WD19 . .40 BW50
Barningham Way, NW9 . . . . . .62 CR58
Barn Lea, Rick. (Mill End)
  WD3 . . . . .38 BG46
Barnlea Cl, Felt. TW13 . . . . . .116 BY89
Barn Mead, Epp. (They.B.)
  CM16 . . . . .33 ES36
  Ongar CM5 . . . . .19 FE29

Barnmead, Wok. (Chobham)
  GU24 . . . . .150 AT110
Barnmead Gdns, Dag. RM9 . .70 EZ64
Barn Meadow, Epp. CM16
  off Upland Rd 17 ET25
Barn Meadow La, Lthd. (Bkhm.)
  KT23 . . . . .170 BZ124
Barnmead Rd, Beck. BR3 . . . .143 DY95
  Dagenham RM9 . . . . .70 EZ64
Barn Ms, Har. HA2 . . . . .60 CA62
Barnock Cl, Dart. DA1
  off Lower Sta Rd 127 FE86
Barnsbury Cl, N.Mal. KT3 . . .138 CQ98
Barnsbury Cres, Surb. KT5 . .138 CQ102
Barnsbury Est, N1
  off Barnsbury Rd 83 DN67
Barnsbury Gro, N7 . . . . .83 DN66
Barnsbury La, Surb. KT5 . . . .138 CP103
Barnsbury Pk, N1 . . . . .83 DN66
Barnsbury Rd, N1 . . . . .83 DN68
Barnsbury Sq, N1 . . . . .83 DN66
Barnsbury St, N1 . . . . .83 DN66
Barnsbury Ter, N1 . . . . .83 DM66
Barnscroft, SW20 . . . . .139 CV97
Barnsdale Av, E14 . . . . .204 A8
Barnsdale Cl, Borwd. WD6 . . .26 CM99
Barnsdale Rd, W9 . . . . .81 CZ70
Barnsfield Pl, Uxb. UB8 . . . . .76 BJ66
Barnsley Rd, Rom. RM3 . . . . .52 FM52
Barnsley St, E1 . . . . .84 DV70
Barnstaple Path, Rom. RM3 . .52 FJ50
Barnstaple Rd, Rom. RM3 . . . .52 FJ50
  Ruislip HA4 . . . . .60 BW62
Barnston Wk, N1
  off Popham St 84 DQ67
Barnston Way, Brwd. CM13 . . .55 GC43
Barn St, N16 off Stoke
  Newington Ch St 66 DS62
Barnsway, Kings L. WD4 . . . . .6 BL28
Barnway, Egh. (Eng.Grn.)
  TW20 . . . . .112 AW92
Barn Way, Wem. HA9 . . . . .62 CN60
Barnwell Rd, SW2 . . . . .121 DN85
  Dartford DA1 . . . . .108 FM83
Barnwood Cl, W9 . . . . .82 DB70
  Ruislip HA4
  off Lysander Rd 59 BR61
Barnyard, The, Tad. KT20 . . .173 CU124
Baron Cl, N11
  off Balmoral Av 44 DG50
  Sutton SM2 . . . . .158 DB110
Baroness Rd, E2
  off Diss St 84 DT69
Baronet Gro, N17
  off St. Paul's Rd 46 DU53
Baronet Rd, N17 . . . . .46 DU53
Baron Gdns, Ilf. IG6 . . . . .69 EQ55
Baron Gro, Mitch. CR4 . . . . . .140 DE98
Baron Rd, Dag. RM8 . . . . .70 EX60
Barons, The, Twick. TW1 . . . .117 CH86
⊕ Barons Court
  off Whelan Way 141 DK104
Barons Ct Rd, W14 . . . . .99 CY78
Baronsfield Rd, Twick. TW1 . .117 CH86
Barons Gate, Barn. EN4 . . . . .28 DE44
Barons Hurst, Epsom KT18 . .172 CQ116
Barons Keep, W14 . . . . .99 CY78
Barons Mead, Har. HA1 . . . . . .61 CE56
Baronsmead Rd, SW13 . . . . . .99 CU81
Baronsmede, W5 . . . . .98 CM75
Baronsmere Rd, N2 . . . . .64 DE56
Barons Pl, SE1 . . . . .200 E5
Baron St, N1 . . . . .83 DN68
Barons Wk, Croy. CR0 . . . . . .143 DY100
Barons Way, Egh. TW20 . . . . .113 BD93
Baron Wk, E16 . . . . .86 EF71
  Mitcham CR4 . . . . .140 DE98
Barque Ms, SE8
  off Watergate St 103 EA79
Barrack Path, Wok. GU21 . . .166 AT118
Barrack Rd, Houns. TW4 . . . . .96 BX84
Barrack Row, Grav. DA11 . . . .131 GH86
Barracks, The, Add. KT15 . . .134 BH104
Barracks La, Barn. EN5
  off High St 27 CY41
Barra Hall Circ, Hayes UB3 . . .77 BS72
Barra Hall Rd, Hayes UB3 . . . .77 BS73
Barras Cl, Enf. EN3
  off Government Row 31 EA38
Barratt Av, N22 . . . . .45 DM54
Barratt Ind Pk, Sthl. UB1 . . . .96 CA75
Barratt Way, Har. HA3
  off Tudor Rd 61 CD55
Barrenger Rd, N10 . . . . .44 DF53
Barrens Brae, Wok. GU22 . . .167 BA118
Barrens Cl, Wok. GU22 . . . . .167 BA118
Barrens Pk, Wok. GU22 . . . . .167 BA118
Barrett Cl, Rom. RM3 . . . . . . .51 FH52
Barrett Rd, E17 . . . . .67 EC56
  Leatherhead (Fetch.) KT22 .170 CC124
Barrett Grn Rd, NW10 . . . . . . .80 CQ68
Barretts Gro, N16 . . . . .66 DS64
Barretts Rd, Sev. (Dunt.Grn.)
  TN13 . . . . .181 FD120
Barrett St, W1 . . . . .194 G9
Barrhill Rd, SW2 . . . . .121 DL89
Barricane, Wok. GU21 . . . . . .166 AV119
Barrie Cl, Couls. CR5 . . . . . . .175 DJ115
Barriedale, SE14 . . . . .103 DY81
Barrie Est, W2
  off Craven Ter 82 DD73
Barrie Ho, W3 . . . . .98 CQ75
Barrier App, SE7 . . . . .104 EK76
Barrier Pt Rd, E16 . . . . .86 EJ74
Barringer Sq, SW17 . . . . .120 DG91
Barrington Cl, NW5 . . . . .64 DG64
  Ilford IG5 . . . . .49 EM53
  Loughton IG10
  off Barrington Rd 33 EQ42
Barrington Ct, Brwd. CM13 . . .55 GC44
Barrington Dr, Uxb. (Hare.)
  UB9 .38 BG52
Barrington Grn, Loug. IG10 . . .33 EQ42
Barrington Lo, Wey. KT13 . . .153 BQ106

Barrington Pk Gdns, Ch.St.G.
  HP8 .36 AX46
Barrington Rd, E12 . . . . .87 EN65
  N8 . . . . .65 DK57
  SW9 . . . . .101 DP83
  Bexleyheath DA7 . . . . .106 EX82
  Loughton IG10 . . . . .33 EQ41
  Purley CR8 . . . . .159 DJ112
  Sutton SM3 . . . . .140 DA102
Barrington Vil, SE18 . . . . . . .105 EN81
Barrow Av, Cars. SM5 . . . . . .158 DF108
Barrow Cl, N21 . . . . .45 DP48
Barrowdene Cl, Pnr. HA5
  off Paines La 40 BY54
Barrowell Grn, N21 . . . . .45 DP47
Barrowfield Cl, N9 . . . . .46 DV48
Barrowgate Rd, W4 . . . . .98 CQ78
Barrow Grn Rd, Oxt. RH8 . . .187 EC128
Barrow Hedges Cl, Cars.
  SM5 . . . . .158 DE108
Barrow Hedges Way, Cars.
  SM5 . . . . .158 DE108
Barrow Hill, Wor.Pk. KT4 . . .138 CS103
Barrow Hill Cl, Wor.Pk. KT4
  off Barrow Hill 138 CS103
Barrow Hill Est, NW8
  off Barrow Hill Rd 82 DE68
Barrow Hill Rd, NW8 . . . . . . .194 B1
Barrow La, Wal.Cr. (Chsht.)
  EN7 .14 DT30
Barrow Pt Av, Pnr. HA5 . . . . . .40 BY54
Barrow Pt La, Pnr. HA5 . . . . . .40 BY54
Barrow Rd, SW16 . . . . .121 DK93
  Croydon CR0 . . . . .159 DN106
Barrowsfield, S.Croy. CR2 . . .160 DT112
Barrow Wk, Brent. TW8
  off Glenhurst Rd 97 CJ78
Barr Rd, Grav. DA12 . . . . .131 GM89
  Potters Bar EN6 . . . . .12 DC33
Barrs Rd, NW10 . . . . .80 CR66
Barry Av, N15 . . . . .66 DT58
  Bexleyheath DA7 . . . . .106 EY80
Barry Cl, Grays RM16 . . . . . . .111 GG75
  Orpington BR6 . . . . .145 ES104
  St. Albans AL2 . . . . .8 CB25
Barry Rd, E6 . . . . .86 EL72
  NW10 . . . . .80 CQ66
  SE22 . . . . .122 DU86
Barset Rd, SE15 . . . . .102 DW83
Barson Cl, SE20 . . . . .122 DW94
Barston Rd, SE27 . . . . .122 DQ90
Barstow Cres, SW2 . . . . .121 DM88
Barter St, WC1 . . . . .196 A7
Barters Wk, Pnr. HA5
  off High St 60 BY55
Bartholomew Cl, EC1 . . . . . . .197 H7
  SW18 . . . . .100 DC84
Bartholomew Dr, Rom.
  (Harold Wd.) RM3 . . . . .52 FK54
Bartholomew La, EC2 . . . . . . .197 L9
Bartholomew Pl, EC1 . . . . . . .197 H7
Bartholomew Rd, NW5 . . . . . .83 DJ65
Bartholomew Sq, E1
  off Coventry Rd 84 DV70
  EC1 . . . . .197 J4
Bartholomew St, SE1 . . . . . . .201 K7
Bartholomew Vil, NW5 . . . . . .83 DJ65
Bartholomew Way, Swan.
  BR8 . . . . .147 FE97
Barth Rd, SE18 . . . . .105 ES77
Bartle Av, E6 . . . . .86 EL68
Bartle Rd, W11 . . . . .81 CY72
Bartlett Cl, E14 . . . . .85 EA72
Bartlett Ct, EC4 . . . . .196 E8
Bartlett Rd, Grav. DA11 . . . . .131 GG88
  Westerham TN16 . . . . .189 EQ126
Bartlett St, S.Croy. CR2 . . . . .160 DR106
Bartlow Gdns, Rom. RM5 . . . .51 FD53
Barton, The, Cob. KT11 . . . . .154 BX112
Barton Av, Rom. RM7 . . . . . . .71 FB60
Barton Cl, E6 . . . . .87 EM72
  E9 off Churchill Wk 66 DW64
  NW4 . . . . .63 CU56
  SE15 off Kirkwood Rd 102 DV83
  Addlestone KT15 . . . . .152 BG107
  Bexleyheath DA6 . . . . .126 EY85
  Chigwell IG7 . . . . .49 EQ47
  Shepperton TW17 . . . . .135 BP100
Barton Grn, N.Mal. KT3 . . . . .138 CR96
Barton Meadows, Ilf. IG6 . . . .69 EQ56
Barton Rd, W14 . . . . .99 CY78
  Dartford (Sutt.H.) DA4 . . . .148 FP95
  Hornchurch RM12 . . . . .71 FG60
  Sidcup DA14 . . . . .126 EY93
  Slough SL3 . . . . .93 AZ75
Bartons, The, Borwd. (Elstree)
  WD6 . . . . .25 CK44
Barton St, SW1 . . . . .199 P6
Bartonway, NW8
  off Queen's Ter 82 DD68
Barton Way, Borwd. WD6 . . . .26 CN40
  Rickmansworth (Crox.Grn.)
  WD3 . . . . .23 BP43
Bartram Cl, Uxb. UB8
  off Lees Rd 77 BP70
Bartram Rd, SE4 . . . . .123 DY85
Bartrams La, Barn. EN4 . . . . . .28 DC38
Bartrop Cl, Wal.Cr. EN7
  off Poppy Wk 14 DR28
Barts Cl, Beck. BR3 . . . . .143 EA99
Barville Cl, SE4
  off St. Norbert Rd 123 DY84
Barwell Business Pk, Chess.
  KT9 . . . . .155 CK109
Barwick Dr, Uxb. UB8
  off Harlington Rd 77 BP71
Barwick Rd, E7 . . . . .68 EH63
Barwood Av, W.Wick. BR4 . . .143 EB102
Bascombe Gro, Dart. DA1
  off Lower Sta Rd 127 FE86
Bascombe St, SW2 . . . . .121 DN86
Basden Gro, Felt. TW13 . . . . .116 CA89
Basedale Rd, Dag. RM9 . . . . . .88 EV66
Baseing Cl, E6 . . . . .87 EN73
Basevi Way, SE8 . . . . .103 EB79

Bashley Rd, NW10 . . . . .80 CR70
Basil Av, E6 . . . . .86 EL68
Basildene Rd, Houns. TW4 . . .96 BX82
Basildon Av, Ilf. IG5 . . . . .49 EN53
Basildon Cl, Sutt. SM2 . . . . . .158 DB109
  Watford WD18 . . . . .23 BQ44
Basildon Rd, SE2 . . . . .106 EU78
Basil Gdns, SE27 . . . . .122 DQ92
  Croydon CR0
  off Primrose La 143 DX102
Basilon Rd, Bexh. DA7 . . . . . .106 EY82
Basil St, SW3 . . . . .198 D6
Basin App, E14
  off Commercial Rd 85 DY72
Basing Ct, SE15 . . . . .102 DT81
Basingdon Way, SE5 . . . . .102 DR84
Basing Dr, Bex. DA5 . . . . .126 EZ86
Basingfield Rd, T.Ditt. KT7 . . .137 CF101
Basinghall Av, EC2 . . . . .197 K7
Basinghall Gdns, Sutt. SM2 . .158 DB109
Basinghall St, EC2 . . . . .197 K8
Basing Hill, NW11 . . . . .63 CZ60
  Wembley HA9 . . . . .62 CM61
Basing Ho, Bark. IG11
  off St. Margarets 87 ER67
Basing Ho Yd, E2 . . . . .197 N2
Basing Pl, E2 . . . . .197 N2
Basing Rd, Bans. SM7 . . . . . .157 CZ114
  Rickmansworth (Mill End)
  WD3 . . . . .37 BF46
Basing St, W11 . . . . .81 CZ72
Basing Way, N3 . . . . .64 DA55
  Thames Ditton KT7 . . . . . . .137 CF101
Basire St, N1 . . . . .84 DQ67
Baskerville Rd, SW18 . . . . . . .120 DE87
Basket Gdns, SE9 . . . . .124 EL85
Baslow Cl, Har. HA3 . . . . .41 CD53
Baslow Wk, E5
  off Overbury St 67 DX63
Basnett Rd, SW11 . . . . .100 DG83
Basque Ct, SE16 . . . . .203 H5
Bassano St, SE22 . . . . .122 DT85
Bassant Rd, SE18 . . . . .105 ET79
Bassein Pk Rd, W12 . . . . .99 CT75
Basset Cl, Add. (New Haw)
  KT15 . . . . .152 BH110
Bassett Cl, Sutt. SM2 . . . . . . .158 DB109
  Reigate RH2 . . . . .184 DA133
Bassett Dr, Reig. RH2 . . . . . .184 DA133
Bassett Flds, Epp. (N.Wld.) CM16
   . . . . .19 FD25
Bassett Gdns, Epp. (N.Wld.Bas.)
  CM16 . . . . .19 FB26
  Isleworth TW7 . . . . .96 CC80
Bassett Ho, Dag. RM9 . . . . . . .88 EV67
Bassett Rd, W10 . . . . .81 CX72
  Uxbridge UB8
  off New Windsor St 76 BJ66
  Woking GU21 . . . . .167 BC116
Bassetts Cl, Orp. BR6 . . . . . . .163 EP105
Bassett St, NW5 . . . . .82 DG65
Bassetts Way, Orp. BR6 . . . . .163 EP105
Bassett Way, Grnf. UB6 . . . . . .78 CB72
Bassingham Rd, SW18 . . . . . .120 DC87
  Wembley HA0 . . . . .79 CK65
Bassishaw Highwalk, EC2
  off London Wall 84 DQ71
Basswood Cl, SE15
  off Linden Gro 102 DV83
Bastable Av, Bark. IG11 . . . . . .87 ES68
Bastion Highwalk, EC2
  off London Wall 84 DQ71
Bastion Ho, EC2
  off London Wall 84 DQ71
Bastion Rd, SE2 . . . . .106 EU78
Baston Manor Rd, Brom.
  BR2 . . . . .144 EH104
Baston Rd, Brom. BR2 . . . . . .144 EH102
Bastwick St, EC1 . . . . .197 H4
Basuto Rd, SW6 . . . . .100 DA81
⇌ Bat & Ball 191 FJ121
Bat & Ball Rd, Sev. TN14 . . . .191 FJ121
Batavia Cl, Sun. TW16 . . . . . .136 BW95
Batavia Ms, SE14
  off Goodwood Rd 103 DY80
Batavia Rd, SE14 . . . . .103 DY80
  Sunbury-on-Thames
  TW16 . . . . .135 BV95
Batchelor St, N1 . . . . .83 DN68
Batchwood Grn, Orp. BR5 . . .146 EU97
BATCHWORTH, Rick. 38 BM47
BATCHWORTH HEATH, Rick. .38 BN49
Batchworth Heath Hill, Rick.
  WD3 . . . . .38 BN49
Batchworth Hill, Rick. WD3 . . .38 BM48
Batchworth La, Nthwd. HA6 . .39 BS50
Batchworth Roundabout, Rick.
  WD3 . . . . .38 BK46
Bateman Cl, Bark. IG11
  off Glenny Rd 87 EQ65
Bateman Ho, SE17
  off Otto St 101 DP79
Bateman Rd, E4 . . . . .47 EA51
  Rickmansworth (Crox.Grn.)
  WD3 . . . . .22 BN44
Bateman's Bldgs, W1 . . . . . . .195 M9
Bateman's Row, EC2 . . . . .197 N4
Bateman St, W1 . . . . .195 M9
Bates Cl, Slou. (Geo.Grn.)
  SL3 .74 AY72
Bates Cres, SW16 . . . . .121 DJ94
  Croydon CR0 . . . . .159 DN106
Bates Ind Est, Rom. (Harold Wd.)
  RM3 . . . . .52 FP52
Bateson St, SE18 . . . . .105 ES77
Bateson Way, Wok. GU21 . . .151 BC114
Bates Pt, E13 off Pelly Rd 86 EG67
Bates Rd, Rom. RM3 . . . . .52 FN52
Bate St, E14 off Three Colt St .85 DZ73
Bates Wk, Add. KT15 . . . . . . .152 BJ108
B.A.T. Export Ho, Wok. GU21 .166 AY117
Bath Cl, SE15 off Asylum Rd .102 DV80
Bath Ct, EC1 . . . . .196 D5
Bath Ho Rd, Croy. CR0 . . . . . .141 DL102
Bath Pas, Kings.T. KT1
  off St. James Rd 137 CK96

Bath Pl, EC2 . . . . .197 M3
  Barnet EN5 . . . . .27 CZ41
Bath Rd, E7 . . . . .86 EK65
  N9 . . . . .46 DV47
  W4 . . . . .98 CS77
  Dartford DA1 . . . . .127 FH87
  Hayes UB3 . . . . .95 BQ81
  Hounslow TW3, TW5,
  TW5, TW6 . . . . .96 BX82
  Mitcham CR4 . . . . .140 DD97
  Romford RM6 . . . . .70 EY58
  Slough (Colnbr.) SL3 . . . . . .93 BB79
  West Drayton UB7 . . . . .94 BK81
  West Drayton. Brom. BR2 .144 EK98
Bath St, EC1 . . . . .197 J3
  Gravesend DA11 . . . . .131 GH86
Bath Ter, SE1 . . . . .201 H7
Bathurst Av, SW19
  off Brisbane Av 140 DB95
Bathurst Cl, Iver SL0 . . . . .93 BF75
Bathurst Gdns, NW10 . . . . . . .81 CV68
Bathurst Ms, W2
  off Sussex Pl 82 DD73
Bathurst Rd, Ilf. IG1 . . . . .69 EP60
Bathurst St, W2 . . . . .82 DD73
Bathurst Wk, Iver SL0 . . . . . . .93 BE75
Bathway, SE18 . . . . .105 EN77
Batley Cl, Mitch. CR4 . . . . . . .140 DF101
Batley Pl, N16 . . . . .66 DT62
Batley Rd, N16 off Stoke
  Newington High St 66 DT62
  Enfield EN2 . . . . .30 DQ39
Batman Cl, W12 . . . . .81 CV74
Baton Cl, Purf. RM19
  off Brimfield Rd 109 FR77
Batoum Gdns, W6 . . . . .99 CW76
Batson St, W12 . . . . .99 CU75
Batsworth Rd, Mitch. CR4 . . .140 DD97
Batten Av, Wok. GU21 . . . . . .166 AS119
Battenburg Wk, SE19
  off Brabourne Cl 122 DS92
Batten Cl, E6
  off Savage Gdns 87 EM72
Batten St, SW11 . . . . .100 DE83
Battersby Rd, SE6 . . . . .123 ED89
BATTERSEA, SW11 . . . . .101 DH81
Battersea Br, SW3 . . . . .100 DD80
  SW11 . . . . .100 DD80
Battersea Br Rd, SW11 . . . . . .100 DE80
Battersea Ch Rd, SW11 . . . . .100 DD81
★ Battersea Dogs Home,
  SW8 . . . . .101 DH80
Battersea High St, SW11 . . . .100 DD81
★ Battersea Park, SW11 . . . .100 DF80
⇌ Battersea Park 101 DH80
Battersea Pk, SW11 . . . . .100 DF80
Battersea Pk Rd, SW8 . . . . . .101 DH81
  SW11 . . . . .100 DE82
Battersea Ri, SW11 . . . . .120 DE85
Battersea Sq, SW11
  off Battersea High St 100 DD81
Battery Rd, SE28 . . . . .105 ES75
Battis, The, Rom. RM1
  off Waterloo Rd 71 FE58
Battishill Gdns, N1
  off Waterloo Ter 83 DP66
Battishill St, N1
  off Waterloo Ter 83 DP66
Battlebridge Ct, N1
  off Wharfdale Rd 83 DL68
Battle Br La, SE1 . . . . .201 M3
Battlebridge La, Red. RH1 . . .185 DH130
Battle Br Rd, NW1 . . . . .195 P1
Battle Cl, SW19 off North Rd .120 DC93
Battledean Rd, N5 . . . . .65 DP64
Battle Rd, Belv. DA17 . . . . . . .107 FC77
  Erith DA8 . . . . .107 FC77
Battlers Grn Dr, Rad. WD7 . . .25 CE37
Batts Hill, Red. RH1 . . . . .184 DE132
  Reigate RH2 . . . . .184 DD132
Batty St, E1 . . . . .84 DU72
Baudwin Rd, SE6 . . . . .124 EE89
Baugh Rd, Sid. DA14 . . . . . . .126 EW92
Baulk, The, SW18 . . . . .120 DA87
Bavant Rd, SW16 . . . . .141 DL96
Bavaria Rd, N19 . . . . .65 DL61
Bavdene Ms, NW4
  off The Burroughs 63 CV56
Bavent Rd, SE5 . . . . .102 DQ82
Bawdale Rd, SE22 . . . . .122 DT85
Bawdsey Av, Ilf. IG2 . . . . .69 ET56
Bawtree Cl, Sutt. SM2 . . . . . .158 DC110
Bawtree Rd, SE14 . . . . .103 DY80
  Uxbridge UB8 . . . . .76 BK65
Bawtry Rd, N20 . . . . .44 DF48
Baxendale, N20 . . . . .44 DC47
Baxendale St, E2 . . . . .84 DU69
Baxter Av, Red. RH1 . . . . .184 DE134
Baxter Cl, Slou. SL1 . . . . .92 AS76
  Southall UB2 . . . . .96 CB75
  Uxbridge UB10 . . . . .77 BP69
Baxter Gdns, Rom. (Noak Hill) RM3
  off Cummings Hall La 52 FJ48
Baxter Rd, E16 . . . . .86 EJ72
  N1 . . . . .84 DR65
  N18 .46 DV49
  NW10 . . . . .80 CS70
  Ilford IG1 . . . . .69 EP64
Bayards, Warl. CR6 . . . . .176 DW118
Bay Ct, W5 off Popes La 98 CL76
Baycroft Cl, Pnr. HA5 . . . . .60 BW55
Baydon Ct, Brom. BR2 . . . . . .144 EF97
Bayes Cl, SE26 . . . . .122 DW92
Bayeux, Tad. KT20 . . . . .173 CX122
Bayfield Rd, SE9 . . . . .104 EK84
Bayford Ms, E8 off Bayford St .84 DV66
Bayford Rd, NW10 . . . . .81 CX69
Bayford St, E8 . . . . .84 DV66
Bayham Pl, NW1 . . . . .83 DJ67
Bayham Rd, W4 . . . . .98 CR76
  W13 .79 CH73
  Morden SM4 . . . . .140 DB98
  Sevenoaks TN13 . . . . .191 FJ123
Bayham St, NW1 . . . . .83 DJ67
Bayhurst Dr, Nthwd. HA6 . . . . .39 BT51
★ Bayhurst Wood Country Pk,
  Uxb. (Hare.) UB9 . . . . .58 BM56

Bayleys Mead, Brwd. CM13 . .55 GC47
Bayley St, WC1 . . . . .195 M7
Bayley Wk, SE2
   off Woolwich Rd 106 EY78
Baylin Rd, SW18 . . . . .120 DB86
   off Garratt La 120 DB86
Baylis Av, SE1 . . . . .200 D5
Bayliss Av, SE28 . . . . .88 EX73
Bayliss Cl, N21 . . . . .29 DL43
Bayly Rd, Dart. DA1 . . . . . .128 FN86
Bay Manor La, Grays RM20 .109 FT79
Baymans Wd, Brwd. CM15 . .54 FY47
Bayne Cl, E6 off Savage Gdns .87 EM72
Baynes Cl, Enf. EN1 . . . . . . .30 DU40
Baynes Ms, NW3
   off Belsize La 82 DD65
Baynes St, NW1 . . . . .83 DJ66
Baynham Cl, Bex. DA5 . . . .126 EZ86
Bayonne Rd, W6 . . . . .99 CY79
Bayshill Ri, Nthlt. UB5 . . . . .78 CB65
Bayston Rd, N16 . . . . .66 DT62
BAYSWATER, W2 . . . . . . .82 DC72
    Bayswater 82 DB73
Bayswater Rd, W2 . . . . . . .194 A10
Baythorne St, E3 . . . . .85 DZ71
Bay Tree Av, Lthd. KT22 . . .171 CG120
Bay Tree Cl, Brom. BR1 . . . .144 EJ95
Baytree Cl, St.Alb. (Park St.)
   AL2 . . . . .8 CB27
   Sidcup DA15 . . . . .125 ET88
   Waltham Cross EN7 . . . . .14 DT27
Baytree Ho, SE4 off Dells Cl .47 DZ71
Baytree Rd, SW2 . . . . .101 DM84
Baytree Wk, Wat. WD17 . . . .23 BT38
Baywood Sq, Chig. IG7 . . . . .50 EV49
Bazalgette Cl, N.Mal. KT3 . .138 CR99
Bazalgette Gdns, N.Mal. KT3 138 CR99
Bazely St, E14 . . . . .85 EC73
Bazile Rd, N21 . . . . .29 DN44
Beacham Cl, SE7 . . . . .104 EK78
Beachborough Rd, Brom.
   BR1 . . . . .123 EC91
Beachcroft Rd, E11 . . . . . . .68 EE62
Beachcroft Way, N19 . . . . . .65 DK60
Beach Gro, Felt. TW13 . . . .116 CA89
Beachy Rd, E3 . . . . .85 EA66
Beacon Cl, Bans. SM7 . . . .173 CX116
   Gerrards Cross (Chal.St.P.)
   SL9 . . . . .36 AY52
   Uxbridge UB8 . . . . .58 BK64
  Beacon Country Pk, Dart.
   (Bean) DA2 . . . . .129 FV91
Beacon Dr, Dart. (Bean) DA2 .129 FV90
Beaconfield Av, Epp. CM16 . .17 ET29
Beaconfield Rd, Epp. CM16 . .17 ET29
Beaconfields, Sev. TN13 . . .190 FF126
Beaconfield Way, Epp. CM16 .17 ET29
Beacon Gate, SE14 . . . . . . .103 DX83
Beacon Gro, Cars. SM5 . . . .158 DG105
Beacon Hill, N7 . . . . .65 DL64
   Purfleet RM19 . . . . .108 FP78
   Woking GU21 . . . . .166 AW118
Beacon Ri, Sev. TN13 . . . . .190 FG126
Beacon Rd, SE13 . . . . .123 ED86
   Erith DA8 . . . . .107 FH80
   Hounslow (Hthrw.Air.)
   TW6 . . . . .114 BN86
Beacon Rd Roundabout, Houns.
   (Hthrw.Air.) TW6 . . . . .115 BP86
Beacons Cl, E6
   off Oliver Gdns 86 EL71
Beaconsfield Cl, N11 . . . . . .44 DG49
   SE3 . . . . .104 EG79
   W4 . . . . .98 CQ78
Beaconsfield Par, SE9
   off Beaconsfield Rd 124 EL91
Beaconsfield Pl, Epsom
   KT17 . . . . .156 CS112
Beaconsfield Rd, E10 . . . . . .67 EC61
   E16 . . . . .86 EF70
   E17 . . . . .67 DZ58
   N9 . . . . .46 DU49
   N11 . . . . .44 DG48
   N15 . . . . .66 DS56
   NW10 . . . . .81 CT65
   SE3 . . . . .104 EF80
   SE9 . . . . .124 EL89
   SE17 . . . . .102 DR78
   W4 . . . . .98 CR76
   W5 . . . . .97 CJ75
   Bexley DA5 . . . . .127 FE88
   Bromley BR1 . . . . .144 EK97
   Croydon CR0 . . . . .142 DR100
   Enfield EN3 . . . . .31 DX37
   Epsom KT18 . . . . .172 CR119
   Esher (Clay.) KT10 . . . . .155 CE108
   Hayes UB4 . . . . .78 BW74
   New Malden KT3 . . . . .138 CR96
   Southall UB1 . . . . .78 BX74
   Surbiton KT5 . . . . .138 CM101
   Twickenham TW1 . . . . .117 CH86
   Woking GU22 . . . . .167 AZ120
Beaconsfield Ter, Rom. RM6 . .70 EX58
Beaconsfield Ter Rd, W14 . . .99 CY76
Beaconsfield Wk, E6
   off East Ham Manor Way . .87 EN72
   SW6 . . . . .99 CZ81
Beacontree Av, E17 . . . . . . .47 ED53
Beacontree Rd, E11 . . . . . . .68 EF59
Beacon Way, Bans. SM7 . . .173 CX116
   Rickmansworth WD3 . . . .38 BG45
Beadles La, Oxt. RH8 . . . . .187 ED130
Beadlow Cl, Cars. SM5
   off Olveston Wk 140 DD100
Beadman Pl, SE27
   off Norwood High St 121 DP91
Beadman St, SE27 . . . . . . .121 DP91
Beadnell Rd, SE23 . . . . . . .123 DX88
Beadon Rd, W6 . . . . .99 CW77
   Bromley BR2 . . . . .144 EG98
Beads Hall La, Brwd. CM15 . .54 FV42
Beaford Gro, SW20 . . . . . .139 CY97
Beagle Cl, Felt. TW13 . . . . .115 BV91
   Radlett WD7 . . . . .25 CF37
Beagles Cl, Orp. BR5 . . . . .146 EX103
Beak St, W1 . . . . .195 L10

Beal Cl, Well. DA16 . . . . . .106 EU81
Beale Cl, N13 . . . . .45 DP50
Beale Pl, E3 . . . . .85 DZ68
Beale Rd, E3 . . . . .85 DZ67
Beales La, Wey. KT13 . . . . .134 BN104
Beal Rd, Ilf. IG1 . . . . .69 EN61
Beam Av, Dag. RM10 . . . . . .89 FB67
Beaminster Gdns, Ilf. IG6 . . .49 EP54
Beamish Cl, Epp. (N.Wld.Bas.)
   CM16 . . . . .19 FC25
Beamish Dr, Bushey (Bushey Hth.)
   WD23 . . . . .40 CC46
Beamish Rd, N9 . . . . .46 DU46
   Orpington BR5 . . . . . . .146 EW101
Beam Way, Dag. RM10 . . . . .89 FD66
BEAN, Dart. 129 FV90
Beanacre Cl, E9 . . . . .85 DZ65
Beane Cft, Grav. DA12
   off Damigos Rd 131 GM88
Bean La, Dart. (Bean) DA2 . .129 FV89
Bean Rd, Bexh. DA6 . . . . . .106 EX84
   Greenhithe DA9 . . . . . .129 FU88
Beanshaw, SE9 . . . . .125 EN91
Beansland Gro, Rom. RM6 . . .52 EY54
Bear All, EC4 . . . . .196 F8
Bear Cl, Rom. RM7 . . . . . . .71 FB58
Beardell St, SE19 . . . . .122 DT93
Beardow Gro, N14 . . . . .29 DJ44
Beard Rd, Kings.T. KT2 . . . .118 CM92
Beardsfield, E13
   off Valetta Gro 86 EG67
Beard's Hill, Hmptn. TW12 . .136 CA95
Beard's Hill Cl, Hmptn. TW12
   off Beard's Hill 136 CA95
Beardsley Ter, Dag. RM8
   off Fitzstephen Rd 70 EV64
Beardsley Way, W3 . . . . . . .98 CR75
Beards Rd, Ashf. TW15 . . . .115 BS93
Bearfield Rd, Kings.T. KT2 . .118 CL94
Bear Gdns, SE1 . . . . .201 H2
Bearing Cl, Chig. IG7 . . . . . .50 EU49
Bearing Way, Chig. IG7 . . . . .50 EU49
Bear La, SE1 . . . . .200 G2
Bear Rd, Felt. TW13 . . . . . .116 BX92
Bears Den, Tad. (Kgswd.)
   KT20 . . . . .173 CZ122
Bears Rails Pk, Wind. (Old Wind.)
   SL4 . . . . .112 AT87
Bearstead Ri, SE4 . . . . . . .123 DZ85
Bearsted Ter, Beck. BR3 . . .143 EA95
Bear St, WC2 . . . . .195 N10
Bearwood Cl, Add. KT15
   off Ongar Pl 152 BG107
   Potters Bar EN6 . . . . . . .12 DD31
Beasley's Ait La, Sun. TW16 .135 BT100
Beasleys Yd, Uxb. UB8
   off Warwick Pl 76 BJ66
Beaton Cl, SE15 off Kelly Av .102 DT80
   Greenhithe DA9 . . . . . .109 FV84
Beatrice Av, SW16 . . . . . . .141 DM97
   Wembley HA9 . . . . .62 CL64
Beatrice Cl, E13
   off Chargeable La 86 EG70
   Pinner HA5 off Reid Cl . . .59 BU56
Beatrice Ct, Buck.H. IG9 . . . .48 EK47
Beatrice Gdns, Grav. (Nthflt.)
   DA11 . . . . .130 GE89
Beatrice Pl, W8 . . . . .100 DB76
Beatrice Rd, E17 . . . . .67 EA57
   N4 . . . . .65 DN59
   N9 . . . . .46 DW45
   SE1 . . . . .202 C9
   Oxted RH8 . . . . .188 EE129
   Richmond TW10
   off Albert Rd 118 CM85
   Southall UB1 . . . . .78 BZ74
Beatson Wk, SE16 . . . . . . .203 K2
Beattie Cl, Felt. TW14 . . . . .115 BT88
   Leatherhead (Bkhm.)
   KT23 . . . . .170 BZ124
Beattock Ri, N10 . . . . .65 DH56
Beatty Rd, N16 . . . . .66 DS63
   Stanmore HA7 . . . . .41 CJ51
   Waltham Cross EN8 . . . . .15 DZ34
Beatty St, NW1 . . . . .83 DJ68
Beattyville Gdns, Ilf. IG6 . . . .69 EN55
Beauchamp Cl, W4
   off Church Path 98 CQ76
Beauchamp Gdns, Rick. (Mill End)
   WD3 . . . . .38 BG46
Beauchamp Pl, SW3 . . . . . .198 C6
Beauchamp Rd, E7 . . . . .86 EH66
   SE19 . . . . .142 DR95
   SW11 . . . . .100 DE84
   East Molesey KT8 . . . . .136 CB99
   Sutton SM1 . . . . .158 DA106
   Twickenham TW1 . . . . .117 CG87
   West Molesey KT8 . . . . .136 CB99
Beauchamp St, EC1 . . . . . .196 D7
Beauchamp Ter, SW15
   off Dryburgh Rd 99 CV83
Beauclare Cl, Lthd. KT22
   off Hatherwood 171 CK121
Beauclerc Rd, W6 . . . . .99 CV76
Beauclerk Cl, Felt. TW13
   off Florence Rd 115 BV88
Beaudesert Ms, West Dr. UB7 .94 BL75
Beaufort, E6
   off Newark Knok 87 EN71
Beaufort Av, Har. HA3 . . . . . .62 CG56
Beaufort Cl, E4
   off Higham Sta Av 47 EB51
   SW15 . . . . .119 CV87
   W5 . . . . .80 CM71
   Epping (N.Wld.Bas.) CM16 .18 FA27
   Grays (Chaff.Hun.) RM16
   off Clifford Rd 110 FZ76
   Reigate RH2 . . . . .183 CZ133
   Romford RM7 . . . . .71 FC56
   Woking GU22 . . . . .167 BC116
Beaufort Ct, Rich. TW10
   off Beaufort Rd 117 CJ91
   SW6 off Lillie Rd 99 CZ79
Beaufort Dr, NW11 . . . . .64 DA56
Beaufort Gdns, SW3 . . . . . .198 C6

Beaufort Gdns, SW16 . . . . .121 DM94
   Hounslow TW5 . . . . .96 BY81
   Ilford IG1 . . . . .69 EN60
Beaufort Ms, SW6
   off Lillie Rd 99 CZ79
Beaufort Pk, NW11 . . . . .64 DA56
Beaufort Rd, W5 . . . . .80 CM71
   Kingston upon Thames
   KT1 . . . . .138 CL98
   Reigate RH2 . . . . .183 CZ133
   Richmond TW10 . . . . . .117 CJ91
   Ruislip HA4
   off Lysander Rd 59 BR61
   Twickenham TW1 . . . . .117 CJ87
   Woking GU22 . . . . .167 BC116
Beauforts, Egh. (Eng.Grn.)
   TW20 . . . . .112 AW92
Beaufort St, SW3 . . . . .100 DD79
Beaufort Way, Epsom KT17 . .157 CU108
Beaufoy Rd, N17 . . . . .46 DS52
Beaufoy Wk, SE11 . . . . . . .200 C9
Beaulieu Av, E16 . . . . .205 P2
   SE26 . . . . .122 DV91
Beaulieu Cl, NW9 . . . . .62 CS56
   SE5 . . . . .102 DR83
   Hounslow TW4 . . . . . . .116 BZ85
   Mitcham CR4 . . . . .140 DG95
   Slough (Datchet) SL3 . . . .92 AV82
   Twickenham TW1 . . . . .117 CK87
   Watford WD19 . . . . .40 BW46
Beaulieu Dr, Pnr. HA5 . . . . . .60 BX58
   Waltham Abbey EN9 . . . .15 ED33
Beaulieu Gdns, N21 . . . . . . .46 DQ45
Beaulieu Pl, W4
   off Rothschild Rd 98 CQ76
Beauly Way, Rom. RM1 . . . . .51 FE53
Beaumanor Gdns, SE9 . . . .125 EN91
Beaumaris Dr, Wdf.Grn. IG8 . .48 EK52
Beaumaris Grn, NW9
   off Goldsmith Av 62 CS58
Beaumont Av, W14 . . . . .99 CZ78
   Harrow HA2 . . . . .60 CB58
   Richmond TW9 . . . . .98 CM83
   Wembley HA0 . . . . .61 CJ64
Beaumont Cl, Kings.T. KT2 . .118 CN94
   Romford RM2 . . . . .52 FJ54
Beaumont Cres, W14 . . . . . .99 CZ78
   Rainham RM13 . . . . .89 FG65
Beaumont Dr, Ashf. TW15 . .115 BR92
   Gravesend (Nthflt.) DA11 .130 GE87
Beaumont Gdns, NW3 . . . . . .64 DA62
   Brentwood CM13
   off Bannister Dr 55 GC44
Beaumont Gate, Rad. WD7
   off Shenley Hill 25 CH35
Beaumont Gro, E1 . . . . .85 DX70
Beaumont Ms, W1 . . . . . . .194 G6
Beaumont Pl, W1 . . . . .195 L4
   Barnet EN5 . . . . .27 CZ39
   Isleworth TW7 . . . . . . .117 CF85
Beaumont Ri, N19 . . . . .65 DK60
Beaumont Rd, E10 . . . . .67 EB59
   E13 . . . . .86 EH69
   SE19 . . . . .122 DQ93
   SW19 . . . . .119 CY87
   W4 . . . . .98 CQ76
   Orpington BR5 . . . . . . .145 ER100
   Purley CR8 . . . . .159 DN113
Beaumont Sq, E1 . . . . .85 DX70
Beaumont St, W1 . . . . .194 G6
Beaumont Vw, Wal.Cr. (Chsht.)
   EN7 . . . . .14 DR26
Beaumont Wk, NW3 . . . . . . .82 DF66
Beauvais Ter, Nthlt. UB5 . . . .78 BX69
Beauval Rd, SE22 . . . . .122 DT86
Beaverbank Rd, SE9 . . . . . .125 ER88
Beaverbrook Roundabout, Lthd.
   KT22 . . . . .172 CL123
Beaver Cl, SE20
   off Lullington Rd 122 DU94
   Hampton TW12 . . . . . . .136 CB95
Beaver Gro, Nthlt. UB5
   off Jetstar Way 78 BY69
Beaver Rd, Ilf. IG6 . . . . .50 EW50
Beavers Cres, Houns. TW4 . . .96 BW84
Beavers La, Houns. TW4 . . . .96 BW83
Beavers La Camp, Houns. TW4
   off Beavers La 96 BW83
Beaverwood Rd, Chis. BR7 . .125 ES93
Beavor Gro, W6 off Beavor La .99 CU77
Beavor La, W6 . . . . .99 CU77
Bebbington Rd, SE18 . . . . . .105 ES77
Bebletts Cl, Orp. BR6 . . . . .163 ET106
Beccles Dr, Bark. IG11 . . . . . .87 ES65
Beccles St, E14 . . . . .85 DZ73
Bec Cl, Ruis. HA4 . . . . .60 BX62
Beck Cl, SE13 . . . . .103 EB81
Beck Ct, Beck. BR3 . . . . . . .143 DX97
BECKENHAM 143 EA95
Beckenham Business Cen, Beck.
   BR3 . . . . .123 DY93
Beckenham Gdns, N9 . . . . . .46 DS46
Beckenham Gro, Brom. BR2 .143 ED96
Beckenham Hill Rd, SE6 . . . .123 EC92
   Beckenham Hill 123 EC92
Beckenham Hill Rd, SE6 . . . .123 EB92
   Beckenham BR3 . . . . . .123 EB92
   Beckenham Hosp, Beck.
   BR3 . . . . .143 DZ96
   Beckenham Junction 143 EA95
Beckenham La, Brom. BR2 . .144 EF96
Beckenham Pl Pk, Beck. BR3 .123 EB94
   Beckenham Road 143 DY95
Beckenham Rd, Beck. BR3 . .143 DX95
   West Wickham BR4 . . . .143 EB101
Beckenshaw Gdns, Bans.
   SM7 . . . . .174 DE115
Beckers, The, N16
   off Rectory Rd 66 DU62
Becket Av, E6 off Courtfield Cres .61 CF57
Becket Cl, SE25 . . . . .142 DU100
   Brentwood CM13 . . . . . . .53 FW51
Becket Fold, Har. HA1
   off Courtfield Cres 61 CF57
Becket Rd, N18 . . . . .46 DW49
Becket St, SE1 . . . . .201 K6
Beckett Av, Ken. CR8 . . . . .175 DP115

Beckett Cl, NW10 . . . . .80 CR65
   SW16 . . . . .121 DK89
   Belvedere DA17
   off Tunstock Way 106 EY76
Becketts Cl, Felt. TW14 . . . .115 BV86
Becketts Pl, Kings.T. KT1 . . .137 CK95
Beckett Wk, Beck. BR3 . . . .123 DY93
Beckford Dr, Orp. BR5 . . . .145 ER101
Beckford Pl, SE17
   off Walworth Rd 102 DQ78
Beckford Rd, Croy. CR0 . . . .142 DT100
Beck La, Beck. BR3 . . . . . . .143 DX97
Becklow Gdns, W12
   off Becklow Rd 99 CU75
Becklow Ms, W12
   off Becklow Rd 99 CT75
Becklow Rd, W12 . . . . .99 CU75
Beckman Rd, Sev. (Halst.)
   TN14 . . . . .181 FC115
Beck River Pk, Beck. BR3 . . .143 DZ95
Beck Rd, E8 . . . . .84 DV67
Becks Rd, Sid. DA14 . . . . . .126 EU90
BECKTON, E6 . . . . .87 EN71
  Beckton 87 EN71
  Beckton Park 87 EM73
Beckton Pk Roundabout, E16
   off Royal Albert Way 87 EM73
Beckton Retail Pk, E6 . . . . . .87 EN71
Beckton Triangle Retail Pk, E6 .87 EN70
Beck Way, Beck. BR3 . . . . . .143 DZ97
Beckway Rd, SW16 . . . . . . .141 DK96
Beckway St, SE17 . . . . .201 L9
Beckwith Rd, SE24 . . . . . . .122 DQ86
Beclands Rd, SW17 . . . . . . .120 DG93
Becmead Av, SW16 . . . . . . .121 DK91
   Harrow HA3 . . . . .61 CH57
Becondale Rd, SE19 . . . . . .122 DS93
BECONTREE, Dag. 70 EY62
  Becontree 88 EW66
Becontree Av, Dag. RM8 . . . .70 EV63
BECONTREE HEATH, Dag. . . .70 FA60
Bective Pl, SW15
   off Bective Rd 99 CZ84
Bective Rd, E7 . . . . .68 EG63
   SW15 . . . . .99 CZ84
Bedale Rd, Enf. EN2 . . . . . . .30 DQ38
   Romford RM3 . . . . .52 FN50
Bedale St, SE1 . . . . .201 K3
BEDDINGTON, Wall. 141 DK103
BEDDINGTON CORNER,
   Mitch. 140 DG101
Beddington Cross, Croy.
   CR0 . . . . .141 DK102
Beddington Fm Rd, Croy.
   CR0 . . . . .141 DL102
Beddington Gdns, Cars.
   SM5 . . . . .158 DG107
   Wallington SM6 . . . . . .159 DH107
Beddington Grn, Orp. BR5 . .145 ET95
Beddington Gro, Wall. SM6 . .159 DK106
  Beddington Lane 141 DJ100
Beddington La, Croy. CR0 . . .141 DJ99
Beddington Path, Orp. BR5 . .145 ET95
Beddington Trd Pk W, Croy.
   CR0 . . . . .141 DL102
Bedenham Way, SE15 . . . . .102 DT80
   off Daniel Gdns 102 DT80
Bedens Rd, Sid. DA14 . . . . .126 EY93
Bede Rd, Rom. RM6 . . . . . . .70 EW58
Bedfont Cl, Felt. TW14 . . . . .115 BQ86
   Mitcham CR4 . . . . .140 DG96
Bedfont Ct, Stai. TW19 . . . . .94 BH84
Bedfont Ct Est, Stai. TW19 . . .94 BG83
Bedfont Grn Cl, Felt. TW14 . .115 BT87
Bedfont La, Felt. TW13, TW14 .115 BT87
Bedfont Rd, Felt. TW13,
   TW14 . . . . .115 BS89
   Staines (Stanw.) TW19 . .114 BL86
Bedford Av, W1 . . . . .195 N7
   Amersham HP6 . . . . . . .20 AW39
   Barnet EN5 . . . . .27 CZ43
   Hayes UB4 . . . . .77 BV72
Bedfordbury, WC2 . . . . . . .195 P10
Bedford Cl, N10 . . . . .44 DG52
   W4 . . . . .98 CS79
   Rickmansworth (Chenies)
   WD3 . . . . .21 BB38
   Woking GU21 . . . . .166 AW115
Bedford Cor, W4
   off The Avenue 98 CS77
Bedford Ct, WC2 . . . . .199 P1
Bedford Cres, Enf. EN3 . . . . .31 DY35
Bedford Gdns, W8 . . . . .82 DA74
   Hornchurch RM12 . . . . . .72 FJ61
Bedford Hill, SW12 . . . . . . .121 DH88
   SW16 . . . . .121 DH88
  Bedford Hill Gall, SW12 . .121 DH88
Bedford Ho, SW4 . . . . .101 DL84
Bedford Ms, N2
   off Bedford Rd 64 DE55
BEDFORD PARK, W4 . . . . . . .98 CR76
Bedford Pk, Croy. CR0 . . . . .142 DQ102
Bedford Pk Cor, W4
   off Bath Rd 98 CS77
Bedford Pas, SW6
   off Dawes Rd 99 CY80
Bedford Pl, WC1 . . . . .195 P6
   Croydon CR0 . . . . .142 DR102
Bedford Rd, E6 . . . . .87 EN67
   E17 . . . . .47 EA54
   E18 . . . . .48 EG54
   N2 . . . . .64 DE55
   N8 . . . . .65 DK58
   N9 . . . . .46 DV45
   N15 . . . . .66 DS56
   N22 . . . . .45 DL53
   NW7 . . . . .42 CS48
   SW4 . . . . .101 DL83
   W4 . . . . .98 CR76

Bedford Rd, W13 . . . . .79 CH73
   Dartford DA1 . . . . .128 FN87
Bedford Rd, Grav. (Nthflt.)
   DA11 . . . . .131 GF89
   Grays RM17 . . . . .110 GB78
   Harrow HA1 . . . . .60 CC58
   Ilford IG1 . . . . .69 EP62
   Northwood HA6 . . . . . . .39 BQ48
   Orpington BR6 . . . . . . .146 EV101
   Ruislip HA4 . . . . .59 BT63
   Sidcup DA15 . . . . .125 ES90
   Twickenham TW2 . . . . .117 CD90
   Worcester Park KT4 . . . .139 CW103
Bedford Row, WC1 . . . . . . .196 C6
Bedford Sq, WC1 . . . . .195 N7
Bedford St, WC2 . . . . .195 P10
   Watford WD24 . . . . .23 BV39
Bedford Ter, SW2
   off Lyham Rd 121 DL85
Bedford Way, WC1 . . . . . . .195 N5
Bedgebury Gdns, SW19 . . . .119 CY89
Bedgebury Rd, SE9 . . . . . . .104 EK84
Bedivere Rd, Brom. BR1 . . . .124 EG90
Bedlam Ms, SE11 . . . . .200 C8
Bedlow Way, Croy. CR0 . . . .159 DM100
BEDMOND, Abb.L. 7 BS27
Bedmond La, Abb.L. WD5 . . . .7 BV25
Bedmond Rd, Abb.L. WD5 . . . .7 BT29
Bedonwell Rd, SE2 . . . . . . .106 EY79
   Belvedere DA17 . . . . . .106 FA79
   Bexleyheath DA7 . . . . . .106 FA79
Bedser Cl, SE11
   off Harleyford Rd 101 DM79
   Thornton Heath CR7 . . . .142 DQ97
   Woking GU21 . . . . .167 BA116
Bedser Dr, Grnf. UB6 . . . . . .61 CD64
Bedster Gdns, W.Mol. KT8 . .136 CB96
Bedwardine Rd, SE19 . . . . .122 DS94
Bedwell Rd, Hayes UB3 . . . . .95 BS78
Bedwell Rd, N17 . . . . .46 DS53
   Belvedere DA17 . . . . . .106 FA78
Beeby Rd, E16 . . . . .86 EH71
Beech Av, N20 . . . . .44 DE46
   W3 . . . . .80 CS74
   Brentford TW8 . . . . .97 CH80
   Brentwood CM13 . . . . . .55 FZ48
   Buckhurst Hill IG9 . . . . . .48 EH47
   Enfield EN2 . . . . .29 DN35
   Radlett WD7 . . . . .9 CG33
   Ruislip HA4 . . . . .59 BV60
   Sidcup DA15 . . . . .126 EU87
   South Croydon CR2 . . . .160 DR111
   Swanley BR8 . . . . .147 FF98
   Upminster RM14 . . . . . .72 FP62
   Westerham (Tats.) TN16 .178 EK119
Beech Cl, N9 . . . . .30 DU44
   SE8 off Clyde St 103 DZ79
   SW15 . . . . .119 CU87
   SW19 . . . . .119 CW93
   Ashford TW15 . . . . .115 BR92
   Carshalton SM5 . . . . . .140 DF103
   Cobham KT11 . . . . .154 CA112
   Hornchurch RM12 . . . . . .71 FH62
   Loughton IG10 off Cedar Dr .33 EP40
   Staines (Stanw.) TW19
   off St. Mary's Cres 114 BK87
   Sunbury-on-Thames TW16
   off Harfield Rd 136 BX96
   Walton-on-Thames KT12 .136 BW105
   West Byfleet (Byfleet)
   KT14 . . . . .152 BL112
   West Drayton UB7 . . . . .94 BN76
Beech Cl Ct, Cob. KT11 . . . .154 BZ111
Beech Copse, Brom. BR1 . . .145 EM96
   South Croydon CR2 . . . .160 DS106
Beech Ct, E17 . . . . .67 EC55
   SE9 . . . . .124 EL86
   Ilford IG1 off Riverdene . .69 EN62
   Surbiton KT6 . . . . .138 CL101
Beech Cres, Tad. KT20 . . . .182 CQ130
Beechcroft, Ashtd. KT21 . . .172 CM119
   Chislehurst BR7 . . . . . .125 EN94
Beechcroft Av, NW11 . . . . . . .63 CZ59
   Bexleyheath DA7 . . . . . .107 FD81
   Harrow HA2 . . . . .60 CA59
   Kenley CR8 . . . . .176 DR115
   New Malden KT3 . . . . .138 CQ95
   Rickmansworth (Crox.Grn.)
   WD3 . . . . .23 BQ44
   Southall UB1 . . . . .78 BZ74
Beechcroft Cl, Houns. TW5 . . .96 BY80
   Orpington BR6 . . . . . . .163 ER105
Beechcroft Gdns, Wem. HA9 . .62 CM61
Beechcroft Lo, Sutt. SM2
   off Devonshire Rd 158 DC108
Beechcroft Manor, Wey.
   KT13 . . . . .135 BR104
Beechcroft Rd, E18 . . . . .48 EH54
   SW14 off Elm Rd 98 CQ83
   SW17 . . . . .120 DE89
   Bushey WD23 . . . . .24 BY43
   Chessington KT9 . . . . . .138 CM104
   Orpington BR6 . . . . . . .163 ER105
Beechdale, N21 . . . . .45 DM47
Beechdale Rd, SW2 . . . . . . .121 DM86
Beech Dell, Kes. BR2 . . . . . .163 EM105
Beechdene, Tad. KT20 . . . . .173 CV122
Beech Dr, N2 . . . . .64 DF55
   Borehamwood WD6 . . . . .26 CM40
   Reigate RH2 . . . . .184 DD134
   Tadworth (Kgswd.) KT20 .173 CZ122
   Woking (Ripley) GU23 . . .168 BG124
Beechen Cliff Way, Islw. TW7
   off Henley Cl 97 CF81
Beechen Gro, Pnr. HA5 . . . . .60 BZ55
   Watford WD17 . . . . .24 BW42
Beechen La, Tad. KT20 . . . .182 CZ125
Beechenlea La, Swan. BR8 . .147 FH97
Beeches, The, Bans. SM7 . . .174 DB116
   Brentwood CM14 . . . . . .54 FV48
   Hounslow TW3 . . . . .96 CB81
   Leatherhead (Fetch.) KT22 .171 CE124
   Rickmansworth (Chorl.)
   WD3 . . . . .21 BF43

Bee - Ben

Beeches, The, St.Alb. (Park St.)
  AL2 ....9 CE27
Beeches, The, Til. RM18 ...111 GH82
Beeches Av, Cars. SM5 ...158 DE108
Beeches Cl, SE20
  off Genoa Rd 142 DW95
  Tadworth (Kgswd.) KT20 ..174 DA123
Beeches Rd, SW17 ....120 DE90
  Sutton SM3 ....139 CY102
Beeches Wk, Cars. SM5 ....158 DD109
Beeches Wd, Tad. KT20 ...174 DA122
Beech Fm Rd, Warl. CR6 ...177 EC120
Beechfield, Bans. SM7 ....158 DB113
  Kings Langley WD4 ....6 BM30
Beechfield Cl, Borwd. WD6 ..26 CL40
Beechfield Cotts, Brom. BR1
  off Widmore Rd 144 EJ96
Beechfield Gdns, Rom. RM7 .71 FC59
Beechfield Rd, N4 ....66 DQ58
  SE6 ....123 DZ88
  Bromley BR1 ....144 EJ96
  Erith DA8 ....107 FE80
Beechfield Wk, Wal.Abb. EN9 .31 ED35
Beech Gdns, EC2
  off Aldersgate St 84 DQ71
  W5 ....98 CL75
  Dagenham RM10 ....89 FB66
  Woking GU21 ....166 AY115
Beech Gro, Add. KT15 ....152 BH105
  Caterham CR3 ....186 DS126
  Croydon CR0 ....160 DV110
  Epsom KT18 ....173 CV117
  Ilford IG6 ....49 ES51
  Mitcham CR4 ....141 DK98
  New Malden KT3 ....138 CR97
  South Ockendon (Aveley)
    RM15 ....90 FQ74
  Woking (Mayford) GU22 ..166 AX123
Beech Hall, Cher. (Ott.) KT16 .151 BC108
Beech Hall Cres, E4 ....47 ED52
Beech Hall Rd, E4 ....47 EC52
  Woking GU22 ....166 AX123
Beech Hill Av, Barn. EN4 ...28 DC39
Beech Hill Gdns, Wal.Abb.
  EN9 ....32 EH37
Beechhill Rd, SE9 ....125 EN85
Beech Holt, Lthd. KT22 ...171 CJ122
Beech Ho, Croy. CR0 .....161 EB107
Beech Ho Rd, Croy. CR0 ..142 DR104
Beech La, Beac. (Jordans)
  HP9 ....36 AS52
  Buckhurst Hill IG9 ....48 EH47
Beech Lawns, N12 ....44 DD50
Beech Lo, Stai. TW18
  off Farm Cl 113 BE92
Beechmeads, Cob. KT11 ..154 BX113
Beechmont Av, Vir.W. GU25 .132 AX99
Beechmont Cl, Brom. BR1 ..124 EE92
Beechmont Rd, Sev. TN13 ..191 FH125
Beechmore Gdns, Sutt. SM3 .139 CX103
Beechmore Rd, SW11 ....100 DF83
Beechmount Av, W7 ....79 CD71
Beecholme, Bans. SM7 ....157 CY114
Beecholme Av, Mitch. CR4 ..141 DH95
Beecholme Est, E5
  off Prout Rd 66 DV62
Beecholm Ms, Wal.Cr. EN8 ..15 DX28
Beech Pk, Amer. HP6 ....20 AV39
Beechpark Way, Wat. WD17 ..23 BS37
Beech Pl, Epp. CM16 ....17 ET31
Beech Rd, N11 ....45 DL51
  SW16 ....141 DL96
  Dartford DA1 ....128 FK88
  Epsom KT17 ....173 CT115
  Feltham TW14 ....115 BS87
  Orpington BR6 ....164 EU108
  Redhill RH1 ....185 DJ126
  Reigate RH2 ....184 DA131
  Sevenoaks TN13
    off Victoria Rd 191 FH125
  Slough SL3 ....92 AY75
  Watford WD24 ....23 BU37
  Westerham (Bigg.H.) TN16 .178 EH118
  Weybridge KT13
    off St. Marys Rd 153 BR105
Beech Row, Rich. TW10 ....118 CL91
Beech St, EC2 ....197 H6
  Romford RM7 ....71 FC56
Beechtree Av, Egh. (Eng.Grn.)
  TW20 ....112 AV93
Beech Tree Cl, Stan. HA7 ...41 CJ50
Beech Tree Glade, E4
  off Forest Side 48 EF46
Beech Tree La, Stai. TW18
  off Staines Rd 134 BH96
Beech Tree Pl, Sutt. SM1
  off St. Nicholas Way ..158 DB106
Beech Vale, Wok. GU22
  off Hill Vw Rd 167 AZ118
Beechvale Cl, N12 ....44 DE50
Beech Wk, NW7 ....42 CS51
  Dartford DA1 ....107 FG84
  Epsom KT17 ....157 CU111
Beech Way, NW10 ....80 CR66
Beechway, Bex. DA5 ....126 EX86
Beech Way, Epsom KT17 ...173 CT115
  South Croydon CR2 .....161 DX113
  Twickenham TW2 ....116 CA90
Beech Waye, Ger.Cr. SL9 ...57 AZ59
Beechwood Av, N3 ....63 CZ55
  Amersham HP6 ....20 AW38
  Coulsdon CR5 ....175 DH115
  Greenford UB6 ....78 CB69
  Harrow HA2 ....60 CB62
  Hayes UB3 ....77 BR73
  Orpington BR6 ....163 ES106
  Potters Bar EN6 ....12 DB33
  Richmond TW9 ....98 CN81
  Rickmansworth (Chorl.)
    WD3 ....21 BB42
  Ruislip HA4 ....59 BT61
  Staines TW18 ....114 BH93
  Sunbury-on-Thames TW16 .115 BU93

Beechwood Av, Tad. (Kgswd.)
  KT20 ....174 DA121
  Thornton Heath CR7 ....141 DP98
  Uxbridge UB8 ....76 BN72
  Weybridge KT13 ....153 BS105
Beechwood Circle, Har. HA2
  off Beechwood Gdns 60 CB62
Beechwood Cl, NW7 ....42 CR50
  Amersham HP6 ....20 AW39
  Waltham Cross (Chsht.)
    EN7 ....14 DS26
  Weybridge KT13 ....153 BS105
  Woking (Knap.) GU21 ..166 AS117
Beechwood Ct, Cars. SM5 ..158 DF105
  Sunbury-on-Thames TW16 .115 BU93
Beechwood Cres, Bexh. DA7 .106 EX83
Beechwood Dr, Cob. KT11 ..154 CA115
  Keston BR2 ....162 EK105
  Woodford Green IG8 ....48 EF50
Beechwood Gdns, NW10
  off St. Annes Gdns 80 CM69
  Caterham CR3 ....176 DU122
  Harrow HA2 ....60 CB62
  Ilford IG5 ....69 EM57
  Rainham RM13 ....89 FH71
  Slough SL1 ....92 AS75
Beechwood Gro, W3
  off East Acton La 81 CS73
  Surbiton KT6 ....137 CJ101
Beechwood La, Warl. CR6 ..177 DX119
Beechwood Manor, Wey.
  KT13 ....153 BS105
Beechwood Ms, N9 ....46 DU47
Beechwood Pk, E18 ....68 EG55
  Leatherhead KT22 ....171 CJ123
  Rickmansworth (Chorl.) WD3
    off Rickmansworth Rd ..21 BF42
Beechwood Ri, Chis. BR7 ..125 EP91
  Watford WD24 ....23 BV36
Beechwood Rd, E8 ....84 DT65
  N8 ....65 DK66
  Caterham CR3 ....176 DU122
  South Croydon CR2 ....160 DS109
  Virginia Water GU25 ...132 AU101
  Woking (Knap.) GU21 ..166 AS117
Beechwoods Ct, SE19
  off Crystal Palace Par .122 DT92
Beechworth Cl, NW3 ....64 DA91
Beecot La, Walt. KT12 ....136 BW103
Beecroft Rd, SE4 ....123 DY85
Beehive Cl, E8 ....84 DT66
  Borehamwood (Elstree)
    WD6 ....25 CK44
  Uxbridge UB10
    off Honey Hill 76 BM66
Beehive La, Ilf. IG1, IG4 ..69 EM58
Beehive Pas, EC3 ....197 M9
Beehive Pl, SW9 ....101 DN83
Beehive Rd, Stai. TW18 ...113 BF92
  Waltham Cross (Chsht.)
    EN7 ....13 DP28
Beeken Dene, Orp. BR6
  off Isabella Dr 163 EQ105
Beel Cl, Amer. HP7 ....20 AW39
Beeleigh Rd, Mord. SM4 ..140 DB98
Beesfield La, Dart. (Fnghm.)
  DA4 ....148 FN101
Beeston Cl, E8 off Ferncliff Rd .66 DU64
  Watford WD19 ....40 BX49
Beeston Dr, Wal.Cr. EN8 ....15 DX27
Beeston Pl, SW1 ....199 J7
Beeston Rd, Barn. EN4 ....28 DD44
Beeston Way, Felt. TW14 ..116 BW86
Beethoven Rd, Borwd. (Elstree)
  WD6 ....25 CK44
Beethoven St, W10 ....81 CY69
Beeton Cl, Pnr. HA5 ....40 CA52
Begbie Rd, SE3 ....104 EJ81
Beggars Bush La, Wat. WD18 .23 BR43
Beggars Hill, Epsom KT17 ..157 CT108
Beggars Hollow, Enf. EN2 ..30 DR37
Beggars La, West. TN16 ...189 ER125
Beggars Roost La, Sutt. SM1 .158 DA107
Begonia Cl, E6 ....86 EL71
Begonia Pl, Hmptn. TW12
  off Gresham Rd 116 CA93
Begonia Wk, W12
  off Du Cane Rd 81 CT72
Beira St, SW12 ....121 DH87
Beken Ct, Wat. WD25 .....24 BW35
Bekesbourne St, E14
  off Ratcliffe La 85 DY72
Bekesbourne Twr, Orp. BR5 .146 EY102
Belcroft Cl, Brom. BR1
  off Hope Pk 124 EF94
Beldam Haw, Sev. (Halst.)
  TN14 ....164 FA112
Beldham Gdns, W.Mol. KT8 .136 CB97
Belfairs Dr, Rom. RM6 ....70 EW59
Belfairs Grn, Wat. WD19
  off Heysham Dr 40 BX50
Belfast Rd, N16 ....66 DT61
  SE25 ....142 DV98
Belfield Rd, Epsom KT19 ..156 CR109
Belfont Wk, N7 ....65 DL63
Belford Gro, SE18 ....105 EN77
Belford Rd, Borwd. WD6 ...26 CM38
Belfort Rd, SE15 ....102 DW82
Belfour Ter, N3 ....44 DB54
Belfry Av, Uxb. (Hare.) UB9 .38 BG53
Belfry Cl, SE16 ....202 E10
Belfry La, Rick. WD3 ....38 BJ46
Belfry Shop Cen, The, Red.
  RH1 ....184 DF133
Belgrade Rd, N16 ....66 DS63
  Hampton TW12 ....136 CB95
Belgrave Av, Rom. RM2 ....72 FJ55
  Watford WD18 ....23 BT43
Belgrave Cl, N14
  off Prince George Av ..29 DJ43
  NW7 ....42 CR50
  W3 off Avenue Rd 98 CQ75
  Orpington BR5 ....146 EW98
  Walton-on-Thames KT12 .153 BV105
Belgrave Ct, E14 ....203 N1

Belgrave Cres, Sun. TW16 ..135 BV95
Belgrave Dr, Kings L. WD4 ..7 BQ28
Belgrave Gdns, N14 ....29 DK67
  NW8 ....82 DB67
  Stanmore HA7
    off Copley Rd 41 CJ50
Belgrave Hts, E11 ....68 EG60
Belgrave Manor, Wok. GU22 ..166 AY119
Belgrave Ms N, SW1 ....198 F5
Belgrave Ms S, SW1 ....198 G6
Belgrave Ms W, SW1 ....198 F6
Belgrave Pl, SW1 ....198 G6
  Slough SL1 off Clifton Rd .92 AV75
Belgrave Rd, E10 ....67 EC60
  E11 ....68 EG61
  E13 ....86 EJ70
  E17 ....67 EA57
  SE25 ....142 DT98
  SW1 ....199 K9
  SW13 ....99 CT80
  Hounslow TW4 ....96 BZ83
  Ilford IG1 ....69 EM60
  Mitcham CR4 ....140 DD97
  Slough SL1 ....74 AS73
  Sunbury-on-Thames
    TW16 ....135 BV95
Belgrave Sq, SW1 ....198 F6
Belgrave St, E1 ....85 DX72
Belgrave Ter, Wdf.Grn. IG8 ..48 EG48
Belgrave Walk, Mitch. CR4 ..140 DD97
Belgrave Wk, Mitch. CR4 ..140 DD97
Belgrave Yd, SW1 ....199 H7
BELGRAVIA, SW1 ....198 F7
Belgravia Cl, Barn. EN5 ....27 CZ41
Belgravia Gdns, Brom. BR1 ..124 EE93
Belgravia Ho, SW4 ....121 DL86
Belgravia Ms, Kings.T. KT1 ..137 CK98
Belgrove St, WC1 ....195 P2
Belham Rd, Kings L. WD4 ....6 BM28
Belham Wk, SE5
  off D'Eynsford Rd 102 DR81
Belhaven Ct, Borwd. WD6 ...26 CM39
Belhus Pk, S.Ock. (Aveley)
  RM15 ....91 FR71
Belinda Rd, SW9 ....101 DP83
Belitha Vil, N1 ....83 DM66
Bellamy Cl, E14 ....203 P4
  W14 off Aisgill Av 99 CZ78
  Edgware HA8 ....42 CQ48
  Uxbridge UB10 ....58 BN62
  Watford WD17 ....23 BU39
Bellamy Dr, Stan. HA7 .....41 CH53
Bellamy Rd, E4 ....47 EB51
  Enfield EN2 ....30 DR40
  Waltham Cross (Chsht.)
    EN8 ....15 DY29
Bellamy St, SW12 ....121 DH87
Bellasis Av, SW2 ....121 DL89
Bell Av, Rom. RM3 ....51 FH53
  West Drayton UB7 ....94 BM77
Bell Br Rd, Cher. KT16 ....133 BF102
Bell Cl, Abb.L. (Bedmond)
  WD5 ....7 BT27
  Greenhithe DA9 ....129 FT85
  Pinner HA5 ....60 BW55
  Ruislip HA4 ....59 BT62
  Slough SL2 ....74 AV71
Bellclose Rd, West Dr. UB7 ..94 BL75
BELL COMMON, Epp. 17 ER32
Bell Common, Epp. CM16 ...17 ES32
Bell Common Tunnel, Epp.
  CM16 ....17 ER33
Bell Ct, Surb. KT5
  off Barnsbury La 138 CP103
Bell Cres, Couls. CR5
  off Maple Way 175 DH121
Bell Dr, SW18 ....119 CX87
Bellefield Rd, Orp. BR5 ...146 EV99
Bellefields Rd, SW9 ....101 DM83
Bellegrove Cl, Well. DA16 ..105 ET82
Bellegrove Par, Well. DA16
  off Bellegrove Rd 105 ET83
Bellegrove Rd, Well. DA16 ..105 ER82
Bellenden Rd, SE15 ....102 DT82
Bellestaines Pleasaunce, E4 .47 EA47
Belleville Rd, SW11 ....120 DF85
Belle Vue, Grnf. UB6 ....79 CD67
Belle Vue Est, NW4 off Bell La .63 CW56
Belle Vue La, Bushey (Bushey Hth.)
  WD23 ....41 CD46
Bellevue Ms, N11 ....44 DG50
Bellevue Par, SW17
  off Bellevue Rd 120 DE88
Belle Vue Pk, Th.Hth. CR7 ..142 DQ97
Bellevue Pl, E1 ....84 DW70
  Slough SL1 off Albert St .92 AT76
Belle Vue Rd, E17 ....47 ED54
Bellevue Rd, N11 ....44 DG49
Belle Vue Rd, NW4 off Bell La .63 CW56
Bellevue Rd, SW13 ....99 CU82
  SW17 ....120 DE88
  W13 ....79 CH70
  Bexleyheath DA6 ....126 EZ85
  Hornchurch RM11 ....72 FM60
  Kingston upon Thames
    KT1 ....138 CL97
Belle Vue Rd, Orp. BR6
  off Standard Rd 163 EN110
Bellevue Rd, Rom. RM5 ....51 FC51
Bellew St, SW17 ....120 DC90
Bell Fm Av, Dag. RM10 ....71 FC62
Bellfield, Croy. CR0 ....161 DY109
Bellfield Av, Har. HA3 .....40 CC51
Bellflower Cl, E6
  off Sorrel Gdns 86 EL71
Bellflower Path, Rom. RM3 ..52 FJ52
Bell Gdns, E10 off Church Rd .67 EA60
  E17 off Markhouse Rd ..67 DZ57
  Orpington BR5 ....146 EW99
Bellgate Ms, NW5 off York Ri .65 DH62
BELL GREEN, SE6 ....123 DZ90
Bell Grn, SE26 ....123 DZ90

Bell Grn, Hem. H. (Bov.) HP3 ..5 BB27
Bell Grn La, SE26 ....123 DY92
Bell Hill, Croy. CR0
  off Surrey St 142 DQ104
Bellhouse La, Brwd. CM14 ..54 FS43
Bell Ho Rd, Rom. RM7 ....71 FC60
BELLINGHAM, SE6 ....123 EB90
  ≠ Bellingham 123 EB90
Bellingham Ct, Bark. IG11
  off Renwick Rd 88 EV69
Bellingham Grn, SE6 ......123 EA90
Bellingham Rd, SE6 ....123 EB90
Bell Inn Yd, EC3 ....197 L9
Bell La, E1 ....197 P7
  E16 ....205 M2
  NW4 ....63 CX56
  Abbots Langley (Bedmond)
    WD5 ....7 BT27
  Amersham HP6, HP7 ....20 AW39
  Enfield EN3 ....31 DX38
  Hatfield (Brook.Pk.) AL9 ..12 DA25
  Leatherhead (Fetch.) KT22 .171 CD123
  St. Albans (Lon.Col.) AL2 ..10 CL29
  Twickenham TW1
    off The Embankment ...117 CG88
  Wembley HA9
    off Magnet Rd 61 CK61
Bell La, Lthd. (Fetch.)
  KT22 ....171 CD123
Bellmaker Ct, E3
  off St. Pauls Way 85 DZ71
Bellman Av, Grav. DA12 ..131 GL88
Bellmarsh Rd, Add. KT15 ..152 BH105
Bell Meadow, SE19
  off Dulwich Wd Av 122 DS91
  Godstone RH9 ....186 DV132
Bellmount Wd Av, Wat. WD17 ..23 BS39
Bello Cl, SE24 ....121 DP87
Bellot Gdns, SE10 ....205 J10
Bellot St, SE10 ....205 J10
Bellring Cl, Belv. DA17 ..106 FA79
Bell Rd, E.Mol. KT8 ....137 CD99
  Enfield EN1 ....30 DR39
  Hounslow TW3 ....96 CB84
Bells All, SW6 ....100 DA82
Bells Gdn Est, SE15
  off Buller Cl 102 DU80
Bell's Hill, Slou. (Stoke P.) SL2 .74 AU67
Bells Hill Grn, Slou. (Stoke P.)
  SL2 ....74 AU66
Bells La, Slou. (Horton) SL3 ..93 BB83
Bell St, NW1 ....194 B6
  SE18 ....104 EL81
  Reigate RH2 ....184 DA134
Bellswood La, Iver SL0 ....75 BB71
Belltrees Gro, SW16 ....121 DM92
Bell Water Gate, SE18 ....105 EN76
Bell Weir Cl, Stai. TW19 ..113 BB89
Bell Wf La, EC4 ....197 J10
Bellwood Rd, SE15 ....103 DX84
Bell Yd, WC2 ....196 D8
Belmarsh Rd, SE28
  off Western Way 105 ES75
BELMONT, Har. 41 CG54
BELMONT, Sutt. 158 DB111
  ≠ Belmont 158 DA110
Belmont Av, N9 ....46 DU46
  N13 ....45 DL50
  N17 ....66 DQ55
  Barnet EN4 ....28 DF43
  New Malden KT3 ....139 CU99
  Southall UB2 ....96 BY76
  Upminster RM14 ....72 FM61
  Welling DA16 ....105 ES83
  Wembley HA0 ....80 CM67
Belmont Circle, Har. HA3 ..41 CH53
Belmont Cl, E4 ....47 ED50
  N20 ....44 DB46
  SW4 ....101 DJ83
  Barnet EN4 ....28 DF42
  Uxbridge UB8 ....76 BK65
  Woodford Green IG8 ....48 EH49
Belmont Cotts, Slou. (Colnbr.)
  SL3 off High St 93 BC80
Belmont Ct, NW11 ....63 CZ57
Belmont Gro, SE13 ....103 ED83
  W4 off Belmont Rd 98 CR77
Belmont Hall Ct, SE13
  off Belmont Gro 103 ED83
Belmont Hill, SE13 ....103 ED83
Belmont La, Chis. BR7 ....125 EQ92
  Stanmore HA7 ....41 CJ52
Belmont Ms, SW19
  off Chapman Sq 119 CX89
Belmont Pk, SE13 ....103 ED84
Belmont Pk Cl, SE13
  off Belmont Pk 103 ED84
Belmont Pk Rd, E10 ....67 EB58
Belmont Ri, Sutt. SM2 ....157 CZ107
Belmont Rd, N15 ....66 DQ56
  N17 ....66 DQ56
  SE25 ....142 DV99
  SW4 ....101 DJ83
  W4 ....98 CR77
  Beckenham BR3 ....143 DZ96
  Bushey WD23 ....24 BY43
  Chislehurst BR7 ....125 EP92
  Erith DA8 ....106 FA80
  Grays RM17 ....110 FZ78
  Harrow HA3 ....61 CF55
  Hornchurch RM12 ......72 FK62
  Ilford IG1 ....69 EQ62
  Leatherhead KT22 .....171 CG122
  Sutton SM2 ....158 DA110
  Twickenham TW2 ....117 CD89
  Uxbridge UB8 ....76 BK66
  Wallington SM6 ....159 DH105
Belmont St, NW1 ....82 DG66
Belmont Ter, W4
  off Belmont Rd 98 CR77
Belmor, Borwd. (Elstree) WD6 .26 CN43
Belmore Av, Hayes UB4 ...77 BU72
  Woking GU22 ....167 BD116
Belmore La, N7 ....65 DK64
Belmore St, SW8 ....101 DK81
Beloe Cl, SW15 ....99 CU83

Belper Ct, E5 off Pedro St 67 DX63
Belsham St, E9 ....84 DW65
BELSIZE, Rick. 5 BF33
Belsize Av, N13 ....45 DM51
  NW3 ....82 DD65
  W13 ....97 CH76
Belsize Ct, NW3
  off Belsize La 64 DE64
Belsize Cres, NW3 ....64 DD64
Belsize Gdns, Sutt. SM1 ..158 DB105
Belsize Gro, NW3 ....82 DE65
Belsize La, NW3 ....82 DD65
Belsize Ms, NW3
  off Belsize La 82 DD65
BELSIZE PARK, NW3 ....82 DE65
  ⊖ Belsize Park 64 DE64
Belsize Pk, NW3 ....82 DD65
Belsize Pk Gdns, NW3 ....82 DE65
Belsize Pk Ms, NW3
  off Belsize La 82 DD65
Belsize Pl, NW3 off Belsize La .82 DD65
Belsize Rd, NW6 ....82 DB67
  Harrow HA3 ....41 CD52
Belsize Sq, NW3 ....82 DD65
Belsize Ter, NW3 ....82 DD65
Belson Rd, SE18 ....105 EM77
Belswains La, Hem.H. HP3 ..6 BM25
Beltana Dr, Grav. DA12 ..131 GL91
Beltane Dr, SW19 ....119 CX90
Belthorn Cres, SW12 ....121 DJ87
Beltinge Rd, Rom. RM3 ....72 FM55
Beltona Gdns, Wal.Cr. (Chsht.)
  EN8 ....15 DX27
Belton Rd, E7 ....86 EH66
  E11 ....68 EE63
  N17 ....66 DS55
  NW2 ....81 CU65
  Sidcup DA14 ....126 EU91
Belton Way, E3 ....85 EA71
Beltran Rd, SW6 ....100 DB82
Beltwood Rd, Belv. DA17 ..107 FC77
BELVEDERE 107 FB77
  ≠ Belvedere 106 FA76
Belvedere Av, SW19 ....119 CY92
  Ilford IG5 ....49 EP54
Belvedere Bldgs, SE1 .....200 G5
Belvedere Cl, Esher KT10 ..154 CB106
  Gravesend DA12 ....131 GJ88
  Teddington TW11 ....117 CE92
  Weybridge KT13 ....152 BN106
Belvedere Ct, N2 ....64 DD57
Belvedere Dr, SW19 ....119 CY92
Belvedere Gdns, St.Alb. AL2 ..8 CA27
  West Molesey KT8 ......136 BZ99
Belvedere Gro, SW19 .....119 CY92
Belvedere Ho, Felt. TW13 ..115 BU88
Belvedere Ind Est, Belv.
  DA17 ....107 FC76
Belvedere Ms, SE3
  off Langton Way 104 EF81
  SE15 ....102 DV83
Belvedere Pl, SE1 ....200 G5
  SW2 off Acre La 101 DM84
Belvedere Rd, E10 ....67 DY60
  SE1 ....200 C4
  SE2 ....88 EX74
  SE19 ....122 DT94
  W7 ....97 CF76
  Bexleyheath DA7 ....106 EZ83
  Brentwood CM14 ....54 FT48
  Westerham (Bigg.H.) TN16 ..179 EM118
Belvedere Sq, SW19 ....119 CY92
Belvedere Strand, NW9 ....43 CT54
Belvedere Twr, The, SW10 ..100 DC81
Belvedere Way, Har. HA3 ...62 CL58
Belvoir Cl, SE9 ....124 EL90
Belvoir Rd, SE22 ....122 DU87
Belvue Cl, Nthlt. UB5 ....78 CA66
Belvue Rd, Nthlt. UB5 ....78 CA66
Bembridge Cl, NW6 ....81 CY66
Bembridge Ct, Slou. SL1
  off Park St 92 AT76
Bembridge Gdns, Ruis. HA4 ..59 BR61
Bemerton Est, N1 ....83 DM66
Bemerton St, N1 ....83 DM67
Bemish Rd, SW15 ....99 CX83
Bempton Dr, Ruis. HA4 ....59 BV61
Bemsted Rd, E17 ....67 DZ55
Benares Rd, SE18 ....105 ET77
Benbow Rd, W6 ....99 CV76
Benbow St, SE8 ....103 EA79
Benbow Waye, Uxb. UB8 ...76 BJ71
Benbury Cl, Brom. BR1 ....123 EC92
Bence, The, Egh. TW20 ....133 BB97
Bench Fld, S.Croy. CR2 ..160 DT107
Bench Manor Cres, Ger.Cr.
  (Chal.St.P.) SL9 ....36 AW54
Bencombe Rd, Pur. CR8 ..159 DN114
Bencroft, Wal.Cr. (Chsht.) EN7 .14 DU26
Bencroft Rd, SW16 ....121 DJ94
Bencurtis Pk, W.Wick. BR4 ..143 ED104
Bendall Ms, NW1 ....194 C6
Bendemeer Rd, SW15 .....99 CX83
Bendish Rd, E6 ....86 EL66
Bendmore Av, SE2 ....106 EU78
Bendon Valley, SW18 .....120 DB87
Bendysh Rd, Bushey WD23 ..24 BY41
Benedict Cl, Belv. DA17
  off Tunstock Way 106 EY76
  Orpington BR6 ....145 ES104
Benedict Dr, Felt. TW14 ..115 BR87
Benedictine Gate, Wal.Cr.
  EN8 ....15 DY27
Benedict Rd, SW9 ....101 DM83
  Mitcham CR4 ....140 DD97
Benedict Way, N2 ....64 DC55
Benenden Grn, Brom. BR2 ..144 EG99
Benen-Stock Rd, Stai. TW19 ..113 BF85
Benets Rd, Horn. RM11 ....72 FN60
Benett Gdns, SW16 ....141 DL96
Benfleet Cl, Cob. KT11 ...154 BZ112
  Sutton SM1 ....140 DC104
Benfleet Way, N11 ....44 DG47
Bengal Ct, EC3 off Birchin La .84 DR72
Bengal Rd, Ilf. IG1 ....69 EP63
Bengarth Dr, Har. HA3 ....41 CD54
Bengarth Rd, Nthlt. UB5 ..78 BX67

Bengeworth Rd, SE5 . . . . . .102 DQ83
Harrow HA1 . . . . .61 CG61
Ben Hale Cl, Stan. HA7 . . . . .41 CH49
Benham Cl, SW11 . . . . . . .100 DD83
Chessington KT9
off Merritt Gdns 155 CJ107
Coulsdon CR5 . . . . . . .175 DP118
Benham Gdns, Houns. TW4 . .88 BZ85
Benham Rd, W7 . . . . .79 CE71
Benhams Pl, NW3
off Holly Wk 64 DC63
Benhill Av, Sutt. SM1 . . . . .158 DB105
Benhill Rd, SE5 . . . . .102 DR80
Sutton SM1 . . . . .140 DC104
BENHILTON, Sutt. 140 DB103
Benhilton Gdns, Sutt. SM1 . .140 DB104
Benhurst Av, Horn. RM12 . . .71 FH62
Benhurst Cl, S.Croy. CR2 . . .161 DX110
Benhurst Ct, SW16 . . . . . .121 DN92
Benhurst Gdns, S.Croy. CR2 .160 DW110
Benhurst La, SW16 . . . . . .121 DN92
Benin St, SE13 . . . . .123 ED87
Benison Ct, Slou. SL1
off Osborne St 92 AT76
Benjafield Cl, N18
off Brettenham Rd 46 DV49
Benjamin Cl, E8 . . . . .84 DU67
Hornchurch RM11 . . . . . .71 FG58
Benjamin St, EC1 . . . . . . .196 F6
Ben Jonson Rd, E1 . . . . . . .85 DY71
Benledi St, E14 . . . . .85 ED72
Benn Cl, Oxt. RH8 . . . . . .188 EG134
Bennelong Cl, W12 . . . . . . .81 CV73
Bennerley Rd, SW11 . . . . .120 DE85
Bennetsfield Rd, Uxb. UB11 . .77 BP74
Bennet's Hill, EC4 . . . . . .196 G10
Bennett Cl, Cob. KT11 . . . .153 BU113
Kingston upon Thames
KT1 . . . . .137 CJ95
Northwood HA6 . . . . . . .39 BT52
Welling DA16 . . . . .106 EU82
Bennett Gro, SE13 . . . . . .103 EB81
Bennett Pk, SE3 . . . . . . .104 EF83
Bennett Rd, E13 . . . . .86 EJ70
N16 . . . . .66 DS63
Romford RM6 . . . . .70 EY58
Bennetts Av, Croy. CR0 . . .143 DY103
Greenford UB6 . . . . .79 CE67
Bennetts Castle La, Dag. RM8 .70 EW63
Bennetts Cl, N17 . . . . .46 DT51
Mitcham CR4 . . . . .141 DH95
Bennetts Copse, Chis. BR7 . .124 EL93
Bennett St, SW1 . . . . . . .199 K2
W4 . . . . .98 CS79
Bennetts Way, Croy. CR0 . .143 DY103
Bennetts Yd, SW1 . . . . . .199 N7
Uxbridge UB8 off High St . .76 BJ66
Bennett Way, Dart. (Lane End)
DA2 . . . . .129 FR91
Benningholme Rd, Edg. HA8 . .42 CS51
Bennington Rd, N17 . . . . . .46 DS53
Woodford Green IG8 . . . . .48 EE52
Bennions Cl, Horn. RM12
off Franklin Rd 90 FK65
Bennison Dr, Rom. (Harold Wd.)
RM3 . . . . .52 FK54
Benn St, E9 . . . . .85 DY65
Benn's Wk, Rich. TW9
off Rosedale Rd 98 CL84
Benrek Cl, Ilf. IG6 . . . . .49 EQ53
Bensbury Cl, SW15 . . . . . .119 CV87
Bensham Cl, Th.Hth. CR7 . . .142 DQ98
Bensham Gro, Th.Hth. CR7 . .142 DQ96
Bensham La, Croy. CR0 . . . .141 DP101
Thornton Heath CR7 . . . . .141 DP98
Bensham Manor Rd, Th.Hth.
CR7 . . . . .142 DQ98
Bensington Ct, Felt. TW14 . .115 BR86
Benskin Rd, Wat. WD18 . . . .23 BU43
Benskins La, Rom. (Noak Hill)
RM4 . . . . .52 FK46
Bensley Cl, N11 . . . . .44 DF50
Ben Smith Way, SE16 . . . . .202 C6
Benson Av, E6 . . . . .86 EJ68
Benson Cl, Houns. TW3 . . . .96 CA84
Slough SL2 . . . . .74 AU74
Uxbridge UB8 . . . . .76 BL71
Benson Quay, E1 . . . . . . .202 F1
Benson Rd, SE23 . . . . . . .122 DW88
Croydon CR0 . . . . .141 DN104
Grays RM17 . . . . .110 GB79
Bentalls Cen, Kings.T. KT1 . .138 CL96
Bentfield Gdns, SE9
off Aldersgrove Av 124 EJ90
Benthal Gdns, Ken. CR8 . . .176 DQ116
Benthal Rd, N16 . . . . .66 DU61
Bentham Av, Wok. GU21 . . .167 BC115
Bentham Ct, N1
off Rotherfield St 84 DQ66
Bentham Rd, E9 . . . . .85 DX65
SE28 . . . . .88 EV73
Bentham Wk, NW10 . . . . . .62 CQ64
Ben Tillet Cl, Bark. IG11 . . . .88 EU66
Ben Tillett Cl, E16
off Newland St 87 EM74
Bentinck Cl, Ger.Cr. SL9 . . . .56 AX57
Bentinck Ms, W1 . . . . . . .194 G8
Bentinck Pl, NW8 . . . . . . .194 B1
Bentinck Rd, West Dr. UB7 . .76 BK74
Bentinck St, W1 . . . . .194 G8
Bentley Dr, NW2 . . . . .63 CZ62
Ilford IG2 . . . . .69 ES58
Weybridge KT13 . . . . . .152 BN109
BENTLEY HEATH, Barn. 27 CZ35
Bentley Heath La, Barn. EN5 . .11 CY34
Bentley Ms, Enf. EN1 . . . . . .30 DR44
★ Bentley Priory, Stan. HA7 . . .41 CE48
Bentley Rd, N1
off Tottenham Rd 84 DS66
Bentley Way, Grav. DA12 . . .131 GJ86
Bentley Way, Stan. HA7 . . . .41 CG50
Woodford Green IG8 . . . . .48 EG48
Benton Rd, Ilf. IG1 . . . . . . .69 ER60
Watford WD19 . . . . .40 BX50
Bentons La, SE27 . . . . . . .122 DQ91
Bentons Ri, SE27 . . . . . . .122 DR92

Bentry Cl, Dag. RM8 . . . . . .70 EY61
Bentry Rd, Dag. RM8 . . . . . .70 EY61
Bentworth Rd, W12 . . . . . . .81 CV72
Benwell Ct, Sun. TW16 . . . .135 BU95
Benwell Rd, N7 . . . . .65 DN65
Benworth St, E3 . . . . .85 DZ69
Benyon Path, S.Ock. RM15
off Tyssen Pl 91 FW68
Benyon Rd, N1
off Southgate Rd 84 DR67
Beomonds Row, Cher. KT16
off Heriot Rd 134 BG101
Berberis Wk, West Dr. UB7 . .94 BL77
Berber Pl, E14
off Birchfield St 85 EA73
Berber Rd, SW11 . . . . . . .120 DF85
Berberry Cl, Edg. HA8
off Larkspur Gro 42 CQ49
Berceau Wk, Wat. WD17 . . . .23 BS39
Bercta Rd, SE9 . . . . .125 EQ89
Beredens La, Brwd. CM13 . . .73 FT55
Berenger Wk, SW10
off Blantyre St 100 DD80
Berens Rd, NW10 . . . . .81 CX69
Orpington BR5 . . . . . . .146 EX99
Berens Way, Chis. BR7 . . . .145 ET98
Beresford Av, N20 . . . . .44 DF47
W7 . . . . .79 CD71
Slough SL2 . . . . .74 AW74
Surbiton KT5 . . . . .138 CP102
Twickenham TW1 . . . . . .117 CJ86
Wembley HA0 . . . . .80 CM67
Beresford Dr, Brom. BR1 . . .144 EK97
Woodford Green IG8 . . . . .48 EJ49
Beresford Gdns, Enf. EN1 . . .30 DS42
Hounslow TW4 . . . . .116 BZ85
Romford RM6 . . . . .70 EY57
Beresford Rd, E4 . . . . .48 EE46
E17 . . . . .47 EB53
N2 . . . . .64 DE55
N5 . . . . .66 DQ64
N8 . . . . .65 DN57
Gravesend (Nthflt.) DA11 . .130 GE87
Harrow HA1 . . . . .61 CD57
Kingston upon Thames
KT2 . . . . .138 CM95
New Malden KT3 . . . . . .138 CQ98
Rickmansworth (Mill End)
WD3 . . . . .37 BF46
Southall UB1 . . . . .78 BX74
Sutton SM2 . . . . .157 CZ108
Beresford Sq, SE18 . . . . . .105 EP77
Beresford St, SE18 . . . . . .105 EP76
Beresford Ter, N5 . . . . .66 DQ64
Berestede Rd, W6 . . . . .99 CT78
Bere St, E1 off Cranford St . . .85 DX73
Bergen Sq, SE16 . . . . .203 L6
Berger Cl, Orp. BR5 . . . . . .145 ER100
Berger Rd, E9 . . . . .85 DX65
Berghem Ms, W14
off Blythe Rd 99 CX76
Berglen Ct, E14 off Branch Rd .85 DY72
Bering Sq, E14 off Napier Av .103 EA78
Berisford Ms, SW18 . . . . . .120 DC86
Berkeley Av, Bexh. DA7 . . . .106 EX81
Greenford UB6 . . . . .79 CE65
Hounslow TW4 . . . . .95 BU82
Ilford IG5 . . . . .49 EN54
Romford RM5 . . . . .51 FC52
Berkeley Cl, Abb.L. WD5 . . . . .7 BT32
Borehamwood (Elstree)
WD6 . . . . .26 CN43
Hornchurch RM11 . . . . . .72 FP61
Kingston upon Thames
KT2 . . . . .118 CL94
Orpington BR5 . . . . . . .145 ES101
Potters Bar EN6 . . . . . . .11 CY32
Ruislip HA4 . . . . .59 BU62
Staines TW19 . . . . .113 BD89
Berkeley Ct, N14 . . . . .29 DJ44
Rickmansworth (Crox.Grn.)
WD3 off Mayfare 23 BR43
Wallington SM6 . . . . . . .141 DJ104
Weybridge KT13 . . . . . .153 BR103
Berkeley Cres, Barn. EN4 . . .28 DD43
Dartford DA1 . . . . .128 FM88
Berkeley Dr, Horn. RM11 . . . .72 FN60
West Molesey KT8 . . . . . .136 BZ97
Berkeley Gdns, N21 . . . . . . .46 DR45
W8 off Brunswick Gdns . . .82 DA74
Esher (Clay.) KT10 . . . . .155 CG107
Walton-on-Thames KT12 . .135 BT101
West Byfleet KT14 . . . . . .151 BF114
Berkeley Ho, E3 . . . . .85 EA70
Berkeley Ms, W1 . . . . .194 E8
Berkeley Pl, SW19 . . . . . . .119 CX93
Epsom KT18 . . . . .172 CR115
Berkeley Rd, E12 . . . . .68 EL64
N8 . . . . .65 DK57
N15 . . . . .66 DR58
NW9 . . . . .62 CN56
SW13 . . . . .99 CU81
Uxbridge UB10 . . . . .77 BQ66
Berkeleys, The, Lthd. (Fetch.)
KT22 . . . . .171 CE124
Berkeley Sq, W1 . . . . .199 J1
Berkeley St, W1 . . . . .199 J1
Berkeley Wk, N7
off Durham Rd 65 DM61
Berkeley Waye, Houns. TW5 . .96 BX80
Berkhampstead Rd, Belv.
DA17 . . . . .106 FA78
Berkhamsted Av, Wem. HA9 . .80 CM65
Berkley Av, Wal.Cr. EN8 . . . .15 DX34
Berkley Cres, Grav. DA12
off Milton Rd 131 GJ86
Berkley Gro, NW1
off Berkley Rd 82 DF66
Berkley Rd, NW1 . . . . .82 DF66
Gravesend DA12 . . . . . .131 GH86
Berks Hill, Rick. (Chorl.) WD3 . .21 BC43

Berkshire Cl, Cat. CR3 . . . .176 DR122
Berkshire Gdns, N13 . . . . . .45 DN51
N18 . . . . .46 DV50
Berkshire Rd, E9 . . . . .85 DZ65
Berkshire Sq, Mitch. CR4
off Berkshire Way 141 DL98
Berkshire Way, Horn. RM11 . .72 FN57
Mitcham CR4 . . . . .141 DL98
Bermans Cl, Brwd. CM13
off Hanging Hill La 55 GB47
Bermans Way, NW10 . . . . . .62 CS63
BERMONDSEY, SE1 . . . . . .201 P7
⊖ Bermondsey 202 C6
★ Bermondsey Leather Mkt,
SE1 . . . . .201 M5
Bermondsey Sq, SE1 . . . . .201 N6
Bermondsey St, SE1 . . . . .201 M3
Bermondsey Wall E, SE16 . .202 C5
Bermondsey Wall W, SE16 . .202 B4
Bermuda Rd, Til. RM18 . . . .111 GG82
Bernal Cl, SE28
off Haldane Rd 88 EX73
Bernard Ashley Dr, SE7 . . . .104 EH78
Bernard Av, W13 . . . . .97 CH76
Bernard Cassidy St, E16 . . . .86 EF71
Bernard Gdns, SW19 . . . . .119 CZ92
Bernard Gro, Wal.Abb. EN9
off Beaulieu Dr 15 EB33
Bernard Rd, N15 . . . . .66 DT57
Romford RM7 . . . . .71 FC59
Wallington SM6 . . . . . . .159 DH105
Bernards Cl, Ilf. IG6 . . . . . .49 EQ51
Bernard St, WC1 . . . . .195 P5
Bernato Cl, W.Byf. KT14
off Viscount Gdns 152 BL112
Bernays Cl, Stan. HA7 . . . . .41 CJ51
Bernays Gro, SW9 . . . . . . .101 DM84
Bernel Dr, Croy. CR0 . . . . .143 DZ104
Berne Rd, Th.Hth. CR7 . . . .142 DQ99
Berners Dr, W13 . . . . .79 CG72
Bernersmede, SE3
off Blackheath Pk 104 EG83
Berners Ms, W1 . . . . .195 L7
Berners Pl, W1 . . . . .195 L8
Berners Rd, N1 . . . . .83 DN67
N22 . . . . .45 DN53
Berners St, W1 . . . . .195 L7
Berney Rd, Croy. CR0 . . . . .142 DR101
Bernhardt Cres, NW8 . . . . .194 B4
Bernhart Cl, Edg. HA8 . . . . .42 CQ52
Bernice Cl, Rain. RM13 . . . . .90 FJ70
Bernville Way, Har. HA3
off Kenton Rd 62 CM57
Bernwell Rd, E4 . . . . .48 EE48
Berridge Grn, Edg. HA8 . . . .42 CN52
Berridge Ms, NW6
off Hillfield Rd 64 DA64
Berridge Rd, SE19 . . . . . . .122 DR92
Berriman Rd, N7 . . . . .65 DM62
Berrington Dr, Lthd. (E.Hors.)
KT24 . . . . .169 BT124
Berriton Rd, Har. HA2 . . . . .60 BZ60
Berry Av, Wat. WD24 . . . . . .23 BU36
Berrybank Cl, E4
off Greenbank Cl 47 EC47
Berry Cl, N21 . . . . .45 DP46
NW10 . . . . .80 CS66
Dagenham RM10 . . . . . . .70 FA64
Hornchurch RM12
off Airfield Way 72 FJ64
Rickmansworth WD3 . . . . .38 BH45
Berry Ct, Houns. TW4 . . . . .116 BZ85
Berrydale Rd, Hayes UB4 . . .78 BY70
Berryfield, Slou. SL2 . . . . . .74 AW72
Berryfield Cl, E17 . . . . .67 EB56
Bromley BR1 . . . . .144 EL95
Berryfield Rd, SE17 . . . . . .200 G10
Berry Gro La, Wat. WD25 . . .24 CA39
Berryhill, SE9 . . . . .105 EP84
Berryhill Gdns, SE9 . . . . . .105 EP84
BERRYLANDS, Surb. 138 CM99
⇌ Berrylands 138 CN98
Berrylands, SW20 . . . . . . .139 CW97
Orpington BR6 . . . . . . .146 EW104
Surbiton KT5 . . . . .138 CN99
Berrylands Rd, Surb. KT5 . . .138 CM100
Berry La, SE21 . . . . .122 DR91
Rickmansworth WD3 . . . . .38 BH46
Walton-on-Thames KT12
off Burwood Rd 154 BX106
Berryman Cl, Dag. RM8
off Bennetts Castle La 70 EW62
Berrymans La, SE26 . . . . . .123 DX91
Berry Meade, Ashtd. KT21 . .172 CM117
Berry Meade Cl, Ashtd. KT21
off Berry Meade 172 CM117
Berrymead Gdns, W3 . . . . . .80 CQ74
Berrymede Rd, W4 . . . . . . .98 CR76
Berry Pl, EC1 . . . . .196 G3
Berryscroft Ct, Stai. TW18
off Berryscroft Rd 114 BJ94
Berryscroft Rd, Stai. TW18 . .114 BJ94
BERRY'S GREEN, West. 179 EP116
Berry's Grn Rd, West.
(Berry's Grn.) TN16 . . . . .179 EP116
Berry's Hill, West. (Berry's Grn.)
TN16 . . . . .179 EP115
Berrys La, W.Byf. (Byfleet)
KT14 . . . . .152 BK111
Berry St, EC1 . . . . .196 G4
Berry Wk, Ashtd. KT21 . . . .172 CM119
Berry Way, W5 . . . . .98 CL76
Rickmansworth WD3 . . . . .38 BH45
Bersham La, Grays (Bad.Dene)
RM17 . . . . .110 FZ77
Bertal Rd, SW17 . . . . .120 DD91
Berther Rd, Horn. RM11 . . . .72 FK59
Berthold Ms, Wal.Abb. EN9 . .15 EB33
Berthon St, SE8 . . . . .103 EA80
Bertie Rd, NW10 . . . . .81 CU65
SE26 . . . . .123 DX93
Bertram Cotts, SW19
off Hartfield Rd 120 DA94
Bertram Rd, NW4 . . . . .63 CU58
Enfield EN1 . . . . .30 DU42

Bertram Rd, Kings.T. KT2 . . .118 CN94
Bertram St, N19 . . . . .65 DH61
Bertram Way, Enf. EN1 . . . . .30 DT42
Bertrand St, SE13 . . . . . . .103 EB83
Bertrand Way, SE28 . . . . . . .88 EV73
Bert Rd, Th.Hth. CR7 . . . . .142 DQ99
Bert Way, Enf. EN1
off Percival Rd 30 DT42
Berwick Av, Hayes UB4 . . . . .78 BX72
Berwick Cl, Stan. HA7
off Gordon Av 41 CF52
Waltham Cross EN8 . . . . . .15 EA34
Berwick Cres, Sid. DA15 . . .125 ES86
Berwick La, Ong. CM5 . . . . .35 FF36
Berwick Pond Cl, Rain. RM13 .90 FK68
Berwick Pond Rd, Rain. RM13 .90 FL68
Upminster RM14 . . . . . . .90 FM66
Berwick Rd, E16 . . . . .86 EH72
N22 . . . . .45 DP53
Borehamwood WD6 . . . . .26 CM38
Rainham RM13 . . . . .90 FK68
Welling DA16 . . . . .106 EV81
Berwick St, W1 . . . . .195 M9
Berwick Way, Orp. BR6 . . . .146 EU102
Sevenoaks TN14 . . . . . .191 FH121
Berwyn Av, Houns. TW3 . . . .96 CB81
Berwyn Rd, SE24 . . . . .121 DP88
Richmond TW10 . . . . .98 CP84
Beryl Av, E6 . . . . .86 EL71
Beryl Rd, E18 off Spinel Cl . .105 ET78
Beryl Rd, W6 . . . . .99 CX78
Berystede, Kings.T. KT2 . . . .118 CP94
Besant Ct, N1
off Newington Grn Rd 66 DR64
Besant Rd, NW2 . . . . .63 CY63
Besant Wk, N7 off Newington
Barrow Way 65 DM61
Besant Way, NW10 . . . . . . .62 CQ64
Besley St, SW16 . . . . .121 DJ93
Bessant Dr, Rich. TW9 . . . . .98 CP81
Bessborough Pl, SW1 . . . . .199 M10
Bessborough Rd, SW15 . . . .119 CU88
Harrow HA1 . . . . .61 CD60
Bessborough St, SW1 . . . . .199 M10
BESSELS GREEN, Sev. 190 FC124
Bessels Grn Rd, Sev. TN13 . .190 FD123
Bessels Meadow, Sev. TN13 .190 FD124
Bessels Way, Sev. TN13 . . . .190 FC124
Bessemer Rd, SE5 . . . . . . .102 DQ82
Bessie Lansbury Cl, E6 . . . . .87 EN72
Bessingby Rd, Ruis. HA4 . . . .59 BU61
Bessingham Wk, SE4
off Frendsbury Rd 103 DX84
Besson St, SE14 . . . . .102 DW81
Bessy St, E2 off Roman Rd . . .84 DW69
Bestwood St, SE8 . . . . . . .203 J9
Beswick Ms, NW6
off Lymington Rd 82 DB65
Betam Rd, Hayes UB3 . . . . .95 BR75
⇌ Betchworth 182 CR134
Betchworth Cl, Sutt. SM1
off Turnpike La 158 DD106
Betchworth Rd, Ilf. IG3 . . . . .69 ES61
Betchworth Way, Croy.
(New Adgtn.) CR0 . . . . . .161 EC109
Betenson Av, Sev. TN13 . . . .190 FF122
Bethany Waye, Felt. TW14 . . .115 BS87
Bethecar Rd, Har. HA1 . . . . .61 CE57
Bethell Av, E16 . . . . .86 EF70
Ilford IG1 . . . . .69 EN59
Bethel Rd, Sev. TN13 . . . . .191 FJ123
Welling DA16 . . . . .106 EW83
Bethersden Cl, Beck. BR3 . . .123 DZ94
Ⓗ Bethlehem Royal Hosp, Beck.
BR3 . . . . .143 EA101
BETHNAL GREEN, E2 . . . . . .84 DU68
⇌ Bethnal Green 84 DV70
⊖ Bethnal Green, E2 . . . . .84 DW69
Bethnal Grn Est, E2 . . . . . . .84 DW69
★ Bethnal Green Mus of
Childhood, E2 . . . . .84 DV69
Bethnal Grn Rd, E1 . . . . . .197 P4
E2 . . . . .197 P4
Bethune Av, N11 . . . . .44 DF49
Bethune Rd, N16 . . . . .66 DR59
NW10 . . . . .80 CR70
Bethwin Rd, SE5 . . . . .101 DP80
Betjeman Cl, Couls. CR5 . . .175 DM117
Pinner HA5 . . . . .60 CA56
Waltham Cross EN7
off Rosedale Way 14 DU28
Betley Ct, Walt. KT12 . . . . .135 BV104
Betony Cl, Croy. CR0
off Primrose La 143 DX102
Betony Rd, Rom. RM3
off Cloudberry Rd 52 FK51
Betoyne Av, E4 . . . . .48 EE49
BETSHAM, Dart. 130 FY91
BETSHAM, Grav. 130 FY91
Betsham Rd, Erith DA8 . . . .107 FF81
Gravesend (Sthflt.) DA13 . .129 FX92
Swanscombe DA10 . . . . .130 FY87
Betstyle Rd, N11 . . . . .45 DH49
Betterton Dr, Sid. DA14 . . . .126 EY89
Betterton Rd, Rain. RM13 . . .89 FE69
Betterton St, WC2 . . . . . . .195 P9
Bettles Cl, Uxb. UB8
off Wescott Way 76 BJ68
Bettons Pk, E15 . . . . .86 EE67
Bettridge Rd, SW6 . . . . . . .99 CZ82
Betts Cl, Beck. BR3
off Kendall Rd 143 DY96
Betts Ms, E17 off Queen's Rd .67 DZ58
Betts Rd, E16
off Victoria Dock Rd 86 EH73
Betts St, E1 . . . . .202 D1
Betts Way, SE20 . . . . .142 DV95
Surbiton KT6 . . . . .137 CH102
Betula Cl, Ken. CR8 . . . . . .176 DR115
Betula Wk, Rain. RM13 . . . . .90 FK69

Between Sts, Cob. KT11 . . . .153 BU114
Beulah Av, Th.Hth. CR7
off Beulah Rd 141 DM98
Beulah Cl, Edg. HA8 . . . . . .42 CP48
Beulah Cres, Th.Hth. CR7 . . .142 DQ96
Beulah Gro, Croy. CR0 . . . .142 DQ100
Beulah Hill, SE19 . . . . .121 DP93
Beulah Path, E17
off Addison Rd 67 EB57
Beulah Rd, E17 . . . . .67 EB57
SW19 . . . . .119 CZ94
Epping CM16 . . . . .18 EU29
Hornchurch RM12 . . . . . .72 FJ62
Sutton SM1 . . . . .158 DA105
Thornton Heath CR7 . . . .142 DQ97
Beulah Wk, Cat. (Wold.) CR3 .177 DY120
Beult Rd, Dart. DA1 . . . . . .107 FG83
Bevan Av, Bark. IG11 . . . . . .88 EU66
Bevan Ct, Croy. CR0 . . . . . .159 DN106
Bevan Ho, Grays RM16
off Laird Av 110 GD75
Bevan Pl, Swan. BR8 . . . . .147 FF98
Bevan Rd, SE2 . . . . .106 EV78
Barnet EN4 . . . . .28 DF42
Bevans Cl, Green. DA9
off Johnsons Way 129 FW86
Bevan St, N1 . . . . .84 DQ67
Bevan Way, Horn. RM12 . . . .72 FM63
Bev Callender Cl, SW8
off Daley Thompson Way . .101 DH83
Bevenden St, N1 . . . . .197 L2
Bevercote Wk, Belv. DA17
off Osborne Rd 106 EZ79
Beverley Rd, NW10
off Curzon Cres 80 CS66
Beverley Av, SW20 . . . . . . .139 CT95
Hounslow TW4 . . . . .96 BZ84
Sidcup DA15 . . . . .125 ET87
Beverley Cl, N21 . . . . .46 DQ46
SW11 off Maysoule Rd . . .100 DD84
SW13 . . . . .99 CT82
Addlestone KT15 . . . . . .152 BK106
Chessington KT9 . . . . . .155 CJ105
Enfield EN1 . . . . .30 DS42
Epsom KT17 . . . . .157 CW111
Hornchurch RM11 . . . . . .72 FM59
Weybridge KT13 . . . . . .135 BS103
Beverley Cotts, SW15
off Kingston Vale 118 CR91
Beverley Ct, N14 . . . . .45 DJ45
N20 off Farnham Cl 44 DC45
SE4 . . . . .103 DZ83
Slough SL1 off Dolphin Rd . .92 AV75
Beverley Cres, Wdf.Grn. IG8 . .48 EH53
Beverley Dr, Edg. HA8 . . . . .62 CP55
Beverley Gdns, NW11 . . . . .63 CY59
SW13 . . . . .99 CT83
Hornchurch RM11 . . . . . .72 FM59
Stanmore HA7 . . . . .41 CG53
Waltham Cross (Chsht.)
EN7 . . . . .14 DT30
Wembley HA9 . . . . .62 CM60
Worcester Park KT4
off Green La 139 CU102
Beverley Hts, Reig. RH2 . . . .184 DB132
Beverley Ho, NW8 . . . . . . .194 B3
Beverley La, SW15 . . . . . . .119 CT90
Kingston upon Thames
KT2 . . . . .118 CS94
Beverley Ms, E4
off Beverley Rd 47 ED51
Beverley Path, SW13 . . . . . .99 CT82
Beverley Rd, E4 . . . . .47 ED51
E6 . . . . .86 EK69
SE20 off Wadhurst Cl 142 DV96
SW13 . . . . .99 CT83
W4 . . . . .99 CT78
Bexleyheath DA7 . . . . . .107 FC82
Bromley BR2 . . . . .144 EL103
Dagenham RM9 . . . . . . .70 EY63
Kingston upon Thames
KT1 . . . . .137 CJ95
Mitcham CR4 . . . . .141 DK98
New Malden KT3 . . . . . .139 CU98
Ruislip HA4 . . . . .59 BU61
Southall UB2 . . . . .96 BY76
Sunbury-on-Thames
TW16 . . . . .135 BT95
Whyteleafe CR3 . . . . . . .176 DS116
Worcester Park KT4 . . . . .139 CW103
Beverley Trd Est, Mord. SM4
off Garth Rd 139 CX101
Beverley Way, SW20 . . . . . .139 CT95
New Malden KT3 . . . . . .139 CT95
Beversbrook Rd, N19 . . . . . .65 DK62
Beverstone Rd, SW2 . . . . . .121 DM85
Thornton Heath CR7 . . . .141 DN98
Beverston Ms, W1 . . . . . . .194 D7
Bevill Allen Cl, SW17 . . . . . .120 DF92
Bevill Cl, SE25 . . . . .142 DU97
Bevin Cl, SE16 . . . . .203 K2
Bevin Ct, WC1 off Holford St . .83 DN69
Bevington Path, SE1
off Tanner St 102 DT75
Bevington Rd, W10 . . . . . . .81 CY71
Beckenham BR3 . . . . . . .143 EB96
Bevington St, SE16 . . . . . .202 C5
Bevin Rd, Hayes UB4 . . . . . .77 BU69
Bevin Sq, SW17 . . . . .120 DF90
Bevin Way, WC1 . . . . .196 D2
Bevis Cl, Dart. DA2 . . . . . .128 FQ87
Bevis Marks, EC3 . . . . . . .197 N8
Bewcastle Gdns, Enf. EN2 . . .29 DL42
Bewdley St, N1 . . . . .83 DN66
Bewick St, SW8 . . . . .101 DH82
Bewley Cl, Wal.Cr. (Chsht.)
EN8 . . . . .15 DX31
Bewley St, E1 off Dellow St . .84 DV73
Bewley St, SW19 . . . . .120 DC93
off East Rd
Bewlys Rd, SE27 . . . . .121 DP92
Bexhill Cl, Felt. TW13 . . . . .116 BY89
Bexhill Rd, N11 . . . . .45 DK50
SE4 . . . . .123 DZ87

A B C D E F G H I J K L M N O P Q R S T U V W X Y Z

Bex - Bla

Bexhill Rd, SW14 . . . . .98 CQ83
Bexhill Wk, E15 off Mitre Rd . .86 EE68
BEXLEY 126 FA86
⇌ Bexley 126 FA88
Bexley Cl, Dart. DA1 . . . . . . .127 FE85
Bexley Gdns, N9 . . . . .46 DR48
 Romford (Chad.Hth.) RM6 . .70 EV57
BEXLEYHEATH 126 EZ85
⇌ Bexleyheath 106 EY82
Bexley High St, Bex. DA5 . .126 FA87
Bexley La, Dart. DA1 . . . . . . .127 FE85
 Sidcup DA14 . . . . .126 EW90
Bexley Rd, SE9 . . . . .125 EP85
 Erith DA8 . . . . .107 FC80
Beynon Rd, Cars. SM5 . . . . .158 DF106
Bianca Ho, N1 off Crondall St .84 DS42
Bianca Rd, SE15 . . . . .102 DT79
Bibsworth Rd, N3 . . . . .43 CZ54
Bibury Cl, SE15 . . . . .102 DS79
Bicester Rd, Rich. TW9 . . . . . .98 CN83
Bickenhall St, W1 . . . . .194 E6
Bickersteth Rd, SW17 . . . . . .120 DF93
Bickerton Rd, N19 . . . . .65 DJ61
BICKLEY, Brom. 145 EM97
⇌ Bickley 144 EL97
Bickley Cres, Brom. BR1 . . . .144 EL98
Bickley Pk Rd, Brom. BR1 . . .144 EL97
Bickley Rd, E10 . . . . .67 EB59
 Bromley BR1 . . . . .144 EK96
Bickley St, SW17 . . . . .120 DE92
Bicknell Rd, SE5 . . . . .102 DQ83
Bickney Way, Lthd. (Fetch.)
 KT22 . . . . .170 CC122
Bicknoller Cl, Sutt. SM2 . . . .158 DB110
Bicknoller Rd, Enf. EN1 . . . . .30 DT39
Bicknor Rd, Orp. BR6 . . . . . .145 ES101
Bidborough Cl, Brom. BR2 . .144 EF99
Bidborough St, WC1 . . . . . . .195 P3
Biddenden Way, SE9 . . . . . . .125 EN91
 Gravesend (Istead Rise)
 DA13 . . . . .130 GE94
Biddenham Turn, Wat. WD25 . .24 BW35
Bidder St, E16 . . . . .86 EE71
Biddestone Rd, N7 . . . . .65 DM63
Biddulph Rd, W9 . . . . .82 DB69
 South Croydon CR2 . . . . . .160 DQ109
Bideford Av, Grnf. UB6 . . . . . .79 CH68
Bideford Cl, Edg. HA8 . . . . . . .42 CN53
 Feltham TW13 . . . . .116 BZ90
 Romford RM3 . . . . .52 FJ53
Bideford Gdns, Enf. EN1 . . . . .46 DS45
Bideford Rd, Brom. BR1 . . . .124 EF90
 Enfield EN3 . . . . .31 DZ38
 Ruislip HA4 . . . . .59 BV62
 Welling DA16 . . . . .106 EV80
Bidhams Cres, Tad. KT20 . . .173 CW121
Bidwell Gdns, N11 . . . . .45 DJ52
Bidwell St, SE15 . . . . .102 DV81
★ Big Ben (St. Stephens Twr),
 SW1 . . . . .200 A5
Bigbury Cl, N17
 off Weir Hall Rd 46 DR52
Bigbury Rd, N17
 off Barkham Rd 46 DS52
Big Common La, Red. (Bletch.)
 RH1 . . . . .185 DP133
Biggerstaff Rd, E15 . . . . .85 EC67
Biggerstaff St, N4 . . . . .65 DN61
Biggin Av, Mitch. CR4 . . . . . .140 DF95
BIGGIN HILL, West. 178 EH116
Biggin Hill, SE19 . . . . .121 DP94
Biggin Hill Business Pk, West.
 TN16 . . . . .178 EK115
Biggin Hill Cl, Kings.T. KT2 . .117 CJ92
Biggin La, Grays RM16 . . . . .111 GH79
Biggin Way, SE19 . . . . .121 DP94
Bigginwood Rd, SW16 . . . . . .121 DP94
Biggs Gro Rd, Wal.Cr. (Chsht.)
 EN7 . . . . .14 DR27
Biggs Row, SW15
 off Felsham Rd 99 CX83
Big Hill, E5 . . . . .66 DV60
Bigland St, E1 . . . . .84 DV72
Bignell Rd, SE18 . . . . .105 EP78
Bignold Rd, E7 . . . . .68 EG63
Bigwood Rd, NW11 . . . . .64 DB57
Biko Cl, Uxb. UB8
 off Sefton Way 76 BJ72
Billet Cl, Rom. RM6 . . . . .70 EX55
Billet La, Horn. RM11 . . . . . . .72 FK60
 Iver SL0 . . . . .75 BB69
 Slough SL3 . . . . .75 BB73
Billet Rd, E17 . . . . .47 DX54
 Romford RM6 . . . . .70 EV55
 Staines TW18
 off Farnell Rd 114 BG90
Billets Hart Cl, W7 . . . . .97 CE75
Billet Wks, E17 . . . . .47 DZ53
Bill Hamling Cl, SE9 . . . . . . .125 EM89
Billingford Cl, SE4 . . . . .103 DX84
Billing Pl, SW10 . . . . .100 DB80
Billing Rd, SW10 . . . . .100 DB80
Billings Cl, Dag. RM9
 off Ellerton Rd 88 EW66
★ Billingsgate Fish Mkt,
 E14 . . . . .204 C2
Billing St, SW10 . . . . .100 DB80
Billington Rd, SE14 . . . . .103 DX80
Billiter Sq, EC3 . . . . .197 N10
Billiter St, EC3 . . . . .197 N9
Bill Nicholson Way, N17
 off High Rd 46 DT52
Billockby Cl, Chess. KT9 . . . .156 CM107
Billson St, E14 . . . . .204 E9
Billy Lows La, Pot.B. EN6 . . . .12 DA31
Bilsby Gro, SE9 . . . . .124 EK91
Bilton Cl, Slou. (Poyle) SL3 . . .93 BE82
Bilton Rd, Erith DA8 . . . . . . .107 FG80
 Greenford UB6 . . . . .79 CH67
Bilton Way, Enf. EN3 . . . . .31 DY39
 Hayes UB3 . . . . .95 BV75
Bina Gdns, SW5 . . . . .100 DC77
Bincote Rd, Enf. EN2 . . . . .29 DM41
Binden Rd, W12 . . . . .99 CT76

Bindon Grn, Mord. SM4 . . . .140 DB98
Binfield Rd, SW4 . . . . .101 DL81
 South Croydon CR2 . . . . . .160 DT106
 West Byfleet (Byfleet)
 KT14 . . . . .152 BL112
Bingfield St, N1 . . . . .83 DL67
Bingham Cl, S.Ock. RM15 . . . .91 FV72
Bingham Ct, N1
 off Halton Rd 83 DP66
Bingham Dr, Stai. TW18 . . . .114 BK94
 Woking GU21 . . . . .166 AT118
Bingham Pl, W1 . . . . .194 F6
Bingham Rd, Cars. SM5
 off Whitworth Pl 105 EP77
 Croydon CR0 . . . . .142 DU102
Bingham St, N1 . . . . .84 DR65
Bingley Rd, E16 . . . . .86 EJ72
 Greenford UB6 . . . . .78 CC71
 Sunbury-on-Thames TW16 .115 BU94
Binley Ho, SW15
 off Highcliffe Dr 119 CU86
Binney St, W1 . . . . .194 G10
Binns Rd, W4 . . . . .98 CS78
Binns Ter, W4 off Binns Rd . . .98 CS78
Binsey Wk, SE2 . . . . .88 EW74
Binyon Cres, Stan. HA7 . . . . .41 CF50
Birbetts Rd, SE9 . . . . .125 EM89
Bircham Path, SE4
 off St. Norbert Rd 103 DX84
Birchanger Rd, SE25 . . . . . . .142 DU99
Birch Av, N13 . . . . .46 DQ48
 Caterham CR3 . . . . .176 DR124
 Leatherhead KT22 . . . . . . .171 CF120
 West Drayton UB7 . . . . .76 BM72
Birch Cl, E16 . . . . .86 EE71
 N19 off Hargrave Rd 65 DJ61
 SE15 off Bournemouth Rd . .102 DU82
 Addlestone (New Haw)
 KT15 . . . . .152 BK109
 Amersham HP6 . . . . .20 AS37
 Brentford TW8 . . . . .97 CH80
 Buckhurst Hill IG9 . . . . .48 EK48
 Dartford (Eyns.) DA4 . . . . .148 FK104
 Hounslow TW3 . . . . .97 CD83
 Iver SL0 . . . . .75 BD68
 Romford RM7 . . . . .71 FB55
 Sevenoaks TN13 . . . . .191 FH123
 South Ockendon RM15 . . . . .91 FX69
 Teddington TW11 . . . . .117 CG92
 Woking GU21 . . . . .166 AW119
Birch Copse, St.Alb. (Brick.Wd.)
 AL2 .8 BY30
Birch Ct, Nthwd. HA6
 off Rickmansworth Rd 39 BQ51
Birch Cres, Horn. RM11 . . . . .72 FL56
 South Ockendon RM15 . . . . .91 FX69
 Uxbridge UB10 . . . . .76 BM67
Birchcroft Cl, Cat. CR3 . . . . .186 DQ125
Birchdale, Ger.Cr. SL9 . . . . . .56 AX60
Birchdale Cl, W.Byf. KT14 . . .152 BJ111
Birchdale Gdns, Rom. RM6 . . .70 EX59
Birchdale Rd, E7 . . . . .68 EJ64
Birchdene Dr, SE28 . . . . .106 EU75
Birchen Cl, NW9 . . . . .62 CR61
Birchend Cl, S.Croy. CR2 . . .160 DR107
Birchen Gro, NW9 . . . . .62 CR61
Birches, The, N21 . . . . .29 DM44
 SE7 . . . . .104 EH79
 Brentwood CM13 . . . . .54 FY48
 Bushey WD23 . . . . .24 CC43
 Epping (N.Wld.Bas.) CM16 . .19 FB26
 Orpington BR6 . . . . .163 EN105
 Swanley BR8 . . . . .147 FE96
 Woking GU22
 off Heathside Rd 167 AZ118
Birches Cl, Epsom KT18 . . . .172 CS115
 Mitcham CR4 . . . . .140 DF97
 Pinner HA5 . . . . .60 BY57
Birches, The, Wal.Abb. EN9
 off Honey La 16 EF34
Birchfield Cl, Add. KT15 . . . .152 BH105
 Coulsdon CR5 . . . . .175 DM116
Birchfield Gro, Epsom KT17 .157 CW110
Birchfield Rd, Wal.Cr. (Chsht.)
 EN8 . . . . .14 DV29
Birchfield St, E14 . . . . .85 EA73
Birch Gdns, Amer. HP7 . . . . . .20 AS39
 Dagenham RM10 . . . . .71 FC62
Birchgate Ms, Tad. KT20
 off Bidhams Cres 173 CW121
Birch Grn, NW9
 off Clayton Fld 42 CS52
 Staines TW18 . . . . .114 BG91
Birch Gro, E11 . . . . .68 EE62
 SE12 . . . . .124 EF87
 W3 .80 CN74
 Cobham KT11 . . . . .154 BW114
 Potters Bar EN6 . . . . .12 DA32
 Shepperton TW17 . . . . .135 BS96
 Tadworth KT20 . . . . .173 CY124
 Welling DA16 . . . . .106 EU88
 Woking GU22 . . . . .167 BD115
★ Birch Hall, Epp. (They.B.)
 CM16 . . . . .33 EQ36
Birch Hill, Croy. CR0 . . . . . . .161 DX106
Birchington Cl, Bexh. DA7 . . .107 FB81
 Orpington BR5
 off Hart Dyke Rd 146 EW102
Birchington Rd, N8 . . . . .65 DK58
 NW6 . . . . .82 DA67
 Surbiton KT5 . . . . .138 CM101
Birchin La, EC3 . . . . .197 L9
Birchlands Av, SW12 . . . . . . .120 DF87
Birch La, Hem.H. (Flaun.) HP3 . .5 BB33
 Purley CR8 . . . . .159 DL111
Birch Mead, Orp. BR6 . . . . . .145 EN103
Birchmead, Wat. WD17 . . . . . .23 BT38
Birchmead Av, Pnr. HA5 . . . . .60 BW56
Birchmere Row, SE3 . . . . . . .104 EF82
Birchmore Wk, N5 . . . . .66 DQ62
Birch Pk, Har. HA3 . . . . .40 CC52
Birch Pl, Green. DA9 . . . . . . .129 FS86
Birch Rd, Felt. TW13 . . . . . . .116 BX92
 Romford RM7 . . . . .71 FB55
Birch Row, Brom. BR2 . . . . . .145 EN101
Birch Tree Av, W.Wick. BR4 . .162 EF106

Birch Tree Gro, Chesh. (Ley Hill)
 HP5 .4 AV30
Birch Tree Wk, Wat. WD17 . . .23 BT37
Birch Tree Way, Croy. CR0 . .142 DV103
Birch Vale, Cob. KT11 . . . . . .154 CA112
Birch Vw, Epp. CM16 . . . . . . .18 EV29
Birchville Ct, Bushey (Bushey Hth.)
 WD23 off Heathbourne Rd .41 CE46
Birch Wk, Borwd. WD6 . . . . . .26 CN39
 Erith DA8 . . . . .107 FC79
 Mitcham CR4 . . . . .141 DH95
 West Byfleet KT14 . . . . . . .152 BG112
Birchway, Hayes UB3 . . . . . . .77 BU74
Birch Way, St.Alb. (Lon.Col.)
 AL2 .8 CK27
 Warlingham CR6 . . . . .177 DY118
Birch Wd, Rad. (Shenley) WD7 .10 CN34
Birchwood, Wal.Abb. EN9
 off Roundhills 16 EE34
Birchwood Av, N10 . . . . .64 DG55
 Beckenham BR3 . . . . .143 DZ98
 Sidcup DA14 . . . . .126 EV89
 Wallington SM6 . . . . .140 DG104
Birchwood Cl, Brwd. CM13
 off Canterbury Way 53 FW51
 Morden SM4 . . . . .140 DB98
Birchwood Ct, N13 . . . . .45 DP50
 Edgware HA8 . . . . .42 CQ54
Birchwood Dr, NW3 . . . . .64 DB62
 Dartford DA2 . . . . .127 FE91
 West Byfleet KT14 . . . . . . .152 BG112
Birchwood Gro, Hmptn.
 TW12 . . . . .116 CA93
Birchwood Rd, Cat. CR3 . . . .185 DP125
 Esher KT10 . . . . .155 CD110
 Leatherhead KT22 . . . . . . .155 CD110
 Sevenoaks (Knock.) TN14 . .222 EZ115
Birchwood Pk Av, Swan.
 BR8 . . . . .147 FE97
Birchwood Rd, SW17 . . . . . . .121 DH92
 Dartford DA2 . . . . .127 FE92
 Orpington BR5 . . . . .145 ER98
 Swanley BR8 . . . . .147 FC95
 West Byfleet KT14 . . . . . . .152 BG112
Birchwood Ter, Swan. BR8
 off Birchwood Rd 147 FC95
Birchwood Way, St.Alb. (Park St.)
 AL2 .8 CB28
Birdbrook Cl, Brwd. CM13 . . . .55 GB44
 Dagenham RM10 . . . . .89 FC66
Birdbrook Rd, SE3 . . . . .104 EJ83
Birdcage Wk, SW1 . . . . .199 L5
Birdham Cl, Brom. BR1 . . . . .144 EL99
Birdhouse La, Orp. BR6 . . . . .179 EN115
Birdhurst Av, S.Croy. CR2 . . .160 DR105
Birdhurst Gdns, S.Croy. CR2 .160 DR105
Birdhurst Ri, S.Croy. CR2 . . .160 DS106
Birdhurst Rd, SW18 . . . . .100 DC84
 SW19 . . . . .120 DE93
 South Croydon CR2 . . . . . .160 DS106
Bird in Bush Rd, SE15 . . . . . .102 DU80
Bird-in-Hand La, Brom. BR1 .144 EK96
Bird-in-Hand Pas, SE23
 off Dartmouth Rd 122 DW89
Bird La, Brwd. CM13 . . . . .73 FX55
 Upminster RM14 . . . . .73 FR57
 Uxbridge (Hare.) UB9 . . . . . .38 BJ54
Birds Fm Av, Rom. RM5 . . . . .51 FB53
Birdsfield La, E3 . . . . .85 DZ67
Birds Hill Dr, Lthd. (Oxshott)
 KT22 . . . . .155 CD113
Birds Hill Ri, Lthd. (Oxshott)
 KT22 . . . . .155 CD113
Birds Hill Rd, Lthd. (Oxshott)
 KT22 . . . . .155 CD112
Bird St, W1 . . . . .194 G9
Birdswood Dr, Wok. GU21 . . .166 AS119
Bird Wk, Twick. TW2 . . . . . . .116 BZ88
Birdwood Cl, S.Croy. CR2 . . .161 DX111
 Teddington TW11 . . . . .117 CE91
⇌ Birkbeck 142 DW97
⇌ Birkbeck 142 DW97
Birkbeck Av, W3 . . . . .80 CQ73
 Greenford UB6 . . . . .78 CC67
Birkbeck Gdns, Wdf.Grn. IG8 .48 EF47
Birkbeck Gro, W3 . . . . .98 CR75
Birkbeck Hill, SE21 . . . . .121 DP89
Birkbeck Ms, E8
 off Sandringham Rd 66 DT64
Birkbeck Pl, SE21 . . . . .122 DQ88
Birkbeck Rd, E8 . . . . .66 DT64
 N8 .65 DL56
 N12 .44 DC50
 N17 .46 DT53
 NW7 . . . . .43 CT50
 SW19 . . . . .120 DB92
 W3 .80 CR74
 W5 .97 CJ77
 Beckenham BR3 . . . . .142 DW96
 Brentwood CM13 . . . . .55 GD44
 Enfield EN2 . . . . .30 DR39
 Ilford IG2 . . . . .69 ER57
 Romford RM7 . . . . .71 FD60
 Sidcup DA14 . . . . .126 EU90
Birkbeck St, E2 . . . . .84 DV69
Birkbeck Way, Grnf. UB6 . . . . .78 CC67
Birkdale Av, Pnr. HA5 . . . . . . .60 CA55
 Romford RM3 . . . . .52 FM52
Birkdale Cl, SE16
 off Masters Dr 102 DV78
 Orpington BR6 . . . . .145 ER101
Birkdale Gdns, Croy. CR0 . . .161 DX105
 Watford WD19 . . . . .40 BX48
Birkdale Rd, SE2 . . . . .106 EU77
 W5 .80 CL70
Birkenhead Av, Kings.T. KT2 .138 CM96
Birkenhead St, WC1 . . . . . . .196 A2
Birken Ms, Nthwd. HA6 . . . . . .39 BP50
Birkett Way, Ch.St.G. HP8 . . .20 AX41
Birkhall Rd, SE6 . . . . .123 ED88
Birkheads Rd, Reig. RH2 . . . .184 DA133
Birklands La, St.Alb. AL1 . . . . .9 CH25
Birkwood Cl, SW12 . . . . .121 DK87
Birley Rd, N20 . . . . .44 DC47
Birley St, SW11 . . . . .100 DG82
Birling Rd, Erith DA8 . . . . . . .107 FD80
Birnam Rd, N4 . . . . .65 DM61

Birnham Cl, Wok. (Send M.)
 GU23 . . . . .168 BG123
Birrell Ho, SW9
 off Stockwell Rd 101 DM82
Birse Cres, NW10 . . . . .62 CS63
Birstall Grn, Wat. WD19 . . . . .40 BX49
Birstall Rd, N15 . . . . .66 DS57
Birtley Path, Borwd. WD6 . . . .26 CL39
Biscay Rd, W6 . . . . .99 CX78
Biscoe Cl, Houns. TW5 . . . . . .96 CA79
Biscoe Way, SE13 . . . . .103 ED83
Bisenden Rd, Croy. CR0 . . . .142 DS103
Bisham Cl, Cars. SM5 . . . . . .140 DF102
Bisham Gdns, N6 . . . . .64 DG60
Bishop Butt Cl, Orp. BR6
 off Stapleton Rd 145 ET104
Bishop Cl, W4 . . . . .98 CQ78
Bishop Duppa's Pk, Shep.
 TW17 . . . . .135 BR101
Bishop Fox Way, W.Mol. KT8 .136 BZ98
Bishop Ken Rd, Har. HA3 . . . . .41 CF54
Bishop Kings Rd, W14 . . . . . .99 CY77
Bishop Rd, N14 . . . . .45 DH45
Bishop's Av, E13 . . . . .86 EH67
 SW6 . . . . .99 CX82
Bishops Av, Borwd. (Elstree)
 WD6 . . . . .26 CM43
 Bromley BR1 . . . . .144 EJ96
 Northwood HA6 . . . . .39 BS49
 Romford RM6 . . . . .70 EW58
Bishops Av, The, N2 . . . . .64 DD59
Bishops Br, W2 . . . . .82 DC71
Bishops Br Rd, W2 . . . . .82 DC72
Bishops Cl, E17 . . . . .67 EB56
 N19 off Wyndham Cres 65 DJ62
 SE9 . . . . .125 EQ89
 Barnet EN5 . . . . .27 CX44
Bishop's Cl, Couls. CR5 . . . . .175 DN118
Bishops Cl, Enf. EN1
 off Central Av 30 DV40
 Richmond TW10 . . . . .117 CK90
Bishops Cl, Sutt. SM1 . . . . . .140 DA104
 Swanley BR8 . . . . .147 FC95
 Uxbridge UB10 . . . . .76 BN68
Bishop's Cl, EC4 . . . . .196 F8
 WC2 . . . . .196 D8
Bishops Ct, Green. DA9 . . . . .129 FS85
 Waltham Cross EN8
 off Churchgate 14 DV30
Bishops Dr, Felt. TW14 . . . . .115 BR86
 Northolt UB5 . . . . .78 BY67
Bishopsford Rd, Mord. SM4 .140 DC101
Bishopsgate, EC2 . . . . .197 M9
Bishopsgate Arc, EC2 . . . . . .197 N7
Bishopsgate Chyd, EC2 . . . . .197 M8
Bishopsgate Rd, Egh. (Eng.Grn.)
 TW20 . . . . .112 AT90
Bishops Gro, N2 . . . . .64 DD58
 Hampton TW12 . . . . .116 BZ91
Bishop's Hall, Kings.T. KT1 . .137 CK96
Bishops Hall Rd, Brwd. CM15 .54 FV44
Bishops Hill, Walt. KT12 . . . .135 BU101
Bishop's Pk, SW6 . . . . .99 CX82
Bishop's Pk Rd, SW6 . . . . . . .99 CX82
Bishops Pk Rd, SW16 . . . . . .141 DL95
Bishops Pl, Sutt. SM1
 off Lind Rd 158 DC106
Bishops Rd, N6 . . . . .64 DG59
 SW6 . . . . .99 CZ81
 W7 .97 CE75
 Croydon CR0 . . . . .141 DP101
 Hayes UB3 . . . . .77 BQ71
 Slough SL1 . . . . .92 AU75
Bishops Ter, SE11 . . . . .200 E8
Bishopsthorpe Rd, SE26 . . . .123 DX91
Bishop St, N1 . . . . .84 DQ67
Bishops Wk, Chis. BR7 . . . . .145 EQ95
 Croydon CR0 . . . . .161 DX106
Bishop's Wk, Pnr. HA5
 off High St 60 BY55
Bishops Way, E2 . . . . .84 DV68
 Egham TW20 . . . . .113 BD93
Bishops Wd, Wok. GU21 . . . .166 AS122
ℍ Bishopswood Private Hosp,
 Nthwd. HA6 . . . . .39 BP51
Bishopswood Rd, N6 . . . . .64 DF59
Bishop Way, NW10 . . . . .80 CS66
Bishop Wilfred Wd Cl, SE15
 off Moncrieff St 102 DU82
Biskra, Wat. WD17 . . . . .23 BU39
Bisley Cl, Wal.Cr. EN8 . . . . . . .15 DX33
 Worcester Park KT4 . . . . . .139 CW102
Bisley Ho, SW19 . . . . .119 CX89
Bispham Rd, NW10 . . . . .80 CM69
Bisson Rd, E15 . . . . .85 EC68
Bisterne Av, E17 . . . . .67 ED55
Bittacy Cl, NW7 . . . . .43 CX51
Bittacy Hill, NW7 . . . . .43 CX51
Bittacy Pk Av, NW7 . . . . .43 CX51
Bittacy Ri, NW7 . . . . .43 CW51
Bittacy Rd, NW7 . . . . .43 CX51
Bittams La, Cher. KT16 . . . . .151 BE105
Bittern Cl, Hayes UB4 . . . . . . .78 BX71
 Hemel Hempstead HP3
 off Belswains La 6 BM25
 Waltham Cross (Chsht.)
 EN7 . . . . .14 DQ25
Bitterne Dr, Wok. GU21 . . . . .166 AT117
Bittern St, SE1 . . . . .201 H5
Bittoms, The, Kings.T. KT1 . .137 CK97
Bixley Cl, Sthl. UB2 . . . . .96 BZ77
Black Acre Cl, Amer. HP7 . . . .20 AS39
Blackacre Rd, Epp. (They.B.)
 CM16 . . . . .33 ES37
Blackall St, EC2 . . . . .197 M4
Blackberry Cl, Shep. TW17
 off Cherry Way 135 BS98
Blackberry Fld, Orp. BR5 . . . .146 EU95
Blackbird Hill, NW9 . . . . .62 CQ61
Blackbirds La, Wat. (Ald.)
 WD25 . . . . .25 CD35
Blackbird Yd, E2
 off Ravenscroft St 84 DT69
Blackborne Rd, Dag. RM10 . . .88 FA65

Blackborough Cl, Reig. RH2 .184 DC134
Black Boy La, N15 . . . . .66 DQ57
Black Boy Wd, St.Alb. (Brick.Wd.)
 AL2 .8 CA30
Blackbridge Rd, Wok. GU22 .166 AX119
Blackbrook La, Brom. BR1,
 BR2 . . . . .145 EN97
Blackburn, The, Lthd. (Bkhm.) KT23
 off Little Bookham St 170 BZ124
Blackburne's Ms, W1 . . . . . . .194 F10
Blackburn Rd, NW6 . . . . .82 DB65
Blackburn Trd Est, Stai. (Stanw.)
 TW19 . . . . .114 BM86
Blackbury Cl, Pot.B. EN6 . . . . .12 DC31
Blackbush Av, Rom. RM6 . . . .70 EX57
Blackbush Cl, Sutt. SM2 . . . .158 DB108
Blackdale, Wal.Cr. (Chsht.)
 EN7 . . . . .14 DU27
Blackdown Av, Wok. GU22 . . .167 BE115
Blackdown Cl, N2 . . . . .44 DC54
 Woking GU22 . . . . .167 BC116
Blackdown Ter, SE18 . . . . . . .105 EN80
Black Eagle Cl, West. TN16 . .189 EQ127
Blackett Cl, Stai. TW18 . . . . .133 BE96
Blackett St, SW15 . . . . .99 CX83
Blacketts Wd Dr, Rick. (Chorl.)
 WD3 . . . . .21 BB43
Black Fan Cl, Enf. EN2 . . . . . .30 DQ39
BLACKFEN, Sid. 125 ET87
Blackfen Rd, Sid. DA15 . . . . .125 ES85
Blackford Cl, S.Croy. CR2 . . .159 DP109
Blackford Rd, Wat. WD19 . . . .40 BX50
Blackford's Path, SW15
 off Roehampton High St . . .119 CU87
⇌ Blackfriars 196 G10
⇌ Blackfriars 196 G10
Blackfriars Br, EC4 . . . . .196 F10
 SE1 . . . . .196 F10
Black Friars Ct, EC4 . . . . . . .196 F10
Blackfriars Pas, EC4 . . . . . . .196 F10
Blackfriars Rd, SE1 . . . . .200 F5
Black Gates, Pnr. HA5
 off Church La 60 BZ55
Blackhall La, Sev. TN15 . . . . .191 FK123
Blackhall Pl, Sev. TN15
 off Blackhall La 191 FL124
BLACKHEATH, SE3 . . . . .104 EE81
★ Blackheath, SE3 . . . . .103 ED81
⇌ Blackheath 104 EE83
Blackheath Av, SE10 . . . . . . .104 ED80
Blackheath Gro, SE3 . . . . . . .104 EF82
Blackheath Hill, SE10 . . . . . .103 EC81
ℍ Blackheath Hosp, The,
 SE3 . . . . .104 EF83
BLACKHEATH PARK, SE3 . . .104 EF84
Blackheath Pk, SE3 . . . . .104 EF83
Blackheath Ri, SE13 . . . . . . .103 EC82
Blackheath Rd, SE10 . . . . . . .103 EB81
Blackheath Vale, SE3 . . . . . .104 EE82
Blackheath Village, SE3 . . . .104 EF82
Blackhills, Esher KT10 . . . . . .154 CA109
Blackhorse Cl, Amer. HP6 . . . .20 AS38
Black Horse Cl, SE1 . . . . .201 L6
Blackhorse Cres, Amer. HP6 . .20 AS38
⇌ Blackhorse Lane 142 DU101
Blackhorse La, E17 . . . . .67 DX56
 Croydon CR0 . . . . .142 DU101
 Epping (N.Wld.Bas.) CM16 . .19 FD25
 Potters Bar EN6 . . . . .10 CS30
 Reigate RH2 . . . . .184 DB129
Blackhorse Ms, E17
 off Blackhorse La 67 DX55
Black Horse Pl, Uxb. UB8
 off Waterloo Rd 76 BJ67
⇌ Blackhorse Road 67 DX56
⇌ Blackhorse Road 67 DX56
Blackhorse Rd, E17 . . . . .67 DX56
 SE8 . . . . .103 DY78
 Sidcup DA14 . . . . .126 EU91
 Woking GU22 . . . . .166 AS122
Black Lake Cl, Egh. TW20 . . .133 BA95
Blacklands Dr, Hayes UB4 . . . .77 BQ70
Blacklands Meadow, Red.
 (Nutfld.) RH1 . . . . .185 DL133
Blacklands Rd, SE6 . . . . .123 EC91
Blacklands Ter, SW3 . . . . . . .198 D9
Blackley Cl, Wat. WD17 . . . . . .23 BT37
Black Lion Hill, Rad. (Shenley)
 WD7 . . . . .10 CL32
Black Lion La, W6 . . . . .99 CU77
Black Lion Ms, W6
 off Black Lion La 99 CU77
Blackmans Cl, Dart. DA1 . . . .128 FJ88
Blackmans La, Warl. CR6 . . . .162 EE114
Blackmans Yd, E2
 off Cheshire St 84 DU70
Blackmead, Sev. (Rvrhd.)
 TN13 . . . . .190 FE121
Blackmoor La, Wat. WD18 . . . .23 BR43
Blackmore Av, Sthl. UB1 . . . . .79 CD74
Blackmore Cl, Grays RM17 . .110 GC78
Blackmore Ct, Wal.Abb. EN9 . .16 EG33
Blackmore Cres, Wok. GU21 .167 BB115
Blackmore Rd, Buck.H. IG9 . . .48 EL45
Blackmores Gro, Tedd. TW11 .117 CG93
Blackness La, Kes. BR2 . . . . .162 EK109
 Woking GU22 . . . . .166 AY119
★ Black Park Country Pk, Slou.
 SL3 . . . . .75 AZ67
Black Pk Rd, Slou. SL3 . . . . . .75 AZ68
Black Path, E10 . . . . .67 DX59
Blackpool Gdns, Hayes UB4 . .77 BS70
Blackpool Rd, SE15 . . . . .102 DV82
Black Prince Cl, W.Byf. (Byfleet)
 KT14 . . . . .152 BM114
Black Prince Rd, SE1 . . . . . . .200 B9
 SE11 . . . . .200 C9
Black Rod Cl, Hayes UB3 . . . . .95 BT76
Blackshaw Pl, N1
 off Hertford Rd 84 DS66
Blackshaw Rd, SW17 . . . . . . .120 DC91
Blackshots La, Grays RM16 . .110 GD75
Blacksmith Cl, Ashtd. KT21
 off Rectory La 172 CM119

Blacksmith Row, Slou. SL3 . . .93 BA77
Blacksmiths Cl, Rom. RM6 . . . .70 EW58
Blacksmiths Hill, S.Croy.
CR2 . . . . .160 DU113
Blacksmiths La, Cher. KT16 . .134 BG101
Orpington BR5 . . . . .146 EW99
Rainham RM13 . . . . .89 FF67
Staines TW18 . . . . .134 BH97
Uxbridge (Denh.) UB9 . . .57 BC61
Blacks Rd, W6
off Queen Caroline St 99 CW77
Blackstock Ms, N4
off Blackstock Rd 65 DP61
Blackstock Rd, N4 . . . . .65 DP61
N5 .65 DP61
Blackstone Est, E8 . . . . .84 DV66
Blackstone Hill, Red. RH1 . .184 DE134
Blackstone Rd, NW2 . . . . . . .63 CW64
Black Swan Yd, SE1 . . . . . . .201 N4
Black's Yd, Sev. TN13
off Bank St 191 FJ125
Blackthorn Av, West Dr. UB7 .94 BN77
Blackthorn Cl, Wat. WD25 . . .7 BV32
Blackthorn Ct, Houns. TW5 . .96 BY80
Blackthorn Dell, Slou. SL3 . . .92 AW76
Blackthorne Av, Croy. CR0 . .142 DW101
Blackthorne Cres, Slou. (Colnbr.)
SL3 . . . . .93 BE83
Blackthorne Dr, E4 . . . . .47 ED49
Blackthorne Rd, Slou. (Colnbr.)
SL3 . . . . .93 BE83
Westerham (Bigg.H.) TN16 .178 EK116
Blackthorn Gro, Bexh. DA7 . .106 EX83
Blackthorn St, E3 . . . . .85 EA70
Blackthorn Way, Brwd. CM14 .54 FX50
Blacktree Ms, SW9 . . . . .101 DN83
[DLR] Blackwall 204 E1
Blackwall La, SE10 . . . . .205 J10
Blackwall Pier, E14 . . . . .205 H1
Blackwall Trd Est, E14 . . . . . .85 ED71
Blackwall Tunnel, E14 . . . . . .204 F1
Blackwall Tunnel App, SE10 .205 H5
Blackwall Tunnel Northern App,
E3 .85 EA68
E14 . . . . .85 EA68
Blackwall Way, E14 . . . . .204 E1
Blackwater Cl, E7 . . . . .68 EF63
Rainham RM13 . . . . .89 FE71
Blackwater Rd, Sutt. SM1
off High St 158 DB105
Blackwater St, SE22 . . . . . . .122 DT85
Blackwell Cl, E5 . . . . .67 DX63
Harrow HA3 . . . . .41 CD52
Blackwell Dr, Wat. WD19 . . . .84 BW44
Blackwell Gdns, Edg. HA8 . . .42 CN48
Blackwell Hall La, Chesh. HP5 . .4 AW33
Blackwell Rd, Kings L. WD4 . . .6 BN29
Blackwood Cl, W.Byf. KT14 . .152 BJ112
Blackwood Ct, Brox. EN10
off Groom Rd 15 DZ26
Blackwood St, SE17 . . . . . . .201 K10
Blade Ms, SW15
off Deodar Rd 99 CZ84
Bladen Cl, Wey. KT13 . . . . . .153 BR107
Blades Cl, Lthd. KT22 . . . . . .171 CK120
Blades Ct, SW15
off Deodar Rd 99 CZ84
Bladindon Dr, Bex. DA5 . . . .126 EW87
Bladon Gdns, Har. HA2 . . . . .60 CB58
Blagdens Cl, N14 . . . . .45 DJ47
Blagdens La, N14 . . . . .45 DK47
Blagdon Rd, SE13 . . . . .123 EB86
New Malden KT3 . . . . . . .139 CT98
Blagdon Wk, Tedd. TW11 . . .117 CJ93
Blagrove Rd, W10 . . . . .81 CY71
Blair Av, NW9 . . . . .62 CS59
Esher KT10 . . . . .136 CC103
Blair Cl, N1 . . . . .84 DQ65
Hayes UB3 . . . . .95 BU77
Sidcup DA15 . . . . .125 ES85
Blairderry Rd, SW2 . . . . .121 DL89
Blair Dr, Sev. TN13 . . . . .191 FH123
Blairhead Dr, Wat. WD19 . . . .39 BV48
Blair Rd, Slou. SL1 . . . . .74 AS74
Blair St, E14 . . . . .85 EC72
Blake Av, Bark. IG11 . . . . . . .87 ES67
Blakeborough Dr, Rom.
(Harold Wd.) RM3 . . . . . .52 FL54
Blake Cl, W10 . . . . .81 CW71
Carshalton SM5 . . . . .140 DE101
Rainham RM13 . . . . .89 FF67
Welling DA16 . . . . .105 ES81
Blakeden Dr, Esher (Clay.)
KT10 . . . . .155 CF107
Blake Gdns, SW6 . . . . .100 DB81
Dartford DA1 . . . . .108 FM84
Blake Hall Cres, E11 . . . . . . .68 EG60
Blake Hall Rd, E11 . . . . .68 EG59
Blake Ho, Beck. BR3 . . . . . . .123 EA93
Blakehall Rd, Cars. SM5 . . . .158 DF107
Blake Ho, Ong. CM5 . . . . . . .19 FG25
Blake St, SE8 . . . . .123 DZ78
Blakeley Cotts, SE10
off Tunnel Av 103 ED75
Blakemore Rd, SW16 . . . . . . .121 DL90
Thornton Heath CR7 . . . .141 DM99
Blakemore Way, Belv. DA17 . .106 EY76
Blakeney Av, Beck. BR3 . . . .143 DZ95
Blakeney Cl, E8
off Ferncliff Rd 84 DU64
N20 . . . . .44 DC46
NW1
off Rossendale Way 83 DK66
Epsom KT19 . . . . .156 CR111
Blakeney Rd, Beck. BR3 . . . .123 DZ94
Blakenham Rd, SW17 . . . . . .120 DF91
Blaker Ct, SE7 off Fairlawn . . .104 EJ80
Blake Rd, E16 . . . . .86 EF70
N11 . . . . .45 DJ52
Croydon CR0 . . . . .142 DS103
Mitcham CR4 . . . . .140 DE97
Blaker Rd, E15 . . . . .85 EC67
Blakes Av, N.Mal. KT3 . . . . .139 CT99
Blake's Grn, W.Wick. BR4 . . .143 EC102
Blakes La, N.Mal. KT3 . . . . .139 CT99
Blakesley Av, W5 . . . . .79 CJ72
Blakesley Wk, SW20
off Kingston Rd 139 CZ96

Blakes Rd, SE15 . . . . .102 DS80
Blakes Ter, N.Mal. KT3 . . . . .139 CU99
Blake St, SE8
off Watergate St 103 EA79
Blakesware Gdns, N9 . . . . . . .46 DR45
Blakes Way, Til. RM18
off Coleridge Rd 111 GJ82
Blakewood Cl, Felt. TW13 . . .116 BW91
Blanchard Chase, Horn. RM12
off Upper Rainham Rd . . .71 FF61
Blanchard Cl, SE9 . . . . .124 EL90
Blanchard Gro, Enf. EN3
off Government Row 31 EA37
Blanchard Way, E8 . . . . .84 DU65
Blanch Cl, SE15
off Culmore Rd 102 DW80
Blanchedowne, SE5 . . . . . . .102 DR84
Blanche La, Pot.B. EN6 . . . . .11 CT34
Blanche St, E16 . . . . .86 EF70
Blanchland Rd, Mord. SM4 . .140 DB99
Blanchmans Rd, Warl. CR6 . .177 DY118
Blandfield Rd, SW12 . . . . . . .120 DG86
Blandford Av, Beck. BR3 . . . .143 DY96
Twickenham TW2 . . . . . . .116 CB88
Blandford Cl, N2 . . . . .64 DC56
Croydon CR0 . . . . .141 DL104
Romford RM7 . . . . .71 FB56
Slough SL3 . . . . .92 AX76
Woking GU22 . . . . .167 BB117
Blandford Ct, Slou. SL3
off Blandford Rd S 92 AX76
Blandford Cres, E4 . . . . .47 EC45
Blandford Rd, W4 . . . . .98 CS76
W5 . . . . .97 CK75
Beckenham BR3 . . . . . . .142 DW96
Southall UB2 . . . . .96 CA77
Teddington TW11 . . . . . . .117 CD92
Blandford Rd N, Slou. SL3 . . .92 AX76
Blandford Rd S, Slou. SL3 . . .92 AX76
Blandford Sq, NW1 . . . . .194 C5
Blandford St, W1 . . . . .194 F8
Blandford Waye, Hayes UB4 . .78 BW72
Bland St, SE9 . . . . .104 EK84
Blaney Cres, E6 . . . . .87 EP69
Blanmerle Rd, SE9 . . . . .125 EP88
Blann Cl, SE9 . . . . .124 EK86
Blantyre St, SW10 . . . . .100 DD80
Blantyre Wk, SW10
off Blantyre St 100 DD80
Blashford, NW3 . . . . .82 DF66
Blashford St, SE13 . . . . .123 ED87
Blasker Wk, E14 . . . . .204 A10
Blattner Cl, Borwd. (Elstree)
WD6 . . . . .26 CL42
Blawith Rd, Har. HA1 . . . . . . .61 CE56
Blaxland Ter, Wal.Cr. (Chsht.)
EN8 off Davison Dr 15 DX28
Blaydon Cl, N17 . . . . .46 DV52
Ruislip HA4 . . . . .59 BS59
Blaydon Wk, N17 . . . . .46 DV52
Blays Cl, Egh. (Eng.Grn.)
TW20 . . . . .112 AW93
Blays La, Egh. (Eng.Grn.)
TW20 . . . . .112 AW93
Bleak Hill La, SE18 . . . . .105 ET79
Blean Gro, SE20 . . . . .122 DW94
Bleasdale Av, Grnf. UB6 . . . .79 CG68
Blechynden St, W10
off Bramley Rd 81 CX73
Bleddyn Cl, Sid. DA15 . . . . .126 EW86
Bledlow Cl, SE28 . . . . .88 EW73
Bledlow Ri, Grnf. UB6 . . . . . .78 CC68
Bleeding Heart Yd, EC1 . . . . .196 E7
Blegborough Rd, SW16 . . . . .121 DJ93
Blencarn Cl, Wok. GU21 . . . .166 AT116
Blendon Dr, Bex. DA5 . . . . . .126 EX86
Blendon Path, Brom. BR1 . . .124 EF94
Blendon Rd, Bex. DA5 . . . . .126 EX86
Blendon Ter, SE18 . . . . .105 EQ78
Blendworth Pt, SW15
off Wanborough Dr 119 CV88
Blendworth Way, SE15
off Daniel Gdns 102 DS80
Blenheim Av, Ilf. IG2 . . . . . . .69 EN58
Blenheim Cl, N21
off Elm Pk Rd 46 DQ46
SE12 off Guibal Rd 124 EH88
SW20 . . . . .139 CW97
Dartford DA1 . . . . .128 FJ86
Greenford UB6
off Leaver Gdns 79 CD68
Romford RM7 . . . . .71 FC56
Slough SL3 . . . . .75 AZ74
Upminster RM14 . . . . . . .73 FS60
Wallington SM6 . . . . .159 DJ108
Watford WD19 . . . . .40 BX45
West Byfleet KT14
off Madeira Rd 151 BF113
Blenheim Ct, N19
off Marlborough Rd 65 DL61
Sidcup DA14 . . . . .125 ER90
Sutton SM2
off Wellesley Rd 158 DC107
Woodford Green IG8
off Navestock Cres 48 EJ52
Blenheim Cres, W11 . . . . . . .81 CY72
Ruislip HA4 . . . . .59 BR61
South Croydon CR2 . . . . .160 DQ108
Blenheim Dr, Well. DA16 . . . .105 ET81
Blenheim Gdns, NW2 . . . . . .63 CW64
SW2 . . . . .121 DM86
Kingston upon Thames
KT2 . . . . .118 CP94
South Croydon CR2 . . . . .160 DU112
South Ockendon (Aveley)
RM15 . . . . .90 FP74
Wallington SM6 . . . . .159 DJ107
Wembley HA9 . . . . .62 CL62
Woking GU22 . . . . .166 AV119
Blenheim Gro, SE15 . . . . . . .102 DU82
Blenheim Pas, NW8
off Blenheim Ter 82 DC68
Blenheim Pk Rd, S.Croy.
CR2 . . . . .160 DQ109
Blenheim Ri, N15
off Talbot Rd 66 DT56
Blenheim Rd, E6 . . . . .86 EK69

Blenheim Rd, E15 . . . . .68 EE63
E17 . . . . .67 DX55
NW8 . . . . .82 DC68
SE20 off Maple Rd 122 DW94
SW20 . . . . .139 CW97
W4 . . . . .98 CS76
Abbots Langley WD5 . . . .7 BU33
Barnet EN5 . . . . .27 CX41
Brentwood CM15 . . . . . . .54 FU44
Bromley BR1 . . . . .144 EL98
Dartford DA1 . . . . .128 FJ86
Epsom KT19 . . . . .156 CR111
Harrow HA2 . . . . .60 CB58
Northolt UB5 . . . . .78 CB65
Orpington BR6 . . . . .146 EW103
Sidcup DA15 . . . . .126 EW88
Slough SL3 . . . . .92 AX77
Sutton SM1 . . . . .140 DA104
Blenheim Shop Cen, SE20 . .122 DW94
Blenheim St, W1 . . . . .195 H9
Blenheim Ter, NW8 . . . . .82 DC68
Blenheim Way, Epp. (N.Wld.Bas.)
CM16 . . . . .18 FA27
Isleworth TW7 . . . . .97 CG81
Blenkarne Rd, SW11 . . . . . . .120 DF86
Bleriot Rd, Houns. TW5 . . . . .96 BW80
Blessbury Rd, Edg. HA8 . . . .42 CQ53
Blessing Way, Bark. IG11 . . . .88 EW69
BLETCHINGLEY, Red. 186 DQ132
Bletchingley Cl, Red. RH1 . . .185 DJ129
Thornton Heath CR7 . . . .141 DP98
Bletchingley Rd, Gdse. RH9 . .186 DU131
Redhill (Bletch.) RH1 . . . .185 DN133
Redhill (S.Merst.) RH1 . . .185 DJ129
Bletchley Ct, N1 . . . . .197 K1
Bletchley St, N1 . . . . .197 J1
Bletchmore Cl, Hayes UB3 . . .95 BR78
Bletsoe Wk, N1 off Cropley St .84 DQ68
Blewbury Ho, SE2
off Yarnton Way 106 EX75
Bligh Rd, Grav. DA11 . . . . . .131 GG86
Bligh's Rd, Sev. TN13 . . . . . .191 FH125
Blincoe Cl, SW19 . . . . .119 CR53
Blinco La, Slou. (Geo.Grn.)
SL3 . . . . .74 AY72
Blind La, Bans. SM7 . . . . . . .174 DE115
Loughton (High Beach)
IG10 . . . . .32 EE40
Waltham Abbey EN9 . . . . .16 EJ33
Blindman's La, Wal.Cr. (Chsht.)
EN8 . . . . .15 DX30
Bliss Cres, SE13
off Coldbath St 103 EB82
Blissett St, SE10 . . . . .103 EC81
Bliss Ms, W10 off Third Av . . .81 CY69
Blisworth Cl, Hayes UB4
off Braunston Dr 78 BY70
Blithbury Rd, Dag. RM9 . . . . .88 EV65
Blithdale Rd, SE2 . . . . .106 EU77
Blithfield St, W8 . . . . .100 DB76
Blockhouse Rd, Grays RM17 .110 GC79
Blockley Rd, Wem. HA0 . . . . .61 CH61
Bloemfontein Av, W12 . . . . . .81 CV74
Bloemfontein Rd, W12 . . . . . .81 CV73
Blomfield Rd, W9 . . . . .82 DC71
Blomfield St, EC2 . . . . .197 L7
Blomfield Vil, W2 . . . . .82 DB71
Blomville Rd, Dag. RM8 . . . . .70 EY62
Blondell Cl, West Dr. UB7 . . . .94 BK79
Blondel St, SW11 . . . . .100 DG82
Blondin Av, W5 . . . . .97 CJ77
Blondin St, E3 . . . . .85 EA68
Bloomburg St, SW1 . . . . .199 L9
Bloomfield Cl, Wok. (Knap.)
GU21 . . . . .166 AS118
Bloomfield Cres, Ilf. IG2 . . . . .69 EP58
Bloomfield Pl, W1 . . . . .195 J10
Bloomfield Rd, N6 . . . . .64 DG58
SE18 . . . . .105 EP78
Bromley BR2 . . . . .144 EK99
Kingston upon Thames
KT1 . . . . .138 CL98
Waltham Cross (Chsht.)
EN7 . . . . .14 DQ25
Westerham TN16 . . . . . . .189 ES125
Bloom Gro, SE27 . . . . .121 DP90
Bloomhall Rd, SE19 . . . . . . .122 DR92
Bloom Pk Rd, SW6 . . . . .99 CZ80
BLOOMSBURY, WC1 . . . . . .195 N7
Bloomsbury Cl, W5 . . . . .80 CM73
Epsom KT19 . . . . .156 CR110
Bloomsbury Ct, WC1 . . . . . . .196 A7
Pinner HA5 . . . . .60 BZ55
Bloomsbury Ho, SW4 . . . . . .121 DK86
Bloomsbury Pl, SW18
off Fullerton Rd 120 DC85
WC1 . . . . .196 A6
Bloomsbury Sq, WC1 . . . . . .196 A7
Bloomsbury St, WC1 . . . . . . .195 N7
Bloomsbury Way, WC1 . . . . .195 P8
Blore Cl, SW8
off Thessaly Rd 101 DK81
Blore Ct, W1 . . . . .195 M9
Blossom Cl, W5
off Almond Av 98 CL75
Dagenham RM9 . . . . .88 EZ67
South Croydon CR2 . . . . .160 DT106
Blossom La, Enf. EN2 . . . . . .30 DQ39
Blossom Pl, E1 . . . . .197 N5
Blossom St, E1 . . . . .197 N6
Blossom Way, Uxb. UB10 . . . .76 BM66
West Drayton UB7 . . . . . . .94 BM77
Blossom Waye, Houns. TW5 . .96 BY80
Blount St, E14 . . . . .85 DY72
Bloxam Gdns, SE9 . . . . .124 EL85
Bloxhall Rd, E10 . . . . .67 DZ60
Bloxham Cres, Hmptn. TW12 .116 BZ94
Bloxworth Cl, Wall. SM6 . . . .141 DJ104
Blucher Rd, SE5 . . . . .102 DQ80
Blue Anchor All, Rich. TW9
off Kew Rd 98 CL84
Blue Anchor La, SE16 . . . . . .202 C8
Tilbury (W.Til.) RM18 . . . .111 GL77
Blue Anchor Yd, E1 . . . . .84 DU73

Blue Ball La, Egh. TW20 . . . .113 AZ92
Blue Ball Yd, SW1 . . . . .199 K3
Blue Barn La, Wey. KT13 . . . .152 BN111
Bluebell Av, E12 . . . . .68 EK64
Bluebell Cl, E9 off Moulins Rd .84 DW67
SE26 . . . . .122 DT91
Orpington BR5 . . . . .145 EQ103
Romford (Rush Grn.) RM7 .71 FE61
Wallington SM6 . . . . .141 DH102
Bluebell Ct, Wok. GU22 . . . .166 AX119
Bluebell Dr, Abb.L. (Bedmond)
WD5 . . . . .7 BT27
Waltham Cross EN7 . . . . .14 DR28
Bluebell Way, Ilf. IG1 . . . . . . .87 EP65
Orpington BR6 . . . . .146 EW103
Blueberry Cl, Wdf.Grn. IG8 . .48 EG51
Blueberry Gdns, Couls. CR5 .175 DM116
Blueberry La, Sev. (Knock.)
TN14 . . . . .180 EW116
Bluebird La, Dag. RM10 . . . . .88 FA66
Bluebird Way, SE28 . . . . .105 ER75
St. Albans AL2 . . . . .8 CB26
Bluebridge Av, Hat. AL9 . . . .11 CZ27
Bluebridge Rd, Hat. AL9 . . . .11 CY26
Blue Cedars, Bans. SM7 . . . .157 CX114
Blue Cedars Pl, Cob. KT11 . .154 BX112
Bluefield Cl, Hmptn. TW12 . .116 CA92
Bluegates, Epsom (Ewell)
KT17 . . . . .157 CU108
Bluehouse Gdns, Oxt. RH8 . .188 EG128
Bluehouse La, Oxt. RH8 . . . .188 EG127
Bluehouse Rd, E4 . . . . .48 EE48
Blue Leaves Av, Couls. CR5
off Netherne La 175 DK122
Bluelion Pl, SE1 . . . . .201 M6
Bluett Rd, St.Alb. (Lon.Col.)
AL2 . . . . .9 CK27
Bluewater Ho, SW18
off Smugglers Way 100 DB84
Bluewater Parkway, Green.
(Bluewater) DA9 . . . . . . .129 FS87
Bluewater Shop Cen, Green.
DA9 . . . . .129 FT88
Blundel La, Cob. (Stoke D'Ab.)
KT11 . . . . .154 CB114
Blundell Rd, Edg. HA8 . . . . . .42 CR53
Blundell St, N7 . . . . .83 DL66
Blunden Cl, Dag. RM8 . . . . . .70 EW60
Blunden Dr, Slou. SL3 . . . . . .93 BB77
Blunesfield, Pot.B. EN6 . . . . .12 DD31
Blunt Rd, S.Croy. CR2 . . . . .160 DR106
Blunts Av, West Dr. UB7 . . . .94 BN80
Blunts Rd, SE9 . . . . .125 EN85
Blurton Rd, E5 . . . . .66 DW63
Blyth Cl, E14 . . . . .204 F8
Borehamwood WD6 . . . . .26 CM39
Twickenham TW1
off Grimwood Rd 117 CF86
Blythe Cl, SE6 . . . . .123 DZ87
Iver SL0 . . . . .75 BF72
Blythe Hill, SE6 . . . . .123 DZ87
Orpington BR5 . . . . .145 ET95
Blythe Hill La, SE6 . . . . .123 DZ87
Blythe Rd, W14 . . . . .99 CX76
Blythe St, E2 . . . . .84 DV69
Blythe Vale, SE6 . . . . .123 DZ88
Blyth Rd, E17 . . . . .67 DZ59
SE28 . . . . .88 EW73
Bromley BR1 . . . . .144 EF95
Hayes UB3 . . . . .95 BS75
Blyth's Wf, E14 . . . . .203 L1
Blythswood Rd, Ilf. IG3 . . . . .70 EU60
Blyth Wk, Upmin. RM14 . . . . .73 FS58
Blyth Wd Pk, Brom. BR1
off Blyth Rd 144 EF95
Blythwood Rd, N4 . . . . .65 DL59
Pinner HA5 . . . . .40 BX53
Boades Ms, NW3
off New End 64 DD63
Boadicea St, N1
off Copenhagen St 83 DM67
Boakes Cl, NW9 . . . . .62 CQ56
Boakes Meadow, Sev. (Shore.)
TN14 . . . . .165 FF111
Boar Cl, Chig. IG7 . . . . .50 EU50
Boardman Av, E4 . . . . .31 EB43
Boardman Cl, Barn. EN5 . . . .27 CY43
Board Sch Rd, Wok. GU21 . .167 AZ116
Boardwalk Pl, E14 . . . . .204 D2
Boar's Head Yd, Brent. TW8
off Brent Way 97 CK80
Boathouse Wk, SE15 . . . . . . .102 DT80
Richmond TW9 . . . . .98 CL81
Boat Lifter Way, SE16 . . . . . .203 L8
Bob Anker Ct, E13
off Chesterton Rd 86 EG69
Bobbin Cl, SW4 . . . . .101 DJ83
Bobby Moore Way, N10 . . . . .44 DF52
Bob Marley Way, SE24
off Mayall Rd 101 DN84
Bobs La, Rom. RM1 . . . . .51 FG52
Bocketts La, Lthd. KT22 . . . .171 CF124
Bockhampton Rd, Kings.T.
KT2 . . . . .118 CM94
Bocking St, E8 . . . . .84 DV67
Boddicott Cl, SW19 . . . . .119 CY89
Bodell Cl, Grays RM16 . . . . .110 GB76
Bodiam Cl, Enf. EN1 . . . . . . .30 DR40
Bodiam Rd, SW16 . . . . .121 DK94
Bodicea Ms, Houns. TW4 . . .116 BZ87
Bodle Av, Swans. DA10 . . . .130 FY87
Bodley Cl, Epp. CM16 . . . . . .17 ET30
New Malden KT3 . . . . . . .138 CS99
Bodley Manor Way, SW2
off Papworth Way 121 DN87
Bodley Rd, N.Mal. KT3 . . . . .138 CR100
Bodmin Cl, Har. HA2 . . . . . . .60 BZ62
Orpington BR5 . . . . .146 EW102
Bodmin Gro, Mord. SM4 . . . .140 DB99
Bodmin St, SW18 . . . . .119 CZ88
Bodnant Gdns, SW20 . . . . . .139 CU97
Bodney Rd, E8 . . . . .66 DV64
Boeing Way, Sthl. UB2 . . . . . .95 BW76
Boevey Path, Belv. DA17 . . . .106 EZ79
Bogey La, Orp. BR6 . . . . .163 EN108
Bognor Gdns, Wat. WD19
off Bowring Grn 40 BW50

Bognor Rd, Well. DA16 . . . . .106 EX81
Bohemia Pl, E8 . . . . .84 DV65
Bohn Rd, E1 . . . . .85 DY71
Bohun Gro, Barn. EN4 . . . . . .28 DE44
Boileau Par, W5
off Boileau Rd 80 CM72
Boileau Rd, SW13 . . . . .99 CU80
W5 . . . . .80 CM72
Bois Hall Rd, Add. KT15 . . . .152 BK105
Bois Hill, Chesh. HP5 . . . . . . .4 AS34
Bolden St, SE8 . . . . .103 EB82
Bolderwood Way, W.Wick.
BR4 . . . . .143 EB103
Boldmere Rd, Pnr. HA5 . . . . .60 BW59
Epsom KT17 . . . . .157 CV110
Boleyn Av, Enf. EN1 . . . . .30 DV39
Boleyn Cl, E17 . . . . .67 EA56
Grays (Chaff.Hun.) RM16
off Clifford Rd 110 FZ76
Loughton IG10
off Roding Gdns 32 EL44
Staines TW18 . . . . .113 BE92
Boleyn Ct, Buck.H. IG9 . . . . .48 EG46
Broxbourne EN10
off Chertsey La 113 BE92
Boleyn Dr, Ruis. HA4 . . . . . . .60 BX61
West Molesey KT8 . . . . . .136 BZ97
Boleyn Gdns, Brwd. CM13 . . .55 GA48
Dagenham RM10 . . . . . . .89 FC66
West Wickham BR4 . . . . .143 EB103
Boleyn Gro, W.Wick. BR4 . . .143 EC103
Boleyn Rd, E6 . . . . .86 EK68
E7 . . . . .86 EG66
N16 . . . . .66 DS64
Boleyn Wk, Lthd. KT22 . . . . .171 CF120
Boleyn Way, Barn. EN5 . . . . .28 DC41
Ilford IG6 . . . . .49 EQ51
Swanscombe DA10 . . . . .130 FY87
Bolina Rd, SE16 . . . . .202 G10
Bolingbroke Gro, SW11 . . . . .100 DE84
[H] Bolingbroke Hosp, SW11 .120 DE85
Bolingbroke Rd, W14 . . . . . . .99 CX76
Bolingbroke Wk, SW11 . . . . .100 DD81
Bolingbroke Way, Hayes UB3 .77 BR74
Bolliger Ct, NW10
off Park Royal Rd 80 CQ70
Bollo Br Rd, W3 . . . . .98 CP76
Bollo La, W3 . . . . .98 CP75
W4 . . . . .98 CQ77
Bolney Gate, SW7 . . . . .198 B5
Bolney St, SW8 . . . . .101 DM80
Bolney Way, Felt. TW13 . . . . .116 BY90
Bolsover Gro, Red. RH1 . . . .185 DL129
Bolsover St, W1 . . . . .195 J5
Bolstead Rd, Mitch. CR4 . . . .141 DH95
Bolt Cellar La, Epp. CM16 . . .17 ES29
Bolt Ct, EC4 . . . . .196 F9
Bolters La, Bans. SM7 . . . . . .157 CZ114
Boltmore Cl, NW4 . . . . .63 CX55
Bolton Cl, SE20
off Selby Rd 142 DU96
Chessington KT9 . . . . . . .155 CK107
Bolton Cres, SE5 . . . . .101 DP79
Bolton Gdns, NW10 . . . . .81 CX68
SW5 . . . . .100 DB78
Bromley BR1 . . . . .124 EF93
Teddington TW11 . . . . . . .117 CG93
Bolton Gdns Ms, SW10 . . . . .100 DB78
Bolton Rd, E15 . . . . .86 EF65
N18 . . . . .46 DT50
NW8 . . . . .82 DB67
NW10 . . . . .80 CS67
W4 . . . . .98 CQ80
Chessington KT9 . . . . . . .155 CK107
Harrow HA1 . . . . .60 CC56
Boltons, The, SW10 . . . . .100 DC78
Wembley HA0 . . . . .61 CF63
Woodford Green IG8 . . . . .48 EG49
Boltons Cl, Wok. GU22 . . . . .168 BG116
Boltons La, Hayes UB3 . . . . .95 BQ80
Woking GU22 . . . . .168 BG116
Boltons Pl, SW5 . . . . .100 DC78
Bolton St, W1 . . . . .199 J2
Bolton Wk, N7 off Durham Rd .65 DM61
Bombay St, SE16 . . . . .202 D8
Bombers La, West. TN16 . . . .179 ER119
Bomer Cl, West Dr. UB7 . . . . .94 BN80
Bomore Rd, W11 . . . . .81 CX73
Bonar Pl, Chis. BR7 . . . . . . .124 EL94
Bonar Rd, SE15 . . . . .102 DU80
Bonaventure Ct, Grav. DA12 .131 GM91
Bonchester Cl, Chis. BR7 . . .125 EN94
Bonchurch Cl, Sutt. SM2 . . . .158 DB108
Bonchurch Rd, W10 . . . . .81 CY71
W13 . . . . .79 CH74
Bond Cl, West. (Knock.) TN14 .180 EX115
West Drayton UB7 . . . . . . .76 BM72
Bond Ct, EC4 . . . . .197 K9
Bondfield Av, Hayes UB4 . . . .77 BU69
Bondfield Rd, E6
off Lovage App 86 EL71
Bondfield Wk, Dart. DA1 . . . .108 FM84
Bond Gdns, Wall. SM6 . . . . .159 DJ105
Bonding Yd Wk, SE16 . . . . . .203 L5
Bond Rd, Mitch. CR4 . . . . . .140 DE96
Surbiton KT6 . . . . .138 CM103
Warlingham CR6 . . . . . . .177 DX118
Bond St, E15 . . . . .68 EE64
W4 . . . . .98 CS77
W5 . . . . .79 CK73
Egham (Eng.Grn.) TW20 .112 AV92
Grays RM17 . . . . .110 GC79
 Bond Street 194 G9
Bondway, SW8 . . . . .101 DL79
Bone Mill La, Gdse. RH9
off Eastbourne Rd 187 DY134
Boneta Rd, SE18 . . . . .105 EM76
Bonfield Rd, SE13 . . . . .103 EC84
Bonham Gdns, Dag. RM8 . . . .70 EX61
Bonham Rd, SW2 . . . . .121 DM85
Dagenham RM8 . . . . .70 EX61
Bonheur Rd, W4 . . . . .98 CR75
Bonhill St, EC2 . . . . .197 L5
Boniface Gdns, Har. HA3 . . . .40 CB52
Boniface Rd, Uxb. UB10 . . . .59 BP62

Bon - Bra

Boniface Wk, Har. HA3 . . . . . . .40 CB52
Bonington Ho, Enf. EN1
 off Ayley Cft 30 DU43
Bonington Rd, Horn. RM12 . .72 FK64
Bon Marche Ter Ms, SE27
 off Gipsy Rd 122 DS91
Bonner Hill Rd, Kings.T. KT1 .138 CM97
Bonner Rd, E2 . . . . .84 DW68
Bonners Cl, Wok. GU22 . . .166 AY122
Bonnersfield Cl, Har. HA1 . . .61 CF58
Bonnersfield La, Har. HA1 . . .61 CG58
Bonner St, E2 . . . . .84 DW68
Bonner Wk, Grays RM16
 off Clifford Rd 110 FZ76
Bonnett Ms, Horn. RM11 . . .72 FL60
Bonneville Gdns, SW4 . . . . .121 DJ86
Bonney Gro, Wal.Cr. (Chsht.)
 EN7 . . . . .14 DU30
Bonney Way, Swan. BR8 . . .147 FE96
Bonningtons, Brwd. CM13 . . .55 GB48
Bonnington Sq, SW8 . . . . . .101 DM79
Bonnington Twr, Brom. BR2 .144 EL100
Bonny St, NW1 . . . . .83 DJ66
Bonser Rd, Twick. TW1 . . . .117 CF89
Bonsey Cl, Wok. GU22 . . . .166 AY121
Bonsey La, Wok. GU22 . . . .166 AY121
Bonseys La, Wok. (Chobham)
 GU24 . . . . .151 AZ110
Bonsor Dr, Tad. KT20 . . . . .173 CY122
Bonsor St, SE5 . . . . .102 DS80
Bonville Gdns, NW4
 off Handowe Cl 63 CU56
Bonville Rd, Brom. BR1 . . . .124 EF92
Bookbinders' Cotts, N20
 off Manor Dr 44 DF48
Booker Cl, E14
 off Wallwood St 85 DZ71
Booker Rd, N18 . . . . .46 DU50
⇌ Bookham 170 BZ123
Bookham Ct, Lthd. KT23
 off Church Rd 170 BZ123
Bookham Ind Est, Lthd. (Bkhm.)
 KT23 . . . . .170 BZ123
Bookham Rd, Cob. (Down.)
 KT11 . . . . .170 BW119
Book Ms, WC2 . . . . .195 N9
Boone Ct, N9 . . . . .46 DW48
Boones Rd, SE13 . . . . . . .104 EE84
Boone St, SE13 . . . . .104 EE84
Boord St, SE10 . . . . .205 J4
Boothby Rd, N19 . . . . . . .65 DK61
Booth Cl, E9
 off Victoria Pk Rd 84 DV67
 SE28 . . . . .88 EV73
Booth Dr, Stai. TW18 . . . . .114 BK93
Booth Rd, NW9 . . . . .42 CS54
 Croydon CR0
 off Waddon New Rd 141 DP103
Booth's Ct, Brwd. (Hutton)
 CM13 . . . . .55 GB44
Booth's Pl, W1 . . . . .195 L7
Boot St, N1 . . . . .197 M3
Bordars Rd, W7 . . . . .79 CE71
Bordars Wk, W7 . . . . .79 CE71
Borden Av, Enf. EN1 . . . . .30 DR44
Border Cres, SE26 . . . . . .122 DV92
Border Gdns, Croy. CR0 . . .161 EB105
Bordergate, Mitch. CR4 . . . .140 DE95
Border Rd, SE26 . . . . . . .122 DV92
Borderside, Slou. SL2 . . . . .74 AU72
Borders La, Loug. IG10 . . . .33 EN42
Bordesley Rd, Mord. SM4 . .140 DB98
Bordon Wk, SW15 . . . . . .119 CU87
Boreas Wk, N1 . . . . .196 G1
Boreham Av, E16 . . . . . . .86 EG72
Boreham Cl, E11
 off Hainault Rd 67 EC60
Boreham Holt, Borwd. (Elstree)
 WD6 . . . . .26 CM42
Boreham Rd, N22 . . . . . . .46 DQ54
BOREHAMWOOD 26 CP41
Borehamwood Ind Pk, Borwd.
 WD6 . . . . .26 CP40
Borgard Rd, SE18 . . . . . .105 EM77
Borkwood Pk, Orp. BR6 . . .163 ET105
Borkwood Way, Orp. BR6 . .163 ES105
Borland Cl, Green. DA9
 off Steele Av 129 FU85
Borland Rd, SE15 . . . . . .102 DW84
 Teddington TW11 . . . . . .117 CH93
Bornedene, Pot.B. EN6 . . . .11 CY31
Borneo St, SW15 . . . . . . .99 CW83
⊖ Borough 201 J5
BOROUGH, THE, SE1 . . . .201 H5
Borough High St, SE1 . . . .201 H5
Borough Hill, Croy. CR0 . . .141 DP104
★ Borough Mkt, SE1 . . . .201 K3
Borough Rd, SE1 . . . . . . .201 F6
 Isleworth TW7 . . . . . . .97 CE81
 Kingston upon Thames
 KT2 . . . . .138 CN95
 Mitcham CR4 . . . . .140 DE96
 Westerham (Tats.) TN16 . .178 EK121
Borough Sq, SE1 . . . . . . .201 H5
Borough Way, Pot.B. EN6 . .11 CY32
Borrett Cl, SE17
 off Penrose St 102 DQ78
Borrodaile Rd, SW18 . . . . .120 DB86
Borrowdale Av, Har. HA3 . . .41 CG54
Borrowdale Cl, Egh. TW20
 off Derwent Rd 113 BB94
 Ilford IG4 . . . . .68 EL56
 South Croydon CR2 . . . .160 DT113
Borrowdale Ct, Enf. EN2 . . .30 DQ39
Borrowdale Dr, S.Croy. CR2 .160 DT112
Borthwick Ms, E15
 off Borthwick Rd 68 EE63
Borthwick Rd, E15 . . . . . .68 EE63
 NW9 off West Hendon Bdy ..63 CT58
Borthwick St, SE8 . . . . . .103 EA78
Borwick Av, E17 . . . . . . .67 DZ55
Bosanquet Cl, Uxb. UB8 . . .76 BK70
Bosbury Rd, SE6 . . . . . . .123 EC90
Boscastle Rd, NW5 . . . . .65 DH62

Boscobel Pl, SW1 . . . . . . .198 G8
Boscobel St, NW8 . . . . . .194 A5
Bosco Cl, Orp. BR6
 off Strickland Way 163 ET105
Boscombe Av, E10 . . . . . .67 ED59
 Grays RM17 . . . . .110 GD77
 Hornchurch RM11 . . . . .72 FK60
Boscombe Cl, E5 . . . . . . .67 DY64
 Egham TW20 . . . . .133 BC95
Boscombe Gdns, SW16 . . .121 DL93
Boscombe Rd, SW17 . . . .120 DG93
 SW19 . . . . .140 DB95
 W12 . . . . .99 CU75
 Worcester Park KT4 . . .139 CW102
Bose Cl, N3 off Claremont Pk . .43 CY53
Bosgrove, E4 . . . . .47 EC46
Boshers Gdns, Egh. TW20 .113 AZ93
Bostall Heath, SE2 . . . . . .106 EW78
Bostall Hill, SE2 . . . . . . .106 EU78
Bostall La, SE2 . . . . .106 EU78
Bostall Manorway, SE2 . . .106 EV77
Bostall Pk Av, Bexh. DA7 . .106 EY80
Bostall Rd, Orp. BR5 . . . . .126 EV94
Bostal Row, Bexh. DA7
 off Harlington Rd 106 EZ83
Boston Gdns, W4 . . . . . . .98 CS79
 W7 . . . . .97 CG77
 Brentford TW8 . . . . . . .97 CG77
Boston Gro, Ruis. HA4 . . . .59 BQ58
★ Boston Manor, Brent.
 TW8 . . . . .97 CH78
⊖ Boston Manor 97 CH77
Boston Manor Rd, Brent. TW8 .97 CH77
Boston Pk Rd, Brent. TW8 . .97 CJ78
Boston Pl, NW1 . . . . . . .194 D5
Boston Rd, E6 . . . . .86 EL69
 E17 . . . . .67 EA58
 W7 . . . . .79 CE74
 Croydon CR0 . . . . . . .141 DM100
 Edgware HA8 . . . . .42 CQ52
Boston St, E2 off Audrey St . .84 DU68
Bostonthorpe Rd, W7 . . . .97 CE75
Boston Vale, W7 . . . . . . .97 CG77
Bosun Cl, E14 . . . . .204 A4
Bosville Av, Sev. TN13 . . .190 FG123
Bosville Dr, Sev. TN13 . . .190 FG123
Bosville Rd, Sev. TN13 . . .190 FG123
Boswell Ct, WC1 . . . . . . .196 A6
 off Killewarren Way 146 EW100
 Radlett (Shenley) WD7 . . .10 CL32
Boswell Path, Hayes UB3
 off Croyde Av 95 BT77
Boswell Rd, Th.Hth. CR7 . .142 DQ98
Boswell St, WC1 . . . . . . .196 A6
Bosworth Cl, E17 . . . . . . .47 DZ53
Bosworth Cres, Rom. RM3 . .52 FJ51
Bosworth Rd, N11 . . . . . .45 DK51
 W10 . . . . .81 CY70
 Barnet EN5 . . . . .28 DA41
 Dagenham RM10 . . . . .70 FA63
BOTANY BAY, Enf. 29 DK36
Botany Bay La, Chis. BR7 . .145 EQ97
Botany Cl, Barn. EN4 . . . . .28 DE42
Botany Rd, Grav. (Nthflt.)
 DA11 . . . . .110 GA83
Botany Way, Purf. RM19 . . .108 FP78
Boteley Cl, E4 . . . . .47 ED47
Botery's Cross, Red. RH1 . .185 DP133
Botham Cl, Edg. HA8
 off Pavilion Way 42 CQ52
Botham Dr, Slou. SL1 . . . . .92 AS76
Botha Rd, E13 . . . . .86 EH71
Bothwell Cl, E16 . . . . . . .86 EF71
Bothwell Rd, Croy. (New Adgtn.)
 CR0 . . . . .161 EC110
Bothwell St, W6
 off Delorme St 99 CX79
BOTLEY, Chesh. 4 AV30
Botley La, Chesh. HP5 . . . .4 AU30
Botley Rd, Chesh. HP5 . . . .4 AT30
Botolph All, EC3 . . . . . . .197 M10
Botolph La, EC3 . . . . . . .197 M10
Botsford Rd, SW20 . . . . .139 CY96
Bottom Ho Fm La, Ch.St.G.
 HP8 . . . . .36 AT45
Bottom La, Chesh. HP5 . . . .4 AT34
 Kings Langley WD4 . . . .22 BH35
Bottrells Cl, Ch.St.G. HP8 . .36 AT47
Bottrells La, Ch.St.G. HP8 . .36 AT47
Bott Rd, Dart. (Hawley) DA2 .128 FM91
Botts Ms, W2
 off Chepstow Rd 82 DA72
Botts Pas, W2
 off Chepstow Rd 82 DA72
Botwell Common Rd, Hayes
 UB3 . . . . .77 BR73
Botwell Cres, Hayes UB3 . . .77 BS73
Botwell La, Hayes UB3 . . . .77 BS74
Boucher Cl, Tedd. TW11 . . .117 CF92
Boucher Dr, Grav. (Nthflt.)
 DA11 . . . . .131 GF90
Bouchier Wk, Rain. RM13
 off Deere Av 89 FG65
Boughton Av, Brom. BR2 . .144 EF101
Boughton Business Pk, Amer.
 HP6 . . . . .20 AV39
Boughton Hall Av, Wok. (Send)
 GU23 . . . . .167 BF124
Boughton Rd, SE28 . . . . .105 ES76
Boughton Way, Amer. HP6 .20 AW38
Boulcott St, E1 . . . . .85 DX72
Boulevard, The, SW6
 off Balham High Rd . . .120 DG89
 Pinner HA5
 off Pinner Rd 60 CA56
 Watford WD18 . . . . . . .23 BR43
 Woodford Green IG8 . . .49 EN52
Boulevard 25 Retail Pk, Borwd.
 WD6 . . . . .26 CN41
Boulmer Rd, Uxb. UB8 . . . .76 BJ69
Boulogne Rd, Croy. CR0 . .142 DQ100
Boulter Gdns, Rain. RM13 . .89 FG65
Boulthurst Way, Oxt. RH8 . .188 EH132
Boulton Ho, Brent. TW8
 off Green Dragon La . . .98 CL78

Boulton Rd, Dag. RM8 . . . .70 EY62
Boultwood Rd, E6 . . . . . .87 EM72
Bounce Hill, Rom. (Nave.) RM4
 off Mill La 35 FH38
Bounces La, N9 . . . . .46 DV47
Bounces Rd, N9 . . . . .46 DV46
Boundaries Rd, SW12 . . . .120 DF89
 Feltham TW13 . . . . . . .116 BW88
Boundary Av, E17 . . . . . .67 DZ59
Boundary Cl, SE20
 off Haysleigh Gdns . . .142 DU96
 Barnet EN5 . . . . .27 CZ39
 Ilford IG3 off Loxford La . .69 ES63
 Kingston upon Thames
 KT1 . . . . .138 CP97
 Southall UB2 . . . . .96 CA78
Boundary Dr, Brwd. CM13 . .55 GE45
Boundary La, E13 . . . . . .86 EK69
 SE17 . . . . .102 DQ79
Boundary Pas, E2 . . . . . .197 P4
Boundary Rd, E13 . . . . . .86 EJ68
 E17 . . . . .67 DZ59
 N9 . . . . .30 DW44
 N22 . . . . .65 DP55
 NW8 . . . . .82 DB67
 SW19 . . . . .120 DD93
 Ashford TW15 . . . . . . .114 BJ92
 Barking IG11 . . . . .87 EQ68
 Carshalton SM5 . . . . .159 DH107
 Gerrards Cross (Chal.St.P.)
 SL9 . . . . .36 AX52
 Pinner HA5 . . . . .60 BX58
 Romford RM1 . . . . .71 FG58
 Sidcup DA15 . . . . .125 ES85
 Upminster RM14 . . . . .72 FN62
 Wallington SM6 . . . . .159 DH107
 Wembley HA9 . . . . .62 CL62
 Woking GU21 . . . . . . .167 BA116
Boundary Row, SE1 . . . . .200 F4
Boundary St, E2 . . . . . . .197 P3
 Erith DA8 . . . . .107 FF80
Boundary Way, Croy. CR0 . .161 EA106
 Watford WD25 . . . . . . .7 BV32
 Woking GU21 . . . . . . .167 BA115
Boundary Yd, Wok. GU21
 off Boundary Rd 167 BA116
Boundfield Rd, SE6 . . . . .124 EE90
⊖ Bounds Green 45 DK51
Bounds Grn Rd, N11 . . . .45 DJ51
 N22 . . . . .45 DJ51
Bourchier Cl, Sev. TN13 . .191 FH126
Bourchier St, W1 . . . . . .195 M10
Bourdon Pl, W1 . . . . . . .195 J10
Bourdon Rd, SE20 . . . . .142 DW96
Bourdon St, W1 . . . . . . .195 J10
Bourke Cl, NW10 off Mayo Rd .80 CS65
 SW4 . . . . .121 DL86
Bourke Hill, Couls. CR5 . . .174 DF118
Bourlet Cl, W1 . . . . .195 K7
Bourn Av, N15 . . . . .66 DR56
 Barnet EN4 . . . . .28 DD43
 Uxbridge UB8 . . . . . . .76 BN70
Bournbrook Rd, SE3 . . . .104 EK83
Bourne, The, N14 . . . . . .45 DK47
 Hemel Hempstead (Bov.)
 HP3 . . . . .5 BA27
Bourne Av, N14 . . . . . . .45 DL47
 Chertsey KT16 . . . . . .134 BG97
 Hayes UB3 . . . . .95 BQ76
 Ruislip HA4 . . . . .60 BW64
Bournebridge Cl, Brwd. CM13 .55 GE45
Bournebridge La, Rom. (Stap.Abb.)
 RM4 . . . . .50 EZ45
Bourne Cl, T.Ditt. KT7 . . .137 CF103
 West Byfleet KT14 . . . .152 BH113
Bourne Ct, Ruis. HA4 . . . .59 BV64
Bourne Dr, Mitch. CR4 . . .140 DD96
Bourne End, Horn. RM11 . .72 FN59
Bourne End Rd, Nthwd. HA6 .39 BS49
Bourne Est, EC1 . . . . . . .196 D6
Bournefield Rd, Whyt. CR3
 off Godstone Rd 176 DT118
Bourne Gdns, E4 . . . . . . .47 EB49
Bourne Gro, Ashtd. KT21 . .171 CK119
Bournehall Av, Bushey WD23 .24 CA43
Bournehall La, Bushey WD23 .24 CA44
⇌ Bournehall Rd, Bushey WD23 .24 CA44
Bourne Hill, N13 . . . . . .45 DL46
Bourne Ind Pk, Dart. DA1
 off Bourne Rd 127 FE85
Bourne La, Cat. CR3 . . . .176 DR121
Bourne Mead, Bex. DA5 . .127 FD85
Bournemead Av, Nthlt. UB5 .77 BU68
Bournemead Cl, Nthlt. UB5 . .77 BU68
Bourne Meadow, Egh. TW20 .133 BB98
Bournemead Way, Nthlt. UB5 .77 BV68
Bournemouth Cl, SE15 . . .102 DU82
Bournemouth Rd, SE15 . . .102 DU82
 SW19 . . . . .140 DA95
Bourne Pk Cl, Ken. CR8 . .176 DS115
Bourne Pl, W4 off Dukes Av . .98 CR78
Bourne Rd, E7 . . . . .68 EF62
 N8 . . . . .65 DL58
 Bexley DA5 . . . . .127 FB86
 Bromley BR2 . . . . . . .144 EK98
 Dartford DA1 . . . . . . .127 FC86
 Gravesend DA12 . . . . .131 GM89
 Redhill RH1 . . . . .185 DJ130
 Virginia Water GU25 . . .132 AX99
Bourneside, Vir.W. GU25 . .132 AU101
Bourneside Cres, N14 . . . .45 DK46
Bourneside Gdns, SE6 . . .123 EC92
Bourneside Rd, Add. KT15 .152 BK105
Bourne St, SW1 . . . . . . .198 F9
 Croydon CR0
 off Waddon New Rd . . .141 DP103
Bourne Ter, W2 . . . . .82 DB71
Bourne Vale, Brom. BR2 . .144 EG101
Bournevale Rd, SW16 . . . .121 DL91
Bourne Vw, Grnf. UB6 . . . .79 CF65
 Kenley CR8 . . . . .176 DR115
Bourne Way, Add. KT15 . .152 BJ106
 Bromley BR2 . . . . . . .144 EF103
 Epsom KT19 . . . . . . .156 CQ105

Bourne Way, Sutt. SM1 . . .157 CZ106
 Swanley BR8 . . . . . . .147 FC97
 Woking GU22 . . . . . . .166 AX122
Bournewood Rd, SE18 . . .106 EU80
 Orpington BR5 . . . . . .126 EV101
Bournville Rd, SE6 . . . . .123 EA87
Bournwell Cl, Barn. EN4 . . .28 DF89
Bourton Cl, Hayes UB3
 off Avondale Dr 77 BU74
Bousfield Rd, SE14 . . . . .103 DX82
Bousley Ri, Cher. (Ott.) KT16 .151 BD108
Boutflower Rd, SW11 . . . .100 DE84
Bouverie Gdns, Har. HA3 . .61 CK58
 Purley CR8 . . . . .159 DL114
Bouverie Ms, N16
 off Bouverie Rd 66 DS61
Bouverie Pl, W2 . . . . . . .194 A8
Bouverie Rd, N16 . . . . . .66 DS61
 Coulsdon CR5 . . . . . .174 DG118
 Harrow HA1 . . . . .60 CC59
Bouverie St, EC4 . . . . . .196 E9
Bouverie Way, Slou. SL3 . .92 AY78
Bouvier Rd, Enf. EN3 . . . .30 DW38
Boveney Rd, SE23 . . . . . .123 DX87
Bovey Way, S.Ock. RM15 . .91 FV71
Bovill Rd, SE23 . . . . . . .123 DX87
BOVINGDON, Hem.H. 5 BA28
Bovingdon Av, Wem. HA9 . .80 CN65
Bovingdon Cl, N19
 off Brookside Rd 65 DJ61
Bovingdon Cres, Wat. WD25 . .8 BX34
Bovingdon La, NW9 . . . . .42 CS53
Bovingdon Rd, SW6 . . . . .100 DB81
Bovingdon Sq, Mitch. CR4
 off Leicester Av 141 DL98
BOW, E3 . . . . .85 DZ68
Bow Arrow La, Dart.
 DA1, DA2 . . . . .128 FN86
Bowater Cl, NW9 . . . . . .62 CR57
 SW2 . . . . .121 DL86
Bowater Gdns, Sun. TW16 .135 BV96
Bowater Pl, SE3 . . . . . . .104 EH80
Bowater Ridge, Wey. KT13 .153 BR110
Bowater Rd, SE18 . . . . . .104 EK76
Bow Br Est, E3 . . . . .85 EB69
ᴅᴸʀ Bow Church 85 EA69
Bow Chyd, EC4 . . . . .197 J9
Bow Common La, E3 . . . .85 DZ70
Bowden Cl, Felt. TW14 . . .115 BS88
Bowden Dr, Horn. RM11 . . .72 FL60
Bowden St, SE11 . . . . . .101 DN78
Bowditch, SE8 . . . . .203 M10
Bowdon Rd, E17 . . . . . . .67 EA59
Bowen Dr, SE21 . . . . . . .122 DS90
Bowen Rd, Har. HA1 . . . .60 CC59
Bowen St, E14 . . . . .85 EB72
Bowens Wd, Croy. CR0 . .161 DZ109
Bower Av, SE10 . . . . . . .104 EE81
Bower Cl, Nthlt. UB5 . . . .78 BW68
 Romford RM5 . . . . . . .51 FB52
Bower Ct, Epp. CM16 . . . .18 EU32
 off Princess Rd 167 BB116
Bowerdean St, SW6 . . . .100 DB81
Bower Fm Rd, Rom. (Hav.at.Bow.)
 RM4 . . . . .51 FC48
BOWER HILL, Epp. 18 EU31
Bower Hill, Epp. CM16 . . . .18 EU32
Bower Hill Ind Est, Epp.
 CM16 . . . . .18 EU32
Bower La, Dart. (Eyns.) DA4 .148 FL103
Bowerman Av, SE14 . . . .103 DY79
Bowerman Rd, Grays RM16 .111 GG77
Bower Rd, Swan. BR8 . . . .127 FG94
Bowers Av, Grav. (Nthflt.)
 DA11 . . . . .131 GF91
Bowers Rd, Sev. (Shore.)
 TN14 . . . . .165 FF111
Bower St, E1 . . . . .85 DX72
Bowers Wk, E6 . . . . .86 EL72
Bower Ter, Epp. CM16
 off Bower Hill 18 EU32
Bower Vale, Epp. CM16 . . .18 EU32
Bowes Cl, Sid. DA15 . . . .126 EV86
BOWES PARK, N22 . . . . .45 DL51
⇌ Bowes Park 45 DL51
Bowes Rd, N11 . . . . . . .45 DH50
 N13 . . . . .45 DL50
 W3 . . . . .80 CS73
 Dagenham RM8 . . . . .70 EW63
 Staines TW18 . . . . . . .113 BE92
 Walton-on-Thames KT12 .135 BV103
Bowfell Rd, W6 . . . . . . .99 CW79
Bowford Av, Bexh. DA7 . . .106 EY81
Bowhay, Brwd. CM13 . . . .55 GA47
Bowhill Cl, SW9 . . . . . . .101 DN80
Bowie Cl, SW4 . . . . .121 DK87
Bow Ind Pk, E15 . . . . . . .86 EA66
Bowland Rd, SW4 . . . . . .101 DK84
 Woodford Green IG8 . . .48 EJ51
Bowland Yd, SW1 . . . . . .198 E5
Bow La, EC4 . . . . .197 J9
 N12 . . . . .44 DC53
 Morden SM4 . . . . . . .139 CY100
Bowl Ct, EC2 . . . . .197 N5
Bowlers Orchard, Ch.St.G.
 HP8 . . . . .36 AU48
Bowles Grn, Enf. EN1 . . . .30 DV36
Bowles Rd, SE1
 off Old Kent Rd 102 DU79
Bowley Cl, SE19 . . . . . . .122 DT93
Bowley La, SE19 . . . . . .122 DT92
Bowling Cl, Uxb. UB10
 off Birch Cres 76 BM67
Bowling Grn Cl, SW15 . . .119 CV87
Bowling Grn La, EC1 . . . .196 E4
Bowling Grn Pl, SE1 . . . .201 K4
Bowling Grn Rd, Wok. (Chobham)
 GU24 . . . . .150 AS109
Bowling Grn Row, SE18
 off Samuel St 105 EM76
Bowling Grn St, SE11 . . .101 DN79
Bowling Grn Wk, N1 . . . .197 M2
Bowls, The, Chig. IG7 . . . .49 ES49
Bowls Cl, Stan. HA7 . . . .41 CH50
Bowman Av, E16 . . . . . . .86 EF73

Bowman Ms, SW18 . . . . .119 CZ88
Bowmans Cl, W13 . . . . . .79 CH74
 Potters Bar EN6 . . . . . .12 DD32
Bowmans Grn, Wat. WD25 . .24 BX36
Bowmans Lea, SE23 . . . .122 DW87
Bowmans Meadow, Wall.
 SM6 . . . . .141 DH104
Bowmans Ms, E1
 off Hooper St 84 DU72
 N7 off Seven Sisters Rd . .65 DL62
Bowmans Pl, N7
 off Holloway Rd 65 DL62
Bowman's Trd Est, NW9
 off Westmoreland Rd . . .62 CM55
Bowmead, SE9 . . . . .125 EM89
Bowmont Cl, Brwd. CM13 . .55 GB44
Bowmore Wk, NW1
 off St. Paul's Cres 83 DK66
Bown Cl, Til. RM18 . . . . .111 GH82
Bowness Cl, E8
 off Beechwood Rd 84 DT65
Bowness Cres, SW15 . . . .118 CS92
Bowness Dr, Houns. TW4 . .96 BY84
Bowness Rd, SE6 . . . . . .123 EB87
 Bexleyheath DA7 . . . . .107 FB82
Bowness Way, Horn. RM12 .71 FG64
Bowood Rd, SW11 . . . . .100 DG84
 Enfield EN3 . . . . .31 DX40
Bowring Grn, Wat. WD19 . .40 BW50
⊖ Bow Road 85 DZ69
Bow Rd, E3 . . . . .85 DZ69
Bowrons Av, Wem. HA0 . . .79 CK66
Bowry Dr, Stai. (Wrays.)
 TW19 . . . . .113 AZ86
Bowsley Ct, Felt. TW13
 off Highfield Rd 115 BU88
Bowsprit, The, Cob. KT11 . .170 BW115
Bowsprit Pt, E14 . . . . . .103 EA76
Bow St, E15 . . . . .68 EE64
 WC2 . . . . .196 A9
Bowstridge La, Ch.St.G. HP8 . .36 AW51
Bowyer Cl, E6 . . . . .87 EM71
Bowyer Cres, Uxb. (Denh.)
 UB9 . . . . .57 BF58
Bowyer Pl, SE5 . . . . . . .102 DR80
Bowyers Cl, Ashtd. KT21 . .172 CM118
Bowyer St, SE5 . . . . . . .102 DQ80
Boxall Rd, SE21 . . . . . . .122 DS86
Boxford Cl, S.Croy. CR2 . .161 DX112
Boxgrove Rd, SE2 . . . . . .106 EW76
BOX HILL, Tad. 182 CP131
Boxhill Dr, Grays RM20 . . .110 FY79
Boxhill Rd, Dor. RH4 . . . .182 CL133
 Tadworth KT20 . . . . . .182 CP131
Box La, Bark. IG11 . . . . . .88 EV68
Boxley Rd, Mord. SM4 . . .140 DC98
Boxley St, E16 . . . . .205 P3
Boxmoor Rd, Har. HA3 . . .61 CH56
 Romford RM5 . . . . . . .51 FC50
Boxoll Rd, Dag. RM9 . . . .70 EZ63
Box Ridge Av, Pur. CR8 . . .159 DM112
Boxted Cl, Buck.H. IG9 . . .48 EL46
Boxtree La, Har. HA3 . . . .40 CC53
Boxtree Rd, Har. HA3 . . . .41 CD52
Boxtree Wk, Orp. BR5 . . .146 EX102
Boxwood Cl, West Dr. UB7
 off Hawthorne Way 94 BM75
Boxwood Way, Warl. CR6 .177 DX117
Boxworth Cl, N12 . . . . . .44 DD50
Boxworth Gro, N1 . . . . . .83 DM67
Boyard Rd, SE18 . . . . . .105 EP78
Boyce Cl, Borwd. WD6 . . .26 CL39
Boyce St, SE1 . . . . .200 C3
Boyce Way, E13 . . . . . . .86 EG70
Boycroft Av, NW9 . . . . . .62 CQ58
Boyd Av, Sthl. UB1 . . . . .78 BZ74
Boyd Cl, Kings.T. KT2
 off Crescent Rd 118 CN94
Boydell Ct, NW8
 off St. John's Wd Pk . . .82 DD66
Boyd Rd, SW19 . . . . . . .120 DD93
Boyd St, E1 . . . . .84 DU72
Boyfield St, SE1 . . . . . . .200 G5
Boyland Rd, Brom. BR1 . .124 EF92
Boyle Av, Stan. HA7 . . . .41 CG51
Boyle Cl, Uxb. UB10 . . . .76 BM68
Boyle Fm Island, T.Ditt. KT7 .137 CG100
Boyle Fm Rd, T.Ditt. KT7 . .137 CG100
Boyle St, W1 . . . . .195 K10
Boyne Av, NW4 . . . . . . .63 CX56
Boyne Rd, SE13 . . . . . . .103 EC83
 Dagenham RM10 . . . . .70 FA62
Boyne Ter Ms, W11 . . . . .81 CZ74
Boyseland Ct, Edg. HA8 . . .42 CQ47
Boyson Rd, SE17 . . . . . .102 DR79
Boyton Cl, E1
 off Stayner's Rd 85 DX70
 N8 . . . . .65 DL55
Boyton Rd, N8 . . . . .65 DL55
Brabant Ct, EC3 . . . . . . .197 M10
Brabant Rd, N22 . . . . . . .45 DM54
Brabazon Av, Wall. SM6 . .159 DL108
Brabazon Rd, Houns. TW5 . .96 BW80
 Northolt UB5 . . . . .78 CA68
Brabazon St, E14 . . . . . .85 EB72
Brabourne Cl, SE19 . . . .122 DS92
Brabourne Cres, Bexh. DA7 .106 EZ79
Brabourne Hts, NW7 . . . .42 CS48
Brabourne Ri, Beck. BR3 . .143 EC99
Brabourn Gro, SE15 . . . .102 DW82
Brace Cl, Wal.Cr. (Chsht.) EN7 .13 DP25
Bracewell Av, Grnf. UB6 . . .61 CF64
Bracewell Rd, W10 . . . . .81 CW71
Bracewood Gdns, Croy. CR0 .142 DT104
Bracey Ms, N4
 off Bracey St 65 DL61
Bracey St, N4 . . . . .65 DL61
Bracken, The, E4
 off Hortus Rd 47 EC47
Bracken Av, SW12 . . . . .120 DG86
 Croydon CR0 . . . . . . .143 EB104
Brackenbridge Dr, Ruis. HA4 .60 BX62
Brackenbury Gdns, W6 . . .99 CV76
Brackenbury Rd, N2 . . . .64 DC55
 W6 . . . . .99 CV76

Bre - Bro

Brent Grn Wk, Wem. HA9 . . . . 62 CQ62
Brentham Way, W5 . . . . .79 CK70
Brenthouse Rd, E9 . . . . .84 DV66
Brenthurst Rd, NW10 . . . . .81 CT65
Brentlands Dr, Dart. DA1 . . . .128 FN88
Brent La, Dart. DA1 . . . . .128 FM87
Brent Lea, Brent. TW8 . . . . . .97 CJ80
Brentmead Cl, W7 . . . . .79 CE73
Brentmead Gdns, NW10 . . . .80 CM68
Brentmead Pl, NW11
    off North Circular Rd 63 CX58
Brenton St, E14 . . . . .85 DY72
Brent Pk, NW10 . . . . .62 CR64
Brent Pk Rd, NW4 . . . . .63 CV59
    NW9 . . . . .63 CU60
Brent Pl, Barn. EN5 . . . . .28 DA43
Brent Rd, E16 . . . . .86 EG71
    SE18 . . . . .105 EP80
    Brentford TW8 . . . . .97 CJ79
    South Croydon CR2 . . . . . .160 DV109
    Southall UB2 . . . . .96 BW76
Brent Side, Brent. TW8 . . . . . .97 CJ79
Brentside Cl, W13 . . . . .79 CG70
Brentside Executive Cen, Brent.
    TW8 . . . . .97 CH79
Brent St, NW4 . . . . .63 CW56
Brent Ter, NW2 . . . . .63 CW61
Brentvale Av, Sthl. UB1 . . . . . .79 CD74
    Wembley HA0 . . . . .80 CM67
Brent Vw Rd, NW9 . . . . .63 CU59
Brent Way, N3 . . . . .44 DA51
    Brentford TW8 . . . . .97 CK80
    Dartford DA2 . . . . .128 FP86
    Wembley HA9 . . . . .80 CP65
Brentwick Gdns, Brent. TW8 . .98 CL77
BRENTWOOD 54 FV47
⇌ Brentwood 54 FW48
Brentwood Bypass, Brwd.
    CM14, CM15 . . . . .53 FR49
Brentwood Cl, SE9 . . . . .125 EQ88
ℍ Brentwood Comm Hosp & Minor
    Injuries Unit, Brwd. CM15 . . .54 FY46
Brentwood Ct, Add. KT15 . . .152 BH105
Brentwood Ho, SE18
    off Shooter's Hill Rd 104 EK80
★ Brentwood Mus, Brwd.
    CM14 . . . . .54 FW49
Brentwood Pl, Brwd. CM15 . . .54 FW46
Brentwood Rd, Brwd. CM13 . .55 GA49
    Grays RM16 . . . . .111 GH77
    Romford RM1, RM2 . . . . . . .71 FF58
Brereton Rd, N17 . . . . .46 DT52
Bressenden Pl, SW1 . . . . . . .199 J6
Bressey Av, Enf. EN1 . . . . . . .30 DU39
Bressey Gro, E18 . . . . .48 EF54
Bretlands Rd, Cher. KT16 . . . .133 BE103
Brett Cl, N16 off Yoakley Rd . . .66 DS61
    Northolt UB5
    off Broomcroft Av 78 BX69
Brett Ct, N9 . . . . .46 DW47
Brett Cres, NW10 . . . . .80 CR66
Brettell St, SE17
    off Merrow St 102 DR78
Brettenham Av, E17 . . . . .47 EA54
Brettenham Rd, E17 . . . . .47 EA54
    N18 . . . . .46 DV49
Brett Gdns, Dag. RM9 . . . . . . .88 EY66
Brettgrave, Epsom KT19 . . . .156 CQ110
Brett Ho Cl, SW15
    off Putney Heath La 119 CX86
Brett Pas, E8 off Kenmure Rd . .66 DV64
Brett Pl, Wat. WD24
    off The Harebreaks 23 BU37
    Barnet EN5 . . . . .27 CW43
Brevet Cl, Purf. RM19 . . . . . . .109 FR77
Brewer's Fld, Dart. DA2 . . . . .128 FJ90
Brewer's Grn, SW1 . . . . .199 M6
Brewers Hall Gdns, EC2 . . . . .197 J7
Brewers La, Rich. TW9 . . . . . .117 CK85
Brewer St, W1 . . . . .195 L10
    Redhill (Bletch.) RH1 . . . . .186 DQ131
Brewery Cl, Wem. HA0 . . . . . .61 CG64
Brewery La, Sev. TN13
    off High St 191 FJ125
    Twickenham TW1 . . . . .117 CF87
    West Byfleet (Byfleet)
    KT14 . . . . .152 BL113
Brewery Rd, N7 . . . . .83 DL66
    SE18 . . . . .105 ER78
    Bromley BR2 . . . . .144 EL102
    Woking GU21 . . . . .166 AX117
Brewery Sq, SE1
    off Horselydown La 84 DT74
Brewery Wk, Rom. RM1 . . . . . .71 FE57
Brewhouse La, E1 . . . . .202 E3
Brewhouse Rd, SE18 . . . . . . .105 EM77
Brewhouse St, SW15 . . . . .99 CY83
Brewhouse Wk, SE16 . . . . . . .203 K3
Brewhouse Yd, EC1 . . . . .196 F4
    Gravesend DA12
    off Queen St 131 GH86
Brewood Rd, Dag. RM8 . . . . . .88 EV65
Brewster Gdns, W10 . . . . .81 CW71
Brewster Ho, E14 . . . . .85 DZ73
Brewster Rd, E10 . . . . .67 EB60
Brian Av, S.Croy. CR2 . . . . . .160 DS112
Brian Cl, Horn. RM12 . . . . . . .71 FH63
Briane Rd, Epsom KT19 . . . . .156 CQ110
Brian Rd, Rom. RM6 . . . . .70 EW57
Briants Cl, Pnr. HA5 . . . . .40 BZ54
Briant St, SE14 . . . . .103 DX81
Briar Av, SW16 . . . . .121 DM94
Briar Banks, Cars. SM5 . . . . .158 DG109
Briar Cl, N2 . . . . .64 DB55
    N13 . . . . .46 DQ48
    Buckhurst Hill IG9 . . . . .48 EK47
    Hampton TW12 . . . . .116 BZ92
    Isleworth TW7 . . . . .117 CF85
    Waltham Cross (Chsht.)
    EN8 . . . . .14 DW29
    Warlingham CR6 . . . . .177 EA116
    West Byfleet KT14 . . . . . . .152 BJ111

Briar Ct, Sutt. SM3 . . . . .157 CW105
Briar Cres, Nthlt. UB5 . . . . . . .78 CB65
Briardale Gdns, NW3 . . . . .64 DA62
Briarfield Av, N3 . . . . .44 DB54
Briar Gdns, Brom. BR2 . . . . . .144 EF102
Briar Gro, S.Croy. CR2 . . . . . .160 DU113
Briar Hill, Pur. CR8 . . . . .159 DL111
Briaris Cl, N17 . . . . .46 DV52
Briar La, Cars. SM5 . . . . .158 DG109
    Croydon CR0 . . . . .161 EB105
Briar Pas, SW16 . . . . .141 DL97
Briar Pl, SW16 . . . . .141 DM97
Briar Rd, NW2 . . . . .63 CW63
    SW16 . . . . .141 DL97
    Bexley DA5 . . . . .127 FD90
    Harrow HA3 . . . . .61 CJ57
    Romford RM3 . . . . .52 FJ52
    Shepperton TW17 . . . . . . .134 BM99
    Twickenham TW2 . . . . .117 CE88
    Watford WD25 . . . . .7 BU34
    Woking (Send) GU23 . . . . .167 BB123
Briars, The, Bushey (Bushey Hth.)
    WD23 . . . . .41 CE45
    Rickmansworth (Sarratt)
    WD3 . . . . .22 BH36
    Slough SL3 . . . . .93 AZ78
    Waltham Cross (Chsht.)
    EN8 . . . . .15 DY31
Briars Ct, Lthd. KT22 . . . . . . .155 CD114
Briars Wk, Rom. RM3 . . . . . . .52 FL54
Briarswood Way, Orp. BR6 . . .163 ET106
Briar Wk, SW15 . . . . .99 CV84
    W10 off Droop St 81 CY70
    Edgware HA8 . . . . .42 CQ52
    West Byfleet KT14 . . . . . . .152 BG112
Briar Way, West Dr. UB7 . . . . .94 BN75
Briarwood, Bans. SM7
    off High St 174 DA115
Briarwood Cl, NW9 . . . . .62 CQ58
    Feltham TW13 . . . . .115 BS90
Briarwood Dr, Nthwd. HA6 . . . .39 BU54
Briarwood Rd, SW4 . . . . .121 DK85
    Epsom KT17 . . . . .157 CU107
Briary Cl, NW3 off Fellows Rd . .82 DE66
Briary Ct, Sid. DA14 . . . . .126 EV92
Briary Gdns, Brom. BR1 . . . . .124 EH92
Briary Gro, Edg. HA8 . . . . .42 CP54
Briary La, N9 . . . . .46 DT48
Brick Ct, EC4 . . . . .196 D9
    Grays RM17
    off Columbia Wf Rd 110 GA79
Brickcroft, Brox. EN10 . . . . . . .15 DY26
Brickenden Ct, Wal.Abb. EN9 . .16 EF33
Brickett Cl, Ruis. HA4 . . . . . . .59 BQ57
BRICKET WOOD, St.Alb. 8 BZ29
⇌ Bricket Wood 8 CA30
Brickfield Cl, Brent. TW8 . . . . .97 CJ80
Brickfield Cotts, SE18 . . . . . .105 ET79
Brickfield Fm Gdns, Orp.
    BR6 . . . . .163 EQ105
Brickfield La, Barn. EN5 . . . . . .27 CT44
    Hayes UB3 . . . . .95 BR79
Brickfield Rd, SW19 . . . . .120 DB91
    Epping CM16 . . . . .18 EX29
    Thornton Heath CR7 . . . . . .141 DP95
Brickfields, Har. HA2 . . . . .61 CD61
Brickfields La, Epp. CM16
    off Brickfield Rd 18 EX29
Brickfields Way, West Dr. UB7 . .94 BM76
Brick Kiln Cl, Wat. WD19 . . . . .24 BY44
Brick Kiln La, Oxt. RH8 . . . . . .188 EJ131
Brick La, E1 . . . . .84 DT71
    E2 . . . . .84 DT69
    Enfield EN1, EN3 . . . . .30 DV40
    Stanmore HA7
    off Honeypot La 41 CK52
Bricklayer's Arms Distribution
    Cen, SE1 . . . . .201 N9
Bricklayer's Arms Roundabout,
    SE1 off Old Kent Rd 102 DR76
Brickwall La, Ruis. HA4 . . . . . .59 BS60
Brickwood Cl, SE26 . . . . .122 DV90
Brickwood Rd, Croy. CR0 . . . .142 DS103
Brideale Cl, SE15
    off Colegrove Rd 102 DT80
Bride Ct, EC4 . . . . .196 F9
Bride La, EC4 . . . . .196 F9
Bridel Ms, N1
    off Colebrooke Row 83 DP67
Bride St, N7 . . . . .83 DM65
Bridewain St, SE1 . . . . .201 P6
Bridewell Pl, E1 . . . . .202 E3
    EC4 . . . . .196 F9
Bridford Ms, W1 . . . . .195 J6
Bridge, The, Har. HA3 . . . . . . .61 CE55
Bridge App, NW1 . . . . .82 DG66
Bridge Av, W6 . . . . .99 CW78
    W7 . . . . .79 CD71
    Upminster RM14 . . . . .72 FN61
Bridge Cl, W10
    off Kingsdown Cl 81 CX72
    Brentwood CM13 . . . . .55 FZ49
    Dartford DA2 . . . . .109 FR83
    Enfield EN1 . . . . .30 DV40
    Romford RM7 . . . . .71 FE58
    Staines TW18 . . . . .113 BE91
    Teddington TW11
    off Shacklegate La 117 CF91
    Walton-on-Thames KT12 . . .135 BT101
    West Byfleet (Byfleet)
    KT14 . . . . .152 BM112
    Woking GU21 . . . . .166 AW117
Bridge Cotts, Upmin. RM14 . . .73 FU64
Bridge Ct, Wok. GU21 . . . . . . .166 AX117
Bridge Dr, N13 . . . . .45 DM49
Bridge End, E17 . . . . .47 EC53
    Brentwood CM15
    off Hutton Rd 55 GE44
Bridgefield Cl, Bans. SM7 . . . .173 CW115
Bridgefield Rd, Sutt. SM1 . . . .158 DA107
Bridgefoot, SE1 . . . . .101 DL78
    Pot.B. EN6 . . . . .11 CX33
Bridge Gdns, Ashf. TW15 . . . .115 BQ94
    East Molesey KT8 . . . . .137 CD98

Bridge Gate, N21 off Ridge Av .46 DQ45
Bridgeham Cl, Wey. KT13
    off Mayfield Rd 152 BN106
Bridge Hill, Epp. CM16 . . . . . . .17 ET33
Bridge Ho Quay, E14 . . . . . . .204 E3
Bridgeland Rd, E16 . . . . .86 EG73
Bridge La, NW11 . . . . .63 CY57
    SW11 . . . . .100 DE81
    Virginia Water GU25 . . . . . .132 AY99
Bridgeman Rd, N1 . . . . .83 DM66
    Teddington TW11 . . . . .117 CG93
Bridgeman St, NW8 . . . . .194 B1
Bridge Meadows, SE14 . . . . . .103 DX79
Bridge Ms, Wok. GU21
    off Bridge Barn La 166 AX117
Bridgend Rd, SW18 . . . . .100 DC84
    Enfield EN1 . . . . .30 DW35
Bridgenhall Rd, Enf. EN1 . . . . .30 DT39
Bridgen Rd, Bex. DA5 . . . . . . .126 EY86
Bridge Pk, SW18 . . . . .120 DA85
Bridge Pl, SW1 . . . . .199 J8
    Amersham HP6 . . . . .20 AT38
    Croydon CR0 . . . . .142 DR101
    Watford WD17 . . . . .24 BX43
Bridgepoint Pl, E1 . . . . .202 C2
Bridge Rd, E6 . . . . .87 EM66
    E15 . . . . .85 ED66
    E17 . . . . .67 DZ59
    N9 off The Broadway 46 DU48
    N22 . . . . .45 DL53
    NW10 . . . . .80 CS65
    Beckenham BR3 . . . . .123 DZ94
    Bexleyheath DA7 . . . . .106 EY82
    Chertsey KT16 . . . . .134 BH101
    Chessington KT9 . . . . .156 CL106
    East Molesey KT8 . . . . .137 CE98
    Epsom KT17 . . . . .157 CT112
    Erith DA8 . . . . .107 FF81
    Grays RM17 . . . . .110 GB78
    Hounslow TW3 . . . . .97 CD82
    Isleworth TW7 . . . . .97 CD80
    Kings Langley WD4 . . . . .7 BQ33
    Orpington BR5 . . . . .146 EV100
    Rainham RM13 . . . . .89 FF70
    Southall UB2 . . . . .96 BZ75
    Sutton SM2 . . . . .158 DB107
    Twickenham TW1 . . . . .117 CH86
    Uxbridge UB8 . . . . .76 BJ68
    Wallington SM6 . . . . .159 DJ106
    Wembley HA9 . . . . .62 CN62
    Weybridge KT13 . . . . .152 BM105
Bridge Row, Croy. CR0
    off Cross Rd 142 DR102
Bridges Cl, SW11 . . . . .100 DD83
Bridges Dr, Dart. DA1 . . . . . . .128 FP85
Bridges La, Croy. CR0 . . . . . .159 DL105
Bridges Pl, SW6 . . . . .99 CZ81
Bridges Rd, SW19 . . . . .120 DB93
    Stanmore HA7 . . . . .41 CF50
Bridges Rd Ms, SW19
    off Bridges Rd 120 DB93
Bridge St, SW1 . . . . .199 P5
    W4 . . . . .98 CR77
    Leatherhead KT22 . . . . . . .171 CG122
    Pinner HA5 . . . . .60 BX55
    Richmond TW9 . . . . .117 CK85
    Slough (Colnbr.) SL3 . . . . . .93 BD80
    Staines TW18 . . . . .113 BE91
    Walton-on-Thames KT12 . . .135 BT102
Bridge Ter, E15 off Bridge Rd . .85 ED66
Bridgetown Cl, SE19
    off St. Kitts Ter 122 DS92
Bridge Vw, W6 . . . . .99 CW78
Bridgeview Ct, Ilf. IG6 . . . . . . .49 ER51
Bridgewater Cl, Chis. BR7 . . . .145 ES97
Bridgewater Ct, Slou. SL3 . . . .93 BA78
Bridgewater Gdns, Edg. HA8 . .42 CM54
Bridgewater Rd, Ruis. HA4 . . . .59 BU63
    Wembley HA0 . . . . .79 CJ66
    Weybridge KT13 . . . . .153 BR107
Bridgewater Sq, EC2 . . . . . . .197 H6
Bridgewater St, EC2 . . . . .197 H6
Bridgewater Way, Bushey
    WD23 . . . . .24 CB44
Bridge Way, N11
    off Pymmes Grn Rd 45 DJ48
    NW11 . . . . .63 CZ57
Bridgeway, Bark. IG11 . . . . . . .87 ET66
Bridge Way, Cob. KT11 . . . . . .153 BT113
    Coulsdon CR5 . . . . .174 DE119
    Twickenham TW2 . . . . .116 CC87
    Uxbridge UB10 . . . . .59 BP64
Bridgeway, Wem. HA0 . . . . . . .80 CL66
Bridgeway St, NW1 . . . . .195 M1
Bridge Wf, Cher. KT16 . . . . . .134 BJ102
Bridge Wf Rd, Islw. TW7
    off Church St 97 CH83
Bridgewood Cl, SE20 . . . . . . .122 DV94
Bridgewood Rd, SW16 . . . . . .121 DK94
    Worcester Park KT4 . . . . . .157 CU105
Bridge Wks, Uxb. UB8 . . . . . . .76 BJ70
Bridgford St, SW18 . . . . .120 DC90
Bridgman Rd, W4 . . . . .98 CQ76
Bridgwater Cl, Rom. RM3 . . . . .52 FK50
Bridgwater Rd, E15 . . . . .85 EC67
    Romford RM3 . . . . .52 FJ50
Bridgwater Wk, Rom. RM3 . . . .52 FK50
Bridle Cl, Enf. EN3 . . . . .31 DZ37
    Epsom KT19 . . . . .156 CR106
    Kingston upon Thames
    KT1 . . . . .137 CK98
    Sunbury-on-Thames TW16
    off Forge La 135 BU97
Bridle End, Epsom KT17 . . . . .157 CT114
Bridle La, W1 . . . . .195 L10
    Cobham KT11 . . . . .170 CB115
    Leatherhead KT22 . . . . . . .170 CB115
    Rickmansworth (Loud.)
    WD3 . . . . .22 BK41
    Twickenham TW1
    off Crown Rd 117 CH86
Bridle Path, Croy. CR0 . . . . . .141 DM104
    Watford WD17 . . . . .23 BV40
Bridle Path, The, Epsom
    KT17 . . . . .157 CV110

Bridle Path, The, Wdf.Grn. IG8 . .48 EE52
Bridlepath Way, Felt. TW14 . . .115 BS88
Bridle Rd, Croy. CR0 . . . . .143 EA104
    Epsom KT17 . . . . .157 CT113
    Esher (Clay.) KT10 . . . . . . .155 CH107
    Pinner HA5 . . . . .60 BW58
Bridle Rd, The, Pur. CR8 . . . . .159 DL110
Bridle Way, Croy. CR0 . . . . . . .161 EA106
    Orpington BR6 . . . . .163 EQ105
Bridle Way, The, Croy. CR0 . . .161 DY110
Bridleway, The, Wall. SM6 . . . .159 DJ105
Bridleway Cl, Epsom KT17 . . .157 CW110
Bridlington Cl, West. (Bigg.H.)
    TN16 . . . . .178 EH119
Bridlington Rd, N9 . . . . .46 DV46
    Watford WD19 . . . . .40 BX48
Bridport Av, Rom. RM7 . . . . . . .71 FB58
Bridport Pl, N1 . . . . .84 DR68
Bridport Rd, N18 . . . . .46 DS50
    Greenford UB6 . . . . .78 CB67
    Thornton Heath CR7 . . . . . .141 DN97
Bridport Ter, SW8
    off Wandsworth Rd 101 DK81
Bridstow Pl, W2 off Talbot Rd .82 DA72
Brief St, SE5 . . . . .101 DP81
Brier Lea, Tad. (Lwr.Kgswd.)
    KT20 . . . . .183 CZ126
Brierley, Croy. (New Adgtn.)
    CR0 . . . . .161 EB107
Brierley Av, N9 . . . . .46 DW46
Brierley Cl, SE25 . . . . .142 DU98
    Hornchurch RM11 . . . . .72 FJ58
Brierley Rd, E11 . . . . .67 ED63
    SW12 . . . . .121 DJ89
Brierly Gdns, E2
    off Royston St 84 DW68
Brier Rd, Tad. KT20 . . . . .173 CV119
Briery Ct, Rick. (Chorl.) WD3 . .22 BG42
Briery Fld, Rick. (Chorl.) WD3 . .22 BG42
Briery Way, Amer. HP6 . . . . . . .20 AS37
Brigade Cl, Har. HA2 . . . . .61 CD61
Brigade Pl, Cat. CR3 . . . . . . .176 DQ122
Brigade St, SE3
    off Royal Par 104 EF82
Brigadier Av, Enf. EN2 . . . . . . .30 DQ39
Brigadier Hill, Enf. EN2 . . . . . .30 DQ38
Briggeford Cl, E5
    off Geldeston Rd 66 DU61
Briggs Cl, Mitch. CR4 . . . . . . .141 DH95
Bright Cl, Belv. DA17 . . . . . . .106 EX77
Brightfield Rd, SE12 . . . . .124 EF85
Brightlands, Grav. (Nthflt.)
    DA11 . . . . .130 GE91
Brightlands Rd, Reig. RH2 . . . .184 DC132
Brightling Rd, SE4 . . . . .123 DZ86
Brightlingsea Pl, E14 . . . . .85 DZ73
Brightman Rd, SW18 . . . . .120 DD88
Brighton Av, E17 . . . . .67 DZ57
Brighton Cl, Add. KT15 . . . . . .152 BJ106
    Uxbridge UB10 . . . . .77 BP66
Brighton Dr, Nthlt. UB5 . . . . . . .78 CA65
Brighton Gro, SE14 . . . . .103 DY81
Brighton Rd, E6 . . . . .87 EN69
    N2 . . . . .44 DC54
    N16 . . . . .66 DS63
    Addlestone KT15 . . . . .152 BJ105
    Banstead SM7 . . . . .157 CZ114
    Coulsdon CR5 . . . . .175 DJ119
    Purley CR8 . . . . .160 DQ110
    South Croydon CR2 . . . . . .160 DQ106
    Surbiton KT6 . . . . .137 CJ100
    Sutton SM2 . . . . .158 DB109
    Tadworth KT20 . . . . .173 CV119
    Watford WD24 . . . . .23 BU38
Brighton Ter, SW9 . . . . .101 DM84
Brights Av, Rain. RM13 . . . . . . .89 FH70
Brightside, The, Enf. EN3 . . . . .31 DX39
Brightside Av, Stai. TW18 . . . .114 BJ94
Brightside Rd, SE13 . . . . .123 ED86
Bright St, E14 . . . . .85 EB72
Brightview Cl, St.Alb. (Brick.Wd.)
    AL2 . . . . .8 BY29
Brightwell Cl, Croy. CR0
    off Sumner Rd 141 DN102
Brightwell Cres, SW17 . . . . . .120 DF92
Brightwell Rd, Wat. WD18 . . . . .23 BU43
Brig Ms, SE8
    off Watergate St 103 EA79
Brigstock Rd, Belv. DA17 . . . .107 FB77
    Coulsdon CR5 . . . . .175 DH115
    Thornton Heath CR7 . . . . . .141 DN99
Brill Pl, NW1 . . . . .195 N1
Brimfield Rd, Purf. RM19 . . . . .109 FR77
Brim Hill, N2 . . . . .64 DC56
Brimpsfield Cl, SE2 . . . . .106 EV76
BRIMSDOWN, Enf. 31 DY41
⇌ Brimsdown 31 DY41
Brimsdown Av, Enf. EN3 . . . . . .31 DY41
Brimsdown Ind Est, Enf. EN3 . .31 DZ40
Brimshot La, Wok. (Chobham)
    GU24 . . . . .150 AS109
Brimstone Cl, Orp. BR6 . . . . . .164 EW108
Brindle Gate, Sid. DA15 . . . . .125 ES88
Brindles, Horn. RM11 . . . . .72 FL56
Brindles, The, Bans. SM7 . . . .173 CZ117
Brindley Cl, Bexh. DA7 . . . . . .107 FB83
    Wembley HA0 . . . . .79 CJ67
Brindley Ho, SW2
    off New Pk Rd 121 DL87
Brindley St, SE14 . . . . .103 DZ81
Brindley Way, Brom. BR1 . . . .124 EG92
    Southall UB1 . . . . .78 CB73
Brindwood Rd, E4 . . . . .47 DZ48
Brinkburn Cl, SE2 . . . . .106 EU77
    Edgware HA8 . . . . .42 CP54
Brinkburn Gdns, Edg. HA8 . . . .62 CN55
Brinkley, Kings.T. KT1
    off Burritt Rd 138 CN96
Brinkley Rd, Wor.Pk. KT4 . . . .139 CV103
Brinklow Cres, SE18 . . . . .105 EP80
Brinklow Ho, W2 . . . . .82 DB71
Brinkworth Rd, Ilf. IG5 . . . . . . .68 EL55
Brinkworth Way, E9 . . . . .85 DZ65
Brinley Cl, Wal.Cr. (Chsht.)
    EN8 . . . . .15 DX31
Brinsdale Rd, NW4 . . . . .63 CX56
Brinsley Rd, Har. HA3 . . . . .41 CD54

Brinsley St, E1
    off Watney St 84 DV72
Brinsmead, St.Alb. (Park St.)
    AL2 . . . . .9 CD27
Brinsmead Rd, Rom. RM3 . . . .52 FN54
Brinsworth Cl, Twick. TW2 . . . .117 CD89
Brinton Wk, SE1 . . . . .200 F3
Brion Pl, E14 . . . . .85 EC71
Brisbane Av, SW19 . . . . .140 DB95
Brisbane Ct, N10
    off Sydney Rd 45 DH52
Brisbane Ho, Til. RM18
    off Leicester Rd 111 GF81
Brisbane Rd, E10 . . . . .67 EB61
    W13 . . . . .97 CG75
    Ilford IG1 . . . . .69 EP59
Brisbane St, SE5 . . . . .102 DR80
Briscoe Cl, E11 . . . . .68 EF61
Briscoe Rd, SW19 . . . . .120 DD93
    Rainham RM13 . . . . .90 FJ68
Briset Rd, SE9 . . . . .104 EK83
Briset St, EC1 . . . . .196 F6
Briset Way, N7 . . . . .65 DM61
Brisson Cl, Esher KT10 . . . . . .154 BZ107
Bristol Cl, Stai. (Stanw.)
    TW19 . . . . .114 BL86
Bristol Gdns, SW15
    off Portsmouth Rd 119 CW87
    W9 . . . . .82 DB70
Bristol Ms, W9
    off Bristol Gdns 82 DB70
Bristol Pk Rd, E17 . . . . .67 DY56
Bristol Rd, E7 . . . . .86 EJ65
    Gravesend DA12 . . . . .131 GK90
    Greenford UB6 . . . . .78 CB67
    Morden SM4 . . . . .140 DC99
Bristol Way, Slou. SL1 . . . . . . .74 AT74
Briston Gro, N8 . . . . .65 DL58
Briston Ms, NW7 . . . . .43 CU52
Bristow Rd, SE19 . . . . .122 DS92
    Bexleyheath DA7 . . . . .106 EY81
    Croydon CR0 . . . . .159 DL105
    Hounslow TW3 . . . . .96 CC83
★ Britain at War Experience,
    SE1 . . . . .201 M3
Britannia Cl, SW4
    off Bowland Rd 101 DK84
    Erith DA8 off Manor Rd 107 FF79
    Northolt UB5 . . . . .78 BX69
Britannia Dr, Grav. DA12 . . . . .131 GM92
Britannia Gate, E16 . . . . .205 N2
Britannia Ind Est, Slou. (Colnbr.)
    SL3 . . . . .93 BE82
Britannia La, Twick. TW2 . . . . .116 CC87
Britannia Rd, E14 . . . . .204 A8
    N12 . . . . .44 DC48
    SW6 . . . . .100 DB80
    Brentwood CM14 . . . . .54 FW50
    Ilford IG1 . . . . .69 EP62
    Surbiton KT5 . . . . .138 CM101
    Waltham Cross EN8 . . . . . . .15 DZ34
Britannia Row, N1 . . . . .83 DP67
Britannia St, WC1 . . . . .196 B2
Britannia Wk, N1 . . . . .197 K2
Britannia Way, NW10 . . . . .80 CP70
    SW6 off Britannia Rd 100 DB81
    Staines (Stanw.) TW19 . . . .114 BK87
★ British Dental Association
    Mus, W1 off Wimpole St . .195 H7
British Gro, W4 . . . . .99 CT78
British Gro Pas, W4 . . . . .99 CT78
British Gro S, W4
    off British Gro Pas 99 CT78
British Legion Rd, E4 . . . . .48 EF47
British Leyland, NW1 . . . . . . .195 N2
★ British Lib Newspaper
    Collection, NW9 . . . . .62 CS55
★ British Medical Association,
    WC1 . . . . .195 N4
★ British Mus, WC1 . . . . .195 P7
British St, E3 . . . . .85 DZ69
Briton Cl, S.Croy. CR2 . . . . . .160 DS111
Briton Cres, S.Croy. CR2 . . . .160 DS111
Briton Hill Rd, S.Croy. CR2 . . .160 DS110
Brittain Rd, Dag. RM8 . . . . . . .70 EY62
    Walton-on-Thames KT12 . . .154 BX106
Brittains La, Sev. TN13 . . . . . .190 FF123
Britten Cl, NW11 . . . . .64 DB60
    Borehamwood (Elstree) WD6
    off Rodgers Cl 25 CK44
Brittenden Cl, Orp. BR6 . . . . . .163 ES107
Britten Dr, Sthl. UB1 . . . . .78 CA72
Britten St, SW3 . . . . .100 DE78
Britton Cl, SE6
    off Brownhill Rd 123 ED87
Britton St, EC1 . . . . .196 F5
Brixham Cres, Ruis. HA4 . . . . .59 BU60
Brixham Gdns, Ilf. IG3 . . . . . . .69 ES64
Brixham Rd, Well. DA16 . . . . . .106 EX81
Brixham St, E16 . . . . .87 EM74
BRIXTON, SW2 . . . . .101 DL84
⇌ Brixton 101 DN84
⊖ Brixton 101 DN84
★ Brixton Academy, The,
    SW9 . . . . .101 DM83
Brixton Est, Edg. HA8 . . . . . . .42 CP54
Brixton Hill, SW2 . . . . .121 DL87
Brixton Hill Pl, SW2
    off Brixton Hill 121 DL87
Brixton Oval, SW2 . . . . .101 DN84
Brixton Rd, SW9 . . . . .101 DN84
    Watford WD24 . . . . .23 BV39
Brixton Sta Rd, SW9 . . . . . . .101 DN84
Brixton Water La, SW2 . . . . . .121 DM85
Broad Acre, St.Alb. (Brick.Wd.)
    AL2 . . . . .8 BY30
Broadacre, Stai. TW18 . . . . . .114 BG92
Broadacre Cl, Uxb. UB10 . . . . .59 BP62
Broadbent Cl, N6 . . . . .65 DH60
Broadbent St, W1 . . . . .195 H10
Broadberry Ct, N18 . . . . .46 DV50
Broadbridge Cl, SE3 . . . . .104 EG80
Broad Cl, Walt. KT12 . . . . .136 BX104
Broadcoombe, S.Croy. CR2 . . .160 DW108
Broad Ct, WC2 . . . . .196 A9
Broadcroft Av, Stan. HA7 . . . . .41 CK54
Broadcroft Rd, Orp. BR5 . . . . .145 ER101

Broad Ditch Rd, Grav. (Sthflt.)
DA13 . . . . .130 GC94
Broadeaves Cl, S.Croy. CR2 .160 DS106
Broadfield Cl, NW2 . . . . . . .63 CW62
Croydon CR0
off Progress Way 141 DM103
Romford RM1 . . . . .71 FF57
Tadworth KT20 . . . . . . .173CW120
Broadfield Ct, Bushey
(Bushey Hth.) WD23 . . . .41 CE47
Broadfield La, NW1 . . . . . . .83 DL66
Broadfield Rd, SE6 . . . . . . .124 EE87
Broadfields, E.Mol. KT8 . . . .137 CD100
Harrow HA2 . . . . .40 CB54
Waltham Cross (Chsht.)
EN7 . . . . .13 DP29
Broadfields Av, N21 . . . . . . .45 DN45
Edgware HA8 . . . . .42 CP49
Broadfields Hts, Edg. HA8 . . .42 CP49
Broadfields La, Wat. WD19 . . .39 BV46
Broadfield Sq, Enf. EN1 . . . . .30 DV40
Broadfields Way, N6 . . . . . . .63 CT64
Broadfield Way, Buck.H. IG9 . .48 EJ48
Broadford La, Wok. (Chobham)
GU24 . . . . .150 AT112
BROADGATE, EC2 . . . . . . .197 L6
Broadgate, E13 . . . . .86 EJ68
EC2 off Liverpool St 84 DS71
Waltham Abbey EN9 . . . . .16 EF33
Broadgate Circle, EC2 . . . . .197 M6
Broadgate Rd, E16 . . . . .86 EK72
Broadgates Av, Barn. EN4 . . .28 DB39
Broadgates Rd, SW18
off Ellerton Rd 120 DD88
BROAD GREEN, Croy. 141 DN100
Broad Grn Av, Croy. CR0 . . .141 DP101
Broadgreen Rd, Wal.Cr. (Chsht.)
EN7 . . . . .14 DR26
Broadham Grn Rd, Oxt. RH8 .187 ED132
Broadham Pl, Oxt. RH8 . . . .187 ED131
Broadhead Strand, NW9 . . . .43 CT53
Broadheath Dr, Chis. BR7 . . .125 EM92
Broad Highway, Cob. KT11 . .154 BX114
Broadhinton Rd, SW4 . . . . .101 DH83
Broadhurst, Ashtd. KT21 . . .172 CL116
Broadhurst Av, Edg. HA8 . . .42 CP49
Ilford IG3 . . . . .69 ET63
Broadhurst Cl, NW6
off Broadhurst Gdns 82 DC65
Richmond TW10
off Lower Gro Rd 118 CM85
Broadhurst Gdns, NW6 . . . .82 DB65
Chigwell IG7 . . . . .49 EQ49
Ruislip HA4 . . . . .60 BW61
Broadhurst Wk, Rain. RM13 . .89 FG65
Broadlake Cl, St.Alb. (Lon.Col.)
AL2 . . . . .9 CK27
Broadlands, Felt. TW13 . . . .116 BZ90
Grays (Bad.Dene) RM17
off Bankfoot 110 FZ78
Broadlands Av, SW16 . . . . .121 DL89
Enfield EN3 . . . . .30 DV41
Shepperton TW17 . . . . . .135 BQ100
Broadlands Cl, N6 . . . . .64 DG59
SW16 . . . . .121 DL89
Enfield EN3 . . . . .30 DV41
Waltham Cross EN8 . . . . .15 DX34
Broadlands Dr, Warl. CR6 . . .176 DW119
Broadlands Rd, N6 . . . . .64 DF59
Bromley BR1 . . . . .124 EH91
Broadlands Way, N.Mal. KT3 .139 CT100
Broad La, EC2 . . . . .197 M6
N8 off Tottenham La 65 DM57
N15 . . . . .66 DT56
Dartford DA2 . . . . .127 FG91
Hampton TW12 . . . . . . .116 CA93
Broad Lawn, SE9 . . . . .125 EN89
Broadlawns Ct, Har. HA3 . . .41 CF53
Broadley Gdns, Rad. (Shenley)
WD7 off Queens Way 10 CL32
Broadley St, NW8 . . . . . . .194 A6
Broadley Ter, NW1 . . . . . . .194 C5
Broadmark Rd, Slou. SL2 . . .74 AV73
Broadmayne, SE17 . . . . . . .201 K10
Broadmead, SE6 . . . . .123 EA90
Broad Mead, Ashtd. KT21 . . .172 CM117
Broadmead Av, Wor.Pk. KT4 .139 CU101
Broadmead Cl, Hmptn. TW12 .116 CA93
Pinner HA5 . . . . .40 BY52
Broadmead Est, Wdf.Grn. IG8 .48 EJ52
Broadmead Rd, Hayes UB4 . . .78 BY70
Northolt UB5 . . . . .78 BY70
Woking (Old Wok.) GU22,
GU23 . . . . .167 BB122
Woodford Green IG8 . . . . .48 EG51
Broadmeads, Wok. (Send)
GU23 off Broadmead Rd .167 BB122
Broad Oak, Sun. TW16 . . . .115 BT93
Woodford Green IG8 . . . . .48 EH50
Broadoak Av, Enf. EN3 . . . . .31 DX35
Broad Oak Cl, E4
off Royston Av 47 EA50
Broadoak Cl, Dart. (Sutt.H.)
DA4 . . . . .128 FN93
Broad Oak Cl, Orp. BR5 . . . .146 EU96
Broadoak Rd, Erith DA8 . . . .107 FD80
Broadoaks, Epp. CM16 . . . .17 ET31
Surbiton KT6 . . . . .138 CP102
Broadoaks Cres, W.Byf. KT14 .152 BH114
Broadoaks Way, Brom. BR2 . .144 EF99
Broad Platts, Slou. SL3 . . . . .92 AX76
Broad Ride, Egh. TW20 . . . .132 AU96
Virginia Water GU25 . . . .132 AU96
Broad Rd, Swans. DA10 . . . .130 FY86
Broad Sanctuary, SW1 . . . . .199 N5
Broadstone Pl, W1 . . . . . . .194 F7
Broadstone Rd, Horn. RM12 . .71 FG61
Broad St, Dag. RM10 . . . . . .88 FA66
Teddington TW11 . . . . . .117 CF93
Broad St Av, EC2 . . . . .197 M7
Broad St Pl, EC2 . . . . .197 L7
Broadstrood, Loug. IG10 . . . .33 EN38
Broadvw, NW9 . . . . .62 CN58
Broadview Av, Grays RM16 . .110 GD75
Broadview Rd, SW16 . . . . . .121 DK94
Broadwalk, E18 . . . . .68 EF55
Broad Wk, N21 . . . . .45 DM47

Broad Wk, NW1 . . . . .195 H3
SE3 . . . . .104 EJ83
W1 . . . . .198 F2
Caterham CR3 . . . . .176 DT122
Coulsdon CR5 . . . . .174 DG123
Croydon CR0 . . . . .161 DY110
Epsom KT18 off Chalk La .172 CS117
Epsom (Burgh Hth.) KT18 .173 CX119
Broadwalk, Har. HA2 . . . . . .60 CA57
Broad Wk, Houns. TW5 . . . .96 BX81
Orpington BR6 . . . . .146 EX104
Richmond TW9 . . . . .98 CM80
Sevenoaks TN15 . . . . . .191 FL128
Broad Wk, The, W8 . . . . . . .82 DB74
East Molesey KT8 . . . . . .137 CF97
Broadwalk, The, Nthwd. HA6 .39 BQ54
Broadwalk Ct, W8 . . . . .82 DA74
Broad Wk La, NW11 . . . . . .63 CZ59
Broad Wk N, The, Brwd.
CM13 . . . . .55 GA49
Broadwalk Shop Cen, Edg.
HA8 . . . . .42 CP51
Broad Wk S, The, Brwd. CM13 .55 GA49
Broadwall, SE1 . . . . .200 E2
Broadwater, Pot.B. EN6 . . . .12 DB30
Broadwater Cl, Stai. (Wrays.)
TW19 . . . . .113 AZ87
Walton-on-Thames KT12 .153 BU106
Woking GU21 . . . . .151 BD112
Broad Water Cres, Wey. KT13
off Churchill Av 135 BQ104
Broadwater Gdns, Orp. BR6 .163 EP105
Uxbridge (Hare.) UB9 . . . .58 BH56
Broadwater La, Uxb. (Hare.)
UB9 . . . . .58 BH56
Broadwater Pk, Uxb. (Denh.)
UB9 . . . . .58 BG58
Broadwater Pl, Wey. KT13
off Oatlands Dr 135 BS103
Broadwater Rd, N17 . . . . . .46 DS53
SE28 . . . . .105 ER76
SW17 . . . . .120 DE91
Broadwater Rd N, Walt.
KT12 . . . . .153 BT106
Broadwater Rd S, Walt.
KT12 . . . . .153 BT106
Broadway, E15 . . . . .85 ED66
SW1 . . . . .199 M6
W13 . . . . .79 CG74
Barking IG11 . . . . .87 EQ66
Bexleyheath DA6 . . . . . .106 EY84
Grays RM17 . . . . .110 GC79
Rainham RM13 . . . . .89 FG70
Romford RM2 . . . . .71 FG55
Staines TW18
off Kingston Rd 114 BH92
Surbiton KT6 . . . . .138 CP102
Swanley BR8 . . . . .147 FC100
Tilbury RM18 . . . . .111 GF82
Broadway, The, E4 . . . . .47 EC51
E13 . . . . .86 EH68
N8 . . . . .65 DL58
N9 . . . . .46 DU48
N14 off Winchmore Hill Rd .45 DK46
N22 . . . . .45 DN54
NW7 . . . . .42 CS50
SW13 off The Terrace 98 CS82
SW19 . . . . .119 CZ93
W5 . . . . .79 CK73
W7 . . . . .79 CE74
Addlestone (New Haw)
KT15 . . . . .152 BG110
Croydon CR0
off Croydon Rd 159 DL105
Dagenham RM8 . . . . . . .70 EZ61
Greenford UB6 . . . . .78 CC70
Harrow HA2 . . . . .41 CE54
Hornchurch RM12 . . . . . .71 FH63
Loughton IG10 . . . . .33 EQ42
Pinner HA5 . . . . .40 BZ52
Southall UB1 . . . . .78 BX73
Staines (Laleham) TW18 .134 BJ97
Stanmore HA7 . . . . .41 CJ50
Sutton (Cheam) SM3 . . . .157 CY107
Thames Ditton KT7
off Hampton Ct Way . . .137 CE102
Watford WD17 . . . . .24 BW41
Wembley HA9 off East La . .62 CL62
Woking GU21 . . . . .167 AZ117
Woodford Green IG8 . . . . .48 EH51
Broadway Av, Croy. CR0 . . .142 DR99
Twickenham TW1 . . . . . .117 CH86
Broadway Cl, S.Croy. CR2 . . .160 DV114
Woodford Green IG8 . . . . .48 EH51
Broadway Ct, SW19
off The Broadway 120 DA93
Broadway E, Uxb. (Denh.)
UB9 . . . . .58 BG58
Broadway Gdns, Mitch. CR4 .140 DE98
Broadway Ho, Brom. BR1
off Elmfield Pk 144 EG97
Broadway Mkt, E8 . . . . .84 DV67
Broadway Mkt Ms, E8
off Brougham Rd 84 DU67
Broadway Ms, E5 . . . . .66 DT59
N13 off Elmdale Rd 45 DM50
N21 off Compton Rd 45 DP46
Broadway Par, N8 . . . . .65 DL58
Hayes UB3
off Coldharbour La 77 BU74
Hornchurch RM12
off The Broadway 71 FH63
Broadway Pl, SW19
off Hartfield Rd 119 CZ93
Broadway Shop Cen, W6
off Hammersmith Bdy 99 CW77
Bexleyheath DA6 . . . . . .106 FA84
Broadwick St, W1 . . . . .195 L10
Broadwood, Grav. DA11 . . . .131 GH92
Broadwood Av, Ruis. HA4 . . .59 BS58
Broadwood Ter, W8
off Pembroke Rd 99 CZ77
Broad Yd, EC1 . . . . .196 F5
Brocas St, SL4 . . . .
Brockbridge Ho, SW15
off Tangley Gro 119 CT86

Brockdish Av, Bark. IG11 . . . .69 ET64
Brockenhurst, W.Mol. KT8 . .136 BZ100
Brockenhurst Av, Wor.Pk.
KT4 . . . . .138 CS102
Brockenhurst Gdns, NW7 . . .42 CS50
Ilford IG1 . . . . .69 EQ64
Brockenhurst Ms, N18
off Lyndhurst Rd 46 DU49
Brockenhurst Rd, Croy. CR0 .142 DV101
Brockenhurst Way, SW16 . .141 DK96
Brocket Cl, Chig. IG7
off Burrow Rd 49 ET50
Brocket Rd, Grays RM16 . . .111 GG76
Brocket Way, Chig. IG7 . . . . .49 ES50
Brock Grn, S.Ock. RM15
off Cam Grn 91 FV72
Brockham Cl, SW19 . . . . . .119 CZ92
Brockham Cres, Croy.
(New Adgtn.) CR0 . . . . .161 ED108
Brockham Dr, SW2
off Fairview Pl 121 DM87
Ilford IG2 . . . . .69 EP58
Brockham Hill Pk, Tad. KT20 .182 CQ131
Brockham La, Bet. (Brock.)
RH3 . . . . .182 CN134
Brockham St, SE1 . . . . .201 J6
Brockhurst Cl, Stan. HA7 . . .41 CF51
Brockill Cres, SE4 . . . . .103 DY84
Brocklebank Ct, Whyt. CR3 .176 DU118
Brocklebank Rd, SE7 . . . . .205 P9
SW18 . . . . .120 DC87
Brocklehurst St, SE14 . . . . .103 DX80
Brocklesby Cl, Wat. WD24 . .24 BW41
Brocklesby Rd, SE25 . . . . . .142 DV98
BROCKLEY, SE4 . . . . .103 DY85
⇌ Brockley 103 DY83
Brockley Av, Stan. HA7 . . . . .42 CL48
Brockley Cl, Stan. HA7 . . . . .42 CL49
Brockley Combe, Wey. KT13 .153 BR105
Brockley Cres, Rom. RM5 . . .51 FC52
Brockley Cross, SE4
off Endwell Rd 103 DY83
Brockley Footpath, SE15 . . .102 DW84
Brockley Gdns, SE4 . . . . . .103 DZ82
Brockley Gro, SE4 . . . . . . .123 DZ85
Brockley Hall Rd, SE4 . . . . .123 DY86
Brockley Hill, Stan. HA7 . . . .41 CJ46
Brockley Ms, SE4 . . . . .123 DY85
Brockley Pk, SE23 . . . . .123 DY87
Brockley Ri, SE23 . . . . .123 DY87
Brockley Rd, SE4 . . . . .103 DZ83
Brockleyside, Stan. HA7 . . . .41 CK49
Brockley Vw, SE23 . . . . . . .123 DY87
Brockley Way, SE4 . . . . . . .123 DX85
Brockman Ri, Brom. BR1 . . .123 ED91
Brock Pl, E3 . . . . .85 EB70
Brock Rd, E13 . . . . .86 EH71
Brocks Dr, Sutt. SM3 . . . . . .139 CY104
Brockshot Cl, Brent. TW8 . . .97 CK79
Brocksparkwood, Brwd.
CM13 . . . . .55 GB48
Brock St, SE15
off Evelina Rd 102 DW83
Brockton Cl, Rom. RM1 . . . .71 FF56
Brockway Cl, E11 . . . . .68 EE60
Brockway Ho, Slou. SL3 . . . .93 BB78
Brockwell Cl, Orp. BR5 . . . .145 ET99
★ Brockwell Park, SE24 . . .121 DP86
Brockwell Pk Gdns, SE24 . . .121 DN87
Brockwell Pk Row, SW2 . . . .121 DN87
Brodewater Rd, Borwd. WD6 .26 CP40
Brodia Rd, N16 . . . . .66 DS62
Brodie Rd, E4 . . . . .47 EC46
Enfield EN2 . . . . .30 DQ38
Brodie St, SE1 . . . . .202 A10
Brodlove La, E1 . . . . .85 DX73
Brodrick Gro, SE2 . . . . .106 EV77
Brodrick Rd, SW17 . . . . . . .120 DE89
Brograve Gdns, Beck. BR3 . .143 EB96
Broke Fm Dr, Orp. BR6 . . . .164 EW109
Brokengate La, Uxb. (Denh.)
UB9 . . . . .57 BC60
Broken Wf, EC4 . . . . .197 H10
Brokes Cres, Reig. RH2 . . . .184 DA132
Brokesley St, E3 . . . . .85 DZ70
Brokes Rd, Reig. RH2 . . . . .184 DA132
Broke Wk, E8 . . . . .84 DU67
Bromar Rd, SE5 . . . . .102 DS83
Bromborough Grn, Wat.
WD19 . . . . .40 BW50
Brokdene Av, Wat. WD19 . . .39 BV45
Brokdene Rd, SE18 . . . . . . .105 ET77
Brook Dr, SE11 . . . . .200 E7
Harrow HA1 . . . . .60 CC56
Radlett WD7 . . . . .9 CF33
Ruislip HA4 . . . . .59 BS58
Sunbury-on-Thames TW16
off Chertsey Rd 115 BS92
Brooke Av, Har. HA2 . . . . . . .60 CC62
Brooke Cl, Bushey WD23 . . .40 CC45
Brookehowse Rd, SE6 . . . . .123 EB90
Brookend Rd, Sid. DA15 . . .125 ES88
Brooke Rd, E5 . . . . .66 DU62
E17 . . . . .67 EC56
N16 . . . . .66 DT62
Grays RM17 . . . . .110 GA78
Brooker Rd, Wal.Abb. EN9 . .15 EC34
Brookers Cl, Ashtd. KT21 . . .171 CJ117
Brooke's Ct, EC1 . . . . .196 D6
Brookes Mkt, EC1 . . . . .196 E6
Brooke St, EC1 . . . . .196 D7
Brooke Way, Bushey WD23
off Richfield Rd 40 CC45
Brook Fm Rd, Cob. KT11 . . .170 BX115
Brookfield, N6 . . . . .64 DG62
Epping (Thnwd.) CM16 . . .18 EW25
Woking GU21 . . . . .166 AV116
Brookfield Av, E17 . . . . .67 EC56
NW7 . . . . .43 CV51
W5 . . . . .79 CK70
Sutton SM1 . . . . .158 DD105
Brookfield Cen, Wal.Cr. (Chsht.)
EN8 off Halfhide La 15 DX27
Brookfield Cl, NW7 . . . . .43 CV51

Bromley Hill, Brom. BR1 . . .124 EE92
Ⓗ Bromley Hosp., Brom.
BR2 . . . . .144 EH98
Bromley La, Chis. BR7 . . . . .125 EQ94
Bromley Mall, The, Brom.
BR1 . . . . .144 EG97
★ Bromley Mus., Orp. BR6 .146 EV101
≷ Bromley North 144 EG95
BROMLEY PARK, Brom. . . .144 EE95
Bromley Pk, Brom. BR1
off London Rd 144 EF95
Bromley Pl, W1 . . . . .195 K6
Bromley Rd, E10 . . . . .67 EB58
E17 . . . . .47 EA54
N17 . . . . .46 DR48
N18 . . . . .46 DT53
SE6 . . . . .123 EB88
Beckenham BR3 . . . . . . .143 EB95
Bromley (Downham) BR1 .123 EC91
Bromley (Short.) BR2 . . . .143 EC96
Chislehurst BR7 . . . . . . .145 EP95
≷ Bromley South 144 EG97
Bromley St, E1 . . . . .85 DX71
BROMPTON, SW3 . . . . . . .198 B7
Brompton Arc, SW3 . . . . . .198 D5
Brompton Cl, SE20
off Selby Rd 142 DU96
Hounslow TW4 . . . . . . .116 BZ85
Brompton Dr, Erith DA8 . . . .107 FH80
Brompton Gro, N2 . . . . .64 DE56
★ Brompton Oratory, SW7
off Brompton Rd 198 B7
Brompton Pk Cres, SW6 . . .100 DB79
Brompton Pl, SW3 . . . . . . .198 C6
Brompton Rd, SW1 . . . . . . .198 C6
SW3 . . . . .198 B8
SW7 . . . . .198 C6
Brompton Sq, SW3 . . . . . . .198 B6
Brompton Ter, SE18
off Prince Imperial Rd . . .105 EN81
Bromwich Av, N6 . . . . .64 DG61
Bromyard Av, W3 . . . . .80 CS74
Bromyard Ho, SE15 . . . . . .102 DV80
BRONDESBURY, NW2 . . . . .81 CY66
⇌ Brondesbury 81 CZ66
Brondesbury Ct, NW2 . . . . .81 CW65
Brondesbury Ms, NW6
off Willesden La 82 DA66
BRONDESBURY PARK, NW6 .81 CX67
≷ Brondesbury Park 81 CX67
Brondesbury Pk, NW2 . . . . .81 CV65
NW6 . . . . .81 CX66
Brondesbury Rd, NW6 . . . . .81 CZ68
Brondesbury Vil, NW6 . . . . .81 CZ68
Bronsart Rd, SW6 . . . . .99 CY80
Bronson Way, Uxb. (Denh.)
UB9 . . . . .57 BF61
Bronson Rd, SW20 . . . . . . .139 CX96
Bronte Cl, E7 off Bective Rd . .68 EG63
Erith DA8 . . . . .107 FB80
Ilford IG2 . . . . .69 EN57
Tilbury RM18 . . . . .111 GJ82
Bronte Gro, Dart. DA1 . . . . .108 FM84
Bronte Ho, NW6 . . . . .82 DA69
Bronte Vw, Grav. DA12 . . . .131 GJ88
Bronti Cl, SE17 . . . . .102 DQ78
Bronze Age Way, Belv. DA17 .107 FC76
Erith DA8 . . . . .107 FC76
Bronze St, SE8 . . . . .103 EA80
Brook Av, Dag. RM10 . . . . . .89 FB66
Edgware HA8 . . . . .42 CP51
Wembley HA9 . . . . .62 CN62
Brookbank Av, W7 . . . . .79 CD71
Brookbank Rd, SE13 . . . . . .103 EA83
Brook Cl, NW7 off Frith Ct . . .43 CY52
SW17 . . . . .120 DG89
SW20 . . . . .139 CV97
W3 off West Lo Av 80 CN74
Borehamwood WD6 . . . . .26 CP41
Epsom KT19 . . . . .156 CS109
Romford RM2 . . . . .51 FF53
Ruislip HA4 . . . . .59 BS59
Staines (Stanw.) TW19 . .114 BM87
Brook Ct, Buck.H. IG9 . . . . .48 EH46
Brook Cres, E4 . . . . .47 EA49
N9 . . . . .46 DV49
Brookdale, N11 . . . . .45 DJ49
Brookdale Av, Upmin. RM14 .72 FN62
Brookdale Cl, Upmin. RM14 .72 FP62
Brookdale Rd, E17 . . . . .67 EA55
SE6 . . . . .123 EB86
Bexley DA5 . . . . .126 EY86
Brookdene Av, Wat. WD19 . .39 BV45
Brookdene Dr, Nthwd. HA6 . .39 BT52
Brookdene Rd, SE18 . . . . . .105 ET77
Brook Dr, SE11 . . . . .200 E7
Harrow HA1 . . . . .60 CC56
Radlett WD7 . . . . .9 CF33
Ruislip HA4 . . . . .59 BS58
Sunbury-on-Thames TW16
off Chertsey Rd 115 BS92
Brooke Av, Har. HA2 . . . . . . .60 CC62
Brooke Cl, Bushey WD23 . . .40 CC45
Brookehowse Rd, SE6 . . . . .123 EB90
Brookend Rd, Sid. DA15 . . .125 ES88
Brooke Rd, E5 . . . . .66 DU62
E17 . . . . .67 EC56
N16 . . . . .66 DT62
Grays RM17 . . . . .110 GA78
Brooker Rd, Wal.Abb. EN9 . .15 EC34
Brookers Cl, Ashtd. KT21 . . .171 CJ117
Brooke's Ct, EC1 . . . . .196 D6
Brookes Mkt, EC1 . . . . .196 E6
Brooke St, EC1 . . . . .196 D7
Brooke Way, Bushey WD23
off Richfield Rd 40 CC45
Brook Fm Rd, Cob. KT11 . . .170 BX115
Brookfield, N6 . . . . .64 DG62
Epping (Thnwd.) CM16 . . .18 EW25
Woking GU21 . . . . .166 AV116
Brookfield Av, E17 . . . . .67 EC56
NW7 . . . . .43 CV51
W5 . . . . .79 CK70
Sutton SM1 . . . . .158 DD105
Brookfield Cen, Wal.Cr. (Chsht.)
EN8 off Halfhide La 15 DX27
Brookfield Cl, NW7 . . . . .43 CV51

Brookfield Cl, Brent. CM13 . . .55 GC44
Chertsey (Ott.) KT16 . . . .151 BD107
Brookfield Ct, Grnf. UB6 . . . .78 CC69
Harrow HA3 . . . . .61 CK57
Brookfield Cres, NW7 . . . . . .43 CV51
Harrow HA3 . . . . .62 CL57
Brookfield Gdns, Esher (Clay.)
KT10 . . . . .155 CF107
Waltham Cross (Chsht.)
EN8 . . . . .15 DX27
Brookfield La, Wal.Cr. (Chsht.)
EN8 . . . . .15 DX27
Brookfield La W, Wal.Cr. (Chsht.)
EN8 . . . . .14 DV28
Brookfield Pk, NW5 . . . . . . .65 DH62
Brookfield Path, Wdf.Grn.
IG8 . . . . .48 EE51
Brookfield Retail Pk, Wal.Cr.
(Chsht.) EN8 . . . . .15 DX26
Brookfield Rd, E9 . . . . .85 DY65
N9 . . . . .46 DU48
W4 . . . . .98 CR75
Brookfields, Enf. EN3 . . . . . .31 DX42
Brookfields Av, Mitch. CR4 . .140 DE96
Brook Gdns, E4 . . . . .47 EB49
SW13 . . . . .99 CT83
Kingston upon Thames
KT2 . . . . .138 CQ95
Brook Gate, W1 . . . . .194 E1
Brook Grn, W6 . . . . .99 CX77
Woking (Chobham) GU24
off Brookleys 150 AT110
Brook Hill, Oxt. RH8 . . . . . .187 EC130
Barnet EN4 . . . . .28 DE43
Brookhill Cl, SE18 . . . . .105 EP78
Barnet EN4 . . . . .28 DE43
Brookhill Rd, SE18 . . . . . . .105 EP78
Barnet EN4 . . . . .28 DE43
Brookhouse Gdns, E4 . . . . . .48 EE49
Brookhurst Rd, Add. KT15 . .152 BH107
Brook Ind Est, Hayes UB4 . . .78 BX74
Brooking Rd, E7 . . . . .68 EG64
Brookland Cl, NW11 . . . . . . .64 DA56
Brookland Garth, NW11 . . . .64 DB56
Brookland Hill, NW11 . . . . . .64 DA56
Brookland Ri, NW11 . . . . . . .64 DA56
BROOKLANDS, Wey. 152 BM109
Brooklands, Dart. DA1 . . . . .128 FL88
Brooklands App, Rom. RM1 . .71 FD56
Brooklands Av, SW19 . . . . .120 DB89
Sidcup DA15 . . . . .125 ER89
Brooklands Business Pk, Wey.
KT13 . . . . .152 BN110
Brooklands Cl, Cob. KT11 . . .170 BY115
Romford RM7
off Marshalls Rd 71 FD56
Sunbury-on-Thames
TW16 . . . . .135 BS95
Brooklands Ct, Add. (New Haw)
KT15 . . . . .152 BK110
Brooklands Dr, Grnf. UB6 . . .79 CK67
Brooklands Gdns, Horn.
RM11 . . . . .72 FJ57
Potters Bar EN6 . . . . . . .11 CY32
Brooklands Ind Pk, Wey.
KT13 . . . . .152 BL110
Brooklands La, Rom. RM7 . . .71 FD56
Weybridge KT13 . . . . . .152 BM107
★ Brooklands Mus., Wey.
KT13 . . . . .152 BN109
Brooklands Pk, SE3 . . . . . .104 EG83
Brooklands Rd, Rom. RM7 . .71 FD56
Thames Ditton KT7 . . . . .137 CF102
Weybridge KT13 . . . . . .153 BP107
Brooklands Way, Red. RH1 .184 DE132
Brook La, SE3 . . . . .104 EH82
Bexley DA5 . . . . .126 EX86
Bromley BR1 . . . . .124 EG93
Woking (Send) GU23 . . . .167 BE122
Brook La N, Brent. TW8 . . . .97 CK78
Brooklea Cl, NW9 . . . . .42 CS53
Brookleys, Wok. (Chobham)
GU24 . . . . .150 AT110
Brooklyn Av, SE25 . . . . . . .142 DV98
Loughton IG10 . . . . .32 EL42
Brooklyn Cl, Cars. SM5 . . . .140 DE103
Woking GU22 . . . . .166 AY119
Brooklyn Ct, Wok. GU22
off Brooklyn Rd 166 AY119
Brooklyn Gro, SE25 . . . . . .142 DV98
Brooklyn Rd, SE25 . . . . . . .142 DV98
Bromley BR2 . . . . .144 EK99
Woking GU22 . . . . .166 AY119
Brooklyn Way, West Dr. UB7 . .94 BK76
Brookmans Av, Hat. AL9 . . . .11 CY26
Brookmans Cl, Upmin. RM14 .73 FS59
BROOKMANS PARK, Hat. . . .11 CY26
≷ Brookmans Park 11 CX27
Brookmarsh Ind Est, SE10
off Norman Rd 103 EB80
Brook Mead, Epsom KT19 . .156 CS107
Brookmead Av, Brom. BR1 . .145 EM99
Brookmead Cl, Orp. BR5 . . .146 EV101
Brook Meadow, N12 . . . . . .44 DB49
Brook Meadow Cl, Wdf.Grn.
IG8 . . . . .48 EE51
Brookmeadow Way, Wal.Abb. EN9
off Breach Barn Mobile
Home Pk 16 EH30
Brookmead Rd, Croy. CR0 . .141 DJ100
Brookmeads Est, Mitch. CR4 .140 DE99
Brookmead Way, Orp. BR5 . .146 EV100
Brook Ms N, W2
off Craven Ter 82 DD73
Brookmill Cl, Wat. WD19
off Brookside Rd 39 BV45
Brookmill Rd, SE8 . . . . . . .103 EA81
Brook Par, Chig. IG7
off High Rd 49 EP48
Brook Pk Cl, N21 . . . . .29 DP44
Brook Path, Loug. IG10 . . . . .32 EL42
Brook Ri, Chig. IG7 . . . . . . .49 EN48
Brook Rd, N8 . . . . .65 DL56
N22 . . . . .65 DM55

Bro - Buf

Brook Rd, NW2 . . . . .63 CU61
  Borehamwood WD6 . . . . . . .26 CN40
  Brentwood CM14 . . . . .54 FT48
  Buckhurst Hill IG9 . . . . .48 EG47
  Epping CM16 . . . . .18 EU33
  Gravesend (Nthflt.) DA11 . .130 GE88
  Ilford IG2 . . . . .69 ES58
  Loughton IG10 . . . . .32 EL43
  Redhill (Merst.) RH1 . . . . .185 DJ129
  Romford RM2 . . . . .51 FF53
  Surbiton KT6 . . . . .138 CL103
  Swanley BR8 . . . . .147 FD97
  Thornton Heath CR7 . . . . .142 DQ98
  Twickenham TW1 . . . . . . .117 CG86
  Waltham Cross EN8 . . . . . .15 DZ34
Brook Rd S, Brent. TW8 . . . . .97 CK79
Brooks Av, E6 . . . . .87 EM70
Brooksbank St, E9 . . . . .85 DX65
Brooksby Ms, N1
  off Brooksby St 83 DN66
Brooksby St, N1 . . . . .83 DN66
Brooksby's Wk, E9 . . . . .67 DX64
Brooks Cl, SE9 . . . . .125 EN89
  Weybridge KT13 . . . . .152 BN110
Brooks Ct, E15
  off Clays La 67 EB64
Brookscroft, Croy. CR0 . . . .161 DY110
Brookscroft Rd, E17 . . . . . . .47 EB53
Brookshill, Har. HA3 . . . . . . .41 CD50
Brookshill Av, Har. HA3 . . . . .41 CD50
Brookshill Dr, Har. HA3 . . . . .41 CD50
Brookside, N21 . . . . .29 DM44
  Barnet EN4 . . . . .28 DE44
  Carshalton SM5 . . . . .158 DG106
  Chertsey KT16 . . . . .133 BE101
  Hornchurch RM11 . . . . . . .72 FL57
  Ilford IG6 . . . . .49 EQ51
  Orpington BR6 . . . . .145 ET101
  Potters Bar EN6 . . . . .11 CU32
  Slough (Colnbr.) SL3 . . . . .93 BC80
  Uxbridge UB10 . . . . .76 BM66
  Waltham Abbey EN9
  off Broomstick Hall Rd . . .16 EE33
Brookside Av, Ashf. TW15 . .114 BJ92
  Staines (Wrays.) TW19 . . . .92 AY83
Brookside Cl, Barn. EN5 . . . .27 CY44
  Feltham TW13
  off Sycamore Cl 115 BU90
  Harrow (Kenton) HA2 . . . . .61 CK57
  Harrow (S.Har.) HA3 . . . . . .60 BY63
Brookside Cres, Pot.B. (Cuffley)
  EN6 . . . . .13 DL27
  Worcester Park KT4
  off Green La 139 CU102
Brookside Gdns, Enf. EN1 . .30 DV37
Brookside Rd, N9 . . . . .46 DV49
  N19 . . . . .65 DJ61
  NW11 . . . . .63 CY58
  Gravesend (Istead Rise)
  DA13 . . . . .131 GF94
  Hayes UB4 . . . . .78 BW73
  Watford WD19 . . . . .39 BV45
Brookside S, Barn. EN4 . . . . .44 DG45
Brookside Wk, N3 . . . . .43 CY54
  N12 . . . . .44 DA51
  NW4 . . . . .63 CY56
  NW11 . . . . .63 CY56
Brookside Way, Croy. CR0 . .143 DX100
Brooks La, W4 . . . . .98 CN78
Brook's Ms, W1 . . . . .195 H10
Brook Sq, SE18
  off Shooter's Hill Rd 104 EL81
Brooks Rd, E13 . . . . .86 EG67
  W4 . . . . .98 CN78
BROOK STREET, Brwd. 54 FS49
Brook St, N17 *off High Rd* . .46 DT54
  W1 . . . . .194 G10
  W2 . . . . .194 A10
  Belvedere DA17 . . . . .107 FB78
  Brentwood CM14 . . . . .54 FS50
  Erith DA8 . . . . .107 FB79
  Kingston upon Thames
  KT1 . . . . .138 CL96
Brooksville Av, NW6 . . . . . . .81 CY67
Brooks Way, Orp. BR5 . . . . .146 EW96
Brook Vale, Erith DA8 . . . . .107 FB81
Brookview Rd, SW16 . . . . . .121 DJ92
Brookville Rd, SW6 . . . . .99 CZ80
Brook Wk, N2 . . . . .44 DD53
  Edgware HA8 . . . . .42 CR51
Brookway, SE3 . . . . .104 EG83
Brook Way, Chig. IG7 . . . . . .49 EN48
  Leatherhead KT22 . . . . . .171 CG118
  Rainham RM13 . . . . .89 FH71
Brookwood Av, SW13 . . . . . .99 CT82
Brookwood Cl, Brom. BR2 . .144 EF98
Brookwood Rd, SW18 . . . . .119 CZ88
  Hounslow TW3 . . . . .96 CB81
Broom Av, Orp. BR5 . . . . . . .146 EV96
Broom Cl, Brom. BR2 . . . . . .144 EL100
  Esher KT10 . . . . .154 CB106
  Teddington TW11 . . . . . . .117 CK94
  Waltham Cross (Chsht.)
  EN7 . . . . .14 DU27
Broomcroft Av, Nthlt. UB5 . . .78 BW69
Broomcroft Cl, Wok. GU22 . .167 BD116
Broomcroft Dr, Wok. GU22 . .167 BD115
Broome Cl, Epsom (Headley)
  KT18 . . . . .182 CQ126
Broome Pl, S.Ock. (Aveley)
  RM15 . . . . .91 FR74
Broome Rd, Hmptn. TW12 . .116 BZ94
Broomer Pl, Wal.Cr. EN8 . . . .14 DW29
Broome Way, SE5 . . . . .102 DQ80
Broomfield, E17 . . . . .67 DZ59
  St. Albans (Park St.) AL2 . . . .8 CC27
  Staines TW18 . . . . .114 BG93
  Sunbury-on-Thames
  TW16 . . . . .135 BU95
Broomfield Av, N13 . . . . .45 DM50
  Broxbourne EN10 . . . . .15 DY26
  Loughton IG10 . . . . .33 EM44
Broomfield Cl, Rom. RM5 . . . .51 FD52
Broomfield Ct, Wey. KT13 . .153 BP107

Broomfield La, N13 . . . . .45 DM49
Broomfield Pl, W13
  off Broomfield Rd 79 CH74
Broomfield Ride, Lthd. (Oxshott)
  KT22 . . . . .155 CD112
Broomfield Ri, Abb.L. WD5 . . .7 BR32
Broomfield Rd, N13 . . . . .45 DL50
  W13 . . . . .79 CH74
  Addlestone (New Haw)
  KT15 . . . . .152 BH111
  Beckenham BR3 . . . . .143 DY97
  Bexleyheath DA6 . . . . . . .126 FA85
  Richmond TW9 . . . . .98 CM81
  Romford RM6 . . . . .70 EX59
  Sevenoaks TN13 . . . . . . .190 FF122
  Surbiton KT5 . . . . .138 CM102
  Swanscombe DA10 . . . . . .130 FY86
  Teddington TW11
  off Melbourne Rd 117 CJ93
Broomfields, Esher KT10 . . .154 CC106
Broomfield St, E14 . . . . .85 EA71
Broom Gdns, Croy. CR0 . . . .143 EA104
Broom Gro, Wat. WD17 . . . . .23 BU38
Broomgrove Gdns, Edg. HA8 .42 CN53
Broomgrove Rd, SW9 . . . . . .101 DM82
Broom Hall, Lthd. (Oxshott)
  KT22 . . . . .155 CD114
Broomhall End, Wok. GU21
  off Broomhall La 166 AY116
Broomhall La, Wok. GU21 . . .166 AY116
Broomhall Rd, S.Croy. CR2 . .160 DR109
  Woking GU21 . . . . .166 AY116
Broom Hill, Slou. (Stoke P.)
  SL2 . . . . .74 AU66
Broomhill Ct, Wdf.Grn. IG8
  off Broomhill Rd 48 EG51
Broomhill Ri, Bexh. DA6 . . . .126 FA85
Broomhill Rd, SW18 . . . . . . .120 DA85
  Dartford DA1 . . . . .127 FH86
  Ilford IG3 . . . . .70 EU61
  Orpington BR6 . . . . .146 EU101
  Woodford Green IG8 . . . . . .48 EG51
Broomhills, Grav. (Sthflt.)
  DA13 *off Betsham Rd* . . .130 FY91
Broomhill Wk, Wdf.Grn. IG8 . .48 EF52
Broomhouse La, SW6 . . . . . .100 DA82
Broomhouse Rd, SW6 . . . . .100 DA82
Broomlands La, Oxt. RH8 . . .188 EJ125
Broom La, Wok. (Chobham)
  GU24 . . . . .150 AS109
Broomloan La, Sutt. SM1 . . .140 DA103
Broom Lock, Tedd. TW11 . . .117 CJ93
Broom Mead, Bexh. DA6 . . .126 FA85
Broom Pk, Tedd. TW11 . . . . .117 CK94
Broom Rd, Croy. CR0 . . . . . .143 EA104
  Teddington TW11 . . . . . . .117 CJ93
Broomsleigh St, NW6 . . . . . .63 CZ64
Broomstick Hall Rd, Wal.Abb.
  EN9 . . . . .16 EE33
Broomstick La, Chesh. HP5 . . .4 AU30
Broom Water, Tedd. TW11 . .117 CJ93
Broom Water W, Tedd. TW11 .117 CJ92
Broom Way, Wey. KT13 . . . .153 BS105
Broomwood Cl, Croy. CR0 . .143 DX99
Broomwood Gdns, Brwd.
  CM15 . . . . .54 FU44
Broomwood Rd, SW11 . . . . .120 DF86
  Orpington BR5 . . . . .146 EV96
Broseley Gdns, Rom. RM3 . . .52 FL49
Broseley Gro, SE26 . . . . . . .123 DY92
Broseley Rd, Rom. RM3 . . . . .52 FL49
Broster Gdns, SE25 . . . . . . .142 DT97
Brougham Rd, E8 . . . . .84 DU67
  W3 . . . . .80 CQ72
Brougham St, SW11 . . . . . . .100 DF82
Brough Cl, SW8
  off Kenchester Cl 101 DL80
  Kingston upon Thames
  KT2 . . . . .117 CK92
Broughinge Rd, Borwd. WD6 . .26 CP40
Broughton Av, N3 . . . . .63 CY55
  Richmond TW10 . . . . .117 CH90
Broughton Dr, SW9 . . . . .101 DN84
Broughton Gdns, N6 . . . . . . .65 DJ58
Broughton Rd, SW6 . . . . . . .100 DB82
  W13 . . . . .79 CH73
  Orpington BR6 . . . . .146 EU103
  Sevenoaks (Otford) TN14 . .181 FG116
  Thornton Heath CR7 . . . . .141 DN100
Broughton Rd App, SW6
  off Wandsworth Br Rd . . .100 DB82
Broughton St, SW8 . . . . .100 DG82
Broughton Way, Rick. WD3 . . .38 BG45
Brouncker Rd, W3 . . . . .98 CQ75
Brow, The, Ch.St.G. HP8 . . . .36 AX48
  Watford WD25 . . . . .7 BV33
Brow Cl, Orp. BR5
  off Brow Cres 146 EX101
Brow Cres, Orp. BR5 . . . . . .146 EW102
Browells La, Felt. TW13 . . . .115 BV89
Brownacres Towpath, Wey.
  KT13 . . . . .135 BP102
Brown Cl, Wall. SM6 . . . . . . .159 DL108
Browne Cl, Brwd. CM14 . . . . .54 FV46
  Romford RM5
  off Bamford Way 51 FB50
Brownfield St, E14 . . . . .85 EB72
Browngraves Rd, Hayes
  UB3 . . . . .95 BQ80
Brown Hart Gdns, W1 . . . . . .194 G10
Brownhill Rd, SE6 . . . . .123 EB87
Browning Av, W7 . . . . .79 CF72
  Sutton SM1 . . . . .158 DE105
  Worcester Park KT4 . . . . .139 CV102
Browning Cl, E17 . . . . .67 EC56
  W9 *off Randolph Av* 82 DC70
  Hampton TW12 . . . . .116 BZ91
  Romford (Coll.Row) RM5 . . .50 EZ52
  Welling DA16 . . . . .105 ES81
Browning Ho, W12
  off Wood La 81 CW72
Browning Ms, W1 . . . . .195 H7
Browning Rd, E11 . . . . .68 EF59
  E12 . . . . .87 EM65
  Dartford DA1 . . . . .108 FM84
  Enfield EN2 . . . . .30 DR38
Browning St, SE17 . . . . .201 J10

Browning Wk, Til. RM18
  off Coleridge Rd 111 GJ82
Browning Way, Houns. TW5 . .96 BX81
Brownlea Gdns, Ilf. IG3 . . . . .70 EU61
Brownlow Ms, WC1 . . . . . . .196 C5
Brownlow Rd, E7
  off Woodford Rd 68 EH63
  E8 . . . . .84 DT67
  N3 . . . . .44 DB52
  N11 . . . . .45 DL51
  NW10 . . . . .80 CS66
  W13 . . . . .79 CG74
  Borehamwood WD6 . . . . . .26 CN42
  Croydon CR0 . . . . .160 DS105
  Redhill RH1 . . . . .184 DE134
Brownlow St, WC1 . . . . .196 C7
  W5 . . . . .79 CK76
  Bexleyheath DA6 . . . . . . .106 EX84
  Enfield EN3 . . . . .31 EA38
  Kingston upon Thames
  KT2 . . . . .138 CN95
  Sutton SM1 . . . . .158 DB105
Brown's Bldgs, EC3 . . . . . . .197 N9
Brownsea Wk, NW7
  off Sanders La 43 CX51
Browns La, NW5 . . . . .65 DH64
Brownspring Dr, SE9 . . . . . .125 EP91
Browns Rd, E17 . . . . .67 EA55
  Surbiton KT5 . . . . .138 CM101
Brown St, W1 . . . . .194 D8
Brownswell Rd, N2 . . . . .44 DD54
Brownswood Rd, N4 . . . . . . .65 DP62
Broxash Rd, SW11 . . . . .120 DG86
Broxbourne Av, E18 . . . . .68 EH56
Broxbourne Rd, E7 . . . . .68 EG62
  Orpington BR6 . . . . .145 ET101
Broxburn Dr, S.Ock. RM15 . . .91 FV73
Broxburn Par, S.Ock. RM15
  off Broxburn Dr 91 FV73
Broxholme Cl, SE25
  off Whitehorse La 142 DR98
Broxholm Rd, SE27 . . . . . . .121 DN90
Broxted Ms, Brwd. CM13 . . . .55 GC44
Broxted Rd, SE6 . . . . .123 DZ89
Broxwood Way, NW8 . . . . . . .82 DE67
Bruce Av, Horn. RM12 . . . . . .72 FK61
  Shepperton TW17 . . . . . .135 BQ100
★ **Bruce Castle Mus**, N17
  (Tottenham) 46 DS53
Bruce Castle Rd, N17 . . . . . .46 DT53
Bruce Cl, W10
  off Ladbroke Gro 81 CY71
  Welling DA16 . . . . .106 EV81
  West Byfleet (Byfleet)
  KT14 . . . . .152 BK113
Bruce Dr, S.Croy. CR2 . . . . .161 DX109
Bruce Gdns, N20
  off Balfour Gro 44 DF48
⮤ **Bruce Grove** 46 DT54
Bruce Gro, N17 . . . . .46 DS53
  Orpington BR6 . . . . .146 EU102
  Watford WD24 . . . . .24 BW38
Bruce Hall Ms, SW17
  off Brudenell Rd 120 DG91
Bruce Rd, E3 . . . . .85 EB69
  NW10 . . . . .80 CR66
  SE25 . . . . .142 DR98
  Barnet EN5
  off St. Albans Rd 27 CY41
  Harrow HA3 . . . . .41 CE54
  Mitcham CR4 . . . . .120 DG94
Bruce's Wf Rd, Grays RM17 . .110 GA79
Bruce Way, Wal.Cr. EN8 . . . . .15 DX33
Bruckner St, W10 . . . . .81 CZ69
Brudenell Rd, SW17 . . . . . . .120 DF90
Bruffs Meadow, Nthlt. UB5 . . .78 BY65
Bruges Pl, NW1
  off Randolph St 83 DJ66
Brumana Cl, Wey. KT13
  off Elgin Rd 153 BP106
Brumfield Rd, Epsom KT19 . .156 CQ106
Brummel Cl, Bexh. DA7 . . . . .107 FC83
★ **Brunei Gall**, WC1
  off Russell Sq 195 N5
Brunel Cl, SE19 . . . . .122 DT93
  Hounslow TW5 . . . . .95 BV80
  Northolt UB5 . . . . .78 BZ69
  Romford RM1 . . . . .71 FE56
  Tilbury RM18 . . . . .111 GH83
★ **Brunel Engine Ho**, SE16 . . .202 F4
Brunel Est, W2 . . . . .82 DA71
Brunel Pl, Sthl. UB1 . . . . .78 CB72
Brunel Rd, E17 . . . . .67 DY58
  SE16 . . . . .202 F5
  W3 . . . . .80 CS71
  Woodford Green IG8 . . . . . .49 EM50
Brunel St, E16
  off Victoria Dock Rd 86 EF72
Brunel Wk, N15 . . . . .66 DS56
  Twickenham TW2
  off Stephenson Rd 116 CA87
Brunel Way, Slou. SL1 . . . . .74 AT74
Brune St, E1 . . . . .197 P7
Brunner Cl, NW11 . . . . .64 DC57
Brunner Ct, Cher. (Ott.) KT16 .151 BC106
Brunner Rd, E17 . . . . .67 DZ57
  W5 . . . . .79 CK70
Bruno Pl, NW9 . . . . .62 CQ61
Brunswick Av, N11 . . . . .44 DG48
  Upminster RM14 . . . . .73 FS59
Brunswick Cl, Bexh. DA6 . . .106 EX84
  Pinner HA5 . . . . .60 BY58
  Thames Ditton KT7 . . . . . .137 CF102
  Twickenham TW2 . . . . . . .117 CD90
  Walton-on-Thames KT12 . .136 BW102
Brunswick Ct, EC1
  off Northampton Sq 83 DP69
  SE1 . . . . .201 N5
  Barnet EN4 . . . . .28 DD43
  Upminster RM14
  off Waycross Rd 73 FS59
Brunswick Cres, N11 . . . . . . .44 DG48
Brunswick Gdns, W5 . . . . . . .80 CL69
  W8 . . . . .82 DA74
  Ilford IG6 . . . . .49 EQ52
Brunswick Gro, N11 . . . . .44 DG48
  Cobham KT11 . . . . .154 BW113
Brunswick Ind Pk, N11 . . . . . .45 DH49

Brunswick Ms, SW16 . . . . . .121 DK93
  W1 . . . . .194 E8
BRUNSWICK PARK, N11 . . . .44 DF47
Brunswick Pk, SE5 . . . . . . .102 DR81
Brunswick Pk Gdns, N11 . . . .44 DG47
Brunswick Pk Rd, N11 . . . . . .44 DG47
Brunswick Pl, N1 . . . . .197 L3
  NW1 . . . . .194 G4
  SE19 . . . . .122 DU94
Brunswick Quay, SE16 . . . . .203 J7
Brunswick Rd, E10 . . . . .67 EC60
  E14 *off Blackwall Tunnel*
  Northern App 85 EC72
  N15 . . . . .66 DS57
  W5 . . . . .79 CK70
  Bexleyheath DA6 . . . . . . .106 EX84
  Enfield EN3 . . . . .31 EA38
  Kingston upon Thames
  KT2 . . . . .138 CN95
  Sutton SM1 . . . . .158 DB105
Brunswick Shop Cen, WC1 . .195 P4
Brunswick Sq, N17 . . . . .46 DT51
  WC1 . . . . .196 A5
Brunswick St, E17 . . . . .67 EC57
Brunswick Vil, SE5 . . . . .102 DS81
Brunswick Wk, Grav. DA12 . .131 GK87
Brunswick Way, N11 . . . . . . .45 DH49
Brunton Pl, E14 . . . . .85 DY72
Brushfield St, E1 . . . . .197 N7
Brushrise, Wat. WD24 . . . . . .23 BU36
Brushwood Dr, Rick. (Chorl.)
  WD3 . . . . .21 BC42
Brussels Rd, SW11 . . . . .100 DD84
Bruton Cl, Chis. BR7 . . . . . . .125 EM94
Bruton La, W1 . . . . .199 J1
Bruton Pl, W1 . . . . .199 J1
  Morden SM4 . . . . .140 DC99
Bruton Rd, Mord. SM4 . . . . .140 DC99
Bruton St, W1 . . . . .199 J1
Bruton Way, W13 . . . . .79 CG71
Bryan Av, NW10 . . . . .81 CV66
Bryan Cl, Sun. TW16 . . . . . . .115 BU94
Bryan Rd, SE16 . . . . .203 M4
Bryan's All, SW6
  off Wandsworth Br Rd . . .100 DB82
Bryanston Av, Twick. TW2 . . .116 CB88
Bryanston Cl, Sthl. UB2 . . . . .96 BZ77
Bryanstone Ct, Sutt. SM1
  off Oakhill Rd 158 DC105
Bryanstone Rd, N8 . . . . .65 DK57
  Waltham Cross EN8 . . . . . .15 DZ34
Bryanston Ms E, W1 . . . . . . .194 D7
Bryanston Ms W, W1 . . . . . .194 D7
Bryanston Pl, W1 . . . . .194 D7
Bryanston Rd, Til. RM18 . . . .111 GJ82
Bryanston Sq, W1 . . . . .194 D7
Bryanston St, W1 . . . . .194 D9
Bryant Av, Rom. RM3 . . . . . . .52 FK53
Bryant Cl, Barn. EN5 . . . . . . .27 CZ43
Bryant Ct, E2 . . . . .84 DT68
Bryant Rd, Nthlt. UB5 . . . . . . .78 BW69
Bryant Row, Rom. (Noak Hill)
  RM3 *off Cummings Hall La* .52 FJ48
Bryant St, E15 . . . . .85 ED66
Bryantwood Rd, N7 . . . . .65 DN64
Brycedale Cres, N14 . . . . . . .45 DK49
Bryce Rd, Dag. RM8 . . . . . . .70 EW63
Bryden Cl, SE26 . . . . .123 DY92
Brydges Pl, WC2 . . . . .199 P1
Brydges Rd, E15 . . . . .67 ED64
Brydon Wk, N1
  off Outram Pl 83 DL67
Bryer Ct, EC2
  off Aldersgate St 84 DQ71
Bryett Rd, N7 . . . . .65 DL62
Brymay Cl, E3 . . . . .85 EA68
Brynford Cl, Wok. GU21 . . . .166 AY115
Brynmaer Rd, SW11 . . . . . . .100 DF81
Bryn-y-Mawr Rd, Enf. EN1 . . .30 DT42
Bryony Cl, Loug. IG10 . . . . . . .33 EP42
  Uxbridge UB8 . . . . .76 BM71
Bryony Rd, W12 . . . . .81 CU73
Bryony Way, Sun. TW16 . . . .115 BT93
Bubblestone Rd, Sev. (Otford)
  TN14 . . . . .181 FH116
Buccleuch Rd, Slou. (Datchet)
  SL3 . . . . .92 AU80
Buchanan Cl, N21 . . . . .29 DM43
  South Ockendon (Aveley)
  RM15 . . . . .90 FQ74
Buchanan Ct, Borwd. WD6 . . .26 CQ40
Buchanan Gdns, NW10 . . . . .81 CV68
Buchan Cl, Uxb. UB8 . . . . . . .76 BJ69
Buchan Rd, SE15 . . . . .102 DW83
Bucharest Rd, SW18 . . . . . .120 DC87
Buckbean Path, Rom. RM3
  off Clematis Cl 52 FJ52
Buckden Cl, N2
  off Southern Rd 64 DF56
  SE12 *off Upwood Rd* 124 EF86
Buckettsland La, Borwd. WD6 .26 CR38
Buckfast Rd, Mord. SM4 . . . .140 DB99
Buckfast St, E2 . . . . .84 DU69
Buckham Thorns Rd, West.
  TN16 . . . . .189 EQ126
Buckhold Rd, SW18 . . . . . . .120 DA86
Buckhurst Av, Cars. SM5 . . .140 DE102
  Sevenoaks TN13 . . . . . . .191 FJ125
Buckhurst Cl, Red. RH1 . . . .184 DE132
BUCKHURST HILL 48 EH45
⊖ **Buckhurst Hill** 48 EK47
Buckhurst La, Sev. TN13 . . . .191 FL125
Buckhurst Rd, West. TN16 . .179 EN121
Buckhurst St, E1 . . . . .84 DV70
Buckhurst Way, Buck.H. IG9 . .48 EK49
Buckingham Arc, WC2 . . . . . .200 A1
Buckingham Av, N20 . . . . . . .44 DC46
  Feltham TW14 . . . . .115 BV86
  Greenford UB6 . . . . .79 CG67
  Thornton Heath CR7 . . . . .141 DN95
  Welling DA16 . . . . .105 ES84
  West Molesey KT8 . . . . . .136 CB97
Buckingham Cl, W5 . . . . .79 CJ71
  Enfield EN1 . . . . .30 DS40
  Hampton TW12 . . . . .116 BZ92
  Hornchurch RM11 . . . . . . .72 FK58

Buckingham Cl, Orp. BR5 . . .145 ES101
Buckingham Ct, NW4 . . . . . . .63 CU55
  Loughton IG10
  off Rectory La 33 EN40
Buckingham Dr, Chis. BR7 . .125 EP92
Buckingham Gdns, Edg. HA8 .42 CM52
  Slough SL1 . . . . .92 AT75
  Thornton Heath CR7 . . . . .141 DN96
  West Molesey KT8
  off Buckingham Av 136 CB96
Buckingham Gate, SW1 . . . .199 K5
Buckingham Gro, Uxb. UB10 .76 BN68
Buckingham La, SE23 . . . . . .123 DY87
Buckingham Ms, N1
  off Buckingham Rd 84 DS65
  NW10 *off Buckingham Rd* .81 CT68
  SW1 . . . . .199 K6
★ **Buckingham Palace**, SW1 . .199 J5
Buckingham Palace Rd, SW1 .199 H9
Buckingham Pl, SW1 . . . . . .199 K6
Buckingham Rd, E10 . . . . . . .67 EB60
  E11 . . . . .68 EJ57
  E15 . . . . .68 EF64
  E18 . . . . .48 EF53
  N1 . . . . .84 DS65
  N22 . . . . .45 DL53
  NW10 . . . . .81 CT68
  Borehamwood WD6 . . . . . .26 CR42
  Edgware HA8 . . . . .42 CM52
  Gravesend DA11
  off Dover Rd 130 GD87
  Hampton TW12 . . . . .116 BZ91
  Harrow HA1 . . . . .61 CD57
  Ilford IG1 . . . . .69 ER61
  Kingston upon Thames
  KT1 . . . . .138 CM98
  Mitcham CR4 . . . . .141 DL99
  Richmond TW10 . . . . .117 CK89
  Watford WD24 . . . . .24 BW37
Buckingham St, WC2 . . . . . .200 A1
Buckingham Way, Wall. SM6 .159 DJ109
BUCKLAND, Bet. 183 CU133
Buckland Av, Slou. SL3 . . . . .92 AV77
Buckland Ct Gdns, Bet. RH3 .183 CU133
Buckland Cres, NW3 . . . . . . .82 DD66
Buckland Gate, Slou. (Wexham)
  SL2 . . . . .74 AV68
Buckland La, Bet. RH3 . . . . .183 CT129
  Tadworth KT20 . . . . .183 CT129
Buckland Ri, Pnr. HA5 . . . . . .40 BW53
Buckland Rd, E10 . . . . .67 EC61
  Chessington KT9 . . . . . . .156 CM106
  Orpington BR6 . . . . .163 ES105
  Reigate RH2 . . . . .183 CX133
  Sutton SM2 . . . . .157 CW110
  Tadworth (Lwr.Kgswd.)
  KT20 . . . . .183 CZ128
Bucklands, The, Rick. WD3 . . .38 BG45
Bucklands Rd, Tedd. TW11 . .117 CJ93
Buckland St, N1 . . . . .197 L1
Buckland Wk, W3 . . . . .98 CQ75
  Morden SM4 . . . . .140 DC98
Buckland Way, Wor.Pk. KT4 .139 CW102
Buck La, NW9 . . . . .62 CR57
Buckleigh Av, SW20 . . . . . . .139 CY97
Buckleigh Rd, SW16 . . . . . . .121 DK93
Buckleigh Way, SE19 . . . . . .142 DT95
Buckler Gdns, SE9
  off Southold Ri 125 EM90
Bucklers All, SW6 . . . . .99 CZ79
Bucklersbury, EC4 . . . . .197 K9
Bucklersbury Pas, EC4 . . . . .197 K9
Bucklers Way, Cars. SM5 . . .140 DF104
Buckles Ct, Belv. DA17
  off Fendyke Rd 106 EX76
Buckles La, S.Ock. RM15 . . . .91 FW71
Buckle St, E1
  off Leman St 84 DT72
Buckley Cl, Dart. DA1 . . . . . .107 FF82
  Forest Hill SE23 . . . . .122 DW87
Buckley Rd, NW6 . . . . .81 CZ66
Buckley St, SE1 . . . . .200 D3
Buckmaster Cl, SW9
  off Stockwell Pk Rd 101 DM83
Buckmaster Rd, SW11 . . . . .100 DE84
Bucknalls Cl, Wat. WD25 . . . . .8 BY32
Bucknalls Dr, St.Alb. (Brick.Wd.)
  AL2 . . . . .8 BZ31
Bucknalls La, Wat. WD25 . . . . .8 BX32
Bucknall St, WC2 . . . . .195 N8
Bucknall Way, Beck. BR3 . . .143 EB98
Bucknell Cl, SW2 . . . . .101 DM84
Buckner Rd, SW2 . . . . .101 DM84
Bucknills Cl, Epsom KT18 . . .156 CP114
Buckrell Rd, E4 . . . . .47 ED47
Bucks Av, Wat. WD19 . . . . . . .40 BY45
Bucks Cl, W.Byf. KT14 . . . . . .152 BH114
Bucks Cross Rd, Grav. (Nthflt.)
  DA11 . . . . .131 GF90
  Orpington BR6 . . . . .164 EY106
★ **BUCKS HILL**, Kings L. 6 BK34
Bucks Hill, Kings L. WD4 . . . . .6 BK34
Buckstone Cl, SE23 . . . . . . .122 DW86
Buckstone Rd, N18 . . . . .46 DU51
Buck St, NW1 . . . . .83 DH66
Buckters Rents, SE16 . . . . . .203 K3
Buckthorne Ho, Chig. IG7 . . . .50 EV49
Buckthorne Rd, SE4 . . . . . . .123 DY86
Buckton Rd, Borwd. WD6 . . . .26 CM38
Buck Wk, E17 *off Wood St* . . .67 ED56
Budd Cl, N12 . . . . .44 DB49
Buddings Circle, Wem. HA9 . . .62 CQ62
Budd's All, Twick. TW1
  off Arlington Cl 117 CJ85
Budebury Rd, Stai. TW18 . . .114 BG92
Bude Cl, E17 . . . . .67 DZ57
Budge La, Mitch. CR4 . . . . . .140 DF101
Budge Row, EC4 . . . . .197 K10
Budge's Wk, W2 . . . . .82 DC73
Budgin's Hill, Orp. BR6 . . . . .164 EW112
Budleigh Cres, Well. DA16 . .106 EW81
Budoch Ct, Ilf. IG3 . . . . .70 EU61
Budoch Dr, Ilf. IG3 . . . . .70 EU61
Buer Rd, SW6 . . . . .99 CY82
Buff Av, Bans. SM7 . . . . .158 DB114

★ Place of interest   ⮤ Railway station   ⊖ London Underground station   **DLR** Docklands Light Railway station   ◆ Tramlink station   Ⓗ Hospital

Buffers La, Lthd. KT22
off Kingston Rd 171 CG119
Bug Hill, Cat. (Wold.) CR3 . .177 DX120
Bugsby's Way, SE7 . . . .104 EG77
SE10 . . . . . .205 K8
Bulganak Rd, Th.Hth. CR7 . .142 DQ98
Bulinga St, SW1 . . . . .199 N9
Bulkeley Cl, Egh. (Eng.Grn.)
TW20 . . . . .112 AW91
Bullace La, Dart. DA1
off High St 128 FL86
Bullace Row, SE5 . . . .102 DR80
Bull All, Well. DA16
off Welling High St 106 EV83
Bullards Pl, E2 . . . .85 DX69
Bullbanks Rd, Belv. DA17 . .107 FC77
Bullbeggars La, Gdse. RH9 . .186 DW132
Woking GU21 . . . .166 AV116
Bull Cl, Grays RM16 . . . .110 FZ75
Bullen St, SW11 . . . .100 DE82
Buller Cl, SE15 . . . .102 DU80
Buller Rd, N17 . . . .46 DU54
N22 . . . . .45 DN54
NW10
off Chamberlayne Rd 81 CX69
Barking IG11 . . . .87 ES66
Thornton Heath CR7 . . . .142 DR96
Bullers Cl, Sid. DA14 . . . .126 EY92
Bullers Wd Dr, Chis. BR7 . .124 EL94
Bullescroft Rd, Edg. HA8 . .42 CN48
Bullfinch Cl, Sev. TN13 . .190 FD122
Bullfinch Dene, Sev. TN13 . .190 FD122
Bullfinch La, Sev. TN13 . .190 FD122
Bullfinch Rd, S.Croy. CR2 . .161 DX110
Bullhead Rd, Borwd. WD6 . .26 CQ41
Bull Hill, Dart. (Hort.Kir.)
DA4 . . . . .148 FQ98
Leatherhead KT22 . . . .171 CG121
Bullied Way, SW1 . . . .199 J9
Bull Inn Ct, WC2 . . . .200 A1
Bullivant Cl, Green. DA9 . .129 FU85
Bullivant St, E14 . . . .85 EC73
Bull La, N18 . . . .46 DS50
Chislehurst BR7 . . . .125 ER94
Dagenham RM10 . . . .71 FB82
Gerrards Cross (Chal.St.P)
SL9 . . . . .56 AX55
Bull Rd, E15 . . . .86 EF68
Bullrush Cl, Croy. CR0 . .142 DS100
Bullrush Gro, Uxb. UB8 . .76 BJ70
Bull's All, SW14 . . . .98 CR82
Bulls Br Ind Est, Sthl. UB2 . .95 BV77
Bulls Br Rd, Sthl. UB2 . . . .95 BV76
Bullsbrook Rd, Hayes UB4 . .78 BW74
BULLS CROSS, Wal.Cr. 30 DT35
Bulls Cross, Enf. EN2 . . . .30 DU37
Bulls Cross Ride, Wal.Cr. EN7 . .30 DU35
Bulls Gdns, SW3 . . . .198 C8
Bull's Head Pas, EC3 . . . .197 M9
Bullsland Gdns, Rick. (Chorl.)
WD3 . . . . .21 BB44
Bullsland La, Ger.Cr. SL9 . .37 BB45
Rickmansworth (Chorl.)
WD3 . . . . .21 BB44
BULLSMOOR, Enf. 30 DV37
Bullsmoor Cl, Wal.Cr. EN8 . .30 DW35
Bullsmoor Gdns, Wal.Cr. EN8 . .30 DV35
Bullsmoor La, Enf. EN1, EN3 . .30 DV35
Waltham Cross EN7 . . . .30 DU35
Bullsmoor Ride, Wal.Cr. EN8 . .30 DW35
Bullsmoor Way, Wal.Cr. EN8 . .30 DW35
Bullwell Cres, Wal.Cr. (Chsht.)
EN8 . . . . .15 DY29
Bull Wf La, EC4 . . . .197 J10
Bull Yd, Grav. DA12
off High St 131 GH86
Bulmer Gdns, Har. HA3 . .61 CK59
Bulmer Ms, W11
off Ladbroke Rd 82 DA73
Bulmer Pl, W11 . . . .82 DA74
Bulmer Wk, Rain. RM13 . .90 FJ68
Bulow Est, SW6
off Broughton Rd 100 DB82
Bulrush Cl, Cars. SM5
off Fellowes Rd 140 DE103
Bulstrode Av, Houns. TW3 . .96 BZ82
Bulstrode Ct, Ger.Cr. SL9 . .56 AX58
Bulstrode Gdns, Houns. TW3 . .96 BZ83
Bulstrode La, Hem.H. (Felden)
HP3 . . . . .6 BG27
Kings Langley (Chipper.)
WD4 . . . . .5 BE29
Bulstrode Pl, W1 . . . .194 G6
Slough SL1 . . . .92 AT76
Bulstrode Rd, Houns. TW3 . .96 CA83
Bulstrode St, W1 . . . .194 G8
Bulstrode Way, Ger.Cr. SL9 . .56 AX57
Bulwer Ct Rd, E11 . . . .67 ED60
Bulwer Gdns, Barn. EN5
off Bulwer Rd 28 DC42
Bulwer Rd, E11 . . . .67 ED59
N18 . . . . .46 DS49
Barnet EN5 . . . .28 DB42
Bulwer St, W12 . . . .81 CW74
Bumbles Grn La, Wal.Abb.
EN9 . . . . .16 EH25
Bunby Way, Epsom KT17 . .173 CV116
Bunby Rd, Slou. (Stoke P.)
SL2 . . . . .74 AT66
Bunce Dr, Cat. CR3 . .176 DR123
Bunces La, Wdf.Grn. IG8 . .48 EF52
Bundys Way, Stai. TW18 . .113 BF93
Bungalow Rd, SE25 . .142 DS98
Woking GU23 . .169 BQ124
Bungalows, The, SW16 . .121 DH94
Wallington SM6 . .159 DH106
Bunhill Row, EC1 . . . .197 K4
Bunhouse Pl, SW1 . . . .198 F10
Bunkers Hill, NW11 . . . .64 DC59
Belvedere DA17 . .106 FA77
Sidcup DA14 . .126 EZ90
Bunning Way, N7 . . . .83 DL66
Bunns La, NW7 . . . .43 CT51
Bunn's La, Chesh. HP5 . .4 AU34
Bunsen St, E3
off Kenilworth Rd 85 DY68
Buntingbridge Rd, Ilf. IG2 . .69 ER57

Bunting Cl, N9
off Dunnock Cl 47 DX46
Mitcham CR4 . .140 DF99
Bunton St, SE18 . .105 EN76
Bunyan Ct, EC2
off Beech St 84 DQ71
Bunyan Rd, E17 . . . .67 DY55
Bunyard Dr, Wok. GU21 . .151 BC114
Bunyons Cl, Brwd. CM13
off Essex Way 53 FW51
Buonaparte Ms, SW1 . .199 M10
H BUPA Bushey Hosp, Bushey
WD23 . . . .41 CF46
H BUPA Hartswood Hosp, Brwd.
CM13 . . . .53 FV51
Burbage Rd, SE1 . .201 K7
Hayes UB3 . . . .77 BR72
Waltham Cross (Chsht.)
EN8 . . . . .15 DZ31
Burbage Rd, SE21 . .122 DR86
SE24 . . . .122 DQ86
Burberry Cl, N.Mal. KT3 . .138 CS96
Burbidge Rd, Shep. TW17 . .134 BN98
Burbridge Way, N17 . . . .46 DT54
Burcham St, E14 . . . .85 EB72
Burcharbro Rd, SE2 . .106 EX79
Burchell Ct, Bushey WD23
off Catsey La 40 CC45
Burchell Rd, E10 . . . .67 EB60
SE15 . . . .102 DV81
Burchetts Way, Shep. TW17 . .135 BP100
Burchett Way, Rom. RM6 . .70 EZ58
Burch Rd, Grav. (Nthflt.)
DA11 . . . .131 GF86
Burchwall Cl, Rom. RM5 . .51 FC52
Burcote, Wey. KT13 . .153 BR107
Burcote Rd, SW18 . .120 DD88
Burcott Gdns, Add. KT15 . .152 BJ107
Burcott Rd, Pur. CR8 . .159 DN114
Burden Cl, Brent. TW8 . . . .97 CJ78
Burdenshott Av, Rich. TW10 . .98 CP84
Burdenshott Rd, Wok. GU22 . .166 AU124
Burden Way, E11
off Brading Cres 68 EH61
Burder Cl, N1 . . . .84 DS65
Burder Rd, N1
off Balls Pond Rd 84 DS65
Burdett Av, SW20 . .139 CU95
Burdett Cl, W7
off Cherington Rd 97 CF75
Sidcup DA14 . .126 EY92
Burdett Ms, NW3
off Belsize Cres 82 DD65
W2
off Hatherley Gro 82 DB72
Burdett Rd, E3 . . . .85 DZ70
E14 . . . .85 DZ70
Croydon CR0 . .142 DR100
Richmond TW9 . . . .98 CM83
Burdetts Rd, Dag. RM9 . .88 EZ67
Burdett St, SE1 . .200 D6
Burdock Cl, Croy. CR0 . .143 DX102
Burdock Rd, N17 . . . .66 DU55
Burdon La, Sutt. SM2 . .157 CY108
Burdon Pk, Sutt. SM2 . .157 CZ109
Burfield Cl, SW17 . .120 DD91
Burfield Dr, Warl. CR6 . .176 DW119
Burfield Rd, Rick. (Chorl.)
WD3 . . . .21 BB43
Windsor (Old Wind.) SL4 . .112 AU86
Burford Cl, Dag. RM8 . . . .70 EW62
Ilford IG6 . . . .69 EQ56
Uxbridge UB10 . . . .58 BL63
Burford Gdns, N13 . . . .45 DM48
Burford La, Epsom KT17 . .157 CW111
Burford Rd, E6 . . . .86 EL69
E15 . . . .85 ED66
SE6 . . . .123 DZ89
Brentford TW8 . . . .98 CL78
Bromley BR1 . .144 EL98
Sutton SM1 . .140 DA103
Worcester Park KT4 . .139 CT101
Burford Wk, SW6
off Cambria St 100 DB80
Burford Way, Croy. (New Adgtn.)
CR0 . . . .161 EC107
Burgate Cl, Dart. DA1 . .107 FF83
Burges Cl, Horn. RM11 . .72 FM58
Burges Ct, E6 . . . .87 EN66
Burges Gro, SW13 . . . .99 CV80
Burges Rd, E6 . . . .86 EL66
Burgess Av, NW9 . . . .62 CR58
Burgess Cl, Felt. TW13 . .116 BY91
Waltham Cross (Chsht.)
EN7 . . . .14 DQ25
Burgess Ct, Borwd. WD6
off Belford Rd 26 CM38
Burgess Hill, NW2 . . . .64 DA63
Burgess Rd, E15 . . . .68 EE63
Sutton SM1 . .158 DB105
Burgess St, E14 . . . .85 EA71
Burge St, SE1 . .201 L7
Burges Way, Stai. TW18 . .114 BG92
Burghfield, Epsom KT17 . .173 CT115
Burghfield Rd, Grav. (Istead Rise)
DA13 . . . .131 GF94
BURGH HEATH, Tad. . .173 CX119
Burgh Heath Rd, Epsom
KT17 . . . .156 CS114
★ Burgh Ho (Hampstead Mus),
NW3 . . . .64 DD63
Burghill Rd, SE26 . .123 DY91
Burghley Av, Borwd. WD6 . .26 CQ43
New Malden KT3 . .138 CR95
Burghley Hall Cl, SW19 . .119 CY87
Burghley Ho, SW19 . .119 CY90
Burghley Pl, Mitch. CR4 . .140 DG99
Burghley Rd, E11 . . . .68 EE60
N8 . . . .65 DN55
NW5 . . . .65 DH64
SW19 . . . .119 CX91
Grays (Chaff.Hun.) RM16 . .109 FW76
Burghley Twr, W3 . . . .81 CT73
Burgh Mt, Bans. SM7 . .173 CZ115
Burgh St, N1 . . . .83 DP68
Burgh Wd, Bans. SM7 . .173 CY115
Burgon St, EC4 . . . .196 G9

Burgos Cl, Croy. CR0 . .159 DN107
Burgos Gro, SE10 . .103 EB81
Burgoyne Rd, N4 . . . .65 DP58
SE25 . . . .142 DT98
SW9 . . . .101 DM83
Sunbury-on-Thames TW16 . .115 BT93
Burham Cl, SE20
off Maple Rd 122 DW94
Burhill Gro, Pnr. HA5 . . . .60 BY54
Burhill Rd, Walt. KT12 . .154 BW107
Burke Cl, SW15 . . . .98 CS84
Burke St, E16 . . . .86 EF72
Burket Cl, Sthl. UB2
off Kingsbridge Rd 96 BZ77
Burland Rd, SW11 . .120 DF85
Brentwood CM15 . . . .54 FX46
Romford RM5 . . . .51 FC51
Burlea Cl, Walt. KT12 . .153 BV106
Burleigh Av, Sid. DA15 . .125 ET85
Wallington SM6 . .140 DG104
Burleigh Cl, Add. KT15 . .152 BH106
Ashford TW15 . .115 BQ92
Burleigh Gdns, N14 . . . .45 DJ46
Ashford TW15 . .115 BQ92
Burleigh Ho, W10
off St. Charles Sq 81 CX71
Burleigh Pk, Cob. KT11 . .154 BY112
Burleigh Pl, SW15 . .119 CX85
Burleigh Rd, Add. KT15 . .152 BH105
Enfield EN1 . . . .30 DS42
Sutton SM3 . .139 CY102
Uxbridge UB10 . . . .77 BP67
Waltham Cross (Chsht.)
EN8 . . . .15 DY32
Burleigh St, WC2 . .196 B10
Burleigh Wk, SE6
off Muirkirk Rd 123 EC88
Burleigh Way, Enf. EN2
off Church St 30 DR41
Potters Bar (Cuffley) EN6 . .13 DL30
Burley Cl, E4 . . . .47 EA50
SW16 . . . .141 DK96
Burley Orchard, Cher. KT16 . .134 BG100
Burley Rd, E16 . . . .86 EJ72
Burlings La, Sev. (Knock.)
TN14 . . . .179 ET118
Burlington Arc, W1 . .199 K1
Burlington Av, Rich. TW9 . .98 CN81
Romford RM7 . . . .71 FB58
Slough SL1 . . . .92 AS75
Burlington Cl, E6
off Northumberland Rd . .86 EL72
W9 . . . .81 CZ70
Feltham TW14 . .115 BR87
Orpington BR6 . .145 EP103
Pinner HA5 . . . .59 BV55
Burlington Gdns, W1 . .199 K1
W3 . . . .80 CQ74
W4 . . . .98 CQ78
Romford RM6 . . . .70 EY59
Burlington La, W4 . . . .98 CS80
Burlington Ms, SW15 . .119 CZ85
W3 . . . .80 CQ74
Burlington Pl, SW6
off Burlington Rd 99 CY82
Reigate RH2 . .184 DA134
Woodford Green IG8 . .48 EG48
Burlington Ri, Barn. EN4 . .44 DE46
Burlington Rd, N10
off Tetherdown 44 DG54
N17 . . . .46 DU53
SW6 . . . .99 CY82
W4 . . . .98 CQ78
Enfield EN2 . . . .30 DR39
Isleworth TW7 . . . .97 CD81
New Malden KT3 . .139 CU98
Slough SL1 . . . .92 AS75
Thornton Heath CR7 . .142 DQ96
Burman Cl, Dart. DA2 . .128 FQ87
Burma Rd, N16 . . . .66 DR63
Chertsey (Longcr.) KT16 . .132 AT104
Burmester Rd, SW17 . .120 DC90
Burnaby Cres, W4 . . . .98 CP79
Burnaby Gdns, W4 . . . .98 CQ79
Burnaby St, SW10 . .100 DC80
Burnbrae Cl, N12 . . . .44 DB51
Burnbury Rd, SW12 . .121 DJ88
Burn Cl, Add. KT15 . .152 BK105
Leatherhead (Oxshott)
KT22 . . . .170 CC115
Burncroft Av, Enf. EN3 . .30 DW40
Burne Jones Ho, N14 . . . .99 CZ77
Burnell Av, Rich. TW10 . .117 CJ92
Welling DA16 . .106 EU82
Burnell Gdns, Stan. HA7 . .41 CK53
Burnell Rd, Sutt. SM1 . .158 DB105
Burnell Wk, SE1 . .202 A10
Brentwood CM13 . . . .53 FW51
Burnels Av, E6 . . . .87 EN69
Burness Cl, N7
off Roman Way 83 DM65
Uxbridge UB8
off Whitehall Rd 76 BK68
Burne St, NW1 . .194 B6
Burnet Gro, Epsom KT19 . .156 CQ113
Burnett Cl, E9 . . . .66 DW64
Burnett Rd, Erith DA8 . .108 FK79
Burney Av, Surb. KT5 . .138 CM99
Burney Dr, Loug. IG10 . .33 EP40
Burney St, SE10 . .103 EC80
Burnfoot Av, SW6 . . . .99 CY81
Burnfoot Ct, SE22 . .122 DV88
Burnham, NW3 . . . .82 DE66
Burnham Av, Uxb. UB10 . .59 BQ63
Burnham Cl, NW7 . . . .43 CU52
SE1 . . . .202 A9
Enfield EN1 . . . .30 DS38
Harrow (Wldste.) HA3 . .61 CG56
Burnham Cres, E11 . . . .68 EJ56
Dartford DA1 . .108 FJ84
Burnham Dr, Reig. RH2 . .184 DA133
Worcester Park KT4 . .139 CX103
Burnham Gdns, Croy. CR0 . .142 DT101
Hayes UB3 . . . .95 BR76
Hounslow TW4 . . . .95 BV81

Burnham Rd, E4 . . . .47 DZ50
Dagenham RM9 . . . .88 EV66
Dartford DA1 . .108 FJ84
Morden SM4 . .140 DB99
Romford RM7 . . . .71 FD55
Sidcup DA14 . .126 EY89
Burnhams Rd, Lthd. (Bkhm.)
KT23 . . . .170 BY124
Burnham St, E2 . . . .84 DW69
Kingston upon Thames
KT2 . . . .138 CN95
Burnham Way, SE26 . .123 DZ92
W13 . . . .97 CH77
Burnhill Rd, Beck. BR3 . .143 EA96
Burnley Cl, Wat. WD19 . .40 BW50
Burnley Rd, NW10 . . . .63 CU64
SW9 . . . .101 DM82
Grays RM20 . .109 FT81
Burnsall St, SW3 . .198 C10
Burns Av, Felt. TW14 . .115 BU86
Romford (Chad.Hth.) RM6 . .70 EW59
Sidcup DA15 . .126 EV86
Southall UB1 . . . .78 CA73
Burns Cl, E17 . . . .67 EC56
SW19 . . . .120 DD93
Carshalton SM5
off Kenny Dr 158 DG109
Erith DA8 . .107 FF81
Hayes UB4 . . . .77 BT71
Welling DA16 . .105 ET81
Burns Dr, Bans. SM7 . .157 CY114
Burn Side, N9 . . . .46 DW48
Burnside, Ashtd. KT21 . .172 CM118
Burnside Av, E4 . . . .47 DZ51
Burnside Cl, SE16 . .203 J2
Barnet EN5 . . . .28 DA41
Twickenham TW1 . .117 CG86
Burnside Cres, Wem. HA0 . .79 CK67
Burns Pl, Til. RM18 . .111 GH81
Burns Rd, NW10 . . . .81 CT67
SW11 . . . .100 DF82
W13 . . . .97 CH75
Wembley HA0 . . . .79 CK68
Burns Way, Brwd. CM13 . .55 GD45
Hounslow TW5 . . . .96 BX82
Burnt Ash Hill, SE12 . .124 EF86
Burnt Ash La, Brom. BR1 . .124 EG93
Burnt Ash Rd, SE12 . .124 EF85
Burnt Fm Ride, Enf. EN2 . .13 DP34
Waltham Cross EN7 . . . .13 DP31
Burnt Ho La, Dart. (Hawley)
DA2 . . . .128 FL91
Burnthwaite Rd, SW6 . .100 DA80
BURNT OAK, Edg. 42 CQ52
⊖ Burnt Oak 42 CQ53
Burnt Oak Bdy, Edg. HA8 . .42 CP52
Burnt Oak Flds, Edg. HA8 . .42 CQ53
Burnt Oak La, Sid. DA15 . .126 EU86
Burntwood, Brwd. CM14 . .54 FW48
Burntwood Av, Horn. RM11 . .72 FK58
Burntwood Cl, SW18 . .120 DD88
Caterham CR3 . .176 DU121
Burntwood Gra Rd, SW18 . .120 DD88
Burntwood Gro, Sev. TN13 . .191 FH127
Burntwood La, SW17 . .120 DE89
Caterham CR3 . .176 DU121
Burntwood Rd, Sev. TN13 . .191 FH128
Burntwood Vw, SE19
off Bowley La 122 DT92
Burnway, Horn. RM11 . .72 FL59
Buross St, E1
off Commercial Rd 84 DV72
Burrage Pl, SE18 . .105 EQ77
Burrage Rd, SE18 . .105 EQ79
Burrard Rd, E16 . . . .86 EH72
NW6 . . . .64 DA64
Burr Cl, E1 . .202 B2
Bexleyheath DA7 . .106 EZ83
St. Albans (Lon.Col.) AL2 . .10 CL27
Burrell Cl, Croy. CR0 . .143 DY100
Edgware HA8 . . . .42 CP47
Burrell Row, Beck. BR3
off High St 143 EA96
Burrell St, SE1 . .200 F2
Burrells Wf Sq, E14 . .204 B10
Burrell Twr, E10 . . . .67 EA59
Burrfield Dr, Orp. BR5 . .146 EX99
Burr Hill La, Wok. (Chobham)
GU24 . . . .150 AS109
Burritt Rd, Kings.T. KT1 . .138 CN96
Burroughs, The, NW4 . . . .63 CV57
Burroughs Gdns, NW4 . . . .63 CV56
Burroughs Par, NW4
off The Burroughs 63 CV56
Burroway Rd, Slou. SL3 . .93 BB76
Burrow Cl, Chig. IG7
off Burrow Rd 49 ET50
Burrow Grn, Chig. IG7 . . . .49 ET50
BURROWHILL, Wok. . .150 AS108
Burrow Rd, SE22 . .102 DS84
Chigwell IG7 . . . .49 ET50
Burrows Chase, Wal.Abb.
EN9 . . . .31 ED36
Burrows Cl, Lthd. (Bkhm.)
KT23 . . . .170 BZ124
Burrows Hill Cl, Houns.
(Hthrw.Air.) TW6 . . . .94 BJ84
Burrows Hill La, Houns.
(Hthrw.Air.) TW6 . . . .94 BH84
Burrows Ms, SE1 . .200 F4
Burrows Rd, NW10 . . . .81 CW69
Burrow Wk, SE21
off Rosendale Rd 122 DQ87
Burr Rd, SW18 . .120 DA87
Bursar St, SE1 . .201 M3
Bursdon Cl, Sid. DA15 . .125 ET89
Burses Way, Brwd. CM13 . .55 GB45
Bursland Rd, Enf. EN3 . .31 DX42
Burslem Av, Ilf. IG6 . .50 EU51
Burslem St, E1 . . . .84 DU72
Burstead Cl, Cob. KT11 . .154 BX113
Burstock Rd, SW15 . . . .99 CY84
Burston Dr, St.Alb. (Park St.)
AL2 . . . .8 CC28
Burston Rd, SW15 . .119 CX85

Buf - Bus

Burston Vil, SW15
off St. John's Av 119 CX85
Burstow Rd, SW20 . .139 CY95
Burtenshaw Rd, T.Ditt. KT7 . .137 CG101
Burtley Cl, N4 . . . .66 DQ60
Burton Av, Wat. WD18 . .23 BU42
Burton Cl, Chess. KT9 . .155 CK108
Thornton Heath CR7 . .142 DR97
Burton Ct, SW3
off Franklin's Row 100 DF78
Burton Dr, Enf. EN3
off Government Row 31 EA37
Burton Gdns, Houns. TW5 . .96 BZ81
Burton Gro, SE17
off Portland St 102 DR78
Burtonhole Cl, NW7 . . . .43 CX49
Burtonhole La, NW7 . . . .43 CY49
Burton La, SW9 . . . .101 DN82
Waltham Cross (Chsht.)
EN7 . . . .14 DS29
Burton Ms, SW1 . .198 G9
Burton Pl, WC1 . .195 N3
Burton Rd, E18 . . . .68 EH55
NW6 . . . .81 CZ66
SW9 . . . .101 DP82
Kingston upon Thames
KT2 . . . .118 CL94
Loughton IG10 . . . .33 EQ42
Burtons La, Ch.St.G. HP8 . .21 AZ43
Rickmansworth WD3 . .21 AZ43
Burtons Rd, Hmptn. (Hmptn.H.)
TW12 . . . .116 CB91
Burton St, WC1 . .195 N3
Burtons Way, Ch.St.G. HP8 . .20 AW40
Burt Rd, E16 . . . .86 EJ74
Burtwell La, SE27 . .122 DR91
Burwash Ct, Orp. BR5
off Rookery Gdns 146 EW99
Burwash Ho, SE1 . .201 L5
Burwash Rd, SE18 . .105 ER78
Burway Cres, Cher. KT16 . .134 BG97
Burwell Av, Grnf. UB6 . .79 CE65
Burwell Cl, E1 off Bigland St . .84 DV72
Burwell Ind Est, E10 . . . .67 DY60
Burwell Rd, E10 . . . .67 DY60
Burwell Wk, E3 . . . .85 EA70
Burwood Av, Brom. BR2 . .144 EH103
Kenley CR8 . .159 DP114
Pinner HA5 . . . .60 BW57
Burwood Cl, Reig. RH2 . .184 DD134
Surbiton KT6 . .138 CN102
Walton-on-Thames KT12 . .154 BW107
Burwood Gdns, Rain. RM13 . .89 FF69
Burwood Ho, SW9 . . . .101 DP83
BURWOOD PARK, Walt. . .153 BT106
Burwood Pk Rd, Walt. KT12 . .153 BV105
Burwood Pl, W2 . .194 C8
Burwood Rd, Walt. KT12 . .153 BV107
Bury Av, Hayes UB4 . . . .77 BS68
Ruislip HA4 . . . .59 BQ58
Bury Cl, SE16 . .203 J2
Woking GU21 . .166 AX116
Bury Ct, EC3 . .197 N8
Burydell La, St.Alb. (Park St.)
AL2 . . . .9 CD27
BURY GREEN, Wal.Cr. . .14 DV31
Bury Grn Rd, Wal.Cr. (Chsht.)
EN7 . . . .14 DU31
Bury Gro, Mord. SM4 . .140 DB99
Bury La, Epp. CM16 . .17 ES31
Rickmansworth WD3 . .38 BK46
Woking GU21 . .166 AW116
Bury Meadows, Rick. WD3 . .38 BK46
Bury Pl, WC1 . .195 P7
Bury Ri, Hem.H. HP3 . .5 BD25
Bury Rd, E4 . . . .32 EE43
N22 . . . .65 DN55
Dagenham RM10 . . . .71 FB64
Epping CM16 . .17 ES31
Bury St, EC3 . .197 N9
N9 . . . .46 DU46
SW1 . .199 K2
Ruislip HA4 . . . .59 BQ58
Bury St W, N9 . . . .46 DR45
Bury Wk, SW3 . .198 B9
Busbridge Ho, E14
off Brabazon St 85 EA71
Busby Ms, NW5
off Torriano Av 83 DK65
Busby Pl, NW5 . . . .83 DK65
Busby St, E2 off Chilton St . .84 DT70
Bushbaby Cl, SE1 . .201 M7
Bushbarns, Wal.Cr. (Chsht.)
EN7 . . . .14 DU29
Bushberry Rd, E9 . . . .85 DY65
Bush Cl, Add. KT15 . .152 BJ106
Ilford IG2 . . . .69 ER57
Bush Cotts, SW18
off Putney Br Rd 120 DA85
Bush Ct, W12
off Shepherds Bush Grn . .99 CX75
Bushell Cl, SW2 . .121 DM86
Bushell Grn, Bushey (Bushey Hth.)
WD23 . . . .41 CD47
Bushell St, E1 . .202 C3
Bushell Way, Chis. BR7 . .125 EN92
Bush Elms Rd, Horn. RM11 . .71 FG59
Bushetts Gro, Red. RH1 . .185 DH129
BUSHEY 40 CA45
⇌ Bushey 24 BX44
Bushey Av, E18 . . . .68 EF55
Orpington BR5 . .145 ER101
Bushey Cl, E4 . . . .47 EC48
Kenley CR8 . .176 DS116
Uxbridge UB10 . . . .59 BP61
Bushey Ct, SW20 . .139 CV96
Bushey Cft, Oxt. RH8 . .187 EC130
Bushey Down, SW12
off Bedford Hill 121 DH89
Bushey Gro Rd, Bushey
WD23 . . . .24 BX42
Bushey Hall Dr, Bushey
WD23 . . . .24 BY42
Bushey Hall Rd, Bushey
WD23 . . . .24 BX42

★ Place of interest   ⇌ Railway station   ⊖ London Underground station   DLR Docklands Light Railway station   ◇ Tramlink station   H Hospital

Bus - Cam

BUSHEY HEATH, Bushey . . .41 CE46
Bushey Hill Rd, SE5 . . . . . .102 DS81
Bushey La, Sutt. SM1 . . . . .158 DA105
Bushey Lees, Sid. DA15
  off Fen Gro 125 ET86
BUSHEY MEAD, SW20 . . . .139 CX97
Bushey Mill Cres, Wat. WD24 .24 BW37
Bushey Mill La, Bushey WD23 .24 BZ40
  Watford WD24 . . . . .24 BW37
Bushey Rd, E13 . . . . .86 EJ68
  N15 . . . . .66 DS58
  SW20 . . . . .139 CV97
  Croydon CR0 . . . . .143 EA103
  Hayes UB3 . . . . .95 BS77
  Sutton SM1 . . . . .158 DA105
  Uxbridge UB10 . . . . .58 BN61
Bushey Shaw, Ashtd. KT21 . .171 CH117
Bushey Vw Wk, Wat. WD24 . .24 BX40
Bushey Way, Beck. BR3 . . . .143 ED100
Bushfield Cl, Edg. HA8 . . . . .42 CP47
Bushfield Cres, Edg. HA8 . . .42 CP47
Bushfield Rd, Hem.H. (Bov.)
  HP3 . . . . .5 BC25
Bushfields, Loug. IG10 . . . . .33 EN43
Bushfield Wk, Swans. DA10 . .130 FY86
Bush Gro, NW9 . . . . .62 CQ59
  Stanmore HA7 . . . . .41 CK53
Bushgrove Rd, Dag. RM8 . . .70 EX63
Bush Hill, N21 . . . . .46 DQ45
BUSH HILL PARK, Enf. 30 DS43
  ₹ Bush Hill Park 30 DT44
Bush Hill Rd, N21 . . . . .30 DR44
  Harrow HA3 . . . . .62 CM58
Bush Ind Est, NW10 . . . . . .80 CR70
Bush La, EC4 . . . . .197 K10
  Woking (Send) GU23 . . . . .167 BD124
Bushmead Cl, N15
  off Copperfield Dr 66 DT56
Bushmoor Cres, SE18 . . . . .105 EQ80
Bushnell Rd, SW17 . . . . . . .121 DH89
Bush Rd, E8 . . . . .84 DV67
  E11 . . . . .68 EF59
  SE8 . . . . .203 J8
  Buckhurst Hill IG9 . . . . . .48 EK49
  Richmond TW9 . . . . .98 CM79
  Shepperton TW17 . . . . . .134 BM99
Bushway, Dag. RM8 . . . . . .70 EX63
Bushwood, E11 . . . . .68 EF60
Bushwood Dr, SE1 . . . . . . .202 A9
Bushwood Rd, Rich. TW9 . . .98 CN79
★ Bushy Park, Tedd. TW11 . .137 CF95
Bushy Pk, Hmptn. (Hmptn.H.)
  TW12 . . . . .137 CF95
  Teddington TW11 . . . . . . .137 CF95
Bushy Pk Gdns, Tedd. TW11 .117 CG92
Bushy Pk Rd, Tedd. TW11 . . .117 CH94
Bushy Rd, Lthd. (Fetch.)
  KT22 . . . . .170 CB122
  Teddington TW11 . . . . . . .117 CF93
★ Business Design Cen, N1 . .83 DN67
Business Village, The, Slou.
  SL2 . . . . .74 AV74
Butcher Row, E1 . . . . .85 DX73
  E14 . . . . .85 DX73
Butchers La, Sev. TN15 . . . .149 FX103
Butchers Rd, E16 . . . . .86 EG72
Butcher Wk, Swans. DA10 . .130 FY87
Bute Av, Rich. TW10 . . . . . .118 CL89
Bute Ct, Wall. SM6
  off Bute Rd 159 DJ106
Bute Gdns, W6 . . . . .99 CX77
  Wallington SM6 . . . . .159 DJ106
Bute Gdns W, Wall. SM6 . . .159 DJ106
Bute Ms, NW11 off Northway .64 DC56
Bute Rd, Croy. CR0 . . . . . . .141 DN102
  Ilford IG6 . . . . .69 EP57
  Wallington SM6 . . . . .159 DJ105
Bute St, SW7 . . . . .100 DD77
Bute Wk, N1
  off Marquess Rd 84 DR65
Butler Av, Har. HA1 . . . . . . .61 CD59
Butler Ct, Wem. HA0
  off Harrow Rd 61 CG63
Butler Ho, Grays RM17
  off Argent St 110 GA79
Butler Pl, SW1 . . . . .199 M6
Butler Rd, NW10
  off Curzon Cres 81 CT66
  Dagenham RM8 . . . . .70 EV63
  Harrow HA1 . . . . .60 CC59
Butlers Ct, Wal.Cr. EN8
  off Trinity La 15 DY32
BUTLERS CROSS, Beac. . . .36 AT49
Butlers Dene Rd, Cat. (Wold.)
  CR3 . . . . .177 DZ120
Butlers Dr, E4 . . . . .31 EC38
Butler St, E2
  off Knottisford St 84 DW69
  Uxbridge UB10 . . . . .77 BP70
Butlers Wf, SE1 . . . . .202 A3
Butler Wk, Grays RM17
  off Palmers Dr 110 GD77
Buttell Cl, Grays RM17 . . . .110 GD78
Buttercross La, Epp. CM16 . .18 EU30
Buttercup Cl, Rom. RM3
  off Copperfields Way 52 FK53
Buttercup Sq, Stai. (Stanw.)
  TW19 off Diamedes Av . . .114 BK88
Butterfield Cl, N17
  off Devonshire Rd 46 DQ51
  SE16 . . . . .202 D5
  Twickenham TW1
  off Rugby Rd 117 CF86
Butterfields, E17 . . . . .67 EC57
Butterfield Sq, E6
  off Harper Rd 87 EM72
Butterfly La, SE9 . . . . .185 EP86
  Borehamwood (Elstree)
  WD6 . . . . .25 CG41
Butterfly Wk, SE5
  off Denmark Hill 102 DR81
  Warlingham CR6 . . . . . . .176 DW120
Butter Hill, Cars. SM5 . . . . .140 DG104
  Wallington SM6 . . . . .140 DG104

Butteridges Cl, Dag. RM9 . . .88 EZ67
Butterly Av, Dart. DA1 . . . . .128 FM89
Buttermere Cl, E15 . . . . . . .67 ED63
  SE1 . . . . .201 P8
  Feltham TW14 . . . . .115 BT88
  Morden SM4 . . . . .139 CX100
Buttermere Dr, SW15 . . . . .119 CY85
Buttermere Gdns, Pur. CR8 . .160 DR113
Buttermere Rd, Orp. BR5 . . .146 EX98
Buttermere Wk, E8 . . . . . . .84 DT65
Buttermere Way, Egh. TW20
  off Keswick Rd 113 BB94
Butterwick, W6 . . . . .99 CW77
  Watford WD25 . . . . .24 BY36
Butterworth Gdns, Wdf.Grn.
  IG8 . . . . .48 EG51
Buttesland St, N1 . . . . .197 L2
Buttfield Cl, Dag. RM10 . . . .89 FB65
Buttlehide, Rick. (Map.Cr.)
  WD3 . . . . .37 BD50
Buttmarsh Cl, SE18 . . . . . .105 EP78
Button Rd, Grays RM17 . . . .110 FZ77
Button St, Swan. BR8 . . . . .148 FJ96
Butts, The, Brent. TW8 . . . . .97 CK79
  Sevenoaks (Otford) TN14 . .181 FH116
  Sunbury-on-Thames TW16
  off Elizabeth Gdns 136 BW97
Buttsbury Rd, Ilf. IG1 . . . . . .69 EQ64
Butts Cotts, Felt. TW13 . . . .116 BZ90
Butts Cres, Felt. TW13 . . . . .116 CA90
Butts Grn Rd, Horn. RM11 . .72 FK58
Buttsmead, Nthwd. HA6 . . . .39 BQ52
Butts Piece, Nthlt. UB5
  off Longhook Gdns 77 BV68
Butts Rd, Brom. BR1 . . . . . .124 EE92
  Woking GU21 . . . . .166 AY117
Buxhall Cres, E9 . . . . .85 DZ65
Buxted Rd, E8 . . . . .84 DT66
  N12 . . . . .44 DE50
  SE22 . . . . .102 DS84
Buxton Av, Cat. CR3 . . . . . .176 DS121
Buxton Cl, Wdf.Grn. IG8 . . . .48 EK51
Buxton Ct, N1 . . . . .197 J2
Buxton Cres, Sutt. SM3 . . . .157 CY105
Buxton Dr, E11 . . . . .68 EE56
  New Malden KT3 . . . . . . .138 CR96
Buxton Gdns, W3 . . . . .80 CP73
Buxton La, Cat. CR3 . . . . . .176 DR120
Buxton Path, Wat. WD19 . . .40 BW48
Buxton Rd, E4 . . . . .47 ED45
  E6 . . . . .86 EL69
  E15 . . . . .68 EE64
  E17 . . . . .67 DY56
  N19 . . . . .65 DK60
  NW2 . . . . .81 CV65
  SW14 . . . . .98 CS83
  Ashford TW15 . . . . .114 BK92
  Epping (They.B.) CM16 . . .33 ES36
  Erith DA8 . . . . .107 FD80
  Grays RM16 . . . . .110 GE75
  Ilford IG2 . . . . .69 ES58
  Thornton Heath CR7 . . . .141 DP99
  Waltham Abbey EN9 . . . . .16 EG32
Buxton St, E1 . . . . .84 DT70
Buzzard Creek Ind Est, Bark.
  IG11 . . . . .87 ET71
Byam, St, SW6 . . . . .100 DC82
Byards Cft, SW16 . . . . .141 DK95
Byatt Wk, Hmptn. TW12
  off Victors Dr 116 BY93
Bychurch End, Tedd. TW11
  off Church Rd 117 CF92
Bycliffe Ter, Grav. DA11 . . . .131 GF87
Bycroft Rd, Sthl. UB1 . . . . . .78 CA70
Bycroft St, SE20
  off Parish La 123 DX94
Bycullah Av, Enf. EN2 . . . . .29 DP41
Bycullah Rd, Enf. EN2 . . . . .29 DP41
Bye, The, W3 . . . . .80 CS72
Byegrove Rd, SW19 . . . . . .120 DD93
Byers Cl, Pot.B. EN6 . . . . . .12 DC34
Byewaters, Wat. WD18 . . . . .23 BQ44
Bye Way, The, Har. HA3 . . . .41 CE53
Byeway, The, SW14 . . . . . . .98 CQ83
Byeway, The, Rick. WD3 . . . .38 BL47
Byeways, Twick. TW2 . . . . .116 CB90
Byeways, The, Ashtd. KT21
  off Skinners La 171 CK118
  Surbiton KT5 . . . . .138 CN99
Byfeld Gdns, SW13 . . . . . . .99 CU81
Byfield Cl, SE16 . . . . .203 L4
Byfield Pas, Islw. TW7 . . . . .97 CG83
Byfield Rd, Islw. TW7 . . . . . .97 CG83
BYFLEET, W.Byf. 152 BM113
  ₹ Byfleet & New Haw 152 BK110
Byfleet Rd, Add. (New Haw)
  KT15 . . . . .152 BK108
  Cobham KT11 . . . . .153 BS113
  West Byfleet (Byfleet)
  KT14 . . . . .152 BN112
Byfleet Technical Cen, W.Byf.
  (Byfleet) KT14 . . . . .152 BK111
Byford Cl, E15 . . . . .86 EE66
Bygrove, Croy. (New Adgtn.)
  CR0 . . . . .161 EB107
Bygrove St, E14 . . . . .85 EB72
Byland Cl, N21 . . . . .45 DM45
  SE2 . . . . .167 BA119
Bylands, Wok. GU22 . . . . . .167 BA119
Bylands Cl, SE2
  off Finchale Rd 106 EV76
  SE16 . . . . .203 J2
Byne Rd, SE26 . . . . .122 DW93
  Carshalton SM5 . . . . . . .140 DE103
Bynes Rd, S.Croy. CR2 . . . .160 DR108
Byng Dr, Pot.B. EN6 . . . . . .12 DA31
Byng Pl, WC1 . . . . .195 M5
Byng Rd, Barn. EN5 . . . . . .27 CX41
Byng St, E14 . . . . .203 P4
Bynon Av, Bexh. DA7 . . . . .106 EY83
Byre, The, N14
  off Farm La 29 DH44
Byre Rd, N14
  off Farm La 28 DG44
Byrne Rd, SW12 . . . . .121 DH88
Byron Av, E12 . . . . .86 EL65
  E18 . . . . .68 EF55
  NW9 . . . . .62 CP56

Byron Av, Borwd. WD6 . . . .26 CN43
  Coulsdon CR5 . . . . .175 DL115
  Hounslow TW4 . . . . .95 BU82
  New Malden KT3 . . . . . . .139 CU99
  Sutton SM1 . . . . .158 DD105
  Watford WD24 . . . . .24 BX39
Byron Av E, Sutt. SM1 . . . . .158 DD105
Byron Cl, E8 . . . . .84 DU67
  SE26 off Porthcawe Rd . . .123 DY91
  SE28 . . . . .88 EW74
  Hampton TW12 . . . . .116 BZ91
  Waltham Cross EN7
  off Allard Cl 14 DT27
  Walton-on-Thames KT12 . .136 BY102
  Woking (Knap.) GU21 . . . .166 AS117
Byron Ct, W9 off Lanhill Rd . .82 DA70
  Enfield EN2
  off Bycullah Rd 29 DP40
  Harrow HA1 . . . . .61 CE58
Byron Dr, N2 . . . . .64 DD58
  Erith DA8 . . . . .107 FB80
Byron Gdns, Sutt. SM1 . . . .158 DD105
  Tilbury RM18 . . . . .111 GJ81
Byron Hill Rd, Har. HA2 . . . .61 CD60
Byron Ho, Beck. BR3 . . . . .123 EA93
  Slough SL3 . . . . .93 BB78
Byron Ms, NW3 . . . . .64 DE64
  W9 off Shirland Rd 82 DA70
Byron Pl, Lthd. KT22 . . . . . .171 CH122
Byron Rd, E10 . . . . .67 EB60
  E17 . . . . .67 EA56
  NW2 . . . . .63 CV61
  NW7 . . . . .43 CU50
  W5 . . . . .80 CM74
  Addlestone KT15 . . . . . . .152 BL105
  Brentwood CM13 . . . . . . .55 GD45
  Dartford DA1 . . . . .108 FP84
  Harrow HA1 . . . . .61 CE58
  Harrow (Wldste.) HA3 . . . .41 CF54
  South Croydon CR2 . . . . .160 DV110
  Wembley HA0 . . . . .61 CJ62
Byron St, E14
  off St. Leonards Rd 85 EC72
Byron Ter, N9 . . . . .46 DW45
Byron Way, Hayes UB4 . . . .77 BT70
  Northolt UB5 . . . . .78 BY69
  Romford RM3 . . . . .52 FJ53
  West Drayton UB7 . . . . . .94 BM77
Bysouth Cl, N15 . . . . .66 DR56
  Ilford IG5 . . . . .49 EP53
By the Wd, Wat. WD19 . . . .40 BX47
Bythorn St, SW9 . . . . .101 DM83
Byton Rd, SW17 . . . . .120 DF93
Byward Av, Felt. TW14 . . . .116 BW86
Byward St, EC3 . . . . .201 N1
Bywater Pl, SE16 . . . . .203 L2
Bywater St, SW3 . . . . .198 D10
Byway, The, Epsom KT19 . . .157 CT105
  Potters Bar EN6 . . . . . . .12 DA33
  Sutton SM2 . . . . .158 DD109
Bywell Pl, W1 . . . . .195 K7
Bywood Av, Croy. CR0 . . . .142 DW100
Bywood Cl, Ken. CR8 . . . . .175 DP115
By-Wood End, Ger.Cr. (Chal.St.P.)
  SL9 . . . . .37 AZ50
Byworth Wk, N19
  off Courtauld Rd 65 DK60

Cabbell Pl, Add. KT15 . . . . .152 BJ105
Cabbell St, NW1 . . . . .194 B7
Caberfeigh Pl, Red. RH1 . . .184 DE134
★ Cabinet War Rooms,
  SW1 . . . . .199 N4
Cabinet Way, E4 . . . . .47 DZ51
Cable Pl, SE10
  off Diamond Ter 103 EC81
Cable St, E1 . . . . .84 DU73
Cable Trade Pk, SE7 . . . . . .104 EJ77
Cabot Pl, E14 . . . . .204 A2
Cabot Sq, E14 . . . . .204 A2
Cabot Way, E6 off Parr Rd . .86 EK67
Cabrera Av, Vir.W. GU25 . . .132 AW100
Cabrera Cl, Vir.W. GU25 . . . .132 AX100
Cabul Rd, SW11 . . . . .100 DE82
Cacket's Cotts, Sev. TN14
  off Cackets La 179 ES115
Cackets La, Sev. (Cudham)
  TN14 . . . . .179 ER115
Cactus Cl, SE15
  off Lyndhurst Gro 102 DS82
Cactus Wk, W12
  off Du Cane Rd 81 CT72
Cadbury Cl, Islw. TW7 . . . . .97 CG81
  Sunbury-on-Thames TW16 .115 BS94
Cadbury Rd, Sun. TW16 . . . .115 BS94
Cadbury Way, SE16 . . . . . .202 A7
Caddington Cl, Barn. EN4 . . .28 DE43
Caddington Rd, NW2 . . . . . .63 CY62
Caddis Cl, Stan. HA7
  off Daventer Dr 41 CF52
Caddy Cl, Egh. TW20 . . . . .113 BA92
Cade La, Sev. TN13 . . . . . .191 FJ128
Cadell Cl, E2
  off Shipton St 84 DT69
Cade Rd, SE10 . . . . .103 ED81
Cader Rd, SW18 . . . . .120 DC86
Cadet Dr, SE1 . . . . .202 A10
Cadet Pl, SE10 . . . . .205 H10
Cadiz Ct, Dag. RM10
  off Rainham Rd S 89 FD66
Cadiz Rd, Dag. RM10 . . . . .89 FC66
Cadiz St, SE17 . . . . .102 DQ78
Cadley Ter, SE23 . . . . .122 DW89
Cadlocks Hill, Sev. (Halst.)
  TN14 . . . . .164 EZ110
Cadman Cl, SW9
  off Langton Rd 101 DP80
Cadmer Cl, N.Mal. KT3 . . . .138 CS98
Cadmore La, Wal.Cr. (Chsht.)
  EN8 . . . . .15 DX28
Cadmus Cl, SW4
  off Aristotle Rd 101 DK83

Cadnam Pt, SW15
  off Dilton Gdns 119 CV88
Cadogan Av, Dart. DA2 . . . .129 FR87
Cadogan Cl, E9
  off Cadogan Ter 85 DZ66
  Beckenham BR3
  off Albemarle Rd 143 ED63
  Harrow HA2 . . . . .60 CB63
  Teddington TW11 . . . . . . .117 CE92
Cadogan Ct, Sutt. SM2 . . . .158 DB107
Cadogan Gdns, E18 . . . . . .68 EH55
  N3 . . . . .44 DB53
  N21 . . . . .29 DN43
  SW3 . . . . .198 E8
Cadogan Gate, SW1 . . . . . .198 E8
Cadogan La, SW1 . . . . .198 F7
Cadogan Pl, SW1 . . . . .198 E6
Cadogan Rd, Surb. KT6 . . . .137 CK99
Cadogan Sq, SW1 . . . . . . .198 E7
Cadogan St, SW3 . . . . .198 D9
Cadogan Ter, E9 . . . . .85 DZ65
Cadoxton Av, N15 . . . . .66 DT58
Cadwallon Rd, SE9 . . . . . . .125 EP89
Caedmon Rd, N7 . . . . .65 DM63
Caenshill Rd, Wey. KT13 . . .152 BN108
Caenwood Cl, Wey. KT13 . . .152 BN107
Caen Rd Rd, Ashtd. KT21 . . .171 CJ118
Caerleon Cl, Sid. DA14 . . . .126 EW92
Caerleon Ter, SE2
  off Blithdale Rd 106 EV77
Caernarvon Cl, Horn. RM11 . .72 FN60
  Mitcham CR4 . . . . .141 DL97
Caernarvon Dr, Ilf. IG5 . . . . .49 EN53
Caesars Wk, Mitch. CR4 . . .140 DF99
Caesars Way, Shep. TW17 . .135 BR100
Cage Pond Rd, Rad. (Shenley)
  WD7 . . . . .10 CM33
Cage Yd, Reig. RH2
  off High St 184 DA134
Cahill St, EC1 . . . . .197 J5
Cahir St, E14 . . . . .204 B9
Caillard Rd, W.Byf. (Byfleet)
  KT14 . . . . .152 BL111
Cains La, Felt. TW14 . . . . . .115 BS85
Caird St, W10 . . . . .81 CY69
Cairn Av, W5 . . . . .79 CK74
Cairndale Cl, Brom. BR1 . . .124 EF94
Cairnes Ms, SE18
  off Shooter's Hill Rd 104 EL81
Cairnfield Av, NW2 . . . . . . .62 CS62
Cairngorm Cl, Tedd. TW11
  off Vicarage Rd 117 CG92
Cairns Av, Wdf.Grn. IG8 . . . .48 EL51
Cairns Cl, Dart. DA1 . . . . . .128 FK85
Cairns Rd, SW11 . . . . .120 DE85
Cairn Way, Stan. HA7 . . . . .41 CF51
Cairo New Rd, Croy. CR0 . . .141 DP103
Cairo Rd, E17 . . . . .67 EA56
Caishowe Rd, Borwd. WD6 . .26 CP39
Caistor Ms, SW12
  off Caistor Rd 121 DH87
Caistor Pk Rd, E15 . . . . . . .86 EF67
Caistor Rd, SW12 . . . . .121 DH87
Caithness Gdns, Sid. DA15 . .125 ET86
Caithness Rd, W14 . . . . . . .99 CX77
  Mitcham CR4 . . . . .121 DH94
Calabria Rd, N5 . . . . .83 DP65
Calais Cl, Wal.Cr. EN7
  off Argent Way 14 DR26
Calais Gate, SE5
  off Calais St 101 DP81
Calais St, SE5 . . . . .101 DP81
Calbourne Av, Horn. RM12 . .71 FH64
Calbourne Rd, SW12 . . . . . .120 DF87
Calcott Cl, Brwd. CM14 . . . .54 FV46
Calcott Wk, SE9 . . . . .124 EK91
Calcutta Rd, Til. RM18 . . . . .111 GF82
Caldbeck, Wal.Abb. EN9 . . . .15 ED34
Caldbeck Av, Wor.Pk. KT4 . .139 CU103
Caldecot Av, Wal.Cr. EN7 . . .14 DT29
Caldecote Gdns, Bushey
  WD23 . . . . .25 CE44
Caldecote La, Bushey WD23 .25 CF45
Caldecot Rd, SE5 . . . . .102 DQ82
Caldecott Way, E5 . . . . .67 DX62
Calder Av, Grnf. UB6 . . . . . .79 CF68
  Hatfield AL9 . . . . .12 DB26
Calder Cl, Enf. EN1 . . . . . . .30 DS41
Calder Ct, Slou. SL3 . . . . . .93 AZ78
Calder Gdns, Edg. HA8 . . . .62 CN55
Calder Rd, Mord. SM4 . . . . .140 DC99
Caldervale Rd, SW4 . . . . . .121 DK85
Calder Way, Slou. (Colnbr.)
  SL3 . . . . .93 BF83
Calderwood, Grav. DA12 . . . .131 GL92
Calderwood St, SE18 . . . . .105 EN77
Caldicot Gm, NW9
  off Snowdon Dr 62 CS58
Caldwell Rd, Wat. WD19 . . . .40 BX49
Caldwell St, SW9 . . . . .101 DM80
Caldwell Yd, EC4
  off Upper Thames St 84 DQ73
Caldy Rd, Belv. DA17 . . . . .107 FB76
Caldy Wk, N1
  off Clephane Rd 84 DQ65
Caleb St, SE1 . . . . .201 H4
Caledonian Cl, Ilf. IG3 . . . . .70 EV60
⊖ Caledonian Road 83 DL65
Caledonian Rd, N1 . . . . . . .196 A1
  N7 . . . . .65 DM64
₹ Caledonian Road &
  Barnsbury 83 DM66
Caledonian Wf, E14 . . . . . .204 F9
Caledonia Rd, Stai. TW19 . . .114 BL88
Caledonia St, N1 . . . . .196 A1
Caledon Rd, E6 . . . . .86 EL67
  St. Albans (Lon.Col.) AL2 . .9 CK26
  Wallington SM6 . . . . .158 DG105
Cale St, SW3 . . . . .198 B10
Caletock Way, SE10 . . . . . .205 K10
Calfstock La, Dart. (S.Darenth)
  DA4 . . . . .148 FL98
Calico Row, SW11
  off York Pl 100 DC83

Calidore Cl, SW2
  off Endymion Rd 121 DM86
California La, Bushey (Bushey Hth.)
  WD23 . . . . .41 CD46
California Rd, N.Mal. KT3 . . .138 CQ98
Caliph Cl, Grav. DA12 . . . . .131 GM90
Callaby Ter, N1
  off Wakeham St 84 DR65
Callaghan Cl, SE13
  off Glenton Rd 104 EE84
Callander Rd, SE6 . . . . . . .123 EB89
Callan Gro, S.Ock. RM15 . . .91 FV73
Callard Av, N13 . . . . .45 DP50
Callcott Rd, NW6 . . . . .81 CZ66
Callcott St, W8
  off Hillgate Pl 82 DA74
Callendar Rd, SW7 . . . . . . .100 DD76
Calley Down Cres, Croy.
  (New Adgtn.) CR0 . . . . . .161 ED110
Callingham Cl, E14
  off Wallwood St 85 DZ71
Callis Fm Cl, Stai. (Stanw.)
  TW19 off Bedfont Rd 114 BL86
Callis Rd, E17 . . . . .67 DZ58
Callow Fld, Pur. CR8 . . . . . .159 DN113
Callow Hill, Vir.W. GU25 . . . .132 AW97
Callowland Cl, Wat. WD24 . . .23 BV38
Callow St, SW3 . . . . .100 DD79
Calluna Ct, Wok. GU22
  off Heathside Rd 167 AZ118
Calmont Rd, Brom. BR1 . . . .123 ED93
Calmore Cl, Horn. RM12 . . .72 FJ64
Calne Av, Ilf. IG5 . . . . .49 EP53
Calonne Rd, SW19 . . . . . . .119 CX91
Calshot Av, Grays (Chaff.Hun.)
  RM16 . . . . .110 FZ75
Calshot Rd, Houns. (Hthrw.Air.)
  TW6 . . . . .94 BN82
Calshot St, N1 . . . . .83 DM68
Calshot Way, Enf. EN2 . . . . .29 DP41
  Hounslow (Hthrw.Air.) TW6
  off Calshot Rd 95 BP82
Calthorpe Gdns, Edg. HA8
  off Jesmond Way 42 CL50
  Sutton SM1 . . . . .140 DC104
Calthorpe St, WC1 . . . . . . .196 C4
Calton Av, SE21 . . . . .122 DS85
Calton Rd, Barn. EN5 . . . . .28 DC44
Calverley Cl, Beck. BR3 . . . .123 EB93
Calverley Cres, Dag. RM10 . .70 FA61
Calverley Gdns, Har. HA3 . . .61 CK59
Calverley Gro, N19 . . . . . . .65 DK60
Calverley Rd, Epsom KT17 . .157 CU107
Calvert Av, E2 . . . . .197 N3
Calvert Cl, Belv. DA17 . . . . .106 FA77
  Sidcup DA14 . . . . .126 EY93
Calverton, SE5 . . . . .102 DS79
Calverton Rd, E6 . . . . .87 EN67
Calvert Rd, SE10 . . . . .104 EF78
  Barnet EN5 . . . . .27 CX40
Calvert's Bldgs, SE1 . . . . . .201 K3
Calvert St, NW1
  off Chalcot Rd 82 DG67
Calvin Cl, Orp. BR5 . . . . . . .146 EX97
Calvin St, E1 . . . . .197 P5
Calydon Rd, SE7 . . . . .104 EH78
Calypso Way, SE16 . . . . . . .203 M7
Camac Rd, Twick. TW2 . . . .117 CD88
Cambalt Rd, SW15 . . . . . . .119 CX85
Camberley Av, SW20 . . . . . .139 CV96
  Enfield EN1 . . . . .30 DS42
Camberley Cl, Sutt. SM3 . . .139 CX104
Camberley Rd, Houns. (Hthrw.Air.)
  TW6 . . . . .94 BN83
Cambert Way, SE3 . . . . . . .104 EH84
CAMBERWELL, SE5 . . . . . .102 DQ80
Camberwell Ch St, SE5 . . . .102 DR81
Camberwell Glebe, SE5 . . . .102 DR82
Camberwell Grn, SE5 . . . . .102 DR81
Camberwell Gro, SE5 . . . . .102 DR81
Camberwell New Rd, SE5 . . .101 DN80
Camberwell Pas, SE5
  off Camberwell Grn 102 DQ81
Camberwell Rd, SE5 . . . . . .102 DQ79
Camberwell Sta Rd, SE5 . . .102 DQ81
Cambeys Rd, Dag. RM10 . . .71 FB64
Camborne Av, W13 . . . . . . .97 CH75
  Romford RM3 . . . . .52 FL52
Camborne Cl, Houns. (Hthrw.Air.)
  TW6 off Camborne Rd S . .94 BN83
Camborne Ms, W11
  off St. Marks Rd 81 CY72
Camborne Rd, SW18 . . . . .120 DA87
  Croydon CR0 . . . . .142 DU101
  Morden SM4 . . . . .139 CX99
  Sidcup DA14 . . . . .126 EW90
  Sutton SM2 . . . . .158 DA108
  Welling DA16 . . . . .105 ET82
Camborne Rd N, Houns. (Hthrw.Air.)
  TW6 off Camborne Rd S . .94 BN83
Camborne Rd S, Houns. (Hthrw.Air.)
  TW6 . . . . .94 BN83
Camborne Way, Houns. TW5 .96 CA81
  Hounslow (Hthrw.Air.) TW6
  off Camborne Rd S 94 BN83
  Romford RM3 . . . . .52 FL52
Cambourne Av, N9 . . . . . . .47 DX45
Cambray Rd, SW12 . . . . . .121 DJ88
  Orpington BR6 . . . . .145 ET101
Cambria Cl, Houns. TW3 . . .96 CA84
  Sidcup DA15 . . . . .125 ER88
Cambria Ct, Felt. TW14
  off Hounslow Rd 115 BV87
  Slough SL3 off Turner Rd . .92 AW75
Cambria Cres, Grav. DA12 . .131 GL91
Cambria Gdns, Stai. TW19 . .114 BL87
Cambrian Av, Ilf. IG2 . . . . . .69 ES57
Cambrian Cl, SE27 . . . . . . .121 DP90
Cambrian Gm, NW9
  off Snowdon Dr 62 CS57
Cambrian Gro, Grav. DA11 . .131 GG87
Cambrian Rd, E10 . . . . .67 EA59
  Richmond TW10 . . . . . . .118 CM86
Cambria Rd, SE5 . . . . .102 DQ83
Cambria St, SW6 . . . . .100 DB80
Cambridge Av, NW6 . . . . . .82 DA68
  Greenford UB6 . . . . .61 CF64

Cam - Car

Cambridge Av, N.Mal. KT3 ...139 CT96
  Romford RM2 ....72 FJ55
  Welling DA16 ....105 ET84
Cambridge Barracks Rd,
  SE18 ....105 EM75
Cambridge Circ, WC2 ....195 N9
Cambridge Cl, E17 ....67 DZ58
  N22 off Pellatt Gro 45 DN53
  NW10 off Lawrence Way 62 CQ62
  SW20 ....139 CV95
  Hounslow TW4 ....96 BY84
  Waltham Cross (Chsht.)
  EN8 ....14 DW29
  West Drayton UB7 ....94 BK79
  Woking GU21
   off Bingham Dr 166 AT118
Cambridge Cotts, Rich. TW9 .98 CN79
Cambridge Cres, E2 ....84 DV68
  Teddington TW11 ....117 CG92
Cambridge Dr, SE12 ....124 EG85
  Potters Bar EN6 ....11 CX31
  Ruislip HA4 ....60 BW61
Cambridge Gdns, N10 ....45 DH53
  N13 ....45 DN50
  N17 off Gt. Cambridge Rd .46 DR52
  N21 ....46 DR45
  NW6 ....82 DA68
  W10 ....81 CY72
  Enfield EN1 ....30 DU40
  Grays RM16 ....111 GG77
  Kingston upon Thames
  KT1 ....138 CN96
Cambridge Gate, NW1 ....195 J3
Cambridge Gate Ms, NW1 ...195 J3
Cambridge Grn, SE9 ....125 EP88
Cambridge Gro, SE20 ....142 DV95
  W6 ....99 CV77
Cambridge Gro Rd, Kings.T.
  KT1 ....138 CN96
≷ Cambridge Heath 84 DV68
Cambridge Heath Rd, E1 ....84 DV68
  E2 ....84 DV68
Cambridge Mans, SW11
  off Cambridge Rd 100 DF81
Cambridge Par, Enf. EN1
  off Great Cambridge Rd 30 DU39
Cambridge Pk, E11 ....68 EG59
  Twickenham TW1 ....117 CK87
Cambridge Pk Rd, E11
  off Cambridge Pk 68 EF59
Cambridge Pl, W8 ....100 DB75
Cambridge Rd, E4 ....47 ED46
  E11 ....68 EF58
  NW6 ....82 DA69
  SE20 ....142 DV97
  SW11 ....100 DF81
  SW13 ....99 CT82
  SW20 ....139 CU95
  W7 ....97 CF75
  Ashford TW15 ....115 BQ94
  Barking IG11 ....87 EQ66
  Bromley BR1 ....124 EG94
  Carshalton SM5 ....158 DE107
  Hampton TW12 ....116 BZ94
  Harrow HA2 ....60 CA57
  Hounslow TW4 ....96 BY84
  Ilford IG3 ....69 ES60
  Kingston upon Thames
  KT1 ....138 CM96
  Mitcham CR4 ....141 DJ97
  New Malden KT3 ....138 CS98
  Richmond TW9 ....98 CN80
  Sidcup DA14 ....125 ES91
  Southall UB1 ....78 BZ74
  Teddington TW11 ....117 CF91
  Twickenham TW1 ....117 CK86
  Uxbridge UB8 ....76 BK65
  Walton-on-Thames KT12 .135 BV100
  Watford WD18 ....24 BW42
  West Molesey KT8 ....136 BZ98
Cambridge Rd N, W4 ....98 CP78
Cambridge Rd S, W4 ....98 CP78
Cambridge Row, SE18 ....105 EP78
Cambridge Sq, W2 ....194 B8
Cambridge St, SW1 ....199 J9
Cambridge Ter, N13 ....45 DN50
  NW1 ....195 J3
Cambridge Ter Ms, NW1 ...195 J3
Cambstone Cl, N11 ....44 DG47
Cambus Cl, Hayes UB4 ....78 BY71
Cambus Rd, E16 ....86 EG71
Camdale Rd, SE18 ....105 ET80
★ Camden Arts Cen, NW3 ....64 DC64
Camden Av, Felt. TW13 ....116 BW89
  Hayes UB4 ....78 BW73
Camden Cl, Chis. BR7 ....125 EQ94
  Gravesend DA11 ....130 GC88
  Grays RM16 ....111 GH77
Camden Gdns, NW1
  off Kentish Town Rd 83 DH66
  Sutton SM1 ....158 DB106
  Thornton Heath CR7 ....141 DP97
Camden Gro, Chis. BR7 ....125 EP93
Camden High St, NW1 ....83 DH67
Camden Hill Rd, SE19 ....122 DS93
Camdenhurst St, E14 ....85 DY72
Camden La, N7
  off Rowstock Gdns 83 DK65
★ Camden Lock Mkt &
  Waterbuses, NW1 ....83 DH66
Camden Lock Pl, NW1
  off Chalk Fm Rd 83 DH66
Camden Ms, NW1 ....83 DK65
  Chislehurst BR7 ....125 EM94
Camden Pas, N1 ....83 DP67
≷ Camden Road 83 DJ66
Camden Rd, E11 ....68 EH58
  E17 ....67 DZ56
  N7 ....65 DK64
  NW1 ....83 DJ66
  Bexley DA5 ....126 EZ88
  Carshalton SM5 ....158 DF105
  Grays RM16 ....110 FY76
  Sevenoaks TN13 ....191 FH122
  Sutton SM1 ....158 DA106
Camden Row, SE3 ....104 EE82

Camden Sq, NW1 ....83 DK65
  SE15 off Watts St 102 DT81
Camden St, NW1 ....83 DJ66
Camden Ter, NW1
  off North Vil 83 DK65
CAMDEN TOWN, NW1 ....83 DJ67
⊖ Camden Town 83 DH67
Camden Wk, N1 ....83 DP67
Camden Way, Chis. BR7 ....125 EM94
  Thornton Heath CR7 ....141 DP97
Camelford Wk, W11
  off Lancaster Rd 81 CY72
Camel Gro, Kings.T. KT2 ...117 CK92
Camellia Cl, Rom. RM3
  off Columbine Way 52 FL53
Camellia Ct, Wdf.Grn. IG8
  off The Bridle Path 48 EE52
Camellia Pl, Twick. TW2 ....116 CB87
Camellia St, SW8 ....101 DL80
Camelot Cl, SE28 ....105 ER75
  SW19 ....120 DA91
  Westerham (Bigg.H.) TN16 .178 EJ116
Camelot Ho, N9
  off Salisbury Rd 46 DU48
Camelot St, SE15
  off Bird in Bush Rd 102 DV80
Camera Pl, SW10 ....100 DD79
Camera Rd, E16 ....86 EK74
Cameron Cl, N18 ....46 DV49
  N20 off Myddelton Pk 44 DE47
  Bexley DA5 ....127 FD90
  Brentwood CM14 ....54 FW49
Cameron Dr, Wal.Cr. EN8 ....15 DX34
Cameron Pl, E1
  off Varden St 84 DV72
Cameron Rd, SE6 ....123 DZ89
  Bromley BR2 ....144 EG98
  Croydon CR0 ....141 DP100
  Ilford IG3 ....69 ES60
Camerton Cl, E8
  off Buttermere Wk 84 DT65
Camgate Cen, Stai. (Stanw.)
  TW19 ....114 BM86
Cam Grn, S.Ock. RM15 ....91 FV72
Camilla Cl, Sun. TW16 ....115 BS93
Camilla Rd, SE16 ....202 D9
Camille Cl, SE25 ....142 DU97
Camlan Rd, Brom. BR1 ....124 EF91
Camlet St, E2 ....197 P4
Camlet Way, Barn. EN4 ....28 DA42
Camley St, NW1 ....83 DK66
★ Camley St Natural Pk,
  NW1 ....83 DL68
Camm Gdns, Kings.T. KT1
  off Church Rd 138 CM96
  Thames Ditton KT7 ....137 CE101
Camms Ter, Dag. RM10 ....71 FC64
Camomile Av, Mitch. CR4 ....140 DF95
Camomile Rd, Rom. (Rush Grn.)
  RM7 ....71 FD61
Camomile St, EC3 ....197 M8
Camomile Way, West Dr. UB7 .76 BL72
Campana Rd, SW6 ....100 DA81
Campbell Av, Ilf. IG6 ....69 EQ56
  Woking GU22 ....167 AZ121
Campbell Cl, SE18
  off Moordown 105 EN81
  SW16 ....121 DK91
  Romford (Hav.at.Bow.)
  RM1 ....51 FE51
  Ruislip HA4 ....59 BU58
  Twickenham TW2 ....117 CD89
Campbell Ct, N17 ....46 DT53
Campbell Cft, Edg. HA8 ....42 CN50
Campbell Gordon Way, NW2 .63 CV63
Campbell Rd, E3 ....85 EA69
  E6 ....86 EL67
  E15 off Trevelyan Rd 68 EF63
  E17 ....67 DZ56
  N17 ....46 DU53
  W7 ....79 CE73
  Caterham CR3 ....176 DR121
  Croydon CR0 ....141 DP101
  East Molesey KT8
   off Hampton Ct Rd 137 CF97
  Gravesend DA11 ....131 GF88
  Twickenham TW2 ....117 CD89
  Weybridge KT13 ....152 BN108
Campbell Wk, N1
  off Outram Pl 83 DL67
Campdale Rd, N7 ....65 DK62
Campden Cres, Dag. RM8 ....70 EV63
  Wembley HA0 ....61 CH61
Campden Gro, W8 ....100 DA75
Campden Hill Ct, W8
  off Campden Hill Rd 100 DA75
Campden Hill Gdns, W8 ....82 DA74
Campden Hill Gate, W8
  off Duchess of Bedford's Wk .100 DA75
Campden Hill Pl, W11
  off Holland Pk Av 81 CZ74
Campden Hill Rd, W8 ....82 DA74
Campden Hill Sq, W11 ....81 CZ74
Campden Hill Twrs, W11
  off Notting Hill Gate 82 DA74
Campden Ho Cl, W8
  off Hornton St 100 DA75
Campden Rd, S.Croy. CR2 ..160 DS106
  Uxbridge UB10 ....58 BM62
Campden St, W8 ....82 DA74
Campen Cl, SW19 ....119 CY89
Camperdown St, E1
  off Leman St 84 DT72
Campfield Rd, SE9 ....124 EK87
Camphill Ct, W.Byf. KT14 ...152 BG112
Camphill Ind Est, W.Byf.
  KT14 ....152 BH111
Camphill Rd, W.Byf. KT14 ...152 BG112
Campine Cl, Wal.Cr. (Chsht.) EN8
  off Welsummer Way 15 DX28
Campion Cl, E6 ....87 EM73
  Croydon CR0 ....160 DS105
  Gravesend (Nthflt.) DA11 ..130 GE91
  Harrow HA3 ....62 CM58

Campion Cl, Rom. (Rush Grn.)
  RM7 ....71 FD61
  Uxbridge (Denh.) UB9
   off Lindsey Rd 58 BG62
  Uxbridge (Hlgdn.) UB8 ....76 BM71
  Watford WD25 ....7 BU33
Campion Ct, Grays RM17 ...110 GD79
Campion Gdns, Wdf.Grn. IG8 .48 EG50
Campion Pl, SE28 ....88 EV74
Campion Rd, SW15 ....99 CW84
  Isleworth TW7 ....97 CF81
Campions, Epp. CM16 ....18 EU28
  Loughton IG10 ....33 EN38
Campions, The, Borwd. WD6 .26 CN38
Campions Cl, Borwd. WD6 ...26 CP37
Campion Ter, NW2 ....63 CX62
Campion Way, Edg. HA8 ......42 CQ49
Cample La, S.Ock. RM15 .....91 FU73
Camplin Rd, Har. HA3 ....62 CL57
Camplin St, SE14 ....103 DX80
Camp Rd, SW19 ....119 CW92
  Caterham (Wold.) CR3 ....177 DY120
  Gerrards Cross SL9 ....56 AX59
Campsbourne, The, N8
  off High St 65 DL56
Campsbourne Rd, N8 ....65 DL55
Campsey Gdns, Dag. RM9 ....88 EV66
Campsey Rd, Dag. RM9 ....88 EV66
Campsfield Rd, N8
  off Campsbourne Rd 65 DL55
Campshill Pl, SE13
  off Campshill Rd 123 EC85
Campshill Rd, SE13 ....123 EC85
Campus Rd, E17 ....67 DZ58
Campus Way, NW4
  off Greyhound Hill 63 CV55
Camp Vw, SW19 ....119 CV92
Cam Rd, E15 ....85 ED67
Camrose Av, Edg. HA8 ....42 CM53
  Erith DA8 ....107 FB79
  Feltham TW13 ....115 BV91
Camrose Cl, Croy. CR0 ....143 DY101
  Morden SM4 ....140 DA98
Camrose St, SE2 ....106 EU78
Canada Av, N18 ....46 DQ51
Canada Cres, W3 ....80 CQ71
Canada Est, SE16 ....202 G6
Canada Fm Rd, Dart. (S.Darenth)
  DA4 ....149 FU98
  Longfield DA3 ....149 FU99
Canada Gdns, SE13 ....123 EC85
Canada La, Brox. EN10 .....15 DY25
Canada Rd, W3 ....80 CQ70
  Cobham KT11 ....154 BW113
  Erith DA8 ....107 FH80
  Slough SL1 ....92 AV75
  West Byfleet (Byfleet)
  KT14 ....152 BK111
Canadas, The, Brox. EN10 ...15 DY25
Canada Sq, E14 ....204 B2
⊖ Canada Water 202 G5
Canada Way, W12 ....81 CV73
Canadian Av, SE6 ....123 EB88
Canadian Memorial Av, Egh.
  TW20 ....132 AT96
Canal App, SE8 ....103 DY79
Canal Basin, Grav. DA12 ....131 GK86
Canal Cl, E1 ....85 DY70
  W10 ....81 CX70
Canal Est, Slou. (Langley)
  SL3 ....93 BA75
Canal Gro, SE15 ....102 DU79
Canal Path, E2 ....84 DT67
Canal Rd, Grav. DA12 ....131 GJ86
Canal Side, Uxb. (Hare.) UB9
  off Summerhouse La 38 BG51
Canal St, SE5 ....102 DR79
Canal Wk, N1 ....84 DR67
  SE26 ....122 DW92
  Croydon CR0 ....142 DS100
Canal Way, N1
  off Packington Sq 84 DQ68
  NW1 ....194 B3
  NW8 ....194 A4
  NW10 ....81 CT70
  W10 ....81 CX70
Canal Way Wk, N1 ....81 CX70
Canal Wf, Slou. SL3 ....93 BA75
⊖ Canary Wharf 204 A2
DLR Canary Wharf 204 A2
Canberra Cl, NW4 ....63 CU55
  Dagenham RM10 ....89 FD66
  Hornchurch RM12 ....72 FJ63
Canberra Cres, Dag. RM10 ...89 FD66
Canberra Dr, Hayes UB4 ......78 BW69
  Northolt UB5 ....78 BW69
Canberra Rd, E6
  off Barking Rd 87 EM67
  SE7 ....104 EJ79
  W13 ....79 CG74
  Bexleyheath DA7 ....106 EX79
  Hounslow (Hthrw.Air.)
  TW6 ....94 BN83
Canberra Sq, Til. RM18 .....111 GG82
Canbury Av, Kings.T. KT2 ...138 CM95
Canbury Ms, SE26
  off Wells Pk Rd 122 DU90
Canbury Pk Rd, Kings.T. KT2 .138 CL95
Canbury Pas, Kings.T. KT2 ..137 CK95
Canbury Path, Orp. BR5 .....146 EU98
Cancell Rd, SW9 ....101 DN81
Candahar Rd, SW11 ....100 DE82
Cander Way, S.Ock. RM15 ....91 FV73
Candle St, N15 ....66 DR58
Candlerush Cl, Wok. GU22 ..167 BB117
Candlestick La, Wal.Cr. EN7
  off Park La 14 DQ27
Candover Cl, West Dr. UB7 ...94 BK80
Candover Rd, Horn. RM12 ...71 FH60
Candover St, W1 ....195 K7
Candy St, E3 ....85 DZ67
Cane Hill, Rom. (Harold Wd.)
  RM3 off Bennison Dr .52 FK54
Caneland Ct, Wal.Abb. EN9 ...16 EF34

Canewdon Cl, Wok. GU22
  off Guildford Rd 166 AY119
Caney Ms, NW2
  off Claremont Rd 63 CX61
Canfield Dr, Ruis. HA4 ....59 BV64
Canfield Gdns, NW6 ....82 DC66
Canfield Pl, NW6
  off Canfield Gdns 82 DC65
Canfield Rd, Rain. RM13 .....89 FF67
  Woodford Green IG8 ....48 EL52
Canford Av, Nthlt. UB5 ....78 BY67
Canford Cl, Enf. EN2 ....29 DN40
Canford Dr, Add. KT15 ....134 BH103
Canford Gdns, N.Mal. KT3 ..138 CR100
Canford Pl, Tedd. TW11 ....117 CH93
Canford Rd, SW11 ....120 DG85
Canham Rd, SE25 ....142 DS97
  W3 ....98 CS75
Cann Hall Rd, E11 ....68 EE63
Canning Cres, N22 ....45 DM53
Canning Cross, SE5 ....102 DS82
Canning Pas, W8 ....100 DC76
Canning Pl, W8 ....100 DC76
Canning Pl Ms, W8
  off Canning Pl 100 DC76
Canning Rd, E15 ....86 EE68
  E17 ....67 DY56
  N5 ....65 DP62
  Croydon CR0 ....142 DT103
  Harrow HA3 ....61 CF55
CANNING TOWN, E16 ....86 EG72
⊖ Canning Town 86 EE72
DLR Canning Town 86 EE72
Cannizaro Rd, SW19 ....119 CW93
Cannonbury Av, Pnr. HA5 ....60 BX58
Cannon Cl, SW20 ....139 CW97
  Hampton TW12
   off Hanworth Rd 116 CB93
Cannon Cres, Wok. (Chobham)
  GU24 ....150 AS111
Cannon Dr, E14 ....203 P1
Cannon Gro, Lthd. (Fetch.)
  KT22 ....171 CE121
Cannon Hill, N14 ....45 DK48
  NW6 ....64 DA64
Cannon Hill La, SW20 ....139 CY97
Cannon La, NW3 ....64 DD62
  Pinner HA5 ....60 BY60
Cannon Ms, Wal.Abb. EN9 ....15 EB33
Cannon Pl, NW3 ....64 DD62
  SE7 ....104 EL78
Cannon Rd, N14 ....45 DL48
  Bexleyheath DA7 ....106 EY81
  Watford WD18 ....24 BW43
Cannonside, Lthd. (Fetch.)
  KT22 ....171 CE122
⊖ Cannon Street 201 K1
⊖ Cannon Street 201 K1
Cannon St, EC4 ....197 H9
Cannon St Rd, E1 ....84 DV72
Cannon Trd Est, Wem. HA9 ..62 CP63
Cannon Way, Lthd. (Fetch.)
  KT22 ....171 CE121
  West Molesey KT8 ....136 CA98
Cannon Wf Business Cen,
  SE8 ....103 DY77
Cannon Workshops, E14 .....203 P1
Canon Av, Rom. RM6 ....70 EW57
Canon Beck Rd, SE16 ....202 G4
Canonbie Rd, SE23 ....122 DW87
CANONBURY, N1 ....84 DQ65
≷ Canonbury 66 DQ64
Canonbury Cres, N1 ....84 DQ66
Canonbury Gro, N1 ....84 DQ66
Canonbury La, N1 ....83 DP66
Canonbury Pk N, N1 ....84 DQ65
Canonbury Pk S, N1 ....84 DQ65
Canonbury Pl, N1 ....83 DP65
Canonbury Rd, N1 ....83 DP65
  Enfield EN1 ....30 DS39
Canonbury Sq, N1 ....83 DP66
Canonbury St, N1 ....84 DQ66
Canonbury Vil, N1 ....83 DP66
Canonbury Yd, N1
  off New N Rd 84 DQ67
Canonbury Yd W, N1
  off Compton Rd 83 DP65
Canon Mohan Cl, N14
  off Farm La 29 DH44
Canon Rd, Brom. BR1 ....144 EJ97
Canon Row, SW1 ....199 P5
Canons Cl, N2 ....64 DD59
  Edgware HA8 ....42 CM51
  Radlett WD7 ....25 CH35
  Reigate RH2 ....183 CZ133
Canons Cor, Edg. HA8 ....42 CL49
Canons Dr, Edg. HA8 ....42 CL51
Canons Gate, Wal.Cr. (Chsht.)
  EN8 ....15 DZ26
Canon's Hill, Couls. CR5 ....175 DN117
Canons La, Tad. KT20 ....173 CY118
Canonsleigh Rd, Dag. RM9 ...88 EV66
CANONS PARK, Edg. 42 CL52
⊖ Canons Park 42 CL52
Canons Pk Cl, Edg. HA8
  off Donnefield Av 42 CL52
Canon St, N1 ....84 DQ67
Canons Wk, Croy. CR0 ....143 DX104
Canopus Way, Nthwd. HA6 ...39 BU49
  Staines TW19 ....114 BL87
Canrobert St, E2 ....84 DV69
Cantelowes Rd, NW1 ....83 DK65
Canterbury Av, Ilf. IG1 ....68 EL59
  Sidcup DA15 ....126 EW89
  Upminster RM14 ....73 FT60
Canterbury Cl, E6
  off Harper Rd 87 EM72
  Amersham HP7 ....20 AS39
  Beckenham BR3 ....143 EB95
  Chigwell IG7 ....49 ET48
  Dartford DA1 ....128 FN87
  Greenford UB6 ....78 CB72
  Northwood HA6 ....39 BT51

Canterbury Cres, SW9 ....101 DN83
Canterbury Gro, SE27 ....121 DP90
Canterbury Ho, Borwd. WD6 .26 CN40
Canterbury Ms, Lthd. (Oxshott)
  KT22 off Steels La 154 CC113
Canterbury Par, S.Ock. RM15 .91 FW69
Canterbury Pl, SE17 ....200 G9
Canterbury Rd, E10 ....67 EC59
  NW6 ....82 DA68
  Borehamwood WD6 ....26 CN40
  Croydon CR0 ....141 DM101
  Feltham TW13 ....116 BY90
  Gravesend DA12 ....131 GJ89
  Harrow HA1, HA2 ....60 CB57
  Morden SM4 ....140 DC99
  Watford WD17 ....23 BV40
Canterbury Ter, NW6 ....82 DA68
Canterbury Way, Brwd. CM13 .53 FW51
  Purfleet RM19 ....109 FS80
  Rickmansworth (Crox.Grn.)
  WD3 ....23 BQ41
Cantley Gdns, SE19 ....142 DT95
  Ilford IG2 ....69 EQ58
Cantley Rd, W7 ....97 CG76
Canton St, E14 ....85 EA72
Cantrell Rd, E3 ....85 DZ70
Cantwell Rd, SE18 ....105 EP80
Canute Gdns, SE16 ....203 H8
Canvey St, SE1 ....200 G2
Cape Cl, Bark. IG11
  off North St 87 EQ65
Capel Av, Wall. SM6 ....159 DM106
Capel Cl, N20 ....44 DC48
  Bromley BR2 ....144 EL102
Capel Ct, EC2 ....197 L9
  SE20 off Melvin Rd 142 DW95
Capel Gdns, Ilf. IG3 ....69 ET63
  Pinner HA5 ....60 BZ56
Capella Rd, Nthwd. HA6 .....39 BT50
Capel La, Rick. (Chorl.) WD3 .21 BC43
Capel Pt, E7 ....68 EH63
Capel Rd, E7 ....68 EH63
  E12 ....68 EJ63
  Barnet EN4 ....28 DE44
  Enfield EN1 ....30 DV36
  Watford WD19 ....24 BY44
Capel Vere Wk, Wat. WD17 ...23 BS39
Capener's Cl, SW1 ....198 F5
Capern Rd, SW18
  off Cargill Rd 120 DC88
Cape Rd, N17
  off High Cross Rd 66 DU55
Cape Yd, E1 ....202 C2
Capital Business Cen, Wem.
  HA0 ....79 CK68
Capital Ind Est, Mitch. CR4
  off Willow La 140 DF99
Capital Interchange Way, Brent.
  TW8 ....98 CN78
Capital Pk, Wok. (Old Wok.)
  GU22 ....167 BB121
Capitol Ind Pk, NW9 ....62 CQ55
Capitol Way, NW9 ....62 CQ55
Capland St, NW8 ....194 A4
Caple Par, NW10
  off Harley Rd 80 CS68
Caple Rd, NW10 ....81 CT68
Capon Cl, Brwd. CM14 ....54 FV46
Capper St, WC1 ....195 L5
Caprea Cl, Hayes UB4
  off Triandra Way 78 BX71
Capri Rd, Croy. CR0 ....142 DT102
Capstan Cen, Til. RM18 .....110 GD80
Capstan Cl, Rom. RM6 ....70 EV58
Capstan Ct, Dart. DA2 ....108 FQ84
Capstan Ms, Grav. DA11
  off Rosherville Way 130 GE87
Capstan Ride, Enf. EN2 ....29 DN40
Capstan Rd, SE8 ....203 M8
Capstan Sq, E14 ....204 E5
Capstan's Wf, Wok. (St. John's)
  GU21 ....166 AT118
Capstan Way, SE16 ....203 L3
Capstone Rd, Brom. BR1 ....124 EF91
Captain Cook Cl, Ch.St.G.
  HP8 ....36 AU49
Capthorne Av, Har. HA2 ....60 BY60
Capuchin Cl, Stan. HA7 ....41 CH51
Capulet Ms, E16 ....205 N2
Capworth St, E10 ....67 EA60
Caractacus Cottage Vw, Wat.
  WD18 ....39 BU45
Caractacus Grn, Wat. WD18 ..23 BT44
Caradoc Cl, W2 ....82 DA72
Caradoc St, SE10 ....205 H10
Caradon Cl, E11
  off Brockway Cl 68 EE61
  Woking GU21 ....166 AV118
Caradon Way, N15 ....66 DR56
Caravan La, Rick. WD3 ....38 BL45
Caravel Cl, E14
  off Tiller Rd 103 EA76
  Grays RM16 ....110 FZ76
Caravelle Gdns, Nthlt. UB5
  off Javelin Way 78 BX69
Caravel Ms, SE8
  off Watergate St 103 EA79
Caraway Cl, E13 ....86 EH71
Caraway Pl, Wall. SM6 ....141 DH104
Carberry Rd, SE19 ....122 DS93
Carbis Cl, E4 ....47 ED46
Carbis Rd, E14 ....85 DZ72
Carbone Hill, Hert. (Newgate St.)
  SG13 ....13 DK26
  Potters Bar (Cuffley) EN6 ..13 DJ27
Carbuncle Pas Way, N17 .....46 DU54
Carburton St, W1 ....195 J6
Carbury Cl, Horn. RM12 .....90 FJ65
Cardale St, E14 ....204 D6

★ Place of interest   ≷ Railway station   ⊖ London Underground station   DLR Docklands Light Railway station   ◇ Tramlink station   Ⓗ Hospital

Car - Cas

Carden Rd, SE15 . . . . .102 DV83
Cardiff Rd, W7 . . . . .97 CG76
  Enfield EN3 . . . . .30 DV42
  Watford WD18 . . . . .23 BV44
Cardiff St, SE18 . . . . .105 ES80
Cardiff Way, Abb.L. WD5 . . . .7 BU32
Cardigan Cl, Wok. GU21
  off Bingham Dr 166 AS118
Cardigan Gdns, Ilf. IG3 . . . .70 EU61
Cardigan Rd, E3 . . . . .85 DZ68
  SW13 . . . . .99 CU82
  SW19 off Haydons Rd . . .120 DC93
  Richmond TW10 . . . . . . .118 CL86
Cardigan St, SE11 . . . . .200 D10
Cardigan Wk, N1
  off Ashby Gro 84 DQ66
Cardinal Av, Borwd. WD6 . . . .26 CP41
  Kingston upon Thames
  KT2 . . . . .118 CL92
  Morden SM4 . . . . .139 CY100
Cardinal Bourne St, SE1 . . .201 L7
Cardinal Cl, Chis. BR7 . . . . .145 ER95
  Edgware HA8
  off Abbots Rd 42 CR52
  Morden SM4 . . . . .139 CY101
  South Croydon CR2 . . . .160 DU113
  Waltham Cross (Chsht.) EN7
  off Adamsfield 14 DT26
  Worcester Park KT4 . . . .157 CU105
Cardinal Ct, Borwd. WD6
  off Cardinal Av 26 CP41
Cardinal Cres, N.Mal. KT3 . .138 CQ96
Cardinal Dr, Ilf. IG6 . . . . . . .49 EQ51
  Walton-on-Thames KT12 .136 BX102
Cardinal Hinsley Cl, NW10 . .81 CU68
Cardinal Pl, SW15 . . . . .99 CX84
Cardinal Rd, Felt. TW13 . . . .115 BW88
  Ruislip HA4 . . . . .60 BX60
Cardinals Wk, Hmptn. TW12 .116 CC94
  Sunbury-on-Thames TW16 .115 BS93
Cardinals Way, N19 . . . . . . .65 DK60
Cardinal Way, Har. HA3
  off Wolseley Rd 61 CE55
  Rainham RM13 . . . . .90 FK68
Cardine Ms, SE15 . . . . .102 DV80
Cardingham, Wok. GU21 . . .166 AU117
Cardington Sq, Houns. TW4 . .96 BX84
Cardington St, NW1 . . . . . . .195 K2
Cardinham Rd, Orp. BR6 . . .163 ET105
Cardozo Rd, N7 . . . . .65 DL64
Cardrew Av, N12 . . . . .44 DD50
Cardrew Cl, N12 . . . . .44 DE50
Cardross St, W6 . . . . .99 CV76
Cardwell Rd, N7 . . . . .65 DL63
Carew Cl, N7 . . . . .65 DM61
  Coulsdon CR5 . . . . .175 DP119
Carew Ct, Sutt. SM2 . . . . . .158 DB109
Carew Rd, N17 . . . . .46 DU54
  W13 . . . . .97 CJ75
  Ashford TW15 . . . . .115 BQ93
  Mitcham CR4 . . . . .140 DG96
  Northwood HA6 . . . . .39 BS51
  Thornton Heath CR7 . . . .141 DP97
  Wallington SM6 . . . . . . .159 DJ107
Carew St, SE5 . . . . .102 DQ82
Carew Way, Wat. WD19 . . . .40 BZ48
Carey Ct, Bexh. DA6 . . . . . .127 FB85
Carey Gdns, SW8 . . . . .101 DJ81
Carey La, EC2 . . . . .197 H8
Carey Pl, SW1 . . . . .199 M9
Carey Rd, Dag. RM9 . . . . . . .70 EY63
Carey's Fld, Sev. (Dunt.Grn.)
  TN13 . . . . .181 FE120
Carey St, WC2 . . . . .196 C9
Carey Way, Wem. HA9 . . . . .62 CP63
Carfax Pl, SW4
  off Holwood Pl 101 DK84
Carfax Rd, Hayes UB3 . . . . .95 BT78
  Hornchurch RM12 . . . . . .71 FF63
Carfree Cl, N1 off Bewdley St .83 DN66
Cargill Rd, SW18 . . . . .120 DB88
Cargreen Pl, SE25
  off Cargreen Rd 142 DT98
Cargreen Rd, SE25 . . . . . . .142 DT98
Carholme Rd, SE23 . . . . . . .123 DZ88
Carisbrooke Av, Bex. DA5 . .126 EX88
  Watford WD24 . . . . .24 BX39
Carisbrooke Cl, Enf. EN1 . . . .30 DT39
  Hornchurch RM11 . . . . . .72 FN60
  Stanmore HA7 . . . . .41 CK54
Carisbrooke Ct, Slou. SL1 . . .74 AT73
Carisbrooke Gdns, SE15
  off Commercial Way 102 DT80
Carisbrooke Rd, E17 . . . . . . .67 DY56
  Bromley BR2 . . . . .144 EJ98
  Mitcham CR4 . . . . .141 DK98
  St. Albans AL2 . . . . .8 CB26
Carisbrook Rd, Brwd. CM15 .54 FV44
Carker's La, NW5 . . . . .65 DH64
Carl Ekman Ho, Grav. DA11 .130 GD87
Carleton Av, Wall. SM6 . . . .159 DK109
Carleton Cl, Esher KT10 . . . .137 CD102
Carleton Pl, Dart. (Hort.Kir.)
  DA4 . . . . .148 FQ98
Carleton Rd, N7 . . . . .65 DK64
  Dartford DA1 . . . . .128 FN87
  Waltham Cross (Chsht.)
  EN8 . . . . .15 DX28
Carleton Vil, NW5
  off Leighton Gro 65 DJ64
Carlile Cl, E3 . . . . .85 DZ68
Carlina Gdns, Wdf.Grn. IG8 . .48 EH50
Carlingford Gdns, Mitch.
  CR4 . . . . .120 DG94
Carlingford Rd, N15 . . . . . . .65 DP55
  NW3 . . . . .64 DD63
  Morden SM4 . . . . .139 CX100
Carlisle Av, EC3 . . . . .197 N9
  W3 . . . . .80 CS72
Carlisle Cl, Kings.T. KT2 . . . .138 CN95
  Pinner HA5 . . . . .60 BY59
Carlisle Gdns, Har. HA3 . . . .61 CK59
  Ilford IG1 . . . . .68 EL58
Carlisle La, SE1 . . . . .200 C7

Carlisle Ms, NW8 . . . . .194 A6
Carlisle Pl, N11 . . . . .45 DH49
  SW1 . . . . .199 K7
Carlisle Rd, E10 . . . . .67 EA60
  N4 . . . . .65 DN59
  NW6 . . . . .81 CY67
  NW9 . . . . .62 CQ55
  Dartford DA1 . . . . .128 FN86
  Hampton TW12 . . . . . . .116 CB94
  Romford RM1 . . . . .71 FG57
  Sutton SM1 . . . . .157 CZ106
Carlisle St, W1 . . . . .195 M9
Carlisle Wk, E8 off Laurel St . .84 DT65
Carlisle Way, SW17 . . . . . . .120 DG92
Carlos Pl, W1 . . . . .198 G1
Carlow St, NW1
  off Arlington Rd 83 DJ68
Carlton Av, N14 . . . . .29 DK43
  Feltham TW14 . . . . .116 BW86
  Greenhithe DA9 . . . . . . .129 FS86
  Harrow HA3 . . . . .61 CH57
  Hayes UB3 . . . . .95 BS77
  South Croydon CR2 . . . .160 DS108
Carlton Av E, Wem. HA9 . . . .62 CL60
Carlton Av W, Wem. HA0 . . . .61 CH61
Carlton Cl, NW3 . . . . .64 DA61
  Borehamwood WD6 . . . . .26 CR42
  Chessington KT9 . . . . . .155 CK107
  Edgware HA8 . . . . .42 CN50
  Northolt UB5
  off Whitton Av W 60 CC64
  Upminster RM14 . . . . . . .72 FP61
  Woking GU21 . . . . .151 AZ114
Carlton Ct, SW9 . . . . .101 DP81
  Ilford IG6 . . . . .69 ER55
  Uxbridge UB8 . . . . .76 BK71
Carlton Cres, Sutt. SM3 . . . .157 CY105
Carlton Dr, SW15 . . . . .119 CY85
  Ilford IG6 . . . . .69 ER55
Carlton Gdns, SW1 . . . . . . .199 M3
  W5 . . . . .79 CJ72
Carlton Grn, Red. RH1 . . . . .184 DE131
Carlton Gro, SE15 . . . . .102 DV81
Carlton Hill, NW8 . . . . .82 DB68
Carlton Ho, Felt. TW14 . . . . .115 BT87
Carlton Ho Ter, SW1 . . . . . .199 M3
  Sevenoaks TN13
  off St. John's Hill 191 FJ122
Carlton Pk Av, SW20 . . . . . .139 CW96
Carlton Rd, Nthwd. HA6 . . . .39 BP50
  Weybridge KT13
  off Castle Vw Rd 153 BP105
Carlton Rd, E11 . . . . .68 EF60
  E12 . . . . .68 EK63
  E17 . . . . .47 DY53
  N4 . . . . .65 DN59
  N11 . . . . .44 DG50
  SW14 . . . . .98 CQ83
  W4 . . . . .98 CR75
  W5 . . . . .79 CJ73
  Erith DA8 . . . . .107 FB79
  Grays RM16 . . . . .111 GF75
  New Malden KT3 . . . . . .138 CS96
  Redhill RH1 . . . . .184 DF131
  Reigate RH2 . . . . .184 DD132
  Romford RM2 . . . . .71 FG57
  Sidcup DA14 . . . . .125 ET92
  Slough SL2 . . . . .74 AV73
  South Croydon CR2 . . . .160 DR107
  Sunbury-on-Thames TW16 .115 BT93
  Walton-on-Thames KT12 .135 BV101
  Welling DA16 . . . . .106 EV83
  Woking GU21 . . . . .151 BA114
Carlton Sq, E1 off Argyle Rd .85 DX70
Carlton St, SW1 . . . . .199 M1
Carlton Ter, E11 . . . . .68 EH57
  N18 . . . . .46 DR48
  SE26 . . . . .122 DW90
Carlton Twr Pl, SW1 . . . . . .198 E6
Carlton Vale, NW6 . . . . .82 DB68
Carlton Vil, SW15
  off St. John's Av 119 CW85
Carlwell St, SW17 . . . . .120 DE92
Carlyle Av, Brom. BR1 . . . . .144 EK97
  Southall UB1 . . . . .78 BZ73
Carlyle Cl, N2 . . . . .64 DC58
  NW10 . . . . .80 CR67
  West Molesey KT8 . . . . .136 CB96
Carlyle Gdns, Sthl. UB1 . . . .78 BZ73
Carlyle Lo, Barn. (New Barn.)
  EN5 off Richmond Rd 28 DC43
Carlyle Ms, E1
  off Alderney Rd 85 DX70
Carlyle Pl, SW15 . . . . .99 CX84
Carlyle Rd, E12 . . . . .68 EL63
  SE28 . . . . .88 EV73
  W5 . . . . .97 CJ78
  Croydon CR0 . . . . .142 DU103
  Staines TW18 . . . . .113 BF94
★ Carlyle's Ho, SW3 . . . . . . .100 DE79
Carlyle Sq, SW3 . . . . .100 DD78
Carlyon Av, Har. HA2 . . . . . . .60 BZ63
Carlyon Cl, Wem. HA0 . . . . . .80 CL67
Carlyon Rd, Hayes UB4 . . . . .78 BW72
  Wembley HA0 . . . . .80 CL68
Carmalt Gdns, SW15 . . . . . .99 CW84
  Walton-on-Thames KT12 .154 BW106
Carmarthen Grn, NW9
  off Snowdon Dr 62 CS58
Carmarthen Rd, Slou. SL1 . . .74 AS73
Carmel Cl, Wok. GU22 . . . . .166 AY118
Carmel Ct, W8 off Holland St .100 DB75
  Wembley HA9 . . . . .62 CP61
Carmelite Cl, Har. HA3 . . . . .40 CC53
Carmelite Rd, Har. HA3 . . . . .40 CC53
Carmelite St, EC4 . . . . .196 E10
Carmelite Wk, Har. HA3 . . . .40 CC53
Carmelite Way, Har. HA3 . . . .40 CC54
Carmen Ct, Borwd. WD6
  off Belford Rd 26 CM38
Carmen St, E14 . . . . .85 EB72
Carmichael Cl, SW11
  off Darien Rd 100 DD83
  Ruislip HA4 . . . . .59 BU63
Carmichael Ms, SW18 . . . . .120 DD87
Carmichael Rd, SE25 . . . . . .142 DU99

Carminia Rd, SW17 . . . . . . .121 DH89
Carnaby St, W1 . . . . .195 K9
Carnach Grn, S.Ock. RM15 . . .91 FV73
Carnac St, SE27 . . . . .122 DR91
Carnanton Rd, E17 . . . . .47 ED53
Carnarvon Av, Enf. EN1 . . . . .30 DT41
Carnarvon Dr, Hayes UB3 . . .95 BQ76
Carnarvon Rd, E10 . . . . .67 EC58
  E15 . . . . .86 EF65
  E18 . . . . .48 EF53
  Barnet EN5 . . . . .27 CY41
Carnation Cl, Rom. (Rush Grn.)
  RM7 . . . . .71 FE61
Carnation St, SE2 . . . . .106 EV76
Carnbrook Rd, SE3 . . . . . . .104 EK83
Carnecke Gdns, SE9 . . . . . .124 EL85
Carnegie Cl, Enf. EN3
  off Government Row 31 EA37
  Surbiton KT6
  off Fullers Av 138 CM103
Carnegie Pl, SW19 . . . . . . .119 CX90
Carnegie St, N1 . . . . .83 DM67
Carnet Cl, Dart. DA1
  off Lower Sta Rd 127 FE86
Carnforth Cl, Epsom KT19 . .156 CP107
Carnforth Gdns, Horn. RM12 . .71 FG64
Carnforth Rd, SW16 . . . . . .121 DK94
Carnie Lo, SW17
  off Manville Rd 121 DH90
Carnoustie Dr, N1 . . . . .83 DM66
Carnwath Rd, SW6 . . . . . . .100 DA83
Carol Cl, NW4 . . . . .63 CX56
Carolina Cl, E15 . . . . .68 EE64
Carolina Rd, Th.Hth. CR7 . . .141 DP96
Caroline Cl, N10
  off Alexandra Pk Rd 45 DH54
  SW16 . . . . .121 DM91
  W2 off Bayswater Rd 82 DB73
  Croydon CR0
  off Brownlow Rd 160 DS105
  Isleworth TW7 . . . . .97 CD80
  West Drayton UB7 . . . . . .94 BK75
Caroline Ct, Ashf. TW15 . . . .115 BP93
  Stanmore HA7
  off The Chase 41 CG51
Caroline Gdns, SE15 . . . . . .102 DV80
Caroline Pl, SW11 . . . . .100 DG83
  W2 . . . . .82 DB73
  Hayes UB3 . . . . .95 BS80
  Watford WD19 . . . . .24 BY44
Caroline Pl Ms, W2
  off Orme La 82 DB73
Caroline Rd, SW19 . . . . . . .119 CZ94
Caroline St, E1 . . . . .85 DX72
Caroline Ter, SW1 . . . . .198 F9
Caroline Wk, W6 . . . . .99 CY79
Carol St, NW1 . . . . .83 DJ67
Carolyn Cl, Wok. GU21 . . . .166 AT119
Carolyn Dr, Orp. BR6 . . . . . .146 EU104
Caroon Dr, Rick. (Sarratt)
  WD3 . . . . .22 BH36
Carpenders Av, Wat. WD19 . .40 BY48
CARPENDERS PARK, Wat. . . .40 BZ47
⇌ Carpenders Park 40 BX48
Carpenders Pk, Wat. WD19 . .40 BY47
Carpenter Cl, Epsom KT17
  off West St 157 CT109
Carpenter Gdns, N21 . . . . . .45 DP47
Carpenter Path, Brwd. CM13 . .55 GD43
Carpenters Arms La, Epp. (Thnwd.)
  CM16 . . . . .18 EV25
Carpenters Arms Path, SE9
  off Eltham High St 125 EM86
Carpenters Cl, Twick. TW2 . .117 CE89
Carpenters Pl, SW4 . . . . . . .101 DK84
Carpenters Rd, E15 . . . . . . .85 BE65
  Enfield EN1 . . . . .30 DW36
Carpenter St, W1 . . . . .194 H1
Carpenters Wd Dr, Rick. (Chorl.)
  WD3 . . . . .21 BB42
Carpenter Way, Pot.B. EN6 . .12 DC33
Carrara Wk, SW9 . . . . .101 DP84
Carrara Wf, SW6 . . . . .99 CY83
Carr Gro, SE18 . . . . .104 EL77
Carriage Dr E, SW11 . . . . . .100 DG80
Carriage Dr N, SW11 . . . . . .100 DG79
Carriage Dr S, SW11 . . . . . .100 DF81
Carriage Dr W, SW11 . . . . . .100 DF80
Carriage Ms, Ilf. IG1 . . . . . . .69 EQ61
Carriage Pl, N16 . . . . .66 DR62
  SW16 off Eardley Rd 121 DJ92
Carriageway, The, West.
  TN16 . . . . .180 EX124
Carrick Cl, Islw. TW7 . . . . . . .97 CG83
Carrick Dr, Ilf. IG6 . . . . .49 EQ53
  Sevenoaks TN13 . . . . . .191 FH123
Carrick Gdns, N17
  off Flexmere Rd 46 DS52
Carrick Gate, Esher KT10 . . .136 CC104
Carrick Ms, SE8
  off Watergate St 103 EA79
Carrill Way, Belv. DA17 . . . .106 EX77
Carrington Av, Borwd. WD6 . .26 CP43
  Hounslow TW3 . . . . .116 CB85
Carrington Cl, Barn. EN5 . . . .27 CU43
  Borehamwood WD6 . . . . .26 CQ43
  Croydon CR0 . . . . .143 DY101
  Kingston upon Thames
  KT2 . . . . .118 CQ92
  Redhill RH1 . . . . .184 DF133
Carrington Gdns, E7
  off Woodford Rd 68 EH63
Carrington Pl, Esher KT10 . . .154 CC105
Carrington Rd, Dart. DA1 . . .128 FM86
Carrington Sq, Har. HA3 . . . .40 CC52
Carrington St, W1 . . . . .199 H3
Carrol Cl, NW5 . . . . .65 DH63
Carroll Cl, E15 . . . . .68 EF64
Carroll Hill, Loug. IG10 . . . . .33 EM41
Carron Cl, E14 . . . . .85 EB72
Carroun Rd, SW8 . . . . .101 DM80
Carroway La, Grnf. UB6
  off Cowgate Rd 79 CD66
Carrow Rd, Dag. RM9 . . . . . .88 EV66

Carrow Rd, Walt. KT12
  off Kenilworth Dr 136 BX104
Carr Rd, E17 . . . . .47 DZ54
  Northolt UB5 . . . . .78 CA65
Carrs La, N21 . . . . .30 DQ43
Carr St, E14 . . . . .85 DY71
CARSHALTON 158 DD105
⇌ Carshalton 158 DF105
CARSHALTON BEECHES,
  Cars. 158 DD109
⇌ Carshalton Beeches 158 DF107
Carshalton Gro, Sutt. SM1 . .158 DD105
CARSHALTON ON THE HILL,
  Cars. 158 DG109
Carshalton Pk Rd, Cars.
  SM5 . . . . .158 DF106
Carshalton Pl, Cars. SM5 . . .158 DG105
Carshalton Rd, Bans. SM7 . .158 DF114
  Carshalton SM5 . . . . . . .158 DC106
  Mitcham CR4 . . . . .140 DG98
  Sutton SM1 . . . . .158 DC106
🏥 Carshalton War Mem Hosp,
  Cars. SM5 . . . . .158 DF107
Carsington Gdns, Dart. DA1 .128 FK89
Carslake Rd, SW15 . . . . . . .119 CW86
Carson Rd, E16 . . . . .86 EG70
  SE21 . . . . .122 DR89
  Barnet EN4 . . . . .28 DF42
Carstairs Rd, SE6 . . . . .123 EC90
Carston Cl, SE12 . . . . .124 EF85
Carswell Cl, Ilf. IG4
  off Roding La S 68 EK56
Carswell Rd, SE6 . . . . .123 EC87
Cartbridge Cl, Wok. (Send)
  GU23 off Send Rd 167 BB123
Cartel Cl, Purf. RM19 . . . . . .109 FR77
Carter Cl, Rom. RM5 . . . . . . .51 FB52
  Wallington SM6 . . . . . . .159 DK108
Carter Ct, EC4
  off Carter La 83 DP72
Carter Dr, Rom. RM5 . . . . . . .51 FB52
Carteret St, SW1 . . . . .199 M5
Carteret Way, SE8 . . . . .203 L9
Carterhatch La, Enf. EN1 . . . .30 DU40
Carterhatch Rd, Enf. EN3 . . .30 DW40
Carter La, EC4 . . . . .196 G9
Carter Pl, SE17 . . . . .102 DQ78
Carter Rd, E13 . . . . .86 EH67
  SW19 . . . . .120 DD93
Carters Cl, Wor.Pk. KT4 . . . .139 CX103
Cartersfield Rd, Wal.Abb. EN9 .15 EC34
Carters Hill, Sev. (Undrvr.)
  TN15 . . . . .191 FP127
Carters Hill Cl, SE9 . . . . . . .124 EJ88
Carters La, SE23 . . . . .123 DY89
  Woking GU22 . . . . .167 BC120
Carters Rd, Epsom KT17 . . .173 CT115
Carters Row, Grav. (Nthflt.)
  DA11 . . . . .131 GF88
Carter St, SE17 . . . . .102 DQ79
Carters Yd, SW18
  off Wandsworth High St . .120 DA85
Carthew Rd, W6 . . . . .99 CV76
Carthew Vil, W6 . . . . .99 CV76
Carthouse La, Wok. GU21 . .150 AS114
Carthusian St, EC1 . . . . . . .197 H6
Cartier Circle, E14 . . . . .204 C3
Carting La, WC2 . . . . .200 A1
Cart La, E4 . . . . .47 ED45
Cartmel Cl, N17
  off Heybourne Rd 46 DV52
  Reigate RH2 . . . . .184 DE133
Cartmel Gdns, Mord. SM4 . .140 DC99
Cartmel Rd, Bexh. DA7 . . . .106 FA81
Carton St, W1 . . . . .194 E8
Cartwright Gdns, WC1 . . . . .195 P3
Cartwright Rd, Dag. RM9 . . . .88 EZ66
Cartwright St, E1 . . . . .84 DT73
Cartwright Way, SW13 . . . . .99 CV80
Carver Cl, W4 . . . . .98 CQ76
Carver Rd, SE24 . . . . .122 DQ86
Carville Cres, Brent. TW8 . . . .98 CL77
Cary Rd, E11 . . . . .68 EE63
Carysfort Rd, N8 . . . . .65 DK57
  N16 . . . . .66 DR62
Cary Wk, Rad. WD7 . . . . .9 CH34
Cascade Av, N10 . . . . .65 DJ56
Cascade Cl, Buck.H. IG9
  off Cascade Rd 48 EK47
  Orpington BR5 . . . . .146 EW97
Cascade Rd, Buck.H. IG9 . . . .48 EK47
Cascades, Croy. CR0 . . . . . .161 DZ110
Caselden Cl, Add. KT15 . . . .152 BJ106
Casella Rd, SE14 . . . . .103 DX80
Casewick Rd, SE27 . . . . . . .121 DP91
Casey Cl, NW8 . . . . .194 B3
Casino Av, SE24 . . . . .122 DQ85
Caspian St, SE5 . . . . .102 DR80
Caspian Wk, E16 . . . . .86 EK72
Caspian Wf, E3 off Violet Rd . .85 EB71
Cassandra Cl, Nthlt. UB5 . . . .61 CD63
Cassandra Gate, Wal.Cr. EN8 .15 DZ27
Casselden Rd, NW10 . . . . . . .80 CR66
🏥 Cassel Hosp, The, Rich.
  TW10 . . . . .117 CK91
Cassidy Rd, SW6 . . . . .100 DA80
Cassilda Rd, SE2 . . . . .106 EU77
Cassilis Rd, Twick. TW1 . . . .117 CH85
Cassio Pl, Wat. WD18 . . . . . .23 BT42
Cassiobridge, Wat. WD18 . . .23 BR42
Cassiobridge Rd, Wat. WD18 .23 BS42
Cassiobury Av, Felt. TW14 . .115 BT86
Cassiobury Ct, Wat. WD17 . . .23 BT40
Cassiobury Dr, Wat. WD17 . . .23 BT40
★ Cassiobury Park, Wat.
  WD18 . . . . .23 BS41
Cassiobury Pk, Wat. WD18 . . .23 BS41
Cassiobury Pk Av, Wat. WD18 .23 BS41
Cassiobury Rd, E17 . . . . .67 DX57
Cassio Rd, Wat. WD18 . . . . . .23 BV41
Cassis Ct, Loug. IG10 . . . . . .33 EQ42
Cassland Rd, E9 . . . . .84 DW66
  Thornton Heath CR7 . . . .142 DR98
Casslee Rd, SE6 . . . . .123 DZ87
Cassocks Sq, Shep. TW17 . .135 BR100

Casson St, E1 . . . . .84 DU71
Casstine Cl, Swan. BR8 . . . .127 FF94
Castalia Sq, E14
  off Roserton St 103 EC75
Castalia St, E14
  off Plevna St 103 EC75
Castano Ct, Abb.L. WD5 . . . . .7 BS31
Castellain Rd, W9 . . . . .82 DB70
Castellan Av, Rom. RM2 . . . .71 FH55
Castellane Cl, Stan. HA7
  off Daventer Dr 41 CF52
Castello Av, SW15 . . . . .119 CW85
Castell Rd, Loug. IG10 . . . . . .33 EQ39
CASTELNAU, SW13 . . . . .99 CU79
Castelnau, SW13 . . . . .99 CV79
Castelnau Gdns, SW13
  off Arundel Ter 99 CV79
Castelnau Pl, SW13
  off Castelnau 99 CV79
Castelnau Row, SW13
  off Lonsdale Rd 99 CV79
Casterbridge, NW6 . . . . .82 DB67
Casterbridge Rd, SE3 . . . . . .104 EG83
Casterton St, E8
  off Wilton Way 84 DV65
Castile Rd, SE18 . . . . .105 EN77
Castillon Rd, SE6 . . . . .124 EE89
Castlands Rd, SE6 . . . . .123 DZ89
Castle Av, E4 . . . . .47 ED50
  Epsom KT17 . . . . .157 CU109
  Rainham RM13 . . . . .89 FE66
  Slough (Datchet) SL3 . . . .92 AU79
  West Drayton UB7 . . . . . .76 BL73
Castlebar Hill, W5 . . . . .79 CH71
Castlebar Ms, W5 . . . . .79 CJ71
⇌ Castle Bar Park 79 CF71
Castlebar Pk, W5 . . . . .79 CH70
Castlebar Rd, W5 . . . . .79 CJ71
Castle Baynard St, EC4 . . . .196 G10
Castlebrook Cl, SE11 . . . . . .200 F8
Castle Cl, E9
  off Swinnerton St 67 DY64
  SW19 . . . . .119 CX90
  W3 . . . . .98 CP75
  Bromley BR2 . . . . .144 EE97
  Bushey WD23 . . . . .24 CB44
  Redhill (Bletch.) RH1 . . . .186 DQ133
  Romford RM3 . . . . .52 FJ48
  Sunbury-on-Thames TW16
  off Mill Fm Av 115 BS94
Castlecombe Dr, SW19 . . . .119 CX87
Castlecombe Rd, SE9 . . . . .124 EL91
Castle Ct, EC3 . . . . .197 L9
  SE26 off Champion Rd . . .123 DY91
Castledine Rd, SE20 . . . . . .122 DV94
Castle Dr, Ilf. IG4 . . . . .68 EL58
Castle Fm Rd, Sev. (Shore.)
  TN14 . . . . .165 FF109
Castlefield Rd, Reig. RH2 . . .184 DA133
Castleford Av, SE9 . . . . . . .125 EP88
Castleford Cl, N17 . . . . .46 DT51
Castle Gdns, Dor. RH4 . . . . .182 CM134
Castlegate, Rich. TW9 . . . . . .98 CM83
Castle Grn, Wey. KT13 . . . . .135 BS104
Castle Gro Rd, Wok. (Chobham)
  GU24 . . . . .150 AS113
Castlehaven Rd, NW1 . . . . . .83 DH66
Castle Hill, Long. (Fawk.)
  DA3 . . . . .149 FX99
Castle Hill Av, Croy. (New Adgtn.)
  CR0 . . . . .161 EB109
Castle Hill Rd, Egh. TW20 . . .112 AV91
Castle La, SW1 . . . . .199 L6
Castleleigh Ct, Enf. EN2 . . . .30 DR43
Castlemaine Av, Epsom
  KT17 . . . . .157 CV109
  South Croydon CR2 . . . .160 DT106
Castlemaine Twr, SW11 . . . .100 DF81
Castle Ms, N12
  off Castle Rd 44 DC50
  NW1 off Castle Rd 83 DH65
Castle Par, Epsom KT17
  off Ewell Bypass 157 CU108
Castle Pl, NW1 . . . . .83 DH65
  W4 off Windmill Rd 98 CS77
Castle Pt, E13 . . . . .86 EJ68
Castlereagh St, W1 . . . . . . .194 D8
Castle Rd, N12 . . . . .44 DC50
  NW1 . . . . .83 DH65
  Coulsdon CR5 . . . . .174 DE120
  Dagenham RM9 . . . . .88 EV67
  Dartford (Eyns.) DA4 . . . .165 FH107
  Enfield EN3 . . . . .31 DY39
  Epsom KT18 . . . . .172 CP115
  Grays RM17 . . . . .110 FZ79
  Isleworth TW7 . . . . .97 CF82
  Northolt UB5 . . . . .78 CB65
  Sevenoaks (Shore.) TN14 .165 FG108
  Southall UB2 . . . . .96 BZ76
  Swanscombe DA10 . . . . .130 FZ86
  Weybridge KT13 . . . . . . .135 BS104
  Woking GU21 . . . . .151 AZ114
Castle Sq, Red. (Bletch.) RH1 .186 DQ133
Castle St, E6 . . . . .86 EJ68
  Greenhithe DA9 . . . . . . .129 FU85
  Kingston upon Thames
  KT1 . . . . .138 CL96
  Redhill (Bletch.) RH1 . . . .185 DP133
  Slough SL1 . . . . .92 AT76
  Swanscombe DA10 . . . . .130 FZ86
Castleton Av, Bexh. DA7 . . . .107 FD81
  Wembley HA9 . . . . .62 CL63
Castleton Cl, Bans. SM7 . . . .174 DA115
  Croydon CR0 . . . . .143 DY100
Castleton Dr, Bans. SM7 . . . .174 DA115
Castleton Gdns, Wem. HA9 . .62 CL62
Castleton Rd, E17 . . . . .47 ED54
  SE9 . . . . .124 EK91
  Ilford IG3 . . . . .70 EU60
  Mitcham CR4 . . . . .141 DK98
  Ruislip HA4 . . . . .60 BX60
Castletown Rd, W14 . . . . . . .99 CY78
Castle Vw, Epsom KT18 . . . .156 CP114
Castleview Cl, N4 . . . . .66 DQ60
Castleview Gdns, Ilf. IG1 . . . .68 EL58
Castleview Rd, Slou. SL3 . . . .92 AW77
Castle Vw Rd, Wey. KT13 . . .153 BP105

Castle Wk, Reig. RH2
  off High St 184 DA134
Sunbury-on-Thames TW16
  off Elizabeth Gdns 136 BW97
Castle Way, SW19 . . . . .119 CX90
Epsom KT17
  off Castle Av 157 CU109
Feltham TW13 . . . . .116 BW91
Castlewood Dr, SE9 . . . . . .105 EM82
Castlewood Rd, N15 . . . . . . .66 DU58
N16 .66 DU59
Barnet EN4 . . . . .28 DD41
H Castlewood Therapy Cen,
  SE18 . . . . .105 EN81
Castle Yd, N6 off North Rd . .64 DG59
SE1 . . . . .200 G2
Richmond TW10 off Hill St . .117 CK85
Castor La, E14 . . . . .204 B1
Catalina Av, Grays (Chaff.Hun.)
  RM16 . . . . .110 FZ75
Catalin Ct, Wal.Abb. EN9
  off Howard Cl 15 ED33
CATERHAM 176 DU123
⇌ Caterham 176 DU124
Caterham Av, Ilf. IG5 . . . . .49 EM54
Caterham Bypass, Cat. CR3 . .176 DV120
Caterham Cl, Cat. CR3 . . . .176 DS120
Caterham Cl, Wal.Abb. EN9 . .16 EF34
H Caterham Dene Hosp, Cat.
  CR3 . . . . .176 DT123
Caterham Dr, Couls. CR5 . .175 DP118
CATERHAM-ON-THE-HILL,
  Cat. 176 DT122
Caterham Rd, SE13 . . . . . .103 EC83
CATFORD, SE6 . . . . .123 EB88
⇌ Catford 123 EA87
⇌ Catford Bridge 123 EA87
Catford Bdy, SE6 . . . . .123 EB87
Catford Hill, SE6 . . . . .123 DZ89
Catford Ms, SE6
  off Holbeach Rd 123 EB87
Catford Rd, SE6 . . . . .123 EA87
Cathall Rd, E11 . . . . .67 ED62
Cathay St, SE16 . . . . .202 E5
Cathay Wk, Nthlt. UB5
  off Brabazon Rd 78 CA68
Cathcart Dr, Orp. BR6 . . . .145 ES103
Cathcart Hill, N19 . . . . . . .65 DJ62
Cathcart Rd, SW10 . . . . . .100 DC79
Cathcart St, NW5 . . . . .83 DH65
Cathedral Piazza, SW1 . . .199 K7
Cathedral Pl, EC4 . . . . . . .197 H8
Cathedral St, SE1 . . . . . . .201 K2
Catherall Rd, N5 . . . . .66 DQ62
Catherine Cl, Brwd. CM15 . .54 FU43
Grays RM16 . . . . .110 FZ75
Loughton IG10
  off Roding Gdns 33 EM44
West Byfleet (Byfleet)
  KT14 . . . . .152 BL114
Catherine Ct, N14
  off Conisbee Ct 29 DJ43
Sunbury-on-Thames TW16 .115 BT93
Catherine Gdns, Houns. TW3 . .97 CD84
Catherine Griffiths Ct, EC1 . .196 E4
Catherine Gro, SE10 . . . . .103 EB81
Catherine Howard Ct, Wey.
  KT13 off Old Palace Rd . .135 BP104
Catherine Pl, SW1 . . . . . . .199 K6
Harrow HA1 . . . . .61 CF57
Catherine Rd, Enf. EN3 . . .31 DY36
Romford RM2 . . . . .71 FH57
Surbiton KT6 . . . . .137 CK99
Catherine's Cl, West Dr. UB7
  off Money La 94 BK76
Catherine St, WC2 . . . . . . .196 B10
Catherine Wheel All, E1 . .197 N7
Catherine Wheel Rd, Brent.
  TW8 . . . . .97 CK80
Catherine Wheel Yd, SW1 . .199 K3
Cat Hill, Barn. EN4 . . . . . .28 DE44
Cathles Rd, SW12 . . . . . . .121 DH86
Cathnor Rd, W12 . . . . .99 CV75
Catisfield Rd, Enf. EN3 . . .31 DY37
Catlin Cres, Shep. TW17 . .135 BR99
Catlin Gdns, Gdse. RH9 . . .186 DV130
Catling Cl, SE23 . . . . .122 DW90
Catlins La, Pnr. HA5 . . . . .59 BV55
Catlin St, SE16 . . . . .202 C10
Cator Cl, Croy. (New Adgtn.)
  CR0 . . . . .162 EE111
Cator Cres, Croy. (New Adgtn.)
  CR0 . . . . .161 ED111
Cator La, Beck. BR3 . . . . .143 DZ96
Cato Rd, SW4 . . . . .101 DK83
Cator Rd, SE26 . . . . .123 DX93
Carshalton SM5 . . . . .158 DF106
Cator St, SE15 . . . . .102 DT79
Cato St, W1 . . . . .194 C7
Catsey La, Bushey WD23 . .40 CC45
Catsey Wds, Bushey WD23 . .40 CC45
Catterick Cl, N11 . . . . .44 DG51
Catterick Way, Borwd. WD6 . .26 CM39
Cattistock Rd, SE9 . . . . . . .124 EL92
CATTLEGATE, Enf. 13 DL33
Cattlegate Hill, Pot.B. (Northaw)
  EN6 . . . . .13 DK31
Cattlegate Rd, Enf. EN2 . .13 DL34
Potters Bar EN6 . . . . .13 DK31
Cattley Cl, Barn. EN5
  off Wood St 27 CY42
Cattlins Cl, Wal.Cr. EN7 . .14 DT29
Catton St, WC1 . . . . .196 B7
Caulfield Rd, E6 . . . . .87 EM66
SE15 . . . . .102 DV82
Causeway, The, N2 . . . . . . .64 DE56
SW18 . . . . .100 DB84
SW19 . . . . .119 CX92
Carshalton SM5 . . . . .140 DG104
Chessington KT9 . . . . . . .156 CL105
Esher (Clay.) KT10 . . . . .155 CF108
Feltham TW14 . . . . .95 BU84
Hounslow TW4 . . . . .95 BU84
Potters Bar EN6 . . . . .12 DC31
Staines TW18 . . . . .113 BC91

Causeway, The, Sutt. SM2 . .158 DC109
Teddington TW11
  off Broad St 117 CF93
Causeway Cl, Pot.B. EN6 . .12 DD31
Causeway Ct, Wok. GU21
  off Bingham Dr 166 AT118
Causeyware Rd, N9 . . . . . . .46 DV46
Causton Rd, N6 . . . . .65 DH59
Causton Sq, Dag. RM10 . . .88 FA66
Causton St, SW1 . . . . .199 N9
Cautley Av, SW4 . . . . .121 DJ85
Cavalier Cl, Rom. RM6 . . . .70 EX56
Cavalier Gdns, Hayes UB3
  off Hanover Circle 77 BR72
Cavalry Barracks, Houns. TW4 . .96 BX83
Cavalry Cres, Houns. TW4 . .96 BX84
Cavalry Gdns, SW15 . . . . .119 CY85
Cavaye Pl, SW10
  off Fulham Rd 100 DC78
Cavell Cres, Dart. DA1 . . .108 FN84
Romford (Harold Wd.) RM3 . .52 FL54
Cavell Dr, Enf. EN2 . . . . . .29 DN40
Cavell Rd, N17 . . . . .46 DR52
Waltham Cross (Chsht.)
  EN7 . . . . .14 DT27
Cavell St, E1 . . . . .84 DV71
Cavell Way, Epsom KT19 . .156 CN112
Cavendish Av, N3 . . . . .44 DA54
NW8 . . . . .194 A1
W13 . . . . .79 CG71
Erith DA8 . . . . .107 FC79
Harrow HA1 . . . . .61 CD63
Hornchurch RM12 . . . . . . .89 FH65
New Malden KT3 . . . . . . .139 CV99
Ruislip HA4 . . . . .59 BV64
Sevenoaks TN13 . . . . . . .190 FG122
Sidcup DA15 . . . . .126 EU87
Welling DA16 . . . . .105 ET83
Woodford Green IG8 . . . .48 EH53
Cavendish Cl, N18 . . . . . . .46 DV50
NW6 off Cavendish Rd . .81 CZ66
NW8 . . . . .194 A2
Amersham HP6 . . . . .20 AV39
Hayes UB4
  off Westacott 77 BS71
Sunbury-on-Thames TW16 .115 BT93
Cavendish Ct, EC3 . . . . . .197 N8
Rickmansworth (Crox.Grn.)
  WD3 off Mayfare 23 BR43
Sunbury-on-Thames TW16 .115 BT93
WD6 . . . . .26 CN42
Hornchurch RM12 . . . . . . .89 FH65
Cavendish Dr, E11 . . . . . . .67 ED60
Edgware HA8 . . . . .42 CM51
Esher (Clay.) KT10 . . . . .155 CE106
Cavendish Gdns, Bark. IG11 . .69 ES64
Ilford IG1 . . . . .69 EN60
Redhill RH1 . . . . .184 DG133
Romford RM6 . . . . .70 EY57
Cavendish Ms N, W1 . . . . .195 J6
Cavendish Ms S, W1 . . . . .195 J7
Cavendish Par, Houns. TW4
  off Bath Rd 96 BY82
Cavendish Pl, W1 . . . . .195 J8
Cavendish Rd, E4 . . . . .47 EC51
N4 .65 DN58
N18 . . . . .46 DV50
NW6 . . . . .81 CY66
SW12 . . . . .121 DH86
SW19 . . . . .120 DD94
W4 . . . . .98 CQ81
Barnet EN5 . . . . .27 CW41
Croydon CR0 . . . . .141 DP102
New Malden KT3 . . . . . . .139 CT99
Redhill RH1 . . . . .184 DG134
Sunbury-on-Thames TW16 .115 BT93
Sutton SM2 . . . . .158 DC108
Weybridge KT13 . . . . . . .153 BQ108
Woking GU22 . . . . .166 AX119
Cavendish Sq, W1 . . . . . . .195 J8
Cavendish St, N1 . . . . .197 K1
Cavendish Ter, Felt. TW13
  off High St 115 BU89
Cavendish Way, W.Wick. BR4 . .143 EB102
Cavenham Gdns, Horn. RM11 . .72 FJ57
Ilford IG1 . . . . .69 ER62
Caverleigh Way, Wor.Pk. KT4 . .139 CU102
Cave Rd, E13 . . . . .86 EH68
Richmond TW10 . . . . .117 CJ91
Caversham Av, N13 . . . . . .45 DN48
Sutton SM3 . . . . .139 CY103
Caversham Ct, N11 . . . . . .44 DG48
Caversham Flats, SW3
  off Caversham St 100 DF79
Caversham Rd, N15 . . . . .66 DQ56
NW5 . . . . .83 DJ65
Kingston upon Thames
  KT1 . . . . .138 CM96
Caversham St, SW3 . . . . .100 DF79
Caverswall St, W12 . . . . .81 CW72
Caveside Cl, Chis. BR7 . . .145 EN95
Cave St, N1 off Carnegie St . .83 DM68
Cavill's Wk, Chig. IG7 . . . .50 EW47
Romford RM4 . . . . .50 EX47
Cawdor Av, S.Ock. RM15 . .91 FU73
Cawdor Cres, W7 . . . . .97 CG77
Cawnpore St, SE19 . . . . . .122 DS92
Cawsey Way, Wok. GU21 . .166 AY117
Caxton Av, Add. KT15 . . . .152 BG107
Caxton Dr, Uxb. UB8
  off Chiltern Vw Rd 76 BK68
Caxton Gro, E3 . . . . .85 EA69
★ Caxton Hall, SW1 . . . . .199 L6
Caxton La, Oxt. RH8 . . . . .188 EL131
Caxton Ms, Brent. TW8
  off The Butts 97 CK79
Caxton Rd, N22 . . . . .45 DM54
SW19 . . . . .120 DC92
W12 . . . . .99 CX75
Southall UB2 . . . . .96 BX76
Caxton St, SW1 . . . . .199 L6
Caxton St N, E16
  off Victoria Dock Rd . . .86 EF73

Caxton Way, Rom. RM1 . . .71 FE56
Watford WD18 . . . . .23 BR44
Cayenne Ct, SE1 . . . . .202 A3
Caygill Cl, Brom. BR2 . . . .144 EF98
Cayley Cl, Wall. SM6 . . . . .159 DL108
Cayley Rd, Sthl. UB2
  off McNair Rd 96 CB76
Cayton Pl, EC1 . . . . .197 K3
Cayton Rd, Couls. CR5 . . .175 DJ122
Greenford UB6 . . . . .79 CE98
Cayton St, EC1 . . . . .197 K3
Cazenove Rd, E17 . . . . . . .47 EA53
N16 . . . . .66 DT61
Cearns Ho, E6 . . . . .86 EK67
Cearn Way, Couls. CR5 . . .175 DM115
Cecil Av, Bark. IG11 . . . . .87 ER66
Enfield EN1 . . . . .30 DT42
Grays RM16 . . . . .110 FZ75
Hornchurch RM11 . . . . . .72 FL55
Wembley HA9 . . . . .62 CM64
Cecil Cl, W5 off Helena Rd . .79 CK71
Ashford TW15 . . . . .115 BQ93
Chessington KT9 . . . . . . .155 CK105
Cecil Ct, WC2 . . . . .199 N1
Barnet EN5 . . . . .27 CX41
Cecile Pk, N8 . . . . .65 DL58
Cecilia Cl, N2 . . . . .64 DC55
★ Cecilia Coleman Gall, NW8
  off St. John's Wd High St . .82 DD68
Cecilia Rd, E8 . . . . .66 DU64
Cecil Pk, Pnr. HA5 . . . . . . .60 BY56
Cecil Pl, Mitch. CR4 . . . . .140 DF99
Cecil Rd, E11 . . . . .68 EE62
E13 . . . . .86 EG67
E17 . . . . .47 EA53
N10 . . . . .45 DH54
N14 . . . . .45 DJ46
NW9 . . . . .62 CS55
NW10 . . . . .80 CS67
SW19 . . . . .120 DB94
W3 . . . . .80 CQ71
Ashford TW15 . . . . .115 BQ94
Croydon CR0 . . . . .141 DM100
Enfield EN2 . . . . .30 DR42
Gravesend DA11 . . . . . . .131 GF88
Harrow HA3 . . . . .61 CE55
Hounslow TW3 . . . . .96 CC82
Ilford IG1 . . . . .69 EP63
Iver SL0 . . . . .75 BE72
Potters Bar EN6 . . . . . . .11 CU32
Romford RM6 . . . . .70 EX59
Sutton SM1 . . . . .157 CZ107
Waltham Cross (Chsht.)
  EN8 . . . . .15 DX32
★ Cecil Sharp Ho, NW1 . . .82 DG67
Cecil St, Wat. WD24 . . . . .23 BV38
Cecil Way, Brom. BR2 . . . .144 EG102
Cedar Av, Barn. EN4 . . . . .44 DE45
Cobham KT11 . . . . .170 BW115
Enfield EN3 . . . . .30 DW40
Gravesend DA12 . . . . . . .131 GJ91
Hayes UB3 . . . . .77 BU72
Romford RM6 . . . . .70 EY57
Ruislip HA4 . . . . .78 BW65
Sidcup DA15 . . . . .126 EU87
Twickenham TW2 . . . . . .116 CB86
Upminster RM14 . . . . . . .72 FN63
Waltham Cross EN8 . . . .15 DX33
West Drayton UB7 . . . . .76 BM74
Cedar Cl, SE21 . . . . .122 DQ88
SW15 . . . . .118 CR91
Borehamwood WD6 . . . .26 CP42
Brentwood CM13 . . . . . .55 GD45
Bromley BR2 . . . . .144 EL104
Buckhurst Hill IG9 . . . . .48 EK47
Carshalton SM5 . . . . . . .158 DF107
East Molesey KT8
  off Cedar Rd 137 CE98
Epsom KT17 . . . . .157 CT114
Esher KT10 . . . . .154 BZ108
Iver SL0 off Thornbridge Rd . .75 BC66
Potters Bar EN6 . . . . . . .12 DA30
Romford RM7 . . . . .71 FC56
Staines TW18 . . . . .134 BJ97
Swanley BR8 . . . . .147 FC96
Warlingham CR6 . . . . . .177 DY118
Cedar Copse, Brom. BR1 . .145 EM96
Cedar Ct, E8 . . . . .84 DU70
  off Grosvenor Rd 68 EH57
N1 off Essex Rd 84 DQ66
SE9 . . . . .124 EL86
SW19 . . . . .119 CX90
Egham TW20 . . . . .113 BA91
Epping CM16 . . . . .18 EU31
Cedar Cres, Brom. BR2 . . .144 EL104
Cedarcroft Rd, Chess. KT9 . .156 CM105
Cedar Dr, N2 . . . . .64 DE56
Dartford (Sutt.H.) DA4 . .148 FP96
Leatherhead (Fetch.) KT22 . .171 CE123
Loughton IG10 . . . . .33 EP40
Pinner HA5 . . . . .40 CA51
Cedar Gdns, Sutt. SM2 . . .158 DC107
Upminster RM14 . . . . . . .72 FQ62
Woking GU21
  off St. John's Rd 166 AV118
Cedar Gro, W5 . . . . .98 CL76
Bexley DA5 . . . . .126 EW86
Southall UB1 . . . . .78 CA71
Weybridge KT13 . . . . . . .153 BQ105
Cedar Hts, Rich. TW10 . . .118 CL88
Cedar Hill, Epsom KT18 . .172 CQ116
Cedar Ho, Croy. CR0 . . . . .161 EB107
Sunbury-on-Thames TW16 .115 BT94
Cedarhurst, Brom. BR1
  off Elstree Hill 124 EE94
Cedarhurst Dr, SE9 . . . . . .124 EJ85
Cedar Lawn Av, Barn. EN5 . .27 CY43
Cedar Mt, SE9 . . . . .124 EK88
Cedarne Rd, SW6 . . . . . . .100 DB80
Cedar Pk, Cat. CR3 . . . . . .176 DS121
Chigwell IG7
  off High Rd 49 EP49
Cedar Pk Gdns, Rom. RM6 . .70 EX59
Cedar Pk Rd, Enf. EN2 . . .30 DQ38
Cedar Pl, SE7 off Floyd Rd . .104 EJ78
Northwood HA6 . . . . .39 BQ51
Cedar Ri, N14 . . . . .44 DG45

Cedar Ri, S.Ock. RM15
  off Sycamore Way 91 FX70
Cedar Rd, N17 . . . . .46 DT53
NW2 . . . . .63 CW63
Brentwood CM13 . . . . . .55 GD44
Bromley BR1 . . . . .144 EJ96
Cobham KT11 . . . . .153 BV114
Croydon CR0 . . . . .142 DS103
Dartford DA1 . . . . .128 FK88
East Molesey KT8 . . . . .137 CE98
Enfield EN2 . . . . .29 DP38
Erith DA8 . . . . .107 FG81
Feltham TW14 . . . . .115 BR86
Grays RM16 . . . . .111 GG76
Hornchurch RM12 . . . . . .72 FJ62
Hounslow TW4 . . . . .96 BW82
Romford RM7 . . . . .71 FC56
Sutton SM2 . . . . .158 DC107
Teddington TW11 . . . . . .117 CG92
Watford WD19 . . . . .24 BW44
Weybridge KT13 . . . . . . .152 BN105
Woking GU22 . . . . .166 AV120
Cedars, Bans. SM7 . . . . . .158 DF114
Cedars, The, E15 off Portway . .86 EF67
W13 off Heronsforde . . .79 CJ72
Buckhurst Hill IG9 . . . . .48 EG46
Leatherhead KT22 . . . . .172 CL121
Reigate RH2 . . . . .184 DD134
Teddington TW11
  off Adelaide Rd 117 CF93
West Byfleet (Byfleet)
  KT14 . . . . .152 BM112
Cedars Av, E17 . . . . .67 EA57
Mitcham CR4 . . . . .140 DG98
Rickmansworth WD3 . . .38 BJ46
Cedars Cl, NW4 . . . . .63 CX55
Gerrards Cross (Chal.St.P.)
  SL9 . . . . .36 AY50
Cedars Ct, N9 off Church St . .46 DS47
Cedars Dr, Uxb. UB10 . . . .76 BM68
Cedars Ms, SW4
  off Cedars Rd 101 DH84
Cedars Rd, E15 . . . . .86 EE65
N9 off Church St 46 DU47
N21 . . . . .45 DP47
SW4 . . . . .101 DH83
SW13 . . . . .99 CT82
W4 . . . . .98 CQ78
Beckenham BR3 . . . . . . .143 DY96
Croydon CR0 . . . . .141 DL104
Kingston upon Thames
  KT1 . . . . .137 CJ95
Morden SM4 . . . . .140 DA98
Cedar Ter, Rich. TW9 . . . .98 CL84
Cedar Ter Rd, Sev. TN13 . .191 FJ123
Cedar Tree Gro, SE27 . . . .121 DP92
Cedarville Gdns, SW16 . . .121 DM93
Cedar Vista, Rich. TW9
  off Kew Rd 98 CL81
Cedar Wk, Esher (Clay.)
  KT10 . . . . .155 CF107
Kenley CR8 . . . . .176 DQ116
Tadworth (Kgswd.) KT20 . .173 CY120
Waltham Abbey EN9 . . . .15 ED34
Cedar Way, NW1 . . . . .83 DK66
Slough SL3 . . . . .92 AV73
Sunbury-on-Thames TW16 .115 BS94
Cedar Wd Dr, Wat. WD25 . .23 BV35
Cedra Ct, N16 . . . . .66 DU60
Cedric Av, Rom. RM1 . . . .71 FE55
Cedric Rd, SE9 . . . . .125 EQ90
Celadon Cl, Enf. EN3 . . . .31 DY41
Celandine Cl, E14 . . . . . . .85 EA71
South Ockendon RM15 . .91 FW70
Celandine Dr, E8 . . . . . . .84 DT66
SE28 . . . . .88 EV74
Celandine Rd, Walt. KT12 . .154 BY105
Celandine Way, E15 . . . . .86 EE69
Celbridge Ms, W2
  off Porchester Rd 82 DB72
Celedon Cl, Grays RM16 . .110 FY75
Celestial Gdns, SE13 . . . .103 ED84
Celia Cres, Ashf. TW15 . .114 BK93
Celia Rd, N19 . . . . .65 DJ63
Cell Fm Av, Wind. (Old Wind.)
  SL4 . . . . .112 AV85
Celtic Av, Brom. BR2 . . . .144 EE97
Celtic Rd, W.Byf. (Byfleet)
  KT14 . . . . .152 BL114
Celtic St, E14 . . . . .85 EB71
Cement Block Cotts, Grays
  RM17 . . . . .110 GC79
Cemetery La, SE7 . . . . . . .104 EL79
Shepperton TW17 . . . . .135 BP101
Waltham Abbey EN9 . . . .16 EF25
Cemetery Rd, E7 . . . . . . .68 EF63
N17 . . . . .46 DS52
SE2 . . . . .106 EV80
Cenacle Cl, NW3 . . . . .64 DA62
★ Cenotaph, The, SW1 . . .199 P4
Centaurs Business Cen, Islw.
  TW7 . . . . .97 CG79
Centaur St, SE1 . . . . .200 C6
Centaury Ct, Grays RM17 . .110 GD79
Centenary Est, Enf. EN3 . .31 DZ42
Centenary Rd, Enf. EN3 . .31 DZ42
Centenary Wk, Loug. IG10 . .32 EH41
Centenary Way, Amer. HP6 . .20 AT38
Centennial Av, Borwd. (Elstree)
  WD6 . . . . .41 CH45
Centennial Pk, Borwd. (Elstree)
  WD6 . . . . .41 CJ45
Central Av, E11 . . . . .67 ED61
N2 .44 DD54
N9 .46 DS48
SW11 . . . . .100 DF80
Enfield EN3 . . . . .30 DV40
Gravesend DA12 . . . . . . .131 GH89
Grays RM20 . . . . .109 FT77
Hayes UB3 . . . . .77 BU73
Hounslow TW3 . . . . .96 CC84
Pinner HA5 . . . . .60 BZ58
South Ockendon (Aveley)
  RM15 . . . . .108 FQ75
Tilbury RM18 . . . . .111 GG81
Wallington SM6 . . . . . . .159 DL106

Cas - Cha

Central Av, Wal.Cr. EN8 . . .15 DY33
Welling DA16 . . . . .105 ET82
West Molesey KT8 . . . . .136 BZ98
Central Circ, NW4
  off Hendon Way 63 CV57
★ Central Criminal Ct
  (Old Bailey), EC4 . . . . .196 G8
Central Dr, Horn. RM12 . . .72 FL62
Central Gdns, Mord. SM4
  off Central Rd 140 DB99
Central Hill, SE19 . . . . . . .122 DR92
Central Mkts, EC1 . . . . . .196 G7
H Central Middlesex Hosp,
  NW10 . . . . .80 CQ69
Central Par, Croy. (New Adgtn.)
  CR0 . . . . .161 EC110
Feltham TW14 . . . . .116 BW87
Greenford UB6 . . . . .79 CG99
Hounslow TW5
  off Heston Rd 96 CA80
Surbiton KT6
  off St. Mark's Hill 138 CL100
Central Pk Av, Dag. RM10 . .71 FB62
Central Pk Est, Houns. TW4 . .116 BX85
Central Pk Rd, E6 . . . . . .86 EK68
Central Pl, SE25
  off Portland Rd 142 DV98
Central Rd, Dart. DA1 . . .128 FL85
Morden SM4 . . . . .140 DA99
Wembley HA0 . . . . .61 CH64
Worcester Park KT4 . . .139 CU103
Central Sch Footpath, SW14 . .98 CQ83
Central Sq, NW11 . . . . . .64 DB58
Wembley HA9
  off Station Gro 62 CL64
West Molesey KT8 . . . . .136 BZ98
Central St, EC1 . . . . .197 H3
Central Way, NW10 . . . . .80 CQ69
SE28 . . . . .88 EU73
Carshalton SM5 . . . . . . .158 DE108
Feltham TW14 . . . . .115 BV85
Oxted RH8 . . . . .187 ED127
Centre, The, Felt. TW13 . .115 BU89
Walton-on-Thames KT12 . .135 BT102
Centre at the Circ, W1 . . .199 L1
Centre Av, W3 . . . . .80 CR74
W10 off Harrow Rd 81 CW69
Epping CM16 . . . . .17 ET32
Centre Cl, Epp. CM16
  off Centre Av 17 ET32
Centre Common Rd, Chis.
  BR7 . . . . .125 EQ93
Centre Ct Shop Cen, SW19 . .119 CZ93
Centre Dr, Epp. CM16 . . .17 ET32
Centre Grn, Epp. CM16
  off Centre Av 17 ET32
Centrepoint, WC1 . . . . . .195 N8
Centre Rd, E7 . . . . .68 EG61
E11 . . . . .68 EG61
Dagenham RM10 . . . . . .89 FB68
Centre St, E2 . . . . .84 DV68
Centre Way, E17 . . . . . . .47 EC52
N9 .46 DW47
Centreway, Ilf. IG1 . . . . .69 EQ61
Centric Cl, NW1
  off Oval Rd 83 DH67
Centurion Cl, N7 . . . . . . .83 DM66
Centurion Ct, Wall. SM6
  off Wandle Rd 141 DH103
Centurion La, E3
  off Libra Rd 85 DZ68
Centurion Way, Erith DA18 . .106 FA76
Purfleet RM19 . . . . .108 FM77
Century Cl, NW4 . . . . . . .63 CX57
Century Ct, Wok. GU21 . .167 AZ116
Century Ms, E5
  off Lower Clapton Rd . .66 DW63
Century Pk, Wat. WD17 . .24 BW43
Century Rd, E17 . . . . . . .67 DY55
Staines TW18 . . . . .113 BC92
Cephas Av, E1 . . . . .84 DW70
Cephas St, E1 . . . . .84 DW70
Ceres Rd, SE18 . . . . .105 ET77
Cerise Rd, SE15 . . . . . . .102 DU81
Cerne Cl, Hayes UB4 . . . .78 BX73
Cerne Rd, Grav. DA12 . . .131 GL91
Morden SM4 . . . . .140 DC100
Cerney Ms, W2
  off Gloucester Ter 82 DD73
Cerotus Pl, Cher. KT16 . .133 BF101
Cervantes Ct, W2
  off Inverness Ter 82 DB72
Northwood HA6
  off Green La 39 BT52
Cervia Way, Grav. DA12 . .131 GM90
Cester St, E2 off Whiston Rd . .84 DU67
Ceylon Rd, W14 . . . . .99 CX76
Chace Av, Pot.B. EN6 . . .12 DD32
Chadacre Av, Ilf. IG5 . . . .69 EM55
Chadacre Rd, Epsom KT17 . .157 CV107
Chadbourn St, E14 . . . . . .85 EB71
Chadd Dr, Brom. BR1 . . .144 EL97
Chadd Grn, E13 . . . . .86 EG67
Chadfields, Til. RM18 . . .111 GG80
Chadview Ct, Rom. (Chad.Hth.)
  RM6 . . . . .70 EX59
Chadville Gdns, Rom. RM6 . .70 EX57
Chadway, Dag. RM8 . . . . .70 EV60
Chadwell, Rom. RM6 . . . .70 EV59
Waltham Cross (Chsht.)
  EN8 . . . . .14 DW28
Chadwell Bypass, Grays
  RM16 . . . . .111 GF78
CHADWELL HEATH, Rom. . .70 EX58
⇌ Chadwell Heath 70 EX56
Chadwell Heath La, Rom.
  RM6 . . . . .70 EV57
Chadwell Hill, Grays RM16 . .111 GH78
Chadwell Rd, Grays RM17 . .110 GC77
CHADWELL ST. MARY, Grays . .111 GJ76
Chadwell St, EC1 . . . . . . .196 E2
Chadwick Av, E4 . . . . . . .47 EC49
N21 . . . . .29 DM43
SW19 . . . . .120 DA93

A B C D E F G H I J K L M N O P Q R S T U V W X Y Z

Cha - Cha

Chadwick Cl, SW15 . . . . .119 CT87
 W7 off Westcott Cres 79 CF71
 Gravesend (Nthflt.) DA11 . .130 GE89
 Teddington TW11 . . . . . . .117 CG93
Chadwick Dr, Rom. (Harold Wd.)
 RM3 . . . . .52 FK54
Chadwick Pl, Surb. KT6 . . . .137 CJ101
Chadwick Rd, E11 . . . . .68 EE59
 NW10 . . . . .81 CT67
 SE15 . . . . .102 DT82
 Ilford IG1 . . . . .69 EP62
Chadwick St, SW1 . . . . .199 N7
Chadwick Way, SE28 . . . . . . .88 EX73
Chadwin Rd, E13 . . . . .86 EH71
Chadworth Way, Esher (Clay.)
 KT10 . . . . .155 CD106
Chaffers Mead, Ashtd. KT21 . .172 CM116
Chaffinch Av, Croy. CR0 . . . .143 DX100
Chaffinch Cl, N9 . . . . .47 DX46
 Croydon CR0 . . . . .143 DX100
 Surbiton KT6 . . . . .138 CN104
Chaffinch La, Wat. WD18 . . . .39 BT45
Chaffinch Rd, Beck. BR3 . . . .143 DY95
CHAFFORD HUNDRED,
 Grays 110 FY76
 ⇌ Chafford Hundred 109 FV77
Chafford Wk, Rain. RM13 . . . .90 FJ68
Chafford Way, Rom. RM6 . . . .70 EW56
Chagford St, NW1 . . . . .194 D5
Chailey Av, Enf. EN1 . . . . . . .30 DT40
Chailey Cl, Houns. TW5
 off Springwell Rd 96 BX81
Chailey Pl, Walt. KT12 . . . . .154 BY105
Chailey St, E5 . . . . .66 DW62
Chairmans Av, Uxb. (Denh.)
 UB9 . . . . .57 BF58
Chalbury Wk, N1 . . . . .83 DM68
Chalcombe Rd, SE2 . . . . . . .106 EV76
Chalcot Cl, Sutt. SM2 . . . . . .158 DA108
Chalcot Cres, NW1 . . . . .82 DF67
Chalcot Gdns, NW3 . . . . .82 DF65
Chalcot Ms, SW16 . . . . .121 DL90
Chalcot Rd, NW1 . . . . .82 DG66
Chalcot Sq, NW1 . . . . .82 DG66
Chalcott Gdns, Surb. KT6 . . .137 CJ102
Chalcroft Rd, SE13 . . . . .124 EE85
CHALDON, Cat. 175 DN124
Chaldon Common Rd, Cat.
 CR3 . . . . .176 DQ124
Chaldon Path, Th.Hth. CR7 . .141 DP98
Chaldon Rd, SW6 . . . . .99 CY80
 Caterham CR3 . . . . .176 DR124
Chaldon Way, Couls. CR5 . . .175 DL117
Chale Rd, SW2 . . . . .121 DL86
Chalet Cl, Bex. DA5 . . . . . . .127 FD91
Chalet Est, NW7 . . . . .43 CU49
Chale Wk, Sutt. SM2
 off Hulverston Cl 158 DB109
 ⇌ Chalfont & Latimer 20 AW39
 ⊖ Chalfont & Latimer 20 AW39
Chalfont Av, Amer. HP6 . . . . .20 AX39
 Wembley HA9 . . . . .80 CP65
CHALFONT COMMON, Ger.Cr. 37 AZ49
Chalfont Ct, NW9 . . . . .63 CT58
Chalfont Grn, N9 . . . . .46 DS48
Chalfont La, Ger.Cr. SL9 . . . . .37 BC51
 Rickmansworth (Chorl.)
 WD3 . . . . .21 BB43
 Rickmansworth (Map.Cr.)
 WD3 . . . . .37 BC51
Chalfont Pk, Ger.Cr. (Chal.St.P.)
 SL9 . . . . .57 AZ55
Chalfont Rd, N9 . . . . .46 DS48
 SE25 . . . . .142 DT97
 Gerrards Cross SL9 . . . . . .37 BB48
 Hayes UB3 . . . . .95 BU75
 Rickmansworth (Map.Cr.)
 WD3 . . . . .37 BD49
CHALFONT ST. GILES, Ger.Cr. .36 AV47
CHALFONT ST. PETER, Ger.Cr. 37 AZ53
 H Chalfonts & Gerrards Cross
 Hosp, Ger.Cr. SL9 . . . . . .36 AX53
Chalfont Sta Rd, Amer. HP7 . .20 AW40
Chalfont Wk, Pnr. HA5
 off Willows Cl 40 BW54
Chalfont Way, W13 . . . . .97 CH76
Chalford Cl, W.Mol. KT8 . . . .136 CA98
Chalforde Gdns, Rom. RM2 . .71 FH56
Chalford Rd, SE21 . . . . .122 DR91
Chalford Wk, Wdf.Grn. IG8 . . .48 EK53
Chalgrove Av, Mord. SM4 . . .140 DA99
Chalgrove Cres, Ilf. IG5 . . . . .48 EL54
Chalgrove Gdns, N3 . . . . . . .63 CY55
Chalgrove Rd, N17 . . . . .46 DV53
 Sutton SM2 . . . . .158 DD108
Chalice Cl, Wall. SM6
 off Lavender Vale 159 DK107
Chalice Way, Green. DA9 . . . .129 FS85
Chalkenden Cl, SE20 . . . . . .122 DV94
 ⊖ Chalk Farm 82 DG66
Chalk Fm Rd, NW1 . . . . .82 DG66
Chalk Hill, Wat. WD19 . . . . . .24 BX44
Chalk Hill Rd, W6
 off Shortlands 99 CX77
Chalkhill Rd, Wem. HA9 . . . . .62 CP62
Chalklands, Wem. HA9 . . . . . .62 CQ62
Chalk La, Ashtd. KT21 . . . . .172 CM119
 Barnet EN4 . . . . .28 DF42
 Epsom KT18 . . . . .172 CR115
Chalkley Cl, Mitch. CR4 . . . .140 DF96
Chalkmill Dr, Enf. EN1 . . . . . .30 DV41
Chalk Paddock, Epsom KT18 .172 CR115
Chalk Pit Av, Orp. BR5 . . . . .146 EW97
Chalkpit La, Bet. RH3 . . . . . .182 CP133
 Oxted RH8 . . . . .187 EC125
Chalk Pit Rd, Bans. SM7 . . . .174 DA117
 Epsom KT18 . . . . .172 CQ119
Chalk Pit Way, Sutt. SM1 . . .158 DC106
Chalkpit Wd, Oxt. RH8 . . . . .187 ED127
Chalk Rd, E13 . . . . .86 EH71
Chalkstone Cl, Well. DA16 . . .106 EU81
Chalkwell Pk Av, Enf. EN1 . . .30 DS42
Chalky Bk, Grav. DA11 . . . . .131 GG91
Chalky La, Chess. KT9 . . . . .155 CK109

Challacombe Cl, Brwd. CM13 .55 GB46
Challenge Cl, Grav. DA12 . . .131 GM91
Challenge Ct, Lthd. KT22 . . .171 CH115
Challenge Rd, Ashf. TW15 . . .115 BQ90
Challice Way, SW2 . . . . .121 DM88
Challin St, SE20 . . . . .142 DW95
Challis Rd, Brent. TW8 . . . . . .97 CK78
Challock Cl, West. (Bigg.H.)
 TN16 . . . . .178 EJ116
Challoner Cl, N2 . . . . .44 DD54
Challoner Cres, W14
 off Challoner St 99 CZ78
Challoners Cl, E.Mol. KT8 . . .137 CD98
Challoner St, W14 . . . . .99 CZ78
Chalmers Ct, Rick. (Crox.Grn.)
 WD3 . . . . .22 BM44
Chalmers Rd, Ashf. TW15 . . .115 BP91
 Banstead SM7 . . . . .174 DD115
Chalmers Rd E, Ashf. TW15 . .115 BP91
Chalmers Wk, SE17
 off Hillingdon St 101 DP79
Chalmers Way, Felt. TW14 . . .115 BU85
Chaloner Ct, SE1 . . . . .201 K4
Chalsey Rd, SE4 . . . . .103 DZ84
Chalton Dr, N2 . . . . .64 DC58
Chalton St, NW1 . . . . .195 N2
Chalvey Gdns, Slou. SL1 . . . .92 AS75
Chalvey Pk, Slou. SL1 . . . . . .92 AS75
Chalvey Rd E, Slou. SL1 . . . . .92 AS75
Chalvey Rd W, Slou. SL1 . . . .92 AS75
Chamberlain Cl, SE28
 off Broadwater Rd 105 ER76
Chamberlain Cotts, SE5
 off Camberwell Gro 102 DR81
Chamberlain Cres, W.Wick.
 BR4 . . . . .143 EB102
Chamberlain Gdns, Houns.
 TW3 . . . . .96 CC81
Chamberlain La, Pnr. HA5 . . . .59 BU56
Chamberlain Pl, E17 . . . . .67 DY55
Chamberlain Rd, N2 . . . . .44 DC54
 N9 . . . . .46 DU48
 W13 off Midhurst Rd 97 CG75
Chamberlain St, NW1
 off Regents Pk Rd 82 DF66
Chamberlain Wk, Felt. TW13
 off Burgess Cl 116 BY91
Chamberlain Way, Pnr. HA5 . . .59 BV55
 Surbiton KT6 . . . . .138 CL101
Chamberlayne Av, Wem. HA9 .62 CL61
Chamberlayne Rd, NW10 . . . .81 CX69
Chambersbury La, Hem.H. HP3 .6 BN25
Chambers Cl, Green. DA9 . . .129 FU85
Chambers Gdns, N2 . . . . .44 DD53
Chambers La, NW10 . . . . . . .81 CV66
Chambers Pl, S.Croy. CR2
 off Rolleston Rd 160 DR108
Chambers Rd, N7 . . . . .65 DL63
Chambers St, SE16 . . . . .202 B4
Chamber St, E1 . . . . .84 DT73
Chambon Pl, W6
 off Beavor La 99 CU77
Chambord St, E2 . . . . .84 DT69
Champion Cres, SE26 . . . . . .123 DY91
Champion Gro, SE5 . . . . . . .102 DR83
Champion Hill, SE5 . . . . .102 DR83
Champion Hill Est, SE5 . . . . .102 DS83
Champion Pk, SE5 . . . . .102 DR82
Champion Pk Est, SE5
 off Denmark Hill 102 DR83
Champion Rd, SE26 . . . . . . .123 DY91
 Upminster RM14 . . . . .72 FP61
Champness Cl, SE27
 off Rommany Rd 122 DR91
Champness Rd, Bark. IG11 . . .87 ET65
Champneys Cl, Sutt. SM2 . . .157 CZ108
Chance Cl, Grays RM16 . . . .110 FZ76
Chancellor Gdns, S.Croy.
 CR2 . . . . .159 DP109
Chancellor Gro, SE21 . . . . . .122 DQ89
Chancellor Pas, E14 . . . . . . .204 A3
Chancellor Pl, NW9 . . . . .43 CT54
Chancellors Rd, W6 . . . . .99 CW78
Chancellors St, W6 . . . . .99 CW78
Chancellor Way, Sev. TN13 . .190 FG122
Chancelot Rd, SE2 . . . . .106 EV77
Chancery Ct, Dart. DA1 . . . . .128 FN87
 ⊖ Chancery Lane 196 D7
Chancery La, WC2 . . . . .196 D8
 Beckenham BR3 . . . . .143 EB96
Chancery Ms, SW17 . . . . . . .120 DE89
Chance St, E1 . . . . .197 P4
 E2 . . . . .197 P4
Chanctonbury Chase, Red.
 RH1 . . . . .185 DH134
Chanctonbury Cl, SE9 . . . . . .125 EP90
Chanctonbury Gdns, Sutt.
 SM2 . . . . .158 DB108
Chanctonbury Way, N12 . . . . .43 CZ49
Chandler Av, E16 . . . . .86 EG71
Chandler Cl, Hmptn. TW12 . . .136 CA95
Chandler Rd, Loug. IG10 . . . . .33 EP39
Chandlers Cl, Felt. TW14 . . . .115 BT87
Chandlers Dr, Erith DA8 . . . .107 FD77
Chandler's La, Rick. WD3 . . . .22 BL37
Chandlers Ms, E14 . . . . .203 P4
Chandlers St, E1 . . . . .202 E2
Chandlers Way, SW2 . . . . . . .121 DN87
 Romford RM1 . . . . .71 FE57
Chandler Way, SE15 . . . . . . .102 DT80
Chandon Lo, Sutt. SM2
 off Devonshire Rd 158 DC108
Chandos Av, E17 . . . . .47 EA54
 N14 . . . . .45 DJ48
 N20 . . . . .44 DC46
 W5 . . . . .97 CJ77
Chandos Cl, Amer. HP6 . . . . .20 AW38
 Buckhurst Hill IG9 . . . . .48 EH47
Chandos Cres, Edg. HA8 . . . .42 CM52
Chandos Mall, Slou. SL1
 off High St 92 AT75
Chandos Par, Edg. HA8
 off Chandos Cres 42 CM52
Chandos Pl, WC2 . . . . .199 P1
Chandos Rd, E15 . . . . .67 ED64

Chandos Rd, N2 . . . . .44 DD54
 N17 . . . . .46 DS54
 NW2 . . . . .63 CW64
 NW10 . . . . .80 CS70
 Borehamwood WD6 . . . . . .26 CM40
 Harrow HA1 . . . . .60 CC57
 Pinner HA5 . . . . .60 BW59
 Staines TW18 . . . . .113 BD92
Chandos St, W1 . . . . .195 J7
Chandos Way, NW11 . . . . . . .64 DB60
Change All, EC3 . . . . .197 L9
Chanlock Path, S.Ock. RM15
 off Carnach Grn 91 FV73
Channel Cl, Houns. TW5 . . . . .96 CA81
Channel Gate Rd, NW10
 off Old Oak La 81 CT69
Channelsea Rd, E15 . . . . .85 ED67
Channing Cl, Horn. RM11 . . . .72 FM59
Channings, Wok. (Horsell)
 GU21 . . . . .166 AY115
Chanton Dr, Epsom KT17 . . .157 CW110
 Sutton SM2 . . . . .157 CW110
Chantress Cl, Dag. RM10 . . . .89 FC67
Chantrey Cl, Ashtd. KT21 . . .171 CJ119
Chantrey Rd, SW9 . . . . .101 DM83
Chantreywood, Brwd. CM13 . .55 GA48
Chantry, The, Uxb. UB8 . . . . .76 BM69
Chantry Cl, NW7
 off Hendon Wd La 27 CT44
 W9 off Elgin Av 82 CZ70
 Enfield EN2 off Bedale Rd . .30 DQ38
 Harrow HA3 . . . . .62 CM57
 Kings Langley WD4 . . . . . . .6 BN29
 Sidcup DA14
 off Ellenborough Rd 126 EY92
 Sunbury-on-Thames TW16 .135 BU94
 West Drayton UB7 . . . . . . .76 BK73
Chantry Ct, Cars. SM5 . . . . .140 DE104
Chantry Ho, Rain. RM13
 off Chantry Way 89 FD68
Chantry Hurst, Epsom KT18 .172 CR115
Chantry La, Brom. BR2
 off Bromley Common 144 EK99
 St. Albans (Lon.Col.) AL2 . . .9 CK26
Chantry Pl, Har. HA3 . . . . . . .40 CB53
Chantry Rd, Cher. KT16 . . . .134 BJ101
 Chessington KT9 . . . . . . .156 CM106
 Harrow HA3 . . . . .40 CB53
Chantry Sq, W8
 off St. Mary's Pl 100 DB76
Chantry St, N1 . . . . .83 DP67
Chantry Way, Mitch. CR4 . . .140 DD97
 Rainham RM13 . . . . .89 FD68
Chant Sq, E15 . . . . .85 ED66
Chant St, E15 . . . . .85 ED66
Chapel Av, Add. KT15 . . . . . .152 BH105
Chapel Cl, Dart. DA1 . . . . . . .127 FE85
 Grays RM20 . . . . .109 FV79
 Hatfield AL9 . . . . .12 DD27
 Watford WD25 . . . . .7 BT34
Chapel Ct, N2 . . . . .64 DE55
 SE1 . . . . .201 K4
Chapel Cft, Kings L. (Chipper.)
 WD4 . . . . .6 BG31
Chapel End, Ger.Cr. (Chal.St.P.)
 SL9 off Austenwood La 36 AX54
Chapel Fm Rd, SE9 . . . . . . .125 EM90
Chapel Gro, Add. KT15 . . . . .152 BH105
 Epsom KT18 . . . . .173 CW119
Chapel High Shop Prec, Brwd.
 CM14 . . . . .54 FW47
Chapel Hill, Dart. DA1 . . . . . .127 FE85
Chapel Ho St, E14 . . . . .204 C10
Chapel La, Chig. IG7 . . . . . . .49 ET48
 Pinner HA5 . . . . .60 BX55
 Romford RM6 . . . . .70 EX59
 Slough (Stoke P.) SL2 . . . . .74 AV66
 Uxbridge UB8 . . . . .76 BN72
Chapel Mkt, N1 . . . . .83 DN68
Chapel Ms, Wdf.Grn. IG8 . . . .49 EN51
Chapelmount Rd, Wdf.Grn.
 IG8 . . . . .49 EM51
Chapel Pk Rd, Add. KT15 . . .152 BH105
Chapel Path, E11 . . . . .68 EG58
Chapel Pl, EC2 . . . . .197 M3
 N1 off Chapel Mkt 83 DN68
 N17 off White Hart La 46 DT52
 W1 . . . . .195 H9
Chapel Rd, SE27 . . . . .121 DP91
 W13 . . . . .79 CH74
 Bexleyheath DA7 . . . . . . .106 FA84
 Epping CM16 . . . . .17 ET30
 Hounslow TW3 . . . . .96 CB83
 Ilford IG1 . . . . .69 EN62
 Oxted RH8 . . . . .188 EJ130
 Redhill RH1 . . . . .184 DF134
 Tadworth KT20 . . . . .173 CW123
 Twickenham TW1 . . . . . . .117 CH87
 Warlingham CR6 . . . . .177 DX118
Chapel Row, Uxb. (Hare.)
 UB9 . . . . .38 BJ53
Chapel Side, W2 . . . . .82 DB73
Chapel Sq, Vir.W. GU25 . . . .132 AY98
Chapel Stones, N17 . . . . .46 DT53
Chapel St, NW1 . . . . .194 B7
 SW1 . . . . .198 G6
 W1 . . . . .199 H2
 Enfield EN2 . . . . .30 DQ41
 Slough SL1 . . . . .92 AT75
 Uxbridge UB8
 off Trumper Way 76 BJ67
 Woking GU21 . . . . .167 AZ117
Chapel Ter, Loug. IG10
 off Forest Rd 32 EL42
Chapel Vw, S.Croy. CR2 . . . .160 DV107
Chapel Way, N4 . . . . .63 CV56
 Croydon CR0
 off Wellesley Rd 142 DQ103
Chapel Yd, N7
 off Sussex Way 65 DM62
 Abbots Langley (Bedmond)
 WD5 . . . . .7 BT27
 Epsom KT18 . . . . .173 CW119
Chapel Yd, SW18
 off Wandsworth High St . .120 DA85
Chaplaincy Gdns, Horn. RM11 .72 FL60
Chaplin Cl, SE1 . . . . .200 E4
Chaplin Cres, Sun. TW16 . . .115 BS93

Chaplin Rd, E15 . . . . .86 EE68
 N17 . . . . .66 DT55
 NW2 . . . . .81 CU65
 Dagenham RM9 . . . . .88 EY66
 Wembley HA0 . . . . .79 CJ65
Chaplin Sq, N12 . . . . .44 DD52
Chapman Cl, West Dr. UB7 . . .94 BM76
Chapman Cres, Har. HA3 . . . .62 CL57
Chapman Pk Ind Est, NW10 . .81 CT65
Chapman Pl, N4 . . . . .65 DP61
Chapman Rd, E9 . . . . .85 DZ65
 Belvedere DA17 . . . . .106 FA78
 Croydon CR0 . . . . .141 DN102
Chapman's La, SE2 . . . . .106 EW77
 Belvedere DA17 . . . . .106 EX77
Chapmans La, Orp. BR5 . . . .146 EX96
Chapman Sq, SW19 . . . . . . .119 CX89
Chapmans Rd, Sev. (Sund.)
 TN14 . . . . .180 EY124
Chapman St, E1 . . . . .84 DV73
Chapmans Yd, Wat. WD25
 off New Rd 24 BW42
Chapone Pl, W1 . . . . .195 M9
Chapter Cl, W4
 off Beaumont Rd 98 CQ76
 Uxbridge UB10 . . . . .76 BM66
Chapter Ho Ct, EC4 . . . . . . .197 H9
Chapter Rd, NW2 . . . . .63 CU64
 SE17 . . . . .101 DP78
Chapter St, SW1 . . . . .199 M9
Chapter Way, Hmptn. TW12 .116 CA91
Chara Pl, W4 . . . . .98 CR79
Charcot Ho, SW15 . . . . .119 CT86
Charcroft Gdns, Enf. EN3 . . . .31 DX42
Chardin Rd, W4
 off Elliott Rd 98 CS77
Chardmore Rd, N16 . . . . .66 DU60
Chard Rd, Houns. (Hthrw.Air.) TW6
 off Heathrow Tunnel App . .94 BN83
Chardwell Cl, E6
 off Northumberland Rd 86 EL72
Charecroft Way, W12 . . . . . . .99 CX75
Charfield Ct, W9
 off Shirland Rd 82 DB70
Charford Rd, E16 . . . . .86 EG71
Chargate Cl, Walt. KT12 . . . .153 BT107
Chargeable La, E13 . . . . .86 EF70
Chargeable St, E16 . . . . .86 EF70
Chargrove Cl, SE16 . . . . .203 J4
Charing Cl, Orp. BR6 . . . . . .163 ET105
 ⇌ Charing Cross 199 P2
 ⊖ Charing Cross 199 P2
Charing Cross, SW1 . . . . . . .199 P2
Charing Cross Rd, WC2 . . . .195 N8
 H Charing Cross Hosp, W6 . .99 CX79
Charlbert St, NW8 . . . . .82 DE68
Charlbury Av, Stan. HA7 . . . . .41 CK50
Charlbury Cl, Rom. RM3 . . . . .52 FJ51
Charlbury Cres, Rom. RM3 . . .52 FJ51
Charlbury Gdns, Ilf. IG3 . . . . .69 ET61
Charlbury Gro, W5 . . . . .79 CJ72
Charlbury Rd, Uxb. UB10 . . . .58 BM62
Charldane Rd, SE9 . . . . .125 EP90
Charlecote Gro, SE26 . . . . . .122 DV90
Charlecote Rd, Dag. RM8 . . . .70 EY62
Charlemont Rd, E6 . . . . .87 EM69
Charles Babbage Cl, Chess.
 KT9 . . . . .155 CJ108
Charles Barry Cl, SW4 . . . . .101 DJ83
Charles Burton Ct, E5
 off Ashenden Rd 67 DY64
Charles Cl, Sid. DA14 . . . . . .126 EV91
Charles Cobb Gdns, Croy.
 CR0 . . . . .159 DN106
Charles Coveney Rd, SE15 . .102 DT81
Charles Cres, Har. HA1 . . . . . .61 CD59
Charles Dickens Ho, E2 . . . . .84 DV69
Charles Dickens Ter, SE20
 off Maple Rd 122 DW94
Charlesfield, SE9 . . . . .124 EJ90
Charles Flemwell Ms, E16 . . .205 N3
Charles Gdns, Slou. SL2 . . . .74 AV72
Charles Grinling Wk, SE18 . .105 EN77
Charles Haller St, SW2
 off Tulse Hill 121 DN87
Charles Ho, N17 off Love La . .46 DT52
Charles La, NW8 . . . . .194 A1
Charles Pl, NW1 . . . . .195 L3
Charles Rd, E7 off Lens Rd . . .86 EJ66
 SW19 . . . . .140 DA95
 W13 . . . . .79 CG72
 Dagenham RM10 . . . . .89 FD65
 Romford RM6 . . . . .70 EX59
 Sevenoaks (Bad.Mt.) TN14 .165 FB110
 Staines TW18 . . . . .114 BK93
Charles II Pl, SW3
 off King's Rd 100 DF78
Charles II St, SW1 . . . . .199 M2
Charles Sevright Dr, NW7 . . .43 CX50
Charles Sq, N1 . . . . .197 L3
Charles Sq Est, N1
 off Pitfield St 84 DR69
Charles St, E16 . . . . .86 EK74
 SW13 . . . . .98 CS82
 W1 . . . . .199 H2
 Chertsey KT16 . . . . .133 BF102
 Croydon CR0 . . . . .142 DQ104
 Enfield EN1 . . . . .30 DT43
 Epping CM16 . . . . .18 EU32
 Grays RM17 . . . . .110 GB79
 Greenhithe DA9 . . . . .129 FT85
 Hounslow TW3 . . . . .96 BZ82
 Uxbridge UB10 . . . . .77 BP70
Charleston Cl, Felt. TW13
 off Vineyard Rd 115 BU90
Charleston St, SE17 . . . . . . .201 J9
Charles Townsend Ho, EC1 . .196 E3
Charles Whincup Rd, E16 . . .205 P2
Charleville Circ, SE26 . . . . . .122 DU92
Charleville Rd, W14 . . . . .99 CY78
Charlie Chaplin Wk, SE1
 off Waterloo Rd 83 DN74
Charlieville Rd, Erith DA8
 off Northumberland Pk 107 FC80
Charlmont Rd, SW17 . . . . . . .120 DF93
Charlock Way, Wat. WD18 . . .23 BT44

Charlotte Av, Slou. SL2 . . . . .74 AT73
Charlotte Cl, Bexh. DA6 . . . .126 EY85
 Ilford IG6 off Connor Cl 49 EQ53
Charlotte Despard Av, SW11 .100 DG81
Charlotte Gdns, Rom. RM5 . . .51 FB51
Charlotte Ms, W1 . . . . .195 L6
 W10 . . . . .81 CY72
 W14 off Munden St 99 CY77
Charlotte Pl, NW9
 off Uphill Dr 62 CQ57
 SW1 . . . . .199 K9
 W1 . . . . .195 L7
 Grays RM20 . . . . .109 FV79
Charlotte Rd, EC2 . . . . .197 M4
 SW13 . . . . .99 CT81
 Dagenham RM10 . . . . .89 FB65
 Wallington SM6 . . . . .159 DJ107
Charlotte Row, SW4 . . . . . . .101 DJ83
Charlotte Sq, Rich. TW10
 off Greville Rd 118 CM86
Charlotte St, W1 . . . . .195 L6
Charlotte Ter, N1 . . . . .83 DM67
Charlow Cl, SW6
 off Townmead Rd 100 DC82
CHARLTON, SE7 . . . . .104 EJ79
 ⇌ Charlton 104 EH78
 ★ Charlton Athletic FC, SE7 .104 EJ78
Charlton Av, Walt. KT12 . . . .153 BV105
Charlton Ch La, SE7 . . . . . . .104 EJ78
Charlton Cl, Uxb. UB10 . . . . .59 BP61
Charlton Cres, Bark. IG11 . . . .87 ET68
Charlton Dene, SE7 . . . . .104 EJ80
Charlton Dr, West. (Bigg.H.)
 TN16 . . . . .178 EK117
Charlton Gdns, Couls. CR5 . .175 DJ118
Charlton Kings, Wey. KT13 . .135 BS104
Charlton Kings Rd, NW5 . . . . .65 DK64
Charlton La, SE7 . . . . .104 EK78
Charlton Pk La, SE7 . . . . . . .104 EK80
Charlton Pk Rd, SE7 . . . . . . .104 EK79
Charlton Pl, N1 . . . . .83 DP68
Charlton Rd, N9 . . . . .47 DX46
 NW10 . . . . .80 CS67
 SE3 . . . . .104 EG80
 SE7 . . . . .104 EH80
 Harrow HA3 . . . . .61 CK56
 Shepperton TW17 . . . . . .135 BQ97
 Wembley HA9 . . . . .62 CM60
Charlton St, Grays RM20 . . . .109 FX79
Charlton Way, SE3 . . . . .104 EE81
Charlwood, Croy. CR0 . . . . . .161 DZ109
Charlwood Cl, Har. HA3
 off Kelvin Cres 41 CE52
 KT22 . . . . .171 CD115
Charlwood Dr, Lthd. (Oxshott)
 KT22 . . . . .171 CD115
Charlwood Pl, SW1 . . . . .199 L9
Charlwood Rd, SW15 . . . . . . .99 CX85
Charlwood Sq, Mitch. CR4 . .140 DD97
Charlwood St, SW1 . . . . .199 L9
Charlwood Ter, SW15
 off Cardinal Pl 99 CX84
Charman Rd, Red. RH1 . . . . .184 DE134
Charmian Av, Stan. HA7 . . . . .61 CK55
Charminster Av, SW19 . . . . .140 DB96
Charminster Ct, Surb. KT6 . .137 CK101
Charminster Rd, SE9 . . . . . . .124 EK91
 Worcester Park KT4 . . . . .139 CX102
Charmouth Rd, Well. DA16 . .106 EW81
Charmwood La, Orp. BR6 . . .164 EV109
Charne, The, Sev. (Otford)
 TN14 . . . . .181 FG117
Charnock, Swan. BR8 . . . . . .147 FE98
Charnock Rd, E5 . . . . .66 DV62
Charnwood Av, SW19 . . . . . .140 DA96
Charnwood Cl, N.Mal. KT3 . .138 CS98
Charnwood Dr, E18 . . . . .68 EH55
Charnwood Gdns, E14 . . . . . .204 A8
Charnwood Pl, N20 . . . . .44 DC48
Charnwood Rd, SE25 . . . . . .142 DR99
 Enfield EN1 . . . . .30 DV36
 Uxbridge UB10 . . . . .76 BN68
Charnwood St, E5 . . . . .66 DU61
Charrington Rd, Croy. CR0
 off Drayton Rd 141 DP103
Charrington St, NW1 . . . . . . .83 DK68
Charsley Cl, Amer. HP6 . . . . .20 AW39
Charsley Rd, SE6 . . . . .123 EB89
Charta Rd, Egh. TW20 . . . . . .113 BC92
Chart Cl, Brom. BR2 . . . . . . .144 EE95
 Croydon CR0
 off Stockbury Rd 142 DW100
Charter Av, Ilf. IG2 . . . . .69 ER60
Charter Cl, Slou. SL1
 off Osborne St 92 AT76
Charter Cres, Houns. TW4 . . .96 BY84
Charter Dr, Amer. HP6 . . . . . .20 AT38
 Bexley DA5 . . . . .126 EY87
 ★ Chartered Insurance
 Institutes Mus,
 EC2 off Aldermanbury 197 J8
 ★ Charterhouse, EC1 . . . . .196 G6
Charterhouse Av, Wem. HA0 . .61 CJ63
Charterhouse Bldgs, EC1 . . .196 G5
Charterhouse Dr, Sev. TN13 .190 FG123
Charterhouse Ms, EC1 . . . . .196 G6
Charterhouse Rd, Orp. BR6 . .146 EU104
Charterhouse Sq, EC1 . . . . . .196 G6
Charterhouse St, EC1 . . . . . .196 E7
Charteris Rd, N4 . . . . .65 DN60
 NW6 . . . . .81 CZ67
 Woodford Green IG8 . . . . . .48 EH52
 H Charter Nightingale Hosp,
 NW1 . . . . .194 C6
Charter Pl, Stai. TW18 . . . . .114 BG93
 Uxbridge UB8 . . . . .76 BK66
 Watford WD17 . . . . .24 BW41
Charter Rd, Kings.T. KT1 . . . .138 CP97
Charter Rd, The, Wdf.Grn. IG8 .48 EE51
Charters Cl, SE19 . . . . .122 DS92
Charter Sq, Kings.T. KT1 . . . .138 CP96
Charter Way, N3 . . . . .63 CZ56
 N14 . . . . .29 DJ44
Chartfield Av, SW15 . . . . .119 CV85
Chartfield Pl, Wey. KT13
 off Hanger Hill 153 BP106

Chartfield Sq, SW15 . . . . . . .119 CX85
Chartham Gro, SE27
   off Royal Circ DN90
Chartham Rd, SE25 . . . . . . .142 DV97
Chart Hills SE28
   off Fairway Dr 88 EY72
Chart La, Reig. RH2 . . . . . .184 DB134
Chartley Av, NW2 . . . . .62 CS62
  Stanmore HA7 . . . . .41 CF51
Charton Cl, Belv. DA17
   off Nuxley Rd 106 EZ79
Chartridge Cl, Barn. EN5 . . . .27 CU43
  Bushey WD23 . . . . .24 CC44
Chart St, N1 . . . . .197 L2
Chartway, Reig. RH2 . . . . . .184 DB133
  Sevenoaks TN13 . . . . . .191 FJ124
★ Chartwell, West. TN16 . . .189 ET131
Chartwell Cl, SE9 . . . . .125 EQ89
  Croydon CR0 . . . . .142 DR102
  Greenford UB6 . . . . .78 CB67
  Waltham Abbey EN9 . . . . .16 EE33
Chartwell Dr, Orp. BR6 . . . .163 ER106
Chartwell Gdns, Sutt. SM3 . .157 CY105
Chartwell Pl, Epsom KT18 . .156 CS114
  Harrow HA2 . . . . .61 CD61
  Sutton SM3 . . . . .157 CZ105
Chartwell Way, SE20 . . . . . .142 DV95
Charville La, Hayes UB4 . . . . .77 BS68
Charville La W, Uxb. UB10 . . .77 BP69
Charwood, SW16 . . . . .121 DN91
Charwood Cl, Rad. (Shenley)
  WD7 . . . . .10 CL33
Chase, The, E12 . . . . .68 EK63
  SW4 . . . . .101 DH83
  SW16 . . . . .121 DM94
  SW20 . . . . .139 CY95
  Ashtead KT21 . . . . .171 CJ118
  Bexleyheath DA7 . . . . . .107 FB83
  Brentwood (Cromwell Rd)
   CM14 . . . . .54 FV49
  Brentwood (Ingrave) CM13 .55 GC50
  Brentwood (Seven Arches Rd)
   CM14 . . . . .54 FX48
  Brentwood (Woodman Rd)
   CM14 . . . . .54 FX50
  Bromley BR1 . . . . .144 EH97
  Chigwell IG7 . . . . .49 EQ49
  Coulsdon CR5 . . . . .159 DJ114
  Edgware HA8 . . . . .42 CP53
  Grays RM20 . . . . .109 FX79
  Hornchurch RM12 . . . . . .71 FE62
  Leatherhead (Oxshott)
   KT22 . . . . .170 CC115
  Loughton IG10 . . . . .48 EJ45
  Pinner HA5 . . . . .60 BZ56
  Pinner (Eastcote) HA5 . . . .60 BW58
  Radlett WD7 . . . . .25 CF35
  Reigate RH2 . . . . .184 DD134
  Romford RM1 . . . . .71 FE55
  Romford (Chad.Hth.) RM6 . .70 EY58
  Romford (Rush Grn.) RM7 . .71 FD62
  Stanmore HA7 . . . . .41 CG50
  Sunbury-on-Thames TW16 135 BV95
  Tadworth (Kgswd.) KT20 . .174 DA122
  Upminster RM14 . . . . .73 FS62
  Uxbridge UB10 . . . . .58 BN64
  Wallington SM6 . . . . . . .159 DL106
  Waltham Cross (Goffs Oak)
   EN7 . . . . .13 DP28
  Watford WD18 . . . . .23 BS42
Chase Ct Gdns, Enf. EN2 . . . .30 DQ41
CHASE CROSS, Rom. 51 FE51
Chase Cross Rd, Rom. RM5 . . .51 FC52
Chase End, Epsom KT19 . . . .156 CR112
H Chase Farm Hosp, Enf.
  EN2 . . . . .29 DN38
Chasefield Rd, SW17 . . . . . .120 DF91
Chase Gdns, E4 . . . . .47 EA49
  Twickenham TW2 . . . . . .117 CD86
Chase Grn, Enf. EN2 . . . . . . .30 DQ41
Chase Grn Av, Enf. EN2 . . . . .29 DP40
Chase Hill, Enf. EN2 . . . . . . .30 DQ41
Chase Ho Gdns, Horn. RM11
   off Great Nelmes Chase . .72 FM57
Chase La, Chig. IG7 . . . . .50 EU48
  Ilford IG6 . . . . .69 ER57
Chaseley Dr, W4
   off Wellesley Rd 98 CP81
  South Croydon CR2 . . . . .160 DR110
Chaseley St, E14 . . . . .85 DY72
Chasemore Cl, Mitch. CR4 . . .140 DF101
Chasemore Gdns, Croy. CR0
   off Thorneloe Gdns 159 DP106
Chase Ridings, Enf. EN2 . . . . .29 DN40
Chase Rd, N14 . . . . .29 DJ44
  NW10 . . . . .80 CR70
  W3 . . . . .80 CR70
  Brentwood CM14 . . . . . . .54 FW48
  Epsom KT19 . . . . .156 CR112
Chase Side, N14 . . . . .28 DG44
  Enfield EN2 . . . . .30 DQ41
Chase Side Av, SW20 . . . . . .139 CY95
  Enfield EN2 . . . . .30 DQ40
Chaseside Cl, Rom. RM1 . . . . .51 FE51
Chase Side Cres, Enf. EN2 . . .30 DQ39
Chaseside Gdns, Cher. KT16 .134 BH101
Chase Side Pl, Enf. EN2
   off Chase Side 30 DQ40
Chase Sq, Grav. DA11
   off High St 131 GH86
Chaseville Pk Rd, N21 . . . . . .29 DL43
Chase Way, N14 . . . . .45 DH47
Chasewood Av, Enf. EN2 . . . .29 DP40
Chasewood Pk, Har. HA1 . . . .61 CF62
Chastilian Rd, Dart. DA1 . . . .127 FF87
Chatfield Ct, Cat. CR3
   off Yorke Road 176 DR122
Chatfield Rd, SW11 . . . . . . .100 DC83
  Croydon CR0 . . . . .141 DP102
Chatham Av, Brom. BR2 . . . .144 EF101
Chatham Cl, NW11 . . . . .64 DA57
  Sutton SM3 . . . . .139 CZ101
Chatham Hill Rd, Sev. TN14 .191 FJ121
Chatham Pl, E9 . . . . .84 DW65
Chatham Rd, E17 . . . . .67 DY55
  E18 off Grove Hill 48 EF54

Chatham Rd, SW11 . . . . . . .120 DF86
  Kingston upon Thames
   KT1 . . . . .138 CN96
  Orpington BR6 . . . . .163 EQ106
Chatham St, SE17 . . . . .201 K8
Chatsfield, Epsom KT17 . . . .157 CU110
Chatsworth Av, NW4 . . . . . . .43 CW54
  SW20 . . . . .139 CY95
  Bromley BR1 . . . . .124 EH91
  Sidcup DA15 . . . . .126 EU88
  Wembley HA9 . . . . .62 CM64
Chatsworth Cl, NW4 . . . . . . .43 CW54
  Borehamwood WD6 . . . . .26 CN41
  West Wickham BR4 . . . . .144 EF103
Chatsworth Ct, W8 . . . . .100 DA77
  Stanmore HA7
   off Marsh La 41 CJ50
Chatsworth Cres, Houns. TW3 .97 CD84
Chatsworth Dr, Enf. EN1 . . . . .46 DU45
Chatsworth Est, E5
   off Elderfield Rd 67 DX63
Chatsworth Gdns, W3 . . . . . .80 CP73
  Harrow HA2 . . . . .60 CB60
  New Malden KT3 . . . . . . .139 CT99
Chatsworth Par, Orp. BR5
   off Queensway 145 EQ99
Chatsworth Pl, Lthd. (Oxshott)
   KT22 . . . . .155 CD112
  Mitcham CR4 . . . . .140 DF97
  Teddington TW11 . . . . . .117 CG91
Chatsworth Ri, W5 . . . . .80 CM70
Chatsworth Rd, E5 . . . . .66 DW62
  E15 . . . . .68 EF64
  NW2 . . . . .81 CX65
  W4 . . . . .98 CQ79
  W5 . . . . .80 CM70
  Croydon CR0 . . . . .160 DR105
  Dartford DA1 . . . . .128 FJ85
  Hayes UB4 . . . . .77 BV70
  Sutton SM3 . . . . .157 CX106
Chatsworth Way, SE27 . . . . .121 DP90
Chatteris Av, Rom. RM3 . . . . .52 FJ51
Chattern Hill, Ashf. TW15 . . .115 BP91
Chattern Rd, Ashf. TW15 . . . .115 BQ91
Chatterton Ms, N4
   off Chatterton Rd 65 DP62
Chatterton Rd, N4 . . . . .65 DP62
  Bromley BR2 . . . . .144 EK98
Chatto Rd, SW11 . . . . .120 DF85
Chaucer Av, Hayes UB4 . . . . .77 BU71
  Hounslow TW4 . . . . .95 BV82
  Richmond TW9 . . . . .98 CN82
  Weybridge KT13 . . . . . . .152 BN108
Chaucer Cl, N11 . . . . .45 DJ50
  Banstead SM7 . . . . .157 CY114
  Tilbury RM18 . . . . .111 GJ82
Chaucer Ct, N16 . . . . .66 DS63
Chaucer Dr, SE1 . . . . .202 A9
Chaucer Gdns, Sutt. SM1 . . . .140 DA104
Chaucer Grn, Croy. CR0 . . . .142 DV101
Chaucer Ho, Sutt. SM1 . . . . .140 DA104
Chaucer Pk, Dart. DA1 . . . . .128 FM87
Chaucer Rd, E7 . . . . .86 EG65
  E11 . . . . .68 EG58
  E17 . . . . .47 EC54
  SE24 . . . . .121 DN85
  W3 . . . . .80 CQ74
  Ashford TW15 . . . . .114 BL91
  Gravesend (Nthflt.) DA11 . .130 GD90
  Romford RM3 . . . . .51 FH52
  Sidcup DA15 . . . . .126 EW88
  Sutton SM1 . . . . .158 DA105
  Welling DA16 . . . . .105 ES81
Chaucer Way, SW19 . . . . . . .120 DD93
  Addlestone KT15 . . . . . . .152 BG107
  Dartford DA1 . . . . .108 FN84
  Slough SL1 . . . . .74 AT74
Chauncey Cl, N9 . . . . .46 DU48
Chauncy Av, Pot.B. EN6 . . . . .12 DC33
Chaundrye Cl, SE9 . . . . .124 EL86
Chauntler Cl, E16 . . . . .86 EH72
Chavecroft Ter, Epsom KT18 .173 CW119
Chave Rd, Dart. DA2 . . . . . . .128 FL90
Chaworth Cl, Cher. KT16 . . . .151 BC107
Chaworth Rd, Cher. (Ott.)
  KT16 . . . . .151 BC107
CHEAM, Sutt. 157 CX107
⇌ Cheam 157 CY108
Cheam Cl, Tad. KT20
   off Waterfield 173 CV121
Cheam Common Rd, Wor.Pk.
  KT4 . . . . .139 CV103
Cheam Mans, Sutt. SM3 . . . .157 CY108
Cheam Pk Way, Sutt. SM3 . . .157 CY107
Cheam Rd, Epsom KT17 . . . .157 CU109
  Sutton SM1 . . . . .157 CZ107
  Sutton (E.Ewell) SM2 . . . .157 CX110
Cheam St, SE15
   off Evelina Rd 102 DV83
Cheapside, EC2 . . . . .197 J9
  N13 off Taplow Rd 46 DQ49
  Woking GU21 . . . . .150 AX114
Cheapside La, Uxb. (Denh.)
  UB9 . . . . .57 BF61
Cheddar Cl, N11
   off Martock Gdns 44 DG51
Cheddar Rd, Houns. (Hthrw.Air.)
   TW6 off Cromer Rd 94 BN82
Cheddar Waye, Hayes UB4 . . .77 BV72
Cheddington Rd, N18 . . . . . . .46 DS48
Chedworth Cl, E16
   off Hallsville Rd 86 EF71
Cheeseman Cl, Hmptn.
  TW12 . . . . .116 BY93
Cheesemans Ter, W14 . . . . . .99 CZ78
Cheldon Av, NW7
   off Bittacy Hill 43 CY52
Chelford Rd, Brom. BR1 . . . .123 ED92
Chelmer Cres, Bark. IG11 . . . .88 EV68
Chelmer Dr, Brwd. CM13 . . . .55 GE44
  South Ockendon RM15 . . . .91 FW73
Chelmer Rd, E9 . . . . .67 DX64
  Grays RM16 . . . . .111 GG78
  Upminster RM14 . . . . .73 FR58
Chelmsford Av, Rom. RM5 . . .51 FD52

Chelmsford Cl, E6
   off Guildford Rd 87 EM72
  W6 . . . . .99 CX79
  Sutton SM2 . . . . .158 DA109
Chelmsford Dr, Upmin. RM14 .72 FM62
Chelmsford Gdns, Ilf. IG1 . . . .68 EL59
Chelmsford Rd, E11 . . . . .67 ED60
  E17 . . . . .67 EA58
  E18 . . . . .48 EF53
  N14 . . . . .45 DJ45
  Brentwood CM15 . . . . . . .55 FZ44
Chelmsford Sq, NW10 . . . . . .81 CW67
CHELSEA, SW3 . . . . .100 DD79
H Chelsea & Westminster
  Hosp, SW10 . . . . .100 DC79
★ Chelsea Antique Mkt,
  SW3 . . . . .100 DD79
Chelsea Br, SW1 . . . . .101 DH79
  SW8 . . . . .101 DH79
Chelsea Br Rd, SW1 . . . . . . .198 F10
Chelsea Cloisters, SW3
   off Lucan Pl 100 DE77
Chelsea Cl, NW10 . . . . .80 CR67
  Edgware HA8 . . . . .42 CN54
  Hampton (Hmptn.H.)
   TW12 . . . . .116 CC92
  Worcester Park KT4 . . . . .139 CU101
Chelsea Cres, SW10
   off Harbour Av 100 DC81
Chelsea Embk, SW3 . . . . . . .100 DE79
★ Chelsea FC, SW6 . . . . . . .100 DB80
Chelsea Gdns, W13
   off Hathaway Gdns 79 CF71
  Sutton SM3 . . . . .157 CY105
Chelsea Harbour, SW10 . . . .100 DC81
Chelsea Harbour Dr, SW10 . .100 DC81
Chelsea Manor Ct, SW3 . . . .100 DE79
   off Chelsea Manor St 100 DE79
Chelsea Manor Gdns, SW3 . .100 DE79
Chelsea Manor St, SW3 . . . .100 DE78
Chelsea Ms, Horn. RM11
   off St. Leonards Way 71 FH60
Chelsea Pk Gdns, SW3 . . . . .100 DD79
★ Chelsea Physic Gdn,
  SW3 . . . . .100 DF79
Chelsea Sq, SW3 . . . . .198 A10
Chelsea Wf, SW10 . . . . .100 DC80
CHELSFIELD, Orp. 164 EW106
⇌ Chelsfield 164 EV106
Chelsfield Av, N9 . . . . .47 DX45
Chelsfield Gdns, SE26 . . . . . .122 DW90
Chelsfield Grn, N9
   off Chelsfield Av 47 DX45
Chelsfield Hill, Orp. BR6 . . . .164 EW109
Chelsfield La, Orp. BR5, BR6 .164 EX101
  Orpington (Maypole) BR6 . .164 FA108
  Sevenoaks TN14 . . . . . . .165 FC109
H Chelsfield Park Hosp, Orp.
  BR6 . . . . .164 EZ106
Chelsfield Rd, Orp. BR5 . . . .146 EW100
CHELSHAM, Warl. 177 EA117
Chelsham Cl, Warl. CR6 . . . .177 DY118
Chelsham Common Rd, Warl.
  CR6 . . . . .177 EA116
Chelsham Ct Rd, Warl. CR6 . .177 ED118
Chelsham Rd, SW4 . . . . .101 DK83
  South Croydon CR2 . . . . .160 DR107
  Warlingham CR6 . . . . . . .177 EA117
Chelston App, Ruis. HA4 . . . . .59 BU61
Chelston Rd, Ruis. HA4 . . . . . .59 BU60
Chelsworth Cl, Rom. RM3
   off Chelsworth Dr 52 FM53
Chelsworth Dr, SE18 . . . . . . .105 ER79
  Romford RM3 . . . . .52 FL53
Cheltenham Av, Twick. TW1 . .117 CG87
Cheltenham Cl, Grav. DA12 . .131 GJ92
  New Malden KT3
   off Northcote Rd 138 CQ97
  Northolt UB5 . . . . .78 CB65
Cheltenham Gdns, E6 . . . . . . .86 EL68
  Loughton IG10 . . . . .32 EL44
Cheltenham Pl, W3 . . . . .80 CP74
  Harrow HA3 . . . . .62 CL56
Cheltenham Rd, E10 . . . . .67 EC58
  SE15 . . . . .102 DW84
  Orpington BR6 . . . . .146 EU104
Cheltenham Ter, SW3 . . . . . .198 E10
Cheltenham Vil, Stai. TW19 . .113 BF90
Chelverton Rd, SW15 . . . . . . .99 CX84
Chelwood, N20
   off Oakleigh Rd N 44 DD47
Chelwood Cl, E4 . . . . .31 EB44
  Coulsdon CR5
   off Starrock Rd 175 DJ119
  Epsom KT17 . . . . .157 CT112
  Northwood HA6 . . . . .39 BQ52
Chelwood Gdns, Rich. TW9 . . .98 CN82
Chelwood Gdns Pas, Rich. TW9
   off Chelwood Gdns 98 CN82
Chelwood Wk, SE4 . . . . .103 DY84
Chenappa Cl, E13 . . . . .86 EG69
Chenduit Way, Stan. HA7 . . . .41 CF50
Cheney Rd, NW1 . . . . .197 P1
Cheney Row, E17 . . . . .47 DZ53
Cheneys Rd, E11 . . . . .68 EE62
Cheney St, Pnr. HA5 . . . . .60 BW57
CHENIES, Rick. 21 BB38
Chenies, The, Dart. DA2 . . . .127 FE91
  Orpington BR6 . . . . .145 ES100
Chenies Av, Amer. HP6 . . . . . .20 AW39
Chenies Hill, Hem.H. (Flaun.)
  HP3 . . . . .5 BB34
Chenies Ms, WC1 . . . . .195 M5
Chenies Par, Amer. HP7 . . . . .20 AW40
Chenies Pl, NW1 . . . . .83 DK68
Chenies Rd, Rick. (Chorl.)
  WD3 . . . . .21 BD40
Chenies St, WC1 . . . . .195 M6
Chenies Way, Wat. WD18 . . . .39 BS45
Cheniston Cl, W.Byf. KT14 . . .152 BG112
Cheniston Gdns, W8 . . . . . . .100 DB76
Chepstow Av, Horn. RM12 . . . .72 FL62
Chepstow Cl, SW15
   off Lytton Gro 119 CY86
Chepstow Cres, W11 . . . . .82 DA73

Chepstow Cres, Ilf. IG3 . . . . .69 ES58
Chepstow Gdns, Sthl. UB1 . . .78 BZ72
Chepstow Pl, W2 . . . . .82 DA72
Chepstow Ri, Croy. CR0 . . . .142 DS104
Chepstow Rd, W2 . . . . .82 DA72
  W7 . . . . .97 CG76
  Croydon CR0 . . . . .142 DS104
Chepstow Vil, W11 . . . . .81 CZ73
Chepstow Way, SE15 . . . . . .102 DT80
Chequers, Buck.H. IG9
   off Hills Rd 48 EH46
Chequers Cl, NW9 . . . . .62 CS55
  Orpington BR5 . . . . .145 ET98
  Tadworth KT20 . . . . .183 CU125
Chequers Gdns, N13 . . . . .45 DP50
Chequers La, Dag. RM9 . . . . .88 EZ70
  Tadworth KT20 . . . . .183 CU125
  Watford WD25 . . . . .8 BW30
Chequers Orchard, Iver SL0 . .75 BF72
Chequers Par, SE9
   off Eltham High St 125 EM86
  Dagenham RM9 . . . . .88 EZ70
Chequers Rd, Brwd. CM14 . . .52 FM46
  Loughton IG10 . . . . .33 EN43
  Romford RM3 . . . . .52 FL47
Chequers Sq, Uxb. UB8
   off High St 76 BJ66
Chequer St, EC1 . . . . .197 J5
Chequers Wk, Wal.Abb. EN9 . .16 EF33
Chequers Way, N13 . . . . .46 DQ50
Chequer Tree Cl, Wok. (Knap.)
  GU21 . . . . .166 AS116
Cherbury Cl, SE28 . . . . .88 EX72
Cherbury Ct, N1 . . . . .197 L1
Cherbury St, N1 . . . . .197 L1
Cherchefelle Ms, Stan. HA7 . .41 CH50
Cherimoya Gdns, W.Mol. KT8
   off Kelvinbrook 136 CB97
Cherington Rd, W7 . . . . .79 CF74
Cheriton Av, Brom. BR2 . . . . .144 EF99
  Ilford IG5 . . . . .49 EM54
Cheriton Cl, W5 . . . . .79 CJ71
  Barnet EN4 . . . . .28 DF41
Cheriton Ct, Walt. KT12
   off St. Johns Dr 136 BW102
Cheriton Dr, SE18 . . . . .105 ER80
Cheriton Sq, SW17 . . . . .120 DG89
Cherries, The, Slou. SL2 . . . . .74 AV72
Cherry Acre, Ger.Cr. (Chal.St.P.)
  SL9 . . . . .36 AX49
Cherry Av, Brwd. CM13 . . . . . .54 FZ48
  Slough SL3 . . . . .92 AX75
  Southall UB1 . . . . .78 BX74
  Swanley BR8 . . . . .147 FD97
Cherry Blossom Cl, N13 . . . . .45 DP50
Cherry Cl, E17
   off Eden Rd 67 EB56
  NW9 . . . . .42 CS54
  SW2 off Tulse Hill 121 DN87
  W5 . . . . .97 CK76
  Banstead SM7 . . . . .157 CX114
  Carshalton SM5 . . . . . . .140 DF103
  Morden SM4 . . . . .139 CY98
  Ruislip HA4
   off Roundways 59 BT62
Cherrycot Hill, Orp. BR6 . . . .163 ER105
Cherrycot Ri, Orp. BR6 . . . . .163 EQ105
Cherry Cres, Brent. TW8 . . . . .97 CH80
Cherry Cft, Rick. (Crox.Grn.)
  WD3 . . . . .22 BN44
Cherrycroft Gdns, Pnr. HA5
   off Westfield Pk 40 BZ52
Cherrydale, Wat. WD18 . . . . . .23 BT42
Cherrydown Av, E4 . . . . .47 DZ48
Cherrydown Cl, E4 . . . . .47 DZ48
Cherrydown Rd, Sid. DA14 . .126 EX89
Cherrydown Wk, Rom. RM7 . . .51 FB54
Cherry Gdns, Dag. RM9 . . . . .70 EZ64
  Northolt UB5 . . . . .78 CB66
Cherry Gdn St, SE16 . . . . . . .202 D5
Cherry Garth, Brent. TW8 . . . .97 CK77
Cherry Gro, Hayes UB3 . . . . . .77 BV74
  Uxbridge UB8 . . . . .77 BP71
Cherry Hill, Barn. EN5 . . . . . .28 DB44
  Harrow HA3 . . . . .41 CE51
  Rickmansworth (Loud.)
   WD3 . . . . .22 BH41
  St. Albans AL2 . . . . .8 CA25
Cherry Hill Gdns, Croy. CR0 . .159 DM105
Cherry Hills, Wat. WD19 . . . . .40 BY50
Cherry Hollow, Abb.L. WD5 . . .7 BT31
Cherrylands Cl, NW9 . . . . .62 CQ61
Cherry La, West Dr. UB7 . . . . .94 BM77
Cherry La Roundabout, West Dr.
  UB7 . . . . .95 BP77
Cherry Laurel Wk, SW2
   off Beechdale Rd 121 DM86
Cherry Orchard, Amer. HP6 . . .20 AS37
  Ashtead KT21 . . . . .172 CP118
  Slough (Stoke P.) SL2 . . . .74 AV66
  Staines TW18 . . . . .114 BG92
  West Drayton UB7 . . . . . . .94 BL75
Cherry Orchard Cl, Orp. BR5 .146 EW99
Cherry Orchard Gdns, Croy.
  CR0 off Oval Rd 142 DR103
  West Molesey KT8 . . . . . .136 BZ97
Cherry Orchard Rd, Brom.
  BR2 . . . . .144 EL103
  Croydon CR0 . . . . .142 DR103
  West Molesey KT8 . . . . . .136 CA97
Cherry Ri, Ch.St.G. HP8 . . . . .36 AX47
Cherry Rd, Enf. EN3 . . . . .30 DW38
Cherry St, Rom. RM7 . . . . . . .71 FD57
  Woking GU21 . . . . .166 AY118
Cherry Tree Av, St.Alb. (Lon.Col.)
  AL2 . . . . .3 CK26
  Staines TW18 . . . . .114 BH93
  West Drayton UB7 . . . . . . .76 BM72
Cherry Tree Cl, E9
   off Moulins Rd 84 DW67
  Grays RM17 . . . . .110 GC79
  Rainham RM13 . . . . .89 FG68
  Wembley HA0 . . . . .61 CF63
Cherry Tree Ct, NW9 . . . . . . .62 CQ56
  Coulsdon CR5 . . . . .175 DM117
  South Ockendon RM15 . . . .91 FX70
Cherry Tree Grn, S.Croy. CR2 .160 DV114

Cherry Tree La, Dart. DA2 . . . .127 FF90
  Epsom KT19
   off Christ Ch Rd 156 CN112
  Ger.Cr. (Chal.St.P.)
   SL9 . . . . .36 AX54
Cherry Tree La, Iver SL0 . . . . .76 BG67
  Potters Bar EN6 . . . . .12 DB34
  Rainham RM13 . . . . .89 FE69
  Rickmansworth (Herons.)
   WD3 . . . . .37 BC46
  Slough (Fulmer) SL3 . . . . .75 AZ65
Cherry Tree Ri, Buck.H. IG9 . . .48 EJ49
Cherry Tree Rd, E15 . . . . .68 EE63
   off Wingfield Rd 68 EE63
  N2 . . . . .64 DF56
  Watford WD24 . . . . .23 BV36
Cherry Tree Wk, EC1 . . . . . . .197 J5
  Beckenham BR3 . . . . . . .143 DZ98
  West Wickham BR4 . . . . .162 EF105
Cherry Tree Way, Stan. HA7 . . .41 CH51
  Brom. BR2 . . . . .144 EG102
  Grays RM16 . . . . .111 GG76
  Rainham RM13 . . . . .89 FF68
  Rickmansworth (Loud.)
   WD3 . . . . .22 BJ40
Cherry Way, Epsom KT19 . . . .156 CR107
  Shepperton TW17 . . . . . .135 BR98
  Slough (Horton) SL3 . . . . .93 BC83
Cherrywood Av, Egh. (Eng.Grn.)
  TW20 . . . . .112 AV93
Cherrywood Cl, E3 . . . . .85 DY69
  Kingston upon Thames
   KT2 . . . . .118 CN94
Cherrywood Dr, SW15 . . . . . .119 CX85
  Gravesend (Nthflt.) DA11 . .130 GE90
Cherrywood La, Mord. SM4 . .139 CY98
Cherry Wd Way, W5
   off Hanger Vale La 80 CN71
Cherston Gdns, Loug. IG10
   off Cherston Rd 33 EN42
Cherston Rd, Loug. IG10 . . . . .33 EN42
CHERTSEY 134 BG102
⇌ Chertsey 133 BF102
Chertsey Br Rd, Cher. KT16 . .134 BK101
Chertsey Cl, Ken. CR8 . . . . . .175 DP115
Chertsey Cres, Croy. (New Adgtn.)
  CR0 . . . . .161 EC110
Chertsey Dr, Sutt. SM3 . . . . .139 CY103
Chertsey La, Cher. KT16 . . . .133 BE95
  Epsom KT19 . . . . .156 CN112
  Staines TW18 . . . . .113 BE92
★ Chertsey Mus, Cher. KT16 .134 BG100
   off Windsor St 134 BG100
Chertsey Rd, E11 . . . . .67 ED60
  Addlestone KT15 . . . . . . .134 BH103
  Ashford TW15 . . . . .115 BR94
  Feltham TW13 . . . . .115 BS92
  Ilford IG1 . . . . .69 ER63
  Shepperton TW17 . . . . . .134 BN101
  Sunbury-on-Thames TW16 .115 BR94
  Twickenham TW1, TW2 . . .117 CF86
  West Byfleet (Byfleet)
   KT14 . . . . .152 BK111
  Woking GU21 . . . . .151 BA113
  Woking (Chobham) GU24 . .150 AY110
Chertsey St, SW17 . . . . .120 DG92
Chervil Cl, Felt. TW13 . . . . . .115 BU90
Chervil Ms, SE28 . . . . .88 EV74
Cherwell Cl, Rick. (Crox.Grn.)
  WD3 . . . . .22 BN43
  Slough SL3 off Tweed Rd . .93 BB79
Cherwell Ct, Epsom KT19 . . .156 CQ105
Cherwell Gro, S.Ock. RM15 . . .91 FV73
Cherwell Way, Ruis. HA4 . . . . .59 BQ58
Cheryls Cl, SW6 . . . . .100 DB81
Cheseman St, SE26 . . . . .122 DV90
Chesfield Rd, Kings.T. KT2 . . .118 CL94
Chesham Av, Orp. BR5 . . . . .145 EP100
Chesham Cl, SW1 . . . . .198 F7
  Romford RM7 . . . . .71 FD56
  Sutton SM2 . . . . .157 CY110
Chesham Ct, Nthwd. HA6
   off Frithwood Av 39 BT51
Chesham Cres, SE20 . . . . . . .142 DW96
Chesham La, Ch.St.G. HP8 . . .36 AY48
  Gerrards Cross (Chal.St.P.)
   SL9 . . . . .36 AY49
Chesham Ms, SW1 . . . . .198 F6
Chesham Pl, SW1 . . . . .198 F7
Chesham Rd, SE20 . . . . .142 DW96
  SW19 . . . . .120 DD92
  Hemel Hempstead (Bov.)
   HP3 . . . . .4 AY27
  Kingston upon Thames
   KT1 . . . . .138 CN95
Chesham St, NW10 . . . . .62 CR62
  SW1 . . . . .198 F7
Chesham Ter, W13 . . . . .97 CH75
Chesham Way, Wat. WD18 . . .23 BS44
Cheshire Cl, E17 . . . . .47 EB53
  SE4 . . . . .103 DZ82
  Chertsey (Ott.) KT16 . . . .151 BC107
  Hornchurch RM11 . . . . . . .72 FN57
  Mitcham CR4 . . . . .141 DL97
Cheshire Ct, EC4 . . . . .196 E9
  Slough SL1
   off Clements Cl 92 AV75
Cheshire Dr, Wat. WD25
   off Ashfields 7 BT34
Cheshire Gdns, Chess. KT9 . .155 CK107
Cheshire Ho, N18 . . . . .46 DV49
Cheshire Rd, N22 . . . . .45 DM52
Cheshire St, E2 . . . . .84 DT70
Chesholm Rd, N16 . . . . .66 DS62
CHESHUNT, Wal.Cr. 15 DX31
⇌ Cheshunt 15 DZ30
H Cheshunt Comm Hosp,
  Wal.Cr. EN8 . . . . .15 DY31
Cheshunt Link Rd, Wal.Cr. (Chsht.)
  EN8 . . . . .14 DW33
Cheshunt Pk, Wal.Cr. (Chsht.)
  EN7 . . . . .14 DV26
Cheshunt Rd, E7 . . . . .86 EH65
  Belvedere DA17 . . . . . . .106 FA78

Cheshunt Wash, Wal.Cr. (Chsht.)
  EN8 . . . .15 DY27
Chesil Ct, E2 . . . .84 DW68
Chesilton Rd, SW6 . . . .99 CZ81
Chesil Way, Hayes UB4 . . .77 BT69
Chesley Gdns, E6 . . . .86 EK68
Cheslyn Gdns, Wat. WD17 . .23 BT37
Chesney Cres, Croy. (New Adgtn.)
  CR0 . . . .161 EC108
Chesney St, SW11 . . . .100 DG81
Chesnut Est, N17 . . . .66 DT55
Chesnut Gro, N17
  off Chesnut Rd . . .66 DT55
Chesnut Rd, N17 . . . .66 DT55
Chess Cl, Chesh. (Latimer)
  HP5 . . . .20 AX36
  Rickmansworth (Loud.)
  WD3 . . . .22 BK42
Chessfield Pk, Amer. HP6 . .20 AY39
Chess Hill, Rick. (Loud.) WD3 .22 BK42
Chessholme Ct, Sun. TW16 .115 BS94
Chessholme Rd, Ashf. TW15 .115 BQ93
CHESSINGTON 156 CL107
Chessington Av, N3 . . . .63 CY55
  Bexleyheath DA7 . . .106 EY80
Chessington Cl, Epsom
  KT19 . . . .156 CQ107
Chessington Ct, Pnr. HA5 . .60 BZ56
Chessington Hall Gdns, Chess.
  KT9 . . . .155 CK108
Chessington Hill Pk, Chess.
  KT9 . . . .156 CN106
Chessington Lo, N3 . . . .63 CZ55
⇌ Chessington North 156 CL106
Chessington Rd, Epsom
  KT17, KT19 . . . .157 CT109
⇌ Chessington South 155 CK108
Chessington Way, W.Wick.
  BR4 . . . .143 EB103
★ Chessington World of
  Adventure, Chess. KT9 . .155 CJ110
Chess La, Rick. (Loud.) WD3 .22 BK42
Chesson Rd, W14 . . . .99 CZ79
Chess Vale Ri, Rick. (Crox.Grn.)
  WD3 . . . .22 BK42
Chess Valley Wk, Chesh. HP5 .20 AU35
  Rickmansworth WD3 . . .22 BL44
Chess Way, Rick. (Chorl.) WD3 .22 BG42
Chesswood Way, Pnr. HA5 . .40 BX54
Chester Av, Rich. TW10 . . .118 CM85
  Twickenham TW2 . . .116 BZ88
  Upminster RM14 . . .73 FS61
Chester Cl, SW1 . . . .198 G5
  SW13 . . . .99 CV83
  Ashford TW15 . . .115 BR92
  Loughton IG10 . . .33 EQ39
  Potters Bar EN6 . . .12 DB29
  Sutton SM1 . . .140 DA103
  Uxbridge UB8
    off Dawley Av . . .77 BP72
Chester Cl N, NW1 . . . .195 J2
Chester Cl S, NW1 . . . .195 J3
Chester Cotts, SW1 . . . .198 F9
Chester Ct, NW1 . . . .195 J2
  SE5 . . . .102 DR80
Chester Cres, E8
  off Ridley Rd . . .84 DT65
Chester Dr, Har. HA2 . . . .60 BZ58
Chesterfield Cl, Orp. BR5 . .146 EX98
Chesterfield Dr, Dart. DA1 . .127 FH85
  Esher KT10 . . .137 CG103
  Sevenoaks TN13 . . .190 FD122
Chesterfield Gdns, N4 . . . .65 DP57
  SE10 off Crooms Hill . . .103 ED80
  W1 . . .199 H2
Chesterfield Gro, SE22 . . . .122 DT85
Chesterfield Hill, W1 . . . .199 H1
Chesterfield Ms, N4
  off Chesterfield Gdns . . .65 DP57
  Ashford TW15
    off Chesterfield Rd . . .114 BL91
Chesterfield Rd, E10 . . . .67 EC58
  N3 . . .44 DA51
  W4 . . .98 CQ79
  Ashford TW15 . . .114 BL91
  Barnet EN5 . . .27 CX43
  Enfield EN3 . . .31 DY37
  Epsom KT19 . . .156 CR108
Chesterfield St, W1 . . . .199 H2
Chesterfield Wk, SE10 . . . .103 ED81
Chesterfield Way, SE15 . . .102 DW80
  Hayes UB3 . . .95 BU75
Chesterford Gdns, NW3 . . .64 DB63
Chesterford Ho, SE18
  off Shooter's Hill Rd . . .104 EK80
Chesterford Rd, E12 . . . .69 EM64
Chester Gdns, W13 . . . .79 CG72
  Enfield EN3 . . .30 DV44
  Morden SM4 . . .140 DC100
Chester Gate, NW1 . . . .195 H3
Chester Gibbons Grn, St.Alb.
  AL2 off High St . . .9 CK26
Chester Grn, Loug. IG10 . . .33 EQ39
Chester Ms, SW1 . . . .199 H6
Chester Path, Loug. IG10 . . .33 EQ39
Chester Pl, NW1 . . . .195 J2
Chester Rd, E7 . . . .86 EK66
  E11 . . .68 EH58
  E16 . . .86 EE70
  E17 . . .67 DX57
  N9 . . .46 DV46
  N17 . . .66 DR55
  N19 . . .65 DH61
  NW1 . . .194 G3
  SW19 . . .119 CW93
  Borehamwood WD6 . . .26 CQ41
  Chigwell IG7 . . .49 EN48
  Hounslow TW4 . . .95 BW83
  Hounslow (Hthrw.Air.) TW6 .94 BN83
  Ilford IG3 . . .69 ET60
  Loughton IG10 . . .33 EP40
  Northwood HA6 . . .39 BS52
  Sidcup DA15 . . .125 ES85

Chester Rd, Wat. WD18 . . . .23 BU43
Chester Row, SW1 . . . .198 F9
Chesters, The, N.Mal. KT3 . .138 CS95
Chester Sq, SW1 . . . .199 H8
Chester Sq Ms, SW1 . . . .199 H7
  SW1 . . .198 G6
Chester St, E2 . . . .84 DU70
  SW1 . . .198 G6
Chester Ter, NW1 . . . .195 H2
Chesterton Cl, SW18
  off Ericsson Cl . . .120 DA85
  Greenford UB6 . . .78 CB68
Chesterton Dr, Red. RH1 . .185 DL128
  Staines TW19 . . .114 BM88
Chesterton Rd, E13 . . . .86 EG69
  W10 . . .81 CX71
Chesterton Sq, W8
  off Pembroke Rd . . .99 CZ77
Chesterton Ter, E13 . . . .86 EG69
  Kingston upon Thames
  KT1 . . .138 CN96
Chesterton Way, Til. RM18 . .111 GJ82
Chester Way, SE11 . . . .200 E9
Chesthunte Rd, N17 . . . .46 DQ53
Chestnut All, SW6
  off Lillie Rd . . .99 CZ79
Chestnut Av, E7 . . . .68 EH63
  N8 . . .65 DL57
  SW14 off Thornton Rd . . .98 CR83
  Brentford TW8 . . .97 CK77
  Brentwood CM14 . . .54 FS45
  Buckhurst Hill IG9 . . .48 EK48
  East Molesey KT8 . . .137 CF97
  Edgware HA8 . . .42 CL51
  Epsom KT19 . . .156 CS105
  Esher KT10 . . .137 CD101
  Grays RM16 . . .110 GB75
  Greenhithe (Bluewater)
  DA9 . . .129 FT87
  Hampton TW12 . . .116 CA94
  Hornchurch RM12 . . .71 FF61
  Northwood HA6 . . .39 BT54
  Rickmansworth WD3 . . .22 BG43
  Slough SL3 . . .92 AX75
  Teddington TW11 . . .137 CF96
  Virginia Water GU25 . . .132 AT98
  Walton-on-Thames KT12 . .153 BS109
  Wembley HA0 . . .61 CH64
  West Drayton UB7 . . .76 BM73
  West Wickham BR4 . . .162 EE106
  Westerham TN16 . . .178 EK122
  Weybridge KT13 . . .153 BQ108
Chestnut Av N, E17 . . . .67 EC56
Chestnut Av S, E17 . . . .67 EC56
Chestnut Cl, N14 . . . .29 DJ43
  N16 off Lordship Gro . . .66 DR61
  SE6 . . .123 EC92
  SE14 off Shardeloes Rd . .103 DZ83
  SW16 . . .121 DN91
  Addlestone KT15 . . .152 BK106
  Ashford TW15 . . .115 BP91
  Buckhurst Hill IG9 . . .48 EK47
  Carshalton SM5 . . .140 DF102
  Egham (Eng.Grn.) TW20 . .112 AW93
  Gerrards Cross (Chal.St.P.)
  SL9 . . .37 AZ52
  Gravesend (Nthflt.) DA11
    off Burch Rd . . .131 GF86
  Hayes UB3 . . .77 BS73
  Hornchurch RM12
    off Lancaster Dr . . .72 FJ63
  Orpington BR6 . . .164 EU106
  Sidcup DA15 . . .126 EU88
  Sunbury-on-Thames TW16 .115 BT93
  Tadworth KT20 . . .174 DA123
  West Drayton UB7 . . .95 BP80
  Woking (Ripley) GU23 . . .168 BL61
Chestnut Copse, Oxt. RH8 . .188 EG132
Chestnut Ct, SW6
  off North End Rd . . .99 CZ79
  Amersham HP6 . . .20 AS37
  Surbiton KT6
    off Penners Gdns . . .138 CL101
Chestnut Cres, Walt. KT12
  off Chestnut Av . . .153 BS109
Chestnut Dr, E11 . . . .68 EG58
  Bexleyheath DA7 . . .106 EX83
  Egham (Eng.Grn.) TW20 . .112 AX93
  Harrow HA3 . . .41 CF52
  Pinner HA5 . . .60 BX57
Chestnut Glen, Horn. RM12 . .71 FF61
Chestnut Gro, SE20 . . . .122 DW94
  SW12 . . .120 DG87
  W5 . . .97 CK76
  Barnet EN4 . . .28 DF43
  Brentwood CM14 . . .54 FW47
  Dartford DA2 . . .127 FD91
  Ilford IG6 . . .49 ES51
  Isleworth TW7 . . .97 CG84
  Mitcham CR4 . . .141 DK98
  New Malden KT3 . . .138 CR97
  South Croydon CR2 . . .160 DV108
  Staines TW18 . . .114 BJ93
  Wembley HA0 . . .61 CH64
  Woking GU22 . . .166 AY120
Chestnut La, N20 . . . .43 CY46
  Sevenoaks TN13 . . .191 FH124
  Weybridge KT13 . . .153 BP106
Chestnut Manor Cl, Stai.
  TW18 . . .114 BH92
Chestnut Mead, Red. RH1
  off Oxford Rd . . .184 DE133
Chestnut Pl, Ashtd. KT21 . .172 CL119
  Epsom KT17 . . .157 CU116
Chestnut Ri, SE18 . . . .105 ER79
  Bushey WD23 . . .40 CB45
Chestnut Rd, SE27 . . . .121 DP90
  SW20 . . .139 CX96
  Ashford TW15 . . .115 BP91
  Dartford DA1 . . .128 FK88
  Enfield EN3 . . .31 DY36
  Kingston upon Thames
  KT2 . . .118 CL94
  Twickenham TW2 . . .117 CE89
Chestnut Row, N3
  off Nether St . . .44 DA52
Chestnuts, Brwd. CM13 . . . .55 GB46
Chestnuts, The, SE14 . . . .103 DZ81

Chestnuts, The, Rom. (Abridge)
  RM4 . . .34 EV41
  Walton-on-Thames KT12 . .135 BU102
Chestnut Wk, Ger.Cr. (Chal.St.P.)
  SL9 . . .36 AY52
  Sevenoaks TN15 . . .191 FL129
  Shepperton TW17 . . .135 BS99
  Walton-on-Thames KT12
    off Octagon Rd . . .153 BS109
  Watford WD24 . . .23 BU37
  West Byfleet (Byfleet) KT14
    off Royston Rd . . .152 BL112
  Woodford Green IG8 . . .48 EG50
Chestnut Way, Felt. TW13 . .115 BV90
Cheston Av, Croy. CR0 . . . .143 DY103
Chestwood Gro, Uxb. UB10 . .76 BM66
Cheswick Cl, Dart. DA1 . . .107 FF84
Chesworth Cl, Erith DA8 . . .107 FE81
Chettle Cl, SE1 . . . .201 K6
Chettle Ct, N8 . . . .65 DN58
Chetwode Dr, Epsom KT18 . .173 CX118
Chetwode Rd, SW17 . . . .120 DF90
  Tadworth KT20 . . .173 CW119
Chetwood Wk, E6 . . . .86 EL72
Chetwynd Av, Barn. EN4 . . . .44 DF46
Chetwynd Dr, Uxb. UB10 . . . .76 BM68
Chetwynd Rd, NW5 . . . .65 DH63
Chevalier Cl, Stan. HA7 . . . .42 CL49
Cheval Pl, SW7 . . . .198 C6
Cheval St, E14 . . . .203 P6
Cheveley Cl, Rom. RM3
  off Chevington Way . . .52 FM53
Chevely Cl, Epp. CM16 . . . .18 EX29
Cheveney Wk, Brom. BR2
  off Marina Cl . . .144 EG97
CHEVENING, Sev. 180 EZ119
Chevening Cross, Sev. (Chev.)
  TN14 . . .180 FA120
Chevening La, Sev. (Knock.)
  TN14 . . .180 EY115
Chevening Rd, NW6 . . . .81 CX68
  SE10 . . .104 EF78
  SE19 . . .122 DR93
  Sevenoaks (Chev.) TN14 . .180 EZ119
  Sevenoaks (Sund.) TN14 . .180 EY123
Chevenings, The, Sid. DA14 . .126 EW90
Cheverton Rd, N19 . . . .65 DK60
Chevet St, E9
  off Kenworthy Rd . . .67 DY64
Chevington Way, Horn. RM12 . .72 FK63
Cheviot Cl, Bans. SM7 . . . .174 DB115
  Bexleyheath DA7 . . .107 FE82
  Bushey WD23 . . .24 CC44
  Enfield EN1 . . .30 DR40
  Hayes UB3 . . .95 BR80
  Sutton SM2 . . .158 DD109
Cheviot Gdns, NW2 . . . .63 CX61
  SE27 . . .121 DP91
Cheviot Gate, NW2 . . . .63 CY61
Cheviot Rd, SE27 . . . .121 DN92
  Hornchurch RM11 . . .71 FG60
  Slough SL3 . . .93 BA78
Cheviot Way, Ilf. IG2 . . . .69 ES56
Chevron Cl, E16 . . . .86 EG72
Chevy Rd, Sthl. UB2 . . . .96 CC75
Chewton Rd, E17 . . . .67 DY56
Cheyham Gdns, Sutt. SM2 . .157 CX110
Cheyham Way, Sutt. SM2 . .157 CY110
Cheyne Av, E18 . . . .68 EF55
  Twickenham TW2 . . .116 BZ88
Cheyne Cl, NW4 . . . .63 CW57
  Bromley BR2
    off Cedar Cres . . .144 EL104
  Gerrards Cross SL9 . . .56 AY60
Cheyne Ct, SW3
  off Flood St . . .100 DF79
  Banstead SM7
    off Park Rd . . .174 DB115
Cheyne Gdns, SW3 . . . .100 DE79
Cheyne Hill, Surb. KT5 . . . .138 CM98
Cheyne Ms, SW3 . . . .100 DE79
Cheyne Path, W7 . . . .79 CF71
Cheyne Pl, SW3 . . . .100 DF79
Cheyne Rd, Ashf. TW15 . . .115 BR93
Cheyne Row, SW3 . . . .100 DE79
Cheyne Wk, N21 . . . .29 DP43
  NW4 . . .63 CW58
  SW3 . . .100 DE79
  SW10 . . .100 DD80
  Croydon CR0 . . .142 DU103
  Longfield DA3
    off Cavendish Sq . . .149 FX97
Cheyneys Av, Edg. HA8 . . . .41 CK51
Chichele Gdns, Croy. CR0
  off Brownlow Rd . . .160 DT105
Chichele Rd, NW2 . . . .63 CX64
  Oxted RH8 . . .188 EE128
Chicheley Gdns, Har. HA3 . . .40 CC52
Chicheley Rd, Har. HA3 . . . .40 CC52
Chicheley St, SE1 . . . .200 C4
Chichester Av, Ruis. HA4 . . .59 BR61
Chichester Cl, E6 . . . .86 EL72
  SE3 . . .104 EJ81
  Hampton TW12
    off Maple Cl . . .116 BZ93
  South Ockendon (Aveley)
  RM15 . . .90 FQ74
Chichester Ct, Epsom KT17 . .157 CT109
  Slough SL1 . . .3 AU75
  Stanmore HA7 . . .62 CL55
Chichester Dr, Pur. CR8 . . .159 DM112
  Sevenoaks TN13 . . .190 FF125
Chichester Gdns, Ilf. IG1 . . .68 EL59
Chichester Ms, SE27 . . . .121 DN91
Chichester Rents, WC2 . . . .196 D8
Chichester Ri, Grav. DA12 . .131 GK91
Chichester Rd, E11 . . . .68 EE62
  N9 . . .46 DU46
  NW6 . . .82 DA68
  W2 . . .82 DB71
  Croydon CR0 . . .142 DS104
  Greenhithe DA9 . . .129 FW86
Chichester St, SW1 . . . .101 DJ78
Chichester Way, E14 . . . .204 F8
  Feltham TW14 . . .115 BV87
  Watford WD25 . . .8 BY33
Chicksand St, E1 . . . .84 DT71

Chiddingfold, N12 . . . .44 DA48
Chiddingstone Av, Bexh.
  DA7 . . .106 EZ80
Chiddingstone Cl, Sutt. SM2 .158 DA110
Chiddingstone St, SW6 . . . .100 DA82
Chieftan Dr, Purf. RM19 . . .108 FM77
Chieveley Rd, Bexh. DA7 . .107 FB84
Chiffinch Gdns, Grav. (Nthflt.)
  DA11 . . .130 GE90
Chignell Pl, W13
  off Broadway . . .79 CG74
CHIGWELL 49 EP48
⊖ Chigwell 49 EP49
Chigwell Hill, E1
  off Pennington St . . .202 D1
Chigwell Hurst Ct, Pnr. HA5 . .60 BX55
Chigwell La, Loug. IG10 . . . .33 EQ43
Chigwell Pk, Chig. IG7 . . . .49 EP48
Chigwell Pk Dr, Chig. IG7 . . .49 EN48
Chigwell Ri, Chig. IG7 . . . .49 EN47
Chigwell Rd, E18 . . . .68 EH55
  Woodford Green IG8 . . .48 EJ54
CHIGWELL ROW, Chig. . . .50 EU47
Chigwell Vw, Rom. RM5
  off Lodge La . . .50 FA51
Chilberton Dr, Red. RH1 . . .185 DJ130
Chilbrook Rd, Cob. (Down.)
  KT11 . . .169 BU118
Chilcombe Ho, SW15
  off Fontley Way . . .119 CU87
Chilcot Cl, E14
  off Grundy St . . .85 EB72
Chilcote La, Amer. (Lt.Chal.)
  HP7 . . .20 AV39
Chilcott Rd, Wat. WD24 . . . .23 BS36
Childebert Rd, SW17 . . . .121 DH89
Childeric Rd, SE14 . . . .103 DY80
Childerley, Kings.T. KT1
  off Burritt Rd . . .138 CN97
Childerley St, SW6
  off Fulham Palace Rd . . .99 CX81
Childers, The, Wdf.Grn. IG8 . .49 EM50
Childers St, SE8 . . . .103 DY79
Child La, SE10 . . . .205 L7
Childs Av, Uxb. (Hare.) UB9 . .38 BJ54
Childs Cl, Horn. RM11 . . . .72 FJ58
Childs Cres, Swans. DA10 . .129 FX86
CHILDS HILL, NW2 . . . .64 DA61
Childs Hill Wk, NW2 . . . .63 CZ62
Childs La, SE19
  off Westow St . . .122 DS93
Child's Ms, SW5 . . . .100 DA77
Child's Pl, SW5 . . . .100 DA77
Child's St, SW5 . . . .100 DA77
Child's Wk, SW5
  off Child's St . . .100 DA77
Childs Way, NW11 . . . .63 CZ57
Chilham Cl, Bex. DA5 . . . .126 EZ87
  Greenford UB6 . . .79 CG68
Chilham Rd, SE9 . . . .124 EL91
Chilham Way, Brom. BR2 . .144 EG101
Chillerton Rd, SW17 . . . .120 DG92
Chillingworth Gdns, Twick.
  TW1 off Tower Rd . . .117 CF90
Chillingworth Rd, N7 . . . .65 DM64
Chilmark Gdns, N.Mal. KT3 . .139 CT101
  Redhill RH1 . . .185 DL129
Chilmark Rd, SW16 . . . .141 DK96
Chilmead La, Red. (Nutfld.)
  RH1 . . .185 DK132
Chilsey Grn Rd, Cher. KT16 . .133 BE100
Chiltern Av, Bushey WD23 . . .24 CC44
  Twickenham TW2 . . .116 CA88
Chiltern Business Village, Uxb.
  UB8 . . .76 BH68
Chiltern Cl, Bexh. DA7
  off Cumbrian Av . . .107 FE81
  Borehamwood WD6 . . .26 CM40
  Bushey WD23 . . .24 CB44
  Croydon CR0 . . .142 DS104
  Uxbridge (Ickhm.) UB10 . .59 BP61
  Waltham Cross (Chsht.)
  EN7 . . .13 DP27
  Woking GU22 . . .166 AW122
  Worcester Park KT4
    off Cotswold Way . . .139 CW103
Chiltern Dene, Enf. EN2 . . . .29 DM42
Chiltern Dr, Rick. (Mill End)
  WD3 . . .37 BF45
  Surbiton KT5 . . .138 CP99
Chiltern Gdns, NW2 . . . .63 CX62
  Bromley BR2 . . .144 EF98
  Hornchurch RM12 . . .72 FJ62
Chiltern Hts, Amer. HP7 . . . .20 AU39
Chiltern Hill, Ger.Cr. (Chal.St.P.)
  SL9 . . .36 AY53
★ Chiltern Open Air Mus,
  Ch.St.G. HP8 . . .37 AZ47
Chiltern Rd, E3 . . . .85 EA70
  Gravesend (Nthflt.) DA11 . .130 GE90
  Ilford IG2 . . .69 ES56
  Pinner HA5 . . .60 BW57
  Sutton SM2 . . .158 DB109
Chilterns, The, Sutt. SM2
  off Gatton Cl . . .158 DB109
Chiltern St, W1 . . . .194 F6
Chiltern Vw Rd, Uxb. UB8 . . .76 BJ68
Chiltern Way, Wdf.Grn. IG8 . .48 EG48
Chilthorne Cl, SE6
  off Ravensbourne Pk Cres .123 DZ87
Chilton Av, W5 . . . .97 CK77
Chilton Ct, Walt. KT12 . . . .153 BU105
Chilton Gro, SE8 . . . .203 J9
Chiltonian Ind Est, SE12 . . .124 EF86
Chilton Rd, Edg. HA8
  off Manor Pk Cres . . .42 CN51
  Grays RM16 . . .111 GG76
  Richmond TW9 . . .98 CN83
Chiltons, The, E18
  off Grove Hill . . .48 EG54
Chiltons Cl, Bans. SM7
  off High St . . .174 DB115
Chilton St, E2 . . . .84 DT70
Chilver St, SE10 . . . .205 L10
Chilwell Gdns, Wat. WD19 . .40 BW49

Chilworth Ct, SW19
  off Windlesham Gro . . .119 CX88
Chilworth Gdns, Sutt. SM1 . .140 DC104
Chilworth Ms, W2 . . . .82 DC72
Chilworth St, W2 . . . .82 DC72
Chimes Av, N13 . . . .45 DN50
Chimes Shop Cen, The, Uxb.
  UB8 . . .76 BK66
China Ms, SW2 off Craster Rd .121 DM87
★ Chinatown, W1
  off Gerrard St . . .195 M10
Chinbrook Cres, SE12 . . . .124 EH90
Chinbrook Est, SE9 . . . .124 EH90
Chinbrook Rd, SE12 . . . .124 EH90
Chinchilla Dr, Houns. TW4 . .96 BW82
Chindits La, Brwd. CM14 . . . .54 FW50
Chine, The, N10 . . . .65 DJ56
  N21 . . .29 DP44
  Wembley HA0 . . .61 CH64
Ching Ct, WC2 . . . .195 P9
Chingdale Rd, E4 . . . .48 EE48
CHINGFORD, E4 . . . .47 EB46
⇌ Chingford 48 EE45
Chingford Av, E4 . . . .47 EB48
CHINGFORD GREEN, E4 . . .48 EF46
Chingford Ind Cen, E4 . . . .47 DY50
Chingford La, Wdf.Grn. IG8 . .48 EE49
Chingford Mt Rd, E4 . . . .47 EA49
Chingford Rd, E4 . . . .47 EA51
  E17 . . .47 EB53
Chingley Cl, Brom. BR1 . . .124 EE93
Ching Way, E4 . . . .47 DZ51
Chinnery Cl, Enf. EN1
  off Garnault Rd . . .30 DT39
Chinnor Cres, Grnf. UB6 . . .78 CB68
Chipka St, E14 . . . .204 D5
Chipley St, SE14 . . . .103 DY79
Chipmunk Gro, Nthlt. UB5
  off Argus Way . . .78 BY69
Chippendale All, Uxb. UB8
  off Chippendale Waye . . .76 BK66
Chippendale St, E5 . . . .67 DX62
Chippendale Waye, Uxb. UB8 .76 BK66
Chippenham Av, Wem. HA9 . .62 CP64
Chippenham Cl, Pnr. HA5 . . .59 BT56
  Romford RM3
    off Chippenham Rd . . .52 FK50
Chippenham Gdns, NW6 . . . .82 DA69
  Romford RM3 . . .52 FK50
Chippenham Ms, W9 . . . .82 DA70
Chippenham Rd, W9 . . . .82 DA70
  Romford RM3 . . .52 FK51
Chippenham Wk, Rom. RM3
  off Chippenham Rd . . .52 FK51
CHIPPERFIELD, Kings L. . . .6 BG31
Chipperfield Cl, Upmin. RM14 .73 FS60
Chipperfield Rd, Hem.H. (Bov.)
  HP3 . . .5 BB27
  Kings Langley WD4 . . .6 BK30
  Orpington BR5 . . .146 EU95
CHIPPING BARNET, Barn. . .27 CY42
Chipping Cl, Barn. EN5
  off St. Albans Rd . . .27 CY41
CHIPSTEAD, Couls. 174 DG119
CHIPSTEAD, Sev. 190 FC122
⇌ Chipstead 174 DF118
Chipstead Av, Th.Hth. CR7 . .141 DP98
CHIPSTEAD BOTTOM, Couls. .174 DE121
Chipstead Cl, SE19 . . . .122 DT94
  Coulsdon CR5 . . .174 DG116
  Sutton SM2 . . .158 DB109
Chipstead Ct, Wok. (Knap.)
  GU21 off Creston Av . . .166 AS117
Chipstead Gdns, NW2 . . . .63 CV61
Chipstead Gate, Couls. CR5
  off Woodfield Cl . . .175 DJ119
  Coulsdon, Couls. CR5 . . .174 DB124
  Sevenoaks TN13 . . .190 FC122
  Tadworth KT20 . . .183 CZ125
Chipstead Pk, Sev. TN13 . . .190 FD122
Chipstead Pk Cl, Sev. TN13 .190 FC122
Chipstead Pl Gdns, Sev. TN13 .190 FC122
Chipstead Rd, Bans. SM7 . .173 CZ117
  Erith DA8 . . .107 FE80
Chipstead Sta Par, Couls.
  (Chipstead) CR5
  off Station App . . .174 DF118
Chipstead St, SW6 . . . .100 DA81
Chipstead Valley Rd, Couls.
  CR5 . . .175 DH116
Chipstead Way, Bans. SM7 . .174 DF115
Chip St, SW4 . . . .101 DK83
Chirk Cl, Hayes UB4
  off Braunston Dr . . .78 BY70
Chirton Wk, Wok. GU21
  off Shilburn Way . . .166 AU118
Chisenhale Rd, E3 . . . .85 DY68
Chisholm Rd, Croy. CR0 . . .142 DS103
  Richmond TW10 . . .118 CM86
CHISLEHURST 125 EN94
⇌ Chislehurst 145 EN96
Chislehurst Av, N12 . . . .44 DC52
★ Chislehurst Caves, Chis.
  BR7 off Caveside Cl . . .145 EN95
Chislehurst Rd, Brom. BR1 . .144 EK96
  Chislehurst BR7 . . .144 EK96
  Orpington BR5, BR6 . . .145 ES98
  Richmond TW10 . . .118 CL86
  Sidcup DA14 . . .126 EU92
CHISLEHURST WEST, Chis. .125 EM92
Chislet Cl, Beck. BR3
  off Abbey La . . .123 EA94
Chisley Rd, N15 . . . .66 DS58
Chiswell Ct, Wat. WD24 . . . .24 BW38
CHISWELL GREEN, St.Alb. . .8 CA26
Chiswell Grn La, St.Alb. AL2 . .8 BX25
Chiswell Sq, SE3
  off Brook La . . .104 EH82
Chiswell St, EC1 . . . .197 J6
CHISWICK, W4 . . . .98 CR79
⇌ Chiswick 98 CQ80
Chiswick Br, SW14 . . . .98 CQ82
  W4 . . .98 CQ82
Chiswick Cl, Croy. CR0 . . . .141 DM104

Chiswick Common Rd, W4 . .98 CR77
Chiswick Ct, Pnr. HA5 . . . . . .60 BZ55
Chiswick Gm Studios, W4
  off Evershed Wk 98 CQ79
Chiswick High Rd, W4 . . . . .98 CR77
  Brentford TW8 . . . . .98 CM78
★ Chiswick Ho, W4 . . . . . . .98 CS79
Chiswick Ho Grds, W4 . . . . .98 CS79
Chiswick La, W4 . . . . .98 CS78
Chiswick La S, W4 . . . . .99 CT78
Ⓗ Chiswick Lo Hosp, W4 . .99 CT79
Chiswick Mall, W4 . . . . .98 CT79
  W6 . . . . .99 CT79
⊖ Chiswick Park 98 CQ77
Chiswick Quay, W4 . . . . . . .98 CQ81
Chiswick Rd, N9 . . . . .46 DU47
  W4 . . . . .98 CQ77
Chiswick Roundabout, W4
  off Chiswick High Rd 98 CN78
Chiswick Sq, W4
  off Hogarth Roundabout . . .98 CS79
Chiswick Staithe, W4 . . . . . .98 CQ81
Chiswick Ter, W4 off Acton La .98 CQ77
Chiswick Village, W4 . . . . . .98 CP78
Chiswick Wf, W4 . . . . .99 CT79
Chittenden Cotts, Wok. (Wisley)
  GU23 . . . . .168 BL116
Chitterfield Gate, West Dr.
  UB7 . . . . .94 BN80
Chitty's La, Dag. RM8 . . . . .70 EX61
Chitty St, W1 . . . . .195 L6
Chivalry Rd, SW11 . . . . . . .120 DE85
Chivenor Gro, Kings.T. KT2 . .117 CK92
Chivers Rd, E4 . . . . .47 EB48
Choats Manor Way, Bark.
  IG11 . . . . .88 EW70
Choats Rd, Bark. IG11 . . . . .88 EW68
  Dagenham RM9 . . . . .88 EW68
CHOBHAM, Wok. 150 AT111
Chobham Cl, Cher. (Ott.)
  KT16 . . . . .151 BB107
★ Chobham Common NNR,
  Wok. GU24 . . . . .150 AS105
Chobham Gdns, SW19 . . . . .119 CX89
Chobham La, Cher. (Longcr.)
  KT16 . . . . .132 AV102
Chobham Pk La, Wok. (Chobham)
  GU24 . . . . .150 AU110
Chobham Rd, E15 . . . . .67 ED64
  Chertsey (Ott.) KT16 . . . .151 BA108
  Woking GU21 . . . . .150 AY116
  Woking (Horsell) GU21 . . .150 AW113
Choir Gm, Wok. (Knap.) GU21
  off Semper Cl 166 AS117
Cholmeley Cres, N6 . . . . . . .65 DH59
Cholmeley Pk, N6 . . . . .65 DH60
Cholmley Gdns, NW6
  off Fortune Grn Rd 64 DA64
Cholmley Rd, T.Ditt. KT7 . . .137 CH100
Cholmondeley Av, NW10 . . . .81 CU68
Cholmondeley Wk, Rich.
  TW9 . . . . .117 CJ85
Choppins Ct, E1 . . . . .202 E2
Chopwell Ct, E15
  off Bryant St 85 ED66
CHORLEYWOOD, Rick. 21 BE43
⇌ Chorleywood 21 BD42
⊖ Chorleywood 21 BD42
CHORLEYWOOD BOTTOM,
  Rick. 21 BD44
Chorleywood Bottom, Rick. (Chorl.)
  WD3 . . . . .21 BD43
Chorleywood Cl, Rick. WD3
  off Nightingale Rd 38 BK45
Chorleywood Common, Rick.
  (Chorl.) WD3 . . . . .21 BE42
Chorleywood Cres, Orp. BR5 .145 ET96
Chorleywood Ho Dr, Rick. (Chorl.)
  WD3 . . . . .21 BE41
Chorleywood Lo La, Rick. (Chorl.)
  WD3 off Rickmansworth Rd .21 BK41
Chorleywood Rd, Rick. WD3 . .22 BG42
Choumert Gro, SE15 . . . . . .102 DU81
Choumert Rd, SE15 . . . . . . .102 DT83
Choumert Sq, SE15 . . . . . . .102 DU82
Chow Sq, E8 off Arcola St . . .66 DT64
Chrislaine Cl, Stai. (Stanw.)
  TW19 off High St 114 BK86
Chrisp St, E14 . . . . .85 EB71
Christchurch Av, N12 . . . . . .44 DC55
  NW6 . . . . .81 CY66
  Erith DA8 . . . . .107 FD79
  Harrow HA3 . . . . .61 CH56
  Rainham RM13 . . . . .89 FF68
  Teddington TW11 . . . . . . .117 CG92
  Wembley HA0 . . . . .80 CL65
Christchurch Cl, SW19 . . . . .120 DD94
  Enfield EN2 . . . . .30 DQ40
Christchurch Ct, NW6 . . . . . .81 CY66
Christchurch Cres, Grav. DA12
  off Christchurch Rd 131 GJ87
  Radlett WD7 . . . . .25 CG36
Christchurch Gdns, Epsom
  KT19 . . . . .156 CP111
  Harrow HA3 . . . . .61 CG56
Christchurch Av, Wem. HA0 . .80 CL65
Christchurch Hill, NW3 . . . . .64 DD62
Christchurch La, Barn. EN5 . .27 CY40
Christ Ch Mt, Epsom KT19 . .156 CP112
Christchurch Pk, Sutt. SM2 . .158 DC108
Christ Ch Pas, EC1 . . . . . . .196 G8
Christchurch Pas, NW3 . . . . .64 DC62
  Barnet EN5 . . . . .27 CY41
Christ Ch Path, Hayes UB3 . .95 BQ76
Christchurch Pl, Epsom
  KT19 . . . . .156 CP111
Christchurch Rd, N8 . . . . . . .65 DL58
  SW2 . . . . .121 DM88
  SW14 . . . . .118 CP85
  SW19 . . . . .140 DD95
Christ Ch Rd, Beck. BR3
  off Fairfield Rd 143 EA96
Christchurch Rd, Dart. DA1 . .128 FJ87
Christ Ch Rd, Epsom KT19 . .156 CL112
Christchurch Rd, Grav. DA12 .131 GJ88
  Hounslow (Hthrw.Air.) TW6
  off Courtney Rd 94 BN83

  Christchurch Rd, Ilf. IG1 . . . .69 EP60
  Purley CR8 . . . . .159 DP110
  Sidcup DA15 . . . . .125 ET91
Christ Ch Rd, Surb. KT5 . . . .138 CM100
Christchurch Rd, Til. RM18 . .111 GG81
  Virginia Water GU25 . . . . .132 AU97
Christchurch Sq, E9
  off Victoria Pk Rd 84 DW67
Christchurch St, SW3 . . . . . .100 DF79
Christchurch Ter, SW3
  off Christchurch St 100 DF79
Christchurch Way, SE10 . . . .205 J9
  Woking GU21
  off Church St E 167 AZ117
Christian Ct, SE16 . . . . .203 M3
Christian Flds, SW16 . . . . . .121 DN94
Christian Flds Av, Grav.
  DA12 . . . . .131 GJ91
Christian St, E1 . . . . .84 DU72
Christie Dr, Croy. CR0 . . . . .142 DU99
Christie Gdns, Rom. RM6 . . .70 EV58
Christie Rd, E9 . . . . .85 DY65
  Waltham Abbey EN9
  off Deer Pk Way 31 EB36
Christies Av, Sev. (Bad.Mt.)
  TN14 . . . . .164 FA110
Christie Wk, Cat. CR3
  off Hambledon Rd 176 DR122
Christina Sq, N4
  off Adolphus Rd 65 DP60
Christina St, EC2 . . . . .197 M4
Christine Worsley Cl, N21
  off Highfield Rd 45 DP47
Christopher Av, W7 . . . . . . .97 CG76
Christopher Cl, SE16 . . . . . .203 H4
  Hornchurch RM12
  off Chevington Way 72 FK63
  Sidcup DA15 . . . . .125 ET85
Christopher Ct, Tad. KT20
  off High St 173 CW123
Christopher Gdns, Dag. RM9
  off Wren Rd 70 EX64
Christopher Pl, NW1 . . . . . .195 N3
Christopher Rd, Sthl. UB2 . . .95 BV77
Christopher's Ms, W11
  off Penzance St 81 CY74
Christopher St, EC2 . . . . . . .197 L5
Christy Rd, West. (Bigg.H.)
  TN16 . . . . .178 EJ115
Chryssell Rd, SW9 . . . . . . .101 DN80
Chubworthy St, SE14 . . . . . .103 DY79
Chucks La, Tad. KT20 . . . . .173 CV124
Chudleigh Cres, Ilf. IG3 . . . . .69 ES63
Chudleigh Gdns, Sutt. SM1 . .140 DC104
Chudleigh Rd, NW6 . . . . . . .81 CX66
  SE4 . . . . .123 DZ85
  Romford RM3 . . . . .52 FL49
  Twickenham TW2 . . . . . . .117 CF87
Chudleigh St, E1 . . . . .85 DX72
Chudleigh Way, Ruis. HA4 . . .59 BU60
Chulsa Rd, SE26 . . . . .122 DV92
Chumleigh St, SE5 . . . . . . .102 DS79
Chumleigh Wk, Surb. KT5 . . .138 CM98
Church All, Croy. CR0 . . . . .141 DN102
  Gravesend DA11
  off High St 131 GH86
  Watford (Ald.) WD25 . . . . .24 CC38
Church App, SE21 . . . . .122 DR90
  Egham TW20 . . . . .133 BC97
  Sevenoaks (Cudham) TN14
  off Cudham La S 179 EQ115
  Staines (Stanw.) TW19 . . .114 BK86
Church Av, E4 . . . . .47 ED51
  NW1 off Kentish Town Rd . .83 DH65
  SW14 . . . . .98 CR83
  Beckenham BR3 . . . . . . .143 EA95
  Northolt UB5 . . . . .78 BZ66
  Pinner HA5 . . . . .60 BY58
  Ruislip HA4 . . . . .59 BR60
  Sidcup DA14 . . . . .126 EU92
  Southall UB2 . . . . .96 BY76
Churchbury Cl, Enf. EN1 . . . .30 DS40
Churchbury La, Enf. EN1 . . . .30 DR41
Churchbury Rd, SE9 . . . . . .124 EK87
  Enfield EN1 . . . . .30 DR40
Church Cl, N20 . . . . .44 DE48
  W8 off Kensington Ch St . .100 DB75
  Addlestone KT15 . . . . . . .152 BH105
  Edgware HA8 . . . . .42 CQ50
  Hayes UB4 . . . . .77 BR71
  Leatherhead (Fetch.)
  KT22 . . . . .171 CD124
  Loughton IG10 . . . . .33 EM40
  Northwood HA6 . . . . .39 BT52
  Potters Bar (Cuffley) EN6 . .13 DL29
  Radlett WD7 . . . . .25 CG36
  Staines TW18
  off The Broadway 134 BJ97
  Tadworth KT20
  off Buckland Rd 183 CZ127
  Uxbridge UB8 . . . . .76 BH68
  West Drayton UB7 . . . . . . .94 BL76
  Woking (Horsell) GU21 . . .166 AX116
Church Ct, Reig. RH2 . . . . .184 DB134
  Richmond TW9
  off George St 117 CK85
Church Cres, E9 . . . . .85 DX66
  N3 . . . . .43 CZ53
  N10 . . . . .65 DH56
  N20 . . . . .44 DE48
  South Ockendon RM15 . . .91 FW69
Churchcroft Cl, SW12
  off Endlesham Rd 120 DG87
Churchdown, Brom. BR1 . . .124 EE91
Church Dr, NW9 . . . . .62 CR60
  Harrow HA2 . . . . .60 BZ58
  West Wickham BR4 . . . . .144 EE104
Church Elm La, Dag. RM10 . .88 FA65
CHURCH END, N3 . . . . .43 CZ53
CHURCH END, NW10 . . . . . .80 CS65
Church End, E17 . . . . .67 EB56
  NW4 . . . . .63 CV56
Church Entry, EC4 . . . . .196 G9
Church Fm La, Swan. BR8 . .147 FC100
★ Church Farm Ho Mus,
  NW4 (Hendon) 63 CV55
Church Fm La, Sutt. SM3 . . .157 CY107

Church Fm Way, Wat. (Ald.)
  WD25 . . . . .24 CB38
Church Fld, Dart. DA2 . . . . .128 FK89
  Epping CM16 . . . . .18 EU29
  Radlett WD7 . . . . .25 CG36
  Sevenoaks TN13 . . . . . . .190 FE122
Churchfield Av, N12 . . . . . . .44 DC51
Churchfield Cl, Har. HA2 . . . .60 CC56
  Hayes UB3 off West Av . . .77 BT73
Churchfield Ms, Slou. SL2 . . .74 AU72
Churchfield Path, Wal.Cr. (Chsht.)
  EN8 . . . . .14 DW29
Churchfield Rd, W3 . . . . .80 CQ74
  W7 . . . . .97 CE75
  W13 . . . . .79 CH74
  Gerrards Cross (Chal.St.P.)
  SL9 . . . . .36 AX53
  Reigate RH2 . . . . .184 DA133
  Walton-on-Thames KT12 . .135 BU102
  Welling DA16 . . . . .106 EU83
  Weybridge KT13 . . . . . . .152 BN105
Churchfields, E18 . . . . .48 EG53
  SE10 off Roan St 103 EC79
  Loughton IG10 . . . . .32 EL42
  West Molesey KT8 . . . . . .136 CA97
  Woking (Horsell) GU21 . . .166 AY116
Churchfields Av, Felt. TW13 . .116 BZ90
  Weybridge KT13 . . . . . . .153 BP105
Churchfields Rd, Beck. BR3 . .143 DX96
  Watford WD24 . . . . .23 BT36
Church Gdns, W5 . . . . .97 CK75
  Wembley HA0 . . . . .61 CG63
Church Gate, SW6 . . . . .99 CY83
Church Grn, Hayes UB3 . . . . .77 BT77
  Walton-on-Thames KT12 . .154 BW107
Church Gro, SE13 . . . . .103 EB84
  Kingston upon Thames
  KT1 . . . . .137 CJ95
  Slough (Wexham) SL3 . . . .74 AW71
Church Hill, E17 . . . . .67 EA56
  N21 . . . . .45 DM45
  SE18 . . . . .105 EM76
  SW19 . . . . .119 CZ92
  Abbots Langley (Bedmond)
  WD5 . . . . .7 BT26
  Carshalton SM5 . . . . . . .158 DF106
  Caterham CR3 . . . . .176 DT124
  Dartford DA2 . . . . .128 FK90
  Dartford (Cray.) DA2 . . . .107 FE84
  Epping CM16 . . . . .18 EU29
  Greenhithe DA9 . . . . . . .129 FS85
  Harrow HA1 . . . . .61 CE60
  Loughton IG10 . . . . .32 EL41
  Orpington BR6 . . . . .146 EU101
  Purley CR8 . . . . .159 DL110
  Redhill (Merst.) RH1 . . . .185 DH126
  Redhill (Nutfld.) RH1 . . . .185 DM133
  Sevenoaks (Plaxtol) TN15 .179 EQ115
  Uxbridge (Hare.) UB9 . . . .58 BJ55
  Westerham (Tats.) TN16 . .178 EK122
  Woking (Horsell) GU21 . . .166 AX116
  Woking (Pyrford) GU22 . . .167 BF117
Church Hill Rd, E17 . . . . . . .67 EB56
  Barnet EN4 . . . . .44 DF45
  Surbiton KT6 . . . . .138 CL99
  Sutton SM3 . . . . .157 CX105
Church Hill Wd, Orp. BR5 . . .145 ET99
Church Hollow, Purf. RM19 . .108 FN78
Church Hyde, SE18
  off Old Mill Rd 105 ES79
Churchill Av, Har. HA3 . . . . . .61 CH58
  Uxbridge UB10 . . . . .77 BP69
Churchill Cl, Dart. DA1 . . . . .128 FP88
  Feltham TW14 . . . . .115 BT88
  Leatherhead (Fetch.) KT22 .171 CE123
  Uxbridge UB10 . . . . .77 BP69
  Warlingham CR6 . . . . . . .176 DW117
Churchill Ct, W5 . . . . .80 CM70
  Northolt UB5 . . . . .64 CA64
  Staines TW18
  off Chestnut Gro 114 BJ93
Churchill Dr, Wey. KT13 . . . .135 BQ104
Churchill Gdns, SW1 . . . . . .101 DJ78
  W3 . . . . .80 CN72
Churchill Gdns Rd, SW1 . . . .101 DH78
Churchill Ms, Wdf.Grn. IG8
  off High Rd Woodford Grn . .48 EF51
Churchill Pl, E14 . . . . .204 C2
  Harrow HA1
  off Sandridge Cl 61 CE56
Churchill Rd, E16 . . . . .86 EJ72
  NW2 . . . . .81 CV65
  NW5 . . . . .65 DH63
  Dartford (Hort.Kir.) DA4 . .148 FQ98
  Edgware HA8 . . . . .42 CM51
  Epsom KT19 . . . . .156 CN111
  Gravesend DA11 . . . . . . .131 GF88
  Grays RM17 . . . . .110 GD79
  Slough SL3 . . . . .93 AZ77
  South Croydon CR2 . . . . .160 DQ109
Churchill Ter, E4 . . . . .47 EA49
Churchill Wk, E9 . . . . .66 DW64
Churchill Way, Brom. BR1
  off Ethelbert Rd 144 EG97
  Sunbury-on-Thames TW16 .115 BU92
  Westerham (Bigg.H.) TN16 .162 EK113
Church Island, Stai. TW18 . . .113 BD91
  E17 . . . . .67 EB56
Church La, E11 . . . . .68 EE60
  N2 . . . . .64 DD55
  N8 . . . . .65 DM56
  N9 . . . . .46 DU47
  N17 . . . . .46 DS53
  NW9 . . . . .62 CQ61
  SW17 . . . . .121 DH91
  SW19 . . . . .139 CZ95
  W5 . . . . .97 CJ75
  Banstead (Nork) SM7 . . . .173 CX117
  Brentwood (Gt.Warley)
  CM13 . . . . .73 FW58
  Brentwood (Hutton) CM13 . .55 GE46
  Bromley BR2 . . . . .144 EL102

Church La, Caterham CR3 . . .175 DN123
  Chessington KT9 . . . . . . .156 CM107
  Chislehurst BR7 . . . . . . .145 EQ95
  Coulsdon CR5 . . . . .174 DG122
  Dagenham RM10 . . . . . . .89 FB65
  Enfield EN1 . . . . .30 DR41
  Epping (N.Wld.Bas.) CM16 .19 FB27
  Epsom (Headley) KT18 . . .172 CQ124
  Gerrards Cross (Chal.St.P.)
  SL9 . . . . .36 AX53
  Godstone RH9 . . . . .187 DX132
  Harrow HA3 . . . . .41 CF53
  Hemel Hempstead (Bov.)
  HP3 . . . . .5 BB27
  Kings Langley WD4 . . . . . .6 BN29
  Loughton IG10 . . . . .33 EM41
  Oxted RH8 . . . . .188 EE129
  Pinner HA5 . . . . .60 BY55
  Potters Bar (Northaw) EN6 .12 DG30
  Purfleet RM19
  off London Rd Purfleet . . .108 FN78
  Rainham (Wenn.) RM13 . . .90 FK72
  Redhill (Bletch.) RH1 . . . .186 DR133
  Richmond TW10 . . . . . . .118 CL88
  Rickmansworth (Mill End)
  WD3 . . . . .38 BG46
  Rickmansworth (Sarratt)
  WD3 . . . . .21 BF38
  Romford RM1 . . . . .71 FE57
  Romford (Abridge) RM4 . . .34 EY40
  Romford (Noak Hill) RM4 . .52 FK46
  Slough (Stoke P.) SL2 . . . .74 AT69
  Slough (Wexham) SL3 . . . .74 AW71
  Teddington TW11 . . . . . . .117 CF92
  Thames Ditton KT7 . . . . .137 CF100
  Twickenham TW1 . . . . . . .117 CG88
  Upminster (N.Ock.) RM14 . .73 FV64
  Uxbridge UB8 . . . . .76 BH68
  Wallington SM6 . . . . .141 DK104
  Waltham Cross (Chsht.) EN8 .14 DV29
  Warlingham CR6 . . . . . . .177 DX117
  Warlingham (Chel.) CR6 . . .177 DZ118
  Watford (Ald.) WD25 . . . . .24 CB38
  Westerham TN16 . . . . . . .178 EK122
  Weybridge KT13 . . . . . . .152 BN105
Church La Av, Couls. CR5 . . .175 DH122
Church La Dr, Couls. CR5 . . .175 DH122
Churchley Rd, SE26 . . . . . . .122 DV91
Church Manor Est, SW9
  off Vassall Rd 101 DN80
Church Manorway, SE2 . . . .105 ET77
  Erith DA8 . . . . .107 FD76
Church Manorway Ind Est, Erith
  DA8 . . . . .107 FC76
Churchmead, Barn. EN4 . . . .28 DF44
Church Meadow, Surb. KT6 . .137 CJ103
Churchmead Rd, NW10 . . . . .81 CU65
Church Ms, Add. KT15 . . . . .152 BJ105
Churchmore Rd, SW16 . . . . .141 DJ95
Church Mt, N2 . . . . .64 DD57
Church Paddock Ct, Wall.
  SM6 . . . . .141 DK104
Church Pas, EC2
  off Gresham St 197 J8
  Barnet EN5 off Wood St . . .27 CZ42
  Surbiton KT6 . . . . .138 CL99
Church Path, E11 . . . . .68 EG57
  E17 off St. Mary Rd 67 EB56
  N12 . . . . .44 DC50
  N17 off White Hart La 46 DS52
  N20 . . . . .44 DC49
  NW10 . . . . .80 CS66
  SW14 . . . . .98 CR83
  SW19 . . . . .140 DA96
  W4 . . . . .98 CQ76
  W7 . . . . .79 CE74
  Cobham KT11 . . . . .153 BV114
  Coulsdon CR5 . . . . .175 DN118
  Gravesend (Nthflt) DA11 . .130 GC86
  Grays RM17 . . . . .110 GA79
  Greenhithe DA9 . . . . . . .129 FT85
  Mitcham CR4 . . . . .140 DE97
  Southall UB1 . . . . .78 CA74
  Southall (Sthl.Grn.) UB2 . . .96 BZ76
  Woking GU21 off High St . .167 AZ117
Church Pl, SW1 . . . . .199 L1
  W5 off Church Gdns 97 CK75
  Mitcham CR4 . . . . .140 DE97
  Twickenham TW1
  off Church St 117 CH88
  Uxbridge (Ickhm.) UB10 . . .59 BQ62
Church Ri, SE23 . . . . .123 DX88
  Chessington KT9 . . . . . . .156 CM107
Church Rd, E10 . . . . .67 EB61
  E12 . . . . .68 EL64
  E17 . . . . .47 DY54
  N6 . . . . .64 DG59
  N17 . . . . .46 DS53
  NW4 . . . . .63 CV56
  NW10 . . . . .80 CS65
  SE19 . . . . .142 DS95
  SW13 . . . . .99 CT82
  SW19 (Wimbledon) 119 CY91
  W3 . . . . .98 CQ75
  W7 . . . . .79 CF74
  Addlestone KT15 . . . . . . .152 BG106
  Ashford TW15 . . . . .114 BM90
  Ashtead KT21 . . . . .171 CK117
  Barking IG11 . . . . .87 EQ65
  Bexleyheath DA7 . . . . . . .106 EZ82
  Bromley BR2 . . . . .144 EG96
  Bromley (Short.) BR2 . . . .144 EE97
  Buckhurst Hill IG9 . . . . . . .48 EH46
  Caterham CR3 . . . . .176 DT123
  Caterham (Wold.) CR3 . . .177 DX122
  Croydon CR0 . . . . .141 DP104
  Dartford (Sutt.H.) DA4 . . .128 FL94
  East Molesey KT8 . . . . . .137 CD98
  Egham TW20 . . . . .113 BA92
  Enfield EN3 . . . . .30 DW44
  Epsom KT17 . . . . .156 CS112
  Epsom (W.Ewell) KT19 . . .156 CR108
  Erith DA8 . . . . .107 FD78
  Esher (Clay.) KT10 . . . . .155 CF107
  Feltham TW13 . . . . .116 BX92
  Gravesend (Cobham)
  DA12, DA13 . . . . .131 GJ94

Church Rd, Green. DA9 . . . .129 FS85
  Hayes UB3 . . . . .77 BT72
  Hounslow (Cran.) TW5 . . . .95 BV78
  Hounslow (Heston) TW5 . . .96 CA80
  Ilford IG2 . . . . .69 ER58
  Isleworth TW7 . . . . .97 CD81
  Iver SL0 . . . . .75 BC69
  Kenley CR8 . . . . .176 DR115
  Keston BR2 . . . . .162 EK108
  Kingston upon Thames
  KT1 . . . . .138 CM96
  Leatherhead KT22 . . . . . .171 CH122
  Leatherhead (Bkhm.)
  KT23 . . . . .170 BZ124
  Loughton (High Beach)
  IG10 . . . . .32 EH40
  Mitcham CR4 . . . . .140 DD96
  Northolt UB5 . . . . .78 BZ66
  Northwood HA6 . . . . .39 BT52
  Orpington (Chels.) BR6 . . .164 EY106
  Orpington (Farnboro.)
  BR6 . . . . .163 EQ106
  Potters Bar EN6 . . . . .12 DB30
  Purley CR8 . . . . .159 DL110
  Richmond TW9, TW10 . . .118 CL85
  Richmond (Ham) TW10 . . .117 CK90
  Romford (Harold Wd.) RM3 .52 FN53
  Romford (Noak Hill) RM4 . .52 FK46
  Sevenoaks (Halst.) TN14 . .164 EY111
  Sevenoaks (Seal) TN15 . . .191 FM121
  Shepperton TW17 . . . . . .135 BP101
  Sidcup DA14 . . . . .126 EU91
  Southall UB2 . . . . .96 BZ76
  Stanmore HA7 . . . . .41 CH50
  Surbiton KT6 . . . . .137 CJ103
  Sutton SM3 . . . . .157 CY107
  Swanley BR8 . . . . .147 FK95
  Swanley (Crock.) BR8 . . .147 FD101
  Swanscombe DA10 . . . . .130 FZ86
  Teddington TW11 . . . . . . .117 CE91
  Tilbury RM18 . . . . .111 GF81
  Tilbury (W.Til.) RM18 . . . .111 GL79
  Uxbridge (Cowley) UB8 . . .76 BK70
  Uxbridge (Hare.) UB9 . . . .58 BJ55
  Wallington SM6 . . . . .141 DJ104
  Warlingham CR6 . . . . . . .176 DW117
  Watford WD17 . . . . .23 BU39
  Welling DA16 . . . . .106 EV82
  West Byfleet (Byfleet)
  KT14 . . . . .152 BM113
  West Drayton UB7 . . . . . . .94 BK76
  Westerham (Bigg.H.) TN16 .178 EK117
  Westerham (Brasted)
  TN16 . . . . .180 EV124
  Whyteleafe CR3 . . . . . . .176 DT118
  Windsor (Old Wind.) SL4 . .112 AV85
  Woking (Horsell) GU21 . . .166 AY116
  Woking (St. John's) GU21 .166 AU119
  Worcester Park KT4 . . . . .138 CS102
Church Rd Merton, SW19 . . .140 DD95
Church Rd Ind Twr Block, Stan. HA7
  off Church Rd 41 CJ50
Church Row, NW3 . . . . .64 DC63
  Chislehurst BR7 . . . . . . .125 EQ94
Church Side, Epsom KT18 . . .156 CP113
Churchside Cl, West. (Bigg.H.)
  TN16 . . . . .178 EJ117
Church Sq, Shep. TW17 . . . .135 BP101
⊖ Church Street 141 DP103
Church St, E15 . . . . .86 EE67
  E16 . . . . .88 EP74
  N9 . . . . .46 DS47
  NW8 . . . . .194 A6
  W2 . . . . .194 A6
  W4 . . . . .98 CS79
  Cobham KT11 . . . . .169 BV115
  Croydon CR0 . . . . .142 DQ103
  Dagenham RM10 . . . . . . .89 FB65
  Enfield EN2 . . . . .30 DR41
  Epsom KT17 . . . . .156 CS113
  Epsom (Ewell) KT17 . . . .157 CU109
  Esher KT10 . . . . .154 CB105
  Gravesend DA11 . . . . . . .131 GH86
  Gravesend (Sthflt.) DA13 . .130 GA92
  Grays RM17 . . . . .110 GC79
  Hampton TW12 . . . . .136 CC95
  Hemel Hempstead (Bov.)
  HP3 . . . . .5 BB27
  Isleworth TW7 . . . . .97 CH83
  Kingston upon Thames
  KT1 . . . . .137 CK96
  Leatherhead KT22 . . . . . .171 CH122
  Reigate RH2 . . . . .184 DA134
  Rickmansworth WD3 . . . . .38 BL46
  Sevenoaks (Seal) TN15 . . .191 FN121
  Sevenoaks (Shore.) TN14 .165 FF111
  Slough SL1 . . . . .92 AT76
  Staines TW18 . . . . .113 BE91
  Sunbury-on-Thames
  TW16 . . . . .135 BV97
  Sutton SM1 off High St . . .158 DB106
  Twickenham TW1 . . . . . . .117 CG88
  Waltham Abbey EN9 . . . . .15 EC33
  Walton-on-Thames KT12 . .135 BU102
  Watford WD18 . . . . .24 BW42
  Weybridge KT13 . . . . . . .152 BN105
  Woking (Old Wok.) GU22 . .167 BC121
Church St E, Wok. GU21 . . . .167 AZ117
Church St Est, NW8 . . . . . . .194 A5
Church St N, E15 . . . . .86 EE67
Church St Pas, E15
  off Church St 86 EE67
Church St W, Wok. GU21 . . .167 AY117
Church Stretton Rd, Houns.
  TW3 . . . . .116 CC85
Church Ter, NW4 . . . . .63 CV55
  SE13 . . . . .104 EE83
  SW8 . . . . .101 DK82
  Richmond TW10 . . . . . . .117 CJ89
CHURCH TOWN, Gdse. 187 DX131
Church Trd Est, The, Erith
  DA8 . . . . .107 FG80
Church Vale, N2 . . . . .64 DF55
  SE23 . . . . .122 DW89

A B C D E F G H I J K L M N O P Q R S T U V W X Y Z

Chu - Cle

Church Vw, S.Ock. (Aveley)
  RM15 ....108 FQ75
Swanley BR8 off Lime Rd .147 FD97
Upminster RM14 .....72 FN61
Churchview Rd, Twick. TW2 .117 CD88
Church Vil, Sev. TN13
  off Church Fld 190 FE122
Church Wk, N6 off Swains La .64 DG62
  N16 ....66 DR63
  NW2 ....63 CZ62
  NW4 ....63 CW55
  NW9 ....62 CR61
  SW13 ....99 CU81
  SW15 ....119 CV85
  SW16 ....141 DJ96
  SW20 ....139 CW97
  Brentford TW8 ....97 CJ79
  Bushey WD23 off High St .24 CA44
  Caterham CR3 ....176 DU124
  Chertsey KT16 ......134 BG101
  Dartford DA2 ....128 FK90
  Dartford (Eyns.) DA4 .....148 FL104
  Enfield EN2 off Church La ...30 DR41
  Gravesend DA12 .....131 GK88
  Hayes UB3 ....77 BD73
  Leatherhead KT22
    off The Crescent 171 CH122
  Redhill (Bletch.) RH1 ...186 DR133
  Reigate RH2
    off Reigate Rd 184 DC134
  Richmond TW9 59
    off Red Lion St 117 CK85
  Thames Ditton KT7 ...137 CF100
  Walton-on-Thames KT12 ...135 BU102
  Weybridge KT13
    off Beales La 135 BP103
Church Wk Shop Cen, Cat. CR3
  off Church Wk 176 DU124
Churchway, N20 ....44 DD48
Churchway, NW1 ......195 N2
Church Way, Barn. EN4 ...28 DF42
  Edgware HA8 ....42 CN51
  Oxted RH8 ....188 EF132
  South Croydon CR2 ...160 DT110
Churchwell Path, E9 ....66 DW64
Churchyard Path, Wdf.Grn.
  IG8 ....48 EJ48
Churchyard Row, SE11 ...200 G8
Church Yd Wk, W2
  off St. Marys Sq 82 DD71
Churston Av, E13 ......86 EH67
Churston Cl, SW2
  off Tulse Hill 121 DP88
Churston Dr, Mord. SM4 .139 CX99
Churston Gdns, N11 ....45 DJ51
Churton Pl, SW1 ......199 L9
Churton St, SW1 ......199 L9
Chusan Pl, E14
  off Commercial Rd 85 DZ72
Chuters Cl, W.Byf. (Byfleet)
  KT14 ....152 BL112
Chuters Gro, Epsom KT17 ...157 CT112
Chyne, The, Ger.Cr. SL9 ...57 AZ57
Chyngton Cl, Sid. DA15 ...125 ET90
Cibber Rd, SE23 ......123 DX89
Cicada Rd, SW18 ......120 DC85
Cicely Rd, SE15 ......102 DU81
Cimba Wd, Grav. DA12 ...131 GL91
Cinderella Path, NW11
  off North End Rd 64 DB60
Cinderford Way, Brom. BR1 .124 EE91
Cinder Path, Wok. GU22 ...166 AW119
Cinema Par, W5
  off Ashbourne Rd 80 CM70
Cinnabar Wf, E1 ......202 C3
Cinnamon Cl, Croy. CR0 ...141 DL101
Cinnamon Row, SW11 ...100 DC83
Cinnamon St, E1 ......202 E3
Cintra Pk, SE19 ......122 DT94
Circle, The, NW2 ......62 CS62
  NW7 ....42 CR50
  SE1 ....201 P4
  Tilbury RM18
    off Toronto Rd 111 GG81
Circle Gdns, SW19 ....140 DA96
  West Byfleet (Byfleet) KT14
    off High Rd 152 BM112
Circle Rd, Walt. KT12 ...153 BS110
Circuits, The, Pnr. HA5 ...60 BW56
Circular Rd, N17 ......46 DT55
Circular Way, SE18 ....105 EM79
Circus Ms, W1 ....194 D6
Circus Pl, EC2 ....197 L7
Circus Rd, NW8 ....82 DD69
Circus St, SE10 ......103 EC80
Cirencester St, W2 ....82 DB71
Cirrus Cres, Grav. DA12 ...131 GL92
Cissbury Ring N, N12 ...43 CZ50
Cissbury Ring S, N12 ...43 CZ50
Cissbury Rd, N15 ......66 DR57
Citadel Pl, SE11 ......200 B10
Citizen Ho, N7
  off Harvist Est 65 DN63
Citizen Rd, N7 ....65 DN63
C.I. Twr, N.Mal. KT3 ...138 CS97
Citron Ter, SE15
  off Nunhead La 102 DV83
City Forum, EC1 ......197 H2
City Gdn Row, N1 ......196 G1
City Gate Ho, Ilf. IG2 ...69 EP58
City Ho, Croy. CR0 ....PD101
★ City of Westminster Archives Cen,
  SW1 off St. Ann's St 197 N6
City Pt, EC2 ....197 K7
City Rd, EC1 ....196 F1
⇌ City Thameslink 196 F9
★ City Uni, EC1 ......196 F3
Civic Sq, Til. RM18 ....111 GG82
Civic Way, Ilf. IG6 .....69 EQ56
  Ruislip HA4 ....60 BX64
Clabon Ms, SW1 ......198 D7
Clacket La, West. TN16 ...178 EL124
Clack St, SE16 ....202 G5

Clacton Rd, E6 ....86 EK69
  E17 ....67 DY58
  N17 off Sperling Rd 46 DT54
Claigmar Gdns, N3 .....44 DB53
Claire Ct, N12 ....44 DC48
  Bushey (Bushey Hth.)
    WD23 ....41 CD46
  Pinner HA5 off Westfield Pk .40 BZ52
Claire Gdns, Stan. HA7 ...41 CJ50
Claire Pl, E14 ....204 A6
Clairvale, Horn. RM11 ...72 FL59
Clairvale Rd, Houns. TW5 ...96 BX81
Clairview Rd, SW16 ...121 DH92
Clairville Ct, Reig. RH2 ...184 DD134
Clairville Gdns, W7 ....79 CF74
Clairville Pt, SE23 ....123 DX90
Clammas Way, Uxb. UB8 ...76 BJ71
Clamp Hill, Stan. HA7 ...41 CD49
Clancarty Rd, SW6 ....100 DA82
Clandon Av, Egh. TW20 ...113 BC94
Clandon Cl, W3
  off Avenue Rd 98 CP75
  Epsom KT17 ....157 CT107
Clandon Gdns, N3 ....64 DA55
Clandon Rd, Ilf. IG3 ....69 ES61
Clandon St, SE8 ......103 EA82
Clanfield Way, SE15
  off Diamond St 102 DS80
Clanricarde Gdns, W2 ...82 DA73
CLAPHAM, SW4 ....101 DH83
  ★ Clapham Common, SW4 .100 DG84
  ⊖ Clapham Common 101 DJ84
Clapham Common N Side,
  SW4 ....101 DH84
Clapham Common S Side,
  SW4 ....101 DH85
Clapham Common W Side,
  SW4 ....100 DG84
Clapham Cres, SW4 ...101 DK84
Clapham High St, SW4 .100 DE84
  ⇌ Clapham High Street ...101 DK83
  Clapham High St, SW4 .101 DK84
  ⊖ Clapham Junction 100 DD84
Clapham Manor St, SW4 .101 DJ83
  ⊖ Clapham North 101 DL83
CLAPHAM PARK, SW4 ...121 DK86
Clapham Pk Est, SW4 ...121 DK86
Clapham Pk Rd, SW4 ...101 DK84
Clapham Rd, SW9 .....101 DL83
Clapham Rd Est, SW4 ...101 DK83
  ⊖ Clapham South 121 DH86
Clap La, Dag. RM10 ....71 FB62
Claps Gate La, E6 .....87 EP70
  ⇌ Clapton 66 DV61
Clapton Common, E5 ...66 DT59
CLAPTON PARK, E5 ....67 DY63
Clapton Pk Est, E5
  off Blackwell Cl 67 DY63
Clapton Pas, E5 ......66 DW64
Clapton Sq, E5 ....66 DW64
Clapton Ter, N16
  off Oldhill St 66 DU60
Clapton Way, E5 ......66 DU63
Clare Cl, N2
  off Thomas More Way ...64 DC55
  Borehamwood (Elstree)
    WD6 ....26 CM44
  West Byfleet KT14 ...152 BG113
Clare Cor, SE9 ....125 EP87
Clare Cotts, Red. (Bletch.)
  RH1 ....185 DP133
Clare Ct, Cat. (Wold.) CR3 ...177 EA123
  Northwood HA6 ....39 BS50
Clare Cres, Lthd. KT22 ...171 CG118
Claredale, Wok. GU22
  off Claremont Av 166 AY119
Claredale St, E2 ......84 DU68
Clare Gdns, E7 ....68 EG63
  W11 off Westbourne Pk Rd .81 CY72
  Barking IG11 ....87 ET65
  Egham TW20
    off Mowbray Cres 113 BA92
Clare Hill, Esher KT10 ...154 CB107
Clare Ho, E3 ....85 DZ67
Clare La, N1 ....84 DQ66
Clare Lawn Av, SW14 ...118 CR85
Clare Mkt, WC2 ....196 B9
Clare Ms, SW6
  off Waterford Rd 100 DB80
Claremont, St.Alb. (Brick.Wd.)
  AL2 ....8 CA31
  Waltham Cross (Chsht.)
    EN7 ....14 DT29
Claremont Av, Esher KT10 ...154 BZ107
  Harrow HA3 ....62 CL57
  New Malden KT3 ......139 CU99
  Sunbury-on-Thames
    TW16 ....135 BV95
  Walton-on-Thames KT12 ...154 BX105
  Woking GU22 ....166 AY119
Claremont Cl, E16 .....87 EN74
  N1 ....196 E1
  SW2 off Streatham Hill ...121 DL88
  Grays RM16
    off Premier Av 110 GC76
  Orpington BR6 ......163 EN105
  South Croydon CR2 ...176 DV115
  Walton-on-Thames KT12 ...154 BW106
Claremont Ct, Surb. KT6
  off St. James Rd 137 CK100
Claremont Cres, Dart. DA1 ...107 FE84
  Rickmansworth (Crox.Grn.)
    WD3 ....23 BQ43
Claremont Dr, Esher KT10 ...154 CB108
  Shepperton TW17 ...135 BP100
  Woking GU22 ....166 AY119
Claremont End, Esher KT10 ...154 CB107
Claremont Gdns, Ilf. IG3 ...69 ES61
  Surbiton KT6 ....138 CL99
  Upminster RM14 ....73 FR60
Claremont Gro, W4
  off Edensor Gdns 98 CS80
  Woodford Green IG8 ...48 EJ51
★ Claremont Landscape Gdns,
  Esher KT10 ....154 BZ108

Claremont La, Esher KT10 ...154 CB105
CLAREMONT PARK, Esher ...154 CB108
Claremont Pk, N3 .....43 CY53
Claremont Pk Rd, Esher
  KT10 ....154 CB107
Claremont Pl, Grav. DA11
  off Cutmore St 131 GH87
Claremont Rd, E7 .....68 EH64
  E17 ....47 DY54
  N6 ....65 DJ59
  NW2 ....63 CX62
  W9 ....81 CY68
  W13 ....79 CG71
  Barnet EN4 ....28 DD37
  Bromley BR1 ....144 EL98
  Croydon CR0 ....142 DU102
  Esher (Clay.) KT10 ...155 CE108
  Harrow HA3 ....41 CE54
  Hornchurch RM11 ...71 FG58
  Redhill RH1 ....184 DG131
  Staines TW18 ....113 BD92
  Surbiton KT6 ....138 CL100
  Swanley BR8 ....127 FE94
  Teddington TW11 ...117 CF92
  Twickenham TW1 ...117 CJ86
  West Byfleet KT14 ...152 BG112
Claremont Sq, N1 .....196 D1
Claremont St, E16 ....87 EN74
  N18 ....46 DU51
  SE10 ....103 EB79
Claremont Way, NW2 ...63 CW60
Claremount Cl, Epsom KT18 .173 CW117
Claremount Gdns, Epsom
  KT18 ....173 CW117
Clarence Av, SW4 .....121 DK86
  Bromley BR1 ....144 EL98
  Ilford IG2 ....69 EN58
  New Malden KT3 ......138 CQ96
  Upminster RM14 ....72 FN61
Clarence Cl, Barn. EN4 ...28 DD43
  Bushey (Bushey Hth.)
    WD23 ....41 CF45
  Walton-on-Thames KT12 ...154 BW105
Clarence Ct, Egh. TW20
  off Clarence St 113 AZ93
Clarence Cres, SW4 ...121 DK86
  Sidcup DA14 ....126 EV90
Clarence Dr, Egh. (Eng.Grn.)
  TW20 ....112 AW91
Clarence Gdns, NW1 ...195 J3
Clarence Gate, Wdf.Grn. IG8 .49 EN51
Clarence Gate Gdns, NW1
  off Glentworth St 82 DF70
  ★ Clarence Ho, SW1 .....199 L4
Clarence La, SW15 ....118 CS86
Clarence Ms, E5 ......66 DV64
  SE16 ....203 H3
  SW12 ....121 DH87
Clarence Pas, NW1 ....195 P1
Clarence Pl, E5 ....66 DV64
Clarence Rd, E5 ......66 DV63
  E12 ....68 EK64
  E16 ....86 EE70
  E17 ....47 DX54
  N15 ....66 DQ57
  N22 ....45 DL52
  NW6 ....81 CZ66
  SE9 ....124 EL89
  SW19 ....120 DB93
  W4 ....98 CN78
  Bexleyheath DA6 ...106 EY84
  Brentwood CM15 ...54 FV44
  Bromley BR1 ....144 EK97
  Croydon CR0 ....142 DR101
  Enfield EN3 ....30 DV43
  Grays RM17 ....110 GA79
  Richmond TW9 ......98 CM81
  Sidcup DA14 ....126 EV90
  Sutton SM1 ....158 DB105
  Teddington TW11 ...117 CF93
  Wallington SM6 ...159 DH106
  Walton-on-Thames KT12 ...153 BV105
  Westerham (Bigg.H.) TN16 ...179 EM118
Clarence Row, Grav. DA12 ...131 GH87
Clarence St, Egh. TW20 ...113 AZ93
  Kingston upon Thames
    KT1 ....138 CL96
  Richmond TW9 ......98 CL84
  Southall UB2 ....96 BX76
  Staines TW18 ....113 BE91
Clarence Ter, NW1 ....194 E4
  Hounslow TW3 ......96 CB84
Clarence Wk, SW4 ....101 DL82
Clarence Way, NW1 ...83 DH66
Clarence Way Est, NW1 .83 DH66
Clarendon Cl, E9 .....84 DW66
  W2 ....194 B10
  Orpington BR5 ....146 EU97
Clarendon Ct, Slou. SL2 ...74 AV73
Clarendon Cres, Twick. TW2 ...117 CD90
Clarendon Cross, W11
  off Portland Rd 81 CY73
Clarendon Dr, SW15 ...99 CW84
Clarendon Gdns, NW4 ...63 CV55
  W9 ....82 DC70
  Dartford DA2 ....129 FR87
  Ilford IG1 ....69 EM60
  Wembley HA9 ....62 CL63
Clarendon Gate, Cher. (Ott.)
  KT16 ....151 BD107
Clarendon Grn, Orp. BR5 ...146 EU98
Clarendon Gro, NW1 ...195 M2
  Mitcham CR4 ....140 DF97
  Orpington BR5 ......146 EU97
Clarendon Ms, W2 ....194 B9
  Ashtead KT21 ......172 CL119
  Bexley DA5 ....127 FB88
  Borehamwood WD6
    off Clarendon Rd 26 CN41
Clarendon Path, Orp. BR5 ...146 EU97
Clarendon Pl, W2 .....194 B10
Clarendon Ri, SE13 ...103 EC83
Clarendon Rd, E11 ....67 ED60

Clarendon Rd, E17 ....67 EB58
  E18 ....68 EG55
  N8 ....65 DM55
  N15 ....65 DP56
  N18 ....46 DU51
  N22 ....45 DM54
  SW19 ....120 DE94
  W5 ....80 CL70
  W11 ....81 CY73
  Ashford TW15 ......114 BM91
  Borehamwood WD6 ...26 CN41
  Croydon CR0 ....141 DP100
  Gravesend DA12 ...131 GJ86
  Harrow HA1 ....61 CE58
  Hayes UB3 ....95 BT75
  Redhill RH1 ....184 DF133
  Sevenoaks TN13 ...190 FG121
  Wallington SM6 ...159 DJ107
  Waltham Cross (Chsht.)
    EN8 ....15 DX29
  Watford WD17 ......23 BV40
Clarendon St, SW1 ....101 DH78
Clarendon Ter, W9
  off Lanark Pl 82 DC70
Clarendon Way, N21 ...30 DQ44
  Chislehurst BR7 ...145 ET97
  Orpington BR5 ......145 ET97
Clarens St, SE6 ......123 DZ89
Clare Pk, Amer. HP7 ...20 AS40
Clare Pl, SW15
  off Minstead Gdns 119 CT87
Clare Pt, NW2
  off Claremont Rd 63 CX60
Clare Rd, E11 ....68 ED58
  NW10 ....81 CU66
  SE14 ....103 DZ81
  Greenford UB6 ....79 CD65
  Hounslow TW4 ......96 BZ83
  Staines (Stanw.) TW19 ...114 BL87
Clare St, E2 ....84 DV68
Claret Gdns, SE25 ....142 DS98
Clareville Gro, SW7 ...100 DC77
Clareville Rd, Cat. CR3 ...176 DU124
  Orpington BR5 ......145 EQ103
Clareville St, SW7 ....100 DC77
Clarewood Wk, SW9 ...101 DN84
Clarges Ms, W1 ......199 H2
Clarges St, W1 ....199 J2
Claribel Rd, SW9 .....101 DP82
Clarice Way, Wall. SM6 ...159 DL109
Claridge Rd, Dag. RM8 ...70 EX60
Clarina Rd, SE20
  off Evelina Rd 123 DX94
Clarissa Rd, Rom. RM6 ...70 EX59
Clarissa St, E8 ....84 DT67
Clark Cl, Erith DA8
  off Forest Rd 107 FG81
Clarkebourne Dr, Grays
  RM17 ....110 GD79
Clarke Grn, Wat. WD25 ...23 BU35
Clarke Ms, N9
  off Plevna Rd 46 DV48
Clarke Path, N16 .....66 DU60
Clarkes Av, Wor.Pk. KT4 ...139 CX102
Clarkes Dr, Uxb. UB8 ...76 BL70
Clarke's Ms, W1 ......194 G6
Clarke Way, Wat. WD25 ...23 BU35
Clarkfield, Rick. (Mill End)
  WD3 ....38 BH46
Clark Lawrence Ct, SW11
  off Winstanley Rd 100 DD83
Clarks La, Epp. CM16 ...17 ET31
  Sevenoaks (Halst.) TN14 ...164 EZ112
  Warlingham CR6 ...178 EF123
  Westerham TN16 ...178 EK123
Clarks Mead, Bushey WD23 ...40 CC45
Clarkson Rd, E16 .....86 EF72
Clarkson Row, NW1 ...195 J1
Clarksons, The, Bark. IG11 ...87 EQ68
Clarkson St, E2 ......84 DV69
Clarks Pl, EC2 ....197 M8
Clark Rd, E1 ....84 DV71
Clark Way, Houns. TW5 ...96 BX80
Classon Cl, West Dr. UB7 ...94 BL75
Claston Cl, Dart. DA1
  off Iron Mill La 107 FE84
CLATTERFORD END, Ong. ...19 FG30
Claude Rd, E10 ......67 EC61
  E13 ....86 EH67
  SE15 ....102 DV82
Claude St, E14 ....203 P8
Claudia Jones Way, SW2 ...121 DL86
Claudian Way, Grays RM16 .111 GH76
Claudia Pl, SW19 ....119 CY88
Claughton Rd, E13 ...86 EJ68
Claughton Way, Brwd. CM13 ..55 GD44
Clauson Av, Nthlt. UB5 ...60 CB64
Clavell St, SE10 ......103 EC79
Claverdale Rd, SW2 ...121 DM87
Claverhambury Rd, Wal.Abb.
  EN9 ....16 EF29
Clavering Av, SW13 ...99 CV79
Clavering Cl, Twick. TW1 ...117 CG91
Clavering Rd, E12 ....68 EK60
Claverings Ind Est, N9 ...47 DX47
  off Poplar Dr 55 GC44
Claverley Gro, N3 .....44 DA52
Claverley Vil, N3
  off Claverley Gro 44 DB52
Claverton Cl, Hem.H. (Bov.)
  HP3 ....5 BA28
Claverton St, SW1 ...101 DJ78
Clave St, E1 ....202 F3
Claxton Gro, W6 .....99 CX78
Clay Av, Mitch. CR4 ...141 DH96
Claybank Gro, SE13
  off Algernon Rd 103 EB83
Clayborne Ms, SE19
  off Church Rd 122 DS94
Claybridge Rd, SE12 ...124 EJ91

Claybrook Cl, N2 .....64 DD55
Claybrook Rd, W6 ....99 CX79
Clayburn Gdns, S.Ock. RM15 .91 FV73
Claybury, Bushey WD23 ...40 CB45
Claybury Bdy, Ilf. IG5 ...68 EL55
Claybury Rd, Wdf.Grn. IG8 .48 EL52
Claydon Dr, Croy. CR0 ...159 DL105
Claydon End, Ger.Cr. (Chal.St.P.)
  SL9 ....56 AY55
Claydon La, Ger.Cr. (Chal.St.P.)
  SL9 ....56 AY55
Claydown Ms, SE18
  off Woolwich New Rd ...105 EN78
Clayfarm Rd, SE9 ....125 EQ89
CLAYGATE, Esher 155 CE108
  ⇌ Claygate 155 CD107
Claygate Cl, Horn. RM12 ...71 FG63
Claygate Cres, Croy. (New Adgtn.)
  CR0 ....161 EC107
Claygate La, Esher KT10 ...137 CG103
  Thames Ditton KT7 ...137 CG102
  Waltham Abbey EN9 ...15 ED30
Claygate Lo Cl, Esher (Clay.)
  KT10 ....155 CE108
CLAYHALL, Ilf. 49 EM54
Clayhall Av, Ilf. IG5 ...68 EL55
Clayhall La, Wind. (Old Wind.)
  SL4 ....112 AT85
CLAY HILL, Enf. 30 DQ37
Clay Hill, Enf. EN2 ....30 DQ37
Clayhill, Surb. KT5 ...138 CN99
Clayhill Cres, SE9 ....124 EK91
Claylands Pl, SW8 ...101 DN80
Claylands Rd, SW8 ...101 DM79
Clay La, Bushey (Bushey Hth.)
  WD23 ....41 CE45
  Edgware HA8 ....42 CN46
  Epsom (Headley) KT18 ...172 CP124
  Staines (Stanw.) TW19 ...114 BM87
Claymill Ho, SE18 ....105 EQ78
Claymore, Hem.H. (Hem.H.)
Claymore Cl, Mord. SM4 ...140 DA101
Claymore Ct, E17
  off Billet Rd 47 DY53
Claypit Hill, Wal.Abb. EN9 ...32 EJ36
Claypole Dr, Houns. TW5 ...96 BY81
Claypole Rd, E15 .....85 EC68
Clayponds Av, Brent. TW8 ...98 CL77
Clayponds Gdns, W5 ...97 CK77
  ℍ Clayponds Hosp, W5 ...98 CL77
Clayponds La, Brent. TW8 ...98 CL78
Clay Rd, The, Loug. IG10 ...32 EL39
Clayside, Chig. IG7 ...49 EQ51
Clay's La, Loug. IG10 ...33 EN39
Clays La, E15 ....67 EB64
Clays La Cl, E15 ......67 EB64
Clay St, W1 ....194 E7
Clayton Av, Upmin. RM14 ...72 FP64
  Wembley HA0 ....80 CL66
Clayton Cl, E6
  off Brandreth Rd 87 EM72
Clayton Cres, N1 .....83 DL67
  Brentford TW8 ......97 CK78
Clayton Cft Rd, Dart. DA2 ...127 FG89
Clayton Fld, NW9 .....42 CS52
Clayton Mead, Gdse. RH9 ...186 DV130
Clayton Ms, SE10 ....103 ED81
Clayton Rd, SE15 ....102 DU81
  Chessington KT9 ...155 CJ105
  Epsom KT17 ....156 CS113
  Hayes UB3 ....95 BS75
  Isleworth TW7 ......97 CE83
  Romford RM7 ....71 FC60
Clayton St, SE11 .....101 DN79
Clayton Ter, Hayes UB4
  off Jollys La 78 BX71
Clayton Wk, Amer. HP7 ...20 AW39
Clayton Way, Uxb. UB8 ...76 BK70
Clay Tye Rd, Upmin. RM14 ...73 FW63
Claywood Cl, Orp. BR6 ...145 ES101
Claywood La, Dart. (Bean)
  DA2 ....129 FX90
Clayworth Cl, Sid. DA15 ...126 EV86
Cleall Av, Wal.Abb. EN9
  off Quaker La 15 EC34
Cleanthus Cl, SE18 ...105 EP81
Cleanthus Rd, SE18 ...105 EP81
Clearbrook Way, E1
  off West Arbour St 85 DX72
Cleardown, Wok. GU22 ...167 BB118
Clearmount, Wok. (Chobham)
  GU24 ....150 AS107
Clears, The, Reig. RH2 ...183 CY132
Clearwater Ter, W11
  off Lorne Gdns 99 CX75
Clearwell Dr, W9 .....82 DB70
Cleave Av, Hayes UB3 ...95 BS77
  Orpington BR6 ......163 ES107
Cleaveland Rd, Surb. KT6 ...137 CK99
Cleave Prior, Couls. CR5 ...174 DE119
Cleaverholme Cl, SE25 ...142 DV100
Cleaver Sq, SE11 .....200 E10
Cleaver St, SE11 .....200 E10
Cleeve Ct, Felt. TW14
  off Kilross Rd 115 BS88
Cleeve Hill, SE23 ....122 DV88
Cleeve Pk Gdns, Sid. DA14 ...126 EV89
Cleeve Rd, Lthd. KT22 ...171 CF120
Cleeve Way, SW15
  off Danebury Av 119 CT87
Clegg Ho, SE3 off Pinto Way .104 EH84
Clegg St, E1 ....202 E2
  E13 ....86 EG68
Cleland Path, Loug. IG10 ...33 EP39
Cleland Rd, Ger.Cr. (Chal.St.P.)
  SL9 ....36 AX54
Clematis Cl, Rom. RM3 ...52 FJ52
Clematis Gdns, Wdf.Grn. IG8 .48 EG50
Clematis St, W12 .....81 CT73
Clem Attlee Ct, SW6 ...99 CZ79
Clem Attlee Est, SW6
  off Lillie Rd 99 CZ79
Clem Attlee Par, SW6
  off Clem Attlee Ct 99 CZ79

★ Place of interest   ⇌ Railway station   ⊖ London Underground station   DLR Docklands Light Railway station   ⊷ Tramlink station   ℍ Hospital

Clemence Rd, Dag. RM10 . . .89 FC67
Clemence St, E14 . . . . .85 DZ71
Clement Av, SW4 . . . . .101 DK84
Clement Cl, NW6 . . . . .81 CW66
  W4 off Acton La 98 CR77
  Purley CR8
   off Croftleigh Av 175 DP116
Clement Gdns, Hayes UB3 . .95 BS77
Clementhorpe Rd, Dag. RM9 .88 EW65
Clementina Rd, E10 . . . . .67 DZ60
H Clementine Churchill Hosp,
  Har. HA1 . . . . .61 CF62
Clementine Cl, W13
  off Balfour Rd 97 CH75
Clement Rd, SW19 . . . . . . .119 CY92
  Beckenham BR3 . . . . .143 DX96
  Waltham Cross (Chsht.)
   EN8 . . . . .21 DY27
Clements Av, E16 . . . . .86 EG73
Clements Cl, Slou. SL1 . . . . .92 AV75
Clements Ct, Houns. TW4 . . .96 BX84
  Ilford IG1 off Clements La .69 EP62
Clement's Inn, WC2 . . . . . . .196 C9
Clement's Inn Pas, WC2 . . . .196 C9
Clements La, EC4 . . . . .197 L10
  Ilford IG1 . . . . .69 EP62
Clements Mead, Lthd. KT22 .171 CG119
Clements Pl, Brent. TW8 . . . .97 CK78
Clements Rd, E6 . . . . .87 EM66
  SE16 . . . . .202 C7
  Ilford IG1 . . . . .69 EP62
  Rickmansworth (Chorl.)
   WD3 . . . . .21 BD43
  Walton-on-Thames KT12 .135 BV103
Clement St, Swan. BR8 . . . .128 FK93
Clement Way, Upmin. RM14 . .72 FM62
Clenches Fm La, Sev. TN13 .190 FG126
Clenches Fm La, Sev. TN13 .190 FG126
Clendon Way, SE18
  off Polthorne Gro 105 ER77
Clennam St, SE1 . . . . .201 J4
Clensham Ct, Sutt. SM1
  off Sutton Common Rd . .140 DA103
Clensham La, Sutt. SM1 . . . .140 DA103
Clenston Ms, W1 . . . . .194 D8
★ Cleopatra's Needle, WC2 .200 B1
Clephane Rd, N1 . . . . .84 DQ65
Clere St, EC2 . . . . .197 L4
Clerics Wk, Shep. TW17
  off Gordon Rd 135 BR100
CLERKENWELL, EC1 . . . . . .196 F5
Clerkenwell Cl, EC1 . . . . . . .196 E4
Clerkenwell Grn, EC1 . . . . . .196 E5
Clerkenwell Rd, EC1 . . . . . .196 D5
Clerks Cft, Red. (Bletch.) RH1 .186 DR133
Clerks Piece, Loug. IG10 . . . .33 EM41
Clermont Rd, E9 . . . . .84 DW67
Clevedon, Wey. KT13 . . . . . .153 BQ106
Clevedon Cl, N16
  off Smalley Cl 66 DT62
Clevedon Gdns, Hayes UB3 . .95 BR76
  Hounslow TW5 . . . . .95 BV81
Clevedon Rd, SE20 . . . . . . .143 DX95
  Kingston upon Thames
   KT1 . . . . .138 CN96
  Twickenham TW1 . . . . . .117 CK86
Clevehurst Cl, Slou. (Stoke P.)
  SL2 . . . . .74 AT65
Cleveland Av, SW20 . . . . . . .139 CZ96
  W4 . . . . .99 CT77
  Hampton TW12 . . . . .116 BZ94
Cleveland Cl, Walt. KT12 . . .135 BV104
Cleveland Cres, Borwd. WD6 .26 CQ43
Cleveland Dr, Stai. TW18 . . .134 BH96
Cleveland Gdns, N4 . . . . .66 DQ57
  NW2 . . . . .63 CX61
  SW13 . . . . .99 CT82
  W2 . . . . .82 DC72
  Worcester Park KT4 . . . .138 CS103
Cleveland Gro, E1
  off Cleveland Way 84 DW70
Cleveland Ms, W1 . . . . .195 K6
Cleveland Pk, Stai. TW19
  off Northumberland Cl . .114 BL86
Cleveland Pk Av, E17 . . . . . .67 EA56
Cleveland Pk Cres, E17 . . . . .67 EA56
Cleveland Pl, SW1 . . . . .199 L2
Cleveland Ri, Mord. SM4 . . .139 CX101
Cleveland Rd, E18 . . . . .68 EG55
  N1 . . . . .84 DR66
  N9 . . . . .46 DV45
  SW13 . . . . .99 CT82
  W4 off Antrobus Rd 98 CQ76
  W13 . . . . .79 CH71
  Ilford IG1 . . . . .69 EP62
  Isleworth TW7 . . . . .97 CG84
  New Malden KT3 . . . . . .138 CS98
  Uxbridge UB8 . . . . .76 BK68
  Welling DA16 . . . . .105 ET82
  Worcester Park KT4 . . . .138 CS103
Cleveland Row, SW1 . . . . . .199 K3
Cleveland Sq, W2 . . . . .82 DC72
Cleveland St, W1 . . . . .195 K5
Cleveland Ter, W2 . . . . .82 DC72
Cleveland Way, E1 . . . . .84 DW70
Cleveley Cl, SE7 . . . . .104 EK77
Cleveley Cres, W5 . . . . .80 CL68
Cleveleys Rd, E5 . . . . .66 DV62
Cleverly Est, W12 . . . . .81 CU74
Cleve Rd, NW6 . . . . .82 DA66
  Sidcup DA14 . . . . .126 EX90
Cleves Av, Brwd. CM14 . . . . .54 FV46
  Epsom KT17 . . . . .157 CV109
Cleves Cl, Cob. KT11 . . . . . .153 BV114
  Loughton IG10 . . . . .32 EL44
Cleves Cres, Croy. (New Adgtn.)
  CR0 . . . . .161 EC111
Cleves Rd, E6 . . . . .86 EK67
  Richmond TW10 . . . . . . .117 CJ90
Cleves Wk, Ilf. IG6 . . . . .49 EQ52
Cleves Way, Hmptn. TW12 . .116 BZ94
  Ruislip HA4 . . . . .60 BX60
  Sunbury-on-Thames TW16 .115 BT93
Cleves Wd, Wey. KT13 . . . . .153 BS105
Clewer Cres, Har. HA3 . . . . . .41 CD53
Clewer Ho, SE2
  off Wolvercote Rd 106 EX75

Clichy Est, E1 . . . . .84 DW71
Clifden Rd, E5 . . . . .66 DW64
  Brentford TW8 . . . . .97 CK79
  Twickenham TW1 . . . . . .117 CF88
Cliff End, Pur. CR8 . . . . .159 DP112
Cliffe Rd, S.Croy. CR2 . . . . .160 DR106
Cliffe Wk, Sutt. SM1
  off Turnpike La 158 DC106
Clifford Av, SW14 . . . . .98 CP83
  Chislehurst BR7 . . . . . . .125 EM93
  Ilford IG5 . . . . .49 EP53
  Wallington SM6 . . . . .159 DJ105
Clifford Cl, Nthlt. UB5 . . . . . .78 BY67
Clifford Dr, SW9 . . . . .101 DP84
Clifford Gdns, NW10 . . . . . . .81 CW68
  Hayes UB3 . . . . .95 BR77
Clifford Rd, E16 . . . . .86 EF70
  E17 . . . . .47 EC54
  N9 . . . . .30 DW44
  SE25 . . . . .142 DU98
  Barnet EN5 . . . . .28 DB41
  Grays (Chaff.Hun.) RM16 .110 FZ75
  Hounslow TW4 . . . . .96 BX83
  Richmond TW10 . . . . . . .117 CK89
  Wembley HA0 . . . . .79 CK67
Clifford's Inn Pas, EC4 . . . . .196 D9
Clifford St, W1 . . . . .199 K1
Clifford Way, NW10 . . . . .63 CT63
Cliff Pl, S.Ock. RM15 . . . . . . .91 FX69
Cliff Reach, Green. (Bluewater)
  DA9 . . . . .129 FS87
Cliff Rd, NW1 . . . . .83 DK65
Cliff Ter, SE8 . . . . .103 EA82
Cliffview Rd, SE13 . . . . .103 EA83
Cliff Vil, NW1 . . . . .83 DK65
Cliff Wk, E16 . . . . .86 EF71
Clifton Av, E17 . . . . .67 DX55
  N3 . . . . .43 CZ53
  W12 . . . . .81 CT74
  Feltham TW13 . . . . .116 BW90
  Stanmore HA7 . . . . .41 CH54
  Sutton SM2 . . . . .158 DB111
  Wembley HA9 . . . . .80 CM65
Clifton Cl, Add. KT15 . . . . . .134 BH103
  Caterham CR3 . . . . .176 DR123
  Orpington BR6 . . . . .163 EQ106
  Waltham Cross (Chsht.)
   EN8 . . . . .15 DY29
Clifton Ct, N4 off Playford Rd .65 DN61
  NW8 off Edgware Rd 82 DD70
  Woodford Green IG8
   off Snakes La W 48 EG51
Clifton Cres, SE15 . . . . .102 DV80
Clifton Est, SE15
  off Consort Rd 102 DV81
Clifton Gdns, N15 . . . . .66 DT58
  NW11 . . . . .63 CZ58
  W4 off Dolman Rd 98 CR77
  W9 . . . . .82 DC70
  Enfield EN2 . . . . .29 DL42
  Uxbridge UB10 . . . . .77 BP68
Clifton Gro, E8 . . . . .84 DU65
  Gravesend DA11 . . . . . . .131 GH87
Clifton Hill, NW8 . . . . .82 DB68
Clifton Marine Par, Grav.
  DA11 . . . . .131 GF86
Clifton Pk Av, SW20 . . . . . . .139 CW96
Clifton Pl, SE16 . . . . .202 G4
  W2 . . . . .194 A10
  Banstead SM7
   off Court Rd 174 DA116
Clifton Ri, SE14 . . . . .103 DY80
Clifton Rd, E7 . . . . .86 EK65
  E16 . . . . .86 EE71
  N3 . . . . .44 DC53
  N8 . . . . .65 DK58
  N22 . . . . .45 DJ53
  NW10 . . . . .81 CU68
  SE25 . . . . .142 DS98
  SW19 . . . . .119 CX93
  W9 . . . . .82 DC70
  Coulsdon CR5 . . . . .175 DH115
  Gravesend DA11 . . . . . . .131 GG86
  Greenford UB6 . . . . .78 CC70
  Harrow HA3 . . . . .62 CM57
  Hornchurch RM11 . . . . . .71 FG58
  Hounslow (Hthrw.Air.) TW6
   off Inner Ring E 95 BP83
  Ilford IG2 . . . . .69 ER58
  Isleworth TW7 . . . . .97 CD82
  Kingston upon Thames
   KT2 . . . . .118 CM94
  Loughton IG10 . . . . .32 EL42
  Sidcup DA14 . . . . .125 ES91
  Slough SL1 . . . . .92 AV75
  Southall UB2 . . . . .96 BY77
  Teddington TW11 . . . . . .117 CE91
  Wallington SM6 . . . . .159 DH106
  Watford WD18 . . . . .23 BV43
  Welling DA16 . . . . .106 EW83
Cliftons La, Reig. RH2 . . . . .183 CX131
Clifton St, EC2 . . . . .197 M6
Clifton Ter, N4 . . . . .65 DN61
Clifton Vil, W9 . . . . .82 DB71
Clifton Wk, E6 . . . . .86 EL72
  W6 off King St 99 CV77
  Dartford DA2
   off Osbourne Rd 128 FP86
Clifton Way, SE15 . . . . .102 DV80
  Borehamwood WD6 . . . . .26 CN39
  Brentwood CM13 . . . . . . .53 GD46
  Wembley HA0 . . . . .80 CL67
  Woking GU21 . . . . .166 AT117
Climb, The, Rick. WD3 . . . . . .22 BH44
Clinch Ct, E16 . . . . .86 EG71
Cline Rd, N11 . . . . .45 DJ51
Clinger Ct, N1 off Pitfield St . .84 DS67
★ Clink Prison Mus, SE1 . . .201 K2
Clink St, SE1 . . . . .201 J2
Clinton Av, E.Mol. KT8 . . . . .136 CC98
  Welling DA16 . . . . .105 ET84
Clinton Cres, Ilf. IG6 . . . . . . .49 ES51
Clinton Rd, E3 . . . . .85 DY69
  E7 . . . . .68 EG63
  N15 . . . . .66 DR56
  Leatherhead KT22 . . . . . .171 CJ123

Clinton Ter, Sutt. SM1
  off Manor La 158 DC105
Clipper Boul, Dart. DA2 . . . .109 FS83
Clipper Boul W, Dart. DA2 . .109 FR83
Clipper Cl, SE16 . . . . .203 H4
Clipper Cres, Grav. DA12 . . .131 GM91
Clipper Way, SE13 . . . . .103 EC84
Clippesby Cl, Chess. KT9 . . .156 CM108
Clipstone Ms, W1 . . . . .195 K6
Clipstone Rd, Houns. TW3 . . .96 CA83
Clipstone St, W1 . . . . .195 J6
Clissold Cl, N2 . . . . .64 DF55
Clissold Ct, N4 . . . . .66 DQ61
Clissold Cres, N16 . . . . .66 DR62
Clissold Rd, N16 . . . . .66 DR62
Clitheroe Av, Har. HA2 . . . . . .60 CA60
Clitheroe Gdns, Wat. WD19 . .40 BX48
Clitheroe Rd, SW9 . . . . .101 DL82
  Romford RM5 . . . . .51 FC50
Clitherow Av, W7 . . . . .97 CG76
Clitherow Pas, Brent. TW8 . . .97 CJ78
Clitherow Rd, Brent. TW8 . . . .97 CJ78
Clitterhouse Cres, NW2 . . . . .63 CW60
Clitterhouse Rd, NW2 . . . . . .63 CW60
Clive Av, N18
  off Claremont St 46 DU51
  Dartford DA1 . . . . .127 FF86
Clive Cl, Pot.B. EN6 . . . . .11 CZ31
Cliveden Cl, N12
  off Woodside Av 44 DC49
  Brentwood CM15 . . . . . . .55 FZ45
Cliveden Pl, SW1 . . . . .198 F8
  Shepperton TW17 . . . . . .135 BP100
Cliveden Rd, SW19 . . . . . . .139 CZ95
Cliveden Ct, W13 . . . . .79 CH71
Clivedon Rd, E4 . . . . .48 EE50
Clive Par, Nthwd. HA6
  off Maxwell Rd 39 BS52
Clive Pas, SE21 off Clive Rd .122 DR90
Clive Rd, SE21 . . . . .122 DR90
  SW19 . . . . .120 DE93
  Belvedere DA17 . . . . . . .106 FA77
  Brentwood CM13 . . . . . . .53 FW52
  Enfield EN1 . . . . .30 DU42
  Esher KT10 . . . . .154 CB105
  Feltham TW14 . . . . .115 BU86
  Gravesend DA11 . . . . . . .131 GH86
  Romford RM2 . . . . .71 FH57
  Twickenham TW1 . . . . . .117 CF91
Clivesdale Dr, Hayes UB3 . . .77 BV74
Clive Way, Enf. EN1 . . . . .30 DU42
  Watford WD24 . . . . .24 BW39
Cloak La, EC4 . . . . .197 J10
⇌ Clock House 143 DY96
Clockhouse Av, Bark. IG11 . . .87 EQ67
Clockhouse Cl, SW19 . . . . . .119 CW90
Clock Ho Cl, W.Byf. (Byfleet)
  KT14 . . . . .152 BM112
Clockhouse La, Ashf. TW15 . .114 BN91
  Feltham TW14 . . . . .115 BP89
  Grays RM16 . . . . .91 FX74
  Romford RM5 . . . . .51 FB52
Clock Ho Mead, Lthd. (Oxshott)
  KT22 . . . . .154 CB114
Clockhouse Ms, Rick. (Chorl.) WD3
  off Chorleywood Ho Dr . .21 BE41
Clockhouse Pl, SW15 . . . . . .119 CY85
  Feltham TW14 . . . . .115 BQ88
Clock Ho Rd, Beck. BR3 . . . .143 DY97
Clockhouse Roundabout, Felt.
  TW14 . . . . .115 BP88
★ Clockmakers Company Collection,
  Guildhall Lib, EC2 . . . . .197 J8
Clock Twr Ms, N1
  off Arlington Av 84 DQ67
  SE28 . . . . .88 EV73
Clock Twr Pl, N7 . . . . .83 DL65
Clock Twr Rd, Islw. TW7 . . . .97 CF83
Cloister Cl, Rain. RM13 . . . . .89 FH70
  Teddington TW11 . . . . . .117 CH92
Cloister Gdns, SE25 . . . . . . .142 DV100
  Edgware HA8 . . . . .42 CQ50
Cloister Rd, NW2 . . . . .63 CZ62
  W3 . . . . .80 CQ71
Cloisters, The, Bushey WD23 .24 BZ42
  Rickmansworth WD3 . . . .38 BL45
  Woking GU22 . . . . .167 BB111
Cloisters Av, Brom. BR2 . . . .145 EM99
Cloisters Business Cen, SW8
  off Battersea Pk Rd 101 DH80
Cloisters Mall, Kings.T. KT1
  off Union St 137 CK96
Clonard Way, Pnr. HA5 . . . . .40 CA51
Clonbrock Rd, N16 . . . . .66 DS63
Cloncurry St, SW6 . . . . .99 CX82
Clonmel Cl, Har. HA2 . . . . . . .61 CD60
Clonmell Rd, N17 . . . . .66 DR55
Clonmel Rd, SW6 . . . . .99 CZ80
  Teddington TW11 . . . . . .117 CD91
Clonmore St, SW18 . . . . . . .119 CZ88
Cloonmore Av, Orp. BR6 . . . .163 ET105
Clorane Gdns, NW3 . . . . .64 DA62
Close, The, E4
  off Beech Hall Rd 47 EC52
  N14 . . . . .45 DK47
  N20 . . . . .43 CZ47
  SE3 off Heath La 103 ED82
  Barnet EN4 . . . . .28 DF44
  Beckenham BR3 . . . . . . .143 DY98
  Bexley DA5 . . . . .126 FA86
  Brentwood CM14 . . . . . . .54 FW48
  Bushey WD23 . . . . .24 CB43
  Carshalton SM5 . . . . . . .158 DE109
  Dartford DA2 . . . . .128 FJ90
  Grays RM16 . . . . .110 GC75
  Harrow HA2 . . . . .40 CC54
  Hatfield AL9 . . . . .11 CY26
  Iver SL0 . . . . .75 BC69
  Mitcham CR4 . . . . .140 DF98
  New Malden KT3 . . . . . .138 CQ96
  Orpington BR5 . . . . .145 ES100
  Pinner (Eastcote) HA5 . . .60 BW59

Close, The, Pnr. (Rayners La)
  HA5 . . . . .60 BZ59
  Potters Bar EN6 . . . . .12 DA32
  Purley (Pampisford Rd)
   CR8 . . . . .159 DP110
  Purley (Russ.Hill) CR8 . . .159 DM110
  Radlett WD7 . . . . .9 CF33
  Richmond TW9 . . . . .98 CP83
  Rickmansworth WD3 . . . .38 BJ46
  Romford RM6 . . . . .70 EY58
  Sevenoaks TN13 . . . . . . .190 FE124
  Sidcup DA14 . . . . .126 EV92
  Sutton SM3 . . . . .139 CZ101
  Uxbridge UB10 . . . . .76 BL66
  Uxbridge (Hlgdn.) UB10 . .76 BN67
  Virginia Water GU25 . . . .132 AW99
  Wembley (Barnhill Rd) HA9 .62 CQ62
  Wembley (Uxb.Pk Av) HA0 .80 CL65
  West Byfleet KT14 . . . . . .152 BG113
  Westerham (Berry's Grn.)
   TN16 . . . . .179 EP116
Closemead Cl, Nthwd. HA6 . .39 BQ51
Cloth Ct, EC1 . . . . .196 G7
Cloth Fair, EC1 . . . . .196 G7
Clothier St, E1 . . . . .197 N8
Cloth St, EC1 . . . . .197 H6
Clothworkers Rd, SE18 . . . . .105 ER80
Cloudberry Rd, Rom. RM3 . . .52 FK51
Cloudesdale Rd, SW17 . . . . .121 DH89
Cloudesley Pl, N1 . . . . .83 DN67
Cloudesley Rd, N1 . . . . .83 DN67
  Bexleyheath DA7 . . . . . .106 EZ81
  Erith DA8 . . . . .107 FF81
Cloudesley Sq, N1 . . . . .83 DN67
Cloudesley St, N1 . . . . .83 DN67
Clouston Cl, Wall. SM6 . . . . .159 DL106
Clova Rd, E7 . . . . .86 EF65
Clove Cres, E14 . . . . .85 ED73
Clove Hitch Quay, SW11 . . . .100 DC83
Clovelly Av, NW9 . . . . .63 CT56
  Uxbridge UB10 . . . . .59 BQ63
  Warlingham CR6 . . . . . . .176 DV118
Clovelly Cl, Pnr. HA5 . . . . . . .59 BV55
  Uxbridge UB10 . . . . .59 BQ63
Clovelly Ct, Horn. RM11 . . . . .72 FN61
Clovelly Gdns, SE19 . . . . . . .142 DT95
  Enfield EN1 . . . . .46 DS45
  Romford RM7 . . . . .51 FB53
Clovelly Rd, N8 . . . . .65 DK56
  W4 . . . . .98 CQ75
  W5 . . . . .97 CJ75
  Bexleyheath DA7 . . . . . . .106 EY79
  Hounslow TW3 . . . . .96 CA82
Clovelly Way, E1
  off Jamaica St 84 DW72
  Harrow HA2 . . . . .60 BZ61
  Orpington BR6 . . . . .145 ET100
Clover Cl, E11 off Norman Rd .67 ED61
Clover Ct, Grays RM17
  off Churchill Rd 110 GD79
  Woking GU22 . . . . .166 AX118
Cloverdale Gdns, Sid. DA15 .125 ET86
Clover Fld, The, Bushey WD23 .24 BZ44
Clover Hill, Couls. CR5 . . . . .175 DH121
Clover Leas, Epp. CM16 . . . . .17 ET30
Cloverleys, Loug. IG10 . . . . . .32 EK43
Clover Ms, SW3 off Dilke St .100 DF79
Clovers, The, Grav. (Nthflt.)
  DA11 . . . . .130 GE91
Clover Way, Wall. SM6 . . . . .140 DG102
Clove St, E13 off Barking Rd .86 EG70
Clowders Rd, SE6 . . . . .123 DZ90
Clowser Cl, Sutt. SM1
  off Turnpike La 158 DC106
Cloysters Grn, E1 . . . . .202 B2
Cloyster Wd, Edg. HA8 . . . . .41 CK52
Club Gdns Rd, Brom. BR2 . . .144 EG101
Club Row, E1 . . . . .197 P4
  E2 . . . . .197 P4
Clump, The, Rick. WD3 . . . . .22 BG43
Clump Av, Tad. KT20 . . . . . .182 CQ131
Clumps, The, Ashf. TW15 . . .115 BR93
Clunas Gdns, Rom. RM2 . . . .72 FK55
Clunbury Av, Sthl. UB2 . . . . . .96 BZ78
Clunbury St, N1 . . . . .197 L1
Cluny Est, SE1 . . . . .201 M6
Cluny Ms, SW5 . . . . .100 DA77
Cluny Pl, SE1 . . . . .201 M6
Cluse Ct, N1 off Dame St 84 DQ68
Clutterbucks, Rick. (Sarratt)
  WD3 . . . . .22 BG36
Clutton St, E14 . . . . .85 EB71
Clydach Rd, Enf. EN1 . . . . . . .30 DT42
Clyde Av, S.Croy. CR2 . . . . .176 DV115
Clyde Circ, N15 . . . . .66 DS56
Clyde Cl, Red. RH1 . . . . .184 DG133
Clyde Ct, Red. RH1
  off Clyde Cl 184 DG133
Clyde Cres, Upmin. RM14 . . .73 FS58
Clyde Pl, E10 . . . . .67 EB59
Clyde Rd, N15 . . . . .66 DS56
  N22 . . . . .45 DK53
  Croydon CR0 . . . . .142 DT102
  Staines (Stanw.) TW19 . .114 BK88
  Sutton SM1 . . . . .158 DA106
  Wallington SM6 . . . . .159 DJ106
Clydesdale, Enf. EN3 . . . . . . .31 DX42
Clydesdale Av, Stan. HA7 . . . .61 CK55
Clydesdale Cl, Borwd. WD6 . .26 CR43
  Isleworth TW7 . . . . .97 CF83
Clydesdale Gdns, Rich. TW10 .98 CP84
Clydesdale Ho, Erith DA18
  off Kale Rd 106 EY75
Clydesdale Rd, W11 . . . . .81 CZ72
  Hornchurch RM11 . . . . . .71 FF60
Clydesdale Wk, Brox. EN10
  off Tarpan Way 15 DZ25
Clyde St, SE8 . . . . .103 DZ79
Clyde Ter, SE23 . . . . .122 DW89
Clyde Vale, SE23 . . . . .122 DW89
Clyde Way, Rom. RM1 . . . . . .51 FE53
Clydon Cl, Erith DA8 . . . . . . .107 FE79
Clyfford Rd, Ruis. HA4 . . . . . .59 BT63
Clymping Dene, Felt. TW14 . .115 BV87
Clyston Rd, Wat. WD18 . . . . .23 BT44
Clyston St, SW8 . . . . .101 DJ82
Clyve Way, Stai. TW18 . . . . .133 BE95

Coach & Horses Yd, W1 . . . .195 J10
Coach Ho La, N5
  off Highbury Hill 65 DP63
  SW19 . . . . .119 CX91
Coach Ho Ms, SE14
  off Waller Rd 103 DX82
Coachhouse Ms, SE20 . . . . .122 DV94
Coach Ho Ms, SE23 . . . . . . .123 DX86
Coach Ho Yd, SW18
  off Ebner St 100 DB84
Coachmaker Ms, SW4
  off Fenwick Pl 101 DL83
Coach Rd, Bet. (Brock.) RH3 .182 CL134
  Chertsey (Ott.) KT16 . . . .151 BC107
Coach Yd Ms, N19
  off Trinder Rd 65 DL60
Coal Ct, Grays RM17
  off Columbia Wf Rd 110 GA79
Coaldale Wk, SE21
  off Lairdale Cl 122 DQ87
Coalecroft Rd, SW15 . . . . . . .99 CW84
Coal Rd, Til. RM18 . . . . .111 GL82
Coal Wf Rd, W12
  off Sterne St 99 CX75
Coates Av, SW18 . . . . .120 DE86
Coates Dell, Wat. WD25 . . . . .8 BY33
Coates Hill Rd, Brom. BR1 . .145 EN96
Coates Rd, Borwd. (Elstree)
  WD6 . . . . .41 CK45
Coate St, E2 . . . . .84 DU68
Coates Wk, Brent. TW8 . . . . .98 CL78
Coates Way, Wat. WD25 . . . . .8 BX33
Cobb Cl, Borwd. WD6 . . . . . .26 CQ43
  Slough (Datchet) SL3 . . . .92 AX81
Cobbett Cl, Enf. EN3 . . . . . . .30 DW36
Cobbett Rd, SE9 . . . . .104 EL83
  Twickenham TW2 . . . . . .116 CA88
Cobbetts Av, Ilf. IG4 . . . . .68 EK57
Cobbetts Cl, Wok. GU21 . . . .166 AV117
Cobbetts Hill, Wey. KT13 . . .153 BP107
Cobbett St, SW8 . . . . .101 DM80
Cobb Grn, Wat. WD25 . . . . . .7 BV32
Cobbins, The, Wal.Abb. EN9 . .16 EE33
Cobbinsend Rd, Wal.Abb.
  EN9 . . . . .16 EK29
Cobble La, N1
  off Edwards Ms 83 DP66
Cobble Ms, N5 . . . . .66 DQ62
Cobblers Wk, E.Mol. KT8 . . .137 CG95
  Hampton TW12 . . . . .116 CC94
  Kingston upon Thames
   KT2 . . . . .137 CG95
  Teddington TW11 . . . . . .137 CG95
Cobbles, The, Brwd. CM15 . . .54 FY47
  Upminster RM14 . . . . . . .73 FT59
Cobblestone Pl, Croy. CR0
  off Oakfield Rd 142 DQ102
Cobbold Est, NW10 . . . . .81 CT65
Cobbold Ms, W12
  off Cobbold Rd 99 CT75
Cobbold Rd, E11 . . . . .68 EF62
  NW10 . . . . .81 CT65
  W12 . . . . .98 CS75
Cobb's Ct, EC4
  off Carter La 83 DP72
Cobb's Rd, Houns. TW4 . . . . .96 BZ84
Cobb St, E1 . . . . .197 P7
Cobden Cl, Uxb. UB8 . . . . . . .76 BJ67
Cobden Hill, Rad. WD7 . . . . .25 CH36
Cobden Rd, E11 . . . . .68 EE62
  SE25 . . . . .142 DU99
  Orpington BR6 . . . . .163 ER105
  Sevenoaks TN13 . . . . . . .191 FJ123
COBHAM 169 BV115
Cobham, Grays RM16 . . . . . .110 GB75
⇌ Cobham & Stoke
  D'Abernon 170 BY117
Cobham Av, N.Mal. KT3 . . . .139 CU99
★ Cobham Bus Mus, Cob.
  KT11 . . . . .153 BQ112
Cobham Cl, SW11 . . . . .120 DE86
  Bromley BR2 . . . . .144 EL101
  Edgware HA8 . . . . .42 CP54
  Enfield EN1 . . . . .30 DU41
  Sidcup DA15
   off Park Mead 126 EV86
  Wallington SM6 . . . . .159 DL107
Cobham Gate, Cob. KT11 . . .153 BV114
Cobham Ho, Bark. IG11
  off St. Margarets 87 EQ67
Cobham Ms, NW1
  off Agar Gro 83 DK66
Cobham Pk Rd, Cob. KT11 . .169 BV117
Cobham Pl, Bexh. DA6 . . . . .126 EX85
Cobham Rd, E17 . . . . .47 EC53
  N22 . . . . .45 DP55
  Cobham (Stoke D'Ab.)
   KT11 . . . . .170 CA118
  Hounslow TW5 . . . . .96 BW80
  Ilford IG3 . . . . .69 ES61
  Kingston upon Thames
   KT1 . . . . .138 CN95
  Leatherhead (Fetch.) KT22 .171 CE122
Cobham St, Grav. DA11 . . . .131 GG87
Cobill Cl, Horn. RM11 . . . . . . .72 FJ56
Cobland Rd, SE12 . . . . .124 EJ91
Coborn Rd, E3 . . . . .85 DZ69
Coborn St, E3 . . . . .85 DZ69
Cobourg Rd, SE5 . . . . .102 DT79
Cobourg St, NW1 . . . . .195 L3
Cobsdene, Grav. DA12 . . . . .131 GK93
Cobs Way, Add. (New Haw)
  KT15 . . . . .152 BJ110
Coburg Cl, SW1 . . . . .199 L8
Coburg Cres, SW2 . . . . .121 DM88
Coburg Gdns, Ilf. IG5 . . . . . . .48 EK54
Coburg Rd, N22 . . . . .45 DM55
Cochrane Ms, NW8 . . . . .194 A1
Cochrane Rd, SW19 . . . . . . .119 CZ94
Cochrane St, NW8 . . . . .194 A1
Cockayne Way, SE8 . . . . . . .203 L10
Cockerell Rd, E17 . . . . .67 DY59

Coc - Com

Cockerhurst Rd, Sev. (Shore.)
TN14 . . . . .165 FD107
Cocker Rd, Enf. EN1 . . . . . . .30 DV36
Cockett Rd, Slou. SL3 . . . . . .92 AY76
COCKFOSTERS, Barn. 28 DE42
⊖ Cockfosters 28 DG42
Cockfosters Rd, Barn. EN4 . . .28 DF40
Cock Hill, E1 . . . . .197 N7
Cock La, E1 . . . . .196 F7
  Leatherhead (Fetch.)
  KT22 . . . . .170 CC122
Cockle Way, Rad. (Shenley)
  WD7 . . . . .10 CL33
Cockmannings La, Orp. BR5 .146 EX102
Cockmannings Rd, Orp. BR5 .146 EX101
Cockpit Steps, SW1 . . . . . . .199 N5
Cockpit Yd, WC1 . . . . .196 C6
Cocks Cres, N.Mal. KT3 . . . .139 CT98
Cocksett Av, Orp. BR6 . . . . .163 ES107
Cockspur Ct, SW1 . . . . .199 N2
Cockspur St, SW1 . . . . .199 N2
Cocksure La, Sid. DA14 . . . . .126 FA90
Cock's Yd, Uxb. UB8
  off Bakers Rd 76 BJ66
Code St, E1 . . . . .84 DT70
Codham Hall La, Brwd. CM13 .73 FV56
Codicote Dr, Wat. WD25 . . . . .8 BX34
Codicote Ter, N4
  off Green Las 66 DQ61
Codling Cl, E1 . . . . .202 C2
Codling Way, Wem. HA0 . . . .61 CK63
CODMORE, Chesh. 4 AS29
Codmore Cres, Chesh. HP5 . . .4 AS29
Codmore Wd Rd, Chesh. HP5 . .4 AW33
Codrington Ct, Wok. GU21
  off Raglan Rd 166 AS118
Codrington Cres, Grav.
  DA12 . . . . .131 GJ92
Codrington Gdns, Grav.
  DA12 . . . . .131 GK92
Codrington Hill, SE23 . . . . . .123 DY87
Codrington Ms, W11
  off Blenheim Cres 81 CY72
Cody Cl, Har. HA3 . . . . .61 CK55
  Wallington SM6
  off Alcock Cl 159 DK108
Cody Rd, E16 . . . . .85 ED70
Cody Rd Business Cen, E16 . .85 ED70
Coe Av, SE25 . . . . .142 DU100
Coe's All, Barn. EN5
  off Wood St 27 CY42
Coftards, Slou. SL2 . . . . .74 AW72
Cogan Av, E17 . . . . .47 DY53
Cohen Cl, Wal.Cr. EN8 . . . . . .15 DY31
Coin St, SE1 . . . . .200 D2
Coity Rd, NW5 . . . . .82 DG65
Cokers La, SE21 off Perifield .122 DR88
Coke's Fm La, Ch.St.G. HP8 . .20 AV41
Coke's La, Amer. HP7 . . . . . . .20 AU42
  Chalfont St. Giles HP8 . . . . .20 AU42
Coke St, E1 . . . . .84 DU72
Colas Ms, NW6
  off Birchington Rd 82 DA67
Colbeck Ms, SW7 . . . . .100 DB77
Colbeck Rd, Har. HA1 . . . . . .60 CC59
Colberg Pl, N16 . . . . .66 DS59
Colborne Way, Wor.Pk. KT4 .139 CW104
Colbrook Av, Hayes UB3 . . . .95 BR76
Colbrook Cl, Hayes UB3 . . . .95 BR76
Colburn Av, Cat. CR3 . . . . . .176 DT124
  Pinner HA5 . . . . .40 BY51
Colburn Way, Sutt. SM1 . . . .140 DD104
Colby Ms, SE19
  off Gipsy Hill 122 DS92
Colby Rd, SE19 . . . . .122 DS92
  Walton-on-Thames KT12
  off Winchester Rd 135 BU102
Colchester Av, E12 . . . . .69 EM62
Colchester Dr, Pnr. HA5 . . . .60 BX57
Colchester Rd, E10 . . . . .67 EC59
  E17 . . . . .67 EA58
  Edgware HA8 . . . . .42 CQ52
  Northwood HA6 . . . . .39 BU54
  Romford RM3 . . . . .52 FK53
Colchester St, E1
  off Braham St 84 DT72
Colcokes Rd, Bans. SM7 . . . .174 DA116
Cold Arbor Rd, Sev. TN13 . . .190 FD124
Coldbath Sq, EC1 . . . . .196 D4
Coldbath St, SE13 . . . . .103 EB81
COLDBLOW, Bex. 127 FC89
Cold Blow Cres, Bex. DA5 . . .127 FD88
Cold Blow La, SE14 . . . . . . .103 DX80
Cold Blows, Mitch. CR4 . . . .140 DG97
Coldershaw Rd, W13 . . . . . . .79 CG74
Coldfall Av, N10 . . . . .44 DF54
Coldham Gro, Enf. EN3 . . . . .31 DY37
Cold Harbour, E14 . . . . .204 E3
Coldharbour Cl, Egh. TW20 .133 BC97
Coldharbour Crest, SE9
  off Great Harry Dr 125 EN90
Coldharbour La, SE5 . . . . . .101 DN84
  SW9 . . . . .101 DN84
  Bushey WD23 . . . . .24 CB44
  Egham TW20 . . . . .133 BC97
  Hayes UB3 . . . . .77 BU73
  Purley CR8 . . . . .159 DN110
  Rainham RM13 . . . . .89 FE72
  Redhill (Bletch.) RH1 . . . . .186 DT134
  Woking GU22 . . . . .167 BF115
Coldharbour Pl, SE5
  off Denmark Hill 102 DQ82
Coldharbour Rd, Croy. CR0 .159 DN106
  Gravesend (Nthflt.) DA11 . .130 GE89
  West Byfleet KT14 . . . . . . .151 BF114
  Woking GU22 . . . . .167 BF115
Coldharbour Way, Croy. CR0 .159 DN106
Coldshott, Oxt. RH8 . . . . . . .188 EG133
Coldstream Gdns, SW18 . . . .119 CZ86
Coldstream Rd, Cat. CR3 . . . .176 DQ121
Cole Av, Grays RM16 . . . . . .111 GJ77
Colebeck Ms, N1 . . . . .83 DP65
Colebert Av, E1 . . . . .84 DW70
Colebrook, Cher. (Ott.) KT16 .151 BD107

Colebrook Cl, NW7
  off Bittacy Hill 43 CY52
  SW15 off West Hill 119 CX87
Colebrooke Av, W13 . . . . . . .79 CH72
Colebrooke Dr, E11 . . . . .68 EH59
Colebrooke Pl, N1
  off St. Peters St 83 DP67
Colebrooke Rd, Brom. BR2 . .144 EE96
  Redhill RH1 . . . . .184 DE132
Colebrooke Row, N1 . . . . . . .196 F1
Colebrook Gdns, Loug. IG10 . .33 EP40
Colebrook Ho, E14
  off Brabazon St 85 EB72
Colebrook La, Loug. IG10 . . . .33 EP40
Colebrook Path, Loug. IG10 . .33 EP40
Colebrook Pl, Cher. (Ott.)
  KT16 . . . . .151 BB108
Colebrook Rd, SW16 . . . . . .141 DL95
Colebrook Way, N11 . . . . . . .45 DH50
Coleby Path, SE5
  off Harris St 102 DR80
Cole Cl, SE28 . . . . .88 EV74
Coledale Dr, Stan. HA7 . . . . .41 CJ53
Coleford Rd, SW18 . . . . .120 DC85
Cole Gdns, Houns. TW5 . . . . .95 BU80
Colegrave Rd, E15 . . . . .67 ED64
Colegrove Rd, SE15 . . . . . . .102 DT80
Coleherne Ct, SW5 . . . . .100 DB78
Coleherne Ms, SW10 . . . . . .100 DB78
Coleherne Rd, SW10 . . . . . . .100 DB78
Colehill Gdns, SW6
  off Fulham Palace Rd 99 CY82
Colehill La, SW6 . . . . .99 CY81
Coleman Cl, SE25 . . . . .142 DU96
Coleman Flds, N1 . . . . .84 DQ67
Coleman Rd, SE5 . . . . .102 DS80
  Belvedere DA17 . . . . .106 FA77
  Dagenham RM9 . . . . .88 EY65
Colemans Heath, SE9 . . . . . .125 EP90
Colemans La, Ong. CM5 . . . .19 FH30
Coleman's La, Wal.Abb. EN9 . .15 ED26
Coleman St, EC2 . . . . .197 K8
Colenso Dr, NW7 . . . . .43 CU52
Colenso Rd, E5 . . . . .66 DW63
  Ilford IG2 . . . . .69 ES60
Cole Pk Gdns, Twick. TW1 . .117 CG86
Cole Pk Rd, Twick. TW1 . . . .117 CG86
Cole Pk Vw, Twick. TW1
  off Hill Vw Rd 117 CG86
Colepits Wd Rd, SE9 . . . . . .125 EQ85
Coleraine Rd, N8 . . . . .65 DN55
  SE3 . . . . .104 EF79
Coleridge Av, E12 . . . . .86 EL65
  Sutton SM1 . . . . .158 DE104
Coleridge Cl, SW8 . . . . .101 DH82
  Waltham Cross (Chsht.) EN7
  off Peakes La 14 DT27
Coleridge Cres, Slou. (Colnbr.)
  SL3 . . . . .93 BE81
Coleridge Gdns, NW6
  off Fairhazel Gdns 82 DC66
Coleridge La, N8
  off Coleridge Rd 65 DL58
Coleridge Rd, E17 . . . . .67 DZ56
  N4 .65 DN61
  N8 .65 DK58
  N12 . . . . .44 DC50
  Ashford TW15 . . . . .114 BL91
  Croydon CR0 . . . . .142 DW101
  Dartford DA1 . . . . .108 FN84
  Romford RM3 . . . . .51 FH52
  Tilbury RM18 . . . . .111 GJ82
Coleridge Sq, W13
  off Berners Dr 79 CG72
  Brentwood CM13 . . . . .55 GD44
Coleridge Wk, NW11 . . . . . . .64 DA56
Coleridge Way, Hayes UB4 . . .77 BU72
  Orpington BR6 . . . . .146 EU100
  West Drayton UB7 . . . . .94 BM77
Cole Rd, Twick. TW1 . . . . . . .117 CG86
  Watford WD17
  off Stamford St 23 BV39
Colesburg Rd, Beck. BR3 . . .143 DZ97
Coles Cres, Har. HA2 . . . . . . .60 CB61
Colescroft Hill, Pur. CR8 . . .175 DN115
Colesdale, Pot.B. (Cuffley)
  EN6 . . . . .13 DL30
Coles Grn, Bushey (Bushey Hth.)
  WD23 . . . . .40 CC46
  Loughton IG10 . . . . .33 EN39
Coles Grn Ct, NW2 . . . . .63 CU61
Coles Grn Rd, NW2 . . . . .63 CU60
Coleshill Rd, Tedd. TW11 . . .117 CE93
Coles La, West. (Brasted)
  TN16 . . . . .180 EW123
Colesmead Rd, Red. RH1 . . .184 DF131
COLES MEADS, Red. 184 DF131
Cole St, SE1 . . . . .201 J5
Colet Cl, N13 . . . . .45 DP61
Colet Gdns, W14 . . . . .99 CX77
Colet Rd, Brwd. CM13 . . . . . .55 GC43
Colets Orchard, Sev. (Otford)
  TN14 . . . . .181 FH116
Coley Av, Wok. GU22 . . . . . .167 BA118
Coley St, WC1 . . . . .196 C5
Colfe Rd, SE23 . . . . .123 DY88
Colgate Pl, Enf. EN3
  off Government Row 31 EA38
Colham Av, West Dr. UB7 . . . .76 BL74
Colham Grn Rd, Uxb. UB8 . . . .76 BN71
Colham Mill Rd, West Dr. UB7 .94 BK75
Colham Rd, Uxb. UB8 . . . . . . .76 BM70
Colham Roundabout, Uxb.
  UB8 . . . . .76 BN73
Colina Ms, N15
  off Harringay Rd 65 DP57
Colina Rd, N15 . . . . .65 DP57
Colin Cl, NW9 . . . . .62 CS56
  Croydon CR0 . . . . .143 DZ104
  Dartford DA2 . . . . .128 FP86
  West Wickham BR4 . . . . . .144 EF104
Colin Cres, NW9 . . . . .63 CT56
⊖ Colindale 62 CS55
Colindale Av, NW9 . . . . .62 CR55
Colindale Business Pk, NW9 .62 CQ55
Ⓗ Colindale Hosp, NW9 . . . .42 CS54

Colindeep Gdns, NW4 . . . . . .63 CU57
Colindeep La, NW4 . . . . .62 CS55
  NW9 . . . . .62 CS55
Colinette Rd, SW15 . . . . .99 CW84
Colin Gdns, NW9 . . . . .63 CT57
Colin Par, NW9
  off Edgware Rd 62 CS56
Colin Pk Rd, NW9 . . . . .62 CS56
Colin Rd, NW10 . . . . .81 CU65
  Caterham CR3 . . . . .176 DU123
Colinton Rd, Ilf. IG3 . . . . .70 EV61
Coliston Pas, SW18
  off Coliston Rd 120 DA87
Coliston Rd, SW18 . . . . .120 DA87
Collamore Av, SW18 . . . . . . .120 DE88
Collapit Cl, Har. HA1 . . . . . . .60 CB57
Collard Av, Loug. IG10 . . . . . .33 EQ40
Collard Grn, Loug. IG10
  off Collard Av 33 EQ40
Collard Pl, NW1
  off Harmood St 83 DH66
College App, SE10 . . . . .103 EC79
College Av, Egh. TW20 . . . . .113 BB93
  Epsom KT17 . . . . .157 CT114
  Grays RM17 . . . . .110 GC77
  Harrow HA3 . . . . .41 CE53
  Slough SL1 . . . . .92 AS76
College Cl, E9 off Median Rd . .66 DW66
  N18 . . . . .46 DT50
  Addlestone KT15 . . . . .134 BK104
  Grays RM17 . . . . .110 GC77
  Harrow HA3 . . . . .41 CE52
  Twickenham TW2
  off Meadway 117 CD88
College Ct, Wal.Cr. (Chsht.)
  EN8 . . . . .14 DW30
College Cres, NW3 . . . . .82 DD65
  Redhill RH1 . . . . .184 DG131
College Cross, N1 . . . . .83 DN66
College Dr, Ruis. HA4 . . . . . .59 BU59
  Thames Ditton KT7 . . . . . .137 CE101
College Gdns, E4 . . . . .47 EB45
  N18 . . . . .46 DT50
  SE21 . . . . .122 DS88
  SW17 . . . . .120 DE89
  Enfield EN2 . . . . .30 DR39
  Ilford IG4 . . . . .68 EL57
  New Malden KT3 . . . . .139 CT99
College Grn, SE19 . . . . .122 DS94
College Gro, NW1
  off St. Pancras Way 83 DK67
College Hill, EC4 . . . . .197 J10
College Hill Rd, Har. HA3 . . .41 CF53
College La, NW5 . . . . .65 DH63
  Woking GU22 . . . . .166 AW119
College Ms, SW1 . . . . .199 P6
  SW18 off St. Ann's Hill . . .120 DB85
★ College of Arms, EC4 . . . .196 G10
College Pk Cl, SE13 . . . . . . .103 ED84
College Pk Rd, N17
  off College Rd 46 DT51
College Pl, E17 . . . . .86 EE56
  NW1 . . . . .83 DJ67
  SW10 off Hortensia Rd 100 DC80
College Pt, E15 . . . . .86 EF65
College Rd, E17 . . . . .67 EC57
  N17 . . . . .46 DT51
  N21 . . . . .45 DN47
  NW10 . . . . .81 CW68
  SE19 . . . . .122 DT92
  SE21 . . . . .122 DS87
  SW19 . . . . .120 DD93
  W13 . . . . .79 CH72
  Abbots Langley WD5 . . . . . .7 BT31
  Bromley BR1 . . . . .124 EG94
  Croydon CR0 . . . . .142 DR103
  Enfield EN2 . . . . .30 DR40
  Epsom KT17 . . . . .157 CU114
  Gravesend (Nthflt.) DA11 . .130 GB85
  Grays RM17 . . . . .110 GC77
  Harrow (Har.Hill) HA1 . . . . .61 CE58
  Harrow (Har.Wld.) HA3 . . . .41 CE53
  Isleworth TW7 . . . . .97 CF81
  Swanley BR8 . . . . .147 FE95
  Waltham Cross (Chsht.)
  EN8 . . . . .14 DV30
  Wembley HA9 . . . . .61 CK60
  Woking GU22 . . . . .167 BB116
College Row, E9 . . . . .67 DX64
College Slip, Brom. BR1 . . . .144 EG95
College St, EC4 . . . . .197 J10
College Ter, E3 . . . . .85 DZ69
  N3 off Hendon La 43 CZ54
College Vw, SE9 . . . . .124 EK88
College Wk, Kings.T. KT1
  off Grange Rd 138 CL96
College Way, Ashf. TW15 . . .114 BM91
  Hayes UB3 . . . . .77 BU73
  Northwood HA6 . . . . .39 BR51
College Yd, NW5
  off College La 65 DH63
Collent St, E9 . . . . .84 DW65
Coller Cres, Dart. (Lane End)
  DA2 . . . . .129 FS91
Colless Rd, N15 . . . . .66 DT57
Collet Cl, Wal.Cr. (Chsht.) EN8 .15 DX28
Collet Gdns, Wal.Cr. (Chsht.)
  EN8 off Collet Cl 15 DX28
Collett Rd, SE16 . . . . .202 C7
Collett Way, Sthl. UB2 . . . . . .78 CB74
Colley Hill La, Slou. (Hedg.)
  SL2 . . . . .56 AT62
Colleyland, Rick. (Chorl.) WD3 .21 BD42
Colley La, Reig. RH2 . . . . . . .183 CY132
Colley Manor Dr, Reig. RH2 .183 CX133
Colley Way, Reig. RH2 . . . . .183 CY131
Collier Cl, E6 off Trader Rd . . .87 EP72
  Epsom KT19 . . . . .156 CN111
Collier Dr, Edg. HA8 . . . . . . .42 CN54
COLLIER ROW, Rom. 50 FA53
Collier Row La, Rom. RM5 . . .51 FB52
Collier Row Rd, Rom. RM5 . . .50 EZ53
Colliers, Cat. CR3 . . . . .186 DU125
Colliers Cl, Wok. GU21 . . . . .166 AV117
Colliers Shaw, Kes. BR2 . . . .162 EK105

Collier St, N1 . . . . .196 B1
Colliers Water La, Th.Hth.
  CR7 . . . . .141 DN99
COLLIER'S WOOD, SW19 . . .120 DD94
⊖ Colliers Wood 120 DD94
Collindale Av, Erith DA8 . . . .107 FB79
  Sidcup DA15 . . . . .126 EU80
Collingbourne Rd, W12 . . . . .81 CV74
Collingham Gdns, SW5 . . . .100 DB77
Ⓗ Collingham Gardens Hosp,
  SW5 . . . . .100 DB77
Collingham Pl, SW5 . . . . . . .100 DB77
Collingham Rd, SW5 . . . . . .100 DB77
Collings Cl, N22
  off Whittington Rd 45 DM51
Collington St, SE10 . . . . .103 ED78
Collingtree Rd, SE26 . . . . . . .122 DW91
Collingwood Av, N10 . . . . . . .64 DG55
  Surbiton KT5 . . . . .138 CQ102
Collingwood Cl, SE20 . . . . . .142 DV95
  Twickenham TW2 . . . . .116 CA86
Collingwood Dr, St.Alb. (Lon.Col.)
  AL2 .8 CK25
Collingwood Pl, Walt. KT12 . .135 BU104
Collingwood Rd, E17 . . . . . . .67 EA58
  N15 . . . . .66 DS56
  Mitcham CR4 . . . . .140 DE96
  Sutton SM1 . . . . .140 DA104
  Uxbridge UB8 . . . . .77 BP70
Collingwood St, E1 . . . . .84 DV70
Collins Av, Stan. HA7 . . . . . . .42 CL54
Collins Dr, Ruis. HA4 . . . . . . .60 BW61
Collinson St, SE1 . . . . .201 H5
Collinson Wk, SE1 . . . . .201 H5
Collins Rd, N5 . . . . .66 DQ63
Collins Sq, SE3
  off Tranquil Vale 104 EF82
Collins St, SE3 . . . . .104 EE82
Collins Way, Brwd. CM13 . . .55 GE43
Collin's Yd, N1
  off Islington Grn 83 DP67
Collinwood Av, Enf. EN3 . . . .30 DW41
Collinwood Gdns, Ilf. IG5 . . . .69 EM57
Collis All, Twick. TW2
  off The Green 117 CE88
Colls Rd, SE15 . . . . .102 DW81
Collyer Av, Croy. CR0 . . . . . .159 DL105
Collyer Pl, SE15
  off Peckham High St 102 DU81
Collyer Rd, Croy. CR0 . . . . . .159 DL105
  St. Albans (Lon.Col.) AL2 . . .9 CJ27
Colman Cl, Epsom KT18 . . . .173 CW117
Colman Rd, E16 . . . . .86 EJ71
Colman Way, Red. RH1 . . . .184 DE132
Colmar Cl, E1 off Alderney Rd .85 DX70
Colmer Pl, Har. HA3 . . . . . . .41 CD52
Colmer Rd, SW16 . . . . .141 DL95
Colmore Ms, SE15 . . . . .102 DV81
Colmore Rd, Enf. EN3 . . . . . .30 DW42
COLNBROOK, Slou. 93 BE81
Colnbrook Bypass, Slou. SL3 .93 BF80
  West Drayton UB7 . . . . .93 BF80
Colnbrook Cl, St.Alb. (Lon.Col.)
  AL2 . . . . .10 CL28
Colnbrook Ct, Slou. SL3 . . . .93 BF81
Colnbrook St, SE1 . . . . .200 F7
Colndale Rd, Slou. (Colnbr.)
  SL3 . . . . .93 BE82
Colne Av, Rick. (Mill End)
  WD3 . . . . .38 BG47
  Watford WD19 . . . . .23 BV44
  West Drayton UB7 . . . . .94 BJ75
Colne Bk, Slou. (Horton) SL3 .93 BC83
Colnebridge Cl, Stai. TW18
  off Clarence St 113 BE91
Colne Cl, S.Ock. RM15 . . . . .91 FW73
Colne Ct, Epsom KT19 . . . . .156 CQ105
Colnedale Rd, Uxb. UB8 . . . .58 BK64
Colne Dr, Rom. RM3 . . . . . . .52 FM51
  Walton-on-Thames KT12 . .136 BX104
Colne Gdns, St.Alb. (Lon.Col.)
  AL2 . . . . .10 CL27
Colne Ho, Bark. IG11 . . . . . . .87 EP65
Colne Mead, Rick. (Mill End) WD3
  off Uxbridge Rd 38 BG47
Colne Orchard, Slou. SL0 . . . .75 BF72
Colne Pk Caravan Site, West Dr.
  UB7 . . . . .94 BJ77
Colne Reach, Stai. TW19 . . .113 BF85
Colne Rd, E5 . . . . .67 DY63
  N21 . . . . .46 DR45
  Twickenham TW1, TW2 . . .117 CE88
Colne St, E13 . . . . .86 EG69
  off Grange Rd 86 EG69
Colne Valley, Upmin. RM14 . .73 FS58
Colne Way, Stai. TW19 . . . . .113 BB90
  Watford WD24, WD25 . . . . .24 BY37
Colney Hatch La, N10 . . . . . .44 DG52
  N11 . . . . .44 DF51
Colney Rd, Dart. DA1 . . . . . .128 FM86
COLNEY STREET, St.Alb. 9 CE31
Cologne Rd, SW11 . . . . .100 DD84
Colombo Rd, Ilf. IG1 . . . . .69 EQ60
Colombo St, SE1 . . . . .200 F3
Colomb St, SE10 . . . . .104 EE78
Colonels La, Cher. KT16 . . . .134 BG100
Colonels Wk, Enf. EN2 . . . . . .29 DP41
Colonial Av, Twick. TW2 . . . .116 CC85
  Slough SL1 . . . . .92 AU75
Colonial Way, Wat. WD24 . . .24 BX39
Colonnade, WC1 . . . . .195 P5
Colonnades, The, W2 . . . . . . .82 DB72
Colonnade Wk, SW1 . . . . . . .199 H9
Colosseum Ter, NW1
  off Albany St 83 DH70
Colson Gdns, Loug. IG10
  off Colson Rd 33 EP42
Colson Path, Loug. IG10 . . . .33 EN42
Colson Rd, Croy. CR0 . . . . . .142 DS103
  Loughton IG10 . . . . .33 EP42
Colson Way, SW16 . . . . .121 DJ91
Colsterworth Rd, N15 . . . . . .66 DT56
Colston Av, Cars. SM5 . . . . .158 DE105

Colston Cl, Cars. SM5
  off West St 158 DF105
Colston Cres, Wal.Cr. (Chsht.)
  EN7 . . . . .13 DP27
Colston Rd, E7 . . . . .86 EK65
  SW14 . . . . .98 CQ84
Colthurst Cres, N4 . . . . .66 DQ61
Colthurst Dr, N9
  off Plevna Rd 46 DV48
Coltishall Rd, Horn. RM12 . . .90 FJ65
Colt Ms, Enf. EN3
  off Government Row 31 EA37
Coltness Cres, SE2 . . . . .106 EV78
Colton Gdns, N17 . . . . .66 DQ55
Colton Rd, Har. HA1 . . . . .61 CE57
Coltsfoot Ct, Grays RM17 . . .110 GD79
Coltsfoot Dr, West Dr. UB7 . . .76 BL72
Coltsfoot La, Oxt. RH8 . . . . .188 EF133
Coltsfoot Path, Rom. RM3 . . .52 FJ52
Columbia Av, Edg. HA8 . . . . .42 CP53
  Ruislip HA4 . . . . .59 BV60
  Worcester Park KT4 . . . . . .139 CT101
Columbia Pt, SE16 . . . . .202 G6
Columbia Rd, E2 . . . . .197 P2
  E13 . . . . .86 EF70
Columbia Sq, SW14
  off Upper Richmond Rd W .98 CQ84
Columbia Wf Rd, Grays
  RM17 . . . . .110 GA79
Columbine Av, E6 . . . . .86 EL71
  South Croydon CR2 . . . . . .159 DP108
Columbine Way, SE13 . . . . . .103 EC82
  Romford RM3 . . . . .52 FL53
Columbus Ct, E1
  off Rotherhithe St 84 DW74
Columbus Ctyd, E14 . . . . . . .203 P2
Columbus Gdns, Nthwd. HA6 .39 BU53
Columbus Sq, Erith DA8 . . . .107 FF79
Colva Wk, N19
  off Chester Rd 65 DH61
Colvestone Cres, E8 . . . . .66 DT64
Colview Ct, SE9
  off Mottingham La 124 EK88
Colville Est, N1 . . . . .84 DS67
Colville Gdns, W11 . . . . .81 CZ72
Ⓗ Colville Hos, W11 . . . . . . .81 CZ72
Colville Ms, W11
  off Lonsdale Rd 81 CZ72
Colville Pl, W1 . . . . .195 L7
Colville Rd, E11 . . . . .67 EC62
  E17 . . . . .47 DY54
  N9 .46 DV46
  W3 .98 CP76
  W11 . . . . .81 CZ72
Colville Sq, W11 . . . . .81 CZ72
Colville Ter, W11 . . . . .81 CZ72
Colvin Cl, SE26 . . . . .122 DW92
Colvin Gdns, E4 . . . . .47 EC48
  E11 . . . . .68 EH56
  Ilford IG6 . . . . .49 EQ53
  Waltham Cross EN8 . . . . . . .31 DX35
Colvin Rd, E6 . . . . .86 EL66
  Thornton Heath CR7 . . . . . .141 DN99
Colwall Gdns, Wdf.Grn. IG8 . .48 EG50
Colwell Rd, SE22 . . . . .122 DT85
Colwick Cl, N6 . . . . .65 DK59
Colwith Rd, W6 . . . . .99 CW79
Colwood Gdns, SW19 . . . . . .120 DD94
Colworth Gro, SE17 . . . . . . .201 J9
Colworth Rd, E11 . . . . .68 EE58
  Croydon CR0 . . . . .142 DU102
Colwyn Av, Grnf. UB6 . . . . . .79 CF68
Colwyn Cl, SW16 . . . . .121 DJ92
Colwyn Cres, Houns. TW3 . . .96 CC81
Colwyn Grn, NW9
  off Snowdon Dr 62 CS58
Colwyn Rd, NW2 . . . . .63 CV62
Colyer Cl, N1 . . . . .83 DM68
  SE9 . . . . .125 EP89
Colyer Rd, Grav. (Nthflt.)
  DA11 . . . . .130 GC89
Colyers Cl, Erith DA8 . . . . . .107 FD81
Colyers La, Erith DA8 . . . . . .107 FC81
Colyers Wk, Erith DA8
  off Colyers La 107 FE81
Colyton Cl, Well. DA16 . . . . .106 EX81
  Wembley HA0
  off Bridgewater Rd 79 CJ65
  Woking GU21 . . . . .166 AW118
Colyton Rd, SE22 . . . . .122 DV85
Colyton Way, N18 . . . . .46 DU50
Combe Av, SE3 . . . . .104 EF80
Combe Bk Dr, Sev. (Sund.)
  TN14 . . . . .180 EY122
Combedale Rd, SE10 . . . . . . .205 M10
Combe La, Walt. KT12 . . . . .153 BT109
Combe Lo, SE7
  off Elliscombe Rd 104 EJ79
Combe Martin, Kings.T. KT2 .118 CQ92
Combemartin Rd, SW18 . . . .119 CY87
Combe Ms, SE3 . . . . .104 EF80
Comber Cl, NW2 . . . . .63 CV62
Comber Gro, SE5 . . . . .102 DQ81
Combermere Rd, SW9 . . . . .101 DM83
  Morden SM4 . . . . .140 DB100
Comberton Rd, E5 . . . . .66 DV61
Combeside, SE18 . . . . .105 ET80
Combwell Cres, SE2 . . . . . . .106 EU76
Comely Bk Rd, E17 . . . . .67 EC57
Comeragh Cl, Wok. GU22 . . .166 AU120
Comeragh Ms, W14 . . . . .99 CY78
Comeragh Rd, W14 . . . . .99 CY78
Comer Cres, Sthl. UB2
  off Windmill Av 96 CC75
Comerford Rd, SE4 . . . . .103 DY84
Comet Cl, E12 . . . . .68 EK63
  Purfleet RM19 . . . . .108 FN77
  Watford WD25 . . . . .7 BT34
Comet Pl, SE8 . . . . .103 EA80
Comet Rd, Stai. (Stanw.)
  TW19 . . . . .114 BK87
Comet St, SE8 . . . . .103 EA80
Comforts Fm Av, Oxt. RH8 . .188 EF133
Comfort St, SE15
  off St. Georges Way 102 DT79
Comfrey Ct, Grays RM17 . . .110 GD79

★ Place of interest   ⇌ Railway station   ⊖ London Underground station   DLR Docklands Light Railway station   ⬥ Tramlink station   Ⓗ Hospital

Commerce Rd, N22 . . . . .45 DM53
Brentford TW8 . . . . .97 CJ80
Commerce Way, Croy. CR0 . .141 DM103
Commercial Pl, Grav. DA12 .131 GJ86
Commercial Rd, E1 . . . . .84 DU72
E14 . . . . .84 DU72
N17 . . . . .46 DS51
N18 . . . . .46 DS50
Staines TW18 . . . . .114 BG93
Commercial St, E1 . . . . .197 P5
Commercial Way, NW10 . . . .80 CP68
SE15 . . . . .102 DT80
Woking GU21 . . . . .167 AZ117
Commerell St, SE10 . . . . . . .205 J10
Commodity Quay, E1 . . . . . .202 A1
Commodore St, E1 . . . . .85 DY70
Common, The, E15 . . . . .86 EE65
W5 . . . . .80 CL73
Kings Langley (Chipper.)
WD4 . . . . .6 BG32
Richmond TW10 . . . . .117 CK90
Southall UB2 . . . . .96 BW77
Stanmore HA7 . . . . .41 CE47
West Drayton UB7 . . . . . . .94 BJ77
Common Cl, Wok. GU21 . . .150 AX114
Commondale, SW15 . . . . . . .99 CW83
Commonfield La, SW17
off Tooting Gro 120 DE92
Commonfield Rd, Bans. SM7 158 DA114
Common Gate Rd, Rick. (Chorl.)
WD3 . . . . .21 BP43
Common La, Add. (New Haw)
KT15 . . . . .152 BJ109
Dartford DA2 . . . . .127 FG89
Esher (Clay.) KT10 . . . . . .155 CG108
Kings Langley WD4 . . . . . .6 BM28
Radlett WD7 . . . . .25 CE39
Watford (Let.Hth.) WD25 . . .25 CE39
Commonmeadow La, Wat. (Ald.)
WD25 . . . . .8 CB33
Common Mile Cl, SE4
off Crescent La 121 DK85
Common Rd, SW13 . . . . . . .99 CU83
Brentwood CM13 . . . . . . .55 GC50
Esher (Clay.) KT10 . . . . . .155 CG107
Leatherhead KT23 . . . . . .170 BY121
Rickmansworth (Chorl.)
WD3 . . . . .21 BD42
Slough (Langley) SL3 . . . . .93 BA77
Stanmore HA7 . . . . .41 CD49
Commonside, Epsom KT18 ..172 CN115
Keston BR2 . . . . .162 EJ105
Leatherhead (Bkhm.) KT23 170 CA122
Commonside Cl, Couls. CR5
off Coulsdon Rd 175 DP120
Sutton SM2 off Downs Rd .158 DB110
Commonside E, Mitch. CR4 .140 DF97
Commonside W, Mitch. CR4 .140 DF97
Commonwealth Av, W12 . . . .81 CV73
Hayes UB3 . . . . .77 BR72
★ Commonwealth Institute,
W8 . . . . .99 CZ76
Commonwealth Rd, N17 . . . .46 DU52
Caterham CR3 . . . . .176 DU123
Commonwealth Way, SE2 . .106 EV78
COMMONWOOD, Kings L. . . .6 BH34
Commonwood La, Kings L.
WD4 . . . . .22 BH35
Community Cl, Houns. TW5 . .95 BV81
Uxbridge UB10 . . . . .59 BQ62
Community La, N7 . . . . .65 DK64
Community Rd, E15 . . . . . . .67 ED64
Greenford UB6 . . . . .78 CC67
Community Wk, Esher KT10
off High St 154 CC105
Community Way, Rick. (Crox.Grn.)
WD3 off Barton Way 23 BP43
Como Rd, SE23 . . . . .123 DY89
Como St, Rom. RM7 . . . . . .71 FD57
Compass Hill, Rich. TW10 . .117 CK86
Compass Ho, SW18
off Smugglers Way 100 DB84
Compayne Gdns, NW6 . . . . .82 DB66
Comport Grn, Croy. (New Adgtn.)
CR0 . . . . .162 EE112
Compton Av, E6 . . . . .86 EK68
N1 . . . . .83 DP65
N6 . . . . .64 DE59
Brentwood CM13 . . . . . . .55 GC46
Romford RM2 . . . . .71 FH55
Compton Cl, E3 . . . . .85 EA71
NW1 . . . . .195 J3
NW11 off The Vale 63 CX62
W13 . . . . .79 CG72
Edgware HA8
off Pavilion Way 42 CQ52
Esher KT10 . . . . .154 CC106
Compton Ct, SE19
off Victoria Cres 122 DS92
Compton Cres, N17 . . . . . . .46 DQ52
W4 . . . . .98 CQ79
Chessington KT9 . . . . . .156 CL107
Northolt UB5 . . . . .78 BX67
Compton Gdns, Add. KT15
off Monks Cres 152 BH106
St. Albans AL2 . . . . .8 CB26
Compton Pas, EC1 . . . . . . .196 G4
Compton Pl, WC1 . . . . .195 P4
Erith DA8 . . . . .107 FF70
Watford WD19 . . . . .40 BY48
Compton Ri, Pnr. HA5 . . . . .60 BY57
Compton Rd, N1 . . . . .83 DP65
N21 . . . . .45 DN46
NW10 . . . . .81 CX69
SW19 . . . . .119 CZ93
Croydon CR0 . . . . .142 DV102
Hayes UB3 . . . . .77 BS73
Compton St, EC1 . . . . .196 F4
Compton Ter, N1 . . . . .83 DP65
Computer Ho, Brent. TW8 . . .97 CJ79
Comreddy Cl, Enf. EN2 . . . . .29 DP39
Comus Pl, SE17 . . . . .201 M9
Comyne Rd, Wat. WD24 . . . .23 BT36
Comyn Rd, SW11 . . . . .100 DE84
Comyns Cl, E16 . . . . .86 EF71

Comyns Rd, Dag. RM9 . . . . .88 FA66
Conant Ms, E1 off Back Ch La .84 DU73
Conaways Cl, Epsom KT17 . .157 CU110
Concanon Rd, SW2 . . . . . .101 DM84
Concert Hall App, SE1 . . . . .200 C3
Concord Cl, Nthlt. UB5
off Britannia Cl 78 BX69
Concorde Cl, Houns. TW3
off Lampton Rd 96 CB82
Uxbridge UB10 . . . . .76 BL68
Concorde Dr, E6 . . . . .87 EM71
Concord Wk, Horn. RM12
off Heron Flight Av 89 FH66
Concord Rd, W3 . . . . .80 CP70
Enfield EN3 . . . . .30 DW43
Concourse, The, N9
off New Rd 46 DU47
NW9 . . . . .43 CT53
Concrete Cotts, Wok. (Wisley)
GU23 off Wisley La 168 BL116
Condell Rd, SW8 . . . . .101 DJ81
Conder St, E14 off Salmon La .85 DY72
Conderton Rd, SE5 . . . . . . .102 DQ83
Condor Path, Nthlt. UB5
off Brabazon Rd 78 CA68
Condor Rd, Stai. TW18 . . . .134 BH97
Condover Cres, SE18 . . . . .105 EP80
Condray Pl, SW11 . . . . . . .100 DE80
Conduit, The, Red. (Bletch.)
RH1 . . . . .186 DS129
Conduit Av, SE10
off Crooms Hill 103 ED81
Conduit Ct, WC2 . . . . .195 P10
Conduit La, N18 . . . . .46 DW50
Croydon CR0 . . . . .160 DU106
Enfield EN3 off Morson Rd .31 DY44
South Croydon CR2 . . . . .160 DU106
Conduit Ms, SE18 . . . . . . .105 EP78
W2 . . . . .82 DD72
Conduit Pas, W2
off Conduit Pl 82 DD72
Conduit Pl, W2 . . . . .82 DD72
Conduit Rd, SE18 . . . . . . .105 EP78
Slough SL3 . . . . .92 AY78
Conduit St, W1 . . . . .195 J10
Conduit Way, NW10 . . . . . . .80 CQ66
Conegar Ct, Slou. SL1 . . . . .74 AS74
Conewood St, N5 . . . . .65 DP62
Coney Acre, SE21 . . . . . . .122 DQ88
Coney Burrows, E4
off Wyemead Cres 48 EE47
Coneybury, Red. (Bletch.)
RH1 . . . . .186 DS134
Coneybury Cl, Warl. CR6 . . .176 DV119
Coney Gro, Uxb. UB8 . . . . . .76 BN69
Coneygrove Path, Nthlt. UB5
off Arnold Rd 78 BY65
CONEY HALL, W.Wick. 144 EF104
Coney Hill Rd, W.Wick. BR4 .144 EE103
Coney Way, SW8 . . . . .101 DM79
Conference Cl, E4
off Greenbank Cl 47 EC47
★ Conference Forum, The,
E1 . . . . .84 DU72
Conference Rd, SE2 . . . . . .106 EW77
Congleton Gro, SE18 . . . . .105 EQ78
Congo Rd, SE18 . . . . .105 ER78
Congress Rd, SE2 . . . . . . .106 EW77
Congreve Rd, SE9 . . . . . . .105 EM83
Waltham Abbey EN9 . . . . .16 EE33
Congreve St, SE17 . . . . . . .201 M8
Congreve Wk, E16 . . . . .86 EK71
Conical Cor, Enf. EN2 . . . . . .30 DQ40
Conifer Av, Rom. RM5 . . . . .51 FB50
Conifer Cl, Orp. BR6 . . . . . .163 ER105
Reigate RH2 . . . . .184 DA132
Waltham Cross EN7 . . . . .14 DT29
Conifer Dr, Brwd. CM14 . . . .54 FX50
Conifer Gdns, SW16 . . . . . .121 DL90
Enfield EN1 . . . . .30 DS44
Sutton SM1 . . . . .140 DB103
Conifer La, Egh. TW20 . . . .113 BC92
Conifers, Wey. KT13 . . . . . .153 BS105
Conifers, The, Wat. WD25 . . .24 BW35
Conifers Cl, Tedd. TW11 . . .117 CH94
Conifer Way, Hayes UB3
off Longmead Rd 77 BU73
Swanley BR8 . . . . .147 FC95
Wembley HA0 . . . . .61 CJ62
Coniger Rd, SW6 . . . . .100 DA82
Coningesby Dr, Wat. WD17 . .23 BS39
Coningham Ms, W12
off Percy Rd 81 CU74
Coningham Rd, W12 . . . . . .99 CV75
Coningsby Cotts, W5
off Coningsby Rd 97 CK75
Coningsby Dr, Pot.B. EN6 . . .12 DD33
Coningsby Gdns, E4 . . . . . .47 EB51
Coningsby Rd, N4 . . . . .65 DP59
W5 . . . . .97 CJ75
South Croydon CR2 . . . . .160 DQ109
Conington Rd, SE13 . . . . . .103 EB82
Conisbee Ct, N14 . . . . .29 DJ43
Conisborough Cres, SE6 . . .123 EC90
Coniscliffe Cl, Chis. BR7 . . .145 EN95
Coniscliffe Rd, N13 . . . . . . .46 DQ48
Conista Ct, Wok. GU21
off Roundthorn Way 166 AT116
Coniston Av, Bark. IG11 . . . .87 ES66
Greenford UB6 . . . . .79 CH69
Upminster RM14 . . . . . . .72 FQ63
Welling DA16 . . . . .105 ES83
Coniston Cl, N20 . . . . .44 DC48
SW13 off Lonsdale Rd 99 CT80
SW20 . . . . .139 CX100
W4 . . . . .98 CQ81
Barking IG11
off Albert Rd 86 EL74
Bexleyheath DA7 . . . . . .107 FC81
Dartford DA1 . . . . .127 FH88
Erith DA8 . . . . .107 FE80
Coniston Ct, SW16
off Coniston Av 87 ES66
Bexleyheath DA7 . . . . . .107 FC81
Coniston Gdns, N9 . . . . . . .46 DW46
NW9 . . . . .62 CR57
Ilford IG4 . . . . .68 EL56
Pinner HA5 . . . . .59 BU56
Sutton SM2 . . . . .158 DD107

Coniston Gdns, Wem. HA9 . . .61 CJ60
Coniston Ho, SE5 . . . . .102 DQ80
Coniston Rd, N10 . . . . .45 DH54
N17 . . . . .46 DU51
Bexleyheath DA7 . . . . . .107 FC81
Bromley BR1 . . . . .124 EE93
Coulsdon CR5 . . . . .175 DJ116
Croydon CR0 . . . . .142 DU101
Kings Langley WD4 . . . . . .6 BM28
Twickenham TW2 . . . . . .116 CB86
Woking GU22 . . . . .167 BB120
Coniston Wk, E9 . . . . .66 DW64
off Clifden Rd 66 DW64
Coniston Way, Chess. KT9 . .138 CL104
Egham TW20 . . . . .113 BB94
Hornchurch RM12 . . . . . .71 FG64
Reigate RH2 . . . . .184 DE133
Conlan St, W10 . . . . .81 CY70
Conley Rd, NW10 . . . . .80 CS65
Conley St, SE10 . . . . .205 J10
Connaught Av, E4 . . . . .47 ED45
SW14 . . . . .98 CQ83
Ashford TW15 . . . . .114 BL91
Barnet EN4 . . . . .44 DF46
Enfield EN1 . . . . .30 DS40
Grays RM16 . . . . .110 GB75
Hounslow TW4 . . . . .116 BY85
Loughton IG10 . . . . .32 EK42
Connaught Br, E16 . . . . .86 EK74
Connaught Business Cen, Mitch.
CR4 off Wandle Way 140 DF99
Connaught Cl, E10 . . . . .67 DY61
W2 . . . . .194 B9
Enfield EN1 . . . . .30 DS40
Sutton SM1 . . . . .140 DD103
Uxbridge UB8 off New Rd . .77 BQ70
Connaught Ct, E17
off Orford Rd 67 EB56
Buckhurst Hill IG9 . . . . . .48 EH46
Connaught Dr, NW11 . . . . . .64 DA56
Weybridge KT13 . . . . . . .152 BN111
Connaught Gdns, N10 . . . . .65 DH57
N13 . . . . .45 DP49
Morden SM4 . . . . .140 DC98
Connaught Hill, Loug. IG10 . .32 EK42
Connaught La, Ilf. IG1
off Connaught Rd 69 ER61
Connaught Ms, SE18 . . . . . .105 EN78
Ilford IG1
off Connaught Rd 69 ER61
Connaught Pl, W2 . . . . .194 D10
Connaught Rd, E4 . . . . .48 EE45
E11 . . . . .67 ED60
E16 . . . . .86 EK74
E17 . . . . .67 EA57
N4 . . . . .65 DN59
NW10 . . . . .80 CS67
SE18 . . . . .105 EN78
W13 . . . . .79 CH73
Barnet EN5 . . . . .27 CX44
Harrow HA3 . . . . .47 CF53
Hornchurch RM12 . . . . . .72 FK62
Ilford IG1 . . . . .69 ER61
New Malden KT3 . . . . . .138 CS98
Richmond TW10
off Albert Rd 118 CM85
Slough SL1 . . . . .92 AV75
Sutton SM1 . . . . .140 DD103
Teddington TW11 . . . . . .117 CD92
Connaught Roundabout, E16
off Connaught Br 86 EK73
Connaught Sq, W2 . . . . . . .194 D9
Connaught St, W2 . . . . . . .194 B9
Connaught Way, N13 . . . . . .45 DP49
Connell Cres, W5 . . . . .80 CM70
Connemara Cl, Borwd. WD6
off Percheron Rd 26 CR44
Connington Cres, E4 . . . . . .47 ED48
Connop Rd, Enf. EN3 . . . . . .31 DX38
Connor Cl, E11 . . . . .68 EE59
Ilford IG6 . . . . .49 EP53
Connor Rd, Dag. RM9 . . . . . .70 EZ63
Connor St, E9
off Lauriston Rd 85 DX67
Conolly Rd, W7 . . . . .79 CE74
Conquest Rd, Add. KT15 . . .152 BG106
Conrad Cl, Grays RM16 . . . .110 GB75
Conrad Dr, Wor.Pk. KT4 . . . .139 CW102
Conrad Gdns, Grays RM16 . .110 GA75
Conrad Ho, N16 . . . . .66 DS64
Consfield Av, N.Mal. KT3 . . .139 CU98
Consort Cl, Brwd. CM14 . . . .54 FW50
Consort Ms, Islw. TW7 . . . . .117 CD85
Consort Rd, SE15 . . . . .102 DV81
Consort Way, Uxb. (Denh.) UB9
off Knowland Way 57 BF58
Cons St, SE1 . . . . .200 E4
Constable Av, E16 . . . . .205 P2
Constable Cl, NW11 . . . . . . .64 DB58
Hayes UB4
off Charville La 77 BQ69
Constable Cres, N15 . . . . . .66 DU57
Constable Gdns, Edg. HA8 . .42 CN53
Isleworth TW7 . . . . .117 CD85
Constable Ms, Dag. RM8
off Stonard Rd 70 EV63
Constable Rd, Grav. (Nthflt.)
DA11 . . . . .130 GE90
Constable Wk, SE21 . . . . . .122 DT90
Constance Cres, Brom. BR2 .144 EF101
Constance Rd, Croy. CR0 . . .141 DP101
Enfield EN1 . . . . .30 DS44
Sutton SM1 . . . . .158 DC105
Twickenham TW2 . . . . . .116 CB87
Constance St, E16
off Albert Rd 86 EL74
Constantine Pl, Uxb. (Hlgdn.)
UB10 . . . . .76 BM67
Constantine Rd, NW3 . . . . . .64 DE63
Constitution Hill, SW1 . . . . .199 H4
Gravesend DA12 . . . . . .131 GJ88
Woking GU21 . . . . .166 AY119
Constitution Ri, SE18 . . . . .105 EN81
Consul Av, Dag. RM9 . . . . . .89 FC69
W13 off Northcroft Rd 97 CH76
Consul Gdns, Swan. BR8 . . .127 FG94
Content St, SE17 . . . . .201 J9
Contessa Cl, Orp. BR6 . . . . .163 ES106

Control Twr Rd, Houns. (Hthrw.Air.)
TW6 . . . . .94 BN83
Convair Wk, Nthlt. UB5
off Kittiwake Rd 78 BX69
Convent Cl, Beck. BR3 . . . . .123 EC94
Convent Gdns, W5 . . . . .97 CJ77
W11 off Kensington Pk Rd . .81 CZ72
Convent Hill, SE19 . . . . . . .122 DQ93
Convent La, Cob. KT11
off Seven Hills Rd 153 BS111
Convent Rd, Ashf. TW15 . . .114 BN92
Convent Way, Sthl. UB2 . . . .96 BW77
Conway Cl, Rain. RM13 . . . . .89 FG66
Stanmore HA7 . . . . .41 CG51
Conway Cres, Grnf. UB6 . . . .79 CE68
Romford RM6 . . . . .70 EW59
Conway Dr, Ashf. TW15 . . . .115 BQ93
Hayes UB3 . . . . .95 BQ76
Sutton SM2 . . . . .158 DB107
Conway Gdns, Enf. EN2 . . . .30 DS38
Grays RM17 . . . . .110 GB80
Mitcham CR4 . . . . .141 DK98
Wembley HA9 . . . . .61 CJ59
Conway Gro, W3 . . . . .80 CR71
Conway Ms, W1 . . . . .195 K5
Conway Rd, N14 . . . . .45 DL48
N15 . . . . .65 DP57
NW2 . . . . .63 CW61
SE18 . . . . .105 ER77
SW20 . . . . .139 CW95
Feltham TW13 . . . . .116 BX92
Hounslow TW4 . . . . .116 BZ87
Hounslow (Hthrw.Air.) TW6
off Inner Ring E 95 BP83
Conway St, E13 . . . . .86 EG70
W1 . . . . .195 K5
Conway Wk, Hmptn. TW12
off Fearnley Cres 116 BZ93
Conybeare, NW3
off King Henry's Rd 82 DE66
Conybury Cl, Wal.Abb. EN9 . .16 EG32
Cony Cl, Wal.Cr. (Chsht.) EN7 .14 DS26
Conyers Cl, Wal. KT12 . . . . .154 BX106
Woodford Green IG8 . . . . .48 EE51
Conyers Rd, SW16 . . . . . . .121 DK92
Conyer St, E3 . . . . .85 DY68
Conyers Way, Loug. IG10 . . .33 EP41
Cooden Cl, Brom. BR1
off Plaistow La 124 EH94
Cook Ct, SE16
off Rotherhithe St 84 DW74
Cooke Cl, E14 off Cabot Sq . .85 EA74
Cookes Cl, E11 . . . . .68 EF61
Cookes La, Sutt. SM3 . . . . .157 CY107
Cookham Cl, Sthl. UB2 . . . . .96 CB75
Cookham Cres, SE16 . . . . . .203 H4
Cookham Dene Cl, Chis.
BR7 . . . . .145 ER95
Cookham Hill, Orp. BR6 . . . .146 FA104
Cookham Rd, Sid. DA14 . . . .126 FA94
Swanley BR8 . . . . .146 FA95
Cookhill Rd, SE2 . . . . .106 EV75
Cook Rd, Dag. RM9 . . . . . . .88 EY67
Cooks Cl, Rom. RM5 . . . . . .51 FC53
Cook's Hole Rd, Enf. EN2 . . .29 DP38
Cooks Mead, Bushey WD23 . .24 CB44
Cookson Gro, Erith DA8 . . . .107 FB80
Cook Sq, Erith DA8 . . . . . . .107 FF80
Cook's Rd, E15 . . . . .85 EB68
Cooks Rd, SE17 . . . . .101 DP79
Coolfin Rd, E16 . . . . .86 EG72
Coolgardie Av, E4 . . . . .47 EC50
Chigwell IG7 . . . . .49 EN48
Coolgardie Rd, Ashf. TW15 . .115 BQ92
Coolhurst Rd, N8 . . . . .65 DK58
Cool Oak La, NW9 . . . . .62 CS59
Coomassie Rd, W9
off Bravington Rd 81 CZ70
COOMBE, Kings.T. 118 CQ94
Coombe, The, Bet. RH3 . . . .182 CR131
Coombe Av, Croy. CR0 . . . .160 DS105
Sevenoaks TN14 . . . . . .181 FH120
Coombe Bk, Kings.T. KT2 . . .138 CS95
Coombe Cl, Edg. HA8 . . . . . .42 CM54
Hounslow TW3 . . . . .96 CA84
Coombe Cor, N21 . . . . .45 DP46
Coombe Cres, Hmptn. TW12 .116 BZ94
Coombe Dr, Add. KT15 . . . .151 BF107
Kingston upon Thames
KT2 . . . . .118 CR94
Ruislip HA4 . . . . .59 BV60
Coombe End, Kings.T. KT2 . .118 CR94
Coombefield Cl, N.Mal. KT3 .138 CS99
Coombe Gdns, SW20 . . . . .139 CU96
New Malden KT3 . . . . . .139 CT98
Coombe Hts, Kings.T. KT2 . .118 CS94
Coombe Hill Glade, Kings.T.
KT2 . . . . .118 CS94
Coombe Hill Rd, Kings.T.
KT2 . . . . .118 CS94
Rickmansworth (Mill End)
WD3 . . . . .38 BG45
Coombe Ho Chase, N.Mal.
KT3 . . . . .138 CR95
Coombehurst Cl, Barn. EN4 . .28 DF40
Coombelands La, Add. KT15 .152 BG107
◆ Coombe Lane 160 DW106
Coombe La, SW20 . . . . . . .139 CU95
Croydon CR0 . . . . .160 DV106
Coombe La W, Kings.T. KT2 .118 CR94
Coombe Lea, Brom. BR1 . . .144 EL97
Coombe Neville, Kings.T.
KT2 . . . . .118 CR94
Coombe Pk, Kings.T. KT2 . . .118 CR92
Coombe Ridings, Kings.T.
KT2 . . . . .118 CQ92
Coombe Ri, Brwd. CM15 . . . .55 FZ46
Kingston upon Thames
KT2 . . . . .138 CQ95
Coombe Rd, N22 . . . . .45 DN53
NW10 . . . . .62 CR62
SE26 . . . . .122 DV91
W4 . . . . .98 CS78
W13 off Northcroft Rd 97 CH76
Bushey WD23 . . . . .24 CC45
Croydon CR0 . . . . .160 DR105
Gravesend DA12 . . . . . .131 GJ89

Coombe Rd, Hmptn. TW12 . .116 BZ93
Kings.T. KT2 . . . . .138 CN95
New Malden KT3 . . . . . .138 CS96
Romford RM3 . . . . .72 FM55
Coomber Way, Croy. CR0 . . .141 DK101
Coombes Rd, Dag. RM9 . . . .88 EZ67
St. Albans (Lon.Col.) AL2 . . .9 CH26
Coombe Vale, Ger.Cr. SL9 . . .56 AY60
Coombe Wk, Sutt. SM1 . . . .140 DB104
Coombe Wd, W.Byf. (Byfleet)
KT14 . . . . .152 BM112
Coombewood Dr, Rom. RM6 .70 EZ58
Coombe Wd Hill, Pur. CR8 . .160 DQ112
Coombe Wd Rd, Kings.T.
KT2 . . . . .118 CQ92
Coombfield Dr, Dart. (Lane End)
DA2 . . . . .129 FR91
Coombs St, N1 . . . . .196 G1
Coomer Ms, SW6
off Coomer Pl 99 CZ79
Coomer Pl, SW6 . . . . .99 CZ79
Coomer Rd, SW6
off Coomer Pl 99 CZ79
Cooms Wk, Edg. HA8
off East Rd 42 CQ53
Cooperage Cl, N17
off Brantwood Rd 46 DT51
Cooper Av, E17 . . . . .47 DX53
Cooper Cl, SE1 . . . . .200 E5
Greenhithe DA9 . . . . . . .129 FT85
Cooper Cr, E15 off Clays La . .67 EB64
Cooper Cres, Cars. SM5 . . .140 DF104
Cooper Rd, NW4 . . . . .63 CX58
NW10 . . . . .63 CU64
Croydon CR0 . . . . .159 DN105
COOPERSALE, Epp. 18 EX29
off King Henry's Rd 82 DE66
CM16 . . . . .18 EX28
Coopersale La, Epp. CM16 . .34 EU37
Coopersale Rd, E9 . . . . .67 DX64
Coopersale St, Epp. CM16 . .18 EW32
Coopersall Rd, Wdf.Grn. IG8
off Navestock Cres 48 EJ52
Coopers Cl, E1 . . . . .84 DW70
Chigwell IG7 . . . . .50 EV47
Dagenham RM10 . . . . . . .89 FB65
Dartford (S.Darenth) DA4 . .148 FQ96
Staines TW18 . . . . .113 BE92
Coopers Cres, Borwd. WD6 . .26 CQ39
Coopers Hill La, Egh. TW20 .112 AY91
Coopers Hill Rd, Red. (Nutfld.)
RH1 . . . . .185 DM133
Coopers La, E10 . . . . .67 EB60
NW1 . . . . .83 DK68
SE12 . . . . .124 EH89
Potters Bar EN6 . . . . . . .12 DD31
Coopers La, Pot.B. EN6 . . . .12 DD31
Coopers La Rd, Pot.B. EN6 . .12 DE31
Coopers Ms, Wat. WD25
off High Elms La 8 BW31
Coopers Rd, SE1 . . . . .102 DT78
Gravesend (Nthflt.) DA11 . .130 GE88
Potters Bar EN6 . . . . . . .12 DC30
Coopers Row, EC3 . . . . . . .197 P10
Coopers Row, Iver SL0 . . . . .75 BC70
Coopers Shaw Rd, Til. RM18 .111 GK80
Cooper St, E16
off Lawrence St 86 EF71
Coopers Wk, E15 . . . . .67 ED64
off Maryland St 67 ED64
Waltham Cross (Chsht.)
EN8 . . . . .15 DX28
Cooper's Yd, SE19
off Westow Hill 122 DS93
Coote Gdns, Dag. RM8 . . . . .70 EZ62
Coote Rd, Bexh. DA7 . . . . . .106 EZ81
Dagenham RM8 . . . . .70 EZ62
Copeland Dr, E14 . . . . .204 A8
Copeland Rd, E17 . . . . .67 EB57
SE15 . . . . .102 DU82
Copeman Cl, SE26 . . . . . . .122 DW92
Copenhagen Gdns, W4 . . . . .98 CQ75
Copenhagen Pl, E14 . . . . . . .85 DZ72
Copenhagen St, N1 . . . . . . .83 DL67
Copenhagen Way, Walt.
KT12 . . . . .135 BV104
Cope Pl, W8 . . . . .100 DA76
Copers Cope Rd, Beck. BR3 .123 DZ93
Cope St, SE16 . . . . .203 H8
Copford Cl, Wdf.Grn. IG8 . . .48 EL51
Copford Wk, N1
off Popham St 84 DQ67
Copgate Path, SW16 . . . . . .121 DM93
Copinger Wk, Edg. HA8
off North Rd 42 CP53
Copland Av, Wem. HA0 . . . . .61 CK64
Copland Cl, Wem. HA0 . . . . .61 CJ64
Copland Ms, Wem. HA0
off Copland Rd 80 CL65
Copland Rd, Wem. HA0 . . . . .80 CL65
Copleigh Dr, Tad. KT20 . . . .173 CY120
Copleston Ms, SE15
off Copleston Rd 102 DT82
Copleston Pas, SE15 . . . . . .102 DT83
Copleston Rd, SE15 . . . . . .102 DT83
Copley Cl, SE17
off Hillingdon St 101 DP79
W7 . . . . .79 CF71
Redhill RH1 . . . . .184 DE132
Woking GU21 . . . . .166 AS119
Copley Dene, Brom. BR1 . . .144 EK95
Copley Pk, SW16 . . . . .121 DM93
Copley Rd, Stan. HA7 . . . . . .41 CJ50
Copley St, E1 . . . . .85 DX71
Copley Way, Tad. KT20 . . . .173 CX120
Copmans Wick, Rick. (Chorl.)
WD3 . . . . .21 BD43
Copnor Way, SE15
off Diamond St 102 DS80
Coppard Gdns, Chess. KT9 .155 CJ107
Copped Hall, SE21
off Glazebrook Cl 122 DR89
Coppelia Rd, SE3 . . . . .104 EF84
Coppen Rd, Dag. RM8 . . . . . .70 EZ59

Cop - Cou

Copperas St, SE8 ....103 EB79
Copperbeech Cl, NW3
  off Akenside Rd 64 DD64
Copper Beech Cl, NW3
  off Daleham Ms 82 DD65
  Gravesend DA12 .....131 GK87
  Ilford IG5 ....49 EN53
  Orpington BR5
    off Rookery Gdns ...146 EW99
  Woking GU22 ......166 AV121
Copper Beech Ct, Loug. IG10 .33 EN39
Copper Beeches, Islw. TW7
  off Eversley Cres 97 CD81
Copper Beech Rd, S.Ock.
  RM15 ....91 FW69
Copper Cl, SE19
  off Auckland Rd 122 DT94
Copperdale Rd, Hayes UB3 ..95 BU75
Copperfield, Chig. IG7 ....49 ER51
Copperfield App, Chig. IG7 ..49 ER51
Copperfield Av, Uxb. UB8 ...76 BN71
Copperfield Cl, S.Croy. CR2 .160 DQ111
Copperfield Ct, Lthd. KT22
  off Kingston Rd 171 CG121
  Pinner HA5
    off Copperfield Way ...60 BZ56
Copperfield Dr, N15 ....66 DT56
Copperfield Gdns, Brwd.
  CM14 ....54 FV46
Copperfield Ms, N18 ......46 DS50
Copperfield Ri, Add. KT15 ..151 BF106
Copperfield Rd, E3 ....85 DY70
  SE28 ....88 EW72
Copperfields, Dart. DA1
  off Spital St 128 FL86
  Leatherhead (Fetch.) KT22 .170 CC122
Copperfield St, SE1 ......200 G4
Copperfields Way, Rom.
  RM3 ....52 FK53
Copperfield Ter, Slou. SL2
  off Mirador Cres 74 AV73
  Pinner HA5 ....60 BZ56
Coppergate Cl, Brom. BR1 ..144 EH95
Coppergate Ct, Wal.Abb. EN9
  off Farthingale La 16 EG34
Copper Mead Cl, NW2 .....63 CW62
Copper Mill Dr, Islw. TW7 ..97 CF82
Coppermill La, E17 ....66 DW58
Copper Mill La, SW17 ....120 DC91
Coppermill La, Rick. WD3 ...37 BE52
  Uxbridge (Hare.) UB9 ..37 BE52
Coppermill Rd, Stai. (Wrays.)
  TW19 ....113 BA86
Copper Ridge, Ger.Cr. (Chal.St.P.)
  SL9 ....37 AZ50
Copper Row, SE1 ....201 P3
Coppetts Cl, N12 ....44 DE52
Coppetts Rd, N10 ....44 DG54
H Coppetts Wood Hosp, N10 .44 DF53
Coppice, The, Ashf. TW15
  off School Rd 115 BP93
  Enfield EN2 ....29 DP42
  Watford WD19 ......24 BW44
  West Drayton UB7 ....76 BL72
Coppice Cl, SW20 ....139 CW97
  Beckenham BR3 .....143 EB98
  Ruislip HA4 ....59 BR58
  Stanmore HA7 ....41 CF51
Coppice Dr, SW15 ......119 CV86
  Staines (Wrays.) TW19 ..112 AX87
Coppice End, Wok. GU22 ..167 BE116
Coppice La, Reig. RH2 ....183 CZ132
Coppice Path, Chig. IG7 ....50 EV49
Coppice Row, Epp. (They.B.)
  CM16 ....33 EM36
Coppice Wk, N20 ....44 DA48
Coppice Way, E18 ....68 EF56
Coppies Gro, N11 ....44 DG49
Copping Cl, Croy. CR0
  off Tipton Dr 160 DS105
Coppins, The, Croy. (New Adgtn.)
  CR0 ....161 EB107
  Harrow HA3 ....41 CE51
Coppins La, Iver SL0 ......75 BF71
Coppock Cl, SW11 ......100 DE82
Coppsfield, W.Mol. KT8
  off Hurst Rd 136 CA97
Copse, The, E4 ....48 EF46
  Caterham CR3
    off Tupwood La 186 DU126
  Leatherhead (Fetch.) KT22 .170 CB123
Copse Av, W.Wick. BR4 ...143 EB104
Copse Cl, SE7 ....104 EH79
  Northwood HA6 ......39 BQ54
  West Drayton UB7 ....94 BK76
Copse Edge Av, Epsom KT17 .157 CT113
Copse Glade, Surb. KT6 ...137 CK102
COPSE HILL, SW20 ......119 CU94
Copse Hill, SW20 ....119 CU94
  Purley CR8 ....159 DL113
  Sutton SM2 ....158 DB108
Copse La, Beac. (Jordans)
  HP9 ....36 AS52
Copsem Dr, Esher KT10 ...154 CB107
Copsem La, Esher KT10 ...154 CB107
  Leatherhead (Oxshott)
  KT22 ....154 CC111
Copsem Way, Esher KT10 ..154 CC107
Copsen Wd, Lthd. KT22 ...154 CC111
Copse Rd, Cob. KT11 .....153 BV113
  Woking GU21 ......166 AT118
Copse Vw, S.Croy. CR2 ...161 DX109
Copse Wd, Iver SL0 ......75 BD67
Copsewood Cl, Sid. DA15 ..125 ES86
Copse Wd Ct, Reig. RH2
  off Green La 184 DE132
Copsewood Rd, Wat. WD24 .23 BV39
Copse Wd Way, Nthwd. HA6 .39 BQ52
Coptefield Dr, Belv. DA17 ..106 EX76
Coptfold Rd, Brwd. CM14 ..54 FW47
Copthall Av, EC2 ....197 L8
Copthall Bldgs, EC2 ......197 K8
Copthall Cl, EC2 ....197 K8

Copthall Cl, Ger.Cr. (Chal.St.P.)
  SL9 ....37 AZ52
Copthall Cor, Ger.Cr. (Chal.St.P.)
  SL9 ....36 AY52
Copthall Ct, EC2 ....84 DR72
Copthall Dr, NW7 ....43 CU52
Copthall Gdns, NW7 ......43 CU52
  Twickenham TW1 ....117 CF88
Copthall La, Ger.Cr. (Chal.St.P.)
  SL9 ....36 AY52
Copthall Rd E, Uxb. UB10 ..58 BN61
Copthall Rd W, Uxb. UB10 ..58 BN61
Copthall Way, Add. (New Haw)
  KT15 ....151 BF110
Copt Hill La, Tad. KT20 ...173 CY120
Copthorne Av, SW12 .....121 DK87
  Bromley BR2 ....145 EM103
  Ilford IG6 ....49 EP51
Copthorne Chase, Ashf. TW15
  off Ford Rd 114 BM91
Copthorne Cl, Rick. (Crox.Grn.)
  WD3 ....22 BM43
  Shepperton TW17 ...135 BQ100
Copthorne Gdns, Horn.
  RM11 ....72 FN57
Copthorne Ms, Hayes UB3 ..95 BS77
Copthorne Ri, S.Croy. CR2 .160 DR113
Copthorne Rd, Lthd. KT22 .171 CH120
  Rickmansworth (Crox.Grn.)
  WD3 ....22 BM44
Coptic St, WC1 ....195 P7
Copwood Cl, N12 ....44 DD49
Coral Cl, Rom. RM6 ......70 EW56
Coraline Cl, Sthl. UB1 .....78 BZ69
Coralline Wk, SE2 ......106 EW75
Coral Row, SW11
  off Gartons Way 100 DC83
Coral St, SE1 ....200 E5
Coram Grn, Brwd. CM13 ...55 GD44
Coram St, WC1 ....195 P5
Coran Cl, N9 ....47 DX45
Corban Rd, Houns. TW3 ....96 CA83
Corbar Cl, Barn. EN4 ......28 DD38
Corbden Cl, SE15 ....102 DT81
Corbet Cl, Wall. SM6 ....140 DG102
Corbet Ct, EC3 ....197 L9
Corbet Pl, E1 ....197 P6
Corbet Rd, Epsom KT17 ...156 CS110
Corbets Av, Upmin. RM14 ..72 FP64
CORBETS TEY, Upmin. 72 FQ65
Corbets Tey Rd, Upmin. RM14 .72 FP63
Corbett Cl, Croy. CR0 ....161 ED112
Corbett Gro, N22 ....45 DL52
Corbett Ho, Wat. WD19 ....40 BW48
Corbett Rd, E11 ....68 EJ58
  E17 ....67 EC55
Corbetts La, SE16 ......202 F9
Corbetts Pas, SE16 .....202 F9
Corbicum, E11 ....68 EE59
Corbiere Ct, SW19
  off Thornton Rd 119 CX93
Corbiere Ho, N1 ....84 DS67
Corbins La, Har. HA2 .....60 CB62
Corbridge Cres, E2 ......84 DV68
Corby Cl, Egh. (Eng.Grn.)
  TW20 ....112 AW93
  St. Albans AL2 ......8 CA25
Corby Cres, Enf. EN2 .....29 DL42
Corby Dr, Egh. (Eng.Grn.)
  TW20 ....112 AV93
Corbylands Rd, Sid. DA15 ..125 ES87
Corbyn St, N4 ....65 DL60
Corby Rd, NW10 ....80 CR68
Corby Way, E3 off Knapp Rd ..85 EA70
Corcorans, Brwd. CM15 ....54 FV44
Cordelia Cl, SE24 ......101 DP84
Cordelia Gdns, Stai. TW19 ..114 BL87
Cordelia Rd, Stai. TW19 ..114 BL87
Cordelia St, E14 ....85 EB72
Cordell Cl, Wal.Cr. (Chsht.)
  EN8 ....15 DY28
Cordell Ho, N15
  off Newton Rd 66 DT57
Corderoy Pl, Cher. KT16 ...133 BE100
Cordingley Rd, Ruis. HA4 ...59 BR61
Cording St, E14 off Chrisp St ..85 EB71
Cordons Cl, Ger.Cr. (Chal.St.P.)
  SL9 ....36 AX53
Cordova Rd, E3 ....85 DY69
Cordrey Gdns, Couls. CR5 .175 DL115
Cordwainers Wk, E13
  off Clegg St 86 EG68
Cord Way, E14 ....204 A6
Cordwell Rd, SE13 ......124 EE85
Corefield Cl, N11
  off Benfleet Way 44 DG47
Corelli Rd, SE3 ....104 EL82
Corfe Av, Har. HA2 ......60 CA63
Corfe Cl, Ashtd. KT21 ....171 CJ118
  Borehamwood WD6
    off Chester Rd 26 CR41
  Hayes UB4 ....78 BW72
Corfe Twr, W3 ....98 CP75
Corfield Rd, N21 ....29 DM43
Corfield St, E2 ....84 DV69
Corfton Rd, W5 ....80 CL72
Coriander Av, E14 ....85 ED72
Cories Cl, Dag. RM8 ......70 EX61
Corinium Cl, Wem. HA9 ...62 CM63
Corinium Ind Est, Amer. HP6 .20 AT38
Corinne Rd, N19 ....65 DJ63
Corinthian Manorway, Erith
  DA8 ....107 FD77
Corinthian Rd, Erith DA8 ..107 FD77
Corinthian Way, Stai. (Stanw.)
  TW19 off Clare Rd ...114 BK87
Corker Wk, N7 ....65 DM61
Corkran Rd, Surb. KT6 ...137 CK101
Corkscrew Hill, W.Wick. BR4 .143 ED103
Cork Sq, E1 ....202 D2
Cork St, W1 ....199 K1
Cork St Ms, W1 ....199 K1
Cork Tree Way, E4 ......47 DY50
Corlett St, NW1 ....194 B6
Cormongers La, Red. (Nutfld.)
  RH1 ....185 DK131

Cormont Rd, SE5 ....101 DP81
Cormorant Cl, E17
  off Banbury Rd 47 DX53
Cormorant Ho, Enf. EN3
  off Alma Rd 31 DX43
Cormorant Pl, Sutt. SM1 ..157 CZ106
Cormorant Rd, E7 ....86 EF63
Cormorant Wk, Horn. RM12
  off Heron Flight Av ...89 FH65
Cornbury Rd, Edg. HA8 ....41 CK52
Cornelia Pl, Erith DA8
  off Queen St 107 FE79
Cornelia St, N7 ....83 DM65
Cornell Cl, Sid. DA14 ....126 EY93
Cornell Way, Rom. RM5 ...50 FA50
Corner, The, W5, Byf. KT14 ..152 BG113
Corner Fm Cl, Tad. KT20 ..173 CW122
Corner Grn, SE3 ....104 EG82
Corner Ho St, WC2 ......199 P2
Corner Mead, NW9 ......43 CT57
Cornerside, Ashf. TW15 ..115 BQ94
Corney Reach Way, W4 ...98 CS80
Corney Rd, W4 ....98 CS79
Cornfield Cl, Uxb. UB8
  off The Greenway 76 BK68
Cornfield Rd, Bushey WD23 ..24 CB42
Cornflower Cl, Croy. CR0 ..143 DX102
Cornflower La, Croy. CR0 ..143 DX102
Cornflower Ter, SE22 ....122 DV86
Cornflower Way, Rom. RM3 ..52 FL53
Cornford Cl, Brom. BR2 ...144 EG99
Cornford Gro, SW12 ....121 DH89
Cornhill, EC3 ....197 L9
Cornhill Cl, Add. KT15 ....134 BH103
Cornhill Dr, Enf. EN3
  off Ordnance Rd 31 DY37
Cornish Ct, N9 ....46 DV45
Cornish Gro, SE20 ......122 DV94
Cornish Ho, SE17
  off Otto St 101 DP79
  Brentford TW8
    off Green Dragon La ..98 CM78
Cornmill, Wal.Abb. EN9 ....15 EB33
Corn Mill Dr, Orp. BR6 ...145 ET101
Cornmill La, SE13 ......103 EB83
Cornmill Ms, Wal.Abb. EN9
  off Highbridge St 15 EB33
Commow Rd, NW10 ......63 CT64
Cornshaw Rd, Dag. RM8 ...70 EX60
Cornsland, Brwd. CM14 ....54 FX48
Cornsland Ct, Brwd. CM14 ..54 FW48
Cornthwaite Rd, E5 ......66 DW62
Cornwall Av, E2 ....84 DW69
  N3 ....44 DA52
  N22 ....45 DL53
  Esher (Clay.) KT10
    off The Causeway ...155 CF108
  Southall UB1 ....78 BZ71
  Welling DA16 ......105 ES83
  West Byfleet (Byfleet)
  KT14 ....152 BM114
Cornwall Cl, Bark. IG11 ....87 ET65
  Hornchurch RM11 .....72 FN56
  Waltham Cross EN8 ...15 DY33
Cornwall Cres, W11 ......81 CY73
Cornwall Dr, Orp. BR5 ....126 EW94
Cornwall Gdns, NW10 .....81 CV65
  SW7 ....100 DB76
Cornwall Gdns Wk, SW7
  off Cornwall Gdns ...100 DB76
Cornwall Gate, Purf. RM19
  off Fanns Ri 108 FN77
Cornwall Gro, W4 ....98 CS78
Cornwallis Av, N9 ....46 DV47
  SE9 ....125 ER89
Cornwallis Cl, Cat. CR3 ...176 DQ122
  Erith DA8 ....107 FF79
Cornwallis Gro, N9 ......46 DV47
Cornwallis Rd, E17 ......67 DX56
  N9 ....46 DV47
  N19 ....65 DL61
  Dagenham RM9 ......70 EX63
Cornwallis Sq, N19 ......65 DL61
Cornwallis Wk, SE9 ......125 EM83
Cornwall Ms S, SW7 .....100 DC76
Cornwall Ms W, SW7
  off Cornwall Gdns ...100 DB76
Cornwall Rd, N4 ....65 DN59
  N15 ....66 DR57
  N18 off Fairfield Rd ..46 DU50
  SE1 ....200 D2
  Brentwood CM15 .....54 FV43
  Croydon CR0 ......141 DP103
  Dartford DA1 ......128 FM83
  Esher (Clay.) KT10 ...155 CG108
  Harrow HA1 ....60 CC58
  Pinner HA5 ....40 BZ52
  Ruislip HA4 ....59 BT62
  Sutton SM2 ....157 CZ108
  Twickenham TW1 ....117 CG88
  Uxbridge UB8 ....76 BK65
  Windsor SL4 ....112 AU86
Cornwall Sq, SE11 ......200 F10
Cornwall St, E1 off Watney St ..84 DV73
Cornwall Ter, NW1 ......194 E5
Cornwall Ter Ms, NW1 ....194 E5
Cornwall Way, Stai. TW18 ..113 BE93
Corn Way, E11 ....67 ED62
Cornwell Av, Grav. DA12 ..131 GJ90
Cornwood Cl, N1 ....84 DD57
Cornwood Dr, E1 ....84 DW72
Cornworthy Rd, Dag. RM8 ..70 EW64
Corona Rd, SE12 ......124 EG87
Coronation Av, N16
  off Victorian Rd 66 DT62
  Slough (Geo.Grn.) SL3 ..74 AY72
  Windsor SL4 ....41 AT81
Coronation Cl, Bex. DA5 ..126 EX86
  Ilford IG6 ....49 EQ56
Coronation Dr, Horn. RM12 ..71 FH63
Coronation Hill, Epp. CM16 ..17 ET30
Coronation Rd, E13 ......86 EJ69
  NW10 ....80 CM69
  Hayes UB3 ....95 BT77
Coronation Wk, Twick. TW2 ..116 CA86
Coronet St, N1 ....197 M3
Corporation Av, Houns. TW4 ..96 BY84

Corporation Row, EC1 ....196 E4
Corporation St, E15 ......86 EE68
  N7 ....65 DL64
Corrance Rd, SW2 ......101 DL84
Corran Way, S.Ock. RM15 ..91 FV73
Corri Av, N14 ....45 DK49
Corrib Dr, Sutt. SM1 .....158 DE106
Corrie Gdns, Vir.W. GU25 ..132 AW101
Corrie Rd, Add. KT15 ....152 BK105
  Woking GU22 ......167 BC120
Corrigan Av, Couls. CR5 ..158 DG114
Corrigan Cl, NW4 ....63 CW55
Corringham Ct, NW11
  off Corringham Rd ...64 DB59
Corringham Rd, NW11 ....64 DA59
  Wembley HA9 ....62 CN61
Corringway, NW11 ......64 DB59
  W5 ....80 CN70
Corris Grn, NW9
  off Snowdon Dr 62 CS58
Corsair Cl, Stai. TW19 ....114 BK87
Corsair Rd, Stai. TW19 ...114 BL87
Corscombe Cl, Kings.T. KT2 ..118 CQ92
Corsehill St, SW16 ......121 DJ93
Corsham St, N1 ....197 L3
Corsica St, N5 ....83 DP65
Cortayne Rd, SW6 ....99 CZ82
Cortis Rd, SW15 ....119 CV86
Cortis Ter, SW15 ....119 CV86
Cortland Cl, Dart. DA1
  off Lower Sta Rd 127 FE86
Corunna Rd, SW8 ....101 DJ81
Corunna Ter, SW8 ......101 DJ81
Corve La, S.Ock. RM15 ....91 FV73
Corvette Sq, SE10
  off Feathers Pl 103 ED79
Corwell La, Uxb. UB8 .....77 BQ72
Cory Dr, Brwd. CM13 .....55 GB45
Coryton Path, W9
  off Ashmore Rd 81 CZ70
Cosbycote Av, SE24 .....122 DQ85
Cosdach Av, Wall. SM6 ...159 DK108
Cosedge Cres, Croy. CR0 ..159 DN106
Cosgrove Cl, N21 ....46 DQ47
  Hayes UB4
    off Kingsash Dr 78 BY70
Cosmo Pl, WC1 ....196 A6
Cosmur Cl, W12 ....99 CT76
Cossall Wk, SE15 ....102 DV81
Cossar Ms, SW2
  off Tulse Hill 121 DN86
Cosser St, SE1 ....200 D6
Costa St, SE15 ....102 DU82
Costead Manor Rd, Brwd.
  CM14 ....54 FV46
Costell's Meadow, West.
  TN16 ....189 ER126
Costons Av, Grnf. UB6 ....79 CD69
Costons La, Grnf. UB6 ....79 CD69
Coston Wk, SE4
  off Frendsbury Rd ...103 DX84
Cosway St, NW1 ....194 C6
Cotall St, E14 ....85 EA72
Coteford Cl, Loug. IG10 ....33 EP40
  Pinner HA5 ....59 BU57
Coteford St, SW17 .....120 DF91
Cotelands, Croy. CR0 ....142 DS104
Cotesbach Rd, E5 ....66 DW62
Cotesmore Gdns, Dag. RM8 ..70 EW63
Cotford Rd, Th.Hth. CR7 ..142 DQ98
Cotham St, SE17 ....201 J9
Cotherstone, Epsom KT19 ..156 CR110
Cotherstone Rd, SW2 ....121 DM88
Cotlandswick, St.Alb. (Lon.Col.)
  AL2 ....9 CJ26
Cotleigh Av, Bex. DA5 ....126 EX89
Cotleigh Rd, NW6 ....82 DA66
  Romford RM7 ....71 FD58
Cotman Cl, NW11 ....64 DC58
  SW15 off Westleigh Av ..119 CX86
Cotmandene Cres, Orp. BR5 .146 EU96
Cotman Gdns, Edg. HA8 ...42 CN54
Cotman Ms, Dag. RM8
  off Highgrove Rd 70 EW64
Cotmans Cl, Hayes UB3 ...77 BU74
Coton Rd, Well. DA16 ....106 EU83
Cotsford Av, N.Mal. KT3 ..138 CQ99
Cotswold Av, Bushey WD23 ..24 CC44
Cotswold Cl, Bexh. DA7 ..107 FE82
  Esher KT10 ....137 CF104
  Kingston upon Thames
  KT2 ....118 CP93
  Staines TW18 ......114 BG92
  Uxbridge UB8 ....76 BJ67
Cotswold Ct, EC1 ....197 H4
  N11 ....44 DG49
Cotswold Gdns, E6 ......86 EK69
  NW2 ....63 CX61
  Brentwood CM13 .....55 GE45
  Ilford IG2 ....69 ER59
Cotswold Gate, NW2
  off Cotswold Gdns ...63 CY60
Cotswold Grn, Enf. EN2
  off Cotswold Way 29 DM42
Cotswold Ms, SW11
  off Battersea High St ..100 DD81
Cotswold Ri, Orp. BR6 ...145 ET100
Cotswold Rd, Grav. (Nthflt.)
  DA11 ....130 GE90
  Hampton TW12 ......116 CA93
  Romford RM3 ....52 FM54
  Sutton SM2 ....158 DB110
Cotswold St, SE27
  off Norwood High St ..121 DP91
Cotswold Way, Enf. EN2 ...29 DM42
  Worcester Park KT4 ..139 CW103
Cottage Av, Brom. BR2 ...144 EL102
Cottage Cl, Cher. (Ott.) KT16 .151 BC107
  Rickmansworth (Crox.Grn.)
  WD3 off Scots Hill ...22 BM44
  Ruislip HA4 ....59 BR60
  Watford WD17 ......23 BT40
Cottage Fm Way, Egh. TW20
  off Green Rd 133 BC97
Cottage Fld Cl, Sid. DA14 ..126 EW88
Cottage Gdns, Wal.Cr. EN8 ..14 DW29

Cottage Grn, SE5 ....102 DR80
Cottage Gro, SW9 ......101 DL83
  Surbiton KT6 ......137 CK100
Cottage Homes, NW7 ....43 CU49
Cottage Pl, SW3 ....198 B6
Cottage Rd, Epsom KT19 ..156 CR108
Cottage St, E14 ....85 EB73
Cottage Wk, N16
  off Smalley Cl 66 DT62
Cottenham Dr, NW9 ......63 CT55
  SW20 ....119 CV94
Cottenham Par, SW20
  off Durham Rd 139 CV96
COTTENHAM PARK, SW20 ..119 CV95
Cottenham Pk Rd, SW20 ..119 CV94
Cottenham Pl, SW20 .....119 CV94
Cottenham Rd, E17 ......67 DZ56
Cotterill Rd, Surb. KT6 ...138 CL103
Cottesbrooke Cl, Slou. (Colnbr.)
  SL3 ....93 BD81
Cottesbrook St, SE14
  off Nynehead St 103 DY80
Cottesloe Ms, SE1 ......200 E6
Cottesmore Av, Ilf. IG5 ...49 EN54
Cottesmore Gdns, W8 ...100 DB76
Cottimore Av, Walt. KT12 .135 BV102
Cottimore Cres, Walt. KT12 .135 BV101
Cottimore La, Walt. KT12 ..135 BW102
Cottimore Ter, Walt. KT12 .135 BV101
Cottingham Chase, Ruis. HA4 .59 BU62
Cottingham Rd, SE20 ....123 DX94
  SW8 ....101 DM80
Cottington Rd, Felt. TW13 ..116 BX91
Cottington St, SE11 .....200 E10
Cottle Way, SE16 ....202 F5
Cotton Av, W3 ....80 CR72
Cotton Cl, Dag. RM9
  off Flamstead Rd 88 EW66
Cottongrass Cl, Croy. CR0
  off Cornflower La ...143 DX102
Cotton Hill, Brom. BR1 ...123 ED91
Cotton La, Dart. DA2 ....128 FQ86
  Greenhithe DA9 .....128 FQ85
Cotton Rd, Pot.B. EN6 ....12 DC31
Cotton Row, SW11 .....100 DC83
Cottons App, Rom. RM7 ...71 FD57
Cottons Ct, Rom. RM7 ....71 FD57
Cottons Gdns, E2 ......197 N2
Cottons La, SE1 ....201 L2
Cotton St, E14 ....85 EC73
Cottrell Ct, SE10
  off Greenroof Way ...104 EF76
Cotts Cl, W7
  off Westcott Cres 79 CF71
Couchmore Av, Esher KT10 .137 CE103
  Ilford IG5 ....49 EN64
Coulgate St, SE4 ....103 DY83
COULSDON 175 DJ116
Coulsdon Common, Cat.
  CR3 ....176 DQ121
Coulsdon Ct Rd, Couls. CR5 .175 DM116
Coulsdon La, Couls. CR5 ..174 DF119
Coulsdon Pl, Cat. CR3 ...176 DR122
Coulsdon Ri, Couls. CR5 ..175 DL117
Coulsdon Rd, Cat. CR3 ...176 DQ122
  Coulsdon CR5 ......175 DM115
⇌ Coulsdon South 175 DK116
Coulson Cl, Dag. RM8 ....70 EW59
Coulson Ct, SW3 ....198 D10
Coulter Cl, Hayes UB4
  off Berrydale Rd 78 BY70
  Potters Bar (Cuffley) EN6 ..13 DK27
Coulter Rd, W6 ....99 CV76
Coulton Av, Grav. (Nthflt.)
  DA11 ....130 GE87
Council Av, Grav. (Nthflt.)
  DA11 ....130 GC86
Council Cotts, Wok. (Wisley)
  GU23 off Wisley La ..168 BK115
Councillor St, SE5 ......102 DQ80
Counter Ct, SE1
  off Southwark St 84 DR74
Counter St, SE1 ....201 M3
Countess Cl, Uxb. (Hare.)
  UB9 ....38 BJ54
Countess Rd, NW5 ......65 DJ64
Countisbury Av, Enf. EN1 ..46 DT45
Countisbury Gdns, Add. KT15
  off Addlestone Pk ...152 BH106
Country Way, Felt. TW13 ..115 BV94
  Sunbury-on-Thames TW16 .115 BV94
County Gate, SE9 ....125 EQ90
  Barnet EN5 ....28 DB44
County Gro, SE5 ....102 DQ81
★ County Hall, SE1 ......200 B4
County Rd, E6 ....87 EP71
  Thornton Heath CR7 ..141 DP96
County St, SE1 ....201 J7
Coupland Pl, SE18 ......105 EQ78
Courage Cl, Horn. RM11 ...72 FJ58
Courage Wk, Brwd. CM13 ..55 GD44
Courcy Rd, N8 ....65 DN55
Courier Rd, Dag. RM9 ....89 FC70
Courland Gro, SW8 .....101 DK81
Courland Rd, Add. KT15 ..134 BH104
Courland St, SW8 ......101 DK81
Course, The, SE9 ....125 EN90
Coursers Rd, St.Alb. (Coln.Hth.)
  AL4 ....10 CN27
Court, The, Ruis. HA4 ....60 BY63
  Warlingham CR6 ....177 DY118
Courtauld Cl, SE28
  off Pitfield Cres 88 EU74
★ Courtauld Gall, WC2 ...196 B10
Courtauld Rd, N19 ......65 DK60
Courtaulds, Kings L. (Chipper.)
  WD4 ....6 BH30
Court Av, Belv. DA17 ....106 EZ78
  Coulsdon CR5 ......175 DN118
  Romford RM3 ....52 FN52
Court Bushes Rd, Whyt. CR3 .176 DU120
Court Cl, Har. HA3 ......62 CL55
  Twickenham TW2 ....116 CB90
  Wallington SM6 ....159 DK108
Court Cl Av, Twick. TW2 ..116 CB90
Court Cres, Chess. KT9 ..155 CK106
  Swanley BR8 ....147 FE98

Court Downs Rd, Beck. BR3 .143 EB96
★ Court Dress Collection,
  Kensington Palace, W8 ..100 DB75
Court Dr, Croy. CR0 ......159 DM105
  Stanmore HA7 ....42 CL49
  Sutton SM1 ....158 DE105
  Uxbridge UB10 ....76 BM67
Courtenay Av, N6 ....64 DE59
  Harrow HA3 ....40 CC53
  Sutton SM2 ....158 DA109
Courtenay Dr, Beck. BR3 .143 ED96
  Grays (Chaff.Hun.) RM16
    off Clifford Rd 110 FZ76
Courtenay Gdns, Har. HA3 ..40 CC54
  Upminster RM14 ....72 FQ60
Courtenay Ms, E17
    off Cranbrook Ms 67 DY57
Courtenay Pl, E17 ....67 DY57
Courtenay Rd, E11 ....68 EF62
  E17 ....67 DX56
  SE20 ....123 DX94
  Wembley HA9 ....61 CK63
  Woking GU21 ....167 BA116
  Worcester Park KT4 ....139 CW104
Courtenay Sq, SE11
    off Courtenay St 101 DN78
Courtenay St, SE11 ......200 D10
Courtens Ms, Stan. HA7 ....41 CJ52
Court Fm Av, Epsom KT19 .156 CR106
Court Fm Rd, SE9 ....124 EK89
  Northolt UB5 ....78 CA66
  Warlingham CR6 ....176 DU118
Courtfield, W5
    off Castlebar Hill 79 CJ71
Courtfield Av, Har. HA1 ....61 CF57
Courtfield Cres, Har. HA1 ..61 CF57
Courtfield Gdns, SW5 ....100 DB77
  W13 ....79 CG72
  Ruislip HA4 ....59 BT61
  Uxbridge (Denh.) UB9 ...58 BG62
Courtfield Ms, SW5
    off Courtfield Gdns ...100 DB77
Courtfield Ri, W.Wick. BR4 .143 ED104
Courtfield Rd, SW7 ......100 DB77
  Ashford TW15 ....115 BP93
Court Gdns, N7 ....83 DN65
Court Grn Hts, Wok. GU22 .166 AW120
Court Haw, Bans. SM7 ....174 DE115
Court Hill, Couls. CR5 ....174 DE118
  South Croydon CR2 ....160 DS112
Courthill Rd, SE13 ....103 EC84
Courthope Rd, NW3 ....64 DF63
  SW19 ....119 CY92
  Greenford UB6 ....79 CD68
Courthope Vil, SW19 .....119 CY94
Court Ho Gdns, N3 ....44 DA54
Courthouse Rd, N12 ....44 DB51
Courtland Av, E4 ....48 EF47
  NW7 ....42 CR48
  SW16 ....121 DM94
  Ilford IG1 ....69 EM61
Courtland Gro, SE28 ....88 EX73
Courtland Rd, E6
    off Harrow Rd 86 EL67
Courtlands, Rich. TW10 ....98 CN84
Courtlands Av, SE12 .....124 EH85
  Bromley BR2 ....144 EF102
  Esher KT10 ....154 BZ107
  Hampton TW12 ....116 BZ93
  Richmond TW9 ....98 CP82
  Slough SL3 ....92 AX77
Courtlands Cl, Ruis. HA4 ...59 BT59
  South Croydon CR2 ....160 DT110
  Watford WD24 ....23 BS35
Courtlands Cres, Bans. SM7 .174 DA116
Courtlands Dr, Epsom KT19 .156 CS107
  Watford WD17, WD24 ...23 BS37
Courtlands Rd, Surb. KT5 .138 CN101
Court La, SE21 ....122 DS86
  Epsom KT19 ....156 CQ113
  Iver SL0 ....76 BG74
Court La Gdns, SE21 .....122 DS87
Courtleas, Cob. KT11 ....154 CA116
Courtleet Dr, Erith DA8 ...107 FB81
Courtleigh Av, Barn. EN4 ..28 DD38
Courtleigh Gdns, NW11 ....63 CY56
Courtman Rd, N17 ....46 DQ52
Court Mead, Nthlt. UB5 ....78 BZ69
Courtmead Cl, SE24 .....122 DQ86
Courtnell St, W2 ....82 DA72
Courtney Cl, SE19 ....122 DS93
Courtney Cres, Cars. SM5 .158 DF108
Courtney Pl, Cob. KT11 ...154 BZ112
  Croydon CR0 ....141 DN104
Courtney Rd, N7
    off Bryantwood Rd 65 DN64
  SW19 ....120 DE94
  Croydon CR0 ....141 DN104
  Grays RM16 ....111 GJ75
  Hounslow (Hthrw.Air.) TW6 .94 BN83
Courtney Way, Houns. (Hthrw.Air.)
  TW6 off Courtney Rd 94 BN82
Court Par, Wem. HA0 ......61 CH62
Courtrai Rd, SE23 ....123 DY86
Court Rd, SE9 ....124 EL89
  SE25 ....142 DT96
  Banstead SM7 ....174 DA116
  Caterham CR3 ....176 DR123
  Dartford (Lane End) DA2 .129 FS92
  Godstone RH9 ....186 DW131
  Orpington BR6 ....146 EV101
  Southall UB2 ....96 BZ77
  Uxbridge UB10 ....59 BP64
Courtside, N8 ....65 DK58
Court St, E1 off Durward St .84 DV71
  Bromley BR1 ....144 EG96
Court Way, NW9 ....62 CS56
  W3 ....80 CQ71
  Ilford IG6 ....69 EQ55
  Romford RM3 ....52 FL54
  Twickenham TW2 ......117 CF87
Courtway, Wdf.Grn. IG8 ....48 EJ50
Courtway, The, Wat. WD19 ..40 BY47
Court Wd Dr, Sev. TN13 ...190 FG124
Court Wd Gro, Croy. CR0 ..161 DZ110
Court Wd La, Croy. CR0 ...161 DZ111

Court Yd, SE9 ....124 EL86
Courtyard, The, N1 ....83 DM66
Courtyard, The, SL3
    off Waterside Dr 93 BA75
Cousin La, EC4 ....201 K1
Cousins Cl, West Dr. UB7 ..76 BL73
Couthurst Rd, SE3 ....104 EH79
Coutts Av, Chess. KT9 ....156 CL106
Coutts Cres, NW5 ....64 DG62
Coval Gdns, SW14 ....98 CP84
Coval La, SW14 ....98 CP84
Coval Rd, SW14 ....98 CP84
Coveham Cres, Cob. KT11 .153 BU113
Covelees Wall, E6 ....87 EN72
Covell Ct, SE8
    off Reginald Sq 103 EA80
Covenbrook, Brwd. CM13 ...55 GB48
★ Covent Garden, WC2 ....196 A10
◉ Covent Garden 195 P10
Covent Gdn, WC2 ....196 A10
Coventry Cl, E6 off Harper Rd .87 EM72
  NW6 off Kilburn High Rd .82 DA67
Coventry Cross, E3
    off Gillender St 85 EC70
Coventry Rd, E1 ....84 DV70
  E2 ....84 DV70
  SE25 ....142 DU98
  Ilford IG1 ....69 EP60
Coventry St, W1 ....199 M1
Coverack Cl, N14 ....29 DJ44
  Croydon CR0 ....143 DY101
Coverdale Cl, Stan. HA7 ....41 CH50
Coverdale Ct, Enf. EN3
    off Raynton Rd 31 DY37
Coverdale Gdns, Croy. CR0
    off Park Hill Ri 142 DT104
Coverdale Rd, N11 ....44 DG51
  NW2 ....81 CX66
  W12 ....81 CV74
Coverdales, The, Bark. IG11 .87 ER68
Coverley Cl, E1 ....84 DU71
  Brentwood CM13
    off Wilmot Grn 53 FW51
Covert, The, Nthwd. HA6 ...39 BQ53
  Orpington BR6 ....145 ES100
Coverton Rd, SW17 ......120 DE92
Covert Rd, Ilf. IG6 ....49 ET51
Coverts, The, Brwd. CM13 ..58 GA46
Coverts Rd, Esher (Clay.)
  KT10 ....155 CF109
Covert Way, Barn. EN4 ....28 DC40
Covet Wd Cl, Orp. BR5
    off Lockesley Dr 145 ET100
Covey Cl, SW19 ....140 DB96
Covington Gdns, SW16 ...121 DP94
Covington Way, SW16 ....121 DM93
Cowan Cl, E6 off Oliver Gdns .86 EL71
Cowbridge La, Bark. IG11 ..87 EP66
Cowbridge Rd, Har. HA3 ...62 CM56
Cowcross St, EC1 ....196 F6
Cowdenbeath Path, N1 ....83 DM67
Cowden Rd, Orp. BR6 ....145 ET101
Cowden St, SE6 ....123 EA91
Cowdray Rd, Uxb. UB10 ...77 BQ67
Cowdray Way, Horn. RM12 ..71 FF63
Cowdrey Cl, Enf. EN1 .....30 DS40
Cowdrey Ct, Dart. DA1 ...127 FH87
Cowdrey Rd, SW19 ......120 DB92
Cowdry Rd, E9 off Wick Rd .85 DY65
Cowen Av, Har. HA2 ......60 CC61
Cowgate Rd, Grnf. UB6 ....79 CD68
Cowick Rd, SW17 ....120 DF91
Cowings Mead, Nthlt. UB5 ..78 BY66
Cowland Av, Enf. EN3 .....30 DW42
Cow La, Grnf. UB6 ....79 CD68
    Watford WD25 ....24 BW36
Cow Leaze, E6 ....87 EN72
Cowleaze Rd, Kings.T. KT2 .138 CL95
Cowles, Wal.Cr. (Chsht.) EN7 .14 DT27
COWLEY, Uxb. 76 BJ70
  Greenhithe DA9 ....129 FT85
Cowley Av, Cher. KT16 ...133 BF101
  Greenhithe DA9 ....129 FT85
Cowley Business Pk, Uxb.
  UB8 ....76 BJ70
Cowley Cl, S.Croy. CR2 ..160 DW109
Cowley Cres, Uxb. UB8 ....76 BJ71
  Walton-on-Thames KT12 .154 BW105
Cowley Hill, Borwd. WD6 ...26 CP37
Cowley La, E11 off Cathall Rd .68 EE62
  Chertsey KT16 ....133 BF101
Cowley Mill Rd, Uxb. UB8 ..76 BH68
Cowley Pl, NW4 ....63 CW57
Cowley Rd, E11 ....68 EH57
  SW9 ....101 DN81
  SW14 ....98 CS83
  W3 ....81 CT74
  Ilford IG1 ....69 EM59
  Romford RM3 ....51 FH52
  Uxbridge UB8 ....76 BJ68
Cowley St, SW1 ....199 P6
Cowling Cl, W11
    off Wilsham St 81 CY74
Cowper Av, E6 ....86 EL66
  Sutton SM1 ....158 DD105
  Tilbury RM18 ....111 GH81
Cowper Cl, Brom. BR2 ....144 EK98
  Chertsey KT16 ....133 BF100
  Welling DA16 ....126 EU85
Cowper Ct, Wat. WD24 ....23 BU37
Cowper Gdns, N14 ....29 DJ44
  Wallington SM6 ......159 DJ107
Cowper Rd, N14 ....45 DH46
  N16 ....66 DS64
  N18 ....46 DU50
  SW19 ....120 DC93
  W3 ....80 CR74
  W7 ....79 CF73
  Belvedere DA17 ......106 FA77
  Bromley BR2 ....144 EK98
  Kingston upon Thames
    KT2 ....118 CM92
  Rainham RM13 ....89 FG70
Cowper St, EC2 ....197 L4
Cowper Ter, W10
    off St. Marks Rd 81 CX71
Cowslip Cl, Uxb. UB10 ....76 BL66
Cowslip La, Wok. GU21 ...166 AV115

Cowslip Rd, E18 ....48 EH54
Cowthorpe Rd, SW8 ......101 DK81
Cox Cl, Rad. (Shenley) WD7 .10 CM32
Coxdean, Epsom KT18 ....173 CW119
Coxe Pl, Har. (Wldste.) HA3 .61 CG56
Cox La, Chess. KT9 ......156 CM105
  Epsom KT19 ....156 CP106
Coxley Ri, Pur. CR8 ......160 DQ113
Coxmount Rd, SE7 ....104 EK78
Coxson Way, SE1 ....201 P5
Cox's Wk, SE21 ....122 DU88
Coxwell Rd, SE18 ....105 ER78
  SE19 ....122 DS94
Coxwold Path, Chess. KT9
    off Garrison La 156 CL108
Crabbs Cft Cl, Orp. BR6
    off Ladycroft Way 163 EQ106
Crab Hill, Beck. BR3 .....123 ED94
Crab La, Wat. (Ald.) WD25 ..24 CB35
Crabtree Av, Rom. RM6 ....70 EX56
  Wembley HA0 ....80 CL68
Crabtree Cl, E2 ....197 P1
  Bushey WD23 ....24 CB43
Crabtree Cor, Egh. TW20 .133 BB95
Crabtree Ct, E15
    off Clays La 67 EB64
Crabtree Dr, Lthd. KT22 ..171 CJ124
Crabtree Hill, Rom. (Abridge)
  RM4 ....50 EZ45
Crabtree La, SW6 ....99 CX80
Crabtree Manorway Ind Est, Belv.
  DA17 ....107 FB76
Crabtree Manorway N, Belv.
  DA17 ....107 FC75
Crabtree Manorway S, Belv.
  DA17 ....107 FC76
Crabtree Rd, Egh. TW20 ..133 BC96
Crace St, NW1 ....195 M2
Craddock Rd, Enf. EN1 ....30 DT41
Craddocks Av, Ashtd. KT21 .172 CL117
Craddocks Par, Ashtd. KT21 .172 CL117
Craddock St, NW5
    off Prince of Wales Rd ..82 DG65
Cradley Rd, SE9 ....125 ER88
Cragg Av, Rad. WD7 ......25 CF36
Craigdale Rd, Horn. RM11 ..71 FF58
Craig Dr, Uxb. UB8 ....77 BP72
Craigen Av, Croy. CR0 ...142 DV102
Craigerne Rd, SE3 ....104 EH80
Craig Gdns, E18 ....48 EF54
Craigholm, SE18 ....105 EN82
Craigmore Twr, Wok. GU22
    off Guildford Rd 166 AY119
Craig Mt, Rad. WD7 ......25 CH35
Craigmuir Pk, Wem. HA0 ...80 CM67
Craignair Rd, SW2 ......121 DN87
Craignish Av, SW16 .....141 DM96
Craig Pk Rd, N18 ....46 DV50
Craig Rd, Rich. TW10 ....117 CJ91
Craigs Ct, SW1 ....199 P2
Craigs Wk, Wal.Cr. (Chsht.)
  EN8 off Davison Dr 15 DX28
Craigton Rd, SE9 ....105 EM84
Craigweil Av, Rad. WD7 ...25 CH35
Craigweil Cl, Stan. HA7 ....41 CK50
Craigweil Dr, Stan. HA7 ....41 CK50
Craigwell Av, Felt. TW13 ..115 BU90
Craigwell Cl, Stai. TW18 ..133 BE95
Craik Ct, NW6
    off Carlton Vale 81 CZ68
Crail Row, SE17 ....201 L9
Cramer Ct, N.Mal. KT3
    off Warwick Rd 138 CQ97
Cramer St, W1 ....194 G7
Crammerville Wk, Rain. RM13 .89 FH70
Cramond Cl, W6 ....99 CY79
Cramond Ct, Felt. TW14
    off Kilross Rd 115 BR88
Crampshaw La, Ashtd. KT21 .172 CM119
Crampton Rd, SE20 .....122 DW93
Cramptons Rd, Sev. TN14 .181 FH120
Crampton St, SE17 ......201 H9
Cranberry Cl, Nthlt. UB5
    off Parkfield Av 78 BX68
Cranberry La, E16 ....86 EE70
Cranborne Av, Sthl. UB2 ...96 CA77
  Surbiton KT6 ....138 CN104
Cranborne Cl, Pot.B. EN6 ..11 CY31
Cranborne Cres, Pot.B. EN6 .11 CY31
Cranborne Gdns, Upmin.
  RM14 ....72 FP61
Cranborne Ind Est, Pot.B. EN6 .11 CY30
Cranborne Rd, Barking IG11 .87 ER67
  Potters Bar EN6 ....11 CY30
  Waltham Cross (Chsht.)
    EN8 ....15 DX32
Cranborne Waye, Hayes UB4 .78 BW73
Cranbourn All, WC2 .....195 N10
Cranbourne Av, E11 ......68 EH56
Cranbourne Cl, SW16 ....141 DL97
Cranbourne Dr, Pnr. HA5 ...60 BX57
Cranbourne Gdns, NW11 ...63 CY57
  Ilford IG6 ....69 EQ55
Cranbourne Rd, E12
    off High St N 68 EL64
  E15 ....67 EC63
  N10 ....45 DH54
  Northwood HA6 ....59 BT55
Cranbourn Pas, SE16
    off Marigold St 102 DV75
Cranbourn St, WC2 .....195 N10
CRANBROOK, Ilf. 69 EM60
Cranbrook Cl, Brom. BR2 ..144 EG100
Cranbrook Dr, Esher KT10 .136 CC102
  Romford RM2 ....71 FH56
  Twickenham TW2 ......116 CB88
Cranbrook Ms, E17 ....67 DY57
Cranbrook Pk, N22 ....45 DM53
Cranbrook Ri, Ilf. IG1 .....69 EM59
Cranbrook Rd, SE8 ......103 EA81
  SW19 ....119 CY94
  W4 ....98 CS78
  Barnet EN4 ....28 DD44
  Bexleyheath DA7 .....106 EZ81
  Hounslow TW4 ....96 BZ84
  Ilford IG1, IG2, IG6 ....69 EN59

Cranbrook Rd, Th.Hth. CR7 .142 DQ96
Cranbrook St, E2
    off Mace St 85 DX68
Cranbury Rd, SW6 ....100 DB82
Crane Av, W3 ....80 CQ73
  Isleworth TW7 ....117 CG85
Cranebrook, Twick. TW2
    off Manor Rd 116 CC89
Crane Ct, EC4 ....196 E9
  Epsom KT19 ....156 CQ105
Cranefield Dr, Wat. WD25 ...8 BY32
Craneford Cl, Twick. TW2 ..117 CF87
Craneford Way, Twick. TW2 .117 CE87
Crane Gdns, Hayes UB3 ...95 BT77
Cranell Grn, S.Ock. RM15 ..91 FV74
Crane Lo Rd, Houns. TW5 ..95 BV79
Crane Mead, SE16 ....203 H9
Crane Pk Rd, Twick. TW2 ..116 CB89
Crane Rd, Twick. TW2 ....117 CE88
Cranesbill Cl, NW9
    off Colindale Av 62 CR55
Cranes Dr, Surb. KT5 ....138 CL98
Cranes Pk, Surb. KT5 ....138 CL98
Cranes Pk Av, Surb. KT5 ..138 CL98
Cranes Pk Cres, Surb. KT5 .138 CM98
Crane St, SE10 ....103 ED78
  SE15 ....102 DT81
Craneswater, Hayes UB3 ...95 BT80
Craneswater Pk, Sthl. UB2 .96 BZ78
Cranes Way, Borwd. WD6 ..26 CQ43
Crane Way, Twick. TW2 ...116 CC87
Cranfield Cl, SE27
    off Dunelm Gro 122 DQ90
Cranfield Dr, NW9 ....42 CS52
Cranfield Rd, SE4 ....103 DZ83
Cranfield Rd E, Cars. SM5 .158 DG109
Cranfield Rd W, Cars. SM5 .158 DF109
Cranfield Row, SE1 ......200 E6
CRANFORD, Houns. 95 BU80
Cranford Av, N13 ....45 DL50
  Staines TW19 ....114 BL87
Cranford Cl, SW20 ......139 CV95
  Purley CR8 ....160 DQ113
  Staines TW19
    off Canopus Way 114 BL87
Cranford Cotts, E1
    off Cranford St 85 DX73
Cranford Dr, Hayes UB3 ...95 BT77
Cranford La, Hayes UB3 ...95 BR79
  Hounslow (Hthrw.Air.) TW6 .95 BT83
  Hounslow (Hthrw.Air.N.)
    TW6 ....95 BT81
  Hounslow (Heston) TW5 ..96 BX80
Cranford Ri, Esher KT10 ...154 CC106
Cranford St, E1 ....85 DX73
Cranford Way, N8 ....65 DM57
CRANHAM, Upmin. 73 FS59
Cranham Gdns, Upmin.
  RM14 ....73 FS60
Cranham Rd, Horn. RM11 ...71 FH58
Cranhurst Rd, NW2 ....63 CW64
Cranleigh Cl, SE20 ......142 DV96
  Bexley DA5 ....127 FB86
  Orpington BR6 ....146 EU104
  South Croydon CR2 ....160 DU112
  Waltham Cross (Chsht.)
    EN7 ....14 DU28
Cranleigh Dr, Swan. BR8 ..147 FE98
Cranleigh Gdns, N21 ......29 DN43
  SE25 ....142 DS97
  Barking IG11 ....87 ER66
  Harrow HA3 ....62 CL57
  Kingston upon Thames
    KT2 ....118 CM93
  Loughton IG10 ....33 EM44
  South Croydon CR2 ....160 DU112
  Southall UB1 ....78 BZ72
  Sutton SM1 ....140 DB103
Cranleigh Gdns Ind Est, Sthl.
  UB1 off Cranleigh Gdns .78 BZ72
Cranleigh Ms, SW11 .....100 DE82
Cranleigh Rd, N15 ....66 DQ57
  SW19 ....140 DA97
  Esher KT10 ....136 CC102
  Feltham TW13 ....115 BT91
Cranleigh St, NW1 ......195 L1
Cranley Dene Ct, N10 ......65 DH56
Cranley Dr, Ilf. IG2 ....69 EQ59
  Ruislip HA4 ....59 BT61
Cranley Gdns, N10 ....65 DJ56
  N13 ....45 DM48
  SW7 ....100 DC78
  Wallington SM6 ......159 DJ108
Cranley Ms, SW7 ....100 DC78
Cranley Par, SE9
    off Beaconsfield Rd ...124 EL91
Cranley Pl, SW7 ....100 DD77
Cranley Rd, E13 ....86 EH71
  Ilford IG2 ....69 EQ58
  Walton-on-Thames KT12 .153 BS106
Cranmer Av, W13 ....97 CH76
Cranmer Cl, Mord. SM4 ...139 CX100
  Potters Bar EN6 ....12 DB30
  Ruislip HA4 ....60 BX60
  Stanmore HA7 ....41 CJ52
  Warlingham CR6 ......177 DY117
  Weybridge KT13 ......152 BN108
Cranmer Ct, SW3 ....198 C9
  SW4 ....101 DK83
  Hampton (Hmptn.H.) TW12
    off Cranmer Rd 116 CB92
Cranmer Fm Cl, Mitch. CR4 .140 DF98
Cranmer Gdns, Dag. RM10 .71 FC63
  Warlingham CR6 ......177 DY117
Cranmer Rd, E7 ....68 EH63
  SW9 ....101 DN80
  Croydon CR0 ....141 DP104
  Edgware HA8 ....42 CP48

Cranmer Rd,Hmptn. (Hmptn.H.)
  TW12 ....116 CB92
  Hayes UB3 ....77 BR72
  Kingston upon Thames
    KT2 ....118 CL92
  Mitcham CR4 ....140 DF98
  Sevenoaks TN13 .....190 FE123
Cranmer Ter, SW17 ......120 DD92
Cranmore Av, Islw. TW7 ...96 CC80
Cranmore Rd, Brom. BR1 ..124 EE90
  Chislehurst BR7 ......125 EM92
Cranmore Way, N10 ....65 DJ56
Cranston Cl, Houns. TW3 ..96 BY82
  Uxbridge UB10 ....59 BR61
Cranston Est, N1 ....197 L1
Cranston Gdns, E4 ....47 EB50
Cranston Pk Av, Upmin.
  RM14 ....72 FP63
Cranston Rd, SE23 ......123 DY88
Cranswick Rd, SE16 .....202 E10
Crantock Rd, SE6 ....123 EB89
Cranwell Cl, E3 ....85 EB70
Cranwell Gro, Shep. TW17 .134 BM98
Cranwich Av, N21 ....46 DR45
Cranwich Rd, N16 ....66 DR59
Cranwood St, EC1 ....197 K3
Cranworth Cres, E4 ....47 ED46
Cranworth Gdns, SW9 ....101 DN81
Craster Rd, SW2 ....121 DM87
Crathie Rd, SE12 ....124 EH86
Cravan Av, Felt. TW13 ...115 BU89
Craven Av, W5 ....79 CJ73
  Southall UB1 ....78 BZ71
Craven Cl, Hayes UB4 .....77 BU72
Craven Gdns, SW19 .....120 DA92
  Barking IG11 ....87 ES68
  Ilford IG6 ....49 ER54
  Romford (Coll.Row) RM5 .50 FA50
  Romford (Harold Wd)
    RM3 ....52 FQ51
Craven Hill, W2 ....82 DC73
Craven Hill Gdns, W2 .....82 DC73
Craven Hill Ms, W2 ....82 DC73
Craven Ms, SW11
    off Taybridge Rd 100 DG83
Craven Pk, NW10 ....80 CS67
Craven Pk Ms, NW10 ......80 CS67
Craven Pk Rd, N15 ....66 DT58
  NW10 ....80 CS67
Craven Pas, WC2 ....199 P2
Craven Rd, NW10 ....80 CR67
  W2 ....82 DC73
  W5 ....79 CJ73
  Croydon CR0 ....142 DV102
  Kingston upon Thames
    KT2 ....138 CM95
  Orpington BR6 ....146 EX104
Craven St, WC2 ....199 P2
Craven Ter, W2 ....82 DC73
Craven Wk, N16 ....66 DU59
Crawford Av, Wem. HA0 ...61 CK64
Crawford Cl, Islw. TW7 ....97 CE82
Crawford Compton Cl, Horn.
  RM12 ....90 FJ65
Crawford Est, SE5 ....102 DQ82
Crawford Gdns, N13 ......45 DP48
  Northolt UB5 ....78 BZ69
Crawford Ms, W1 ....194 D7
Crawford Pas, EC1 ......196 D5
Crawford Pl, W1 ....194 C8
Crawford Rd, SE5 ....102 DQ81
Crawford St, NW10 ......80 CR66
  W1 ....194 D7
Crawley Rd, E10 ....67 EB60
  N22 ....46 DQ54
  Enfield EN1 ....46 DS45
Crawshaw Rd, Cher. (Ott.)
  KT16 ....151 BD107
Crawshaw Rd, Sev. TN13 ..190 FG123
Crawshay Ct, SW9
    off Eythorne Rd 101 DN81
Crawthew Gro, SE22 ....102 DT84
Cray Av, Ashtd. KT21 ....172 CL116
  Orpington BR5 ....146 EV99
Craybrooke Rd, Sid. DA14 .126 EV91
Crayburne, Grav. (Sthflt.)
  DA13 ....130 FZ92
Craybury End, SE9 ......125 EQ89
Cray Cl, Dart. DA1 ....107 FG84
Craydene Rd, Erith DA8 ...107 FF81
Crayfield Ind Pk, Orp. BR5 .146 EW99
CRAYFORD, Dart. 127 FD85
⇌ Crayford 127 FE86
Crayford Cl, E6
    off Neatscourt Rd 86 EL71
Crayford High St, Dart. DA1 .127 FE84
Crayford Rd, N7 ....65 DK63
  Dartford DA1 ....127 FF85
Crayford Way, Dart. DA1 ..127 FF85
Crayke Hill, Chess. KT9 ...156 CL108
Craylands, Orp. BR5 .....146 EW97
Craylands La, Swans. DA10 .129 FX85
Craylands Sq, Swans.
  DA10 ....129 FX85
Craymill Sq, Dart. DA1 ...107 FF82
Crayonne Cl, Sun. TW16 ..135 BS95
Cray Riverway, Dart. DA1 .127 FG85
Cray Rd, Belv. DA17 .....106 FA79
  Sidcup DA14 ....126 EW94
  Swanley BR8 ....147 FB100
Crayside Ind Est, Dart. DA1
    off Thames Rd 107 FH84
Cray Valley Rd, Orp. BR5 .146 EU99
Crealock Gro, Wdf.Grn. IG8 .48 EF50
Crealock St, SW18 ......120 DB86
Creasey Cl, Horn. RM11 ...72 FK61
Creasy Cl, Abb.L. WD5 ....7 BT31
Creasy Est, SE1 ....201 M7
Crebor St, SE22 ....122 DU86
Credenhall Dr, Brom. BR2 .145 EM102
Credenhill St, SW16 .....121 DJ93
Crediton Hill, NW6 ....64 DB64

Cre - Cro

Crediton Rd, E16
off Pacific Rd 86 EG72
NW10 ....81 CX67
Crediton Way, Esher (Clay.)
KT10 ....155 CG106
Credon Rd, E13 ....86 EJ68
SE16 ....202 E10
Credo Way, Grays RM20 .109 FV79
Creechurch La, EC3 .....197 N9
Creechurch Pl, EC3 .....197 N9
Creed Ct, EC4
off Ludgate Hill 83 DP72
Creed La, EC4 ....196 G9
Creek, The, Grav. DA11 .130 GB85
Sunbury-on-Thames
TW16 ....135 BU99
CREEKMOUTH, Bark. 88 EU70
Creek Rd, SE8 ....103 EA79
SE10 ....103 EA79
Barking IG11 ....87 ET69
East Molesey KT8 .....137 CE98
Creekside, SE8 ....103 EB80
Rainham RM13 ....89 FE70
Creeland Gro, SE6
off Catford Hill 123 DZ88
Cree Way, Rom. RM1 .....51 FE52
Crefeld Cl, W6 ....99 CX79
Creffield Rd, W3 ....80 CM73
W5 ....80 CM73
Creighton Av, E6 ....86 EK68
N2 ....64 DE55
N10 ....64 DE55
Creighton Cl, W12
off Bloemfontein Rd ...81 CV73
Creighton Rd, N17 ......46 DS52
NW6 ....81 CX68
W5 ....97 CK76
Cremer St, E2 ....197 P1
Cremorne Est, SW10
off Milman's St 100 DD79
Cremorne Gdns, Epsom
KT19 ....156 CR109
Cremorne Rd, SW10 ....100 DC80
Gravesend (Nthflt.) DA11 .131 GF87
Crescent, EC3 ....197 P10
Crescent, The, E17 ......67 DY57
N11 ....44 DF49
NW2 ....63 CV62
SW13 ....99 CT82
SW19 ....120 DA90
W3 ....80 CS72
Abbots Langley WD5 ....7 BT30
Ashford TW15 ....114 BM92
Barnet EN5 ....28 DB41
Beckenham BR3 ......143 EA95
Bexley DA5 ....126 EW87
Caterham CR3 ....177 EA123
Chertsey KT16
off Western Av 134 BG97
Croydon CR0 ....142 DR99
Egham TW20 ....112 AY93
Epping CM16 ....17 ET32
Epsom KT18 ....156 CN114
Gravesend (Nthflt.) DA11 .131 GF87
Greenhithe DA9 ......129 FW85
Harrow HA2 ....61 CD60
Hayes UB3 ....95 BQ80
Ilford IG2 ....69 EN58
Leatherhead KT22 ...171 CH122
Loughton IG10 ....32 EK43
New Malden KT3 .....138 CQ96
Reigate RH2 off Chartway .184 DB134
Rickmansworth (Crox.Grn.)
WD3 ....23 BP44
St. Albans (Brick.Wd.) AL2 ..8 CA30
Sevenoaks TN13 .....191 FK121
Shepperton TW17 ....135 BT101
Sidcup DA14 ....125 ET91
Slough SL1 ....92 AS75
Southall UB1 ....96 BZ75
Surbiton KT6 ....138 CL99
Sutton SM1 ....158 DD105
Sutton (Belmont) SM2 .158 DA111
Upminster RM14 ......73 FS59
Watford WD18 ....24 BW42
Watford (Ald.) WD25 ..24 CB37
Wembley HA0 ....61 CH61
West Molesey KT8 ...136 CA98
West Wickham BR4 ...144 EE100
Weybridge KT13 .....134 BN104
Crescent Av, Grays RM17 .110 GD78
Hornchurch RM12 .....71 FF61
Crescent Cotts, Sev. TN13 .191 FE120
Crescent Ct, Surb. KT6 .137 CK99
Crescent Dr, Brwd. CM15 ..54 FY46
Orpington BR5 ....145 EP100
Crescent E, Barn. EN4 ...28 DC38
Crescent Gdns, SW19 ...120 DA90
Ruislip HA4 ....59 BV58
Swanley BR8 ....147 FC96
Crescent Gro, SW4 .....101 DJ84
Mitcham CR4 ....140 DE98
Crescent Ho, SE13
off Ravensbourne Pl ...103 EB82
Crescent La, SW4 ......121 DK85
Crescent Ms, N22
off Palace Gates Rd ...45 DL53
Crescent Pl, SW3 ......198 B8
Crescent Ri, N22 ....45 DK53
Barnet EN4 ....28 DE43
Crescent Rd, E4 ....48 EE45
E6 ....86 EJ67
E10 ....67 EB61
E13 ....86 EG67
E18 ....48 EJ54
N3 ....43 CZ53
N8 ....65 DK59
N9 ....46 DU46
N11 ....44 DF49
N15 off Carlingford Rd .65 DP55
N22 ....45 DK53
SE18 ....105 EP78
SW20 ....139 CX95
Barnet EN4 ....28 DE43

Crescent Rd, Beck. BR3 ...143 EB96
Brentwood CM14 ....54 FV49
Bromley BR1 ....124 EG94
Caterham CR3 ....176 DU124
Dagenham RM10 ....71 FB63
Enfield EN2 ....29 DP41
Erith DA8 ....107 FF79
Kingston upon Thames
KT2 ....118 CN94
Redhill (Bletch.) RH1 .186 DQ133
Shepperton TW17 ....135 BQ99
Sidcup DA15 ....125 ET90
South Ockendon (Aveley)
RM15 ....108 FQ75
Crescent Row, EC1 .....197 H5
Crescent Stables, SW15
off Upper Richmond Rd .99 CY84
Crescent St, N1 ....83 DM66
Crescent Vw, Loug. IG10 .32 EK44
Crescent Wk, S.Ock. (Aveley)
RM15 ....108 FQ75
Crescent Way, N12 ......44 DE51
SE4 ....103 EA83
SW16 ....121 DM94
Orpington BR6 ......163 ES106
South Ockendon (Aveley)
RM15 ....91 FR74
Crescent W, Barn. EN4 ...28 DC38
Cresford Rd, SW6 ......100 DB81
Crespigny Rd, NW4 ......63 CV58
Cressage Cl, Sthl. UB1 ...78 CA70
Cressall Cl, Lthd. KT22 .171 CH120
Cressall Mead, Lthd. KT22 .171 CH120
Cress End, Rick. WD3
off Springwell Av 38 BG46
Cresset Rd, E9 ....84 DW65
Cresset St, SW4 ....101 DK83
Cressfield Cl, NW5 ......64 DG64
Cressida Rd, N19 ....65 DJ60
Cressingham Gro, Sutt.
SM1 ....158 DC105
Cressingham Rd, SE13 .103 EC83
Edgware HA8 ....42 CR51
Cressington Cl, N16
off Wordsworth Rd 66 DS64
Cresswell Gdns, SW5 ...100 DC78
Cresswell Pk, SE3 ....104 EF83
Cresswell Pl, SW10 ....100 DC78
Cresswell Rd, SE25 ....142 DU98
Feltham TW13 ....116 BY91
Twickenham TW1 ....117 CK86
Cresswell Way, N21 .....45 DN45
Cressy Ct, E1 off Cressy Pl .84 DW71
W6 ....99 CV76
Cressy Pl, E1 ....84 DW71
Cressy Rd, NW3 ....64 DF64
Crest, The, N13 ....45 DN49
NW4 ....63 CW57
Surbiton KT5 ....138 CN99
Waltham Cross (Chsht.) EN7
off Orchard Way 13 DP27
Cresta Dr, Add. (Woodham)
KT15 ....151 BF110
Crest Av, Grays RM17 .110 GB80
Crestbrook Av, N13 .....45 DP48
Crestbrook Pl, N13 ......45 DP48
Crest Cl, Sev. (Bad.Mt.) TN14 .165 FB111
Crest Dr, Enf. EN3 ......30 DW38
Crestfield St, WC1 .....196 A2
Crest Gdns, Ruis. HA4 ...60 BW62
Cresthill Av, Grays RM17 .110 GC77
Creston Av, Wok. (Knap.)
GU21 ....166 AS116
Creston Way, Wor.Pk. KT4 .139 CX102
Crest Rd, NW2 ....63 CT62
Bromley BR2 ....144 EF101
South Croydon CR2 ..160 DV108
Crest Vw, Green. DA9
off Woodland Way 109 FU84
Pinner HA5 ....60 BX56
Crest Vw Dr, Orp. BR5 .145 EP99
Crestway, SW15 ....119 CV86
Crestwood Way, Houns. TW4 .116 BZ85
Creswick Rd, W3 ....80 CP73
Creswick Wk, E3
off Malmesbury Rd 85 EA69
NW11 ....63 CZ56
Crete Hall Rd, Grav. DA11 .130 GD86
Creton St, SE18 ....105 EN76
Crewdson Rd, SW9 .....101 DN80
Crewe Pl, NW10 ....81 CT69
Crewe's Av, Warl. CR6 .176 DW116
Crewe's Cl, Warl. CR6 .176 DW116
Crewe's Fm La, Warl. CR6 .177 DX116
Crewe's La, Warl. CR6 .177 DX116
CREWS HILL, Enf. 29 DP35
⇌ Crews Hill 13 DM34
Crews St, E14 ....203 P8
Crewys Rd, NW2 ....63 CX61
SE15 ....102 DV82
Crichton Av, Wall. SM6 .159 DK106
Crichton Rd, Cars. SM5 .158 DF107
Crichton St, SW8
off Westbury St 101 DJ82
Cricketers Arms Rd, Enf. EN2 .30 DQ40
Cricketers Cl, N14 ......45 DJ45
Chessington KT9 ....155 CK105
Erith DA8 ....107 FE78
Cricketers Ct, SE11 ....200 F9
Cricketers Ms, SW18
off East Hill 120 DB85
Cricketers Ter, Cars. SM5
off Wrythe La 140 DE104
Cricketfield Rd, E5 .....66 DV63
Cricket Fld Rd, Uxb. UB8 ..76 BK67
Cricketfield Rd, West Dr. UB7 .94 BJ77
Cricket Grn, Mitch. CR4 .140 DF97
Cricket Grd Rd, Chis. BR7 .145 EP95
Cricket La, Beck. BR3 ..123 DY93
Cricket Way, Wey. KT13 .135 BS103
Cricklade Av, SW2 .....121 DL89
Romford RM3 ....52 FK51
CRICKLEWOOD, NW2 ....63 CX62
⇌ Cricklewood 63 CX63
Cricklewood Bdy, NW2 ..63 CX62
Cricklewood La, NW2 ...63 CX63

Cridland St, E15 off Church St .86 EF67
Crieff Ct, Tedd. TW11 .117 CJ94
Crieff Rd, SW18 ....120 DC86
Criffel Av, SW2 ....121 DK89
Crimp Hill, Egh. (Eng.Grn.)
TW20 ....112 AU90
Crimp Hill Rd, Wind. (Old Wind.)
SL4 ....112 AT87
Crimscott St, SE1 .....201 N7
Crimsworth Rd, SW8 ....101 DK81
Crinan St, N1 ....83 DL68
Cringle St, SW8 ....101 DJ80
Cripplegate St, EC2 ...197 H6
Cripps Grn, Hayes UB4
off Stratford Rd 77 BV70
Crispe Ho, Bark. IG11
off Dovehouse Mead ...87 ER68
Crispen Rd, Felt. TW13 .116 BY91
Crispian Cl, NW10 ......62 CS63
Crispin Cl, Ashtd. KT21 .172 CM118
Croydon CR0
off Harrington Cl ...141 DL103
Crispin Cres, Croy. CR0 .141 DK104
Crispin Rd, Edg. HA8 ...42 CQ51
Crispin St, E1 ....197 P7
Crisp Rd, W6 ....99 CW78
Criss Cres, Ger.Cr. (Chal.St.P.)
SL9 ....36 AW54
Criss Gro, Ger.Cr. (Chal.St.P.)
SL9 ....36 AW54
Cristowe Rd, SW6 ......99 CZ82
Criterion Ms, N19 ......65 DK61
Crittall's Cor, Sid. DA14 .126 EW94
Crockenhill Way, Grav.
(Istead Rise) DA13 ...130 GE94
CROCKENHILL, Swan. ...147 FD101
Crockenhill La, Dart. (Eyns.)
DA4 ....148 FJ102
Swanley BR8 ....147 FG101
Crockenhill Rd, Orp. BR5 .146 EX99
Swanley BR8 ....146 EZ100
Crockerton Rd, SW17 ..120 DF89
Crockford Cl, Add. KT15 .152 BJ105
Crockford Pk Rd, Add. KT15 .152 BJ106
CROCKHAM HILL, Eden. .189 EQ133
Crockham Way, SE9 ...125 EN91
Crocus Cl, Croy. CR0
off Cornflower La 143 DX102
Crocus Fld, Barn. EN5 ...27 CZ44
Croffets, Tad. KT20 ....173 CX121
Croft, The, E4 ....48 EE47
NW10 ....81 CT68
W5 ....80 CL71
Barnet EN5 ....27 CX42
Hounslow TW5 ....96 BY79
Loughton IG10 ....33 EN40
Pinner HA5 off Rayners La .60 BZ59
Ruislip HA4 ....60 BW63
St. Albans AL2 ....8 CA25
Swanley BR8 ....147 FC97
Wembley HA0 ....61 CJ64
Croft Av, W.Wick. BR4 .143 EC102
Croft Cl, NW7 ....42 CS48
Belvedere DA17 .....106 EZ78
Chislehurst BR7 .....125 EM91
Hayes UB3 ....95 BQ80
Kings Langley (Chipper.)
WD4 ....6 BG30
Uxbridge UB10 ....76 BN66
Croft Ct, Borwd. WD6
off Kensington Way ...26 CR41
Croftdown Rd, NW5 .....64 DG62
Croft End Cl, Chess. KT9
off Ashcroft Rd 138 CM104
Croft End Rd, Kings L. (Chipper.)
WD4 ....6 BG30
Crofters, The, Wind. SL4 .112 AU86
Crofters Cl, Islw. TW7
off Ploughmans End .117 CD85
Crofters Ct, SE8
off Croft St 103 DY77
Crofters Mead, Croy. CR0 .161 DZ109
Crofters Rd, Nthwd. HA6 .39 BS49
Crofters Way, NW1 .....83 DK67
Croft Fld, Kings L. (Chipper.)
WD4 ....6 BG30
Croft Gdns, W7 ....97 CG75
Ruislip HA4 ....59 BT60
Croft La, Kings L. (Chipper.)
WD4 ....6 BG30
Croft Lo Cl, Wdf.Grn. IG8 .48 EH51
Croft Meadow, Kings L. (Chipper.)
WD4 ....6 BG30
Croft Ms, N12 ....44 DC48
Crofton, Ashtd. KT21 ..172 CL118
Crofton Av, W4 ....98 CR80
Bexley DA5 ....126 EX87
Orpington BR6 ......145 EQ103
Walton-on-Thames KT12 .136 BW104
Crofton Cl, Cher. (Ott.) KT16 .151 BC108
Croftongate Way, SE4 ..123 DY85
Crofton Gro, E4 ....47 ED49
Crofton La, Orp. BR5, BR6 .145 ER101
Crofton Pk Rd, SE4 ...123 DZ86
Crofton Rd, E13 ....86 EH70
SE5 ....102 DS81
Grays RM16 ....110 GE76
Orpington BR6 ......145 EN104
Crofton Ter, E5 off Studley Cl .67 DY64
Richmond TW9 ....98 CM84
Crofton Way, Barn. EN5
off Wycherley Cres ...28 DB44
Enfield EN2 ....29 DN40
Croft Rd, SW16 ....141 DN95
SW19 ....120 DC94
Bromley BR1 ....124 EG93
Caterham (Wold.) CR3 .177 DZ122
Enfield EN3 ....31 DY39
Gerrards Cross (Chal.St.P.)
SL9 ....36 AY54
Sutton SM1 ....158 DE106
Westerham TN16 ....189 EP126
Crofts, The, Shep. TW17 .135 BS98
Croftside, SE25
off Sunny Bk 142 DU97

Crofts La, N22
off Glendale Av 45 DN52
Crofts Rd, Har. HA1 .....61 CG58
Crofts St, E1 ....202 B1
Croft St, SE8 ....203 K9
Croftway, NW3 ....64 DA63
Richmond TW10 .....117 CH90
Croft Way, Sev. TN13 .190 FF125
Sidcup DA15 ....125 ES90
Crogsland Rd, NW1 ......82 DG66
Croham Cl, S.Croy. CR2 .160 DS107
Croham Manor Rd, S.Croy.
CR2 ....160 DS106
Croham Mt, S.Croy. CR2 .160 DS108
Croham Pk Av, S.Croy. CR2 .160 DT106
Croham Rd, S.Croy. CR2 .160 DR106
Croham Valley Rd, S.Croy.
CR2 ....160 DT107
Croindene Rd, SW16 ...141 DL95
Cromartie Rd, N19 ......65 DK59
Cromarty Rd, Edg. HA8 ..42 CP47
Crombie Cl, Ilf. IG4 .....69 EM57
Crombie Rd, Sid. DA15 .125 ER88
Cromer Cl, Uxb. UB8
off Dawley Av 77 BQ72
Cromer Pl, Orp. BR6
off Andover Rd 145 ER102
Cromer Rd, E10
off James La 67 ED58
N17 ....46 DU54
SE25 ....142 DV97
SW17 ....120 DG93
Barnet EN5 ....28 DC42
Hornchurch RM11 .....72 FK59
Hounslow (Hthrw.Air.) TW6 .94 BN83
Romford RM7 ....71 FC58
Romford (Chad.Hth.) RM6 .70 EY58
Watford WD24 ....24 BW38
Woodford Green IG8 ...48 EG49
Cromer Rd W, Houns. (Hthrw.Air.)
TW6 ....94 BN83
Cromer St, WC1 ....196 A3
Cromer Ter, E8 off Ferncliff Rd .66 DU64
Cromer Vil Rd, SW18 ..119 CZ86
Cromford Cl, Orp. BR6 .145 ES104
Cromford Path, E5
off Overbury St 67 DX63
Cromford Rd, SW18 ...120 DA85
Cromford Way, N.Mal. KT3 .138 CR95
Cromlix Cl, Chis. BR7 ..145 EP96
Crompton Pl, Enf. EN3
off Government Row ...31 EA37
Crompton St, W2 ....82 DD70
Cromwell Av, N6 ....65 DH60
W6 ....99 CV78
Bromley BR2 ....144 EH98
New Malden KT3 .....139 CT99
Waltham Cross (Chsht.)
EN7 ....14 DU30
Cromwell Cl, E1
off Vaughan Way 84 DU74
N2 ....64 DD56
W3 off High St 80 CQ74
Bromley BR2 ....144 EH98
Chalfont St. Giles HP8 ..36 AW48
Walton-on-Thames KT12 .135 BV102
Cromwell Cres, SW5 ....100 DA77
Cromwell Dr, Slou. SL1 ..74 AS72
Cromwell Gdns, SW7 ..198 A8
Cromwell Gro, W6 ......99 CW76
Caterham CR3 ....176 DQ121
Cromwell Highwalk, EC2
off Beech St 84 DQ71
🏥 Cromwell Hosp, The,
SW5 ....100 DB77
Cromwell Ind Est, E10 ...67 DY60
Cromwell Ms, SW7 .....198 A8
Cromwell Pl, N6 ....65 DH60
SW7 ....198 A8
SW14 ....98 CQ83
W3 off Grove Pl 80 CQ74
Cromwell Rd, E7 ....86 EJ66
E17 ....67 EC57
N3 ....44 DC53
N10 ....44 DG52
SW5 ....100 DB77
SW7 ....100 DB77
SW9 ....101 DP81
SW19 ....120 DA92
Beckenham BR3 ......143 DY96
Borehamwood WD6 ....26 CL39
Brentwood CM14 ....54 FV49
Caterham CR3 ....176 DQ121
Croydon CR0 ....142 DR101
Feltham TW13 ....115 BV88
Grays RM17 ....110 GA77
Hayes UB3 ....77 BR72
Hounslow TW3 ....96 CA84
Kingston upon Thames
KT2 ....138 CL95
Redhill RH1 ....184 DF133
Teddington TW11 ....117 CG93
Waltham Cross (Chsht.)
EN7 ....14 DV28
Walton-on-Thames KT12 .135 BV102
Wembley HA0 ....80 CL68
Worcester Park KT4 .138 CR104
Cromwells Mere, Rom. RM1
off Havering Rd 51 FD51
Cromwell St, Houns. TW3 .96 CA84
Cromwell Twr, EC2 .....197 J6
Cromwell Wk, Red. RH1 .184 DF134
Crondace Rd, SW6 .....100 DA81
Crondall Ct, N1 ....197 M1
Crondall Ho, SW15
off Fontley Way 119 CU88
Crondall St, N1 ....197 L1
Cronin St, SE15 ....102 DT80
Crooked Billet, SW19
off Woodhayes Rd ...119 CW93
Crooked Billet Roundabout, 🅿
E17 ....48 EA52
Staines TW18 ....114 BG91
Crooked Billet Yd, E2
off Kingsland Rd 84 DS69
Crooked La, Grav. DA12 .131 GH86
Crooked Mile, Wal.Abb. EN9 .15 EC33

Crooked Mile Roundabout,
Wal.Abb. EN9 ....15 EC33
Crooked Usage, N3 ......63 CY55
Crooke Rd, SE8 ....203 K10
Crookham Rd, SW6 ......99 CZ81
Crook Log, Bexh. DA6 ..106 EX83
Crookston Rd, SE9 .....105 EN83
Coombs Rd, E16 ....86 EJ71
Crooms Hill, SE10 .....103 EC80
Crooms Hill Gro, SE10 .103 EC80
Cropley Ct, N1 off Cropley St .84 DR68
Cropley St, N1 ....84 DR68
Croppath Rd, Dag. RM10 .70 FA63
Cropthorne Ct, W9
off Maida Vale 82 DC69
Crosby Cl, Felt. TW13 .116 BY91
Crosby Ct, SE1 ....201 K4
Crosby Rd, E7 ....86 EG65
Dagenham RM10 ......89 FB68
Crosby Row, SE1 ......201 K5
Crosby Sq, EC3 ....197 M9
Crosby Wk, E8 off Laurel St .84 DT65
SW2 ....121 DN87
Crosier Cl, SE3 ....104 EL81
Crosier Rd, Uxb. (Ickhm.)
UB10 ....59 BQ63
Crosier Way, Ruis. HA4 ..59 BS62
Crosland Pl, SW11
off Taybridge Rd 100 DG83
Crossacres, Wok. GU22 .167 BE115
Cross Av, SE10 ....103 ED79
Crossbow Rd, Chig. IG7 ..49 ET50
Crossbrook Rd, SE3 ...104 EL82
Crossbrook St, Wal.Cr. (Chsht.)
EN8 ....15 DX31
Cross Cl, SE15
off Gordon Rd 102 DV81
Cross Deep, Twick. TW1 .117 CF89
Cross Deep Gdns, Twick. TW1 .117 CF89
Crossfield Pl, Wey. KT13 .153 BP108
Crossfield Rd, N17 ......66 DQ55
NW3 ....82 DD66
Crossfields, Loug. IG10 .33 EP43
Crossfield St, SE8 .....103 EA80
Crossford St, SW9 .....101 DM82
Crossgate, Edg. HA8 ....42 CN48
Greenford UB6 ....79 CH65
🅳 Crossharbour & London
Arena 204 C6
Crossing Rd, Epp. CM16 .18 EU32
Cross Keys Cl, N9
off Balham Rd 46 DU47
W1 ....194 G7
Sevenoaks TN13 ....190 FG127
Cross Keys Sq, EC1 ...197 H7
Cross Lances Rd, Houns. TW3 .96 CB84
Crossland Rd, Red. RH1 .184 DG134
Thornton Heath CR7 ..141 DP100
Crosslands, Cher. KT16 .133 BE104
Crosslands Av, W5 ......80 CM74
Southall UB2 ....96 BZ78
Crosslands Rd, Epsom KT19 .156 CR107
Cross La, EC3 ....201 N1
N8 ....65 DM56
Bexley DA5 ....126 EZ87
Chertsey (Ott.) KT16 .151 BB107
Cross La E, Grav. DA12 .131 GH89
Cross La W, Grav. DA11 .131 GH89
Cross Las, Ger.Cr. (Chal.St.P.)
SL9 ....36 AY50
Cross Las Cl, Ger.Cr. (Chal.St.P.)
SL9 off Cross Las 37 AZ50
Crosslet St, SE17 .....201 L8
Crosslet Vale, SE10 ...103 EB81
Crossley Cl, West. (Bigg.H.)
TN16 ....178 EK115
Crossleys, Ch.St.G. HP8 ..36 AW49
Crossley St, N7 ....83 DN65
Crossmead, SE9 ....125 EM88
Watford WD19 ....23 BV44
Crossmead Av, Grnf. UB6 .78 CA69
Crossmount Ho, SE5 ...102 DQ80
Crossness La, SE28 ....88 EX73
★ Crossness Pumping Sta,
SE2 ....88 EY72
Crossness Rd, Bark. IG11 .87 ET69
Crossoaks La, Borwd. WD6 .26 CR35
Potters Bar (S.Mimms)
EN6 ....10 CS34
Crosspath, The, Rad. WD7 .25 CG35
Cross Rd, E4 ....48 EE46
N11 ....45 DH50
N22 ....45 DN52
SE5 ....102 DS82
SW19 ....120 DA94
Bromley BR2 ....144 EL103
Croydon CR0 ....142 DR102
Dartford DA1 ....128 FJ86
Dartford (Hawley) DA2 .128 FM91
Enfield EN1 ....30 DS42
Feltham TW13 ....116 BY91
Gravesend (Nthflt.) DA11 .131 GF86
Harrow HA1 ....61 CD56
Harrow (S.Har.) HA2 ...60 CB62
Harrow (Wldste.) HA3 ..41 CG54
Kingston upon Thames
KT2 ....118 CM94
Orpington BR5 ......146 EV99
Purley CR8 ....159 DP113
Romford RM7 ....70 FA55
Romford (Chad.Hth.) RM6 .70 EW59
Sidcup DA14
off Sidcup Hill 126 EV91
Sutton SM2 ....158 DD106
Sutton (Belmont) SM2 .158 DA110
Tadworth KT20 ......173 CW122
Uxbridge UB8
off New Windsor St ...76 BJ66
Waltham Cross EN8 ...15 DY33
Watford WD19 ....24 BY44
Weybridge KT13 .....135 BR104
Woodford Green IG8 ...49 EM51
Cross Rds, Loug. (High Beach)
IG10 ....32 EH40
Cross St, N1 ....83 DP67
SW13 ....98 CS82
Erith DA8 off Bexley Rd .107 FE78

★ Place of interest ⇌ Railway station ⊖ London Underground station 🅳 Docklands Light Railway station ◈ Tramlink station 🏥 Hospital

Cross St, Hmptn. (Hmptn.H.)
  TW12 ....116 CC92
  Uxbridge UB8 ....76 BJ66
  Watford WD17 ....24 BW41
Cross Ter, Wal.Abb. EN9
  off Stonyshotts 16 EE34
Crossthwaite Av, SE5 ....102 DR84
Crosswall, EC3 ....197 P10
Crossway, N12 ....44 DD51
  N16 ....66 DS64
  NW9 ....63 CT56
  SE28 ....88 EW72
  SW20 ....139 CW98
  W13 ....79 CG70
  Chesham HP5 ....4 AS30
  Dagenham RM8 ....70 EW62
  Enfield EN1 ....46 DS45
  Hayes UB3 ....77 BU74
  Orpington BR5 ....145 ER98
  Pinner HA5 ....39 BV54
  Ruislip HA4 ....60 BW63
  Walton-on-Thames KT12 ..135 BV103
  Woodford Green IG8 ....48 EJ49
Crossway, The, N22 ....45 DP52
  SE9 ....124 EK89
Cross Way, The, Har. HA3 ....41 CE54
Crossway, The, Uxb. UB10 ..76 BN68
Crossways, N21 ....30 DQ44
  Brentwood CM15 ....55 GA44
  Egham TW20 ....113 BD93
  Romford RM7 ....71 FH55
  South Croydon CR2 ....161 DY108
  Sunbury-on-Thames TW16 .115 BT94
  Sutton SM2 ....158 DD109
  Westerham (Tats.) TN16 ..138 EJ121
Crossways, The, Couls. CR5 .175 DM119
  Hounslow TW5 ....96 BZ80
  Redhill RH1 ....185 DJ130
  Wembley HA9 ....62 CN61
Crossways Boul, Dart. DA2 ..108 FQ84
  Greenhithe DA9 ....109 FT84
Crossways Business Pk, Dart.
  DA2 ....108 FQ84
Crossways La, Reig. RH2 ....184 DC128
Crossways Rd, Beck. BR3 ....143 EA98
  Mitcham CR4 ....141 DH97
Crosswell Cl, Shep. TW17 ..135 BQ96
Croston St, E8 ....84 DU67
Crothall Cl, N13 ....45 DM48
Crouch Av, Bark. IG11 ....88 EV68
Crouch Cft, Beck. BR3
  off Abbey La 123 EA93
Crouch Cft, SE9 ....125 EN90
CROUCH END, N8 ....65 DJ58
Crouch End Hill, N8 ....65 DK59
Crouch Hall Rd, N8 ....65 DK58
⇌ **Crouch Hill** 65 DM59
Crouch Hill, N4 ....65 DL58
  N8 ....65 DL58
Crouch La, Wal.Cr. (Chsht.)
  EN7 ....14 DQ28
Crouchman's Cl, SE26 ....122 DT90
Crouch Oak La, Add. KT15 ..152 BJ105
Crouch Rd, NW10 ....80 CR66
  Grays RM16 ....111 GG78
Crouch Valley, Upmin. RM14 .73 FS57
Crowborough Cl, Warl. CR6 .177 DY117
Crowborough Dr, Warl. CR6 .177 DY118
Crowborough Path, Wat. WD19
  off Prestwick Rd 40 BX49
Crowborough Rd, SW17 ....120 DG93
Crowden Way, SE28 ....88 EW73
Crowder St, E1 ....84 DU73
Crow Dr, Sev. (Halst.) TN14 .181 FC115
Crowfoot Cl, E9
  off Lee Conservancy Rd ...67 DZ64
CROW GREEN, Brwd. 54 FT41
Crow Grn La, Brwd. CM15 ..54 FT43
Crow Grn Rd, Brwd. CM15 ..54 FT43
Crowhurst Cl, SW9 ....101 DN82
Crowhurst Mead, Gdse. RH9 .186 DW130
Crowhurst Way, Orp. BR5 ..146 EW99
Crowland Av, Hayes UB3 ....95 BS77
Crowland Gdns, N14 ....45 DL45
Crowland Rd, N15 ....66 DT57
  Thornton Heath CR7 ....142 DR98
Crowlands Av, Rom. RM7 ....71 FB58
Crowland Ter, N1 ....84 DR66
Crowland Wk, Mord. SM4 ..140 DB100
Crow La, Rom. RM7 ....70 EZ59
Crowley Cres, Croy. CR0 ....159 DN106
Crowline Wk, N1
  off Clephane Rd 84 DR65
Crowmarsh Gdns, SE23
  off Tyson Rd 122 DW87
Crown Arc, Kings.T. KT1
  off Union St 137 CK96
Crown Ash Hill, West. TN16 .162 EH114
Crown Ash La, Warl. CR6 ...178 EG116
  Westerham TN16 ....178 EG116
Crown Cl, E3 ....85 EA67
  NW6 ....82 DB65
  NW7 ....43 CT47
  Hayes UB3 ....95 BT75
  Orpington BR6 ....164 EU105
  Slough (Colnbr.) SL3 ....93 BC80
  Walton-on-Thames KT12 ..136 BW101
Crown Ct, EC2 ....197 J9
  SE12 ....124 EH86
  WC2 ....196 A9
  Bromley BR2
  off Victoria Rd 144 EK99
Crown Dale, SE19 ....121 DP93
Crowndale Rd, NW1 ....83 DJ68
Crownfield Av, Ilf. IG2 ....69 ES57
Crownfield Rd, E15 ....67 ED64
Crownfields, Sev. TN13 ....191 FH125
Crown Hill, Croy. CR0
  off Church St 142 DQ103
  Epping CM16 ....17 EM33
  Waltham Abbey EN9 ....17 EM33
Crownhill Rd, NW10 ....81 CT67
  Woodford Green IG8 ....48 EL52
Crown Ho, Bark. IG11
  off Linton Rd 87 EQ66
Crown La, N14 ....45 DJ46
  SW16 ....121 DN92

Crown La, Brom. BR2 ....144 EK99
  Chislehurst BR7 ....145 EQ95
  Morden SM4 ....140 DB97
  Virginia Water GU25 ....132 AX100
Crown La Gdns, SW16
  off Crown La 121 DN92
Crown La Spur, Brom. BR2 ..144 EK100
Crown Meadow, Slou. (Colnbr.)
  SL3 ....93 BB80
Crownmead Way, Rom. RM7 .71 FB56
Crown Ms, E13 ....86 EJ67
  W6 ....99 CU77
Crown Office Row, EC4 ....196 D10
Crown Pas, SW1 ....199 L3
  Kingston upon Thames KT1
  off Church St 137 CK96
  Watford WD18
  off The Crescent 24 BW42
Crown Pt, EC2 ....197 M6
  NW5 off Kentish Town Rd .83 DH65
Crown Pt Par, SE19
  off Beulah Hill 121 DP93
Crown Ri, Cher. KT16 ....133 BF102
  Watford WD25 ....8 BW34
Crown Rd, N10 ....44 DG52
  Borehamwood WD6 ....26 CN39
  Enfield EN1 ....30 DV42
  Grays RM17 ....110 GA79
  Ilford IG6 ....69 ER56
  Morden SM4 ....140 DB98
  New Malden KT3 ....138 CQ95
  Orpington BR6 ....164 EU106
  Ruislip HA4 ....60 BX64
  Sevenoaks (Shore.) TN14 ..165 FF110
  Sutton SM1 ....158 DB105
  Twickenham TW1 ....117 CH86
  Virginia Water GU25 ....132 AW100
Crown Sq, Wok. GU21
  off Commercial Way 167 AZ117
Crownstone Rd, SW2 ....121 DN85
Crown St, SE5 ....102 DQ80
  W3 ....80 CP74
  Brentwood CM14 ....54 FW47
  Dagenham RM10 ....89 FC65
  Egham TW20 ....113 BA92
  Harrow HA2 ....61 CD60
Crown Ter, Rich. TW9 ....98 CM84
Crowntree Cl, Islw. TW7 ....97 CF79
Crown Wk, Uxb. UB8
  off Oxford Rd 76 BJ66
  Wembley HA9 ....62 CM62
Crown Way, West Dr. UB7 ...76 BM74
Crown Wds La, SE9 ....105 EP82
  SE18 ....105 EP82
Crown Wds Way, SE9 ....125 ER85
Crown Wks, E2
  off Temple St 84 DV68
Crown Yd, Houns. TW3
  off High St 96 CC83
Crowshott Av, Stan. HA7 ....41 CJ53
Crows Rd, E15 ....85 ED69
  Barking IG11 ....87 EP65
  Epping CM16 ....17 ET30
Crowstone Rd, Grays RM16 ..110 GC75
Crowther Av, Brent. TW8 ....98 CL77
Crowther Rd, SE25 ....142 DU98
Croxdale Rd, Borwd. WD6 ...26 CM40
Croxden Cl, Edg. HA8 ....62 CM55
Croxden Wk, Mord. SM4 ....140 DC100
Croxford Gdns, N22 ....45 DP52
Croxford Way, Rom. RM7
  off Horace Av 71 FD60
⇌ **Croxley** 23 BP44
Croxley Business Pk, Wat.
  WD18 ....23 BR43
Croxley Cl, Orp. BR5 ....146 EV96
CROXLEY GREEN, Rick. 22 BN43
⇌ **Croxley Green (closed)** 23 BR43
Croxley Grn, Orp. BR5 ....146 EV95
Croxley Rd, W9 ....81 CZ69
Croxley Vw, Wat. WD18 ....23 BS44
Croxted Cl, SE21 ....122 DQ87
Croxted Rd, SE21 ....122 DQ87
  SE24 ....122 DQ87
Croyde Av, Grnf. UB6 ....78 CC69
  Hayes UB3 ....95 BS77
Croyde Cl, Sid. DA15 ....125 ER87
CROYDON 142 DR103
Croydon Flyover, Croy. CR0 .159 DP105
Croydon Gro, Croy. CR0 ....141 DP102
Croydon La, Bans. SM7 ....158 DB114
Croydon La S, Bans. SM7 ...158 DB114
★ **Croydon Mus**, Croy. CR0 .142 DQ104
Croydon Rd, E13 ....86 EF70
  SE20 ....142 DV96
  Beckenham BR3 ....143 DY98
  Bromley BR2 ....144 EF104
  Caterham CR3 ....176 DU122
  Croydon (Bedd.) CR0 ....159 DL105
  Hounslow (Hthrw.Air.) TW6 .95 BP82
  Keston BR2 ....144 EJ104
  Mitcham CR4 ....140 DG98
  Reigate RH2 ....184 DB134
  Wallington SM6 ....159 DH105
  Warlingham CR6 ....177 ED122
  West Wickham BR4 ....144 EE104
  Westerham TN16 ....179 EM123
Croyland Rd, N9 ....46 DU46
Croylands Dr, Surb. KT6 ....138 CL101
Croysdale Av, Sun. TW16 ...135 BU97
Crozier Dr, S.Croy. CR2 ....160 DV110
Crozier Ter, E9 ....67 DX64
Crozier Ho, SE3
  off Ebdon Way 104 EH83
Crucible Cl, Rom. RM6 ....70 EV58
Crucifix La, SE1 ....201 M4
Cruden Ho, SE3
  off Hillingdon St 101 DP79
Cruden Rd, Grav. DA12 ....131 GM90
Cruden St, N1 ....83 DP67
Cruick Av, S.Ock. RM15 ....91 FW73
Cruikshank Rd, E15 ....68 EE63
Cruikshank St, WC1 ....196 D2
Crummock Gdns, NW9 ....62 CS57

Crumpsall St, SE2 ....106 EW77
Crundale Av, NW9 ....62 CN57
Crundel Twr, Orp. BR5 ....146 EW100
Crunden Rd, S.Croy. CR2 ...160 DR108
Crusader Cl, Purf. RM19
  off Centurion Way 108 FN77
Crusader Gdns, Croy. CR0
  off Cotelands 142 DS104
Crusader Way, Wat. WD18 ...23 BT44
Crusoe Ms, N16 ....66 DR61
Crusoe Rd, Erith DA8 ....107 FD78
  Mitcham CR4 ....120 DF94
Crutched Friars, EC3 ....197 N10
Crutches La, Beac. (Jordans)
  HP9 ....36 AS51
Crutchfield La, Walt. KT12 ..135 BV103
Crutchley Rd, SE6 ....124 EE89
Crystal Av, Horn. RM12 ....72 FL63
Crystal Ct, SE19
  off College Rd 122 DT92
Crystal Ho, SE18
  off Spinel Cl 105 ET78
✦ **Crystal Palace** 122 DU93
★ **Crystal Palace FC**, SE25 .142 DS98
★ **Crystal Palace National
  Sport Cen**, SE19 ....122 DU93
Crystal Palace Par, SE19 ...122 DT93
★ **Crystal Palace Pk**, SE19 ..122 DT92
Crystal Palace Pk Rd, SE26 .122 DU92
Crystal Palace Rd, SE22 ...102 DU84
Crystal Palace Sta Rd, SE19
  off Anerley Hill 122 DU93
Crystal Ter, SE19 ....122 DR93
Crystal Vw Ct, Brom. BR1
  off Winlaton Rd 123 ED91
Crystal Way, Dag. RM8 ....70 EW60
  Harrow HA1 ....61 CF57
Cuba Dr, Enf. EN3 ....30 DW40
Cuba St, E14 ....203 P4
Cubitt Sq, Sthl. UB2
  off Windmill Av 78 CC74
Cubitt Steps, E14 ....204 A2
Cubitt St, WC1 ....196 B3
  Croydon CR0 ....159 DM106
Cubitt Ter, SW4 ....101 DJ83
Cubitts Yd, WC2 ....196 A10
CUBITT TOWN, E14 ....204 E6
Cuckmans Dr, St.Alb. AL2 ...8 CA25
Cuckoo Av, W7 ....79 CE70
Cuckoo Dene, W7 ....79 CD71
Cuckoo Hall La, N9 ....46 DW45
Cuckoo Hill, Pnr. HA5 ....60 BW55
Cuckoo Hill Dr, Pnr. HA5 ....60 BW55
Cuckoo Hill Rd, Pnr. HA5 ...60 BW56
Cuckoo La, W7 ....79 CE73
Cuckoo Pound, Shep. TW17 .135 BS99
Cudas Cl, Epsom KT19 ....157 CT105
Cuddington Av, Wor.Pk. KT4 .139 CT104
Cuddington Cl, Tad. KT20 ...173 CW120
Cuddington Pk Cl, Bans.
  SM7 ....157 CZ113
Cuddington Way, Sutt. SM2 .157 CX112
CUDHAM, Sev. 179 ER115
Cudham Cl, Sutt. (Belmont)
  SM2 ....158 DA110
Cudham Dr, Croy. (New Adgtn.)
  CR0 ....161 EC110
Cudham La N, Orp. BR6 ....163 ES110
  Sevenoaks (Cudham)
  TN14 ....163 ER112
Cudham La S, Sev. (Cudham)
  TN14 ....179 EQ115
Cudham Pk Rd, Sev. (Cudham)
  TN14 ....163 ES110
Cudham Rd, Orp. BR6 ....163 EN111
  Westerham (Tats.) TN16 ...178 EL120
Cudham St, SE6 ....123 EC87
Cudworth St, E1 ....84 DV70
Cuff Cres, SE9 ....124 EK86
Cuff Pt, E2 ....197 P2
Cugley Rd, Dart. DA2 ....128 FQ87
Culford Gdns, SW3 ....198 E9
Culford Gro, N1 off Culford Rd .84 DS65
Culford Ms, N1 off Culford Rd .84 DS65
Culford Rd, N1 ....84 DS66
  Grays RM16 ....110 GC75
Culgaith Gdns, Enf. EN2 ....29 DL42
Cullen Sq, S.Ock. RM15 ....91 FW73
Cullen Way, NW10 ....80 CQ70
Cullera Cl, Nthwd. HA6 ....39 BT51
Cullerne Cl, Epsom (Ewell)
  KT17 ....157 CT110
Cullesden Rd, Ken. CR8 ....175 DP115
Culling Rd, SE16 ....202 F6
Cullings Ct, Wal.Abb. EN9 ..16 EF33
Cullington Cl, Har. HA3 ....61 CG56
Cullingworth Rd, NW10 ....63 CU64
Culloden Cl, SE16 ....102 DU78
Culloden Rd, Enf. EN2 ....30 DP40
Culloden St, E14 ....85 EC72
Cullum St, EC3 ....197 M10
Culmington Rd, W13 ....97 CJ75
  South Croydon CR2 ....160 DQ109
Culmore Cross, SW12 ....121 DH88
Culmore Rd, SE15 ....102 DV80
Culmstock Rd, SW11 ....120 DG85
Culpeper Cl, Ilf. IG6 ....49 EP51
Culross Cl, N15 ....66 DQ56
Culross St, W1 ....198 G1
Culsac Rd, Surb. KT6 ....138 CL103
Culverden Rd, SW12 ....121 DJ89
  Watford WD19 ....40 BW48
Culver Dr, Oxt. RH8 ....188 EE130
Culver Gro, Stan. HA7 ....41 CJ54
Culverhay, Ashtd. KT21 ....172 CL116
Culverhouse Gdns, SW16 ...121 DM90
Culverlands Cl, Stan. HA7 ...41 CH49
Culverley Rd, SE6 ....123 EB88
Culvers Av, Cars. SM5 ....140 DF103
Culvers Retreat, Cars. SM5 .140 DF102
Culverstone Cl, Brom. BR2 .144 EF100

Culvers Way, Cars. SM5 ....140 DF103
Culvert La, Uxb. UB8 ....76 BH68
Culvert Pl, SW11 ....100 DG82
Culvert Rd, N15 ....66 DS57
  SW11 ....100 DF82
Culworth St, NW8 ....194 B1
Cumberland Av, NW10 ....80 CP69
  Gravesend DA12 ....131 GJ87
  Hornchurch RM12 ....72 FL62
  Welling DA16 ....105 ES83
Cumberland Cl, E8 ....84 DT65
  SW20 off Lansdowne Rd ..119 CX94
  Amersham HP7 ....20 AV39
  Epsom KT19 ....156 CS110
  Hornchurch RM12 ....72 FL62
  Ilford IG6 off Carrick Dr ...49 EQ53
  Twickenham TW1
  off Westmorland Cl 117 CH86
Cumberland Cres, W14 ....99 CY77
Cumberland Dr, Bexh. DA7 ..106 EY80
  Chessington KT9 ....138 CM106
  Dartford DA1 ....128 FM87
  Esher KT10 ....137 CG103
Cumberland Gdns, NW4 ....43 CY54
  WC1 ....196 C2
Cumberland Gate, W1 ....194 D10
Cumberland Mkt, NW1 ....195 J2
Cumberland Mkt Est, NW1 ..195 J2
Cumberland Mills Sq, E14 ..204 F10
Cumberland Pk, NW10 ....81 CU69
  W3 ....80 CQ73
  SE6 ....124 EF88
  Sunbury-on-Thames
  TW16 ....135 BU98
Cumberland Pl, NW1 ....195 H2
  SE6 ....124 EF88
  Sunbury-on-Thames
  TW16 ....135 BU98
Cumberland Rd, E12 ....68 EK63
  E13 ....86 EH71
  E17 ....47 DY54
  N9 ....46 DW46
  N22 ....45 DM54
  SE25 ....142 DV100
  SW13 ....99 CT81
  W3 ....80 CQ73
  W7 ....97 CF75
  Ashford TW15 ....114 BK90
  Bromley BR2 ....144 EE98
  Grays (Chaff.Hun.) RM16 ..110 FY75
  Harrow HA1 ....60 CB57
  Richmond TW9 ....98 CN80
  Stanmore HA7 ....62 CM55
Cumberlands, Ken. CR8 ....176 DR115
Cumberland St, SW1 ....199 J10
  Staines TW18 ....113 BD92
Cumberland Ter, NW1 ....195 H2
Cumberland Ter Ms, NW1 ..195 H1
Cumberland Vil, W3
  off Cumberland Rd 80 CQ73
Cumberlow Av, SE25 ....142 DT97
Cumbernauld Gdns, Sun.
  TW16 ....115 BT92
Cumberton Rd, N17 ....46 DR53
Cumbrae Cl, Slou. SL2
  off St. Pauls Av 74 AU74
Cumbrae Gdns, Surb. KT6 ..137 CK103
Cumbria Ho, SE26
  off High Level Dr 122 DU91
Cumbrian Av, Bexh. DA7 ....107 FE81
Cumbrian Gdns, NW2 ....63 CX61
Cumbrian Way, Uxb. UB8
  off Chippendale Waye 76 BK66
★ **Cuming Mus**, SE17 ....201 H9
Cumley Rd, Ong. CM5 ....19 FE30
Cummings Hall La, Rom.
  (Noak Hill) RM3 ....52 FJ48
Cumming St, N1 ....196 B1
Cumnor Gdns, Epsom KT17 .157 CU109
Cumnor Ri, Ken. CR8 ....176 DQ117
Cumnor Rd, Sutt. SM2 ....158 DC107
Cunard Cres, N21 ....30 DR44
Cunard Pl, EC3 ....197 N9
Cunard Rd, NW10 ....80 CR69
Cunard St, SE5
  off Albany Rd 102 DS79
Cunard Wk, SE16 ....203 J8
Cundy Rd, E16 ....86 EJ72
Cundy St, SW1 ....198 G9
Cundy St Est, SW1 ....198 G9
Cunliffe Cl, Epsom (Headley)
  KT18 ....172 CP124
Cunliffe Rd, Epsom KT19 ...157 CT105
Cunliffe St, SW16 ....121 DJ93
Cunningham Av, Enf. EN3 ...31 DY36
Cunningham Cl, Rom. RM6 ..70 EW57
  West Wickham BR4 ....143 EB103
Cunningham Pk, Har. HA1 ...60 CC57
Cunningham Pl, NW8 ....194 A4
Cunningham Ri, Epp. (N.Wld.Bas.)
  CM16 ....19 FC25
Cunningham Rd, N15 ....66 DU56
  Banstead SM7 ....174 DD115
  Waltham Cross (Chsht.)
  EN8 ....15 DY27
Cunnington St, W4 ....98 CQ76
Cupar Rd, SW11 ....100 DG81
Cupola Cl, Brom. BR1 ....124 EH92
Curates Wk, Dart. DA1 ....128 FK90
Cureton St, SW1 ....199 N9
Curfew Bell Rd, Cher. KT16 .133 BF101
Curfew Ho, Bark. IG11
  off St. Ann's 87 EQ67
Curie Gdns, NW9
  off Pasteur St 42 CS54
Curlew Cl, SE28 ....88 EX73
  South Croydon CR2 ....161 DX111
Curlew Ct, Surb. KT6 ....138 CM104
Curlew Ho, Enf. EN3
  off Allington Ct 31 DX43
Curlews, The, Grav. DA12 ...131 GK89
Curlew St, SE1 ....201 P4
Curlew Ter, Ilf. IG5
  off Tiptree Cres 69 EN55
Curlew Way, Hayes UB4 ....78 BX71
Curling La, Grays (Bad.Dene)
  RM17 ....110 FZ78

Curnock Est, NW1
  off Plender St 83 DJ67
Curran Av, Sid. DA15 ....125 ET85
  Wallington SM6 ....140 DG104
Curran Cl, Uxb. UB8 ....76 BJ70
Currey Rd, Grnf. UB6 ....79 CD65
Curricle St, W3 ....80 CS74
Currie Hill Cl, SW19 ....119 CZ91
Curry Ri, NW7 ....43 CX51
Cursitor St, EC4 ....196 D8
Curtain Pl, EC2
  off Curtain Rd 84 DS69
Curtain Rd, EC2 ....197 M5
Curthwaite Gdns, Enf. EN2 ..29 DK42
Curtis Cl, Rick. (Mill End)
  WD3 ....38 BG46
Curtis Dr, W3 ....80 CR72
  Watford WD25 off Ashfields .7 BT34
Curtis Fld Rd, SW16 ....121 DM91
Curtis La, Wem. HA0
  off Montrose Cres 80 CL65
Curtismill Cl, Orp. BR5 ....146 EV97
Curtis Mill Grn, Rom. (Nave.)
  RM4 ....35 FF42
Curtis Mill La, Rom. (Nave.)
  RM4 ....35 FF42
Curtismill Way, Orp. BR5 ....146 EV97
Curtis Rd, Epsom KT19 ....156 CQ105
  Hornchurch RM11 ....72 FM60
  Hounslow TW4 ....116 BZ87
Curtis St, SE1 ....201 P8
Curtis Way, SE1 ....201 P8
  SE28 off Tawney Rd 88 EV73
Curvan Cl, Epsom KT17 ....157 CT110
Curve, The, W12 ....81 CU73
Curwen Av, E7
  off Woodford Rd 68 EH63
Curwen Rd, W12 ....99 CU75
Curzon Av, Enf. EN3 ....31 DX43
  Stanmore HA7 ....41 CG53
Curzon Cl, Orp. BR6 ....163 ER105
  Weybridge KT13
  off Curzon Rd 152 BN105
Curzon Cres, NW10 ....81 CT66
  Barking IG11 ....87 ET68
Curzon Dr, Grays RM17 ....110 GC80
Curzon Gate, W1 ....198 G3
Curzon Mall, Slou. SL1
  off High St 92 AT75
Curzon Pl, Pnr. HA5 ....60 BW57
Curzon Rd, N10 ....45 DH54
  W5 ....79 CH70
  Thornton Heath CR7 ....141 DN100
  Weybridge KT13 ....152 BN105
Curzon Sq, W1 ....198 G3
Curzon St, W1 ....198 G3
Cusack Cl, Twick. TW1
  off Waldegrave Rd 117 CF91
Cussons Cl, Wal.Cr. (Chsht.)
  EN7 ....14 DU29
CUSTOM HOUSE, E16 ....86 EK72
★ **Custom House**, EC3 ....201 M1
⇌ **Custom House** 86 EH73
DLR **Custom House** 86 EH73
Custom Ho Quay, EC3
  off Lower Thames St 84 DS73
Custom Ho Reach, SE16 ....203 M5
Custom Ho Wk, EC3 ....201 M1
Cut, The, SE1 ....200 E4
Cutcombe Rd, SE5 ....102 DQ82
Cuthberga Cl, Bark. IG11
  off George St 87 EQ66
Cuthbert Gdns, SE25 ....142 DS97
Cuthbert Rd, E17 ....67 EC55
  N18 off Fairfield Rd 46 DU50
  Croydon CR0 ....141 DP103
Cuthberts Cl, Wal.Cr. EN7 ...14 DT29
Cuthbert St, W2 ....82 DD70
Cut Hills, Egh. TW20 ....132 AV95
  Virginia Water GU25 ....132 AV95
Cuthill Wk, SE5 ....102 DR81
Cutlers Gdns, E1 ....197 N8
Cutlers Gdns Arc, EC2
  off Cutler St 84 DS72
Cutlers Sq, E14 ....204 A9
Cutlers Ter, N1
  off Balls Pond Rd 84 DR65
Cutler St, E1 ....197 N8
Cutmore St, Grav. DA11 ....131 GH87
Cutthroat All, Rich. TW10
  off Ham St 117 CJ89
★ **Cutty Sark**, SE10 ....103 EC79
DLR **Cutty Sark** 103 EC79
Cutty Sark Ct, Green. DA9
  off Low Cl 129 FU85
Cutty Sark Gdns, SE10
  off King William Wk 103 EC79
Cuxton Cl, Bexh. DA6 ....126 EY85
Cyclamen Cl, Hmptn. TW12
  off Gresham Rd 116 CA93
Cyclamen Rd, Swan. BR8 ...147 FD98
Cyclamen Way, Epsom KT19 .156 CP106
Cyclops Ms, E14 ....203 P8
Cygnet Av, Felt. TW14 ....116 BW87
Cygnet Cl, NW10 ....62 CR64
  Borehamwood WD6 ....26 CQ39
  Northwood HA6 ....39 BQ52
  Woking GU21 ....166 AV116
Cygnet Gdns, Grav. (Nthflt.)
  DA11 ....131 GF89
Cygnets, The, Felt. TW13 ...116 BY91
  Staines TW18
  off Edgell Rd 113 BF92
Cygnets Cl, Red. RH1 ....184 DG132
Cygnet St, E1
  off Sclater St 84 DT70
Cygnet Vw, Grays RM20 ....109 FT77
Cygnet Way, Hayes UB4 ....78 BX71
Cygnus Business Cen, NW10 .81 CT65
Cymbeline Ct, Har. HA1 ....61 CF58
Cynthia St, N1 ....196 C1
Cyntra Pl, E8 ....84 DV66
Cypress Av, Enf. EN2 ....29 DN35
  Twickenham TW2 ....116 CC87

★ Place of interest   ⇌ Railway station   ● London Underground station   DLR Docklands Light Railway station   ◇ Tramlink station   H Hospital

Cyp - Dau

Cypress CI, Wal.Abb. EN9 . . . . .15 ED34
Cypress Ct, Vir.W. GU25 . . . . . .132 AY98
Cypress Gro, Ilf. IG6 . . . . .49 ES51
Cypress Path, Rom. RM3 . . . . . .52 FK52
Cypress PI, W1 . . . . .195 L5
Cypress Rd, SE25 . . . . .142 DS96
  Harrow HA3 . . . . .41 CD54
Cypress Tree CI, Sid. DA15
  off White Oak Gdns 125 ET87
Cypress Wk, Egh. (Eng.Grn.)
  TW20 . . . . .112 AV93
  Watford WD25
  off Cedar Wd Dr 23 BV35
Cypress Way, Bans. SM7 . . . . .157 CX114
DLR Cyprus 87 EN73
Cyprus Av, N3 . . . . .43 CY54
Cyprus CI, N4
  off Atterbury Rd 65 DP58
Cyprus Gdns, N3 . . . . .43 CY54
Cyprus PI, E2 . . . . .84 DW68
  E6 . . . . .87 EN73
Cyprus Rd, N3 . . . . .43 CZ54
  N9 . . . . .46 DT47
Cyprus Roundabout, E16
  off Royal Albert Way 87 EN73
Cyrena Rd, SE22 . . . . .122 DT86
Cyril Mans, SW11 . . . . .100 DF81
Cyril Rd, Bexh. DA7 . . . . .106 EY82
  Orpington BR6 . . . . .146 EU101
Cyrus St, EC1 . . . . .196 G4
Czar St, SE8 . . . . .103 EA79

D

Dabbling CI, Erith DA8 . . . . . .107 FH80
Dabbs Hill La, Nthlt. UB5 . . . . .60 CB64
D'Abernon CI, Esher KT10 . . . .154 CA105
D'Abernon Dr, Cob. (Stoke D'Ab.)
  KT11 . . . . .170 BY116
Dabin Cres, SE10 . . . . .103 EC81
Dacca St, SE8 . . . . .103 DZ79
Dace Rd, E3 . . . . .85 EA66
Dacre Av, Ilf. IG5 . . . . .49 EN54
  South Ockendon (Aveley)
  RM15 . . . . .91 FR74
Dacre CI, Chig. IG7 . . . . .49 EQ49
  Greenford UB6 . . . . .78 CB68
Dacre Cres, S.Ock. (Aveley)
  RM15 . . . . .91 FR74
Dacre Gdns, SE13 . . . . .104 EE84
  Borehamwood WD6 . . . . . .26 CR43
  Chigwell IG7 . . . . .49 EQ49
Dacre Pk, SE13 . . . . .104 EE83
Dacre PI, SE13 . . . . .104 EE83
Dacre Rd, E11 . . . . .68 EF60
  E13 . . . . .86 EH67
  Croydon CR0 . . . . .141 DL101
Dacres Rd, SE23 . . . . .123 DX90
Dacre St, SW1 . . . . .199 M6
Dade Way, Sthl. UB2 . . . . .96 BZ78
Daerwood CI, Brom. BR2 . . . . .124 EM102
Daffodil Av, Brwd. CM15 . . . . . .54 FV43
Daffodil CI, Croy. CR0
  off Primrose La 143 DX102
Daffodil Gdns, Ilf. IG1 . . . . .69 EP64
Daffodil PI, Hmptn. TW12
  off Gresham Rd 116 CA93
Daffodil St, W12 . . . . .81 CT73
Dafforne Rd, SW17 . . . . .120 DG90
DAGENHAM 88 FA65
Dagenham Av, Dag. RM9 . . . . . .88 EY67
  ⇌ Dagenham Dock 88 EZ68
  ⬤ Dagenham East 71 FC64
  ⬤ Dagenham Heathway 88 EZ65
Dagenham Rd, E10 . . . . .67 DZ60
  Dagenham RM10 . . . . .71 FC63
  Rainham RM13 . . . . .89 FD66
  Romford RM7 . . . . .71 FD62
Dagger La, Borwd. (Elstree)
  WD6 . . . . .25 CG44
Dagmar Av, Wem. HA9 . . . . . . .62 CM63
Dagmar Gdns, NW10 . . . . .81 CX68
Dagmar Ms, Sthl. UB2
  off Dagmar Rd 96 BY76
Dagmar Pas, N1
  off Cross St 83 DP67
Dagmar Rd, N4 . . . . .65 DN59
  N15 off Cornwall Rd 66 DR56
  N22 . . . . .45 DK53
  SE5 . . . . .102 DS81
  SE25 . . . . .142 DS99
  Dagenham RM10 . . . . .89 FC66
  Kingston upon Thames
  KT2 . . . . .138 CM95
  Southall UB2 . . . . .96 BY76
Dagmar Ter, N1 . . . . .83 DP67
Dagnall Cres, Uxb. UB8 . . . . . . .76 BJ71
Dagnall Pk, SE25 . . . . .142 DS100
Dagnall Rd, SE25 . . . . .142 DS99
Dagnall St, SW11 . . . . .100 DF82
Dagnam Pk CI, Rom. RM3 . . . . .52 FN50
Dagnam Pk Dr, Rom. RM3 . . . . .52 FL50
Dagnam Pk Gdns, Rom.
  RM3 . . . . .52 FN51
Dagnam Pk Sq, Rom. RM3 . . . . .52 FP51
Dagnan Rd, SW12 . . . . .121 DH87
Dagonet Gdns, Brom. BR1 . . . .124 EG90
Dagonet Rd, Brom. BR1 . . . . . .124 EG90
Dahlia CI, Wal.Cr. (Chsht.)
  EN7 . . . . .14 DQ25
Dahlia Dr, Swan. BR8 . . . . . . .147 FF96
Dahlia Gdns, Ilf. IG1 . . . . .87 EP65
  Mitcham CR4 . . . . .141 DK98
Dahlia Rd, SE2 . . . . .106 EV77
Dahomey Rd, SW16 . . . . .121 DJ93
Daiglen Dr, S.Ock. RM15 . . . . . .91 FU72
Daimler Way, Wall. SM6 . . . . . .159 DL108
Daines CI, E12
  off Colchester Av 69 EM62
  South Ockendon RM15 . . . . .91 FU70

Dainford CI, Brom. BR1 . . . . . .123 ED92
Dainton CI, Brom. BR1 . . . . . . .144 EH95
Daintry CI, Har. HA3 . . . . .61 CG56
Daintry Lo, Nthwd. HA6 . . . . . . .39 BT52
Daintry Way, E9
  off Osborne Rd 85 DZ65
Dairsie Rd, SE9 . . . . .105 EN83
Dairy CI, NW10 . . . . .81 CU67
  Dartford (Sutt.H.) DA4 . . . .128 FP94
  Thornton Heath CR7 . . . . .142 DQ96
Dairyglen Av, Wal.Cr. EN8 . . . . .15 DY31
Dairy La, SE18 . . . . .105 EM77
  Edenbridge (Crock.H.) TN8 .189 EN134
Dairyman CI, NW2
  off Claremont Rd 63 CY62
Dairy Ms, SW9 . . . . .101 DL83
Dairy Wk, SW19 . . . . .119 CY91
Dairy Way, Abb.L. WD5 . . . . . . .7 BT29
Daisy CI, Croy. CR0
  off Primrose La 143 DX102
Daisy Dobbins Wk, N19
  off Hillrise Rd 65 DL59
Daisy La, SW6 . . . . .100 DA83
Daisy Rd, E16
  off Cranberry La 86 EE70
  E18 . . . . .48 EH54
Dakota CI, Wall. SM6
  off Handley Page Rd 159 DM108
Dakota Gdns, E6 . . . . .86 EL70
  Northolt UB5
  off Argus Way 78 BY69
Dalberg Rd, SW2 . . . . .121 DN85
Dalberg Way, SE2
  off Lanridge Rd 106 EX76
Dalby Rd, SW18 . . . . .100 DC84
Dalby St, NW5 . . . . .83 DH65
Dalcross Rd, Houns. TW4 . . . . . .96 BY82
Dale, The, Kes. BR2 . . . . .162 EK105
  Waltham Abbey EN9 . . . . . .16 EE34
Dale Av, Edg. HA8 . . . . .42 CM53
  Hounslow TW4 . . . . .96 BY83
Dalebury Rd, SW17 . . . . .120 DE89
Dale CI, SE3 . . . . .104 EG83
  Addlestone KT15 . . . . .152 BH106
  Barnet EN5 . . . . .28 DB44
  Dartford DA1 . . . . .127 FF86
  Pinner HA5 . . . . .39 BV53
  South Ockendon RM15 . . . . .91 FU72
Dale Dr, Hayes UB4 . . . . .77 BT70
Dale End, Dart. DA1
  off Dale Rd 127 FF86
Dale Gdns, Wdf.Grn. IG8 . . . . . .48 EH49
Dalegarth Gdns, Pur. CR8 . . . .160 DR113
Dale Grn Rd, N11 . . . . .45 DH48
Dale Gro, N12 . . . . .44 DC50
Daleham Av, Egh. TW20 . . . . . .113 BA93
Daleham Dr, Uxb. UB8 . . . . .77 BP72
Daleham Gdns, NW3 . . . . .64 DD64
Daleham Ms, NW3 . . . . .82 DD65
Dalehead, NW1 . . . . .195 K1
Dalemain Ms, E16 . . . . .205 N2
Dale Pk Av, Cars. SM5 . . . . . . .140 DF103
Dale Pk Rd, SE19 . . . . .142 DQ95
Dale Rd, NW5 off Grafton Rd . . .64 DG64
  SE17 . . . . .101 DP79
  Dartford DA1 . . . . .127 FF86
  Gravesend (Sthflt.) DA13 . .130 GA91
  Greenford UB6 . . . . .78 CB71
  Purley CR8 . . . . .159 DN112
  Sunbury-on-Thames TW16 .135 BT94
  Sutton SM1 . . . . .157 CZ105
  Swanley BR8 . . . . .147 FC96
  Walton-on-Thames KT12 . . .135 BT101
Dale Row, W11
  off St. Marks Rd 81 CY72
Daleside, Ger.Cr. SL9 . . . . .56 AY60
  Orpington BR6 . . . . .164 EU106
Daleside CI, Orp. BR6 . . . . . . .164 EU107
Daleside Dr, Pot.B. EN6 . . . . . . .11 CZ32
Daleside Gdns, Chig. IG7 . . . . . .49 EQ48
Daleside Rd, SW16 . . . . .121 DH92
  Epsom KT19 . . . . .156 CR107
Dales Path, Borwd. WD6
  off Farriers Way 26 CR43
Dales Rd, Borwd. WD6 . . . . . . .26 CR43
Dalestone Ms, Rom. RM3 . . . . . .51 FH51
Dale St, W4 . . . . .98 CS78
Dale Vw, Epsom (Headley)
  KT18 . . . . .172 CP123
  Erith DA8 . . . . .107 FF82
  Woking GU21 . . . . .166 AU118
Dale Vw Av, E4 . . . . .47 EC47
Dale Vw Cres, E4 . . . . .47 EC47
Dale Vw Gdns, E4 . . . . .47 ED48
Daleview Rd, N15 . . . . .66 DS58
Dale Wk, Dart. DA2 . . . . .128 FQ88
Dalewood CI, Horn. RM11 . . . . . .72 FM59
Dalewood Gdns, Wor.Pk.
  KT4 . . . . .139 CV103
Dale Wd Rd, Orp. BR6 . . . . . . .145 ES101
Daley St, E9 . . . . .85 DX65
Daley Thompson Way, SW8 . . .101 DH82
Dalgarno Gdns, W10 . . . . .81 CW71
Dalgarno Way, W10 . . . . .81 CW70
Dalgleish St, E14 . . . . .85 DY72
Daling Way, E3 . . . . .85 DY67
Dalkeith Gro, Stan. HA7 . . . . . . .41 CK50
Dalkeith Rd, SE21 . . . . .122 DQ88
  Ilford IG1 . . . . .69 EQ62
Dallas Rd, NW4 . . . . .63 CU59
  SE26 . . . . .122 DV91
  W5 . . . . .80 CM71
  Sutton SM3 . . . . .157 CY107
Dallas Ter, Hayes UB3 . . . . .95 BT76
Dallega CI, Hayes UB3
  off Dawley Rd 77 BR73
Dallinger Rd, SE12 . . . . .124 EF86
Dalling Rd, W6 . . . . .99 CV76
Dallington CI, Walt. KT12 . . . . .154 BW107
Dallington Sq, EC1
  off Dallington St 83 DP70
Dallington St, EC1 . . . . .196 G4
Dallin Rd, SE18 . . . . .105 EP80
  Bexleyheath DA6 . . . . . . .106 EX84
Dalmain CI, SE23 . . . . .123 DX88
Dalmally Rd, Croy. CR0 . . . . . . .142 DT101
Dalmeny Av, N7 . . . . .65 DK63

Dalmeny Av, SW16 . . . . .141 DN96
Dalmeny CI, Wem. HA0 . . . . . . .79 CJ65
Dalmeny Cres, Houns. TW3 . . . .97 CD84
Dalmeny Rd, N7 . . . . .65 DK62
  Barnet EN5 . . . . .28 DC44
  Carshalton SM5 . . . . .158 DG108
  Erith DA8 . . . . .107 FB81
  Worcester Park KT4 . . . . . .139 CV104
Dalmeyer Rd, NW10 . . . . .81 CT65
Dalmore Av, Esher (Clay.)
  KT10 . . . . .155 CF107
Dalmore Rd, SE21 . . . . .122 DQ89
Dalroy CI, S.Ock. RM15 . . . . . . .91 FU72
Dalrymple CI, N14 . . . . .45 DK45
Dalrymple Rd, SE4 . . . . .103 DY84
DALSTON, E8 . . . . .84 DU66
Dalston Cross Shop Cen, E8 . . . .84 DT65
Dalston Gdns, Stan. HA7 . . . . . .42 CL53
  ⇌ Dalston Kingsland 84 DS65
Dalston La, E8 . . . . .84 DT65
Dalton Av, Mitch. CR4 . . . . .140 DE96
Dalton CI, Hayes UB4 . . . . .77 BR70
  Orpington BR6 . . . . .145 ES104
  Purley CR8 . . . . .160 DQ112
Dalton Rd, Har. (Har.Wld.)
  HA3 . . . . .41 CD54
Daltons Rd, Orp. BR6 . . . . .147 FB104
  Swanley BR8 . . . . .147 FC102
Dalton St, SE27 . . . . .121 DP89
Dalton Way, Wat. WD17 . . . . . . .24 BX43
Dalwood St, SE5 . . . . .102 DS81
Daly Ct, E15 . . . . .67 EC64
Dalyell Rd, SW9 . . . . .101 DM83
Damascene Wk, SE21
  off Lovelace Rd 122 DQ88
Damask Cres, E16
  off Cranberry La 86 EE70
Damer Ter, SW10
  off Tadema Rd 100 DC80
Dames Rd, E7 . . . . .68 EG62
Dame St, N1 . . . . .84 DQ68
Dameswick Vw, St.Alb. AL2 . . . . .8 CA27
Damien CI, E1 . . . . .84 DV72
Damigos Rd, Grav. DA12 . . . . . .131 GM88
Damon CI, Sid. DA14 . . . . .126 EV90
Damson Ct, Swan. BR8 . . . . . . .147 FD98
Damson Dr, Hayes UB3 . . . . . . .77 BU74
Damson Way, Cars. SM5 . . . . . .158 DF110
Damsonwood Rd, Sthl. UB2 . . . .96 CA76
Danbrook Rd, SW16 . . . . .141 DL95
Danbury CI, Brwd. CM15 . . . . . .54 FT43
  Romford RM6 . . . . .70 EX55
Danbury Cres, S.Ock. RM15 . . . .91 FV72
Danbury Ms, Wall. SM6 . . . . . .159 DH105
Danbury Rd, Loug. IG10 . . . . . . .48 EL45
  Rainham RM13 . . . . .89 FF67
Danbury St, N1 . . . . .83 DP68
Danbury Way, Wdf.Grn. IG8 . . . .48 EJ51
Danby St, SE15 . . . . .102 DT83
Dancer Rd, SW6 . . . . .99 CZ81
  Richmond TW9 . . . . .98 CN83
DANCERS HILL, Barn. 27 CW35
Dancers Hill Rd, Barn. EN5 . . . . .27 CY36
Dancers La, Barn. EN5 . . . . .27 CW35
Dandelion CI, Rom. (Rush Grn.)
  RM7 . . . . .71 FE61
Dando Cres, SE3 . . . . .104 EH83
Dandridge CI, SE10 . . . . .205 L10
Dandridge CI, SE10 . . . . .205 L10
  Slough SL3 . . . . .92 AX76
Danebury, Croy. (New Adgtn.)
  CR0 . . . . .161 EB107
Danebury Av, SW15 . . . . .118 CS86
Daneby Rd, SE6 . . . . .123 EB89
Dane CI, Amer. HP7 . . . . .20 AT41
  Bexley DA5 . . . . .126 FA87
  Orpington BR6 . . . . .163 ER106
Dane Ct, Wok. GU22 . . . . .167 BF115
Danecourt Gdns, Croy. CR0 . . . .142 DT104
Danecroft Rd, SE24 . . . . .122 DQ85
Danehill Wk, Sid. DA14
  off Hatherley Rd 126 EU90
Danehurst CI, Egh. TW20 . . . . .112 AY93
Danehurst Gdns, Ilf. IG4 . . . . . . .68 EL57
Danehurst St, SW6 . . . . .99 CY81
Daneland, Barn. EN4 . . . . .28 DF44
Danemead Gro, Nthlt. UB5 . . . . .60 CB64
Danemere St, SW15 . . . . .99 CW83
Dane PI, E3 off Roman Rd 85 DY68
Dane Rd, N18 . . . . .46 DW48
  SW19 . . . . .140 DC95
  W13 . . . . .79 CJ74
  Ashford TW15 . . . . .115 BQ93
  Ilford IG1 . . . . .69 EQ64
  Sevenoaks (Otford) TN14 . .181 FE117
  Southall UB1 . . . . .78 BY73
  Warlingham CR6 . . . . .177 DX117
Danes, The, St.Alb. (Park St.)
  AL2 . . . . .8 CC28
Danesbury Rd, Felt. TW13 . . . . .115 BV88
Danes CI, Grav. (Nthflt.)
  DA11 . . . . .130 GC90
  Leatherhead (Oxshott)
  KT22 . . . . .154 CC114
Danescombe, SE12
  off Winn Rd 124 EG88
Danes Ct, Wem. HA9 . . . . .62 CP62
Danescourt Cres, Sutt. SM1 . . . .140 DC103
Danescroft, NW4 . . . . .63 CX57
Danescroft Av, NW4 . . . . .63 CX57
Danescroft Gdns, NW4 . . . . .63 CX57
Danesdale Rd, E9 . . . . .85 DY65
Danesfield, SE5 . . . . .102 DS79
  Woking GU23
  off Polesden La 167 BF123
Danesfield CI, Walt. KT12 . . . . .135 BV104
Danes Gate, Har. HA1 . . . . .61 CE55
Daneshill, Red. RH1 . . . . .184 DE133
Daneshill CI, Red. RH1 . . . . . . .184 DE133
Danes Rd, Rom. RM7 . . . . .71 FC59
Dane St, WC1 . . . . .196 B7
Daney Way, Brwd. CM15 . . . . . .54 FU43
  Leatherhead (Oxshott)
  KT22 . . . . .155 CD114
Daneswood Av, SE6 . . . . .123 EC90
Daneswood CI, Wey. KT13 . . . . .153 BP106

Danethorpe Rd, Wem. HA0 . . . . .79 CK65
Danetree CI, Epsom KT19 . . . . .156 CQ108
Danetree Rd, Epsom KT19 . . . . .156 CQ108
Danette Gdns, Dag. RM10 . . . . .70 EZ61
Daneville Rd, SE5 . . . . .102 DR81
Dangan Rd, E11 . . . . .68 EG58
Daniel Bolt CI, E14
  off Uamvar St 85 EB71
Daniel CI, N18 . . . . .46 DW49
  SW17 . . . . .120 DE93
  Grays RM16 . . . . .111 GH76
  Grays (Chaff.Hun.) RM16 . .110 FY75
  Hounslow TW4
  off Harvey Rd 116 BZ87
Daniel Gdns, SE15 . . . . .102 DT80
Daniell Way, Croy. CR0 . . . . . . .141 DL102
Daniel PI, NW4 . . . . .63 CV58
Daniel Rd, W5 . . . . .80 CM73
Daniels La, Warl. CR6 . . . . .177 DZ116
Daniels Ms, SE4 . . . . .103 DZ84
Daniels Rd, SE15 . . . . .102 DW83
Daniel Way, Bans. SM7 . . . . . . .158 DB114
Dan Leno Wk, SW6
  off Britannia Rd 100 DB80
Dansey PI, W1 . . . . .195 M10
Dansington Rd, Well. DA16 . . . .106 EU84
Danson Cres, Well. DA16 . . . . .106 EV83
Danson La, Well. DA16 . . . . . . .106 EU84
Danson Mead, Well. DA16 . . . . .106 EW84
★ Danson Park, Well. DA16 . . . .106 EW84
Danson Pk, Bexh. DA6 . . . . . . .106 EW84
Danson Rd, Bex. DA5 . . . . .126 EX85
  Bexleyheath DA6 . . . . . . .126 EX85
Danson Underpass, Sid. DA15
  off Danson Rd 126 EW86
Dante PI, SE11 . . . . .200 G8
Dante Rd, SE11 . . . . .200 F8
Danube St, SW3 . . . . .198 C10
Danvers Rd, N8 . . . . .65 DK56
Danvers St, SW3 . . . . .100 DD79
Danvers Way, Cat. CR3 . . . . . . .176 DQ123
Danziger Way, Borwd. WD6 . . . . .26 CQ39
Daphne Gdns, E4
  off Gunners Gro 47 EC48
Daphne St, SW18 . . . . .120 DC86
Daplyn St, E1
  off Hanbury St 84 DU71
Darby CI, Cat. CR3
  off Fairbourne La 176 DQ122
Darby Cres, Sun. TW16 . . . . . . .136 BW96
Darby Dr, Wal.Abb. EN9 . . . . . . .15 EC33
Darby Gdns, Sun. TW16 . . . . . .136 BW96
D'Arcy Av, Wall. SM6 . . . . .159 DJ105
D'Arcy CI, Brwd. CM13 . . . . . . .55 GB45
D'Arcy CI, Couls. CR5 . . . . .175 DP119
  Waltham Cross (Chsht.)
  EN8 . . . . .15 DY31
D'Arcy Dr, Har. HA3 . . . . .61 CK56
D'Arcy Gdns, Dag. RM9 . . . . . . .88 EZ67
  Harrow HA3 . . . . .62 CL56
D'Arcy PI, Ashtd. KT21 . . . . . . .172 CM117
  Bromley BR2 . . . . .144 EG98
Darcy Rd, SW16 . . . . .141 DL96
D'Arcy Rd, Ashtd. KT21 . . . . . . .172 CM117
Darcy Rd, Islw. TW7
  off London Rd 97 CG81
D'Arcy Rd, Sutt. SM3 . . . . .157 CX105
Dare Gdns, Dag. RM8
  off Grafton Rd 70 EY62
Darell Rd, Rich. TW9 . . . . .98 CN83
DARENTH, Dart. 128 FQ91
Darenth CI, Sev. TN13 . . . . . . .190 FC122
Darenth Gdns, West. TN16
  off Quebec Av 189 ER126
Darenth Hill, Dart. (Darenth)
  DA2 . . . . .128 FQ92
Darenth La, Sev. (Dunt.Grn.)
  TN13 . . . . .190 FE121
  South Ockendon RM15 . . . . .91 FU72
Darenth Pk Av, Dart. DA2 . . . . .129 FR89
Darenth Rd, N16 . . . . .66 DT59
  Dartford DA1 . . . . .128 FM87
  Dartford (Darenth) DA2 . . .128 FP91
  Welling DA16 . . . . .106 EU81
Darenth Way, Sev. (Shore.)
  TN14 . . . . .165 FG111
Darenth Wd Rd, Dart. DA2 . . . .129 FS89
Darent Ind Pk, Erith DA8 . . . . .108 FJ79
Darent Mead, Dart. (Sutt.H.)
  DA4 . . . . .148 FP95
Darent Valley Path, Dart. DA1,
  DA2, DA4 . . . . .128 FM89
  Sevenoaks TN13, TN14 . . .181 FG115
Darfield Rd, SE4 . . . . .123 DZ85
Darfield Way, W10 . . . . .81 CX72
Darfur St, SW15 . . . . .99 CX83
Dargate CI, SE19
  off Chipstead CI 122 DT94
Darien Rd, SW11 . . . . .100 DD83
Darkes La, Pot.B. EN6 . . . . .12 DA32
Dark Ho Wk, EC3
  off King William St 84 DS73
Dark La, Brwd. CM14 . . . . .53 FU52
  Waltham Cross (Chsht.)
  EN7 . . . . .14 DU31
Darlands Dr, Barn. EN5 . . . . . . .27 CX43
Darlan Rd, SW6 . . . . .99 CZ80
Darlaston Rd, SW19 . . . . .119 CX94
Darley CI, Add. KT15 . . . . .152 BJ106
  Croydon CR0 . . . . .143 DY100
Darley Cft, St.Alb. AL2 . . . . .8 CB28
Darley Dr, N.Mal. KT3 . . . . . . .138 CR96
Darley Gdns, Mord. SM4 . . . . . .140 DB100
Darley Rd, N9 . . . . .46 DT46
  SW11 . . . . .120 DF86
Darling Rd, SE4 . . . . .103 EA83
Darling Row, E1 . . . . .84 DV70
Darlington Path, Rom. RM3
  off Darlington Gdns 52 FK50
Darlington Gdns, Rom. RM3 . . . .52 FK50
Darlington Rd, SE27 . . . . .121 DP92
Darlton CI, Dart. DA1 . . . . .107 FF83
Darmaine CI, S.Croy. CR2
  off Churchill Rd 160 DQ108

Darnaway PI, E14
  off Abbott Rd 85 EC72
Darndale CI, E17 . . . . .47 DZ54
Darnets Fld, Sev. (Otford)
  TN14 . . . . .181 FF117
Darnhills, Rad. WD7 . . . . .25 CG35
Darnicle Hill, Wal.Cr. (Chsht.)
  EN7 . . . . .13 DM25
Darnley Ho, E14 . . . . .85 DY72
Darnley Pk, Wey. KT13 . . . . . . .135 BP104
Darnley Rd, E9 . . . . .84 DV65
  Gravesend DA11 . . . . .131 GG88
  Grays RM17
  off Stanley Rd 110 GB79
  Woodford Green IG8 . . . . . .48 EG53
Darnley St, Grav. DA11 . . . . . . .131 GG87
Darnley Ter, W11
  off St. James's Gdns 81 CY74
Darns Hill, Swan. BR8 . . . . .147 FC101
Darrell CI, Slou. SL3 . . . . .93 AZ77
Darrell Rd, SE22 . . . . .122 DU85
Darren CI, N4 . . . . .65 DM59
Darrick Wd Rd, Orp. BR6 . . . . .145 ER103
Darrington Rd, Borwd. WD6 . . . .26 CL39
Darris CI, Hayes UB4 . . . . .78 BY70
Darsley Dr, SW8 . . . . .101 DL81
Dart CI, Slou. SL3 . . . . .93 BB78
  Upminster RM14 . . . . .73 FR58
Dartfields, Rom. RM3 . . . . .52 FK51
DARTFORD 128 FJ87
  ⇌ Dartford 128 FL86
Dartford Av, N9 . . . . .30 DW44
Dartford Bypass, Dart. DA2 . . . .127 FE88
Dartford Gdns, Rom. (Chad.Hth.)
  RM6 off Heathfield Pk Dr . . .70 EV58
★ Dartford Heath, Dart. DA1 . . .127 FG88
★ Dartford Mus, Dart. DA1 . . . .128 FL87
Dartford Northern Bypass, Dart.
  DA1 . . . . .108 FN83
Dartford Rd, Bex. DA5 . . . . . . .127 FC88
  Dartford DA1 . . . . .127 FG86
  Dartford (Fngham.) DA4 . . .148 FP95
  Sevenoaks TN13 . . . . .191 FJ124
Dartford St, SE17 . . . . .102 DQ79
Dartford Trade Pk, Dart. DA1 . . .128 FL89
Dartford Tunnel, Dart. DA1 . . . .109 FR83
  Purfleet RM19 . . . . .109 FR83
Dartford Tunnel App Rd, Dart.
  DA1 . . . . .128 FN86
Dart Grn, S.Ock. RM15 . . . . .91 FV71
Dartmouth Av, Wok. GU21 . . . .151 BC114
Dartmouth CI, W11 . . . . .81 CZ72
Dartmouth Grn, Wok. GU21 . . . .151 BD114
Dartmouth Gro, SE10 . . . . .103 EC81
Dartmouth Hill, SE10 . . . . .103 EC81
DARTMOUTH PARK, NW5 . . . . .65 DH62
Dartmouth Pk Av, NW5 . . . . . . .65 DH62
Dartmouth Pk Hill, N19 . . . . . . .65 DH60
  NW5 . . . . .65 DH60
Dartmouth Pk Rd, NW5 . . . . . . .65 DH63
Dartmouth Path, Wok.
  GU21 . . . . .151 BD114
Dartmouth PI, SE23
  off Dartmouth Rd 122 DW89
  W4 . . . . .98 CS79
Dartmouth Rd, E16
  off Fords Pk Rd 86 EG72
  NW2 . . . . .81 CX65
  NW4 . . . . .63 CU58
  SE23 . . . . .122 DW90
  SE26 . . . . .122 DW90
  Bromley BR2 . . . . .144 EG101
  Ruislip HA4 . . . . .59 BU62
Dartmouth Row, SE10 . . . . .103 EC82
Dartmouth St, SW1 . . . . .199 M5
Dartmouth Ter, SE10 . . . . .103 ED81
Dartnell Av, W.Byf. KT14 . . . . . .152 BH112
Dartnell CI, W.Byf. KT14 . . . . . .152 BH112
Dartnell Cres, W.Byf. KT14 . . . .152 BH112
DARTNELL PARK, W.Byf. 152 BJ112
Dartnell Pk Rd, W.Byf. KT14 . . .152 BJ111
Dartnell PI, W.Byf. KT14 . . . . . .152 BH112
Dartnell Rd, Croy. CR0 . . . . . . .142 DT101
Dartrey Wk, SW10
  off World's End Est 100 DD80
Dart St, W10 . . . . .81 CY69
Dartview CI, Grays RM17 . . . . . .110 GE77
Darvel CI, Wok. GU21 . . . . .166 AU116
Darville Rd, N16 . . . . .66 DT62
Darwell CI, E6 . . . . .87 EN68
Darwin CI, N11 . . . . .45 DH48
  Orpington BR6 . . . . .163 ER106
Darwin Dr, Sthl. UB1 . . . . .78 CB72
Darwin Gdns, Wat. WD19
  off Barnhurst Path 40 BW50
Darwin Rd, N22 . . . . .45 DP53
  W5 . . . . .97 CJ78
  Slough SL3 . . . . .93 AZ75
  Tilbury RM18 . . . . .111 GF81
  Welling DA16 . . . . .105 ET83
Darwin St, SE17 . . . . .201 L8
Daryngton Dr, Grnf. UB6 . . . . . .79 CD68
Dashwood CI, Bexh. DA6 . . . . . .126 FA85
  Slough SL3 . . . . .92 AW77
  West Byfleet KT14 . . . . . . .152 BJ112
Dashwood Rd, N8 . . . . .65 DM58
  Gravesend DA11 . . . . .131 GG89
Dassett Rd, SE27 . . . . .121 DP92
DATCHET, Slou. 92 AW81
  ⇌ Datchet 92 AV81
Datchet PI, Slou. (Datchet)
  SL3 . . . . .92 AV81
Datchet Rd, SE6 . . . . .123 DZ90
  Slough SL3 . . . . .92 AT76
  Slough (Horton) SL3 . . . . . .92 AZ83
  Windsor (Old Wind.) SL4 . . .92 AU84
Datchworth Ct, N4
  off Queens Dr 66 DQ62
Date St, SE17 . . . . .102 DQ78
Daubeney Gdns, N17 . . . . .46 DQ52
Daubeney Rd, E5 . . . . .67 DY63
  N17 . . . . .46 DQ52
Daubeney Twr, SE8 . . . . .203 M9
Dault Rd, SW18 . . . . .120 DC86

Davall Ho, Grays RM17
  off Argent St 110 GA79
Davema CI, Chis. BR7
  off Brenchley CI 145 EN95
Davenant Rd, N19 . . . . . .65 DK61
  Croydon CR0
  off Duppas Hill Rd . . .159 DP105
Davenant St, E1 . . . . . .84 DU71
Davenham Av, Nthwd. HA6 . .39 BT49
Davenport CI, Tedd. TW11 . .117 CG93
Davenport Rd, SE6 . . . . . .123 EB86
  Sidcup DA14 . . . . . .126 EX89
Daventer Dr, Stan. HA7 . . . .41 CF52
Daventry Av, E17 . . . . . .67 EA57
Daventry CI, Slou. (Colnbr.)
  SL3 . . . . .93 BF81
Daventry Gdns, Rom. RM3 . .52 FJ50
Daventry Grn, Rom. RM3
  off Hailsham Rd 52 FJ50
Daventry Rd, Rom. RM3 . . . .52 FJ50
Daventry St, NW1 . . . . . .194 B6
Davern CI, SE10 . . . . . .205 K9
Davey CI, N7 . . . . . .83 DM65
Davey Rd, E9 . . . . . .85 EA66
Davey St, SE15 . . . . . .102 DT79
David Av, Grnf. UB6 . . . . . .79 CE69
David CI, Hayes UB3 . . . . . .95 BR80
David Dr, Rom. RM3 . . . . . .52 FN51
Davidge St, SE1 . . . . . .200 F5
David Lee Pt, E15 . . . . . .86 EE67
David Ms, W1 . . . . . .194 E6
David Rd, Dag. RM8 . . . . . .70 EY61
  Slough (Colnbr.) SL3 . .93 BF82
Davidson Gdns, SW8 . . . . . .101 DL80
Davidson La, Har. HA1
  off Grove Hill 61 CF59
Davidson Rd, Croy. CR0 . . . .142 DT100
Davidson Way, Rom. RM7 . .71 FE58
Davids Rd, SE23 . . . . . .122 DW88
David St, E15 . . . . . .85 ED65
David's Way, Ilf. IG6 . . . . . .49 ES52
David Twigg CI, Kings.T. KT2 .138 CL95
Davies CI, Croy. CR0 . . . . . .142 DU100
  Rainham RM13 . . . . . .90 FJ69
Davies La, E11 . . . . . .68 EE61
Davies Ms, W1 . . . . . .195 H10
Davies St, W1 . . . . . .195 H10
Davington Gdns, Dag. RM8 . .70 EV64
Davington Rd, Dag. RM8 . . . .88 EV65
Davinia CI, Wdf.Grn. IG8
  off Deacon Way 49 EM51
Davis Av, Grav. (Nthflt.)
  DA11 . . . . .130 GE88
Davis CI, Sev. TN13 . . . . . .191 FJ122
Davison CI, Wal.Cr. EN8 . . . .15 DX28
Davison Dr, Wal.Cr. (Chsht.)
  EN8 . . . . .15 DX28
Davis Rd, W3 . . . . . .81 CT74
  Chessington KT9 . . . . . .156 CN105
  Grays (Chaff.Hun.) RM16 . .110 FZ76
  South Ockendon (Aveley)
  RM15 . . . . .91 FR74
  Weybridge KT13 . . . . . .152 BM110
Davis St, E13 . . . . . .86 EH68
Davisville Rd, W12 . . . . . .99 CU75
Davos CI, Wok. GU22 . . . . . .166 AY119
Davys PI, Grav. DA12 . . . . . .131 GL93
Dawell Dr, West. (Bigg.H.)
  TN16 . . . . .178 EJ117
Dawes Av, Horn. RM12 . . . .72 FK62
  Isleworth TW7 . . . . . .117 CG85
Dawes CI, Green. DA9 . . . . . .129 FT85
Dawes Ct, Esher KT10 . . . . . .154 CB105
Dawes Ho, SE17 . . . . . .201 L9
Dawes La, Rick. (Sarratt) WD3 .21 BE37
Dawes Moor CI, Slou. SL2 . .74 AW72
Dawes Rd, SW6 . . . . . .99 CY80
  Uxbridge UB10 . . . . . .76 BL68
Dawes St, SE17 . . . . . .201 L10
Dawley Av, Uxb. UB8 . . . . . .77 BQ71
Dawley Grn, S.Ock. RM15 . .91 FU72
Dawley Par, Hayes UB3
  off Dawley Rd 77 BQ73
Dawley Ride, Slou. (Colnbr.)
  SL3 . . . . .93 BE81
Dawley Rd, Hayes UB3 . . . . . .95 BS76
Dawlish Av, N13 . . . . . .45 DL49
  SW18 . . . . .120 DB89
  Greenford UB6 . . . . . .79 CG68
Dawlish Dr, Ilf. IG3 . . . . . .69 ES63
  Pinner HA5 . . . . . .60 BY57
  Ruislip HA4 . . . . . .59 BU61
Dawlish Rd, E10 . . . . . .67 EC61
  N17 . . . . .66 DU55
  NW2 . . . . .81 CX65
Dawlish Wk, Rom. RM3 . . . .52 FJ53
Dawnay Gdns, SW18 . . . . . .120 DD89
Dawnay Rd, SW18 . . . . . .120 DC88
Dawn CI, Houns. TW4 . . . . . .96 BY83
Dawn Cres, E15 . . . . . .85 ED67
  off Bridge Rd 85 ED67
Dawn Redwood CI, Slou. (Horton)
  SL3 . . . . .93 BA83
Dawpool Rd, NW2 . . . . . .63 CT61
Daws Hill, E4 . . . . . .31 EC41
Daws La, NW7 . . . . . .43 CT50
Dawson Av, Bark. IG11 . . . .87 ES66
  Orpington BR5 . . . . . .146 EV96
Dawson CI, SE18 . . . . . .105 EQ77
  Hayes UB3 . . . . . .77 BR71
Dawson Dr, Rain. RM13 . . . .89 FH66
  Swanley BR8 . . . . . .127 FE94
Dawson Gdns, Bark. IG11
  off Dawson Av 87 ET66
Dawson Hts, SE22 . . . . . .122 DU87
Dawson PI, W2 . . . . . .82 DA73
Dawson Rd, NW2 . . . . . .63 CW64
  Kingston upon Thames
  KT1 . . . . .138 CM97
  West Byfleet (Byfleet)
  KT14 . . . . .152 BK111
Dawson St, E2 . . . . . .84 DT68
Dax Ct, Sun. TW16
  off Thames St 136 BW97
Daybrook Rd, SW19 . . . . . .140 DB96
Daylesford Av, SW15 . . . . . .99 CU84
Daylop Dr, Chig. IG7 . . . . . .50 EV48

Daymer Gdns, Pnr. HA5 . . . .59 BV56
Daymerslea Ridge, Lthd.
  KT22 . . . . .171 CJ121
Days Acre, S.Croy. CR2 . . . .160 DT110
Daysbrook Rd, SW2 . . . . . .121 DM88
Days La, Brwd. CM15 . . . . . .54 FU42
  Sidcup DA15 . . . . . .125 ES87
Dayton Dr, Erith DA8 . . . . . .108 FK78
Dayton Gro, SE15 . . . . . .102 DW81
Deacon CI, Cob. (Down.)
  KT11 . . . . .169 BV119
  Purley CR8 . . . . . .159 DL109
Deacon Ms, N1 . . . . . .84 DR66
Deacon Rd, Cat. CR3 . . . . . .176 DQ123
  Kingston upon Thames
  KT2 . . . . .138 CM95
Deacons CI, Borwd. (Elstree)
  WD6 . . . . .26 CN42
  Pinner HA5 . . . . . .39 BV54
Deacons Hill, Wat. WD19 . .24 BW44
Deacon's Hill Rd, Borwd. (Elstree)
  WD6 . . . . .26 CM42
Deacons Leas, Orp. BR6 . . . .163 ER105
Deacons Ri, N2 . . . . . .64 DD57
Deacons Wk, Hmptn. TW12
  off Bishops Gro 116 BZ91
Deacon Way, SE17 . . . . . .201 H8
  Woodford Green IG8 . . . .49 EM52
Deadhearn La, Ch.St.G. HP8 . .36 AY46
Deadman's Ash La, Rick. (Sarratt)
  WD3 . . . . .22 BH36
Deakin CI, Wat. WD18
  off Chenies Way 39 BS45
Deal Ms, W5
  off Darwin Rd 97 CK77
Deal Porters Way, SE16 . . . .202 G6
Deal Rd, SW17 . . . . . .120 DG93
Deal's Gateway, SE10
  off Blackheath Rd 103 EB81
Deal St, E1 . . . . . .84 DU71
Dealtry Rd, SW15 . . . . . .99 CW84
Deal Wk, SW9
  off Mandela St 101 DN80
Deanacre CI, Ger.Cr. (Chal.St.P.)
  SL9 . . . . .36 AY51
DEAN BOTTOM, Dart. 149 FV97
Dean Bradley St, SW1 . . . . . .199 P7
Dean CI, E9 off Churchill Wk . .84 DW64
  SE16 . . . . .203 J3
  Uxbridge UB10 . . . . . .76 BM66
  Woking GU22 . . . . . .167 BE115
Dean Ct, Wem. HA0 . . . . . .61 CH62
Deancroft Rd, Ger.Cr. (Chal.St.P.)
  SL9 . . . . .36 AY51
Deancross St, E1 . . . . . .84 DW72
Dean Dr, Stan. HA7 . . . . . .42 CL54
Deane Av, Ruis. HA4 . . . . . .60 BW64
Deane Cft Rd, Pnr. HA5 . . . .59 BV58
Deanery CI, N2 . . . . . .64 DE56
Deanery Ms, W1 . . . . . .198 G2
Deanery Rd, E15 . . . . . .86 EE65
  Edenbridge (Crock.H.) TN8 .189 EQ134
Deanery St, W1 . . . . . .198 G2
Deane Way, Ruis. HA4 . . . . . .59 BV58
Dean Farrar St, SW1 . . . . . .199 M6
Dean Fld, Hem.H. (Bov.) HP3 . .5 BA27
Dean Gdns, E17 . . . . . .67 ED56
  W13 off Northfield Av 79 CH74
Deanhill Rd, SW14 . . . . . .98 CP84
Dean La, Red. RH1 . . . . . .175 DH123
Dean Rd, NW2 . . . . . .81 CW65
  SE28 . . . . .88 EU73
  Croydon CR0 . . . . . .160 DR105
  Hampton TW12 . . . . . .116 CA92
  Hounslow TW3 . . . . . .116 CB85
Dean Ryle St, SW1 . . . . . .199 P8
Deansbrook CI, Edg. HA8 . . . .42 CQ52
Deansbrook Rd, Edg. HA8 . .42 CQ51
Deans Bldgs, SE17 . . . . . .201 K9
Deans CI, W4 . . . . . .98 CP79
  Abbots Langley WD5 . . . .7 BR32
  Amersham HP6 . . . . . .20 AT37
Dean's CI, Croy. CR0 . . . . . .142 DT104
  Edgware HA8 . . . . . .42 CQ51
  Slough (Stoke P.) SL2 . . . .74 AV67
  Tadworth KT20
  off Deans La 173 CV124
Deans Ct, EC4 . . . . . .196 G9
Deanscroft Av, NW9 . . . . . .62 CQ61
Deans Dr, N13 . . . . . .45 DP51
  Edgware HA8 . . . . . .42 CR50
Deansfield, Cat. CR3 . . . . . .186 DT125
Dean's Gate CI, SE23 . . . . . .123 DX90
Deans La, W4 . . . . . .98 CP79
  Edgware HA8 . . . . . .42 CQ51
  Redhill (Nutfld.) RH1 . . . .185 DN133
  Tadworth KT20 . . . . . .173 CV124
Deans Ms, W1 . . . . . .195 J8
Dean's PI, SW1 . . . . . .199 M10
Deans Rd, W7 . . . . . .79 CF74
  Brentwood CM14 . . . . . .54 FV49
  Redhill RH1 . . . . . .185 DJ130
  Sutton SM1 . . . . . .140 DB104
Dean Stanley St, SW1 . . . . . .199 P7
Dean St, E7 . . . . . .68 EG64
  W1 . . . . .195 M8
Deans Wk, Couls. CR5 . . . . . .175 DN118
Deansway, N2 . . . . . .64 DD56
  N9 . . . . .46 DS48
Deans Way, Edg. HA8 . . . . . .42 CQ50
Dean's Yd, SW1 . . . . . .199 N6
Dean Trench St, SW1 . . . . . .199 P7
Dean Wk, Edg. HA8
  off Deansbrook Rd 42 CQ51
Deanway, Ch.St.G. HP8 . . . .36 AU48
Dean Way, Sthl. UB2 . . . . . .96 CB75
De'Arn Gdns, Mitch. CR4 . .140 DE97
Dearsley Ho, Rain. RM13 . . .89 FF68
Dearsley Rd, Enf. EN1 . . . . . .30 DU41
Deason St, E15
  off High St 85 EC67
De Barowe Ms, N5
  off Leigh Rd 65 DP63
DEBDEN, Loug. 33 ER41
⊖ Debden 33 EQ42

Debden CI, Kings.T. KT2 . . . .117 CK92
  Woodford Green IG8 . . . . . .48 EJ52
DEBDEN GREEN, Loug. 33 EQ38
Debden Grn, Loug. IG10 . . . .33 EP38
Debden La, Loug. IG10 . . . .33 EP38
Debden Rd, Loug. IG10 . . . .33 EP38
Debden Wk, Horn. RM12 . . . .89 FH65
De Beauvoir Cres, N1 . . . . . .84 DS67
De Beauvoir Est, N1 . . . . . .84 DR67
De Beauvoir Rd, N1 . . . . . .84 DS67
De Beauvoir Sq, N1 . . . . . .84 DS66
DE BEAUVOIR TOWN, N1 . . . .84 DR67
Debenham Rd, Wal.Cr. (Chsht.)
  EN7 . . . . .14 DV27
De Bohun Av, N14 . . . . . .29 DH44
Deborah CI, Islw. TW7 . . . . . .97 CE81
Deborah Cres, Ruis. HA4 . . .59 BR59
Debrabant CI, Erith DA8 . . .107 FD79
De Brome Rd, Felt. TW13 . .116 BW88
De Burgh Gdns, Tad. KT20 .173 CX119
De Burgh Pk, Bans. SM7 . . .174 DB115
Deburgh Rd, SW19 . . . . . .120 DC94
Decies Way, Slou. (Stoke P.)
  SL2 . . . . .74 AU67
Decima St, SE1 . . . . . .201 M6
Deck CI, SE16 . . . . . .203 J4
Decoy Av, NW11 . . . . . .63 CY57
De Crespigny Pk, SE5 . . . . . .102 DR82
Dee CI, Upmin. RM14 . . . . . .73 FS58
Deeley Rd, SW8 . . . . . .101 DK81
Deena CI, W3 . . . . . .80 CM72
Deepdale, SW19 . . . . . .119 CX91
Deepdale Av, Brom. BR2 . . .144 EF98
Deepdale CI, N11
  off Ribblesdale Av 44 DG51
Deepdene, W5 . . . . . .80 CM70
  Potters Bar EN6 . . . . . .11 CX31
Deepdene Av, Croy. CR0 . . .142 DT104
Deepdene CI, E11 . . . . . .68 EG56
Deepdene Ct, N21 . . . . . .29 DP44
Deepdene Gdns, SW2 . . . . . .121 DM87
Deepdene Path, Loug. IG10 . .33 EN42
Deepdene Pt, SE23
  off Dacres Rd 123 DX90
Deepdene Rd, SE5 . . . . . .102 DR84
  Loughton IG10 . . . . . .33 EN42
  Welling DA16 . . . . . .106 EU83
Deep Fld, Slou. (Datchet) SL3 .92 AV80
Deepfield Way, Couls. CR5 .175 DL116
Deep Pool La, Wok. (Chobham)
  GU24 . . . . .150 AV114
Deepwell CI, Islw. TW7 . . . . . .97 CG84
Deepwood La, Grnf. UB6
  off Cowgate Rd 79 CD69
Deerbrook Rd, SE24 . . . . . .121 DP88
Deerdale Rd, SE24 . . . . . .102 DQ84
Deere Av, Rain. RM13 . . . . . .89 FG65
Deerhurst CI, Felt. TW13 . .115 BU91
Deerhurst Cres, Hmptn. (Hmptn.H.)
  TW12 . . . . .116 CC92
Deerhurst Rd, NW2 . . . . . .81 CX65
  SW16 . . . . .121 DM92
Deerings Dr, Pnr. HA5 . . . . . .59 BU57
Deerings Rd, Reig. RH2 . . . .184 DB134
Deerleap Gro, E4 . . . . . .31 EB43
Deerleap La, Sev. TN14 . . . .164 EX115
Dee Rd, Rich. TW9 . . . . . .98 CM84
Deer Pk CI, Kings.T. KT2 . .118 CP94
Deer Pk Gdns, Mitch. CR4 .140 DD97
Deer Pk Rd, SW19 . . . . . .140 DB96
Deer Pk Wk, Chesh. HP5 . . . .4 AS28
Deer Pk Way, Wal.Abb. EN9 . .31 EC36
  West Wickham BR4 . . . . . .144 EF103
Deers Fm CI, Wok. (Wisley)
  GU23 . . . . .168 BL116
Deerswood CI, Cat. CR3 . . .176 DU124
Deeside Rd, SW17 . . . . . .120 DD90
Dee St, E14 . . . . . .85 EC72
Deeves Hall La, Pot.B. EN6 . .11 CS33
Dee Way, Epsom KT19 . . . . . .156 CS110
  Romford RM1 . . . . . .51 FE53
Defiance Wk, SE18 . . . . . .105 EM76
Defiant Way, Wall. SM6 . . . .159 DL108
Defoe Av, Rich. TW9 . . . . . .98 CN80
Defoe CI, SE16 . . . . . .203 M5
  SW17 . . . . .120 DE93
  Erith DA8 off Selkirk Dr . .107 FE81
Defoe Ho, EC2 . . . . . .197 J6
Defoe Par, Grays RM16 . . . .111 GH76
Defoe PI, EC2 off Beech St . .84 DQ71
  SW17 off Lessingham Av . .120 DF91
Defoe Rd, N16 . . . . . .66 DS61
Defoe Way, Rom. RM5 . . . . . .51 FB51
De Frene Rd, SE26 . . . . . .123 DX91
De Gama PI, E14
  off Maritime Quay 103 EA78
Degema Rd, Chis. BR7 . . . . . .125 EP92
Dehar Cres, NW9 . . . . . .63 CT59
Dehavilland CI, Nthlt. UB5 . .78 BX69
De Havilland Ct, Rad. (Shenley)
  WD7 off Armstrong Gdns .10 CL32
De Havilland Dr, Wey. KT13 .152 BL111
★ De Havilland Mosquito
  Aircraft Mus., St.Alb.
  (Lon.Col.) AL2 . . . . . .10 CP29
De Havilland Rd, Edg. HA8 . .42 CP54
  Hounslow TW5 . . . . . .96 BW80
  Wallington SM6 . . . . . .159 DL108
De Havilland Way, Abb.L. WD5 .7 BT32
  Staines (Stanw.) TW19 . . .114 BK86
Dekker Rd, SE21 . . . . . .122 DS86
Delabole Rd, Red. RH1 . . . .185 DL129
Delacourt Rd, SE3
  off Old Dover Rd 104 EH80
Delafield Rd, SE7 . . . . . .104 EH80
  Grays RM17 . . . . . .110 GD78
Delaford CI, Iver SL0 . . . . . .75 BF72
Delaford Rd, SE16 . . . . . .202 E10
Delaford St, SW6 . . . . . .99 CY80
Delagarde Rd, West. TN16 .189 EQ126
Delamare Cres, Croy. CR0 .142 DW100
Delamare Rd, Wal.Cr. (Chsht.)
  EN8 . . . . .15 DZ30
Delamere Gdns, NW7 . . . . . .42 CR51
Delamere Rd, SW20 . . . . . .139 CX95
  W5 . . . . .80 CL74

Delamere Rd, Borwd. WD6 . .26 CP39
  Hayes UB4 . . . . . .78 BX73
Delamere Ter, W2 . . . . . .82 DB71
Delancey Pas, NW1
  off Delancey St 83 DH67
Delancey St, NW1 . . . . . .83 DH67
Delaporte CI, Epsom KT17 .156 CS112
De Lapre CI, Orp. BR5 . . . . . .146 EX101
De Lara Way, Wok. GU21 . . .166 AX118
De Laune St, SE17 . . . . . .101 DP78
Delaware Rd, W9 . . . . . .82 DB70
Delawyk Cres, SE24 . . . . . .122 DQ86
Delcombe Av, Wor.Pk. KT4 .139 CW102
Delderfield, Lthd. KT22 . . . .171 CK123
Delft Way, SE22
  off East Dulwich Gro . . .122 DS85
Delhi Rd, Enf. EN1 . . . . . .46 DT45
Delhi St, N1 . . . . . .83 DL67
Delia St, SW18 . . . . . .120 DB87
Delisle Rd, SE28 . . . . . .87 ES74
Delius CI, Borwd. (Elstree)
  WD6 . . . . .25 CJ44
Delius Gro, E15 . . . . . .85 ED68
Dell, The, SE2 . . . . . .106 EU78
  SE19 . . . . .142 DT95
  Bexley DA5 . . . . . .127 FE88
  Brentford TW8 . . . . . .97 CJ79
  Brentwood (Gt.Warley)
  CM13 . . . . .53 FV51
  Feltham TW14
  off Harlington Rd W . . .115 BV87
  Gerrards Cross (Chal.St.P.)
  SL9 . . . . .36 AY51
  Northwood HA6 . . . . . .39 BS47
  Pinner HA5 . . . . . .40 BX54
  Radlett WD7 . . . . . .25 CG36
  Reigate RH2 . . . . . .184 DA133
  Tadworth KT20 . . . . . .173 CW121
  Waltham Abbey EN9
  off Greenwich Way 31 EC36
  Wembley HA0 . . . . . .61 CH64
  Woking GU21 . . . . . .166 AW118
  Woodford Green IG8 . . . . . .48 EH48
Della Path, E5
  off Napoleon Rd 66 DV62
Dellbow Rd, Felt. TW14
  off Central Way 115 BV85
Dell CI, E15 . . . . . .85 ED67
  Leatherhead (Fetch.) KT22 .171 CE123
  Wallington SM6 . . . . . .159 DK105
  Woodford Green IG8 . . . . . .48 EH48
Dell Fm Rd, Ruis. HA4 . . . . . .59 BR57
Dellfield CI, Beck. BR3
  off Foxgrove Rd 123 EC94
  Radlett WD7 . . . . . .25 CE35
  Watford WD17 . . . . . .23 BU40
Dellfield Cres, Uxb. UB8 . . . .76 BJ70
Dellfield Par, Uxb. (Cowley) UB8
  off High St 76 BJ70
Dell La, Epsom KT17 . . . . . .157 CU106
Dellmeadow, Abb.L. WD5 . . . .7 BS30
Dellors CI, Barn. EN5 . . . . . .27 CX43
Dellow CI, Ilf. IG2 . . . . . .69 ER59
Dellow St, E1 . . . . . .84 DV73
Dell Ri, St.Alb. (Park St.) AL2 . .8 CB26
Dell Rd, Enf. EN3 . . . . . .30 DW38
  Epsom KT17 . . . . . .157 CU107
  Grays RM17 . . . . . .110 GB79
  Watford WD24 . . . . . .23 BU37
  West Drayton UB7 . . . . . .94 BM76
Dells CI, E4 . . . . . .47 EB45
  Teddington TW11
  off Middle La 117 CF93
Dellside, Uxb. (Hare.) UB9 . .58 BJ57
Dell Side, Wat. WD24
  off The Harebreaks 23 BU37
Dell's Ms, SW1 . . . . . .199 L9
Dell Wk, N.Mal. KT3 . . . . . .138 CS96
Dell Way, W13 . . . . . .79 CJ72
Dellwood Gdns, Ilf. IG5 . . . .69 EN55
Delmare CI, SW9
  off Brighton Ter 101 DM84
Delme Cres, SE3 . . . . . .104 EH82
Delmey CI, Croy. CR0
  off Radcliffe Rd 142 DT104
Deloraine St, SE8 . . . . . .103 EA81
Delorme St, W6 . . . . . .99 CX79
Delta CI, Wok. (Chobham)
  GU24 . . . . .150 AT110
  Worcester Park KT4 . . . . . .139 CT104
Delta Ct, NW2 . . . . . .63 CU61
Delta Gain, Wat. WD19 . . . .40 BX47
Delta Gro, Nthlt. UB5 . . . . . .78 BX69
Delta Rd, Brwd. CM13 . . . . . .55 GD44
  Woking GU21 . . . . . .167 BA116
  Woking (Chobham) GU24 .150 AT110
  Worcester Park KT4 . . . . . .138 CS104
Delta St, E2
  off Wellington Row 84 DU69
Delta Way, Egh. TW20 . . . . . .133 BC95
De Luci Rd, Erith DA8 . . . . . .107 FC78
De Lucy St, SE2 . . . . . .106 EV77
Delvan CI, SE18
  off Ordnance Rd 105 EN80
Delvers Mead, Dag. RM10 . .71 FC63
Delverton Rd, SE17 . . . . . .101 DP78
Delves, Tad. KT20
  off Heathcote 173 CX121
Delvino Rd, SW6 . . . . . .100 DA81
De Mandeville Gate, Enf. EN1
  off Southbury Rd 30 DU42
De Mel CI, Epsom KT19
  off Abbots Av 156 CN112
Demesne Rd, Wall. SM6 . . .159 DK106
Demeta CI, Wem. HA9 . . . . . .62 CQ62
De Montfort Par, SW16
  off Streatham High Rd . .121 DL90
De Montfort Rd, SW16 . . . .121 DL90
De Morgan Rd, SW6 . . . . . .100 DB83
Dempster CI, Surb. KT6 . . .137 CJ102
Dempster Rd, SW18 . . . . . .120 DC85
Denbar Par, Rom. RM7
  off Mawney Rd 71 FC56
Denberry Dr, Sid. DA14 . . .126 EV90
Denbigh CI, NW10 . . . . . .80 CS66

Denbigh CI, W11 . . . . . .81 CZ73
  Chislehurst BR7 . . . . . .125 EM93
  Hornchurch RM11 . . . . . .72 FN56
  Ruislip HA4 . . . . . .59 BT61
  Southall UB1 . . . . . .78 BZ72
  Sutton SM1 . . . . . .157 CZ106
Denbigh Dr, Hayes UB3 . . . .95 BQ75
Denbigh Gdns, Rich. TW10 .118 CM85
Denbigh Ms, SW1 . . . . . .199 K9
Denbigh PI, SW1 . . . . . .199 K10
Denbigh Rd, E6 . . . . . .86 EK69
  W11 . . . . .81 CZ73
  W13 . . . . .79 CH73
  Hounslow TW3 . . . . . .96 CB82
  Southall UB1 . . . . . .78 BZ72
Denbigh St, SW1 . . . . . .199 K9
Denbigh Ter, W11 . . . . . .81 CZ73
Denbridge Rd, Brom. BR1 .145 EM96
Denby Rd, Cob. KT11 . . . . . .154 BW113
Den CI, Beck. BR3 . . . . . .143 ED97
Dendridge CI, Enf. EN1 . . . .30 DV37
Dene, The, W13 . . . . . .79 CH71
  Croydon CR0 . . . . . .161 DX105
  Sevenoaks TN13 . . . . . .191 FH126
  Sutton SM2 . . . . . .157 CZ111
  Wembley HA9 . . . . . .62 CL63
  West Molesey KT8 . . . . . .136 BZ99
Dene Av, Houns. TW3 . . . . . .96 BZ83
  Sidcup DA15 . . . . . .126 EV87
Dene CI, SE4 . . . . . .103 DY83
  Bromley BR2 . . . . . .144 EF102
  Coulsdon CR5 . . . . . .174 DE119
  Dartford DA2 . . . . . .127 FE91
  Worcester Park KT4 . . . . . .139 CT103
Dene Ct, Stan. HA7
  off Marsh La 41 CJ50
Denecroft Cres, Uxb. UB10 . .77 BP67
Denecroft Gdns, Grays RM17 .110 GD76
Dene Dr, Orp. BR6 . . . . . .146 EV104
Denefield Dr, Ken. CR8 . . . .176 DR115
Dene Gdns, Stan. HA7 . . . . . .41 CJ50
  Thames Ditton KT7 . . . . . .137 CG103
Dene Holm Rd, Grav. (Nthflt.)
  DA11 . . . . .130 GD90
Denehurst Gdns, NW4 . . . . . .63 CW58
  W3 . . . . .80 CP74
  Richmond TW10 . . . . . .98 CN84
  Twickenham TW2 . . . . . .117 CD87
  Woodford Green IG8 . . . . . .48 EH49
Dene Path, S.Ock. RM15 . . .91 FU72
Dene PI, Wok. GU21 . . . . . .166 AV118
Dene Rd, N11 . . . . . .44 DF46
  Ashtead KT21 . . . . . .172 CM119
  Buckhurst Hill IG9 . . . . . .48 EK46
  Dartford DA1 . . . . . .128 FM87
  Northwood HA6 . . . . . .39 BS51
Denewood, Barn. EN5 . . . . . .28 DC43
Denewood CI, Wat. WD17 . .23 BT37
Denewood Rd, N6 . . . . . .64 DF58
Dengie Wk, N1 off Basire St . .84 DQ67
DENHAM, Uxb. 58 BG62
⇌ Denham 58 BG59
★ Denham Aerodrome, Uxb.
  UB9 . . . . .57 BD57
Denham Av, Uxb. (Denh.)
  UB9 . . . . .57 BF61
Denham CI, Uxb. (Denh.) UB9 .58 BG62
  Welling DA16
  off Park Vw Rd 106 EW83
Denham Ct Dr, Uxb. (Denh.)
  UB9 . . . . .58 BH63
Denham Cres, Mitch. CR4 .140 DF98
Denham Dr, Ilf. IG2 . . . . . .69 EQ58
Denham Gdn Village, Uxb. UB9
  off Denham Grn La 58 BF58
⇌ Denham Golf Club 57 BD59
DENHAM GREEN, Uxb. 57 BE58
Denham Grn CI, Uxb. (Denh.)
  UB9 . . . . .58 BG59
Denham Grn La, Uxb. (Denh.)
  UB9 . . . . .57 BE57
Denham La, Ger.Cr. (Chal.St.P.)
  SL9 . . . . .37 BA53
Denham Lo, Uxb. UB9 . . . . . .76 BJ65
Denham Rd, N20 . . . . . .44 DF48
  Egham TW20 . . . . . .113 BA91
  Epsom KT17 . . . . . .157 CT112
  Feltham TW14 . . . . . .116 BW86
  Iver SL0 . . . . . .75 BE65
  Uxbridge (Denh.) UB9 . . . .75 BE65
Denham St, SE10 . . . . . .205 M10
Denham Wk, Ger.Cr. (Chal.St.P.)
  SL9 . . . . .37 AZ51
Denham Way, Bark. IG11 . . .87 ES67
  Borehamwood WD6 . . . . . .26 CR39
  Rickmansworth (Map.Cr.)
  WD3 . . . . .37 BE52
  Uxbridge (Denh.) UB9 . . . .58 BG62
Denholme Rd, W9 . . . . . .81 CZ69
Denholme Wk, Rain. RM13
  off Ryder Gdns 89 FF65
Denison CI, N2 . . . . . .64 DC55
Denison Rd, SW19 . . . . . .120 DD93
  W5 . . . . .79 CJ70
  Feltham TW13 . . . . . .115 BT91
Deniston Av, Bex. DA5 . . . .126 EY88
Denleigh Gdns, N21 . . . . . .45 DN46
  Thames Ditton KT7 . . . . . .137 CE100
Denman Dr, NW11 . . . . . .64 DA57
  Ashford TW15 . . . . . .115 BP93
  Esher (Clay.) KT10 . . . . . .155 CG106
Denman Dr N, NW11 . . . . . .64 DA57
Denman Dr S, NW11 . . . . . .64 DA57
Denman PI, W1
  off Great Windmill St . . .83 DK73
Denman Rd, SE15 . . . . . .102 DT81
Denman St, W1 . . . . . .199 M1
Denmark Ct, Mord. SM4 . . .140 DA99
Denmark Gdns, Cars. SM5 .140 DF104
Denmark Gro, N1 . . . . . .83 DN68
⇌ Denmark Hill 102 DR82
Denmark Hill, SE5 . . . . . .102 DR81
Denmark Hill Dr, NW9 . . . . . .63 CT56

Den - Dit

Denmark Hill Est, SE5 ....102 DR84
Denmark Pl, WC2 ....195 N8
Denmark Rd, N8 ....65 DM56
  NW6 ....81 CZ68
  SE5 ....102 DU99
  SE25 ....142 DU99
  SW19 ....119 CX93
  W13 ....79 CH73
  Bromley BR1 ....144 EH95
  Carshalton SM5 ....140 DF104
  Kingston upon Thames
    KT1 ....138 CL97
  Twickenham TW2 ....117 CD90
Denmark St, E11 ....68 EE62
  off High Rd Leytonstone .68 EE62
  E13 ....86 EH71
  N17 ....46 DV53
  WC2 ....195 N8
  Watford WD17 ....23 BV40
Denmark Wk, SE27 ....122 DQ91
Denmead Cl, Ger.Cr. SL9 ..56 AY59
Denmead Ho, SW15
  off Highcliffe Dr 119 CT86
Denmead Rd, Croy. CR0 ..141 DP102
Denmead Way, SE15
  off Pentridge St 102 DT80
Dennan Rd, Surb. KT6 ...138 CM102
Dennard Way, Orp. BR6 ..163 EP105
Denner Rd, E4 ....47 EA47
Denne Ter, E8 ....84 DT67
Dennett Rd, Croy. CR0 ..141 DN102
Dennetts Gro, SE14
  off Dennetts Rd 103 DX82
Dennettsland Rd, Eden. (Crock.H.)
  TN8 ....189 EQ134
Dennetts Rd, SE14 ......102 DW81
Denning Av, Croy. CR0 ..159 DN105
Denning Cl, NW8 ....82 DC69
  Hampton TW12 ....116 BZ93
Denning Rd, NW3 ....64 DD63
Dennington Cl, E5
  off Detmold Rd 66 DV61
Dennington Pk Rd, NW6 ..82 DA65
Denningtons, The, Wor.Pk.
  KT4 ....138 CS103
Dennis Av, Wem. HA9 ....62 CM64
Dennis Cl, Ashf. TW15 ..115 BR93
  Redhill RH1 ....184 DE132
Dennises La, Upmin. RM14 ..91 FS67
Dennis Gdns, Stan. HA7 ..41 CJ50
Dennis La, Stan. HA7 ...41 CH48
Dennison Pt, E15 ....85 EC66
Dennis Pk Cres, SW20 ..139 CY95
Dennis Reeve Cl, Mitch.
  CR4 ....140 DF95
Dennis Rd, E.Mol. KT8 ..136 CC98
  Gravesend DA11 ....131 GG90
  South Ockendon RM15 ..91 FU66
Dennis Way, SW4
  off Gauden Rd 101 DK83
Denny Av, Wal.Abb. EN9 ..15 ED34
Denny Cl, E6 off Linton Gdns .86 EL71
Denny Cres, SE11 ....200 E9
Denny Gdns, Dag. RM9
  off Canonsleigh Rd 88 EV66
Denny Gate, Wal.Cr. EN8 ..15 DZ27
Denny Rd, N9 ....46 DV46
  Slough SL3 ....93 AZ77
Denny St, SE11 ....200 E10
Den Rd, Brom. BR2 .....143 ED97
Densham Dr, Pur. CR8 ..159 DN114
Densham Rd, E15 ....86 EE67
Densole Cl, Beck. BR3
  off Kings Hall Rd 143 DY95
Densworth Gro, N9 ......46 DW47
Dent Cl, S.Ock. RM15 ...91 FU72
DENTON, Grav. 131 GL87
Denton Cl, Barn. EN5 ...27 CW43
Denton Ct Rd, Grav. DA12 .131 GL87
Denton Gro, Walt. KT12 .136 BX103
Denton Rd, N8 ....65 DM57
  N18 ....46 DS49
  Bexley DA5 ....127 FE89
  Dartford DA1 ....127 FE88
  Twickenham TW1 ......117 CK86
  Welling DA16 ....106 EW80
Denton St, SW18 ....120 DB86
  Gravesend DA12 ......131 GL87
Denton Ter, Bex. DA5
  off Denton Rd 127 FE89
Denton Way, E5 ....67 DX62
  Woking GU21 ....166 AT118
Dents Gro, Tad. KT20 ..183 CZ128
Dents Rd, SW11 ....120 DF86
Denvale Wk, Wok. GU21 .166 AU118
Denver Cl, Orp. BR6 ...145 ES100
Denver Ind Est, Rain. RM13 .89 FF71
Denver Rd, N16 ....66 DS59
  Dartford DA1 ....127 FG87
Denyer St, SW3 ....198 C9
Denziloe Av, Uxb. UB10 .77 BP69
Denzil Rd, NW10 ......63 CT64
Deodara Cl, N20 ......44 DE48
Deodar Rd, SW15 .....99 CY84
★ Department for Environment,
  Food & Rural Affairs
  (DEFRA), SW1 ....199 P2
★ Department for Transport,
  Local Government & Regions
  (DTLR), SW1 ....199 K6
★ Department of Health &
  Department for Work & Pensions
  (DWP), SW1 ....199 P4
Depot App, NW2 ....63 CX63
Depot Rd, Epsom KT17 .156 CS113
  Hounslow TW3 ....97 CD83
DEPTFORD, SE8 ....103 DZ78
⇌ Deptford 103 DZ80
🚈 Deptford Bridge 103 EA81
Deptford Br, SE8 .....103 EA81
Deptford Bdy, SE8 ....103 EA81
Deptford Ch St, SE8 ..103 EA79
Deptford Ferry Rd, E14 .204 A9
Deptford Grn, SE8 ....103 EA79

Deptford High St, SE8 ..103 EA79
Deptford Strand, SE8 ..203 N9
Deptford Wf, SE8 ......203 M8
De Quincey Ms, E16 ....205 N2
De Quincey Rd, N17 ....46 DR53
Derby Arms Rd, Epsom
  KT18 ....173 CT117
Derby Av, N12 ....44 DC50
  Harrow HA3 ....41 CD53
  Romford RM7 ....71 FC58
  Upminster RM14 ......72 FM62
Derby Cl, Epsom KT18 ..173 CV119
Derby Ct, E5
  off Overbury St 67 DX63
Derby Gate, SW1 ......199 P4
Derby Hill, SE23 .....122 DW89
Derby Hill Cres, SE23 .122 DW89
Derby Rd, E7 ....86 EJ66
  E9 ....85 DX67
  E18 ....48 EF53
  N18 ....46 DW50
  SW14 ....98 CP84
  SW19 off Russell Rd ..120 DA94
  Croydon CR0 ....141 DP103
  Enfield EN3 ....30 DV43
  Grays RM17 ....110 GB78
  Greenford UB6 ....78 CB67
  Hounslow TW3 ....96 CB84
  Surbiton KT5 ....138 CN102
  Sutton SM1 ....157 CZ107
  Uxbridge UB8 ....76 BJ68
  Watford WD17 ....24 BW41
Derby Rd Br, Grays RM17 .110 GB79
Derbyshire St, E2 ....84 DU69
Derby Stables Rd, Epsom
  KT18 ....172 CS117
Derby St, W1 ....198 G3
  Romford RM5 ....51 FB51
Dereham Pl, EC2 ......197 N3
Dereham Rd, Bark. IG11 .87 ET65
Derek Av, Epsom KT19 ..156 CN106
  Wallington SM6 ......159 DH105
  Wembley HA9 ....80 CP66
Derek Cl, Epsom (Ewell)
  KT19 ....156 CP106
Derek Walcott Cl, SE24
  off Shakespeare Rd ..121 DP85
Derham Gdns, Upmin. RM14 .72 FQ62
Deri Av, Rain. RM13 ...89 FH70
Dericote St, E8 ......84 DU67
Deridene Cl, Stai. (Stanw.) TW19
  off Bedfont Rd 114 BL86
Derifall Cl, E6 ......87 EM71
Dering Pl, Croy. CR0 ..160 DQ105
Dering Rd, Croy. CR0 ..160 DQ105
Dering St, W1 ....195 H9
Dering Way, Grav. DA12 .131 GM88
Derinton Rd, SW17 ....120 DF91
Derley Rd, Sthl. UB2 ..96 BW76
Dermody Gdns, SE13 ..123 ED85
Dermody Rd, SE13 ....123 ED85
Deronda Rd, SE24 ....121 DP88
De Ros Pl, Egh. TW20 ..113 BA93
Deroy Cl, Cars. SM5 ..158 DF107
Derrick Av, S.Croy. CR2 .160 DQ110
Derrick Gdns, SE7
  off Anchor & Hope La ..104 EJ77
Derrick Rd, Beck. BR3 ..143 DZ97
Derry Av, S.Ock. RM15 .91 FU72
Derrydown, Wok. GU22 ..166 AW121
Derry Rd, Croy. CR0 ..141 DL104
Derry St, W8 ....100 DB75
Dersingham Av, E12 ..69 EN64
Dersingham Rd, NW2 ..63 CY63
Derwent Av, N18 .....46 DR50
  NW7 ....42 CR50
  SW15 ....118 CS91
  Barnet EN4 ....44 DF46
  Pinner HA5 ....40 BY51
  Uxbridge UB10 ......58 BN62
Derwent Cl, Add. KT15 .152 BK106
  Amersham HP7 ....20 AV39
  Dartford DA1 ....127 FH88
  Esher (Clay.) KT10 ..155 CE107
  Feltham TW14 ....115 BT88
Derwent Cres, N20 ...44 DC48
  Bexleyheath DA7 ....106 FA82
  Stanmore HA7 ......41 CJ54
Derwent Dr, NW9 ....42 CS57
  Hayes UB4 ....77 BS71
  Orpington BR5 ......145 ER101
  Purley CR8 ....160 DR113
Derwent Gdns, Ilf. IG4 .68 EL56
  Wembley HA9 ....61 CJ59
Derwent Gro, SE22 ..102 DT84
Derwent Par, S.Ock. RM15 .91 FV72
Derwent Ri, NW9 ....62 CS58
Derwent Rd, N13 ....45 DM49
  SE20 ....142 DU96
  SW20 ....139 CX100
  W5 ....97 CJ76
  Egham TW20 ....113 BB94
  Southall UB1 ......78 CA72
  Twickenham TW2 ...116 CB86
Derwent St, SE10 ...205 H10
Derwent Wk, Wall. SM6 .159 DH108
Derwentwater Rd, W3 ..80 CQ74
Derwent Way, Horn. RM12 .71 FH64
Derwent Yd, W5
  off Northfield Av ...97 CJ76
De Salis Rd, Uxb. UB10 .77 BQ70
Desborough Cl, W2 ..82 DB71
  Shepperton TW17 ...134 BN101
Desborough St, W2
  off Cirencester St ..82 DB71
Desenfans Rd, SE21 ..122 DS86
Desford Ct, Ashf. TW15
  off Desford Way 114 BM89
Desford Ms, E16
  off Desford Rd 86 EE70
Desford Rd, E16 ....86 EE70
Desford Way, Ashf. TW15 .114 BM89
★ Design Mus, SE1 ..202 A3
Desmond Rd, Wat. WD24 .23 BT36
Desmond St, SE14 ...103 DY79

Despard Rd, N19 ......65 DJ60
Detillens La, Oxt. RH8 ..188 EG129
Detling Cl, Horn. RM12 .72 FJ64
Detling Rd, Brom. BR1 ..124 EG92
  Erith DA8 ....107 FD80
  Gravesend (Nthflt.) DA11 .130 GD88
Detmold Rd, E5 ....66 DW61
Devalls Cl, E6 ....87 EN73
Devana End, Cars. SM5 .140 DF104
Devas Rd, SW20 ......139 CW95
Devas St, E3 ....85 EB70
Devenay Rd, E15 ....86 EF66
Devenish Rd, SE2 ....106 EU75
Deventer Cres, SE22 .122 DS85
De Vere Cotts, W8
  off Canning Pl 100 DC76
De Vere Gdns, W8 ...100 DC75
  Ilford IG1 ....69 EM61
Deverell St, SE1 ...201 K7
De Vere Ms, W8
  off Canning Pl 100 DC76
Devereux Ct, WC2 ...196 D9
Devereux Dr, Wat. WD17 .23 BS38
Devereux La, SW13 ..99 CV80
Devereux Rd, SW11 ..120 DF86
  Grays RM16 ....110 GB78
De Vere Wk, Wat. WD17 .23 BS40
Deverill Ct, SE20 ...142 DW95
Deverills Way, Slou. SL3 .93 BC77
Deveron Gdns, S.Ock. RM15 .91 FU71
Deveron Way, Rom. RM1 .51 FE53
Devey Cl, Kings.T. KT2 .118 CS94
Devils La, Egh. TW20 .113 BD94
Devitt Cl, Ashtd. KT21 .172 CN116
Devizes St, N1 off Poole St .84 DR67
Devoke Way, Walt. KT12 .136 BX103
Devon Av, Twick. TW2 .116 CC88
Devon Cl, N17 ....66 DT55
  Buckhurst Hill IG9 ..48 EH47
  Greenford UB6 ......79 CJ67
  Kenley CR8 ....176 DT116
Devon Ct, Buck.H. IG9 ..48 EH46
  Dartford (Sutt.H.) DA4 .148 FP95
Devon Cres, Red. RH1 .184 DD134
Devoncroft Gdns, Twick. TW1 .C87
Devonhurst Pl, W4
  off Heathfield Ter ..98 CR78
Devonia Gdns, N18 ..46 DQ51
Devonia Rd, N1 .....83 DP68
Devonport Gdns, Ilf. IG1 .69 EM58
Devonport Ms, W12
  off Devonport Rd ...81 CV74
Devonport Rd, W12 ..99 CV75
  Grays RM16 ....110 GB78
Devonport St, E1 ...84 DW72
Devon Ri, N2 ....64 DD56
Devon Rd, Bark. IG11 ..87 ES67
  Dartford (Sutt.H.) DA4 .148 FP95
  Redhill RH1 ....185 DJ130
  Sutton SM2 ....157 CY109
  Walton-on-Thames KT12 .154 BW105
  Watford WD24 ....24 BX39
Devons Estate, E3 ..85 EB69
Devonshire Av, Dart. DA1 .127 FH86
  Sutton SM2 ....158 DC108
  Tadworth KT20 .....182 CQ131
  Woking GU21 ....151 BC114
Devonshire Cl, E15 ..68 EE63
  N13 ....45 DN49
  W1 ....195 H6
Devonshire Cres, NW7 .43 CX52
Devonshire Dr, SE10 ..103 EB80
  Surbiton KT6 ......137 CK102
Devonshire Gdns, N17 .46 DQ51
  N21 ....46 DQ45
  W4 ....98 CQ80
Devonshire Gro, SE15 .102 DV79
Devonshire Hill La, N17 .46 DQ51
Devonshire Ho, Sutt. SM2
  off Devonshire Av ..158 DC108
Devonshire Ms, SW10
  off Park Wk 100 DD79
  W4 off Glebe St 98 CS78
Devonshire Ms N, W1 .195 H6
Devonshire Ms S, W1 .195 H6
Devonshire Ms W, W1 .195 H5
Devonshire Pas, W4 ..98 CS78
Devonshire Pl, NW2 ..64 DA62
  W1 ....194 G5
  W4 ....98 CS78
  W8 off St. Mary's Pl ..100 DB76
Devonshire Pl Ms, W1 .194 G5
Devonshire Rd, E16 ..86 EH72
  E17 ....67 EA58
  N9 ....46 DW46
  N13 ....45 DM49
  N17 ....46 DQ51
  NW7 ....43 CX52
  SE9 ....124 EL89
  SE23 ....122 DW88
  SW19 ....120 DE94
  W4 ....98 CS78
  W5 ....97 CJ76
  Bexleyheath DA6 ....106 EY84
  Carshalton SM5 ....158 DG105
  Croydon CR0 ....142 DR101
  Feltham TW13 ......116 BY90
  Gravesend DA12 ....131 GH88
  Grays RM16 ....110 FY77
  Harrow HA1 ....61 CD58
  Hornchurch RM12 ...72 FJ61
  Ilford IG2 ....69 ER59
  Orpington BR6 .....146 EU101
  Pinner (Eastcote) HA5 .60 BW58
  Pinner (Hatch End) HA5 .40 BZ53
  Southall UB1 ......78 CA71
  Sutton SM2 ....158 DC108
  Weybridge KT13 ...152 BN105
Devonshire Row, EC2 .197 N7
Devonshire Row Ms, W1 .195 J5
Devonshire Sq, EC2 ..197 N8
  Bromley BR2 ....144 EH98
Devonshire St, W1 ...194 G6
  W4 ....98 CS78
Devonshire Ter, W2 ..82 DC72
  Hayes UB4 ....77 BV74

Devons Road 85 EB70
Devons Rd, E3 ......85 EA71
Devon St, SE15 .....102 DV79
Devon Way, Chess. KT9 .155 CJ106
  Epsom KT19 ....156 CP106
  Uxbridge UB10 .....76 BM68
Devon Waye, Houns. TW5 .96 BZ80
De Walden St, W1 ...194 G7
Dewar St, SE15 .....102 DU83
Dewberry Gdns, E6 ..86 EL71
Dewberry St, E14 ...85 EC71
Dewey Path, Horn. RM12 .90 FJ65
Dewey Rd, N1 ....83 DN68
  Dagenham RM10 ...89 FB65
Dewey St, SW17 ....120 DF92
Dewgrass Gro, Wal.Cr. EN8 .31 DX35
Dewhurst Rd, W14 ..99 CX76
  Waltham Cross (Chsht.)
    EN8 ....14 DW29
Dewlands, Gdse. RH9 ..186 DW131
Dewlands Av, Dart. DA2 .128 FP87
Dewlands Ct, NW4
  off Holders Hill Rd ..43 CX54
Dewsbury Cl, Pnr. HA5 .60 BZ58
  Romford RM3 ....52 FL51
Dewsbury Ct, W4
  off Chiswick Rd 98 CQ77
Dewsbury Gdns, Rom. RM3 .52 FK51
  Worcester Park KT4 .139 CU104
Dewsbury Rd, NW10 .63 CU64
  Romford RM3 ....52 FK51
Dewsbury Ter, N1
  off Camden High St ..83 DH67
Dexter Cl, Grays RM17 .110 GA76
Dexter Ho, Erith DA18
  off Kale Rd 106 EY76
  Uxbridge (Hare.) UB9 .38 BJ54
Dexter Rd, Barn. EN5 .27 CX44
Deynecourt Gdns, Upmin.
  RM14 ....72 FQ61
Deyncourt Rd, N17 ..46 DQ53
Deynecourt Gdns, E11 .68 EJ56
D'Eynsford Rd, SE5 ..102 DR81
Diadem Ct, W1 .....195 M9
Dial Cl, Green. DA9
  off Knockhall Rd ..129 FX85
Dialmead, Pot.B. EN6
  off Crossoaks La ...11 CT34
Dial Wk, The, W8 ..100 DB75
Diameter Rd, Orp. BR5 .145 EP101
Diamond Cl, Dag. RM8 .70 EW60
  Grays RM16 ....110 FZ76
Diamond Rd, Ruis. HA4 .60 BX63
  Slough SL1 ....92 AU75
  Watford WD24 ......23 BU38
Diamond St, NW10 ..80 CR66
  SE15 ....102 DS80
Diamond Ter, SE10 ..103 EC81
Diamond Way, SE8
  off Deptford High St ..103 EA80
Diana Cl, E18 ....48 EH53
  SE8 off Staunton St ..103 DZ79
  Grays (Chaff.Hun.) RM16 .110 FZ76
  Slough (Geo.Grn.) SL3 .74 AY72
Diana Gdns, Surb. KT6 ..138 CM103
Diana Ho, SW13 ....99 CT81
Diana Pl, NW1 .....195 J4
Diana Rd, E17 ......67 DZ55
Dianne Way, Barn. EN4 .28 DE43
Dianthus Cl, SE2
  off Carnation St ...106 EV78
  Chertsey KT16 .....133 BE101
Dianthus Ct, Wok. GU22 .166 AX118
Diban Av, Horn. RM12 ..71 FH63
Dibden La, Sev. (Ide Hill)
  TN14 ....190 FE126
Dibden Row, SE1
  off Gerridge St 101 DN76
Dibden St, N1 .....83 DP67
Dibdin Cl, Sutt. SM1 .140 DA104
Dibdin Rd, Sutt. SM1 .140 DA104
Diceland Rd, Bans. SM7 .173 CZ116
Dicey Av, NW2 .....63 CW64
Dickens Av, N3 ....44 DC53
  Dartford DA1 ......108 FN84
  Tilbury RM18 ......111 GH81
  Uxbridge UB8 .....77 BP72
Dickens Cl, Erith DA8 .107 FB80
  Hayes UB3 off Croyde Av .95 BS77
  Richmond TW10 ....118 CL89
  Waltham Cross EN7 ..14 DU26
Dickens Ct, Add. KT15 .151 BF107
Dickens Est, SE1 ..202 B5
  SE16 ....202 B5
★ Dickens Ho, WC1 ..196 C5
Dickens Ho, NW6 ..82 DA69
Dickens La, N18 ..46 DS50
Dickenson Cl, N9
  off Croyland Rd ...46 DU46
Dickenson Rd, N8 ..65 DL59
  Feltham TW13 ......116 BW92
Dickensons La, SE25 .142 DU99
Dickensons Pl, SE25 .142 DU100
Dickenson St, NW5
  off Dalby St 83 DH65
Dickens Ri, Chig. IG7 ..49 EN48
Dickens Rd, E6 .....86 EK68
  Gravesend DA12 ...131 GL88
Dickens Sq, SE1 ...201 J6
Dickens St, SW8 ...101 DH82
Dickens Way, Rom. RM1 .71 FE56
Dickenswood Cl, SE19 .121 DP94
Dickerage La, N.Mal. KT3 .138 CQ97
Dickerage Rd, Kings.T. KT1 .138 CQ95
  New Malden KT3 ..138 CQ95
Dickinson Av, Rick. (Crox.Grn.)
  WD3 ....22 BN44
Dickinson Sq, Rick. (Crox.Grn.)
  WD3 ....22 BN44
Dickson, Wal.Cr. (Chsht.) EN7 .14 DT27
Dickson Fold, Pnr. HA5 ..60 BX56
Dickson Rd, SE9 ..104 EL83

Dick Turpin Way, Felt. TW14 ..95 BT84
Didsbury Cl, E6
  off Barking Rd 87 EM67
Digby Cres, N4 ....66 DQ61
Digby Gdns, Dag. RM10 ..88 FA67
Digby Pl, Croy. CR0 ..142 DT104
Digby Rd, E9 ....85 DX65
  Barking IG11 ......87 ET66
Digby St, E2 ......84 DW69
Digby Wk, Horn. RM12
  off Pembrey Way ..90 FJ65
Digby Way, W.Byf. (Byfleet) KT14
  off High Rd 152 BM112
Dig Dag Hill, Wal.Cr. (Chsht.)
  EN7 ....14 DT27
Digdens Ri, Epsom KT18 .172 CQ115
Diggon St, E1
  off Stepney Way ..85 DX71
Dighton Ct, SE5 ..102 DQ79
Dighton Rd, SW18 .120 DC85
Dignum St, N1
  off Cloudesley Rd ..83 DN68
Digswell Cl, Borwd. WD6 ..26 CN38
Digswell Rd, N8 ..65 DN65
Dilhorne Cl, SE12 .124 EH90
Dilke St, SW3 .....100 DF79
Dilloway Yd, Sthl. UB2
  off The Green 96 BY75
Dillwyn Cl, SE26 ..123 DY91
Dilston Cl, Nthlt. UB5
  off Yeading La 78 BW69
Dilston Gro, SE16 ..202 F8
Dilston Rd, Lthd. KT22 .171 CG119
Dilton Gdns, SW15 .119 CU88
Dilwyn Ct, E17 off Hillyfield ..67 DY55
Dimes Pl, W6 off King St ..99 CV77
Dimmock Dr, Grnf. UB6 ..61 CD64
Dimmocks La, Rick. (Sarratt)
  WD3 ....22 BH36
Dimond Cl, E7 .....68 EG63
Dimsdale Dr, NW9 ..62 CQ60
  Enfield EN1 ....30 DU44
Dimsdale Wk, E13
  off Stratford Rd ..86 EG67
Dimson Cres, E3 ..85 EA70
Dingle, The, Uxb. UB10 ..77 BP68
Dingle Cl, Barn. EN5 ..27 CT44
Dingle Gdns, E14 .204 A1
Dingle Rd, Ashf. TW15 .115 BP92
Dingley La, SW16 .121 DK89
Dingley Pl, EC1 ...197 J3
Dingley Rd, EC1 ..197 H3
Dingwall Av, Croy. CR0 .142 DQ103
Dingwall Gdns, NW11 .64 DA58
Dingwall Rd, SW18 .120 DC87
  Carshalton SM5 ..158 DF109
  Croydon CR0 ......142 DR103
Dinmont St, E2
  off Coate St 84 DV68
Dinmore, Hem.H. (Bov.) HP3 .5 AZ28
Dinsdale Cl, Wok. GU22 .167 BA118
Dinsdale Gdns, SE25 .142 DS99
  Barnet EN5 ....28 DB43
Dinsdale Rd, SE3 ..104 EF79
Dinsmore Rd, SW12 .121 DH87
Dinton Rd, SW19 ..120 DD93
  Kingston upon Thames
    KT2 ....118 CM94
Diploma Av, N2 ...64 DE56
Diploma Ct, N2
  off Diploma Av ...64 DE56
Dirdene Cl, Epsom KT17 .157 CT112
Dirdene Gdns, Epsom KT17 .157 CT112
Dirdene Gro, Epsom KT17 .156 CS112
Dirleton Rd, E15 ..86 EF67
Disbrowe Rd, W6 ..99 CY79
Discovery Business Pk, SE16
  off St. James's Rd .102 DU76
Discovery Wk, E1 ..202 D1
Dishforth La, NW9 ..42 CS53
Disney Ms, N4
  off Chesterfield Gdns ..65 DP57
Disney Pl, SE1 ...201 J4
Disney St, SE1 ...201 J4
Dison Cl, Enf. EN3 ..31 DX39
Disraeli Cl, SE28 ..88 EW74
  W4 off Acton La ...98 CR77
Disraeli Ct, Slou. SL3
  off Sutton Pl 93 BB79
Disraeli Gdns, SW15
  off Fawe Pk Rd ...99 CZ84
Disraeli Rd, E7 ...86 EG65
  NW10 ....80 CQ68
  SW15 ....99 CY84
  W5 ....79 CK74
Diss St, E2 ....197 P2
Distaff La, EC4 ..197 H10
Distillery La, W6
  off Fulham Palace Rd ..99 CW78
Distillery Rd, W6 ..99 CW78
Distillery Wk, Brent. TW8 ..98 CL79
Distin St, SE11 ...200 D9
District Rd, Wem. HA0 ..61 CH64
Ditch All, SE10 ...103 EB81
Ditchburn St, E14 .204 E1
Ditches La, Cat. CR3 ..175 DM122
  Coulsdon CR5 ....175 DL120
Ditches Ride, The, Loug.
  IG10 ....33 EN37
Ditchfield Rd, Hayes UB4 ..78 BY70
Dittisham Rd, SE9 ..124 EL91
Ditton Cl, T.Ditt. KT7 ..137 CG101
Dittoncroft Cl, Croy. CR0 .160 DS105
Ditton Gra Cl, Surb. KT6 .137 CK102
Ditton Gra Dr, Surb. KT6 .137 CK102
Ditton Hill, Surb. KT6 ..137 CJ102
Ditton Hill Rd, Surb. KT6 .137 CJ102
Ditton Lawn, T.Ditt. KT7 .137 CG102
Ditton Pk, Slou. SL3 ..92 AX78
Ditton Pk Rd, Slou. SL3 ..92 AX79
Ditton Pl, SE20 ...142 DV95
Ditton Reach, T.Ditt. KT7 .137 CH100
Ditton Rd, Bexh. DA6 ..126 EX85
  Slough SL3 ....93 AZ79
  Slough (Datchet) SL3 ..92 AX81
  Southall UB2 ......96 BZ77

★ Place of interest   ⇌ Railway station   ⊖ London Underground station   🚈 Docklands Light Railway station   ◈ Tramlink station   Ⓗ Hospital

Dow - Dun

Downsview Cl, Swan. BR8 . .147 FF97
Downsview Gdns, SE19 . .121 DP94
Downsview Rd, SE19 . . . . .122 DQ94
　Sevenoaks TN13 . . . . .190 FF125
Downs Way, Epsom KT18 . .173 CT116
Downsway, Orp. BR6 . . . . .163 ES106
Downsway, Oxt. RH8 . . . . .188 EE127
Downsway, S.Croy. CR2 . . .160 DS111
Downsway, Tad. KT20 . . . .173 CV121
Downsway, Whyt. CR3 . . . .176 DT116
Downsway, The, Sutt. SM2 .158 DC109
Downs Way Cl, Tad. KT20 . .173 CU121
Downs Wd, Epsom KT18 . . .173 CV117
Downswood, Reig. RH2 . . . .184 DE133
Downton Av, SW2 . . . . . . .121 DL89
Downview Cl, Cob. KT11 . . .169 BV119
Downway, N12 . . . . .44 DE52
Down Way, Nthlt. UB5 . . . . .77 BV69
Dowrey St, N1
　off Richmond Av 83 DN67
Dowry Wk, Wat. WD17 . . . .23 BT38
Dowsett Rd, N17 . . . . .46 DT54
Dowson Cl, SE5 . . . . .102 DR84
Doyce St, SE1 . . . . .201 H4
Doyle Cl, Erith DA8 . . . . . .107 FE81
Doyle Gdns, NW10 . . . . . . .81 CU67
Doyle Rd, SE25 . . . . .142 DU98
Doyle Way, Til. RM18
　off Coleridge Rd 111 GJ82
D'Oyley St, SW1 . . . . .198 F8
D'Oyly Carte Island, Wey.
　KT13 . . . . .135 BP102
Doynton St, N19 . . . . .65 DH61
Draco St, SE17 . . . . .102 DQ79
Dragonfly Cl, E13
　off Hollybush St 86 EH69
Dragon La, Wey. KT13 . . . .152 BN110
Dragon Rd, SE15 . . . . .102 DS79
Dragoon Rd, SE8 . . . . .103 DZ78
Dragor Rd, NW10 . . . . .80 CQ70
Drake Av, Cat. CR3 . . . . . .176 DQ122
　Slough SL3 . . . . .92 AX77
　Staines TW18 . . . . .113 BF92
Drake Cl, SE16 . . . . .203 J4
　Brentwood CM14 . . . . .54 FX50
Drake Ct, SE19 . . . . .122 DT92
　W12 . . . . .99 CW75
　Harrow HA2 . . . . .60 BZ60
Drake Cres, SE28 . . . . .88 EW72
Drakefell Rd, SE4 . . . . . . .103 DX82
　SE14 . . . . .103 DX82
Drakefield Rd, SW17 . . . . .120 DG90
Drakeley Ct, N5
　off Highbury Hill 65 DP63
Drake Ms, Horn. RM12
　off Fulmar Rd 89 FG66
Drake Rd, SE4 . . . . .103 EA83
　Chessington KT9 . . . . . . .156 CN106
　Croydon CR0 . . . . .141 DM101
　Grays (Chaff.Hun.) RM16 . .110 FY75
　Harrow HA2 . . . . .60 BZ61
　Mitcham CR4 . . . . .140 DG100
Drakes Cl, Esher KT10 . . . .154 CA106
　Waltham Cross (Chsht.)
　EN8 . . . . .15 DX28
Drakes Ctyd, NW6 . . . . . . .81 CZ66
Drakes Dr, Nthwd. HA6 . . . .39 BP53
Drakes Rd, Amer. HP7 . . . . .20 AS39
Drake St, WC1 . . . . .196 B7
　Enfield EN2 . . . . .30 DR39
Drakes Wk, E6 . . . . .87 EM67
Drakes Way, Wok. GU22 . . .166 AX122
Drakewood Rd, SW16 . . . .121 DK94
Draper Cl, Belv. DA17 . . . .106 EZ77
　Isleworth TW7 . . . . .97 CD82
Draper Pl, N1 off Dagmar Ter . .83 DP67
Drapers Gdns, EC2
　off Copthall Av 84 DR72
Drapers Rd, E15 . . . . .67 ED63
　N17 . . . . .66 DT55
　Enfield EN2 . . . . .29 DP40
Drappers Way, SE16 . . . . .202 C8
Draven Cl, Brom. BR2 . . . .144 EF101
Drawdock Rd, SE10 . . . . . .204 G3
Drawell Cl, SE18 . . . . .105 ES78
Drax Av, SW20 . . . . .119 CV94
Draxmont, SW19 . . . . .119 CY93
Draycot Rd, E11 . . . . .68 EH58
　Surbiton KT6 . . . . .138 CN102
Draycott Av, SW3 . . . . . . .198 C8
　Harrow HA3 . . . . .61 CH58
Draycott Cl, NW2 . . . . .63 CX62
　Harrow HA3 . . . . .61 CH58
Draycott Ms, SW6
　off New Kings Rd 99 CZ82
Draycott Pl, SW3 . . . . .198 D9
Draycott Ter, SW3 . . . . . . .198 E8
Drayford Cl, W9 . . . . .81 CZ70
Dray Gdns, SW2 . . . . .121 DM85
Draymans Way, Islw. TW7 . .97 CF83
Drayside Ms, Sthl. UB2
　off Kingston Rd 96 BZ75
Drayson Cl, Wal.Abb. EN9 . .16 EE32
Drayson Ms, W8 . . . . .100 DA75
Drayton Av, W13 . . . . .79 CG73
　Loughton IG10 . . . . .33 EM44
　Orpington BR6 . . . . .145 EP102
　Potters Bar EN6 . . . . .11 CY32
Drayton Br Rd, W7 . . . . . . .79 CF73
　W13 . . . . .79 CF73
Drayton Cl, Houns. TW4
　off Bramley Way 116 BZ85
　Ilford IG1 . . . . .69 ER60
　Leatherhead (Fetch.) KT22 .171 CE124
Drayton Ford, Rick. WD3 . . .38 BG48
Drayton Gdns, N21 . . . . . . .45 DP45
　SW10 . . . . .100 DC78
　W13 . . . . .79 CG73
　West Drayton UB7 . . . . . . .94 BL75
⇌ Drayton Green 79 CF72
Drayton Grn, W13 . . . . .79 CG73
Drayton Grn Rd, W13 . . . . .79 CH73
Drayton Gro, W13 . . . . .79 CG73

⇌ Drayton Park 65 DN63
Drayton Pk, N5 . . . . .65 DN64
Drayton Pk Ms, N5
　off Drayton Pk 65 DN64
Drayton Rd, E11 . . . . .67 ED60
　N17 . . . . .46 DS54
　NW10 . . . . .81 CT67
　W13 . . . . .79 CG73
　Borehamwood WD6 . . . . . .26 CN42
　Croydon CR0 . . . . .141 DP103
Drayton Waye, Har. HA3 . . . .61 CH58
Drenon Sq, Hayes UB3 . . . .77 BT73
Dresden Cl, NW6 . . . . .82 DB65
Dresden Rd, N19 . . . . .65 DK60
Dresden Way, Wey. KT13 . .153 BQ106
Dressington Av, SE4 . . . . . .123 EA86
Drew Av, NW7 . . . . .43 CY51
Drew Gdns, Grnf. UB6 . . . . .79 CF65
Drew Pl, Cat. CR3 . . . . . . .176 DR123
Drew Rd, E16 . . . . .86 EL74
Drewstead Rd, SW16 . . . . .121 DK89
Drey, The, Ger.Cr. (Chal.St.P.)
　SL9 . . . . .36 AY50
Driffield Rd, E3 . . . . .85 DY68
Drift, The, Brom. BR2 . . . . .144 EK104
Drift La, Cob. KT11 . . . . . .170 BZ117
Drift Way, Rich. TW10 . . . .118 CM88
　Slough (Colnbr.) SL3 . . . . .93 BC81
Driftway, The, Bans. SM7 . .173 CW115
　Leatherhead KT22
　off Downs La 171 CH123
　Mitcham CR4 . . . . .140 DG95
Driftwood Av, St.Alb. AL2 . . .8 CA26
Driftwood Dr, Ken. CR8 . . .175 DP117
Drill Hall Rd, Cher. KT16 . .134 BG101
Drinkwater Rd, Har. HA2 . . .60 CB61
Drive, The, E4 . . . . .47 ED45
　E17 . . . . .67 EB56
　E18 . . . . .68 EG56
　N3 . . . . .44 DA52
　N6 . . . . .64 DF57
　N11 . . . . .45 DJ51
　NW10 off Longstone Av . . .81 CT67
　NW11 . . . . .63 CY59
　SW6 off Fulham Rd 99 CY82
　SW16 . . . . .141 DM97
　SW20 . . . . .119 CW94
　W3 . . . . .80 CQ72
　Ashford TW15 . . . . .115 BR94
　Banstead SM7 . . . . .173 CY117
　Barking IG11 . . . . .87 ET66
　Barnet (High Barn.) EN5 . . .27 CY41
　Barnet (New Barn.) EN5 . . .28 DC44
　Beckenham BR3 . . . . .143 EA96
　Bexley DA5 . . . . .126 EW86
　Brentwood CM14 . . . . .54 FW50
　Buckhurst Hill IG9 . . . . . . .48 EJ45
　Chislehurst BR7 . . . . .145 ET97
　Chislehurst (Scad.Pk.)
　BR7 . . . . .145 ES95
　Cobham KT11 . . . . .154 BY114
　Coulsdon CR5 . . . . .159 DL114
　Edgware HA8 . . . . .42 CN50
　Enfield EN2 . . . . .30 DR39
　Epsom KT19 . . . . .156 CP111
　Epsom (Headley) KT18 . . .172 CN124
　Erith DA8 . . . . .107 FB80
　Esher KT10 . . . . .136 CC102
　Feltham TW14 . . . . .116 BW87
　Gerrards Cross (Chal.St.P.)
　SL9 . . . . .36 AY52
　Gravesend DA12 . . . . . . .131 GK91
　Harrow HA2 . . . . .60 CA59
　Hatfield (Brook.Pk.) AL9 . . .12 DA25
　Hounslow TW3 . . . . .97 CD82
　Ilford IG1 . . . . .69 EM60
　Isleworth TW7 . . . . .97 CD82
　Kingston upon Thames
　KT2 . . . . .118 CQ94
　Leatherhead (Fetch.) KT22 .171 CE122
　Leatherhead (Tyr.Wd.)
　KT22 . . . . .172 CN124
　Loughton IG10 . . . . .32 EL41
　Morden SM4 . . . . .140 DD99
　Northwood HA6 . . . . .39 BS54
　Orpington BR6 . . . . .145 ET103
　Potters Bar EN6 . . . . .11 CZ33
　Radlett WD7 . . . . .9 CG34
　Rickmansworth WD3 . . . . .22 BJ44
　Romford (Coll.Row) RM5 . . .51 FC53
　Romford (Harold Wd) RM3 . .52 FL53
　St. Albans (Lon.Col.) AL2 . . .9 CG26
　Sevenoaks TN13 . . . . . . .191 FH124
　Sidcup DA14 . . . . .126 EX90
　Slough SL3 . . . . .92 AY75
　Slough (Datchet) SL3 . . . . .92 AX81
　Staines (Wrays.) TW19 . . .112 AX85
　Surbiton KT6 . . . . .138 CL101
　Sutton SM2 . . . . .157 CZ112
　Thornton Heath CR7 . . . . .142 DR98
　Uxbridge UB10 . . . . .58 BL63
　Virginia Water GU25 . . . . .133 AZ99
　Wallington SM6 . . . . .159 DJ110
　Waltham Cross (Chsht.)
　EN7 . . . . .13 DP28
　Watford WD17 . . . . .23 BR37
　Wembley HA9 . . . . .62 CQ61
　West Wickham BR4 . . . . . .143 ED101
　Woking GU22 . . . . .166 AU120
Drive Mead, Couls. CR5 . . .159 DL114
Drive Rd, Couls. CR5 . . . . .175 DM119
Drive Spur, Tad. KT20 . . . .174 DB121
Driveway, The, E17
　off Hoe St 67 EB58
　Potters Bar (Cuffley) EN6 . .13 DL28
Droitwich Cl, SE26 . . . . . . .122 DU90
Dromey Gdns, Har. HA3 . . . .41 CF52
Dromore Rd, SW15 . . . . . .119 CY86
Dronfield Gdns, Dag. RM8 . .70 EW64
Droop St, W10 . . . . .81 CY70
Drop La, St.Alb. (Brick.Wd.)
　AL2 . . . . .8 CB30
Drover La, SE15 . . . . .102 DV80
Drovers Pl, SE15 . . . . .102 DV80
Drovers Rd, S.Croy. CR2 . .160 DR106
Droveway, Loug. IG10 . . . . .33 EP40

Drove Way, The, Grav. (Istead Rise)
　DA13 . . . . .130 GE94
Druce Rd, SE21 . . . . .122 DS86
Drudgeon Way, Dart. (Bean)
　DA2 . . . . .129 FV90
Druids Cl, Ashtd. KT21 . . . .172 CM120
Druid St, SE1 . . . . .201 N4
Druids Way, Brom. BR2 . . .143 ED98
Drumaline Ridge, Wor.Pk.
　KT4 . . . . .138 CS103
Drummond Av, Rom. RM7 . . .71 FD56
Drummond Cen, Croy. CR0 .142 DQ103
Drummond Cl, Erith DA8 . . .107 FE81
Drummond Cres, NW1 . . . .195 M2
Drummond Dr, Stan. HA7 . . .41 CF52
Drummond Gdns, Epsom
　KT19 . . . . .156 CP111
Drummond Gate, SW1 . . . .199 N10
Drummond Pl, Rich. TW9 . . .98 CL84
　Twickenham TW1 . . . . . . .117 CH86
Drummond Rd, E11 . . . . . . .68 EJ58
　SE16 . . . . .202 D6
　Croydon CR0 . . . . .142 DQ103
　Romford RM7 . . . . .71 FD56
Drummonds, The, Buck.H. IG9 .48 EH47
　Epping CM16 . . . . .18 EU30
Drummond St, NW1 . . . . . .195 K4
Drum St, E1
　off Whitechapel High St . . .84 DT72
Drury Cres, Croy. CR0 . . . .141 DN103
Drury La, WC2 . . . . .196 A9
Drury Rd, Har. HA1 . . . . . . .60 CC59
Drury Way, NW10 . . . . .62 CQ64
Drury Way Ind Est, NW10 . .62 CQ64
Dryad St, SW15 . . . . .99 CX83
Dryburgh Gdns, NW9 . . . . .62 CN55
Dryburgh Rd, SW15 . . . . . .99 CV83
Dryden Av, W7 . . . . .79 CF72
Dryden Cl, Ilf. IG6 . . . . .49 ET51
Dryden Ct, SE11 . . . . .200 E9
Dryden Pl, Til. RM18
　off Fielding Av 111 GH81
Dryden Rd, SW19 . . . . .120 DC93
　Enfield EN1 . . . . .30 DS44
　Harrow HA3 . . . . .41 CF53
　Welling DA16 . . . . .105 ES81
Dryden St, WC2 . . . . .196 A9
Dryden Twrs, Rom. RM3 . . . .51 FH52
Dryden Way, Orp. BR6 . . . .146 EU102
Dryfield Cl, NW10 . . . . .80 CQ65
Dryfield Rd, Edg. HA8 . . . . .42 CQ51
Dryfield Wk, SE8
　off New King St 103 EA79
Dryhill La, Sev. (Sund.) TN14 .190 FB123
Dryhill Rd, Belv. DA17 . . . .106 EZ79
Dryland Av, Orp. BR6 . . . . .163 ET105
Drylands Rd, N8 . . . . .65 DL58
Drynham Pk, Wey. KT13 . . .135 BS104
Drysdale Av, E4 . . . . .47 EB45
Drysdale Cl, Nthwd. HA6
　off Northbrook Dr 39 BS52
Drysdale Pl, N1 . . . . .197 N2
Drysdale St, N1 . . . . .197 N2
Duarte Pl, Grays RM16 . . . .110 FZ76
Dublin Av, E8 . . . . .84 DU67
Du Burstow Ter, W7 . . . . . .97 CE75
Ducal St, E2 off Brick La . . .84 DT69
Du Cane Cl, W12 . . . . .81 CW72
Du Cane Ct, SW17 . . . . . . .120 DG88
Du Cane Rd, W12 . . . . .81 CT72
Duchess Cl, N11 . . . . .45 DH50
　Sutton SM1 . . . . .158 DC105
Duchess Gro, Buck.H. IG9 . .48 EH47
Duchess Ms, W1 . . . . .195 J7
Duchess of Bedford's Wk,
　W8 . . . . .100 DA75
Duchess St, W1 . . . . .195 J7
Duchess Wk, Sev. TN15 . . .191 FL125
Duchy Rd, Barn. EN4 . . . . . .28 DD38
Duchy St, SE1 . . . . .200 E2
Ducie St, SW4 . . . . .101 DM84
Duckett Ms, N4
　off Duckett Rd 65 DP58
Duckett Rd, N4 . . . . .65 DP58
Ducketts Rd, Dart. DA1 . . .127 FF85
Duckett St, E1 . . . . .85 DX70
Ducking Stool Ct, Rom. RM1 .71 FE56
Duck La, W1 . . . . .195 M9
　Epping (Thnwd.) CM16 . . . .18 EW26
Duck Lees La, Enf. EN3 . . . .31 DY42
Ducks Hill, Nthwd. HA6 . . . .39 BP54
Ducks Hill Rd, Nthwd. HA6 . .39 BP54
　Ruislip HA4 . . . . .39 BP54
DUCKS ISLAND, Barn. 27 CX44
Ducks Wk, Twick. TW1 . . . .117 CJ85
Du Cros Dr, Stan. HA7 . . . . .41 CK51
Du Cros Rd, W3 off The Vale .80 CS74
Dudden Hill La, NW10 . . . . .63 CT63
Duddington Cl, SE9 . . . . . .124 EK91
Dudley Av, Har. HA3 . . . . . .61 CJ55
　Waltham Cross EN8 . . . . . .15 DX32
Dudley Cl, Add. KT15 . . . . .134 BJ104
　Grays (Chaff.Hun.) RM16 . .110 FY75
　Hemel Hempstead (Bov.)
　HP3 . . . . .5 BA27
Dudley Ct, NW11 . . . . .63 CZ56
　Slough SL1 off Upton Rd . . .92 AU76
Dudley Dr, Mord. SM4 . . . .139 CY101
　Ruislip HA4 . . . . .59 BV64
Dudley Gdns, W13 . . . . . . .97 CH75
　Harrow HA2 . . . . .60 CD60
　Romford RM3
　off Dudley Rd 52 FK51
Dudley Gro, Epsom KT18 . .156 CQ114
Dudley Ms, SW2
　off Bascombe St 121 DN86
Dudley Rd, E17 . . . . .47 EA54
　N3 . . . . .44 DB54
　NW6 . . . . .81 CY68
　SW19 . . . . .120 DA93
　Ashford TW15 . . . . .114 BM92
　Feltham TW14 . . . . .115 BQ88
　Gravesend (Nthflt.) DA11 . .130 GE87
　Harrow HA2 . . . . .60 CC61
　Ilford IG1 . . . . .69 EP63
　Kingston upon Thames
　KT1 . . . . .138 CM97

Dudley Rd, Rich. TW9 . . . . .98 CM82
　Romford RM3 . . . . .52 FK51
　Southall UB2 . . . . .96 BX75
　Walton-on-Thames KT12 . .135 BU100
Dudley St, W2 . . . . .82 DD71
Dudlington Rd, E5 . . . . .66 DW61
Dudmaston Ms, SW3 . . . . .198 A10
Dudsbury Rd, Dart. DA1 . . .127 FG86
　Sidcup DA14 . . . . .126 EV93
Dudset La, Houns. TW5 . . . .95 BU81
Dufferin Av, EC1 . . . . .197 K5
Dufferin St, EC1 . . . . .197 J5
Duffield Cl, Grays (Daniel Cl)
　RM16 . . . . .110 FY75
　Grays (Davis Rd) RM16 . . .110 FZ76
　Harrow HA1 . . . . .61 CF57
Duffield Dr, N15
　off Copperfield Dr 66 DT56
Duffield La, Slou. (Stoke P.)
　SL2 . . . . .74 AT65
Duffield Pk, Slou. (Stoke P.)
　SL2 . . . . .74 AT69
Duffield Rd, Tad. KT20 . . . .173 CV124
Duffins Orchard, Cher. (Ott.)
　KT16 . . . . .151 BC108
Duff St, E14 . . . . .85 EB72
Dufour's Pl, W1 . . . . .195 L9
Dugard Way, SE11 . . . . . . .200 F8
Dugdale Hill La, Pot.B. EN6 .11 CY33
Dugdales, Rick. (Crox.Grn.)
　WD3 . . . . .22 BN42
Duke Gdns, Ilf. IG6
　off Duke Rd 69 ER56
Duke Humphrey Rd, SE3 . . .104 EE81
Duke of Cambridge Cl, Twick.
　TW2 . . . . .117 CD86
Duke of Edinburgh Rd, Sutt.
　SM1 . . . . .140 DD103
Duke of Wellington Pl, SW1 .198 G4
Duke of York St, SW1 . . . . .199 L2
Duke Rd, W4 . . . . .98 CR78
　Ilford IG6 . . . . .69 ER56
Dukes Av, N3 . . . . .44 DB53
　N10 . . . . .65 DJ55
　W4 . . . . .98 CR78
　Edgware HA8 . . . . .42 CM51
　Epping (They.B.) CM16 . . . .33 ES35
　Grays RM17 . . . . .110 GA75
　Harrow HA1 . . . . .61 CE56
　Harrow (N.Har.) HA2 . . . . .60 BZ58
　Hounslow TW4 . . . . .96 BY84
　Kingston upon Thames
　KT2 . . . . .117 CJ91
　New Malden KT3 . . . . . . .139 CT97
　Northolt UB5 . . . . .78 BY66
　Richmond TW10 . . . . .117 CJ91
Dukes Cl, Ashf. TW15 . . . . .115 BQ91
　Epping (N.Wld.Bas.) CM16 . .19 FB27
　Gerrards Cross SL9 . . . . . .56 AX60
　Hampton TW12 . . . . .116 BZ92
Dukes Ct, E6 . . . . .87 EN67
　Woking GU21 . . . . .167 AZ117
Dukes Grn Av, Felt. TW14 . .115 BU85
Dukes Head Yd, N6
　off Highgate High St 65 DH60
Dukes Hill, Cat. (Wold.) CR3 .177 DY120
Duke Shore Pl, E14 . . . . . . .203 M1
Duke Shore Wf, E14
　off Narrow St 85 DZ73
Dukes Kiln Dr, Ger.Cr. SL9 . .56 AW60
Dukes La, W8 . . . . .100 DA75
　Gerrards Cross SL9 . . . . . .56 AY59
Dukes Lo, Nthwd. HA6
　off Eastbury Av 39 BS50
Duke's Meadows, W4
　off Great Chertsey Rd 98 CQ82
Dukes Ms, N10 off Dukes Av .65 DH55
Duke's Ms, W1 . . . . .194 G8
Dukes Orchard, Bex. DA5 . .127 FC88
Duke's Pas, E17 . . . . .67 EC56
Dukes Pl, EC3 . . . . .197 N9
Dukes Ride, Ger.Cr. SL9 . . .56 AY60
　Uxbridge UB10 . . . . .58 BL63
Dukes Rd, E6 . . . . .87 EN67
　W3 . . . . .80 CN71
Duke's Rd, WC1 . . . . .195 N3
Dukesthorpe Rd, SE26 . . . .123 DX91
Duke St, SW1 . . . . .199 L2
　W1 . . . . .194 G8
　Richmond TW9 . . . . .97 CK84
　Sutton SM1 . . . . .158 DD106
　Watford WD17 . . . . .24 BW41
　Woking GU21 . . . . .167 AZ117
Duke St Hill, SE1 . . . . .201 L2
Dukes Valley, Ger.Cr. SL9 . .56 AV61
Dukes Way, Uxb. UB8
　off Waterloo Rd 76 BJ67
　West Wickham BR4 . . . . . .144 EE104
Dukes Wd Av, Ger.Cr. SL9 . .56 AY60
Dukes Wd Dr, Ger.Cr. SL9 . .56 AW60
Duke's Yd, W1 . . . . .194 G10
Dulas St, N4 off Everleigh St .65 DM60
Dulford St, W11 . . . . .81 CY73
Dulka Rd, SW11 . . . . .120 DF85
Dulverton Rd, SE9 . . . . . . .125 EQ89
　Romford RM3 . . . . .52 FK51
　Ruislip HA4 . . . . .59 BU60
　South Croydon CR2 . . . . .160 DW110
DULWICH, SE21 . . . . .122 DS87
★ Dulwich Coll Picture Gall,
　SE21 . . . . .122 DS86
Dulwich Common, SE21 . . .122 DS88
　SE22 . . . . .122 DS88
Dulwich Lawn Cl, SE22
　off Colwell Rd 122 DT85
Dulwich Oaks, The, SE21 . .122 DS90
Dulwich Rd, SE24 . . . . .121 DN85
Dulwich Village, SE21 . . . .122 DS86
Dulwich Village, Rick. (Crox.Grn.)
　WD3 . . . . .22 BN43
Dulwich Wd Av, SE19 . . . . .122 DS91
Dulwich Wd Pk, SE19 . . . . .122 DS91

Dumbletons, The, Rick. (Map.Cr.)
　WD3 . . . . .37 BE49
Dumbreck Rd, SE9 . . . . . . .105 EM84
Dumfries Cl, Wat. WD19 . . . .39 BT48
Dumont Rd, N16 . . . . .66 DS62
Dumpton Pl, NW1
　off Gloucester Av 82 DG66
Dumville Dr, Gdse. RH9 . . .186 DV131
Dunally Pk, Shep. TW17 . . .135 BR101
Dunbar Av, SW16 . . . . .141 DN96
　Beckenham BR3 . . . . .143 DY98
　Dagenham RM10 . . . . .70 FA62
Dunbar Cl, Hayes UB4 . . . .77 BU71
Dunbar Cl, Slou. SL2 . . . . . .74 AU72
Dunbar Ct, Sutt. SM1 . . . . .158 DD106
　Walton-on-Thames KT12 . .136 BW103
Dunbar Gdns, Dag. RM10 . . .70 FA64
Dunbar Rd, E7 . . . . .86 EG65
　N22 . . . . .45 DN53
　New Malden KT3 . . . . . . .138 CQ98
Dunbar St, SE27 . . . . .122 DQ90
Dunblane Cl, Edg. HA8
　off Tayside Dr 42 CP47
Dunblane Rd, SE9 . . . . .104 EL83
Dunboe Pl, Shep. TW17 . . .135 BQ101
Dunboyne Rd, NW3 . . . . . . .64 DF64
Dunbridge Ho, SW15
　off Highcliffe Dr 119 CT86
Dunbridge St, E2 . . . . .84 DU70
Duncan Cl, Barn. EN5 . . . . .28 DC42
Duncan Gdns, Stai. TW18
　off Burges Way 114 BG92
Duncan Gro, W3 . . . . .80 CS72
Duncan Rd, E8 . . . . .84 DV67
　Richmond TW9 . . . . .98 CL84
　Tadworth KT20 . . . . .173 CY119
Duncan St, N1 . . . . .83 DP68
Duncan Ter, N1 . . . . .196 F1
Duncan Way, Bushey WD23 . .24 BZ40
Dunch St, E1 off Watney St . .84 DV72
Duncombe Cl, Amer. HP6 . . .20 AS38
Duncombe Ct, Stai. TW18 . .113 BF94
Duncombe Hill, SE23 . . . . .123 DY87
Duncombe Rd, N19 . . . . . . .65 DK60
Duncrievie Rd, SE13 . . . . . .123 ED86
Duncroft, SE18 . . . . .105 ES80
Duncroft Cl, Reig. RH2 . . . .183 CZ133
Dundalk Rd, SE4 . . . . .103 DY83
Dundas Gdns, W.Mol. KT8 . .136 CB97
Dundas Ms, Enf. EN3
　off Government Row 31 EA37
Dundas Rd, SE15 . . . . .102 DW83
Dundee Rd, E13 . . . . .86 EH68
　SE25 . . . . .142 DV99
Dundee St, E1 . . . . .202 D3
Dundee Way, Enf. EN3 . . . . .31 DY41
Dundela Gdns, Wor.Pk. KT4 .157 CV105
Dundonald Cl, E6
　off Northumberland Rd 86 EL72
◆ Dundonald Road 119 CZ94
Dundonald Rd, NW10 . . . . .81 CX67
　SW19 . . . . .119 CY94
Dundrey Cres, Red. RH1 . . .185 DL129
Dunedin Dr, Cat. CR3 . . . . .186 DS125
Dunedin Rd, E16
　off Manwood St 87 EM74
　E10 . . . . .67 EB62
　Ilford IG1 . . . . .69 EQ60
　Rainham RM13 . . . . .89 FF69
Dunedin Way, Hayes UB4 . . .78 BW70
Dunelm Gro, SE27 . . . . . . .122 DQ91
Dunelm St, E1 . . . . .85 DX72
Dunfee Way, W.Byf. KT14 . .152 BL112
Dunfield Gdns, SE6 . . . . . .123 EB91
Dunfield Rd, SE6 . . . . .123 EB92
Dunford Rd, N7 . . . . .65 DM63
Dungarvan Av, SW15 . . . . . .99 CU84
Dungates La, Bet. (Buckland)
　RH3 . . . . .183 CU133
Dunheved Cl, Th.Hth. CR7 . .141 DN100
Dunheved Rd N, Th.Hth. CR7 .141 DN100
Dunheved Rd S, Th.Hth. CR7 .141 DN100
Dunheved Rd W, Th.Hth.
　CR7 . . . . .141 DN100
Dunhill Pt, SW15
　off Dilton Gdns 119 CV88
Dunholme Grn, N9 . . . . .46 DT48
Dunholme La, N9
　off Dunholme Rd 46 DT48
Dunholme Rd, N9 . . . . .46 DT48
Dunkeld Rd, SE25 . . . . .142 DR98
　Dagenham RM8 . . . . .70 EV61
Dunkellin Gro, S.Ock. RM15
　off Dunkellin Way 91 FU72
Dunkellin Way, S.Ock. RM15 .91 FU72
Dunkery Rd, SE9 . . . . .124 EK91
Dunkin Rd, Dart. DA1 . . . . .108 FN84
Dunkirk Cl, Grav. DA12 . . . .131 GJ92
Dunkirk St, SE27
　off Waring St 122 DQ91
Dunlace Rd, E5 . . . . .66 DW63
Dunleary Cl, Houns. TW4 . .116 BZ87
Dunley Dr, Croy. (New Adgtn.)
　CR0 . . . . .161 EB108
Dunlin Ho, W13 . . . . .79 CF70
Dunloe Av, N17 . . . . .66 DR55
Dunloe St, E2 . . . . .197 P1
Dunlop Pl, SE16 . . . . .202 A7
Dunlop Rd, Til. RM18 . . . . .111 GF81
Dunmore Pt, E2 . . . . .197 P3
Dunmore Rd, NW6 . . . . .81 CY67
　SW20 . . . . .139 CW95
Dunmow Cl, Felt. TW13 . . . .116 BY91
　Loughton IG10 . . . . .32 EL44
　Romford RM6 . . . . .70 EW57
Dunmow Dr, Rain. RM13 . . . .89 FF67
Dunmow Ho, Dag. RM9 . . . .88 EV67
Dunmow Rd, E15 . . . . .67 ED63
Dunmow Wk, N1
　off Popham St 84 DQ67
Dunnage Cres, SE16 . . . . . .203 L8
Dunnets, Wok. (Knap.) GU21 .166 AS117
Dunning Cl, S.Ock. RM15
　off Dent Cl 91 FU72
Dunningford Cl, Horn. RM12 .71 FF64

Dunn Mead, NW9
  off Field Mead 43 CT52
Dunnock Cl, N9 ....47 DX46
  Borehamwood WD6 ...26 CN42
Dunnock Rd, E6 ....86 EL72
Dunns Pas, WC1 ....196 A8
Dunn St, E8 ....66 DT64
Dunny La, Kings L. (Chipper.)
  WD4 ....5 BE32
Dunnymans Rd, Bans. SM7 .173 CZ115
Dunollie Pl, NW5
  off Dunollie Rd 65 DJ64
Dunollie Rd, NW5 ....65 DJ64
Dunoon Rd, SE23 ....122 DW87
Dunraven Dr, Enf. EN2 ...29 DN40
Dunraven Rd, W12 ....81 CU74
Dunraven St, W1 ....194 E10
Dunsany Rd, W14 ....99 CX76
Dunsborough Pk, Wok. (Ripley)
  GU23 ....168 BJ120
Dunsbury Cl, Sutt. SM2
  off Nettlecombe Cl 158 DB109
Dunsfold Ri, Couls. CR5 ...159 DK113
Dunsfold Way, Croy. (New Adgtn.)
  CR0 ....161 EB108
  SW15 off Dover Pk Dr ...119 CV86
Dunsmore Cl, Bushey WD23 .25 CD44
  Hayes UB4
  off Kingsash Dr 78 BY70
Dunsmore Rd, Walt. KT12 .135 BV100
Dunsmore Way, Bushey
  WD23 ....25 CD44
Dunsmure Rd, N16 ....66 DS60
Dunspring La, Ilf. IG5 ...49 EP54
Dunstable Ms, W1 ....194 G6
Dunstable Rd, Rich. TW9 ..98 CL84
  Romford RM3 ....52 FK51
  West Molesey KT8 ......136 BZ98
Dunstall Grn, Wok. (Chobham)
  GU24 ....150 AW109
Dunstall Rd, SW20 ....139 CV93
Dunstall Way, W.Mol. KT8 .136 CB97
Dunstan Cl, N2
  off Thomas More Way ...64 DC55
Dunstan Rd, NW11 ....63 CZ60
  Coulsdon CR5 ....175 DK117
Dunstans Gro, SE22 ....122 DV86
Dunstans Rd, SE22 ....122 DU87
Dunster Av, Mord. SM4 ...139 CX102
Dunster Cl, Barn. EN5 ...27 CX42
  Romford RM5 ....51 FC54
  Uxbridge (Hare.) UB9 ...38 BH53
Dunster Ct, EC3 ....197 M10
  Borehamwood WD6
  off Kensington Way 26 CR41
Dunster Cres, Horn. RM11 .72 FN61
Dunster Dr, NW9 ....62 CQ60
Dunster Gdns, NW6 ....81 CZ66
Dunsterville Way, SE1 ...201 L5
Dunster Way, Har. HA2 ...60 BY62
  Wallington SM6
  off London Rd 140 DG102
Dunston Rd, E8 ....84 DT67
  SW11 ....100 DG82
Dunston St, E8 ....84 DT67
Duntshill Rd, SW18 ....120 DB88
Dunvegan Cl, W.Mol. KT8 .136 CB98
Dunvegan Rd, SE9 ....105 EM84
Dunwich Rd, Bexh. DA7 ...106 EZ81
Dunworth Ms, W11
  off Portobello Rd 81 CZ72
Duplex Ride, SW1 ....198 E5
Dupont Rd, SW20 ....139 CX96
Duppas Av, Croy. CR0
  off Violet La 159 DP105
Duppas Cl, Shep. TW17
  off Green La 135 BR99
Duppas Hill La, Croy. CR0
  off Duppas Hill Rd ...159 DP105
Duppas Hill Rd, Croy. CR0 .159 DP105
Duppas Hill Ter, Croy. CR0 .141 DP104
Duppas Rd, Croy. CR0 ...141 DN104
Dupre Cl, Grays (Chaff.Hun.)
  RM16 ....110 FY76
Dupree Rd, SE7 ....205 P10
Dura Den Cl, Beck. BR3 ...123 EB94
Durand Cl, Cars. SM5 ...140 DF102
Durand Gdns, SW9 ....101 DM81
Durand Way, NW10 ....80 CQ66
Durants Pk Av, Enf. EN3 ...31 DX42
Durants Rd, Enf. EN3 ...30 DW42
Durant St, E2 ....84 DU68
Durban Gdns, Dag. RM10 ..89 FC66
Durban Rd, E15 ....86 EE69
  E17 ....47 DZ53
  N17 ....46 DS51
  SE27 ....122 DQ91
  Beckenham BR3 ....143 DZ96
  Ilford IG2 ....69 ES60
Durban Rd E, Wat. WD18 ...23 BU42
Durban Rd W, Wat. WD18 ...23 BU42
Durbin Rd, Chess. KT9 ...156 CL105
Durdans Rd, Sthl. UB1 ...78 BZ72
Durell Gdns, Dag. RM9 ...70 EX64
Durell Rd, Dag. RM9 ...70 EX64
Durfold Dr, Reig. RH2 ...184 DC134
Durford Cres, SW15 ....119 CV88
Durham Av, Brom. BR2 ...144 EF98
  Hounslow TW5 ....96 BZ78
  Romford RM2 ....72 FJ56
  Woodford Green IG8 ...48 EK56
Durham Cl, SW20
  off Durham Rd 139 CV96
Durham Hill, Brom. BR1 ...124 EF91
Durham Ho St, WC2 ....200 A1
Durham Pl, SW3
  off Smith St 100 DF78

Durham Pl, Ilf. IG1
  off Eton Rd 69 EQ63
Durham Ri, SE18 ....105 EQ78
Durham Rd, E12 ....68 EK63
  E16 ....86 EE70
  N2 ....64 DE55
  N7 ....65 DM61
  N9 ....46 DU47
  SW20 ....139 CV95
  W5 ....97 CK75
  Borehamwood WD6 ...26 CQ41
  Bromley BR2 ....144 EF97
  Dagenham RM10 ....71 FC64
  Feltham TW14 ....116 BW87
Durham Rd, Har. HA1 ...60 CB57
  Sidcup DA14 ....126 EV92
Durham Row, E1 ....85 DY71
Durham St, SE11 ....101 DM78
Durham Ter, W2 ....82 DB72
Durham Wf, Brent. TW8
  off London Rd 97 CJ80
Durham Yd, E2
  off Teesdale St 84 DV69
Duriun Way, Erith DA8 ...107 FH80
Durley Av, Pnr. HA5 ...60 BY59
Durley Gdns, Orp. BR6 ...164 EV105
Durley Rd, N16 ....66 DS59
Durlston Rd, E5 ....66 DU61
  Kingston upon Thames
  KT2 ....118 CL93
Durndale La, Grav. (Nthflt.)
  DA11 ....131 GF91
Durnell Way, Loug. IG10 ...33 EN41
Durnford St, N15 ....66 DS57
  SE10 off Greenwich Ch St .103 EC79
Durnsford Av, SW19 ....120 DA89
Durnsford Rd, N11 ....45 DK53
  SW19 ....120 DA89
Durrants Cl, Rain. RM13 ...90 FJ68
Durrants Dr, Rick. (Crox.Grn.)
  WD3 ....23 BQ42
Durrant Way, Orp. BR6 ...163 ER106
  Swanscombe DA10 ....130 FY87
Durrell Rd, SW6 ....99 CZ81
Durrell Way, Shep. TW17 ..135 BR100
Durrington Av, SW20 ....139 CW95
Durrington Pk Rd, SW20 ...119 CW94
Durrington Rd, E5 ....67 DY63
Durrington Twr, SW8
  off Westbury St 101 DJ82
Dursley Cl, SE3 ....104 EJ82
Dursley Gdns, SE3 ....104 EK81
Dursley Rd, SE3 ....104 EJ82
Durward St, E1 ....84 DV71
Durweston Ms, W1 ....194 E6
Durweston St, W1 ....194 E6
Dury Falls Cl, Horn. RM11 .72 FM60
Dury Rd, Barn. EN5 ....27 CZ39
Dutch Barn Cl, Stai. (Stanw.)
  TW19 ....114 BK86
Dutch Elm Av, Wind. SL4 ...92 AT80
Dutch Gdns, Kings.T. KT2
  off Windmill Ri 118 CP93
Dutch Yd, SW18
  off Wandsworth High St .120 DA85
Duthie St, E14 ....204 E1
Dutton St, SE10 ....103 EC81
Dutton Way, Iver SL0 ...75 BE72
Duxberry Cl, Brom. BR2
  off Southborough La ...144 EL99
Duxford Cl, Horn. RM12 ...89 FH65
Duxford Ho, SE2
  off Wolvercote Rd 106 EX75
Dwight Ct, SW6
  off Burlington Rd 99 CY82
Dwight Rd, Wat. WD18 ...39 BR45
Dye Ho La, E3 ....85 EA67
Dyer's Bldgs, EC1 ....196 D7
Dyers Hall Rd, E11 ....68 EE60
Dyers La, SW15 ....99 CV84
Dyers Way, Rom. RM3 ...51 FH52
Dyke Dr, Orp. BR5 ....146 EW102
Dykes Path, Wok. GU21
  off Bracken Av 167 BC115
Dykes Way, Brom. BR2 ...144 EF97
Dykewood Cl, Bex. DA5 ...127 FE90
Dylan Cl, Borwd. (Elstree) WD6
  off Coates Rd 41 CK45
Dylan Rd, SE24 ....101 DP84
  Belvedere DA17 ....106 FA76
Dylan Thomas Ho, N8 ...65 DM56
Dylways, SE5 ....102 DR84
Dymchurch Cl, Ilf. IG5 ...49 EN54
  Orpington BR6 ....163 ES105
Dymes Path, SW19
  off Queensmere Rd ...119 CX89
Dymock St, SW6 ....100 DB83
Dymoke Rd, Horn. RM11 ...71 FF59
Dymond Est, SW17
  off Glenburnie Rd 120 DE90
Dyneley Rd, SE12 ....124 EJ91
Dyne Rd, NW6 ....81 CZ66
Dynevor Rd, N16 ....66 DS62
  Richmond TW10 ....118 CL85
Dynham Rd, NW6 ....82 DA66
Dyott St, WC1 ....195 P8
Dyrham La, Barn. EN5 ...27 CU36
Dysart Av, Kings.T. KT2 ...117 CJ92
Dysart St, EC2 ....197 M5
Dyson Rd, E11 ....68 EE58
  E15 ....86 EF65
Dysons Cl, Wal.Cr. EN8 ...15 DX33
Dysons Rd, N18 ....46 DV50

E

Eade Rd, N4 ....66 DQ59
Eagans Cl, N2 off Market Pl ..64 DE55
Eagle Av, Rom. RM6 ...70 EY58
Eagle Cl, SE16 off Varcoe Rd .102 DW78
  Amersham HP6 ....20 AT37
  Enfield EN3 ....30 DW42
  Hornchurch RM12 ....89 FH65

Eagle Cl, Wall. SM6 ....159 DL107
  Waltham Abbey EN9 ...16 EG34
Eagle Ct, EC1 ....196 F6
Eagle Dr, NW9 ....42 CS54
Eagle Hill, SE19 ....122 DR93
Eagle La, E11 ....68 EG56
Eagle Ms, N1
  off Tottenham Rd 84 DS65
Eagle Pl, SW1 ....199 L1
  SW7 off Old Brompton Rd .100 DC78
Eagle Rd, Wem. HA0 ...80 CL67
Eagles Dr, West. (Tats.) TN16 .178 EK118
Eaglesfield Rd, SE18 ....105 EP80
Eagles Rd, Green. DA9 ...109 FV84
Eagle St, WC1 ....196 B7
Eagle Ter, Wdf.Grn. IG8 ...48 EH52
Eagle Trd Est, Mitch. CR4
  off Willow La 140 DF100
Eagle Way, Brwd. CM13 ...53 FV67
  Gravesend (Nthflt.) DA11 .130 GA85
Eagle Wf, E14
  off Broomfield St 85 EB71
Eagle Wf Rd, N1 ....84 DQ68
Ealdham Sq, SE9 ....104 EJ84
EALING, W5 ....79 CJ73
≠ Ealing Broadway 79 CK73
⊖ Ealing Broadway 79 CK73
Ealing Bdy Shop Cen, W5 ...79 CK73
Ealing Cl, Borwd. WD6 ...26 CR39
Ealing Common, W5 ....80 CL74
★ Ealing Common 80 CM74
⊖ Ealing Common 80 CM74
Ealing Downs Ct, Grnf. UB6
  off Perivale La 79 CG69
Ealing Grn, W5 ....79 CK74
🏥 Ealing Hosp NHS Trust, Sthl.
  UB1 ....79 CD74
Ealing Pk Gdns, W5 ....97 CJ77
Ealing Rd, Brent. TW8 ...97 CK78
  Northolt UB5 ....78 CA66
  Wembley HA0 ....80 CL67
Ealing Village, W5 ....80 CL72
Eamont Cl, Ruis. HA4
  off Allonby Dr 59 BP59
Eamont St, NW8 ....82 DE68
Eardemont Cl, Dart. DA1 ...107 FF84
Eardley Cres, SW5 ....100 DA78
Eardley Pt, SE18
  off Wilmount St 105 EP77
Eardley Rd, SW16 ....121 DJ92
  Belvedere DA17 ....106 FA78
  Sevenoaks TN13 ....191 FH124
Earl Cl, N11 ....45 DH50
Earldom Rd, SW15 ....99 CW84
Earle Gdns, Kings.T. KT2 ...118 CL93
Earlewood, Cob. KT11 ...154 BX112
Earlham Gro, E7 ....68 EF64
  N22 ....45 DM52
Earlham St, WC2 ....195 N9
Earl Ri, SE18 ....105 ER77
Earl Rd, SW14 off Elm Rd ..98 CQ84
  Gravesend (Nthflt.) DA11 .130 GE89
EARLS COURT, SW5 ....99 CZ78
⊖ Earls Court 100 DA78
★ Earls Court Exhibition Cen,
  SW5 ....100 DA78
Earls Ct Gdns, SW5 ....100 DB77
Earls Ct Rd, SW5 ....100 DA77
  W8 ....100 DA76
Earls Ct Sq, SW5 ....100 DB78
Earls Cres, Har. HA1 ...61 CE56
Earlsdown Ho, Bark. IG11
  off Wheelers Cross 87 ER68
Earlsferry Way, N1 ....83 DM66
EARLSFIELD, SW18 ....120 DC88
≠ Earlsfield 120 DC88
Earlsfield Rd, SW18 ....120 DC88
Earlshall Rd, SE9 ....105 EM84
Earls La, Pot.B. EN6 ...12 CS32
Earlsmead, Har. HA2 ...60 BZ63
Earlsmead Rd, N15 ....66 DT57
  NW10 ....81 CW69
Earl's Path, Loug. IG10 ...32 EJ40
Earls Ter, W8 ....99 CZ76
Earlsthorpe Ms, SW12 ...120 DG86
Earlsthorpe Rd, SE26 ...123 DX91
Earlstoke St, EC1 ....196 F2
Earlston Gro, E9 ....84 DV67
Earl St, EC2 ....197 M6
  Watford WD17 ....24 BW41
Earls Wk, W8 ....100 DA76
  Dagenham RM8 ....70 EV63
Earls Way, Orp. BR6
  off Station Rd 145 ET103
Earlswood Av, Th.Hth. CR7 .141 DN99
Earlswood Cl, SE10
  off Earlswood St 104 EE78
Earlswood Gdns, Ilf. IG5 ...69 EN55
Earlswood St, SE10 ....104 EE78
Early Ms, NW1
  off Arlington Rd 83 DH67
Earnshaw St, WC2 ....195 N8
Earsby St, W14 ....99 CY77
Easby Cres, Mord. SM4 ...140 DB100
Easebourne Rd, Dag. RM8 ..70 EW64
Easedale Dr, Horn. RM12 ...71 FG64
Easedale Ho, Islw. TW7
  off Summerwood Rd ...117 CF85
Eashing Pt, SW15
  off Wanborough Dr ...119 CV88
Easington Way, S.Ock. RM15 .91 FU71
Easley's Ms, W1 ....194 G8
EAST ACTON, W3 ....80 CR74
⊖ East Acton 81 CT72
East Acton La, W3 ....80 CS73
East Arbour St, E1 ....85 DX72
East Av, E12 ....86 EL66
  E17 ....67 EC57
  Hayes UB3 ....95 BT75
  Southall UB1 ....78 BZ73
  Wallington SM6 ....159 DM106
  Walton-on-Thames KT12
  off Octagon Rd 153 BT110
East Bk, N16 ....66 DS59
Eastbank Rd, Hmptn. (Hmptn.H.)
  TW12 ....116 CC92
EAST BARNET, Barn. 28 DE44
East Barnet Rd, Barn. EN4 ..28 DD44

EAST BEDFONT, Felt. 115 BS88
Eastbourne Av, W3 ....80 CR72
Eastbourne Gdns, SW14 ...98 CQ83
Eastbourne Ms, W2 ....82 DC72
Eastbourne Rd, E6 ....87 EN69
  E15 ....86 EE67
  N15 ....66 DS58
  SW17 ....120 DG93
  W4 ....98 CQ79
  Brentford TW8 ....97 CJ78
  Feltham TW13 ....116 BX89
  Godstone RH9 ....186 DW132
Eastbournia Av, N9 ....46 DV48
Eastbridge, Slou. SL2
  off Victoria Rd 74 AV74
Eastbrook Av, N9 ....46 DW46
  Dagenham RM10 ....71 FC63
Eastbrook Cl, Wok. GU21 ...167 BA116
Eastbrook Dr, Rom. RM7 ...71 FE62
Eastbrook Rd, SE3 ....104 EH80
  Waltham Abbey EN9 ...16 EE33
EASTBURY, Nthwd. 39 BS49
Eastbury Av, Bark. IG11 ...87 ES67
  Enfield EN1 ....30 DS39
  Northwood HA6 ....39 BS50
Eastbury Ct, Bark. IG11 ...87 ES67
Eastbury Gro, W4 ....98 CS78
Eastbury Ho, Bark. IG11 ...87 ET67
★ Eastbury Ho, Bark. IG11 ...87 ET67
Eastbury Rd, E6 ....87 EN70
  Kingston upon Thames
  KT2 ....118 CL94
  Northwood HA6 ....39 BS51
  Orpington BR5 ....145 ER100
  Romford RM7 ....71 FD58
  Watford WD19 ....39 BV45
Eastbury Sq, Bark. IG11 ...87 ET67
Eastbury Ter, E1 ....85 DX70
Eastcastle St, W1 ....195 K8
Eastcheap, EC3 ....197 L10
East Churchfield Rd, W3 ...80 CR74
Eastchurch Rd, Houns. (Hthrw.Air.)
  TW6 ....95 BS82
East Cl, W5 ....80 CN70
  Barnet EN4 ....28 DG42
  Greenford UB6 ....78 CC68
  Rainham RM13 ....89 FH70
  St. Albans AL2 ....8 CB25
Eastcombe Av, SE7 ....104 EH79
East Common, Ger.Cr. SL9 ...56 AY59
EASTCOTE, Pnr. 60 BW58
⊖ Eastcote 60 BW59
Eastcote, Orp. BR6 ....145 ET102
Eastcote Av, Grnf. UB6 ...61 CG64
  Harrow HA2 ....60 CB61
  West Molesey KT8 ....136 BZ99
Eastcote La, Har. HA2 ...60 CA62
  Northolt UB5 ....78 CA66
Eastcote La N, Nthlt. UB5 ...78 BZ65
Eastcote Pl, Pnr. HA5 ...59 BV58
Eastcote Rd, Har. HA2 ...60 CC62
  Pinner HA5 ....60 BX57
  Pinner (Eastcote Vill.) HA5 .59 BU58
  Ruislip HA4 ....59 BS59
  Welling DA16 ....105 ER82
Eastcote St, SW9 ....101 DM82
Eastcote Vw, Pnr. HA5 ...60 BW56
EASTCOTE VILLAGE, Pnr. ...59 BV57
Eastcourt, Sun. TW16 ....136 BW96
East Ct, Wem. HA0 ....61 CJ61
East Cres, N11 ....44 DF49
  Enfield EN1 ....30 DT43
East Cres Rd, Grav. DA12 ..131 GJ86
Eastcroft Rd, Epsom KT19 ..156 CS108
East Cross Cen, E15 ....85 EA65
East Cross Route, E3 ....85 DZ66
  E9 ....85 DZ65
≠ East Croydon 142 DR103
⊖ East Croydon 142 DR103
Eastdean Av, Epsom KT18 ..156 CP113
East Dene Dr, Rom. (Harold Hill)
  RM3 ....52 FK50
Eastdown Pk, SE13 ....103 ED84
East Dr, Cars. SM5 ....158 DE109
  Northwood HA6 ....39 BS47
  Orpington BR5 ....146 EV100
  Slough (Stoke P.) SL2 ...74 AS69
  Virginia Water GU25 ....132 AU101
  Watford WD25 ....23 BV35
East Duck Lees La, Enf. EN3 .31 DY42
EAST DULWICH, SE22 ....122 DU86
≠ East Dulwich 102 DS84
East Dulwich Gro, SE22 ...122 DS86
East Dulwich Rd, SE15 ...102 DT84
  SE22 ....102 DT84
East End Rd, N2 ....64 DC55
  N3 ....44 DA54
East End Way, Pnr. HA5 ...60 BY56
East Entrance, Dag. RM10 ..89 FB68
Eastern Av, E11 ....68 EJ58
  Chertsey KT16 ....134 BG97
  Grays (W.Thur.) RM20 ...109 FT78
  Ilford IG2, IG4 ....68 EL58
  Pinner HA5 ....60 BX59
  Romford RM6 ....70 EW56
  South Ockendon (Aveley)
  RM15 ....90 FQ74
  Waltham Cross EN8 ...15 DY33
Eastern Av E, Rom. RM1,
  RM2, RM3 ....71 FD55
Eastern Av W, Rom. RM1,
  RM5, RM6, RM7 ....70 EY56
Eastern Ind Est, Erith DA18 .106 FA75
Eastern Pathway, Horn.
  RM12 ....90 FJ67
Eastern Perimeter Rd Houns.
  (Hthrw.Air.) TW6 ....95 BT83
Eastern Rd, E13 ....86 EH68
  E17 ....67 EC57
  N2 ....64 DF56
  N22 ....45 DL53
  SE4 ....103 EA84
  Grays RM17 ....110 GD77
  Romford RM1 ....71 FE57

Eastern Vw, West. (Bigg.H.)
  TN16 ....178 EJ117
Easternville Gdns, Ilf. IG2 ...69 EQ58
Eastern Way, SE2 ....88 EX74
  SE28 ....106 EU75
  Belvedere DA17 ....107 FB75
  Erith DA18 ....88 EX74
  Grays RM17 ....110 GA79
EAST EWELL, Sutt. 157 CX110
East Ferry Rd, E14 ....204 C8
Eastfield Av, Wat. WD24 ...24 BX39
Eastfield Cl, Slou. SL1
  off St. Laurence Way 92 AU76
Eastfield Cotts, Hayes UB3 ..95 BS78
Eastfield Gdns, Dag. RM10 ..70 FA63
Eastfield Par, Pot.B. EN6 ...12 DD32
Eastfield Rd, E17 ....47 EA56
  N8 ....65 DL55
  Brentwood CM14 ....54 FX47
  Dagenham RM9, RM10 ...70 FA63
  Enfield EN3 ....31 DX38
  Waltham Cross EN8 ...15 DY32
Eastfields, Pnr. HA5 ....60 BW57
Eastfields Rd, W3 ....80 CQ71
  Mitcham CR4 ....140 DG96
Eastfield St, E14 ....85 DY71
EAST FINCHLEY, N2 ....64 DD56
⊖ East Finchley 64 DE56
East Gdns, SW17 ....120 DE93
Eastgate, Bans. SM7 ....157 CY114
Eastgate Cl, SE28 ....88 EX72
Eastglade, Nthwd. HA6 ...39 BS50
  Pinner HA5 ....60 BY55
East Gorse, Croy. CR0 ...161 DY112
East Grn, Hem.H. HP3 ...6 BM25
East Hall La, Rain. (Wenn.)
  RM13 ....90 FK72
East Hall Rd, Orp. BR5 ...146 EY101
EAST HAM, E6 ....86 EL68
⊖ East Ham 86 EL66
Eastham Cl, Barn. EN5 ...27 CY43
Eastham Cres, Brwd. CM13 ..55 GA49
East Ham Ind Est, E6 ....86 EL70
East Ham Manor Way, E6 ...87 EN72
🏥 East Ham Mem Hosp, E7 ..86 EK66
East Ham Shop Hall, E6
  off Myrtle Rd 86 EL67
East Harding St, EC4 ....196 E8
East Heath Rd, NW3 ....64 DD62
East Hill, SW18 ....120 DB85
  Dartford DA1 ....128 FM87
  Dartford (S.Darenth) DA4 .148 FQ95
  Oxted RH8 ....188 EE129
  South Croydon CR2 ...160 DS110
  Wembley HA9 ....62 CN61
  Westerham (Bigg.H.) TN16 .178 EH118
  Woking GU22 ....167 BC116
East Hill Dr, Dart. DA1 ...128 FM87
East Hill Rd, Oxt. RH8 ...188 EE129
Eastholm, NW11 ....64 DB56
East Holme, Erith DA8 ...107 FD81
Eastholme, Hayes UB3 ...77 BU74
DLR East India 85 ED73
East India Dock Rd, E14 ...85 EA72
East Kent Av, Grav. (Nthflt.)
  DA11 ....130 GC86
Eastlake Rd, SE5 ....101 DP82
Eastlands Cl, Oxt. RH8
  off Eastlands Way 187 ED127
Eastlands Cres, SE21 ....122 DT86
Eastlands Way, Oxt. RH8 ...187 ED127
East La, SE16 ....202 B5
  Abbots Langley WD5 ...7 BU29
  Dartford (S.Darenth) DA4 .149 FR96
  Kingston upon Thames KT1
  off High St 137 CK97
  Wembley HA0, HA9 ....61 CK62
Eastlea Av, Wat. WD25 ...24 BY37
Eastlea Ms, E16
  off Desford Rd 86 EE70
Eastleigh Av, Har. HA2 ...60 CB61
Eastleigh Cl, NW2 ....62 CS62
  Sutton SM2 ....158 DB108
Eastleigh Rd, E17 ....47 DZ54
  Bexleyheath DA7 ....107 FC82
  Hounslow (Hthrw.Air.) TW6
  off Cranford La 95 BT83
Eastleigh Wk, SW15 ....119 CU87
Eastleigh Way, Felt. TW14 ..115 BU88
East Lo La, Enf. EN2 ...29 DK36
🏥 Eastman Dental Hosp,
  WC1 ....196 B4
Eastman Rd, W3 ....80 CR74
East Mascalls, SE7
  off Mascalls Rd 104 EJ79
East Mead, Ruis. HA4 ...60 BX62
Eastmead, Wok. GU21 ...166 AV117
Eastmead Av, Grnf. UB6 ...78 CB69
Eastmead Cl, Brom. BR1 ...144 EL96
Eastmearn Rd, SE21 ....122 DQ89
East Mill, Grav. DA11 ...131 GF86
East Milton Rd, Grav. DA12 .131 GK87
EAST MOLESEY 137 CD98
Eastmont Rd, Esher KT10 ..137 CE103
Eastmoor Pl, SE7
  off Eastmoor St 104 EK76
Eastmoor St, SE7 ....104 EK76
East Mt St, E1 ....84 DV71
Eastney Rd, Croy. CR0 ...141 DP102
Eastney St, SE10 ....103 ED78
Eastnor, Hem.H. (Bov.) HP3 ...5 BA28
Eastnor Rd, SE9 ....125 EQ88
Easton Gdns, Borwd. WD6 ..26 CR42
Easton St, WC1 ....196 D3
East Pk Cl, Rom. RM6 ...70 EX57
East Parkside, SE10 ....205 K5
  Warlingham CR6 ....177 EA116
East Pas, EC1 ....196 G6
East Pier, E1 ....202 D3
East Pl, SE27 off Pilgrim Hill .122 DQ91
East Poultry Av, EC1 ....196 F7
⊖ East Putney 119 CY85
East Ramp, Houns. (Hthrw.Air.)
  TW6 ....95 BP81

★ Place of interest   ≠ Railway station   ⊖ London Underground station   DLR Docklands Light Railway station   ◇ Tramlink station   🏥 Hospital

Eas - Eld

East Ridgeway, Pot.B. (Cuffley)
EN6 . . . . . .13 DK29
East Rd, E15 . . . . . .86 EG67
N1 . . . . . .197 K3
SW19 . . . . . .120 DC93
Barnet EN4 . . . . . .44 DG66
Edgware HA8 . . . . . .42 CP53
Enfield EN3 . . . . . .30 DW38
Feltham TW14 . . . . . .115 BR87
Kingston upon Thames
KT2 . . . . . .138 CL95
Reigate RH2 . . . . . .183 CZ133
Romford (Chad.Hth.) RM6 . .70 EY57
Romford (Rush Grn.) RM7 . .71 FD59
Welling DA16 . . . . . .106 EV82
West Drayton UB7 . . . . . .94 BM77
Weybridge KT13 . . . . . .153 BR108
East Rochester Way, SE9 . . .105 ES84
Bexley DA5 . . . . . .127 FC87
Sidcup DA15 . . . . . .105 ES84
East Row, E11 . . . . . .68 EG58
W10 . . . . . .81 CY70
Eastry Av, Brom. BR2 . . .144 EF100
Eastry Rd, Erith DA8 . . .106 FA80
EAST SHEEN, SW14 . . . .98 CR84
East Sheen Av, SW14 . . .98 CR84
Eastside Rd, NW11 . . . .63 CZ56
East Smithfield, E1 . . .202 A1
East St, SE17 . . . . . .201 J10
Barking IG11 . . . . . .87 EQ66
Bexleyheath DA7 . . . .106 FA84
Brentford TW8 . . . . . .97 CJ80
Bromley BR1 . . . . . .144 EG96
Chertsey KT16 . . . . . .134 BG101
Epsom KT17 . . . . . .156 CS113
Grays RM17 . . . . . .110 GC79
Grays (S.Stfd.) RM20 . . .110 FY79
East Surrey Gro, SE15 . . .102 DT80
★ East Surrey Mus, Cat.
CR3 . . . . . .176 DU124
East Tenter St, E1 . . . . . .84 DT72
East Ter, Grav. DA12 . . .131 GJ86
East Thurrock Rd, Grays
RM17 . . . . . .110 GB79
East Twrs, Pnr. HA5 . . .60 BX57
East Vw, E4 . . . . . .47 EC50
Barnet EN5 . . . . . .27 CZ41
Eastview Av, SE18 . . . .105 ES80
Eastville Av, NW11 . . . .63 CZ58
East Wk, Barn. EN4 . . . .44 DG46
Hayes UB3 . . . . . .77 BU74
Reigate RH2 . . . . . .184 DB134
Eastway, E9 . . . . . .85 DZ65
East Way, E11 . . . . . .68 EH57
Bromley BR2 . . . . . .144 EG101
Croydon CR0 . . . . . .143 DY103
Eastway, Epsom KT19 . . .156 CQ112
East Way, Hayes UB3 . . .77 BU74
Eastway, Mord. SM4 . . .139 CX99
East Way, Ruis. HA4 . . .59 BU60
Eastway, Wall. SM6 . . .159 DJ105
Eastway Commercial Cen, E9 .67 EA64
Eastwell Cl, Beck. BR3 . . .143 DY95
Eastwick Ct, SW19
off Victoria Dr 119 CX88
Eastwick Cres, Rick. (Mill End)
WD3 . . . . . .37 BF47
Eastwick Dr, Lthd. (Bkhm.)
KT23 . . . . . .170 CA123
EAST WICKHAM, Well. . . .106 EU80
Eastwick Pk Av, Lthd. (Bkhm.)
KT23 . . . . . .170 CB124
Eastwick Rd, Walt. KT12 . .153 BV106
Eastwood Cl, E18
off George La 48 EG54
N7 off Eden Gro 65 DN64
N17
off Northumberland Gro . .46 DV52
Eastwood Dr, Rain. RM13 . .89 FH72
Eastwood Rd, E18 . . . . . .48 EG54
N10 . . . . . .44 DG54
Ilford IG3 . . . . . .70 EU59
West Drayton UB7 . . . . . .94 BN75
East Woodside, Bex. DA5 . .126 EY88
Eastwood St, SW16 . . . .121 DJ93
Eastworth Rd, Cher. KT16 . .134 BG102
Eatington Rd, E10 . . . .67 ED57
Eaton Cl, SW1 . . . . . .198 F9
Stanmore HA7 . . . . . .41 CH49
Eaton Dr, SW9 . . . . . .101 DP84
Kingston upon Thames
KT2 . . . . . .118 CN94
Romford RM5 . . . . . .51 FB52
Eaton Gdns, Dag. RM9 . . .88 EY66
Eaton Gate, SW1 . . . . . .198 F8
Northwood HA6 . . . . . .39 BQ51
Eaton Ho, E14
off Westferry Circ 85 EA74
Eaton La, SW1 . . . . . .199 J7
Eaton Ms N, SW1 . . . . . .198 F8
Eaton Ms S, SW1 . . . . . .198 G8
Eaton Ms W, SW1 . . . . . .198 G8
Eaton Pk, Cob. KT11 . . . .154 BY114
Eaton Pk Rd, N13 . . . . . .45 DN47
Cobham KT11 . . . . . .154 BY114
Eaton Pl, SW1 . . . . . .198 F7
Eaton Ri, E11 . . . . . .68 EJ57
W5 . . . . . .79 CK72
Eaton Rd, NW4 . . . . . .63 CW57
Enfield EN1 . . . . . .30 DS41
Hounslow TW3 . . . . . .97 CD84
Sidcup DA14 . . . . . .126 EX89
Sutton SM2 . . . . . .158 DD107
Upminster RM14 . . . . . .73 FS61
Eaton Row, SW1 . . . . . .199 H7
Eatons Mead, E4 . . . . . .47 EA47
Eaton Sq, SW1 . . . . . .199 H6
Longfield DA3
off Bramblefield Cl 149 FX97
Eaton Ter, SW1 . . . . . .198 F8
Eaton Ter Ms, SW1 . . . . . .198 F8
Eatonville Rd, SW17 . . . .120 DF89
Eatonville Vil, SW17
off Eatonville Rd 120 DF89

Ebbas Way, Epsom KT18 . .172 CP115
Ebbisham Cl, SW8 . . . . . .101 DM79
Ebbisham La, Tad. KT20 . .173 CT121
Ebbisham Rd, Epsom KT18 .156 CP114
Worcester Park KT4 . . .139 CW103
Ebbsfleet Ind Est, Grav. (Nthflt.)
DA11 . . . . . .130 GA85
Ebbsfleet Rd, NW2 . . . .63 CY63
Ebbsfleet Wk, Grav. (Nthflt.)
DA11 . . . . . .130 GB86
Ebdon Way, SE3 . . . . . .104 EH83
Ebenezer Ho, SE11 . . . .200 E9
Ebenezer St, N1 . . . . . .197 K2
Ebenezer Wk, SW16 . . . .141 DJ95
Ebley Cl, SE15 . . . . . .102 DT79
Ebner St, SW18 . . . . . .120 DB85
Ebor St, E1 . . . . . .197 P4
Ebrington Rd, Har. HA3 . .61 CK58
Ebsworth St, SE23 . . . .123 DX87
Eburne Rd, N7 . . . . . .65 DL62
Ebury Br, SW1 . . . . . .199 H10
Ebury Br Est, SW1 . . . . . .199 H10
Ebury Br Rd, SW1 . . . . . .100 DG78
Ebury Cl, Kes. BR2 . . . .144 EL104
Northwood HA6 . . . . . .39 BQ50
Ebury Ms, SE27 . . . . . .121 DP90
SW1 . . . . . .198 G8
Ebury Ms E, SW1 . . . . . .199 H8
Ebury Rd, Rick. WD3 . . . .38 BK46
Watford WD17 . . . . . .24 BW41
Ebury Sq, SW1 . . . . . .198 G9
Ebury St, SW1 . . . . . .199 H8
Ebury Way Cycle Path, The, Rick.
WD3 . . . . . .39 BP45
Watford WD18 . . . . . .39 BP45
Ecclesbourne Cl, N13 . . . .45 DN50
Ecclesbourne Gdns, N13 . .45 DN50
Ecclesbourne Rd, N1 . . . .84 DQ66
Thornton Heath CR7 . . .142 DQ99
Eccles Rd, SW11 . . . . . .100 DF84
Eccleston Br, SW1 . . . . . .199 J8
Eccleston Cl, Barn. EN4 . .28 DF42
Orpington BR6 . . . . . .145 ER102
Eccleston Cres, Rom. RM6 . .70 EU59
Eccleston Ct, Wem. HA9
off St. John's Rd 62 CL64
Eccleston Pl, Wem. HA9 . .62 CM64
Eccleston Ms, SW1 . . . . . .198 G7
Eccleston Pl, SW1 . . . . . .199 H8
Eccleston Rd, W13 . . . . . .79 CG73
Eccleston Sq, SW1 . . . . . .199 J9
Eccleston Sq Ms, SW1 . . .199 K9
Eccleston St, SW1 . . . . . .199 H7
Echelforde Dr, Ashf. TW15 .114 BN91
Echo Hts, E4
off Mount Echo Dr 47 EB46
Echo Sq, Grav. DA12
off Old Rd E 131 GJ89
Eckersley St, E1 off Buxton St .84 DU70
Eckford St, N1 . . . . . .83 DN68
Eckington Ho, N15
off Fladbury Rd 66 DR58
Eckstein Rd, SW11 . . . .100 DE84
Eclipse Rd, E13 . . . . . .86 EH71
Ecton Rd, Add. KT15 . . .152 BH105
Ector Rd, SE6 . . . . . .124 EE89
Edbrooke Rd, W9 . . . . . .82 DA70
Eddiscombe Rd, SW6 . . . .99 CZ82
Eddy Cl, Rom. RM7 . . . .71 FB58
Eddystone Rd, SE4 . . . .123 DY85
Eddystone Twr, SE8 . . . .103 DY77
Eddystone Wk, Stai. TW19 .114 BL87
Ede Cl, Houns. TW3 . . . .96 BZ83
Edenbridge Cl, SE16
off Masters Dr 102 DV78
Orpington BR5 . . . . . .146 EX98
Edenbridge Rd, E9 . . . . . .85 DX66
Enfield EN1 . . . . . .30 DS44
Eden Cl, NW3 . . . . . .64 DA61
W8 off Adam & Eve Ms . .100 DA76
Addlestone (New Haw)
KT15 . . . . . .152 BH110
Bexley DA5 . . . . . .127 FD91
Enfield EN3
off Government Row 31 EA38
Slough SL3 . . . . . .93 BA78
Wembley HA0 . . . . . .79 CK67
Edencourt Rd, SW16 . . . .121 DH93
Edendale Rd, Bexh. DA7 . .107 FD81
Eden Dr, Enf. EN3
off Government Row 31 EA37
Edenfield Gdns, Wor.Pk. KT4 .139 CT104
Eden Grn, S.Ock. RM15
off Bovey Way 91 FV71
Eden Gro, E17 . . . . . .67 EB57
N7 . . . . . .65 DM64
Eden Gro Rd, W.Byf. (Byfleet)
KT14 . . . . . .152 BL113
Edenhall Cl, Rom. RM3 . . .52 FJ50
Edenhall Glen, Rom. RM3 . .52 FJ50
Edenhall Rd, Rom. RM3 . . .52 FJ50
Edenham Way, W10
off Elkstone Rd 81 CZ71
Edenhurst Av, SW6 . . . .99 CZ83
Eden Ms, SW17
off Huntspill St 120 DC90
EDEN PARK, Beck. 143 EA99
⇌ Eden Park 143 EA99
Eden Pk Av, Beck. BR3 . .143 DY98
Eden Pl, Grav. DA12
off Lord St 131 GH87
Eden Rd, E17 . . . . . .67 EB57
SE27 . . . . . .121 DP92
Beckenham BR3 . . . . . .143 DY98
Bexley DA5 . . . . . .127 FC91
Croydon CR0 . . . . . .160 DR105
Edenside Rd, Lthd. (Bkhm.)
KT23 . . . . . .170 BZ124
Edensor Gdns, W4 . . . . . .98 CS80
Edensor Rd, W4 . . . . . .98 CS80
Eden St, Kings.T. KT1 . . .137 CK96
Edenvale Cl, Mitch. CR4
off Edenvale Rd 120 DG94
Edenvale Rd, Mitch. CR4 . .120 DG94
Edenvale St, SW6 . . . . . .100 DB82
Eden Wk, Kings.T. KT1
off Eden St 138 CL96

Eden Wk Shop Cen, Kings.T.
KT1 . . . . . .138 CL96
Eden Way, Beck. BR3 . . .143 DZ99
Warlingham CR6 . . . . . .177 DY118
Ederline Av, SW16 . . . .141 DM97
Edgar Cl, Swan. BR8 . . . .147 FF97
Edgar Kail Way, SE22 . . .102 DS84
Edgarley Ter, SW6 . . . .99 CY81
Edgar Rd, E3 . . . . . .85 EB69
Hounslow TW4 . . . . . .116 BZ87
Romford RM6 . . . . . .70 EX59
South Croydon CR2 . . .160 DR109
West Drayton UB7 . . . .76 BL73
Westerham (Tats.) TN16 .178 EK121
Edgbaston Dr, Rad. (Shenley)
WD7 . . . . . .10 CL32
Edgbaston Rd, Wat. WD19 . .39 BV48
Edgeborough Way, Brom.
BR1 . . . . . .124 EK94
Edgebury, Chis. BR7 . . . .125 EP91
Edgebury Wk, Chis. BR7 . .125 EQ91
Edge Cl, Wey. KT13 . . . .152 BN108
Edgecombe Ho, SW19 . . .119 CY88
Edgecoombe, S.Croy. CR2 .160 DW108
Edgecoombe Cl, Kings.T.
KT2 . . . . . .118 CR94
Edgecote Cl, W3
off Cheltenham Pl 80 CQ74
Edgecot Gro, N15
off Oulton Rd 66 DR57
Edgefield Av, Bark. IG11 . .87 ET66
Edgefield Cl, Dart. DA1 . .128 FP88
Edge Hill, SE18 . . . . . .105 EP79
SW19 . . . . . .119 CX94
Edge Hill Av, N3 . . . . . .64 DA55
Edge Hill Ct, SW19 . . . .119 CX94
Edgehill Cl, Walt. KT12
off St. Johns Dr 136 BW102
Edgehill Gdns, Dag. RM10 . .70 FA63
Edgehill Rd, W13 . . . . . .79 CJ71
Chislehurst BR7 . . . . . .125 EQ90
Mitcham CR4 . . . . . .141 DH95
Purley CR8 . . . . . .159 DN110
Edgeley, Lthd. (Bkhm.) KT23 .170 BY124
Edgeley La, SW4
off Edgeley Rd 101 DK83
Edgeley Rd, SW4 . . . . . .101 DK83
Edgell Cl, Vir.W. GU25 . . .133 AZ97
Edgell Rd, Stai. TW18 . . .113 BF92
Edgel St, SW18
off Ferrier St 100 DB84
Edgepoint Cl, SE27
off Knights Hill 121 DP92
Edge St, W8
off Kensington Ch St 82 DA74
Edgewood Dr, Orp. BR6 . .163 ET106
Edgewood Grn, Croy. CR0 .143 DX102
Edgeworth Av, NW4 . . . .63 CU57
Edgeworth Cl, NW4 . . . .63 CU57
Whyteleafe CR3 . . . . . .176 DU118
Edgeworth Cres, NW4 . . .63 CU57
Edgeworth Rd, SE9 . . . .104 EJ84
Barnet EN4 . . . . . .28 DE42
Edgington Rd, SW16 . . . .121 DK93
Edgington Way, Sid. DA14 .126 EW94
EDGWARE 42 CP50
⊖ Edgware 42 CP51
Edgwarebury Gdns, Edg. HA8 .42 CN50
Edgwarebury La, Borwd. (Elstree)
WD6 . . . . . .42 CL45
Edgware HA8 . . . . . .42 CN49
H Edgware Comm Hosp, Edg.
HA8 . . . . . .42 CP52
Edgware Ct, Edg. HA8
off Cavendish Dr 42 CN51
⊖ Edgware Road 194 D7
Edgware Rd, NW2 . . . . . .63 CV60
NW9 . . . . . .62 CR55
W2 . . . . . .194 C7
Edgware Rd Subway, W2
off Edgware Rd 82 DE71
Edgware Way, Edg. HA8 . .42 CM49
Edinburgh Av, Rick. (Mill End)
WD3 . . . . . .22 BG44
Edinburgh Cl, E2
off Russia La 84 DW68
Pinner HA5 . . . . . .60 BX59
Uxbridge UB10 . . . . . .59 BP63
Edinburgh Ct, SW20 . . . .139 CX99
Edinburgh Cres, Wal.Cr. EN8 . .15 DY33
Edinburgh Dr, Abb.L. WD5 . .7 BU32
Romford RM7
off Eastern Av W 71 FC56
Staines TW18 . . . . . .114 BK93
Uxbridge (Denh.) UB9 . . .57 BF58
Uxbridge (Ickhm.) UB10 . .59 BP63
Edinburgh Gate, SW1 . . .198 D4
Edinburgh Ho, W9 . . . . . .82 DC69
Edinburgh Ms, Til. RM18 . .111 GH82
Edinburgh Rd, E13 . . . . . .86 EH68
E17 . . . . . .67 EA57
N18 . . . . . .46 DU50
W7 . . . . . .97 CF75
Sutton SM1 . . . . . .140 DC103
Edington Rd, SE2 . . . . . .106 EV76
Enfield EN3 . . . . . .30 DW40
Edison Av, Horn. RM12 . . .71 FF61
Edison Cl, E17 off Exeter Rd . .67 EA57
Hornchurch RM12
off Edison Av 71 FF60
Edison Ct, SE10 . . . . . .205 L8
Edison Dr, Sthl. UB1 . . . .78 CB72
Wembley HA9 . . . . . .62 CL61
Edison Gro, SE18 . . . . . .105 ET80
Edison Rd, N8 . . . . . .65 DK58
Bromley BR2 . . . . . .144 EG96
Enfield EN3 . . . . . .31 DZ40
Welling DA16 . . . . . .105 ET81
Edis St, NW1 . . . . . .82 DG67
Edith Cavell Cl, N19
off Hornsey Ri Gdns 65 DK59
Edith Gdns, Surb. KT5 . . .138 CP101
Edith Gro, SW10 . . . . . .100 DC79
Edithna St, SW9 . . . . . .101 DL83
Edith Rd, E6 . . . . . .86 EK66
E15 off Chandos Rd 67 ED64
N11 . . . . . .45 DK52

Edith Rd, SE25 . . . . . .142 DR99
SW19 . . . . . .120 DB93
W14 . . . . . .99 CY78
Orpington BR6 . . . . . .164 EU106
Romford RM6 . . . . . .70 EX58
Edith Row, SW6 . . . . . .100 DB81
Edith St, E2 . . . . . .84 DU68
Edith Summerskill Ho, SW6
off Clem Attlee Ct 99 CZ80
Edith Ter, SW10 . . . . . .100 DC80
Edith Vil, SW15
off Bective Rd 99 CY84
W14 . . . . . .99 CZ77
Edith Yd, SW10
off World's End Est 100 DC80
Edmansons Cl, N17
off Bruce Gro 46 DS53
Edmeston Cl, E9 . . . . . .85 DY65
Edmond Halley Way, SE10 .205 H5
Edmonds Ct, W.Mol. KT8
off Avern Rd 136 CB98
EDMONTON, N9 . . . . . .46 DU49
⇌ Edmonton Green 46 DU47
Edmonton Grn, N9
off Hertford Rd 46 DV47
Edmund Gro, Felt. TW13 . .116 BZ89
Edmund Hurst Dr, E6 . . . .87 EP71
Edmund Rd, Grays (Chaff.Hun.)
RM16 . . . . . .109 FX75
Mitcham CR4 . . . . . .140 DE97
Orpington BR5 . . . . . .146 EW100
Rainham RM13 . . . . . .89 FE68
Welling DA16 . . . . . .106 EU83
Edmunds Av, Orp. BR5 . .146 EX97
Edmunds Cl, Hayes UB4 . .78 BW71
Edmund St, SE5 . . . . . .102 DR80
Edmunds Wk, N2 . . . . . .64 DE56
Edna Rd, SW20 . . . . . .139 CX96
Edna St, SW11 . . . . . .100 DE81
Edrich Ho, SW4 . . . . . .101 DL81
Edrick Rd, Edg. HA8 . . . .42 CQ51
Edrick Wk, Edg. HA8 . . . .42 CQ51
Edric Rd, SE14 . . . . . .103 DX80
Edridge Cl, Bushey WD23 . .24 CC43
Hornchurch RM12 . . . . . .72 FK64
Edridge Rd, Croy. CR0 . . .142 DQ104
Edulf Rd, Borwd. WD6 . . .26 CP39
Edward Amey Cl, Wat. WD25 . .24 BW36
Edward Av, E4 . . . . . .47 EB51
Morden SM4 . . . . . .140 DD99
Edward Cl, N9 . . . . . .46 DT45
NW2 . . . . . .63 CX63
Abbots Langley WD5 . . . .7 BT32
Grays (Chaff.Hun.) RM16 .109 FX76
Hampton (Hmptn.H.) TW12
off Edward Rd 116 CC92
Northolt UB5 . . . . . .78 BW68
Edward Ct, E16
off Alexandra St 86 EG71
Staines TW18 . . . . . .114 BJ93
Waltham Abbey EN9 . . . .16 EF33
Edwardes Pl, W8
off Edwardes Sq 99 CZ76
Edwardes Sq, W8 . . . . . .100 DA76
Edward Ms, NW1 . . . . . .195 J1
Edward Pauling Ho, Felt. TW14
off Westmacott Dr 115 BT87
Edward Pl, SE8 . . . . . .103 DZ79
Edward Rd, E17 . . . . . .67 DX56
SE20 . . . . . .123 DX94
Barnet EN4 . . . . . .28 DD43
Bromley BR1 . . . . . .124 EH94
Chislehurst BR7 . . . . . .125 EP92
Coulsdon CR5 . . . . . .175 DK115
Croydon CR0 . . . . . .142 DS101
Feltham TW14 . . . . . .115 BR85
Hampton (Hmptn.H.)
TW12 . . . . . .116 CC92
Harrow HA2 . . . . . .60 CC55
Northolt UB5 . . . . . .78 BW68
Romford RM6 . . . . . .70 EY58
Westerham (Bigg.H.) TN16 .178 EL118
Edward's Av, Ruis. HA4 . . .77 BV65
Edwards Cl, Brwd. CM13 . .55 GE44
Worcester Park KT4 . . .139 CX103
Edwards Cotts, N1
off Compton Av 83 DP65
Edwards Ct, Slou. SL1 . . .92 AS75
Waltham Cross EN8
off Turners Hill 15 DX31
Edwards Dr, N11
off Gordon Rd 45 DK52
Edward II Av, W.Byf. (Byfleet)
KT14 . . . . . .152 BM114
Edwards Gdns, Swan. BR8
off Ladds Way 147 FD98
Edwards La, N16 . . . . . .66 DR61
Edwards Ms, N1 . . . . . .83 DN66
W1 . . . . . .194 F9
Edward Sq, N1
off Caledonian Rd 83 DM67
SE16 . . . . . .203 L2
Edwards Rd, Belv. DA17 . .106 FA77
Edward St, E16 . . . . . .86 EG70
SE8 . . . . . .103 DZ79
SE14 . . . . . .103 DY80
Edwards Way, Brwd. CM13 .55 GE44
Edwards Yd, Wem. HA0
off Mount Pleasant 80 CL67
Edward Temme Av, E15 . . .86 EF66
Edward Tyler Rd, SE12 . . .124 EH89
Edward Way, Ashf. TW15 . .114 BM89
Edwina Gdns, Ilf. IG4 . . . .68 EL57
Edwin Av, E6 . . . . . .87 EN68
Edwin Cl, Bexh. DA7 . . . .106 EZ79
Rainham RM13 . . . . . .89 FF69
Edwin Pl, Croy. CR0
off Cross Rd 142 DR102
Edwin Rd, Dart. DA2 . . . .127 FH90
Edgware HA8 . . . . . .42 CR51
Twickenham TW1, TW2 . .117 CF88
Edwin's Mead, E9
off Lindisfarne Way 67 DY63

Edwin St, E1 . . . . . .84 DW70
E16 . . . . . .86 EG71
Gravesend DA12 . . . . . .131 GH87
Edwyn Cl, Barn. EN5 . . . .27 CW44
Eel Brook Studios, SW6
off Moore Pk Rd 100 DA80
Eel Pie Island, Twick. TW1 .117 CH88
Effie Pl, SW6 . . . . . .100 DA80
Effie Rd, SW6 . . . . . .100 DA80
Effingham Cl, Sutt. SM2 . .158 DB108
Effingham Common, Lthd. (Eff.)
KT24 . . . . . .169 BU123
Effingham Common Rd, Lthd.
(Eff.) KT24 . . . . . .169 BU123
Effingham Ct, Wok. GU22
off Constitution Hill 166 AY118
⇌ Effingham Junction 169 BU123
Effingham Rd, N8 . . . . . .65 DN57
SE12 . . . . . .124 EE85
Croydon CR0 . . . . . .141 DM101
Surbiton KT6 . . . . . .137 CH101
Effort St, SW17 . . . . . .120 DE92
Effra Par, SW2 . . . . . .121 DN85
Effra Rd, SW2 . . . . . .101 DN84
SW19 . . . . . .120 DB93
Egan Way, Hayes UB3 . . .77 BS73
Egbert St, NW1 . . . . . .82 DG67
Egbury Ho, SW15
off Tangley Gro 119 CT86
Egdean Wk, Sev. TN13 . . .191 FJ123
Egerton Av, Swan. BR8 . . .127 FF94
Egerton Cl, Dart. DA1 . . .127 FH88
Pinner HA5 . . . . . .59 BU56
Egerton Cres, SW3 . . . .198 C8
Egerton Dr, SE10 . . . . . .103 EB81
Egerton Gdns, NW4 . . . .63 CV56
NW10 . . . . . .81 CW67
SW3 . . . . . .198 B7
W13 . . . . . .79 CH72
Ilford IG3 . . . . . .69 ET62
Egerton Gdns Ms, SW3 . .198 C7
Egerton Pl, SW3 . . . . . .198 C7
Weybridge KT13 . . . . . .153 BQ107
Egerton Rd, N16 . . . . . .66 DT59
SE25 . . . . . .142 DS97
New Malden KT3 . . . . . .139 CT98
Twickenham TW2 . . . . . .117 CE87
Wembley HA0 . . . . . .80 CM66
Weybridge KT13 . . . . . .153 BQ107
Egerton Ter, SW3 . . . . . .198 C7
Egerton Way, Hayes UB3 . .95 BP80
Eggardon Ct, Nthlt. UB5
off Lancaster Rd 78 CC65
Egg Fm La, Kings L. WD4
off Station Rd 7 BP30
Egg Hall, Epp. CM16 . . . .18 EU29
EGHAM 113 BA93
⇌ Egham 113 BA92
Egham Bypass, Egh. TW20 .113 AZ92
Egham Cl, SW19
off Winterfold Cl 119 CY89
Sutton SM3 . . . . . .139 CY103
Egham Cres, Sutt. SM3 . .139 CX104
Egham Hill, Egh. TW20 . . .112 AX93
EGHAM HYTHE, Stai. . . .113 BE93
★ Egham Mus, Egh. TW20 .113 BA92
Egham Rd, E13 . . . . . .86 EH71
EGHAM WICK, Egh. 112 AU94
Eglantine La, Dart. (Hort.Kir.)
DA4 . . . . . .148 FN101
Eglantine Rd, SW18 . . . .120 DC85
Egleston Rd, Mord. SM4 . .140 DB100
Egley Dr, Wok. GU22 . . . .166 AX122
Egley Rd, Wok. GU22 . . . .166 AX122
Eglington Ct, SE17
off Carter St 102 DQ79
Eglington Rd, E4 . . . . . .47 ED45
Eglinton Hill, SE18 . . . . . .105 EP79
Eglinton Rd, SE18 . . . . . .105 EN79
Swanscombe DA10 . . . .130 FZ86
Eglise Rd, Warl. CR6 . . . .177 DY117
Egliston Ms, SW15 . . . . . .99 CW83
Egliston Rd, SW15 . . . . . .99 CW83
Eglon Ms, NW1
off Berkley Rd 82 DF66
Egmont Av, Surb. KT6 . . .138 CM102
Egmont Pk Rd, Tad. KT20 .183 CU125
Egmont Rd, N.Mal. KT3 . .139 CT98
Surbiton KT6 . . . . . .138 CM102
Sutton SM2 . . . . . .158 DC108
Walton-on-Thames KT12 .135 BV101
Egmont St, SE14 . . . . . .103 DX80
Egmont Way, Tad. KT20
off Oatlands Dr 173 CY119
Egremont Ho, SE13 . . . . . .103 EB82
Egremont Rd, SE27 . . . .121 DN90
Egret Way, Hayes UB4 . . .78 BX71
Eider Cl, E7 . . . . . .68 EF64
Hayes UB4
off Cygnet Way 78 BX71
Eighteenth Rd, Mitch. CR4 .141 DL98
Eighth Av, E12 . . . . . .69 EM63
Hayes UB3 . . . . . .77 BU74
Eileen Rd, SE25 . . . . . .142 DR99
Eindhoven Cl, Cars. SM5 .140 DG102
Eisenhower Dr, E6 . . . . . .86 EL71
Elaine Gro, NW5 . . . . . .64 DG64
Elam Cl, SE5 . . . . . .101 DP82
Elam St, SE5 . . . . . .101 DP82
Eland Pl, Croy. CR0
off Eland Rd 141 DP104
Eland Rd, SW11 . . . . . .100 DF83
Croydon CR0 . . . . . .141 DP104
Elan Rd, S.Ock. RM15 . . .91 FU71
Elba Pl, SE17 . . . . . .201 J8
Elberon Av, Croy. CR0 . . .141 DJ100
Elbe St, SW6 . . . . . .100 DC82
Elborough Rd, SE25 . . . .142 DU99
Elborough St, SW18 . . . .120 DA88
Elbow Meadow, Slou. (Colnbr.)
SL3 . . . . . .93 BF81
Elbury Dr, E16 . . . . . .86 EG72
Elcho St, SW11 . . . . . .100 DE80
Elcot Av, SE15 . . . . . .102 DV80
Elder Av, N8 . . . . . .65 DL57
Elderbek Cl, Wal.Cr. EN7 . .14 DU28

Elm - Esh

Elmsleigh Ct, Sutt. SM1 . . . . .**140** DB104
Elmsleigh Rd, Stai. TW18 . . . . .**113** BF92
  Twickenham TW2 . . . .**117** CD89
Elmslie Cl, Epsom KT18 . . . . .**156** CQ114
  Woodford Green IG8 . . . . .**49** EM51
Elmslie Pt, E3 . . . .**85** DZ71
Elms Ms, W2 . . . .**82** DD73
Elms Pk Av, Wem. HA0 . . . . . .**61** CG63
Elms Rd, SW4 . . . .**121** DJ85
  Gerrards Cross (Chal.St.P.)
    SL9 . . . .**36** AY52
  Harrow HA3 . . . .**41** CE52
ELMSTEAD, Chis. **124** EK92
Elmstead Av, Chis. BR7 . . . . .**125** EM92
  Wembley HA9 . . . .**62** CL60
Elmstead Cl, N20 . . . .**44** DA47
  Epsom KT19 . . . .**156** CS106
  Sevenoaks TN13 . . . .**190** FE122
Elmstead Cres, Well. DA16 . . .**106** EW79
Elmstead Gdns, Wor.Pk.
  KT4 . . . .**139** CU104
Elmstead Glade, Chis. BR7 . . .**125** EM93
Elmstead La, Chis. BR7 . . . . . .**125** EM92
Elmstead Rd, Erith DA8 . . . . . .**107** FE81
  Ilford IG3 . . . .**69** ES61
  West Byfleet KT14 . . . .**152** BG113
★ Elmstead Woods **124** EL93
Elmstone Rd, SW6 . . . .**100** DA81
Elmsway, Ashf. TW15 . . . .**114** BM92
Elmswood, Lthd. (Bkhm.)
  KT23 . . . .**170** BZ124
Elmsworth Av, Houns. TW3 . . .**96** CB82
Elm Ter, NW2 . . . .**64** DA62
  NW3
    off Constantine Rd **64** DE63
  SE9 . . . .**125** EN86
  Grays RM20 . . . .**109** FV79
  Harrow HA3 . . . .**41** CD52
Elmton Way, E5
  off Rendlesham Rd **66** DU62
Elm Tree Av, Esher KT10 . . . .**137** CD101
Elm Tree Cl, NW8 . . . .**82** DD69
  Ashford TW15
    off Convent Rd **115** BP92
  Chertsey KT16 . . . .**133** BE103
  Northolt UB5 . . . .**78** BZ68
Elmtree Cl, W.Byf. (Byfleet)
  KT14 . . . .**152** BL113
Elm Tree Rd, NW8 . . . .**82** DD69
Elmtree Rd, Tedd. TW11 . . . . .**117** CE91
Elm Tree Wk, Rick. (Chorl.)
  WD3 . . . .**21** BF42
Elm Wk, NW3 . . . .**64** DA61
  SW20 . . . .**139** CW98
  Orpington BR6 . . . .**145** EM104
  Radlett WD7 . . . .**25** CF36
  Romford RM2 . . . .**71** FG55
Elm Way, N11 . . . .**44** DG51
  NW10 . . . .**62** CS63
  Brentwood CM14 . . . .**54** FU48
  Epsom KT19 . . . .**156** CR106
  Rickmansworth WD3 . . . . .**38** BH46
  Worcester Park KT4 . . . . .**139** CW104
Elmwood Av, N13 . . . .**45** DL50
  Borehamwood WD6 . . . . .**26** CP42
  Feltham TW13 . . . .**115** BU89
  Harrow HA3 . . . .**61** CG57
Elmwood Cl, Ashtd. KT21 . . . .**171** CK117
  Epsom KT17 . . . .**157** CU108
  Wallington SM6 . . . .**140** DG103
Elmwood Ct, SW11 . . . .**101** DH81
  Ashtead KT21
    off Elmwood Cl **171** CK117
  Wembley HA0 . . . .**61** CG62
Elmwood Cres, NW9 . . . .**62** CQ56
Elmwood Dr, Bex. DA5 . . . . . .**126** EY87
  Epsom KT17 . . . .**157** CU107
Elmwood Gdns, W7 . . . .**79** CE72
Elmwood Pk, Ger.Cr. SL9 . . . .**56** AY60
Elmwood Rd, SE24 . . . .**122** DR85
  W4 . . . .**98** CQ79
  Croydon CR0 . . . .**141** DP101
  Mitcham CR4 . . . .**140** DF97
  Redhill RH1 . . . .**184** DG130
  Slough SL2 . . . .**74** AV73
Elmworth Gro, SE21 . . . .**122** DR89
Elnathan Ms, W9
  off Shirland Rd **82** DB70
Elphinstone Rd, E17 . . . .**47** DZ54
Elphinstone St, N5
  off Avenell Rd **65** DP63
Elrick Cl, Erith DA8
  off Queen St **107** FE79
Elrington Rd, E8 . . . .**84** DU65
  Woodford Green IG8 . . . . .**48** EG50
Elruge Cl, West Dr. UB7 . . . . .**94** BK76
Elsa Rd, Well. DA16 . . . .**106** EV82
Elsa St, E1 . . . .**85** DY71
Elsdale St, E9 . . . .**84** DW65
Elsden Ms, E2
  off Old Ford Rd **84** DW68
Elsden Rd, N17 . . . .**46** DT53
Elsdon Rd, Wok. GU21 . . . . .**166** AU117
Elsenham Rd, E12 . . . .**69** EN64
Elsenham St, SW18 . . . .**119** CZ88
Elsham Rd, E11 . . . .**68** EE62
  W14 . . . .**99** CY75
Elsham Ter, W14 . . . .**99** CY75
Elsiedene Rd, N21 . . . .**46** DQ45
Elsiemaud Rd, SE4 . . . .**123** DZ85
Elsie Rd, SE22 . . . .**102** DT84
Elsinge Rd, Enf. EN1 . . . .**30** DV36
Elsinore Av, Stai. TW19 . . . . . .**114** BL87
Elsinore Gdns, NW2 . . . .**63** CY62
Elsinore Rd, SE23 . . . .**123** DY88
Elsinore Way, Rich. TW9
  off Lower Richmond Rd . . .**98** CP83
Elsley Rd, SW11 . . . .**100** DF83
Elspeth Rd, SW11 . . . .**100** DF84
  Wembley HA0 . . . .**62** CL64
Elsrick Av, Mord. SM4
  off Chalgrove Av **140** DA99
Elstan Way, Croy. CR0 . . . . . .**143** DY101

Elstead Ct, Sutt. SM3
  off Stonecot Hill **139** CY102
Elsted St, SE17 . . . .**201** L9
Elstow Cl, SE9 . . . .**125** EN85
  Ruislip HA4 . . . .**60** BX59
Elstow Gdns, Dag. RM9 . . . . . .**88** EY67
Elstow Rd, Dag. RM9 . . . .**88** EY66
ELSTREE, Borwd. **25** CK43
★ Elstree Aerodrome, Borwd.
  WD6 . . . .**25** CG44
≷ Elstree & Borehamwood . .**26** CM42
Elstree Gdns, N9 . . . .**46** DV46
  Belvedere DA17 . . . .**106** EY77
  Ilford IG1 . . . .**69** EQ64
Elstree Hill, Brom. BR1 . . . . . .**124** EE94
Elstree Hill N, Borwd. (Elstree)
  WD6 . . . .**25** CK44
Elstree Hill S, Borwd. (Elstree)
  WD6 . . . .**41** CJ45
Elstree Pk, Borwd. WD6 . . . . . .**26** CR44
Elstree Rd, Borwd. (Elstree)
  WD6 . . . .**25** CG44
  Bushey (Bushey Hth.)
    WD23 . . . .**41** CD45
Elstree Way, Borwd. WD6 . . . .**26** CP41
Elswick Rd, SE13 . . . .**103** EB82
Elswick St, SW6 . . . .**100** DC82
Elsworth Cl, Felt. TW14 . . . . .**115** BS88
Elsworthy, T.Ditt. KT7 . . . . . .**137** CE100
Elsworthy Ri, NW3 . . . .**82** DE66
Elsworthy Rd, NW3 . . . .**82** DE67
Elsworthy Ter, NW3 . . . .**82** DE66
Elsynge Rd, SW18 . . . .**120** DD85
ELTHAM, SE9 . . . .**124** EK86
≷ Eltham **125** EM85
Eltham Grn, SE9 . . . .**124** EJ85
Eltham Grn Rd, SE9 . . . .**104** EJ84
Eltham High St, SE9 . . . .**125** EM86
Eltham Hill, SE9 . . . .**124** EK85
★ Eltham Palace, SE9 . . . . . .**124** EL87
Eltham Palace Rd, SE9 . . . . . .**124** EJ86
Eltham Pk Gdns, SE9 . . . .**105** EN84
Eltham Rd, SE9 . . . .**124** EF85
  SE12 . . . .**124** EF85
Elthiron Rd, SW6 . . . .**100** DA81
Elthorne Av, W7 . . . .**97** CF75
Elthorne Ct, Felt. TW13 . . . . .**116** BW88
Elthorne Pk Rd, W7 . . . .**97** CF75
Elthorne Rd, N19 . . . .**65** DK61
  NW9 . . . .**62** CR59
  Uxbridge UB8 . . . .**76** BK68
Elthorne Way, NW9 . . . .**62** CR58
Elthruda Rd, SE13 . . . .**123** ED86
Eltisley Rd, Ilf. IG1 . . . .**69** EP63
Elton Av, Barn. EN5 . . . .**27** CZ43
  Greenford UB6 . . . .**79** CF65
  Wembley HA0 . . . .**61** CH64
Elton Cl, Kings.T. KT1 . . . .**117** CJ94
Elton Ho, E3 . . . .**85** DZ67
Elton Pk, Wat. WD17 . . . .**23** BV40
Elton Pl, N16 . . . .**66** DS64
Elton Rd, Kings.T. KT2 . . . . . .**138** CM95
  Purley CR8 . . . .**159** DJ112
Elton Way, Wat. WD25 . . . .**24** CB44
Eltringham St, SW18 . . . .**100** DC84
Elvaston Ms, SW7 . . . .**100** DC76
Elvaston Pl, SW7 . . . .**100** DC76
Elveden Pl, NW10 . . . .**80** CN68
Elveden Rd, NW10 . . . .**80** CN68
Elvedon Rd, Cob. KT11 . . . . . .**153** BV111
Elvendon Rd, N13 . . . .**45** DL51
Elver Gdns, E2
  off St. Peter's Cl **84** DU68
Elverson Rd, SE8 . . . .**103** EB82
ᴰᴸᴿ Elverson Road **103** EB82
Elverton St, SW1 . . . .**199** M8
Elvet Av, Rom. RM2 . . . .**72** FJ56
Elvington Grn, Brom. BR2 . . . .**144** EF99
Elvington La, NW9 . . . .**42** CS53
Elvino Rd, SE26 . . . .**123** DY92
Elvis Rd, NW2 . . . .**81** CW65
Elwell Cl, Egh. TW20
  off Mowbray Cres **113** BA92
Elwick Rd, S.Ock. RM15 . . . . .**91** FW72
Elwill Way, Beck. BR3 . . . . . .**143** EC98
Elwin St, E2 . . . .**84** DU69
Elwood St, N5 . . . .**65** DP62
Elwyn Gdns, SE12 . . . .**124** EG87
Ely Cl, Amer. HP7 . . . .**20** AS39
  New Malden KT3 . . . .**139** CT96
Ely Ct, EC1 . . . .**196** E7
Ely Gdns, Borwd. WD6 . . . .**26** CR43
  Dagenham RM10 . . . .**71** FC62
  Ilford IG1
    off Canterbury Av **68** EL59
Elyne Rd, N4 . . . .**65** DN58
Ely Pl, EC1 . . . .**196** E7
  Woodford Green IG8 . . . . .**49** EN51
Ely Rd, E10 . . . .**67** EC58
  Croydon CR0 . . . .**142** DR99
  Hounslow (Hthrw.Air.) TW6
    off Eastern Perimeter Rd . .**95** BT82
  Hounslow (Houns.W.) TW4 . .**96** BW82
Elysian Av, Orp. BR5 . . . .**145** ET100
Elysium Pl, SW6
  off Fulham Pk Gdns **99** CZ82
Elysium St, SW6
  off Fulham Pk Gdns **99** CZ82
Elystan Business Cen, Hayes
  UB4 . . . .**78** BW73
Elystan Cl, Wall. SM6 . . . . . .**159** DH109
Elystan Pl, SW3 . . . .**198** C10
Elystan St, SW3 . . . .**198** B9
Elystan Wk, N1
  off Cloudesley Rd **83** DN67
Emanuel Av, W3 . . . .**80** CQ72
Emanuel Dr, Hmptn. TW12 . . .**116** BZ92
⊖ Embankment **200** A2
Embankment, The, Stai. (Wrays.)
  TW19 . . . .**112** AW87
  Twickenham TW1 . . . .**117** CG88
Embankment Gdns, SW3 . . . .**100** DF79
Embankment Pl, WC2 . . . .**200** A2
Embassy Ct, Sid. DA14 . . . . . .**126** EV90

Embassy Ct, Well. DA16
  off Welling High St **106** EV83
Embassy Gdns, Beck. BR3 . . .**143** DZ95
Emba St, SE16 . . . .**202** C5
Ember Cen, Walt. KT12 . . . . .**136** BY103
Ember Cl, Add. KT15 . . . .**152** BK106
  Orpington BR5 . . . .**145** EQ101
Embercourt Rd, T.Ditt. KT7 . .**137** CE100
Ember Fm Av, E.Mol. KT8 . . .**137** CD100
Ember Fm Way, E.Mol. KT8 . .**137** CD100
Ember Gdns, T.Ditt. KT7 . . . .**137** CE101
Ember La, E.Mol. KT8 . . . . . .**137** CD101
  Esher KT10 . . . .**137** CD101
Ember Rd, Slou. SL3 . . . .**93** BB76
Emberson Way, Epp. (N.Wld.Bas.)
  CM16 . . . .**19** FC26
Emberton, SE5 . . . .**102** DS79
Embleton Rd, SE13 . . . .**103** EB83
  Watford WD19 . . . .**39** BU48
Embleton Wk, Hmptn. TW12
  off Fearnley Cres **116** BZ93
Embry Cl, Stan. HA7 . . . .**41** CG49
Embry Dr, Stan. HA7 . . . .**41** CG51
Embry Way, Stan. HA7 . . . .**41** CG50
Emden Cl, West Dr. UB7 . . . . .**94** BN75
Emden St, SW6 . . . .**100** DB81
Emerald Cl, E16 . . . .**86** EL72
Emerald Ct, Slou. SL1 . . . .**92** AS75
Emerald Gdns, Dag. RM8 . . . . .**70** FA60
Emerald Sq, Sthl. UB2 . . . .**96** BX76
Emerald St, WC1 . . . .**196** B6
Emerson Dr, Horn. RM11 . . . . .**72** FK59
Emerson Gdns, Har. HA3 . . . . .**62** CM58
EMERSON PARK, Horn. **72** FL58
≷ Emerson Park **72** FL59
Emerson Rd, Ilf. IG1 . . . .**69** EN59
Emersons Av, Swan. BR8 . . . .**127** FF94
Emerson St, SE1 . . . .**201** H2
Emerton Cl, Bexh. DA6 . . . . . .**106** EY84
Emerton Rd, Lthd. KT22 . . . . .**170** CC120
Emery Hill St, SW1 . . . .**199** L7
Emery St, SE1 . . . .**200** E6
Emes Rd, Erith DA8 . . . .**107** FC80
Emilia Cl, Enf. EN3 . . . .**30** DV43
Emily Davidson Dr, Epsom
  KT18 . . . .**173** CV118
Emily Jackson Cl, Sev. TN13 .**191** FH124
Emily Pl, N7 . . . .**65** DN63
Emley Rd, Add. KT15 . . . .**134** BG104
Emlyn Gdns, W12 . . . .**98** CS75
Emlyn La, Lthd. KT22 . . . .**171** CG122
Emlyn Rd, W12 . . . .**98** CS75
Emmanuel Lo, Wal.Cr. (Chsht.)
  EN8 off College Rd **14** DW30
Emmanuel Rd, SW12 . . . .**121** DJ88
  Northwood HA6 . . . .**39** BT52
Emma Rd, E13 . . . .**86** EF68
Emma St, E2 . . . .**84** DV68
Emmaus Way, Chig. IG7 . . . . . .**49** EN50
Emmett Cl, Rad. (Shenley)
  WD7 . . . .**10** CL33
Emmetts Cl, Wok. GU21 . . . .**166** AW117
Emmott Av, Ilf. IG6 . . . .**69** EQ57
Emmott Cl, E1 . . . .**85** DY70
  NW11 . . . .**64** DC58
Emms Pas, Kings.T. KT1
  off High St **137** CK96
Emperor's Gate, SW7 . . . .**100** DB76
Empire Av, N18 . . . .**46** DQ50
Empire Ct, Wem. HA9 . . . .**62** CP62
Empire Rd, Grnf. UB6 . . . .**79** CJ67
Empire Sq, N7 . . . .**65** DL62
  SE20 off High St **123** DX94
Empire Way, Wem. HA9 . . . . . .**62** CM63
Empire Wf Rd, E14 . . . .**204** F9
Empress Av, E4 . . . .**47** EA52
  E12 . . . .**68** EJ61
  Ilford IG1 . . . .**69** EM61
  Woodford Green IG8 . . . . .**48** EF52
Empress Dr, Chis. BR7 . . . . . .**125** EP93
Empress Pl, SW6 . . . .**100** DA78
Empress Rd, Grav. DA12 . . . .**131** GL87
Empress St, SE17 . . . .**102** DQ79
Empson St, E3 . . . .**85** EB70
Emsworth Cl, N9 . . . .**46** DW46
Emsworth Rd, Ilf. IG6 . . . .**49** EP54
Emsworth St, SW2 . . . .**121** DM89
Emu Rd, SW8 . . . .**101** DH82
Ena Rd, SW16 . . . .**141** DL97
Enborne Grn, S.Ock. RM15
  off Elan Rd **91** FU71
Enbrook St, W10 . . . .**81** CY69
Endale Cl, Cars. SM5 . . . .**140** DF103
Endeavour Ho, Barn. EN5 . . . .**28** DC42
Endeavour Rd, Wal.Cr. (Chsht.)
  EN8 . . . .**15** DY27
Endeavour Way, SW19 . . . . . .**120** DB91
  Barking IG11 . . . .**88** EU68
  Croydon CR0 . . . .**141** DK101
Endell St, WC2 . . . .**195** P8
Enderby St, SE10 . . . .**205** H10
Enderley Cl, Har. HA3
  off Enderley Rd **41** CE53
Enderley Rd, Har. HA3 . . . .**41** CE53
Endersby Rd, Barn. EN5 . . . . .**27** CW43
Endersleigh Gdns, NW4 . . . . . .**63** CU56
Endlebury Rd, E4 . . . .**47** EB47
Endlesham Rd, SW12 . . . .**120** DG87
Endsleigh Cl, S.Croy. CR2 . . .**160** DW110
Endsleigh Gdns, WC1 . . . . . .**195** M4
  Ilford IG1 . . . .**69** EM61
  Surbiton KT6 . . . .**137** CJ100
  Walton-on-Thames
    KT12 . . . .**154** BW106
Endsleigh Pl, WC1 . . . .**195** N4
Endsleigh Rd, W13 . . . .**79** CG73
  Redhill RH1 . . . .**185** DJ129
  Southall UB2 . . . .**96** BY77
Endsleigh St, WC1 . . . .**195** M4
Endway, Surb. KT5 . . . .**138** CN101
Endwell Rd, SE4 . . . .**103** DY82
Endymion Rd, N4 . . . .**65** DN59
  SW2 . . . .**121** DM86
Energen Cl, NW10 . . . .**80** CS65
ENFIELD **30** DT41
≷ Enfield Chase **30** DQ41

Enfield Cl, Uxb. UB8
  off Villier St **76** BK68
ENFIELD HIGHWAY, Enf. **30** DW41
ENFIELD LOCK, Enf. **31** DZ37
≷ Enfield Lock **31** DY37
Enfield Retail Pk, Enf. EN1 . . . .**30** DV41
Enfield Rd, N1 . . . .**84** DS66
  W3 . . . .**98** CP75
  Brentford TW8 . . . .**97** CK78
  Enfield EN2 . . . .**29** DK42
  Hounslow (Hthrw.Air.) TW6
    off Eastern Perimeter Rd . .**95** BS82
ENFIELD TOWN, Enf. **30** DR40
≷ Enfield Town **30** DS42
Enfield Wk, Brent. TW8 . . . . . .**97** CK78
ENFIELD WASH, Enf. **31** DX38
Enford St, W1 . . . .**194** D6
Engadine Cl, Croy. CR0 . . . . .**142** DT104
Engadine St, SW18 . . . .**119** CZ88
Engate St, SE13 . . . .**103** EC84
Engayne Gdns, Upmin. RM14 .**72** FP60
Engel Pk, NW7 . . . .**43** CW51
Engineer Cl, SE18 . . . .**105** EN79
Engineers Way, Wem. HA9 . . . .**62** CN63
Englands La, NW3 . . . .**82** DF65
  Loughton IG10 . . . .**33** EN40
England Way, N.Mal. KT3 . . . .**138** CP98
Englefield Cl, Croy. CR0
  off Queen's Rd **142** DQ100
  Egham (Eng.Grn.) TW20
    off Alexandra Rd **112** AW93
  Enfield EN2 . . . .**29** DN40
  Orpington BR5 . . . .**145** ET98
Englefield Cres, Orp. BR5 . . .**145** ET98
ENGLEFIELD GREEN, Egh. . .**112** AV92
Englefield Grn, Egh. (Eng.Grn.)
  TW20 . . . .**112** AW91
Englefield Path, Orp. BR5 . . .**145** ET98
Englefield Rd, N1 . . . .**84** DR65
  Orpington BR5 . . . .**146** EU98
Engleheart Dr, Felt. TW14 . . .**115** BT86
Engleheart Rd, SE6 . . . .**123** EB87
Englehurst, Egh. (Eng.Grn.)
  TW20 . . . .**112** AW93
Englemere Pk, Lthd. (Oxshott)
  KT22 . . . .**154** CB114
Englewood Rd, SW12 . . . .**121** DH86
Engliff La, Wok. GU22 . . . . . .**167** BF116
English Gdns, Stai. (Wrays.)
  TW19 . . . .**92** AX84
English Grds, SE1 . . . .**201** M3
English St, E3 . . . .**85** DZ70
Enid Cl, St.Alb. (Brick.Wd.)
  AL2 . . . .**8** BZ31
Enid St, SE16 . . . .**202** A6
Enmore Av, SE25 . . . .**142** DU99
Enmore Gdns, SW14 . . . .**118** CR85
Enmore Rd, SE25 . . . .**142** DU99
  SW15 . . . .**99** CW84
  Southall UB1 . . . .**78** CA70
Ennerdale Av, Horn. RM12 . . . .**71** FG64
  Stanmore HA7 . . . .**61** CJ55
Ennerdale Cl, Felt. TW14 . . . .**115** BT88
  Sutton (Cheam) SM1 . . . .**157** CZ105
Ennerdale Dr, NW9 . . . .**62** CS57
Ennerdale Gdns, Wem. HA9 . . .**61** CK60
Ennerdale Ho, E3 . . . .**85** DZ70
Ennerdale Rd, Bexh. DA7 . . .**106** FA81
  Richmond TW9 . . . .**98** CM82
Ennersdale Rd, SE13 . . . .**123** ED85
Ennis Rd, N4 . . . .**65** DN60
  SE18 . . . .**105** EQ79
Ennismore Av, W4 . . . .**99** CT77
  Greenford UB6 . . . .**79** CE65
Ennismore Gdns, SW7 . . . . . .**198** B6
  Thames Ditton KT7 . . . . .**137** CE100
Ennismore Gdns Ms, SW7 . . .**198** B6
Ennismore Ms, SW7 . . . .**198** B5
Ennismore St, SW7 . . . .**198** B6
Ensign Cl, Pur. CR8 . . . .**159** DN110
  Staines (Stanw.) TW19 . . .**114** BK88
Ensign Dr, N13 . . . .**46** DQ48
Ensign St, E1 . . . .**84** DU73
Ensign Way, Stai. (Stanw.)
  TW19 . . . .**114** BK88
Enslin Rd, SE9 . . . .**125** EN86
Ensor Ms, SW7
  off Cranley Gdns **100** DD78
Enstone Rd, Enf. EN3 . . . .**31** DY41
  Uxbridge UB10 . . . .**58** BM62
Enterdent Rd, Gdse. RH9 . . .**186** DW134
Enterprise Cl, Croy. CR0 . . . .**141** DN102
Enterprise Way, NW10 . . . .**81** CU69
  SW18 . . . .**100** DA84
  Teddington TW11 . . . .**117** CF92
Enterprize Way, SE8 . . . .**203** M8
Eothen Cl, Cat. CR3 . . . .**176** DU124
Eothen Hts, Cat. CR3 . . . .**176** DU124
Epirus Ms, SW6 . . . .**100** DA80
Epirus Rd, SW6 . . . .**99** CZ80
EPPING **17** ES31
⊖ Epping **18** EU31
Epping Cl, E14 . . . .**204** A8
  Romford RM7 . . . .**71** FB55
★ Epping Forest,
  Epp. & Loug. **32** EJ39
★ Epping Forest District Mus,
  Wal.Abb. EN9 off Sun St . .**15** EC33
Epping Glade, E4 . . . .**31** EC44
Epping La, Rom. (Stap.Taw.)
  RM4 . . . .**34** EV40
Epping New Rd, Buck.H. IG9 . .**48** EH47
  Loughton IG10 . . . .**32** EH43
Epping Pl, N1
  off Liverpool Rd **83** DN65
Epping Rd, Epp. (Epp.Grn.) CM16 .**17** ER27
  Epping (N.Wld.Bas.) CM16 .**18** EW27
  Ongar (Toot Hill) CM5 . . . . .**19** FC30
Epping Way, E4 . . . .**31** EB44
Epple Rd, SW6 . . . .**99** CZ81
EPSOM **156** CQ114
≷ Epsom **156** CR112
Ⓗ Epsom & Ewell New Cottage
  Hosp, Epsom KT19 . . . . . .**156** CL111
Epsom Cl, Bexh. DA7 . . . .**107** FB83
  Northolt UB5 . . . .**60** BZ64

≷ Epsom Downs **173** CV115
Epsom Downs, Epsom **173** CU118
Epsom Downs Metro Cen, Tad.
  KT20 off Waterfield **173** CV120
Ⓗ Epsom Gen Hosp, Epsom
  KT18 . . . .**172** CQ115
Epsom Gap, Lthd. KT22 . . . . .**171** CH115
Epsom La N, Epsom KT18 . . .**173** CV118
  Tadworth KT20 . . . .**173** CV118
Epsom La S, Tad. KT20 . . . . .**173** CW121
★ Epsom Racecourse, Epsom
  KT18 . . . .**173** CT118
Epsom Rd, E10 . . . .**67** EC58
  Ashtead KT21 . . . .**172** CM118
  Croydon CR0 . . . .**159** DN105
  Epsom KT17 . . . .**157** CT110
  Ilford IG3 . . . .**69** ES58
  Leatherhead KT22 . . . . . .**171** CH121
  Morden SM4 . . . .**139** CZ101
  Sutton SM3 . . . .**139** CZ101
Epsom Sq, Houns. (Hthrw.Air.) TW6
  off Eastern Perimeter Rd . .**95** BT82
Epsom Way, Horn. RM12 . . . . .**72** FM63
Epstein Rd, SE28 . . . .**88** EU74
Epworth Rd, Islw. TW7 . . . .**97** CH80
Epworth St, EC2 . . . .**197** L5
Equity Sq, E2
  off Shacklewell St **84** DT69
Erasmus St, SW1 . . . .**199** N9
Erconwald St, W12 . . . .**81** CT72
Eresby Dr, Beck. BR3 . . . .**143** EA102
Eresby Pl, NW6 . . . .**82** DA66
Erica Ct, Swan. BR8
  off Azalea Dr **147** FE98
  Woking GU22 . . . .**166** AX118
Erica Gdns, Croy. CR0 . . . . . .**161** EB105
Erica St, W12 . . . .**81** CU73
Eric Clarke La, Bark. IG11 . . . .**87** EP70
Eric Cl, E7 . . . .**68** EG63
Ericcson Cl, SW18 . . . .**120** DA85
Eric Rd, E7 . . . .**68** EG63
  NW10 off Church Rd **81** CT65
  Romford RM6 . . . .**70** EX59
Eric Steele Ho, St.Alb. AL2 . . . .**8** CB27
Eridge Grn Cl, Orp. BR5
  off Petten Gro **146** EW102
Eridge Rd, W4 . . . .**98** CR76
Erin Cl, Brom. BR1 . . . .**124** EE94
  Ilford IG3 . . . .**70** EU58
Erindale, SE18 . . . .**105** ER79
Erindale Ter, SE18 . . . .**105** ER79
Eriswell Cres, Walt. KT12 . . .**153** BS107
Eriswell Rd, Walt. KT12 . . . . .**153** BT105
ERITH **107** FD79
≷ Erith **107** FE78
Ⓗ Erith & District Hosp, Erith
  DA8 . . . .**107** FD79
Erith Ct, Purf. RM19 . . . .**108** FN77
  off Thamley **108** FN77
Erith Cres, Rom. RM5 . . . .**51** FC53
Erith High St, Erith DA8 . . . . .**107** FE78
★ Erith Lib & Mus, Erith DA8
  off Walnut Tree Rd **107** FE78
Erith Rd, Belv. DA17 . . . .**106** FA78
  Bexleyheath DA7 . . . .**107** FB84
  Erith DA8 . . . .**107** FB84
Erkenwald Cl, Cher. KT16 . . .**133** BC100
Erlanger Rd, SE14 . . . .**103** DX81
Erlesmere Gdns, W13 . . . .**97** CG76
Ermine Cl, Houns. TW4 . . . . . .**96** BW82
  Waltham Cross (Chsht.)
    EN7 . . . .**14** DV31
Ermine Ho, N17
  off Moselle St **46** DT52
Ermine Rd, N15 . . . .**66** DT58
  SE13 . . . .**103** EB83
Ermine Side, Enf. EN1 . . . .**30** DU43
Ermington Rd, SE9 . . . .**125** EQ89
Ermyn Cl, Lthd. KT22 . . . .**171** CK121
Ermyn Way, Lthd. KT22 . . . . .**171** CK121
Ernald Av, E6 . . . .**86** EL68
Ernan Cl, S.Ock. RM15 . . . . . .**91** FU71
Ernan Rd, S.Ock. RM15 . . . . . .**91** FU71
Erncroft Way, Twick. TW1 . . . .**117** CF86
Ernest Av, SE27 . . . .**121** DP91
Ernest Cl, Beck. BR3 . . . .**143** EA99
Ernest Gdns, W4 . . . .**98** CP79
Ernest Gro, Beck. BR3 . . . . . .**143** DZ99
Ernest Rd, Horn. RM11 . . . . . .**72** FL58
  Kingston upon Thames
    KT1 . . . .**138** CP96
Ernest Sq, Kings.T. KT1 . . . . .**138** CP96
Ernest St, E1 . . . .**85** DX70
Erne Rd, SW20 . . . .**139** CV94
Ernshaw Pl, SW15
  off Carlton Dr **119** CY85
★ Eros, W1 . . . .**199** M1
Erpingham Rd, SW15 . . . .**99** CW83
Erridge Rd, SW19 . . . .**140** DA96
Erriff Dr, S.Ock. RM15 . . . .**91** FT71
Errington Cl, Grays RM16
  off Cedar Rd **111** GH76
Errington Rd, W9 . . . .**81** CZ70
Errol Gdns, Hayes UB4 . . . . . .**77** BV70
  New Malden KT3 . . . .**139** CU98
Erroll Rd, Rom. RM1 . . . .**71** FF56
Errol St, EC1 . . . .**197** J5
Erskine Cl, Sutt. SM1 . . . .**140** DE104
Erskine Cres, N17 . . . .**66** DV56
Erskine Hill, NW11 . . . .**64** DA57
Erskine Ms, NW3
  off Erskine Rd **82** DF66
Erskine Rd, E17 . . . .**67** DZ56
  NW3 . . . .**82** DF66
  Sutton SM1 . . . .**158** DD105
  Watford WD19 . . . .**40** BW48
Erwood Rd, SE7 . . . .**104** EL78
Esam Way, SW16 . . . .**121** DN92
Escott Gdns, SE9 . . . .**124** EL91
Escott Pl, Cher. (Ott.) KT16 . .**151** BC107
Escot Way, Barn. EN5 . . . .**27** CW43
Escreet Gro, SE18 . . . .**105** EN77
Esdaile Gdns, Upmin. RM14 . . .**73** FR59
ESHER **154** CB105
≷ Esher **137** CD103

★ Place of interest   ≷ Railway station   ⊖ London Underground station   ᴰᴸᴿ Docklands Light Railway station   ⬩ Tramlink station   Ⓗ Hospital

Esher Av, Rom. RM7 . . . . .71 FC58
Sutton SM3 . . . . .139 CX104
Walton-on-Thames KT12 . .135 BU101
Esher Bypass, Chess. KT9 . .155 CH108
Cobham KT11 . . . . .153 BU112
Esher KT10 . . . . .155 CH108
Esher Cl, Bex. DA5 . . . . . . .126 EY88
Esher KT10 . . . . .154 CB106
Esher Cres, Houns. (Hthrw.Air.) TW6
off Eastern Perimeter Rd . .95 BS82
Esher Gdns, SW19 . . . . . . .119 CX89
Esher Grn, Esher KT10 . . . .154 CB105
Esher Ms, Mitch. CR4 . . . . .140 DF97
Esher Pk Av, Esher KT10 . . .154 CC105
Esher Pl Av, Esher KT10 . . .154 CB105
Esher Rd, E.Mol. KT8 . . . . .137 CD100
Ilford IG3 . . . . .69 ES62
Walton-on-Thames KT12 . .154 BX106
Eskdale, St.Alb. (Lon.Col.)
AL2 . . . . .10 CM27
Eskdale Av, Nthlt. UB5 . . . . .78 BZ67
Wembley HA9 . . . . .61 CK61
Eskdale Gdns, Pur. CR8 . . . .160 DR114
Eskdale Rd, Bexh. DA7 . . . .106 FA82
Uxbridge UB8 . . . . .76 BH68
Eskley Gdns, S.Ock. RM15 . .91 FV70
Eskmont Ridge, SE19 . . . . .122 DS94
Esk Rd, E13 . . . . .86 EG70
Esk Way, Rom. RM1 . . . . . . .51 FD52
Esmar Cres, NW9 . . . . .63 CU59
Esme Ho, SW15 . . . . .99 CT84
Esmeralda Rd, SE1 . . . . . . .202 C9
Esmond Cl, Rain. RM13
off Dawson Dr 89 FH66
Esmond Rd, NW6 . . . . .81 CZ67
W4 . . . . .98 CR77
Esmond St, SW15 . . . . .99 CY84
Esparto St, SW18 . . . . .120 DB87
Essendene Cl, Cat. CR3 . . . .176 DS123
Essendene Rd, Cat. CR3 . . . .176 DS123
Essenden Rd, Belv. DA17 . . .106 FA78
South Croydon CR2 . . . . .160 DS108
Essendine Rd, W9 . . . . .82 DA70
Essex Av, Islw. TW7 . . . . . . .97 CE83
Essex Cl, E17 . . . . .67 DY56
Addlestone KT15 . . . . . . .152 BJ105
Morden SM4 . . . . .139 CX101
Romford RM7 . . . . .71 FB56
Ruislip HA4 . . . . .60 BX60
Essex Ct, EC4 . . . . .196 D9
SW13 . . . . .99 CT82
Essex Gdns, N4 . . . . .65 DP58
Hornchurch RM11 . . . . . .72 FM57
Essex Gro, SE19 . . . . .122 DR93
Essex Ho, E14 off Giraud St . .85 EB72
Essex La, Kings L. WD4 . . . . .7 BS33
H Essex Nuffield Hosp, Brwd.
CM15 . . . . .54 FY46
Essex Pk, N3 . . . . .44 DB51
Essex Pk Ms, W3 . . . . .80 CS74
Essex Pl, W4 . . . . .98 CQ77
Essex Pl Sq, W4
off Chiswick High Rd 98 CR77
≷ Essex Road 84 DQ66
Essex Rd, E4 . . . . .48 EE46
E10 . . . . .67 EC58
E12 . . . . .68 EL64
E17 . . . . .67 DY58
E18 . . . . .48 EH54
N1 . . . . .83 DP67
NW10 . . . . .80 CS66
W3 . . . . .80 CQ73
W4 off Belmont Rd 98 CR77
Barking IG11 . . . . .87 ER66
Borehamwood WD6 . . . . .26 CN41
Dagenham RM10 . . . . . . .71 FC64
Dartford DA1 . . . . .128 FK86
Enfield EN2 . . . . .30 DR42
Gravesend DA11 . . . . . . .131 GG88
Grays RM20 . . . . .109 FU79
Longfield DA3 . . . . .149 FX96
Romford RM7 . . . . .71 FB56
Romford (Chad.Hth.) RM6 . .70 EW59
Watford WD17 . . . . .23 BU40
Essex Rd S, E11 . . . . .67 ED59
Essex St, E7 . . . . .68 EG64
WC2 . . . . .196 D10
Essex Twr, SE20 . . . . .142 DV95
Essex Vil, W8 . . . . .100 DA75
Essex Way, Brwd. CM13 . . . .53 FW51
Epping CM16 . . . . .18 EV32
Ongar CM5 . . . . .19 FF29
Essex Wf, E5 . . . . .66 DW61
Essian St, E1 . . . . .85 DY71
Essoldo Way, Edg. HA8 . . . .62 CM55
Estate Way, E10 . . . . .67 DZ60
Estcourt Rd, SE25 . . . . . . .142 DV100
SW6 . . . . .99 CZ80
Watford WD17 . . . . .24 BW41
Estella Av, N.Mal. KT3 . . . . .139 CV98
Estelle Rd, NW3 . . . . .64 DF63
Esterbrooke St, SW1 . . . . . .199 M9
Este Rd, SW11 . . . . .100 DE83
Esther Cl, N21 . . . . .45 DN45
Esther Rd, E11 . . . . .68 EE59
Estoria Cl, SW2 . . . . .121 DN87
★ Estorick Collection of
Modern Italian Art, N1 . . . .83 DP65
Estreham Rd, SW16 . . . . . .121 DK93
Estridge Cl, Houns. TW3 . . . .96 CA84
Estuary Cl, Bark. IG11 . . . . .88 EV69
Eswyn Rd, SW17 . . . . .120 DF91
Etchingham Pk Rd, N3 . . . . .44 DB52
Etchingham Rd, E15 . . . . . .67 EC63
Eternit Wk, SW6 . . . . .99 CW81
Etfield Gro, Sid. DA14 . . . . .126 EV92
Ethel Bailey Cl, Epsom KT19 .156 CN112
Ethelbert Cl, Brom. BR1 . . . .144 EG97
Ethelbert Gdns, Ilf. IG2 . . . . .69 EM57
Ethelbert Rd, SW20 . . . . . .139 CX95
Bromley BR1 . . . . .144 EG97
Dartford (Hawley) DA2 . . .128 FL91
Erith DA8 . . . . .107 FC80
Orpington BR5 . . . . .146 EX97
Ethelbert St, SW12
off Fernlea Rd 121 DH88

Ethelburga Rd, Rom. RM3 . . .52 FM53
Ethelburga St, SW11 . . . . . .100 DE81
Etheldene Av, N10 . . . . .65 DJ56
Ethelden Rd, W12 . . . . .81 CV74
Ethel Rd, E16 . . . . .86 EH72
Ashford TW15 . . . . .114 BL92
Ethel St, SE17 . . . . .201 H9
Ethel Ter, Orp. BR6 . . . . . . .164 EW109
Ethelwine Pl, Abb.L. WD5
off The Crescent 7 BT30
Etheridge Grn, Loug. IG10
off Etheridge Rd 33 EQ41
Etheridge Rd, NW2 . . . . . . .63 CW59
Loughton IG10 . . . . .33 EP40
Etherley Rd, N15 . . . . .66 DQ57
Etherow St, SE22 . . . . .122 DU86
Etherstone Grn, SW16 . . . . .121 DN91
Etherstone Rd, SW16 . . . . . .121 DN91
Ethnard Rd, SE15 . . . . .102 DV79
Ethorpe Cl, Ger.Cr. SL9 . . . . .56 AY57
Ethorpe Cres, Ger.Cr. SL9 . . .56 AY57
Ethronvi Rd, Bexh. DA7 . . . .106 EY83
Etloe Rd, E10 . . . . .67 EA61
Eton Av, N12 . . . . .44 DC52
NW3 . . . . .82 DD66
Barnet EN4 . . . . .28 DE44
Hounslow TW5 . . . . .96 BZ79
New Malden KT3 . . . . . . .138 CR99
Wembley HA0 . . . . .61 CH63
Eton Cl, SW18 . . . . .120 DB87
Slough (Datchet) SL3 . . . .92 AU79
Eton Coll Rd, NW3 . . . . .82 DF65
Eton Ct, NW3 off Eton Av . . .82 DD66
Staines TW18
off Richmond Rd 113 BF92
Wembley HA0
off Eton Av 61 CJ63
Eton Garages, NW3
off Lambolle Pl 82 DE65
Eton Gro, NW9 . . . . .62 CN55
SE13 . . . . .104 EE83
Eton Hall, NW3
off Eton Coll Rd 82 DF65
Eton Pl, NW3
off Haverstock Hill 82 DG66
Eton Ri, NW3
off Eton Coll Rd 82 DF65
Eton Rd, NW3 . . . . .82 DF66
Hayes UB3 . . . . .95 BT80
Ilford IG1 . . . . .69 EQ64
Orpington BR6 . . . . .164 EV105
Slough (Datchet) SL3 . . . .92 AT78
Eton St, Rich. TW9 . . . . . . .118 CL85
Eton Vil, NW3 . . . . .82 DF65
Eton Way, Dart. DA1 . . . . . .108 FJ84
Etta St, SE8 . . . . .103 DY79
Ettrick St, E14 . . . . .85 EC78
Etwell Pl, Surb. KT5 . . . . . .138 CM100
Euclid Way, Grays RM20 . . . .109 FU78
Euesden Cl, N9
off Plevna Rd 46 DV48
Eugene Cl, Rom. RM2 . . . . . .72 FJ56
Eugenia Rd, SE16 . . . . .202 G9
Eureka Rd, Kings.T. KT1
off Washington Rd 138 CN96
Europa Pl, EC1 . . . . .197 H3
Europa Trd Est, Erith DA8 . . .107 FD78
Europe Rd, SE18 . . . . .105 EM76
Eustace Rd, E6 . . . . .86 EL69
SW6 . . . . .100 DA80
Romford RM6 . . . . .70 EX59
≷ Euston 195 L2
⊖ Euston 199 L2
Euston Av, Wat. WD18 . . . . . .23 BT43
Euston Cen, NW1
off Triton Sq 83 DJ70
Euston Gro, NW1 . . . . .195 M3
Euston Rd, N1 . . . . .195 P2
NW1 . . . . .195 J5
Croydon CR0 . . . . .141 DN102
⊖ Euston Square 195 L4
Euston Sq, NW1 . . . . .195 M3
Euston Sta Colonnade, NW1 .195 M3
Euston St, NW1 . . . . .195 L4
Euston Twr, NW1 . . . . .83 DJ70
Evandale Rd, SW9 . . . . .101 DN82
Evangelist Rd, NW5 . . . . . . .65 DH63
Evans Av, Wat. WD25 . . . . . .23 BT35
Evans Cl, E8
off Buttermere Wk 84 DT65
Greenhithe DA9 . . . . . . .129 FU85
Rickmansworth (Crox.Grn.) WD3
off New Rd 22 BN43
Evansdale, Rain. RM13
off New Zealand Way 89 FF69
Evans Gro, Felt. TW13 . . . . .116 CA89
Evans Rd, SE6 . . . . .124 EE89
Evanston Av, E4 . . . . .47 EC52
Evanston Gdns, Ilf. IG4 . . . . .68 EL58
Eva Rd, Rom. RM6 . . . . .70 EW59
Evelina Rd, SE15 . . . . .102 DW83
SE20 . . . . .123 DX94
Eveline Lowe Est, SE16 . . . .202 B7
Eveline Rd, Mitch. CR4 . . . . .140 DF95
Evelyn Av, NW9 . . . . .62 CR56
Ruislip HA4 . . . . .59 BT58
Evelyn Cl, Twick. TW2 . . . . .116 CB87
Woking GU22 . . . . .166 AX120
Evelyn Ct, N1 . . . . .197 K1
Evelyn Cres, Sun. TW16 . . . .135 BT95
Evelyn Denington Rd, E6 . . . .86 EL70
Evelyn Dr, Pnr. HA5 . . . . . . .40 BX52
Evelyn Fox Ct, W10 . . . . . . .81 CW71
Evelyn Gdns, SW7 . . . . .100 DD78
Godstone RH9 . . . . .186 DW130
Richmond TW9
off Kew Rd 98 CL84
Evelyn Gro, W5 . . . . .80 CM74
Southall UB1 . . . . .78 BZ72
Evelyn Rd, E16 . . . . .205 P2
E17 . . . . .67 EC66
SW19 . . . . .120 DB92
W4 . . . . .98 CR76
Barnet EN4 . . . . .28 DF42
Richmond TW9 . . . . .98 CL83
Richmond (Ham) TW10 . . .117 CJ90

Evelyns Cl, Uxb. UB8 . . . . . .76 BN72
Evelyn Sharp Cl, Rom. RM2
off Amery Gdns 72 FK55
Evelyn St, SE8 . . . . .203 K9
Evelyn Ter, Rich. TW9 . . . . . .98 CL83
Evelyn Wk, N1 . . . . .197 K1
Brentwood CM13 . . . . . . .53 FW51
Evelyn Way, Cob. (Stoke D'Ab.)
KT11 . . . . .170 BZ116
Epsom KT19 off Queen
Alexandra's Way 156 CN111
Sunbury-on-Thames
TW16 . . . . .135 BT95
Wallington SM6 . . . . .159 DK105
Evelyn Yd, W1 . . . . .195 M8
Evening Hill, Beck. BR3 . . . .123 EC94
Evensyde, Wat. WD18 . . . . . .23 BR44
Evenwood Cl, SW15 . . . . . . .119 CY85
Everard Av, Brom. BR2 . . . .144 EG102
Slough SL1 . . . . .92 AS75
Everard La, Cat. CR3
off Tillingdown Hill 176 DU122
Everard Way, Wem. HA9 . . . .62 CL62
Everatt Cl, SW18
off Amerland Rd 119 CZ86
Everdon Rd, SW13 . . . . .99 CU79
Everest Cl, Grav. (Nthflt.)
DA11 . . . . .130 GE90
Everest Ct, Wok. GU21
off Langmans Way 166 AS116
Everest Pl, E14 . . . . .85 EC71
Swanley BR8 . . . . .147 FD98
Everest Rd, SE9 . . . . .125 EM85
Staines (Stanw.) TW19 . . . .114 BK87
Everett Cl, Bushey (Bushey Hth.)
WD23 . . . . .41 CE46
Pinner HA5 . . . . .59 BT55
Waltham Cross (Chsht.)
EN7 . . . . .14 DQ25
Everett Wk, Belv. DA17
off Osborne Rd 106 EZ78
Everglade, West. (Bigg.H.)
TN16 . . . . .178 EK118
Everglade Strand, NW9 . . . . .43 CT53
Evergreen Ct, Stai. (Stanw.) TW19
off Evergreen Way 114 BK87
Evergreen Oak Av, Wind. SL4 .92 AU83
Evergreen Sq, E8 . . . . .84 DT66
Evergreen Way, Hayes UB3 . .77 BT73
Staines (Stanw.) TW19 . . . .114 BK87
Everilda St, N1 . . . . .83 DM67
Evering Rd, E5 . . . . .66 DT62
N16 . . . . .66 DT62
Everington Rd, N10 . . . . .44 DF54
Everington St, W6 . . . . .99 CX79
Everitt Rd, NW10 . . . . .80 CR69
Everlands Cl, Wok. GU22 . . . .166 AY118
Everleigh St, N4 . . . . .65 DM60
Eve Rd, E11 . . . . .68 EE63
E15 . . . . .86 EE68
N17 . . . . .66 DS55
Isleworth TW7 . . . . .97 CG84
Woking GU21 . . . . .167 BB115
Eversfield Gdns, NW7 . . . . . .42 CS52
Eversfield Rd, Reig. RH2 . . . .184 DB134
Richmond TW9 . . . . .98 CM82
Evershed Wk, W4 . . . . .98 CR77
Eversholt St, NW1 . . . . .83 DJ68
Evershot Rd, N4 . . . . .65 DM60
Eversleigh Gdns, Upmin.
RM14 . . . . .73 FR60
Eversleigh Rd, E6 . . . . .86 EK67
N3 . . . . .43 CZ52
SW11 . . . . .100 DF83
Barnet EN5 . . . . .28 DC43
Eversley Av, Bexh. DA7 . . . .107 FD82
Wembley HA9 . . . . .62 CN61
Eversley Cl, N21 . . . . .29 DM44
Loughton IG10
off The Broadway 33 EQ41
Eversley Cres, N21 . . . . .29 DM44
Isleworth TW7 . . . . .97 CD81
Ruislip HA4 . . . . .59 BS61
Eversley Cross, Bexh. DA7 . .107 FE82
Eversley Mt, N21 . . . . .29 DM44
Eversley Pk, SW19 . . . . .119 CV92
Eversley Pk Rd, N21 . . . . . . .29 DM44
Eversley Rd, SE7 . . . . .104 EH79
SE19 . . . . .122 DR94
Surbiton KT5 . . . . .138 CM98
Eversley Way, Croy. CR0 . . . .161 EA105
Egham TW20 . . . . .133 BC96
Everthorpe Rd, SE15 . . . . . .102 DT83
Everton Bldgs, NW1 . . . . . .195 K3
Everton Dr, Stan. HA7 . . . . . .62 CM55
Everton Rd, Croy. CR0 . . . . .142 DU102
Evesham Av, E17 . . . . .47 EA54
Evesham Cl, Grnf. UB6 . . . . .78 CB68
Reigate RH2 . . . . .183 CZ133
Sutton SM2 . . . . .158 DA108
Evesham Grn, Mord. SM4 . . .140 DB100
Evesham Rd, E15 . . . . .86 EF67
N11 . . . . .45 DJ50
Gravesend DA12 . . . . . . .131 GK89
Morden SM4 . . . . .140 DB100
Reigate RH2 . . . . .183 CZ134
Evesham Rd N, Reig. RH2 . . .183 CZ133
Evesham St, W11 . . . . .81 CX73
Evesham Wk, SE5
off Love Wk 102 DR82
SW9 . . . . .101 DN82
Evesham Way, SW11 . . . . . .100 DG83
Ilford IG5 . . . . .69 EN55
Ewald Rd, SW6 . . . . .99 CZ82
Ewanrigg Ter, Wdf.Grn. IG8 . .48 EJ50
Ewan Rd, Rom. (Harold Wd.)
RM3 . . . . .52 FK54
Ewart Gro, N22 . . . . .45 DN53
Ewart Pl, E3
off Roman Rd 85 DZ68
Ewart Rd, SE23 . . . . .123 DX87
Ewe Cl, N7 . . . . .83 DL65
EWELL, Epsom 157 CU110
Ewell Bypass, Epsom KT17 . .157 CU108
Ewell Ct Av, Epsom KT19 . . .156 CS106

Ewell Downs Rd, Epsom
KT17 . . . . .157 CU111
≷ Ewell East 157 CU111
Ewell Ho Gro, Epsom KT17 . .157 CT110
Ewell Pk Gdns, Epsom KT17 .157 CU108
Ewell Pk Way, Epsom (Ewell)
KT17 . . . . .157 CU107
Ewell Rd, Surb. KT6 . . . . . .138 CL100
Surbiton (Long Dit.) KT6 . .137 CH101
Sutton SM3 . . . . .157 CY107
≷ Ewell West 156 CS109
Ewelme Rd, SE23 . . . . .122 DW88
Ewen Cres, SW2 . . . . .121 DN87
Ewer St, SE1 . . . . .201 H3
Ewhurst Av, S.Croy. CR2 . . . .160 DT109
Ewhurst Cl, E17 . . . . .48 DW71
Sutton SM2 . . . . .157 CW109
Ewhurst Rd, SE4 . . . . .123 DZ86
Exbury Rd, SE6 . . . . .123 EA89
★ ExCeL, E16 . . . . .86 EH73
Excel Ct, WC2 . . . . .199 N1
Excelsior Cl, Kings.T. KT1
off Washington Rd 138 CN96
Excelsior Gdns, SE13 . . . . .103 EC82
Exchange Arc, EC2 . . . . . . .197 N6
Exchange Bldgs, E1
off Cutler St 84 DS72
Exchange Cl, N11
off Benfleet Way 44 DG47
Exchange Ct, WC2 . . . . . . .200 A1
Exchange Pl, EC2 . . . . .197 M6
Exchange Rd, Wat. WD18 . . . .23 BV42
Exchange Sq, EC2 . . . . .197 M6
Exchange St, Rom. RM1 . . . .71 FE57
Exchange III Shop Cen, The, Ilf.
IG1 . . . . .69 EP61
Exeforde Av, Ashf. TW15 . . . .114 BN91
Exeter Cl, E6
off Harper Rd 87 EM72
Watford WD24 . . . . .24 BW40
Exeter Gdns, Ilf. IG1 . . . . . . .68 EL60
Exeter Ho, SW15
off Putney Heath 119 CW86
Exeter Ms, NW6
off West Hampstead Ms . . .82 DB65
SW6 off Farm La 100 DA80
Exeter Rd, E16 . . . . .86 EG71
E17 . . . . .67 EA57
N9 . . . . .46 DW47
N14 . . . . .45 DH46
NW2 . . . . .63 CY64
Croydon CR0 . . . . .142 DS101
Dagenham RM10 . . . . . . .89 FB65
Enfield EN3 . . . . .31 DX41
Feltham TW13 . . . . .116 BZ90
Gravesend DA12 . . . . . . .131 GK90
Harrow HA2 . . . . .60 BY61
Hounslow (Hthrw.Air.) TW6 .95 BS82
Welling DA16 . . . . .105 ET82
Exeter St, WC2 . . . . .196 A10
Exeter Way, SE14 . . . . .103 DZ80
Hounslow (Hthrw.Air.) TW6 .95 BS83
Exford Gdns, SE12 . . . . . . .124 EH88
Exford Rd, SE12 . . . . .124 EH89
Exhibition Cl, W12 . . . . .81 CW73
Exhibition Rd, SW7 . . . . . . .198 A5
Exmoor Cl, Ilf. IG6 . . . . .49 EQ53
Exmoor St, W10 . . . . .81 CX70
Exmouth Mkt, EC1 . . . . . . .196 D4
Exmouth Ms, NW1 . . . . . . .195 L3
Exmouth Pl, E8 . . . . .84 DV66
Exmouth Rd, E17 . . . . .67 DZ57
Bromley BR2 . . . . .144 EH97
Grays RM17 . . . . .110 GB79
Hayes UB4 . . . . .77 BS69
Ruislip HA4 . . . . .60 BW62
Welling DA16 . . . . .106 EW81
Exmouth St, E1
off Commercial Rd 84 DW72
Exning Rd, E16 . . . . .86 EF70
Exon St, SE17 . . . . .201 N10
Explorer Av, Stai. TW19 . . . .114 BL88
Explorer Dr, Wat. WD18 . . . . .23 BT44
Express Dr, Ilf. IG3 . . . . .70 EV60
Exton Cres, NW10 . . . . .80 CQ66
Exton Gdns, Dag. RM8 . . . . .70 EW64
Exton St, SE1 . . . . .200 D3
Eyebright Cl, Croy. CR0
off Primrose La 143 DX102
Eyhurst Av, Horn. RM12 . . . . .71 FG62
Eyhurst Cl, NW2 . . . . .63 CU61
Tadworth (Kgswd.) KT20 . .173 CZ123
Eyhurst Pk, Tad. KT20 . . . . .174 DC123
Eyhurst Spur, Tad. KT20 . . . .173 CZ124
Eylewood Rd, SE27 . . . . . . .122 DQ92
Eynella Rd, SE22 . . . . .122 DT87
Eynham Rd, W12 . . . . .81 CW72
EYNSFORD, Dart. 148 FL103
★ Eynsford Castle, Dart.
DA4 . . . . .148 FK103
Eynsford Cl, Orp. BR5 . . . . .145 EQ101
Eynsford Cres, Bex. DA5 . . . .126 EW88
Eynsford Rd, Dart. (Fngham.)
DA4 . . . . .148 FM102
Greenhithe DA9 . . . . . . .129 FW85
Ilford IG3 . . . . .69 ES61
Sevenoaks TN14 . . . . . . .165 FH108
Swanley BR8 . . . . .147 FD100
Eynsham Dr, SE2 . . . . .106 EU77
Eynswood Dr, Sid. DA14 . . . .126 EV92
Eyot Gdns, W6 . . . . .99 CT78
Eyot Grn, W4
off Chiswick Mall 99 CT79
Evry Rd, Sid. DA14 . . . . . . .126 EW93
Eyre Cl, Rom. RM2 . . . . .71 FH56
Eyre Ct, NW8 off Finchley Rd .82 DC68
Eyre St Hill, EC1 . . . . .196 D5
Eyston Dr, Wey. KT13 . . . . . .152 BN110
Eythorne Rd, SW9 . . . . .101 DN81
Ezra St, E2 . . . . .84 DT69

F

Fabian Rd, SW6 . . . . .99 CZ80
Fabian St, E6 . . . . .87 EM70
Fackenden La, Sev. (Shore.)
TN14 . . . . .165 FH113
Factory La, N17 . . . . .46 DT54
Croydon CR0 . . . . .141 DN102
Factory Rd, E16 . . . . .86 EL74
Gravesend (Nthflt.) DA11 . .130 GC86
Factory Sq, SW16 . . . . .121 DL93
Factory Yd, W7
off Uxbridge Rd 79 CE74
Faesten Way, Bex. DA5 . . . .127 FE90
Faggotts Cl, Rad. WD7 . . . . .25 CJ35
Faggs Rd, Felt. TW14 . . . . .115 BU85
Fagus Av, Rain. RM13 . . . . . .90 FK69
Faints Cl, Wal.Cr. EN7 . . . . . .14 DT29
Fairacre, N.Mal. KT3 . . . . . .138 CS97
Fairacres, SW15 . . . . .99 CU84
Fair Acres, Brom. BR2 . . . . .144 EG99
Fairacres, Cob. KT11 . . . . . .154 BX112
Croydon CR0 . . . . .161 DZ109
Ruislip HA4 . . . . .59 BT59
Tadworth KT20 . . . . .173 CW121
Fairacres Cl, Pot.B. EN6 . . . .11 CZ33
Fairbairn Cl, Pur. CR8 . . . . .159 DN111
Fairbairn Grn, SW9 . . . . . . .101 DN81
Fairbank Av, Orp. BR6 . . . . .145 EP103
Fairbank Est, N1 off East Rd . .84 DR68
Fairbanks Rd, N17 . . . . .66 DT55
Fairbourne, Cob. KT11 . . . . .154 BX113
Fairbourne, Wok. GU21
off Abercorn Way 166 AU118
Fairbourne La, Cat. CR3 . . . .176 DQ122
Fairbourne Rd, N17 . . . . .66 DS55
Fairbridge Rd, N19 . . . . .65 DK61
Fairbrook Cl, N13 . . . . .45 DN50
Fairbrook Rd, N13 . . . . .45 DN51
Fairburn Cl, Borwd. WD6 . . . .26 CN39
Fairburn Ct, SW15
off Mercier Rd 119 CY85
Fairby Rd, SE12 . . . . .124 EH85
Faircharm Trd Est, SE8 . . . . .103 EB80
Fairchild Cl, SW11 off Wye St .100 DD82
Fairchildes Av, Croy. (New Adgtn.)
CR0 . . . . .161 ED112
Fairchildes La, Warl. CR6 . . .161 ED114
Fairchild Pl, EC2 . . . . .197 N5
Fairchild St, EC2 . . . . .197 N5
Fair Cl, Bushey WD23
off Claybury 40 CB45
Fairclough St, E1 . . . . .84 DU72
Faircross Av, Bark. IG11 . . . . .87 EQ65
Romford RM5 . . . . .51 FD52
Fairdale Gdns, SW15 . . . . . . .99 CV84
Hayes UB3 . . . . .77 BU74
Fairdene Rd, Couls. CR5 . . . .175 DK117
Fairey Av, Hayes UB3 . . . . . .95 BT77
Fairfax Av, Epsom KT17 . . . .157 CV109
Redhill RH1 . . . . .184 DE133
Fairfax Cl, Walt. KT12 . . . . .135 BV102
Fairfax Gdns, SE3 . . . . .104 EK81
Fairfax Ms, E16 . . . . .205 P2
SW15 . . . . .99 CW84
Fairfax Pl, NW6 . . . . .82 DC66
W14 off Holland Rd 99 CY76
Fairfax Rd, N8 . . . . .65 DN56
NW6 . . . . .82 DC66
W4 . . . . .98 CS76
Grays RM17 . . . . .110 GB78
Teddington TW11 . . . . . .117 CG93
Tilbury RM18 . . . . .111 GF81
Woking GU22 . . . . .167 BB120
Fairfax Way, N10
off Cromwell Rd 44 DG52
Fairfield App, Stai. (Wrays.)
TW19 . . . . .112 AX86
Fairfield Av, NW4 . . . . .63 CV58
Edgware HA8 . . . . .42 CP51
Ruislip HA4 . . . . .59 BQ59
Slough (Datchet) SL3 . . . .92 AW80
Staines TW18 . . . . .113 BF91
Twickenham TW2 . . . . . .116 CB88
Upminster RM14 . . . . . . .72 FQ62
Watford WD19 . . . . .40 BW48
Fairfield Cl, N12 . . . . .44 DC49
Enfield EN3
off Scotland Grn Rd N 31 DY42
Epsom (Ewell) KT19 . . . . .156 CS106
Hornchurch RM12 . . . . . .71 FG60
Mitcham CR4 . . . . .120 DE94
Northwood HA6
off Thirlmere Gdns 39 BP50
Radlett WD7 . . . . .25 CE37
Sidcup DA15 . . . . .125 ET86
Slough (Datchet) SL3 . . . .92 AX80
Fairfield Ct, NW10 . . . . .81 CU67
Northwood HA6
off Windsor Cl 39 BU54
Fairfield Cres, Edg. HA8 . . . .42 CP51
Fairfield Dr, SW18 . . . . .120 DB85
Greenford UB6 . . . . .79 CJ67
Harrow HA2 . . . . .60 CC55
Fairfield E, Kings.T. KT1 . . . .138 CL96
Fairfield Gdns, N8
off Elder Av 65 DL57
Fairfield Gro, SE7 . . . . .104 EK78
Fairfield Ind Est, Kings.T.
KT1 . . . . .138 CM97
Fairfield N, Kings.T. KT1 . . . .138 CL96
Fairfield Pk, Cob. KT11 . . . . .154 BX114
Fairfield Path, Croy. CR0 . . . .142 DR104
Fairfield Pathway, Horn.
RM12 . . . . .90 FJ66
Fairfield Rd, E3 . . . . .85 EA68
E17 . . . . .47 DY54
N8 . . . . .65 DL57
N18 . . . . .46 DU49
W7 . . . . .97 CG76
Beckenham BR3 . . . . . . .143 EA96
Bexleyheath DA7 . . . . . . .106 EZ82
Brentwood CM14 . . . . . . .54 FW48
Bromley BR1 . . . . .124 EG94

Fai - Far

Fairfield Rd, Croy. CR0 . . . . . .142 DS104
 Epping CM16 . . . . .18 EV29
 Ilford IG1 . . . . .87 EP65
 Kingston upon Thames
  KT1 . . . . .138 CL96
 Leatherhead KT22 . . . . . .171 CH121
 Orpington BR5 . . . . .145 ER100
 Southall UB1 . . . . .78 BZ72
 Staines (Wrays.) TW19 . . .112 AX86
 Uxbridge UB8 . . . . .76 BK65
 West Drayton UB7 . . . . . . .76 BL74
 Woodford Green IG8 . . . . . .48 EG51
Fairfields, Cher. KT16 . . . . .134 BG102
 Gravesend DA12 . . . . .131 GL92
Fairfields CI, NW9 . . . . .62 CQ57
Fairfields Cres, NW9 . . . . . . .62 CQ56
Fairfields Rd, Houns. TW3 . . .96 CC83
Fairfield St, SW18 . . . . .120 DB85
Fairfield Wk, Lthd. KT22
 off Fairfield Rd 171 CH121
 Waltham Cross (Chsht.)
  EN8 . . . . .15 DY28
Fairfield Way, Barn. EN5 . . . .28 DA43
 Coulsdon CR5 . . . . .159 DK114
 Epsom KT19 . . . . .156 CS106
Fairfield W, Kings.T. KT1 . . .138 CL96
Fairfolds, Wat. WD25 . . . . . . .24 BY36
Fairfoot Rd, E3 . . . . .85 EA70
Fairford Av, Bexh. DA7 . . . . .107 FD81
 Croydon CR0 . . . . .143 DX99
Fairford CI, Croy. CR0 . . . . . .143 DY99
 Reigate RH2 . . . . .184 DC132
 Romford RM3
  off Fairford Way 52 FP51
 West Byfleet KT14 . . . . . .151 BF114
Fairford Ct, Sutt. SM2
 off Grange Rd 158 DB108
Fairford Gdns, Wor.Pk. KT4 .139 CT104
Fairford Ho, SE11 . . . . .200 E9
Fairford Way, Rom. RM3 . . . .52 FP51
Fairgreen, Barn. EN4 . . . . . . .28 DF41
Fairgreen E, Barn. EN4 . . . . .28 DF41
Fairgreen Par, Mitch. CR4
 off London Rd 140 DF97
Fairgreen Rd, Th.Hth. CR7 . .141 DP99
Fairham Av, S.Ock. RM15 . . .91 FU73
Fairhaven, Egh. TW20 . . . . .113 AZ92
Fairhaven Av, Croy. CR0 . . . .143 DX100
Fairhaven Cres, Wat. WD19 . .39 BU48
Fairhaven Rd, Red. RH1 . . . .184 DG130
Fairhazel Gdns, NW6 . . . . . . .82 DB65
Fairholme, Felt. TW14 . . . . . .115 BR87
Fairholme Av, Rom. RM2 . . . .71 FG57
Fairholme CI, N3 . . . . .63 CY56
Fairholme Cres, Ashtd.
 KT21 . . . . .171 CJ117
 Hayes UB4 . . . . .77 BT70
Fairholme Gdns, N3 . . . . .63 CY55
 Upminster RM14 . . . . .73 FT59
Fairholme Rd, W14 . . . . .99 CY78
 Ashford TW15 . . . . .114 BL92
 Croydon CR0 . . . . .141 DN101
 Harrow HA1 . . . . .61 CF57
 Ilford IG1 . . . . .69 EM59
 Sutton SM1 . . . . .157 CZ107
Fairholt CI, N16 . . . . .66 DS60
Fairholt Rd, N16 . . . . .66 DR60
Fairholt St, SW7 . . . . .198 C6
Fairkytes Av, Horn. RM11 . . .72 FK60
Fairland Rd, E15 . . . . .86 EF65
Fairlands Av, Buck.H. IG9 . . .48 EG47
 Sutton SM1 . . . . .140 DA103
 Thornton Heath CR7 . . . . .141 DM98
Fairlands Ct, SE9
 off North Pk 125 EN86
Fair La, Couls. CR5 . . . . . . .184 DC125
Fairlawn, SE7 . . . . .104 EJ79
 Leatherhead (Bkhm.)
  KT23 . . . . .170 BZ124
Fairlawn Av, N2 . . . . .64 DE56
 W4 . . . . .98 CQ77
 Bexleyheath DA7 . . . . . . .106 EX82
Fairlawn CI, N14 . . . . .29 DJ44
 Esher (Clay.) KT10 . . . . . .155 CF107
 Feltham TW13 . . . . .116 BZ91
 Kingston upon Thames
  KT2 . . . . .118 CQ93
Fairlawn Dr, Wdf.Grn. IG8 . . .48 EG52
Fairlawnes, Wall. SM6
 off Maldon Rd 159 DH106
Fairlawn Gdns, Sthl. UB1 . . .78 BZ73
Fairlawn Gro, W4 . . . . .98 CQ77
 Banstead SM7 . . . . .158 DD113
Fairlawn Pk, SE26 . . . . .123 DY92
 Woking GU21 . . . . .150 AY114
Fairlawn Rd, SW19 . . . . .119 CZ94
 Banstead SM7 . . . . .158 DD112
 Carshalton SM5 . . . . .158 DC111
Fairlawns, Add. (Woodham)
 KT15 . . . . .151 BF111
 Brentwood CM14 . . . . .54 FU48
 Pinner HA5 . . . . .40 BW54
 Sunbury-on-Thames
  TW16 . . . . .135 BU97
 Twickenham TW1 . . . . . . .117 CJ86
 Watford WD17
  off Langley Rd 23 BT38
 Weybridge KT13 . . . . .153 BS106
Fairlawns CI, Horn. RM11 . . .72 FM59
 Staines TW18 . . . . .114 BH93
Fairlea PI, W5 . . . . .79 CK70
Fairlie Gdns, SE23 . . . . .122 DW87
Fairlight Av, E4 . . . . .47 ED47
 NW10 . . . . .80 CS68
 Woodford Green IG8 . . . . . .48 EG51
Fairlight CI, E4 . . . . .47 ED47
 Worcester Park KT4 . . . . .157 CW105
Fairlight Dr, Uxb. UB8 . . . . . .76 BK65
Fairlight Rd, SW17 . . . . .120 DD91
⊖ Fairlop 49 ER53
Fairlop CI, Horn. RM12 . . . . .89 FH65

Fairlop Gdns, Ilf. IG6 . . . . . . .49 EQ52
Fairlop Rd, E11 . . . . .67 ED59
 Ilford IG6 . . . . .49 EQ54
Fairmark Dr, Uxb. UB10 . . . . .76 BN65
Fairmead, Brom. BR1 . . . . . .145 EM99
 Surbiton KT5 . . . . .138 CP102
 Woking GU21 . . . . .166 AW118
Fairmead CI, Brom. BR1 . . . .145 EM98
 Hounslow TW5 . . . . .96 BX80
 New Malden KT3 . . . . . . .138 CR97
Fairmead Cres, Edg. HA8 . . .42 CQ48
Fairmead Gdns, Ilf. IG4 . . . . .68 EL57
Fairmead Rd, N19 . . . . .65 DK62
 Croydon CR0 . . . . .141 DM102
 Loughton IG10 . . . . .32 EH42
Fairmeads, Cob. KT11 . . . . .154 BZ113
 Loughton IG10 . . . . .33 EP40
Fairmead Side, Loug. IG10 . .32 EJ43
FAIRMILE, Cob. 154 BZ112
Fairmile Av, SW16 . . . . .121 DK92
 Cobham KT11 . . . . .154 BY114
Fairmile Ho, Tedd. TW11
 off Twickenham Rd 117 CG91
Fairmile La, Cob. KT11 . . . . .154 BX112
Fairmile Pk Copse, Cob.
 KT11 . . . . .154 BZ112
Fairmile Pk Rd, Cob. KT11 . .154 BZ113
Fairmont CI, Belv. DA17
 off Lullingstone Rd 106 EZ78
Fairmont Rd, SW2 . . . . .121 DM86
Fairoak CI, Ken. CR8 . . . . . .175 DP115
 Leatherhead (Oxshott)
  KT22 . . . . .155 CD112
 Orpington BR5 . . . . .145 EP101
Fairoak Dr, SE9 . . . . .125 ER85
Fairoak Gdns, Rom. RM1 . . . .51 FE54
Fairoak La, Chess. KT9 . . . . .155 CF111
 Leatherhead (Oxshott)
  KT22 . . . . .155 CF111
Fairseat CI, Bushey (Bushey Hth.)
 WD23 off Hive Rd 41 CE47
Fairs Rd, Lthd. KT22 . . . . . .171 CG119
Fairstead Wk, N1
 off Popham Rd 84 DQ67
Fair St, SE1 . . . . .201 N4
 Hounslow TW3 off High St .96 CC83
Fairthorn Rd, SE7 . . . . .205 N10
Fairtrough Rd, Orp. BR6 . . . .164 EV112
Fairview, Epsom KT17 . . . . .157 CW111
 Erith DA8 off Guild Rd . . .107 FF80
 Potters Bar EN6
  off Hawkshead Rd 12 DB29
Fairview Av, Brwd. CM13 . . . .55 GE45
 Rainham RM13 . . . . .90 FK68
 Wembley HA0 . . . . .79 CK65
 Woking GU22 . . . . .166 AY118
Fairview CI, E17 . . . . .47 DY53
 Chigwell IG7 . . . . .49 ES49
 Woking GU22
  off Fairview Av 167 AZ118
Fairview Ct, Ashf. TW15 . . . .114 BN92
Fairview Cres, Har. HA2 . . . .60 CA60
Fairview Dr, Chig. IG7 . . . . . .49 ES49
 Orpington BR6 . . . . .163 ER105
 Shepperton TW17 . . . . . .134 BM99
 Watford WD17 . . . . .23 BS36
Fairview Gdns, Wdf.Grn. IG8 .48 EH53
Fairview Ind Est, Oxt. RH8 . .188 EG133
Fairview Ind Pk, Rain. RM13 . .89 FE71
Fairview PI, SW2 . . . . .121 DM87
Fairview Rd, N15 . . . . .66 DT57
 SW16 . . . . .141 DM95
 Chigwell IG7 . . . . .49 ES49
 Enfield EN2 . . . . .29 DN39
 Epsom KT17 . . . . .157 CT111
 Gravesend (Istead Rise)
  DA13 . . . . .130 GD94
 Sutton SM1 . . . . .158 DD106
Fairview Way, Edg. HA8 . . . . .42 CN49
Fairwater Av, Well. DA16 . . . .106 EU84
Fairwater Dr, Add. (New Haw)
 KT15 . . . . .152 BK109
Fairway, SW20 . . . . .139 CW97
 Bexleyheath DA6 . . . . . . .126 EY85
 Carshalton SM5 . . . . .158 DC111
 Chertsey KT16 . . . . .134 BH102
 Orpington BR5 . . . . .145 ER99
 Virginia Water GU25 . . . . .132 AV100
 Woodford Green IG8 . . . . . .48 EJ50
Fairway, The, N13 . . . . .46 DQ48
 N14 . . . . .29 DH44
 NW7 . . . . .42 CR48
 W3 . . . . .80 CS72
 Abbots Langley WD5 . . . . . .7 BR32
 Barnet EN5 . . . . .28 DB44
 Bromley BR1 . . . . .145 EM99
 Gravesend DA11 . . . . .131 GG89
 Leatherhead KT22 . . . . . .171 CG118
 New Malden KT3 . . . . . . .138 CR95
 Northolt UB5 . . . . .78 CC65
 Northwood HA6 . . . . .39 BS49
 Ruislip HA4 . . . . .60 BX62
 Upminster RM14 . . . . .72 FQ59
 Uxbridge UB10 . . . . .76 BM68
 Wembley HA0 . . . . .61 CH62
 West Molesey KT8 . . . . . .136 CB97
 Weybridge KT13 . . . . .152 BN111
Fairway Av, NW9 . . . . .62 CP55
 Borehamwood WD6 . . . . . .26 CP40
 West Drayton UB7 . . . . . . .76 BJ74
Fairway CI, NW11 . . . . .64 DC59
 Croydon CR0 . . . . .143 DY99
 Epsom KT19 . . . . .156 CQ105
 Hounslow TW4 . . . . .116 BW85
 St. Albans (Park St.) AL2 . . .8 CC27
 West Drayton UB7
  off Fairway Av 76 BK74
 Woking GU22 . . . . .166 AU119
Fairway Ct, NW7
 off The Fairway 42 CR48
Fairway Dr, SE28 . . . . .88 EX72
 Dartford DA2 . . . . .128 FP87
 Greenford UB6 . . . . .78 CB66
Fairway Gdns, Beck. BR3 . . .143 ED100
 Ilford IG1 . . . . .69 EQ64
Fairways, Ashf. TW15 . . . . . .115 BP93
 Kenley CR8 . . . . .176 DQ117

Fairways, Stan. HA7 . . . . . . .42 CL54
 Teddington TW11 . . . . . . .117 CK94
 Waltham Abbey EN9 . . . . . .16 EE34
 Waltham Cross (Chsht.)
  EN8 . . . . .15 DX26
Fairweather CI, N15 . . . . .66 DS56
Fairweather Rd, N16 . . . . .66 DU58
Fairwyn Rd, SE26 . . . . .123 DY91
Fakenham CI, NW7 . . . . .43 CU52
 Northolt UB5
  off Goodwood Dr 78 CA65
Fakruddin St, E1 . . . . .84 DU70
Falaise, Egh. TW20 . . . . .112 AY92
Falcon Av, Brom. BR1 . . . . . .144 EL98
 Grays RM17 . . . . .110 GB79
Falconberg Ct, W1 . . . . .195 N8
Falconberg Ms, W1 . . . . .195 M8
Falcon CI, SE1 . . . . .200 G2
 W4 off Sutton La S 98 CQ79
 Dartford DA1 . . . . .128 FM85
 Northwood HA6 . . . . .39 BS52
 Waltham Abbey EN9
  off Kestrel Rd 16 EG34
Falcon Ct, EC4 . . . . .196 D9
 Woking GU21 . . . . .151 BC113
Falcon Cres, Enf. EN3 . . . . . .31 DX43
Falcon Dr, Stai. (Stanw.)
 TW19 . . . . .114 BK86
Falconer Rd, Bushey WD23 . .24 BZ44
 Ilford IG6 . . . . .50 EV50
Falconer Wk, N7
 off Newington Barrow Way .65 DM61
Falcon Gro, SW11 . . . . .100 DE83
Falcon Ho, W13 . . . . .79 CF70
Falconhurst, Lthd. (Oxshott)
 KT22 . . . . .171 CD115
Falcon La, SW11 . . . . .100 DE83
Falcon Ms, Grav. DA11 . . . . .130 GE88
Falcon Pk Ind Est, NW10 . . . .63 CT64
Falcon Rd, SW11 . . . . .100 DE83
 Enfield EN3 . . . . .31 DX43
 Hampton TW12 . . . . .116 BZ94
Falcons CI, West. (Bigg.H.)
 TN16 . . . . .178 EK117
Falcon St, E13 . . . . .86 EG70
Falcon Ter, SW11 . . . . .100 DE83
Falcon Way, E11 . . . . .68 EG56
 E14 . . . . .204 C8
 NW9 . . . . .42 CS54
 Feltham TW14 . . . . .115 BV85
 Harrow HA3 . . . . .62 CL57
 Hornchurch RM12 . . . . . . .89 FG66
 Sunbury-on-Thames
  TW16 . . . . .135 BS96
 Watford WD25 . . . . .8 BY34
FALCONWOOD, Well. 105 ER83
⇌ Falconwood 106 EQ84
Falconwood, Egh. TW20 . . . .112 AY92
 Leatherhead (E.Hors.)
  KT24 . . . . .171 CF120
Falconwood Av, Well. DA16 . .105 ER82
Falconwood Par, Well. DA16 .105 ES84
Falconwood Rd, Croy. CR0 . .161 EA108
Falcourt CI, Sutt. SM1 . . . . . .158 DB106
Falkland Av, N3 . . . . .44 DA53
 N11 . . . . .44 DG49
Falkland Ho, W9 . . . . .82 DB69
Falkirk Gdns, Wat. WD19
 off Blackford Rd 40 BX50
Falkirk Ho, W9 . . . . .82 DB69
Falkirk St, N1 . . . . .197 N1
Falkland Av, N3 . . . . .44 DA53
 N11 . . . . .44 DG49
Falkland Pk Av, SE25 . . . . . .142 DS97
Falkland PI, NW5
 off Falkland Rd 65 DJ64
Falkland Rd, N8 . . . . .65 DN56
 NW5 . . . . .65 DJ64
 Barnet EN5 . . . . .27 CY40
Fallaize Av, Ilf. IG1
 off Riverdene Rd 69 EP63
Falling La, West Dr. UB7 . . . .76 BL73
Falloden Way, NW11 . . . . . . .64 DA56
Fallow CI, Chig. IG7 . . . . .49 ET50
Fallow Ct, SE16
 off Argyle Way 102 DU78
Fallow Ct Av, N12 . . . . .44 DC52
Fallowfield, Dart. (Bean)
 DA2 . . . . .129 FV90
 Stanmore HA7 . . . . .41 CG48
Fallowfield Ct, Stan. HA7 . . . .41 CG48
Fallow Flds, Loug. IG10 . . . . .48 EJ45
Fallowfields Dr, N12 . . . . . . .44 DE51
Fallows CI, N2 . . . . .44 DC54
Fallsbrook Rd, SW16 . . . . . .121 DJ94
Falman CI, N9
 off Croyland Rd 46 DU46
Falmer Rd, E17 . . . . .67 EB55
 N15 . . . . .66 DQ57
 Enfield EN1 . . . . .30 DS42
Falmouth Av, E4 . . . . .47 ED50
Falmouth CI, N22 off Truro Rd .45 DM52
 SE12 . . . . .124 EF85
Falmouth Gdns, Ilf. IG4 . . . . .68 EL57
Falmouth Rd, SE1 . . . . .201 J6
 Walton-on-Thames KT12 . .154 BW105
Falmouth St, E15 . . . . .67 ED64
Falmouth Way, E17
 off Gosport Rd 67 DZ57
Falstaff CI, Dart. DA1
 off Lower Sta Rd 127 FE86
Falstaff Ms, Hmptn. (Hmptn.H.)
 TW12 off Hampton Rd . . .117 CD92
Falstone, Wok. GU21 . . . . . .166 AV118
Fambridge CI, SE26 . . . . . . .123 DZ91
Fambridge Rd, Dag. RM8 . . . .70 FA60
Famet Av, Pur. CR8 . . . . .160 DQ113
Famet CI, Pur. CR8 . . . . .160 DQ113
Famet Wk, Pur. CR8 . . . . . . .160 DQ113
★ Family Records Cen, Public
 Record Office, EC1 . . . . .196 E3
Fane St, W14 . . . . .99 CZ79
 off North End Rd 99 CZ79
Fangrove Pk, Cher. (Lyne)
 KT16 . . . . .133 BB102
★ Fan Mus, SE10 . . . . .103 EC80
Fanns Ri, Purf. RM19 . . . . . .108 FN77

Fann St, EC1 . . . . .197 H5
 EC2 . . . . .197 H5
Fanshawe Av, Bark. IG11 . . . .87 EQ65
Fanshawe Cres, Dag. RM9 . . .70 EY64
 Hornchurch RM11 . . . . . . .72 FK58
Fanshawe Rd, Grays RM16 . .111 GG76
 Richmond TW10 . . . . .117 CJ91
Fanshaw St, N1 . . . . .197 M2
Fanthorpe St, SW15 . . . . . . .99 CW83
Faraday Av, Sid. DA14 . . . . .126 EU89
Faraday CI, N7
 off Bride St 83 DM65
 Watford WD18 . . . . .23 BR44
★ Faraday Mus, W1
 off Albemarle St 199 K1
Faraday Rd, E15 . . . . .86 EF65
 SW19 . . . . .120 DA93
 W3 . . . . .80 CQ73
 W10 . . . . .81 CY71
 Southall UB1 . . . . .78 CB73
 Welling DA16 . . . . .106 EU83
 West Molesey KT8 . . . . . .136 CA98
Faraday Way, SE18 . . . . .104 EK76
 Croydon CR0
  off Ampere Way 141 DM102
 Orpington BR5 . . . . .146 EV98
Fareham Rd, Felt. TW14 . . . .116 BW87
Fareham St, W1 . . . . .195 M8
Farewell PI, Mitch. CR4 . . . . .140 DE95
Faringdon Av, Brom. BR2 . . .145 EP100
 Romford RM3 . . . . .52 FJ53
Faringford CI, Pot.B. EN6 . . . .12 DD31
Faringford Rd, E15 . . . . .86 EE66
Farington Acres, Wey. KT13 .135 BR104
Faris Barn Dr, Add. (Woodham)
 KT15 . . . . .151 BF112
Faris La, Add. (Woodham)
 KT15 . . . . .151 BF111
Farjeon Rd, SE3 . . . . .104 EK81
FARLEIGH, Warl. 161 DZ114
Farleigh Av, Brom. BR2 . . . . .144 EF100
Farleigh Border, Croy. CR0 . .161 DY112
Farleigh Ct Rd, Warl. CR6 . . .161 DZ114
Farleigh Dean Cres, Croy.
 CR0 . . . . .161 EB111
Farleigh PI, N16
 off Farleigh Rd 66 DT63
Farleigh Rd, N16 . . . . .66 DT63
 Addlestone (New Haw)
  KT15 . . . . .152 BG111
 Warlingham CR6 . . . . . . .177 DX118
Farleton CI, Wey. KT13 . . . . .153 BR107
Farley Common, West. TN13 .189 EQ126
Farleycroft, West. TN16 . . . .189 EQ126
Farley Dr, Ilf. IG3 . . . . .69 ES60
Farley La, West. TN16 . . . . . .189 EP127
Farley Ms, SE6 . . . . .123 EC87
Farley Nursery, West. TN16 . .189 EQ127
Farley Pk, Oxt. RH8 . . . . . . .187 ED130
Farley PI, SE25 . . . . .142 DU98
Farley Rd, SE6 . . . . .123 EB87
 Gravesend DA12 . . . . .131 GM88
 South Croydon CR2 . . . . .160 DV108
Farlington PI, SW15
 off Roehampton La 119 CV87
Farlow CI, Grav. (Nthflt.)
 DA11 . . . . .131 GF90
Farlow Rd, SW15 . . . . .99 CX83
Farlton Rd, SW18 . . . . .120 DB87
Farman Gro, Nthlt. UB5
 off Wayfarer Rd 78 BX69
Farm Av, NW2 . . . . .63 CY62
 SW16 . . . . .121 DL91
 Harrow HA2 . . . . .60 BZ59
 Swanley BR8 . . . . .147 FC97
 Wembley HA0 . . . . .79 CJ65
Farmborough CI, Har. HA1
 off Pool Rd 61 CD59
Farm CI, SW6 off Farm La . . .100 DA80
 Amersham HP6 . . . . .20 AX39
 Barnet EN5 . . . . .27 CW43
 Borehamwood WD6 . . . . . .25 CK38
 Brentwood CM13 . . . . .55 GC45
 Buckhurst Hill IG9 . . . . . . .48 EJ48
 Chertsey (Lyne) KT16 . . . .133 BA100
 Coulsdon CR5 . . . . .174 DF120
 Dagenham RM10 . . . . .89 FC66
 Leatherhead (Fetch.) KT22 .171 CD124
 Potters Bar (Cuffley) EN6 . .13 DK27
 Radlett WD7 . . . . .10 CL30
 Shepperton TW17 . . . . . .134 BN101
 Southall UB1 . . . . .78 CB73
 Staines TW18 . . . . .113 BE92
 Sutton SM2 . . . . .158 DD108
 Uxbridge UB10 . . . . .59 BP61
 Wallington SM6 . . . . .159 DJ110
 Waltham Cross (Chsht.)
  EN8 . . . . .14 DW30
 West Byfleet (Byfleet)
  KT14 . . . . .152 BM112
 West Wickham BR4 . . . . . .144 EE104
Farmcote Rd, SE12 . . . . .124 EG88
Farm Ct, NW4 . . . . .63 CU55
Farm Cres, Slou. SL2 . . . . . . .74 AV71
Farmcroft, Grav. DA11 . . . . . .131 GG89
Farmdale Rd, SE10 . . . . .205 N10
 Carshalton SM5 . . . . .158 DE108
Farm Dr, Croy. CR0 . . . . .143 DZ103
 Purley CR8 . . . . .159 DK112
Farm End, E4 . . . . .32 EE43
 Northwood HA6
  off Drakes Dr 39 BP53
Farmer Rd, E10 . . . . .67 EB60
Farmers CI, Wat. WD25 . . . . . .7 BV33
Farmers Rd, SE5 . . . . .101 DP80
 Staines TW18 . . . . .113 BE92
Farmer St, W8
 off Uxbridge St 82 DA74
Farm Fld, Wat. WD17 . . . . . . .23 BS38
Farmfield Rd, Brom. BR1 . . . .124 EE92
Farm Flds, S.Croy. CR2 . . . .160 DS111
Farm Hill Rd, Wal.Abb. EN9 . .15 EC34
Farm Ho CI, Brox. EN10 . . . . .15 DZ25
Farmhouse CI, Wok. GU22 . .167 BD115
Farmhouse Rd, SW16 . . . . . .121 DJ94

Farmilo Rd, E17 . . . . .67 DZ59
Farmington Av, Sutt. SM1 . . .140 DD104
Farmlands, Enf. EN2 . . . . .29 DN39
 Pinner HA5 . . . . .59 BU56
Farmlands, The, Nthlt. UB5 . .78 BZ65
Farmland Wk, Chis. BR7 . . . .125 EP92
Farm La, N14 . . . . .28 DG44
 SW6 . . . . .100 DA79
 Addlestone KT15 . . . . . . .152 BG107
 Ashtead KT21 . . . . .172 CN116
 Carshalton SM5 . . . . .158 DF110
 Croydon CR0 . . . . .143 DZ103
 Epsom KT18 . . . . .172 CP119
 Purley CR8 . . . . .159 DJ110
 Rickmansworth (Loud.)
  WD3 . . . . .22 BH41
 Woking (Send) GU23 . . . .167 BC124
Farmleigh, N14 . . . . .45 DJ45
Farmleigh Gro, Walt. KT12 . .153 BT106
Farm PI, W8 off Uxbridge St . .82 DA74
 Dartford DA1 . . . . .107 FG84
Farm Rd, N21 . . . . .45 DP46
 NW10 off Mordaunt Rd 80 CR67
 Edgware HA8 . . . . .42 CP51
 Esher KT10 . . . . .136 CB102
 Grays (Orsett) RM16 . . . .111 GF75
 Hounslow TW5 . . . . .116 BY88
 Morden SM4 . . . . .140 DB99
 Northwood HA6 . . . . .39 BQ50
 Rainham RM13 . . . . .90 FJ69
 Rickmansworth (Chorl.)
  WD3 . . . . .21 BA42
 Sevenoaks TN14 . . . . . . .191 FJ121
 Staines TW18 . . . . .114 BH93
 Sutton SM2 . . . . .158 DD108
 Warlingham CR6 . . . . . . .177 DY119
 Woking GU22 . . . . .167 BB120
Farmstead Rd, SE6 . . . . .123 EB91
 Harrow HA3 . . . . .41 CD53
Farm St, W1 . . . . .199 H1
Farm Vale, Bex. DA5 . . . . . . .127 FB86
Farmview, Cob. KT11 . . . . . .170 BX116
Farm Vw, Tad. (Lwr.Kgswd.)
 KT20 . . . . .183 CZ127
Farm Wk, NW11 . . . . .63 CZ57
Farm Way, Buck.H. IG9 . . . . .48 EJ49
 Bushey WD23 . . . . .24 CB42
Farmway, Dag. RM8 . . . . .70 EW63
Farm Way, Horn. RM12 . . . . .71 FH63
 Northwood HA6 . . . . .39 BS49
 Staines TW19 . . . . .113 BF86
 Worcester Park KT4 . . . . .139 CW104
Farnaby Dr, Sev. TN13 . . . . .190 FF126
Farnaby Rd, SE9 . . . . .104 EJ84
 Bromley BR1, BR2 . . . . . .123 ED94
Farnan Av, E17 . . . . .47 EA54
Farnan Rd, SW16 . . . . .121 DL92
FARNBOROUGH, Orp. 163 EQ106
Farnborough Av, E17 . . . . . . .67 DY55
 South Croydon CR2 . . . . .161 DX108
Farnborough CI, Wem. HA9
 off Chalkhill Rd 62 CP61
Farnborough Common, Orp.
 BR6 . . . . .145 EM104
Farnborough Cres, Brom. BR2
 off Saville Row 144 EF102
 South Croydon CR2 . . . . .161 DY109
Farnborough Hill, Orp. BR6 . .163 ER106
Ⓗ Farnborough Hosp, Orp.
 BR6 . . . . .145 EN104
Farnborough Ho, SW15
 off Fontley Way 119 CU88
Farnborough Way, SE15
 off Chandler Way 102 DT80
 Orpington BR6 . . . . .163 EQ105
Farncombe St, SE16 . . . . . . .202 C5
Farndale Av, N13 . . . . .45 DP48
Farndale Cres, Grnf. UB6 . . . .78 CC69
Farnell Ms, SW5
 off Earls Ct Sq 100 DB78
Farnell Rd, Islw. TW7 . . . . . . .97 CD83
 Staines TW18 . . . . .114 BG90
Farnes Dr, Rom. RM2 . . . . . . .52 FJ54
Farnham CI, N20 . . . . .44 DC45
 Hemel Hempstead (Bov.)
  HP3 . . . . .5 BA28
Farnham Gdns, SW20 . . . . . .139 CV96
Farnham PI, SE1 . . . . .200 G3
Farnham Rd, Ilf. IG3 . . . . .69 ET59
 Romford RM3 . . . . .52 FK50
 Welling DA16 . . . . .106 EW82
Farnham Royal, SE11 . . . . . .101 DM78
FARNINGHAM, Dart. 148 FN100
Farningham Cres, Cat. CR3
 off Commonwealth Rd . . .176 DU123
Farningham Hill Rd, Dart. (Fnghm.)
 DA4 . . . . .148 FJ99
⇌ Farningham Road 148 FP96
Farningham Rd, N17 . . . . .46 DU52
 Caterham CR3 . . . . .176 DU123
Farnley, Wok. GU21 . . . . . . .166 AT117
Farnley Rd, E4 . . . . .48 EE45
 SE25 . . . . .142 DR98
Farnol Rd, Dart. DA1 . . . . . . .108 FN84
Faro CI, Brom. BR1 . . . . .145 EN96
Faroe Rd, W14 . . . . .99 CX76
Faroma Wk, Enf. EN2 . . . . . . .29 DN39
Farquhar Rd, SE19 . . . . .122 DT92
 SW19 . . . . .120 DA90
Farquharson Rd, Croy. CR0 . .142 DQ102
Farraline Rd, Wat. WD18 . . . .23 BV42
Farrance Rd, Rom. RM6 . . . . .70 EY58
Farrance St, E14 . . . . .85 DZ72
Farrans Ct, Har. HA3 . . . . . . .61 CH59
Farrant Av, N22 . . . . .45 DN54
Farrant CI, Orp. BR6 . . . . . . .164 EU108
Farrant Way, Borwd. WD6 . . .26 CL39
Farrell Ho, E1 . . . . .84 DW72
Farren Rd, SE23 . . . . .123 DY89
Farrer Ms, N8 off Farrer Rd . .65 DJ56
Farrer Rd, N8 . . . . .65 DJ56
 Harrow HA3 . . . . .62 CL57
Farrer's PI, Croy. CR0 . . . . . .161 DX105
Farrier CI, Sun. TW16 . . . . . .135 BU98
 Uxbridge UB8
  off Horseshoe Dr 76 BN72

Farrier Rd, Nthlt. UB5 . . . .78 CA68
Farriers Cl, Epsom KT17 . . .156 CS111
Gravesend DA12 . . . . . . .131 GM88
Hemel Hempstead (Bov.) HP3
off Chipperfield Rd 5 BB28
Farriers Ct, Sutt. SM3
off Forge La 157 CY108
Watford WD25 . . . . .7 BV32
Farriers End, Brox. EN10 . . .15 DZ26
Farriers Rd, Epsom KT17 . . .156 CS112
Farrier St, NW1 . . . . .83 DH66
Farriers Way, Borwd. WD6 . .26 CQ44
Farrier Wk, SW10 . . . . . . .100 DC79
⇌ Farringdon 196 E6
⊖ Farringdon 196 E6
Farringdon La, EC1 . . . . . .196 E5
Farringdon Rd, EC1 . . . . . .196 D4
Farringdon St, EC4 . . . . . .196 F8
Farringford Cl, St.Alb. AL2 . . .8 CA26
Farrington Av, Orp. BR5 . . .146 EV97
Farrington Pl, Chis. BR7 . . .125 ER94
Northwood HA6 . . . . .39 BT49
Farrins Rents, SE16 . . . . . .203 K3
Farrow La, SE14 . . . . .102 DW80
Farrow Pl, SE16 . . . . .203 K6
Farr Rd, Enf. EN2 . . . . .30 DR39
Farthingale Ct, Wal.Abb. EN9 .16 EG34
Farthingale La, Wal.Abb. EN9 .16 EG34
Farthingale Wk, E15 . . . . . .85 ED66
Farthing All, SE1 . . . . .202 B5
Farthing Cl, Dart. DA1 . . . .108 FM84
Farthing Flds, E1 . . . . .202 E2
Farthing Grn La, Slou. (Stoke P.)
SL2 . . . . .74 AU68
Farthings, Wok. (Knap.)
GU21 . . . . .166 AS116
Farthings, The, Kings.T. KT2
off Brunswick Rd 138 CN95
Farthings Cl, E4 . . . . .48 EE48
Pinner HA5 . . . . .59 BV55
Farthing St, Orp. BR6 . . . . .163 EM108
Farwell Rd, Sid. DA14 . . . . .126 EV90
Farwig La, Brom. BR1 . . . . .144 EF95
Fashion St, E1 . . . . .197 P7
Fashoda Rd, Brom. BR2 . . .144 EK98
Fassett Rd, E8 . . . . .84 DU65
Kingston upon Thames
KT1 . . . . .138 CL98
Fassett Sq, E8 . . . . .84 DU65
Fassnidge Way, Uxb. UB8
off Oxford Rd 76 BJ66
Fauconberg Rd, W4 . . . . . . .98 CQ79
Faulkner Cl, Dag. RM8 . . . . .70 EX59
Faulkner's All, EC1 . . . . . . .196 F6
Faulkners Rd, Walt. KT12 . . .154 BW100
Faulkner St, SE14 . . . . . . .102 DW81
Fauna Cl, Rom. RM6 . . . . . .70 EW59
Faunce St, SE17
off Harmsworth St 101 DP78
Favart Rd, SW6 . . . . .100 DA81
Faverolle Grn, Wal.Cr. EN8 . .15 DX28
Faversham Av, E4 . . . . .48 EE46
Enfield EN1 . . . . .30 DR44
Faversham Cl, Chig. IG7 . . . .50 EV47
Faversham Rd, SE6 . . . . . .123 DZ87
Beckenham BR3 . . . . .143 DZ96
Morden SM4 . . . . .140 DB100
Fawcett Cl, SW11 . . . . . . .100 DD82
SW16 . . . . .121 DN91
Fawcett Est, E5 . . . . .66 DU60
Fawcett Rd, NW10 . . . . . . .81 CT67
Croydon CR0 . . . . .142 DQ104
Fawcett St, SW10 . . . . . . .100 DC79
Fawcus Cl, Esher (Clay.) KT10
off Dalmore Av 155 CF107
Fawe Pk Rd, SW15 . . . . . . .99 CZ84
Fawe St, E14 . . . . .85 EB71
Fawke Common, Sev. (Undrvr.)
TN15 . . . . .191 FP127
Fawke Common Rd, Sev.
TN15 . . . . .191 FP126
Fawkes Av, Dart. DA1 . . . . .128 FM89
FAWKHAM GREEN, Long. . . .149 FV104
Fawkham Grn Rd, Long.
(Fawk.Grn.) DA3 . . . . . . .149 FV104
Ⓗ Fawkham Manor Hosp,
Long. DA3 . . . . .149 FW102
Fawkham Rd, Long. DA3 . . .149 FX97
Fawley Rd, NW6 . . . . .64 DB64
Fawnbrake Av, SE24 . . . . . .121 DP85
Fawn Rd, E13 . . . . .86 EJ68
Chigwell IG7 . . . . .50 ET50
Fawns Manor Cl, Felt. TW14 .115 BQ88
Fawns Manor Rd, Felt. TW14 .115 BR88
Fawood Av, NW10 . . . . .80 CR66
Fawsley Cl, Slou. (Colnbr.)
SL3 . . . . .93 BE80
Fawters Cl, Brwd. CM13 . . . .55 GD44
Fayerfield, Pot.B. EN6 . . . . .12 DD31
Faygate Cres, Bexh. DA6 . . .126 FA85
Faygate Rd, SW2 . . . . .121 DM89
Fay Grn, Abb.L. WD5 . . . . . . .7 BR33
Fayland Av, SW16 . . . . . . .121 DJ92
Faymore Gdns, S.Ock. RM15 . .91 FU72
Fearney Mead, Rick. (Mill End)
WD3 . . . . .38 BG46
Fearnley Cres, Hmptn. TW12 .116 BY92
Fearnley St, Wat. WD18 . . . .23 BV42
Fearns Mead, Brwd. CM14
off Bucklers Ct 54 FW50
Fearon St, SE10 . . . . .205 N10
Featherbed La, Abb.L. (Bedmond)
WD5 off Sergehill La 7 BV26
Croydon CR0 . . . . .161 DZ108
Romford RM4 . . . . .50 EY45
Warlingham CR6 . . . . .161 ED113
Feathers, Stai. (Wrays.)
TW19 . . . . .113 BA89
Feathers Pl, SE10 . . . . . . .103 ED79
Featherstone Av, SE23 . . . .122 DV89
Featherstone Gdns, Borwd.
WD6 . . . . .26 CQ42
Featherstone Ind Est, Sthl.
UB2 . . . . .96 BY75
Featherstone Rd, NW7 . . . . .43 CV51
Southall UB2 . . . . .96 BY76
Featherstone St, EC1 . . . . .197 K4

Featherstone Ter, Sthl. UB2 . .96 BY76
Federal Rd, Grnf. UB6 . . . . .79 CJ68
Federal Way, Wat. WD24 . . .24 BW38
Federation Rd, SE2 . . . . . .106 EV77
Fee Fm Rd, Esher (Clay.)
KT10 . . . . .155 CF108
Feenan Highway, Til. RM18 .111 GH80
Felbridge Av, Stan. HA7 . . . .41 CG53
Felbridge Cl, SW16 . . . . . .121 DN91
Sutton SM2 . . . . .158 DC109
Felbrigge Rd, Ilf. IG3 . . . . . .69 ET61
Felday Rd, SE13 . . . . .123 EB86
Felden Cl, Pnr. HA5 . . . . . . .40 BY52
Watford WD25 . . . . .8 BX34
Felden St, SW6 . . . . .99 CZ81
Feldman Cl, N16 . . . . .66 DU60
Felgate Ms, W6 . . . . .99 CV77
Felhampton Rd, SE9 . . . . . .125 EP89
Felhurst Cres, Dag. RM10 . . .71 FB65
Felipe Rd, Grays (Chaff.Hun.)
RM16 . . . . .109 FW76
Felix Av, N8 . . . . .65 DL58
Felix La, Shep. TW17 . . . . .135 BS100
Felix Rd, W13 . . . . .79 CG73
Walton-on-Thames KT12 . . .135 BU100
Felixstowe Ct, E16
off Fishguard Way 105 EP75
Felixstowe Rd, N9 . . . . .46 DU49
N17 . . . . .66 DT55
NW10 . . . . .81 CV69
SE2 . . . . .106 EV76
Fellbrigg Rd, SE22 . . . . . . .122 DT85
Fellbrigg St, E1
off Headlam St 84 DV70
Fellbrook, Rich. TW10 . . . . .117 CH90
Fellmongers Path, SE1 . . . .201 N5
Fellmongers Yd, Croy. CR0
off Surrey St 142 DQ103
Fellowes Cl, Hayes UB4
off Paddington Cl 78 BX70
Fellowes Rd, Cars. SM5 . . . .140 DE104
Fellows Ct, E2 . . . . .197 P1
Fellows Rd, NW3 . . . . .82 DD66
Fell Rd, Croy. CR0 . . . . . . .142 DQ104
Felltram Way, SE7 . . . . . . .205 N10
Fell Wk, Edg. HA8
off East Rd 42 CP53
Felmersham Cl, SW4
off Haselrigge Rd 101 DK84
Felmingham Rd, SE20 . . . . .142 DW96
Felnex Trd Est, Wall. SM6 . . .140 DG103
Felsberg Rd, SW2 . . . . . . .121 DL86
Fels Cl, Dag. RM10 . . . . . . .71 FB62
Fels Fm Av, Dag. RM10 . . . .71 FC62
Felsham Rd, SW15 . . . . . . .99 CX83
Felspar Cl, SE18 . . . . .105 ER78
Felstead Av, Ilf. IG5 . . . . . . .49 EN53
Felstead Cl, Brwd. CM13 . . . .55 GC44
Felstead Gdns, E14
off Ferry St 103 EC78
Felstead Rd, E11 . . . . .68 EG59
Epsom KT19 . . . . .156 CR111
Loughton IG10 . . . . .48 EL45
Orpington BR6 . . . . .146 EU103
Romford RM5 . . . . .51 FC51
Waltham Cross EN8 . . . . . .15 DY32
Felsted Rd, E16 . . . . .86 EK72
FELTHAM 115 BU89
⇌ Feltham 115 BV88
Felthambrook Way, Felt.
TW13 . . . . .115 BV90
Feltham Business Complex, Felt.
TW13 . . . . .115 BV89
FELTHAMHILL, Felt. 115 BT92
Feltham Hill Rd, Ashf. TW15 .115 BP92
Feltham TW13 . . . . .115 BP91
Feltham Rd, Ashf. TW15 . . .115 BP91
Mitcham CR4 . . . . .140 DF96
Felton Cl, Borwd. WD6 . . . . .26 CL38
Broxbourne EN10 . . . . .15 DZ25
Orpington BR5 . . . . .145 EP100
Felton Gdns, Bark. IG11
off Sutton Rd 87 ES67
Felton Ho, SE3
off Ryan Cl 104 EH84
Felton Lea, Sid. DA14 . . . . .125 ET92
Felton Rd, W13
off Camborne Av 97 CJ75
Barking IG11
off Sutton Rd 87 ES68
Felton St, N1 . . . . .84 DR67
Fencepiece Rd, Chig. IG7 . . .49 EQ50
Ilford IG6 . . . . .49 EQ50
Fenchurch Av, EC3 . . . . . . .197 M9
Fenchurch Bldgs, EC3 . . . . .197 N9
Fenchurch Pl, EC3 . . . . . . .197 N10
⇌ Fenchurch Street 197 N10
Fenchurch St, EC3 . . . . . . .197 N10
Fen Cl, Brwd. CM15 . . . . . . .55 GC42
Fen Ct, EC3 . . . . .197 M10
Fendall Rd, Epsom KT19 . . .156 CQ106
Fendall St, SE1 . . . . .201 N7
Fendt Cl, E16
off Bowman Av 86 EF73
Fendyke Rd, Belv. DA17 . . .106 EX76
Fenelon Pl, W14 . . . . .99 CZ77
Fengates Rd, Red. RH1 . . . .184 DE134
Fen Gro, Sid. DA15 . . . . . .125 ET86
Fen La, Upmin. (N.Ock.)
RM14 . . . . .73 FW64
Fenman Ct, N17
off Shelbourne Rd 46 DV53
Fenman Gdns, Ilf. IG3 . . . . . .70 EV60
Fenn Cl, Brom. BR1 . . . . . .124 EG93
Fennel Cl, E16
off Cranberry La 86 EE70
Croydon CR0
off Primrose La 143 DX102
Fennells Mead, Epsom KT17 .157 CT109
Fennel St, SE18 . . . . .105 EN79

Fenner Cl, SE16 . . . . .202 E8
Fenner Ho, Walt. KT12 . . . .153 BU105
Fenner Sq, SW11
off Thomas Baines Rd 100 DD83
Fenning St, SE1 . . . . .201 M4
Fenn St, E9 . . . . .66 DW64
Fenns Way, Wok. GU21 . . . .166 AY115
Fen St, E16
off Victoria Dock Rd 86 EF73
Fens Way, Swan. BR8 . . . . .127 FG93
Fenswood Cl, Bex. DA5 . . . .126 FA85
Fentiman Rd, SW8 . . . . . . .101 DL79
Fentiman Way, Horn. RM11 . .72 FL60
Fenton Cl, E8 off Laurel St . . .84 DT65
SW9 . . . . .101 DM82
Chislehurst BR7 . . . . .125 EM92
Redhill RH1 . . . . .184 DG134
Fentons Av, E13 . . . . .86 EH68
Fenwick Cl, SE18 off Ritter St .105 EN79
Woking GU21 . . . . .166 AV118
Fenwick Gro, SE15 . . . . . . .102 DU82
Fenwick Path, Borwd. WD6 . .26 CM38
Fenwick Pl, SW9 . . . . .101 DL83
South Croydon CR2
off Columbine Av 159 DP108
Fenwick Rd, SE15 . . . . . . .102 DU83
Ferdinand Pl, NW1
off Ferdinand St 82 DG66
Ferdinand St, NW1 . . . . . . .82 DG65
Ferguson Av, Grav. DA12 . . .131 GJ91
Romford RM2 . . . . .52 FJ54
Surbiton KT5 . . . . .138 CM99
Ferguson Cl, E14 . . . . .203 P9
Bromley BR2 . . . . .143 EC97
Ferguson Ct, Rom. RM2 . . . .52 FK54
Ferguson Dr, W3 . . . . .80 CR72
Fergus Rd, N5
off Calabria Rd 65 DP64
Ferme Pk Rd, N4 . . . . .65 DL57
N8 . . . . .65 DL57
Fermor Rd, SE23 . . . . .123 DY88
Fermoy Rd, W9 . . . . .81 CZ70
Greenford UB6 . . . . .78 CB70
Fern Av, Mitch. CR4 . . . . . .141 DK98
Fernbank, Buck.H. IG9 . . . . .48 EH46
Fernbank Av, Horn. RM12 . . .72 FJ63
Walton-on-Thames KT12 . . .136 BY101
Wembley HA0 . . . . .61 CF63
Fernbank Ms, SW12 . . . . . .121 DJ86
Fernbank Rd, Add. KT15 . . .152 BG106
off Blackfen Rd 125 ES85
Fernbrook Av, Sid. DA15
Fernbrook Cres, SE13 . . . . .124 EE86
Fernbrook Dr, Har. HA2 . . . .60 CB59
Fernbrook Rd, SE13 . . . . . .124 EE86
Ferncliff Rd, E8 . . . . .66 DU64
Fern Cl, Erith DA8
off Hollywood Way 107 FH81
Warlingham CR6 . . . . .177 DY118
Ferncroft Av, N12 . . . . .44 DE51
NW3 . . . . .64 DA62
Ruislip HA4 . . . . .60 BW61
Ferndale, Brom. BR1 . . . . . .144 EJ96
Ferndale Av, E17 . . . . .67 ED57
Chertsey KT16 . . . . .133 BE104
Hounslow TW4 . . . . .96 BY83
Ferndale Cl, Bexh. DA7 . . . .106 EY81
Ferndale Ct, SE3 . . . . .104 EF80
Ferndale Cres, Uxb. UB8 . . . .76 BJ69
Ferndale Rd, E7 . . . . .86 EH66
E11 . . . . .68 EE61
N15 . . . . .66 DT58
SE25 . . . . .142 DV99
SW4 . . . . .101 DL84
SW9 . . . . .101 DM83
Ashford TW15 . . . . .114 BK92
Banstead SM7 . . . . .173 CZ116
Enfield EN3 . . . . .31 DY37
Gravesend DA12 . . . . .131 GH89
Romford RM5 . . . . .51 FC54
Woking GU21 . . . . .167 AZ116
Ferndale St, E6 . . . . .87 EP73
Ferndale Ter, Har. HA1 . . . . .61 CF56
Ferndale Way, Orp. BR6 . . .163 ER106
Ferndell Av, Bex. DA5 . . . . .127 FD90
Fern Dene, W13
off Templewood 79 CH71
Ferndene, St.Alb. (Brick.Wd.)
AL2 . . . . .8 BZ31
Ferndene Rd, SE24 . . . . . .122 DQ84
Ferndown, Horn. RM11 . . . . .72 FN58
Northwood HA6 . . . . .39 BU54
Ferndown Av, Orp. BR6 . . . .145 ER102
Ferndown Cl, Pnr. HA5 . . . . .40 BY52
Sutton SM2 . . . . .158 DD107
Ferndown Gdns, Cob. KT11 .154 BW113
Ferndown Rd, SE9 . . . . . . .124 EK87
Watford WD19 . . . . .40 BW48
Fernery, The, Stai. TW18 . . .113 BE92
Ferney Ct, W.Byf. (Byfleet) KT14
off Ferney Rd 152 BK112
Ferney Meade Way, Islw. TW7 .97 CG82
Ferney Rd, Barn. EN4 . . . . . .44 DG45
Waltham Cross (Chsht.)
EN7 . . . . .14 DR26
West Byfleet (Byfleet)
KT14 . . . . .152 BK112
Fern Gro, Felt. TW14 . . . . . .115 BV87
Ferngrove Cl, Lthd. (Fetch.)
KT22 . . . . .171 CE122
Fernhall Dr, Ilf. IG4 . . . . .68 EK57
Fernhall La, Wal.Abb. EN9 . . .16 EK31
Fernham Rd, Th.Hth. CR7 . . .142 DQ97
Fernhead Rd, W9 . . . . .81 CZ70
Fernheath Way, Dart. DA2 . .127 FD92
Fernhill, Lthd. (Oxshott)
KT22 . . . . .155 CD114

Fernhill Cl, Wok. GU22 . . . .166 AW120
Fernhill Ct, E17 . . . . .47 ED54
Fernhill Gdns, Kings.T. KT2 .117 CK92
Fernhill Pk, Wok. GU22 . . . .166 AW120
Fernhills, Kings L. WD4 . . . . .7 BR33
Fernhill St, E16 . . . . .87 EM74
Fernholme Rd, SE15 . . . . . .123 DX85
Fernhurst Gdns, Edg. HA8 . . .42 CN51
Fernhurst Rd, SW6 . . . . . . .99 CY81
Ashford TW15 . . . . .115 BQ91
Croydon CR0 . . . . .142 DU101
Fernie Cl, Chig. IG7 . . . . . . .50 EU50
Fernihough Cl, Wey. KT13 . .152 BN111
Fernlands Cl, Cher. KT16 . . .133 BE104
Fern La, Houns. TW5 . . . . . .96 BZ78
Fernlea, Lthd. (Bkhm.) KT23 .170 CB123
Fernlea Rd, SW12 . . . . . . .121 DH88
Mitcham CR4 . . . . .140 DG96
Fernleigh Cl, W9 . . . . .81 CZ69
Croydon CR0
off Stafford Rd 159 DN105
Walton-on-Thames KT12 . . .135 BV100
Fernleigh Ct, Har. HA2 . . . . .40 CB54
Wembley HA9 . . . . .62 CL61
Fernleigh Rd, N21 . . . . .45 DN47
Fernsbury St, WC1 . . . . . . .196 D3
Ferns Cl, Enf. EN3 . . . . .31 DY36
South Croydon CR2 . . . . . .160 DV110
Fernshaw Rd, SW10 . . . . . .100 DC79
Fernside, NW11
off Finchley Rd 64 DA61
Buckhurst Hill IG9 . . . . . . .48 EH46
Fernside Av, NW7 . . . . .42 CR48
Feltham TW13 . . . . .115 BV91
Fernside La, Sev. TN13 . . . .191 FJ129
Fernside Rd, SW12 . . . . . . .120 DF88
Fernsleigh Cl, Ger.Cr. (Chal.St.P.)
SL9 . . . . .36 AY51
Ferns Rd, E15 . . . . .86 EF65
Fern St, E3 . . . . .85 EA70
Fernthorpe Rd, SW16 . . . . .121 DJ93
Ferntower Rd, N5 . . . . .66 DR64
Fern Twrs, Cat. CR3 . . . . . .186 DU125
Fern Wk, SE16
off Argyle Way 102 DU78
Ashford TW15
off Ferndale Rd 114 BK92
Fern Way, Wat. WD25 . . . . . .23 BU35
Fernways, Ilf. IG1
off Cecil Rd 69 EP63
Fernwood, SW19 . . . . .119 CZ88
Fernwood Av, SW16 . . . . . .121 DK91
Wembley HA0
off Bridgewater Rd 61 CJ64
Fernwood Cl, Brom. BR1 . . .144 EJ96
Fernwood Cres, N20 . . . . . . .44 DF48
Ferny Hill, Barn. EN4 . . . . . .28 DF38
Ferranti Cl, SE18 . . . . .104 EK76
Ferraro Cl, Houns. TW5 . . . . .96 CA79
Ferrers Av, Wall. SM6 . . . . .159 DK105
West Drayton UB7 . . . . . . .94 BK75
Ferrers Rd, SW16 . . . . .121 DK92
Ferrestone Rd, N8 . . . . .65 DM56
Ferriby Cl, N1
off Bewdley St 83 DN66
Ferrier Pt, E16
off Forty Acre La 86 EH71
Ferrier St, SW18 . . . . .100 DB84
Ferriers Way, Epsom KT18 . .173 CW119
Ferring Cl, Har. HA2 . . . . . . .60 CC60
Ferrings, SE21 . . . . .122 DS89
Ferris Av, Croy. CR0 . . . . . .143 DZ104
Ferris Rd, SE22 . . . . .102 DU84
Ferron Rd, E5 . . . . .66 DV62
Ferro Rd, Rain. RM13 . . . . . .89 FG70
Ferrour Ct, N2 . . . . .64 DD55
Ferry Av, Stai. TW18 . . . . . .113 BE94
Ferryhills Cl, Wat. WD19 . . . .40 BW48
Ferry La, N17 . . . . .66 DU56
SW13 . . . . .99 CT79
Brentford TW8 . . . . .98 CL79
Chertsey KT16 . . . . .134 BH98
Rainham RM13 . . . . .89 FE72
Richmond TW9 . . . . .98 CM79
Shepperton TW17 . . . . . . .134 BN102
Staines (Laleham) TW18 . . .134 BJ97
Staines (Wrays.) TW19 . . . .113 BB89
Ferryman's Quay, SW6 . . . .100 DC82
Ferrymead Av, Grnf. UB6 . . . .78 CA69
Ferrymead Dr, Grnf. UB6 . . . .78 CA69
Ferrymead Gdns, Grnf. UB6 . .78 CC68
Ferrymoor, Rich. TW10 . . . .117 CH90
Ferry Pl, SE18
off Woolwich High St 105 EN76
Ferry Rd, SW13 . . . . .99 CU80
Teddington TW11 . . . . . . .117 CH92
Thames Ditton KT7 . . . . . .137 CH100
Tilbury RM18 . . . . .111 GG83
Twickenham TW1 . . . . . . .117 CH88
West Molesey KT8 . . . . . . .136 CA97
Ferry Sq, Brent. TW8 . . . . . .98 CL79
Shepperton TW17 . . . . . . .135 BP101
Ferry St, E14 . . . . .204 D10
Feryby Rd, Grays RM16 . . . .111 GH76
Festing Rd, SW15 . . . . .99 CX83
Festival Cl, Bex. DA5 . . . . . .126 EX88
Erith DA8 off Betsham Rd . .107 FF80
Uxbridge UB10 . . . . .77 BP67
Festival Path, Wok. GU21 . . .166 AT119
Festival Wk, Cars. SM5 . . . .158 DF106
FETCHAM, Lthd. 171 CD123
Fetcham Common La, Lthd.
(Fetch.) KT22 . . . . .170 CB121
Fetcham Pk Dr, Lthd. (Fetch.)
KT22 . . . . .171 CE123
Fetherstone Cl, Pot.B. EN6 . .12 DD32
Fetter La, EC4 . . . . .196 E9
Ffinch St, SE8 . . . . .103 EA80
Fiddicroft Av, Bans. SM7 . . .158 DB114
Fiddlers Cl, Green. DA9 . . . .109 FV84
FIDDLERS HAMLET, Epp. . . .18 EW32
Fidler Pl, Bushey WD23
off Ashfield Av 24 CB44
Field Cl, E4 . . . . .47 EB51
NW2 . . . . .63 CU61
Bromley BR1 . . . . .144 EJ96

Field Cl, Buck.H. IG9 . . . . . .48 EJ48
Chesham HP5 . . . . .4 AS28
Chessington KT9 . . . . .155 CJ106
Hayes UB3 . . . . .95 BQ80
Hounslow TW4 . . . . .95 BV81
Romford (Abridge) RM4 . . . .34 EV41
Ruislip HA4 off Field Way . . .59 BQ60
South Croydon CR2 . . . . . .160 DV114
West Molesey KT8 . . . . . . .136 CB99
Fieldcommon La, Walt. KT12 .136 BZ101
Field Ct, WC1 . . . . .196 C7
Oxted RH8
off Silkham Rd 188 EE127
Field End, Barn. EN5 . . . . . .27 CV42
Coulsdon CR5 . . . . .159 DK114
Northolt UB5 . . . . .78 BX65
Ruislip HA4 . . . . .78 BW65
Twickenham TW1 . . . . . . .117 CF91
Field End Cl, Wat. WD19 . . . .40 BY45
Fieldend Rd, SW16 . . . . . . .141 DJ95
Field End Rd, Pnr. HA5 . . . . .59 BV58
Ruislip HA4 . . . . .60 BY63
Fielders Cl, Enf. EN1
off Woodfield Cl 30 DS42
Harrow HA2 . . . . .60 CC60
Fielders Way, Rad. (Shenley)
WD7 . . . . .10 CL33
Fieldfare Rd, SE28 . . . . .88 EW73
Fieldgate La, Mitch. CR4 . . .140 DE97
Fieldgate St, E1 . . . . .84 DU71
Fieldhouse Cl, E18 . . . . .48 EG53
Fieldhouse Rd, SW12 . . . . .121 DJ88
Fieldhurst, Slou. SL3 . . . . . .93 AZ78
Fieldhurst Cl, Add. KT15 . . .152 BH106
Fielding Av, Til. RM18 . . . . .111 GH81
Twickenham TW2 . . . . . . .116 CC90
Fielding Gdns, Slou. SL3 . . . .92 AW75
Fielding Ho, NW6 . . . . .82 DA69
Fielding Ms, SW13
off Castelnau 99 CV79
Fielding Rd, W4 . . . . .98 CR76
W14 . . . . .99 CX76
Fieldings, The, SE23 . . . . . .122 DW88
Banstead SM7 . . . . .173 CZ117
Woking GU21 . . . . .166 AT116
Fieldings Rd, Wal.Cr. (Chsht.)
EN8 . . . . .15 DZ29
Fielding St, SE17 . . . . .102 DQ79
Fielding Wk, W13 . . . . .97 CH76
Fielding Way, Brwd. CM13 . . .55 GC44
Field La, Brent. TW8 . . . . . . .97 CJ80
Teddington TW11 . . . . . . .117 CG92
Field Mead, NW7 . . . . .42 CS52
NW9 . . . . .42 CS52
Field Rd, E7 . . . . .68 EF63
N17 . . . . .66 DR55
W6 . . . . .99 CY78
Feltham TW14 . . . . .115 BV86
South Ockendon (Aveley)
RM15 . . . . .90 FQ74
Uxbridge (Denh.) UB9 . . . . .57 BE63
Watford WD19 . . . . .24 BY44
Fields Ct, Pot.B. EN6 . . . . . .12 DD33
Fieldsend Rd, Sutt. SM3 . . .157 CY106
Fields Est, E8 . . . . .84 DU66
Fieldside Cl, Orp. BR6
off State Fm Av 163 EQ105
Fieldside Rd, Brom. BR1 . . .123 ED92
Fields Pk Cres, Rom. RM6 . . .70 EX57
Field St, WC1 . . . . .196 B2
Fieldview, SW18 . . . . .120 DD88
Field Vw, Egh. TW20 . . . . . .113 BC92
Feltham TW13 . . . . .115 BR91
Fieldview Ct, Stai. TW18
off Burges Way 114 BG93
Field Vw Ri, St.Alb. (Brick.Wd.)
AL2 . . . . .8 BY29
Field Vw Rd, Pot.B. EN6 . . . .12 DA33
⊖ Fieldway 161 EB108
Field Way, NW10
off Twybridge Way 80 CQ66
Croydon CR0 . . . . .161 EB107
Fieldway, Dag. RM8 . . . . . . .70 EV63
Field Way, Ger.Cr. (Chal.St.P.)
SL9 . . . . .36 AX52
Greenford UB6 . . . . .78 CB67
Hemel Hempstead (Bov.)
HP3 . . . . .5 BA27
Fieldway, Orp. BR5 . . . . . . .145 ER100
Field Way, Rick. WD3 . . . . . .38 BH46
Ruislip HA4 . . . . .59 BQ60
Uxbridge UB8 . . . . .76 BK70
Fieldway Cres, N5 . . . . .65 DN64
Fiennes Cl, Dag. RM8 . . . . . .70 EW60
Fiennes Way, Sev. TN13 . . .191 FJ127
Fiesta Dr, Dag. RM9 . . . . . . .89 FC70
Fifehead Cl, Ashf. TW15 . . .114 BL93
Fife Rd, E16 . . . . .86 EG71
N22 . . . . .45 DP52
SW14 . . . . .118 CQ85
Kingston upon Thames
KT1 . . . . .138 CL96
Fife Ter, N1 . . . . .83 DM68
Fifield Path, SE23
off Bampton Rd 123 DX90
Fifth Av, E12 . . . . .69 EM63
W10 . . . . .81 CY69
Grays RM20 . . . . .109 FU79
Hayes UB3 . . . . .77 BT74
Watford WD25 . . . . .24 BX35
Fifth Cross Rd, Twick. TW2 . .117 CD89
Fifth Way, Wem. HA9 . . . . . .62 CP63
Figges Rd, Mitch. CR4 . . . . .120 DG94
Fig St, Sev. TN14 . . . . .190 FF129
Fig Tree Cl, NW10
off Craven Pk 80 CS67
Filby Rd, Chess. KT9 . . . . . .156 CM107
Filey Av, N16 . . . . .66 DU60
Filey Cl, Sutt. SM2 . . . . . . .158 DC108
Westerham (Bigg.H.) TN16 .178 EH119
Filey Waye, Ruis. HA4 . . . . . .59 BU61
Filigree Ct, SE16 . . . . .203 L3
Fillebrook Av, Enf. EN1 . . . . .30 DS40

Fil - Fol

Fillebrook Rd, E11 . . . . .67 ED60
Filmer La, Sev. TN14 . . . . . . .191 FL121
Filmer Rd, SW6 . . . . .99 CY81
Filston La, Sev. TN14 . . . . . .165 FE113
Filston Rd, Erith DA8
  off Riverdale Av 107 FB78
Finborough Rd, SW10 . . . . . . .100 DB78
  SW17 . . . . .120 DF93
Finchale Rd, SE2 . . . . .106 EU76
Fincham Cl, Uxb. UB10
  off Aylsham Dr 59 BQ61
Finch Av, SE27 . . . . .122 DR91
Finch Cl, NW10 . . . . .62 CR64
  Barnet EN5 . . . . .28 DA43
Finchdean Ho, SW15
  off Tangley Gro 119 CT87
Finch Dr, Felt. TW14 . . . . . . .116 BX87
Finch Gdns, E4 . . . . .47 EA50
Finch Grn, Rick. (Chorl.) WD3 . .21 BF42
Finchingfield Av, Wdf.Grn.
  IG8 . . . . .48 EJ52
Finch La, EC3 . . . . .197 L9
  Amersham HP7 . . . . .20 AV40
  Bushey WD23 . . . . .24 CA43
FINCHLEY, N3 . . . . .44 DB53
  ● Finchley Central 44 DA53
Finchley Cl, Dart. DA1 . . . . . .128 FN86
Finchley Ct, N3 . . . . .44 DB51
Finchley La, NW4 . . . . .63 CW56
  □ Finchley Mem Hosp, N12 . .44 DC52
Finchley Pk, N12 . . . . .44 DC49
  ● Finchley Pl, NW8 . . . . .82 DD68
  ● Finchley Road 82 DC65
Finchley Rd, NW2 . . . . .64 DA62
  NW3 . . . . .82 DC65
  NW8 . . . . .82 DD67
  NW11 . . . . .63 CZ58
  Grays RM17 . . . . .110 GB79
  ≍ Finchley Road & Frognal . . .64 DC64
Finchley Way, N3 . . . . .44 DA53
Finch Ms, SE15 . . . . .102 DT80
Finck St, SE1 . . . . .200 C5
Finden Rd, E7 . . . . .68 EH64
Findhorn Av, Hayes UB4 . . . . .77 BV71
Findhorn St, E14 . . . . .85 EC72
Findon Cl, SW18
  off Wimbledon Pk Rd 120 DA86
  Harrow HA2 . . . . .60 CB62
Findon Ct, Add. KT15
  off Spinney Hill 151 BF106
Findon Gdns, Rain. RM13 . . . .89 FG71
Findon Rd, N9 . . . . .46 DV46
  W12 . . . . .99 CU75
Fine Bush La, Uxb. (Hare.)
  UB9 . . . . .59 BP58
Fingal St, SE10 . . . . .205 L10
Finglesham Cl, Orp. BR5
  off Westwell Cl 146 EX102
Finians Cl, Uxb. UB10 . . . . . . .76 BM66
Finland Quay, SE16 . . . . .203 L7
Finland Rd, SE4 . . . . .103 DY83
Finland St, SE16 . . . . .203 L7
Finlay Gdns, Add. KT15 . . . . .152 BJ105
Finlays Cl, Chess. KT9 . . . . . .156 CN106
Finlay St, SW6 . . . . .99 CX81
Finnart Cl, Wey. KT13 . . . . . .153 BQ105
Finnart Ho Dr, Wey. KT13
  off Vaillant Rd 153 BQ105
Finney La, Islw. TW7 . . . . .97 CG81
Finnis St, E2 . . . . .84 DV69
Finnymore Rd, Dag. RM9 . . . .88 EY66
FINSBURY, EC1 . . . . .196 E2
Finsbury Av, EC2 . . . . .197 L7
Finsbury Circ, EC2 . . . . .197 L7
Finsbury Cotts, N22
  off Clarence Rd 45 DL52
Finsbury Ct, Wal.Cr. EN8
  off Parkside 15 DY34
Finsbury Est, EC1 . . . . .196 F3
Finsbury Ho, N22 . . . . .45 DL53
Finsbury Mkt, EC2 . . . . .197 M5
FINSBURY PARK, N4 . . . . . . .65 DN60
  ★ Finsbury Park, N4 . . . . . . .65 DP59
  ≍ Finsbury Park 65 DN61
  ● Finsbury Park 65 DN61
Finsbury Pk Av, N4 . . . . .66 DQ58
Finsbury Pk Rd, N4 . . . . .65 DP61
Finsbury Pavement, EC2 . . . .197 L6
Finsbury Rd, N22 . . . . .45 DM53
Finsbury Sq, EC2 . . . . .197 L6
Finsbury St, EC2 . . . . .197 K6
Finsbury Twr, EC1 . . . . .197 K5
Finsbury Way, Bex. DA5 . . . . .126 EZ86
Finsen Rd, SE5 . . . . .102 DQ83
Finstock Rd, W10 . . . . .81 CX72
Finucane Dr, Orp. BR5 . . . . . .146 EW101
Finucane Gdns, Rain. RM13 . .89 FG65
Finucane Ri, Bushey (Bushey Hth.)
  WD23 . . . . .40 CC47
Finway Ct, Wat. WD18
  off Whippendell Rd 23 BT43
Fiona Ct, Lthd. (Bkhm.)
  KT23 . . . . .170 CA124
Firbank Cl, E16 . . . . .86 EK71
  Enfield EN2
  off Gladbeck Way 30 DQ42
Firbank Dr, Wat. WD19 . . . . . .40 BY45
  Woking GU21 . . . . .166 AV119
Firbank La, Wok. GU21 . . . . . .166 AV119
Firbank Pl, Egh. (Eng.Grn.)
  TW20 . . . . .112 AV93
Firbank Rd, SE15 . . . . .102 DV82
  Romford RM5 . . . . .51 FB50
Fir Cl, Walt. KT12 . . . . .135 BU101
Fircroft Ct, Wok. GU22
  SL2 . . . . .74 AU65
  Woking GU22 . . . . .167 AZ118
Fircroft Gdns, Har. HA1 . . . . . .61 CE62
Fircroft Rd, SW17 . . . . .120 DF89
  Chessington KT9 . . . . .156 CM105
Fir Dene, Orp. BR6 . . . . .145 EM104
Firdene, Surb. KT5 . . . . .138 CQ102

Fire Bell All, Surb. KT6 . . . . . .138 CL100
Firecrest Dr, NW3 . . . . .64 DB62
Firefly Cl, Wall. SM6 . . . . .159 DL108
Firefly Gdns, E6
  off Jack Dash Way 86 EL71
Fire Sta All, Barn. EN5
  off Christchurch La 27 CZ40
Firethorn Cl, Edg. HA8
  off Larkspur Gro 42 CQ49
Firfield Rd, Add. KT15 . . . . . .152 BG105
Firfields, Wey. KT13 . . . . .153 BP107
Fir Gra Av, Wey. KT13 . . . . . .153 BP106
Fir Gro, N.Mal. KT3 . . . . .139 CT100
  Woking GU21 . . . . .166 AU119
Firham Pk Av, Rom. RM3 . . . .52 FN62
Firhill Rd, SE6 . . . . .123 EA91
Firlands, Wey. KT13 . . . . .153 BS107
Firmingers Rd, Orp. BR6 . . . .165 FB106
Firmin Rd, Dart. DA1 . . . . . . .128 FJ85
  Sutton SM3 . . . . .139 CZ102
Firs, The, E17 off Leucha Rd . .67 DY57
  N20 . . . . .44 DD46
  W5 . . . . .79 CK71
  Bexley DA5
  off Dartford Rd 127 FD88
  Brentwood (Pilg.Hat.)
  CM15 . . . . .54 FU44
  Caterham CR3
  off Yorke Gate Rd 176 DR122
  Leatherhead (Bkhm.)
  KT23 . . . . .170 CC124
  Tadworth KT20
  off Brighton Rd 183 CZ126
  Waltham Cross (Chsht.)
  EN7 . . . . .14 DS27
Firs Av, N10 . . . . .64 DG55
  N11 . . . . .44 DG51
  SW14 . . . . .98 CQ84
Firsby Av, Croy. CR0 . . . . . . .143 DX102
Firsby Rd, N16 . . . . .66 DT60
Firs Cl, N10 off Firs Av 64 DG55
  SE23 . . . . .123 DX87
  Esher (Clay.) KT10 . . . . . . .155 CE108
  Iver SL0 off Thornbridge Rd .75 BC67
  Mitcham CR4 . . . . .141 DH96
Firscroft, N13 . . . . .46 DQ48
Firsdene Cl, Cher. (Ott.) KT16
  off Slade Rd 151 BD107
Firs Dr, Houns. TW5 . . . . .95 BV80
  Loughton IG10 . . . . .33 EN39
  Slough SL3 . . . . .75 AZ74
Firs End, Ger.Cr. (Chal.St.P.)
  SL9 . . . . .56 AY55
Firsgrove Cres, Brwd. CM14 . .54 FV49
Firsgrove Rd, Brwd. CM14 . . . .54 FV49
Firside Gro, Sid. DA15 . . . . . .125 ET88
Firs La, N13 . . . . .46 DQ48
  N21 . . . . .46 DQ47
  Potters Bar EN6 . . . . .12 DB33
Firs Pk Av, N21 . . . . .46 DR46
Firs Pk Gdns, N21 . . . . .46 DQ46
Firs Rd, Ken. CR8 . . . . .175 DP115
First Av, E12 . . . . .68 EL63
  E13 . . . . .86 EG69
  E17 . . . . .67 EA57
  N18 . . . . .46 DW49
  NW4 . . . . .63 CW56
  SW14 . . . . .98 CS83
  W3 . . . . .81 CT74
  W10 . . . . .81 CZ70
  Bexleyheath DA7 . . . . .106 EW80
  Dagenham RM10 . . . . .89 FB68
  Enfield EN1 . . . . .30 DT44
  Epsom KT19 . . . . .156 CS109
  Gravesend (Nthflt.) DA11 . .130 GE88
  Grays RM20 . . . . .109 FU79
  Greenford UB6 . . . . .79 CH74
  Hayes UB3 . . . . .77 BT74
  Romford RM6 . . . . .70 EW57
  Tadworth (Lwr.Kgswd.)
  KT20 . . . . .183 CY125
  Waltham Abbey EN9 off Breach
  Barn Mobile Home Pk 16 EH30
  Walton-on-Thames KT12 . . .135 BV100
  Watford WD25 . . . . .24 BW35
  Wembley HA9 . . . . .61 CK61
  West Molesey KT8 . . . . . . .136 BZ98
First Cl, W.Mol. KT8 . . . . .136 CC97
First Cross Rd, Twick. TW2 . . .117 CE89
First Dr, NW10 . . . . .80 CQ66
First Slip, Lthd. KT22 . . . . . . .171 CG118
First St, SW3 . . . . .198 C8
Firstway, SW20 . . . . .139 CW96
First Way, Wem. HA9 . . . . . . .62 CP63
Firs Wk, Nthwd. HA6 . . . . .39 BR51
  Woodford Green IG8 . . . . . .48 EG50
Firswood Av, Epsom KT19 . . .157 CT106
Firs Wd Cl, Pot.B. EN6 . . . . . .12 DF32
Firth Gdns, SW6 . . . . .99 CY81
Fir Tree Av, Mitch. CR4 . . . . .140 DG96
  Slough (Stoke P.) SL2 . . . . .74 AT70
  West Drayton UB7 . . . . .94 BN76
Fir Tree Cl, SW16 . . . . .121 DJ92
  W5 . . . . .80 CL72
  Epsom KT17 . . . . .173 CW115
  Epsom (Ewell) KT19 . . . . . .157 CT105
  Esher KT10 . . . . .154 CC106
  Grays RM17 . . . . .110 GD79
  Leatherhead KT22 . . . . . . .171 CJ123
  Orpington BR6
  off Highfield Av 163 ET106
  Romford RM1 . . . . .71 FD55
Firtree Ct, Borwd. (Elstree)
  WD6 . . . . .26 CM42
Fir Tree Gdns, Croy. CR0 . . . .161 EA105
Fir Tree Gro, Cars. SM5 . . . . .158 DF108
Fir Tree Hill, Rick. WD3 . . . . . .22 BM38
Fir Tree Pl, Ashf. TW15
  off Percy Av 114 BN92
Fir Tree Rd, Bans. SM7 . . . . . .157 CW114
  Epsom KT17 . . . . .173 CV116
  Hounslow TW4 . . . . .96 BY84
  Leatherhead KT22 . . . . . . .171 CJ123
Fir Trees, Rom. (Abridge) RM4 .34 EV41
Fir Trees Cl, SE16 . . . . .203 L3

Fir Tree Wk, Dag. RM10
  off Wheel Fm Dr 71 FC62
  Enfield EN1 . . . . .30 DR41
  Reigate RH2 . . . . .184 DD134
Firwood Cl, Wok. GU21 . . . . .166 AS119
Firwood Rd, Vir.W. GU25 . . . .132 AS100
Fisher Cl, Croy. CR0
  off Grant Rd 142 DT102
  Enfield EN3
  off Government Row 31 EA37
  Greenford UB6
  off Gosling Cl 78 CA69
  Kings Langley WD4 . . . . . . .6 BN29
  Walton-on-Thames KT12 . . .153 BV105
Fisherman Cl, Rich. TW10
  off Locksmeade Rd 117 CJ91
Fishermans Dr, SE16 . . . . . . .203 J4
Fishermans Hill, Grav. DA11 . .130 GB85
Fisherman's Wk, E14 . . . . . . .203 P2
Fisher Rd, Har. HA3 . . . . .41 CF54
Fishers Cl, SW16
  off Garrad's Rd 121 DK90
  Bushey WD23 . . . . .24 BY41
  Waltham Cross EN8 . . . . . . .15 EA34
Fishers Ct, SE14
  off Besson St 103 DX81
Fishersdene, Esher (Clay.)
  KT10 . . . . .155 CG108
Fishers Grn La, Wal.Abb. EN9 .15 EB29
Fishers La, W4 . . . . .98 CR77
  Epping CM16 . . . . .17 ES32
Fisher St, E16 . . . . .86 EG71
  WC1 . . . . .196 A7
Fishers Way, Belv. DA17 . . . . .89 FC74
Fisherton St, NW8 . . . . .82 DD70
Fishguard Spur, Slou. SL1 . . . .92 AV75
Fishguard Way, E16 . . . . .105 EP75
Fishing Temple, Stai. TW18 . .133 BF95
Fishponds Rd, SW17 . . . . . . .120 DE91
  Keston BR2 . . . . .162 EK106
Fish St Hill, EC3 . . . . .197 L10
Fitzalan Rd, N3 . . . . .63 CY55
  Esher (Clay.) KT10 . . . . . . .155 CE108
Fitzalan St, SE11 . . . . .200 C8
Fitzgeorge Av, W14 . . . . .99 CY77
  New Malden KT3 . . . . .138 CR95
Fitzgerald Av, SW14 . . . . .98 CS83
Fitzgerald Cl, E11
  off Fitzgerald Rd 68 EG57
Fitzgerald Ho, E14 . . . . .85 EB72
  Hayes UB3 . . . . .77 BV74
Fitzgerald Rd, E11 . . . . .68 EG57
  SW14 . . . . .98 CR83
  Thames Ditton KT7 . . . . . . .137 CG100
Fitzhardinge St, W1 . . . . .194 F8
Fitzherbert Ho, Rich. TW10
  off Kingsmead 118 CM86
Fitzhugh Gro, SW18 . . . . .120 DD86
Fitzjames Av, W14 . . . . .99 CY77
  Croydon CR0 . . . . .142 DU103
Fitzjohn Av, Barn. EN5 . . . . . . .27 CY43
Fitzjohn's Av, NW3 . . . . .64 DD64
Fitzmaurice Pl, W1 . . . . .199 J2
Fitzneal St, W12 . . . . .81 CT72
Fitzrobert Pl, Egh. TW20 . . . . .113 BA93
Fitzroy Cl, N6 . . . . .64 DF60
Fitzroy Ct, W1 . . . . .195 L5
Fitzroy Cres, W4 . . . . .98 CR80
Fitzroy Gdns, SE19 . . . . .122 DS94
Fitzroy Ms, W1 . . . . .195 K5
Fitzroy Pk, N6 . . . . .64 DF60
Fitzroy Rd, NW1 . . . . .82 DG67
Fitzroy Sq, W1 . . . . .195 K5
Fitzroy St, W1 . . . . .195 K5
Fitzroy Yd, NW1
  off Fitzroy Rd 82 DG67
Fitzstephen Rd, Dag. RM8 . . . .70 EV64
Fitzwarren Gdns, N19 . . . . . . .65 DJ60
Fitzwilliam Av, Rich. TW9 . . . . .98 CM82
Fitzwilliam Ms, E16 . . . . .205 M2
Fitzwilliam Rd, SW4 . . . . .101 DJ83
Fitzwygram Cl, Hmptn. (Hmptn.H.)
  TW12 . . . . .116 CC92
Five Acre, NW9 . . . . .43 CT53
Fiveacre Cl, Th.Hth. CR7 . . . .141 DN100
Five Acres, Kings L. WD4 . . . . .6 BM29
  St. Albans (Lon.Col.) AL2 . . .9 CK25
Five Acres Av, St.Alb. (Brick.Wd.)
  AL2 . . . . .8 BZ29
Fiveash Rd, Grav. DA11 . . . . .131 GF87
Five Bell All, E14
  off Three Colt St 85 DZ73
Five Elms Rd, Brom. BR2 . . . .144 EH104
  Dagenham RM9 . . . . .70 EZ62
Five Flds Cl, Wat. WD19 . . . . .40 BZ48
Five Oaks, Add. KT15 . . . . . .151 BF107
Five Oaks La, Chig. IG7 . . . . . .50 EY51
Five Points, Iver SL0 . . . . .75 BC69
Fives Ct, SE11 . . . . .200 F8
Five Ways Cor, NW4 . . . . .43 CV53
Fiveways Rd, SW9 . . . . .101 DN82
Five Wents, Swan. BR8 . . . . .147 FG96
Fladbury Rd, N15 . . . . .66 DR58
Fladgate Rd, E11 . . . . .68 EE58
Flag Cl, Croy. CR0 . . . . .143 DX102
Flagstaff Cl, Wal.Abb. EN9 . . .15 EB33
Flagstaff Rd, Wal.Abb. EN9 . . .15 EB33
Flag Wk, Pnr. HA5
  off Eastcote Rd 59 BU58
Flambard Rd, Har. HA1 . . . . . .61 CG58
Flamborough Cl, West. (Bigg.H.)
  TN16 . . . . .178 EH119
Flamborough Rd, Ruis. HA4 . . .59 BU62
Flamborough St, E14 . . . . .85 DY72
Flamborough Wk, E14
  off Flamborough St 85 DY72
Flamingo Gdns, Nthlt. UB5
  off Jetstar Way 78 BY69
Flamingo Wk, Horn. RM12 . . . .89 FG65
FLAMSTEAD END, Wal.Cr. . . .14 DU28
Flamstead End Rd, Wal.Cr. (Chsht.)
  EN8 . . . . .14 DV28
Flamstead Gdns, Dag. RM9
  off Flamstead Rd 88 EW63

Flamstead Rd, Dag. RM9 . . . .88 EW66
Flamsted Av, Wem. HA9 . . . . .80 CN65
  ★ Flamsteed House Mus,
  SE10 . . . . .103 ED80
Flamsteed Rd, SE7 . . . . .104 EL78
Flanchford Rd, W12 . . . . .99 CT76
  Reigate RH2 . . . . .183 CX134
Flanders Ct, Egh. TW20 . . . . .113 BC92
Flanders Cres, SW17 . . . . . . .120 DF94
Flanders Rd, E6 . . . . .87 EM68
  W4 . . . . .98 CS77
Flanders Way, E9 . . . . .85 DX65
Flank St, E1 off Dock St 84 DU73
Flash La, Enf. EN2 . . . . .29 DP37
Flask Cotts, NW3
  off New End Sq 64 DD63
Flask Wk, NW3 . . . . .64 DD63
Flat Iron Sq, SE1 off Union St .84 DQ74
FLAUNDEN, Hem.H. BB33
Flaunden Bottom, Chesh.
  HP5 . . . . .20 AY36
  Hemel Hempstead (Flaun.)
  HP3 . . . . .20 AY35
Flaunden Hill, Hem.H. (Flaun.)
  HP3 . . . . .5 AZ33
Flaunden La, Hem.H. (Bov.)
  HP3 . . . . .5 BB32
  Rickmansworth WD3 . . . . . .5 BD33
Flaunden Pk, Hem.H. (Flaun.)
  HP3 . . . . .5 BA32
Flavell Ms, SE10 . . . . .205 J10
Flaxen Cl, E4 off Flaxen Rd . . .47 EB48
Flaxen Rd, E4 . . . . .47 EB48
Flaxley Rd, Mord. SM4 . . . . . .140 DB100
Flaxman Ct, W1 . . . . .195 M9
Flaxman Rd, SE5 . . . . .101 DP82
Flaxman Ter, WC1 . . . . .195 N3
Flaxton Rd, SE18 . . . . .105 ER81
Flecker Cl, Stan. HA7 . . . . .41 CF50
Fleece Dr, N9 . . . . .46 DU49
Fleece Rd, Surb. KT6 . . . . . . .137 CJ102
Fleece Wk, N7
  off Manger Rd 83 DL65
Fleeming Cl, E17
  off Pennant Ter 47 DZ54
Fleeming Rd, E17 . . . . .47 DZ54
Fleet Av, Dart. DA2 . . . . .128 FQ88
  Upminster RM14 . . . . .73 FR58
Fleet Cl, Ruis. HA4 . . . . .59 BQ58
  Upminster RM14 . . . . .73 FR58
  West Molesey KT8 . . . . . . .136 BZ99
Fleetdale Par, Dart. DA2
  off Fleet Av 128 FQ88
Fleet Pl, EC4
  off Farringdon St 83 DN72
Fleet Rd, NW3 . . . . .64 DE64
  Dartford DA2 . . . . .128 FQ88
  Gravesend (Nthflt.) DA11 . .130 GC90
Fleetside, W.Mol. KT8 . . . . . . .136 BZ100
Fleet Sq, WC1 . . . . .196 B3
Fleet St, EC4 . . . . .196 D9
Fleet St Hill, E1
  off Weaver St 84 DU70
Fleetway, Egh. TW20 . . . . . . .133 BC97
Fleetway Business Pk, Grnf.
  UB6 . . . . .79 CH68
Fleetwood Cl, E16 . . . . .86 EK71
  Chalfont St. Giles HP8 . . . . .36 AU49
  Chessington KT9 . . . . .155 CK108
  Croydon CR0 . . . . .142 DT104
  Tadworth KT20 . . . . .173 CW120
Fleetwood Ct, E6
  off Evelyn Denington Rd . . .87 EM71
  West Byfleet KT14 . . . . . . .152 BG113
Fleetwood Gro, W3
  off East Acton La 80 CS73
Fleetwood Rd, NW10 . . . . .63 CU64
  Kingston upon Thames
  KT1 . . . . .138 CP97
  Slough SL2 . . . . .74 AT74
Fleetwood Sq, Kings.T. KT1 . .138 CP97
Fleetwood St, N16 off Stoke
  Newington Ch St 66 DS61
Fleetwood Way, Wat. WD19 . . .40 BW49
Fleming Cl, W9
  off Chippenham Rd 82 DA70
  Waltham Cross (Chsht.)
  EN7 . . . . .14 DU26
Fleming Ct, W2
  off St. Marys Ter 82 DD71
  Croydon CR0 . . . . .159 DN106
Fleming Dr, N21 . . . . .29 DM43
Fleming Gdns, Rom. (Harold Wd.)
  RM3 off Bartholomew Dr . .52 FK54
  Tilbury RM18
  off Fielding Av 111 GJ81
Fleming Mead, Mitch. CR4 . . .120 DE94
Fleming Rd, SE17 . . . . .101 DP79
  Grays (Chaff.Hun.) RM16 . .109 FW77
  Southall UB1 . . . . .78 CB72
  Waltham Abbey EN9
  off Sewardstone Rd 31 ED35
Flemings, Brwd. CM13 . . . . . .53 FW51
Fleming Wk, NW9
  off Pasteur Cl 42 CS54
Fleming Way, SE28 . . . . .88 EX73
  Isleworth TW7 . . . . .97 CF83
Flemish Flds, Cher. KT16 . . . .134 BG101
Flemming Av, Ruis. HA4 . . . . . .59 BV60
Flempton Rd, E10 . . . . .67 DY60
Fletcher Cl, E6 off Trader Rd . .87 EP72
  Chertsey (Ott.) KT16 . . . . .151 BE107
Fletcher La, E10 . . . . .67 EC59
Fletcher Path, SE8
  off New Butt La 103 EA80
Fletcher Rd, W4 . . . . .98 CQ76
  Chertsey (Ott.) KT16 . . . . .151 BD107
  Chigwell IG7 . . . . .49 ET50
Fletchers Cl, Brom. BR2 . . . . .144 EH98
Fletcher St, E1 off Cable St . . .84 DU73
Fletching Rd, E5 . . . . .66 DW62
  SE7 . . . . .104 EJ79
Fletton Rd, N11 . . . . .45 DL52
Fleur de Lis St, E1 . . . . .197 N5
Fleur Gates, SW19
  off Princes Way 119 CX87

Flexmere Gdns, N17
  off Flexmere Rd 46 DR53
Flexmere Rd, N17 . . . . .46 DR53
Flight App, NW9 . . . . .43 CT54
Flimwell Cl, Brom. BR1 . . . . . .124 EE92
Flint Cl, Bans. SM7 . . . . .158 DB114
  Redhill RH1 . . . . .184 DF133
Flint Down Cl, Orp. BR5 . . . . .146 EU95
Flintlock Cl, Stai. TW19 . . . . . .94 BG84
Flintmill Cres, SE3 . . . . .104 EL82
Flinton St, SE17 . . . . .201 N10
Flint St, SE17 . . . . .201 L9
  Grays RM20 . . . . .109 FV79
Flitcroft St, WC2 . . . . .195 N8
Floats, The, Sev. (Rvrhd.)
  TN13 . . . . .190 FE121
Flock Mill Pl, SW18 . . . . .120 DB88
Flockton St, SE16 . . . . .202 B5
Flodden Rd, SE5 . . . . .102 DQ81
Flood La, Twick. TW1
  off Church La 117 CG88
Flood Pas, SE18
  off Samuel St 105 EM77
Flood St, SW3 . . . . .100 DE78
Flood Wk, SW3 . . . . .100 DE79
Flora Cl, E14 . . . . .85 EB72
Flora Gdns, W6
  off Ravenscourt Rd 99 CV77
  Croydon CR0 . . . . .161 EC111
  Romford RM6 . . . . .70 EW58
Floral Ct, Ashtd. KT21 . . . . . .171 CJ118
  off Rosedale 171 CJ118
Floral Dr, St.Alb. (Lon.Col.)
  AL2 . . . . .9 CK26
Floral St, WC2 . . . . .195 P10
Flora St, Belv. DA17
  off Victoria St 106 EZ78
Florence Av, Add. (New Haw)
  KT15 . . . . .152 BG111
  Enfield EN2 . . . . .30 DQ41
  Morden SM4 . . . . .140 DC99
Florence Cantwell Wk, N19
  off Hillrise Rd 65 DL59
Florence Cl, Grays RM20 . . . .110 FY79
  Hornchurch RM12 . . . . .72 FL61
  Walton-on-Thames KT12
  off Florence Rd 135 BV101
  Watford WD25 . . . . .23 BU35
Florence Dr, Enf. EN2 . . . . . . .30 DQ41
Florence Elson Cl, E12 . . . . . .69 EN63
  off Grantham Rd 69 EN63
Florence Gdns, W4 . . . . .98 CQ79
  Romford RM6 off Roxy Av . . .70 EW59
  Staines TW18 . . . . .114 BH94
Florence Nightingale Ho, N1
  off Clephane Rd 84 DR65
  ★ Florence Nightingale Mus,
  SE1 . . . . .200 B5
Florence Rd, E6 . . . . .86 EJ67
  E13 . . . . .86 EF68
  N4 .65 DN60
  SE2 . . . . .106 EW76
  SE14 . . . . .103 DZ81
  SW19 . . . . .120 DB93
  W4 . . . . .98 CR76
  W5 . . . . .80 CL73
  Beckenham BR3 . . . . .143 DX96
  Bromley BR1 . . . . .144 EG95
  Feltham TW13 . . . . .115 BV88
  Kingston upon Thames
  KT2 . . . . .118 CM94
  South Croydon CR2 . . . . . .160 DR109
  Southall UB2 . . . . .96 BX77
  Walton-on-Thames KT12 . . .135 BV101
Florence St, E16 . . . . .86 EF70
  N1 .83 DP66
  NW4 . . . . .63 CW56
Florence Ter, SE14 . . . . .103 DZ81
Florence Way, SW12 . . . . . . .120 DF88
  Uxbridge UB8
  off Wyvern Way 76 BJ67
Florfield Pas, E8
  off Reading La 84 DV65
Florfield Rd, E8
  off Reading La 84 DV65
Florian Av, Sutt. SM1 . . . . . . .158 DD105
Florian Rd, SW15 . . . . .99 CY84
Florida Cl, Bushey (Bushey Hth.)
  WD23 . . . . .41 CD47
Florida Rd, Th.Hth. CR7 . . . . .141 DP95
Florida St, E2 . . . . .84 DU69
Florin Ct, SE1 off Tanner St . .201 DT75
Floris Pl, SW4
  off Fitzwilliam Rd 101 DJ83
Floriston Av, Uxb. UB10 . . . . . .77 BQ66
Floriston Cl, Stan. HA7 . . . . . . .41 CH53
Floriston Ct, Nthlt. UB5 . . . . . .60 CB64
Floriston Gdns, Stan. HA7 . . . .41 CH53
Floss St, SW15 . . . . .99 CW82
Flower & Dean Wk, E1
  off Thrawl St 84 DT71
Flower Cres, Cher. (Ott.)
  KT16 . . . . .151 BB107
Flowerfield, Sev. (Otford)
  TN14 . . . . .181 FF117
Flowerhill Way, Grav. (Istead Rise)
  DA13 . . . . .130 GE94
Flower La, NW7 . . . . .43 CT50
  Godstone RH9 . . . . .187 DY128
  ★ Flower Mkt, New Covent
  Garden Mkt, SW8 . . . . . . .101 DK79
Flower Ms, NW11 . . . . .63 CY58
Flower Pot Cl, N15
  off St. Ann's Rd 66 DT58
Flowers Cl, NW2 . . . . .63 CU62
Flowersmead, SW17 . . . . . . .120 DG89
Flowers Ms, N19
  off Archway Rd 65 DJ61
Floyd Rd, SE7 . . . . .104 EJ78
Floyds La, Wok. GU22 . . . . . .168 BG116
Fludyer St, SE13 . . . . .104 EE84
Flux's La, Epp. CM16 . . . . .18 EU33
Flyer's Way, The, West. TN16 .189 ER126
Fogerty Cl, Enf. EN3
  off Government Row 31 EA37
Foley Ms, Esher (Clay.) KT10 .155 CE108

Foley Rd, Esher (Clay.) KT10 .155 CE108
 Westerham (Bigg.H.) TN16 .178 EK118
Foley St, W1 . . . . .195 K7
Folgate St, E1 . . . . .197 N6
Foliot St, W12 . . . . .81 CT72
Folkes La, Upmin. RM14 . . . .73 FT57
Folkestone Cl, Slou. SL3 . . . .93 BA78
Folkestone Rd, E6 . . . . .87 EN68
 E17 . . . . .67 EB56
 N18 . . . . .46 DU49
Folkingham La, NW9 . . . . . .42 CR53
Folkington Cor, N12 . . . . . . .43 CZ50
Follet Dr, Abb.L. WD5 . . . . . .7 BT31
Follett Cl, Wind. (Old Wind.)
 SL4 . . . . .112 AV86
Follett St, E14 . . . . .85 EC72
Folly Cl, Rad. WD7 . . . . .25 CF36
Follyfield Rd, Bans. SM7 . . .158 DA114
Folly La, E4 . . . . .47 DZ52
 E17 . . . . .47 DY53
Folly Ms, W11
 off Portobello Rd 81 CZ72
Folly Pathway, Rad. WD7 . . . .25 CF35
Folly Wall, E14 . . . . .204 E5
Fontaine Rd, SW16 . . . . . . .121 DM94
Fontarabia Rd, SW11 . . . . .100 DG84
Fontayne Av, Chig. IG7 . . . . .49 EQ49
 Rainham RM13 . . . . .89 FE66
 Romford RM1 . . . . .51 FE54
Fontenoy Rd, SW12 . . . . . .121 DH89
Fonteyne Gdns, Wdf.Grn. IG8
 off Lechmere Av 48 EK54
Fonthill Cl, SE20
 off Selby Rd 142 DU96
Fonthill Ms, N4
 off Lennox Rd 65 DN61
Fonthill Rd, N4 . . . . .65 DM60
Font Hills, N2 . . . . .44 DC54
Fontley Way, SW15 . . . . . .119 CU87
Fontmell Cl, Ashf. TW15 . . .114 BN92
Fontmell Pk, Ashf. TW15 . . .114 BM92
Fontwell Cl, Har. HA3 . . . . . .41 CE52
 Northolt UB5 . . . . .78 CA65
Fontwell Dr, Brom. BR2 . . . .145 EN99
Fontwell Pk Gdns, Horn.
 RM12 . . . . .72 FL63
Foord Cl, Dart. DA2 . . . . . .129 FS89
Football La, Har. HA1 . . . . . .61 CE60
Footbury Hill Rd, Orp. BR6 . .146 EU101
Footpath, The, SW15 . . . . .119 CU85
FOOTS CRAY, Sid. 126 EV93
Foots Cray High St, Sid.
 DA14 . . . . .126 EW93
Foots Cray La, Sid. DA14 . . .126 EW88
Footscray Rd, SE9 . . . . . . .125 EN86
Footway, The, SE9 . . . . . . .125 EQ87
Forbench Cl, Wok. (Ripley)
 GU23 . . . . .168 BH122
Forbes Av, Pot.B. EN6 . . . . .12 DD33
Forbes Cl, NW2 . . . . .63 CU62
 Hornchurch RM11
 off St. Leonards Way 71 FH60
Forbes Ct, SE19 . . . . .122 DS92
Forbes St, E1 off Ellen St . . .84 DU72
Forbes Way, Ruis. HA4 . . . . .59 BV61
Forburg Rd, N16 . . . . .66 DU60
FORCE GREEN, West. 179 ER124
Force Grn La, West. TN16 . .179 ER124
Fordbridge Cl, Cher. KT16 . .134 BH102
Fordbridge Rd, Ashf. TW15 .114 BL93
 Shepperton TW17 . . . . . .135 BS100
 Sunbury-on-Thames
 TW16 . . . . .135 BS100
Ford Cl, E3
 off Roman Rd 85 DY68
 Ashford TW15 . . . . .114 BL93
 Bushey WD23 . . . . .24 CC42
 Harrow HA1 . . . . .61 CD59
 Rainham RM13 . . . . .89 FF66
 Shepperton TW17 . . . . . .134 BN98
 Thornton Heath CR7 . . . . .141 DP100
Fordcroft Rd, Orp. BR5 . . . .146 EV99
Forde Av, Brom. BR1 . . . . .144 EJ97
Fordel Rd, SE6 . . . . .123 ED88
Ford End, Uxb. (Denh.) UB9 . .57 BF61
 Woodford Green IG8 . . . . . .48 EH51
Fordham Cl, Barn. EN4 . . . . .28 DE41
 Hornchurch RM11 . . . . . . .71 FN59
Fordham Rd, Barn. EN4 . . . . .28 DE41
Fordham St, E1 . . . . .84 DU72
Fordhook Av, W5 . . . . .80 CM73
Fordingley Rd, W9 . . . . .82 CZ69
Fordington Rd, N6 . . . . .64 DF57
Ford La, Iver SL0 . . . . .75 BG72
 Rainham RM13 . . . . .89 FF66
Fordmill Rd, SE6 . . . . .123 EA89
Ford Rd, E3 . . . . .85 DY67
 Ashford TW15 . . . . .114 BM91
 Chertsey KT16 . . . . .134 BH102
 Dagenham RM9, RM10 . . . .88 EZ66
 Gravesend (Nthflt.) DA11 . .130 GB85
 Woking (Old Wok.) GU22 . .167 BB120
Fords Gro, N21 . . . . .46 DQ46
Fords Pk Rd, E16 . . . . .86 EG72
Ford Sq, E1 . . . . .84 DV71
Ford St, E3 . . . . .85 DY67
 E16 . . . . .86 EF72
Fordwater Rd, Cher. KT16 . .134 BH102
Fordwater Trd Est, Cher.
 KT16 . . . . .134 BJ102
Fordwich Cl, Orp. BR6 . . . .145 ET101
Fordwych Rd, NW2 . . . . . . .63 CY64
Fordyce Cl, Horn. RM11 . . . .72 FM59
Fordyce Ho, SW16
 off Colson Way 121 DJ91
Fordyce Rd, SE13 . . . . . . .123 EC86
Fordyke Rd, Dag. RM8 . . . . .70 EZ61
Forefield, St.Alb. AL2 . . . . . .8 CA27
★ Foreign & Commonwealth
 Office, SW1 . . . . .199 P4
Foreland Ct, NW4 . . . . .43 CY53
Foreland St, SE18
 off Plumstead Rd 105 ER77
Foreman Ct, W6
 off Hammersmith Bdy 99 CW77
Foremark Cl, Ilf. IG6 . . . . . .49 ET50
Foreshore, SE8 . . . . .203 N9

Forest, The, E11 . . . . .68 EE56
Forest App, E4 . . . . .48 EE45
 Woodford Green IG8 . . . . . .48 EF52
Forest Av, E4 . . . . .48 EE45
 Chigwell IG7 . . . . .49 EN50
Forest Business Pk, E17 . . . .67 DX59
Forest Cl, E11 . . . . .68 EF57
 Chislehurst BR7 . . . . .145 EN95
 Waltham Abbey EN9 . . . . . .32 EH37
 Woking GU22 . . . . .167 BD115
 Woodford Green IG8 . . . . . .48 EH48
Forest Ct, E4 . . . . .48 EF46
 E11 . . . . .68 EE56
Forest Cres, Ashtd. KT21 . . .172 CN116
Forest Cft, SE23 . . . . .122 DV89
FORESTDALE, Croy. 161 EA109
Forestdale, N14 . . . . .45 DK49
Forest Dr, E12 . . . . .68 EK62
 Epping (They.B.) CM16 . . . .33 ES36
 Keston BR2 . . . . .162 EL105
 Sunbury-on-Thames
 TW16 . . . . .115 BT94
 Tadworth (Kgswd.) KT20 . .173 CZ121
 Woodford Green IG8 . . . . . .47 ED52
Forest Dr E, E11 . . . . .67 ED59
Forest Dr W, E11 . . . . .67 EC59
Forest Edge, Buck.H. IG9 . . . .48 EJ49
Forester Rd, SE15 . . . . . . .102 DV84
Foresters Cl, Wall. SM6 . . . .159 DK108
 Waltham Cross EN7 . . . . . .14 DS27
 Woking GU21 . . . . .166 AT118
Foresters Cres, Bexh. DA7 . .107 FB84
Foresters Dr, E17 . . . . .67 ED56
 Wallington SM6 . . . . .159 DK108
Forest Gdns, N17 . . . . .46 DT54
FOREST GATE, E7 . . . . .68 EG64
⇌ Forest Gate 68 EG64
Forest Gate, NW9 . . . . .62 CS57
Forest Glade, E4 . . . . .48 EE49
 E11 . . . . .68 EE58
 Epping (N.Wld.Bas.) CM16 .18 EV27
Forest Gro, E8 . . . . .84 DT66
Forest Hts, Buck.H. IG9 . . . . .48 EG47
FOREST HILL, SE23 . . . . . .123 DX88
⇌ Forest Hill 122 DW89
Forest Hill Business Cen,
 SE23 . . . . .122 DW89
Forest Hill Ind Est, SE23
 off Perry Vale 122 DW89
Forest Hill Rd, SE22 . . . . . .122 DV85
 SE23 . . . . .122 DV85
Forestholme Cl, SE23 . . . . .122 DW89
Forest Ind Pk, Ilf. IG6 . . . . . .49 ES53
Forest La, E7 . . . . .68 EE64
 E15 . . . . .68 EE64
 Chigwell IG7 . . . . .49 EN50
 Leatherhead (E.Hors.)
 KT24 . . . . .169 BT124
Forest Mt Rd, Wdf.Grn. IG8 . .47 ED52
Fore St, EC2 . . . . .197 J7
 N9 . . . . .46 DU50
 N18 . . . . .46 DT51
 Pinner HA5 . . . . .59 BU57
Fore St Av, EC2 . . . . .197 K7
Forest Ridge, Beck. BR3 . . . .143 EA97
 Keston BR2 . . . . .162 EL105
Forest Ri, E17 . . . . .67 ED57
Forest Rd, E7 . . . . .68 EG63
 E8 . . . . .84 DT66
 E11 . . . . .67 ED59
 E17 . . . . .66 DW56
 N9 . . . . .46 DV46
 N17 . . . . .66 DW56
 Enfield EN3 . . . . .31 DY36
 Erith DA8 . . . . .107 FG81
 Feltham TW13 . . . . .116 BW89
 Ilford IG6 . . . . .49 ES53
 Leatherhead (E.Hors.)
 KT24 . . . . .169 BU123
 Loughton IG10 . . . . .32 EK41
 Richmond TW9 . . . . .98 CN80
 Romford RM7 . . . . .71 FB55
 Sutton SM3 . . . . .140 DA102
 Waltham Cross (Chsht.)
 EN8 . . . . .15 DX29
 Watford WD25 . . . . .7 BV33
 Woking GU22 . . . . .167 BD115
 Woodford Green IG8 . . . . . .48 EG48
Forest Side, E4 . . . . .48 EF45
 E7 off Capel Rd 68 EH63
 Buckhurst Hill IG9 . . . . . . .48 EJ46
 Epping CM16 . . . . .17 ER33
 Waltham Abbey EN9 . . . . . .32 EJ36
 Worcester Park KT4 . . . . .139 CT102
Forest St, E7 . . . . .68 EG64
 WD6 . . . . .25 CK44
Forest Vw, E4 . . . . .47 ED45
 E11
 off High Rd Leytonstone . . .68 EF59
Forest Vw Av, E10 . . . . .67 ED57
Forest Vw Rd, E12 . . . . .68 EL63
 E17 . . . . .47 EC53
 Loughton IG10 . . . . .32 EK42
Forest Wk, Bushey WD23
 off Millbrook Rd 24 BZ39
Forest Way, N19
 off Hargrave Pk 65 DJ61
 Ashtead KT21 . . . . .172 CM117
 Loughton IG10 . . . . .32 EL41
 Orpington BR5 . . . . .145 ET99
 Sidcup DA15 . . . . .125 ER87
 Waltham Abbey EN9 . . . . . .32 EK35
 Woodford Green IG8 . . . . . .48 EH49
Forfar Rd, N22 . . . . .45 DP53
 SW11 . . . . .100 DG81
Forge Av, Couls. CR5 . . . . .175 DN120
Forge Br La, Couls. CR5 . . . .175 DH121
Forge Cl, Brom. BR2 . . . . . .144 EG102
 Hayes UB3 off High St 95 BR79
 Kings Langley (Chipper.)
 WD4 . . . . .6 BG31
Forge Cotts, W5
 off Ealing Grn 79 CK74
Forge Dr, Esher (Clay.) KT10 .155 CG108
Forge End, St.Alb. AL2 . . . . . .8 CA26
 Woking GU21 . . . . .166 AY117
Forgefield, West. (Bigg.H.) TN16
 off Main Rd 178 EK116

Forge La, Dart. (Hort.Kir.)
 DA4 . . . . .148 FQ98
 Feltham TW13 . . . . .116 BY92
 Gravesend DA12 . . . . .131 GM89
 Northwood HA6 . . . . .39 BS52
 Sunbury-on-Thames
 TW16 . . . . .135 BU97
 Sutton SM3 . . . . .157 CY108
Forge Ms, Sun. TW16
 off Forge La 135 BU97
Forge Pl, NW1
 off Malden Cres 82 DG65
Forge Way, Sev. (Shore.)
 TN14 . . . . .165 FF111
Forlong Path, Nthlt. UB5
 off Arnold Rd 78 BY65
Forman Pl, N16
 off Farleigh Rd 66 DT63
Formation, The, E16
 off Woolwich Manor Way . .105 EP75
Formby Av, Stan. HA7 . . . . . .61 CJ55
Formby Cl, Slou. SL3 . . . . . .93 BC77
Formosa St, W9 . . . . .82 DB70
Formunt Cl, E16
 off Vincent St 86 EF71
Forres Gdns, NW11 . . . . . . .64 DA58
Forrester Path, SE26 . . . . . .123 DX91
Forrest Gdns, SW16 . . . . . .141 DM97
Forris Av, Hayes UB3 . . . . . .77 BT74
Forset St, W1 . . . . .194 C8
Forstal Cl, Brom. BR2
 off Ridley Rd 144 EG97
Forster Cl, E17 . . . . .47 ED52
Forster Rd, E17 . . . . .67 DY58
 N17 . . . . .66 DT55
 SW2 . . . . .121 DL87
 Beckenham BR3 . . . . .143 DY97
 Croydon CR0
 off Windmill Rd 142 DQ101
Forsters Cl, Rom. RM6 . . . . . .70 EZ58
Forster's Way, SW18 . . . . . .120 DB88
Forsters Way, Hayes UB4 . . . .77 BV72
Forston St, N1 off Cropley St .84 DR68
Forsyte Cres, SE19 . . . . . . .142 DS95
Forsyth Gdns, SE17 . . . . . .101 DP79
Forsythia Cl, Ilf. IG1 . . . . . . .69 EP64
Forsythia Gdns, Slou. SL3 . . .92 AY76
Forsyth Path, Wok. GU21 . . .151 BD113
Forsyth Pl, Enf. EN1 . . . . . . .30 DS43
Forsyth Rd, Wok. GU21 . . . .151 BC114
Forterie Gdns, Ilf. IG3 . . . . . .70 EU62
Fortescue Av, E8
 off Mentmore Ter 84 DV66
 Twickenham TW2 . . . . . . .116 CC90
Fortescue Rd, SW19 . . . . . .120 DD94
 Edgware HA8 . . . . .42 CR53
 Weybridge KT13 . . . . .152 BM105
Fortess Gro, NW5
 off Fortess Rd 65 DH64
Fortess Rd, NW5 . . . . .65 DH64
Fortess Wk, NW5
 off Fortess Rd 65 DH64
Forthbridge Rd, SW11 . . . . .100 DG84
Forth Rd, Upmin. RM14 . . . . .73 FR58
Fortin Path, S.Ock. RM15 . . . .91 FU73
Fortin Way, S.Ock. RM15 . . . .91 FU73
Fortis Cl, E16 . . . . .86 EJ72
FORTIS GREEN, N2 . . . . . . .64 DF56
Fortis Grn, N2 . . . . .64 DE56
 N10 . . . . .64 DE56
Fortis Grn Av, N2 . . . . .64 DF56
Fortis Grn Rd, N10 . . . . .64 DG55
Fortismere Av, N10 . . . . .64 DG55
Fort La, Reig. RH2 . . . . .184 DB130
Fort Rd, SE1 . . . . .202 A9
 Northolt UB5 . . . . .78 CA66
 Sevenoaks (Halst.) TN14 . .181 FC115
 Tadworth KT20 . . . . .182 CP131
 Tilbury RM18 . . . . .111 GH84
Fortrose Gdns, SW2
 off New Pk Rd 121 DK88
Fortrye Cl, Grav. (Nthflt.)
 DA11 . . . . .130 GE89
Fort St, E1 . . . . .197 N7
 E16 . . . . .86 EH73
Fortuna Cl, N7 off Vulcan Way .83 DM65
Fortune Gate Rd, NW10 . . . . .80 CS67
Fortune Grn Rd, NW6 . . . . . .64 DA63
Fortune La, Borwd. (Elstree)
 WD6 . . . . .25 CK44
Fortunes Mead, Nthlt. UB5 . . .78 BY65
Fortune St, EC1 . . . . .197 J5
Fortune Wk, SE28
 off Broadwater Rd 105 ER76
Fortune Way, NW10 . . . . . . .81 CU69
Forty Acre La, E16 . . . . .86 EG71
Forty Av, Wem. HA9 . . . . . . .62 CM62
Forty Cl, Wem. HA9 . . . . . . .62 CM61
Forty Footpath, SW14 . . . . . .98 CQ83
Fortyfoot Rd, Lthd. KT22 . . . .171 CJ121
★ Forty Hall & Mus, Enf.
 EN2 . . . . .30 DT38
FORTY HILL, Enf. 30 DS37
Forty Hill, Enf. EN2 . . . . .30 DT38
Forty La, Wem. HA9 . . . . . . .62 CP61
Forum, The, W.Mol. KT8 . . . .136 CB98
★ Forum Club, NW5 . . . . . . .65 DH64
Forum Magnum Sq, SE1 . . . .200 B4
Forumside, Edg. HA8
 off High St 42 CN51
Forum Way, Edg. HA8
 off High St 42 CN51
Forval Cl, Mitch. CR4 . . . . . .140 DF99
Fosbury Ms, W2
 off Inverness Ter 82 DB73
Foscote Ms, W9
 off Amberley Rd 82 DA71
Foscote Rd, NW4 . . . . .63 CV58
Foskett Rd, SW6 . . . . .99 CZ82
Foss Av, Croy. CR0 . . . . . . .159 DN106

Fossdene Rd, SE7 . . . . .104 EH78
Fossdyke Cl, Hayes UB4 . . . .78 BY71
Fosse Way, W13 . . . . .79 CG71
 West Byfleet KT14
 off Brantwood Dr 151 BF113
Fossil Rd, SE13 . . . . .103 EA83
Fossington Rd, Belv. DA17 . .106 EX77
Foss Rd, SW17 . . . . .120 DD90
Fossway, Dag. RM8 . . . . . . .70 EW61
Foster La, EC2 . . . . .197 H8
Foster Rd, E13 . . . . .86 EG70
 W3 . . . . .80 CS73
 W4 . . . . .98 CR78
Fosters Cl, E18 . . . . .48 EH53
 Chislehurst BR7 . . . . .125 EM92
Foster St, NW4 . . . . .63 CW56
Foster Wk, NW4
 off New Brent St 63 CW56
Fothergill Cl, E13 . . . . .86 EG68
Fothergill Dr, N21 . . . . .29 DL43
Fotheringham Rd, Enf. EN1 . . .30 DT42
Fotherley Rd, Rick. (Mill End)
 WD3 . . . . .37 BF47
Foubert's Pl, W1 . . . . .195 K9
Foulden Rd, N16 . . . . .66 DT63
Foulden Ter, N16
 off Foulden Rd 66 DT63
Foulis Ter, SW7 . . . . .198 A10
Foulser Rd, SW17 . . . . .120 DF90
Foulsham Rd, Th.Hth. CR7 . .142 DQ97
Founder Cl, E6 off Trader Rd . .87 EP72
Founders Ct, EC2 . . . . .197 K8
Founders Dr, Uxb. (Denh.)
 UB9 . . . . .57 BF58
Founders Gdns, SE19 . . . . .122 DQ94
Foundry Cl, SE16 . . . . .203 K2
Foundry La, Slou. (Horton)
 SL3 . . . . .93 BB83
Foundry Ms, NW1 . . . . .195 L4
Fountain Ct, EC4 . . . . .196 D10
Fountain Dr, SE19 . . . . .122 DT91
 Carshalton SM5 . . . . .158 DF109
Fountain Grn Sq, SE16 . . . . .202 C4
Fountain La, Sev. TN15 . . . .191 FP122
Fountain Ms, N5
 off Kelross Rd 66 DQ63
 NW3 off Haverstock Hill 82 DF65
Fountain Pl, SW9 . . . . .101 DN81
 Waltham Abbey EN9 . . . . . .16 EC34
Fountain Rd, SW17 . . . . . . .120 DD92
 Thornton Heath CR7 . . . . .142 DQ96
Fountains, The, Loug. IG10
 off Fallow Flds 48 EK45
Fountains Av, Felt. TW13 . . .116 BZ90
Fountains Cl, Felt. TW13 . . .116 BZ89
Fountains Cres, N14 . . . . . . .45 DL45
Fountain Sq, SW1 . . . . .199 H8
Fountain St, E2
 off Columbia Rd 84 DT69
Fountain Wk, Grav. (Nthflt.)
 DA11 . . . . .130 GE86
Fountayne Rd, N15 . . . . . . .66 DU56
 N16 . . . . .66 DU61
Fount St, SW8 . . . . .101 DK80
Fouracres, SW12
 off Little Dimocks 121 DH89
 Enfield EN3 . . . . .31 DY39
Fouracre Way, Cob. KT11 . . .154 BY113
Fourland Wk, Edg. HA8 . . . . .42 CQ51
Fournier St, E1 . . . . .197 P6
Four Seasons Cl, E3 . . . . . . .85 EA68
Fourth Av, E12 . . . . .69 EM63
 W10 . . . . .81 CY70
 Grays RM20 . . . . .109 FU79
 Hayes UB3 . . . . .77 BT74
 Romford RM7 . . . . .71 FD60
 Watford WD25 . . . . .24 BX35
Fourth Cross Rd, Twick. TW2 .117 CD89
Fourth Dr, Couls. CR5 . . . . .175 DK116
Fourth Way, Wem. HA9 . . . . .62 CQ63
Four Tubs, The, Bushey WD23 .41 CD45
Four Wents, Cob. KT11 . . . .153 BV113
Four Wents, The, E4
 off Kings Rd 47 ED47
Fowey Av, Ilf. IG4 . . . . .68 EK57
Fowey Cl, E1 . . . . .202 D2
Fowler Cl, SW11 . . . . .100 DD83
Fowler Rd, E7 . . . . .68 EG63
 N1 off Halton Rd 83 DP66
 Ilford IG6 . . . . .50 EV51
 Mitcham CR4 . . . . .140 DG96
Fowlers Cl, Sid. DA14
 off Thursland Rd 126 EY92
Fowlers Mead, Wok. (Chobham)
 GU24 off Windsor Rd 150 AS109
Fowlers Wk, W5 . . . . .79 CK70
Fowley Cl, Wal.Cr. EN8 . . . . .15 DZ34
Fowley Mead Pk, Wal.Cr. EN8 .15 EA34
Fownes St, SW11 . . . . .100 DE83
Foxacre, Cat. CR3
 off Town End Cl 176 DS122
Foxberry Rd, SE4 . . . . .103 DY83
Foxberry Wk, Grav. (Nthflt.)
 DA11 off Rowmarsh Cl 130 GD91
Foxborough Cl, Slou. SL3 . . . .93 AZ78
Foxborough Gdns, SE4 . . . . .123 EA86
Foxbourne Rd, SW17 . . . . . .120 DG89
Foxburrow Rd, Chig. IG7 . . . .50 EX50
Foxbury Av, Chis. BR7 . . . . .125 ER93
Foxbury Cl, Brom. BR1 . . . .124 EH93
 Orpington BR6
 off Foxbury Dr 164 EU106
Foxbury Dr, Orp. BR6 . . . . .164 EU107
Foxbury Rd, Brom. BR1 . . . .124 EH93

Fox Cl, Wey. KT13 . . . . .153 BR106
 Woking GU22 . . . . .167 BD115
Foxcombe, Croy. (New Adgtn.)
 CR0 . . . . .161 EB107
Foxcombe Cl, E6
 off Boleyn Rd 86 EK68
Foxcombe Rd, SW15 . . . . . .119 CU88
Foxcote, SE5 . . . . .102 DS78
Fox Covert, Lthd. (Fetch.)
 KT22 . . . . .171 CD124
Foxcroft Rd, SE18 . . . . . . .105 EP81
Foxdell, Nthwd. HA6 . . . . . . .39 BR51
Foxdell Way, Ger.Cr. (Chal.St.P.)
 SL9 . . . . .36 AY50
Foxearth Cl, West. (Bigg.H.)
 TN16 . . . . .178 EL118
Foxearth Rd, S.Croy. CR2 . . .160 DW110
Foxearth Spur, S.Croy. CR2 . .160 DW109
Foxes Dale, SE3 . . . . .104 EG83
 Bromley BR2 . . . . .143 ED97
Foxes Dr, Wal.Cr. EN7 . . . . . .14 DU29
Foxes Grn, Grays (Orsett)
 RM16 . . . . .111 GG75
Foxes La, Pot.B. (Cuffley)
 EN6 . . . . .13 DL28
Foxfield Cl, Nthwd. HA6 . . . . .39 BT51
Foxfield Rd, Orp. BR6 . . . . .145 ER103
Foxglove Cl, Sthl. UB1 . . . . . .78 BY73
 Staines (Stanw.) TW19 . . . .114 BK88
Foxglove Gdns, E11 . . . . . . .68 EJ56
 Purley CR8 . . . . .159 DL111
Foxglove La, Chess. KT9 . . . .156 CN105
Foxglove Rd, Rom. (Rush Grn.)
 RM7 . . . . .71 FE61
 South Ockendon RM15 . . . .91 FW71
Foxglove St, W12 . . . . .81 CT73
Foxglove Way, Wall. SM6 . . .141 DH102
Foxgrove, N14 . . . . .45 DL48
Fox Gro, Walt. KT12 . . . . . .135 BV101
Foxgrove Av, Beck. BR3 . . . .123 EB94
Foxgrove Dr, Wok. GU21 . . . .167 BA115
Foxgrove Path, Wat. WD19 . . .40 BX50
Foxgrove Rd, Beck. BR3 . . . .123 EB94
Foxhall Rd, Upmin. RM14 . . . .72 FQ64
Foxham Rd, N19 . . . . .65 DK62
Foxhanger Gdns, Wok. GU22
 off Oriental Rd 167 BA116
Foxherne, Slou. SL3 . . . . . . .92 AW75
Fox Hill, SE19 . . . . .122 DT94
 Keston BR2 . . . . .162 EJ106
Foxhill, Wat. WD24 . . . . .23 BU36
Fox Hill Gdns, SE19 . . . . . .122 DT94
Foxhills, Wok. GU21 . . . . . .166 AW117
Foxhills Cl, Cher. (Ott.) KT16 .151 BB107
Foxhills Ms, Cher. KT16 . . . .133 BB104
Foxhills Rd, Cher. (Ott.) KT16 .151 BA105
Foxhole Rd, SE9 . . . . .124 EL85
Fox Hollow Cl, SE18 . . . . . .105 ES78
Fox Hollow Dr, Bexh. DA7 . . .106 EX83
Foxholt Gdns, NW10 . . . . . . .80 CQ66
Foxhome Cl, Chis. BR7 . . . . .125 EN93
Foxhounds La, Grav. DA13 . .130 GA90
Fox Ho Rd, Belv. DA17 . . . . .107 FB77
Foxlake Rd, W.Byf. (Byfleet)
 KT14 . . . . .152 BM112
Foxlands Cl, Wat. WD25 . . . . .7 BU34
Foxlands Cres, Dag. RM10 . . .71 FC64
Foxlands La, Dag. RM10 . . . .71 FC64
Foxlands Rd, Dag. RM10 . . . .71 FC64
Fox La, N13 . . . . .45 DM48
 W5 . . . . .80 CL70
 Caterham CR3 . . . . .175 DP121
 Keston BR2 . . . . .162 EH106
 Leatherhead (Bkhm.)
 KT23 . . . . .170 BY124
 Reigate RH2 . . . . .184 DB131
Fox La N, Cher. KT16 . . . . . .133 BF102
Fox La S, Cher. KT16
 off Guildford St 133 BF102
Foxlees, Wem. HA0 . . . . . . .61 CG63
Foxley Cl, E8
 off Ferncliff Rd 66 DU64
 Loughton IG10 . . . . .33 EP40
Foxley Ct, Sutt. SM2 . . . . . .158 DC108
Foxley Gdns, Pur. CR8 . . . . .159 DP113
Foxley Hill Rd, Pur. CR8 . . . .159 DN112
Foxley La, Pur. CR8 . . . . . . .159 DK111
Foxley Rd, SW9 . . . . .101 DN80
 Kenley CR8 . . . . .159 DP114
 Thornton Heath CR7 . . . . .141 DP98
Foxleys, Wat. WD19 . . . . . . .40 BY48
Foxley Sq, SW9
 off Cancell Rd 101 DP80
Fox Manor Way, Grays
 RM20 . . . . .109 FV79
Foxmead Cl, Enf. EN2 . . . . . .29 DM41
Foxmoor Ct, Uxb. (Denh.) UB9
 off North Orbital Rd 58 BG58
Foxmore St, SW11 . . . . . . .100 DF81
Foxon Cl, Cat. CR3 . . . . . . .176 DS121
Foxon La, Cat. CR3 . . . . . . .176 DR121
Foxon La Gdns, Cat. CR3 . . .176 DS121
Fox Rd, E16 . . . . .86 EF71
 Slough SL3 . . . . .92 AX77
Fox's Path, Mitch. CR4 . . . . .140 DE96
Foxton Gro, Mitch. CR4 . . . .140 DD96
Foxton, Grays RM20 . . . . . .109 FX79
Foxwarren, Esher (Clay.)
 KT10 . . . . .155 CF109
Foxwell Ms, SE4
 off Foxwell St 103 DY83
Foxwell St, SE4 . . . . .103 DY83
Foxwood Chase, Wal.Abb.
 EN9 . . . . .31 ED35
Foxwood Cl, NW7 . . . . .42 CS49
 Feltham TW13 . . . . .115 BV90
Foxwood Grn Cl, Enf. EN1 . . .30 DS44
Foxwood Gro, Grav. (Nthflt.)
 DA11 . . . . .130 GE88
 Orpington BR6 . . . . .164 EW110
Foxwood Rd, SE3 . . . . .104 EF84
 Dartford (Bean) DA2 . . . . .129 FV90

Foy - Fur

Foyle Dr, S.Ock. RM15 ....91 FU71
Foyle Rd, N17 ....46 DU53
SE3 ....104 EE79
Frailey Cl, Wok. GU22 ....167 BB116
Frailey Hill, Wok. GU22 ...167 BB116
Framewood Rd, Slou. SL2,
SL3 ....74 AW66
Framfield Cl, N12 ......44 DA48
Framfield Ct, Enf. EN1 ....30 DS44
Framfield Rd, N5 ......65 DP64
W7 ....79 CE72
Mitcham CR4 ....120 DG94
Framlingham Cl, E5
off Detmold Rd 66 DW61
Framlingham Cres, SE9 ...124 EL91
Frampton Cl, Sutt. SM2 ...158 DA108
Frampton Pk Rd, E9 .....84 DW65
Frampton Rd, Epp. CM16 ...18 EU28
Hounslow TW4 ....116 BY85
Potters Bar EN6 ......12 DC30
Frampton St, NW8 .....82 DD70
Francemary Rd, SE4 ....123 EA85
Frances Av, Grays (Chaff.Hun.)
RM16 ....109 FW77
Frances Gdns, S.Ock. RM15 ..91 FT72
Frances Rd, E4 ....47 EA51
Frances St, SE18 ......105 EM77
Franche Ct Rd, SW17 ....120 DC90
Francis Av, Bexh. DA7 ...106 FA82
Feltham TW13 ....115 BU90
Ilford IG1 ....69 ER61
Francis Barber Cl, SW16
off Well Cl 121 DM91
Franciscan Rd, SW17 ....120 DF92
Francis Chichester Way,
SW11 ....100 DG81
Francis Cl, E14 ....204 F8
Epsom KT19 ....156 CR105
Shepperton TW17 ....134 BN98
Francisco Cl, Grays (Chaff.Hun.)
RM16 ....109 FW76
Francis Gro, SW19 .....119 CZ93
Francis Rd, E10 ......67 EC60
N2 off Lynmouth Rd 64 DF56
Caterham CR3 ......176 DR122
Croydon CR0 ....141 DP101
Dartford DA1 ....128 FK85
Greenford UB6 ......79 CJ67
Harrow HA1 ....61 CG57
Hounslow TW4 ......96 BX82
Ilford IG1 ....69 ER61
Orpington BR5 ......146 EX97
Pinner HA5 ....60 BW57
Wallington SM6 .....159 DJ107
Watford WD18 ......23 BV42
Francis St, E15 ....68 EE64
SW1 ....199 K8
Ilford IG1 ....69 ER61
Francis Ter, N19
off Junction Rd 65 DJ62
Francis Wk, N1
off Bingfield St 83 DM67
Francklyn Gdns, Edg. HA8 ..42 CN48
Francombe Gdns, Rom. RM1 .71 FG58
Franconia Rd, SW4 .....121 DJ85
Frank Bailey Wk, E12
off Gainsborough Av 69 EN64
Frank Burton Cl, SE7
off Victoria Way 104 EH78
Frank Dixon Cl, SE21 ....122 DS88
Frank Dixon Way, SE21 ...122 DS88
Frankfurt Rd, SE24 .....122 DQ85
Frankham St, SE8 .....103 EA80
Frankland Cl, SE16 .....202 E7
Rickmansworth (Crox.Grn.)
WD3 ....38 BN45
Woodford Green IG8 ....48 EJ50
Frankland Rd, E4 ......47 EA50
SW7 off Armstrong Rd ...100 DD76
Rickmansworth (Crox.Grn.)
WD3 ....23 BP44
Franklands Dr, Add. KT15 ..151 BF108
Franklin Av, Wal.Cr. (Chsht.)
EN7 ....14 DU30
Franklin Cl, N20 ......44 DC45
SE13 ....103 EB83
SE27 ....121 DP90
Kingston upon Thames
KT1 ....138 CN97
Franklin Cres, Mitch. CR4 ..141 DJ98
Franklin Ho, NW9 ......63 CT59
Franklin Pas, SE9 .....104 EL83
Franklin Rd, SE20 .....122 DW94
Bexleyheath DA7 .....106 EY81
Gravesend DA12 .....131 GK92
Hornchurch RM12 .....90 FJ65
Watford WD17 ......23 BW40
Franklins Ms, Har. HA2 ...60 CC61
Franklin Sq, W14
off Marchbank Rd 99 CZ78
Franklin's Row, SW3 ....198 E10
Franklin St, E3
off St. Leonards St 85 EB69
N15 ....66 DS58
Franklin Way, Croy. CR0 ..141 DL101
Franklyn Gdns, Ilf. IG6 ....49 ER51
Franklyn Rd, NW10 .....81 CT66
Walton-on-Thames KT12 .135 BU100
Frank Martin Ct, Wal.Cr.
EN7 ....14 DU30
Franks Av, N.Mal. KT3 ...138 CQ98
Franks La, Dart. (Hort.Kir.)
DA4 ....148 FN98
Frank St, E13 ....86 EG70
Frankswood Av, Orp. BR5 ..145 EP99
West Drayton UB7 .....76 BM72
Frank Towell Ct, Felt. TW14 .115 BU88
Franlaw Cres, N13 .....46 DQ49
Franmil Rd, Horn. RM12 ...71 FG60
Fransfield Gro, SE26 ....122 DV90
Frant Cl, SE20 ....122 DW94
Franthorne Way, SE6 ....123 EB89
Frant Rd, Th.Hth. CR7 ...141 DP99
Fraser Cl, E6 off Linton Gdns ..86 EL72

Fraser Cl, Bex. DA5
off Dartford Rd 127 FC88
Fraser Ho, Brent. TW8
off Green Dragon La 98 CM78
Fraser Rd, E17 ....67 EB57
N9 ....46 DV48
Erith DA8 ....107 FC78
Greenford UB6 ......79 CH67
Waltham Cross (Chsht.)
EN8 ....15 DY28
Fraser St, W4 ....98 CS78
Frating Cres, Wdf.Grn. IG8 ..48 EG51
Frays Av, West Dr. UB7 ...94 BK75
Frays Cl, West Dr. UB7 ...94 BK76
Frays Lea, Uxb. UB8 ....76 BJ68
Frays Waye, Uxb. UB8 ...76 BJ67
Frazer Av, Ruis. HA4 ....60 BW64
Frazer Cl, Rom. RM1 ....71 FF59
Frazier St, SE1 ....200 D5
Frean St, SE16 ....202 B6
Freda Corbett Cl, SE15
off Bird in Bush Rd 102 DU80
Frederica Rd, E4 ......47 ED45
Frederica St, N7
off Caledonian Rd 83 DM66
Frederick Andrews Ct, Grays
RM17 ....110 GD79
Frederick Cl, W2 ......194 D10
Sutton SM1 ....157 CZ105
Frederick Ct, NW2
off Douglas Ms 63 CY62
Frederick Cres, SW9 ....101 DP80
Enfield EN3 ....30 DW40
Frederick Gdns, Sutt. SM1 .157 CZ106
Frederick Pl, SE18 .....105 EP78
Frederick Rd, SE17
off Chapter Rd 101 DP78
Rainham RM13 ......89 FD68
Sutton SM1 ....157 CZ106
Frederick's Pl, EC2 ....197 K9
Fredericks Pl, N12 .....44 DC49
Frederick Sq, SE16 ....203 K1
Frederick's Row, EC1 ...196 F2
Frederick St, WC1 .....196 B3
Frederick Ter, E8
off Haggerston Rd 84 DT67
Frederick Vil, W7
off Lower Boston Rd 79 CE74
Frederic Ms, SW1 .....198 E5
Fredericks St, E17 .....67 DY57
Fred White Wk, N7
off Market Rd 83 DL65
Fred Wigg Twr, E11 ....68 EF61
Freeborne Gdns, Rain. RM13
off Mungo Pk Rd 89 FG65
Freedom Cl, E17 ......67 DY56
Freedom Rd, N17 .....46 DR54
Freedom St, SW11 .....100 DF82
Freedown La, Sutt. SM2 ..158 DC113
Freegrove Rd, N7 .....65 DL64
Freeland Pk, NW4 .....43 CY54
Freeland Rd, W5 ......80 CM73
Freelands Av, S.Croy. CR2 .161 DX109
Freelands Gro, Brom. BR1 .144 EH95
Freelands Rd, Brom. BR1 ..144 EH95
Cobham KT11 ....153 BV114
Freeland Way, Erith DA8
off Slade Grn Rd 107 FG81
Freeling St, N1
off Caledonian Rd 83 DM66
Freeman Cl, Nthlt. UB5 ...78 BY66
Shepperton TW17 ....135 BS98
Freeman Ct, N7
off Tollington Way 65 DL62
Freeman Dr, W.Mol. KT8 ..136 BZ97
Freeman Rd, Grav. DA12 ..131 GL90
Morden SM4 ....140 DD99
Freemans Cl, Slou. (Stoke P.)
SL2 ....74 AT65
Freemans La, Hayes UB3 ..77 BS73
Freemantle Av, Enf. EN3 ..31 DX43
Freemantle St, SE17 ....201 M10
Freeman Way, Horn. RM11 .72 FL58
★ Freemason's Hall (United
Grand Lodge of England),
WC2 ....196 A8
Freemasons Rd, E16 ....86 EH71
Croydon CR0 ....142 DS102
Free Prae Rd, Cher. KT16 .134 BG102
Freesia Cl, Orp. BR6
off Briarswood Way 163 ET106
Freethorpe Cl, SE19 ....142 DR95
Free Trade Wf, E1
off The Highway 86 EF73
Freezeland Way, Uxb. UB10
off Western Av 76 BN65
FREEZY WATER, Wal.Cr. ...31 DY35
★ Freightliners City Fm,
N7 ....83 DM65
Freightmaster Est, Rain.
RM13 ....107 FG76
Freke Rd, SW11 ......100 DG83
Fremantle Ho, Til. RM18
off Leicester Rd 111 GF81
Fremantle Rd, Belv. DA17 .106 FA77
Ilford IG6 ....49 EQ54
Fremont St, E9 ....84 DW67
French Apartments, The, Pur. CR8
off Lansdowne Rd 159 DN112
Frenchaye, Add. KT15 ...152 BJ106
Frenches, The, Red. RH1 ..184 DG132
Frenches Ct, Red. RH1
off Frenches Rd 184 DG132
Frenches Dr, Red. RH1
off The Frenches 184 DG132
Frenches Rd, Red. RH1 ...184 DG132
Frenchs, Cob. KT11 ....154 BW114
French Ordinary Ct, EC3 ..197 N10
French Pl, E1 ....197 N3
French St, Sun. TW16 ...136 BW96
Westerham TN16 .....189 ES128
French's Wells, Wok. GU21 .166 AV117
Frendsbury Rd, SE4 ....103 DY84
Frensham, Wal.Cr. (Chsht.)
EN7 ....14 DT27
Frensham Cl, Sthl. UB1 ...78 BZ70

Frensham Ct, Mitch. CR4
off Phipps Br Rd 140 DD97
Frensham Dr, SW15 ....119 CU89
Croydon (New Adgtn.)
CR0 ....161 EC108
Frensham Rd, SE9 .....125 ER89
Kenley CR8 ....159 DP114
Frensham St, SE15 ....102 DU80
Frensham Way, Epsom KT17 .173 CW116
Frere St, SW11 ....100 DE82
Freshfield Av, E8 ......84 DT66
Freshfield Cl, SE13
off Mischal Rd 103 ED84
Freshfield Dr, N14 .....45 DH45
Freshfields, Croy. CR0 ...143 DZ101
Freshfields Av, Upmin.
RM14 ....72 FP64
Freshford St, SW18 ....120 DC90
Freshmount Gdns, Epsom
KT19 ....156 CP111
Freshwater Cl, SW17 ....120 DG93
Freshwater Rd, SW17 ...120 DG93
Dagenham RM8 ......70 EX60
Fresh Wf Rd, Bark. IG11 ..87 EP67
Freshwood Cl, Beck. BR3 .143 EB95
Freshwood Way, Wall. SM6 .159 DH109
Freston Gdns, Barn. EN4 ..28 DG43
Freston Pk, N3 ....43 CZ54
Freston Rd, W10 ......81 CX73
W11 ....81 CX73
Freta Rd, Bexh. DA6 ....126 EZ85
★ Freud Mus, NW3 ......82 DC65
Frewin Rd, SW18 .....120 DD88
Friar Ms, SE27
off Prioress Rd 121 DP90
Friar Rd, Hayes UB4 ....78 BX70
Orpington BR5 ......146 EU99
Friars, The, Chig. IG7 ....49 ES49
Friars Av, N20 ....44 DE48
SW15 ....119 CT90
Brentwood CM15 .....55 GA46
Friars Cl, E4 ....47 EC48
N2 ....64 DD56
SE1 off Bear La 83 DP74
Brentwood (Shenf.) CM15 .55 FZ45
Ilford IG1 off Leeds Rd ..69 ER60
Northolt UB5
off Broomcroft Av 78 BX69
Friars Gdns, W3
off St. Dunstans Av 80 CR72
Friars Gate Cl, Wdf.Grn. IG8 .48 EG49
Friars La, Rich. TW9 ....117 CK85
Friars Mead, E14 .....204 D7
Friars Ms, SE9 ....125 EN85
Friars Orchard, Lthd. (Fetch.)
KT22 ....171 CD121
Friars Pl La, W3 ......80 CR73
Friars Ri, Wok. GU22 ...167 BA118
Friars Rd, E6 ....86 EK67
Virginia Water GU25 ...132 AX98
Friars Stile Pl, Rich. TW10
off Friars Stile Rd 118 CL86
Friars Stile Rd, Rich. TW10 .118 CL86
Friar St, EC4 ....196 G9
Friars Wk, N14 ....45 DH46
SE2 ....106 EX78
Friars Way, W3 ....80 CR72
Bushey WD23 ....24 BZ39
Chertsey KT16 ......134 BG100
Kings Langley WD4 ....6 BN30
Friars Wd, Croy. CR0 ...161 DY109
Friary, The, Wind. (Old Wind.)
SL4 ....112 AV86
Friary Cl, N12 ....44 DE50
Friary Ct, SW1 ....199 L3
Woking GU21 ....166 AT118
Friary Est, SE15 ......102 DU79
Friary Island, Stai. (Wrays.)
TW19 ....112 AW86
Friary La, Wdf.Grn. IG8 ..48 EG49
Friary Rd, N12 ....44 DD49
SE15 ....102 DU80
W3 ....80 CR72
Staines (Wrays.) TW19 ..112 AW86
Friary Way, N12 ......44 DE49
FRIDAY HILL, E4 ......47 ED47
Friday Hill, E4 ....48 EE47
Friday Hill E, E4 ......48 EE48
Friday Hill W, E4 ......48 EE47
Friday Rd, Erith DA8 ...107 FD78
Mitcham CR4 ....120 DF94
Friday St, EC4 ....197 H9
Frideswide Pl, NW5
off Islip St 65 DJ64
Friendly Pl, SE13
off Lewisham Rd 103 EB81
Friendly St, SE8 ......103 EA81
Friendly St Ms, SE8
off Friendly St 103 EA82
Friends Av, Wal.Cr. EN8 ..15 DX31
Friends Rd, Croy. CR0 ...142 DR104
Purley CR8 ....159 DP112
Friend St, EC1 ....196 F2
Friends Wk, Stai. TW18 ..113 BF92
Uxbridge UB8
off Bakers Rd 76 BK66
Friern Barnet La, N11 ...44 DE49
FRIERN BARNET, N11 ...44 DE49
Friern Barnet La, N11 ...44 DE49
N20 ....44 DE49
Friern Barnet Rd, N11 ...44 DF50
Friern Br Retail Pk, N11 ..45 DH51
Friern Ct, N20 ....44 DD48
Friern Mt Dr, N20 .....44 DC45
Friern Pk, N12 ....44 DC50
Friern Rd, SE22 ......122 DU86
Friern Watch Av, N12 ...44 DC49
Frigate Ms, SE8
off Watergate St 103 EA79
Frimley Av, Horn. RM11 ..72 FN60
Wallington SM6 .....159 DL106
Frimley Cl, SW19 .....119 CY89
Croydon (New Adgtn.)
CR0 ....161 EC108
Frimley Ct, Sid. DA14 ...126 EV92

Frimley Cres, Croy. (New Adgtn.)
CR0 ....161 EC108
Frimley Gdns, Mitch. CR4 ..140 DE97
Frimley Rd, Chess. KT9 ..156 CL106
Ilford IG3 ....69 ES62
Frimley Way, E1 ......85 DX70
Fringewood Cl, Nthwd. HA6 .39 BP53
Frinstead Ho, W10 .....81 CX73
Frinsted Cl, Orp. BR5 ...146 EX98
Frinsted Rd, Erith DA8 ...107 FD80
Frinton Cl, Wat. WD19 ...39 BV47
Frinton Dr, Wdf.Grn. IG8 ..47 ED52
Frinton Ms, Ilf. IG2
off Bramley Cres 69 EN58
Frinton Rd, E6 ....86 EK69
N15 ....66 DS58
SW17 ....120 DG93
Romford RM5 ....50 EZ52
Sidcup DA14 ....126 EY89
Friston Path, Chig. IG7 ...49 ES50
Friston St, SW6 ......100 DB82
Friswell Pl, Bexh. DA6 ...106 FA84
Fritham Cl, N.Mal. KT3 ..138 CS100
Frith Ct, NW7 ....43 CY52
Frith Knowle, Walt. KT12 .153 BV106
Frith La, NW7 ....43 CY52
Frith Rd, E11 ....67 EC63
Croydon CR0 ....142 DQ103
Frith St, W1 ....195 M9
Frithville Gdns, W12 ....81 CW74
Frithwald Rd, Cher. KT16 .133 BF101
Frithwood Av, Nthwd. HA6 .39 BS51
Frizlands La, Dag. RM10 ..71 FB63
Frobisher Cl, Bushey WD23 .24 CA44
Kenley CR8 off Hayes La .176 DR117
Pinner HA5 ....60 BX59
Frobisher Cres, EC2
off Beech St 84 DQ71
Staines TW19 ......114 BL87
Frobisher Gdns, Stai. TW19 .114 BL87
Frobisher Pas, E14 ....204 A2
Frobisher Rd, E6 .....87 EM72
N8 ....65 DN56
Erith DA8 ....107 FF80
Frobisher St, SE10 ....104 EE79
Frobisher Way, Grav. DA12 .131 GL92
Greenhithe DA9 .....109 FV84
Froggy La, (Uxb.) (Denh.) UB9 .57 BD62
Froghall La, Chig. IG7 ...49 ER49
FROGHOLE, Eden. 189 ER133
Froghole La, Eden. TN8 ..189 ER132
Frogley Rd, SE22 .....102 DT84
Frogmoor La, Rick. WD3 ..38 BK47
FROGMORE, St.Alb. 9 CE28
Frogmore, SW18 .....120 DA85
St. Albans AL2 ......9 CD27
Frogmore Av, Hayes UB4 ..77 BS69
Frogmore Cl, Sutt. SM3 ..139 CX104
Frogmore Dr, Wind. SL4 ..92 AS81
Frogmore Est, Ruis. HA4 ..60 BX64
Frogmore Gdns, Hayes UB4 .77 BS70
Sutton SM3 ....157 CY105
Frogmore Home Pk, St.Alb.
AL2 ....9 CD28
Frogmore Ind Est, NW10 ..80 CQ69
Hayes UB3 ....95 BR75
Frognal, NW3 ....64 DC64
Frognal Av, Har. HA1 ...61 CF56
Sidcup DA14 ....126 EU92
Frognal Cl, NW3 ......64 DC64
Frognal Ct, NW3 ......82 DC65
Frognal Gdns, NW3 ....64 DC63
Frognal La, NW3 ......64 DB64
Frognal Par, NW3
off Frognal Ct 82 DC65
Frognal Pl, Sid. DA14 ...126 EU93
Frognal Ri, NW3 ......64 DC63
Frognal Way, NW3 ....64 DC63
Froissart Rd, SE9 .....124 EK85
Frome Rd, N22
off Westbury Av 65 DP55
Frome St, N1 ....84 DQ68
Fromondes Rd, Sutt. SM3 .157 CY106
Front La, Upmin. RM14 ...73 FS59
Frostic Wk, E1 ....84 DT71
Froude St, SW8 ......101 DH82
Frowyke Cres, Pot.B. EN6 ..11 CU32
Fruen Rd, Felt. TW14 ...115 BT87
Fruiterers Pas, EC4
off Southwark Br 84 DQ73
Fryatt Rd, N17 ....46 DR52
Fry Cl, Rom. RM5 .....50 FA50
Fryent Cl, NW9 ....62 CN58
Fryent Cres, NW9 .....62 CS58
Fryent Flds, NW9 .....62 CS58
Fryent Gro, NW9 ......62 CS58
Fryent Way, NW9 .....62 CN57
Fryern Wd, Cat. CR3 ...176 DQ124
Frye's Bldgs, N1 off Upper St ..83 DN68
Frying Pan All, E1 .....197 P7
Fry Rd, E6 ....86 EK66
NW10 ....81 CT67
Fryston Av, Couls. CR5 ..159 DH114
Croydon CR0 ....142 DU103
Fuchsia Cl, Rom. (Rush Grn.)
RM7 ....71 FE61
Fuchsia St, SE2 ......106 EV78
Fulbeck Dr, NW9 ......42 CS53
Fulbeck Wk, Edg. HA8
off Knightswood Cl 42 CP47
Fulbeck Way, Har. HA2 ...40 CC54
Fulbourne Cl, Red. RH1
off Dennis Cl 184 DE132
Fulbourne Rd, E17 ....47 EC53
Fulbourne St, E1
off Durward St 84 DV71
Fulbrook Av, Add. (New Haw)
KT15 ....152 BG111
Fulbrook La, S.Ock. RM15 ..91 FT73
Fulbrook Rd, N19
off Junction Rd 65 DJ63
Fulford Gro, Wat. WD19 ..39 BV47
Fulford Rd, Cat. CR3 ...176 DR121
Epsom KT19 ....156 CR108
Fulford St, SE16 .....202 E5
FULHAM, SW6 ....99 CY82

⊖ Fulham Broadway 100 DA80
Fulham Bdy, SW6 .....100 DA80
Fulham Cl, Uxb. UB10
off Uxbridge Rd 77 BQ70
Fulham Ct, SW6
off Shottendane Rd ...100 DA80
★ Fulham FC (share Loftus Rd
Stadium with QPR FC)SW6 .99 CX81
Fulham High St, SW6 ...99 CY82
Fulham Palace Mus, SW6 .99 CX82
Fulham Palace Rd, SW6 ..99 CX80
W6 ....99 CW78
Fulham Pk Gdns, SW6 ...99 CZ82
Fulham Pk Rd, SW6 ....99 CZ82
Fulham Rd, SW3 ......100 DC79
SW6 ....99 CY82
SW10 ....100 DC79
Fullarton Cres, S.Ock. RM15 .91 FT72
Fullbrooks Av, Wor.Pk. KT4 .139 CT102
Fuller Cl, E2
off St. Matthew's Row ...84 DU70
Orpington BR6 ......163 ET106
Fuller Gdns, Wat. WD24
off Fuller Rd 23 BV37
Fuller Rd, Dag. RM8 ....70 EV62
Watford WD24 ......23 BV37
Fullers Av, Surb. KT6 ...138 CM103
Woodford Green IG8 ...48 EF52
Fullers Cl, Rom. RM5 ...51 FC52
Waltham Abbey EN9 ...16 EG33
★ Fuller's Griffin Brewery,
W4 ....99 CT79
Fullers Hill, West. TN16
off High St 189 ER126
Fullers La, Rom. RM5 ...51 FC52
Fullers Rd, E18 ......48 EF53
Fuller St, NW4 ....63 CW56
Fullers Way N, Surb. KT6 .138 CM104
Fullers Way S, Chess. KT9 .156 CL105
Fullers Wd, Croy. CR0 ...161 EA106
Fullers Wd La, Red. (S.Nutfld.)
RH1 ....185 DJ134
Fuller Ter, Ilf. IG1
off Oaktree Gro 69 EQ64
Fullerton Cl, W.Byf. (Byfleet)
KT14 ....152 BM114
Fullerton Dr, W.Byf. (Byfleet)
KT14 ....152 BL114
Fullerton Rd, SW18 ....120 DC85
Carshalton SM5 .....158 DE109
Croydon CR0 ....142 DT101
West Byfleet (Byfleet)
KT14 ....152 BM114
Fullerton Way, W.Byf. (Byfleet)
KT14 ....152 BL114
Fuller Way, Hayes UB3 ..95 BT78
Rickmansworth (Crox.Grn.)
WD3 ....22 BN43
Fullmer Way, Add. (Woodham)
KT15 ....151 BF110
Fullwell Av, Ilf. IG5, IG6 ..49 EM53
FULLWELL CROSS, Ilf. ...49 ER53
Fullwell Cross Roundabout, Ilf. IG6
off Fencepiece Rd 49 ER54
Fullwoods Ms, N1 .....197 L2
Fulmar Cl, Surb. KT5 ...138 CM100
Fulmar Rd, Horn. RM12 ..89 FG66
Fulmead St, SW6 .....100 DB81
FULMER, Slou. 56 AX63
Fulmer Cl, Hmptn. TW12 .116 BY92
Fulmer Common Rd, Iver SL0 .75 AZ65
Slough (Fulmer) SL3 ...75 AZ65
Fulmer Dr, Ger.Cr. SL9 ..56 AW60
Fulmer La, Ger.Cr. SL9 ..57 BB60
Slough (Fulmer) SL3 ...56 AY62
Fulmer Ri Est, Slou. SL3 ..75 AZ65
Fulmer Rd, E16 ......86 EK71
Gerrards Cross SL9 ...56 AY62
Slough (Fulmer) SL3 ...56 AY63
Fulmer Way, W13 .....97 CH76
Gerrards Cross SL9 ...56 AY58
Fulready Rd, E10 .....67 ED57
Fulstone Cl, Houns. TW4 ..96 BZ84
Fulthorp Rd, SE3 .....104 EF82
Fulton Ms, W2
off Porchester Ter 82 DC73
Fulton Rd, Wem. HA9 ...62 CN62
⇌ Fulwell, ...117 CD91
Fulwell Pk Av, Twick. TW2 .116 CB89
Fulwell Rd, Tedd. TW11 ..117 CD91
Fulwich Rd, Dart. DA1 ...128 FM86
Fulwood Av, Wem. HA0 ..80 CM67
Fulwood Cl, Hayes UB3 ..77 BT72
Fulwood Gdns, Twick. TW1 .117 CF86
Fulwood Pl, WC1 .....196 C7
Fulwood Wk, SW19 ....119 CY88
Furber St, W6 ....99 CV76
Furham Feild, Pnr. HA5 ..40 CA52
Furley Rd, SE15 ......102 DU80
Furlong Cl, Wall. SM6 ...140 DG102
Furlong Rd, N7 ......83 DN65
Furlough, The, Wok. GU22
off Pembroke Rd 167 BA117
Furmage St, SW18 ....120 DB87
Furneaux Av, SE27 ....121 DP92
Furner Cl, Dart. DA1 ...107 FF83
Furness Cl, Grays RM16 ..111 GH78
Furness Rd, NW10 ....81 CU68
SW6 ....100 DB82
Harrow HA2 ....60 CB59
Morden SM4 ....140 DB101
Furness Way, Horn. RM12 .71 FG64
Furnival Cl, Vir.W. GU25 ..132 AX100
Furnival St, EC4 ......196 D8
Furrow La, E9 ....66 DW64
Furrows, The, Uxb. (Hare.)
UB9 ....58 BJ57
Walton-on-Thames KT12 .136 BW103
Furrows Pl, Cat. CR3 ...176 DT123
Fursby Av, N3 ....44 DA51
Further Acre, NW9 ....43 CT54
Furtherfield, Abb.L. WD5 ..7 BS32
Furtherfield Cl, Croy. CR0 .141 DN100
Further Grn Rd, SE6 ...124 EE87
Furzebushes La, St.Alb. AL2 ..8 BY25
Furze Cl, Red. RH1 ...184 DF133
Watford WD19 ......40 BW50

Furzedown, SW17 . . . . .120 DG92
Furzedown Cl, Egh. TW20 . .112 AY93
Furzedown Dr, SW17 . . . . .121 DH92
Furzedown Rd, SW17 . . . . .121 DH92
  Sutton SM2 . . . . .158 DC107
Furze Fm Cl, Rom. RM6 . . . .50 EY54
Furze Fld, Lthd. (Oxshott)
  KT22 . . . . .155 CD113
Furzefield, Wal.Cr. (Chsht.)
  EN8 . . . . .14 DV28
Furzefield Cl, Chis. BR7 . . .125 EP93
Furzefield Rd, SE3 . . . . . . .104 EH79
Furzeground Way, Uxb. UB11 .77 BQ74
Furze Gro, Tad. KT20 . . . .173 CZ121
Furze Hill, Pur. CR8 . . . . . .159 DL111
  Redhill RH1
    off Linkfield La 184 DE133
  Tadworth (Kgswd.) KT20 .173 CZ120
Furzehill Rd, Borwd. WD6 . . .26 CN42
Furzehill Sq, Orp. (St.M.Cray)
  BR5 . . . . .146 EV98
Furze La, Pur. CR8 . . . . . . .159 DL111
Furze Rd, Add. KT15 . . . . .151 BF107
  Thornton Heath CR7 . . . . .142 DQ97
Furze St, E3 . . . . .85 EA71
Furze Vw, Rick. (Chorl.) WD3 .21 BC44
Furzewood, Sun. TW16 . . . .135 BU95
Fuschia Ct, Wdf.Grn. IG8
  off The Bridle Path 48 EE52
Fusedale Way, S.Ock. RM15 .91 FT73
Fyfe Way, Brom. BR1
  off Widmore Rd 144 EG96
Fyfield Cl, Brom. BR2 . . . . .143 ED98
Fyfield Ct, E7 . . . . .86 EG65
Fyfield Rd, E17 . . . . .67 ED55
  SW9 . . . . .101 DN83
  Enfield EN1 . . . . .30 DS41
  Rainham RM13 . . . . .89 FF67
  Woodford Green IG8 . . . . . .48 EJ52
Fynes St, SW1 . . . . .199 M8

G

Gabion Av, Purf. RM19 . . . .109 FR77
Gable Cl, Abb.L. WD5 . . . . . . .7 BS32
  Dartford DA1 . . . . .127 FG85
  Pinner HA5 . . . . .40 CA52
Gable Ct, SE26
  off Lawrie Pk Av 122 DV92
Gables, The, Bans. SM7 . . .173 CZ117
  Leatherhead (Oxshott)
    KT22 . . . . .154 CC112
  Wembley HA9 . . . . .62 CM62
Gables Av, Ashf. TW15 . . . .114 BM92
  Borehamwood WD6 . . . . . .26 CM41
Gables Cl, SE5 . . . . .102 DS81
  SE12 . . . . .124 EG88
  Gerrards Cross (Chal.St.P.)
    SL9 . . . . .36 AY49
  Slough (Datchet) SL3 . . . . .92 AU79
  Woking (Kgfld.) GU22
    off Kingfield Rd 167 AZ120
Gables Way, Bans. SM7 . . .173 CZ117
Gabriel Cl, Felt. TW13 . . . .116 BX91
  Grays (Chaff.Hun.) RM16 . .109 FW76
  Romford RM5 . . . . .51 FC52
Gabrielle Cl, Wem. HA9 . . . .62 CM62
Gabrielle Ct, NW3 . . . . .82 DD65
Gabriels Gdns, Grav. DA12 .131 GL92
Gabriel Spring Rd, Long.
  (Fawk.Grn.) DA3 . . . . . . .149 FR103
Gabriel Spring Rd (East), Long.
  (Fawk.Grn.) DA3 . . . . . . .149 FS103
Gabriel St, SE23 . . . . .123 DX87
Gabriel's Wf, SE1 . . . . .200 D2
Gad Cl, E13 . . . . .86 EH69
Gaddesden Av, Wem. HA9 . . .62 CM65
Gaddesden Cres, Wat. WD25 . .8 BX34
Gade Av, Wat. WD18 . . . . . .23 BS42
Gade Bk, Rick. (Crox.Grn.)
  WD3 . . . . .23 BR42
Gade Cl, Hayes UB3 . . . . . . .77 BV74
  Watford WD18 . . . . .23 BS42
Gadesden Rd, Epsom KT19 .156 CQ107
Gadeside, Wat. WD25
  off North Western Av 23 BS35
Gade Twr, Hem.H. HP3 . . . . . .6 BN25
Gade Valley Cl, Kings L. WD4 . .6 BN28
Gade Vw Gdns, Kings L. WD4 . .7 BQ32
Gadsbury Cl, NW9 . . . . .63 CT58
Gadsden Cl, Upmin. RM14 . .73 FS58
Gadswell Cl, Wat. WD25 . . . .24 BX36
Gadwall Cl, E16
  off Freemasons Rd 86 EH72
Gadwall Way, SE28 . . . . . .105 ER75
Gage Rd, E16
  off Malmesbury Rd 86 EE71
Gage St, WC1 . . . . .196 A6
Gainford Cl, N1
  off Richmond Av 83 DN67
Gainsborough Gdns, Grnf. UB6 .61 CE64
Gainsborough Av, E12 . . . . .69 EN64
  Dartford DA1 . . . . .128 FJ85
  Tilbury RM18 . . . . .111 GG81
Gainsborough Cl, Beck. BR3 .123 EA94
  Esher KT10
    off Lime Tree Av 137 CE102
Gainsborough Ct, N12 . . . . .44 DB50
  W12
    off Lime Gro 99 CW75
  Walton-on-Thames
    KT12 . . . . .153 BU105
Gainsborough Dr, Grav. (Nthflt.)
  DA11 . . . . .130 GD90
  South Croydon CR2 . . . . . .160 DU113
Gainsborough Gdns, NW3 . . .64 DD62
  NW11 . . . . .63 CZ59
  Edgware HA8 . . . . .42 CM54
  Isleworth TW7 . . . . .117 CD85
Gainsborough Ho, Enf. EN1
  off Ayley Cft 30 DU43

Gainsborough Ms, SE26
  off Panmure Rd 122 DV90
Gainsborough Pl, Chig. IG7 . .49 ET48
Gainsborough Rd, E11 . . . . . .68 EE59
  E15 . . . . .86 EE69
  N12 . . . . .44 DB50
  W4 . . . . .99 CT77
  Dagenham RM8 . . . . .70 EV63
  Epsom KT19 . . . . .156 CQ110
  New Malden KT3 . . . . . . .138 CR101
  Rainham RM13 . . . . .89 FG67
  Richmond TW9 . . . . .98 CM83
  Woodford Green IG8 . . . . . .48 EL51
Gainsborough Sq, Bexh. DA6
  off Regency Way 106 EX83
Gainsford Rd, E17 . . . . .67 DZ56
Gainsford St, SE1 . . . . .201 P4
Gairloch Rd, SE5 . . . . .102 DS82
Gaisford St, NW5 . . . . .83 DJ65
Gaist Av, Cat. CR3 . . . . . . .176 DU122
Gaitskell Ct, SW11 . . . . . . .100 DE82
Gaitskell Rd, SE9 . . . . .125 EQ88
Galahad Rd, Brom. BR1 . . .124 EG90
  N9 . . . . .46 DU47
Galata Rd, SW13 . . . . .99 CU80
Galatea Sq, SE15
  off Scylla Rd 102 DV83
Galbraith St, E14 . . . . .204 D6
Galdana Av, Barn. EN5 . . . . .28 DC41
Galeborough Av, Wdf.Grn.
  IG8 . . . . .47 ED52
Gale Cl, Hmptn. TW12
  off Stewart Cl 116 BY93
  Mitcham CR4 . . . . .140 DD97
Gale Cres, Bans. SM7 . . . . .174 DA117
Galena Ho, SE18
  off Grosmont Rd 105 ET78
Galena Rd, W6 . . . . .99 CV77
Galen Cl, Epsom KT19
  off Williams Evans Rd 156 CN111
Galen Pl, WC1 . . . . .196 A7
Galesbury Rd, SW18 . . . . . .120 DC86
Gales Gdns, E2 . . . . .84 DV69
Gale St, E3 . . . . .85 EA71
  Dagenham RM9 . . . . .88 EX67
Gales Way, Wdf.Grn. IG8 . . . .48 EL52
Galey Grn, S.Ock. RM15
  off Bovey Way 91 FV71
Galgate Cl, SW19 . . . . .119 CY88
Gallants Fm Rd, Barn. EN4 . .44 DE45
Galleon Boul, Dart. DA2 . . .109 FR84
Galleon Cl, SE16 . . . . .202 G4
  Erith DA8 . . . . .107 FD77
Galleon Ms, Grav. DA11
  off Rosherville Way 130 GE87
Galleon Wk, Grays (Chaff.Hun.)
  RM16 . . . . .109 FW77
Galleons Dr, Bark. IG11 . . . .88 EU69
Galleons La, Slou. (Geo.Grn.)
  SL3 . . . . .74 AX71
Gallery Gdns, Nthlt. UB5 . . . .78 BX68
Gallery Rd, SE21 . . . . .122 DR88
Galley Hill, Wal.Abb. EN9 . . . .16 EF30
Galley Hill Rd, Grav. (Nthflt.)
  DA11 . . . . .130 FZ85
  Swanscombe DA10 . . . . . .130 FZ85
Galley La, Barn. EN5 . . . . . . .27 CV41
Galleymead Rd, Slou. (Colnbr.) .
  SL3 . . . . .93 BF81
Galleywall Rd, SE16 . . . . . .202 D9
Galleywood Cres, Rom. RM5 .51 FD51
Galliard Cl, N9 . . . . .30 DW44
Galliard Rd, N9 . . . . .46 DU46
Gallia Rd, N5 . . . . .65 DP64
Gallions Cl, Bark. IG11 . . . . .88 EU69
Gallions Reach 87 EP72
Gallions Rd, SE7 . . . . .104 EH77
Gallions Roundabout, E16 . . .87 EP73
Gallions Vw Rd, SE28
  off Goldfinch Rd 105 ES75
Gallon Cl, SE7 . . . . .104 EJ77
Gallop, The, S.Croy. CR2 . . .160 DV108
  Sutton SM2 . . . . .158 DC108
Gallops, The, Tad. KT20 . . .183 CV126
Gallosson Rd, SE18 . . . . . .105 ES77
Galloway Chase, Slou. SL2 . . .74 AU73
Galloway Cl, Brox. EN10 . . . .15 DZ26
Galloway Dr, Dart. DA1
  off Lower Sta Rd 127 FE86
Galloway Path, Croy. CR0 . . .160 DR105
Galloway Rd, W12 . . . . .81 CU74
Gallows Cor, Rom. (Harold Wd.)
  RM3 . . . . .52 FK53
Gallows Hill, Kings L. WD4 . . . .7 BQ31
Gallows Hill La, Abb.L. WD5 . . .7 BQ32
Gallus Cl, N21 . . . . .29 DM44
Gallus Sq, SE3 . . . . .104 EH83
Galpins Rd, Th.Hth. CR7 . . .141 DM98
Galsworthy Av, E14 . . . . . . .85 DY71
  Romford RM6 . . . . .70 EV58
Galsworthy Cl, SE28 . . . . . . .88 EV74
Galsworthy Cres, SE3
  off Merriman Rd 104 EJ81
Galsworthy Rd, NW2 . . . . . . .63 CY63
  Chertsey KT16 . . . . .134 BG101
  Kingston upon Thames
    KT2 . . . . .118 CP94
Galsworthy Ter, N16
  off Hawksley Rd 66 DS62
Galton St, W10 . . . . .81 CY70
Galva Cl, Barn. EN4 . . . . . . .28 DG42
Galvani Way, Croy. CR0
  off Ampere Way 141 DM102
Galveston Rd, SW15 . . . . . .119 CZ85
Galway Cl, SE16
  off Masters Dr 102 DV78
Galway St, EC1 . . . . .197 J3
Gambetta St, SW8 . . . . . . .101 DH82
Gambia St, SE1 . . . . .200 G3
Gambles La, Wok. (Ripley)
  GU23 . . . . .168 BJ124
Gamble Rd, SW17 . . . . .120 DE91
Games Rd, Barn. EN4 . . . . . .28 DF41
Garford St, E14 . . . . .203 P1
Garganey Wk, SE28 . . . . . . .88 EX73
Gargery Cl, Grav. DA12
  off Damigos Rd 131 GM88
Gammons Fm Cl, Wat. WD24 .23 BT36
Gammons La, Brox. EN10 . . . .14 DT25

Gammons La, Wat. WD24 . . . .23 BV38
Gamuel Cl, E17 . . . . .67 EA58
Gander Grn Cres, Hmptn.
  TW12 . . . . .136 CA95
Gander Grn La, Sutt. SM1,
  SM3 . . . . .139 CY103
Ganders Ash, Wat. WD25 . . . .7 BU33
Gandhi Cl, E17 . . . . .67 EA58
Gandolfi St, SE15
  off St. Georges Way . . . . .102 DS
Gangers Hill, Cat. (Wold.)
  CR3 . . . . .187 EA127
  Godstone RH9 . . . . .187 EA127
Gant Ct, Wal.Abb. EN9 . . . . .16 EF34
Ganton St, W1 . . . . .195 K10
Ganton Wk, Wat. WD19
  off Woodhall La 40 BY49
GANTS HILL, Ilf. 69 EN57
Gants Hill 69 EN58
Gants Hill, Ilf. IG2 . . . . .69 EN58
Gantshill Cres, Ilf. IG2 . . . . . .69 EN57
GANWICK CORNER, Barn. . . .28 DB35
Gap Rd, SW19 . . . . .120 DA92
Garage Rd, W3 . . . . .80 CN72
Garbrand Wk, Epsom KT17 .157 CT109
Garbutt Pl, W1 . . . . .194 G6
Garbutt Rd, Upmin. RM14 . . .72 FQ61
Garden Av, Bexh. DA7 . . . . .106 FA83
  Mitcham CR4 . . . . .121 DH94
Garden City, Edg. HA8 . . . . . .42 CN51
Garden Cl, E4 . . . . .47 EA50
  SE12 . . . . .124 EH90
  SW15 . . . . .119 CV87
  Addlestone KT15 . . . . .152 BK105
  Ashford TW15 . . . . .115 BQ93
  Banstead SM7 . . . . .174 DA115
  Barnet EN5 . . . . .27 CW42
  Hampton TW12 . . . . .116 BZ92
  Leatherhead KT22 . . . . . .171 CJ124
  Northolt UB5 . . . . .78 BY67
  Ruislip HA4 . . . . .59 BS61
  Wallington SM6 . . . . .159 DL106
  Watford WD17 . . . . .23 BT40
Garden Cotts, Orp. BR5
  off Main Rd 146 EW96
Garden Ct, EC4 . . . . .196 D10
  N12 off Holden Rd 44 DB50
  Richmond TW9
    off Lichfield Rd 98 CM81
  Stanmore HA7
    off Marsh La 41 CJ50
  West Molesey KT8
    off Avern Rd 136 CB98
Garden End, Amer. HP6 . . . . .20 AS37
Gardeners Cl, N11 . . . . .44 DG47
Gardeners Rd, Croy. CR0 . . .141 DP102
Gardenia Rd, Enf. EN1 . . . . . .30 DS44
Gardenia Way, Wdf.Grn. IG8 . .48 EG50
Garden La, SW2
  off Christchurch Rd 121 DM88
  Bromley BR1 . . . . .124 EH93
Garden Ms, W2
  off Linden Gdns 82 DA73
  Slough SL1
    off Littledown Rd 74 AT74
Garden Pl, Dart. DA2 . . . . . .128 FK90
Garden Reach, Ch.St.G. HP8 . .20 AX41
Garden Rd, NW8 . . . . .82 DC69
  SE20 . . . . .142 DW95
  Abbots Langley WD5 . . . . . . .7 BS31
  Bromley BR1 . . . . .124 EH94
  Richmond TW9 . . . . .98 CN83
  Sevenoaks TN13 . . . . .191 FK122
  Walton-on-Thames KT12 . .135 BV100
Garden Row, SE1 . . . . .200 F7
  Gravesend (Nthflt.) DA11 . .131 GF90
Gardens, The, SE22 . . . . . .102 DU84
  Beckenham BR3 . . . . .143 EC96
  Esher KT10 . . . . .154 CA105
  Feltham TW14 . . . . .115 BR85
  Harrow HA1 . . . . .60 CC58
  Hatfield AL9 . . . . .11 CY27
  Pinner HA5 . . . . .60 BZ58
  Watford WD17 . . . . .23 BT40
Gardens of the Rose, St.Alb.
  AL2 . . . . .8 BY26
Garden St, E1 . . . . .85 DX71
Garden Ter, SW1 . . . . .199 M10
Garden Wk, EC2 . . . . .197 M3
  Beckenham BR3
    off Hayne Rd 143 DZ95
  Coulsdon CR5 . . . . .175 DH123
Garden Way, NW10 . . . . .80 CQ65
  Loughton IG10 . . . . .33 EN38
Gardiner Av, NW2 . . . . .63 CW64
Gardiner Cl, Dag. RM8 . . . . . .70 EX63
  Enfield EN3 . . . . .31 DX44
  Orpington BR5 . . . . .146 EW96
Gardner Cl, E11 . . . . .68 EH58
Gardner Gro, Felt. TW13 . . .116 BZ89
Gardner Pl, Felt. TW14 . . . .115 BW86
Gardner Rd, E13 . . . . .86 EH70
Gardners La, EC4 . . . . .197 H10
Gardnor Rd, NW3
  off Flask Wk 64 DD63
Gard St, EC1 . . . . .196 G2
Garendon Gdns, Mord. SM4 .140 DB101
Garendon Rd, Mord. SM4 . .140 DB101
Gareth Cl, Wor.Pk. KT4
  off Burnham Dr 139 CX103
Gareth Gro, Brom. BR1 . . . .124 EG91
Garfield Ms, SW11
  off Garfield Rd 100 DG83
Garfield Rd, E4 . . . . .47 ED46
  E13 . . . . .86 EF70
  SW11 . . . . .100 DG83
  SW19 . . . . .120 DC92
  Addlestone KT15 . . . . .152 BJ106
  Enfield EN3 . . . . .30 DW42
  Twickenham TW1 . . . . . . .117 CG88

Garibaldi St, SE18 . . . . .105 ES77
Garland Cl, Wal.Cr. EN8 . . . .15 DY31
Garland Rd, SE18 . . . . .105 ER80
  Stanmore HA7 . . . . .42 CL53
Garlands Ct, Croy. CR0
  off Chatsworth Rd 160 DR105
Garlands Rd, Lthd. KT22 . . .171 CH121
Garland Way, Cat. CR3 . . . .176 DR122
  Hornchurch RM11 . . . . . . .72 FL56
Garlichill Rd, Epsom KT18 . .173 CV117
Garlick Hill, EC4 . . . . .J10
Garlies Rd, SE23 . . . . .123 DY90
Garlinge Rd, NW2 . . . . .81 CZ65
Garman Cl, N18 . . . . .46 DR50
Garman Rd, N17 . . . . .46 DW52
Garnault Ms, EC1 . . . . .196 E3
Garnault Pl, EC1 . . . . .196 E3
Garnault Rd, Enf. EN1 . . . . . .30 DT38
Garner Cl, Dag. RM8 . . . . . . .70 EX60
Garner Dr, Brox. EN10 . . . . . .9 DY26
Garner Rd, E17 . . . . .47 EC53
Garners Cl, Ger.Cr. (Chal.St.P.)
  SL9 . . . . .36 AY51
Garners End, Ger.Cr. (Chal.St.P.)
  SL9 . . . . .36 AY51
Garners Rd, Ger.Cr. (Chal.St.P.)
  SL9 . . . . .36 AY51
Garner St, E2 off Coate St . . .84 DU68
Garnet Rd, NW10 . . . . .80 CS65
  Thornton Heath CR7 . . . . .142 DR98
Garnet St, E1 . . . . .F1
Garnett Cl, SE9 . . . . .105 EM83
  Watford WD24 . . . . .24 BX37
Garnett Dr, St.Alb. (Brick.Wd.)
  AL2 . . . . .8 BZ29
Garnett Rd, NW3 . . . . .64 DF64
Garnett Way, E17
  off McEntee Av 47 DY53
Garnet Wk, E6
  off Kingfisher St 86 EL71
Garnham Cl, N16
  off Garnham St 66 DT61
Garnham St, N16 . . . . .66 DT61
Garnies Cl, SE15 . . . . .102 DT80
Garnon Mead, Epp. CM16 . . .18 EX28
Garrad's Rd, SW16 . . . . . . .121 DK90
Garrard Cl, Bexh. DA7 . . . . .106 FA83
  Chislehurst BR7 . . . . .125 EP92
Garrard Wk, NW10
  off Garnet Rd 80 CS65
Garratt Cl, Croy. CR0 . . . . . .159 DL105
Garratt La, SW17 . . . . .120 DD91
  SW18 . . . . .120 DB86
Garratt Rd, Edg. HA8 . . . . . .42 CN52
Garratts La, Bans. SM7 . . . .173 CZ116
Garratts Rd, Bushey WD23 . . .40 CC45
Garratt Ter, SW17 . . . . .120 DE91
Garrett Cl, W3
  off Jenner Av 80 CR71
Garrett St, EC1 . . . . .197 J4
Garrick Av, NW11 . . . . .63 CY58
Garrick Cl, SW18 . . . . .100 DC84
  W5 . . . . .80 CL70
  Richmond TW9
    off The Green 117 CK85
  Staines TW18 . . . . .114 BG94
  Walton-on-Thames KT12 . .136 BW103
Garrick Cres, Croy. CR0 . . . .142 DS103
Garrick Dr, NW4 . . . . .43 CW54
  SE28 off Broadwater Rd 105 ER76
Garrick Gdns, W.Mol. KT8 . .136 CA97
Garrick Pk, NW4 . . . . .43 CX54
Garrick Rd, NW9 . . . . .63 CT58
  Greenford UB6 . . . . .78 CB70
  Richmond TW9 . . . . .98 CN82
Garrick St, WC2 . . . . .195 P10
  Gravesend DA11
    off Barrack Row 131 GH86
Garrick Way, NW4 . . . . .63 CX56
Garrison Cl, SE18
  off Red Lion La 105 EN80
  Hounslow TW4 . . . . .116 BZ85
Garrison La, Chess. KT9 . . . .155 CK108
Garrison Par, Purf. RM19
  off Comet Cl 108 FN77
Garrolds Cl, Swan. BR8 . . . .147 FD96
Garron La, S.Ock. RM15 . . . .91 FT72
Garry Cl, Rom. RM1 . . . . . . .51 FE52
Garry Way, Rom. RM1 . . . . . .51 FE52
Garsdale Cl, N11 . . . . .44 DG51
Garside Cl, SE28
  off Goosander Way 105 ER76
  Hampton TW12 . . . . .116 CB93
Garsington Ms, SE4 . . . . . . .103 DZ83
Garsmouth Way, Wat. WD25 . .24 BX36
Garson Cl, Esher KT10
  off Garson Rd 154 BZ107
Garson La, Stai. (Wrays.)
  TW19 . . . . .112 AX87
Garson Mead, Esher KT10 . .154 BZ106
Garson Rd, Esher KT10 . . . .154 BZ107
GARSTON, Wat. 24 BW35
Garston 24 BX35
Garston Cres, Wat. WD25 . . . .8 BW34
Garston Dr, Wat. WD25 . . . . . .8 BW34
Garston Gdns, Ken. CR8
  off Godstone Rd 176 DR115
Garston La, Ken. CR8 . . . . . .160 DR114
  Watford WD25 . . . . .8 BX34
Garston Pk Par, Wat. WD25 . . .8 BX34
Garter Way, SE16 . . . . .203 H5
Garth, The, N12
  off Holden Rd 44 DB50
  Abbots Langley WD5 . . . . . . .7 BR33
  Cobham KT11 . . . . .154 BY113
  Hampton (Hmptn.H.) TW12
    off Uxbridge Rd 116 CB93
  Harrow HA3 . . . . .62 CM58
Garth Cl, W4 . . . . .98 CR78
  Kingston upon Thames
    KT2 . . . . .118 CM92
  Morden SM4 . . . . .139 CX101
  Ruislip HA4 . . . . .60 BX60
Garth Ct, W4
  off Garth Rd 98 CR78
Garthland Dr, Barn. EN5 . . . .27 CV43

Garth Ms, W5
  off Greystoke Gdns 80 CL70
Garthorne Rd, SE23 . . . . . .123 DX87
Garth Rd, NW2 . . . . .63 CZ61
  W4 . . . . .98 CR79
  Kingston upon Thames
    KT2 . . . . .118 CM92
  Morden SM4 . . . . .139 CW100
  Sevenoaks TN13 . . . . .191 FJ128
  South Ockendon RM15 . . . .91 FW70
Garth Rd Ind Cen, Mord.
  SM4 . . . . .139 CX101
Garthside, Rich. TW10 . . . . .118 CL92
Garthway, N12 . . . . .44 DE51
Gartlett Rd, Wat. WD17 . . . . .24 BW41
Gartmoor Gdns, SW19 . . . .119 CZ88
Gartmore Rd, Ilf. IG3 . . . . . . .69 ET60
Garton Pl, SW18 . . . . .120 DC86
Gartons Cl, Enf. EN3 . . . . . . .30 DW43
Gartons Way, SW11 . . . . . .100 DC83
Garvary Rd, E16 . . . . .86 EH72
Garvock Dr, Sev. TN13 . . . .190 FG126
Garway Rd, W2 . . . . .82 DB72
Gascoigne Gdns, Wdf.Grn.
  IG8 . . . . .48 EE52
Gascoigne Pl, E2 . . . . .197 P3
Gascoigne Rd, Bark. IG11 . . .87 EQ67
  Croydon (New Adgtn.)
    CR0 . . . . .161 EC110
  Weybridge KT13 . . . . .135 BP104
Gascony Av, NW6 . . . . .82 DA66
Gascoyne Cl, Pot.B. EN6 . . . .11 CU32
  Romford RM3 . . . . .52 FK52
Gascoyne Dr, Dart. DA1 . . . .107 FF82
Gascoyne Rd, E9 . . . . .85 DX66
Gaselee St, E14 . . . . .204 E1
Gasholder Pl, SE11
  off Kennington La 101 DM78
Gaskarth Rd, SW12 . . . . . . .121 DH86
  Edgware HA8 . . . . .42 CQ53
Gaskell Rd, N6 . . . . .64 DF58
Gaskell St, SW4 . . . . .101 DL82
Gaskin St, N1 . . . . .83 DP67
Gaspar Cl, SW5
  off Courtfield Gdns 100 DB77
Gaspar Ms, SW5
  off Courtfield Gdns 100 DB77
Gassiot Rd, SW17 . . . . .120 DF91
Gassiot Way, Sutt. SM1 . . . .140 DD104
Gasson Rd, Swans. DA10 . . .130 FY86
Gastein Rd, W6 . . . . .99 CX79
Gaston Bell Cl, Rich. TW9 . . .98 CM83
Gaston Br Rd, Shep. TW17 . .135 BS99
Gaston Rd, Mitch. CR4 . . . .140 DG97
Gaston Way, Shep. TW17 . . .135 BR99
Gataker St, SE16 . . . . .202 E6
Gatcombe Ms, W5 . . . . .80 CM73
Gatcombe Rd, E16 . . . . .205 N2
  N19 . . . . .65 DK62
Gatcombe Way, Barn. EN4 . . .28 DF41
Gate Cl, Borwd. WD6 . . . . . . .26 CQ39
Gate End, Nthwd. HA6 . . . . . .39 BU52
Gateforth St, NW8 . . . . .194 B5
Gatehill Rd, Nthwd. HA6 . . . .39 BT52
Gatehope Dr, S.Ock. RM15 . .91 FT72
Gatehouse Cl, Kings.T. KT2 . .118 CQ94
Gatehouse Sq, SE1
  off Southwark Br Rd 84 DQ74
Gateley Rd, SW9 . . . . .101 DM83
Gate Ms, SW7 . . . . .198 C5
Gater Dr, Enf. EN2 . . . . .30 DR39
Gatesborough St, EC2 . . . . .197 M4
Gatesden Cl, Lthd. (Fetch.)
  KT22 . . . . .170 CC123
Gatesden Rd, Lthd. (Fetch.)
  KT22 . . . . .170 CC123
Gates Grn Rd, Kes. BR2 . . . .162 EG105
  West Wickham BR4 . . . . . .144 EF104
Gateshead Rd, Borwd. WD6 . .26 CM39
Gateside Rd, SW17 . . . . . . .120 DF90
Gatestone Rd, SE19 . . . . . .122 DS93
Gate St, WC2 . . . . .196 B8
Gateway, SE17 . . . . .102 DQ79
  Weybridge KT13
    off Palace Dr 135 BP104
Gateway, The, Wok. GU21 . .151 BB114
Gateway Arc, N1
  off Islington High St 83 DP68
Gateway Cl, Nthwd. HA6 . . . .39 BQ51
Gateway Ho, Bark. IG11
  off St. Ann's Rd 87 EQ67
Gateway Ind Est, NW10 . . . . .81 CT69
Gateway Ms, E8 . . . . .66 DT64
  off Shacklewell La 66 DT64
Gateway Retail Pk, E6 . . . . . .87 EP70
Gateway Rd, E10 . . . . .67 EB62
Gateways, The, SW3 . . . . . .198 C9
  Waltham Cross EN7 . . . . . . .14 DR28
Gatward Cl, N21 . . . . .29 DP44
Gatward Grn, N9 . . . . .46 DS47
Gatwick Rd, SW18 . . . . .119 CZ87

Gat - Gla

Gatwick Rd, Grav. DA12 ....131 GH90
Gatwick Way, Horn. RM12
  off Haydock Cl 72 FM63
Gauden Cl, SW4 ....101 DK83
Gauden Rd, SW4 ....101 DK82
Gaumont App, Wat. WD17 ..23 BV41
Gaumont Ter, W12
  off Lime Gro 99 CW75
Gauntlet Cl, Nthlt. UB5 ....78 BY66
Gauntlet Cres, Ken. CR8 ..176 DR120
Gauntlett Ct, Wem. HA0 ....61 CH64
Gauntlett Rd, Sutt. SM1 ..158 DD106
Gaunt St, SE1 ....200 G6
Gautrey Rd, SE15 ....102 DW82
Gautrey Sq, E6 ....87 EM72
Gavell Rd, Cob. KT11 .....153 BU113
Gavel St, SE17 ....201 L8
Gavenny Path, S.Ock. RM15 ..91 FT72
Gaveston Cl, W.Byf. (Byfleet)
  KT14 ....152 BM113
Gavestone Cres, SE12 ....124 EH87
Gavestone Rd, SE12 ......124 EH87
Gaveston Rd, Lthd. KT22 ..171 CG120
Gaviller Pl, E5 off Clarence Rd .66 DV63
Gavina Cl, Mord. SM4 ....140 DE99
Gavin St, SE18 ....105 ES77
Gaviots Cl, Ger.Cr. SL9 ....57 AZ60
Gaviots Grn, Ger.Cr. SL9 ..56 AY60
Gaviots Way, Ger.Cr. SL9 ..56 AY59
Gawber St, E2 ....84 DW69
Gawsworth Cl, E15
  off Ash Rd 68 EE64
Gawthorne Av, NW7
  off Lane App 43 CY50
Gawthorne Ct, E3
  off Mostyn Gro 85 EA68
Gay Cl, NW2 ....63 CV64
Gaydon Ho, W2 ....82 DB71
Gaydon La, NW9 ....42 CS53
Gayfere Rd, Epsom KT17 ..157 CU106
  Ilford IG5 ....69 EM55
Gayfere St, SW1 ....199 P7
Gayford Rd, W12 ....99 CT75
Gay Gdns, Dag. RM10 .....71 FC63
Gayhurst, SE17
  off Hopwood Rd 102 DR79
Gayhurst Rd, E8 ....84 DU66
Gayler Cl, Red. (Bletch.) RH1 .186 DT133
Gaylor Rd, Nthlt. UB5 .....60 BZ64
  Tilbury RM18 ....110 GE81
Gaynes Ct, Upmin. RM14 ..72 FP63
Gaynesford Rd, SE23 .....123 DX89
  Carshalton SM5 ....158 DF108
Gaynes Hill Rd, Wdf.Grn. IG8 .48 EL51
Gaynes Pk, Epp. CM16 .....19 EY31
Gaynes Pk Rd, Upmin. RM14 .72 FN63
Gaynes Rd, Upmin. RM14 ..72 FP61
Gay Rd, E15 ....85 ED68
Gaysham Av, Ilf. IG2 ......69 EN57
Gaysham Hall, Ilf. IG5 .....69 EP55
Gay St, SW15 ....99 CX83
Gayton Cl, Amer. HP6 .....20 AS35
  Ashtead KT21 ....172 CL118
Gayton Ct, Har. HA1 ......61 CF58
Gayton Cres, NW3 ....64 DD63
Gayton Rd, NW3 ....64 DD63
  SE2 off Florence Rd 106 EW76
  Harrow HA1 ....61 CF58
Gayville Rd, SW11 ....120 DF86
Gaywood Av, Wal.Cr. (Chsht.)
  EN8 ....15 DX30
Gaywood Cl, SW2 ....121 DM88
Gaywood Est, SE1 ....200 G7
Gaywood Rd, E17 ....67 EA55
  Ashtead KT21 ....172 CM118
Gaywood St, SE1 ....200 G7
Gaza St, SE17
  off Braganza St 101 DP78
Gazelle Glade, Grav. DA12 .131 GM92
Geariesville Gdns, Ilf. IG6 ..69 EP56
Geary Dr, Brwd. CM14 ....54 FW46
Geary Rd, NW10 ....63 CU64
Geary St, N7 ....65 DM64
G.E.C. Est, Wem. HA9 .....61 CK62
Geddes Pl, Bexh. DA6
  off Market Pl 106 FA84
Geddes Rd, Bushey WD23 ..24 CC42
Gedeney Rd, N17 ....46 DQ53
Gedling Pl, SE1 ....202 A6
Geere Rd, E15 ....86 EF67
Gees Ct, W1 ....194 G9
Gee St, EC1 ....197 H4
Geffrye Ct, N1 ....197 N1
Geffrye Est, N1
  off Stanway St 84 DS68
★ Geffrye Mus, E2 ....197 N1
Geffrye St, E2 ....84 DT68
Geisthorp Ct, Wal.Abb. EN9
  off Winters Way 16 EG33
Geldart Rd, SE15 ....102 DW80
Geldeston Rd, E5 ....66 DU61
Gellatly Rd, SE14 ....102 DW82
Gell Cl, Uxb. UB10 ....58 BM62
Gelsthorpe Rd, Rom. RM5 ..51 FB52
Gemini Gro, Nthlt. UB5
  off Javelin Way 78 BY69
General Gordon Pl, SE18 ..105 EP77
Generals Wk, The, Enf. EN3 .31 DY37
General Wolfe Rd, SE10 ...103 ED81
Genesis Business Pk, Wok.
  GU21 ....167 BC115
Genesis Cl, Stai. (Stanw.)
  TW19 ....114 BM88
Genesta Rd, SE18 ....105 EP79
Geneva Cl, Shep. TW17 ...135 BS99
Geneva Dr, SW9 ....101 DN84
Geneva Gdns, Rom. RM6 ..70 EY57
Geneva Rd, Kings.T. KT1 ..138 CL98
  Thornton Heath CR7 ....142 DQ99
Genever Cl, E4 ....47 EA50
Genista Rd, N18 ....46 DV50
Genoa Av, SW15 ....119 CW85
Genoa Rd, SE20 ....142 DW95
Genotin Rd, Enf. EN1 .....30 DR41

Genotin Ter, Enf. EN1
  off Genotin Rd 30 DR41
Gentian Row, SE13 ....103 EC81
Gentlemans Row, Enf. EN2 .30 DQ41
Gentry Gdns, E13
  off Whitwell Rd 86 EG70
Geoffrey Av, Rom. RM3 ....52 FN51
Geoffrey Cl, SE5 ....102 DQ82
Geoffrey Gdns, E6 ....86 EL68
Geoffrey Rd, SE4 ....103 DZ83
George Avey Cft, Epp. (N.Wld.Bas.)
  CM16 ....19 FB26
George Beard Rd, SE8 ....203 M9
George Comberton Wk, E12
  off Gainsborough Av 69 EN64
George Ct, WC2 ....200 A1
George Cres, N10 ....44 DG52
George Crook's Ho, Grays RM17
  off New Rd 110 GB79
George Downing Est, N16
  off Cazenove Rd 66 DT61
George V Av, Pnr. HA5 ....60 CA55
  off George V Av 60 CA55
George V Cl, Pnr. HA5
  off George V Av 60 CA55
  Rickmansworth (Sarratt)
  WD3 ....82 BG36
George Gange Way, Har. (Wldste.)
  HA3 ....61 CE55
GEORGE GREEN, Slou. 74 AX72
George Grn Dr, Slou. (Geo.Grn.)
  SL3 ....75 AZ71
George Grn Rd, Slou. (Geo.Grn.)
  SL3 ....74 AX72
George Gro Rd, SE20 .....142 DU95
★ George Inn, SE1
  off Borough High St 201 K3
George Inn Yd, SE1 ....201 K3
Georgelands, Wok. (Ripley)
  GU23 ....168 BH121
George La, E18 ....48 EG54
  SE13 ....123 EC86
  Bromley BR2 ....144 EH102
George Lansbury Ho, N22
  off Progress Way 45 DN53
George Loveless Ho, E2
  off Diss St 84 DT69
George Lovell Dr, Enf. EN3
  off Government Row 31 EA37
George Lowe Ct, W2
  off Bourne Ter 82 DB71
George Mathers Rd, SE11 ..200 F8
George Ms, NW1 ....195 K3
  Enfield EN2 off Sydney Rd .30 DR41
George Pl, N17
  off Dongola Rd 66 DS55
George Rd, E4 ....47 EA51
  Kingston upon Thames
  KT2 ....118 CP94
  New Malden KT3 ....139 CT98
George Row, SE16 ....202 B5
Georges Cl, Orp. BR5 .....146 EW97
Georges Dr, Brwd. CM15 ..54 FT43
Georges Mead, Borwd. (Elstree)
  WD6 ....25 CK44
George Sq, SW19
  off Mostyn Rd 139 CZ97
George's Rd, N7 ....65 DM64
Georges Rd, West. (Tats.)
  TN16 ....178 EK120
Georges Sq, SW6
  off North End Rd 99 CZ79
Georges Ter, Cat. CR3
  off Coulsdon Rd 176 DQ122
◆ George Street 142 DQ103
George St, E16 ....86 EF72
  W1 ....194 E8
  W7 off The Broadway ...79 CE74
  Barking IG11 ....87 EQ66
  Croydon CR0 ....142 DR103
  Grays RM17 ....110 GA79
  Hounslow TW3 ....96 BZ82
  Richmond TW9 ....117 CK85
  Romford RM1 ....71 FF58
  Southall UB2 ....96 BY77
  Staines TW18 ....113 BF91
  Uxbridge UB8 ....76 BK66
  Watford WD18 ....24 BW42
George's Wd Rd, Hat. AL9 ..12 DA26
George Tilbury Ho, Grays
  RM16 ....111 GH75
Georgetown Cl, SE19
  off St. Kitts Ter 122 DR92
Georgette Pl, SE10
  off King George St 103 EC80
Georgeville Gdns, Ilf. IG6 ..69 EP56
Georgewyver Cl, SW19
  off Beaumont Rd 119 CY87
George Yd, EC3 ....197 L9
  W1 ....194 G10
Georgiana St, NW1 ....83 DJ67
Georgian Cl, Brom. BR2 ..144 EH101
  Staines TW18 ....114 BH91
  Stanmore HA7 ....41 CG52
  Uxbridge UB10 ....58 BL63
Georgian Ct, SW16
  off Gleneldon Rd 121 DL91
  Wembley HA9 ....80 CN65
Georgian Way, Har. HA1 ..61 CD61
Georgia Rd, N.Mal. KT3 ..138 CQ98
  Thornton Heath CR7 ....141 DP95
Georgina Gdns, E2
  off Columbia Rd 84 DT69
Geraint Rd, Brom. BR1 ...124 EG91
Geraldine Rd, SW18 ......120 DC85
  W4 ....98 CN79
Geraldine St, SE11 ....200 F7
Gerald Ms, SW1 ....198 G8
Gerald Rd, E16 ....86 EF70
  SW1 ....198 G8
  Dagenham RM8 ....70 EZ61
  Gravesend DA12 ....131 GL87
Geralds Gro, Bans. SM7 ..157 CX114
Gerard Av, Houns. TW4
  off Redfern Av 116 CA87

Gerard Gdns, Rain. RM13 ..89 FE68
Gerard Rd, SW13 ....99 CT81
  Harrow HA1 ....61 CG58
Gerards Cl, SE16 ....102 DW78
Gerda Rd, SE9 ....125 EQ89
Gerdview Dr, Dart. DA2 ..128 FJ91
Germander Way, E15 ......86 EE69
Gernigan Ho, SW18 ....120 DD86
Gernon Cl, Rain. RM13
  off Jordans Way 90 FK68
Gernon Rd, E3 ....85 DY68
Geron Way, NW2 ....63 CV60
Gerpins La, Upmin. RM14 ..90 FM68
Gerrard Gdns, Pnr. HA5 ...59 BU57
Gerrard Pl, W1 ....195 N10
Gerrard Rd, N1 ....83 DP68
Gerrards Cl, N14 ....29 DJ43
GERRARDS CROSS 56 AX58
⇌ Gerrards Cross 56 AY57
Gerrards Cross Rd, Slou. (Stoke P.)
  SL2 ....74 AU66
Gerrards Mead, Bans. SM7
  off Garratts La 173 CZ117
Gerridge St, SE1 ....200 E5
Gerry Raffles Sq, E15
  off Great Eastern Rd 85 ED65
Gertrude Rd, Belv. DA17 ..106 FA77
Gertrude St, SW10 ....100 DC79
Gervase Cl, Wem. HA9 ....62 CQ62
Gervase Rd, Edg. HA8 .....42 CQ53
Gervase St, SE15 ....102 DV80
Gews Cor, Wal.Cr. (Chsht.)
  EN8 ....15 DX29
Ghent St, SE6 ....123 EA88
Ghent Way, E8 off Tyssen St .84 DT65
Giant Arches Rd, SE24 ....122 DQ87
Giant Tree Hill, Bushey (Bushey Hth.) .41 CD46
Gibbard Ms, SW19 ....119 CX92
Gibbfield Cl, Rom. RM6 ...70 EY55
Gibbins Rd, E15 ....85 EC66
Gibbon Rd, SE15 ....102 DW82
  W3 ....80 CS73
  Kingston upon Thames
  KT2 ....138 CL95
Gibbons Cl, Borwd. WD6 ..26 CL39
Gibbons Rents, SE1
  off Magdalen St 84 DS74
Gibbon Wk, SW15
  off Swinburne Rd 99 CU84
Gibbs Av, SE19 ....122 DR92
Gibbs Cl, SE19 ....122 DR92
  Waltham Cross (Chsht.)
  EN8 ....15 DX29
Gibbs Couch, Wat. WD19 ..40 BX48
Gibbs Grn, W14 ....99 CZ78
  Edgware HA8 ....42 CQ50
Gibbs Rd, N18 ....46 DW49
Gibbs Sq, SE19 ....122 DR92
Gibraltar Cl, Brwd. CM13
  off Essex Way 53 FW51
Gibraltar Cres, Epsom KT19 .156 CS110
Gibraltar Ho, Brwd. CM13 ..53 FW51
Gibraltar Wk, E2 ....84 DT69
Gibson Cl, E1 off Colebert Av .84 DW70
  N21 ....29 DN44
  Chessington KT9 ....155 CJ107
  Epping (N.Wld.Bas.) CM16
  off Beamish Cl 19 FC25
  Gravesend (Nthflt.) DA11 .131 GF90
  Isleworth TW7 ....97 CD83
Gibson Ct, Slou. SL3 .....93 AZ78
Gibson Gdns, N16
  off Northwold Rd 66 DT61
Gibson Pl, Stai. (Stanw.)
  TW19 ....114 BJ86
Gibson Rd, SE11 ....200 C9
  Dagenham RM8 ....70 EW60
  Sutton SM1 ....158 DB106
  Uxbridge UB10 ....58 BM63
Gibson's Hill, SW16 ......121 DN93
Gibson Sq, N1 ....83 DN67
Gibson St, SE10 ....104 EE78
Gidd Hill, Couls. CR5 .....174 DG116
Gidea Av, Rom. RM2 .....71 FG55
Gidea Cl, Rom. RM2 ......71 FG55
  South Ockendon RM15
  off Tyssen Pl 91 FW69
GIDEA PARK, Rom. 71 FG55
⇌ Gidea Park 72 FG56
Gideon Cl, Belv. DA17 ....107 FB77
Gideon Ms, W5 ....97 CK75
Gideon Rd, SW11 ....100 DG83
Gidian Ct, St.Alb. AL2 .....9 CD27
Giesbach Rd, N19 ....65 DJ61
Giffard Rd, N18 ....46 DS50
Giffin St, SE8 ....103 EA80
Gifford Gdns, W7 ....79 CD71
Gifford Pl, Brwd. CM14
  off Blackthorn Way 54 FX50
Giffordside, Grays RM16 ..111 GH78
Gifford St, N1 ....83 DL66
Gift La, E15 ....86 EE67
Giggs Hill, Orp. BR5 .....146 EU96
Giggs Hill Gdns, T.Ditt. KT7 .137 CG102
Giggs Hill Rd, T.Ditt. KT7 ..137 CG101
Gilbert Cl, SE18 ....105 EM81
  Swanscombe DA10 ......129 FX86
Gilbert Gro, Edg. HA8 .....42 CR53
Gilbert Ho, EC2
  off The Barbican 84 DQ71
  SE8 off McMillan St 103 EA79
Gilbert Pl, WC1 ....195 P7
Gilbert Rd, SE11 ....200 E9
  SW19 ....120 DC94
  Belvedere DA17 ....106 FA76
  Bromley BR1 ....124 EG94
  Grays (Chaff.Hun.) RM16 .109 FW76
  Pinner HA5 ....60 BX56
  Romford RM1 ....71 FF56
  Uxbridge (Hare.) UB9 ...38 BK54
Gilbert St, E15 ....68 EE63
  W1 ....194 G9

Gilbert St, Enf. EN3 ....30 DW37
  Hounslow TW3
  off High St 96 CC83
Gilbert Way, Croy. CR0
  off Beddington Fm Rd ...141 DL102
Gilbey Cl, Uxb. UB10 ......59 BP63
Gilbey Rd, SW17 ....120 DE91
Gilbeys Yd, NW1 ....82 DG66
Gilbourne Rd, SE18 ......105 ET79
Gilda Av, Enf. EN3 ....31 DY43
Gilda Cres, N16 ....66 DU60
Gildea Cl, Pnr. HA5 ....40 CA52
Gildea St, W1 ....195 J7
Gilden Cres, NW5 ....64 DG64
Gildenhill Rd, Swan. BR8 ..128 FJ94
Gildersome St, SE18
  off Nightingale Vale 105 EN79
Gilders Rd, Chess. KT9 ...156 CM107
Giles Cl, Rain. RM13 ......90 FK68
Giles Coppice, SE19 ......122 DT91
Giles Travers Cl, Egh. TW20 .133 BC97
Gilfrid Cl, Uxb. UB8
  off Craig Dr 77 BP72
Gilhams Av, Bans. SM7 ...157 CY112
Gilkes Cres, SE21 ....122 DS86
Gilkes Pl, SE21 ....122 DS86
Gillam Way, Rain. RM13 ..89 FG65
Gillan Grn, Bushey (Bushey Hth.)
  WD23 ....40 CC47
Gillards Ms, E17
  off Gillards Way 67 EA56
Gillards Way, E17 ....67 EA56
Gill Av, E16 ....86 EG72
Gill Cl, Wat. WD18 ....23 BQ44
Gill Cres, Grav. (Nthflt.)
  DA11 ....131 GF90
Gillender St, E3 ....85 EC70
  E14 ....85 EC70
Gillespie Rd, N5 ....65 DN62
Gillett Av, E6 ....86 EL68
Gillette Cor, Islw. TW7 ....97 CG80
Gillett Pl, N16 off Gillett St ..66 DS64
Gillett Rd, Th.Hth. CR7 ...142 DR98
Gillett St, N16 ....66 DS64
Gillfoot, NW1 ....195 L1
Gillham Ter, N17 ....46 DU51
Gilliam Gro, Pur. CR8 ....159 DN110
Gillian Cres, Rom. RM2 ...52 FJ54
Gillian Pk Rd, Sutt. SM3 ..139 CZ102
Gillian St, SE13 ....123 EB85
Gilliat Cl, Iver SL0
  off Dutton Way 75 BE72
Gilliat Rd, Slou. SL1 ......74 AS73
Gilliat's Grn, Rick. (Chorl.)
  WD3 ....21 BD42
Gillies St, NW5 ....64 DG64
Gilling Ct, NW3 ....82 DE65
Gillingham Ms, SW1 ......199 K8
Gillingham Rd, NW2 ......63 CY62
Gillingham Row, SW1 .....199 K8
Gillingham St, SW1 ......199 K8
Gillison Wk, SE16 ....202 C6
Gillman Dr, E15 ....86 EF67
Gillmans Rd, Orp. BR5 ...146 EV102
Gills Hill, Rad. WD7 ......25 CF35
Gills Hill La, Rad. WD7 ...25 CF36
Gills Hollow, Rad. WD7 ...25 CF36
Gill's Rd, Dart. (S.Darenth)
  DA2, DA4 ....149 FS95
Gill St, E14 ....85 DZ72
Gillum Cl, Barn. EN4 ......44 DF46
Gilmore Cl, Slou. SL3 .....92 AW75
  Uxbridge UB10 ....58 BN62
Gilmore Cres, Ashf. TW15 .114 BN92
Gilmore Rd, SE13 ....103 ED84
Gilmour Cl, Wal.Cr. EN7 ..30 DU35
Gilpin Av, SW14 ....98 CR84
Gilpin Cl, W2 off Porteus Rd .82 DC71
  Mitcham CR4 ....140 DE96
Gilpin Cres, N18 ....46 DT50
  Twickenham TW2 ....116 CB87
Gilpin Rd, E5 ....67 DY63
Gilpin Way, Hayes UB3 ...95 BR80
Gilroy Cl, Rain. RM13 .....89 FF65
Gilroy Way, Orp. BR5 ....146 EV101
Gilsland, Wal.Abb. EN9 ...32 EE35
Gilsland Rd, Th.Hth. CR7 ..142 DR98
Gilstead Ho, Bark. IG11 ...88 EV68
Gilstead Rd, SW6 ....100 DB82
Gilston Rd, SW10 ....100 DC78
Gilton Rd, SE6 ....124 EE90
Giltspur St, EC1 ....196 G8
Gilwell Cl, E4 off Antlers Hill .31 EB42
Gilwell La, E4 ....31 EC42
Gilwell Pk, E4 ....31 EC41
Gimcrack Hill, Lthd. KT22
  off Dorking Rd 171 CH123
Gippeswyck Cl, Pnr. HA5
  off Uxbridge Rd 40 BX53
⇌ Gipsy Hill 122 DS92
Gipsy Hill, SE19 ....122 DS92
Gipsy La, SW15 ....99 CU83
  Grays RM17 ....110 GC79
Gipsy Rd, SE27 ....122 DQ91
  Welling DA16 ....106 EX81
Gipsy Rd Gdns, SE27 ....122 DQ91
Giralda Cl, E16 off Fulmer Rd .86 EK71
Giraud St, E14 ....85 EB72
Girdlers Rd, W14 ....99 CX77
Girdwood Rd, SW18 ......119 CY87
Girling Way, Felt. TW14 ..95 BU83
Girona Cl, Grays (Chaff.Hun.)
  RM16 ....109 FW76
Gironde Rd, SW6 ....99 CZ80
Girtin Rd, Bushey WD23 ..24 CB43
Girton Av, NW9 ....62 CN55
Girton Cl, Nthlt. UB5 .....78 CC65
Girton Ct, Wal.Cr. EN8 ...15 DY30
Girton Gdns, Croy. CR0 ..143 EA104
Girton Rd, SE26 ....123 DX92
  Northolt UB5 ....78 CC65
Girton Vil, W10 ....81 CX72
Girton Way, Rick. (Crox.Grn.)
  WD3 ....23 BQ43
Gisborne Gdns, Rain. RM13 .89 FF69

Gisbourne Cl, Wall. SM6 ..141 DK104
Gisburne Way, Wat. WD24 ..23 BU37
Gisburn Rd, N8 ....65 DM56
Gissing Wk, N1 off Lofting Rd .83 DN65
Gittens Cl, Brom. BR1 ....124 EF91
Given Wilson Wk, E13 .....86 EF68
Glacier Way, Wem. HA0 ...79 CK68
Gladbeck Way, Enf. EN2 ..29 DP42
Gladding Rd, E12 ....68 EK63
  Waltham Cross (Chsht.)
  EN7 ....13 DP25
Glade, The, N21 ....29 DM44
  SE7 ....104 EJ80
  Brentwood CM13 ....55 GA46
  Bromley BR1 ....144 EK96
  Coulsdon CR5 ....175 DN119
  Croydon CR0 ....143 DX99
  Enfield EN2 ....29 DN41
  Epsom KT17 ....157 CU106
  Gerrards Cross SL9 .....56 AX60
  Ilford IG5 ....49 EM53
  Leatherhead (Fetch.) KT22 .170 CA122
  Sevenoaks TN13 ....191 FH123
  Staines TW18 ....114 BH94
  Sutton SM2 ....157 CY109
  Tadworth KT20 ....174 DA121
  Upminster RM14 ....72 FQ64
  West Byfleet KT14 .....151 BE113
  West Wickham BR4 ....143 EB104
  Woodford Green IG8 ...48 EH48
Glade Cl, Surb. KT6 ......137 CK103
Glade Ct, Ilf. IG5
  off The Glade 49 EM53
Glade Gdns, Croy. CR0 ...143 DY101
Glade La, Sthl. UB2 ......96 CB75
Glades, The, Grav. DA12 ..131 GK93
Gladeside, N21 ....29 DM44
  Croydon CR0 ....143 DX100
Gladeside Cl, Chess. KT9
  off Leatherhead Rd 155 CK108
Gladeside Ct, Warl. CR6 ..176 DV120
Glademore Rd, N15 ......66 DT58
Glade Spur, Tad. KT20 ...174 DB121
Glades Shop Cen, The, Brom.
  BR1 ....144 EG96
Gladeswood Rd, Belv. DA17 .107 FB77
Gladeway, The, Wal.Abb. EN9 .15 ED33
Gladiator St, SE23 ....123 DY86
Glading Ter, N16 ....66 DT62
Gladioli Cl, Hmptn. TW12
  off Gresham Rd 116 CA93
Gladsdale Dr, Pnr. HA5 ...59 BU56
Gladsmuir Cl, Walt. KT12 ..136 BW103
Gladsmuir Rd, N19 ....65 DJ60
  Barnet EN5 ....27 CY40
Gladstone Av, E12 ....86 EL66
  N22 ....45 DN54
  Feltham TW14 ....115 BU86
  Twickenham TW2 ......117 CD87
Gladstone Ct, SW19
  off Gladstone Rd 120 DA94
Gladstone Gdns, Houns. TW3
  off Palmerston Rd 96 CC81
Gladstone Ms, N22
  off Pelham Rd 45 DN54
  NW6 off Cavendish Rd ..81 CZ66
  SE20 ....122 DW94
Gladstone Par, NW2
  off Edgware Rd 63 CV60
Gladstone Pk Gdns, NW2 ..63 CV62
Gladstone Pl, E3
  off Roman Rd 85 DZ68
  Barnet EN5 ....27 CX42
Gladstone Rd, SW19 ......120 DA94
  W4 off Acton La 98 CR76
  Ashtead KT21 ....171 CK118
  Buckhurst Hill IG9 .....48 EH46
  Croydon CR0 ....142 DR101
  Dartford DA1 ....128 FM86
  Kingston upon Thames
  KT1 ....138 CN97
  Orpington BR6 ....163 EQ106
  Southall UB2 ....96 BY76
  Surbiton KT6 ....137 CK103
  Watford WD17 ....24 BW41
Gladstone St, SE1 ....200 F6
Gladstone Ter, SE27 .....122 DQ91
  SW8 ....101 DH81
Gladstone Way, Har. (Wldste.)
  HA3 ....61 CE55
Gladwell Rd, N8 ....65 DM58
  Bromley BR1 ....124 EG93
Gladwyn Rd, SW15 ....99 CX83
Gladys Rd, NW6 ....82 DA66
Glaisher St, SE8 ....103 EB79
Glaisyer Way, Iver SL0 ....75 BC68
Glamis Cl, Wal.Cr. (Chsht.)
  EN7 ....14 DU29
Glamis Cres, Hayes UB3 ..95 BQ76
Glamis Dr, Horn. RM11 ...72 FL60
Glamis Pl, E1 ....84 DW73
Glamis Rd, E1 ....84 DW73
Glamis Way, Nthlt. UB5 ...78 CC65
Glamorgan Cl, Mitch. CR4 .141 DL97
Glamorgan Rd, Kings.T. KT1 .117 CJ94
Glanfield Rd, Beck. BR3 ..143 DZ98
Glanleam Rd, Stan. HA7 ..41 CK49
Glanmead, Brwd. CM15 ...54 FY46
Glanmor Rd, Slou. SL2 ...74 AV73
Glanthams Cl, Brwd. CM15 .54 FY47
Glanthams Rd, Brwd. CM15 .55 FZ47
Glanty, The, Egh. TW20 ..113 BB91
Glanville Dr, Horn. RM11 ..72 FM60
Glanville Rd, SW2 ....121 DL85
  Bromley BR2 ....144 EH97
Glasbrook Av, Twick. TW2 .116 BZ88
Glasbrook Rd, SE9 ....124 EK87
Glaserton Rd, N16 ....66 DS59
Glasford St, SW17 ....120 DF93
Glasgow Ho, W9 ....82 DB68
Glasgow Rd, E13 ....86 EH68
  N18 off Aberdeen Rd ...46 DV50
Glasgow Ter, SW1 ....101 DJ78
Glasse Cl, W13 ....79 CG73
Glasshill St, SE1 ....200 G4
Glasshouse Cl, Uxb. UB8
  off Harlington Rd 77 BP71

Glasshouse Flds, E1 . . . . .85 DX73
Glasshouse St, W1 . . . . .199 L1
Glasshouse Wk, SE11 . . . . .200 A10
Glasshouse Yd, EC1 . . . . .197 H6
Glasslyn Rd, N8 . . . . .65 DK63
Glassmill La, Brom. BR2 . . . . . . .144 EF96
Glass St, E2 off Coventry Rd .84 DV70
Glass Yd, SE18
  off Woolwich High St 105 EN76
Glastonbury Av, Wdf.Grn. IG8 .48 EK52
Glastonbury Cl, Orp. BR5 .146 EW102
Glastonbury Pl, E1
  off Sutton St 84 DW72
Glastonbury Rd, N9 . . . . .46 DU46
  Morden SM4 . . . . .140 DA101
Glastonbury St, NW6 . . . . .63 CZ64
Glaucus St, E3 . . . . .85 EB71
Glazbury Rd, W14 . . . . .99 CY77
Glazebrook Cl, SE21 . . . . .122 DR89
Glazebrook Rd, Tedd. TW11 .117 CF94
Glebe, The, SE3 . . . . .104 EE83
  SW16 . . . . .121 DK91
  Chislehurst BR7 . . . . .145 EQ95
  Kings Langley WD4 . . . . . . .6 BN29
  Watford WD25 . . . . .8 BW33
  West Drayton UB7 . . . . .94 BM77
  Worcester Park KT4 . . . . . .139 CT102
Glebe Av, Enf. EN2 . . . . .29 DP41
  Harrow HA3 . . . . .62 CL55
  Mitcham CR4 . . . . .140 DE96
  Ruislip HA4 . . . . .77 BV65
  Uxbridge UB10 . . . . .59 BQ63
  Woodford Green IG8 . . . . . . .48 EG51
Glebe Cl, W4 off Glebe St 98 CS78
  Gerrards Cross (Chal.St.P)
    SL9 . . . . .36 AX52
  South Croydon CR2 . . . . . .160 DT111
  Uxbridge UB10 . . . . .59 BQ63
Glebe Cotts, Sutt. SM1
  off Vale Rd 158 DB105
  Westerham (Brasted)
    TN16 . . . . .180 EV123
Glebe Ct, W7 . . . . .79 CD73
  Coulsdon CR5
    off Whitethorn Av 175 DH115
  Mitcham CR4 . . . . .140 DF97
  Sevenoaks TN13 . . . . .191 FH126
  Stanmore HA7
    off Oak La 41 CJ50
Glebe Cres, NW4 . . . . .63 CW56
  Harrow HA3 . . . . .62 CL55
Glebefield, The, Sev. TN13 .190 FF123
Glebe Gdns, N.Mal. KT3 . . . .138 CS101
  West Byfleet (Byfleet)
    KT14 . . . . .152 BK114
Glebe Ho Dr, Brom. BR2 .144 EH102
Glebe Hyrst, SE19
  off Giles Coppice 122 DT91
  South Croydon CR2 . . . . . .160 DT112
Glebeland Gdns, Shep.
  TW17 . . . . .135 BQ100
Glebelands, Chig. IG7 . . . . . . .50 EV48
  Dartford DA1 . . . . .107 FF84
  Esher (Clay.) KT10 . . . . . . .155 CF109
  West Molesey KT8 . . . . . . .136 CB99
Glebelands Av, E18 . . . . .48 EG54
  Ilford IG2 . . . . .69 ER59
Glebelands Cl, SE5
  off Grove Hill Rd 102 DS83
  Woodford Green IG8 . . . . . . .48 EG51
Glebe La, Barn. EN5 . . . . .27 CU43
  Harrow HA3 . . . . .62 CL56
  Sevenoaks TN13 . . . . .191 FH126
Glebe Path, Mitch. CR4 . . . . .140 DE97
Glebe Pl, SW3 . . . . .100 DE79
  Dartford (Hort.Kir.) DA4 .148 FQ98
Glebe Rd, E8
  off Middleton Rd 84 DT66
  N3 . . . . .44 DC53
  N8 . . . . .65 DM56
  NW10 . . . . .81 CT65
  SW13 . . . . .99 CU82
  Ashtead KT21 . . . . .171 CK118
  Bromley BR1 . . . . .144 EG95
  Carshalton SM5 . . . . .158 DF107
  Dagenham RM10 . . . . .89 FB65
  Egham TW20 . . . . .113 BC93
  Gerrards Cross (Chal.St.P)
    SL9 . . . . .36 AW53
  Gravesend DA11 . . . . .131 GF88
  Hayes UB3 . . . . .77 BT74
  Rainham RM13 . . . . .90 FJ69
  Redhill RH1 . . . . .175 DH124
  Staines TW18 . . . . .114 BH93
  Stanmore HA7 . . . . .41 CJ50
  Sutton SM2 . . . . .157 CY109
  Uxbridge UB8 . . . . .76 BJ68
  Warlingham CR6 . . . . .177 DX117
  Windsor (Old Wind.) SL4 .112 AV85
Glebe Side, Twick. TW1 . . . . .117 CF86
Glebe St, W4 . . . . .98 CS78
Glebe Ter, E3 off Bow Rd 85 EA69
Glebe Way, Erith DA8 . . . . . . .107 FE78
  Feltham TW13 . . . . .116 CA90
  Hornchurch RM11 . . . . .72 FL59
  South Croydon CR2 . . . . . .160 DT111
  West Wickham BR4 . . . . . .E6 EC103
Glebeway, Wdf.Grn. IG8 . . . . .48 EJ50
Gledhow Gdns, SW5 . . . . .100 DC77
Gledhow Wd, Tad. KT20 .174 DB121
Gledstanes Rd, W14 . . . . .99 CY78
Gledwood Av, Hayes UB4 ..77 BT71
Gledwood Cres, Hayes UB4 .77 BT71
Gledwood Dr, Hayes UB4 ..77 BT71
Gledwood Gdns, Hayes UB4 .77 BT71
Gleed Av, Bushey (Bushey Hth.)
  WD23 . . . . .41 CD47
Gleeson Dr, Orp. BR6 . . . . . . .163 ET106
Gleeson Ms, Add. KT15 .152 BJ105
Glegg Pl, SW15 . . . . .99 CX84
Glen, The, Add. KT15 . . . . . . .151 BF106
  Bromley BR2 . . . . .144 EE96
  Croydon CR0 . . . . .143 DX103
  Enfield EN2 . . . . .29 DP42
  Northwood HA6 . . . . .39 BR52
  Orpington BR6 . . . . .145 EM104

Glen, The, Pnr. HA5 . . . . .60 BY59
  Pinner (Eastcote) HA5 . . . . .59 BV57
  Rainham RM13 . . . . .90 FJ70
  Slough SL3 . . . . .92 AW77
  Southall UB2 . . . . .96 BZ78
  Wembley HA9 . . . . .61 CK63
Glenaffric Av, E14 . . . . .204 F9
Glen Albyn Rd, SW19 . . . . . . .119 CX89
Glenalla Rd, Ruis. HA4 . . . . . .59 BT59
Glenalmond Rd, Har. HA3 ..62 CL56
Glenalvon Way, SE18 . . . . . . .104 EL77
Glena Mt, Sutt. SM1 . . . . .158 DC105
Glenarm Rd, E5 . . . . .66 DW64
Glen Av, Ashf. TW15 . . . . .114 BN91
Glenavon Cl, Esher (Clay.)
  KT10 . . . . .155 CG108
Glenavon Gdns, Slou. SL3 ..92 AW77
Glenavon Rd, E15 . . . . .86 EE66
Glenbarr Cl, SE9
  off Dumbreck Rd 105 EP83
Glenbow Rd, Brom. BR1 .124 EE93
Glenbrook N, Enf. EN2 . . . . . .29 DM42
Glenbrook Rd, NW6 . . . . .64 DA64
Glenbrook S, Enf. EN2 . . . . . .29 DM42
Glenbuck Ct, Surb. KT6
  off Glenbuck Rd 137 CK100
Glenbuck Rd, Surb. KT6 .137 CK100
Glenburnie Rd, SW17 . . . . . . .120 DF90
Glencairn Dr, W5 . . . . .79 CH70
Glencairn Rd, SW16 . . . . .141 DL95
Glen Cl, Shep. TW17 . . . . .134 BN98
  Tadworth (Kgswd.) KT20 .173 CY123
Glencoe Av, Ilf. IG2 . . . . .69 ER59
Glencoe Dr, Dag. RM10 . . . . .70 FA63
Glencoe Rd, Bushey WD23 ..24 CA44
  Hayes UB4 . . . . .78 BX71
  Weybridge KT13 . . . . .134 BN104
Glencorse Grn, Wat. WD19
  off Caldwell Rd 40 BX49
Glen Ct, Stai. TW18
  off Riverside Dr 113 BF94
Glen Cres, Wdf.Grn. IG8 . . . . .48 EH51
Glendale, Swan. BR8 . . . . .147 FF99
Glendale Av, N22 . . . . .45 DN52
  Edgware HA8 . . . . .42 CM49
  Romford RM6 . . . . .70 EW59
Glendale Cl, SE9
  off Dumbreck Rd 105 EN83
  Brentwood CM15 . . . . .54 FY45
  Woking GU21 . . . . .166 AW118
Glendale Dr, SW19 . . . . .119 CZ92
Glendale Gdns, Wem. HA9 ..61 CK60
Glendale Ms, Beck. BR3 . . . . .143 EB95
Glendale Ri, Ken. CR8 . . . . . .175 DP115
Glendale Rd, Erith DA8 . . . . . .107 FC77
  Gravesend (Nthflt.) DA11 .130 GE91
Glendale Wk, Wal.Cr. (Chsht.)
  EN8 . . . . .15 DY30
Glendale Way, SE28 . . . . .88 EW73
Glendall St, SW9 . . . . .101 DM84
Glendarvon St, SW15 . . . . . . .99 CX83
Glendevon Cl, Edg. HA8
  off Tayside Dr 42 CP48
Glendish Rd, N17 . . . . .46 DU53
Glendor Gdns, NW7 . . . . .42 CR49
Glendower Cres, Orp. BR6 .146 EU100
Glendower Gdns, SW14
  off Glendower Rd 98 CR83
Glendower Pl, SW7 . . . . .100 DD77
Glendower Rd, E4 . . . . .47 ED46
  SW14 . . . . .98 CR83
Glendown Rd, SE2 . . . . .106 EU78
Glendun Rd, W3 . . . . .80 CS73
Gleneagle Ms, SW16
  off Ambleside Av 121 DK92
Gleneagle Rd, SW16 . . . . .121 DK92
Gleneagles, Stan. HA7 . . . . . .41 CH51
Gleneagles Cl, SE16
  off Ryder Dr 102 DV78
  Orpington BR6 . . . . .145 ER102
  Romford RM3 . . . . .52 FM52
  Staines (Stanw.) TW19 .114 BK86
  Watford WD19 . . . . .40 BX49
Gleneagles Grn, Orp. BR6
  off Tandridge Dr 145 ER102
Gleneagles Twr, Sthl. UB1 ..78 CC72
Gleneldon Ms, SW16 . . . . . . .121 DL91
Gleneldon Rd, SW16 . . . . .121 DL91
Glenelg Rd, SW2 . . . . .121 DL85
Glenesk Rd, SE9 . . . . .105 EN83
Glenfarg Rd, SE6 . . . . .123 ED88
Glenfield Cres, Ruis. HA4 ..59 BR59
Glenfield Rd, SW12 . . . . .121 DJ88
  W13 . . . . .97 CH75
  Ashford TW15 . . . . .115 BP93
  Banstead SM7 . . . . .174 DB115
Glenfield Ter, W13 . . . . .97 CH75
Glenfinlas Way, SE5 . . . . .101 DP80
Glenforth St, SE10 . . . . .205 L10
Glengall Causeway, E14 ..203 P6
Glengall Gro, E14 . . . . .204 D6
Glengall Rd, NW6 . . . . .81 CZ67
  SE15 . . . . .102 DT79
  Bexleyheath DA7 . . . . .106 EY83
  Edgware HA8 . . . . .42 CP48
  Woodford Green IG8 . . . . . .48 EG51
Glengall Ter, SE15 . . . . .102 DT79
Glen Gdns, Croy. CR0 . . . . . .141 DN104
Glengarnock Av, E14 . . . . . . .204 E9
Glengarry Rd, SE22 . . . . .122 DS85
Glenham Dr, Ilf. IG2 . . . . .69 EP57
Glenhaven Av, Borwd. WD6 ..26 CN41
Glenhead Cl, SE9
  off Dumbreck Rd 105 EP83
Glenhill Cl, Lthd. KT22
  off Glenheadon Ri 171 CK123
Glenheadon Cl, Lthd. KT22
  off Glenheadon Ri 171 CK123
Glenheadon Ri, Lthd. KT22 .171 CK123
Glenhill Cl, N3 . . . . .44 DA54
Glenhouse Rd, SE9 . . . . .125 EN85
Glenhurst Av, NW5 . . . . .64 DG63
  Bexley DA5 . . . . .126 EZ88
  Ruislip HA4 . . . . .59 BQ59
Glenhurst Ct, SE19 . . . . .122 DT92
Glenhurst Ri, SE19 . . . . .122 DQ94
Glenhurst Rd, N12 . . . . .44 DD50
  Brentford TW8 . . . . .97 CJ79

Glenilla Rd, NW3 . . . . .82 DE65
Glenister Ho, Hayes UB3 ..77 BV74
Glenister Pk Rd, SW16 .121 DK94
Glenister Rd, SE10 . . . . .205 K10
Glenister St, E16 . . . . .87 EN74
Glenkerry Ho, E14
  off Burcham St 85 EC72
Glenlea Rd, SE9 . . . . .125 EM85
Glenlion Ct, Wey. KT13 .135 BS104
Glenloch Rd, NW3 . . . . .82 DE65
  Enfield EN3 . . . . .30 DW40
Glenluce Rd, SE3 . . . . .104 EG80
Glenlyon Rd, SE9 . . . . .125 EN85
Glenmere Av, NW7 . . . . .43 CU52
Glen Ms, E17 off Glen Rd ..67 DZ57
Glenmill, Hmptn. TW12 . . . . . .116 BZ92
Glenmore Cl, Add. KT15 .134 BH104
Glenmore Gdns, Abb.L. WD5
  off Stewart Cl 7 BU32
Glenmore Rd, NW3 . . . . .82 DE65
  Welling DA16 . . . . .105 ET81
Glenmore Way, Bark. IG11 ..88 EU69
Glenmount Path, SE18
  off Raglan Rd 105 EQ78
Glenn Av, Pur. CR8 . . . . .159 DP111
Glennie Rd, SE27 . . . . .121 DN90
Glenny Rd, Bark. IG11 . . . . . .87 EQ65
Glenorchy Cl, Hayes UB4 ..78 BY71
Glenparke Rd, E7 . . . . .86 EH65
Glen Ri, Wdf.Grn. IG8 . . . . . . .48 EH51
Glen Rd, E13 . . . . .86 EJ70
  E17 . . . . .67 DZ57
  Chessington KT9 . . . . .138 CL104
Glen Rd End, Wall. SM6 .159 DH109
Glenrosa Gdns, Grav. DA12 .131 GM92
Glenrosa St, SW6 . . . . .100 DC82
Glenrose Ct, Sid. DA14 . . . . . .126 EV92
Glenroy St, W12 . . . . .81 CW72
Glensdale Rd, SE4 . . . . .103 DZ83
Glenshee Cl, Nthwd. HA6
  off Rickmansworth Rd 39 BQ51
Glenshiel Rd, SE9 . . . . .125 EN85
Glenside, Chig. IG7 . . . . .49 EP51
Glenside Cotts, Slou. SL1 ..92 AT76
Glentanner Way, SW17
  off Aboyne Rd 120 DD90
Glentham Gdns, SW13
  off Glentham Rd 99 CV79
Glentham Rd, SW13 . . . . .99 CU79
Glenthorne Av, Croy. CR0 .142 DV102
Glenthorne Cl, Sutt. SM3 .140 DA102
  Uxbridge UB10
    off Uxbridge Rd 76 BN69
Glenthorne Gdns, Ilf. IG6 ..69 EN55
  Sutton SM3 . . . . .140 DA102
Glenthorne Ms, W6
  off Glenthorne Rd 99 CV77
Glenthorne Rd, E17 . . . . .67 DY57
  N11 . . . . .44 DF50
  W6 . . . . .99 CW77
  Kingston upon Thames
    KT1 . . . . .138 CM98
Glenthorpe Rd, Mord. SM4 .139 CX99
Glenton Cl, Rom. RM1 . . . . . .51 FE51
Glenton Rd, SE13 . . . . .104 EE84
Glenton Way, Rom. RM1 ..51 FE58
Glentrammon Av, Orp. BR6 .163 ET107
Glentrammon Cl, Orp. BR6 .163 ET107
Glentrammon Gdns, Orp.
  BR6 . . . . .163 ET107
Glentrammon Rd, Orp. BR6 .163 ET107
Glentworth St, NW1 . . . . .194 E5
Glenure Rd, SE9 . . . . .125 EN85
Glenview, SE2 . . . . .106 EX79
Glen Vw, Grav. DA12 . . . . . . .131 GJ88
Glenview Rd, Brom. BR1 .144 EK96
Glenville Av, Enf. EN2 . . . . . .30 DQ38
Glenville Ct, SE19
  off Lymer Av 122 DT92
Glenville Gro, SE8 . . . . .103 DZ80
Glenville Ms, SW18 . . . . .120 DB87
Glenville Rd, Kings.T. KT2 .138 CN95
Glen Wk, Islw. TW7 . . . . .117 CD85
Glen Way, Wat. WD17 . . . . . .23 BS38
Glenwood Av, NW9 . . . . .62 CS60
  Rainham RM13 . . . . .89 FH70
Glenwood Cl, Har. HA1 . . . . . .61 CF57
Glenwood Ct, E18
  off Clarendon Rd 68 EG55
Glenwood Dr, Rom. RM2 ..71 FG56
Glenwood Gdns, Ilf. IG2 . . . . .69 EN57
Glenwood Gro, NW9 . . . . .62 CQ60
Glenwood Rd, N15 . . . . .65 DP57
  NW7 . . . . .42 CS48
  SE6 . . . . .123 DZ88
  Epsom KT17 . . . . .157 CU107
  Hounslow TW3 . . . . .97 CD83
Glenwood Way, Croy. CR0 .143 DX100
Glenworth Av, E14 . . . . .204 F9
Gliddon Rd, W14 . . . . .99 CY77
Glimpsing Grn, Erith DA18 .106 EY76
Glisson Rd, Uxb. UB10 . . . . . .76 BN68
Gload Cres, Orp. BR5 . . . . . .146 EX103
Global App, SE1
  off Hancock Rd 85 EB68
Globe Ind Estates, Grays
  RM17 . . . . .110 GC78
Globe Pond Rd, SE16 . . . . . .203 K3
Globe Rd, E1 . . . . .84 DW68
  E2 .84 DW69
  E15 . . . . .68 EF64
  Hornchurch RM11 . . . . .71 FG58
  Woodford Green IG8 . . . . . .48 EJ51
Globe Rope Wk, E14 . . . . . . .204 D9
Globe St, SE1 . . . . .201 J6
Globe Ter, E2 off Globe Rd ..84 DW69
Globe Yd, W1 . . . . .195 H9
Glossop Rd, S.Croy. CR2 .160 DR109
Gloster Rd, N.Mal. KT3 . . . . .138 CS98
Gloucester Arc, SW7
  off Gloucester Rd 100 DC77
Gloucester Av, NW1 . . . . .82 DG66
  Grays RM16 . . . . .110 GC75
  Hornchurch RM11 . . . . .72 FN56
  Sidcup DA15 . . . . .125 ES89

Gloucester Av, Wal.Cr. EN8 ..15 DY33
  Welling DA16 . . . . .105 ET84
Gloucester Circ, SE10 . . . . . .103 EC80
Gloucester Cl, NW10 . . . . .80 CR66
  Thames Ditton KT7 . . . . . .137 CG102
Gloucester Ct, EC3 . . . . .201 N1
  Richmond TW9 . . . . .98 CN80
  Tilbury RM18
    off Dock Rd 111 GF82
  Uxbridge (Denh.) UB9
    off Moorfield 58 BG58
Gloucester Cres, NW1 . . . . . .83 DH67
  Staines TW18 . . . . .114 BK93
Gloucester Dr, N4 . . . . .65 DP61
  NW11 . . . . .64 DA56
  Staines TW18 . . . . .113 BC90
Gloucester Gdns, NW11 . . . . .63 CZ59
  W2 off Bishops Br Rd 82 DC72
  Barnet EN4 . . . . .28 DG42
  Ilford IG1 . . . . .68 EL59
  Sutton SM1 . . . . .140 DB103
Gloucester Gate, NW1 . . . . . .83 DH68
Gloucester Gate Ms, NW1
  off Gloucester Gate 83 DH68
Gloucester Gro, Edg. HA8 ..42 CR53
Gloucester Gro Est, SE15 .102 DS79
Gloucester Ho, NW6 . . . . .82 DA68
Gloucester Ms, E10
  off Gloucester Rd 67 EA59
  W2 . . . . .82 DC72
Gloucester Ms W, W2 . . . . . .82 DC72
Gloucester Par, Sid. DA15 .126 EU85
Gloucester Pk, SW7
  off Courtfield Rd 100 DC77
Gloucester Pl, NW1 . . . . .194 D4
  W1 . . . . .194 E6
  Enfield EN2
    off Chase Side 30 DQ40
Gloucester Pl Ms, W1 . . . . . .194 E7
● Gloucester Road 100 DC77
Gloucester Rd, E10 . . . . .67 EA59
  E11 . . . . .68 EH57
  E12 . . . . .69 EM62
  E17 . . . . .47 DX54
  N17 . . . . .46 DR54
  N18 . . . . .46 DT50
  SW7 . . . . .100 DC76
  W3 . . . . .98 CQ75
  W5 . . . . .97 CJ75
  Barnet EN5 . . . . .28 DC43
  Belvedere DA17 . . . . .106 EZ78
  Brentwood (Pilg.Hat.)
    CM15 . . . . .54 FV43
  Croydon CR0 . . . . .142 DR100
  Dartford DA1 . . . . .127 FH87
  Enfield EN2 . . . . .30 DQ38
  Feltham TW13 . . . . .116 BW88
  Gravesend DA12 . . . . .131 GJ91
  Hampton TW12 . . . . .116 CB94
  Harrow HA1 . . . . .60 CB57
  Hounslow TW4 . . . . .96 BY84
  Kingston upon Thames
    KT1 . . . . .138 CP96
  Redhill RH1 . . . . .184 DF133
  Richmond TW9 . . . . .98 CN80
  Romford RM1 . . . . .71 FE58
  Teddington TW11 . . . . .117 CE92
  Twickenham TW2 . . . . .116 CC88
Gloucester Sq, E2
  off Whiston Rd 84 DU67
  W2 . . . . .194 A9
  Woking GU21
    off Church St E 166 AY117
Gloucester St, SW1 . . . . .101 DJ78
Gloucester Ter, W2 . . . . .82 DD73
Gloucester Wk, W8 . . . . .100 DA75
  Woking GU21 . . . . .167 AZ117
Gloucester Way, EC1 . . . . . . .196 E3
Glover Cl, SE2 . . . . .106 EW77
  Waltham Cross EN7
    off Allwood Rd 14 DT27
Glover Dr, N18 . . . . .46 DW51
Glover Rd, Pnr. HA5 . . . . .60 BX58
Glovers Gro, Ruis. HA4 . . . . .59 BP59
Gloxinia Rd, Grav. (Sthflt.)
  DA13 . . . . .130 GB93
Gloxinia Wk, Hmptn. TW12 .116 CA93
Glycena Rd, SW11 . . . . .100 DF83
Glyn Av, Barn. EN4 . . . . .28 DD42
Glyn Cl, SE25 . . . . .142 DS96
  Epsom KT17 . . . . .157 CU109
Glyn Ct, SW16 . . . . .121 DN90
Glyn Davies Cl, Sev. (Dunt.Grn.)
  TN13 . . . . .181 FE120
Glyndebourne Pk, Orp. BR6 .145 EP103
Glynde Ms, SW3 . . . . .198 C7
Glynde Rd, Bexh. DA7 . . . . . .106 EX83
Glynde St, SE4 . . . . .123 DZ86
Glyndon Rd, SE18 . . . . .105 EQ77
Glyn Dr, Sid. DA14 . . . . .126 EV91
Glynfield Rd, NW10 . . . . .80 CS66
Glynne Rd, N22 . . . . .45 DN54
Glyn Rd, E5 . . . . .67 DX62
  Enfield EN3 . . . . .30 DW42
  Worcester Park KT4 . . . . . .139 CX103
Glyn St, SE11
  off Kennington La 101 DM78
Glynswood, Ger.Cr. (Chal.St.P.)
  SL9 . . . . .37 AZ52
Glynwood Ct, SE23 . . . . .122 DW89
Goaters All, SW6 . . . . .99 CZ80
GOATHURST COMMON, Sev. .190 FB130
Goat La, Enf. EN1 . . . . .30 DT38
  Surbiton KT6 . . . . .137 CJ103
Goat Rd, Mitch. CR4 . . . . . . .140 DG101
Goatsfield Rd, West. (Tats.)
  TN16 . . . . .178 EJ120
Goat St, SE1 . . . . .201 P4
Goatswood La, Rom. (Nave.)
  RM4 . . . . .51 FH45
Goat Wf, Brent. TW8 . . . . . . .98 CL79
Gobions Av, Rom. RM5 . . . . .51 FD52
Gobions Way, Pot.B. EN6
  off Swanley Bar La 12 DB28
Godalming Av, Wall. SM6 .159 DL106
Godalming Rd, E14 . . . . .85 EB71

Godbold Rd, E15 . . . . .86 EE69
Goddard Cl, Shep. TW17
  off Magdalene Rd 134 BM97
Goddard Pl, N19 . . . . .65 DJ62
Goddard Rd, Beck. BR3 . . . . .143 DX98
Goddards Way, Ilf. IG1 . . . . . .69 ER60
GODDEN GREEN, Sev. 191 FN125
H Godden Green Clinic, Sev.
  TN15 . . . . .191 FP125
GODDINGTON, Orp. 146 EW104
Goddington Chase, Orp.
  BR6 . . . . .164 EV105
Goddington La, Orp. BR6 .146 EU104
Godfrey Av, Nthlt. UB5 . . . . . .78 BY67
  Twickenham TW2 . . . . .117 CD87
Godfrey Hill, SE18 . . . . .104 EL77
Godfrey Rd, SE18 . . . . .105 EM77
Godfrey St, E15 . . . . .85 EC68
  SW3 . . . . .198 C10
Godfrey Way, Houns. TW4 .116 BZ87
Goding St, SE11 . . . . .101 DL78
Godley Rd, SW18 . . . . .120 DD88
  West Byfleet (Byfleet)
    KT14 . . . . .152 BM113
Godliman St, EC4 . . . . .197 H9
Godman Rd, SE15 . . . . .102 DV82
  Grays RM16 . . . . .111 GG76
Godolphin Cl, N13 . . . . .45 DP51
  Sutton SM3 . . . . .157 CZ111
Godolphin Pl, W3
  off Vyner Rd 80 CR73
Godolphin Rd, W12 . . . . .99 CV75
  Weybridge KT13 . . . . .153 BR107
Godric Cres, Croy. (New Adgtn.)
  CR0 . . . . .161 ED110
Godson Rd, Croy. CR0 . . . . . .141 DN104
Godson St, N1 . . . . .83 DN68
GODSTONE 186 DV131
Godstone Bypass, Gdse.
  RH9 . . . . .186 DW129
Godstone Grn, Gdse. RH9 .186 DV131
Godstone Grn Rd, Gdse.
  RH9 . . . . .186 DV131
Godstone Hill, Gdse. RH9 .186 DV127
Godstone Rd, Cat. CR3 . . . . .176 DU124
  Kenley CR8 . . . . .159 DN112
  Oxted RH8 . . . . .187 EA131
  Purley CR8 . . . . .159 DN112
  Redhill (Bletch.) RH1 . . . . .186 DR133
  Sutton SM1 . . . . .158 DC105
  Twickenham TW1 . . . . .117 CG86
  Whyteleafe CR3 . . . . .176 DT116
Godstow Rd, SE2 . . . . .106 EW75
Godwin Cl, E4 . . . . .31 EC38
  N1 off Napier Gro 84 DQ68
  Epsom KT19 . . . . .156 CQ107
Godwin Ct, NW1
  off Crowndale Rd 83 DJ68
Godwin Rd, E7 . . . . .68 EH63
  Bromley BR2 . . . . .144 EJ97
Goffers Rd, SE3 . . . . .103 ED81
Goffs Cres, Wal.Cr. (Chsht.)
  EN7 . . . . .13 DP29
Goffs La, Wal.Cr. (Chsht.) EN7 .14 DU29
GOFFS OAK, Wal.Cr. (Chsht.) ..14 DQ29
Goffs Oak Av, Wal.Cr. (Chsht.)
  EN7 . . . . .13 DP28
Goffs Rd, Ashf. TW15 . . . . . .115 BR93
Gogmore Fm Cl, Cher. KT16 .133 BF101
Gogmore La, Cher. KT16 .134 BG101
Goidel Cl, Wall. SM6 . . . . . . .159 DK105
Golborne Gdns, W10
  off Golborne Rd 81 CZ70
Golborne Ms, W10
  off Portobello Rd 81 CY71
Golborne Rd, W10 . . . . .81 CY71
Goldace, Grays RM17 . . . . . .110 FZ79
Golda Cl, Barn. EN5 . . . . .27 CX44
Goldbeaters Gro, Edg. HA8 ..42 CS51
Goldcliff Cl, Mord. SM4 .140 DA100
Goldcrest Cl, E16
  off Sheerwater Rd 86 EK71
  SE28 . . . . .88 EW73
Goldcrest Ms, W5
  off Montpelier Av 79 CK71
Goldcrest Way, Bushey WD23 .40 CC46
  Croydon (New Adgtn.)
    CR0 . . . . .161 ED109
  Purley CR8 . . . . .159 DK110
Golden Ct, Rich. TW9
  off George St 117 CK85
Golden Cres, Hayes UB3 . . . .77 BT74
Golden Cross Ms, W11
  off Basing St 81 CZ72
★ Golden Hinde, SE1
  off Cathedral St 201 K2
Golden La, EC1 . . . . .197 H5
Golden La Est, EC1 . . . . .197 H5
Golden Manor, W7 . . . . .79 CE73
Golden Plover Cl, E16
  off Maplin Rd 86 EH72
Golden Sq, W1 . . . . .195 L10
Golden Yd, NW3
  off Heath St 64 DC63
Golders Cl, Edg. HA8 . . . . . . .42 CP50
Golders Gdns, NW11 . . . . . . .63 CY59
GOLDERS GREEN, NW11 . . .64 DA59
● Golders Green 64 DA59
Golders Grn Cres, NW11 . . . .63 CZ59
Golders Grn Rd, NW11 . . . . . .63 CY58
Golders Manor Dr, NW11 ..63 CX58
Golders Pk Cl, NW11 . . . . . . .64 DB60
Golders Ri, NW4 . . . . .63 CX57
Golders Way, NW11 . . . . .63 CY59
Goldfinch Cl, Orp. BR6 . . . . . .164 EU106
  South Croydon CR2 . . . . . .161 DX111
Goldfinch Rd, SE28 . . . . .105 ER76
  South Croydon CR2 . . . . . .161 DY110
Goldfinch Way, Borwd. WD6 .26 CN42
Goldfort Wk, Wok. GU21
  off Langmans Way 166 AS116
Goldhawk Ms, W12
  off Devonport Rd 99 CV75
● Goldhawk Road 99 CW75
Goldhawk Rd, W6 . . . . .99 CT77

Gol - Gra

Goldhawk Rd, W12 . . . . .99 CU76
Goldhaze Cl, Wdf.Grn. IG8 . . .48 EK52
Gold Hill, Edg. HA8 . . . . .42 CR51
Gold Hill E, Ger.Cr. (Chal.St.P.)
  SL9 . . . . .36 AX54
Gold Hill N, Ger.Cr. (Chal.St.P.)
  SL9 . . . . .36 AW53
Gold Hill W, Ger.Cr. (Chal.St.P.)
  SL9 . . . . .36 AW53
Goldhurst Ter, NW6 . . . . .82 DB66
H Goldie Leigh Hosp, SE2 .106 EW79
Golding Cl, Chess. KT9
  off Coppard Gdns 155 CJ107
Goldingham Av, Loug. IG10 . .33 EQ40
Golding Rd, Sev. TN13 . . . . .191 FJ122
Goldings, The, Wok. GU21 . .166 AT116
Goldings Hill, Loug. IG10 . . .33 EN39
Goldings Ri, Loug. IG10 . . . .33 EN39
Goldings Rd, Loug. IG10 . . . .33 EN39
Golding St, E1 . . . . .84 DU72
Golding Ter, SW11
  off Longhedge St 100 DG82
Goldington Cres, NW1 . . . . .83 DK68
Goldington St, NW1 . . . . . . .83 DK68
Gold La, Edg. HA8 . . . . .42 CR51
Goldman Cl, E2 . . . . .84 DU70
Goldmark Ho, SE3
  off Lebrun Sq 104 EH83
Goldney Rd, W9 . . . . .82 DA70
Goldrill Dr, N11 . . . . .44 DG47
Goldrings Rd, Lthd. (Oxshott)
  KT22 . . . . .154 CC113
Goldsboro Rd, SW8 . . . . . . .101 DK81
Goldsborough Cres, E4 . . . . .47 EC47
Goldsdown Cl, Enf. EN3 . . . .31 DY40
Goldsdown Rd, Enf. EN3 . . . .31 DX40
Goldsel Rd, Swan. BR8 . . . .147 FD99
Goldsmid St, SE18
  off Sladedale Rd 105 ES78
Goldsmith, Grays RM17 . . . .110 FZ79
Goldsmith Av, E12 . . . . .86 EL65
  NW9 . . . . .63 CT58
  W3 . . . . .80 CR73
  Romford RM7 . . . . .70 FA59
Goldsmith Cl, W3
  off East Acton La 80 CS74
  Harrow HA2 . . . . .60 CB60
Goldsmith La, NW9 . . . . .62 CP56
Goldsmith Rd, E10 . . . . .67 EA60
  E17 . . . . .47 DX54
  N11 . . . . .44 DF50
  SE15 . . . . .102 DU81
  W3 . . . . .80 CR74
Goldsmiths Bottom, Sev.
  TN14 . . . . .190 FE127
Goldsmiths Cl, Wok. GU21 . .166 AW118
★ Goldsmiths' Hall, EC2 . . .197 J8
Goldsmith's Row, E2 . . . . . . .84 DU68
Goldsmith's Sq, E2 . . . . .84 DU68
Goldsmith St, EC2 . . . . .197 J8
Goldsworth Orchard, Wok. GU21
  off St. John's Rd 166 AU118
GOLDSWORTH PARK, Wok. .166 AU117
Goldsworth Pk Trd Est, Wok.
  GU21 . . . . .166 AV116
Goldsworth Rd, Wok. GU21 . .166 AW118
Goldsworthy Gdns, SE16 . . .202 G9
Goldwell Rd, Th.Hth. CR7 . . .141 DM98
Goldwin Cl, SE14 . . . . .102 DW81
Goldwing Cl, E16 . . . . .86 EG72
Golf Cl, Bushey WD23 . . . . . .24 BX41
  Stanmore HA7 . . . . .41 CJ52
  Thornton Heath CR7
   off Kensington Av 141 DN95
  Woking GU22 . . . . .151 BE114
Golf Club Dr, Kings.T. KT2 . .118 CR94
Golf Club Rd, Hat. AL9 . . . . .12 DA26
  Weybridge KT13 . . . . .153 BP109
  Woking GU22 . . . . .166 AU120
Golfe Rd, Ilf. IG1 . . . . .69 ER62
Golf Ho Rd, Oxt. RH8 . . . . . .188 EJ129
Golf Links Av, Grav. DA11 . . .131 GH92
Golf Ride, Enf. EN2 . . . . .29 DN35
Golf Rd, W5 off Boileau Rd . . .80 CM72
  Bromley BR1 . . . . .145 EN97
  Kenley CR8 . . . . .176 DR118
Golf Side, Sutt. SM2 . . . . . . .157 CY111
  Twickenham TW2 . . . . . . .117 CD90
Golfside Cl, N20 . . . . .44 DE48
  New Malden KT3 . . . . . . .138 CS96
Goliath Cl, Wall. SM6 . . . . . .159 DL108
Gollogly Ter, SE7 . . . . .104 EJ78
Gomer Gdns, Tedd. TW11 . . .117 CG93
Gomer Pl, Tedd. TW11 . . . . .117 CG93
Gomm Rd, SE16 . . . . .202 F7
Gomshall Av, Wall. SM6 . . . .159 DL106
Gomshall Gdns, Ken. CR8 . .176 DS115
Gomshall Rd, Sutt. SM2 . . . .157 CW110
Gondar Gdns, NW6 . . . . .63 CZ64
Gonson Pl, SE8 . . . . .103 EA79
Gonson St, SE8 . . . . .103 EB79
Gonston Cl, SW19
  off Boddicott Cl 119 CY89
Gonville Av, Rick. (Crox.Grn.)
  WD3 . . . . .23 BP44
Gonville Cres, Nthlt. UB5 . . . .78 CB65
Gonville Rd, Th.Hth. CR7 . . .141 DM99
Gonville St, SW6
  off Putney Br App 99 CY83
Goodall Rd, E11 . . . . .67 EC62
Gooden Ct, Har. HA1 . . . . . . .61 CE62
Goodenough Cl, Couls. CR5 .175 DN120
Goodenough Rd, SW19 . . . . .119 CZ94
Goodenough Way, Couls.
  CR5 . . . . .175 DM120
Gooderham Ho, Grays RM16 .111 GH75
Goodge Pl, W1 . . . . .195 L7
⊖ Goodge Street 195 L6
Goodge St, W1 . . . . .195 L7
Goodhall St, NW10 . . . . .80 CS69
Goodhart Pl, E14 . . . . .85 DY73
Goodhart Way, W.Wick. BR4 .144 EE101
Goodhew Rd, Croy. CR0 . . . .142 DU100
Gooding Cl, N.Mal. KT3 . . . .138 CQ98

Goodinge Cl, N7 . . . . .83 DL65
Goodlake Ct, Uxb. (Denh.)
  UB9 . . . . .57 BF59
GOODLEY STOCK, West. . . .189 EP130
Goodley Stock, West. TN16 . .189 EP129
Goodley Stock Rd, Eden. (Crock.H.)
  TN8 . . . . .189 EP131
  Westerham TN16 . . . . . . .189 EP128
Goodman Cres, SW2 . . . . . .121 DK89
Goodman Pk, Slou. SL2 . . . . .74 AW74
Goodman Pl, Stai. TW18 . . . .113 BF91
Goodman Rd, E10 . . . . .67 EC59
Goodmans Ct, E1 . . . . .197 P10
  Wembley HA0 . . . . .61 CK63
Goodman's Stile, E1 . . . . . . .84 DU72
Goodmans Yd, E1 . . . . .197 P10
GOODMAYES, Ilf. 70 EV61
⇌ Goodmayes 70 EU60
Goodmayes Av, Ilf. IG3 . . . . .70 EU60
Goodmayes La, Ilf. IG3 . . . . .70 EU63
Goodmayes Rd, Ilf. IG3 . . . . .70 EU63
Goodmead Rd, Orp. BR6 . . .146 EU101
Goodrich Cl, Wat. WD25 . . . .23 BU35
Goodrich Rd, SE22 . . . . .122 DT86
Goodson Rd, NW10 . . . . .80 CS66
Goods Way, NW1 . . . . .83 DL68
Goodway Gdns, E14 . . . . . . .85 ED72
Goodwin Cl, SE16 . . . . .202 A7
  Mitcham CR4 . . . . .140 DD97
Goodwin Ct, Barn. EN4 . . . . .28 DE44
  Waltham Cross EN8 . . . . . .15 DY28
Goodwin Dr, Sid. DA14 . . . . .126 EX90
Goodwin Gdns, Croy. CR0 . .159 DP107
Goodwin Rd, N9 . . . . .46 DW46
  W12 . . . . .99 CU75
  Croydon CR0 . . . . .159 DP106
Goodwins Ct, WC2 . . . . .195 P10
Goodwin St, N4
  off Fonthill Rd 65 DN61
Goodwood Av, Brwd. CM13 . .55 GE47
  Enfield EN3 . . . . .30 DW37
  Hornchurch RM12 . . . . . . .72 FL63
  Watford WD24 . . . . .23 BS35
Goodwood Cl, Mord. SM4 . . .140 DA98
  Stanmore HA7 . . . . .41 CJ50
Goodwood Cres, Grav. DA12 .131 GJ93
Goodwood Dr, Nthlt. UB5 . . . .78 CA65
Goodwood Path, Borwd. WD6
  off Stratfield Rd 26 CN41
Goodwood Rd, SE14 . . . . . . .103 DY80
  Redhill RH1 . . . . .184 DF132
Goodwyn Av, NW7 . . . . .42 CS50
Goodwyns Vale, N10 . . . . . . .44 DG53
Goodyers Av, Rad. WD7 . . . . .9 CF33
Goodyers Gdns, NW4 . . . . . .63 CX57
Goosander Way, SE28 . . . . .105 ER76
Goose Acre, Chesh. HP5 . . . . .4 AT30
Gooseacre La, Har. HA3 . . . . .61 CK57
Goosefields, Rick. WD3 . . . . .22 BJ44
Goose Grn, Cob. KT11 . . . . .169 BU119
Goose Grn Cl, Orp. BR5 . . . .146 EU96
Gorse Wk, West Dr. UB7 . . . .76 BL72
Gooseley La, E6 . . . . .87 EN69
Goosens Cl, Sutt. SM1
  off Turnpike La 158 DC106
Goose Sq, E6 off Harper Rd . .87 EM72
Gooshays Dr, Rom. RM3 . . . .52 FL50
Gooshays Gdns, Rom. RM3 . .52 FL51
Gophir La, EC4 . . . . .197 K10
Gopsall St, N1 . . . . .84 DR67
Goral Mead, Rick. WD3 . . . . .38 BK46
Gordon Av, E4 . . . . .48 EE51
  SW14 . . . . .98 CS84
  Hornchurch RM12 . . . . . . .71 FF61
  South Croydon CR2 . . . . .160 DQ110
  Stanmore HA7 . . . . .41 CH51
  Twickenham TW1 . . . . . . .117 CG85
Gordonbrock Rd, SE4 . . . . . .123 EA85
Gordon Cl, E17 . . . . .67 EA58
  N19 off Highgate Hill 65 DJ60
  Chertsey KT16 . . . . .133 BE104
  Staines TW18 . . . . .114 BH93
Gordon Ct, W12 . . . . .81 CW72
Gordon Cres, Croy. CR0 . . . .142 DS102
  Hayes UB3 . . . . .95 BU76
Gordondale Rd, SW19 . . . . .120 DA89
Gordon Dr, Cher. KT16 . . . . .133 BE104
  Shepperton TW17 . . . . . .135 BR100
Gordon Gdns, Edg. HA8 . . . .42 CP54
Gordon Gro, SE5 . . . . .101 DP82
⇌ Gordon Hill 29 DP39
Gordon Hill, Enf. EN2 . . . . . .30 DQ39
H Gordon Hosp, SW1 . . . . . .199 M9
Gordon Ho, E1 off Glamis Rd .84 DW73
Gordon Ho Rd, NW5 . . . . . . .64 DG63
Gordon Pl, W8 . . . . .100 DA75
  Gravesend DA12
   off East Ter 131 GJ86
Gordon Prom, Grav. DA12 . .131 GJ86
Gordon Prom E, Grav. DA12 .131 GJ86
Gordon Rd, E4 . . . . .48 EE45
  E11 . . . . .68 EG58
  E15 . . . . .67 EC63
  E18 . . . . .48 EH53
  N3 . . . . .43 CZ52
  N9 . . . . .46 DV47
  N11 . . . . .45 DK52
  SE15 . . . . .102 DV82
  W4 . . . . .98 CP79
  W5 . . . . .79 CJ73
  W13 . . . . .79 CH73
  Ashford TW15 . . . . .114 BL90
  Barking IG11 . . . . .87 ES67
  Beckenham BR3 . . . . .143 DZ97
  Belvedere DA17 . . . . .107 FC77
  Brentwood CM15 . . . . .55 GA46
  Carshalton SM5 . . . . .158 DF107
  Caterham CR3 . . . . .176 DR121
  Dartford DA1 . . . . .128 FK87
  Enfield EN2 . . . . .30 DQ39
  Esher (Clay.) KT10 . . . . . .155 CE107
  Gravesend (Nthflt.) DA11 . .130 GE87
  Grays RM16 . . . . .111 GF75
  Harrow HA3 . . . . .61 CE55
  Hounslow TW3 . . . . .96 CC84
  Ilford IG1 . . . . .69 ER62

Gordon Rd, Kings.T. KT2 . . .138 CM95
  Redhill RH1 . . . . .184 DG131
  Richmond TW9 . . . . .98 CM82
  Romford RM6 . . . . .70 EZ58
  Sevenoaks TN13 . . . . . . .191 FH125
  Shepperton TW17 . . . . . .135 BR100
  Sidcup DA15 . . . . .125 ES85
  Southall UB2 . . . . .96 BY77
  Staines TW18 . . . . .113 BC91
  Surbiton KT5 . . . . .138 CM101
  Waltham Abbey EN9 . . . . .15 EA34
  West Drayton UB7 . . . . . . .76 BL73
Gordon Sq, WC1 . . . . .195 N5
Gordon St, E13
  off Grange Rd 86 EG69
  WC1 . . . . .195 M4
Gordons Way, Oxt. RH8 . . . .187 ED128
Gordon Way, Barn. EN5 . . . . .27 CZ42
  Bromley BR1 . . . . .144 EG95
  Chalfont St. Giles HP8 . . . .36 AV48
Gore Cl, Uxb. (Hare.) UB9 . . .58 BH56
Gore Ct, NW9 . . . . .62 CN57
Gorefield Pl, NW6 . . . . .82 DA68
Gorelands La, Ch.St.G. HP8 . .37 AZ47
Gore Rd, E9 . . . . .84 DW67
  SW20 . . . . .139 CW96
  Dartford DA2 . . . . .128 FQ90
Goresbrook Rd, Dag. RM9 . . .88 EV67
Goresbrook Village, Dag. RM9
  off Goresbrook Rd 88 EV67
Gore St, SW7 . . . . .100 DC76
Gorham Pl, W11 off Mary Pl . .81 CY73
Goring Cl, Rom. RM5 . . . . . . .51 FC53
Goring Gdns, Dag. RM8 . . . . .70 EW62
Goring Rd, N11 . . . . .45 DL51
  Dagenham RM10 . . . . .89 FD65
  Staines TW18 . . . . .113 BD92
Gorings Sq, Stai. TW18 . . . . .113 BE91
Goring St, EC3 . . . . .197 N8
Goring Way, Grnf. UB6 . . . . . .78 CC68
Gorle Cl, Wat. WD25 . . . . .7 BU34
Gorleston Rd, N15 . . . . .66 DR57
Gorleston St, W14 . . . . .99 CY77
Gorman Rd, SE18 . . . . .105 EM77
Gorringe Av, Dart. (S.Darenth)
  DA4 . . . . .149 FR96
Gorringe Pk Av, Mitch. CR4 . .120 DF97
Gorse Cl, E16 . . . . .86 EG72
  Tadworth KT20 . . . . .173 CV120
Gorse Hill, Dart. (Fngham).
  DA4 . . . . .148 FL100
Gorse Hill La, Vir.W. GU25 . .132 AX98
Gorse Hill Rd, Vir.W. GU25 . .132 AX98
Gorselands Cl, W.Byf. KT14 . .152 BJ111
Gorse La, Wok. (Chobham)
  GU24 . . . . .150 AS108
Gorse Ri, SW17 . . . . .120 DG92
Gorse Rd, Croy. CR0 . . . . . .161 EA105
  Orpington BR5 . . . . .146 FA103
Gorseway, Rom. RM7 . . . . . . .71 FD61
Gorst Rd, NW10 . . . . .80 CQ70
  SW11 . . . . .120 DF86
Gorsuch Pl, E2 . . . . .197 P2
Gorsuch St, E2 . . . . .197 P2
Gosberton Rd, SW12 . . . . . .120 DG88
Gosbury Hill, Chess. KT9 . . .156 CL105
Gosfield Rd, Dag. RM8 . . . . .70 FA61
  Epsom KT19 . . . . .156 CR112
Gosfield St, W1 . . . . .195 K6
Gosford Gdns, Ilf. IG4 . . . . . .69 EM57
Gosforth La, Wat. WD19 . . . . .40 BW48
Gosforth Path, Wat. WD19 . . .39 BU48
Goshawk Gdns, Hayes UB4 . .77 BS69
Goslett Ct, Bushey WD23
  off Bournehall Av 24 CA43
Goslett Yd, WC2 . . . . .195 N9
Gosling Cl, Grnf. UB6 . . . . . . .78 CA69
Gosling Grn, Slou. SL3 . . . . .92 AY76
Gosling Rd, Slou. SL3 . . . . . .92 AY76
Gosling Way, SW9 . . . . .101 DN81
Gospatrick Rd, N17 . . . . .46 DQ52
GOSPEL OAK, NW5 . . . . . . .64 DG63
⇌ Gospel Oak 64 DG63
Gospel Oak Est, NW5 . . . . . .64 DF64
Gosport Dr, Horn. RM12 . . . . .90 FJ65
Gosport Rd, E17 . . . . .67 DZ57
Gosport Wk, N17
  off Yarmouth Cres 66 DV57
Gosport Way, SE15
  off Pentridge St 102 DT80
Gossage Rd, SE18
  off Ancona Rd 105 ER78
  Uxbridge UB10 . . . . .76 BM66
Gossamers, The, Wat. WD25 . .24 BY36
Gosset St, E2 . . . . .84 DT69
Goss Hill, Dart. DA2 . . . . . . .128 FJ93
  Swanley BR8 . . . . .128 FJ93
Gosshill Rd, Chis. BR7 . . . . .145 EN96
Gossington Cl, Chis. BR7
  off Beechwood Ri 125 EP91
Gosterwood St, SE8 . . . . . . .103 DY79
Gostling Rd, Twick. TW2 . . . .116 CA88
Goston Gdns, Th.Hth. CR7 . .141 DN97
Goswell Rd, EC1 . . . . .197 H5
Gothic Cl, Dart. DA1 . . . . . . .128 FK90
Gothic Ct, Hayes UB3
  off Sipson La 95 BR79
Gothic Rd, Twick. TW2 . . . . .117 CD89
Gottfried Ms, NW5
  off Fortess Rd 65 DJ63
Gouch Ho, E5 . . . . .66 DV62
Goudhurst Rd, Brom. BR1 . . .124 EE92
Gouge Av, Grav. (Nthflt.)
  DA11 . . . . .130 GE88
Gough Rd, E15 . . . . .68 EF63
  Enfield EN1 . . . . .30 DV40
Gough Sq, EC4 . . . . .196 E8
Gough St, WC1 . . . . .196 C4
Gough Wk, E14 . . . .
  off Saracen St 85 EA72
Gould Ct, SE19 . . . . .122 DT92
Goulden Ho App, SW11 . . . .100 DE82
Goulding Gdns, Th.Hth. CR7 .141 DP96
Gould Rd, Felt. TW14 . . . . . .115 BS87
  Twickenham TW2 . . . . . . .117 CE88
Goulds Grn, Uxb. UB8 . . . . . .77 BP71

Gould Ter, E8 off Kenmure Rd .66 DV64
Goulston St, E1 . . . . .197 P8
Goulton Rd, E5 . . . . .66 DV63
Gourley Pl, N15
  off Gourley St 66 DS57
Gourley St, N15 . . . . .66 DS57
Gourock Rd, SE9 . . . . .125 CK85
Govan St, E2 off Whiston Rd . .84 DU67
Government Row, Enf. EN3 . . .31 EA38
Governors Av, Uxb. (Denh.)
  UB9 . . . . .57 BF57
Governors Cl, Amer. HP6 . . . .20 AT37
Govett Av, Shep. TW17 . . . . .135 BQ99
Govier Cl, E15 . . . . .86 EE66
Gowan Av, SW6 . . . . .99 CY81
Gowan Rd, NW10 . . . . .81 CV65
Gowar Fld, Pot.B. EN6 . . . . . .11 CU32
Gower, The, Egh. TW20 . . . .133 BB97
Gower Cl, SW4 . . . . .121 DJ86
Gower Ct, WC1 . . . . .195 M4
Gower Ms, WC1 . . . . .195 M7
Gower Pl, WC1 . . . . .195 L4
Gower Rd, E7 . . . . .86 EG65
  Isleworth TW7 . . . . .97 CF79
  Weybridge KT13 . . . . .153 BR107
Gowers, The, Amer. HP6 . . . .20 AS36
Gowers La, Grays (Orsett)
  RM16 . . . . .111 GF75
Gower St, WC1 . . . . .195 M5
Gower's Wk, E1 . . . . .84 DU72
Gowland Pl, Beck. BR3 . . . . .143 DZ96
Gowlett Rd, SE15 . . . . .102 DU83
Gowrie Pl, Cat. CR3 . . . . . . .176 DQ122
Gowrie Rd, SW11 . . . . .100 DG83
Graburn Way, E.Mol. KT8 . . .137 CD97
Grace Av, Bexh. DA7 . . . . . . .106 EZ82
  Radlett (Shenley) WD7 . . . .9 CK33
Grace Business Cen, Mitch.
  CR4 . . . . .140 DF99
Gracechurch St, EC3 . . . . . .197 L10
Grace Cl, SE9 . . . . .124 EK90
  Borehamwood WD6 . . . . . .26 CR39
  Edgware HA8
   off Pavilion Way 42 CQ52
  Ilford IG6 . . . . .49 ET51
Gracedale Rd, SW16 . . . . . .121 DH92
Gracefield Gdns, SW16 . . . .121 DL90
Grace Jones Cl, E8
  off Parkholme Rd 84 DU65
Grace Path, SE26 . . . . .122 DW91
Grace Pl, E3
  off St. Leonards St 85 EB69
Grace's All, E1 . . . . .84 DU73
Grace's Ms, SE5 . . . . .102 DS82
Graces Rd, SE5 . . . . .102 DS82
Grace St, E3 . . . . .85 EB69
Gracious La, Sev. TN13 . . . .190 FG130
Gracious La End, Sev. TN14 .190 FF130
Gracious Pond Rd, Wok.
  (Chobham) GU24 . . . . . . .150 AT108
Gradient, The, SE26 . . . . . . .122 DU91
Graduate Pl, SE1 off Long La .102 DS76
Graeme Rd, Enf. EN1 . . . . . . .30 DR40
Graemesdyke Av, SW14 . . . . .98 CP83
Grafton Cl, W13 . . . . .79 CG72
  Hounslow TW4 . . . . .116 BY88
  Slough (Geo.Grn.) SL3 . . . .74 AY72
  West Byfleet KT14
   off Madeira Rd 151 BF113
  Worcester Park KT4 . . . . .138 CS104
Grafton Ct, Felt. TW14
  off Loxwood Cl 115 BR88
Grafton Cres, NW1 . . . . .83 DH65
Grafton Gdns, N4 . . . . .66 DQ58
  Dagenham RM8 . . . . .70 EY61
Grafton Ho, E3 . . . . .85 EA69
Grafton Ms, W1 . . . . .195 K5
Grafton Pk Rd, Wor.Pk. KT4 .138 CS103
Grafton Pl, NW1 . . . . .195 M3
Grafton Rd, NW5 . . . . .64 DG64
  W3 . . . . .80 CQ73
  Croydon CR0 . . . . .141 DN102
  Dagenham RM8 . . . . .70 EY61
  Enfield EN2 . . . . .30 DM41
  Harrow HA1 . . . . .60 CC57
  New Malden KT3 . . . . . . .138 CS97
  Worcester Park KT4 . . . . .138 CR104
Graftons, The, NW2
  off Hermitage La 64 DA62
Grafton Sq, SW4 . . . . .101 DJ83
Grafton St, W1 . . . . .199 J1
Grafton Ter, NW5 . . . . .64 DF64
Grafton Way, W1 . . . . .195 K5
  WC1 . . . . .195 K5
  West Molesey KT8 . . . . . .136 BZ98
Grafton Yd, NW5
  off Prince of Wales Rd 83 DH65
Graham Av, W13 . . . . .97 CH75
  Mitcham CR4 . . . . .140 DG95
Graham Cl, Brwd. CM13 . . . . .55 GC43
  Croydon CR0 . . . . .143 EA103
Grahame Pk Est, NW9 . . . . . .42 CS53
Grahame Pk Way, NW7 . . . . .43 CT52
  NW9 . . . . .42 CT54
Graham Gdns, Surb. KT6 . . .138 CL102
Graham Rd, E8 . . . . .84 DU65
  E13 . . . . .86 EG70
  N15 . . . . .45 DP55
  NW4 . . . . .63 CV58
  SW19 . . . . .119 CZ94
  W4 . . . . .98 CR76
  Bexleyheath DA6 . . . . . . .106 FA84
  Hampton TW12 . . . . .116 CA91
  Harrow HA3 . . . . .61 CE55
  Mitcham CR4 . . . . .140 DG95
  Purley CR8 . . . . .159 DN113
Graham St, N1 . . . . .197 G1
Graham Ter, SW1 . . . . .198 F9
Grainger Cl, Nthlt. UB5
  off Lancaster Rd 60 CC64
Grainger Rd, N22 . . . . .46 DQ53
  Isleworth TW7 . . . . .97 CF82
Grainge's Yd, Uxb. UB8
  off Cross St 76 BJ66
Gramer Cl, E11
  off Norman Rd 67 ED61

Grampian Cl, Hayes UB3 . . . .95 BR80
  Orpington BR6
   off Cotswold Ri 145 ET100
  Sutton SM2
   off Devonshire Rd 158 DC108
Grampian Gdns, NW2 . . . . . .63 CY60
Grampian Ho, N9
  off Plevna Rd 46 DV47
Grampian Way, Slou. SL3 . . .93 BA78
Granard Av, SW15 . . . . .119 CV85
Granard Rd, SW12 . . . . .120 DF87
Granaries, The, Wal.Abb. EN9 .16 EE34
Granary Cl, N9 off Turin Rd . . .46 DW45
Granary Rd, E1 . . . . .84 DV70
Granary St, NW1 . . . . .83 DK67
Granby Pk Rd, Wal.Cr. (Chsht.)
  EN7 . . . . .14 DT28
Granby Pl, SE1 . . . . .200 D5
Granby Rd, SE9 . . . . .105 EM82
  Gravesend DA11 . . . . .130 GC86
Granby St, E2 . . . . .84 DT70
Granby Ter, NW1 . . . . .195 K1
Grand Arc, N12
  off Ballards La 44 DC50
Grand Av, EC1 . . . . .196 G6
  N10 . . . . .64 DG56
  Surbiton KT5 . . . . .138 CP99
  Wembley HA9 . . . . .62 CN64
Grand Av E, Wem. HA9 . . . . .62 CP64
Grand Depot Rd, SE18 . . . . .105 EN78
Grand Dr, SW20 . . . . .139 CW96
  Southall UB2 . . . . .96 CC75
Granden Rd, SW16 . . . . .141 DL96
Grandfield Av, Wat. WD17 . . .23 BT39
Grandis Cotts, Wok. (Ripley)
  GU23 . . . . .168 BH122
Grandison Rd, SW11 . . . . . .120 DF85
  Worcester Park KT4 . . . . .139 CW103
Grand Junct Wf, N1 . . . . . . .197 H1
Grand Par Ms, SW15
  off Upper Richmond Rd . .119 CY85
Grand Stand Rd, Epsom
  KT18 . . . . .173 CT117
Grand Union Canal Wk, W7 . .97 CE76
Grand Union Cl, W9
  off Woodfield Rd 81 CZ71
Grand Union Cres, E8 . . . . . .84 DU66
Grand Union Ind Est, NW10 . .80 CP68
Grand Union Wk, NW1 . . . . . .83 DH66
Grand Vw Av, West. (Bigg.H.)
  TN16 . . . . .178 EJ117
Grand Wk, E1 off Solebay St . .85 DY70
Granfield St, SW11 . . . . .100 DD81
Grange, The, N2
  off Central Av 44 DD54
  N20 . . . . .44 DC46
  SE1 . . . . .201 P6
  SW19 . . . . .119 CX93
  Croydon CR0 . . . . .143 DZ103
  Dartford (S.Darenth) DA4 .149 FR95
  Walton-on-Thames KT12 . .135 BV103
  Wembley HA0 . . . . .80 CN66
  Windsor (Old Wind.) SL4 . .112 AV85
  Woking (Chobham) GU24 . .150 AS110
  Worcester Park KT4 . . . . .138 CT104
Grange Av, N12 . . . . .44 DC50
  N20 . . . . .43 CY45
  SE25 . . . . .142 DS96
  Barnet EN4 . . . . .44 DE46
  Stanmore HA7 . . . . .41 CH54
  Twickenham TW2 . . . . . . .117 CE89
  Woodford Green IG8 . . . . .48 EG51
Grangecliffe Gdns, SE25 . . .142 DS96
Grange Cl, Brwd. CM13 . . . . .55 GC50
  Edgware HA8 . . . . .42 CQ50
  Gerrards Cross (Chal.St.P.)
   SL9 . . . . .36 AY53
  Hayes UB3 . . . . .77 BS71
  Hounslow TW5 . . . . .96 BZ79
  Leatherhead KT22 . . . . . .171 CK120
  Redhill (Bletch.) RH1 . . . .186 DR133
  Redhill (Merst.) RH1 . . . . .185 DH128
  Sidcup DA15 . . . . .126 EU90
  Staines (Wrays.) TW19 . . .112 AY86
  Watford WD17 . . . . .23 BU39
  West Molesey KT8 . . . . . .136 CB98
  Westerham TN16 . . . . . . .189 EQ126
  Woodford Green IG8 . . . . .48 EG52
Grange Ct, WC2 . . . . .196 C9
  Chigwell IG7 . . . . .49 EQ47
  Loughton IG10 . . . . .32 EK43
  Northolt UB5 . . . . .78 BW68
  Staines TW18 . . . . .114 BG92
  Waltham Abbey EN9 . . . . .15 EC34
  Walton-on-Thames KT12 . .135 BU103
Grangecourt Rd, N16 . . . . . . .66 DS60
Grange Cres, SE28 . . . . .88 EW72
  Chigwell IG7 . . . . .49 ER50
  Dartford DA2 . . . . .128 FP86
Grangedale Cl, Nthwd. HA6 . .39 BS53
Grange Dr, Chis. BR7 . . . . . .124 EL93
  Orpington BR6
   off Rushmore Hill 164 EW109
  Redhill (Merst.) RH1
   off London Rd S 185 DH128
  Woking GU21 . . . . .150 AY114
Grange Fm Cl, Har. HA2 . . . .60 CC61
Grange Flds, Ger.Cr. (Chal.St.P.)
  SL9 off Lower Rd 36 AY53
Grange Gdns, N14 . . . . .45 DK46
  NW3 . . . . .64 DB62
  SE25 . . . . .142 DS96
  Banstead SM7 . . . . .158 DB113
  Pinner HA5 . . . . .60 BZ56
Grange Gro, N1 . . . . .83 DP65
GRANGE HILL, Chig. 49 ER51
⊖ Grange Hill 49 ER49
Grange Hill, SE25 . . . . .142 DS96
  Edgware HA8 . . . . .42 CQ50
Grangehill Pl, SE9
  off Westmount Rd 105 EM83
Grangehill Rd, SE9 . . . . .105 EM83
Grange Ho, Bark. IG11
  off St. Margarets 87 ER67
  Erith DA8 . . . . .107 FE82
Grange La, SE21 . . . . .122 DT89
  Watford (Let.Hth.) WD25 . .25 CD39

★ Place of interest   ⇌ Railway station   ⊖ London Underground station   DLR Docklands Light Railway station   ⬦ Tramlink station   H Hospital

Grange Mans, Epsom KT17 . .157	CT108
Grange Meadow, Bans. SM7 .158	DB113
Grange Ms, SE10	
off Crooms Hill 103	ED80
Grangemill Rd, SE6 123	EA90
Grangemill Way, SE6 123	EA89
Grangemount, Lthd. KT22 . .171	CK120
★ Grange Mus of Comm History,	
NW10 off Neasden La 62	CS63
GRANGE PARK, N21 29	DP43
⇌ Grange Park 29	DP43
Grange Pk, W5 80	CL74
Woking GU21 166	AY115
Grange Pk Av, N21 29	DP44
Grange Pk Pl, SW20 119	CV94
Grange Pk Rd, E10 67	EB60
Thornton Heath CR7 142	DR98
Grange Pl, NW6 82	DA66
Staines TW18 134	BJ96
Walton-on-Thames KT12 . .135	BU103
Grange Rd, E10 67	EA60
E13 86	EF69
E17 67	DY57
N6 64	DG58
N17 46	DU51
N18 46	DU51
NW10 81	CV65
SE1 201	N6
SE19 142	DR98
SE25 142	DR98
SW13 99	CU81
W4 98	CP78
W5 79	CK74
Addlestone (New Haw)	
KT15 152	BG110
Borehamwood (Elstree)	
WD6 26	CM43
Bushey WD23 24	BY43
Caterham CR3 186	DU125
Chessington KT9 156	CL105
Edgware HA8 42	CR51
Egham TW20 113	AZ92
Gerrards Cross (Chal.St.P.)	
SL9 36	AY53
Gravesend DA11 131	GG87
Grays RM17 110	GB79
Harrow HA1 61	CG58
Harrow (S.Har.) HA2 61	CD61
Hayes UB3 77	BS72
Ilford IG1 69	EP63
Kingston upon Thames	
KT1 138	CL97
Leatherhead KT22 171	CK120
Orpington BR6 145	EQ103
Romford RM3 51	FH51
Sevenoaks TN13 190	FG127
South Croydon CR2 160	DQ110
South Ockendon (Aveley)	
RM15 90	FQ74
Southall UB1 96	BY75
Sutton SM2 158	DA108
Thornton Heath CR7 . . .142	DR98
Walton-on-Thames KT12 .154	BY105
West Molesey KT8 136	CB98
Woking GU21 150	AY114
Granger Way, Rom. RM1 71	FG58
Grange St, N1 84	DR67
Grange Vale, Sutt. SM2 158	DB108
Grange Vw Rd, N20 44	DC46
Grange Wk, SE1 201	N6
Grangeway, N12 44	DB49
NW6 off Messina Av 82	DA66
Grange Way, Erith DA8 107	FH80
Iver SL0 75	BF72
Grangeway, Wdf.Grn. IG8 . . .48	EJ49
Grangeway, The, N21 29	DP44
Grangeway Gdns, Ilf. IG4 . . .68	EL57
Grangeways Cl, Grav. (Nthflt.)	
DA11 131	GF91
Grangewood, Bex. DA5	
off Hurst Rd 126	EZ88
Potters Bar EN6 12	DB30
Slough (Wexham) SL3 . . .74	AW71
Grangewood Av, Grays	
RM16 110	GE76
Rainham RM13 90	FJ70
Grangewood Cl, Brwd. CM13	
off Knight's Way 55	GA48
Pinner HA5 59	BU57
Grangewood Dr, Sun. TW16	
off Forest Rd 115	BT94
Grangewood La, Beck. BR3 . .123	DZ93
Grangewood St, E6 86	EJ67
Grangewood Ter, SE25	
off Grange Rd 142	DR97
Grange Yd, SE1 201	P7
Granham Gdns, N9 46	DT47
Granite St, SE18 105	ET78
Granleigh Rd, E11 68	EE61
Gransden Av, E8 84	DV66
Gransden Rd, W12	
off Wendell Rd 99	CT75
Grant Av, Slou. SL1 74	AS72
Grantbridge St, N1 83	DP68
Grantchester Cl, Har. HA1 . . .61	CF62
Grant Cl, N14 45	DJ45
Shepperton TW17 135	BP100
Grantham Cl, Edg. HA8 42	CL48
Grantham Gdns, Rom. RM6 . .70	EZ58
Grantham Grn, Borwd. WD6 . .26	CQ43
Grantham Pl, W1 199	H3
Grantham Rd, E12 69	EN63
SW9 101	DL82
W4 98	CS80
Grantley Pl, Esher KT10 154	CB106
Grantley Rd, Houns. TW4 . . .96	BW82
Grantley St, E1 85	DX69
Grantock Rd, E17 47	ED53
Granton Av, Upmin. RM14 . . .72	FM61
Granton Rd, SW16 141	DJ95
Ilford IG3 70	EU60
Sidcup DA14 126	EW93
Grant Pl, Croy. CR0 142	DT102
Grant Rd, SW11 100	DD84
Croydon CR0 142	DT102
Harrow HA3 61	CE55
Grants Cl, NW7 43	CW52

Grants La, Oxt. RH8 188	EJ132
Grant's Quay Wf, EC3 201	L1
Grant St, E13 86	EG69
N1 off Chapel Mkt 83	DN68
Grantully Rd, W9 82	DB69
Grant Way, Islw. TW7 97	CG79
Granville Av, N9 46	DW48
Feltham TW13 115	BU89
Hounslow TW3 116	CA85
Granville Cl, Croy. CR0 142	DS103
West Byfleet (Byfleet) KT14	
off Church Rd 152	BM113
Weybridge KT13 153	BQ107
Granville Ct, N1 84	DR67
Granville Dene, Hem.H. (Bov.)	
HP3 5	BA27
Granville Gdns, SW16 141	DM95
W5 80	CM74
Granville Gro, SE13 103	EC83
Granville Ms, Sid. DA14 126	EU91
Granville Pk, SE13 103	EC83
Granville Pl, N12 (N.Finchley)	
off High Rd 44	DC52
SW6 off Maxwell Rd 100	DB80
W1 194	F9
Pinner HA5 60	BX55
Granville Rd, E17 67	EB58
E18 48	EH54
N4 65	DM58
N12 44	DB52
N13 off Russell Rd 45	DM51
N22 45	DP53
NW2 63	CZ61
NW6 82	DA68
SW18 120	DA87
SW19 off Russell Rd 120	DA94
Barnet EN5 27	CW42
Epping CM16 18	EV29
Gravesend DA11 131	GF87
Hayes UB3 95	BT77
Ilford IG1 69	EP60
Oxted RH8 188	EF129
Sevenoaks TN13 190	FG124
Sidcup DA14 126	EU91
Uxbridge UB10 77	BP65
Watford WD18 24	BW42
Welling DA16 106	EW83
Westerham TN16 189	EQ126
Weybridge KT13 153	BQ107
Woking GU22 167	AZ120
Granville Sq, SE15 102	DS80
WC1 196	C3
Granville St, WC1 196	C3
Grape St, WC2 195	P8
Graphite Sq, SE11 200	B10
Grapsome Cl, Chess. KT9	
off Nigel Fisher Way 155	CJ108
Grasdene Rd, SE18 106	EU80
Grasholm Way, Slou. SL3 . . .93	BC77
Grasmere Av, SW15 118	CR91
SW19 140	DA97
W3 80	CQ73
Hounslow TW3 116	CB86
Orpington BR6 145	EP104
Ruislip HA4 59	BQ59
Slough SL2 74	AU73
Wembley HA9 61	CK59
Grasmere Cl, Egh. TW20	
off Keswick Rd 113	BB94
Feltham TW14 115	BT88
Loughton IG10 33	EM46
Watford WD25 7	BV32
Grasmere Ct, N22	
off Palmerston Rd 45	DM51
Grasmere Gdns, Har. HA3 . . .41	CG54
Ilford IG4 69	EM57
Orpington BR6 145	EP104
Grasmere Pt, SE15	
off Ilderton Rd 102	DW80
Grasmere Rd, E13 86	EG68
N10 45	DH53
N17 46	DU51
SE25 142	DV100
SW16 121	DM92
Bexleyheath DA7 107	FC81
Bromley BR1 144	EF95
Orpington BR6 145	EP104
Purley CR8 159	DP111
Grasmere Way, W.Byf. (Byfleet)	
KT14 152	BM112
Grassfield Cl, Couls. CR5 . . .175	DH119
Grasshaven Way, SE28 87	ET74
Grassingham End, Ger.Cr.	
(Chal.St.P.) SL9 36	AY52
Grassingham Rd, Ger.Cr.	
(Chal.St.P.) SL9 36	AY52
Grassington Cl, N11	
off Ribblesdale Av 44	DG51
St. Albans (Brick.Wd.) AL2 . .8	CA30
Grassington Rd, Sid. DA14 . .126	EU91
Grassmere Rd, Horn. RM11 . .72	FM56
Grassmount, SE23 122	DV89
Purley CR8 159	DJ110
Grass Pk, N3 43	CZ53
Grassway, Wall. SM6 159	DJ105
Grassy La, Sev. TN13 191	FH126
Grasvenor Av, Barn. EN5 28	DA44
Grately Way, SE15	
off Daniel Gdns 102	DT80
Gratton Rd, W14 99	CY76
Gratton Ter, NW2 63	CX62
Gravel Cl, Chig. IG7 50	EU47
Graveley, Kings.T. KT1	
off Willingham Way 138	CN96
Graveley Av, Borwd. WD6 . . .26	CQ42
◆ Gravel Hill 161	DY108
Gravel Hill, N3 43	CZ54
Bexleyheath DA6 127	FB85
Croydon CR0 161	DX107
Gerrards Cross (Chal.St.P.)	
SL9 36	AY53
Leatherhead KT22	
off North St 171	CH121
Loughton (High Beach)	
IG10 32	EG38
Uxbridge UB8 58	BK64
Gravel Hill Cl, Bexh. DA6 . . .127	FB85

Gravel La, E1 197	P8
Chigwell IG7 50	EU46
Gravelly Hill, Cat. CR3 186	DS120
Gravelly Ride, SW19 119	CV91
Gravel Pit La, SE9 125	EQ85
Gravel Pit Way, Orp. BR6 . . .146	EU103
Gravel Rd, Brom. BR2 144	EL103
Dartford (Sutt.H.) DA4 . .128	FP94
Twickenham TW2 117	CE88
Gravelwood Cl, Chis. BR7 . . .125	EQ90
Graveney Gro, SE20 122	DW94
Graveney Rd, SW17 120	DE91
⇌ Gravesend 131	GG87
GRAVESEND 131	GJ85
⊞ Gravesend & North Kent	
Hosp, Grav. DA11 131	GG86
Gravesend Rd, W12 81	CU73
Gravesham Ct, Grav. DA12	
off Clarence Row 131	GH87
★ Gravesham Mus, Grav.	
DA11 131	GH86
Gray Av, Dag. RM8 70	EZ60
Grayburn Cl, Ch.St.G. HP8 . . .36	AU47
Gray Gdns, Rain. RM13 89	FG65
Grayham Cres, N.Mal. KT3 . .138	CR98
Grayham Rd, N.Mal. KT3 . . .138	CR98
Grayland Cl, Brom. BR1 144	EK95
Graylands, Epp. (They.B.)	
CM16 33	ER37
Woking GU21 166	AY116
Graylands Cl, Wok. GU21 . . .166	AY116
Grayling Cl, E16	
off Cranberry La 86	EE70
Grayling Rd, N16 66	DR81
Graylings, The, Abb.L. WD5 . . .7	BR33
Grayling Sq, E2 84	DU69
GRAYS 110	GA78
⇌ Grays 110	GA79
Grayscroft Rd, SW16 121	DK94
Grays End Cl, Grays RM17 . . .110	GA76
Grays Fm Rd, Orp. BR5 146	EV95
Grayshott Rd, SW11 100	DG82
★ Gray's Inn, WC1 196	C6
Gray's Inn Rd, WC1 196	C6
Gray's Inn Pl, WC1 196	C7
Gray's Inn Rd, WC1 196	B3
Gray's Inn Sq, WC1 196	D6
Grays La, Ashf. TW15 115	BP91
Gray's La, Ashtd. KT21 172	CM119
Epsom KT18	
off Shepherds' Wk 172	CP121
Grays Pk Rd, Slou. (Stoke P.)	
SL2 74	AU68
Grays Pl, Slou. SL2 74	AT74
Grays Rd, Slou. SL1 74	AT74
Uxbridge UB10 76	BL67
Westerham TN16 179	EP121
Gray St, SE1 200	E5
Grays Wk, Brwd. CM13 55	GD45
Grayswood Gdns, SW20	
off Farnham Gdns 139	CV96
Grayswood Pt, SW15	
off Norley Vale 119	CU88
Gray's Yd, W1 194	G9
Graywood Ct, N12 44	DC52
Grazebrook Rd, N16 66	DR61
Grazeley Cl, Bexh. DA6 127	FC85
Grazeley Ct, SE19	
off Gipsy Hill 122	DS91
Great Acre Ct, SW4	
off St. Alphonsus Rd 101	DK84
Great Bell All, EC2 197	K8
Great Benty, West Dr. UB7 . . .94	BL77
★ Great Bookham Common,	
Lthd. KT23 170	BZ121
Great Brownings, SE21 122	DT91
Great Bushey Dr, N20 44	DB46
Great Cambridge Rd, N9 46	DS46
N17 46	DR50
N18 46	DR50
Broxbourne EN10 15	DY26
Enfield EN1 30	DU42
Waltham Cross (Chsht.)	
EN8 14	DW34
Great Castle St, W1 195	J8
Great Cen Av, Ruis. HA4 60	BW64
Great Cen St, NW1 194	D6
Great Cen Way, NW10 62	CS64
Wembley HA9 62	CQ63
Great Chapel St, W1 195	M8
Great Chertsey Rd, W4 98	CQ82
Feltham TW13 116	CA90
Great Ch La, W6 99	CX78
Great Coll St, SW1 199	P6
Great Cross Av, SE10 104	EE80
Great Cullings, Rom. RM7 . . .71	FE61
Great Cumberland Ms, W1 . .194	D9
Great Cumberland Pl, W1 . . .194	D8
Great Dover St, SE1 201	J5
Greatdown Rd, W7 79	CF70
Great Eastern Rd, E15 85	ED66
Brentwood CM14 54	FW49
Great Eastern St, EC2 197	M3
Great Eastern Wk, EC2 197	N7
Great Ellshams, Bans. SM7 . .174	DA116
Great Elms Rd, Brom. BR2 . .144	EJ98
Great Fld, NW9 42	CS53
Greatfield Av, E6 87	EM70
Greatfield Cl, N19	
off Warrender Rd 65	DJ63
SE4 103	EA84
Greatfields Dr, Uxb. UB8 76	BN71
Greatfields Rd, Bark. IG11 . . .87	ER67
Great Fleete Way, Bark. IG11	
off Choats Rd 88	EW68
Great Galley Cl, Bark. IG11 . . .88	EV69
Great Gdns Rd, Horn. RM11 . .71	FH58
Great Gatton Cl, Croy. CR0 . .143	DY101
Great George St, SW1 199	N5
Great Gregories La, Epp.	
CM16 17	ES33
Great Gro, Bushey WD23 24	CB42
Great Gros, Wal.Cr. EN7 14	DS28

Great Guildford St, SE1 201	H2
Greatham Rd, Bushey WD23 . .24	BX41
Greatham Wk, SW15 119	CU88
Greathurst End, Lthd. (Bkhm.)	
KT23 170	BZ124
Great James St, WC1 196	B5
Great Julians, Rick. WD3	
off Grove Cres 22	BN42
Great Marlborough St, W1 . .195	K9
Great Maze Pond, SE1 201	L4
Great Nelmes Chase, Horn.	
RM11 72	FM57
Great Newport St, WC2	
off Cranbourn St 83	DK73
Great New St, EC4 196	E8
Great N Rd, N2 64	DE56
N6 64	DE56
Barnet EN5 27	CZ38
Barnet (New Barn.) EN5 . .28	DA43
Hatfield AL9 12	DB27
Potters Bar EN6 12	DB27
Great N Way, NW4 43	CW56
Great Oaks, Brwd. CM13 55	GB44
Chigwell IG7 49	EQ49
Greatorex St, E1 84	DU71
Great Ormond St, WC1 196	A6
⊞ Great Ormond St Hosp for	
Children, WC1 196	A5
Great Owl Rd, Chig. IG7 49	EN48
Great Pk, Kings L. WD4 6	BM30
Great Percy St, WC1 196	C2
Great Peter St, SW1 199	M7
Great Pettits Ct, Rom. RM1 . .51	FE54
⊖ Great Portland Street 195	J5
Great Portland St, W1 195	J6
Great Pulteney St, W1 195	L10
Great Queen St, WC2 196	A9
Dartford DA1 128	FM87
Great Ropers La, Brwd. CM13 .53	FU51
Great Russell St, WC1 195	N8
Great St. Helens, EC3 197	M8
Great St. Thomas Apostle,	
EC4 197	J10
Great Scotland Yd, SW1 199	P3
Great Slades, Pot.B. EN6 11	CZ33
Great Smith St, SW1 199	N6
Great South-West Rd, Felt.	
TW14 115	BQ87
Hounslow TW4 95	BT84
Great Spilmans, SE22 122	DS85
Great Stockwood Rd, Wal.Cr.	
(Chsht.) EN7 14	DR26
Great Strand, NW9 43	CT53
Great Suffolk St, SE1 200	G3
Great Sutton St, EC1 196	G5
Great Swan All, EC2 197	K8
Great Tattenhams, Epsom	
KT18 173	CV118
Great Thrift, Orp. BR5 145	EQ98
Great Till Cl, Sev. (Otford)	
TN14 181	FE116
Great Titchfield St, W1 195	K8
Great Twr St, EC3 197	M10
Great Trinity La, EC4 197	J10
Great Turnstile, WC1 196	C7
GREAT WARLEY, Brwd. 53	FV53
Great Warley St, Brwd. CM13 .53	FU53
Great Western Rd, W2 81	CZ71
W9 81	CZ71
W11 81	CZ71
Great W Rd, W4 98	CP78
W6 99	CT78
Brentford TW8 98	CP78
Hounslow TW5 96	BX82
Isleworth TW7 97	CE80
Great Wf Rd, E14	
off Churchill Pl 85	EB74
Great Winchester St, EC2 . . .197	L8
Great Windmill St, W1 195	M10
Greatwood, Chis. BR7 125	EN94
Greatwood Cl, Cher. (Ott.)	
KT16 151	BC109
Great Woodcote Dr, Pur.	
CR8 159	DK110
Great Woodcote Pk, Pur.	
CR8 159	DK110
Greaves Cl, Bark. IG11	
off Norfolk Rd 87	ES66
Greaves Pl, SW17 120	DE91
Grebe Av, Hayes UB4	
off Cygnet Way 78	BX72
Grebe Cl, E7	
off Cormorant Rd 68	EF64
E17 47	DY52
Barking IG11 88	EU70
Grebe Ct, Sutt. SM1 157	CZ106
Grebe Crest, Grays RM20 . . .109	FU77
Grecian Cres, SE19 121	DP93
Greding Wk, Brwd. CM13 55	GB47
Gredo Ho, Bark. IG11 88	EV69
Greek Ct, W1 195	N9
Greek St, W1 195	N9
Greek Yd, WC2 195	P10
Green, The, E4 47	EC46
E11 68	EH58
E15 85	EE65
N9 46	DU47
N14 45	DK48
N21 45	DN45
SW14 98	CQ83
SW19 119	CX92
W3 80	CS72
W5 off High St 79	CK74
Bexleyheath DA7 106	FA81
Bromley BR1	
off Downham Way 124	EG90
Bromley (Hayes) BR2 . . .144	EG101
Carshalton SM5 158	DG105
Caterham (Wold.) CR3 . .177	EA123
Chalfont St. Giles HP8	
off High St 36	AW47
Croydon CR0 161	DZ109
Dartford DA2 129	FR89

Green, The, Epp. (They.B.)	
CM16 33	ES37
Epsom KT17 157	CU111
Esher (Clay.) KT10 155	CF107
Feltham TW13 115	BV89
Hayes UB3	
off Wood End 77	BS72
Hemel Hempstead (Bov.)	
HP3 5	BA29
Hounslow TW5	
off Heston Rd 96	CA79
Leatherhead (Fetch.) KT22 .171	CD124
Morden SM4 139	CY98
New Malden KT3 138	CQ97
Orpington (Pr.Bot.) BR6	
off Rushmore Hill 164	EW110
Orpington (St.P.Cray) BR5	
off The Avenue 126	EV94
Rainham (Wenn.) RM13 . .90	FL73
Richmond TW9 117	CK85
Rickmansworth (Crox.Grn.)	
WD3 22	BN44
Rickmansworth (Sarratt)	
WD3 22	BG35
Romford (Hav.at.Bow.)	
RM4 51	FE48
Sevenoaks TN13 191	FK122
Shepperton TW17 135	BS98
Sidcup DA14 126	EU101
Slough (Datchet) SL3 . . .92	AV80
South Ockendon RM15 . .91	FW69
Southall UB2 96	BY76
Staines (Wrays.) TW19 . .112	AY86
Sutton SM1 140	DB104
Tadworth (Burgh Hth.)	
KT20 173	CY119
Tilbury (W.Til.) RM18 . . .111	GL79
Twickenham TW2 117	CG88
Uxbridge (Hare.) UB9 . . .38	BJ53
Uxbridge (Ickhm.) UB10 . .59	BQ61
Waltham Abbey EN9	
off Sewardstone Rd . . .15	EC34
Waltham Cross (Chsht.)	
EN8 14	DW28
Walton-on-Thames KT12	
off Octagon Rd 153	BS110
Warlingham CR6 177	DX117
Watford (Let.Hth.) WD25 . .25	CE39
Welling DA16 105	ES84
Wembley HA0 61	CG61
West Drayton UB7 94	BK76
Westerham TN16 189	ER126
Woking (Ripley) GU23 . . .168	BH121
Woodford Green IG8 48	EG50
Greenacre, Dart. DA1	
off Oakfield La 128	FL89
Woking (Knap.) GU21	
off Mead Ct 166	AS116
Greenacre Cl, Barn. EN5 27	CZ38
Northolt UB5 60	BZ64
Swanley BR8 147	FE98
Greenacre Ct, Egh. (Eng.Grn.)	
TW20 112	AW93
Greenacre Gdns, E17 67	EC56
Greenacre Pl, Wall. (Hackbr.) SM6	
off Park Rd 141	DH103
Greenacres, N3 43	CY54
SE9 125	EN86
Bushey (Bushey Hth.)	
WD23 41	CD47
Green Acres, Croy. CR0 142	DT104
Greenacres, Epp. CM16 17	ET29
Leatherhead (Bkhm.)	
KT23 170	CB124
Oxted RH8 188	EE127
Greenacres Av, Uxb. UB10 . . .58	BM62
Greenacres Cl, Orp. BR6 163	EQ105
Rainham RM13 90	FL69
Greenacres Dr, Stan. HA7 . . .41	CH52
Greenacre Sq, SE16 203	J4
Greenacre Wk, N14 45	DL48
Greenall Cl, Wal.Cr. (Chsht.)	
EN8 15	DY30
Green Arbour Ct, EC1 196	F8
Green Av, NW7 42	CR49
W13 97	CH76
Greenaway Gdns, NW3 64	DB63
Green Bk, E1 202	D3
N12 44	DB49
Greenbank, Wal.Cr. (Chsht.)	
EN8 14	DV28
Greenbank Av, Wem. HA0 61	CG64
Greenbank Cl, E4 47	EC47
Romford RM3 52	FK48
Greenbank Cres, NW4 63	CY59
Greenbank Rd, Wat. WD17 . . .23	BR36
Greenbanks, Dart. DA1 128	FL89
Upminster RM14 73	FS60
Greenbay Rd, SE7 104	EK80
Greenberry St, NW8 194	B1
Greenbrook Av, Barn. EN4 . . .28	DC39
Greenbury Cl, Rick. (Chorl.)	
WD3 21	BC41
Green Cl, NW9 62	CQ58
NW11 64	DC59
Bromley BR2 144	EE97
Carshalton SM5 140	DF103
Feltham TW13 116	BY92
Hatfield AL9	
off Station Rd 11	CY26
Waltham Cross (Chsht.)	
EN8 15	DY32
Greencoat Pl, SW1 199	L8
Greencoat Row, SW1 199	L7
Greencourt Av, Croy. CR0 . . .142	DV103
Edgware HA8 42	CP53
Greencourt Gdns, Croy. CR0 .142	DV103
Greencourt Rd, Orp. BR5 . . .145	ER99
Green Ct Rd, Swan. BR8 . . .147	FD99
Greencrest Pl, NW2	
off Dollis Hill La 63	CU62
Green Cft, Edg. HA8	
off Deans La 42	CQ50
Greencroft Av, Ruis. HA4 60	BW61

A B C D E F G H I J K L M N O P Q R S T U V W X Y Z

Gre - Gri

Greencroft Cl, E6
off Neatscourt Rd 86 EL71
Greencroft Gdns, NW6 ...82 DB66
Enfield EN1 ....30 DS41
Greencroft Rd, Houns.TW5 ..96 BZ81
Green Curve, Bans. SM7 ...157 CZ114
Green Dale, SE5 ....102 DR84
SE22 ....122 DS85
Green Dale Cl, SE22
off Green Dale 122 DS85
Greendale Ms, Slou. SL2 ...74 AU73
Greendale Wk, Grav. (Nthflt.)
DA11 ....130 GE90
Green Dragon Ct, SE1 .....201 K2
Green Dragon La, N21 ......29 DP44
Brentford TW8 ....98 CL78
Green Dragon Yd, E1
off Old Montague St 84 DU71
Southall UB1 ....78 CA74
Woking (Ripley) GU23 ..167 BF123
Green E Rd, Beac. (Jordans)
HP9 ....36 AS52
Green Edge, Wat. WD25
off Clarke Grn 23 BU35
Greene Fielde End, Stai.
TW18 ....114 BK94
Green End, N21 ....45 DP47
Chessington KT9 ....156 CL105
Green End Business Cen, Rick.
WD3 off Church La 22 BG37
Greenend Rd, W4 ....98 CS75
Greenfarm Cl, Orp. BR6 ...163 ET106
Greenfield Av, Surb. KT5 ..138 CP101
Watford WD19 ....40 BX47
Greenfield End, Ger.Cr. (Chal.St.P.)
SL9 ....36 AY51
Greenfield Gdns, NW2 .....63 CY61
Dagenham RM9 ....88 EX67
Orpington BR5 ....145 ER101
Greenfield Link, Couls. CR5 ..175 DL115
Greenfield Rd, E1 ....84 DU71
Dagenham RM9 ....88 EW67
N15 ....36 DS57
Dagenham RM9 ....88 EW67
Dartford DA2 ....127 FD92
Greenfields, Loug. IG10 ....33 EN42
Potters Bar (Cuffley) EN6
off South Dr 13 DL30
Greenfields Cl, Brwd. CM13
off Essex Way 53 FW51
Loughton IG10 ....33 EN42
Greenfield St, Wal.Abb. EN9 ..15 EC34
Greenfield Way, Har. HA2 ...60 CB55
GREENFORD 78 CB69
≥ Greenford 79 CD67
⊖ Greenford 79 CD67
Greenford Av, W7 ....79 CE70
Southall UB1 ....78 BZ73
Greenford Gdns, Grnf. UB6 ..78 CB69
Greenford Rd, Grnf. UB6 ....78 CC71
Harrow HA1 ....61 CE64
Southall UB1 ....78 CC74
Sutton SM1 ....158 DB105
Green Gdns, Orp. BR6 .....163 EQ106
Greengate, Grnf. UB6 ......79 CH65
Greengate St, E13 ....86 EH68
Green Glade, Epp. (They.B.)
CM16 ....33 ES37
Green Glades, Horn. RM11 ...72 FM58
Greenham Cl, SE1 ....200 D5
Greenham Cres, E4 ....47 DZ51
Greenham Rd, N10 ....44 DG54
Greenham Wk, Wok. GU21 ..166 AW118
Greenhaven Dr, SE28 .....88 EV72
Greenhayes Av, Bans. SM7 ..158 DA114
Greenhayes Cl, Reig. RH2 ...184 DC134
Greenhayes Gdns, Bans.
SM7 ....174 DA115
Greenheys Cl, Nthwd. HA6 ...39 BS53
Greenheys Dr, E18 ....68 EF55
Greenheys Pl, Wok. GU22
off White Rose La 167 AZ118
Greenhill, NW3
off Hampstead High St ..64 DD63
SE18 ....105 EM78
Green Hill, Buck.H. IG9 ....48 EJ46
Orpington BR6 ....162 EL112
Greenhill, Sutt. SM1 ......140 DC103
Wembley HA9 ....62 CP61
Greenhill Av, Cat. CR3 ....176 DV121
Greenhill Cres, Wat. WD18 ..23 BS44
Greenhill Gdns, Nthlt. UB5 ..78 BZ68
Greenhill Gro, E12 ....68 EL63
Green Hill La, Warl. CR6 ...177 DY117
Greenhill Pk, NW10 ......80 CS67
Barnet EN5 ....28 DB43
Greenhill Rd, NW10 ......80 CS67
Gravesend (Nthflt.) DA11 ..131 GF89
Harrow HA1 ....61 CE58
Greenhills Cl, Rick. WD3 ...22 BH43
Greenhill's Rents, EC1 .....196 G6
Greenhill Ter, N1
off Baxter Rd 84 DH65
Greenhill Ter, SE18 ....105 EM78
Northolt UB5 ....78 BZ68
Greenhill Way, Croy. CR0 ...161 DX111
Harrow HA1 ....61 CE58
Wembley HA9 ....62 CP61
GREENHITHE 129 FV85
≥ Greenhithe 129 FU85
Greenhithe Cl, Sid. DA15 ...125 ES87
Greenholm Rd, SE9 ......125 EP85
Green Hundred Rd, SE15 ...102 DU79
Greenhurst Rd, Oxt. RH8 ...188 EG132
Greenhurst Rd, SE27 .....121 DN92
Greening St, SE2 ....106 EW77
Greenlake Ter, Stai. TW18 ..113 BF94
Greenland Cres, Sthl. UB2 ..96 BW76
Greenland Ms, SE8
off Trundleys Rd 103 DX78
Greenland Pl, NW1
off Greenland Rd 83 DH67
Greenland Quay, SE16 ....203 J8

Greenland Rd, NW1 ....83 DJ67
Barnet EN5 ....27 CW44
Greenlands, Cher. KT16 ....133 BC104
Greenlands Rd, Stai. TW18 ..114 BG91
Weybridge KT13 ....135 BP104
Greenland St, NW1
off Camden High St 83 DH67
Green La, E4 ....32 EE41
NW4 ....63 CX57
SE9 ....125 EN89
SE20 ....123 DX94
SW16 ....121 DM94
W7 ....97 CE75
Addlestone KT15 ......134 BG104
Amersham HP6 ....20 AS38
Ashtead KT21 ....171 CJ117
Brentford (Pilg.Hat.)
CM15 ....54 FV43
Brentwood (Warley) CM14 ..53 FV52
Caterham CR3 ....176 DQ122
Chertsey KT16 ....133 BE103
Chesham HP5 ....4 AV33
Chessington KT9 ......156 CL109
Chigwell IG7 ....49 ER47
Chislehurst BR7 ....125 EP91
Cobham KT11 ....154 BY112
Coulsdon CR5 ....184 DA125
Dagenham RM8 ....70 EU60
Edgware HA8 ....42 CN50
Egham TW20 ....113 BB91
Egham (Thorpe)TW20 ..133 BD95
Feltham TW13 ....116 BY92
Harrow HA1 ....61 CE62
Hemel Hempstead (Bov.)
HP3 ....5 AZ28
Hounslow TW4 ....95 BV83
Ilford IG1, IG3 ....69 EQ61
Leatherhead KT22 .....171 CK121
Morden SM4 ....140 DB100
New Malden KT3 ......138 CQ99
Northwood HA6 ....39 BT52
Purley CR8 ....159 DJ111
Redhill RH1 ....184 DE132
Redhill (Bletch.) RH1 ...186 DS131
Reigate RH2 ....183 CZ134
Rickmansworth (Crox.Grn.)
WD3 ....22 BM43
Shepperton TW17 .....135 BQ100
Slough (Datchet) SL3 ...92 AV81
South Ockendon RM15 ..91 FR69
Staines TW18 ....133 BE95
Stanmore HA7 ....41 CH49
Sunbury-on-Thames TW16 ..115 BT94
Tadworth KT20 ....183 CZ126
Thornton Heath CR7 ...141 DN95
Upminster RM14 ......91 FR68
Uxbridge UB8 ....77 BQ71
Waltham Abbey EN9 ....16 EJ34
Walton-on-Thames KT12 ..153 BV107
Warlingham CR6 ......177 DY116
Watford WD19 ....40 BW46
West Byfleet (Byfleet)
KT14 ....152 BM112
West Molesey KT8 ....136 CB99
Woking (Chobham) GU24 ..150 AT110
Woking (Mayford) GU24
off Copper Beech Cl ...166 AV121
Woking (Ockham) GU23 ..169 BP124
Worcester Park KT19 ...139 CU102
Green La Av, Walt. KT12 ...154 BW106
Green La Cl, Cher. KT16 ...133 BE103
West Byfleet (Byfleet)
KT14 ....152 BM112
Green La Gdns, Th.Hth. CR7 ..142 DQ96
Green Las, N4 ....66 DQ60
N8 ....65 DP55
N13 ....45 DM51
N15 ....65 DP55
N16 ....66 DQ62
N21 ....45 DP46
Epsom KT19 ....156 CS109
Greenlaw Gdns, N.Mal. KT3 ..139 CT101
Green Lawns, Ruis. HA4 ....60 BW60
Greenlaw St, SE18 ....105 EN76
Green Leaf Av, Wall. SM6 ..159 DK105
Greenleaf Cl, SW2
off Tulse Hill 121 DN87
Greenleafe Dr, Ilf. IG6 .....69 EP56
Greenleaf Rd, E6
off Redclyffe Rd 86 EJ67
E17 ....67 DZ55
Greenlea Pk, SW19 ......140 DD95
Green Leas, Sun. TW16 ....115 BT93
Waltham Abbey EN9
off Roundhills 15 ED34
Green Leas Cl, Sun. TW16
off Green Leas 115 BT93
Greenleaves Ct, Ashf. TW15
off Redleaves Av 115 BP93
Greenleigh Av, Orp. BR5 ...146 EV98
Green Man Gdns, W13 ....79 CG73
Green Man La, W13 ......79 CG74
Feltham TW14 ....95 BU84
Green Man Pas, W13 .....79 CG73
Green Man Roundabout, E11 ..68 EF59
Greenman St, N1 ....84 DQ66
Green Mead, Esher KT10
off Winterdown Gdns ..154 BZ107
Greenmead Cl, SE25 .....142 DU99
Green Meadow, Pot.B. EN6 ..12 DA30
Greenmeads, Wok. GU22 ..166 AY122
Green Moor Link, N21 ....45 DP45
Greenmoor Rd, Enf. EN3 ...30 DW40
Green N Rd, Beac. (Jordans)
HP9 ....36 AS51
Greenoak Pl, Barn. EN4 ...28 DF40
Greenoak Ri, West. (Bigg.H.)
TN16 ....178 EJ118
Greenoak Way, SW19 ....119 CX91
Greenock Rd, SW16 ......141 DK95
W3 ....98 CP76
Greenock Way, Rom. RM1 ..51 FE51
Greeno Cres, Shep. TW17 ..134 BN99
★ Green Park, SW1 ......199 J4
⊖ Green Park 199 K3

Green Pk, Stai. TW18 .....113 BE90
Greenpark Ct, Wem. HA0 ...79 CJ66
Green Pk Way, Grnf. UB6 ...79 CE67
Green Pl, Dart. DA1 ......127 FE85
Green Pt, E15 ....86 EE65
Green Pond Cl, E17 ......67 DZ55
Green Pond Rd, E17 .....67 DY55
Green Ride, Epp. CM16 ...33 EP35
Loughton IG10 ....32 EG43
Green Rd, N14 ....29 DH44
N20 ....44 DC48
Egham (Thorpe) TW20 ..133 BB98
Greenroof Way, SE10 ....205 L7
Greensand Cl, Red. (S.Merst.)
RH1 ....185 DK128
Green Sand Rd, Red. RH1 ..184 DG133
Greens Cl, The, Loug. IG10 ..33 EN40
Green's Ct, W1 ....195 M10
Green's End, SE18 ......105 EP77
Greenshank Cl, E17
off Banbury Rd 47 DY52
Greenshaw, Brwd. CM14 ...54 FV46
Greenshields Ind Est, E16 ..205 P3
Greenside, Bex. DA5 .....126 EY88
Borehamwood WD6 ....26 CM39
Dagenham RM8 ....70 EW60
Swanley BR8 ....147 FD96
Greenside Cl, N20 ......44 DD47
SE6 ....123 ED89
Greenside Dr, Ashtd. KT21 ..171 CH118
Greenside Rd, W12 ......99 CU76
Croydon CR0 ....141 DN100
Weybridge KT13 ....135 BP104
Greenside Wk, West. (Bigg.H.)
TN16 off Kings Rd 178 EH118
Greenslade Av, Ashtd. KT21 ..172 CP119
Greenslade Rd, Bark. IG11 ..87 ER66
Green Slip Rd, Barn. EN5 ...27 CZ40
Greenstead Av, Wdf.Grn.
IG8 ....48 EJ52
Greenstead Cl, Brwd. CM13 ..55 GE45
Woodford Green IG8
off Greenstead Gdns ..48 EJ51
Greenstead Gdns, SW15 ..119 CU85
Woodford Green IG8 ...48 EJ51
GREENSTED GREEN, Ong. ..19 FH28
Greensted Rd, Loug. IG10 ..48 EL45
Ongar CM5 ....19 FG28
Greenstone Ms, E11 ......68 EG58
GREEN STREET, Borwd. ...26 CP37
Green St, E7 ....86 EH65
E13 ....86 EJ67
W1 ....194 E10
Borehamwood WD6 ....26 CN36
Enfield EN3 ....30 DW40
Radlett (Shenley) WD7 ..26 CN36
Rickmansworth (Chorl.)
WD3 ....21 BC40
Sunbury-on-Thames
TW16 ....135 BU95
GREEN STREET GREEN,
Dart. 129 FU93
GREEN STREET GREEN,
Orp. 163 ES107
Green St Grn Rd, Dart.
DA1, DA2 ....128 FP88
Greensward, Bushey WD23 ..24 CB44
Green Ter, EC1 ....196 E3
Green Tiles La, Uxb. (Denh.)
UB9 ....57 BF58
Greentrees, Epp. CM16 ...18 EU31
Green Vale, W5 ....80 CM72
Bexleyheath DA6 ......126 EX85
Greenvale Rd, SE9 ......105 EM84
Green Verges, Stan. HA7 ...41 CK52
Green Vw, Chess. KT9 ....156 CM108
Greenview Av, Beck. BR3 ..143 DY100
Croydon CR0 ....143 DY100
Greenview Cl, W3 ......80 CS74
Green Vw Cl, Hem.H. (Bov.)
HP3 ....5 BA29
Greenview Ct, Ashf. TW15
off Village Way 114 BM91
Green Wk, NW4 ....63 CX57
SE1 ....201 M7
Buckhurst Hill IG9 ....48 EL45
Dartford DA1 ....107 FF84
Hampton TW12
off Orpwood Cl 116 BZ93
Ruislip HA4 ....59 BT60
Southall UB2 ....96 CA78
Woodford Green IG8 ...48 EL51
Green Wk, The, E4 ......47 EC46
Greenway, N14 ....45 DL47
N20 ....44 DA47
Greenway, SE9 ....124 EK85
Greenway, SW20 ....139 CW98
Brentwood CM13 ......55 GA45
Green Way, Brom. BR2 ...144 EL100
Greenway, Chis. BR7 ....125 EN92
Dagenham RM8 ....70 EW61
Harrow HA3 ....62 CL57
Hayes UB4 ....77 BV70
Leatherhead KT23 .....170 CB123
Pinner HA5 ....39 BV54
Green Way, Red. RH1 ....184 DE132
Greenway, Rom. RM3 ....52 FP51
Green Way, Sun. TW16 ...135 BU98
Greenway, Wall. SM6 ....159 DJ105
Westerham (Tats.) TN16 ..178 EJ120
Woodford Green IG8 ...48 EJ50
Greenway, The, NW9 ....42 CR56
Enfield EN3 ....31 DX35
Epsom KT18 ....172 CN115
Gerrards Cross (Chal.St.P.)
SL9 ....56 AX55
Harrow HA3 ....41 CE53
Hounslow TW4 ....96 BZ84
Orpington BR5 ....146 EV100
Oxted RH8 ....188 EH131
Pinner HA5 ....60 BZ58
Potters Bar EN6 ......12 DA33
Rickmansworth (Mill End)
WD3 ....38 BG45
Uxbridge UB8 ....76 BJ68
Uxbridge (Ickhm.) UB10 ..59 BQ61
Greenway Av, E17 ......67 ED56

Greenway Cl, N4 ....66 DQ61
N11 ....44 DG51
N15 off Copperfield Dr ..66 DT56
N20 ....44 DA47
NW9 ....42 CR56
West Byfleet KT14 .....152 BG113
Greenway Dr, Stai. TW18 ..134 BK95
Greenway Gdns, NW9 ....42 CR56
Croydon CR0 ....143 DZ104
Greenford UB6 ....78 CA69
Harrow HA3 ....41 CE54
Greenways, Abb.L. WD5 ....7 BS32
Beckenham BR3 ....143 EA96
Egham TW20 ....112 AY93
Esher KT10 ....155 CE105
Tadworth KT20 ....183 CV125
Waltham Cross (Chsht.)
EN7 ....13 DP29
Woking GU21 ....166 AS120
Greenways, The, Twick. TW1
off South Western Rd ..117 CG86
Greenwell Cl, Gdse. RH9 ..186 DV130
Greenwell St, W1 ......195 J5
Green W Rd, Beac. (Jordans)
HP9 ....36 AS52
GREENWICH, SE10 ......103 ED79
≥ Greenwich 103 EB80
DLR Greenwich 103 EB80
★ Greenwich Borough Mus, SE18
off Plumstead High St ..105 ET78
Greenwich Ch St, SE10 ...103 EC79
Greenwich Ct, Wal.Cr. EN8
off Parkside 15 DY34
Greenwich Cres, E6
off Swan App 86 EL71
Greenwich Foot Tunnel, E14 ..103 EC78
SE10 ....103 EC78
Greenwich High Rd, SE10 ..103 EB81
Greenwich Ind Est, SE7 ...205 P9
Greenwich Mkt, SE10
off King William Wk ...103 EC79
★ Greenwich Park, SE10 ..103 ED80
Greenwich Pk, SE10 .....104 EE80
★ Greenwich Pk St, SE10 ..103 ED78
★ Greenwich Pier, SE10 ...103 EC79
Greenwich S St, SE10 ....103 EB81
Greenwich Vw Pl, E14 ....204 B7
Greenwich Way, Wal.Abb.
EN9 ....31 EC36
Greenwood Av, Dag. RM10 ..71 FB63
Enfield EN3 ....31 DY40
Waltham Cross (Chsht.)
EN7 ....14 DV31
Greenwood Cl, Add. (Woodham)
KT15 ....151 BF111
Amersham HP6 ....20 AS37
Bushey (Bushey Hth.) WD23
off Langmead Dr 41 CE45
Morden SM4 ....139 CY98
Orpington BR5 ....145 ES100
Sidcup DA15
off Hurst Rd 126 EU89
Thames Ditton KT7 ....137 CG102
Waltham Cross (Chsht.) EN7
off Greenwood Av 14 DV31
Greenwood Ct, SW1 .....199 K10
Greenwood Dr, E4
off Avril Way 47 EC50
Watford WD25 ....7 BV33
Greenwood Gdns, N13 ...45 DP48
Caterham CR3 ....186 DU125
Ilford IG6 ....49 EQ52
Oxted RH8 ....188 EG134
Radlett (Shenley) WD7 ...10 CL33
Greenwood Ho, Grays RM17
off Argent St 110 GA79
Greenwood La, Hmptn. (Hmptn.H.)
TW12 ....116 CB92
Greenwood Pk, Kings.T. KT2 ..118 CS94
Greenwood Pl, NW5
off Highgate Rd 65 DH64
Greenwood Rd, E8 ......84 DU65
E13 off Maud Rd 86 EF68
Bexley DA5 ....127 FD91
Chigwell IG7 ....50 EV49
Croydon CR0 ....141 DP101
Isleworth TW7 ....97 CE83
Mitcham CR4 ....141 DK97
Thames Ditton KT7 ....137 CG102
Woking GU21 ....166 AS120
Greenwoods, The, Har. (S.Har.)
HA2 ....60 CC61
Greenwood Vw Ter, NW10 ..80 CR82
Greenwood Way, Sev. TN13 ..190 FF125
Green Wrythe Cres, Cars.
SM5 ....140 DE102
Green Wrythe La, Cars. SM5 ..140 DD100
Greenyard, Wal.Abb. EN9 ..15 EC33
Greer Rd, Har. HA3 .....40 CC53
Greet St, SE1 ....200 E3
Greg Cl, E10 ....67 EC58
Gregor Ms, SE3 ....104 EG80
Gregory Av, Pot.B. EN6 ...12 DC33
Gregory Cl, Wok. GU21 ...166 AW117
Gregory Cres, SE9 ......124 EK87
Gregory Dr, Wind. (Old Wind.)
SL4 ....112 AV86
Gregory Ms, Wal.Abb. EN9
off Beaulieu Dr 15 EB33
Gregory Pl, W8 ....100 DB75
Gregory Rd, Rom. RM6 ...70 EX56
Southall UB2 ....96 CA76
Gregson Cl, Borwd. WD6 ..26 CQ39
Gregson's Ride, Loug. IG10 ..33 EN38
Greig Cl, N8 ....65 DL57
Greig Ter, SE17
off Lorrimore Sq 101 DP79
Grenaby Av, Croy. CR0 ...142 DR101
Grenaby Rd, Croy. CR0 ...142 DR101
Grenade St, E14 ....85 DZ73
Grenadier Pl, Cat. CR3 ...176 DQ122
Grenadier St, E16 ......87 EN74
Grenadine Cl, Wal.Cr. EN7
off Allwood Rd 14 DT27
Grena Gdns, Rich. TW9 ...98 CM84

Grena Rd, Rich. TW9 .....98 CM84
Grendon Gdns, Wem. HA9 ..62 CN61
Grendon St, NW8 ......194 B4
Grenfell Av, Horn. RM12 ...71 FF60
Grenfell Cl, Borwd. WD6 ...26 CQ39
Grenfell Gdns, Har. HA3 ...62 CL59
Grenfell Rd, W11 ....81 CX73
Mitcham CR4 ....120 DF93
Grenfell Twr, W11 ......81 CX73
Grenfell Wk, W11 ....81 CX73
Grennell Cl, Sutt. SM1 ...140 DD103
Grennell Rd, Sutt. SM1 ...140 DC103
Grenoble Gdns, N13 .....45 DN51
Grenville Cl, N3 ....43 CZ53
Cobham KT11 ....154 BX113
Surbiton KT5 ....138 CQ102
Waltham Cross EN8 ....15 DY34
Grenville Gdns, Wdf.Grn. IG8 ..48 EJ53
Grenville Ms, N19 ......100 DC77
Hampton TW12 ....116 CB92
Grenville Pl, NW7 ......42 CR50
SW7 ....100 DC76
Grenville Rd, N19 ......65 DL60
Croydon (New Adgtn.)
CR0 ....161 EC109
Grays (Chaff.Hun.) RM16 ..109 FV78
Grenville St, WC1 ......196 A5
Gresham Av, N20 ......44 DF49
Warlingham CR6 ......177 DY118
Gresham Cl, Bex. DA5 ...126 EY86
Brentwood CM14 ......54 FW48
Enfield EN2 ....30 DQ41
Oxted RH8 ....188 EF128
Gresham Dr, Rom. RM6 ...70 EV57
Gresham Gdns, NW11 ....63 CY60
Gresham Rd, E6 ....87 EM68
E16 ....86 EH72
NW10 ....62 CR64
SE25 ....142 DU98
SW9 ....101 DN83
Beckenham BR3 ....143 DY96
Brentwood CM14 ......54 FW48
Edgware HA8 ....42 CM51
Hampton TW12 ....116 CA93
Hounslow TW3 ....96 CC81
Oxted RH8 ....188 EF128
Staines TW18 ....113 BF92
Uxbridge UB10 ....76 BN68
Gresham St, EC2 ....197 H8
Gresham Way, SW19 ....120 DA90
Gresley Cl, E17 ....67 DY58
N15 off Clinton Rd 66 DR56
Gresley Ct, Pot.B. EN6 ...12 DC29
Gresley Rd, N19 ....65 DJ60
Gressenhall Rd, SW18 ...119 CZ86
Gresse St, W1 ....195 M7
Gresswell Cl, Sid. DA14 ..126 EU90
Greswell St, SW6 ......99 CX81
Gretton Rd, N17 ....46 DS52
Greville Av, S.Croy. CR2 ..161 DX110
Greville Cl, Ashtd. KT21 ..172 CL119
Twickenham TW1 .....117 CH87
Greville Hall, NW6 ......82 DB68
Greville Ms, NW6
off Greville Rd 82 DB68
Greville Pk Av, Ashtd. KT21 ..172 CL118
Greville Pk Rd, Ashtd. KT21 ..172 CL118
Greville Pl, NW6 ....82 DB68
Greville Rd, E17 ....67 EC56
NW6 ....82 DB67
Richmond TW10 ......118 CM86
Greville St, EC1 ....196 E7
Grey Alders, Bans. SM7
off High Beeches 157 CW114
Greycaine Rd, Wat. WD24 ..24 BX37
Grey Cl, NW11 ....64 DC58
Greycoat Pl, SW1 ......199 M7
Greycoat St, SW1 ......199 M7
Greycot Rd, Beck. BR3 ...123 EA92
Grey Eagle St, E1 ......197 P6
Greyfell Cl, Stan. HA7
off Coverdale Cl 41 CH50
Greyfields Cl, Pur. CR8 ...159 DP113
Greyfriars, Brwd. CM13 ...55 GB45
Greyfriars Pas, EC1 .....196 G8
Greyfriars, Wok. (Ripley)
GU23 ....168 BG124
Greyhound Hill, NW4 ....63 CU55
Greyhound La, SW16 ....121 DK93
Grays (Orsett) RM16 ....111 GG75
Potters Bar EN6 ......11 CU33
Greyhound Rd, N17 .....66 DS55
NW10 ....81 CV69
W6 ....99 CX79
W14 ....99 CY79
Sutton SM1 ....158 DC106
Greyhound Ter, SW16 ...141 DJ95
Greyhound Way, Dart. DA1 ..127 FE86
Greys Pk Cl, Kes. BR2 ...162 EJ106
Greystead Rd, SE23 ....122 DW87
Greystoke Av, Pnr. HA5 ..60 CA55
Greystoke Dr, Ruis. HA4 ..59 BP58
Greystoke Gdns, W5 ....80 CL70
Enfield EN2 ....29 DK42
Greystoke Pk Ter, W5 ...79 CK69
Greystoke Pl, EC4 ......196 D8
Greystone Cl, S.Croy. CR2 ..160 DW111
Greystone Gdns, Har. HA3 ..61 CJ58
Ilford IG6 ....49 EQ54
Greystone Path, E11
off Grove Rd 68 EF59
Greystones Dr, Reig. RH2 ..184 DC132
Greyswood St, SW16 ....121 DH93
Greythorne Rd, Wok. GU21 ..166 AU118
Grey Twrs Av, Horn. RM11 ..72 FK60
Grey Twrs Gdns, Horn. RM11
off Grey Twrs Av 72 FK60
Grice Av, West. (Bigg.H.)
TN16 ....162 EH113
Gridiron Pl, Upmin. RM14 ..72 FP62
Grierson Rd, SE23 ......123 DX87
Grieves Rd, Grav. (Nthflt.)
DA11 ....131 GF90
Griffin Av, Upmin. RM14 ...73 FS58
Griffin Cen, The, Felt. TW14 ..115 BV85
Griffin Cl, NW10 ....63 CV64
Griffin Manor Way, SE28 ..105 ER76

Griffin Rd, N17 .....46 DS54
SE18 .....105 ER78
Griffins, The, Grays RM16 .....110 GB75
Griffin Wk, Green. DA9
  off Church Rd 129 FT85
Griffin Way, Sun. TW16 .....135 BU96
Griffith Rd, Dag. RM8
  off Gibson Rd 70 EW60
Griffiths Cl, Wor.Pk. KT4 .....139 CV103
Griffiths Rd, SW19 .....120 DA94
Griffon Way, Wat. WD25
  off Ashfields 7 BT34
Grifon Rd, Grays (Chaff.Hun.)
RM16 .....109 FW76
Griggs App, Ilf. IG1 .....69 EQ61
Griggs Gdns, Horn. RM12
  off Tylers Cres 72 FJ64
Griggs Pl, SE1 .....201 N7
Griggs Rd, E10 .....67 EC58
Grilse Cl, N9 .....46 DV49
Grimsby Gro, E16 .....87 EP74
Grimsby St, E2
  off Cheshire St 84 DU70
Grimsdyke Cres, Barn. EN5 .....27 CW41
Grimsdyke Rd, Pnr. HA5 .....40 BY52
Grimsel Path, SE5
  off Laxley Cl 101 DP80
Grimshaw Cl, N6 .....64 DG59
Grimshaw Way, Rom. RM1 .....71 FF57
Grimstone Cl, Rom. RM5 .....51 FB51
Grimston Rd, SW6 .....99 CZ82
Grimwade Av, Croy. CR0 .....142 DU104
Grimwade Cl, SE15 .....102 DW83
Grimwood Rd, Twick. TW1 .....117 CF87
Grindall Cl, Croy. CR0
  off Hillside Rd 159 DP105
Grindal St, SE1 .....200 D5
Grindleford Av, N11 .....44 DG47
Grindley Gdns, Croy. CR0 .....142 DT100
Grinling Pl, SE8 .....103 EA79
Grinstead Rd, SE8 .....103 DY78
Grisedale Cl, Pur. CR8 .....160 DS114
Grisedale Gdns, Pur. CR8 .....160 DS114
Grittleton Av, Wem. HA9 .....80 CP65
Grittleton Rd, W9 .....82 DA70
Grizedale Ter, SE23 .....122 DV89
Grobars Av, Wok. GU21 .....166 AW115
Grocer's Hall Ct, EC2 .....197 K9
Grogan Cl, Hmptn. TW12 .....116 BZ93
Groombridge Cl, Walt. KT12 .....153 BV106
  Welling DA16 .....126 EU85
Groombridge Rd, E9 .....85 DX66
Groom Cl, Brom. BR2 .....144 EH98
Groom Cres, SW18 .....120 DD87
Groomfield Cl, SW17 .....120 DG91
Groom Pl, SW1 .....198 G6
Groom Rd, Brox. EN10 .....15 DZ26
Grooms Cotts, Chesh. HP5 .....4 AV30
Grooms Dr, Pnr. HA5 .....59 BU57
Grosmont Rd, SE18 .....105 ET78
Grosse Way, SW15 .....119 CV86
Grosvenor Av, N5 .....66 DQ64
SW14 .....98 CS83
  Carshalton SM5 .....158 DF107
  Harrow HA2 .....60 CB58
  Hayes UB4 .....77 BS68
  Kings Langley WD4 .....7 BQ28
  Richmond TW10
  off Grosvenor Rd 118 CL85
Grosvenor Cl, Iver SL0 .....75 BD69
  Loughton IG10 .....33 EP39
Grosvenor Cotts, SW1 .....198 F8
Grosvenor Ct, N14 .....45 DJ45
NW6 .....81 CX67
  Rickmansworth (Crox.Grn.) WD3
  off Mayfare 23 BR43
  Slough SL1
  off Stoke Poges La 74 AS72
Grosvenor Cres, NW9 .....62 CN56
SW1 .....198 G5
  Dartford DA1 .....128 FK85
  Uxbridge UB10 .....77 BP66
Grosvenor Cres Ms, SW1 .....198 F5
Grosvenor Dr, Horn. RM11 .....72 FJ60
  Loughton IG10 .....33 EP39
Grosvenor Est, SW1 .....199 N8
Grosvenor Gdns, E6 .....86 EK69
N10 .....65 DJ55
N14 .....29 DK43
NW2 .....63 CW64
NW11 .....63 CZ58
SW1 .....199 H6
SW14 .....98 CS83
  Kingston upon Thames
  KT2 .....117 CK93
  Upminster RM14 .....73 FR60
  Wallington SM6 .....159 DJ108
  Woodford Green IG8 .....48 EG51
Grosvenor Gdns Ms E, SW1 .....199 J6
Grosvenor Gdns Ms N, SW1 .....199 H7
Grosvenor Gdns Ms S, SW1 .....199 J7
Grosvenor Gate, W1 .....198 F1
Grosvenor Hill, SW19 .....119 CY93
W1 .....195 H10
Grosvenor Pk, SE5 .....102 DQ79
Grosvenor Pk Rd, E17 .....67 EA57
Grosvenor Path, Loug. IG10 .....33 EP39
Grosvenor Pl, SW1 .....198 G5
  Weybridge KT13
  off Vale Rd 135 BR104
Grosvenor Ri E, E17 .....67 EB57
Grosvenor Rd, E6 .....86 EK67
E7 .....86 EH65
E10 .....67 EC60
E11 .....68 EG57
N3 .....43 CZ52
N9 .....46 DV46
N10 .....45 DH53
SE25 .....142 DU98
SW1 .....101 DH79
W4 .....98 CP78
W7 .....79 CG74
  Belvedere DA17 .....106 FA79
  Bexleyheath DA6 .....126 EX85
  Borehamwood WD6 .....26 CN41
  Brentford TW8 .....97 CK79
  Dagenham RM8 .....70 EZ60

Grosvenor Rd, Epsom KT18 .172 CR119
  Hounslow TW3 .....96 BZ83
  Ilford IG1 .....69 EQ62
  Northwood HA6 .....39 BT50
  Orpington BR5 .....145 ES100
  Richmond TW10 .....118 CL85
  Romford RM7 .....71 FD59
  Southall UB2 .....96 BZ76
  Staines TW18 .....114 BG46
  Twickenham TW1 .....117 CG87
  Wallington SM6 .....159 DH107
  Watford WD17 .....24 BW42
  West Wickham BR4 .....143 EB102
Grosvenor Sq, W1 .....194 G10
  Kings Langley WD4
  off Grosvenor Av 7 BQ28
Grosvenor St, W1 .....195 H10
Grosvenor Ter, SE5 .....101 DP80
Grosvenor Vale, Ruis. HA4 .....59 BT61
Grosvenor Way, E5 .....66 DW61
Grosvenor Wf Rd, E14 .....204 F9
Grote's Bldgs, SE3 .....104 EE82
Grote's Pl, SE3 .....104 EE82
Grotto Pas, W1 .....194 G6
Grotto Rd, Twick. TW1 .....117 CF89
  Weybridge KT13 .....135 BP104
Grove, The, E15 .....86 EE65
N3 .....44 DA53
N4 .....65 DM59
N6 .....64 DG60
N8 .....65 DK57
N13 .....45 DN50
N14 .....29 DJ43
NW9 .....62 CR57
NW11 .....63 CY59
W5 .....79 CK74
  Addlestone KT15 .....152 BH104
  Bexleyheath DA6 .....106 EX84
  Brentwood CM14 .....54 FT49
  Caterham CR3 .....175 DP121
  Chesham HP5 .....20 AX36
  Coulsdon CR5 .....175 DK115
  Edgware HA8 .....42 CP49
  Egham TW20 .....113 BA92
  Enfield EN2 .....29 DN40
  Epsom KT17 .....156 CS113
  Esher KT10 .....136 CB102
  Gravesend DA12 .....131 GH87
  Greenford UB6 .....78 CC72
  Hatfield AL9 .....12 DA27
  Isleworth TW7 .....97 CE81
  Potters Bar EN6 .....12 DC32
  Radlett WD7 .....9 CG34
  Sidcup DA14 .....126 EY91
  Slough SL1 .....92 AU75
  Stanmore HA7 .....41 CG47
  Swanley BR8 .....147 FF97
  Swanscombe DA10 .....130 FZ85
  Teddington TW11 .....117 CG91
  Twickenham TW1
  off Bridge Rd 117 CH86
  Upminster RM14 .....72 FP63
  Uxbridge UB10 .....58 BN64
  Walton-on-Thames KT12 .135 BV101
  Watford WD17 .....23 BQ37
  West Wickham BR4 .....143 EB104
  Westerham (Bigg.H.) TN16 .178 EK118
  Woking GU21 .....167 AZ116
Grove Av, N3 .....44 DA52
N10 .....45 DJ54
N7 .....65 CE72
  Epsom KT17 .....156 CS113
  Pinner HA5 .....60 BY56
  Sutton SM1 .....158 DA107
  Twickenham TW1 .....117 CF88
Grove Bk, Wat. WD19 .....40 BX46
Grovebarns, Stai. TW18 .....114 BG93
Grovebury Cl, Erith DA8 .....107 FD79
Grovebury Gdns, St.Alb. (Park St.)
AL2 .....8 CC27
Grovebury Rd, SE2 .....106 EV75
Grove Cl, N14 off Avenue Rd .45 DH45
SE23 .....123 DX88
  Bromley BR2 .....144 EG103
  Feltham TW13 .....116 BY91
  Gerrards Cross (Chal.St.P.) SL9
  off Grove La 36 AW53
  Kingston upon Thames
  KT1 .....138 CM98
  Slough SL1 off Alpha St S .92 AU76
  Uxbridge UB10 .....58 BN64
  Windsor (Old Wind.) SL4 .112 AV87
Grove Cotts, SW3 .....100 DE79
Grove Ct, SE3 .....104 EG81
  Barnet EN5 off High St .27 CZ41
  East Molesey KT8
  off Walton Rd 137 CD99
  Waltham Abbey EN9
  off Highbridge St 15 EB33
Grove Cres, E18 .....48 EF54
NW9 .....62 CQ56
SE5 .....102 DS82
  Feltham TW13 .....116 BY91
  Kingston upon Thames
  KT1 .....138 CL97
  Rickmansworth (Crox.Grn.)
  WD3 .....22 BN42
  Walton-on-Thames KT12 .135 BV101
Grove Cres Rd, E15 .....85 ED65
Grovedale Cl, Wal.Cr. (Chsht.)
EN7 .....14 DT30
Grovedale Rd, N19 .....65 DK61
Grove End, E18
  off Grove Hill 48 EF54
NW5 off Chetwynd Rd 65 DH63
  Gerrards Cross (Chal.St.P.)
  SL9 .....36 AW53
Grove End Gdns, NW8
  off Grove End Rd 82 DD68
Grove End La, Esher KT10 .137 CD102
Grove End Rd, NW8 .....82 DD69
Grove Fm Ct, Mitch. CR4
  off Brookfields Av 140 DF98
Grove Fm Pk, Nthwd. HA6 .....39 BR50
Grove Footpath, Surb. KT5 .138 CL98

Grove Gdns, NW4 .....63 CU56
NW8 .....194 C3
  Dagenham RM10 .....71 FC62
  Enfield EN3 .....31 DX39
  Teddington TW11 .....117 CG91
Grove Grn Rd, E11 .....67 EC62
Grove Hall Ct, NW8
  off Hall Rd 82 DC69
Grove Hall Rd, Bushey WD23 .24 BY42
Grove Heath, Wok. (Ripley)
GU23 .....168 BJ124
Grove Heath Ct, Wok. (Ripley)
GU23 .....168 BJ124
Grove Heath N, Wok. (Ripley)
GU23 .....168 BH122
Grove Heath Rd, Wok. (Ripley)
GU23 .....168 BJ123
Groveherst Rd, Dart. DA1 .....108 FM83
Grove Hill, E18 .....48 EF54
  Gerrards Cross (Chal.St.P.)
  SL9 .....36 AW52
  Harrow HA1 .....61 CE59
Grove Hill Rd, SE5 .....102 DS83
  Harrow HA1 .....61 CE59
Grovehill Rd, Red. RH1 .....184 DE134
Grove Ho Rd, N8 .....65 DL56
Groveland Av, SW16 .....121 DM94
Groveland Ct, EC4 .....197 J9
Groveland Rd, Beck. BR3 .....143 DZ97
Grovelands, St.Alb. (Park St.)
AL2 .....8 CB27
  West Molesey KT8 .....136 CA98
Grovelands Cl, SE5 .....102 DS82
  Harrow HA2 .....60 CB62
Grovelands Ct, N14 .....45 DK45
Grovelands Rd, N13 .....45 DM49
N15 .....66 DU58
  Orpington BR5 .....126 EU94
  Purley CR8 .....159 DL112
Grovelands Way, Grays
RM17 .....110 FZ78
Groveland Way, N.Mal. KT3 .138 CQ99
Grove La, SE5 .....102 DR81
  Chesham HP5 .....20 AV27
  Chigwell IG7 .....49 ET48
  Coulsdon CR5 .....158 DG113
  Epping CM16 off High St .18 EU30
  Gerrards Cross (Chal.St.P.)
  SL9 .....36 AW53
  Kingston upon Thames
  KT1 .....138 CL98
  Uxbridge UB8 .....76 BM70
Grove La Ter, SE5
  off Grove La 102 DS83
Groveley Rd, Sun. TW16 .....115 BT92
Grove Mkt Pl, SE9 .....125 EM86
Grove Ms, W6 .....99 CW76
W11 off Portobello Rd 81 CZ72
Grove Mill La, Wat. WD17 .....23 BP37
Grove Mill Pl, Cars. SM5 .140 DG104
GROVE PARK, SE12 .....124 EG89
GROVE PARK, W4 .....98 CP80
Grove Park 124 EG90
Grove Pk, E11 .....68 EH58
NW9 .....62 CQ56
SE5 .....102 DS82
Grove Pk Av, E4 .....47 EB52
Grove Pk Br, W4 .....98 CQ80
Grove Pk Gdns, W4 .....98 CP79
Grove Pk Ms, W4 .....98 CQ80
Grove Pk Rd, N15 .....66 DS56
SE9 .....124 EJ90
W4 .....98 CP80
  Rainham RM13 .....89 FG67
Grove Pk Ter, W4 .....98 CP79
Grove Pas, E2 .....84 DV68
  Teddington TW11 .....117 CG92
Grove Path, Wal.Cr. (Chsht.)
EN7 .....14 DU31
Grove Pl, NW3
  off Christchurch Hill 64 DD63
SW12 off Cathles Rd 121 DH86
W3 .....80 CQ74
W5 off The Grove 79 CK74
  Banstead SM7 .....158 DF112
  Barking IG11
  off Clockhouse Av 87 EQ67
  Watford WD25 .....24 CB39
  Weybridge KT13
  off Princes Rd 153 BQ106
Grove Rd, E3 .....85 DX67
E4 .....47 EB49
E11 .....68 EF59
E17 .....67 EB58
E18 .....48 EF54
N11 .....45 DH50
N12 .....44 DD50
N15 .....66 DS57
NW2 .....81 CW65
SW13 .....99 CT82
SW19 .....120 DC94
W3 .....80 CQ74
W5 .....79 CK73
  Amersham HP6 .....20 AT37
  Ashtead KT21 .....172 CM118
  Barnet EN4 .....28 DC41
  Belvedere DA17 .....106 EZ79
  Bexleyheath DA7 .....107 FC84
  Borehamwood WD6 .....26 CN39
  Brentford TW8 .....97 CJ78
  Chertsey KT16 .....133 BF100
  East Molesey KT8 .....137 CD98
  Edgware HA8 .....42 CN51
  Epsom KT17 .....156 CS113
  Gravesend (Nthflt.) DA11 .130 GB85
  Grays RM17 .....110 GC79
  Hounslow TW3 .....96 CB84
  Isleworth TW7 .....97 CE81
  Mitcham CR4 .....141 DH96
  Northwood HA6 .....39 BR50
  Oxted RH8
  off Southlands La .187 EC134
  Pinner HA5 .....60 BZ57
  Richmond TW10 .....118 CM86
  Rickmansworth (Mill End)
  WD3 .....38 BG47
  Romford RM6 .....70 EY59

Grove Rd, Sev. TN14 .....191 FJ121
  Sevenoaks (Seal) TN15 .191 FN122
  Shepperton TW17 .....135 BQ100
  Surbiton KT6 .....137 CK99
  Sutton SM1 .....158 DB107
  Thornton Heath CR7 .....141 DN98
  Twickenham TW2 .....117 CD90
  Uxbridge UB8 .....76 BK66
  Westerham (Tats.) TN16 .178 EJ120
  Woking GU21 .....167 AZ116
Grove Rd W, Enf. EN3 .....30 DW37
Grover Rd, Wat. WD19 .....40 BX45
Grove Shaw, Tad. (Kgswd.)
KT20 .....173 CY124
Groveside Cl, W3 .....80 CN72
  Carshalton SM5 .....140 DE103
Groveside Rd, E4 .....48 EE47
Grovestile Waye, Felt. TW14 .115 BR87
Grove St, N18 .....46 DT51
SE8 .....203 M8
Grove Ter, NW5 .....65 DH62
  Teddington TW11 .....117 CG91
Grove Ter Ms, NW5
  off Grove Ter 65 DH62
Grove Vale, SE22 .....102 DS84
  Chislehurst BR7 .....125 EN93
Grove Vil, E14 .....85 EB72
Groveway, SW9 .....101 DM81
  Dagenham RM8 .....70 EX63
Grove Way, Esher KT10 .....136 CC101
  Rickmansworth (Chorl.)
  WD3 .....21 BB42
  Uxbridge UB8 .....76 BK66
  Wembley HA9 .....62 CP64
Grovewood, Rich. TW9
  off Sandycombe Rd 98 CN81
Grovewood Cl, Rick. (Chorl.)
WD3 .....21 BB43
Grove Wd Hill, Couls. CR5 .159 DK114
Grovewood Pl, Wdf.Grn. IG8 .49 EM53
Grubb St, Oxt. RH8 .....188 EJ128
Grummant Rd, SE15 .....102 DT81
Grundy St, E14 .....85 EB72
Gruneisen Rd, N3 .....44 DB52
Guardian Cl, Horn. RM11 .....71 FH60
Guards Av, Cat. CR3 .....176 DQ122
Guards Mus, SW1 .....199 L5
Gubbins La, Rom. RM3 .....52 FM52
Gubyon Av, SE24 .....121 DP85
Guerin Sq, E3 .....85 DZ69
Guernsey Cl, Houns. TW5 .....96 CA81
Guernsey Fm Dr, Wok. GU21 .166 AX115
Guernsey Gro, SE24 .....122 DQ87
Guernsey Ho, Enf. EN3
  off Eastfield Rd 31 DX38
Guernsey Rd, E11 .....67 ED60
Guibal Rd, SE12 .....124 EH88
Guildersfield Rd, SW16 .....121 DL94
Guildford Av, Felt. TW13 .....115 BT89
Guildford Gdns, Rom. RM3 .....52 FL51
Guildford Gro, SE10 .....103 EB81
Guildford La, Wok. GU22 .166 AX120
Guildford Rd, E6 .....86 EL72
E17 .....47 EC53
SW8 .....101 DL81
  Chertsey KT16 .....133 BE102
  Croydon CR0 .....142 DR100
  Ilford IG3 .....69 ES61
  Leatherhead (Fetch.) KT22 .171 CG122
  Romford RM3 .....52 FL51
  Woking GU22 .....166 AY119
  Woking (Mayford) GU22 .166 AX122
Guildford St, Cher. KT16 .134 BG101
  Staines TW18 .....114 BG93
Guildford Way, Wall. SM6 .159 DL106
Guildhall, The, EC2 .....197 K8
Guildhall Art Gall,
  Guildhall Lib, EC2 .....197 J8
Guildhall Bldgs, EC2
  off Basinghall St 84 DR72
Guildhall Yd, EC2 .....197 K8
Guildhouse St, SW1 .....199 K8
Guildown Av, N12 .....44 DB49
Guild Rd, SE7 .....104 EK78
  Erith DA8 .....107 FF80
Guildsway, E17 .....47 DZ53
Guileshill La, Wok. (Ockham)
GU23 .....168 BL123
Guilford Av, Surb. KT5 .....138 CM99
Guilford Pl, WC1 .....196 B5
Guilford St, WC1 .....195 P5
Guilford Vil, Surb. KT5
  off Alpha Rd 138 CM100
Guilsborough Cl, NW10 .....80 CS66
Guinevere Gdns, Wal.Cr. EN8 .15 DY31
Guinness Cl, E9 .....85 DY66
  Hayes UB3 .....95 BR76
Guinness Ct, Wok. GU21
  off Iveagh Rd 166 AT118
Guinness Sq, SE1 .....201 M8
Guinness Trust Bldgs, SE1
  off Snowsfields 102 DS75
SE11 .....200 G10
SW3 .....198 D9
SW9 .....101 DP84
Guinness Trust Est, N16
  off Holmleigh Rd 66 DS60
Guion Rd, SW6 .....99 CZ82
Gulland Cl, Bushey WD23 .....24 CC43
Gulland Wk, N1
  off Clephane Rd 84 DQ65
Gull Cl, Wall. SM6 .....159 DL108
Gullet Wd Rd, Wat. WD25 .....23 BU35
Gulliver Cl, Nthlt. UB5 .....78 BZ67
Gulliver Rd, Sid. DA15 .....125 ES89
Gulliver St, SE16 .....203 M6
Gull Wk, Horn. RM12
  off Heron Flight Av 89 FH66
Gulston Wk, SW3 .....198 E9
Gumleigh Rd, W5 .....97 CJ77
Gumley Gdns, Islw. TW7 .....97 CG83
Gumley Rd, Grays RM20 .....109 FX79
Gumping Rd, Orp. BR5 .....145 EQ103
Gundulph Rd, Brom. BR2 .....144 EJ97
Gunfleet Cl, Grav. DA12 .....131 GL87
Gun Hill, Til. (W.Til.) RM18 .111 GK79

Gunmakers La, E3 .....85 DY67
Gunnell Cl, SE26 .....122 DU92
  Croydon CR0 .....142 DU100
Gunner Dr, Enf. EN3
  off Government Row 31 EA37
Gunner La, SE18 .....105 EN78
GUNNERSBURY, W4 .....98 CP77
Gunnersbury 98 CP78
Gunnersbury 98 CP78
Gunnersbury Av, W3 .....98 CN76
W4 .....98 CP78
W5 .....80 CM74
Gunnersbury Cl, W4
  off Grange Rd 98 CP78
Gunnersbury Ct, W3
  off Bollo La 98 CP75
Gunnersbury Cres, W3 .....98 CN75
Gunnersbury Dr, W5 .....98 CM75
Gunnersbury Gdns, W3 .....98 CN75
Gunnersbury La, W3 .....98 CN76
Gunnersbury Ms, W4
  off Chiswick High Rd 98 CP78
Gunnersbury Park, W3
  (Ealing) 98 CM75
Gunnersbury Pk, W3 .....98 CM77
W5 .....98 CM77
Gunnersbury Park Mus &
  Art Cen, W3 .....98 CN76
Gunners Gro, E4 .....47 EC48
Gunners Rd, SW18 .....120 DD89
Gunning Rd, Grays RM17 .110 GD78
Gunning St, SE18 .....105 ES77
Gunn Rd, Swans. DA10 .....130 FY86
Gunpowder Sq, EC4 .....196 E8
Gunstor Rd, N16 .....66 DS63
Gun St, E1 .....197 P7
Gunter Gro, SW10 .....100 DC79
  Edgware HA8 .....42 CR53
Gunterstone Rd, W14 .....99 CY77
Gunthorpe St, E1 .....84 DT71
Gunton Rd, E5 .....66 DV62
SW17 .....120 DG93
Gunwhale Cl, SE16 .....203 J3
Gurdon Rd, SE7 .....104 EG78
Gurnard Cl, West Dr. UB7
  off Trout Rd 76 BK73
Gurnell Gro, W13 .....79 CF70
Gurney Cl, E15
  off Gurney Rd 68 EE64
E17 .....47 DX53
  Barking IG11 .....87 EP65
Gurney Cres, Croy. CR0 .141 DM102
Gurney Dr, N2 .....64 DC57
Gurney Rd, E15 .....68 EE64
  Carshalton SM5 .....158 DG105
  Northolt UB5 .....77 BV69
Guthrie St, SW3 .....198 B10
Gutteridge La, Rom. (Stap.Abb.)
RM4 .....35 FC44
Gutter La, EC2 .....197 J8
Guyatt Gdns, Mitch. CR4
  off Ormerod Gdns 140 DG96
Guy Barnett Gro, SE3
  off Casterbridge Rd 104 EG83
Guy Rd, Wall. SM6 .....141 DK104
Guyscliff Rd, SE13 .....123 EC85
Guysfield Cl, Rain. RM13 .....89 FG67
Guysfield Dr, Rain. RM13 .....89 FG67
Guy's Hosp, SE1 .....201 L4
Guy St, SE1 .....201 L4
Gwalior Rd, SW15 .....99 CX84
Gwendolen Av, SW15 .....119 CX85
Gwendolen Cl, SW15 .....119 CX85
Gwendoline Av, E13 .....86 EH67
Gwendwr Rd, W14 .....99 CY78
Gwent Cl, Wat. WD25 .....8 BX34
Gwillim Cl, Sid. DA15 .....126 EU85
Gwydor Rd, Beck. BR3 .....143 DX98
Gwydyr Rd, Brom. BR2 .....144 EF97
Gwyn Cl, SW6 .....100 DC80
Gwynne Av, Croy. CR0 .....143 DX101
Gwynne Cl, W4
  off Pumping Sta Rd 99 CT79
Gwynne Pk Av, Wdf.Grn. IG8 .49 EM51
Gwynne Pl, WC1 .....196 C3
Gwynne Rd, SW11 .....100 DD82
  Caterham CR3 .....176 DR123
Gwynn Rd, Grav. (Nthflt.)
DA11 .....130 GC89
Gyfford Wk, Wal.Cr. EN7 .....14 DV31
Gylcote Cl, SE5 .....102 DR84
Gyles Pk, Stan. HA7 .....41 CJ53
Gyllyngdune Gdns, Ilf. IG3 .69 ET61
Gypsy La, Kings L. WD4 .....23 BR35
  Slough (Stoke P.) SL2 .....56 AS63

H

Haarlem Rd, W14 .....99 CX76
Haberdasher Est, N1
  off Haberdasher St 84 DR69
Haberdasher Pl, N1 .....197 L2
Haberdasher St, N1 .....197 L2
Habgood Rd, Loug. IG10 .....32 EL41
Haccombe Rd, SW19
  off Haydons Rd 120 DC93
HACKBRIDGE, Wall. 141 DH103
Hackbridge 141 DH103
Hackbridge Grn, Wall. SM6 .140 DG103
Hackbridge Pk Gdns, Cars.
SM5 .....140 DG103
Hackbridge Rd, Wall. SM6 .140 DG103
Hacketts La, Wok. GU22 .151 BF114
Hackford Rd, SW9 .....101 DM81
Hackforth Cl, Barn. EN5 .....27 CW43
Hackington Cres, Beck. BR3 .123 EA93
HACKNEY 84 DV65
Hackney Central 84 DV65
Hackney City Fm, E2 .....84 DU68
Hackney Cl, Borwd. WD6 .....26 CR43

★ Place of interest   ≒ Railway station   ⊖ London Underground station   DLR Docklands Light Railway station   ◇ Tramlink station   H Hospital

Hac - Ham

⇌ Hackney Downs 66 DV64
Hackney Gro, E8
　off Reading La 84 DV65
★ Hackney Marsh, E9 . . . . .67 DY62
★ Hackney Mus, E8 . . . . . . .84 DV65
Hackney Rd, E2 . . . . .197 P3
HACKNEY WICK, E9 . . . . . .67 EA64
⇌ Hackney Wick 85 EA65
Hackworth Pt, E3
　off Rainhill Way 85 EB69
HACTON, Rain. 72 FM64
Hacton Dr, Horn. RM12 . . .72 FK63
Hacton La, Horn. RM12 . . .72 FM62
　Upminster RM14 . . . . .72 FM64
Hadden Rd, SE28 . . . . . . .105 ES76
Hadden Way, Grnfd. UB6 . . .79 CD65
Haddestoke Gate, Wal.Cr. (Chsht.)
　EN8 . . . . .15 DZ26
Haddington Rd, Brom. BR1 .123 ED90
Haddon Cl, Borwd. WD6 . . .26 CN41
　Enfield EN1 . . . . .30 DU44
　New Malden KT3 . . . . . . .139 CT99
　Weybridge KT13 . . . . . . .135 BR104
Haddonfield, SE8 . . . . . . .203 J9
Haddon Gro, Sid. DA15 . . .126 EU87
Haddon Rd, Orp. BR5 . . . .146 EW99
　Rickmansworth (Chorl.)
　WD3 . . . . .21 BC43
　Sutton SM1 . . . . .158 DB105
Haddo St, SE10 . . . . .103 EB79
Hadfield Cl, Sthl. UB1
　off Adrienne Av 78 BZ69
Hadfield Rd, Stai. (Stanw.)
　TW19 . . . . .114 BK86
Hadlands Cl, Hem.H. (Bov.)
　HP3 . . . . .5 AZ26
Hadleigh Cl, E1
　off Mantus Rd 84 DW70
　SW20 . . . . .139 CZ96
Hadleigh Dr, Sutt. SM2 . . .158 DA109
Hadleigh Rd, N9 . . . . .46 DV45
Hadleigh St, E2 . . . . .84 DW70
Hadleigh Wk, E6 . . . . .86 EL72
HADLEY, Barn. 27 CZ40
Hadley Cl, N21 . . . . .29 DN44
　Borehamwood (Elstree)
　WD6 . . . . .26 CM44
Hadley Common, Barn. EN5 .28 DA40
Hadley Gdns, W4 . . . . .98 CR78
　Southall UB2 . . . . .96 BZ78
Hadley Grn, Barn. EN5 . . . .27 CZ40
Hadley Grn Rd, Barn. EN5 . .27 CZ40
Hadley Grn W, Barn. EN5 . .27 CZ40
Hadley Gro, Barn. EN5 . . . .27 CY40
Hadley Highstone, Barn.
　EN5 . . . . .27 CZ39
Hadley Pl, Wey. KT13 . . . .152 BN102
Hadley Ridge, Barn. EN5 . . .27 CZ41
Hadley Rd, Barn. (Had.Wd.)
　EN4 . . . . .29 DH38
　Barnet (New Barn.) EN5 . .28 DB42
　Belvedere DA17 . . . . . . .106 EZ77
　Enfield EN2 . . . . .29 DL38
　Mitcham CR4 . . . . .141 DK98
Hadley St, NW1 . . . . .83 DH65
Hadley Way, N21 . . . . .29 DN44
HADLEY WOOD, Barn. 28 DD38
⇌ Hadley Wood 28 DC38
Hadley Wd Ri, Ken. CR8 . .175 DP115
Hadlow Pl, SE19 . . . . .122 DU94
Hadlow Rd, Sid. DA14 . . . .126 EU91
　Welling DA16 . . . . .106 EW80
Hadlow Way, Grav. (Istead Rise)
　DA13 . . . . .130 GE94
Hadrian Cl, Stai. TW19
　off Hadrian Way 114 BL88
　Wallington SM6 . . . . . . .159 DL108
Hadrian Ct, Sutt. SM2
　off Stanley Rd 158 DB108
Hadrian Est, E2 . . . . .84 DU68
Hadrian Ms, N7
　off Roman Way 83 DM66
Hadrians Ride, Enf. EN1 . . .30 DT43
Hadrian St, SE10 . . . . . . .104 EE78
Hadrian Way, Stai. (Stanw.)
　TW19 . . . . .114 BL87
Hadyn Pk Rd, W12 . . . . . . .99 CU75
Hafer Rd, SW11 . . . . .100 DF84
Hafton Rd, SE6 . . . . .124 EE88
Hagden La, Wat. WD18 . . . .23 BT43
HAGGERSTON, E2 . . . . . . .84 DT68
Haggerston Rd, E8 . . . . . . .84 DT66
　Borehamwood WD6 . . . . .26 CL38
Hague St, E2
　off Derbyshire St 84 DU69
Ha-Ha Rd, SE18 . . . . .105 EM78
Haig Gdns, Grav. DA12 . . .131 GJ87
Haig Pl, Mord. SM4
　off Green La 140 DA100
Haig Rd, Grays RM16 . . . .111 GG76
　Stanmore HA7 . . . . .41 CJ50
　Uxbridge UB8 . . . . .77 BP71
　Westerham (Bigg.H.) TN16 .178 EL117
Haig Rd E, E13 . . . . .86 EJ69
Haig Rd W, E13 . . . . .86 EJ69
Haigville Gdns, Ilf. IG6 . . . .69 EP56
Hailes Cl, SW19 . . . . .120 DC93
　off North La
Hailey Rd, Erith DA18 . . . .106 FA75
Haileybury Av, Enf. EN1 . . .30 DT44
Haileybury Rd, Orp. BR6 . .164 EU105
Hailey Rd, Erith DA18 . . . .106 FA75
Hailsham Av, SW2 . . . . . .121 DM89
Hailsham Cl, Rom. RM3 . . .52 FJ50
　Surbiton KT6 . . . . .137 CK101
Hailsham Dr, Har. HA1 . . . .61 CD55
Hailsham Gdns, Rom. RM3 . .52 FJ50
Hailsham Rd, SW17 . . . . .120 DG93
　Romford RM3 . . . . .52 FJ50
Hailsham Ter, N18 . . . . . . .46 DQ50
Haimo Rd, SE9 . . . . .124 EK85
HAINAULT, Ilf. 49 ES52
⊖ Hainault 49 ES52
Hainault Ct, E17 . . . . .67 ED56

★ Hainault Forest Country Pk,
　Chig. IG7 . . . . .50 EW47
Hainault Gore, Rom. RM6 . .70 EY57
Hainault Gro, Chig. IG7 . . .49 EQ49
Hainault Ind Est, Ilf. IG6 . . .50 EW50
Hainault Rd, E11 . . . . .67 EC60
　Chigwell IG7 . . . . .49 EP48
　Romford RM5 . . . . .51 FC54
　Romford (Chad.Hth.) RM6 .70 EZ58
　Romford (Lt.Hth.) RM6 . . .70 EV55
　Ilford IG1 . . . . .69 EP61
Haines Ct, Wey. KT13
　off St. George's Lo 153 BR106
Haines Wk, Mord. SM4
　off Dorchester Rd 140 DB101
Haines Way, Wat. WD25 . . .7 BU34
Hainford Cl, SE4 . . . . .103 DX84
Haining Cl, W4
　off Wellesley Rd 98 CN78
Hainthorpe Rd, SE27 . . . .121 DP90
Hainton Cl, E1 . . . . .84 DV72
Halberd Ms, E5
　off Knightland Rd 66 DV61
Halbutt Gdns, Dag. RM9 . . .70 EZ62
Halbutt St, Dag. RM9 . . . . .70 EZ63
Halcomb St, N1 . . . . .84 DS67
Halcrow St, E1
　off Newark St 84 DV71
Halcyon Way, Horn. RM11 . .72 FM60
Haldane Cl, N10 . . . . .45 DH52
　Enfield EN3
　off Government Row 31 EA37
Haldane Gdns, Grav. DA11 .130 GC88
Haldane Pl, SW18 . . . . . . .120 DB88
Haldane Rd, E6 . . . . .86 EK69
　SE28 . . . . .88 EX73
　SW6 . . . . .99 CZ80
　Southall UB1 . . . . .78 CC72
Haldan Rd, E4 . . . . .47 EC51
Haldon Cl, Chig. IG7
　off Arrowsmith Rd 49 ES50
Haldon Rd, SW18 . . . . . . .119 CZ85
Hale, The, E4 . . . . .47 ED50
　N17 . . . . .66 DU56
Hale Cl, E4 . . . . .47 EC48
　Edgware HA8 . . . . .42 CQ50
　Orpington BR6 . . . . .163 EQ105
Hale Dr, NW7 . . . . .42 CQ51
HALE END, E4 . . . . .47 ED51
Hale End, Rom. RM3 . . . . .51 FH51
Hale End Cl, Ruis. HA4 . . . .59 BU58
Hale End Rd, E4 . . . . .47 ED51
　E17 . . . . .47 ED52
　Woodford Green IG8 . . . . .47 ED52
Halefield Rd, N17 . . . . .46 DU53
Hale Gdns, N17 . . . . .66 DU55
　W3 . . . . .80 CN74
Hale Gro Gdns, NW7 . . . . .42 CR50
Hale La, NW7 . . . . .42 CR50
　Edgware HA8 . . . . .42 CP50
　Sevenoaks (Otford) TN14 .181 FE117
Hale Path, SE27 . . . . .121 DP91
Hale Rd, E6 . . . . .86 EL70
　N17 . . . . .66 DU55
Hales Ct, E9
　off Deptford High St 103 EA80
Hale St, E14 . . . . .85 EB73
　Staines TW18 . . . . .113 BE91
Haleswood, Cob. KT11 . . . .153 BV114
Halesworth Cl, E5
　off Theydon Rd 66 DW61
　Romford RM3 . . . . .52 FL51
Halesworth Rd, SE13 . . . .103 EB83
　Romford RM3 . . . . .52 FL51
Hale Wk, W7 . . . . .79 CE71
Haley Rd, NW4 . . . . .63 CW58
Half Acre, Brent. TW8 . . . . .97 CK79
Halfacre Hill, Ger.Cr. (Chal.St.P.)
　SL9 . . . . .36 AY53
Half Acre Rd, W7 . . . . .79 CE74
Halfhide La, Brox. (Turnf.)
　EN10 . . . . .15 DY26
　Waltham Cross (Chsht.)
　EN8 . . . . .15 DX27
Halfhides, Wal.Abb. EN9 . . .15 ED33
Half Moon Ct, EC1 . . . . . .197 H7
Half Moon Cres, N1 . . . . . .83 DM68
Half Moon La, SE24 . . . . .122 DQ86
　Epping CM16 . . . . .17 ET31
Half Moon Pas, E1
　off Braham St 84 DT72
Half Moon St, W1 . . . . . . .199 J2
Halford Cl, Edg. HA8 . . . . .42 CP54
Halford Rd, E10 . . . . .67 ED57
　SW6 . . . . .100 DA79
　Richmond TW10 . . . . . . .118 CL85
　Uxbridge UB10 . . . . .58 BN64
Halfway La, Purf. RM19
　off Thamley 108 FN77
Halfway Grn, Walt. KT12 . .135 BV104
Halfway St, Sid. DA15 . . . .125 ER87
Haliburton Rd, Twick. TW1 .117 CG85
Haliday Wk, N1
　off Balls Pond Rd 84 DR65
Halidon Cl, E9 off Urswick Rd .66 DW64
Halidon Ri, Rom. RM3 . . . .52 FP51
Halifax Cl, St.Alb. AL2 . . . . .8 BZ30
　Watford WD25 off Ashfields .7 BT34
Halifax Rd, Enf. EN2 . . . . . .30 DQ40
　Greenford UB6 . . . . .78 CB67
　Rickmansworth (Herons.)
　WD3 . . . . .37 BC45
Halifax St, SE26 . . . . .122 DV91
Halifield Dr, Belv. DA17 . . .106 EY76
Haling Down Pas, S.Croy.
　CR2 . . . . .160 DQ109
Haling Gro, S.Croy. CR2 . .160 DQ108
Haling Pk, S.Croy. CR2 . . .160 DQ108
Haling Pk Gdns, S.Croy. CR2 .159 DP107
Haling Pk Rd, S.Croy. CR2 .159 DP107
Halings La, Uxb. (Denh.) UB9 .57 BE56
Halkin Arc, SW1 . . . . .198 F6

Halkingcroft, Slou. SL3 . . . .92 AW75
Halkin Ms, SW1 . . . . .198 F6
Halkin Pl, SW1 . . . . .198 F6
Halkin St, SW1 . . . . .198 G5
Hall, The, SE3 . . . . .104 EG83
Hallam Cl, Chis. BR7 . . . . .125 EM92
　Watford WD24 . . . . .24 BW40
Hallam Gdns, Pnr. HA5 . . . .40 BY52
Hallam Ms, W1 . . . . .195 J6
Hallam Rd, N15 . . . . .65 DP56
　SW13 . . . . .99 CV83
Hallam St, W1 . . . . .195 J5
Halland Way, Nthwd. HA6 . .39 BR51
Hall Av, N18
　off Weir Hall Av 46 DR51
　South Ockendon (Aveley)
　RM15 . . . . .90 FQ74
Hall Cl, W5 . . . . .80 CL71
　Rickmansworth (Mill End)
　WD3 . . . . .38 BG46
Hall Ct, Slou. (Datchet) SL3 .92 AV80
　Teddington TW11
　off Teddington Pk 117 CF92
Hall Cres, S.Ock. (Aveley)
　RM15 . . . . .108 FQ75
Hall Dr, SE26 . . . . .122 DW92
　W7 . . . . .79 CE72
　Uxbridge (Hare.) UB9 . . . .38 BJ53
Halley Gdns, SE13 . . . . . .103 ED84
Halley Rd, E7 . . . . .86 EJ65
　E12 . . . . .86 EK65
　Waltham Abbey EN9 . . . . .31 EB36
Halleys App, Wok. GU21 . .166 AU118
Halleys Ct, Wok. GU21
　off Halleys App 166 AU118
Halley St, E14 . . . . .85 DY71
Halleys Wk, Add. KT15 . . .152 BJ108
Hall Fm Cl, Stan. HA7 . . . .41 CH49
Hall Fm Dr, Twick. TW2 . . .117 CD87
Hallfield Est, W2 . . . . .82 DC72
Halford Way, Dart. DA1 . . .128 FJ85
Hall Gdns, E4 . . . . .47 DZ49
Hall Gate, NW8 off Hall Rd .82 DC69
Hall Grn La, Brwd. CM13 . . .55 GC45
Hall Hill, Oxt. RH8 . . . . . . .187 ED131
　Sevenoaks (Seal) TN15 . .191 FP123
Halliards, The, Walt. KT12
　off Felix La 135 BU100
Halliday Cl, Rad. (Shenley)
　WD7 . . . . .10 CL32
Halliday Sq, Sthl. UB2 . . . .79 CD74
Halliford Cl, Shep. TW17 . .135 BR98
Halliford Rd, Shep. TW17 . .135 BS99
　Sunbury-on-Thames
　TW16 . . . . .135 BS99
Hallingbury Ct, E17 . . . . . .67 EB55
Hallington Cl, Wok. GU21 .166 AV117
Halliwell Rd, SW2 . . . . . . .121 DM86
Halliwick Rd, N10 . . . . .44 DG53
Hall La, E4 . . . . .47 DY50
　NW4 . . . . .43 CU53
　Brentwood (Shenf.) CM15 .55 FZ44
　Hayes UB3 . . . . .95 BR80
　South Ockendon RM15 . . .91 FX68
　Upminster RM14 . . . . . . .72 FQ60
Hallmark Trd Est, NW10
　off Great Cen Way 62 CQ63
Hallmead Rd, Sutt. SM1 . .140 DB104
Hall Oak Wk, NW6
　off Barlow Rd 81 DZ66
Hallowell Av, Croy. CR0 . .159 DL105
Hallowell Cl, Mitch. CR4 . .140 DG97
Hallowell Rd, Nthwd. HA6 . .39 BS52
Hallowes Cres, Wat. WD19
　off Hayling Rd 39 BU48
Hallowfield Way, Mitch. CR4 .140 DD98
Hallows Gro, Sun. TW16 . .115 BT92
Hall Pk Av, Upmin. RM14 . .72 FQ64
★ Hall Pl, Bex. DA5 . . . . . .127 FC86
Hall Pl, W2 . . . . .82 DD70
　Woking GU21 . . . . .167 BA116
Hall Pl Cres, Bex. DA5 . . .127 FC85
Hall Pl Dr, Wey. KT13 . . . .153 BS106
Hall Rd, E6 . . . . .87 EM67
　E15 . . . . .67 ED63
　NW8 . . . . .82 DC69
　SE16 . . . . .203 L5
　Barnet EN4 . . . . .28 DE42
　Chertsey KT16 . . . . .133 BF102
　Epsom KT19 . . . . .156 CQ112
　Feltham TW13 . . . . .115 BT92
　Potters Bar EN6 . . . . .11 CU33
　Purley CR8 . . . . .159 DP112
　St. Albans (Brick.Wd.) AL2 . .8 CA30
　Stanmore HA7 . . . . .41 CF47
Hamilton Cl, N17 . . . . . . .66 DT55
　NW8 . . . . .82 DD69
　SE16 . . . . .203 L5
　Barnet EN4 . . . . .28 DE42
　Chertsey KT16 . . . . .133 BF102
　Epsom KT19 . . . . .156 CQ112
　Feltham TW13 . . . . .115 BT92
　Potters Bar EN6 . . . . .11 CU33
　Purley CR8 . . . . .159 DP112
　St. Albans (Brick.Wd.) AL2 . .8 CA30
　Stanmore HA7 . . . . .41 CF47
Hamilton Ct, W5 . . . . .80 CM73
　W9 off Maida Vale 82 DC69
Hamilton Cres, N13 . . . . . .45 DN49
　Brentwood CM14 . . . . . . .54 FW49
　Harrow HA2 . . . . .60 BZ62
　Hounslow TW3 . . . . .116 CB85
Hamilton Dr, Rom. RM3 . . .52 FL54
Hamilton Gdns, NW8 . . . . .82 DC69
Hamilton La, N5
　off Hamilton Pk 65 DP63
Hamilton Mead, Hem.H. (Bov.)
　HP3 . . . . .5 BA27
Hamilton Ms, SW18
　off Merton Rd 120 DA88
　W1 . . . . .199 H4
Hamilton Pk, N5 . . . . .65 DP63
Hamilton Pk W, N5 . . . . . . .65 DP63
Hamilton Pl, N19
　off Wedmore St 65 DK62
　W1 . . . . .198 G3
　Sunbury-on-Thames TW16 .115 BV94
　Tadworth (Kgswd.) KT20 .173 CZ122
Hamilton Rd, E15 . . . . .86 EE69
　E17 . . . . .47 DY54
　N2 . . . . .64 DC55
　N9 . . . . .46 DU45
　NW10 . . . . .63 CU64
　NW11 . . . . .63 CX59
　SE27 . . . . .122 DR91
　SW19 . . . . .120 DB94

Hamilton Rd, W4 . . . . .98 CS75
　W5 . . . . .80 CL73
　Barnet EN4 . . . . .28 DE42
　Bexleyheath DA7 . . . . . .106 EY82
　Brentford TW8 . . . . .97 CK79
　Feltham TW13 . . . . .115 BT91
　Harrow HA1 . . . . .61 CF57
　Hayes UB3 . . . . .77 BV73
　Ilford IG1 . . . . .69 EP63
　Kings Langley WD4 . . . . . .7 BQ33
　Romford RM2 . . . . .71 FH57
　Sidcup DA15 . . . . .126 EU91
　Southall UB1 . . . . .78 BZ74
　Thornton Heath CR7 . . . .142 DR97
　Twickenham TW2 . . . . . .117 CE88
　Uxbridge UB8 . . . . .76 BK71
　Watford WD19 . . . . .39 BV48
Hamilton Rd Ind Est, SE27 .122 DR91
Hamilton Sq, N12
　off Sandringham Gdns . . .44 DD51
　SE1 . . . . .201 L4
Hamilton St, SE8
　off Deptford High St 103 EA79
　Watford WD18 . . . . .24 BW43
Hamilton Ter, NW8 . . . . . . .82 DB68
Hamilton Wk, Erith DA8 . .107 FF80
Hamilton Way, N3 . . . . .44 DA51
　N13 . . . . .45 DP49
　Wallington SM6 . . . . . . .159 DK109
Ham Island, Wind. (Old Wind.)
　SL4 . . . . .92 AX84
Ham La, Egh. (Eng.Grn.)
　TW20 . . . . .112 AV91
　Windsor (Old Wind.) SL4 . .92 AX84
Hamlea Cl, SE12 . . . . .124 EF85
Hamlet, The, SE5 . . . . . . .102 DR83
Hamlet Cl, SE13 off Old Rd .104 EE84
　Romford RM5 . . . . .50 FA52
　St. Albans AL2 . . . . .8 BZ30
Hamlet Gdns, W6 . . . . .99 CU77
Hamlet Rd, SE19 . . . . .122 DT94
　Romford RM5 . . . . .50 FA52
Hamlet Sq, NW2 . . . . .63 CY62
Hamlets Way, E3 . . . . .85 DZ70
Hamlet Way, SE1 . . . . . . .201 L4
★ Hamleys, W1 . . . . .195 K10
Hamlin Cres, Pnr. HA5 . . . .60 BW57
Hamlyn Cl, Har. HA3 . . . . .40 BZ52
Hamlyn Cl, Edg. HA8 . . . . .42 CL48
Hamm Ct, Wey. KT13 . . . .134 BL103
Hamlyn Gdns, SE19 . . . . .122 DS94
Hammelton Grn, SW9
　off Cromwell Rd 101 DP81
Hammelton Rd, Brom. BR1 .144 EF95
Hammers Gate, St.Alb. AL2 . .8 CA25
Hammers La, NW7 . . . . . . .43 CU50
HAMMERSMITH, W6 . . . . .99 CW78
⊖ Hammersmith 99 CW77
Hammersmith Br, SW13 . . .99 CV78
Hammersmith Br Rd, W6 . . .99 CW78
　W6 . . . . .99 CW78
Hammersmith Bdy, W6 . . . .99 CW77
Hammersmith Flyover, W6 . .99 CW78
Hammersmith Gro, W6 . . . .99 CW76
Ⓗ Hammersmith Hosp, W12 .81 CV72
Hammersmith Rd, W6 . . . . .99 CX77
　W14 . . . . .99 CX77
Hammersmith Ter, W6 . . . . .99 CU77
Hammet Cl, Hayes UB4
　off Willow Tree La 78 BX71
Hammett St, EC3 . . . . . . .197 P10
Hamm Moor La, Add. KT15 .152 BL106
Hammond Av, Mitch. CR4 .141 DH96
Hammond Cl, Barn. EN5 . . .27 CY43
　Greenford UB6
　off Lilian Board Way 61 CD64
　Hampton TW12 . . . . . . .136 CA95
　Waltham Cross (Chsht.)
　EN7 . . . . .14 DS26
　Woking GU21 . . . . .166 AW115
Hammond Rd, Enf. EN1 . . .30 DV40
　Southall UB2 . . . . .96 BY76
　Woking GU21 . . . . .166 AW115
Hammonds Cl, Dag. RM8 . .70 EW62
Hammonds La, Brwd. CM13 .53 FV51
HAMMOND STREET, Wal.Cr. .14 DR26
Hammond St, NW5 . . . . . . .83 DJ65
Hammondstreet Rd, Wal.Cr.
　(Chsht.) EN7 . . . . .14 DR26
Hammond Way, SE28
　off Oriole Way 88 EV73
Hamond Cl, S.Croy. CR2 . .159 DP109
Hamonde Cl, Edg. HA8 . . . .42 CP47
Ham Pk Rd, E7 . . . . .86 EF66
　E15 . . . . .86 EF66
Hampden Av, Beck. BR3 . .143 DY96
Hampden Cl, NW1 . . . . . . .195 N1
　Epping (N.Wld.Bas.) CM16 .18 FA27
　Slough (Stoke P.) SL2 . . . .74 AU69
Hampden Cres, Brwd. CM14 .54 FW49
　Waltham Cross (Chsht.)
　EN7 . . . . .14 DV31
Hampden Gurney St, W1 . .194 D9
Hampden La, N17 . . . . .46 DT53
Hampden Pl, St.Alb. (Frog.)
　AL2 . . . . .9 CE29
Hampden Rd, N8 . . . . .65 DN56
　N10 . . . . .44 DG52
　N17 . . . . .46 DU53
　N19 off Holloway Rd 65 DK61
　Beckenham BR3 . . . . . . .143 DY96
　Gerrards Cross (Chal.St.P.)
　SL9 . . . . .36 AX53
　Grays RM17 . . . . .110 GB78
　Harrow HA3 . . . . .40 CC53
　Kingston upon Thames
　KT1 . . . . .138 CN97
　Romford RM5 . . . . .51 FB52
　Slough SL3 . . . . .93 AZ76
Hampden Sq, N14
　off Osidge La 45 DH46
Hampden Way, N14 . . . . . .45 DH47
　Watford WD17 . . . . .23 BS36
Hampermill La, Wat. WD19 . .39 BT47
Hampshire Cl, N18
　off Berkshire Gdns 46 DV50

Har - Haw

Harrier Av, E11
  off Eastern Av 68 EH58
Harrier Cl, Horn. RM12 . . . .89 FH65
Harrier Ms, SE28 . . . . .105 EC56
Harrier Rd, NW9 . . . . .42 CS54
Harriers Cl, W5 . . . . .80 CL73
Harrier Way, E6 . . . . .87 EM71
  Waltham Abbey EN9 . . .16 EG34
Harriescourt, Wal.Abb. EN9 . .16 EG32
Harries Rd, Hayes UB4 . . . .78 BW70
Harriet Cl, E8 . . . . .84 DU67
Harriet Gdns, Croy. CR0 . .142 DU103
Harriet St, SW1 . . . . .198 E5
Harriet Tubman Cl, SW2 . . .121 DN87
Harriet Wk, SW1 . . . . .198 E5
Harriet Walker Way, Rick. WD3
  off Thellusson Way 37 BF45
Harriet Way, Bushey WD23 . .41 CD45
HARRINGAY, N8 . . . . .65 DN57
⇌ Harringay 65 DN58
Harringay Gdns, N8 . . . . . . .65 DP56
⇌ Harringay Green Lanes . .65 DP58
Harringay Rd, N15 . . . . .65 DP57
Harrington Cl, NW10 . . . . . .62 CR62
  Croydon CR0 . . . . .141 DL103
Harrington Ct, W10
  off Dart St 81 CZ69
Harrington Gdns, SW7 . . . .100 DB77
Harrington Hill, E5 . . . . . . .66 DV60
❖ Harrington Road 142 DW97
Harrington Rd, E11 . . . . . . .68 EE60
  SE25 . . . . .142 DU98
  SW7 . . . . .100 DD77
Harrington Sq, NW1 . . . . . .195 K1
Harrington St, NW1 . . . . . .195 K2
Harrington Way, SE18 . . . .104 EK76
Harriott Cl, SE10 . . . . .205 K9
Harriotts Cl, Ashtd. KT21
  off Harriotts La 171 CJ120
Harriotts La, Ashtd. KT21 . .171 CJ119
Harris Cl, Enf. EN2 . . . . . . .29 DP39
  Gravesend (Nthflt.) DA11 . .130 GE90
  Hounslow TW3 . . . . .96 CA81
  Romford RM3 . . . . .52 FL52
Harris La, Rad. (Shenley) WD7 .10 CN34
Harrison Cl, N20 . . . . .44 DE46
  Brentwood CM13 . . . . . . .55 GD43
  Northwood HA6 . . . . .39 BQ51
Harrison Ct, Shep. TW17
  off Greeno Cres 135 BP99
Harrison Dr, Epp. (N.Wld.Bas.)
  CM16 . . . . .19 FB26
Harrison Rd, Dag. RM10 . . .89 FB65
Harrisons Ri, Croy. CR0 . . .141 DP104
Harrison St, WC1 . . . . .196 A3
Harrisons Wf, Purf. RM19 . .108 FN78
Harrison Wk, Wal.Cr. (Chsht.)
  EN8 . . . . .15 DX30
Harrison Way, Sev. TN13 . . .190 FG122
  Waltham Abbey EN9
  off Greenwich Way 31 EC36
Harris Rd, Bexh. DA7 . . . . .106 EY81
  Dagenham RM9 . . . . .70 EZ64
  Watford WD25 . . . . .23 BU35
Harris St, E17 . . . . .67 DZ59
  SE5 . . . . .102 DR80
Harris Way, Sun. TW16 . . .135 BS95
★ Harrods, SW1 . . . . .198 D6
Harrogate Ct, N11
  off Coverdale Rd 44 DG51
  Slough SL3 . . . . .93 BA78
Harrogate Rd, Wat. WD19 . .40 BW48
Harrold Rd, Dag. RM8 . . . .70 EV64
HARROW 61 CD59
⇌ Harrow & Wealdstone . .61 CE56
⊖ Harrow & Wealdstone . .61 CE56
★ Harrow Arts Cen, Pnr.
  HA5 . . . . .40 CB52
Harrow Av, Enf. EN1 . . . . .30 DT44
Harroway Rd, SW11 . . . . . .100 DD82
Harrow Bottom Rd, Vir.W.
  GU25 . . . . .133 AZ100
Harrowby Gdns, Grav. (Nthflt.)
  DA11 . . . . .130 GE89
Harrowby St, W1 . . . . .194 C8
Harrow Cl, Add. KT15 . . . .134 BH103
  Chessington KT9 . . . . . . .155 CK108
Harrow Cres, Rom. RM3 . .51 FH52
Harrowdene Cl, Wem. HA0 . .61 CK63
Harrowdene Gdns, Tedd.
  TW11 . . . . .117 CG93
Harrowdene Rd, Wem. HA0 . .61 CK62
Harrow Dr, N9 . . . . .46 DT46
  Hornchurch RM11 . . . . . .71 FH60
Harrowes Meade, Edg. HA8 . .42 CN48
Harrow Flds Gdns, Har. HA1 . .61 CE62
Harrow Gdns, Orp. BR6 . .164 EV105
  Warlingham CR6 . . . . . . .177 DZ115
Harrowgate Rd, E9 . . . . . .85 DY65
Harrow Grn, E11
  off Harrow Rd 68 EE62
Harrow La, E14 . . . . .204 D1
Harrow Manorway, SE2 . . .88 EW74
Harrow Mkt, Slou. SL3 . . .93 BA76
★ Harrow Mus & Heritage Cen,
  Har. HA2 . . . . .60 CC55
HARROW ON THE HILL, Har. . .61 CE61
⇌ Harrow on the Hill 61 CE58
⊖ Harrow on the Hill 61 CE58
Harrow Pk, Har. HA1 . . . . .61 CE61
Harrow Pas, Kings.T. KT1
  off Market Pl 137 CK96
Harrow Pl, E1 . . . . .197 N8
Harrow Rd, E6 . . . . .86 EL67
  E11 . . . . .68 EE62
  NW10 . . . . .81 CV69
  W2 .81 CZ70
  W9 .81 CZ70
  W10 . . . . .81 CX70
  Barking IG11 . . . . .87 ES67
  Carshalton SM5 . . . . . . .158 DE106
  Feltham TW14 . . . . .114 BN88
  Ilford IG1 . . . . .69 EQ63
  Sevenoaks (Knock.) TN14 . .180 EY115

Harrow Rd, Slou. SL3 . . . . .93 AZ76
  Warlingham CR6 . . . . . . .177 DZ115
  Wembley HA0 . . . . .61 CJ64
  Wembley (Tkgtn.) HA9 . .62 CM64
★ Harrow Sch 61 CE60
Harrow Vw, Har. HA1, HA2 . .61 CD56
  Hayes UB3 . . . . .77 BU72
  Uxbridge UB10 . . . . .77 BQ69
Harrow Vw Rd, W5 . . . . . .79 CH70
Harrow Way, Shep. TW17 . .135 BQ96
  Watford WD19 . . . . .40 BY48
HARROW WEALD, Har. . . .41 CD53
Harrow Weald Pk, Har. HA3 . .41 CD51
Harston Dr, Enf. EN3 . . . . .31 EA38
Hart Cl, Red. (Bletch.) RH1 . .186 DT134
Hart Cor, Grays RM20 . . . .109 FX78
Hart Cres, Chig. IG7 . . . . .49 ET50
Hart Dyke Cres, Swan. BR8
  off Hart Dyke Rd 147 FD97
Hart Dyke Rd, Orp. BR5 . .146 EW102
  Swanley BR8 . . . . .147 FD97
Harte Rd, Houns. TW3 . . .96 BZ82
Hartfield Av, Borwd. (Elstree)
  WD6 . . . . .26 CN43
  Northolt UB5 . . . . .77 BV68
Hartfield Cl, Borwd. (Elstree)
  WD6 . . . . .26 CN43
Hartfield Cres, SW19 . . . .119 CZ94
  West Wickham BR4 . . . .144 EG104
Hartfield Gro, SE20 . . . . .142 DV95
Hartfield Pl, Grav. (Nthflt.)
  DA11 . . . . .130 GD87
Hartfield Rd, SW19 . . . . . .119 CZ94
  Chessington KT9 . . . . . . .155 CK106
  West Wickham BR4 . . . .162 EG105
Hartfield Ter, E3 . . . . .85 EA68
Hartford Av, Har. HA3 . . . .61 CG55
Hartforde Rd, Borwd. WD6 . .26 CN40
Hartford Rd, Bex. DA5 . . .126 FA86
  Epsom KT19 . . . . .156 CN107
Hart Gro, W5 . . . . .80 CN74
  Southall UB1 . . . . .78 CA71
Harthall La, Hem.H. HP3 . . .7 BS26
  Kings Langley WD4 . . . . .7 BP28
Hartham Cl, N7 . . . . .65 DL64
  Isleworth TW7 . . . . .97 CG81
Hartham Rd, N7 . . . . .65 DL64
  N17 . . . . .46 DT54
  Isleworth TW7 . . . . .97 CF81
Harting Rd, SE9 . . . . .124 EL91
Hartington Cl, Har. HA1 . .61 CE63
Hartington Ct, W4 . . . . . .98 CP80
Hartington Pl, Reig. RH2 . .184 DA132
Hartington Rd, E16 . . . . . .86 EH72
  E17 . . . . .67 DY58
  SW8 . . . . .101 DL81
  W4 .98 CP80
  W13 . . . . .79 CH73
  Southall UB2 . . . . .96 BY75
  Twickenham TW1 . . . . . .117 CH87
Hartismere Rd, SW6 . . . . .99 CZ80
Hartlake Rd, E9 . . . . .85 DX65
Hartland Cl, N21
  off Elmscott Gdns 30 DQ44
  Addlestone (New Haw)
  KT15 . . . . .152 BJ110
  Edgware HA8 . . . . .42 CN47
Hartland Dr, Edg. HA8 . . .42 CN47
  Ruislip HA4 . . . . .59 BV62
Hartland Rd, E15 . . . . .86 EF66
  N11 . . . . .44 DF60
  NW1 . . . . .83 DH66
  NW6 . . . . .81 CZ68
  Addlestone KT15 . . . . . .152 BG108
  Epping CM16 . . . . .18 EU31
  Hampton (Hmptn.H.)
  TW12 . . . . .116 CB91
  Hornchurch RM12 . . . . . .71 FG61
  Isleworth TW7 . . . . .97 CG83
  Morden SM4 . . . . .140 DA101
  Waltham Cross (Chsht.)
  EN8 . . . . .15 DX30
Hartlands Cl, Bex. DA5 . .126 EZ86
Hartland Way, Croy. CR0 . .143 DY103
  Morden SM4 . . . . .139 CZ101
Hartlepool Ct, E16
  off Fishguard Way 105 EP75
Hartley Av, E6 . . . . .86 EL67
  NW7 . . . . .43 CT50
Hartley Cl, NW7 . . . . .43 CT50
  Bromley BR1 . . . . .145 EM96
  Slough (Stoke P.) SL3 . . .74 AW67
Hartley Copse, Wind. (Old Wind.)
  SL4 . . . . .112 AU86
Hartley Down, Pur. CR8 . .159 DM113
Hartley Fm Est, Pur. CR8 . .175 DM115
HARTLEY GREEN, Long. . .149 FX99
Hartley Hill, Pur. CR8 . . .175 DM115
Hartley Old Rd, Pur. CR8 . .159 DM114
Hartley Rd, E11 . . . . .68 EF60
  Croydon CR0 . . . . .141 DP101
  Welling DA16 . . . . .106 EW80
  Westerham TN16 . . . . . .189 ER125
Hartley St, E2 . . . . .84 DW69
Hartley Way, Pur. CR8 . . .175 DM115
Hartmann Rd, E16 . . . . . . .86 EK74
Hartmoor Ms, Enf. EN3 . . .31 DX37
Hartnoll St, N7 off Eden Gro . .65 DM64
Harton Cl, Brom. BR1 . . . .144 EK95
Harton Rd, N9 . . . . .46 DV47
Harton St, SE8 . . . . .103 EA81
Hart Rd, W.Byf. (Byfleet)
  KT14 . . . . .152 BL113
Hartsbourne Av, Bushey
  (Bushey Hth.) WD23 . . . .40 CC47
Hartsbourne Cl, Bushey
  (Bushey Hth.) WD23 . . . .41 CD47
Hartsbourne Rd, Bushey
  (Bushey Hth.) WD23 . . . .41 CD47
Harts Cl, Bushey WD23 . . .24 CA40
Harts Gro, Wdf.Grn. IG8 . . .48 EG50
Hartshill Cl, Uxb. UB10 . . .76 BN65
Hartshill Rd, Grav. (Nthflt.)
  DA11 . . . . .131 GF89
Hartshill Wk, Wok. GU21 . .166 AV116
Hartshorn All, EC3 . . . . . .197 N9

Hartshorn Gdns, E6 . . . . . .87 EN70
Hartslands Rd, Sev. TN13 . .191 FJ123
Harts La, SE14 . . . . .103 DY80
  Barking IG11 . . . . .87 EP65
Hartslock Dr, SE2 . . . . . . .88 EX75
Hartsmead Rd, SE9 . . . . .125 EM89
Hartspring La, Bushey WD23 . .24 CA39
  Watford WD25 . . . . .24 CA39
Hart St, EC3 . . . . .197 N10
  Brentwood CM14 . . . . . .54 FW47
Hartsway, Enf. EN3 . . . . . .30 DW42
Hartswood Cl, Brwd. CM14 . .54 FY49
Hartswood Gdns, W12 . . .99 CT76
Hartswood Grn, Bushey
  (Bushey Hth.) WD23 . . . .41 CD47
Hartswood Rd, W12 . . . . .99 CT75
  Brentwood CM14 . . . . . .54 FY49
Hartsworth Cl, E13 . . . . . .86 EF68
Hartville Rd, SE18 . . . . . .105 ES77
Hartwell Dr, E4 . . . . .47 EC51
Hartwell St, E8 off Dalston La . .84 DT65
Harvard Hill, W4 . . . . . . .98 CP79
Harvard La, W4 . . . . .98 CP78
Harvard Rd, SE13 . . . . . . .123 EC85
  W4 .98 CP78
  Isleworth TW7 . . . . .97 CE81
Harvard Wk, Horn. RM12 . .71 FG63
Harvel Cl, Orp. BR5 . . . . .146 EU97
Harvel Cres, SE2 . . . . . . .106 EX78
Harvest Bk Rd, W.Wick. BR4 . .144 EF104
Harvest Ct, Shep. TW17 . .134 BN98
Harvest End, Wat. WD25 . .24 BX36
Harvester Rd, Epsom KT19 . .156 CR110
Harvesters Cl, Islw. TW7 . .117 CD85
Harvest La, Loug. IG10 . . .48 EK45
  Thames Ditton KT7 . . . .137 CG100
Harvest Rd, Bushey WD23 . .24 CB42
  Egham (Eng.Grn.) TW20 . .112 AX92
  Feltham TW13 . . . . .115 BU91
Harvest Way, Swan. BR8 . .147 FD101
Harvey Gdns, E11
  off Harvey Rd 68 EF60
  SE7 . . . . .104 EK77
  Loughton IG10 . . . . .33 EP41
Harvey Ho, Brent. TW8
  off Green Dragon La 98 CL78
Harvey Pt, E16 off Fife Rd . .86 EH71
Harvey Rd, E11 . . . . .68 EE60
  N8 .65 DM57
  SE5 . . . . .102 DR81
  Hounslow TW4 . . . . .116 BZ87
  Ilford IG1 . . . . .69 EP64
  Northolt UB5 . . . . .78 BW66
  Rickmansworth (Crox.Grn.)
  WD3 . . . . .22 BN44
  St. Albans (Lon.Col.) AL2 . .9 CJ26
  Slough SL3 . . . . .93 BB76
  Uxbridge UB10 . . . . .76 BN68
  Walton-on-Thames KT12 . .135 BU101
Harveys La, Rom. RM7 . . .71 FD61
Harvey St, N1 . . . . .84 DR67
Harvill Rd, Sid. DA14 . . . .126 EX92
Harvil Rd, Uxb. (Hare.) UB9 . .58 BK58
  Uxbridge (Ickhm.) UB10 . .58 BL60
Harvington Wk, E8
  off Wilman Gro 84 DU66
Harvist Est, N7 . . . . .66 DN63
Harvist Rd, NW6 . . . . .81 CX68
Harwater Dr, Loug. IG10 . .33 EM40
Harwell Cl, Ruis. HA4 . . . .59 BR60
Harwell Pas, N2 . . . . .64 DF56
Harwich La, EC2 . . . . .197 N6
Harwood Av, Brom. BR1 . .144 EH96
  Hornchurch RM11 . . . . . .72 FL55
  Mitcham CR4 . . . . .140 DE97
Harwood Cl, N12
  off Summerfields Av 44 DE51
  Wembley HA0
  off Harrowdene Rd 61 CK63
Harwood Dr, Uxb. UB10 . .76 BM67
Harwood Gdns, Wind. (Old Wind.)
  SL4 . . . . .112 AV87
Harwood Hall La, Upmin.
  RM14 . . . . .90 FP65
Harwood Rd, SW6 . . . . . .100 DA80
Harwoods Rd, Wat. WD18 . .23 BU42
Harwoods Yd, N21
  off Wades Hill 45 DN45
Harwood Ter, SW6 . . . . . .100 DB81
Hascombe Ter, SE5
  off Love Wk 102 DR82
Haselbury Rd, N9 . . . . . . .46 DS49
  N18 . . . . .46 DS49
Haseldine Rd, St.Alb. (Lon.Col.)
  AL2 . . . . .9 CK26
Haseley End, SE23
  off Tyson Rd 122 DW87
Haselrigge Rd, SW4 . . . . .101 DK84
Haseltine Rd, SE26 . . . . .123 DZ91
Haselwood Dr, Enf. EN2 . .29 DP42
Haskard Rd, Dag. RM9 . . .70 EX63
Haskell Ho, NW10 . . . . . .80 CR67
Hasker St, SW3 . . . . .198 C8
Haslam Av, Sutt. SM3 . . .139 CY102
Haslam Cl, N1 . . . . .83 DN66
  Uxbridge UB10 . . . . .59 BQ61
Haslam St, SE15 . . . . . . .102 DT80
Haslemere Av, NW4 . . . .63 CX58
  SW18 . . . . .120 DB89
  W7 .97 CG76
  W13 . . . . .97 CG76
  Barnet EN4 . . . . .44 DF46
  Hounslow TW5 . . . . .96 BW82
  Mitcham CR4 . . . . .140 DD96
Haslemere Business Cen, Enf.
Haslemere Cl, Hmptn. TW12 . .116 BZ92
  Wallington SM6
  off Stafford Rd 159 DL106
Haslemere Gdns, N3 . . . .63 CZ55
Haslemere Heathrow Est, Houns.
  TW4 . . . . .95 BV82
Haslemere Rd, N8 . . . . . .65 DK59
  N21 . . . . .45 DP47
  Bexleyheath DA7 . . . . . .106 EZ82
  Ilford IG3 . . . . .69 ET61

Haslemere Rd, Th.Hth. CR7 . .141 DP99
Hasler Cl, SE28 . . . . .88 EV73
Haslett Rd, Shep. TW17 . .135 BS96
Hasluck Gdns, Barn. EN5 . .28 DC44
Hassard St, E2
  off Hackney Rd 84 DT68
Hassendean Rd, SE3 . . . .104 EH79
Hassett Rd, E9 . . . . .85 DX65
Hassocks Cl, SE26 . . . . . .122 DV90
Hassocks Rd, SW16 . . . .141 DK95
Hassock Wd, Kes. BR2 . .162 EK105
Hassop Rd, NW2 . . . . .63 CX63
Hassop Wk, SE9 . . . . .124 EL91
Hasted Cl, Green. DA9 . .129 FW86
Hasted Rd, SE7 . . . . .104 EK78
Hastings Av, Ilf. IG6 . . . .69 EQ56
Hastings Cl, SE15 . . . . . .102 DU80
  Barnet EN5 off Leicester Rd . .28 DC43
  Grays RM17 . . . . .110 FY79
Hastings Dr, Surb. KT6 . .137 CJ100
Hastings Ho, SE18 . . . . . .105 EM77
Hastings Rd, N11 . . . . . . .45 DJ50
  N17 . . . . .66 DR55
  W13 . . . . .79 CH73
  Bromley BR2 . . . . .144 EL102
  Croydon CR0 . . . . .142 DT102
  Romford RM2 . . . . .71 FH57
Hastings St, WC1 . . . . . . .195 P3
Hastings Way, Bushey WD23 . .24 BY42
  Rickmansworth (Crox.Grn.)
  WD3 . . . . .23 BQ42
Hastingwood Trd Est, N18 . .47 DX51
Hastoe Cl, Hayes UB4
  off Kingsash Dr 78 BY70
Hat & Mitre Ct, EC1 . . . .196 G5
Hatch, The, Enf. EN3 . . . .31 DX39
Hatcham Pk Ms, SE14
  off Hatcham Pk Rd 103 DX81
Hatcham Pk Rd, SE14 . . .103 DX81
Hatcham Rd, SE15 . . . . .102 DW79
Hatchard Rd, N19 . . . . . .65 DK61
Hatch Cl, Add. KT15 . . . .134 BH104
Hatch Gdns, Tad. KT20 . .173 CX120
Hatch Gro, Rom. RM6 . . .70 EY56
Hatchlands Rd, Red. RH1 . .184 DE134
Hatch La, E4 . . . . .47 ED49
  Cobham KT11 . . . . .169 BP119
  Coulsdon CR5 . . . . .174 DG115
  West Drayton UB7 . . . . .94 BK80
  Woking (Ockham) GU23 . .169 BP120
Hatch Pl, Kings.T. KT2 . .118 CM92
Hatch Rd, SW16 . . . . . . .141 DL96
  Brentwood CM15 . . . . . .54 FU43
Hatch Side, Chig. IG7 . . .49 EN50
Hatchwood Cl, Wdf.Grn. IG8
  off Sunset Av 48 EF49
Hatcliffe Cl, SE3 . . . . . . .104 EF83
Hatcliffe St, SE10 . . . . . .205 K10
Hatfield Cl, SE14
  off Reaston St 103 DX80
  Brentwood CM13 . . . . . .55 GD45
  Hornchurch RM12 . . . . .72 FK64
  Ilford IG6 . . . . .69 EP55
  Mitcham CR4 . . . . .140 DD98
  Sutton SM2 . . . . .158 DA109
  West Byfleet KT14 . . . .152 BH112
Hatfield Mead, Mord. SM4
  off Central Rd 140 DA99
Hatfield Rd, E15 . . . . .68 EE64
  W4 .98 CR75
  W13 . . . . .79 CG74
  Ashtead KT21 . . . . .172 CM119
  Dagenham RM9 . . . . .88 EY65
  Grays (Chaff.Hun.) RM16 . .109 FX77
  Potters Bar EN6 . . . . . . .12 DC30
  Slough SL1 . . . . .92 AU75
  Watford WD24 . . . . .23 BV39
Hatfields, SE1 . . . . .200 E2
  Loughton IG10 . . . . .33 EP41
Hathaway Cl, Brom. BR2 . .145 EM102
  Ruislip HA4 off Stafford Rd . .59 BT63
  Stanmore HA7 . . . . .41 CG50
Hathaway Cres, E12 . . . .87 EM65
Hathaway Gdns, W13 . . .79 CF71
  Grays RM17
  off Hathaway Rd 110 GB76
  Romford RM6 . . . . .70 EX57
Hathaway Rd, Croy. CR0 . .141 DP101
  Grays RM17 . . . . .110 GB77
Hatherleigh Cl, NW7
  off Bittacy Hill 43 CY52
  Chessington KT9 . . . . . . .155 CK106
  Morden SM4 . . . . .140 DA98
Hatherleigh Gdns, Pot.B. EN6 . .12 DD32
Hatherleigh Rd, Ruis. HA4 . .59 BU61
Hatherleigh Way, Rom. RM3 . .52 FK53
Hatherley Cres, Sid. DA14 . .126 EU89
Hatherley Gdns, E6 . . . . .86 EK68
  N8 .65 DL58
Hatherley Gro, W2 . . . . .82 DB72
Hatherley Ms, E17 . . . . .67 EA56
Hatherley Rd, E17 . . . . . .67 EA56
  Richmond TW9 . . . . .98 CM82
  Sidcup DA14 . . . . .126 EU91
Hatherley St, SW1 . . . . .199 L8
Hathern Gdns, SE9 . . . . .125 EN91
Hatherop Rd, Hmptn. TW12 . .116 BZ94
Hatherwood, Lthd. KT22 . .171 CK121
Hathorne Cl, SE15 . . . . .102 DV82
Hathway St, SE15
  off Gibbon Rd 102 DW82
Hathway Ter, SE14
  off Kitto Rd 102 DW82
Hatley Av, Ilf. IG6 . . . . . .69 EQ56
Hatley Cl, N11 . . . . .44 DF49
Hatley Rd, N4 . . . . .65 DM61
Hatteraick St, SE16 . . . .202 G4
Hattersfield Cl, Belv. DA17 . .106 EZ77
Hatters La, Wat. WD18 . .23 BR44
HATTON, Felt. 95 BT84
Hatton Cl, SE18 . . . . .105 ER80
  Gravesend (Nthflt.) DA11 . .130 GE90

Hatton Cl, Grays (Chaff.Hun.)
  RM16 . . . . .109 FX76
Hatton Ct, E5 off Gilpin Rd . .67 DY63
⊖ Hatton Cross 95 BT84
Hatton Gdn, EC1 . . . . . . .196 E6
Hatton Gdns, Mitch. CR4 . .140 DF99
Hatton Grn, Felt. TW14 . .95 BU84
Hatton Gro, West Dr. UB7 . .94 BK75
Hatton Ho, E1
  off Wellclose Sq 84 DU73
Hatton Pl, EC1 . . . . .196 E5
Hatton Rd, Croy. CR0 . . .141 DN102
  Feltham TW14 . . . . .115 BS85
  Waltham Cross (Chsht.)
  EN8 . . . . .15 DX29
Hatton Row, NW8 . . . . . .194 A5
Hatton St, NW8 . . . . .194 A5
Hatton Wall, EC1 . . . . . .196 D6
Haunch of Venison Yd, W1 . .195 H9
Havana Cl, Rom. RM1
  off Exchange St 71 FE57
Havana Rd, SW19 . . . . . .120 DA89
Havannah St, E14 . . . . . .204 A5
Havant Rd, E17 . . . . .67 EC55
Havant Way, SE15
  off Daniel Gdns 102 DT80
Havelock Pl, Har. HA1 . . .61 CE58
Havelock Rd, N17 . . . . . .46 DU54
  SW19 . . . . .120 DC92
  Belvedere DA17 . . . . . . .106 EZ77
  Bromley BR2 . . . . .144 EJ98
  Croydon CR0 . . . . .142 DT102
  Dartford DA1 . . . . .127 FH87
  Gravesend DA11 . . . . . .131 GF88
  Harrow HA3 . . . . .61 CE55
  Kings Langley WD4 . . . .6 BN28
  Southall UB2 . . . . .96 BZ76
Havelock St, N1 . . . . .83 DL67
  Ilford IG1 . . . . .69 EP61
Havelock Ter, SW8 . . . . .101 DH80
Havelock Wk, SE23 . . . .122 DW88
Haven, The, SE26
  off Springfield Rd 122 DV92
  Grays RM16 . . . . .111 GF78
  Richmond TW9 . . . . .98 CN83
  Sunbury-on-Thames TW16 . .115 BU94
Haven Cl, SE9 . . . . .125 EM90
  SW19 . . . . .119 CX90
  Gravesend (Istead Rise)
  DA13 . . . . .131 GF94
  Hayes UB4 . . . . .77 BS71
  Sidcup DA14 . . . . .126 EW93
  Swanley BR8 . . . . .147 FF96
Havengore Av, Grav. DA12 . .131 GL87
Haven Grn, W5 . . . . .79 CK72
Haven Grn Ct, W5 . . . . . .79 CK72
  off Haven Grn
Havenhurst Ri, Enf. EN2 . .29 DN40
Haven La, W5 . . . . .80 CL72
Haven Ms, E3
  off St. Pauls Way 85 DZ71
Haven Pl, W5
  off The Broadway 79 CK73
  Grays RM16 . . . . .110 GC75
Haven Rd, Ashf. TW15 . .115 BP91
Havensfield, Kings L. (Chipper.)
  WD4 . . . . .6 BH31
Haven St, NW1
  off Castlehaven Rd 83 DH66
Haven Ter, W5
  off The Broadway 79 CK73
Havenwood, Wem. HA9 . .62 CP62
Havenwood Cl, Brwd. CM13
  off Wilmot Grn 53 FW51
Haverfield Gdns, Rich. TW9 . .98 CN80
Haverfield Rd, E3 . . . . . .85 DY69
Haverford Way, Edg. HA8 . .42 CM53
Haverhill Rd, E4 . . . . .47 EC46
  SW12 . . . . .121 DJ88
HAVERING-ATTE-BOWER,
  Rom. 51 FE48
Havering Dr, Rom. RM1 . .71 FE56
Havering Gdns, Rom. RM6 . .70 EW57
HAVERING PARK, Rom. . . .50 FA50
Havering Rd, Rom. RM1 . .71 FD55
Havering St, E1
  off Devonport St 85 DX72
Havering Way, Bark. IG11 . .88 EV69
Havers Av, Walt. KT12 . .154 BX106
Haversfield Est, Brent. TW8 . .98 CL78
Haversham Cl, Twick. TW1 . .117 CK86
Haversham Pl, N6 . . . . . .64 DF61
Haverstock Ct, Orp. BR5 . .146 EU96
Haverstock Hill, NW3 . . .64 DE64
Haverstock Pl, N1
  off Haverstock St 83 DP68
Haverstock Rd, NW5 . . .64 DG64
Haverstock St, N1 . . . . .196 G1
Haverthwaite Rd, Orp. BR6 . .145 ER103
Havil St, SE5 . . . . .102 DS80
Havisham Pl, SE19 . . . . .121 DP93
Hawarden Gro, SE24 . . .122 DQ87
Hawarden Hill, NW2 . . .63 CU62
Hawarden Rd, E17 . . . . .67 DX56
  Caterham CR3 . . . . .176 DQ121
Hawbridge Rd, E11 . . . .67 ED60
Hawes Cl, Nthwd. HA6 . . .39 BT52
Hawes La, E4 . . . . .31 EC38
  West Wickham BR4 . . . .143 ED102
Hawes Rd, N18 . . . . .46 DV51
  Bromley BR1 . . . . .144 EH95
  Tadworth KT20
  off Hatch Gdns 173 CX120
Hawes St, N1 . . . . .83 DP66
Haweswater Dr, Wat. WD25 . .8 BW33
Haweswater Ho, Islw. TW7
  off Summerwood Rd 117 CF85
Hawfield Bk, Orp. BR6 . .146 EX104
Hawfield Gdns, St.Alb. (Park St.)
  AL2 . . . . .9 CD26
Hawgood St, E3 . . . . .85 EA71
Hawk Cl, Wal.Abb. EN9 . .16 EG34
Hawkdene, E4 . . . . .31 EB44
Hawke Pk Rd, N22 . . . . .65 DP55
Hawke Pl, SE16 . . . . .203 J4
Hawker Cl, Wall. SM6 . .159 DL108
Hawke Rd, SE19 . . . . . . .122 DS93

Hawkesbury Rd, SW15 . . . .119 CV85
Hawkes Cl, Grays RM17
  off New Rd 110 GB79
Hawkesfield Rd, SE23 . . . .123 DY89
Hawkesley Cl, Twick. TW1 . .117 CG91
Hawke's Pl, Sev. TN13 . . . .190 FG127
Hawkes Rd, Felt. TW14 . . . .115 BU87
  Mitcham CR4 . . . . .140 DE95
Hawkesworth Cl, Nthwd. HA6 .39 BS52
Hawke Twr, SE14
  off Nynehead St 103 DY79
Hawkewood Rd, Sun. TW16 .135 BU97
Hawkhirst Rd, Ken. CR8 . . .176 DR115
Hawkhurst, Cob. KT11 . . . .154 CA114
Hawkhurst Gdns, Chess.
  KT9 . . . . .156 CL105
  Romford RM5 . . . . .51 FD51
Hawkhurst Rd, SW16 . . . . .141 DK95
Hawkhurst Way, N.Mal. KT3 .138 CR99
  West Wickham BR4 . . . . .143 EB103
Hawkinge Wk, Orp. BR5 . . .146 EV97
Hawkinge Way, Horn. RM12 . .90 FJ65
Hawkins Av, Grav. DA12 . . .131 GJ91
Hawkins Cl, NW7 off Hale La . .42 CR50
  Borehamwood WD6
  off Banks Rd 26 CQ40
  Harrow HA1 . . . . .61 CD59
Hawkins Dr, Grays (Chaff.Hun.)
  RM16 . . . . .109 FX75
Hawkins Rd, Tedd. TW11 . . .117 CH93
Hawkins Way, SE6 . . . . . . .123 EA92
  Hemel Hempstead (Bov.)
  HP3 . . . . .5 BA26
Hawkley Gdns, SE27 . . . . .121 DP89
Hawkridge Cl, Rom. RM6 . . .70 EW59
Hawkridge Dr, Grays RM17 . .110 GD78
Hawksbrook La, Beck. BR3 . .143 EB100
Hawkshaw Cl, SW2
  off Tierney Rd 121 DL87
Hawkshead Cl, Brom. BR1 . .124 EE94
Hawkshead La, Hat. AL9 . . . .11 CW28
Hawkshead Rd, NW10 . . . . .81 CT66
  W4 . . . . .98 CS75
  Potters Bar EN6 . . . . .12 DB29
Hawks Hill, Epp. (N.Wld.Bas.)
  CM16 . . . . .18 FA27
Hawk's Hill, Lthd. KT22 . . .171 CF123
Hawkshill Cl, Esher KT10 . .154 CA107
Hawks Hill Cl, Lthd. (Fetch.)
  KT22 . . . . .171 CF122
Hawkshill Way, Esher KT10 .154 BZ107
Hawkslade Rd, SE15 . . . . .123 DX85
Hawksley Rd, N16 . . . . .66 DS62
Hawksmead Cl, Enf. EN3 . . . .31 DX35
Hawks Ms, SE10 off Luton Pl .103 EC80
Hawksmoor, Rad. (Shenley)
  WD7 . . . . .10 CN33
Hawksmoor Cl, E6
  off Allhallows Rd 86 EL72
  SE18 . . . . .105 ES78
Hawksmoor Grn, Brwd. CM13 .55 GD43
Hawksmoor Ms, E1
  off Cable St 84 DV73
Hawksmoor St, W6 . . . . . . .99 CX79
Hawksmouth, E4 . . . . .47 EB45
Hawks Rd, Kings.T. KT1 . . .138 CM96
Hawkstone Rd, SE16 . . . . .202 G9
Hawksview, Cob. KT11 . . . .154 BZ113
Hawksway, Stai. TW18 . . . .113 BF90
Hawkswell Cl, Wok. GU21 . .166 AT117
Hawkswell Wk, N1
  off Lockfield Dr 166 AS117
Hawkswood Gro, Slou. (Fulmer)
  SL3 . . . . .75 AZ65
Hawkswood La, Ger.Cr. SL9 . .57 AZ64
Hawk Ter, Ilf. IG5
  off Tiptree Cres 69 EN55
Hawkwell Ct, E4
  off Colvin Gdns 47 EC48
Hawkwell Ho, Dag. RM8 . . . .70 FA60
Hawkwell Wk, N1
  off Basire St 84 DQ67
Hawkwood Cres, E4 . . . . . . .31 EB44
Hawkwood La, Chis. BR7 . . .145 EQ95
Hawkwood Mt, E5 . . . . .66 DV60
Hawlands Dr, Pnr. HA5 . . . . .60 BY59
HAWLEY, Dart. 128 FM92
Hawley Cl, Hmptn. TW12 . . .116 BZ93
Hawley Cres, NW1 . . . . .83 DH66
Hawley Ms, NW1
  off Hawley St 83 DH66
Hawley Mill, Dart. DA2 . . . .128 FN91
Hawley Rd, N18 . . . . .47 DX50
  NW1 . . . . .83 DH66
  Dartford DA1, DA2 . . . . . .128 FL89
HAWLEY'S CORNER, West. . .179 EN121
Hawley St, NW1 . . . . .83 DH66
Hawley Ter, Dart. DA2
  off Hawley Vale 128 FN92
Hawley Vale, Dart. DA2 . . . .128 FN92
Hawley Way, Ashf. TW15 . . .114 BN92
Haws La, Stai. TW19 . . . . . .114 BG86
Hawstead La, Orp. BR6 . . . .164 EZ106
Hawstead Rd, SE6 . . . . . . .123 EB86
Hawsted, Buck.H. IG9 . . . . . .48 EH45
Hawthorn Av, E3 . . . . .85 DZ67
  N13 . . . . .45 DL50
  Brentwood CM13 . . . . .55 FZ48
  Carshalton SM5 . . . . . . .158 DG108
  Rainham RM13 . . . . .89 FH70
  Richmond TW9
  off Kew Rd 98 CL82
  Thornton Heath CR7 . . . . .141 DP95
Hawthorn Cen, Har. HA1 . . . .61 CF56
Hawthorn Cl, Abb.L. WD5 . . . .7 BU32
  Banstead SM7 . . . . .157 CY114
  Gravesend DA12 . . . . . . .131 GH91
  Hampton TW12 . . . . .116 CA92
  Hounslow TW5 . . . . .95 BV80
  Iver SL0 . . . . .75 BD68
  Orpington BR5 . . . . .145 ER100
  Watford WD17 . . . . .23 BT38
  Woking GU22 . . . . .166 AY120
Hawthorn Cotts, Well. DA16
  off Hook La 106 EU83
Hawthorn Ct, Rich. TW9
  off West Hall Rd 98 CP81

Hawthorn Cres, SW17 . . . . .120 DG92
  South Croydon CR2 . . . . .160 DW111
Hawthornden Cl, N12
  off Fallowfields Dr 44 DE51
Hawthornden Cl, Brom.
  BR2 . . . . .144 EF103
Hawthornden Rd, Brom.
  BR2 . . . . .144 EF103
Hawthorn Dr, Har. HA2 . . . . .60 BZ58
  Uxbridge (Denh.) UB9 . . . .76 BJ65
  West Wickham BR4 . . . . .162 EE105
Hawthorne Av, Har. HA3 . . . .61 CG58
  Mitcham CR4 . . . . .140 DD96
  Ruislip HA4 . . . . .59 BV58
  Waltham Cross (Chsht.)
  EN7 . . . . .14 DV31
  Westerham (Bigg.H.) TN16 .178 EK115
Hawthorne Cl, N1 . . . . .84 DS65
  Bromley BR1 . . . . .145 EM97
  Sutton SM1
  off Aultone Way 140 DB103
  Waltham Cross (Chsht.)
  EN7 . . . . .14 DV31
Hawthorne Ct, Nthwd. HA6
  off Ryefield Cres 39 BU54
  Walton-on-Thames KT12
  off Ambleside Av 136 BX103
Hawthorne Cres, Slou. SL1 . .74 AS71
  West Drayton UB7 . . . . . . .94 BM75
Hawthorne Fm Av, Nthlt. UB5 .78 BY67
Hawthorne Gro, NW9 . . . . . .62 CQ59
Hawthorne Ms, Grnf. UB6
  off Greenford Rd 78 CC72
Hawthorne Pl, Epsom KT17 .156 CS112
  Hayes UB3 . . . . .77 BT73
Hawthorne Rd, E17 . . . . . . .67 EA55
  Bromley BR1 . . . . .144 EL97
  Radlett WD7 . . . . .9 CG34
  Staines TW18 . . . . .113 BC92
Hawthorne Way, N9 . . . . . . .46 DS46
  Staines (Stanw.) TW19 . . .114 BK87
Hawthorn Gdns, W5 . . . . . . .97 CK76
Hawthorn Gro, SE20 . . . . . .122 DV94
  Barnet EN5 . . . . .27 CT44
  Enfield EN2 . . . . .30 DR38
Hawthorn Hatch, Brent. TW8 . .97 CH80
Hawthorn La, Sev. TN13 . . . .190 FF122
Hawthorn Ms, NW7
  off Holders Hill Rd 43 CY53
Hawthorn Pl, Erith DA8 . . . .107 FC78
Hawthorn Rd, N8 . . . . .65 DK55
  N18 . . . . .46 DT50
  NW10 . . . . .81 CU66
  Bexleyheath DA6 . . . . . . .106 EZ84
  Brentford TW8 . . . . .97 CH80
  Buckhurst Hill IG9 . . . . . . .48 EK49
  Dartford DA1 . . . . .128 FK88
  Sutton SM1 . . . . .158 DE107
  Wallington SM6 . . . . .159 DH108
  Woking GU22 . . . . .166 AX120
  Woking (Send M.) GU23 . . .168 BG124
Hawthorns, Wdf.Grn. IG8 . . . .48 EG48
Hawthorns, The, Ch.St.G.
  HP8 . . . . .20 AW40
  Epsom KT17
  off Ewell Bypass 157 CT107
  Loughton IG10 . . . . .33 EN42
  Oxted RH8 . . . . .188 EG133
  Rickmansworth (Map.Cr.)
  WD3 . . . . .37 BD50
  Slough (Colnbr.) SL3 . . . . .93 BF81
Hawthorn Wk, W10
  off Droop St 81 CY70
Hawthorn Way, Add. (New Haw)
  KT15 . . . . .152 BJ110
  Shepperton TW17 . . . . . .135 BR98
Hawtrees, Rad. WD7 . . . . . .25 CF35
Hawtrey Av, Nthlt. UB5 . . . . .78 BX68
Hawtrey Cl, Slou. SL1 . . . . . .92 AV75
Hawtrey Dr, Ruis. HA4 . . . . . .59 BU59
Hawtrey Rd, NW3 . . . . .82 DE66
Haxted Rd, Brom. BR1
  off North Rd 144 EH95
Hayburn Way, Horn. RM12 . . .71 FF60
Hay Cl, E15 . . . . .86 EE66
  Borehamwood WD6 . . . . . .26 CQ40
Haycroft Cl, Couls. CR5
  off Caterham Dr 175 DP118
Haycroft Gdns, NW10 . . . . . .81 CU67
Haycroft Rd, SW2 . . . . .121 DL85
  Surbiton KT6 . . . . .138 CL104
Hay Currie St, E14 . . . . .85 EB72
Hayday Rd, E16 . . . . .86 EG71
Hayden Ct, Add. (New Haw)
  KT15 . . . . .152 BH111
Hayden Rd, Wal.Abb. EN9 . . .31 EC35
Haydens Cl, Orp. BR5 . . . . .146 EV100
Haydens Pl, W11
  off Portobello Rd 81 CZ72
Hayden Way, Rom. RM5 . . . .51 FC54
Haydn Av, Pur. CR8 . . . . . .159 DN114
Haydns Ms, W3 . . . . .80 CQ72
Haydock Av, Nthlt. UB5 . . . . .78 CA65
Haydock Cl, Horn. RM12 . . . .72 FM63
Haydock Grn, Nthlt. UB5
  off Haydock Av 78 CA65
Haydon Cl, NW9 . . . . .62 CQ56
  Enfield EN1
  off Mortimer Dr 30 DS44
Haydon Dr, Pnr. HA5 . . . . . . .59 BU56
Haydon Pk Rd, SW19 . . . . . .120 DB92
Haydon Rd, Dag. RM8 . . . . . .70 EW61
  Watford WD19 . . . . .24 BY44
⇌ Haydons Road 120 DC92
Haydons Rd, SW19 . . . . . . .120 DB92
Haydon St, EC3 . . . . .197 P10
Haydon Wk, E1 off Mansell St .84 DT73
Haydon Way, SW11 . . . . . . .100 DD84
HAYES, Brom. 144 EG103
HAYES 77 BS72
⇌ Hayes 144 EF102
Hayes, The, Epsom KT18 . . .172 CR119
⇌ Hayes & Harlington 95 BT76
Hayes Barton, Wok. GU22 . .167 BD116
Hayes Bypass, Hayes UB3,
  UB4 . . . . .78 BX70

Hayes Chase, W.Wick. BR4 . .144 EE99
Hayes Cl, Brom. BR2 . . . . .144 EG103
  Grays RM20 . . . . .109 FW79
Hayes Ct, SW2 . . . . .121 DL88
Hayes Cres, NW11 . . . . .63 CZ57
  Sutton SM3 . . . . .157 CX105
Hayes Dr, Rain. RM13 . . . . . .89 FH66
HAYES END, Hayes 77 BQ71
Hayes End Cl, Hayes UB4 . . .77 BR70
Hayes End Dr, Hayes UB4 . . .77 BR70
Hayes End Rd, Hayes UB4 . . .77 BR70
Hayesford Pk Dr, Brom. BR2 .144 EF99
Hayes Gdn, Brom. BR2 . . . .144 EG103
H Hayes Grove Priory Hosp,
  Brom. BR2 . . . . .144 EG103
Hayes Hill, Brom. BR2 . . . .144 EE102
Hayes Hill Rd, Brom. BR2 . .144 EF102
Hayes La, Beck. BR3 . . . . .143 EC97
  Bromley BR2 . . . . .144 EG99
  Kenley CR8 . . . . .160 DQ114
Hayes Mead Rd, Brom. BR2 .144 EE102
Hayes Metro Cen, Hayes UB4 .78 BW73
Hayes Pk, Hayes UB4 . . . . . .77 BS70
Hayes Pl, NW1 . . . . .194 C5
Hayes Rd, Brom. BR2 . . . . .144 EG98
  Greenhithe DA9 . . . . .129 FS87
  Southall UB2 . . . . .95 BV77
Hayes St, Brom. BR2 . . . . .144 EH102
HAYES TOWN, Hayes 95 BS75
Hayes Wk, Brox. EN10
  off Landau Way 15 DZ25
  Potters Bar EN6
  off Hyde Av 12 DB33
Hayes Way, Beck. BR3 . . . .143 EC98
Hayes Wd Av, Brom. BR2 . . .144 EH102
Hayfield Cl, Bushey WD23 . . .24 CB42
Hayfield Pas, E1
  off Stepney Grn 84 DW70
Hayfield Rd, Orp. BR5 . . . . .146 EU99
Hayfield Yd, E1
  off Mile End Rd 84 DW70
Haygarth Pl, SW19 . . . . . . .119 CX92
Haygreen Cl, Kings.T. KT2 . .118 CP93
Hay Hill, W1 . . . . .199 J1
Hayland Cl, NW9 . . . . .62 CR56
Hay La, NW9 . . . . .62 CR56
  Slough (Fulmer) SL3 . . . . .56 AX63
Hayles St, SE11 . . . . .200 F8
Haylett Gdns, Kings.T. KT1
  off Anglesea Rd 137 CK98
Hayling Av, Felt. TW13 . . . .115 BU90
Hayling Cl, N16
  off Pellerin Rd 66 DS64
Hayling Rd, Wat. WD19 . . . . .39 BV47
Haymaker Cl, Uxb. UB10
  off Honey Hill 76 BM66
Hayman Cres, Hayes UB4 . . .77 BR68
Hayman St, N1 off Cross St . .83 DP66
Haymarket, SW1 . . . . .199 M1
Haymarket Arc, SW1 . . . . . .199 M1
Haymeads Dr, Esher KT10 . .154 CC107
Haymer Gdns, Wor.Pk. KT4 .139 CU104
Haymerle Rd, SE15 . . . . . .102 DU79
Haymill Cl, Grnf. UB6 . . . . . .79 CF69
Hayne Rd, Beck. BR3 . . . . .143 DZ96
Haynes Cl, N11 . . . . .44 DG48
  N17 . . . . .46 DV52
  SE3 . . . . .104 EE83
  Slough SL3 . . . . .93 AZ78
  Woking (Ripley) GU23 . . . .168 BH122
Haynes Dr, N9 off Plevna Rd . .46 DV48
Haynes La, SE19 . . . . .122 DS93
Haynes Rd, Grav. (Nthflt.)
  DA11 . . . . .131 GF90
  Hornchurch RM11 . . . . . . .72 FK57
  Wembley HA0 . . . . .80 CL66
Hayne St, EC1 . . . . .196 G6
Haynt Wk, SW20 . . . . .139 CY97
★ Hay's Galleria, SE1 . . . . .201 M2
Hay's Galleria, SE1 . . . . . .201 M2
Hay's La, SE1 . . . . .201 M3
Haysleigh Gdns, SE20 . . . .142 DU96
Hay's Ms, W1 . . . . .199 H1
Haysoms Cl, Rom. RM1 . . . .71 FE56
Haystall Cl, Hayes UB4 . . . . .77 BS68
Hay St, E2 . . . . .84 DU67
Hays Wk, Sutt. SM2 . . . . . .157 CX110
Hayter Ct, E11 . . . . .68 EH61
Hayter Rd, SW2 . . . . .121 DL85
Hayton Cl, E8
  off Buttermere Wk 84 DT65
Haywain, Oxt. RH8 . . . . . . .187 ED130
Hayward Cl, SW19 . . . . . . .140 DB95
  Dartford DA1 . . . . .127 FD85
Hayward Dr, Dart. DA1 . . . .128 FM89
Hayward Gdns, SW15 . . . . .119 CW86
Hayward Rd, N20 . . . . .44 DC47
  Thames Ditton KT7 . . . . . .137 CG102
★ Hayward Gall, SE1 . . . . .200 C2
Haywards Cl, Brwd. CM13 . . .53 GE44
  Romford (Chad.Hth.) RM6 . .70 EV57
Hayward's Pl, EC1 . . . . . . .196 F5
Haywood Cl, Pnr. HA5 . . . . . .40 BX54
Haywood Ct, Wal.Abb. EN9 . .16 EF34
Haywood Dr, Rick. WD3
  off Haywood Pk 21 BF43
Haywood Pk, Rick. (Chorl.)
  WD3 . . . . .21 BF43
Haywood Ri, Orp. BR6 . . . .163 ES105
Haywood Rd, Brom. BR2 . . .144 EK98
Hayworth Cl, Enf. EN3
  off Green St 31 DY40
Hazel Av, West Dr. UB7 . . . . .94 BN76
Hazelbank, Surb. KT5 . . . . .138 CQ102
Hazelbank Rd, Cher. KT16 . .134 BJ102
  SE6 . . . . .123 ED89
  Chertsey KT16 . . . . .134 BJ102
Hazelbourne Rd, SW12 . . . .121 DH86
Hazelbrouck Gdns, Ilf. IG6 . . .49 ER52
Hazelbury Av, Abb.L. WD5 . . . .7 BQ32
Hazelbury Cl, SW19 . . . . . .140 DA96
Hazelbury Grn, N9 . . . . .46 DS48
Hazelbury La, N9 . . . . .46 DS48
Hazel Cl, N13 . . . . .46 DA48
  N19 off Hargrave Pk 65 DJ61
  SE15 . . . . .102 DU82
  Brentford TW8 . . . . .97 CH80

Hazel Cl, Croy. CR0 . . . . . .143 DX101
  Egham (Eng.Grn.) TW20 . .112 AV93
  Hornchurch RM12 . . . . . . .71 FH62
  Mitcham CR4 . . . . .141 DK98
  Twickenham TW2 . . . . . . .116 CC87
  Waltham Cross EN7
  off The Laurels 14 DS26
Hazelcroft, Pnr. HA5 . . . . . . .40 CA51
Hazelcroft Cl, Uxb. UB10 . . . .76 BM66
Hazeldean Rd, NW10 . . . . . .80 CR66
Hazeldene, Add. KT15 . . . . .152 BJ106
  Waltham Cross EN8 . . . . . .15 DY32
Hazeldene Ct, Ken. CR8 . . .176 DR115
Hazeldene Dr, Pnr. HA5 . . . .60 BW55
Hazeldene Gdns, Uxb. UB10 . .77 BQ67
Hazeldene Rd, Ilf. IG3 . . . . . .70 EV61
  Welling DA16 . . . . .106 EW82
Hazeldon Rd, SE4 . . . . .123 DY85
Hazel Dr, Erith DA8 . . . . . .107 FH81
  South Ockendon RM15 . . . .91 FW69
Hazeleigh, Brwd. CM13 . . . . .55 GB48
Hazeleigh Gdns, Wdf.Grn. IG8 .48 EL50
Hazel End, Swan. BR8 . . . . .147 FE99
Hazel Gdns, Edg. HA8 . . . . . .42 CP49
  Grays RM16 . . . . .110 GE76
Hazelgreen Cl, N21 . . . . .45 DP46
Hazel Gro, SE26 . . . . .123 DX91
  Enfield EN1
  off Dimsdale Dr 30 DU44
  Orpington BR6 . . . . .145 EP103
  Romford RM6 . . . . .70 EY55
  Staines TW18 . . . . .114 BH93
  Watford WD25
  off Cedar Wd Dr 23 BV35
  Wembley HA0
  off Carlyon Rd 80 CL67
Hazel Gro Est, SE26 . . . . . .123 DX91
Hazelhurst, Beck. BR3 . . . .143 ED95
Hazelhurst Rd, SW17 . . . . .120 DC91
Hazel La, Rich. TW10 . . . . .118 CL89
Hazell Cres, Rom. RM5 . . . . .51 FB53
Hazells Rd, Grav. DA13 . . . .130 GD92
Hazellville Rd, N19 . . . . .65 DK59
Hazell Way, Slou. (Stoke P.)
  SL2 . . . . .74 AT65
Hazel Mead, Barn. EN5 . . . . .27 CV43
  Epsom KT17 . . . . .157 CU110
Hazelmere Cl, Felt. TW14 . . .115 BR86
  Northolt UB5 . . . . .78 BZ68
Hazelmere Dr, Nthlt. UB5 . . . .78 BZ68
Hazelmere Gdns, Horn. RM11 .71 FH57
Hazelmere Rd, NW6 . . . . . . .82 DA67
  Northolt UB5 . . . . .78 BZ68
  Orpington BR5 . . . . .145 EQ98
Hazelmere Wk, Nthlt. UB5 . . .78 BZ68
Hazelmere Way, Brom. BR2 .144 EG100
Hazel Ms, N22
  off Alexandra Rd 65 DN55
Hazel Ri, Horn. RM11 . . . . . .72 FJ58
Hazel Rd, E15
  off Wingfield Rd 68 EE64
  NW10 . . . . .81 CW69
  Dartford DA1 . . . . .128 FK89
  Erith DA8 . . . . .107 FG81
  St. Albans (Park St.) AL2 . . .8 CB28
  West Byfleet KT14 . . . . . .152 BG114
Hazeltree La, Nthlt. UB5 . . . .78 BY69
Hazel Tree Rd, Wat. WD24 . . .23 BV37
Hazel Wk, Brom. BR2 . . . . .145 EN100
Hazel Way, E4 . . . . .47 DZ51
  SE1 . . . . .201 P8
  Coulsdon CR5 . . . . .174 DF119
  Leatherhead (Fetch.) KT22 .170 CC122
HAZELWOOD, Sev. 163 ER111
Hazelwood, Loug. IG10 . . . . .32 EK43
Hazelwood Av, Mord. SM4 . .140 DB98
Hazelwood Cl, W5 . . . . .98 CL75
  Harrow HA2 . . . . .60 CB56
Hazelwood Ct, NW10
  off Neasden La N 62 CS62
Hazelwood Cres, N13 . . . . . .45 DN49
Hazelwood Cft, Surb. KT6 . .138 CL100
Hazelwood Dr, Pnr. HA5 . . . .39 BV54
Hazelwood Gdns, Brwd.
  CM15 . . . . .54 FU44
Hazelwood Gro, S.Croy. CR2 .160 DV113
Hazelwood Hts, Oxt. RH8 . . .188 EG131
Hazelwood La, N13 . . . . .45 DN49
  Abbots Langley WD5 . . . . . .7 BQ32
  Coulsdon CR5 . . . . .174 DF119
Hazelwood Pk Cl, Chig. IG7 . .49 ES50
Hazelwood Rd, E17 . . . . .67 DY57
  Enfield EN1 . . . . .30 DT44
  Oxted RH8 . . . . .188 EH132
  Rickmansworth (Crox.Grn.)
  WD3 . . . . .23 BQ44
  Sevenoaks (Cudham)
  TN14 . . . . .163 ER112
  Woking (Knap.) GU21 . . . .166 AS118
Hazlebury Rd, SW6 . . . . . .100 DB82
Hazledean Rd, Croy. CR0 . .142 DR103
Hazledene Rd, W4 . . . . .98 CQ79
Hazlemere Gdns, Wor.Pk.
  KT4 . . . . .139 CV102
Hazlemere Rd, Slou. SL2 . . . .74 AW74
Hazlewell Rd, SW15 . . . . . .119 CV85
Hazlewood Cl, E5
  off Mandeville St 67 DY62
Hazlewood Cres, W10 . . . . . .81 CY70
Hazlitt Cl, Felt. TW13 . . . . .116 BY91
Hazlitt Ms, W14 off Hazlitt Rd .99 CY76
Hazlitt Rd, W14 . . . . .99 CY76
Hazon Way, Epsom KT19 . . .156 CR112
Heacham Av, Uxb. UB10 . . . .59 BQ62
Headcorn Pl, Th.Hth. CR7
  off Headcorn Rd 141 DM98
Headcorn Rd, N17 . . . . .46 DT52
  Bromley BR1 . . . . .124 EF92
  Thornton Heath CR7 . . . . .141 DM98
Headfort Pl, SW1 . . . . .198 G5
Headingley Cl, IG6 . . . . .49 ET51
  Radlett (Shenley) WD7 . . . .10 CL32
  Waltham Cross (Chsht.)
  EN7 . . . . .14 DT26
Headington Rd, SW18 . . . . .120 DC89
Headlam Rd, SW4 . . . . .121 DK86

Headlam St, E1 . . . . .84 DV70
HEADLEY, Epsom 182 CQ125
Headley App, Ilf. IG2 . . . . . . .69 EN57
Headley Av, Wall. SM6 . . . . .159 DM106
Headley Chase, Brwd. CM14 . .54 FW49
Headley Cl, Epsom KT19 . . .156 CN107
Headley Common, Brwd. CM13
  off Warley Gap 53 FV52
Headley Common Rd, Epsom
  (Headley) KT18 . . . . .182 CR127
  Tadworth KT20 . . . . .182 CR127
Headley Ct, SE26 . . . . .122 DV92
Headley Dr, Croy. (New Adgtn.)
  CR0 . . . . .161 EB108
  Epsom KT18 . . . . .173 CV119
  Ilford IG2 . . . . .69 EP58
Headley Gro, Tad. KT20 . . . .173 CV120
★ Headley Heath, Epsom
  KT18 . . . . .182 CP128
Headley Heath App, Dor. (Mick.)
  RH5 off Ashurst Dr 182 CP130
  Tadworth KT20 . . . . .182 CP130
Headley Rd, Epsom (Tyr.Wd.)
  KT18 . . . . .172 CN123
  Epsom (Woodcote) KT18 . .172 CP118
  Leatherhead KT22 . . . . . .171 CK123
Head's Ms, W11
  off Artesian Rd 82 DA72
HEADSTONE, Har. 60 CC56
Headstone Dr, Har. HA1, HA3 .61 CE55
Headstone Gdns, Har. HA2 . . .60 CC56
⇌ Headstone Lane 40 CB53
Headstone La, Har. HA2, HA3 .60 CB56
Headstone Rd, Har. HA1 . . . .61 CE57
Head St, E1 . . . . .85 DX72
Headway, The, Epsom KT17 .157 CT109
Headway Cl, Rich. TW10
  off Locksmeade Rd 117 CJ91
Heald St, SE14 . . . . .103 DZ81
Healey Dr, Orp. BR6 . . . . . .163 ET105
Healey Rd, Wat. WD18 . . . . .23 BT44
Healey St, NW1 . . . . .83 DH65
Heanor Ct, E5 off Pedro St . . .67 DX62
Heards La, Brwd. CM15 . . . . .55 FZ41
Hearne Ct, Ch.St.G. HP8
  off Gordon Way 36 AV48
Hearne Rd, W4 . . . . .98 CN79
Hearn Ri, Nthlt. UB5 . . . . . . .78 BX65
Hearn Rd, Rom. RM1 . . . . . .71 FF58
Hearn's Bldgs, SE17 . . . . . .201 L9
Hearn's Rd, Orp. BR5 . . . . .146 EW98
Hearn St, EC2 . . . . .197 N5
Hearnville Rd, SW12 . . . . . .120 DG88
H Heart Hosp, The, W1 . . . .194 G7
Heath, The, W7
  off Lower Boston Rd 79 CE74
  Caterham CR3 . . . . .176 DQ124
  Radlett WD7 . . . . .9 CG33
Heathacre, Slou. (Colnbr.) SL3
  off Park Av 93 BE81
Heatham Pk, Twick. TW2 . . .117 CF87
Heath Av, Bexh. DA7 . . . . .106 EX79
Heathbourne Rd, Bushey
  (Bushey Hth.) WD23 . . . . . .41 CE47
  Stanmore HA7 . . . . .41 CE47
Heathbridge, Wey. KT13 . . .152 BN108
Heath Brow, NW3
  off North End Way 64 DC62
Heath Cl, NW11 . . . . .64 DB59
  W5 . . . . .80 CM70
  Banstead SM7 . . . . .158 DB114
  Hayes UB3 . . . . .95 BR80
  Orpington BR5
  off Sussex Rd 146 EW100
  Potters Bar EN6 . . . . .12 DA30
  Romford RM2 . . . . .71 FG55
  Staines TW19 . . . . .114 BJ86
  Virginia Water GU25 . . . . .132 AX98
Heathclose Av, Dart. DA1 . . .127 FH87
Heathclose Rd, Dart. DA1 . . .127 FG88
Heathcock Ct, WC2
  off Strand 83 DL73
Heathcote, Tad. KT20 . . . . .173 CX121
Heathcote Av, Ilf. IG5 . . . . . .49 EM54
Heathcote Ct, Ilf. IG5
  off Heathcote Av 49 EM54
Heathcote Gro, E4 . . . . .47 EC48
Heathcote Pt, E9
  off Wick Rd 85 DX65
Heathcote Rd, Epsom KT18 .156 CR114
  Twickenham TW1 . . . . . . .117 CH86
Heathcote St, WC1 . . . . . . .196 B4
Heathcote Way, West Dr. UB7
  off Tavistock Rd 76 BK74
Heath Cotts, Pot.B. EN6
  off Heath Rd 12 DB30
Heath Ct, Houns. TW4 . . . . . .96 BZ84
  Uxbridge UB8 . . . . .76 BL66
Heathcroft, NW11 . . . . .64 DB60
  W5 . . . . .80 CM70
Heathcroft Av, Sun. TW16 . .115 BT94
Heathcroft Gdns, E17 . . . . . .47 ED53
Heathdale Av, Houns. TW4 . . .96 BY83
Heathdene, Tad. KT20
  off Canons La 173 CY119
Heathdene Dr, Belv. DA17 . .107 FB77
Heathdene Rd, SW16 . . . . .121 DM94
  Wallington SM6 . . . . .159 DH108
Heathdown Rd, Wok. GU22 .167 BD115
Heath Dr, NW3 . . . . .64 DB63
  SW20 . . . . .139 CW98
  Epping (They.B.) CM16 . . . .33 ES35
  Potters Bar EN6 . . . . .12 DA30
  Romford RM2 . . . . .51 FG53
  Sutton SM2 . . . . .158 DC109
  Tadworth KT20 . . . . .183 CU125
  Woking (Send) GU23 . . . .167 BB122
Heathedge, SE26 . . . . .122 DV89
Heath End Rd, Bex. DA5 . . .127 FE88
Heather Av, Rom. RM1 . . . . .51 FD54
Heatherbank, SE9 . . . . . . .105 EM82
  Chislehurst BR7 . . . . . . .145 EN96
Heatherbank Cl, Dart. DA1 . .127 FE86
Heather Cl, E6 . . . . .87 EP72

A B C D E F G H I J K L M N O P Q R S T U V W X Y Z

Hea - Her

Heather Cl, N7 off Newington
  Barrow Way 65 DM62
SE13 . . . . .123 ED87
SW8 . . . . .101 DH83
  Abbots Langley WD5 . . . . . . .7 BU32
  Addlestone (New Haw)
    KT15 . . . . .152 BH110
  Brentwood CM15 . . . . .54 FV43
  Hampton TW12 . . . . .136 BZ95
  Isleworth TW7
    off Harvesters Cl 117 CD85
  Redhill RH1 . . . . .185 DH130
  Romford RM1 . . . . .51 FD53
  Tadworth KT20 . . . . .173 CY122
  Uxbridge UB8
    off Violet Av 76 BM71
  Woking GU21 . . . . .166 AW115
Heatherdale Cl, Kings.T. KT2 .118 CN93
Heatherdene Cl, N12
  off Bow La 44 DC53
  Mitcham CR4 . . . . .140 DE98
Heatherden Grn, Iver SL0 . . . .75 BC67
Heather Dr, Dart. DA1 . . . . . .127 FG87
  Enfield EN2
    off Chasewood Av 29 DP40
  Romford RM1 . . . . .51 FD54
Heather End, Swan. BR8 . . . .147 FD98
Heatherfields, Add. (New Haw)
  KT15 . . . . .152 BH110
Heatherfold Way, Pnr. HA5 . . .59 BT55
Heather Gdns, NW11 . . . . . . .63 CY58
  Romford RM1 . . . . .51 FD54
  Sutton SM2 . . . . .158 DA100
  Waltham Abbey EN9 . . . . . . .31 EC36
Heather Glen, Rom. RM1 . . . . .51 FD64
Heatherlands, Sun. TW16 . . . .115 BU93
Heather La, Wat. WD24 . . . . . .23 BT35
  West Drayton UB7 . . . . .76 BL72
Heatherley Dr, Ilf. IG5 . . . . . . .68 EL55
Heather Pk Dr, Wem. HA0 . . . .80 CN66
Heather Pl, Esher KT10
  off Park Rd 154 CB105
Heather Ri, Bushey WD23 . . . .24 BZ40
Heather Rd, E4 . . . . .47 DZ51
  NW2 . . . . .63 CT61
  SE12 . . . . .124 EG89
Heathers, The, Stai. TW19 . . . .114 BM87
Heatherset Cl, Esher KT10 . . .154 CC106
Heatherset Gdns, SW16 . . . . .121 DM94
Heatherside Dr, Vir.W. GU25 . .132 AU100
Heatherside Rd, Epsom
  KT19 . . . . .156 CR108
  Sidcup DA14 off Wren Rd . . .126 EW90
Heatherton Ter, N3 . . . . .44 DB54
Heathervale Caravan Pk, Add.
  (New Haw) KT15 . . . . .152 BJ110
Heathervale Rd, Add. (New Haw)
  KT15 . . . . .152 BH110
Heather Wk, W10 off Droop St .81 CY70
  Edgware HA8 . . . . .42 CP50
  Twickenham TW2
    off Stephenson Rd 116 CA87
  Walton-on-Thames KT12
    off Octagon Rd 153 BT110
Heather Way, Pot.B. EN6 . . . . .11 CZ32
  Romford RM1 . . . . .51 FD54
  South Croydon CR2 . . . . . .161 DX109
  Stanmore HA7 . . . . .41 CF51
  Woking (Chobham) GU24 . . .150 AS108
Heatherwood Cl, E12 . . . . .68 EJ61
Heatherwood Dr, Hayes UB4
  off Charville La 77 BR68
Heath Fm Ct, Wat. WD17
  off Grove Mill La 23 BR37
Heathfield, E4 . . . . .47 EC48
  Chislehurst BR7 . . . . .125 EQ93
  Cobham KT11 . . . . .154 CA114
Heathfield Av, SW18
  off Heathfield Rd 120 DD87
  South Croydon CR2 . . . . . .161 DY109
Heathfield Cl, E16 . . . . .86 EK71
  Keston BR2 . . . . .162 EJ106
  Potters Bar EN6 . . . . .12 DB30
  Watford WD19 . . . . .40 BW45
  Woking GU22 . . . . .167 BA118
Heathfield Dr, Mitch. CR4 . . . .140 DE95
Heathfield Gdns, NW11 . . . . . .63 CX58
  SE3 . . . . .104 EE82
  SW18 off Heathfield Rd 120 DD86
  W4 . . . . .98 CQ78
  Croydon CR0
    off Coombe Rd 160 DR105
Heathfield La, Chis. BR7 . . . . .125 EP93
Heathfield N, Twick. TW2 . . . .117 CF87
Heathfield Pk, NW2 . . . . .63 CW65
Heathfield Pk Dr, Rom. (Chad.Hth.)
  RM6 . . . . .70 EV57
Heathfield Ri, Ruis. HA4 . . . . . .59 BQ59
Heathfield Rd, SW18 . . . . . . .120 DC86
  W3 . . . . .98 CP75
  Bexleyheath DA6 . . . . .106 EZ84
  Bromley BR1 . . . . .124 EF94
  Bushey WD23 . . . . .24 BY42
  Croydon CR0 . . . . .160 DR105
  Keston BR2 . . . . .162 EJ106
  Sevenoaks TN13 . . . . .190 FF122
  Walton-on-Thames KT12 . . .154 BY105
  Woking GU22 . . . . .167 BA118
Heathfields Cl, Ashtd. KT21 . . .171 CJ118
Heathfields Ct, Houns. TW4
  off Frampton Rd 116 BY85
Heathfield S, Twick. TW2 . . . .117 CF87
Heathfield Sq, SW18 . . . . . . .120 DD87
Heathfield St, W11
  off Portland Rd 81 CY73
  W4 . . . . .98 CP78
Heathfield Ter, SE18 . . . . . . .105 ET79
  W4 . . . . .98 CP78
Heathfield Vale, S.Croy. CR2 .161 DX109
Heath Gdns, Twick. TW1 . . . . .117 CF88
Heathgate, NW11 . . . . .64 DB58
Heathgate Pl, NW3
  off Agincourt Rd 64 DF64
Heath Gro, SE20
  off Maple Rd 122 DW94

Heath Gro, Sun. TW16 . . . . . .115 BT94
Heath Hurst Rd, NW3 . . . . . . .64 DE63
Heathhurst Rd, S.Croy. CR2 . .160 DS109
Heathland Rd, N16 . . . . .66 DS60
Heathlands, Tad. KT20 . . . . . .173 CX122
Heathlands Cl, Sun. TW16 . . . .135 BU96
  Twickenham TW1 . . . . .117 CF89
  Woking GU21 . . . . .150 AY114
Heathlands Ri, Dart. DA1 . . . .127 FH86
Heathlands Way, Houns.
  TW4 . . . . .116 BY85
Heath La, SE3 . . . . .103 ED82
  Dartford (Lower) DA1 . . . . .128 FJ88
  Dartford (Upper) DA1 . . . . .127 FG89
Heathlee Rd, SE3 . . . . .104 EF84
  Dartford DA1 . . . . .127 FE86
Heathley End, Chis. BR7 . . . . .125 EQ93
Heath Mead, SW19 . . . . .119 CX90
Heath Pk Ct, Rom. RM2
  off Heath Pk Rd 71 FG57
Heath Pk Dr, Brom. BR1 . . . . .144 EL97
Heath Pk Rd, Rom. RM2 . . . . .71 FG57
Heath Pas, NW3 . . . . .64 DB61
Heath Ri, SW15 . . . . .119 CX86
  Bromley BR2 . . . . .144 EF100
  Virginia Water GU25 . . . . . .132 AX98
  Woking (Ripley) GU23 . . . . .168 BH123
Heath Rd, SW8 . . . . .101 DH82
  Bexley DA5 . . . . .127 FC88
  Caterham CR3 . . . . .176 DR123
  Dartford DA1 . . . . .127 FF86
  Grays RM16 . . . . .111 GG75
  Harrow HA1 . . . . .60 CC59
  Hounslow TW3 . . . . .96 CB84
  Leatherhead (Oxshott)
    KT22 . . . . .154 CC112
  Potters Bar EN6 . . . . .12 DA30
  Romford RM6 . . . . .70 EX59
  Thornton Heath CR7 . . . . . .142 DQ97
  Twickenham TW1, TW2 . . . .117 CF88
  Uxbridge UB10 . . . . .77 BQ70
  Watford WD19 . . . . .40 BX45
  Weybridge KT13 . . . . .152 BN106
  Woking GU21 . . . . .167 AZ115
★ Heathrow Airport (London),
  Houns. TW6 . . . . .95 BP81
Heathrow Cl, West Dr. UB7 . . .94 BH81
Heathrow Interchange, Hayes
  UB4 . . . . .78 BW74
Heathrow Int Trd Est, Houns.
  TW4 . . . . .95 BV83
⊁ Heathrow Terminal 4 . . . . . .115 BP85
⊕ Heathrow Terminal 4 . . . . . .115 BP85
⊁ Heathrow Terminals 1,2,3 . . .95 BP83
⊕ Heathrow Terminals 1,2,3 . . .95 BP83
Heathrow Tunnel App, Houns.
  (Hthrw.Air.) TW6 . . . . .95 BP83
Heathrow Vehicle Tunnel, Houns.
  (Hthrw.Air.) TW6 . . . . .95 BP81
Heaths Cl, Enf. EN1 . . . . .30 DS40
Heath Side, NW3 . . . . .64 DD63
Heathside, Esher KT10 . . . . . .137 CE104
  Hounslow TW4 . . . . .116 BZ87
Heath Side, Orp. BR5 . . . . . . .145 EQ102
Heathside, Wey. KT13 . . . . . .153 BP106
Heathside Av, Bexh. DA7 . . . .106 EY81
Heathside Cl, Esher KT10 . . . .137 CE104
  Ilford IG2 . . . . .69 ER57
Heathside Ct, Tad. KT20 . . . . .173 CV123
Heathside Cres, Wok. GU22 . .167 AZ117
Heathside Gdns, Wok. GU22 .167 BA117
Heathside Pk Rd, Wok.
  GU22 . . . . .167 AZ118
Heathside Pl, Epsom KT18 . . .173 CX118
Heathside Rd, Nthwd. HA6 . . . .39 BR49
  Woking GU22 . . . . .167 AZ118
Heathstan Rd, W12 . . . . .81 CU72
Heath St, NW3 . . . . .64 DC63
  Dartford DA1 . . . . .128 FK87
Heath Vw, N2 . . . . .64 DC56
Heathview Av, Dart. DA1 . . . .127 FE86
Heath Vw Cl, N2 . . . . .64 DC56
Heathview Ct, SW19 . . . . . . .119 CX89
Heathview Cres, Dart. DA1 . . .127 FG88
Heathview Dr, SE2 . . . . .106 EX79
Heathview Gdns, SW15 . . . . .119 CW87
Heath Vw Gdns, Grays
  RM16 . . . . .110 GC75
Heath Vw Rd, Grays RM16 . . .110 GC75
Heathview Rd, Th.Hth. CR7 . . .141 DN98
Heath Vil, SE18 . . . . .105 ET78
  SW18 off Cargill Rd 120 DC88
Heathville Rd, N19 . . . . .65 DL59
Heathwall St, SW11 . . . . .100 DF83
Heathway, SE3 . . . . .104 EF80
  Caterham CR3 . . . . .186 DQ125
  Croydon CR0 . . . . .143 DZ104
  Dagenham RM9, RM10 . . . . .88 FA66
  Heath Way, Erith DA8 . . . . .107 FC81
  Heathway, Iver SL0 . . . . . . .75 BD68
  Leatherhead (E.Hors.)
    KT24 . . . . .169 BT124
  Woodford Green IG8 . . . . . . .48 EJ49
Heathway Ind Est, Dag. RM10
  off Manchester Way 71 FB63
Heathwood Gdns, SE7 . . . . . .104 EL77
  Swanley BR8 . . . . .147 FC96
Heathwood Pt, SE23
  off Dacres Rd 123 DX90
Heathwood Wk, Bex. DA5 . . . .127 FE88
Heaton Av, Rom. RM3 . . . . . . .52 FJ52
Heaton Cl, E4 . . . . .47 EC48
  Romford RM3 . . . . .52 FJ52
Heaton Ct, Wal.Cr. (Chsht.)
  EN8 . . . . .15 DX29
Heaton Gra Rd, Rom. RM2 . . . .51 FF54
Heaton Rd, SE15 . . . . .102 DU83
  Mitcham CR4 . . . . .120 DG94
Heaton Way, Rom. RM3 . . . . . .52 FJ52
Heaver Rd, SW11 off Wye St .100 DD83
Heavitree Cl, SE18 . . . . .105 ER78
Heavitree Rd, SE18 . . . . .105 ER78
Hebden Ct, E2
  off Laburnum St 84 DT67

Hebden Ter, N17
  off Commercial Rd 46 DS51
Hebdon Rd, SW17 . . . . .120 DE90
Heber Rd, NW2 . . . . .63 CX64
  SE22 . . . . .122 DT86
Hebron Rd, W6 . . . . .99 CV76
Hecham Cl, E17 . . . . .47 DY54
Heckfield Pl, SW6
  off Fulham Rd 100 DA80
Heckford Cl, Wat. WD18 . . . . .23 BQ44
Heckford St, E1
  off The Highway 85 DX73
Hector St, SE18 . . . . .105 ES77
Heddington Gro, N7 . . . . .65 DM64
Heddon Cl, Islw. TW7 . . . . .97 CG84
Heddon Ct Av, Barn. EN4 . . . . .28 DF43
Heddon Rd, Barn. EN4 . . . . . . .28 DF43
Heddon St, W1 . . . . .195 K10
Hedgeley, Ilf. IG4 . . . . .69 EM56
Hedgemans Rd, Dag. RM9 . . . .88 EX66
Hedgemans Way, Dag. RM9 . . .88 EY65
Hedge Pl Rd, Green. DA9 . . . .129 FT86
Hedgerley Gdns, Grnf. UB6 . . .78 CC68
Hedgerley Grn, Slou. (Hedg.)
  SL2 . . . . .56 AT58
Hedgerley La, Ger.Cr. SL9 . . . .56 AV59
  Slough SL2 . . . . .56 AS58
Hedgerow La, Barn. EN5 . . . . .27 CV43
Hedgerows, The, Grav. (Nthflt.)
  DA11 . . . . .130 GE89
Hedgerow Wk, Wal.Cr. EN8 . . .15 DX30
Hedgers Cl, Loug. IG10
  off Newmans La 33 EN42
Hedgers Gro, E9 . . . . .85 DY65
Hedger St, SE11 . . . . .200 F8
Hedgeside Rd, Nthwd. HA6 . . .39 BQ50
Hedge Wk, SE6 . . . . .123 EB91
Hedgewood Gdns, Ilf. IG5 . . . .69 EN57
Hedgley St, SE12 . . . . .124 EF85
Hedingham Cl, N1
  off Popham Rd 84 DQ66
Hedingham Rd, Dag. RM8 . . . .70 EV64
  Grays (Chaff.Hun.) RM16 . . .109 FW78
  Hornchurch RM11 . . . . .72 FN60
Hedley Av, Grays RM20 . . . . . .109 FW80
Hedley Cl, Rom. RM1
  off High St 71 FE57
Hedley Rd, Twick. TW2 . . . . . .116 CA87
Hedley Row, N5
  off Poets Rd 66 DR64
Hedworth Av, Wal.Cr. EN8 . . . .15 DX33
Heenan Cl, Bark. IG11
  off Glenny Rd 87 DQ65
Heene Rd, Enf. EN2 . . . . .30 DR39
Heideck Gdns, Brwd. CM13
  off Victors Cres 55 GB47
Heidegger Cres, SW13
  off Trinity Ch Rd 99 CV79
Heigham Rd, E6 . . . . .86 EK66
Heighton Gdns, Croy. CR0 . . .159 DP106
Heights, The, SE7 . . . . .104 EJ78
  Beckenham BR3 . . . . .123 EC96
  Loughton IG10 . . . . .33 EM40
  Northolt UB5 . . . . .60 BZ64
  Waltham Abbey (Nazeing)
    EN9 . . . . .16 EH25
  Weybridge KT13 . . . . .152 BN110
Heights Cl, SW20 . . . . .119 CV94
  Banstead SM7 . . . . .173 CY116
★ Heinz Gall, RIBA, W1 . . . . . .194 F8
Heiron St, SE17 . . . . .101 DP79
Helby Rd, SW4 . . . . .121 DK86
Helder Gro, SE12 . . . . .124 EF87
Helder St, S.Croy. CR2 . . . . . .160 DR107
Heldmann Cl, Houns. TW3 . . . .97 CD84
Helegon Cl, Orp. BR6 . . . . . . .163 ET105
Helena Cl, Barn. EN4 . . . . .28 DD38
  Wallington SM6
    off Kingsford Av 159 DL108
Helena Pl, E9 off Fremont St . . .84 DW67
Helena Rd, E13 . . . . .86 EF68
  E17 . . . . .67 EA57
  NW10 . . . . .63 CV64
  W5 . . . . .79 CK71
Helena Sq, SE16 . . . . .203 K1
Helen Av, Felt. TW14 . . . . . . .115 BV87
Helen Cl, N2
  off Thomas More Way 64 DC55
  Dartford DA1 . . . . .127 FH87
  West Molesey KT8 . . . . . . .136 CB98
Helen Rd, Horn. RM11 . . . . . . .72 FK55
Helens Gate, Wal.Cr. EN8 . . . .15 DZ26
Helenslea Av, NW11 . . . . .63 CZ60
Helen's Pl, E2 off Roman Rd . . .84 DW69
Helen St, SE18
  off Wilmount St 105 EP77
Helford Cl, Ruis. HA4
  off Chichester Av 59 BS61
Helford Wk, Wok. GU21 . . . . .166 AU118
Helford Way, Upmin. RM14 . . .73 FR58
Helgiford Gdns, Sun. TW16 . . .115 BS94
Helios Rd, Wall. SM6
  off London Rd 140 DG102
Helix Gdns, SW2
  off Helix Rd 121 DM86
Helix Rd, SW2 . . . . .121 DM86
Helleborine, Grays (Bad.Dene)
  RM17 . . . . .110 FZ78
Hellings St, E1 . . . . .202 C3
Helm Cl, Epsom KT19 . . . . . . .156 CN112
Helme Cl, SW19 . . . . .119 CZ92
Helmet Row, EC1 . . . . .197 J4
Helmore Rd, Bark. IG11 . . . . . .87 ET66
Helmsdale, Wok. GU21
  off Winnington Way 166 AV118
Helmsdale Cl, Hayes UB4 . . . .78 BY70
  Romford RM1 . . . . .51 FE52
Helmsdale Rd, SW16 . . . . . . .141 DJ95
  Romford RM1 . . . . .51 FE52
Helmsley Pl, E8 . . . . .84 DV66
Helsinki Sq, SE16 . . . . .203 L6
Helston Cl, Pnr. HA5 . . . . .40 BZ52

Helston Pl, Abb.L. WD5
  off Shirley Rd 7 BT32
Helvellyn Cl, Egh. TW20 . . . . .113 BB96
Helvetia St, SE6 . . . . .123 DZ89
Hemans St, SW8 . . . . .101 DK80
Hemberton Rd, SW9 . . . . .101 DL83
Hemery Rd, Grnf. UB6 . . . . . . .61 CD60
Hemingford Cl, N12 . . . . .44 DD50
Hemingford Rd, N1 . . . . .83 DM67
  Sutton SM3 . . . . .157 CW105
  Watford WD17 . . . . .23 BS36
Heming Rd, Edg. HA8 . . . . . . .42 CP52
Hemington Av, N11 . . . . .44 DF50
Hemlock Cl, Tad. (Kgswd.)
  KT20 . . . . .173 CY123
Hemlock Rd, W12 . . . . .81 CT73
Hemmen La, Hayes UB3 . . . . .77 BT72
Hemming Cl, Hmptn. TW12
  off Chandler Cl 136 CA95
Hemming St, E1 . . . . .84 DU70
Hemming Way, Wat. WD25 . . .23 BU35
Hemnall St, Epp. CM16 . . . . . .17 ET31
Hempshaw Av, Bans. SM7 . . .174 DF116
Hempson Av, Slou. SL3 . . . . . .92 AW76
Hempstead Cl, Buck.H. IG9 . . .48 EG47
Hempstead Rd, E17 . . . . .47 DC54
  Hemel Hempstead HP3 . . . . .5 BA27
  Kings Langley WD4 . . . . .6 BM26
  Watford WD17 . . . . .23 BT39
Hemp Wk, SE17 . . . . .201 L8
Hemsby Rd, Chess. KT9 . . . . .156 CM107
Hemstal Rd, NW6 . . . . .82 DA66
Hemsted Rd, Erith DA8 . . . . . .107 FE80
Hemswell Dr, NW9 . . . . .42 CS53
Hemsworth Cl, N1
  off Hemsworth St 84 DS68
Hemsworth St, N1 . . . . .84 DS68
Hemus Pl, SW3
  off Chelsea Manor St 100 DE78
Hen & Chicken Ct, EC4
  off Fleet St 83 DN72
Henbane Path, Rom. RM3
  off Clematis Cl 52 FK52
Henbit Cl, Tad. KT20 . . . . .173 CV119
Henbury Way, Wat. WD19 . . . .40 BX48
Henchman St, W12 . . . . .81 CT72
Hencroft St N, Slou. SL1 . . . . .92 AT75
Hencroft St S, Slou. SL1 . . . . .92 AT76
Hendale Av, NW4 . . . . .63 CU55
Henderson Cl, NW10 . . . . .80 CQ65
  Hornchurch RM11 . . . . .71 FH61
Henderson Dr, NW8
  off Cunningham Pl 82 DD70
  Dartford DA1 . . . . .108 FM84
Ⓗ Henderson Hosp., Sutt.
  SM2 . . . . .158 DB109
Henderson Pl, Abb.L. (Bedmond)
  WD5 . . . . .7 BT27
Henderson Rd, E7 . . . . .86 EJ65
  N9 . . . . .46 DV46
  SW18 . . . . .120 DE87
  Croydon CR0 . . . . .142 DR100
  Hayes UB4 . . . . .77 BU69
  Westerham (Bigg.H.) TN16 .162 EJ112
Hendham Rd, SW17 . . . . .120 DE89
HENDON, NW4 . . . . .63 CV56
⊁ Hendon 63 CU58
Hendon Av, N3 . . . . .43 CY53
⊕ Hendon Central 63 CW57
Hendon Gdns, Rom. RM5 . . . . .51 FC51
Hendon Hall Ct, NW4
  off Parson St 63 CX55
Hendon La, N3 . . . . .63 CY55
Hendon Pk Row, NW11 . . . . . .63 CZ58
Hendon Rd, N9 . . . . .46 DU47
Hendon Way, NW2 . . . . .63 CZ62
  NW4 . . . . .63 CV58
  Staines (Stanw.) TW19 . . . .114 BK86
Hendon Wd La, NW7 . . . . .27 CT44
Hendren Cl, Grnf. UB6
  off Dimmock Dr 61 CD64
Hendre Rd, SE1 . . . . .201 N9
Hendrick Av, SW12 . . . . .120 DF86
Heneage Cres, Croy. (New Adgtn.)
  CR0 . . . . .161 EC110
Heneage La, EC3 . . . . .197 N9
Heneage St, E1 . . . . .84 DT71
Henfield Cl, N19 . . . . .65 DJ60
  Bexley DA5 . . . . .126 FA86
Henfield Rd, SW19 . . . . .139 CZ95
Hengelo Gdns, Mitch. CR4 . . .140 DD98
Hengist Rd, SE12 . . . . .124 EH87
  Erith DA8 . . . . .107 FB80
Hengist Way, Brom. BR2 . . . .144 EE98
Hengrave Rd, SE23 . . . . .122 DX87
Hengrove Ct, Bex. DA5
  off Hurst Rd 126 EY88
Hengrove Cres, Ashf. TW15 . .114 BK90
Henhurst Rd, Grav. (Cobham)
  DA12 . . . . .131 GK94
Henley Av, Sutt. SM3 . . . . . . .139 CY104
Henley Cl, Grnf. UB6 . . . . .78 CC68
  Isleworth TW7 . . . . .97 CF81
Henley Ct, N14 . . . . .45 DJ45
  Woking GU22 . . . . .167 BB120
Henley Cross, SE3 . . . . .104 EH83
Henley Deane, Grav. (Nthflt.)
  DA11 . . . . .130 GE91
Henley Dr, SE1 . . . . .202 A8
  Kingston upon Thames
    KT2 . . . . .119 CT94
Henley Gdns, Pnr. HA5 . . . . . .59 BV55
  Romford RM6 . . . . .70 EY57
Henley Rd, E16 . . . . .105 EM75
  N18 . . . . .46 DS49
  NW10 . . . . .81 CW67
  Ilford IG1 . . . . .69 EQ63
Henley St, SW11 . . . . .100 DG82
Henley Way, Felt. TW13 . . . . .116 BX92
Henlow Pl, Rich. TW10
  off Sandpits Rd 117 CK89
Hennel Cl, SE23 . . . . .122 DW90
Hennessy Ct, Wok. GU21 . . . .151 BC113
Henniker Gdns, E6 . . . . .86 EK69
Henniker Ms, SW3
  off Callow St 100 DD79

Henniker Pt, E15 . . . . .68 EE64
Henniker Rd, E15 . . . . .67 ED64
Henning St, SW11 . . . . .100 DE81
Henrietta Ms, WC1 . . . . .196 A4
Henrietta Pl, W1 . . . . .195 H9
Henrietta St, E15 . . . . .67 EC64
  WC2 . . . . .196 A10
Henriques St, E1 . . . . .84 DU72
Henry Addlington Cl, E6 . . . . . .87 EP71
Henry Cl, Enf. EN2 . . . . .30 DS38
Henry Cooper Way, SE9 . . . . .124 EK90
Henry Darlot Dr, NW7 . . . . . . .43 CX50
Henry De Gray Cl, Grays
  RM17 . . . . .110 FZ77
Henry Dickens Ct, W11 . . . . . .81 CX74
Henry Doulton Dr, SW17 . . . . .121 DH91
Henry Jackson Rd, SW15 . . . . .99 CX83
Henry Macaulay Av, Kings.T.
  KT2 . . . . .137 CK95
Henry Rd, E6 . . . . .86 EL68
  N4 . . . . .66 DQ60
  Barnet EN4 . . . . .28 DD43
Henry's Av, Wdf.Grn. IG8 . . . . .48 EF50
Henryson Rd, SE4 . . . . .124 EA85
Henry St, Brom. BR1 . . . . . . .144 EH95
Grays RM17
  off East Thurrock Rd 110 GC79
Henry's Wk, Ilf. IG6 . . . . .49 ER51
Hensford Gdns, SE26
  off Wells Pk Rd 122 DV91
Henshall St, N1 . . . . .84 DR65
Henshawe Rd, Dag. RM8 . . . . .70 EX62
Henshaw St, SE17 . . . . .201 K8
Henshill Pt, E3
  off Bromley High St 85 EB69
Hensley Pt, E9
  off Wick Rd 85 DX65
Henslowe Rd, SE22 . . . . .122 DU85
Henslow Way, Wok. GU21 . . . .151 BD114
Henson Av, NW2 . . . . .63 CW64
Henson Cl, Orp. BR6 . . . . .145 EP103
Henson Path, Har. HA3 . . . . . .61 CK55
Henson Pl, Nthlt. UB5 . . . . . . .78 BW67
Henstridge Pl, NW8 . . . . .82 DE68
Hensworth Rd, Ashf. TW15 . . .114 BK93
Henty Cl, SW11 . . . . .100 DE80
Henty Wk, SW15 . . . . .119 CV85
Henville Rd, Brom. BR1 . . . . . .144 EH96
Henwick Rd, SE9 . . . . .104 EK83
Henwood Side, Wdf.Grn. IG8
  off Love La 49 EM51
Hepburn Cl, Grays (Chaff.Hun.)
  RM16 . . . . .109 FX77
  Bromley. Brom. BR2 . . . . . .144 EE102
Hepburn Ms, SW11
  off Webbs Rd 120 DF85
Hepple Cl, Islw. TW7 . . . . .97 CH82
Hepplestone Cl, SW15
  off Dover Pk Dr 119 CV86
Hepscott Rd, E9 . . . . .85 EA66
Hepworth Ct, Bark. IG11 . . . . .70 EU64
  Hayes UB4 . . . . .77 BU69
Hepworth Gdns, Bark. IG11 . . .70 EU64
Hepworth Rd, SW16 . . . . .121 DL94
Hepworth Wk, NW3
  off Haverstock Hill 64 DE64
Hepworth Way, Walt. KT12 . . .135 BT102
Heracles Cl, Wall. SM6 . . . . . .159 DL108
Herald Gdns, Wall. SM6 . . . . .141 DH104
Herald's Ct, SE11 . . . . .200 F9
Herald's Pl, SE11 . . . . .200 E8
Herald St, E2
  off Three Colts La 84 DV70
Herald Wk, Dart. DA1
  off Temple Hill Sq 128 FM85
Herbal Hill, EC1 . . . . .196 E5
Herbert Cres, SW1 . . . . .198 E6
  Woking (Knap.) GU21 . . . . .166 AS117
Herbert Gdns, NW10 . . . . .81 CV68
  W4 off Magnolia Rd 98 CP79
  Romford RM6 . . . . .70 EX59
  St. Albans AL2 . . . . .8 CB29
Herbert Ms, SW2
  off Bascombe St 121 DN86
Herbert Morrison Ho, SW6
  off Clem Attlee Ct 99 CZ79
Herbert Pl, SE18 off Plumstead
  Common Rd 105 EP79
Herbert Rd, E12 . . . . .68 EL63
  E17 . . . . .67 DZ59
  N11 . . . . .45 DL52
  N15 . . . . .66 DT57
  NW9 . . . . .63 CU58
  SE18 . . . . .105 EN80
  SW19 . . . . .119 CZ94
  Bexleyheath DA7 . . . . .106 EY82
  Bromley BR2 . . . . .144 EK99
  Hornchurch RM11 . . . . .72 FL59
  Ilford IG3 . . . . .69 ES61
  Kingston upon Thames
    KT1 . . . . .138 CM97
  Southall UB1 . . . . .78 BZ74
  Swanley BR8 . . . . .127 FH93
  Swanscombe DA10 . . . . . .130 FZ86
Herbert St, E13 . . . . .86 EG68
  NW5 . . . . .82 DG65
Herbert Ter, SE18
  off Herbert Rd 105 EP79
Herbrand St, WC1 . . . . .195 P4
Hercies Rd, Uxb. UB10 . . . . . .76 BM66
Hercules Pl, N7
  off Hercules St 65 DL62
Hercules Rd, SE1 . . . . .200 C7
Hercules St, N7 . . . . .65 DL62
Hereford Av, Barn. EN4 . . . . . .44 DF46
Hereford Cl, Epsom KT18 . . . .156 CR113
  Staines TW18 . . . . .134 BH95
Hereford Copse, Wok. GU22 . .166 AV119
Hereford Ct, Sutt. SM2
  off Worcester Rd 158 DA108
Hereford Gdns, SE13
  off Longhurst Rd 124 EE85
  Ilford IG1 . . . . .68 EL59
  Pinner HA5 . . . . .60 BY57
  Twickenham TW2 . . . . .116 CC88
Hereford Ho, NW6 . . . . .82 DA68

Hereford Ms, W2
  off Hereford Rd 82 DA72
Hereford Pl, SE14 . . . . .103 DZ80
Hereford Retreat, SE15
  off Bird in Bush Rd 102 DU80
  W2 . . . . .82 DA72
  E11 . . . . .68 EH57
  W3 . . . . .80 CP73
  W5 . . . . .97 CJ76
  Feltham TW13 . . . . .116 BW88
Hereford Sq, SW7 . . . . .100 DC77
Hereford St, E2 . . . . .84 DU70
Hereford Way, Chess. KT9 . .155 CJ106
Herent Dr, Ilf. IG5 . . . . .69 EM55
Hereward Av, Pur. CR8 . . . . .159 DN111
Hereward Cl, Wal.Abb. EN9 . .15 ED32
Hereward Gdns, N13 . . . . . . .45 DN50
Hereward Grn, Loug. IG10 . . .33 EQ39
Hereward Rd, SW17 . . . . . . .120 DF91
Herga Ct, Har. HA1 . . . . .61 CE62
  Watford WD17 . . . . .23 BU40
Herga Rd, Har. HA3 . . . . .61 CF56
Herington Gro, Brwd. CM13 . .55 GA45
Heriot Av, E4 . . . . .47 EA47
Heriot Rd, NW4 . . . . .63 CW57
  Chertsey KT16 . . . . .134 BG101
Heriots Cl, Stan. HA7 . . . . . . .41 CG49
Heritage Cl, SW9 . . . . .101 DP83
  Uxbridge UB8 . . . . .76 BJ70
Heritage Hill, Kes. BR2 . . . . .162 EJ106
Heritage Pl, SW18
  off Earlsfield Rd 120 DC88
Heritage Vw, Har. HA1 . . . . . .61 CF62
Heritage Wk, Rick. (Chorl.) WD3
  off Chenies Rd 21 BE41
Herkomer Cl, Bushey WD23 . .24 CB44
Herkomer Rd, Bushey WD23 . .24 CA43
Herlwyn Av, Ruis. HA4 . . . . . .59 BS62
Herlwyn Gdns, SW17 . . . . . .120 DF91
Hermes Cl, W9
  off Chippenham Rd 82 DA70
Hermes St, N1 . . . . .196 D1
Hermes Way, Nthlt. UB5
  off Hotspur Rd 78 CA68
Hermes Way, Wall. SM6 . . . .159 DK108
Herm Ho, Enf. EN3
  off Eastfield Rd 31 DX38
Hermiston Av, N8 . . . . .65 DL57
Hermitage, The, SE23 . . . . . .122 DW88
  SW13 . . . . .99 CT81
  Feltham TW13 . . . . .115 BT90
  Richmond TW10 . . . . . . .117 CK85
  Uxbridge UB8 . . . . .76 BL65
Hermitage Cl, E18 . . . . .68 EF56
  Enfield EN2 . . . . .29 DP40
  Esher (Clay.) KT10 . . . . .155 CG107
  Shepperton TW17 . . . . . .134 BN98
  Slough SL3 . . . . .92 AW76
Hermitage Ct, E18 . . . . .68 EG56
  NW2 *off Hermitage La* . . .64 DA62
  Potters Bar EN6
    off Southgate Rd 12 DC33
Hermitage Gdns, NW2 . . . . . .64 DA62
  SE19 . . . . .122 DQ93
Hermitage La, N18 . . . . .46 DR50
  NW2 . . . . .64 DA62
  SE25 . . . . .142 DU100
  SW16 . . . . .121 DM94
  Croydon CR0 . . . . .142 DU100
Hermitage Path, SW16 . . . . .141 DL95
Hermitage Rd, N4 . . . . .65 DP59
  N15 . . . . .65 DP59
  SE19 . . . . .122 DQ94
  Kenley CR8 . . . . .176 DQ116
  Woking GU21 . . . . .166 AT119
Hermitage Row, E8 . . . . .66 DU64
Hermitage St, W2 . . . . .82 DD71
Hermitage Wk, E18 . . . . .68 EF56
Hermitage Wall, E1 . . . . .202 C3
Hermitage Waterside, E1 . . . .202 B2
Hermitage Way, Stan. HA7 . . .41 CG53
Hermitage Wds Cres, Wok.
  GU21 . . . . .166 AS119
Hermit Pl, NW6
  off Belsize Rd 82 DB67
Hermit Rd, E16 . . . . .86 EF71
Hermit St, EC1 . . . . .196 F2
Hermon Gro, Hayes UB3 . . . .77 BU74
Hermon Hill, E11 . . . . .68 EG57
  E18 . . . . .68 EG57
Herndon Cl, Egh. TW20 . . . .113 BA91
Herndon Rd, SW18 . . . . .120 DC85
Herne Cl, NW10
  off North Circular Rd 62 CR64
HERNE HILL, SE24 . . . . .122 DQ85
  ⇌ Herne Hill, SE24 . . . . .121 DP86
Herne Hill, SE24 . . . . .122 DQ86
Herne Hill Ho, SE24
  off Railton Rd 121 DP86
Herne Hill Rd, SE24 . . . . . . .102 DQ83
Herne Ms, N18 . . . . .46 DU49
Herne Pl, SE24 . . . . .121 DP85
Herne Rd, Bushey WD23 . . . .24 CB44
  Surbiton KT6 . . . . .137 CK103
Heron Cl, E17 . . . . .47 DZ54
  NW10 . . . . .80 CS65
  Buckhurst Hill IG9 . . . . . .48 EG46
  Hemel Hempstead HP3
    off Belswains La 6 BM25
  Rickmansworth WD3 . . . .38 BK47
  Sutton SM1
    off Sandpiper Rd 157 CZ106
  Uxbridge UB8 . . . . .76 BK65
Heron Ct, Brom. BR2 . . . . . .144 EJ98
Heron Cres, Sid. DA14 . . . . .125 ES90
Heron Dale, Add. KT15 . . . . .152 BK106
Herondale, S.Croy. CR2 . . . .161 DX109
Herondale Av, SW18 . . . . . . .120 DD88
Heron Dr, N4 . . . . .66 DQ61
  Slough SL3 . . . . .93 BB77
Heronfield, Egh. (Eng.Grn.)
  TW20 . . . . .112 AV93
  Potters Bar EN6 . . . . .12 DC30
Heron Flight Av, Horn. RM12 . .89 FG66
Herongate Rd, E12 . . . . .68 EJ61
  Swanley BR8 . . . . .127 FE93

Herongate Rd, Wal.Cr. (Chsht.)
  EN8 . . . . .15 DY27
Heron Hill, Belv. DA17 . . . . . .106 EZ77
Heron Ms, Ilf. IG1
  off Balfour Rd 69 EP61
Heron Pl, SE16 . . . . .203 L2
Heron Quay, E14 . . . . .203 P3
DLR Heron Quays 204 A3
Heron Rd, SE24 . . . . .102 DQ84
  Croydon CR0
    off Tunstall Rd 142 DS103
  Twickenham TW1 . . . . . . .97 CG84
Heronry, The, Walt. KT12 . . .153 BU107
Herons, The, E11 . . . . .68 EF58
Herons Cft, Wey. KT13 . . . . .153 BR107
Heronsforde, W13 . . . . .79 CJ72
HERONSGATE, Rick. (Chorl.)
  WD3 . . . . .21 BB44
Heronsgate, Edg. HA8 . . . . . .42 CN50
Heronsgate Rd, Rick. (Chorl.) WD3
  off Alliance Rd 80 CP70
Heronslea, Wat. WD25 . . . . . .24 BW36
Heronslea Dr, Stan. HA7 . . . .42 CL50
Heron's Pl, Islw. TW7 . . . . . . .97 CH83
Heron Sq, Rich. TW9
  off Bridge St 117 CK85
Herons Ri, Barn. EN4 . . . . . . .28 DE42
Heronswood, Wal.Abb. EN9
  off Roundhills 16 EE34
Heron Trd Est, W3
  off Heyford Av 80 CP70
Heron Wk, Nthwd. HA6 . . . . .39 BS49
  Woking GU21
    off Blackmore Cres 151 BC114
Heronway, Brwd. CM13 . . . . .55 GA46
Heron Way, Felt. TW14
  off The Causeway 95 BU84
  Grays RM20 . . . . .109 FV78
  Upminster RM14 . . . . . . .73 FS60
Heronway, Wdf.Grn. IG8 . . . .48 EJ49
Herrick Rd, N5 . . . . .66 DQ62
Herrick St, SW1 . . . . .199 M9
Herries St, W10 . . . . .81 CY68
Herringham Rd, SE7 . . . . . . .104 EJ76
Herrings La, Cher. KT16 . . . .134 BG100
Herrongate Cl, Enf. EN1 . . . . .30 DT40
Hersant Cl, NW10 . . . . .81 CU67
Herschell Rd, SE23 . . . . .123 DY87
Herschel Pk Dr, Slou. SL1 . . .92 AT75
Herschel St, Slou. SL1 . . . . . .92 AT75
HERSHAM, Walt. 154 BX107
  ⇌ Hersham 136 BY104
Hersham Bypass, Walt. KT12 .153 BV106
Hersham Cl, SW15 . . . . .119 CU87
Hersham Gdns, Walt. KT12 . .154 BW105
Hersham Rd, Walt. KT12 . . . .154 BW105
Hertford Av, SW14 . . . . .118 CS85
Hertford Cl, Barn. EN4 . . . . . .28 DD41
Hertford Pl, W1 . . . . .195 K5
Hertford Rd, N1 . . . . .84 DS67
  N2 . . . . .64 DE55
  N9 . . . . .46 DV47
  Barking IG11 . . . . .87 EP66
  Barnet EN4 . . . . .28 DC41
  Enfield EN3 . . . . .30 DW41
  Ilford IG2 . . . . .69 ES58
  Waltham Cross EN8 . . . . .31 DX37
Hertford Sq, Mitch. CR4
  off Hertford Way 141 DL98
Hertford St, W1 . . . . .199 H2
Hertford Wk, Belv. DA17
  off Hoddesdon Rd 106 FA78
Hertford Way, Mitch. CR4 . . .141 DL98
Hertslet Rd, N7 . . . . .65 DM62
Hertsmere Rd, E14 . . . . .203 P1
Hervey Cl, N3 . . . . .44 DA53
Hervey Pk Rd, E17 . . . . .67 DY56
Hervey Rd, SE3 . . . . .104 EH81
Hesa Rd, Hayes UB3 . . . . . . .77 BU72
Hesewall Cl, SW4
  off Brayburne Av 101 DJ82
Hesiers Hill, Warl. CR6 . . . . .178 EE117
Hesiers Rd, Warl. CR6 . . . . . .178 EE117
Hesketh Pl, W11 . . . . .81 CY73
Hesketh Rd, E7 . . . . .68 EG62
Heslop Rd, SW12 . . . . .120 DF88
Hesper Ms, SW5 . . . . .100 DB78
Hesperus Cres, E14 . . . . . . .204 B9
Hessel Rd, W13 . . . . .97 CG75
Hessel St, E1 . . . . .84 DV72
Hesselyn Dr, Rain. RM13 . . . .89 FH66
Hessle Gro, Epsom KT17 . . .157 CT111
Hestercombe Av, SW6 . . . . . .99 CY82
Hesterman Way, Croy. CR0 . .141 DL102
Hester Rd, N18 . . . . .46 DU50
  SW11 . . . . .100 DE80
Hester Ter, Rich. TW9
  off Chilton Rd 98 CN83
HESTON, Houns. 96 BZ80
Heston Av, Houns. TW5 . . . . .96 BY80
Heston Gra La, Houns. TW5 . .96 BZ79
Heston Ind Mall, Houns. TW5 .96 BZ80
Heston Rd, Houns. TW5 . . . . .96 CA80
  SE14 . . . . .103 DZ81
Heswall Grn, Wat. WD19
  off Fairhaven Cres 39 BU48
Hetherington Rd, SW4 . . . . .101 DL84
  Shepperton TW17 . . . . . .135 BQ96
Hetherington Way, Uxb. UB10 .58 BL63
Hethersett Rd, Reig. RH2 . . .184 DC131
Hetley Gdns, SE19
  off Fox Hill 122 DT94
Hetley Rd, W12 . . . . .81 CV74
Heton Gdns, NW4 . . . . .63 CU56
Heusden Way, Ger.Cr. SL9 . . .57 AZ60
Hevelius Cl, SE10 . . . . .205 K10
Hever Ct Rd, Grav. DA12 . . . .131 GK93
Hever Gdns, Brom. BR1 . . . .145 EN97
Heversham Rd, Bexh. DA7 . .106 FA82
Hewens Rd, Hayes UB4 . . . . .77 BQ70
  Uxbridge UB10 . . . . .77 BQ70
Hewer St, W10 . . . . .81 CX71
Hewers Way, Tad. KT20 . . . .173 CV120
Hewett Cl, Stan. HA7 . . . . . . .41 CH49
Hewett Pl, Swan. BR8 . . . . . .147 FD98

Hewett Rd, Dag. RM8 . . . . . . .70 EX64
Hewett St, EC2 . . . . .197 N5
Hewins Cl, Wal.Abb. EN9
  off Broomstick Hall Rd . . .16 EE33
Hewish Rd, N18 . . . . .46 DS49
Hewison St, E3 . . . . .85 DZ68
Hewitt Av, N22 . . . . .45 DP54
Hewitt Cl, Croy. CR0 . . . . . . .143 EA104
Hewitt Rd, N8 . . . . .65 DN57
Hewitts Rd, Orp. BR6 . . . . . .164 EZ108
Hexagon, The, N6 . . . . .64 DF60
Hexal Rd, SE6 . . . . .124 EE90
Hexham Gdns, Islw. TW7 . . . .97 CG80
Hexham Rd, SE27 . . . . .122 DQ89
  Barnet EN5 . . . . .28 DB42
  Morden SM4 . . . . .140 DB101
HEXTABLE, Swan. 127 FG94
Hextalls La, Red. (Bletch.)
  RH1 . . . . .186 DR128
Heybourne Rd, N17 . . . . .46 DV52
Heybridge Av, SW16 . . . . . . .121 DL94
Heybridge Dr, Ilf. IG6 . . . . . . .49 ER54
Heybridge Way, E10 . . . . .67 DY59
Heyford Av, SW8 . . . . .101 DL80
  SW20 . . . . .139 CZ97
Heyford Rd, Mitch. CR4 . . . .140 DE96
  Radlett WD7 . . . . .25 CF37
Heyford Ter, SW8
  off Heyford Av 101 DL80
Heygate St, SE17 . . . . .201 H9
Heylyn Sq, E3
  off Malmesbury Rd 85 DZ69
Heymede, Lthd. KT22 . . . . . .171 CJ123
Heynes Rd, Dag. RM8 . . . . . .70 EW63
Heysham Dr, Wat. WD19 . . . .40 BW50
Heysham La, NW3 . . . . .64 DB62
Heysham Rd, N15 . . . . .66 DR58
Heythorp Cl, Wok. GU21 . . . .166 AT117
Heythorp St, SW18 . . . . .119 CZ88
Heythrop Dr, Uxb. (Ickhm.)
  UB10 . . . . .58 BM63
Heywood Av, NW9 . . . . .42 CS53
Heyworth Rd, E5 . . . . .66 DV63
  E15 . . . . .68 EF64
Hibbert Av, Wat. WD24 . . . . . .24 BX38
Hibbert Lo, Ger.Cr. (Chal.St.P.) SL9
  off Gold Hill E 36 AX54
Hibbert Rd, E17 . . . . .67 DZ59
  Harrow HA3 . . . . .41 CF54
Hibbert St, SW11 . . . . .100 DC83
Hibberts Way, Ger.Cr. SL9
  off North Pk 56 AY56
Hibbs Cl, Swan. BR8 . . . . . . .147 FD96
Hibernia Dr, Grav. DA12 . . . .131 GM90
Hibernia Gdns, Houns. TW3 . .96 CA84
Hibernia Pt, SE2
  off Wolvercote Rd 106 EX75
Hibernia Rd, Houns. TW3 . . . .96 CA84
Hibiscus Cl, Edg. HA8
  off Campion Way 42 CQ49
Hichisson Rd, SE15 . . . . .122 DW85
Hickin Cl, SE7 . . . . .104 EK77
Hickin St, E14 . . . . .204 D6
Hickling Rd, Ilf. IG1 . . . . .69 EP64
Hickman Av, E4 . . . . .47 EC51
Hickman Cl, E16 . . . . .86 EK71
Hickman Rd, Rom. RM6 . . . . .70 EW59
Hickmans Cl, Gdse. RH9 . . . .186 DW132
Hickmore Wk, SW4 . . . . .101 DJ83
Hickory Cl, N9 . . . . .46 DU45
Hicks Av, Grnf. UB6 . . . . .79 CD68
Hicks Cl, SW11 . . . . .100 DE83
Hicks St, SE8 . . . . .203 K10
Hidcote Cl, Wok. GU22 . . . . .167 BB116
Hidcote Gdns, SW20 . . . . . .139 CV97
Hide, E6 *off Downings* 87 EN72
Hideaway, The, Abb.L. WD5 . . .7 BU31
Hide Pl, SW1 . . . . .199 M9
Hide Rd, Har. HA1 . . . . .61 CD56
Hides St, N7
  off Sheringham Rd 83 DM65
Hide Twr, SW1 . . . . .199 M9
Higgins Rd, Wal.Cr. (Chsht.)
  EN7 . . . . .14 DR27
Higgins Wk, Hmptn. TW12
  off Abbott Cl 116 BY93
High Acres, Abb.L. WD5 . . . . .7 BR32
  Enfield EN2 *off Old Pk Vw* . .29 DP41
HIGHAM HILL, E17 . . . . .47 DY54
Higham Hill Rd, E17 . . . . .47 DY54
Higham Pl, E17 . . . . .67 DY55
Higham Rd, N17 . . . . .66 DR55
  Woodford Green IG8 . . . . .48 EG49
Highams Ct, E4 *off Friars Cl* . .47 ED48
Highams Lo Business Cen,
  E17 . . . . .67 DY55
HIGHAMS PARK, E4 . . . . .47 ED50
  ⇌ Highams Park 47 ED51
Highams Pk Ind Est, E4 . . . . .47 EC51
Higham Sta Av, E4 . . . . .47 EB51
Higham St, E17 . . . . .67 DY55
Higham Vw, Epp. (N.Wld.Bas.)
  CM16 . . . . .19 FB26
Highbanks Cl, Well. DA16 . . .106 EV80
Highbanks Rd, Pnr. HA5 . . . . .40 CB50
Highbank Way, N8 . . . . .65 DN58
HIGH BARNET, Barn. 27 CX40
  ⊖ High Barnet 28 DA42
Highbarns, Hem.H. HP3 . . . . . .6 BN25
Highbarrow Rd, Croy. CR0 . .142 DU101
HIGH BEACH, Loug. 32 EG39
High Beech, S.Croy. CR2 . . . .160 DS108
High Beeches, Bans. SM7 . . .157 CX114
  Gerrards Cross SL9 . . . . . .AX60
  Orpington BR6 . . . . .164 EU107
  Sidcup DA14 . . . . .126 EY92
High Beeches Cl, Pur. CR8 . .159 DK110
High Beech Rd, Loug. IG10 . . .32 EK42
High Br, SE10 . . . . .103 ED78
Highbridge Ind Est, Uxb. UB8 .76 BJ67
Highbridge Rd, Bark. IG11 . . .87 EP66
Highbridge St, Wal.Abb. EN9 .15 EA33
High Br Wf, SE10 . . . . .103 ED78
Highbrook Rd, SE3 . . . . .104 EK83
High Broom Cres, W.Wick.
  BR4 . . . . .143 EB101

HIGHBURY, N5 . . . . .65 DP64
  ⇌ Highbury & Islington . . .83 DP65
  ⊖ Highbury & Islington . . .83 DP65
Highbury Av, Th.Hth. CR7 . . .141 DN96
Highbury Cl, N.Mal. KT3 . . . .138 CQ98
  West Wickham BR4 . . . . .143 EB103
Highbury Cor, N5 . . . . .83 DN65
Highbury Cres, N5 . . . . .65 DN64
Highbury Est, N5 . . . . .66 DQ64
Highbury Gdns, Ilf. IG3 . . . . . .69 ES61
Highbury Gra, N5 . . . . .65 DP64
Highbury Gro, N5 . . . . .83 DP65
Highbury Hill, N5 . . . . .65 DN65
Highbury Ms, N7
  off Holloway Rd 83 DN65
Highbury New Pk, N5 . . . . . . .66 DQ64
Highbury Pk, N5 . . . . .65 DP64
Highbury Pk Ms, N5
  off Highbury Gra 66 DQ63
Highbury Pl, N5 . . . . .83 DP65
Highbury Quad, N5 . . . . .66 DQ62
Highbury Rd, SW19 . . . . .119 CY92
Highbury Sta Rd, N1 . . . . .83 DN65
Highbury Ter, N5 . . . . .65 DP65
Highbury Ter Ms, N5 . . . . . . .65 DP64
High Canons, Borwd. WD6 . . .26 CQ37
High Cedar Dr, SW20 . . . . . .119 CV94
Highclere Cl, Ken. CR8 . . . . .176 DQ115
Highclere Rd, N.Mal. KT3 . . .138 CR97
Highclere St, SE26 . . . . .123 DY91
Highcliffe Dr, SW15 . . . . .119 CT86
Highcliffe Gdns, Ilf. IG4 . . . . .68 EL57
High Cl, Rick. WD3 . . . . .22 BJ43
Highcombe, SE7 . . . . .104 EH79
Highcombe Cl, SE9 . . . . .124 EK88
High Coombe Pl, Kings.T.
  KT2 . . . . .118 CR94
Highcroft, NW9 . . . . .62 CS57
Highcroft Av, Wem. HA0 . . . . .80 CN67
Highcroft Ct, Lthd. (Bkhm.)
  KT23 . . . . .170 CA124
Highcroft Gdns, NW11 . . . . . .63 CZ58
Highcroft Rd, N19 . . . . .65 DL59
  Hemel Hempstead (Felden)
  HP3 . . . . .6 BG25
High Cross, Wat. (Ald.) WD25 .25 CD37
High Cross Cen, N15 . . . . . . .66 DU56
High Cross Rd, N17 . . . . .66 DU55
Highcross Rd, Grav. (Sthflt.)
  DA13 . . . . .129 FX92
Highcross Way, SW15 . . . . . .119 CU88
Highdaun Dr, SW16 . . . . .141 DM98
Highdown, Wor.Pk. KT4 . . . .138 CS103
Highdown La, Sutt. SM2 . . . .158 DB111
Highdown Rd, SW15 . . . . . . .119 CV86
High Dr, Cat. (Wold.) CR3 . . .177 DZ122
  Leatherhead (Oxshott)
  KT22 . . . . .155 CD114
  New Malden KT3 . . . . . . .138 CQ95
High Elms, Chig. IG7 . . . . . . .49 ES49
  Upminster RM14 . . . . . . .73 FS60
  Woodford Green IG8 . . . . .48 EG50
High Elms Cl, Nthwd. HA6 . . .39 BR51
High Elms La, Wat. WD25 . . . .7 BV31
High Elms Rd, Orp. BR6 . . . .163 EP110
HIGHER DENHAM, Uxb. 57 BB59
Higher Dr, Bans. SM7 . . . . . .157 CX112
  Purley CR8 . . . . .159 DN113
Higher Grn, Epsom KT17 . . .157 CU113
Highfield, Bans. SM7 . . . . . . .174 CE117
  Bushey (Bushey Hth.) WD23
  off High Rd 41 CE47
  Chalfont St. Giles HP8 . . .36 AX47
  Feltham TW13 . . . . .115 BU88
  Kings Langley WD4 . . . . . .6 BL28
  Watford WD19 . . . . .40 BZ48
Highfield Av, NW9 . . . . .62 CQ57
  NW11 . . . . .63 CX59
  Erith DA8 . . . . .107 FB79
  Greenford UB6 . . . . .61 CE64
  Orpington BR6 . . . . .163 ET106
  Pinner HA5 . . . . .60 BZ57
  Wembley HA9 . . . . .62 CM64
Highfield Cl, N22 . . . . .45 DN53
  NW9 . . . . .62 CQ57
  SE13 . . . . .123 ED87
  Egham (Eng.Grn.) TW20 .112 AW93
  Leatherhead (Oxshott)
  KT22 . . . . .155 CD111
  Northwood HA6 . . . . .39 BS53
  Romford RM5 . . . . .51 FC51
  Surbiton KT6 . . . . .137 CJ102
  West Byfleet KT14 . . . . . .152 BG113
Highfield Ct, N14 . . . . .29 DJ44
Highfield Cres, Horn. RM12 . .72 FM61
  Northwood HA6 . . . . .39 BS53
Highfield Dr, Brom. BR2 . . . .144 EE98
  Caterham CR3 . . . . .176 DU122
  Epsom KT19 . . . . .157 CT108
  Uxbridge (Ickhm.) UB10 . .58 BL63
  West Wickham BR4 . . . . .143 EB103
Highfield Gdns, NW11 . . . . . .63 CY58
  Grays RM16 . . . . .110 GD78
Highfield Grn, Epp. CM16 . . .17 ES31
Highfield Link, Rom. RM5 . . . .51 FC51
Highfield Ms, NW6
  off Compayne Gdns 82 DB66
Highfield Pl, Epp. CM16 . . . . .17 ES31
Highfield Rd, N21 . . . . .45 DP47
  NW11 . . . . .63 CY58
  W3 . . . . .80 CP71
  Bexleyheath DA6 . . . . . .126 EZ85
  Bromley BR1 . . . . .145 EM98
  Bushey WD23 . . . . .24 BY43
  Caterham CR3 . . . . .176 DU122
  Chertsey KT16 . . . . .134 BG102
  Chislehurst BR7 . . . . . . .145 ET97
  Dartford DA1 . . . . .128 FK87
  Feltham TW13 . . . . .115 BU89
  Hornchurch RM12 . . . . . .72 FM61
  Isleworth TW7 . . . . .97 CF81
  Northwood HA6 . . . . .39 BS53
  Purley CR8 . . . . .159 DM110
  Romford RM5 . . . . .51 FC51
  Sunbury-on-Thames
  TW16 . . . . .135 BT98

Highfield Rd, Surb. KT5 . . . .138 CQ101
  Sutton SM1 . . . . .158 DE106
  Waltham Cross (Chsht.)
  EN7 . . . . .14 DS26
  Walton-on-Thames KT12 .135 BU102
  West Byfleet KT14 . . . . . .152 BG113
  Westerham (Bigg.H.) TN16 .178 EJ117
  Woodford Green IG8 . . . . .48 EL52
Highfield Rd S, Dart. DA1 . . .128 FK87
Highfields, Ashtd. KT21 . . . . .171 CK119
  Leatherhead (Fetch.) KT22 .171 CD124
  Potters Bar (Cuffley) EN6 . .13 DL28
  Radlett WD7 . . . . .25 CF35
Highfields Gro, N6 . . . . .64 DF60
Highfield Twr, Rom. RM5 . . . .51 FD50
Highfield Way, Horn. RM12 . . .72 FM61
  Potters Bar EN6 . . . . .12 DB32
  Rickmansworth WD3 . . . .22 BH44
High Firs, Rad. WD7 . . . . .25 CF35
  Swanley BR8 . . . . .147 FE98
High Foleys, Esher (Clay.)
  KT10 . . . . .155 CH108
High Gables, Loug. IG10 . . . . .32 EK43
High Garth, Esher KT10 . . . . .154 CC107
HIGHGATE, N6 . . . . .64 DG61
Highgate Av, N6 . . . . .65 DH58
  ★ Highgate Cem, N6 . . . .64 DG60
Highgate Cl, N6 . . . . .64 DG59
Highgate High St, N6 . . . . . . .64 DG60
Highgate Hill, N6 . . . . .64 DH60
  N19 . . . . .64 DH60
Highgate Rd, NW5 . . . . .65 DH63
Highgate Wk, SE23 . . . . .122 DW89
Highgate W Hill, N6 . . . . .64 DG61
High Gro, SE18 . . . . .105 ER80
Highgrove, Brwd. CM15 . . . . .54 FV44
High Gro, Brom. BR1 . . . . . .144 EJ95
Highgrove Cl, N11
  off Balmoral Av 44 DG50
  Chislehurst BR7 . . . . . . .144 EL95
Highgrove Ms, Cars. SM5 . . .140 DF104
  Grays RM17 . . . . .110 GC78
Highgrove Rd, Dag. RM8 . . . .70 EW64
Highgrove Way, Ruis. HA4 . . .59 BU58
High Hill Est, E5
  off Mount Pleasant La 66 DV60
High Hill Ferry, E5 . . . . .66 DV60
High Hill Rd, Warl. CR6 . . . . .177 EC115
High Holborn, WC1 . . . . .196 A8
High Ho La, Grays (Orsett)
  RM16 . . . . .111 GJ75
  Tilbury (W.Til.) RM18 . . . .111 GK77
Highland Av, W7 . . . . .79 CE72
  Brentwood CM15 . . . . . . .54 FW46
  Dagenham RM10 . . . . . . .71 FC62
  Loughton IG10 . . . . .32 EL44
Highland Cotts, Wall. SM6 . . .159 DH105
Highland Ct, E18 . . . . .48 EH53
Highland Cft, Beck. BR3 . . . .123 EB92
Highland Dr, Bushey WD23 . . .40 CC45
  Hemel Hempstead HP3 . . . .6 BK22
Highland Pk, Felt. TW13 . . . .115 BT91
Highland Rd, SE19 . . . . .122 DS93
  Bexleyheath DA6 . . . . . .126 FA85
  Bromley BR1, BR2 . . . . . .144 EF95
  Northwood HA6 . . . . .39 BT54
  Purley CR8 . . . . .159 DN114
  Sevenoaks (Bad.Mt.) TN14 .165 FB111
Highlands, Ashtd. KT21 . . . . .171 CJ119
  Watford WD19 . . . . .40 BW46
Highlands, The, Edg. HA8 . . . .42 CP54
  Potters Bar EN6 . . . . .28 DB43
  Rickmansworth WD3 . . . .38 BH45
Highlands Av, N21 . . . . .29 DM43
  W3 . . . . .80 CQ73
  Leatherhead KT22 . . . . . .171 CJ122
Highlands Cl, N4
  off Mount Vw Rd 65 DL59
  Gerrards Cross (Chal.St.P.)
  SL9 . . . . .37 AZ52
  Hounslow TW3 . . . . .96 CB81
  Leatherhead KT22 . . . . . .171 CH122
Highlands End, Ger.Cr. (Chal.St.P.)
  SL9 . . . . .36 AY52
Highlands Gdns, Ilf. IG1 . . . . .69 EM60
Highlands Heath, SW15 . . . . .119 CW87
Highlands Hill, Swan. BR8 . . .147 FG96
Highlands La, Ger.Cr. (Chal.St.P.)
  SL9 . . . . .37 AZ51
  Woking GU22 . . . . .166 AY122
Highlands Rd, Lthd. KT22 . . .171 CK123
  Sevenoaks (Seal) TN15 . .191 FL121
Highlands Rd, Barn. EN5 . . . .28 DA43
  Leatherhead KT22 . . . . . .171 CH122
  Orpington BR5 . . . . .146 EV101
  Reigate RH2 . . . . .184 DD133
High La, W7 . . . . .79 CD72
  Caterham CR3 . . . . .177 DZ119
  Warlingham CR6 . . . . . . .177 DZ118
High Lawns, Har. HA1 . . . . . .61 CE62
Highlea Cl, NW9 . . . . .42 CS53
High Level Dr, SE26 . . . . . . .122 DU91
Highlever Rd, W10 . . . . .81 CW71
Highmead, SE18 . . . . .105 ET80
High Mead, Chig. IG7 . . . . . . .49 EQ47
  Harrow HA1 . . . . .61 CE57
  West Wickham BR4 . . . . .143 ED103
Highmead Cres, Wem. HA0 . .80 CM66
High Meadow Cl, Pnr. HA5
  off Daymer Gdns 59 BV56
High Meadow Cres, NW9 . . . .62 CR57
High Meadow Pl, Cher. KT16 .133 BF100
High Meadows, Chig. IG7 . . . .49 ER50
High Meads Rd, E16 . . . . .86 EK72
Highmore Rd, SE3 . . . . .104 EE80
High Mt, NW4 . . . . .63 CU58
High Oaks, Enf. EN2 . . . . . . .29 DM38
High Pk Av, Rich. TW9 . . . . . .98 CN81
High Pk Rd, Rich. TW9 . . . . . .98 CN81
High Path, SW19 . . . . .140 DB95
High Pine Cl, Wey. KT13 . . . .153 BQ106
High Pines, Warl. CR6 . . . . . .176 DW119
High Pt, N6 . . . . .64 DG59
  SE9 . . . . .125 EP90

Hig - Hil

High Pt, Wey. KT13 . . .152 BN106
High Ridge, Pot.B. (Cuffley)
  EN6 . . . . .13 DL27
Highridge Cl, Epsom KT18 . .172 CS115
High Ridge Cl, Hem.H. HP3 . .6 BK25
High Ridge Rd, Hem.H. HP3 . .6 BK25
High Rd, N2 . . . . . .44 DD53
  N11 . . . . . . .45 DH50
  N12 . . . . . . .44 DC51
  N15 . . . . . . .66 DT58
  N17 . . . . . . .46 DT53
  N20 . . . . . . .44 DC45
  N22 . . . . . . .65 DN55
  NW10 (Willesden) . . .81 CV65
  Buckhurst Hill IG9 . . .48 EH47
  Bushey (Bushey Hth.)
    WD23 . . . . .41 CD46
  Chigwell IG7 . . . .49 EM50
  Coulsdon CR5 . . .174 DF121
  Dartford (Wilm.) DA2 . . .128 FJ90
  Epping CM16 . . . .17 ER32
  Epping (N.Wld.Bas.) CM16 .19 FB27
  Epping (Thnwd.) CM16 . .18 EV28
  Harrow (Har.Wld.) HA3 . .41 CE52
  Ilford IG1 . . . . .69 EP62
  Ilford (Seven Kings) IG3 . .69 ET60
  Loughton IG10 . . .48 EJ45
  Pinner HA5 . . . .59 BV56
  Reigate RH2 . . .184 DD126
  Romford (Chad.Hth.) RM6 . .70 EV60
  Uxbridge UB8 . . .76 BJ71
  Watford WD25 . . .23 BT35
  Wembley HA0, HA9 . . .61 CK64
  West Byfleet (Byfleet)
    KT14 . . . . .152 BM112
High Rd Ickenham, Uxb.
  UB10 . . . . . .59 BP62
High Rd Leyton, E10 . . .67 EB60
  E15 . . . . . . .67 EC62
High Rd Leytonstone, E11 . .68 EE63
  E15 . . . . . . .68 EE63
High Rd Turnford, Brox.
  EN10 . . . . . .15 DY25
High Rd Woodford Grn, E18 .48 EF52
  Woodford Green IG8 . . .48 EF52
Highshore Rd, SE15 . . .102 DT82
High Silver, Loug. IG10 . . .32 EK42
High Standing, Cat. CR3 . .186 DQ125
Highstead Cres, Erith DA8 .107 FE81
Highstone Av, E11 . . .68 EG58
High St, E11 . . . . .68 EG57
  E13 . . . . . . .86 EG68
  E15 . . . . . . .85 EC68
  E17 . . . . . . .67 DZ57
  N8 . . . . . . .65 DL56
  N14 . . . . . . .45 DK46
  NW7 . . . . . . .43 CV49
  NW10 (Harlesden) . . .81 CT68
  SE20 . . . . . .122 DV93
  SE25 (S.Norwood) . . .142 DT98
  W3 . . . . . . .80 CP74
  W5 . . . . . . .79 CK73
  Abbots Langley WD5 . . .6 BN29
  Abbots Langley (Bedmond)
    WD5 . . . . . .7 BS31
  Addlestone KT15 . . .152 BH105
  Banstead SM7 . . .174 DA115
  Barnet EN5 . . . .27 CY41
  Beckenham BR3 . . .143 EA96
  Borehamwood (Elstree)
    WD6 . . . . .25 CK44
  Brentford TW8 . . .97 CK79
  Brentwood CM14 . . .54 FV47
  Bromley BR1 . . .144 EG96
  Bushey WD23 . . .24 CA44
  Carshalton SM5 . . .158 DG105
  Caterham CR3 . . .176 DS123
  Chalfont St. Giles HP8 . .36 AW48
  Chislehurst BR7 . . .125 EP93
  Cobham KT11 . . .153 BV114
  Croydon CR0 . . .142 DQ103
  Dartford DA1 . . .128 FL86
  Dartford (Bean) DA2 . . .129 FV90
  Dartford (Eyns.) DA4 . . .148 FL103
  Dartford (Fngham.) DA4 . .148 FM100
  Edgware HA8 . . .42 CN51
  Egham TW20 . . .113 BA92
  Enfield (Pond.End) EN3 . .30 DW42
  Epping CM16 . . . .17 ET31
  Epsom KT19 . . .156 CR113
  Epsom (Ewell) KT17 . . .157 CT109
  Esher KT10 . . .154 CB105
  Esher (Clay.) KT10 . . .155 CF107
  Feltham TW13 . . .115 BT90
  Gerrards Cross (Chal.St.P.)
    SL9 . . . . .36 AY53
  Godstone RH9 . . .186 DV131
  Gravesend DA11 . . .131 GH86
  Gravesend (Nthflt.) DA11 .130 GB86
  Grays RM17 . . .110 GA79
  Greenhithe DA9 . . .109 FV84
  Hampton TW12 . . .116 CC93
  Harrow HA1, HA2 . . .61 CE60
  Harrow (Wldste.) HA3 . .61 CE55
  Hayes UB3 . . . .95 BS78
  Hemel Hempstead (Bov.)
    HP3 . . . . . .5 BA27
  Hornchurch RM11, RM12 . .72 FK60
  Hounslow TW3 . . .96 CC83
  Hounslow (Cran.) TW5 . .95 BV80
  Ilford (Barkingside) IG6 . .49 EQ54
  Iver SL0 . . . . .75 BE72
  Kings Langley WD4 . . .7 BT27
  Kingston upon Thames
    KT1 . . . . .137 CK96
  Kingston upon Thames
    (Hmptn.W.) KT1 . . .137 CJ95
  Leatherhead KT22 . . .171 CH122
  Leatherhead (Oxshott)
    KT22 . . . . .155 CD113
  New Malden KT3 . . .138 CS97
  Northwood HA6 . . .39 BT53
  Orpington BR6 . . .146 EU102
  Orpington (Downe) BR6 . .163 EN111

High St, Orp. (Farnboro.)
  BR6 . . . . . .163 EP106
  Orpington (Grn.St.Grn.)
  BR6 . . . . . .163 ET108
  Orpington (St.M.Cray)
  BR5 . . . . . .146 EW98
  Oxted RH8 . . .187 ED130
  Oxted (Lmpfld.) RH8 . . .188 EG128
  Pinner HA5 . . . .60 BY55
  Potters Bar EN6 . . .12 DC33
  Purfleet RM19
    off London Rd Purfleet . .108 FN78
  Purley CR8 . . .159 DN111
  Redhill RH1 . . .184 DF134
  Redhill (Bletch.) RH1 . . .186 DQ133
  Redhill (Merst.) RH1 . . .185 DH128
  Redhill (Nutfld.) RH1 . . .185 DM133
  Reigate RH2 . . .184 DA134
  Rickmansworth WD3 . . .38 BK46
  Romford RM1 . . .71 FE57
  Ruislip HA4 . . . .59 BS59
  St. Albans (Lon.Col.) AL2 . .9 CJ25
  Sevenoaks TN13 . . .191 FJ125
  Sevenoaks (Chipstead)
    TN13 . . . . .190 FC122
  Sevenoaks (Otford) TN14 .181 FF116
  Sevenoaks (Seal) TN15 . .191 FL121
  Sevenoaks (Shore.) TN14 .165 FF110
  Shepperton TW17 . . .135 BP100
  Slough SL1 . . . .92 AU75
  Slough (Colnbr.) SL3 . . .92 BC80
  Slough (Datchet) SL3 . . .92 AV81
  Slough (Langley) SL3 . . .93 AZ78
  South Ockendon (Aveley)
    RM15 . . . . .91 FR74
  Southall UB1 . . . .78 BZ74
  Staines TW18 . . .114 BG91
  Staines (Stanw.) TW19 . .114 BK86
  Staines (Wrays.) TW19 . .112 AZ86
  Sutton SM1 . . .158 DB105
  Sutton (Cheam) SM3 . . .157 CY107
  Swanley BR8 . . .147 FF98
  Swanscombe DA10 . . .130 FZ85
  Tadworth KT20 . . .173 CW123
  Teddington TW11 . . .117 CG92
  Thames Ditton KT7 . . .137 CG101
  Thornton Heath CR7 . . .142 DQ98
  Twickenham (Whitton)
    TW2 . . . . .116 CC87
  Uxbridge UB8 . . .76 BK67
  Uxbridge (Cowley) UB8 . .76 BJ70
  Uxbridge (Hare.) UB9 . . .38 BJ54
  Waltham Cross EN8 . . .15 DY34
  Waltham Cross (Chsht.)
    EN8 . . . . . .15 DX29
  Walton-on-Thames KT12 .135 BU102
  Watford WD17 . . . .23 BV41
  Wembley HA9 . . .62 CM63
  West Drayton (Harm.) UB7 .94 BK79
  West Drayton (Yiew.) UB7 .76 BK74
  West Molesey KT8 . . .136 CA98
  West Wickham BR4 . . .143 EB102
  Westerham TN16 . . .189 EQ127
  Westerham (Brasted)
    TN16 . . . . .180 EV124
  Weybridge KT13 . . .152 BN105
  Woking GU21 . . .166 AY117
  Woking (Chobham) GU24 .150 AS111
  Woking (Horsell) GU21 . .166 AV115
  Woking (Old Wok.) GU22 .167 BB121
  Woking (Ripley) GU23 . .168 BJ121
High St Colliers Wd, SW19 .120 DD94
High St Ms, SW19 . . .119 CY92
⊖ High Street Kensington . .100 DB75
High St N, E6 . . . . .86 EL67
  E12 . . . . . . .68 EL64
High St S, E6 . . . . .87 EM68
High St Wimbledon, SW19 .119 CX92
High Timber St, EC4 . . .197 H10
High Tor Cl, Brom. BR1
  off Babbacombe Rd . . .124 EH94
High Tree Cl, Add. KT15 . .151 BF106
High Tree Ct, W7 . . .79 CE73
High Trees, SW2 . . .121 DN88
  Barnet EN5 . . . .28 DE43
  Croydon CR0 . . .143 DY102
High Trees Cl, Cat. CR3 . .176 DT123
High Trees Ct, Brwd. CM14
  off Warley Mt 54 FW49
Highview, Cat. CR3 . . .176 DS124
High Vw, Ch.St.G. HP8 . . .36 AX47
Highview, Nthlt. UB5 . . .78 BY69
High Vw, Pnr. HA5 . . .60 BW56
  Rickmansworth (Chorl.)
    WD3 . . . . .22 BG42
  Sutton SM2 . . .157 CZ111
  Watford WD18 . . . .23 BT44
Highview Av, Edg. HA8 . . .42 CQ49
High Vw Av, Grays RM17 . .110 GC78
Highview Av, Wall. SM6 . . .159 DM106
High Vw Caravan Pk, Kings L.
  WD4 . . . . . .7 BR28
High Vw Cl, SE19 . . .142 DT96
  Loughton IG10 . . .32 EJ43
Highview Cl, Pot.B. EN6 . . .12 DC33
Highview Cres, Brwd. CM13 .53 GC44
Highview Gdns, N3 . . .63 CY55
  N11 . . . . . . .45 DJ50
  Edgware HA8 . . .42 CQ49
High Vw Gdns, Grays RM17 .110 GC78
Highview Gdns, Pot.B. EN6 . .12 DC33
  Upminster RM14 . . .72 FP61
Highview Ho, Rom. RM6 . . .70 EY56
Highview Path, Bans. SM7 .174 DA115
High Vw Rd, E18 . . .68 EF55
Highview Rd, SE19 . . .122 DR93
  W13 . . . . . . .79 CG71
  Sidcup DA14 . . .126 EV91
Highway, The, E1 . . .202 C1
  E14 . . . . . .202 C1
  Orpington BR6 . . .164 EW106
  Stanmore HA7 . . . .41 CF53
  Sutton SM2 . . .158 DC109
Highwold, Couls. CR5 . . .174 DG118
Highwood, Brom. BR2 . . .144 EE97

Highwood Av, N12 . . .44 DC49
  Bushey WD23 . . . .24 BZ39
Highwood Cl, Brwd. CM14 . .54 FV45
  Kenley CR8 . . .176 DQ117
  Orpington BR6 . . .145 EQ103
Highwood Dr, Orp. BR6 . . .145 EQ103
Highwood Gdns, Ilf. IG5 . . .69 EM57
Highwood Gro, NW7 . . .42 CR50
Highwood Hall La, Hem.H.
  HP3 . . . . . .7 BQ25
HIGHWOOD HILL, NW7 . . .43 CU47
Highwood Hill, NW7 . . .43 CT47
⊞ Highwood Hosp, Brwd.
    CM15 . . . . .54 FW45
Highwood La, Loug. IG10 . .33 EN43
Highwood Rd, N19 . . .65 DL62
Highwoods, Cat. CR3 . . .186 DS125
  Leatherhead KT22 . . .171 CJ121
High Worple, Har. HA2 . . .60 BZ59
Highworth Rd, N11 . . .45 DK51
Hilary Av, Mitch. CR4 . . .140 DG97
Hilary Cl, SW6 . . . .100 DB80
  Erith DA8 . . . .107 FC81
  Hornchurch RM12 . . .72 FK64
Hilary Rd, W12 . . . .81 CT72
  Slough SL3 . . . .92 AY76
Hilbert Rd, Sutt. SM3 . . .139 CX104
Hilborough Way, Orp. BR6 .163 ER106
Hilda May Av, Swan. BR8 . .147 FE97
Hilda Rd, E6 . . . . .86 EK66
  E16 . . . . . . .86 EE70
Hilda Ter, SW9 . . . .101 DN82
Hilda Vale Cl, Orp. BR6 . . .163 EP105
Hilda Vale Rd, Orp. BR6 . .163 EN105
Hildenborough Gdns, Brom.
  BR1 . . . . . .124 EE93
Hilden Dr, Erith DA8 . . .107 FH80
Hildenlea Pl, Brom. BR2 . .144 EE96
Hildenley Cl, Red. RH1
  off Malmstone Av . . .185 DK128
Hilders, The, Ashtd. KT21 .172 CP117
Hildreth St, SW12 . . .121 DH88
Hildyard Rd, SW6 . . .100 DA79
Hiley Rd, NW10 . . . .81 CW69
Hilfield La, Wat. (Ald.) WD25 .25 CF41
Hilfield La S, Bushey WD23 . .25 CF44
Hilgrove Rd, NW6 . . .82 DC66
Hiliary Gdns, Stan. HA7 . . .41 CJ54
Hiljon Cres, Ger.Cr. (Chal.St.P.)
  SL9 . . . . . .36 AY53
Hilley Fld La, Lthd. (Fetch.)
  KT22 . . . . .170 CC122
Hill Brow, Brom. BR1 . . .144 EK95
  Dartford DA1 . . .127 FF86
Hillbrow, N.Mal. KT3 . . .139 CT97
  Hillbrow, Bex. DA5 . . .127 FD91
Hillbrow Cotts, Gdse. RH9 .186 DW132
Hillbrow Rd, Brom. BR1 . .124 EE94
  Esher KT10 . . .154 CC105
Hillbury Av, Har. HA3 . . .61 CH57
Hillbury Cl, Warl. CR6 . . .176 DV118
Hillbury Gdns, Warl. CR6 . .176 DW118
Hillbury Rd, SW17 . . .121 DH90
  Warlingham CR6 . . .176 DU117
  Whyteleafe CR3 . . .176 DU117
Hill Cl, NW2 . . . . .63 CV62
  NW11 . . . . . .64 DA58
  Barnet EN5 . . . .27 CW43
  Chislehurst BR7 . . .125 EP92
  Cobham KT11 . . .154 CA112
  Gravesend (Istead Rise)
    DA13 . . . . .130 GE94
  Harrow HA1 . . . .61 CE62
  Purley CR8 . . .160 DQ113
  Stanmore HA7 . . . .41 CH49
  Woking GU21 . . .166 AX115
Hillcote Av, SW16 . . .121 DN94
Hill Ct, Nthlt. UB5 . . .60 CA64
Hillcourt Av, N12 . . .44 DB51
Hillcourt Est, N16 . . .66 DR60
Hillcourt Rd, SE22 . . .122 DV86
Hill Cres, N20 . . . .44 DB47
  Bexley DA5 . . .127 FC88
  Harrow HA1 . . . .61 CG57
  Hornchurch RM11 . . .72 FK58
  Surbiton KT5 . . .138 CM99
  Worcester Park KT4 . . .139 CW103
Hillcrest, N6 . . . . .64 DG59
  N21 . . . . . . .45 DP45
Hill Crest, Pot.B. EN6 . . .12 DC34
  Sevenoaks TN13 . . .190 FG122
  Sidcup DA15 . . .126 EU87
Hillcrest, Wey. KT13 . . .153 BP105
Hillcrest Av, NW11 . . .63 CY57
  Chertsey KT16 . . .151 BE105
  Edgware HA8 . . .42 CP49
  Grays RM20 . . .109 FU79
  Pinner HA5 . . . .60 BX56
Hillcrest Caravan Pk, Tad.
  KT20 . . . . .182 CQ131
Hillcrest Cl, SE26 . . .122 DU91
  Beckenham BR3 . . .143 DZ99
  Epsom KT18 . . .173 CT115
Hillcrest Ct, Sutt. SM2
  off Eaton Rd . . .158 DD107
Hillcrest Dr, Green. DA9
  off Riverview Rd . . .129 FV85
Hillcrest Gdns, N3 . . .63 CY56
  NW2 . . . . . . .63 CU62
  Esher KT10 . . .137 CF104
Hillcrest Par, Couls. CR5 . .159 DH114

Hillcrest Rd, E17 . . .47 ED54
  E18 . . . . . . .48 EF54
  W3 . . . . . . .80 CN74
  W5 . . . . . . .80 CL71
  Bromley BR1 . . .124 EG92
  Dartford DA1 . . .127 FF87
  Hornchurch RM11 . . .71 FG59
  Loughton IG10 . . .32 EK44
  Ongar CM5 . . . .19 FE30
  Orpington BR6 . . .146 EU101
  Purley CR8 . . .159 DM110
  Radlett (Shenley) WD7 . .10 CN33
  Westerham (Bigg.H.) TN16 .178 EK116
  Whyteleafe CR3 . . .176 DT117
Hillcrest Vw, Beck. BR3 . .143 DZ100
Hillcrest Way, Epp. CM16 . .18 EU31
Hillcrest Waye, Ger.Cr. SL9 . .57 AZ59
Hillcroft, Loug. IG10 . . .33 EN40
Hillcroft Av, Pnr. HA5 . . .60 BZ58
  Purley CR8 . . .159 DJ113
Hillcroft Cres, W5 . . .80 CL72
  Ruislip HA4 . . . .60 BX62
  Watford WD19 . . .39 BV46
  Wembley HA9 . . .62 CM63
Hillcroft Rd, E6 . . . .87 EP71
Hillcroome Rd, Sutt. SM2 . .158 DD107
Hillcross Av, Mord. SM4 . .139 CZ99
Hilldeane Rd, Pur. CR8 . . .159 DN109
Hilldene Av, Rom. RM3 . . .52 FJ51
Hilldene Cl, Rom. RM3 . . .52 FK50
Hilldown Rd, SW16 . . .121 DL94
  Bromley BR2 . . .144 EE102
Hill Dr, NW9 . . . . .62 CQ60
  SW16 . . . . . .141 DM97
Hilldrop Cres, N7 . . .65 DK64
Hilldrop Est, N7 . . .65 DK64
Hilldrop La, N7 . . . .65 DK64
Hilldrop Rd, N7 . . . .65 DK64
  Bromley BR1 . . .124 EG93
HILL END, Uxb. 38 BH51
Hillend, SE18 . . . .105 EN81
Hill End, Orp. BR6
  off The Approach . . .145 ET103
Hill End Rd, Uxb. (Hare.) UB9 .38 BH51
Hillersdon, Slou. SL2 . . .74 AV71
Hillersdon Av, SW13 . . .99 CU82
  Edgware HA8 . . .42 CM50
Hillery Cl, SE17 . . .201 L9
Hilley Fld La, Lthd. (Fetch.)
  KT22 . . . . .170 CC122
Hill Fm Av, Wat. WD25 . . .7 BU33
Hill Fm Cl, Wat. WD25 . . .7 BU33
Hill Fm Ind Est, Wat. WD25 . .7 BT33
Hill Fm La, Ch.St.G. HP8 . .36 AT46
Hill Fm Rd, W10 . . . .81 CW71
  Gerrards Cross (Chal.St.P.)
    SL9 . . . . .36 AY52
  Uxbridge UB10
    off Austin's La . . .59 BR63
Hillfield Av, N8 . . . .65 DL57
  NW9 . . . . . . .62 CS57
  Wembley HA0 . . .80 CL66
Hillfield Cl, Har. HA2 . . .60 CC56
  Redhill RH1 . . .184 DG134
Hillfield Ct, NW3 . . .64 DE64
Hillfield Par, Mord. SM4 . .140 DE100
Hillfield Pk, N10 . . .65 DH56
  N21 . . . . . . .45 DN47
Hillfield Pk Ms, N10 . . .65 DH56
Hillfield Rd, NW6 . . .63 CZ64
  Gerrards Cross (Chal.St.P.)
    SL9 . . . . .36 AY52
  Hampton TW12 . . .116 BZ94
  Redhill RH1 . . .184 DG134
  Sevenoaks (Dunt.Grn.)
    TN13 . . . . .181 FE120
Hillfield Sq, Ger.Cr. (Chal.St.P.)
  SL9 . . . . . .36 AY52
Hillfoot Av, Rom. RM5 . . .51 FC53
Hillfoot Rd, Rom. RM5 . . .51 FC53
Hillgate Pl, SW12 . . .121 DH87
  W8 . . . . . . .82 DA74
Hillgate St, W8 . . . .82 DA74
Hill Gro, Felt. TW13
  off Watermill Way . . .116 BZ89
Hillgrove, Ger.Cr. (Chal.St.P.)
  SL9 . . . . . .37 AZ53
Hill Hall, Epp. CM16 . . .34 EZ35
Hillhouse, Wal.Abb. EN9 . .16 EF33
Hill Ho Av, Stan. HA7 . . .41 CF52
Hill Ho Cl, N21 . . . .45 DN45
  Gerrards Cross (Chal.St.P.) SL9 .36 AY52
Hill Ho Dr, Hmptn. TW12 . .136 CA95
  Weybridge KT13 . . .152 BN111
Hill Ho Rd, SW16 . . .121 DM92
Hillhouse Rd, Dart. DA2 . .128 FQ87
Hillhurst Gdns, Cat. CR3 . .176 DS120
Hilliard Rd, Nthwd. HA6 . . .39 BT53
Hilliards Ct, E1 . . . .202 E2
Hilliards Rd, Uxb. UB8 . . .76 BK72
Hillier Cl, Barn. EN5 . . .28 DB44
Hillier Gdns, Croy. CR0
  off Crowley Cres . . .159 DN106
Hillier Pl, Chess. KT9 . . .155 CJ107
Hillier Rd, SW11 . . .120 DF86
Hilliers Av, Uxb. UB8
  off Harlington Rd . . .76 BN69
Hilliers La, Croy. CR0 . . .141 DL104
Hillingdale, West. (Bigg.H.)
  TN16 . . . . .178 EH118
HILLINGDON, Uxb. 76 BN69
⊖ Hillingdon 58 BN64
Hillingdon Av, Sev. TN13 . .191 FJ121
  Staines TW19 . . .114 BL88
Hillingdon Hill, Uxb. UB10 . .76 BL68
⊞ Hillingdon Hosp, Uxb.
    UB8 . . . . .76 BM71
Hillingdon Ri, Sev. TN13 . .191 FK122
Hillingdon Rd, Bexh. DA7 . .107 FC82
  Gravesend DA11 . . .131 GG89
  Uxbridge UB10 . . .76 BL67
  Watford WD25 . . . .8 BU34
Hillingdon St, SE5 . . .101 DP79
  SE17 . . . . . .101 DP79

Hillington Gdns, Wdf.Grn. IG8 .48 EK54
Hill La, Ruis. HA4 . . .59 BQ60
  Tadworth (Kgswd.) KT20 .173 CY121
Hill Leys, Pot.B. (Cuffley)
  EN6 . . . . . .13 DL28
Hillman Cl, Horn. RM11 . . .72 FK55
  Uxbridge UB8 . . .58 BL64
Hillman Dr, W10 . . . .81 CW70
Hillman St, E8 . . . .84 DV65
Hillmarton Rd, N7 . . .65 DL64
Hillmead Dr, SW9 . . .101 DP84
Hillmont Rd, Esher KT10 . .137 CE104
Hillmore Gro, SE26 . . .123 DX92
Hillmount, Wok. GU22
  off Constitution Hill . . .166 AY119
Hill Pk Dr, Lthd. KT22 . . .171 CF119
Hill Path, SW16
  off Valley Rd . . .121 DM92
Hillpoint, Rick. (Loud.) WD3 . .22 BJ43
Hillreach, SE18 . . . .105 EM78
Hill Ri, N9 . . . . . .30 DV44
  NW11 . . . . . .64 DB56
  SE23 off London Rd . . .122 DV88
  Dartford (Lane End) DA2 .129 FR92
  Esher KT10 . . .137 CH103
  Gerrards Cross (Chal.St.P.)
    SL9 . . . . .36 AX54
  Greenford UB6 . . .78 CC66
  Potters Bar EN6 . . .12 DC34
  Richmond TW10 . . .117 CK85
  Rickmansworth WD3 . . .22 BH44
  Ruislip HA4 . . . .59 BQ60
  Slough SL3 . . . .93 BA79
  Upminster RM14 . . .72 FN61
Hillrise, Walt. KT12 . . .135 BT101
Hillrise Av, Wat. WD24 . . .24 BX38
Hill Ri Cres, Ger.Cr. (Chal.St.P.)
  SL9 . . . . . .36 AY54
Hillrise Rd, N19 . . .65 DL59
  Romford RM5 . . .51 FC51
Hill Rd, N10 . . . . .44 DF53
  NW8 . . . . . . .82 DC68
  Brentwood CM14 . . .54 FU48
  Carshalton SM5 . . .158 DE107
  Dartford DA2 . . .128 FL89
  Epping (They.B.) CM16 . .33 ES37
  Harrow HA1 . . . .61 CG57
  Leatherhead (Fetch.) KT22 .170 CB122
  Mitcham CR4 . . .141 DH95
  Northwood HA6 . . .39 BR51
  Pinner HA5 . . . .60 BY57
  Purley CR8 . . .159 DM112
  Sutton SM1 . . .158 DB106
  Wembley HA0 . . .61 CH62
Hillsborough Grn, Wat. WD19
  off Ashburnham Dr . . .39 BU48
Hillsborough Rd, SE22 . . .122 DS85
Hills Chace, Brwd. CM14 . .54 FW48
Hillsgrove, Well. DA16 . . .106 EW80
Hillside, NW9 . . . . .62 CR56
  NW10 . . . . . .80 CQ67
  SW19 . . . . . .119 CX93
  Banstead SM7 . . .173 CY115
  Barnet EN5 . . . .28 DC43
  Dartford (Fngham.) DA4 . .148 FM101
  Dartford (Lane End) DA2 .129 FS92
  Erith DA8 . . . .107 FD77
  Grays RM17 . . .110 GD77
  Slough SL1 . . . .93 AS75
  Uxbridge (Hare.) UB9 . . .58 BJ57
  Virginia Water GU25 . . .132 AW100
  Woking GU22 . . .166 AX120
Hillside, The, Orp. BR6 . . .164 EV109
Hillside Av, N11 . . .44 DF51
  Borehamwood WD6 . . .26 CP42
  Gravesend DA12 . . .131 GK89
  Purley CR8 . . .159 DP113
  Waltham Cross (Chsht.)
    EN8 . . . . . .15 DX31
  Wembley HA9 . . .62 CM63
  Woodford Green IG8 . . .48 EJ50
Hillside Cl, NW8 . . .82 DB68
  Abbots Langley WD5 . . .8 BS32
  Banstead SM7 . . .173 CY116
  Chalfont St. Giles HP8 . .36 AV48
  Gerrards Cross (Chal.St.P.)
    SL9 . . . . .36 AY51
  Morden SM4 . . .139 CY98
  Woodford Green IG8 . . .48 EJ50
Hillside Ct, Swan. BR8 . . .147 FG98
Hillside Cres, Enf. EN2 . . .30 DR38
  Harrow HA2 . . . .60 CC60
  Northwood HA6 . . .39 BU53
  Waltham Cross (Chsht.)
    EN8 . . . . . .15 DX31
  Watford WD19 . . .24 BY44
Hillside Dr, Edg. HA8 . . .42 CN51
  Gravesend DA12 . . .131 GK89
Hillside Est, N15 . . .66 DT58
Hillside Gdns, E17 . . .67 ED55
  N6 . . . . . . .64 DG58
  SW2 . . . . . .121 DN89
  Addlestone KT15 . . .151 BF107
  Barnet EN5 . . . .27 CY42
  Betchworth (Brock.) RH3 .182 CN134
  Edgware HA8 . . .42 CM49
  Harrow HA3 . . . .62 CL59
  Northwood HA6 . . .39 BU52
  Wallington SM6 . . .159 DJ108
Hillside Gro, N14 . . .45 DK45
  NW7 . . . . . . .43 CU52
Hillside La, Brom. BR2 . . .144 EG103
Hillside Pas, SW2 . . .121 DM89
Hillside Ri, Nthwd. HA6 . . .39 BU52
Hillside Rd, N15 . . .66 DS59
  SW2 . . . . . .121 DN89
  W5 . . . . . . .80 CL71
  Ashtead KT21 . . .172 CM117
  Bromley BR2 . . .144 EF97
  Bushey WD23 . . . .24 BY43
  Coulsdon CR5 . . .175 DM118
  Croydon CR0 . . .159 DP106
  Dartford DA1 . . .127 FG86
  Epsom KT17 . . .157 CW110
  Northwood HA6 . . .39 BU52
  Pinner HA5 . . . .39 BV54

Hillside Rd, Radlett WD7 .....25 CH35
  Rickmansworth (Chorl.)
    WD3 ....21 BC43
  Sevenoaks TN13 .191 FK123
  Southall UB1 ....78 CA70
  Surbiton KT5 ....138 CM99
  Sutton SM2 ....157 CZ108
  Westerham (Tats.) TN16 ..178 EL119
  Whyteleafe CR3 ....176 DU118
Hillside Wk, Brwd. CM14 ...54 FU48
Hills La, Nthwd. HA6 ....39 BS53
Hillsmead Way, S.Croy. CR2 .160 DU113
Hills Ms, W5 ....80 CL73
Hills Pl, W1 ....195 K9
Hills Rd, Buck.H. IG9 ....48 EH46
Hillstowe St, E5 ....66 DW61
Hill St, W1 ....198 G2
  Richmond TW9 ....117 CK85
Hillswood Business Pk, Cher.
  KT16 ....151 BC105
Hillswood Dr, Cher. KT16 ..151 BC105
Hill Top, NW11 ....64 DB56
  Loughton IG10 ....33 EN40
  Morden SM4 ....140 DA100
  Sutton SM3 ....139 CZ101
Hilltop Cl, Lthd. KT22 .....171 CJ123
Hill Top Cl, Loug. IG10 .....33 EN41
Hilltop Cl, Wal.Cr. (Chsht.)
  EN7 ....14 DT26
Hilltop Gdns, NW4 ....43 CV54
  Dartford DA1 ....128 FM85
  Orpington BR6 ....145 ES103
Hilltop La, Cat. CR3 .....185 DN126
  Redhill RH1 ....185 DN126
Hill Top Pl, Loug. IG10 .....33 EN41
Hilltop Rd, NW6 ....82 DA66
  Grays RM20 ....109 FV79
  Kings Langley WD4 ....7 BR27
  Whyteleafe CR3 ....176 DS117
Hill Top Vw, Wdf.Grn. IG8 ...49 EM51
Hilltop Wk, Cat. CR3 .....177 DY120
Hilltop Way, Stan. HA7 .....41 CG48
Hillview, SW20 ....119 CV94
  Mitcham CR4 ....141 DL98
  Whyteleafe (Wold.) CR3 ..176 DT117
Hillview Av, Har. HA3 .....61 CL57
  Hornchurch RM11 ....72 FJ58
Hillview Cl, Pnr. HA5 ....40 BZ51
  Purley CR8 ....159 DP111
Hill Vw Cl, Tad. KT20
  off Shelvers Way 173 CW121
Hillview Cl, Wem. HA9 .....62 CM61
Hillview Ct, Wok. GU22 ....167 AZ118
Hillview Cres, Ilf. IG1 .....69 EM58
Hill Vw Cres, Orp. BR6 ....145 ET102
Hill Vw Dr, Well. DA16 ....105 ES82
Hillview Gdns, NW4 ....63 CX56
Hill Vw Gdns, NW9 ....62 CR57
Hillview Gdns, Har. HA2 ...60 CA55
  Waltham Cross (Chsht.)
    EN8 ....15 DX27
Hillview Rd, NW7 ....43 CX49
  Chislehurst BR7 ....125 EN92
Hill Vw Rd, Esher (Clay.)
  KT10 ....155 CG108
  Orpington BR6 ....145 ET102
Hillview Rd, Pnr. HA5 ....40 BZ52
Hill Vw Rd, Stai. (Wrays.)
  TW19 ....112 AX86
Hillview Rd, Sutt. SM1 ....140 DC104
Hill Vw Rd, Twick. TW1 ...117 CG86
  Woking GU22 ....167 AZ118
Hillway, N6 ....64 DG61
  NW9 ....62 CS60
Hill Waye, Ger.Cr. SL9 .....57 AZ58
Hillwood Cl, Brwd. CM13 ...55 GB46
Hillwood Gro, Brwd. CM13 .55 GB46
Hillworth Rd, SW2 ....121 DN87
Hillyard Rd, W7 ....79 CE71
Hillyard St, SW9 ....101 DN81
Hillyfield, E17 ....47 DY54
Hillyfields, Loug. IG10 .....33 EN40
Hilly Flds Cres, SE4 ....103 EA83
Hilperton Rd, Slou. SL1 .....92 AS75
Hilsea St, SW15
  off Wanborough Dr 119 CV88
Hilsea St, E5 ....66 DW63
Hilton Av, N12 ....44 DD50
Hilton Way, S.Croy. CR2 ...176 DV115
Hilversum Cres, SE22
  off East Dulwich Gro 122 DS85
Himalayan Way, Wat. WD18 ..23 BT44
Himley Rd, SW17 ....120 DE92
Hinchcliffe Cl, Wall. SM6 ..159 DM108
Hinchley Cl, Esher KT10 ...137 CF104
Hinchley Dr, Esher KT10 ...137 CF104
Hinchley Way, Esher KT10 ..137 CG104
HINCHLEY WOOD, Esher ..137 CF104
⇌ Hinchley Wood 137 CF104
Hinckley Rd, SE15 ....102 DU84
Hind Cl, Chig. IG7 ....49 ET50
Hind Ct, EC4 ....196 E9
Hind Cres, Erith DA8 .....107 FD79
Hinde Ms, W1
  off Marylebone La 82 DG72
Hindes Rd, Har. HA1 ....61 CD57
Hinde St, W1 ....194 G8
Hind Gro, E14 ....85 EA72
Hindhead Cl, N16 ....66 DS60
  Uxbridge UB8
    off Aldenham Dr 77 BP71
Hindhead Gdns, Nthlt. UB5 ..78 BY67
Hindhead Grn, Wat. WD19 ..40 BW50
Hindhead Pt, SW15
  off Wanborough Dr 119 CV88
Hindhead Way, Wall. SM6 ..159 DL106
Hind Ho, N7 off Harvist Est .65 DN63
Hindmans Rd, SE22 ....122 DU86
Hindmans Way, Dag. RM9 ..88 EZ70
Hindmarsh Cl, E1
  off Cable St 84 DU73
Hindrey Rd, E5 ....66 DV64
Hindsley's Pl, SE23 ....122 DW89
Hind Ter, Grays RM20
  off Mill La 109 FX78

Hine Cl, Couls. CR5 ....175 DJ122
Hinkler Cl, Wall. SM6 .....159 DL108
Hinkler Rd, Har. HA3 ....61 CK55
Hinkley Cl, Uxb. (Hare.) UB9 .58 BJ56
Hinksey Cl, Slou. SL3 ....93 BB76
Hinksey Path, SE2 ....106 EX76
Hinstock Rd, SE18 ....105 EQ79
Hinton Av, Houns. TW4 .....96 BX84
Hinton Cl, SE9 ....124 EL88
Hinton Rd, N18 ....46 DS49
  SE24 ....101 DP83
  Uxbridge UB8 ....76 BJ67
  Wallington SM6 ....159 DJ107
Hipley St, Wok. GU22 .....167 BB121
Hippodrome Ms, W11
  off Portland Rd 81 CY73
Hippodrome Pl, W11 ....81 CY73
Hiscocks Ho, NW10 ....80 CQ66
Hitcham Rd, E17 ....67 DZ59
Hitchcock Cl, Shep. TW17 ..134 BM97
Hitchen Hatch La, Sev. TN13 .190 FG124
Hitchin Cl, Rom. RM3 .....52 FJ49
Hitchin Sq, E3 ....85 DY68
Hitherbroom Rd, Hayes UB3 .77 BU74
Hither Fm Rd, SE3 ....104 EJ83
Hitherfield Rd, SW16 .....121 DM89
  Dagenham RM8 ....70 EY61
HITHER GREEN, SE13 .....124 EE86
⇌ Hither Green 124 EE86
Hither Grn La, SE13 .....123 EC85
Hitherlands, SW12 ....121 DH89
Hither Meadow, Ger.Cr. (Chal.St.P.)
  SL9 off Lower Rd 36 AY53
Hithermoor Rd, Stai. TW19 ..114 BG85
Hitherwell Dr, Har. HA3 .....41 CD53
Hitherwood Cl, Horn. RM12
  off Swanbourne Dr 72 FK63
  Reigate RH2 ....184 DD132
Hitherwood Dr, SE19 .....122 DT91
Hive, The, Grav. (Nthflt.) DA11
  off Fishermans Hill 130 GB85
Hive Cl, Brwd. CM14 ....54 FU47
  Bushey (Bushey Hth.)
    WD23 ....41 CD47
Hive La, Grav. (Nthflt.) DA11 .130 GB86
Hive Rd, Bushey (Bushey Hth.)
  WD23 ....41 CD47
★ HMS Belfast, SE1 ....201 N2
★ HMS President, EC4 .....196 E10
★ HM Treasury, SW1 ....199 P4
Hoadly Rd, SW16 ....121 DK90
Hobart Cl, N20
  off Oakleigh Rd N 44 DE47
  Hayes UB4 ....78 BX70
Hobart Dr, Hayes UB4 ....78 BX70
Hobart Gdns, Th.Hth. CR7 ..142 DR97
Hobart La, Hayes UB4 ....78 BX70
Hobart Pl, SW1 ....199 H6
  Richmond TW10
    off Chisholm Rd 118 CM86
Hobart Rd, Dag. RM9 ....70 EX63
  Hayes UB4 ....78 BX70
  Ilford IG6 ....49 EQ54
  Tilbury RM18 ....111 GG81
  Worcester Park KT4 .....139 CV104
Hobarts Dr, Uxb. (Denh.) UB9 .57 BF58
Hobbayne Rd, W7 ....79 CD72
Hobbes Wk, SW15 ....119 CV85
Hobbs Cl, Wal.Cr. (Chsht.)
  EN8 ....15 DX29
  West Byfleet KT14 .....152 BH113
Hobbs Cross Rd, Epp. CM16 ..34 EW35
Hobbs Grn, N2 ....64 DC55
Hobbs Ms, Ilf. IG3
  off Ripley Rd 69 ET61
Hobbs Pl Est, N1
  off Pitfield St 84 DS67
Hobbs Rd, SE27 ....122 DQ91
Hobby Horse Cl, Wal.Cr.
  (Chsht.) EN7
  off Great Stockwood Rd ..14 DR26
Hobday St, E14 ....85 EB71
Hobill Wk, Surb. KT5 .....138 CM100
Hoblands End, Chis. BR7 ...125 ES93
Hobsons Pl, E1 off Hanbury St .84 DU71
Hobury St, SW10 ....100 DC79
Hockenden La, Swan. BR8 ..147 FB96
Hockering Gdns, Wok. GU22 .167 BA117
Hockering Rd, Wok. GU22 ..167 BA118
Hocker St, E2 ....197 P3
Hockett Cl, SE8 ....203 L8
Hockley Av, E6 ....86 EL68
Hockley Cl, E18
  off Churchfields 48 EG53
Hockley Dr, Rom. RM2 .....51 FH54
Hockley La, Slou. (Stoke P.)
  SL2 ....74 AV67
Hockley Ms, Bark. IG11 .....87 ES68
Hockley Rd, Slou. (Stoke P.)
  SL2 ....74 AV67
Hocroft Av, NW2 ....63 CZ62
Hocroft Rd, NW2 ....63 CZ63
Hocroft Wk, NW2 ....63 CZ62
Hodder Dr, Grnf. UB6 ....79 CF68
Hoddesdon Rd, Belv. DA17 ..106 FA78
  Broxbourne EN10 ....15 DX27
Hodford Rd, NW11 ....63 CZ61
Hodgemoor Vw, Ch.St.G.
  HP8 ....36 AT48
Hodges Way, Wat. WD18 ....23 BU44
Hodgkin Cl, SE28
  off Fleming Way 88 EX73
Hodister Cl, SE5
  off Badsworth Rd 102 DQ80
Hodnet Gro, SE16 ....203 H8
Hodsoll Ct, Orp. BR5 .....146 EX100
Hodson Cl, Har. HA2 ....60 BZ62
Hodson Cres, Orp. BR5 ....146 EX100
Hodson Pl, Enf. EN3 ....31 EA37
Hoe, The, Wat. WD19 ....40 BX47
Hoebrook Cl, Wok. GU22 ...166 AX121
Hoe La, Enf. EN1, EN3 ....30 DU38
  Romford (Abridge) RM4 ....34 EV43
Hoe St, E17 ....67 EA56
Hofland Rd, W14 ....99 CX76
Hogan Ms, W2
  off Porteus Rd 82 DD71

Hogan Way, E5
  off Geldeston Rd 66 DU61
  Brentwood CM15 ....54 FY48
Hogarth Business Pk, W4 ...98 CS79
Hogarth Cl, E16 ....86 EK71
  W5 ....80 CL71
Hogarth Ct, EC3 ....197 N10
  SE19 off Fountain Dr 122 DT91
  Bushey WD23
    off Steeplands 40 CB45
Hogarth Cres, SW19 ....140 DD95
  Croydon CR0 ....142 DQ101
Hogarth Gdns, Houns. TW5 ..96 CA80
Hogarth Hill, NW11 ....63 CZ56
Hogarth La, W4 ....98 CS79
Hogarth Pl, SW5
  off Hogarth Rd 100 DB77
Hogarth Reach, Loug. IG10 ..33 EM43
Hogarth Rd, SW5 ....100 DB77
  Dagenham RM8 ....70 EV64
  Edgware HA8 ....42 CN54
  Romford RM7 ....71 FC57
  Stanmore HA7 ....41 CH50
Hogarth Roundabout, W4 ...98 CS79
Hogarth Roundabout Flyover, W4
  off Burlington La 98 CS79
Hogarth Way, Hmptn. TW12 .136 CC95
Hogg End La, Hem.H. (Flaun.)
  HP3 ....5 BB32
  St. Albans AL3 ....5 BB32
Hogg La, Borwd. (Elstree)
  WD6 ....25 CG42
  Grays RM16, RM17 ....110 GA76
Hogg La Roundabout, Grays
  RM16 ....110 FZ75
Hog Hill Rd, Rom. RM5 .....50 FA52
Hog Pits, Hem.H. (Flaun.)
  HP3 ....5 BB32
HOGPITS BOTTOM, Hem.H. ..5 BA31
Hogpits Bottom, Hem.H. (Flaun.)
  HP3 ....5 BA32
Hogscross La, Couls. CR5 ..174 DF123
Hogshead Pas, E1 ....202 E1
Hogshill La, Cob. KT11 ....154 BX112
Hogs La, Grav. DA11 ....130 GD90
Hogsmill Way, Epsom KT19 .156 CQ106
Hogs Orchard, Swan. BR8 ..147 FH95
Hogtrough Hill, West. (Brasted)
  TN16 ....179 ET120
Hogtrough La, Gdse. RH9 ...187 EA128
  Oxted RH8 ....187 EB128
Holbeach Gdns, Sid. DA15 ..125 ES86
Holbeach Ms, SW12
  off Harberson Rd 121 DH88
Holbeach Rd, SE6 ....123 EA87
Holbeck La, Wal.Cr. (Chsht.)
  EN7 ....14 DT26
Holbeck Row, SE15 ....102 DU80
Holbein Gate, Nthwd. HA6 ...39 BS50
Holbein Ms, SW1 ....198 F10
Holbein Pl, SW1 ....198 F9
Holbein Ter, Dag. RM8
  off Marlborough Rd 70 EV63
Holberton Gdns, NW10 .....81 CV69
HOLBORN, WC2 ....196 B8
⊖ Holborn 196 A7
Holborn, EC1 ....196 D7
Holborn Circ, EC1 ....196 E7
Holborn Pl, WC1 ....196 B7
Holborn Rd, E13 ....86 EH70
Holborn Viaduct, EC1 .....196 E7
Holborn Way, Mitch. CR4 ..140 DF96
Holbreck Pl, Wok. GU22
  off Heathside Rd 167 AZ118
Holbrook Cl, N19
  off Dartmouth Pk Hill 65 DH60
  Enfield EN1 ....30 DT39
Holbrooke Ct, N7 ....65 DL63
Holbrooke Pl, Rich. TW10
  off Hill Ri 117 CK85
Holbrook La, Chis. BR7 ....125 ER94
Holbrook Meadow, Egh.
  TW20 ....113 BC93
Holbrook Rd, E15 ....86 EF68
Holbrook Way, Brom. BR2 ..145 EM100
Holburne Cl, SE3 ....104 EJ81
Holburne Gdns, SE3 ....104 EK81
Holburne Rd, SE3 ....104 EJ81
Holcombe Hill, NW7 ....43 CU48
Holcombe Rd, N17 ....66 DT55
  Ilford IG1 ....69 EN59
Holcombe St, W6 ....99 CV78
Holcon Ct, Red. RH1 .....184 DG131
Holcote Cl, Belv. DA17
  off Blakemore Way 106 EY76
Holcroft Rd, E9 ....84 DW66
HOLDBROOK, Wal.Cr. 15 EA34
Holdbrook N, Wal.Cr. EN8
  off Eleanor Way 15 DZ34
Holdbrook S, Wal.Cr. EN8
  off Queens Way 15 DZ34
Holdbrook Way, Rom. RM3 ..52 FM54
Holden Av, N12 ....44 DB50
  NW9 ....62 CQ60
Holdenby Rd, SE4 ....123 DY85
Holden Cl, Dag. RM8 ....70 EV62
Holden Gdns, Brwd. CM14 ..54 FX50
Holdenhurst Av, N12 ....44 DB52
Holden Pt, E15 ....85 ED65
Holden Rd, N12 ....44 DB50
Holden St, SW11 ....100 DG82
Holden Way, Upmin. RM14 ..73 FR59
Holder Cl, N3 ....44 DB52
Holdernesse Cl, Islw. TW7 ...97 CG81
Holdernesse Rd, SW17 ....120 DF90
Holderness Way, SE27 ....121 DP92
HOLDERS HILL, NW4 ....43 CX54
Holders Hill Av, NW4 ....43 CX54
Holders Hill Circ, NW7
  off Dollis Rd 43 CY52
Holders Hill Cres, NW4 .....43 CX54
Holders Hill Dr, NW4 ....43 CX55
Holders Hill Gdns, NW4 ....43 CY54
Holders Hill Rd, NW4 ....43 CX54
  NW7 ....43 CX54

Holecroft, Wal.Abb. EN9 ....16 EE34
Hole Fm La, Brwd. CM13 ...73 FV55
Holford Ms, WC1
  off Cruikshank St 83 DN69
Holford Pl, WC1 ....196 C2
Holford Rd, NW3 ....64 DC62
  Grays RM16 ....111 GK76
  Stanford-le-Hope (Linford)
    SS17 ....111 GL75
  Tilbury RM18 ....111 GK76
Holford St, WC1 ....196 D2
Holford Yd, WC1
  off Cruikshank St 83 DN69
Holgate Av, SW11 ....100 DD83
Holgate Gdns, Dag. RM10 ..70 FA64
Holgate Rd, Dag. RM10 .....70 FA64
HOLLAND, Oxt. 188 EG134
Holland Av, SW20 ....139 CT95
  Sutton SM2 ....158 DA109
Holland Cl, Barn. EN5 .....44 DD45
  Bromley BR2 ....144 EF103
  Redhill RH1 ....184 DF134
  Romford RM7 ....71 FC57
  Stanmore HA7 ....41 CH50
Holland Ct, E17
  off Evelyn Rd 67 EC56
  NW7 off Page St 43 CU51
Holland Cres, Oxt. RH8 ....188 EG133
Holland Dr, SE23 ....123 DY90
Holland Gdns, W14 ....99 CY76
  Egham TW20 ....133 BF96
  Watford WD25 ....24 BW35
Holland Gro, SW9 ....101 DN80
★ Holland Ho & Pk, W8 .....99 CZ75
⊖ Holland Park 99 CY74
Holland Pk, W11 ....99 CY75
  W11 ....99 CY75
Holland Pk Av, W11 ....99 CY75
  Ilford IG3 ....69 ES58
Holland Pk Gdns, W14 .....99 CY74
Holland Pk Ms, W11 ....81 CY74
Holland Pk Rd, W14 ....99 CZ76
Holland Pas, N1 off Basire St .84 DQ67
Holland Pl, W8
  off Kensington Ch St 100 DB75
Holland Rd, E6 ....87 EM67
  E15 ....86 EE69
  NW10 ....81 CU67
  SE25 ....142 DU99
  W14 ....99 CX75
  Oxted RH8 ....188 EG133
  Wembley HA0 ....79 CK65
Hollands, The, Felt. TW13 ..116 BX91
  Woking GU22
    off Montgomery Rd 166 AY118
  Worcester Park KT4 .....139 CT102
Holland St, SE1 ....200 G2
  W8 ....100 DA75
Holland Vil Rd, W14 ....99 CY75
Holland Wk, N19
  off Duncombe Rd 65 DK60
  W8 ....99 CZ75
  Stanmore HA7 ....41 CG50
Holland Way, Brom. BR2 ..144 EF103
Hollar Rd, N16 off Stoke
  Newington High St 66 DT62
Hollen St, W1 ....195 M8
Holles Cl, Hmptn. TW12 ...116 CA93
Holles St, W1 ....195 J8
Holley Rd, W3 ....98 CS75
Hollickwood Av, N12 ....44 DF51
Holliday Sq, SW11
  off Fowler Cl 100 DD83
Hollidge Way, Dag. RM10 ...89 FB65
Hollies, The, N20 off Oakleigh Pk N .44 DD46
  Gravesend DA12 ....131 GK93
  Harrow HA3 ....61 CG56
  Hemel Hempstead (Bov.)
    HP3 ....5 BA29
Hollies Av, Sid. DA15 .....125 ET89
  West Byfleet KT14 .....151 BF113
Hollies Cl, SW16 ....121 DN93
  Twickenham TW1 ....117 CF89
Hollies Ct, Add. KT15 .....152 BJ106
Hollies End, NW7 ....43 CV50
Hollies Rd, W5 ....97 CJ77
Hollies Way, SW12
  off Bracken Av 120 DG87
  Potters Bar EN6 ....12 DC31
Holligrave Rd, Brom. BR1 ..144 EG95
Hollingbourne Av, Bexh.
  DA7 ....106 EZ80
Hollingbourne Gdns, W13 ...79 CH71
Hollingbourne Rd, SE24 ...122 DQ85
Hollingbourne Twr, Orp. BR5 .146 EX102
Hollingsworth Rd, Croy. CR0 .160 DV107
Hollington Cres, N.Mal. KT3 .139 CT100
Hollington Rd, E6 ....87 EM69
  N17 ....46 DU54
Hollingworth Cl, W.Mol. KT8 .136 BZ98
Hollingworth Rd, Orp. BR5 ..145 EP100
Hollingworth Way, West.
  TN16 ....189 ER126
Hollis Pl, Grays RM17
  off Ward Av 110 GA77
Hollman Gdns, SW16 .....121 DP93
Hollow, The, Wdf.Grn. IG8 ...48 EF49
HOLLOWAY, N7 ....65 DL63
Holloway Cl, West Dr. UB7 ...94 BL78
Holloway Dr, Vir.W. GU25 ..132 AY98
Holloway Hill, Cher. KT16 ..133 BC104
Holloway La, Rick. (Chenies)
  WD3 ....21 BD36
  West Drayton UB7 ....94 BL79
⊖ Holloway Road 65 DM64
Holloway Rd, E6 ....87 EM69
  E11 ....68 EE62
  N7 ....65 DK61
  N19 ....65 DK61
Holloway St, Houns. TW3 ...96 CB83
Hollow Cotts, Purf. RM19 ..108 FN78
Hollowfield Wk, Nthlt. UB5 ..78 BY65
Hollow Hill La, Iver SL0 .....75 BB73
Hollow La, Vir.W. GU25 ....132 AY97

Hollows, The, Brent. TW8
  off Kew Br Rd 98 CM79
Hollow Wk, Rich. TW9
  off Kew Rd 98 CL80
Hollow Way La, Amer. HP6 ..20 AS35
  Chesham HP5 ....20 AS35
Holly Av, Add. (New Haw)
  KT15 ....152 BG110
  Stanmore HA7 ....42 CL54
  Walton-on-Thames KT12 ..136 BX102
Hollybank Cl, Hmptn. TW12 .116 CA93
Hollybank Rd, W.Byf. KT14 .152 BG114
Holly Bk Rd, Wok. GU22 ...166 AV121
Hollyberry La, NW3
  off Holly Wk 64 DC63
Hollybrake Cl, Chis. BR7 ...125 ER94
Hollybush Cl, E11 ....68 EG57
  Harrow HA3 ....41 CE53
  Sevenoaks TN13 ....191 FJ124
  Watford WD19 ....40 BW45
Hollybush Ct, Sev. TN13 ...191 FJ124
Hollybush Gdns, E2 ....84 DV69
★ Hollybush Ho, W4
  off Holly Wk 64 DC63
Holly Bush Hill, NW3 ....64 DC63
Hollybush Hill, E11 ....68 EF58
Holly Bush Hill, NW3 ....64 DC63
  SL2 ....74 AU66
Holly Bush La, Hmptn. TW12 .116 BZ94
Hollybush La, Iver SL0 .....75 BB72
  Orpington BR6 ....164 FA107
Holly Bush La, Sev. TN13 ..191 FJ123
Hollybush La, Uxb. (Denh.)
  UB9 ....57 BE63
  Woking (Ripley) GU23 ....168 BK119
Hollybush Pl, E2
  off Bethnal Grn Rd 84 DV69
Hollybush Rd, Grav. DA12 ..131 GJ89
  Kingston upon Thames
    KT2 ....118 CL92
Holly Bush Steps, NW3
  off Heath St 64 DC63
Hollybush St, E13 ....86 EH69
Holly Bush Vale, NW3
  off Heath St 64 DC63
Hollybush Wk, SW9 ....101 DP84
Hollybush Way, Wal.Cr. EN7 ..14 DU28
Holly Cl, NW10 ....80 CS66
  Beckenham BR3 ....143 EC98
  Buckhurst Hill IG9 ....48 EK48
  Chertsey (Longcr.) KT16 ..132 AU104
  Egham (Eng.Grn.) TW20 ..112 AV93
  Feltham TW13 ....116 BY92
  Wallington SM6 ....159 DH108
  Woking GU21 ....166 AV119
Hollycombe, Egh. (Eng.Grn.)
  TW20 ....112 AW91
Holly Cottage Ms, Uxb. UB8
  off Pield Heath Rd 76 BN71
Holly Ct, Sutt. SM2
  off Worcester Rd 158 DA108
Hollycroft Av, NW3 ....64 DA62
  Wembley HA9 ....62 CM61
Hollycroft Cl, S.Croy. CR2 ..160 DS106
  West Drayton UB7 ....94 BN79
Hollycroft Gdns, West Dr. UB7 .94 BN79
Hollydale Cl, Nthlt. UB5
  off Dorchester Rd 60 CB63
Hollydale Dr, Brom. BR2 ..145 EM104
Hollydale Rd, SE15 ....102 DW81
Hollydene, SE15 ....102 DV81
Hollydown Way, E11 ....67 ED62
Holly Dr, E4 ....47 EB45
  Brentford TW8 ....97 CG79
  Potters Bar EN6 ....12 DB33
  South Ockendon RM15 ....91 FX70
  Windsor SL4 ....112 AS85
Holly Fm Rd, Sthl. UB2 .....96 BY78
Hollyfield Av, N11 ....44 DF50
Hollyfield Rd, Surb. KT5 ...138 CM101
Hollyfields, Brox. EN10 .....15 DY26
Holly Gdns, West Dr. UB7 ...94 BM75
Holly Grn, Wey. KT13 .....135 BR104
Holly Gro, NW9 ....62 CQ59
  SE15 ....102 DT82
  Bushey WD23 ....41 CD45
  Pinner HA5 ....40 BY53
Hollyhedge Rd, Cob. KT11 ..153 BV114
Holly Hedges La, Hem.H. (Bov.)
  HP3 ....5 BC30
  Rickmansworth WD3 ....5 BC30
Holly Hedge Ter, SE13 .....123 ED85
Holly Hill, N21 ....29 DM44
  NW3 ....64 DC63
Holly Hill Dr, Bans. SM7 ..174 DA116
Holly Hill Pk, Bans. SM7 ..174 DA117
Holly Hill Rd, Belv. DA17 ..107 FB78
  Erith DA8 ....107 FB78
Holly Ho, Brox. EN10
  off Sawyers Hall La 54 FX46
Ⓗ Holly House Hosp, Buck.H.
  IG9 ....48 EH47
Holly La, Bans. SM7 ....174 DA116
Holly La E, Bans. SM7 .....174 DA116
Holly La W, Bans. SM7 ....174 DA117
Holly Lo Gdns, N6 ....64 DG61
Holly Lo Mobile Home Pk, Tad.
  KT20 ....183 CY126
Hollymead, Cars. SM5 ....140 DF104
Hollymead Rd, Couls. CR5 .174 DG118
Hollymeaoak Rd, Couls. CR5 .175 DH119
Holly Ms, SW10
  off Drayton Gdns 100 DC78
Hollymoor La, Epsom KT19 .156 CR110
Holly Mt, NW3
  off Holly Bush Hill 64 DC63
Hollymount Cl, SE10 .....103 EC81
Holly Pk, N3 ....63 CZ55
  N4 ....65 DM59
Holly Pk Est, N4
  off Blythwood Rd 65 DM59
Holly Pk Gdns, N3 ....63 DA55
Holly Pk Rd, N11 ....44 DG50
  W7 ....79 CF74

A B C D E F G H I J K L M N O P Q R S T U V W X Y Z

★ Place of interest   ⇌ Railway station   ⊖ London Underground station   DLR Docklands Light Railway station   ◆ Tramlink station   Ⓗ Hospital

Hol - Hor

Hornsey La Est, N19		
off Hornsey La	.65	DK59
Hornsey La Gdns, N6	.65	DJ59
Hornsey Pk Rd, N8	.65	DM55
Hornsey Ri, N19	.65	DK59
Hornsey Ri Gdns, N19	.65	DK59
Hornsey Rd, N7	.65	DL61
N19	.65	DL61
Hornsey St, N7	.65	DM66
HORNS GREEN, Sev.	179	ES117
Hornshay St, SE15	102	DW79
Horns Rd, Ilf. IG2, IG6	.69	EQ57
Hornton Pl, W8	100	DA75
Hornton St, W8	100	DA75
Horsa Cl, Wall. SM6	159	DL108
Horsa Rd, SE12	124	EJ87
Erith DA8	107	FC80
Horse & Dolphin Yd, W1	195	N10
Horsecroft, Bans. SM7		
off Lyme Regis Rd	173	CZ117
Horsecroft Cl, Orp. BR6	146	EV102
Horsecroft Rd, Edg. HA8	.42	CR52
Horse Fair, Kings.T. KT1	137	CK96
Horseferry Pl, SE10	103	EC79
Horseferry Rd, E14	.85	DY73
SW1	199	M7
Horse Guards Av, SW1	199	P3
★ Horse Guards Par, SW1	199	N3
★ Horse Guards Rd, SW1	199	N3
Horse Hill, Chesh. HP5	..4	AX32
Horse Leaze, E6	.87	EN72
HORSELL, Wok.	166	AV116
Horsell Birch, Wok. GU21	166	AV115
Horsell Common, Wok.		
GU21	150	AX114
Horsell Common Rd, Wok.		
GU21	150	AW114
Horsell Ct, Cher. KT16		
off Stepgates	134	BH101
Horsell Moor, Wok. GU21	166	AX117
Horsell Pk, Wok. GU21	166	AX116
Horsell Pk Cl, Wok. GU21	166	AX116
Horsell Ri, Wok. GU21	166	AX115
Horsell Ri Cl, Wok. GU21	166	AX115
Horsell Rd, N5	.65	DN64
Orpington BR5	146	EV95
Horsell Vale, Wok. GU21	166	AY115
Horsell Way, Wok. GU21	166	AW116
Horselydown La, SE1	201	P4
Horselydown Old Stairs,		
SE1	201	P3
Horseman Side, Brwd. (Nave.S.)		
CM14	.51	FH45
Horsemans Ride, St.Alb. AL2	..8	CA26
Horsemongers Ms, SE1	201	J5
Horsemoor Cl, Slou. SL3		
off Parlaunt Rd	.93	BA77
Horsenden Av, Grnf. UB6	.61	CE64
Horsenden Cres, Grnf. UB6	.61	CF64
Horsenden La N, Grnf. UB6	.79	CF65
Horsenden La S, Grnf. UB6	.79	CG67
Horse Ride, SW1	199	M3
Tadworth KT20	183	CY125
Horse Rd, E7 off Centre Rd	.68	EH62
Horseshoe, The, Bans. SM7	173	CZ115
Coulsdon CR5	159	DK113
Horseshoe Cl, E14	204	D10
NW2	.63	CV61
Waltham Abbey EN9	.16	EG34
Horse Shoe Cres, Nthlt. UB5	.78	CA68
Horseshoe Dr, Uxb. UB8	.76	BN72
Horse Shoe Grn, Sutt. SM1		
off Aultone Way	140	DB103
Horseshoe Hill, Wal.Abb. EN9	.16	EJ33
Horseshoe La, N20	.43	CX46
Enfield EN2 off Chase Side	.30	DQ41
Watford WD25	..7	BV32
Horseshoe Ridge, Wey. KT13	153	BQ111
Horse Yd, N1 off Essex Rd	.83	DP67
Horsfeld Gdns, SE9	124	EL85
Horsfeld Rd, SE9	124	EK85
Horsfield Cl, Dart. DA2	128	FQ87
Horsford Rd, SW2	121	DM85
Horsham Av, N12	.44	DE50
Horsham Rd, Bexh. DA6	126	FA85
Feltham TW14	115	BQ86
Horsley Cl, Epsom KT19	156	CR113
Horsley Dr, Croy. (New Adgtn.)		
CR0	161	EC108
Kingston upon Thames		
KT2	117	CK92
Horsley Rd, E4	.47	EC47
Bromley BR1		
off Palace Rd	144	EH95
Cobham KT11	169	BV119
Horsleys, Rick. (Map.Cr.) WD3	.37	BD50
Horsley St, SE17	102	DR79
Horsmonden Cl, Orp. BR6	145	ES101
Horsmonden Rd, SE4	123	DZ85
Hortensia Rd, SW10	100	DC80
Horticultural Pl, W4		
off Heathfield Ter	.98	CR78
HORTON, Epsom	156	CP110
HORTON, Slou.	.93	BA83
Horton Av, NW2	.63	CY63
Horton Br Rd, West Dr. UB7	.76	BM74
Horton Cl, West Dr. UB7	.76	BM74
★ Horton Country Pk, Epsom		
KT19	156	CM110
Horton Footpath, Epsom		
KT19	156	CQ111
Horton Gdns, Epsom KT19		
off Horton Hill	156	CQ111
Horton Hill, Epsom KT19	156	CQ111
Horton Ind Pk, West Dr. UB7	.76	BM74
HORTON KIRBY, Dart.	149	FR98
Horton La, Epsom KT19	156	CP110
★ Horton Park Children's Fm,		
Epsom KT19	156	CN110
Horton Rd, E8	.84	DV65
Dartford (Hort.Kir.) DA4	148	FQ97
Slough (Colnbr.) SL3	.93	BA81
Slough (Datchet) SL3	.92	AW81
Slough (Poyle) SL3	.93	BE83
Staines TW19	114	BG85
West Drayton UB7	.76	BN74

Horton St, SE13	103	EB83
Hortons Way, West. TN16	189	ER126
Horton Way, Croy. CR0	143	DX99
Dartford (Fngham.) DA4	148	FM101
Hortus Rd, E4	.47	EC47
Southall UB2	.96	BZ75
Horvath Cl, Wey. KT13	153	BR105
Horwood Cl, Rick. WD3		
off Thellusson Rd	.38	BG45
Horwood Ct, Wat. WD24	.24	BX37
Hosack Rd, SW17	120	DF89
Hoser Av, SE12	124	EG89
Hosey Common La, West.		
TN16	189	ES130
Hosey Common Rd, Eden.		
TN8	189	EQ133
Westerham TN16	189	ER130
HOSEY HILL, West.	189	ES127
Hosey Hill, West. TN16	189	ER127
Hosier La, EC1	196	F7
Hoskins Cl, E16	.86	EJ72
Hayes UB3		
off Cranford Dr	.95	BT78
Hoskins Rd, Oxt. RH8	188	EE129
Hoskins St, SE10	103	ED78
Hoskins Wk, Oxt. RH8	188	EE129
Hospital Br Rd, Twick. TW2	116	CB87
Ⓗ Hospital of St. John & St.		
Elizabeth, NW8	.82	DD68
Hospital Rd, E9		
off Homerton Row	.67	DX64
Hounslow TW3	.96	CA83
Sevenoaks TN13	191	FJ121
Hotham Cl, Dart. (Sutt.H.)		
DA4	128	FP94
Swanley BR8	147	FH95
West Molesey KT8		
off Garrick Gdns	136	CA97
Hotham Rd, SW15	.99	CW83
SW19	120	DC94
Hotham Rd Ms, SW19		
off Haydons Rd	120	DC94
Hotham St, E15	.86	EE67
Hothfield Pl, SE16	202	G7
Hotspur Rd, Nthlt. UB5	.78	CA68
Hotspur St, SE11	200	D10
Houblon Rd, Rich. TW10	118	CL85
Houghton Cl, E8		
off Buttermere Wk	.84	DT65
Hampton TW12	116	BY93
Houghton Rd, N15		
off West Grn Rd	.66	DT57
Houghton St, WC2	196	C9
Houlder Cres, Croy. CR0	159	DP107
Houndsden Rd, N21	.29	DM44
Houndsditch, EC3	197	N8
Houndsfield Rd, N9	.46	DV45
HOUNSLOW	.96	BZ84
⇌ Hounslow	116	CB85
Hounslow Av, Houns. TW3	.96	CB85
Hounslow Business Pk, Houns.		
TW3	.96	CA84
● Hounslow Central	.96	CA83
● Hounslow East	.96	CC82
Hounslow Gdns, Houns.		
TW3	116	CB85
★ Hounslow Heath, Houns.		
TW4	116	BY86
Hounslow Rd, Felt. (Feltham)		
TW14	115	BV88
Feltham (Han.) TW13	116	BX91
Twickenham TW2	116	CC86
HOUNSLOW WEST, Houns.	.96	BX83
● Hounslow West	.96	BY82
Houseman Way, SE5		
off Hopewell St	102	DR80
★ Houses of Parliament,		
SW1	200	A5
Houston Pl, Esher KT10		
off Lime Tree Av	137	CE102
Houston Rd, SE23	123	DY89
Surbiton KT6	137	CH100
Hove Av, E17	.67	DZ57
Hove Cl, Brwd. CM13	.55	GC47
Grays RM17		
off Argent St	110	GA79
Hoveden Rd, NW2	.63	CY64
Hove Gdns, Sutt. SM1	140	DB102
Hoveton Rd, SE28	.88	EW72
Howard Agne Cl, Hem.H. (Bov.)		
HP3	..5	BA27
Howard Av, Bex. DA5	126	EW88
Epsom KT17	157	CU110
Howard Business Pk, Wal.Abb.		
EN9 off Howard Cl	.15	ED33
Howard Cl, N11	.44	DG47
NW2	.63	CY63
W3	.80	CP72
Ashtead KT21	172	CM118
Bushey (Bushey Hth.)		
WD23	.41	CE45
Hampton TW12	116	CC93
Leatherhead KT22	171	CJ123
Loughton IG10	.32	EL44
Sunbury-on-Thames TW16		
off Catherine Dr	115	BT93
Tadworth KT20	183	CT125
Waltham Abbey EN9	.15	ED34
Watford WD24	.23	BU37
Howard Ct, Reig. RH2	184	DC133
Howard Dr, Borwd. WD6	.26	CR42
Howard Ms, N5		
off Hamilton Pk	.65	DP63
Slough SL3		
off Laburnum Gro	.93	BB79
Howard Pl, SW1	199	K7
Reigate RH2	184	DA132
Howard Rd, E6	.87	EM68
E11	.68	EE62
E17	.67	EA55
N15	.66	DS58
N16	.66	DR63
NW2	.63	CX63
SE20	142	DW95
SE25	142	DU99
Barking IG11	.87	ER67

Howard Rd, Brom. BR1	124	EG94
Coulsdon CR5	175	DJ115
Dartford DA1	128	FN86
Grays (Chaff.Hun.) RM16	109	FW76
Ilford IG1	.69	EP63
Isleworth TW7	.97	CF83
Leatherhead (Eff.Junct.)		
KT24	169	BU122
New Malden KT3	138	CS97
Southall UB1	.78	CB72
Surbiton KT6	138	CM100
Upminster RM14	.72	FQ61
Howards Cl, Pnr. HA5	.39	BV54
Woking GU22	167	BA120
Howards Crest Cl, Beck. BR3	143	EC96
Howards La, SW15	.99	CV84
Addlestone KT15	151	BE107
Howards Rd, E13	.86	EG69
Woking GU22	167	AZ120
Howards Thicket, Ger.Cr.		
SL9	.56	AW61
Howard St, T.Ditt. KT7	137	CH101
Howards Wd Dr, Ger.Cr. SL9	.56	AX61
Howard Wk, N2	.64	DC56
Howard Way, Barn. EN5	.27	CX43
Hayes UB3	.77	BV73
Howarth Ct, E15		
off Clays La	.67	EC64
Howarth Rd, SE2	106	EU78
Howberry Cl, Edg. HA8	.41	CK51
Howberry Rd, Edg. HA8	.41	CK51
Stanmore HA7	.41	CK51
Thornton Heath CR7	142	DR95
Howbury La, Erith DA8	107	FG82
Howbury Rd, SE15	102	DW83
Howcroft Cres, N3	.44	DA52
Howcroft La, Grnf. UB6		
off Cowgate Rd	.79	CD69
Howden Cl, SE28	.88	EX73
Howden Rd, SE25	142	DT96
Howden St, SE15	102	DU83
Howe Cl, Rad. (Shenley) WD7	.10	CL32
Romford RM7	.50	FA53
Howe Dr, Cat. CR3	176	DR122
Howell Cl, Rom. RM6	.70	EX57
Howell Hill Cl, Epsom KT17	157	CW111
Howell Hill Gro, Epsom		
KT17	157	CW110
Howell Wk, SE1	200	G9
Howes Cl, N3	.64	DA55
Howfield Pl, N17	.66	DT55
Howgate Rd, SW14	.98	CR83
Howick Pl, SW1	199	L7
Howie St, SW11	100	DE80
Howitt Cl, N16 off Allen Rd	.66	DS63
NW3 off Howitt Rd	.82	DE65
Howitt Rd, NW3	.82	DE65
Howitts Cl, Esher KT10	154	CA107
Howland Est, SE16	202	G6
Howland Ms E, W1	195	L6
Howland St, W1	195	L6
Howland Way, SE16	203	L5
How La, Couls. CR5	174	DG117
Howletts La, Ruis. HA4	.59	BQ57
Howletts Rd, SE24	122	DQ86
Howley Pl, W2	.82	DC71
Howley Rd, Croy. CR0	141	DP104
Hows Cl, Uxb. UB8		
off Hows Rd	.76	BJ67
Howse Rd, Wal.Abb. EN9		
off Deer Pk Way	.31	EB35
Howsman Rd, SW13	.99	CU79
Howson Rd, SE4	103	DY84
Howson Ter, Rich. TW10	118	CL86
Hows Rd, Uxb. UB8	.76	BJ67
Hows St, E2	.84	DT68
Howton Pl, Bushey (Bushey Hth.)		
WD23	.41	CD46
HOW WOOD, St.Alb.	..8	CC27
⇌ How Wood	..8	CC28
How Wd, St.Alb. (Park St.) AL2	..8	CC28
HOXTON, N1	197	M1
Hoxton Mkt, N1	197	M3
Hoxton Sq, N1	197	M3
Hoxton St, N1	197	N3
Hoylake Cres, Uxb. (Ickhm.)		
UB10	.58	BN60
Hoylake Gdns, Mitch. CR4	141	DJ97
Romford RM3	.52	FN53
Ruislip HA4	.59	BV60
Watford WD19	.40	BX49
Hoylake Rd, W3	.80	CS72
Hoyland Cl, SE15		
off Commercial Way	102	DV80
Hoyle Rd, SW17	120	DE92
Hoy St, E16	.86	EF72
Hoy Ter, Grays RM20	109	FX78
★ HQS Wellington, Master		
Mariners' Hall, WC2	196	D10
Hubbard Dr, Chess. KT9	155	CJ107
Hubbard Rd, SE27	122	DQ91
Hubbards Chase, Horn. RM11	.72	FN57
Hubbards Cl, Horn. RM11	.72	FN57
Uxbridge UB8	.77	BP72
Hubbard's Hill, Sev. (Sev.Wld.)		
TN13	191	FH130
Hubbards Rd, Rick. (Chorl.)		
WD3	.21	BD43
Hubbard St, E15	.86	EE67
Hubbinet Ind Est, Rom. RM7	.71	FC55
Hubert Gro, SW9	101	DL83
Hubert Rd, E6	.86	EK69
Brentwood CM14	.54	FV48
Rainham RM13	.89	FF69
Slough SL3	.93	AX76
Hucknall Cl, Rom. RM3	.52	FM51
Huddart St, E3	.85	DZ71
Huddleston Cl, E2	.84	DW68
Huddlestone Cres, Red. RH1	185	DK128
Huddlestone Rd, E7	.68	EF63
NW2	.81	CV65
Huddleston Rd, N7	.65	DK63
Hudons Cl, Grays RM20	109	FT78
Hudson Av, Uxb. (Denh.) UB9	.57	BF58
Hudson Cl, Wat. WD24	.23	BT36
Hudson Ct, E14		
off Maritime Quay	103	EA78
SW19	120	DB94

Hudson Gdns, Orp. BR6		
off Superior Dr	163	ET107
Hudson Pl, SE18	105	EQ78
Hudson Rd, Bexh. DA7	106	EZ82
Hayes UB3	.95	BR79
Hudsons, Tad. KT20	173	CX121
Hudson's Pl, SW1	199	J8
off Gratton Ter	.63	CX62
Huggin Ct, EC4	197	J10
Huggin Hill, EC4	197	J10
Huggins Pl, SW2		
off Roupell Rd	121	DM88
Hughan Rd, E15	.67	ED64
Hugh Dalton Av, SW6	.99	CZ80
Hughenden Av, Har. HA3	.61	CH57
Hughenden Gdns, Nthlt.		
UB5	.78	BW69
Hughenden Rd, Wor.Pk. KT4	139	CU101
Hughendon Ter, E15		
off Westdown Rd	.67	EC63
Hughes Cl, N12		
off Coleridge Rd	.44	DC50
Hughes Rd, Ashf. TW15	115	BQ94
Grays RM16	111	GG76
Hayes UB3	.77	BV73
Hughes Wk, Croy. CR0		
off St. Saviours Rd	142	DQ101
Hugh Gaitskell Cl, SW6	.99	CZ79
Hugh Ms, SW1	199	J9
Hugh Pl, SW1	199	M8
Hugh St, SW1	199	J9
Hugo Gdns, Rain. RM13	.89	FF65
Hugo Gryn Way, Rad. (Shenley)		
WD7 off Farm Cl	.10	CL31
Hugon Rd, SW6	100	DB83
Hugo Rd, N19	.65	DJ63
Huguenot Pl, E1	.84	DT71
SW18	120	DC85
Huguenot Sq, SE15		
off Scylla Rd	102	DV83
HULBERIDGE, Swan.	147	FG103
Hullbridge Ms, N1		
off Sherborne St	.84	DR67
Hull Cl, SE16	203	J4
Sutton SM2		
off Yarbridge Cl	158	DB110
Waltham Cross (Chsht.)		
EN7	.14	DR26
Hull Pl, E16		
off Fishguard Way	105	EP75
Hull St, EC1	197	H3
Hulme Pl, SE1	201	J5
Hulse Av, Bark. IG11	.87	ER65
Romford RM7	.51	FB55
Hulse Ter, Ilf. IG1		
off Buttsbury Rd	.69	EQ64
Hulsewood Cl, Dart. DA2	127	FH90
Hulton Cl, Lthd. KT22	171	CJ123
Hulverston Cl, Sutt. SM2	158	DB110
Humber Av, S.Ock. RM15	.91	FT72
Humber Cl, West Dr. UB7	.76	BK74
Humber Dr, W10	.81	CX70
Upminster RM14	.73	FR58
Humber Rd, NW2	.63	CV61
SE3	104	EF79
Dartford DA1	128	FK85
Humberstone Rd, E13	.86	EJ69
Humberton Cl, E9		
off Marsh Hill	.67	DY64
Humber Way, Slou. SL3	.93	BA77
Humbolt Rd, W6	.99	CY79
Hume Av, Til. RM18	111	GG83
Hume Ter, E16		
off Prince Regent La	.86	EJ72
Hume Way, Ruis. HA4	.59	BU58
Hummer Rd, Egh. TW20	113	BA91
Humphrey Cl, Ilf. IG5	.49	EM53
Leatherhead (Fetch.) KT22	170	CC122
Humphrey St, SE1	201	P10
Humphries Cl, Dag. RM9	.70	EZ63
Hundred Acre, NW9	.43	CT54
Hungerdown, E4	.47	EC46
Hungerford Av, Slou. SL2	.74	AS71
Hungerford Br, SE1	200	A2
WC2	200	A2
Hungerford La, WC2	199	P2
Hungerford Rd, N7	.65	DK64
Hungerford Sq, Wey. KT13		
off Rosslyn Pk	153	BR105
Hungerford St, E1		
off Commercial Rd	.84	DV72
Hungry Hill, Wok. (Ripley) GU23		
off Hungry Hill La	168	BK124
Hungry Hill La, Wok. (Send)		
GU23	168	BK124
Hunsdon Cl, Dag. RM9	.88	EY65
Hunsdon Dr, Sev. TN13	191	FH123
Hunsdon Rd, SE14	103	DX79
Hunslett St, E2		
off Royston St	.84	DW68
Hunstanton Cl, Slou. (Colnbr.)		
SL3	.93	BC80
Hunston Rd, Mord. SM4	140	DB102
Hunter Av, Brwd. CM15	.55	GA44
Hunter Cl, SE1	201	L7
SW12 off Balham Pk Rd	120	DG88
Borehamwood WD6	.26	CQ43
Potters Bar EN6	.12	DC33
Huntercombe Gdns, Wat.		
WD19	.40	BW50
Hunter Dr, Horn. RM12	.72	FJ63
Hunter Ho, Felt. TW13	115	BU48
Hunter Rd, SW20	139	CW95
Ilford IG1	.69	EP64
Thornton Heath CR7	142	DR97
Hunters, The, Beck. BR3	143	EC95
Hunters Cl, Bex. DA5	127	FE90
Epsom KT19		
off Marshalls Cl	156	CQ113
Hemel Hempstead (Bov.)		
HP3	..5	BA29
Hunters Ct, Rich. TW9		
off Friars La	117	CK85
Huntersfield Cl, Reig. RH2	184	DB131

Hunters Gate, Wat. WD25		
off Hunters La	..7	BU33
Hunters Gro, Har. HA3	.61	CJ56
Hayes UB3	.77	BU74
Orpington BR6	163	EP105
Romford RM5	.51	FB50
Hunters Hall Rd, Dag. RM10	.70	FA63
Hunters Hill, Ruis. HA4	.60	BW62
Hunters La, Wat. WD25	..7	BT33
Hunters Meadow, SE19		
off Dulwich Wd Av	122	DS92
Hunters Reach, Wal.Cr. EN7	.14	DT29
Hunters Ride, St.Alb. (Brick.Wd.)		
AL2	..8	CA31
Hunters Rd, Chess. KT9	138	CL104
Hunters Sq, Dag. RM10	.70	FA63
Hunter St, WC1	196	A4
Hunters Wk, Sev. (Knock.)		
TN14	164	EY114
Hunters Way, Croy. CR0		
off Brownlow Rd	160	DS105
Enfield EN2	.29	DN39
Hunter Wk, E13	.86	EG68
Borehamwood WD6		
off Hunter Cl	.26	CQ43
Hunting Cl, Esher KT10	154	CA105
Huntingdon Gdns, W4	.98	CQ80
Worcester Park KT4	139	CW104
Huntingdon Rd, N2	.64	DE55
N9	.46	DW46
Redhill RH1	184	DF134
Woking GU21	166	AT117
Huntingdon St, E16	.86	EF72
N1	.83	DM66
Huntingfield, Croy. CR0	161	DZ108
Huntingfield Rd, SW15	.99	CU84
Huntingfield Way, Egh. TW20	113	BD94
Hunting Gate Cl, Enf. EN2	.29	DN41
Hunting Gate Dr, Chess.		
KT9	156	CL108
Hunting Gate Ms, Sutt. SM1	140	DB104
Twickenham TW2		
off Colne Rd	117	CE88
Huntings Rd, Dag. RM10	.88	FA65
Huntland Cl, Rain. RM13	.89	FH71
Huntley Av, Grav. (Nthflt.)		
DA11	130	GB86
Ⓗ Huntley Cen, WC1	195	M5
Huntley Cl, Stai. (Stanw.) TW19		
off Cambria Gdns	114	BL87
Huntley Dr, N3	.44	DA51
Huntley St, WC1	195	L5
Huntley Way, SW20	139	CU96
Huntly Rd, SE25	142	DS98
HUNTON BRIDGE, Kings L.	..7	BP33
Hunton Br Hill, Kings L. WD4	..7	BQ32
Hunton St, E1	.84	DU70
Hunt Rd, Grav. (Nthflt.) DA11	130	GE90
Southall UB2	.96	CA76
Hunt's Cl, SE3	104	EG82
Hunt's Ct, WC2	199	N1
Hunts La, E15	.85	EC68
Huntsman Cl, Warl. CR6	176	DW119
Huntsman Rd, Ilf. IG6	.50	EU51
Huntsmans Cl, Felt. TW13	115	BV91
Leatherhead (Fetch.) KT22		
off The Green	171	CD124
Huntsmans Dr, Upmin. RM14	.72	FQ64
Huntsman St, SE17	201	L9
Hunts Mead, Enf. EN3	.31	DX41
Hunts Mead Cl, Chis. BR7	125	EM94
Huntsmoor Rd, Epsom KT19	156	CR106
Huntspill St, SW17	120	DC90
Hunts Slip Rd, SE21	122	DS90
Huntsworth Ms, NW1	194	D5
Hunt Way, SE15		
off Dulwich Common	122	DU88
Hurcules Way, Wat. WD25	..7	BT33
Hurdwick Pl, NW1		
off Harrington Sq	.83	DJ83
Hurley Cl, Walt. KT12	135	BV103
Hurley Cres, SE16	203	J4
Hurley Ho, SE11	200	E9
Hurley Rd, Grnf. UB6	.78	CB72
Hurlfield, Dart. DA2	128	FJ90
Hurlford, Wok. GU21	166	AU117
Hurlingham Business Pk,		
SW6	100	DA83
Hurlingham Ct, SW6	.99	CZ83
Hurlingham Gdns, SW6	.99	CZ83
★ Hurlingham Ho, SW6	100	DA83
★ Hurlingham Park, SW6	.99	CZ82
Hurlingham Retail Pk, SW6		
off Carnwath Rd	100	DB83
Hurlingham Rd, SW6	.99	CZ82
Bexleyheath DA7	106	EZ80
Hurlingham Sq, SW6	100	DA83
off Peterborough Rd		
Hurlock St, N5	.65	DP62
Hurlstone Rd, SE25	142	DR99
Hurn Ct Rd, Houns. TW4		
off Renfrew Rd	.96	BX82
Humford Rd, S.Croy. CR2	160	DS110
Huron Cl, Orp. BR6		
off Winnipeg Dr	163	ET107
Huron Rd, SW17	120	DG89
Hurren Cl, SE3	104	EE83
Hurricane Rd, Wall. SM6	159	DM108
Hurricane Way, Abb.L. WD5		
off Abbey Dr	..7	BU32
Epping (N.Wld.Bas.) CM16	.18	EZ27
Slough SL3	.93	BB78
Hurry Cl, E15	.86	EE66
Hursley Rd, Chig. IG7		
off Tufter Rd	.49	ET50
Hurst Av, E4	.47	EA49
N6	.65	DJ58
Hurstbourne, Esher (Clay.)		
KT10	155	CF107
Hurstbourne Gdns, Bark. IG11	.87	ES65
Hurstbourne Ho, SW15		
off Tangley Gro	119	CT86
Hurstbourne Rd, SE23	123	DY88

Hur - Isl

Hurst Cl, E4 ....47 EA48
  NW11 ....64 DB58
  Bromley BR2 ....144 EF102
  Chessington KT9 ......156 CN106
  Northolt UB5 ....78 BZ65
  Woking GU22 ....151 BA116
Hurstcourt Rd, Sutt. SM1 ..140 DB103
Hurstdene Av, Brom. BR2 ..144 EF102
  Staines TW18 ....114 BH93
Hurstdene Gdns, N15 ......66 DS59
Hurst Dr, Tad. KT20 ......183 CU126
  Waltham Cross EN8 ......15 DX34
Hurst Est, SE2 ....106 EX78
Hurstfield, Brom. BR2 ....144 EG99
Hurstfield Cres, Hayes UB4 ..77 BS70
Hurstfield Rd, W.Mol. KT8 ..136 CA97
HURST GREEN, Oxt. 188 EG132
  ⇌ Hurst Green 188 EF132
Hurst Grn Cl, Oxt. RH8 ....188 EG132
Hurst Grn Rd, Oxt. RH8 ....188 EF132
Hurst Gro, Walt. KT12 ....135 BT102
Hurstlands, Oxt. RH8 ......188 EG132
Hurstlands Cl, Horn. RM11 ..72 FJ59
Hurst La, SE2 ....106 EX78
  East Molesey KT8 ......136 CC98
  Egham TW20 ....133 BA96
  Epsom (Headley) KT18 ..172 CQ124
Hurstleigh Cl, Red. RH1 ..184 DF132
Hurstleigh Dr, Red. RH1 ..184 DF132
Hurstleigh Gdns, Ilf. IG5 ..49 EM53
Hurstmead Ct, Edg. HA8 ....42 CP49
Hurst Pk Av, Horn. RM12
  off Newmarket Way 72 FL63
Hurst Pl, Nthwd. HA6 ......39 BP53
Hurst Ri, Barn. EN5 ....28 DA41
Hurst Rd, E17 ....67 EB55
  N21 ....45 DN46
  Bexley DA5 ....126 EX88
  Buckhurst Hill IG9 ......48 EK46
  Croydon CR0 ....160 DR106
  East Molesey KT8 ......136 CA97
  Epsom KT19 ....156 CR111
  Epsom (Headley) KT18 ..172 CR123
  Erith DA8 ....107 FC80
  Sidcup DA15 ....126 EU89
  Tadworth KT20 ....172 CR123
  Walton-on-Thames KT12 ..136 BW99
  West Molesey KT8 ......136 BY97
Hurst Springs, Bex. DA5 ..126 EY88
Hurst St, SE24 ....121 DP86
Hurst Vw Rd, S.Croy. CR2 ..160 DS108
Hurst Way, Sev. TN13 ....191 FJ127
  South Croydon CR2 ....160 DS109
  Woking (Pyrford) GU22 ..151 BE114
Hurstway Wk, E11 ....81 CX73
Hurstwood Av, E18 ....68 EH56
  Bexley DA5 ....126 EY88
  Bexleyheath DA7 ......107 FE81
  Brentwood CM15
    off Ongar Rd 54 FV45
  Erith DA8 ....107 FE81
Hurstwood Ct, Upmin. RM14 ..72 FQ60
Hurstwood Dr, Brom. BR1 ..145 EM97
Hurstwood Rd, NW11 ......63 CY56
Hurtwood Rd, Walt. KT12 ..136 BZ101
Hurworth Av, Slou. SL3 ....92 AW76
Huson Cl, NW3 ....82 DE66
Hussars Cl, Houns. TW4 ....96 BY83
Husseywell Cres, Brom. BR2 ..144 EG102
Hutchinsons Rd, Croy.
  (New Adgtn.) CR0 ......161 EC111
Hutchings St, E14 ....203 P5
Hutchings Wk, NW11 ......64 DB56
Hutchins Cl, E15
  off Gibbins Rd 85 EC66
  Hornchurch RM12 ......72 FL62
Hutchinson Ter, Wem. HA9 ..61 CK62
Hutchins Rd, SE28 ....88 EU73
Hutson Ter, Purf. RM19
  off London Rd Purfleet ..109 FR78
HUTTON, Brwd. 55 GD44
Hutton Cl, Grnf. UB6
  off Mary Peters Dr 61 CD64
  Woodford Green IG8 ......48 EH51
Hutton Dr, Brwd. CM13 ....55 GD45
Hutton Gdns, Har. HA3 ....40 CC52
Hutton Gate, Brwd. CM13 ..55 GB45
Hutton Gro, N12 ....44 DB50
Hutton La, Har. HA3 ......40 CC52
HUTTON MOUNT, Brwd. 55 GB46
Hutton Rd, Brwd. CM15 ....55 FZ45
Hutton Row, Edg. HA8
  off Pavilion Way 42 CQ52
Hutton St, EC4 ....196 E9
Hutton Village, Brwd. CM13 ..55 GE45
Hutton Wk, Har. HA3 ......40 CC52
Huxbear St, SE4 ....123 DZ85
Huxbear Cl, Nthlt. UB5 ....78 BY67
  Uxbridge UB8 ....76 BK70
Huxley Dr, Rom. RM6 ......70 EV59
Huxley Gdns, NW10 ......80 CM69
Huxley Par, N18 ....46 DR50
Huxley Pl, N13 ....45 DP49
Huxley Rd, E10 ....67 EC61
  N18 ....46 DR49
  Welling DA16 ....105 ET83
Huxley Sayze, N18 ....46 DR50
Huxley St, W10 ....81 CY69
Hyacinth Cl, Hmptn. TW12
  off Gresham Rd 116 CA93
  Ilford IG1 ....87 EP65
Hyacinth Ct, Pnr. HA5
  off Tulip Ct 60 BW55
Hyacinth Dr, Uxb. UB10 ....76 BL66
Hyacinth Rd, SW15 ......119 CU88
Hyburn Cl, St.Alb. (Brick.Wd.)
  AL2 ....8 BZ30
Hycliffe Gdns, Chig. IG7 ..49 EQ49
HYDE, THE, NW9 ....63 CT56
Hyde, The, NW9 ....62 CS57
Hyde Av, Pot.B. EN6 ......12 DB33
Hyde Cl, E13 ....86 EG68
  Ashford TW15 off Hyde Ter ..115 BS93
  Barnet EN5 ....27 CZ41

Hyde Cl, Grays (Chaff.Hun.)
  RM16 ....109 FX76
Hyde Ct, N20 ....44 DD48
  Waltham Cross EN8
    off Parkside 15 DY34
Hyde Cres, NW9 ....62 CS57
Hyde Dr, Orp. BR5 ......146 EV98
Hyde Est Rd, NW9 ....63 CT57
Hyde Fm Ms, SW12
  off Telferscot Rd 121 DK88
Hydefield Cl, N21 ....46 DR46
Hydefield Ct, N9 ....46 DS47
Hyde Ho, NW9 ....62 CS57
Hyde La, SW11
  off Battersea Br Rd 100 DE81
  Hemel Hempstead HP3 ....7 BR26
  Hemel Hempstead (Bov.)
    HP3 ....5 BA27
  St. Albans (Frog.) AL2 ....9 CE28
  Woking (Ockham) GU23 ..168 BN120
Hyde Meadows, Hem.H. (Bov.)
  HP3 ....5 BA28
★ Hyde Park, W2 ....198 B2
Hyde Pk, SW7 ....198 B2
  W1 ....198 B2
  W2 ....198 B2
Hyde Pk Av, N21 ....46 DQ47
⊖ Hyde Park Corner 198 F4
Hyde Pk Cor, W1 ....198 G4
Hyde Pk Cres, W2 ......194 B9
Hyde Pk Gdns, N21 ......46 DQ46
  W2 ....194 A10
Hyde Pk Gdns Ms, W2 ....194 A10
Hyde Pk Gate, SW7 ......100 DC75
Hyde Pk Gate Ms, SW7
  off Hyde Pk Gate 100 DC75
Hyde Pk Pl, W2 ....194 C10
Hyde Pk Sq, W2 ....194 B9
Hyde Pk Sq Ms, W2 ......194 B9
Hyde Pk St, W2 ....194 B9
Hyderabad Way, E15 ......86 EE66
Hyde Rd, N1 ....84 DR67
  Bexleyheath DA7 ......106 EZ82
  Richmond TW10
    off Albert Rd 118 CM85
  South Croydon CR2 ....160 DS113
  Watford WD17 ....23 BU40
Hyder Rd, Grays RM16 ....111 GJ76
Hydeside Gdns, N9 ....46 DT47
Hydes Pl, N1
  off Compton Av 83 DP66
Hyde St, SE8
  off Deptford High St 103 EA79
Hyde Ter, Ashf. TW15 ....115 BS93
Hydethorpe Av, N9 ....46 DT47
Hydethorpe Rd, SW12 ....121 DJ88
Hyde Vale, SE10 ....103 EC80
Hyde Wk, Mord. SM4 ....140 DA101
Hyde Way, N9 ....46 DT47
  Hayes UB3 ....95 BT77
Hyland Cl, Horn. RM11 ....71 FH59
Hylands Cl, Epsom KT18 ..172 CQ115
Hylands Ms, Epsom KT18 ..172 CQ115
Hylands Rd, E17 ....47 ED54
  Epsom KT18 ....172 CQ115
Hyland Way, Horn. RM11 ..71 FH59
Hylton St, SE18 ....105 ET77
Hyndewood, SE23 ....123 DX90
Hyndman St, SE15 ......102 DV79
Hynton Rd, Dag. RM8 ....70 EW61
Hyperion Pl, Epsom KT19 ..156 CR109
Hyrons Cl, Amer. HP6 ....20 AS38
Hyrstdene, S.Croy. CR2 ..159 DP105
Hyson Rd, SE16 ....202 E10
Hythe, The, Stai. TW18 ..113 BE92
Hythe Av, Bexh. DA7 ....106 EZ80
Hythe Cl, N18 ....46 DU49
  Orpington BR5
    off Sandway Rd 146 EW98
HYTHE END, Stai. 113 BB90
Hythe End Rd, Stai. (Wrays.)
  TW19 ....113 BA89
Hythe Fld Av, Egh. TW20 ..113 BD93
Hythe Pk Rd, Egh. TW20 ..113 BC92
Hythe Path, Th.Hth. CR7 ..142 DR97
Hythe Rd, NW10 ....81 CU70
  Staines TW18 ....113 BD92
  Thornton Heath CR7 ....142 DR96
Hythe Rd Ind Est, NW10 ..81 CU69
Hythe St, Dart. DA1 ....128 FL86
Hythe St Lwr, Dart. DA1 ..128 FL85
Hyver Hill, NW7 ....26 CR44

I

Ian Sq, Enf. EN3
  off Lansbury Rd 31 DX39
Ibbetson Path, Loug. IG10 ..33 EP41
Ibbotson Av, E16 ....86 EF72
Ibbott St, E1 off Mantus Rd ..84 DW70
Iberian Av, Wall. SM6 ....159 DK105
Ibis La, W4 ....98 CQ81
Ibis Way, Hayes UB4
  off Cygnet Way 78 BX72
Ibscott Cl, Dag. RM10 ....89 FC65
Ibsley Gdns, SW15 ......119 CU88
Ibsley Way, Barn. EN4 ....28 DE43
Icehouse Wd, Oxt. RH8 ..188 EE131
Iceland Rd, E3 ....85 EA67
Iceni Ct, E3 off Roman Rd ..85 DZ67
Ice Wf, N1 off New Wf Rd ..83 DL68
Ice Wf Marina, N1
  off New Wf Rd 83 DL68
Ickburgh Est, E5
  off Ickburgh Rd 66 DV62
Ickburgh Rd, E5 ....66 DV62
ICKENHAM, Uxb. 59 BQ62
⊖ Ickenham 59 BQ63
Ickenham Cl, Ruis. HA4 ....59 BR61
Ickenham Rd, Ruis. HA4 ....59 BR60
  Uxbridge (Ickhm.) UB10 ..59 BQ61
Ickleton Rd, SE9 ....124 EL91
Icklingham Gate, Cob. KT11 ..154 BW112
Icklingham Rd, Cob. KT11 ..154 BW112

Icknield Dr, Ilf. IG2 ......69 EP57
Ickworth Pk Rd, E17 ......67 DY56
Ida Rd, N15 ....66 DR57
Ida St, E14 ....85 EC72
Iden Cl, Brom. BR2 ......144 EE97
Idlecombe Rd, SW17 ....120 DG93
Idmiston Rd, E15 ....68 EF64
  SE27 ....122 DQ90
  Worcester Park KT4 ....139 CT101
Idmiston Sq, Wor.Pk. KT4 ..139 CT101
Idol La, EC3 ....201 M1
Idonia St, SE8 ....103 DZ80
Iffley Cl, Uxb. UB8 ......76 BK66
Iffley Rd, W6 ....99 CV76
Ifield Cl, Red. RH1 ......184 DE134
Ifield Rd, SW10 ....100 DB79
Ifield Way, Grav. DA12 ..131 GK93
Ifor Evans Pl, E1
  off Mile End Rd 85 DX70
Ightham Rd, Erith DA8 ..106 FA80
Ikea Twr, NW10 ....62 CR64
Ikona Ct, Wey. KT13 ....153 BQ106
Ilbert St, W10 ....81 CX69
Ilchester Gdns, W2 ......82 DB73
Ilchester Pl, W14 ....99 CZ76
Ilchester Rd, Dag. RM8 ..70 EV64
Ildersly Gro, SE21 ......122 DR89
Ilderton Rd, SE15 ......102 DW80
  SE16 ....202 E10
Ilex Cl, Egh. (Eng.Grn.) TW20 ..112 AV92
  Sunbury-on-Thames TW16
    off Oakington Dr 136 BW96
Ilex Ho, N4 ....65 DM59
Ilex Rd, NW10 ....81 CT65
Ilex Way, SW16 ....121 DN92
ILFORD 69 EQ62
⇌ Ilford 69 EN62
Ilford Hill, Ilf. IG1 ......69 EN62
Ilford La, Ilf. IG1 ......69 EP62
Ilfracombe Cres, Horn. RM12 ..72 FJ63
Ilfracombe Gdns, Rom. RM6 ..70 EV59
Ilfracombe Rd, Brom. BR1 ..124 EF90
Iliffe St, SE17 ....200 G10
Iliffe Yd, SE17 ....200 G10
Ilkeston Ct, E5
  off Overbury St 67 DX63
Ilkley Cl, SE19 ....122 DR93
Ilkley Rd, E16 ....86 EJ71
  Watford WD19 ....40 BX50
Illingworth Cl, Mitch. CR4 ..140 DD97
Illingworth Way, Enf. EN1 ..30 DS42
Ilmington Rd, Har. HA3 ..61 CK58
Ilminster Gdns, SW11 ..100 DE84
Ilsom Cl, N14 ....45 DJ45
  Esher KT10 off Ember La ..137 CD102
Imber Ct Trd Est, E.Mol. KT8 ..137 CD100
Imber Gro, Esher KT10 ..137 CD101
Imber Pk Rd, Esher KT10 ..137 CD102
Imber St, N1 ....84 DR67
Imer Pl, T.Ditt. KT7 ....137 CF101
Imperial Av, N16
  off Victorian Rd 66 DT62
Imperial Business Est, Grav.
  DA11 ....131 GF86
Imperial Cl, Har. HA2 ....60 CA58
★ Imperial Coll, Uni of
  London, SW7 ....100 DD76
Imperial Coll Rd, SW7 ..100 DD76
Imperial Cres, Wey. KT13
  off Churchill Dr 135 BQ104
Imperial Dr, Grav. DA12 ..131 GM92
  Harrow HA2 ....60 CA59
Imperial Gdns, Mitch. CR4 ..141 DH97
Imperial Ms, E6
  off Central Pk Rd 86 EJ68
Imperial Pk, Wat. WD24 ..24 BW39
Imperial Retail Pk, Grav.
  DA11 ....131 GG86
Imperial Rd, N22 ....45 DL53
  SW6 ....100 DB81
  Feltham TW14 ....115 BS87
Imperial Sq, SW6 ......100 DB81
Imperial St, E3 ....85 EC69
★ Imperial War Mus, SE1 ..200 E7
Imperial Way, Chis. BR7 ..125 EQ90
  Croydon CR0 ....159 DM107
  Harrow HA3 ....62 CL58
  Watford WD24 ....24 BW39
Imprimo Pk, Loug. IG10
  off Lenthall Rd 33 ER42
Imre Cl, W12 off Ellerslie Rd ..81 CV74
Inca Dr, SE9 ....125 EP87
Ince Rd, Walt. KT12 ....153 BS107
Inchmery Rd, SE6 ......123 EB89
Inchwood, Croy. CR0 ..161 EB105
Independent Pl, E8
  off Downs Pk Rd 66 DT64
Independents Rd, SE3
  off Blackheath Village ..104 EF83
India Pl, WC2 ....196 B10
India Rd, Slou. SL1 ......92 AV75
India St, EC3 ....197 P9
India Way, W12 ....81 CV73
Indigo Ms, E14 off Ashton St ..85 CE73
  N16 ....66 DR62
Indus Rd, SE7 ....104 EJ80
Industry Ter, SW9
  off Canterbury Cres 101 DN83
Ingal Rd, E13 ....86 EG70
Ingate Pl, SW8 ....101 DH81
Ingatestone Rd, E12 ......68 EJ60
  SE25 ....142 DV98
  Woodford Green IG8 ......48 EG52
Ingelow Rd, SW8 ....101 DH82
Ingels Mead, Epp. CM16 ..17 ET29
Ingersoll Rd, W12 ......81 CV74
  Enfield EN3 ....30 DW38
Ingestre Pl, W1 ....195 L9
Ingestre Rd, E7 ....68 EG63
  NW5 ....65 DH63
Ingham Cl, S.Croy. CR2 ..161 DX109
Ingham Rd, NW6 ....64 DA63
  South Croydon CR2 ....160 DW109
Inglebert St, EC1 ......196 D2
Ingleboro Dr, Pur. CR8 ..160 DR113
Ingleborough St, SW9 ..101 DN82

Ingleby Dr, Har. HA1 ......61 CD62
Ingleby Gdns, Chig. IG7 ..50 EV48
Ingleby Rd, N7 off Bryett Rd ..65 DL62
  Dagenham RM10 ....89 FB65
  Grays RM16 ....111 GH76
  Ilford IG1 ....69 EP60
Ingleby Way, Chis. BR7 ..125 EN92
  Wallington SM6 ......159 DK109
Ingle Cl, Pnr. HA5 ....60 BY56
Ingledew Rd, SE18 ......105 ER78
Inglefield, Pot.B. EN6 ....12 DA30
Ingleglen, Horn. RM11 ....72 FN59
Inglehurst, Add. (New Haw)
  KT15 ....152 BH110
Inglehurst Gdns, Ilf. IG4 ..69 EM57
Inglemere Rd, SE23 ....123 DX90
  Mitcham CR4 ....120 DF94
Ingleside, Slou. (Colnbr.)
  SL3 ....93 BE81
Ingleside Cl, Beck. BR3 ..123 EA94
Ingleside Gro, SE3 ......104 EF79
Inglethorpe St, SW6 ......99 CX81
Ingleton Av, Well. DA16 ..126 EU85
Ingleton Rd, N18 ....46 DU51
  Carshalton SM5 ......158 DE109
Ingleton St, SW9 ......101 DN82
Ingleway, N12 ....44 DD51
Inglewood, Croy. CR0 ..161 DY109
  Woking GU21 ....166 AV118
Inglewood Cl, E14 ......204 A8
  Hornchurch RM12 ......72 FK63
  Ilford IG6 ....49 ET51
Inglewood Copse, Brom.
  BR1 ....144 EL96
Inglewood Rd, NW6 ......64 DA64
  Bexleyheath DA7 ......107 FD84
Inglis Barracks, NW7 ....43 CX50
Inglis Rd, W5 ....80 CM73
  Croydon CR0 ....142 DT102
Inglis St, SE5 ....101 DP81
Ingoldsby Rd, Grav. DA12 ..131 GL88
Ingram Av, NW11 ....64 DC59
Ingram Cl, SE11 ....200 C8
  Stanmore HA7 ....41 CJ50
Ingram Rd, N2 ....64 DE56
  Dartford DA1 ....128 FL88
  Grays RM17 ....110 GD77
  Thornton Heath CR7 ....142 DQ95
Ingrams Cl, Walt. KT12 ..154 BW106
Ingram Way, Grnf. UB6 ..79 CD67
Ingrave Ho, Dag. RM9 ....88 EV67
Ingrave Rd, Brwd. CM13,
  CM15 ....54 FX47
  Romford RM1 ....71 FD56
Ingrave St, SW11 ......100 DD83
Ingrebourne Gdns, Upmin.
  RM14 ....72 FQ60
Ingrebourne Rd, Rain. RM13 ..89 FH70
Ingrebourne Valley Grn Way, Horn.
  RM12 ....72 FK64
Ingress Gdns, Green. DA9 ..129 FX85
Ingress St, W4
  off Devonshire Rd 98 CS78
Ingreway, Rom. RM3 ......52 FP52
Inigo Jones Rd, SE7 ....104 EL80
Inigo Pl, WC2 ....195 P10
Inkerman Rd, NW5 ....83 DH65
  Woking (Knap.) GU21 ..166 AS118
Inkerman Ter, W8
  off Allen St 100 DA76
Inkerman Way, Wok. GU21 ..166 AS118
Inks Grn, E4 ....47 EC50
Inman Rd, NW10 ....80 CS67
  SW18 ....120 DC87
Inmans Row, Wdf.Grn. IG8 ..48 EG49
Inner Circle, NW1 ......194 F3
Inner Pk Rd, SW19 ......119 CX88
Inner Ring E, Houns. (Hthrw.Air.)
  TW6 ....95 BP83
Inner Ring W, Houns. (Hthrw.Air.)
  TW6 ....94 BN83
Inner Temple La, EC4 ....196 D9
Innes Cl, SW20 ....139 CY96
Innes Gdns, SW15 ......119 CV86
Innes Yd, Croy. CR0
  off Whitgift St 142 DQ104
Inniskilling Rd, E13 ......86 EJ68
Innova Pk, Enf. EN3 ......31 DZ36
Innovation Cl, Wem. HA0 ..80 CL67
Innova Way, Enf. EN3 ....31 DZ36
Inskip Cl, E10 ....67 EB61
Inskip Dr, Horn. RM11 ....72 FL60
Inskip Rd, Dag. RM8 ......70 EX60
Institute of Contemporary
★ Arts (ICA), SW1 ......199 N2
Institute Pl, E8
  off Amhurst Rd 66 DV64
Institute Rd, Epp. CM16 ..18 EX29
Instone Cl, Wall. SM6 ..159 DL108
Instone Rd, Dart. DA1 ..128 FK87
Integer Gdns, E11
  off Forest Rd 67 ED59
Interchange E Ind Est, E5
  off Theydon Rd 66 DW60
International Av, Houns. TW5 ..96 BW78
International Trd Est, Sthl.
  UB2 ....95 BV76
Inveraray Pl, SE18 ......105 ER79
  off Old Mill Rd 105 ER79
Inver Cl, E5 off Theydon Rd ..66 DW61
Inverclyde Gdns, Rom. RM6 ..70 EW56
Inver Ct, W2 off Inverness Ter ..82 DB72
Inveresk Gdns, Wor.Pk. KT4 ..139 CT104
Inverforth Cl, NW3
  off North End Way 64 DC61
Inverforth Rd, N11 ......45 DH50
Inverine Rd, SE7 ....104 EH78
Invermore Pl, SE18 ....105 EQ77
Inverness Av, Enf. EN1 ..30 DS39
Inverness Dr, Ilf. IG6 ....49 ES51
Inverness Gdns, W8
  off Vicarage Gate 82 DB74
Inverness Ms, E16 ......87 EM74
  W2 off Inverness Ter 82 DB73
Inverness Pl, W2 ....82 DB73

Inverness Rd, N18
  off Aberdeen Rd 46 DV50
  Hounslow TW3 ....96 BZ84
  Southall UB2 ....96 BY77
  Worcester Park KT4 ....139 CX102
Inverness St, NW1 ......83 DH67
Inverness Ter, W2 ....82 DB73
Inverton Rd, SE15 ......103 DX84
Invicta Cl, Chis. BR7 ....125 EN92
  Feltham TW14
    off Westmacott Dr 115 BT88
Invicta Gro, Nthlt. UB5 ..78 BZ69
Invicta Plaza, SE1 ......200 F2
Invicta Rd, SE3 ....104 EG80
  Dartford DA2 ....128 FP86
Inville Rd, SE17 ....102 DR78
Inwen Ct, SE8 ....103 DY78
Inwood Av, Couls. CR5 ..175 DN120
  Hounslow TW3 ....96 CC83
Inwood Cl, Croy. CR0 ..143 DY103
Inwood Ct, Walt. KT12 ..136 BW103
Inwood Rd, Houns. TW3 ..96 CB84
Inworth St, SW11 ......100 DE82
Inworth Wk, N1
  off Popham St 84 DQ67
Iona Cl, SE6 ....123 EA87
  Morden SM4 ....140 DB101
Ion Sq, E2 off Hackney Rd ..84 DU68
Ipswich Rd, SW17 ......120 DG93
Ireland Cl, E6
  off Bradley Stone Rd 87 EM71
Ireland Pl, N22
  off Whittington Rd 45 DL52
Ireland Yd, EC4 ....196 G9
Irene Rd, SW6 ....100 DA81
  Cobham (Stoke D'Ab.)
    KT11 ....154 CA114
  Orpington BR6 ....145 ET101
Ireton Av, Walt. KT12 ..135 BS103
Ireton Cl, N10 ....44 DG52
Ireton Pl, Grays RM17
  off Russell Rd 110 GA77
Ireton St, E3 off Tidworth Rd ..85 EA70
Iris Av, Bex. DA5 ......126 EY85
Iris Cl, E6 ....86 EL70
  Brentwood CM15 ......54 FV43
  Croydon CR0 ....143 DX102
  Surbiton KT6 ....138 CM101
Iris Ct, Pnr. HA5 ....60 BW55
Iris Cres, Bexh. DA7 ....106 EZ79
Iris Path, Rom. RM3
  off Clematis Cl 52 FJ52
Iris Rd, Epsom (W.Ewell)
  KT19 ....156 CP106
Iris Wk, Edg. HA8 off Ash Cl ..42 CQ49
Iris Way, E4 ....47 DZ51
Irkdale Av, Enf. EN1 ......30 DT39
Iron Br Cl, NW10 ....62 CS64
  Southall UB2 ....78 CC74
Iron Br Rd, Uxb. UB11 ....94 BN75
  West Drayton UB7 ......94 BN75
Iron Mill La, Dart. DA1 ..107 FE84
Iron Mill Pl, SW18
  off Garratt La 120 DB86
  Dartford DA1 ....107 FF84
Iron Mill Rd, SW18 ......120 DB86
Ironmonger La, EC2 ....197 K9
Ironmonger Pas, EC1 ....197 J4
Ironmonger Row, EC1 ....197 J4
Ironmongers Pl, E14 ....204 A9
Ironside Cl, SE16 ......203 H4
Irons Way, Rom. RM5 ....51 FC52
Irvine Av, Har. HA3 ......61 CG55
Irvine Cl, N20 ....44 DE47
Irvine Gdns, S.Ock. RM15 ..91 FT72
Irvine Pl, Vir.W. GU25 ..132 AY99
Irvine Way, Orp. BR6 ..145 ET101
Irving Av, Nthlt. UB5 ....78 BX67
Irving Gro, SW9 ....101 DM82
Irving Ms, N1 off Alwyne Rd ..84 DQ65
Irving Rd, W14 ....99 CX76
Irving St, WC2 ....195 N10
Irving Wk, Swans. DA10 ..130 FY87
Irving Way, NW9 ....63 CT57
  Swanley BR8 ....147 FD96
Irwin Av, SE18 ....105 ES80
Irwin Cl, Uxb. UB10 ......58 BN62
Irwin Gdns, NW10 ....81 CV67
Isabel Gate, Wal.Cr. (Chsht.)
  EN8 ....15 DZ26
Isabel Hill Cl, Hmptn. TW12
  off Upper Sunbury Rd ..136 CB95
Isabella Cl, N14 ....45 DJ45
Isabella Ct, Rich. TW10
  off Grove Rd 118 CM86
Isabella Dr, Orp. BR6 ..163 EQ105
Isabella Rd, E9 ....66 DW64
Isabella St, SE1 ....200 F3
Isabelle Cl, Wal.Cr. EN7 ..13 DQ29
Isambard Cl, Uxb. UB8 ..76 BK69
Isambard Ms, E14 ......204 E7
Isambard Pl, SE16 ......202 G3
Isbell Gdns, Rom. RM1 ..51 FE52
Isel Way, SE22
  off East Dulwich Gro ..122 DS85
Isham Rd, SW16 ....141 DL96
Isis Cl, SW15 ....99 CW84
  Ruislip HA4 ....58 BQ58
Isis Dr, Upmin. RM14 ....73 FS58
Isis St, SW18 ....120 DC89
Island, The, Stai. (Wrays.)
  TW19 ....113 BA90
  West Drayton UB7 ......94 BH81
Island Cl, Stai. TW18 ..113 BE91
Island Fm Av, W.Mol. KT8 ..136 BZ99
Island Fm Rd, W.Mol. KT8 ..136 BZ99
ᴰᴸᴿ Island Gardens 204 D9
Island Rd, Mitch. CR4 ..120 DF94
Island Row, E14 ....85 DZ72
Isla Rd, SE18 ....105 EQ79
Islay Gdns, Houns. TW4 ..116 BX85
Islay Wk, N1 off Douglas Rd ..84 DQ66
Isledon Rd, N7 ....65 DN62
Islehurst Cl, Chis. BR7 ..145 EN95
ISLEWORTH 97 CF83
⇌ Isleworth 97 CF82

Isleworth Business Complex, Islw.
  TW7 off St. John's Rd . . .97 CF82
Isleworth Prom, Twick. TW1 . .97 CH84
ISLINGTON, N1 . . .83 DM67
Islington Grn, N1 . . .83 DP67
Islington High St, N1 . . .196 E1
Islington Pk Ms, N1
  off Islington Pk St . . .83 DN66
Islington Pk St, N1 . . .83 DN66
Islip Gdns, Edg. HA8 . . .42 CR52
  Northolt UB5 . . .78 BY66
Islip Manor Rd, Nthlt. UB5 . . .78 BY66
Islip St, NW5 . . .65 DJ64
Ismailia Rd, E7 . . .86 EH66
★ Ismaili Cen & Zamana Gall,
  SW7 . . .198 A8
Ismay Ct, Slou. SL2
  off Elliman Av . . .74 AS73
Isom Cl, E13
  off Belgrave Rd . . .86 EJ70
ISTEAD RISE, Grav. . . .130 GE94
Istead Ri, Grav. DA13 . . .131 GF94
Itchingwood Common Rd, Oxt.
  RH8 . . .188 EJ133
Ivanhoe Cl, Uxb. UB8 . . .76 BK71
Ivanhoe Dr, Har. HA3 . . .61 CG55
Ivanhoe Rd, SE5 . . .102 DT83
  Hounslow TW4 . . .96 BX83
Ivatt Pl, W14 . . .99 CZ78
Ivatt Way, N17 . . .65 DP55
Iveagh Av, NW10 . . .80 CN68
Iveagh Cl, E9 . . .85 DX67
  NW10 . . .80 CN68
  Northwood HA6 . . .39 BP53
Iveagh Rd, Wok. GU21 . . .166 AT118
Iveagh Ter, NW10
  off Iveagh Av . . .80 CN68
Ivedon Rd, Well. DA16 . . .106 EW82
Ive Fm Cl, E10 . . .67 EA61
Ive Fm La, E10 . . .67 EA61
Iveley Rd, SW4 . . .101 DJ82
IVER . . .75 BF72
⇌ Iver . . .93 BF75
Iverdale Cl, Iver SL0 . . .75 BC73
Ivere Dr, Barn. EN5 . . .28 DB44
IVER HEATH, Iver . . .75 BD69
Iverhurst Cl, Bexh. DA6 . . .126 EX85
Iver La, Iver SL0 . . .76 BH71
  Uxbridge UB8 . . .76 BH71
Iverna Ct, W8 . . .100 DA76
Iverna Gdns, W8 . . .100 DA76
  Feltham TW14 . . .115 BR88
Iver Rd, Brwd. CM15 . . .54 FV44
  Iver SL0 . . .76 BG72
Iverson Rd, NW6 . . .81 CZ65
Ivers Way, Croy. (New Adgtn.)
  CR0 . . .161 EB108
Ives Rd, Rom. RM1
  off Sims Cl . . .71 FF56
Ives Rd, E16 . . .86 EE71
  Slough SL3 . . .93 AZ76
Ives St, SW3 . . .198 C8
Ivestor Ter, SE23 . . .122 DW87
Ivimey St, E2 . . .84 DU69
Ivinghoe Cl, Enf. EN1 . . .30 DS40
  Watford WD25 . . .24 BX35
Ivinghoe Rd, Bushey WD23 . .41 CD45
  Dagenham RM8 . . .70 EV64
  Rickmansworth (Mill End)
  WD3 . . .38 BG45
Ivor Gro, SE9 . . .125 EP88
Ivor Pl, NW1 . . .194 D5
Ivor St, NW1 . . .83 DJ66
Ivorydown, Brom. BR1 . . .124 EG91
Ivory Sq, SW11
  off Gartons Way . . .100 DC83
Ivy Bower Cl, Green. DA9
  off Riverview Rd . . .129 FV85
Ivybridge Cl, Twick. TW1 . . .117 CG86
  Uxbridge UB8 . . .76 BL69
Ivybridge Est, Islw. TW7 . . .117 CF85
Ivybridge La, WC2 . . .200 A1
IVY CHIMNEYS, Epp. . . .17 ES32
Ivy Chimneys Rd, Epp. CM16 .17 ES32
Ivychurch Cl, SE20 . . .122 DW94
Ivychurch La, SE17 . . .201 P10
Ivy Cl, Dart. DA1 . . .128 FN87
  Gravesend DA12 . . .131 GJ90
  Harrow HA2 . . .60 BZ63
  Pinner HA5 . . .60 BW59
  Sunbury-on-Thames
  TW16 . . .136 BW96
Ivy Cotts, E14 off Grove Vil . .85 EB73
Ivy Ct, SE16 off Argyle Way . .202 D7
Ivy Cres, W4 . . .98 CQ77
Ivydale Rd, SE15 . . .103 DX83
  Carshalton SM5 . . .140 DF103
Ivyday Gro, SW16 . . .121 DM90
Ivydene, W.Mol. KT8 . . .136 BZ99
Ivydene Cl, Sutt. SM1 . . .158 DC105
Ivy Gdns, N8 . . .65 DL58
  Mitcham CR4 . . .141 DK97
Ivy Ho La, Sev. TN14 . . .181 FD118
Ivyhouse Rd, Dag. RM9 . . .88 EX65
Ivy Ho Rd, Uxb. UB10 . . .59 BP62
Ivy La, Houns. TW4 . . .96 BZ84
  Sevenoaks (Knock.) TN14 . .180 EY116
  Woking GU22 . . .167 BB118
Ivy Lea, Rick. WD3
  off Springwell Av . . .38 BG46
Ivy Lo La, Rom. RM3 . . .52 FP53
Ivy Mill Cl, Gdse. RH9 . . .186 DV132
Ivy Mill La, Gdse. RH9 . . .186 DU132
Ivymount Rd, SE27 . . .121 DN90
Ivy Pl, Surb. KT5
  off Alpha Rd . . .138 CM100
Ivy Rd, E16 off Pacific Rd . . .86 EG72
  E17 . . .67 EA58
  N14 . . .45 DJ45
  NW2 . . .63 CW63
  SE4 . . .103 DZ84
  SW17 off Tooting High St . .120 DE92
  Hounslow TW3 . . .96 CB84
  Surbiton KT6 . . .138 CN102
Ivy St, N1 . . .84 DS68
Ivy Wk, Dag. RM9 . . .88 EY65
Ixworth Pl, SW3 . . .198 B10

Izane Rd, Bexh. DA6 . . .106 EZ84

J

Jacaranda Cl, N.Mal. KT3 . . .138 CS97
Jacaranda Gro, E8 . . .84 DT66
Jackass La, Kes. BR2 . . .162 EH107
  Oxted (Tand.) RH8 . . .187 DZ131
Jack Barnett Way, N22 . . .45 DM54
Jack Clow Rd, E15 . . .86 EE68
Jack Cornwell St, E12 . . .69 EN63
Jack Dash Way, E6 . . .86 EL70
Jackets La, Nthwd. HA6 . . .39 BP53
  Uxbridge (Hare.) UB9 . . .38 BN52
Jacketts Fld, Abb.L. WD5 . . .7 BT31
Jack Goodchild Way, Kings.T. KT1
  off Kingston Rd . . .138 CP97
Jacklin Grn, Wdf.Grn. IG8 . . .48 EG49
Jackman Ms, NW10 . . .62 CS62
Jackmans La, Wok. GU21 . . .166 AU119
Jackman St, E8 . . .84 DV67
Jacks La, Uxb. (Hare.) UB9 . . .38 BG53
Jackson Cl, E9 . . .84 DW66
  Epsom KT18 . . .156 CR114
  Greenhithe DA9
  off Cowley Av . . .129 FU85
  Hornchurch RM11 . . .72 FM56
  Uxbridge UB10
  off Jackson Rd . . .76 BL66
Jackson Ct, E11
  off Brading Cres . . .68 EH60
Jackson Rd, N7 . . .65 DM63
  Barking IG11 . . .87 ER67
  Barnet EN4 . . .28 DE44
  Bromley BR2 . . .144 EL103
  Uxbridge UB10 . . .76 BL66
Jacksons Dr, Wal.Cr. EN7 . . .14 DU28
Jacksons La, N6 . . .64 DG59
Jacksons Pl, Croy. CR0
  off Cross Rd . . .142 DR102
Jackson St, SE18 . . .105 EN79
Jacksons Way, Croy. CR0 . . .143 EA104
Jackson Way, Sthl. UB2 . . .96 CB75
Jack Walker Ct, N5 . . .65 DP63
Jacob Ho, Erith DA18
  off Kale Rd . . .106 EX75
Jacobs Av, Rom. (Harold Wd.)
  RM3 . . .52 FL54
Jacobs Cl, Dag. RM10 . . .71 FB65
Jacobs Ho, E13 . . .86 EJ69
Jacobs La, Dart. (Hort.Kir.)
  DA4 . . .148 FQ97
Jacob St, SE1 . . .202 A4
Jacob's Well Ms, W1 . . .194 G8
Jacqueline Cl, Nthlt. UB5
  off Canford Av . . .78 BZ67
Jade Cl, E16 . . .86 EK72
  NW2 off Marble Dr . . .63 CX59
  Dagenham RM8 . . .70 EW60
Jaffe Rd, Ilf. IG1 . . .69 EQ60
Jaffray Pl, SE27
  off Chapel Rd . . .121 DP91
Jaffray Rd, Brom. BR2 . . .144 EK98
Jaggard Way, SW12 . . .120 DF87
Jagger Cl, Dart. DA2 . . .128 FQ87
Jago Cl, SE18 . . .105 EQ79
Jago Wk, SE5 . . .102 DR80
Jail La, West. (Bigg.H.) TN16 .178 EK116
Jamaica Rd, SE1 . . .202 A5
  SE16 . . .202 D6
  Thornton Heath CR7 . . .141 DP100
Jamaica St, E1 . . .84 DW72
James Av, NW2 . . .63 CW64
  Dagenham RM8 . . .70 EZ60
James Bedford Cl, Pnr. HA5 . .40 BW54
James Boswell Cl, SW16
  off Curtis Fld Rd . . .121 DN91
James Cl, E13
  off Richmond St . . .86 EG68
  NW11 off Woodlands . . .63 CY58
  Bushey WD23
  off Aldenham Rd . . .24 BY43
  Romford RM2 . . .71 FG57
James Collins Cl, W9
  off Fermoy Rd . . .81 CZ70
James Ct, N1
  off Morton Rd . . .84 DQ66
James Dudson Ct, NW10 . . .80 CQ66
James Gdns, N22 . . .45 DP52
James Hammett Ho, E2
  off Ravenscroft St . . .84 DT69
James Joyce Wk, SE24
  off Shakespeare Rd . . .101 DP84
James La, E10 . . .68 ED59
  E11 . . .67 ED58
James Lee Sq, Enf. EN3
  off Government Row . . .31 EA37
James Martin Cl, Uxb. (Denh.)
  UB9 . . .58 BG58
James Newman Ct, SE9
  off Great Harry Dr . . .125 EN90
Jameson Cl, W3
  off Acton La . . .98 CQ75
Jameson Ct, E2 . . .84 DW68
Jameson St, W8 . . .82 DA74
Jameson Wk, Wdf.Grn. IG8
  off Baddow Cl . . .48 EK51
James Pl, N17 . . .46 DT53
James Rd, Dart. DA1 . . .127 FG87
James's Cotts, Rich. TW9
  off Kew Rd . . .98 CN80
James Sinclair Pt, E13 . . .86 EJ67
James St, W1 . . .194 G8
  WC2 . . .196 A10
  Barking IG11 . . .87 EQ66
  Enfield EN1 . . .30 DT43
  Epping CM16 . . .17 ET28
  Hounslow TW3 . . .97 CD83
James Ter, SW14
  off Mullins Path . . .98 CR83
Jamestown Rd, NW1 . . .83 DH67
Jamestown Way, E14 . . .204 G1
James Watt Way, Erith DA8 . .107 FF79
James Yd, E4 . . .47 ED51

Jamieson Ho, Houns. TW4 . . .116 BZ87
Jamnagar Cl, Stai. TW18 . . .113 BF93
Jamuna Cl, E14 . . .85 DY71
Jane St, E1
  off Commercial Rd . . .84 DV72
Janet St, E14 . . .204 A6
Janeway Pl, SE16 . . .202 D5
Janeway St, SE16 . . .202 C5
Janice Ms, Ilf. IG1
  off Oakfield Rd . . .69 EP62
Janmead, Brwd. CM13 . . .55 GB45
Janoway Hill La, Wok. GU21 .166 AW119
Jansen Wk, SW11
  off Hope St . . .100 DD84
Janson Cl, E15 off Janson Rd . .68 EE64
  NW10 . . .62 CR62
Janson Rd, E15 . . .68 EE64
Jansons Rd, N15 . . .66 DS55
Japan Cres, N4 . . .65 DM59
Japan Rd, Rom. RM6 . . .70 EX58
Japonica Cl, Wok. GU21 . . .166 AW118
Jardine Ho, E1
  off London Rd Purfleet . . .109 FR79
Jarrah Cotts, Purf. RM19
  off London Rd Purfleet . . .109 FR79
Jarrett Cl, SW2 . . .121 DP88
Jarrow Cl, Mord. SM4 . . .140 DB99
Jarrow Rd, N17 . . .66 DV56
  SE16 . . .202 F9
  Romford RM6 . . .70 EW58
Jarrow Way, E9 . . .67 DY63
Jarvis Cleys, Wal.Cr. (Chsht.)
  EN7 . . .14 DT26
Jarvis Cl, Bark. IG11
  off Westbury Rd . . .87 ER67
  Barnet EN5 . . .27 CX43
Jarvis Rd, SE22 . . .102 DS84
  South Croydon CR2 . . .160 DR107
Jarvis Way, Rom. (Harold Wd.)
  RM3 . . .52 FL54
Jasmin Cl, Nthwd. HA6 . . .39 BT53
Jasmine Cl, Ilf. IG1 . . .69 EP64
  Orpington BR6 . . .145 EP102
  Southall UB1 . . .78 BY73
  Woking GU21 . . .166 AT116
Jasmine Gdns, Croy. CR0 . . .143 EB104
  Harrow HA2 . . .60 CA61
Jasmine Gro, SE20 . . .142 DV95
Jasmine Rd, Rom. (Rush Grn.)
  RM7 . . .71 FE61
Jasmine Ter, West Dr. UB7 . . .94 BN75
Jasmine Way, E.Mol. KT8
  off Hampton Ct Way . . .137 CE98
Jasmin Rd, Epsom KT19 . . .156 CP106
Jason Cl, Brwd. CM14 . . .54 FT49
  Weybridge KT13 . . .153 BQ106
Jason Ct, W1
  off Marylebone La . . .82 DG72
Jasons Hill, Chesh. HP5 . . .4 AV30
Jason Wk, SE9 . . .125 EN91
Jasper Cl, Enf. EN3 . . .30 DW38
Jasper Pas, SE19 . . .122 DT93
Jasper Rd, E16 . . .86 EK72
  SE19 . . .122 DT92
Jasper Wk, N1 . . .197 K2
Javelin Way, Nthlt. UB5 . . .78 BX69
Jaycroft, Enf. EN2
  off The Ridgeway . . .29 DN39
Jay Gdns, Chis. BR7 . . .125 EM91
Jay Ms, SW7 . . .100 DC75
Jays Covert, Couls. CR5 . . .174 DG119
Jean Batten Cl, Wall. SM6
  off Lancastrian Rd . . .159 DM108
Jebb Av, SW2 . . .121 DL86
Jebb St, E3 . . .85 EA68
Jedburgh Rd, E13 . . .86 EJ69
Jedburgh St, SW11 . . .100 DG84
Jeddo Rd, W12 . . .99 CT75
Jefferson Cl, W13 . . .97 CH76
  Ilford IG2 . . .69 EP57
  Slough SL3 . . .93 BA77
Jefferson Wk, SE18
  off Kempt St . . .105 EN79
Jeffreys Pl, NW1
  off Jeffreys St . . .83 DJ66
Jeffreys Rd, SW4 . . .101 DL82
  Enfield EN3 . . .31 DZ41
Jeffreys St, NW1 . . .83 DH66
Jeffreys Wk, SW4 . . .101 DL82
Jeffries Ho, NW10 . . .80 CR67
Jeffs Cl, Hmptn. TW12
  off Uxbridge Rd . . .116 CB93
Jeffs Rd, Sutt. SM1 . . .157 CZ105
Jeger Av, E2 . . .84 DT67
Jeken Rd, SE9 . . .104 EJ84
Jelf Rd, SW2 . . .121 DN86
Jellicoe Av, Grav. DA12 . . .131 GJ90
Jellicoe Av W, Grav. DA12
  off Kitchener Av . . .131 GJ90
Jellicoe Gdns, Stan. HA7 . . .41 CF51
Jellicoe Rd, E13
  off Jutland Rd . . .86 EG70
  N17 . . .46 DR52
  Watford WD18 . . .23 BU44
Jemmett Cl, Kings.T. KT2 . . .138 CP96
Jengar Cl, Sutt. SM1 . . .158 DB105
Jenkins La, E6 . . .87 EN68
  Barking IG11 . . .87 EP68
Jenkins Rd, E13 . . .86 EH70
Jenner Av, W3 . . .80 CR71
Jenner Ho, SE3 . . .104 EE79
Jenner Pl, SW13 . . .99 CV79
Jenner Rd, N16 . . .66 DT61
Jennett Rd, Croy. CR0 . . .141 DN104
Jennifer Rd, Brom. BR1 . . .124 EF90
Jennings Cl, Add. (New Haw)
  KT15 off Woodham La . . .152 BJ109
  Surbiton KT6 . . .137 CJ101
Jennings Rd, SE22 . . .122 DT86
Jennings Way, Barn. EN5 . . .27 CW41
Jenningtree Rd, Erith DA8 . . .107 FH80
Jenningtree Way, Belv. DA17 .107 FC75
Jenny Hammond Cl, E11
  off Newcomen Rd . . .68 EF62
Jenny Path, Rom. RM3 . . .52 FK52

Jennys Way, Couls. CR5 . . .175 DJ122
Jenson Way, SE19 . . .122 DT94
Jenton Av, Bexh. DA7 . . .106 EY81
Jephson Rd, E7 . . .86 EJ66
Jephson St, SE5
  off Grove La . . .102 DR81
Jeppos La, Mitch. CR4 . . .140 DF98
Jepps Cl, Wal.Cr. EN7
  off Little Gro Av . . .14 DS27
Jerdan Pl, SW6 . . .100 DA80
Jeremiah St, E14 . . .85 EB72
Jeremys Grn, N18 . . .46 DV49
Jermyn St, SW1 . . .199 K2
Jerningham Av, Ilf. IG5 . . .49 EP54
  NW10 . . .62 CR62
Jerningham Rd, SE14 . . .103 DY82
Jerome Cres, NW8 . . .194 B4
Jerome Pl, Kings.T. KT1
  off Wadbrook St . . .137 CK96
Jerome St, E1 . . .197 P6
Jerrard St, N1 . . .197 N1
  SE13 . . .103 EB83
Jersey Av, Stan. HA7 . . .41 CH54
Jersey Cl, Cher. KT16 . . .133 BF104
Jersey Dr, Orp. BR5 . . .145 ER100
Jersey Ho, Enf. EN3
  off Eastfield Rd . . .31 DX38
Jersey Par, Houns. TW5 . . .96 CB81
Jersey Rd, E11 . . .67 ED60
  E16 off Prince Regent La . . .86 EJ72
  SW17 . . .121 DH93
  W7 . . .97 CG75
  Hounslow TW3, TW5 . . .96 CB81
  Ilford IG1 . . .69 EP63
  Isleworth TW7 . . .97 CE79
  Rainham RM13 . . .89 FG66
Jersey St, E2
  off Bethnal Grn Rd . . .84 DV69
Jerviston Gdns, SW16 . . .121 DN93
Jervis Av, Enf. EN3 . . .31 DY35
Jervis Ct, W1 . . .195 J9
Jesmond Av, Wem. HA9 . . .80 CM65
Jesmond Cl, Mitch. CR4 . . .141 DH97
Jesmond Rd, Croy. CR0 . . .142 DT101
Jesmond Way, Stan. HA7 . . .42 CL50
Jessam Av, E5 . . .66 DV60
Jessamine Pl, Dart. DA2 . . .128 FQ87
Jessamine Rd, W7 . . .79 CE74
Jessamine Ter, Swan. BR8
  off Birchwood Rd . . .147 FC95
Jessamy Rd, Wey. KT13 . . .135 BP103
Jessel Dr, Loug. IG10 . . .33 EQ39
Jesse Rd, E10 . . .67 EC60
Jessett Cl, Erith DA8
  off West St . . .107 FD77
Jessica Rd, SW18 . . .120 DC86
Jessie Blythe La, N19 . . .65 DL59
Jessiman Ter, Shep. TW17 . . .134 BN99
Jessop Av, Sthl. UB2 . . .96 BZ77
Jessop Rd, SE24
  off Milkwood Rd . . .101 DP84
Jessop Sq, E14
  off Heron Quay . . .85 EA74
Jessops Way, Croy. CR0 . . .141 DJ100
Jessup Cl, SE18 . . .105 EQ77
Jetstar Way, Nthlt. UB5 . . .78 BY69
Jetty Wk, Grays RM17 . . .110 GA79
Jevington Way, SE12 . . .124 EH88
Jewel Rd, E17 . . .67 EA55
Jewels Hill, West. (Bigg.H.)
  TN16 . . .162 EG112
★ Jewel Twr, Houses of
  Parliament, SW1 . . .199 P6
✡ Jewish Mus, NW1 . . .83 DH67
Jewry St, EC3 . . .197 P9
Jew's Row, SW18 . . .100 DB84
Jews Wk, SE26 . . .122 DV91
Jeymer Av, NW2 . . .63 CV64
Jeymer Dr, Grnf. UB6 . . .78 CC67
Jeypore Pas, SW18
  off Jeypore Rd . . .120 DC86
Jeypore Rd, SW18 . . .120 DC86
Jillian Cl, Hmptn. TW12 . . .116 CA94
Jim Bradley Cl, SE18
  off John Wilson St . . .105 EN77
Jim Griffiths Ho, SW6
  off Clem Attlee Ct . . .99 CZ79
Joan Cres, SE9 . . .124 EK87
Joan Gdns, Dag. RM8 . . .70 EY61
Joan Rd, Dag. RM8 . . .70 EY61
Joan St, SE1 . . .200 F3
Jocelyn Rd, Rich. TW9 . . .98 CL83
Jocelyn St, SE15 . . .102 DU81
Jockey's Flds, WC1 . . .196 C6
Jodane St, SE8 . . .203 M9
Jodrell Cl, Islw. TW7 . . .97 CG81
Jodrell Rd, E3 . . .85 DZ67
Jodrell Way, Grays (W.Thur.)
  RM20 . . .109 FT78
Joel St, Nthwd. HA6 . . .59 BU55
  Pinner HA5 . . .59 BU55
Johanna St, SE1 . . .200 D5
John Adam St, WC2 . . .200 A1
John Aird Ct, W2 . . .82 DC71
John Archer Way, SW18 . . .120 DD86
John Ashby Cl, SW2 . . .121 DL86
John Austin Cl, Kings.T. KT2
  off Queen Elizabeth Rd . . .138 CM95
John Barnes Wk, E15 . . .86 EF65
John Bradshaw Rd, N14
  off High St . . .45 DK46
John Burns Dr, Bark. IG11 . . .87 ES66
Johnby Cl, Enf. EN3
  off Manly Dixon Dr . . .31 DY37
John Campbell Rd, N16 . . .66 DS64
John Carpenter St, EC4 . . .196 F10
John Cobb Rd, Wey. KT13 . . .152 BN108
John Cornwell VC Ho, E12 . . .69 EN64
John Drinkwater Cl, E11
  off Browning Rd . . .68 EF59
John Felton Rd, SE16 . . .202 B5
John Fisher St, E1 . . .84 DU73
John Gooch Dr, Enf. EN2 . . .29 DP39
John Harrison Way, SE10 . . .205 K7
John Horner Ms, N1
  off Frome St . . .84 DQ68

John Islip St, SW1 . . .199 P9
John Keats Ho, N22 . . .45 DM52
John Maurice Cl, SE17 . . .201 K8
John McKenna Wk, SE16 . . .202 C6
John Newton Ct, Well. DA16
  off Danson La . . .106 EV83
John Parker Cl, Dag. RM10 . . .89 FB66
John Parker Sq, SW11
  off Thomas Baines Rd . . .100 DD83
John Penn St, SE13 . . .103 EB81
John Perrin Pl, Har. HA3 . . .62 CL59
John Princes St, W1 . . .195 J8
John Rennie Wk, E1 . . .202 E2
John Roll Way, SE16 . . .202 D7
John Ruskin St, SE5 . . .101 DP80
Johns Av, NW4 . . .63 CW56
Johns Cl, Ashf. TW15 . . .115 BQ91
Johns Ct, Sutt. SM2
  off Mulgrave Rd . . .158 DB107
Johnsdale, Oxt. RH8 . . .188 EF129
John Silkin La, SE8 . . .203 J9
Johns La, Mord. SM4 . . .140 DC99
John's Ms, WC1 . . .196 C5
John Smith Av, SW6 . . .99 CZ80
Johnson Cl, E8 . . .84 DU67
  Gravesend (Nthflt.) DA11 . .130 GD90
Johnson Rd, NW10
  off Milton Av . . .80 CR67
  Bromley BR2 . . .144 EK99
  Croydon CR0 . . .142 DR101
  Hounslow TW5 . . .96 BW80
Johnsons Av, Sev. (Bad.Mt.)
  TN14 . . .181 FB110
Johnsons Cl, Cars. SM5 . . .140 DF104
Johnson's Ct, EC4
  off Fleet St . . .83 DN72
Johnsons Ct, Sev. (Seal) TN15
  off School La . . .191 FM121
Johnsons Dr, Hmptn. TW12 . .136 CC95
Johnson's Pl, SW1 . . .101 DJ78
Johnson St, E1 off Cable St . . .84 DW73
  Southall UB2 . . .96 BW76
Johnsons Way, NW10 . . .80 CP70
  Greenhithe DA9 . . .129 FW86
Johnson's Yd, Uxb. UB8
  off Redford Way . . .76 BJ66
John's Pl, E1
  off Damien St . . .84 DV72
Johns Rd, West. (Tats.) TN16 .178 EK120
John's Ter, Croy. CR0 . . .142 DR102
  Romford RM3 . . .52 FP51
Johnston Cl, SW9
  off Hackford Rd . . .101 DM81
Johnstone Rd, E6 . . .87 EM69
Johnston Rd, Wdf.Grn. IG8 . . .48 EG50
Johnston Ter, NW2
  off Kara Way . . .63 CX62
John St, E15 . . .86 EF67
  SE25 . . .142 DU98
  WC1 . . .196 C5
  Enfield EN1 . . .30 DT43
  Grays RM17 . . .110 GC79
  Hounslow TW3 . . .96 BY82
Johns Wk, Whyt. CR3 . . .176 DU119
John Trundle Ct, EC2
  off The Barbican . . .84 DQ71
John Walsh Twr, E11 . . .68 EF61
John Williams Cl, SE14 . . .103 DX79
  Kingston upon Thames KT2
  off Henry Macaulay Av . . .137 CK95
John Wilson St, SE18 . . .105 EN76
John Woolley Cl, SE13 . . .104 EE84
Joiner's Arms Yd, SE5
  off Denmark Hill . . .102 DR81
Joiners Cl, Chesh. (Ley Hill)
  HP5 . . .4 AV30
  Gerrards Cross (Chal.St.P.)
  SL9 . . .37 AZ52
Joiners La, Ger.Cr. (Chal.St.P.)
  SL9 . . .36 AY53
Joiners Pl, N5
  off Leconfield Rd . . .66 DR63
Joiner St, SE1 . . .201 L3
Joiners Way, Ger.Cr. (Chal.St.P.)
  SL9 . . .36 AY52
Joinville Pl, Add. KT15 . . .152 BK105
Jolliffe Rd, Red. RH1 . . .185 DJ126
Jollys La, Har. HA2 . . .61 CD60
  Hayes UB4 . . .78 BX71
Jonathan Ct, W4
  off Windmill Rd . . .98 CS77
Jonathan St, SE11 . . .200 B10
Jones Rd, E13 . . .86 EH70
  off Holborn Rd
  Waltham Cross (Chsht.)
  EN7 . . .13 DP30
Jones St, W1 . . .199 H1
Jones Wk, Rich. TW10
  off Pyrland Rd . . .118 CM86
Jonquil Gdns, Hmptn. TW12
  off Partridge Rd . . .116 BZ93
Jonson Cl, Hayes UB4 . . .77 BU71
  Mitcham CR4 . . .141 DH98
Jordan Cl, Dag. RM10
  off Muggeridge Rd . . .71 FB63
  Harrow HA2
  off Hamilton Cres . . .60 BZ62
  South Croydon CR2 . . .160 DT111
  Watford WD25 . . .23 BT35
Jordan Ct, SW15
  off Charlwood Rd . . .99 CX84
Jordan Rd, Grnf. UB6 . . .79 CH67
JORDANS, Beac. . . .36 AT52
Jordans Cl, Islw. TW7 . . .97 CE81
  Staines (Stanw.) TW19 . . .114 BJ87
Jordans La, Beac. (Jordans)
  HP9 . . .36 AS53
Jordans Rd, Rick. WD3 . . .38 BG45
Jordans Way, Beac. (Jordans)
  HP9 . . .36 AT51
  Rainham RM13 . . .90 FK68
  St. Albans (Brick.Wd.) AL2 . . .8 BZ30
Joseph Av, W3 . . .80 CR72
Josephine Av, SW2 . . .121 DM85

A B C D E F G H I J K L M N O P Q R S T U V W X Y Z

Jos - Ken

Kennel La, Lthd. (Fetch.)	
KT22 . . . . .170 CC122	
Kennelwood Cres, Croy.	
(New Adgtn.) CR0 . . . .161 ED111	

Kennel La, Lthd. (Fetch.)
  KT22 . . . . .170 CC122
Kennelwood Cres, Croy.
  (New Adgtn.) CR0 . . . . . .161 ED111
Kennet Cl, SW11
  off Maysoule Rd 100 DD84
  Upminster RM14 . . . . .73 FS58
Kennet Grn, S.Ock. RM15 . . .73 FV73
Kenneth Av, Ilf. IG1 . . . . . .69 EP63
Kenneth Cres, NW2 . . . . . . .63 CV64
Kenneth Gdns, Stan. HA7 . . .41 CG51
Kenneth More Rd, Ilf. IG1
  off Oakfield Rd 69 EP62
Kenneth Rd, Bans. SM7 . . .174 DD115
  Romford RM6 . . . . .70 EX59
Kenneth Robbins Ho, N17 . .46 DV52
Kennet Rd, W9 . . . . .81 CZ70
  Dartford DA1 . . . . .107 FG83
  Isleworth TW7 . . . . .97 CF83
Kennet Sq, Mitch. CR4 . . . .140 DE95
Kennet St, E1 . . . . .202 C2
Kennett Ct, Swan. BR8 . . . .147 FE97
Kennett Dr, Hayes UB4 . . . .78 BY71
Kennett Rd, Slou. SL3 . . . . .93 BB76
Kennet Wf La, EC4 . . . . . .197 J10
Kenninghall Rd, E5 . . . . . . .66 DU62
  N18 . . . . .46 DW50
Kenning St, SE16 . . . . . . .202 G4
Kennings Way, SE11 . . . . . .200 F10
Kenning Ter, N1 . . . . .84 DS67
KENNINGTON, SE11 . . . . . .101 DN79
⊖ Kennington 200 F10
Kennington Grn, SE11
  off Montford Pl 101 DN78
Kennington Gro, SE11
  off Oval Way 101 DM79
Kennington La, SE11 . . . . . .200 E10
Kennington Oval, SE11 . . . .101 DM79
Kennington Pk Est, SE11
  off Harleyford Rd 101 DN79
Kennington Pk Gdns, SE11 . .101 DP79
Kennington Pk Pl, SE11 . . . .101 DN79
Kennington Pk Rd, SE11 . . .101 DN79
Kennington Rd, SE1 . . . . . .200 D6
  SE11 . . . . .200 D7
Kenny Dr, Cars. SM5 . . . . . .158 DF109
Kenny Rd, NW7 . . . . .43 CY50
Kenrick Pl, W1 . . . . .194 F6
Kenrick Sq, Red. (Bletch.)
  RH1 . . . . .186 DS133
KENSAL GREEN, NW10 . . . . .81 CW69
≷ Kensal Green 81 CW69
⊖ Kensal Green 81 CW69
★ Kensal Green Cem, W10 . .81 CW69
KENSAL RISE, NW6 . . . . . . .81 CX68
≷ Kensal Rise 81 CX68
Kensal Rd, W10 . . . . .81 CY70
KENSAL TOWN, W10 . . . . . .81 CX69
KENSINGTON, W8 . . . . .99 CZ75
Kensington Av, E12 . . . . . . .86 EL65
  Thornton Heath CR7 . . . . .141 DN95
  Watford WD18 . . . . .23 BT42
Kensington Ch Ct, W8 . . . . .100 DB75
Kensington Ch St, W8 . . . . .82 DA74
Kensington Ch Wk, W8 . . . .100 DB75
Kensington Cl, N11 . . . . . . .44 DG51
Kensington Ct, NW7
  off Grenville Pl 42 CR50
  W8 . . . . .100 DB75
Kensington Ct Gdns, W8
  off Kensington Ct Pl 100 DB76
Kensington Ct Ms, W8
  off Kensington Ct Pl 100 DB76
Kensington Ct Pl, W8 . . . . .100 DB76
Kensington Dr, Wdf.Grn. IG8 . .48 EK53
★ Kensington Gdns, W2 . . . .82 DC74
Kensington Gdns, W2 . . . . . .82 DB74
  Ilford IG1 . . . . .69 EM61
  Kingston upon Thames KT1
  off Portsmouth Rd 137 CK97
Kensington Gdns Sq, W2 . . .82 DB72
Kensington Gate, W8 . . . . . .100 DC76
Kensington Gore, SW7 . . . . .100 DD75
Kensington Hall Gdns, W14
  off Beaumont Av 99 CZ78
Kensington High St, W8 . . . .100 DA76
  W14 . . . . .99 CY77
Kensington Mall, W8 . . . . . .82 DA74
≷ Kensington (Olympia) 99 CY76
⊖ Kensington (Olympia) 99 CY76
★ Kensington Palace, W8 . . .100 DB75
Kensington Palace Gdns, W8 . .82 DB74
Kensington Pk Gdns, W11 . . .81 CZ73
Kensington Pk Ms, W11
  off Kensington Pk Rd 81 CZ72
Kensington Pk Rd, W11 . . . .81 CZ73
Kensington Pl, W8 . . . . .82 DA74
Kensington Rd, SW7 . . . . . .198 A5
  W8 . . . . .100 DB75
  Brentwood CM15 . . . . .54 FU44
  Northolt UB5 . . . . .78 CA69
  Romford RM7 . . . . .71 FC58
Kensington Sq, W8 . . . . . . .100 DB75
Kensington Ter, S.Croy. CR2
  off Sanderstead Rd 160 DR108
Kensington Way, Borwd. WD6 .26 CR41
Kent Av, W13 . . . . .79 CH71
  Dagenham RM9 . . . . .88 FA70
  Welling DA16 . . . . .125 ET85
Kent Cl, Borwd. WD6 . . . . . .26 CR38
  Mitcham CR4 . . . . .141 DL98
  Orpington BR6 . . . . .163 ES107
  Staines TW18 . . . . .114 BK93
  Uxbridge UB8 . . . . .76 BJ65
Kent Dr, Barn. EN4 . . . . . . .28 DG42
  Hornchurch RM12 . . . . .72 FK63
  Teddington TW11 . . . . . . .117 CE92
Kentford Way, Nthlt. UB5 . . .78 BY67
Kent Gdns, W13 . . . . .79 CH71
  Ruislip HA4 . . . . .59 BV58
Kent Gate Way, Croy. CR0 . .161 EA106
KENT HATCH, Eden. 189 EP131
Kent Hatch Rd, Eden. (Crock.H.)
  TN8 . . . . .189 EM131
  Oxted RH8 . . . . .188 EJ129
≷ Kent House 143 DY95
Kent Ho La, Beck. BR3 . . . .123 DY92

Kent Ho Rd, SE26 . . . . .143 DX95
  Beck. BR3 . . . . .123 DY92
Kentish Bldgs, SE1 . . . . . . .201 K3
Kentish La, Hat. AL9 . . . . . .12 DC25
Kentish Rd, Belv. DA17 . . . .106 FA77
KENTISH TOWN, NW5 . . . . . .83 DJ65
≷ Kentish Town 65 DJ64
⊖ Kentish Town 65 DJ64
Kentish Town Rd, NW1 . . . . .83 DH66
  NW5 . . . . .83 DH66
≷ Kentish Town West 82 DG65
Kentish Way, Brom. BR1 . . .144 EG96
Kentlea Rd, SE28 . . . . .105 ES75
Kentmere Rd, SE18 . . . . . . .105 ES77
KENTON, Har. 61 CH57
≷ Kenton 61 CH58
⊖ Kenton 61 CH58
Kenton Av, Har. HA1 . . . . . .61 CF59
  Southall UB1 . . . . .78 CA73
  Sunbury-on-Thames
  TW16 . . . . .136 BY96
Kenton Ct, W14
  off Kensington High St 99 CZ76
Kenton Gdns, Har. HA3 . . . .61 CJ57
Kenton La, Har. HA3 . . . . . .61 CJ55
Kenton Pk Av, Har. HA3 . . . .61 CK56
Kenton Pk Cl, Har. HA3 . . . .61 CJ56
Kenton Pk Cres, Har. HA3 . .61 CK56
Kenton Pk Rd, Har. HA3 . . . .61 CJ56
Kenton Rd, E9 . . . . .85 DX65
  Harrow HA1, HA3 . . . . . . .61 CK57
Kenton St, WC1 . . . . .195 P4
Kenton Way, Hayes UB4
  off Exmouth Rd 77 BS69
  Woking GU21 . . . . .166 AT117
Kent Pas, NW1 . . . . .194 D4
Kent Rd, N21 . . . . .46 DR46
  W4 . . . . .98 CQ76
  Dagenham RM10 . . . . .71 FB64
  Dartford DA1 . . . . .128 FK86
  East Molesey KT8 . . . . . . .136 CC98
  Gravesend DA11 . . . . .131 GG88
  Grays RM17 . . . . .110 GC79
  Kingston upon Thames KT1
  off The Bittoms 137 CK97
  Longfield DA3 . . . . .149 FX96
  Orpington BR5 . . . . .146 EV100
  Richmond TW9 . . . . .98 CN80
  West Wickham BR4 . . . . . .143 EB102
  Woking GU22 . . . . .167 BB116
Kents Pas, Hmptn. TW12 . . .136 BZ95
Kent St, E2 . . . . .84 DT68
  E13 . . . . .86 EJ69
Kent Ter, NW1 . . . . .194 C3
Kent Twr, SE20 . . . . .122 DV94
Kent Vw, S.Ock. (Aveley)
  RM15 . . . . .108 FQ75
Kent Vw Gdns, Ilf. IG3 . . . . .69 ES61
Kent Wk, SW9
  off Moorland Rd 101 DP84
Kent Way, Surb. KT6 . . . . . .138 CL104
Kentwode Grn, SW13 . . . . . .99 CU80
Kent Yd, SW7 . . . . .198 C5
Kenver Av, N12 . . . . .44 DD51
Kenward Rd, SE9 . . . . .124 EJ85
Kenway, Rain. RM13 . . . . . .90 FJ69
Kenway Cl, Rain. RM13
  off Kenway 90 FJ69
Kenway Dr, Amer. HP7 . . . . .20 AV39
Kenway Rd, SW5 . . . . .100 DB77
Kenway Wk, Rain. RM13
  off Kenway 90 FK69
Kenwood Av, N14 . . . . .29 DK43
  SE14 *off Besson St* 103 DX81
Kenwood Cl, NW3 . . . . .64 DD60
  West Drayton UB7 . . . . . . .94 BN79
Kenwood Dr, Beck. BR3 . . . .143 EC97
  Rickmansworth (Mill End)
  WD3 . . . . .37 BF47
  Walton-on-Thames KT12 . .153 BV107
Kenwood Gdns, E18 . . . . . . .68 EH55
  Ilford IG2 . . . . .69 EN56
★ Kenwood Ho (The Iveagh
  Bequest), NW3 . . . . .64 DE60
Kenwood Pk, Wey. KT13 . . .153 BR107
Kenwood Ridge, Ken. CR8 . .175 DP117
Kenwood Rd, N6 . . . . .64 DF58
  N9 . . . . .46 DU46
Kenworth Cl, Wal.Cr. EN8 . . .15 DX33
Kenworthy Rd, E9 . . . . .67 DY64
Kenwyn Dr, NW2 . . . . .62 CS62
Kenwyn Rd, SW4 . . . . .101 DK84
  SW20 . . . . .139 CW95
  Dartford DA1 . . . . .128 FK85
Kenya Rd, SE7 . . . . .104 EK80
Kenyngton Dr, Sun. TW16 . .115 BU92
Kenyngton Pl, Har. HA3 . . . .61 CJ57
Kenyon St, SW6 . . . . .99 CX81
Keogh Rd, E15 . . . . .86 EE65
Kepler Rd, SW4 . . . . .101 DL84
Keppel Rd, E6 . . . . .87 EM66
  Dagenham RM9 . . . . .70 EY63
Keppel Row, SE1 . . . . .201 H3
Keppel Spur, Wind. (Old Wind.)
  SL4 . . . . .112 AV87
Keppel St, WC1 . . . . .195 N6
Kerbela St, E2 *off Cheshire St* .84 DU70
Kerbey St, E14 . . . . .85 EB72
Kerdistone Cl, Pot.B. EN6 . . .12 DB30
Kerfield Cres, SE5 . . . . .102 DR81
Kerfield Pl, SE5 . . . . .102 DR81
Kernow Cl, Horn. RM12 . . . .72 FL61
Kerri Cl, Barn. EN5 . . . . . . .27 CW42
Kerridge Ct, N1 . . . . .84 DS65
Kerrill Av, Couls. CR5 . . . . .175 DN119
Kerrison Rd, E15 . . . . .85 ED67
  SW11 . . . . .100 DE83
  W5 . . . . .79 CK74
Kerrison Vil, W5
  off Kerrison Pl 79 CK74
Kerry Av, S.Ock. (Aveley)
  RM15 . . . . .108 FM75
  Stanmore HA7 . . . . .41 CK49
Kerry Cl, E16 . . . . .86 EH72

Kerry Cl, N13 . . . . .45 DM47
  Upminster RM14 . . . . .73 FT59
Kerry Ct, Stan. HA7 . . . . . . .41 CK49
Kerry Dr, Upmin. RM14 . . . .73 FT59
Kerry Path, SE14
  off Kerry Rd 103 DZ79
Kerry Rd, SE14 . . . . .103 DZ79
Kerry Ter, Wok. GU21 . . . . .167 BB116
Kersey Dr, S.Croy. CR2 . . . .160 DW112
Kersey Gdns, SE9 . . . . .124 EK85
  Romford RM3 . . . . .52 FL53
Kersfield Rd, SW15 . . . . . . .119 CX86
Kershaw Cl, SW18 . . . . .100 DD86
  Grays (Chaff.Hun.) RM16 . .109 FW77
  Hornchurch RM11 . . . . . . .72 FL59
Kershaw Rd, Dag. RM10 . . . .70 FA62
Kersley Ms, SW11 . . . . .100 DF82
Kersley Rd, N16 . . . . .66 DS63
Kersley St, SW11 . . . . .100 DF82
Kerstin Cl, Hayes UB3
  off St. Mary's Rd 77 BT73
Kerswell Cl, N15 . . . . .66 DS57
Kerwick Cl, N7
  off Sutterton St 83 DM66
Keslake Rd, NW6 . . . . .81 CX68
Kessock Cl, N17 . . . . .66 DV57
Kesteven Cl, Ilf. IG6 . . . . . . .49 ET51
Kestlake Rd, Bex. DA5
  off East Rochester Way . . .126 EW86
KESTON 162 EJ106
Keston Av, Add. (New Haw)
  KT15 . . . . .152 BG111
  Coulsdon CR5 . . . . .175 DN119
  Keston BR2 . . . . .162 EJ106
Keston Cl, N18 . . . . .46 DR48
  Welling DA16 . . . . .106 EW80
Keston Gdns, Kes. BR2 . . . .162 EJ105
Keston Ms, Wat. WD17
  off Nascot Rd 23 BV40
Keston Pk Cl, Kes. BR2 . . . .145 EM104
Keston Rd, N17 . . . . .66 DR55
  SE15 . . . . .102 DU83
  Thornton Heath CR7 . . . . .141 DN100
Kestral Ct, Wall. SM6
  off Carew Rd 159 DJ106
Kestrel Av, E6 *off Swan App* .86 EL71
  SE24 . . . . .121 DP85
  Staines TW18 . . . . .113 BF90
Kestrel Cl, NW9 . . . . .42 CS54
  NW10 . . . . .62 CR64
  Epsom KT19
  off Abbots Av 156 CN111
  Hornchurch RM12 . . . . . . .89 FH66
  Ilford IG6 . . . . .50 EW49
  Kingston upon Thames
  KT2 . . . . .117 CK91
  Watford WD25 . . . . .8 BY34
Kestrel Ho, EC1 . . . . .197 H2
  W13 . . . . .79 CF70
  Enfield EN3 *off Alma Rd* . . .31 DX43
Kestrel Pl, SE14
  off Milton Ct Rd 103 DY79
Kestrel Rd, Wal.Abb. EN9 . . .16 EG34
Kestrels, The, St.Alb. AL2
  off Bucknalls Dr 8 BZ31
Kestrel Way, Croy. (New Adgtn.)
  CR0 . . . . .161 ED109
  Hayes UB3 *off Betam Rd* . . .95 BR75
Keswick Av, SW15 . . . . .118 CS92
  SW19 . . . . .140 DA96
  Hornchurch RM11 . . . . . . .72 FK60
Keswick Bdy, SW15
  off Upper Richmond Rd . . .119 CY85
Keswick Cl, Sutt. SM1 . . . . .158 DC105
Keswick Ct, Slou. SL2
  off Stoke Rd 74 AT73
Keswick Dr, Enf. EN3 . . . . . .30 DW36
Keswick Gdns, Ilf. IG4 . . . . .68 EL57
  Ruislip HA4 . . . . .59 BR58
  Wembley HA9 . . . . .62 CL63
Keswick Ms, W5 . . . . .80 CL74
Keswick Rd, SW15 . . . . .119 CY85
  Bexleyheath DA7 . . . . .126 FA82
  Egham TW20 . . . . .113 BB94
  Leatherhead (Fetch.) KT22 .170 CC124
  Orpington BR6 . . . . .145 ET102
  Twickenham TW2 . . . . . . .116 CC86
  West Wickham BR4 . . . . . .144 EE103
Kettering Rd, Enf. EN3
  off Beaconsfield Rd 31 DX37
  Romford RM3 . . . . .52 FL52
Kettering St, SW16 . . . . . . .121 DJ93
Kett Gdns, SW2 . . . . .121 DM85
Kettlebaston Rd, E10 . . . . . .67 DZ60
Kettlewell Cl, N11 . . . . .44 DG51
  Woking GU21 . . . . .150 AX114
Kettlewell Ct, Swan. BR8 . . .147 FF96
Kettlewell Dr, Wok. GU21 . .150 AY114
Kettlewell Hill, Wok. GU21 . .150 AY114
Ketton Grn, Red. RH1
  off Malmstone Av 185 DK128
Kevan Dr, Wok. (Send) GU23 .167 BE124
Kevan Ho, SE5 . . . . .102 DQ80
Kevelioc Rd, N17 . . . . .46 DQ53
Kevin Cl, Houns. TW4 . . . . . .96 BX82
Kevington Cl, Orp. BR5 . . . .145 ET98
Kevington Dr, Chis. BR7 . . . .145 ET98
  Orpington BR5 . . . . .145 ET98
KEW, Rich. 98 CN79
≷ Kew Bridge 98 CM78
Kew Br, Brent. TW8 . . . . . . .98 CM79
  Richmond TW9 . . . . .98 CM79
Kew Br Arches, Rich. TW9
  off Kew Br 98 CM79
Kew Br Ct, W4 . . . . .98 CN78
Kew Br Rd, Brent. TW8 . . . . .98 CM79
★ Kew Bridge Steam Mus,
  Brent. TW8 . . . . .98 CM78
Kew Cres, Sutt. SM3 . . . . . .139 CY104
Kewferry Dr, Nthwd. HA6 . . .39 BP50
Kewferry Rd, Nthwd. HA6 . . .39 BQ51
Kew Foot Rd, Rich. TW9 . . . .98 CL84
⊖ Kew Gardens 98 CM81
≷ Kew Gardens 98 CM81
Kew Gdns Rd, Rich. TW9 . . .98 CM80
Kew Grn, Rich. TW9 . . . . . . .98 CN79

Kew Meadow Path, Rich. TW9 .98 CN81
★ Kew Observatory,
  Rich. TW9 . . . . .97 CH83
★ Kew Palace, Royal Botanic
  Gdns, Rich. TW9 . . . . .98 CL80
Kew Palace, Rich. TW9 . . . . .98 CL80
Kew Rd, Rich. TW9 . . . . .98 CN79
Keybridge Ho, SW8 . . . . . . .101 DL79
Key Cl, E1 . . . . .84 DV70
Keyes Rd, NW2 . . . . .63 CX64
  Dartford DA1 . . . . .108 FM84
Keymer Cl, West. (Bigg.H.)
  TN16 . . . . .178 EK116
Keymer Rd, SW2 . . . . .121 DM89
Keynes Cl, N2 . . . . .64 DF55
Keynsham Av, Wdf.Grn. IG8 . .48 EE49
Keynsham Gdns, SE9 . . . . . .124 EL85
Keynsham Rd, SE9 . . . . . . .124 EK85
  Morden SM4 . . . . .140 DB102
Keynsham Wk, Mord. SM4 . .140 DB102
Keys, The, CM13
  off Eagle Way 53 FW51
Keyse Rd, SE1 . . . . .201 P7
Keysham Av, Houns. TW5
  off The Avenue 95 BU81
Keys Ho, Enf. EN3
  off Beaconsfield Rd 31 DX37
Keystone Cres, N1 . . . . .196 A1
Keywood Dr, Sun. TW16 . . . .115 BU93
Keyworth Cl, E5 . . . . .67 DY63
Keyworth St, SE1 . . . . .200 G6
Kezia St, SE8
  off Trundleys Rd 103 DY78
Khalsa Av, Grav. DA12 . . . .131 GJ87
Khalsa Ct, N22
  off Acacia Rd 45 DP53
Khama Rd, SW17 . . . . .120 DE91
Khartoum Pl, Grav. DA12 . . .131 GJ86
Khartoum Rd, E13 . . . . .86 EH69
  SW17 . . . . .120 DD91
  Ilford IG1 . . . . .69 EP64
Khyber Rd, SW11 . . . . .100 DE82
Kibworth St, SW8 . . . . .101 DM80
KIDBROOKE, SE3 . . . . .104 EH83
≷ Kidbrooke 104 EH83
Kidbrooke Gdns, SE3 . . . . .104 EG82
Kidbrooke Gro, SE3 . . . . . .104 EG81
Kidbrooke La, SE9 . . . . . . .104 EL84
Kidbrooke Pk Cl, SE3 . . . . .104 EH81
Kidbrooke Pk Rd, SE3 . . . . .104 EH82
Kidbrooke Way, SE3 . . . . . .104 EH82
Kidderminster Pl, Croy. CR0
  off Kidderminster Rd 141 DP102
Kidderminster Rd, Croy. CR0 .141 DP102
Kidderpore Av, NW3 . . . . . . .64 DA63
Kidderpore Gdns, NW3 . . . . .64 DA63
Kidd Pl, SE7 . . . . .104 EL78
Kidlington Way, NW9 . . . . . .42 CS54
Kielder Cl, Ilf. IG6 . . . . .49 ET51
Kiffen St, EC2 . . . . .197 L4
Kilberry Cl, Islw. TW7 . . . . . .97 CD81
KILBURN, NW6 . . . . .82 DA68
⊖ Kilburn 81 CZ65
  Beckenham BR3 . . . . .143 DX96
  Croydon CR0 . . . . .141 DP100
Kilburn Br, NW6
  off Kilburn High Rd 81 CZ66
Kilburn Gate, NW6
  off Kilburn Priory 82 DB68
≷ Kilburn High Road 82 DA67
Kilburn High Rd, NW6 . . . . . .81 CZ66
  W10 . . . . .81 CX69
⊖ Kilburn Park 82 DA68
Kilburn La, W9 . . . . .81 CX69
  W10 . . . . .81 CX69
Kilburn Pk Rd, NW6 . . . . . . .82 DA68
Kilburn Pl, NW6 . . . . .82 DA67
Kilburn Priory, NW6 . . . . . . .82 DB67
Kilburn Sq, NW6
  off Kilburn High Rd 82 DA67
Kilburn Vale, NW6
  off Belsize Rd 82 DB67
Kilby Cl, Wat. WD25 . . . . . . .24 BX35
Kilby Ter, Wdf.Grn. IG8
  off Baddow Cl 48 EK51
Kilcorral Cl, Epsom KT17 . . .157 CU114
Kildare Cl, Ruis. HA4 . . . . . .60 BW60
Kildare Gdns, W2 . . . . .82 DA72
Kildare Rd, E16 . . . . .86 EG71
Kildare Ter, W2 . . . . .82 DA72
Kildare Wk, E14
  off Farrance St 85 EA72
Kildonan Rd, Wat. WD17 . . . .23 BT39
Kildoran Rd, SW2 . . . . .121 DL85
Kildowan Rd, Ilf. IG3 . . . . . .70 EU60
Kilgour Rd, SE23 . . . . .123 DY86
Kilkie St, SW6 . . . . .100 DC82
Killarney Rd, SW18 . . . . . . .120 DC86
Killasser Ct, Tad. KT20 . . . .173 CW123
Killburns Mill Cl, Wall. SM6
  off London Rd 159 DH105
Killearn Rd, SE6 . . . . .123 ED88
Killester Gdns, Wor.Pk. KT4 .157 CV105
Killewarren Way, Orp. BR5 . .146 EW100
Killick Cl, Sev. (Dunt.Grn.)
  TN13 . . . . .190 FE121
Killick St, N1 . . . . .83 DM68
Killieser Av, SW2 . . . . .121 DL89
Killip Cl, E16 . . . . .86 EF72
Killowen Av, Nthlt. UB5 . . . .60 CC64
Killowen Rd, E9 . . . . .85 DX65
Killy Hill, Wok. (Chobham)
  GU24 . . . . .150 AS108
Killyon Rd, SW8 . . . . .101 DJ82
Killyon Ter, SW8 . . . . .101 DJ82
Kilmaine Rd, SW6 . . . . .99 CY80
Kilmarnock Gdns, Dag. RM8
  off Lindsey Rd 70 EW62
Kilmarnock Pk, Reig. RH2 . .184 DB133
Kilmarnock Rd, Wat. WD19 . .40 BX49
Kilmarsh Rd, W6 . . . . .99 CW77
Kilmartin Av, SW16 . . . . . . .141 DM97
Kilmartin Rd, Ilf. IG3 . . . . . .70 EU61
Kilmartin Way, Horn. RM12 . .71 FH64
Kilmeston Way, SE15
  off Daniel Gdns 102 DT80
Kilmington Cl, Brwd. CM13 . .55 GB47
Kilmington Rd, SW13 . . . . . .99 CU79
Kilmiston Av, Shep. TW17 . .135 BQ100
Kilmorey Gdns, Twick. TW1 . .117 CH85

Kilmorey Rd, Twick. TW1 . . . .97 CH84
Kilmorie Rd, SE23 . . . . .123 DY88
Kiln Av, Amer. HP6 . . . . .20 AW38
Kiln Cl, Hayes UB3
  off Brickfield La 95 BR79
Kilndown, Grav. DA12 . . . . .131 GK93
Kilner St, E14 . . . . .85 EA71
Kiln La, Bet. (Brock.) RH3 . .182 CQ134
  Chesham (Ley Hill) HP5 . . . .4 AV31
  Epsom KT17 . . . . .156 CS111
  Woking (Ripley) GU23 . . . .168 BH124
Kiln Ms, SW17 . . . . .120 DD92
Kiln Pl, NW5 . . . . .64 DG64
Kiln Rd, Epp. (N.Wld.Bas.)
  CM16 . . . . .18 FA27
Kilnside, Esher (Clay.) KT10 .155 CG108
Kiln Wd La, Rom. (Hav.at.Bow.)
  RM4 . . . . .51 FD50
Kilpatrick Way, Hayes UB4 . .78 BY71
Kilravock St, W10 . . . . .81 CY69
Kilross Rd, Felt. TW14 . . . . .115 BR88
Kilrue La, Walt. KT12 . . . . . .153 BT105
Kilrush Ter, Wok. GU21 . . . .167 BA116
Kilsby Wk, Dag. RM9
  off Rugby Rd 88 EV65
Kilsha Rd, Walt. KT12 . . . . .135 BV100
Kilsmore La, Wal.Cr. (Chsht.)
  EN8 . . . . .15 DX28
Kilvinton Dr, Enf. EN2 . . . . . .30 DR38
Kilworth Av, Brwd. CM15 . . . .55 GA44
Kimball Gdns, SW6 . . . . .99 CY81
Kimbell Pl, SE3
  off Tudway Rd 104 EJ84
Kimberley Av, E6 . . . . .86 EL68
  SE15 . . . . .102 DV82
  Ilford IG2 . . . . .69 ER59
  Romford RM7 . . . . .71 FC58
Kimberley Cl, Slou. SL3 . . . .93 AZ77
Kimberley Dr, Sid. DA14 . . . .126 EX89
Kimberley Gdns, N4 . . . . . . .65 DP57
  Enfield EN1 . . . . .30 DT41
Kimberley Gate, Brom. BR1
  off Oaklands Rd 124 EF94
Kimberley Ind Est, E17 . . . . .47 DZ53
Kimberley Pl, Pur. CR8
  off Brighton Rd 159 DN111
Kimberley Ride, Cob. KT11 . .154 CB113
Kimberley Rd, E4 . . . . .48 EE46
  E11 . . . . .67 ED61
  E16 . . . . .86 EF70
  E17 . . . . .47 DZ53
  N17 . . . . .46 DU55
  N18 . . . . .46 DV51
  NW6 . . . . .81 CY67
  SW9 . . . . .101 DL82
  Beckenham BR3 . . . . .143 DX96
  Croydon CR0 . . . . .141 DP100
Kimber Rd, SW18 . . . . .120 DA87
Kimble Cl, Wat. WD18 . . . . . .23 BS44
Kimble Cres, Bushey WD23 . .40 CB45
Kimble Rd, SW19 . . . . .120 DD93
Kimbolton Cl, SE12 . . . . . . .124 EF86
Kimbolton Grn, Borwd. WD6 . .26 CQ42
Kimbolton Row, SW3 . . . . . .198 B9
Kimmeridge Gdns, SE9 . . . .124 EL91
Kimmeridge Rd, SE9 . . . . . .124 EL91
Kimpton Av, Brwd. CM15 . . . .54 FV45
Kimpton Ho, SW15
  off Fontley Way 119 CU87
Kimpton Pl, Wat. WD25 . . . . .8 BX34
Kimpton Rd, SE5 . . . . .102 DR81
  Sutton SM3 . . . . .139 CZ103
Kimptons Cl, Pot.B. EN6 . . . .11 CX33
Kimptons Mead, Pot.B. EN6 . .11 CX32
Kimpton Trade Business Cen,
  Sutt. SM3 . . . . .139 CZ103
Kinburn Dr, Egh. TW20 . . . .112 AY92
Kinburn St, SE16 . . . . .203 H4
Kincaid Rd, SE15 . . . . .102 DV80
Kincardine Gdns, W9
  off Harrow Rd 81 CZ70
Kinch Gro, Wem. HA9 . . . . . .62 CM59
Kincraig Dr, Sev. TN13 . . . .190 FG124
Kinder Cl, SE28 . . . . .88 EX73
Kindersley Way, Abb.L. WD5 . .7 BQ31
Kinder St, E1
  off Cannon St Rd 84 DV72
Kinetic Cres, Enf. EN3 . . . . .31 DZ36
Kinfauns Av, Horn. RM11 . . .72 FJ58
Kinfauns Rd, SW2 . . . . .121 DN89
  Ilford IG3 . . . . .70 EU60
Kingaby Gdns, Rain. RM13 . .89 FG66
King Acre Ct, Stai. TW18
  off Moor La 113 BE90
King Alfred Av, SE6 . . . . . . .123 EA90
King Alfred Rd, Rom. RM3 . . .52 FM54
King & Queen Cl, SE9
  off St. Keverne Rd 124 EL91
King & Queen St, SE17 . . . .201 J9
King Arthur Cl, SE15 . . . . . .102 DW80
King Arthur Ct, Wal.Cr. EN8 . .15 DX31
King Charles Cres, Surb.
  KT5 . . . . .138 CM101
King Charles Rd, Rad. (Shenley)
  WD7 . . . . .10 CL32
  Surbiton KT5 . . . . .138 CM99
King Charles St, SW1 . . . . . .199 N4
King Charles Ter, E1 . . . . . .202 E1
King Charles Wk, SW19
  off Princes Way 119 CY88
Kingcup Cl, Croy. CR0
  off Primrose La 143 DX102
King David La, E1 . . . . .84 DW73
Kingdon Rd, NW6 . . . . .82 DA65
King Edward Dr, Dart. DA1 . .108 FK85
  Rainham RM13 . . . . .90 FK68
King Edward Rd, Chess. KT9
  off Kelvin Gro 138 CL104
  Grays RM16 . . . . .110 GE75

Kin - Kin

King Edward Ms, SW13 . . . . . .99 CU81
King Edward Rd, E10 . . . . . .67 EC60
E17 . . . . .67 DY55
Barnet EN5 . . . . .28 DA42
Brentwood CM14 . . . . . .54 FW48
Greenhithe DA9 . . . . . .129 FU85
Radlett (Shenley) WD7 . . .10 CL30
Romford RM1 . . . . .71 FF58
Waltham Cross EN8 . . . . .15 DY33
Watford WD19 . . . . .24 BY44
King Edward VII Av, Wind.
SL4 . . . . .92 AS80
Ⓗ King Edward VII Hosp
for Officers, W1 . . . . . .194 G6
King Edwards Gro, Tedd.
TW11 . . . . .117 CH93
King Edward's Pl, W3
off King Edward's Gdns . . .80 CN74
King Edwards Rd, E9 . . . . .84 DV67
N9 . . . . .46 DV45
Barking IG11 . . . . .87 ER67
King Edward's Rd, Enf. EN3 . .31 DX42
King Edwards Rd, Ruis. HA4 . .59 BR60
King Edward St, EC1 . . . . .197 H8
King Edward III Ms, SE16 . . .202 E5
King Edward Wk, SE1 . . . . .200 E6
Kingfield Cl, Wok. GU22 . . .167 AZ120
Kingfield Dr, Wok. GU22 . . .167 AZ120
Kingfield Gdns, Wok. GU22 . .167 AZ120
Kingfield Grn, Wok. GU22 . . .167 AZ120
Kingfield Rd, W5 . . . . .79 CK70
Woking GU22 . . . . . . .166 AY120
Kingfield St, E14 . . . . . . .204 E9
Kingfisher Av, E11
off Eastern Av 68 EH58
Kingfisher Cl, SE28 . . . . . .88 EW73
Brentwood CM13 . . . . . .53 GA45
Harrow (Har.Wld.) HA3 . . .41 CF52
Northwood HA6 . . . . . . .39 BP53
Orpington BR5 . . . . . . .146 EX98
Walton-on-Thames KT12
off Old Esher Rd 154 BY106
Kingfisher Ct, SW19
off Queensmere Rd 119 CY89
Enfield EN2 off Mount Vw . .29 DM38
Surbiton KT6 off Ewell Rd . .138 CM101
Sutton SM1
off Sandpiper Rd 157 CZ106
Woking GU21
off Vale Fm Rd 166 AY117
Woking (Sheer.) GU21
off Blackmore Cres 151 BC114
Kingfisher Dr, Hem.H. HP3
off Belswains La 6 BM25
Redhill RH1 . . . . .184 DG131
Richmond TW10 . . . . . .117 CH91
Staines TW18 . . . . .113 BF91
Kingfisher Gdns, S.Croy.
CR2 . . . . .161 DX111
Kingfisher Lure, Kings L. WD4 . .7 BP29
Rickmansworth (Loud.)
WD3 . . . . .22 BH42
Kingfisher Rd, Upmin. RM14 . .73 FT60
Kingfisher Sq, SE8 . . . . . .103 DZ79
Kingfisher St, E6 . . . . .86 EL71
Kingfisher Wk, NW9
off Eagle Dr 42 CS54
Kingfisher Way, NW10 . . . . .62 CR64
Beckenham BR3 . . . . . . .143 DX99
King Frederik IX Twr, SE16 . .203 M6
King Gdns, Croy. CR0 . . . . .159 DP106
King George Av, E16 . . . . . .86 EK72
Bushey WD23 . . . . .24 CB44
Ilford IG2 . . . . .69 ER57
Walton-on-Thames KT12 . .136 BX102
King George Cl, Rom. RM7 . . .71 FC55
Sunbury-on-Thames
TW16 . . . . .115 BS92
Ⓗ King George Hosp
(Eastern Av), Ilf. IG2 . . . .69 ER58
Ⓗ King George Hosp
(Barley La), Ilf. IG3 . . . . .70 EV57
King George Rd, Wal.Abb.
EN9 . . . . .15 EC34
King Georges Av, Wat. WD18 . .23 BS43
King Georges Dr, Add. (New Haw)
KT15 . . . . .152 BG110
Southall UB1 . . . . .78 BZ71
King George VI Av, Mitch.
CR4 . . . . .140 DF98
Westerham TN16 . . . . . .178 EK116
King George Sq, Rich. TW10 . .118 CM86
King Georges Sq, Brwd.
CM15 . . . . .54 FV44
King George's Trd Est, Chess.
KT9 . . . . .156 CN105
King George St, SE10 . . . . .103 EC80
Kingham Cl, SW18 . . . . . .120 DC87
W11 . . . . .99 CY75
King Harolds Way, Bexh.
DA7 . . . . .106 EX80
King Henry Ms, Orp. BR6
off Osgood Av 163 ET106
King Henry's Ct, Wal.Abb. EN9
off Deer Pk Way 31 EC36
✦ King Henry's Drive, Croy.
(New Adgtn.) CR0 . . . . .161 EC109
King Henry's Dr, Croy.
(New Adgtn.) CR0 . . . . .161 EC109
King Henry's Ms, Enf. EN3 . . .31 EA37
King Henry's Reach, W6 . . . .99 CW79
King Henry's Wk, N1 . . . . . .84 DS65
King Henry's Wk, NW3 . . . . .82 DE66
Kingston upon Thames
KT1 . . . . .138 CP97
King Henry St, N16 . . . . . . .66 DS64
King Henry's Wk, N1 . . . . . .84 DS65
King Henry Ter, E1 . . . . . . .202 E1
Kinghorn St, EC1 . . . . . . .197 H7
King James Av, Pot.B. (Cuffley)
EN6 . . . . .13 DL29
King James Ct, SE1
off Borough Rd 101 DP75
King James St, SE1 . . . . . .200 G5
King John Ct, EC2 . . . . . . .197 N4

King John's Cl, Stai. (Wrays.)
TW19 . . . . .112 AW86
King John St, E1 . . . . .85 DX71
King Johns Wk, SE9 . . . . . .124 EK88
Kinglake Ct, Wok. GU21
off Raglan Rd 166 AS118
Kinglake Est, SE17 . . . . . .201 N10
Kinglake St, SE17 . . . . . . .102 DS78
Kingly Ct, W1 . . . . .195 K10
Kingly St, W1 . . . . .195 K9
Kingsand Rd, SE12 . . . . . .124 EG89
Kings Arbour, Sthl. UB2 . . . .96 BY78
Kings Arms Ct, E1
off Old Montague St 84 DU71
Kings Arms Yd, EC2 . . . . . .197 K8
Kingsash Dr, Hayes UB4 . . . .78 BY70
Kings Av, N10 . . . . .64 DG55
N21 . . . . .45 DP46
King's Av, SW4 . . . . .121 DK87
SW12 . . . . .121 DK88
Kings Av, W5 . . . . .79 CK72
Bromley BR1 . . . . .124 EF93
Buckhurst Hill IG9 . . . . . .48 EK47
Carshalton SM5 . . . . . .158 DE108
Greenford UB6 . . . . .78 CB72
Hounslow TW3 . . . . .96 CB81
New Malden KT3 . . . . . .138 CS98
Romford RM6 . . . . .70 EZ58
Sunbury-on-Thames TW16 . .115 BT92
Watford WD18 . . . . .23 BT42
West Byfleet (Byfleet)
KT14 . . . . .152 BK112
Woodford Green IG8 . . . . .48 EH51
Kings Bench St, SE1 . . . . . .200 G4
Kings Bench Wk, EC4 . . . . .196 E9
Kingsbridge Av, W3 . . . . . .98 CM75
Kingsbridge Circ, Rom. RM3 . .52 FL51
Kingsbridge Cl, Rom. RM3 . . .52 FL51
Kingsbridge Ct, E14
off Dockers Tanner Rd . . .103 EA77
Kingsbridge Cres, Sthl. UB1 . .78 BZ71
Kingsbridge Dr, NW7
off Bittacy Hill 43 CY52
Kingsbridge Rd, W10 . . . . . .81 CW72
Barking IG11 . . . . .87 ER68
Morden SM4 . . . . .139 CX101
Romford RM3 . . . . .52 FL51
Southall UB2 . . . . .96 BY78
Walton-on-Thames KT12 . .135 BV101
Kingsbridge Way, Hayes UB4 . .77 BS69
Kingsbrook, Lthd. KT22
off Ryebrook Rd 171 CG118
KINGSBURY, NW9 . . . . . . .62 CP58
◆ Kingsbury 62 CN57
Kingsbury Circle, NW9 . . . . .62 CN57
Kingsbury Cres, Stai. TW18 . .113 BD91
Kingsbury Dr, Wind. (Old Wind.)
SL4 . . . . .112 AV86
Ⓗ Kingsbury Hosp, NW9 . . . .62 CN56
Kingsbury Rd, N1 . . . . .84 DS65
NW9 . . . . .62 CP57
Kingsbury Ter, N1 . . . . .84 DS65
Kingsbury Trd Est, NW9 . . . .62 CR58
Kings Chace Vw, Enf. EN2
off Crofton Way 29 DN40
Kings Chase, Brwd. CM14 . . .54 FV48
East Molesey KT8 . . . . .136 CC97
Kingsclere Cl, SW15 . . . . . .119 CU87
Kingsclere Ct, Barn. EN5
off Gloucester Rd 28 DC43
Kingsclere Pl, Enf. EN2
off Chase Side 30 DQ40
Kingscliffe Gdns, SW19 . . . .119 CZ88
Kings Cl, E10 . . . . .67 EB59
NW4 . . . . .63 CX56
Chalfont St. Giles HP8 . . . .36 AX47
Dartford DA1 . . . . .107 FE84
Kings Langley (Chipper.)
WD4 . . . . .6 BH31
Northwood HA6 . . . . . . .39 BT51
Staines TW18 . . . . .114 BK94
Thames Ditton KT7 . . . .137 CG100
Walton-on-Thames KT12 . .135 BV102
King's Cl, Wat. WD18
off Lady's Cl 23 BV42
Ⓗ King's Coll Hosp, SE5 . . . .102 DR82
Ⓗ King's Coll Hosp Dulwich,
SE22 . . . . .102 DS84
Kings Coll Rd, NW3 . . . . . .82 DE66
Ruislip HA4 . . . . .59 BT58
Kingscote Rd, W4 . . . . .98 CR76
Croydon CR0 . . . . .142 DV101
New Malden KT3 . . . . . .138 CR97
Kingscote St, EC4 . . . . . . .196 F10
Kings Ct, E13 . . . . .86 EH67
W6 off King St 99 CU77
Tadworth KT20 . . . . . . .173 CW122
Wembley HA9 . . . . .62 CP61
Kingscourt Rd, SW16 . . . . .121 DK90
Kings Ct S, SW3
off Chelsea Manor Gdns . .100 DE78
Kings Cres, N4 . . . . .66 DQ62
Kings Cres Est, N4 . . . . . . .66 DQ61
Kingscroft Rd, NW2 . . . . . .81 CZ65
Banstead SM7 . . . . . . .174 DD115
Leatherhead KT22 . . . . .171 CH120
KING'S CROSS, N1 . . . . . . .83 DK67
⇌ King's Cross 196 A1
⇌ King's Cross 195 P1
King's Cross Br, N1 . . . . . .196 A2
King's Cross Rd, WC1 . . . . .196 C2
⊖ King's Cross St. Pancras . . .196 A1
⇌ King's Cross Thameslink . . .196 A1
Kingsdale Ct, Wal.Abb. EN9
off Lamplighters Cl 16 EG34
Kingsdale Gdns, W11 . . . . . .81 CX74
Kingsdale Rd, SE18 . . . . . .105 ET80
SE20 . . . . .123 DX94
Kingsdene, Tad. KT20 . . . . .173 CV121
Kingsdown Av, W3 . . . . . . .80 CS73
W13 . . . . .97 CH75
South Croydon CR2 . . . .159 DP109
Kingsdown Cl, SE16
off Masters Dr 102 DV78
W10 . . . . .81 CX72
Gravesend DA12
off Farley Rd 131 GM88
Kingsdowne Rd, Surb. KT6 . .138 CL101

Kingsdown Rd, E11 . . . . . . .68 EE62
N19 . . . . .65 DL61
Epsom KT17 . . . . .157 CU113
Sutton SM3 . . . . .157 CY106
Kingsdown Way, Brom. BR2 . .144 EG101
Kings Dr, Edg. HA8 . . . . . . .42 CM49
Gravesend DA12 . . . . . .131 GH90
Surbiton KT5 . . . . .138 CN102
Teddington TW11 . . . . . .117 CD92
Thames Ditton KT7 . . . .137 CH100
Wembley HA9 . . . . .62 CP61
Kings Dr, The, Walt. KT12 . . .153 BT110
Kingsend, Ruis. HA4 . . . . . .59 BR60
KINGS FARM, Grav. 131 GJ90
Kings Fm Av, Rich. TW10 . . . .98 CN84
Kings Fm Rd, Rick. (Chorl.)
WD3 . . . . .21 BD44
Kingsfield Av, Har. HA2 . . . . .60 CB56
Kingsfield Ct, Wat. WD19 . . . .40 BX45
Kingsfield Dr, Enf. EN3 . . . . .31 DX35
Kingsfield Ho, SE9 . . . . . . .124 EK90
Kingsfield Rd, Har. HA1 . . . . .61 CD59
Watford WD19 . . . . .40 BX45
Kingsfield Ter, Dart. DA1
off Priory Rd S 128 FK86
Kingsfield Way, Enf. EN3 . . . .31 DX35
Kingsford St, NW5 . . . . . . .64 DF64
Kingsford Way, E6 . . . . . . .87 EM71
Kings Gdns, NW6
off West End La 82 DA66
Ilford IG1 . . . . .69 ER60
Upminster RM14 . . . . . .73 FS59
King's Garth Ms, SE23
off London Rd 122 DW89
Kingsgate, Wem. HA9 . . . . .62 CQ62
Kingsgate Av, N3 . . . . .64 DA55
Kingsgate Cl, Bexh. DA7 . . . .106 EY81
Orpington BR5
off Main Rd 146 EW97
Kingsgate Pl, NW6 . . . . . . .82 DA66
Kingsgate Rd, NW6 . . . . . .82 DA66
Kingston upon Thames
KT2 . . . . .138 CL95
Kings Grn, Loug. IG10 . . . . .32 EL41
Kingsground, SE9 . . . . . . .124 EL87
Kings Gro, SE15 . . . . .102 DV80
Romford RM1 . . . . .71 FG57
Kingshall Ms, SE13
off Lewisham Rd 103 EC83
Kings Hall Rd, Beck. BR3 . . .123 DY94
Kings Head La, W.Byf. (Byfleet)
KT14 . . . . .152 BK111
Kings Head Yd, SE1 . . . . . .201 K3
Kings Highway, SE18 . . . . .105 ES79
Kings Hill, Loug. IG10 . . . . .32 EL40
Kingshill Av, Har. HA3 . . . . .61 CH56
Hayes UB4 . . . . .77 BS69
Northolt UB5 . . . . .77 BU69
Romford RM5 . . . . .51 FC51
Worcester Park KT4 . . . .139 CU101
Kingshill Dr, Har. HA3 . . . . .61 CH55
Kingshold Est, E9
off Victoria Pk Rd 84 DW67
Kingshold Rd, E9 . . . . .84 DW66
Kingsholm Gdns, SE9 . . . . .104 EK84
Kingshurst Rd, SE12 . . . . .124 EG87
Kingside Business Pk, SE18
off Woolwich Ch St 104 EL76
Kings Keep, Kings.T. KT1
off Beaufort Rd 138 CL98
KINGSLAND, N1 . . . . .84 DS65
Kingsland, NW8
off Broxwood Way 82 DE67
Potters Bar EN6 . . . . . . .11 CZ33
Kingsland Grn, E8 . . . . . . .84 DS65
Kingsland High St, E8 . . . . .66 DT64
Kingsland Pas, E8
off Kingsland Grn 84 DS65
Kingsland Rd, E2 . . . . .197 N2
E8 . . . . .84 DS68
E13 . . . . .86 EJ69
Kings La, Egh. (Eng.Grn.)
TW20 . . . . .112 AU92
Kings Langley (Chipper.)
WD4 . . . . .6 BG31
Sutton SM1 . . . . .158 DD107
KINGS LANGLEY 6 BM30
⇌ Kings Langley 7 BQ30
Kings Langley Bypass, Kings L.
WD4 . . . . .6 BK28
Kingslawn Cl, SW15
off Howards La 119 CV85
Kingslea, Lthd. KT22 . . . . .171 CG120
Kingsleigh Pl, Mitch. CR4
off Chatsworth Pl 140 DF97
Kingsleigh Wk, Brom. BR2
off Stamford Dr 144 EF98
Kingsley Av, W13 . . . . .79 CG72
Banstead SM7 . . . . . . .174 DA115
Borehamwood WD6 . . . . .26 CM40
Dartford DA1 . . . . .128 FN85
Egham (Eng.Grn.) TW20 . .112 AV93
Hounslow TW3 . . . . .96 CC82
Southall UB1 . . . . .78 CA73
Sutton SM1 . . . . .158 DD105
Waltham Cross (Chsht.)
EN8 . . . . .14 DV29
Kingsley Cl, N2 . . . . .64 DC57
Dagenham RM10 . . . . . . .71 FB63
Kingsley Ct, Edg. HA8 . . . . .42 CP47
Kingsley Dr, Wor.Pk. KT4
off Badgers Copse 139 CT103
Kingsley Flats, SE1
off Old Kent Rd 102 DS77
Kingsley Gdns, E4 . . . . . . .47 EA50
Hornchurch RM11 . . . . . .72 FK56
Kingsley Ms, E1 . . . . .202 E1
W8 off Stanford Rd 100 DB76
Chislehurst BR7 . . . . . . .125 EP93
Kingsley Pl, N6 . . . . .64 DG59
Kingsley Rd, E7 . . . . .86 EG66
E17 . . . . .47 EC54
N13 . . . . .45 DN49
NW6 . . . . .81 CZ67
SW19 . . . . .120 DB92

Kingsley Rd, Brwd CM13 . . . .55 GD45
Croydon CR0 . . . . .141 DN102
Harrow HA2 . . . . .60 CC63
Hounslow TW3 . . . . .96 CC82
Ilford IG6 . . . . .49 EQ53
Loughton IG10 . . . . .33 ER41
Orpington BR6 . . . . . . .163 ET108
Pinner HA5 . . . . .60 BZ56
Kingsley St, SW11 . . . . . . .100 DF83
Kingsley Wk, Grays RM16 . . .111 GG77
Kingsley Way, N2 . . . . .64 DC58
Kingsley Wd Dr, SE9 . . . . . .125 EM90
Kingslyn Cres, SE19 . . . . . .142 DS95
Kings Lynn Ct, Rom. RM3
off Kings Lynn Dr 52 FK51
Kings Lynn Dr, Rom. RM3 . . .52 FK51
Kings Lynn Path, Rom. RM3
off Kings Lynn Dr 52 FK51
Kings Mall, W6 . . . . .99 CW77
Kingsman Par, SE18
off Woolwich Ch St 105 EM76
Kingsman St, SE18 . . . . . .105 EM76
Kingsmead, Barn. EN5 . . . . .28 DA43
Potters Bar (Cuffley) EN6 . .13 DL28
Richmond TW10 . . . . . .118 CM86
Waltham Cross EN8 . . . . .15 DX28
Westerham (Bigg.H.)
TN16 . . . . .178 EK116
Kingsmead Av, N9 . . . . . . .46 DV46
NW9 . . . . .62 CR59
Mitcham CR4 . . . . .141 DJ97
Romford RM1 . . . . .71 FE58
Sunbury-on-Thames
TW16 . . . . .136 BW97
Surbiton KT6 . . . . .138 CN103
Worcester Park KT4 . . . .139 CV104
Kingsmead Cl, Epsom KT19 . .156 CR108
Sidcup DA15 . . . . .126 EU89
Teddington TW11 . . . . . .117 CG93
Kingsmead Dr, Nthlt. UB5 . . .78 BZ66
Kingsmead Est, E9
off Kingsmead Way 67 DY63
Kings Meadow, Kings L. WD4 . .6 BN28
Kingsmead Rd, SW2 . . . . . .121 DN89
Kingsmead Way, E9 . . . . . . .67 DY63
Kingsmere Cl, SW15
off Felsham Rd 99 CY83
Kingsmere Pk, NW9 . . . . . .62 CP60
Kingsmere Pl, N16 . . . . . . .66 DR60
Kingsmere Rd, SW19 . . . . .119 CX89
Kings Ms, SW4 off King's Av . .121 DL85
Kings Ms, WC1 . . . . .196 C5
Kings Ms, Chig. IG7 . . . . . . .49 EQ47
Kingsmill Gdns, Dag. RM9 . . .70 EZ64
Kingsmill Rd, Dag. RM9 . . . .70 EZ64
Kingsmill Ter, NW8 . . . . . . .82 DD68
Kingsnympton Pk, Kings.T.
KT2 . . . . .118 CP93
Kings Oak, Rom. RM7 . . . . .70 FA55
King's Orchard, SE9 . . . . . .124 EL86
Kings Paddock, Hmptn.
TW12 . . . . .136 CC95
Kings Par, Cars. SM5
off Wrythe La 140 DE104
Kingspark Ct, E18 . . . . .68 EG55
Kings Pas, E11 . . . . .68 EE59
Kings Pas, Kings.T. KT1 . . . .137 CK96
Kings Pl, SE1 . . . . .201 H5
W4 . . . . .98 CQ78
Buckhurst Hill IG9 . . . . . .48 EJ47
Loughton IG10 . . . . .48 EK45
Kings Sq, EC1 . . . . .197 H3
King's Reach Twr, SE1 . . . . .200 E2
Kings Ride Gate, Rich. TW10 . .98 CN84
Kingsridge, SW19 . . . . . . .119 CY89
Kingsridge Gdns, Dart. DA1 . .128 FK86
Kings Rd, E4 . . . . .47 ED46
E6 . . . . .86 EJ67
E11 . . . . .68 EE59
King's Rd, N17 . . . . .46 DT53
Kings Rd, N18 . . . . .46 DU50
N22 . . . . .45 DM53
NW10 . . . . .81 CV66
SE25 . . . . .142 DU97
King's Rd, SW1 . . . . .198 C10
SW3 . . . . .198 C10
SW6 . . . . .100 DB81
SW10 . . . . .100 DB81
Kings Rd, SW14 . . . . .98 CR83
SW19 . . . . .120 DA93
W5 . . . . .79 CK71
Addlestone (New Haw)
KT15 . . . . .152 BH110
Barking IG11 off North St . .87 EQ66
Barnet EN5 . . . . .27 CW41
Brentwood CM14 . . . . . .54 FW48
Chalfont St. Giles HP8 . . . .36 AX47
Egham TW20 . . . . .113 BA91
Feltham TW13 . . . . .116 BW88
Harrow HA2 . . . . .60 BZ61
Kingston upon Thames
KT2 . . . . .118 CL94
Mitcham CR4 . . . . .140 DG97
Orpington BR6 . . . . . . .163 ET105
Richmond TW10 . . . . . .118 CM85
Romford RM1 . . . . .71 FG57
St. Albans (Lon.Col.) AL2 . . .9 CJ26
Slough SL1 . . . . .92 AS76
Surbiton KT6 . . . . .137 CJ102
Sutton SM2 . . . . .158 DA110
Teddington TW11 . . . . . .117 CD92
Twickenham TW1 . . . . . .117 CH86
King's Rd, Uxb. UB8 . . . . . .76 BK68
Kings Rd, Wal.Cr. EN8 . . . . .15 DY34
Walton-on-Thames KT12 . .135 BV103
West Drayton UB7 . . . . . .94 BM75
Westerham (Bigg.H.) TN16 . .178 EJ116
Woking GU21 . . . . .167 BA116
Kings Rd Bungalows, Har. HA2
off Kings Rd 60 BZ62
King's Scholars' Pas, SW1 . . .199 K8
King Stairs Cl, SE16 . . . . . .202 E4
King's Ter, NW1 off Plender St . .83 DJ67

Kings Ter, Islw. TW7
off Worple Rd 97 CG83
Kingsthorpe Rd, SE26 . . . . .123 DX91
⇌ Kingston 138 CL95
Kingston Av, Felt. TW14 . . . .115 BS86
Leatherhead KT22 . . . . .171 CH121
Sutton SM3 . . . . .139 CY104
West Drayton UB7 . . . . . .76 BM75
Kingston Br, Kings.T. KT1 . . .137 CK96
Kingston Bypass, SW15 . . . .118 CS91
SW20 . . . . .118 CS91
Esher KT10 . . . . .137 CG104
New Malden KT3 . . . . . .139 CT95
Surbiton KT5, KT6 . . . . .138 CP103
Kingston Cl, Nthlt. UB5 . . . .78 BZ67
Romford RM6 . . . . .70 EY55
Teddington TW11 . . . . . .117 CH93
Kingston Ct, N4
off Wiltshire Gdns 66 DQ58
Gravesend (Nthflt.) DA11 . .130 GB85
Kingston Cres, Ashf. TW15 . . .114 BJ92
Beckenham BR3 . . . . . .143 DZ95
Kingston Gdns, Croy. CR0
off Wandle Rd 141 DL104
Kingston Hall Rd, Kings.T.
KT1 . . . . .137 CK97
Kingston Hill, Kings.T. KT2 . .118 CQ93
Kingston Hill Av, Rom. RM6 . .70 EY55
Kingston Hill Pl, Kings.T. KT2 . .118 CQ91
Ⓗ Kingston Hosp, Kings.T.
KT2 . . . . .138 CP95
Kingston Ho Gdns, Lthd. KT22
off Upper Fairfield Rd . . .171 CG121
Kingston La, Tedd. TW11 . . .117 CG92
Uxbridge UB8 . . . . .76 BL69
West Drayton UB7 . . . . . .94 BM75
✦ Kingston Mus & Heritage
Cen, Kings.T. KT1 . . . . . .138 CL96
Kingston Pk Est, Kings.T.
KT2 . . . . .118 CP93
Kingston Pl, Har. HA3
off Richmond Gdns 41 CF52
Kingston Ri, Add. (New Haw)
KT15 . . . . .152 BG110
Kingston Rd, N9 . . . . .46 DU47
SW15 . . . . .119 CU88
SW19 . . . . .139 CZ95
SW20 . . . . .139 CW96
Ashford TW15 . . . . .114 BL93
Barnet EN4 . . . . .28 DD43
Epsom KT17, KT19 . . . . .156 CS106
Ilford IG1 . . . . .69 EP63
Kingston upon Thames
KT1 . . . . .138 CP97
Leatherhead KT22 . . . . .171 CG117
New Malden KT3 . . . . . .138 CR98
Romford RM1 . . . . .71 FF56
Southall UB2 . . . . .96 BZ75
Staines TW18 . . . . .114 BH93
Surbiton KT5 . . . . .138 CP103
Teddington TW11 . . . . . .117 CH92
Worcester Park KT4 . . . .138 CP103
Kingston Sq, SE19 . . . . . . .122 DR92
KINGSTON UPON THAMES . .138 CL96
KINGSTON VALE, SW15 . . . .118 CS91
Kingston Vale, SW15 . . . . .118 CR91
Kingstown St, NW1 . . . . . . .82 DG67
King St, E13 . . . . .86 EG70
EC2 . . . . .197 J9
N2 . . . . .64 DD55
N17 . . . . .46 DT53
SW1 . . . . .199 L3
W3 . . . . .80 CP74
W6 . . . . .99 CU77
WC2 . . . . .195 P10
Chertsey KT16 . . . . . . .134 BG102
Gravesend DA12 . . . . . .131 GH86
Richmond TW9 . . . . . . .117 CK85
Southall UB2 . . . . .96 BY76
Twickenham TW1 . . . . . .117 CG88
Watford WD18 . . . . .24 BW42
Kings Wk, Grays RM17 . . . .110 GA79
King's Wk, Kings.T. KT2 . . . .137 CK95
Kings Wk, S.Croy. CR2 . . . .160 DV114
Kings Wk Shop Mall, SW3
off King's Rd 100 DF78
Kings Warren, Lthd. (Oxshott)
KT22 . . . . .154 CC111
Kingswater Pl, SW11
off Battersea Ch Rd 100 DE80
Kingsway, N12 . . . . .44 DC51
SW14 . . . . .98 CP83
WC2 . . . . .196 B8
Croydon CR0 . . . . .159 DM106
Enfield EN3 . . . . .30 DV43
Gerrards Cross (Chal.St.P.)
SL9 . . . . .56 AY55
Kings Way, Har. HA1 . . . . . .61 CE56
Kingsway, Hayes UB3 . . . . .77 BQ71
Iver SL0 off High St 75 BE72
New Malden KT3 . . . . . .139 CW98
Orpington BR5 . . . . . . .145 ES99
Potters Bar (Cuffley) EN6 . .13 DL30
Staines TW19 . . . . .114 BK88
Watford WD25 . . . . .8 BW34
Wembley HA9 . . . . .62 CL63
West Wickham BR4 . . . .144 EE104
Woking GU21 . . . . .166 AX118
Woodford Green IG8 . . . . .48 EJ50
Kingsway, The, Epsom KT17 . .157 CT111
Kingsway Av, S.Croy. CR2 . .160 DW109
Woking GU21 . . . . .166 AX118
Kingsway Business Pk, Hmptn.
TW12 . . . . .136 BZ95
Kingsway Cres, Har. HA2 . . . .60 CC56
Kingsway Pl, EC1 . . . . .196 E4
Kingsway Rd, Sutt. SM3 . . . .157 CY108
Kingsway Shop Cen, NW3
off Hampstead High St . . .64 DC63
Kingswear Rd, NW5 . . . . . .65 DH62
Ruislip HA4 . . . . .59 BU61
Kingswell Ride, Pot.B. (Cuffley)
EN6 . . . . .13 DL30
Kingswick Business Pk, Wok.
GU21 . . . . .151 BC114
KINGSWOOD, Tad. 173 CY123
KINGSWOOD, Wat. 7 BV34

⇌ Kingswood 173 CZ121
Kingswood Av, NW6 . . . . . .81 CY67
  Belvedere DA17 . . . . . . .106 EZ77
  Bromley BR2 . . . . .144 EE97
  Hampton TW12 . . . . . . .116 CB93
  Hounslow TW3 . . . . .96 BZ81
  South Croydon CR2 . . . .176 DV115
  Swanley BR8 . . . . .147 FF98
  Thornton Heath CR7 . . . .141 DN99
Kingswood Cl, N20 . . . . . . .28 DC44
  SW8 . . . . .101 DL80
  Dartford DA1 . . . . .128 FJ86
  Egham (Eng.Grn.) TW20 . .112 AX91
  Enfield EN1 . . . . .30 DS43
  New Malden KT3
    off Motspur Pk 139 CT100
  Orpington BR6 . . . . . . .145 ER101
  Surbiton KT6 . . . . .138 CL101
  Weybridge KT13 . . . . . .153 BP108
Kingswood Creek, Stai. (Wrays.)
  TW19 . . . . .112 AX85
Kingswood Dr, SE19 . . . . . .122 DS91
  Carshalton SM5 . . . . . .140 DF102
  Sutton SM2 . . . . .158 DB109
Kingswood Est, SE21
  off Bowen Dr 122 DS91
Kingswood La, S.Croy. CR2 . .160 DW113
  Warlingham CR6 . . . . . .176 DW115
Kingswood Ms, N15
  off Harringay Rd 65 DP57
Kingswood Pk, N3 . . . . .43 CZ54
Kingswood Pl, SE13 . . . . . .104 EE84
Kingswood Ri, Egh. (Eng.Grn.)
  TW20 . . . . .112 AX92
Kingswood Rd, E11
  off Grove Grn Rd 67 ED61
  SE20 . . . . .122 DW93
  SW2 . . . . .121 DL86
  SW19 . . . . .119 CZ94
  W4 . . . . .98 CQ76
  Bromley BR2 . . . . .143 ED98
  Ilford IG3 . . . . .70 EU60
  Sevenoaks (Dunt.Grn.)
    TN13 . . . . .181 FE120
  Tadworth KT20 . . . . . . .173 CV121
  Watford WD25 . . . . .7 BV34
  Wembley HA9 . . . . .62 CN62
Kingswood Ter, W4
  off Kingswood Rd 98 CQ76
Kingswood Way, S.Croy.
  CR2 . . . . .160 DW113
  Wallington SM6 . . . . . . .159 DL106
Kingsworth Cl, Beck. BR3 . . .143 DY99
Kingsworthy Cl, Kings.T.
  KT1 . . . . .138 CM97
King's Yd, SW15
  off Stanbridge Rd 99 CW83
Kingthorpe Rd, NW10 . . . . . .80 CR66
Kingthorpe Ter, NW10 . . . . . .80 CR65
Kingwell Rd, Barn. EN4 . . . . .28 DD38
Kingweston Cl, NW2
  off Windmill Dr 63 CY62
King William Ct, Wal.Abb. EN9
  off Deer Pk Way 31 EB36
King William IV Gdns, SE20
  off St. John's Rd 122 DW93
King William La, SE10
  off Orlop St 104 EE78
King William St, EC4 . . . . . .201 L1
King William Wk, SE10 . . . . .103 EC79
Kingwood Rd, SW6 . . . . .99 CX81
Kinlet Rd, SE18 . . . . .105 EQ81
Kinloch Dr, NW9 . . . . .62 CS59
Kinloch St, N7
  off Hornsey Rd 65 DM62
Kinloss Ct, N3
  off Haslemere Gdns 63 CZ56
Kinloss Gdns, N3 . . . . .63 CZ56
Kinloss Rd, Cars. SM5 . . . . .140 DC101
Kinnaird Av, W4 . . . . .98 CQ80
  Bromley BR1 . . . . .124 EF93
Kinnaird Cl, Brom. BR1 . . . .124 EF93
Kinnaird Way, Wdf.Grn. IG8 . .49 EM51
Kinnear Rd, W12 . . . . .99 CT75
Kinnerton Pl N, SW1 . . . . . .198 E5
Kinnerton Pl S, SW1 . . . . . .198 E5
Kinnerton St, SW1 . . . . . . .198 F5
Kinnerton Yd, SW1 . . . . . . .198 E5
Kinnoul Rd, W6 . . . . .99 CY79
Kinross Av, Wor.Pk. KT4 . . . .139 CU103
Kinross Cl, Edg. HA8
  off Tayside Dr 42 CP47
  Harrow HA3 . . . . .62 CL58
  Sunbury-on-Thames TW16 .115 BT92
Kinross Dr, Sun. TW16 . . . . .115 BT92
Kinross Ter, E17 . . . . .47 DZ54
Kinsale Rd, SE15 . . . . .102 DU83
Kintore Way, SE1 . . . . .201 P8
Kintyre Cl, SW16 . . . . .141 DM94
Kinveachy Gdns, SE7 . . . . . .104 EL78
Kinver Rd, SE26 . . . . .122 DW91
Kipings, Tad. KT20 . . . . . . .173 CX122
Kipling Av, Til. RM18 . . . . . .111 GH81
Kipling Dr, SW19 . . . . .120 DD93
Kipling Est, SE1 . . . . .201 L5
Kipling Pl, Stan. HA7
  off Uxbridge Rd 41 CF51
Kipling Rd, Bexh. DA7 . . . . .106 EY81
  Dartford DA1 . . . . .128 FP85
Kipling St, SE1 . . . . .201 L5
Kipling Ter, N9 . . . . .46 DR48
Kipling Twrs, Rom. RM3 . . . . .51 FH52
KIPPINGTON, Sev. 190 FG126
Kippington Cl, Sev. TN13 . . .190 FF124
Kippington Dr, SE9 . . . . . . .124 EK88
Kippington Ho, Sev. TN13
  off Kippington Rd 190 FG126
Kippington Rd, Sev. TN13 . . .190 FG124
Kirby Cl, Epsom KT19 . . . . .157 CT106
  Ilford IG6 . . . . .49 ES51
  Loughton IG10 . . . . .48 EL45
  Northwood HA6 . . . . .39 BT51
  Romford RM3 . . . . .52 FN50
Kirby Est, SE16 . . . . .202 D6
Kirby Gro, SE1 . . . . .201 M4
Kirby Rd, Dart. DA2 . . . . . . .128 FQ87
  Woking GU21 . . . . .166 AW117

Kirby St, EC1 . . . . .196 E6
Kirby Way, Walt. KT12 . . . . .136 BW100
Kirchen Rd, W13 . . . . .79 CH73
Kirkby Cl, N11
  off Coverdale Rd 44 DG51
Kirkcaldy Grn, Wat. WD19
  off Trevose Way 40 BW48
Kirk Ct, Sev. TN13 . . . . . . .190 FG123
Kirkdale, SE26 . . . . .122 DV89
Kirkdale Rd, E11 . . . . .68 EE60
Kirkfield Cl, W13
  off Broomfield Rd 79 CH74
Kirkham Rd, E6 . . . . .86 EL72
Kirkham St, SE18 . . . . .105 ES79
Kirkland Av, Ilf. IG5 . . . . .49 EN54
  Woking GU21 . . . . .166 AS116
Kirkland Cl, Sid. DA15 . . . . .125 ES86
Kirkland Dr, Enf. EN2 . . . . . .29 DP39
Kirkland Wk, E8 . . . . .84 DT65
Kirk La, SE18 . . . . .105 EQ79
Kirkleas Rd, Surb. KT6 . . . . .138 CL102
Kirklees Rd, Dag. RM8 . . . . .70 EW64
  Thornton Heath CR7 . . . .141 DN99
Kirkley Rd, SW19 . . . . .140 DA95
Kirkly Cl, S.Croy. CR2 . . . . .160 DS109
Kirkman Pl, W1 . . . . .195 M7
Kirkmichael Rd, E14
  off Dee St 85 EC72
Kirk Ri, Sutt. SM1 . . . . .140 DB104
Kirk Rd, E17 . . . . .67 DZ58
Kirkside Rd, SE3 . . . . .104 EG79
Kirks Pl, E14
  off Rhodeswell Rd 85 DZ71
Kirkstall Av, N17 . . . . .66 DR56
Kirkstall Gdns, SW2 . . . . . .121 DK88
Kirkstall Rd, SW2 . . . . .121 DK88
Kirkstead Ct, E5
  off Mandeville St 67 DY62
Kirksted Rd, Mord. SM4 . . . .140 DB102
Kirkstone Way, Brom. BR1 . .124 EE94
Kirk St, WC1
  off Northington St 83 DM70
Kirkton Rd, N15 . . . . .66 DS56
Kirkwall Pl, E2 . . . . .84 DW69
Kirkwall Spur, Slou. SL1 . . . .73 AS71
Kirkwood Rd, SE15 . . . . . . .102 DV82
Kirn Rd, W13 off Kirchen Rd . .79 CH73
Kirrane Cl, N.Mal. KT3 . . . . .139 CT99
Kirtley Rd, SE26 . . . . .123 DY91
Kirtling St, SW8 . . . . .101 DJ80
Kirton Cl, W4 off Dolman Rd . .98 CR77
  Hornchurch RM12 . . . . . .90 FJ65
Kirton Gdns, E2
  off Chambord St 84 DT69
Kirton Rd, E13 . . . . .86 EJ68
Kirton Wk, Edg. HA8 . . . . . . .42 CQ52
Kirwyn Way, SE5 . . . . .101 DP80
Kitcat Ter, E3 . . . . .85 EA69
Kitchener Av, Grav. DA12 . . .131 GJ90
Kitchener Rd, E7 . . . . .86 EH65
  E17 . . . . .47 EB53
  N2 . . . . .64 DE55
  N17 . . . . .66 DR55
  Dagenham RM10 . . . . . .89 FB65
  Thornton Heath CR7 . . . .142 DR97
Kitchenride Cor, Cher.
  KT16 . . . . .151 BA105
Kite Pl, E2 off Nelson Gdns . . .84 DU69
Kite Yd, SW11
  off Cambridge Rd 100 DF81
Kitley Gdns, SE19 . . . . .142 DT95
Kitsmead La, Cher. (Longcr.)
  KT16 . . . . .132 AX103
Kitson Rd, SE5 . . . . .102 DR80
  SW13 . . . . .99 CU81
Kitswell Way, Rad. WD7 . . . . .9 CF33
Kitters Grn, Abb.L. WD5
  off High St 7 BS31
Kittiwake Cl, S.Croy. CR2 . . .161 DY110
Kittiwake Pl, Sutt. SM1
  off Sandpiper Rd 157 CZ106
Kittiwake Rd, Nthlt. UB5 . . . .78 BX69
Kittiwake Way, Hayes UB4 . . .78 BX71
Kitto Rd, SE14 . . . . .103 DX82
KITT'S END, Barn. 27 CY37
Kitt's End Rd, Barn. EN5 . . . .27 CX36
Kiver Rd, N19 . . . . .65 DK61
Kiwi Cl, Twick. TW1
  off Crown Rd 117 CH86
Klea Av, SW4 . . . . .121 DJ86
Knapdale Cl, SE23 . . . . .122 DV89
Knapmill Rd, SE6 . . . . .123 EA89
Knapmill Way, SE6 . . . . . . .123 EB89
Knapp Cl, NW10 . . . . .80 CS65
Knapp Rd, E3 . . . . .85 EA70
  Ashford TW15 . . . . .114 BM91
Knapton Ms, SW17
  off Seely Rd 120 DG93
Knaresborough Dr, SW18 . . .120 DB88
Knaresborough Pl, SW5 . . . .100 DB77
Knatchbull Rd, NW10 . . . . . .80 CR67
  SE5 . . . . .102 DQ81
Knebworth Av, E17 . . . . .47 EA53
Knebworth Path, Borwd.
  WD6 . . . . .26 CR42
Knebworth Rd, N16
  off Nevill Rd 66 DS63
Knee Hill, SE2 . . . . .106 EW77
Knee Hill Cres, SE2 . . . . . . .106 EW77
Kneller Gdns, Islw. TW7 . . . .117 CD85
Kneller Rd, SE4 . . . . .103 DY84
  New Malden KT3 . . . . . .138 CS101
  Twickenham TW2 . . . . . .116 CC86
Knighten St, E1 . . . . .202 C3
Knighthead Pt, E14 . . . . . . .103 EA76
Knightland Rd, E5 . . . . .66 DV61
Knighton Cl, Rom. RM7 . . . . .71 FD58
  South Croydon CR2 . . . .159 DP108
  Woodford Green IG8 . . . . .48 EH49
Knighton Dr, Wdf.Grn. IG8 . . .48 EG49
Knighton Grn, Buck.H. IG9
  off High Rd 48 EH47
Knighton La, Buck.H. IG9 . . . .48 EH47
Knighton Pk Rd, SE26 . . . . .123 DX92
Knighton Rd, E7 . . . . .68 EG62
  Romford RM7 . . . . .71 FC58
  Sevenoaks (Otford) TN14 . .181 FF116

Knighton Way La, Uxb. (Denh.)
  UB9 . . . . .76 BH65
Knightrider Ct, EC4 . . . . . . .197 H10
Knightrider St, EC4
  off Godliman St 84 DQ73
Knights Arc, SW1 . . . . .198 D5
Knights Av, W5 . . . . .98 CL75
⊖ Knightsbridge 198 E5
Knightsbridge, SW1 . . . . . . .198 E5
  SW7 . . . . .198 E5
Knightsbridge Ct, Slou. (Langley)
  SL3 off High St 93 BA77
Knightsbridge Cres, Stai.
  TW18 . . . . .114 BH93
Knightsbridge Gdns, Rom.
  RM7 . . . . .71 FD57
Knightsbridge Grn, SW1 . . . .198 D5
Knights Cl, E9
  off Churchill Wk 66 DW64
  Egham TW20 . . . . .113 BA92
  Kingston upon Thames KT1 .138 CL97
  Romford RM6 . . . . .70 EY58
Knights Hill, SE27 . . . . .121 DP92
Knights Hill Sq, SE27
  off Knights Hill 121 DP91
Knights La, N9 . . . . .46 DU48
Knights Manor Way, Dart.
  DA1 . . . . .128 FM86
Knights Ms, Sutt. SM2
  off York Rd 158 DA108
Knights Pk, Kings.T. KT1 . . . .138 CL97
Knights Pl, Red. RH1
  off Noke Dr 184 DG133
Knights Ridge, Orp. BR6
  off Stirling Dr 164 EV106
Knights Rd, E16 . . . . .205 N4
  Stanmore HA7 . . . . .41 CJ49
Knights Wk, SE11 . . . . .200 F9
  Romford (Abridge) RM4 . . .34 EV41
Knight's Way, Brwd. CM13 . . .55 GA48
Knightswood, Wok. GU21 . . .166 AT118
Knightswood Cl, Edg. HA8 . . .42 CQ47
Knightwood Cres, N.Mal.
  KT3 . . . . .138 CS100
Knipp Hill, Cob. KT11 . . . . . .154 BZ113
Knivet Rd, SW6 . . . . .100 DA79
Knobs Hill Rd, E15 . . . . .85 EB67
KNOCKHALL, Green. 129 FW85
Knockhall Chase, Green.
  DA9 . . . . .129 FV85
Knockhall Rd, Green. DA9 . . .129 FW86
KNOCKHOLT, Sev. 180 EU116
Knockholt Cl, Sutt. SM2 . . . .158 DB110
KNOCKHOLT POUND, Sev. . .180 EX115
Knockholt Main Rd, Sev. (Knock.)
  TN14 . . . . .180 EY115
Knockholt Rd, SE9 . . . . .124 EK85
  Sevenoaks (Halst.) TN14 . .164 EZ113
Knole, The, SE9 . . . . .125 EN91
  Gravesend (Istead Rise)
    DA13 . . . . .130 GE94
Knole Cl, Croy. CR0
  off Stockbury Rd 142 DW100
Knole Gate, Sid. DA15
  off Woodside Cres 125 ES90
★ Knole Ho & Pk, Sev.
  TN15 . . . . .191 FL126
Knole La, Sev. TN13, TN15 . .191 FJ126
Knole Rd, Dart. DA1 . . . . . . .127 FG87
  Sevenoaks TN13 . . . . . .191 FK123
Knole Way, Sev. TN13 . . . . .191 FJ125
  off Batavia Rd 135 BV95
Knoll, The, W13 . . . . .79 CJ71
  Beckenham BR3 . . . . . .143 EB95
  Bromley BR2 . . . . .144 EG103
  Chertsey KT16 . . . . .133 BF102
  Cobham KT11 . . . . .154 CA113
  Leatherhead KT22 . . . . .171 CJ120
Knoll Ct, SE19 . . . . .122 DT92
Knoll Cres, Nthwd. HA6 . . . . .39 BS53
Knoll Dr, N14 . . . . .44 DG45
Knoll Pk Rd, Cher. KT16 . . . .133 BF102
Knoll Ri, Orp. BR6 . . . . .145 ET102
Knoll Rd, SW18 . . . . .120 DC85
  Bexley DA5 . . . . .126 FA87
  Sidcup DA14 . . . . .126 EV92
Knolls, The, Epsom KT17 . . .173 CW116
Knolls Cl, Wor.Pk. KT4 . . . . .139 CV104
Knollys Cl, SW16 . . . . .121 DN90
Knollys Rd, SW16 . . . . .121 DN90
Knolton Way, Slou. SL2 . . . . .74 AW72
Knottisford St, E2 . . . . .84 DW69
Knotts Grn Ms, E10 . . . . . . .67 EB58
Knotts Grn Rd, E10 . . . . . . .67 EB58
Knotts Pl, Sev. TN13 . . . . . .190 FG124
Knowland Way, Uxb. (Denh.)
  UB9 . . . . .57 BF58
Knowle, The, Tad. KT20 . . . .173 CW121
Knowle Av, Bexh. DA7 . . . . .106 EY80
Knowle Cl, SW9 . . . . .101 DN83
Knowle Gdns, W.Byf. KT14
  off Madeira Rd 151 BF113
Knowle Grn, Stai. TW18 . . . .114 BG92
Knowle Gro, Vir.W. GU25 . . .132 AW101
Knowle Gro Cl, Vir.W. GU25 . .132 AW101
Knowle Hill, Vir.W. GU25 . . . .132 AV101
Knowle Pk, Cob. KT11 . . . . .170 BY115
Knowle Pk Av, Stai. TW18 . . .114 BH93
Knowle Rd, Brom. BR2 . . . . .144 EL103
  Twickenham TW2 . . . . . .117 CE88
Knowles Cl, West Dr. UB7 . . .76 BL74
Knowles Hill Cres, SE13 . . . .123 ED85
Knowles Wk, SW4 . . . . .101 DJ83
Knowl Hill, Wok. GU22 . . . . .167 BB119
Knowl Pk, Borwd. (Elstree)
  WD6 . . . . .26 CL43
Knowlton Grn, Brom. BR2 . . .144 EF99
Knowl Way, Borwd. (Elstree)
  WD6 . . . . .26 CL42
Knowsley Av, Sthl. UB1 . . . . .78 CA74
Knowsley Rd, SW11 . . . . . . .100 DF82
Knoxfield Caravan Pk, Dart.
  DA2 . . . . .129 FS90
Knox Rd, E7 . . . . .86 EF65
Knox St, W1 . . . . .194 D6

Knoyle St, SE14
  off Chubworthy St 103 DY79
Knutsford Av, Wat. WD24 . . . .24 BX38
Kohat Rd, SW19 . . . . .120 DB92
Koh-i-noor Av, Bushey
  WD23 . . . . .24 CA44
Koonowla Cl, West. (Bigg.H.)
  TN16 . . . . .178 EK115
Kooringa, Warl. CR6 . . . . . . .176 DV119
Korda Cl, Shep. TW17 . . . . .134 BM97
Kossuth St, SE10 . . . . .205 H10
Kotree Way, SE1 . . . . .202 C9
Kramer Ms, SW5
  off Kempsford Gdns 100 DA78
Kreedman Wk, E8 . . . . .66 DU64
Kreisel Wk, Rich. TW9 . . . . . .98 CM79
Kuala Gdns, SW16 . . . . .141 DM95
Kydbrook Cl, Orp. BR5 . . . . .145 ER101
Kylemore Cl, E6 off Parr Rd . .86 EK68
Kylemore Rd, NW6 . . . . .82 DA66
Kymberley Rd, Har. HA1 . . . . .61 CE58
Kyme Rd, Horn. RM11 . . . . . .71 FF58
Kynance Cl, Rom. RM3 . . . . .52 FJ48
Kynance Gdns, Stan. HA7 . . .41 CJ53
Kynance Ms, SW7 . . . . .100 DB76
Kynance Pl, SW7 . . . . .100 DC76
Kynaston Av, N16
  off Dynevor Rd 66 DT62
  Thornton Heath CR7 . . . .142 DQ99
Kynaston Cl, Har. HA3 . . . . . .41 CD52
Kynaston Cres, Th.Hth. CR7 . .142 DQ99
Kynaston Rd, N16 . . . . .66 DS62
  Bromley BR1 . . . . .124 EG92
  Enfield EN2 . . . . .30 DR39
  Orpington BR5 . . . . .146 EV101
  Thornton Heath CR7 . . . .142 DQ99
Kynaston Wd, Har. HA3 . . . . .41 CD52
Kynersley Cl, Cars. SM5
  off William St 140 DF104
Kynock Rd, N18 . . . . .46 DW49
Kyrle Rd, SW11 . . . . .120 DG85
Kytes Dr, Wat. WD25 . . . . . . .8 BX33
Kytes Est, Wat. WD25 . . . . . .8 BX33
Kyverdale Rd, N16 . . . . .66 DT61

Laburnham Cl, Upmin. RM14 .73 FU59
  Wembley HA0
    off Highcroft Av 80 CN67
Laburnham Gdns, Upmin.
  RM14 . . . . .73 FT59
Laburnum Av, N9 . . . . .46 DS47
  N17 . . . . .46 DR52
  Dartford DA1 . . . . .128 FJ88
  Hornchurch RM12 . . . . . .71 FF62
  Sutton SM1 . . . . .140 DE104
  Swanley BR8 . . . . .147 FC96
  West Drayton UB7 . . . . . .76 BM73
Laburnum Cl, E4 . . . . .47 DZ51
  N11 . . . . .44 DG51
  SE15 off Clifton Way 102 DW80
  Waltham Cross (Chsht.)
    EN8 . . . . .15 DX31
Laburnum Ct, E2
  off Laburnum St 84 DT67
  Stanmore HA7 . . . . .41 CJ49
Laburnum Cres, Sun. TW16
  off Batavia Rd 135 BV95
Laburnum Gdns, N21 . . . . . .46 DQ47
  Croydon CR0 . . . . .143 DX101
Laburnum Gro, N21 . . . . . . .46 DQ47
  NW9 . . . . .62 CQ59
  Gravesend (Nthflt.) DA11 . .130 GD87
  Hounslow TW3 . . . . .96 BZ84
  New Malden KT3 . . . . . .138 CR96
  Ruislip HA4 . . . . .59 BR58
  St. Albans AL2 . . . . .8 CB25
  Slough SL3 . . . . .93 BB79
  South Ockendon RM15 . . .91 FW69
  Southall UB1 . . . . .78 BZ70
Laburnum Ho, Dag. RM10
  off Bradwell Av 70 FA61
Laburnum Rd, Egh. (Eng.Grn.)
  TW20 . . . . .112 AV93
  SW19 . . . . .120 DC94
  Chertsey KT16 . . . . .134 BG102
  Epping CM16 . . . . .18 EW29
  Epsom KT18 . . . . .156 CS113
  Hayes UB3 . . . . .95 BT77
  Mitcham CR4 . . . . .140 DG96
  Woking GU22 . . . . .166 AX120
Laburnum St, E2 . . . . .84 DT67
Laburnum Wk, Horn. RM12 . . .72 FJ64
Laburnum Way, Brom. BR2 . .145 EN101
  Staines TW19 . . . . .114 BM88
  Waltham Cross (Chsht.) EN7
    off Millcrest Rd 13 DP28
Lacebark Cl, Sid. DA15 . . . . .125 ET87
Lacey Av, Couls. CR5 . . . . . .175 DN120
Lacey Cl, N9 . . . . .46 DU47
  Egham TW20 . . . . .113 BD94
Lacey Dr, Couls. CR5 . . . . . .175 DN120
  Dagenham RM8 . . . . . . .70 EV63
  Edgware HA8 . . . . .42 CL49
  Hampton TW12 . . . . . . .136 BZ95
Lacey Grn, Couls. CR5 . . . . .175 DN120
Lacey Wk, E3 . . . . .85 EA68
Lackford Rd, Couls. CR5 . . . .174 DF118
Lackington St, EC2 . . . . . . .197 L6
Lackmore Rd, Enf. EN1 . . . . .30 DW35
Lacock Cl, SW19 . . . . .120 DC93
Lacon Rd, SE22 . . . . .102 DU84
Lacy Rd, SW15 . . . . .99 CX84
Ladas Rd, SE27 . . . . .122 DQ91
Ladbroke Ct, Red. RH1 . . . . .184 DG132
Ladbroke Cres, W11
  off Ladbroke Gro 81 CY72
Ladbroke Gdns, W11 . . . . . . .81 CZ73
◉ Ladbroke Grove 81 CY72
Ladbroke Gro, W10 . . . . .81 CX70
  W11 . . . . .81 CY72
  Redhill RH1 . . . . .184 DG133

Ladbroke Ms, W11
  off Ladbroke Rd 81 CY74
Ladbroke Rd, W11 . . . . .81 CZ74
  Enfield EN1 . . . . .30 DT44
  Epsom KT18 . . . . .156 CR114
  Redhill RH1 . . . . .184 DG133
Ladbroke Sq, W11 . . . . .81 CZ73
Ladbroke Ter, W11 . . . . .81 CZ73
Ladbroke Wk, W11 . . . . .81 CZ74
Ladbrook Cl, Pnr. HA5 . . . . . .60 BZ57
Ladbrooke Cl, Pot.B. EN6
  off Strafford Gate 12 DA32
Ladbrooke Cres, Sid. DA14 . .126 EX90
Ladbrooke Dr, Pot.B. EN6 . . . .12 DA32
Ladbrook Rd, SE25 . . . . . . .142 DR97
Ladderstile Ride, Kings.T. KT2 .118 CP92
Ladderswood Way, N11 . . . . .45 DJ50
Ladds Way, Swan. BR8 . . . . .147 FD98
Lady Booth Rd, Kings.T. KT1 .138 CL96
Ladybower Ct, E5
  off Gilpin Rd 67 DY63
Ladycroft Gdns, Orp. BR6 . . .163 EQ106
Ladycroft Rd, SE13 . . . . . . .103 EB83
Ladycroft Wk, Stan. HA7 . . . .41 CK53
Ladycroft Way, Orp. BR6 . . . .163 EQ106
Lady Dock Path, SE16 . . . . .203 K5
Ladyfield Cl, Loug. IG10 . . . . .33 EP42
Ladyfields, Grav. (Nthflt.)
  DA11 . . . . .131 GF91
  Loughton IG10 . . . . .33 EP42
Ladygate La, Ruis. HA4 . . . . .59 BP58
Ladygrove, Croy. CR0 . . . . . .161 DY109
Lady Hay, Wor.Pk. KT4 . . . . .139 CT103
Lady Margaret Rd, N19 . . . . .65 DJ63
  NW5 . . . . .65 DJ64
  Southall UB1 . . . . .78 BZ71
Ladymeadow, Kings L. WD4 . . .6 BK27
Lady's Cl, Wat. WD18 . . . . . .23 BV42
Ladysmith Av, E6 . . . . .86 EL68
  Ilford IG2 . . . . .69 ER59
Ladysmith Cl, NW7
  off Colenso Dr 43 CU52
Ladysmith Rd, E16 . . . . .86 EF69
  N17 . . . . .46 DU54
  N18 . . . . .46 DV50
  SE9 . . . . .125 EN86
  Enfield EN1 . . . . .30 DS41
  Harrow HA3 . . . . .41 CE54
Lady Somerset Rd, NW5 . . . .65 DH63
Ladythorpe Cl, Add. KT15
  off Church Rd 152 BH105
Ladywalk, Rick. (Map.Cr.)
  WD3 . . . . .37 BE50
LADYWELL, SE13 . . . . .123 EA85
⇌ Ladywell 123 EB85
Ladywell Cl, SE4
  off Adelaide Av 103 DZ84
Ladywell Hts, SE4 . . . . .123 DZ86
H Ladywell Mental Health Unit -
  Uni Hosp Lewisham, SE4 .123 EA86
Ladywell Rd, SE13 . . . . .123 EA85
Ladywell St, E15
  off Plaistow Gro 86 EF67
Ladywood Av, Orp. BR5 . . . .145 ES99
Ladywood Cl, Rick. WD3 . . . .22 BH41
Ladywood Rd, Dart. (Lane End)
  DA2 . . . . .129 FS92
  Surbiton KT6 . . . . .138 CN103
Lady Yorke Pk, Iver SL0 . . . . .75 BD65
Lafone Av, Felt. TW13
  off Alfred Rd 116 BW88
Lafone St, SE1 . . . . .201 P4
Lagado Ms, SE16 . . . . .203 J3
Lagger, The, Ch.St.G. HP8 . . .36 AV48
Lagger Cl, Ch.St.G. HP8 . . . . .36 AV48
Laglands Cl, Reig. RH2 . . . . .184 DC132
Lagonda Av, Ilf. IG6 . . . . .49 ET51
Lagonda Way, Dart. DA1 . . . .108 FJ84
Lagoon Rd, Orp. BR5 . . . . . .146 EV99
Laidlaw Dr, N21 . . . . .29 DM42
Laing Cl, Ilf. IG6 . . . . .49 ER51
Laing Dean, Nthlt. UB5 . . . . .78 BW67
Lainlock Pl, Houns. TW3
  off Spring Gro Rd 96 CB81
Lainson St, SW18 . . . . .120 DA87
Laitwick Cl, SE21 . . . . .122 DQ88
Laird Av, Grays RM16 . . . . . .110 GD75
Laird Ho, SE5 . . . . .102 DQ80
Lairs Cl, N7 off Manger Rd . . .83 DL65
Laitwood Rd, SW12 . . . . . . .121 DH88
Lake, The, Bushey (Bushey Hth.)
  WD23 . . . . .40 CC46
Lake Av, Brom. BR1 . . . . . . .124 EG93
  Rainham RM13 . . . . .90 FK68
Lake Cl, SW19 off Lake Rd . . .119 CZ92
  West Byfleet (Byfleet)
    KT14 . . . . .152 BK112
Lakedale Rd, SE18 . . . . . . .105 ES79
Lake Dr, Bushey (Bushey Hth.)
  WD23 . . . . .40 CC47
Lakefield Cl, SE20
  off Limes Av 122 DV94
Lakefield Rd, N22 . . . . .45 DP54
Lakefields Cl, Rain. RM13 . . . .90 FK68
Lake Gdns, Dag. RM10 . . . . .70 FA64
  Richmond TW10 . . . . . . .117 CH89
  Wallington SM6 . . . . . . .141 DH104
Lakehall Gdns, Th.Hth. CR7 . .141 DP99
Lakehall Rd, Th.Hth. CR7 . . . .141 DP99
Lakeland Cl, Chig. IG7 . . . . . .50 EV49
  Harrow HA3 . . . . .41 CD51
Lakenheath, N14 . . . . .29 DK44
Lake Ri, Grays RM20 . . . . . .109 FU77
  Romford RM1 . . . . .71 FF55
Lake Rd, E10
  Croydon CR0 . . . . .143 DZ103
  Romford RM6 . . . . .70 EX56
  Virginia Water GU25 . . . .132 AV98
Laker Pl, SW15 . . . . .119 CZ86
Lakers Ri, Bans. SM7 . . . . . .174 DE116
Lakeside, N3 . . . . .44 DB54

Lak - Lan

Lakeside, W13 *off Edgehill Rd* .79 CJ72
  Beckenham BR3 . . . . .143 EB97
  Enfield EN2 . . . . .29 DK42
  Rainham RM13 . . . . .90 FL68
  Redhill RH1 . . . . .184 DG132
  Wallington SM6
    off Derek Av 141 DH104
  Weybridge KT13 . . . . . . .135 BQ104
  Woking GU21 . . . . .166 AS119
Lakeside Av, SE28 . . . . .88 EU74
  Ilford IG4 . . . . .68 EK56
Lakeside Cl, SE25 . . . . .142 DU96
  Chigwell IG7 . . . . .49 ET49
  Ruislip HA4 . . . . .59 BR56
  Sidcup DA15 . . . . .126 EW86
  Woking GU21 . . . . .166 AS119
Lakeside Ct, N4 . . . . .65 DP61
  Borehamwood (Elstree) WD6
    off Cavendish Cres 26 CN43
Lakeside Cres, Barn. EN4 . . .28 DF43
  Brentwood CM14 . . . . . . .54 FX48
  Weybridge KT13
    off Churchill Dr 135 BQ104
Lakeside Dr, Brom. BR2 . . .144 EL104
  Esher KT10 . . . . .154 CC107
  Slough (Stoke P.) SL2 . . . . .74 AS67
Lakeside Gra, Wey. KT13 . . .135 BQ104
Lakeside Pl, St.Alb. (Lon.Col.)
  AL2 . . . . .9 CK27
Lakeside Rd, N13 . . . . .45 DM48
  W14 . . . . .99 CX76
  Slough SL3 . . . . .93 BF80
  Waltham Cross (Chsht.)
    EN8 . . . . .14 DW28
Lakeside Way, Wem. HA9 . . .62 CN62
Lakes Rd, Kes. BR2 . . . . . . .162 EJ106
Lakeswood Rd, Orp. BR5 . . .145 EP100
Lake Vw, Edg. HA8 . . . . .42 CM50
  Potters Bar EN6 . . . . .12 DC33
Lakeview Ct, SW19
  off Victoria Dr 119 CY89
Lakeview Rd, SE27 . . . . . . .121 DN92
Lake Vw Rd, Sev. TN13 . . . .190 FG122
Lakeview Rd, Well. DA16 . . .106 EV84
Lakis Cl, NW3 *off Flask Wk* . .64 DC63
LALEHAM, Stai. 134 BJ97
Laleham Av, NW7 . . . . .42 CR48
Laleham Cl, Stai. TW18
  off Worple Rd 134 BH95
★ **Laleham Heritage Cen**, Stai.
  TW18 . . . . .134 BJ97
Laleham Pk, Stai. TW18 . . . .134 BJ98
Laleham Reach, Cher. KT16 .134 BH96
Laleham Rd, SE6 . . . . .123 EC86
  Shepperton TW17 . . . . . .134 BM98
  Staines TW18 . . . . .113 BF92
Lalor St, SW6 . . . . .99 CY82
Lambarde Av, SE9 . . . . .62 CN65
Lambarde Dr, Sev. TN13 . . . .190 FG123
Lambarde Rd, Sev. TN13 . . .190 FG123
Lambardes Cl, Orp. BR6 . . . .164 EW110
Lamb Cl, Til. RM18
  off Coleridge Rd 111 GJ82
  Watford WD25 . . . . .8 BX34
Lamberhurst Cl, Orp. BR5 . . .146 EX102
Lamberhurst Rd, SE27 . . . .121 DN91
  Dagenham RM8 . . . . .70 EZ60
Lambert Av, Rich. TW9 . . . . .98 CP83
  Slough SL3 . . . . .92 AY75
Lambert Cl, West. (Bigg.H.)
  TN16 . . . . .178 EK116
Lambert Ct, Bushey WD23 . . .24 BX42
Lambert Jones Ms, EC2
  off The Barbican 84 DQ71
Lambert Rd, E16 . . . . .86 EH72
  N12 . . . . .44 DD50
  SW2 . . . . .121 DL85
  Banstead SM7 . . . . .158 DA114
Lamberts Pl, Croy. CR0 . . . .142 DR102
Lamberts Rd, Surb. KT5 . . . .138 CL99
Lambert St, N1 . . . . .83 DN66
Lambert Wk, Wem. HA9 . . . .61 CK62
Lambert Way, N12
  off Woodhouse Rd 44 DC50
LAMBETH, SE1 . . . . .200 B6
Lambeth Br, SE1 . . . . .200 A8
  SW1 . . . . .200 A8
Lambeth High St, SE1 . . . . .200 B9
Lambeth Hill, EC4 . . . . .197 H10
⊖ **Lambeth North** 200 D5
★ **Lambeth Palace**, SE1 . . . .200 B7
Lambeth Palace Rd, SE1 . . .200 B7
Lambeth Rd, SE1 . . . . .200 C7
  SE11 . . . . .200 C7
  Croydon CR0 . . . . .141 DN101
Lambeth Wk, SE11 . . . . . . .200 C8
Lamb La, E8 . . . . .84 DV66
Lamble St, NW5 . . . . .64 DG64
Lambley Rd, Dag. RM9 . . . . .88 EV65
Lambly Hill, Vir.W. GU25 . . .132 AY97
Lambolle Pl, NW3 . . . . .82 DE65
Lambolle Rd, NW3 . . . . .82 DE65
Lambourn Chase, Rad. WD7 .25 CF36
Lambourn Cl, W7 . . . . .97 CF75
Lambourne Av, SW19 . . . . .119 CZ91
Lambourne Cl, Chig. IG7 . . . .50 EV48
Lambourne Ct, Wdf.Grn. IG8
  off Navestock Cres 48 EJ52
Lambourne Cres, Chig. IG7 . .50 EV47
  Woking GU21 . . . . .151 BD113
Lambourne Dr, Brwd. CM13 . .55 GE45
  Cobham KT11 . . . . .170 BX115
LAMBOURNE END, Rom. . . .48 EX44
Lambourne Gdns, E4 . . . . . . .47 EA47
  Barking IG11
    off Lambourne Rd 87 ET66
  Enfield EN1 . . . . .30 DT40
  Hornchurch RM12 . . . . . . .72 FK61
Lambourne Gro, Kings.T. KT1
  off Kenley Rd 138 CP96
Lambourne Pl, SE3
  off Shooter's Hill Rd 104 EH81
Lambourne Rd, E11 . . . . . . .67 EC59

Lambourne Rd, Bark. IG11 . . .87 ES66
  Chigwell IG7 . . . . .49 ES49
  Ilford IG3 . . . . .69 ES61
Lambourn Rd, SW4 . . . . . . .101 DH83
Lambrook Ter, SW6 . . . . .99 CY81
Lamb's Bldgs, EC1 . . . . . . .197 K5
Lambs Cl, Pot.B. (Cuffley)
  EN6 . . . . .13 DM29
Lambs Conduit Pas, WC1 . . .196 B6
Lamb's Conduit St, WC1 . . . .196 B5
Lambscroft Av, SE9 . . . . . . .124 EJ90
Lambscroft Way, Ger.Cr. (Chal.St.P.)
  SL9 . . . . .36 AY54
Lambs La N, Rain. RM13 . . . .90 FJ70
Lambs La S, Rain. RM13 . . . .89 FH71
Lambs Meadow, Wdf.Grn.
  IG8 . . . . .48 EK54
Lambs Ms, N1
  off Colebrooke Row 83 DP67
Lamb's Pas, EC1 . . . . .197 K5
Lambs Ter, N9 . . . . .46 DR47
Lamb St, E1 . . . . .197 P6
Lambs Wk, Enf. EN2 . . . . . . .30 DQ40
Lambton Pl, W11
  off Westbourne Gro 81 CZ72
Lambton Rd, N19 . . . . .65 DL60
  SW20 . . . . .139 CW95
Lamb Wk, SE1 . . . . .201 M5
Lamerock Rd, Brom. BR1 . . .124 EF91
Lamerton Rd, Ilf. IG6 . . . . . . .49 EP54
Lamerton St, SE8 . . . . .103 EA79
Lamford Cl, N17 . . . . .46 DR52
Lamington St, W6 . . . . .99 CV77
Lamlash St, SE11 . . . . .200 F8
Lammas Av, Mitch. CR4 . . . .140 DG96
Lammas Cl, Stai. TW18 . . . . .113 BE90
Lammas Ct, Stai. TW19 . . . .113 BD89
Lammas Dr, Stai. TW18 . . . .113 BD90
Lammas Grn, SE26 . . . . . . .122 DV90
Lammas Pk, W5 . . . . .97 CJ75
Lammas Pk Gdns, W5 . . . . . .97 CJ75
Lammas Pk Rd, W5 . . . . .79 CJ74
Lammas Rd, E9 . . . . .85 DX66
  E10 . . . . .67 DY61
  Richmond TW10 . . . . . . .117 CJ91
  Watford WD18 . . . . .24 BW43
Lammermoor Rd, SW12 . . . .121 DH87
Lamont Rd, SW10 . . . . .100 DC79
Lamont Rd Pas, SW10
  off Lamont Rd 100 DD79
LAMORBEY, Sid. 125 ET88
Lamorbey Cl, Sid. DA15 . . . .125 ET88
Lamorna Av, Grav. DA12 . . . .131 GJ90
Lamorna Cl, E17 . . . . .47 EC53
  Orpington BR6 . . . . .146 EU101
  Radlett WD7 . . . . .9 CH34
Lamorna Gro, Stan. HA7 . . . .41 CK53
Lampard Gro, N16 . . . . .66 DT60
Lampern Sq, E2
  off Nelson Gdns 84 DU69
Lampeter Cl, NW9 . . . . .62 CS58
  Woking GU22 . . . . .166 AY118
Lampeter Sq, W6
  off Humbolt Rd 99 CY79
Lamplighter Cl, E1 . . . . .84 DW70
Lamplighters Cl, Dart. DA1 . .128 FM86
  Waltham Abbey EN9 . . . . .16 EG34
Lampmead Rd, SE12 . . . . . .124 EE85
Lamp Office Ct, WC1 . . . . . .196 B5
Lamport Cl, SE18 . . . . .105 EM77
LAMPTON, Houns. 96 CB81
Lampton Av, Houns. TW3 . . . .96 CB81
Lampton Ho Cl, SW19 . . . . .119 CX91
Lampton Pk Rd, Houns. TW3 .96 CB82
Lampton Rd, Houns. TW3 . . . .96 CB82
Lamson Rd, Rain. RM13 . . . .89 FF70
Lanacre Av, NW9 . . . . .43 CT53
Lanark Cl, W5 . . . . .79 CJ71
Lanark Ms, W9 *off Lanark Rd* .82 DC69
Lanark Pl, W9 . . . . .82 DC70
Lanark Rd, W9 . . . . .82 DB68
Lanark Sq, E14 . . . . .204 C6
Lanata Wk, Hayes UB4
  off Ramulis Dr 78 BX70
Lanbury Rd, SE15 . . . . .103 DX84
Lancashire Ct, W1 . . . . .195 J10
Lancaster Av, E18 . . . . .68 EH56
  SE27 . . . . .121 DP89
  SW19 . . . . .119 CX92
  Barking IG11 . . . . .87 ES66
  Barnet EN4 . . . . .28 DD38
  Mitcham CR4 . . . . .141 DL99
Lancaster Cl, N1
  off Hertford Rd 84 DS66
  N17 *off Park La* 46 DU52
  NW9 . . . . .43 CT52
  Brentwood CM15 . . . . . . .54 FU43
  Bromley BR2 . . . . .144 EF98
  Egham TW20 . . . . .112 AX92
  Kingston upon Thames
    KT2 . . . . .117 CK92
  Staines (Stanw.) TW19 . . .114 BL86
  Woking GU21 . . . . .167 BA116
Lancaster Cotts, Rich. TW10
  off Lancaster Pk 118 CL86
Lancaster Ct, SE27 . . . . . . .121 DP89
  SW6 . . . . .99 CZ80
  W2 *off Lancaster Gate* 82 DC73
  Banstead SM7 . . . . .157 CZ114
  Walton-on-Thames KT12 .135 BU101
Lancaster Dr, E14 . . . . .204 E3
  NW3 . . . . .82 DE65
  Hemel Hempstead (Bov.)
    HP3 . . . . .5 AZ27
  Hornchurch RM12 . . . . . . .71 FH64
  Loughton IG10 . . . . .32 EL44
Lancaster Gdns, SW19 . . . .119 CY92
  W13 . . . . .97 CH75
  Bromley BR1
    off Southborough Rd . . .144 EL99
  Kingston upon Thames
    KT2 . . . . .117 CK92
⊖ **Lancaster Gate** 82 DD73

Lancaster Gate, W2 . . . . . . .82 DC73
Lancaster Gro, NW3 . . . . . . .82 DD65
★ **Lancaster Ho**, SW1 . . . . . .199 K4
Lancaster Ms, SW18
  off East Hill 120 DB85
  W2 . . . . .82 DC73
  Richmond TW10
    off Richmond Hill 118 CL86
Lancaster Pk, Rich. TW10 . . .118 CL85
Lancaster Pl, SW19
  off Lancaster Rd 119 CX92
  WC2 . . . . .196 B10
  Hounslow TW4 . . . . .96 BW82
  Ilford IG1 *off Staines Rd* . . .69 EQ64
  Twickenham TW1 . . . . . .117 CG86
Lancaster Rd, E7 . . . . .86 EG65
  E11 . . . . .68 EE61
  E17 . . . . .47 DX54
  N4 . . . . .65 DN59
  N11 . . . . .45 DK51
  N18 . . . . .46 DT50
  NW10 . . . . .63 CU64
  SE25 . . . . .142 DT96
  SW19 . . . . .119 CX92
  W11 . . . . .81 CY72
  Barnet EN4 . . . . .28 DD43
  Enfield EN2 . . . . .30 DR39
  Epping (N.Wld.Bas.) CM16 .18 FA26
  Grays (Chaff.Hun.) RM16 .109 FX78
  Harrow HA2 . . . . .60 CA57
  Northolt UB5 . . . . .78 CC65
  Southall UB1 . . . . .78 BY73
  Uxbridge UB8 . . . . .76 BK65
Lancaster St, SE1 . . . . .200 G5
Lancaster Ter, W2 . . . . .82 DD73
Lancaster Wk, W2 . . . . .82 DC74
  Hayes UB3 . . . . .77 BQ72
Lancaster Way, Abb.L. WD5 . .7 BT31
Lancaster W, W11
  off Grenfell Rd 81 CX73
Lancastrian Rd, Wall. SM6 . .159 DL108
Lancefield St, W10 . . . . .81 CZ69
Lancell St, N16 *off Stoke*
  Newington Ch St 66 DS61
Lancelot Av, Wem. HA0 . . . . .61 CK63
Lancelot Cres, Wem. HA0 . . . .61 CK63
Lancelot Gdns, Barn. EN4 . . .44 DG45
Lancelot Ho, N9 *off Barbot Cl* .46 DU48
Lancelot Pl, SW7 . . . . .198 D5
Lancelot Rd, Ilf. IG6 . . . . .49 ES51
  Welling DA16 . . . . .106 EU83
  Wembley HA0 . . . . .61 CK64
Lance Rd, Har. HA1 . . . . .60 CC59
Lancer Sq, W8 *off Old Ct Pl* . .100 DB75
Lancey Cl, SE7
  off Cleveley Cl 104 EK77
Lanchester Rd, N6 . . . . .64 DF57
Lancing Gdns, N9 . . . . .46 DT46
Lancing Rd, W13
  off Drayton Grn Rd 79 CH73
  Croydon CR0 . . . . .141 DM100
  Feltham TW13 . . . . .115 BT89
  Ilford IG2 . . . . .69 ER58
  Orpington BR6 . . . . .146 EU103
  Romford RM3 . . . . .52 FL52
Lancing St, NW1 . . . . .195 M3
Lancing Way, Rick. (Crox.Grn.)
  WD3 . . . . .23 BP43
Lancresse Cl, Uxb. UB8 . . . . .76 BK65
Lancresse Ct, N1 . . . . .84 DS67
Landale Gdns, Dart. DA1 . . .128 FJ87
Landau Way, Brox. EN10 . . . .15 DZ26
  Erith DA8 . . . . .108 FK78
Landcroft Rd, SE22 . . . . . . .122 DT86
Landells Rd, SE22 . . . . .122 DT86
Lander Rd, Grays RM17 . . . .110 GD78
Landford Cl, Rick. WD3 . . . . .38 BL47
Landford Rd, SW15 . . . . .99 CW83
Landgrove Rd, SW19 . . . . . .120 DA92
Landmann Way, SE14 . . . . .103 DX79
Landmead Rd, Wal.Cr. (Chsht.)
  EN8 . . . . .15 DY29
Landon Pl, SW1 . . . . .198 D6
Landons Cl, E14 . . . . .204 E2
Landon Wk, E14
  off Cottage St 85 EB73
Landon Way, Ashf. TW15
  off Courtfield Rd 115 BP93
Landor Rd, SW9 . . . . .101 DL83
Ⓗ **Landor Rd Unit**, SW9 . . . .101 DL83
Landor Wk, W12 . . . . .99 CU75
Landport Way, SE15
  off Daniel Gdns 102 DT80
Landra Gdns, N21 . . . . .29 DP44
Landridge Dr, Enf. EN1 . . . . .30 DV38
Landridge Rd, SW6 . . . . .99 CZ82
Landrock Rd, N8 . . . . .65 DL58
Landscape Rd, Warl. CR6 . . .176 DV119
  Woodford Green IG8 . . . . .48 EH52
Landseer Av, E12 . . . . .69 EN64
  Gravesend (Nthflt.) DA11 .130 GD90
Landseer Cl, SW19
  off Brangwyn Cres 140 DC95
  Edgware HA8 . . . . .42 CN54
  Hornchurch RM11 . . . . . . .71 FH60
Landseer Rd, N19 . . . . .65 DL62
  Enfield EN1 . . . . .30 DU43
  New Malden KT3 . . . . . . .138 CR101
  Sutton SM1 . . . . .158 DA107
Lands End, Borwd. (Elstree)
  WD6 . . . . .25 CK44
Landstead Rd, SE18 . . . . . .105 ER80
Landway, The, Orp. BR5 . . . .146 EW97
Lane, The, NW8
  off Marlborough Pl 82 DC68
  SE3 . . . . .104 EG83
  Chertsey KT16 . . . . .134 BG97
  Virginia Water GU25 . . . . .132 AY97
Lane App, NW7 . . . . .43 CY79
Lane Av, Green. DA9 . . . . . . .129 FW86
Lane Cl, NW2 . . . . .63 CV62
  Addlestone KT15 . . . . . . .152 BG106
LANE END, Dart. 129 FR92
  off Lane End 107 FB83
Lane End, Bexh. DA7 . . . . . .107 FB83
  Epsom KT18 . . . . .156 CP114
Lane Gdns, Bushey (Bushey Hth.)
  WD23 . . . . .41 CE45

Lane Ms, E12
  off Colchester Av 69 EM62
Lanercost Av, SW2 . . . . .121 DN89
Lanercost Gdns, N14 . . . . . .45 DL45
Lanercost Rd, SW2 . . . . .121 DN89
Lanes Av, Grav. (Nthflt.)
  DA11 . . . . .131 GG90
Lanesborough Pl, SW1 . . . . .198 F4
Laneside, Chis. BR7 . . . . . . .125 EQ92
  Edgware HA8 . . . . .42 CQ50
Laneside Av, Dag. RM8 . . . . .70 EZ59
Laneway, SW15 . . . . .119 CV85
Lanfranc Rd, E3 . . . . .85 DY68
Lanfrey Pl, W14
  off North End Rd 99 CZ78
Langaller La, Lthd. KT22 . . . .170 CB123
Langbourne Av, N6 . . . . .64 DG61
Langbourne Pl, E14 . . . . . . .204 B10
Langbourne Way, Esher (Clay.)
  KT10 . . . . .155 CG107
Langbrook Rd, SE3 . . . . . . .104 EK83
Langcroft Cl, Cars. SM5 . . . .140 DF104
Langdale Av, Mitch. CR4 . . . .140 DF97
Langdale Cl, SE17 . . . . .102 DQ79
  SW14 . . . . .98 CP84
  Dagenham RM8 . . . . .70 EW60
  Orpington BR6
    off Grasmere Rd 145 EP104
  Woking GU21 . . . . .166 AV119
Langdale Cres, Bexh. DA7 . .106 FA80
Langdale Dr, Hayes UB4 . . . .77 BS68
Langdale Gdns, Grnf. UB6 . . .79 CH69
  Hornchurch RM11 . . . . . . .71 FG64
  Waltham Cross EN8 . . . . .31 DX35
Langdale Rd, SE10 . . . . .103 EC80
  Thornton Heath CR7 . . . .141 DN98
Langdale St, E1
  off Burslem St 84 DV72
Langdale Wk, Grav. (Nthflt.)
  DA11 *off Landseer Av* . . .130 GE90
Langdon Ct, NW10 . . . . .80 CS67
Langdon Cres, E6 . . . . .87 EN68
Langdon Dr, NW9 . . . . .62 CQ60
Langdon Pk Rd, N6 . . . . .65 DJ59
Langdon Pl, SW14
  off Rosemary La 98 CQ83
Langdon Rd, E6 . . . . .87 EN67
  Bromley BR2 . . . . .144 EH97
  Morden SM4 . . . . .140 DC99
Langdon Shaw, Sid. DA14 . . .125 ET92
Langdons Ct, Sthl. UB2 . . . . .96 CA76
Langdon Way, SE1 . . . . .202 C7
Langford Cl, E8 . . . . .66 DU64
  N15 . . . . .66 DS58
  NW8 *off Langford Pl* 82 DC68
  W3 . . . . .98 CP75
Langford Ct, NW8 . . . . .82 DC68
Langford Cres, Barn. EN4 . . .28 DF42
Langford Grn, SE5 . . . . .102 DS83
  Brentwood CM13 . . . . . . .55 GC44
Langford Pl, NW8 . . . . .82 DC68
  Sidcup DA14 . . . . .126 EU90
Langford Rd, SW6 . . . . .100 DB82
  Barnet EN4 . . . . .28 DE42
  Woodford Green IG8 . . . . .48 EJ51
Langfords, Buck.H. IG9 . . . . .48 EK47
Langfords Way, Croy. CR0 . . .161 DY111
Langham Cl, N15
  off Langham Rd 65 DP55
Langham Ct, Horn. RM11 . . . .72 FK59
Langham Dene, Ken. CR8 . . .175 DP115
Langham Dr, Rom. RM6 . . . . .70 EV59
Langham Gdns, N21 . . . . . . .29 DN43
  W13 . . . . .79 CH73
  Edgware HA8 . . . . .42 CQ52
  Richmond TW10 . . . . . . .117 CJ91
  Wembley HA0 . . . . .61 CJ61
Langham Ho Cl, Rich. TW10 .117 CK91
Langham Pk Pl, Brom. BR2 . .144 EF98
Langham Pl, N15 . . . . .65 DP55
  W1 . . . . .195 J7
  W4
    off Hogarth Roundabout . .98 CS79
  Egham TW20 . . . . .113 AZ92
Langham Rd, N15 . . . . .65 DP55
  SW20 . . . . .139 CW95
  Edgware HA8 . . . . .42 CQ51
  Teddington TW11 . . . . . .117 CH92
Langham St, W1 . . . . .195 J7
Langhedge Cl, N18
  off Langhedge La 46 DT50
Langhedge La, N18 . . . . .46 DT50
Langhedge La Ind Est, N18 . .46 DT51
Langholm Cl, SW12
  off King's Av 121 DK87
Langholme, Bushey WD23 . . .40 CC46
Langhorn Dr, Twick. TW2 . . . .117 CE87
Langhorne Rd, Dag. RM10 . . .88 FA66
Langland Ct, Nthwd. HA6 . . . .39 BQ52
Langland Cres, Stan. HA7 . . .62 CL54
Langland Gdns, NW3 . . . . . . .64 DB64
  Croydon CR0 . . . . .143 DZ103
Langlands Dr, Dart. (Lane End)
  DA2 . . . . .129 FS92
Langlands Ri, Epsom KT19
  off Burnet Gro 156 CQ113
LANGLEY, Slou. 93 BA76
⊖ **Langley** 93 BA75
Langley Av, Ruis. HA4 . . . . . .59 BV60
  Surbiton KT6 . . . . .137 CK102
  Worcester Park KT4 . . . . .139 CX103
Langley Broom, Slou. SL3 . . .93 BA77
LANGLEYBURY, Kings.L. 7 BP34
Langleybury La, Kings.L. WD4 .23 BP37
Langley Business Cen, Slou.
  (Langley) SL3 . . . . .93 BA75
Langley Cl, Epsom KT18 . . . .172 CR119
  Romford RM3 . . . . .52 FK52
Langley Cor, Slou. (Fulmer)
  SL3 . . . . .75 AZ65
Langley Ct, SE9 . . . . .125 EN86
  WC2 . . . . .195 P10

Langley Ct, Beck. BR3 . . . . . .143 EB99
Langley Cres, E11 . . . . .68 EJ59
  Dagenham RM9 . . . . .88 EW66
  Edgware HA8 . . . . .42 CQ48
  Hayes UB3 . . . . .95 BT80
  Kings Langley WD4 . . . . . .6 BN30
Langley Dr, E11 . . . . .68 EH59
  W3 . . . . .98 CP75
  Brentwood CM14 . . . . . . .54 FU38
Langley Gdns, Brom. BR2 . . .144 EJ98
  Dagenham RM9 . . . . .88 EW66
  Orpington BR5 . . . . .145 EP100
Langley Gro, N.Mal. KT3 . . . .138 CS96
Langley Hill, Kings L. WD4 . . .6 BM29
Langley Hill Cl, Kings L. WD4 . .6 BN29
Langley La, SW8 . . . . .101 DM79
  Abbots Langley WD5 . . . . .7 BT31
  Epsom (Headley) KT18 . . .182 CP125
Langley Lo La, Kings L. WD4 . .6 BN31
Langley Meadow, Loug. IG10 .33 ER40
Langley Oaks Av, S.Croy.
  CR2 . . . . .160 DU110
Langley Pk, NW7 . . . . .42 CS51
★ **Langley Park Country Pk**,
  Slou. SL3 . . . . .75 BA70
Langley Pk Rd, Iver SL0 . . . . .75 BC72
  Slough SL3 . . . . .93 BA75
  Sutton SM1, SM2 . . . . . .158 DC106
Langley Quay, Slou. (Langley)
  SL3 . . . . .93 BA75
Langley Rd, SW19 . . . . .139 CZ95
  Abbots Langley WD5 . . . . .7 BS31
  Beckenham BR3 . . . . . . .143 DY98
  Isleworth TW7 . . . . .97 CF82
  Kings Langley (Chipper.)
    WD4 . . . . .6 BH30
  Slough SL3 . . . . .92 AW75
  South Croydon CR2 . . . . .161 DX109
  Staines TW18 . . . . .113 BF93
  Surbiton KT6 . . . . .138 CL101
  Watford WD17 . . . . .23 BU39
  Welling DA16 . . . . .106 EW79
Langley Row, Barn. EN5 . . . .27 CZ39
Langley St, WC2 . . . . .195 P9
LANGLEY VALE, Epsom 172 CR120
Langley Vale Rd, Epsom
  KT18 . . . . .172 CR118
Langley Wk, Wok. GU22
  off Midhope Rd 166 AY119
Langley Way, Wat. WD17 . . . .23 BS40
  West Wickham BR4 . . . . .143 ED102
Langmans La, Wok. GU21 . . .166 AV118
Langmans Way, Wok. GU21 .166 AS116
Langmead Dr, Bushey
  (Bushey Hth.) WD23 . . . . .41 CD46
Langmead St, SE27
  off Beadman St 121 DP91
Langmore Ct, Bexh. DA6
  off Regency Way 106 EX83
Langport Ct, Walt. KT12 . . . .136 BW102
Langridge Ms, Hmptn. TW12
  off Oak Av 116 BZ93
Langroyd Rd, SW17 . . . . . . .120 DF89
Langshott Cl, Add. (Woodham)
  KT15 . . . . .151 BE111
Langside Av, SW15 . . . . .99 CU84
Langside Cres, N14 . . . . .45 DK48
Langston Hughes Cl, SE24
  off Shakespeare Rd 101 DP84
Langston Rd, Loug. IG10 . . . .33 EQ43
Lang St, E1 . . . . .84 DW70
Langthorn Ct, EC2 . . . . .197 K8
Langthorne Cres, Grays
  RM17 . . . . .110 GC77
Langthorne Rd, E11 . . . . .67 ED62
Langthorne St, SW6 . . . . . . .99 CX80
Langton Av, E6 . . . . .87 EN69
  N20 . . . . .44 DC45
  Epsom KT17 . . . . .157 CT111
Langton Cl, WC1 . . . . .196 C3
  Addlestone KT15 . . . . . . .134 BH104
  Woking GU21 . . . . .166 AT117
Langton Gro, Nthwd. HA6 . . . .39 BQ50
Langton Ho, SW16
  off Colson Way 121 DJ91
Langton Ho, SW18
  off Merton Rd 120 DA88
Langton Ri, SE23 . . . . .122 DV87
Langton Rd, NW2 . . . . .63 CW62
  SW9 . . . . .101 DP80
  Harrow HA3 . . . . .40 CC52
  West Molesey KT8 . . . . . .136 CC98
Langton St, SW10 . . . . .100 DC79
Langton Way, SE3 . . . . .104 EF81
  Croydon CR0 . . . . .160 DS105
  Egham TW20 . . . . .113 BC93
  Grays RM16 . . . . .111 GJ77
Langtry Pl, SW6
  off Seagrave Rd 100 DA79
Langtry Rd, NW8 . . . . .82 DB67
  Northolt UB5 . . . . .78 BX68
Langtry Wk, NW8
  off Alexandra Pl 82 DC66
Langwood Chase, Tedd.
  TW11 . . . . .117 CJ93
Langwood Cl, Ashtd. KT21 . .172 CN117
Langwood Gdns, Wat. WD17 .23 BU39
Langworth Cl, Dart. DA2 . . . .128 FK90
Langworth Dr, Hayes UB4 . . .77 BU72
Lanhill Rd, W9 . . . . .82 DA70
Lanier Rd, SE13 . . . . .123 EC86
Lanigan Dr, Houns. TW3 . . . .116 CB85
Lankaster Gdns, N2 . . . . . . .44 DD53
Lankers Dr, Har. HA2 . . . . . . .60 BZ58
Lankton Cl, Beck. BR3 . . . . . .143 EC95
Lannock Rd, Hayes UB3 . . . . .77 BS74
Lannoy Rd, SE9 . . . . .125 EQ88
Lanrick Rd, E14 . . . . .85 ED72
Lanridge Rd, SE2 . . . . .106 EX76
Lansbury Av, N18 . . . . .46 DR50
  Barking IG11 . . . . .88 EU66
  Feltham TW14 . . . . .115 BV86
  Romford RM6 . . . . .70 EY57
Lansbury Cl, NW10 . . . . .62 CQ64
Lansbury Cres, Dart. DA1 . . .128 FN85
Lansbury Dr, Hayes UB4 . . . .77 BT71
Lansbury Est, E14 . . . . .85 EB72

Lansbury Gdns, E14 . . . . .85 ED72
Tilbury RM18 . . . . .111 GG81
Lansbury Rd, Enf. EN3 . . . . .31 DX39
Lansbury Way, N18 . . . . . . .46 DS50
Lanscombe Wk, SW8 . . . . . .101 DL81
Lansdell Rd, Mitch. CR4 . . . .140 DG96
Lansdown Cl, Walt. KT12
off St. Johns Dr 136 BW102
Woking GU21 . . . . .166 AT119
Lansdowne Av, Bexh. DA7 . .106 EX80
Orpington BR6 . . . . . . .145 EP102
Slough SL1 . . . . .74 AS74
Lansdowne Cl, SW20 . . . . . .119 CX94
Surbiton KT5
off Kingston Rd 138 CP103
Twickenham TW1
off Lion Rd 117 CF88
Watford WD25 . . . . .8 BX34
Lansdowne Copse, Wor.Pk. BR1
off The Avenue 139 CU103
Lansdowne Ct, Pur. CR8 . . . .159 DP110
Slough SL1 . . . . .74 AS74
Worcester Park KT4
off The Avenue 139 CU103
Lansdowne Cres, W11 . . . . . .81 CY73
Lansdowne Dr, E8 . . . . .62 DU65
Lansdowne Gdns, SW8 . . . . .101 DL81
Lansdowne Grn, SW8
off Hartington Rd 101 DL81
Lansdowne Gro, NW10 . . . . . .62 CS63
Lansdowne Hill, SE27 . . . . . .121 DP90
Lansdowne La, SE7 . . . . . . .104 EK79
Lansdowne Ms, SE7 . . . . . . .104 EK78
W11 off Lansdowne Rd 81 CZ74
Lansdowne Pl, SE1 . . . . . . .201 L7
SE19 . . . . .122 DT94
Lansdowne Ri, W11 . . . . . . .81 CY73
Lansdowne Rd, E4 . . . . .47 EA47
E11 . . . . .68 EF61
E17 . . . . .67 EA57
E18 . . . . .68 EG55
N3 . . . . .43 CZ52
N10 . . . . .45 DJ54
N17 . . . . .46 DT53
SW20 . . . . .119 CW94
W11 . . . . .81 CY73
Bromley BR1 . . . . .124 EG94
Croydon CR0 . . . . .142 DR103
Epsom KT19 . . . . .156 CQ108
Harrow HA1 . . . . .61 CE59
Hounslow TW3 . . . . . . .96 CB83
Ilford IG3 . . . . .69 ET60
Purley CR8 . . . . .159 DN112
Sevenoaks TN13 . . . . . .191 FK122
Staines TW18 . . . . . . .114 BH94
Stanmore HA7 . . . . .41 CJ51
Tilbury RM18 . . . . . . .111 GF82
Uxbridge UB8 . . . . .77 BP72
Lansdowne Row, W1 . . . . . . .199 J2
Lansdowne Sq, Grav. (Nthflt.)
DA11 . . . . .131 GF86
Lansdowne Ter, WC1 . . . . . .196 A5
Lansdowne Wk, W11 . . . . . . .81 CY74
Lansdowne Way, SW8 . . . . . .101 DL81
Lansdowne Wd Cl, SE27 . . . .121 DP90
Lansdown Pl, Grav. (Nthflt.)
DA11 . . . . .131 GF88
Lansdown Rd, E7 . . . . .86 EJ66
Gerrards Cross (Chal.St.P.)
SL9 . . . . .36 AX53
Sidcup DA14 . . . . .126 EV90
Lansfield Av, N18 . . . . .46 DU49
Lantern Cl, SW15 . . . . .99 CU84
Wembley HA0 . . . . .61 CK64
Lanterns Ct, E14 . . . . .204 A5
Lantern Way, West Dr. UB7 . . .94 BL75
Lant St, SE1 . . . . .201 H4
Lanvanor Rd, SE15 . . . . . . .102 DW82
Lapford Cl, W9 . . . . .81 CZ70
La Plata Gro, Brwd. CM14 . . .54 FV48
Lapponum Wk, Hayes UB4
off Lochan Cl 78 BX71
Lapse Wd Wk, SE23 . . . . . .122 DV88
Lapstone Gdns, Har. HA3 . . . .61 CJ58
Lapwing Cl, Erith DA8 . . . . .107 FH80
South Croydon CR2 . . . .161 DY110
Lapwing Ct, Surb. KT6
off Chaffinch Cl 138 CN104
Lapwings, The, Grav. DA12 . .131 GK89
Lapwing Twr, SE8
off Abinger Gro 103 DZ79
Lapwing Way, Abb.L. WD5 . . . .7 BU31
Hayes UB4 . . . . .78 BX72
Lapworth Cl, Orp. BR6 . . . . .146 EW103
Lara Cl, SE13 . . . . .123 EC86
Chessington KT9 . . . . . .156 CL108
Larbert Rd, SW16 . . . . . . .141 DJ95
Larby Pl, Epsom KT17 . . . . .156 CS110
Larch Av, W3 . . . . .80 CS74
St. Albans (Brick.Wd.) AL2 . .8 BY30
Larch Cl, E13 . . . . .86 EH70
N11 . . . . .44 DG52
N19 off Bredgar Rd 65 DJ61
SE8 off Clyde St 103 DZ79
SW12 . . . . .121 DH89
Tadworth KT20 . . . . . .174 DC121
Waltham Cross EN7
off The Firs 14 DS27
Warlingham CR6 . . . . . .177 DY119
Larch Cres, Epsom KT19 . . . .156 CP107
Hayes UB4 . . . . .78 BW70
Larchdene, Orp. BR6 . . . . . .145 EN103
Larch Dr, W4
off Gunnersbury Av 98 CN78
Larches, The, N13 . . . . .46 DQ48
Amersham HP6 . . . . . . .20 AV38
Bushey WD23 . . . . .24 BY43
Northwood HA6
off Rickmansworth Rd . . .39 BQ51
Uxbridge UB10 . . . . . . .77 BP69
Woking GU21 . . . . . . .166 AY116
Larches Av, SW14 . . . . .98 CR84
Enfield EN1 . . . . .30 DW35
Larch Grn, NW9
off Clayton Fld 42 CS53
Larch Gro, Sid. DA15 . . . . . .125 ET88
Larch Rd, E10 off Walnut Rd . .67 EA61

Larch Rd, NW2 . . . . .63 CW63
Dartford DA1 . . . . .128 FK87
Larch Tree Way, Croy. CR0 . .143 EA104
Larch Wk, Swan. BR8 . . . . . .147 FD96
Larch Way, Brom. BR2 . . . . .145 EN101
Larchwood Av, Rom. RM5 . . . .51 FB51
Larchwood Cl, Bans. SM7 . . .173 CY116
Romford RM5 . . . . .51 FC51
Larchwood Dr, Egh. (Eng.Grn.)
TW20 . . . . .112 AV93
Larchwood Gdns, Brwd.
CM15 . . . . .54 FU44
Larchwood Rd, SE9 . . . . . . .125 EP89
Larcombe Cl, Croy. CR0 . . . .160 DT105
Larcom St, SE17 . . . . .201 J9
Larden Rd, W3 . . . . .80 CS74
Largewood Av, Surb. KT6 . . .138 CN103
Largo Wk, Erith DA8
off Selkirk Dr 107 FE81
Larissa St, SE17 . . . . .201 L10
Lark Av, Stai. TW18
off Kestrel Av 113 BF90
Larkbere Rd, SE26 . . . . . . .123 DY91
Larken Cl, Bushey WD23
off Larken Dr 40 CC46
Larken Dr, Bushey WD23 . . . .40 CC46
Larkfield Av, Har. HA3 . . . . . .61 CH55
Larkfield Cl, Brom. BR2 . . . .144 EF103
Larkfield Rd, Rich. TW9 . . . . .98 CL84
Sevenoaks TN13 . . . . . .190 FC123
Sidcup DA14 . . . . .125 ET90
Larkfields, Grav. (Nthflt.)
DA11 . . . . .130 GE90
Larkhall Cl, Walt. KT12 . . . .154 BW107
Larkhall La, SW4 . . . . .101 DK82
Larkhall Ri, SW4 . . . . .101 DJ83
Larkham Cl, Felt. TW13 . . . .115 BS90
Larkhill Ter, SE18 . . . . . . .105 EN81
Larkin Cl, Brwd. CM13 . . . . .55 GC45
Coulsdon CR5 . . . . . . .175 DM117
Larkings La, Slou. (Stoke P.)
SL2 . . . . .74 AV67
Lark Row, E2 . . . . .84 DW67
Larksfield, Egh. (Eng.Grn.)
TW20 . . . . .112 AW94
Larksfield Gro, Enf. EN1 . . . .30 DV39
Larks Gro, Bark. IG11 . . . . . .87 ES66
Larkshall Ct, Rom. RM7 . . . . .51 FC54
Larkshall Cres, E4 . . . . .47 EC49
Larkshall Rd, E4 . . . . .47 EC50
Larkspur Cl, E6 . . . . .86 EL71
N17 off Fryatt Rd 46 DR52
NW9 . . . . .62 CP57
Orpington BR6 . . . . . . .146 EW103
Ruislip HA4 . . . . .59 BQ59
South Ockendon RM15 . . .91 FW69
Larkspur Gro, Edg. HA8 . . . . .42 CQ49
Larkspur Way, Epsom KT19 . .156 CQ106
Larkswood Cl, Erith DA8 . . . .107 FG81
Larkswood Ct, E4 . . . . .47 ED50
Larkswood Ri, Pnr. HA5 . . . . .60 BW56
Larkswood Rd, E4 . . . . .47 EA49
Lark Way, Cars. SM5 . . . . . .140 DE101
Larkway Cl, NW9 . . . . .62 CR56
Larmans Rd, Enf. EN3 . . . . . .30 DW36
Larnach Rd, W6 . . . . .99 CX79
Larne Rd, Ruis. HA4 . . . . . . .59 BT59
Larner Rd, Erith DA8 . . . . . .107 FE80
La Roche Cl, Slou. SL3 . . . . .92 AW76
Larpent Av, SW15 . . . . .119 CW85
Larsen Dr, Wal.Abb. EN9 . . . .15 ED34
Larwood Rd, Grnf. UB6 . . . . .61 CD64
Lascelles Av, Har. HA1 . . . . . .61 CD59
Lascelles Cl, E11 . . . . .67 ED61
Brentwood CM15 . . . . . .54 FU43
Lascelles Rd, Slou. SL3 . . . . .92 AV76
Lascotts Rd, N22 . . . . .45 DM51
Las Palmas Est, Shep. TW17 .135 BQ101
Lassa Rd, SE9 . . . . .124 EL85
Lassell St, SE10 . . . . .103 ED78
Lasseter Pl, SE3
off Vanbrugh Hill 104 EF79
Lasswade Rd, Cher. KT16 . . .133 BF101
Latchett Rd, E18 . . . . .48 EH53
Latchford Pl, Chig. IG7
off Manford Way 50 EV49
Latching Ct, Rom. RM3
off Troopers Dr 52 FK49
Latchingdon Ct, E17 . . . . . . .67 DX56
Latchingdon Gdns, Wdf.Grn.
IG8 . . . . .48 EL51
Latchmere Cl, Rich. TW10 . . .118 CL92
Latchmere La, Kings.T. KT2 . .118 CM93
Latchmere Pas, SW11
off Cabul Rd 100 DE82
Latchmere Rd, SW11 . . . . . .100 DF82
Kingston upon Thames
KT2 . . . . .118 CL94
Latchmere St, SW11 . . . . . .100 DF82
Latchmoor Av, Ger.Cr. (Chal.St.P.)
SL9 . . . . .56 AX56
Latchmoor Gro, Ger.Cr. (Chal.St.P.)
SL9 . . . . .56 AX56
Latchmoor Way, Ger.Cr. (Chal.St.P.)
SL9 . . . . .56 AX56
Lateward Rd, Brent. TW8 . . . .97 CK79
Latham Cl, E6
off Oliver Gdns 86 EL72
Dartford DA2 . . . . . . .129 FS89
Twickenham TW1 . . . . .117 CG87
Westerham (Bigg.H.) TN16 .178 EJ116
Latham Ho, E1 . . . . .85 DX72
Latham Rd, Bexh. DA6 . . . . .126 FA85
Twickenham TW1 . . . . .117 CF87
Lathams Way, Croy. CR0 . . . .141 DM102
Lathkill Cl, Enf. EN1 . . . . . . .46 DU45
Lathom Rd, E6 . . . . .87 EM66
LATIMER, Chesh. 20 AY36
Latimer, SE17
off Beaconsfield Rd 102 DS78
Latimer Av, E6 . . . . .87 EM67
Latimer Cl, Amer. HP6 . . . . . .20 AW39
Pinner HA5 . . . . .40 BW53
Watford WD18 . . . . . . .39 BS45
Woking GU22 . . . . . . .167 BB116
Worcester Park KT4 . . . .157 CV105

🄷 Latimer Day Hosp, W1 . .195 K6
Latimer Dr, Horn. RM12 . . . . .72 FK62
Latimer Gdns, Pnr. HA5 . . . . .40 BW53
Latimer Pl, W10 . . . . .81 CW72
⊖ Latimer Road 81 CX73
Latimer Rd, E7 . . . . .68 EH63
N15 . . . . .66 DS58
SW19 . . . . .120 DB93
W10 . . . . .81 CW72
Barnet EN5 . . . . .28 DB41
Chesham HP5 . . . . .20 AU36
Croydon CR0
off Abbey Rd 141 DP104
Rickmansworth (Chenies)
WD3 . . . . .21 BB38
Teddington TW11 . . . . .117 CF92
Latona Dr, Grav. DA12 . . . . .131 GM92
Latona Rd, SE15 . . . . .102 DU79
La Tourne Gdns, Orp. BR6 . . .145 EQ104
Lattimer Pl, W4 . . . . .98 CS79
Latton Cl, Esher KT10 . . . . .154 CB105
Walton-on-Thames KT12 .136 BY101
Latymer Cl, Wey. KT13 . . . . .153 BQ105
Latymer Ct, W6 . . . . .99 CX77
Latymer Rd, N9 . . . . .46 DT46
Latymer Way, N9 . . . . .46 DR47
Lauder Cl, Nthlt. UB5 . . . . . .78 BX68
Lauderdale Dr, Rich. TW10 . .117 CK90
Lauderdale Pl, EC2
off Beech St 84 DQ71
Lauderdale Rd, W9 . . . . .82 DB69
Kings Langley WD4 . . . . .7 BQ33
Lauderdale Twr, EC2 . . . . . .197 H6
Laud St, SE11 . . . . .200 B10
Croydon CR0 . . . . .142 DQ104
Laughton Ct, Borwd. WD6
off Banks Rd 26 CR40
Laughton Rd, Nthlt. UB5 . . . .78 BX67
Launcelot Rd, Brom. BR1 . . .124 EG91
Launcelot St, SE1 . . . . . . .200 D5
Launceston Cl, Rom. RM3 . . . .52 FJ53
Launceston Gdns, Grnf. UB6 . .79 CJ67
Launceston Pl, W8 . . . . . . .100 DC76
Launceston Rd, Grnf. UB6 . . . .79 CJ67
Launch St, E14 . . . . .204 D6
Laundress La, N16 . . . . .66 DU62
Laundry La, N1
off Greenman St 84 DQ67
Waltham Abbey EN9 . . . .16 EE25
Laundry Rd, W6 . . . . .99 CY79
Laura Cl, E11 . . . . .68 EJ57
Enfield EN1 . . . . .30 DS43
Lauradale Rd, N2 . . . . .64 DF56
Laura Dr, Swan. BR8 . . . . . .127 FG94
Laura Pl, E5 . . . . .66 DW63
Laurel Av, Egh. (Eng.Grn.)
TW20 . . . . .112 AV92
Gravesend DA12 . . . . . .131 GJ89
Potters Bar EN6 . . . . . .11 CZ32
Slough SL3 . . . . .92 AY75
Twickenham TW1 . . . . .117 CF88
Laurel Bk Gdns, SW6
off New Kings Rd 99 CZ82
Laurel Bk Rd, Enf. EN2 . . . . .30 DQ39
Laurel Bk Vil, W7
off Lower Boston Rd 79 CE74
Laurel Cl, N19
off Hargrave Pk 65 DJ61
SW17 . . . . .120 DE92
Brentwood CM13 . . . . . .55 GB43
Dartford DA1
off Willow Rd 128 FJ88
Ilford IG6 . . . . .49 EQ51
Sidcup DA14 . . . . .126 EU90
Slough (Colnbr.) SL3 . . . .93 BE80
Woking GU21 . . . . . . .151 BD113
Laurel Ct, Pot.B. (Cuffley) EN6
off Station Rd 13 DM29
Laurel Cres, Croy. CR0 . . . .143 EA104
Romford RM7 . . . . .71 FE60
Woking GU21 . . . . . . .151 BC113
Laurel Dr, N21 . . . . .45 DN45
Oxted RH8 . . . . .188 EF131
South Ockendon RM15 . . .91 FX70
Laurel Flds, Pot.B. EN6 . . . . .11 CZ31
Laurel Gdns, E4 . . . . .47 EB45
NW7 . . . . .42 CR48
W7 . . . . .79 CE74
Addlestone (New Haw)
KT15 . . . . .152 BH110
Bromley BR1
off Southborough Rd . . .144 EL98
Hounslow TW4 . . . . . . .96 BY84
Laurel Gro, SE20 . . . . .122 DV94
SE26 . . . . .123 DX91
Laurel La, Horn. RM12
off Station La 72 FL61
West Drayton UB7 . . . . .94 BL77
Laurel Lo La, Barn. EN5 . . . . .27 CW36
Laurel Manor, Sutt. SM2
off Devonshire Rd 158 DC108
Laurel Pk, Har. HA3 . . . . . . .41 CF52
Laurel Rd, SW13 . . . . .99 CU82
SW20 . . . . .139 CV95
Gerrards Cross (Chal.St.P.)
SL9 . . . . .36 AX53
Hampton (Hmptn.H.)
TW12 . . . . .117 CD92
Laurels, The, Bans. SM7 . . . .173 CZ117
Cobham KT11 . . . . . . .170 BY115
Dartford DA2 . . . . . . .128 FJ90
Waltham Cross EN7 . . . . .14 DS27
Weybridge KT13 . . . . . .135 BR104
Laurels Rd, Iver SL0 . . . . . .75 BD68
Laurel St, E8 . . . . .84 DT65
Laurel Vw, N12 . . . . .44 DB48
Laurel Way, E18 . . . . .68 EF56
N20 . . . . .44 DA48
Laurence Ms, W12
off Askew Rd 99 CU75
Laurence Pountney Hill, EC4 .197 K10
Laurence Pountney La, EC4 . .197 K10
Laurie Gro, SE14 . . . . .103 DY81
Laurie Rd, W7 . . . . .79 CE71
Laurier Rd, NW5 . . . . .65 DH62
Croydon CR0 . . . . .142 DT101

Laurie Wk, Rom. RM1 . . . . . .71 FE57
Laurimel Cl, Stan. HA7
off September Way 41 CH51
Laurino Pl, Bushey (Bushey Hth.)
WD23 . . . . .40 CC47
Lauriston Rd, E9 . . . . .85 DX67
SW19 . . . . .119 CX93
Lausanne Rd, N8 . . . . .65 DN56
SE15 . . . . .102 DW81
Lauser Rd, Stai. (Stanw.)
TW19 . . . . .114 BJ87
Lavell St, N16 . . . . .66 DR63
Lavender Av, NW9 . . . . .62 CQ60
Brentwood CM15 . . . . . .54 FV43
Mitcham CR4 . . . . . . .140 DE95
Worcester Park KT4 . . . .139 CW104
Lavender Cl, SW3 . . . . .100 DD79
Bromley BR2 . . . . . . .144 EL100
Carshalton SM5 . . . . . .158 DG105
Caterham CR3 . . . . . . .186 DQ125
Coulsdon CR5 . . . . . . .175 DJ119
Leatherhead KT22 . . . . .171 CJ123
Romford RM3 . . . . .52 FK52
Waltham Cross (Chsht.)
EN7 . . . . .14 DT27
Lavender Ct, W.Mol. KT8
off Molesham Way 136 CB97
Lavender Dr, Uxb. UB8 . . . . .76 BM71
Lavender Gdns, SW11 . . . . . .100 DF84
Enfield EN2 . . . . .29 DP39
Harrow HA3
off Uxbridge Rd 41 CE51
Lavender Gate, Lthd. KT22 . .154 CB113
Lavender Gro, E8 . . . . .84 DT66
Mitcham CR4 . . . . . . .140 DE95
Lavender Hill, SW11 . . . . . .100 DE84
Enfield EN2 . . . . .29 DN39
Swanley BR8 . . . . .147 FD97
Lavender Pk Rd, W.Byf. KT14 .152 BG112
Lavender Pl, Ilf. IG1 . . . . . . .69 EP64
Lavender Ri, West Dr. UB7 . . .94 BN75
Lavender Rd, SE16 . . . . . . .203 K2
SW11 . . . . .100 DD83
Carshalton SM5 . . . . . .158 DG105
Croydon CR0 . . . . .141 DM100
Enfield EN2 . . . . .30 DR39
Epsom KT19 . . . . .156 CP106
Sutton SM1 . . . . .158 DD105
Uxbridge UB8 . . . . .76 BM71
Woking GU22 . . . . . . .167 BB116
Lavender Sq, E11
off Anglian Rd 67 ED62
Lavender St, E15
off Manbey Gro 86 EE65
Lavender Sweep, SW11 . . . . .100 DF84
Lavender Ter, SW11
off Falcon Rd 100 DE83
Lavender Vale, Wall. SM6 . . .159 DK107
Lavender Wk, SW11 . . . . . . .100 DF84
Mitcham CR4 . . . . . . .140 DG97
Lavender Way, Croy. CR0 . . .143 DX100
Lavengro Rd, SE27 . . . . . . .122 DQ89
Lavenham Rd, SW18 . . . . . .119 CZ88
Lavernock Rd, Bexh. DA7 . . .106 FA82
Lavers Rd, N16 . . . . .66 DS62
Laverstoke Gdns, SW15 . . . .119 CU87
Laverton Ms, SW5
off Laverton Pl 100 DB77
Laverton Pl, SW5 . . . . .100 DB77
Lavidge Rd, SE9 . . . . .124 EL89
Lavina Gro, N1
off Wharfdale Rd 83 DM68
Lavington Cl, E9 . . . . .85 DZ65
Lavington Rd, W13 . . . . .79 CH74
Croydon CR0 . . . . .141 DM104
Lavington St, SE1 . . . . . . .200 G3
Lavinia Av, Wat. WD25 . . . . . .8 BX34
Lavinia Rd, Dart. DA1 . . . . .128 FM86
Lavrock La, Rick. WD3 . . . . .38 BM45
Lawdons Gdns, Croy. CR0 . . .159 DP105
Lawford Av, Rick. (Chorl.)
WD3 . . . . .21 BC44
Lawford Cl, Horn. RM12 . . . . .72 FJ63
Rickmansworth (Chorl.)
WD3 . . . . .21 BC44
Wallington SM6 . . . . . .159 DL109
Lawford Gdns, Dart. DA1 . . .128 FJ85
Kenley CR8 . . . . .176 DQ116
Lawford Rd, N1 . . . . .84 DS66
NW5 . . . . .83 DJ65
W4 . . . . .98 CQ80
Law Ho, Bark. IG11 . . . . . . .88 EU68
Lawless St, E14 . . . . .85 EB73
Lawley Rd, N14 . . . . .45 DH45
Lawley St, E5 . . . . .66 DW63
Lawn, The, Sthl. UB2 . . . . . .96 CA78
Lawn Av, West Dr. UB7 . . . . .94 BJ75
Lawn Cl, N9 . . . . .46 DT45
Bromley BR1 . . . . .124 EH93
New Malden KT3 . . . . . .138 CS96
Ruislip HA4 . . . . .59 BT62
Slough (Datchet) SL3 . . . .92 AW80
Swanley BR8 . . . . .147 FC96
Lawn Cres, Rich. TW9 . . . . . .98 CN82
Lawn Fm Gro, Rom. RM6 . . . .70 EY56
Lawnfield, NW2
off Coverdale Rd 81 CX66
Lawn Gdns, W7 . . . . .79 CE74
Lawn Ho Cl, E14 . . . . .204 D4
Lawn La, SW8 . . . . .101 DL79
Lawn Pk, Sev. TN13 . . . . . .191 FH127
Lawn Rd, NW3 . . . . .64 DF64
Beckenham BR3 . . . . . .123 DZ94
Gravesend DA11 . . . . . .130 GC86
Uxbridge UB8
off New Windsor St 76 BJ66
Lawns, The, E4 . . . . .47 EA50
SE3 off Lee Ter 104 EE83
SE19 . . . . .142 DR95
Pinner HA5 . . . . .60 CB52
Radlett (Shenley) WD7 . . .10 CL33
Sidcup DA14 . . . . .126 EV91
Sutton SM2 . . . . .157 CY108
Lawns Ct, Wem. HA9
off The Avenue 62 CM61
Lawns Cres, Grays RM17 . . .110 GD79

Lawnside, SE3 . . . . .104 EF84
Lawns Way, Rom. RM5 . . . . . .51 FC52
Lawn Ter, SE3 . . . . .104 EE83
Lawn Vale, Pnr. HA5 . . . . . . .60 BX54
Lawrance Gdns, Wal.Cr. (Chsht.)
EN8 . . . . .15 DX28
Lawrence Av, E12 . . . . .69 EN63
E17 . . . . .47 DX53
N13 . . . . .45 DP49
NW7 . . . . .42 CS49
New Malden KT3 . . . . . .138 CR100
Lawrence Bldgs, N16 . . . . . .66 DT62
Lawrence Campe Cl, N20
off Friern Barnet La 44 DD48
Lawrence Cl, E3 . . . . .85 EA68
N15 off Lawrence Rd 66 DS55
Lawrence Ct, NW7 . . . . .42 CS50
Woodford Green IG8
off Baddow Cl 48 EJ51
Lawrence Cres, Dag. RM10 . . .71 FB62
Edgware HA8 . . . . .42 CN54
Lawrence Dr, Uxb. UB10 . . . .59 BQ63
Lawrence Gdns, NW7 . . . . . .43 CT48
Tilbury RM18 . . . . . . .111 GH80
Lawrence Hill, E4 . . . . .47 EA47
Lawrence Hill Gdns, Dart.
DA1 . . . . .128 FJ86
Lawrence Hill Rd, Dart. DA1 .128 FJ86
Lawrence La, EC2 . . . . .197 J9
Betchworth (Buckland)
RH3 . . . . .183 CV131
Lawrence Orchard, Rick. (Chorl.)
WD3 . . . . .21 BD43
Lawrence Pl, N1 off Outram Pl .83 DL67
Lawrence Rd, E6 . . . . .86 EK67
E13 . . . . .86 EH67
N15 . . . . .46 DS56
N18 . . . . .46 DV49
SE25 . . . . .142 DT98
W5 . . . . .97 CK77
Erith DA8 . . . . .107 FB80
Hampton TW12 . . . . . .116 BZ94
Hayes UB4 . . . . .77 BQ68
Hounslow TW4 . . . . . . .96 BW84
Pinner HA5 . . . . .60 BX57
Richmond TW10 . . . . . .117 CJ91
Romford RM2 . . . . .71 FH57
West Wickham BR4 . . . .162 EG105
Lawrence Sq, Grav. DA11
off Haynes Rd 131 GF90
Lawrence St, E16 . . . . .86 EF71
NW7 . . . . .43 CT48
SW3 . . . . .100 DE79
Lawrence Way, NW10 . . . . . .62 CQ62
Lawrence Weaver Cl, Mord. SM4
off Green La 140 DB100
Lawrie Pk Av, SE26 . . . . . . .122 DV92
Lawrie Pk Cres, SE26 . . . . . .122 DV92
Lawrie Pk Gdns, SE26 . . . . . .122 DV91
Lawrie Pk Rd, SE26 . . . . . . .122 DV93
Lawson Cl, E16 . . . . .86 EJ71
SW19 . . . . .119 CX90
Lawson Est, SE1 . . . . .201 K7
Lawson Gdns, Dart. DA1 . . . .128 FK85
Pinner HA5 . . . . .59 BV55
Lawson Rd, Dart. DA1 . . . . .108 FK84
Enfield EN3 . . . . .30 DW39
Southall UB1 . . . . .78 BZ70
Lawson Wk, Cars. SM5 . . . . .158 DF110
Law St, SE1 . . . . .201 L6
Lawton Rd, E3 . . . . .85 DY69
E10 . . . . .67 EC60
Barnet EN4 . . . . .28 DD41
Loughton IG10 . . . . . . .33 EP41
Laxcon Cl, NW10 . . . . .62 CQ64
Laxey Rd, Orp. BR6 . . . . . . .163 ET107
Laxley Cl, SE5 . . . . .101 DP80
Laxton Gdns, Red. (Shenley) WD7
off Porters Pk Dr 10 CL32
Redhill RH1 . . . . .185 DK128
Laxton Pl, NW1 . . . . .195 J4
Layard Rd, SE16 . . . . .202 E8
Enfield EN1 . . . . .30 DT39
Thornton Heath CR7 . . . .142 DR96
Layard Sq, SE16 . . . . .202 D8
Layborne Av, Rom. RM3
off Cummings Hall La 52 FJ48
Layburn Cres, Slou. SL3 . . . .93 BB79
Laycock St, N1 . . . . .83 DN65
Layer Gdns, W3 . . . . .80 CN73
Layfield Cl, NW4 . . . . .63 CV59
Layfield Cres, NW4 . . . . .63 CV59
Layfield Rd, NW4 . . . . .63 CV59
Layhams Rd, Kes. BR2 . . . . .162 EF106
West Wickham BR4 . . . .143 ED104
Laymarsh Cl, Belv. DA17 . . . .106 EZ76
Laymead Cl, Nthlt. UB5 . . . . .78 BY65
Laystall St, EC1 . . . . .196 D5
Layters Av, Ger.Cr. (Chal.St.P.)
SL9 . . . . .36 AW54
Layters Av S, Ger.Cr. (Chal.St.P.)
SL9 . . . . .36 AW54
Layters Cl, Ger.Cr. (Chal.St.P.)
SL9 . . . . .36 AW54
Layters End, Ger.Cr. (Chal.St.P.)
SL9 . . . . .36 AW54
LAYTER'S GREEN, Ger.Cr. 36 AW54
Layters Grn La, Ger.Cr. (Chal.St.P.)
SL9 . . . . .56 AU55
Layter's Grn Mobile Home Pk,
Ger.Cr. (Chal.St.P.) SL9
off Layters Grn La 36 AV54
Layters Way, Ger.Cr. SL9 . . . .56 AX56
Layton Cr, Wey. KT13
off Castle Vw Rd 153 BP105
Layton Cres, Croy. CR0 . . . .159 DN106
Layton Pl, Rich. TW9
off Station Av 98 CN81
Layton Rd, Brent. TW8 . . . . .97 CK78
Hounslow TW3 . . . . . . .96 CB84
Laytons Bldgs, SE1 . . . . . . .201 J4
Laytons La, Sun. TW16 . . . . .135 BT96
Layzell Wk, SE9
off Mottingham La 124 EK88

A B C D E F G H I J K L M N O P Q R S T U V W X Y Z

★ Place of interest   ⇄ Railway station   ⊖ London Underground station   [DLR] Docklands Light Railway station   ⬦ Tramlink station   🄷 Hospital

Laz - Lew

Lazar Wk, N7 *off Briset Way* 65 DM61
Lea, The, Egh. TW20 . . . . .133 BB95
Leabank Cl, Har. HA1 . . . . .61 CE62
Leabank Sq, E9 . . . . .85 EA65
Leabank Vw, N15 . . . . .66 DU58
Leabourne Rd, N16 . . . . .66 DU58
LEA BRIDGE, E5 . . . . .67 DX62
Lea Br Business Cen, E10
   off Burwell Rd 67 DY60
Lea Br Rd, E5 . . . . .66 DW62
   E10 . . . . .67 DY60
   E17 . . . . .67 ED56
Lea Bushes, Wat. WD25 . . . . . .24 BY35
Leachcroft, Ger.Cr. (Chal.St.P.)
   SL9 . . . . .36 AV53
Leach Gro, Lthd. KT22 . . . . . . .171 CJ122
Lea Cl, Bushey WD23 . . . . .24 CB43
   Twickenham TW2 . . . . .116 BZ87
Lea Cres, Ruis. HA4 . . . . .59 BT63
Leacroft, Stai. TW18 . . . . .114 BH91
Leacroft Av, SW12 . . . . .120 DF87
Leacroft Cl, Ken. CR8 . . . . . . .176 DQ116
   Staines TW18 . . . . .114 BH91
   West Drayton UB7 . . . . .76 BL72
Leacroft Rd, Iver SL0 . . . . .75 BD72
Leadale Av, E4 . . . . .47 EA47
Leadale Rd, N15 . . . . .66 DU58
   N16 . . . . .66 DU58
Leadbeaters Cl, N11
   off Goldsmith Rd 44 DF50
★ **Leadenhall Mkt**, EC3 . . . . . .197 M9
Leadenhall Mkt, EC3 . . . . . . .197 M9
Leadenhall Pl, EC3 . . . . .197 M9
Leadenhall St, EC3 . . . . .197 M9
Leader Av, E12 . . . . .69 EN64
Leadings, The, Wem. HA9 . . . . .62 CQ62
Leaf Cl, Nthwd. HA6 . . . . .39 BR52
   Thames Ditton KT7 . . . . . . .137 CE99
Leaf Gro, SE27 . . . . .121 DN90
Leafield Cl, SW16 . . . . .121 DP93
   Woking GU21
   off Winnington Way 166 AV118
Leafield La, Sid. DA14 . . . . . . .126 EZ91
Leafield Rd, SW20 . . . . .139 CZ97
   Sutton SM1 . . . . .140 DA103
Leaford Cres, Wat. WD24 . . . . .23 BT37
Leaforis Rd, Wal.Cr. EN7 . . . . .14 DU28
Leafy Gro, Croy. CR0 . . . . .161 DY111
   Keston BR2 . . . . .162 EJ106
Leafy Oak Rd, SE12 . . . . .124 EJ90
Leafy Way, Brwd. CM13 . . . . . .55 GD46
   Croydon CR0 . . . . .142 DT103
Lea Gdns, Wem. HA9 . . . . .62 CL63
Leagrave St, E5 . . . . .66 DW62
Lea Hall Rd, E10 . . . . .67 EA60
Leaholme Way, Ruis. HA4 . . . . .59 BP58
Leahurst Rd, SE13 . . . . .123 ED85
Leake St, SE1 . . . . .200 C4
Lealand Rd, N15 . . . . .66 DT58
Leamington Av, E17 . . . . .67 EA57
   Bromley BR1 . . . . .124 EJ92
   Morden SM4 . . . . .139 CZ98
   Orpington BR6 . . . . .163 ES105
Leamington Cl, E12 . . . . .68 EL64
   Bromley BR1 . . . . .124 EJ92
   Hounslow TW3 . . . . .116 CC85
   Romford RM3 . . . . .52 FM51
Leamington Cres, Har. HA2 . . . .60 BY62
Leamington Gdns, Ilf. IG3 . . . . .69 ET61
Leamington Pk, W3 . . . . .80 CR71
Leamington Pl, Hayes UB4 . . . . .77 BT70
Leamington Rd, Rom. RM3 . . . .52 FN50
   Southall UB2 . . . . .96 BX77
Leamington Rd Vil, W11 . . . . . . .81 CZ71
Leamore St, W6 . . . . .99 CV77
Lea Mt, Wal.Cr. EN7 . . . . .14 DS28
Leamouth Rd, E6
   off Remington Rd 86 EL72
   E14 . . . . .85 ED72
Leander Ct, SE8 . . . . .103 EA83
Leander Dr, Grav. DA12 . . . . . .131 GM91
Leander Gdns, Wat. WD25 . . . .24 BY37
Leander Rd, SW2 . . . . .121 DM86
   Northolt UB5 . . . . .78 CA68
   Thornton Heath CR7 . . . . . .141 DM98
Learner Dr, Har. HA2 . . . . .60 CA61
Lea Rd, Beck. BR3
   off Fairfield Rd 143 EA96
   Enfield EN2 . . . . .30 DR39
   Grays RM16 . . . . .111 GG78
   Sevenoaks TN13 . . . . .191 FJ127
   Southall UB2 . . . . .96 BY77
   Waltham Abbey EN9 . . . . . .15 EA34
Learoyd Gdns, E6 . . . . .87 EN73
Leas, The, Bushey WD23 . . . . .24 BZ39
   Staines TW18
   off Raleigh Ct 114 BG91
   Upminster RM14 . . . . .73 FR59
Leas Cl, Chess. KT9 . . . . .156 CM108
Leas Dale, SE9 . . . . .125 EN90
Leas Dr, Iver SL0 . . . . .75 BE72
Leas Grn, Chis. BR7 . . . . .125 ET93
Leaside, Lthd. (Bkhm.) KT23 . . .170 CA123
Leaside Av, N10 . . . . .64 DG55
Leaside Ct, Uxb. UB10
   off The Larches 77 BP69
Leaside Rd, E5 . . . . .66 DW60
Leasowes Rd, E10 . . . . .67 EA60
Leas Rd, Warl. CR6 . . . . .177 DX118
Leasway, Brwd. CM14 . . . . .54 FX48
   Upminster RM14 . . . . .72 FQ62
Leathart Cl, Horn. RM12
   off Dowding Way 89 FH66
Leatherbottle Grn, Erith
   DA18 . . . . .106 EZ76
Leather Bottle La, Belv.
   DA17 . . . . .106 EY77
Leather Cl, Mitch. CR4 . . . . . . .140 DG96
Leatherdale St, E1
   off Portelet Rd 85 DX70
Leather Gdns, E15
   off Abbey Rd 86 EE67
LEATHERHEAD 171 CF121

⇌ **Leatherhead** 171 CG121
Leatherhead Bypass Rd, Lthd.
   KT22 . . . . .171 CH120
LEATHERHEAD COMMON,
   Lthd. 171 CF119
H **Leatherhead Hosp**, Lthd.
   KT22 . . . . .171 CJ122
★ **Leatherhead Mus of Local**
   History, Lthd. KT22 . . . . . .171 CH122
Leatherhead Rd, Ashtd.
   KT21 . . . . .171 CK121
   Chessington KT9 . . . . .155 CJ111
   Leatherhead KT22 . . . . . . .171 CK121
   Leatherhead (Oxshott)
   KT22 . . . . .155 CD114
Leather La, EC1 . . . . .196 E7
   Hornchurch RM11
   off North St 72 FK60
Leathermarket Ct, SE1 . . . . . .201 M5
Leathermarket St, SE1 . . . . . .201 M5
Leathersellers Cl, Barn. EN5
   off The Avenue 27 CY42
Leathsail Rd, Har. HA2 . . . . . . .60 CB62
Leathwaite Rd, SW11 . . . . . . .100 DF84
Leathwell Rd, SE8 . . . . .103 EB82
Lea Vale, Dart. DA1 . . . . .107 FD84
Lea Valley Rd, E4 . . . . .31 DX43
   Enfield EN3 . . . . .31 DX43
Lea Valley Trd Est, N18 . . . . . . .47 DX50
Lea Valley Viaduct, E4 . . . . . . .47 DX50
   N18 . . . . .47 DX50
Lea Valley Wk, E3 . . . . .85 EC70
   E5 .67 DY62
   E9 .67 DY62
   E10 . . . . .67 DY62
   E14 . . . . .85 EB71
   E15 . . . . .85 EC69
   E17 . . . . .46 DW53
   N9 .47 DY46
   N15 . . . . .66 DU58
   N16 . . . . .66 DU58
   N17 . . . . .46 DW53
   N18 . . . . .46 DW53
   Enfield EN3 . . . . .31 DZ41
   Waltham Abbey EN9 . . . . . .15 DZ30
   Waltham Cross EN8 . . . . . . .15 DZ30
Leaveland Cl, Beck. BR3 . . . . .143 EA98
Leaver Gdns, Grnf. UB6 . . . . . .79 CD68
LEAVESDEN GREEN, Wat. 7 BT34
   Watford WD24 . . . . .23 BV38
Leavesden Rd, Stan. HA7 . . . . .41 CG51
   Weybridge KT13 . . . . .153 BP106
LEAVES GREEN, Kes. 162 EK109
Leaves Grn Cres, Kes. BR2 . . .162 EJ111
Leaves Grn Rd, Kes. BR2 . . . . .162 EK111
Leaview, Wal.Abb. EN9 . . . . . .15 EB33
Lea Vw Hos, E5
   off Springfield 66 DV60
Leaway, E10 . . . . .67 DV60
Leazes Av, Cat. CR3 . . . . .175 DN123
Leazes La, Cat. CR3 . . . . .175 DN123
Lebanon Av, Felt. TW13 . . . . . .116 BX92
Lebanon Cl, Wat. WD17 . . . . . .23 BR36
Lebanon Ct, Dob. KT11 . . . . . .154 CA113
Lebanon Gdns, SW18 . . . . . . .120 DA86
   Westerham (Bigg.H.) TN16 . .178 EK117
Lebanon Pk, Twick. TW1 . . . . .117 CH87
⇌ **Lebanon Road** 142 DS103
Lebanon Rd, SW18 . . . . .120 DA85
   Croydon CR0 . . . . .142 DS102
Lebrun Sq, SE3 . . . . .104 EH83
Lechmere App, Wdf.Grn. IG8 . . .48 EJ54
Lechmere Av, Chig. IG7 . . . . . .49 EQ49
   Woodford Green IG8 . . . . . .48 EK54
Lechmere Rd, NW2 . . . . .81 CV65
Leckford Rd, SW18 . . . . .120 DC89
Leckwith Av, Bexh. DA7 . . . . . .106 EY79
Lecky St, SW7 . . . . .100 DD78
Leclair Ho, SE3 *off Gallus Sq* . .104 EH83
Leconfield Av, SW13 . . . . .99 CT83
Leconfield Rd, N5 . . . . .66 DR63
Leconfield Wk, Horn. RM12
   off Airfield Way 90 FJ65
Leda Av, Enf. EN3 . . . . .31 DX39
Leda Rd, SE18 . . . . .105 EM76
Ledbury Est, SE15 . . . . .102 DV80
Ledbury Ms N, W11
   off Ledbury Rd 82 DA73
Ledbury Ms W, W11
   off Ledbury Rd 82 DA73
Ledbury Pl, Croy. CR0
   off Ledbury Rd 160 DQ105
Ledbury Rd, W11 . . . . .81 CZ72
   Croydon CR0 . . . . .160 DQ105
   Reigate RH2 . . . . .183 CZ133
Ledbury St, SE15 . . . . .102 DU80
Ledger Dr, Add. KT15 . . . . .151 BF106
Ledgers Rd, Slou. SL1 . . . . . . .92 AS75
   Warlingham CR6 . . . . .177 EB117
Ledrington Rd, SE19
   off Anerley Hill 122 DU93
Ledway Dr, Wem. HA9 . . . . .62 CM59
LEE, SE12 . . . . .124 EE84
⇌ **Lee** 124 EG86
Lee, The, Nthwd. HA6 . . . . .39 BT50
Lee Av, Rom. RM6 . . . . .70 EY58
Lee Br, SE13 . . . . .103 EC83
Lee Cl, E17 . . . . .47 DX53
   Barnet EN5 . . . . .28 DC42
Lee Conservancy Rd, E9 . . . . . .67 DY64
Leecroft Rd, Barn. EN5 . . . . . . .27 CY43
Leeds Cl, Orp. BR6 . . . . .146 EX103
Leeds Pl, N4 *off Tollington Pk* . .65 DM61
Leeds Rd, Ilf. IG1 . . . . .69 ER60
   Slough SL1 . . . . .74 AS73
Leeds St, N18 . . . . .46 DU50
Lee Fm Cl, Chesh. HP5 . . . . .4 AU30

Leefern Rd, W12 . . . . .99 CU75
Lee Gdns Av, Horn. RM11 . . . . .72 FN60
Leegate, SE12 . . . . .124 EF85
Leegate Cl, Wok. GU21
   off Sythwood 166 AV116
Lee Grn, SE12
   off Lee High Rd 124 EF85
Lee Grn La, Epsom KT18 . . . . .172 CP124
Lee Gro, Chig. IG7 . . . . .49 EN47
Lee High Rd, SE12 . . . . .103 ED83
   SE13 . . . . .103 ED83
Leeke St, WC1 . . . . .196 B2
Leeland Rd, W13 . . . . .79 CG74
Leeland Ter, W13 . . . . .79 CG74
Leeland Way, NW10 . . . . .63 CT63
Leeming Rd, Borwd. WD6 . . . . .26 CM39
Lee Pk, SE3 . . . . .104 EF84
Lee Pk Way, N9 . . . . .47 DX49
   N18 . . . . .47 DX49
Leerdam Dr, E14 . . . . .204 E7
Lee Rd, NW7 . . . . .43 CX52
   SE3 . . . . .104 EF83
   SW19 . . . . .140 DB95
   Enfield EN1 . . . . .30 DU44
   Greenford UB6 . . . . .79 CJ67
Lees, The, Croy. CR0 . . . . .143 DZ103
Lees Av, Nthwd. HA6 . . . . .39 BT53
Leeside, Barn. EN5 . . . . .27 CY43
   Potters Bar EN6
   off Wayside 12 DD31
Leeside Ct, SE16 . . . . .203 H2
Leeside Cres, NW11 . . . . .63 CZ58
Leeside Rd, N17 . . . . .46 DV51
Leeson Rd, SE24 . . . . .101 DN84
Leesons Hill, Chis. BR7 . . . . . .145 ES97
   Orpington BR5 . . . . .146 EU97
Leesons Way, Orp. BR5 . . . . . .145 ET96
Lees Pl, W1 . . . . .194 F10
Lees Rd, Uxb. UB8 . . . . .77 BP70
Lee St, E8 . . . . .84 DT67
Lee Ter, SE3 . . . . .104 EE83
   SE13 . . . . .104 EE83
Lee Valley Cycle Route, Wal.Abb.
   EN9 . . . . .15 EC26
★ **Lee Valley Pk**, E10 . . . . .15 DZ31
Lee Valley Pathway, E9 . . . . . .67 DZ62
   E10 . . . . .66 DW59
   E17 . . . . .66 DW59
   Waltham Abbey EN9 . . . . . .15 EA31
Lee Valley Technopark, N17 . . . .66 DU55
Lee Vw, Enf. EN2 . . . . .29 DP39
Leeward Gdns, SW19 . . . . . . .119 CZ93
Leeway, SE8 . . . . .203 M10
Leeway Cl, Pnr. HA5 . . . . .40 BZ52
Leewood Cl, SE12
   off Upwood Rd 124 EF86
Leewood Rd, Swan. BR8 . . . . .147 FD98
Lefevre Wk, E3 . . . . .85 EA67
Lefroy Rd, W12 . . . . .99 CT75
Legard Rd, N5 . . . . .65 DP62
Legatt Rd, SE9 . . . . .124 EK85
Leggatt Rd, E15 . . . . .85 EC68
Leggatts Cl, Wat. WD24 . . . . . .23 BT36
Leggatts Ri, Wat. WD25 . . . . . .23 BU35
Leggatts Way, Wat. WD24 . . . . .23 BT36
Leggatts Wd Av, Wat. WD24 . . .23 BV36
Legge St, SE13 . . . . .123 EC85
Leghorn Rd, NW10 . . . . .81 CT68
   SE18 . . . . .105 ER78
Legion Cl, N1 . . . . .83 DN65
Legion Ct, Mord. SM4 . . . . . . .140 DA100
Legion Rd, Grnf. UB6 . . . . .78 CC67
Legion Ter, E3 *off Lefevre Wk* . .85 DZ67
Legion Way, N12 . . . . .44 DE52
Legon Av, Rom. RM7 . . . . .71 FC60
Legrace Av, Houns. TW4 . . . . . .96 BX82
Leicester Av, Mitch. CR4 . . . . .141 DL98
Leicester Cl, Wor.Pk. KT4 . . . . .157 CW105
Leicester Ct, WC2 . . . . .195 N10
Leicester Gdns, Ilf. IG3 . . . . . . .69 ES59
Leicester Ms, N2
   off Leicester Rd 64 DE55
Leicester Pl, WC2 . . . . .195 N10
Leicester Rd, E11 . . . . .68 EH57
   N2 .64 DE55
   Barnet EN5 . . . . .28 DB43
   Croydon CR0 . . . . .142 DS101
   Tilbury RM18 . . . . .111 GF81
★ **Leicester Square** 195 N10
Leicester Sq, WC2 . . . . .199 N1
Leicester St, WC2 . . . . .195 N10
Leigham Av, SW16 . . . . .121 DL90
Leigham Ct, Wall. SM6
   off Stafford Rd 159 DJ107
Leigham Ct Rd, SW16 . . . . . . .121 DL89
Leigham Dr, Islw. TW7 . . . . . . .97 CE80
Leigham Vale, SW2 . . . . .121 DM90
   SW16 . . . . .121 DM90
Leigh Av, Ilf. IG4 . . . . .68 EK56
Leigh Cl, Add. KT15 . . . . .151 BF108
   New Malden KT3 . . . . .138 CR98
Leigh Cor, Cob. KT11
   off Leigh Hill Rd 154 BW114
Leigh Ct, SE4
   off Lewisham Way 103 EA82
   Borehamwood WD6
   off Banks Rd 26 CR40
   Harrow HA2 . . . . .61 CE60
Leigh Ct Cl, Cob. KT11 . . . . . . .154 BW114
Leigh Cres, Croy. (New Adgtn.)
   CR0 . . . . .161 EB108
Leigh Dr, Rom. RM3 . . . . .52 FK49
Leigh Gdns, NW10 . . . . .81 CW68
Leigh Hill Rd, Cob. KT11 . . . . .154 BW114
Leigh Hunt Dr, N14 . . . . .45 DK46
Leigh Hunt St, SE1 . . . . .201 H4
Leigh Orchard Cl, SW16 . . . . . .121 DM90
Leigh Pk, Slou. (Datchet) SL3 . .92 AV80
Leigh Pl, EC1 . . . . .196 E6
   Cobham KT11 . . . . .170 BW115
   Dartford DA2
   off Hawley Rd 128 FN92
   Welling DA16 . . . . .106 EU82
Leigh Pl La, Gdse. RH9 . . . . . .187 DY132
Leigh Rd, E6 . . . . .87 EN65

Leigh Rd, E10 . . . . .67 EC59
   N5 .65 DP63
   Cobham KT11 . . . . .153 BV113
   Gravesend DA11 . . . . .131 GH89
   Hounslow TW3 . . . . .97 CD84
Leigh Rodd, Wat. WD19 . . . . . . .40 BZ48
Leigh St, WC1 . . . . .196 P4
Leigh Ter, Orp. BR5
   off Saxville Rd 146 EV97
Leighton Av, E12 . . . . .69 EN64
   Pinner HA5 . . . . .60 BY55
Leighton Cl, Edg. HA8 . . . . .42 CN54
Leighton Cres, NW5
   off Leighton Gro 65 DJ64
Leighton Gdns, NW10 . . . . .81 CV68
   South Croydon CR2 . . . . . .160 DV113
   Tilbury RM18 . . . . .111 GG80
★ **Leighton Ho Mus**, W14 . . . . .99 CZ76
Leighton Pl, NW5 . . . . .65 DJ64
Leighton Rd, NW5 . . . . .65 DK64
   W13 . . . . .97 CG75
   Enfield EN1 . . . . .30 DT43
   Harrow (Har.Wld.) HA3 . . . . .41 CD54
   Croydon CR0 . . . . .141 DP102
Leighton Way, Epsom KT18 . . .156 CR114
Leila Parnell Pl, SE7 . . . . .104 EJ79
Leinster Av, SW14 . . . . .98 CQ83
Leinster Gdns, W2 . . . . .82 DC72
Leinster Ms, W2 . . . . .82 DC73
Leinster Pl, W2 . . . . .82 DC72
Leinster Rd, N10 . . . . .65 DH56
Leinster Sq, W2 . . . . .82 DA72
Leinster Ter, W2 . . . . .82 DC73
Leiston Spur, Slou. SL1 . . . . . . .74 AS72
Leisure La, W.Byf. KT14 . . . . . .152 BH112
Leisure Way, N12 . . . . .44 DD52
Leith Cl, NW9 . . . . .62 CR60
   Slough SL1 . . . . .74 AU74
Leithcote Gdns, SW16 . . . . . . .121 DM91
Leithcote Path, SW16 . . . . . . .121 DM90
Leith Hill, Orp. BR5 . . . . .146 EU95
Leith Hill Grn, Orp. BR5
   off Leith Hill 146 EU95
Leith Pk Rd, Grav. DA12 . . . . .131 GH88
Leith Rd, N22 . . . . .45 DP53
   Epsom KT17 . . . . .156 CS112
Leith Yd, NW6 *off Quex Rd* 82 DA67
Lela Av, Houns. TW4 . . . . .96 BW82
Lelitia Cl, E8 *off Pownall Rd* . . .84 DU67
Leman St, E1 . . . . .84 DT72
Lemark Cl, Stan. HA7 . . . . .41 CJ50
Le May Av, SE12 . . . . .124 EH90
Lemmon Rd, SE10 . . . . .104 EE79
Lemna Rd, E11 . . . . .68 EE59
Lemonfield Dr, Wat. WD25 . . . . .8 BY32
Lemonwell Ct, SE9
   off Lemonwell Dr 125 EQ85
Lemonwell Dr, SE9 . . . . .125 EQ85
Lemsford Cl, N15 . . . . .66 DU57
Lemsford Ct, N4
   off Brownswood Rd 66 DQ61
   Borehamwood WD6 . . . . . .26 CQ42
Lemuel St, SW18 . . . . .120 DB86
Lena Gdns, W6 . . . . .99 CW76
Lena Kennedy Cl, E4 . . . . .47 EB51
Lenanton Steps, E14 . . . . .204 A4
Lendal Ter, SW4 . . . . .101 DK83
Lenelby Rd, Surb. KT6 . . . . . . .138 CN102
Len Freeman Pl, SW6
   off John Smith Av 99 CZ80
Lenham Rd, SE12 . . . . .104 EF84
   Bexleyheath DA7 . . . . .106 EZ79
   Sutton SM1 . . . . .158 DB106
   Thornton Heath CR7 . . . . . .142 DR98
Lenmore Av, Grays RM17 . . . . .110 GC76
Lennard Av, W.Wick. BR4 . . . . .144 EE103
Lennard Cl, W.Wick. BR4 . . . . .144 EE103
Lennard Rd, SE20 . . . . .122 DW93
   Beckenham BR3 . . . . .123 DX93
   Bromley BR2 . . . . .145 EM102
   Croydon CR0 . . . . .142 DQ102
   Sevenoaks (Dunt.Grn.)
   TN13 . . . . .181 FE120
Lennard Row, S.Ock. (Aveley)
   RM15 . . . . .91 FR74
Lennon Rd, NW2 . . . . .63 CW64
Lennox Av, Grav. DA11 . . . . . .131 GF86
Lennox Cl, Grays (Chaff.Hun.)
   RM16 . . . . .109 FW77
   Romford RM1 . . . . .71 FF58
Lennox Gdns, NW10 . . . . .63 CU65
   SW1 . . . . .198 D7
   Croydon CR0 . . . . .159 DP105
   Ilford IG1 . . . . .69 EM60
Lennox Gdns Ms, SW1 . . . . . .198 D7
Lennox Rd, E17 . . . . .67 DZ58
   N4 .65 DM61
   Gravesend DA11 . . . . .131 GF86
Lennox Rd E, Grav. DA11 . . . . .131 GG87
Lenor Cl, Bexh. DA6 . . . . .106 EY84
Lensbury Cl, Wal.Cr. (Chsht.) EN8
   off Ashdown Cres 15 DY28
Lensbury Way, SE2 . . . . .106 EW76
Lens Rd, E7 . . . . .86 EJ66
Lenthall Av, Grays RM17 . . . . .110 GA75
Lenthall Rd, E8 . . . . .84 DU66
   Loughton IG10 . . . . .33 ER42
Lenthorp Rd, SE10 . . . . .205 K10
Lentmead Rd, Brom. BR1 . . . . .124 EF90
Lenton Path, SE18 . . . . .105 ER79
Lenton Ri, Rich. TW9
   off Evelyn Ter 98 CL83
Lenton St, SE18 . . . . .105 ER77
Leof Cres, SE6 . . . . .123 EB92
Leominster Rd, Mord. SM4 . . . .140 DC100
Leominster Wk, Mord. SM4 . . . .140 DC100
Leonard Av, Mord. SM4 . . . . . .140 DC99
   Romford RM7 . . . . .71 FD60
   Sevenoaks (Otford) TN14 . .181 FH116
   Swanscombe DA10 . . . . . .130 FY87
Leonard Pl, N16 *off Allen Rd* . . .66 DS63
Leonard Rd, E4 . . . . .47 EA51
   E7 .68 EG63
   N9 .46 DT48
   SW16 . . . . .141 DJ95
   Southall UB2 . . . . .96 BX76

Leonard Robbins Path, SE28
   off Tawney Rd 88 EV73
Leonard St, E16 . . . . .86 EL74
   EC2 . . . . .197 L4
Leonard Way, Brwd. CM14 . . . .54 FS49
Leontine Cl, SE15 . . . . .102 DU80
Leopold Av, SW19 . . . . .119 CZ92
Leopold Dr, Slou. SL1 . . . . .74 AS71
Leopold Ms, E9
   off Fremont St 84 DW67
Leopold Rd, E17 . . . . .67 EA57
   N2 .64 DD55
   N18 . . . . .46 DV50
   NW10 . . . . .80 CS66
   SW19 . . . . .119 CZ91
   W5 .80 CM74
Leopold St, E3 . . . . .85 DZ71
Leopold Ter, SW19
   off Dora Rd 120 DA92
Leo St, SE15 . . . . .102 DV80
Leo Yd, EC1 . . . . .196 G5
Le Personne Rd, Cat. CR3 . . . .176 DR122
Leppoc Rd, SW4 . . . . .121 DK85
Leret Way, Lthd. KT22 . . . . . . .171 CH121
Leroy St, SE1 . . . . .201 M8
Lerwick Dr, Slou. SL1 . . . . .74 AS71
Lescombe Cl, SE23 . . . . .123 DY90
Lescombe Rd, SE23 . . . . .123 DY90
Lesley Cl, Bex. DA5 . . . . .127 FB87
   Gravesend (Istead Rise)
   DA13 . . . . .131 GF94
   Swanley BR8 . . . . .147 FD97
Leslie Gdns, Sutt. SM2 . . . . . .158 DA108
Leslie Gro, Croy. CR0 . . . . . . .142 DS102
Leslie Gro Pl, Croy. CR0
   off Leslie Gro 142 DR102
Leslie Pk Rd, Croy. CR0 . . . . . .142 DS102
Leslie Rd, E11 . . . . .67 EC63
   E16 . . . . .86 EH72
   N2 .64 DD55
   Woking (Chobham) GU24 . .150 AS110
Leslie Smith Sq, SE18
   off Nightingale Vale 105 EN79
★ **Lesnes Abbey (ruins)**, Erith
   DA18 . . . . .106 EX77
Lesney Fm Est, Erith DA8 . . . .107 FD80
Lesney Pk, Erith DA8 . . . . .107 FD79
Lesney Pk Rd, Erith DA8 . . . . .107 FD79
Lessar Av, SW4 . . . . .121 DJ85
Lessingham Av, SW17 . . . . . . .120 DF91
   Ilford IG5 . . . . .69 EN55
Lessing St, SE23 . . . . .123 DY87
Lessington Av, Rom. RM7 . . . . .71 FC58
LESSNESS HEATH, Belv. 107 FB78
Lessness Av, Bexh. DA7 . . . . .106 EX80
Lessness Pk, Belv. DA17 . . . . .106 EZ78
Lessness Rd, Belv. DA17
   off Stapley Rd 106 FA78
   Morden SM4 . . . . .140 DC100
Lester Av, E15 . . . . .86 EE69
Leston Cl, Rain. RM13 . . . . .89 FG69
Leswin Pl, N16 *off Leswin Rd* . .66 DT62
Leswin Rd, N16 . . . . .66 DT62
Letchfield, Chesh. (Ley Hill)
   HP5 . . . . .4 AV31
Letchford Gdns, NW10 . . . . . . .81 CU69
Letchford Ms, NW10
   off Letchford Gdns 81 CU69
Letchford Ter, Har. HA3 . . . . . . .40 CB53
LETCHMORE HEATH, Wat. 25 CD38
Letchmore Rd, Rad. WD7 . . . . .25 CG36
Letchworth Av, Felt. TW14 . . . .115 BT87
Letchworth Cl, Brom. BR2 . . . .144 EG99
   Watford WD19 . . . . .40 BX50
Letchworth Dr, Brom. BR2 . . . .144 EG99
Letchworth St, SW17 . . . . .120 DF91
Lethbridge Cl, SE13 . . . . .103 EC81
Letter Box La, Sev. TN13 . . . . .191 FJ129
Letterstone Rd, SW6
   off Varna Rd 99 CZ80
Lettice St, SW6 . . . . .99 CZ81
Lett Rd, E15 . . . . .85 ED66
Lettsom St, SE5 . . . . .102 DS82
Lettsom Wk, E13 . . . . .86 EG68
Leucha Rd, E17 . . . . .67 DY57
Levana Cl, SW19 . . . . .119 CY88
Levehurst Way, SW4 . . . . .101 DL82
Leven Cl, Wal.Cr. EN8 . . . . .15 DX33
   Watford WD19 . . . . .40 BX50
Levendale Rd, SE23 . . . . .123 DY89
Leven Dr, Wal.Cr. EN8 . . . . .15 DX33
Leven Rd, E14 . . . . .85 EC71
Leven Way, Hayes UB3 . . . . . . .77 BS72
Leveret Cl, Croy. (New Adgtn.)
   CR0 . . . . .161 ED111
   Watford WD25 . . . . .7 BU34
Leverett St, SW3 . . . . .198 C8
Leverholme Gdns, SE9 . . . . . .125 EN90
Leverson St, SW16 . . . . .121 DJ93
Leverton Pl, NW5 . . . . .65 DJ64
Leverton St, NW5 . . . . .65 DJ64
Leverton Way, Wal.Abb. EN9 . . .15 EC33
Leveson Rd, Grays RM16 . . . . .111 GH76
Levett Gdns, Ilf. IG3 . . . . .69 ET63
Levett Rd, Bark. IG11 . . . . .87 ES65
   Leatherhead KT22 . . . . . . .171 CH120
Levine Gdns, Bark. IG11 . . . . . .88 EX68
Levison Way, N19
   off Grovedale Rd 65 DK61
Lewes Cl, Grays RM17 . . . . . . .110 GA79
   Northolt UB5 . . . . .78 CA65
Lewesdon Cl, SW19 . . . . .119 CX88
Lewes Rd, N12 . . . . .44 DE50
   Bromley BR1 . . . . .144 EK96
   Romford RM3 . . . . .52 FJ49
Leweston Pl, N16 . . . . .66 DT59
Lewes Way, Rick. (Crox.Grn.)
   WD3 . . . . .23 BQ42
Lewey Ho, E3 . . . . .85 DZ70
Lewgars Av, NW9 . . . . .62 CQ58
Lewin Rd, SW14 . . . . .98 CR83
   SW16 . . . . .121 DK93
   Bexleyheath DA6 . . . . .106 EY84
Lewins Rd, Epsom KT18 . . . . . .156 CP114

Lewins Rd, Ger.Cr. (Chal.St.P.)
  SL9 . . . . .56 AX55
Lewis Av, E17 . . . . .47 EA53
Lewis Cl, N14 off Orchid Rd . .45 DJ45
  Addlestone KT15 . . . . .152 BJ105
  Brentwood CM15 . . . . .55 FZ45
  Uxbridge (Hare.) UB9 . . . . . .38 BJ54
Lewis Cres, NW10 . . . . .62 CQ64
Lewis Gdns, N2 . . . . .44 DD54
Lewis Gro, SE13 . . . . .103 EC83
LEWISHAM, SE13 . . . . .103 EB84
≷ Lewisham 103 EC83
ⅅⅬⅡ Lewisham 103 EC83
Lewisham Cen, SE13 . . . . . . .103 EC83
Lewisham High St, SE13 . . . .103 EC83
Lewisham Hill, SE13 . . . . . . .103 EC82
Lewisham Pk, SE13 . . . . .123 EB86
Lewisham Rd, SE13 . . . . .103 EB81
Lewisham St, SW1 . . . . .199 N5
Lewisham Way, SE4 . . . . .103 DZ81
  SE14 . . . . .103 DZ81
Lewis La, Ger.Cr. (Chal.St.P.)
  SL9 . . . . .36 AY53
Lewis Pl, E8 . . . . .66 DU64
Lewis Rd, Horn. RM11 . . . . . . .72 FJ58
  Mitcham CR4 . . . . .140 DD96
  Richmond TW10
   off Red Lion St 117 CK85
  Sidcup DA14 . . . . .126 EW90
  Southall UB1 . . . . .96 BY75
  Sutton SM1 . . . . .158 DB105
  Swanscombe DA10 . . . . . .130 FY86
  Welling DA16 . . . . .106 EW83
Lewis St, NW1 . . . . .83 DH65
Lewis Way, Dag. RM10 . . . . . . .89 FB65
Lexden Dr, Rom. RM6 . . . . .70 EV58
Lexden Rd, W3 . . . . .80 CP73
  Mitcham CR4 . . . . .141 DK98
Lexham Ct, Grnf. UB6 . . . . .79 CD67
Lexham Gdns, W8 . . . . .100 DB76
Lexham Gdns Ms, W8 . . . . . .100 DB76
Lexham Ho, Bark. IG11
  off St. Margarets 87 ER67
Lexham Ms, W8 . . . . .100 DA77
Lexham Wk, W8
  off Lexham Gdns 100 DB76
Lexington, The, EC1 . . . . .197 K4
Lexington Cl, Borwd. WD6 . . . .26 CM41
Lexington Ct, Pur. CR8 . . . . . .160 DQ110
Lexington St, W1 . . . . .195 L9
Lexington Way, Barn. EN5 . . . .27 CX42
  Upminster RM14 . . . . .73 FT58
Lexton Gdns, SW12 . . . . .121 DK88
Leyborne Av, W13 . . . . .97 CH75
Leyborne Pk, Rich. TW9 . . . . . .98 CN81
Leybourne Av, W.Byf. (Byfleet)
  KT14 . . . . .152 BM113
Leybourne Cl, Brom. BR2 . . . .144 EG100
  West Byfleet (Byfleet) KT14
   off Leybourne Av 152 BM113
Leybourne Rd, E11 . . . . .68 EF60
  NW1 . . . . .83 DH66
  NW9 . . . . .62 CN57
  Uxbridge UB10 . . . . .77 BQ67
Leybourne St, NW1
  off Hawley St 83 DH66
Leybridge Ct, SE12 . . . . .124 EG85
Leyburn Cres, Rom. RM3 . . . . .52 FL52
Leyburn Gdns, Croy. CR0 . . . .142 DS103
Leyburn Gro, N18 . . . . .46 DU51
Leyburn Rd, N18 . . . . .46 DU51
  Romford RM3 . . . . .52 FL52
Leycroft Cl, Loug. IG10 . . . . . . .33 EN43
Leycroft Gdns, Erith DA8 . . . .107 FH81
Leydenhatch La, Swan. BR8 . .147 FC95
Leydon Cl, SE16 . . . . .203 J3
Leyfield, Wor.Pk. KT4 . . . . . . .138 CS102
Leyhill Cl, Swan. BR8 . . . . . . .147 FE97
Ley Hill Rd, Hem.H. (Bov.) HP3 .4 AX30
Leyland Av, Enf. EN3 . . . . .31 DY40
Leyland Cl, Wal.Cr. (Chsht.)
  EN8 . . . . .14 DW28
Leyland Gdns, Wdf.Grn. IG8 . . .48 EJ50
Leyland Rd, SE12 . . . . .124 EG85
Leylands La, Stai. TW19 . . . . .113 BF85
Leylang Rd, SE14 . . . . .103 DX80
Leys, The, N2 . . . . .64 DC56
  Harrow HA3 . . . . .62 CM58
Leys Av, Dag. RM10 . . . . .89 FC66
Leys Cl, Dag. RM10 . . . . .89 FC66
  Harrow HA1 . . . . .61 CD57
  Uxbridge (Hare.) UB9 . . . . . .38 BK53
Leysdown Av, Bexh. DA7 . . . .107 FC84
Leysdown Rd, SE9 . . . . .124 EL89
Leysfield Rd, W12 . . . . .99 CU75
Leys Gdns, Barn. EN4 . . . . . . .28 DG43
Leyspring Rd, E11 . . . . .68 EF60
Leys Rd, Lthd. (Oxshott)
  KT22 . . . . .155 CD112
Leys Rd E, Enf. EN3 . . . . .31 DY39
Leys Rd W, Enf. EN3 . . . . .31 DY39
Ley St, Ilf. IG1, IG2 . . . . .69 EP61
Leyswood Dr, Ilf. IG2 . . . . .69 ER58
Leythe Rd, W3 . . . . .98 CQ75
LEYTON, E11 . . . . .67 EB60
◉ Leyton 67 EC62
Leyton Business Cen, E10 . . . .67 EA61
Leyton Cross Rd, Dart. DA2 . .127 FF90
Leyton Gra, E10
  off Goldsmith Rd 67 EB60
Leyton Gra Est, E10 . . . . .67 EB60
Leyton Grn Rd, E10 . . . . .67 EC58
Leyton Ind Village, E10 . . . . . . .67 DX59
≷ Leyton Midland Road 67 EC60
★ Leyton Orient FC, E10 . . . . . .67 EB62
Leyton Pk Rd, E10 . . . . .67 EC62
Leyton Rd, E15 . . . . .67 ED64
  SW19 . . . . .120 DC94
LEYTONSTONE, E11 . . . . .67 ED59
◉ Leytonstone 68 EE60
≷ Leytonstone High Road 68 EE61
Leytonstone Rd, E15 . . . . .68 EE64
Leyton Way, E11 . . . . .68 EE59
Leywick St, E15 . . . . .86 EE68
Lezayre Rd, Orp. BR6 . . . . . . .163 ET107

Liardet St, SE14 . . . . .103 DY79
Liberia Rd, N5 . . . . .83 DP65
★ Liberty, W1 . . . . .195 K9
Liberty, The, Rom. RM1 . . . . . .71 FE57
Liberty Av, SW19 . . . . .140 DD95
Liberty Hall Rd, Add. KT15 . . .152 BG106
Liberty La, Add. KT15 . . . . . . .152 BG106
Liberty Ms, SW12 . . . . .121 DH86
Liberty Ri, Add. KT15 . . . . . . .152 BG107
Liberty St, SW9 . . . . .101 DM81
Libra Rd, E3 . . . . .85 DZ67
  E13 . . . . .86 EG68
Library Hill, Brwd. CM14
  off Coptfold Rd 54 FX47
Library Pl, E1 off Cable St 84 DV73
Library St, SE1 . . . . .200 F5
Library Way, Twick. TW2
  off Nelson Rd 116 CC87
Licenced Victuallers National
  Homes, Uxb. (Denh.) UB9
  off Denham Grn La 57 BF58
Lichfield Cl, Barn. EN4 . . . . . . .28 DF41
Lichfield Ct, Rich. TW9
  off Sheen Rd 98 CL84
Lichfield Gdns, Rich. TW9 . . . .98 CL84
Lichfield Gro, N3 . . . . .44 DA53
Lichfield Rd, E3 . . . . .85 DY69
  E6 . . . . .86 EK69
  N9 off Winchester Rd 46 DU47
  NW2 . . . . .63 CY63
  Dagenham RM8 . . . . .70 EV63
  Hounslow TW4 . . . . .96 BW83
  Northwood HA6 . . . . .59 BU55
  Richmond TW9 . . . . .98 CM81
  Woodford Green IG8 . . . . . .48 EE49
Lichfield Ter, Upmin. RM14 . . . .73 FT61
Lichfield Way, S.Croy. CR2 . . .161 DX110
Lichlade Cl, Orp. BR6 . . . . . . .163 ET105
Lidbury Rd, NW7 . . . . .43 CY51
Lidcote Gdns, SW9 . . . . .101 DN82
Liddall Way, West Dr. UB7 . . . .76 BM74
Liddell Cl, Har. HA3 . . . . .61 CK55
Liddell Gdns, NW10 . . . . .81 CW68
Liddell Rd, NW6 . . . . .82 DA65
Lidding Rd, Har. HA3 . . . . .61 CK57
Liddington Rd, E15 . . . . .86 EF67
Liddon Rd, E13 . . . . .86 EH69
  Bromley BR1 . . . . .144 EJ97
Liden Cl, E17 off Hitcham Rd . .67 DZ60
Lidfield Rd, N16 . . . . .66 DR63
Lidgate Rd, SE15
  off Chandler Way 102 DT80
Lidiard Rd, SW18 . . . . .120 DC89
Lidlington Pl, NW1 . . . . .195 K1
Lidstone Cl, Wok. GU21 . . . . .166 AV117
Lidyard Rd, N19 . . . . .65 DJ60
Lieutenant Ellis Way, Wal.Cr.
  EN7, EN8 . . . . .14 DT31
★ Lifetimes Mus, Croy.
  CR0 . . . . .142 DQ104
Liffler Rd, SE18 . . . . .105 ES78
Liffords Pl, SW13 . . . . .99 CT82
Lifford St, SW15 . . . . .99 CX84
Lightcliffe Rd, N13 . . . . .45 DN49
Lighter Cl, SE16 . . . . .203 L8
Lighterman Ms, E1 . . . . .85 DX72
Lightermans Rd, E14 . . . . . . .204 A5
Lightfoot Rd, N8 . . . . .65 DL57
Lightley Cl, Wem. HA0
  off Stanley Av 80 CM66
Lightswood Cl, Wal.Cr. (Chsht.)
  EN7 . . . . .14 DR27
Ligonier St, E2 . . . . .197 P4
Lilac Av, Enf. EN1 . . . . .30 DW36
  Woking GU22 . . . . .166 AX120
Lilac Cl, E4 . . . . .47 DZ51
  Brentwood CM15
   off Magnolia Way 54 FV43
  Waltham Cross (Chsht.) EN7
   off Greenwood Av 14 DV31
Lilac Gdns, W5 . . . . .97 CK76
  Croydon CR0 . . . . .143 EA104
  Hayes UB3 . . . . .77 BS72
  Romford RM7 . . . . .71 FE60
  Swanley BR8 . . . . .147 FD97
Lilac Ms, N8 off Courcy Rd 65 DN55
Lilac Pl, SE11 . . . . .200 B9
  West Drayton UB7
   off Cedar Av 76 BM73
Lilac St, W12 . . . . .81 CU73
Lila Pl, Swan. BR8 . . . . .147 FE98
Lilburne Gdns, SE9 . . . . .124 EL85
Lilburne Rd, SE9 . . . . .124 EL85
Lilburne Wk, NW10 . . . . .80 CQ65
Lile Cres, W7 . . . . .79 CE71
Lilestone Est, NW8
  off Fisherton St 82 DD70
Lilestone St, NW8 . . . . .194 B4
Lilford Rd, SE5 . . . . .101 DP82
Lilian Barker Cl, SE12 . . . . . . .124 EG85
Lilian Board Way, Grnf. UB6 . . .61 CD64
Lilian Cl, N16
  off Barbauld Rd 66 DS62
Lilian Cres, Brwd. CM13 . . . . . .55 GC47
Lilian Gdns, Wdf.Grn. IG8 . . . . .48 EH53
Lilian Rd, SW16 . . . . .141 DJ95
Lilleshall Rd, Mord. SM4 . . . . .140 DD100
Lilley Cl, E1 . . . . .202 C3
  Brentwood CM14 . . . . .54 FT49
Lilley Dr, Tad. (Kgswd.) KT20 .174 DB122
Lilley La, NW7 . . . . .42 CR50
Lillian Av, W3 . . . . .98 CN75
Lillian Rd, SW13 . . . . .99 CU79
Lillie Rd, SW6 . . . . .99 CY80
  Westerham (Bigg.H.) TN16 .178 EK118
Lillieshall Rd, SW4 . . . . .101 DH83
Lillie Yd, SW6 . . . . .100 DA79
Lillington Gdns Est, SW1 . . . .199 L9
Lillington Ho, N7
  off Harvist Est 65 DN63
Lilliots La, Lthd. KT22
  off Kingston Rd 171 CG119
Lilliput Av, Nthlt. UB5 . . . . .78 BZ67
Lilliput Rd, Rom. RM7 . . . . .71 FD59
Lily Cl, W14 . . . . .99 CY77

Lily Dr, West Dr. UB7 . . . . .94 BK77
Lily Gdns, Wem. HA0 . . . . .79 CJ68
Lily Pl, EC1 . . . . .196 E6
Lily Rd, E17 . . . . .67 EA58
Lilyville Rd, SW6 . . . . .99 CZ81
Lime Av, Brwd. CM13 . . . . .55 FZ48
  Gravesend (Nthflt.) DA11 . .130 GD87
  Upminster RM14 . . . . .72 FN63
  West Drayton UB7 . . . . .76 BM73
  Windsor SL4 . . . . .92 AT80
Limeburner La, EC4 . . . . .196 F9
Limebush Cl, Add. (New Haw)
  KT15 . . . . .152 BJ109
Lime Cl, E1 . . . . .202 C2
  Bromley BR1 . . . . .144 EL98
  Buckhurst Hill IG9 . . . . .48 EK48
  Carshalton SM5 . . . . .140 DF103
  Harrow HA3 . . . . .41 CF54
  Pinner HA5 . . . . .59 BT55
  Romford RM7 . . . . .71 FC56
  South Ockendon RM15 . . . . .91 FW69
  Watford WD19 . . . . .40 BX45
Lime Ct, Mitch. CR4
  off Lewis Rd 140 DD96
Lime Cres, Sun. TW16 . . . . . .136 BW96
Limecroft Cl, Epsom KT19 . . . .156 CR108
Limedene Cl, Pnr. HA5 . . . . . . .40 BX53
Lime Gro, E4 off Burnside Av . .47 EA49
  N20 . . . . .43 CZ46
  W12 . . . . .99 CW75
  Addlestone KT15 . . . . .152 BG105
  Hayes UB3 . . . . .77 BR73
  Ilford IG6 . . . . .49 ET51
  New Malden KT3 . . . . .138 CR97
  Orpington BR6 . . . . .145 EP103
  Ruislip HA4 . . . . .59 BV59
  Sidcup DA15 . . . . .125 ET86
  Twickenham TW1 . . . . .117 CF86
  Warlingham CR6 . . . . .177 DY118
  Woking GU22 . . . . .166 AY121
Limeharbour, E14 . . . . .204 C5
LIMEHOUSE, E14 . . . . .85 DY73
≷ Limehouse 85 DY72
ⅅⅬⅡ Limehouse 85 DY72
Limehouse Causeway, E14 . . .85 DZ73
Limehouse Flds Est, E14 . . . . .85 DY71
Limehouse Link, E14 . . . . .85 DY73
Limekiln Dr, SE7 . . . . .104 EH79
Limekiln Pl, SE19 . . . . .122 DT94
Lime Meadow Av, S.Croy.
  CR2 . . . . .160 DU113
Lime Pit La, Sev. TN14 . . . . . .181 FC117
Limerick Cl, SW12 . . . . .121 DJ87
Limerick Gdns, Upmin. RM14 . .73 FT59
Lime Rd, Epp. CM16 . . . . .17 ET31
  Richmond TW9
   off St. Mary's Gro 98 CM84
  Swanley BR8 . . . . .147 FD97
Lime Row, Erith DA18
  off Northwood Pl 106 EZ76
Limerston St, SW10 . . . . .100 DC79
Limes, The, W2
  off Linden Gdns 82 DA73
  Brentwood CM13 . . . . .55 FZ48
  Bromley BR2 . . . . .144 EL103
  Purfleet RM19
   off Tank Hill Rd 108 FN78
  Woking GU22 . . . . .166 AX115
Limes Av, E11 . . . . .68 EH56
  N12 . . . . .44 DC49
  NW7 . . . . .42 CS51
  NW11 . . . . .63 CY59
  SE20 . . . . .122 DV94
  SW13 . . . . .99 CT82
  Carshalton SM5 . . . . .140 DF102
  Chigwell IG7 . . . . .49 ER51
  Croydon CR0 . . . . .141 DN104
Limes Av, The, N11 . . . . .45 DH50
Limes Cl, Ashf. TW15 . . . . . . .114 BN92
Limes Ct, Brwd. CM15
  off Sawyers Hall La 54 FX46
Limesdale Gdns, Edg. HA8 . . .42 CQ54
Limes Fld Rd, SW14
  off White Hart La 98 CS83
Limesford Rd, SE15 . . . . .103 DX84
Limes Gdns, SW18 . . . . .120 DA86
Limes Gro, SE13 . . . . .103 EC84
Limes Pl, Croy. CR0 . . . . .142 DR101
Limes Rd, Beck. BR3 . . . . . . .143 EB96
  Croydon CR0 . . . . .142 DR100
  Egham TW20 . . . . .113 AZ92
  Waltham Cross (Chsht.)
   EN8 . . . . .15 DX32
  Weybridge KT13 . . . . .152 BN105
Limes Row, Orp. BR6
  off Orchard Rd 163 EP106
Limestone Wk, Erith DA18 . . .106 EX76
Lime St, E17 . . . . .67 DY56
  EC3 . . . . .197 M10
Lime St Pas, EC3 . . . . .197 M9
Limes Wk, SE15 . . . . .102 DV84
  W5 off Chestnut Gro 97 CK75
Lime Ter, W7 off Manor Ct Rd . .79 CE73
Lime Tree Av, Esher KT10 . . . .137 CD102
  Greenhithe (Bluewater)
   DA9 . . . . .129 FU88
  Thames Ditton KT7 . . . . . .137 CD102
Lime Tree Cl, Lthd. (Bkhm.)
  KT23 . . . . .170 CA124
Lime Tree Gro, Croy. CR0 . . . .143 DZ104
Lime Tree Pl, Mitch. CR4 . . . . .141 DH95
Lime Tree Rd, Houns. TW5 . . . .96 CB81
  off Winterstoke Rd 123 DZ88
Limetree Ter, Well. DA16
  off Hook La 106 EU83
Lime Tree Wk, SW17 . . . . .120 DG92
  Amer. HP7 . . . . .20 AT39
  Bushey (Bushey Hth.)
   WD23 . . . . .41 CE46
  Enfield EN2 . . . . .30 DQ38
  Rickmansworth WD3 . . . . . .22 BH43
  Sevenoaks TN13 . . . . .191 FH123

Lime Tree Wk, Vir.W. GU25 . . .132 AY98
  West Wickham BR4 . . . . . .162 EF105
Lime Wk, E15 off Church St N . .86 EE67
  Uxbridge (Denh.) UB9 . . . . .58 BJ64
Limewood Cl, E17 . . . . .67 DZ56
  W13 off St. Stephens Rd . . .79 CH72
  Beckenham BR3 . . . . .143 EC99
Limewood Ct, Ilf. IG4 . . . . .69 EM57
Limewood Rd, Erith DA8 . . . .107 FC80
Lime Wks Rd, Red. (Merst.)
  RH1 . . . . .185 DJ126
LIMPSFIELD, Oxt. 188 EG128
Limpsfield Av, SW19 . . . . .119 CX89
  Thornton Heath CR7 . . . . . .141 DM99
LIMPSFIELD CHART, Oxt. 188 EL130
Limpsfield Rd, S.Croy. CR2 . . .160 DU112
  Warlingham CR6 . . . . .176 DW116
Linacre Ct, W6 . . . . .99 CX78
Linacre Rd, NW2 . . . . .81 CV65
Linberry Wk, SE8 . . . . .203 M9
Linchfield Rd, Slou. (Datchet)
  SL3 . . . . .92 AW81
Linchmere Rd, SE12 . . . . .124 EF87
Lincoln Av, N14 . . . . .45 DJ48
  SW19 . . . . .119 CX90
  Romford RM7 . . . . .71 FD60
  Twickenham TW2 . . . . .116 CB89
Lincoln Cl, SE25
  off Woodside Grn 142 DU100
  Erith DA8 . . . . .107 FF82
  Greenford UB6 . . . . .78 CC67
  Harrow HA2 . . . . .60 BZ57
  Hornchurch RM11 . . . . .72 FN57
Lincoln Ct, N16 . . . . .66 DR59
  Borehamwood WD6 . . . . . . .26 CR43
Lincoln Cres, Enf. EN1 . . . . . . .30 DS43
Lincoln Dr, Rick. (Crox.Grn.)
  WD3 . . . . .23 BP42
  Watford WD19 . . . . .40 BW48
  Woking GU22 . . . . .167 BE115
Lincoln Gdns, Ilf. IG1 . . . . .68 EL59
Lincoln Grn Rd, Orp. BR5 . . . .145 ET99
Lincoln Ms, NW6
  off Willesden La 81 CZ67
  SE21 . . . . .122 DR88
Lincoln Pk, Amer. HP7 . . . . . . .20 AS39
Lincoln Rd, E7 . . . . .86 EK65
  E13 . . . . .86 EH70
  E18 off Grove Rd 48 EG53
  N2 . . . . .64 DE55
  SE25 . . . . .142 DV99
  Enfield EN1, EN3 . . . . .30 DU43
  Erith DA8 . . . . .107 FF82
  Feltham TW13 . . . . .116 BZ90
  Gerrards Cross (Chal.St.P.)
   SL9 . . . . .AY53
  Harrow HA2 . . . . .60 BZ57
  Mitcham CR4 . . . . .141 DL99
  New Malden KT3 . . . . .138 CQ97
  Northwood HA6 . . . . .59 BT55
  Sidcup DA14 . . . . .126 EV92
  Wembley HA0 . . . . .79 CK65
  Worcester Park KT4 . . . . . .139 CV102
Lincolns, The, NW7 . . . . .43 CT48
Lincolns Fld, Epp. CM16 . . . . . .17 ET29
Lincolnshott, Grav. (Sthflt.)
  DA13 . . . . .130 GB92
★ Lincoln's Inn, WC2 . . . . .196 C8
Lincoln's Inn, WC2 . . . . .196 C8
Lincoln's Inn Flds, WC2 . . . . .196 B8
Lincoln St, E11 . . . . .68 EE61
  SW3 . . . . .198 D9
Lincoln Wk, Epsom KT19
  off Hollymoor La 156 CR110
Lincoln Way, Enf. EN1 . . . . . . .30 DV43
  Rickmansworth (Crox.Grn.)
   WD3 . . . . .23 BP42
  Sunbury-on-Thames
   TW16 . . . . .135 BS95
Lincombe Rd, Brom. BR1 . . . .124 EF90
Lindal Cres, Enf. EN2 . . . . .29 DL42
Lindale Cl, Vir.W. GU25 . . . . . .132 AT98
Lindales, The, N17
  off Brantwood Rd 46 DT51
Lindal Rd, SE4 . . . . .123 DZ85
Lindberg Rd, Wall. SM6 . . . . . .159 DL109
Linden Av, NW10 . . . . .81 CX68
  Coulsdon CR5 . . . . .175 DH116
  Dartford DA1 . . . . .128 FJ88
  Enfield EN1 . . . . .30 DU39
  Hounslow TW3 . . . . .116 CB85
  Ruislip HA4 . . . . .59 BU60
  Thornton Heath CR7 . . . . . .141 DP98
  Wembley HA9 . . . . .62 CM64
Linden Chase Rd, Sev. TN13 . .191 FH122
Linden Cl, N14 . . . . .29 DJ44
  Addlestone (New Haw)
   KT15 . . . . .152 BG110
  Orpington BR6 . . . . .164 EU106
  Purfleet RM19 . . . . .108 FQ79
  Ruislip HA4 . . . . .59 BU60
  Stanmore HA7 . . . . .41 CH50
  Tadworth KT20 . . . . .173 CX120
  Thames Ditton KT7 . . . . . .137 CF101
  Waltham Cross EN7 . . . . . .14 DU30
Linden Ct, W12 . . . . .81 CW74
  Egham (Eng.Grn.) TW20 . . .112 AV93
  Leatherhead KT22 . . . . . . .171 CH121
Linden Cres, Grnf. UB6 . . . . . .79 CF65
  Kingston upon Thames
   KT1 . . . . .138 CM96
  Woodford Green IG8 . . . . . .48 EH51
Linden Dr, Cat. CR3 . . . . .176 DQ124
  Gerrards Cross (Chal.St.P.) SL9
   off Woodside Hill 36 AY54
Lindenfield, Chis. BR7 . . . . . . .145 EP96
Linden Gdns, W2 . . . . .82 DA73
  W4 . . . . .98 CR78
  Enfield EN1 . . . . .30 DU39
  Leatherhead KT22 . . . . . . .171 CJ121
Linden Gro, SE15 . . . . .102 DV83
  SE26 . . . . .122 DW93
  New Malden KT3 . . . . .138 CS97
  Teddington TW11
   off Waldegrave Rd 117 CF92
  Walton-on-Thames KT12 . . .135 BT103
  Warlingham CR6 . . . . .177 DY118

Linden Ho, Slou. SL3 . . . . .93 BB78
Linden Lawns, Wem. HA9 . . . . .62 CM63
Linden Lea, N2 . . . . .64 DC57
  Watford WD25 . . . . .7 BU33
Linden Leas, W.Wick. BR4 . . . .143 ED103
Linden Ms, N1
  off Mildmay Gro N 66 DR64
  W2 off Linden Gdns 82 DA73
Linden Pas, W4 . . . . .98 CR78
Linden Pit Path, Lthd. KT22 . . .171 CH121
Linden Pl, Epsom KT17
  off East St 156 CS112
  Mitcham CR4 . . . . .140 DE98
Linden Ri, Brwd. CM14 . . . . . . .54 FX50
Linden Rd, E17 off High St 67 DZ57
  N10 . . . . .65 DH56
  N11 . . . . .44 DF47
  N15 . . . . .66 DQ56
  Hampton TW12 . . . . .116 CA94
  Leatherhead KT22 . . . . . . .171 CH121
  Weybridge KT13 . . . . .153 BQ109
Lindens, The, N12 . . . . .44 DD50
  W4 off Hartington Rd 98 CQ81
  Croydon (New Adgtn.)
   CR0 . . . . .161 EC107
  Loughton IG10 . . . . .33 EM43
Linden Sq, Sev. TN13
  off London Rd 190 FE122
Linden St, Rom. RM7 . . . . .71 FD56
Linden Wk, N19
  off Hargrave Pk 65 DJ61
Linden Way, N14 . . . . .29 DJ44
  Purley CR8 . . . . .159 DJ110
  Shepperton TW17 . . . . . . .135 BQ99
  Woking GU22 . . . . .167 AZ121
  Woking (Send M.) GU23 . . .167 BF124
Lindeth Cl, Stan. HA7
  off Old Ch La 41 CJ51
Lindfield Gdns, NW3 . . . . .64 DB64
  Greenford UB6 . . . . .79 CJ70
  Croydon CR0 . . . . .142 DT100
  Romford RM3 . . . . .52 FL50
Lindfield St, E14 . . . . .85 EA72
Lindhill Cl, Enf. EN3 . . . . .31 DX39
Lindisfarne Cl, Grav. DA12
  off St. Benedict's Av 131 GL89
Lindisfarne Rd, SW20 . . . . . . .119 CU94
  Dagenham RM8 . . . . .70 EW62
Lindisfarne Way, E9 . . . . .67 DY63
Lindley Est, SE15
  off Bird in Bush Rd 102 DU80
Lindley Pl, Rich. TW9 . . . . .98 CN81
Lindley Rd, E10 . . . . .67 EB61
  Godstone RH9 . . . . .186 DW130
  Walton-on-Thames KT12 . . .136 BX104
Lindley St, E1 . . . . .84 DW71
Lindore Rd, SW11 . . . . .100 DF84
Lindores Rd, Cars. SM5 . . . . .140 DC101
Lindo St, SE15
  off Selden Rd 102 DW82
Lind Rd, Sutt. SM1 . . . . .158 DC106
Lindrop St, SW6 . . . . .100 DC82
Lindsay Cl, Chess. KT9 . . . . . .156 CL108
  Epsom KT19 . . . . .156 CQ113
  Staines (Stanw.) TW19 . . . .114 BK85
Lindsay Dr, Har. HA3 . . . . .62 CL58
  Shepperton TW17 . . . . . . .135 BR100
Lindsay Pl, Wal.Cr. EN7 . . . . . .14 DV30
Lindsay Rd, Add. (New Haw)
  KT15 . . . . .152 BG110
  Hampton (Hmptn.H.)
   TW12 . . . . .116 CB91
  Worcester Park KT4 . . . . . .139 CV103
Lindsay Sq, SW1 . . . . .199 N10
Lindsell St, SE10 . . . . .103 EC81
Lindsey Cl, Brwd. CM14 . . . . . .54 FU49
  Bromley BR1 . . . . .144 EK97
  Mitcham CR4 . . . . .141 DL98
Lindsey Gdns, Felt. TW14 . . . .115 BR87
Lindsey Ms, N1 . . . . .84 DQ66
Lindsey Rd, Dag. RM8 . . . . . . .70 EW63
  Uxbridge (Denh.) UB9 . . . . .58 BG62
Lindsey St, EC1 . . . . .196 G6
  Epping CM16 . . . . .17 ER28
Lindsey Way, Horn. RM11 . . . . .72 FJ57
Lind St, SE8 . . . . .103 EB82
Lindum Rd, Tedd. TW11 . . . . . .117 CJ94
Lindvale, Wok. GU21 . . . . .167 AY115
Lindway, SE27 . . . . .121 DP92
Lindwood Cl, E6
  off Northumberland Rd 86 EL71
Linfield Cl, NW4 . . . . .63 CW55
  Walton-on-Thames KT12 . . .153 BV106
Linfields, Amer. HP7 . . . . .20 AW40
LINFORD, S.le H. 111 GM75
Linford Rd, E17 . . . . .67 EC55
  Grays RM16 . . . . .111 GH78
Linford St, SW8 . . . . .101 DJ81
Lingards Rd, SE13 . . . . .103 EC84
Lingey Cl, Sid. DA15 . . . . .125 ET89
Lingfield Av, Dart. DA2 . . . . . .128 FP87
  Kingston upon Thames
   KT1 . . . . .138 CL98
  Upminster RM14 . . . . .72 FM62
Lingfield Cl, Enf. EN1 . . . . .30 DS44
  Northwood HA6 . . . . .59 BS52
Lingfield Cres, SE9 . . . . .105 ER84
Lingfield Gdns, N9 . . . . .46 DV45
  Coulsdon CR5 . . . . .175 DP119
Lingfield Rd, SW19 . . . . .119 CX92
  Gravesend DA12 . . . . .131 GH89
  Worcester Park KT4 . . . . . .139 CW104
Lingfield Way, Wat. WD17 . . . . .23 BT38
Lingham St, SW9 . . . . .101 DL82
Lingholm Way, Barn. EN5 . . . . .27 CX43
Lingmere Cl, Chig. IG7 . . . . . . .49 EQ47
Lingmoor Dr, Wat. WD25 . . . . . .8 BW33
Ling Rd, E16 . . . . .86 EG71
  Erith DA8 . . . . .107 FC79
Lingrove Gdns, Buck.H. IG9
  off Beech La 48 EH47
Lings Coppice, SE21 . . . . .122 DR89
Lingwell Rd, SW17 . . . . .120 DE90

Lin - Lod

Lingwood Gdns, Islw. TW7 . . .97 CE80
Lingwood Rd, E5 . . . . .66 DU59
Linhope St, NW1 . . . . .194 D4
Linington Av, Chesh. HP5 . . . . .4 AU30
Link, The, SE9 . . . . .125 EN90
W3 . . . . .80 CP72
Enfield EN3 . . . . .31 DY39
Northolt UB5
off Eastcote La 60 BZ64
Pinner HA5 . . . . .60 BW59
Slough SL2 . . . . .74 AV72
Wembley HA0
off Nathans Rd 61 CJ60
Link Av, Wok. GU22 . . . . . . .167 BD115
Linkfield, Brom. BR2 . . . . . . .144 EG100
West Molesey KT8 . . . . .136 CA97
Linkfield Cor, Red. RH1
off Hatchlands Rd 184 DE133
Linkfield Gdns, Red. RH1
off Hatchlands Rd 184 DE134
Linkfield La, Red. RH1 . . . . .184 DE133
Linkfield Rd, Islw. TW7 . . . . .97 CF82
Linkfield St, Red. RH1 . . . . .184 DE134
Link La, Wall. SM6 . . . . .159 DK107
Linklea Cl, NW9 . . . . .44 CS52
Link Rd, N11 . . . . .44 DG49
Addlestone KT15
off Weybridge Rd 152 BL105
Dagenham RM9 . . . . .89 FB68
Feltham TW14 . . . . .115 BT87
Rickmansworth (Chenies)
WD3 . . . . .21 BA37
Slough (Datchet) SL3 . . . . . .92 AW80
Wallington SM6 . . . . .140 DG102
Watford WD24 . . . . .24 BX40
Links, The, E17 . . . . .67 DY56
Waltham Cross (Chsht.)
EN8 . . . . .15 DX26
Walton-on-Thames KT12 . . .135 BU103
Links Av, Mord. SM4 . . . . . .140 DA98
Romford RM2 . . . . .51 FH54
Links Brow, Lthd. (Fetch.)
KT22 . . . . .171 CE124
Links Cl, Ashtd. KT21 . . . . .171 CJ117
Linkscroft Av, Ashf. TW15 . .115 BP93
Links Dr, N20 . . . . .44 DA46
Borehamwood (Elstree)
WD6 . . . . .26 CM41
Radlett WD7 . . . . .9 CF33
Links Gdns, SW16 . . . . .121 DN94
Links Grn Way, Cob. KT11 . .154 CA114
Linkside, N12 . . . . .43 CZ51
Chigwell IG7 . . . . .49 EQ50
New Malden KT3 . . . . .138 CS96
Linkside Cl, Enf. EN2 . . . . . .29 DM41
Linkside Gdns, Enf. EN2 . . . .29 DM41
Links Pl, Ashtd. KT21 . . . . .171 CK117
Links Rd, NW2 . . . . .63 CT61
SW17 . . . . .120 DF93
W3 . . . . .80 CN72
Ashford TW15 . . . . .114 BL92
Ashtead KT21 . . . . .171 CJ118
Epsom KT17 . . . . .157 CU113
West Wickham BR4 . . . . . .143 EC102
Woodford Green IG8 . . . . . .48 EG50
Links Side, Enf. EN2 . . . . . .29 DM41
Link St, E9 . . . . .84 DW65
Links Vw, N3 . . . . .43 CZ52
Dartford DA1 . . . . .128 FJ88
Links Vw Av, Bet. (Brock.)
RH3 . . . . .182 CN134
Links Vw Cl, Stan. HA7 . . . . .41 CG51
Links Vw Rd, Croy. CR0 . . . .143 EA104
Hampton (Hmptn.H.)
TW12 . . . . .116 CC92
Linksway, NW4 . . . . .43 CX54
Links Way, Beck. BR3 . . . . .143 EA100
Linksway, Nthwd. HA6 . . . . .39 BQ53
Links Way, Rick. (Crox.Grn.)
WD3 . . . . .23 BQ41
Links Yd, E off Spelman St . . .84 DU71
Linkway, N4 . . . . .66 DQ59
SW20 . . . . .139 CV97
Link Way, Brom. BR2 . . . . .144 EL101
Linkway, Dag. RM8 . . . . . . .70 EW63
Link Way, Horn. RM11 . . . . .72 FL60
Pinner HA5 . . . . .40 BX53
Linkway, Rich. TW10 . . . . . .117 CH89
Link Way, Stai. TW18 . . . . .114 BH93
Uxbridge (Denh.) UB9 . . . . .58 BG58
Linkway, Wok. GU22 . . . . . .167 BC117
Linkway, The, Barn. EN5 . . . .28 DB44
Sutton SM2 . . . . .158 DC109
Link Way Rd, Brwd. CM14 . . .54 FT48
Linkwood Wk, NW1
off Maiden La 83 DK66
Linley Cres, Rom. RM7 . . . . .71 FB55
Linley Rd, N17 . . . . .46 DS54
★ Linley Sambourne Ho,
W8 . . . . .100 DA75
Linnell Cl, NW11 . . . . .64 DB58
Linnell Dr, NW11 . . . . .64 DB58
Linnell Rd, N18
off Fairfield Rd 46 DU50
SE5 . . . . .102 DS82
Linnet Cl, N9 . . . . .47 DX46
SE28 . . . . .88 EW73
Bushey WD23 . . . . .40 CC45
South Croydon CR2 . . . . . .161 DX110
Linnet Ms, SW12 . . . . .120 DG87
Linnet Rd, Abb.L. WD5 . . . . .7 BU31
Linnett Cl, E4 . . . . .47 EC49
Linnet Ter, Ilf. IG5
off Tiptree Cres 69 EN55
Linnet Way, Purf. RM19 . . . .108 FP78
Linom Rd, SW4 . . . . .101 DL84
Linscott Rd, E5 . . . . .66 DW63
Linsey St, SE16 . . . . .202 B8
Linslade Cl, Houns. TW4
off Frampton Rd 116 BY85
Pinner HA5 . . . . .59 BV55
Linslade Rd, Orp. BR6 . . . . .164 EU107
Linstead Ct, SE9 . . . . .125 ES86

Linstead St, NW6 . . . . .82 DA66
Linstead Way, SW18 . . . . . .119 CY87
Linster Gro, Borwd. WD6 . . . .26 CQ43
Lintaine Cl, W6 off Moylan Rd .99 CY79
Linthorpe Av, Wem. HA0 . . . .79 CJ65
Linthorpe Rd, N16 . . . . .66 DS59
Barnet EN4 . . . . .28 DE41
Linton Av, Borwd. WD6 . . . . .26 CM39
Linton Cl, Mitch. CR4 . . . . .140 DF101
Welling DA16
off Anthony Rd 106 EV81
Linton Gdns, E6 . . . . .86 EL72
Linton Glade, Croy. CR0 . . . .161 DY109
Linton Gro, SE27 . . . . .121 DP92
Linton Rd, Bark. IG11 . . . . . .87 EQ66
Lintons, The, Bark. IG11 . . . .87 EQ66
Lintons La, Epsom KT17 . . . .156 CS112
Linton St, N1 . . . . .84 DQ67
Lintott Ct, Stai. (Stanw.)
TW19 . . . . .114 BK86
Linver Rd, SW6 . . . . .100 DA82
Linwood Cl, SE5 . . . . .102 DT82
Linwood Cres, Enf. EN1 . . . .30 DU39
Linwood Way, SE15
off Daniel Gdns 102 DT80
Linzee Rd, N8 . . . . .65 DL56
Lion Av, Twick. TW1
off Lion Rd 117 CF88
Lion Cl, SE4 . . . . .123 EA86
Shepperton TW17 . . . . . . .134 BL97
Lion Ct, Borwd. WD6 . . . . . .26 CQ39
Lionel Gdns, SE9 . . . . .124 EK85
Lionel Ms, W10 off Telford Rd .81 CY71
Lionel Oxley Ho, Grays RM17
off New Rd 110 GB79
Lionel Rd, SE9 . . . . .124 EK85
Lionel Rd N, Brent. TW8 . . . .98 CL77
Lionel Rd S, Brent. TW8 . . . .98 CM78
Lion Gate Gdns, Rich. TW9 . .98 CM83
Lion Grn Rd, Couls. CR5 . . . .175 DK115
Lion La, Red. RH1 . . . . .184 DF133
Lion Pk Av, Chess. KT9 . . . . .156 CN105
Lion Plaza, EC2
off Threadneedle St 84 DR72
Lion Rd, E6 . . . . .87 EM71
N9 . . . . .46 DU47
Bexleyheath DA6 . . . . .106 EZ84
Croydon CR0 . . . . .142 DQ99
Twickenham TW1 . . . . .117 CF88
Lions Cl, SE9 . . . . .124 EJ90
Lion Way, Brent. TW8 . . . . . .97 CK80
Lion Wf Rd, Islw. TW7 . . . . . .97 CH83
Lion Yd, SW4
off Tremadoc Rd 101 DK84
Liphook Cl, Horn. RM12
off Petworth Way 71 FF63
Liphook Cres, SE23 . . . . . . .122 DW87
Liphook Rd, Wat. WD19 . . . . .40 BX49
Lippitts Hill, Loug. (High Beach)
IG10 . . . . .32 EF38
Lipsham Cl, Bans. SM7 . . . . .158 DD113
Lipton Cl, SE28 off Aisher Rd .88 EW73
Lipton Rd, E1 off Bower St . . .85 DX72
Lisbon Av, Twick. TW2 . . . . .116 CC89
Lisburne Rd, NW3 . . . . .64 DF63
Lisford St, SE15 . . . . .102 DT81
Lisgar Ter, W14 . . . . .99 CZ77
Liskeard Cl, Chis. BR7 . . . . .125 EQ93
Liskeard Gdns, SE3 . . . . . . .104 EG81
Lister Av, Rom. RM3 . . . . . . .52 FK54
Lisle Cl, SW17 . . . . .121 DH91
Lisle Pl, Grays RM17 . . . . . .110 GA76
Lisle St, WC2 . . . . .195 N10
Lismore Circ, NW5 . . . . .64 DG64
Lismore Cl, Islw. TW7 . . . . . .97 CG82
Lismore Pk, Slou. SL2 . . . . . .74 AT72
Lismore Rd, N17 . . . . .66 DR55
South Croydon CR2 . . . . . .160 DS107
Lismore Wk, N1
off Clephane Rd 84 DQ65
Lissenden Gdns, NW5 . . . . . .64 DG63
Lissoms Rd, Couls. CR5 . . . .174 DG118
Lisson Grn Est, NW8 . . . . . .194 B3
LISSON GROVE, NW8 . . . . .194 A5
Lisson Gro, NW1 . . . . .194 B4
NW8 . . . . .194 A3
Lisson St, NW1 . . . . .194 B6
Liss Way, SE15
off Pentridge St 102 DT80
Lister Av, Rom. RM3 . . . . . . .52 FK54
Lister Cl, W3 . . . . .80 CR71
Mitcham CR4 . . . . .140 DE95
Lister Ct, NW9 off Pasteur Cl . .42 CS54
Lister Gdns, N18 . . . . .46 DQ50
Ⓗ Lister Hosp, SW1 . . . . . .101 DH78
Lister Ho, SE3 . . . . .104 EE79
E1 . . . . .68 EE60
Tilbury RM18 . . . . .111 GG82
Lister Wk, SE28
off Haldane Rd 88 EX73
Liston Rd, N17 . . . . .46 DU53
SW4 . . . . .101 DJ83
Liston Way, Wdf.Grn. IG8 . . . .48 EJ52
Listowel Cl, SW9
off Mandela St 101 DN80
Listowel Rd, Dag. RM10 . . . .70 FA62
Listria Pk, N16 . . . . .66 DS61
Litchfield Av, E15 . . . . .86 EE65
Morden SM4 . . . . .139 CZ101
Litchfield Gdns, NW10 . . . . .81 CU65
Litchfield Rd, Sutt. SM1 . . . .158 DC105
Litchfield St, WC2 . . . . .195 N10
Litchfield Way, NW11 . . . . . .64 DB57
Lithos Rd, NW3 . . . . .82 DB65
Little Acre, Beck. BR3 . . . . .143 EA97
Little Albany St, NW1 . . . . .195 J4
Little Argyll St, W1 . . . . . . .195 K9
Little Aston Rd, Rom. RM3 . . .52 FM52
Little Belhus Cl, S.Ock. RM15 .91 FU70
Little Benty, West Dr. UB7 . . .94 BK78
Little Birch Cl, Add. (New Haw)
KT15 . . . . .152 BK109
Little Birches, Sid. DA15 . . . .125 ES89
Little Boltons, The, SW5 . . . .100 DB78

Little Boltons, The, SW10 . . . .100 DB78
Little Bookham Common, Lthd.
(Bkhm.) KT23 . . . . .170 BY122
Little Bookham St, Lthd. (Bkhm.)
KT23 . . . . .170 BZ124
Little Bornes, SE21 . . . . . . .122 DS91
Little Britain, EC1 . . . . .197 H8
Littlebrook Cl, Croy. CR0 . . . .143 DX100
Littlebrook Gdns, Wal.Cr. (Chsht.)
EN8 . . . . .14 DW30
Littlebrook Manor Way, Dart.
DA1 . . . . .128 FN85
Little Brownings, SE23 . . . . .122 DV89
Littlebury Rd, SW4 . . . . . . .101 DK83
Little Bury St, N9 . . . . .46 DR46
Little Bushey La, Bushey
WD23 . . . . .25 CD44
Little Bushey La Footpath, Bushey
WD23 off Little Bushey La . .41 CD45
Little Cedars, N12
off Woodside Av 44 DC49
Hayes UB3 . . . . .95 BT75
LITTLE CHALFONT, Amer. . . .20 AW40
LITTLE CHALFONT, Ch.St.G. . .20 AW40
Little Chester St, SW1 . . . . .198 G6
Little Cloisters, SW1
off Tufton St 101 DK76
Little Coll La, EC4
off Garlick Hill 84 DR73
Little Coll St, SW1 . . . . .199 P6
Littlecombe, SE7 . . . . .104 EH79
Littlecombe Cl, SW15 . . . . . .119 CX86
Little Common, Stan. HA7 . . .41 CG48
Little Common La, Red. (Bletch.)
RH1 . . . . .185 DP132
Littlecote Cl, SW19 . . . . . . .119 CX87
Littlecote Pl, Pnr. HA5 . . . . . .40 BY53
Little Ct, W.Wick. BR4 . . . . .144 EE103
Littlecourt Rd, Sev. TN13 . . .190 FG124
Littlecroft, SE9 . . . . .105 EN83
Gravesend (Istead Rise)
DA13 . . . . .130 GE94
Littlecroft Rd, Egh. TW20 . . .113 AZ92
Littledale, SE2 . . . . .106 EU79
Dartford DA2 . . . . .128 FQ90
Little Dean's Yd, SW1 . . . . .199 P6
Little Dimocks, SW12 . . . . . .121 DH89
Little Dormers, Ger.Cr. SL9 . . .57 AZ56
Little Dorrit Ct, SE1 . . . . . . .201 J4
Littledown Rd, Slou. SL1 . . . .74 AT74
Little Dragons, Loug. IG10 . . .32 EK42
LITTLE EALING, W5 . . . . . . .97 CJ77
Little Ealing La, W5 . . . . .97 CJ77
Little Edward St, NW1 . . . . .195 J2
Little Elms, Hayes UB3 . . . . .95 BR80
Little Essex St, WC2 . . . . . .196 D10
Little Ferry Rd, Twick. TW1
off Ferry Rd 117 CH88
Littlefield Cl, N19
off Tufnell Pk Rd 65 DJ63
Kingston upon Thames KT1
off Fairfield W 138 CL96
Littlefield Rd, Edg. HA8 . . . . .42 CQ52
Little Friday Rd, E4 . . . . .48 EE47
Little Gaynes Gdns, Upmin.
RM14 . . . . .72 FP63
Little Gaynes La, Upmin.
RM14 . . . . .72 FM63
Little Gearies, Ilf. IG6 . . . . . .69 EP56
Little George St, SW1 . . . . .199 P5
Little Gerpins La, Upmin.
RM14 . . . . .90 FM67
Little Gra, Grnf. UB6
off Perivale La 79 CG69
Little Graylings, Abb.L. WD5 . .7 BS33
Little Grn, Rich. TW9 . . . . . . .97 CK84
Little Grn La, Cher. KT16 . . .133 BE104
Rickmansworth (Crox.Grn.)
WD3 . . . . .23 BP41
Little Grn St, NW5
off College La 65 DH63
Little Gregories La, Epp. (They.B.)
CM16 . . . . .33 ER35
Littlegrove, Barn. EN4 . . . . . .28 DE44
Little Gro, Bushey WD23 . . . .24 CB42
Little Gro Av, Wal.Cr. (Chsht.)
EN7 . . . . .14 DS27
Little Halliards, Walt. KT12
off Felix Rd 135 BU100
Little Hayes, Kings L. WD4 . . .6 BN29
Little Heath, SE7 . . . . .104 EL79
Romford (Chad.Hth.) RM6 . .70 EV56
Littleheath La, Cob. KT11 . . .154 CA114
Little Heath La, Wok. (Chobham)
GU24 . . . . .150 AS109
Little Heath Rd, Bexh. DA7 . .106 EZ81
Littleheath Rd, S.Croy. CR2 . .160 DV108
Little Heath Rd, Wok. (Chobham)
GU24 . . . . .150 AS109
Little Highwood Hosp,
Brwd. CM15 . . . . .54 FV45
Little Hill, Rick. (Herons.) WD3 .21 BC44
★ Little Holland Ho, Cars.
SM5 . . . . .158 DE108
Little How Cft, Abb.L. WD5 . . .7 BQ31
LITTLE ILFORD, E12 . . . . . . .68 EL64
Little Ilford La, E12 . . . . .69 EM63
Littlejohn Rd, W7 . . . . .79 CF72
Orpington BR5 . . . . .146 EU100
Little Julians Hill, Sev. TN13 .190 FG128
Little London, Uxb. UB8
off Harlington Rd 77 BP71
Little Marlborough St, W1 . . .195 K9
Little Martins, Bushey WD23 . .24 CB43
Littlemead, Esher KT10 . . . .155 CD105
Little Mead, Wok. GU21 . . . .166 AT116
Littlemede, SE9 . . . . .125 EM86
Littlemoor Rd, Ilf. IG1 . . . . . .69 ER62
Little Moreton Cl, W.Byf.
KT14 . . . . .152 BH112
Little Moss La, Pnr. HA5 . . . .40 BY54
Little Newport St, WC2 . . . .195 N10
Little New St, EC4 . . . . .196 E8
Little Orchard, Add. (Woodham)
KT15 . . . . .151 BF111
Woking GU21 . . . . .151 BA114
Little Orchard Cl, Abb.L. WD5 .7 BR32

Little Orchard Cl, Pin. HA5
off Barrow Pt La 40 BY54
Little Oxhey La, Wat. WD19 . .40 BY48
Little Pk, Hem.H. (Bov.) HP3 . .5 BA28
Little Pk Dr, Felt. TW13 . . . . .116 BX89
Little Pk Gdns, Enf. EN2 . . . .30 DQ41
Little Pipers Cl, Wal.Cr. (Chsht.)
EN7 . . . . .13 DP29
Little Plucketts Way, Buck.H.
IG9 . . . . .48 EJ46
Little Portland St, W1 . . . . . .195 K8
Littleport Spur, Slou. SL1 . . . .74 AS72
Little Potters, Bushey WD23 . .41 CD45
Little Queen St, Dart. DA1 . . .128 FM87
Little Queens Rd, Tedd. TW11 .117 CF93
Little Redlands, Brom. BR1 . .144 EL96
Little Riding, Wok. GU22 . . . .167 BB116
Little Rd, Croy. CR0 off Lower
Addiscombe Rd 142 DS102
Hayes UB3 . . . . .95 BT75
Little Roke Av, Ken. CR8 . . . .159 DP114
Little Roke Rd, Ken. CR8 . . . .160 DQ114
Littlers Cl, SW19
off Runnymede 140 DD95
Little Russell St, WC1 . . . . .195 P7
Little Russets, Brwd. CM13
off Hutton Village 55 GE45
Little St. James's St, SW1 . . .199 K3
Little St. Leonards, SW14 . . . .98 CQ83
Little Sanctuary, SW1 . . . . .199 N5
Little Smith St, SW1 . . . . . .199 N6
Little Somerset St, E1 . . . . .197 N9
Littlestock Rd, Wal.Cr. (Chsht.)
EN7 . . . . .14 DR26
Littlestone Cl, Beck. BR3
off Abbey La 123 EA93
Little Strand, NW9 . . . . .43 CT54
Little Stream Cl, Nthwd. HA6 .39 BS50
Little St, Wal.Abb. EN9
off Greenwich Way 31 EB36
Little Sutton La, Slou. SL3 . . .93 BC78
Little Thrift, Orp. BR5 . . . . . .145 EQ98
LITTLE THURROCK, Grays . . .110 GD76
Little Titchfield St, W1 . . . . .195 K7
LITTLETON, Shep. 135 BP97
Littleton Av, E4 . . . . .48 EF46
Littleton Cres, Har. HA1 . . . . .61 CF61
Littleton La, Shep. TW17 . . . .134 BK101
Littleton Rd, Ashf. TW15 . . . .115 BQ94
Harrow HA1 . . . . .61 CF61
Littleton St, SW18 . . . . .120 DC89
Little Trinity La, EC4 . . . . . . .197 J10
Little Turnstile, WC1 . . . . . .196 B8
★ Little Venice (Waterbuses),
W2 . . . . .82 DC71
Littlewick Rd, Wok. GU21 . . .150 AW114
Little Windmill Hill, Kings L.
(Chipper.) WD4 . . . . .5 BE32
Littlewood, SE13 . . . . .123 EC85
Sevenoaks TN13 . . . . .191 FJ122
Littlewood Cl, W13 . . . . .97 CH76
Little Wd Cl, Orp. BR5 . . . . .146 EU95
LITTLE WOODCOTE, Cars. . . .158 DG111
Little Woodcote Est, Cars. SM5
off Woodmansterne La 158 DG111
Wallington SM6
off Woodmansterne La 158 DG111
Little Woodcote La, Cars.
SM5 . . . . .159 DH112
Purley CR8 . . . . .159 DH112
Wallington SM6 . . . . .159 DH112
Littleworth Av, Esher KT10 . .155 CD106
Littleworth Common Rd, Esher
KT10 . . . . .137 CD104
Littleworth La, Esher KT10 . .155 CD105
Littleworth Pl, Esher KT10 . .155 CD105
Littleworth Rd, Esher KT10 . .155 CD105
Livermere Rd, E8 . . . . .84 DT67
Liverpool Gro, SE17 . . . . . . .102 DR78
Liverpool Rd, E10 . . . . .67 EC58
E16 . . . . .86 EE71
N1 . . . . .83 DN68
N7 . . . . .65 DN64
W5 . . . . .97 CK75
Kingston upon Thames
KT2 . . . . .118 CN94
Thornton Heath CR7 . . . . . .142 DQ97
Watford WD18 . . . . .23 BV43
⇌ Liverpool Street 197 M7
⊖ Liverpool Street 197 M7
Liverpool St, EC2 . . . . .197 M7
Livesey Cl, Kings.T. KT1 . . . .138 CM97
★ Livesey Mus, SE15 . . . . . .102 DV79
Livesey Pl, SE15
off Peckham Pk Rd 102 DU79
Livingstone Ct, E10
off Matlock Rd 67 EC58
Barnet EN5
off Christchurch La 27 CY40
Livingstone Gdns, Grav.
DA12 . . . . .131 GK92
Ⓗ Livingstone Hosp, Dart.
DA1 . . . . .128 FM87
Livingstone Pl, E14
off Ferry St 103 EC78
Livingstone Rd, E15 . . . . . . .85 EC67
E17 . . . . .67 EB58
N13 . . . . .45 DL51
SW11 off Winstanley Rd . . .100 DD83
Caterham CR3 . . . . .176 DR122
Gravesend DA12 . . . . .131 GK92
Hounslow TW3 . . . . .96 CC84
Southall UB1 . . . . .78 BX73
Thornton Heath CR7 . . . . . .142 DQ96
Livingstone Ter, Rain. RM13 . .89 FE67
Livingstone Wk, SW11 . . . . .100 DD83
Livonia St, W1 . . . . .195 L9
Lizard St, EC1 . . . . .197 J3
Lizban St, SE3 . . . . .104 EH80
Llanbury Cl, Ger.Cr. (Chal.St.P.)
SL9 . . . . .36 AY52
Llanelly Rd, NW2 . . . . .63 CZ61
Llanover Rd, SE18 . . . . .105 EN79
Wembley HA9 . . . . .61 CK63
Llanthony Rd, Mord. SM4 . . .140 DD100
Llanvanor Rd, NW2 . . . . .63 CZ61

Llewellyn St, SE16 . . . . .202 C5
Lloyd Av, SW16 . . . . .141 DL95
Coulsdon CR5 . . . . .158 DG114
Lloyd Baker St, WC1 . . . . . .196 C3
Lloyd Ct, Pnr. HA5 . . . . .60 BX57
Lloyd Ms, Enf. EN3
off Government Row 31 EA37
◇ Lloyd Park 160 DT105
Lloyd Pk Av, Croy. CR0 . . . . .160 DT105
Lloyd Rd, E6 . . . . .87 EM67
E17 . . . . .67 DX56
Dagenham RM9 . . . . .88 EZ65
Worcester Park KT4 . . . . . .139 CW104
★ Lloyds of London, EC3 . . .197 M9
Lloyds Av, EC3 . . . . .197 N9
Lloyds Pl, SE3 . . . . .104 EE82
Lloyd Sq, WC1 . . . . .196 D2
Lloyd's Row, EC1 . . . . .196 E3
Lloyd St, WC1 . . . . .196 D2
Lloyds Way, Beck. BR3 . . . . .143 DY99
Loampit Hill, SE13 . . . . .103 EA82
Loampit Vale, SE13 . . . . . . .103 EB83
Loanda Cl, E8 off Clarissa St . .84 DT67
Loates La, Wat. WD17 . . . . . .24 BW41
Loats Rd, SW2 . . . . .121 DL86
Lobelia Cl, E6 off Sorrel Gdns .86 EL71
Local Board Rd, Wat. WD17 . .24 BW43
Locarno Rd, W3 off High St . . .80 CQ74
Greenford UB6 . . . . .78 CC70
Lochaber Rd, SE13 . . . . .104 EE84
Lochaline St, W6 . . . . .99 CW79
Lochan Cl, Hayes UB4 . . . . . .78 BY70
Lochinvar St, SW12 . . . . . . .121 DH87
Lochmere Cl, Erith DA8 . . . . .107 FB79
Loch Chase, SE3 . . . . .104 EE83
Lochnagar St, E14 . . . . .85 EC71
Lock Cl, Add. (Woodham)
KT15 . . . . .151 BE113
Southall UB2
off Navigator Dr 96 CC75
Locke Cl, Rain. RM13 . . . . . .89 FF65
Locke Gdns, Slou. SL3 . . . . . .92 AW75
Locke King Cl, Wey. KT13 . . .152 BN108
Locke King Rd, Wey. KT13 . . .152 BN108
Lockesfield Pl, E14 . . . . .204 C10
Lockesley Dr, Orp. BR5 . . . . .145 ET100
Lockesley Sq, Surb. KT6 . . . .137 CK100
Locket Rd, Har. HA3 . . . . . . .61 CE55
Locke Way, Wok. GU21
off The Broadway 167 AZ117
Lockfield Av, Enf. EN3 . . . . . .31 DY40
Lockfield Dr, Wok. GU21 . . . .166 AT118
Lockgate Cl, E9
off Lee Conservancy Rd 67 DZ64
Lockhart Cl, N7 . . . . .83 DM65
Enfield EN3 off Derby Rd . . .30 DV43
Lockhart St, E3 . . . . .85 DZ70
Lockhurst St, E5 . . . . .67 DX63
Lockie Pl, SE25 . . . . .142 DU97
Lock Island, Shep. TW17 . . . .134 BN103
Lockington Rd, SW8 . . . . . . .101 DH81
Lock La, Wok. GU22 . . . . . . .168 BH116
Lockmead Rd, N15 . . . . .66 DU58
SE13 . . . . .103 EC83
Lock Rd, Rich. TW10 . . . . . .117 CJ91
Locks La, Mitch. CR4 . . . . . .140 DF95
Locksley Dr, Wok. GU21
off Robin Hood Rd 166 AT118
Locksley Est, E14 . . . . .85 DZ72
Locksley St, E14 . . . . .85 DZ71
Locksmeade Rd, Rich. TW10 .117 CJ91
Lockswood Cl, Barn. EN4 . . . .28 DF42
Lockwood Cl, SE26 . . . . .123 DX91
Lockwood Ind Pk, N17 . . . . . .66 DV55
Lockwood Path, Wok. GU21 . .151 BD113
Lockwood Sq, SE16 . . . . . . .202 D6
Lockwood Wk, E17 . . . . .47 DZ54
Lockwood Way, E17 . . . . . . .47 DX54
Chessington KT9 . . . . .156 CN106
Lockyer Est, SE1 . . . . .201 L4
Lockyer Rd, Purf. RM19 . . . .108 FQ79
Lockyer St, SE1 . . . . .201 L5
Loddiges Rd, E9 . . . . .84 DW66
Loddon Spur, Slou. SL1 . . . . .74 AS73
Loder Cl, Wok. GU21 . . . . . .151 BD113
Loder St, SE15 . . . . .102 DW81
Lodge Av, SW14 . . . . .98 CS83
Borehamwood (Elstree)
WD6 . . . . .26 CM43
Croydon CR0 . . . . .141 DN104
Dagenham RM8, RM9 . . . . .88 EU67
Dartford DA1 . . . . .128 FJ86
Harrow HA3 . . . . .62 CL56
Romford RM2 . . . . .71 FG56
Lodgebottom Rd, Lthd.
KT22 . . . . .182 CM127
Lodge Cl, N18 . . . . .46 DQ50
Brentwood (Hutton) CM13 . .55 GE45
Chigwell IG7 . . . . .50 EU48
Cobham (Stoke D'Ab.)
KT11 . . . . .170 BZ115
Edgware HA8 . . . . .42 CM51
Egham (Eng.Grn.) TW20 . . .112 AX92
Epsom KT17
off Howell Hill Gro 157 CW110
Isleworth TW7 . . . . .97 CH81
Leatherhead (Fetch.) KT22 . .171 CD122
Orpington BR6 . . . . .146 EV102
Uxbridge UB8 . . . . .76 BJ70
Wallington SM6 . . . . .140 DG102
Lodge Ct, Horn. RM12 . . . . . .72 FL61
Wembley HA0 . . . . .62 CL64
Lodge Cres, Orp. BR6 . . . . .146 EV102
Waltham Cross EN8 . . . . . .15 DX34
Lodge Dr, N13 . . . . .45 DN49
Rickmansworth (Loud.)
WD3 . . . . .22 BJ42
Lodge End, Rad. WD7 . . . . . .9 CH34
Rickmansworth (Crox.Grn.)
WD3 . . . . .23 BR42
Lodge Gdns, Beck. BR3 . . . .143 DZ99
Lodge Hill, SE2 . . . . .106 EV80
Ilford IG4 . . . . .68 EL56
Purley CR8 . . . . .175 DN115
Welling DA16 . . . . .106 EV80

Lodgehill Pk Cl, Har. HA2 . . . .60 CB61
Lodge La, N12 . . . . .44 DC50
  Bexley DA5 . . . . .126 EX86
  Chalfont St. Giles HP8 . . . . .21 AZ41
  Croydon (New Adgtn.)
    CR0 . . . . .161 EA107
  Grays RM16, RM17 . . . . . .110 GA75
  Romford RM5 . . . . .50 FA52
  Waltham Abbey EN9 . . . . . .31 ED35
  Westerham TN16 . . . . . . .189 EQ127
Lodge Pl, Sutt. SM1 . . . . . . .158 DB106
Lodge Rd, NW4 . . . . .63 CW56
  NW8 . . . . .194 A3
  Bromley BR1 . . . . .124 EH94
  Croydon CR0 . . . . .141 DP100
  Leatherhead (Fetch.) KT22 .170 CC122
  Sutton SM1
    off Throwley Way 158 DB106
  Wallington SM6 . . . . .159 DH106
Lodge Vil, Wdf.Grn. IG8 . . . . .48 EF52
Lodge Wk, Warl. CR6 . . . . . . .177 EA116
Lodge Way, Ashf. TW15 . . . . .114 BL89
  Shepperton TW17 . . . . . . .135 BQ96
Lodore Gdns, NW9 . . . . .62 CS57
Lodore Grn, Uxb. UB10 . . . . . .58 BL62
Lodore St, E14 . . . . .85 EC72
Loewen Rd, Grays RM16 . . . . .111 GG76
Lofthouse Pl, Chess. KT9 . . . .155 CJ107
Loftie St, SE16 . . . . .202 C5
Lofting Rd, N1 . . . . .83 DM66
Loftus Rd, W12 . . . . .81 CV74
Logan Cl, Enf. EN3 . . . . .31 DX39
  Hounslow TW4 . . . . .96 BZ83
Logan Ct, Rom. RM1
  off Logan Ms 71 FE57
Logan Ms, W8 . . . . .100 DA77
  Romford RM1 . . . . .71 FE57
Logan Pl, W8 . . . . .100 DA77
Logan Rd, N9 . . . . .46 DV47
  Wembley HA9 . . . . .62 CL61
Loggetts, The, SE21 . . . . . . .122 DS89
Logs Hill, Brom. BR1 . . . . . . .124 EL94
  Chislehurst BR7 . . . . .124 EL94
Logs Hill Cl, Chis. BR7 . . . . . .144 EL95
Lois Dr, Shep. TW17 . . . . . . .135 BP99
Lolesworth Cl, E1
  off Commercial St 84 DT71
Lollard St, SE11 . . . . .200 C8
Loman Path, S.Ock. RM15 . . . .91 FT72
Loman St, SE1 . . . . .200 G4
Lomas Cl, Croy. CR0 . . . . . . .161 EC108
Lomas Dr, E8 . . . . .84 DT66
Lomas St, E1 . . . . .84 DU71
Lombard Av, Enf. EN3 . . . . . . .30 DW39
  Ilford IG3 . . . . .69 ES60
Lombard Business Pk, SW19 .140 DC96
Lombard Ct, EC3 . . . . .197 L10
  W3 off Crown St 80 CP74
Lombard La, EC4 . . . . .196 E9
Lombard Rd, N11 . . . . .45 DH50
  SW11 . . . . .100 DD82
  SW19 . . . . .140 DB96
Lombards, The, Horn. RM11 . . .72 FM59
Lombard St, EC3 . . . . .197 L9
  Dartford (Hort.Kir.) DA4 . . .148 FQ99
Lombard Wall, SE7 . . . . .205 P7
Lombardy Cl, Wok. GU21
  off Nethercote Av 166 AT117
Lombardy Pl, W2 off Bark Pl . .82 DB73
Lombardy Retail Pk, Hayes
  UB3 . . . . .77 BV73
Lombardy Way, Borwd. WD6 . . .26 CL39
Lomond Cl, N15 . . . . .66 DS66
  Wembley HA0 . . . . .80 CM66
Lomond Gdns, S.Croy. CR2 . . .161 DY108
Lomond Gro, SE5 . . . . .102 DR80
Loncin Mead Av, Add. (New Haw)
  KT15 . . . . .152 BJ109
Loncroft Rd, SE5 . . . . .102 DS79
Londesborough Rd, N16 . . . . .66 DS63
★ London Aquarium, SE1 . . . .200 B4
★ London Arena, E14 . . . . . .204 C6
★ London Biggin Hill Airport,
  West.TN16 . . . . .162 EK113
★ London Brass Rubbing Cen, St.
  Martin-in-the-Fields Church,
  WC2 . . . . .199 P1
⇌ London Bridge 201 M3
⊖ London Bridge 201 M3
London Br, EC4 . . . . .201 L2
  SE1 . . . . .201 L2
Ⓗ London Bridge Hosp,
  SE1 . . . . .201 L2
London Br St, SE1 . . . . .201 K3
London Br Wk, SE1 . . . . .201 L2
★ London Broncos RLC (share
  Griffin Pk with Brentford FC),
  Brent. TW8 . . . . .97 CK79
★ London Butterfly Ho, Syon Pk,
  Brent. TW8 . . . . .97 CH81
★ London Canal Mus, The,
  N1 . . . . .83 DL68
★ London Cen Mosque,
  NW8 . . . . .194 C3
Ⓗ London Chest Hosp, E2 . . .84 DW68
★ London City Airport, E16 . . .86 EL74
London City Airport, E16 . . . . .87 EM74
Ⓗ London Clinic, The, W1 . . .194 G5
LONDON COLNEY, St.Alb. . . .10 CL26
London Colney Bypass, St.Alb.
  AL2 . . . . .9 CK25
★ London Commodity
  Exchange, E1 . . . . .202 A1
★ London Dungeon, SE1 . . . .201 L3
⊖ London Eye, SE1 . . . . . . .200 B4
⇌ London Fields 84 DV66
London Flds, E8 . . . . .84 DV66
London Flds E Side, E8 . . . . . .84 DV66
London Flds W Side, E8 . . . . . .84 DU66
★ London Fire Brigade Mus,
  SE1 . . . . .201 H4
Ⓗ London Foot Hosp & Sch of
  Podiatric Medicine, W1 . . .195 K5
★ London Heathrow Airport,
  Houns. TW6 . . . . .95 BP81
Ⓗ London Independent Hosp,
  E1 . . . . .85 DX71

London La, E8 . . . . .84 DV66
  Bromley BR1 . . . . .124 EF94
★ London Metropolitan
  Archives, EC1 . . . . .196 E4
London Ms, W2 . . . . .194 A9
★ London Palladium, W1 . . . .195 K9
★ London Peace Pagoda,
  SW11 . . . . .100 DF79
★ London Regatta Cen, E16 . .86 EK73
London Rd, E13 . . . . .86 EG68
  SE1 . . . . .200 F6
  SE23 . . . . .122 DU88
  SW16 . . . . .141 DM95
  SW17 . . . . .140 DF96
  Ashford TW15 . . . . .114 BH90
  Barking IG11 . . . . .87 EP66
  Borehamwood WD6 . . . . . .10 CN34
  Brentford TW8 . . . . .97 CJ80
  Brentwood CM14 . . . . .54 FT49
  Bromley BR1 . . . . .124 EF94
  Bushey WD23 . . . . .24 BY44
  Caterham CR3 . . . . .176 DR123
  Chalfont St. Giles HP8 . . . . .36 AW47
  Croydon CR0 . . . . .141 DP100
  Dartford (Cray.) DA1 . . . . .127 FD85
  Dartford (Fnghm.) DA4 . . .148 FL100
  Dartford (Stone) DA2 . . . . .128 FP87
  Egham (Eng.Grn.) TW20 . .132 AV95
  Enfield EN2 . . . . .30 DR41
  Epsom KT17 . . . . .157 CT109
  Feltham TW14 . . . . .114 BH90
  Gravesend (Nthflt.) DA11 . .130 GD86
  Grays RM17, RM20 . . . . . .109 FW79
  Greenhithe DA9 . . . . .129 FS86
  Harrow HA1 . . . . .61 CE61
  Hounslow TW3 . . . . .96 CC83
  Isleworth TW7 . . . . .97 CF82
  Kingston upon Thames
    KT2 . . . . .138 CM96
  Mitcham CR4 . . . . .140 DF96
  Mitcham (Bedd.Cor.) CR4 . .140 DG101
  Morden SM4 . . . . .140 DA99
  Ongar CM5 . . . . .35 FH36
  Radlett (Shenley) WD7 . . . .10 CM33
  Redhill RH1 . . . . .184 DG132
  Reigate RH2 . . . . .184 DA134
  Rickmansworth WD3 . . . . . .38 BM47
  Romford (Abridge) RM4 . . . .33 ET42
  Romford (Chad.Hth.)
    RM6, RM7 . . . . .70 FA58
  Romford (Stap.Taw.) RM4 . .35 FC40
  Sevenoaks TN13 . . . . . . .190 FF123
  Sevenoaks (Halst.) TN14 . .165 FB112
  Sevenoaks (Longford)
    TN13 . . . . .181 FD117
  Slough SL3 . . . . .93 AZ78
  Slough (Datchet) SL3 . . . . .92 AX80
  South Ockendon (Aveley)
    RM15 . . . . .90 FM74
  Staines TW18 . . . . .113 BF91
  Stanmore HA7 . . . . .41 CJ50
  Sutton SM3 . . . . .139 CX104
  Swanley BR8 . . . . .147 FC95
  Swanscombe DA10 . . . . . .129 FV85
  Thornton Heath CR7 . . . . .141 DN99
  Tilbury RM18 . . . . .111 GH82
  Twickenham TW1 . . . . . . .117 CG85
  Virginia Water GU25 . . . . .132 AV95
  Wallington SM6 . . . . .159 DH105
  Wembley HA9 . . . . .80 CL65
  Westerham TN16 . . . . . . .189 ER125
London Rd E, Amer. HP7 . . . . .20 AT42
London Rd N, Red. (Merst.)
  RH1 . . . . .185 DH125
London Rd Purfleet, Purf.
  RM20 . . . . .109 FS79
London Rd W Thurrock, Grays
  RM20 . . . . .109 FS79
Londons Cl, Upmin. RM14 . . . .72 FQ64
★ London Shop Pavilion, W1 . .199 M1
★ London Silver Vaults,
  WC2 . . . . .196 D7
London Silver Vaults, WC2 . . .196 D7
London Stile, W4
  off Wellesley Rd 98 CN78
★ London Stone, EC4 . . . . . .197 K10
London St, EC3 . . . . .197 N10
  W2 . . . . .82 DD72
  Chertsey KT16 . . . . .134 BG101
★ London Transport Mus, WC2
  off Covent Gdn 196 A10
London Wall, EC2 . . . . .197 J7
London Wall Bldgs, EC2 . . . . .197 L7
★ London Wildlife Trust,
  NW1 . . . . .83 DK67
★ London Zoo, NW1 . . . . .82 DG68
Lonesome Way, SW16 . . . . . .141 DH95
Long Acre, WC2 . . . . .195 P10
  Orpington BR6 . . . . .206 EX103
Longacre Pl, Cars. SM5
  off Beddington Gdns 158 DG107
Longacre Rd, E17 . . . . .47 ED53
Longaford Way, Brwd. CM13 . .55 GB46
Long Barn Cl, Wat. WD25 . . . . .7 BV32
Longbeach Rd, SW11 . . . . . . .100 DF83
Longberrys, NW2 . . . . .63 CZ62
Longboat Row, Sthl. UB1 . . . . .78 BZ72
Longbourne Way, Cher.
  KT16 . . . . .133 BF100
Longboyds, Cob. KT11 . . . . . .153 BV114
Longbridge Rd, Bark. IG11 . . . .87 EQ66
  Dagenham RM8 . . . . .70 EU63
Longbridge Way, SE13 . . . . . .123 DC85
  Uxbridge UB8 . . . . .76 BH68
Longbury Cl, Orp. BR5 . . . . . .146 EV97
Longbury Dr, Orp. BR5 . . . . . .146 EV97
Longcliffe Path, Wat. WD19
  off Gosforth La 39 BU48
Long Copse Cl, Lthd. (Bkhm.)
  KT23 . . . . .170 CB123
Long Ct, Purf. RM19
  off Thamley 108 FN77
Longcroft, SE9 . . . . .125 EM90
  Watford WD19 . . . . .39 BV45
Longcroft Av, Bans. SM7 . . . .158 DC114

Longcroft Dr, Wal.Cr. EN8 . . . .15 DZ34
Longcrofte Rd, Edg. HA8 . . . . .41 CK52
Longcroft La, Hem.H. (Bov.)
  HP3 . . . . .5 BC28
Longcroft Ri, Loug. IG10 . . . . .33 EN43
Longcroft Rd, Rick. (Map.Cr.)
  WD3 . . . . .37 BD50
Longcrofts, Wal.Abb. EN9
  off Roundhills 16 EE34
LONGCROSS, Cher. 132 AU104
⇌ Longcross 132 AT102
Longcross Rd, Cher. (Longcr.)
  .132 AY104
Long Deacon Rd, E4 . . . . .48 EE46
LONG DITTON, Surb. 137 CJ102
Longdown Wd, Bex. BR2 . . . .162 EL105
Longdown La N, Epsom
  KT17 . . . . .157 CU114
Longdown La S, Epsom
  KT17 . . . . .157 CU114
Longdown Rd, SE6 . . . . .123 EA91
  Epsom KT17 . . . . .157 CU114
Long Dr, W3 . . . . .80 CS72
  Greenford UB6 . . . . .78 CB67
  Ruislip HA4 . . . . .60 BX63
Long Elmes, Har. HA3 . . . . . . .40 CB53
Long Elms, Abb.L. WD5 . . . . . . .7 BR33
Long Elms Cl, Abb.L. WD5
  off Long Elms 7 BR33
Long Fallow, St.Alb. AL2 . . . . . .8 CA27
Longfellow Dr, Brwd. CM13 . . .55 GC45
Longfellow Rd, E17 . . . . .67 DZ58
  Worcester Park KT4 . . . . . .139 CU103
Longfellow Way, SE1 . . . . . . .202 A9
Long Fld, NW9 . . . . .42 CS52
Longfield, Brom. BR1 . . . . . . .144 EF95
  Loughton IG10 . . . . .32 EJ43
Longfield Av, E17 . . . . .67 DY56
  NW7 . . . . .43 CU52
  W5 . . . . .79 CJ73
  Enfield EN3 . . . . .30 DW37
  Hornchurch RM11 . . . . .71 FF59
  Wallington SM6 . . . . .140 DG102
  Wembley HA9 . . . . .62 CL64
Longfield Cres, SE26 . . . . . . .122 DW90
  Tadworth KT20 . . . . .173 CW120
Longfield Dr, SW14 . . . . .118 CP85
  Mitcham CR4 . . . . .120 DE94
Longfield Est, SE1 . . . . .202 A9
Longfield La, Wal.Cr. (Chsht.)
  EN7 . . . . .14 DU27
Longfield Rd, W5 . . . . .79 CJ73
Longfield St, SW18 . . . . .120 DA87
Longfield Wk, W5 . . . . .79 CJ72
LONGFORD, Sev. 181 FD120
LONGFORD, West Dr. 94 BH81
Longford Av, Felt. TW14 . . . . .115 BS86
  Southall UB1 . . . . .78 CA73
  Staines TW19 . . . . .114 BL88
Longford Cl, Hmptn. (Hmptn.H.)
  TW12 . . . . .116 CA91
  Hayes UB4
    off Longford Gdns 78 BX73
Longford Ct, E5 off Pedro St . .67 DX63
  NW4 . . . . .63 CX56
  Epsom KT19 . . . . .156 CQ105
Longford Gdns, Hayes UB4 . . .78 BX73
  Sutton SM1 . . . . .140 DC104
Longford Rd, Twick. TW2 . . . .116 CA88
Longford Roundabout, West Dr.
  UB7 . . . . .94 BH81
Longford St, NW1 . . . . .195 J4
Longford Wk, SW2
  off Papworth Way 121 DN87
Longford Way, Stai. TW19 . . .114 BL88
Long Grn, Chig. IG7 . . . . .49 ES49
Long Gro, Rom. (Harold Wd.)
  RM3 . . . . .52 FL54
Long Gro Rd, Epsom KT19 . . .156 CP110
Longhayes Av, Rom. RM6 . . . .70 EX56
Longhayes Ct, Rom. RM6
  off Longhayes Av 70 EX56
Longheath Gdns, Croy. CR0 . .142 DW99
Longhedge Ho, SE26 . . . . . . .122 DV89
Long Hedges, Houns. TW3 . . . .96 CA81
Longhedge St, SW11 . . . . . . .100 DG82
Long Hill, Cat. (Wold.) CR3 . . .177 DX121
Longhill Rd, SE6 . . . . .124 ED89
Longhook Gdns, Nthlt. UB5 . . .77 BU68
Longhope Cl, SE15 . . . . .102 DS79
Longhouse Rd, Grays RM16 . .111 GH76
Longhurst Rd, SE13 . . . . .123 ED85
  Croydon CR0 . . . . .142 DV100
Longland Ct, SE1 . . . . .202 B10
Longland Dr, N20 . . . . .44 DB48
LONGLANDS, Chis. 125 EQ90
Longlands Av, Couls. CR5 . . . .158 DG114
Longlands Cl, Wal.Cr. (Chsht.)
  EN8 . . . . .15 DX32
Longlands Ct, W11
  off Portobello Rd 81 CZ73
  Mitcham CR4
    off Summerhill Way 140 DG95
Longlands Pk Cres, Sid.
  DA15 . . . . .125 ES90
Longlands Rd, Sid. DA15 . . . .125 ES90
Long La, EC1 . . . . .196 G6
  N2 . . . . .44 DC54
  N3 . . . . .44 DB54
  SE1 . . . . .201 K5
  Bexleyheath DA7 . . . . . . .106 EX80
  Croydon CR0 . . . . .142 DW99
  Grays RM16 . . . . .110 GA75
  Hemel Hempstead (Bov.)
    HP3 . . . . .5 AZ31
  Rickmansworth (Herons.)
    WD3 . . . . .21 BC44
  Rickmansworth (Mill End)
    WD3 . . . . .37 BF47
  Staines (Stanw.) TW19 . . .114 BM87
  Uxbridge UB10 . . . . .76 BN69
Longleat Ms, Orp. BR5
  off High St 146 EW98
Longleat Rd, Enf. EN1 . . . . . . .30 DS43
Longleat Way, Felt. TW14 . . . .115 BR87
Longlees, Rick. (Map.Cr.) WD3 .37 BC50
Longleigh La, SE2 . . . . .106 EW77

Longleigh La, Bexh. DA7 . . . .106 EW79
Longlents Ho, NW10 . . . . .80 CR67
Longley Av, Wem. HA0 . . . . . . .80 CM67
Longley Rd, SW17 . . . . .120 DE93
  Croydon CR0 . . . . .141 DP101
  Harrow HA1 . . . . .60 CC57
Longleys, E4 . . . . .47 EB51
Longley St, SE1 . . . . .202 B9
Longley Way, NW2 . . . . .63 CW63
Long Lo Dr, Walt. KT12 . . . . .136 BW104
Longmans Cl, Wat. WD18 . . . .23 BQ44
Long Mark Rd, E16
  off Fulmer Rd 86 EK71
Longmarsh Vw, Dart. (Sutt.H.)
  DA4 . . . . .148 FP95
Long Mead, NW9 . . . . .43 CT53
Longmead, Chis. BR7 . . . . . . .145 EN96
  Epsom KT19 . . . . .156 CR110
Longmead Business Pk, Epsom
  KT19 . . . . .156 CR111
Longmead Cl, Brwd. CM15 . . . .54 FY46
  Caterham CR3 . . . . .176 DS122
Longmead Dr, Sid. DA14 . . . .126 EX89
Longmeade, Grav. DA12
  off Damigos Rd 131 GM88
Long Meadow, NW5
  off Torriano Av 65 DK64
  Brentwood CM13 . . . . .55 GC47
  Romford (Noak Hill) RM3 . .52 FJ48
  Sevenoaks (Rvrhd.) TN13 .190 FD121
Long Meadow, W.Wick.
  BR4 . . . . .143 EC101
Longmeadow Rd, Sid. DA15 .125 ES88
Longmead Rd, SW17 . . . . . . .120 DF92
  Epsom KT19 . . . . .156 CR111
  Hayes UB3 . . . . .77 BT73
  Thames Ditton KT7 . . . . . .137 CE101
Longmere Gdns, Tad. KT20 . .173 CW119
Longmoor, Wal.Cr. (Chsht.)
  EN8 . . . . .15 DY29
Longmoore St, SW1 . . . . .199 K9
Longmoor Pt, SW15
  off Norley Vale 119 CV88
Longmore Av, Barn. EN4, EN5 .28 DC44
Longmore Cl, Rick. (Map.Cr.)
  WD3 . . . . .37 BF49
Longmore Rd, Walt. KT12 . . . .154 BY105
Longnor Rd, E1 . . . . .85 DX69
Long Pond Rd, SE3 . . . . .104 EE81
Longport Cl, Ilf. IG6 . . . . .50 EU51
Long Reach, Wok. (Ockham)
  GU23 . . . . .168 BN123
Long Reach Ct, Bark. IG11 . . . .87 ER68
Longreach Rd, Bark. IG11 . . . .87 ET70
  Erith DA8 . . . . .107 FH80
Longridge Gro, Wok. GU22
  off Old Woking Rd 151 BE114
Longridge La, Sthl. UB1 . . . . . .78 CB73
Longridge Rd, SW5 . . . . .100 DA77
Long Ridings Av, Brwd.
  CM13 . . . . .55 GB43
Long Rd, SW4 . . . . .101 DH84
Longs Cl, Wok. GU22 . . . . . . .168 BG116
Long's Ct, WC2 . . . . .195 M10
Longs Ct, Rich. TW9
  off Crown Ter 98 CM84
Longsdon Way, Cat. CR3 . . . .176 DU124
Long Shaw, Lthd. KT22 . . . . .171 CG119
Longshaw Rd, E4 . . . . .47 ED48
Longshore, SE8 . . . . .203 M9
Longspring, Wat. WD24 . . . . . .23 BV38
Longspring Wd, Sev. TN14 . . .190 FF130
Longstaff Cres, SW18 . . . . . .120 DA86
Longstaff Rd, SW18 . . . . .120 DA86
Longstone Av, NW10 . . . . .81 CT66
Longstone Rd, SW17 . . . . . . .121 DH92
  Iver SL0 . . . . .75 BC68
Long St, E2 . . . . .197 P2
  Waltham Abbey EN9 . . . . . .16 EL32
Longthornton Rd, SW16 . . . . .141 DJ96
Longton Av, SE26 . . . . .122 DU91
Longton Gro, SE26 . . . . .122 DV91
Longtown Cl, Rom. RM3 . . . . .52 FJ50
Longtown Rd, Rom. RM3 . . . . .52 FJ50
Longview Way, Rom. RM5 . . . .51 FD53
Longville Rd, SE11 . . . . .200 F8
Long Wk, SE1 . . . . .201 N6
  SE18 . . . . .105 EP79
  SW13 . . . . .98 CS82
  Chalfont St. Giles HP8 . . . .20 AX41
  Epsom KT18 . . . . .173 CX119
  New Malden KT3 . . . . .138 CQ97
  Waltham Abbey EN9 . . . . . .15 EA30
  West Byfleet KT14 . . . . . .152 BJ114
Longwalk Rd, Uxb. UB11 . . . . .77 BP74
Longwood Business Pk, Sun.
  TW16 . . . . .135 BT99
Longwood Cl, Upmin. RM14 . .72 FQ64
Longwood Dr, SW15 . . . . .119 CU86
Long Wd Dr, Beac. (Jordans)
  HP9 . . . . .36 AT51
Longwood Gdns, Ilf. IG5, IG6 . .69 EM56
Longwood Rd, Ken. CR8 . . . . .176 DR116
Longworth Cl, SE28 . . . . .88 EX72
Long Yd, WC1 . . . . .196 B5
Loning, The, NW9 . . . . .62 CS56
  Enfield EN3 . . . . .30 DW38
Lonsdale Av, E6 . . . . .86 EK69
  Brentwood CM13 . . . . .55 GD44
  Romford RM7 . . . . .71 FC58
  Wembley HA9 . . . . .62 CL64
Lonsdale Cl, E6
  off Lonsdale Av 86 EL70
  SE9 . . . . .124 EK90
  Edgware HA8
    off Orchard Dr 42 CM50
  Pinner HA5 . . . . .40 BY52
  Uxbridge UB8
    off Dawley Av 77 BQ71

Lonsdale Pl, N1
  off Barnsbury St 83 DN66
Lonsdale Rd, E11 . . . . .68 EF59
  NW6 . . . . .81 CZ68
  SE25 . . . . .142 DV98
  SW13 . . . . .99 CU79
  W4 . . . . .99 CT77
  W11 . . . . .81 CZ72
  Bexleyheath DA7 . . . . . . .106 EZ82
  Southall UB2 . . . . .96 BX76
  Weybridge KT13 . . . . .152 BN108
Lonsdale Sq, N1 . . . . .83 DN66
Loobert Rd, N15 . . . . .66 DS55
Looe Gdns, Ilf. IG6 . . . . .69 EP55
Loom Ct, E1 . . . . .197 N5
Loom La, Rad. WD7 . . . . .25 CG37
Loom Pl, Rad. WD7 . . . . .25 CG36
Loop Rd, Chis. BR7 . . . . .125 EQ93
  Epsom KT18
    off Woodcote Side 172 CQ116
  Waltham Abbey EN9 . . . . . .15 EB32
  Woking GU22 . . . . .167 AZ121
Lopen Rd, N18 . . . . .46 DS49
Loraine Cl, Enf. EN3 . . . . .30 DW43
Loraine Gdns, Ashtd. KT21 . .172 CL117
Loraine Rd, N7 . . . . .65 DM63
  W4 . . . . .98 CP79
Lorane Ct, Wat. WD17 . . . . . . .23 BU40
Lord Amory Way, E14 . . . . . . .204 D4
Lord Av, Ilf. IG5 . . . . .69 EM56
Lord Chancellor Wk, Kings.T.
  KT2 . . . . .138 CQ95
Lord Chatham's Ride, Sev.
  TN14 . . . . .180 EX117
Lordell Pl, SW19 . . . . .119 CW93
Lorden Wk, E2 . . . . .84 DU69
Lords Cl, Ilf. IG5 . . . . .68 EL56
Lord Hills Br, W2
  off Porchester Rd 82 DB71
Lord Hills Rd, W2 . . . . .82 DB71
Lord Holland La, SW9
  off St. Lawrence Way 101 DN81
Lord Knyvett Cl, Stai. (Stanw.)
  TW19 . . . . .114 BK86
Lord Napier Pl, W6
  off Upper Mall 99 CU78
Lord N St, SW1 . . . . .199 P7
Lord Roberts Ms, SW6
  off Moore Pk Rd 100 DB80
Lord Roberts Ter, SE18 . . . . . .105 EN78
★ Lord's, Middlesex County
  Cricket Club & Mus, NW8 .194 A2
Lordsbury Fld, Wall. SM6 . . . .159 DJ110
Lord's Cl, SE21 . . . . .122 DQ89
Lords Cl, Felt. TW13 . . . . .116 BY89
  Radlett (Shenley) WD7 . . . .10 CL32
Lordsgrove Cl, Tad. KT20
  off Whitegate Way 173 CV120
Lordship Cl, Brwd. CM13 . . . . .55 GD46
Lordship Gro, N16 . . . . .66 DR61
Lordship La, N17 . . . . .46 DQ53
  N22 . . . . .45 DN54
  SE22 . . . . .122 DT86
Lordship La Est, SE22 . . . . . .122 DU88
Lordship Pk, N16 . . . . .66 DQ61
Lordship Pk Ms, N16
  off Allerton Rd 66 DQ61
Lordship Pl, SW3
  off Cheyne Row 100 DE79
Lordship Rd, N16 . . . . .66 DR61
  Northolt UB5 . . . . .78 BY66
  Waltham Cross (Chsht.)
    EN7 . . . . .14 DV30
Lordship Ter, N16 . . . . .66 DR61
Lordsmead Rd, N17 . . . . .46 DS53
Lord St, E16 . . . . .86 EL74
  Gravesend DA12 . . . . .131 GH87
  Watford WD17 . . . . .24 BW41
Lord's Vw, NW8 . . . . .194 A3
Lordswood Cl, Dart. (Lane End)
  DA2 . . . . .129 FS91
Lords Wd Ho, Couls. CR5 . . . .175 DK122
Lord Warwick St, SE18 . . . . . .105 EM76
Lorenzo St, WC1 . . . . .196 B2
Loretto Gdns, Har. HA3 . . . . . .62 CL56
Lorian Cl, N12 . . . . .44 DB49
Lorian Dr, Reig. RH2 . . . . . . .184 DC133
Loriners Cl, Cob. KT11
  off Between Sts 153 BU114
Loring Rd, N20 . . . . .44 DE47
  Isleworth TW7 . . . . .97 CF82
Loris Rd, W6 . . . . .99 CW76
Lorn Ct, SW9 . . . . .101 DN82
Lorne Av, Croy. CR0 . . . . .143 DX101
Lorne Cl, NW8 . . . . .194 C3
Lorne Gdns, E11 . . . . .68 EJ56
  W11 . . . . .99 CX75
  Croydon CR0 . . . . .143 DX101
Lorne Rd, E7 . . . . .68 EH63
  E17 . . . . .67 EA57
  N4 . . . . .65 DM60
  Brentwood CM14 . . . . .54 FW49
  Harrow HA3 . . . . .41 CF54
  Richmond TW10
    off Albert Rd 118 CM85
Lorn Rd, SW9 . . . . .101 DM82
Lorraine Chase, S.Ock. RM15 .108 FM75
Lorraine Pk, Har. HA3 . . . . . . .41 CE52
Lorrimore Rd, SE17 . . . . .101 DP79
Lorrimore Sq, SE17 . . . . .101 DP79
Lorton Cl, Grav. DA12 . . . . . . .131 GL89
Loseberry Rd, Esher (Clay.)
  KT10 . . . . .155 CD106
Lossie Dr, Iver SL0 . . . . .75 BB73
Lothair Rd, W5 . . . . .97 CK75
Lothair Rd N, N4 . . . . .65 DP58
Lothair Rd S, N4 . . . . .65 DN59
Lothbury, EC2 . . . . .197 K8
Lothian Av, Hayes UB4 . . . . . .77 BV71
Lothian Cl, Wem. HA0 . . . . . . .61 CG63
Lothian Rd, SW9 . . . . .101 DP81
Lothian Wd, Tad. KT20 . . . . . .173 CV122
Lothrop St, W10 . . . . .81 CY69
Lots Rd, SW10 . . . . .100 DC80

Lot - Lyn

Lotus Cl, SE21 . . . .**122** DQ90
Lotus Rd, West. (Bigg.H.)
TN16 . . . .**179** EM118
Loubet St, SW17 . . . .**120** DF93
Loudhams Rd, Amer. HP7 . . .**20** AW39
Loudhams Wd La, Ch.St.G.
HP8 . . . .**20** AX40
Loudoun Av, Ilf. IG6 . . . .**69** EP57
Loudoun Rd, NW8 . . . .**82** DC66
off Loudoun Rd **82** DC67
LOUDWATER, Rick. **22** BK41
Loudwater Cl, Sun. TW16 . . .**135** BU98
Loudwater Dr, Rick. (Loud.)
WD3 . . . .**22** BJ42
Loudwater Hts, Rick. (Loud.)
WD3 . . . .**22** BH41
Loudwater La, Rick. WD3 . . . .**22** BK42
Loudwater Ridge, Rick. (Loud.)
WD3 . . . .**22** BJ42
Loudwater Rd, Sun. TW16 . . .**135** BU98
Loughborough Est, SW9
off Loughborough Rd **101** DP82
⇌ Loughborough Junction .**101** DP83
Loughborough Pk, SW9 . . . .**101** DP84
Loughborough Rd, SW9 . . . .**101** DN82
Loughborough St, SE11 . . . .**200** C10
Lough Rd, N7 . . . .**83** DM65
LOUGHTON **33** EM43
⊖ Loughton **32** EL43
Loughton Ct, Wal.Abb. EN9 . .**16** EH33
Loughton La, Epp. (They.B.)
CM16 . . . .**33** ER38
Loughton Way, Buck.H. IG9 . .**48** EK46
Louisa Gdns, E1
off Louisa St **85** DX70
Louisa Ho, SW15 . . . .**98** CS84
Louisa St, E1 . . . .**85** DX70
Louise Aumonier Wk, N19
off Hillrise Rd **65** DL59
Louise Bennett Cl, SE24
off Shakespeare Rd **101** DP84
Louise Ct, E11
off Grosvenor Rd **68** EH57
Louise Gdns, Rain. RM13 . . .**89** FE69
Louise Rd, E15 . . . .**86** EE65
Louise Wk, Hem.H. (Bov.) HP3 .**5** BA28
Louis Ms, N10 . . . .**45** DH53
Louisville Rd, SW17 . . . .**120** DG92
Louvaine Rd, SW11 . . . .**100** DD84
Louvain Rd, Green. DA9 . . . .**129** FS87
Louvain Way, Wat. WD25 . . . .**7** BV32
Lovage App, E6 . . . .**86** EL71
Lovat Cl, NW2 . . . .**63** CT62
Lovat La, EC3 . . . .**201** M1
Lovatt Cl, Edg. HA8 . . . .**42** CP51
Lovatt Dr, Ruis. HA4 . . . .**59** BU57
Lovatts, Rick. (Crox.Grn.)
WD3 . . . .**22** BN42
Lovat Wk, Houns. TW5
off Cranford La **96** BY80
Loveday Rd, W13 . . . .**79** CH74
Lovegrove St, SE1 . . . .**102** DU78
Lovegrove Wk, E14 . . . .**204** D3
Love Hill La, Slou. SL3 . . . . . .**75** BA73
Lovekyn Cl, Kings.T. KT2
off Queen Elizabeth Rd . .**138** CM96
Lovelace Av, Brom. BR2 . . . .**145** EN100
Lovelace Cl, Lthd. (Eff.Junct.)
KT24 . . . .**169** BU123
Lovelace Dr, Wok. GU22 . . . .**167** BF115
Lovelace Gdns, Bark. IG11 . . .**70** EU63
Surbiton KT6 . . . .**137** CK101
Walton-on-Thames KT12 . .**154** BW106
Lovelace Grn, SE9 . . . .**105** EM83
Lovelace Rd, SE21 . . . .**122** DQ89
Barnet EN4 . . . .**44** DE45
Surbiton KT6 . . . .**137** CJ101
Lovelands La, Tad. KT20 . . . .**184** DB127
Love La, EC2 . . . .**197** J8
N17 . . . .**46** DT52
SE18 . . . .**105** EP77
SE25 . . . .**142** DV99
Abbots Langley WD5 . . . .**7** BT30
Bexley DA5 . . . .**126** EZ86
Godstone RH9 . . . .**186** DW132
Gravesend DA12 . . . .**131** GJ87
Iver SL0 . . . .**75** BD72
Kings Langley WD4 . . . .**6** BL29
Mitcham CR4 . . . .**140** DE97
Morden SM4 . . . .**140** DA101
Pinner HA5 . . . .**60** BY55
South Ockendon (Aveley)
RM15 . . . .**108** FQ75
Surbiton KT6 . . . .**137** CK103
Sutton SM3 . . . .**157** CY106
Tadworth KT20 . . . .**183** CT126
Woodford Green IG8 . . . . . .**49** EM51
Lovel Av, Well. DA16 . . . .**106** EU82
Lovel End, Ger.Cr. (Chal.St.P.)
SL9 . . . .**36** AW52
Lovelinch Cl, SE15 . . . .**102** DW79
Lovell Ho, E8 . . . .**84** DU67
Lovell Pl, SE16 . . . .**203** L6
Lovell Rd, Enf. EN1 . . . .**30** DV35
Richmond TW10 . . . .**117** CJ90
Southall UB1 . . . .**78** CB72
Lovell Wk, Rain. RM13 . . . . .**89** FG65
Lovel Mead, Ger.Cr. (Chal.St.P.)
SL9 . . . .**36** AW52
Lovelock Cl, Ken. CR8 . . . . .**176** DQ117
Lovel Rd, Ger.Cr. (Chal.St.P.)
SL9 . . . .**36** AW52
Loveridge Ms, NW6
off Loveridge Rd **81** CZ65
Loveridge Rd, NW6 . . . .**81** CZ65
Lovering Rd, Wal.Cr. (Chsht.)
EN7 . . . .**14** DQ26
Lovers La, Green. DA9 . . . . .**109** FX84
Lovers Wk, N3 . . . .**44** DA52
NW7 . . . .**43** CZ51
SE10 . . . .**104** EE79
Lover's Wk, W1 . . . .**198** F2

Lovett Dr, Cars. SM5 . . . . . .**140** DC101
Lovett Rd, Stai. TW18 . . . . . .**113** BB91
Uxbridge (Hare.) UB9 . . . . . .**58** BJ55
Lovett's Pl, SW18
off Old York Rd **100** DB84
Lovett Way, NW10 . . . .**62** CQ64
Love Wk, SE5 . . . .**102** DR82
Lovibonds Av, Orp. BR6 . . . .**163** EP105
West Drayton UB7 . . . .**76** BM72
Lowbell La, St.Alb. (Lon.Col.)
AL2 . . . .**10** CL27
Lowbrook Rd, Ilf. IG1 . . . .**69** EP64
Low Cl, Green. DA9 . . . .**129** FU85
Low Cross Wd La, SE21 . . . .**122** DT90
Lowden Rd, N9 . . . .**46** DV46
SE24 . . . .**101** DP84
Southall UB1 . . . .**78** BY73
Lowe, The, Chig. IG7 . . . .**50** EU50
Lowe Av, E16 . . . .**86** EG71
Lowe Cl, Chig. IG7 . . . .**50** EU50
Lowell St, E14 . . . .**85** DY72
Lowen Rd, Rain. RM13 . . . . .**89** FD68
Lower Addiscombe Rd, Croy.
CR0 . . . .**142** DS102
Lower Addison Gdns, W14 . . .**99** CY75
Lower Alderton Hall La, Loug.
IG10 . . . .**33** EN43
LOWER ASHTEAD, Ashtd. . .**171** CJ119
Lower Barn Rd, Pur. CR8 . . .**160** DR112
Lower Bedfords Rd, Rom.
RM1 . . . .**51** FE51
Lower Belgrave St, SW1 . . . .**199** H7
Lower Boston Rd, W7 . . . . . .**79** CE74
Lower Br Rd, Red. RH1 . . . . .**184** DF134
Lower Broad St, Dag. RM10 . .**88** FA67
Lower Bury La, Epp. CM16 . . .**17** ES31
Lower Camden, Chis. BR7 . . .**125** EM94
Lower Ch Hill, Green. DA9 . . .**129** FS85
Lower Ch St, Croy. CR0
off Waddon New Rd **141** DP103
LOWER CLAPTON, E5 . . . . . .**67** DX63
Lower Clapton Rd, E5 . . . . . .**66** DV64
Lower Clarendon Wk, W11
off Lancaster Rd **81** CY72
Lower Common S, SW15 . . . .**99** CV83
Lower Coombe St, Croy.
CR0 . . . .**160** DQ105
Lower Ct Rd, Epsom KT19 . .**156** CQ111
Lower Cft, Swan. BR8 . . . . . .**147** FF98
Lower Downs Rd, SW20 . . . .**139** CX95
Lower Drayton Pl, Croy. CR0
off Drayton Rd **141** DP103
Lower Dunnymans, Bans. SM7
off Basing Rd **157** CZ114
LOWER EDMONTON, N9 . . . .**46** DT46
Lower Fm Rd, Lthd. (Eff.)
KT24 . . . .**169** BV124
LOWER FELTHAM, Felt. **115** BS90
Lower George St, Rich. TW9
off George St **117** CK85
LOWER GREEN, Esher **136** CA103
Lower Grn Rd, Esher KT10 . .**136** CB103
Lower Grn W, Mitch. CR4 . . .**140** DE97
Lower Grosvenor Pl, SW1 . . .**199** H6
Lower Gro Rd, Rich. TW10 . .**118** CM86
Lower Guild Hall, Green.
(Bluewater) DA9
off Bluewater Parkway . .**129** FU88
Lower Hall La, E4 . . . .**47** DY50
Lower Hampton Rd, Sun.
TW16 . . . .**136** BW97
Lower Ham Rd, Kings.T. KT2 .**117** CK94
Lower Higham Rd, Grav.
DA12 . . . .**131** GM88
Lower High St, Wat. WD17 . . .**24** BX44
Lower Hill Rd, Epsom KT19 . .**156** CP112
Lower James St, W1 . . . . . .**195** L10
Lower John St, W1 . . . .**195** L10
Lower Kenwood Av, Enf. EN2 .**29** DK43
LOWER KINGSWOOD, Tad. . .**184** DA127
Lower Lea Crossing, E14 . . .**86** EE73
Lower Maidstone Rd, N11
off Telford Rd **45** DJ51
Lower Mall, W6 . . . .**99** CV78
Lower Mardyke Av, Rain.
RM13 . . . .**89** FC68
Lower Marsh, SE1 . . . .**200** D5
Lower Marsh La, Kings.T. KT1 .**138** CM98
Lower Mead, Iver SL0 . . . . . .**75** BD69
Lower Meadow, Wal.Cr. EN8 . .**15** DX27
Lower Morden La, Mord.
SM4 . . . .**139** CW100
Lower Mortlake Rd, Rich.
TW9 . . . .**98** CL84
Lower Noke Cl, Brwd. CM14 . .**52** FL47
Lower Northfield, Bans.
SM7 . . . .**157** CZ114
Lower Paddock Rd, Wat.
WD19 . . . .**24** BY44
Lower Pk Rd, N11 . . . .**45** DJ50
Belvedere DA17 . . . .**106** FA76
Coulsdon CR5 . . . .**174** DE118
Loughton IG10 . . . .**32** EK43
Lower Pillory Down, Cars.
SM5 . . . .**158** DG113
Lower Plantation, Rick. (Loud.)
WD3 . . . .**22** BJ41
Lower Queens Rd, Buck.H.
IG9 . . . .**48** EK47
Lower Range Rd, Grav.
DA12 . . . .**131** GL87
Lower Richmond Rd, SW14 . .**98** CP83
SW15 . . . .**99** CW83
Richmond TW9 . . . .**98** CN83
Lower Rd, SE8 . . . .**202** F6
SE16 . . . .**203** H8
Belvedere DA17 . . . .**106** FA76
Brentwood (Mtnsg.)
CM13, CM15 . . . .**55** GD41
Erith DA8 . . . .**107** FD77
Gerrards Cross SL9 . . . .**36** AY53
Gravesend (Nthflt.) DA11 . . .**110** FY84

Lower Rd, Har. HA2 . . . .**61** CD61
Hemel Hempstead HP3 . . . . . .**6** BN25
Kenley CR8 . . . .**159** DP113
Leatherhead (Fetch.) KT22 . .**171** CD123
Loughton IG10 . . . .**33** EN48
Orpington BR5 . . . .**146** EV101
Rickmansworth (Chorl.)
WD3 . . . .**21** BC42
Sutton SM1 . . . .**158** DC105
Swanley BR8 . . . .**127** FF94
Tilbury RM18 . . . .**111** GG84
Uxbridge (Denh.) UB9 . . . . . .**57** BC59
Lower Robert St, WC2
off John Adam St **83** DL73
Lower Rose Gallery, Green.
(Bluewater) DA9
off Bluewater Parkway . .**129** FU88
Lower Sandfields, Wok. (Send)
GU23 . . . .**167** BD124
Lower Sand Hills, T.Ditt. KT7 .**137** CJ101
Lower Sawley Wd, Bans. SM7
off Upper Sawley Wd . . .**157** CZ114
Lower Shott, Wal.Cr. (Chsht.)
EN7 . . . .**14** DT26
Lower Sloane St, SW1 . . . . .**198** F9
Lower Sq, Islw. TW7 . . . .**97** CH83
Lower Sta Rd, Dart. (Cray.)
DA1 . . . .**127** FE86
Lower Strand, NW9 . . . .**43** CT54
Lower Sunbury Rd, Hmptn.
TW12 . . . .**136** BZ96
Lower Swaines, Epp. CM16 . .**17** ES30
LOWER SYDENHAM, SE26 . .**123** DX91
⇌ Lower Sydenham **123** DZ92
Lower Sydenham Ind Est,
SE26 . . . .**123** DZ92
Lower Tail, Wat. WD19 . . . . . .**40** BY48
Lower Talbot Wk, W11
off Lancaster Rd **81** CY72
Lower Teddington Rd, Kings.T.
KT1 . . . .**137** CK95
Lower Ter, NW3 . . . .**64** DC62
Lower Thames St, EC3 . . . . .**201** L1
Lower Thames Wk, Green.
(Bluewater) DA9
off Bluewater Parkway . . .**129** FU88
Lower Tub, Bushey WD23 . . . .**41** CD45
Lower Wd Rd, Esher (Clay.)
KT10 . . . .**155** CG107
Lowestoft Cl, E5
off Theydon Rd **66** DW61
Lowestoft Ms, E16 . . . .**105** EP75
Lowestoft Rd, Wat. WD24 . . .**23** BV39
Loweswater Cl, Wat. WD25 . . .**8** BW33
Wembley HA9 . . . .**61** CK61
Lowfield Rd, NW6 . . . .**82** DA66
W3 . . . .**80** CQ72
Lowfield St, Dart. DA1 . . . . . .**128** FL89
Low Hall Cl, E4 . . . .**47** EA45
Low Hall La, E17 . . . .**67** DY58
Lowick Rd, Har. HA1 . . . .**61** CE56
Lowlands Dr, Stai. (Stanw.)
TW19 . . . .**114** BK85
Lowlands Gdns, Rom. RM7 . .**71** FB58
Lowlands Rd, Har. HA1 . . . . .**61** CE59
Pinner HA5 . . . .**60** BW59
South Ockendon (Aveley)
RM15 . . . .**90** FP74
Lowman Rd, N7 . . . .**65** DM63
Lowndes Cl, SW1 . . . .**198** G7
Lowndes Ct, W1
off Carnaby St **195** L9
Bromley BR1
off Queens Rd **144** EG96
Lowndes Pl, SW1 . . . .**198** F7
Lowndes Sq, SW1 . . . .**198** E5
Lowndes St, SW1 . . . .**198** E6
Lowood Ct, SE19 . . . .**122** DT92
Lowood St, E1 *off Dellow St* . .**84** DV73
Lowry Cl, Erith DA8 . . . .**107** FD77
Lowry Cres, Mitch. CR4 . . . .**140** DE96
Lowry Rd, Dag. RM8 . . . .**70** EV63
Lowshoe La, Rom. RM5 . . . . .**51** FB53
Lowson Gro, Wat. WD19 . . . .**40** BY45
LOW STREET, Til. **111** GM79
Low St La, Til. (E.Til.) RM18 . .**111** GM78
Lowswood Cl, Nthwd. HA6 . . .**39** BQ53
Lowther Cl, Borwd. (Elstree)
WD6 . . . .**26** CM43
Lowther Dr, Enf. EN2 . . . .**29** DL42
Lowther Gdns, SW7 . . . .**198** A5
Lowther Hill, SE23 . . . .**123** DY87
Lowther Rd, E17 . . . .**47** DY54
N7 *off Mackenzie Rd* **65** DN64
SW13 . . . .**99** CT81
Kingston upon Thames
KT2 . . . .**138** CM95
Stanmore HA7 . . . .**62** CM55
Lowthorpe, Wok. GU21
off Shilburn Way **166** AU118
Lowton Rd, SE5 . . . .**102** DQ82
LOXFORD, Ilf. **69** EQ64
Loxford Av, E6 . . . .**86** EK68
Loxford La, Ilf. IG1, IG3 . . . . .**69** EQ64
Loxford Rd, Bark. IG11 . . . . .**87** EP65
Caterham CR3 . . . .**186** DT125
Loxford Ter, Bark. IG11
off Fanshawe Av **87** EQ65
Loxford Way, Cat. CR3 . . . . .**186** DT125
Loxham Rd, E4 . . . .**47** EA52
Loxham St, WC1 . . . .**196** A3
Loxley Cl, SE26 . . . .**123** DX92
Loxley Rd, SW18 . . . .**120** DD88
Hampton TW12 . . . .**116** BZ91
Loxton Rd, SE23 . . . .**123** DX88
Loxwood Cl, Felt. TW14 . . . .**115** BS88
Orpington BR5 . . . .**146** EX103
Loxwood Rd, N17 . . . .**66** DS55
Lubbock Rd, Chis. BR7 . . . .**125** DS93
Lubbock St, SE14 . . . .**102** DW80
Lucan Pl, SW3 . . . .**198** B9
Lucan Rd, Barn. EN5 . . . .**27** CY41
Lucas Av, E13 . . . .**86** EH67
Harrow HA2 . . . .**60** CA61
Lucas Cl, NW10 *off Pound La* .**81** CU66
Lucas Ct, Har. HA2 . . . .**60** CA60
Waltham Abbey EN9 . . . .**16** EF33

Lucas Gdns, N2 . . . .**44** DC54
Lucas Rd, SE20 . . . .**122** DW93
Grays RM17 . . . .**110** GA76
Lucas Sq, NW11
off Hampstead Way **64** DA58
Lucas St, SE8 . . . .**103** EA81
Lucern Cl, Wal.Cr. (Chsht.)
EN7 . . . .**14** DS27
Lucerne Cl, N13 . . . .**45** DL49
Woking GU22 . . . .
off Claremont Av **166** AY119
Lucerne Ct, Erith DA18
off Middle Way **106** EY76
Lucerne Gro, E17 . . . .**67** ED56
Lucerne Ms, W8
off Kensington Mall **82** DA74
Lucerne Rd, N5 . . . .**65** DP63
Orpington BR6 . . . .**145** ET102
Thornton Heath CR7 . . . . . .**141** DP99
Lucerne Way, Rom. RM3 . . . .**52** FK51
Lucey Rd, SE16 . . . .**202** B7
Lucey Way, SE16 . . . .**202** C7
Lucie Av, Ashf. TW15 . . . . . .**115** BP93
Lucien Rd, SW17 . . . .**120** DG91
SW19 . . . .**120** DB89
Lucknow St, SE18 . . . .**105** ES80
Lucorn Cl, SE12 . . . .**124** EF86
Lucton Ms, Loug. IG10 . . . . . .**33** EP42
Luctons Av, Buck.H. IG9 . . . .**48** EJ46
Lucy Cres, W3 . . . .**80** CQ71
Lucy Gdns, Dag. RM8
off Grafton Rd **70** EY62
Luddesdon Rd, Erith DA8 . . .**106** FA80
Luddington Av, Vir.W. GU25 . .**133** AZ96
Ludford Cl, NW9
off Warrington Rd **159** DP105
Ludgate Bdy, EC4 . . . .**196** F9
Ludgate Circ, EC4 . . . .**196** F9
Ludgate Hill, EC4 . . . .**196** F9
Ludgate Sq, EC4 . . . .**196** G9
Ludham Cl, SE28
off Rollesby Way **88** EW72
Ludlow Cl, Brom. BR2
off Aylesbury Rd **144** EG97
Harrow HA2 . . . .**60** BZ63
Ludlow Mead, Wat. WD19 . . .**39** BV48
Ludlow Pl, Grays RM17 . . . .**110** GB76
Ludlow Rd, W5 . . . .**79** CJ70
Feltham TW13 . . . .**115** BU91
Ludlow St, EC1 . . . .**197** H4
Ludlow Way, N2 . . . .**64** DC56
Rickmansworth (Crox.Grn.)
WD3 . . . .**23** BQ42
Ludovick Wk, SW15 . . . .**98** CS84
Ludwick Ms, SE14 . . . .**103** DY80
Luffield Rd, SE2 . . . .**106** EV76
Luffman Rd, SE12 . . . .**124** EH90
Lugard Rd, SE15 . . . .**102** DV82
Lugg App, E12 . . . .**69** EN62
Luke Ho, E1 . . . .**84** DV72
Luke St, EC2 . . . .**197** M4
Lukin Cres, E4 . . . .**47** ED48
Lukin St, E1 . . . .**84** DW72
Lukintone Cl, Loug. IG10 . . . .**32** EL44
Lullarook Cl, West. (Bigg.H.)
TN16 . . . .**178** EJ116
Lullingstone Av, Swan. BR8 . .**147** FF97
Lullingstone Cl, Orp. BR5
off Lullingstone Cres **126** EV94
Lullingstone Cres, Orp. BR5 .**126** EU94
Lullingstone La, SE13 . . . . . .**123** ED87
Dartford (Eyns.) DA4 . . . . .**148** FJ104
★ Lullingstone Park Visitor
Cen, Dart. (Eyns.) DA4 . . .**165** FG107
Lullingstone Rd, Belv. DA17 . .**106** EZ79
★ Lullingstone Roman Villa, Dart.
DA4 . . . .**147** FH104
Lullington Garth, N12 . . . . . .**43** CZ50
Borehamwood WD6 . . . .**26** CP43
Bromley BR1 . . . .**124** EE94
Lullington Rd, SE20 . . . .**122** DU94
Dagenham RM9 . . . .**88** EY66
Lulot Gdns, N19 . . . .**65** DH61
Lulworth, NW1
off Wrotham Rd **83** DJ66
SE17 . . . .**201** K10
Lulworth Av, Houns. TW5 . . . .**96** CB80
Waltham Cross (Chsht.)
EN7 . . . .**13** DP29
Wembley HA9 . . . .**61** CJ59
Lulworth Cl, Har. HA2 . . . . . .**60** BZ62
Lulworth Cres, Mitch. CR4 . .**140** DE96
Lulworth Dr, Pnr. HA5 . . . . . .**60** BX59
Romford RM5 . . . .**51** FB50
Lulworth Gdns, Har. HA2 . . . .**60** BY61
Lulworth Rd, SE9 . . . .**124** EL89
SE15 . . . .**102** DV82
Welling DA16 . . . .**105** ET82
Lulworth Waye, Hayes UB4 . .**78** BW72
Lumen Rd, Wem. HA9 . . . . . .**61** CK61
Lumley Cl, Belv. DA17 . . . . .**106** FA79
Lumley Ct, WC2 . . . .**200** A1
Lumley Gdns, Sutt. SM3 . . . .**157** CY106
Lumley Rd, Sutt. SM3 . . . . . .**157** CY107
Lumley St, W1 . . . .**194** G9
Lunar Cl, West. (Bigg.H.)
TN16 . . . .**178** EK116
Luna Rd, Th.Hth. CR7 . . . . . .**142** DQ97
Lundin Wk, Wat. WD19
off Woodhall La **40** BX49
Lundy Dr, Hayes UB3 . . . . . .**95** BS77
Lundy Wk, N1
off Clephane Rd **84** DQ65
Lunedale Rd, Dart. DA2 . . . .**128** FQ88
Lunedale Wk, Dart. DA2
off Lunedale Rd **128** FP88
Lunghurst Rd, Cat. (Wold.)
CR3 . . . .**177** DZ120
Lunham Rd, SE19 . . . .**122** DS93
Lupin Cl, SW2 *off Palace Rd* .**121** DP89
Croydon CR0
off Primrose La **143** DX102
Romford (Rush Grn.) RM7 . .**71** FD61
West Drayton UB7
off Magnolia St **94** BK78
Lupin Cres, Ilf. IG1
off Bluebell Way **69** EP64
Luppit Cl, Brwd. CM13 . . . . . .**55** GA46

Lupton Cl, SE12 . . . .**124** EH90
Lupton St, NW5 . . . .**65** DJ63
Lupus St, SW1 . . . .**101** DH79
Luralda Gdns, E14 . . . .**204** E10
Lurgan Av, W6 . . . .**99** CX79
Lurline Gdns, SW11 . . . .**100** DG81
Luscombe Ct, Brom. BR2 . . .**144** EE96
Luscombe Way, SW8 . . . . . .**101** DL80
Lushes Ct, Loug. IG10
off Lushes Rd **33** EP43
Lushes Rd, Loug. IG10 . . . . .**33** EP43
Lushington Dr, Cob. KT11 . . .**153** BV112
Lushington Rd, NW10 . . . . . .**81** CV68
SE6 . . . .**123** EB92
Lushington Ter, E8
off Wayland Av **66** DU64
Lusted Hall La, West. (Tats.)
TN16 . . . .**178** EJ120
Lusted Rd, Sev. TN13 . . . . . .**181** FE120
Luther Cl, Edg. HA8 . . . .**42** CQ47
Luther King Cl, E17 . . . .**67** DY58
Luther Rd, Tedd. TW11 . . . . .**117** CF92
Luton Pl, SE10 . . . .**103** EC80
Luton Rd, E17 . . . .**67** DZ55
Sidcup DA14 . . . .**126** EW90
Luton St, NW8 . . . .**194** A5
Lutton Ter, NW3 *off Flask Wk* .**64** DD63
Luttrell Av, SW15 . . . .**119** CV85
Lutwyche Rd, SE6 . . . .**123** DZ89
Luxborough La, Chig. IG7 . . .**48** EL48
Luxborough St, W1 . . . .**194** F6
Luxemburg Gdns, W6 . . . . . .**99** CX77
Luxfield Rd, SE9 . . . .**124** EL88
Luxford St, SE16 . . . .**203** H9
Luxmore St, SE4 . . . .**103** DZ81
Luxor St, SE5 . . . .**102** DQ83
Luxted Rd, Orp. BR6 . . . . . .**163** EN112
Lyall Av, SE21 . . . .**122** DS90
Lyall Ms, SW1 . . . .**198** F7
Lyall Ms W, SW1 . . . .**198** F7
Lyall St, SW1 . . . .**198** F7
Lyal Rd, E3 . . . .**85** DY68
Lycett Pl, W12 *off Becklow Rd* .**99** CU75
Lych Gate, Wat. WD25 . . . .**8** BX33
Lych Gate Rd, Orp. BR6 . . . .**146** EU102
Lych Gate Wk, Hayes UB3 . . .**77** BT73
Lych Way, Wok. GU21 . . . . .**166** AX116
Lyconby Gdns, Croy. CR0 . . .**143** DY101
Lycrome Rd, Chesh. HP5 . . . . .**4** AS28
Lydd Cl, Sid. DA14 . . . .**125** ES90
Lydden Ct, SE9 . . . .**125** ES86
Lydden Gro, SW18 . . . .**120** DB87
Lydden Rd, SW18 . . . .**120** DB87
Lydd Rd, Bexh. DA7 . . . .**106** EZ80
Lydeard Rd, E6 . . . .**87** EM66
Lydele Cl, Wok. GU21 . . . . . .**167** AZ115
Lydford, N16 . . . .
off Pellerin Rd **66** DS64
Lydford Rd, N15 . . . .**66** DR57
NW2 . . . .**81** CX65
W9 . . . .**81** CZ70
Lydhurst Av, SW2 . . . .**121** DM89
Lydia Rd, Erith DA8 . . . .**107** FF79
Lydney Cl, SE15 . . . .**102** DS80
SW19 *off Princes Way* . . .**119** CY89
Lydon Rd, SW4 . . . .**101** DJ83
Lydstep Rd, Chis. BR7 . . . . .**125** EN91
Lye, The, Tad. KT20 . . . .**173** CW122
LYE GREEN, Chesh. **4** AT27
Lye La, St.Alb. (Brick.Wd.) AL2 . .**8** CA30
Lyfield, Lthd. (Oxshott) KT22 .**154** CB114
Lyford Rd, SW18 . . . .**120** DD87
Lygon Pl, SW1 . . . .**199** H7
Lyham Cl, SW2 . . . .**121** DL86
Lyham Rd, SW2 . . . .**121** DL85
Lyle Cl, Mitch. CR4 . . . .**140** DG101
Lyle Pk, Sev. TN13 . . . .**191** FH123
Lymbourne Cl, Sutt. SM2 . . .**158** DA110
Lyme Gro, E9
off St. Thomas's Sq **84** DW66
Lymer Av, SE19 . . . .**122** DT92
Lyme Regis Rd, Bans. SM7 . .**173** CZ117
Lyme Rd, Well. DA16 . . . . . .**106** EV81
Lymescote Gdns, Sutt. SM1 .**140** DA103
Lyme St, NW1 . . . .**83** DJ66
Lyme Ter, NW1
off Royal Coll St **83** DJ66
Lyminge Cl, Sid. DA14 . . . . .**125** ET91
Lyminge Gdns, SW18 . . . . . .**120** DE88
Lymington Av, N22 . . . .**45** DN54
Lymington Cl, E6
off Valiant Way **87** EM71
SW16 . . . .**141** DK96
Lymington Dr, Ruis. HA4 . . . .**59** BR61
Lymington Gdns, Epsom
KT19 . . . .**157** CT106
Lymington Rd, NW6 . . . .**82** DB65
Dagenham RM8 . . . .**70** EX60
Lympstone Gdns, SE15 . . . .**102** DU80
Lynbridge Gdns, N13 . . . . . .**45** DP49
Lynbrook Cl, SE15
off Blakes Rd **102** DS80
Rainham RM13 . . . .**89** FD68
Lynceley Gra, Epp. CM16 . . . .**18** EU29
Lynch, The, Uxb. UB8
off New Windsor St **76** BJ67
Lynch Cl, Uxb. UB8
off New Windsor St **76** BJ66
Lynchen Cl, Houns. TW5
off The Avenue **95** BU81
Lynch Wk, SE8 *off Prince St* .**103** DZ79
Lyncott Cres, SW4 . . . .**101** DH84
Lyncroft Av, Pnr. HA5 . . . . . .**60** BY57
Lyncroft Gdns, NW6 . . . .**64** DA64
W13 . . . .**97** CJ75
Epsom KT17 . . . .**157** CT109
Hounslow TW3 . . . .**96** CC84
Lyndale, NW2 . . . .**63** CZ63
Lyndale Av, NW2 . . . .**63** CZ62
Lyndale Cl, SE3 . . . .**104** EF79
Lyndale Ct, W.Byf. KT14 . . . .
off Parvis Rd **152** BG113
Lyndale Est, Grays RM20 . . .**109** FV79
Lyndale Rd, Red. RH1 . . . . .**184** DF131
Lynden Way, Swan. BR8 . . . .**147** FC97
Lyndhurst Av, N12 . . . .**44** DF51

Lyndhurst Av, NW7 . . . . .42 CS51
SW16 . . . . .141 DK96
Pinner HA5 . . . . .39 BV53
Southall UB1 . . . . .78 CB74
Sunbury-on-Thames
TW16 . . . . .135 BU97
Surbiton KT5 . . . . .138 CP102
Twickenham TW2 . . . . . . .116 BZ88
Lyndhurst Cl, NW10 . . . . .62 CR62
Bexleyheath DA7 . . . . .107 FB83
Croydon CR0 . . . . .142 DT104
Orpington BR6 . . . . .163 EP105
Woking GU21 . . . . .166 AX115
Lyndhurst Ct, E18
off Churchfields 48 EG53
Sutton SM2
off Overton Rd 158 DA108
Lyndhurst Dr, E10 . . . . .67 EC59
Hornchurch RM11 . . . . .72 FJ60
New Malden KT3 . . . . .138 CS100
Sevenoaks TN13 . . . . .190 FE124
Lyndhurst Gdns, N3 . . . . .43 CY53
NW3 . . . . .64 DD64
Barking IG11 . . . . .87 ES65
Enfield EN1 . . . . .30 DS42
Ilford IG2 . . . . .69 ER58
Pinner HA5 . . . . .39 BV53
Lyndhurst Gro, SE15 . . . . . . .102 DS82
Lyndhurst Ho, SW15
off Ellisfield Dr 119 CU87
Lyndhurst Ri, Chig. IG7 . . . . . .49 EN49
Lyndhurst Rd, E4 . . . . .47 EC52
N18 . . . . .46 DU49
N22 . . . . .45 DM51
NW3 . . . . .64 DD64
Bexleyheath DA7 . . . . .107 FB83
Coulsdon CR5 . . . . .174 DG116
Greenford UB6 . . . . .78 CB70
Thornton Heath CR7 . . . . . .141 DN98
Lyndhurst Sq, SE15 . . . . .102 DT81
Lyndhurst Ter, NW3 . . . . .64 DD64
Lyndhurst Way, SE15 . . . . . . .102 DT81
Brentwood CM13 . . . . .55 GC45
Chertsey KT16 . . . . .133 BE144
Sutton SM2 . . . . .158 DA108
Lyndon Av, Pnr. HA5 . . . . .40 BY51
Sidcup DA15 . . . . .125 ET85
Wallington SM6 . . . . .140 DG104
Lyndon Rd, Belv. DA17 . . . . . .106 FA77
Lyndwood Dr, Wind. (Old Wind.)
SL4 . . . . .112 AU86
LYNE, Cher. 133 BA102
Lyne Cl, Vir.W. GU25 . . . . . . .133 AZ100
Lyne Cres, E17 . . . . .47 DZ53
Lyne Crossing Rd, Cher. (Lyne)
KT16 . . . . .133 BA100
Lynegrove Av, Ashf. TW15 . . . .115 BQ92
Lyneham Wk, E5 . . . . .67 DY64
Pinner HA5 . . . . .59 BT55
Lyne La, Cher. (Lyne) KT16 . . .133 BA100
Egham TW20 . . . . .133 BA99
Virginia Water GU25 . . . . . .133 BA100
Lyne Rd, Vir.W. GU25 . . . . . . .132 AX100
Lynette Av, SW4 . . . . .121 DH86
Lynford Cl, Barn. EN5
off Rowley La 27 CT43
Edgware HA8 . . . . .42 CQ52
Lynford Gdns, Edg. HA8 . . . . . .42 CP48
Ilford IG3 . . . . .69 ET61
Lynhurst Cres, Uxb. UB10 . . . . .77 BQ66
Lynhurst Rd, Uxb. UB10 . . . . . .77 BQ66
Lynmere Rd, Well. DA16 . . . . .106 EV82
Lyn Ms, E3 off Tredegar Sq . . .85 DZ69
N16 . . . . .66 DS63
Lynmouth Av, Enf. EN1 . . . . . . .30 DT44
Morden SM4 . . . . .139 CX101
Lynmouth Dr, Ruis. HA4 . . . . . .59 BV61
Lynmouth Gdns, Grnf. UB6 . . . .79 CH67
Hounslow TW5 . . . . .96 BX81
Lynmouth Ri, Orp. BR5 . . . . . .146 EV98
Lynmouth Rd, E17 . . . . .67 DY58
N2 . . . . .64 DF55
N16 . . . . .66 DT60
Greenford UB6 . . . . .79 CH67
Lynn Cl, Ashf. TW15
off Goffs Rd 115 BR92
Harrow HA3 . . . . .41 CD54
Lynne Cl, Orp. BR6 . . . . .163 ET107
South Croydon CR2 . . . . . . .160 DW111
Lynne Wk, Esher KT10 . . . . . .154 CC106
Lynne Way, NW10 . . . . .80 CS65
Northolt UB5 . . . . .78 BX68
Lynn Ms, E11 off Lynn Rd 68 EE61
Lynn Rd, E11 . . . . .68 EE61
SW12 . . . . .121 DH87
Ilford IG2 . . . . .69 ER59
Lynn St, Enf. EN2 . . . . .30 DR39
Lynross Cl, Rom. RM3 . . . . . . .52 FM54
Lynscott Way, S.Croy. CR2 . . . .159 DP109
Lynsted Cl, Bexh. DA6 . . . . . .127 FB85
Bromley BR1 . . . . .144 EJ96
Lynsted Ct, Beck. BR3
off Churchfields Rd 143 DY96
Lynsted Gdns, SE9 . . . . .104 EK83
Lynton Av, N12 . . . . .44 DD49
NW9 . . . . .63 CT56
W13 . . . . .79 CG72
Orpington BR5 . . . . .146 EV98
Romford RM7 . . . . .50 FA53
Lynton Cl, NW10 . . . . .62 CS64
Chessington KT9 . . . . .156 CL105
Isleworth TW7 . . . . .97 CF84
Lynton Cres, Ilf. IG2 . . . . .69 EP58
Lynton Crest, Pot.B. EN6
off Strafford Gate 12 DA32
Lynton Est, SE1 . . . . .202 B9
Lynton Gdns, N11 . . . . .45 DK51
Enfield EN1 . . . . .46 DS45
Lynton Mead, N20 . . . . .44 DA48
Lynton Par, Wal.Cr. EN8
off Turners Hill 15 DX30
Lynton Rd, E4 . . . . .47 EB50
N8 . . . . .65 DK57
NW6 . . . . .81 CZ67
SE1 . . . . .202 A9
W3 . . . . .80 CN73

Lynton Rd, Croy. CR0 . . . . . . .141 DN100
Gravesend DA11 . . . . .131 GG88
Harrow HA2 . . . . .60 BY61
New Malden KT3 . . . . .138 CR99
Lynton Rd S, Grav. DA11 . . . .131 GG88
Lynton Ter, W3
off Lynton Rd 80 CQ72
Lynton Wk, Hayes UB4 . . . . . .77 BS69
Lynwood Av, Couls. CR5 . . . . .175 DH115
Egham TW20 . . . . .112 AY93
Epsom KT17 . . . . .157 CT114
Slough SL3 . . . . .92 AX76
Lynwood Cl, E18 . . . . .48 EJ53
Harrow HA2 . . . . .60 BY62
Romford RM5 . . . . .51 FB51
Woking GU21 . . . . .151 BD113
Lynwood Dr, Nthwd. HA6 . . . . .39 BT53
Romford RM5 . . . . .51 FB51
Worcester Park KT4 . . . . . . .139 CU103
Lynwood Gdns, Croy. CR0 . . . .159 DM105
Southall UB1 . . . . .78 BZ72
Lynwood Gro, N21 . . . . .45 DN46
Orpington BR6 . . . . .145 ES101
Lynwood Hts, Rick. WD3 . . . . .22 BH43
Lynwood Rd, SW17 . . . . .120 DF90
W5 . . . . .80 CL70
Epsom KT17 . . . . .157 CT114
Redhill RH1 . . . . .184 DG132
Thames Ditton KT7 . . . . . . .137 CF103
Lyon Business Pk, Bark. IG11 . .87 ES68
Lyon Meade, Stan. HA7 . . . . . .41 CJ53
Lyon Pk Av, Wem. HA0 . . . . . .80 CL65
Lyon Rd, SW19 . . . . .140 DC95
Harrow HA1 . . . . .61 CF58
Romford RM1 . . . . .71 FF59
Walton-on-Thames KT12 . . . .136 BY103
Lyonsdene, Tad. KT20 . . . . . .183 CZ127
Lyonsdown Av, Barn. EN5 . . . . .28 DC44
Lyonsdown Rd, Barn. EN5 . . . . .28 DC44
Lyons Pl, NW8 . . . . .82 DD70
Lyon St, N1
off Caledonian Rd 83 DM66
Lyons Wk, W14 . . . . .99 CY77
Lyon Way, Grnf. UB6 . . . . .79 CE67
Lyoth Rd, Orp. BR5 . . . . .145 EQ103
Lyric Dr, Grnf. UB6 . . . . .78 CB70
Lyric Ms, SE26 . . . . .122 DW91
Lyric Rd, SW13 . . . . .99 CT81
Lysander Cl, Hem.H. (Bov.)
HP3 . . . . .5 AZ27
Lysander Gdns, Surb. KT6
off Ewell Rd 138 CM100
Lysander Gro, N19 . . . . .65 DK60
Lysander Ms, N19
off Lysander Gro 65 DJ60
Lysander Rd, Croy. CR0 . . . . .159 DM107
Ruislip HA4 . . . . .59 BR61
Lysander Way, Abb.L. WD5 . . . . .7 BU32
Orpington BR6 . . . . .145 EQ104
Lysias Rd, SW12 . . . . .120 DG86
Lysia St, SW6 . . . . .99 CX80
Lysley Pl, Hat. AL9 . . . . .12 DC27
Lyster Ms, Cob. KT11 . . . . . . .153 BV113
Lytchet Rd, Brom. BR1 . . . . . .124 EH94
Lytchet Way, Enf. EN3 . . . . . . .30 DW39
Lytchgate Cl, S.Croy. CR2 . . . .160 DS108
Lytcott Dr, W.Mol. KT8
off Freeman Dr 136 BZ97
Lytcott Gro, SE22 . . . . .122 DT85
Lyte St, E2 off Bishops Way . . .84 DW68
Lytham Av, Wat. WD19 . . . . . . .40 BX50
Lytham Cl, SE28 . . . . .88 EY72
Lytham Gro, W5 . . . . .80 CL69
Lytham St, SE17 . . . . .102 DR78
Lyttelton Cl, NW3 . . . . .82 DE66
Lyttelton Rd, E10 . . . . .67 EB62
N2 . . . . .64 DC57
Lyttleton Rd, N8 . . . . .65 DN55
Lytton Av, N13 . . . . .45 DN47
Enfield EN3 . . . . .31 DY38
Lytton Cl, N2 . . . . .64 DD57
Loughton IG10 . . . . .33 ER41
Northolt UB5 . . . . .78 BZ66
Lytton Gdns, Wall. SM6 . . . . . .159 DK105
Lytton Gro, SW15 . . . . .119 CX85
Lytton Pk, Cob. KT11 . . . . . . .154 BZ112
Lytton Rd, E11 . . . . .68 EE59
Barnet EN5 . . . . .28 DC42
Grays RM16 . . . . .111 GG77
Pinner HA5 . . . . .40 BY52
Romford RM2 . . . . .71 FH57
Woking GU22 . . . . .167 BB116
Lytton Strachey Path, SE28
off Titmuss Av 88 EV73
Lyveden Rd, SE3 . . . . .104 EH80
SW17 . . . . .120 DE93
Lywood Cl, Tad. KT20 . . . . . . .173 CW122

M section:

Mabbotts, Tad. KT20 . . . . . . .173 CX121
Mabbutt Cl, St.Alb. (Brick.Wd.)
AL2 . . . . .8 BY30
Mabel Rd, Swan. BR8 . . . . . . .127 FG93
Mabel St, Wok. GU21 . . . . . . .166 AX117
Maberley Cres, SE19 . . . . . . .122 DU94
Maberley Rd, SE19 . . . . .142 DT95
Beckenham BR3 . . . . .143 DX97
Mabledon Pl, WC1 . . . . .195 N3
Mablethorpe Rd, SW6 . . . . . . .99 CY80
Mabley St, E9 . . . . .85 DY65
McAdam Dr, Enf. EN2
off Rowantree Rd 29 DP40
Macaret Cl, N20 . . . . .44 DB45
MacArthur Cl, E7 . . . . .86 EG65
MacArthur Ter, SE7 . . . . .104 EL78
Macaulay Av, Esher KT10 . . . . .137 CE103
Macaulay Ct, SW4 . . . . .101 DH83
Macaulay Rd, E6 . . . . .86 EK68
SW4 . . . . .101 DH83
Caterham CR3 . . . . .176 DS122
Macaulay Sq, SW4 . . . . .101 DH84

Macaulay Way, SE28
off Booth Cl 88 EV73
McAuley Cl, SE1 . . . . .200 D6
SE9 . . . . .125 EP85
Macauley Ms, SE13 . . . . .103 EC82
Macbean St, SE18 . . . . .105 EN76
Macbeth St, W6 . . . . .99 CV78
McCall Cl, SW4
off Jeffreys Rd 101 DL82
McCall Cres, SE7 . . . . .104 EL78
McCarthy Rd, Felt. TW13 . . . .116 BX92
Macclesfield Br, NW1 . . . . . . .82 DE68
Macclesfield Rd, EC1 . . . . . . .197 H2
SE25 . . . . .142 DV99
McClintock Pl, Enf. EN3
off Government Row 31 EA37
McCoid Way, SE1 . . . . .201 H5
McCrone Ms, NW3
off Belsize La 82 DD65
McCudden Rd, Dart. DA1
off Cornwall Rd 108 FM83
McCullum Rd, E3 . . . . .85 DZ67
McDermott Cl, SW11 . . . . . . .100 DE83
McDermott Rd, SE15 . . . . . . .102 DU83
Macdonald Av, Dag. RM10 . . . .71 FB62
Hornchurch RM11 . . . . .72 FL56
Macdonald Rd, E7 . . . . .68 EG63
E17 . . . . .47 EC54
N11 . . . . .44 DF50
N19 . . . . .65 DJ61
Macdonald Way, Horn. RM11 . .72 FL56
Macdonnell Gdns, Wat. WD25
off High Rd 23 BT35
McDonough Cl, Chess. KT9 . . .156 CL106
McDowall Cl, E16 . . . . .86 EF71
McDowall Rd, SE5 . . . . .102 DQ81
Macduff Rd, SW11 . . . . .100 DG81
Mace Cl, E1 . . . . .202 D2
Mace Ct, Grays RM17 . . . . . . .110 GE79
Mace Gateway, E16 . . . . .205 M1
Mace La, Sev. (Cudham)
TN14 . . . . .163 ER113
McEntee Av, E17 . . . . .47 DY53
Mace St, E2 . . . . .85 DX68
McEwen Way, E15 . . . . .85 ED67
MacFarlane La, Islw. TW7 . . . . .97 CF79
Macfarlane Rd, W12 . . . . .81 CW74
Macfarren Pl, NW1 . . . . .194 G5
McGrath Rd, E15 . . . . .68 EF64
McGredy, Wal.Cr. (Chsht.)
EN7 . . . . .14 DV29
Macgregor Rd, E16 . . . . .86 EJ71
McGregor Rd, W11 . . . . .81 CZ72
Machell Rd, SE15 . . . . .102 DW83
McIntosh Cl, Rom. RM1 . . . . . .71 FE55
Wallington SM6 . . . . .159 DL108
Macintosh Cl, Wal.Cr. EN7 . . . .14 DR26
McIntosh Rd, Rom. RM1 . . . . .71 FE55
Mackay Rd, SW4 . . . . .101 DH83
McKay Rd, SW20 . . . . .119 CV94
McKay Trd Est, Slou. (Colnbr.)
SL3 . . . . .93 BE82
McKellar Cl, Bushey (Bushey Hth.)
WD23 . . . . .40 CC47
Mackennal St, NW8 . . . . .194 C1
Mackenzie Mall, Slou. SL1
off High St 92 AT75
Mackenzie Rd, N7 . . . . .83 DM65
Beckenham BR3 . . . . .142 DW96
Mackenzie St, Slou. SL1 . . . . . .74 AT74
Mackenzie Wk, E14 . . . . .204 A3
Mackenzie Way, Grav. DA12 . .131 GK93
McKerrell Rd, SE15 . . . . .102 DU81
Mackeson Rd, NW3 . . . . .64 DF63
Mackie Rd, SW2 . . . . .121 DN87
Mackintosh La, E9
off Homerton High St 67 DX64
Macklin St, WC2 . . . . .196 A8
Mackrow Wk, E14
off Robin Hood La 85 EC73
Macks Rd, SE16 . . . . .202 C8
Mackworth St, NW1 . . . . .195 K2
Maclaren Ms, SW15
off Clarendon Dr 99 CW84
Maclean Rd, SE23 . . . . .123 DY86
Maclennan Av, Rain. RM13 . . . .90 FK69
Macleod Cl, Grays RM17 . . . . .110 GD77
Macleod Rd, N21 . . . . .29 DL43
McLeod Rd, SE2 . . . . .106 EV77
McLeod's Ms, SW7
off Emperor's Gate 100 DB76
Macleod St, SE17 . . . . .102 DQ78
Maclise Rd, W14 . . . . .99 CY76
McMillan Cl, Grav. DA12 . . . . .131 GJ91
Macmillan Gdns, Dart. DA1 . . .108 FN84
McMillan St, SE8 . . . . .103 EA79
Macmillan Way, SW17
off Church La 121 DH92
McNair Rd, Sthl. UB2 . . . . .96 CB75
McNeil Rd, SE5 . . . . .102 DS82
McNicol Dr, NW10 . . . . .80 CQ68
Macoma Rd, SE18 . . . . .105 ER79
Macoma Ter, SE18 . . . . .105 ER79
Maconochies Rd, E14 . . . . . .204 B10
Macon Way, Upmin. RM14 . . . .73 FT59
Macquarie Way, E14 . . . . . . .204 C9
McRae La, Mitch. CR4 . . . . . .140 DF101
Macroom Rd, W9 . . . . .81 CZ69
Mac's Pl, EC4 off Norwich St . .83 DN72
★ Madame Tussaud's, NW1 . .194 F5
Madan Rd, West. TN16 . . . . . .189 ER125
Madans Wk, Epsom KT18 . . . .156 CR114
Mada Rd, Orp. BR6 . . . . .145 EP104
Maddams St, E3 . . . . .85 EB70
Madden Cl, Swans. DA10 . . . .129 FX86
Maddison Cl, Tedd. TW11 . . . .117 CF93
Maddock Way, SE17 . . . . .101 DP79
Maddox La, Lthd. (Bkhm.)
KT23 . . . . .170 BY123
Maddox Pk, Lthd. (Bkhm.)
KT23 . . . . .170 BY123
Maddox St, W1 . . . . .195 J10
Madeira Av, Brom. BR1 . . . . . .124 EE94
Madeira Rd, E.Byf. KT14
off Brantwood Gdns 152 BG113

Madeira Cres, W.Byf. KT14
off Brantwood Gdns 152 BG113
Madeira Gro, Wdf.Grn. IG8 . . . .48 EJ51
Madeira Rd, E11 . . . . .67 ED60
N13 . . . . .45 DP49
SW16 . . . . .121 DL92
Mitcham CR4 . . . . .140 DF98
West Byfleet KT14 . . . . . . .151 BF113
Madeira Wk, Brwd. CM15 . . . .54 FY48
Reigate RH2 . . . . .184 DD133
Madeley Rd, W5 . . . . .80 CL72
Madeline Gro, Ilf. IG1 . . . . . . .69 ER64
Madeline Rd, SE20 . . . . .142 DU95
Madells, Epp. CM16 . . . . .17 ET31
Madge Gill Way, E6
off Ron Leighton Way 86 EL67
Madinah Rd, E8 . . . . .84 DU65
Madingley, Kings.T. KT1
off St. Peters Rd 138 CN96
Madison Cres, Bexh. DA7 . . . .106 EW80
Madison Gdns, Bexh. DA7 . . . .106 EW80
Bromley BR2 . . . . .144 EF97
Madison Way, Sev. TN13 . . . . .190 FF123
Madras Pl, N7 . . . . .83 DN65
Madras Rd, Ilf. IG1 . . . . .69 EP63
Madresfield Ct, Rad. (Shenley)
WD7 off Russet Dr 10 CL32
Madrid Rd, SW13 . . . . .99 CU81
Madrigal La, SE5 . . . . .101 DP80
Madron St, SE17 . . . . .201 N10
Maesmaur Rd, West. (Tats.)
TN16 . . . . .178 EK121
Mafeking Av, E6 . . . . .86 EK68
Brentford TW8 . . . . .98 CL79
Ilford IG2 . . . . .69 ER59
Mafeking Rd, E16 . . . . .86 EF70
N17 . . . . .46 DU54
Enfield EN1 . . . . .30 DT41
Staines (Wrays.) TW19 . . . .113 BB89
Magazine Pl, Lthd. KT22 . . . . .171 CH122
Magazine Rd, Cat. CR3 . . . . . .175 DP122
Magdala Av, N19 . . . . .65 DH61
Magdala Rd, Islw. TW7 . . . . . .97 CG83
South Croydon CR2
off Napier Rd 160 DR108
Magdalen Cl, W.Byf. (Byfleet)
KT14 . . . . .152 BL114
Magdalen Cres, W.Byf. (Byfleet)
KT14 . . . . .152 BL114
Magdalene Cl, SE15
off Heaton Rd 102 DV82
Magdalene Gdns, E6 . . . . .87 EN70
Magdalene Rd, Shep. TW17 . . .134 BM98
Magdalen Gdns, Brwd. CM13 . .55 GE44
Magdalen Gro, Orp. BR6 . . . . .164 EV105
Magdalen Pas, E1
off Prescot St 84 DT72
Magdalen Rd, SW18 . . . . . . .120 DC88
SW6 . . . . .201 M3
Magee St, SE11 . . . . .101 DN79
Magellan Pl, E14
off Maritime Quay 103 EA78
Magna Carta La, Stai. (Wrays.)
TW19 . . . . .112 AX88
Magna Rd, Egh. (Eng.Grn.)
TW20 . . . . .112 AX89
★ Magna Carta Monument, Egh.
(Runny.) TW20 . . . . .112 AX89
Magnaville Rd, Bushey
(Bushey Hth.) WD23 . . . . . .41 CE45
Magnet Est, Grays RM20 . . . .109 FW78
Magnet Rd, Grays RM20 . . . .109 FW79
Wembley HA9 . . . . .61 CK61
Magnin Cl, E8 off Wilde Cl 84 DU67
Magnolia Av, Abb.L. WD5 . . . . .7 BU32
Magnolia Cl, E10 . . . . .67 EA61
Kingston upon Thames
KT2 . . . . .118 CQ93
St. Albans (Park St.) AL2 . . . . .9 CD27
Magnolia Ct, Har. HA3 . . . . . . .62 CM59
Richmond TW9
off West Hall Rd 98 CP81
Wallington SM6
off Parkgate Rd 159 DH106
Magnolia Dr, West. (Bigg.H.)
TN16 . . . . .178 EK116
Magnolia Gdns, Edg. HA8 . . . . .42 CQ49
Slough SL3 . . . . .92 AW76
Magnolia Pl, SW4 . . . . .121 DL85
W5 off Montpelier Rd 80 CL71
Magnolia Rd, W4 . . . . .98 CP79
Magnolia St, West Dr. UB7 . . . .94 BK77
Magnolia Way, Epsom KT19 . . .156 CQ106
Brwd. CM15 . . . . .54 FV43
Magnum Cl, Rain. RM13 . . . . . .90 FJ70
Magpie All, EC4 . . . . .196 E9
Magpie Cl, E7 . . . . .68 EF64
NW9 off Eagle Dr 42 CS54
Coulsdon CR5
off Ashbourne Cl 175 DJ118
Enfield EN1 . . . . .30 DU39
Magpie Hall Cl, Brom. BR2 . . .144 EL100
Magpie Hall La, Brom. BR2 . . .145 EM99
Magpie Hall Rd, Bushey
(Bushey Hth.) WD23 . . . . . .41 CE47
Magpie La, Brwd. CM13 . . . . . .53 FW54
Magpie Pl, SE14
off Milton Ct Rd 103 DY73
Magri Wk, E1 off Ashfield St . . .84 DW71
Maguire Dr, Rich. TW10 . . . . .117 CJ91
Maguire St, SE1 . . . . .202 A4
Mahatma Gandhi Ho, Wem.
HA9 . . . . .62 CN64
Mahlon Av, Ruis. HA4 . . . . . . .59 BV64
Mahogany Cl, SE16 . . . . .203 L3
Mahon Cl, Enf. EN1 . . . . .30 DT39
Maida Av, E4 . . . . .47 EB45
W2 . . . . .82 DC71
MAIDA HILL, W9 . . . . .81 CZ70
Maida Rd, Belv. DA17 . . . . . . .106 FA76
MAIDA VALE, W9 . . . . .82 DB70
⊖ Maida Vale 82 DC69
Maida Vale, W9 . . . . .82 DB68
Maida Vale Rd, Dart. DA1 . . . .127 FG85
Maida Way, E4 . . . . .47 EB45
Maiden Erlegh Av, Bex. DA5 . . .126 EY87
Maiden La, NW1 . . . . .83 DK66

Maiden La, SE1 . . . . .201 J2
WC2 . . . . .200 A1
Dartford DA1 . . . . .107 FG83
Maiden Rd, E15 . . . . .86 EE66
Maidenshaw Rd, Epsom KT19 .156 CR112
Maidenstone Hill, SE10 . . . . . .103 EC81
Maids of Honour Row, Rich. TW9
off The Green 117 CK85
Maidstone Av, Rom. RM5 . . . . .51 FC54
Maidstone Bldgs, SE1 . . . . . .201 J3
Maidstone Ho, E14
off Carmen St 85 EB72
Maidstone Rd, N11 . . . . .45 DJ51
Grays RM17 . . . . .110 GA79
Sevenoaks TN13 . . . . .190 FE122
Sevenoaks (Seal) TN15 . . . .191 FN121
Sidcup DA14 . . . . .126 EX93
Swanley BR8 . . . . .147 FB95
Maidstone St, E2
off Audrey St 84 DU68
Main Av, Enf. EN1 . . . . .30 DT43
Northwood HA6 . . . . .39 BQ48
Main Dr, Ger.Cr. SL9 . . . . .56 AW57
Iver SL0 . . . . .93 BE77
Wembley HA9 . . . . .61 CK62
Main Par, Rick. (Chorl.) WD3
off Whitelands Av 21 BC42
Main Par Flats, Rick. (Chorl.) WD3
off Whitelands Av 21 BC42
Main Ride, Egh. TW20 . . . . . .112 AS93
Mainridge Rd, Chis. BR7 . . . . .125 EN91
Main Rd, Dart. (Fnghm.)
DA4 . . . . .148 FL100
Dartford (Sutt.H.) DA4 . . . . .128 FP93
Edenbridge (Crock.H.) TN8 . .189 EQ134
Longfield DA3 . . . . .149 FX96
Orpington BR5 . . . . .146 EW95
Romford RM1, RM2 . . . . . . .71 FF56
Sevenoaks (Knock.) TN14 . . .187 ET119
Sevenoaks (Sund.) TN14 . . .180 EX124
Sidcup DA14 . . . . .125 ES90
Swanley (Crock.) BR8 . . . . .147 FD100
Swanley (Hext.) BR8 . . . . . .127 FF94
Westerham TN16 . . . . .162 EJ113
Main St, Felt. TW13 . . . . .116 BX92
Maisemore St, SE15
off Peckham Pk Rd 102 DU80
Maisie Webster Cl, Stai. (Stanw.)
TW19 off Lauser Rd 114 BK87
Maitland Cl, SE10 . . . . .103 EB80
Hounslow TW4 . . . . .96 BZ83
Walton-on-Thames KT12 . . . .136 BY103
West Byfleet KT14 . . . . . . .152 BG113
Maitland Pk Est, NW3 . . . . . . .82 DF65
Maitland Pk Rd, NW3 . . . . .82 DF65
Maitland Pk Vil, NW3 . . . . .82 DF65
Maitland Pl, E5
off Clarence Rd 66 DV63
Maitland Rd, E15 . . . . .86 EF65
SE26 . . . . .123 DX93
Maizey Ct, Brwd. CM15
off Danes Way 54 FU43
Majendie Rd, SE18 . . . . .105 ER78
Majestic Way, Mitch. CR4 . . . .140 DF96
Major Rd, E15 . . . . .67 EC64
SE16 . . . . .202 C6
Majors Fm Rd, Slou. SL3 . . . . .92 AX80
Makepeace Av, N6 . . . . .64 DG61
Makepeace Rd, E11 . . . . .68 EG56
Northolt UB5 . . . . .78 BY68
Makins St, SW3 . . . . .198 C9
Malabar St, E14 . . . . .203 P5
Malam Gdns, E14
off Wades Pl 85 EB73
Malan Cl, West. (Bigg.H.)
TN16 . . . . .178 EL117
Malan Sq, Rain. RM13 . . . . . . .89 FH65
Malbrook Rd, SW15 . . . . .99 CV84
Malcolm Ct, Stan. HA7 . . . . . . .41 CJ50
Malcolm Cres, NW4 . . . . .63 CU58
Malcolm Dr, Surb. KT6 . . . . . .138 CL102
Malcolm Pl, E2 . . . . .84 DW70
Malcolm Rd, E1 . . . . .84 DW70
SE20 . . . . .122 DW94
SE25 . . . . .142 DU100
SW19 . . . . .119 CY93
Coulsdon CR5 . . . . .175 DK115
Uxbridge UB10 . . . . .58 BM63
Malcolms Way, N14 . . . . .29 DJ43
Malcolm Way, E11 . . . . .68 EG57
Malden Av, SE25 . . . . .142 DV98
Greenford UB6 . . . . .61 CE64
Malden Cl, Amer. HP6 . . . . . . .20 AT38
Malden Cres, NW1 . . . . .82 DG65
Malden Grn Av, Wor.Pk. KT4 . .139 CT102
Malden Hill, N.Mal. KT3 . . . . .139 CT97
Malden Hill Gdns, N.Mal.
KT3 . . . . .139 CT97
⇌ Malden Manor 138 CS101
Malden Pk, N.Mal. KT3 . . . . . .139 CT100
Malden Pl, NW5
off Grafton Ter 64 DG64
Malden Rd, NW5 . . . . .64 DG64
Borehamwood WD6 . . . . . . .26 CN41
New Malden KT3 . . . . .138 CS99
Sutton SM3 . . . . .157 CX105
Watford WD17 . . . . .23 BU40
Worcester Park KT4 . . . . . . .139 CT101
MALDEN RUSHETT, Chess. . . .155 CH111
Malden Way, N.Mal. KT3 . . . . .139 CT99
Maldon Cl, E15 off David St . . .67 ED64
N1 off Popham Rd 84 DQ67
SE5 . . . . .102 DS83
Maldon Ct, Wall. SM6
off Maldon Rd 159 DJ106
Maldon Rd, N9 . . . . .46 DT48
W3 . . . . .80 CQ73
Romford RM7 . . . . .71 FC59
Wallington SM6 . . . . .159 DH106
Maldon Wk, Wdf.Grn. IG8 . . . . .48 EJ51
Malet Cl, Egh. TW20 . . . . . . .113 BD93
Malet Pl, WC1 . . . . .195 M5
Malet St, WC1 . . . . .195 M5
Maley Av, SE27 . . . . .121 DP89

★ Place of interest   ⇌ Railway station   ⊖ London Underground station   DLR Docklands Light Railway station   ◆ Tramlink station   H Hospital

A B C D E F G H I J K L M N O P Q R S T U V W X Y Z

Mal - Man

Malford Ct, E18 .....48 EG54
Malford Gro, E18 .....68 EF56
Malfort Rd, SE5 .....102 DS83
Malham Cl, N11
Malham Rd, SE23 .....123 DX88
Malins Cl, Barn. EN5 .....27 CV43
Mall, The, E15 .....85 ED66
  N14 .....45 DL48
  SW1 .....199 L4
  SW14 .....118 CQ85
  W5 .....80 CL73
  Croydon CR0 .....142 DQ103
  Harrow HA3 .....62 CM58
  Hornchurch RM11 .....71 FH60
  St. Albans (Park St.) AL2 .....8 CC27
  Surbiton KT6 .....137 CK99
Mallams Ms, SW9
  off St. James's Cres 101 DP83
Mallard Cl, E9
  off Berkshire Rd 85 DZ65
  NW6 .....82 DA68
  W7 .....97 CE75
  Barnet EN5 off The Hook 28 DD44
  Dartford DA1 .....128 FM85
  Redhill RH1 .....184 DG131
  Twickenham TW2
    off Stephenson Rd 116 CA87
  Upminster RM14 .....73 FT59
Mallard Path, SE28 .....105 ER76
Mallard Pl, Twick. TW1 .....117 CG90
Mallard Pt, E3
  off Rainhill Way 85 EB69
Mallard Rd, Abb.L. WD5 .....7 BU31
  South Croydon CR2 .....161 DX110
Mallards, The, Hem.H. HP3
  off Belswains La 6 BM25
  Staines TW18
    off Thames Side 134 BH96
Mallards Reach, Wey. KT13 .....135 BR103
Mallards Rd, Bark. IG11 .....88 EU70
  Woodford Green IG8 .....48 EH52
Mallard Wk, Beck. BR3 .....143 DX99
  Sidcup DA14 .....126 EW92
Mallard Way, NW9 .....62 CQ59
  Brentwood CM13 .....55 GB45
  Northwood HA6 .....39 BQ52
  Wallington SM6 .....159 DJ109
  Watford WD25 .....24 BY37
Mallet Dr, Nthlt. UB5 .....60 BZ64
Mallet Rd, SE13 .....123 ED86
★ Mall Galleries, SW1 .....199 N2
Malling, SE13 .....123 EC85
Malling Cl, Croy. CR0 .....142 DW100
Malling Gdns, Mord. SM4 .....140 DC100
Malling Way, Brom. BR2 .....144 EF101
Mallinson Cl, Horn. RM12 .....72 FJ64
Mallinson Rd, SW11 .....120 DE85
  Croydon CR0 .....141 DK104
Mallion Ct, Wal.Abb. EN9 .....16 EF33
Mallord St, SW3 .....100 DD79
Mallory Cl, SE4 .....103 DY84
Mallory Gdns, Barn. EN4 .....44 DG45
Mallory St, NW8 .....194 C4
Mallow Cl, Croy. CR0
  off Marigold Way 143 DX102
  Gravesend (Nthflt.) DA11 .....130 GE91
  Tadworth KT20 .....173 CV119
Mallow Ct, Grays RM17 .....110 GD79
Mallow Mead, NW7 .....43 CY52
Mallows, The, Uxb. UB10 .....59 BP62
Mallow St, EC1 .....197 K4
Mallow Wk, Wal.Cr. EN7 .....14 DR28
Mall Rd, W6 .....99 CV78
Mallys Pl, Dart. (S.Darenth)
  DA4 .....148 FQ95
Malmains Cl, Beck. BR3 .....143 ED99
Malmains Way, Beck. BR3 .....143 EC98
Malm Cl, Rick. WD3 .....38 BK47
Malmesbury Cl, Pnr. HA5 .....59 BT56
Malmesbury Rd, E3 .....85 DZ69
  E16 .....86 EE71
  E18 .....48 EF53
  Morden SM4 .....140 DC101
Malmesbury Ter, E16 .....86 EF71
Malmstone Av, Red. RH1 .....185 DJ128
Malpas Dr, Pnr. HA5 .....60 BX57
Malpas Rd, E8 .....84 DV65
  SE4 .....103 DZ82
  Dagenham RM9 .....88 EX65
  Grays RM16 .....111 GJ76
  Slough SL2 .....74 AV73
Malta Rd, E10 .....67 EA60
  Tilbury RM18 .....111 GF82
Malta St, EC1 .....196 G4
Maltby Cl, Orp. BR6
  off Vinson Cl 146 EU102
Maltby Dr, Enf. EN1 .....30 DV38
Maltby Rd, Chess. KT9 .....156 CN107
Maltby St, SE1 .....201 P5
Malt Hill, Egh. TW20 .....112 AY92
Malt Ho Cl, Wind. (Old Wind.)
  SL4 .....112 AV87
Malthouse Dr, W4 .....98 CS79
  Feltham TW13 .....116 BX92
Malthouse Pas, SW13
  off The Terrace 98 CS82
Malthouse Pl, Rad. WD7 .....9 CG34
Malthus Path, SE28
  off Owen Cl 88 EW74
Malting Ho, E14 .....85 DZ73
Maltings, The, Kings L. WD4 .....7 BQ33
  Orpington BR6 .....145 ET102
  Oxted RH8 .....188 EF131
  Romford RM1 .....71 FF59
  Staines TW18
    off Church St 113 BE91
  West Byfleet (Byfleet)
    KT14 .....152 BM113
Maltings Cl, SW13
  off Cleveland Gdns 98 CS82
Maltings Dr, Epp. CM16
  off Palmers Hill 18 EU29
Maltings La, Epp. CM16 .....18 EU29

Maltings Ms, Sid. DA15
  off Station Rd 126 EU90
Maltings Pl, SW6 .....100 DB81
Malting Way, Islw. TW7 .....97 CF83
Malt La, Rad. WD7 .....25 CG35
Maltmans La, Ger.Cr. (Chal.St.P.)
  SL9 .....56 AW55
Malton Ms, SE18
  off Malton St 105 ES79
  W10 off Cambridge Gdns 81 CY72
Malton Rd, W10
  off St. Marks Rd 81 CY72
Malton St, SE18 .....105 ES79
Maltravers St, WC2 .....196 C10
Malt St, SE1 .....102 DU79
Malus Cl, Add. KT15 .....151 BF108
Malus Dr, Add. KT15 .....151 BF107
Malva Cl, SW18
  off St. Ann's Hill 120 DB85
Malvern Av, E4 .....47 ED52
  Bexleyheath DA7 .....106 EY80
  Harrow HA2 .....60 BY62
Malvern Cl, SE20
  off Derwent Rd 142 DU96
  W10 .....81 CZ71
  Bushey WD23 .....24 CC44
  Chertsey (Ott.) KT16 .....151 BC107
  Mitcham CR4 .....141 DJ97
  Surbiton KT6 .....138 CL102
  Uxbridge UB10 .....59 BP61
Malvern Ct, SE14
  off Avonley Rd 102 DW80
  SW7 .....100 A9
  Slough SL3 off Hill Ri 93 BA79
  Sutton SM2
    off Overton Rd 158 DA108
Malvern Dr, Felt. TW13 .....116 BX92
  Ilford IG3 .....69 ET63
  Woodford Green IG8 .....48 EJ50
Malvern Gdns, NW2 .....63 CY61
  NW6 off Carlton Vale 81 CZ68
  Harrow HA3 .....62 CL55
  Loughton IG10 .....33 EM44
Malvern Ms, NW6
  off Malvern Rd 82 DA69
Malvern Pl, NW6 .....81 CZ69
Malvern Rd, E6 .....86 EL67
  E8 .....84 DU66
  E11 .....68 EE61
  N8 .....65 DM55
  N17 .....66 DU55
  NW6 .....82 DA69
  Enfield EN3 .....31 DY37
  Grays RM17 .....110 GD77
  Hampton TW12 .....116 CA94
  Hayes UB3 .....95 BS80
  Hornchurch RM11 .....71 FG58
  Orpington BR6 .....164 EV105
  Surbiton KT6 .....138 CL103
  Thornton Heath CR7 .....141 DN98
Malvern Ter, N1 .....83 DN67
  N9 off Latymer Rd 46 DT46
Malvern Way, W13
  off Templewood 79 CH71
Rickmansworth (Crox.Grn.)
  WD3 .....23 BP43
Malvina Av, Grav. DA12 .....131 GH89
Malwood Rd, SW12 .....121 DH86
Malyons, The, Shep. TW17
  off Gordon Rd 135 BR100
Malyons Rd, SE13 .....123 EB85
  Swanley BR8 .....127 FF94
Malyons Ter, SE13 .....123 EB85
Managers St, E14 .....204 E3
Manatee Pl, Wall. SM6
  off Croydon Rd 141 DK104
Manaton Cl, SE15 .....102 DV83
Manaton Cres, Sthl. UB1 .....78 CA72
Manbey Gro, E15 .....86 EE65
Manbey Pk Rd, E15 .....86 EE65
Manbey Rd, E15 .....86 EE65
Manbey St, E15 .....86 EE65
Manbre Rd, W6 .....99 CW79
Manbrough Av, E6 .....87 EM69
Manchester Ct, E16 .....86 EH72
Manchester Dr, W10 .....81 CY70
Manchester Gro, E14 .....204 D10
Manchester Ms, W1 .....194 F7
Manchester Rd, E14 .....204 D10
  N15 .....66 DR58
  Thornton Heath CR7 .....142 DQ97
Manchester Sq, W1 .....194 F8
Manchester St, W1 .....194 F7
Manchester Way, Dag. RM10 .....71 FB63
Manchuria Rd, SW11 .....120 DG86
Manciple St, SE1 .....201 K5
Mandalay Rd, SW4 .....121 DJ85
Mandarin St, E14 off Salter St 85 EA73
Mandarin Way, Hayes UB4 .....78 BX71
Mandela Cl, NW10 .....80 CQ66
Mandela Rd, E16 .....86 EG72
Mandela St, NW1 .....83 DJ67
  SW9 .....101 DN80
Mandela Way, SE1 .....201 N8
Mandeville Cl, SE3
  off Vanbrugh Pk 104 EF80
  SW20 .....139 CY95
  Watford WD17 .....23 BT38
Mandeville Ct, E4 .....47 DY49
  Egham TW20 .....113 BA91
Mandeville Dr, Surb. KT6 .....137 CK102
Mandeville Ms, SW4
  off Clapham Pk Rd 101 DL84
Mandeville Pl, W1 .....194 G8
Mandeville Rd, N14 .....45 DH47
  Enfield EN3 .....31 DX36
  Isleworth TW7 .....97 CG82
  Northolt UB5 .....78 CA66
  Potters Bar EN6 .....12 DC32
  Shepperton TW17 .....134 BN99
Mandeville St, E5 .....67 DY62
Mandeville Wk, Brwd. CM13 .....55 GE44
Mandrake Rd, SW17 .....120 DF90
Mandrake Way, E15 .....86 EE66
Mandrell Rd, SW2 .....121 DL85
Manette St, W1 .....195 N9
Manford Cl, Chig. IG7 .....50 EU49

Manford Cross, Chig. IG7 .....50 EU50
Manford Ind Est, Chig. IG7 .....49 ES49
Manfred Rd, SW15 .....119 CZ85
Manger Rd, N7 .....83 DL65
Mangold Way, Erith DA18 .....106 EY76
Manhattan Wf, E16 .....205 M4
Manilla St, E14 .....203 P4
Manister Rd, SE2 .....106 EU76
Manitoba Ct, SE16
  off Renforth St 102 DW75
Manitoba Gdns, Orp. BR6
  off Superior Dr 163 ET107
Manley Ct, N16 off Stoke
  Newington High St 66 DT62
Manley St, NW1 .....82 DG67
Manly Dixon Dr, Enf. EN3 .....31 DY37
Mannamead, Epsom KT18 .....172 CS119
Mannamead Cl, Epsom KT18
  off Mannamead 172 CS119
Mann Cl, Croy. CR0
  off Salem Pl 142 DQ104
Manningford Cl, EC1 .....196 F2
Manning Gdns, Har. HA3 .....61 CK59
Manning Pl, Rich. TW10
  off Grove Rd 118 CM86
Manning Rd, E17
  off Southcote Rd 67 DY57
  Dagenham RM10 .....88 FA65
  Orpington BR5 .....146 EX99
  RM15 .....90 FQ74
Manning St, S.Ock. (Aveley)
  RM15 .....90 FQ74
Manningtree Cl, SW19 .....119 CY88
Manningtree Rd, Ruis. HA4 .....59 BV63
Manningtree St, E1
  off White Ch La 84 DU72
Mannin Rd, Rom. RM6 .....70 EV59
Mannock Dr, Loug. IG10 .....33 EQ40
Mannock Rd, N22 .....65 DP55
  Dartford DA1
    off Barnwell Rd 108 FM83
Manns Cl, Islw. TW7 .....117 CF85
Manns Rd, Edg. HA8 .....42 CN51
Manoel Rd, Twick. TW2 .....116 CC89
Manor Av, SE4 .....103 DZ82
  Caterham CR3 .....176 DS124
  Hornchurch RM11 .....72 FJ57
  Hounslow TW4 .....96 BX83
  Northolt UB5 .....78 BZ66
Manorbrook, SE3 .....104 EG84
Manor Chase, Wey. KT13 .....153 BP106
Manor Cl, E17
  off Manor Rd 47 DY55
  NW7 off Manor Dr 42 CR50
  NW9 .....62 CP57
  SE28 .....88 EW72
  Barnet EN5 .....27 CY42
  Dagenham RM10 .....89 FD65
  Dartford (Cray.) DA1 .....107 FD84
  Dartford (Wilm.) DA2 .....127 FG90
  Romford RM1
    off Manor Rd 71 FG57
  Ruislip HA4 .....59 BT60
  South Ockendon (Aveley)
    RM15 .....90 FQ74
  Warlingham CR6 .....177 DY117
  Woking GU22 .....167 BF116
  Worcester Park KT4 .....138 CS102
Manor Cl S, S.Ock. (Aveley)
  RM15 off Manor Cl 90 FQ74
Manor Cotts, Nthwd. HA6 .....39 BT53
Manor Cotts App, N2 .....44 DC54
Manor Ct, E10
  off Grange Pk Rd 67 EB60
  N2 .....64 DF57
  SW6 off Bagley's La 100 DB81
  Enfield EN1 .....30 DV36
  Radlett WD7 .....25 CF38
  Twickenham TW2 .....116 CC89
  Wembley HA9 .....62 CL64
  Weybridge KT13 .....153 BP105
Manor Ct Rd, W7 .....79 CE73
Manor Cres, Epsom KT19
  off Abbots Av 156 CN112
  Hornchurch RM11 .....72 FJ57
  Surbiton KT5 .....138 CN100
  West Byfleet (Byfleet)
    KT14 .....152 BM113
Manorcrofts Rd, Egh. TW20 .....113 BA93
Manordene Cl, T.Ditt. KT7 .....137 CG102
Manordene Rd, SE28 .....88 EW72
Manor Dr, N14 .....45 DH45
  N20 .....44 DE48
  NW7 .....42 CR50
  Addlestone (New Haw)
    KT15 .....152 BG110
  Epsom KT19 .....156 CS107
  Esher KT10 .....137 CF103
  Feltham TW13
    off Lebanon Av 116 BX92
  St. Albans AL2 .....8 CA27
  Sunbury-on-Thames
    TW16 .....135 BU96
  Surbiton KT5 .....138 CM100
  Wembley HA9 .....62 CM63
Manor Dr, The, Wor.Pk. KT4 .....138 CS102
Manor Dr N, N.Mal. KT3 .....138 CR101
  Worcester Park KT4 .....138 CS102
Manor Est, SE16 .....202 D9
Manor Fm, Dart. (Fnghm.)
  DA4 .....148 FM101
Manor Fm Av, Shep. TW17 .....135 BP100
Manor Fm Cl, Wor.Pk. KT4 .....138 CS102
Manor Fm Dr, E4 .....48 EE48
Manor Fm Est, Stai. (Wrays.)
  TW19 .....112 AX86
Manor Fm La, Egh. TW20 .....113 BA92
Manor Fm Rd, Enf. EN1 .....30 DV35
  Thornton Heath CR7 .....141 DN96
  Wembley HA0 .....79 CK68
Manorfield Cl, N19
  off Junction Rd 65 DJ63
Manor Flds, SW15 .....119 CX86
Manorfields Cl, Chis. BR7 .....145 ET97
Manor Gdns, N7 .....65 DL62
  SW20 .....139 CZ96
  W3 .....98 CN71

Manor Gdns, W4
  off Devonshire Rd 98 CS78
  Hampton TW12 .....116 CB94
  Richmond TW9 .....98 CM84
  Ruislip HA4 .....60 BW64
  South Croydon CR2 .....160 DT107
  Sunbury-on-Thames
    TW16 .....135 BU96
Manor Gate, Nthlt. UB5 .....78 BY66
Manorgate Rd, Kings.T. KT2 .....138 CN95
Manor Grn Rd, Epsom KT19 .....156 CP113
Manor Gro, SE15 .....102 DW79
  Beckenham BR3 .....143 EB96
  Richmond TW9 .....98 CN84
Manor Hall Av, NW4 .....43 CX54
Manor Hall Dr, NW4 .....43 CX54
Manorhall Gdns, E10 .....67 EA60
✚ Manor House 65 DP59
Manor Ho Ct, Epsom KT18 .....156 CQ113
  Shepperton TW17 .....135 BP101
Manor Ho Dr, NW6 .....81 CX66
  Northwood HA6 .....39 BP52
  Walton-on-Thames KT12 .....153 BT107
Manor Ho Est, Stan. HA7
  off Old Ch La 41 CH51
Manor Ho Gdns, Abb.L. WD5 .....7 BT31
Manor Ho La, Slou. (Datchet)
  SL3 .....92 AV80
Manor Ho Way, Islw. TW7 .....97 CH83
Manor La, SE12 .....124 EE86
  SE13 .....104 EE84
  Feltham TW13 .....115 BU89
  Gerrards Cross SL9 .....56 AX59
  Hayes UB3 .....95 BR79
  Longfield (Fawk.Grn.) DA3 .....149 FW101
  Sevenoaks TN15 .....149 FW103
  Sunbury-on-Thames
    TW16 .....135 BU96
  Sutton SM1 .....158 DC106
  Tadworth KT20 .....184 DA129
Manor La Ter, SE13 .....104 EE84
Manor Leaze, Egh. TW20 .....113 BB92
Manor Ms, NW6
  off Cambridge Av 82 DA68
  SE4 .....103 DZ82
Manor Mt, SE23 .....122 DW88
Manor Par, NW10
  off Station Rd 81 CT68
Manor Pk, SE13 .....103 ED84
  Chislehurst BR7 .....145 ER96
  Richmond TW9 .....98 CM84
  Staines TW18 .....113 BD90
MANOR PARK, E12 .....68 EL63
≷ Manor Park 68 EK63
Manor Pk Cl, W.Wick. BR4 .....143 EB102
Manor Pk Cres, Edg. HA8 .....42 CN51
Manor Pk Dr, Har. HA2 .....60 CB55
Manor Pk Gdns, Edg. HA8 .....42 CN50
Manor Pk Par, SE13
  off Lee High Rd 103 ED84
Manor Pk Rd, E12 .....68 EK63
  N2 .....64 DD55
  NW10 .....81 CT67
  Chislehurst BR7 .....145 EQ95
  Sutton SM1 .....158 DC106
  West Wickham BR4 .....143 EB102
Manor Pl, SE17 .....101 DP78
  Chislehurst BR7 .....145 ER95
  Dartford DA1
    off Highfield Rd S 128 FL88
  Feltham TW14 .....115 BU88
  Mitcham CR4 .....141 DJ97
  Staines TW18 .....114 BH92
  Sutton SM1 .....158 DB105
  Walton-on-Thames KT12
    off Manor Rd 135 BT101
Manor Rd, E10 .....67 EA59
  E15 .....86 EE69
  E16 .....86 EE69
  E17 .....47 DY54
  N16 .....66 DR61
  N17 .....46 DU53
  N22 .....45 DL51
  SE25 .....142 DU98
  SW20 .....139 CZ96
  W13 .....79 CG73
  Ashford TW15 .....114 BM92
  Barking IG11 .....87 ET65
  Barnet EN5 .....27 CY43
  Beckenham BR3 .....143 EB96
  Bexley DA5 .....127 FB88
  Chigwell IG7 .....49 EP50
  Dagenham RM10 .....89 FC65
  Dartford DA1 .....107 FE84
  East Molesey KT8 .....137 CD98
  Enfield EN2 .....30 DR40
  Erith DA8 .....107 FF79
  Gravesend DA12 .....131 GH86
  Grays RM17 .....110 GC79
  Grays (W.Thur.) RM20 .....109 FW79
  Harrow HA1 .....61 CG58
  Hayes UB3 .....77 BU72
  Loughton IG10 .....32 EH44
  Loughton (High Beach)
    IG10 .....32 EH38
  Mitcham CR4 .....141 DJ98
  Potters Bar EN6 .....11 CZ31
  Redhill RH1 .....185 DJ129
  Reigate RH2 .....183 CZ132
  Richmond TW9 .....98 CM83
  Romford RM1 .....71 FG57
  Romford (Chad.Hth.) RM6 .....70 EX58
  Romford (Lamb.End) RM4 .....50 EX58
  Ruislip HA4 .....59 BR60
  St. Albans (Lon.Col.) AL2 .....9 CJ26
  Sevenoaks (Sund.) TN14 .....180 EX124
  Sidcup DA15 .....125 ET90
  Sutton SM2 .....157 CZ108
  Swanscombe DA10 .....129 FX86
  Teddington TW11 .....117 CH92
  Tilbury RM18 .....111 GG82
  Twickenham TW2 .....116 CC89
  Wallington SM6 .....159 DH105
  Waltham Abbey EN9 .....15 ED33
  Walton-on-Thames KT12 .....135 BT101
  Watford WD17 .....23 BV39
  West Wickham BR4 .....143 EB103

Manor Rd, West. (Tats.) TN16 .....178 EL120
  Woking GU21 .....166 AW116
  Woking (Send M.) GU23 .....167 BF123
  Woodford Green IG8 .....49 EM51
Manor Rd N, Esher KT10 .....137 CF104
  Thames Ditton KT7 .....137 CG103
  Wallington SM6 .....159 DH105
Manor Rd S, Esher KT10 .....155 CE105
Manorside, Barn. EN5 .....27 CY42
Manorside Cl, SE2 .....106 EW77
Manor Sq, Dag. RM8 .....70 EX61
Manor Vale, Brent. TW8 .....97 CJ78
Manor Vw, N3 .....44 DB54
Manor Wk, Wey. KT13 .....153 BP106
Manor Way, E4 .....47 ED49
  NW9 .....62 CS55
  SE3 .....104 EF84
  SE28 .....88 EW74
  Banstead SM7 .....174 DF116
  Beckenham BR3 .....143 EA96
  Bexley DA5 .....126 FA88
  Bexleyheath DA7 .....107 FD83
  Borehamwood WD6 .....26 CQ42
  Brentwood CM14 .....54 FU48
  Bromley BR2 .....144 EL100
  Egham TW20 .....113 AZ93
Manorway, Enf. EN1 .....46 DS45
Manor Way, Grays RM17 .....110 GB80
  Harrow HA2 .....60 CB56
  Leatherhead (Oxshott)
    KT22 .....170 CC115
  Mitcham CR4 .....141 DJ97
  Orpington BR5 .....145 EQ98
  Potters Bar EN6 .....12 DA30
  Purley CR8 .....159 DL112
  Rainham RM13 .....89 FE71
  Rickmansworth (Crox.Grn.)
    WD3 .....22 BN42
  Ruislip HA4 .....59 BS59
  South Croydon CR2 .....160 DS107
  Southall UB2 .....96 BX77
  Swanscombe DA10 .....109 FX84
  Waltham Cross (Chsht.) EN8
    off Russells Ride 15 DY31
  Woking GU22 .....167 BB121
Manorway, Wdf.Grn. IG8 .....48 EJ50
Manor Way, Wor.Pk. KT4 .....138 CS102
Manor Way, The, Wall. SM6 .....159 DH105
Manor Waye, Uxb. UB8 .....76 BK67
Manor Way Ind Est, Grays
  RM17 .....110 GC80
Manor Wd Rd, Pur. CR8 .....159 DL113
Manpreet Ct, E12
  off Morris Av 69 EM64
Manresa Rd, SW3 .....100 DE78
Mansard Beeches, SW17 .....120 DG92
Mansard Cl, Horn. RM12 .....71 FG61
  Pinner HA5 .....60 BX55
Mansbridge Way, NW7
  off Bittacy Hill 43 CY52
Manse Cl, Hayes UB3 .....95 BR79
Mansel Cl, Slou. SL2 .....74 AV71
Mansel Gro, E17 .....47 EA53
Mansell Rd, W3 .....98 CR75
  Greenford UB6 .....78 CB71
Mansell St, E1 .....202 A1
Mansell Way, Cat. CR3 .....176 DR122
Mansel Rd, SW19 .....119 CY93
Mansergh Cl, SE18 .....104 EL80
Manse Rd, N16 .....66 DT62
Manser Rd, Rain. RM13 .....89 FE69
Manse Way, Swan. BR8 .....147 FG98
Mansfield Av, N15 .....66 DR56
  Barnet EN4 .....28 DF44
  Ruislip HA4 .....59 BV60
Mansfield Cl, N9 .....30 DU44
  Orpington BR5 .....146 EX101
  Weybridge KT13 .....153 BP106
Mansfield Dr, Hayes UB4 .....77 BS70
  Redhill RH1 .....185 DK128
Mansfield Gdns, Horn.
  RM12 .....72 FK61
Mansfield Hill, E4 .....47 EB46
Mansfield Ms, W1 .....195 H7
Mansfield Pl, NW3
  off New End 64 DC63
Mansfield Rd, E11 .....68 EH58
  E17 .....67 DZ56
  NW3 .....64 DF64
  W3 .....80 CP70
  Chessington KT9 .....155 CJ106
  Ilford IG1 .....69 EN61
  South Croydon CR2 .....160 DR107
  Swanley BR8 .....127 FE93
Mansfield St, W1 .....195 H7
Mansford St, E2 .....84 DU68
Manship Rd, Mitch. CR4 .....120 DG94
Mansion Cl, SW9
  off Cowley Rd 101 DN81
Mansion Gdns, NW3 .....64 DB62
★ Mansion Ho, EC4 .....197 K9
✚ Mansion House 197 J10
Mansion Ho, EC4 .....197 K9
Mansion Ho Pl, EC4 .....197 K9
Mansion Ho St, EC4 .....197 K9
Mansion La, Iver SL0 .....75 BC74
Manson Ms, SW7 .....100 DC77
Manson Pl, SW7 .....100 DD77
Manstead Gdns, Rain. RM13 .....89 FH72
Mansted Gdns, Rom. RM6 .....70 EW59
Manston Av, Sthl. UB2 .....96 CA77
Manston Cl, SE20
  off Garden Rd 142 DW95
  Waltham Cross (Chsht.)
    EN8 .....14 DW30
Manstone Rd, NW2 .....63 CY64
Manston Gro, Kings.T. KT2 .....117 CK92
Manston Way, Horn. RM12 .....89 FH65
Manthorp Rd, SE18 .....105 EQ78
Mantilla Rd, SW17 .....120 DG91
Mantle Rd, SE4 .....103 DY83
Mantlet Cl, SW16 .....121 DJ94
Mantle Way, E15
  off Romford Rd 86 EE66
Manton Av, W7 .....97 CF75
Manton Cl, Hayes UB3 .....77 BS73
Manton Rd, SE2 .....106 EU77

Manton Rd, Enf. EN3
  off Government Row **31** EA37
Mantua St, SW11 . . . .**100** DD83
Mantus Cl, E1 off Mantus Rd .**84** DW70
Mantus Rd, E1 . . . .**84** DW70
Manus Way, N20
  off Blakeney Cl **44** DC47
Manville Gdns, SW17 . . . . . .**121** DH89
Manville Rd, SW17 . . . .**120** DG89
Manwood Rd, SE4 . . . .**123** DZ85
Manwood St, E16 . . . .**87** EM74
Manygate La, Shep. TW17 . .**135** BQ101
Manygates, SW12 . . . .**121** DH89
Mapesbury Rd, NW2 . . . .**81** CY65
Mapeshill Pl, NW2 . . . .**81** CW65
Mape St, E2 . . . .**84** DV70
Maple Av, E4 . . . .**47** DZ50
  W3 . . . .**80** CS74
  Harrow HA2 . . . .**60** CB81
  Upminster RM14 . . . .**72** FP62
  West Drayton UB7 . . . .**76** BL73
Maple Cl, N3 . . . .**44** DA51
  N16 . . . .**66** DU58
  SW4 . . . .**121** DK86
  Brentwood CM13
    off Cherry Av **55** FZ48
  Buckhurst Hill IG9 . . . .**48** EK48
  Bushey WD23 . . . .**24** BY40
  Epping (They.B.) CM16
    off Loughton La **33** ER37
  Hampton TW12 . . . .**116** BZ93
  Hayes UB4 . . . .**78** BX69
  Hornchurch RM12 . . . .**71** FH62
  Ilford IG6 . . . .**49** ES50
  Mitcham CR4 . . . .**141** DH95
  Orpington BR5 . . . .**146** ER99
  Ruislip HA4 . . . .**59** BV58
  Swanley BR8 . . . .**147** FE96
  Whyteleafe CR3 . . . .**176** DT117
Maple Ct, Egh. (Eng.Grn.) TW20
    off Ashwood Rd **112** AV93
  New Malden KT3 . . . .**138** CS97
Maple Cres, Sid. DA15 . . . . .**126** EU86
  Slough SL2 . . . .**74** AV73
Maplecroft Cl, E6
    off Allhallows Rd **86** EL72
MAPLE CROSS, Rick. **37** BD49
Maple Cross Ind Est, Rick.
  (Map.Cr.) WD3 . . . .**37** BF49
Mapledale Av, Croy. CR0 . . .**142** DU103
Mapledene, Chis. BR7
    off Kemnal Rd **125** EQ92
Mapledene Rd, E8 . . . .**84** DT66
Maple Dr, S.Ock. RM15 . . . . .**91** FX70
Maplefield, St.Alb. (Park St.)
  AL2 . . . .**8** CB29
Maplefield La, Ch.St.G. HP8 .**20** AV41
Maple Gdns, Edg. HA8 . . . . .**42** CS52
  Staines TW19 . . . .**114** BL89
Maple Gate, Loug. IG10 . . . .**33** EN40
Maple Gro, NW9 . . . .**62** CQ59
  W5 . . . .**97** CK76
  Brentford TW8 . . . .**97** CH80
  Southall UB1 . . . .**78** BZ71
  Watford WD17 . . . .**23** BU39
  Woking GU22 . . . .**166** AY121
Maple Hill, Hem.H. (Bov.) HP3
    off Ley Hill Rd **5** AX30
Maplehurst, Lthd. KT22 . . . .**171** CD123
Maplehurst Cl, Kings.T. KT1 .**138** CL98
Maple Ind Est, Felt. TW13
    off Maple Way **115** BU90
Maple Leaf Cl, Abb.L. WD5 . . .**7** BU32
Mapleleaf Cl, S.Croy. CR2 . .**161** DX111
Maple Leaf Cl, West. (Bigg.H.)
  TN16 off Main Rd **178** EK116
Maple Leaf Dr, Sid. DA15 . . .**125** ET88
Mapleleafe Gdns, Ilf. IG6 . . .**69** EP55
Maple Leaf Sq, SE16 . . . . . .**203** J4
Maple Lo Cl, Rick. (Map.Cr.)
  WD3 . . . .**37** BE49
Maple Ms, NW6
    off Kilburn Pk Rd **82** DB68
  SW16 . . . .**121** DM92
Maple Pl, W1 . . . .**195** L5
  Banstead SM7 . . . .**157** CX114
  West Drayton UB7
    off Maple Av **76** BM73
Maple Rd, E11 . . . .**68** EE58
  SE20 . . . .**142** DV95
  Ashtead KT21 . . . .**171** CK119
  Dartford DA1 . . . .**128** FJ88
  Gravesend DA12 . . . .**131** GJ91
  Grays RM17 . . . .**110** GC79
  Hayes UB4 . . . .**78** BW69
  Surbiton KT6 . . . .**138** CL99
  Whyteleafe CR3 . . . .**176** DT117
  Woking (Ripley) GU23 . . . .**168** BG124
Maples, The, Bans. SM7 . . . .**158** DB114
  Chertsey (Ott.) KT16 . . . . .**151** BB107
  Esher (Clay.) KT10 . . . .**155** CG108
  Waltham Cross (Goffs Oak)
  EN7 . . . .**14** DS28
Maplescombe La, Dart. (Fnghm.)
  DA4 . . . .**148** FN104
Maples Pl, E1
    off Raven Row **84** DV71
Maple Springs, Wal.Abb.
  EN9 . . . .**16** EG33
Maplestead Rd, SW2 . . . . . .**121** DM87
  Dagenham RM9 . . . .**88** EV67
Maple St, W1 . . . .**195** K6
  Romford RM7 . . . .**71** CF56
Maplethorpe Rd, Th.Hth.
  CR7 . . . .**141** DP98
Mapleton Cl, Brom. BR2 . . . .**144** EG100
Mapleton Cres, SW18 . . . . . .**120** DB86
  Enfield EN3 . . . .**30** DW38
Mapleton Rd, E4 . . . .**47** EC48
  SW18 . . . .**120** DB86
  Edenbridge TN8 . . . .**189** ET133
  Enfield EN1 . . . .**30** DV40
  Westerham TN16 . . . .**189** ES130
Maple Wk, W10
    off Droop St **81** CX70
  Sutton SM2 . . . .**158** DB110
Maple Way, Couls. CR5 . . . .**175** DH121
  Feltham TW13 . . . .**115** BU90

Maple Way, Wal.Abb. EN9 off Breach
  Barn Mobile Home Pk . .**16** EH30
Maplin Cl, N21 . . . .**29** DM44
Maplin Ho, SE2
    off Wolvercote Rd **106** EX75
Maplin Pk, Slou. SL3 . . . .**93** BC78
Maplin Rd, E16 . . . .**86** EG72
Maplin St, E3 . . . .**85** DZ69
Mapperley Dr, Wdf.Grn. IG8
    off Forest Dr **48** EE52
Maran Way, Erith DA18 . . . .**106** EX75
Marban Rd, W9 . . . .**81** CZ69
★ **Marble Arch**, W1 . . . .**194** E10
  Marble Arch, W1 . . . .**194** E10
Marble Cl, W3 . . . .**80** CP74
Marble Dr, NW2 . . . .**63** CX60
Marble Hill Cl, Twick. TW1 . .**117** CH87
Marble Hill Gdns, Twick. TW1 .**117** CH87
★ **Marble Hill Ho**, Twick.
  TW1 . . . .**117** CJ87
Marble Ho, SE18
    off Felspar Cl **105** ET78
Marble Quay, E1 . . . .**202** B2
Marbles Way, Tad. KT20 . . . .**173** CX119
Marbrook Ct, SE12 . . . .**124** EJ90
Marcella Rd, SW9 . . . .**101** DN82
Marcellina Way, Orp. BR6 . .**145** ES104
Marcet Rd, Dart. DA1 . . . . . .**128** FJ85
Marchant Rd, E11 . . . .**67** ED61
Marchant St, SE14
    off Sanford St **103** DY79
Marchbank Rd, W14 . . . .**99** CZ79
Marchmont Gdns, Rich. TW10
    off Marchmont Rd **118** CM85
Marchmont Rd, Rich. TW10 .**118** CM85
  Wallington SM6 . . . .**159** DJ108
Marchmont St, WC1 . . . .**195** P4
March Rd, Twick. TW1 . . . . . .**117** CG87
  Weybridge KT13 . . . .**152** BN106
Marchside Cl, Houns. TW5
    off Springwell Rd **96** BX81
Marchwood Cl, SE5 . . . .**102** DS80
Marchwood Cres, W5 . . . .**79** CJ72
Marcia Rd, SE1 . . . .**201** N9
Marcilly Rd, SW18 . . . .**120** DD85
Marconi Rd, E10 . . . .**67** EA60
  Gravesend (Nthflt.) DA11 .**130** GD90
Marconi Way, Sthl. UB1 . . . . .**78** CB72
Marcon Pl, E8 . . . .**84** DV65
Marco Rd, W6 . . . .**99** CW76
Marcourt Lawns, W5 . . . .**80** CL70
Marcus Ct, E15 . . . .**86** EE67
Marcus Garvey Ms, SE22
    off St. Aidan's Rd **122** DV85
Marcus Garvey Way, SE24 . .**101** DN84
Marcus Rd, Dart. DA1 . . . . . .**127** FG87
Marcus St, E15 . . . .**86** EE67
  SW18 . . . .**120** DB86
Marcus Ter, SW18 . . . .**120** DB86
Mardale Dr, NW9 . . . .**62** CR57
Mardell Rd, Croy. CR0 . . . . . .**143** DX99
Marden Av, Brom. BR2 . . . . .**144** EG100
Marden Cl, Chig. IG7 . . . .**50** EV47
Marden Cres, Bex. DA5 . . . .**127** FC85
  Croydon CR0 . . . .**141** DM100
Marden Pk, Cat. (Wold.) CR3 .**187** DZ125
Marden Rd, N17 . . . .**66** DS55
  Croydon CR0 . . . .**141** DM100
  Romford RM1 . . . .**71** FE58
Marden Sq, SE16 . . . .**202** D7
Marder Rd, W13 . . . .**97** CG75
Mardyke Cl, Rain. RM13
    off Lower Mardyke Av **89** FC68
Mardyke Ho, Rain. RM13
    off Lower Mardyke Av **89** FD68
Marechal Niel Av, Sid. DA15 .**125** ER90
Maresfield, Croy. CR0 . . . . . .**142** DS104
Maresfield Gdns, NW3 . . . . . .**64** DC64
Mare St, E8 . . . .**84** DV67
Marfleet Cl, Cars. SM5 . . . . .**140** DE103
Margaret Av, E4 . . . .**31** EB44
  Brentwood CM15 . . . .**55** FZ45
Margaret Bondfield Av, Bark.
  IG11 . . . .**88** EU66
Margaret Bldgs, N16
    off Margaret Rd **66** DT60
Margaret Cl, Abb.L. WD5 . . . . .**7** BT32
  Epping CM16
    off Margaret Rd **18** EU29
  Potters Bar EN6 . . . .**12** DC33
  Romford RM2
    off Margaret Rd **71** FH57
  Staines TW18
    off Charles Rd **114** BK93
  Waltham Abbey EN9 . . . . .**15** ED33
Margaret Ct, W1 . . . .**195** K8
Margaret Dr, Horn. RM11 . . . .**72** FM60
Margaret Gardner Dr, SE9 . .**125** EM89
Margaret Ingram Cl, SW6
    off John Smith Av **99** CZ80
Margaret Lockwood Cl, Kings.T.
  KT1 . . . .**138** CM98
Margaret Rd, N16 . . . .**66** DT60
  Barnet EN4 . . . .**28** DD42
  Bexley DA5 . . . .**126** EX86
  Epping CM16 . . . .**18** EU29
  Romford RM2 . . . .**71** FH57
Margaret Sq, Uxb. UB8 . . . . .**76** BJ67
Margaret St, W1 . . . .**195** J8
Margaretta Ter, SW3 . . . . . .**100** DE79
Margaretting Rd, E12 . . . . . .**68** EJ61
  Ilford IG4 . . . .**68** EL58
Margeholes, Wat. WD19 . . . . .**40** BY47
MARGERY, Tad. **184** DA129
Margery Gro, Tad. KT20 . . . .**183** CY129
Margery La, Tad. KT20 . . . . .**183** CZ129
Margery Pk Rd, E7 . . . .**86** EG65
Margery Rd, Dag. RM8 . . . . .**70** EX62
Margery St, WC1 . . . .**196** D3
Margery Wd La, Tad. KT20 . .**183** CZ129
Margherita Pl, Wal.Abb. EN9 .**16** EF34
Margherita Rd, Wal.Abb. EN9 .**16** EG34

Margin Dr, SW19 . . . .**119** CX92
Margravine Gdns, W6 . . . .**99** CX78
Margravine Rd, W6 . . . .**99** CX78
Marham Gdns, SW18 . . . . . .**120** DE88
  Morden SM4 . . . .**140** DC100
Maria Cl, SE1 . . . .**202** D8
Mariam Gdns, Horn. RM12 . . .**72** FM61
Marian Cl, Hayes UB4 . . . . . .**78** BX70
Marian Ct, Sutt. SM1 . . . . . .**158** DB106
Marian Pl, E2 . . . .**84** DV68
Marian Rd, SW16 . . . .**141** DJ95
Marian Sq, E2
    off Pritchard's Rd **84** DU68
Marian St, E2 off Hackney Rd .**84** DV68
Marian Way, NW10 . . . .**81** CT66
Maria Ter, E1 . . . .**85** DX70
Maria Theresa Cl, N.Mal.
  KT3 . . . .**138** CR99
Maricas Av, Har. HA3 . . . .**41** CD53
H **Marie Curie Cen**, Cat.
  CR3 . . . .**186** DT125
Marie Lloyd Gdns, N19
    off Hornsey Ri Gdns **65** DL59
Marie Lloyd Wk, E8
    off Forest Rd **84** DU65
Mariette Way, Wall. SM6 . . .**159** DL109
Marigold All, SE1 . . . .**200** F1
Marigold Cl, Sthl. UB1
    off Lancaster Rd **78** BY73
Marigold Rd, N17 . . . .**46** DW52
Marigold St, SE16 . . . .**202** D5
Marigold Way, E4
    off Silver Birch Av **47** DZ51
  Croydon CR0 . . . .**143** DX102
Marina App, Hayes UB4 . . . . .**78** BY71
Marina Av, N.Mal. KT3 . . . . .**139** CV99
Marina Cl, Brom. BR2 . . . . . .**144** EG97
  Chertsey KT16 . . . .**134** BH102
Marina Dr, Dart. DA1 . . . . . .**128** FN88
  Gravesend (Nthflt.) DA11 . .**131** GF87
  Welling DA16 . . . .**105** ES82
Marina Gdns, Rom. RM7 . . . .**71** FC58
  Waltham Cross (Chsht.)
  EN8 . . . .**14** DW30
Marina Way, Iver SL0 . . . .**75** BF73
  Teddington TW11
    off Fairways **117** CK94
Marine Dr, SE18 . . . .**105** EM77
  Barking IG11 . . . .**88** EV70
Marinefield Rd, SW6 . . . . . .**100** DB82
Mariner Gdns, Rich. TW10 . .**117** CJ90
Mariner Rd, E12
    off Dersingham Av **69** EM63
Mariners Ct, Green. DA9
    off High St **109** FV84
Mariners Ms, E14 . . . .**204** F8
Mariners Wk, Erith DA8
    off Frobisher Rd **107** FF79
Mariners Way, Grav. DA11
    off Rosherville Way **130** GE87
Marine St, SE16 . . . .**202** B6
Marine Twr, SE8
    off Abinger Gro **103** DZ79
Marion Av, Shep. TW17 . . . . .**135** BP99
Marion Cl, Bushey WD23 . . . .**24** BZ39
  Ilford IG6 . . . .**49** ER52
Marion Cres, Orp. BR5 . . . . .**146** EU99
Marion Gro, Wdf.Grn. IG8 . . .**48** EE50
Marion Rd, NW7 . . . .**43** CU50
  Thornton Heath CR7 . . . . .**142** DQ99
Marischal Rd, SE13 . . . .**103** ED83
Marisco Cl, Grays RM16 . . . .**111** GH77
Marish La, Uxb. (Denh.) UB9 .**57** BC56
Marish Wf, Slou. (Mdgrn.)
  SL3 . . . .**93** AY75
Maritime Cl, Green. DA9 . . . .**129** FV85
Maritime Gate, Grav. DA11
    off Rosherville Way **130** GE87
Maritime Ho, Bark. IG11
    off Linton Rd **87** EQ66
Maritime Quay, E14 . . . .**204** A10
Maritime St, E3 . . . .**85** DZ70
Marius Pas, SW17
    off Marius Rd **120** DG89
Marius Rd, SW17 . . . .**120** DG89
Marjorams Av, Loug. IG10 . . .**33** EM40
Marjorie Gro, SW11 . . . .**100** DF84
Marjorie Ms, E1
    off Arbour Sq **85** DX72
Markab Rd, Nthwd. HA6 . . . . .**39** BT50
Mark Av, E4 . . . .**31** EB44
Mark Cl, Bexh. DA7 . . . .**106** EY81
  Southall UB1
    off Longford Av **78** CB74
Mark Dr, Ger.Cr. (Chal.St.P.)
  SL9 . . . .**36** AX49
Marke Cl, Kes. BR2 . . . .**162** EL105
Markedge La, Couls. CR5 . . .**174** DE124
  Redhill RH1 . . . .**184** DF128
Markeston Grn, Wat. WD19 . .**40** BX49
Market Ct, W1 . . . .**195** K8
Market Est, N7 . . . .**83** DL65
Marketfield Rd, Red. RH1 . . .**184** DF134
Marketfield Way, Red. RH1 . .**184** DF134
Market Hill, SE18 . . . .**105** EN76
Market La, Edg. HA8 . . . .**42** CQ53
  Iver SL0 . . . .**93** BC75
  Slough SL3 . . . .**93** BC75
Market Link, Rom. RM1 . . . . .**71** FE56
Market Meadow, Orp. BR5 . .**146** EW98
Market Ms, W1 . . . .**199** H3
Market Pl, N2 . . . .**64** DE55
  NW11 . . . .**64** DC56
  SE16 . . . .**202** C8
  W1 . . . .**195** K8
  W3 . . . .**80** CQ74
  Bexleyheath DA6 . . . .**106** FA84
  Brentford TW8 . . . .**97** CJ80
  Dartford DA1
    off Market St **128** FL87
  Enfield EN2 off The Town . .**30** DR41
  Gerrards Cross (Chal.St.P.)
  SL9 . . . .**36** AX53
  Kingston upon Thames
  KT1 . . . .**137** CK96

Market Pl, Rom. RM1 . . . .**71** FE57
  Romford (Abridge) RM4 . . .**34** EV41
  Tilbury RM18 . . . .**111** GF82
Market Rd, N7 . . . .**83** DL65
  Richmond TW9 . . . .**98** CN83
Market Row, SW9
    off Atlantic Rd **101** DN84
Market Sq, E2 . . . .**197** P2
  E14 off Chrisp St **85** EB72
  N9 off New Rd **46** DU47
  Bromley BR1 . . . .**144** EG96
  Staines TW18
    off Clarence St **113** BE91
  Uxbridge UB8 off High St . .**76** BJ66
  Waltham Abbey EN9
    off Leverton Way **15** EC33
  Westerham TN16 . . . .**189** EQ127
  Woking GU21
    off Cawsey Way **166** AY117
Market St, E6 . . . .**87** EM68
  SE18 . . . .**105** EN77
  Dartford DA1 . . . .**128** FL87
  Watford WD18 . . . .**23** BV42
Market Way, E14
    off Kerbey St **85** EB72
  Wembley HA0
    off Turton Rd **62** CL64
  Westerham TN16
    off Costell's Meadow **189** ER126
Markfield, Croy. CR0 . . . .**161** DZ110
Markfield Gdns, E4 . . . .**47** EB45
Markfield Rd, N15 . . . .**66** DU56
  Caterham CR3 . . . .**186** DV126
Markham Pl, SW3 . . . .**198** D10
H **Markham Rd**, Brwd.
  CM13 . . . .**53** FX51
Markham Sq, SW3 . . . .**198** D10
Markham St, SW3 . . . .**198** C10
Markhole Cl, Hmptn. TW12
    off Priory Rd **116** BZ94
Markhouse Av, E17 . . . .**67** DY58
Markhouse Rd, E17 . . . .**67** DZ57
Markland Ho, W10 . . . .**81** CX73
Mark La, EC3 . . . .**201** N1
  Gravesend DA12 . . . .**131** GL86
Markmanor Av, E17 . . . .**67** DY59
Mark Oak La, Lthd. KT22 . . . .**170** CA122
Mark Rd, N22 . . . .**45** DP54
Marksbury Av, Rich. TW9 . . . .**98** CN83
MARK'S GATE, Rom. **50** EY54
Mark Sq, EC2 . . . .**197** M4
Marks Rd, Rom. RM7 . . . .**71** FC57
  Warlingham CR6 . . . .**177** DY118
Marks Sq, Grav. (Nthflt.)
  DA11 . . . .**131** GF91
Mark St, E15 . . . .**86** EE66
  EC2 . . . .**197** M4
  Reigate RH2 . . . .**184** DB133
Markville Gdns, Cat. CR3 . . .**186** DU125
Markway, Sun. TW16 . . . .**136** BW96
Mark Way, Swan. BR8 . . . . . .**147** FG99
Markwell Cl, SE26
    off Longton Gro **122** DV91
Markyate Rd, Dag. RM8 . . . . .**70** EV64
Marlands Rd, Ilf. IG5 . . . .**68** EL55
Marlborough, SW3 . . . .**198** C8
Marlborough Av, E8 . . . .**84** DU67
  N14 . . . .**45** DJ48
  Edgware HA8 . . . .**42** CP48
  Ruislip HA4 . . . .**59** BQ58
Marlborough Cl, N20
    off Marlborough Gdns **44** DF48
  SE17 . . . .**200** G9
  SW19 . . . .**120** DE93
  Grays RM16 . . . .**110** GC75
  Orpington BR6
    off Aylesham Rd **145** ET101
  Upminster RM14 . . . .**73** FS60
  Walton-on-Thames KT12
    off Arch Rd **136** BX104
Marlborough Ct, W1 . . . .**195** K9
  W8 . . . .**100** DA77
  Wallington SM6
    off Cranley Gdns **159** DJ108
Marlborough Cres, W4 . . . . . .**98** CR76
  Sevenoaks TN13 . . . .**190** FE124
Marlborough Dr, Ilf. IG5 . . . . .**68** EL55
  Weybridge KT13 . . . .**135** BQ104
Marlborough Gdns, N20 . . . . .**44** DF48
  Upminster RM14 . . . .**73** FR60
Marlborough Gate Ho, W2
    off Elms Ms **82** DD73
Marlborough Gro, SE1 . . . . .**102** DU78
Marlborough Hill, NW8 . . . . . .**82** DC67
  Harrow HA1 . . . .**61** CF56
★ **Marlborough Ho**, SW1 . . . .**199** L3
Marlborough La, SE7 . . . . . .**104** EJ79
Marlborough Ms, Bans. SM7
    off Court Rd **174** DA115
Marlborough Pk Av, Sid.
  DA15 . . . .**126** EU87
Marlborough Pl, NW8 . . . .**82** DC68
Marlborough Rd, E4 . . . .**47** EA51
  E7 . . . .**86** EJ66
  E15 off Borthwick Rd **68** EE63
  E18 . . . .**68** EG55
  N9 . . . .**46** DT46
  N19 . . . .**65** DK61
  N22 . . . .**45** DL52
  SW1 . . . .**199** L3
  SW19 . . . .**120** DD93
  W4 . . . .**98** CQ78
  W5 . . . .**97** CK75
  Ashford TW15 . . . .**114** BK92
  Bexleyheath DA7 . . . .**106** EX83
  Brentwood (Pilg.Hat.)
  CM15 . . . .**54** FU44
  Bromley BR2 . . . .**144** EJ98
  Dagenham RM8 . . . .**70** EV63
  Dartford DA1 . . . .**128** FJ86
  Feltham TW13 . . . .**116** BX89
  Hampton TW12 . . . .**116** CA93
  Isleworth TW7 . . . .**97** CH81
  Richmond TW10 . . . .**118** CL86
  Romford RM7 . . . .**71** FA56
  Slough SL3 . . . .**92** AX77
  South Croydon CR2 . . . . . .**160** DQ108

Marlborough Rd, Sthl. UB2 . . .**96** BW76
  Sutton SM1 . . . .**140** DA104
  Uxbridge UB10 . . . .**77** BP70
  Watford WD18 . . . .**23** BV42
  Woking GU21 . . . .**167** BA116
Marlborough St, SW3 . . . . . .**198** B9
Marlborough Yd, N19 . . . .**65** DK61
Marld, The, Ashtd. KT21 . . . .**172** CM118
Marle Gdns, Wal.Abb. EN9 . . .**15** EC32
Marler Rd, SE23 . . . .**123** DY88
Marley Av, Bexh. DA7 . . . . . .**106** EX79
Marley Cl, N15
    off Stanmore Rd **65** DP56
  Addlestone KT15 . . . .**151** BF107
  Greenford UB6 . . . .**78** CA69
Marley Wk, NW2
    off Lennon Rd **63** CW64
Marlin Cl, Sun. TW16 . . . .**115** BT93
Marlingdene Cl, Hmptn.
  TW12 . . . .**116** CA93
Marlings Cl, Chis. BR7 . . . . .**145** ES98
  Whyteleafe CR3 . . . .**176** DS117
Marlings Pk Av, Chis. BR7 . .**145** ES98
Marling Way, Grav. DA12 . . .**131** GL92
Marlins, The, Nthwd. HA6 . . .**39** BT51
Marlins Cl, Rick. (Chorl.) WD3 .**21** BE40
  Sutton SM1
    off Turnpike La **158** DC106
Marlins Meadow, Wat. WD18 .**23** BR44
Marloes Cl, Wem. HA0 . . . . . .**61** CK63
Marloes Rd, W8 . . . .**100** DB76
Marlow Av, Purf. RM19 . . . . .**108** FN77
Marlow Cl, SE20 . . . .**142** DV97
Marlow Ct, NW6 . . . .**81** CX66
  NW9 . . . .**63** CT55
Marlow Cres, Twick. TW1 . . .**117** CF86
Marlow Dr, Sutt. SM3 . . . . . .**139** CX103
Marlowe Cl, Chis. BR7 . . . . .**125** ER93
  Ilford IG6 . . . .**49** EQ53
Marlowe Ct, SE19
    off Lymer Av **122** DT92
Marlowe Gdns, SE9 . . . .**125** EN86
  Romford RM3
    off Shenstone Gdns **52** FJ53
Marlowe Rd, E17 . . . .**67** EC56
Marlowes, The, NW8 . . . .**82** DD67
  Dartford DA1 . . . .**107** FD84
Marlowe Sq, Mitch. CR4 . . . .**141** DJ98
Marlowe Way, Croy. CR0 . . .**141** DL103
Marlow Gdns, Hayes UB3 . . .**95** BR76
Marlow Rd, E6 . . . .**87** EM69
  SE20 . . . .**142** DV97
  Southall UB2 . . . .**96** BZ76
Marlow Way, SE16 . . . .**203** H4
Marlpit Av, Couls. CR5 . . . . .**175** DL117
Marlpit La, Couls. CR5 . . . . .**175** DK116
Marl Rd, SW18 . . . .**100** DB84
Marl St, SW18 off Marl Rd . . .**100** DC84
Marlton St, SE10 . . . .**205** L10
Marlwood Cl, Sid. DA15 . . . .**125** ES89
Marlyon Rd, Ilf. IG6 . . . .**50** EV50
Marmadon Rd, SE18 . . . .**105** ET77
Marmion App, E4 . . . .**47** EA49
Marmion Av, E4 . . . .**47** DZ49
Marmion Cl, E4 . . . .**47** DZ49
Marmion Ms, SW11
    off Taybridge Rd **100** DG84
Marmion Rd, SW11 . . . .**100** DG84
Marmont Rd, SE15 . . . .**102** DU81
Marmora Rd, SE22 . . . .**122** DW86
Marmot Rd, Houns. TW4 . . . . .**96** BX83
Marne Av, N11 . . . .**45** DH49
  Welling DA16 . . . .**106** EU83
Marnell Way, Houns. TW4 . . .**96** BX83
Marne St, W10 . . . .**81** CY69
Marney Rd, SW11 . . . .**100** DG84
Marneys Cl, Epsom KT18 . . .**172** CN115
Marnfield Cres, SW2 . . . .**121** DM88
Marnham Av, NW2 . . . .**63** CY63
Marnham Cres, Grnf. UB6 . . .**78** CB69
Marnock Rd, SE4 . . . .**123** DY85
Maroon St, E14 . . . .**85** DY71
Maroons Way, SE6 . . . .**123** EA92
Marquess Rd, N1 . . . .**84** DR65
Marquis Cl, Wem. HA0 . . . . . .**80** CM66
Marquis Rd, N4 . . . .**65** DM60
  N22 . . . .**45** DM51
  NW1 . . . .**83** DK65
Marrabon Cl, Sid. DA15 . . . .**126** EU88
Marram Ct, Grays RM17
    off Medlar Rd **110** GE79
Marrick Cl, SW15 . . . .**99** CU84
Marrilyne Av, Enf. EN3 . . . . . .**31** DZ38
Marriots Cl, NW9 . . . .**63** CT58
Marriott Cl, Felt. TW14 . . . . .**115** BR86
Marriot Ter, Rick. (Chorl.) WD3 .**21** BF42
Marriott Lo Cl, Add. KT15 . . .**152** BJ105
Marriott Rd, E15 . . . .**86** EE67
  N4 . . . .**65** DM60
  N10 . . . .**44** DF53
  Barnet EN5 . . . .**27** CX41
  Dartford DA1 . . . .**128** FN87
Mar Rd, S.Ock. RM15 . . . .**91** FW70
Marrowells, Wey. KT13 . . . . .**135** BS104
Marryat Pl, SW19 . . . .**119** CY91
Marryat Rd, SW19 . . . .**119** CX92
  Enfield EN1 . . . .**30** DV35
Marryat Sq, SW6 . . . .**99** CY81
Marsala Rd, SE13 . . . .**103** EB84
Marsden Rd, N9 . . . .**46** DV47
  SE15 . . . .**102** DT83
Marsden St, NW5 . . . .**82** DG65
Marsden Way, Orp. BR6 . . . .**163** ET105
Marshall Cl, SW18
    off Allfarthing La **120** DC86
  Harrow HA1
    off Bowen Rd **61** CD59
  Hounslow TW4 . . . .**116** BZ85
  South Croydon CR2 . . . . . .**160** DU113
Marshall Dr, Hayes UB4 . . . . .**77** BT71
Marshall Path, SE28
    off Attlee Rd **88** EV73

Mar - May

Marshall Pl, Add. (New Haw)
KT15 . . . . .152 BJ109
Marshall Rd, E10 . . . . .67 EB62
N17 . . . . .46 DR83
Marshalls Cl, N11 . . . . .45 DH49
Epsom KT19 . . . . .156 CQ113
Marshalls Dr, Rom. RM1 . . .71 FE55
Marshall's Gro, SE18 . . . . .104 EL77
Marshalls Pl, SE16 . . . . . . .202 A7
Marshalls Rd, Rom. RM7 . . .71 FD56
Marshall's Rd, Sutt. SM1 . . .158 DB105
Marshall St, W1 . . . . .195 L9
Marshalsea Rd, SE1 . . . . . .201 J4
Marsham Cl, Chis. BR7 . . . .125 EP92
Marsham La, Ger.Cr. SL9 . . .56 AY58
Marsham Lo, Ger.Cr. SL9 . . .56 AY58
Marsham St, SW1 . . . . . . .199 N7
Marsham Way, Ger.Cr. SL9 . .56 AY57
Marsh Av, Epsom KT19 . . . .156 CS110
Mitcham CR4 . . . . .140 DG96
Marshbrook Cl, SE3 . . . . . .104 EK83
Marsh Cl, NW7 . . . . .43 CT48
Waltham Cross EN8 . . . . .15 DZ33
Marsh Ct, SW19 . . . . .140 DC95
Marshcroft Dr, Wal.Cr. (Chsht.)
EN8 . . . . .15 DY30
Marsh Dr, NW9 . . . . .63 CT58
Marshe Cl, Pot.B. EN6 . . . . .12 DD32
Marsh Fm Rd, Twick. TW2 . . .117 CF88
Marshfield, Slou. (Datchet)
SL3 . . . . .92 AW81
Marshfield St, E14 . . . . . . .204 D6
Marshfoot Rd, Grays RM16,
RM17 . . . . .110 GE78
Marshgate La, E15 . . . . . . .85 EB67
Marshgate Path, SE28
off Tom Cribb Rd 105 EQ77
Marshgate Sidings, E15
off Marshgate La 85 EB66
Marsh Grn Rd, Dag. RM10 . .88 FA67
Marsh Hill, E9 . . . . .67 DY64
Marsh La, E10 . . . . .67 EA61
N17 . . . . .46 DV52
NW7 . . . . .42 CS49
Addlestone KT15 . . . . . .152 BH105
Stanmore HA7 . . . . .41 CJ50
Marsh Rd, Pnr. HA5 . . . . . .60 BY56
Wembley HA0 . . . . .79 CK68
Marshside Cl, N9 . . . . .46 DW46
Marsh St, E14 . . . . .204 B9
Dartford DA1 . . . . .108 FN82
Marsh Ter, Orp. BR5
off Buttermere Rd 146 EX98
Marsh Vw, Grav. DA12
off Damigos Rd 131 GM88
Marsh Wall, E14 . . . . .203 P3
Marsh Way, Rain. RM13 . . . .89 FD70
Marsland Cl, SE17 . . . . . . .101 DP78
Marston, Epsom KT19 . . . . .156 CQ110
Marston Av, Chess. KT9 . . . .156 CL107
Dagenham RM10 . . . . . .70 FA61
Marston Cl, NW6
off Fairfax Rd 82 DC66
Dagenham RM10 . . . . . .70 FA62
Marston Ct, Walt. KT12
off St. Johns Dr 136 BW102
Marston Dr, Warl. CR6 . . . .177 DY118
Marston Ho, Grays RM17 . . .110 GA79
Marston Rd, Ilf. IG5 . . . . . .48 EL53
Teddington TW11 . . . . . .117 CH90
Woking GU21 . . . . .166 AV117
Marston Way, SE19 . . . . . .121 DP94
Marsworth Av, Pnr. HA5 . . . .40 BX53
Marsworth Cl, Hayes UB4 . . .78 BY71
Watford WD18 . . . . .23 BS44
Martaban Rd, N16 . . . . . . .66 DS61
Martello St, E8 . . . . .84 DV66
Martello Ter, E8 . . . . .84 DV66
Martell Rd, SE21 . . . . .122 DR90
Marten Rd, E17 . . . . .47 EA54
Martens Av, Bexh. DA7 . . . .107 FC84
Martens Cl, Bexh. DA7 . . . .107 FC84
Martham Cl, SE28 . . . . . . .88 EX73
Martha Rd, E4 . . . . .47 DZ51
E15 . . . . .86 EE65
Martha's Bldgs, EC1 . . . . . .197 K4
Martha St, E1 . . . . .84 DV72
Marthorne Cres, Har. HA3 . .41 CD54
Martina Ter, Chig. IG7
off Manford Way 49 ET50
Martin Bowes Rd, SE9 . . . .105 EM83
Martinbridge Trd Est, Enf.
EN1 . . . . .30 DU43
Martin Cl, N9 . . . . .47 DX46
South Croydon CR2 . . . .161 DX111
Uxbridge UB10
off Valley Rd 76 BL68
Warlingham CR6 . . . . . .176 DV116
Martin Cres, Croy. CR0 . . . .141 DN102
Martindale, SW14 . . . . . . .118 CQ85
Iver SL0 . . . . .75 BD70
Martindale Av, E16 . . . . . . .86 EG73
Orpington BR6 . . . . . . .164 EU106
Martindale Rd, SW12 . . . . .121 DH87
Hounslow TW4 . . . . .96 BY83
Woking GU21 . . . . .166 AT118
Martin Dene, Bexh. DA6 . . .126 EZ85
Martin Dr, Dart. (Stone) DA2 .128 FQ86
Northolt UB5 . . . . .60 BZ64
Rainham RM13 . . . . .89 FH70
Martineau Cl, Esher KT10 . .155 CD105
Martineau Ms, N5
off Martineau Rd 65 DP63
Martineau Rd, N5 . . . . .65 DP63
Martineau St, E1 . . . . .84 DW73
Martingale Cl, Sun. TW16 . .135 BU98
Martingales Cl, Rich. TW10 . .117 CK90
Martin Gdns, Dag. RM8 . . . .70 EW63
Martin Gro, Mord. SM4 . . . .140 DA97
Martini Dr, Enf. EN3
off Government Row 31 EA37
Martin La, EC4 . . . . .197 L10

Martin Ri, Bexh. DA6 . . . .126 EZ85
Martin Rd, Dag. RM8 . . . . .70 EW63
Dartford DA2 . . . . .128 FJ90
Slough SL1 . . . . .92 AS76
South Ockendon (Aveley)
RM15 . . . . .91 FR73
Martins Cl, Orp. BR5 . . . . .146 EW49
Radlett WD7 . . . . .25 CE36
West Wickham BR4 . . . .143 ED102
Martins Dr, Wal.Cr. (Chsht.)
EN8 . . . . .15 DY28
Martins Mt, Barn. EN5 . . . .28 DA42
Martin's Plain, Slou. (Stoke P.)
SL2 . . . . .74 AS69
Martins Shaw, Sev. (Chipstead)
TN13 . . . . .190 FC122
Martinstown Cl, Horn. RM11 .72 FN58
Martin St, SE28 . . . . .87 ES74
Martins Wk, N10 . . . . .44 DG53
Borehamwood WD6
off Siskin Cl 26 CN42
Martinsyde, Wok. GU22 . . .167 BC117
Martin Way, SW20 . . . . . . .139 CY97
Morden SM4 . . . . .139 CY97
Woking GU21 . . . . .166 AU118
Martlesham Cl, Horn. RM12 .72 FJ64
Martlet Gro, Nthlt. UB5
off Javelin Way 78 BX69
Martlett Ct, WC2 . . . . .196 A9
Martley Dr, Ilf. IG2 . . . . . . .69 EP57
Martock Cl, Har. HA3 . . . . .61 CG56
Marton Cl, SE6 . . . . .123 EA90
Marton Rd, N16 . . . . .66 DS61
MARTYR'S GREEN, Wok. . .169 BR120
Martyrs La, Wok. GU21 . . . .151 BP114
Martys Yd, NW3
off Hampstead High St . . .64 DD63
Marvell Av, Hayes UB4 . . . .77 BU71
Marvels Cl, SE12 . . . . .124 EH89
Marvels La, SE12 . . . . .124 EH89
Marville Rd, SW6 . . . . .99 CZ80
Marvin St, E8
off Sylvester Rd 84 DV65
Marwell, West. TN16 . . . . .189 EP126
Marwell Cl, Rom. RM1 . . . .71 FG57
West Wickham BR4
off Deer Pk Way 144 EF103
Marwood Cl, Kings L. WD4 . .6 BN29
Welling DA16 . . . . .106 EV83
Marwood Dr, NW7
off Bittacy Hill 43 CY52
Mary Adelaide Cl, SW15 . . .118 CS91
Mary Ann Gdns, SE8 . . . . .103 EA79
Maryatt Av, Har. HA2 . . . . .60 CB61
Marybank, SE18 . . . . .105 EM77
Mary Cl, Stan. HA7 . . . . . . .62 CM56
Mary Datchelor Cl, SE5 . . . .102 DR81
Marygold Wk, Amer. HP6 . . .20 AV39
Mary Grn, NW8 . . . . .82 DB67
Maryhill Cl, Ken. CR8 . . . . .176 DQ117
⇌ Maryland 86 EE65
Maryland Ind Est, E15
off Maryland Rd 67 ED64
Maryland Pk, E15 . . . . .68 EE64
Maryland Pt, E15
off Leytonstone Rd 86 EE65
Maryland Rd, E15 . . . . .67 ED64
N22 . . . . .45 DM51
Thornton Heath CR7 . . . .141 DP95
Maryland Sq, E15 . . . . .68 EE64
Marylands Rd, W9 . . . . . . .82 DA70
Maryland St, E15 . . . . .67 ED64
Maryland Wk, N1
off Popham St 84 DQ67
Mary Lawrenson Pl, SE3 . . .104 EF80
MARYLEBONE, NW1 . . . . .194 D8
⇌ Marylebone 194 D5
⊖ Marylebone 194 D5
Marylebone Flyover, NW1 . .194 A7
W2 . . . . .194 A7
Marylebone High St, W1 . . .194 G6
Marylebone La, W1 . . . . . .195 H9
Marylebone Ms, W1 . . . . . .195 H7
Marylebone Pas, W1 . . . . . .195 L8
Marylebone Rd, NW1 . . . . .194 C6
Marylebone St, W1 . . . . . .194 G7
Marylee Way, SE11 . . . . . .200 C10
Mary Macarthur Ho, W6
off Field Rd 99 CY79
Maryon Gro, SE7 . . . . .104 EL77
Maryon Ms, NW3
off South End Rd 64 DE63
Maryon Rd, SE7 . . . . .104 EL77
SE18 . . . . .104 EL77
Mary Peters Dr, Grnf. UB6 . .61 CD64
Mary Pl, W11 . . . . .81 CY73
Mary Rose Cl, Grays (Chaff.Hun.)
RM16 . . . . .109 FW77
Hampton TW12
off Ashley Rd 136 CA95
Mary Rose Mall, E6
off Frobisher Rd 87 EN71
Maryrose Way, N20 . . . . . . .44 DD46
Mary Seacole Cl, E8
off Clarissa St 84 DT67
Maryside, Slou. SL3 . . . . . .92 AY75
Mary's Ter, Twick. TW1 . . . .117 CG87
Mary St, E16 off Barking Rd . .86 EF71
N1 . . . . .84 DQ67
Mary Ter, NW1 . . . . .83 DH67
Masbro Rd, W14 . . . . .99 CX76
Mascalls Ct, SE7
off Victoria Way 104 EJ79
Mascalls Gdns, Brwd. CM14 .54 FT49
Mascalls La, Brwd. CM14 . . .54 FT49
Mascalls Rd, SE7 . . . . .104 EJ79
Mascotte Rd, SW15 . . . . . .99 CX84
Mascotts Cl, NW2 . . . . . . .63 CV62
Masefield Av, Borwd. WD6 . .26 CP43
Southall UB1 . . . . .78 CA73
Stanmore HA7 . . . . .41 CF50
Masefield Cl, Erith DA8 . . . .107 FF81

Masefield Cl, Rom. RM3 . . .52 FJ53
Masefield Ct, Brwd. CM14 . .54 FW49
Masefield Cres, N14 . . . . . .29 DJ44
Romford RM3 . . . . .52 FJ53
Masefield Dr, Upmin. RM14 . .72 FQ59
Masefield Gdns, E6 . . . . . . .87 EN70
Masefield La, Hayes UB4 . . .77 BV70
Masefield Rd, Dart. DA1 . . .128 FP85
Gravesend (Nthflt.) DA11 . .130 GD90
Grays RM16 . . . . .110 GE75
Hampton TW12
off Wordsworth Rd 116 BZ91
Masefield Vw, Orp. BR6 . . .145 EQ104
Masefield Way, Stai. TW19 . .114 BM88
Masham Ho, Erith DA18
off Kale Rd 106 EX75
Mashie Rd, W3 . . . . .80 CS72
Mashiters Hill, Rom. RM1 . . .51 FD53
Mashiters Wk, Rom. RM1 . . .71 FE55
Maskall Cl, SW2 . . . . .121 DN88
Maskani Wk, SW16
off Bates Cres 121 DJ94
Maskell Rd, SW17 . . . . . . .120 DC90
Maskelyne Cl, SW11 . . . . . .100 DE81
Mason Bradbear Ct, N1
off St. Paul's Rd 84 DR65
Mason Cl, E16 . . . . .86 EG73
SE16 . . . . .202 C10
SW20 . . . . .139 CX95
Bexleyheath DA7 . . . . . .107 FB83
Borehamwood WD6 . . . . .26 CQ40
Hampton TW12 . . . . . . .136 BZ95
Mason Dr, Rom. (Harold Wd.) RM3
off Whitmore Av 52 FL54
Masonic Hall Rd, Cher. KT16 .133 BF100
Mason Rd, Sutt. SM1
off Manor Pl 158 DB106
Woodford Green IG8 . . . .48 EE49
Masons Arms Ms, W1 . . . . .195 J9
Masons Av, EC2 . . . . .197 K8
Croydon CR0 . . . . .142 DQ104
Harrow HA3 . . . . .61 CF56
Masons Ct, Wem. HA9
off Mayfields 62 CN61
Masons Grn La, W3 . . . . . .80 CN71
Masons Hill, SE18 . . . . . . .105 EP77
Bromley BR1, BR2 . . . . .144 EG97
Mason's Pl, EC1 . . . . .196 G2
Masons Pl, Mitch. CR4 . . . .140 DF95
Masons Pl, Enf. EN1 . . . . . .30 DW36
Mason St, SE17 . . . . .201 L8
Mason's Yd, SW1 . . . . .199 L2
SW19
off High St Wimbledon . . .119 CX92
Mason Way, Wal.Abb. EN9 . .16 EF34
Massey Cl, N11 off Grove Rd . .45 DH50
Massey Ct, E6 . . . . .86 EJ67
Massie Rd, E8 off Graham Rd . .84 DU65
Massinger St, SE17 . . . . . .201 M9
Massingberd Way, SW17 . . .121 DH91
Massingham St, E1 . . . . . . .85 DX70
Masson Av, Ruis. HA4 . . . . .78 BW65
Master Cl, Oxt. RH8
off Church La 188 EE129
Master Gunner Pl, SE18 . . .104 EL80
Masterman Ho, SE5 . . . . . .102 DR80
Masterman Rd, E6 . . . . . . .86 EL69
Masters Cl, SW16
off Blegborough Rd 121 DJ93
Masters Dr, SE16 . . . . .102 DV78
Masters St, E1 . . . . .85 DX71
Masthead Cl, Dart. DA2 . . . .108 FQ84
Mast Ho Ter, E14 . . . . .204 A9
Mast Leisure Pk, SE16 . . . .203 J7
Mastmaker Rd, E14 . . . . . .204 A4
Maswell Pk Cres, Houns.
TW3 . . . . .116 CC85
Maswell Pk Rd, Houns. TW3 .116 CB85
Matcham Rd, E11 . . . . .68 EE62
Matchless Dr, SE18 . . . . . .105 EN80
Matfield Cl, Brom. BR2 . . . .144 EG99
Matfield Rd, Belv. DA17 . . .106 FA79
Matham Gro, SE22 . . . . . .102 DT84
Matham Rd, E.Mol. KT8 . . .137 CD99
Matheson Rd, W14 . . . . . . .99 CZ77
Mathews Av, E6 . . . . .87 EN68
Mathews Pk Av, E15 . . . . . .86 EF65
Mathias Cl, Epsom KT18 . . .156 CQ113
Mathisen Way, Slou. (Colnbr.)
SL3 . . . . .93 BE81
Matilda Cl, SE19
off Elizabeth Way 122 DR94
Matilda St, N1 . . . . .83 DM67
Matlock Cl, SE24 . . . . .102 DQ84
Barnet EN5 . . . . .27 CX43
Matlock Ct, SE5
off Denmark Hill Est 102 DR84
Matlock Cres, Sutt. SM3 . . .157 CY105
Watford WD19 . . . . .40 BW48
Matlock Gdns, Horn. RM12 . .72 FL62
Sutton SM3 . . . . .157 CY105
Matlock Pl, Sutt. SM3 . . . . .157 CY105
Matlock Rd, E10 . . . . .67 EC58
Caterham CR3 . . . . . . .176 DS121
Matlock St, E14 . . . . .85 DY71
Matlock Way, N.Mal. KT3 . . .138 CR95
Matrimony Pl, SW8 . . . . . .101 DJ82
Matson Ct, Wdf.Grn. IG8
off The Bridle Path 48 EE52
Matthew Arnold Cl, Cob.
KT11 . . . . .153 BU114
Staines TW18
off Elizabeth Av 114 BJ93
Matthew Cl, W10 . . . . .81 CX70
Matthew Ct, Mitch. CR4 . . .141 DK99
Matthew Parker St, SW1 . . .199 N5
Matthews Ct, Rom. (Hav.at.Bow.)
RM3 off Oak Rd 52 FM53
Matthews Gdns, Croy.
(New Adgtn.) CR0 . . . . .161 ED111
Matthews Rd, Grnf. UB6 . . .61 CD64
Matthews St, SW11 . . . . . .100 DF82
Matthews Yd, WC2 . . . . . . .195 P9
Matthias Rd, N16 . . . . .66 DR64
Mattingley Way, SE15
off Daniel Gdns 102 DT80
Mattison Rd, N4 . . . . .65 DN58

Mattock La, W5 . . . . .79 CH74
W13 . . . . .79 CH74
Maud Cashmore Way, SE18 .105 EM76
Maude Cres, Wat. WD24 . . .23 BV37
Maude Rd, E17 . . . . .67 DY57
SE5 . . . . .102 DS81
Swanley BR8 . . . . .127 FG93
Maudesville Cotts, W7
off The Broadway 79 CE74
Maude Ter, E17 . . . . .67 DY56
Maud Gdns, E13 . . . . .86 EF67
Barking IG11 . . . . .87 ET68
Maudlin's Grn, E1 . . . . . . .202 B2
Maud Rd, E10 . . . . .67 EC62
E13 . . . . .86 EF68
Maudslay Rd, SE9 . . . . . . .105 EM83
⊞ Maudsley Hosp, The, SE5 .102 DR82
Maudsley Ho, Brent. TW8
off Green Dragon La 98 CL78
Maud St, E16 . . . . .86 EF71
Maud Wilkes Cl, NW5 . . . . .65 DJ64
Mauleverer Rd, SW2 . . . . .121 DL85
Maunder Rd, W7 . . . . .79 CF74
Maunsel St, SW1 . . . . .199 M8
Maurice Av, N22 . . . . .45 DP54
Caterham CR3 . . . . . . .176 DR122
Maurice Brown Cl, NW7 . . .43 CX50
Maurice St, W12 . . . . .81 CV72
Maurice Wk, NW11 . . . . . . .64 DC56
Maurier Cl, Nthlt. UB5 . . . . .78 BW67
Mauritius Rd, SE10 . . . . . .205 J9
Maury Rd, N16 . . . . .66 DU61
Mavelstone Cl, Brom. BR1 . .144 EL95
Mavelstone Rd, Brom. BR1 . .144 EL95
Maverton Rd, E3 . . . . .85 EA67
Mavis Av, Epsom KT19 . . . .156 CS106
Mavis Cl, Epsom KT19 . . . .156 CS106
Mavis Gro, Horn. RM12 . . . .72 FL61
Mavis Wk, E6 . . . . .86 EL71
Mawbey Est, SE1 . . . . .102 DU78
Mawbey Pl, SE1 . . . . .102 DT78
Mawbey Rd, SE1
off Old Kent Rd 102 DT78
Chertsey (Ott.) KT16 . . . .151 BD107
Mawbey St, SW8 . . . . .101 DL80
Mawney Cl, Rom. RM7 . . . .51 FB54
Mawney Rd, Rom. RM7 . . . .71 FC56
Mawson Cl, SW20 . . . . . . .139 CY96
Mawson La, W4
off Great W Rd 99 CT79
Maxey Gdns, Dag. RM9 . . . .70 EY63
Maxey Rd, SE18 . . . . .105 EQ77
Dagenham RM9 . . . . . . .70 EY63
Maxfield Cl, N20 . . . . .44 DC45
Maxilla Gdns, W10
off Cambridge Gdns 81 CX72
Maxilla Wk, W10
off Kingsdown Cl 81 CX72
Maximfeldt Rd, Erith DA8 . .107 FE78
Maxim Rd, N21 . . . . .29 DN44
Dartford DA1 . . . . .127 FE85
Erith DA8 . . . . .107 FE77
Maxted Pk, Har. HA1 . . . . .61 CE59
Maxted Rd, SE15 . . . . .102 DT83
Maxwell Cl, Croy. CR0 . . . .141 DL102
Hayes UB3 . . . . .77 BU73
Rickmansworth (Mill End)
WD3 . . . . .38 BG47
Maxwell Dr, W.Byf. KT14 . . .152 BJ111
Maxwell Gdns, Orp. BR6 . . .145 ET104
Maxwell Ri, Wat. WD19 . . . .40 BY45
Maxwell Rd, SW6 . . . . .100 DB80
Ashford TW15 . . . . .115 BQ93
Borehamwood WD6 . . . . .26 CP41
Northwood HA6 . . . . . . .39 BR52
Welling DA16 . . . . .106 EU83
West Drayton UB7 . . . . .94 BM77
Maxwelton Av, NW7 . . . . . .42 CR50
Maxwelton Cl, NW7 . . . . . .42 CR50
Maya Angelou Ct, E4
off Bailey Cl 47 EC49
Maya Cl, SE15 . . . . .102 DV82
Mayall Rd, SE24 . . . . .121 DP85
Maya Rd, N2 . . . . .64 DC56
May Av, Grav. (Nthflt.) DA11
off Lansdown Pl 131 GF88
Orpington BR5 . . . . . . .146 EV99
May Av Ind Est, Grav. DA11
off Lansdown Pl 131 GF88
Maybank Av, E18 . . . . .48 EH54
Hornchurch RM12 . . . . . .71 FH64
Wembley HA0 . . . . .61 CF64
Maybank Gdns, Pnr. HA5 . . .59 BU57
Maybank Lo, Horn. RM12 . . .72 FJ64
Maybank Rd, E18 . . . . .48 EH53
May Bate Av, Kings.T. KT2 . .137 CK95
Maybells Commercial Est, Bark.
IG11 . . . . .88 EX68
Mayberry Pl, Surb. KT5 . . . .138 CM101
Maybourne Cl, SE26 . . . . .122 DV92
Maybourne Ri, Wok. GU22 . .166 AX124
Maybrick Rd, Horn. RM11 . .72 FJ58
Maybrook Meadow Est, Bark.
IG11 . . . . .88 EU66
MAYBURY, Wok. 167 BB117
Maybury Av, Dart. DA2 . . . .128 FQ88
Waltham Cross (Chsht.)
EN8 . . . . .14 DW28
Maybury Cl, Enf. EN1 . . . . .30 DV38
Loughton IG10 . . . . .33 EP42
Orpington BR5 . . . . . . .145 EP99
Tadworth KT20
off Ballards Grn 173 CY119
Maybury Gdns, NW10 . . . . .81 CV65
Maybury Hill, Wok. GU22 . . .167 BB116
Maybury Ms, N6 . . . . .65 DJ59
Maybury Rd, E13 . . . . .86 EJ70
Barking IG11 . . . . .87 ET68
Woking GU21 . . . . .167 AZ117
Maybury St, SW17 . . . . . . .120 DE92
Maybush Rd, Horn. RM11 . .72 FL59
Maychurch Cl, Stan. HA7 . . .41 CK52
May Cl, Chess. KT9 . . . . . .156 CM107
Maycock Gro, Nthwd. HA6 . .39 BT51

May Cotts, Wat. WD18 . . . .24 BW43
May Ct, SW19 . . . . .140 DC100
Grays RM17 off Medlar Rd .110 GE79
Maycroft, Pnr. HA5 . . . . . . .39 BV54
Maycroft Av, Grays RM17 . . .110 GD78
Maycroft Gdns, Grays RM17 .110 GD78
Maycroft Rd, Wal.Cr. (Chsht.)
EN7 . . . . .14 DS26
Maycross Av, Mord. SM4 . . .139 CZ97
⊞ Mayday Hosp, Th.Hth.
CR7 . . . . .141 DP100
Mayday Rd, Th.Hth. CR7 . . .141 DP100
Maydwell Lo, Borwd. WD6 . .26 CM40
Mayell Cl, Lthd. KT22 . . . . .171 CJ123
Mayerne Rd, SE9 . . . . .124 EK85
Mayer Rd, Wal.Abb. EN9
off Deer Pk Way 31 EB36
Mayesbrook Rd, Bark. IG11 . .87 ET67
Dagenham RM8 . . . . . . .70 EU62
Ilford IG3 . . . . .70 EU62
Mayes Cl, Swan. BR8 . . . . .147 FG98
Warlingham CR6 . . . . . .177 DX118
Mayesford Rd, Rom. RM6 . . .70 EW59
Mayes Rd, N22 . . . . .45 DN54
Mayeswood Rd, SE12 . . . . .124 EJ90
MAYFAIR, W1 . . . . .199 H1
Mayfair Av, Bexh. DA7 . . . .106 EX81
Ilford IG1 . . . . .69 EM61
Romford RM6 . . . . .70 EX58
Twickenham TW2 . . . . . .116 CC87
Worcester Park KT4 . . . .139 CU102
Mayfair Cl, Beck. BR3 . . . . .143 EB95
Surbiton KT6 . . . . .138 CL102
Mayfair Gdns, N17 . . . . . . .46 DR51
Woodford Green IG8 . . . .48 EG52
Mayfair Ms, NW1
off Regents Pk Rd 82 DF66
Mayfair Pl, W1 . . . . .199 J2
Mayfair Rd, Dart. DA1 . . . . .128 FK85
Mayfair Ter, N14 . . . . .45 DK47
Mayfare, Rick. (Crox.Grn.)
WD3 . . . . .23 BR43
Mayfield, Bexh. DA7 . . . . . .106 EZ83
Leatherhead KT22 . . . . .171 CJ121
Waltham Abbey EN9 . . . .15 ED34
Mayfield Av, N12 . . . . .44 DC49
N14 . . . . .45 DK47
W4 . . . . .98 CS77
W13 . . . . .97 CH76
Addlestone (New Haw)
KT15 . . . . .152 BH110
Gerrards Cross SL9 . . . . .56 AX56
Harrow HA3 . . . . .61 CH57
Orpington BR6 . . . . . . .145 ET102
Woodford Green IG8 . . . .48 EG52
Mayfield Cl, E8 off Forest Rd .84 DT65
SW4 . . . . .121 DK85
Addlestone (New Haw)
KT15 . . . . .152 BJ110
Ashford TW15 . . . . .115 BP93
Thames Ditton KT7 . . . . .137 CH102
Uxbridge UB10 . . . . . . .77 BP69
Walton-on-Thames KT12 . .153 BU105
Mayfield Cres, N9 . . . . .30 DV44
Thornton Heath CR7 . . . .141 DM98
Mayfield Dr, Pnr. HA5 . . . . .60 BZ56
Mayfield Gdns, NW4 . . . . . .63 CX58
W7 . . . . .79 CD72
Brentwood CM14 . . . . . .54 FV46
Staines TW18 . . . . .113 BF93
Walton-on-Thames KT12 . .153 BU105
Mayfield Mans, SW15
off West Hill 119 CX87
Mayfield Pk, West Dr. UB7 . .94 BJ76
Mayfield Rd, E4 . . . . .47 EC47
E8 . . . . .84 DT66
E13 . . . . .86 EF70
E17 . . . . .47 DY54
N8 . . . . .65 DM58
SW19 . . . . .139 CZ95
W3 . . . . .80 CP73
W12 . . . . .98 CS75
Belvedere DA17 . . . . . .107 FC77
Bromley BR1 . . . . .144 EL99
Dagenham RM8 . . . . . . .70 EW60
Enfield EN3 . . . . .31 DX40
Gravesend DA11 . . . . . .131 GF87
South Croydon CR2 . . . .160 DR109
Sutton SM2 . . . . .158 DD107
Thornton Heath CR7 . . . .141 DM98
Walton-on-Thames KT12 . .153 BU105
Weybridge KT13 . . . . . .152 BM106
Mayfields, Grays RM16 . . . .110 GC75
Swanscombe DA10
off Madden Cl 130 FY86
Wembley HA9 . . . . .62 CN61
Mayfields Cl, Wem. HA9 . . . .62 CN61
Mayflower Cl, SE16 . . . . . .203 J8
Ruislip HA4
off Leaholme Way 59 BQ58
South Ockendon RM15 . . .91 FW70
Mayflower Ct, SE16
off St. Marychurch St 102 DW75
Mayflower Rd, SW9 . . . . . .101 DL83
Grays (Chaff.Hun.) RM16 . .109 FW78
St. Albans (Park St.) AL2 . .8 CB27
Mayflower St, SE16 . . . . . .202 F5
May Fly Cl, Orp. BR5 . . . . .146 EX98
Pinner HA5 . . . . .60 BW59
Mayfly Gdns, Nthlt. UB5
off Ruislip Rd 78 BX69
MAYFORD, Wok. 166 AW122
Mayford, SW12 . . . . .120 DF87
Beckenham BR3 . . . . . .143 DX59
Woking GU22 . . . . .166 AX122
Mayford Grn, Wok. GU22
off Smarts Heath Rd . . .166 AW122
Mayford Rd, SW12 . . . . . . .120 DF87
May Gdns, Borwd. (Elstree)
WD6 . . . . .25 CK44
Wembley HA0 . . . . .79 CJ68
Maygood Cl, Uxb. UB8 . . . .76 BK71
Maygoods Cl, Uxb. UB8
off Worcester Rd 76 BK71
Maygoods Grn, Uxb. UB8
off Worcester Rd 76 BK71
Maygoods La, Uxb. UB8 . . . .76 BK71
Maygood St, N1 . . . . .83 DM68

★ Place of interest ⇌ Railway station ⊖ London Underground station [DLR] Docklands Light Railway station ⬦ Tramlink station ⊞ Hospital

Maygoods Vw, Uxb. UB8
 off Benbow Waye 76 BJ71
Maygreen Cres, Horn. RM11 .71 FG59
Maygrove Rd, NW6 ......81 CZ65
Mayhew Cl, E4 ......47 EA48
Mayhill Rd, SE7 ......104 EH79
 Barnet EN5 ......27 CY44
Mayhurst Av, Wok. GU22 .167 BC116
Mayhurst Cl, Wok. GU22 .167 BC116
Mayhurst Cres, Wok. GU22 .167 BC116
Maylands Av, Horn. RM12 .71 FH63
Maylands Dr, Sid. DA14 ..126 EX90
 Uxbridge UB8 ......76 BK65
Maylands Rd, Wat. WD19 .40 BW49
Maylands Way, Rom. RM3 .52 FQ51
Maynard Cl, N15
 off Brunswick Rd 66 DS56
 SW6 off Cambria St 100 DB83
 Erith DA8 ......107 FF80
Maynard Ct, Wal.Abb. EN9 .16 EF34
Maynard Path, E17 ......67 EC57
Maynard Pl, Pot.B. EN6 ..13 DL29
Maynard Rd, E17 ......67 EC57
Maynards, Horn. RM11 ..72 FL59
Maynards Quay, E1 ......202 F1
Maynooth Gdns, Cars. SM5 .140 DF101
Mayo Cl, Wal.Cr. (Chsht.)
 EN8 ......14 DW28
Mayola Rd, E5 ......66 DW63
Mayo Rd, NW10 ......80 CS65
 Croydon CR0 ......142 DR99
 Walton-on-Thames KT12 .135 BT101
Mayor's La, Dart. DA2 ....128 FJ92
Mayow Rd, SE23 ......123 DX90
 SE26 ......123 DX91
Mayplace Av, Dart. DA1 ..107 FG84
Mayplace Cl, Bexh. DA7 ..107 FB83
Mayplace La, SE18 ......105 EP80
Mayplace Rd E, Bexh. DA7 .107 FB83
 Dartford DA1 ......107 FC83
Mayplace Rd W, Bexh. DA7 .107 FA84
MAYPOLE, Orp. 164 EZ106
Maypole Cres, Erith DA8 ..108 FK79
 Ilford IG6 ......49 ER52
Maypole Dr, Chig. IG7 ....50 EU48
Maypole Rd, Grav. DA12 ..131 GM88
 Orpington BR6 ......164 EZ106
May Rd, E4 ......47 EA51
 E13 ......86 EG68
 Dartford (Hawley) DA2 ..128 FM91
 Twickenham TW2 ......117 CE88
Mayroyd Av, Surb. KT6 ....138 CN103
Mays Cl, Wey. KT13 ......152 BM110
Mays Ct, WC2 ......199 P1
Maysfield Rd, Wok. (Send)
 GU23 ......167 BD123
MAY'S GREEN, Cob. 169 BT120
Mays Gro, Wok. (Send)
 GU23 ......167 BD123
Mays Hill Rd, Brom. BR2 ..144 EE96
Mays La, E4 ......47 ED47
 Barnet EN5 ......27 CY43
Maysoule Rd, SW11 ......100 DD84
Mays Rd, Tedd. TW11 ....117 CD92
Mayston Ms, SE10
 off Westcombe Hill 104 EG78
May St, W14
 off North End Rd 99 CZ78
Mayswood Rd, Dag. RM10 .89 FC65
Maythorne Cl, Wat. WD18 .23 BS42
Mayton St, N7 ......65 DM62
Maytree Cl, Edg. HA8 ....42 CQ48
 Rainham RM13 ......89 FE68
Maytree Cres, Wat. WD24 .23 BT35
Maytree Gdns, W5
 off South Ealing Rd 97 CK75
May Tree La, Stan. HA7 ..41 CF52
Maytrees, Rad. WD7 ......25 CG37
Maytree Wk, SW2 ......121 DN89
Mayville Est, N16
 off King Henry St 66 DS64
Mayville Rd, E11 ......68 EE61
 Ilford IG1 ......69 EP64
May Wk, E13 ......86 EH68
Maywater Cl, S.Croy. CR2 .160 DR111
Maywin Dr, Horn. RM11 ..72 FM60
Maywood Cl, Beck. BR3 ..123 EB94
⇌ Maze Hill 104 EE79
Maze Hill, SE3 ......104 EE79
 SE10 ......104 EE79
Mazenod Av, NW6 ......82 DA66
Maze Rd, Rich. TW9 ......98 CN80
Mead, The, N2 ......44 DC54
 W13 ......79 CH71
 Ashtead KT21 ......172 CL119
 Beckenham BR3 ......143 EC95
 Uxbridge UB10 ......58 BN61
 Wallington SM6 ......159 DK107
 Waltham Cross (Chsht.)
 EN8 ......14 DW29
 Watford WD19 ......40 BY48
 West Wickham BR4 ......143 ED102
Mead Av, Slou. SL3 ......93 BB75
Mead Cl, Egh. TW20 ......113 BB93
 Grays RM16 ......110 GB75
 Harrow HA3 ......41 CD53
 Loughton IG10 ......33 EQ40
 Redhill RH1 ......184 DG131
 Romford RM2 ......51 FG54
 Slough SL3 ......93 BB75
 Swanley BR8 ......147 FG95
 Uxbridge (Denh.) UB9 ..58 BG61
Mead Ct, NW9 ......62 CQ57
 Egham TW20
 off Holbrook Meadow ..113 BC93
 Waltham Abbey EN9 ....15 EB34
 Woking (Knap.) GU21 ..166 AS116
Mead Cres, E4 ......47 EC49
 Dartford DA1
 off Beech Rd 128 FJ85
 Sutton SM1 ......158 DE105
Meadcroft Rd, SE11 ......101 DP79
Meade Cl, W4 ......98 CN79
Meade Ct, Tad. KT20 ......173 CU124
Mead End, Ashtd. KT21 ..172 CM116
Meades, The, Wey. KT13 ..153 BQ107
Meadfield, Edg. HA8 ......42 CP47

Mead Fld, Har. HA2
 off Kings Rd 60 BZ62
Meadfield Av, Slou. SL3 ..93 BA76
Meadfield Grn, Edg. HA8 ..42 CP47
Meadfield Rd, Slou. SL3 ..93 BA76
Meadfoot Rd, SW16 ......121 DJ94
Meadgate Av, Wdf.Grn. IG8 .48 EL50
Mead Gro, Rom. RM6 ......70 EY55
Mead Ho La, Hayes UB4 ..77 BR70
Meadhurst Rd, Cher. KT16 .134 BH102
Meadlands Dr, Rich. TW10 .117 CK89
Mead La, Cher. KT16 ......134 BH102
Mead La Caravan Pk, Cher.
 KT16 ......134 BJ102
Meadow, The, Chis. BR7 ..125 EQ93
Meadow Av, Croy. CR0 ....143 DX99
Meadow Bk, N21 ......29 DM44
Meadowbank, NW3 ......82 DF66
 SE3 ......104 EF83
 Kings Langley WD4 ......6 BN30
 Surbiton KT5 ......138 CM100
 Watford WD19 ......40 BW45
Meadowbank Cl, SW6 ......99 CW80
Meadowbank Gdns, Houns.
 TW5 ......95 BU82
Meadowbank Rd, NW9 ....62 CR59
Meadowbanks, Barn. EN5 .27 CT43
Meadowbrook, Oxt. RH8 ..187 EC130
Meadowbrook Cl, Slou. (Colnbr.)
 SL3 ......93 BF82
Meadow Cl, E4
 off Mount Echo Av 47 EB46
 E9 ......67 DZ64
 SE6 ......123 EA82
 SW20 ......139 CW98
 Barnet EN5 ......27 CZ44
 Bexleyheath DA6 ......126 EZ85
 Chislehurst BR7 ......125 EP92
 Enfield EN3 ......31 DY38
 Esher KT10 ......137 CF104
 Hounslow TW4 ......116 CA86
 Northolt UB5 ......78 CA68
 Purley CR8 ......159 DK113
 Richmond TW10 ......118 CL88
 Ruislip HA4 ......59 BS59
 St. Albans (Brick.Wd.) AL2 ..8 CA29
 St. Albans (Lon.Col.) AL2 ..9 CK27
 Sevenoaks TN13 ......190 FG123
 Sutton SM1
 off Aultone Way 140 DB103
 Walton-on-Thames KT12 .154 BZ105
 Windsor (Old Wind.) SL4 .112 AV86
Meadow Ct, Epsom KT18 .156 CQ113
 Redhill RH1 ......185 DK130
 Staines TW18 ......113 BE90
Meadowcourt Rd, SE3 ....104 EF84
Meadowcroft, Brom. BR1 ..145 EM97
 Bushey WD23 ......24 CB44
 Gerrards Cross (Chal.St.P.)
 SL9 ......36 AX54
Meadowcroft Rd, N13 ......45 DN47
Meadowcross, Wal.Abb. EN9 .16 EE34
Meadow Dr, N10 ......65 DH55
 NW4 ......43 CW54
 Amersham HP6 ......20 AS37
 Woking (Ripley) GU23 ..167 BF123
Meadow Gdns, Edg. HA8 ..42 CP51
 Staines TW18 ......113 BD92
Meadow Garth, NW10 ....80 CQ65
Meadow Hill, Couls. CR5 ..159 DJ113
 New Malden KT3 ......138 CS100
 Purley CR8 ......159 DJ113
Meadowlands, Cob. KT11 ..153 BU113
 Hornchurch RM11 ......72 FL59
 Oxted RH8 ......188 EG134
Meadowlands Pk, Add. KT15 .134 BL104
Meadow La, SE12 ......124 EH90
 Leatherhead (Fetch.) KT22 .170 CC121
Meadowlea Cl, West Dr. UB7 .94 BK79
Meadow Ms, SW8 ......101 DM79
Meadow Pl, SW8 ......101 DL80
 W4 off Edensor Rd 98 CS80
Meadow Ri, Couls. CR5 ..159 DK113
Meadow Rd, SW8 ......101 DM79
 SW19 ......120 DC94
 Ashford TW15 ......115 BR92
 Ashtead KT21 ......172 CL117
 Barking IG11 ......87 ET66
 Borehamwood WD6 ....26 CP40
 Bromley BR2 ......144 EE95
 Bushey WD23 ......24 CB43
 Dagenham RM9 ......88 EZ65
 Epping CM16 ......17 ET29
 Esher (Clay.) KT10 ......155 CE107
 Feltham TW13 ......116 BY89
 Gravesend DA11 ......131 GG85
 Loughton IG10 ......32 EL43
 Pinner HA5 ......60 BX57
 Romford RM7 ......71 FC60
 Slough SL3 ......92 AY77
 Southall UB1 ......78 BZ73
 Sutton SM1 ......158 DE106
 Virginia Water GU25 ....132 AS99
 Watford WD25 ......7 BU34
Meadow Row, SE1 ......201 J7
Meadows, The, Amer. HP7 .20 AS39
 Orpington BR6 ......164 EW107
 Sevenoaks (Halst.) TN14 .164 EZ113
 Warlingham CR6 ......177 DX117
Meadows Cl, E10 ......67 EA61
Meadows End, Sun. TW16 .135 BU95
Meadowside, SE9 ......104 EJ84
 Beaconsfield (Jordans) HP9 .36 AT52
 Dartford DA1 ......128 FK88
 Leatherhead (Bkhm.)
 KT23 ......170 CA123
 Walton-on-Thames KT12 .136 BW103
Meadow Side, Wat. WD25 ..7 BV31
Meadowside Rd, Sutt. SM2 .157 CY109
 Upminster RM14 ......72 FQ64
Meadows Leigh Cl, Wey.
 KT13 ......135 BQ104
Meadow Stile, Croy. CR0
 off High St 142 DQ104
Meadowsweet Cl, E16 ....86 EK71
 off Monarch Dr 86 EK71
Meadow Vw, Ch.St.G. HP8 .36 AU48

Meadow Vw, Har. HA1 ....61 CE60
Meadowview, Orp. BR5 ..146 EW97
Meadow Vw, Sid. DA15 ..126 EV87
 Staines TW19 ......113 BF85
Meadowview Rd, SE6 ....123 DZ92
 Bexley DA5 ......126 EY86
 Epsom KT19 ......156 CS109
Meadow Vw Rd, Hayes UB4 .77 BQ70
 Thornton Heath CR7 ....141 DP99
Meadow Wk, E18 ......68 EG56
 Dagenham RM9 ......88 EZ65
 Dartford DA2 ......128 FJ91
 Epsom KT17, KT19 ......156 CS107
 Tadworth KT20 ......173 CV124
 Wallington SM6 ......141 DH104
Meadow Way, NW9 ......62 CR57
 Abbots Langley (Bedmond)
 WD5 ......7 BT27
 Addlestone KT15 ......152 BH105
 Chessington KT9 ......156 CL106
 Chigwell IG7 ......49 EQ48
 Dartford DA2 ......128 FQ87
 Kings Langley WD4 ......6 BN30
 Leatherhead (Bkhm.)
 KT23 ......170 CB123
 Orpington BR6 ......145 EN104
 Potters Bar EN6 ......12 DA34
 Rickmansworth WD3 ....38 BJ45
 Ruislip HA4 ......59 BV58
 Tadworth KT20 ......173 CV118
 Upminster RM14 ......72 FQ62
 Wembley HA9 ......61 CK63
 Windsor (Old Wind.) SL4 .112 AV86
Meadow Way, The, Har. HA3 .41 CE53
Meadow Waye, Houns. TW5 .96 BY79
Mead Path, SW17 ......120 DC92
Mead Pl, E9 ......84 DW65
 Croydon CR0 ......141 DP102
 Rickmansworth WD3 ....38 BH46
Mead Plat, NW10 ......80 CQ65
Mead Rd, Cat. CR3 ......176 DT123
 Chislehurst BR7 ......125 EQ93
 Dartford DA1 ......128 FK88
 Edgware HA8 ......42 CN51
 Gravesend DA11 ......131 GH88
 Radlett (Shenley) WD7 ..10 CM33
 Richmond TW10 ......117 CJ90
 Uxbridge UB8 ......76 BK66
 Walton-on-Thames KT12 .154 BY105
Mead Row, SE1 ......200 D6
Meads, The, Edg. HA8 ....42 CR51
 St. Albans (Brick.Wd.) AL2 ..8 BZ30
 Sutton SM3 ......139 CY104
 Upminster RM14 ......73 FS61
 Uxbridge UB8 ......76 BL70
Meads La, Ilf. IG3 ......69 ES59
Meads Rd, N22 ......45 DP54
 Enfield EN3 ......31 DY39
Meadsway, Brwd. CM13 ..53 FV51
Mead Ter, Wem. HA9
 off Meadow Way 61 CK63
Meadvale Rd, W5 ......79 CH70
 Croydon CR0 ......142 DT101
Mead Wk, Slou. SL3 ......93 BB75
Meadway, N14 ......45 DK47
 NW11 ......64 DB58
 SW20 ......139 CW98
 Ashford TW15 ......114 BN91
 Barnet EN5 ......28 DA42
 Beckenham BR3 ......143 EC95
Mead Way, Brom. BR2 ....144 EF100
 Bushey WD23 ......24 BY40
 Coulsdon CR5 ......175 DL118
 Croydon CR0 ......143 DY103
Meadway, Enf. EN3 ......30 DW36
 Epsom KT19 ......156 CQ112
 Esher KT10 ......154 CB109
 Grays RM17 ......110 GD77
 Ilford IG3 ......69 ES63
 Leatherhead (Oxshott)
 KT22 ......155 CD114
 Romford RM2 ......51 FG54
 Ruislip HA4 ......59 BR58
 Sevenoaks (Halst.) TN14 .164 EZ113
 Staines TW18 ......114 BG94
 Surbiton KT5 ......138 CQ102
 Twickenham TW2 ......117 CD88
 Warlingham CR6 ......176 DW115
 Woodford Green IG8 ....48 EJ50
Meadway, The, SE3
 off Heath La 103 ED82
 Buckhurst Hill IG9 ......48 EK46
 Loughton IG10 ......33 EM44
 Orpington BR6 ......164 EV106
 Potters Bar (Cuffley) EN6 .13 DM28
 Sevenoaks TN13 ......190 FF122
Meadway Cl, NW11 ......64 DB58
 Barnet EN5 ......28 DA42
 Pinner HA5
 off Highbanks Rd 40 CB51
 Staines TW18 ......113 BF94
Meadway Ct, NW11 ......64 DB58
Meadway Dr, Add. KT15 ..152 BJ108
 Woking GU21 ......166 AW116
Meadway Gdns, Ruis. HA4 ..59 BR58
Meadway Gate, NW11 ....64 DA58
Meaford Way, SE20 ......122 DV94
Meakin Est, SE1 ......201 M6
Meanley Rd, E12 ......68 EL63
Meard St, W1 ......195 M9
Meare Cl, Tad. KT20 ......173 CW123
Meath Cl, Orp. BR5 ......146 EV99
Meath Rd, E15 ......86 EF68
 Ilford IG1 ......69 EQ62
Meath St, SW11 ......101 DH81
Mecklenburgh Pl, WC1 ..196 B4
Mecklenburgh Sq, WC1 ..196 B4
Mecklenburgh St, WC1 ..196 B4
Medburn St, NW1 ......195 N1
Medbury Rd, Grav. DA12 ..131 GM88
Medcalf Rd, Enf. EN3 ....31 DZ37
Medcroft Gdns, SW14 ....98 CQ84
 off High St 142 DQ104
Medebourne Cl, SE3 ......104 EG83
Mede Fld, Lthd. KT22 ....171 CD124
Medesenge Way, N13 ....45 DP51

Medfield St, SW15 ......119 CV87
★ Medici Gall, W1
 off Arbery Rd 85 DY68
 Woking (Chobham) GU24 .150 AT109
Medhurst Cres, Grav. DA12 .131 GM90
Medhurst Gdns, Grav. DA12 .131 GM90
Median Rd, E5 ......66 DW64
Medick Ct, Grays RM17 ..110 GE79
Medina Av, Esher KT10 ..137 CE104
Medina Gro, N7
 off Medina Rd 65 DN62
Medina Rd, N7 ......65 DN62
 Grays RM17 ......110 GD77
Medland Cl, Wall. SM6 ..140 DG102
Medland Ho, E14
 off Branch Rd 85 DY73
Medlar Cl, Nthlt. UB5
 off Parkfield Av 78 BY68
Medlar Rd, Grays RM17 ..110 GD79
Medlar St, SE5 ......102 DQ81
Medley Rd, NW6 ......82 DA65
Medman Cl, Uxb. UB8
 off Chiltern Vw Rd 76 BJ68
Medora Rd, SW2 ......121 DM87
 Romford RM7 ......71 FD56
Medow Mead, Rad. WD7 ..9 CF33
Medusa Cl, SE6 ......123 EB86
Medway Bldgs, E3
 off Medway Rd 85 DY68
Medway Cl, Croy. CR0 ....142 DW100
 Ilford IG1 ......69 EQ64
 Watford WD25 ......8 BW34
Medway Dr, Grnf. UB6 ....79 CF68
Medway Gdns, Wem. HA0 ..61 CG63
Medway Ms, E3
 off Medway Rd 85 DY68
Medway Par, Grnf. UB6 ..79 CF68
Medway Rd, E3 ......85 DY68
 Dartford DA1 ......107 FG83
Medway St, SW1 ......199 N7
Medwin St, SW4 ......101 DM84
Meerbrook Rd, SE3 ......104 EJ83
Meeson Rd, E15 ......86 EF67
Meeson St, E5 ......67 DY63
Meesons La, Grays RM17 ..110 FZ77
Meeting Flds Path, E9
 off Morning La 84 DW65
Meeting Ho All, E1 ......202 E2
Meeting Ho La, SE15 ......102 DV81
Megg La, Kings L. (Chipper.)
 WD4 ......6 BH29
Mehetabel Rd, E9 ......84 DW65
Meister Cl, Ilf. IG1 ......69 ER60
Melancholy Wk, Rich. TW10 .117 CJ89
Melanda Cl, Chis. BR7 ..125 EM92
Melanie Cl, Bexh. DA7 ..106 EY81
Melba Gdns, Til. RM18 ..111 GG80
Melba Way, SE13 ......103 EB81
Melbourne Av, N13 ......45 DM51
 W13 ......79 CG74
 Pinner HA5 ......60 CB55
Melbourne Cl, Orp. BR6 ..145 ES101
 Uxbridge UB10 ......58 BN63
 Wallington SM6
 off Melbourne Rd 159 DJ106
Melbourne Ct, E5
 off Daubeney Rd 67 DY63
 N10 off Sydney Rd 45 DH52
 SE20 ......122 DU94
Melbourne Gdns, Rom. RM6 .70 EY57
Melbourne Gro, SE22 ....102 DS84
Melbourne Ho, Hayes UB4 .78 BW70
Melbourne Ms, SE6 ......123 EC87
 SW9 ......101 DN81
Melbourne Pl, WC2 ......196 C10
Melbourne Rd, E6 ......87 EM67
 E10 ......67 EB59
 E17 ......67 DY56
 SW19 ......140 DA95
 Bushey WD23 ......24 CB44
 Ilford IG1 ......69 EP60
 Teddington TW11 ......117 CJ93
 Tilbury RM18 ......110 GE81
 Wallington SM6 ......159 DH106
Melbourne Sq, SW9
 off Melbourne Ms 101 DN81
Melbourne Ter, SW6
 off Waterford Rd 100 DB80
Melbourne Way, Enf. EN1 ..30 DT44
Melbury Av, Sthl. UB2 ....96 CB76
Melbury Cl, Cher. KT16 ..134 BG101
 Chislehurst BR7 ......125 EM93
 Esher (Clay.) KT10 ......155 CH107
 West Byfleet KT14 ......152 BG114
Melbury Ct, W8 ......99 CZ76
Melbury Dr, SE5
 off Sedgmoor Pl 102 DS80
Melbury Gdns, SW20 ....139 CV95
Melbury Rd, W14 ......99 CZ76
 Harrow HA3 ......62 CM57
Melcombe Gdns, Har. HA3 .62 CM58
Melcombe Pl, NW1 ......194 D6
Melcombe St, NW1 ......194 E5
Meldex Cl, NW7 ......43 CW51
Meldon Cl, SW6
 off Bagley's La 100 DB81
Meldone Cl, Surb. KT5 ..138 CP100
Meldrum Cl, Orp. BR5
 off Killewarren Way ..146 EW100
 Oxted RH8 ......188 EG132
Melfield Gdns, SE6 ......123 EB91
Melford Av, Bark. IG11 ..87 ES65
Melford Cl, Chess. KT9 ..156 CM106
Melford Rd, E6 ......87 EM70
 E11 ......68 EE61
 E17 ......67 DY56
 SE22 ......122 DU87
 Ilford IG1 ......69 ER61
Melfort Av, Th.Hth. CR7 ..141 DP97
Melfort Rd, Th.Hth. CR7 ..141 DP97

Melgund Rd, N5 ......65 DN64
Melina Cl, Hayes UB3
 off Middleton Rd 77 BR71
Melina Pl, NW8 ......82 DD69
Melina Rd, W12 ......99 CV75
Melior Pl, SE1 ......201 M4
Melior St, SE1 ......201 L4
Meliot Rd, SE6 ......123 ED89
Melksham Gdns, Rom. RM3 .52 FL52
Melksham Dr, Rom. RM3
 off Melksham Gdns 52 FL52
Melksham Gdns, Rom. RM3 .52 FL52
Melksham Grn, Rom. RM3
 off Melksham Gdns 52 FM52
Meller Cl, Croy. CR0 ......141 DL104
Melling Dr, Enf. EN1 ......30 DU39
Melling St, SE18 ......105 ES79
Mellish Cl, Bark. IG11 ....87 ET67
Mellish Gdns, Wdf.Grn. IG8 .48 EG50
Mellish Ind Est, SE18 ....104 EL76
Mellish St, E14 ......203 P6
Mellison Rd, SW17 ......120 DE92
Melliss Av, Rich. TW9 ....98 CP81
Mellitus St, W12 ......81 CT72
Mellor Cl, Walt. KT12 ....136 BZ101
Mellow Cl, Bans. SM7 ..158 DB114
Mellow La E, Hayes UB4 ..77 BQ69
Mellow La W, Uxb. UB10 ..77 BQ69
Mellows Rd, Ilf. IG5 ......69 EM55
 Wallington SM6 ......159 DK106
Mells Cres, SE9 ......125 EM91
Mell St, SE10
 off Trafalgar Rd 104 EE78
Melody La, N5 ......65 DP64
Melody Rd, SW18 ......120 DC85
 Westerham (Bigg.H.) TN16 .178 EJ118
Melon Pl, W8
 off Kensington Ch St ..100 DA75
Melon Rd, E11 ......68 EE62
 SE15 ......102 DU81
Melrose Av, N22 ......45 DP53
 NW2 ......63 CV64
 SW16 ......141 DM97
 SW19 ......120 DA89
 Borehamwood WD6 ....26 CP43
 Dartford DA1
 off Lower Sta Rd 127 FE86
 Greenford UB6 ......78 CB68
 Mitcham CR4 ......121 DH94
 Potters Bar EN6 ......12 DB32
 Twickenham TW2 ......116 CB87
Melrose Cl, SE12 ......124 EG88
 Greenford UB6 ......78 CB68
 Hayes UB4 ......77 BU71
Melrose Cres, Orp. BR6 ..163 ER105
Melrose Dr, Sthl. UB1 ....78 CA74
Melrose Gdns, W6 ......99 CW76
 Edgware HA8 ......42 CP54
 New Malden KT3 ......138 CR97
 Walton-on-Thames KT12 .154 BW106
Melrose Pl, Wat. WD17
 off Wentworth Cl 23 BT38
Melrose Rd, SW13 ......99 CT82
 SW18 ......119 CZ86
 SW19 ......140 DA96
 W3 off Stanley Rd 98 CQ76
 Coulsdon CR5 ......175 DH115
 Pinner HA5 ......60 BZ56
 Westerham (Bigg.H.) TN16 .178 EJ116
 Weybridge KT13 ......152 BN106
Melrose Ter, W6 ......99 CW76
Melsa Rd, Mord. SM4 ....140 DC100
Melstock Av, Upmin. RM14 .72 FQ63
Melthorne Dr, Ruis. HA4 ..60 BW62
Melthorpe Gdns, SE3 ....104 EL81
Melton Cl, Ruis. HA4 ......60 BW60
Melton Ct, SW7 ......198 A9
 Sutton SM2 ......158 DC108
Melton Flds, Epsom KT19 .156 CR109
Melton Gdns, Rom. RM1 ..71 FF59
Melton Pl, Epsom KT19 ..156 CR109
Melton Rd, Red. RH1 ....185 DJ130
Melton St, NW1 ......195 L3
Melville Av, SW20 ......119 CU94
 Greenford UB6 ......61 CF64
 South Croydon CR2 ....160 DT106
Melville Cl, Uxb. UB10 ..59 BR62
Melville Gdns, N13 ......45 DP50
Melville Pl, N1 off Essex Rd .83 DP67
Melville Rd, E17 ......67 DZ55
 NW10 ......80 CR66
 SW13 ......99 CU81
 Rainham RM13 ......89 FG70
 Romford RM5 ......51 FB52
 Sidcup DA14 ......126 EW89
Melville Vil Rd, W3
 off High St 80 CR74
Melvin Rd, SE20 ......142 DW95
Melvinshaw, Lthd. KT22 ..171 CJ121
Melvyn Cl, Wal.Cr. (Chsht.)
 EN7 ......13 DP28
Melyn Cl, N7 off Anson Rd .65 DJ63
Memel Cl, EC1 ......197 H5
Memel St, EC1 ......197 H5
Memess Path, SE18 ......105 EN79
Memorial Av, E15 ......86 EE69
Memorial Cl, Houns. TW5 ..96 BZ79
H Memorial Hosp, SE18 ..105 EN82
Mendip Cl, SE26 ......122 DW91
 Hayes UB3 ......95 BR80
 Slough SL3 ......93 BA78
 Worcester Park KT4 ....139 CW102
Mendip Dr, NW2 ......63 CX61
Mendip Ho, N9
 off New Rd 46 DU48
Mendip Rd, SW11 ......100 DC83
 Bexleyheath DA7 ......107 FE81
 Bushey WD23 ......24 CC44
 Hornchurch RM11 ......71 FG59
 Ilford IG2 ......69 ES57

Men - Mil

Millennium Wf, Rick. WD3
  off Wharf La 38 BL45
Miller Av, Enf. EN3
  off Government Row 31 EA37
Miller Cl, Mitch. CR4 . . . . .140 DF104
  Pinner HA5 . . . . .60 BW54
Miller Pl, Ger.Cr. SL9 . . . . .56 AX57
Miller Rd, SW19 . . . . .120 DD93
  Croydon CR0 . . . . .141 DM102
Miller's Av, E8 . . . . .66 DT64
Millers Cl, NW7 . . . . .43 CU49
  Chigwell IG7 . . . . .50 EV47
  Rickmansworth (Chorl.)
  WD3 . . . . .21 BE41
  Staines TW18 . . . . .114 BH92
Millers Copse, Epsom KT18 .172 CR119
Millers Ct, W4
  off Chiswick Mall 99 CT78
Millers Grn Cl, Enf. EN2 . . .29 DP41
Millers La, Chig. IG7 . . . . . .50 EV46
Millers La, Wind. SL4 . . . . .112 AT86
Millers Meadow Cl, SE3
  off Meadowcourt Rd 124 EF85
Miller's Ter, E8 . . . . .66 DT64
Miller St, NW1 . . . . .83 DJ68
Millers Way, W6 . . . . .99 CW75
Millet Rd, Grnf. UB6 . . . . . .78 CB69
Mill Fm Av, Sun. TW16 . . . .115 BS94
Mill Fm Cl, Pnr. HA5 . . . . . .40 BW54
Mill Fm Cres, Houns. TW4 . .116 BY88
Millfield, Sun. TW16 . . . . . .135 BR95
Millfield Av, E17 . . . . .47 DY53
Millfield Dr, Grav. (Nthflt.)
  DA11 . . . . .130 GE89
Millfield La, N6 . . . . .64 DF61
  Tadworth KT20 . . . . . . .183 CZ125
Millfield Pl, N6 . . . . .64 DG61
Millfield Rd, Edg. HA8 . . . . .42 CQ54
  Hounslow TW4 . . . . . . .116 BY88
Millfields Cl, Orp. BR5 . . . .146 EV97
Millfields Cotts, Orp. BR5
  off Millfields Cl 146 EV98
Millfields Est, E5
  off Denton Way 67 DX62
Millfields Rd, E5 . . . . .66 DW63
Millford, Wok. GU21 . . . . . .166 AV117
Mill Gdns, SE26 . . . . .122 DV91
Mill Grn, Mitch. CR4
  off London Rd 140 DG101
Mill Grn Business Pk, Mitch. CR4
  off Mill Grn Rd 140 DG101
Mill Grn Rd, Mitch. CR4 . . .140 DF101
Millgrove St, SW11 . . . . . .100 DG82
Millharbour, E14 . . . . .204 B5
Millhaven Cl, Rom. RM6 . . .70 EV58
Millhedge Cl, Cob. KT11 . . .170 BY116
MILL HILL, NW7 . . . . .43 CU50
Mill Hill, SW13
  off Mill Hill Rd 99 CU82
  Brentwood CM15 . . . . . .54 FY45
≷ **Mill Hill Broadway** 42 CS51
Mill Hill Circ, NW7
  off Watford Way 43 CT50
⊖ **Mill Hill East** 43 CX52
Mill Hill Gro, W3
  off Mill Hill Rd 80 CP74
Mill Hill La, Bet. (Brock.) RH3 .182 CP134
Mill Hill Rd, SW13 . . . . . . .99 CU82
  W3 . . . . .98 CP75
Millhoo Ct, Wal.Abb. EN9 . .16 EF34
Mill Ho Cl, Dart. (Eyns.) DA4
  off Mill La 148 FL102
Millhouse La, Abb.L. (Bedmond)
  WD5 . . . . .7 BT27
Mill Ho La, Cher. KT16 . . . .133 BB98
  Egham TW20 . . . . .133 BB98
Millhouse Pl, SE27 . . . . . .121 DP91
Millicent Rd, E10 . . . . .67 DZ60
Milligan St, E14 . . . . .203 N1
Milliners Ct, Loug. IG10
  off The Croft 33 EN40
Milling Rd, Edg. HA8 . . . . . .42 CR52
Millington Rd, Hayes UB3 . .95 BS76
Mill La, E4 . . . . .31 EB41
  NW6 . . . . .63 CZ64
  SE18 . . . . .105 EN78
  Carshalton SM5 . . . . . .158 DF105
  Chalfont St. Giles HP8 . . .36 AU47
  Croydon CR0 . . . . .141 DM104
  Dartford (Eyns.) DA4 . . .148 FL102
  Egham TW20 . . . . .133 BC98
  Epsom KT17 . . . . .157 CT109
  Gerrards Cross SL9 . . . . .57 AZ58
  Grays RM20 . . . . .109 FX78
  Kings Langley WD4 . . . . .6 BN29
  Leatherhead (Fetch.) KT22 .171 CG122
  Ongar (Toot Hill) CM5 . . .19 FE29
  Orpington (Downe) BR6 . .163 EN110
  Oxted RH8 . . . . .188 EF132
  Oxted (Lmpfld.Ch.) RH8 . .189 EM131
  Redhill RH1 . . . . .185 DJ131
  Rickmansworth (Crox.Grn.)
  WD3 . . . . .23 BQ44
  Romford (Chad.Hth.) RM6 .70 EY58
  Romford (Nave.) RM6 . . . .35 FH40
  Sevenoaks TN14 . . . . . .191 FJ121
  Sevenoaks (Shore.) TN14 .165 FF110
  Slough (Horton) SL3 . . . .93 BB83
  Waltham Cross EN8 . . . . .15 DY28
  West Byfleet (Byfleet)
  KT14 . . . . .152 BM113
  Westerham TN16 . . . . . .189 EQ127
  Woking (Ripley) GU23 . . .168 BK119
  Woodford Green IG8 . . . .48 EF50
Mill La Trd Est, Croy. CR0 . .141 DM104
Millman Ms, WC1 . . . . .196 B5
Millman Pl, WC1
  off Millman St 83 DM70
Millman St, WC1 . . . . .196 B5
Millmark Gro, SE14 . . . . . .103 DY82
Millmarsh La, Enf. EN3 . . . .31 DY40
Mill Mead, Stai. TW18 . . . .113 BF91
Millmead, W.Byf. (Byfleet)
  KT14 . . . . .152 BM112
Mill Mead Rd, N17 . . . . . . .66 DV56

Mill Pl, E14
  off East India Dock Rd . . .85 DZ72
  Chislehurst BR7 . . . . . .145 EP95
  Dartford DA1 . . . . .107 FG84
  Kingston upon Thames
  KT1 . . . . .138 CM97
  Slough (Datchet) SL3 . . . .92 AX82
Mill Pl Caravan Pk, Slou. (Datchet)
  SL3 . . . . .92 AW82
Mill Plat, Islw. TW7 . . . . . . .97 CG83
Mill Plat Av, Islw. TW7 . . . . .97 CG82
Mill Pond Cl, SW8
  off Crimsworth Rd 101 DK80
Millpond Ct, Add. KT15 . . .152 BL106
Millpond Est, SE16 . . . . . .202 D5
Mill Pond Rd, Dart. DA1 . . .128 FL86
Mill Ridge, Edg. HA8 . . . . . .42 CM50
Mill Rd, E16 . . . . .86 EH74
  SW19 . . . . .120 DC94
  Cobham KT11 . . . . . . .170 BW115
  Dartford (Hawley) DA2 . .128 FM91
  Epsom KT17 . . . . .157 CT112
  Erith DA8 . . . . .107 FC80
  Esher KT10 . . . . .136 CA103
  Gravesend (Nthflt.) DA11 .130 GE87
  Ilford IG1 . . . . .69 EN62
  Purfleet RM19 . . . . . . .108 FP79
  Sevenoaks (Dunt.Grn.)
  TN13 . . . . .190 FE121
  South Ockendon (Aveley)
  RM15 . . . . .90 FQ73
  Tadworth KT20 . . . . . . .173 CX123
  Twickenham TW2 . . . . .116 CC89
  West Drayton UB7 . . . . . .94 BJ76
Mill Row, N1 . . . . .84 DS67
Mills Cl, Uxb. UB10 . . . . . . .76 BN68
Mills Ct, EC2 . . . . .197 N3
Mills Gro, E14
  off Dewberry St 85 EC71
  NW4 . . . . .63 CX55
Mill Shaw, Oxt. RH8 . . . . . .188 EF132
Mill Shot Cl, SW6 . . . . .99 CW80
Millside, Cars. SM5 . . . . . .140 DF103
Millside Ct, Iver SL0 . . . . . .94 BH75
Millside Ind Est, Dart. DA1 .108 FK84
Millside Pl, Islw. TW7 . . . . . .97 CH82
Millsmead Way, Loug. IG10 . .33 EM40
Millson Cl, N20 . . . . .44 DD47
Mills Rd, Walt. KT12 . . . . . .154 BW106
Mills Row, W4 . . . . .98 CR77
Mills Spur, Wind. (Old Wind.)
  SL4 . . . . .112 AV87
Millstead Cl, Tad. KT20 . . .173 CV122
Millstone Cl, Dart. (S.Darenth)
  DA4 . . . . .148 FQ96
Millstone Ms, Dart. (S.Darenth)
  DA4 . . . . .148 FQ95
Millstream Cl, N13 . . . . . . .45 DN50
Millstream Rd, SE1 . . . . . .201 P5
Mill St, SE1 . . . . .202 A5
  W1 . . . . .195 J10
  Kingston upon Thames
  KT1 . . . . .138 CL97
  Slough SL2 . . . . .74 AT74
  Slough (Colnbr.) SL3 . . . .93 BD80
  Westerham TN16 . . . . . .189 ER127
Mills Way, Brwd. CM13 . . . .55 GC46
Millthorne Cl, Rick. (Crox.Grn.)
  WD3 . . . . .22 BM43
Mill Vale, Brom. BR2 . . . . .144 EF96
Mill Vw, St.Alb. (Park St.) AL2
  off Park St 9 CD27
Mill Vw Cl, Epsom (Ewell)
  KT17 . . . . .157 CT108
Millview Cl, Reig. RH2 . . . .184 DD132
Mill Vw Gdns, Croy. CR0 . . .143 DX104
MILLWALL, E14 . . . . .204 B8
Millwall Dock Rd, E14 . . . .203 P6
★ **Millwall FC**, SE16 . . . . .102 DW78
Millway, NW7 . . . . .42 CS50
Mill Way, Bushey WD23 . . . .24 BY40
  Feltham TW14 . . . . . . .115 BV85
  Leatherhead KT22 . . . . .172 CM124
Millway, Reig. RH2 . . . . . .184 DD131
Mill Way, Rick. (Mill End) WD3 .37 BF46
Millway Gdns, Nthlt. UB5 . . .78 BZ65
Millwell Cres, Chig. IG7 . . . .49 ER50
Millwood Rd, Houns. TW3 . .116 CC85
  Orpington BR5 . . . . . . .146 EW97
Millwood St, W10
  off St. Charles Sq 81 CY71
Mill Yd, E1
  off Cable St 84 DU73
Milman Cl, Pnr. HA5 . . . . . .60 BX55
Milman Rd, NW6 . . . . .81 CY68
Milman's St, SW10 . . . . . .100 DD79
Milmead Ind Cen, N17 . . . . .46 DV54
Milne Ct, E18
  off Churchfields 48 EG53
Milne Feild, Pnr. HA5 . . . . . .40 CA52
Milne Gdns, SE9 . . . . .124 EL85
Milne Pk E, Croy. (New Adgtn.)
  CR0 . . . . .161 ED111
Milne Pk W, Croy. (New Adgtn.)
  CR0 . . . . .161 ED111
Milner App, Cat. CR3 . . . . .176 DU121
Milner Cl, Cat. CR3 . . . . . .176 DT121
  Watford WD25 . . . . .7 BV34
Milner Ct, Bushey WD23 . . .24 CB44
Milner Dr, Cob. KT11 . . . . .154 BZ112
  Twickenham TW2 . . . . . .117 CD87
Milner Pl, N1 . . . . .83 DN67
  Carshalton SM5
  off High St 158 DG105
Milner Rd, E15 . . . . .86 EE69
  SW19 . . . . .140 DB95
  Caterham CR3 . . . . . . .176 DU122
  Dagenham RM8 . . . . . . .70 EW61
  Kingston upon Thames
  KT1 . . . . .137 CK97
  Morden SM4 . . . . .140 DD99
  Thornton Heath CR7 . . . .142 DR97
Milner Sq, N1 . . . . .83 DP66
Milner St, SW3 . . . . .198 D8
Milner Wk, SE9 . . . . .125 ER89
Milne Way, Uxb. (Hare.) UB9 .38 BH53

Milnthorpe Rd, W4 . . . . . . .98 CR79
Milo Rd, SE22 . . . . .122 DT86
Milroy Av, Grav. (Nthflt.)
  DA11 . . . . .130 GE89
Milroy Wk, SE1 . . . . .200 F2
Milson Rd, W14 . . . . .99 CY76
MILTON, Grav. 131 GK86
Milton Av, E6 . . . . .86 EK66
  N6 . . . . .65 DJ59
  NW9 . . . . .62 CQ55
  NW10 . . . . .80 CQ67
  Barnet EN5 . . . . .27 CZ43
  Croydon CR0 . . . . .142 DR101
  Gerrards Cross (Chal.St.P.)
  SL9 . . . . .56 AX56
  Gravesend DA12 . . . . . .131 GJ88
  Hornchurch RM12 . . . . . .71 FF61
  Sevenoaks (Bad.Mt.) TN14 .165 FB110
  Sutton SM1 . . . . .140 DD104
Milton Cl, N2 . . . . .64 DC57
  SE1 . . . . .201 P9
  Hayes UB4 . . . . .77 BU72
  Slough (Horton) SL3 . . . .93 BA83
  Sutton SM1 . . . . .140 DD104
Milton Ct, EC2 . . . . .197 K6
  Romford (Chad.Hth.) RM6
  off Cross Rd 70 EW59
  Uxbridge UB10 . . . . . . .59 BP62
  Waltham Abbey EN9 . . . .15 EC34
Milton Ct Rd, SE14 . . . . . .103 DY79
Milton Cres, Ilf. IG2 . . . . . . .69 EQ59
Milton Dr, Borwd. WD6 . . . .26 CP43
  Shepperton TW17 . . . . .134 BL98
Milton Flds, Ch.St.G. HP8 . .36 AV48
Milton Gdn Est, N16
  off Milton Gro 66 DS63
Milton Gdns, Epsom KT18 . .156 CS114
  Staines TW19
  off Chesterton Dr 114 BM88
  Tilbury RM18 . . . . .111 GH81
Milton Gro, N11 . . . . .45 DJ50
  N16 . . . . .66 DR63
Milton Hall Rd, Grav. DA12 .131 GK88
Milton Hill, Ch.St.G. HP8 . . .36 AV48
Milton Pk, N6 . . . . .65 DJ59
Milton Pl, N7 *off George's Rd* .66 DN64
  Gravesend DA12 . . . . . .131 GJ86
Milton Rd, E17 . . . . .67 EA56
  N6 . . . . .65 DJ59
  N15 . . . . .65 DP56
  NW7 . . . . .43 CU50
  NW9 *off West Hendon Bdy* .63 CU59
  SE24 . . . . .121 DP86
  SW14 . . . . .98 CR83
  SW19 . . . . .120 DC93
  W3 . . . . .80 CR74
  W7 . . . . .79 CF73
  Addlestone KT15 . . . . . .152 BG107
  Belvedere DA17 . . . . . .106 FA77
  Brentwood CM14 . . . . . .54 FV49
  Caterham CR3 . . . . . . .176 DR121
  Croydon CR0 . . . . .142 DR102
  Egham TW20 . . . . .113 AZ92
  Gravesend DA12 . . . . . .131 GJ86
  Grays RM17 . . . . .110 GB78
  Hampton TW12 . . . . . . .116 CA94
  Harrow HA1 . . . . .61 CE56
  Mitcham CR4 . . . . .120 DG94
  Romford RM1 . . . . .71 FG58
  Sevenoaks (Dunt.Grn.)
  TN13 . . . . .190 FE121
  Sutton SM1 . . . . .140 DA104
  Swanscombe DA10 . . . .130 FY86
  Uxbridge UB10 . . . . . . .58 BN63
  Wallington SM6 . . . . . .159 DJ107
  Walton-on-Thames KT12 .136 BX104
  Welling DA16 . . . . .105 ET81
Milton St, EC2 . . . . .197 K6
  Swanscombe DA10 . . . .129 FX86
  Waltham Abbey EN9 . . . .15 EC34
  Watford WD24 . . . . .23 BV38
Milton Way, West Dr. UB7 . .94 BM77
Milverton Dr, Uxb. UB10 . . .59 BQ63
Milverton Gdns, Ilf. IG3 . . . .69 ET61
Milverton Ho, SE23 . . . . . .123 DY90
Milverton Rd, NW6 . . . . . . .81 CW66
Milverton St, SE11 . . . . . . .101 DN78
Milverton Way, SE9 . . . . . .125 EN91
Milward St, E1 . . . . .84 DV71
Milward Wk, SE18
  off Spearman St 105 EN79
MIMBRIDGE, Wok. 150 AV113
Mimms Hall Rd, Pot.B. EN6 .11 CX31
Mimms La, Pot.B. (S.Mimms)
  EN6 . . . . .10 CQ33
  Radlett (Shenley) WD7 . . .10 CN33
Mimosa Cl, Brwd. CM15 . . .54 FV43
  Orpington BR6
  off Berrylands 146 EW104
  Romford RM3 . . . . .52 FJ52
Mimosa Rd, Hayes UB4 . . . .78 BW71
Mimosa St, SW6 . . . . .99 CZ81
Mina Av, Slou. SL3 . . . . . . .92 AX75
Mina Rd, SE17 . . . . .102 DS78
  SW19 . . . . .140 DA95
Minchenden Cres, N14 . . . .45 DJ48
Minchin Cl, Lthd. KT22 . . . .171 CG122
Mincing La, EC3 . . . . .197 M10
  Woking (Chobham) GU24 .150 AT108
Minden Rd, SE20 . . . . .142 DV95
  Sutton SM3 . . . . .139 CZ103
Minehead Rd, SW16 . . . . . .121 DM92
  Harrow HA2 . . . . .60 CA62
Mineral St, SE18 . . . . .105 ES77
Minera Ms, SW1 . . . . .198 G8
Minerva Cl, SW9 . . . . .101 DN80
  Sidcup DA14 . . . . .125 ES90
  Staines TW19 . . . . .114 BG85
Minerva Dr, Wat. WD24 . . . .23 BS36
Minerva Rd, E4 . . . . .47 EB52
  NW10 . . . . .80 CQ70
  Kingston upon Thames
  KT1 . . . . .138 CM96

Minerva St, E2 . . . . .84 DV68
Minet Av, NW10 . . . . .80 CS68
Minet Dr, Hayes UB3 . . . . . .77 BU74
Minet Gdns, NW10 . . . . . . .80 CS68
  Hayes UB3 . . . . .77 BU74
Minet Rd, SW9 . . . . .101 DP82
Minford Gdns, W14 . . . . . . .99 CX75
Mingard Wk, N7
  off Hornsey Rd 65 DM61
Ming St, E14 . . . . .85 EA73
Ministers Gdns, St.Alb. AL2
  off Frogmore 9 CE28
★ **Ministry of Defence**, SW1 .199 P3
Ministry Way, SE9 . . . . . . .125 EM89
Miniver Pl, EC4
  off Garlick Hill 84 DQ73
Mink Ct, Houns. TW4 . . . . . .96 BW83
Minniedale, Surb. KT5 . . . .138 CM99
Minnow St, SE17
  off East St 102 DS77
Minnow Wk, SE17 . . . . . . .201 N9
Minorca Rd, Wey. KT13 . . .152 BN105
Minories, EC3 . . . . .197 P10
Minshull Pl, Beck. BR3 . . . .123 EA94
Minshull St, SW8
  off Wandsworth Rd 101 DK81
Minson Rd, E9 . . . . .85 DX67
Minstead Gdns, SW15 . . . .119 CT87
Minstead Way, N.Mal. KT3 .138 CS100
Minster Av, Sutt. SM1
  off Leafield Cl 140 DA103
Minster Ct, EC3
  off Mincing La 84 DR73
  Hornchurch RM11 . . . . . .72 FN61
  St. Albans (Frog.) AL2 . . .9 CE28
Minster Dr, Croy. CR0 . . . .160 DS105
Minster Gdns, W.Mol. KT8
  off Molesey Av 136 BZ99
Minsterley Av, Shep. TW17 .135 BS98
Minster Pavement, EC3
  off Mincing La 84 DR73
Minster Rd, NW2 . . . . .63 CY64
  Bromley BR1 . . . . .124 EH94
Minster Wk, N8
  off Lightfoot Rd 65 DL56
Minster Way, Horn. RM11 . .72 FN60
  Slough SL3 . . . . .92 AY75
Minstrel Gdns, Surb. KT5 . .138 CM98
Mint Business Pk, E16 . . . . .86 EG71
Mint Cl, Uxb. (Higdn.) UB10 .77 BP69
Minterne Av, Sthl. UB2 . . . . .96 CA77
Minterne Rd, Har. HA3 . . . . .62 CM57
Minterne Waye, Hayes UB4 .78 BW72
Mintern St, N1 . . . . .84 DR68
Minton Ms, NW6
  off Lymington Rd 82 DB65
Mint Rd, Bans. SM7 . . . . . .174 DC116
  Wallington SM6 . . . . . .159 DH105
Mint St, SE1 . . . . .201 H4
Mint Wk, Croy. CR0
  off High St 142 DQ104
  Warlingham CR6 . . . . . .177 DX118
  Woking (Knap.) GU21 . . .166 AS117
Mirabel Rd, SW6 . . . . .99 CZ80
Mirador Cres, Slou. SL2 . . . .74 AV73
Miramar Way, Horn. RM12 . .72 FK64
Miranda Cl, E1 *off Sidney St* .84 DW71
Miranda Ct, W3
  off Queens Dr 80 CM72
Miranda Rd, N19 . . . . .65 DJ60
Mirfield St, SE7 . . . . .104 EK77
Miriam Rd, SE18 . . . . .105 ES78
Mirravale Trd Est, Dag. RM8 .70 EZ59
Mirren Cl, Har. HA2 . . . . . . .82 BZ63
Mirror Path, SE9
  off Lambscroft Av 124 EJ90
Misbourne Av, Ger.Cr. (Chal.St.P.)
  SL9 . . . . .36 AY50
Misbourne Cl, Ger.Cr. (Chal.St.P.)
  SL9 . . . . .36 AY50
Misbourne Ct, Slou. SL3
  off High St 93 BA77
Misbourne Meadows, Uxb. (Denh.)
  UB9 . . . . .57 BC60
Misbourne Rd, Uxb. UB10 . .76 BN67
Misbourne Vale, Ger.Cr. (Chal.St.P.)
  SL9 . . . . .36 AX50
Miskin Rd, Dart. DA1 . . . . .128 FJ87
Miskin Way, Grav. DA12 . . .131 GK93
Missenden Cl, Felt. TW14 . .115 BT88
Missenden Gdns, Mord.
  SM4 . . . . .140 DC100
Mission Gro, E17 . . . . .67 DY57
Mission Pl, SE15 . . . . .102 DU81
Mission Sq, Brent. TW8 . . . .98 CL79
Mistletoe Cl, Croy. CR0
  off Marigold Way 143 DX102
Misty's Fld, Walt. KT12 . . . .136 BW102
Mitali Pas, E1
  off Back Ch La 84 DU72
MITCHAM 140 DG97
⊖ **Mitcham** 140 DE98
Mitcham Gdn Village, Mitch.
  CR4 . . . . .140 DG99
Mitcham Ind Est, Mitch. CR4 .140 DG95
⊖ **Mitcham Junction** 140 DG99
≷ **Mitcham Junction** 140 DG99
Mitcham La, SW16 . . . . . .121 DJ93
Mitcham Pk, Mitch. CR4 . . .140 DF98
Mitcham Rd, E6 . . . . .86 EL69
  SW17 . . . . .120 DF92
  Croydon CR0 . . . . .141 DL100
  Ilford IG3 . . . . .69 ET59
Mitchell Av, Grav. (Nthflt.)
  DA11 . . . . .130 GD89
Mitchellbrook Way, NW10 . .80 CR65
Mitchell Cl, SE2 . . . . .106 EW77
  Abbots Langley WD5 . . . .7 BU32
  Belvedere DA17 . . . . . .107 FC76
  Dartford DA1 . . . . .128 FL89
  Hemel Hempstead (Bov.)
  HP3 . . . . .5 AZ27
  Rainham RM13 . . . . . . .90 FJ68

Mitchell Rd, N13 . . . . .45 DP50
  Orpington BR6 . . . . . . .163 ET105
Mitchell's Pl, SE21
  off Dulwich Village 122 DS87
Mitchell St, EC1 . . . . .197 H4
Mitchell Wk, E6 . . . . .86 EL71
  Amersham HP6 . . . . . . .20 AS38
  Swanscombe DA10 . . . .130 FY87
Mitchell Way, NW10 . . . . . . .80 CQ65
  Bromley BR1 . . . . .144 EG95
Mitchison Rd, N1 . . . . .84 DR65
Mitchley Av, Pur. CR8 . . . . .160 DQ113
  South Croydon CR2 . . . .160 DQ113
Mitchley Gro, S.Croy. CR2 . .160 DU113
Mitchley Hill, S.Croy. CR2 . .160 DT113
Mitchley Rd, N17 . . . . .66 DU55
Mitchley Vw, S.Croy. CR2 . .160 DU113
Mitford Cl, Chess. KT9
  off Merritt Gdns 155 CJ107
Mitford Rd, N19 . . . . .65 DL61
Mitre, The, E14
  off Three Colt St 85 DZ73
Mitre Av, E17
  off Greenleaf Rd 67 DZ55
Mitre Cl, Brom. BR2
  off Beckenham La 144 EF96
  Shepperton TW17
  off Gordon Dr 135 BR100
  Sutton SM2 . . . . .158 DC108
Mitre Ct, EC2 . . . . .197 J8
  EC4 . . . . .196 E9
Mitre Rd, E15 . . . . .86 EE68
  SE1 . . . . .200 E4
Mitre Sq, EC3 . . . . .197 N9
Mitre St, EC3 . . . . .197 N9
Mitre Way, W10 . . . . .81 CV70
Mixbury Gro, Wey. KT13 . . .153 BR107
Mixnams La, Cher. KT16 . . .134 BG97
Mizen Cl, Cob. KT11 . . . . . .154 BX114
Mizen Way, Cob. KT11 . . . .170 BW115
Moat, The, N.Mal. KT3 . . . .138 CS95
  Ongar CM5 . . . . .19 FF29
Moat Cl, Bushey WD23 . . . .24 CB43
  Orpington BR6 . . . . . . .163 ET107
  Sevenoaks (Chipstead)
  TN13 . . . . .190 FB123
Moat Ct, Ashtd. KT21 . . . . .172 CL107
Moat Cres, N3 . . . . .64 DB55
Moat Cft, Well. DA16 . . . . .106 EW83
Moat Dr, E13
  off Boundary Rd 86 EJ68
  Harrow HA1 . . . . .60 CC56
  Ruislip HA4 . . . . .59 BS59
  Slough SL2 . . . . .74 AW71
Moated Fm Dr, Add. KT15 . .152 BJ108
Moat Fm Rd, Nthlt. UB5 . . . .78 BZ65
Moatfield Rd, Bushey WD23 .24 CB43
Moat La, Erith DA8 . . . . . . .107 FG81
Moat Pl, SW9 . . . . .101 DM83
  W3 . . . . .80 CP72
  Uxbridge (Denh.) UB9 . . .57 BH63
Moatside, Enf. EN3 . . . . . . .31 DX42
  Feltham TW13 . . . . . . .116 BW91
Moatview Ct, Bushey WD23 .24 CB43
Moberley Rd, SW4 . . . . . . .121 DK87
Modbury Gdns, NW5
  off Queen's Cres 82 DG65
Modder Pl, SW15 . . . . .99 CX84
Model Cotts, SW14
  off Upper Richmond Rd W .98 CQ84
Model Fm Cl, SE9 . . . . . . .124 EL90
Modling Ho, E2 . . . . .85 DX68
Moelwyn Hughes Ct, N7
  off Hilldrop Cres 65 DK64
Moelyn Ms, Har. HA1 . . . . .61 CG57
Moffat Rd, N13 . . . . .45 DL51
  SW17 . . . . .120 DE91
  Thornton Heath CR7 . . . .142 DQ96
Moffats Cl, Hat. AL9 . . . . . .12 DA26
Moffats La, Hat. AL9 . . . . . .11 CZ26
MOGADOR, Tad. 183 CY129
Mogador Cotts, Tad. KT20
  off Mogador Rd 183 CX128
Mogador Rd, Tad. (Lwr.Kgswd.)
  KT20 . . . . .183 CX128
Mogden La, Islw. TW7 . . . . .117 CE85
Mohmmad Khan Rd, E11
  off Harvey Rd 68 EF60
Moira Cl, N17 . . . . .46 DS54
Moira Rd, SE9 . . . . .105 EM84
Moir Cl, S.Croy. CR2 . . . . . .160 DU109
Moland Mead, SE16 . . . . . .203 H10
Molash Rd, Orp. BR5 . . . . .146 EX98
Molasses Row, SW11
  off Cinnamon Row 100 DC83
Mole Abbey Gdns, W.Mol. KT8
  off New Rd 136 CA97
Mole Business Pk, Lthd.
  KT22 . . . . .171 CG121
Mole Ct, Epsom KT19 . . . . .156 CQ105
Molember Ct, E.Mol. KT8 . .137 CE98
Molember Rd, E.Mol. KT8 . .137 CE99
Mole Rd, Lthd. (Fetch.) KT22 .171 CD121
  Walton-on-Thames KT12 .154 BX106
Molescroft, SE9 . . . . .125 EQ90
Molesey Av, W.Mol. KT8 . . .136 BZ98
Molesey Cl, Walt. KT12 . . . .154 BY105
Molesey Dr, Sutt. SM3 . . . .139 CY103
Ⓗ **Molesey Hosp**, W.Mol.
  KT8 . . . . .136 CA99
Molesey Pk Av, W.Mol. KT8 .136 CB99
Molesey Pk Cl, E.Mol. KT8 .136 CC99
Molesey Pk Rd, E.Mol. KT8 .137 CD99
  West Molesey KT8 . . . . .136 CB99
Molesey Rd, Walt. KT12 . . .154 BX106
  West Molesey KT8 . . . . .136 BY99
Molesford Rd, SW6 . . . . . .100 DA81
Molesham Cl, W.Mol. KT8 . .136 CB97
Molesham Way, W.Mol. KT8 .136 CB97
Moles Hill, Lthd. (Oxshott)
  KT22 . . . . .155 CD111
Molesworth Rd, Cob. KT11 .153 BU113
Molesworth St, SE13 . . . . .103 EC83
Mole Valley Pl, Ashtd. KT21 .171 CK119

Mol - Mor

Mollands La, S.Ock. RM15 ....91 FW70
Mollison Av, Enf. EN3 ....31 DY43
Mollison Dr, Wall. SM6 ....159 DL107
Mollison Ri, Grav. DA12 ...131 GL92
Mollison Way, Edg. HA8 ....42 CN54
Molloy Ct, Wok. GU21
off Courtenay Rd 167 BA116
Molly Huggins Cl, SW12 ...121 DJ87
Molteno Rd, Wat. WD17 .....23 BU39
Molyneaux Av, Hem.H. (Bov.)
HP3 ....5 AZ27
Molyneux Dr, SW17 ....121 DH91
Molyneux Rd, Wey. KT13 ...152 BN106
Molyneux St, W1 ....194 C7
Monahan Av, Pur. CR8 .....159 DM112
Monarch Cl, Felt. TW14 ....115 BS87
Tilbury RM18 ....111 GH82
West Wickham BR4 ....162 EF105
Monarch Dr, E16 ....86 EK71
Monarch Ms, E17 ....67 EB57
SW16 ....121 DN92
Monarch Par, Mitch. CR4
off London Rd 140 DF96
Monarch Pl, Buck.H. IG9 ...48 EJ47
Monarch Rd, Belv. DA17 ...106 FA76
Monarchs Ct, NW7
off Grenville Pl 42 CR50
Monarchs Way, Ruis. HA4 ...59 BR60
Waltham Cross EN8 ....15 DY34
Mona Rd, SE15 ....102 DW82
Monastery Gdns, Enf. EN2 ...30 DR40
Mona St, E16 ....86 EF71
Monaveen Gdns, W.Mol.
KT8 ....136 CA97
Monck St, SW1 ....199 N7
Monclar Rd, SE5 ....102 DR84
Moncorvo Cl, SW7 ....198 B5
Moncrieff Cl, E6 ....86 EL72
off Linton Gdns
Moncrieff Pl, SE15 off Rye La .102 DU82
Moncrieff St, SE15 ....102 DU82
Mondial Way, Hayes UB3 ...95 BQ80
Monega Rd, E7 ....86 EJ65
E12 ....86 EK65
Money Av, Cat. CR3 ....176 DR122
MONEYHILL, Rick. 38 BH46
Moneyhill Par, Rick. WD3
off Uxbridge Rd 38 BH46
Money Hill Rd, Rick. WD3 ...38 BH46
Money La, West Dr. UB7 ....94 BK76
Money Rd, Cat. CR3 ....176 DR122
Mongers La, Epsom KT17 ..157 CT110
Monica Cl, Wat. WD24 .....24 BW40
Monier Rd, E3 ....85 EA66
Monivea Rd, Beck. BR3 ....123 DZ94
Monkchester Cl, Loug. IG10 ..33 EN39
Monk Dr, E16 ....86 EG72
MONKEN HADLEY, Barn. 27 CZ39
Monkfrith Av, N14 ....29 DH44
Monkfrith Cl, N14 ....45 DH45
Monkfrith Way, N14 ....44 DG45
Monkhams Av, Wdf.Grn. IG8 ..48 EG50
Monkhams Dr, Wdf.Grn. IG8 ..48 EH49
Monkhams La, Buck.H. IG9 ..48 EH48
Woodford Green IG8 ......48 EG50
Monkleigh Rd, Mord. SM4 ..139 CY97
Monk Pas, E16 off Monk Dr ..86 EG72
Monks Av, Barn. EN5 ......28 DC44
West Molesey KT8 ....136 BZ99
Monks Chase, Brwd. CM13 ..55 GC50
Monks Cl, SE2 ....106 EX77
Enfield EN2 ....30 DQ40
Harrow HA2 ....60 CB61
Ruislip HA4 ....60 BX63
Monks Cres, Add. KT15 ...152 BH106
Walton-on-Thames KT12 ..135 BV102
Monksdene Gdns, Sutt. SM1 .140 DB104
Monks Dr, W3 ....80 CN71
Monks Grn, Lthd. (Fetch.)
KT22 ....170 CC121
Monksgrove, Loug. IG10 ....33 EN43
Monksmead, Borwd. WD6 ...26 CQ42
MONKS ORCHARD, Croy. ...143 DZ101
Monks Orchard, Dart. DA1 ..128 FJ89
Monks Orchard Rd, Beck.
BR3 ....143 EA102
Monks Pk, Wem. HA9 ......80 CQ65
Monks Pk Gdns, Wem. HA9 ..80 CP65
Monks Pl, Cat. CR3
off Tillingdown Hill 176 DU122
Monk's Ridge, N20 ....43 CV46
Monks Rd, Bans. SM7 .....174 DA116
Enfield EN2 ....30 DQ40
Virginia Water GU25 .....132 AX98
Monk St, SE18 ....105 EN77
Monks Wk, Cher. KT16 ....133 BE98
Gravesend (Sthflt.)
DA13 ....130 GA93
Monk's Wk, Reig. RH2 ....184 DB134
Monks Way, NW11
off Hurstwood Rd 63 CZ56
Beckenham BR3 ....143 EA99
Orpington BR5 ....145 EQ102
Staines TW18 ....114 BK94
West Drayton UB7
off Harmondsworth La ...94 BL79
Monkswell Ct, N10
off Pembroke Rd 44 DG53
Monkswell La, Couls. CR5 ..174 DB124
Monkswood Av, Wal.Abb.
EN9 ....15 ED33
Monkswood Gdns, Borwd.
WD6 ....26 CR42
Ilford IG5 ....69 EN55
Monkton Rd, Well. DA16 ...105 ET82
Monkton St, SE11 ....200 E8
Monkville Av, NW11 ......63 CZ56
Monkwell Sq, EC2 ....197 J7
Monkwood Cl, Rom. RM1 ...71 FG57
Monmouth Av, E18 ....68 EH56
Kingston upon Thames
KT1 ....117 CJ94
Monmouth Cl, W4 ....98 CR78
off Beaumont Rd

Monmouth Cl, Mitch. CR4
off Recreation Way 141 DL98
Welling DA16 ....106 EU84
Monmouth Gro, Brent. TW8
off Sterling Pl 98 CL77
Monmouth Pl, W2
off Monmouth Rd 82 DA72
Monmouth Rd, E6 ....87 EM69
N9 ....46 DV47
W2 ....82 DA72
Dagenham RM9 ....70 EZ64
Hayes UB3 ....95 BS77
Watford WD17 ....23 BV41
Monmouth St, WC2 ....195 P9
Monnery Rd, N19 ....65 DJ62
Monnow Grn, S.Ock. (Aveley)
RM15 off Monnow Rd 90 FQ73
Monnow Rd, SE1 ....202 B10
South Ockendon (Aveley)
RM15 ....90 FQ73
Mono La, Felt. TW13 ......115 BV89
Monoux Gro, E17 ....47 EA53
Monroe Cres, Enf. EN1 ....30 DV39
Monroe Dr, SW14 ....118 CP85
Monro Gdns, Har. HA3 .....41 CE52
Monro Way, E5 off Downs Rd ..66 DU62
Monsal Ct, E5
Monsell Ct, N4
off Monsell Rd 66 DP62
Monsell Gdns, Stai. TW18 ..113 BE92
Monsell Rd, N4 ....66 DP62
Monson Rd, NW10 ....81 CU68
SE14 ....103 DX80
Redhill RH1 ....184 DF130
Mons Wk, Egh. TW20 ......113 BC92
Mons Way, Brom. BR2 .....144 EL100
Montacute Rd, SE6 ....123 DZ87
Bushey (Bushey Hth.)
WD23 ....41 CE45
Croydon (New Adgtn.)
CR0 ....161 EC109
Morden SM4 ....140 DD100
Montagu Cres, N18 ....46 DV49
Montague Av, SE4 ....103 DZ84
W7 ....79 CF74
South Croydon CR2 ......160 DS112
Montague Cl, SE1 ....201 K2
Walton-on-Thames KT12 ..135 BU101
Montague Dr, Cat. CR3
off Drake Av 176 DQ122
Montague Gdns, W3 ......80 CN73
Montague Hall Pl, Bushey
WD23 ....24 CA44
Montague Pl, WC1 ....195 N6
Montague Rd, E8 ....66 DU64
E11 ....68 EF61
N8 ....65 DM57
N15 ....66 DU56
SW19 ....120 DB94
W7 ....79 CF74
W13 ....79 CH72
Croydon CR0 ....141 DP102
Hounslow TW3 ....96 CB83
Richmond TW10 ....118 CL86
Slough SL1 ....74 AT73
Slough (Datchet) SL3 ....92 AV81
Southall UB2 ....96 BY77
Uxbridge UB8 ....76 BK66
Montague Sq, SE15
off Clifton Way 102 DW80
Montague St, EC1 ....197 H7
WC1 ....195 P6
Montague Waye, Sthl. UB2 ..96 BY76
Montagu Gdns, N18 ....46 DV49
Wallington SM6 ....159 DJ105
Montagu Mws, W1 ....194 E6
Montagu Ms N, W1 ....194 E7
Montagu Ms S, W1 ....194 E8
Montagu Ms W, W1 ....194 E8
Montagu Pl, W1 ....194 D7
Montagu Rd, N9 ....46 DW49
N18 ....46 DW49
NW4 ....63 CU58
Montagu Rd Ind Est, N18 ...46 DW49
Montagu Row, W1 ....194 E7
Montagu Sq, W1 ....194 E7
Montagu St, W1 ....194 E8
Montalt Rd, Wdf.Grn. IG8 ...48 EF50
Montana Cl, S.Croy. CR2 ...160 DR109
Montana Gdns, SE26 ......123 DZ92
Sutton SM1 off Lind Rd ...158 DC106
Montana Rd, SW17 ....120 DG91
SW20 ....139 CW95
Montayne Rd, Wal.Cr. (Chsht.)
EN8 ....15 DX32
Montbelle Rd, SE9 ....125 EP90
Montbretia Cl, Orp. BR5 ...146 EW98
Montcalm Cl, Brom. BR2 ...144 EG100
Hayes UB4 off Ayles Rd ...77 BV69
Montcalm Rd, SE7 ....104 EK80
Montclare St, E2 ....197 P3
Monteagle Av, Bark. IG11 ..87 EQ65
Monteagle Way, E5
off Rendlesham Rd 66 DU62
SE15 ....102 DV83
Montefiore St, SW8 ....101 DH82
Montego Cl, SE24
off Railton Rd 101 DN84
Montem Rd, SE23 ....123 DZ87
New Malden KT3 ....138 CS98
Montem St, N4
off Thorpedale Rd 65 DM60
Montenotte Rd, N8 ....65 DJ57
Monterey Cl, Bex. DA5 ....127 FC89
Montesole Ct, Pnr. HA5 ....40 BW54
Montevetro, SW11 ....100 DD81
Montford Pl, SE11 ....101 DN78
Montford Rd, Sun. TW16 ...135 BU98
Montfort Gdns, Ilf. IG6 ....49 EQ51
Montfort Pl, SW19 ....119 CX88
Montgolfier Wk, Nthlt. UB5
off Jetstar Way 78 BY69
Montgomery Av, Esher KT10 .137 CE104
Montgomery Cl, Grays
RM16 ....110 GC75
Mitcham CR4 ....141 DL98

Montgomery Cl, Sid. DA15 ..125 ET86
Montgomery Cres, Rom. RM3 .52 FJ50
Montgomery Dr, Wal.Cr. (Chsht.)
EN8 ....15 DY28
Montgomery Pl, Slou. SL2 ..74 AW72
Montgomery Rd, W4 ......98 CQ77
Dartford (S.Darenth) DA4 .149 FR95
Edgware HA8 ....42 CM51
Woking GU22 ....166 AY118
Montgomery St, E14 ......204 C3
Montholme Rd, SW11 .....120 DF86
Monthope Rd, E1
off Casson St 84 DU71
Montolieu Gdns, SW15 ....119 CV85
Montpelier Av, W5 ....79 CJ71
Bexley DA5 ....126 EX87
Montpelier Cl, Uxb. UB10 ..76 BN67
Montpelier Gdns, E6 ......86 EK69
Romford RM6 ....70 EW59
Montpelier Gro, NW5 .....65 DJ64
Montpelier Ms, SW7 ......198 C6
SW7 ....198 C6
Montpelier Pl, E1 ....84 DW72
SW7 ....198 C6
Montpelier Ri, NW11 ......63 CY59
Wembley HA9 ....61 CK60
Montpelier Rd, N3 ....44 DC53
SE15 ....102 DV81
W5 ....79 CK71
Purley CR8 ....159 DP110
Sutton SM1 ....158 DC105
Montpelier Row, SE3 .....104 EF82
Twickenham TW1 ....117 CH87
Montpelier Sq, SW7 ......198 C5
Montpelier St, SW7 ....198 C5
Montpelier Ter, SW7 ......198 C5
Montpelier Vale, SE3 .....104 EF82
Montpelier Wk, SW7 ......198 C6
Montpelier Way, NW11 ....63 CY59
Montrave Rd, SE20 ....122 DW93
Montreal Pl, WC2 ....196 B10
Montreal Rd, Ilf. IG1 ......69 EQ59
Sevenoaks TN13 ....190 FE123
Tilbury RM18 ....111 GG82
Montrell Rd, SW2 ....121 DL88
Montrose Av, NW6 ....81 CY68
Edgware HA8 ....42 CQ54
Upminster RM14 ....73 FN65
West Drayton UB7 ....94 BJ79
Sidcup DA15 ....125 ET81
Slough (Datchet) SL3 ....92 AW80
Twickenham TW2 ....116 CB87
Welling DA16 ....105 ER83
Woodford Green IG8 .....48 EG49
Montrose Cl, Ashf. TW15 ..115 BQ93
Welling DA16 ....105 ET83
Woodford Green IG8 .....48 EG49
Montrose Ct, SW7 ....198 A5
Montrose Cres, N12 ......44 DC51
Wembley HA0 ....80 CL65
Montrose Gdns, Lthd. (Oxshott)
KT22 ....155 CD112
Mitcham CR4 ....140 DF97
Sutton SM1 ....140 DB103
Montrose Pl, SW1 ....198 G5
Montrose Rd, Felt. TW14 ...115 BR86
Harrow HA3 ....41 CE54
Montrose Wk, Wey. KT13 ..135 BP104
Montrose Way, SE23 ......123 DX88
Slough (Datchet) SL3 ....92 AX81
Montrouge Cres, Epsom
KT17 ....173 CW116
Montserrat Av, Wdf.Grn. IG8 .47 ED52
Montserrat Cl, SE19 ......122 DR92
Montserrat Rd, SW15 .....99 CY84
★ Monument, The, EC3 ...201 L1
⊖ Monument 197 L10
Monument Gdns, SE13 ...123 EC85
Monument Grn, Wey. KT13 .135 BP104
Monument Hill, Wey. KT13 .153 BP105
Monument La, Ger.Cr. (Chal.St.P.)
SL9 ....58 AY51
Monument Rd, Wey. KT13 ..153 BP105
Woking GU21 ....151 BA114
Monument St, EC3 ....197 L10
Monument Way, N17 ......66 DT55
Monument Way E, Wok.
GU21 ....167 BB115
Monument Way W, Wok.
GU21 ....167 BA115
Monza St, E1 ....202 F1
Moodkee St, SE16 ....202 G6
Moody Rd, SE15 ....102 DT80
Moody St, E1 ....85 DX69
Moon La, Barn. EN5 ....27 CZ41
Moon St, N1 ....83 DP67
Moorcroft Gdns, Brom. BR2
off Southborough Rd 144 EL99
Moorcroft La, Uxb. UB8 ....76 BN71
Moorcroft Rd, SW16 ......121 DL90
Moorcroft Way, Pnr. HA5 ..60 BY57
Moordown, SE18 ....105 EN81
Moore Av, Grays RM20 ....110 FY78
Tilbury RM18 ....111 GH82
Moore Cl, SW14
off Little St. Leonards ...98 CQ83
Addlestone KT15 ....152 BH106
Dartford DA2 ....129 FR89
Mitcham CR4 ....141 DH96
Wallington SM6
off Brabazon Av 159 DL109
Moore Cres, Dag. RM9 ....88 EV67
Moorefield Rd, N17 ....46 DT54
Moore Gro Cres, Egh. TW20 .112 AY94
Moorehead Way, SE3 .....104 EH83
Mooreland Rd, Brom. BR1 ..124 EF94
Moore Pk Rd, SW6 ....100 DB80
Moore Rd, SE19 ....122 DQ93
Swanscombe DA10 ......130 FY86
Moores Pl, Brwd. CM14 ...54 FX47
Moore St, SW3 ....198 D8
Moore Wk, E7 off Stracey Rd .68 EG63
Moore Way, SE22 ....122 DU88
Sutton SM2 ....158 DA109
Moorey Cl, E15
off Stephen's Rd 86 EF67
Moorfield Av, W5 ....79 CK70
Moorfield Rd, Chess. KT9 ..156 CL106
Enfield EN3 ....30 DW39

Montgomery Cl, Orp. BR6 ..146 EU101
Uxbridge UB8 ....76 BK72
Uxbridge (Hare.) UB9 ....58 BG59
Moorfields, EC2 ....197 K7
Moorfields Cl, Stai. TW18 ..133 BE95
Ⓗ Moorfields Eye Hosp,
EC1 ....197 K3
off Fore St 84 DR71
⇌ Moorgate 197 K7
Moorgate, EC2 ....197 K7
Moorgate Pl, EC2 ....197 K8
Moorhall Rd, Uxb. (Hare.)
UB9 ....58 BH58
Moorhayes Dr, Stai. TW18 ..134 BJ97
Moorhen Cl, Erith DA8 ....107 FH80
Moorholme, Wok. GU22
off Oakbank 166 AY119
★ MOORHOUSE BANK, West. .189 EM128
Moorhouse Rd, W2 ....82 DA72
Harrow HA3 ....61 CK55
Oxted RH8 ....189 EM131
Westerham TN16 ....189 EM128
Moorhurst Av, Wal.Cr. (Chsht.)
EN7 ....13 DN29
Moorings, SE28 ....88 EV73
Moorings, The, Wind. SL4
off Straight Rd 112 AW87
Moorland Cl, Rom. RM5 ...51 FB52
Twickenham TW2
off Telford Rd 116 CA87
Moorland Rd, SW9 ....101 DP84
West Drayton UB7 ....94 BJ79
Moorlands, St.Alb. (Frog.) AL2
off Frogmore 9 CE28
Moorlands, The, Wok. GU22 .167 AZ121
Moorlands Av, NW7 ......43 CV51
Moorlands Est, SW9 ......101 DN84
Moor La, EC2 ....197 K7
Chessington KT9 ....156 CL106
Rickmansworth WD3 .....38 BM47
Rickmansworth (Sarratt)
WD3 ....21 BE36
Staines TW18, TW19 ....113 BE90
Upminster RM14 ....73 FS60
West Drayton UB7 ....94 BJ79
Woking GU22 ....166 AY119
Moor La Crossing, Wat. WD18 .39 BQ46
Moormead Dr, Epsom KT19 .156 CS106
Moor Mead Rd, Twick. TW1 .117 CG86
Moormede Cres, Stai. TW18 .113 BF91
Moor Mill La, St.Alb. (Coln.St.)
AL2 ....9 CE29
★ MOOR PARK, Nthwd. 39 BQ49
⊖ Moor Park 39 BR48
Moor Pk Est, Nthwd. HA6 ..39 BQ49
Moor Pk Gdns, Kings.T. KT2 .118 CS94
Moor Pk Ind Est, Wat. WD18 .39 BQ45
★ Moor Park Mansion, Rick.
WD3 ....38 BN48
Moor Pk Mansion, Rick. WD3 .38 BN48
Moor Pk Rd, Nthwd. HA6 ...39 BR50
Moor Pl, EC2 ....197 K7
Moor Rd, The, Sev. TN14 ..181 FH102
Moorside Rd, Brom. BR1 ..124 EE90
Moorsom Way, Couls. CR5 .175 DK117
Moorstown Ct, Slou. SL1 ..92 AS75
Moor St, W1 ....195 N9
Moortown Rd, Wat. WD19 ..40 BW49
Moor Vw, Wat. WD18 .....39 BU45
Moot Ct, NW9 ....62 CN57
Moran Cl, St.Alb. (Brick.Wd.)
AL2 ....8 BZ31
Morant Gdns, Rom. RM5 ...51 FB50
Morant Pl, N22
off Commerce Rd 45 DM53
Morant Rd, Grays RM16 ...111 GH76
Morants Ct Cross, Sev. (Dunt.Grn.)
TN14 ....181 FC118
Morants Ct Rd, Sev. (Dunt.Grn.)
TN13 ....181 FC118
Morant St, E14 ....85 EA73
Mora Rd, NW2 ....63 CW63
Mora St, EC1 ....197 J3
Morat St, SW9 ....101 DM81
Moravian Pl, SW10 ....100 DD79
off Milman's St
Moravian St, E2 ....84 DW69
Moray Av, Hayes UB3 .....77 BT74
Moray Cl, Edg. HA8
off Pentland Av 42 CP47
Romford RM1 ....51 FE52
Moray Dr, Slou. SL2 ......74 AU72
Moray Ms, N7 off Durham Rd .65 DM61
Moray Rd, N4 ....65 DM61
Moray Way, Rom. RM1 ....51 FD52
Mordaunt Gdns, Dag. RM9 ..88 EY66
Mordaunt Ho, NW10 ......80 CR67
Mordaunt Rd, NW10 ......80 CR67
Mordaunt St, SW9 ....101 DM83
MORDEN 140 DA97
⊖ Morden 140 DB97
Morden Cl, SE13 ....103 EC82
Tadworth KT20
off Marbles Way 173 CX120
Morden Ct, Mord. SM4 ....140 DB98
Morden Gdns, Grnf. UB6 ...61 CF64
Mitcham CR4 ....140 DD98
★ Morden Hall Park NT, Mord.
SM4 ....140 DB97
Morden Hall Rd, Mord. SM4 .140 DB97
Morden Hill, SE13 ....103 EC82
Morden La, SE13 ....103 EC81
MORDEN PARK, Mord. 139 CY99
⊖ Morden Road 140 DB96
Morden Rd, SE3 ....104 EG82
SW19 ....140 DB95
Mitcham CR4 ....140 DD98
Romford RM6 ....70 EY59
Morden Rd Ms, SE3 ......104 EG82
⇌ Morden South 140 DA99
Morden St, SE13 ....103 EB81
Morden Way, Sutt. SM3 ...140 DA101
Morden Wf Rd, SE10 .....205 H7
Mordon Rd, Ilf. IG3 ....69 ET59
Mordred Rd, SE6 ....124 EE89

Moreau Wk, Slou. (Geo.Grn.) SL3
off Alan Way 74 AY72
Morecambe Cl, E1 ....85 DX71
Hornchurch RM12 ....71 FH64
Morecambe Gdns, Stan. HA7 .41 CK49
Morecambe St, SE17 .....201 J9
SE17 ....201 J9
Morecambe Ter, N18 .....46 DR49
More Cl, E16 ....86 EF72
W14 ....99 CY77
Purley CR8 ....159 DN111
Morecoombe Cl, Kings.T.
KT2 ....118 CP94
Moreland Av, Grays RM16 ..110 GC75
Slough (Colnbr.) SL3 ....93 BC80
Moreland Cl, Slou. (Colnbr.) SL3
off Moreland Av 93 BC80
NW11 ....64 DA60
Moreland Dr, Ger.Cr. SL9 ..57 AZ59
Moreland St, EC1 ....196 G2
Moreland Way, E4 ....47 EB48
More La, Esher KT10 .....136 CB103
Morel Ct, Sev. TN13 ......191 FH122
Morella Cl, Vir.W. GU25 ...132 AW98
Morella Rd, SW12 ....120 DF87
Morell Cl, Barn. EN5
off Galdana Av 28 DC41
Morello Av, Uxb. UB8 .....77 BP71
Morello Cl, Swan. BR8 ....147 FD98
Morello Dr, Slou. SL3 .....75 AZ74
Moremead, Wal.Abb. EN9 ..15 ED33
Moremead Rd, SE6 ....123 DZ91
Morena St, SE6 ....123 EB87
Moresby Av, Surb. KT5 ...138 CP101
Moresby Rd, E5 ....66 DV60
Moresby Wk, SW8 ....101 DJ82
Moretaine Rd, Ashf. TW15
off Hengrove Cres 114 BK90
Moreton Av, Islw. TW7 ....97 CE81
Moreton Cl, E5 ....66 DW61
N15 ....66 DR58
NW7 ....43 CW51
SW1 ....199 L10
Swanley BR8
off Bonney Way 147 FE96
Waltham Cross (Chsht.)
EN7 ....14 DV27
Moreton Gdns, Wdf.Grn. IG8 .48 EL50
Moreton Ind Est, Swan. BR8 .147 FH98
Moreton Pl, SW1 ....199 L10
Moreton Rd, N15 ....66 DR58
South Croydon CR2 ......160 DR106
Worcester Park KT4 .....139 CU103
Moreton St, SW1 ....199 L10
Moreton Ter, SW1 ....199 L10
Moreton Ter Ms N, SW1 ..199 L10
Moreton Ter Ms S, SW1 ..199 L10
Moreton Twr, W3 ....80 CP74
Morewood Cl, Sev. TN13 ..190 FF123
Morewood Cl Ind Pk, Sev. TN13
off Morewood Cl 190 FF123
Morford Cl, Ruis. HA4 .....59 BV59
Morford Way, Ruis. HA4 ...59 BV59
Morgan Av, E17 ....67 ED56
Morgan Cl, Dag. RM10 ....88 FA66
Northwood HA6 ....39 BT51
Morgan Cres, Epp. (They.B.)
CM16 ....33 ER36
Morgan Dr, Green. DA9 ...129 FS87
Morgan Gdns, Wat. (Ald.)
WD25 ....24 CB38
Morgan Rd, N7 ....65 DN64
W10 ....81 CZ71
Bromley BR1 ....124 EG94
Morgans La, SE1 ....201 M3
Hayes UB3 ....77 BR71
Morgan St, E3 ....85 DY69
E16 ....86 EF71
Morgan Way, Rain. RM13 ..90 FJ69
Woodford Green IG8 .....48 EL51
Moriatry Cl, N7 ....65 DL63
Morie St, SW18 ....120 DB85
Morieux Rd, E10 ....67 DZ60
Moring Rd, SW17 ....120 DG91
Morkyns Wk, SE21 ....122 DS90
Morland Av, Croy. CR0 ....142 DS102
Dartford DA1 ....127 FH85
Morland Cl, NW11 ....64 DB60
Hampton TW12 ....116 BZ92
Mitcham CR4 ....140 DE97
Morland Gdns, NW10 .....80 CR66
Southall UB1 ....78 CB74
Morland Ms, N1
off Lofting Rd 83 DN66
Morland Rd, E17 ....67 DX57
SE20 ....123 DX93
Croydon CR0 ....142 DS102
Dagenham RM10 ....88 FA66
Harrow HA3 ....62 CL57
Ilford IG1 ....69 EP61
Sutton SM1 ....158 DC106
Ⓗ Morland Rd Day Hosp, Dag.
RM10 ....88 FA66
Morland Way, Wal.Cr. (Chsht.)
EN8 ....15 DY28
Morley Av, E4 ....47 ED52
N18 ....46 DU49
N22 ....45 DN54
Morley Cl, Orp. BR6 ......145 EP103
Slough SL3 ....93 AZ75
Morley Cres, Edg. HA8 ....42 CQ47
Ruislip HA4 ....60 BW61
Morley Cres E, Stan. HA7 ..41 CJ54
Morley Cres W, Stan. HA7 ..41 CJ54
Morley Hill, Enf. EN2 .....30 DR38
Morley Rd, E10 ....67 EC60
E15 ....86 EF68
SE13 ....103 EC84
Barking IG11 ....87 EQ67
Chislehurst BR7 ....145 EQ95
Romford RM6 ....70 EY57
South Croydon CR2 ......160 DT110
Sutton SM3 ....139 CZ102
Twickenham TW1 ....117 CK86
Morley Sq, Grays RM16 ...111 GG77
Morley St, SE1 ....200 E6
Morna Rd, SE5 ....102 DQ82
Morning La, E9 ....84 DW65

Morning Ri, Rick. (Loud.) WD3	.22	BK41
Morningside Rd, Wor.Pk. KT4	.139	CV103
Mornington Av, W14	.99	CZ77
Bromley BR1	.144	EJ97
Ilford IG1	.69	EN59
Mornington Cl, West. (Bigg.H.) TN16	.178	EK117
Woodford Green IG8	.48	EG68
Mornington Ct, Bex. DA5	.127	FC88
⊖ Mornington Crescent	.83	DJ68
Mornington Cres, NW1	.83	DJ68
Hounslow TW5	.95	BV81
Mornington Gro, E3	.85	EA69
Mornington Ms, SE5	.102	DQ81
Mornington Pl, NW1 off Mornington Ter	.83	DH68
Mornington Rd, E4	.47	ED45
E11	.68	EF60
SE8	.103	DZ80
Ashford TW15	.115	BQ92
Greenford UB6	.78	CB71
Loughton IG10	.33	EQ41
Radlett WD7	.9	CG34
Woodford Green IG8	.48	EF49
Mornington St, NW1	.83	DH68
Mornington Ter, NW1	.83	DH67
Mornington Wk, Rich. TW10	.117	CK91
Morocco St, SE1	.201	M5
Morpeth Av, Borwd. WD6	.26	CM38
Morpeth Gro, E9	.85	DX67
Morpeth Rd, E9	.85	DW67
Morpeth St, E2	.85	DX69
Morpeth Ter, SW1	.199	K7
Morpeth Wk, N17 off West Rd	.46	DV52
Morrab Gdns, Ilf. IG3	.69	ET62
Morrice Cl, Slou. SL3	.93	AZ77
Morris Av, E12	.69	EM64
Morris Cl, Croy. CR0	.143	DY100
Gerrards Cross (Chal.St.P.) SL9	.37	AZ53
Orpington BR6	.145	ES104
Morris Ct, E4 off Flaxen Rd	.47	EB48
Waltham Abbey EN9	.16	EF34
Morris Gdns, SW18	.120	DA87
Dartford DA1	.128	FN85
Morrish Rd, SW2	.121	DL87
Morrison Av, N17	.66	DS55
Morrison Rd, Bark. IG11	.88	EY68
Hayes UB4	.77	BV69
Morrison St, SW11	.100	DG83
Morris Pl, N4	.30	DN61
Morris Rd, E14	.85	EB71
E15	.68	EE63
Dagenham RM8	.70	EZ61
Isleworth TW7	.97	CF83
Romford RM3	.51	FH76
Morris St, E1	.84	DV72
Morriston Cl, Wat. WD19	.40	BW50
Morris Way, St.Alb. (Lon.Col.) AL2	.10	CL26
Morse Cl, E13	.86	EG69
Uxbridge (Hare.) UB9	.38	BJ54
Morshead Rd, W9	.82	DA69
Morson Rd, Enf. EN3	.31	DY44
Morston Cl, Tad. KT20 off Waterfield	.173	CV120
Morston Gdns, SE9	.125	EM91
Morten Cl, SW4	.121	DK86
Morten Gdns, Uxb. (Denh.) UB9	.58	BG59
Mortens Wd, Amer. HP7	.20	AS40
Morteyne Rd, N17	.46	DR53
Mortgramit Sq, SE18 off Powis St	.105	EN76
Mortham St, E15	.85	ED67
Mortimer Cl, NW2	.63	CZ62
SW16	.121	DK89
Bushey WD23	.24	CB44
Mortimer Cres, NW6	.82	DB67
Worcester Park KT4	.138	CR104
Mortimer Dr, Enf. EN1	.30	DR43
Mortimer Est, NW6	.82	DB67
Mortimer Gate, Wal.Cr. EN8	.15	DZ27
Mortimer Ho, W11 off St. Anns Rd	.99	CX74
Mortimer Mkt, WC1	.195	L5
Mortimer Pl, NW6	.82	DB67
Mortimer Rd, E6	.87	EM69
N1	.84	DS66
NW10	.81	CW69
W13	.79	CJ72
Erith DA8	.107	FD79
Mitcham CR4	.140	DF95
Orpington BR6	.146	EU103
Slough SL3	.92	AX76
Westerham (Bigg.H.) TN16	.162	EJ112
Mortimer Sq, W11 off St. Anns Rd	.81	CX73
Mortimer St, W1	.195	K7
Mortimer Ter, NW5 off Gordon Ho Rd	.65	DH63
MORTLAKE, SW14	.98	CQ83
⇌ Mortlake	.98	CQ83
Mortlake Cl, Croy. CR0 off Richmond Rd	.141	DL104
Mortlake Dr, Mitch. CR4	.140	DE95
Mortlake High St, SW14	.98	CR83
Mortlake Rd, E16	.86	EH72
Ilford IG1	.69	EQ63
Richmond TW9	.98	CN80
Mortlake Ter, Rich. TW9 off Kew Rd	.98	CN80
Mortlock Cl, SE15 off Cossall Wk	.102	DV81
Morton, Tad. KT20 off Hudsons	.173	CX121
Morton Cl, Wall. SM6 off Lancastrian Rd	.159	DM108
Woking GU21	.166	AW115
Morton Ct, Nthlt. UB5	.60	CC64
Morton Cres, N14	.45	DK49
Morton Gdns, Wall. SM6	.159	DJ106
Morton Ms, SW5 off Earls Ct Gdns	.100	DB77
Morton Pl, SE1	.200	D7
Morton Rd, E15	.86	EF66
Morton Rd, N1	.84	DQ66
Mordon SM4	.140	DD99
Woking GU21	.166	AW115
Morval Cl, Belv. DA17	.106	EZ77
Morval Rd, SW2	.121	DN85
Morven Cl, Pot.B. EN6	.12	DC31
Morven Rd, SW17	.120	DF90
Morville Ho, SW18 off Fitzhugh Gro	.120	DD86
Morville St, E3	.85	EA68
Morwell St, WC1	.195	N7
Mosbach Gdns, Brwd. CM13	.55	GB47
Moscow Pl, W2 off Moscow Rd	.82	DB73
Moscow Rd, W2	.82	DA73
Moseley Row, SE10	.205	L8
Moselle Av, N22	.45	DN54
Moselle Cl, N8 off Miles Rd	.65	DM55
Moselle Ho, N17 off William St	.46	DT52
Moselle Pl, N17 off High Rd	.46	DT52
Moselle Rd, West. (Bigg.H.) TN16	.178	EL118
Moselle St, N17	.46	DT52
Mospey Cres, Epsom KT17	.173	CT115
Moss Bk, Grays RM17	.110	FZ78
Mossborough Cl, N12	.44	DB51
Mossbury Rd, SW11	.100	DE83
Moss Cl, E1 off Old Montague St	.84	DU71
Pinner HA5	.40	BZ54
Rickmansworth WD3	.38	BK47
Mossdown Cl, Belv. DA17	.106	FA77
Mossendew Cl, Uxb. (Hare.) UB9	.38	BK53
Mossfield, Cob. KT11	.153	BU113
Mossford Ct, Ilf. IG6	.69	EP55
Mossford Grn, Ilf. IG6	.69	EP55
Mossford La, Ilf. IG6	.49	EP54
Mossford St, E3	.85	DZ70
Moss Gdns, Felt. TW13	.115	BU89
South Croydon CR2 off Warren Av	.161	DX108
Moss Hall Ct, N12	.44	DB51
Moss Hall Cres, N12	.44	DB51
Moss Hall Gro, N12	.44	DB51
Mossington Gdns, SE16	.202	F9
Moss La, Pnr. HA5	.60	BZ55
Romford RM1 off Wheatsheaf Rd	.71	FF58
Mosslea Rd, SE20	.122	DW93
Bromley BR2	.144	EK99
Orpington BR6	.145	EQ104
Whyteleafe CR3	.176	DT116
Mossop St, SW3	.198	C8
Moss Rd, Dag. RM10	.88	FA66
South Ockendon RM15	.91	FW71
Watford WD25	.7	BV34
Moss Side, St.Alb. (Brick.Wd.) AL2	.8	BZ30
Mossville Gdns, Mord. SM4	.139	CZ97
Moss Way, Dart. (Lane End) DA2	.129	FR91
Moston Cl, Hayes UB3 off Fuller Way	.95	BT78
Mostyn Av, Wem. HA9	.62	CM64
Mostyn Gdns, NW10	.81	CX68
Mostyn Gro, E3	.85	DZ68
Mostyn Rd, SW9	.101	DN81
SW19	.139	CZ95
Bushey WD23	.24	CC43
Edgware HA8	.42	CR52
Mosul Way, Brom. BR2	.144	EL100
Mosyer Dr, Orp. BR5	.146	EX103
Motcomb St, SW1	.198	E6
Moth Cl, Wall. SM6 off Lancastrian Rd	.159	DL108
Mothers' Sq, E5	.66	DV63
Motherwell Way, Grays RM20	.109	FU78
Motley Av, EC2 off Scrutton St	.84	DS70
Motley St, SW8 off St. Rule St	.101	DJ82
MOTSPUR PARK, N.Mal.	.139	CU100
⇌ Motspur Park	.139	CV99
Motspur Pk, N.Mal. KT3	.139	CT100
MOTTINGHAM, SE9	.124	EJ89
⇌ Mottingham	.124	EL88
Mottingham Gdns, SE9	.124	EK88
Mottingham La, SE9	.124	EJ88
SE12	.124	EJ88
Mottingham Rd, N9	.31	DX44
SE9	.124	EL89
Mottisfont Rd, SE2	.106	EU76
Motts Hill La, Tad. KT20	.173	CU123
Mott St, E4	.31	ED38
Loughton (High Beach) IG10	.32	EF39
Mouchotte Cl, West. (Bigg.H.) TN16	.162	EH112
Moulins Rd, E9	.84	DW67
Moulsford Ho, N7	.65	DK64
Moultain Hill, Swan. BR8	.147	FG98
Moulton Av, Houns. TW3	.96	BY82
Moultrie Way, Upmin. RM14	.73	FS59
Mound, The, SE9	.125	EN90
Moundfield Rd, N16	.66	DU58
Mount, The, N20	.44	DC47
NW3 off Heath St	.64	DC63
W3	.80	CP74
Brentwood CM14	.54	FW48
Coulsdon CR5	.174	DG115
Epsom (Ewell) KT17	.157	CT110
Esher KT10	.154	CA107
Leatherhead (Fetch.) KT22	.171	CE123
New Malden KT3	.139	CT97
Potters Bar EN6	.12	DB30
Rickmansworth WD3	.22	BJ44
Romford RM3	.52	FJ48
Tadworth KT20	.183	CZ126
Virginia Water GU25	.132	AX100
Waltham Cross (Chsht.) EN7	.14	DR26
Warlingham CR6	.176	DU119
Wembley HA9	.62	CP61
Mount, The, Wey. KT13	.135	BS103
Woking GU21	.166	AX118
Woking (St. John's) GU21	.166	AU119
Worcester Park KT4	.157	CV105
Mountacre Cl, SE26	.122	DT91
Mount Adon Pk, SE22	.122	DU87
Mountague Pl, E14	.85	EC73
Mountain Ct, Dart. (Eyns.) DA4 off Pollyhaugh	.148	FL103
Mount Angelus Rd, SW15	.119	CT87
Mount Ararat Rd, Rich. TW10	.118	CL85
Mount Ash Rd, SE26	.122	DV90
Mount Av, E4	.47	EA48
W5	.79	CK71
Brentwood CM13	.55	GA44
Caterham CR3	.176	DQ124
Romford RM3	.52	FQ51
Southall UB1	.78	CA72
Mountbatten Cl, SE18	.105	ES79
SE19	.122	DS92
Slough SL1	.92	AU76
Mountbatten Ct, SE16 off Rotherhithe St	.84	DW74
Buckhurst Hill IG9	.48	EK47
Mountbatten Gdns, Beck. BR3 off Balmoral Av	.143	DY98
Mountbatten Ms, SW18 off Inman Rd	.120	DC88
Mountbel Rd, Stan. HA7	.41	CG53
Mount Cl, W5	.79	CJ71
Barnet EN4	.28	DG42
Bromley BR1	.144	EL95
Carshalton SM5	.158	DG109
Kenley CR8	.176	DQ116
Leatherhead (Fetch.) KT22	.171	CE123
Sevenoaks TN13	.190	FF123
Woking GU22	.166	AV121
Mount Cl, The, Vir.W. GU25	.132	AX100
Mountcombe Cl, Surb. KT6	.138	CL101
Mount Cor, Felt. TW13	.116	BX89
Mount Ct, SW15 off Weimar St	.99	CY83
West Wickham BR4	.144	EE103
Mount Cres, Brwd. CM14	.54	FX49
Mount Culver Av, Sid. DA14	.126	EX93
Mount Dr, Bexh. DA6	.126	EY85
Harrow HA2	.60	BZ57
St. Albans (Park St.) AL2	.9	CD25
Wembley HA9	.62	CQ61
Mount Dr, The, Reig. RH2	.184	DC132
Mountearl Gdns, SW16	.121	DM90
Mount Echo Av, E4	.47	EB47
Mount Echo Dr, E4	.47	EB46
MOUNT END, Epp.	.18	EZ32
Mount Ephraim La, SW16	.121	DK90
Mount Ephraim Rd, SW16	.121	DK90
Mount Est, The, E5 off Mount Pleasant La	.66	DV61
Mount Felix, Walt. KT12	.135	BT102
Mountfield Cl, SE6	.123	ED87
Mountfield Rd, E6	.87	EN68
N3	.64	DA55
W5	.79	CK72
Mountfield Way, Orp. BR5	.146	EW98
Mountford St, E1 off Adler St	.84	DU72
Mountfort Cres, N1 off Barnsbury Sq	.83	DN66
Mountfort Ter, N1 off Barnsbury Sq	.83	DN66
Mount Gdns, SE26	.122	DV90
Mount Grace Rd, Pot.B. EN6	.12	DA31
Mount Gro, Edg. HA8	.42	CQ48
Mountgrove Rd, N5	.65	DP63
Mount Harry Rd, Sev. TN13	.190	FG123
MOUNT HERMON, Wok.	.166	AX118
Mount Hermon Cl, Wok. GU22	.166	AX118
Mount Hermon Rd, Wok. GU22	.166	AX119
Mount Hill La, Ger.Cr. SL9	.56	AV60
Mounthurst Rd, Brom. BR2	.144	EF101
Mountington Pk Cl, Har. HA3	.61	CK58
Mountjoy Cl, SE2	.106	EV75
Mountjoy Ho, EC2 off The Barbican	.84	DQ71
Mount La, Dart. (Denh.) UB9	.57	BD61
Mount Lee, Egh. TW20	.112	AY92
Mount Ms, Hmptn. TW12	.136	CB95
Mount Mills, EC1	.196	G3
Mountnessing Bypass, Brwd. CM15	.55	GD41
Mount Nod Rd, SW16	.121	DM90
Mount Pk, Cars. SM5	.158	DG109
Mount Pk Av, Har. HA1	.61	CD61
South Croydon CR2	.159	DP109
Mount Pk Cres, W5	.79	CK72
Mount Pk Rd, W5	.79	CK71
Harrow HA1	.61	CD62
Pinner HA5	.59	BU57
Mount Pl, W3 off High St	.80	CP74
Mount Pleasant, SE27	.122	DQ91
WC1	.196	C5
Barnet EN4	.28	DE42
Epsom KT17	.157	CT110
Ruislip HA4	.60	BW61
Uxbridge (Hare.) UB9	.38	BG53
Wembley HA0	.80	CL67
Westerham (Bigg.H.) TN16	.178	BK43
Weybridge KT13	.134	BN104
Mount Pleasant Av, Brwd. CM13	.55	GE44
Mount Pleasant Cres, N4	.65	DM59
Mount Pleasant Hill, E5	.66	DV61
Mount Pleasant La, E5	.66	DV61
St. Albans (Brick.Wd.) AL2	.8	BY30
Mount Pleasant Pl, SE18 off Orchard Rd	.105	ER77
Mount Pleasant Rd, E17	.47	DY54
N17	.46	DS54
NW10	.81	CW66
SE13	.123	EB86
W5	.79	CJ70
Caterham CR3	.176	DU123
Chigwell IG7	.49	ER49
Dartford DA1	.128	FM86
New Malden KT3	.138	CQ97
Romford RM5	.51	FD51
Mount Pleasant Vil, N4	.65	DM59
Mount Pleasant Wk, Bex. DA5	.127	FC85
Mount Rd, NW2	.63	CV62
NW4	.63	CU58
SE19	.122	DR93
SW19	.120	DA89
Barnet EN4	.28	DE43
Bexleyheath DA6	.126	EX85
Chessington KT9	.156	CM106
Dagenham RM8	.70	EZ60
Dartford DA1	.127	FF86
Epping CM16	.18	EW32
Feltham TW13	.116	BY90
Hayes UB3	.95	BT75
Ilford IG1	.69	EP64
Mitcham CR4	.140	DE96
New Malden KT3	.138	CR97
Woking GU22	.166	AV121
Woking (Chobham) GU24	.150	AV112
Mount Row, W1	.199	H1
Mountsfield Cl, Stai. TW19	.114	BG86
Mountsfield Ct, SE13	.123	ED86
Mountside, Felt. TW13	.116	BY90
Stanmore HA7	.41	CF53
Mounts Pond Rd, SE3	.103	ED82
Mount Sq, The, NW3 off Heath St	.64	DC62
Mounts Rd, Green. DA9	.129	FV85
Mount Stewart Av, Har. HA3	.61	CK68
Mount St, W1	.198	G1
Mount Ter, E off New Rd	.84	DV71
Mount Vernon, NW3	.64	DC63
Ⓗ Mount Vernon Hosp, Nthwd. HA6	.39	BP51
Mount Vw, NW7	.42	CR48
W5	.79	CK70
Enfield EN2	.29	DM38
Mountview, Nthwd. HA6	.39	BT51
Mount Vw, Rick. WD3	.38	BH46
St. Albans (Lon.Col.) AL2	.10	CL27
Mountview Ct, N8 off Green Las	.65	DP56
Mount Vw Rd, E4	.47	EC45
N4	.65	DL59
NW9	.62	CR56
Mountview Rd, Esher (Clay.) KT10	.155	CH108
Orpington BR6	.146	EU101
Waltham Cross (Chsht.) EN7	.14	DS26
Mount Vil, SE27	.121	DP90
Mountway, Pot.B. EN6	.12	DA30
Mountwood, W.Mol. KT8	.136	CA97
Mountwood Cl, S.Croy. CR2	.160	DV110
Movers La, Bark. SW14	.87	ES68
Mowatt Cl, N19	.65	DK60
Mowbray Av, W.Byf. (Byfleet) KT14	.152	BL113
Mowbray Cres, Egh. TW20	.113	BA92
Mowbray Rd, NW6	.81	CY66
SE19	.142	DT95
Barnet EN5	.28	DC42
Edgware HA8	.42	CN49
Richmond TW10	.117	CJ90
Mowbrays Cl, Rom. RM5	.51	FC54
Mowbrays Rd, Rom. RM5	.51	FC54
Mowbrey Gdns, Loug. IG10	.33	EQ40
Mowlem St, E2	.84	DV68
Mowlem Trd Est, N17	.46	DW52
Mowll St, SW9	.101	DN80
Moxom Av, Wal.Cr. (Chsht.) EN8	.15	DY30
Moxon Cl, E13 off Whitelegg Rd	.86	EF68
Moxon St, W1	.194	F7
Barnet EN5	.27	CZ41
Moye Cl, E2 off Dove Row	.84	DU67
Moyers Rd, E10	.67	EC59
Moylan Rd, W6	.99	CY79
Moyne Cl, Wok. GU21 off Iveagh Rd	.166	AT118
Moyne Pl, NW10	.80	CN68
Moynihan Dr, N21	.29	DL43
Moys Cl, Croy. CR0	.141	DL100
Moyser Rd, SW16	.121	DH92
Mozart St, W10	.81	CZ69
Mozart Ter, SW1	.198	G9
Muchelney Rd, Mord. SM4	.140	DC100
Muckhatch La, Egh. TW20	.133	BB97
MUCKINGFORD, S.le H.	.111	GM76
Muckingford Rd, S.le H. (Linford) SS17	.111	GM77
Tilbury (W.Til.) RM18	.111	GL77
DLR Mudchute	.204	C8
Muddy La, Slou. SL2	.74	AS71
Mud La, W5	.79	CK71
Muggeridge Cl, S.Croy. CR2	.160	DR106
Muggeridge Rd, Dag. RM10	.71	FB63
MUGSWELL, Couls.	.184	DB125
Muirdown Av, SW14	.98	CQ84
Muir Dr, SW18	.120	DD86
Muirfield, W3	.80	CS72
Muirfield Cl, SE16 off Ryder Dr	.102	DV78
Watford WD19	.40	BW49
Muirfield Cres, E14	.204	B6
Muirfield Grn, Wat. WD19	.40	BW49
Muirfield Rd, Wat. WD19	.40	BX49
Woking GU21	.166	AU118
Muirkirk Rd, SE6	.123	EC88
Muir Rd, E5	.66	DU63
Muir St, E16 off Newland St	.87	EM74
Mulberry Av, Stai. TW19	.114	BL88
Windsor SL4	.92	AT83
Mulberry Business Cen, SE16	.203	J5
Mulberry Cl, E4	.47	EA47
N8	.65	DL57
NW3 off Hampstead High St	.64	DD63
NW4	.63	CW55
SE7 off Charlton Pk Rd	.104	EK79
SE22	.122	DU85
Mulberry Cl, SW3 off Beaufort St	.100	DD79
SW16	.121	DJ91
Amersham HP7	.20	AT39
Barnet EN4	.28	DD42
Northolt UB5 off Parkfield Av	.78	BY68
Romford RM2	.71	FH56
St. Albans (Park St.) AL2	.8	CB28
Weybridge KT13	.135	BP104
Woking GU21	.150	AY114
Mulberry Ct, Bark. IG11 off Westrow Dr	.87	ET66
Mulberry Cres, Brent. TW8	.97	CH80
West Drayton UB7	.94	BN75
Mulberry Dr, Purf. RM19	.108	FM77
Slough SL3	.92	AY78
Mulberry Gdns, Rad. (Shenley) WD7	.10	CL33
Mulberry Gate, Bans. SM7	.173	CZ116
West Drayton UB7	.94	BN75
Mulberry Hill, Brwd. CM15	.55	FZ45
Mulberry La, Croy. CR0	.142	DT102
Mulberry Ms, SE14 off Lewisham Way	.103	DZ81
Wallington SM6 off Ross Rd	.159	DJ107
Mulberry Par, West Dr. UB7	.94	BN76
Mulberry Pl, W6 off Chiswick Mall	.99	CU78
Mulberry Rd, E8	.84	DT66
Gravesend (Nthflt.) DA11	.130	GE90
Mulberry St, E1 off Adler St	.84	DU72
Mulberry Trees, Shep. TW17	.135	BQ101
Mulberry Wk, SW3	.100	DD79
Mulberry Way, E18	.48	EH54
Belvedere DA17	.107	FC75
Ilford IG6	.69	EQ56
Mulgrave Rd, NW10	.63	CT63
SE18	.105	EM77
SW6	.99	CZ79
W5	.79	CK69
Croydon CR0	.142	DR104
Harrow HA1	.61	CG61
Sutton SM2	.158	DA107
Mulgrave Way, Wok. (Knap.) GU21	.166	AS118
Mulholland Cl, Mitch. CR4	.141	DH96
Mulkern Rd, N19	.65	DK60
Mullards Cl, Mitch. CR4	.140	DF102
Mullein Ct, Grays RM17	.110	GD79
Mullens Rd, Egh. TW20	.113	BB92
Muller Rd, SW4	.121	DK86
Mullet Gdns, E2 off St. Peter's Cl	.84	DU68
Mullins Path, SW14	.98	CR83
Mullion Cl, Har. HA3	.40	CB53
Mullion Wk, Wat. WD19 off Ormskirk Rd	.40	BX49
Mull Wk, N1 off Clephane Rd	.84	DQ65
Mulready St, NW8	.194	B5
Multi-way, W3 off Valetta Rd	.98	CS75
Multon Rd, SW18	.120	DD87
Mulvaney Way, SE1	.201	L5
Mumford Ct, EC2	.197	J8
Mumford Rd, SE24 off Railton Rd	.121	DP85
Mumfords La, Ger.Cr. (Chal.St.P.) SL9	.56	AU55
Muncaster Cl, Ashf. TW15	.114	BN91
Muncaster Rd, SW11	.120	DF85
Ashford TW15	.115	BP92
Muncies Ms, SE6	.123	EC89
Mundania Rd, SE22	.122	DV86
Munday Rd, E16	.86	EG72
Mundells, Wal.Cr. EN7	.14	DU27
Munden Dr, Wat. WD25	.24	BY37
Munden Gro, Wat. WD24	.24	BW38
Munden St, W14	.99	CY77
Munden Vw, Wat. WD25	.24	BX36
Mundesley Cl, Wat. WD19	.40	BW49
Mundesley Spur, Slou. SL1	.74	AS72
Mundford Rd, E5	.66	DW61
Mundon Gdns, Ilf. IG1	.69	ER60
Mund St, W14	.99	CZ78
Mundy St, N1	.197	M2
Munford Dr, Swans. DA10	.130	FY87
Mungo Pk Cl, Bushey (Bushey Hth.) WD23	.40	CC47
Mungo Pk Rd, Grav. DA12	.131	GK92
Rainham RM13	.89	FG65
Mungo Pk Way, Orp. BR6	.146	EW101
Munnery Way, Orp. BR6	.145	EN104
Munnings Gdns, Islw. TW7	.117	CD85
Munro Dr, N11	.45	DJ51
Munro Ms, W10	.81	CY71
Munro Rd, Bushey WD23	.24	CB43
Munro Ter, SW10	.100	DD80
Munslow Gdns, Sutt. SM1	.158	DD105
Munster Av, Houns. TW4	.96	BZ84
Munster Ct, Tedd. TW11	.117	CJ93
Munster Gdns, N13	.45	DP49
Munster Ms, SW6 off Munster Rd	.99	CY80
Munster Rd, SW6	.99	CZ81
Teddington TW11	.117	CH93
Munster Sq, NW1	.195	J3
Munton Rd, SE17	.201	J8
Murchison Av, Bex. DA5	.126	EX88
Murchison Rd, E10	.67	EC61
Murdoch Cl, Stai. TW18	.114	BG92
Murdock Cl, E16 off Rogers Rd	.86	EF72
Murdock St, SE15	.102	DV79
Murfett Cl, SW19	.119	CY89
Murfitt Way, Upmin. RM14	.72	FN63
Muriel Av, Wat. WD18	.24	BW43
Muriel St, N1	.83	DM68
Murillo Rd, SE13	.103	ED84
Murphy St, SE1	.200	D5
Murray Av, Brom. BR1	.144	EH96
Hounslow TW3	.116	CB85
Murray Business Cen, Orp. BR5	.146	EV97
Murray Cres, Pnr. HA5	.40	BX53

Mur - New

Murray Grn, Wok. GU21
off Bunyard Dr 151 BC114
Murray Gro, N1 . . . . .197 J1
Murray Ms, NW1 . . . . .83 DK66
Murray Rd, SW19 . . . . .119 CX93
W5 . . . . .97 CJ77
Chertsey (Ott.) KT16 . . .151 BC107
Northwood HA6 . . . . .39 BS53
Orpington BR5 . . . . .146 EV97
Richmond TW10 . . . . . . .117 CH89
Murrays La, W.Byf. (Byfleet)
KT14 . . . . .152 BK114
Murray Sq, E16 . . . . .86 EG72
Murray St, NW1 . . . . .83 DK66
Murray Ter, NW3 off Flask Wk . .64 DC63
W5 off Murray Rd 97 CK77
Murrells Wk, Lthd. (Bkhm.)
KT23 . . . . .170 CA123
Murreys, The, Ashtd. KT21 . .171 CK118
Mursell Est, SW8 . . . . .101 DM81
Murthering La, Rom. RM4 . . .35 FG43
Murtwell Dr, Chig. IG7 . . . . .49 EQ51
Musard Rd, W6 . . . . .99 CY79
W14 . . . . .99 CY79
Musbury St, E1 . . . . .84 DW72
Muscal, W6 . . . . .99 CY79
Muscatel Pl, SE5
off Dalwood St 102 DS81
Muschamp Rd, SE15 . . . . . .102 DT83
Carshalton SM5 . . . . . . .140 DE103
Muscovy Ho, Erith DA18
off Kale Rd 106 EY75
Muscovy St, EC3 . . . . .201 N1
★ Museum Interpretative Cen, E6
off Norman Rd 87 EM70
Museum La, SW7
off Exhibition Rd 100 DD76
★ Museum of Artillery,
The Rotunda, SE18 . . . . .105 EM78
★ Museum of Docklands,
E14 . . . . .204 A1
★ Museum of Garden History,
SE1 . . . . .200 B7
★ Museum of Instruments,
Royal Coll of Music, SW7 .100 DD76
★ Museum of London, EC2 .197 H7
★ Museum of Richmond, Rich.
TW9 . . . . .117 CK85
Museum Pas, E2
off Victoria Pk Sq 84 DV69
Museum St, WC1 . . . . .195 P7
Musgrave Cl, Barn. EN4 . . . . .28 DC39
Waltham Cross EN7
off Allwood Rd 14 DT27
Musgrave Cres, SW6 . . . . . .100 DA81
Musgrave Rd, Islw. TW7 . . . .97 CF81
Musgrove Rd, SE14 . . . . . . .103 DX81
★ Musical Mus, Brent. TW8
off High St 98 CL79
Musjid Rd, SW11
off Kambala Rd 100 DD82
Muskalls Cl, Wal.Cr. (Chsht.)
EN7 . . . . .14 DU27
Musket Cl, Barn. EN4
off East Barnet Rd 28 DD43
Musquash Way, Houns. TW4 . .96 BW82
Mussenden La, Dart. (Hort.Kir.)
DA4 . . . . .148 FQ99
Longfield (Fawk.Grn.) DA3 .149 FS101
Muston Rd, E5 . . . . .66 DV61
Mustow Pl, SW6
off Munster Rd 99 CZ82
Muswell Av, N10 . . . . .45 DH54
MUSWELL HILL, N10 . . . . . . .65 DH55
Muswell Hill, N10 . . . . .65 DH55
Muswell Hill Bdy, N10 . . . . . .65 DH55
Muswell Hill Pl, N10 . . . . . . .65 DH55
Muswell Hill Rd, N6 . . . . .64 DG58
N10 . . . . .64 DG56
Muswell Ms, N10
off Muswell Rd 65 DH55
Muswell Rd, N10 . . . . .65 DH55
Mutchetts Cl, Wat. WD25 . . . . .8 BY33
Mutrix Rd, NW6 . . . . .82 DA67
Mutton La, Pot.B. EN6 . . . . . .11 CY31
Mutton Pl, NW1
off Harmood St 83 DH65
Muybridge Rd, N.Mal. KT3 . .138 CQ96
Myatt Rd, SW9 . . . . .101 DP81
Myatt's Flds N, SW9
off Eythorne Rd 101 DN81
Myatt's Flds S, SW9
off Loughborough Rd 101 DN82
Mycenae Rd, SE3 . . . . .104 EG80
Myddelton Av, Enf. EN1 . . . . .30 DS38
Myddelton Cl, Enf. EN1 . . . . .30 DT39
Myddelton Gdns, N21 . . . . . .45 DP45
Myddelton Pas, EC1 . . . . . . .196 E2
Myddelton Pk, N20 . . . . .44 DD48
Myddelton Rd, N8 . . . . .65 DL56
Myddelton Sq, EC1 . . . . . . .196 E2
Myddelton St, EC1 . . . . .196 E3
Myddelton Av, N4 . . . . .66 DQ61
Myddelton Ms, N22 . . . . .45 DL52
Myddelton Path, Wal.Cr. (Chsht.)
EN7 . . . . .14 DV31
Myddleton Rd, N22 . . . . .45 DL52
Uxbridge UB8 . . . . .76 BJ67
Myers La, SE14 . . . . .103 DX79
Mygrove Cl, Rain. RM13 . . . . .90 FK68
Mygrove Gdns, Rain. RM13 . . .90 FK68
Mygrove Rd, Rain. RM13 . . . .90 FK68
Myles Ct, Wal.Cr. EN7 . . . . . .14 DQ29
Mylis Cl, SE26 . . . . .122 DV91
Mylius Cl, SE14
off Kender St 102 DW81
Mylne Cl, Wal.Cr. EN8 . . . . . .14 DW27
Mylne St, EC1 . . . . .196 D1
Mylor Cl, Wok. GU21 . . . . . .150 AY114
Mymms Dr, Hat. AL9 . . . . . . .12 DA26
Mynns Cl, Epsom KT18 . . . .156 CP114
Mynterne Ct, SW19
off Swanton Gdns 119 CX88
Myra St, SE2 . . . . .106 EU78

Myrdle St, E1 . . . . .84 DU71
Myrke, The, Slou. (Datchet)
SL3 . . . . .92 AT77
Myrna Cl, SW19 . . . . .120 DE94
Myron Pl, SE13 . . . . .103 EC83
Myrtle Av, Felt. TW14 . . . . . .95 BS84
Ruislip HA4 . . . . .59 BU59
Myrtleberry Cl, E8
off Beechwood Rd 84 DT65
Myrtle Cl, Barn. EN4 . . . . . . .44 DF46
Erith DA8 . . . . .107 FE81
Slough (Colnbr.) SL3 . . . . .93 BE81
Uxbridge UB8 off Violet Av .76 BM71
West Drayton UB7 . . . . . . .94 BM76
Myrtle Cres, Slou. SL2 . . . . . .74 AT73
Myrtledene Rd, SE2 . . . . . . .106 EU78
Myrtle Gdns, W7 . . . . .79 CE74
Myrtle Gro, Enf. EN2 . . . . . . .30 DR38
New Malden KT3 . . . . . . .138 CQ96
South Ockendon (Aveley)
RM15 . . . . .108 FQ75
Myrtle Pl, Dart. DA2 . . . . . . .129 FR87
Myrtle Rd, E6 . . . . .86 EL67
E17 . . . . .67 DY58
N13 . . . . .46 DQ48
W3 . . . . .80 CQ74
Brentwood CM14 . . . . . . .54 FW49
Croydon CR0 . . . . .143 EA104
Dartford DA1 . . . . .128 FK88
Hampton (Hmptn.H.)
TW12 . . . . .116 CC93
Hounslow TW3 . . . . .96 CC82
Ilford IG1 . . . . .69 EP61
Romford RM3 . . . . .52 FJ51
Sutton SM1 . . . . .158 DC106
Myrtleside Cl, Nthwd. HA6 . . .39 BR52
Myrtle Wk, N1 . . . . .197 M1
Mysore Rd, SW11 . . . . .100 DF83
Myton Rd, SE21 . . . . .122 DR90

N

N1 Shop Cen, N1 . . . . .83 DN68
Nadine Cl, Wall. SM6
off Woodcote Rd 159 DJ109
Nadine St, SE7 . . . . .104 EJ78
Nafferton Ri, Loug. IG10 . . . .32 EK43
Nagle Cl, E17 . . . . .47 ED54
Nag's Head Ct, EC1 . . . . . . .197 H5
Nags Head La, Brwd. CM14 . .53 FR51
Upminster RM14 . . . . . . .52 FQ53
Welling DA16 . . . . .106 EV83
Nags Head Rd, Enf. EN3 . . . .30 DW42
Nags Head Shop Cen, N7 . . .65 DM63
Nailsworth Cres, Red. RH1 . .185 DK129
Nailzee Cl, Ger.Cr. SL9 . . . . .56 AY59
Nairn Ct, Til. RM18
off Dock Rd 111 GF82
Nairne Gro, SE24 . . . . .122 DR85
Nairn Grn, Wat. WD19 . . . . . .39 BU48
Nairn Rd, Ruis. HA4 . . . . . . .78 BW65
Nairn St, E14 . . . . .85 EC71
Naish Ct, N1 . . . . .83 DL67
Nallhead Rd, Felt. TW13 . . . .116 BW92
Namba Roy Cl, SW16 . . . . . .121 DM91
Namton Dr, Th.Hth. CR7 . . . .141 DM98
Nan Clark's La, NW7 . . . . . . .43 CT47
Nancy Downs, Wat. WD19 . . .40 BW45
Nankin St, E14 . . . . .85 EA72
Nansen Rd, SW11 . . . . .100 DG84
Nansen Village, N12 . . . . . . .44 DB49
Nantes Cl, SW18 . . . . .100 DC84
Nantes Pas, E1 . . . . .197 P6
Nant Rd, NW2 . . . . .63 CZ61
Nant St, E2
off Cambridge Heath Rd . .84 DV69
Naoroji St, WC1 . . . . .196 D3
Nap, The, Kings L. WD4 . . . . . .6 BN29
Napier Av, E14 . . . . .204 A10
SW6 . . . . .99 CZ83
Napier Cl, SE8
off Amersham Vale 103 DZ80
W14 off Napier Rd 99 CZ76
Hornchurch RM11 . . . . . . .71 FH60
St. Albans (Lon.Col.) AL2 . . .9 CK25
West Drayton UB7 . . . . . . .94 BM76
Napier Ct, SW6
off Ranelagh Gdns 99 CZ83
Waltham Cross (Chsht.) EN8
off Flamstead End Rd 14 DV28
Napier Dr, Bushey WD23 . . . .24 BY42
Napier Ho, Rain. RM13 . . . . .89 FF69
Napier Gro, N1 . . . . .197 J1
Napier Pl, W14 . . . . .99 CZ76
Napier Rd, E6 . . . . .87 EN67
E11 . . . . .68 EE63
E15 . . . . .86 EE68
N17 . . . . .66 DS55
NW10 . . . . .81 CV69
SE25 . . . . .142 DV98
W14 . . . . .99 CY76
Ashford TW15 . . . . .115 BR94
Belvedere DA17 . . . . . . .106 EZ77
Bromley BR2 . . . . .144 EH98
Enfield EN3 . . . . .31 DX43
Gravesend (Nthflt.) DA11 .131 GF88
Hounslow (Hthrw.Air.) TW6 .94 BK81
Isleworth TW7 . . . . .97 CG84
South Croydon CR2 . . . . .160 DR108
Wembley HA0 . . . . .61 CK64
Napier Ter, N1 . . . . .83 DP66
Napoleon Rd, E5 . . . . .66 DV62
Twickenham TW1 . . . . . .117 CH87
Napsbury Av, St.Alb. (Lon.Col.)
AL2 . . . . .9 CJ26
Napton Cl, Hayes UB4
off Kingsash Dr 78 BY70
Narbonne Av, SW4 . . . . .121 DJ85
Narboro Ct, Rom. RM1
off Manor Rd 71 FG57
Narborough Cl, Uxb. UB10
off Aylsham Dr 59 BQ61
Narborough St, SW6 . . . . . .100 DB82

Narcissus Rd, NW6 . . . . .64 DA64
Narcot La, Ch.St.G. HP8 . . . .36 AU48
Gerrards Cross (Chal.St.P.)
SL9 . . . . .36 AV52
Narcot Rd, Ch.St.G. HP8 . . . .36 AU48
Narcot Way, Ch.St.G. HP8 . . .36 AU49
Nare Rd, S.Ock. (Aveley)
RM15 . . . . .90 FQ73
Naresby Fold, Stan. HA7
off Bernays Cl 41 CJ51
Narford Rd, E5 . . . . .66 DU62
Narrow Boat Cl, SE28
off Ridge Cl 105 ER75
Narrow La, Warl. CR6 . . . . . .176 DV119
Narrow St, E14 . . . . .85 DY73
Narrow Way, Brom. BR2 . . . .144 EL100
Nascot Pl, Wat. WD17 . . . . . .23 BV39
Nascot Rd, Wat. WD17 . . . . . .23 BV40
Nascot St, W12 . . . . .81 CW72
Watford WD17 . . . . .23 BV40
Nascot Wd Rd, Wat. WD17 . . .23 BT37
Naseberry Ct, E4
off Merriam Cl 47 EC50
Naseby Cl, NW6
off Fairfax Rd 82 DC66
Isleworth TW7 . . . . .97 CE81
Naseby Ct, Walt. KT12
off Clements Rd 136 BW103
Naseby Rd, SE19 . . . . .122 DR93
Dagenham RM10 . . . . . . .70 FA62
Ilford IG5 . . . . .49 EM53
Nash Cl, Borwd. (Elstree)
WD6 . . . . .26 CM42
Sutton SM1 . . . . .140 DD104
Nash Ct, E14 . . . . .204 B3
Nash Cft, Grav. (Nthflt.)
DA11 . . . . .130 GE91
Nash Dr, Red. RH1 . . . . .184 DF132
Nash Gdns, Red. RH1 . . . . . .184 DF132
Nash Grn, Brom. BR1 . . . . . .124 EG93
Hemel Hempstead HP3 . . . .6 BM25
Nash La, Kes. BR2 . . . . .162 EG106
Nash Mills La, Hem.H. HP3 . . .6 BM26
Nash Rd, N9 . . . . .46 DW47
SE4 . . . . .103 DY84
Romford RM6 . . . . .70 EX56
Slough SL3 . . . . .93 AZ77
Nash St, NW1 . . . . .195 J3
Nash's Yd, Uxb. UB8
off Bakers Rd 76 BK66
Nash Way, Har. HA3 . . . . .61 CH58
Nasmyth St, W6 . . . . .99 CV76
Nassau Path, SE28
off Disraeli Cl 88 EW74
Nassau Rd, SW13 . . . . .99 CT81
Nassau St, W1 . . . . .195 K7
Nassington Rd, NW3 . . . . . . .64 DE63
Natalie Cl, Felt. TW14 . . . . . .115 BR87
Natalie Ms, Twick. TW2
off Sixth Cross Rd 117 CD90
Natal Rd, N11 . . . . .45 DL51
SW16 . . . . .121 DK93
Ilford IG1 . . . . .69 EP63
Thornton Heath CR7 . . . .142 DR97
Nathan Cl, Upmin. RM14 . . . .73 FS60
Nathaniel Cl, E1
off Thrawl St 84 DT71
Nathans Rd, Wem. HA0 . . . . .61 CJ60
Nathan Way, SE28 . . . . .105 ES77
★ National Army Mus,
SW3 . . . . .100 DF79
Ｈ National Blood Service/
Brentwood Transfusion
Service, Brwd. CM15 . . . . .55 FZ46
★ National Gall, WC2 . . . . . .199 N1
Ｈ National Hosp for Neurology
& Neurosurgery, WC1 . . . .64 DE56
Ｈ National Hosp for Neurology
& Neurosurgery, The, WC1 .196 A5
★ National Maritime Mus,
SE10 . . . . .103 ED79
★ National Portrait Gall,
WC2 . . . . .199 N1
National Ter, SE16
off Bermondsey Wall E . . .102 DV75
Nation Way, E4 . . . . .47 EC46
★ Natural History Mus,
SW7 . . . . .100 DD76
Naunton Way, Horn. RM12 . . .72 FK62
Naval Row, E14 . . . . .85 EC73
Naval Wk, Brom. BR1
off High St 144 EG97
Navarino Gro, E8 . . . . .84 DU65
Navarino Rd, E8 . . . . .84 DU65
Navarre Gdns, Rom. RM5 . . .51 FB51
Navarre Rd, E6 . . . . .86 EL68
Navarre St, E2 . . . . .197 P4
Navenby Wk, E3
off Rounton Rd 85 EA70
Navestock Cl, E4
off Mapleton Rd 47 EC48
Navestock Cres, Wdf.Grn. IG8 .48 EJ53
Navestock Ho, Bark. IG11 . . . .88 EV68
Navigator Dr, Sthl. UB2 . . . . .96 CC75
Navy St, SW4 . . . . .101 DK83
Naylor Gro, Enf. EN3
off South St 31 DX43
Naylor Rd, N20 . . . . .44 DC47
SE15 . . . . .102 DV80
Naylor Ter, Slou. (Colnbr.) SL3
off Vicarage Way 93 BC80
Nazareth Gdns, SE15 . . . . . .102 DV82
NAZEING GATE, Wal.Abb. 16 EJ25
Nazeing Wk, Rain. RM13
off Ongar Way 89 FE67
Nazrul St, E2 . . . . .197 P2
Neagle Ho, Brwd. WD6
off Balcon Way 26 CQ39
Neal Av, Sthl. UB1 . . . . .78 BZ70
Neal Cl, Ger.Cr. SL9 . . . . .57 BB60
Northwood HA6 . . . . .39 BU53
Neal Ct, Wal.Abb. EN9 . . . . . .16 EF33
Nealden St, SW9 . . . . .101 DM83
Neale Cl, N2 . . . . .64 DC55
Neal St, WC2 . . . . .195 P9
Watford WD18 . . . . .24 BW43
Neal's Yd, WC2 . . . . .195 P9

Near Acre, NW9 . . . . .43 CT53
NEASDEN, NW2 . . . . .62 CS62
⊖ Neasden 62 CS64
Neasden Cl, NW10 . . . . .62 CS64
Neasden La, NW10 . . . . .62 CS63
Neasden La N, NW10 . . . . . .62 CR62
Neasham Rd, Dag. RM8 . . . . .70 EV64
Neate St, SE5 . . . . .102 DT79
Neath Gdns, Mord. SM4 . . . .140 DC100
Neats Acre, Ruis. HA4 . . . . . .59 BR59
Neatscourt Rd, E6 . . . . .86 EK71
Neave Cres, Rom. RM3 . . . . .52 FJ53
Neb La, Oxt. RH8 . . . . .187 EC131
Nebraska St, SE1 . . . . .201 K5
Neckinger, SE16 . . . . .202 A6
Neckinger Est, SE16 . . . . . . .202 A6
Neckinger St, SE1 . . . . .202 A5
Nectarine Way, SE13 . . . . . .103 EB82
Needham Rd, W11
off Westbourne Gro 82 DA72
Needham Ter, NW2
off Kara Way 63 CX62
Needleman St, SE16 . . . . . . .203 H5
Needles Bk, Gdse. RH9 . . . .186 DV131
Neela Cl, Uxb. UB10 . . . . . . .59 BP63
Neeld Cres, NW4 . . . . .63 CV57
Wembley HA9 . . . . .62 CN64
Neeld Par, Wem. HA9
off Harrow Rd 62 CN64
Neil Cl, Ashf. TW15 . . . . . . .115 BQ92
Neil Wates Cres, SW2 . . . . . .121 DN88
Nelgarde Rd, SE6 . . . . .123 EA87
Nella Rd, W6 . . . . .99 CX79
Nelldale Rd, SE16 . . . . .202 F8
Nellgrove Rd, Uxb. UB10 . . . .77 BP70
Nell Gwynn Cl, Rad. (Shenley)
WD7 . . . . .10 CL32
Nell Gwynne Av, Shep.
TW17 . . . . .135 BR100
Nell Gwynne Cl, Epsom KT19
off Ripley Way 156 CN111
Nello James Gdns, SE27 . . . .122 DR91
Nelmes Cl, Horn. RM11 . . . . .72 FM57
Nelmes Cres, Horn. RM11 . . .72 FL57
Nelmes Rd, Horn. RM11 . . . .72 FL59
Nelmes Way, Horn. RM11 . . . .72 FL56
Nelson Cl, NW6 . . . . .82 DA68
Brentwood CM14 . . . . . . .54 FV50
Croydon CR0 . . . . .141 DP102
Feltham TW14 . . . . .115 BT88
Romford RM7 . . . . .51 FB53
Slough SL3 . . . . .92 AX77
Uxbridge UB10 . . . . .77 BP69
Walton-on-Thames KT12 . .135 BV102
Westerham (Bigg.H.) TN16 .178 EL117
Nelson Ct, SE16
off Brunel Rd 84 DW74
Nelson Gdns, E2 . . . . .84 DU69
Hounslow TW3 . . . . .116 CA86
Nelson Gro Rd, SW19 . . . . . .140 DB95
Ｈ Nelson Hosp, SW20 . . . .139 CZ96
Nelson La, Uxb. UB10
off Nelson Rd 77 BP69
Nelson Mandela Cl, N10 . . . . .44 DG54
Nelson Mandela Rd, SE3 . . . .104 EJ83
Nelson Pas, EC1 . . . . .197 J3
Nelson Pl, N1 . . . . .196 G1
Sidcup DA14 . . . . .126 EU91
Nelson Rd, E4 . . . . .47 EB51
E11 . . . . .68 EG56
N8 . . . . .65 DM57
N9 . . . . .46 DV47
N15 . . . . .66 DS56
SE10 . . . . .103 EC79
SW19 . . . . .120 DB94
Ashford TW15 . . . . .114 BL92
Belvedere DA17 . . . . . . .106 EZ78
Bromley BR2 . . . . .144 EJ98
Caterham CR3 . . . . .176 DR123
Dartford DA1 . . . . .128 FJ86
Enfield EN3 . . . . .31 DX44
Gravesend (Nthflt.) DA11 .131 GF89
Harrow HA1 . . . . .61 CD60
Hounslow TW3 . . . . .116 CC87
Hounslow (Hthrw.Air.) TW6 .94 BM82
New Malden KT3 . . . . . . .138 CR99
Rainham RM13 . . . . .89 FF68
Sidcup DA14 . . . . .126 EU91
South Ockendon RM15 . . .91 FW68
Stanmore HA7 . . . . .41 CJ51
Twickenham TW2 . . . . . .116 CC86
Uxbridge UB10 . . . . .77 BP69
Nelson's Column, WC2 . . . . .199 P2
Nelson Sq, SE1 . . . . .200 F4
Nelson's Row, SW4 . . . . . . .101 DK84
Nelson St, E1 . . . . .84 DV72
E6 . . . . .87 EM68
E16 off Huntingdon St 86 EF73
Nelsons Yd, NW1
off Mornington Cres 83 DJ68
Nelson Ter, N1 . . . . .196 G1
Nelson Trd Est, SW19 . . . . . .140 DB95
Nelson Wk, SE16 . . . . .203 L3
Nelwyn Av, Horn. RM11 . . . . .72 FM57
Nemoure Rd, W3 . . . . .80 CQ73
Nene Gdns, Felt. TW13 . . . . .116 BZ89
Nene Rd, Houns. (Hthrw.Air.)
TW6 . . . . .95 BP81
Nepaul Rd, SW11 . . . . .100 DE82
Nepean St, SW15 . . . . .119 CU86
Neptune Ct, Borwd. WD6
off Clarendon Rd 26 CN41
Neptune Rd, Har. HA1 . . . . . .61 CD58
Hounslow (Hthrw.Air.) TW6 .95 BR81
Neptune St, SE16 . . . . .202 F6
Neptune Wk, Erith DA8 . . . . .107 FD77
Nesbit Rd, SE9 . . . . .104 EK84
Nesbit Cl, SE3 off Hurren Cl .104 EE83
Nesbitts All, Barn. EN5
off Bath Pl 27 CZ41
Nesbitt Sq, SE19
off Coxwell Rd 122 DS94
Nesham St, E1 . . . . .202 B2
Ness Rd, Erith DA8 . . . . .108 FK79
Ness St, SE16 . . . . .202 B6
Nesta Rd, Wdf.Grn. IG8 . . . . .48 EE51

Nestles Av, Hayes UB3 . . . . . .95 BT76
Neston Rd, Wat. WD24 . . . . . .24 BW37
Nestor Av, N21 . . . . .29 DP44
Nethan Dr, S.Ock. (Aveley)
RM15 . . . . .90 FQ73
Netheravon Rd, W4 . . . . .99 CT77
W7 . . . . .79 CF74
Netheravon Rd S, W4 . . . . . . .99 CT78
Netherbury Rd, W5 . . . . .97 CK76
Netherby Gdns, Enf. EN2 . . . .29 DL42
Netherby Pk, Wey. KT13 . . . .153 BS106
Netherby Rd, SE23 . . . . .122 DW87
Nether Cl, N3 . . . . .44 DA53
Nethercote Av, Wok. GU21 . .166 AT117
Nethercourt Av, N3 . . . . .44 DA51
Netherfield Gdns, Bark. IG11 .87 ER65
Netherfield Rd, N12 . . . . .44 DB50
SW17 . . . . .120 DG90
Netherford Rd, SW4 . . . . . . .101 DJ82
Netherhall Gdns, NW3 . . . . . .82 DC65
Netherhall Way, NW3
off Netherhall Gdns 64 DC64
Netherlands, The, Couls.
CR5 . . . . .175 DJ119
Netherlands Rd, Barn. EN5 . . .28 DD44
Netherleigh Cl, N6 . . . . .65 DH60
Nethern Ct Rd, Cat. (Wold.)
CR3 . . . . .177 EA123
Netherne Dr, Couls. CR5 . . . .175 DH121
Netherne La, Couls. CR5 . . . .175 DK121
Redhill RH1 . . . . .175 DJ123
Netherpark Dr, Rom. RM2 . . .51 FF54
Nether St, N3 . . . . .44 DA53
N12 . . . . .44 DA52
Netherton Gro, SW10 . . . . . .100 DC79
Netherton Rd, N15 . . . . .66 DR58
Twickenham TW1 . . . . . .117 CH85
Netherwood, N2 . . . . .44 DD54
Netherwood Pl, W14
off Netherwood Rd 99 CX76
Netherwood Rd, W14 . . . . . . .99 CX76
Netherwood St, NW6 . . . . . . .81 CZ66
Netherwood St Est, NW6 . . . .81 CZ66
Netley Cl, Croy. (New Adgtn.)
CR0 . . . . .161 EC108
Sutton SM3 . . . . .157 CX106
Netley Dr, Walt. KT12 . . . . . .136 BZ101
Netley Gdns, Mord. SM4 . . . .140 DC101
Netley Rd, E17 . . . . .67 DZ57
Brentford TW8 . . . . .98 CL79
Hounslow (Hthrw.Air.) TW6 .95 BR81
Ilford IG2 . . . . .69 ER57
Morden SM4 . . . . .140 DC101
Netley St, NW1 . . . . .195 K3
Nettlecombe Cl, Sutt. SM2 . .158 DB109
Nettleden Av, Wem. HA9 . . . .80 CN65
Nettlefold Pl, SE27 . . . . .121 DP90
Nettlestead Cl, Beck. BR3
off Copers Cope Rd 123 DZ94
Nettleton Rd, SE14 . . . . .103 DX81
Hounslow (Hthrw.Air.)
TW6 . . . . .95 BP81
Uxbridge UB10 . . . . .58 BM63
Nettlewood Rd, SW16 . . . . . .121 DK94
Neuchatel Rd, SE6 . . . . .123 DZ89
Nevada Cl, N.Mal. KT3
off Georgia Rd 138 CQ98
Nevada St, SE10 . . . . .103 EC79
Nevell Grays RM16 . . . . .111 GH76
Nevern Pl, SW5 . . . . .100 DA77
Nevern Rd, SW5 . . . . .100 DA77
Nevern Sq, SW5 . . . . .100 DA77
Nevil Cl, Nthwd. HA6 . . . . . . .39 BQ50
Neville Av, N.Mal. KT3 . . . . .138 CR95
Neville Cl, E11 . . . . .68 EF62
NW1 . . . . .195 N1
NW6 . . . . .81 CZ68
SE15 . . . . .102 DU80
W3 off Acton La 98 CQ75
Banstead SM7 . . . . .158 DB114
Esher KT10 . . . . .154 BZ107
Hounslow TW3 . . . . .96 CB82
Potters Bar EN6 . . . . .11 CZ31
Sidcup DA15 . . . . .125 ET91
Slough (Stoke P.) SL2 . . . .74 AT65
Neville Dr, N2 . . . . .64 DC58
Neville Gdns, Dag. RM8 . . . . .70 EX62
Neville Gill Cl, SW18 . . . . . .120 DA86
Neville Pl, N22 . . . . .45 DM53
Neville Rd, E7 . . . . .86 EG66
NW6 . . . . .81 CZ68
W5 . . . . .79 CK70
Croydon CR0 . . . . .142 DR101
Dagenham RM8 . . . . .70 EX61
Ilford IG6 . . . . .49 EQ53
Kingston upon Thames
KT1 . . . . .138 CN96
Richmond TW10 . . . . . . .117 CJ90
Neville St, SW7 . . . . .100 DD78
Neville Ter, SW7 . . . . .100 DD78
Neville Wk, Cars. SM5
off Green Wrythe La 140 DE101
Nevill Gro, Wat. WD24 . . . . . .23 BV39
Nevill Rd, N16 . . . . .66 DS63
Nevill Way, Loug. IG10
off Valley Hill 48 EL45
Nevin Dr, E4 . . . . .47 EB46
Nevinson Cl, SW18 . . . . .120 DD86
Nevis Cl, Rom. RM1 . . . . .51 FE51
Nevis Rd, SW17 . . . . .120 DG89
Newacres Rd, SE28 . . . . .87 ES74
NEW ADDINGTON, Croy. 161 ED109
⊖ New Addington 161 EC110
Newall Rd, Houns. (Hthrw.Air.)
TW6 . . . . .95 BQ81
New Arc, Uxb. UB8
off High St 76 BK67
Newark Cl, Wok. (Ripley)
GU23 . . . . .168 BG121
Newark Cotts, Wok. (Ripley)
GU23 . . . . .168 BG121
Newark Ct, Walt. KT12 . . . . .136 BW102
off St. Johns Dr
Newark Cres, NW10 . . . . .80 CR69
Newark Grn, Borwd. WD6 . . . .26 CR41
Newark Knok, E6 . . . . .87 EN72

Newark La, Wok. (Ripley)
GU23 . . . . .167 BF118
Newark Par, NW4
off Greyhound Hill 63 CU55
Newark Rd, S.Croy. CR2 . . .160 DR107
Newark St, E1 . . . . .84 DV71
New Ash Way, NW4 . . . . . . .63 CU56
New Ash Cl, N2
off Oakridge Dr 64 DD55
NEW ASH GREEN, Long. 149 FX103
New Atlas Wf, E14 . . . . . . .203 N7
New Barn Cl, Wall. SM6
off Merlin Cl 159 DM107
NEW BARNET, Barn. 28 DB42
⇌ New Barnet 28 DD43
New Barn La, Beac. HP9 . . . . .36 AS49
Sevenoaks (Cudham) . . . . .
TN14 . . . . .179 EQ116
Westerham TN16 . . . . . . .179 EQ118
Whyteleafe CR3 . . . . .176 DS117
New Barn Rd, Grav. (Sthflt.)
DA13 . . . . .130 GC90
Swanley BR8 . . . . .147 FE95
New Barns Av, Mitch. CR4 . . .141 DK98
New Barn St, E13 . . . . .86 EG70
New Barns Way, Chig. IG7 . . .49 EP48
New Battlebridge La, Red.
RH1 . . . . .185 DH130
NEW BECKENHAM, Beck. . . .123 DZ93
⇌ New Beckenham 123 DZ94
Newberries Av, Rad. WD7 . . . .25 CH35
New Berry La, Walt. KT12 . . .154 BX106
Newbery Rd, Erith DA8 . . . . .107 FF81
Newbiggin Path, Wat. WD19 . . .88 BW49
Newbolt Av, Sutt. SM3 . . . . .157 CW106
Newbolt Rd, Stan. HA7 . . . . .41 CF51
New Bond St, W1 . . . . .195 H9
Newborough Grn, N.Mal.
KT3 . . . . .138 CR98
New Brent St, NW4 . . . . . . .63 CW57
Newbridge Pt, SE23
off Windrush La 123 DX90
New Br St, EC4 . . . . .196 F9
New Broad St, EC2 . . . . . . .197 M7
New Bdy, W5 . . . . .79 CJ73
Hampton (Hmptn.H.) TW12
off Hampton Rd 117 CD92
Newburgh Rd, W3 . . . . .80 CQ74
Grays RM17 . . . . .110 GD78
Newburgh St, W1 . . . . .195 K9
New Burlington Ms, W1 . . . . .195 K10
New Burlington Pl, W1 . . . . .195 K10
New Burlington St, W1 . . . . .195 K10
Newburn St, SE11 . . . . .200 C10
Newbury Av, Enf. EN3 . . . . . .31 DZ38
Newbury Cl, Nthlt. UB5 . . . . .78 BZ65
Romford RM3 . . . . .52 FK51
Newbury Gdns, Epsom
KT19 . . . . .157 CT105
Romford RM3 . . . . .52 FK51
Upminster RM14 . . . . .72 FM62
Newbury Ho, N22 . . . . .45 DL53
Newbury Ms, NW5
off Malden Rd 82 DG65
NEWBURY PARK, Ilf. 69 ER57
⊖ Newbury Park 69 ER58
Newbury Rd, E4 . . . . .47 EC51
Bromley BR2 . . . . .144 EG92
Hounslow (Hthrw.Air.) TW6 . .94 BM81
Ilford IG2 . . . . .69 ER58
Romford RM3 . . . . .52 FK50
Newbury St, EC1 . . . . .197 H7
Newbury Wk, Rom. RM3 . . . . .52 FK50
Newbury Way, Nthlt. UB5 . . . .78 BY65
New Butt La, SE8 . . . . .103 EA80
off Reginald Rd 103 EA80
New Butt La N, SE8
off Reginald Rd 103 EA80
Newby Cl, Enf. EN1 . . . . . . .30 DS40
Newby Pl, E14 . . . . .85 EC73
Newby St, SW8 . . . . .101 DH83
New Caledonian Wf, SE16 . . .203 M6
Newcastle Av, Ilf. IG6 . . . . . .50 EU51
Newcastle Cl, EC4 . . . . . . .196 F8
Newcastle Pl, W2 . . . . .194 A7
Newcastle Row, EC1 . . . . . .196 E4
New Cavendish St, W1 . . . . .195 J6
New Change, EC4 . . . . .197 H9
New Chapel Sq, Felt. TW13 . . .115 BV88
New Charles St, EC1 . . . . . .196 G2
NEW CHARLTON, SE7 . . . . . .104 EJ77
New Ch Ct, SE19
off Waldegrave Rd 122 DU94
New Ch Rd, SE5 . . . . .102 DQ80
New City Rd, E13 . . . . .86 EJ69
New Cl, SW19 . . . . .140 DC97
Feltham TW13 . . . . .116 BY92
New Coll Ct, NW3
off College Cres 82 DC66
New Coll Ms, N1
off Islington Pk St 83 DN66
New Coll Par, NW3
off College Cres 82 DD65
Newcombe Gdns, SW16 . . . .121 DL91
Newcombe Pk, NW7 . . . . . . .42 CS50
Wembley HA0 . . . . .80 CM67
Newcombe Ri, West Dr. UB7 . .76 BL72
Newcombe St, W8
off Kensington Pl 82 DA74
Newcomen Rd, E11 . . . . . . .68 EF62
SW11 . . . . .100 DD83
Newcomen St, SE1 . . . . . . .201 K4
Newcome Path, Rad. (Shenley)
WD7 off Newcome Rd 10 CN34
Newcome Rd, Rad. (Shenley)
WD7 . . . . .10 CN34
New Compton St, WC2 . . . . .195 N9
New Concordia Wf, SE1 . . . . .202 B4
New Coppice, Wok. GU21 . . .166 AS119
New Cotts, Rain. (Wenn.)
RM13 . . . . .90 FJ72
New Ct, EC4 . . . . .196 D10
Addlestone KT15 . . . . . . .134 BJ104
Newcourt, Uxb. UB8 . . . . . . .76 BJ71
Newcourt St, NW8 . . . . . . .194 B1
★ New Covent Garden Mkt,
SW8 . . . . .101 DK80
New Covent Gdn Mkt, SW8 . .101 DK80

New Crane Pl, E1 . . . . .202 F2
Newcroft Cl, Uxb. UB8 . . . . . .76 BM71
NEW CROSS, SE14 . . . . . . .103 DY81
⇌ New Cross 103 DZ80
⊖ New Cross 103 DZ80
NEW CROSS GATE, SE14 . . .103 DX81
⇌ New Cross Gate 103 DY80
⊖ New Cross Gate 103 DY80
New Cross Rd, SE14 . . . . . .102 DW80
Newdales Cl, N9
off Balham Rd 46 DU47
Newdene Av, Nthlt. UB5 . . . . .78 BX68
Newdigate Grn, Uxb. (Hare.)
UB9 . . . . .38 BK53
Newdigate Rd, Uxb. (Hare.)
UB9 . . . . .38 BJ53
Newdigate Rd E, Uxb. (Hare.)
UB9 . . . . .38 BK53
Newell St, E14 . . . . .85 DZ72
NEW ELTHAM, SE9 . . . . . . .125 EN89
⇌ New Eltham 125 EP88
New End, NW3 . . . . .64 DC63
New End Sq, NW3 . . . . .64 DD63
Newent Cl, SE15 . . . . .102 DS80
Carshalton SM5 . . . . .140 DF102
New Era Est, N1
off Phillipp St 84 DS67
New Fm Av, Brom. BR2 . . . . .144 EG98
New Fm Dr, Rom. (Abridge)
RM4 . . . . .34 EV41
New Fm La, Nthwd. HA6 . . . . .39 BS53
New Ferry App, SE18 . . . . . .105 EN76
New Fetter La, EC4 . . . . . . .196 E8
Newfield Cl, Hmptn. TW12
off Percy Rd 136 CA95
Newfield Ri, NW2 . . . . .63 CV62
New Ford Rd, Wal.Cr. EN8 . . . .15 DZ34
New Forest La, Chig. IG7 . . . .49 EN51
Newgale Gdns, Edg. HA8 . . . .42 CM53
New Gdn Dr, West Dr. UB7
off Drayton Gdns 94 BL75
Newgate, Croy. CR0 . . . . . .142 DQ102
Newgate Cl, Felt. TW13 . . . . .116 BY89
Newgate St, E4 . . . . .48 EF48
EC1 . . . . .196 G8
Newgatestreet Rd, Wal.Cr. (Chsht.)
EN7 . . . . .13 DP27
Newgate St Village, Hert.
SG13 . . . . .13 DL25
New Globe Wk, SE1 . . . . . . .201 H2
New Goulston St, E1 . . . . . .197 P8
New Grn Pl, SE19
off Hawke Rd 122 DS93
New Hall Cl, Hem.H. (Bov.)
HP3 . . . . .5 BA27
Newhall Ct, Wal.Abb. EN9 . . . .16 EF33
New Hall Dr, Rom. RM3 . . . . .52 FL53
Newhall Gdns, Walt. KT12
off Rodney Rd 136 BW103
⊞ Newham Gen Hosp, E13 . . .86 EH70
Newhams Row, SE1 . . . . . . .201 N5
Newham Way, E6 . . . . .86 EJ71
E16 . . . . .86 EF71
Newhaven Cl, Hayes UB3 . . . .95 BT77
Newhaven Cres, Ashf. TW15 . .115 BR92
Newhaven Gdns, SE9 . . . . . .104 EK84
Newhaven La, E16 . . . . .86 EF70
Newhaven Rd, SE25 . . . . . . .142 DR99
NEW HAW, Add. 152 BK108
New Haw Rd, Add. KT15 . . . .152 BJ106
New Heston Rd, Houns. TW5 . .96 BZ80
New Horizons Ct, Brent. TW8
off Shield Dr 97 CG79
Newhouse Av, Rom. RM6 . . . .70 EX55
Newhouse Cl, N.Mal. KT3 . . .138 CS101
Newhouse Cres, Wat. WD25 . . .7 BV32
New Ho La, Epp. (N.Wld.Bas.)
CM16 . . . . .19 FC25
Gravesend DA11 . . . . . . .131 GF90
Newhouse Rd, Hem.H. (Bov.)
HP3 . . . . .5 BA26
Newhouse Wk, Mord. SM4 . . .140 DC101
Newick Cl, Bex. DA5 . . . . . .127 FB86
Newick Rd, E5 . . . . .66 DV62
Newing Grn, Brom. BR1 . . . . .144 EK94
NEWINGTON, SE1 . . . . .201 H8
Newington Barrow Way, N7 . . .65 DM62
Newington Butts, SE1 . . . . . .200 G9
SE11 . . . . .200 G9
Newington Causeway, SE1 . . .200 G7
Newington Grn, N1 . . . . .66 DR64
N16 . . . . .66 DR64
Newington Grn Rd, N1 . . . . . .84 DR65
New Inn Bdy, EC2 . . . . .197 N4
New Inn Ms, WC2 . . . . .196 C9
New Inn St, EC2 . . . . .197 N4
New Inn Yd, EC2 . . . . .197 N4
New James Ct, SE15
off Nunhead La 102 DV83
New Jersey Ter, SE15
off Nunhead La 102 DV83
New Jubilee Ct, Wdf.Grn. IG8
off Grange Av 48 EG52
New Kent Rd, SE1 . . . . .201 H7
New Kings Rd, SW6 . . . . . . .99 CZ82
New King St, SE8 . . . . .103 EA79
Newland Cl, Pnr. HA5 . . . . . .40 BY51
Newland Ct, Wem. HA9
off Forty Av 62 CN61
Newland Dr, Enf. EN1 . . . . . .30 DV39
Newland Gdns, W13 . . . . . . .97 CG75
Newland Rd, N8 . . . . .65 DL55
Newlands, Abb.L. (Bedmond)
WD5 . . . . .7 BT26
Newlands, The, Wall. SM6 . . .159 DJ108
Newlands Av, Rad. WD7 . . . . .9 CF34
Thames Ditton KT7 . . . . . .137 CE100
Woking GU22 . . . . .167 AZ121
Newlands Cl, Brwd. CM13 . . . .55 GD45
Edgware HA8 . . . . .42 CL48
Southall UB2 . . . . .96 BY78
Walton-on-Thames KT12 . . .154 BY105
Wembley HA0 . . . . .79 CJ65
Newlands Cl, SE9 . . . . .125 EN86
Newlands Dr, Slou. (Colnbr.)
SL3 . . . . .93 BE83
Newlands Pk, SE26 . . . . . . .123 DX92

Newlands Pl, Barn. EN5 . . . . .27 CX43
Newlands Quay, E1 . . . . . . .202 F1
Newlands Rd, SW16 . . . . . . .141 DL96
Woodford Green IG8 . . . . . .48 EF47
Newlands Wk, Wat. WD25
off Trevellance Way 8 BX33
Newlands Way, Chess. KT9 . . .155 CJ106
Potters Bar EN6 . . . . .12 DB30
Newlands Wd, Croy. CR0 . . . .161 DZ109
New La, Guil. (Sutt.Grn.)
GU4 . . . . .166 AY122
New Lo Dr, Oxt. RH8 . . . . . .188 EF128
New London St, EC3 . . . . . .197 N10
New Lydenburg St, SE7 . . . . .104 EJ76
Newlyn Cl, Orp. BR6 . . . . . .163 ET105
St. Albans (Brick.Wd.) AL2 . . .8 BY30
Uxbridge UB8 . . . . .76 BN71
Newlyn Gdns, Har. HA2 . . . . .60 BZ59
Newlyn Rd, N17 . . . . .46 DT53
NW2 off Tilling Rd 63 CW60
Barnet EN5 . . . . .27 CZ42
Welling DA16 . . . . .105 ET82
NEW MALDEN 138 CR97
⇌ New Malden 138 CS97
Newman Cl, Horn. RM11 . . . .72 FL57
Newman Pas, W1 . . . . .195 L7
Newman Rd, E13 . . . . .86 EH69
E17 off Southcote Rd 67 DX57
Bromley BR1 . . . . .144 EG95
Croydon CR0 . . . . .141 DM102
Hayes UB3 . . . . .77 BV73
Newmans Cl, Loug. IG10 . . . .33 EP41
Newman's Ct, EC3 . . . . .197 L9
Newmans Dr, Brwd. CM13 . . . .55 GC45
Newmans La, Loug. IG10 . . . .33 EN41
Surbiton KT6 . . . . .137 CK100
Newmans Rd, Grav. (Nthflt.)
DA11 . . . . .131 GF89
Newman's Row, WC2 . . . . . .196 C7
Newman St, W1 . . . . .195 L7
Newmans Way, Barn. EN4 . . . .28 DC39
Newnham Av, Ruis. HA4 . . . . .60 BW60
Newnham Cl, Loug. IG10 . . . .32 EK44
Northolt UB5 . . . . .60 CC64
Slough SL2 . . . . .74 AU74
Thornton Heath CR7 . . . . . .142 DQ96
Newnham Gdns, Nthlt. UB5 . . .60 CC64
Newnham Ms, N22
off Newnham Rd 45 DM53
Newnham Pl, Grays RM16 . . .111 GG77
Newnham Rd, N22 . . . . .45 DM53
Newnhams Cl, Brom. BR1 . . .145 EM97
Newnham Ter, SE1 . . . . .200 D6
Newnham Way, Har. HA3 . . . .62 CL57
New Pl, N1 EC2 . . . . .197 M5
New N Rd, N1 . . . . .197 L1
Ilford IG6 . . . . .49 ER52
New N St, WC1 . . . . .196 B6
Newnton Cl, N4 . . . . .66 DR59
New Oak Rd, N2 . . . . .44 DC54
New Orleans Wk, N19 . . . . . .65 DK59
New Oxford St, WC1 . . . . . .195 N8
New Par, Ashf. TW15
off Church Rd 114 BM91
Rickmansworth (Chorl.) WD3
off Whitelands Av 21 BC42
New Par Flats, Rick. (Chorl.) WD3
off Whitelands Av 21 BC42
New Pk Av, N13 . . . . .46 DQ48
New Pk Cl, Nthlt. UB5 . . . . . .78 BY65
New Pk Ct, SW2 . . . . .121 DL87
New Pk Par, SW2
off Doverfield Rd 121 DL86
New Pk Rd, SW2 . . . . .121 DK88
Ashford TW15 . . . . .115 BQ92
Uxbridge (Hare.) UB9 . . . . .38 BJ53
New Peachey La, Uxb. UB8 . . .76 BK72
Newpiece, Loug. IG10 . . . . . .33 EP41
New Pl Gdns, Upmin. RM14 . . .73 FR61
New Pl Sq, SE16 . . . . .202 D6
New Plaistow Rd, E15 . . . . . .86 EE67
Newport Av, E13 . . . . .86 EH70
E14 . . . . .85 ED73
Newport Cl, Enf. EN3 . . . . . .31 DY37
Newport Ct, WC2 . . . . .195 N10
Newport Mead, Wat. WD19
off Kilmarnock Rd 40 BX49
Newport Pl, WC2 . . . . .195 N10
Newport Rd, E10 . . . . .67 EC61
E17 . . . . .67 DY56
SW13 . . . . .99 CU81
Hayes UB4 . . . . .77 BR70
Hounslow (Hthrw.Air.) TW6 . .94 BN81
Newports, Swan. BR8 . . . . . .147 FD101
Newport St, SE11 . . . . .200 B9
New Printing Ho Sq, WC1
off Gray's Inn Rd 83 DM70
New Priory Ct, NW6
off Mazenod Av 82 DA66
Newquay Cres, Har. HA2 . . . .60 BY61
Newquay Gdns, Wat. WD19
off Fulford Gro 39 BV47
Newquay Rd, SE6 . . . . .123 EB89
New Quebec St, W1 . . . . . . .194 E9
New Ride, SW7 . . . . .198 D4
New River Ct, Wal.Cr. (Chsht.) EN7
off Pengelly Cl 14 DV30
New River Cres, N13 . . . . . . .45 DP49
New River Head, EC1 . . . . . .196 E2
New River Trd Est, Wal.Cr. (Chsht.)
EN8 . . . . .15 DX26
New River Wk, N1 . . . . .84 DQ65
New River Way, N4 . . . . .66 DR59

New Rd, E1 . . . . .84 DV71
E4 . . . . .47 EB49
N8 . . . . .65 DL57
N9 . . . . .46 DU48
N17 . . . . .46 DT53
N22 . . . . .46 DQ53
NW7 . . . . .43 CY52
NW7 (Barnet Gate) 43 CT45
SE2 . . . . .106 EX77
Amersham HP6 . . . . .20 AS37
Borehamwood (Elstree)
WD6 . . . . .25 CK44
Brentford TW8 . . . . .97 CK79
Brentwood CM14 . . . . .54 FX47
Chalfont St. Giles HP8 . . . . .20 AY41
Chertsey KT16 . . . . .133 BF101
Dagenham RM9, RM10 . . . .88 FA67
Dartford (S.Darenth) DA4 . .148 FQ96
Epping CM16 . . . . .18 FA32
Esher KT10 . . . . .136 CC104
Esher (Clay.) KT10 . . . . . .155 CF110
Feltham TW14 . . . . .115 BR86
Feltham (E.Bed.) TW14 . . . .115 BV88
Feltham (Han.) TW13 . . . . .116 BY92
Gravesend DA11 . . . . . . .131 GH86
Grays RM17 . . . . .110 GA79
Grays (Manor Way) RM17 . .110 GB79
Harrow HA1 . . . . .61 CF63
Hayes UB3 . . . . .95 BQ80
Hounslow TW3
off Station Rd 96 CB84
Ilford IG3 . . . . .69 ES61
Kings Langley (Chipper.)
WD4 . . . . .5 BF30
Kingston upon Thames
KT2 . . . . .118 CN94
Leatherhead KT22 . . . . . .155 CF110
Mitcham CR4 . . . . .140 DF102
Orpington BR6 . . . . .146 EU101
Oxted (Lmpfld.) RH8 . . . . .188 EH130
Potters Bar (S.Mimms) EN6 . .11 CU33
Radlett WD7 . . . . .25 CE36
Radlett (Shenley) WD7 . . . .10 CN34
Rainham RM13 . . . . .89 FG69
Richmond TW10 . . . . . . .117 CJ91
Rickmansworth (Ch.End)
WD3 . . . . .21 BF39
Rickmansworth (Crox.Grn.)
WD3 . . . . .22 BN43
Romford (Abridge) RM4 . . . .34 EX44
Sevenoaks (Sund.) TN14 . . .180 EX124
Shepperton TW17 . . . . . .135 BP97
Slough (Datchet) SL3 . . . . .92 AX81
Slough (Langley) SL3 . . . . .93 BA76
Staines TW18 . . . . .113 BC92
Swanley BR8 . . . . .147 FF97
Swanley (Hext.) BR8 . . . . .127 FF94
Tadworth KT20 . . . . .173 CW123
Uxbridge UB8 . . . . .77 BQ70
Watford WD17 . . . . .24 BW42
Watford (Let.Hth.) WD25 . . .25 CE39
Welling DA16 . . . . .106 EV82
West Molesey KT8 . . . . . .136 CA97
Weybridge KT13 . . . . . . .153 BQ106
New Rd Hill, Kes. BR2 . . . . .162 EL109
Orpington BR6 . . . . .162 EL109
New Row, WC2 . . . . .195 P10
Newry Rd, Twick. TW1 . . . . . .97 CG84
Newsam Av, N15 . . . . .66 DR57
★ New Scotland Yd, SW1 . . .199 M6
Newsham Rd, Wok. GU21 . . .166 AT117
Newsholme Dr, N21 . . . . . . .29 DM43
NEW SOUTHGATE, N11 . . . . .45 DK49
⇌ New Southgate 45 DH50
New Spring Gdns Wk, SE11
off Goding St 101 DL78
New Sq, WC2 . . . . .196 C8
Feltham TW14 . . . . .115 BQ88
Slough SL1 . . . . .92 AT75
New Sq Pas, WC2
off New Sq 83 DM72
Newstead Av, Orp. BR6 . . . . .145 ER104
Newstead Ri, Cat. CR3 . . . . .186 DV126
Newstead Rd, SE12 . . . . . . .124 EE87
Newstead Wk, Cars. SM5 . . .140 DC101
Newstead Way, SW19 . . . . . .119 CX91
New St, EC2 . . . . .197 N7
Staines TW18 . . . . .114 BG91
Watford WD18 . . . . .24 BW42
Westerham TN16 . . . . . . .189 EQ127
New St Hill, Brom. BR1 . . . . .124 EH92
New St Sq, EC4 . . . . .196 E8
New Swan Yd, Grav. DA12
off Bank St 131 GH86
Newteswell Dr, Wal.Abb.
EN9 . . . . .15 ED32
Newton Abbot Rd, Grav. (Nthflt.)
DA11 . . . . .131 GF89
Newton Av, N10 . . . . .44 DG53
W3 . . . . .98 CQ75
Newton Cl, E17 . . . . .67 DY58
Harrow HA2 . . . . .60 CA61
Slough SL3 . . . . .93 AZ75
Newton Ct, Wind. (Old Wind.)
SL4 . . . . .112 AU86
Newton Cres, Borwd. WD6 . . .26 CQ42
Newton Gro, W4 . . . . .98 CS77
Newton La, Wind. (Old Wind.)
SL4 . . . . .112 AV86
Newton Pl, E14 . . . . .203 P8
Newton Rd, E15 . . . . .67 ED64
N15 . . . . .66 DT57
NW2 . . . . .63 CW62
SW19 . . . . .119 CY94
W2 . . . . .82 DA72
Chigwell IG7 . . . . .50 EV50
Harrow HA3 . . . . .41 CE54
Isleworth TW7 . . . . .97 CF82
Purley CR8 . . . . .159 DJ112
Tilbury RM18 . . . . .111 GG82
Welling DA16 . . . . .106 EU83
Wembley HA0 . . . . .80 CM66
Newtons Cl, Rain. RM13 . . . . .89 FF66
Newtons Ct, Dart. DA2 . . . . .109 FR84
Newtonside Orchard, Wind.
SL4 . . . . .112 AU86
Newton St, WC2 . . . . .196 A8

Newtons Yd, SW18
off Wandsworth High St . . .120 DB85
Newton Wk, Edg. HA8
off North Rd 42 CP53
Newton Way, N18 . . . . .46 DQ50
Newton Wd, Ashtd. KT21 . . . .156 CL114
Newton Wd Rd, Ashtd. KT21 . .172 CM116
NEWTOWN, Dart. 128 FN86
Newtown Rd, Uxb. (Denh.)
UB9 . . . . .76 BH65
Newtown St, SW11
off Strasburg Rd 101 DH81
New Trinity Rd, N2 . . . . .64 DD55
New Turnstile, WC1 . . . . . . .196 B7
New Union Cl, E14 . . . . .204 E6
New Union St, EC2 . . . . . . .197 K7
⊞ New Victoria Hosp, Kings.T.
KT2 . . . . .138 CS95
New Wanstead, E11 . . . . . . .68 EF58
New Way Rd, NW9 . . . . .62 CS56
New Wf Rd, N1 . . . . .83 DL68
New Wickham La, Egh.
TW20 . . . . .113 BA94
New Windsor St, Uxb. UB8 . . .76 BJ67
NEWYEARS GREEN, Uxb. 58 BN59
New Years Grn La, Uxb. (Hare.)
UB9 . . . . .58 BL58
New Years La, Orp. BR6 . . . .164 EU114
Sevenoaks (Knock.) TN14 . .179 ET116
New Zealand Av, Walt. KT12 . .135 BT102
New Zealand Way, W12 . . . . .81 CV73
Rainham RM13 . . . . .89 FF69
Niagara Av, W5 . . . . .97 CJ77
Niagara Cl, N1 off Cropley St . .84 DR68
Waltham Cross (Chsht.)
EN8 . . . . .15 DX29
Nibthwaite Rd, Har. HA1 . . . . .61 CE57
Nicholas Cl, Grnf. UB6 . . . . . .78 CB66
South Ockendon RM15 . . . .91 FW69
Watford WD24 . . . . .23 BV37
Nicholas Ct, E13
off Tunmarsh La 86 EH69
Nicholas Gdns, W5 . . . . .97 CK75
Woking GU22 . . . . .167 BE116
Nicholas La, EC4 . . . . .197 L10
Nicholas Ms, W4 off Short Rd . .98 CS79
Nicholas Pas, EC4 . . . . .197 L10
Nicholas Rd, E1 . . . . .84 DW70
Borehamwood (Elstree)
WD6 . . . . .26 CM44
Croydon CR0 . . . . .159 DL105
Dagenham RM8 . . . . .70 EZ61
Nicholas Wk, Grays RM16
off Godman Rd 111 GH75
Nicholas Way, Nthwd. HA6 . . . .39 BQ53
Nicholay Rd, N19 . . . . .65 DK60
Nichol Cl, N14 . . . . .45 DK46
Nicholes Rd, Houns. TW3 . . . .96 CA84
Nichol La, Brom. BR1 . . . . . .124 EG94
Nicholl Rd, Epp. CM16 . . . . . .17 ET31
Nicholls Av, Uxb. UB8 . . . . . .76 BN70
Nichollsfield Wk, N7
off Hillmarton Rd 65 DM64
Nicholls Pt, E15 off Park Gro . .86 EG67
Nicholl St, E2 . . . . .84 DU67
Nichols Cl, N4
off Osborne Rd 65 DN60
Chessington KT9
off Merritt Gdns 155 CJ107
Nichols Grn, W5
off Montpelier Rd 80 CL71
Nicholson Ms, Egh. TW20
off Nicholson Wk 113 BA92
Nicholson Rd, Croy. CR0 . . . .142 DT102
Nicholson St, SE1 . . . . .200 F3
Nicholson Wk, Egh. TW20 . . .113 BA92
Nicholson Way, Sev. TN13 . . .191 FK122
Nickelby Cl, SE28 . . . . .88 EW72
Uxbridge UB8
off Dickens Av 77 BP72
Nicola Cl, Har. HA3 . . . . .41 CD54
South Croydon CR2 . . . . .160 DQ107
Nicola Ms, Ilf. IG6 . . . . .49 EP52
Nicol Cl, Ger.Cr. (Chal.St.P.)
SL9 . . . . .36 AX53
Twickenham TW1
off Cassilis Rd 117 CH86
Nicol End, Ger.Cr. (Chal.St.P.)
SL9 . . . . .36 AW53
Nicoll Pl, NW4 . . . . .63 CV58
Nicoll Rd, NW10 . . . . .80 CS67
Nicoll Way, Borwd. WD6 . . . . .26 CR43
Nicol Rd, Ger.Cr. (Chal.St.P.)
SL9 . . . . .36 AW53
Nicolson Dr, Bushey (Bushey Hth.)
WD23 . . . . .40 CC46
Nicolson Rd, Orp. BR5 . . . . .146 EX101
Nicosia Rd, SW18 . . . . .120 DE87
Niederwald Rd, SE26 . . . . . .123 DY91
Nield Rd, Hayes UB3 . . . . . . .95 BT75
Nield Way, Rick. WD3
off Thellusson Way 37 BF45
Nigel Cl, Nthlt. UB5
off Church Rd 78 BY67
Nigel Fisher Way, Chess.
KT9 . . . . .155 CJ108
Nigel Ms, Ilf. IG1 . . . . .69 EP63
Nigel Playfair Av, W6
off King St 99 CV77
Nigel Rd, E7 . . . . .68 EJ64
SE15 . . . . .102 DU83
Nigeria Rd, SE7 . . . . .104 EJ80
Nightingale Av, E4 . . . . .48 EE50
Harrow HA1 . . . . .61 CH59
Leatherhead (W.Hors.)
KT24 . . . . .169 BR124
Upminster RM14 . . . . .73 FT60
Nightingale Cl, E4 . . . . .48 EE49
W4 off Grove Pk Ter 98 CQ79
Abbots Langley WD5 . . . . . .7 BU31
Carshalton SM5 . . . . .140 DG103
Cobham KT11 . . . . .154 BX111
Epsom KT19 . . . . .156 CN112
Gravesend (Nthflt.) DA11 . .130 GE91

Nig - Nor

Nightingale CI, Pin. HA5 . . . . .60 BW57
  Radlett WD7 . . . . .25 CF36
Nightingale Ct, E11
  off Nightingale La 68 EH57
  Slough SL1
  off St. Laurence Way 8 AU76
Nightingale Cres, Lthd. (W.Hors.)
  KT24 . . . . .169 BQ124
Nightingale Dr, Epsom KT19 .156 CP107
Nightingale Est, E5 . . . . . . .66 DU62
Nightingale Gro, SE13 . . . . .123 ED85
  Dartford DA1 . . . . .108 FN84
Nightingale La, E11 . . . . . . .68 EG57
  N6 . . . . .64 DE60
  N8 . . . . .65 DL56
  SW4 . . . . .120 DF87
  SW12 . . . . .120 DF87
  Bromley BR1 . . . . .144 EJ96
  Richmond TW10 . . . . . .118 CL87
  Sevenoaks (Ide Hill) TN14 .190 FB130
Nightingale Ms, E3
  off Chisenhale Rd 85 DY68
  E11 . . . . .68 EG57
  SE11 . . . . .200 E8
  Kingston upon Thames KT1
  off South La 137 CK97
Nightingale PI, SE18 . . . . . .105 EN79
  SW10 off Fulham Rd 100 DC79
  Rickmansworth WD3
  off Nightingale Rd 38 BK45
Nightingale Rd, E5 . . . . .66 DV62
  N9 . . . . .30 DW44
  N22 . . . . .45 DL53
  NW10 . . . . .81 CT68
  W7 . . . . .79 CF74
  Bushey WD23 . . . . .24 CA43
  Carshalton SM5 . . . . . . .140 DF104
  Esher KT10 . . . . .154 BZ106
  Hampton TW12 . . . . . . .116 CA92
  Orpington BR5 . . . . . . .145 EQ100
  Rickmansworth WD3 . . . . .38 BJ46
  South Croydon CR2 . . . . .161 DX111
  Waltham Cross (Chsht.)
  EN7 . . . . .14 DQ25
  Walton-on-Thames KT12 . .135 BV101
  West Molesey KT8 . . . . .136 CB99
Nightingales, Wal.Abb. EN9
  off Roundhills 16 EE34
Nightingales, The, Stai. TW19 .114 BM87
Nightingales Cor, Amer. HP7
  off Chalfont Sta Rd 20 AW40
Nightingale Shott, Egh.
  TW20 . . . . .113 AZ93
Nightingales La, Ch.St.G. HP8 . .36 AX46
Nightingale Sq, SW12 . . . . .120 DG87
Nightingale Vale, SE18 . . . . .105 EN79
Nightingale Wk, SW4 . . . . . .121 DH86
Nightingale Way, E6 . . . . . . .86 EL71
  Redhill (Bletch.) RH1 . . . .186 DS134
  Swanley BR8 . . . . .147 FE97
  Uxbridge (Denh.) UB9 . . . .57 BF59
Nile Path, SE18
  off Jackson St 105 EN79
Nile Rd, E13 . . . . .86 EJ68
Nile St, N1 . . . . .197 J2
Nile Ter, SE15 . . . . .102 DT78
Nimbus Rd, Epsom KT19 . . . .156 CR110
Nimegen Way, SE22 . . . . . . .122 DS85
Nimmo Dr, Bushey (Bushey Hth.)
  WD23 . . . . .41 CD45
Nimrod CI, Nthlt. UB5
  off Britannia CI 78 BX69
Nimrod Pas, N1
  off Tottenham Rd 84 DS65
Nimrod Rd, SW16 . . . . .121 DH93
Nina Mackay CI, E15
  off Arthingworth St 86 EE67
Nine Acres CI, E12 . . . . .68 EL64
Nineacres Way, Couls. CR5 . .175 DL116
NINE ELMS, SW8 . . . . .101 DH80
Nine Elms Av, Uxb. UB8 . . . . .76 BK71
Nine Elms CI, Felt. TW14 . . . .115 BT88
  Uxbridge UB8 . . . . .76 BK72
Nine Elms Gro, Grav. DA11 . .131 GG87
Nine Elms La, SW8 . . . . . . .101 DJ79
Ninefields, Wal.Abb. EN9 . . . .16 EF33
Ninehams CI, Cat. CR3 . . . . .176 DR120
Ninehams Gdns, Cat. CR3 . . .176 DR120
Ninehams Rd, Cat. CR3 . . . .176 DR121
  Westerham (Tats.) TN16 . .178 EJ121
Nine Stiles CI, Uxb. (Denh.)
  UB9 . . . . .57 BF61
Nineteenth Rd, Mitch. CR4 . .141 DL98
Ninhams Wd, Orp. BR6 . . . . .163 EN105
Ninnings Rd, Ger.Cr. (Chal.St.P.)
  SL9 . . . . .37 AZ52
Ninnings Way, Ger.Cr. (Chal.St.P.)
  SL9 . . . . .37 AZ52
Ninth Av, Hayes UB3 . . . . . . .77 BU73
Nisbet Ho, E9
  off Homerton High St 67 DX64
Nita Rd, Brwd. CM14 . . . . . . .54 FW50
Nithdale Rd, SE18 . . . . .105 EP80
Nithsdale Gro, Uxb. UB10
  off Tweeddale Gro 59 BQ62
Niton CI, Barn. EN5 . . . . .27 CX44
Niton Rd, Rich. TW9 . . . . .98 CN83
Niton St, SW6 . . . . .99 CX80
Niven CI, Borwd. WD6 . . . . . .26 CQ39
Nixey CI, Slou. SL1 . . . . .92 AU75
N.L.A. Twr, Croy. CR0 . . . . . .142 DR103
NOAK HILL 52 FK47
Noak Hill Rd, Rom. RM3 . . . . .52 FJ49
Nobel Dr, Hayes UB3 . . . . . . .95 BR80
Nobel Rd, N18 . . . . .46 DW50
Noble St, EC2 . . . . .197 H8
  Walton-on-Thames KT12 . .135 BV104
Nobles Way, Egh. TW20 . . . .112 AY93
NOEL PARK, N22 . . . . .45 DN54
Noel Pk Rd, N22 . . . . .45 DN54
Noel Rd, E6 . . . . .86 EL70
  N1 . . . . .83 DP68
  W3 . . . . .80 CP72
Noel Sq, Dag. RM8 . . . . .70 EW63

Noel St, W1 . . . . .195 L9
Noel Ter, SE23
  off Dartmouth Rd 122 DW89
Noke Dr, Red. RH1 . . . . .184 DG133
Noke Fm Barns, Couls. CR5 . .174 DF122
Noke La, St.Alb. AL2 . . . . .8 BY26
Noke Side, St.Alb. AL2 . . . . . . .8 CA27
Nolan Way, E5 . . . . .66 DU63
Nolton PI, Edg. HA8 . . . . .42 CM53
Nonsuch CI, Ilf. IG6 . . . . .49 EP51
Nonsuch Ct Av, Epsom KT17 .157 CV110
Nonsuch Ind Est, Epsom
  KT17 . . . . .156 CS111
★ Nonsuch Mansion Ho, Sutt.
  SM3 . . . . .157 CW107
Nonsuch Wk, Sutt. SM2 . . . .157 CW110
Nora Gdns, NW4 . . . . .63 CX56
NORBITON, Kings.T. 138 CP96
⊖ Norbiton 138 CN95
Norbiton Av, Kings.T. KT1 . . . .8 CN96
Norbiton Common Rd, Kings.T.
  KT1 . . . . .138 CP97
Norbiton Rd, E14 . . . . .85 DZ72
Norbreck Gdns, NW10
  off Lytham Gro 80 CM69
Norbreck Par, NW10
  off Lytham Gro 80 CM69
Norbroke St, W12 . . . . .81 CT73
Norburn St, W10
  off Chesterton Rd 81 CY71
NORBURY, SW16 . . . . .141 DN95
⊖ Norbury 141 DN95
Norbury Av, SW16 . . . . .141 DM95
  Hounslow TW3 . . . . . . .117 CD85
  Thornton Heath CR7 . . . .141 DN96
  Watford WD24 . . . . .24 BW39
Norbury CI, SW16 . . . . .141 DN95
Norbury Ct Rd, SW16 . . . . . .141 DL95
Norbury Cres, SW16 . . . . . .141 DM95
Norbury Cross, SW16 . . . . . .141 DL97
Norbury Gdns, Rom. RM6 . . . .70 EX57
Norbury Gro, NW7 . . . . .42 CS48
Norbury Hill, SW16 . . . . .121 DN94
Norbury Ri, SW16 . . . . .141 DL97
Norbury Rd, E4 . . . . .47 EA50
  Reigate RH2 . . . . .183 CZ134
  Thornton Heath CR7 . . . .142 DQ96
Norcombe Gdns, Har. HA3 . . . .61 CJ58
Norcott CI, Hayes UB4
  off Willow Tree La 78 BW70
Norcott Rd, N16 . . . . .66 DU61
Norcroft Gdns, SE22 . . . . . .122 DU87
Norcutt Rd, Twick. TW2 . . . . .117 CE88
Nordenfeldt Rd, Erith DA8 . . .107 FD78
Nordmann PI, S.Ock. RM15 . . .91 FX70
Norfield Rd, Dart. DA2 . . . . . .127 FC91
Norfolk Av, N13 . . . . .45 DP51
  N15 . . . . .66 DT58
  South Croydon CR2 . . . . .160 DU110
  Watford WD24 . . . . .24 BW38
Norfolk CI, N2 off Park Rd 64 DE55
  N13 . . . . .45 DP51
  Barnet EN4 . . . . .28 DG42
  Dartford DA1 . . . . .128 FN86
  Twickenham TW1
  off Cassilis Rd 117 CH86
Norfolk Cres, W2 . . . . .194 C8
  Sidcup DA15 . . . . .125 ES87
Norfolk Fm CI, Wok. GU22 . . .167 BD116
Norfolk Fm Rd, Wok. GU22 . . .167 BD115
Norfolk Gdns, Bexh. DA7 . . . .106 EZ81
  Borehamwood WD6 . . . . . .26 CR42
Norfolk Ho, SE3 . . . . .104 EE79
Norfolk Ho Rd, SW16 . . . . . .121 DK90
Norfolk Ms, W10
  off Blagrove Rd 81 CZ71
Norfolk PI, W2 . . . . .194 A8
  Welling DA16 . . . . .106 EU82
Norfolk Rd, E6 . . . . .87 EM67
  E17 . . . . .47 DX54
  NW8 . . . . .82 DD67
  NW10 . . . . .80 CS66
  SW19 . . . . .120 DE94
  Barking IG11 . . . . .87 ES66
  Barnet EN5 . . . . .28 DA41
  Dagenham RM10 . . . . . . .71 FB64
  Enfield EN3 . . . . .30 DV44
  Esher (Clay.) KT10 . . . . .155 CE106
  Feltham TW13 . . . . .116 BW88
  Gravesend DA12 . . . . . .131 GK86
  Harrow HA1 . . . . .60 CB57
  Ilford IG3 . . . . .69 ES60
  Rickmansworth WD3 . . . . .38 BL46
  Romford RM7 . . . . .71 FC58
  Thornton Heath CR7 . . . .142 DQ97
  Upminster RM14 . . . . . . .72 FN62
  Uxbridge UB8 . . . . .76 BK65
Norfolk Row, SE1 . . . . .200 B8
Norfolk Sq, W2 . . . . .194 A9
Norfolk Sq Ms, W2 . . . . .194 A9
Norfolk St, E7 . . . . .68 EG63
Norfolk Ter, W6 off Field Rd . . .99 CY78
Norgrove Pk, Ger.Cr. SL9 . . . .56 AY56
Norgrove St, SW12 . . . . .120 DG87
Norheads La, Warl. CR6 . . . . .175 EQ119
  Westerham (Bigg.H.) TN16 .178 EJ116
Norhyrst Av, SE25 . . . . .142 DT97
NORK, Bans. 173 CY115
Nork Gdns, Bans. SM7 . . . . .157 CY114
Nork Ri, Bans. SM7 . . . . .173 CX116
Nork Way, Bans. SM7 . . . . . .173 CY115
Norland Ho, W11 . . . . .81 CX74
Norland PI, W11 . . . . .81 CY74
Norland Rd, W11 . . . . .81 CX74
Norlands Cres, Chis. BR7 . . . .145 EP95
Norlands Gate, Chis. BR7 . . . .145 EP95
Norlands La, Egh. TW20 . . . .133 BE97
Norland Sq, W11 . . . . .81 CY74
Norley Vale, SW15 . . . . .119 CU88
Norlington Rd, E10 . . . . .67 EC60
  E11 . . . . .67 EC60
Norman Av, N22 . . . . .45 DP53
  Epsom KT17 . . . . .157 CT112
  Feltham TW13 . . . . .116 BY89
  South Croydon CR2 . . . . .160 DQ110
  Southall UB1 . . . . .78 BY73
  Twickenham TW1 . . . . . .117 CH87

Normanby CI, SW15
  off Manfred Rd 119 CZ85
Normanby Rd, NW10 . . . . . . .63 CT63
Norman CI, Epsom KT18 . . . .173 CV119
  Orpington BR6 . . . . .145 EQ104
  Romford RM5 . . . . .51 FB54
  Waltham Abbey EN9 . . . . .15 ED33
Norman Ct, Ilf. IG2 . . . . .69 ER59
  Potters Bar EN6 . . . . .12 DC30
  Woodford Green IG8
  off Monkhams Av 48 EH50
Norman Cres, Brwd. CM13 . . .55 GA48
  Hounslow TW5 . . . . .96 BX81
  Pinner HA5 . . . . .40 BW53
Normand Gdns, W14
  off Greyhound Rd 99 CY79
Normand Ms, W14
  off Normand Rd 99 CY79
Normand Rd, W14 . . . . .99 CZ79
Normandy Av, Barn. EN5 . . . . .27 CZ43
Normandy CI, SE26 . . . . .123 DY90
Normandy Dr, Hayes UB3 . . . .77 BQ72
Normandy Rd, SW9 . . . . .101 DN81
Normandy Ter, E16 . . . . .86 EH72
Normandy Wk, Egh. TW20
  off Mullens Rd 113 BC92
Normandy Way, Erith DA8 . . .107 FE81
Norman Gro, E3 . . . . .85 DY68
Normanhurst, Ashf. TW15 . . .114 BN92
  Brentwood CM13 . . . . . . .55 GC44
  St. Albans AL2 . . . . .8 CB25
Normanhurst Av, Bexh. DA7 . .106 EX81
Normanhurst Dr, Twick. TW1
  off St. Margarets Rd 117 CH85
Normanhurst Rd, SW2 . . . . . .121 DM89
  Orpington BR5 . . . . .146 EV96
  Walton-on-Thames KT12 . .136 BX103
Norman Rd, E6 . . . . .87 EM70
  E11 . . . . .67 ED61
  N15 . . . . .66 DT57
  SE10 . . . . .103 EB80
  SW19 . . . . .120 DC94
  Ashford TW15 . . . . .115 BR93
  Belvedere DA17 . . . . . . .107 FB76
  Dartford DA1 . . . . .128 FL88
  Hornchurch RM11 . . . . . . .71 FG59
  Ilford IG1 . . . . .69 EP64
  Sutton SM1 . . . . .158 DA106
  Thornton Heath CR7 . . . .141 DP99
Normans, The, Slou. SL2 . . . . .74 AV72
Norman's Bldgs, EC1
  off Ironmonger Row 84 DQ69
Normans CI, NW10 . . . . .80 CR65
  Gravesend DA11 . . . . . .131 GG87
  Uxbridge UB8 . . . . .76 BL71
Normansfield Av, Tedd. TW11 .117 CJ94
Normansfield CI, Bushey
  WD23 . . . . .40 CB45
Normanshire Av, E4 . . . . .47 EC49
Normanshire Dr, E4 . . . . .47 EA49
Normans Mead, NW10 . . . . . .80 CR65
Norman St, EC1 . . . . .197 H3
Normanton Av, SW19 . . . . . .120 DA89
Normanton Pk, E4 . . . . .48 EE48
Normanton Rd, S.Croy. CR2 . .160 DS107
Normanton St, SE23 . . . . . . .123 DX89
Norman Way, N14 . . . . .45 DL47
  W3 . . . . .80 CP71
Normington CI, SW16 . . . . . .121 DN92
Norrice Lea, N2 . . . . .64 DD57
Norris Rd, Stai. TW18 . . . . . .113 BF91
Norris St, SW1 . . . . .199 M1
Norris Way, Dart. DA1 . . . . . .107 FF83
Norroy Rd, SW15 . . . . .99 CX84
Norrys CI, Barn. EN4 . . . . . . .28 DF43
Norrys Rd, Barn. EN4 . . . . . . .28 DF43
Norseman CI, Ilf. IG3 . . . . . . .70 EV60
Norseman Way, Grnf. UB6
  off Olympic Way 78 CB67
Norstead PI, SW15 . . . . .119 CU89
Norsted La, Orp. BR6 . . . . . .164 EU110
North Access Rd, E17 . . . . . . .67 DX58
North Acre, NW9 . . . . .42 CS53
  Banstead SM7 . . . . .173 CZ116
NORTH ACTON, W3 . . . . .80 CR70
⊖ North Acton 80 CR70
North Acton Rd, NW10 . . . . . .80 CR69
Northallerton Way, Rom. RM3 .52 FK50
Northall Rd, Bexh. DA7 . . . . .107 FC82
Northampton Gro, N1 . . . . . . .66 DR64
Northampton Pk, N1 . . . . .84 DQ65
Northampton Rd, EC1 . . . . . .196 E4
  Croydon CR0 . . . . .142 DU103
  Enfield EN3 . . . . .31 DY42
Northampton Sq, EC1 . . . . . .196 F3
Northampton St, N1 . . . . .84 DQ66
Northanger Rd, SW16 . . . . . .121 DL93
North App, Nthwd. HA6 . . . . . .39 BQ47
  Watford WD25 . . . . .23 BT35
North Arc, Croy. CR0
  off North End 142 DQ103
North Audley St, W1 . . . . . . .194 F9
North Av, N18 . . . . .46 DU49
  W13 . . . . .79 CH72
  Brentwood CM14 . . . . . . .54 FR45
  Carshalton SM5 . . . . . . .158 DF108
  Harrow HA2 . . . . .60 CB58
  Hayes UB3 . . . . .77 BU73
  Radlett (Shenley) WD7 . . . .10 CL32
  Richmond TW9
  off Sandycombe Rd 98 CN81
  Southall UB1 . . . . .78 BZ73
  Walton-on-Thames KT12 . .153 BS109
NORTHAW, Pot.B. 12 DF30
Northaw PI, Pot.B. EN6 . . . . . .12 DF30
  EN6 . . . . .13 DK31
Northaw Rd E, Pot.B. (Cuffley)
  EN6 . . . . .13 DK31
North Bk, NW8 . . . . .194 A3
Northbank Rd, E17 . . . . .47 EC54
NORTH BECKTON, E6 . . . . . . .86 EL70
North Birkbeck Rd, E11 . . . . . .67 ED62
Northborough Rd, SW16 . . . .141 DK97
Northbourne, Brom. BR2 . . . .144 EG101
Northbourne Rd, SW4 . . . . . .101 DK84
North Branch Av, W10
  off Harrow Rd 81 CW69
Northbrook Dr, Nthwd. HA6 . . .39 BS53

Northbrook Rd, N22 . . . . .45 DL52
  SE13 . . . . .123 ED85
  Barnet EN5 . . . . .27 CY44
  Croydon CR0 . . . . .142 DR99
  Ilford IG1 . . . . .69 EN61
Northburgh St, EC1 . . . . .196 G4
North Carriage Dr, W2 . . . . . .194 B10
NORTH CHEAM, Sutt. 139 CW104
Northchurch, SE17 . . . . .201 L10
Northchurch Rd, N1 . . . . .84 DR66
  Wembley HA9 . . . . .80 CM65
Northchurch Ter, N1 . . . . .84 DS66
North Circular Rd, E4 . . . . . . .47 DZ51
  E18 . . . . .48 EJ54
  N3 . . . . .64 DD53
  N12 . . . . .44 DD53
  N13 . . . . .45 DN50
  NW2 . . . . .62 CS62
  NW10 . . . . .80 CP66
  NW11 . . . . .64 CY56
Northcliffe CI, Wor.Pk. KT4 . . .138 CS104
Northcliffe Dr, N20 . . . . .43 CZ46
North CI, Barn. EN5 . . . . .27 CW43
  Bexleyheath DA6 . . . . . .106 EX84
  Chigwell IG7 . . . . .50 EU50
  Dagenham RM10 . . . . . . .88 FA67
  Feltham TW14
  off North Rd 115 BR86
  Morden SM4 . . . . .139 CY98
  St. Albans AL2 . . . . .8 CB25
North Colonnade, E14 . . . . . .204 A2
North Common, Wey. KT13 . .153 BP105
North Common Rd, W5 . . . . . .80 CL73
  Uxbridge UB8 . . . . .58 BK64
Northcote, Add. KT15 . . . . . .152 BK105
  Leatherhead (Oxshott)
  KT22 . . . . .154 CC114
  Pinner HA5 . . . . .40 BW54
Northcote Av, W5 . . . . .80 CL73
  Isleworth TW7 . . . . .117 CG85
  Southall UB1 . . . . .78 BY73
  Surbiton KT5 . . . . .138 CN101
Northcote Ms, SW11
  off Northcote Rd 100 DE84
Northcote Rd, E17 . . . . .67 DY56
  NW10 . . . . .80 CS66
  SW11 . . . . .100 DE84
  Croydon CR0 . . . . .142 DR100
  Gravesend DA11 . . . . . .131 GF88
  New Malden KT3 . . . . . .138 CQ97
  Sidcup DA14 . . . . .125 ES91
  Twickenham TW1 . . . . . .117 CG85
North Cotts, St.Alb. (Lon.Col.)
  AL2 . . . . .9 CG25
North Countess Rd, E17 . . . . .47 DZ54
North Ct, W1 . . . . .195 L6
Northcott Av, N22 . . . . .45 DL53
Northcotts, Abb.L. WD5
  off Long Elms 7 BR33
North Cray Rd, Bex. DA5 . . . .126 EZ90
  Sidcup DA14 . . . . .126 EZ90
North Cres, E16 . . . . .85 ED70
  N3 . . . . .43 DZ54
  WC1 . . . . .195 M6
North Cross Rd, SE22 . . . . . .122 DT85
  Ilford IG6 . . . . .69 EQ56
North Dene, NW7 . . . . .42 CR48
  Hounslow TW3 . . . . .96 CB81
North Dene, Houns. TW3 . . . . .96 CB81
Northdene Gdns, N15 . . . . . . .66 DT58
North Down, S.Croy. CR2 . . . .160 DS111
Northdown CI, Ruis. HA4 . . . . .59 BT62
Northdown Gdns, Ilf. IG2 . . . . .69 ES57
Northdown Rd, Cat. (Wold.)
  CR3 . . . . .177 EA123
  Gerrards Cross (Chal.St.P.)
  SL9 . . . . .36 AY51
  Hornchurch RM11 . . . . . . .71 FH59
  Longfield DA3 . . . . .149 FX96
  Sutton SM2 . . . . .158 DA110
  Welling DA16 . . . . .106 EV82
North Downs Cres, Croy.
  (New Adgtn.) CR0 . . . . . .161 EB110
H North Downs Private Hosp,
  The, Cat. CR3 . . . . .186 DT125
North Downs Rd, Croy.
  (New Adgtn.) CR0 . . . . . .161 EB110
North Downs Way, Bet. RH3 . .183 CU130
  Caterham CR3 . . . . .185 DN126
  Godstone RH9 . . . . .187 DY128
  Oxted RH8 . . . . .188 EE126
  Redhill RH1 . . . . .184 DG128
  Reigate RH2 . . . . .184 DD130
  Sevenoaks TN13, TN14 . . .181 FD118
  Tadworth KT20 . . . . .183 CX130
  Westerham TN16 . . . . . .179 ER121
North Dr, SW16 . . . . .121 DJ91
  Hounslow TW3 . . . . .96 CC82
  Orpington BR6 . . . . .163 ES105
  Romford RM2 . . . . .72 FJ55
  Ruislip HA4 . . . . .59 BS59
  Slough SL2 . . . . .74 AS69
  Virginia Water GU25 . . . .132 AS100
North Dulwich 122 DR85
⊖ North Ealing 80 CM72
North End, NW3 . . . . .64 DC61
  Buck.H. IG9 . . . . .48 EJ45
  Croydon CR0 . . . . .142 DQ103
  Romford (Noak Hill) RM3 . .52 FJ47
North End Av, NW3 . . . . .64 DC61
North End Cres, W14 . . . . . . .99 CZ77

North End Ho, W14 . . . . .99 CY77
North End La, Orp. BR6 . . . . .163 EN110
North End Par, W14
  off North End Rd 99 CY77
North End Rd, NW11 . . . . .64 DA60
  SW6 . . . . .99 CZ79
  W14 . . . . .99 CZ77
Northend Rd, Dart. DA1 . . . . .107 FF80
  Erith DA8 . . . . .107 FF80
North End Rd, Wem. HA9 . . . . .62 CN62
Northend Trd Est, Erith DA8 . .107 FE81
North End Way, NW3 . . . . .64 DC61
Northern Av, N9 . . . . .46 DT47
Northernhay Wk, Mord. SM4 . .139 CY98
Northern Perimeter Rd, Houns.
  (Hthrw.Air.) TW6 . . . . . . .95 BQ81
Northern Perimeter Rd W, Houns.
  (Hthrw.Air.) TW6 . . . . . . .94 BK81
Northern Relief Rd, Bark. IG11 .87 EP66
Northern Service Rd, Barn.
  EN5 . . . . .27 CY41
Northey Av, Sutt. SM2 . . . . . .157 CZ110
North Eyot Gdns, W6 . . . . . . .99 CU78
Northey St, E14 . . . . .85 DY73
Northfield, Loug. IG10 . . . . . . .32 EK42
Northfield Av, W5 . . . . .97 CH75
  W13 . . . . .97 CH75
  Orpington BR5 . . . . .146 EW100
  Pinner HA5 . . . . .60 BX56
Northfield CI, Brom. BR1 . . . .144 EL95
  Hayes UB3 . . . . .95 BT76
Northfield Ct, Stai. TW18 . . . .134 BH95
Northfield Cres, Sutt. SM3 . . .157 CY105
Northfield Gdns, Dag. RM9
  off Northfield Rd 70 EZ63
  Watford WD24 . . . . .24 BW37
Northfield Ind Est, NW10 . . . . .80 CN69
Northfield Pk, Hayes UB3 . . . .95 BT76
Northfield Path, Dag. RM9 . . . .70 EZ62
Northfield PI, Wey. KT13 . . . .153 BP108
Northfield Rd, E6 . . . . .87 EM66
  N16 . . . . .66 DS59
  W13 . . . . .97 CH75
  Barnet EN4 . . . . .28 DE41
  Borehamwood WD6 . . . . . .26 CP39
  Cobham KT11 . . . . .153 BU113
  Dagenham RM9 . . . . .70 EZ63
  Enfield EN3 . . . . .30 DV43
  Hounslow TW5 . . . . .96 BX79
  Staines TW18 . . . . .134 BH95
  Waltham Cross EN8 . . . . . .15 DY32
⊖ Northfields 97 CH76
Northfields, SW18 . . . . .100 DA84
  Ashtead KT21 . . . . .172 CL119
  Grays RM17 . . . . .110 GC77
Northfields Ind Est, Wem.
  HA0 . . . . .80 CN67
Northfields Rd, W3 . . . . .80 CP71
NORTH FINCHLEY, N12 . . . . . .44 DD50
⊖ Northfleet 130 GD86
NORTHFLEET, Grav. 130 GD86
≥ Northfleet 130 GA86
NORTHFLEET GREEN, Grav. . .130 GC92
Northfleet Grn Rd, Grav.
  DA13 . . . . .130 GC93
Northfleet Ind Est, Grav.
  DA11 . . . . .110 FZ84
North Flockton St, SE16 . . . .202 B4
North Gdn, E14
  off Westferry Circ 85 DZ74
North Gdns, SW19 . . . . .120 DD94
Northgate, Nthwd. HA6 . . . . . .39 BQ52
Northgate Dr, NW9 . . . . .62 CS58
Northgate Ind Pk, Rom. RM5 . .50 EZ54
Northgate Path, Borwd. WD6 . .26 CM39
North Glade, The, Bex. DA5 . .126 EZ87
North Gower St, NW1 . . . . . .195 L3
North Grn, NW9
  off Clayton Fld 42 CS52
  Slough SL1 . . . . .74 AS73
⊖ North Greenwich 205 H4
North Gro, N6 . . . . .64 DG59
  N15 . . . . .66 DR57
  Chertsey KT16 . . . . .133 BF100
NORTH HARROW, Har. 60 CA58
⊖ North Harrow 60 CA57
North Hatton Rd, Houns.
  (Hthrw.Air.) TW6 . . . . . . .95 BR81
North Hill, N6 . . . . .64 DF58
  Rickmansworth WD3 . . . . .21 BE40
North Hill Av, N6 . . . . .64 DG58
North Hill Dr, Rom. RM3 . . . . .52 FK48
North Hill Grn, Rom. RM3 . . . .52 FK49
NORTH HILLINGDON, Uxb. 77 BQ66
NORTH HYDE, Sthl. 96 BY77
North Hyde Gdns, Hayes UB3 . .95 BU77
North Hyde La, Houns. TW5 . . .96 BY78
  Southall UB2 . . . . .96 BY78
North Hyde Rd, Hayes UB3 . . .95 BT76
Northiam, N12 . . . . .44 DA48
Northiam St, E9 . . . . .84 DV67
Northington St, WC1 . . . . . . .196 C5
NORTH KENSINGTON, W10 . . .81 CW72
North Kent Av, Grav. (Nthflt.)
  DA11 . . . . .130 GC86
Northlands, Pot.B. EN6 . . . . . .12 DD31
Northlands Av, Orp. BR6 . . . .163 ES105
Northlands St, SE5 . . . . .102 DQ82
North La, Tedd. TW11 . . . . . .117 CF93
North Lo CI, SW15
  off Westleigh Av 119 CX85
H North London Blood
  Transfusion Cen, NW9 . . . .42 CR54
H North London Nuffield Hosp,
  Enf. EN2 . . . . .29 DN40
NORTH LOOE, Epsom 157 CW113
North Mall, N9
  off St. Martins Rd 46 DV47
North Mead, Red. RH1 . . . . . .184 DF131
North Ms, WC1 . . . . .196 C5
H North Middlesex Hosp,
  N18 . . . . .46 DS50
North Mymms Pk, Hat. AL9 . . .11 CT25
NORTH OCKENDON, Upmin. . . .73 FV64
Northolm, Edg. HA8 . . . . .42 CR49
Northolme CI, Grays RM16
  off Premier Av 110 GC76

Oak - Old

★ Place of interest   ⇌ Railway station   ⊖ London Underground station   DLR Docklands Light Railway station   ⬥ Tramlink station   Ⓗ Hospital

Old Ch Path, Esher KT10
  off High St 154 CB105
Oldchurch Ri, Rom. RM7 . . .71 FD59
Old Ch Rd, E1 . . . . .85 DX72
  E4 . . . . .47 EA49
Oldchurch Rd, Rom. RM7 . . .71 FD59
Old Ch St, SW3 . . . . .100 DD78
Old Claygate La, Esher (Clay.)
  KT10 . . . . .155 CG107
Old Clem Sq, SE18
  off Kempt St 105 EN79
Old Coach Rd, Cher. KT16 . .133 BD99
Old Coal Yd, SE28
  off Pettman Cres 105 ER77
Old Common Rd, Cob. KT11 .153 BU112
Old Compton St, W1 . . . . .195 M10
Old Cote Dr, Houns. TW5 . . .96 CA79
OLD COULSDON, Couls. . . .175 DN119
Old Ct, Ashtd. KT21 . . . . .172 CL119
Old Ct Pl, W8 . . . . .100 DB75
★ Old Curiosity Shop, WC2 .196 B9
Old Dairy Ms, SW12
  off Chestnut Gro 120 DG87
Old Dartford Rd, Dart. (Fngham.)
  DA4 . . . . .148 FM100
Old Dean, Hem.H. (Bov.) HP3 . .5 BA27
Old Deer Pk Gdns, Rich. TW9 .98 CL83
Old Devonshire Rd, SW12 . .121 DH87
Old Dock App Rd, Grays
  RM17 . . . . .110 GE77
Old Dock Cl, Rich. TW9
  off Watcombe Cotts 98 CN79
Old Dover Rd, SE3 . . . . . .104 EG80
Olden La, Pur. CR8 . . . . . .159 DN112
Old Esher Cl, Walt. KT12
  off Old Esher Rd 154 BX106
Old Esher Rd, Walt. KT12 . .154 BX106
Old Farleigh Rd, S.Croy. CR2 .160 DW110
  Warlingham CR6 . . . . . .161 DY113
Old Fm Av, N14 . . . . .45 DJ45
  Sidcup DA15 . . . . .125 ER88
Old Fm Cl, Houns. TW4 . . . .96 BZ84
Old Fm Gdns, Swan. BR8 . . .147 FF97
Old Farmhouse Dr, Lthd. (Oxshott)
  KT22 . . . . .155 CD115
Old Fm Pas, Hmptn. TW12 . .136 CC95
Old Fm Rd, N2 . . . . .44 DD53
  Hampton TW12 . . . . . . .116 BZ93
  West Drayton UB7 . . . . . .94 BK75
Old Fm Rd E, Sid. DA15 . . .126 EU89
Old Fm Rd W, Sid. DA15 . . .125 ET89
Old Ferry Dr, Stai. (Wrays.)
  TW19 . . . . .112 AW86
Old Fld Cl, Amer. HP6 . . . . .20 AY39
Oldfield Cl, Brom. BR1 . . . .145 EM98
  Greenford UB6 . . . . .68 CE64
  Stanmore HA7 . . . . .41 CG50
  Waltham Cross (Chsht.)
  EN8 . . . . .15 DY28
Oldfield Dr, Wal.Cr. (Chsht.)
  EN8 . . . . .15 DY28
Oldfield Fm Gdns, Grnf. UB6 .79 CD67
Oldfield Gdns, Ashtd. KT21 .171 CK119
Oldfield Gro, SE16 . . . . . .203 H9
Oldfield La N, Grnf. UB6 . . .79 CE65
Oldfield La S, Grnf. UB6 . . .86 CC70
Oldfield Ms, N6 . . . . .65 DJ59
  NW10 . . . . .81 CT66
  SW19 . . . . .119 CY93
  W3 off Valetta Rd 99 CT75
  Bexleyheath DA7 . . . . . .106 EY82
  Bromley BR1 . . . . .145 EM98
  Hampton TW12 . . . . . . .136 BZ95
  St. Albans (Lon.Col.) AL2 . . .9 CK25
Oldfields Circ, Nthlt. UB5 . . .78 CC65
Oldfields Rd, Sutt. SM1 . . .139 CZ104
Oldfields Trd Est, Sutt. SM1 .140 DA104
Oldfield Wd, Wok. GU22
  off Maybury Hill 167 BB117
Old Fish St Hill, EC4 . . . . .197 H10
Old Fleet La, EC4 . . . . . . .196 F8
Old Fold Cl, Barn. EN5
  off Old Fold La 27 CZ39
Old Fold La, Barn. EN5 . . . .27 CZ39
Old Fold Vw, Barn. EN5 . . . .27 CW41
OLD FORD, E3 . . . . .85 DZ66
Old Ford Rd, E2 . . . . .84 DW68
  E3 . . . . .85 DY68
Old Forge Cl, Stan. HA7 . . . .41 CG49
  Watford WD25 . . . . .BU33
Old Forge Cres, Shep. TW17 .135 BP100
Old Forge Ms, W12
  off Goodwin Rd 99 CV75
Old Forge Rd, Enf. EN1 . . . .30 DT38
Old Forge Way, Sid. DA14 . .126 EV91
Old Fox Cl, Cat. CR3 . . . . .175 DP121
Old Fox Footpath, S.Croy. CR2
  off Essenden Rd 160 DS108
Old Gannon Cl, Nthwd. HA6 . .39 BQ50
Old Gdn, The, Sev. TN13 . . .190 FD123
Old Gloucester St, WC1 . . .196 A6
Old Gro Cl, Wal.Cr. (Chsht.)
  EN7 . . . . .14 DR26
Old Hall Cl, Pnr. HA5 . . . . .40 BY53
Old Hall Dr, Pnr. HA5 . . . . .40 BY53
Oldham Ter, W3 . . . . .80 CQ74
Old Harrow La, West. TN16 .179 EQ119
Old Hatch Manor, Ruis. HA4 . .59 BT59
Old Hill, Chis. BR7 . . . . . .145 EN95
  Orpington BR6 . . . . . . .163 ER107
  Woking GU22 . . . . .166 AX120
Oldhill St, N16 . . . . .66 DU60
Old Homesdale Rd, Brom.
  BR2 . . . . .144 EJ98
Old Hosp Cl, SW12 . . . . . .120 DF88
Old Ho Cl, SW19 . . . . . . .119 CY92
  Epsom KT17 . . . . .157 CT110
Old Ho Gdns, Twick. TW1 . .117 CJ85
Old Ho La, Kings L. WD4 . . . .7 BP28
Old Howlett's La, Ruis. HA4 . .59 BQ58
Old Jamaica Rd, SE16 . . . .202 B6
Old James St, SE15 . . . . .102 DV83
Old Jewry, EC2 . . . . .197 K9
Old Kenton La, NW9 . . . . . .62 CP57
Old Kent Rd, SE1 . . . . . . .201 M8
  SE15 . . . . .102 DS77

Old Kingston Rd, Wor.Pk.
  KT4 . . . . .138 CQ104
Old La, Cob. KT11 . . . . . .169 BP117
  Westerham (Tats.) TN16 . .178 EK121
Old La Gdns, Cob. KT11 . . .169 BT122
  Purley CR8 . . . . .159 DM114
Old Lo La, Ken. CR8 . . . . .175 DN115
Old Lo Pl, Twick. TW1
  off St. Margarets Rd 117 CH86
Old Lo Way, Stan. HA7 . . . .41 CG50
Old London Rd, Epsom
  KT18 . . . . .173 CU118
  Sevenoaks (Bad.Mt.) TN14 .164 FA110
  Sevenoaks (Knock.P.) TN14 .180 EY115
Old Maidstone Rd, Sid.
  DA14 . . . . .126 EZ94
OLD MALDEN, Wor.Pk. . . .138 CR102
Old Malden La, Wor.Pk. KT4 .138 CR103
Old Malt Way, Wok. GU21 . .166 AX117
Old Manor Dr, Grav. DA12 . .131 GJ88
  Isleworth TW7 . . . . .116 CC86
Old Manor Ho Ms, Shep. TW17
  off Squires Br Rd 134 BN97
Old Manor Rd, Sthl. UB2 . . .96 BX77
  Chislehurst BR7 . . . . . .125 EM92
Old Manor Yd, SW5
  off Earls Ct Rd 100 DB77
Old Marylebone Rd, NW1 . .194 C7
Old Mead, Ger.Cr. (Chal.St.P.)
  SL9 . . . . .36 AY51
Old Ms, Har. HA1
  off Hindes Rd 61 CE57
Old Mill Cl, Dart. (Eyns.)
  DA4 . . . . .148 FL102
Old Mill Ct, E18 . . . . .68 EJ55
Old Mill La, Red. RH1 . . . .185 DH128
  Uxbridge UB8 . . . . .76 BH72
Old Mill Pl, Rom. RM7 . . . .71 FD58
Old Mill Rd, SE18 . . . . . .105 ER79
  Kings Langley WD4 . . . . . .7 BQ33
  Uxbridge (Denh.) UB9 . . . .58 BG62
Old Mitre Ct, EC4
  off Fleet St 83 DN72
Old Montague St, E1 . . . . .84 DU71
Old Nichol St, E2 . . . . . . .197 P4
Old N St, WC1 . . . . .196 B6
Old Oak Av, Couls. CR5 . . .174 DE119
Old Oak Cl, Chess. KT9 . . .156 CM105
OLD OAK COMMON, NW10 . .81 CT71
Old Oak Common La, NW10 . .80 CS70
  W3 . . . . .80 CS70
Old Oak La, NW10 . . . . . . .80 CS69
Old Oak Rd, W3 . . . . .81 CT73
Old Oaks, Wal.Abb. EN9 . . .16 EE32
★ Old Operating Thea Mus
  & Herb Garret, SE1 . . . .201 L3
Old Orchard, St.Alb. (Park St.)
  AL2 . . . . .8 CC26
  Sunbury-on-Thames
  TW16 . . . . .136 BW96
  West Byfleet (Byfleet)
  KT14 . . . . .152 BM112
Old Orchard, The, NW3
  off Nassington Rd 64 DF63
Old Orchard Cl, Barn. EN4 . .28 DD38
  Uxbridge UB8 . . . . .76 BN72
Old Otford Rd, Sev. TN14 . .181 FH117
Old Palace La, Rich. TW9 . .117 CJ85
Old Palace Rd, Croy. CR0 . .141 DP104
  Weybridge KT13 . . . . . .135 BP104
Old Palace Ter, Rich. TW9
  off King St 117 CK85
Old Palace Yd, SW1 . . . . .199 P6
  Richmond TW9 . . . . . . .117 CJ85
Old Paradise St, SE11 . . . .200 B8
Old Pk Av, SW12 . . . . . . .120 DG86
  Enfield EN2 . . . . .30 DQ42
Old Pk Gro, Enf. EN2 . . . . .30 DQ42
Old Pk La, W1 . . . . .198 G3
Old Pk Ms, Houns. TW5 . . . .96 BZ80
Old Pk Ride, Wal.Cr. EN7 . . .14 DT33
Old Pk Ridings, N21 . . . . . .29 DP44
Old Pk Rd, N13 . . . . .DM49
  SE2 . . . . .106 EU78
  Enfield EN2 . . . . .29 DP41
Old Pk Rd S, Enf. EN2 . . . . .29 DP42
Old Pk Vw, Enf. EN2 . . . . . .29 DN41
Old Parvis Rd, W.Byf. KT14 .152 BK112
Old Perry St, Chis. BR7 . . .125 ES94
  Gravesend (Nthflt.) DA11 . .130 GE89
Old Polhill, Sev. TN14 . . . .181 FD115
Old Pound Cl, Islw. TW7 . . .97 CG81
Old Priory, Uxb. (Hare.) UB9 . .59 BP59
Old Pye St, SW1 . . . . . . .199 M6
Old Quebec St, W1 . . . . . .194 E9
Old Queen St, SW1 . . . . . .199 N5
Old Rectory Cl, Tad. KT20 . .173 CU124
Old Rectory Gdns, Edg. HA8 . .42 CN51
Old Rectory La, Uxb. (Denh.)
  UB9 . . . . .57 BE59
Old Rectory Rd, Ong. CM5 . .19 FH34
Old Redding, Har. HA3 . . . .40 CC49
Old Reigate Rd, Bet. RH3 . .182 CP134
  Dorking RH4 . . . . .182 CL134
Oldridge Cl, W12 . . . . .81 CT74
Oldridge Rd, SW12 . . . . . .120 DG87
Old Rd, SE13 . . . . .104 EE84
  Addlestone KT15 . . . . . .151 BF108
  Betchworth (Buckland)
  RH3 . . . . .182 CR134
  Dartford DA1 . . . . .107 FD84
  Enfield EN3 . . . . .30 DW39
Old Rd E, Grav. DA12 . . . .131 GH88
Old Rd W, Grav. DA11 . . . .131 GG88
Old Rope Wk, Sun. TW16
  off The Avenue 135 BV97
Old Royal Free Pl, N1
  off Liverpool Rd 83 DN81
Old Royal Free Sq, N1 . . . .83 DN81
Old Ruislip Rd, Nthlt. UB5 . .78 BX68
Olds App, Wat. WD18 . . . . .39 BP46
Old Savill's Cotts, Chig. IG7
  off The Chase 49 EQ49
Old Sch Cl, SE10 . . . . . . .205 J7
  SW19 . . . . .140 DA96

Old Sch Cl, Beck. BR3 . . . .143 DX96
Old Sch Ct, Stai. (Wrays.)
  TW19 . . . . .112 AY87
Old Sch Cres, E7 . . . . .86 EF65
Old Sch Ms, Egh. TW20 . . .113 BD92
  Weybridge KT13 . . . . . .153 BP105
Old Sch Pl, Wok. GU22 . . .166 AY121
Old Sch Rd, Uxb. UB8 . . . . .76 BM70
Old Schools La, Epsom
  KT17 . . . . .157 CT109
Old Sch Sq, E14
  off Pelling St 85 EA72
  Thames Ditton KT7 . . . . .137 CF100
Olds Cl, Wat. WD18 . . . . . .39 BP46
Old Seacoal La, EC4 . . . . .196 F8
Old Shire La, Ger.Cr. SL9 . . .37 BA46
  Rickmansworth (Chorl.)
  WD3 . . . . .21 BB44
  Waltham Abbey EN9 . . . . .32 EG35
Old Slade La, Iver SL0 . . . . .93 BE76
Old Solesbridge La, Rick. (Chorl.)
  WD3 . . . . .22 BG41
Old S Cl, Pnr. HA5 . . . . . . .60 BX53
Old S Lambeth Rd, SW8 . . .101 DL80
★ Old Spitalfields Mkt, E1 . .197 P6
Old Spitalfields Mkt, E1 . . .197 P6
Old Sq, WC2 . . . . .196 C8
Old Sta App, Lthd. KT22 . . .171 CG121
Old Sta Rd, Hayes UB3 . . . .95 BT76
  Loughton IG10 . . . . .32 EL43
Old Sta Yd, Brom. BR2
  off Bourne Way 144 EF102
Oldstead Rd, Brom. BR1 . . .123 ED91
Old Stockley Rd, West Dr.
  UB7 . . . . .95 BP75
⊖ Old Street 197 K3
⊖ Old Street 197 K3
Old St, E13 . . . . .86 EH68
  EC1 . . . . .197 H4
Old Swan Yd, Cars. SM5 . . .158 DF105
Old Tilburstow Rd, Gdse.
  RH9 . . . . .186 DW134
Old Town, SW4 . . . . .101 DJ83
  Croydon CR0 . . . . .141 DP104
Old Tram Yd, SE18
  off Lakedale Rd 105 ES77
Old Tye Av, West. (Bigg.H.)
  TN16 . . . . .178 EL116
Old Uxbridge Rd, Rick. (Map.Cr.)
  WD3 . . . . .37 BE53
Old Wk, The, Sev. (Otford)
  TN14 . . . . .181 FH117
Old Watford Rd, St.Alb. (Brick.Wd.)
  AL2 . . . . .8 BY30
Old Watling St, Grav. DA11 .131 GG92
Old Westhall Cl, Warl. CR6 . .176 DW119
Old Wf Way, Wey. KT13
  off Weybridge Rd 152 BM105
OLD WINDSOR, Wind. 112 AU86
Old Windsor Lock, Wind.
  (Old Wind.) SL4 . . . . . .112 AW85
OLD WOKING, Wok. 167 BA121
Old Woking Rd, W.Byf. KT14 .152 BF113
  Woking GU22 . . . . .167 BE116
Old Woolwich Rd, SE10 . . .103 ED79
Old Yd, The, West. TN16 . . .180 EW124
Old York Rd, SW18 . . . . . .120 DB85
Oleander Cl, Orp. BR6 . . . .163 ER106
O'Leary Sq, E1 . . . . .84 DW71
Olga St, E3 . . . . .85 DY68
Olinda Rd, N16 . . . . .66 DT58
Oliphant St, W10 . . . . .81 CX69
Olive Av, SE25 . . . . .142 DT97
Oliver Cl, W4 . . . . .98 CP79
  Addlestone KT15 . . . . . .152 BG105
  Grays RM20 . . . . .109 FT80
  St. Albans (Park St.) AL2 . . .9 CD27
Oliver Cres, Dart. (Fngham.)
  DA4 . . . . .148 FM101
Oliver Gdns, E6 . . . . .86 EL72
Oliver-Goldsmith Est, SE15 .102 DU81
Oliver Gro, SE25 . . . . . . .142 DT98
Olive Rd, E13 . . . . .86 EJ69
  NW2 . . . . .63 CW63
  SW19 off Norman Rd 120 DC94
  W5 . . . . .97 CK76
  Dartford DA1 . . . . .128 FK88
Oliver Rd, E10 . . . . .67 EB61
  E17 . . . . .67 EC57
  NW10 . . . . .80 CQ68
  Brentwood CM15 . . . . . . .55 GA45
  Grays RM20 . . . . .109 FT81
  New Malden KT3 . . . . . .138 CQ96
  Rainham RM13 . . . . .89 FF67
  Sutton SM1 . . . . .158 DD105
  Swanley BR8 . . . . .147 FD97
Olivers Yd, EC1 . . . . .197 L4
Olive St, Rom. RM7 . . . . . .71 FD57
Olivette St, SW15 . . . . . . .99 CX83
Olivia Gdns, Uxb. (Hare.) UB9 .38 BJ53
Ollards Gro, Loug. IG10 . . . .32 EK42
Olleberrie La, Rick. (Sarratt) WD3
  off Green La 22 BM43
  Sevenoaks (Dunt.Grn.)
  TN13 . . . . .181 FE120
Ollerton Grn, E3 . . . . .85 DZ67
Ollerton Rd, N11 . . . . .45 DK50
Olley Cl, Wall. SM6 . . . . . .159 DL108
Ollgar Cl, W12 . . . . .81 CT74
Olliffe St, E14 . . . . .204 E7
Olmar St, SE1 . . . . .102 DU79
Olney Rd, SE17 . . . . .101 DP79
Olron Cres, Bexh. DA6 . . . .126 EX85
Olven Rd, SE18 . . . . .105 EQ80
Olveston Wk, Cars. SM5 . . .140 DD100
Olwen Ms, Pnr. HA5 . . . . . .40 BX54
Olyffe Av, Well. DA16 . . . . .106 EU82
Olyffe Dr, Beck. BR3 . . . . .143 EC95
★ Olympia, W14 . . . . .99 CY76
Olympia Ms, W2
  off Queensway 82 DB73
Olympia Way, W14 . . . . . . .99 CY76
Olympic Way, Grnf. UB6 . . . .78 CB67
  Wembley HA9 . . . . .62 CN63
Olympus Sq, E5
  off Nolan Way 66 DU63
Oman Av, NW2 . . . . .63 CW63
O'Meara St, SE1 . . . . . . .201 J3
Omega Cl, E14 . . . . .204 B6

Omega Pl, N1 . . . . .196 A1
Omega Rd, Wok. GU21 . . . .167 BA115
Omega St, SE14 . . . . .103 EA81
Ommaney Rd, SE14 . . . . . .103 DX81
Omnibus Way, E17 . . . . . . .47 EA54
Ondine Rd, SE15 . . . . . . .102 DT84
Onega Gate, SE16 . . . . . . .203 K6
O'Neill Path, SE18
  off Kempt St 105 EN79
One Tree Cl, SE23 . . . . . . .122 DW86
Ongar Cl, Add. KT15 . . . . .151 BF107
  Romford RM6 . . . . .70 EW57
Ongar Hill, Add. KT15 . . . .152 BG107
Ongar Pl, Add. KT15 . . . . .152 BG107
Ongar Rd, SW6 . . . . .100 DA79
  Addlestone KT15 . . . . . .152 BG106
  Brentwood CM15 . . . . . . .54 FV45
  Romford RM4 . . . . .34 EW40
Ongar Way, Rain. RM13 . . . .89 FE67
Onra Rd, E17 . . . . .67 EA59
Onslow Av, Rich. TW10 . . . .118 CL85
  Sutton SM2 . . . . .157 CZ110
Onslow Cl, E4 . . . . .47 EC47
  Thames Ditton KT7 . . . . .137 CE102
  Woking GU22 . . . . .167 BA117
Onslow Cres, Chis. BR7 . . .145 EP95
  Woking GU22 . . . . .167 BA117
Onslow Dr, Sid. DA14 . . . .126 EX89
Onslow Gdns, E18 . . . . . . .68 EH55
  N10 . . . . .65 DH57
  N21 . . . . .29 DN43
  SW7 . . . . .100 DD78
  South Croydon CR2 . . . .160 DU112
  Thames Ditton KT7 . . . . .137 CE102
  Wallington SM6 . . . . . . .159 DJ107
Onslow Ms, Cher. KT16 . . .134 BG100
Onslow Ms E, SW7
  off Cranley Pl 100 DD77
Onslow Ms W, SW7
  off Cranley Pl 100 DD77
Onslow Rd, Croy. CR0 . . . .141 DM101
  New Malden KT3 . . . . . .139 CU98
  Richmond TW10 . . . . . .118 CL85
  Walton-on-Thames KT12 . .153 BT105
Onslow Sq, SW7 . . . . . . .100 DD77
Onslow St, EC1 . . . . .196 E5
Onslow Way, T.Ditt. KT7 . . .137 CE102
  Woking GU22 . . . . .167 BF115
Ontario St, SE1 . . . . .200 G7
Ontario Way, E14 . . . . . . .203 P1
On The Hill, Wat. WD19 . . . .40 BY47
Opal Cl, E16 . . . . .86 EK72
Opal Ct, Slou. (Wexham) SL3
  off Wexham St 74 AV70
Opal Ms, NW6
  off Priory Pk Rd 81 CZ67
  Ilford IG1 off Ley St 69 EP61
Opal St, SE11 . . . . .200 F9
Openshaw Rd, SE2 . . . . . .106 EV77
Openview, SW18 . . . . . . .120 DC88
Ophelia Gdns, NW2
  off Hamlet Sq 63 CY62
Ophir Ter, SE15 . . . . .102 DU81
Opossum Way, Houns. TW4 . .96 BW82
Oppenheim Rd, SE13 . . . .103 EC82
Oppidans Ms, NW3
  off Meadowbank 82 DF66
Oppidans Rd, NW3 . . . . . . .82 DF66
Orange Ct, E1 . . . . .202 C3
Orange Ct La, Orp. BR6 . . .163 EN109
Orange Gro, E11 . . . . .68 EE62
  Chigwell IG7 . . . . .49 EQ51
Orange Hill Rd, Edg. HA8 . . .42 CQ52
Orange Pl, SE16 . . . . .202 G7
Orangery, The, Rich. TW10 .117 CJ89
Orangery La, SE9 . . . . . . .125 EM85
Orange Sq, SW1
  off Ebury St 198 G9
Orange St, WC2 . . . . .199 M1
Orange Tree Hill, Rom.
  (Hav.at.Bow.) RM4 . . . . . .51 FD50
Orange Yd, W1 . . . . .195 N9
Oratory La, SW3 . . . . .198 A10
Orbain Rd, SW6 . . . . .99 CY80
Orbel St, SW11 . . . . .100 DE81
Orbital Cres, Wat. WD25 . . . .23 BT35
Orbital One, Dart. DA1 . . . .128 FP89
Orb St, SE17 . . . . .201 K9

Old - Orc

Orchard Cl, E4
  off Chingford Mt Rd 47 EA49
  E11 . . . . .68 EH56
  N1 off Morton Rd 84 DQ66
  NW2 . . . . .63 CU62
  SE23 off Brenchley Gdns . .122 DW86
  SW20 off Grand Dr 139 CW98
  W10 . . . . .81 CY71
  Ashford TW15 . . . . .115 BQ93
  Banstead SM7 . . . . .158 DB114
  Bexleyheath DA7 . . . . . .106 EY81
  Borehamwood (Elstree)
  WD6 . . . . .26 CM42
  Bushey (Bushey Hth.)
  WD23 . . . . .41 CD46
  Edgware HA8 . . . . .42 CL53
  Egham TW20 . . . . .113 BB92
  Epsom (W.Ewell) KT19 . . .156 CP107
  Leatherhead KT22 . . . . .171 CF119
  Leatherhead (E.Hors.)
  KT24 . . . . .169 BT124
  Leatherhead (Fetch.) KT22 .171 CD122
  Northolt UB5 . . . . .60 CC64
  Potters Bar (Cuffley) EN6 . .13 DL28
  Radlett WD7 . . . . .25 CE37
  Rickmansworth (Chorl.)
  WD3 . . . . .21 BD42
  Ruislip HA4 . . . . .59 BQ59
  South Ockendon RM15 . . .91 FW70
  Surbiton KT6 . . . . .137 CH101
  Uxbridge (Denh.) UB9 . . . .76 BH65
  Walton-on-Thames KT12
  off Garden Rd 135 BV101
  Watford WD17 . . . . .23 BT40
  Wembley HA0 . . . . .80 CL67
  Woking GU22 . . . . .167 AZ115
Orchard Ct, Hem.H. (Bov.) HP3 . .5 BA27
  Isleworth TW7
  off Thornbury Av 97 CD81
  Twickenham TW2 . . . . . .117 CD89
  Wallington SM6
  off Parkgate Rd 159 DH106
  Worcester Park KT4
  off The Avenue 139 CU102
Orchard Cres, Edg. HA8 . . . .42 CQ50
  Enfield EN1 . . . . .30 DT39
Orchard Dr, SE3
  off Orchard Rd 104 EE82
  Ashtead KT21 . . . . .171 CK120
  Edgware HA8 . . . . .42 CM50
  Epping (They.B.) CM16 . . .33 ES36
  Grays RM17 . . . . .110 GA75
  Rickmansworth (Chorl.)
  WD3 . . . . .21 BC41
  St. Albans (Park St.) AL2 . . .8 CB27
  Uxbridge UB8 . . . . .76 BK70
  Watford WD17 . . . . .23 BT39
  Woking GU21 . . . . .167 AZ115
Orchard End, Cat. CR3 . . . .176 DS122
  Leatherhead (Fetch.) KT22 .170 CC124
  Weybridge KT13 . . . . . .135 BS103
Orchard End Av, Amer. HP7 . .20 AT39
Orchard Gdns, Chess. KT9 .156 CL105
  Epsom KT18 . . . . .156 CQ114
  Sutton SM1 . . . . .158 DA106
  Waltham Abbey EN9 . . . . .15 EC34
Orchard Gate, NW9 . . . . . .62 CS56
  Esher KT10 . . . . .137 CD102
  Greenford UB6 . . . . .79 CH65
Orchard Grn, Orp. BR6 . . . .145 ES103
Orchard Gro, SE20 . . . . . .122 DU94
  Croydon CR0 . . . . .143 DY101
  Edgware HA8 . . . . .42 CN53
  Gerrards Cross (Chal.St.P.)
  SL9 . . . . .36 AW53
  Harrow HA3 . . . . .62 CM57
  Orpington BR6 . . . . . . .145 ET103
Orchard Hill, SE13
  off Coldbath St 103 EB82
  Carshalton SM5 . . . . . . .158 DF106
  Dartford DA1 . . . . .127 FE85
Orchard Ho, Erith DA8
  off Northend Rd 107 FF81
Orchard La, SW20 . . . . . .139 CV95
  East Molesey KT8 . . . . . .137 CD100
  Woodford Green IG8 . . . . .48 EJ49
Orchard Lea Cl, Wok. GU22 .167 BE115
ORCHARD LEIGH, Chesh. . . .4 AV28
Orchard Leigh, Chesh. HP5 . .4 AU28
Orchardleigh, Lthd. KT22 . .171 CH122
Orchardleigh Av, Enf. EN3 . .30 DW40
Orchard Mains, Wok. GU22 .166 AW119
Orchardmede, N21 . . . . . . .30 DR44
Orchard Ms, N1
  off Southgate Gro 84 DR66
Orchard Path, Slou. SL3 . . .75 BA72
Orchard Pl, E14 . . . . .86 EE73
  N17 . . . . .46 DT52
  Keston BR2 . . . . .162 EJ109
  Sevenoaks (Sund.) TN14 . .180 EY124
  Waltham Cross (Chsht.) EN8
  off Turners Hill 15 DX30
Orchard Ri, Croy. CR0 . . . .143 DY102
  Kingston upon Thames
  KT2 . . . . .138 CQ95
  Pinner HA5 . . . . .59 BT55
  Richmond TW10 . . . . . . .98 CP84
Orchard Ri E, Sid. DA15 . . .125 ET85
Orchard Ri W, Sid. DA15 . . .125 ES85
Orchard Rd, N6 . . . . .65 DH59
  SE3 . . . . .104 EE82
  SE18 . . . . .105 ER77
  Barnet EN5 . . . . .27 CZ42
  Belvedere DA17 . . . . . .106 FA77
  Brentford TW8 . . . . .97 CJ79
  Bromley BR1 . . . . .144 EJ95
  Chalfont St. Giles HP8 . . .36 AW47
  Chessington KT9 . . . . . .156 CL105
  Dagenham RM10 . . . . . . .88 FA67
  Enfield EN3 . . . . .30 DW43
  Gravesend (Nthflt.) DA11 .130 GC89
  Hampton TW12 . . . . . . .116 BZ94
  Hayes UB3 . . . . .77 BT73

Orc - Oxf

Orchard Rd, Houns. TW4 ..116 BZ85
Kingston upon Thames
  KT1 ....138 CL96
  Mitcham CR4 ....140 DG102
  Orpington (Farnboro.)
    BR6 ....163 EP106
  Orpington (Pr.Bot.) BR6 ..164 EW110
  Reigate RH2 ....184 DB134
  Richmond TW9 ....98 CN83
  Romford RM7 ....51 FB53
  Sevenoaks (Otford) TN14 ..181 FF116
  Sevenoaks (Rvrhd.) TN13 .190 FE122
  Sidcup DA14 ....125 ES91
  South Croydon CR2 .....160 DV114
  South Ockendon RM15 ..91 FW70
  Sunbury-on-Thames TW16
    off Hanworth Rd 115 BV94
  Sutton SM1 ....158 DA106
  Swanscombe DA10 .....130 FY85
  Twickenham TW1 ....117 CG85
  Welling DA16 ....106 EV83
  Windsor (Old Wind.) SL4 ..112 AV86
Orchards, The, Epp. CM16 ..18 EU32
Orchards CI, W.Byf. KT14 ..152 BG114
Orchardson St, NW8 ....82 DD70
Orchard Sq, W14 off Sun Rd .99 CZ78
Orchards Residential Pk, The,
  Slou.SL3 ....75 AZ74
Orchards Shop Cen, Dart.
  DA1 ....128 FL86
Orchard St, E17 ....67 DY56
  W1 ....194 F9
  Dartford DA1 ....128 FL86
Orchard Ter, Enf. EN1
  off Great Cambridge Rd ..30 DU44
Orchard Vw, Uxb. UB8 ....76 BK70
Orchard Vil, Sid. DA14
  off Haven CI 106 EW93
Orchard Way, Add. KT15 ..152 BH106
  Ashford TW15 ....114 BM89
  Beckenham BR3 ....143 DY99
  Chigwell IG7 ....50 EU48
  Croydon CR0 ....143 DY102
  Dartford DA2 ....128 FK90
  Enfield EN1 ....30 DS41
  Esher KT10 ....154 CC107
  Hemel Hempstead (Bov.)
    HP3 ....5 BA28
  Oxted RH8 ....188 EG133
  Potters Bar EN6 ....12 DB28
  Rickmansworth (Mill End)
    WD3 ....38 BG45
  Slough SL3 ....74 AY74
  Sutton SM1 ....158 DD105
  Tadworth KT20 ....183 CZ126
  Waltham Cross (Chsht.)
    EN7 ....13 DP27
Orchard Waye, Uxb. UB8 ....76 BK68
Orchehill Av, Ger.Cr. SL9 ...56 AX56
Orchehill Ct, Ger.Cr. SL9 ...56 AY56
Orchehill Ri, Ger.Cr. SL9 ...56 AY57
Orchid CI, E6 ....86 EL71
  Chessington KT9 ....155 CJ108
  Romford (Abridge) RM4 ..34 EV41
  Southall UB1 ....78 BY72
  Waltham Cross EN7
    off Silver St 14 DQ30
Orchid Ct, Egh. TW20 ......113 BB91
  Romford RM7 ....71 FE61
Orchid Rd, N14 ....45 DJ45
Orchid St, W12 ....81 CU73
Orchis Gro, Grays (Bad.Dene)
  RM17 ....110 FZ78
Orchis Way, Rom. RM3 .....52 FM51
Orde Hall St, WC1 ....196 B5
Ordell Rd, E3 ....85 DZ68
Ordnance CI, Felt. TW13 ..115 BU90
Ordnance Cres, SE10 ....204 G4
Ordnance Hill, NW8 ....82 DD67
Ordnance Ms, NW8
  off St. Ann's Ter 82 DD68
Ordnance Rd, E16 ....86 EF71
  SE18 ....105 EN79
  Enfield EN3 ....31 DX37
  Gravesend DA12 ....131 GJ86
Oregano CI, West Dr. UB7
  off Camomile Way 76 BM72
Oregano Dr, E14 ....85 ED72
Oregon Av, E12 ....69 EM63
Oregon CI, N.Mal. KT3
  off Georgia Rd 138 CQ98
Oregon Sq, Orp. BR6 ......145 ER102
Orestes Ms, NW6
  off Aldred Rd 64 DA64
Oreston Rd, Rain. RM13 ....90 FK69
Orford Ct, SE27 ....121 DP89
Orford Gdns, Twick. TW1 ..117 CF89
Orford Rd, E17 ....67 EA57
  E18 ....68 EH55
  SE6 ....123 EB90
Organ Hall Rd, Borwd. WD6 ..26 CL39
Organ La, E4 ....47 EC47
Oriel CI, Mitch. CR4 ....141 DK98
Oriel Ct, NW3 off Heath St ..64 DC63
Oriel Dr, SW13 ....99 CV79
Oriel Gdns, Ilf. IG5 ....69 EM55
Oriel PI, NW3 off Heath St ..64 DC63
Oriel Rd, E9 ....85 DX65
Oriel Way, Nthlt. UB5 ....78 CB66
Oriental CI, Wok. GU22
  off Oriental Rd 167 BA117
Oriental Rd, E16 ....86 EK74
  Woking GU22 ....167 BA117
Oriental St, E14
  off Morant St 85 EA72
Orient Ind Pk, E10 ....67 EA61
Orient St, SE11 ....200 F8
Orient Way, E5 ....67 DX62
  E10 ....67 DY61
Oriole CI, Abb.L. WD5 ....7 BU31
Oriole Way, SE28 ....88 EV73
Orion Rd, N11 ....45 DH51
Orion Way, Nthwd. HA6 ....39 BT49
Orissa Rd, SE18 ....105 ES78

Orkney St, SW11 ....100 DG82
Orlando Gdns, Epsom KT19 .156 CR110
Orlando Rd, SW4 ....101 DJ83
Orleans CI, Esher KT10 ....137 CD103
★ Orleans Ho Gall, Twick.
  TW1 ....117 CH88
Orleans Rd, SE19 ....122 DR93
  Twickenham TW1 ....117 CH87
Orlestone Gdns, Orp. BR6 ..164 EY106
Orleston Ms, N7 ....83 DN65
Orleston Rd, N7 ....83 DN65
Orley Fm Rd, Har. HA1 .....61 CE62
Orlop St, SE10 ....104 EE78
Ormanton Rd, SE26 ....122 DU91
Orme Ct, W2 ....82 DB73
Orme Ct Ms, W2 off Orme La .82 DB73
Orme La, W2 ....82 DB73
Ormeley Rd, SW12 ....121 DH88
Orme Rd, Kings.T. KT1 .....138 CP97
  Sutton SM1 off Grove Rd ..158 DB107
Ormerod Gdns, Mitch. CR4 ..140 DG96
Ormesby CI, SE28
  off Wroxham Rd 88 EX73
Ormesby Dr, Pot.B. EN6 .....11 CX32
Ormesby Way, Har. HA3 .....62 CM58
Orme Sq, W2
  off Bayswater Rd 82 DB73
Ormiston Gro, W12 ....81 CV74
Ormiston Rd, SE10 ....104 EG78
Ormond Av, Hmptn. TW12 ..136 CB95
  Richmond TW10
    off Ormond Rd 117 CK85
Ormond CI, WC1 ....196 A6
  Romford (Harold Wd.) RM3
    off Chadwick St 52 FK54
Ormond Cres, Hmptn. TW12 ..136 CB95
Ormond Dr, Hmptn. TW12 ..116 CB94
Ormonde Av, Epsom KT19 ..156 CR109
  Orpington BR6 ....145 EQ103
Ormonde Gate, SW3 ....100 DF78
Ormonde PI, SW1 ....198 F9
Ormonde Ri, Buck.H. IG9 ....48 EJ46
Ormonde Rd, SW14 ....98 CP83
  Northwood HA6 ....39 BR49
  Woking GU21 ....166 AW116
Ormonde Ter, NW8 ....82 DF67
Ormond Ms, WC1 ....196 A5
Ormond Rd, N19 ....65 DL60
  Richmond TW10 ....117 CK85
Ormond Yd, SW1 ....199 L2
Ormsby, Sutt. SM2
  off Grange Rd 158 DB108
Ormsby Gdns, Grnf. UB6 ....78 CC68
Ormsby PI, N16
  off Victorian Gro 66 DT62
Ormsby St, SE18 ....105 EP77
Ormsby St, E2 ....84 DT68
Ormside St, SE15 ....102 DW79
Ormside Way, Red. RH1 ....185 DH130
Ormskirk Rd, Wat. WD19 ....40 BX49
Ornan Rd, NW3 ....64 DE64
Oronsay Wk, N1
  off Clephane Rd 84 DQ65
Orpen Wk, N16 ....66 DS62
Orphanage Rd, Wat.
  WD17, WD24 ....24 BW40
Orpheus St, SE5 ....102 DR81
ORPINGTON 145 ES102
⇌ Orpington 145 ET103
Orpington Bypass, Orp.
  BR6 ....146 EV103
  Sevenoaks TN14 ....164 FA109
Orpington Gdns, N18 ....46 DS48
🄷 Orpington Hosp, Orp.
  BR6 ....163 ET105
Orpington Rd, N21 ....45 DP46
  Chislehurst BR7 ....145 ES97
Orpin Rd, Red. RH1 ....185 DH130
Orpwood CI, Hmptn. TW12 ..116 BZ92
ORSETT HEATH, Grays 111 GG75
Orsett Heath Cres, Grays
  RM16 ....111 GG76
Orsett Rd, Grays RM17 ....110 GA78
Orsett St, SE11 ....200 C10
Orsett Ter, W2 ....82 DC72
  Woodford Green IG8 ....48 EJ53
Orsman Rd, N1 ....84 DS67
Orton St, E1 ....202 B3
Orville Rd, SW11 ....100 DD82
Orwell CI, Hayes UB3 ....77 BS73
  Rainham RM13 ....89 FD71
Orwell Ct, N5 ....66 DQ63
Orwell Rd, E13 ....86 EJ68
Osbaldeston Rd, N16 ....66 DU61
Osberton Rd, SE12 ....124 EG85
Osbert St, SW1 ....199 M9
Osborn CI, E8 ....84 DU67
Osborne Av, Stai. TW19 ....114 BL88
Osborne CI, Barn. EN4 .....28 DF41
  Beckenham BR3 ....143 DY98
  Feltham TW13 ....116 BX92
  Hornchurch RM11 ....71 FH58
Osborne Ct, Pot.B. EN6 .....12 DB29
Osborne Gdns, Pot.B. EN6 ..12 DB30
  Thornton Heath CR7 .....142 DQ96
Osborne Gro, E17 ....67 DZ56
  N4 ....65 DN60
Osborne Ms, E17
  off Osborne Gro 67 DZ56
Osborne PI, Sutt. SM1 ....158 DD106
Osborne Rd, E7 ....68 EH64
  E9 ....85 DZ65
  E10 ....67 EB62
  N4 ....65 DN60
  N13 ....45 DN48
  NW2 ....81 CV65
  W3 ....98 CP86
  Belvedere DA17 ....106 EZ78
  Brentwood (Pilg.Hat.)
    CM15 ....54 FU44
  Buckhurst Hill IG9 ....48 EH46
  Dagenham RM9 ....70 EZ64
  Egham TW20 ....113 AZ93
  Enfield EN3 ....31 DY40
  Hornchurch RM11 ....71 FH58
  Hounslow TW3 ....96 BZ83

Osborne Rd, Kings.T. KT2 ...118 CL94
  Potters Bar EN6 ....12 DB30
  Redhill RH1 ....184 DG109
  Southall UB1 ....78 CC72
  Thornton Heath CR7 .....142 DQ96
  Uxbridge UB8
    off Oxford Rd 76 BJ66
  Waltham Cross (Chsht.)
    EN8 ....15 DY27
  Walton-on-Thames KT12 ..135 BU102
  Watford WD24 ....24 BW38
Osborne Sq, Dag. RM9 .....70 EZ63
Osborne St, Slou. SL1 .....92 AT75
Osborne Ter, SW17
  off Church La 120 DG92
Osborn Gdns, NW7 ....43 CX52
Osborn La, SE23 ....123 DY87
Osborn St, E1 ....84 DT71
Osborn Ter, SE3 off Lee Rd ..104 EF84
Osbourne Av, NW7
  off Bittacy Hill 43 CY52
  Kings Langley WD4 ....6 BM28
Osbourne Rd, Dart. DA2 ....128 FP86
Oscar St, SE8 ....103 EA81
Oseney Cres, NW5 ....83 DJ65
Osgood Av, Orp. BR6 ....163 ET106
Osgood Gdns, Orp. BR6 ....163 ET106
OSIDGE, N14 ....45 DH46
Osidge La, N14 ....44 DG46
Osier Cres, N10 ....44 DF53
Osier La, SE10 ....205 L7
Osier Ms, W4 ....99 CT79
Osier PI, Egh. TW20 ....113 BC93
Osiers Rd, SW18 ....100 DA84
Osier St, E1 ....84 DW70
Osier Way, E10 ....85 EC67
  Banstead SM7 ....157 CY114
  Mitcham CR4 ....140 DE99
Oslac Rd, SE6 ....123 EB92
Oslo Ct, NW8 ....194 B1
Oslo Sq, SE16 ....203 L6
Osman CI, N15
  off Tewkesbury Rd 66 DR58
Osman Rd, N9 ....46 DU48
  W6 off Batoum Gdns 99 CW76
Osmond CI, Har. HA2 ....60 CC61
Osmond Gdns, Wall. SM6 ..159 DJ106
Osmund St, W12
  off Braybrook St 81 CT72
Osnaburgh St, NW1 ....195 J5
  NW1 (north section)
    off Robert St 83 DH69
Osnaburgh Ter, NW1 ....195 J4
Osney Ho, SE2
  off Hartslock Dr 106 EX75
Osney Wk, Cars. SM5 ......140 DD100
Osney Way, Grav. DA12 ....131 GM89
Osprey CI, E6 off Dove App ..86 EL71
  E11 ....68 EG56
  E17 ....47 DY52
  Sutton SM1
    off Sandpiper Rd 157 CZ106
  Watford WD25 ....8 BY34
  West Drayton UB7 ....94 BK75
Osprey Ct, Wal.Abb. EN9 ....16 EG34
Osprey Gdns, S.Croy. CR2 ..161 DX110
Osprey Ms, Enf. EN3 ....30 DV43
Osprey Rd, Wal.Abb. EN9 ....16 EG34
Ospringe CI, SE20 ....122 DW94
Ospringe Ct, SE9
  off Alderwood Rd 125 ER86
Ospringe Rd, NW5 ....65 DJ63
Osram Ct, W6
  off Lena Gdns 99 CW76
Osram Rd, Wem. HA9 ....61 CK62
Osric Path, N1 ....197 M1
Ossian Ms, N4 ....65 DM59
Ossian Rd, N4 ....65 DM59
Ossington Bldgs, W1 ....194 F6
Ossington CI, W2
  off Ossington St 82 DB73
Ossington St, W2 ....82 DB73
Ossory Rd, SE1 ....102 DU78
Ossulston St, NW1 ....195 M1
Ossulton PI, N2
  off East End Rd 64 DC55
Ossulton Way, N2 ....64 DC56
Ostade Rd, SW2 ....121 DM87
Ostell Cres, Enf. EN3 ....31 EA37
Osten Ms, SW7
  off Emperor's Gate 100 DB76
Osterberg Rd, Dart. DA1 ...108 FM84
OSTERLEY, Islw. 96 CC80
⊖ Osterley 97 CD80
Osterley Av, Islw. TW7 .....97 CD80
Osterley CI, Orp. BR5
  off Leith Hill 146 EU95
Osterley Ct, Islw. TW7 .....97 CD81
Osterley Cres, Islw. TW7 ...97 CE80
Osterley Gdns, Th.Hth. CR7 .142 DQ96
★ Osterley Park Ho, Islw.
  TW7 ....96 CC78
Osterley Pk Rd, Sthl. UB2 ..96 BZ76
Osterley Pk Vw Rd, W7 .....97 CE75
Osterley Rd, N16 ....66 DS63
  Isleworth TW7 ....97 CE80
Osterley Views, Sthl. UB2
  off West Pk Rd 78 CC74
Oster Ter, E17
  off Southcote Rd 67 DX57
Ostliffe Rd, N13 ....46 DQ50
Oswald CI, Lthd. (Fetch.)
  KT22 ....170 CC122
Oswald Rd, Lthd. (Fetch.)
  KT22 ....170 CC122
  Southall UB1 ....78 BY74
Oswald's Mead, E9
  off Lindisfarne Way 67 DY63
Oswald St, E5 ....67 DX62

Oswald Ter, NW2
  off Temple Rd 63 CW62
Osward, Croy. CR0 ....161 DZ109
Osward PI, N9 ....46 DV47
Osward Rd, SW17 ....120 DE89
Oswell Ho, E1 ....202 E2
Oswin St, SE11 ....200 G8
Oswyth Rd, SE5 ....102 DS82
OTFORD, Sev. 181 FG116
Otford CI, SE20 ....142 DW95
  Bexley DA5
    off Southwold Rd 127 FB86
  Bromley BR1 ....145 EN97
Otford Cres, SE4 ....123 DZ86
Otford La, Sev. (Halst.) TN14 .164 EZ112
Otford Rd, Sev. TN14 ......181 FH118
Othello CI, SE11 ....200 F10
Otis St, E3 ....85 EC70
Otley App, Ilf. IG2 ....69 EP58
Otley Dr, Ilf. IG2 ....69 EP57
Otley Rd, E16 ....86 EJ72
Otley Ter, E5 ....67 DX61
Otley Way, Wat. WD19 .....40 BW48
Otlinge CI, Orp. BR5 ....146 EX98
Ottawa Gdns, Dag. RM10 ..89 FD66
Ottawa Rd, Til. RM18 ......111 GG82
Ottaway St, E5
  off Stellman CI 66 DU62
Ottenden CI, Orp. BR6
  off Southfleet Rd 163 ES105
Otterbourne Rd, E4 ....47 ED48
  Croydon CR0 ....142 DQ103
Otterburn Gdns, Islw. TW7 ..97 CG80
Otterburn Ho, SE5 ....102 DQ80
Otterburn St, SW17 ....120 DF93
Otterden St, SE6 ....123 EA91
Otterfield Rd, West Dr. UB7 ..76 BL73
Ottermead La, Cher. (Ott.)
  KT16 ....151 BC107
Otter Meadow, Lthd. KT22 ..171 CF119
Otter Rd, Grnf. UB6 ....78 CC70
Otters CI, Orp. BR5 ....146 EX98
OTTERSHAW, Cher. 151 BC106
Otterspool La, Wat. WD25 ..24 BY38
Otterspool Service Rd, Wat.
  WD25 ....24 BZ39
Otterspool Way, Wat. WD25 ..24 BY39
Otto CI, SE26 ....122 DV90
Ottoman Ter, Wat. WD17
  off Ebury Rd 24 BW41
Otto St, SE17 ....101 DP79
Ottways Av, Ashtd. KT21 ...171 CK119
Ottways La, Ashtd. KT21 ...171 CK120
Otway Gdns, Bushey WD23 ..41 CE45
Otways CI, Pot.B. EN6 .....12 DB32
Oulton CI, E5
  off Mundford Rd 66 DW61
  SE28 off Rollesby Way 88 EW72
Oulton Cres, Bark. IG11 ....87 ET65
  Potters Bar EN6 ....11 CX32
Oulton Rd, N15 ....66 DR57
Oulton Way, Wat. WD19 ....40 BY49
Oundle Av, Bushey WD23 ..24 CC44
Ousden CI, Wal.Cr. (Chsht.)
  EN8 ....15 DY30
Ousden Dr, Wal.Cr. (Chsht.)
  EN8 ....15 DY30
Ouseley Rd, SW12 ....120 DF88
  Staines (Wrays.) TW19 ....112 AW48
  Windsor (Old Wind.) SL4 ..112 AW87
Outer Circle, NW1 ....194 F5
Outfield Rd, Ger.Cr. (Chal.St.P.)
  SL9 ....36 AX52
Outgate Rd, NW10 ....81 CT66
Outlook Dr, Ch.St.G. HP8 ....36 AX48
Outram PI, N1 ....83 DL67
  Weybridge KT13 ....153 BQ106
Outram Rd, E6 ....86 EL67
  N22 ....45 DK53
  Croydon CR0 ....142 DT102
Outwich St, EC3 ....197 N8
Outwood La, Couls. CR5 ....174 DF118
  Tadworth (Kgswd.) KT20 ..174 DB122
★ Oval, The, Surrey County
  Cricket Club, SE11 ....101 DM79
⊖ Oval 101 DN79
Oval, The, E2 ....84 DV68
  Banstead SM7 ....158 DA114
  Broxbourne EN10 ....15 DY25
  Sidcup DA15 ....126 EU87
Oval Gdns, Grays RM17 ....110 GC76
Oval PI, SW8 ....101 DM80
Oval Rd, NW1 ....83 DH67
  Croydon CR0 ....142 DS102
Oval Rd N, Dag. RM10 .....89 FB67
Oval Rd S, Dag. RM10 .....89 FB68
Oval Way, SE11 ....101 DM78
  Gerrards Cross SL9 ....56 AY56
Ovenden Rd, Sev. (Sund.)
  TN14 ....180 EX120
Overbrae, Beck. BR3 ....123 EA93
Overbrook Wk, Edg. HA8 ...42 CN52
Overbury Av, Beck. BR3 ....143 EB97
Overbury Cres, Croy. (New Adgtn.)
  CR0 ....161 EC110
Overbury Rd, N15 ....66 DR58
Overbury St, E5 ....67 DX63
Overcliff Rd, SE13 ....103 EA83
  Grays RM17 ....110 GD78
Overcourt CI, Sid. DA15 ....126 EV86
Overdale, Ashtd. KT21 .....172 CL115
  Redhill (Bletch.) RH1 .....186 DQ133
Overdale Av, N.Mal. KT3 ...138 CQ96
Overdale Rd, W5 ....97 CJ76
Overdown Rd, SE6 ....123 EA91
Overhill, Warl. CR6 ....176 DW119
Overhill Rd, SE22 ....122 DU87
  Purley CR8 ....159 DN109
Overhill Way, Beck. BR3 ...143 ED99
Overlea Rd, E5 ....66 DU59
Overmead, Sid. DA15 ......125 ER87
  Swanley BR8 ....147 FE99
Oversley Ho, W2 ....82 DA71
Overstand CI, Beck. BR3 ...143 EA99

Overstone Gdns, Croy. CR0 ..143 DZ101
Overstone Rd, W6 ....99 CW76
Overstream, Rick. (Loud.)
  WD3 ....22 BH42
Over The Misbourne, Ger.Cr.
  SL9 ....57 BA58
  Uxbridge (Denh.) UB9 .....57 BC58
Overthorpe CI, Wok. (Knap.)
  GU21 ....166 AS117
Overton CI, NW10 ....80 CQ65
  Isleworth TW7
    off Avenue Rd 97 CF81
Overton Ct, E11 ....68 EG59
Overton Dr, E11 ....68 EH59
  Romford RM6 ....70 EW59
Overton Ho, SW15
  off Tangley Gro 119 CT87
Overton Rd, E10 ....67 DY60
  N14 ....29 DL43
  SE2 ....106 EW76
  SW9 ....101 DN82
  Sutton SM2 ....158 DA107
Overton Rd E, SE2 ....106 EX76
Overtons Yd, Croy. CR0 ....142 DQ104
Overy St, Dart. DA1 ....128 FL86
Ovesdon Av, Har. HA2 .....60 BZ60
Ovett CI, SE19 ....122 DS93
Ovex CI, E14 ....204 E5
Ovington Ct, Wok. GU21
  off Roundthorn Way 166 AT116
Ovington Gdns, SW3 ....198 C7
Ovington Ms, SW3 ....198 C7
Ovington Sq, SW3 ....198 C7
Ovington St, SW3 ....198 C7
Owen CI, SE28 ....88 EW74
  Croydon CR0 ....142 DR100
  Hayes UB4 ....77 BV69
  Romford RM5 ....51 FB51
Owen Gdns, Wdf.Grn. IG8 ...48 EL51
Owenite St, SE2 ....106 EV77
Owen PI, Lthd. KT22
  off Church Rd 171 CH122
Owen Rd, N13 ....46 DQ50
  Hayes UB4 ....77 BV69
Owen's Ct, EC1 ....196 F2
Owen's Row, EC1 ....196 F2
Owen St, EC1 ....196 F1
Owens Way, SE23 ....123 DY87
  Rickmansworth (Crox.Grn.)
    WD3 ....22 BN43
Owen Wk, SE20
  off Sycamore Gro 122 DU94
Owen Waters Ho, Ilf. IG5 ...49 EM53
Owen Way, NW10 ....80 CQ65
Owgan CI, SE5
  off Benhill Rd 102 DR80
Owl CI, S.Croy. CR2 ....161 DX110
Owlets Hall CI, Horn. RM11
  off Prospect Rd 72 FM55
Owl Pk, Loug. (High Beach)
  IG10 ....32 EF40
Ownstead Gdns, S.Croy.
  CR2 ....160 DT111
Ownsted Hill, Croy. (New Adgtn.)
  CR0 ....161 EC110
Oxberry Av, SW6 ....99 CY82
Oxdowne CI, Cob. (Stoke D'Ab.)
  KT11 ....154 CB114
Oxenden Wd Rd, Orp. BR6 ..164 EV107
Oxendon St, SW1 ....199 M1
Oxenford St, SE15 ....102 DT83
Oxenholme, NW1 ....195 L1
Oxenpark Av, Wem. HA9 ....62 CL59
Oxestalls Rd, SE8 ....203 L10
Oxford Av, SW20 ....139 CY96
  Grays RM16 ....111 GG77
  Hayes UB3 ....95 BT80
  Hornchurch RM11 ....72 FN56
  Hounslow TW5 ....96 CA78
★ Oxford Circus, W1 ....195 K8
⊖ Oxford Circus 195 K8
Oxford Circ Av, W1 ....195 K9
Oxford CI, N9 ....46 DV47
  Ashford TW15 ....115 BQ94
  Gravesend DA12 ....131 GM89
  Mitcham CR4 ....141 DJ97
  Northwood HA6 ....39 BQ49
  Waltham Cross (Chsht.)
    EN8 ....15 DX29
Oxford Ct, EC4 ....197 K10
  W3 ....80 CN72
  Brentwood (Warley) CM14 ..54 FX49
  Feltham TW13
    off Oxford Way 116 BX91
Oxford Cres, N.Mal. KT3 ...138 CR100
Oxford Dr, SE1 ....201 M3
  Ruislip HA4 ....60 BW61
Oxford Gdns, N20 ....44 DD46
  N21 ....46 DQ45
  W4 ....98 CN78
  W10 ....81 CY72
  Uxbridge (Denh.) UB9 .....57 BF62
Oxford Gate, W6 ....99 CX77
Oxford Ms, Bex. DA5
  off Bexley High St 126 FA87
Oxford PI, NW10
  off Neasden La N 62 CR62
Oxford Rd, E15 ....85 ED65
  N4 ....65 DN60
  N9 ....46 DV47
  NW6 ....82 DA68
  SE19 ....122 DR93
  SW15 ....99 CY84
  W5 ....79 CK73
  Carshalton SM5 ....158 DE100
  Enfield EN3 ....30 DV43
  Gerrards Cross SL9 ....53 BA60
  Harrow HA1 ....60 CC58
  Harrow (Wldste.) HA3 .....61 CF55
  Ilford IG1 ....69 EQ63
  Redhill RH1 ....184 DE133
  Romford RM3 ....52 FM51
  Sidcup DA14 ....126 EV92
  Teddington TW11 ....117 CD92
  Uxbridge UB8, UB9 ....76 BJ65
  Wallington SM6 ....159 DJ106
  Woodford Green IG8 ....48 EJ50

Oxford Rd N, W4 . . . . .98 CP78
Oxford Rd S, W4 . . . . .98 CN78
Oxford Sq, W2 . . . . .194 C9
Oxford St, W1 . . . . .194 F9
  Watford WD18 . . . . .23 BV43
Oxford Wk, Sthl. UB1 . . . . . .78 BZ74
Oxford Way, Felt. TW13 . . . .116 BW90
Oxgate Gdns, NW2 . . . . .63 CV62
Oxgate La, NW2 . . . . .63 CV64
Oxhawth Cres, Brom. BR2 . .145 EN99
OXHEY, Wat. 24 BW44
Oxhey Av, Wat. WD19 . . . . . .40 BX45
Oxhey Dr, Nthwd. HA6 . . . . . .39 BV50
  Watford WD19 . . . . .40 BW48
Oxhey Dr S, Nthwd. HA6 . . . .39 BV50
Oxhey La, Har. HA3 . . . . .40 CA50
  Pinner HA5 . . . . .40 CA50
  Watford WD19 . . . . .40 BW48
Oxhey Ridge Cl, Nthwd. HA6 .39 BU50
Oxhey Rd, Wat. WD19 . . . . . .24 BW44
Ox La, Epsom KT17
  off Church St 157 CU109
Oxleas, E6 . . . . .87 EP72
Oxleas Cl, Well. DA16 . . . . . .105 ER82
Oxleay Ct, Har. HA2 . . . . .60 CA60
Oxleay Rd, Har. HA2 . . . . .60 CA60
Oxleigh Cl, N.Mal. KT3 . . . . .138 CS99
Oxley Cl, SE1 . . . . .202 A10
  Romford RM2 . . . . .52 FJ54
Oxleys Rd, NW2 . . . . .63 CV62
  Waltham Abbey EN9 . . . .16 EG32
Oxlip Cl, Croy. CR0
  off Marigold Way 143 DX102
Oxlow La, Dag. RM9, RM10 . .70 FA63
Oxonian St, SE22 . . . . .102 DT84
Oxo Twr Wf, SE1 . . . . .200 E1
OXSHOTT, Lthd. 155 CD113
⇌ Oxshott 154 CC113
Oxshott Ri, Cob. KT11 . . . . .154 BX113
Oxshott Rd, Lthd. KT22 . . . .171 CE115
Oxshott Way, Cob. KT11 . . . .170 BY115
OXTED 187 ED129
⇌ Oxted 188 EE129
Oxted Cl, Mitch. CR4 . . . . . .140 DD97
Oxted Rd, Gdse. RH9 . . . . . .186 DW130
Oxtoby Way, SW16 . . . . .141 DK96
Oyster Catchers Cl, E16
  off Freemasons Rd 86 EH72
Oyster Catcher Ter, Ilf. IG5
  off Tiptree Cres 69 EN55
Oyster La, W.Byf. (Byfleet)
  KT14 . . . . .152 BK110
Oyster Row, E1 off Lukin St . .84 DW72
Ozolins Way, E16 . . . . .86 EG72

P

Pablo Neruda Cl, SE24
  off Shakespeare Rd 101 DP84
Paceheath Cl, Rom. RM5 . . . .51 FD51
Pace Pl, E1
  off Bigland St 84 DV72
PACHESHAM PARK, Lthd. . . .171 CG116
Pachesham Pk, Lthd. KT22 . .171 CG117
Pacific Cl, Felt. TW14 . . . . . .115 BT88
Pacific Rd, E16 . . . . .86 EG72
Packet Boat La, Uxb. UB8 . . .76 BH72
Packham Cl, Orp. BR6
  off Berrylands 146 EW104
Packham Ct, Wor.Pk. KT4
  off Lavender Av 139 CW104
Packham Rd, Grav. (Nthflt.)
  DA11 . . . . .131 GF90
Packhorse La, Borwd. WD6 . . .26 CS37
  Potters Bar EN6 . . . . . . .10 CR31
Packhorse Rd, Ger.Cr. (Chal.St.P.)
  SL9 . . . . .56 AY58
  Sevenoaks TN13 . . . . . .190 FC123
Packington Rd, W3 . . . . .98 CQ76
Packington Sq, N1 . . . . .84 DQ67
Packington St, N1 . . . . .83 DP67
Packmores Rd, SE9 . . . . . . .125 ER85
Padbrook, Oxt. RH8 . . . . . . .188 EG129
Padbrook Cl, Oxt. RH8 . . . . .188 EH128
Padbury, SE17 . . . . .102 DS78
Padbury Cl, Felt. TW14 . . . . .115 BR88
Padbury Ct, E2 . . . . .84 DT69
Padcroft Rd, West Dr. UB7 . . .76 BK74
Padden Ct, NW7
  off Bittacy Hill 43 CY52
Paddenswick Rd, W6 . . . . . . .99 CU76
PADDINGTON, W2 . . . . .82 DB71
⇌ Paddington 82 DC72
⊖ Paddington 82 DC72
Paddington Cl, Hayes UB4 . . .78 BX70
Paddington Grn, W2 . . . . . . .194 A6
Paddington St, W1 . . . . .194 F6
Paddock, The, Ger.Cr. (Chal.St.P.)
  SL9 . . . . .36 AY50
  Slough (Datchet) SL3 . . . .92 AV81
  Uxbridge (Ickhm.) UB10 . . .59 BP63
  Westerham TN16 . . . . . .189 EQ126
Paddock Cl, SE3 . . . . .104 EG82
  SE26 . . . . .123 DX91
  Dartford (S.Darenth) DA4 .148 FQ95
  Northolt UB5 . . . . .78 CA68
  Orpington BR6
    off State Fm Av 163 EP105
  Oxted RH8 . . . . .188 EF131
  Watford WD19 . . . . .24 BY44
  Worcester Park KT4 . . . .138 CS102
Paddock Gdns, SE19
  off Westow St 122 DS93
Paddock Rd, NW2 . . . . .63 CU62
  Bexleyheath DA6 . . . . . .106 EY84
  Ruislip HA4 . . . . .60 BX62
Paddocks, The, NW7 . . . . . . .43 CY51
  Addlestone (New Haw)
    KT15 . . . . .152 BH110
  Barnet EN4 . . . . .28 DF41
  Rickmansworth (Chorl.)
    WD3 . . . . .21 BF42
  Romford (Stap.Abb.) RM4 .35 FF44
  Sevenoaks TN13 . . . . . .191 FK124

Paddocks, The, Vir.W. GU25 . .132 AY100
  Wembley HA9 . . . . .62 CP61
  Weybridge KT13 . . . . . . .135 BS104
Paddocks Cl, Ashtd. KT21 . . .172 CL118
  Cobham KT11 . . . . .154 BW114
  Harrow HA2 . . . . .60 CB63
  Orpington BR5 . . . . .146 EX103
Paddocks Mead, Wok. GU21 .166 AS116
Paddocks Retail Pk, Wey.
  KT13 . . . . .152 BL111
Paddocks Way, Ashtd. KT21 . .172 CL118
  Chertsey KT16 . . . . .134 BH102
Paddock Wk, Warl. CR6 . . . .176 DV119
Paddock Way, Chis. BR7 . . . .125 ER94
  Oxted RH8 . . . . .188 EF131
  Woking GU21 . . . . .151 BB114
Padfield Rd, SE5 . . . . .102 DQ83
Padgets, The, Wal.Abb. EN9 . .15 ED34
Padley Cl, Chess. KT9
  off Moor La 156 CM106
Padnall Ct, Rom. RM6
  off Padnall Rd 70 EX55
Padnall Rd, Rom. RM6 . . . . . .70 EX55
Padstow Cl, Orp. BR6 . . . . . .163 ET105
  Slough SL3 . . . . .92 AY76
Padstow Rd, Enf. EN2 . . . . . .29 DP40
Padstow Wk, Felt. TW14 . . . .115 BT88
Padua Rd, SE20 . . . . .142 DW95
Pagden St, SW8 . . . . .101 DH84
Pageant Av, NW9 . . . . .42 CR53
Pageant Cl, Til. RM18 . . . . . .111 GJ81
Pageant Cres, SE16 . . . . . . .203 L2
Pageantmaster Ct, EC4 . . . .196 F9
Pageant Wk, Croy. CR0 . . . . .142 DS104
Page Av, Wem. HA9 . . . . .62 CQ62
Page Cl, Dag. RM9 . . . . .70 EY64
  Dartford (Bean) DA2 . . . .129 FW90
  Hampton TW12 . . . . . . .116 BY93
  Harrow HA3 . . . . .62 CM58
Page Cres, Croy. CR0 . . . . . .159 DN106
  Erith DA8 . . . . .107 FF80
Page Grn Rd, N15 . . . . .66 DU58
Page Grn Ter, N15 . . . . .66 DT57
Page Heath La, Brom. BR1 . .144 EK97
Page Heath Vil, Brom. BR1 . .144 EK97
Pagehurst Rd, Croy. CR0 . . . .142 DV101
Page Meadow, NW7 . . . . .43 CU52
Page Rd, Felt. TW14 . . . . . . .115 BR86
Pages Hill, N10 . . . . .44 DG54
Pages La, N10 . . . . .44 DG54
  Romford RM3 . . . . .52 FP54
  Uxbridge UB8 . . . . .76 BJ65
Page St, NW7 . . . . .43 CU53
  SW1 . . . . .199 N8
Pages Wk, SE1 . . . . .201 M8
Pages Yd, W4 off Church St . .98 CS79
Paget Av, Sutt. SM1 . . . . . . .140 DD104
Paget Cl, Hmptn. TW12 . . . . .117 CD91
Paget Gdns, Chis. BR7 . . . . .145 EP95
Paget La, Islw. TW7 . . . . .97 CD83
Paget Pl, Kings.T. KT2 . . . . . .118 CQ93
  Thames Ditton KT7
    off Brooklands Rd 137 CG102
Paget Ri, SE18 . . . . .105 EN80
Paget Rd, N16 . . . . .66 DR60
  Ilford IG1 . . . . .69 EP63
  Slough SL3 . . . . .93 AZ77
  Uxbridge UB10 . . . . .77 BQ70
Paget St, EC1 . . . . .196 F2
Paget Ter, SE18 . . . . .105 EN79
Pagette Way, Grays (Bad.Dene)
  RM17 . . . . .110 GA77
Pagitts Gro, Barn. EN4 . . . . . .28 DB39
Paglesfield, Brwd. CM13 . . . . .55 GC44
Pagnell St, SE14 . . . . .103 DZ80
Pagoda Av, Rich. TW9 . . . . . .98 CM83
Pagoda Gdns, SE3 . . . . .103 ED82
Pagoda Vista, Rich. TW9 . . . .98 CM82
Paignton Rd, N15 . . . . .66 DS58
  Ruislip HA4 . . . . .59 BU62
Paines Brook Rd, Rom. RM3
  off Paines Brook Way 52 FM51
Paines Brook Way, Rom. RM3 .52 FM51
Paines Cl, Pnr. HA5 . . . . .60 BY55
Paines La, Pnr. HA5 . . . . .40 BY53
Pains Cl, Mitch. CR4 . . . . . . .141 DH96
Pains Hill, Oxt. RH8 . . . . .188 EJ132
★ Painshill Park, Cob. KT11 . .153 BS114
Painsthorpe Rd, N16
  off Oldfield Rd 66 DS62
Painters Ash La, Grav. (Nthflt.)
  DA11 . . . . .130 GD90
Painters La, Enf. EN3 . . . . . . .31 DY35
Painters Ms, SE16
  off Macks Rd 102 DU77
Painters Rd, Ilf. IG2 . . . . .69 ET55
Paisley Rd, N22 . . . . .45 DP53
  Carshalton SM5 . . . . . . .140 DD102
Pakeman St, N7 . . . . .65 DM62
Pakenham Cl, SW12
  off Balham Pk Rd 120 DG88
Pakenham St, WC1 . . . . .196 C4
Pakes Way, Epp. (They.B.)
  CM16 . . . . .33 ES37
Palace Av, W8 . . . . .82 DB74
Palace Cl, Kings L. WD4 . . . . .6 BM30
Palace Ct, NW3 . . . . .64 DB64
  W2 . . . . .82 DB73
  Bromley BR1
    off Palace Gro 144 EH95
  Harrow HA3 . . . . .62 CL58
Palace Ct Gdns, N10 . . . . . . .65 DJ55
Palace Dr, Wey. KT13 . . . . . .135 BP104
Palace Gdns, Buck.H. IG9 . . . .48 EK46
Palace Gdns Ms, W8 . . . . . . .82 DA74
Palace Gdns Prec, Enf. EN2
  off Sydney Rd 30 DR41
Palace Gdns Ter, W8 . . . . . . .82 DA74
Palace Gate, W8 . . . . .100 DC75
Palace Grn, W8 . . . . .100 DB75
  Croydon CR0 . . . . .161 DZ108
Palace Gro, SE19 . . . . .122 DT94
  Bromley BR1 . . . . .144 EH95
Palace Ms, E17 . . . . .67 DZ56
  SW1 . . . . .198 G9
  SW6 off Hartismere Rd . . .99 CZ80

Palace of Industry, Wem. HA9 .62 CN63
Palace Par, E17 . . . . .67 EA56
Palace Pl, SW1 . . . . .199 K6
Palace Rd, N8 . . . . .65 DK57
  N11 . . . . .45 DL52
  SE19 . . . . .122 DT94
  SW2 . . . . .121 DM88
  Bromley BR1 . . . . .144 EH95
  East Molesey KT8 . . . . . .137 CD97
  Kingston upon Thames
    KT1 . . . . .137 CK98
  Ruislip HA4 . . . . .60 BY63
  Westerham TN16 . . . . . .179 EN121
Palace Rd Est, SW2 . . . . . . .121 DM88
Palace Sq, SE19 . . . . .122 DT94
Palace St, SW1 . . . . .199 K6
Palace Vw, SE12 . . . . .124 EG89
  Bromley BR1 . . . . .144 EG97
  Croydon CR0 . . . . .161 DZ105
Palace Vw Rd, E4 . . . . .47 EB50
Palace Way, Wey. KT13
  off Palace Dr 135 BP104
Palamos Rd, E10 . . . . .67 EA60
Palatine Av, N16
  off Stoke Newington Rd . .66 DT63
Palatine Rd, N16 . . . . .66 DS63
Palermo Rd, NW10 . . . . .81 CU68
Palestine Gro, SW19 . . . . . .140 DD95
Palewell Cl, Orp. BR5 . . . . . .146 EV96
Palewell Common Dr, SW14 .118 CR85
Palewell Pk, SW14 . . . . .118 CR85
Palfrey Pl, SW8 . . . . .101 DM80
Palgrave Av, Sthl. UB1 . . . . . .78 CA73
Palgrave Gdns, NW1 . . . . . . .194 C4
Palgrave Rd, W12 . . . . .99 CT76
Palissy St, E2 . . . . .197 P3
Palladino Ho, SW17
  off Laurel Cl 120 DE92
Pallant Way, Orp. BR6 . . . . . .145 EN104
Pallet Way, SE18 . . . . .104 EL81
Palliser Dr, Rain. RM13 . . . . . .89 FG71
Palliser Rd, W14 . . . . .99 CY78
  Chalfont St. Giles HP8 . . . .36 AU48
Pall Mall, SW1 . . . . .199 L3
Pall Mall E, SW1 . . . . .199 N2
Palmar Cres, Bexh. DA7 . . . .106 FA83
Palmar Rd, Bexh. DA7 . . . . . .106 FA82
Palmarsh Cl, Orp. BR5
  off Wotton Grn 146 EX98
Palm Av, Sid. DA14 . . . . .126 EX93
Palm Cl, E10 . . . . .67 EB62
Palmeira Rd, Bexh. DA7 . . . .106 EX83
Palmer Av, Bushey WD23 . . . .24 CB43
  Gravesend DA12 . . . . . .131 GK91
  Sutton SM3 . . . . .157 CW105
Palmer Cl, Houns. TW5 . . . . . .96 CA81
  West Wickham BR4 . . . . .143 ED104
Palmer Cres, Cher. (Ott.)
  KT16 . . . . .151 BD107
  Kingston upon Thames
    KT1 . . . . .138 CL97
Palmer Gdns, Barn. EN5 . . . . .27 CX43
Palmer Pl, N7 . . . . .65 DN64
Palmer Rd, E13 . . . . .86 EH70
  Dagenham RM8 . . . . .70 EX60
Palmers Av, Grays RM17 . . . .110 GC78
Palmers Dr, Grays RM17 . . . .110 GC77
Palmersfield Rd, Bans. SM7 .158 DA114
Palmers Gro, W.Mol. KT8 . . . .136 CA98
Palmers Hill, Epp. CM16 . . . . .18 EU29
Palmers La, Enf. EN1, EN3 . . .30 DV39
Palmers Moor La, Iver SL0 . . .76 BG70
Palmers Orchard, Sev. (Shore.)
  TN14 . . . . .165 FF111
Palmers Pas, SW14
  off Palmers Rd 98 CQ83
Palmers Rd, E2 . . . . .85 DX69
  N11 . . . . .45 DJ50
  SW14 . . . . .98 CQ83
  SW16 . . . . .141 DM96
  Borehamwood WD6 . . . . .26 CP39
Palmerston Av, Slou. SL3 . . . .92 AV76
Palmerston Cl, Wok. GU21 . .151 AZ114
Palmerston Cres, N13 . . . . . .45 DM50
  SE18 . . . . .105 EQ79
Palmerstone Rd, Vir.W. GU25
  off Sandhills La 132 AY99
Palmerston Gdns, Grays
  RM20 . . . . .109 FX78
Palmerston Gro, SW19 . . . . .120 DA94
Palmerston Rd, E7 . . . . .68 EH64
  E17 . . . . .67 DZ56
  N22 . . . . .45 DM52
  NW6 . . . . .82 DA66
  SW14 . . . . .98 CQ84
  SW19 . . . . .120 DA94
  W3 . . . . .98 CQ76
  Buckhurst Hill IG9 . . . . . .48 EH47
  Carshalton SM5 . . . . . . .158 DF105
  Croydon CR0 . . . . .142 DR99
  Grays RM20 . . . . .109 FX78
  Harrow HA3 . . . . .61 CF55
  Hounslow TW3 . . . . .96 CC81
  Orpington BR6 . . . . .163 EQ105
  Rainham RM13 . . . . .90 FJ68
  Sutton SM1 off Vernon Rd .158 DC106
  Twickenham TW2 . . . . . .117 CF86
Palmerston Way, SW8
  off Bradmead 101 DH80
Palmer St, SW1 . . . . .199 M5
Palmers Way, Wal.Cr. (Chsht.)
  EN8 . . . . .15 DY29
Palm Rd, Rom. RM7 . . . . .71 FC57
Pamela Gdns, Pnr. HA5 . . . . .59 BV57
Pamela Wk, E8
  off Marlborough Av 84 DU67
Pampisford Rd, Pur. CR8 . . . .159 DN111
  South Croydon CR2 . . . .159 DP108
Pams Way, Epsom KT19 . . . .156 CR106
Pancras La, EC4 . . . . .197 J9
Pancras Rd, NW1 . . . . .83 DK68
Pancroft, Rom. (Abridge)
  RM4 . . . . .34 EV41

Pandora Rd, NW6 . . . . .82 DA65
Panfield Ms, Ilf. IG2
  off Cranbrook Rd 69 EN58
Panfield Rd, SE2 . . . . .106 EU76
Pangbourne Av, W10 . . . . . . .81 CW71
Pangbourne Dr, Stan. HA7 . . .41 CK50
Pangbourne Ho, N7 . . . . .65 DL64
Panhard Pl, Sthl. UB1 . . . . . .78 CB73
Pankhurst Cl, SE14
  off Briant St 103 DX80
  Isleworth TW7 . . . . .97 CF83
Pankhurst Rd, Walt. KT12 . . .136 BW101
Panmuir Rd, SW20 . . . . .139 CV95
Panmure Cl, N5 . . . . .65 DP63
Panmure Rd, SE26 . . . . .122 DV90
Pannells Cl, Cher. KT16 . . . . .133 BF102
Pansy Gdns, W12 . . . . .81 CU73
Panters, Swan. BR8 . . . . . . .127 FF94
Panther Dr, NW10 . . . . .62 CR64
Pantile Rd, Wey. KT13 . . . . . .153 BR105
Pantile Row, Slou. SL3 . . . . . .93 BA77
Pantiles, The, N11
  off Willifield Way 63 CZ57
  Bexleyheath DA7 . . . . . .106 EZ80
  Bromley BR1 . . . . .144 EL97
  Bushey (Bushey Hth.)
    WD23 . . . . .41 CD45
Pantiles Cl, N13 . . . . .45 DP50
  Woking GU21 . . . . .166 AV118
Pantile Wk, Uxb. UB8
  off High St 76 BJ66
Panton St, SW1 . . . . .199 M1
Panyer All, EC4 . . . . .197 H8
Papercourt La, Wok. (Ripley)
  GU23 . . . . .167 BF122
Papermill Cl, Cars. SM5 . . . .158 DG105
Papillons Wk, SE3 . . . . .104 EG82
Papworth Gdns, N7
  off Liverpool Rd 65 DM64
Papworth Way, SW2 . . . . . . .121 DN87
Parade, The, SW11 . . . . .100 DF80
  Brentwood CM14
    off Kings Rd 54 FW48
  Dartford DA1
    off Crayford Way 127 FF85
  Epsom KT18 . . . . .156 CR113
  Esher (Clay.) KT10 . . . . .155 CE107
  Hampton TW12
    off Hampton Rd 117 CD92
  Romford RM3 . . . . .52 FP51
  South Ockendon (Aveley)
    RM15 . . . . .108 FQ75
  Sunbury-on-Thames TW16 .115 BT94
  Virginia Water GU25 . . . .132 AX100
  Watford WD17 . . . . .23 BV41
  Watford (Carp.Pk.) WD19 .40 BY48
  Watford (S.Oxhey) WD19
    off Prestwick Rd 40 BX48
Parade Ms, SE27
  off Norwood Rd 121 DP89
Paradise Cl, Wal.Cr. (Chsht.)
  EN7 . . . . .14 DV28
Paradise Pas, N7 . . . . .65 DN64
Paradise Pl, SE18
  off Woodhill 104 EL77
Paradise Rd, SW4 . . . . .101 DL82
  Richmond TW9 . . . . .117 CK85
  Waltham Abbey EN9 . . . . .15 EC34
Paradise Row, E2
  off Bethnal Grn Rd 84 DV69
Paradise St, SE16 . . . . .202 D5
Paradise Wk, SW3 . . . . .100 DF79
Paragon, The, SE3 . . . . .104 EF82
Paragon Cl, E16 . . . . .86 EG72
Paragon Gro, Surb. KT5 . . . .138 CM100
Paragon Ms, SE1 . . . . .201 L8
Paragon Pl, SE3 . . . . .104 EF82
  Surbiton KT5
    off Berrylands 138 CM100
Paragon Rd, E9 . . . . .84 DW65
Parbury Ri, Chess. KT9 . . . . .156 CL107
Parbury Rd, SE23 . . . . .123 DY86
Parchment Cl, Amer. HP6 . . . .20 AS37
Parchmore Rd, Th.Hth. CR7 . .141 DP96
Parchmore Way, Th.Hth. CR7 .141 DP96
Pardoner St, SE1 . . . . .201 L6
Pardon St, EC1 . . . . .196 G4
Parfett St, E1 . . . . .84 DU71
Parfitt Cl, NW3
  off North End 64 DC61
Parfour Dr, Ken. CR8 . . . . . . .176 DQ116
Parfrey St, W6 . . . . .99 CW79
Parham Dr, Ilf. IG2 . . . . .69 EP58
Parham Way, N10 . . . . .45 DJ54
Paris Gdn, SE1 . . . . .200 F2
Parish Cl, Horn. RM11
  off Saville Rd 72 FH61
  Watford WD25 off Crown Ri .8 BX34
  Parish Gate Dr, Sid. DA15 . .125 ES86
Parish La, SE20 . . . . .123 DX93
Parish Ms, SE20 . . . . .123 DX94
Parish Wf Pl, SE1
  off Woodhill 104 EL77
Park, The, N6 . . . . .64 DG58
  NW11 . . . . .64 DB60
  SE19 . . . . .122 DS94
  SE23 off Park Hill 122 DV88
  W5 . . . . .79 CK74
  Carshalton SM5 . . . . . . .158 DF106
  Leatherhead (Bkhm.)
    KT23 . . . . .170 CA123
  Sidcup DA14 . . . . .125 ET92
Park App, Well. DA16 . . . . . .106 EV84
Park Av, E6 . . . . .87 EN67
  E15 . . . . .86 EE65
  N3 . . . . .44 DB53
  N13 . . . . .45 DN48
  N18 . . . . .46 DU49
  N22 . . . . .45 DL54
  NW2 . . . . .81 CV65
  NW10 . . . . .80 CM69
  NW11 . . . . .64 DB60
  SW14 . . . . .98 CR84
  Barking IG11 . . . . .87 EQ65
  Brentwood CM13 . . . . . . .55 GC46
  Bromley BR1 . . . . .124 EF93

Park Av, Bushey WD23 . . . . . .24 BZ40
  Carshalton SM5 . . . . . . .158 DG107
  Caterham CR3 . . . . .176 DS124
  Egham TW20 . . . . .113 BC93
  Enfield EN1 . . . . .30 DS44
  Gravesend DA12 . . . . . .131 GJ88
  Gravesend (Perry St.) DA11 .130 GE88
  Grays RM20 . . . . .109 FU79
  Hounslow TW3 . . . . .116 CB86
  Ilford IG1 . . . . .69 EN61
  Mitcham CR4 . . . . .121 DH94
  Orpington BR6 . . . . .146 EU103
  Orpington (Farnboro.)
    BR6 . . . . .145 EM104
  Potters Bar EN6 . . . . . . .12 DC34
  Radlett WD7 . . . . .9 CH33
  Rickmansworth (Chorl.)
    WD3 . . . . .22 BG43
  Ruislip HA4 . . . . .59 BR58
  Southall UB1 . . . . .78 CA74
  Staines TW18 . . . . .113 BF93
  Staines (Wrays.) TW19 . .112 AX85
  Upminster RM14 . . . . . . .73 FS59
  Watford WD18 . . . . .23 BU42
  West Wickham BR4 . . . . .143 EC103
  Woodford Green IG8 . . . . .48 EH50
Park Av E, Epsom KT17 . . . .157 CU107
Park Av Ms, Mitch. CR4
  off Park Av 121 DH94
Park Av N, N8 . . . . .65 DK55
  NW10 . . . . .63 CV64
Park Av Rd, N17 . . . . .46 DV52
Park Av S, N8 . . . . .65 DK56
Park Av W, Epsom KT17 . . . .157 CU107
Park Boul, Rom. RM2 . . . . . . .51 FF53
Park Chase, Wem. HA9 . . . . . .62 CM63
Park Cl, E9 . . . . .84 DW67
  NW2 . . . . .63 CV62
  NW10 . . . . .80 CM69
  SW1 . . . . .198 D5
  W4 . . . . .98 CR78
  W14 . . . . .99 CZ76
  Addlestone (New Haw)
    KT15 . . . . .152 BH110
  Bushey WD23 . . . . .24 BX41
  Carshalton SM5 . . . . . . .158 DF107
  Epping (N.Wld.Bas.) CM16 .18 FA27
  Esher KT10 . . . . .154 BZ107
  Hampton TW12 . . . . . . .136 CC95
  Harrow HA3 . . . . .41 CE53
  Hatfield (Brook.Pk.) AL9 . .11 CZ26
  Hounslow TW3 . . . . .116 CC85
  Kingston upon Thames
    KT2 . . . . .138 CN95
  Leatherhead (Fetch.)
    KT22 . . . . .171 CD124
  Oxted RH8 . . . . .188 EF128
  Rickmansworth WD3 . . . . .39 BP49
  Walton-on-Thames KT12 .135 BT103
Park Cor Rd, Grav. (Sthflt.)
  DA13 . . . . .130 FZ91
Park Ct, SE26 . . . . .122 DV93
  Kingston upon Thames
    KT1 . . . . .137 CJ95
  New Malden KT3 . . . . . .138 CR98
  Wembley HA9 . . . . .62 CL64
  West Byfleet KT14 . . . . .152 BG113
  Woking GU22 off Park Dr .167 AZ118
Park Cres, N3 . . . . .44 DB52
  W1 . . . . .195 H5
  Borehamwood (Elstree)
    WD6 . . . . .26 CM41
  Enfield EN2 . . . . .30 DR42
  Erith DA8 . . . . .107 FC79
  Harrow HA3 . . . . .41 CE53
  Hornchurch RM11 . . . . . .71 FG59
  Twickenham TW2 . . . . . .117 CD88
Park Cres Ms E, W1 . . . . . . .195 J5
Park Cres Ms W, W1 . . . . . . .195 H6
Park Cres Rd, Erith DA8 . . . .107 FD79
Park Cft, Edg. HA8 . . . . .42 CQ53
Parkcroft Rd, SE12 . . . . .124 EF87
Park Dale, N11 . . . . .45 DK51
Parkdale Cres, Wor.Pk. KT4 . .138 CR104
Parkdale Rd, SE18 . . . . .105 ES78
Park Dr, N21 . . . . .30 DQ44
  NW11 . . . . .64 DB60
  SE7 . . . . .104 EL79
  SW14 . . . . .98 CR84
  W3 . . . . .98 CN76
  Ashtead KT21 . . . . .172 CN118
  Dagenham RM10 . . . . . . .71 FC62
  Harrow (Har.Wld.) HA3 . . .41 CE51
  Harrow (N.Har.) HA2 . . . .60 CA59
  Potters Bar EN6 . . . . . . .12 DA31
  Romford RM1 . . . . .71 FD56
  Upminster RM14 . . . . . . .72 FQ63
  Weybridge KT13 . . . . . .153 BP106
  Woking GU22 . . . . .167 AZ118
Park Dr Cl, SE7 . . . . .104 EL78
Park End, NW3
  off South Hill Pk 64 DE63
  Bromley BR1 . . . . .144 EF95
Park End Rd, Rom. RM1 . . . . .71 FE56
Parker Av, Til. RM18 . . . . . . .111 GJ81
Parker Cl, E16 . . . . .86 EL74
Parker Ms, WC2 . . . . .196 A8
Parke Rd, SW13 . . . . .99 CU81
  Sunbury-on-Thames
    TW16 . . . . .135 BU98
Parker Rd, Croy. CR0 . . . . . .160 DQ105
  Grays RM17 . . . . .110 FZ78
Parkers Cl, Ashtd. KT21 . . . .172 CL119
Parkers Hill, Ashtd. KT21 . . .172 CL119
Parkers La, Ashtd. KT21 . . . .172 CL119
Parkers Row, SE1 . . . . .202 A5
Parker St, E16 . . . . .86 EL74
  WC2 . . . . .196 A8
  Watford WD24 . . . . .23 BV39
Parkes Rd, Chig. IG7 . . . . . . .49 ES50
Park Fm Cl, N2 . . . . .64 DC55
  Pinner HA5
    off Field End Rd 59 BV57
Park Fm Rd, Brom. BR1 . . . .144 EK95

A B C D E F G H I J K L M N O P Q R S T U V W X Y Z

Par - Pat

Park Fm Rd, Kings.T. KT2 ....118 CL94
  Upminster RM14 ....72 FM64
Parkfield, Rick. (Chorl.) WD3 ..21 BF42
  Sevenoaks TN15 ....191 FM123
Parkfield Av, SW14 ....98 CS84
  Feltham TW13 ....115 BU90
  Harrow HA2 ....40 CC54
  Northolt UB5 ....78 BX68
  Uxbridge (Hlgdn.) UB10 ..77 BP69
Parkfield Cl, Edg. HA8 ....42 CP51
  Northolt UB5 ....78 BY68
Parkfield Cres, Felt. TW13 ...115 BU90
  Harrow HA2 ....40 CC54
  Ruislip HA4 ....60 BY62
Parkfield Dr, Nthlt. UB5 ....78 BX68
Parkfield Gdns, Har. HA2 ......60 CB55
Parkfield Rd, NW10 ....81 CU66
  SE14 ....103 DZ81
  Feltham TW13 ....115 BU90
  Harrow HA2 ....60 CC62
  Northolt UB5 ....78 BY68
  Uxbridge (Ickhm.) UB10 ..59 BP61
Parkfields, SW15 ....99 CW84
  Croydon CR0 ....143 DZ102
  Leatherhead (Oxshott)
    KT22 ....155 CD111
Parkfields Av, NW9 ....62 CR60
  SW20 ....139 CV95
Parkfields Cl, Cars. SM5
  off Devonshire Rd 158 DG105
Parkfields Rd, Kings.T. KT2 ..118 CM92
Parkfield St, N1
  off Berners Rd 83 DN68
Parkfield Vw, Pot.B. EN6 .....12 DB32
Parkfield Way, Brom. BR2 ...145 EM100
Park Gdns, NW9 ....62 CP55
  Erith DA8 off Valley Rd ...107 FD77
  Kingston upon Thames
    KT2 ....118 CM92
Park Gate, N2 ....64 DD55
  N21 ....45 DM45
Parkgate, SE3 ....104 EF83
Park Gate, W5 off Mount Av ...79 CK71
Parkgate Av, Barn. EN4 ....28 DC39
Parkgate Cl, Kings.T. KT2
  off Warboys App 118 CP93
Parkgate Cres, Barn. EN4 .....28 DC40
Parkgate Gdns, SW14 ....118 CR85
Parkgate Ms, N6
  off Stanhope Rd 65 DJ59
Parkgate Rd, SW11 ....100 DE80
  Orpington BR6 ....165 FB105
  Wallington SM6 ....158 DG106
  Watford WD24 ....24 BW37
Park Gates, Har. HA2 ....60 CA63
Park Gra Gdns, Sev. TN13
  off Solefields Rd 191 FJ127
Park Grn, Lthd. (Bkhm.)
  KT23 ....170 CA124
Park Gro, E15 ....86 EG67
  N11 ....45 DK52
  Bexleyheath DA7 ....107 FC84
  Bromley BR1 ....144 EH95
  Chalfont St. Giles HP8 ...20 AX41
  Edgware HA8 ....42 CM50
Park Gro Rd, E11 ....68 EE61
Park Hall Rd, N2 ....64 DE56
  SE21 ....122 DQ90
  Reigate RH2 ....184 DA132
Parkham Ct, Brom. BR2 ......144 EE96
Parkham St, SW11 ....100 DE81
Park Hill, SE23 ....122 DV89
  SW4 ....121 DK85
  W5 ....79 CK71
  Bromley BR1 ....144 EL98
  Carshalton SM5 ....158 DE107
  Loughton IG10 ....32 EK43
  Richmond TW10 ....118 CM86
Park Hill Cl, Cars. SM5 ......158 DE106
Parkhill Cl, Horn. RM12 ....72 FJ62
Park Hill Ct, SW17
  off Beeches Rd 120 DF90
Park Hill Ri, Croy. CR0 ......142 DS103
Parkhill Rd, E4 ....47 EC46
  NW3 ....64 DF64
  Bexley DA5 ....126 EZ87
Park Hill Rd, Brom. BR2 .....144 EE96
  Croydon CR0 ....142 DS103
  Epsom KT17 ....157 CT111
Parkhill Rd, Sid. DA15 ......125 ER90
Park Hill Rd, Wall. SM6 .....159 DH108
Parkhill Wk, NW3 ....64 DF64
Parkholme, E8 ....84 DT65
Park Ho, N21 ....45 DM45
Park Ho Gdns, Twick. TW1 ..117 CJ86
Parkhouse St, SE5 ....102 DR80
Parkhurst, Epsom KT19 .....156 CQ110
Parkhurst Av, E16
  off Wesley Av 86 EH74
Parkhurst Gdns, Bex. DA5 ..126 FA87
Parkhurst Rd, E12 ....69 EN63
  E17 ....67 DY56
  N7 ....65 DL63
  N11 ....44 DG49
  N17 ....46 DU54
  N22 ....45 DM52
  Bexley DA5 ....126 FA87
  Sutton SM1 ....158 DD105
Park Ind Est, St.Alb. (Frog.)
  AL2 ....9 CE27
Parkland Av, Rom. RM1 ......71 FE55
  Slough SL3 ....92 AX77
  Upminster RM14 ....72 FP64
Parkland Cl, Chig. IG7 ....49 EQ48
  Sevenoaks TN13 ....191 FJ129
Parkland Gdns, SW19 ....119 CX88
Parkland Gro, Ashf. TW15 ...114 BN91
Parkland Rd, N22 ....45 DM54
  Ashford TW15 ....114 BN91
  Woodford Green IG8 ....48 EG52
Parklands, N6 ....65 DH59
  Addlestone KT15 ....152 BJ106
  Chigwell IG7 ....49 EQ48
  Epping (Cooper.) CM16 ..18 EX29

Parklands, Lthd. (Bkhm.)
  KT23 ....170 CA123
  Oxted RH8 ....188 EE131
  Surbiton KT5 ....138 CM99
  Waltham Abbey EN9 ....15 ED32
Parklands Cl, SW14 ....118 CQ85
  Barnet EN4 ....28 DD38
  Ilford IG2 ....69 ES84
Parklands Ct, Houns. TW5 ....96 BX82
Parklands Dr, N3 ....63 CY55
Parklands Rd, SW16 ....121 DH92
Parklands Way, Wor.Pk. KT4 .138 CS104
Parkland Wk, N4 ....65 DM59
  N6 ....65 DH59
  N10 ....65 DH56
Park La, E15 off High St 85 ED67
  N9 ....46 DT48
  N17 ....46 DU52
  W1 ....198 G3
  Ashtead KT21 ....172 CM118
  Banstead SM7 ....174 DB118
  Carshalton SM5 ....158 DG105
  Coulsdon CR5 ....175 DK121
  Croydon CR0 ....142 DR104
  Harrow HA2 ....60 CB62
  Hayes UB4 ....77 BS71
  Hornchurch RM11 ....71 FG58
  Hornchurch (Elm Pk.) RM12 .89 FH65
  Hounslow TW5 ....95 BU80
  Richmond TW9 ....97 CK84
  Romford (Chad.Hth.) RM6 ..70 EX58
  Sevenoaks TN13 ....191 FJ124
  Sevenoaks (Seal) TN15 .191 FN121
  Slough SL3 ....92 AV76
  Slough (Horton) SL3 ....93 BA83
  South Ockendon (Aveley)
    RM15 ....91 FR74
  Stanmore HA7 ....41 CG48
  Sutton SM3 ....157 CY107
  Swanley BR8 ....148 FJ96
  Teddington TW11 ....137 CF93
  Uxbridge (Hare.) UB9 ..38 BG53
  Wallington SM6 ....158 DG105
  Waltham Cross EN8 .....14 DW33
  Waltham Cross (Chsht.)
    EN7 ....14 DU26
  Wembley HA9 ....62 CL64
Park La Cl, N17 ....46 DU52
PARK LANGLEY, Beck. 143 EC99
Parklawn Av, Epsom KT18 ...156 CP113
Park Lawn Rd, Wey. KT13 ...153 BQ105
Park Lawns, Wem. HA9 ....62 CM63
Parklea Cl, NW9 ....42 CS53
Parkleigh Rd, SW19 ....140 DB96
Park Ley Rd, Cat. (Wold.)
  CR3 ....177 DX120
Parkleys, Rich. TW10 ....117 CK91
Parkmead, SW15 ....119 CV86
Park Mead, Har. HA2 ....60 CB62
Parkmead, Loug. IG10 ....33 EN43
Park Mead, Sid. DA15 ......126 EV85
Parkmead Gdns, NW7 ....43 CT51
Park Ms, SE24
  off Croxted Rd 122 DQ86
  Chislehurst BR7 ....125 EP93
  East Molesey KT8 ......136 CC98
  Hampton (Hmptn.H.) TW12
    off Park Rd 116 CC92
  Rainham RM13
    off Sowrey Av 89 FG65
Parkmore Cl, Wdf.Grn. IG8 ...48 EG49
Park Nook Gdns, Enf. EN2 ....30 DR37
Park Par, NW10 ....81 CT68
Park Pl, E14 ....203 P2
  SW1 ....199 K3
  W3 ....98 CN77
  W5 ....79 CK74
  Amersham HP6 ....20 AT38
  Gravesend DA12 ....131 GJ86
  Hampton (Hmptn.H.)
    TW12 ....116 CC93
  St. Albans (Park St.) AL2 ..9 CD27
  Sevenoaks TN13 ....190 FD123
  Wembley HA9 ....62 CM63
  Woking GU22
    off Park Dr 167 AZ118
Park Pl Vil, W2 ....82 DC71
Park Ridings, N8 ....65 DN55
Park Ri, SE23 ....123 DY88
  Harrow HA3 ....41 CE53
  Leatherhead KT22 .....171 CH121
Park Ri Cl, Lthd. KT22 ......171 CH121
Park Ri Rd, SE23 ....123 DY88
Park Rd, E6 ....86 EJ67
  E10 ....67 EA60
  E12 ....68 EH60
  E15 ....86 EG67
  E17 ....67 DZ57
  N2 ....64 DD55
  N8 ....65 DJ56
  N11 ....45 DK52
  N14 ....45 DK45
  N15 ....65 DP56
  N18 ....46 DT49
  NW1 ....194 B2
  NW4 ....63 CU59
  NW8 ....194 B2
  NW9 ....62 CR59
  NW10 ....80 CS67
  SE25 ....142 DS98
  SW19 ....120 DD93
  W4 ....98 CQ80
  W7 ....79 CF73
  Amersham HP6 ....20 AT37
  Ashford TW15 ....115 BP92
  Ashtead KT21 ....172 CL118
  Banstead SM7 ....174 DB115
  Barnet EN5 ....27 CZ42
  Barnet (New Barn.) EN4 ..28 DE42
  Beckenham BR3 ....123 DZ94
  Brentwood CM14 ....54 FV46
  Bromley BR1 ....144 EH95
  Bushey WD23 ....24 CA44
  Caterham CR3 ....176 DS123
  Chislehurst BR7 ....125 EP93
  Dartford DA1 ....128 FN87
  East Molesey KT8 ......136 CC98

Park Rd, Egham TW20 ....113 BA91
  Enfield EN3 ....31 DY36
  Esher KT10 ....154 CB105
  Feltham TW13 ....116 BX91
  Gravesend DA11 ....131 GH88
  Grays RM17 ....110 GB78
  Hampton (Hmptn.H.)
    TW12 ....116 CB91
  Hayes UB4 ....77 BS71
  Hounslow TW3 ....96 CC84
  Ilford IG1 ....69 ER62
  Isleworth TW7 ....97 CH81
  Kenley CR8 ....175 DP115
  Kingston upon Thames
    KT2 ....118 CM92
  Kingston upon Thames
    (Hmptn.W.) KT1 ......117 CF93
  New Malden KT3 ....138 CR98
  Orpington BR5 ....146 EW99
  Oxted RH8 ....188 EF128
  Potters Bar EN6 ....12 DG30
  Radlett WD7 ....25 CG35
  Redhill RH1 ....184 DF132
  Richmond TW10 ....118 CM86
  Rickmansworth WD3 ....38 BK45
  Shepperton TW17 .....134 BN102
  Staines (Stanw.) TW19 .114 BH86
  Sunbury-on-Thames
    TW16 ....115 BV94
  Surbiton KT5 ....138 CM99
  Sutton SM3 ....157 CY107
  Swanley BR8 ....147 FF97
  Swanscombe DA10 .....130 FY86
  Teddington TW11 ....137 CJ95
  Twickenham TW1 ......117 CJ86
  Uxbridge UB8 ....76 BL66
  Wallington SM6 ....159 DH106
  Wallington (Hackbr.) SM6 .141 DH103
  Waltham Cross EN8 .....15 DX33
  Warlingham CR6 ....162 EE114
  Watford WD17 ....23 BU39
  Wembley HA0 ....80 CL65
  Woking GU22 ....167 BA111
Park Rd E, W3 ....98 CP75
  Uxbridge UB10
    off Hillingdon Rd 76 BK68
Park Rd N, W3 ....98 CP75
  W4 ....98 CR78
Park Row, SE10 ....103 ED79
Park Royal, NW10 ....80 CN69
  Park Royal 80 CN70
Park Royal Rd, NW10 ....80 CQ69
  W3 ....80 CQ69
Parkshot, Rich. TW9 ....98 CL84
Parkside, N3 ....44 DB53
  NW2 ....63 CU62
  NW7 ....43 CU51
  SE3 ....104 EF80
  SW19 ....119 CX91
  Addlestone (New Haw)
    KT15 ....152 BH110
  Buckhurst Hill IG9 ......48 EH47
  Gerrards Cross (Chal.St.P.) SL9
    off Lower Rd 57 AZ56
  Grays RM16 ....171 GH78
  Hampton (Hmptn.H.) TW12 .117 CD92
  Potters Bar EN6
    off High St 12 DC32
  Sevenoaks (Halst.) TN14 .164 EZ117
  Sidcup DA14 ....126 EV89
  Sutton SM3 ....157 CY107
  Waltham Cross EN8 .....15 DY34
  Watford WD19 ....24 BW44
Parkside Business Est, SE8
  off Rolt St 103 DY79
Parkside Cl, SE20 ....122 DW94
Parkside Ct, Wey. KT13 .....152 BN105
Parkside Cres, N7 ....65 DN62
  Surbiton KT5 ....138 CQ100
Parkside Cross, Bexh. DA7 ..107 FE82
Parkside Dr, Edg. HA8 ....42 CN48
  Watford WD17 ....23 BS40
Parkside Est, E9
  off Rutland Rd 84 DW67
Parkside Gdns, SW19 ....119 CX91
  Barnet EN4 ....44 DF46
  Coulsdon CR5 ....175 DH117
Parkside Hosp, SW19 ....119 CX90
Parkside Ho, Dag. RM10 ......71 FC62
Parkside Rd, SW11 ....100 DG81
  Belvedere DA17 ....107 FC77
  Hounslow TW3 ....116 CB85
  Northwood HA6 ....39 BT50
  Warlingham CR6 ....177 EA116
Parkside Ter, N18
  off Great Cambridge Rd ..46 DR49
Parkside Wk, SE10 ....205 H7
  Slough SL1 ....92 AU76
Parkside Way, Har. HA2 ......60 CB56
Park S, SW11 off Austin Rd .100 DG81
Park Sq, Esher KT10
  off Park Rd 154 CB105
Park Sq E, NW1 ....195 H4
Park Sq Ms, NW1 ....195 H5
Park Sq W, NW1 ....195 H4
Parkstead Rd, SW15 ....119 CU85
Parkstone Av, N18 ....46 DT50
  Hornchurch RM11 ....72 FK58
Parkstone Rd, E17 ....67 EC55
  SE15 off Rye La 102 DU82
PARK STREET, St.Alb. 9 CD26
  Park Street 9 CD26
Park St, SE1 ....201 H2
  W1 ....194 F10
  Croydon CR0 ....142 DQ103
  St. Albans AL2 ....9 CD26
  Slough SL1 ....92 AT76
  Slough (Colnbr.) SL3 ....93 BD80
  Teddington TW11 ....117 CE93
Park St La, St.Alb. (Park St.)
  AL2 ....8 CB30
Park Ter, Green. DA9 ....129 FV85

Park Ter, Sev. (Sund.) TN14
  off Main Rd 180 EX124
  Worcester Park KT4 ....139 CU102
Parkthorne Cl, Har. HA2 ......60 CB58
Parkthorne Dr, Har. HA2 ......60 CA58
Parkthorne Rd, SW12 ....121 DK87
Park Vw, N21 ....45 DM45
  W3 ....80 CQ71
  New Malden KT3 ....139 CT97
  Pinner HA5 ....40 BZ53
  Potters Bar EN6 ....12 DC33
  South Ockendon (Aveley)
    RM15 ....91 FR74
  Wembley HA9 ....62 CP64
Parkview Ct, SW18
  off Broomhill Rd 120 DA86
Park Vw Ct, Ilf. IG2
  off Brancaster Rd 69 ES58
  Woking GU22 ....166 AY119
Park Vw Cres, N11 ....45 DH49
Parkview Dr, Mitch. CR4 .....140 DD96
Park Vw Dr, Mitch. CR4 .....140 DD96
Park Vw Est, E2 ....85 DX68
Park Vw Gdns, NW4 ....63 CW57
  Grays RM17 ....110 GB78
  Ilford IG4 ....69 EM56
Park Vw Ho, SE24
  off Hurst St 121 DP86
Park Vw Rd, N3 ....44 DB53
  N17 ....66 DU55
  NW10 ....63 CT63
Parkview Rd, SE9 ....125 EP89
Park Vw Rd, W5 ....80 CL71
  Caterham (Wold.) CR3 ..177 DY122
Parkview Rd, Croy. CR0 .....142 DU102
Park Vw Rd, Pnr. HA5 ....39 BV52
  Southall UB1 ....78 CA74
  Uxbridge UB8 ....76 BN72
  Welling DA16 ....106 EW83
Park Village E, NW1 ....83 DH68
Park Village W, NW1 ....83 DH68
Parkville Rd, SW6 ....99 CZ80
Park Vil, Rom. RM6 ....70 EX58
Park Vista, SE10 ....103 ED79
Park Wk, N6 off North Rd 64 DG59
  SE10 off Crooms Hill ...103 ED80
  SW10 ....100 DC79
  Ashtead KT21
    off Rectory La 172 CM119
Parkway, N14 ....45 DL47
Park Way, N20 ....44 DF49
Parkway, NW1 ....83 DH67
Park Way, NW11 ....63 CY57
Parkway, SW20 ....139 CX98
  Bexley, Bex. DA5 ......127 FE90
  Brentwood CM15 ......55 FZ46
Parkway, Croy. (New Adgtn.)
  CR0 ....161 EC109
Park Way, Edg. HA8 ....42 CP53
  Enfield EN2 ....29 DN40
Parkway, Erith DA18 ....106 EY76
Park Way, Felt. TW14 ....115 BV87
Parkway, Ilf. IG3 ....69 ET62
Park Way, Lthd. (Bkhm.)
  KT23 ....170 CA123
Parkway, Rain. RM13
  off Upminster Rd S 89 FG70
Park Way, Rick. WD3 ....38 BJ46
  Romford. RM2 ....71 FF55
Park Way, Ruis. HA4 ....59 BU60
Parkway, Uxb. UB10 ....76 BN66
Park Way, W.Mol. KT8 ....136 CB97
Parkway, Wey. KT13 ....153 BR105
  Woodford Green IG8 ....48 EJ50
Parkway, The, Hayes
  UB3, UB4 ....78 BW72
  Hounslow (Cran.)
    TW4, TW5 ....95 BV82
  Iver SL0 ....75 BC68
  Northolt UB5 ....78 BX69
  Southall UB2 ....95 BU78
Parkway Trd Est, Houns. TW5 .96 BW79
Park W, W2 ....194 C9
Park W Pl, W2 ....194 C8
Parkwood, N20 ....44 DF48
  Beckenham BR3 ....143 EA95
Parkwood Av, Esher KT10 ..136 CC102
Parkwood Cl, Bans. SM7 ....173 CX115
Parkwood Gro, Sun. TW16 ..135 BU97
Parkwood Ms, N6 ....65 DH58
Parkwood Rd, SW19 ....119 CZ92
  Banstead SM7 ....173 CX115
  Bexley DA5 ....126 EZ87
  Isleworth TW7 ....97 CF81
  Redhill (Nutfld.) RH1 ...185 DL133
  Westerham (Tats.) TN16 .178 EJ121
Parkwood Vw, Bans. SM7 ...173 CW116
Park Wks Rd, Red. RH1 .....185 DM133
Parley Dr, Wok. GU21 ....166 AW117
Parliament Ct, E1
  off Sandy's Row 84 DS71
Parliament Hill, NW3 ....64 DE63
Parliament Ms, SW14
  off Thames Bk 98 CQ82
Parliament Sq, SW1 ....199 P5
Parliament St, SW1 ....199 P5
Parliament Vw Apartments,
  SE1 ....200 B8
Parma Cres, SW11 ....100 DF84
Parmiter St, E2 ....84 DV68
Parmoor Ct, EC1 ....197 J4
Parnell Cl, Abb.L. WD5 ....7 BT30
  Edgware HA8 ....42 CP53
  Grays (Chaff.Hun.) RM16 .109 FW78
Parnell Gdns, Wey. KT13 ...152 BN111
Parnell Rd, E3 ....85 DZ67
Parnham St, E1 off Blount St .85 DY72
Parolles Rd, N19 ....65 DJ60
Paroma Rd, Belv. DA17 .....106 FA76
Parr Cl, N9 ....46 DV49
  N18 ....46 DV49
  Grays (Chaff.Hun.) RM16 .109 FW77
  Leatherhead KT22 .....171 CF120
Parr Ct, N1 off New N Rd 84 DR68
  Feltham TW13 ....116 BW91
Parrock, The, Grav. DA12 ...131 GJ88

Parrock Av, Grav. DA12 .....131 GJ88
PARROCK FARM, Grav. 131 GK91
Parrock Rd, Grav. DA12 .....131 GJ88
Parrock St, Grav. DA12 .....131 GH87
Parrotts Cl, Rick. (Crox.Grn.)
  WD3 ....22 BN42
Parr Pl, W4
  off Chiswick High Rd 99 CT77
Parr Rd, E6 ....86 EK67
  Stanmore HA7 ....41 CK53
Parrs Cl, S.Croy. CR2
  off Florence Rd 160 DR109
Parrs Pl, Hmptn. TW12 .....116 CA94
Parr St, N1 ....84 DR68
Parry Av, E6 ....87 EM72
Parry Cl, Epsom KT17 ......157 CU108
Parry Grn N, Slou. SL3 ....93 AZ77
Parry Grn S, Slou. SL3 ....93 BA77
Parry Pl, SE18 ....105 EP77
Parry Rd, SE25 ....142 DS97
  W10 ....81 CY69
Parry St, SW8 ....101 DL79
Parsifal Rd, NW6 ....64 DA64
Parsley Gdns, Croy. CR0
  off Primrose La 143 DX102
Parsloes Av, Dag. RM9 ......70 EX63
Parsonage Cl, Abb.L. WD5 ....7 BS30
  Hayes UB3 ....77 BT72
  Warlingham CR6 ....177 DY116
Parsonage Gdns, Enf. EN2 ...30 DQ40
Parsonage La, Dart. (Sutt.H.)
  DA4 ....128 FP93
  Enfield EN1, EN2 ....30 DR40
  Sidcup DA14 ....126 EZ91
Parsonage Manorway, Belv.
  DA17 ....106 FA79
Parsonage Rd, Ch.St.G. HP8 ..36 AV48
  Egham (Eng.Grn.) TW20 .112 AX92
  Grays RM20 ....109 FW79
  Rainham RM13 ....90 FJ69
  Rickmansworth WD3 ....38 BK45
Parsonage St, E14 ....204 E9
Parsons Cres, Edg. HA8 ......42 CN48
Parsonsfield Cl, Bans. SM7 ..173 CX115
Parsonsfield Rd, Bans. SM7 .173 CX116
PARSONS GREEN, SW6 ....99 CZ81
  Parsons Green 99 CZ81
Parsons Grn, SW6 ....100 DA81
Parsons Grn La, SW6 ....100 DA81
Parsons Gro, Edg. HA8 ....42 CN48
Parsons Hill, SE18
  off Powis St 105 EN76
Parsons Ho, SW2
  off New Pk Rd 121 DL87
Parson's Ho, W2 ....82 DD70
Parsons La, Dart. DA2 ......127 FH90
Parson's Mead, Croy. CR0 ..142 DP102
Parsons Mead, E.Mol. KT8 ..136 CC97
Parsons Pightle, Couls. CR5 .175 DN120
Parsons Rd, E13 off Old St ...86 EJ68
Parson St, NW4 ....63 CW56
Parthenia Rd, SW6 ....100 DA81
Parthia Cl, Tad. KT20 ......173 CV119
Partingdale La, NW7 ....43 CX50
Partington Cl, N19 ....65 DK60
Partridge Cl, E16
  off Fulmer Rd 86 EK71
  Barnet EN5 ....27 CW44
  Bushey WD23 ....40 CB46
  Chesham HP5 ....4 AS28
  Stanmore HA7 ....42 CL49
Partridge Ct, EC1
  off Percival St 83 DP70
Partridge Dr, Orp. BR6 .....145 EQ104
Partridge Grn, SE9 ....125 EN90
Partridge Knoll, Pur. CR8 ...159 DP112
Partridge Mead, Bans. SM7 .173 CW116
Partridge Rd, Hmptn. TW12 ..116 BZ93
  Sidcup DA14 ....125 ES90
Partridge Sq, E6
  off Nightingale Way 86 EL71
Partridge Way, N22 ....45 DL53
Parvills, Wal.Abb. EN9 ....15 ED32
Parvin St, SW8 ....101 DK81
Parvis Rd, W.Byf. KT14 .....152 BG113
Pasadena Cl, Hayes UB3 ....95 BV75
Pasadena Cl Trd Est, Hayes UB3
  off Pasadena Cl 95 BV75
Pascal St, SW8 ....101 DK80
Pascoe Rd, SE13 ....123 ED85
Pasfield, Wal.Abb. EN9 ....15 ED33
Pasley Cl, SE17
  off Penrose St 102 DQ78
Pasquier Rd, E17 ....67 DY55
Passey Pl, SE9 ....125 EM86
Passfield Dr, E14 ....85 EB71
  off Uamvar St 85 EB71
Passfield Path, SE28
  off Booth Cl 88 EV73
Passing All, EC1 ....196 G5
Passmore Gdns, N11 ....45 DK51
Passmore St, SW1 ....198 F9
★ Passport Office, SW1 ...199 L6
Pastens Cl, Oxt. RH8 ....188 EJ131
Pasteur Cl, NW9 ....42 CS54
Pasteur Dr, Rom. (Harold Wd.)
  RM3 ....52 FK54
Pasteur Gdns, N18 ....45 DP50
Paston Cl, E5
  off Caldecott Way 67 DX62
  Wallington SM6 ....141 DJ104
Paston Cres, SE12 ....124 EH87
Pastor St, SE11 ....200 G8
Pasture Cl, Bushey WD23 ....40 CC45
  Wembley HA0 ....61 CH62
Pasture Rd, SE6 ....124 EF88
  Dagenham RM9 ....70 EZ63
  Wembley HA0 ....61 CH61
Pastures, The, N20 ....43 CZ46
  Watford WD19 ....40 BW45
Pastures Mead, Uxb. UB10 ...76 BN65
Patch, The, Sev. TN13 ......190 FE122
Patcham Ct, Sutt. SM2 ......158 DC109
Patcham Ter, SW8 ....101 DH81
Patch Cl, Uxb. UB10 ....76 BM67
PATCHETTS GREEN, Wat. 24 CC39

Paternoster Cl, Wal.Abb. EN9 .16 EF33
Paternoster Hill, Wal.Abb.
  EN9 ....16 EF32
Paternoster Row, EC4 .197 H9
  Romford (Noak Hill) RM4 .52 FJ47
Paternoster Sq, EC4 .196 G8
Paterson Rd, Ashf. TW15 .114 BK92
Pater St, W8 ....100 DA76
Pates Manor Dr, Felt. TW14 .115 BR87
Path, The, SW19 .....140 DB95
Pathfield Rd, SW16 ...121 DK93
Pathway, The, Rad. WD7 .25 CF36
  Watford WD19
  off Anthony Cl 40 BX46
Patience Rd, SW11 ...100 DE82
Patio Cl, SW4 ......121 DK86
Patmore Est, SW8 ...101 DJ81
Patmore La, Walt. KT12 .153 BT107
Patmore Rd, Wal.Abbey EN9 .16 EE34
Patmore St, SW8 ....101 DJ81
Patmore Way, Rom. RM5 .51 FB50
Patmos Rd, SW9 .....101 DP80
Paton Cl, E3 ....85 EA69
Paton St, EC1 ......197 H3
Patricia Ct, Chis. BR7
  off Manor Pk Rd ...145 ER95
  Welling DA16 ......106 EV80
Patricia Dr, Horn. RM11 ..72 FL60
Patricia Gdns, Sutt. SM2
  off The Crescent ...158 DA111
Patrick Connolly Gdns, E3
  off Talwin St 85 EB69
Patrick Gro, Wal.Abb. EN9
  off Beaulieu Dr 15 EB33
Patrick Rd, E13 ......86 EJ69
Patrington Cl, Uxb. UB8
  off Boulmer Rd 76 BJ69
Patriot Sq, E2 ....84 DV68
Patrol Pl, SE6 ......123 EB86
Patrons Dr, Uxb. (Denh.) UB9 .57 BF58
Patshull Pl, NW5
  off Patshull Rd 83 DJ65
Patshull Rd, NW5 ....83 DJ65
Patten All, Rich. TW10
  off The Hermitage ..117 CK85
Pattenden Rd, SE6 ..123 DZ88
Patten Rd, SW18 ....120 DE87
Patterdale Cl, Brom. BR1 .124 EF93
Patterdale Rd, SE15 ..102 DW80
  Dartford DA2 ....129 FR88
Patterson Ct, SE19 ..122 DT94
  Dartford DA1 ....128 FN85
Patterson Rd, SE19 ..122 DT93
Pattina Wk, SE16 .....85 DZ74
Pattison Pt, E6 off Fife Rd .86 EG71
Pattison Rd, NW2 .....64 DA62
Pattison Wk, SE18 ...105 EQ78
Paul Cl, E15 ....86 EE66
Paul Gdns, Croy. CR0 .142 DT103
Paulhan Rd, Har. HA3 ..61 CK56
Paulin Dr, N21 ....45 DN45
Pauline Cres, Twick. TW2 .116 CC88
Paulinus Cl, Orp. BR5 .146 EW96
Paul Julius Cl, E14 ..204 F1
Paul Robeson Cl, E6
  off Eastbourne Rd ...87 EN69
Pauls Grn, Wal.Cr. EN8
  off Eleanor Rd 15 DY33
Paul's Pl, Ashtd. KT21 .172 CP119
Paul St, E15 ....85 ED67
  EC2 ....197 L5
Paul's Wk, EC4 ......196 G10
Paultons Sq, SW3 ....100 DD79
Paultons St, SW3 ....100 DD79
Pauntley St, N19 .....65 DJ60
Paved Ct, Rich. TW9 ..117 CK85
Paveley Dr, SW11 ....100 DE80
Paveley St, NW8 .....194 C4
Pavement, The, SW4 ..101 DJ84
  W5 off Popes La 98 CL76
Pavement Ms, Rom. RM6
  off Clarissa Rd 70 EX59
Pavement Sq, Croy. CR0 .142 DU102
Pavet Cl, Dag. RM10 ...89 FB65
Pavilion Gdns, Stai. TW18 .114 BH94
Pavilion La, Beck. BR3
  off Lennard Rd 123 DZ93
Pavilion Ms, N3
  off Windermere Av ...44 DA54
Pavilion Rd, SW1 ....198 E7
  Ilford IG1 ....69 EM59
Pavilions, The, Epp. (N.Wld.Bas.)
  CM16 ....19 FC25
  Uxbridge UB8 ......76 BJ66
Pavilion Shop Cen, The, Wal.Cr.
  EN8 ....15 DX34
Pavilion St, SW1 ....198 E7
Pavilion Ter, E.Mol. KT8 .137 CF98
  Ilford IG2
  off Southdown Cres ..69 ES57
Pavilion Way, Amer. HP6 .20 AW39
  Edgware HA8 ....42 CP52
  Ruislip HA4 ....60 BW61
Pawleyne Cl, SE20 ...122 DW94
Pawsey Cl, E13 off Plashet Rd .86 EG67
Pawson's Rd, Croy. CR0 .142 DQ100
Paxford Rd, Wem. HA0 ..61 CH61
Paxton Cl, Rich. TW9 ..98 CM82
  Walton-on-Thames KT12 .136 BW101
Paxton Gdns, Wok. GU21 .151 BE112
Paxton Pl, SE27 .....122 DS91
Paxton Rd, N17 ....46 DT52
  SE23 ....123 DY90
  W4 ....98 CS79
  Bromley BR1 ....124 EG94
Paxton Ter, SW1 .....101 DH79
Payne Cl, Bark. IG11 ...87 ES66
Paynell Ct, SE3
  off Lawn Ter 104 EE83
Payne Rd, E3 ....85 EB68
Paynesfield Av, SW14 ..98 CR83
Paynesfield Rd, Bushey
  (Bushey Hth.) WD23 ..41 CF45
  Westerham (Tats.) TN16 .178 EJ121
Payne St, SE8 ....103 DZ79
Paynes Wk, W6 ....99 CY79

Peabody Av, SW1 .....199 H10
Peabody Cl, SE10
  off Devonshire Dr ...103 EB81
  SW1 off Lupus St ...101 DH79
  Croydon CR0
  off Shirley Rd 142 DW102
Peabody Dws, WC1 ...195 P4
Peabody Est, EC1 ....197 J5
  N17 ....46 DS53
  SE1 ....200 E3
  SE24 ....122 DQ87
  SW3 off Margaretta Ter .100 DE79
  W6 off The Square ..99 CW78
  W10 ....81 CW71
Peabody Hill, SE21 ..121 DP88
Peabody Hill Est, SE21 .121 DP87
Peabody Sq, N1 off Essex Rd .83 DP67
  SE1 ....200 F5
Peabody Twr, EC1
  off Golden La 84 DQ70
Peabody Trust, SE1 ..201 H3
Peabody Yd, N1
  off Greenman St 84 DQ67
Peace Cl, N14 ....29 DH43
  SE25 ....142 DS98
  Waltham Cross EN7
  off Goffs La 14 DU29
Peace Dr, Wat. WD17 ..23 BU41
Peace Gro, Wem. HA9 ..62 CP62
Peace Prospect, Wat. WD17 .23 BU41
Peace Rd, Iver SL0 ....75 BA68
  Slough SL3 ....75 BA68
Peace St, SE18
  off Nightingale Vale .105 EP79
Peach Cft, Grav. (Nthflt.)
  DA11 ....130 GE90
Peaches Cl, Sutt. SM2 .157 CY108
Peachey Cl, Uxb. UB8 ..76 BK72
Peachey La, Uxb. UB8 ..76 BK71
Peach Rd, W10 ....81 CX69
Peach Tree Av, West Dr. UB7
  off Pear Tree Av 76 BM72
Peachum Rd, SE3 ....104 EF79
Peachwalk Ms, E3
  off Grove Rd 85 DX68
Peacock Av, Felt. TW14 ..115 BR88
Peacock Cl, Horn. RM11 ..72 FL56
Peacock Gdns, S.Croy. CR2 .161 DY110
  GU21 ....166 AY117
Peacock St, SE17 ....200 G9
  Gravesend DA12 ....131 GJ87
Peacock Wk, E16 .....86 EH72
  Abbots Langley WD5 ..7 BU31
  Orpington BR6 .....163 EQ106
  Wembley HA9 ......61 CK62
Peacock Yd, SE17 ...200 G9
Peak, The, SE26 ....122 DW90
Peakes La, Wal.Cr. (Chsht.)
  EN7 ....14 DT27
Peakes Way, Wal.Cr. (Chsht.)
  EN7 ....14 DT27
Peaketon Av, Ilf. IG4 ..68 EK56
Peak Hill, Pur. CR8 ...159 DK110
Peak Hill Av, SE26 ...122 DW91
Peak Hill Gdns, SE26 .122 DW91
Peaks Hill, Pur. CR8 ..159 DK110
Peaks Hill Ri, Pur. CR8 .159 DL110
Pea La, Upmin. RM14 ..91 FU66
Peal Gdns, W13
  off Ruislip Rd E 79 CG79
Peall Rd, Croy. CR0 ..141 DM100
Pearce Cl, Mitch. CR4 .140 DG96
Pearcefield Av, SE23 ..122 DW88
Pearce Rd, W.Mol. KT8 .136 CB97
Pear Cl, NW9 ....62 CR56
  SE14
  off Southgate Way ..103 DY80
Pearcroft Rd, E11 ....67 ED61
Pearcy Cl, Rom. (Harold Hill)
  RM3 ....52 FL52
Peardon St, SW8 ....101 DH82
Peareswood Gdns, Stan. HA7 .41 CK53
Peareswood Rd, Erith DA8 ..107 FF81
Pearfield Rd, SE23 ...123 DY90
Pearl Cl, E6 ....87 EN72
  NW2 off Marble Dr ..63 CX59
Pearl Ct, Wok. GU21
  off Langmans Way ..166 AS116
Pearl Rd, E17 ....67 EA55
Pearl St, E1 ....202 E7
Pearmain Cl, Shep. TW17 .135 BP99
Pearman St, SE1 .....200 E6
Pear Pl, SE1 ....200 D4
Pear Rd, E11 ....67 ED62
Pearscroft Ct, SW6 ..100 DB81
Pearscroft Rd, SW6 ..100 DB81
Pearse St, SE15
  off Dragon Rd 102 DS79
Pearson Cl, SW4
  off Edgeley Rd 101 DK83
Pearsons Av, SE14
  off Tanners Hill 103 EA81
Pearson St, E2 ......84 DS68
Pearson Way, Dart. DA1 .128 FM89
Pears Rd, Houns. TW3 ..96 CC83
Peartree Av, SW17 ...120 DC90
Pear Tree Av, West Dr. UB7 ..76 BM72
Pear Tree Cl, E2 .....84 DT67
  Addlestone KT15
  off Pear Tree Rd ...152 BG106
  Amersham HP7
  off Orchard End Av ..20 AT39
  Chessington KT9 ...156 CN106
Peartree Cl, Erith DA8 .107 FD81
  Mitcham CR4 ......140 DE96
Pear Tree Cl, S.Croy. CR2 .160 DV114
  South Ockendon RM15 ..91 FW68
  Swanley BR8 ......147 FD96
Peartree Ct, E18
  off Churchfields 48 EH53
Pear Tree Ct, EC1 ...196 E5
Peartree Gdns, Dag. RM8 ..70 EV63
  Romford RM7 ......51 FB54
Peartree La, E1 .....202 G1
Pear Tree Rd, Add. KT15 .152 BG106
  Ashford TW15 ......115 BQ92

Peartree Rd, Enf. EN1 ..30 DS41
Pear Tree St, EC1 ....196 G4
Pear Tree Wk, Wal.Cr. (Chsht.)
  EN7 ....14 DR26
Peartree Way, SE10 ..205 M8
Peary Pl, E2 off Kirkwall Pl ..84 DW69
Pease, Horn. RM12
  off Dowding Way 89 FH66
Peatfield Cl, Sid. DA15
  off Woodside Rd ...125 ES90
Peatmore Av, Wok. GU22 .168 BG116
Peatmore Cl, Wok. GU22 .168 BG116
Pebble Cl, Tad. KT20 ..182 CS128
Pebble Hill Rd, Bet. RH3 .182 CS131
  Tadworth KT20 .....182 CS131
Pebble La, Epsom KT18 .172 CN121
  Leatherhead KT22 ..182 CL125
Pebble Way, W3 ......80 CP74
Pebworth Rd, Har. HA1 ..61 CG61
Peckarmans Wd, SE26 .122 DU90
Peckett Sq, N5
  off Highbury Gra ...66 DQ63
Peckford Pl, SW9 ....101 DN82
PECKHAM, SE15 .....102 DU81
Peckham Gro, SE15 ..102 DS80
Peckham High St, SE15 .102 DU81
Peckham Hill St, SE15 .102 DU80
Peckham Pk Rd, SE15 .102 DU80
Peckham Rd, SE5 ....102 DS81
  SE15 ....102 DS81
⇌ Peckham Rye 102 DU82
Peckham Rye, SE15 ..102 DU83
  SE22 ....102 DU84
Pecks Yd, E1 ....197 P6
Peckwater St, NW5 ...65 DJ64
Pedham Pl Ind Est, Swan.
  BR8 ....147 FG99
Pedlars Wk, N7 ......83 DL65
Pedley Rd, Dag. RM8 ..70 EW60
Pedley St, E1 ....84 DT70
Pedro St, E5 ....67 DX62
Pedworth Gdns, SE16 .202 F9
Peek Cres, SW19 ....119 CX92
Peel Cl, E4 ....47 EB47
  N9 off Plevna Rd ...46 DU48
Peel Dr, NW9 ....63 CT55
  Ilford IG5 ....68 EL55
Peel Gro, E2 ....84 DW68
Peel Pas, W8 off Peel St ..82 DA74
Peel Pl, Ilf. IG5 ......48 EL54
Peel Prec, NW6 ......82 DA68
Peel Rd, E18 ....48 EF53
  NW6 ....81 CZ69
  Harrow (Wldste.) HA3 ..61 CF55
  Orpington BR6 ....163 EQ106
  Wembley HA9 ......61 CK62
Peel St, W8 ....82 DA74
Peel Way, Rom. RM3 ...52 FM54
  Uxbridge UB8 ......76 BL71
Peerage Way, Horn. RM11 ..72 FL59
Peerless Dr, Uxb. (Hare.) UB9 .58 BJ57
Peerless St, EC1 ....197 K3
Pegamoid Rd, N18 ...46 DW48
Pegasus Cl, N16
  off Green Las 66 DR63
Pegasus Ct, Abb.L. WD5
  off Furtherfield 7 BT32
  Gravesend DA12 ...131 GJ90
Pegasus Pl, SE11
  off Clayton St 101 DN78
  SW6 off Ackmar Rd .100 DA81
Pegasus Rd, Croy. CR0 .159 DN107
Pegasus Way, N11 ....45 DH51
Pegelm Gdns, Horn. RM11 ..72 FM59
Peggotty Way, Uxb. UB8
  off Dickens Av 77 BP72
Pegg Rd, Houns. TW5 ..96 BX80
Pegley Gdns, SE12 ..124 EG89
Pegmire La, Wat. (Ald.) WD25 .24 CC39
Pegwell St, SE18 ....105 ES80
Peket Cl, Stai. TW18 .133 BE95
Pekin Cl, E14
  off Pekin St 85 EA72
Pekin St, E14 ....85 EA72
Peldon Ct, Rich. TW9 ..98 CM84
Peldon Pas, Rich. TW10
  off Worple Way 98 CM84
Peldon Wk, N1
  off Britannia Row ...83 DP67
Pelham Av, Bark. IG11 ..87 ET67
Pelham Cl, SE5 ......102 DS82
Pelham Cres, SW7 ...198 B9
Pelham Pl, SW7 .....198 B9
  W13 off Ruislip Rd E ..79 CF70
Pelham Rd, E18 ......68 EH55
  N15 ....66 DT56
  N22 ....45 DN54
  SW19 ....120 DA94
  Beckenham BR3 ...142 DW96
  Bexleyheath DA7 ..106 FA83
  Gravesend DA11 ...131 GF88
  Ilford IG1 ....69 ER61
Pelham Rd S, Grav. DA11 .131 GF88
Pelhams, The, Wat. WD25 ..24 BX35
Pelhams Cl, Esher KT10 .154 CA105
Pelham St, SW7 .....198 A8
Pelhams Wk, Esher KT10 .154 CA104
Pelham Ter, Grav. DA11
  off Campbell Rd ...131 GF87
Pelican Est, SE15 ....102 DT81
Pelican Pas, E1
  off Cambridge Heath Rd .84 DW70
Pelican Wk, SW9
  off Loughborough Pk .101 DP84
Pelier St, SE17
  off Langdale Cl 102 DQ79
Pelinore Rd, SE6 ....124 EE89
Pellant Rd, SW6 .....99 CY80
Pellatt Gro, N22 ......45 DN53
Pellatt Rd, SE22 ....122 DT85
  Wembley HA9 ......61 CK61
Pellerin Rd, N16 .....66 DS64
Pelling Hill, Wind. (Old Wind.)
  SL4 ....112 AV87
Pelling St, E14 ......85 EA72
Pellipar Cl, N13 ......45 DN48

Pellipar Gdns, SE18 ..105 EM78
Pelly Ct, Epp. CM16 ..17 ET31
Pelly Rd, E13 ....86 EG68
Pelter St, E2 ....197 P2
Pelton Av, Sutt. SM2 .158 DB110
Pelton Rd, SE10 .....205 H10
Pembar Av, E17 ......67 DY55
Pemberley Chase, Epsom
  (W.Ewell) KT19 ....156 CP106
Pemberley Cl, Epsom (W.Ewell)
  KT19 ....156 CP106
Pember Rd, NW10 ...81 CX69
Pemberton Av, Rom. RM2 .71 FH55
Pemberton Gdns, N19 ..65 DJ62
  Romford RM6 ......70 EY57
  Swanley BR8 ......147 FE97
Pemberton Ho, SE26
  off High Level Dr ...122 DU91
Pemberton Pl, E8
  off Mare St 84 DV66
  Esher KT10
  off Carrick Gate ...136 CC104
Pemberton Rd, N4 ...65 DN57
  East Molesey KT8 ..136 CC98
Pemberton Row, EC4 .196 G8
Pemberton Ter, N19 ..65 DJ62
Pembrey Way, Horn. RM12 ..90 FJ65
Pembridge Av, Twick. TW2 ..116 BZ88
Pembridge Chase, Hem.H. (Bov.)
  HP3 off Pembridge Cl ..5 BA28
Pembridge Cl, Hem.H. (Bov.)
  HP3 ....5 AZ28
Pembridge Cres, W11 ..82 DA73
Pembridge Gdns, W2 ..82 DA73
Pembridge Ms, W11 ..82 DA73
Pembridge Pl, SW15 ..120 DA85
  W2 ....82 DA73
Pembridge Rd, W11 ..82 DA73
  Hemel Hempstead (Bov.)
  HP3 ....5 BA28
Pembridge Sq, W2 ...82 DA73
Pembridge Vil, W2 ...82 DA73
  W11 ....82 DA73
Pembroke Av, N1
  off Bingfield St 83 DL67
  Enfield EN1 ....30 DV38
  Harrow HA3 ....61 CG55
  Pinner HA5 ....60 BX60
  Surbiton KT5 ......138 CP99
  Walton-on-Thames KT12 .154 BX105
Pembroke Cl, SW1 ...198 G5
  Banstead SM7 .....174 DB117
  Erith DA8
  off Pembroke Rd ...107 FD77
  Hornchurch RM11 ..72 FM56
Pembroke Cotts, W8
  off Pembroke Sq ..100 DA76
Pembroke Dr, Wal.Cr. (Chsht.)
  EN7 ....13 DP29
Pembroke Gdns, W8 ..99 CZ77
  Dagenham RM10 ...71 FB62
  Woking GU22 ......167 BA118
Pembroke Gdns Cl, W8 ..100 DA76
Pembroke Ms, E3
  off Morgan St 85 DY69
  N10 off Pembroke Rd ..44 DG53
  W8 off Earls Wk ...100 DA76
  Sevenoaks TN13
  off Pembroke Rd ..191 FH125
Pembroke Pl, W8 ....100 DA76
  Dartford (Sutt.H.) DA4 .148 FP95
  Edgware HA8 ....42 CN52
  Isleworth TW7
  off Thornbury Rd ...97 CE82
Pembroke Rd, E6 ....87 EM71
  E17 ....67 EB57
  N8 ....65 DL56
  N10 ....44 DG53
  N13 ....46 DQ48
  N15 ....66 DT57
  SE25 ....142 DS98
  W8 ....100 DA77
  Bromley BR1 ......144 EJ96
  Erith DA8 ....107 FC78
  Greenford UB6 .....78 CB70
  Ilford IG3 ....69 ET60
  Mitcham CR4 ......140 DG96
  Northwood HA6 ....39 BQ48
  Ruislip HA4 ....59 BS60
  Sevenoaks TN13 ...191 FH125
  Wembley HA9 ......61 CK62
  Woking GU22 ......167 BA118
Pembroke Sq, W8 ...100 DA76
Pembroke St, N1 .....83 DL66
Pembroke Studios, W8 ..99 CZ76
Pembroke Vil, W8 ....100 DA77
  Richmond TW9 .....97 CK84
Pembroke Wk, W8 ...100 DA77
Pembroke Way, Hayes UB3 .95 BQ76
Pembry Cl, SW9 .....101 DN81
Pembury Av, Wor.Pk. KT4 .139 CU101
Pembury Cl, Brom. BR2 .144 EF101
  Coulsdon CR5 .....158 DG114
Pembury Ct, Hayes UB3 ..95 BR79
Pembury Cres, Sid. DA14 ..126 EY89
Pembury Pl, E5 ......66 DV64
Pembury Rd, E5 .....66 DV64
  N17 ....46 DT54
  SE25 ....142 DU98
  Bexleyheath DA7 ..106 EY80
Pemdevon Rd, Croy. CR0 .141 DN101
Pemell Cl, E1 off Colebert Av .84 DW70
Pemerich Cl, Hayes UB3 ..95 BT78
Pempath Pl, Wem. HA9 ..61 CK61
Penally Pl, N1
  off Shepperton Rd ..84 DR67
Penang St, E1 ....202 E2
Penard Rd, Sthl. UB2 ..96 CA76
Penarth St, SE15 ...102 DW79
Penates, Esher KT10 .155 CD105
Penberth Rd, SE6 ...123 EC89
Penbury Rd, Sthl. UB2 ..96 BZ77
Pencombe Ms, W11
  off Denbigh Rd 81 CZ73
Pencraig Way, SE15 .102 DV79
Pencroft Dr, Dart. DA1
  off Shepherds La ..128 FJ87

Pat - Pen

Pendall Cl, Barn. EN4 ..28 DE42
Penda Rd, Erith DA8 ..107 FB80
Pendarves Rd, SW20 .139 CW95
Penda's Mead, E9
  off Lindisfarne Way ..67 DY63
Pendell Av, Hayes UB3 ..95 BT80
Pendell Ct, Red. (Bletch.)
  RH1 ....185 DP131
Pendell Rd, Red. (Bletch.)
  RH1 ....185 DP131
Pendennis Cl, W.Byf. KT14 .152 BG114
Pendennis Rd, N17 ...66 DR55
  SW16 ....121 DL91
  Orpington BR6 ....146 EW103
  Sevenoaks TN13 ...191 FH123
Penderel Rd, Houns. TW3 .116 CA85
Penderry Ri, SE6 ....123 ED89
Penderyn Way, N7 ...65 DK63
Pendle Rd, SW16 ....121 DH93
Pendlestone Rd, E17 ..67 EA57
Pendragon Ho, N9
  off Salisbury Rd 46 DU48
Pendragon Rd, Brom. BR1 .124 EF90
Pendragon Wk, NW9 ..62 CS58
Pendrell Rd, SE4 ....103 DY82
Pendrell St, SE18 ...105 ER80
Pendula Dr, Hayes UB4 ..78 BX70
Pendulum Ms, E8
  off Birkbeck Rd 66 DT64
Penerley Rd, SE6 ....123 EB88
  Rainham RM13 .....89 FH71
Penfold Cl, Croy. CR0
  off Epsom Rd 141 DN104
Penfold La, Bex. DA5 .126 EX89
Penfold Pl, NW1 .....194 B6
Penfold Rd, N9 ......47 DX46
Penfold St, NW1 ....194 A5
  NW8 ....194 A5
Penford Gdns, SE9 ..104 EK83
Penford St, SE5 .....101 DP82
Pengarth Rd, Bex. DA5 .126 EX85
PENGE, SE20 ....122 DW94
⇌ Penge East 122 DW93
Penge Ho, SW11 off Wye St .100 DD83
Penge La, SE20 ......122 DW94
Pengelly Cl, Wal.Cr. (Chsht.)
  EN7 ....14 DV30
Penge Rd, E13 ......86 EJ66
  SE20 ....142 DU97
  SE25 ....142 DU97
⇌ Penge West 122 DV93
Penhale Cl, Orp. BR6 .164 EU105
Penhall Rd, SE7 .....104 EK77
Penhill Rd, Bex. DA5 .126 EW87
Penhurst, Wok. GU21 .151 AZ114
Penhurst Rd, Ilf. IG6 ..49 EP52
Penifather La, Grnf. UB6 ..79 CD69
Peninsular Cl, Felt. TW14 .115 BR86
Peninsular Pk Rd, SE7 .205 N9
Penistone Rd, SW16 .121 DL94
Penistone Wk, Rom. RM3
  off Okehampton Rd ..52 FJ51
Penketh Dr, Har. HA1 ..61 CD62
Penman Cl, St.Alb. AL2 ..8 CA27
Penman's Grn, Kings L. WD4 ..5 BF32
Penmon Rd, SE2 ....106 EU76
Pennack Rd, SE15 ...102 DT79
Pennant Ms, W8 ....100 DB77
Pennant Ter, E17 ....47 DZ54
Pennard Rd, W12 ....99 CW75
Pennards, The, Sun. TW16 .136 BW96
Penn Cl, Grnf. UB6 ...78 CB68
  Harrow HA3 ....61 CJ56
  Rickmansworth (Chorl.)
  WD3 ....21 BD44
  Uxbridge UB8 ......76 BK70
Penn Dr, Uxb. (Denh.) UB9 .57 BF58
Penne Cl, Rad. WD7 ..9 CF34
Penner Cl, SW19
  off Victoria Dr 119 CY89
Penners Gdns, Surb. KT6 .138 CL101
Pennethorne Cl, E9
  off Victoria Pk Rd ...84 DW67
Pennethorne Rd, SE15 .102 DW80
Penney Cl, Dart. DA1 .128 FK87
Penn Gdns, Chis. BR7 .145 EP96
  Romford RM5 ......50 FA52
Penn Gaskell La, Ger.Cr.
  (Chal.St.P.) SL9 ....37 AZ50
Pennine Dr, NW2 .....63 CY61
Pennine Ho, N9
  off Plevna Rd 46 DU48
Pennine La, NW2
  off Pennine Dr 63 CY61
Pennine Way, Bexh. DA7 .107 FE81
  Gravesend (Nthflt.) DA11 .130 GE90
  Hayes UB3 ....95 BR80
Pennington Cl, SE27
  off Hamilton Rd 122 DR91
  Romford RM5 ......50 FA50
Pennington Dr, N21 ..29 DL43
  Weybridge KT13 ...135 BS104
Pennington St, E1 ...202 C1
Pennington Way, SE12 .124 EH89
Pennis La, Long. (Fawk.Grn.)
  DA3 ....149 FX100
Penniston Cl, N17 ...46 DQ54
Penn La, Bex. DA5 ...126 EX85
Penn Meadow, Slou. (Stoke P.)
  SL2 ....74 AT67
Penn Pl, Rick. WD3
  off Northway 38 BK45
Penn Rd, N7 ....65 DL64
  Gerrards Cross (Chal.St.P.)
  SL9 ....36 AX53
  Rickmansworth (Mill End)
  SL9 ....36 AX53
  St. Albans (Park St.) AL2 ..8 CC27
  Slough (Datchet) SL3 ..92 AX43
  Watford WD24 ......23 BV39
Penn St, N1 ....84 DR67

A B C D E F G H I J K L M N O P Q R S T U V W X Y Z

Pen - Pie

Penn Way, Rick. (Chorl.) WD3 .21 BD44
Penny Cl, Rain. RM13 . . . . .89 FH69
Pennycroft, Croy. CR0 . . . . . .161 DY109
Pennyfather La, Enf. EN2 . . . . .30 DQ40
Pennyfield, Cob. KT11 . . . . . .153 BU113
Pennyfields, E14 . . . . .85 EA73
  Brentwood CM14 . . . . .54 FW49
Penny La, Shep. TW17 . . . . . .135 BS101
Pennylets Grn, Slou. (Stoke P.)
  SL2 . . . . .74 AT66
Penny Ms, SW12
  off Caistor Rd 121 DH87
Pennymoor Wk, W9
  off Ashmore Rd 81 CZ69
Pennyroyal Av, E6 . . . . .87 EN72
Penpoll Rd, E8 . . . . .84 DV65
Penpool La, Well. DA16 . . . . .106 EU83
Penrhyn Av, E17 . . . . .47 DZ53
Penrhyn Cres, E17 . . . . .47 EA53
  SW14 . . . . .98 CQ84
Penrhyn Gdns, Kings.T. KT1
  off Surbiton Rd 137 CK98
Penrhyn Gro, E17 . . . . .47 EA53
Penrhyn Rd, Kings.T. KT1 . . .138 CL97
Penrith Cl, SW15 . . . . .119 CY85
  Beckenham BR3
  off Albemarle Rd 143 EB95
  Reigate RH2 . . . . .184 DE133
  Uxbridge UB8
  off Chippendale Waye 76 BK66
Penrith Cres, Rain. RM13 . . . .71 FG64
Penrith Pl, SE27
  off Harpenden Rd 121 DP89
Penrith Rd, N15 . . . . .66 DR57
  Ilford IG6 . . . . .49 ET51
  New Malden KT3 . . . . .138 CR98
  Romford RM3 . . . . .52 FN51
  Thornton Heath CR7 . . . . . .142 DQ96
Penrith St, SW16 . . . . .121 DJ93
Penrose Av, Wat. WD19 . . . . . .40 BX47
Penrose Dr, Epsom KT19
  off Churchill Rd 156 CN111
Penrose Gro, SE17 . . . . .102 DQ78
Penrose Ho, SE17 . . . . .102 DQ78
Penrose Rd, Lthd. (Fetch.)
  KT22 . . . . .170 CC122
Penrose St, SE17 . . . . .102 DQ78
Penryn St, NW1 . . . . .83 DK68
Penry St, SE1 . . . . .201 N9
Pensbury Pl, SW8 . . . . .101 DJ82
Pensbury St, SW8 . . . . .101 DJ82
Penscroft Gdns, Borwd. WD6 . .26 CR42
Pensford Av, Rich. TW9 . . . . . .98 CN83
Penshurst Av, Sid. DA15 . . . .126 EU86
Penshurst Cl, Ger.Cr. (Chal.St.P.)
  SL9 . . . . .36 AX54
Penshurst Gdns, Edg. HA8 . . . .42 CP50
Penshurst Grn, Brom. BR2 . . .144 EF99
Penshurst Rd, E9 . . . . .85 DX66
  N17 . . . . .46 DT52
  Bexleyheath DA7 . . . . .106 EZ81
  Potters Bar EN6 . . . . .12 DD31
  Thornton Heath CR7 . . . . . .141 DP99
Penshurst Wk, Brom. BR2
  off Hayesford Pk Dr 144 EF99
Penshurst Way, Orp. BR5
  off Star La 146 EW98
  Sutton SM2 . . . . .158 DA108
Pensilver Cl, Barn. EN4 . . . . . .28 DE42
Pensons La, Ong. CM5 . . . . . .19 FG28
Penstemon Cl, N3 . . . . .44 DA52
Penstock Footpath, N22 . . . . .65 DL55
Pentavia Retail Pk, NW7
  off Bunns La 43 CT52
Pentelow Gdns, Felt. TW14 . . .115 BU86
Pentire Cl, Upmin. RM14 . . . . .73 FS58
Pentire Rd, E17 . . . . .47 ED53
Pentland Av, Edg. HA8 . . . . . .42 CP47
  Shepperton TW17 . . . . . . .134 BN99
Pentland Cl, NW11 . . . . .63 CY61
Pentland Gdns, SW18
  off St. Ann's Hill 120 DC86
Pentland Pl, Nthlt. UB5 . . . . . .78 BY67
Pentland Rd, Bushey WD23 . . .24 CC44
Pentlands Cl, Mitch. CR4 . . . .141 DH97
Pentland St, SW18 . . . . .120 DC86
Pentland Way, Uxb. UB10 . . . .59 BQ62
Pentlow St, SW15 . . . . .99 CW83
Pentney Rd, E4 . . . . .47 ED46
  SW12 . . . . .121 DJ88
  SW19 off Midmoor Rd 139 CY95
Penton Av, Stai. TW18 . . . . . .113 BF94
Penton Dr, Wal.Cr. (Chsht.)
  EN8 . . . . .15 DX29
Penton Gro, N1 . . . . .196 D1
Penton Hall Dr, Stai. TW18 . . .134 BG95
Penton Hook Rd, Stai. TW18 . .114 BG94
Penton Ho, SE2
  off Hartslock Dr 106 EX75
Penton Pk, Cher. KT16 . . . . . .134 BG97
Penton Pl, SE17 . . . . .200 G10
Penton Ri, WC1 . . . . .196 C2
Penton Rd, Stai. TW18 . . . . . .113 BF94
Penton St, N1 . . . . .83 DN68
PENTONVILLE, N1 . . . . .196 D1
Pentonville Rd, N1 . . . . .196 D1
Pentrich Av, Enf. EN1 . . . . . . .30 DU38
Pentridge St, SE15 . . . . .102 DT80
Pentyre Av, N18 . . . . .46 DR49
Penwerris Av, Islw. TW7 . . . . .96 CC80
Penwith Rd, SW18 . . . . .120 DB89
Penwith Wk, Wok. GU22
  off Wych Hill Pk 166 AX119
Penwood End, Wok. GU22 . . .166 AV121
Penwood Ho, SW15
  off Tunworth Cres 119 CT86
Penwortham Rd, SW16 . . . . . .121 DH93
  South Croydon CR2 . . . . . .160 DQ110
Penylan Pl, Edg. HA8 . . . . . . .42 CN52
Penywern Rd, SW5 . . . . .100 DA78
Penzance Cl, Uxb. (Hare.)
  UB9 . . . . .38 BK53

Penzance Gdns, Rom. RM3 . . .52 FN51
Penzance Pl, W11 . . . . .81 CY74
Penzance Rd, Rom. RM3 . . . . .52 FN51
Penzance St, W11 . . . . .81 CY74
Peony Cl, Brwd. CM15 . . . . . . .54 FV44
Peony Ct, Wdf.Grn. IG8
  off The Bridle Path 48 EE52
Peony Gdns, W12 . . . . .81 CU73
Pepler Ms, SE5
  off Cobourg Rd 102 DT79
Peplins Cl, Hat. AL9 . . . . .11 CY26
Peplins Way, Hat. AL9 . . . . . . .11 CY25
Peploe Rd, NW6 . . . . .81 CX68
Peplow Cl, West Dr. UB7
  off Tavistock Rd 76 BK74
Pepper All, Loug. (High Beach)
  IG10 . . . . .32 EG39
Pepper Cl, E6 . . . . .87 EM71
  Caterham CR3 . . . . .186 DS125
Peppercorn Cl, Th.Hth. CR7 . . .142 DR96
Pepper Hill, Grav. (Nthflt.)
  DA11 . . . . .130 GC90
Pepperhill La, Grav. (Nthflt.)
  DA11 . . . . .130 GC90
Peppermead Sq, SE13 . . . . . .123 EA85
Peppermint Cl, Croy. CR0 . . . .141 DL101
Peppermint Pl, E11
  off Birch Gro 68 EE62
Pepper St, E14 . . . . .204 B6
  SE1 . . . . .201 H4
Peppie Cl, N16
  off Bouverie Rd 66 DS61
Pepys Cl, Ashtd. KT21 . . . . . .172 CN117
  Dartford DA1 . . . . .108 FN84
  Gravesend (Nthflt.) DA11 . . .130 GD90
  Slough SL3 . . . . .93 BB79
  Tilbury RM18 . . . . .111 GJ81
  Uxbridge UB10 . . . . .59 BP63
Pepys Cres, E16 . . . . .205 N2
  Barnet EN5 . . . . .27 CW43
Pepys Ri, Orp. BR6 . . . . .145 ET102
Pepys Rd, SE14 . . . . .103 DX81
  SW20 . . . . .139 CW95
Pepys St, EC3 . . . . .197 N10
Perceval Av, NW3 . . . . .64 DE64
Percheron Cl, Islw. TW7 . . . . .97 CG83
Percheron Rd, Borwd. WD6 . . .26 CR44
Perch St, E8 . . . . .66 DT63
Percival Av, NW9 . . . . .62 CS56
Percival Cl, Lthd. KT22 . . . . . .154 CB111
Percival Ct, N17 off High Rd . . .46 DT52
  Northolt UB5 . . . . .60 CA64
★ Percival David Foundation
  of Chinese Art, WC1
  off Gordon Sqaure 195 N4
Percival Gdns, Rom. RM6 . . . .70 EW58
Percival Rd, SW14 . . . . .98 CQ84
  Enfield EN1 . . . . .30 DT42
  Feltham TW13 . . . . .115 BT89
  Hornchurch RM11 . . . . . . .72 FJ58
  Orpington BR6 . . . . .145 EP103
Percival St, EC1 . . . . .196 G4
Percival Way, Epsom KT19 . . .156 CQ105
Percy Av, Ashf. TW15 . . . . . . .114 BN92
Percy Bryant Rd, Sun. TW16 . .115 BS94
Percy Bush Rd, West Dr. UB7 . .94 BM76
Percy Circ, WC1 . . . . .196 C2
Percy Gdns, Enf. EN3 . . . . . . .31 DX43
  Hayes UB4 . . . . .85 BS69
  Isleworth TW7 . . . . .97 CG82
  Worcester Park KT4 . . . . . .138 CR102
Percy Ms, W1 . . . . .195 M7
Percy Pas, W1 . . . . .195 L7
Percy Pl, Slou. (Datchet) SL3 . .92 AV81
Percy Rd, E11 . . . . .68 EE59
  E16 . . . . .86 EE71
  N12 . . . . .44 DC50
  N21 . . . . .46 DQ45
  SE20 . . . . .143 DX95
  SE25 . . . . .142 DU99
  W12 . . . . .99 CU75
  Bexleyheath DA7 . . . . .106 EY82
  Hampton TW12 . . . . .116 CA94
  Ilford IG3 . . . . .70 EU59
  Isleworth TW7 . . . . .97 CG84
  Mitcham CR4 . . . . .140 DG101
  Romford RM7 . . . . .71 FB55
  Twickenham TW2 . . . . . . .116 CB88
  Watford WD18 . . . . .23 BV42
Percy St, W1 . . . . .195 M7
  Grays RM17 . . . . .110 GC79
Percy Way, Twick. TW2 . . . . . .116 CC88
Percy Yd, WC1 . . . . .196 C2
Peregrine Cl, NW10 . . . . .62 CR64
  Watford WD25 . . . . .8 BY34
Peregrine Ct, SW16
  off Leithcote Gdns 121 DM91
  Welling DA16 . . . . .105 ET81
Peregrine Gdns, Croy. CR0 . . .143 DY103
Peregrine Ho, EC1 . . . . .196 G2
Peregrine Rd, Ilf. IG6 . . . . . . .50 EV50
  Sunbury-on-Thames
  TW16 . . . . .135 BT96
  Waltham Abbey EN9 . . . . . .16 EG34
Peregrine Wk, Horn. RM12
  off Heron Flight Av 89 FH65
Peregrine Way, SW19 . . . . . . .119 CW94
Perham Rd, W14 . . . . .99 CY78
Perham Way, St.Alb. (Lon.Col.)
  AL2 . . . . .9 CK26
Peridot St, E6 . . . . .86 EL71
Perifield, SE21 . . . . .122 DQ88
Perimeade Rd, Grnf. UB6 . . . . .79 CJ68
Periton Rd, SE9 . . . . .104 EK84
PERIVALE, Grnf. 79 CG67
◆ Perivale 79 CG68
Perivale Gdns, W13
  off Bellevue Rd 79 CH70
  Watford WD25 . . . . .7 BV34
Perivale Gra, Grnf. UB6 . . . . . .79 CG69
Perivale Ind Pk, Grnf. UB6 . . . .79 CH68
Perivale La, Grnf. UB6 . . . . . . .79 CG69
Perivale New Business Cen, Grnf.
  UB6 . . . . .79 CH68
Perkin Cl, Wem. HA0 . . . . .61 CH64
Perkins Cl, Green. DA9 . . . . . .129 FT85
Perkins Ct, Ashf. TW15 . . . . . .114 BM92
Perkin's Rents, SW1 . . . . .199 M6

Perkins Rd, Ilf. IG2 . . . . .69 ER57
Perkins Sq, SE1 . . . . .201 J2
Perks Cl, SE3 off Hurren Cl . . .104 EE83
Perleybrooke La, Wok. GU21
  off Bampton Way 166 AU117
Permain Cl, Rad. (Shenley)
  WD7 . . . . .9 CK33
Perpins Rd, SE9 . . . . .125 ES86
Perran Cl, Brox. EN10 . . . . . . .15 DY26
Perran Rd, SW2
  off Christchurch Rd 121 DP89
Perran Wk, Brent. TW8 . . . . . .98 CL78
Perren St, NW5
  off Ryland Rd 83 DH65
Perrers Rd, W6 . . . . .99 CV77
Perrin Cl, Ashf. TW15
  off Fordbridge Rd 114 BM92
Perrin Ct, Wok. GU21
  off Blackmore Cres 167 BB115
Perrin Rd, Wem. HA0 . . . . .61 CG63
Perrins Ct, NW3
  off Hampstead High St 64 DC63
Perrins La, NW3 . . . . .64 DC63
Perrin's Wk, NW3 . . . . .64 DC63
Perriors Cl, Wal.Cr. (Chsht.)
  EN7 . . . . .14 DU27
Perrott St, SE18 . . . . .105 EQ77
Perry Av, W3 . . . . .80 CR72
Perry Cl, Rain. RM13
  off Lowen Rd 89 FD68
  Uxbridge UB8
  off Harlington Rd 77 BQ72
Perry Ct, E14
  off Napier Av 103 EA78
  N15 off Albert Rd 66 DS58
Perryfield Way, NW9 . . . . .63 CT58
  Richmond TW10 . . . . .117 CH89
Perry Gdns, N9
  off Deansway 46 DS46
Perry Garth, Nthlt. UB5 . . . . . .78 BW66
Perry Gro, Dart. DA1 . . . . . . .108 FN84
Perry Hall Cl, Orp. BR6 . . . . . .146 EU101
Perry Hall Rd, Orp. BR6 . . . . .145 ET100
Perry Hill, SE6 . . . . .123 DZ90
Perry Ho, SW2
  off Tierney Rd 121 DL87
  Rainham RM13
  off Lowen Rd 89 FD68
Perry How, Wor.Pk. KT4 . . . . .139 CT102
Perryman Ho, Bark. IG11 . . . . .87 EQ67
Perrymans Fm Rd, Ilf. IG2 . . . .69 ER58
Perry Mead, Bushey WD23 . . . .40 CB45
  Enfield EN2 . . . . .29 DP40
Perrymead St, SW6 . . . . .100 DA81
Perryn Rd, SE16 . . . . .202 D6
  W3 . . . . .80 CR73
Perry Oaks Dr, Houns. (Hthrw.Air.)
  TW6 . . . . .94 BH82
Perry Ri, SE23 . . . . .123 DY90
Perry Rd, Dag. RM9 . . . . .88 EZ70
Perrysfield Rd, Wal.Cr. (Chsht.)
  EN8 . . . . .15 DY27
PERRY STREET, Grav. 130 GE88
Perry St, Chis. BR7 . . . . .125 ER93
  Dartford DA1 . . . . .107 FE84
  Gravesend (Nthflt.) DA11 . . .130 GE88
Perry St Gdns, Chis. BR7
  off Old Perry St 125 ES93
Perry Vale, SE23 . . . . .122 DW89
Perry Way, S.Ock. (Aveley)
  RM15 . . . . .90 FQ73
Persant Rd, SE6 . . . . .124 EE89
Perseverance Cotts, Wok. (Ripley)
  GU23 . . . . .168 BJ121
Perseverance Pl, SW9 . . . . . .101 DN80
  Richmond TW9
  off Shaftesbury Rd 98 CL83
Persfield Cl, Epsom KT17 . . . .157 CU109
Pershore Cl, Ilf. IG2 . . . . .69 EP57
Pershore Gro, Cars. SM5 . . . .140 DD100
Pert Cl, N10 . . . . .45 DH52
Perth Av, NW9 . . . . .62 CR59
  Hayes UB4 . . . . .78 BW70
Perth Cl, SW20
  off Huntley Way 139 CU96
Perth Rd, E10 . . . . .67 DY60
  E13 . . . . .86 EH68
  N4 . . . . .65 DN60
  N22 . . . . .45 DP53
  Barking IG11 . . . . .87 ER68
  Beckenham BR3 . . . . .143 EC96
  Ilford IG2 . . . . .69 EN58
Perth Ter, Ilf. IG2 . . . . .69 EQ59
Perwell Av, Har. HA2 . . . . .60 BZ60
Perwell Ct, Har. HA2 . . . . .60 BZ60
Peter Av, NW10 . . . . .81 CV66
  Oxted RH8 . . . . .187 ED129
Peterboat Cl, SE10 . . . . .205 J8
Peterborough Av, Upmin.
  RM14 . . . . .73 FS60
Peterborough Gdns, Ilf. IG1 . . .68 EL59
Peterborough Ms, SW6 . . . . .100 DA82
Peterborough Rd, E10 . . . . . . .67 EC57
  SW6 . . . . .100 DA82
  Carshalton SM5 . . . . .140 DE100
  Harrow HA1 . . . . .61 CE58
Peterborough Vil, SW6 . . . . . .100 DB81
Peterchurch Ho, SE15
  off Commercial Way 102 DV79
Petergate, SW11 . . . . .100 DC84
Peterhead Ms, Slou. SL3
  off Grampian Way 93 BA78
Peterhill Cl, Ger.Cr. (Chal.St.P.)
  SL9 . . . . .36 AY50
Peterhouse Gdns, SW6
  off Bagley's La 100 DB81
Peter James Business Cen,
  Hayes UB3 . . . . .95 BU75
Peterley Business Cen, E2
  off Hackney Rd 84 DV68
★ Peter Pan Statue, W2 . . . . . .82 DD74
Peters Av, St.Alb. (Lon.Col.)
  AL2 . . . . .9 CJ26
Peters Cl, Dag. RM8 . . . . .70 EX60
  Stanmore HA7 . . . . .41 CK51

Peters Cl, Well. DA16 . . . . . . .105 ES82
Petersfield Av, Rom. RM3 . . . .52 FL51
  Slough SL2 . . . . .74 AU74
  Staines TW18 . . . . .114 BJ92
Petersfield Cl, N18 . . . . .46 DQ50
  Romford RM3 . . . . .52 FN51
Petersfield Ri, SW15 . . . . . . .119 CV88
Petersfield Rd, W3 . . . . .98 CQ75
  Staines TW18 . . . . .114 BJ92
PETERSHAM, Rich. 118 CL88
Petersham Av, W.Byf. (Byfleet)
  KT14 . . . . .152 BL112
Petersham Cl, Rich. TW10 . . .117 CK89
  Sutton SM1 . . . . .158 DA106
  West Byfleet (Byfleet)
  KT14 . . . . .152 BL112
Petersham Dr, Orp. BR5 . . . . .145 ET96
Petersham Gdns, Orp. BR5 . . .145 ET96
Petersham La, SW7 . . . . .100 DC76
Petersham Ms, SW7 . . . . . . .100 DC76
Petersham Pl, SW7 . . . . .100 DC76
Petersham Rd, Rich. TW10 . . .118 CL86
Petersham Ter, Croy. CR0
  off Richmond Grn 141 DL104
Peters Hill, EC4 . . . . .197 H10
Peter's La, EC1 . . . . .196 G6
Peterslea, Kings L. WD4 . . . . . .7 BP29
Petersmead Ri, Tad. KT20 . . . .173 CW122
Peters Path, SE26 . . . . .122 DV91
Peterstone Rd, SE2 . . . . .106 EV76
Peterstow Cl, SW19 . . . . .119 CY89
Peter St, W1 . . . . .195 L10
  Gravesend DA12 . . . . .131 GH87
Peterwood Way, Croy. CR0 . . .141 DM103
Petherton Rd, N5 . . . . .66 DQ64
Petley Rd, W6 . . . . .99 CW79
Peto Pl, NW1 . . . . .195 J4
Peto St N, E16 . . . . .86 EF73
Petrie Cl, NW2 . . . . .81 CY65
★ Petrie Mus of Egyptian
  Archaeology, WC1
  off Malet Pl 195 M5
Pett Cl, Horn. RM11 . . . . .71 FH61
Petten Cl, Orp. BR5 . . . . .146 EX102
Petten Gro, Orp. BR5 . . . . . . .146 EW102
Petters Rd, Ashtd. KT21 . . . . .172 CM116
Petticoat La, E1 . . . . .197 N7
Petticoat Sq, E1 . . . . .197 P8
★ Petticoat La (Mkt), E1 . . . . .197 N7
Pettits Boul, Rom. RM1 . . . . . .51 FE53
Pettits Cl, Rom. RM1 . . . . .51 FE54
Pettits La, Rom. RM1 . . . . .51 FE54
Pettits La N, Rom. RM1 . . . . . .51 FD53
Pettits Pl, Dag. RM10 . . . . . . .70 FA64
Pettits Rd, Dag. RM10 . . . . . . .70 FA64
Pettley Gdns, Rom. RM7 . . . . .71 FD57
Pettman Cres, SE28 . . . . .105 ER76
Pettsgrove Av, Wem. HA0 . . . .61 CJ64
Petts Hill, Nthlt. UB5 . . . . .60 CB64
Petts La, Shep. TW17 . . . . . . .134 BN98
Pett St, SE18 . . . . .104 EL77
Petts Wd Rd, Orp. BR5 . . . . . .145 EQ99
PETTS WOOD, Orp. 145 EQ99
⚇ Petts Wood 145 EQ99
Petty France, SW1 . . . . .199 L6
Pettys Cl, Wal.Cr. (Chsht.)
  EN8 . . . . .15 DX28
Petworth Cl, Couls. CR5 . . . . .175 DJ119
  Northolt UB5 . . . . .78 BZ66
Petworth Gdns, SW20
  off Hidcote Gdns 139 CV97
  Uxbridge UB10 . . . . .77 BQ67
Petworth Rd, N12 . . . . .44 DE50
  Bexleyheath DA6 . . . . .126 FA85
Petworth St, SW11 . . . . .100 DE81
Petworth Way, Horn. RM12 . . . .71 FF63
Petyt Pl, SW3 off Old Ch St . . .100 DE79
Petyward, SW3 . . . . .198 C9
Pevensey Av, N11 . . . . .45 DK50
  Enfield EN1 . . . . .30 DR40
Pevensey Cl, Islw. TW7 . . . . . .96 CC80
Pevensey Rd, E7 . . . . .68 EF63
  SW17 . . . . .120 DD91
  Feltham TW13 . . . . .116 BY90
Peverel, E6 off Downings 87 EN72
Peverel Ho, Dag. RM10 . . . . . .70 FA61
Peveret Cl, N11
  off Woodland Rd 45 DH50
Peveril Dr, Tedd. TW11 . . . . . .117 CD92
Pewsey Cl, E4 . . . . .47 EA50
Peyton Pl, SE10 . . . . .103 EC80
Peyton's Cotts, Red. RH1 . . . .185 DM122
Pharaoh Cl, Mitch. CR4 . . . . .140 DF101
Pharaoh's Island, Shep.
  TW17 . . . . .134 BM103
Pheasant Cl, E16
  off Maplin Rd 86 EG72
  Purley CR8
  off Partridge Knoll 159 DP113
Pheasant Hill, Ch.St.G. HP8 . . .36 AW47
Pheasants Way, Rick. WD3 . . . .38 BH45
Pheasant Wk, Ger.Cr. (Chal.St.P.)
  SL9 . . . . .36 AX49
Phelp St, SE17 . . . . .102 DR79
Phelps Way, Hayes UB3 . . . . . .95 BT77
Phene St, SW3 . . . . .100 DE79
Philan Way, Rom. RM5 . . . . . .51 FD51
Philbeach Gdns, SW5 . . . . . .100 DA78
Phil Brown Pl, SW8
  off Heath Rd 101 DH82
Philchurch Pl, E1
  off Ellen St 84 DU72
Philimore Cl, SE18 . . . . .105 ES78
Philip Av, Rom. RM7 . . . . .71 FD60
  Swanley BR8 . . . . .147 FD98
Philip Cl, Brwd. CM15 . . . . . . .54 FV44
  Romford RM7
  off Philip Av 71 FD60
Philip Gdns, Croy. CR0 . . . . . .143 DZ103
Philip La, N15 . . . . .66 DR56
Philipot Path, SE9 . . . . .125 EM86
Philippa Gdns, SE9 . . . . .124 EK85
Philippa Way, Grays RM16 . . .111 GH77
Philip Rd, Rain. RM13 . . . . . . .89 FE69

Philip Rd, Stai. TW18 . . . . . . .114 BK93
Philips Cl, Cars. SM5 . . . . . . .140 DG102
Philip St, E13 . . . . .86 EG70
Philip Sydney Rd, Grays
  RM16 . . . . .109 FX78
Philip Wk, SE15 . . . . .102 DU83
Phillida Rd, Rom. RM3 . . . . . .52 FN54
Phillimore Gdns, NW10 . . . . . .81 CW67
  W8 . . . . .100 DA75
Phillimore Gdns Cl, W8
  off Phillimore Gdns 100 DA76
Phillimore Pl, W8 . . . . .100 DA75
  Radlett WD7 . . . . .25 CE36
Phillippers, Wat. WD25 . . . . . .24 BY35
Phillipp St, N1 . . . . .84 DS67
Phillips Cl, Dart. DA1 . . . . . . .127 FH86
Philpot La, EC3 . . . . .197 M10
  Woking (Chobham) GU24 . .150 AV113
Philpot Path, Ilf. IG1
  off Sunnyside Rd 69 EQ62
Philpots Cl, West Dr. UB7 . . . .76 BK73
Philpot Sq, SW6
  off Peterborough Rd 100 DB83
Philpot St, E1 . . . . .84 DV72
Phineas Pett Rd, SE9 . . . . . . .104 EL83
◆ Phipps Bridge 140 DC97
Phipps Br Rd, SW19 . . . . . . .140 DC96
  Mitcham CR4 . . . . .140 DC96
Phipps Hatch La, Enf. EN2 . . . .30 DQ38
Phipp's Ms, SW1 . . . . .199 H7
Phipp St, EC2 . . . . .197 M4
Phoebeth Rd, SE4 . . . . .123 EA85
Phoenix Cl, E8 off Stean St . . .84 DT67
  E17 . . . . .47 DZ54
  Epsom KT19 off Queen
  Alexandra's Way 156 CN112
  Northwood HA6 . . . . .39 BT49
  West Wickham BR4 . . . . . .144 EE103
Phoenix Dr, Kes. BR2 . . . . . . .144 EK104
Phoenix Pk, Brent. TW8 . . . . . .97 CK78
Phoenix Pl, WC1 . . . . .196 C4
  Dartford DA1 . . . . .128 FK87
Phoenix Rd, NW1 . . . . .195 M2
  SE20 . . . . .122 DW93
Phoenix St, WC2 . . . . .195 N9
Phoenix Way, Houns. TW5 . . . .96 BW79
Phoenix Wf, SE10 . . . . .205 K4
Phoenix Wf Rd, SE1 . . . . .202 A5
Phoenix Yd, WC1
  off King's Cross Rd 83 DM69
★ Photographers' Gall, WC2
  off Great Newport St 195 N10
Phygtle, The, Ger.Cr. (Chal.St.P.)
  SL9 . . . . .36 AY51
Phyllis Av, N.Mal. KT3 . . . . . .139 CV99
★ Physical Energy Statue,
  W2 . . . . .82 DC74
Physic Pl, SW3
  off Royal Hosp Rd 100 DF79
Piazza, The, WC2
  off Covent Gdn 83 DL73
Picardy Manorway, Belv.
  DA17 . . . . .107 FB76
Picardy Rd, Belv. DA17 . . . . .106 FA77
Picardy St, Belv. DA17 . . . . . .106 FA76
Piccadilly, W1 . . . . .199 J3
Piccadilly Arc, SW1 . . . . .199 K2
◆ Piccadilly Circus 199 L1
Piccadilly Circ, W1 . . . . .199 M1
Piccadilly Pl, W1 . . . . .199 L1
Pickard St, EC1 . . . . .196 G2
Pickering Av, E6 . . . . .87 EN68
Pickering Cl, E9
  off Cassland Rd 85 DX66
Pickering Gdns, N11 . . . . .44 DG51
  Croydon CR0 . . . . .142 DT100
Pickering Ms, W2
  off Bishops Br Rd 82 DB72
Pickering Pl, SW1 . . . . .199 L3
Pickering St, N1 off Essex Rd . .83 DP67
Picketts Cl, Bushey (Bushey Hth.)
  WD23 . . . . .41 CD46
Pickets St, SW12 . . . . .121 DH87
Pickett Cft, Stan. HA7 . . . . . . .41 CK53
Picketts Lock La, N9 . . . . .46 DW47
Pickford Cl, Bexh. DA7 . . . . . .106 EY82
Pickford Dr, Slou. SL3 . . . . . . .75 AZ74
Pickford Gdn, Slou. SL1
  off Stoke Poges La 74 AS74
Pickford La, Bexh. DA7 . . . . . .106 EY82
Pickford Rd, Bexh. DA7 . . . . .106 EY83
Pickfords Wf, N1 . . . . .197 H1
Pick Hill, Wal.Abb. EN9 . . . . . .16 EF32
Pickhurst Grn, Brom. BR2 . . . .144 EF101
Pickhurst La, Brom. BR2 . . . . .144 EF102
  West Wickham BR4 . . . . . .144 EE100
Pickhurst Mead, Brom. BR2 . . .144 EF101
Pickhurst Pk, Brom. BR2 . . . .144 EE99
Pickhurst Ri, W.Wick. BR4 . . . .143 EC101
Pickins Piece, Slou. (Horton)
  SL3 . . . . .93 BA82
Pickle Herring St, SE1
  off Tooley St 84 DS74
Pickmoss La, Sev. (Otford)
  TN14 . . . . .181 FH116
Pickwick Cl, Houns. TW4
  off Dorney Way 116 BY85
Pickwick Ct, SE9
  off West Pk 124 EL88
Pickwick Gdns, Grav. (Nthflt.)
  DA11 . . . . .130 GD90
Pickwick Ms, N18 . . . . .46 DS50
Pickwick Pl, Har. HA1 . . . . .61 CE59
Pickwick Rd, SE21 . . . . .122 DR87
Pickwick St, SE1 . . . . .201 H5
Pickwick Ter, Slou. SL2
  off Maple Cres 74 AV73
Pickwick Way, Chis. BR7 . . . . .125 EQ93
Pickworth Cl, SW8
  off Kenchester Cl 101 DL80
Picquets Way, Bans. SM7 . . . .173 CY116
Picton Pl, W1 . . . . .194 G9
  Surbiton KT6 . . . . .138 CN102
Picton St, SE5 . . . . .102 DR80
Piedmont Rd, SE18 . . . . .105 ER78
Pield Heath Av, Uxb. UB8 . . . . .76 BN70

Pield Heath Rd, Uxb. UB8 . . . .76 BM71
Piercing Hill, Epp. (They.B.)
  CM16 . . . . .33 ER35
Pier Head, E1 . . . . .202 D3
Piermont Grn, SE22 . . . . . . .122 DV86
Piermont Pl, Brom. BR1 . . . .144 EL96
Piermont Rd, SE22 . . . . .122 DV86
Pier Par, E16 off Pier Rd 105 EN75
Pierrepoint Arc, N1
  off Islington High St 83 DP68
Pierrepoint Rd, W3 . . . . .80 CP73
Pierrepoint Row, N1
  off Islington High St 83 DP68
Pier Rd, E16 . . . . .105 EM75
  Erith DA8 . . . . .107 FE79
  Feltham TW14 . . . . .115 BV85
  Gravesend (Nthflt.) DA11 .131 GF86
  Greenhithe DA9 . . . . .109 FV84
Pier St, E14 . . . . .204 E8
Pier Ter, SW18
  off Jew's Row 100 DC84
Pier Wk, Grays RM17 . . . . . .110 GA80
Pier Way, SE28 . . . . .105 ER76
Pigeonhouse La, Couls. CR5 .184 DC125
Pigeon La, Hmptn. TW12 . . . .116 CA91
Piggs Cor, Grays RM17 . . . .110 GC76
Piggy La, Rick. (Chorl.) WD3 . .21 BB44
Pigott St, E14 . . . . .85 EA72
Pike Cl, Brom. BR1 . . . . .124 EH92
  Uxbridge UB10 . . . . .76 BM67
Pike La, Upmin. RM14 . . . . . .73 FT64
Pike Rd, NW7
  off Ellesmere Av 42 CR49
Pikes End, Pnr. HA5 . . . . . . .59 BV55
Pikes Hill, Epsom KT17 . . . .156 CS113
Pikestone Cl, Hayes UB4
  off Berrydale Rd 78 BY70
Pike Way, Epp. (N.Wld.Bas.)
  CM16 . . . . .18 FA27
Pilgrimage St, SE1 . . . . .201 K5
Pilgrim Cl, Mord. SM4 . . . . . .140 DB101
  St. Albans (Park St.) AL2 . . . .8 CC27
Pilgrim Hill, SE27 . . . . .122 DQ91
  Orpington BR5 . . . . .146 EY96
Pilgrims Cl, N13 . . . . .45 DM49
  Brentwood CM15 . . . . .54 FT43
  Northolt UB5 . . . . .60 CC64
  Watford WD25 off Kytes Dr . .8 BX33
Pilgrims Cl, SE3 . . . . .104 EG81
  Dartford DA1 . . . . .128 FN85
PILGRIM'S HATCH, Brwd. 54 FU42
Pilgrims La, Cat. CR3 . . . . .185 DM125
  Grays (N.Stfd.) RM16 . . . . .91 FW74
  Oxted (Titsey) RH8 . . . . . .188 EH125
  Westerham TN16 . . . . .178 EL123
Pilgrims Ms, E14
  off Blackwall Way 85 EC73
Pilgrims Pl, NW3
  off Hampstead High St 64 DD63
  Reigate RH2 . . . . .184 DA132
Pilgrims Ri, Barn. EN4 . . . . . .28 DE43
Pilgrims Rd, Swans. DA10 . . .110 FY84
Pilgrim St, EC4 . . . . .196 F9
Pilgrims Vw, Green. DA9 . . . .129 FW86
Pilgrims Way, E6
  off High St N 86 EL67
  N19 . . . . .65 DK60
Pilgrims' Way, Bet. RH3 . . . .183 CY131
  Caterham CR3 . . . . .185 DN126
Pilgrims' Way, Dart. DA1 . . . .128 FN84
Pilgrims' Way, Red. RH1 . . . .185 DJ127
Pilgrims' Way, Reig. RH2 . . . .184 DA131
  Sevenoaks (Chev.) TN14 . .180 EV121
  South Croydon CR2 . . . . . .160 DT106
Pilgrims' Way, Wem. HA9 . . . .62 CP60
Pilgrims Way, West. TN16 . . .179 EM123
Pilgrims Way W, Sev. (Otford)
  TN14 . . . . .181 FD116
Pilkington Rd, SE15 . . . . . . .102 DV82
  Orpington BR6 . . . . .145 EQ103
Pillions La, Hayes UB4 . . . . . .77 BR70
Pilot Cl, SE8 . . . . .103 DZ79
Pilots Pl, Grav. DA12 . . . . . .131 GJ86
Pilsdon Cl, SW19
  off Inner Pk Rd 119 CX88
Piltdown Rd, Wat. WD19 . . . . .40 BX49
Pilton Est, The, Croy. (Pitlake) CR0
  off Pitlake 141 DP103
Pilton Pl, SE17 . . . . .201 J10
Pimento Ct, W5 off Olive Rd . .97 CK76
PIMLICO, SW1 . . . . .199 K10
⊖ Pimlico 199 M10
Pimlico Rd, SW1 . . . . .198 F10
Pimlico Wk, N1 . . . . .197 M2
Pimpernel Way, Rom. RM3 . . .52 FK51
Pinchbeck Rd, Orp. BR6 . . . .163 ET107
Pinchfield, Rick. (Map.Cr.)
  WD3 . . . . .37 BE50
Pinchin St, E1 . . . . .84 DU73
Pincott Pl, SE4 . . . . .103 DX84
Pincott Rd, SW19 . . . . .120 DC94
  Bexleyheath DA6 . . . . .126 FA85
Pindar St, EC2 . . . . .197 M6
PINDEN, Dart. 149 FW96
Pindock Ms, W9
  off Warwick Av 82 DB70
Pineapple Ct, SW1 . . . . .199 K6
Pineapple Rd, Amer. HP7 . . . .20 AT39
Pine Av, E15 . . . . .67 ED64
  Gravesend DA12 . . . . .131 GK88
  West Wickham BR4 . . . . . .143 EB102
Pine Cl, E10 off Walnut Rd . . .67 EB61
  N14 . . . . .45 DJ45
  N19 off Hargrave Pk 65 DJ61
  SE20 . . . . .142 DW96
  Addlestone (New Haw)
    KT15 . . . . .152 BH111
  Kenley CR8 . . . . .176 DR117
  Stanmore HA7 . . . . .41 CH49
  Swanley BR8 . . . . .147 FF98
  Waltham Cross (Chsht.)
    EN8 . . . . .15 DX28
  Woking GU21 . . . . .166 AW117
Pine Coombe, Croy. CR0 . . . .161 DX109
Pine Ct, Upmin. RM14 . . . . . .72 FN63
Pine Cres, Brwd. CM13 . . . . .55 GD43

Pine Cres, Cars. SM5 . . . . . .158 DD111
Pinecrest Gdns, Orp. BR6 . . .163 EP105
Pinecroft, Brwd. CM13 . . . . . .55 GB45
  Romford (Gidea Pk.) RM2 . .72 FJ56
Pinecroft Cres, Barn. EN5
  off Hillside Gdns 27 CY42
Pinedene, SE15
  off Meeting Ho La 102 DV81
Pinefield Cl, E14 . . . . .85 EA73
Pine Gdns, Ruis. HA4 . . . . . . .59 BV60
  Surbiton KT5 . . . . .138 CN100
Pine Glade, Orp. BR6 . . . . . .163 EM105
Pine Gro, N4 . . . . .65 DL61
  N20 . . . . .43 CZ46
  SW19 . . . . .119 CZ92
  Bushey WD23 . . . . .24 BZ40
  Hatfield AL9 . . . . .12 DB25
  St. Albans (Brick.Wd.) AL2 . . .8 BZ30
  Weybridge KT13 . . . . .153 BP106
Pine Gro Ms, Wey. KT13 . . . .153 BQ106
Pine Hill, Epsom KT18 . . . . . .172 CR115
Pinehurst, Sev. TN14 . . . . . .191 FL121
Pinehurst Cl, Abb.L. WD5 . . . .7 BS32
  Tadworth (Kgswd.) KT20 . .174 DA122
Pinehurst Wk, Orp. BR6 . . . .145 ES102
Pinelands Cl, SE3
  off St. John's Pk 104 EF80
Pinel Cl, Vir.W. GU25 . . . . . .132 AY98
Pinemartin Cl, NW2 . . . . .63 CW62
Pine Ms, NW10
  off Clifford Gdns 81 CX68
Pineneedle La, Sev. TN13 . . .191 FH123
Pine Pl, Bans. SM7 . . . . .157 CX114
  Hayes UB4 . . . . .77 BT70
Pine Ridge, Cars. SM5 . . . . .158 DG109
Pine Rd, N11 . . . . .44 DG47
  NW2 . . . . .63 CW63
  Woking GU22 . . . . .166 AW120
Pines, The, N14 . . . . .29 DJ43
  Borehamwood WD6
    off Anthony Rd 26 CM40
  Coulsdon CR5 . . . . .175 DH118
  Purley CR8 . . . . .159 DP113
  Sunbury-on-Thames
    TW16 . . . . .135 BU97
  Woking GU21 . . . . .151 AZ114
  Woodford Green IG8 . . . . . .48 EG48
Pines Av, Enf. EN1 . . . . .30 DV36
Pines Cl, Nthwd. HA6 . . . . . . .39 BS51
Pines Rd, Brom. BR1 . . . . . .144 EL96
Pine St, EC1 . . . . .196 D4
Pinetree Cl, Ger.Cr. (Chal.St.P.)
  SL9 . . . . .36 AW52
Pine Tree Cl, Houns. TW5 . . . .95 BV81
Pine Tree Hill, Wok. GU22 . . .167 BD116
Pine Trees Dr, Uxb. UB10 . . . .58 BL63
Pine Vw Manor, Epp. CM16 . . .18 EU30
Pine Wk, Bans. SM7 . . . . . . .174 DF117
  Bromley BR1 . . . . .144 EJ95
  Carshalton SM5 . . . . .158 DD110
  Caterham CR3 . . . . .176 DT122
  Cobham KT11 . . . . .154 BX114
  Surbiton KT5 . . . . .138 CN100
Pine Way, Egh. (Eng.Grn.) TW20
  off Ashwood Rd 112 AV93
Pine Wd, Sun. TW16 . . . . . . .135 BU95
Pinewood Av, Add. (New Haw)
  KT15 . . . . .152 BJ109
  Pinner HA5 . . . . .40 CB51
  Rainham RM13 . . . . .89 FH70
  Sevenoaks TN14 . . . . .191 FK121
  Sidcup DA15 . . . . .125 ES88
  Uxbridge UB8 . . . . .76 BM72
Pinewood Cl, Borwd. WD6 . . .26 CR39
  Croydon CR0 . . . . .143 DY104
  Gerrards Cross SL9
    off Dukes Wd Av 56 AY59
  Iver SL0 . . . . .75 BC66
  Northwood HA6 . . . . .39 BV50
  Orpington BR6 . . . . .145 ER102
  Pinner HA5 . . . . .40 CB51
  Watford WD17 . . . . .23 BU39
  Woking GU21 . . . . .151 BA114
Pinewood Dr, Orp. BR6 . . . . .163 ES106
  Potters Bar EN6 . . . . .11 CZ31
  Staines TW18
    off Cotswold Cl 114 BG92
Pinewood Grn, Iver SL0 . . . . .75 BC66
Pinewood Gro, W5 . . . . .79 CJ72
  Addlestone (New Haw)
    KT15 . . . . .152 BH110
Pinewood Ms, Stai. (Stanw.) TW19
  off Oaks Rd 114 BK86
Pinewood Pk, Add. (New Haw)
  KT15 . . . . .152 BH111
Pinewood Ride, Iver SL0 . . . . .75 BA68
  Slough SL3
    off Fulmer Common Rd . . .75 BA65
Pinewood Rd, SE2 . . . . .106 EX79
  Bromley BR2 . . . . .144 EG98
  Feltham TW13 . . . . .115 BV90
  Iver SL0 . . . . .75 BB65
  Romford (Hav.at.Bow.)
    RM4 . . . . .51 FC49
  Virginia Water GU25 . . . . . .132 AU98
Pinewood Way, Brwd. CM13 . .55 GD43
Pinfold Rd, SW16 . . . . .121 DL91
  Bushey WD23 . . . . .24 BZ40
Pinglestone Cl, West Dr. UB7 . .94 BL80
Pinkcoat Cl, Felt. TW13
  off Tanglewood Way 115 BV90
Pinkerton Pl, SW16
  off Riggindale Rd 121 DK91
Pinkham Way, N11 . . . . .44 DG52
Pinks Hill, Swan. BR8 . . . . . .147 FE99
Pinkwell Av, Hayes UB3 . . . . .95 BR77
Pinkwell La, Hayes UB3 . . . . .95 BQ77
Pinley Gdns, Dag. RM9
  off Stamford Rd 88 EV67
Pinnacle Hill, Bexh. DA7 . . . .107 FB84
Pinnacle Hill N, Bexh. DA7 . .107 FB83
Pinnacles, Wal.Abb. EN9 . . . .16 EE34
Pinn Cl, Uxb. UB8
  off High Rd 76 BK72
Pinnell Rd, SE9 . . . . .104 EK84
PINNER 60 BY56
⊖ Pinner 60 BY56

Pinner Ct, Pnr. HA5 . . . . .60 CA56
PINNER GREEN, Pnr. 40 BW53
Pinner Grn, Pnr. HA5 . . . . . . .40 BW54
Pinner Gro, Pnr. HA5 . . . . . . .60 BY56
Pinner Hill, Pnr. HA5 . . . . . . .40 BW53
Pinner Hill Rd, Pnr. HA5 . . . . .40 BW54
Pinner Pk, Pnr. HA5 . . . . .40 CA53
Pinner Pk Av, Har. HA2 . . . . . .60 CB57
Pinner Pk Gdns, Har. HA2 . . . .40 CC54
Pinner Rd, Har. HA1, HA2 . . . .60 CB57
  Northwood HA6 . . . . .39 BT53
  Pinner HA5 . . . . .60 CB55
  Watford WD19 . . . . .24 BX44
Pinner Vw, Har. HA1, HA2 . . . .60 CC58
PINNERWOOD PARK, Pnr. . . .40 BW52
Pinnocks Av, Grav. DA11 . . . .131 GH88
Pinn Way, Ruis. HA4 . . . . .59 BS59
Pinstone Way, Ger.Cr. SL9 . . .57 BB61
Pintail Cl, E6 off Swan App . . .86 EL71
Pintail Rd, Wdf.Grn. IG8 . . . . .48 EH52
Pintail Way, Hayes UB4 . . . . .78 BX71
Pinter Ho, SW9
  off Grantham Rd 101 DL82
Pinto Cl, Borwd. WD6
  off Percheron Rd 26 CR44
Pinto Way, SE3 . . . . .104 EH84
Pioneer Cl, Croy. CR0 . . . . . .161 EA109
Pioneers Ind Pk, Croy. CR0 . .141 DL102
Pioneer St, SE15 . . . . .102 DU81
Pioneer Way, W12
  off Du Cane Rd 81 CV72
  Swanley BR8 . . . . .147 FE97
  Watford WD18 . . . . .23 BT44
Piper Cl, N7 . . . . .65 DM64
Piper Rd, Kings.T. KT1 . . . . . .138 CN97
Pipers Cl, Cob. KT11 . . . . . . .170 BX115
Pipers End, Vir.W. GU25 . . . .132 AX97
Piper's Gdns, Croy. CR0 . . . .143 DY101
Pipers Grn, NW9 . . . . .62 CQ57
Pipers Grn La, Edg. HA8 . . . . .42 CL48
Pipewell Rd, Cars. SM5 . . . . .140 DE100
Pippin Cl, NW2 . . . . .63 CV62
  Croydon CR0 . . . . .143 DZ102
  Radlett (Shenley) WD7 . . . . .9 CK33
Pippins, The, Slou. SL3
  off Pickford Dr 75 AZ74
Pippins Cl, West Dr. UB7 . . . .94 BK76
Pippins Ct, Ashf. TW15 . . . . .115 BP93
Piquet Rd, SE20 . . . . .142 DW96
Pirbright Cres, Croy. (New Adgtn.)
  CR0 . . . . .161 EC107
Pirbright Rd, SW18 . . . . .119 CZ88
Pirie Cl, SE5 off Denmark Hill .102 DR83
Pirie St, E16 . . . . .86 EH74
Pirrip Cl, Grav. DA12 . . . . . . .131 GM89
Pitcairn Cl, Rom. RM7 . . . . . .70 FA56
Pitcairn Rd, Mitch. CR4 . . . . .120 DF94
Pitcairn's Path, Har. HA2
  off Eastcote Rd 60 CC62
Pitchfont La, Oxt. RH8 . . . . . .178 EF124
Pitchford St, E15 . . . . .85 ED66
Pitfield Cres, SE28 . . . . .88 EU74
Pitfield Est, N1 . . . . .197 L2
Pitfield St, N1 . . . . .197 M3
Pitfield Way, NW10 . . . . .80 CQ65
  Enfield EN3 . . . . .30 DW39
Pitfold Cl, SE12 . . . . .124 EG86
Pitfold Rd, SE12 . . . . .124 EG86
Pitlake, Croy. CR0 . . . . .141 DP103
Pitman St, SE5 . . . . .102 DQ80
Pitmaston Ho, SE13
  off Lewisham Rd 103 EC82
Pitsea Pl, E1 off Pitsea St 85 DX72
Pitsea St, E1 . . . . .85 DX72
Pitshanger La, W5 . . . . .79 CH70
★ Pitshanger Manor & Gall,
  W5 (Ealing) 79 CJ74
Pitshanger Pk, W13 . . . . .79 CJ69
Pitson Cl, Add. KT15 . . . . . . .152 BK105
Pitt Cres, SW19 . . . . .120 DB91
Pittman Gdns, Ilf. IG1 . . . . . . .69 EQ64
Pitt Pl, Epsom KT17 . . . . . . .156 CS114
Pitt Rd, Croy. CR0 . . . . .142 DQ99
  Epsom KT17 . . . . .156 CS114
  Orpington BR6 . . . . .163 EQ105
  Thornton Heath CR7 . . . . . .142 DQ99
Pitt's Head Ms, W1 . . . . .198 G3
Pittsmead Av, Brom. BR2 . . . .144 EG101
Pitt St, W8 . . . . .100 DA75
Pittville Gdns, SE25 . . . . .142 DU97
Pittwood, Brwd. CM15 . . . . . .55 GA46
Pitwood Grn, Tad. KT20 . . . . .173 CW121
Pitwood Pk Ind Est, Tad. KT20
  off Waterfield 173 CV120
Pixfield Ct, Brom. BR2
  off Beckenham La 144 EF96
Pixley St, E14 . . . . .85 DZ72
Pixton Way, Croy. CR0 . . . . . .161 DY109
Place Fm Av, Orp. BR6 . . . . .145 ER102
Place Fm Rd, Red. (Bletch.)
  RH1 . . . . .186 DR130
Placehouse La, Couls. CR5 . .175 DM119
Plain, The, Epp. CM16 . . . . . .18 EV29
PLAISTOW, E13 . . . . .86 EF69
PLAISTOW, Brom. 124 EF93
⊖ Plaistow 86 EF68
Plaistow Gro, E15 . . . . .86 EF67
  Bromley BR1 . . . . .124 EH94
ⓗ Plaistow Hosp, E13 . . . . . .86 EJ68
Plaistow La, Brom. BR1 . . . . .124 EH94
Plaistow Pk Rd, E13 . . . . .86 EH68
Plaistow Rd, E13 . . . . .86 EF67
  E15 . . . . .86 EF67
Plaitford Cl, Rick. WD3 . . . . . .38 BL47
Plane, The, Grav. (Nthflt.)
  DA11 . . . . .130 GD87
Planes, The, Cher. KT16 . . . .134 BJ101
Plane St, SE26 . . . . .122 DV90
Plane Tree Cres, Felt. TW13 . .115 BV90
Plane Tree Wk, N2 . . . . .64 DD55
  SE19 off Central Hill 122 DS93
Plantagenet Pl, Wal.Abb. EN9 . .15 EB33
Plantagenet Cl, Wor.Pk. KT4 .156 CR105

Plantagenet Gdns, Rom.
  RM6 . . . . .70 EX59
Plantagenet Pl, Rom. RM6
  off Broomfield Rd 70 EX59
Plantagenet Rd, Barn. EN5 . . .28 DC42
Plantain Gdns, E11
  off Hollydown Way 67 ED62
Plantain Pl, SE1 . . . . .201 K4
Plantation, The, SE3 . . . . . . .104 EG82
Plantation Cl, Green. DA9 . . .129 FT86
Plantation Dr, Orp. BR5 . . . . .146 EX102
Plantation La, Warl. CR6 . . . .177 DY119
Plantation Rd, Amer. HP6 . . . .20 AS37
  Erith DA8 . . . . .107 FG81
  Swanley BR8 . . . . .127 FG94
Plantation Way, Amer. HP6 . . .20 AS37
Plantation Wf, SW11 . . . . . . .100 DC83
Plasel Ct, E13 off Plashet Rd . .86 EG67
Plashet Gdns, Brwd. CM13 . . .55 GA49
Plashet Gro, E6 . . . . .86 EJ67
Plashet Rd, E13 . . . . .86 EG67
Plassy Rd, SE6 . . . . .123 EB87
Platford Grn, Horn. RM11 . . . .72 FL56
Platina St, EC2 . . . . .197 L4
Plato Rd, SW2 . . . . .101 DL84
Platt, The, SW15 . . . . .99 CX83
Platts Av, Wat. WD17 . . . . . . .23 BV41
Platt's Eyot, Hmptn. TW12 . .136 CA96
Platt's La, NW3 . . . . .64 DA62
Platts Rd, Enf. EN3 . . . . .30 DW39
Platt St, NW1 . . . . .83 DK68
Plawsfield Rd, Beck. BR3 . . . .143 DX95
Plaxtol Cl, Brom. BR1 . . . . . .144 EJ95
Plaxtol Rd, Erith DA8 . . . . . .106 FA80
Plaxton Ct, E11
  off Woodhouse Rd 68 EF62
Playfair St, W6
  off Winslow Rd 99 CW78
Playfield Av, Rom. RM5 . . . . .51 FC53
Playfield Cres, SE22 . . . . . . .122 DT85
Playfield Rd, Edg. HA8 . . . . . .42 CQ54
Playford Rd, N4 . . . . .65 DM61
Playgreen Way, SE6 . . . . . . .123 EA91
Playground Cl, Beck. BR3
  off Churchfields Rd 143 DX96
Playhouse Yd, EC4 . . . . .196 F9
Plaza Par, NW6
  off Kilburn High Rd 82 DB68
Plaza Shop Cen, The, W1 . . . .83 DJ72
Plaza W, Houns. TW3 . . . . . . .96 CB81
Pleasance, The, SW15 . . . . . .99 CV84
Pleasance Rd, SW15 . . . . . . .119 CV85
  Orpington BR5 . . . . .146 EV96
Pleasant Gro, Croy. CR0 . . . .143 DZ104
Pleasant Pl, N1 . . . . .83 DP66
  Rickmansworth (Map.Cr.)
    WD3 . . . . .37 BE52
  Walton-on-Thames KT12 . .154 BW107
Pleasant Row, NW1 . . . . .83 DH67
Pleasant Vw, Erith DA8 . . . . .107 FE78
Pleasant Vw Pl, Orp. BR6
  off High St 163 EP106
Pleasant Way, Wem. HA0 . . . .79 CJ68
Pleasure Pit Rd, Ashtd. KT21 .172 CP118
Plender St, NW1 . . . . .83 DJ67
Pleshey Rd, N7 . . . . .65 DK63
Plesman Way, Wall. SM6 . . . .159 DL109
Plevna Cres, N15 . . . . .66 DS58
Plevna Rd, N9 . . . . .46 DU48
  Hampton TW12 . . . . .136 CB95
Plevna Rd Shop Cen, N9
  off Plevna Rd 46 DV47
Plevna St, E14 . . . . .204 D6
Pleydell Av, SE19 . . . . .122 DT94
  W6 . . . . .99 CT77
Pleydell Ct, EC4 . . . . .196 E9
Pleydell Est, EC1
  off Radnor St 84 DQ69
Pleydell St, EC4 . . . . .196 E9
Plimsoll Cl, E14
  off Grundy St 85 EB72
Plimsoll Rd, N4 . . . . .65 DN62
Plough Ct, EC3 . . . . .197 L10
Plough Fm Cl, Ruis. HA4 . . . . .59 BR58
Plough Hill, Pot.B. (Cuffley)
  EN6 . . . . .13 DL28
Plough Ind Est, Lthd. KT22 . .171 CH119
Plough La, SE22 . . . . .122 DT86
  SW17 . . . . .120 DB92
  SW19 . . . . .120 DB92
  Cobham (Down.) KT11 . . . .169 BU116
  Purley CR8 . . . . .159 DL109
  Rickmansworth (Sarratt)
    WD3 . . . . .5 BF33
  Slough (Stoke P.) SL2 . . . . .74 AV67
  Teddington TW11 . . . . .117 CG92
  Uxbridge (Hare.) UB9 . . . . .38 BJ51
  Wallington SM6 . . . . .159 DL105
Plough La Cl, Wall. SM6 . . . . .159 DL106
Ploughlees La, Slou. SL1 . . . .74 AS73
Ploughmans Cl, NW1
  off Crofters Way 83 DK67
Ploughmans End, Islw. TW7 . .117 CD85
Ploughmans Wk, N2
  off Long La 44 DC54
Plough Ms, SW11
  off Plough Ter 100 DD84
Plough Pl, EC4 . . . . .196 E8
Plough Ri, Upmin. RM14 . . . . .73 FS59
Plough Rd, SW11 . . . . .100 DD83
  Epsom KT19 . . . . .156 CR109
Plough St, E1 off Leman St . . .84 DU72
Plough Ter, SW11 . . . . .100 DD84
Plough Way, SE16 . . . . .203 J8
Plough Yd, EC2 . . . . .197 N5
Plover Cl, Stai. TW18
  off Waters Dr 113 BF90
Plover Gdns, Upmin. RM14 . . .73 FT60
Plover Way, SE16 . . . . .203 K6
  Hayes UB4 . . . . .78 BX72
Plowden Bldgs, EC4
  off Middle Temple La 83 DN72
Plowman Cl, N18 . . . . .46 DR50
Plowman Way, Dag. RM8 . . . .70 EW60
Plumbers Row, E1 . . . . .84 DU71
Plumbridge St, SE10
  off Blackheath Hill 103 EC81

Plum Cl, Felt. TW13
  off Highfield Rd 115 BU88
Plum Garth, Brent. TW8 . . . . .97 CK77
Plum La, SE18 . . . . .105 EP80
Plummer La, Mitch. CR4 . . . .140 DF96
Plummer Rd, SW4 . . . . .121 DK87
Plummers Cft, Sev. (Dunt.Grn.)
  TN13 . . . . .190 FE121
Plumpton Av, Horn. RM12 . . . .72 FL63
Plumpton Cl, Nthlt. UB5 . . . . .78 CA65
Plumpton Way, Cars. SM5 . . .140 DE104
PLUMSTEAD, SE18 . . . . .105 ES78
⇌ Plumstead 105 ER77
Plumstead Common Rd,
  SE18 . . . . .105 EP79
Plumstead High St, SE18 . . . .105 ES77
Plumstead Rd, SE18 . . . . . . .105 EP77
Plumtree Cl, Dag. RM10 . . . . .89 FB65
  Wallington SM6 . . . . .159 DK108
Plumtree Ct, EC4 . . . . .196 E8
Plumtree Mead, Loug. IG10 . . .33 EN43
Plymouth Dr, Sev. TN13 . . . .191 FJ124
Plymouth Ho, Rain. RM13 . . . .89 FF69
Plymouth Pk, Sev. TN13 . . . .191 FJ124
Plymouth Rd, E16 . . . . .86 EG71
  Bromley BR1 . . . . .144 EH95
  Grays (Chaff.Hun.) RM16 . .109 FW77
Plympton Av, NW6 . . . . .81 CZ66
Plympton Cl, Belv. DA17
  off Halifield Dr 106 EY76
Plympton Pl, NW8 . . . . .194 B5
Plympton Rd, NW6 . . . . .81 CZ66
Plympton St, NW8 . . . . .194 B5
Plymstock Rd, Well. DA16 . . .106 EW80
Pocketsdell La, Hem.H. (Bov.)
  HP3 . . . . .4 AX28
Pocklington Cl, NW9 . . . . .42 CS54
Pocock Av, West Dr. UB7 . . . .94 BM76
Pococks La, Wind. (Eton) SL4 .92 AS78
Pocock St, SE1 . . . . .200 F4
Podmore Rd, SW18 . . . . .100 DC84
Poets Gate, Wal.Cr. EN7 . . . . .14 DS28
Poets Rd, N5 . . . . .66 DR64
Poets Way, Har. HA1
  off Blawith Rd 61 CE56
Point, The, Ruis. HA4
  off Bedford Rd 59 BU63
Pointalls Cl, N3 . . . . .44 DC54
Point Cl, SE10 off Point Hill . .103 EC81
Pointer Cl, SE28 . . . . .88 EX72
Pointers, The, Ashtd. KT21 . .172 CL120
Pointers Cl, E14 . . . . .204 B10
Pointers Rd, Cob. KT11 . . . . .169 BQ116
Point Hill, SE10 . . . . .103 EC80
Point of Thomas Path, E1 . . .202 G1
Point Pl, Wem. HA9 . . . . .80 CP66
Point Pleasant, SW18 . . . . . .100 DA84
Poland Ho, E15 . . . . .85 ED67
Poland St, W1 . . . . .195 L9
Polebrook Rd, SE3 . . . . .104 EJ83
Pole Cat All, Brom. BR2 . . . .144 EF103
Polecroft La, SE6 . . . . .123 DZ89
Polehamptons, The, Hmptn. TW12
  off High St 116 CC94
Pole Hill Rd, E4 . . . . .47 EC45
  Hayes UB4 . . . . .77 BQ69
  Uxbridge UB10 . . . . .77 BQ69
Polesden Gdns, SW20 . . . . . .139 CV96
Polesden La, Wok. (Send M.)
  GU23 . . . . .167 BF122
Poles Hill, Rick. (Sarratt) WD3 . .5 BE33
Polesteeple Hill, West. (Bigg.H.)
  TN16 . . . . .178 EK117
Polesworth Ho, W2 . . . . .82 DA71
Polesworth Rd, Dag. RM9 . . . .88 EX66
Polhill, Sev. (Halst.) TN14 . . .181 FC115
Police Sta La, Bushey WD23
  off Sparrows Herne 40 CB45
Police Sta Rd, Walt. KT12 . . .154 BW107
★ Polish Institute & Sikorski
  Mus, SW7
  off Princes Gate 198 A5
Pollard Av, Uxb. (Denh.) UB9 . .57 BF58
Pollard Cl, E16 . . . . .86 EG73
  N7 . . . . .65 DM63
  Chigwell IG7 . . . . .50 EU50
  Windsor (Old Wind.) SL4 . .112 AV85
Pollard Rd, N20 . . . . .44 DE47
  Morden SM4 . . . . .140 DD99
  Woking GU22 . . . . .167 BB116
Pollard Row, E2 . . . . .84 DU69
Pollards, Rick. (Map.Cr.) WD3 . .37 BD50
Pollards Cl, Loug. IG10 . . . . . .32 EJ43
  Waltham Cross (Chsht.)
    EN7 . . . . .14 DQ29
Pollards Cres, SW16 . . . . . . .141 DL97
Pollards Hill E, SW16 . . . . . . .141 DM97
Pollards Hill N, SW16 . . . . . . .141 DL97
Pollards Hill S, SW16 . . . . . . .141 DL97
Pollards Hill W, SW16 . . . . . .141 DL97
Pollards Oak Cres, Oxt. RH8 .188 EG132
Pollards Oak Rd, Oxt. RH8 . .188 EG132
Pollard St, E2 . . . . .84 DU69
Pollards Wd Hill, Oxt. RH8 . . .188 EH130
Pollards Wd Rd, SW16 . . . . . .141 DL96
  Oxted RH8 . . . . .188 EH131
Pollard Wk, Sid. DA14 . . . . . .126 EW93
Pollen St, W1 . . . . .195 J9
Pollitt Dr, NW8
  off Cunningham Pl 82 DD70
★ Pollock's Toy Mus, W1 . . .195 L6
Pollyhaugh, Dart. (Eyns.)
  DA4 . . . . .148 FL104
Polperro Cl, Orp. BR6
  off Cotswold Ri 145 ET100
Polperro Ms, SE11 . . . . .200 F8
Polsted Rd, SE6 . . . . .123 DZ87
Polsten Ms, Enf. EN3
  off Government Row 31 EA37
Polthorne Est, SE18 . . . . . . .105 ER78
Polthorne Gro, SE18 . . . . . . .105 EQ77
Polworth Rd, SW16 . . . . .121 DL92

★ Place of interest   ⇌ Railway station   ⊖ London Underground station   🚈 Docklands Light Railway station   ⊙ Tramlink station   ⓗ Hospital

Pol - Pre

Polygon, The, SW4
  off Old Town 101 DJ84
Polygon Rd, NW1 . . . . .195 M1
Polytechnic St, SE18 . . . . . .105 EN77
Pomell Way, E1
  off Commercial St 84 DT72
Pomeroy Cres, Wat. WD24 . . .23 BV36
Pomeroy St, SE14 . . . . .102 DW81
Pomfret Rd, SE5
  off Flaxman Rd 101 DP83
Pomoja La, N19 . . . . .65 DL61
Pompadour Cl, Brwd. CM14
  off Queen St 54 FW50
Pond Cl, N12
  off Summerfields Av 44 DE51
  SE3 . . . . .104 EF82
  Ashtead KT21 . . . . .172 CL117
  Uxbridge (Hare.) UB9 . . . .38 BJ54
  Walton-on-Thames KT12 . .153 BU107
Pond Cottage La, W.Wick.
  BR4 . . . . .143 EA102
Pond Cotts, SE21 . . . . .122 DS88
PONDERS END, Enf. 30 DW43
⇌ Ponders End 31 DX43
Ponders End Ind Est, Enf.
  EN3 . . . . .31 DZ42
Ponder St, N7 . . . . .83 DM66
Pond Fld End, Loug. IG10 . . .48 EJ45
Pondfield La, Brwd. CM13 . . .55 GA49
Pondfield Rd, Brom. BR2 . . .144 EE102
  Dagenham RM10 . . . . . . .71 FB64
  Kenley CR8 . . . . .175 DP116
  Orpington BR6 . . . . .145 EP104
Pond Grn, Ruis. HA4 . . . . . . .59 BS61
Pond Hill Gdns, Sutt. SM3 . .157 CY107
Pond La, Ger.Cr. (Chal.St.P.)
  SL9 . . . . .36 AV53
Pond Lees Cl, Dag. RM10
  off Leys Av 89 FD66
Pond Mead, SE21 . . . . .122 DR86
Pond Path, Chis. BR7
  off Heathfield La 125 EP93
Pond Piece, Lthd. (Oxshott)
  KT22 . . . . .154 CB114
Pond Pl, SW3 . . . . .198 B9
Pond Rd, E15 . . . . .86 EE68
  SE3 . . . . .104 EF82
  Egham TW20 . . . . .113 BC93
  Hemel Hempstead HP3 . . . .6 BN25
  Woking GU22 . . . . .166 AU120
Ponds, The, Wey. KT13
  off Ellesmere Rd 153 BS107
Pondside Cl, Hayes UB3
  off Providence La 95 BR80
Pond Sq, N6 off South Gro . . .64 DG60
Pond St, NW3 . . . . .64 DE64
Pond Wk, Upmin. RM14 . . . . .73 FS61
Pond Way, Tedd. TW11
  off Holmesdale Rd 117 CJ93
Pondwood Ri, Orp. BR6 . . . .145 ES101
Ponler St, E1 . . . . .84 DV72
Ponsard Rd, NW10 . . . . .81 CV69
Ponsford St, E9 . . . . .84 DW65
Ponsonby Pl, SW1 . . . . .199 N10
Ponsonby Rd, SW15 . . . . . .119 CV87
Ponsonby Ter, SW1 . . . . . . .199 N10
Pontefract Rd, Brom. BR1 . . .124 EF92
Pontoise Cl, Sev. TN13 . . . . .190 FF122
Ponton Rd, SW8 . . . . .101 DK79
Pont St, SW1 . . . . .198 D7
Pont St Ms, SW1 . . . . .198 D7
Pontypool Pl, SE1 . . . . .200 F4
Pontypool Wk, Rom. RM3
  off Saddleworth Rd 52 FJ51
Pony Chase, Cob. KT11 . . . .154 BZ113
Poole Cl, Beck. BR3 . . . . . .123 EA92
  West Molesey KT8 . . . . . .136 BZ99
Pool Ct, SE6 . . . . .123 EA89
Poole Cl, Ruis. HA4
  off Chichester Av 59 BS61
Poole Ct Rd, Houns. TW4
  off Vicarage Fm Rd 96 BY82
Poole Ho, Grays RM20 . . . . .111 GJ75
Poole Rd, E9 . . . . .85 DX65
  Epsom KT19 . . . . .156 CR107
  Hornchurch RM11 . . . . . .72 FM59
  Woking GU21 . . . . .166 AY117
Pooles Bldgs, EC1 . . . . .196 D5
Pooles La, SW10 off Lots Rd . .100 DC80
  Dagenham RM9 . . . . .88 EY68
Pooles Pk, N4
  off Seven Sisters Rd 65 DN61
Poole St, N1 . . . . .84 DR67
Poole Way, Hayes UB4 . . . . .77 BR69
Pooley Av, Egh. TW20 . . . . .113 BC92
POOLEY GREEN, Egh. 113 BC92
Pooley Grn Cl, Egh. TW20 . .113 BB92
Pooley Grn Rd, Egh. TW20 . .113 BB92
Pool Gro, Croy. CR0 . . . . . .161 DY112
Pool La, Slou. SL1 . . . . .74 AS73
Poolmans St, SE16 . . . . . . .203 H4
Pool Rd, Har. HA1 . . . . .61 CD59
  West Molesey KT8 . . . . . .136 BZ100
Poolsford Rd, NW9 . . . . .62 CS56
Poonah St, E1
  off Hardinge St 84 DW72
Pootings Rd, Eden. (Crock.H.)
  TN8 . . . . .189 ER134
Pope Cl, SW19 . . . . .120 DD93
  Feltham TW14 . . . . .115 BT88
Pope Rd, Brom. BR2 . . . . . .144 EK99
Popes Av, Twick. TW2 . . . . .117 CE89
Popes Cl, Amer. HP6 . . . . . . .20 AT37
  Slough (Colnbr.) SL3 . . . . .93 BB80
Popes Dr, N3 . . . . .44 DA53
Popes Gro, Croy. CR0 . . . . .143 DZ104
  Twickenham TW1, TW2 . . .117 CE89
Pope's Head All, EC3
  off Cornhill 84 DR72
Popes La, W5 . . . . .97 CK76
  Oxted RH8 . . . . .188 EE134
  Watford WD24 . . . . .23 BV37

Popes Rd, SW9 . . . . .101 DN83
  Abbots Langley WD5 . . . . . .7 BS31
Pope St, SE1 . . . . .201 N5
Popham Cl, Felt. TW13 . . . . .116 BZ90
Popham Gdns, Rich. TW9
  off Lower Richmond Rd 98 CN83
Popham Rd, N1 . . . . .84 DQ67
Popham St, N1 . . . . .83 DP67
POPLAR, E14 . . . . .204 B2
DLR Poplar 204 B2
Poplar Av, Amer. HP7 . . . . . .20 AT39
  Gravesend DA12 . . . . . .131 GJ91
  Leatherhead KT22 . . . . . .171 CH122
  Mitcham CR4 . . . . .140 DF95
  Orpington BR6 . . . . .145 EP103
  Southall UB2 . . . . .96 CB76
  West Drayton UB7 . . . . . .76 BM73
Poplar Bath St, E14
  off Lawless St 85 EB73
Poplar Business Pk, E14 . . . .204 D1
Poplar Cl, E9
  off Lee Conservancy Rd . . .67 DZ64
  Pinner HA5 . . . . .40 BX53
  Slough (Colnbr.) SL3 . . . . .93 BE81
  South Ockendon RM15 . . . .91 FX70
Poplar Ct, SW19 . . . . .120 DA92
Poplar Cres, Epsom KT19 . . .156 CQ107
Poplar Dr, Bans. SM7 . . . . . .157 CX114
  Brentwood CM13 . . . . . . .55 GC44
Poplar Fm Cl, Epsom KT19 . .156 CQ107
Poplar Gdns, N.Mal. KT3 . . .138 CR96
Poplar Gro, N11 . . . . .44 DG51
  W6 . . . . .99 CW75
  New Malden KT3 . . . . . . .138 CR97
  Wembley HA9 . . . . .62 CQ62
  Woking GU22 . . . . .166 AY119
Poplar High St, E14 . . . . . . .85 EA73
Poplar Mt, Belv. DA17 . . . . .107 FB77
Poplar Pl, SE28 . . . . .88 EW73
  W2 . . . . .82 DB73
  Hayes UB3 off Central Av . .77 BU73
Poplar Rd, SE24 . . . . .102 DQ84
  SW19 . . . . .140 DA96
  Ashford TW15 . . . . .115 BQ92
  Leatherhead KT22 . . . . . .171 CH122
  Sutton SM3 . . . . .139 CZ102
  Uxbridge (Denh.) UB9 . . . .58 BJ64
Poplar Rd S, SW19 . . . . . . .140 DA97
Poplar Row, Epp. (They.B.)
  CM16 . . . . .33 ES37
Poplars, The, N14 . . . . .29 DH43
  Gravesend DA12 . . . . . .131 GL87
  Romford (Abridge) RM4
    off Hoe La 34 EV41
  Waltham Cross (Chsht.)
    EN7 . . . . .14 DS26
Poplars Av, NW10 . . . . .81 CW65
Poplars Cl, Ruis. HA4 . . . . . .59 BS60
  Watford WD25 . . . . .7 BV32
Poplar Shaw, Wal.Abb. EN9 . .16 EF33
Poplars Rd, E17 . . . . .67 EB58
Poplar St, Rom. RM7 . . . . . .71 FC56
Poplar Vw, Wem. HA9
  off Magnet Rd 61 CK61
Poplar Wk, SE24 . . . . .102 DQ84
  Caterham CR3 . . . . .176 DS123
  Croydon CR0 . . . . .142 DQ103
Poplar Way, Felt. TW13 . . . .115 BU90
  Ilford IG6 . . . . .69 EQ56
Poppins Ct, EC4 . . . . .196 F9
Poppleton Rd, E11 . . . . .68 EE58
Poppy Cl, Brwd. CM15 . . . . .54 FV43
  Wallington SM6 . . . . .140 DG102
★ Poppy Factory Mus, The, Rich.
  TW10 . . . . .117 CK86
Poppy La, Croy. CR0 . . . . . .142 DW101
Poppy Wk, Wal.Cr. EN7 . . . . .14 DR28
Porchester Cl, SE5 . . . . . . .102 DQ84
  Hornchurch RM11 . . . . . .72 FL58
Porchester Gdns, W2 . . . . . .82 DB73
Porchester Gdns Ms, W2
  off Porchester Gdns 82 DB72
Porchester Mead, Beck. BR3 .123 EB93
Porchester Ms, W2 . . . . .82 DB72
Porchester Pl, W2 . . . . .194 C9
Porchester Rd, W2 . . . . .82 DB71
  Kingston upon Thames
    KT1 . . . . .138 CP96
Porchester Sq, W2 . . . . .82 DB72
Porchester Ter, W2 . . . . .82 DC73
Porchester Ter N, W2 . . . . . .82 DB72
Porchfield Cl, Grav. DA12 . . .131 GJ89
  Sutton SM2 . . . . .158 DB110
Porch Way, N20 . . . . .44 DF48
Porcupine Cl, SE9 . . . . .124 EL89
Porden Rd, SW2 . . . . .101 DM84
Porlock Av, Har. HA2 . . . . . .60 CC60
Porlock Rd, W10
  off Ladbroke Gro 81 CX70
  Enfield EN1 . . . . .46 DT45
Porlock St, SE1 . . . . .201 K4
Porrington Cl, Chis. BR7 . . . .145 EM95
Portal Cl, SE27 . . . . .121 DN90
  Ruislip HA4 . . . . .59 BU63
  Uxbridge UB10 . . . . .76 BL66
Port Av, Green. DA9 . . . . . . .129 FV86
Portbury Cl, SE15
  off Clayton Rd 102 DU81
Port Cres, E13
  off Jenkins Rd 86 EH70
★ Portcullis House - New
Parliamentary Building,
  SW1 . . . . .199 P4
Portcullis Lo Rd, Enf. EN2 . . .30 DR41
Portelet Ct, N1
  off De Beauvoir Est 84 DS67
Portelet Rd, E1 . . . . .85 DX69
Porten Rd, W14 . . . . .99 CY76
Porter Cl, Grays RM20 . . . . .109 FW79
Porter Rd, E6 . . . . .87 EM72
Porters Av, Dag. RM8, RM9 . .88 EV65
Porters Cl, Brwd. CM14 . . . . .54 FU46
Portersfield Rd, Enf. EN1 . . . .30 DS42
Porters Pk Dr, Rad. (Shenley)
  WD7 . . . . .9 CK33
Porter Sq, N19
  off Hornsey Rd 65 DL60

Porter St, SE1 . . . . .201 J2
  W1 . . . . .194 E6
Porters Wk, E1 . . . . .202 F1
Porters Way, West Dr. UB7 . . .94 BM76
Porteus Rd, W2 . . . . .82 DC71
Portgate Cl, W9 . . . . .81 CZ70
Porthallow Cl, Orp. BR6
  off Sevenoaks Rd 145 ET105
Porthcawe Rd, SE26 . . . . . .123 DY91
Port Hill, Orp. BR6 . . . . .164 EV110
Porthkerry Av, Well. DA16 . . .106 EU84
Portia Way, E3 . . . . .85 DZ70
Portinscale Rd, SW15 . . . . . .119 CY85
Portland Av, N16 . . . . .66 DT59
  Gravesend DA12 . . . . . .131 GH89
  New Malden KT3 . . . . . . .139 CT101
  Sidcup DA15 . . . . .126 EU86
Portland Cl, Rom. RM6 . . . . .70 EY57
Portland Cres, SE9 . . . . . . .124 EL89
  Feltham TW13 . . . . .115 BR91
  Greenford UB6 . . . . .78 CB70
  Stanmore HA7 . . . . .41 CK54
Portland Dr, Enf. EN2 . . . . . .30 DS38
  Redhill RH1 . . . . .185 DK129
  Waltham Cross (Chsht.)
    EN7 . . . . .14 DU31
Portland Gdns, N4 . . . . .65 DP58
  Romford RM6 . . . . .70 EX57
Portland Gro, SW8 . . . . .101 DM81
Portland Hts, Nthwd. HA6 . . . .39 BT49
H Portland Hosp for Women
  & Children, The, W1 . . . . .195 J5
Portland Ho, Red. RH1 . . . . .185 DK129
Portland Ms, W1 . . . . .195 L9
Portland Pk, Ger.Cr. SL9 . . . .56 AX58
Portland Pl, W1 . . . . .195 J7
  Epsom KT17 . . . . .156 CS112
Portland Ri, N4 . . . . .66 DP60
Portland Ri Est, N4 . . . . .66 DQ60
Portland Rd, N15 . . . . .66 DT56
  SE9 . . . . .124 EL89
  SE25 . . . . .142 DU98
  W11 . . . . .81 CY73
  Ashford TW15 . . . . .114 BL90
  Bromley BR1 . . . . .124 EJ91
  Gravesend DA12 . . . . . .131 GH88
  Hayes UB4 . . . . .77 BS69
  Kingston upon Thames
    KT1 . . . . .138 CL97
  Mitcham CR4 . . . . .140 DE96
  Southall UB2 . . . . .96 BZ76
Portland Sq, E1 . . . . .202 E2
Portland St, SE17 . . . . .201 K10
Portland Ter, Rich. TW9
  off Portland St 102 DT79
Portley La, Cat. CR3 . . . . . .176 DS121
Portley Wd Rd, Whyt. CR3 . . .176 DT120
Portman Av, SW14 . . . . .98 CR83
Portman Cl, W1 . . . . .194 E8
  Bexley DA5 . . . . .127 FE88
  Bexleyheath DA7
    off Queen Anne's Gate . .106 EX83
Portman Dr, Wdf.Grn. IG8 . . .48 EK54
Portman Gdns, NW9 . . . . . . .42 CR54
  Uxbridge UB10 . . . . .76 BN66
Portman Gate, NW1 . . . . . . .194 C5
Portman Ms S, W1 . . . . .194 F9
Portman Pl, E2 . . . . .84 DW69
Portman Rd, Kings.T. KT1 . . .138 CM96
Portman Sq, W1 . . . . .194 F8
Portman St, W1 . . . . .194 F9
Portmeadow Wk, SE2 . . . . . .106 EX75
Portmeers Cl, E17
  off Lennox Rd 67 DZ58
Portmore Gdns, Rom. RM5 . . .50 FA50
Portmore Pk Rd, Wey. KT13 . .152 BN105
Portmore Quays, Wey. KT13
  off Weybridge Rd 152 BM105
Portmore Way, Wey. KT13 . . .134 BN104
Portnall Dr, Vir.W. GU25 . . . .132 AT99
Portnall Ri, Vir.W. GU25 . . . .132 AT99
Portnall Rd, W9 . . . . .81 CZ68
  Virginia Water GU25 . . . .132 AT99
Portnalls Cl, Couls. CR5 . . . .175 DH116
Portnalls Ri, Couls. CR5 . . . .175 DH116
Portnalls Rd, Couls. CR5 . . . .175 DH118
Portnoi Cl, Rom. RM1 . . . . . .51 FD54
Portobello Ct, W11
  off Westbourne Gro 81 CZ73
Portobello Ms, W11
  off Portobello Rd 82 DA73
Portobello Rd, W10 . . . . .81 CZ72
  W11 . . . . .81 CZ72
Porton Ct, Surb. KT6 . . . . . .137 CJ100
Portpool La, EC1 . . . . .196 D6
Portree Cl, N22
  off Nightingale Rd 45 DM52
Portree St, E14 . . . . .85 ED72
Portsdown, Edg. HA8
  off Rectory La 42 CN50
Portsdown Av, NW11 . . . . . . .63 CZ58
Portsdown Ms, NW11 . . . . . .63 CZ58
Portsea Ms, W2 . . . . .194 C9
Portsea Pl, W2 . . . . .194 C9
Portslade Rd, SW8 . . . . .101 DJ82
Portsmouth Av, T.Ditt. KT7 . . .137 CG101
Portsmouth Ct, Slou. SL1 . . . .74 AS73
Portsmouth Ms, E16
  off Wesley Av 86 EH72
Portsmouth Rd, SW15 . . . . .119 CV87
  Cobham KT11 . . . . .153 BU114
  Esher KT10 . . . . .154 CC105
  Kingston upon Thames
    KT1 . . . . .137 CJ99
  Surbiton KT6 . . . . .137 CJ99
  Thames Ditton KT7 . . . . .137 CE103
  Woking (Ripley) GU23 . . . .168 BM119
Portsmouth St, WC2 . . . . . . .196 B9
Portsoken St, E1 . . . . .197 P10
Portugal Gdns, Twick. TW2
  off Fulwell Pk Av 116 CC89
Portugal Rd, Wok. GU21 . . . .167 BA116
Portugal St, WC2 . . . . .196 B9
Portway, E15 . . . . .86 EF67
  Epsom KT17 . . . . .157 CU110

Portway Cres, Epsom KT17 . .157 CU109
Portway Gdns, SE18
  off Shooter's Hill Rd 104 EK80
Postern Grn, Enf. EN2 . . . . . .29 DN40
Post La, Twick. TW2 . . . . . . .117 CD88
Post Meadow, Iver SL0 . . . . .75 BD68
Postmill Cl, Croy. CR0 . . . . .143 DX104
Post Office App, E7 . . . . .68 EH64
Post Office Ct, EC3 . . . . . . .197 L9
Post Office La, Slou. (Geo.Grn.)
  SL3 . . . . .74 AX72
Post Office Row, Oxt. RH8 . . .188 EL131
Post Office Way, SW8 . . . . . .101 DK80
Post Rd, Sthl. UB2 . . . . .96 CB76
Postway Ms, Ilf. IG1
  off Clements Rd 69 EP62
Potier St, SE1 . . . . .201 L7
Potter Cl, Mitch. CR4 . . . . . .141 DH96
Potterells, Hat. (N.Mymms)
  AL9 . . . . .11 CX25
Potteries, The, Cher. KT16 . .151 BE82
Potterne Cl, SW19 . . . . .119 CX87
POTTERS BAR 12 DA32
⇌ Potters Bar 12 DA32
H Potters Bar Comm Hosp,
  Pot.B. EN6 . . . . .12 DC34
★ Potters Bar Mus, The
  Wyllyotts Cen, Pot.B. EN6 .11 CZ32
Potters Cl, Croy. CR0 . . . . . .143 DY102
  Loughton IG10 . . . . .32 EL40
Potters Ct, Pot.B. EN6
  off Darkes La 12 DA32
Potters Cross, Iver SL0 . . . . .75 BD69
Potters Flds, SE1 off Tooley St .84 DS74
Potters Gro, N.Mal. KT3 . . . .138 CQ98
Potters Hts Cl, Pnr. HA5 . . . .39 BV52
Potters La, SW16 . . . . .121 DK93
  Barnet EN5 . . . . .28 DA42
  Borehamwood WD6 . . . . .26 CQ39
  Woking (Send) GU23 . . . .167 BB123
Potters Ms, Borwd. (Elstree) WD6
  off Elstree Hill N 25 CK44
Potters Rd, SW6 . . . . .100 DC82
  Barnet EN5 . . . . .28 DB42
Potter St, Nthwd. HA6 . . . . . .39 BU53
  Pinner HA5 . . . . .39 BV53
Potter St Hill, Pnr. HA5 . . . . .39 BV51
Pottery La, W11
  off Portland Rd 81 CY73
Pottery Rd, Bex. DA5 . . . . . .127 FC89
  Brentford TW8 . . . . .98 CL79
Pottery St, SE16 . . . . .202 D5
Pott St, E2 . . . . .84 DV69
Poulcott, Stai. (Wrays.) TW19 .112 AY86
Poulett Gdns, Twick. TW1 . . .117 CG88
Poulett Rd, E6 . . . . .87 EM68
Poulner Way, SE15
  off Daniel Gdns 102 DT80
Poulters Wd, Kes. BR2 . . . . .162 EK106
Poultney Cl, Rad. (Shenley)
  WD7 . . . . .10 CM32
Poulton Av, Sutt. SM1 . . . . . .140 DD104
Poulton Cl, E8
  off Spurstowe Ter 66 DV64
Poultry, EC2 . . . . .197 K9
Pound Cl, Orp. BR6 . . . . . . .145 ER103
  Surbiton KT6 . . . . .137 CJ102
Pound Ct, Ashtd. KT21 . . . . .172 CM118
Pound Ct Dr, Orp. BR6 . . . . .145 ER103
Pound Cres, Lthd. (Fetch.)
  KT22 . . . . .171 CD121
Pound Fm Cl, Esher KT10
  off High St 137 CD102
Poundfield, Wat. WD25
  off Ashfields 23 BT35
Poundfield Ct, Wok. GU22
  off High St 167 BC121
Poundfield Gdns, Wok.
  GU22 . . . . .167 BC120
Poundfield Rd, Loug. IG10 . . .33 EN43
Pound La, NW10 . . . . .81 CU65
  Epsom KT19 . . . . .156 CR112
  Radlett (Shenley) WD7 . . . .10 CM33
  Sevenoaks TN13 . . . . . . .190 FE121
  Sevenoaks (Knock.P.) TN14 .191 FH124
Pound Pk Rd, SE7 . . . . .104 EK77
Pound Pl, SE9 . . . . .125 EN86
Pound Rd, Bans. SM7 . . . . . .173 CZ117
  Chertsey KT16 . . . . .134 BH101
Pound St, Cars. SM5 . . . . . .158 DF106
Pound Way, Chis. BR7
  off Royal Par 125 EQ94
Pounsley Rd, Sev. (Dunt.Grn.)
  TN13 . . . . .190 FE121
Pountney Rd, SW11 . . . . . . .100 DG83
POVEREST, Orp. 145 ET99
Poverest Rd, Orp. BR5 . . . . .145 ET99
Powder Mill La, Dart. DA1 . . .128 FL89
  Twickenham TW2 . . . . . .116 BZ88
Powdermill La, Wal.Abb. EN9 .15 EB33
Powdermill Ms, Wal.Abb. EN9
  off Powdermill La 15 EB33
Powdermill Way, Wal.Abb. EN9 15 EB32
Powell Cl, Chess. KT9
  off Coppard Gdns 155 CK106
  Dartford DA2 . . . . .129 FS89
  Edgware HA8 . . . . .42 CM51
  Wallington SM6 . . . . .159 DK108
Powell Gdns, Dag. RM10 . . . .70 FA63
Powell Rd, E5 . . . . .66 DV62
  Buckhurst Hill IG9 . . . . . .48 EJ45
Powell's Wk, W4 . . . . .98 CS79
Powergate Business Pk,
  NW10 . . . . .80 CR69
Power Ind Est, Erith DA8 . . . .107 FG81
Power Rd, W4 . . . . .98 CN77
Powers Ct, Twick. TW1 . . . . .117 CK87
Powerscroft Rd, E5 . . . . .66 DW63
  Sidcup DA14 . . . . .126 EW93
Powis Ct, Pot.B. EN6 . . . . . .12 DC34
Powis Gdns, NW11 . . . . .63 CZ59
  W11 . . . . .81 CZ72
Powis Ms, W11
  off Westbourne Pk Rd 81 CZ72
Powis Pl, WC1 . . . . .196 A5

Powis Rd, E3 . . . . .85 EB69
Powis Sq, W11 . . . . .81 CZ72
Powis St, SE18 . . . . .105 EN76
Powis Ter, W11 . . . . .81 CZ72
Powle Ter, Ilf. IG1
  off Oaktree Gro 69 EQ64
Powlett Pl, NW1
  off Harmood St 83 DH65
Pownall Gdns, Houns. TW3 . . .96 CB84
Pownall Rd, E8 . . . . .84 DT67
  Hounslow TW3 . . . . .96 CB84
Pownsett Ter, Ilf. IG1
  off Buttsbury Rd 69 EQ64
Powster Rd, Brom. BR1 . . . .124 EH92
Powys Cl, Bexh. DA7 . . . . . .106 EX79
Powys Ct, Borwd. WD6
  off Kensington Way 26 CR41
Powys La, N13 . . . . .45 DL50
  N14 . . . . .45 DL49
POYLE, Slou. 93 BE81
Poyle Pk, Slou. (Colnbr.) SL3 .93 BE83
Poyle Rd, Slou. (Colnbr.) SL3 .93 BE83
Poyle Technical Cen, Slou.
  SL3 . . . . .93 BE82
Poynder Rd, Til. RM18 . . . . .111 GH81
Poynders Ct, SW4
  off Poynders Rd 121 DJ86
Poynders Gdns, SW4 . . . . . .121 DJ87
Poynders Rd, SW4 . . . . .121 DJ86
Poynings, The, Iver SL0 . . . . .93 BF77
Poynings Cl, Orp. BR6 . . . . .146 EW103
Poynings Rd, N19 . . . . .65 DJ62
Poynings Way, N12 . . . . .44 DA50
  Romford RM3
    off Arlington Gdns 52 FL53
Poyntell Cres, Chis. BR7 . . . .145 ER95
Poynter Ho, W11 . . . . .81 CX74
Poynter Rd, Enf. EN1 . . . . . . .30 DU43
Poynton Rd, N17 . . . . .46 DU54
Poyser St, E2 . . . . .84 DV68
Prae, The, Wok. GU22 . . . . . .167 BF118
Praed Ms, W2 . . . . .194 A8
Praed St, W2 . . . . .194 B7
Pragel St, E13 . . . . .86 EH68
Pragnell Rd, SE12 . . . . .124 EH89
Prague Pl, SW2 . . . . .121 DL85
Prah Rd, N4 . . . . .65 DN61
Prairie Cl, Add. KT15 . . . . . .134 BH104
Prairie Rd, Add. KT15 . . . . . .134 BH104
Prairie St, SW8 . . . . .100 DG82
Pratt Ms, NW1 off Pratt St . . .83 DJ67
PRATT'S BOTTOM, Orp. 164 EV110
Pratts La, Walt. KT12
  off Molesey Rd 154 BX105
Pratts Pas, Kings.T. KT1
  off Eden St 138 CL96
Pratt St, NW1 . . . . .83 DJ67
Pratt Wk, SE11 . . . . .200 C8
Prayle Gro, NW2 . . . . .63 CX60
Prebend Gdns, W4 . . . . .99 CT76
  W6 . . . . .99 CT76
Prebend St, N1 . . . . .84 DQ67
Precinct, The, W.Mol. KT8
  off Victoria Av 136 CB97
Precinct Rd, Hayes UB3 . . . . .77 BU73
Precincts, The, Mord. SM4
  off Green La 140 DB100
Precinct, The, Egh. TW20 . . .113 BA92
Premier Av, Grays RM16 . . . .110 GC75
Premier Cor, W9
  off Kilburn La 81 CZ68
Premiere Pl, E14 . . . . .203 P1
Premier Pk, NW10 . . . . .80 CP67
Premier Pk Rd, NW10 . . . . . .80 CP68
Premier Pl, SW15
  off Putney High St 99 CY84
Prendergast Rd, SE3 . . . . . .104 EE83
Prentis Rd, SW16 . . . . .121 DK91
Prentiss Ct, SE7 . . . . .104 EK77
Presburg Rd, N.Mal. KT3 . . . .138 CS99
Presburg St, E5 off Glyn Rd . . .67 DX62
Prescelly Pl, Edg. HA8 . . . . . .42 CM53
Prescot St, E1 . . . . .84 DT73
Prescott Av, Orp. BR5 . . . . . .145 EP100
Prescott Cl, SW16 . . . . .121 DL94
  Hornchurch RM11 . . . . . .71 FH60
Prescott Grn, Loug. IG10 . . . .33 EQ41
Prescott Ho, SE17
  off Hillingdon St 101 DP79
Prescott Pl, SW4 . . . . .101 DK83
Prescott Rd, Slou. (Colnbr.)
  SL3 . . . . .93 BE82
  Waltham Cross (Chsht.)
    EN8 . . . . .15 DY27
Presentation Ms, SW2
  off Palace Rd 121 DM88
President Dr, E1 . . . . .202 D2
President St, EC1 . . . . .197 H2
Press Rd, NW10 . . . . .62 CR62
  Uxbridge UB8 . . . . .76 BK65
Prestage Way, E14 . . . . .85 EC73
Prestbury Ct, Wok. GU21 . . . .166 AU118
Prestbury Cres, Bans. SM7 . .174 DF116
Prestbury Rd, E7 . . . . .86 EJ66
Prestbury Sq, SE9 . . . . .125 EM91
Prested Rd, SW11
  off St. John's Hill 100 DE84
Prestige Way, NW4
  off Heriot Rd 63 CW57
PRESTON, Wem. 61 CK59
Preston Av, E4 . . . . .47 ED51
Preston Cl, SE1 . . . . .201 M8
  Twickenham TW2 . . . . . .117 CE90
Preston Ct, Walt. KT12
  off St. Johns Dr 136 BW102
Preston Dr, E11 . . . . .68 EJ57
  Bexleyheath DA7 . . . . . .106 EX81
  Epsom KT19 . . . . .156 CS107
Preston Gdns, NW10
  off Church Rd 80 CS65
  Enfield EN3 . . . . .31 DY37
  Ilford IG1 . . . . .68 EL58
Preston Gro, Ashtd. KT21 . . .171 CJ117
Preston Hill, Har. HA3 . . . . . .62 CM58

Preston La, Tad. KT20 . . . . . .173 CV121
Preston Pl, NW2 . . . . .81 CU65
  Richmond TW10 . . . . .118 CL85
⊖ Preston Road 62 CL60
Preston Rd, E11 . . . . .68 EE58
  SE19 . . . . .121 DP93
  SW20 . . . . .119 CT94
  Gravesend (Nthflt.) DA11 . .130 GE88
  Harrow HA3 . . . . .62 CL59
  Romford RM3 . . . . .52 FK49
  Shepperton TW17 . . . . . . .134 BN99
  Slough SL2 . . . . .74 AW73
  Wembley HA9 . . . . .62 CL61
Prestons Rd, E14 . . . . .204 E3
  Bromley BR2 . . . . .144 EG104
Preston Waye, Har. HA3 . . . .62 CL60
Prestwick Cl, Sthl. UB2
  off Ringway 96 BY78
Prestwick Rd, Wat. WD19 . . .40 BX50
Prestwood Av, Har. HA3 . . . .61 CH56
Prestwood Cl, SE18 . . . . . .106 EU80
  Harrow HA3 . . . . .61 CH56
Prestwood Dr, Rom. RM5 . . .51 FC50
Prestwood Gdns, Croy. CR0 .142 DQ101
Prestwood St, N1 . . . . .197 J1
Pretoria Av, E17 . . . . .67 DY56
Pretoria Cl, N17
  off Pretoria Rd 46 DT52
Pretoria Cres, E4 . . . . .47 EC46
Pretoria Rd, E4 . . . . .47 EC46
  E11 . . . . .67 ED60
  E16 . . . . .86 EF69
  N17 . . . . .46 DT52
  SW16 . . . . .121 DH93
  Chertsey KT16 . . . . .133 BF102
  Ilford IG1 . . . . .69 EP64
  Romford RM7 . . . . .71 FC56
  Watford WD18 . . . . .23 BU42
Pretoria Rd N, N18 . . . . .46 DT51
Pretty La, Couls. CR5 . . . . . .175 DJ121
Prevost Rd, N11 . . . . .44 DG47
Prey Heath, Wok. GU22 . . . .166 AV124
Prey Heath Cl, Wok. GU22 . .166AW124
Prey Heath Rd, Wok. GU22 . .166 AV124
Price Cl, NW7 . . . . .43 CY51
  SW17 . . . . .120 DF90
Price Rd, Croy. CR0 . . . . . .159 DP106
Price's St, SE1 . . . . .200 G3
Price's St, SE1 off Bear La . . .83 DP74
Price Way, Hmptn. TW12
  off Victors Dr 116 BY93
Pricklers Hill, Barn. EN5 . . . .28 DB44
Prickley Wd, Brom. BR2 . . . .144 EF102
Priddy's Yd, Croy. CR0
  off Church St 142 DQ103
Prideaux Pl, W3
  off Friars Pl La 80 CR73
  WC1 . . . . .196 C2
Prideaux Rd, SW9 . . . . .101 DL83
Pridham Rd, Th.Hth. CR7 . . .142 DR98
Priest Ct, EC2 . . . . .197 H8
Priestfield Rd, SE23 . . . . . .123 DY90
Priest Hill, Egh. TW20 . . . . .112 AW90
  Windsor (Old Wind.) SL4 . .112 AW90
Priestlands Pk Rd, Sid. DA15 .125 ET90
Priestley Cl, N16
  off Ravensdale Rd 66 DT59
Priestley Gdns, Rom. RM6 . . .70 EV58
Priestley Rd, Mitch. CR4 . . . .70 DG96
Priestley Way, E17 . . . . .67 DX55
  NW2 . . . . .63 CU60
Priestly Gdns, Wok. GU22 . .167 BA120
Priestman Pt, E3
  off Rainhill Way 85 EB69
Priest Pk Av, Har. HA2 . . . . .60 CA61
Priests Av, Rom. RM1 . . . . . .51 FD54
Priests Br, SW14 . . . . .98 CS83
  SW15 . . . . .98 CS83
Priests Fld, Brwd. CM13 . . . .55 GC50
Priests La, Brwd. CM15 . . . . .54 FY47
Prima Rd, SW9 . . . . .101 DN80
Primrose Av, Enf. EN2 . . . . . .30 DR39
  Romford RM6 . . . . .70 EV59
Primrose Cl, SE6 . . . . .123 EC92
  Harrow HA2 . . . . .60 BZ63
  Wallington SM6 . . . . .141 DH102
Primrose Dr, West Dr. UB7 . . .94 BK77
Primrose Gdns, NW3 . . . . . . .82 DE65
  Bushey WD23 . . . . .40 CB45
  Ruislip HA4 . . . . .60 BW64
Primrose Glen, Horn. RM11 . .72 FL56
PRIMROSE HILL, NW8 . . . . . .82 DF67
Primrose Hill, EC4 . . . . .196 E9
  Brentwood CM14 . . . . .54 FW48
  Kings Langley WD4 . . . . .7 BP28
Primrose Hill Ct, NW3 . . . . . .82 DF66
Primrose Hill Rd, NW3 . . . . . .82 DE66
Primrose Hill Studios, NW1
  off Fitzroy Rd 82 DG67
Primrose La, Croy. CR0 . . . .143 DX102
Primrose Ms, NW1
  off Sharpleshall St 82 DF66
  SE3 . . . . .104 EH80
  W5 off St. Mary's Rd 97 CK75
Primrose Path, Wal.Cr. (Chsht.)
  EN7 . . . . .14 DU31
Primrose Rd, E10 . . . . .67 EB60
  E18 . . . . .48 EH54
  Walton-on-Thames KT12 . . .154 BW106
Primrose St, EC2 . . . . .197 M6
Primrose Wk, SE14
  off Alexandra St 103 DY80
  Epsom KT17 . . . . .157 CT108
Primrose Way, Wem. HA0 . . .79 CK68
Primula St, W12 . . . . .81 CU72
Prince Albert Rd, NW1 . . . . .194 C1
  NW8 . . . . .194 C1
Prince Alberts Wk, Wind. SL4 .92 AU81
Prince Arthur Ms, NW3
  off Perrins La 64 DC63
Prince Arthur Rd, NW3 . . . . .64 DC64
Prince Charles Av, Dart.
  (S.Darenth) DA4 . . . . .149 FR96
Prince Charles Dr, NW4 . . . . .63 CW59

Prince Charles Rd, SE3 . . . . .104 EF81
Prince Charles Way, Wall.
  SM6 . . . . .141 DH104
Prince Consort Dr, Chis. BR7 .145 ER95
Prince Consort Rd, SW7 . . . .100 DC76
Princedale Rd, W11 . . . . .81 CY74
Prince Edward Rd, E9 . . . . . .85 DZ65
Prince George Av, N14 . . . . . .29 DJ42
Prince George Duke of Kent Ct,
  Chis. BR7 off Holbrook La . .125 ER94
Prince George Rd, N16 . . . . . .66 DS63
Prince George's Av, SW20 . . .139 CW96
Prince George's Rd, SW19 . . .140 DD95
Prince Henry Rd, SE7 . . . . . .104 EK80
★ Prince Henry's Room,
  EC4 . . . . .196 D9
Prince Imperial Rd, SE18 . . . .105 EM81
  Chislehurst BR7 . . . . .125 EP94
Prince John Rd, SE9 . . . . . .124 EL85
Princelet St, E1 . . . . .84 DT71
Prince of Orange La, SE10
  off Greenwich High Rd 103 EC80
Prince of Wales Cl, NW4
  off Church Ter 63 CV56
  SW11 . . . . .100 DF81
Prince of Wales Footpath, Enf.
  EN3 . . . . .31 DY38
Prince of Wales Gate, SW7 . .198 B4
Prince of Wales Pas, NW1 . . .195 K3
Prince of Wales Rd, NW5 . . . .82 DG65
  SE3 . . . . .104 EF81
  Sutton SM1 . . . . .140 DD103
Prince of Wales Ter, W4 . . . . .98 CS78
  W8 off Kensington Rd 100 DB75
DLR Prince Regent 86 EJ73
Prince Regent La, E13 . . . . . .86 EH69
  E16 . . . . .86 EJ71
Prince Regent Ms, NW1
  off Hampstead Rd 83 DJ69
Prince Regent Rd, Houns.
  TW3 . . . . .96 CC83
Prince Rd, SE25 . . . . .142 DS99
Prince Rupert Rd, SE9 . . . . .105 EM84
Prince's Arc, SW1 . . . . .199 L2
Princes Av, N3 . . . . .44 DA53
  N10 . . . . .64 DG55
  N13 . . . . .45 DN50
  N22 . . . . .45 DK53
  NW9 . . . . .62 CP56
  W3 . . . . .98 CN76
  Carshalton SM5 . . . . .158 DF108
  Dartford DA2 . . . . .128 FP88
  Enfield EN3 . . . . .31 DY36
  Greenford UB6 . . . . .78 CB72
  Orpington BR5 . . . . .145 ES99
  South Croydon CR2 . . . . . .176 DV115
  Surbiton KT6 . . . . .138 CN102
  Watford WD18 . . . . .23 BT43
  Woodford Green IG8 . . . . . .48 EH49
Princes Cl, N4 . . . . .65 DP60
  NW9 . . . . .62 CN56
  SW4 off Old Town 101 DJ83
  Edgware HA8 . . . . .42 CN50
  Epping (N.Wld.) CM16 . . . . .19 FC25
  Sidcup DA14 . . . . .126 EX90
  South Croydon CR2 . . . . . .176 DV115
  Teddington TW11 . . . . . . .117 CD91
Princes Ct, E1 . . . . .202 E1
  SE16 . . . . .203 M7
  Wembley HA9 . . . . .62 CL64
Princes Dr, Lthd. (Oxshott)
  KT22 . . . . .155 CE112
Princesfield Rd, Wal.Abb. EN9 .16 EH33
Princes Gdns, SW7 . . . . . . .198 A5
  W3 . . . . .80 CN71
  W5 . . . . .79 CJ70
Princes Gate, SW7 . . . . .198 B5
Princes Gate Ct, SW7 . . . . . .198 A5
Princes Gate Ms, SW7 . . . . .198 A6
Princes La, N10 . . . . .65 DH55
Princes Ms, W2
  off Hereford Rd 82 DA73
  W11 . . . . .81 CY74
  off High St 12 DC32
Princes Pk, Rain. RM13 . . . . .89 FG66
Princes Pk Av, NW11 . . . . . . .63 CY58
  Hayes UB3 . . . . .77 BR73
Princes Pk Circle, Hayes UB3 .77 BR73
Princes Pk Cl, Hayes UB3 . . .77 BR73
Princes Pk La, Hayes UB3 . . .77 BR73
Princes Pk Par, Hayes UB3 . . .77 BR73
Princes Pl, SW1 . . . . .199 L2
  W11 . . . . .81 CY74
Princes Plain, Brom. BR2 . . .144 EL101
Princes Ri, SE13 . . . . .103 EC82
Princes Riverside Rd, SE16 . .203 J4
Princes Rd, N18 . . . . .46 DW49
  SE20 . . . . .123 DX93
  SW14 . . . . .98 CR83
  SW19 . . . . .120 DA93
  W13 off Broomfield Rd 79 CH74
  Ashford TW15 . . . . .114 BM92
  Buckhurst Hill IG9 . . . . .48 EJ47
  Dartford DA1, DA2 . . . . . .127 FG86
  Egham TW20 . . . . .113 AZ93
  Feltham TW13 . . . . .115 BT89
  Gravesend DA12 . . . . .131 GJ90
  Ilford IG6 . . . . .69 ER56
  Kingston upon Thames
  KT2 . . . . .118 CN94
  Richmond TW10 . . . . .118 CM85
  Richmond (Kew) TW9 . . . . .98 CM80
  Romford RM1 . . . . .71 FG57
  Swanley BR8 . . . . .147 FG93
  Teddington TW11 . . . . . . .117 CD91
  Weybridge KT13 . . . . .153 BP106
Princess Alice Way, SE28 . . .105 ER75
Princess Av, Wem. HA9 . . . . .62 CL61
Princess Cres, N4 . . . . .65 DP61
Princesses Wk, Rich. TW9
  off Kew Rd 98 CL80
Princess Gdns, Wok. GU22 . .167 BB116
H Princess Grace Hosp, The,
  W1 . . . . .194 F5
Princess La, Ruis. HA4 . . . . . .59 BS60

Princess Louise Cl, W2 . . . . .194 A6
H Princess Louise Hosp,
  W10 . . . . .81 CX71
Princess Mary's Rd, Add.
  KT15 . . . . .152 BJ105
Princess May Rd, N16 . . . . . .66 DS63
Princess Ms, NW3
  off Belsize Cres 82 DD65
Princess Par, Orp. BR6
  off Crofton Rd 145 EN104
Princess Pk Manor, N11 . . . . .44 DG50
Princes Sq, W2 . . . . .82 DB73
Princess Rd, NW1 . . . . .82 DG67
  NW6 . . . . .82 DA68
  Croydon CR0 . . . . .142 DQ100
  Woking GU22 . . . . .167 BB116
Princes St, EC2 . . . . .197 K9
  N17 off Queen St 46 DS51
  W1 . . . . .195 J9
  Bexleyheath DA7 . . . . .106 EZ84
  Gravesend DA11 . . . . .131 GH86
  Richmond TW9
  off Sheen Rd 118 CL85
  Slough SL1 . . . . .92 AV75
  Sutton SM1 . . . . .158 DD105
Princess Way, Red. RH1 . . . .184 DG133
Princes Ter, E13 . . . . .86 EH68
Prince St, SE8 . . . . .103 DZ79
  Watford WD17 . . . . .24 BW41
Princes Vw, Dart. DA1 . . . . .128 FN88
Princes Way, SW19 . . . . . . .119 CX87
  Brentwood CM13 . . . . .55 GA46
  Buckhurst Hill IG9 . . . . .48 EJ47
  Croydon CR0 . . . . .159 DM106
  Ruislip HA4 . . . . .60 BY63
  West Wickham BR4 . . . . . .162 EF105
Princes Yd, W11
  off Princedale Rd 81 CY74
Princethorpe Ho, W2 . . . . . . .82 DB71
Princethorpe Rd, SE26 . . . . .123 DX91
Princeton Ct, SW15
  off Felsham Rd 99 CX83
Princeton St, WC1 . . . . .196 B6
Pringle Gdns, SW16 . . . . . . .121 DJ91
  Purley CR8 . . . . .159 DM110
Printers Inn Ct, EC4 . . . . . . .196 D8
Printers Ms, E3 . . . . .85 DY67
Printer St, EC4 . . . . .196 E8
Printing Ho La, Hayes UB3 . . .95 BS75
Printing Ho Yd, E2 . . . . .197 N2
Print Village, SE15
  off Chadwick Rd 102 DT82
Priolo Rd, SE7 . . . . .104 EJ78
Prior Av, Sutt. SM2 . . . . .158 DE108
Prior Bolton St, N1 . . . . .83 DP65
Prior Chase, Grays (Bad.Dene)
  RM17 . . . . .110 FZ77
Prioress Rd, SE27 . . . . .121 DP90
Prioress St, SE1 . . . . .201 L7
Prior Rd, Ilf. IG1 . . . . .69 EN62
Priors, The, Ashtd. KT21 . . . .171 CK119
Priors Cl, Slou. SL1 . . . . .92 AU76
Priors Ct, Wok. GU21 . . . . . .166 AU118
  Woking GU22 . . . . .167 BA120
Priors Cft, E17 . . . . .47 DY54
Priors Fld, Nthlt. UB5
  off Arnold Rd 78 BY65
Priorsford Av, Orp. BR5 . . . .146 EU98
Priors Gdns, Ruis. HA4 . . . . .60 BW64
Priors Mead, Enf. EN1 . . . . . .30 DS39
Priors Pk, Horn. RM12 . . . . . .72 FJ62
Priors Shop Cen, The, N12
  off Highe Rd 44 DC50
Prior St, SE10 . . . . .103 EC80
Priory, The, SE3 . . . . .104 EF84
  Godstone RH9 . . . . .186 DV131
Priory Av, E4 . . . . .47 DZ48
  E17 . . . . .67 EA57
  N8 . . . . .65 DK56
  W4 . . . . .98 CS77
  Orpington BR5 . . . . .145 ER100
  Sutton SM3 . . . . .157 CX105
  Uxbridge (Hare.) UB9 . . . . .58 BJ56
  Wembley HA0 . . . . .61 CF63
Priory Cl, E4 . . . . .47 DZ48
  E18 . . . . .48 EG53
  N3 off Church Cres 43 CZ53
  N14 . . . . .29 DH43
  N20 . . . . .43 CZ45
  SW19 off High Path 140 DB95
  Beckenham BR3 . . . . .143 DY97
  Brentwood CM15 . . . . .54 FU43
  Chislehurst BR7 . . . . .145 EM95
  Dartford DA1 . . . . .128 FJ85
  Hampton TW12
  off Priory Gdns 136 BZ95
  Hayes UB3 . . . . .77 BV73
  Ruislip HA4 . . . . .59 BT60
  Stanmore HA7 . . . . .41 CF48
  Sunbury-on-Thames TW16
  off Staines Rd E 115 BU94
  Uxbridge (Denh.) UB9 . . . . .58 BG62
  Uxbridge (Hare.) UB9 . . . . .58 BH56
  Walton-on-Thames KT12 . . .135 BU104
  Wembley (Sudbury) HA0 . . .61 CF63
  Woking GU21 . . . . .151 BD113
Priory Ct, E17 . . . . .67 DZ55
  EC4 off Ludgate Hill 83 DP72
  SW8 . . . . .101 DK81
  Bushey WD23
  off Sparrows Herne 40 CC46
  Epsom KT17
  off Old Schools La 157 CT109
Priory Ct Est, E17
  off Priory Ct 47 DZ54
Priory Cres, SE19 . . . . .122 DQ94
  Sutton SM3 . . . . .157 CX105
  Wembley HA0 . . . . .61 CG62
Priory Dr, SE2 . . . . .106 EX78
  Stanmore HA7 . . . . .41 CF48
Priory Fld Dr, Edg. HA8 . . . . .42 CP49
Priory Flds, Dart. (Fngham).
  DA4 . . . . .148 FM103
Priory Gdns, N6 . . . . .65 DH58
  SE25 . . . . .142 DT98
  SW13 . . . . .99 CT83

Priory Gdns, W4 . . . . .98 CS77
  W5 off Hanger La 80 CL69
  Ashford TW15 . . . . .115 BR92
  Dartford DA1 . . . . .128 FK85
  Hampton TW12 . . . . .116 BZ94
  Uxbridge (Hare.) UB9 . . . . .58 BJ56
  Wembley HA0 . . . . .61 CG63
Priory Gate, Wal.Cr. EN8 . . . .15 DZ27
Priory Grn, Stai. TW18 . . . . .114 BH92
Priory Grn Est, N1 . . . . .83 DM68
Priory Gro, SW8 . . . . .101 DL81
  Barnet EN5 . . . . .28 DA43
  Romford RM3 . . . . .52 FL48
Priory Hill, Dart. DA1 . . . . . .128 FK85
  Wembley HA0 . . . . .61 CG63
Priory La, SW15 . . . . .118 CS86
  Dartford (Fngham.) DA4 . . .148 FM102
  Richmond TW9
  off Forest Rd 98 CN80
  West Molesey KT8 . . . . . . .136 CA98
Priory Ms, SW8 . . . . .101 DK81
  Hornchurch RM11 . . . . .71 FH60
  Staines TW18
  off Chestnut Manor Cl 114 BH92
Priory Pk, SE3 . . . . .104 EF83
Priory Pk Rd, NW6 . . . . .81 CZ67
  Wembley HA0 . . . . .61 CG63
Priory Path, Rom. RM3 . . . . . .52 FL48
Priory Pl, Dart. DA1 . . . . . . .128 FK86
  Walton-on-Thames KT12 . . .135 BU104
Priory Rd, E6 . . . . .86 EK67
  N8 . . . . .65 DK56
  NW6 . . . . .82 DB67
  SW19 . . . . .120 DD94
  W4 . . . . .98 CR76
  Barking IG11 . . . . .87 ER66
  Chessington KT9 . . . . .138 CL104
  Croydon CR0 . . . . .141 DN101
  Gerrards Cross (Chal.St.P.)
  SL9 . . . . .56 AW55
  Hampton TW12 . . . . .116 BZ94
  Hounslow TW3 . . . . .116 CC85
  Loughton IG10 . . . . .32 EL42
  Richmond TW9 . . . . .98 CN79
  Romford RM3 . . . . .52 FL48
  Sutton SM3 . . . . .157 CX105
Priory Rd N, Dart. DA1 . . . . .108 FK84
Priory Rd S, Dart. DA1 . . . . .128 FK85
Priory Shop Cen, Dart. DA1 . .128 FL86
Priory St, E3
  off St. Leonards St 85 EB69
Priory Ter, NW6 . . . . .82 DB67
  Sunbury-on-Thames TW16
  off Staines Rd E 115 BU94
Priory Vw, Bushey (Bushey Hth.)
  WD23 . . . . .41 CE45
Priory Wk, SW10 . . . . .100 DC78
Priory Way, Ger.Cr. (Chal.St.P.)
  SL9 . . . . .56 AX55
  Harrow HA2 . . . . .60 CB56
  Slough (Datchet) SL3 . . . . .92 AV80
  Southall UB2 . . . . .96 BX76
  West Drayton UB7 . . . . . . .94 BL79
Pritchard's Rd, E2 . . . . .84 DU67
Pritchett Cl, Enf. EN3
  off Government Row 31 EA37
Priter Rd, SE16 . . . . .202 C7
Priter Way, SE16
  off Dockley Rd 102 DU76
Private Rd, Enf. EN1 . . . . .30 DS43
Probert Rd, SW2 . . . . .121 DN85
Probyn Rd, SW2 . . . . .121 DP89
Procter St, WC1 . . . . .196 B7
Proctor Cl, Mitch. CR4 . . . . .140 DG95
Proctors Cl, Felt. TW14 . . . . .115 BU88
Profumo Rd, Walt. KT12 . . . .154 BX106
Progress Business Pk, Croy.
  CR0 . . . . .141 DM103
Progress Way, N22 . . . . .45 DN53
  Croydon CR0 . . . . .141 DM103
  Enfield EN1 . . . . .30 DU43
Promenade, The, W4 . . . . . . .98 CS81
Promenade App Rd, W4 . . . . .98 CS80
Promenade de Verdun, Pur.
  CR8 . . . . .159 DK111
Promenade Mans, Edg. HA8
  off Hale La 42 CP50
Prospect Business Pk, Loug.
  IG10 . . . . .33 EQ42
Prospect Cl, SE26 . . . . .122 DV91
  Belvedere DA17 . . . . .106 FA77
  Hounslow TW3 . . . . .96 BZ81
  Ruislip HA4 . . . . .60 BX59
Prospect Cotts, SW18
  off Point Pleasant 100 DA84
Prospect Cres, Twick. TW2 . . .116 CC86
Prospect Gro, Grav. DA12 . . .131 GK87
Prospect Hill, E17 . . . . .67 EB56
Prospect La, Egh. (Eng.Grn.)
  TW20 . . . . .112 AT92
Prospect Pl, E1 . . . . .202 F2
  N2 . . . . .64 DD56
  N7 off Parkhurst Rd 65 DL63
  N17 . . . . .46 DS53
  NW2 off Ridge Rd 63 CZ62
  NW3 off Holly Wk 64 DC63
  Bromley BR2 . . . . .144 EH97
  Dartford DA1 . . . . .128 FL86
  Epsom KT17
  off Clayton Rd 156 CS113
  Gravesend DA12 . . . . .131 GK87
  Grays RM17 . . . . .110 GA79
  Romford RM5 . . . . .51 FC54
  Staines TW18 . . . . .113 BF92
Prospect Quay, SW18 . . . . . .100 DA84
Prospect Ring, N2 . . . . .64 DD55
Prospect Rd, NW2 . . . . .63 CZ62
  Barnet EN5 . . . . .28 DA43
  Hornchurch RM11 . . . . .72 FM55
  Sevenoaks TN13 . . . . .191 FJ123
  Surbiton KT6 . . . . .137 CJ100
  Waltham Cross (Chsht.)
  EN8 . . . . .14 DW29
  Woodford Green IG8 . . . . . .48 EJ50
Prospect St, SE16 . . . . .202 E6
Prospect Vale, SE18 . . . . . . .104 EL77
Prospect Way, Brwd. CM13 . . .55 GE42

Pre - Pur

Prospero Rd, N19 . . . . .65 DJ60
Prossers, Tad. KT20
  off Croffets 173 CX121
Protea Cl, E16 off Hermit Rd . .86 EF70
Prothero Gdns, NW4 . . . . . . .63 CV57
Prothero Ho, NW10 . . . . .80 CR66
Prothero Rd, SW6 . . . . .99 CY80
Prout Gro, NW10 . . . . .62 CS63
Prout Rd, E5 . . . . .66 DV62
Provence St, N1
  off St. Peters St 84 DQ68
Providence Ct, W1 . . . . .194 G10
Providence La, Hayes UB3 . . .95 BR80
Providence Pl, N1
  off Upper St 83 DP67
  Epsom KT17 . . . . .156 CS112
  Romford RM5 . . . . .50 EZ54
  Woking GU22 . . . . .152 BG114
Providence Rd, West Dr. UB7 .76 BL74
Providence Row, N1
  off Pentonville Rd 83 DM68
Providence Row Cl, E2
  off Ainsley St 84 DV69
Providence Sq, SE1
  off Jacob St 102 DT75
Providence St, N1
  off St. Peters St 84 DQ68
  Greenhithe DA9 . . . . .129 FU85
Providence Yd, E2
  off Ezra St 84 DU69
Provident Ind Est, Hayes UB3 .95 BU75
Provost Est, N1 . . . . .197 K2
Provost Rd, NW3 . . . . .82 DF66
Provost St, N1 . . . . .197 K3
Prowse Av, Bushey (Bushey Hth.)
  WD23 . . . . .40 CC47
Prowse Pl, NW1 off Bonny St .83 DH66
Pruden Cl, N14 . . . . .45 DJ47
Prudent Pas, EC2 . . . . .197 J8
Prune Hill, Egh. (Eng.Grn.)
  TW20 . . . . .112 AX94
Prusom St, E1 . . . . .202 E3
Pryors, The, NW3 . . . . .64 DD62
★ PS Tattershall Castle,
  SW1 . . . . .200 A3
★ Public Record Office, Rich.
  TW9 . . . . .98 CP80
Puck La, Wal.Abb. EN9 . . . . .15 ED29
Puddenhole Cotts, Bet. RH3 .182 CN133
Pudding La, EC3 . . . . .201 L1
  Chigwell IG7 . . . . .49 ET46
  Sevenoaks (Seal) TN15
  off Church St 191 FN121
DLR Pudding Mill Lane 85 EB67
Pudding Mill La, E15 . . . . . . .85 EB67
Puddle Dock, EC4 . . . . .196 G10
Puddledock La, Dart. DA2 . . .127 FE92
  Westerham TN16 . . . . .189 ET133
Puers La, Beac. (Jordans)
  HP9 . . . . .36 AS51
Puffin Cl, Bark. IG11 . . . . . . .88 EV69
  Beckenham BR3 . . . . .143 DX99
Puffin Ter, Ilf. IG5
  off Tiptree Cres 69 EN55
Pulborough Rd, SW18 . . . . . .119 CZ87
Pulborough Way, Houns. TW4 .96 BW84
Pulford Rd, N15 . . . . .66 DR58
Pulham Av, N2 . . . . .64 DC56
Puller Rd, Barn. EN5 . . . . . . .27 CY40
Pulleyns Av, E6 . . . . .86 EL69
Pullman Cl, SW2 . . . . .121 DL88
Pullman Gdns, SW15 . . . . . .119 CW86
Pullman Pl, SE9 . . . . .124 EL85
Pullmans Pl, Stai. TW18 . . . .114 BG92
Pulross Rd, SW9 . . . . .101 DM83
Pulteney Cl, E3 . . . . .85 DZ67
Pulteney Gdns, E18
  off Pulteney Rd 68 EH55
Pulteney Rd, E18 . . . . .68 EH55
Pulteney Ter, N1 . . . . .83 DM67
Pulton Pl, SW6 . . . . .100 DA80
Puma Ct, E1 . . . . .197 P6
Pump All, Brent. TW8 . . . . . . .97 CK80
Pump Cl, Nthlt. UB5
  off Union Rd 78 CA68
Pump Ct, EC4 . . . . .196 D9
Pumphandle Path, N2
  off Tarling Rd 44 DC54
Pump Hill, Loug. IG10 . . . . . .33 EM40
Pump Ho Cl, SE16 . . . . .202 G5
  Bromley BR2 . . . . .144 EF96
Pumping Sta Rd, W4 . . . . . . .98 CS80
Pump La, SE14 . . . . .102 DW80
  Chesham HP5 . . . . .4 AS32
  Hayes UB3 . . . . .95 BV75
  Orpington BR6 . . . . .165 FB106
Pump Pail N, Croy. CR0
  off Old Town 142 DQ104
Pump Pail S, Croy. CR0
  off Southbridge Rd 142 DQ104
Pundersons Gdns, E2 . . . . . . .84 DV69
Punjab La, Sthl. UB1
  off Herbert Rd 78 BZ74
Purbeck Cl, Red. RH1 . . . . . .185 DK128
Purbeck Dr, NW2 . . . . .63 CY61
  Woking GU21 . . . . .151 AZ114
Purbeck Rd, Horn. RM11 . . . .71 FG60
Purberry Gro, Epsom KT17 . .157 CT110
Purbrook Av, Wat. WD25 . . . .24 BW36
Purbrook Est, SE1 . . . . .201 N5
Purbrook St, SE1 . . . . .201 N5
Purcell Cl, Borwd. WD6 . . . . .25 CK39
  Kenley CR8 . . . . .160 DR114
Purcell Cres, SW6 . . . . .99 CY80
Purcell Ms, NW10
  off Suffolk Rd 80 CS66
Purcell Rd, Grnf. UB6 . . . . . . .78 CB71
Purcells Av, Edg. HA8 . . . . . .42 CN50
Purcells Cl, Ashtd. KT21
  off Albert Rd 172 CM118
Purcell St, N1 . . . . .84 DS68
Purchese St, NW1 . . . . .83 DK68

★ Place of interest   ⇌ Railway station   ⊖ London Underground station   DLR Docklands Light Railway station   ◇ Tramlink station   H Hospital

Pur - Que

Purdy St, E3 .....85 EB70
Purelake Ms, SE13 .....103 ED83
PURFLEET 108 FP77
⇌ Purfleet 108 FN78
Purfleet Bypass, Purf. RM19 .108 FP77
Purfleet Ind Pk, S.Ock. (Aveley)
  .....108 FM75
Purfleet Rd, S.Ock. (Aveley)
  RM15 .....108 FN75
Purfleet Thames Terminal, Purf.
  RM19 .....108 FQ8
Purland Cl, Dag. RM8 .....70 EZ60
Purland Rd, SE28 .....105 ET75
Purleigh Av, Wdf.Grn. IG8 .48 EL51
PURLEY 159 DM111
⇌ Purley 159 DP112
Ⓗ Purley & District War Mem
  Hosp, Pur. CR8 .....159 DN111
Purley Av, NW2 .....63 CY62
Purley Bury Av, Pur. CR8 .160 DQ110
Purley Bury Cl, Pur. CR8 .160 DQ110
Purley Cl, Ilf. IG5 .....49 EN54
Purley Downs Rd, Pur. CR8 .160 DQ110
  South Croydon CR2 .....160 DR111
Purley Hill, Pur. CR8 .....159 DP112
Purley Knoll, Pur. CR8 .....159 DM111
⇌ Purley Oaks 160 DQ109
Purley Oaks Rd, S.Croy. CR2 .160 DR109
Purley Par, Pur. CR8
  off High St 159 DN111
Purley Pk Rd, Pur. CR8 .159 DP110
Purley Pl, N1 .....83 DP66
  off Islington Pk St 83 DP66
Purley Ri, Pur. CR8 .....159 DM112
Purley Rd, N9 .....46 DR48
  Purley CR8 .....159 DN111
  South Croydon CR2 .....160 DR108
Purley Vale, Pur. CR8 .....159 DP113
Purley Way, Croy. CR0 .141 DM101
  Purley CR8 .....159 DN108
Purley Way Cres, Croy. CR0
  .141 DM101
Purlieu Way, Epp. (They.B.)
  CM16 .....33 ES35
Purlings Rd, Bushey WD23 .24 CB43
Purneys Rd, SE9 .....104 EK84
Purrett Rd, SE18 .....105 ET78
Purser's Cross Rd, SW6 .99 CZ81
Pursewardens Cl, W13 .79 CJ74
Pursley Gdns, Borwd. WD6 .26 CN38
Pursley Rd, NW7 .....43 CV52
Purves Rd, NW10 .....81 CW68
Puteaux Ho, E2 .....85 DX68
PUTNEY, SW15 .....99 CY84
⇌ Putney 99 CY84
⊖ Putney Bridge 99 CY83
Putney Br, SW6 .....99 CY83
  SW15 .....99 CY83
Putney Br App, SW6 .99 CY84
Putney Br Rd, SW15 .99 CY83
  SW18 .....120 DA85
Putney Common, SW15 .99 CW83
Putney Ex Shop Cen, SW15 .99 CX84
Putney Gdns, Rom. (Chad.Hth.)
  RM6 off Heathfield Pk Dr .70 EV58
PUTNEY HEATH, SW15 .119 CW86
Putney Heath, SW15 .119 CW86
Putney Heath La, SW15 .119 CX86
Putney High St, SW15 .99 CX84
Putney Hill, SW15 .....119 CX86
Ⓗ Putney Hosp, SW15 .99 CW82
Putney Pk Av, SW15 .99 CU84
Putney Pk La, SW15 .99 CV84
Putney Rd, Enf. EN3 .31 DX36
PUTNEY VALE, SW15 .119 CT90
Puttenham Cl, Wat. WD19 .40 BW48
Pycroft Way, N9 .....46 DU49
Pye Cl, Cat. CR3
  off St. Lawrence Way .176 DR123
Pyecombe Cor, N12 .....43 CZ49
Pyghtle, The, Uxb. (Denh.)
  UB9 .....58 BG60
Pylbrook Rd, Sutt. SM1 .140 DA104
Pyle Hill, Wok. GU22 .166 AX124
Pylon Way, Croy. CR0 .141 DL102
Pym Cl, Barn. EN4 .....28 DD43
Pymers Mead, SE21 .122 DQ88
Pymmes Cl, N13 .....45 DM50
  N17 .....46 DV53
Pymmes Gdns N, N9 .46 DT48
Pymmes Gdns S, N9 .46 DT48
Pymmes Grn Rd, N11 .45 DH49
Pymmes Rd, N13 .....45 DL51
Pymms Brook Dr, Barn. EN4 .28 DE42
Pym Orchard, West. (Brasted)
  TN16 .....180 EW124
Pym Pl, Grays RM17 .110 GA77
Pynchester Cl, Uxb. UB10 .58 BN61
Pyne Rd, Surb. KT6 .138 CN102
Pynest Grn La, Wal.Abb. EN9 .32 EG38
Pyne Ter, SW19
  off Windlesham Gro .119 CX88
Pynfolds, SE16 .....202 E5
Pynham Cl, SE2 .....106 EU76
Pynnacles Cl, Stan. HA7 .41 CH50
Pyrcroft La, Wey. KT13 .153 BP106
Pyrcroft Rd, Cher. KT16 .133 BF101
PYRFORD, Wok. 167 BE115
Pyrford Common Rd, Wok.
  GU22 .....167 BD116
★ Pyrford Ct, Wok. GU22 .167 BE117
Pyrford Ct, Wok. GU22 .167 BE117
PYRFORD GREEN, Wok. .168 BH117
Pyrford Heath, Wok. GU22 .167 BF116
PYRFORD VILLAGE, Wok. .168 BG118
Pyrford Wds Cl, Wok. GU22 .167 BE115
Pyrford Wds Rd, Wok. GU22 .167 BE115
Pyrland Rd, N5 .....66 DR64
  Richmond TW10 .....118 CM86
Pyrles Grn, Loug. IG10 .33 EP39

Pyrles La, Loug. IG10 .....33 EP40
Pyrmont Gro, SE27 .....121 DP90
Pyrmont Rd, W4 .....98 CN79
  Ilford IG1 off High Rd .69 EQ61
Pytchley Cres, SE19 .....122 DQ93
Pytchley Rd, SE22 .....102 DS8

Q

Quadrangle, The, W2 .....194 B8
Quadrangle Ms, Stan. HA7 .41 CJ52
Quadrant, The, SE24
  off Herne Hill 122 DQ85
  SW20 .....139 CY95
  Bexleyheath DA7 .106 EX80
  Epsom KT17 .....156 CS113
  Purfleet RM19 .....108 FQ77
  Richmond TW9 .....98 CL84
  Sutton SM2 .....158 DC107
Quadrant Arc, W1 .....199 L1
  Romford RM1 .....71 FE57
Quadrant Cl, NW4
  off The Burroughs .63 CV57
Quadrant Gro, NW5 .....64 DF64
Quadrant Ho, Sutt. SM2 .158 DC107
Quadrant Rd, Rich. TW9 .97 CK84
  Thornton Heath CR7 .141 DP98
Quadrant Way, Wey. KT13
  off Weybridge Rd .152 BM105
Quad Rd, Wem. HA9
  off Courtenay Rd .61 CK62
Quaggy Wk, SE3 .....104 EG84
Quail Gdns, S.Croy. CR2 .161 DY110
Quainton St, NW10 .....62 CR62
Quaker Cl, Sev. TN13 .191 FK123
Quaker Ct, E1 .....197 P5
Quaker La, Sthl. UB2 .96 CA76
  Waltham Abbey EN9 .15 EC34
Quakers Course, NW9 .43 CT53
Quakers Hall La, Sev. TN13 .191 FJ122
Quakers La, Islw. TW7 .97 CG81
  Potters Bar EN6 .....12 DB30
Quaker's Pl, E7 .....68 EK64
Quaker St, E1 .....197 P5
Quakers Wk, N21 .....30 DR44
Quality Ct, WC2 .....196 D8
Quality St, Red. RH1 .185 DH128
Quantock Cl, Hayes UB3 .95 BR80
  Slough SL3 .....93 BA78
Quantock Dr, Wor.Pk. KT4 .139 CW103
Quantock Gdns, NW2 .63 CX61
Quantock Rd, Bexh. DA7
  off Cumbrian Av .107 FE82
Quarles Cl, Rom. RM5 .50 FA52
Quarley Way, SE15
  off Daniel Gdns .102 DT80
Quarrendon St, SW6 .100 DA82
Quarr Rd, Cars. SM5 .140 DD100
Quarry, The, Bet. RH3
  off Station Rd .182 CS132
Quarry Cl, Lthd. KT22 .171 CK121
  Oxted RH8 .....188 EE130
Quarry Cotts, Sev. TN13 .190 FG123
Quarry Gdns, Lthd. KT22 .171 CK121
Quarry Hill, Grays RM17 .110 GA78
  Sevenoaks TN15 .....191 FK123
Quarry Hill Pk, Reig. RH2 .184 DC131
Quarry Ms, Purf. RM19
  off Fanns Ri .108 FN77
Quarry Pk Rd, Sutt. SM1 .157 CZ107
Quarry Ri, Sutt. SM1 .157 CZ107
Quarry Rd, SW18 .....120 DC86
  Godstone RH9 .186 DW128
  Oxted RH8 .....188 EE130
Quarryside Business Pk, Red.
  RH1 .....185 DH130
Quarterdeck, The, E14 .203 P5
Quartermaine Av, Wok.
  GU22 .....167 AZ122
Quarter Mile La, E10 .67 EB63
Quaves Rd, Slou. SL3 .92 AV76
Quay La, Green. DA9 .109 FV84
Quayside Wk, Kings.T. KT1
  off Bishop's Hall .137 CK96
Quay W, Tedd. TW11 .117 CH92
Quebec Av, West. TN16 .189 ER126
★ Quebec Ho (Wolfe's Ho), West.
  TN16 .....189 ER126
Quebec Ms, W1 .....194 E9
Quebec Rd, Hayes UB4 .78 BW73
  Ilford IG1, IG2 .....69 EP59
  Tilbury RM18 .....111 GG82
Quebec Sq, West. TN16 .189 ER126
Quedgeley Ct, SE15 .....203 J5
Queen Adelaide Rd, SE20 .122 DW93
Queen Alexandra's Ct, SW19 .119 CZ92
Queen Alexandra's Way, Epsom
  KT19 .....156 CN112
Queen Anne Av, N15
  off Suffield Rd .66 DT57
  Bromley BR2 .....144 EF97
Queen Anne Dr, Esher (Clay.)
  KT10 .....155 CE108
Queen Anne Ms, W1 .195 J7
Queen Anne Rd, E9 .85 DX65
Queen Anne's Cl, Twick. TW2 .117 CD90
Queen Anne's Gdns, W4 .98 CS76
  W5 .....98 CL75
  Enfield EN1 .....30 DS44
  Leatherhead KT22
  off Upper Fairfield Rd .171 CH121
Queen Anne's Gdns, Mitch.
  CR4 .....140 DF97
Queen Anne's Gate, SW1 .199 M5
  Bexleyheath DA7 .106 EX83
Queen Anne's Gro, W4 .98 CS76
  W5 .....98 CL75
  Enfield EN1 .....30 DR45
Queen Anne's Ms, Lthd. KT22
  off Fairfield Rd .171 CH121
Queen Annes Pl, Enf. EN1 .30 DS44
Queen Annes Ter, Lthd. KT22
  off Upper Fairfield Rd .171 CH121
Queen Anne St, W1 .195 H8

Queen Anne's Wk, WC1
  off Guilford St .83 DL70
Queen Anne Ter, E1 .202 E1
Queenborough Gdns, Chis.
  BR7 .....125 ER93
  Ilford IG2 .....69 EN56
Queen Caroline Est, W6 .99 CW78
Queen Caroline St, W6 .99 CW77
Ⓗ Queen Charlotte & Chelsea
  Hosp, W6 .....81 CU72
Queendale Ct, Wok. GU21
  off Roundthorn Way .166 AT116
Queen Elizabeth Ct, Brox. EN10
  off Groom Rd 15 DZ26
  Waltham Abbey EN9
  off Greenwich Way .31 EC36
Queen Elizabeth Gdns, Mord.
  SM4 .....140 DA98
★ Queen Elizabeth Hall &
  Purcell Room, SE1 .200 B2
Ⓗ Queen Elizabeth Hosp,
  SE18 .....104 EL80
Queen Elizabeth Pl, Til.
  RM18 .....111 GG84
Queen Elizabeth Rd, E17 .67 DY55
  Kingston upon Thames
  KT2 .....138 CM95
Queen Elizabeths Cl, N16 .66 DR61
Queen Elizabeths Dr, N14 .45 DL46
Queen Elizabeth's Dr, Croy.
  (New Adgtn.) CR0 .161 ED110
Queen Elizabeth II Br, Dart.
  DA1 .....109 FR82
  Purfleet RM19 .....109 FR82
★ Queen Elizabeth II Conf
  Cen, SW1 .....199 N5
Queen Elizabeth's Gdns, Croy.
  (New Adgtn.) CR0
  off Queen Elizabeth's Dr .161 ED110
★ Queen Elizabeth's Hunting
  Lodge, Epping Forest, E4 .48 EF45
Queen Elizabeth St, SE1 .201 N4
Queen Elizabeths Wk, N16 .66 DR61
Queen Elizabeth's Wk, Wall.
  SM6 .....159 DK105
Queen Elizabeth Wk, SW13 .99 CV81
  Windsor SL4 .....92 AS82
Queen Elizabeth Way, Wok.
  GU22 .....167 AZ119
Queenhill Rd, S.Croy. CR2 .160 DV110
Queenhithe, EC4 .....197 J10
Queen Margaret's Gro, N1 .66 DS64
Queen Mary Av, Mord. SM4 .139 CX99
  Surbiton KT6 .....138 CL104
  Woking GU22 .....167 BC116
Queen Mary Cl, Rom. RM1 .71 FF58
  Surbiton KT6 .....138 CM104
  Woking GU22 .....167 BC116
Queen Mary Rd, SE19 .121 DP93
  Shepperton TW17 .135 BQ96
Queen Mary's Av, Cars. SM5 .158 DF107
Queen Marys Av, Wat. WD18 .23 BS42
Queen Marys Av, Wal.Abb. EN9
  off Greenwich Way .31 EC35
Queen Marys Dr, Add. (New Haw)
  KT15 .....151 BF110
★ Queen Mary's Gdns, NW1
  off Regent's Pk .194 F3
Ⓗ Queen Mary's Hosp, NW3 .64 DC62
Ⓗ Queen Mary's Hosp,
  Sid. DA14 .....126 EU93
Ⓗ Queen Mary's Hosp for
  Children, Cars. SM5 .140 DC102
Ⓗ Queen Mary's Uni Hosp
  (Roehampton), SW15 .119 CU86
Queen Mother's Dr, Uxb. (Denh.)
  UB9 .....57 BF58
Queen of Denmark Ct, SE16 .203 M6
Queens Acre, Sutt. SM3 .157 CX108
Queens All, Epp. CM16 .17 ET31
Queens Av, N3 .....44 DC52
  N10 .....64 DG55
  N20 .....44 DD47
Queen's Av, N21 .....45 DP46
Queens Av, Felt. TW13 .116 BW91
  Greenford UB6 .78 CB72
  Stanmore HA7 .....61 CJ55
  Watford WD18 .....23 BT42
  West Byfleet (Byfleet)
  KT14 .....152 BK112
  Woodford Green IG8 .48 EH50
Queensberry Ms W, SW7
  off Queen's Gate .100 DD77
Queensberry Pl, E12 .68 EK64
  SW7 .....100 DD77
  Richmond TW9
  off Friars La .117 CK85
Queensberry Way, SW7
  off Harrington Rd .100 DD77
Queensborough Ms, W2 .82 DC73
Queensborough Pas, W2
  off Porchester Ter .82 DC73
Queensborough S Bldgs, W2
  off Porchester Ter .82 DC73
Queensborough Studios, W2
  off Porchester Ter .82 DC73
Queensborough Ter, W2 .82 DB73
Queensbridge Pk, Islw. TW7 .117 CE85
Queensbridge Rd, E2 .84 DT67
  E8 .....84 DT66
QUEENSBURY, Har. .61 CK55
⊖ Queensbury 62 CM55
Queensbury Circle Par, Har. HA3
  off Streatfield Rd .62 CL55
  Stanmore HA7
  off Streatfield Rd .62 CL55
Queensbury Rd, NW9 .62 CR59
  Wembley HA0 .....80 CM68
Queensbury Sta Par, Edg.
  HA8 .....62 CM55
Queensbury St, N1 .84 DQ66
Queen's Circ, SW8
  off Queenstown Rd .101 DH80
  SW11 off Queenstown Rd .101 DH80
Queens Cl, Edg. HA8 .42 CN50
  Tadworth KT20 .173 CU124
  Wallington SM6
  off Queens Rd .159 DH106

Queens Cl, Wind. (Old Wind.)
  SL4 .....112 AU85
★ Queens Club (Tennis Cen),
  W14 .....99 CY78
Queens Club Gdns, W14 .99 CY79
Queens Ct, SE23 .....122 DW88
  Richmond TW10 .118 CM86
  Slough SL1 .....74 AT73
Queenscourt, Wem. HA9 .62 CL63
Queens Ct, Wey. KT13 .153 BR106
  Woking GU22
  off Hill Vw Rd .167 AZ118
Queens Ct Ride, Cob. KT11 .153 BU113
Queen's Cres, NW5 .82 DG65
Queens Cres, Rich. TW10 .118 CM86
Queenscroft Rd, SE9 .124 EK85
Queensdale Cres, W11 .81 CX74
Queensdale Pl, W11 .81 CY74
Queensdale Rd, W11 .81 CX74
Queensdale Wk, W11 .81 CY74
Queensdown Rd, E5 .66 DV63
Queens Dr, E10 .....67 EA59
  N4 .....65 DP61
  W3 .....80 CM72
  W5 .....80 CM72
  Abbots Langley WD5 .7 BT32
  Leatherhead (Oxshott)
  KT22 .....154 CC111
Queen's Dr, Slou. SL3 .75 AZ66
Queen's Dr, Surb. KT5 .138 CN101
  Thames Ditton KT7 .137 CG101
  Waltham Cross EN8 .15 EA34
Queens Dr, The, Rick. (Mill End)
  WD3 .....37 BF45
Queens Elm Par, SW3
  off Old Ch St .100 DD78
Queen's Elm Sq, SW3
  off Old Ch St .100 DD78
Queensferry Wk, N17
  off Jarrow Rd .66 DV56
★ Queen's Gall, The, SW1 .199 J5
Queens Gdns, NW4 .63 CW57
  W2 .....82 DC73
  W5 .....79 CJ70
  Dartford DA2 .....128 FP88
Queen's Gdns, Houns. TW5 .96 BY81
  Rainham RM13 .89 FD68
  Upminster RM14 .73 FT58
Queen's Gate, SW7 .100 DD77
Queensgate, Cob. KT11 .154 BX112
  Waltham Cross EN8 .15 DZ34
Queen's Gate Gdns, SW7 .100 DC76
Queensgate Gdns, SW15
  off Upper Richmond Rd .119 CY87
Queensgate Gdns, Chis. BR7 .145 ER95
Queen's Gate Ms, SW7 .100 DC75
Queensgate Pl, NW6 .82 DA66
Queen's Gate Pl, SW7 .100 DC76
Queen's Gate Pl Ms, SW7 .100 DC76
Queen's Gate Ter, SW7 .100 DC76
Queens Gro, NW8 .82 DD67
Queens Gro Ms, NW8 .82 DD67
Queens Gro Rd, E4 .47 ED46
Queen's Head St, N1 .83 DP67
Queens Head Yd, SE1 .201 K3
Queens Ho, Tedd. TW11 .117 CF93
★ Queen's Ice Rink, W2
  off Queensway .82 DB73
Queensland Av, N18 .46 DQ51
  SW19 .....140 DB95
Queensland Cl, E17 .47 DZ54
Queensland Ho, E16
  off Rymill St .87 EN74
Queensland Pl, N7
  off Queensland Rd .65 DN63
Queensland Rd, N7 .65 DN63
Queens La, N10 .65 DH55
  Ashford TW15
  off Clarendon Rd .114 BM91
Queens Mkt, E13 off Green St .86 EJ67
Queensmead, NW8 .82 DD67
  Leatherhead KT22 .154 CC111
  Slough (Datchet) SL3 .92 AV81
Queensmead Av, Epsom
  KT17 .....157 CV110
Queensmead Rd, Brom. BR2 .144 EF96
Queensmere Cl, SW19 .119 CX89
Queensmere Rd, SW19 .119 CX89
  Slough SL1
  off Wellington St .92 AU75
Queensmere Shop Cen, Slou.
  SL1 .....92 AT75
Queens Ms, W2 .82 DB73
Queensmill Rd, SW6 .99 CX80
Queens Par, N11
  off Colney Hatch La .44 DF50
  W5 .....80 CM72
Queens Par Cl, N11
  off Colney Hatch La .44 DF50
⇌ Queen's Park 81 CY68
⊖ Queen's Park 81 CY68
Queens Pk Ct, W10 .81 CX69
Queens Pk Gdns, Felt. TW13
  off Vernon Rd .115 BU90
★ Queens Park Rangers FC,
  W12 .....81 CV74
Queens Pk Rd, Cat. CR3 .176 DS123
  Romford RM3 .52 FM53
Queens Pas, Chis. BR7
  off High St .125 EP93
Queens Pl, Mord. SM4 .140 DA98
  Watford WD17 .24 BW41
Queen's Prom, Kings.T. KT1
  off Portsmouth Rd .137 CK97
Queen Sq, WC1 .....196 A5
Queen Sq Pl, WC1 .196 A5
Queens Reach, E.Mol. KT8 .137 CE98
Queens Ride, SW13 .99 CU83
  SW15 .....99 CU83
Queen's Ride, Rich. TW10 .118 CP88
Queens Ri, Rich. TW10 .118 CM86
Queens Rd, E11 .67 ED59
  E13 .....86 EH67
Queen's Rd, E17 .67 DZ58
Queens Rd, N3 .44 DC53
  N9 .....46 DV48
Queen's Rd, N11 .45 DL52

Queens Rd, NW4 .....63 CW57
  SE14 .....102 DV81
  SE15 .....102 DV81
  SW14 .....98 CR83
  SW19 .....119 CZ93
  W5 .....80 CL72
  Barking IG11 .87 EQ66
  Barnet EN5 .27 CX41
  Beckenham BR3 .143 DY96
  Brentwood CM14 .54 FW48
  Bromley BR1 .144 EG96
  Buckhurst Hill IG9 .48 EH47
  Chislehurst BR7 .125 EP93
Queen's Rd, Croy. CR0 .141 DP100
Queens Rd, Egh. TW20 .113 AZ93
  Enfield EN1 .30 DS42
  Epping (N.Wld.Bas.) CM16 .19 FB26
  Erith DA8 .107 FE79
  Felt. TW13 .115 BV88
  Gravesend DA12 .131 GJ90
  Hampton (Hmptn.H.)
  TW12 .....116 CB91
  Hayes UB3 .77 BS72
Queen's Rd, Houns. TW3 .96 CB83
Queens Rd, Kings.T. KT2 .118 CN94
  Loughton IG10 .32 EL41
  Mitcham CR4 .140 DD97
  Morden SM4 .140 DA98
  New Malden KT3 .139 CT98
  Richmond TW10 .118 CL87
Queen's Rd, Slou. SL1 .74 AT73
  SL3 .....92 AU81
  Southall UB2 .96 BX75
  Sutton SM2 .158 DA110
Queen's Rd, Tedd. TW11 .117 CE93
  Thames Ditton KT7 .137 CF99
Queen's Rd, Twick. TW1 .117 CF88
Queen's Rd, Uxb. UB8 .76 BJ69
Queen's Rd, Wall. SM6 .159 DH106
  Waltham Cross EN8 .15 DY34
  Walton-on-Thames KT12 .153 BV106
  Watford WD17 .24 BW42
Queens Rd, Well. DA16 .106 EV82
Queen's Rd, West Dr. UB7 .94 BM75
  Weybridge KT13 .153 BQ105
⇌ Queens Road Peckham .102 DW81
Queens Rd W, E13 .86 EG68
Queen's Row, SE17 .102 DR79
Queens Ter, E13 .86 EH67
Queen's Ter, NW8 .82 DD68
  Islw. TW7 .97 CG84
Queens Ter Cotts, W7
  off Boston Rd .97 CE75
★ Queen's Twr, SW7 .100 DD76
Queenstown Gdns, Rain.
  RM13 .....89 FF69
Queenstown Ms, SW8
  off Queenstown Rd .101 DH82
⇌ Queenstown Road
  (Battersea), SW8 .101 DH81
Queenstown Rd, SW8 .197 J10
  N17 .....46 DS51
  W1 .....199 H2
  Bexleyheath DA7 .106 EZ83
  Brentwood CM14 .54 FW50
  Chertsey KT16 .134 BG102
  Croydon CR0
  off Church Rd .142 DQ104
  Erith DA8 .107 FE79
  Gravesend DA12 .131 GH86
  Kings Langley (Chipper.)
  WD4 .....6 BG32
  Romford RM7 .71 FD58
Queen St Pl, EC4 .201 J1
Queensville Rd, SW12 .121 DK87
Queens Wk, E4
  off The Green Wk .47 ED46
  NW9 .....62 CQ61
Queen's Wk, SE1 .200 B3
  SW1 .....199 K3
Queens Wk, W5 .79 CJ70
  Ashford TW15 .114 BK91
Queen's Wk, Har. HA1 .61 CE56
  Ruislip HA4 .60 BX62
⊖ Queensway 82 DB73
Queens Way, NW4 .63 CW57
Queensway, W2 .82 DB72
Queensway, Croy. CR0 .159 DM107
Queensway, Enf. EN3 .30 DV42
Queensway, Felt. TW13 .116 BW91
Queensway, Orp. BR5 .145 EQ99
Queensway, Rad. (Shenley)
  WD7 .....10 CL32
Queensway, Red. RH1 .184 DF133
  Sunbury-on-Thames
  TW16 .....135 BV96
Queens Way, Wal.Cr. EN8 .15 DZ34
Queensway, W.Wick. BR4 .144 EE104
Queensway, The, Ger.Cr.
  (Chal.St.P.) SL9 .56 AX55
Queensway N, Walt. KT12
  off Robinsway .154 BW104
Queensway S, Walt. KT12
  off Trenchard Cl .154 BW105
Queens Well Av, N20 .44 DE48
Queenswood Av, E17 .47 EC53
  Brentwood CM13 .55 GD43
  Hampton TW12 .116 CB93
  Hounslow TW3 .96 BZ82
  Thornton Heath CR7 .141 DN99
  Wallington SM6 .159 DK105
Queenswood Cres, Wat. WD25 .7 BU33
Queenswood Gdns, E11 .68 EG60
Queenswood Pk, N3 .43 CY54
Queens Wd Rd, N10 .65 DH58
Queenswood Rd, SE23 .123 DX90
  Sidcup DA15 .125 ET85
Queen Victoria Av, Wem. HA0 .79 CK66
★ Queen Victoria Mem,
  SW1 .....199 K4
Queen Victoria's Wk, Wind.
  SL4 .....92 AS81

Rav - Reg

Ravenscroft Cl, E16 ....86 EG71
Ravenscroft Cres, SE9 ...125 EM90
Ravenscroft Pk, Barn. EN5 ...27 CX42
Ravenscroft Pt, E9
  off Kenton Rd 85 DX65
Ravenscroft Rd, E16 ....86 EG71
  W4 ....98 CQ77
  Beckenham BR3 ....142 DW96
  Weybridge KT13 ....153 BQ111
Ravenscroft St, E2 ....84 DT68
Ravensdale Av, N12 ....44 DC49
Ravensdale Gdns, SE19 ...122 DR94
  Hounslow TW4 ....96 BY83
Ravensdale Ms, Stai. TW18
  off Worple Rd 114 BH93
Ravensdale Rd, N16 ....66 DT59
  Hounslow TW4 ....96 BY83
Ravensdon St, SE11 ....101 DN78
Ravensfield, Slou. SL3 ....92 AX75
Ravensfield Cl, Dag. RM9 ....70 EX63
Ravensfield Gdns, Epsom
  KT19 ....156 CS106
Ravenshaw St, NW6 ....63 CZ64
Ravenshead Cl, S.Croy. CR2 ...160 DW111
Ravenshill, Chis. BR7 ....145 EP95
Ravenshurst Av, NW4 ....63 CW56
Ravenside Cl, N18 ....47 DX51
Ravenside Retail Pk, N18 ....47 DX50
Ravenslea Rd, SW12 ....120 DF87
Ravensmead, Ger.Cr. (Chal.St.P.)
  SL9 ....37 AZ50
Ravensmead Rd, Brom. BR2 .123 ED94
Ravensmede Way, W4 ....99 CT77
Ravensmere, Epp. CM16 .....18 EU31
Ravens Ms, SE12
  off Ravens Way 124 EG85
Ravenstone, SE17 ....102 DS78
Ravenstone Rd, N8 ....65 DN55
  NW9
  off West Hendon Bdy ...63 CT58
Ravenstone St, SW12 ......120 DG88
Ravens Way, SE12 ....124 EG85
Ravenswold, Ken. CR8 .....176 DQ115
Ravenswood, Bex. DA5 .....126 EY88
Ravenswood Av, Surb. KT6 .138 CM103
  West Wickham BR4 .....143 EC102
Ravenswood Cl, Cob. KT11 .170 BXI15
  Romford RM5 ....51 FB50
Ravenswood Ct, Kings.T.
  KT2 ....118 CP93
  Woking GU22 ....167 AZ118
Ravenswood Cres, Har. HA2 ..60 BZ61
  West Wickham BR4 .....143 EC102
Ravenswood Gdns, Islw.
  TW7 ....97 CE81
Ravenswood Pk, Nthwd. HA6 .39 BU51
Ravenswood Rd, E17 ....67 EB56
  SW12 ....121 DH87
  Croydon CR0 ....141 DP104
Ravensworth Rd, NW10 ......81 CV69
  SE9 ....125 EM91
Ravent Rd, SE11 ....200 C9
Ravey St, EC2 ....197 M4
Ravine Gro, SE18 ....105 ES79
Rawlings Cl, Orp. BR6 ......163 ET106
Rawlings Cres, Wem. HA9 ....62 CP62
Rawlings St, SW3 ....198 D9
Rawlins Cl, N3 ....63 CY55
  South Croydon CR2 ....161 DY109
Rawnsley Av, Mitch. CR4 ....140 DD99
Rawreth Wk, N1 *off Basire St* .84 DQ67
Rawson St, SW11
  off Strasburg Rd 100 DG81
Rawsthorne Cl, E16
  off Kennard St 87 EM74
Rawstone Wk, E13 ....86 EG68
Rawstorne Pl, EC1 ....196 F2
Rawstorne St, EC1 ....196 F2
Rayburn Rd, Horn. RM11 .....72 FN59
Ray Cl, Chess. KT9
  off Merritt Gdns 155 CJ107
Raydean Rd, Barn. EN5 ......28 DB43
Raydon Rd, Wal.Cr. (Chsht.)
  EN8 ....15 DX32
Raydons Gdns, Dag. RM9 ....70 EY64
Raydons Rd, Dag. RM9 ......70 EY64
Raydon St, N19 ....65 DH61
Rayfield, Epp. CM16 ....18 EU30
Rayfield Cl, Brom. BR2 .....144 EL100
Rayford Av, SE12 ....124 EF87
Rayford Cl, Dart. DA1 ......128 FJ85
Ray Gdns, Bark. IG11 ....88 EU68
  Stanmore HA7 ....41 CH50
Ray Lamb Way, Erith DA8 ...107 FH79
Raylands Mead, Ger.Cr. SL9
  off Bull La 56 AW57
Rayleas Cl, SE18 ....105 EP81
Rayleigh Av, Tedd. TW11 ...117 CE93
Rayleigh Cl, N13
  off Rayleigh Rd 46 DQ48
  Brentwood CM13 ....55 GC44
Rayleigh Ct, Kings.T. KT1 ..138 CM96
Rayleigh Ri, S.Croy. CR2 ...160 DS107
Rayleigh Rd, E16 ....86 EH74
  N13 ....46 DQ48
  SW19 ....139 CZ95
  Brentwood CM13 ....55 GB44
  Woodford Green IG8 .....48 EJ51
Ray Lo Rd, Wdf.Grn. IG8 ....48 EJ51
Ray Massey Way, E6
  off Ron Leighton Way ...86 EL67
Raymead, NW4
  off Tenterden Gro 63 CW56
Raymead Av, Th.Hth. CR7 ...141 DN99
Raymead Cl, Lthd. (Fetch.)
  KT22 ....171 CE122
Raymead Way, Lthd. (Fetch.)
  KT22 ....171 CE122
Raymere Gdns, SE18 ....105 ER80
Raymond Av, E18 ....68 EF55
  W13 ....97 CG76
Raymond Bldgs, WC1 ....196 C6
Raymond Cl, SE26 ....122 DW92
  Abbots Langley WD5 .....7 BR32

Raymond Cl, Slou. (Colnbr.)
  SL3 ....93 BE81
Raymond Ct, N10
  off Pembroke Rd 44 DG52
  Potters Bar EN6
  off St. Francis Cl 12 DC34
  Sutton SM2
  off Mulgrave Rd 158 DB107
Raymond Gdns, Chig. IG7 ...50 EV48
Raymond Rd, E13 ....86 EJ66
  SW19 ....119 CY93
  Beckenham BR3 ....143 DY98
  Ilford IG2 ....69 ER59
  Slough SL3 ....93 BA76
Raymond Way, Esher (Clay.)
  KT10 ....155 CG107
Raymouth Rd, SE16 ....202 E8
Rayne Ct, E18 ....68 EF56
Rayners Cl, Slou. (Colnbr.)
  SL3 ....93 BC80
  Wembley HA0 ....61 CK64
Rayners Cres, Grav. DA11 ...130 GB86
  Harrow HA2 ....60 CA60
Rayners Gdns, Nthlt. UB5 ...77 BV69
RAYNERS LANE, Har. 60 BZ60
  ⊖ Rayners Lane 60 BZ59
Rayners La, Har. HA2 ....60 CB61
  Pinner HA5 ....60 BZ58
Rayners Rd, SW15 ....119 CY85
Rayner Twr, E10 ....67 EA59
Raynes Av, E11 ....68 EJ59
RAYNES PARK, SW20 ......139 CV97
  ⇌ Raynes Park 139 CW96
Raynham Av, N18 ....46 DU51
Raynham Rd, N18 ....46 DU50
  W6 ....99 CV77
Raynham Ter, N18 ....46 DU50
Raynor Cl, Sthl. UB1 ....78 BZ74
Raynor Pl, N1 *off Elizabeth Av* .84 DQ67
Raynton Cl, Har. HA2 ....60 BY60
  Hayes UB4 ....77 BT70
Raynton Dr, Hayes UB4 .....77 BT70
Rays Av, N18 ....46 DW49
  West Molesey KT8 ......136 CB99
Rays Hill, Dart. (Hort.Kir.)
  DA4 ....148 FQ98
Rays Rd, N18 ....46 DW49
  West Wickham BR4 .....143 EC101
Ray St, EC1 ....196 E5
Ray St Br, EC1 ....196 E5
Ray Wk, N7 *off Andover Rd* .65 DM61
Raywood Cl, Hayes UB3 .....95 BQ80
Reachview Cl, NW1
  off Baynes St 83 DJ66
Read Cl, T.Ditt. KT7 ....137 CG101
Read Ct, Wal.Abb. EN9 ......16 EG33
Reade Ct, Slou. SL2
  off Victoria Rd 74 AV72
Readens, The, Bans. SM7 ...174 DF116
Reade Wk, NW10
  off Denbigh Cl 80 CS66
Reading Arch Rd, Red. RH1 .184 DF134
Reading La, E8 ....84 DV65
Reading Rd, Nthlt. UB5 .....60 CB64
  Sutton SM1 ....158 DC106
Readings, The, Rick. (Chorl.)
  WD3 ....21 BF41
Reading Way, NW7 ....43 CX50
Read Rd, Ashtd. KT21 ......171 CK117
Reads Cl, Ilf. IG1
  off Chapel La 69 EP62
Reads Rest La, Tad. KT20 ..173 CZ119
Read Way, Grav. DA12 .....131 GK92
Reapers Cl, NW1
  off Crofters Way 83 DK67
Reapers Way, Islw. TW7
  off Hall Rd 117 CD85
Reardon Ct, N21
  off Cosgrove Cl 46 DQ47
Reardon Path, E1 ....202 E3
Reardon St, E1 ....202 D2
Reaston St, SE14 ....102 DW80
Reckitt Rd, W4 ....98 CS78
Record St, SE15 ....102 DW79
Recovery St, SW17 ....120 DE92
Recreation Av, Rom. RM7 ....71 FC57
  Romford (Harold Wd.) RM3 .52 FM54
Recreation Rd, SE26 ......123 DX91
  Bromley BR2 ....144 EF96
  Sidcup DA15
  off Woodside Rd 125 ES90
  Southall UB2 ....96 BY77
Recreation Way, Mitch. CR4 .141 DK97
Rector St, N1 ....84 DQ67
Rectory Chase, Brwd. (Lt.Warley)
  CM13 ....73 FX56
Rectory Cl, E4 ....47 EA48
  N3 ....43 CZ53
  SW20 ....139 CW97
  Ashtead KT21 ....172 CM119
  Dartford DA1 ....107 FE84
  Shepperton TW17 ......134 BN97
  Sidcup DA14 ....126 EV91
  Stanmore HA7 ....41 CH51
  Surbiton KT6 ....137 CJ102
  West Byfleet (Byfleet)
  KT14 ....152 BL113
Rectory Cres, E11 ....68 EJ58
Rectory Fm Rd, Enf. EN2 ....29 DM38
Rectory Fld Cres, SE7 .....104 EJ80
Rectory Gdns, N8 ....65 DL56
  SW4 *off Fitzwilliam Rd* .101 DJ83
  Chalfont St.Giles HP8 ....36 AV48
  Northolt UB5 ....78 BZ67
  Upminster RM14 ....73 FR61
Rectory Grn, Beck. BR3 ....143 DZ95
Rectory Gro, SW4 ....101 DJ83
  Croydon CR0 ....141 DP103
  Hampton TW12 ....116 BZ91
Rectory La, SW17 ....120 DG93
  Ashtead KT21 ....172 CM118
  Banstead SM7 ....158 DF114
  Betchworth (Buckland)
  RH3 ....183 CT131

Rectory La, Edg. HA8 ....42 CN51
  Kings Langley WD4 ......6 BN28
  Loughton IG10 ....33 EN40
  Radlett (Shenley) WD7 ...10 CN33
  Rickmansworth WD3 .....38 BK46
  Sevenoaks TN13 ....191 FJ126
  Sidcup DA14 ....126 EV91
  Stanmore HA7 ....41 CH50
  Surbiton KT6 ....137 CH102
  Wallington SM6 ....159 DJ105
  West Byfleet (Byfleet)
  KT14 ....152 BL113
  Westerham TN16 ....180 EL121
  Westerham (Brasted)
  TN16 ....180 EW123
Rectory Meadow, Grav. (Sthflt.)
  DA13 ....130 GA93
Rectory Pk, S.Croy. CR2 ...160 DS113
Rectory Pk Av, Nthlt. UB5 ...78 BZ69
Rectory Pl, SE18 ....105 EN77
⇌ Rectory Road 84 DT62
Rectory Rd, E12 ....69 EM64
  E17 ....67 EB55
  N16 ....66 DT62
  SW13 ....99 CU82
  W3 ....80 CP74
  Beckenham BR3 ....143 EA95
  Coulsdon CR5 ....184 DD125
  Dagenham RM10 ....88 FA66
  Grays RM17 ....110 GD76
  Hayes UB3 ....77 BU72
  Hounslow TW4 ....95 BV81
  Keston BR2 ....162 EK108
  Rickmansworth WD3 .....38 BK46
  Southall UB2 ....96 BZ76
  Sutton SM1 ....140 DA104
  Swanscombe DA10 .....130 FY87
  Tilbury (W.Til.) RM18 ...111 GK79
Rectory Sq, E1 ....85 DX71
Rectory Way, Uxb. UB10 ....59 BP62
Reculver Ms, N18
  off Lyndhurst Rd 46 DU49
Reculver Rd, SE16 ....203 H10
Red Anchor Cl, SW3
  off Old Ch St 100 DE79
Redan Pl, W2 ....82 DB72
Redan St, W14 ....99 CX76
Redan Ter, SE5
  off Flaxman Rd 102 DQ82
Redbarn Cl, Pur. CR8
  off Whytecliffe Rd S ...159 DP111
Red Barracks Rd, SE18 ....105 EM77
Redberry Gro, SE26 ....122 DW90
Redbourne Av, N3 ....44 DA53
Redbourne Dr, SE28 ....88 EX72
REDBRIDGE, Ilf. 69 EK58
  ⊖ Redbridge 68 EK58
Redbridge Enterprise Cen, Ilf.
  IG1 ....69 EQ61
Redbridge Gdns, SE5 ......102 DS80
Redbridge La E, Ilf. IG4 ....68 EK58
Redbridge La W, E11 ....68 EH58
Redburn St, SW3 ....100 DF79
Redbury Cl, Rain. RM13
  off Deri Av 89 FH70
Redcar Cl, Nthlt. UB5 ......60 CB64
Redcar Rd, Rom. RM3 ......52 FM50
Redcar St, SE5 ....102 DQ80
Redcastle Cl, E1 ....84 DW73
Red Cedars Rd, Orp. BR6 ..145 ES101
Redchurch St, E2 ....197 P4
Redcliffe Cl, SW5
  off Warwick Rd 100 DB78
Redcliffe Gdns, SW5 ......100 DB78
  SW10 ....100 DB78
  W4 ....98 CP80
  Ilford IG1 ....69 EN60
Redcliffe Ms, SW10 ....100 DB78
Redcliffe Pl, SW10 ....100 DC79
Redcliffe Rd, SW10 ....100 DC78
Redcliffe Sq, SW10 ....100 DB78
Redcliffe St, SW10 ....100 DB79
Redclose Av, Mord. SM4 ...140 DA99
Redclyffe Rd, E6 ....86 EJ67
Red Cottage Ms, Slou. SL3 ..92 AW76
Red Ct, Slou. SL1 ....74 AS74
Redcourt, Wok. GU22 ......167 BD115
Redcroft Rd, Sthl. UB1 .....78 CC73
Redcross Way, SE1 ....201 J4
Redden Ct Rd, Rom. RM3 ....72 FL55
Redding Cl, Dart. DA2 .....129 FS89
Reddings, The, NW7 ....43 CT48
  Borehamwood WD6 ......26 CM41
Reddings Av, Bushey WD23 ..24 CB43
Reddings Cl, NW7 ....43 CT49
Reddington Cl, S.Croy. CR2 .160 DR109
Reddington Dr, Slou. SL3 ....92 AY76
Reddins Rd, SE15 ....102 DU79
Reddons Rd, Beck. BR3 ....123 DY94
Reddown Rd, Couls. CR5 ...175 DK118
Reddy Rd, Erith DA8 ......107 FF79
Rede Ct, Wey. KT13
  off Old Palace Rd 135 BP104
Redenham Ho, SW15
  off Tangley Gro 119 CT87
Rede Pl, W2
  off Chepstow Pl 82 DA72
Redesdale Gdns, Islw. TW7 ..97 CG80
Redesdale St, SW3 ....100 DF79
Redfern Av, Houns. TW4 ...116 CA81
Redfern Gdns, Rom. RM2 ....52 FK54
Redfern Rd, E6 ....86 EL68
  SE6 ....123 EC87
Redfield La, SW5 ....100 DA77
Redfield Ms, SW5
  off Redfield La 100 DA77
Redford Av, Couls. CR5 ....159 DH114
  Thornton Heath CR7 ....141 DM98
  Wallington SM6 ....159 DL107
Redford Cl, Felt. TW13 ....115 BT89
Redford Wk, N1
  off Britannia Row 83 DP67
Redford Way, Uxb. UB8 .....76 BJ66
Redgate Dr, Brom. BR2 ....144 EH103

Redgate Ter, SW15
  off Lytton Gro 119 CX86
Redgrave Cl, Croy. CR0 ....142 DT100
Redgrave Rd, SW15 ....99 CX83
Redhall Ct, Cat. CR3 ......176 DR123
Redhall La, Rick. WD3 ......22 BL39
Redheath Cl, Wat. WD25 ....23 BT35
REDHILL 184 DG134
⇌ Redhill 184 DG133
Red Hill, Chis. BR7 ....125 EN92
  Uxbridge (Denh.) UB9 ...57 BD61
Redhill Dr, Edg. HA8 ....42 CQ54
Redhill Rd, Cob. KT11 .....153 BP113
Redhill St, NW1 ....195 J2
★ Red Ho, The (William Morris
  Ho), Bexh. DA6 ....106 EY84
Red Ho La, Bexh. DA6 .....106 EY84
  Walton-on-Thames KT12 .135 BU103
Redhouse Rd, Croy. CR0 ...141 DK100
  Westerham (Tats.) TN16 .178 EJ120
Red Ho Sq, N1
  off Clephane Rd 84 DQ65
Redington Gdns, NW3 ......64 DB63
Redington Rd, NW3 ....64 DB63
Redland Gdns, W.Mol. KT8
  off Dunstable Rd 136 BZ98
Redlands, Couls. CR5 .....175 DL116
Redlands Ct, Brom. BR1 ...124 EF64
Redlands Rd, Enf. EN3 ......31 DY39
  Sevenoaks TN13 ....190 FF124
Redlands Way, SW2 ....121 DM87
Red La, Esher (Clay.) KT10 .155 CG107
  Oxted RH8 ....188 EH133
Redleaf Cl, Belv. DA17 .....106 FA79
Red Leaf Cl, Slou. SL3
  off Pickford Dr 75 AZ74
Redleaves Av, Ashf. TW15 ..115 BP93
Redlees Cl, Islw. TW7 ......97 CG84
Red Leys, Uxb. UB8
  off Park Rd 76 BL66
Red Lion Cl, SE17
  off Red Lion Row 102 DQ79
  Orpington BR5 ....146 EW100
Red Lion Ct, EC4 ....196 E8
Red Lion Hill, N2 ....44 DD54
Red Lion La, SE18 ....105 EN80
  Hemel Hempstead HP3 ....6 BM26
  Rickmansworth (Sarratt)
  WD3 ....22 BG35
  Woking (Chobham) GU24 .150 AS109
Red Lion Pl, SE17
  off Shooter's Hill Rd ...105 EN81
Red Lion Rd, Surb. KT6 ....138 CM103
  Woking (Chobham) GU24 .150 AS109
Red Lion Row, SE17 ....102 DQ79
Red Lion Sq, SW18
  off Wandsworth High St .120 DA85
  WC1 ....196 B7
Red Lion St, WC1 ....196 B6
  Richmond TW9 ....117 CK85
Red Lion Yd, W1 ....198 G2
  Watford WD17 *off High St* .24 BW42
Red Lo Cres, Bex. DA5 ....127 FD90
Red Lo Rd, Bex. DA5 ......127 FD90
  West Wickham BR4 .....143 EC100
Redman Cl, Nthlt. UB5 ......78 BW68
Redman's Rd, E1 ....84 DW71
Redmead La, E1 ....202 B3
Redmead Rd, Hayes UB3 ....95 BS77
Redmore Rd, W6 ....99 CV77
Red Oak Cl, Orp. BR6 .....145 EP104
Red Oaks Mead, Epp. (They.B.)
  CM16 ....33 ER37
Red Path, E9 ....85 DZ65
Red Pl, W1 ....194 F10
Redpoll Way, Erith DA18 ...106 EX76
Red Post Hill, SE21 ....122 DR85
  SE24 ....102 DR84
Redriffe Rd, E13 ....86 EF67
Redriff Est, SE16 ....203 M6
Redriff Rd, SE16 ....203 J7
  Romford RM7 ....51 FB54
Red Rd, Borwd. WD6 ....26 CM41
  Brentwood CM14 ....54 FV49
Redroofs Cl, Beck. BR3 ....143 EB95
Redruth Cl, N22
  off Palmerston Rd 45 DM52
Redruth Gdns, Rom. RM3 ....52 FM50
Redruth Rd, E9 ....85 DX67
  Romford RM3 ....52 FM50
Redruth Wk, Rom. RM3 .....52 FN50
Redstart Cl, E6
  off Columbine Av 86 EL71
  SE14
  off Southerngate Way ..103 DY80
  Croydon (New Adgtn.)
  CR0 ....161 ED110
Redstone Hill, Red. RH1 ...184 DG134
Redstone Manor, Red. RH1 .184 DG134
Redstone Pk, Red. RH1 ....184 DG134
Redstone Rd, Red. RH1 ....184 DG135
Redston Rd, N8 ....65 DK56
REDSTREET, Grav. 130 GB93
Red St, Grav. (Sthflt.) DA13 .130 GB93
Redvers Rd, N22 ....45 DN54
  Warlingham CR6 ....176 DW118
Redvers St, N1 ....197 N2
Redwald Rd, E5 ....67 DX63
Redway Dr, Twick. TW2 ....116 CC87
Redwing Cl, S.Croy. CR2 ...161 DX111
Redwing Gdns, W.Byf. KT14 .152 BH112
Redwing Gro, Abb.L. WD5 ....7 BU31
Redwing Path, SE28 ....105 ER75
Redwing Rd, Wall. SM6 ....159 DM108
Redwood, Egh. TW20 ......133 BE96
Redwood Chase, S.Ock.
  RM15 ....91 FW70
Redwood Cl, N14 *off The Vale* .45 DK47
  SE16 ....203 L3
  Buckhurst Hill IG9
  off Beech La 48 EH47
  Kenley CR8 ....160 DQ114
  Sidcup DA15 ....126 EU87
  Uxbridge UB10
  off The Larches 77 BP68
  Watford WD19 ....40 BW49

Redwood Ct, NW6
  off The Avenue 81 CY66
Redwood Est, Houns. TW5 ...95 BV79
  Chigwell IG7 ....50 EU50
Redwood Ms, SW4
  off Hannington Rd 101 DH83
  Reigate. RH2 ....184 DA131
Redwood Ri, Borwd. WD6 ....26 CN37
Redwoods, SW15 ....119 CU88
  Addlestone KT15 ....152 BG107
Redwood Wk, Surb. KT6 ...137 CK102
Redwood Way, Barn. EN5 ....27 CX43
Reece Ms, SW7 ....100 DD77
Reed Av, Orp. BR6 ....145 ES104
Reed Cl, E16 ....86 EG71
  SE12 ....124 EG85
  Iver SL0 ....75 BE72
  St. Albans (Lon.Col.) AL2 ...9 CK27
Reede Gdns, Dag. RM10 ....71 FB64
Reede Rd, Dag. RM10 ......88 FA65
Reede Way, Dag. RM10 .....89 FB65
⇌ Reedham 159 DM113
Reedham Cl, N17 ....66 DV56
  St. Albans (Brick.Wd.) AL2 ...8 CA29
Reedham Dr, Pur. CR8 .....159 DN113
Reedham Pk Av, Pur. CR8 ..175 DN116
Reedham St, SE15 ....102 DU82
Reedholm Vil, N16
  off Winston Rd 66 DR63
Reed Pl, SW4 ....101 DK84
West Byfleet KT14 ....151 BE113
Reed Pond Wk, Rom. RM2 ...51 FF54
Reed Rd, N17 ....46 DT54
Reeds Cres, Wat. WD24 .....24 BW40
Reedsfield Cl, Ashf. TW15 .115 BP91
Reedsfield Rd, Ashf. TW15 .115 BP91
Reeds Pl, NW1
  off Royal Coll St 83 DJ66
Reeds Wk, Wat. WD24 ......24 BW40
Reedworth St, SE11 ......200 E9
Ree La Cotts, Loug. IG10
  off Englands La 33 EN40
Reenglass Rd, Stan. HA7 ....41 CK49
Rees Dr, Stan. HA7 ....42 CL49
Rees Gdns, Croy. CR0 .....142 DT100
Reesland Cl, E12 ....87 EN65
Rees St, N1 ....84 DQ67
Reets Fm Cl, NW9 ....62 CS58
Reeves Av, NW9 ....62 CR59
◆ Reeves Corner 141 DP103
Reeves Cor, Croy. CR0
  off Roman Way 141 DP103
Reeves Cres, Swan. BR8 ...147 FD97
Reeves Ms, W1 ....198 F1
Reeves Rd, E3 ....85 EB70
  SE18 ....105 EP79
Reflection, The, E16
  off Woolwich Manor Way .105 EP75
Reform Row, N17 ....46 DT54
Reform St, SW11 ....100 DF82
Regal Cl, E1
  off Old Montague St 84 DU71
  W5 ....79 CK71
Regal Ct, N18
  off College Cl 46 DT50
Regal Cres, Wall. SM6 ....141 DH104
Regal Dr, N11 ....45 DH50
Regal La, NW1
  off Regents Pk Rd 82 DG67
Regal Pl, E3 *off Coborn St* .85 DZ69
  SW6 *off Maxwell Rd* ...100 DB80
Regal Row, SE15
  off Queens Rd 102 DW81
Regal Way, Har. HA3 ......62 CL58
  Watford WD24 ....24 BW38
Regan Way, N1 ....197 M1
Regarder Rd, Chig. IG7 .....50 EU50
Regarth Av, Rom. RM1 .....71 FE58
Regatta Ho, Tedd. TW11
  off Twickenham Rd 117 CG91
Regency Cl, W5 ....80 CL72
  Chigwell IG7 ....49 EQ50
  Hampton TW12 ....116 BZ92
Regency Ct, Brwd. CM14 ....54 FW47
  Sutton SM1
  off Brunswick Rd 158 DB105
Regency Cres, NW4 ....43 CX54
Regency Dr, Ruis. HA4 .....59 BS60
  West Byfleet KT14 .....151 BF113
Regency Gdns, Horn. RM11 ..72 FJ59
  Walton-on-Thames KT12 .136 BW102
Regency Lo, Buck.H. IG9 ....48 EK47
Regency Ms, NW10
  off High Rd 81 CU65
  Beckenham BR3 ....143 EC95
  Isleworth TW7
  off Queensbridge Pk ..117 CE85
Regency Pl, SW1 ....199 N8
  Woodford Green IG8 .....49 EN52
Regency St, SW1 ....199 N8
Regency Ter, SW7
  off Fulham Rd 100 DD78
Regency Wk, Croy. CR0 ....143 DY100
  Richmond TW10
  off Friars Stile Rd 118 CL86
Regency Way, Bexh. DA6 ...106 EX83
  Woking GU22 ....167 BD115
Regent Av, Uxb. UB10 ......77 BP66
Regent Cl, N12 *off Nether St* .44 DC50
  Addlestone (New Haw)
  KT15 ....152 BK109
  Grays RM16 ....110 GC75
  Harrow HA3 ....62 CL58
  Hounslow TW4 ....95 BV81
  Redhill RH1 ....185 DJ129
Regent Ct, Slou. SL1
  off Stoke Poges La 74 AS72
Regent Cres, Red. RH1 ....184 DF132
Regent Gdns, Ilf. IG3 ......70 EU58
Regent Gate, Wal.Cr. EN8 ...15 DY34
Regent Pk, Lthd. KT22 .....171 CG118
Regent Pl, SW19
  off Haydons Rd 120 DB92
  W1 ....195 L10
  Croydon CR0 *off Grant Rd* .142 DT102

Regent Rd, SE24 ....121 DP86
Epping CM16 ....17 ET30
Surbiton KT5 ....138 CM99
Regents Av, N13 ....45 DM50
Regents Br Gdns, SW8 ......101 DL80
Regents Cl, Hayes UB4
off Park Rd 77 BS71
Radlet WD7 ....9 CG34
South Croydon CR2 .....160 DS107
Whyteleafe CR3 ......176 DS118
Regents Dr, Kes. BR2 ....162 EK106
Regents Ms, NW8
off Langford Pl 82 DC68
REGENT'S PARK, NW1 ......194 G1
★ Regent's Park, NW1 ....194 D1
⊖ Regent's Park 195 H5
Regent's Pk, NW1 ....194 E1
Regent's Pk Est, NW1 ....195 K3
Regents Pk Rd, N3 ......63 CZ55
NW1 ....82 DF67
Regent's Pk Ter, NW1
off Oval Rd 83 DH67
Regent's Pl, NW1 ....195 K4
SE3 ....104 EG82
Regents Row, E8 ....84 DU67
Regent Sq, E3 ....85 EB69
WC1 ....196 A3
Belvedere DA17 ......107 FB77
Regents Wf, N1
off All Saints St 83 DM68
Regina Cl, Barn. EN5 ....27 CX41
Reginald Rd, E7 ....86 EG66
SE8 ....103 EA80
Northwood HA6 ....39 BT53
Romford RM3 ....52 FN53
Reginald Sq, SE8 ......103 EA80
Regina Pt, SE16 ....202 G6
Regina Rd, N4 ....65 DM60
SE25 ....142 DU97
W13 ....79 CG74
Southall UB2 ....96 BY77
Regina Ter, W13 ....79 CG74
Regis Pl, SW2 ....101 DM84
Regis Rd, NW5 ....65 DH64
Regnart Bldgs, NW1 ....195 L4
Reid Av, Cat. CR3 .....176 DR121
Reid Cl, Couls. CR5 ....175 DH116
Pinner HA5 ....59 BU56
Reidhaven Rd, SE18 ....105 ES77
REIGATE 184 DA134
⇌ Reigate 184 DA134
Reigate Av, Sutt. SM1 ...140 DA102
Reigate Business Ms, Reig. RH2
off Albert Rd N 183 CZ133
Reigate Hill, Reig. RH2 ..184 DB130
Reigate Hill Cl, Reig. RH2 .184 DA131
Reigate Rd, Bet. RH3 ....CS132
Bromley BR1 ....124 EF90
Epsom KT17, KT18 ....157 CT110
Ilford IG3 ....69 ET61
Leatherhead KT22 ....171 CJ122
Redhill RH1 ....184 DB134
Reigate RH2 ....184 DB134
Tadworth KT20 ......173 CX117
Reigate Way, Wall. SM6 ..159 DL106
Reighton Rd, E5 ....66 DU62
Relay Rd, W12 ....81 CW73
Relf Rd, SE15 ....102 DU83
Relko Ct, Epsom KT19 ...156 CR110
Relko Gdns, Sutt. SM1 ..158 DD106
Relton Ms, SW7 ....198 C6
Rembrandt Cl, E14 .....204 F7
SW1 ....198 F9
Rembrandt Ct, Epsom KT19 .157 CT107
Rembrandt Dr, Grav. (Nthflt.)
DA11 ....130 GD90
Rembrandt Rd, SE13 ....104 EE84
Edgware HA8 ....42 CN54
Rembrandt Way, Walt. KT12 .135 BV104
Remington Rd, E6 ......86 EL72
N15 ....66 DR58
Remington St, N1 ......196 G1
Remnant St, WC2 ......196 B8
Rempstone Ms, N1
off Mintern St 84 DR68
Remus Rd, E3 off Monier Rd ..85 EA66
Renaissance Wk, SE10 ..205 L6
Rendle Cl, Croy. CR0 ...142 DT99
Rendlesham Av, Rad. WD7 ..25 CF37
Rendlesham Rd, E5 .....66 DU63
Enfield EN2 ....29 DP39
Rendlesham Way, Rick. (Chorl.)
WD3 ....21 BC44
Renforth St, SE16 ......202 G5
Renfree Way, Shep. TW17 ..134 BM101
Renfrew Cl, E6 ....87 EN73
Renfrew Rd, SE11 ......200 F8
Hounslow TW4 ....96 BX82
Kingston upon Thames
KT2 ....118 CP94
Renmans, The, Ashtd. KT21 .172 CM116
Renmuir St, SW17 ......120 DF93
Rennell St, SE13 ......103 EC83
Rennets Way, Islw. TW7
off St. John's Rd 97 CE82
Renness Rd, E17 ......67 DY55
Rennets Cl, SE9 ......125 ES85
Rennets Wd Rd, SE9 ...125 ER85
Rennie Cl, Ashf. TW15 ..114 BK90
Rennie Est, SE16 ......202 E9
Rennie St, SE1 ....200 F2
Rennison Cl, Wal.Cr. EN7
off Allwood Rd 14 DT27
Renovation, The, E16
off Woolwich Manor Way .105 EP75
Renown Cl, Croy. CR0 ..141 DP102
Romford RM7 ....50 FA53
Rensburg Rd, E17 ......67 DX57
Renshaw Cl, Belv. DA17
off Grove Rd 106 EZ79

Renters Av, NW4 ....63 CW58
Renton Dr, Orp. BR5 ...146 EX101
Renwick Ind Est, Bark. IG11 ..88 EV67
Renwick Rd, Bark. IG11 ..88 EV70
Repens Way, Hayes UB4
off Stipularis Dr 78 BX70
Rephidim St, SE1 ......201 M7
Replingham Rd, SW18 ..119 CZ88
Reporton Rd, SW6 ......99 CY81
Repository Rd, SE18 ...105 EM79
Repton Av, Hayes UB3 ..95 BR77
Romford RM2 ....71 FG55
Wembley HA0 ....61 CJ63
Repton Cl, Cars. SM5 ..158 DE106
Repton Ct, Beck. BR3 ..143 EB95
Ilford IG5 off Repton Gro ..49 EM53
Repton Dr, Rom. RM2 ..71 FG56
Repton Gdns, Rom. RM2 ..71 FG55
Repton Gro, Ilf. IG5 ...49 EM53
Repton Pl, Amer. HP7 ..20 AU39
Repton Rd, Har. HA3 ...62 CM56
Orpington BR6 ....146 EU104
Repton St, E14 ....85 DY72
Repton Way, Rick. (Crox.Grn.)
WD3 ....22 BN43
Repulse Cl, Rom. RM5 ..51 FB53
Reservoir Cl, Th.Hth. CR7 ..142 DR98
Reservoir Rd, N14 .....29 DJ43
SE4 ....103 DY82
Ruislip HA4 ....59 BQ57
Resolution Wk, SE18 ...105 EM76
Resolution Way, SE8
off Deptford High St ...103 EA80
Restavon Pk, West. (Berry's Grn.)
TN16 ....179 EP116
Restell Cl, SE3 ....104 EE79
Restmor Way, Wall. SM6 ..140 DG103
Reston Cl, Borwd. WD6 ..26 CN38
Reston Path, Borwd. WD6 ..26 CN38
Reston Pl, SW7
off Hyde Pk Gate 100 DC75
Restons Cres, SE9 ....125 ER86
Restormel Cl, Houns. TW3 ..116 CA85
Retcar Cl, N19
off Dartmouth Pk Hill ..65 DH61
Retcar Pl, N19 ....65 DH61
Retford Cl, Borwd. WD6
off The Campions 26 CN38
Romford RM3 ....52 FN51
Retford Path, Rom. RM3 ..52 FN51
Retford Rd, Rom. RM3 ..52 FM51
Retford St, N1 ....197 N1
Retingham Way, E4 ....47 EB47
Retreat, The, NW9 .....62 CR57
SW14
off South Worple Way ..98 CS83
Addlestone KT15 .....152 BK106
Amersham HP6 ....20 AY39
Brentwood CM14
off Costead Manor Rd ..54 FV46
Brentwood (Hutton) CM13 ..55 GB44
Egham TW20 ....112 AX92
Grays RM17 ....110 GB79
Harrow HA2 ....60 CA59
Kings Langley WD4 ....7 BQ31
Orpington BR6 ....164 EV107
Surbiton KT5 ....138 CM100
Thornton Heath CR7 ..142 DR98
Worcester Park KT4 ..139 CV103
Retreat Cl, Har. HA3 ...61 CJ57
Retreat Pl, E9 ....84 DW65
Retreat Rd, Rich. TW9 ..117 CK85
Retreat Way, Chig. IG7 ..50 EV48
Reubens Rd, Brwd. CM13 ..55 GB44
Reunion Row, E1 ......202 E1
Reveley Sq, SE16 ......203 L5
Revell Cl, Lthd. (Fetch.) KT22 ..170 CB122
Revell Dr, Lthd. (Fetch.)
...................170 CB122
Revell Ri, SE18 ....105 ET79
Revell Rd, Kings.T. KT1 ..138 CP95
Sutton SM1 ....157 CZ107
Revelon Rd, SE4 ......103 DY84
Revelstoke Rd, SW18 ..119 CZ89
Reventlow Rd, SE9 ....125 EQ88
Reverdy Rd, SE1 ......202 B9
Reverend Cl, Har. HA2 ..60 CB62
Revesby Rd, Cars. SM5 ..140 DD100
Review Rd, NW2 ....63 CT61
Dagenham RM10 ......89 FB67
Rewell St, SW6 ....100 DC80
Rewley Rd, Cars. SM5 ..140 DD100
Rex Av, Ashf. TW15 ...114 BN93
Rex Cl, Rom. RM5 .....51 FB52
Rex Pl, W1 ....198 G1
Reydon Av, E11 ....68 EJ58
Reynard Cl, SE4
off Foxwell St 103 DY83
Bromley BR1 ....145 EM97
Reynard Dr, SE19 .....122 DT94
Reynard Pl, SE14
off Milton Ct Rd 103 DY79
Reynardson Rd, N17 ...46 DQ52
Reynards Way, St.Alb. (Brick.Wd.)
AL2 ....8 BZ29
Reynolah Gdns, SE7
off Rathmore Rd 104 EH78
Reynolds Av, E12 .....69 EN64
Chessington KT9 .....156 CL108
Romford RM6 ....70 EW59
Reynolds Cl, NW11 ....64 DB59
SW19 ....140 DD95
Carshalton SM5 .....140 DF102
Reynolds Ct, E11
off Cobbold Rd 68 EF62
Romford RM6 ....70 EX55
Reynolds Dr, Edg. HA8 ..62 CM55
Reynolds Pl, SE3 .....104 EH80
Richmond TW10
off Cambrian Rd 118 CM86
Reynolds Rd, SE15 ....122 DW85
W4 ....98 CQ76
Hayes UB4 ....78 BW70
New Malden KT3 .....138 CR101
Reynolds Way, Croy. CR0 ..160 DS105
Rheidol Ms, N1
off Rheidol Ter 84 DQ68

Rheidol Ter, N1 ....83 DP68
Rheingold Way, Wall. SM6 ..159 DL109
Rheola Cl, N17 ....46 DT53
Rhoda St, E2 off Brick La ..84 DT70
Rhodes Av, N22 ....45 DJ53
Rhodes Cl, Egh. TW20
off Mullens Rd 113 BC92
Rhodesia Rd, E11 .....67 ED61
SW9 ....101 DL82
Rhodes Moorhouse Ct, Mord.
SM4 ....140 DA100
Rhodes St, N7
off Mackenzie Rd 65 DM64
Rhodeswell Rd, E14 ...85 DZ72
Rhododendron Ride, Egh.
TW20 ....112 AT94
Slough SL3 ....75 AZ69
Rhodrons Av, Chess. KT9 ..156 CL106
Rhondda Gro, E3 ......85 DY69
Rhyl Rd, Grnf. UB6 ....79 CF68
Rhyl St, NW5 ....82 DG65
Rhys Av, N11 ....45 DK52
Rialto Rd, Mitch. CR4 ..140 DG96
Ribble Cl, Wdf.Grn. IG8
off Prospect Rd 48 EJ51
Ribbledale, St.Alb. (Lon.Col.)
AL2 ....10 CM27
Ribblesdale Av, N11 ...44 DG51
Northolt UB5 ....78 CB65
Ribblesdale Rd, N8 ...65 DM56
SW16 ....121 DH93
Dartford DA2 ....128 FQ88
Ribchester Av, Grnf. UB6 ..79 CF69
Ribston Cl, Brom. BR2 ..145 EM102
Radlett (Shenley) WD7
off Wayside 9 CK33
Ricardo Path, SE28
off Byron Cl 88 EW74
Ricardo Rd, Wind. (Old Wind.)
SL4 ....112 AV86
Ricardo St, E14 ....85 EB72
Ricards Rd, SW19 .....119 CZ92
Richard Cl, SE18 .....104 EL77
Richard Fell Ho, E12
off Walton Rd 69 EN63
Richard Foster Cl, E17 ..67 DZ59
Richard Ho Dr, E16 ....86 EK72
Richards Av, Rom. RM7 ..71 FC57
Richards Cl, Bushey WD23 ..41 CD45
Harrow HA1 ....61 CG57
Hayes UB3 ....95 BR79
Uxbridge UB10 ....76 BN67
Richards Fld, Epsom KT19 ..156 CR109
Richardson Cl, E8
off Clarissa St 84 DT67
Greenhithe DA9
off Steele Av 129 FU85
St. Albans (Lon.Col.) AL2 ..10 CL27
Richardson Cres, Wal.Cr. (Chsht.)
EN7 ....13 DP25
Richardson Rd, E15 ...86 EE68
Richardson's Ms, W1 ..195 K5
Richards Pl, E17 ......67 EA55
SW3 ....198 C8
Richards Rd, Cob. (Stoke D'Ab.)
KT11 ....154 CB114
Richard St, E1
off Commercial Rd 84 DV72
Richbell Cl, Ashtd. KT21 ..171 CK118
Richbell Pl, WC1 ......196 B6
Richborne Ter, SW8 ...101 DM80
Richborough Cl, Orp. BR5 ..146 EX98
Richborough Rd, NW2 ..63 CX63
Richens Cl, Houns. TW3 ..97 CD82
Riches Rd, Ilf. IG1 ....69 EQ61
Richfield Rd, Bushey WD23 ..40 CC45
Richford Rd, E15 .....86 EF67
Richford St, W6 ....99 CW75
RICHINGS PARK, Iver ..93 BE75
Richings Way, Iver SL0 ..93 BF76
Richland Av, Couls. CR5 ..158 DG114
Richlands Av, Epsom KT17 ..157 CU105
Rich La, SW5 off Warwick Rd ..100 DB78
Richmer Rd, Erith DA8 ..107 FG80
RICHMOND 118 CL86
⇌ Richmond 98 CL84
⊖ Richmond 98 CL84
Richmond Av, E4 ......47 ED50
N1 ....83 DM67
NW10 ....81 CW65
SW20 ....139 CY95
Feltham TW14 ....115 BS86
Uxbridge UB10 ....77 BP65
Richmond Br, Rich. TW9 ..117 CK86
Twickenham TW1 .....117 CK86
Richmond Bldgs, W1 ..195 M9
Richmond Cl, E17 .....67 DZ58
Amersham HP6 ....20 AT38
Borehamwood WD6 ...26 CR43
Epsom KT18 ....156 CS114
Leatherhead (Fetch.) KT22 ..170 CC124
Waltham Cross (Chsht.)
EN8 ....14 DW29
Westerham (Bigg.H.) TN16 ..178 EK116
Richmond Ct, Pot.B. EN6 ..12 DC31
Richmond Cres, E4 ....47 ED50
N1 ....83 DM67
N9 ....46 DU46
Slough SL1 ....74 AU74
Staines TW18 ....113 BF92
Richmond Dr, Grav. DA12 ..131 GL89
Shepperton TW17 ....135 BQ100
Watford WD17 ....23 BS39
Richmond Gdns, NW4 ..63 CU57
Harrow HA3 ....41 CF51
Richmond Grn, Croy. CR0 ..141 DL104
Richmond Gro, N1 ....83 DP66
Surbiton KT5 ....138 CM100
Richmond Hill, Rich. TW10 ..118 CL86
Richmond Hill Ct, Rich.
TW10 ....118 CL86
Richmond Ms, W1 .....195 M9
Teddington TW11
off Broad St 117 CF93
★ Richmond Palace (remains),
Rich. TW9 ....117 CJ85

★ Richmond Park, Rich.
TW10 ....118 CN88
Richmond Pk, Kings.T. KT2 ..118 CP88
Loughton IG10
off Fallow Flds 48 EJ45
Richmond TW10 .....118 CP88
Richmond Pk Rd, SW14 ..118 CQ85
Kingston upon Thames
KT2 ....118 CL94
Richmond Pl, SE18 ...105 EQ77
Richmond Rd, E4 .....47 ED46
E7 ....68 EH64
E8 ....84 DT66
E11 ....67 ED61
N2 ....44 DC54
N11 ....45 DL51
N15 ....66 DS58
SW20 ....139 CV95
W5 ....98 CL75
Barnet EN5 ....28 DB43
Coulsdon CR5 ....175 DH115
Croydon CR0 ....141 DL104
Grays RM17 ....110 GC79
Ilford IG1 ....69 EQ62
Isleworth TW7 ....97 CG83
Kingston upon Thames
KT2 ....117 CK92
Potters Bar EN6 ......12 DC31
Romford RM1 ....71 FF58
Staines TW18 ....113 BF92
Thornton Heath CR7 ..141 DP97
Twickenham TW1 .....117 CJ86
Richmond St, E13 .....86 EG68
Richmond Ter, SW1 ...199 P4
Richmond Ter Ms, SW1
off Parliament St 101 DL75
Richmond Way, E11 ...68 EG61
W12 ....99 CX75
W14 ....99 CX76
Leatherhead (Fetch.) KT22 ..170 CB123
Rickmansworth (Crox.Grn.)
WD3 ....23 BQ42
Richmount Gdns, SE3 ..104 EG83
Rich St, E14 ....85 DZ73
Rickard Cl, NW4 ......63 CV56
SW2 ....121 DM88
West Drayton UB7 ....94 BK76
Rickards Cl, Surb. KT6 ..138 CL102
Rickett St, SW6 ......100 DA79
Rickman Cres, Add. KT15 ..134 BH104
Rickman Hill, Couls. CR5 ..175 DH118
Rickman Hill Rd, Couls. CR5 ..175 DH118
Rickmans La, Slou. (Stoke P.)
SL2 ....56 AS64
Rickman St, E1
off Mantus Rd 84 DW69
RICKMANSWORTH 38 BL45
⇌ Rickmansworth 38 BK45
⊖ Rickmansworth 38 BK45
Rickmansworth La, Ger.Cr.
(Chal.St.P.) SL9 ......37 AZ50
Rickmansworth Pk, Rick. WD3 ..38 BK45
Rickmansworth Rd, Nthwd.
HA6 ....39 BR52
Pinner HA5 ....39 BV54
Rickmansworth (Chorl.)
WD3 ....21 BD41
Uxbridge (Hare.) UB9 ..38 BJ53
Watford WD17, WD18 ..23 BS42
Rick Roberts Way, E15 ..85 EC67
Rickthorne Rd, N19
off Landseer Rd 65 DL61
Rickyard Path, SE9 ...104 EL84
Ridding La, Grnf. UB6 ..61 CF64
Riddings, The, Cat. CR3 ..186 DT125
⇌ Riddlesdown 160 DR113
Riddlesdown Av, Pur. CR8 ..160 DQ112
Riddlesdown Rd, Pur. CR8 ..160 DQ111
Riddons Rd, SE12 ....124 EJ90
Ride, The, Brent. TW8 ..97 CH78
Enfield EN3 ....30 DW41
Rideout St, SE18 .....105 EM77
Rider Cl, Sid. DA15 ...125 ES86
Riders Way, Gdse. RH9 ..186 DW131
Ridgdale St, E3 ......85 EB68
RIDGE, Pot.B. 10 CS34
Ridge, The, Bex. DA5 ..126 EZ87
Caterham (Wold.) CR3 ..187 EB126
Coulsdon CR5 ....159 DL114
Epsom KT18 ....172 CP117
Leatherhead (Fetch.) KT22 ..171 CD124
Orpington BR6 ....145 ER103
Purley CR8 ....159 DJ110
Surbiton KT5 ....138 CN99
Twickenham TW2 .....117 CD87
Woking GU22 ....167 BB117
Ridge Av, N21 ....46 DQ45
Dartford DA1 ....127 FF86
Ridgebrook Rd, SE3 ..104 EJ83
Ridge Cl, NW4 ....43 CX54
NW9 ....62 CR56
SE28 ....105 ER75
Woking GU22 ....166 AV121
Ridge Crest, Enf. EN2 ..29 DM39
Ridgecroft Cl, Bex. DA5 ..127 FC88
Ridgefield, Wat. WD17 ..23 BS37
Ridgegate Cl, Reig. RH2 ..184 DD132
RIDGEHILL, Rad. 10 CQ30
Ridge Hill, NW11 .....63 CY60
Ridgehurst Av, Wat. WD25 ..7 BT34
Ridgelands, Lthd. (Fetch.)
KT22 ....171 CD124
Ridge La, Wat. WD17 ..23 BS38
Ridge Langley, S.Croy. CR2 ..160 DU109
Ridgemead Rd, Egh. (Eng.Grn.)
TW20 ....112 AU90
Ridgemont Gdns, Edg. HA8 ..42 CQ49
Ridgemount, Wey. KT13
off Oatlands Dr 135 BS103
Ridgemount Av, Couls. CR5 ..175 DH117
Croydon CR0 ....143 DX102
Ridgemount Cl, SE20
off Anerley Pk 122 DV94
Ridgemount End, Ger.Cr.
(Chal.St.P.) SL9 ......36 AY50

Ridgemount Gdns, Enf. EN2 ..29 DP40
Ridge Pk, Pur. CR8 ...159 DK110
Ridge Rd, N8 ....65 DM58
N21 ....46 DQ46
NW2 ....63 CZ62
Mitcham CR4 ....121 DH94
Sutton SM3 ....139 CY102
Ridge St, Wat. WD24 ..23 BV38
Ridgeview Cl, Barn. EN5 ..27 CX44
Ridgeview Lo, St.Alb. (Lon.Col.)
AL2 ....10 CM28
Ridgeview Rd, N20 ....44 DB48
Ridge Way, SE19
off Central Hill 122 DS93
Ridgeway, SE28 ......105 ER77
off Pettman Cres 105 ER77
Brentwood CM13 .....55 GB46
Bromley BR2 ....144 EG103
Ridge Way, Dart. (Cray.) DA1 ..127 FF86
Ridgeway, Dart. (Lane End)
DA2 ....129 FS92
Epsom KT19 ....156 CQ112
Ridge Way, Felt. TW13 ..116 BY90
Ridgeway, Grays RM17 ..110 GE77
Ridge Way, Iver SL0 ...75 BE74
Ridgeway, Rick. WD3 ..38 BH45
Virginia Water GU25 ..132 AY99
Woking (Horsell) GU21 ..166 AX115
Woodford Green IG8 ..48 EJ49
Ridgeway, The, E4 ...47 EB47
N3 ....44 DB52
N11 ....44 DF49
N14 ....45 DL47
NW7 ....43 CU49
NW9 ....62 CS56
NW11 ....63 CZ60
W3 ....98 CN76
Croydon CR0 ....141 DM104
Enfield EN2 ....29 DN39
Gerrards Cross (Chal.St.P.)
SL9 ....56 AX55
Harrow (Kenton) HA3 ..61 CJ58
Harrow (N.Har.) HA2 ..60 BZ57
Leatherhead (Fetch.) KT22 ..171 CD123
Leatherhead (Oxshott)
KT22 ....154 CC114
Potters Bar EN6 ......12 DD34
Potters Bar (Cuffley) EN6 ..12 DE28
Radlett WD7 ....25 CF37
Romford (Gidea Pk.) RM2 ..71 FG56
Romford (Harold Wd) RM3 ..52 FL53
Ruislip HA4 ....60 CA58
South Croydon CR2 ..160 DS110
Stanmore HA7 ....41 CJ51
Walton-on-Thames KT12 ..135 BT102
Watford WD17 ....23 BS37
Ridgeway Av, Barn. EN4 ..28 DF44
Gravesend DA12 .....131 GH90
Ridgeway Cl, Lthd. (Oxshott)
KT22 ....154 CC114
Woking GU21 ....166 AX116
Ridgeway Ct, Red. RH1 ..184 DE134
Ridgeway Cres, Orp. BR6 ..145 ES104
Ridgeway Cres Gdns, Orp.
BR6 ....145 ES103
Ridgeway Dr, Brom. BR1 ..124 EH91
Ridgeway E, Sid. DA15 ..125 ET85
Ridgeway Est, The, Iver SL0 ..75 BF74
Ridgeway Gdns, N6 ...65 DJ59
Ilford IG4 ....68 EL57
Woking GU21 ....166 AX116
Ridgeway Rd, SW9 ...101 DP83
Isleworth TW7 ....97 CE80
Redhill RH1 ....184 DE134
Ridgeway Rd N, Islw. TW7 ..97 CE79
Ridgeway Wk, Nthlt. UB5
off Fortunes Mead 78 BY65
Ridgeway W, Sid. DA15 ..125 ES85
Ridgewell Cl, N1 off Basire St ..84 DQ67
SE26 ....123 DZ91
Dagenham RM10 .....89 FB67
Ridgmount Gdns, WC1 ..195 M5
Ridgmount Pl, WC1 ...195 M6
Ridgmount Rd, SW18 ..120 DB85
Ridgmount St, WC1 ...195 M6
Ridgway, SW19 ......119 CX93
Woking (Pyrford) GU22 ..167 BF115
Ridgway, The, Sutt. SM2 ..158 DD108
Ridgway Gdns, SW19 ..119 CX94
Ridgway Pl, SW19 ....119 CY93
Ridgway Rd, Wok. (Pyrford)
GU22 ....167 BF115
Ridgwell Rd, E16 .....86 EJ71
Riding, The, NW11
off Golders Grn Rd ...63 CZ59
Woking GU21 ....151 BB114
Riding Ct Rd, Slou. (Datchet)
SL3 ....92 AW80
Riding Hill, S.Croy. CR2 ..160 DU113
Riding Ho St, W1 .....195 K7
Ridings, The, E11
off Malcolm Way 68 EG57
W5 ....80 CM70
Addlestone KT15 .....151 BF107
Ashtead KT21 ....171 CK117
Chesham HP5 ....20 AX36
Chigwell IG7
off Manford Way 50 EV49
Cobham KT11 ....154 CA112
Epsom KT18 ....155 CS115
Epsom (Ewell) KT17 ..157 CT109
Iver SL0 ....93 BF77
Reigate RH2 ....184 DD131
Sunbury-on-Thames
TW16 ....135 BU95
Surbiton KT5 ....138 CN99
Tadworth KT20 ......173 CZ120
Westerham (Bigg.H.) TN16 ..178 EL117
Woking (Ripley) GU23 ..168 BG123
Ridings Av, N21 ......29 DP42
Ridings Cl, N6
off Hornsey La Gdns ..65 DJ59
Ridings La, Wok. GU23 ..168 BN113
Ridlands Gro, Oxt. RH8 ..188 EL130

★ Place of interest   ⇌ Railway station   ⊖ London Underground station   DLR Docklands Light Railway station   ⊗ Tramlink station   H Hospital

Rid - Rod

Rodings, The, Wdf.Grn IG8 . . .48 EJ51
Rodings Row, Barn. EN5
  off Leecroft Rd 27 CY43
Roding Trd Est, Bark. IG11 . .87 EP66
⊖ Roding Valley 48 EK58
Roding Vw, Buck.H. IG9 . . . .48 EK46
Roding Way, Rain. RM13 . . .90 FK68
Rodmarton St, W1 . . . . . . .194 E7
Rodmell Cl, Hayes UB4 . . . .78 BY70
Rodmell Slope, N12 . . . . . . .43 CZ50
Rodmere St, SE10 . . . . . . .104 EE78
Rodmill La, SW2 . . . . .121 DL87
Rodney Cl, Croy. CR0 . . . . .141 DP102
  New Malden KT3 . . . . . .138 CS99
  Pinner HA5 . . . . .60 BY59
  Walton-on-Thames KT12
    off Rodney Rd 136 BW102
Rodney Ct, W9 off Maida Vale .82 DC70
Rodney Gdns, Pnr. HA5 . . . .59 BV57
  West Wickham BR4 . . . . .162 EG105
Rodney Grn, Walt. KT12 . . .136 BW103
Rodney Pl, E17 . . . . .47 DY54
  SE17 . . . . .201 J8
  SW19 . . . . .140 DC95
Rodney Rd, E11 . . . . .68 EH56
  SE17 . . . . .201 J8
  Mitcham CR4 . . . . .140 DE96
  New Malden KT3 . . . . . .138 CS99
  Twickenham TW2 . . . . . .116 CA86
  Walton-on-Thames KT12 .136 BW103
Rodney St, N1 . . . . .83 DM68
Rodney Way, Rom. RM7 . . . .50 FA53
  Slough (Colnbr.) SL3 . . . .93 BE81
Rodona Rd, Wey. KT13 . . . .153 BR111
Rodway Rd, SW15 . . . . . . .119 CU87
  Bromley BR1 . . . . .84 EH95
Rodwell Cl, Ruis. HA4 . . . . .60 BW60
Rodwell Ct, Add. KT15
  off Garfield Rd 152 BJ105
Rodwell Pl, Edg. HA8
  off Whitchurch La 42 CN51
Rodwell Rd, SE22 . . . . . . .122 DT86
Roebourne Way, E16 . . . . .105 EN75
Roebuck Cl, Ashtd. KT21 . .172 CL120
  Feltham TW13 . . . . . . .115 BV91
  Reigate RH2 . . . . .184 DB134
Roebuck La, N17 off High Rd .46 DT51
  Buckhurst Hill IG9 . . . . . .48 EJ45
Roebuck Rd, Chess. KT9 . .156 CN106
  Ilford IG6 . . . . .50 EU50
Roedean Av, Enf. EN3 . . . . .30 DW39
Roedean Cl, Enf. EN3 . . . . .30 DW39
  Orpington BR6 . . . . . . .164 EV105
Roedean Cres, SW15 . . . . .118 CS86
Roedean Rd, Rom. RM1 . . . .71 FE56
Roe End, NW9 . . . . .62 CQ56
Roe Grn, NW9 . . . . .62 CP57
ROEHAMPTON, SW15 . . . .119 CU85
Roehampton Cl, SW15 . . . . .99 CU84
  Gravesend DA12 . . . . . .131 GL87
Roehampton Dr, Chis. BR7 .125 EQ93
Roehampton Gate, SW15 . .118 CS86
Roehampton High St, SW15 .119 CV87
Roehampton La, SW15 . . . . .99 CU84
🏥 Roehampton Priory Hosp,
  SW15 . . . . .99 CT84
Roehampton Vale, SW15 . .118 CS90
Roe La, NW9 . . . . .62 CP56
Roe Way, Wall. SM6 . . . . .159 DL107
Rofant Rd, Nthwd. HA6 . . . .39 BS51
Roffes La, Cat. CR3 . . . . . .176 DR124
Roffey Cl, Pur. CR8 . . . . . .175 DP116
Roffey St, E14 . . . . .204 D5
Roffords, Wok. GU21 . . . . .166 AV117
Rogate Ho, E5 off Muir Rd . .66 DU62
Roger Dowley Ct, E2 . . . . . .84 DW68
Rogers Cl, Cat. CR3
  off Tillingdown Hill 176 DV122
  Coulsdon CR5 . . . . . . .175 DP118
  Waltham Cross (Chsht.)
    EN7 . . . . .14 DR26
Rogers Ct, Swan. BR8 . . . .147 FG98
Rogers Gdns, Dag. RM10 . . .70 FA64
Rogers La, Slou. (Stoke P.) SL2 .74 AT67
  Warlingham CR6 . . . . . .177 DZ118
Rogers Mead, Gdse. RH9
  off Ivy Mill La 186 DV132
Rogers Ruff, Nthwd. HA6 . . .39 BQ53
Roger St, WC1 . . . . .196 C5
Rogers Wk, N12
  off Brook Meadow 44 DB48
Rojack Rd, SE23 . . . . .123 DX88
Rokeby Gdns, Wdf.Grn. IG8 . .48 EG53
Rokeby Pl, SW20 . . . . . . .119 CV94
Rokeby Rd, SE4 . . . . .103 DZ82
Rokeby St, E15 . . . . .86 EE67
Roke Cl, Ken. CR8 . . . . . . .160 DQ114
Roke Lo Rd, Ken. CR8 . . . .159 DP113
Roke Rd, Ken. CR8 . . . . . .160 DQ115
Roker Pk Av, Uxb. UB10 . . .58 BL63
Rokesby Cl, Well. DA16 . . .105 ER82
Rokesby Pl, Wem. HA0 . . . .61 CK64
Rokesly Av, N8 . . . . .65 DL57
Roland Gdns, SW7 . . . . . .100 DC78
  Feltham TW13 . . . . . . .116 BY90
Roland Ms, E1 off Stepney Grn .85 DX71
Roland Rd, E17 . . . . .67 ED56
Roland Way, SE17 . . . . . . .102 DR78
  SW7 off Roland Gdns . . .100 DC78
  Worcester Park KT4 . . . .137 CT103
Roles Gro, Rom. RM6 . . . . .70 EX56
Rolfe Cl, Barn. EN4 . . . . . . .28 DE42
Rolinsden Way, Kes. BR2 . .162 EK105
Rollesby Rd, Chess. KT9 . .156 CN107
Rollesby Way, SE28 . . . . . .88 EW73
Rolleston Av, Orp. BR5 . . . .145 EP100
Rolleston Cl, Orp. BR5 . . . .145 EP101
Rolleston Rd, S.Croy. CR2 .160 DR108
Roll Gdns, Ilf. IG2 . . . . .69 EN57
Rollins St, SE15 . . . . .102 DW79
Rollit Cres, Houns. TW3 . . .116 CA85

Rollit St, N7
  off Hornsey Rd 65 DM64
Rollo Rd, Swan. BR8 . . . . .127 FF94
Rolls Bldgs, EC4 . . . . .196 D8
Rollscourt Av, SE24 . . . . . .122 DQ85
Rolls Pk Av, E4 . . . . .47 EA51
Rolls Pk Rd, E4 . . . . .47 EB50
Rolls Pas, EC4 . . . . .196 D8
Rolls Rd, SE1 . . . . .202 A10
Rolt St, SE8 . . . . .103 DY79
Rolvenden Gdns, Brom. BR1 .124 EK94
Rolvenden Pl, N17
  off Manor Rd 46 DU53
★ Roman Bath, WC2
  off Strand La 196 C10
Roman Cl, W3
  off Avenue Gdns 98 CP75
  Feltham TW14 . . . . .116 BW85
  Rainham RM13 . . . . .89 FD68
  Uxbridge (Hare.) UB9 . . . .38 BH53
Romanfield Rd, SW2 . . . . .121 DM87
Roman Gdns, Kings L. WD4 . .7 BP30
Roman Ho, Rain. RM13
  off Roman Cl 89 FD68
Romanhurst Av, Brom. BR2 .144 EE98
Romanhurst Gdns, Brom.
  BR2 . . . . .144 EE98
Roman Ind Est, Croy. CR0 .142 DS101
Roman Ri, SE19 . . . . .122 DR93
Roman Rd, E2 . . . . .84 DW69
  E3 . . . . .85 DY68
  E6 . . . . .86 EL70
  N10 . . . . .45 DH52
  NW2 . . . . .63 CW62
  W4 . . . . .99 CT77
  Brentwood CM15 . . . . . .54 FW48
  Gravesend (Nthflt.) DA11 .130 GC90
  Ilford IG1 . . . . .87 EP65
Roman Sq, SE28 . . . . .88 EU74
Romans Way, Wok. GU22 . .168 BG115
Roman Vil Rd, Dart. (S.Darenth)
  DA2, DA4 . . . . .128 FQ92
Roman Way, N7 . . . . .83 DM65
  SE15 off Clifton Way 102 DW80
  Carshalton SM5 . . . . . . .158 DF109
  Croydon CR0 . . . . .141 DP103
  Dartford DA1 . . . . .127 FE85
  Enfield EN1 . . . . .30 DT43
  Waltham Abbey EN9 . . . . .31 EB35
Roman Way Ind Est, N1
  off Offord St 83 DM66
Romany Gdns, E17
  off McEntee Av 47 DY53
  Sutton SM3 . . . . .140 DA101
Romany Ri, Orp. BR5 . . . . .145 EQ102
Roma Read Cl, SW15
  off Bessborough Rd 119 CV87
Roma Rd, E17 . . . . .67 DY55
Romberg Rd, SW17 . . . . . .120 DG90
Romborough Gdns, SE13 . .123 EC85
Romborough Way, SE13 . . .123 EC85
Rom Cres, Rom. RM7 . . . . .71 FF59
Romeland, Borwd. (Elstree)
  WD6 . . . . .25 CK44
  Waltham Abbey EN9 . . . . .15 EC33
Romero Cl, SW9
  off Stockwell Rd 101 DM83
Romero Sq, SE3 . . . . .104 EJ84
Romeyn Rd, SW16 . . . . . .121 DM90
ROMFORD 71 FF57
⇌ Romford 71 FE58
Romford Rd, E7 . . . . .68 EH64
  E12 . . . . .68 EL63
  E15 . . . . .86 EE66
  Chigwell IG7 . . . . .50 EU48
  Romford RM5 . . . . .50 EY52
  South Ockendon (Aveley)
    RM15 . . . . .90 FQ73
Romford St, E1 . . . . .84 DU71
Romilly Dr, Wat. WD19 . . . . .40 BY49
Romilly Rd, N4 . . . . .65 DP61
Romilly St, W1 . . . . .195 M10
Rommany Rd, SE27 . . . . . .122 DR91
Romney Chase, Horn. RM11 . .72 FM58
Romney Cl, N17 . . . . .46 DV53
  NW11 . . . . .64 DC60
  SE14 off Kender St 102 DW80
  Ashford TW15 . . . . .115 BQ92
  Chessington KT9 . . . . . .156 CL105
  Harrow HA2 . . . . .60 CA59
Romney Dr, Brom. BR1 . . . .124 EK94
  Harrow HA2 . . . . .60 CA59
Romney Gdns, Bexh. DA7 .106 EZ81
Romney Lock, Wind. SL4 . . .92 AS79
Romney Ms, W1 . . . . .194 F6
Romney Par, Hayes UB4
  off Romney Rd 77 BR68
Romney Rd, SE10 . . . . . . .103 EC79
  Gravesend (Nthflt.) DA11 .130 GE90
  Hayes UB4 . . . . .77 BR68
  New Malden KT3 . . . . . .138 CR100
Romney Row, NW2
  off Brent Ter 63 CX61
Romney St, SW1 . . . . .199 N7
Romola Rd, SE24 . . . . . . .121 DP88
Romsey Cl, Orp. BR6 . . . . .163 EP105
  Slough SL3 . . . . .93 AZ76
Romsey Gdns, Dag. RM9 . . .88 EX67
Romsey Rd, W13 . . . . .79 CG73
  Dagenham RM9 . . . . . . .88 EX67
Rom Valley Way, Rom. RM7 . .71 FE59
Ronald Av, E15 . . . . .86 EE69
Ronald Cl, Beck. BR3 . . . . .143 DZ98
Ronald Ct, St.Alb. AL2 . . . . .8 BY29
Ronald Ho, SE3
  off Cambert Way 104 EJ84
Ronald Rd, Rom. RM3 . . . . .52 FN53
Ronaldsay Spur, Slou. SL1 . .74 AS71
Ronalds Rd, N5 . . . . .65 DN64
  Bromley BR1 . . . . .144 EG95
Ronaldstone Rd, Sid. DA15 .125 ES86
Ronald St, E1 off Devonport St .84 DW72
Rona Rd, NW3 . . . . .64 DG63
Ronart St, Har. (Widste.) HA3
  off Stuart Rd 61 CF55
Rona Wk, N1 off Clephane Rd .84 DR65
Rondu Rd, NW2 . . . . .63 CY64

Ronelean Rd, Surb. KT6 . . .138 CM104
Roneo Cor, Horn. RM12 . . .71 FF60
Roneo Link, Horn. RM12 . . .71 FF60
Ronfearn Av, Orp. BR5 . . . .146 EX99
Ron Leighton Way, E6 . . . . .86 EL68
Ronneby Cl, Wey. KT13 . . .135 BS104
Ronson Way, Lthd. KT22 . .171 CF121
Ronver Rd, SE12 . . . . .124 EF87
Rood La, EC3 . . . . .197 M10
Roof of the World Caravan Pk,
  Tad. KT20 . . . . .182 CP131
Rookby Ct, N21
  off Carpenter Gdns 45 DP47
Rook Cl, Horn. RM12 . . . . .89 FG66
  Wembley HA9 . . . . .62 CP62
Rookdean, Sev. (Chipstead)
  TN13 . . . . .190 FC122
Rookeries Cl, Felt. TW13 . .115 BV90
Rookery, The, Grays RM20 .109 FU79
Rookery Cl, NW9 . . . . .63 CT57
  Leatherhead (Fetch.) KT22 .171 CE124
Rookery Ct, Grays RM20 . .109 FU79
Rookery Cres, Dag. RM10 . .89 FB66
Rookery Dr, Chis. BR7 . . . .145 EN95
Rookery Gdns, Orp. BR5 . .146 EX100
Rookery Hill, Ashtd. KT21 .172 CN118
Rookery La, Brom. BR2 . . .144 EK100
  Grays RM17 . . . . .110 GD78
Rookery Rd, SW4 . . . . . . .101 DJ84
  Orpington BR6 . . . . . . .163 EM110
  Staines TW18 . . . . .114 BH92
Rookery Vw, Grays RM17 . .110 GD78
Rookery Way, NW9 . . . . . . .63 CT57
  Tadworth (Lwr.Kgswd.)
    KT20 . . . . .183 CZ127
Rookesley Rd, Orp. BR5 . . .146 EX101
Rooke Way, SE10 . . . . . . .205 K10
Rookfield Av, N10 . . . . .65 DJ56
Rookfield Cl, N10
  off Cranmore Way 65 DJ56
Rooks Hill, Rick. (Loud.) WD3 . .22 BK42
Rooksmead Rd, Sun. TW16 .135 BT96
Rookstone Rd, SW17 . . . . .120 DF92
Rook Wk, E6
  off Allhallows Rd 86 EL72
Rookwood Av, Loug. IG10 . . .33 EQ41
  New Malden KT3 . . . . . .139 CU98
  Wallington SM6 . . . . . . .159 DK105
Rookwood Cl, Grays RM17 .110 GB77
  Redhill RH1 . . . . .185 DH129
Rookwood Gdns, E4
  off Whitehall Rd 48 EF46
  Loughton IG10 . . . . .33 EQ41
Rookwood Ho, Bark. IG11
  off St. Marys 87 ER68
Rookwood Rd, N16 . . . . . . .66 DT59
Roosevelt Mem, W1
  off Grosvenor Sq 194 G10
Roosevelt Way, Dag. RM10 . .89 FD65
Rootes Dr, W10 . . . . .81 CX70
Ropemaker Rd, SE16 . . . . .203 K5
Ropemakers Flds, E14 . . . .203 M1
Ropemaker St, EC2 . . . . . .197 K6
Roper La, SE1 . . . . .201 N5
Ropers Av, E4 . . . . .47 EC50
Ropers Orchard, SW3
  off Danvers St 100 DE79
Roper St, SE9 . . . . .125 EM86
Ropers Wk, SW2
  off Brockwell Pk Gdns . . .121 DN87
Roper Way, Mitch. CR4 . . . .140 DG96
Ropery St, E3 . . . . .85 DZ70
Rope St, SE16 . . . . .203 L7
Rope Wk, Sun. TW16 . . . . .136 BW97
Rope Wk Gdns, E1
  off Commercial Rd 84 DU72
Ropewalk Ms, E8
  off Middleton Rd 84 DT66
Rope Yd Rails, SE18 . . . . .105 EP76
Ropley St, E2 . . . . .84 DU68
Rosa Alba Ms, N5
  off Kelross Rd 66 DQ63
Rosa Av, Ashf. TW15 . . . . .114 BN91
Rosaline Rd, SW6 . . . . . . .99 CY80
Rosamond St, SE26 . . . . . .122 DV90
Rosamund Cl, S.Croy. CR2 .160 DR105
Rosamun St, Sthl. UB2 . . . .96 BY77
Rosary, The, Egh. TW20 . . .133 BD96
Rosary Cl, Houns. TW3 . . . .96 BY82
Rosary Ct, Pot.B. EN6 . . . .12 DB30
Rosary Gdns, SW7 . . . . . .100 DC77
  Ashford TW15 . . . . .115 BP91
  Bushey WD23 . . . . .41 CE45
Rosaville Rd, SW6 . . . . . . .99 CZ80
Roscoe St, EC1 . . . . .197 J5
Roscoff Cl, Edg. HA8 . . . . .42 CQ53
Roseacre, Oxt. RH8 . . . . . .188 EG134
Roseacre Cl, W13
  off Middlefielde 79 CH71
  Hornchurch RM11 . . . . . .72 FM60
  Shepperton TW17 . . . . .134 BN99
Roseacre Rd, Well. DA16 . .106 EV83
Rose All, SE1 . . . . .201 J2
Rose & Crown Ct, EC2 . . . .197 H8
Rose & Crown Yd, SW1 . . . .199 L2
Roseary Cl, West Dr. UB7 . .94 BK77
Rose Av, E18 . . . . .48 EH54
  Gravesend DA12 . . . . . .131 GL88
  Mitcham CR4 . . . . .140 DF95
  Morden SM4 . . . . .140 DC99
Rose Bk, Brwd. CM14 . . . . .54 FX48
Rosebank, SE20 . . . . .122 DV94
  Epsom KT18 . . . . .156 CQ114
  Waltham Abbey EN9 . . . . .16 EE33
Rosebank Av, Horn. RM12 . .72 FJ64
  Wembley HA0 . . . . .61 CG63
Rosebank Cl, N12 . . . . .44 DE50
  Teddington TW11 . . . . . .117 CG93
Rosebank Gdns, E3 . . . . . .85 DZ68
  Gravesend (Nthflt.) DA11 .130 GE88
Rosebank Gro, E17 . . . . . .67 DZ55
Rosebank Rd, E17 . . . . . . .67 EB58
  W7 . . . . .97 CE75
Rosebank Vil, E17 . . . . . . .67 EA56

Rosebank Wk, NW1
  off Maiden La 83 DK66
  SE18 off Woodhill 104 EL77
Rosebank Way, W3 . . . . . . .80 CR72
Rose Bates Dr, NW9 . . . . . .62 CN56
Roseberry Av, Upmin. RM14 . .73 FT58
Roseberry Ct, Wat. WD17
  off Grandfield Av 23 BU39
Roseberry Gdns, N4 . . . . . .65 DP58
  Dartford DA1 . . . . .128 FJ87
  Orpington BR6 . . . . . . .145 ES104
  Upminster RM14 . . . . . . .73 FT59
Rosebery Av, E12 . . . . .86 EL65
  EC1 . . . . .196 D5
  N17 . . . . .46 DU54
  Epsom KT17 . . . . .156 CS114
  Harrow HA2 . . . . .60 BZ63
  New Malden KT3 . . . . . .139 CT96
  Sidcup DA15 . . . . .125 ES87
  Thornton Heath CR7 . . . .142 DQ96
Rosebery Cl, Mord. SM4 . . .139 CX100
Rosebery Ct, EC1
  off Rosebery Av 83 DN70
  Gravesend (Nthflt.) DA11 .131 GF88
Rosebery Cres, Wok. GU22 .167 AZ121
Rosebery Gdns, N8 . . . . . .65 DL57
  W13 . . . . .79 CG72
  Sutton SM1 . . . . .158 DB105
Rosebery Ms, N10 . . . . . . .45 DJ54
  SW2 off Rosebery Rd . . .121 DL86
Rosebery Rd, N9 . . . . .46 DU48
  N10 . . . . .45 DJ54
  SW2 . . . . .121 DL86
  Bushey WD23 . . . . .40 CB45
  Epsom KT18 . . . . .172 CR119
  Grays RM17 . . . . .110 FY79
  Hounslow TW3 . . . . . . .116 CC85
  Kingston upon Thames KT1 .138 CP96
  Sutton SM1 . . . . .157 CZ107
Rosebery Sq, EC1 . . . . . . .196 D5
  Kingston upon Thames KT1 .138 CP96
Rosebine Av, Twick. TW2 . .117 CD87
Rosebriar Cl, Wok. GU22 . .168 BG116
Rosebriars, Cat. CR3 . . . . .176 DS120
  Esher KT10 . . . . .154 CC106
Rosebriar Wk, Wat. WD24 . .23 BT36
Rosebury Rd, SW6 . . . . . .100 DB82
Rosebury Sq, Wdf.Grn. IG8 . .49 EN52
Rosebury Vale, Ruis. HA4 . .59 BT60
Rose Bushes, Epsom KT17 .173 CV116
Rose Ct, E1 off Sandy's Row .84 DS71
  SE26 . . . . .122 DV89
  Pinner HA5 off Nursery Rd .60 BW55
  Waltham Cross EN7 . . . . .14 DU27
Rosecourt Rd, Croy. CR0 . .141 DM100
Rosecroft Av, NW3 . . . . . . .64 DA62
Rosecroft Cl, Orp. BR5 . . . .146 EW100
  Westerham (Bigg.H.) TN16
    off Lotus Rd 179 EM118
Rosecroft Dr, Wat. WD17 . . .23 BS36
Rosecroft Gdns, NW2 . . . . .63 CU62
  Twickenham TW2 . . . . . .117 CD88
Rosecroft Rd, Sthl. UB1 . . .78 CA70
Rosecroft Wk, Pnr. HA5 . . . .60 BX57
  Wembley HA0 . . . . .61 CK64
Rosedale, Ashtd. KT21 . . . .171 CJ118
  Caterham CR3 . . . . .176 DS123
Rosedale Av, Hayes UB3 . . .77 BR71
  Waltham Cross (Chsht.) EN7 .14 DT29
Rosedale Cl, SE2
  off Finchale Rd 106 EV76
  W7 off Boston Rd 97 CF75
  Dartford DA2 . . . . .128 FP87
  St. Albans (Brick.Wd.) AL2 . .8 BY30
  Stanmore HA7 . . . . .41 CH51
Rosedale Ct, N5 . . . . .65 DP63
Rosedale Gdns, Dag. RM9 . .88 EV66
Rosedale Pl, Croy. CR0 . . . .143 DX101
Rosedale Rd, E7 . . . . .68 EJ64
  Dagenham RM9 . . . . . . .88 EV66
  Epsom KT17 . . . . .157 CU106
  Grays RM17 . . . . .110 GD78
  Richmond TW9 . . . . .98 CL84
  Romford RM1 . . . . .51 FC54
Rosedale Ter, W6
  off Dalling Rd 99 CV76
Rosedale Way, Wal.Cr. (Chsht.)
  EN7 . . . . .14 DU29
Rosedene, NW6 . . . . .81 CX67
Rosedene Av, SW16 . . . . . .121 DM90
  Croydon CR0 . . . . .141 DM101
  Greenford UB6 . . . . .78 CA69
  Morden SM4 . . . . .140 DA99
Rosedene Ct, Dart. DA1
  off Shepherds La 128 FJ87
  Ruislip HA4 . . . . .59 BS60
Rosedene Gdns, Ilf. IG2 . . .69 EN56
Rosedene Ter, E10 . . . . . . .68 EB61
Rosedew Rd, W6 . . . . .99 CX79
Rose Dr, Chesh. HP5 . . . . . .4 AS32
Rose End, Wor.Pk. KT4 . . . .139 CX102
Rosefield, Sev. TN13 . . . . .190 FG124
Rosefield Cl, Cars. SM5 . . .158 DE106
Rosefield Gdns, E14 . . . . . .85 EA73
  Chertsey (Ott.) KT16 . . . .151 BD107
Rosefield Rd, Stai. TW18 . .114 BG91
Rose Gdn Cl, Edg. HA8 . . . .42 CL51
Rose Gdns, W5 . . . . .97 CK76
  Feltham TW13 . . . . .115 BU89
  Southall UB1 . . . . .78 CA70
  Staines (Stanw.) TW19 . .114 BK87
Rose Glen, NW9 . . . . .62 CR56
  Romford RM7 . . . . .71 FE60
Roseheart Ms, W11
  off Westbourne Gro 82 DA72
Rosehatch Av, Rom. RM6 . . .70 EX55
Roseheath Rd, Houns. TW4 .116 BZ85
ROSEHILL, Sutt. SM1 . . . .140 DB102
Rosehill, Esher (Clay.) KT10 .155 CG107
  Hampton TW12 . . . . . . .136 CA95
Rose Hill, Sutt. SM1 . . . . . .140 DB104

Rosehill Av, Sutt. SM1 . . . .140 DC102
  Woking GU21 . . . . .166 AW116
Rosehill Cl, Slou. SL1
  off Yew Tree Rd 92 AU76
Rosehill Fm Meadow, Bans. SM7
  off The Tracery 174 DB115
Rosehill Gdns, Abb.L. WD5 . .7 BQ32
  Greenford UB6 . . . . .61 CF64
  Sutton SM1 . . . . .140 DB103
Rosehill Pk W, Sutt. SM1 . .140 DC102
Rosehill Rd, SW18 . . . . . . .120 DC86
  Westerham (Bigg.H.) TN16 .178 EJ117
Roseland Cl, N17
  off Cavell Rd 46 DR52
Rose La, Rom. RM6 . . . . . .70 EX55
  Woking (Ripley) GU23 . . .168 BG124
Rose Lawn, Bushey (Bushey Hth.)
  WD23 . . . . .40 CC46
Roseleigh Av, N5 . . . . .65 DP63
Roseleigh Cl, Twick. TW1 . .117 CK86
Rosemary Av, N3 . . . . .44 DB54
  N9 . . . . .46 DV46
  Enfield EN2 . . . . .30 DR39
  Hounslow TW4 . . . . .96 BX82
  Romford RM1 . . . . .71 FF55
  West Molesey KT8 . . . . .136 CA97
Rosemary Cl, Croy. CR0 . . .141 DL100
  Oxted RH8 . . . . .188 EG133
  South Ockendon RM15 . . .91 FW69
  Uxbridge UB8 . . . . .76 BN71
Rosemary Dr, E14 . . . . . . .85 ED72
  Ilford IG4 . . . . .68 EK57
Rosemary Gdns, SW14
  off Rosemary La 98 CQ83
  Chessington KT9 . . . . . .156 CL105
  Dagenham RM8 . . . . . . .70 EZ60
Rosemary La, SW14 . . . . . .98 CQ83
  Egham TW20 . . . . .133 BB97
Rosemary Rd, SE15 . . . . . .102 DT80
  SW17 . . . . .120 DC90
  Welling DA16 . . . . .105 ET81
Rosemary St, N1
  off Shepperton Rd 84 DR67
Rosemead, NW9 . . . . .63 CT59
  Chertsey KT16 . . . . .134 BH101
  Potters Bar EN6 . . . . . . .12 DC30
Rosemead Av, Felt. TW13 . .115 BT89
  Mitcham CR4 . . . . .141 DJ96
  Wembley HA9 . . . . .62 CL64
Rosemead Gdns, Brwd. CM13 . .55 GD42
Rosemont Av, N12 . . . . . . .44 DC51
Rosemont Rd, NW3 . . . . . .82 DC65
  W3 . . . . .80 CP73
  New Malden KT3 . . . . . .138 CQ97
  Richmond TW10 . . . . . . .118 CL86
  Wembley HA0 . . . . .80 CL67
Rosemoor St, SW3 . . . . . . .198 D9
Rosemount Av, W.Byf. KT14 .152 BG113
Rosemount Cl, Wdf.Grn. IG8
  off Chapelmount Rd 49 EM51
Rosemount Dr, Brom. BR1 .145 EM98
Rosemount Pt, SE23
  off Dacres Rd 123 DX90
Rosemount Rd, W13 . . . . . .79 CG72
Rosenau Cres, SW11 . . . . .100 DE81
Rosenau Rd, SW11 . . . . . .100 DE81
Rosendale Rd, SE21 . . . . . .122 DQ87
  SE24 . . . . .122 DQ87
Roseneath Av, N21 . . . . . . .45 DP46
Roseneath Cl, Orp. BR6 . . .164 EW108
Roseneath Rd, SW11 . . . . .120 DG86
Roseneath Wk, Enf. EN1 . . .30 DS42
Rosens Wk, Edg. HA8 . . . . .42 CP48
Rosenthal Rd, SE6 . . . . . . .123 EB86
Rosenthorpe Rd, SE15 . . . .123 DX85
Rose Pk Cl, Hayes UB4 . . . .78 BW70
Rosepark Ct, Ilf. IG5 . . . . . .49 EM54
Roserton St, E14 . . . . .204 D5
Rosery, The, Croy. CR0 . . . .143 DX100
Roses, The, Wdf.Grn. IG8 . . .48 EF52
Rose Sq, SW3 . . . . .198 A10
Rose St, WC2 . . . . .195 P10
  Gravesend (Nthflt.) DA11 .130 GB86
★ Rose Thea, SE1
  off Park St 201 J2
Rosethorn Cl, SW12 . . . . . .121 DK88
Rosetta Cl, SW8 . . . . .101 DL80
Rosetti Ter, Dag. RM8
  off Marlborough Rd 70 EV63
Rose Valley, Brwd. CM14 . . .54 FW48
Roseveare Rd, SE12 . . . . . .124 EJ91
Rose Vil, Dart. DA1 . . . . . . .128 FP87
Roseville Av, Houns. TW3 . .116 CA85
Roseville Rd, Hayes UB3 . . .95 BU78
Rosevine Rd, SW20 . . . . . .139 CW95
Rose Wk, Pur. CR8 . . . . . . .159 DK111
  Surbiton KT5 . . . . .138 CP99
  West Wickham BR4 . . . . .143 ED103
Rose Wk, The, Rad. WD7 . . .25 CH37
Rosewarne Cl, Wok. GU21
  off Muirfield Rd 166 AU118
Rose Way, SE12 . . . . .124 EG85
Roseway, SE21 . . . . .122 DR86
Rose Way, Edg. HA8 . . . . . .42 CQ49
Rosewell Cl, SE20 . . . . . . .122 DV94
Rosewood, Dart. DA2 . . . . .127 FE91
  Esher KT10 . . . . .137 CG103
  Sutton SM2 . . . . .158 DC110
  Woking GU22 . . . . .167 BA119
Rosewood Av, Grnf. UB6 . . .61 CG64
  Hornchurch RM12 . . . . . .71 FG64
Rosewood Cl, Sid. DA14 . . .126 EW90
Rosewood Ct, Brom. BR1 . .144 EJ95
  Romford RM6 . . . . .70 EW57
Rosewood Dr, Enf. EN2 . . . .29 DN35
  Shepperton TW17 . . . . .134 BM99
Rosewood Gdns, SE13
  off Lewisham Rd 103 EC82
Rosewood Gro, Sutt. SM1 . .140 DC103
Rosewood Sq, W12
  off Primula St 81 CU72
Rosewood Ter, SE20
  off Laurel Gro 122 DW94
Rosher Cl, E15 . . . . .85 ED66

Ros - Rug

ROSHERVILLE, Grav. **131** GF85
Rosherville Way, Grav. DA11 .**130** GE87
Rosina St, E9 . . . .**67** DX64
Roslin Rd, W3 . . . .**98** CP76
Roslin Way, Brom. BR1 . . . . .**124** EG92
Roslyn Cl, Mitch. CR4 . . . . . .**140** DD96
Roslyn Ct, Wok. GU21
 off St. John's Rd **166** AU118
Roslyn Gdns, Rom. RM2 . . . . .**51** FF54
Roslyn Rd, N15 . . . .**66** DR57
Rosmead Rd, W11 . . . .**81** CY73
Rosoman Pl, EC1 . . . .**196** E4
Rosoman St, EC1 . . . .**196** E3
Rossall Cl, Horn. RM11 . . . .**71** FG58
Rossall Cres, NW10 . . . .**80** CM69
Ross Av, NW7 . . . .**43** CY50
 Dagenham RM8 . . . .**70** EZ61
Ross Cl, Har. HA3 . . . .**40** CC52
 Hayes UB3 . . . .**95** BR77
Ross Ct, SW15 . . . .**119** CX87
Ross Cres, Wat. WD25 . . . .**23** BU35
Rossdale, Sutt. SM1 . . . .**158** DE106
Rossdale Dr, N9 . . . .**30** DW44
 NW9 . . . .**62** CQ60
Rossdale Rd, SW15 . . . .**99** CW84
Rosse Ms, SE3 . . . .**104** EH81
Rossendale St, E5 . . . .**66** DV61
Rossendale Way, NW1 . . . .**83** DJ66
Rossetti Gdns, Couls. CR5 . .**175** DM118
Rossetti Rd, SE16 . . . .**202** D10
Rossignol Gdns, Cars. SM5 .**140** DG103
Rossindel Rd, Houns. TW3 . . .**116** CA85
Rossington Av, Borwd. WD6 . .**26** CL38
Rossington Cl, Enf. EN1 . . . . . .**30** DV38
Rossington St, E5 . . . .**66** DU61
Rossiter Cl, Slou. SL3 . . . .**92** AY77
Rossiter Flds, Barn. EN5 . . . . .**27** CY44
Rossiter Rd, SW12 . . . .**121** DH88
Rossland Cl, Bexh. DA6 . . . . .**127** FB85
Rosslare Cl, West. TN16 . . . . .**189** ER125
Rosslyn Av, E4 . . . .**48** EF47
 SW13 . . . .**98** CS83
 Barnet EN4 . . . .**28** DE44
 Dagenham RM8 . . . .**70** EZ59
 Feltham TW14 . . . .**115** BU86
 Romford RM3 . . . .**52** FM54
Rosslyn Cl, Hayes UB3
 off Morgans La **77** BR71
 Sunbury-on-Thames TW16
 off Cadbury Rd **115** BS93
 West Wickham BR4 . . . .**144** EF104
Rosslyn Cres, Har. HA1 . . . . . .**61** CF57
 Wembley HA9 . . . .**62** CL63
Rosslyn Gdns, Wem. HA9
 off Rosslyn Cres **62** CL62
Rosslyn Hill, NW3 . . . .**64** DD63
Rosslyn Ms, NW3
 off Rosslyn Hill **64** DD63
Rosslyn Pk Ms, NW3
 off Lyndhurst Rd **64** DD64
Rosslyn Rd, E17 . . . .**67** EC56
 Barking IG11 . . . .**87** ER66
 Twickenham TW1 . . . .**117** CJ86
 Watford WD18 . . . .**23** BV41
Rossmore Ct, NW1 . . . .**194** D4
Rossmore Rd, NW1 . . . .**194** C5
Ross Par, Wall. SM6 . . . .**159** DH107
Ross Rd, SE25 . . . .**142** DR97
 Cobham KT11 . . . .**154** BW113
 Dartford DA1 . . . .**127** FG86
 Twickenham TW2 . . . .**116** CB88
 Wallington SM6 . . . .**159** DJ106
Ross Way, SE9 . . . .**104** EL83
 Northwood HA6 . . . .**39** BT49
Rossway Dr, Bushey WD23 . . .**24** CC43
Rosswood Gdns, Wall. SM6 .**159** DJ107
Rostella Rd, SW17 . . . .**120** DD90
Rostrevor Av, N15 . . . .**66** DT58
Rostrevor Gdns, Hayes UB3 . .**77** BS74
 Iver SL0 . . . .**75** BD68
 Southall UB2 . . . .**96** BY78
Rostrevor Ms, SW6 . . . .**99** CZ81
Rostrevor Rd, SW6 . . . .**99** CZ81
 SW19 . . . .**120** DA92
Roswell Cl, Wal.Cr. (Chsht.)
 EN8 . . . .**15** DY30
Rotary St, SE1 . . . .**200** F6
Rothbury Av, Rain. RM13 . . . . .**89** FH71
Rothbury Gdns, Islw. TW7 . . . .**97** CG80
Rothbury Rd, E9 . . . .**85** DZ66
Rothbury Wk, N17 . . . .**46** DU52
Roth Dr, Brwd. CM13 . . . .**55** GB47
Rother Cl, Wat. WD25 . . . .**8** BW34
Rotherfield Rd, Cars. SM5 . . .**158** DG105
 Enfield EN3 . . . .**31** DX37
Rotherfield St, N1 . . . .**84** DQ66
Rotherham Wk, SE1 . . . .**200** F3
Rotherhill Av, SW16 . . . .**121** DK93
ROTHERHITHE, SE16 . . . .**203** H6
⊖ **Rotherhithe** **202** G4
★ **Rotherhithe Heritage Mus.**,
 SE16 . . . .**203** L2
Rotherhithe New Rd, SE16 . .**102** DU78
Rotherhithe Old Rd, SE16 . . .**203** H7
Rotherhithe St, SE16 . . . .**202** G4
Rotherhithe Tunnel, E1 . . . . .**203** H4
Rotherhithe Tunnel App, E14 . .**85** DY73
 SE16 . . . .**202** F5
Rothermere Rd, Croy. CR0 . .**159** DM106
Rotherwick Hill, W5 . . . .**80** CM70
Rotherwick Rd, NW11 . . . .**64** DA59
Rotherwood Cl, SW20 . . . . . .**139** CY96
Rotherwood Rd, SW15 . . . . . .**99** CX83
Rothery St, N1 *off Gaskin St* . .**83** DP67
Rothery Ter, SW9 . . . .**101** DP80
Rothesay Av, SW20 . . . .**139** CY96
 Greenford UB6 . . . .**79** CD65
 Richmond TW10 . . . .**98** CP84
Rothesay Rd, SE25 . . . .**142** DS98
Rothsay Rd, E7 . . . .**86** EJ65
Rothsay St, SE1 . . . .**201** M6
Rothsay Wk, E14 . . . .**204** A8

Rothschild Rd, W4 . . . .**98** CQ77
Rothschild St, SE27 . . . .**121** DP91
Roth Wk, N7 *off Durham Rd* . . .**65** DM62
Rothwell Gdns, Dag. RM9 . . . .**88** EW66
Rothwell Rd, Dag. RM9 . . . . . .**88** EW67
Rothwell St, NW1 . . . .**82** DF67
Rotten Row, SW1 . . . .**198** F4
 SW7 . . . .**198** B4
Rotterdam Dr, E14 . . . .**204** E7
Rouel Rd, SE16 . . . .**202** B7
Rouge La, Grav. DA12 . . . . . .**131** GH88
Rougemont Av, Mord. SM4 . .**140** DA100
Roughetts La, Gdse. RH9 . . .**186** DS129
 Redhill RH1 . . . .**186** DS129
Roughlands, Wok. GU22 . . . . .**167** BE115
Roughs, The, Nthwd. HA6 . . . .**39** BT48
Roughtallys, Epp. (N.Wld.Bas.)
 CM16 . . . .**18** EZ27
Roughwood Cl, Wat. WD17 . . . .**23** BS38
Roughwood La, Ch.St.G. HP8 . .**36** AY45
Roundacre, SW19
 off Inner Pk Rd **119** CX89
Roundaway Rd, Ilf. IG5 . . . .**49** EM54
ROUND BUSH, Wat. **24** CC38
Roundcroft, Wal.Cr. (Chsht.)
 EN7 . . . .**14** DT26
Roundel Cl, SE4
 off Adelaide Av **103** DZ84
Round Gro, Croy. CR0 . . . . . .**143** DX101
Roundhay Cl, SE23 . . . .**123** DX89
Roundhedge Way, Enf. EN2 . . .**29** DM38
Round Hill, SE26 . . . .**122** DW89
Roundhill Dr, Enf. EN2 . . . .**29** DM42
 Woking GU22 . . . .**167** BB118
Roundhills, Wal.Abb. EN9 . . . . .**16** EE34
Roundhill Way, Cob. KT11 . . .**154** CB111
Roundlyn Gdns, Orp. (St.M.Cray)
 BR5 *off Lynmouth Ri* **146** EV98
Roundmead Av, Loug. IG10 . . .**33** EN41
Roundmead Cl, Loug. IG10 . . .**33** EN41
Roundmoor Dr, Wal.Cr. (Chsht.)
 EN8 . . . .**15** DX29
Round Oak Rd, Wey. KT13 . . .**152** BM105
Roundshaw Cen, Wall. SM6
 off Meteor Way **159** DL108
Roundtable Rd, Brom. BR1 . . .**124** EF90
Roundthorn Way, Wok. GU21 .**166** AT116
Roundtree Rd, Wem. HA0 . . . . .**61** CH64
Roundway, The, N17 . . . .**46** DQ53
 Esher (Clay.) KT10 . . . .**155** CF106
 Watford WD18 . . . .**23** BT44
Roundways, Ruis. HA4 . . . .**59** BT62
Roundwood, Chis. BR7 . . . . . .**145** EP96
 Kings Langley WD4 . . . .**6** BL26
Roundwood Av, Brwd. CM13 . .**55** GA46
 Uxbridge UB11 . . . .**77** BQ74
Roundwood Cl, Ruis. HA4 . . . . .**59** BR59
Roundwood Gro, Brwd.
 CM13 . . . .**55** GB45
Roundwood Lake, Brwd. (Hutton)
 CM13 . . . .**55** GB46
Roundwood Rd, NW10 . . . .**81** CT65
 Amersham HP6 . . . .**20** AS38
Roundwood Vw, Bans. SM7 . .**173** CX115
Roundwood Way, Bans. SM7 .**173** CX115
Rounton Rd, E3 . . . .**85** EA70
 Waltham Abbey EN9 . . . .**16** EE33
Roupell Rd, SW2 . . . .**121** DM88
Roupell St, SE1 . . . .**200** E3
Rousden St, NW1 . . . .**83** DJ66
Rousebarn La, Rick. WD3 . . . . .**23** BQ41
Rouse Gdns, SE21 . . . .**122** DS91
Rous Rd, Buck.H. IG9 . . . .**48** EL46
Routemaster Cl, E13 . . . .**86** EH69
Routh Ct, Felt. TW14
 off Loxwood Cl **115** BS88
Routh Rd, SW18 . . . .**120** DE87
Routh St, E6 . . . .**87** EM71
Routledge Cl, N19 . . . .**65** DK60
Rover Av, Ilf. IG6 . . . .**49** ET51
Rowallan Rd, SW6 . . . .**99** CY80
Rowan Av, E4 . . . .**47** DZ51
 Egham TW20 . . . .**113** BC92
Rowan Cl, SW16 . . . .**141** DJ95
 W5 . . . .**98** CL75
 Ilford IG1 . . . .**69** ER64
 New Malden KT3 . . . .**138** CS96
 Radlett (Shenley) WD7
 off Juniper Gdns **10** CL33
 St. Albans (Brick.Wd.) AL2 . . . .**8** CA31
 Stanmore HA7
 off Woodlands Dr **41** CF51
 Wembley HA0 . . . .**61** CG62
Rowan Ct, Borwd. WD6
 off Theobald St **26** CL39
Rowan Cres, SW16 . . . .**141** DJ95
 Dartford DA1 . . . .**128** FJ88
Rowan Dr, NW9 . . . .**63** CU56
 Broxbourne EN10 . . . .**15** DZ25
Rowan Gdns, Croy. CR0
 off Radcliffe Rd **142** DT104
 Iver SL0 . . . .**75** BD68
Rowan Grn, Wey. KT13 . . . . . .**153** BR105
Rowan Grn E, Brwd. CM13 . . . .**55** FZ48
Rowan Grn W, Brwd. CM13 . . . .**55** FZ48
Rowan Gro, Couls. CR5 . . . . . .**175** DH121
Rowan Pl, Amer. HP6 . . . .**20** AT38
 Hayes UB3 *off West Av* **77** BT73
Rowan Rd, SW16 . . . .**141** DJ96
 W6 . . . .**99** CX77
 Bexleyheath DA7 . . . .**106** EY83
 Brentford TW8 . . . .**97** CH80
 Swanley BR8 . . . .**147** FD97
 West Drayton UB7 . . . .**94** BK77
Rowans, The, N13 . . . .**45** DP48
 Gerrards Cross (Chal.St.P.)
 SL9 . . . .**56** AW55
 South Ockendon (Aveley)
 RM15 *off Purfleet Rd* **90** FQ74
 Sunbury-on-Thames TW16 .**135** BT92
 Woking GU22 . . . .**166** AY118
Rowans Cl, Long. DA3 . . . . . .**149** FX96
Rowans Way, Loug. IG10 . . . . .**33** EM42

Rowan Ter, SE20
 off Sycamore Gro **142** DU95
 W6 *off Bute Gdns* **99** CX77
Rowantree Cl, N21 . . . .**46** DR46
Rowantree Rd, N21 . . . .**46** DR46
 Enfield EN2 . . . .**29** DP40
Rowan Wk, N2 . . . .**64** DC58
 N19 *off Bredgar Rd* **65** DJ61
 W10 *off Droop St* **81** CY70
 Barnet EN5 *off Station Rd* **28** DB43
 Bromley BR2 . . . .**145** EM104
 Hornchurch RM11 . . . .**72** FK56
Rowan Way, Rom. RM6 . . . . . .**70** EW55
 South Ockendon RM15 . . . . . .**91** FX70
Rowanwood Av, Sid. DA15 . . .**126** EU88
Rowanwood Ms, Enf. EN2
 off Rowantree Rd **29** DP40
Rowben Cl, N20 . . . .**44** DB46
Rowberry Cl, SW6 . . . .**99** CW80
Rowcross St, SE1 . . . .**201** P10
Rowden Pk Gdns, E4
 off Rowden Rd **47** EA51
Rowden Rd, E4 . . . .**47** EA51
 Beckenham BR3 . . . .**143** DY95
 Epsom KT19 . . . .**156** CP105
Rowditch La, SW11 . . . .**100** DG82
Rowdon Av, NW10 . . . .**81** CV66
Rowdown Cres, Croy.
 (New Adgtn.) CR0 . . . .**161** ED109
Rowdowns Rd, Dag. RM9 . . . . .**88** EZ67
Rowe Gdns, Bark. IG11 . . . . . .**87** ET68
Rowe La, E9 . . . .**66** DW64
Rowena Cres, SW11 . . . .**100** DE82
Rowe Wk, Har. HA2 . . . .**60** CA62
Rowfant Rd, SW17 . . . .**120** DG88
Rowhedge, Brwd. CM13 . . . . . .**55** GA48
Row Hill, Add. KT15 . . . .**151** BF107
Rowhill Rd, E5 . . . .**66** DV63
 Dartford DA2 . . . .**127** FF93
 Swanley BR8 . . . .**127** FF93
Rowhurst Av, Add. KT15 . . . . .**152** BH107
 Leatherhead KT22 . . . .**171** CF117
Rowington Cl, W2 . . . .**82** DB71
Rowland Av, Har. HA3 . . . .**61** CJ56
Rowland Ct, E16 . . . .**86** EF70
Rowland Cres, Chig. IG7 . . . . .**49** ES49
Rowland Gro, SE26
 off Dallas Rd **122** DV90
Rowland Hill Av, N17 . . . .**46** DQ52
Rowland Hill St, NW3 . . . .**64** DE64
Rowlands Av, Pnr. HA5 . . . .**40** CA51
Rowlands Cl, N6 *off North Hill* . .**64** DG58
 NW7 . . . .**43** CU52
 Waltham Cross (Chsht.) EN8 . .**15** DX30
Rowlands Flds, Wal.Cr. (Chsht.)
 EN8 . . . .**15** DX29
Rowlands Rd, Dag. RM8 . . . . . .**70** EZ61
Rowland Wk, Rom. (Hav.at.Bow.)
 RM4 . . . .**51** FE48
Rowland Way, SW19
 off Hayward Cl **140** DB95
 Ashford TW15
 off Littleton Rd **115** BQ94
Rowlatt Cl, Dart. DA2 . . . .**128** FJ91
Rowlatt Rd, Dart. DA2
 off Whitehead Cl **128** FJ91
Rowley Av, Sid. DA15 . . . .**126** EV87
Rowley Cl, Wat. WD19
 off Lower Paddock Rd **24** BY44
 Wembley HA0 . . . .**80** CM66
 Woking (Pyrford) GU22 . . . . .**168** BG116
Rowley Ct, Cat. CR3 . . . .**176** DQ122
Rowley Gdns, N4 . . . .**66** DQ59
 Waltham Cross (Chsht.) EN8
 off Warwick Dr **15** DX28
ROWLEY GREEN, Barn. **27** CT42
Rowley Grn Rd, Barn. EN5 . . . .**27** CT43
Rowley Ind Pk, W3 . . . .**98** CP76
Rowley La, Barn. EN5 . . . .**27** CT43
 Borehamwood WD6 . . . .**26** CR39
 Slough (Wexham) SL3 . . . .**74** AW67
Rowley Mead, Epp. (Thnwd.)
 CM16 . . . .**18** EW25
Rowley Rd, N15 . . . .**66** DQ57
Rowley Way, NW8 . . . .**82** DB67
Rowlheys Pl, West Dr. UB7 . . . .**94** BL76
Rowlls Rd, Kings.T. KT1 . . . . . .**138** CM97
Rowmarsh Cl, Grav. (Nthflt.)
 DA11 . . . .**130** GD91
Rowney Gdns, Dag. RM9 . . . . .**88** EW65
Rowney Rd, Dag. RM9 . . . .**88** EV65
Rowntree Clifford Cl, E13
 off Liddon Rd **86** EH69
Rowntree Path, SE28
 off Booth Cl **88** EV73
Rowntree Rd, Twick. TW2 . . . .**117** CE88
Rowse Cl, E15 . . . .**85** EC66
Rowsley Av, NW4 . . . .**63** CW55
Rowstock Gdns, N7 . . . .**65** DK64
Rowton Rd, SE18 . . . .**105** EQ80
ROW TOWN, Add. **151** BF108
Rowtown, Add. KT15 . . . .**151** BF108
Rowzill Rd, Swan. BR8 . . . .**127** FF93
Roxborough Av, Har. HA1 . . . . .**61** CD59
 Isleworth TW7 . . . .**97** CF80
Roxborough Pk, Har. HA1 . . . . .**61** CE59
Roxborough Rd, Har. HA1 . . . . .**61** CD57
Roxbourne Cl, Nthlt. UB5 . . . . .**78** BX65
Roxburgh Av, Upmin. RM14 . . .**72** FQ62
Roxburgh Rd, SE27 . . . .**121** DP92
Roxburn Way, Ruis. HA4 . . . . . .**59** BT62
Roxby Pl, SW6 . . . .**100** DA80
ROXETH, Har. **61** CD61
 off Pitfield St **84** DS69
Roxeth Grn Av, Har. HA2 . . . . . .**60** CB62
Roxeth Gro, Har. HA2 . . . .**60** CB63
Roxeth Hill, Har. HA2 . . . .**61** CD61
Roxford Cl, Shep. TW17 . . . . .**135** BS99
Roxley Rd, SE13 . . . .**123** EB86
Roxton Gdns, Croy. CR0 . . . . .**161** EA106
Roxwell Gdns, Brwd. CM13 . . .**55** GC42
Roxwell Rd, W12 . . . .**99** CU75
 Barking IG11 . . . .**88** EU68
Roxwell Trd Pk, E10 . . . .**67** DY59
Roxwell Way, Wdf.Grn. IG8 . . . .**48** EJ52
Roxy Av, Rom. RM6 . . . .**70** EW59

★ **Royal Academy of Arts**, W1 .**199** K1
★ **Royal Academy of Dramatic**
 Art (RADA), WC1 . . . .**195** M6
★ **Royal Academy of Music**,
 NW1 . . . .**194** G5
★ **Royal Air Force Museums**,
 NW9 (Hendon) **43** CU54
⊖ **Royal Albert** **86** EL73
Royal Albert Dock, E16 . . . .**87** EM73
★ **Royal Albert Hall**, SW7 . . . .**100** DD75
Royal Albert Roundabout, E16
 off Royal Albert Way **86** EL73
Royal Albert Way, E16 . . . .**86** EK73
Royal Arc, W1 . . . .**199** K1
Royal Artillery Barracks, SE18
 off Repository Rd **105** EN78
Royal Av, SW3 . . . .**198** D10
 Waltham Cross EN8 . . . .**15** DY33
 Worcester Park KT4 . . . .**138** CS103
★ **Royal Botanic Gardens, Kew**,
 Rich. TW9 . . . .**98** CL80
Ⓗ **Royal Brompton Hosp**,
 SW3 . . . .**198** B10
Royal Circ, SE27 . . . .**121** DN90
Royal Cl, N16 *off Manor Rd* . . .**66** DS60
 SE8 . . . .**103** DZ79
 SW19 *off Queensmere Rd* .**119** CX89
 Ilford IG3 . . . .**69** EU59
 Orpington BR6 . . . .**163** EP105
 Uxbridge UB8 . . . .**76** BM72
 Worcester Park KT4 . . . .**138** CS103
★ **Royal Coll of Art**, SW7 . . . .**100** DC75
★ **Royal Coll of Music**, SW7 .**100** DD76
★ **Royal Coll of Surgeons**,
 WC2 . . . .**196** C8
Royal Coll St, NW1 . . . .**83** DJ66
Royal Ct, EC3 *off Cornhill* **84** DR72
 SE16 . . . .**203** M6
★ **Royal Courts of Justice**,
 WC2 . . . .**196** C9
Royal Cres, W11 . . . .**81** CX74
 Ruislip HA4 . . . .**60** BY63
Royal Cres Ms, W11
 off Queensdale Rd **81** CX74
Royal Docks Rd, E6 . . . .**87** EP72
Royal Dr, N11 . . . .**44** DG50
 Epsom KT18 . . . .**173** CV118
Royal Duchess Ms, SW12
 off Dinsmore Rd **121** DH87
Royale Leisure Pk, W3 . . . .**80** CN70
★ **Royal Exchange**, EC3 . . . . .**197** L9
Royal Ex, EC3 . . . .**197** L9
Royal Ex Av, EC3 . . . .**197** L9
Royal Ex Bldgs, EC3 . . . .**197** L9
Royal Ex Steps, EC3
 off Cornhill **84** DR72
★ **Royal Festival Hall**, SE1 . .**200** B2
Ⓗ **Royal Free Hosp, The**, NW3 .**64** DE64
Royal Gdns, W7 . . . .**97** CG76
★ **Royal Geographical Society**,
 SW7 . . . .**100** DD75
Royal Herbert Pavilions, SE18 .**105** EM81
Royal Hill, SE10 . . . .**103** EC80
Royal Horticultural Society Cotts,
 Wok. (Wisley) GU23
 off Wisley La **168** BL116
★ **Royal Horticultural Society**
 Gdns, Wisley, Wok. GU22 .**168** BL118
★ **Royal Horticultural Society**
 (Lawrence Hall), SW1 . . . .**199** M7
★ **Royal Horticultural Society**
 (Lindley Hall), SW1 . . . . . .**199** M8
★ **Royal Hosp Chelsea & Mus.**,
 SW3 . . . .**100** DG78
Ⓗ **Royal Hosp for Neuro-**
 Disability, SW15 . . . .**119** CY86
Ⓗ **Royal Hosp Richmond**, Rich.
 TW9 . . . .**98** CL83
Royal Hosp Rd, SW3 . . . .**100** DF79
Royal La, Uxb. UB8 . . . .**76** BM69
 West Drayton UB7 . . . .**76** BM72
Royal London Est, The, N17 . . .**46** DV51
Ⓗ **Royal London Homeopathic**
 Hosp, WC1 . . . .**196** A6
Ⓗ **Royal London Hosp**
 (Mile End), E1 . . . .**85** DX70
Ⓗ **Royal London Hosp**
 (St. Clements), E3 . . . .**85** DZ69
Ⓗ **Royal London Hosp**
 (Whitechapel), E1 . . . .**84** DV71
Ⓗ **Royal Marsden Hosp**, Sutt.
 SM2 . . . .**158** DC110
Ⓗ **Royal Marsden Hosp**
 (Fulham), SW3 . . . .**198** A10
★ **Royal Mews, The**, SW1 . . .**199** J6
★ **Royal Military Academy**,
 SE18 . . . .**105** EM80
★ **Royal Ms, The**, SW1 . . . . . .**199** J6
Royal Mint Ct, EC3 . . . .**202** A1
Royal Mint Pl, E1
 off Blue Anchor Yd **84** DT73
Royal Mint St, E1 . . . .**84** DT73
Royal Mt Ct, Twick. TW2 . . . . .**117** CE90
Ⓗ **Royal National Orthopaedic**
 Hosp, W1 . . . .**195** J5
Ⓗ **Royal National Orthopaedic**
 Hosp, Stan. HA7 . . . .**41** CJ47
★ **Royal National Theat**, SE1 .**200** C2
Ⓗ **Royal National Throat, Nose**
 & Ear Hosp, WC1 . . . .**196** B2
Royal Naval Pl, SE14 . . . .**103** DZ80
⊖ **Royal Oak** **82** DB71
Royal Oak Ct, N1
 off Pitfield St **84** DS69
Royal Oak Pl, SE22 . . . .**122** DV86
Royal Oak Rd, E8 . . . .**84** DV65
 Bexleyheath DA6 . . . .**126** EZ85
 Woking GU21 . . . .**166** AW118
Royal Opera Arc, SW1 . . . .**199** M2
★ **Royal Opera Ho**, WC2 . . . . .**196** A9
Royal Orchard Cl, SW18 . . . . .**119** CY87
Royal Par, SE3 . . . .**104** EE82
 SW6 *off Dawes Rd* **99** CY80
 W5 *off Western Av* **80** CL69
 Chislehurst BR7 . . . .**125** EQ94
 Richmond TW9
 off Station App **98** CN81

Royal Par Ms, SE3
 off Royal Par **104** EF82
 Chislehurst BR7 . . . .**125** EQ94
Royal Pier Ms, Grav. DA12
 off Royal Pier Rd **131** GH86
Royal Pier Rd, Grav. DA12 . . .**131** GH86
Royal Pl, SE10 . . . .**103** EC80
Royal Rd, E16 . . . .**86** EK72
 SE17 . . . .**101** DP79
 Dartford (Darenth) DA2 . . . . .**128** FN92
 Sidcup DA14 . . . .**126** EX90
 Teddington TW11 . . . .**117** CD92
Royal Route, Wem. HA9 . . . . . .**62** CM63
Royal St, SE1 . . . .**200** C6
Royalty Ms, W1 . . . .**195** M9
ⅅⅬⅭ **Royal Victoria** **86** EG73
Royal Victoria Dock, E16 . . . . .**86** EH73
Royal Victoria Patriotic Building,
 SW18 *off Fitzhugh Gro* **120** DD86
Royal Victoria Pl, E16
 off Wesley Av **86** EH74
Royal Victoria Sq, E16 . . . . . .**205** P1
Royal Victor Pl, E3 . . . .**85** DX68
Royal Wk, Wall. SM6
 off Prince Charles Way **141** DH104
Royce Gro, Wat. WD25
 off Ashfields **7** BT34
Roycraft Av, Bark. IG11 . . . .**87** ET68
Roycraft Cl, Bark. IG11 . . . .**87** ET68
Roycroft Cl, E18 . . . .**48** EH53
 SW2 . . . .**121** DN88
Roydene Rd, SE18 . . . .**105** ES79
Roydon Cl, SW11 *off Reform St* .**100** DF82
 Loughton IG10 . . . .**48** EL45
Roydon Ct, Walt. KT12 . . . .**153** BU105
Roydon St, SW6
 off Southolm St **101** DH81
Roy Gdns, Ilf. IG2 . . . .**69** ES56
Roy Gro, Hmptn. TW12 . . . . . .**116** CB93
Royle Cl, Ger.Cr. (Chal.St.P.)
 SL9 . . . .**37** AZ52
 Romford RM2 . . . .**71** FH57
Royle Cres, W13 . . . .**79** CG70
Roy Rd, Nthwd. HA6 . . . .**39** BT52
Roy Sq, E14 *off Narrow St* **85** DY73
Royston Av, E4 . . . .**47** EA50
 Sutton SM1 . . . .**140** DD104
 Wallington SM6 . . . .**159** DK105
 West Byfleet (Byfleet) KT14 .**152** BL112
Royston Cl, Houns. TW5 . . . . . .**95** BV81
 Walton-on-Thames KT12 . . . .**135** BU102
Royston Ct, SE24
 off Burbage Rd **122** DQ86
 Richmond TW9
 off Lichfield Rd **98** CM81
 Surbiton KT6 *off Hook Ri N* .**138** CN104
Royston Gdns, Ilf. IG1 . . . .**68** EK58
Royston Gro, Pnr. HA5 . . . .**40** BZ51
Royston Par, Ilf. IG1 . . . .**68** EK58
Royston Pk Rd, Pnr. HA5 . . . . .**40** BZ51
Royston Rd, SE20 . . . .**143** DX95
 Dartford DA1 . . . .**127** FF86
 Richmond TW10 . . . .**118** CL85
 Romford RM3 . . . .**52** FN52
 West Byfleet (Byfleet) KT14 .**152** BL112
Roystons, The, Surb. KT5 . . . .**138** CP99
Royston St, E2 . . . .**84** DW68
Rozel Ct, N1 . . . .**84** DS67
Rozel Rd, SW4 . . . .**101** DJ82
Rubastic Rd, Sthl. UB2 . . . .**95** BV76
Rubens Rd, Nthlt. UB5 . . . .**78** BW68
Rubens St, SE6 . . . .**123** DZ89
Rubeus Pl, SW4
 off Dolman St **101** DL84
Rubin Pl, Enf. EN3
 off Government Row **31** EA37
Ruby Ms, E17 *off Ruby Rd* **67** EA55
Ruby Rd, E17 . . . .**67** EA55
Ruby St, NW10 *off Fawood Av* . .**80** CR66
 SE15 . . . .**102** DV79
Ruby Triangle, SE15
 off Sandgate St **102** DV79
Ruckholt Cl, E10 . . . .**67** EB62
Ruckholt Rd, E10 . . . .**67** EA63
Rucklers La, Kings L. WD4 . . . . .**6** BK27
Rucklidge Av, NW10 . . . .**81** CT68
Rudall Cres, NW3
 off Willoughby Rd **64** DD63
Ruddington Cl, E5 . . . .**67** DY63
Ruddock Cl, Edg. HA8 . . . .**42** CQ52
Ruddstreet Cl, SE18 . . . .**105** EP71
Ruden Way, Epsom KT17 . . . .**173** CV116
Rudge Ri, Add. KT15 . . . .**151** BF106
Rudgwick Ter, NW8
 off St. Stephens Cl **82** DE67
Rudland Rd, Bexh. DA7 . . . . . .**107** FB83
Rudloe Rd, SW12 . . . .**121** DJ87
Rudolf Pl, SW8 *off Miles St* . . .**101** DL79
Rudolph Ct, SE22 . . . .**122** DU87
Rudolph Rd, E13 . . . .**86** EF68
 NW6 . . . .**82** DA68
 Bushey WD23 . . . .**24** CA44
Rudsworth Cl, Slou. (Colnbr.)
 SL3 . . . .**93** BD80
Rudyard Gro, NW7 . . . .**42** CQ51
Rue de St. Lawrence, Wal.Abb.
 EN9 *off Quaker La* **15** EC34
Ruffets Wd, Grav. DA12 . . . . .**131** GJ93
Ruffetts, The, S.Croy. CR2 . . .**160** DV108
Ruffetts Cl, S.Croy. CR2 . . . . .**160** DV108
Ruffetts Way, Tad. KT20 . . . . .**173** CY118
Ruffle Cl, West Dr. UB7 . . . .**94** BL75
Rufford Cl, Har. HA3 . . . .**61** CG58
 Watford WD17 . . . .**23** BT37
Rufford St, N1 . . . .**83** DL67
Rufford Twr, W3 . . . .**80** CP74
Rufus Cl, Ruis. HA4 . . . .**60** BY62
Rufus St, N1 . . . .**197** M3
Rugby Av, N9 . . . .**46** DT46
 Greenford UB6 . . . .**79** CD66
 Wembley HA0 . . . .**61** CH64
Rugby Cl, Har. HA1 . . . .**61** CE57
★ **Rugby Football Union**
 Twickenham, Twick. TW2 . . .**117** CE86
Rugby Gdns, Dag. RM9 . . . .**88** EW63
Rugby La, Sutt. SM2
 off Nonsuch Wk **157** CX109

★ Place of interest   ⇌ Railway station   ⊖ London Underground station   ⅅⅬⅭ Docklands Light Railway station   ⬥ Tramlink station   Ⓗ Hospital

Rugby Rd, NW9 . . . . .62 CP56
W4 . . . . .98 CS75
Dagenham RM9 . . . . .88 EV66
Twickenham TW1 . . . . . . .117 CE86
Rugby St, WC1 . . . . .196 B5
Rugby Way, Rick. (Crox.Grn.)
WD3 . . . . .23 BP43
Rugged La, Wal.Abb. EN9 . . .16 EK33
Ruggles-Brise Rd, Ashf. TW15 .114 BK92
Rugg St, E14 . . . . .85 EA73
RUISLIP 59 BS59
✿ Ruislip 59 BS60
Ruislip Cl, Grnf. UB6 . . . . . .78 CB70
RUISLIP COMMON, Ruis. . . .59 BR57
Ruislip Ct, Ruis. HA4
off Courtfield Gdns 59 BT61
RUISLIP GARDENS, Ruis. . . .59 BS63
✿ Ruislip Gardens 59 BU63
RUISLIP MANOR, Ruis. 59 BU61
✿ Ruislip Manor 59 BU60
Ruislip Rd, Grnf. UB6 . . . . . .78 CA69
Northolt UB5 . . . . .78 BX68
Southall UB1 . . . . .78 CA69
Ruislip Rd E, W7 . . . . .79 CD70
W13 . . . . .79 CD70
Greenford UB6 . . . . .79 CD70
Ruislip St, SW17 . . . . .120 DF91
Rumania Wk, Grav. DA12 . . .131 GM90
Rumbold Rd, SW6 . . . . .100 DB80
Rum Cl, E1 . . . . .202 F1
Rumsey Cl, Hmptn. TW12 . . .116 BZ93
Rumsey Ms, N4 off Monsell Rd .65 DP62
Rumsey Rd, SW9 . . . . .101 DM83
Rumsley, Wal.Cr. EN7 . . . . . .14 DU27
Runbury Circle, NW9 . . . . . .62 CR61
Runciman Cl, Orp. BR6 . . . . .164 EW110
Runcorn Cl, N17 . . . . .66 DV56
Runcorn Pl, W11 . . . . .81 CY73
Rundell Cres, NW4 . . . . .63 CV57
Runes Cl, Mitch. CR4 . . . . . .140 DD98
Runnemede Rd, Egh. TW20 . .113 BA91
Running Horse Yd, Brent. TW8
off Pottery Rd 98 CL79
Running Waters, Brwd. CM13 .55 GA46
Runnymede, SW19 . . . . .140 DD95
Runnymede Cl, Twick. TW2 . .116 CB86
Runnymede Ct, Croy. CR0 . . .142 DT103
Egham TW20 . . . . .113 BA91
Runnymede Cres, SW16 . . . .141 DK95
Runnymede Gdns, Grnf. UB6 .79 CD68
Twickenham TW2 . . . . .116 CB86
Ⓗ Runnymede Hosp, Cher.
KT16 . . . . .133 BD104
Runnymede Rd, Twick. TW2 . .116 CB86
Runrig Hill, Amer. HP6 . . . . .20 AS35
Runway, The, Ruis. HA4 . . . . .59 BV64
Rupack St, SE16 . . . . .202 F5
Rupert Av, Wem. HA9 . . . . . .62 CL64
Rupert Ct, W1 . . . . .195 M10
West Molesey KT8
off St. Peter's Rd 136 CA98
Rupert Gdns, SW9 . . . . .101 DP82
Rupert Rd, N19
off Holloway Rd 65 DK62
NW6 . . . . .81 CZ68
W4 . . . . .98 CS76
Rupert St, W1 . . . . .195 M10
Rural Cl, Horn. RM11 . . . . . .72 FH60
Rural Vale, Grav. (Nthflt.) DA11 .130 GE87
Rural Way, SW16 . . . . .121 DH94
Redhill RH1 . . . . .184 DG134
Ruscoe Dr, Wok. GU22
off Pembroke Rd 167 BA117
Ruscoe Rd, E16 . . . . .86 EF72
Ruscombe Dr, St.Alb. (Park St.)
AL2 . . . . .8 CB26
Ruscombe Gdns, Slou. (Datchet)
SL3 . . . . .92 AU80
Ruscombe Way, Felt. TW14 . .115 BT87
Rush, The, SW19
off Kingston Rd 139 CZ95
Rusham Pk Av, Egh. TW20 . .113 AZ93
Rusham Rd, SW12 . . . . .120 DF86
Egham TW20 . . . . .113 AZ93
Rushbrook Cres, E17 . . . . . . .47 DZ53
Rushbrook Rd, SE9 . . . . .125 EQ89
Rush Common, Ms, SW2 . . . .121 DM87
Rushcroft Rd, E4 . . . . .47 EA52
SW2 . . . . .101 DN84
Rushden Cl, SE19 . . . . .122 DR94
Rushdene Av, Barn. EN4 . . . .44 DE45
Rushdene Cl, Nthlt. UB5 . . . .78 BW69
Rushdene Cres, Nthlt. UB5 . .78 BW68
Rushdene Rd, Brwd. CM15 . .54 FW45
Pinner HA5 . . . . .60 BX58
Rushdene Wk, West. (Bigg.H.)
TN16 . . . . .178 EK117
Rushden Gdns, NW7 . . . . . . .43 CW51
Ilford IG5 . . . . .69 EN55
Rushdon Cl, Grays RM17 . . . .110 GA76
Romford RM1 . . . . .71 FG57
Rush Dr, Wal.Abb. EN9 . . . . .31 EC36
Rushen Wk, Cars. SM5
off Paisley Rd 140 DD102
Rushes Mead, Uxb. UB8
off Frays Waye 76 BJ67
Rushet Rd, Orp. BR5 . . . . . . .146 EU96
Rushett Cl, T.Ditt. KT7 . . . . .137 CH102
Rushett La, Chess. KT9 . . . . .155 CJ111
Epsom KT18 . . . . .155 CJ111
Rushett Rd, T.Ditt. KT7 . . . . .137 CH101
Rushey Cl, N.Mal. KT3 . . . . .138 CR98
Rushey Grn, SE6 . . . . .123 EB87
Rushey Hill, Enf. EN2 . . . . . .29 DM42
Rushey Mead, SE4 . . . . .123 EA85
Rushfield, Pot.B. EN6 . . . . . .11 CX33
Rushford Rd, SE4 . . . . .123 DZ86
RUSH GREEN, Rom. 71 FC59
Rush Grn Gdns, Rom. RM7 . .71 FC60
Rush Grn Rd, Rom. RM7 . . . .71 FC60
Rushgrove Av, NW9 . . . . . . .63 CT57
Rush Gro St, SE18 . . . . .105 EM77
Rush Hill Ms, SW11
off Rush Hill Rd 100 DG83
Rush Hill Rd, SW11 . . . . . . .100 DG83

Rushleigh Av, Wal.Cr. (Chsht.)
EN8 . . . . .15 DX31
Rushley Cl, Kes. BR2 . . . . . .162 EK105
Rushmead, E2 off Florida St . .84 DV69
Richmond TW10 . . . . .117 CH90
Rushmead Cl, Croy. CR0 . . . .160 DT105
Rushmere Av, Upmin. RM14 . .72 FQ62
Rushmere Ct, Wor.Pk. KT4
off The Avenue 139 CU103
Rushmere Ho, SW15
off Fontley Way 119 CU88
Rushmere La, Chesh. (Orch.L.)
HP5 . . . . .4 AU28
Rushmere Pl, SW19 . . . . . . .119 CX92
Egham TW20 . . . . .112 AY92
Rushmoor, Pnr. HA5 . . . . . . .59 BV56
Rickmansworth WD3 . . . . . .38 BK47
Rushmore Cl, Brom. BR1 . . . .144 EL97
Rushmore Cres, E5
off Rushmore Rd 67 DX63
Rushmore Hill, Orp. BR6 . . . .164 EW110
Sevenoaks (Knock.) TN14 . .164 EX112
Rushmore Rd, E5 . . . . .66 DW63
E5 . . . . .67 DX63
Rusholme Av, Dag. RM10 . . .70 FA62
Rusholme Gro, SE19 . . . . . .122 DS92
Rusholme Rd, SW15 . . . . . . .119 CX86
Rushout Av, Har. HA3 . . . . . .61 CH58
Rushton Av, Wat. WD25 . . . . .23 BU35
Rushton St, N1 . . . . .84 DR68
Rushworth Av, NW4
off Rushworth Gdns 63 CU55
Rushworth Gdns, NW4 . . . . .63 CU56
Rushworth Rd, Reig. RH2 . . .184 DA133
Rushworth St, SE1 . . . . .200 G4
Rushy Meadow La, Cars. SM5 .140 DE103
Ruskin Av, E12 . . . . .68 EL65
Feltham TW14 . . . . .115 BT86
Richmond TW9 . . . . .98 CN80
Upminster RM14 . . . . .72 FQ59
Waltham Abbey EN9 . . . . . .16 EE34
Welling DA16 . . . . .105 EU83
Ruskin Cl, NW11 . . . . .64 DB58
Waltham Cross (Chsht.) EN7 .14 DS26
Ruskin Dr, Orp. BR6 . . . . . . .145 ES104
Welling DA16 . . . . .106 EU83
Worcester Park KT4 . . . . . .139 CV103
Ruskin Gdns, W5 . . . . .79 CK70
Harrow HA3 . . . . .62 CM56
Romford RM3 . . . . .51 FH52
Ruskin Gro, Dart. DA1 . . . . .128 FN85
Welling DA16 . . . . .106 EU82
Ruskin Pk Ho, SE5 . . . . .102 DR83
Ruskin Rd, N17 . . . . .46 DT53
Belvedere DA17 . . . . .106 FA77
Carshalton SM5 . . . . .158 DF106
Croydon CR0 . . . . .141 DP103
Grays RM16 . . . . .111 GG77
Isleworth TW7 . . . . .97 CF83
Southall UB1 . . . . .78 BY73
Staines TW18 . . . . .113 BF94
Ruskin Wk, N9 off Durham Rd .46 DU47
SE24 . . . . .122 DQ85
Bromley BR2 . . . . .145 EM100
Ruskin Way, SW19 . . . . .140 DD95
Rusland Av, Orp. BR6 . . . . . .145 ER104
Rusland Hts, Har. HA1
off Rusland Pk Rd 61 CE56
Rusland Pk Rd, Har. HA1 . . . .61 CE56
Rusper Cl, NW2 . . . . .63 CW62
Stanmore HA7 . . . . .41 CJ49
Rusper Rd, N22 . . . . .46 DQ54
Dagenham RM9 . . . . .88 EW65
Russell Av, N22 . . . . .45 DP54
Russell Cl, NW10 . . . . .80 CQ66
SE7 . . . . .104 EJ80
W4 . . . . .99 CT79
Amersham HP6 . . . . .20 AX39
Beckenham BR3 . . . . .143 EB97
Bexleyheath DA7 . . . . .106 FA84
Brentwood CM15 . . . . .54 FV45
Dartford DA1 . . . . .107 FG83
Northwood HA6 . . . . .39 BQ50
Ruislip HA4 . . . . .60 BW61
Tadworth KT20 . . . . .183 CU125
Woking GU21 . . . . .166 AW115
Russell Ct, SW1 . . . . .199 L3
Leatherhead KT22 . . . . . . .171 CH122
St. Albans AL2 . . . . .8 CA30
Russell Cres, Wat. WD25
off High Rd 23 BT35
Russell Dr, Stai. (Stanw.)
TW19 . . . . .114 BK86
Russell Gdns, N20 . . . . .44 DE47
NW11 . . . . .63 CY58
W14 . . . . .99 CY76
Richmond TW10 . . . . .117 CJ89
West Drayton UB7 . . . . . . .94 BN78
Russell Gdns Ms, W14 . . . . .99 CY76
Russell Grn Cl, Pur. CR8 . . . .159 DN110
Russell Gro, NW7 . . . . .42 CS50
SW9 . . . . .101 DN80
Russell Hill, Pur. CR8 . . . . . .159 DM110
Russell Hill Pl, Pur. CR8 . . . .159 DN111
Russell Hill Rd, Pur. CR8 . . . .159 DN110
Russell Kerr Cl, W4
off Burlington La 98 CQ80
Russell La, N20 . . . . .44 DE47
Watford WD17 . . . . .23 BR36
Russell Mead, Har. (Har.Wld.)
HA3 . . . . .41 CF53
Russell Par, NW11
off Golders Grn Rd 63 CY58
Russell Pl, NW3 off Aspern Gro .64 DE64
SE16 . . . . .203 K7
Dartford (Sutt.H.) DA4 . . . .148 FN95
Russell Rd, E4 . . . . .47 DZ49
E10 . . . . .67 EB58
E16 . . . . .86 EG72
E17 . . . . .67 DZ55
N8 . . . . .65 DK58
N13 . . . . .45 DM51
N15 . . . . .66 DS57
N20 . . . . .44 DE47
NW9 . . . . .63 CT58
SW19 . . . . .120 DA94
W14 . . . . .99 CY76
Buckhurst Hill IG9 . . . . . . .48 EH46

Russell Rd, Enf. EN1 . . . . . . .30 DT38
Gravesend DA12 . . . . .131 GK86
Grays RM17 . . . . .110 GA77
Mitcham CR4 . . . . .140 DE97
Northolt UB5 . . . . .60 CC64
Northwood HA6 . . . . .39 BQ49
Shepperton TW17 . . . . . . .135 BQ101
Tilbury RM18 . . . . .110 GE81
Twickenham TW1 . . . . . . .117 CF86
Walton-on-Thames KT12 . . .135 BU100
Woking GU21 . . . . .166 AW115
Russells, Tad. KT20 . . . . . . .173 CX122
Russell's Footpath, SW16 . . .121 DL92
Russell Sq, WC1 . . . . .195 P5
off Pasteur Dr 52 FK54
Russell Square 195 P5
Longfield DA3
off Cavendish Sq 149 FX97
Russells Ride, Wal.Cr. (Chsht.)
EN8 . . . . .15 DX31
Russell St, WC2 . . . . .196 A10
Russell Wk, Rich. TW10
off Park Hill 118 CM86
Russell Way, Sutt. SM1 . . . . .158 DA106
Watford WD19 . . . . .39 BV45
Russet Cl, Stai. TW19 . . . . . .113 BF86
Uxbridge UB10
off Uxbridge Rd 77 BQ70
Walton-on-Thames KT12 . . .136 BX104
Russet Cres, N7
off Stock Orchard Cres 65 DM64
Russet Dr, Croy. CR0 . . . . . .143 DY102
Radlett (Shenley) WD7 . . . .10 CL32
Russets, The, Ger.Cr. (Chal.St.P.)
SL9 off Austenwood Cl 36 AX54
Russets Cl, E4 off Larkshall Rd .47 ED49
Russett Cl, Orp. BR6 . . . . . .164 EV106
Russett Ct, Cat. CR3 . . . . . .186 DU125
Russett Hill, Ger.Cr. (Chal.St.P.)
SL9 . . . . .56 AY75
Russetts, Horn. RM11 . . . . . .72 FL56
Russett Way, SE13
off Conington Rd 103 EB82
Swanley BR8 . . . . .147 FD96
Russia Ct, EC2 . . . . .197 J8
Russia Dock Rd, SE16 . . . . . .203 L3
Russia La, E2 . . . . .84 DW68
Russia Row, EC2 . . . . .197 J9
Russia Wk, SE16 . . . . .203 K5
Russington Rd, Shep. TW17 . .135 BR100
Rusthall Av, W4 . . . . .98 CR77
Rusthall Cl, Croy. CR0 . . . . .142 DW100
Rustic Av, SW16 . . . . .121 DH94
Rustic Cl, Upmin. RM14 . . . .73 FS60
Rustic Pl, Wem. HA0 . . . . . . .61 CK63
Rustic Wk, E16 off Lambert Rd .86 EH72
Rustington Wk, Mord. SM4 . .139 CZ101
Ruston Av, Surb. KT5 . . . . . .138 CP101
Ruston Gdns, N14 off Farm La .28 DG44
Ruston Ms, W11
off St. Marks Rd 81 CY72
Ruston Rd, SE18 . . . . .104 EL76
Ruston St, E3 . . . . .85 DZ67
Rust Sq, SE5 . . . . .102 DR80
Rutford Rd, SW16 . . . . .121 DL92
Ruth Cl, Stan. HA7 . . . . .62 CM56
Ruthen Cl, Epsom KT18 . . . .156 CP114
Rutherford Cl, Borwd. WD6 . .26 CQ40
Sutton SM2 . . . . .158 DD107
Uxbridge UB8 . . . . .76 BM70
Rutherford St, SW1 . . . . . . .199 M8
Rutherford Twr, Sthl. UB1 . . .78 CB72
Rutherford Way, Bushey
(Bushey Hth.) WD23 . . . . .41 CD46
Wembley HA9 . . . . .62 CN63
Rutherglen Rd, SE2 . . . . . . .106 EU79
Rutherwick Ri, Couls. CR5 . . .175 DL117
Rutherwick Cl, Epsom KT17 . .157 CU107
Rutherwyk Rd, Cher. KT16 . . .133 BE101
Ruthin Cl, NW9 . . . . .62 CS58
Ruthin Rd, SE3 . . . . .104 EG79
Ruthven Av, Wal.Cr. EN8 . . . .15 DX33
Ruthven St, E9
off Lauriston Rd 85 DX67
Rutland App, Horn. RM11 . . .72 FN57
Rutland Av, Sid. DA15 . . . . . .126 EU87
Rutland Cl, SW14 . . . . .98 CQ83
SW19 off Rutland Rd 120 DE94
Ashtead KT21 . . . . .172 CL117
Bexley DA5 . . . . .126 EX88
Chessington KT9 . . . . .156 CM107
Dartford DA1 . . . . .128 FK87
Epsom KT19 . . . . .156 CR110
Redhill RH1 . . . . .184 DF133
Rutland Ct, Enf. EN3 . . . . . . .30 DW43
Rutland Dr, Horn. RM11 . . . .72 FN57
Morden SM4 . . . . .139 CZ100
Richmond TW10 . . . . .117 CK88
Rutland Gdns, N4 . . . . .65 DP58
SW7 . . . . .198 C5
W13 . . . . .79 CG71
Croydon CR0 . . . . .160 DS105
Dagenham RM8 . . . . .70 EW64
Rutland Gdns Ms, SW7 . . . . .198 C5
Rutland Gate, SW7 . . . . .198 C5
Belvedere DA17 . . . . .107 FB78
Bromley BR2 . . . . .144 EF98
Rutland Gate Ms, SW7 . . . . .198 B5
Rutland Gro, W6 . . . . .99 CV78
Rutland Ms, NW8
off Boundary Rd 82 DB67
Rutland Ms E, SW7 . . . . .198 B6
Rutland Ms S, SW7 . . . . .198 B6
Rutland Ms W, SW7
off Ennismore St 100 DE76
Rutland Pk, NW2 . . . . .81 CW65
SE6 . . . . .123 DZ89
Rutland Pk Gdns, NW2
off Rutland Pk 81 CW65
Rutland Pk Mans, NW2
off Walm La 81 CW65
Rutland Pl, EC1 . . . . .197 H5
Bushey (Bushey Hth.) WD23
off The Rutts 41 CD46
Rutland Rd, E7 . . . . .86 EK66
E9 . . . . .84 DW67

Rutland Rd, E11 . . . . .68 EH57
E17 . . . . .67 EA58
SW19 . . . . .120 DE94
Harrow HA1 . . . . .60 CC58
Hayes UB3 . . . . .95 BR77
Ilford IG1 . . . . .69 EP63
Southall UB1 . . . . .78 CA71
Twickenham TW2 . . . . . . .117 CD89
Rutland St, SW7 . . . . .198 C6
Rutland Wk, SE6 . . . . .123 DZ89
Rutland Way, Orp. BR5 . . . . .146 EW100
Rutley Cl, SE17 off Royal Rd . .101 DP79
Romford (Harold Wd.) RM3
off Pasteur Dr 52 FK54
Rutlish Rd, SW19 . . . . .140 DA95
Rutson Rd, W.Byf. (Byfleet)
KT14 . . . . .152 BM114
Rutter Gdns, Mitch. CR4 . . . .140 DC98
Rutters Cl, West Dr. UB7 . . . .94 BN75
Rutts, The, Bushey (Bushey Hth.)
WD23 . . . . .41 CD46
Rutts Ter, SE14 . . . . .103 DX81
Ruvigny Gdns, SW15 . . . . . . .99 CX83
Ruxbury Rd, Cher. KT16 . . . .133 BC100
Ruxley Cl, Epsom KT19 . . . . .156 CP106
Sidcup DA14 . . . . .126 EX93
Ruxley Cor Ind Est, Sid. DA14 .126 EX93
Ruxley Cres, Esher (Clay.)
KT10 . . . . .155 CH107
Ruxley Gdns, Shep. TW17 . . .135 BQ99
Ruxley La, Epsom KT19 . . . . .156 CR106
Ruxley Ms, Epsom KT19 . . . .156 CP106
Ruxley Ridge, Esher (Clay.)
KT10 . . . . .155 CG108
Ruxton Cl, Swan. BR8 . . . . . .147 FE97
Ryall Cl, St.Alb. (Brick.Wd.) AL2 .8 BY29
Ryalls Ct, N20 . . . . .44 DF48
Ryan Cl, SE3 . . . . .104 EJ84
Ruislip HA4 . . . . .59 BV60
Ryan Dr, Brent. TW8 . . . . . . .97 CG79
Ryan Way, Wat. WD24 . . . . . .24 BW39
Ryarsh Cres, Orp. BR6 . . . . .163 ES105
Rycott Path, SE22
off Lordship La 122 DU87
Rycroft Way, N17 . . . . .66 DT55
Ryculff Sq, SE3 . . . . .104 EF82
Rydal Cl, NW4 . . . . .43 CY53
Purley CR8 . . . . .160 DR113
Rydal Cres, Grnf. UB6 . . . . . .79 CH69
Rydal Dr, Bexh. DA7 . . . . . . .106 FA81
West Wickham BR4 . . . . . .144 EE103
Rydal Gdns, NW9 . . . . .62 CS57
SW15 . . . . .118 CS92
Hounslow TW3 . . . . .116 CB86
Wembley HA9 . . . . .61 CJ60
Rydal Rd, SW16 . . . . .121 DK91
Rydal Way, Egh. TW20 . . . . . .113 BB94
Enfield EN3 . . . . .30 DW44
Ruislip HA4 . . . . .60 BW63
Ryde, The, Stai. TW18 . . . . . .134 BH95
Ryde Cl, Wok. (Ripley) GU23 . .168 BJ121
Ryde Heron, Wok. (Knap.) GU21
off Robin Hood Rd 166 AS117
Rydens Av, Walt. KT12 . . . . .135 BV103
Rydens Cl, Walt. KT12 . . . . . .136 BW103
Rydens Gro, Walt. KT12 . . . .154 BX105
Rydens Pk, Walt. KT12
off Rydens Rd 136 BX103
Rydens Rd, Walt. KT12 . . . . .136 BX103
Rydens Way, Wok. GU22 . . . .167 BA120
Ryde Pl, Twick. TW1 . . . . . . .117 CJ86
Ryder Cl, Brom. BR1 . . . . . . .124 EH92
Bushey WD23 . . . . .24 CB44
Hemel Hempstead (Bov.) HP3 .5 BA28
Ryder Ct, SW1 . . . . .199 L2
Ryder Dr, SE16 . . . . .102 DV78
Ryder Gdns, Rain. RM13 . . . .89 FF65
Ryder Ms, E9
off Homerton High St 66 DW64
Ryders Ter, NW8 . . . . .82 DC68
Ryder St, SW1 . . . . .199 L2
Ryder Yd, SW1 . . . . .199 L2
Rydes Cl, Wok. GU22 . . . . . .167 BC120
Ryde Vale Rd, SW12 . . . . . . .121 DH89
Rydon Business Cen, Lthd.
. . . . .171 CH119
Rydon's La, Couls. CR5 . . . . .176 DQ120
Rydon St, N1 off St. Paul St . .84 DQ67
Rydons Wd Cl, Couls. CR5 . . .176 DQ120
Rydston Cl, N7
off Sutterton St 83 DM66
Rye, The, N14 . . . . .45 DJ45
Ryebridge Cl, Lthd. KT22 . . .171 CG118
Ryebrook Rd, Lthd. KT22 . . .171 CG118
Rye Cl, Bex. DA5 . . . . .127 FB86
Hornchurch RM12 . . . . . . .72 FJ64
Rye Ct, Slou. SL1
off Alpha St S 92 AU76
Rye Cres, Orp. BR5 . . . . .146 EW102
Ryecroft, Grav. DA12 . . . . . .131 GL92
Ryecroft Av, Ilf. IG5 . . . . . . .49 EP54
Twickenham TW2 . . . . . . .116 CB87
Ryecroft Cres, Barn. EN5 . . . .27 CV43
Ryecroft Rd, SE13 . . . . .123 EC85
SW16 . . . . .121 DN93
Orpington BR5 . . . . .145 ER100
Sevenoaks (Otford) TN14 . .181 FG116
Ryecroft St, SW6 . . . . .100 DB81
Ryedale, SE22 . . . . .122 DV86
Ryedale, Sev. TN13
off London Rd 190 FE121
Rye Fld, Ashtd. KT21 . . . . . .171 CK117
Orpington BR5 . . . . .146 EX102
Ryefield Ct, Nthwd. HA6
off Ryefield Cres 39 BU54
Ryefield Cres, Nthwd. HA6 . . .39 BU54
Ryefield Par, Nthwd. HA6
off Ryefield Cres 39 BU54
Ryefield Path, SW15 . . . . . . .119 CU88

Ryefield Rd, SE19 . . . . .122 DQ93
Ryegates, SE15
off Caulfield Rd 102 DV82
Rye Hill Pk, SE15 . . . . .102 DW84
Ryeland Cl, West Dr. UB7 . . . .76 BL72
Ryelands Cl, Cat. CR3 . . . . . .176 DS121
Ryelands Ct, Lthd. KT22 . . . .171 CG118
Ryelands Cres, SE12 . . . . . . .124 EJ86
Ryelands Pl, Wey. KT13 . . . . .135 BS104
Rye La, SE15 . . . . .102 DU81
Sevenoaks (Dunt.Grn.) TN14 .181 FG117
Rye Pas, SE15 . . . . .102 DU83
Rye Rd, SE15 . . . . .103 DX84
Rye Wk, SW15
off Chartfield Av 119 CX85
Rye Way, Edg. HA8
off Canons Dr 42 CM51
Ryfold Rd, SW19 . . . . .120 DA90
Ryhope Rd, N11 . . . . .45 DH49
Rykhill, Grays RM16 . . . . . . .111 GH76
Ryland Cl, Felt. TW13 . . . . . .115 BT91
Rylandes Rd, NW2 . . . . .63 CU62
South Croydon CR2 . . . . . .160 DV109
Ryland Ho, Croy. CR0 . . . . . .142 DQ104
Ryland Rd, NW5 . . . . .83 DH65
Rylett Cres, W12 . . . . .99 CT76
Rylett Rd, W12 . . . . .99 CT75
SW6 . . . . .99 CZ79
Rymer Rd, Croy. CR0 . . . . . .142 DS101
Rymer St, SE24 . . . . .121 DP86
Rymill Cl, Hem.H. (Bov.) HP3 .5 BA28
Rymill St, E16 . . . . .87 EN74
Rysbrack St, SW3 . . . . .198 D6
Rysted La, West. TN16 . . . . .189 EQ126
Rythe Cl, Chess. KT9
off Nigel Fisher Way 155 CJ108
Rythe Ct, T.Ditt. KT7 . . . . . . .137 CG101
Rythe Rd, Esher (Clay.) KT10 .155 CD106
Ryvers Rd, Slou. SL3 . . . . . . .93 AZ76

★ Saatchi Gall, NW8 . . . . . . .82 DB67
Sabah Ct, Ashf. TW15 . . . . . .114 BN91
Sabbarton St, E16
off Victoria Dock Rd 86 EF72
Sabella Ct, E3 . . . . .85 DZ68
Sabina Rd, Grays RM16 . . . . .111 GJ77
Sabine Rd, SW11 . . . . .100 DF83
Sable Cl, Houns. TW4 . . . . . .96 BW83
Sable St, N1 off Canonbury Rd .83 DP66
Sach Rd, E5 . . . . .66 DV61
Sackville Av, Brom. BR2 . . . .144 EG102
Sackville Cl, Har. HA2 . . . . . .61 CD62
Sevenoaks TN13 . . . . .191 FH122
Sackville Ct, Rom. RM3
off Sackville Cres 52 FL53
Sackville Cres, Rom. RM3 . . .52 FL53
Sackville Est, SW16 . . . . . . .121 DL90
Sackville Gdns, Ilf. IG1 . . . . .69 EM60
Sackville Rd, Dart. DA2 . . . . .128 FK89
Sutton SM2 . . . . .158 DA108
Sackville St, W1 . . . . .199 L1
Sackville Way, SE22
off Dulwich Common 122 DU88
Saddington St, Grav. DA12 . .131 GH87
Saddlebrook Pk, Sun. TW16 . .115 BS94
Saddlers Cl, Barn. (Arkley) EN5 .27 CV43
Borehamwood WD6
off Farriers Way 26 CR44
Pinner HA5 . . . . .40 CA51
Saddlers Ms, SW8
off Portland Gro 101 DM81
Kingston upon Thames KT1 .137 CJ95
Wembley HA0
off The Boltons 61 CF63
Saddler's Pk, Dart. (Eyns.)
DA4 . . . . .148 FK104
Saddlers Path, Borwd. WD6 . .26 CR43
Saddlers Way, Epsom KT18 . .172 CR119
Saddlescombe Way, N12 . . . .44 DA50
Saddleworth Rd, Rom. RM3 . .52 FJ51
Saddleworth Sq, Rom. RM3 . .52 FJ51
Saddle Yd, W1 . . . . .199 H2
Sadler Cl, Mitch. CR4 . . . . . .140 DF96
Waltham Cross (Chsht.) EN7
off Markham Rd 14 DQ25
Sadlers Ride, W.Mol. KT8 . . .136 CC96
★ Sadler's Wells Thea, EC1 . .196 F2
Saffron Av, E14 . . . . .85 ED73
Saffron Cl, NW11 . . . . .63 CZ57
Croydon CR0 . . . . .141 DL100
Slough (Langley) SL3 . . . . .92 AV81
Saffron Ct, Felt. TW14
off Staines Rd 115 BQ87
Saffron Hill, EC1 . . . . .196 E5
Saffron Rd, Grays (Chaff.Hun.)
RM16 . . . . .109 FW77
Romford RM5 . . . . .51 FC54
Saffron St, EC1 . . . . .196 E6
Saffron Way, Surb. KT6 . . . . .137 CK102
Sage Cl, E6
off Bradley Stone Rd 87 EM71
Sage St, E1 off Cable St 84 DW73
Sage Way, WC1 . . . . .196 B3
Saigasso Cl, E16 off Royal Rd .86 EK72
Sailmakers Ct, SW6
off William Morris Way . . .100 DC83
Sail St, SE11 . . . . .200 C8
Sainfoin Rd, SW17 . . . . .120 DG92
Sainsbury Rd, SE19 . . . . . . .122 DS92
St. Agatha's Dr, Kings.T. KT2 .118 CM93
St. Agathas Gro, Cars. SM5 . .140 DF102
St. Agnes Pl, SE11 . . . . .101 DN79
St. Agnes Well, EC1 off Old St .84 DR70
St. Aidans Ct, W13
off St. Aidans Rd 97 CH75
Barking IG11
off Choats Rd 88 EV69

St. A- St. J

St. Aidan's Rd, SE22 . . . . .122 DV86
St. Aidans Rd, W13 . . . . . . .97 CH75
St. Aidan's Way, Grav. DA12 .131 GL90
St. Albans Av, E6 . . . . .87 EM69
St. Alban's Av, W4 . . . . . . .98 CR77
St. Albans Av, Felt. TW13 . .116 BX92
Upminster RM14 . . . . . . .73 FS60
Weybridge KT13 . . . . . .134 BN104
St. Albans Cl, NW11 . . . . . .64 DA60
Gravesend DA12 . . . . . .131 GK90
St. Albans Cres, N22 . . . . . .45 DN53
St. Albans Cres, Wdf.Grn. IG8 .48 EG52
St. Alban's Gdns, Grav. DA12 .131 GK90
St. Alban's Gdns, Tedd. TW11 .117 CG92
St. Albans Gro, W8 . . . . . .100 DB76
St. Alban's Gro, N5 . . . . . . .65 DP64
St. Albans La, NW11
  off West Heath Dr 64 DA60
Abbots Langley (Bedmond)
  WD5 . . . . .7 BT26
St. Alban's Pl, N1 . . . . .83 DP67
St. Albans Rd, NW5 . . . . . .64 DG62
  NW10 . . . . .80 CS67
  Barnet EN5 . . . . .27 CX39
  Dartford DA1 . . . . .128 FM87
  Epping CM16 . . . . .18 EX29
  Ilford IG3 . . . . .69 ET60
St. Alban's Rd, Kings.T. KT2 .118 CL93
St. Albans Rd, Pot.B. (Dance.H.)
  EN6 . . . . .27 CV35
  Potters Bar (S.Mimms) EN6 .11 CV34
  Radlett (Shenley) WD7 . . . .10 CQ30
  Reigate RH2 . . . . .184 DA133
  St. Albans (Lon.Col.) AL2 . .10 CN28
St. Alban's Rd, Sutt. SM1 . . .157 CZ105
St. Albans Rd, Wat. WD17,
  WD24, WD25 . . . . .23 BV40
St. Alban's Rd, Wdf.Grn. IG8 . .48 EG52
St. Albans St, SW1 . . . . . .199 M1
St. Albans Ter, W6
  off Margravine Rd 99 CY79
St. Alban's Vil, NW5
  off Highgate Rd 64 DG62
St. Alfege Pas, SE10 . . . . .103 EC79
St. Alfege Rd, SE7 . . . . . .104 EK79
St. Alphage Gdns, EC2 . . . .197 J7
St. Alphage Highwalk, EC2
  off London Wall 84 DR71
St. Alphage Wk, Edg. HA8 . . .42 CQ54
St. Alphege Rd, N9 . . . . . . .46 DW45
St. Alphonsus Rd, SW4 . . . .101 DJ84
St. Amunds Cl, SE6 . . . . . .123 EA91
 H St. Andrew's at Harrow (Bowden
  Ho Hosp), Har. HA1 . . . . .61 CE61
St. Andrews Av, Horn. RM12 . .71 FG64
  Wembley HA0 . . . . .61 CG63
St. Andrew's Cl, N12
  off Woodside Av 44 DC49
St. Andrews Cl, NW2 . . . . . .63 CV62
  SE16 off Ryder Dr 102 DV78
  SE28 . . . . .88 EX72
St. Andrew's Cl, Islw. TW7 . . .97 CD81
St. Andrews Cl, Ruis. HA4 . . .60 BX61
St. Andrew's Cl, Stan. TW17 .135 BR98
  Staines (Wrays.) TW19 . . .112 AY87
St. Andrews Cl, Stan. HA7 . . .41 CJ54
St. Andrew's Cl, Wind. (Old Wind.)
  SL4 . . . . .112 AU86
St. Andrews Cl, Wok. GU21
  off St. Mary's Rd 166 AW117
St. Andrew's Ct, SW18
  off Waynflete St 120 DC89
St. Andrews Ct, Slou. (Colnbr.)
  SL3 off High St 93 BD80
  Watford WD17 . . . . .23 BV39
St. Andrews Dr, Orp. BR5 . . .146 EV100
  Stanmore HA7 . . . . .41 CJ53
St. Andrews Gdns, Cob. KT11 .154 BW113
St. Andrew's Gro, N16 . . . . .66 DR60
St. Andrew's Hill, EC4 . . . .196 G10
 H St. Andrew's Hosp, E3 . . .85 EB70
St. Andrew's Ms, N16 . . . . .66 DS60
St. Andrews Ms, SE3
  off Mycenae Rd 104 EG80
St. Andrews Pl, NW1 . . . . .195 J4
  Brentwood CM15 . . . . . .55 FZ47
St. Andrews Rd, E11 . . . . . .68 EE58
  E13 . . . . .86 EH69
  E17 . . . . .47 DX54
  N9 . . . . .46 DW45
  NW9 . . . . .62 CR60
  NW10 . . . . .81 CV65
  NW11 . . . . .63 CZ58
  W3 . . . . .80 CS73
  W7 off Church Rd 97 CE75
  W14 . . . . .99 CY79
  Carshalton SM5 . . . . . .140 DE104
  Coulsdon CR5 . . . . . . .174 DG116
  Croydon CR0
  off Lower Coombe St . . .160 DQ105
  Enfield EN1 . . . . .30 DR41
St. Andrew's Rd, Grav. DA12 .131 GJ87
St. Andrews Rd, Ilf. IG1 . . . .69 EM59
  Romford RM7 . . . . .71 FD58
  Sidcup DA14 . . . . .126 EX90
St. Andrew's Rd, Surb. KT6 . .137 CK100
St. Andrews Rd, Til. RM18 . .110 GE81
  Uxbridge UB10 . . . . . . .76 BM66
  Watford WD19 . . . . .40 BX48
St. Andrews Sq, W11
  off St. Marks Rd 81 CY72
St. Andrew's Sq, Surb. KT6 .137 CK100
St. Andrews Twr, Sthl. UB1 . .78 CC73
St. Andrew St, EC4 . . . . . .196 E7
St. Andrews Wk, Cob. KT11 .169 BV115
  Oxted RH8 . . . . .188 EL130
St. Andrews Way, E3 . . . . . .85 EB70
St. Anna Rd, Barn. EN5
  off Sampson Av 27 CX43
St. Annes Av, Stai. (Stanw.)
  TW19 . . . . .114 BK87
St. Annes Boul, Red. RH1 . .185 DH132
St. Anne's Cl, N6
  off Highgate W Hill 64 DG62

St. Annes Cl, Wal.Cr. (Chsht.)
  EN7 . . . . .14 DU28
St. Anne's Cl, Wat. WD19 . . .40 BW49
St. Annes Ct, W1 . . . . . . .195 M9
St. Annes Dr, Red. RH1 . . .184 DG133
St. Anne's Dr N, Red. RH1 . .184 DG132
St. Annes Gdns, NW10 . . . . .80 CM69
St. Annes Mt, Red. RH1 . . .184 DG133
St. Annes Pas, E14
  off Newell St 85 DZ72
St. Annes Ri, Red. RH1 . . . .184 DG133
St. Anne's Rd, St.Alb. (Lon.Col.)
  AL2 . . . . .9 CK27
  Uxbridge (Hare.) UB9 . . . .58 BJ55
  Wembley HA0 . . . . .61 CK64
St. Anne's Row, E14
  off Commercial Rd 85 DZ72
St. Anne St, E14
  off Commercial Rd 85 DZ72
St. Anne's Way, Red. RH1
  off St. Anne's Dr 184 DG133
St. Ann's, Bark. IG11 . . . . . .87 EQ67
St. Anns Cl, Cher. KT16 . . .133 BF100
St. Ann's Cres, SW18 . . . . .120 DC86
St. Ann's Gdns, NW5
  off Queen's Cres 82 DG65
St. Ann's Hill, SW18 . . . . . .120 DB85
St. Anns Hill Rd, Cher. KT16 .133 BC100
 H St. Ann's Hosp, N15 . . . .66 DQ57
St. Ann's La, SW1 . . . . . . .199 N6
St. Ann's Pk Rd, SW18 . . . .120 DC86
St. Ann's Pas, SW13 . . . . . .98 CS83
St. Anns Rd, N9 . . . . .46 DT47
St. Ann's Rd, N15 . . . . .65 DP57
  SW13 . . . . .99 CT82
St. Anns Rd, W11 . . . . .81 CX73
St. Ann's Rd, Bark. IG11
  off Axe St 87 EQ67
St. Anns Rd, Cher. KT16 . . .133 BF100
St. Ann's Rd, Har. HA1 . . . . .61 CE58
St. Ann's Shop Cen, Har. HA1 .61 CE58
St. Ann's St, SW1 . . . . . . .199 N6
St. Ann's Ter, NW8 . . . . . . .82 DD68
St. Anns Vil, W11 . . . . .81 CX73
St. Anns Way, S.Croy. CR2 . .159 DP107
  Westerham (Berry's Grn.)
  TN16 . . . . .179 EP116
St. Anselm's Pl, W1 . . . . . .195 H9
St. Anselms Rd, Hayes UB3 . .95 BT75
St. Anthonys Av, Wdf.Grn. IG8 .48 EJ51
St. Anthonys Cl, E1 . . . . . .202 B2
  SW17 off College Gdns . .120 DE89
 H St. Anthony's Hosp, Sutt.
  SM3 . . . . .139 CX102
St. Anthony's Way, Felt. TW14 .95 BT84
St. Antony's Rd, E7 . . . . . . .86 EH66
St. Arvans Cl, Croy. CR0 . . .142 DS104
St. Asaph Rd, SE4 . . . . . .103 DX83
St. Aubyn's Av, SW19 . . . . .119 CZ92
St. Aubyns Av, Houns. TW3 .116 CA85
St. Aubyns Cl, Orp. BR6 . . .145 ET104
St. Aubyns Gdns, Orp. BR6 .145 ET103
St. Aubyn's Rd, SE19 . . . . .122 DT93
St. Audrey Av, Bexh. DA7 . .106 FA82
St. Augustine Rd, Grays RM16 .111 GH77
St. Augustine's Av, W5 . . . . .80 CL68
St. Augustines Av, Brom. BR2 .144 EL99
St. Augustine's Av, S.Croy.
  CR2 . . . . .160 DQ107
St. Augustines Av, Wem. HA9 .62 CL62
St. Augustine's Path, N5 . . . .65 DP64
St. Augustine's Rd, NW1 . . . .83 DK66
St. Augustine's Rd, Belv.
  DA17 . . . . .106 EZ77
St. Austell Cl, Edg. HA8 . . . .42 CM54
St. Austell Rd, SE13 . . . . . .103 EC82
St. Awdry's Rd, Bark. IG11 . . .87 ER66
St. Awdry's Wk, Bark. IG11
  off Station Par 87 EQ66
St. Barnabas Cl, SE22
  off East Dulwich Gro 122 DS85
  Beckenham BR3 . . . . . .143 EC96
St. Barnabas Ct, Har. HA3 . . .40 CC53
St. Barnabas Gdns, W.Mol.
  KT8 . . . . .136 CA99
St. Barnabas Rd, E17 . . . . . .67 EA58
  Mitcham CR4 . . . . .120 DG94
  Sutton SM1 . . . . .158 DD106
  Woodford Green IG8 . . . .48 EH53
St. Barnabas Rd, SW1 . . . .198 G10
St. Barnabas Ter, E9 . . . . . .67 DX64
St. Barnabas Vil, SW8 . . . .101 DL81
St. Bartholomews Cl, SE26 . .122 DW91
 H St. Bartholomew's Hosp,
  EC1 . . . . .196 G7
St. Bartholomew's Rd, E6 . . .86 EL67
 ★ St. Bartholomew-the-Great
  Church, EC1 off Cloth Fair .196 G7
 ★ St. Benedict's Av, Grav. DA12 131 GK89
St. Benedict's Cl, SW17
  off Church La 120 DG92
St. Benet's Cl, SW17
  off College Gdns 120 DE89
St. Benet's Gro, Cars. SM5 . .140 DC101
St. Benet's Pl, EC3 . . . . . . .197 L10
St. Benjamins Dr, Orp. BR6 .164 EW109
St. Bernards, Croy. CR0 . . .142 DS104
St. Bernard's Cl, SE27
  off St. Gothard Rd 122 DR91
 H St. Bernard's Hosp, Sthl.
  UB1 . . . . .97 CD75
St. Bernard's Rd, E6 . . . . . .86 EK67
St. Bernards Rd, Slou. SL3 . . .92 AW76
St. Blaise Av, Brom. BR1 . . .144 EH96
St. Botolph Rd, Grav. DA11 .130 GC90
St. Botolph Row, EC3 . . . . .197 P9
St. Botolph's Av, Sev. TN13 .190 FG124
St. Botolph's Rd, Sev. TN13 .190 FG124
St. Botolph St, EC3 . . . . . .197 P8
St. Bride's Av, EC4
  off New Br St 196 G9
St. Brides Av, Edg. HA8 . . . .42 CM53
 ★ St. Bride's Church & Crypt
  Mus, EC4 . . . . .196 G9
St. Brides Cl, Erith DA18
  off St. Katherines Rd . . .106 EX75

St. Bride's Pas, EC4 . . . . . .196 F9
 ★ St. Bride's Printing Lib, EC4
  off Bride La 196 F9
St. Bride St, EC4 . . . . .196 F8
St. Catherines Cl, SW17
  off College Gdns 120 DE89
St. Catherines Cross, Red.
  (Bletch.) RH1 . . . . .186 DS134
St. Catherines Dr, SE14
  off Kitto Rd 103 DX82
St. Catherines Fm Ct, Ruis.
  HA4 . . . . .59 BQ58
St. Catherines Ms, SW3 . . .198 D8
St. Catherines Rd, E4 . . . . . .47 EA47
  Ruislip HA4 . . . . .59 BR57
St. Catherines Twr, E10
  off Kings Cl 67 EB59
St. Cecilia's Rd, Grays RM16 .111 GH77
St. Cecilia's Cl, Sutt. SM3 . .139 CY102
St. Chads Cl, Surb. KT6 . . . .137 CJ101
St. Chad's Dr, Grav. DA12 . .131 GL90
St. Chad's Pl, WC1 . . . . . .196 A2
St. Chad's Rd, Rom. RM6 . . .70 EY59
  Tilbury RM18 . . . . .111 GG80
St. Chad's St, WC1 . . . . . .196 A2
St. Charles Ct, Wey. KT13 . .152 BN106
St. Charles Pl, W10
  off Chesterton Rd 81 CY71
  Weybridge KT13 . . . . . .152 BN106
St. Charles Rd, Brwd. CM14 . .54 FV46
St. Charles Sq, W10 . . . . . .81 CY71
St. Christopher Rd, Uxb. UB8 .76 BK71
St. Christopher's Cl, Islw. TW7 .97 CE81
St. Christopher's Dr, Hayes
  UB3 . . . . .77 BV73
St. Christophers Gdns, Th.Hth.
  CR7 . . . . .141 DN97
St. Christophers Ms, Wall.
  SM6 . . . . .159 DJ106
St. Christopher's Pl, W1 . . . .194 G8
St. Clair Cl, Oxt. RH8 . . . . .187 EC130
  Reigate RH2 . . . . .184 DC134
St. Clair Dr, Wor.Pk. KT4 . . .139 CV104
St. Clair Rd, E13 . . . . .86 EH68
St. Clair's Rd, Croy. CR0 . . .142 DS103
St. Clare Business Pk, Hmptn.
  TW12 . . . . .116 CC93
St. Clare St, EC3 . . . . .197 P9
St. Clare Cl, Ilf. IG5 . . . . . . .49 EM54
St. Clare St, EC3 . . . . .197 P9
St. Clement Cl, Uxb. UB8 . . .76 BK72
 ★ St. Clement Danes Church,
  WC2 off Strand 196 C9
St. Clements Av, Grays RM20 .109 FU79
St. Clement's Cl, Grav. (Nthflt.)
  DA11 off Coldharbour Rd .131 GF90
St. Clements Ct, EC4
  off Clements La 84 DR73
  N7 off Arundel Sq 83 DN65
  Purfleet RM19 off Thamley .108 FN77
St. Clements Hts, SE26 . . . .122 DU90
St. Clement's La, WC2 . . . .196 C9
St. Clements Rd, Grays
  RM20 . . . . .109 FW80
St. Clements St, N7 . . . . . . .83 DN65
St. Cloud Rd, SE27 . . . . . .122 DQ91
St. Columba's Cl, Grav. DA12 .131 GL90
St. Crispins Cl, NW3 . . . . . .64 DE63
  Southall UB1 . . . . .78 BZ72
St. Crispins Way, Cher. (Ott.)
  KT16 . . . . .151 BC109
St. Cross St, EC1 . . . . .196 E6
St. Cuthberts Cl, Egh. TW20 .112 AX92
St. Cuthberts Gdns, Pnr. HA5
  off Westfield Pk 40 BZ52
St. Cuthberts Rd, N13 . . . . .45 DN51
  NW2 . . . . .81 CZ65
St. Cyprian's St, SW17 . . . .120 DF91
St. David Cl, Uxb. UB8 . . . . .76 BK71
St. Davids, Couls. CR5 . . . .175 DM117
St. Davids Cl, SE16
  off Masters Dr 102 DV78
  Iver SL0 . . . . .75 BD67
St. David's Cl, Reig. RH2 . . .184 DD133
St. Davids Cl, Wem. HA9 . . . .62 CQ62
St. David's Cl, W.Wick. BR4 .143 EB101
St. David's Ct, E17 . . . . .67 EC55
St. Davids Cres, Grav. DA12 .131 GK91
St. Davids Dr, Egh. DA8 . . . .42 CM53
St. David's Dr, Egh.
  TW20 . . . . .112 AW94
St. Davids Ms, E3
  off Morgan St 85 DY69
St. Davids Pl, NW4 . . . . . . .63 CV59
St. Davids Sq, E14 . . . . . .204 C10
St. Denis Rd, SE27 . . . . . .122 DR91
St. Dionis Rd, SW6 . . . . . . .99 CZ82
St. Donatts Rd, SE14 . . . . .103 DZ81
St. Dunstan's All, EC3 . . . .197 M10
St. Dunstans Av, W3 . . . . . .80 CR73
St. Dunstans Cl, Hayes UB3 . .95 BT77
St. Dunstan's Ct, EC4
  off Fleet St 83 DN72
St. Dunstan's Dr, Grav. DA12 .131 GL91
St. Dunstans Gdns, W3
  off St. Dunstans Av 80 CR73
St. Dunstan's Hill, EC3 . . . .201 M1
  Sutton SM1 . . . . .157 CY106
St. Dunstan's La, EC3 . . . . .201 M1
  Beckenham BR3 . . . . . .143 EC100
St. Dunstans Rd, E7 . . . . . . .86 EJ65
St. Dunstans Rd, SE25 . . . .142 DT98
  W6 . . . . .99 CX78
  W7 . . . . .97 CE75
St. Dunstan's Rd, Felt. TW13 .115 BT90
St. Dunstans Rd, Houns. TW4 .96 BW82
 H St. Ebba's Hosp, Epsom
  KT19 . . . . .156 CQ109
St. Edith Cl, Epsom KT18
  off St. Elizabeth Dr 156 CQ114
St. Edmunds Av, Ruis. HA4 . .59 BR58
St. Edmunds Cl, NW8
  off St. Edmunds Ter 82 DF67
  SW17 off College Gdns . .120 DE89

St. Edmunds Cl, Erith DA18
  off St. Katherines Rd . . .106 EX75
St. Edmunds Dr, Stan. HA7 . .41 CG51
St. Edmund's La, Twick. TW2 .116 CB87
St. Edmunds Rd, N9 . . . . . .46 DU85
  Dartford DA1 . . . . .108 FM84
  Ilford IG1 . . . . .69 EM58
St. Edmunds Sq, SW13 . . . .99 CW79
St. Edmunds Ter, NW8 . . . . .82 DE67
St. Edwards Cl, NW11 . . . . .64 DA58
  Croydon (New Adgtn.) CR0 .161 ED111
St. Egberts Way, E4 . . . . . . .47 EC46
St. Elizabeth Dr, Epsom KT18 .156 CQ114
St. Elmo Rd, W12 . . . . .81 CT74
St. Elmos Rd, SE16 . . . . . .203 K4
St. Erkenwald Ms, Bark. IG11
  off St. Erkenwald Rd 87 ER67
St. Erkenwald Rd, Bark. IG11 .87 ER67
St. Ermin's Hill, SW1 . . . . .199 M6
St. Ervans Rd, W10 . . . . . . .81 CY72
St. Fabian Twr, E4 off Iris Way .47 DZ51
St. Faiths Cl, Enf. EN2 . . . . .30 DQ39
St. Faith's Rd, SE21 . . . . . .121 DP88
St. Fidelis Rd, Erith DA8 . . .107 FD77
St. Fillans Rd, SE6 . . . . . . .123 EC88
St. Francis Av, Grav. DA12 . .131 GL91
St. Francis Cl, Orp. BR5 . . .145 ES100
  Potters Bar EN6 . . . . . . .12 DC33
St. Francis Rd, SE22 . . . . . .102 DS84
  Erith DA8 off West St . . .107 FD77
  Uxbridge (Denh.) UB9 . . . .57 BF58
St. Francis Way, Grays RM16 .111 GJ77
  Ilford IG1 . . . . .69 ES63
St. Frideswides Ms, E14
  off Lodore St 85 EC72
St. Gabriel's Cl, E11 . . . . . . .68 EH61
St. Gabriels Rd, NW2 . . . . . .63 CX64
St. Georges Av, E7 . . . . .86 EH66
  N7 . . . . .65 DK63
  NW9 . . . . .62 CQ56
St. George's Av, W5 . . . . . . .97 CK75
St. Georges Av, Grays RM17 .110 GC77
  Hornchurch RM11 . . . . . .72 FM59
  Southall UB1 . . . . .78 BZ73
St. George's Av, Wey. KT13 .153 BP107
St. Georges Cen, Har. HA1
  off St. Ann's Rd 61 CE58
St. Georges Circ, SE1 . . . . .200 F6
St. Georges Cl, NW11 . . . . .63 CZ58
  SE28 off Redbourne Dr . . .88 EX72
St. George's Cl, SW8
  off Patmore Est 101 DJ81
St. Georges Cl, Wem. HA0 . .61 CG62
St. George's Cl, Wey. KT13 .153 BQ106
St. Georges Ct, E6 . . . . .87 EM70
  EC4 . . . . .196 F8
  SW7 off Gloucester Rd . .100 DC76
St. Georges Cres, Grav. DA12 .131 GK91
St. George's Dr, SW1 . . . . .199 K10
St. Georges Dr, Uxb. UB10 . .58 BM62
  Watford WD19 . . . . .40 BY48
St. Georges Flds, W2 . . . . .194 C9
St. Georges Gdns, Epsom KT17
  off Lynwood Rd 157 CT114
St. George's Gdns, Surb. KT6
  off Hamilton Av 138 CP103
St. Georges Gro, SW17 . . . .120 DD90
St. Georges Gro Est, SW17 .120 DD90
ST. GEORGE'S HILL, Wey. . .153 BQ110
 H St. George's Hosp, SW17 .120 DD92
 H St. Georges Hosp, Horn.
  RM12 . . . . .72 FK63
St. Georges Ind Est, Kings.T. KT2
  off Richmond Rd 117 CK92
St. Georges La, EC3 . . . . . .197 M10
St. George's Lo, Wey. KT13 .153 BR106
St. Georges Ms, NW1
  off Regents Pk Rd 82 DF66
St. Georges Pl, Twick. TW1
  off Church St 117 CG88
St. Georges Rd, E7 . . . . . . .86 EH65
  E10 . . . . .67 EC62
  N9 . . . . .46 DU48
  N13 . . . . .45 DM48
  NW11 . . . . .63 CZ58
  SE1 . . . . .200 E6
St. George's Rd, SW19 . . . .119 CZ93
St. Georges Rd, W4 . . . . . . .98 CS75
  W7 . . . . .79 CF74
  Addlestone KT15 . . . . . .152 BJ105
St. George's Rd, Beck. BR3 .143 EB95
St. Georges Rd, Brom. BR1 .145 EM96
  Dagenham RM9 . . . . . . .70 EY64
  Enfield EN1 . . . . .30 DT38
St. George's Rd, Felt. TW13 .116 BX91
St. Georges Rd, Ilf. IG1 . . . . .69 EM59
St. George's Rd, Kings.T. KT2 .118 CN94
  Mitcham CR4 . . . . .141 DH97
  Orpington BR5 . . . . . . .145 ER100
St. Georges Rd, Rich. TW9 . . .98 CM83
  Sevenoaks TN13 . . . . . .191 FH122
  Sidcup DA14 . . . . .126 EX93
St. Georges Rd, Swan. BR8 .147 FF98
  Twickenham TW1 . . . . . .117 CH85
  Wallington SM6 . . . . . . .159 DH106
  Watford WD24 . . . . .23 BV38
St. George's Rd, Wey. KT13 .153 BR107
St. Georges Rd W, Brom. BR1 144 EL95
St. Georges Shop Cen, Grav.
  DA11 . . . . .131 GH86
St. Georges Sq, E7 . . . . . . .86 EH66
  E14 off Narrow St 85 DY73
  SE8 . . . . .203 M8
St. George's Sq, SW1 . . . . .199 M10
  New Malden KT3
  off High St 138 CS97
St. George's Sq Ms, SW1 . . .101 DK78
St. Georges Ter, NW1
  off Regents Pk Rd 82 DF66
St. George St, W1 . . . . . . .195 J9
St. Georges Wk, Croy. CR0 .142 DQ104
St. Georges Way, SE15 . . . .102 DS79
St. George Wf, SW8 . . . . . .101 DL78
St. Gerards Cl, SW4 . . . . . .121 DJ85
St. German's Pl, SE3 . . . . .104 EG81

St. Germans Rd, SE23 . . . . .123 DY88
St. Giles Av, Dag. RM10 . . . .89 FB66
  Potters Bar EN6 . . . . . . .11 CV32
  Uxbridge UB10 . . . . . . .59 BQ63
St. Giles Cl, Dag. RM10
  off St. Giles Av 89 FB66
  Orpington BR6 . . . . . . .163 ER106
St. Giles Ct, WC2
  off St. Giles High St 83 DL72
St. Giles High St, WC2 . . . .195 N8
St. Giles Pas, WC2 . . . . . .195 N9
St. Giles Rd, SE5 . . . . .102 DS80
St. Gilles Ho, E2 . . . . .85 DX68
St. Gothard Rd, SE27 . . . . .122 DR91
St. Gregory Cl, Ruis. HA4 . . .60 BW63
St. Gregorys Cres, Grav.
  DA12 . . . . .131 GL89
St. Helena Rd, SE16 . . . . . .203 H9
St. Helena St, WC1 . . . . . .196 D3
St. Helens Cl, Uxb. UB8 . . . .76 BK72
St. Helens Ct, Epp. CM16
  off Hemnall St 18 EU30
  Rainham RM13 . . . . . . .89 FG70
St. Helens Cres, SW16
  off St. Helens Rd 141 DM95
St. Helens Gdns, W10 . . . . .81 CX72
St. Helens Pl, EC3 . . . . . . .197 M8
St. Helens Rd, SW16 . . . . .141 DM95
St. Helen's Rd, W13
  off Dane Rd 79 CH74
St. Helens Rd, Erith DA18 . .106 EX75
  Ilford IG1 . . . . .69 EM58
ST. HELIER, Cars. 140 DD101
⇌ St. Helier 140 DA100
St. Helier Av, Mord. SM4 . . .140 DC101
 H St. Helier Hosp, Cars.
  SM5 . . . . .140 DC102
St. Heliers Av, Houns. TW3 . .116 CA85
St. Heliers Rd, E10 . . . . . . .67 EC58
St. Hildas Av, Ashf. TW15 . . .114 BL92
St. Hildas Cl, NW6 . . . . . . .81 CX66
  SW17 . . . . .120 DE89
St. Hilda's Rd, SW13 . . . . . .99 CV79
St. Hilda's Way, Grav. DA12 .131 GK91
St. Huberts Cl, Ger.Cr. SL9 . .56 AY60
St. Huberts La, Ger.Cr. SL9 . .57 AZ61
St. Hughe's Cl, SW17
  off College Gdns 120 DE89
St. Hughs Rd, SE20
  off Ridsdale Rd 142 DV95
St. Ives Cl, Rom. RM3 . . . . .52 FM52
St. Ivians Dr, Rom. RM2 . . . .71 FG55
St. James Av, N20 . . . . .44 DE48
  W13 . . . . .79 CG74
  Epsom KT17 . . . . .157 CT111
  Sutton SM1 . . . . .158 DA106
St. James Cl, N20 . . . . .44 DE48
  SE18 off Congleton Gro . .105 EQ78
  Barnet EN4 . . . . .28 DD42
  Epsom KT18 . . . . .156 CS114
  New Malden KT3 . . . . . .139 CT99
  Ruislip HA4 . . . . .60 BW61
  Woking GU21 . . . . .166 AU118
St. James Gdns, Rom. (Lt.Hth.)
  RM6 . . . . .70 EV56
  Wembley HA0 . . . . .79 CK66
St. James Gate, NW1
  off St. Paul's Cres 83 DK66
St. James Gro, SW11
  off Reform St 100 DF82
St. James La, Green. DA9 . . .129 FS88
St. James Ms, E14 . . . . . . .204 E7
  E17 off St. James's St 67 DY57
  Weybridge KT13 . . . . . .153 BP105
St. James Oaks, Grav. DA11
  off Trafalgar Rd 131 GG87
St. James Pl, Dart. DA1
  off Spital St 128 FK86
St. James Rd, E15 . . . . .68 EF64
  N9 off Queens Rd 46 DV47
  Brentwood CM14 . . . . . .54 FW48
  Carshalton SM5 . . . . . .140 DE104
  Kingston upon Thames
  KT1 . . . . .138 CL96
  Mitcham CR4 . . . . .120 DG94
  Purley CR8 . . . . .159 DP113
  Sevenoaks TN13 . . . . . .191 FH122
  Surbiton KT6 . . . . .137 CK100
  Sutton SM1 . . . . .158 DA106
  Waltham Cross (Chsht.) EN7 .14 DQ28
  Watford WD18 . . . . .23 BV43
ST. JAMES'S, SW1 . . . . . .199 L3
St. James's, SE14 . . . . . . .103 DY81
St. James's Av, E2 . . . . .84 DW68
  Beckenham BR3 . . . . . .143 DY97
  Gravesend DA11 . . . . . .131 GG87
  Hampton (Hmptn.H.) TW12 .116 CC92
St. James's Cl, SW17
  off St. James's Dr 120 DF89
St. James's Cotts, Rich. TW9
  off Paradise Rd 117 CK85
St. James's Ct, SW1 . . . . . .199 L6
St. James's Cres, SW9 . . . .101 DN83
St. James's Dr, SW12 . . . . .120 DF88
  SW17 . . . . .120 DF88
St. James's Gdns, W11 . . . . .81 CY74
St. James's La, N10 . . . . . . .65 DH56
St. James's Mkt, SW1 . . . . .199 M1
 ★ St. James's Palace, SW1 .199 L4
 ★ St. James's Palace, SW1 . .199 L4
 ★ St. James's Park, SW1 . . .199 M4
 ◉ St. James's Park 199 M5
 ★ St. James's Pk, SW1 . . . .199 M4
  Croydon CR0 . . . . .142 DQ101
St. James's Pas, EC3 . . . . .197 N9
St. James's Pl, SW1 . . . . . .199 K3
St. James's Rd, SE1 . . . . . .202 C10
  SE16 . . . . .202 C6
  Croydon CR0 . . . . .141 DP101
St. James's Row, EC1 . . . . .196 E4
St. James's Sq, SW1 . . . . . .199 L2
St. James's St, E17 . . . . . . .67 DY57
  SW1 . . . . .199 K2
  Gravesend DA11 . . . . . .131 GG86

St. P - San

St. Paul's Rd, Rich. TW9 .....98 CM83
  Staines TW18 ....113 BD92
  Thornton Heath CR7 ...142 DQ97
St. Pauls Rd, Wok. GU22 ...167 BA117
St. Paul's Shrubbery, N1 ....84 DR65
St. Pauls Sq, Brom. BR2 ..144 EG96
St. Paul's Ter, SE17
  off Westcott Rd 101 DP79
St. Pauls Twr, E10 ....67 EB59
St. Paul St, N1 ....84 DQ67
St. Pauls Wk, Kings.T. KT2
  off Alexandra Rd 118 CN94
St. Pauls Way, E3 ....85 DZ71
  E14 ....85 DZ71
St. Paul's Way, N3 ....44 DB52
St. Pauls Way, Wal.Abb. EN9
  off Rochford Av 15 ED33
  Watford WD24 ....24 BW40
St. Pauls Wd Hill, Orp. BR5 .145 ES96
St. Peter's All, EC3 ....197 L9
St. Peter's Av, E2
  off St. Peter's Cl 84 DU68
  E17 ....68 EE56
St. Peters Av, N18 ....46 DU49
  Westerham (Berry's Grn.)
  TN16 ....179 EP116
St. Petersburgh Ms, W2 ....82 DB73
St. Petersburgh Pl, W2 ....82 DB73
St. Peter's Cl, E2 ....84 DU68
St. Peters Cl, SW17
  off College Gdns 120 DE89
St. Peter's Cl, Barn. EN5 ...27 CV43
St. Peters Cl, Bushey
  (Bushey Hth.) WD23 .....41 CD46
  Chislehurst BR7 ....125 ER94
  Gerrards Cross (Chal.St.P.) SL9
  off Lewis La 36 AY53
  Ilford IG2 ....69 ES56
  Rickmansworth (Mill End)
  WD3 ....38 BH46
St. Peter's Cl, Ruis. HA4 ....60 BX61
St. Peters Cl, Stai. TW18 ...113 BF93
  Swanscombe DA10 ......130 FZ87
  Windsor (Old Wind.) SL4
  off Church Rd 112 AU85
  Woking GU22 ....167 BC120
St. Peter's Ct, NW4 ....63 CW57
St. Peters Ct, SE3
  off Eltham Rd 104 EF84
  SE4 off Wickham Rd ...103 DZ82
  Gerrards Cross (Chal.St.P.) SL9
  off High St 36 AY53
  West Molesey KT8 .....136 CA98
St. Peter's Gdns, SE27 .....121 DN90
St. Peter's Gro, W6 ......99 CU77
Ⓗ St. Peter's Hosp, Cher.
  KT16 ....133 BD104
St. Peters La, Orp. BR5 ...146 EU96
St. Peter's Pl, W9
  off Shirland Rd 82 DB70
St. Peters Rd, N9 ....46 DW46
St. Peter's Rd, W6 ......99 CU78
St. Peters Rd, Brwd. CM14
  off Crescent Rd 54 FV49
St. Peter's Rd, Croy. CR0 .160 DR105
  Grays RM16 ....111 GH77
St. Peters Rd, Kings.T. KT1 .138 CN96
  Southall UB1 ....78 CA71
  Twickenham TW1 ......117 CH85
  Uxbridge UB8 ....76 BK71
St. Peter's Rd, W.Mol. KT8 .136 CA98
St. Peters Rd, Wok. GU22 .167 BB121
St. Peter's Sq, E2
  off St. Peter's Cl 84 DU68
  W6 ....99 CU78
St. Peters St, N1 ....83 DP67
St. Peter's St, S.Croy. CR2 .160 DR106
St. Peters Ter, SW6 .....99 CY80
St. Peter's Vil, W6 ......99 CU77
St. Peter's Way, N1 .....84 DS66
St. Peter's Way, W5 .....79 CK71
St. Peter's Way, Add. KT15 .134 BG104
  Chertsey KT16 ....151 BD105
St. Peters Way, Hayes UB3 ..95 BR78
  Rickmansworth (Chorl.) WD3 .21 BB43
St. Philip's Av, Wor.Pk. KT4 .139 CV103
St. Philips Gate, Wor.Pk. KT4 .139 CV103
St. Philip Sq, SW8 ......101 DH82
St. Philip's Rd, E8 ......84 DU65
St. Philips Rd, Surb. KT6 .137 CK100
St. Philip St, SW8 ......101 DH82
St. Philip's Way, N1
  off Linton St 84 DQ67
St. Pinnock Av, Stai. TW18 .134 BG95
St. Quentin Ho, SW18
  off Fitzhugh Gro 120 DD86
St. Quentin Rd, Well. DA16 .105 ET83
St. Quintin Av, W10 .....81 CW71
St. Quintin Gdns, W10 ...81 CW71
St. Quintin Rd, E13 .....86 EH68
St. Raphael's Way, NW10 .62 CQ64
St. Regis Cl, N10 ....45 DH54
St. Ronan's Cl, Barn. EN4 .28 DD38
St. Ronans Cres, Wdf.Grn. IG8 .48 EG52
St. Rule St, SW8 ....101 DJ82
St. Saviour's Est, SE1 ...201 P6
St. Saviour's Rd, SW2 ...121 DM85
St. Saviours Rd, Croy. CR0 .142 DQ100
Saints Cl, SE27
  off Wolfington Rd 121 DP91
Saints Dr, E7 ....68 EK64
St. Silas Pl, NW5 ......82 DG65
St. Silas St Est, NW5 ...82 DG65
St. Simon's Av, SW15 ...119 CW85
St. Stephens Av, E17 ...67 EC57
  W12 ....99 CV75
  W13 ....79 CH72
St. Stephen's Av, Ashtd. KT21 .172 CL116
St. Stephens Cl, E17 ...67 EB57
  NW8 ....82 DE67
  Southall UB1 ....78 CA71
St. Stephens Cres, W2 ..82 DA72
  Brentwood CM13 .....55 GA49
  Thornton Heath CR7 ..141 DN97

St. Stephens Gdn Est, W2
  off Shrewsbury Rd 82 DA72
St. Stephens Gdns, SW15
  off Manfred Rd 119 CZ85
  W2 ....82 DA72
  Twickenham TW1 ....117 CJ86
St. Stephens Gro, SE13 .103 EC83
St. Stephens Ms, W2
  off Chepstow Rd 82 DA71
St. Stephen's Par, E7
  off Green St 86 EJ66
St. Stephen's Pas, Twick. TW1
  off Richmond Rd 117 CJ86
St. Stephen's Rd, E3 ...85 DZ68
St. Stephens Rd, E6 ....86 EJ66
St. Stephen's Rd, E17
  off Grove Rd 67 EB57
St. Stephen's Rd, W13 .79 CH72
St. Stephens Rd, Barn. EN5 .27 CX43
St. Stephen's Rd, West Dr. UB7 .76 BK74
  Hounslow TW3 ....116 CA86
St. Stephens Row, EC4 .197 K9
St. Stephens Ter, SW8 .101 DM80
St. Stephen's Wk, SW7 .100 DC77
Saints Wk, Grays RM16 .111 GJ77
St. Swithin's La, EC4 ...197 K10
St. Swithun's Rd, SE13 .123 ED85
St. Teresa Wk, Grays RM16 .111 GH76
St. Theresa Cl, Epsom KT18 .156 CQ114
St. Theresa's Rd, Felt. TW14 ..95 BT84
St. Thomas' Cl, Surb. KT6 .138 CM102
St. Thomas Cl, Wok. GU21
  off St. Mary's Rd 166 AW117
St. Thomas Ct, Bex. DA5 .126 FA87
St. Thomas Dr, Orp. BR5 .145 EQ102
St. Thomas' Dr, Pnr. HA5 .40 BY53
St. Thomas Gdns, Ilf. IG1 .87 EQ65
Ⓗ St. Thomas' Hosp, SE1 .200 B6
St. Thomas Pl, NW1
  off Maiden La 83 DK66
St. Thomas Rd, E16 ....86 EG72
  N14 ....45 DK45
St. Thomas' Rd, W4 ....98 CQ79
St. Thomas Rd, Belv. DA17 .107 FC75
  Brentwood CM14 .....54 FX47
  Gravesend (Nthflt.) DA11
  off St. Margaret's Rd .130 GE89
St. Thomas's Av, Grav. DA11 .131 GH88
St. Thomas's Cl, Wal.Abb. EN9 .16 EH33
St. Thomas's Gdns, NW5
  off Queen's Cres 82 DG65
St. Thomas's Pl, E9 ....84 DW66
St. Thomas's Rd, N4 ...65 DN61
  NW10 ....80 CS67
St. Thomas's Sq, E9 ...84 DV66
St. Thomas's St, SE1 ..201 K3
St. Thomas's Way, SW6 .99 CZ80
St. Thomas Wk, Slou. (Colnbr.)
  SL3 ....93 BD80
St. Timothy's Ms, Brom. BR1
  off Wharton Rd 144 EH95
St. Ursula Gro, Pnr. HA5 .60 BX57
St. Ursula Rd, Sthl. UB1 .78 CA72
St. Vincent Cl, SE27 ....121 DP92
St. Vincent Rd, Twick. TW2 .116 CC86
  Walton-on-Thames KT12 .135 BV104
St. Vincents Av, Dart. DA1 .128 FN85
ST. VINCENT'S HAMLET, Brwd.52 FP46
St. Vincents Cl, Dart. DA1 .128 FN86
St. Vincent St, W1 .....194 G7
St. Vincents Way, Pot.B. EN6 .12 DC33
St. Wilfrids Cl, Barn. EN4 .28 DE43
St. Wilfrids Rd, Barn. EN4 .28 DD43
St. Winefride's Av, E12 .69 EM64
St. Winifreds, Ken. CR8 .176 DQ115
St. Winifreds Cl, Chig. IG7 .49 EQ50
St. Winifred's Rd, Tedd. TW11 .117 CH93
  Westerham (Bigg.H.) TN16 .179 EM118
Saladin Dr, Purf. RM19 ..108 FN77
Sala Ho, SE3 off Pinto Way .104 EH84
Salamanca Pl, SE1 .....200 B9
Salamanca St, SE1 .....200 A9
Salamander Cl, Kings.T. KT2 .117 CJ92
Salamander Quay, Uxb. (Hare.)
  UB9 off Coppermill La .38 BG52
Salamons Way, Rain. RM13 .89 FE72
Salcombe Dr, Mord. SM4 .139 CX102
  Romford RM6 ....70 EZ58
Salcombe Gdns, NW7 ...43 CW51
Salcombe Pk, Loug. IG10 .32 EK43
Salcombe Rd, E17 .....67 DZ59
  N16 ....66 DS64
  Ashford TW15 ....114 BL91
Salcombe Way, Hayes UB4
  off Portland Rd 77 BS69
  Ruislip HA4 ....59 BU61
Salcot Cres, Croy. (New Adgtn.)
  CR0 ....161 EC110
Salcote Rd, Grav. DA12 .131 GL92
Salcott Rd, SW11 ......120 DE85
  Croydon CR0 ....141 DL104
Salehurst Cl, Har. HA3 ...62 CL57
Salehurst Rd, SE4 .....123 DZ86
Salem Pl, Croy. CR0 ....142 DQ104
  Gravesend (Nthflt.) DA11 .130 GD87
Salem Rd, W2 ....82 DB73
Sale Pl, W2 ....194 B7
Salesian Gdns, Cher. KT16 .134 BG102
Sale St, E2 off Hereford St .84 DU70
Salford Rd, SW2 ....121 DK88
Salhouse Cl, SE28
  off Rollesby Way 88 EW72
Salisbury Av, N3 ....63 CZ55
  Barking IG11 ....87 ES66
  Sutton SM1 ....157 CZ107
  Swanley BR8 ....147 FG98
Salisbury Cl, SE17 .....201 K8
  Amersham HP7 ....AS39
  Potters Bar EN6 .....12 DC32
  Upminster RM14
  off Canterbury Av ...73 FT61
  Worcester Park KT4 ..139 CT104
Salisbury Ct, EC4 ......196 F9
  EN8 ....15 DX32
Salisbury Cres, Wal.Cr. (Chsht.)
Salisbury Gdns, SW19 ..119 CY94

Salisbury Gdns, Buck.H. IG9 .48 EK47
Salisbury Hall Gdns, E4 ..47 EA51
Salisbury Ho, E14
  off Hobday St 85 EB72
Salisbury Ms, SW6
  off Dawes Rd 99 CZ80
  Bromley BR2
  off Salisbury Rd 144 EL99
Salisbury Pl, SW9 ......101 DP80
  W1 ....194 D6
  West Byfleet KT14 ...152 BJ111
Salisbury Rd, E4 ....47 EA48
  E7 ....86 EG65
  E10 ....67 EC61
  E12 ....68 EK64
  E17 ....67 EC57
  N4 ....65 DP57
  N9 ....46 DU48
  N22 ....45 DP53
  SE25 ....142 DU100
  SW19 ....119 CY95
  W13 ....97 CG75
  Banstead SM7 ....158 DA116
  Barnet EN5 ....27 CY41
  Bexley DA5 ....126 FA88
  Bromley BR2 ....144 EL99
  Carshalton SM5 .....158 DF107
  Dagenham RM10 ......89 FB65
  Dartford DA2 ....128 FQ88
  Enfield EN3 ....31 DZ37
  Feltham TW13 ....116 BW88
  Godstone RH9 ....186 DW131
  Gravesend DA11 .....131 GF88
  Grays RM17 ....110 GC79
  Harrow HA1 ....61 CD57
  Hounslow TW4 ....96 BW83
  Hounslow (Hthrw.Air.)TW6 .115 BQ85
  Ilford IG3 ....69 ES61
  New Malden KT3 .....138 CR97
  Pinner HA5 ....59 BU56
  Richmond TW9 ......98 CL84
  Romford RM2 ....71 FH57
  Southall UB2 ....96 BY77
  Uxbridge UB8 ....76 BH68
  Watford WD24 ....23 BV38
  Woking GU22 ....166 AY119
  Worcester Park KT4 ..139 CT104
Salisbury Sq, EC4 ......196 E9
Salisbury St, NW8 ......194 B5
  W3 ....98 CQ75
Salisbury Ter, SE15 ....102 DW83
Salisbury Wk, N19 .....65 DJ61
Salix Cl, Lthd. (Fetch.) KT22 .170 CB123
  Sunbury-on-Thames TW16
  off Oak Gro 115 BV94
Salix Rd, Grays RM17 ..110 GD79
Salliesfield, Twick. TW2 .117 CD86
Sally Murrey Cl, E12
  off Grantham Rd 69 EN63
Salmen Rd, E13 ....86 EF68
Salmond Cl, Stan. HA7
  off Robb Rd 41 CG51
Salmonds Gro, Brwd. CM13 .55 GC50
Salmon La, E14 ....85 DY72
Salmon Rd, Belv. DA17 .106 FA78
  Dartford DA1 ....108 FM83
Salmons La, Whyt. CR3 .176 DU119
Salmons La W, Cat. CR3 .176 DS120
Salmons Rd, N9 ....46 DU46
  Chessington KT9 ....155 CK107
Salmon St, E14 off Salmon La .85 DZ72
  NW9 ....62 CP60
Salomons Rd, E13 off Chalk Rd .86 EJ71
Salop Rd, E17 ....67 DX58
Saltash Cl, Sutt. SM1 ..157 CZ105
Saltash Rd, Ilf. IG6 ....49 ER52
  Welling DA16 ....106 EW81
Salt Box Hill, West. TN16 .162 EH113
Saltcoats Rd, W4 ......98 CS75
Saltcote Cl, Dart. DA1
  off Lower Sta Rd 127 FE86
Saltcroft Cl, Wem. HA9 .62 CP60
Salter Cl, Har. HA2 ....60 BZ62
Salterford Rd, SW17 ...120 DG93
Salter Rd, SE16 ....203 H3
Salters Cl, Rick. WD3 ...38 BL46
Salters Gdns, Wat. WD17 .23 BU39
Salters Hall Ct, EC4 ...197 K10
Salters Hill, SE19 .....122 DR92
Salters Rd, E17 ....67 ED56
  W10 ....81 CX70
Salter St, E14 ....85 EA73
  NW10 ....81 CU69
Salterton Rd, N7 ......65 DL62
Saltford Cl, Erith DA8 ..107 FE78
Salthill Cl, Uxb. UB8 ...58 BL64
Saltley Cl, E6
  off Dunnock Rd 86 EL72
Saltoun Rd, SW2 ......101 DN84
Saltram Cl, N15 ....66 DT56
Saltram Cres, W9 ......81 CZ69
Saltwell St, E14 ....85 EA73
Saltwood Cl, Orp. BR6 .164 EW105
Saltwood Gro, SE17
  off Merrow St 102 DR78
Salusbury Rd, NW6 ....81 CY67
Salutation Rd, SE10 ...205 J8
Salvia Gdns, Grnf. UB6
  off Selborne Gdns ...79 CG68
Salvin Rd, SW15 ......99 CX83
Salway Cl, Wdf.Grn. IG8 .48 EF52
Salway Pl, E15 off Broadway .86 EE65
Salway Rd, E15
  off Great Eastern Rd .85 ED65
Samantha Cl, E17 .....67 DZ59
Samantha Ms, Rom. (Hav.at.Bow.)
  RM4 ....51 FE48
Sam Bartram Cl, SE7 ...104 EJ78
Sambruck Ms, SE6 .....123 EB88
Samels Ct, W6
  off South Black Lion La .99 CU78
Samford St, NW8 ......194 A5
Samira Cl, E17
  off Colchester Rd 67 EA58
Samos Rd, SE20 ....142 DV96
Samphire Ct, Grays RM17
  off Salix Rd 110 GE80

Sampson Av, Barn. EN5 ..27 CX43
Sampson Cl, Belv. DA17
  off Carrill Way 106 EX76
Sampsons Ct, Shep. TW17
  off Linden Way 135 BQ99
Samson St, E13 ....86 EJ68
Samuel Cl, E8 off Pownall Rd .84 DT67
  SE14 ....103 DX79
  SE18 ....104 EL77
Samuel Gray Gdns, Kings.T.
  KT2 ....137 CK95
Samuel Johnson Cl, SW16
  off Curtis Fld Rd 121 DN91
Samuel Lewis Trust Dws, E8
  off Amhurst Rd 66 DU63
  N1 off Liverpool Rd ..83 DN66
  SW3 ....198 B9
  SW6 ....100 DA80
Samuels Cl, W6
  off South Black Lion La .99 CU78
Samuel St, SE15 ......102 DT80
  SE18 ....105 EM77
Sancroft Cl, NW2 ......63 CV62
Sancroft Rd, Har. HA3 ...41 CF54
Sancroft St, SE11 .....200 C10
Sanctuary, The, SW1 ...199 N5
  Bexley DA5 ....126 EX86
  Morden SM4 ....140 DA100
Sanctuary Cl, Dart. DA1 .128 FM86
  Uxbridge (Hare.) UB9 .38 BJ52
Sanctuary Rd, Houns. (Hthrw.Air.)
  TW6 ....114 BN86
Sanctuary St, SE1 .....201 J5
Sandale Cl, N16 off Stoke
  Newington Ch St 66 DR62
Sandall Cl, W5 ....80 CL70
Sandall Rd, NW5 ......83 DJ65
  W5 ....80 CL70
Sandal Rd, N18 ....46 DU50
  New Malden KT3 ....138 CR99
Sandal St, E15 ....86 EE67
Sandalwood Av, Cher. KT16 .133 BD104
Sandalwood Cl, E1
  off Solebay St 85 DY70
Sandalwood Dr, Ruis. HA4 .59 BQ59
Sandalwood Rd, Felt. TW13 .115 BV90
Sandbach Pl, SE18 ....105 EQ77
Sandbanks, Felt. TW14 .115 BT88
Sandbanks Hill, Dart. (Bean)
  DA2 ....129 FV93
Sandbourne Av, SW19 .140 DB97
Sandbourne Rd, SE4 ...103 DY82
Sandbrook Cl, NW7 ....42 CR51
Sandbrook Rd, N16 ....66 DS62
Sandby Grn, SE9 ......104 EL83
Sandcliff Rd, Erith DA8 .107 FD77
Sandcroft Cl, N13 .....45 DP51
Sandell St, SE1 ....200 D4
Sanders Cl, Hmptn. (Hmptn.H.)
  TW12 ....116 CC92
  St. Albans (Lon.Col.) AL2 ..9 CK27
Sandersfield Gdns, Bans.
  SM7 ....174 DA115
Sandersfield Rd, Bans. SM7 .174 DB115
Sanders La, NW7 ......43 CX52
Sanderson Av, Sev. (Bad.Mt.)
  TN14 ....164 FA110
Sanderson Cl, NW5 ....65 DH63
Sanderson Rd, Uxb. UB8 .76 BJ65
SANDERSTEAD, S.Croy. ..160 DT111
⇌ Sanderstead 160 DR109
Sanderstead Av, NW2 ..63 CY61
Sanderstead Cl, SW12
  off Atkins Rd 121 DJ87
Sanderstead Ct Av, S.Croy.
  CR2 ....160 DU113
Sanderstead Hill, S.Croy. CR2 .160 DS111
Sanderstead Rd, E10 ..67 DY60
  Orpington BR5 ......146 EV100
  South Croydon CR2 ..160 DR108
Sanders Way, N19
  off Sussex Way 65 DK60
Sandes Pl, Lthd. KT22 .171 CG118
Sandfield Gdns, Th.Hth. CR7 .141 DP97
Sandfield Pas, Th.Hth. CR7 .142 DQ97
Sandfield Rd, Th.Hth. CR7 .141 DP97
Sandfields, Wok. (Send) GU23 .167 BD124
Sandford Av, N22 ......46 DQ52
  Loughton IG10 ......33 EQ41
Sandford Cl, E6 ....87 EM70
Sandford Ct, N16 .....66 DS60
Sandford Rd, E6 ......86 EL70
  Bexleyheath DA7 ....106 EY84
  Bromley BR2 ....144 EG98
Sandford St, SW6
  off King's Rd 100 DB80
Sandgate Cl, Rom. RM7 .71 FD59
Sandgate La, SW18 ....120 DE88
Sandgate Rd, Well. DA16 .106 EW80
Sandgate St, SE15 ....102 DV79
Sandham Pt, SE18 off Troy Ct .105 EP77
Sandhills, Wall. SM6 ...159 DK105
Sandhills La, Vir.W. GU25 .132 AY90
Sandhills Meadow, Shep.
  TW17 ....135 BQ101
Sandhurst Av, Har. HA2 .60 CB58
  Surbiton KT5 ....138 CP101
Sandhurst Cl, NW9 ....62 CN55
  South Croydon CR2 ..160 DS109
Sandhurst Dr, Ilf. IG3 ..69 ES63
Sandhurst Rd, N9 .....30 DW44
  NW9 ....62 CN55
  SE6 ....123 ED88
  Bexley DA5 ....126 EX85
  Orpington BR6 ......146 EU104
  Sidcup DA15 ....125 ET90
  Tilbury RM18 ....111 GJ82
Sandhurst Way, S.Croy. CR2 .160 DS108
Sandifer Dr, NW2 .....63 CX62
Sandiford Rd, Sutt. SM3 .139 CZ103
Sandiland Cres, Brom. BR2 .144 EF103
⊷ Sandilands 142 DT103
Sandilands, Croy. CR0 .142 DU103
  Sevenoaks TN13 ....190 FD122
Sandilands Rd, SW6 ...100 DB81

Sandison St, SE15 .....102 DT83
Sandlands Gro, Tad. KT20 .173 CU123
Sandlands Rd, Tad. KT20 .173 CU123
Sandland St, WC1 .....196 C7
Sandling Ri, SE9 ......125 EN90
Sandlings, The, N22 ...45 DN54
Sandlings Cl, SE15
  off Pilkington Rd 102 DV82
Sandmartin Way, Wall. SM6
  off London Rd 140 DG102
Sandmere Rd, SW4 ....101 DL84
Sandon Cl, Esher KT10 .137 CD101
Sandon Rd, Wal.Cr. (Chsht.)
  EN8 ....14 DW30
Sandow Cres, Hayes UB3 .95 BT76
Sandown Av, Dag. RM10 .89 FC65
  Esher KT10 ....154 CC106
  Hornchurch RM12 ...72 FK61
Sandown Cl, Houns. TW5 .95 BU81
Sandown Ct, Sutt. SM2
  off Grange Rd 158 DB108
Sandown Dr, Cars. SM5 .158 DG109
Sandown Gate, Esher KT10 .136 CC104
Sandown Ind Pk, Esher KT10 .136 CA103
★ Sandown Park Racecourse,
  Esher KT10 ....136 CB104
Sandown Rd, SE25 ....142 DV99
  Coulsdon CR5 ......174 DG116
  Esher KT10 ....154 CC105
  Gravesend DA12 ....131 GJ93
  Watford WD24 ......24 BW38
Sandown Way, Nthlt. UB5 .78 BY65
Sandpiper Cl, E17 .....47 DX53
  SE16 ....203 M4
Sandpiper Dr, Erith DA8 .107 FH80
Sandpiper Rd, S.Croy. CR2 .161 DX111
  Sutton SM1 ....157 CZ106
Sandpipers, The, Grav. DA12 .131 GK89
Sandpiper Way, Orp. BR5 .146 EX98
Sandpit Hall Rd, Wok. (Chobham)
  GU24 ....150 AU112
Sandpit La, Brwd. (Pilg.Hat.)
  CM14, CM15 ....54 FT46
Sandpit Pl, SE7 ....104 EL78
Sandpit Rd, Brom. BR1 .124 EE92
  Dartford DA1 ....108 FJ84
Sandpits Rd, Croy. CR0 .161 DX105
  Richmond TW10 ....117 CK89
Sandra Cl, N22 off New Rd .46 DQ53
  Hounslow TW3 .....116 CB85
Sandridge Cl, Har. HA1 .61 CE56
Sandridge St, N19 ....65 DJ61
Sandringham Av, SW20 .139 CY96
Sandringham Cl, SW19 .119 CX88
  Enfield EN1 ....30 DS40
  Ilford IG6 ....69 EQ55
  Woking GU22 ......168 BG116
Sandringham Ct, W9
  off Maida Vale 82 DC69
Sandringham Cres, Har. HA2 .60 CA61
Sandringham Dr, Ashf. TW15 .114 BK91
  Welling DA16 ....105 ES82
Sandringham Gdns, N8 .65 DL58
  N12 ....44 DC51
  Hounslow TW5 .....95 BU81
  Ilford IG6 ....69 EQ55
Sandringham Ms, W5
  off High St 79 CK73
Sandringham Pk, Cob. KT11 .154 BZ112
Sandringham Rd, E7 ...68 EJ64
  E8 ....66 DT64
  E10 ....67 ED58
  N22 ....66 DU55
  NW2 ....81 CV65
  NW11 ....63 CY59
  Barking IG11 ....87 ET65
  Brentwood CM15 ....54 FV43
  Bromley BR1 ....124 EG92
  Hounslow (Hthrw.Air.)TW6 .114 BL85
  Northolt UB5 ....78 CA66
  Potters Bar EN6 ....12 DB30
  Thornton Heath CR7 .142 DQ99
  Watford WD24 ......24 BW37
  Worcester Park KT4 ..139 CU104
Sandringham Way, Wal.Cr.
  EN8 ....15 DX34
Sandrock Pl, Croy. CR0 .161 DX105
Sandrock Rd, SE13 ....103 EA83
Sandroyd Way, Cob. KT11 .154 CA113
SANDS END, SW6 .....100 DC81
Sand's End La, SW6 ...100 DB81
Sandstone Pl, N19 .....65 DH61
Sandstone Rd, SE12 ...124 EH89
Sands Way, Wdf.Grn. IG8 .48 EL51
Sandtoft Rd, SE7 .....104 EH79
Sandway Path, Orp. BR5
  off Okemore Gdns ...146 EW98
Sandway Rd, Orp. BR5 .146 EW98
Sandwell Cres, NW6 ...82 DA65
Sandwich St, WC1 ....195 P3
Sandwick Cl, NW7
  off Sebergham Gro ..43 CU52
Sandy Bk Rd, Grav. DA12 .131 GH88
Sandy Bury, Orp. BR6 .145 ER104
Sandy Cl, Wok. GU22
  off Sandy La 167 BB117
Sandycombe Rd, Felt. TW14 .115 BU88
  Richmond TW9 .....98 CN83
Sandycoombe Rd, Twick. TW1 .117 CJ86
Sandycroft, SE2 ......106 EU79
  Epsom KT17 ....157 CW110
Sandycroft Rd, Amer. HP6 .20 AV39
Sandy Dr, Cob. KT11 ..154 CA111
  Feltham TW14 ......115 BS86
Sandy Hill Av, SE18 ...105 EP78
Sandy Hill Rd, SE18 ...105 EP78
Sandyhill Rd, Ilf. IG1 ..69 EP63
Sandy Hill Rd, Wall. SM6 .159 DJ109
Sandy La, Bushey WD23 .24 CC41
  Cobham KT11 ......154 CA112
  Dartford (Bean) DA2 .129 FW89
  Grays (Chad.St.M) RM16 .111 GH79
  Grays (W.Thur.) RM20
  off London Rd W Thurrock .109 FV79
  Harrow HA3 ....62 CM58
  Kingston upon Thames KT1 .117 CG94
  Leatherhead KT22 ..154 CA112

Sandy La, Mitch. CR4 . . . .140 DG95
Northwood HA6 . . . . .39 BU50
Orpington BR6 . . . . .146 EU101
Orpington (St.P.Cray) BR5 .146 EX95
Oxted RH8 . . . . .187 EC129
Oxted (Lmpfld.) RH8 . . . .188 EH127
Redhill (Bletch.) RH1 . . . .185 DP132
Richmond TW10 . . . . . . .117 CJ89
Sevenoaks TN13 . . . . . . .191 FJ123
Sidcup DA14 . . . . .126 EX94
South Ockendon (Aveley)
RM15 . . . . .90 FM73
Sutton SM2 . . . . .157 CY108
Tadworth (Kgswd.) KT20 .173 CZ124
Teddington TW11 . . . . . .117 CG94
Virginia Water GU25 . . . .132 AY98
Walton-on-Thames KT12 .135 BV100
Watford WD25 . . . . .24 CC41
Westerham TN16 . . . . . .189 ER125
Woking GU22 . . . . .167 BC116
Woking (Chobham) GU24 .150 AS109
Woking (Pyrford) GU22 . . .167 BF117
Woking (Send) GU23 . . . .167 BC123
Sandy La Est, Rich. TW10 .117 CK89
Sandy La N, Wall. SM6 . . .159 DK107
Sandy La S, Wall. SM6 . . .159 DK107
Sandy Lo La, Nthwd. HA6 . .39 BR47
Sandy Lo Rd, Rick. WD3 . . .39 BP47
Sandy Lo Way, Nthwd. HA6 .39 BS50
Sandymount Av, Stan. HA7 . .41 CJ50
Sandy Ridge, Chis. BR7 . . .125 EN93
Sandy Ri, Ger.Cr. (Chal.St.P.)
SL9 . . . . .36 AY53
Sandy Rd, NW3 . . . . .64 DB62
Addlestone KT15 . . . . . .152 BG107
Sandy's Row, E1 . . . . . . .197 N7
Sandy Way, Cob. KT11 . . .154 CA112
Croydon CR0 . . . . .143 DZ104
Walton-on-Thames KT12 .135 BT102
Woking GU22 . . . . .167 BC117
Sanford La, N16
off Lawrence Bldgs 66 DT61
Sanford St, SE14 . . . . . . .103 DY79
Sanford Ter, N16 . . . . . . .66 DT62
Sanford Wk, N16
off Sanford Ter 66 DT61
SE14 off Cold Blow La . . .103 DY79
Sanger Av, Chess. KT9 . . .156 CL106
Sanger Dr, Wok. (Send) GU23 .167 BC123
Sangley Rd, SE6 . . . . . . .123 EB87
SE25 . . . . .142 DS98
Sangora Rd, SW11 . . . . . .100 DD84
Sansom Rd, E11 . . . . .68 EE61
Sansom St, SE5 . . . . .102 DR80
Sans Wk, EC1 . . . . .196 E4
Santers La, Pot.B. EN6 . . . .11 CY33
Santley St, SW4 . . . . . . .101 DM84
Santos Rd, SW18 . . . . . . .120 DA85
Santway, The, Stan. HA7 . . .41 CE50
Sanway Cl, W.Byf. (Byfleet)
KT14 . . . . .152 BL114
Sanway Rd, W.Byf. (Byfleet)
KT14 . . . . .152 BL114
Sapcote Trd Cen, NW10 . . .63 CT64
Saperton Wk, SE11 . . . . .200 C8
Sapho Pk, Grav. DA12 . . . .131 GM91
Saphora Cl, Orp. BR6
off Oleander Cl 163 ER106
Sapperton Ct, EC1 . . . . . .197 H4
Sapphire Cl, E6 . . . . .87 EN72
Dagenham RM8 . . . . . . .70 EW60
Sapphire Rd, SE8 . . . . . . .203 L9
Sappho Ct, Wok. GU21
off Langmans Way 166 AS116
Saracen Cl, Croy. CR0 . . . .142 DR100
Saracen's Head Yd, EC3 . .197 P9
★ Saracens RFC (share
Vicarage Rd with Watford
FC), Wat. WD18 . . . . . . .23 BV43
Saracen St, E14 . . . . .85 EA72
Sara Ct, Beck. BR3
off Albemarle Rd 143 EB95
Sara Cres, Green. DA9 . . . .109 FU84
Sarah Ho, SW15 . . . . .57 CT84
Sara Pk, Grav. DA12 . . . . .131 GL91
Saratoga Rd, E5 . . . . .66 DW63
Sardinia St, WC2 . . . . . . .196 B9
Sargeant Cl, Uxb. UB8
off Ratcliffe Cl 76 BK69
Sarita Cl, Har. HA3 . . . . . .41 CD54
Sarjant Path, SW19
off Queensmere Rd 119 CX89
Sark Cl, Houns. TW5 . . . . .96 CA80
Sark Ho, Enf. EN3
off Eastfield Rd 31 DX38
Sark Wk, E16 . . . . .86 EH72
Sarnesfield Ho, SE15
off Pencraig Way 102 DV79
Sarnesfield Rd, Enf. EN2
off Church St 30 DR41
SARRATT, Rick. 22 BG35
Sarratt Bottom, Rick. (Sarratt)
WD3 . . . . .21 BE36
Sarratt La, Rick. WD3 . . . . .22 BH40
Sarratt Rd, Rick. WD3 . . . .22 BM41
Sarre Av, Horn. RM12 . . . . .90 FJ65
Sarre Rd, NW2 . . . . .63 CZ64
Orpington BR5 . . . . . . .146 EW99
Sarsby Dr, Stai. TW19 . . . .113 BA89
Sarsen Av, Houns. TW3 . . . .96 BZ82
Sarsfeld Rd, SW12 . . . . . .120 DF88
Sarsfield Rd, Grnf. UB6 . . . .79 CH68
Sartor Rd, SE15 . . . . .103 DX84
Sarum Complex, Uxb. UB8 . .76 BH68
Sarum Grn, Wey. KT13 . . . .135 BS104
Sarum Ter, E3 . . . . .85 DZ70
Satanita Cl, E16
off Fulmer Rd 86 EK72
Satchell Mead, NW9 . . . . . .43 CT53
Satchwell Rd, E2 . . . . .84 DU69
Satis Ct, Epsom KT17
off Windmill Av 157 CT111
Sattar Ms, Enf. EN3 off Clissold Rd .66 DR62
Sauls Grn, E11 off Napier Rd .68 EE62
Saunder Cl, Wal.Cr. EN8
off Welsummer Way 15 DX27
Saunders Cl, E14 . . . . . . .203 N1

Saunders Cl, Grav. (Nthflt.)
DA11 . . . . .130 GE89
Saunders Copse, Wok. GU22 .166 AS122
Saunders La, Wok. GU22 . .166 AS122
Saunders Ness Rd, E14 . . .204 N10
Saunders Rd, SE18 . . . . . .105 ET78
Uxbridge UB10 . . . . .76 BM66
Saunders St, SE11 . . . . . .200 D8
Saunders Way, SE28
off Oriole Way 88 EV73
Dartford DA1 . . . . .128 FM89
Saunderton Rd, Wem. HA0 . .61 CH64
Saunton Av, Hayes UB3 . . .95 BT80
Saunton Rd, Horn. RM12 . . .71 FG61
Savage Gdns, E6 . . . . .87 EM72
EC3 . . . . .197 N10
Savay Cl, Uxb. (Denh.) UB9 . .58 BG59
Savay La, Uxb. (Denh.) UB9 . .58 BG58
Savernake Rd, N9 . . . . . . .30 DU44
NW3 . . . . .64 DF63
Savery Dr, Surb. KT6 . . . . .137 CJ101
Savile Cl, N.Mal. KT3 . . . .138 CS99
Thames Ditton KT7 . . . . .137 CF102
Savile Gdns, Croy. CR0 . . .142 DT103
Savile Row, W1 . . . . .195 K10
Savill Cl, Wal.Cr. (Chsht.) EN7
off Markham Rd 14 DQ25
Saville Cres, Ashf. TW15 . .115 BR93
Saville Rd, E16 . . . . .86 EL74
W4 . . . . .98 CR76
Romford RM6 . . . . .70 EZ58
Twickenham TW1 . . . . . .117 CF88
Saville Row, Brom. BR2 . . .144 EF102
Enfield EN3 . . . . .31 DX40
Savill Gdns, SW20
off Bodnant Gdns 139 CU95
Savill Row, Wdf.Grn. IG8 . . .48 EF51
Savona Cl, SW19 . . . . . . .119 CY94
Savona Est, SW8 . . . . . . .101 DJ80
Savona St, SW8 . . . . .101 DJ80
Savoy Av, Hayes UB3 . . . . .95 BS78
Savoy Bldgs, WC2 . . . . . .200 B1
Savoy Cl, E15
off Arthingworth St 86 EE67
Edgware HA8 . . . . .42 CN50
Uxbridge (Hare.) UB9 . . . .38 BK54
Savoy Ct, WC2 . . . . .200 A1
Savoy Hill, WC2 . . . . .200 B1
Savoy Pl, WC2 . . . . .200 A1
Savoy Rd, Dart. DA1 . . . . .128 FK85
Savoy Row, WC2 . . . . . . .196 B10
Savoy Steps, WC2
off Savoy St 83 DM73
Savoy St, WC2 . . . . .200 B1
Savoy Way, WC2 . . . . . . .200 B1
Sawbill Cl, Hayes UB4 . . . .78 BX71
Sawkins Cl, SW19 . . . . . .119 CY89
Sawley Rd, W12 . . . . .81 CU74
Sawmill Yd, E3 . . . . .85 DY67
Sawtry Cl, Cars. SM5 . . . .140 DE101
Sawtry Way, Borwd. WD6 . . .26 CN38
Sawyer Cl, N9
off Lion Rd 46 DU47
Sawyers Chase, Rom. (Abridge)
RM4 . . . . .34 EV41
Sawyers Cl, Dag. RM10 . . . .89 FC65
Sawyers Hall La, Brwd. CM15 .54 FW49
Sawyer's Hill, Rich. TW10 . .118 CP87
Sawyers La, Borwd. (Elstree)
WD6 . . . . .25 CH40
Potters Bar EN6 . . . . . . .11 CX34
Sawyers Lawn, W13 . . . . . .79 CF72
Sawyer St, SE1 . . . . .201 H4
Saxby Rd, SW2 . . . . .121 DL87
Saxham Rd, Bark. IG11 . . . .87 ES68
Saxlingham Rd, E4 . . . . . . .47 ED48
Saxon Av, Felt. TW13 . . . .116 BZ89
Saxonbury Av, Sun. TW16 . .135 BV97
Saxonbury Cl, Mitch. CR4 . .140 DD97
Saxonbury Gdns, Surb. KT6 .137 CJ102
Saxon Cl, E17 . . . . .67 EA59
Brentwood CM13 . . . . . .55 GA48
Gravesend (Nthflt.) DA11 .130 GC90
Romford RM3 . . . . .52 FM54
Sevenoaks (Otford) TN14 .181 FF117
Slough SL3 . . . . .93 AZ75
Surbiton KT6 . . . . .137 CK100
Uxbridge UB8 . . . . .76 BM71
Saxon Ct, Borwd. WD6 . . . .26 CL40
Saxon Dr, W3 . . . . .80 CP72
Saxonfield Cl, SW2 . . . . . .121 DM87
Saxon Gdns, Sthl. UB1
off Saxon Rd 78 BY73
Saxon Pl, Dart. (Hort.Kir.) DA4 .148 FQ98
Saxon Rd, E3 . . . . .85 DZ68
E6 . . . . .87 EM70
N22 . . . . .45 DP53
SE25 . . . . .142 DR99
Ashford TW15 . . . . .115 BR93
Bromley BR1 . . . . .124 EF94
Dartford (Hawley) DA2 . .128 FL91
Ilford IG1 . . . . .87 EP65
Southall UB1 . . . . .78 BY74
Walton-on-Thames KT12 .136 BX104
Wembley HA9 . . . . .62 CQ62
Saxons, Tad. KT20 . . . . . .173 CX121
Saxon Shore Way, Grav.
DA12 . . . . .131 GM86
Saxon Wk, Sid. DA14 . . . .126 EW93
Saxon Way, N14 . . . . .29 DK44
Reigate RH2 . . . . .183 CZ133
Waltham Abbey EN9 . . . . .15 EC33
West Drayton UB7 . . . . . .94 BJ79
Windsor (Old Wind.) SL4 .112 AV86
Saxony Par, Hayes UB3 . . . .77 BQ71
Saxton Cl, SE13 . . . . .103 ED83
Saxton Ms, Wat. WD17
off Dellfield Cl 23 BU40
Saxville Rd, Orp. BR5 . . . .146 EV97
Sayer Cl, Green. DA9 . . . . .109 FU85
Sayers Cl, Lthd. (Fetch.) KT22 .170 CC124
Sayers Wk, Rich. TW10
off Stafford Pl 118 CM87
Sayesbury La, N18 . . . . . . .46 DU50
Sayes Ct, SE8 . . . . .203 N10
off Sayes Ct St 103 DZ78
Addlestone KT15 . . . . . .152 BJ106

Sayes Ct Fm Dr, Add. KT15 .152 BH106
Sayes Ct Rd, Orp. BR5 . . . .146 EU98
Sayes Ct St, SE8 . . . . . . .103 DZ79
Scadbury Pk, Chis. BR7 . . .125 ET93
Scads Hill Cl, Orp. BR6 . . .145 ET100
Scala St, W1 . . . . .195 L6
Scales Rd, N17 . . . . .66 DT55
Scammell Way, Wat. WD18 . .23 BT44
Scampston Ms, W10 . . . . . .81 CX72
Scampton Rd, Houns. (Hthrw.Air.)
TW6 off Southampton Rd . .114 BM86
Scandrett St, E1 . . . . .202 D3
Scarba Wk, N1
off Marquess Rd 84 DR65
Scarborough Cl, Sutt. SM2 .157 CZ111
Westerham (Bigg.H.) TN16 .178 EJ118
Scarborough Rd, E11 . . . . .67 ED60
N4 . . . . .65 DN59
N9 . . . . .46 DW45
Hounslow (Hthrw.Air.) TW6
off Southern Perimeter Rd .115 BQ86
Scarborough St, E1
off West Tenter St 84 DT72
Scarbrook Rd, Croy. CR0 . .142 DQ104
Scarle Rd, Wem. HA0 . . . . .79 CK65
Scarlet Cl, Orp. BR5 . . . . .146 EV98
Scarlet Rd, SE6 . . . . .124 EE90
Scarlett Cl, Wok. GU21
off Bingham Dr 166 AT118
Scarlette Manor Way, SW2
off Papworth Way 121 DN87
Scarsbrook Rd, SE3 . . . . .104 EK83
Scarsdale Pl, W8
off Wrights La 100 DB76
Scarsdale Rd, Har. HA2 . . . .60 CC62
Scarsdale Vil, W8 . . . . . . .100 DA76
Scarth Rd, SW13 . . . . .99 CT83
Scatterdells La, Kings L. (Chipper.)
WD4 . . . . .5 BF30
Scawen Cl, Cars. SM5 . . . .158 DG105
Scawen Rd, SE8 . . . . .103 DY78
Scawfell St, E2 . . . . .84 DT68
Scaynes Link, N12 . . . . . . .44 DA50
Sceaux Est, SE5 . . . . .102 DS81
Sceptre Rd, E2 . . . . .84 DW69
Schofield Wk, SE3
off Dornberg Cl 104 EH80
Scholars Rd, E4 . . . . .47 EC46
SW12 . . . . .121 DJ88
Scholars Wk, Ger.Cr. (Chal.St.P.)
SL9 . . . . .36 AY51
Scholars Way, Amer. HP6 . . .5 AT38
Scholefield Rd, N19 . . . . . .65 DK60
Schonfeld Sq, N16 . . . . . . .66 DR61
Schoolbank Rd, SE10 . . . .205 K8
Schoolbell Ms, E3
off Arbery Rd 85 DY68
School Cres, Dart. (Cray.) DA1 .107 FF84
Schoolfield Rd, Grays RM20 .108 FU79
School Grn La, Epp. (N.Wld.Bas.)
CM16 . . . . .19 FC25
School Hill, Red. RH1 . . . .185 DJ128
Schoolhouse Gdns, Loug. IG10 .33 EP42
Schoolhouse La, E1 . . . . . .85 DX73
School Ho La, Tedd. TW11 . .117 CH94
School La, SE23 . . . . .122 DV89
Addlestone KT15 . . . . . .152 BG105
Bushey WD23 . . . . .40 CB45
Caterham CR3 . . . . . . .186 DT126
Chalfont St. Giles HP8 . . .36 AV47
Chigwell IG7 . . . . .49 ET49
Dartford (Bean) DA2 . . .129 FW90
Dartford (Hort.Kir.) DA4 .148 FQ98
Egham TW20 . . . . .113 BA92
Gerrards Cross (Chal.St.P.)
SL9 . . . . .36 AX54
Kingston upon Thames KT1
off School Rd 137 CJ95
Leatherhead (Fetch.) KT22 .171 CD122
Longfield DA3 . . . . .149 FT100
Pinner HA5 . . . . .60 BY56
St. Albans (Brick.Wd.) AL2 . .8 CA31
Sevenoaks (Seal) TN15 . .191 FM121
Shepperton TW17 . . . . .135 BP100
Slough SL2 . . . . .74 AT73
Slough (Stoke P.) SL2 . . .74 AV67
Surbiton KT6 . . . . .138 CN102
Swanley BR8 . . . . .147 FH95
Tadworth KT20
off Chequers La 183 CU125
Welling DA16 . . . . .106 EV83
Woking (Ockham) GU23 .169 BP122
School Mead, Abb.L. WD5 . . .7 BS32
School Pas, Kings.T. KT1 . .138 CM96
Southall UB1 . . . . .78 BZ74
School Rd, E12 off Sixth Av . .69 EM63
NW10 . . . . .80 CR70
Ashford TW15 . . . . .115 BR93
Chislehurst BR7 . . . . . .145 EQ95
Dagenham RM10 . . . . . . .89 FA67
East Molesey KT8 . . . . .137 CD98
Hampton (Hmptn.H.) TW12 .116 CC93
Hounslow TW3 . . . . . . .96 CC83
Kingston upon Thames KT1 .137 CJ95
Ongar CM5 . . . . .19 FG32
Potters Bar EN6 . . . . . . .12 DC30
West Drayton UB7 . . . . . .94 BK79
School Rd Av, Hmptn. (Hmptn.H.)
TW12 . . . . .116 CC93
School Wk, Slou. SL2
off Grasmere Av 74 AV73
Sunbury-on-Thames TW16 .135 BT98
Schoolway, N12 . . . . .44 DD51
School Way, N12 off High Rd . .44 DD50
Dagenham RM8 . . . . . . .70 EW62
Schooner Cl, E14 . . . . . . .204 F7
SE16 . . . . .203 H4
Barking IG11 . . . . .88 EV69
Schooner Ct, Dart. DA2 . . .108 FQ84
Schroder Ct, Egh. (Eng.Grn.)
TW20 . . . . .112 AV92
Schubert Rd, SW15 . . . . . .119 CZ85
Borehamwood (Elstree)
WD6 . . . . .25 CK44
★ Science Mus, SW7 . . . . .198 A7
Scilla Ct, Grays RM17 . . . .110 GD79
Sclater St, E1 . . . . .197 P4

Scoble Pl, N16 off Amhurst Rd .66 DT63
Scoles Cres, SW2 . . . . . . .121 DN88
Scope Way, Kings.T. KT1 . .138 CL98
Scoresby St, SE1 . . . . . . .200 F3
Scorton Av, Grnf. UB6 . . . . .79 CG68
Scotch Common, W13 . . . . .79 CG71
Scoter Cl, Wdf.Grn. IG8
off Mallards Rd 48 EH52
Scot Gro, Pnr. HA5 . . . . . . .40 BX52
Scotia Rd, SW2 . . . . .121 DN87
Scotland Br Rd, Add. (New Haw)
KT15 . . . . .152 BG111
Scotland Grn, N17 . . . . . . .46 DT54
Scotland Grn Rd, Enf. EN3 . .31 DX43
Scotland Grn Rd N, Enf. EN3 .31 DX42
Scotland Pl, SW1 . . . . . . .199 P2
Scotland Rd, Buck.H. IG9 . . .48 EJ46
Scotney Cl, Orp. BR6 . . . . .163 EN105
Scotney Wk, Horn. RM12
off Bonington Rd 72 FK64
Scotscraig, Rad. WD7 . . . . .25 CF35
Scotshall La, Warl. CR6 . . .161 EC114
Scots Hill, Rick. (Crox.Grn.)
WD3 . . . . .22 BM44
Scots Hill Cl, Rick. WD3
off Scots Hill 22 BM44
Scotsmill La, Rick. (Crox.Grn.)
WD3 . . . . .22 BM44
Scotswood St, EC1 . . . . . .196 E4
Scotswood Wk, N17 . . . . . .46 DU52
Scott Cl, SW16 . . . . .141 DM95
Epsom KT19 . . . . .156 CQ106
West Drayton UB7 . . . . . .94 BM77
Scott Ct, W3
off Petersfield Rd 98 CQ75
Scott Cres, Erith DA8
off Cloudesley Rd 107 FF81
Harrow HA2 . . . . .60 CB60
Scott Ellis Gdns, NW8 . . . . .82 DD69
Scottes La, Dag. RM8
off Valence Av 70 EX60
Scott Fm Cl, T.Ditt. KT7 . .137 CH102
Scott Gdns, Houns. TW5 . . .96 BX80
Scott Ho, N18 . . . . .46 DU50
Scott Lidgett Cres, SE16 . .202 B5
Scott Rd, Grav. DA12 . . . .131 GK92
Grays RM16 . . . . .111 GG77
Scott Russell Pl, E14 . . . . .204 B10
Scotts Av, Brom. BR2 . . . .143 ED96
Sunbury-on-Thames TW16 .115 BS94
Scotts Cl, Horn. RM12
off Rye Cl 72 FJ64
Staines TW19 . . . . .114 BK88
Scotts Dr, Hmptn. TW12 . .116 CB94
Scotts Fm Rd, Epsom KT19 .156 CQ107
Scotts La, Brom. BR2 . . . .143 ED97
Walton-on-Thames KT12 .154 BX105
Scotts Rd, E10 . . . . .67 EC60
W12 . . . . .99 CV75
Bromley BR1 . . . . .124 EG94
Southall UB2 . . . . .96 BW76
Scott St, E1 . . . . .84 DV70
Scotts Way, Sev. TN13 . . . .190 FE122
Sunbury-on-Thames TW16 .115 BS93
Scottswood Cl, Bushey WD23
off Scottswood Rd 24 BY40
Scottswood Rd, Bushey WD23 .24 BY40
Scott's Yd, EC4 . . . . .197 K10
Scott Trimmer Way, Houns.
TW3 . . . . .96 BY82
Scottwell Dr, NW9 . . . . . . .63 CT67
Scoulding Rd, E16 . . . . . . .86 EF72
Scouler St, E14 . . . . .204 F1
Scout App, NW10 . . . . . . .62 CS63
Scout La, SW4 off Old Town .101 DJ83
Scout Way, NW7 . . . . .42 CR49
Scovell Cres, SE1 . . . . . . .201 H5
Scovell Rd, SE1 . . . . .201 H5
Scratchers La, Long. (Fawk.Grn.)
DA3 . . . . .149 FR103
Scrattons Ter, Bark. IG11 . . .88 EX68
Scriven St, E8 . . . . .84 DT67
Scrooby St, SE6 . . . . .123 EB86
Scrubbitts Pk Rd, Rad. WD7 .25 CG35
Scrubbitts Sq, Rad. WD7
off The Dell 25 CG36
Scrubs La, NW10 . . . . .81 CU69
W10 . . . . .81 CU69
Scrutton Cl, SW12 . . . . . .121 DK87
Scrutton St, EC2 . . . . .197 M5
Scudamore La, NW9 . . . . . .62 CQ55
Scudders Hill, Long. (Fawk.Grn.)
DA3 . . . . .149 FV100
Scylla Cres, Houns. (Hthrw.Air.)
TW6 . . . . .115 BP87
Scylla Pl, Wok. (St. John's) GU21
off Church St 166 AU119
Scylla Rd, SE15 . . . . .102 DV83
Hounslow (Hthrw.Air.) TW6 .115 BP86
Seaborough Rd, Grays RM16 .111 GJ76
Seabright St, E2
off Bethnal Grn Rd 84 DV69
Seabrook Dr, W.Wick. BR4 . .144 EE103
Seabrooke Ri, Grays RM17 .110 GB79
Seabrook Gdns, Rom. RM7 . .70 FA59
Seabrook Rd, Dag. RM8 . . . .70 EX62
Kings Langley WD4 . . . . . .7 BR27
Seaburn Cl, Rain. RM13 . . . .89 FE68
Seacole Cl, W3 . . . . .80 CR71
Seacourt Rd, SE2 . . . . . . .106 EX75
Slough SL3 . . . . .93 BB77
Seacroft Gdns, Wat. WD19 . .40 BX48
Seafield Rd, N11 . . . . .45 DK49
Seaford Cl, Ruis. HA4 . . . . .59 BR61
Seaford Rd, E17 . . . . .67 EB55
N15 . . . . .66 DR57
W13 . . . . .79 CH74
Enfield EN1 . . . . .30 DS42
Hounslow (Hthrw.Air.) TW6 .114 BK85
Seaford St, WC1 . . . . .196 A3
Seaforth Av, N.Mal. KT3 . . .139 CV99
Seaforth Cl, Rom. RM1 . . . .51 FE52
Seaforth Cres, N5 . . . . . . .66 DQ64

Seaforth Dr, Wal.Cr. EN8 . . .15 DX34
Seaforth Gdns, N21 . . . . . .45 DM45
Epsom KT19 . . . . .157 CT105
Woodford Green IG8 . . . . .48 EJ50
Seaforth Pl, SW1
off Buckingham Gate 101 DJ76
Seagrave Rd, SW6 . . . . . .100 DA78
Seagry Rd, E11 . . . . .68 EG58
Seagull Cl, Bark. IG11 . . . . .88 EU69
SEAL, Sev. 191 FN121
Sealand Rd, Houns. (Hthrw.Air.)
TW6 . . . . .114 BN86
Sealand Wk, Nthlt. UB5
off Wayfarer Rd 78 BY69
Seal Dr, Sev. (Seal) TN15 . .191 FM121
Seal Hollow Rd, Sev. TN13,
TN15 . . . . .191 FJ124
Seal Rd, Sev. TN14, TN15 . .191 FJ121
Seal St, E8 . . . . .66 DT63
Seaman Cl, St.Alb. (Park St.)
AL2 . . . . .9 CD25
Searches La, Abb.L. (Bedmond)
WD5 . . . . .7 BV28
Searchwood Rd, Warl. CR6 .176 DV118
Searle Rd, N4 off Evershot Rd .65 DM60
Searles Cl, SW11 . . . . . . .100 DE80
Searles Dr, E6 . . . . .87 EP71
Searles Rd, SE1 . . . . .201 L8
Sears St, SE5 . . . . .102 DR80
Seasprite Cl, Nthlt. UB5 . . . .78 BX69
Seaton Av, Ilf. IG3 . . . . . . .69 ES64
Seaton Cl, E13
off New Barn St 86 EH70
SE11 . . . . .200 E10
SW15 . . . . .99 CV88
Twickenham TW2 . . . . . .117 CD86
Seaton Dr, Ashf. TW15 . . . .114 BL89
Seaton Gdns, Ruis. HA4 . . . .59 BU62
Seaton Pt, E5 . . . . .66 DV63
Seaton Rd, Dart. DA1 . . . . .127 FG87
Hayes UB3 . . . . .95 BR77
Mitcham CR4 . . . . .140 DE96
St. Albans (Lon.Col.) AL2 . .9 CK26
Twickenham TW2 . . . . . .116 CC86
Welling DA16 . . . . .106 EW80
Wembley HA0 . . . . .80 CL68
Seaton Sq, NW7
off Bittacy Hill 43 CY52
Seaton St, N18 . . . . .46 DU50
Sebastian Av, Brwd. CM15 . .55 GA44
Sebastian St, EC1 . . . . . . .196 G3
Sebastopol Rd, N9 . . . . . . .46 DU49
Sebbon St, N1 . . . . .83 DP66
Sebergham Gro, NW7 . . . . .43 CU52
Sebert Rd, E7 . . . . .68 EH64
Sebright Pas, E2
off Hackney Rd 84 DU68
Sebright Rd, Barn. EN5 . . . .27 CX40
Secker Cres, Har. HA3 . . . . .40 CC53
Secker St, SE1 . . . . .200 D3
Second Av, E12 . . . . .68 EL63
E13 . . . . .86 EG69
E17 . . . . .67 EA57
N18 . . . . .46 DW49
NW4 . . . . .63 CX56
SW14 . . . . .98 CS83
W3 . . . . .81 CT74
W10 . . . . .81 CY70
Dagenham RM10 . . . . . . .89 FB67
Enfield EN1 . . . . .30 DT43
Grays RM20 . . . . .109 FU79
Hayes UB3 . . . . .77 BT74
Romford RM6 . . . . .70 EW57
Waltham Abbey EN9 off Breach
Barn Mobile Home Pk . . .16 EH30
Walton-on-Thames KT12 .135 BV100
Watford WD25 . . . . .24 BX35
Wembley HA9 . . . . .61 CK61
Second Cl, W.Mol. KT8 . . . .136 CC98
Second Cross Rd, Twick. TW2 .117 CE89
Second Way, Wem. HA9 . . . .62 CP63
Sedan Way, SE17 . . . . . . .201 M10
Sedcombe Cl, Sid. DA14
off Knoll Rd 126 EV91
Sedcote Rd, Enf. EN3 . . . . .30 DW43
Sedding St, SW1 . . . . .198 F8
Seddon Highwalk, EC2
off Beech St 84 DQ71
Seddon Ho, EC2
off The Barbican 84 DQ71
Seddon Rd, Mord. SM4 . . . .140 DD99
Seddon St, WC1 . . . . .196 C3
Sedgebrook Rd, SE3 . . . . .104 EK83
Sedgecombe Av, Har. HA3 . .61 CJ57
Sedge Ct, Grays RM17 . . . .110 GE80
Sedgefield Cl, Rom. RM3 . . .52 FM49
Sedgefield Cres, Rom. RM3 . .52 FM49
Sedgeford Rd, W12 . . . . . . .81 CT74
Sedgehill Rd, SE6 . . . . . . .123 EA91
Sedgemere Av, N2 . . . . . . .64 DC55
Sedgemere Rd, SE2 . . . . . .106 EW76
Sedgemoor Dr, Dag. RM10 . .70 FA63
Sedge Rd, N17 . . . . .46 DW52
Sedgeway, SE6 . . . . .124 EF88
Sedgewick Av, Uxb. UB10 . .77 BP66
Sedgewood Cl, Brom. BR2 .144 EF101
Sedgmoor Pl, SE5 . . . . . . .102 DS80
Sedgwick Rd, E10 . . . . . . .67 EC61
Sedgwick St, E9 . . . . .67 DX64
Sedleigh Rd, SW18 . . . . . .119 CZ86
Sedlescombe Rd, SW6 . . . . .99 CZ79
Sedley, Grav. (Sthflt.) DA13 .130 GA93
Sedley Cl, Enf. EN1 . . . . . .30 DV38
Sedley Gro, Uxb. (Hare.) UB9 .58 BJ56
Sedley Pl, W1 . . . . .195 H9
Sedley Ri, Loug. IG10 . . . . .33 EM40
Sedum Cl, NW9 . . . . .62 CP57
Seeley Dr, SE21 . . . . .122 DS91
Seelig Av, NW9 . . . . .63 CU59
Seely Rd, SW17 . . . . .120 DG93
Seer Grn La, Beac. (Jordans)
HP9 . . . . .36 AS52
Seething La, EC3 . . . . .201 N1
Seething Wells La, Surb. KT6 .137 CJ100

Sef - She

Sefton Av, NW7 . . . . .42 CR50
Harrow HA3 . . . . .41 CD53
Sefton Cl, Orp. BR5 . . . . .145 ET98
Slough (Stoke P.) SL2 . . . . .74 AT66
Sefton Paddock, Slou. (Stoke P.)
SL2 . . . . .74 AU66
Sefton Pk, Slou. (Stoke P.) SL2 .74 AU66
Sefton Rd, Croy. CR0 . . . . . .142 DU102
Epsom KT19 . . . . .156 CR110
Orpington BR5 . . . . .145 ET98
Sefton St, SW15 . . . . .99 CW82
Sefton Way, Uxb. UB8 . . . . . .76 BJ72
Segal Cl, SE23 . . . . .123 DY87
Segrave Cl, W.Mol. KT13 . . . .152 BN108
Sekforde St, EC1 . . . . .196 F5
Sekhon Ter, Felt. TW13 . . . . .116 CA90
Selah Dr, Swan. BR8 . . . . . . .147 FC95
Selan Gdns, Hayes UB4 . . . . .77 BV71
Selbie Av, NW10 . . . . .63 CT64
Selborne Av, E12 off Walton Rd .69 EN63
Bexley DA5 . . . . .126 EY88
Selborne Gdns, NW4 . . . . . . .63 CU56
Greenford UB6 . . . . .79 CG67
Selborne Rd, E17 . . . . .67 DZ56
N14 . . . . .45 DL48
N22 . . . . .45 DM53
SE5 off Denmark Hill 102 DR82
Croydon CR0 . . . . .142 DS104
Ilford IG1 . . . . .69 EN61
New Malden KT3 . . . . . . .138 CS96
Sidcup DA14 . . . . .126 EV91
Selbourne Av, E17 . . . . .67 DZ56
Addlestone (New Haw)
KT15 . . . . .152 BH110
Surbiton KT6 . . . . .138 CM103
Selbourne Cl, Add. (New Haw)
KT15 . . . . .152 BH109
Selbourne Sq, Gdse. RH9 . .186 DW130
Selbourne Wk, E17 off Selbourne
Wk Shop Cen 67 DZ56
Selbourne Wk Shop Cen, E17 .67 DZ56
Selby Chase, Ruis. HA4 . . . . .59 BV61
Selby Cl, E6 off Linton Gdns .86 EL71
Chessington KT9 . . . . . . .156 CL108
Chislehurst BR7 . . . . .125 EN93
Selby Gdns, Sthl. UB1 . . . . . .78 CA70
Selby Grn, Cars. SM5 . . . . . .140 DE101
Selby Rd, E11 . . . . .68 EE62
E13 . . . . .86 EH71
N17 . . . . .46 DS51
SE20 . . . . .142 DU96
W5 . . . . .79 CH70
Ashford TW15 . . . . .115 BQ93
Carshalton SM5 . . . . .140 DE101
Selby St, E1 . . . . .84 DU70
Selby Wk, Wok. GU21
off Wyndham Rd 166 AV118
Selcroft Rd, Pur. CR8 . . . . . .159 DP112
Selden Rd, SE15 . . . . .102 DW82
Selden Wk, N7 off Durham Rd .65 DM61
★ Selfridges, W1 . . . . .194 G9
SELHURST, SE25 . . . . .142 DS100
⇌ Selhurst 142 DS99
Selhurst Cl, SW19 . . . . .119 CX88
Woking GU21 . . . . .167 AZ115
Selhurst New Rd, SE25 . . . . .142 DS100
Selhurst Pl, SE25 . . . . .142 DS100
Selhurst Rd, N9 . . . . .46 DR48
SE25 . . . . .142 DS99
Selinas La, Dag. RM8 . . . . . . .70 EY59
Selkirk Dr, Erith DA8 . . . . . .107 FE81
Selkirk Rd, SW17 . . . . .120 DE91
Twickenham TW2 . . . . . . .116 CC89
Sell Cl, Wal.Cr. (Chsht.) EN7
off Gladding Rd 13 DP26
Sellers Cl, Borwd. WD6 . . . . . .26 CQ39
Sellers Hall Cl, N3 . . . . .44 DA52
Sellincourt Rd, SW17 . . . . . .120 DE92
Sellindge Cl, Beck. BR3 . . . . .123 DZ94
Sellon Ms, SE11 . . . . .200 C9
Sellons Av, NW10 . . . . .81 CT67
Sellwood Dr, Barn. EN5 . . . . .27 CX43
Sellwood St, SW2
off Tulse Hill 121 DN87
SELSDON, S.Croy. 160 DW110
Selsdon Av, S.Croy. CR2
off Selsdon Rd 160 DR107
Selsdon Cl, Rom. RM5 . . . . . .51 FC53
Surbiton KT6 . . . . .138 CL99
Selsdon Cres, S.Croy. CR2 . .160 DW109
Selsdon Pk Rd, S.Croy. CR2 .161 DX109
Selsdon Rd, E11 . . . . .68 EG59
E13 . . . . .86 EJ67
NW2 . . . . .63 CT61
SE27 . . . . .121 DP90
Addlestone (New Haw)
KT15 . . . . .152 BG111
South Croydon CR2 . . . . . .160 DR106
Selsdon Rd Ind Est, S.Croy. CR2
off Selsdon Rd 160 DR107
Selsdon Way, E14 . . . . .204 C7
Selsea Pl, N16
off Crossway 66 DS64
Selsey Cres, Well. DA16 . . . . .106 EX81
Selsey St, E14 . . . . .85 EA71
Selvage La, NW7 . . . . .42 CR50
Selway Cl, Pnr. HA5 . . . . .59 BV56
Selwood Cl, Stai. (Stanw.)
TW19 . . . . .114 BJ86
Selwood Gdns, Stai. (Stanw.)
TW19 . . . . .114 BJ86
Selwood Pl, SW7 . . . . .100 DD78
Selwood Rd, Brwd. CM14 . . . .54 FT98
Chessington KT9 . . . . . . .155 CK105
Croydon CR0 . . . . .142 DU102
Sutton SM3 . . . . .139 CZ102
Woking GU22 . . . . .167 BB120
Selwood Ter, SW7
off Onslow Gdns 100 DD78
Selworthy Cl, E11 . . . . .68 EG57
Selworthy Ho, SW11 . . . . . . .100 DD81
Selworthy Rd, SE6 . . . . .123 DZ90
Selwyn Av, E4 . . . . .47 EC51
Ilford IG3 . . . . .69 ES58

Selwyn Av, Rich. TW9 . . . . . . .98 CL83
Selwyn Cl, Houns. TW4 . . . . .96 BY84
Selwyn Ct, SE3 . . . . .104 EE83
Edgware HA8
off Camrose Av 42 CP52
Selwyn Cres, Well. DA16 . . . .106 EV84
Selwyn Pl, Orp. BR5 . . . . . . .146 EV97
Selwyn Rd, E3 . . . . .85 DZ68
E13 . . . . .86 EH67
NW10 . . . . .80 CR66
New Malden KT3 . . . . . . .138 CR99
Tilbury RM18 off Dock Rd .111 GF82
Semley Pl, SW1 . . . . .198 G9
Semley Rd, SW16 . . . . .141 DL96
Semper Cl, Wok. (Knap.)
GU21 . . . . .166 AS117
Semper Rd, Grays RM16 . . . .111 GJ75
Senate St, SE15 . . . . .102 DW82
Senator Wk, SE28
off Broadwater Rd 105 ER76
SEND, Wok. 167 BC124
Sendall Ct, SW11 . . . . .100 DD83
Send Barns La, Wok. (Send)
GU23 . . . . .167 BD124
Send Cl, Wok. (Send) GU23 . .167 BC123
SEND MARSH, Wok. 167 BF124
Send Marsh Rd, Wok. (Ripley)
GU23 . . . . .167 BF123
Send Par Cl, Wok. (Send) GU23
off Send Rd 167 BC123
Send Rd, Wok. (Send) GU23 .167 BB122
Seneca Rd, Th.Hth. CR7 . . . .142 DQ98
Senga Rd, Wall. SM6 . . . . . .140 DG102
Senhouse Rd, Sutt. SM3 . . . .139 CX104
Senior St, W2 . . . . .82 DB71
Senlac Rd, SE12 . . . . .124 EH88
Sennen Rd, Enf. EN1 . . . . . . .46 DT45
Sennen Wk, SE9 . . . . .124 EL90
Senrab St, E1 . . . . .85 DX72
Sentinel Cl, Nthlt. UB5 . . . . . .78 BY70
Sentinel Sq, NW4 . . . . .63 CW56
Sentis Ct, Nthwd. HA6
off Carew Rd 39 BS51
September Way, Stan. HA7 . . .41 CH51
Sequoia Cl, Bushey (Bushey Hth.)
WD23 off Giant Tree Hill . . .41 CD46
Sequoia Gdns, Orp. BR6 . . . .145 ET101
Sequoia Pk, Pnr. HA5 . . . . . . .40 CB51
Serbin Cl, E10 . . . . .67 EC59
Serenaders Rd, SW9 . . . . . . .101 DN82
Sergeants Grn La, Wal.Abb.
EN9 . . . . .16 EJ33
Sergeants Pl, Cat. CR3
off Coulsdon Rd 176 DQ122
Sergehill La, Abb.L. (Bedmond)
WD5 . . . . .7 BT27
Serjeants Inn, EC4 . . . . .196 E9
Serle St, WC2 . . . . .196 C8
Sermed Ct, Slou. SL2 . . . . . . .74 AW74
Sermon Dr, Swan. BR8 . . . . .147 FC97
Sermon La, EC4 . . . . .197 H9
★ Serpentine, The, W2 . . . . .198 B3
Serpentine Ct, Sev. TN13 . . . .191 FK122
★ Serpentine Gall, W2 . . . . .198 A3
Serpentine Grn, Red. RH1
off Malmstone Av 185 DK129
Serpentine Rd, W2 . . . . .198 D3
Sevenoaks TN13 . . . . .191 FJ123
Service Rd, The, Pot.B. EN6 . . .12 DA32
Serviden Dr, Brom. BR1 . . . .144 EK95
Setchell Rd, SE1 . . . . .201 P8
Setchell Way, SE1 . . . . .201 P8
Seth St, SE16 . . . . .202 G5
Seton Gdns, Dag. RM9 . . . . . .88 EW66
Settle Pt, E13 off London Rd .86 EG68
Settle Rd, E13 off London Rd .86 EG68
Romford RM3 . . . . .52 FN49
Settles St, E1 . . . . .84 DU71
Settrington Rd, SW6 . . . . . . .100 DB82
Seven Acres, Cars. SM5 . . . .140 DE103
Northwood HA6 . . . . .39 BU51
Swanley BR8 . . . . .147 FD100
Seven Arches App, Wey. KT13 .152 BM108
Seven Arches Rd, Brwd. CM14 .54 FX48
Seven Hills Cl, Walt. KT12 . . .153 BS111
Seven Hills Rd, Cob. KT11 . . .153 BS111
Iver SL0 . . . . .75 BC65
Walton-on-Thames KT12 . .153 BS109
Seven Hills Rd S, Cob. KT11 .153 BS113
SEVEN KINGS, Ilf. 69 ES59
⇌ Seven Kings 69 ES60
Seven Kings Rd, Ilf. IG3 . . . . .69 ES61
SEVENOAKS 191 FJ125
⇌ Sevenoaks 190 FG124
Sevenoaks Business Cen, Sev.
TN14 . . . . .191 FJ121
Sevenoaks Bypass, Sev.TN14 .190 FC123
Sevenoaks Cl, Bexh. DA7 . . .107 FC84
Romford RM3 . . . . .52 FJ49
Sutton SM2 . . . . .158 DA110
SEVENOAKS COMMON, Sev. .191 FH129
Sevenoaks Ho, SE25 . . . . . . .142 DU97
Sevenoaks Hosp, Sev.
TN13 . . . . .191 FJ121
★ Sevenoaks Mus, Sev.
TN13 . . . . .191 FJ125
Sevenoaks Rd, SE4 . . . . .123 DY86
Orpington BR6 . . . . .163 ET106
Orpington (Grn.St.Grn.)
BR6 . . . . .163 ET108
Sevenoaks (Otford) TN14 . .181 FH116
Sevenoaks Way, Orp. BR5 . . .126 EW94
Sidcup DA14 . . . . .126 EW94
⇌ Seven Sisters 66 DS57
⊖ Seven Sisters 66 DS57
Seven Sisters Rd, N4 . . . . . . .65 DM62
N7 . . . . .65 DM62
N15 . . . . .66 DQ59
Seven Stars Cor, W12
off Goldhawk Rd 99 CU76
Seventh Av, E12 . . . . .69 EM63
Hayes UB3 . . . . .77 BU74
Severnake Cl, E14 . . . . .204 A8
Severn Av, Rom. RM2 . . . . . . .71 FH55
Severn Cres, Slou. SL3 . . . . . .93 BB78
Severn Dr, Enf. EN1 . . . . .30 DU38

Severn Dr, Esher KT10 . . . . .137 CG103
Upminster RM14 . . . . .73 FR58
Walton-on-Thames KT12 . .136 BX103
Severn Rd, S.Ock. (Aveley)
RM15 . . . . .90 FQ72
Severns Fld, Epp. CM16 . . . . .18 EU29
Severnvale, St.Alb. (Lon.Col.)
AL2 off Thamesdale 10 CM27
Severn Way, NW10 . . . . .63 CT64
Watford WD25 . . . . .8 BW34
Severus Rd, SW11 . . . . .100 DE84
Seville Ms, N1 . . . . .84 DS66
Seville St, SW1 . . . . .198 E5
Sevington Rd, NW4 . . . . .63 CV58
Sevington St, W9 . . . . .82 DB70
Seward Rd, W7 . . . . .97 CG75
Beckenham BR3 . . . . .143 DX96
SEWARDSTONE, E4 . . . . .31 EC39
SEWARDSTONEBURY, E4 . . .32 EE42
Sewardstone Gdns, E4 . . . . . .31 EB43
Sewardstone Grn, E4 . . . . . . .32 EE42
Sewardstone Rd, E2 . . . . .84 DW68
E4 . . . . .47 EB45
Waltham Abbey EN9 . . . . . .31 EC38
Sewardstone Roundabout,
Wal.Abb. EN9 . . . . .31 EC35
Sewardstone St, Wal.Abb. EN9 .15 EC34
Seward St, EC1 . . . . .196 G4
Sewdley St, E5 . . . . .67 DX62
Sewell Cl, Grays (Chaff.Hun.)
RM16 . . . . .109 FW78
Sewell Rd, SE2 . . . . .106 EU76
Sewell St, E13 . . . . .86 EG69
Sextant Av, E14 . . . . .204 F8
Sexton Cl, Rain. RM13
off Blake Cl 89 FF67
Waltham Cross (Chsht.) EN7
off Shambrook Rd 14 DQ25
Sexton Rd, Til. RM18 . . . . . .111 GF81
Seymer Rd, Rom. RM1 . . . . . .71 FD55
Seymour Av, N17 . . . . .46 DU54
Caterham CR3 . . . . .176 DQ123
Epsom KT17 . . . . .157 CV109
Morden SM4 . . . . .139 CX101
Seymour Cl, E.Mol. KT8 . . . .136 CC99
Loughton IG10 . . . . .32 EL44
Pinner HA5 . . . . .40 BZ53
Seymour Ct, E4 . . . . .48 EF47
Seymour Dr, Brom. BR2 . . . .145 EM102
Seymour Gdns, SE4 . . . . . . .103 DY83
Feltham TW13 . . . . .116 BW91
Ilford IG1 . . . . .69 EM60
Ruislip HA4 . . . . .60 BX60
Surbiton KT5 . . . . .138 CM99
Twickenham TW1 . . . . . . .117 CH87
Seymour Ms, W1 . . . . .194 F8
Seymour Pl, SE25 . . . . .142 DV98
W1 . . . . .194 D7
Seymour Rd, E4 . . . . .47 EB46
E6 . . . . .86 EK68
E10 . . . . .67 DZ60
N3 . . . . .44 DB52
N8 . . . . .65 DN57
N9 . . . . .46 DV47
SW18 . . . . .119 CZ87
SW19 . . . . .119 CX89
W4 . . . . .98 CQ77
Carshalton SM5 . . . . .158 DG106
Chalfont St. Giles HP8 . . . .36 AW49
East Molesey KT8 . . . . . .136 CC99
Gravesend (Nthflt.) DA11 .131 GF88
Hampton (Hmptn.H.) TW12 .116 CC92
Kingston upon Thames KT1 .137 CK95
Mitcham CR4 . . . . .140 DG101
Tilbury RM18 . . . . .111 GF81
Seymours, The, Loug. IG10 . . .33 EN39
Seymour St, W1 . . . . .194 D9
W2 . . . . .194 D9
Seymour Ter, SE20 . . . . .142 DV95
Seymour Vil, SE20 . . . . .142 DV95
Seymour Wk, SW10 . . . . .100 DC79
Swanscombe DA10 . . . . . .130 FY87
Seymour Way, Sun. TW16 . . .115 BS93
Seyssel St, E14 . . . . .204 E8
Shaa Rd, W3 . . . . .80 CR73
Shacklands Rd, Sev. (Bad.Mt.)
TN14 . . . . .165 FB110
Shackleford Rd, Wok. GU22 . .167 BA121
Shacklegate La, Tedd. TW11 .117 CE91
Shackleton Cl, SE23
off Featherstone Av 122 DV89
Shackleton Ct, E14
off Maritime Quay 103 EA78
W12 . . . . .99 CV75
Shackleton Rd, Slou. SL1 . . . .74 AT73
Southall UB1 . . . . .78 BZ73
Shackleton Way, Abb.L. WD5
off Lysander Way 7 BU32
SHACKLEWELL, N16 . . . . . . .66 DT63
Shacklewell Grn, E8 . . . . .66 DT63
Shacklewell La, E8 . . . . .66 DT64
Shacklewell Rd, N16 . . . . .66 DT63
Shacklewell Row, E8 . . . . .66 DT63
Shacklewell St, E2 . . . . .84 DT70
Shadbolt Av, E4 . . . . .47 DY50
Shadbolt Cl, Wor.Pk. KT4 . . .157 CT103
Shad Thames, SE1 . . . . .201 P3
SHADWELL, E1 . . . . .202 F1
⊖ Shadwell 84 DW73
DLR Shadwell 84 DW73
Shadwell Ct, Nthlt. UB5
off Shadwell Dr 78 BZ68
Shadwell Dr, Nthlt. UB5 . . . . .78 BZ69
Shadwell Gdns Est, E1
off Martha St 84 DW72
Shadwell Pierhead, E1 . . . . .202 P2
Shadwell Pl, E1 off Sutton St .84 DW73
Shady Bush Cl, Bushey WD23
off Richfield Rd 40 CC45
Shady La, Wat. WD17 . . . . . . .23 BV40
Shaef Way, Tedd. TW11 . . . . .117 CG94
Shafter Rd, Dag. RM10 . . . . . .89 FC65
Shaftesbury, Loug. IG10 . . . . .32 EK41
Shaftesbury Av, W1 . . . . .195 M10
WC2 . . . . .195 M10
Barnet EN5 . . . . .28 DC42
Enfield EN3 . . . . .31 DX40

Shaftesbury Av, Felt. TW14 . .115 BU86
Harrow HA2 . . . . .60 CB60
Harrow (Kenton) HA3 . . . . .61 CK58
Southall UB2 . . . . .96 CA77
Shaftesbury Circle, Har. HA2
off Shaftesbury Av 60 CC60
Shaftesbury Ct, N1
off Shaftesbury St 84 DR68
Shaftesbury Cres, Stai. TW18 .114 BK94
Shaftesbury Gdns, NW10 . . . .80 CS70
Shaftesbury La, Dart. DA1 . . .108 FP84
Shaftesbury Ms, SW4 off Clapham
Common S Side 121 DJ85
W8 off Stratford Rd 100 DA76
Shaftesbury Pt, E13 off High St .86 EH68
Shaftesbury Rd, E4 . . . . .47 ED46
E7 . . . . .86 EJ66
E10 . . . . .67 EA60
E17 . . . . .67 EB58
N18 . . . . .46 DS51
N19 . . . . .65 DL60
Beckenham BR3 . . . . .143 DZ96
Carshalton SM5 . . . . .140 DD101
Epping CM16 . . . . .17 ET29
Richmond TW9 . . . . .98 CL83
Romford RM1 . . . . .71 FF58
Watford WD17 . . . . .24 BW41
Woking GU22 . . . . .167 BA117
Shaftesburys, The, Bark. IG11 .87 EQ67
Shaftesbury St, N1 . . . . .197 J1
Shaftesbury Way, Kings L.WD4 .7 BQ28
Twickenham TW2 . . . . . . .117 CD90
Shaftesbury Waye, Hayes UB4 .77 BV71
Shafto Ms, SW1 . . . . .198 D7
Shafton Rd, E9 . . . . .85 DX67
Shaggy Calf La, Slou. SL2 . . . .74 AU73
Shakespeare Av, N11 . . . . . . .45 DJ50
NW10 . . . . .80 CR67
Feltham TW14 . . . . .115 BU86
Hayes UB4 . . . . .77 BV70
Tilbury RM18 . . . . .111 GH82
Shakespeare Cres, E12 . . . . . .87 EM65
NW10 . . . . .80 CR67
Shakespeare Dr, Har. HA3 . . . .62 CM58
Shakespeare Gdns, N2 . . . . . .64 DF56
Shakespeare Ho, N14
off High St 45 DK47
Shakespeare Rd, E17 . . . . . . .47 DX54
N3 off Popes Dr 44 DA53
NW7 . . . . .43 CT49
SE24 . . . . .121 DP85
W3 . . . . .80 CQ74
W7 . . . . .79 CF73
Addlestone KT15 . . . . . . .152 BK105
Bexleyheath DA7 . . . . . . .106 EY81
Dartford DA1 . . . . .108 FN84
Romford RM1 . . . . .71 FF58
★ Shakespeare's Globe Thea,
SE1 . . . . .201 H1
Shakespeare Sq, Ilf. IG6 . . . . .49 EQ51
Shakespeare St, Wat. WD24 . .23 BV38
Shakespeare Twr, EC2 . . . . . .197 J6
Shakespeare Way, Felt. TW13 .116 BW91
Shakspeare Ms, N16
off Shakspeare Wk 66 DS63
Shakspeare Wk, N16 . . . . .66 DS63
Shalbourne Sq, E9 . . . . .85 DZ65
Shalcomb St, SW10 . . . . . . .100 DC79
Shalcross Dr, Wal.Cr. (Chsht.)
EN8 . . . . .15 DZ31
Shalden Ho, SW15
off Tunworth Cres 119 CT86
Shaldon Dr, Mord. SM4 . . . . .139 CY99
Ruislip HA4 . . . . .60 BW62
Shaldon Rd, Edg. HA8 . . . . . .42 CM53
Shaldon Way, Walt. KT12 . . .136 BW104
Shale Grn, Red. RH1
off Bletchingley Rd 185 DK129
Shalfleet Dr, W10 . . . . .81 CX73
Shalford Cl, Orp. BR6 . . . . . .163 EQ105
Shalimar Gdns, W3 . . . . .80 CQ73
Shalimar Rd, W3
off Hereford Rd 80 CQ73
Shallons Rd, SE9 . . . . .125 EP91
Shalstone Rd, SW14 . . . . .98 CP83
Shalston Vil, Surb. KT6 . . . . .138 CM100
Shambrook Rd, Wal.Cr. (Chsht.)
EN7 . . . . .13 DP25
Shamrock Cl, Lthd. (Fetch.)
KT22 . . . . .171 CD121
Shamrock Ho, SE26
off Talisman Sq 122 DU91
Shamrock Rd, Croy. CR0 . . . .141 DM100
Gravesend DA12 . . . . . . .131 GL87
Shamrock St, SW4 . . . . .101 DK83
Shamrock Way, N14 . . . . .45 DH46
Shandon Rd, SW4 . . . . .121 DJ86
Shand St, SE1 . . . . .201 M4
Shandy St, E1 . . . . .85 DX71
Shanklin Cl, Wal.Cr. EN7
off Hornbeam Way 14 DT29
Shanklin Gdns, Wat. WD19 . . .40 BW49
Shanklin Rd, N8 . . . . .65 DK57
N15 . . . . .66 DU56
Shanklin Way, SE15
off Pentridge St 102 DT80
Shannon Cl, NW2 . . . . .63 CX62
Southall UB2 . . . . .96 BX78
Shannon Gro, SW9 . . . . .101 DM84
Shannon Pl, NW8 . . . . .82 DE68
off Allitsen Rd
Shannon Way, Beck. BR3 . . . .123 EB93
South Ockendon (Aveley)
RM15 . . . . .90 FQ73
Shantock Hall La, Hem.H. (Bov.)
HP3 . . . . .5 AY29
Shantock La, Hem.H. (Bov.) HP3 .4 AX30
Shap Cres, Cars. SM5 . . . . . .140 DF102
Shapland Way, N13 . . . . .45 DM50
Shapwick Cl, N11
off Friern Barnet Rd 44 DF50
Shardcroft Av, SE24 . . . . . . .121 DP85
Shardeloes Rd, SE14 . . . . . .103 DZ83
Sharland Cl, Th.Hth. CR7
off Dunheved Rd N 141 DN100

Sharland Rd, Grav. DA12 . . . .131 GJ89
Sharman Ct, Sid. DA14 . . . . .126 EU91
Sharnbrooke Cl, Well. DA16 . .106 EW83
Sharney Av, Slou. SL3 . . . . . . .93 BB76
Sharon Cl, Epsom KT19 . . . . .156 CQ113
Leatherhead (Bkhm.) KT23 .170 CA124
Surbiton KT6 . . . . .137 CK102
Sharon Gdns, E9 . . . . .84 DW67
Sharon Rd, W4 . . . . .98 CR78
Enfield EN3 . . . . .31 DY40
Sharpe Cl, W7
off Templeman Rd 79 CF71
Sharpleshall St, NW1 . . . . . . .82 DF66
Sharpness Cl, Hayes UB4 . . . .78 BY71
Sharps La, Ruis. HA4 . . . . . . .59 BR60
Sharp Way, Dart. DA1 . . . . . .108 FM83
Sharratt St, SE15 . . . . .102 DW79
Sharsted St, SE17 . . . . .101 DP78
Sharvel La, Nthlt. UB5 . . . . . .77 BU67
Shavers Pl, SW1 . . . . .199 M1
Shaw Av, Bark. IG11 . . . . .88 EY68
Shawbrooke Rd, SE9 . . . . . . .124 EJ85
Shawbury Rd, SE22 . . . . .122 DT85
Shaw Cl, SE28 . . . . .88 EV74
Bushey (Bushey Hth.) WD23 .41 CE47
Chertsey (Ott.) KT16 . . . . .151 BC107
Epsom KT17 . . . . .157 CT111
Hornchurch RM11 . . . . . . .71 FH60
South Croydon CR2 . . . . . .160 DT112
Waltham Cross (Chsht.) EN8 .14 DW28
Shaw Ct, SW11 . . . . .100 DD83
Windsor SL4 . . . . .112 AU85
Shaw Cres, Brwd. CM13 . . . . .55 GD43
South Croydon CR2 . . . . . .160 DT112
Tilbury RM18 . . . . .111 GH81
Shaw Dr, Walt. KT12 . . . . . . .136 BW101
Shawfield Ct, West Dr. UB7 . . .94 BL76
Shawfield Pk, Brom. BR1 . . . .144 EK96
Shawfield St, SW3 . . . . .100 DE78
Shawford Ct, SW15 . . . . .119 CU87
Shawford Rd, Epsom KT19 . .156 CR107
Shaw Gdns, Bark. IG11 . . . . . .88 EY68
Shawley Cres, Epsom KT18 . .173 CW118
Shawley Way, Epsom KT18 . .173 CV118
Shaw Rd, SE22 . . . . .102 DS84
Bromley BR1 . . . . .124 EF90
Enfield EN3 . . . . .31 DX39
Westerham (Tats.) TN16 . .178 EJ120
Shaws Cotts, SE23 . . . . .123 DY90
Shaw Sq, E17 . . . . .47 DY53
Shaw Way, Wall. SM6 . . . . . .159 DL108
Shaxton Cres, Croy. (New Adgtn.)
CR0 . . . . .161 EC109
Shearing Dr, Cars. SM5
off Stavordale Rd 140 DC101
Shearling Way, N7 . . . . .83 DL65
Shearman Rd, SE3 . . . . .104 EF84
Shears Ct, Sun. TW16
off Staines Rd W 115 BS94
Shearsmith Ho, E1
off Cable St 84 DU73
Shearwater Cl, Bark. IG11 . . . .88 EU69
Shearwater Rd, Sutt. SM1 . . .157 CZ106
Shearwater Way, Hayes UB4 . .78 BX72
Shearwood Cres, Dart. DA1 . .107 FF83
Sheath's La, Lthd. KT22 . . . . .154 CB113
Sheaveshill Av, NW9 . . . . .62 CS56
Sheehy Way, Slou. SL2 . . . . . .74 AV73
Sheen Common Dr, Rich.
TW10 . . . . .98 CN84
Sheen Ct, Rich. TW10 . . . . . . .98 CN84
Sheen Ct Rd, Rich. TW10 . . . .98 CN84
Sheendale Rd, Rich. TW9 . . . .98 CM84
Sheenewood, SE26 . . . . .122 DV92
Sheen Gate Gdns, SW14 . . . .98 CQ84
Sheen Gro, N1
off Richmond Av 83 DN67
Sheen La, SW14 . . . . .98 CQ83
Sheen Pk, Rich. TW9 . . . . . . .98 CM84
Sheen Rd, Orp. BR5 . . . . . . .145 ET98
Richmond TW9,TW10 . . . .118 CL85
Sheen Way, Wall. SM6 . . . . . .159 DM106
Sheen Wd, SW14 . . . . .118 CQ85
Sheepbarn La, Warl. CR6 . . . .162 EF112
Sheepcot Dr, Wat. WD25 . . . . .8 BW34
Sheepcote Cl, Houns. TW5 . . .95 BU80
Sheepcote Gdns, Uxb. (Denh.)
UB9 . . . . .58 BG58
Sheepcote La, SW11 . . . . . . .100 DF82
Orpington BR5 . . . . .146 EZ99
Swanley BR8 . . . . .146 EZ98
Sheepcote Rd, Har. HA1 . . . . .61 CF58
Sheepcotes Rd, Rom. RM6 . . .70 EX56
Sheepcot La, Wat. WD25 . . . . .7 BV34
Sheephouse Way, N.Mal. KT3 .138 CS101
Sheep La, E8 . . . . .84 DV67
Sheep Wk, Epsom KT17 . . . .172 CR122
Reigate RH2 . . . . .183 CY131
Shepperton TW17 . . . . . . .134 BM101
Sheep Wk, The, Wok. GU22 . .167 BE118
Sheep Wk Ms, SW19 . . . . . . .119 CX93
Sheerness Ms, E16 . . . . .105 EP75
SHEERWATER, Wok. 151 BC113
Sheerwater Av, Add. (Woodham)
KT15 . . . . .151 BE112
Sheerwater Rd, E16 . . . . .86 EK71
Addlestone (Woodham)
KT15 . . . . .151 BE112
West Byfleet KT14 . . . . . .151 BE112
Sheffield Dr, Rom. RM3 . . . . . .52 FN50
Sheffield Gdns, Rom. RM3 . . . .52 FN50
Sheffield Rd, Houns. (Hthrw.Air.)
TW6 off Southern
Perimeter Rd 115 BR85
Sheffield Sq, E3
off Malmesbury Rd 85 DZ69
Sheffield St, WC2 . . . . .196 B9
Sheffield Ter, W8 . . . . .82 DA74
Shefton Ri, Nthwd. HA6 . . . . .39 BU52
Sheila Cl, Rom. RM5 . . . . .51 FB52
Sheila Rd, Rom. RM5 . . . . . . .51 FB52
Sheilings, The, Horn. RM11 . . .72 FM57
Shelbourne Cl, Pnr. HA5 . . . . .60 BZ55
Shelbourne Pl, Beck. BR3 . . .123 DZ94
Shelbourne Rd, N17 . . . . .46 DV54
Shelburne Dr, Houns. TW4
off Hanworth Rd 116 CA86

Shelburne Rd, N7 . . . . .65 DM63
Shelbury Cl, Sid. DA14 . .126 EU90
Shelbury Rd, SE22 . . . . . .122 DV85
Sheldon Av, N6 . . . . .64 DE59
  Ilford IG5 . . . . .49 EP54
Sheldon Cl, SE12 . . . . . . .124 EH85
  SE20 . . . . .142 DV95
  Waltham Cross (Chsht.) EN7 .14 DS26
Sheldon Rd, N18 . . . . .46 DS49
  NW2 . . . . .63 CX63
  Bexleyheath DA7 . . . . . .106 EZ81
  Dagenham RM9 . . . . .88 EY66
Sheldon St, Croy. CR0
  off Wandle Rd 142 DQ104
Sheldrake Cl, E16 . . . . . . .87 EM74
Sheldrake Pl, W8 . . . . .99 CZ75
Sheldrick Cl, SW19 . . . . . .140 DD96
Shelduck Cl, E15 . . . . .68 EE64
Sheldwich Ter, Brom. BR2 . .144 EL100
Shelford Pl, N16 off Stoke
  Newington Ch St 66 DR62
Shelford Ri, SE19 . . . . . . .122 DT94
Shelford Rd, Barn. EN5 . . . .27 CW44
Shelgate Rd, SW11 . . . . . .120 DE85
Shellbank La, Dart. (Bean)
  DA2 . . . . .129 FU93
★ Shell Cen, SE1 . . . . . . .200 C3
Shell Cl, Brom. BR2 . . . . . .145 EM100
Shellduck Cl, NW9
  off Swan Dr 42 CS54
Shell Est, N16 . . . . .66 DS64
Shelley Av, E12 . . . . .86 EL65
  Greenford UB6 . . . . .79 CD69
  Hornchurch RM12 . . . . . . .71 FF61
Shelley Cl, SE15 . . . . .102 DV82
  Banstead SM7 . . . . .173 CX115
  Coulsdon CR5 . . . . .175 DM117
  Edgware HA8 . . . . .42 CN49
  Greenford UB6 . . . . .79 CD69
  Hayes UB4 . . . . .77 BU71
  Northwood HA6 . . . . .39 BT50
  Orpington BR6 . . . . .145 ES104
  Slough SL3 . . . . .93 AZ78
Shelley Cres, Houns. TW5 . .96 BX82
  Southall UB1 . . . . .78 BZ72
Shelley Dr, Well. DA16 . . . .105 ES81
Shelley Gdns, Wem. HA0 . . .61 CJ61
Shelley Gro, Loug. IG10 . . . .33 EM42
Shelley La, Uxb. (Hare.) UB9 .38 BG53
Shelley Pl, Til. RM18
  off Kipling Av 111 GH81
Shelley Rd, NW10 . . . . . . .80 CR67
  Brentwood CM13 . . . . . . .55 GD45
Shelleys La, Sev. (Knock.)
  TN14 . . . . .179 ET116
Shelley Way, SW19 . . . . . .120 DD93
Shellfield Cl, Stai. TW19 . . .114 BG85
Shellness Rd, E5 . . . . .66 DV64
Shell Rd, SE13 . . . . .103 EB83
Shellwood Rd, SW11 . . . . .100 DF82
Shelmerdine Cl, E3 . . . . . .85 EA71
Shelson Av, Felt. TW13 . . . .115 BT90
Shelton Av, Warl. CR6 . . . .176 DW117
Shelton Cl, Warl. CR6 . . . .176 DW117
Shelton Ct, Slou. SL3
  off London Rd 92 AW76
Shelton Rd, SW19 . . . . . . .140 DA95
Shelton St, WC2 . . . . .195 P9
Shelvers Grn, Tad. KT20 . . .173 CW121
Shelvers Hill, Tad. KT20
  off Ashurst Rd 173 CW121
Shelvers Spur, Tad. KT20 . .173 CW121
Shelvers Way, Tad. KT20 . .173 CW121
Shenden Cl, Sev. TN13 . . . .191 FJ128
Shenden Way, Sev. TN13 . .191 FJ128
SHENFIELD, Brwd. 55 GA45
⇌ Shenfield 55 GA45
Shenfield Cl, Couls. CR5
  off Woodfield Rd 175 DJ119
Shenfield Common, Brwd.
  CM15 . . . . .54 FY48
Shenfield Cres, Brwd. CM15 .54 FY47
Shenfield Gdns, Brwd. CM13 .68 GB44
Shenfield Grn, Brwd. CM15
  off Hutton Rd 55 GA45
Shenfield Ho, SE18
  off Shooter's Hill Rd 104 EK80
Shenfield Pl, Brwd. CM15 . . .54 FY45
Shenfield Rd, Brwd. CM15 . .54 FX46
  Woodford Green IG8 . . . . .48 EH52
Shenfield St, N1 . . . . .197 N1
SHENLEY, Rad. 10 CN33
Shenley Av, Ruis. HA4 . . . . .59 BT61
Shenley Hill, Rad. WD7 . . . .25 CG35
Shenleybury, Rad. (Shenley)
  WD7 . . . . .10 CL30
Shenleybury Cotts, Rad. (Shenley)
  WD7 . . . . .10 CL31
Shenley Hill, Rad. WD7 . . . .25 CG35
Shenley La, St.Alb. (Lon.Col.)
  AL2 . . . . .9 CJ27
Shenley Manor, Rad. (Shenley)
  WD7 . . . . .9 CK33
Shenley Rd, SE5 . . . . .102 DS81
  Borehamwood WD6 . . . . .26 CN42
  Dartford DA1 . . . . .128 FN86
  Hounslow TW5 . . . . .96 BY81
  Radlett WD7 . . . . .9 CH34
Shenstone Cl, Dart. DA1 . . .107 FD84
Shenstone Gdns, Rom. RM3 . .52 FJ53
Shepcot Ho, N14 . . . . .29 DJ44
Shepherd Cl, W1 off Lees Pl .82 DG73
  Abbots Langley WD5 . . . . .7 BT30
Shepherdess Pl, N1 . . . . . .197 J2
Shepherdess Wk, N1 . . . . . .84 DQ68
Shepherd Mkt, W1 . . . . . . .199 H2
SHEPHERD'S BUSH, W12 . . .81 CW75
⊖ Shepherd's Bush 99 CW75
Shepherds Bush Grn, W12 . .99 CW75
Shepherds Bush Mkt, W12 . .99 CW75
Shepherds Bush Pl, W12 . . .99 CX75
Shepherds Bush Rd, W6 . . . .99 CW77
Shepherds Cl, N6 . . . . .65 DH58
  Leatherhead KT22 . . . . . .172 CL124
  Orpington BR6
    off Stapleton Rd 145 ET104
  Romford RM6 . . . . .70 EX57
  Shepperton TW17 . . . . . .135 BP100

Shepherds Cl, Uxb. (Cowley) UB8
  off High St 76 BJ70
Shepherds Ct, W12
  off Shepherds Bush Grn .99 CX75
Shepherds Grn, Chis. BR7 . .125 ER94
Shepherds Hill, N6 . . . . . . .65 DH58
  Redhill RH1 . . . . .185 DU134
  Romford RM3 . . . . .52 FN54
Shepherds La, E9 . . . . .67 DX64
Shepherd's La, Brwd. CM14 .54 FV45
Shepherds La, Dart. DA1 . . .127 FG88
  Rickmansworth WD3 . . . . .37 BH45
Shepherds Path, Nthlt. UB5
  off Fortunes Mead 78 BY65
Shepherd's Pl, W1 . . . . . . .194 F10
Shepherds Rd, Wat. WD18 . .23 BT41
Shepherd St, W1 . . . . .199 H3
  Gravesend (Nthflt.) DA11 .130 GD87
Shepherds Wk, NW2 . . . . . .63 CU61
  NW3 . . . . .64 DD64
  Bushey (Bushey Hth.) WD23 .41 CD47
Shepherds' Wk, Epsom KT18 .172 CP121
Shepherds Way, Hat. (Brook.Pk.)
  AL9 . . . . .12 DC27
  Rickmansworth WD3 . . . . .38 BH45
  South Croydon CR2 . . . . .161 DX108
Shepiston La, Hayes UB3 . . .95 BR77
  West Drayton UB7 . . . . . .95 BQ77
Shepley Cl, Cars. SM5 . . . .140 DG104
  Hornchurch RM12
    off Chevington Way 72 FK64
Shepley Ms, Enf. EN3 . . . . .31 EA37
Sheppard Cl, Enf. EN1 . . . . .30 DV39
  Kingston upon Thames KT1
    off Beaufort Rd 138 CL98
Sheppard Dr, SE16 . . . . . . .202 D10
Sheppard St, E16 . . . . .86 EF70
SHEPPERTON 134 BN101
⇌ Shepperton 135 BQ99
Shepperton Business Pk, Shep.
  TW17 . . . . .135 BQ99
Shepperton Cl, Borwd. WD6 .26 CR39
Shepperton Ct, Shep. TW17 .135 BP100
Shepperton Ct Dr, Shep.
  TW17 . . . . .135 BP99
Shepperton Rd, N1 . . . . . . .84 DQ67
  Orpington BR5 . . . . .145 EQ100
  Staines TW18 . . . . .134 BJ97
Sheppey Cl, Erith DA8 . . . .107 FH80
Sheppey Gdns, Dag. RM9
  off Sheppey Rd 88 EV66
Sheppey Rd, Dag. RM9 . . . .88 EV66
Sheppeys La, Abb.L. (Bedmond)
  WD5 . . . . .7 BS28
Sheppey Wk, N1
  off Clephane Rd 84 DQ66
Sheppy Pl, Grav. DA12 . . . .131 GH87
Sherard Ct, N7 off Manor Gdns .65 DL62
Sherard Rd, SE9 . . . . .124 EL85
Sheraton Business Cen, Grnf.
  UB6 . . . . .79 CH68
Sheraton Cl, Borwd. (Elstree)
  WD6 . . . . .26 CM43
Sheraton Dr, Epsom KT19 . .156 CQ113
Sheraton Ms, Wat. WD18 . . .23 BS42
Sheraton St, W1 . . . . .195 M9
  Southall UB2 . . . . .96 CA77
Sherborne Cl, Epsom KT18 .173 CW117
  Hayes UB4 . . . . .78 BW72
  Slough (Colnbr.) SL3 . . . . .93 BE81
Sherborne Cres, Cars. SM5 .140 DE101
Sherborne Gdns, NW9 . . . . .62 CN55
  W13 . . . . .79 CH72
  Romford RM5 . . . . .50 FA50
Sherborne La, EC4 . . . . . . .197 K10
Sherborne Pl, Nthwd. HA6 . .39 BR51
Sherborne Rd, Chess. KT9 . .156 CL106
  Feltham TW14 . . . . .115 BR87
  Orpington BR5 . . . . .145 ET98
  Sutton SM3 . . . . .140 DA103
Sherborne St, N1 . . . . .84 DR67
Sherborne Wk, Lthd. KT22
  off Windfield 171 CJ121
Sherborne Way, Rick. (Crox.Grn.)
  WD3 . . . . .23 BP42
Sherboro Rd, N15
  off Ermine Rd 66 DT58
Sherbourne Cotts, Wat. WD18
  off Watford Fld Rd 24 BW43
Sherbourne Gdns, Shep.
  TW17 . . . . .135 BS101
Sherbourne Pl, Stan. HA7 . . .41 CG51
Sherbrooke Cl, Bexh. DA6 . .106 FA84
Sherbrooke Rd, SW6 . . . . . .99 CZ80
Sherbrook Gdns, N21 . . . . .45 DP45
Shere Av, Sutt. SM2 . . . . . .CW110
Shere Cl, Chess. KT9 . . . . .155 CK106
Sheredan Rd, E4 . . . . .47 ED50
Shere Rd, Ilf. IG2 . . . . .69 EN57
Sherfield Av, Rick. WD3 . . . .38 BK47
Sherfield Cl, N.Mal. KT3 . . .138 CP98
Sherfield Gdns, SW15 . . . . .119 CT86
Sherfield Rd, Grays RM17 . .110 GB79
Sheridan Cl, Rom. RM3 . . . .51 FH52
  Swanley BR8 off Willow Av .147 FF97
  Uxbridge UB10
    off Alpha Rd 77 BQ70
Sheridan Ct, Houns. TW4
  off Vickers Way 116 BZ85
  Northolt UB5 . . . . .60 CB64
Sheridan Cres, Chis. BR7 . . .145 EP96
Sheridan Dr, Reig. RH2 . . . .184 DB132
Sheridan Gdns, Har. HA3 . . .61 CK58
Sheridan Ms, E11
  off Woodbine Pl 68 EG58
Sheridan Pl, SW13
  off Brookwood Av 99 CT82
  Hampton TW12 . . . . .136 CB95
Sheridan Rd, E7 . . . . .68 EF62
  E12 . . . . .86 EL64
  SW19 . . . . .139 CZ95
  Belvedere DA17 . . . . . . .106 FA77
  Bexleyheath DA7 . . . . . .106 EY83
  Richmond TW10 . . . . . . .117 CJ90
  Watford WD19 . . . . .40 BX45
Sheridan St, E1 off Watney St .84 DV72

Sheridan Ter, Nthlt. UB5
  off Whitton Av W 60 CB64
Sheridan Wk, NW11 . . . . . .64 DA58
  Carshalton SM5
    off Carshalton Pk Rd . . .158 DF106
Sheridan Way, Beck. BR3
  off Turners Meadow Way .143 DZ95
Sheriff Way, Wat. WD25 . . . .7 BU33
Sheringham Av, E12 . . . . . .69 EM63
  N14 . . . . .29 DK43
  Feltham TW13 . . . . .115 BU90
  Romford RM7 . . . . .71 FC58
  Twickenham TW2 . . . . . .116 BZ88
Sheringham Dr, Bark. IG11 . .69 ET64
Sheringham Rd, N7 . . . . . . .83 DM65
  SE20 . . . . .142 DW102
Sheringham Twr, Sthl. UB1 . .78 CB73
Sherington Av, Pnr. HA5 . . . .40 CA52
Sherington Rd, SE7 . . . . . .104 EH79
Sherland Rd, Twick. TW1 . . .117 CF88
Sherlies Av, Orp. BR6 . . . . .145 ES103
★ Sherlock Holmes Mus,
  NW1 . . . . .194 E5
Sherlock Ms, W1 . . . . .194 F6
Sherman Rd, Brom. BR1 . . .144 EG95
  Slough SL1 . . . . .74 AS71
Shernbroke Rd, Wal.Abb. EN9 .16 EF34
Shernhall St, E17 . . . . .67 EC57
Sherrard Rd, E7 . . . . .86 EJ65
  E12 . . . . .86 EK65
Sherrards Way, Barn. EN5 . .28 DA43
Sherrick Grn Rd, NW10 . . . .63 CV64
Sherriff Rd, NW6 . . . . .82 DA65
Sherringham Av, N17 . . . . . .46 DU54
Sherrin Rd, E10 . . . . .67 EA63
Sherrock Gdns, NW4 . . . . . .63 CU56
Sherry Ms, Bark. IG11 . . . . .87 ER66
Sherwin Rd, SE14 . . . . . . .103 DX81
Sherwood Av, E18 . . . . . . .68 EH55
  SW16 . . . . .121 DK94
  Greenford UB6 . . . . .79 CE65
  Hayes UB4 . . . . .77 BV70
  Potters Bar EN6 . . . . . . .11 CY32
  Ruislip HA4 . . . . .59 BS58
Sherwood Cl, SW13
  off Lower Common S 99 CV83
  W13 . . . . .79 CH74
  Bexley DA5 . . . . .126 EX86
  Leatherhead (Fetch.) KT22 .170 CC122
  Slough SL3 . . . . .92 AY76
Sherwood Ct, Slou. (Colnbr.) SL3
  off High St 93 BD80
Sherwood Gdns, E14 . . . . . .204 A8
  SE16 . . . . .102 DU78
  Barking IG11 . . . . .87 ER66
Sherwood Pk Av, Sid. DA15 .126 EU87
Sherwood Pk Rd, Mitch. CR4 .141 DJ98
  Sutton SM1 . . . . .158 DA106
Sherwood Rd, NW4 . . . . . . .63 CW55
  SW19 . . . . .119 CZ94
  Coulsdon CR5 . . . . .175 DJ116
  Croydon CR0 . . . . .142 DV101
  Hampton (Hmptn.H.) TW12 .116 CC92
  Harrow HA2 . . . . .60 CC61
  Ilford IG6 . . . . .69 ER56
  Welling DA16 . . . . .105 ES82
  Woking (Knap.) GU21 . . .166 AS117
Sherwoods Rd, Wat. WD19 . .40 BY45
Sherwood St, N20 . . . . .44 DD48
  W1 . . . . .195 L10
Sherwood Ter, N20
  off Green Rd 44 DD48
Sherwood Way, W.Wick. BR4 .143 EB103
Shetland Cl, Borwd. WD6
  off Percheron Rd 26 CR44
Shetland Rd, E3 . . . . .85 DZ68
Shevon Way, Brwd. CM14 . . .54 FT49
Shewens Rd, Wey. KT13 . . .153 BR105
Shey Copse, Wok. GU22 . . .167 BC117
Shield Dr, Brent. TW8 . . . . .97 CG79
Shieldhall St, SE2 . . . . . . .106 EW77
Shield Rd, Ashf. TW15 . . . .115 BQ91
Shifford Path, SE23 . . . . . .123 DX90
Shilburn Way, Wok. GU21 . .166 AU118
Shillibeer Pl, W1 . . . . .194 C6
Shillibeer Wk, Chig. IG7 . . .49 ET49
Shillingford Cl, NW7
  off Bittacy Hill 43 CY52
Shillingford St, N1
  off Cross St 83 DP66
Shillitoe Av, Pot.B. EN6 . . . .11 CX32
Shillingford Cl, NW7 . . . . . .12 SL54
Shingle Ct, Wal.Abb. EN9 . . .16 EG33
Shinglewell Rd, Erith DA8 . .106 FA80
Shinners Cl, SE25 . . . . . . .142 DU99
Ship All, W4 off Thames Rd . .98 CN79
Ship & Mermaid Row, SE1 . .201 L4
Shipfield Cl, West. (Tats.) TN16 .178 EJ121
Ship Hill, West. (Tats.) TN16 .178 EJ121
Shipka Rd, SW12 . . . . . . .121 DH88
Ship La, SW14 . . . . .98 CQ82
  Brentwood CM13 . . . . . . .55 GF41
  Dartford (Sutt.H.) DA4 . . .148 FK95
  Purfleet RM19 . . . . .109 FS76
  South Ockendon (Aveley)
    RM15 . . . . .109 FR75
  Swanley BR8 . . . . .148 FK95
Ship La Caravan Site, S.Ock.
  RM15 . . . . .109 FR76
Shipman Rd, E16 . . . . .86 EH72
  SE23 . . . . .123 DX89
Ship St, SE8 . . . . .103 EA81
Ship Tavern Pas, EC3 . . . . .197 M10
Shipton Cl, Dag. RM8 . . . . .70 EX62
Shipton St, E2 . . . . .84 DT69
Shipwright Rd, SE16 . . . . . .203 K5
Ship Yd, E14 . . . . .204 B10
  Weybridge KT13
    off High St 153 BP105
Shirburn Cl, SE23
  off Tyson Rd 122 DW87
Shirbutt St, E14 . . . . .85 EB73
Shirebrook Rd, SE3 . . . . . .104 EK83
Shire Cl, Brox. EN10
  off Groom Rd 15 DZ26
Shire Ct, Epsom KT17 . . . . .157 CT108

Shire Ct, Erith DA18
  off St. John Fisher Rd . . .106 EX76
Shirehall Cl, NW4 . . . . .63 CX58
Shirehall Gdns, NW4 . . . . . .63 CX58
Shirehall La, NW4 . . . . .63 CX58
Shirehall Pk, NW4 . . . . .63 CX58
Shirehall Rd, Dart. DA2 . . . .128 FK92
Shire Horse Way, Islw. TW7 . .97 CF83
Shire La, Ger.Cr. (Chal.St.P.)
  SL9 . . . . .37 BD54
  Keston BR2 . . . . .163 EM108
  Orpington BR6 . . . . .163 ER107
  Rickmansworth (Chorl.) WD3 .21 BB43
  Uxbridge (Denh.) UB9 . . . .57 BE55
Shiremeade, Borwd. (Elstree)
  WD6 . . . . .26 CM43
Shire Pl, SW18
  off Whitehead Cl 120 DC87
Shires, The, Rich. TW10 . . .118 CL91
  Watford WD25
    off High Elms La 8 BW31
Shires Cl, Ashtd. KT21 . . . .171 CK118
Shires Ho, W.Byf. (Byfleet) KT14
  off Eden Gro Rd 152 BL113
Shirland Ms, W9 . . . . .81 CZ69
Shirland Rd, W9 . . . . .82 DA69
SHIRLEY, Croy. 143 DX104
Shirley Av, Bex. DA5 . . . . .126 EX87
  Coulsdon CR5 . . . . .175 DP119
  Croydon CR0 . . . . .142 DW102
  Sutton SM1 . . . . .158 DE105
  Sutton (Cheam) SM2 . . . .157 CZ109
Shirley Ch Rd, Croy. CR0 . . .143 DX104
Shirley Cl, E17
  off Addison Rd 67 EB57
  Dartford DA1 . . . . .108 FJ84
  Hounslow TW3 . . . . .116 CC85
  Waltham Cross (Chsht.) EN8 .14 DW29
Shirley Ct, Croy. CR0 . . . . .143 DX104
Shirley Cres, Beck. BR3 . . .143 DY98
Shirley Dr, Houns. TW3 . . . .116 CC85
Shirley Gdns, W7 . . . . .79 CF74
  Barking IG11 . . . . .87 ES65
  Hornchurch RM12 . . . . . .72 FJ61
Shirley Gro, N9 . . . . .46 DW46
  SW11 . . . . .100 DG83
Shirley Hts, Wall. SM6 . . . .159 DJ109
Shirley Hills Rd, Croy. CR0 .161 DX106
Shirley Ho Dr, SE7 . . . . . . .104 EJ80
Ⓗ Shirley Oaks Hosp, Croy.
  CR0 . . . . .142 DW101
Shirley Oaks Rd, Croy. CR0 .143 DX102
Shirley Pk Rd, Croy. CR0 . . .142 DV102
Shirley Rd, E15 . . . . .86 EE66
  W4 . . . . .98 CR75
  Abbots Langley WD5 . . . . .7 BT32
  Croydon CR0 . . . . .142 DV101
  Enfield EN2 . . . . .30 DQ41
  Sidcup DA15 . . . . .125 ES90
  Wallington SM6 . . . . . . .159 DJ109
Shirley St, E16 . . . . .86 EF72
Shirley Way, Croy. CR0 . . . .143 DY104
Shirlock Rd, NW3 . . . . .64 DF63
Shirwell Cl, NW7
  off Bittacy Hill 43 CY52
Shobden Rd, N17 . . . . .46 DR53
Shobroke Cl, NW2 . . . . .63 CW62
Shoebury Rd, E6 . . . . .87 EM66
Shoe La, EC4 . . . . .196 E8
Sholden Gdns, Orp. BR5 . . .146 EW99
Sholto Rd, Houns. (Hthrw.Air.)
  TW6 . . . . .114 BM85
Shonks Mill Rd, Rom. (Nave.)
  RM4 . . . . .35 FG37
Shooters Av, Har. HA3 . . . . .61 CJ56
SHOOTER'S HILL, SE18 . . .105 EQ81
Shooter's Hill, SE18 . . . . . .105 EN81
  Welling DA16 . . . . .105 EN81
Shooter's Hill Rd, SE3 . . . .104 EF81
  SE10 . . . . .104 EF81
  SE18 . . . . .104 EH80
Shooters Rd, Enf. EN2 . . . . .29 DP39
Shoot Up Hill, NW2 . . . . . . .63 CY64
Shord Hill, Ken. CR8 . . . . .176 DR116
Shore, The, Grav. (Nthflt.)
  DA11 . . . . .130 GC85
  Gravesend (Rosh.) DA11 .131 GF86
Shore Cl, Felt. TW14 . . . . .115 BU87
  Hampton TW12
    off Stewart Cl 116 BY92
SHOREDITCH, E1 . . . . . . .197 P5
⊖ Shoreditch 84 DT70
Shoreditch High St, E1 . . . .197 N3
Shoreditch Ho, N1 . . . . . . .197 L3
Shore Gro, Felt. TW13 . . . .116 CA89
SHOREHAM, Sev. 165 FG111
⇌ Shoreham 165 FG111
Shoreham Cl, SW18
  off Ram St 120 DB85
  Bexley DA5
    off Stansted Cres 126 EX88
  Croydon CR0 . . . . .142DW100
Shoreham La, Orp. BR6 . . . .164 FA107
  Sevenoaks TN13 . . . . . .190 FF122
  Sevenoaks (Halst.) TN14 .164 EZ112
Shoreham Pl, Sev. (Shore.)
  TN14 . . . . .165 FG112
Shoreham Rd, Orp. BR5 . . . .146 EV95
  Sevenoaks (Otford) TN14 .165 FH111
Shoreham Rd E, Houns.
  (Hthrw.Air.) TW6 . . . . . .114 BL85
Shoreham Rd W, Houns.
  (Hthrw.Air.) TW6 . . . . . .114 BL85
Shoreham Way, Brom. BR2 .144 EG100
Shore Pl, E9 . . . . .84 DW66
Shore Rd, E9 . . . . .84 DW66
Shores Rd, Wok. GU21 . . . .150 AY114
Shorncliffe Rd, SE1 . . . . . .201 P10
Shorndean St, SE6 . . . . . . .123 EC88
Shorne Cl, Orp. BR5 . . . . . .146 EX98
  Sidcup DA15 . . . . .126 EV86
Shornefield Cl, Brom. BR1 . .145 EN97
Shornells Way, SE2 . . . . . . .106 EW78
  off Willrose Cres
Shorrolds Rd, SW6 . . . . . . .99 CZ80
Shortacres, Red. RH1 . . . . .185 DM133

Shortcroft Rd, Epsom KT17 . .157 CT108
Shortcrofts Rd, Dag. RM9 . . .88 EZ65
Shorter Av, Brwd. CM15 . . . .55 FZ44
Shorter St, E1 . . . . .197 P10
Shortfern, Slou. SL2 . . . . . .74 AW72
Shortgate, N12 . . . . .43 CZ49
Short Hedges, Houns.
  TW3, TW5 . . . . .96 CB81
Short Hill, Har. HA1
  off High St 61 CE60
SHORTLANDS, Brom. 144 EE97
⇌ Shortlands 144 EE96
Shortlands, W6 . . . . .99 CX77
  Hayes UB3 . . . . .95 BR79
Shortlands Cl, N18 . . . . . . .46 DR48
  Belvedere DA17 . . . . . . .106 EZ76
Shortlands Gdns, Brom. BR2 .144 EE96
Shortlands Gro, Brom. BR2 .143 ED97
Shortlands Rd, E10 . . . . . . .67 EB59
  Bromley BR2 . . . . .143 ED97
  Kingston upon Thames KT2 .118 CM94
Short La, Oxt. RH8 . . . . . . .188 EH132
  St. Albans (Brick.Wd.) AL2 . .8 BZ30
  Staines TW19 . . . . .114 BM88
Shortmead Dr, Wal.Cr. (Chsht.)
  EN8 . . . . .15 DY31
Short Path, SE18
  off Westdale Rd 105 EP79
Short Rd, E11 . . . . .68 EE61
  E15 . . . . .85 ED67
  W4 . . . . .98 CS79
  Hounslow (Hthrw.Air.) TW6 .114 BL86
Shorts Cft, NW9 . . . . .62 CP56
Shorts Gdns, WC2 . . . . . . .195 P9
Shorts Rd, Cars. SM5 . . . . .158 DE105
Short St, NW4
  off New Brent St 63 CW56
  SE1 . . . . .200 E4
Short Wall, E15 . . . . .85 EC69
Shortway, N12 . . . . .44 DE51
Short Way, SE9 . . . . .104 EL83
  Twickenham TW2 . . . . . .116 CC87
Shortwood Av, Stai. TW18 . .114 BH90
Shortwood Common, Stai.
  TW18 . . . . .114 BH91
Shotfield, Wall. SM6 . . . . . .159 DH107
Shothanger Way, Hem.H. (Bov.)
  HP3 . . . . .5 BC26
Shott Cl, Sutt. SM1
  off Turnpike La 158 DC106
Shottendane Rd, SW6 . . . . .100 DA81
Shottery Cl, SE9 . . . . .124 EL90
Shottfield Av, SW14 . . . . . . .98 CS84
Shoulder of Mutton All, E14
  off Narrow St 85 DY73
Shouldham St, W1 . . . . . . .194 C7
Showers Way, Hayes UB3 . . .77 BU74
Shrapnel Cl, SE18 . . . . . . .104 EL80
Shrapnel Rd, SE9 . . . . . . .105 EM83
SHREDING GREEN, Iver 75 BB72
Shrewsbury Av, SW14 . . . . .98 CQ84
  Harrow HA3 . . . . .62 CL56
Shrewsbury Cl, Surb. KT6 . .138 CL103
Shrewsbury Ct, EC1
  off Whitecross St 84 DQ70
Shrewsbury Cres, NW10 . . . .80 CR67
Shrewsbury La, SE18 . . . . .105 EP81
Shrewsbury Ms, W2
  off Chepstow Rd 82 DA71
Shrewsbury Rd, E7 . . . . . . .68 EK64
  N11 . . . . .45 DJ51
  W2 . . . . .82 DA72
  Beckenham BR3 . . . . . . .143 DY97
  Carshalton SM5 . . . . . . .140 DE100
  Hounslow (Hthrw.Air.) TW6 .115 BQ86
  Redhill RH1 . . . . .184 DE134
Shrewsbury St, W10 . . . . . .81 CW70
Shrewsbury Wk, Islw. TW7
  off South St 97 CG83
Shrewton Rd, SW17 . . . . . .120 DF94
Shroffold Rd, Brom. BR1 . . .124 EE91
Shropshire Cl, Mitch. CR4 . .141 DL98
Shropshire Ho, N18
  off Cameron Cl 46 DV50
Shropshire Pl, WC1 . . . . . .195 L5
Shropshire Rd, N22 . . . . . . .45 DM52
Shroton St, NW1 . . . . .194 B6
Shrubberies, The, E18 . . . . .48 EG54
  Chigwell IG7 . . . . .49 EQ50
Shrubbery, The, E11 . . . . . .68 EH57
  Upminster RM14 . . . . . . .72 FQ62
Shrubbery Cl, N1
  off St. Paul St 84 DQ67
Shrubbery Gdns, N21 . . . . . .45 DP45
Shrubbery Rd, N9 . . . . .46 DU48
  SW16 . . . . .121 DL91
  Dartford (S.Darenth) DA4 .149 FR95
  Gravesend DA12 . . . . . .131 GH88
  Southall UB1 . . . . .78 BZ74
Shrubland Gro, Wor.Pk. KT4 .139 CW104
Shrubland Rd, E8 . . . . .84 DU67
  E10 . . . . .67 EA59
  E17 . . . . .67 EA57
  Banstead SM7 . . . . .173 CZ116
Shrublands, Hat. AL9 . . . . . .12 DB26
Shrublands, The, Pot.B. EN6 .11 CY33
Shrublands Av, Croy. CR0 . .161 EA105
Shrublands Cl, N20 . . . . . . .44 DD46
  SE26 . . . . .122 DW90
  Chigwell IG7 . . . . .49 EQ51
Shrubsall Cl, SE9 . . . . .124 EL88
Shrubs Rd, Rick. WD3 . . . . .38 BM51
Shuna Wk, N1
  off St. Paul's Rd 84 DR65
Shurland Av, Barn. EN4 . . . .28 DD44
Shurland Gdns, SE15
  off Rosemary Rd 102 DT80
Shurlock Av, Swan. BR8 . . .147 FD96
Shurlock Dr, Orp. BR6 . . . .163 EQ105
Shuters Sq, W14
  off Sun Rd 99 CZ78
Shuttle Cl, Sid. DA15 . . . . .125 ET87
Shuttlemead, Bex. DA5 . . . .126 EZ87
Shuttle Rd, Dart. DA1 . . . . .107 FG83

Shu - Som

Shuttle St, E1 off Buxton St . .84 DU70
Shuttleworth Rd, SW11 . . . . .100 DE82
Siamese Ms, N3 off Station Rd .44 DA53
Sibella Rd, SW4 . . . . .101 DK82
Sibley Cl, Bexh. DA6 . . . . . . .126 EY85
Sibley Gro, E12 . . . . .86 EL66
Sibthorpe Rd, SE12 . . . . .124 EH86
Sibton Rd, Cars. SM5 . . . . . . .140 DE101
Sicilian Av, WC1 . . . . .196 A7
Sicklefield Cl, Wal.Cr. (Chsht.)
  EN7 . . . . .14 DT26
Sidbury St, SW6 . . . . .99 CY81
SIDCUP 125 ET91
⇌ Sidcup 126 EU89
Sidcup Bypass, Chis. BR7 . . .125 EP89
  Orpington BR5 . . . . .126 EX94
  Sidcup DA14 . . . . .125 ES91
Sidcup High St, Sid. DA14 . . .126 EU91
Sidcup Hill, Sid. DA14 . . . . . .126 EV91
Sidcup Hill Gdns, Sid. DA14
  off Sidcup Hill 126 EW92
Sidcup Pl, Sid. DA14 . . . . . . .126 EU92
Sidcup Rd, SE9 . . . . .124 EK87
  SE12 . . . . .124 EH85
Sidcup Technology Cen, Sid.
  DA14 . . . . .126 EX92
Siddeley Dr, Houns. TW4 . . . .96 BY83
Siddons La, NW1 . . . . .194 E5
Siddons Rd, N17 . . . . .46 DU53
  SE23 . . . . .123 DY89
  Croydon CR0 . . . . .141 DN104
Side Rd, E17 . . . . .67 DZ57
  Uxbridge (Denh.) UB9 . . . . .57 BD59
Sidewood Rd, SE9 . . . . .125 ER88
Sidford Pl, SE1 . . . . .200 C7
Sidings, The, E11 . . . . .67 EC60
  Loughton IG10 . . . . .32 EL44
  Staines TW18 off Leacroft . .114 BH91
Sidings Ms, N7 . . . . .65 DN62
Sidmouth Av, Islw. TW7 . . . . .97 CE82
Sidmouth Cl, Wat. WD19 . . . .39 BV47
Sidmouth Dr, Ruis. HA4 . . . . .59 BU62
Sidmouth Par, NW2
  off Sidmouth Rd 81 CW66
Sidmouth Rd, E10 . . . . .67 EC62
  NW2 . . . . .81 CW66
  Orpington BR5 . . . . .146 EV99
  Welling DA16 . . . . .106 EW80
Sidmouth St, WC1 . . . . .196 A3
Sidney Av, N13 . . . . .45 DM50
Sidney Elson Way, E6
  off Edwin Av 87 EN68
Sidney Gdns, Brent. TW8 . . . .97 CJ79
Sidney Gro, EC1 . . . . .196 F1
Sidney Rd, E7 . . . . .68 EG62
  N22 . . . . .45 DM52
  SE25 . . . . .142 DU99
  SW9 . . . . .101 DM82
  Beckenham BR3 . . . . .143 DY96
  Epping (They.B.) CM16 . . . .33 ER36
  Harrow HA2 . . . . .60 CC55
  Staines TW18 . . . . .114 BG91
  Twickenham TW1 . . . . .117 CG86
  Walton-on-Thames KT12 . . .135 BU101
Sidney Sq, E1 . . . . .84 DW72
Sidney St, E1 . . . . .84 DV71
Sidworth St, E8 . . . . .84 DV66
Siebert Rd, SE3 . . . . .104 EG79
Siemens Rd, SE18 . . . . .104 EK76
Sigdon Rd, E8 . . . . .66 DU64
Sigers, The, Pnr. HA5 . . . . . . .59 BV58
Signmakers Yd, NW1
  off Delancey St 83 DH67
Sigrist Sq, Kings.T. KT2 . . . . .138 CL95
Silbury Av, Mitch. CR4 . . . . . .140 DE95
Silbury St, N1 . . . . .197 K2
Silchester Rd, W10 . . . . .81 CX72
Silecroft Rd, Bexh. DA7 . . . . .106 FA81
Silesia Bldgs, E8 off London La .66 DV66
Silex St, SE1 . . . . .200 G5
Silk Cl, SE12 . . . . .124 EG85
Silkfield Rd, NW9 . . . . .62 CS57
Silkham Rd, Oxt. RH8 . . . . . .187 ED127
Silkin Ho, Wat. WD19 . . . . . . .40 BW48
Silk Mill Ct, Wat. WD19
  off Silk Mill Rd 39 BV45
Silk Mill Rd, Wat. WD19 . . . . .39 BV45
Silk Mills Cl, Sev. TN14 . . . . .191 FJ121
Silk Mills Path, SE13
  off Lewisham Rd 103 EC82
Silkmills Sq, E9 . . . . .85 DZ65
Silkstream Rd, Edg. HA8 . . . .42 CQ53
Silk St, EC2 . . . . .197 J6
Silsden Cres, Ch.St.G. HP8
  off London Rd 36 AX48
Silsoe Rd, N22 . . . . .45 DM54
Silver Birch Av, E4 . . . . .47 DZ51
  Epping (N.Wld.Bas.) CM16 . .18 EY27
Silver Birch Cl, N11 . . . . .44 DG51
  SE28 . . . . .88 EU74
  Addlestone (Woodham)
  KT15 . . . . .151 BE112
  Dartford DA2 . . . . .127 FE91
  Uxbridge UB10 . . . . .58 BL63
Silver Birches, Brwd. CM13 . . .55 GA46
Silver Birch Gdns, E6 . . . . . . .87 EM70
Silver Birch Ms, Ilf. IG6
  off Fencepiece Rd 49 EQ51
Silverbirch Wk, NW3
  off Queen's Cres 82 DG65
Silvercliffe Gdns, Barn. EN4 . .28 DE42
Silver Cl, SE14
  off Southerngate Way 103 DY80
  Harrow HA3 . . . . .41 CD52
  Tadworth (Kgswd.) KT20 . . .173 CY124
Silver Cres, W4 . . . . .98 CP77
Silverdale, SE26 . . . . .122 DW91
  Enfield EN2 . . . . .29 DL42
Silverdale Av, Ilf. IG3 . . . . . . .69 ES57
  Leatherhead (Oxshott) KT22 .154 CC114
  Walton-on-Thames KT12 . . .135 BT104
Silverdale Cl, W7 . . . . .79 CE74
  Northolt UB5 . . . . .60 BZ64
  Sutton SM1 . . . . .157 CZ105

Silverdale Ct, Stai. TW18 . . . .114 BH92
Silverdale Dr, SE9 . . . . .124 EL89
  Hornchurch RM12 . . . . .71 FH64
  Sunbury-on-Thames TW16 . .135 BV96
Silverdale Gdns, Hayes UB3 . .95 BU75
Silverdale Rd, E4 . . . . .47 ED51
  Bexleyheath DA7 . . . . .107 FB82
  Bushey WD23 . . . . .24 BY43
  Hayes UB3 . . . . .95 BU75
  Orpington (Petts Wd) BR5 . .145 EQ98
  Orpington (St.P.Cray) BR5 . .146 EU97
Silver Dell, Wat. WD24 . . . . . .23 BT35
Silverglade Business Pk, Chess.
  KT9 . . . . .155 CJ112
Silverhall St, Islw. TW7 . . . . .97 CG83
Silver Hill, Ch.St.G. HP8 . . . . .36 AV47
Silverholme Rd, Har. HA3 . . . .61 CK59
Silver Jubilee Way, Houns.
  TW4 . . . . .95 BV82
Silverland St, E16 . . . . .87 EM74
Silver La, Pur. CR8 . . . . .159 DK112
  West Wickham BR4 . . . . . . .143 ED103
Silverleigh Rd, Th.Hth. CR7 . .141 DM98
Silverlocke Rd, Grays RM17 . .110 GD79
Silvermead, E18
  off Churchfields 48 EG52
Silvermere Av, Rom. RM5 . . . .51 FB51
Silvermere Rd, SE6 . . . . .123 EB86
Silversmiths Way, Wok. GU21 .166 AW118
Silver Spring Cl, Erith DA8 . . .107 FB79
Silverstead La, West. TN16 . . .179 ER121
Silverstone Cl, Red. RH1
  off Goodwood Rd 184 DF132
Silverston Way, Stan. HA7 . . .41 CJ51
⇌ Silver Street 46 DT50
Silver St, N18 . . . . .46 DS49
  Enfield EN1 . . . . .30 DR41
  Romford (Abridge) RM4 . . . .34 EV41
  Waltham Abbey EN9 . . . . . .15 EC34
  Waltham Cross (Goffs Oak)
  EN7 . . . . .14 DR30
Silverthorne Rd, SW8 . . . . . .101 DH82
Silverthorn Gdns, E4 . . . . . . .47 EA47
Silverton Rd, W6 . . . . .99 CX79
SILVERTOWN, E16 . . . . .104 EJ75
⇌ Silvertown & London City
  Airport 86 EK74
Silvertown Way, E16 . . . . . . .86 EF72
Silver Tree Cl, Walt. KT12 . . .135 BU104
Silvertree La, Grnf. UB6
  off Cowgate Rd 79 CD69
Silvertrees, St.Alb. (Brick.Wd.)
  AL2 off West Riding 8 BZ30
Silver Wk, SE16 . . . . .203 M3
Silver Way, Rom. RM7 . . . . . .71 FB55
  Uxbridge UB10
  off Oakdene Rd 77 BP68
Silverwood Cl, Beck. BR3 . . .123 EA94
  Croydon CR0 . . . . .161 DZ109
  Northwood HA6 . . . . .39 BQ53
Silvester Rd, SE22 . . . . .122 DT85
Silvester St, SE1 . . . . .201 J5
Silvocea Way, E14 . . . . .85 ED72
Silwood Est, SE16 . . . . .202 G9
Silwood St, SE16 . . . . .202 G9
Simla Cl, SE14 . . . . .103 DY79
Simla Ho, SE1 . . . . .201 L5
Simmil Rd, Esher (Clay.) KT10 .155 CE106
Simmons Cl, N20 . . . . .44 DE46
  Chessington KT9 . . . . .155 CJ108
  Slough SL3 off Common Rd .93 BA77
Simmons La, E4 . . . . .47 ED47
Simmons Pl, Stai. TW18
  off Chertsey La 113 BE92
Simmons Rd, SE18 . . . . .105 EP78
Simmons Way, N20 . . . . .44 DE47
Simms Cl, Cars. SM5 . . . . . .140 DE103
Simms Gdns, N2 . . . . .44 DC54
Simms Rd, SE1 . . . . .202 B9
Simnel Rd, SE12 . . . . .124 EH87
Simon Cl, W11
  off Portobello Rd 81 CZ73
Simon Dean, Hem.H. (Bov.) HP3 .5 BA27
Simonds Rd, E10 . . . . .67 EA61
Simone Cl, Brom. BR1 . . . . . .144 EK95
Simone Dr, Ken. CR8 . . . . . .176 DQ116
Simons Cl, Cher. (Ott.) KT16 .151 BC107
Simons Wk, E15
  off Waddington Rd 67 ED64
  Egham (Eng.Grn.) TW20 . . .112 AW94
Simplemarsh Ct, Add. KT15
  off Simplemarsh Rd 152 BH105
Simplemarsh Rd, Add. KT15 .152 BG105
Simpson Cl, N21
  off Macleod Rd 29 DL43
Simpson Dr, W3 . . . . .80 CR72
Simpson Rd, Houns. TW4 . . . .116 BZ86
  Rainham RM13 . . . . .89 FF65
  Richmond TW10 . . . . .117 CJ91
Simpsons Rd, E14 . . . . .204 C1
  Bromley BR2 . . . . .144 EG97
Simpson St, SW11 . . . . .100 DE82
Simrose Ct, SW18
  off Wandsworth High St . . .120 DA85
Sims Cl, Rom. RM1 . . . . .71 FF56
Sims Wk, SE3 . . . . .104 EF84
Sinclair Cl, Beck. BR3 . . . . . .123 EA94
Sinclair Dr, Sutt. SM2 . . . . . .158 DB109
Sinclair Gdns, W14 . . . . .99 CX75
Sinclair Gro, NW11 . . . . .63 CX58
Sinclair Rd, E4 . . . . .47 DZ50
  W14 . . . . .99 CX75
Sinclair Way, Dart. (Lane End)
  DA2 . . . . .129 FR91
Sinclare Cl, Enf. EN1 . . . . . . .30 DT39
Sincots Rd, Red. RH1
  off Lower Br Rd 184 DF134
Sinderby Cl, Borwd. WD6 . . . .26 CL39
Singapore Rd, W13 . . . . .79 CG74
Singer St, EC2 . . . . .197 L3
Singles Cross La, Sev. (Knock.)
  TN14 . . . . .164 EW114
SINGLE STREET, West. 179 EN115

Single St, West. (Berry's Grn.)
  TN16 . . . . .179 EP115
Singleton Cl, SW17 . . . . .120 DF94
  Croydon CR0
  off St. Saviours Rd 142 DQ101
  Hornchurch RM12
  off Carfax Rd 71 FF63
Singleton Rd, Dag. RM9 . . . . .70 EZ64
Singleton Scarp, N12 . . . . . . .44 DA50
SINGLEWELL, Grav. 131 GK93
Singlewell Rd, Grav. DA11 . . .131 GH89
Singret Pl, Uxb. (Cowley) UB8
  off High St 76 BJ70
Sinnott Rd, E17 . . . . .47 DX53
Sion Rd, Twick. TW1 . . . . . . .117 CH88
SIPSON, West Dr. 94 BN79
Sipson Cl, West Dr. UB7 . . . . .94 BN79
Sipson La, Hayes UB3 . . . . . .94 BN79
  West Drayton UB7 . . . . .94 BN79
Sipson Rd, West Dr. UB7 . . . .94 BN78
Sipson Way, West Dr. UB7 . . .94 BN80
Sir Alexander Cl, W3 . . . . . . .81 CT74
Sir Alexander Rd, W3 . . . . . . .81 CT74
Sir Cyril Black Way, SW19 . . .120 DA94
Sirdar Rd, N22 . . . . .65 DP55
  W11 . . . . .81 CX73
  Mitcham CR4
  off Grenfell Rd 120 DG93
Sirdar Strand, Grav. DA12 . . .131 GM92
Sir Francis Way, Brwd. CM14 . .54 FV47
Sirinham Pt, SW8 . . . . .101 DM79
Sirius Rd, Nthwd. HA6 . . . . . .39 BU50
★ Sir John Soane's Mus, WC2
  off Lincoln's Inn Flds 196 B8
Sir Thomas More Est, SW3
  off Beaufort St 100 DD79
Sise La, EC4 . . . . .197 K9
Siskin Cl, Borwd. WD6 . . . . . .26 CN42
  Bushey WD23 . . . . .24 BY42
Sisley Rd, Bark. IG11 . . . . . . .87 ES67
Sispara Gdns, SW18 . . . . . . .119 CZ86
Sissinghurst Rd, Croy. CR0 . .142 DU101
Sissulu Ct, E6 . . . . .86 EJ67
Sister Mabel's Way, SE15
  off Radnor Rd 102 DU80
Sisters Av, SW11 . . . . .100 DF84
Sistova Rd, SW12 . . . . .121 DH88
Sisulu Pl, SW9 . . . . .101 DN83
Sittingbourne Av, Enf. EN1 . . .30 DR44
Sitwell Gro, Stan. HA7 . . . . . .41 CF50
Siverst Cl, Nthlt. UB5 . . . . . . .78 CB65
Sivill Ho, E2 . . . . .84 DT69
Siviter Way, Dag. RM10 . . . . .89 FB66
Siward Rd, N17 . . . . .46 DR53
  SW17 . . . . .120 DC90
  Bromley BR2 . . . . .144 EH97
Six Acres Est, N4 . . . . .65 DN61
Six Bells La, Sev. TN13 . . . . .191 FJ126
Six Bridges Trd Est, SE1 . . . .102 DU78
Sixth Av, E12 . . . . .69 EM63
  W10 . . . . .81 CY69
  Hayes UB3 . . . . .77 BT74
  Watford WD25 . . . . .24 BX35
Sixth Cross Rd, Twick. TW2 . .116 CC90
Skardu Rd, NW2 . . . . .63 CY64
Skarnings Ct, Wal.Abb. EN9 . .16 EG33
Skeena Hill, SW18 . . . . .119 CY87
Skeet Hill La, Orp. BR5, BR6 .146 EY103
Skeffington Rd, E6 . . . . .86 EL67
Skelbrook St, SW18 . . . . .120 DB89
Skelgill Rd, SW15 . . . . .99 CZ84
Skelley Rd, E15 . . . . .86 EF66
Skelton Cl, E8
  off Buttermere Wk 84 DT65
Skelton Rd, E7 . . . . .86 EG65
Skeltons La, E10 . . . . .67 EB59
Skelwith Rd, W6 . . . . .99 CW79
Skenfrith Ho, SE15
  off Commercial Way 102 DV79
Skerne Rd, Kings.T. KT2 . . . .137 CK95
Skerries Ct, Slou. (Langley) SL3
  off Blacksmith Row 93 BA77
Sketchley Gdns, SE16 . . . . . .203 H10
Sketty Rd, Enf. EN1 . . . . .30 DS41
Skibbs La, Orp. BR5, BR6 . . .146 EZ103
Skid Hill La, Warl. CR6 . . . . . .162 EF113
Skidmore Way, Rick. WD3 . . .38 BL46
Skiers St, E15 . . . . .86 EE67
Skiffington Cl, SW2 . . . . .121 DN88
Skillet Hill, Wal.Abb. EN9 . . . .32 EH35
Skinner Ct, E2 off Parmiter St .84 DV68
Skinner Pl, SW1 . . . . .198 F9
★ Skinners' Hall, EC4
  off Dowgate Hill 197 K10
Skinners La, EC4 . . . . .197 J10
  Ashtead KT21 . . . . .171 CK118
  Hounslow TW5 . . . . .96 CB81
Skinner St, EC1 . . . . .196 E3
Skinney La, Dart. (Hort.Kir.)
  DA4 . . . . .148 FQ97
Skip La, Uxb. (Hare.) UB9 . . . .58 BL60
Skippers Cl, Green. DA9 . . . .129 FV85
Skips Cor, Epp. (N.Wld.Bas.)
  CM16 . . . . .19 FD25
Skipsea Ho, SW18
  off Fitzhugh Gro 120 DD86
Skipsey Av, E6 . . . . .87 EM69
Skipton Cl, N11
  off Ribblesdale Av 44 DG51
Skipton Dr, Hayes UB3 . . . . . .95 BQ76
Skipworth Rd, E9 . . . . .84 DW67
Skomer Wk, N1
  off Clephane Rd 84 DQ65
Skylark Rd, Uxb. (Denh.) UB9 .57 BC60
Skylines Village, E14 . . . . . . .204 D5
Sky Peals Rd, Wdf.Grn. IG8 . .47 ED53
Skyport Dr, West Dr. UB7 . . . .94 BK80
Slade, The, SE18 . . . . .105 ES79
Sladebrook Rd, SE3 . . . . . . .104 EK83
Slade Ct, Cher. (Ott.) KT16 . . .151 BD107
  Radlett WD7 . . . . .25 CG35
Sladedale Rd, SE18 . . . . .105 ES78
Slade End, Epp. (They.B.)
  CM16 . . . . .33 ES36
Slade Gdns, Erith DA8 . . . . . .107 FF81
⇌ Slade Green 107 FG81
Slade Grn Rd, Erith DA8 . . . .107 FG80

Slade Ho, Houns. TW4 . . . . . .116 BZ86
Slade Oak La, Ger.Cr. SL9 . . .57 BB55
  Uxbridge (Denh.) UB9 . . . . .57 BD59
Slade Rd, Cher. (Ott.) KT16 . .151 BD107
Slades Cl, Enf. EN2 . . . . .29 DN41
Slades Dr, Chis. BR7 . . . . . . .125 EQ90
Slades Gdns, Enf. EN2 . . . . . .29 DN40
Slades Hill, Enf. EN2 . . . . . . .29 DN41
Slades Ri, Enf. EN2 . . . . .29 DN41
Slade Twr, E10 . . . . .67 EB61
Slade Wk, SE17 off Heiron St .101 DP79
Slagrove Pl, SE13 . . . . .123 EB85
Slaidburn St, SW10 . . . . .100 DC79
Slaithwaite Rd, SE13 . . . . . . .103 EC84
Slaney Pl, N7 off Hornsey Rd .65 DN64
Slaney Rd, Rom. RM1 . . . . . . .71 FE57
Slapleys, Wok. GU22 . . . . . . .166 AX120
Slater Cl, SE18
  off Woolwich New Rd 105 EN78
Slattery Rd, Felt. TW13 . . . . .116 BW88
Sleaford Grn, Wat. WD19 . . . .40 BX48
Sleaford St, SW8 . . . . .101 DJ80
Sledmere Ct, Felt. TW14
  off Kilross Rd 115 BS88
Sleepers Fm Rd, Grays RM16 .111 GH75
Slewins Cl, Horn. RM11 . . . . .72 FJ57
Slewins La, Horn. RM11 . . . . .72 FJ57
Slievemore Cl, SW4
  off Voltaire Rd 101 DK83
Slines Oak Rd, Cat. (Wold.)
  CR3 . . . . .177 EA123
  Warlingham CR6 . . . . .177 AA119
Slingsby Pl, WC2 . . . . .195 P10
Slip, The, West. TN16 . . . . . .189 EQ126
Slippers Pl, SE16 . . . . .202 E6
Slipshoe St, Reig. RH2
  off West St 183 CZ134
Sloane Av, SW3 . . . . .198 B8
Sloane Ct E, SW3 . . . . .198 F10
Sloane Ct W, SW3 . . . . .198 F10
Sloane Gdns, SW1 . . . . .198 F9
  Orpington BR6 . . . . .145 EQ104
H Sloane Hosp, The, Beck.
  BR3 . . . . .143 ED95
⊖ Sloane Square 198 F9
Sloane Sq, SW1 . . . . .198 F9
Sloane St, SW1 . . . . .198 E6
Sloane Ter, SW1 . . . . .198 E8
Sloane Wk, Croy. CR0 . . . . . .143 DZ100
Slocock Hill, Wok. GU21 . . . .166 AW117
Slocum Cl, SE28 . . . . .88 EW73
SLOUGH 74 AS74
⇌ Slough 74 AT74
Slough La, NW9 . . . . .62 CQ58
  Betchworth (Buckland) RH3 .183 CU133
  Epsom (Headley) KT18 . . . .182 CQ125
★ Slough Mus, Slou. SL1 . . . .92 AU75
Slough Rd, Iver SL0 . . . . .75 BC69
  Slough (Datchet) SL3 . . . . .92 AU78
Slowmans Cl, St.Alb. (Park St.)
  AL2 . . . . .8 CC28
Sly St, E1 off Cannon St Rd . .84 DV72
Smaldon Cl, West Dr. UB7
  off Walnut Av 94 BN76
Smallberry Av, Islw. TW7 . . . .97 CF82
Smallbrook Ms, W2
  off Craven Rd 82 DD72
Smalley Cl, N16 . . . . .66 DT63
Smalley Rd Est, N16
  off Smalley Cl 66 DT62
Small Grains, Long. (Fawk.Grn.)
  DA3 . . . . .149 FV104
Smallholdings Rd, Epsom
  KT17 . . . . .157 CW114
Smallwood Rd, SW17 . . . . . .120 DD91
Smardale Rd, SW18
  off Alma Rd 120 DC85
Smarden Cl, Belv. DA17
  off Essenden Rd 106 FA78
Smarden Gro, SE9 . . . . .125 EM91
Smart Cl, Rom. RM3 . . . . .51 FH53
Smarts Grn, Wal.Cr. (Chsht.)
  EN7 . . . . .14 DT27
Smarts Heath La, Wok. GU22 .166 AU121
Smarts Heath Rd, Wok. GU22 .166 AT123
Smarts La, Loug. IG10 . . . . . .32 EK42
Smarts Pl, N18 off Fore St . . .46 DU50
Smart's Pl, WC2 . . . . .196 A8
Smart St, E2 . . . . .85 DX69
Smeaton Cl, Chess. KT9
  off Merritt Gdns 155 CK107
  Waltham Abbey EN9 . . . . . .16 EE32
Smeaton Rd, SW18 . . . . .120 DA87
  Enfield EN3 . . . . .31 EA37
  Woodford Green IG8 . . . . . .49 EM50
Smeaton St, E1 . . . . .202 D2
Smedley St, SW4 . . . . .101 DK82
  SW8 . . . . .101 DK82
Smeed Rd, E3 . . . . .85 EA66
Smiles Pl, SE13 . . . . .103 EC82
⇌ Smitham 175 DL115
Smitham Bottom La, Pur.
  CR8 . . . . .159 DJ111
Smitham Downs Rd, Pur.
  CR8 . . . . .159 DK113
Smith Cl, SE16 . . . . .203 H3
★ Smithfield Cen Mkt, EC1 . . .196 G7
Smithfield St, EC1 . . . . .196 F7
Smithies Ct, E15 . . . . .67 EC64
Smithies Rd, SE2 . . . . .106 EV77
Smiths Caravan Site, Iver SL0 .75 BC74
Smith's Ct, W1 . . . . .195 L10
Smiths Fm Est, Nthlt. UB5 . . .78 CA68
Smiths La, Eden. (Crock.H.)
  TN8 . . . . .189 EQ133
  Waltham Cross (Chsht.) EN7 .14 DR26
Smithson Rd, N17 . . . . .46 DR53
Smiths Pt, E13 off Brooks Rd .86 EG67
Smiths Yd, SW18
  off Summerley St 120 DC89
Smith's Yd, Croy. CR0
  off St. Georges Wk 142 DQ104

Smith Ter, SW3 . . . . .100 DF78
Smithwood Cl, SW19 . . . . . . .119 CY88
Smithy Cl, Tad. (Lwr.Kgswd.)
  KT20 . . . . .183 CZ126
Smithy La, Tad. (Lwr.Kgswd.)
  KT20 . . . . .183 CZ127
Smithy St, E1 . . . . .84 DW71
Smock Wk, Croy. CR0 . . . . . .142 DQ100
Smokehouse Yd, EC1 . . . . . . .196 G6
Smugglers Wk, Green. DA9 . .129 FV85
Smugglers Way, SW18 . . . . . .100 DB84
Smug Oak Grn Business Cen,
  St.Alb. AL2 . . . . .8 CB30
Smug Oak La, St.Alb. (Brick.Wd.)
  AL2 . . . . .8 CB30
Smyrks Rd, SE17 . . . . .102 DS78
Smyrna Rd, NW6 . . . . .82 DA66
Smythe Cl, Dart. (Sutt.H.)
  DA4 . . . . .148 FN95
Smythe St, E14 . . . . .85 EB73
Snag La, Sev. (Cudham) TN14 .163 ES109
Snakes La, Barn. EN4 . . . . . . .29 DH41
Snakes La E, Wdf.Grn. IG8 . . .48 EJ51
Snakes La W, Wdf.Grn. IG8 . . .48 EG51
Snape Spur, Slou. SL1 . . . . . .74 AS72
SNARESBROOK, E11 . . . . . . .68 EE57
⊖ Snaresbrook 68 EG57
Snaresbrook Dr, Stan. HA7 . . .41 CK49
Snaresbrook Rd, E11 . . . . . . .68 EE56
Snarsgate St, W10 . . . . .81 CW71
Snatts Hill, Oxt. RH8 . . . . . . .188 EF129
Sneath Av, NW11 . . . . .63 CZ59
Snelling Av, Grav. (Nthflt.)
  DA11 . . . . .130 GE89
Snellings Rd, Walt. KT12 . . . .154 BW106
Snells La, Amer. HP7 . . . . . . .20 AV39
Snells Pk, N18 . . . . .46 DT51
Snells Wd Ct, Amer. HP7 . . . .20 AW40
Sneyd Rd, NW2 . . . . .63 CW63
Snipe Cl, Erith DA8 . . . . .107 FH80
Snodland Cl, Orp. BR6
  off Mill La 163 EN110
Snowberry Cl, E15 . . . . .67 ED63
Snowbury Rd, SW6 . . . . .100 DB82
Snowden Av, Uxb. UB10 . . . . .77 BP68
Snowden St, EC2 . . . . .197 M5
Snowdon Cres, Hayes UB3 . . .95 BQ76
Snowdon Dr, NW9 . . . . .62 CS58
Snowdon Rd, Houns. (Hthrw.Air.)
  TW6 off Southern
  Perimeter Rd 115 BQ85
Snowdown Cl, SE20 . . . . .143 DX95
Snowdrop Cl, Hmptn. TW12
  off Gresham Rd 116 CA93
Snowdrop Path, Rom. RM3 . . .52 FK52
Snow Hill, EC1 . . . . .196 F7
Snow Hill Ct, EC1 . . . . .196 G8
Snowman Ho, NW6 . . . . .82 DB67
Snowsfields, SE1 . . . . .201 L4
Snowshill Rd, E12 . . . . .68 EL64
Snowy Fielder Waye, Islw. TW7 .97 CH82
Soames St, SE15 . . . . .102 DT83
Soames Wk, N.Mal. KT3 . . . .138 CS95
Soap Ho La, Brent. TW8 . . . . .98 CL80
Socket La, Brom. BR2 . . . . . .144 EH100
SOCKETT'S HEATH, Grays . . .110 GD76
Soham Rd, Enf. EN3 . . . . .31 DZ37
SOHO, W1 . . . . .195 M10
Soho Sq, W1 . . . . .195 M8
Soho St, W1 . . . . .195 M8
Sojourner Truth Cl, E8
  off Richmond Rd 84 DV65
Solander Gdns, E1
  off Dellow St 84 DV73
Solar Way, Enf. EN3 . . . . .31 DZ36
Solebay St, E1 . . . . .85 DY70
Sole Fm Cl, Lthd. (Bkhm.)
  KT23 . . . . .170 BZ124
Solefields Rd, Sev. TN13 . . . .191 FH128
Solent Ri, E13 . . . . .86 EG69
Solent Rd, NW6 . . . . .64 DA64
  Hounslow (Hthrw.Air.) TW6 . .114 BM86
Soleoak Dr, Sev. TN13 . . . . . .191 FH127
Solesbridge Cl, Rick. (Chorl.) WD3
  off Solesbridge La 21 BF41
Solesbridge La, Rick. WD3 . . .22 BG40
Soley Ms, WC1 . . . . .196 D2
Solna Av, SW15 . . . . .119 CW85
Solna Rd, N21 . . . . .46 DR46
Solomon Av, N9 . . . . .46 DU49
Solomons Hill, Rick. WD3
  off Northway 38 BK45
Solomon's Pas, SE15 . . . . . .102 DV84
Solomon's Ct Rd, Bans. SM7 .174 DE117
Solon New Rd, SW4 . . . . . . .101 DL84
Solon New Rd Est, SW4
  off Solon New Rd 101 DL84
Solon Rd, SW2 . . . . .101 DL84
Solway Cl, E8
  off Buttermere Wk 84 DT65
  Hounslow TW4 . . . . .96 BY83
Solway Rd, N22 . . . . .45 DP53
  SE22 . . . . .102 DU84
Somaford Gro, Barn. EN4 . . . .28 DD44
Somali Rd, NW2 . . . . .63 CZ63
Somborne Ho, SW15
  off Fontley Way 119 CU87
Somerby Rd, Bark. IG11 . . . . .87 ER66
Somercoates Cl, Barn. EN4 . .28 DE41
Somerden Rd, Orp. BR5 . . . . .146 EX101
Somerfield Cl, Tad. KT20 . . . .173 CY119
Somerfield Rd, N4 . . . . .65 DP61
Somerford Cl, Pnr. HA5 . . . . . .59 BU56
Somerford Gro, N16 . . . . .66 DT63
  N17 . . . . .46 DU52
Somerford Gro Est, N16
  off Somerford Gro 66 DT63
Somerford St, E1 . . . . .84 DV70
Somerford Way, SE16 . . . . . .203 K5
Somerhill Av, Well. DA16 . . . .106 EV82
Somerhill Rd, Well. DA16 . . . .106 EV82
Somerleyton Pas, SW9 . . . . .101 DP84
Somerleyton Rd, SW9 . . . . . .101 DN84
Somersby Gdns, Ilf. IG4 . . . . .69 EM57
Somers Cl, NW1 off Platt St . .83 DK68
Somerset Av, SW20 . . . . .139 CV96
  Reigate RH2 . . . . .184 DA133
Somers Cres, W2 . . . . .194 B9

Somerset Av, SW20 . . . . .139 CV96
Chessington KT9 . . . . . . .155 CK105
Welling DA16 . . . . .125 ET85
Somerset Cl, N17 . . . . . . .46 DR54
Epsom KT19 . . . . . . .156 CS109
New Malden KT3 . . . . . .138 CS100
Walton-on-Thames KT12
off Queens Rd 153 BV106
Woodford Green IG8 . . . .48 EG53
Somerset Est, SW11 . . . . . .100 DD81
Somerset Gdns, N6 . . . . . .64 DG59
N17 . . . . .46 DS52
SE13 . . . . .103 EB82
SW16 . . . . .141 DM97
Hornchurch RM11 . . . . .72 FN60
Teddington TW11 . . . . . .117 CE92
★ Somerset Ho, WC2 . . . . .196 B10
Somerset Ho, SW19 . . . . . .119 CX90
Somerset Rd, E17 . . . . . . .67 EA57
N17 . . . . .66 DT55
N18 . . . . .46 DT50
NW4 . . . . .63 CW56
SW19 . . . . .119 CY91
W4 . . . . .98 CR76
W13 . . . . .79 CH74
Barnet EN5 . . . . .28 DB43
Brentford TW8 . . . . . . .97 CJ79
Dartford DA1 . . . . . . .127 FH86
Enfield EN3 . . . . . . .31 EA38
Harrow HA1 . . . . .60 CC57
Kingston upon Thames KT1 .138 CM96
Orpington BR6 . . . . . . .146 EU101
Southall UB1 . . . . . . .78 BZ71
Teddington TW11 . . . . . .117 CE92
Somerset Sq, W14 . . . . . . .99 CY75
Somerset Way, Iver SL0 . . . .93 BF75
Somerset Waye, Houns. TW5 .96 BY79
Somersham Rd, Bexh. DA7 . .106 EY82
Somers Ms, W2 . . . . . . .194 B9
Somers Pl, SW2 . . . . . . .121 DM87
Reigate RH2 . . . . . . .184 DA133
Somers Rd, E17 . . . . . . .67 DZ56
SW2 . . . . .121 DM86
Reigate RH2 . . . . . . .183 CZ133
SOMERS TOWN, NW1 . . . . .195 M2
Somers Way, Bushey WD23 . .40 CC45
Somerton Av, Rich. TW9 . . . .98 CP83
Somerton Cl, Pur. CR8 . . . .175 DN115
Somerton Rd, NW2 . . . . . .63 CY62
SE15 . . . . .102 DV84
Somertrees Av, SE12 . . . . .124 EH89
Somervell Rd, Har. HA2 . . . .60 BZ64
Somerville Av, SW13 . . . . . .99 CV79
Somerville Rd, SE20 . . . . . .123 DX94
Cobham KT11 . . . . . . .154 CA114
Dartford DA1 . . . . . . .128 FM86
Romford RM6 . . . . . . .70 EW58
Sonderburg Rd, N7 . . . . . .65 DM61
Sondes St, SE17 . . . . . . .102 DR79
Sonia Cl, Wat. WD19 . . . . . .40 BW45
Sonia Ct, Har. HA1 . . . . . .61 CF58
Sonia Gdns, N12
off Woodside Av 44 DC49
NW10 . . . . .63 CT63
Hounslow TW5 . . . . . .96 CA80
Sonnet Wk, West. (Bigg.H.) TN16
off Kings Rd 178 EH118
Sonning Gdns, Hmptn. TW12 .116 BY93
Sonning Rd, SE25 . . . . . .142 DU100
Soper Cl, E4 . . . . .47 DZ50
Soper Dr, Cat. CR3
off Hambledon Rd 176 DR123
Soper Ms, Enf. EN3
off Harston Dr 31 EA38
Sopers Rd, Pot.B. (Cuffley) EN6 .13 DM29
Sophia Cl, N7
off Mackenzie Rd 83 DM65
Sophia Rd, E10 . . . . . . .67 EB60
E16 . . . . .86 EH72
Sophia Sq, SE16 . . . . . . .203 K1
Sopwith Av, Chess. KT9 . . . .156 CL106
Sopwith Cl, Kings.T. KT2 . . .118 CM92
Westerham (Bigg.H.) TN16 .178 EK116
Sopwith Dr, W.Byf. KT14 . . .152 BL111
Weybridge KT13 . . . . . .152 BL111
Sopwith Rd, Houns. TW5 . . .96 BW80
Sopwith Way, SW8 . . . . . .101 DH80
Kingston upon Thames KT2 .138 CL95
Sorbie Cl, Wey. KT13 . . . . .153 BR107
Sorrel Bk, Croy. CR0 . . . . .161 DY110
Sorrel Cl, SE28 . . . . . . .88 EU74
Sorrel Ct, Grays RM17
off Salix Rd 110 GD79
Sorrel Gdns, E6 . . . . . . .86 EL71
Sorrel La, E14 . . . . . . .85 ED72
Sorrell Cl, SE14
off Southerngate Way 103 DY80
Sorrel Wk, Rom. RM1 . . . . .71 FF55
Sorrel Way, Grav. (Nthflt.)
DA11 . . . . .130 GE91
Sorrento Rd, Sutt. SM1 . . . .140 DB104
Sotheby Rd, N5 . . . . . . .65 DP62
Sotheran Cl, E8 . . . . . . .84 DU67
Sotheron Rd, SW6 . . . . . .100 DB80
Watford WD17 . . . . . . .24 BW40
Soudan Rd, SW11 . . . . . .100 DF81
Souldern Rd, W14 . . . . . .99 CX76
Souldern St, Wat. WD18 . . . .23 BU43
Sounds Lo, Swan. BR8 . . . .147 FC100
South Access Rd, E17 . . . . .67 DY59
Southacre Way, Pnr. HA5 . . .40 BW53
SOUTH ACTON, W3 . . . . . .98 CN76
⇌ South Acton 98 CQ76
South Africa Rd, W12 . . . . .81 CV74
South Albert Rd, Reig. RH2 . .183 CZ133
SOUTHALL 78 BX74
⇌ Southall 78 BZ75
Southall La, Houns. TW5 . . . .96 BV79
Southall UB2 . . . . . . .95 BV79
Southall Pl, SE1 . . . . . . .201 K5
Southall Way, Brwd. CM14 . . .54 FT49
Southampton Bldgs, WC2 . . .196 D8
Southampton Gdns, Mitch.
CR4 . . . . .141 DL99
Southampton Ms, E16 . . . . .205 P2
Southampton Pl, WC1 . . . . .196 A7
Southampton Rd, NW5 . . . . .64 DF64

Southampton Rd, Houns.
(Hthrw.Air.) TW6 . . . . . . .114 BN86
Southampton Row, WC1 . . . .196 A6
Southampton St, WC2 . . . . .196 A10
Southampton Way, SE5 . . . .102 DR80
South App, Nthwd. HA6 . . . .39 BR48
South Audley St, W1 . . . . .198 G1
South Av, E4 . . . . .47 EB45
Carshalton SM5 . . . . . .158 DF108
Egham TW20 . . . . . . .113 BC93
Richmond TW9
off Sandycombe Rd 98 CN82
Southall UB1 . . . . . . .78 BZ73
Walton-on-Thames KT12 . .153 BS110
South Av Gdns, Sthl. UB1 . . .78 BZ73
South Bk, Chis. BR7 . . . . .125 EQ91
Surbiton KT6 . . . . . . .138 CL100
Southbank, T.Ditt. KT7 . . . .137 CH101
South Bk, West. TN16 . . . . .189 ER126
South Bk Ter, Surb. KT6 . . . .138 CL100
SOUTH BEDDINGTON, Wall. .159 DK107
⇌ South Bermondsey 202 F10
South Birkbeck Rd, E11 . . . .67 ED62
South Black Lion La, W6 . . . .99 CU77
South Bolton Gdns, SW5 . . .100 DB78
South Border, The, Pur. CR8 .159 DK111
SOUTHBOROUGH, Brom. . . .145 EM100
Southborough Cl, Surb. KT6 .137 CK102
Southborough La, Brom. BR2 .144 EL99
Bromley BR1 . . . . . . .144 EL97
Surbiton KT6 . . . . . . .138 CL102
Southbourne, Brom. BR2 . . .144 EG101
Southbourne Av, NW9 . . . . .42 CQ54
Southbourne Cl, Pnr. HA5 . . .60 BY59
Southbourne Cres, NW4 . . . .63 CY56
Southbourne Gdns, SE12 . . .124 EH85
Ilford IG1 . . . . .69 EQ64
Ruislip HA4 . . . . .59 BV60
Southbridge Pl, Croy. CR0 . .160 DQ105
Southbridge Rd, Croy. CR0 . .160 DQ105
Southbridge Way, Sthl. UB2 . .96 BY75
Southbrook Dr, Wal.Cr. (Chsht.)
EN8 . . . . .15 DX28
Southbrook Ms, SE12 . . . . .124 EF86
Southbrook Rd, SE12 . . . . .124 EF86
SW16 . . . . .141 DL95
⇌ Southbury 30 DV42
Southbury Av, Enf. EN1 . . . .30 DU43
Southbury Cl, Horn. RM12 . . .72 FK64
Southbury Rd, Enf. EN1, EN3 .30 DR41
SW7 . . . . .198 A5
South Carriage Dr, SW1 . . . .198 D4
SOUTH CHINGFORD, E4 . . . .47 DZ50
Southchurch Rd, E6 . . . . . .87 EM68
Southcliffe Dr, Ger.Cr. (Chal.St.P.)
SL9 . . . . .36 AY50
South Cl, N6 . . . . .65 DH58
Barnet EN5 . . . . .27 CZ41
Bexleyheath DA6 . . . . .106 EX84
Dagenham RM10 . . . . . .88 FA67
Morden SM4 off Green La .140 DB100
Pinner HA5 . . . . .60 BZ59
St. Albans AL2 . . . . . . .8 CB25
Twickenham TW2 . . . . .116 CA90
West Drayton UB7 . . . . .94 BM76
Woking GU21 . . . . . .166 AW116
South Cl Grn, Red. RH1 . . . .185 DH129
South Colonnade, E14 . . . . .204 A2
Southcombe St, W14 . . . . . .99 CY77
South Common Rd, Uxb. UB8 .76 BL65
Southcote, Wok. GU21 . . . .166 AX115
Southcote Av, Felt. TW13 . . .115 BT89
Surbiton KT5 . . . . . . .138 CP101
Southcote Ri, Ruis. HA4 . . . .59 BR59
Southcote Rd, E17 . . . . . .67 DX57
N19 . . . . .65 DJ63
SE25 . . . . .142 DV100
Redhill RH1 . . . . . . .185 DJ129
South Croydon CR2 . . . .160 DS110
South Cottage Dr, Rick. (Chorl.)
WD3 . . . . .21 BF43
South Cottage Gdns, Rick. (Chorl.)
WD3 . . . . .21 BF43
South Countess Rd, E17 . . . .67 DZ55
South Cres, E16 . . . . . . .85 ED70
WC1 . . . . .195 M7
South Cft, Egh. (Eng.Grn.)
TW20 . . . . .112 AV92
Southcroft Av, Well. DA16 . . .105 ES83
West Wickham BR4 . . . .143 EC103
Southcroft Rd, SW16 . . . . .120 DG93
SW17 . . . . .120 DG93
Orpington BR6 . . . . . .145 ES104
South Cross Rd, Ilf. IG6 . . . .69 EQ57
SOUTH CROYDON 160 DQ107
⇌ South Croydon 160 DR106
Southdale, Chig. IG7 . . . . . .49 ER51
SOUTH DARENTH, Dart. . . .149 FR95
Southdean Gdns, SW19 . . . .119 CZ89
South Dene, NW7 . . . . . . .42 CR48
Southdene, Sev. (Halst.) TN14 .164 EY113
Southdown Av, W7 . . . . . .97 CG76
Southdown Cres, Har. HA2 . . .60 CB60
Ilford IG2 . . . . .69 ES57
Southdown Dr, SW20
off Crescent Rd 119 CX94
Southdown Rd, SW20 . . . . .139 CX95
Carshalton SM5 . . . . . .158 DG109
Caterham (Wold.) CR3 . . .177 DZ122
Hornchurch RM11 . . . . .71 FH59
Walton-on-Thames KT12 . .154 BY105
Southdowns, Dart. (S.Darenth)
DA4 . . . . .149 FR96
South Dr, Bans. SM7 . . . . .158 DE113
Brentwood CM14 . . . . .54 FX49
Coulsdon CR5 . . . . . .175 DK115
Orpington BR6 . . . . . .163 ES106
Potters Bar (Cuffley) EN6 . .13 DL30
Romford RM2 . . . . . . .72 FJ55
Ruislip HA4 . . . . .59 BS60
Sutton SM2 . . . . . . .157 CY110
Virginia Water GU25 . . . .132 AU102
⇌ South Ealing 97 CJ76
South Ealing Rd, W5 . . . . . .97 CK75

South Eastern Av, N9 . . . . . .46 DT48
South Eaton Pl, SW1 . . . . .198 G8
South Eden Pk Rd, Beck. BR3 .143 EB60
South Edwardes Sq, W8 . . . .99 CZ76
SOUTHEND, SE6 . . . . . . .123 EB91
South End, W8
off St. Albans Gro 100 DB76
Croydon CR0 . . . . . . .160 DQ105
Southend Arterial Rd, Brwd.
CM13 . . . . .73 FV57
Hornchurch RM11 . . . . .52 FK54
Romford RM2, RM3 . . . .52 FK54
Upminster RM14 . . . . . .73 FR57
South End Cl, NW3 . . . . . .64 DE63
Southend Cl, SE9 . . . . . . .125 EP86
Southend Cres, SE9 . . . . . .125 EN86
South End Grn, NW3
off South End Rd 64 DE63
Southend La, SE6 . . . . . . .123 DZ91
SE26 . . . . .123 DZ91
Waltham Abbey EN9 . . . .16 EH34
Southend Rd, E4 . . . . . . .47 DY50
E6 . . . . .87 EM66
E17 . . . . .47 EB53
E18 . . . . .48 EG53
South End Rd, NW3 . . . . . .64 DE63
Beckenham BR3 . . . . . .123 EA94
Grays RM17 . . . . . . .110 GC77
South End Rd, Horn. RM12 . .89 FH65
Rainham RM13 . . . . . .89 FG67
Southend Rd, Wdf.Grn. IG8 . .48 EJ54
South End Row, W8 . . . . . .100 DB76
Southerland Cl, Wey. KT13 . .153 BQ105
Southern Av, SE25 . . . . . .142 DT97
Feltham TW14 . . . . . .115 BU88
Southern Dr, Loug. IG10 . . . .33 EM44
Southern Gro, E3 . . . . . . .85 DZ69
Southernhay, Loug. IG10 . . . .32 EK43
Southern Perimeter Rd, Houns.
(Hthrw.Air.) TW6 . . . . . . .115 BR85
Southern Pl, Swan. BR8 . . . .147 FD98
Southern Rd, E13 . . . . . . .86 EH68
N2 . . . . .64 DF56
Southern Row, W10 . . . . . .81 CY70
Southerns La, Couls. CR5 . . .184 DC125
Southern St, N1 . . . . . . .83 DM68
Southern Way, SE10 . . . . . .205 L8
Romford RM7 . . . . . . .70 FA58
Southerton Rd, W6 . . . . . .99 CW76
Southerton Way, Rad. (Shenley)
WD7 . . . . .10 CL33
South Esk Rd, E7 . . . . . . .86 EJ65
Southey Ms, E16 . . . . . . .205 N2
Southey Rd, N15 . . . . . . .66 DS57
SW9 . . . . .101 DN81
SW19 . . . . .120 DA94
Southey St, SE20 . . . . . . .123 DX94
Southey Wk, Til. RM18 . . . .111 GH81
Southfield, Barn. EN5 . . . . .27 CX43
Southfield Av, Wat. WD24 . . .24 BW38
Southfield Cotts, W7
off Oaklands Rd 97 CF75
Southfield Gdns, Twick. TW1 .117 CF91
Southfield Pk, Har. HA2 . . . .60 CB56
Southfield Pl, Wey. KT13 . . .153 BP108
Southfield Rd, N17
off The Avenue 46 DS54
W4 . . . . .98 CS76
Chislehurst BR7 . . . . . .145 ET97
Enfield EN3 . . . . . . .30 DV44
Waltham Cross EN8 . . . .15 DY32
SOUTHFIELDS, SW18 . . . . .120 DA88
⊖ Southfields 119 CZ88
Southfields, NW4 . . . . . . .63 CU55
East Molesey KT8 . . . . .137 CE100
Swanley BR8 . . . . . . .127 FE97
Southfields Av, Ashf. TW15 . .115 BP93
Southfields Ct, SW19 . . . . .119 CY88
Sutton SM1
off Sutton Common Rd . .140 DA103
Southfields Pas, SW18 . . . .120 DA86
Southfields Rd, SW18 . . . . .120 DA86
Caterham (Wold.) CR3 . . .177 EB123
SOUTHFLEET, Grav. 130 GB93
Southfleet Rd, Dart. (Bean)
DA2 . . . . .129 FW91
Gravesend (Nthflt.) DA11 . .131 GF89
Orpington BR6 . . . . . .145 ES104
Swanscombe DA10 . . . .130 FZ87
Sutton Gdns, SW19 . . . .120 DA94
SOUTHGATE, N14 . . . . . . .45 DJ47
⊖ Southgate 45 DJ46
Southgate, Purf. RM19 . . . .108 FQ77
Southgate Av, Felt. TW13 . . .115 BR91
Southgate Circ, N14
off The Bourne 45 DK46
Southgate Gro, N1 . . . . . .84 DR66
Southgate Rd, N1 . . . . . . .84 DR67
Potters Bar EN6 . . . . . .12 DC33
South Gipsy Rd, Well. DA16 . .106 EX83
South Glade, The, Bex. DA5 . .126 EZ88
South Gro, NW9
off Clayton Fld 42 CS53
Slough SL1 . . . . .74 AS73
⇌ South Greenford 79 CE69
South Gro, E17 . . . . . . .67 DZ57
N6 . . . . .64 DG60
N15 . . . . .66 DR57
Chertsey KT16 . . . . . .133 BF100
South Gro Ho, N6
off Highgate W Hill 64 DG60
SOUTH HACKNEY, E9 . . . . .84 DW66
South Hall Cl, Dart. (Fngham.)
DA4 . . . . .148 FM101
South Hall Dr, Rain. RM13 . . .89 FH71
SOUTH HAMPSTEAD, NW6 . .82 DC66
⇌ South Hampstead 82 DC66
SOUTH HAREFIELD, Uxb. . . .58 BJ56
SOUTH HARROW, Har. 60 CB62
⇌ South Harrow 60 CC62
South Hill, Chis. BR7 . . . . .125 EM93
South Hill Av, Har. HA1, HA2 . .60 CC62
South Hill Gro, Har. HA1 . . . .61 CE63
South Hill Pk, NW3 . . . . . .64 DE63
South Hill Pk Gdns, NW3 . . . .64 DE63

South Hill Rd, Brom. BR2 . . .144 EE97
Gravesend DA12 . . . . . .131 GH88
Southholme Cl, SE19 . . . . .142 DS95
SOUTH HORNCHURCH, Rain. .89 FE67
South Huxley, N18 . . . . . .46 DR50
Southill La, Pnr. HA5 . . . . .59 BU56
Southill Rd, Chis. BR7 . . . . .124 EL94
South Island Pl, SW9 . . . . .101 DM80
SOUTH KENSINGTON, SW7 . .100 DB76
⊖ South Kensington 198 A8
South Kensington Sta Arc, SW7
off Pelham St 100 DD77
DA11 . . . . .130 GC86
⇌ South Kenton 61 CJ60
⊖ South Kenton 61 CJ60
SOUTH LAMBETH, SW8 . . . .101 DL81
South Lambeth Pl, SW8 . . . .101 DL79
South Lambeth Rd, SW8 . . . .101 DL79
Southland Rd, SE18 . . . . . .105 ET80
Southlands Av, Orp. BR6 . . .163 ER105
Southlands Cl, Couls. CR5 . .175 DM117
Southlands Dr, SW19 . . . . .119 CX89
Southlands Gro, Brom. BR1 . .144 EL97
Southlands La, Oxt. (Tand.)
RH8 . . . . .187 EB134
Southlands Rd, Brom.
BR1, BR2 . . . . .144 EJ99
Iver SL0 . . . . .57 BF64
Uxbridge (Denh.) UB9 . . .57 BF63
Southland Way, Houns. TW3 .117 CD85
South La, Kings.T. KT1 . . . .137 CK97
New Malden KT3 . . . . .138 CR98
South La W, N.Mal. KT3 . . . .138 CR98
SOUTHLEA, Slou. 92 AV82
Southlea Rd, Slou. (Datchet)
SL3 . . . . .92 AV81
Windsor SL4 . . . . . . .92 AU84
South Lo Av, Mitch. CR4 . . . .141 DL98
South Lo Cres, Enf. EN2 . . . .29 DK42
South Lo Dr, N14 . . . . . . .29 DL43
South Lo Rd, Walt. KT12 . . .153 BU109
★ South London Art Gall,
SE5 . . . . .102 DS81
Southly Cl, Sutt. SM1 . . . . .140 DA104
South Mall, N9 off Plevna Rd .46 DU48
South Mead, NW9 . . . . . . .43 CT53
Epsom KT19 . . . . . . .156 CS108
Redhill RH1 . . . . . . .184 DF131
Southmead Cres, Wal.Cr. (Chsht.)
EN8 . . . . .15 DY30
South Meadows, Wem. HA9 . .62 CM64
Southmead Rd, SW19 . . . . .119 CY88
SOUTH MERSTHAM, Red. . . .185 DJ130
⇌ South Merton 139 CZ97
SOUTH MIMMS, Pot.B. 11 CT32
South Molton La, W1 . . . . .195 H9
South Molton Rd, E16 . . . . .86 EG72
South Molton St, W1 . . . . .195 H9
Southmont Rd, Esher KT10 . .137 CE103
Southmoor Way, E9 . . . . . .85 DZ65
SOUTH NORWOOD, SE25 . . .142 DT97
South Norwood Hill, SE25 . .142 DS96
South Oak Rd, SW16 . . . . .121 DM91
SOUTH OCKENDON 91 FW70
Southold Ri, SE9 . . . . . . .125 EM90
Southolm St, SW11 . . . . . .101 DH81
South Ordnance Rd, Enf. EN3 .31 EA37
SOUTH OXHEY, Wat. 40 BW48
South Par, SW3 . . . . . . .198 A10
W4 . . . . .98 CR77
Waltham Abbey EN9
off Sun St 15 EC33
South Pk, SW6 . . . . .100 DA82
Gerrards Cross SL9 . . . .57 AZ57
Sevenoaks TN13 . . . . .191 FH125
South Pk Av, Rick. (Chorl.)
WD3 . . . . .21 BF43
South Pk Cres, SE6 . . . . . .124 EE88
Gerrards Cross SL9 . . . .56 AY56
Ilford IG1 . . . . .69 ER62
South Pk Dr, Bark. IG11 . . . .69 ES63
Gerrards Cross SL9 . . . .56 AY56
Ilford IG1 . . . . .69 ER62
South Pk Gro, N.Mal. KT3 . .138 CQ98
South Pk Hill Rd, S.Croy. CR2 .160 DR106
South Pk Ms, SW6 . . . . . .100 DB83
South Pk Rd, SW19 . . . . . .120 DA93
Ilford IG1 . . . . .69 ER62
South Pk Ter, Ilf. IG1 . . . . .69 ER62
South Pk Vw, Ger.Cr. SL9 . . .57 AZ56
South Pk Way, Ruis. HA4 . . .78 BW65
South Penge Pk Est, SE20 . .142 DV96
South Perimeter Rd, Uxb. UB8
off Kingston La 76 BL69
South Pl, EC2 . . . . .197 L6
Enfield EN3 . . . . . . .30 DW43
Surbiton KT5 . . . . . . .138 CM101
South Pl Ms, EC2 . . . . . .197 L7
South Pt, Sutt. SM1 . . . . . .158 DC107
Southport Rd, SE18 . . . . . .105 ER77
DLR South Quay 204 B4
South Ridge, Wey. KT13 . . .153 BP110
Southridge Pl, SW20 . . . . .119 CX94
South Riding, St.Alb. (Brick.Wd.)
AL2 . . . . .8 CA30
South Ri, Cars. SM5 . . . . .158 DE109
South Ri Way, SE18 . . . . . .105 ER78
South Rd, N9 . . . . .46 DU46
SE23 . . . . .123 DX89
SW19 . . . . .120 DC93
W5 . . . . .97 CK77
Edgware HA8 . . . . . . .42 CP53
Egham (Eng.Grn.) TW20 . .112 AW93
Erith DA8 . . . . .107 FF79
Feltham TW13 . . . . . .116 BX92
Hampton TW12 . . . . . .116 BY93
Rickmansworth (Chorl.) WD3 .21 BE43
Romford (Chad.Hth.) RM6 . .70 EY58
Romford (Lt.Hth.) RM6 . . .70 EW57
South Ockendon RM15 . . .91 FW72
Southall UB1 . . . . . . .96 BZ75
Twickenham TW2 . . . . .117 CD90
West Drayton UB7 . . . . .94 BM76

South Rd, Wey. KT13 . . . . .153 BQ106
Weybridge (St.Geo.H.)
KT13 . . . . .153 BP109
Woking GU21 . . . . . .150 AX114
South Row, SE3 . . . . . . .104 EF82
SOUTH RUISLIP, Ruis. 60 BW63
⇌ South Ruislip 60 BW63
⊖ South Ruislip 60 BW63
Southsea Av, Wat. WD18 . . .23 BU42
Southsea Rd, Kings.T. KT1 . .138 CL98
South Sea St, SE16 . . . . . .203 M6
South Side, W6 . . . . . . .99 CT76
Southside, Ger.Cr. (Chal.St.P.)
SL9 . . . . .56 AX55
Southside Common, SW19 . .119 CW93
Southspring, Sid. DA15 . . . .125 ER87
South Sq, NW11 . . . . . . .64 DB58
WC1 . . . . .196 D7
SOUTH STIFFORD, Grays . . .109 FW78
SOUTH STREET, West. 179 EM119
South St, W1 . . . . .198 G2
Brentwood CM14 . . . . .54 FW47
Bromley BR1 . . . . . . .144 EG96
Enfield EN3 . . . . . . .31 DX43
Epsom KT18 . . . . . . .156 CR113
Gravesend DA12 . . . . . .131 GH87
Isleworth TW7 . . . . . . .97 CG83
Rainham RM13 . . . . . .89 FC68
Romford RM1 . . . . . . .71 FF58
Staines TW18 . . . . . . .113 BF92
South Tenter St, E1 . . . . . .84 DT73
South Ter, SW7 . . . . . . .198 B8
Surbiton KT6 . . . . . . .138 CL100
SOUTH TOTTENHAM, N15 . . .66 DS57
⇌ South Tottenham 66 DT57
South Vale, SE19 . . . . . . .122 DS93
Harrow HA1 . . . . .61 CE63
Southvale Rd, SE3 . . . . . .104 EE82
South Vw, Brom. BR1 . . . . .144 EH96
Southview Av, NW10 . . . . . .63 CT64
South Vw Av, Til. RM18 . . . .111 GG81
Southview Cl, SW17 . . . . . .120 DG92
Bexley DA5 . . . . .126 EZ86
Swanley BR8 . . . . . . .147 FF98
Waltham Cross (Chsht.) EN7 .14 DS26
South Vw Ct, Wok. GU22
off Constitution Hill 166 AY118
Southview Cres, Ilf. IG2 . . . .69 EP58
South Vw Dr, E18 . . . . . . .68 EH55
Upminster RM14 . . . . . .72 FN62
Southview Gdns, Wall. SM6 .159 DJ108
South Vw Rd, N8 . . . . . . .65 DK55
Ashtead KT21 . . . . . . .171 CK119
Southview Rd, Brom. BR1 . . .123 ED91
Caterham (Wold.) CR3 . . .177 EB124
South Vw Rd, Dart. DA2 . . .128 FK90
Gerrards Cross SL9 . . . .56 AX56
Grays RM20 . . . . . . .109 FW79
Loughton IG10 . . . . . . .33 EM44
Pinner HA5 . . . . .39 BV51
Southviews, S.Croy. CR2 . . .161 DX109
South Vil, NW1 . . . . . . .83 DK65
Southville, SW8 . . . . . . .101 DK81
Southville Cl, Epsom KT19 . .156 CR109
Feltham TW14 . . . . . .115 BS88
Southville Cres, Felt. TW14 . .115 BS88
Southville Rd, Felt. TW14 . . .115 BS88
Thames Ditton KT7 . . . .137 CH101
South Wk, Hayes UB3
off Middleton Rd 77 BR71
Reigate RH2 off Church St .184 DB134
West Wickham BR4 . . . .144 EE104
SOUTHWARK, SE1 . . . . . .200 G3
⊖ Southwark 200 F3
Southwark Br, EC4 . . . . . .201 J2
SE1 . . . . .201 J2
Southwark Br Rd, SE1 . . . . .200 G6
★ Southwark Cathedral,
SE1 . . . . .201 K2
Southwark Gro, SE1 . . . . . .201 H3
Southwark Pk Est, SE16 . . .202 D8
Southwark Pk Rd, SE16 . . . .202 A8
Southwark Pl, Brom. BR1
off St. Georges Rd 145 EM97
Southwark St, SE1 . . . . . .200 G2
Southwater Cl, E14 . . . . . .85 DZ72
Beckenham BR3 . . . . . .123 EB94
South Way, N9 . . . . .46 DW47
N11 off Ringway 45 DJ51
Southway, N20 . . . . .44 DA47
NW11 . . . . .64 DB58
SW20 . . . . .139 CW98
South Way, Abb.L. WD5 . . . . .7 BT33
Bromley BR2 . . . . . . .144 EG101
Southway, Cars. SM5 . . . . .158 DD110
South Way, Croy. CR0 . . . . .143 DY104
Harrow HA2 . . . . .60 CA56
Purfleet RM19 . . . . . . .109 FS76
Southway, Wall. SM6 . . . . .159 DJ105
South Way, Wem. HA9 . . . . .62 CN64
SOUTH WEALD, Brwd. 54 FS47
South Weald Dr, Wal.Abb. EN9 .15 ED33
South Weald Rd, Brwd. CM14 .54 FU48
Southwell Av, Nthlt. UB5 . . .78 CA65
Southwell Gdns, SW7 . . . . .100 DC77
Southwell Gro Rd, E11 . . . . .68 EE61
Southwell Rd, SE5 . . . . . .102 DQ83
Croydon CR0 . . . . . . .141 DN100
Harrow HA3 . . . . .61 CK58
South Western Rd, Twick. TW1 .117 CG86
Southwest Rd, E11 . . . . . .67 ED60
Southwick Ms, W2 . . . . . .194 A8
Southwick Pl, W2 . . . . . . .194 B9
Southwick St, W2 . . . . . . .194 B8
SOUTH WIMBLEDON, SW19 . .120 DB94
⊖ South Wimbledon 120 DB94
Southwold Dr, Bark. IG11 . . .70 EU64
Southwold Rd, E5 . . . . . . .66 DV61
Bexley DA5 . . . . .127 FB86
Watford WD24 . . . . . . .24 BW38
Southwold Spur, Slou. SL3 . .93 BC75
Southwood Av, N6 . . . . . .65 DH59

★ Place of interest   ⇌ Railway station   ⊖ London Underground station   DLR Docklands Light Railway station   ⊷ Tramlink station   H Hospital

Sou - Sta

Southwood Av, Cher. (Ott.)
 KT16 . . . . .151 BC108
 Coulsdon CR5 . . . . . .175 DJ115
 Kingston upon Thames KT2 .138 CQ95
Southwood Cl, Brom. BR1 .145 EM98
 Worcester Park KT4 . . . .139 CX102
Southwood Dr, Surb. KT5 .138 CQ101
SOUTH WOODFORD, E18 . .48 EF54
⊖ South Woodford 48 EG54
South Woodford to Barking
 Relief Rd, E11 . . . . . .68 EJ56
 E12 . . . . .69 EN62
 E18 . . . . .68 EJ56
 Barking IG11 . . . . . . .69 EN62
 Ilford IG1, IG4 . . . . . .69 EN62
Southwood Gdns, Esher
 KT10 . . . . .137 CG104
 Ilford IG2 . . . . .69 EP56
H Southwood Hosp, N6 . . .64 DG59
Southwood La, N6 . . . . . .64 DG59
Southwood Lawn Rd, N6 . .64 DG59
Southwood Rd, SE9 . . . .125 EP89
 SE28 . . . . .88 EV74
Southwood Smith St, N1
 off Old Royal Free Sq . . .83 DN67
South Worple Av, SW14 . . .98 CS83
South Worple Way, SW14 . .98 CS83
Soval Ct, Nthwd. HA6
 off Maxwell Rd 39 BR52
Sovereign Cl, E1 . . . . . .202 E1
 W5 . . . . .79 CJ71
 Purley CR8 . . . . .159 DM110
 Ruislip HA4 . . . . .59 BS60
Sovereign Ct, Brom. BR2 .145 EM99
 West Molesey KT8 . . . .136 BZ98
Sovereign Cres, SE16 . . .203 K1
Sovereign Gro, Wem. HA0 .61 CK62
Sovereign Ms, E2
 off Pearson St 84 DT68
 Barnet EN4
 off Bournwell Cl 28 DF41
Sovereign Pk, NW10 . . . .80 CP70
Sovereign Pl, Kings L. WD4 . .6 BN29
Sovereign Rd, Bark. IG11 . .88 EW69
Sowerby Cl, SE9 . . . . . .124 EL85
Sowrey Av, Rain. RM13 . . .89 FF65
Soyer Ct, Wok. GU21
 off Raglan Rd 166 AS118
Space Waye, Felt. TW14 . .115 BU85
Spa Cl, SE25 . . . . .142 DS95
Spa Dr, Epsom KT18 . . . .156 CN114
Spafield St, EC1 . . . . . .196 D4
Spa Grn Est, EC1 . . . . .196 E2
Spa Hill, SE19 . . . . . . .142 DR95
Spalding Cl, Edg. HA8
 off Blundell Rd 42 CS52
Spalding Rd, NW4 . . . . .63 CW58
 SW17 . . . . .121 DH93
Spalt Cl, Brwd. CM13 . . . .55 GB47
Spanby Rd, E3 . . . . . . .85 EA70
Spaniards Cl, NW11 . . . . .64 DD60
Spaniards End, NW3 . . . . .64 DC60
Spaniards Rd, NW3 . . . . .64 DC61
Spanish Pl, W1 . . . . . . .194 G8
Spanish Rd, SW18 . . . . .120 DC85
Spareleaze Hill, Loug. IG10 . .33 EM43
Sparepenny La, Dart. (Eyns.)
 DA4 . . . . .148 FL102
Sparkbridge Rd, Har. HA1 . .61 CE56
Sparkford Gdns, N11
 off Friern Barnet Rd . . .44 DG50
Sparkford Ho, SW11 . . . .100 DD81
Sparks Cl, W3 off St. Joseph Av .80 CR72
 Dagenham RM8 . . . . . .70 EX61
 Hampton TW12
 off Victors Dr 116 BY93
Spa Rd, SE16 . . . . .201 P7
Sparrow Cl, Hmptn. TW12 .116 BY93
Sparrow Dr, Orp. BR5 . . .145 EQ102
Sparrow Fm Dr, Felt. TW14 .116 BX87
Sparrow Fm Rd, Epsom KT17 .157 CU105
Sparrow Grn, Dag. RM10 . .71 FB62
Sparrows Herne, Bushey
 WD23 . . . . .40 CB45
Sparrows La, SE9 . . . . .125 EQ87
Sparrows Mead, Red. RH1 .184 DG131
Sparrows Way, Bushey WD23
 off Sparrows Herne 40 CC46
Sparsholt Rd, N19 . . . . . .65 DM60
 Barking IG10 . . . . . . .87 ES67
Sparta St, SE10 . . . . . .103 EB81
★ Speaker's Cor, W2 . . . .194 E10
Speaker's Ct, Croy. CR0
 off St. James's Rd 142 DR102
Spearman St, SE18 . . . .105 EN79
Spear Ms, SW5 . . . . . . .100 DA77
Spearpoint Gdns, Ilf. IG2 . .69 ET56
Spears Rd, N19 . . . . . . .65 DL60
Speart La, Houns. TW5 . . .96 BY80
Spedan Cl, NW3 . . . . . . .64 DB62
Speechly Ms, E8
 off Alvington Cres 66 DT64
Speedbird Way, West Dr. UB7 .94 BH80
Speedgate Hill, Long. (Fawk.Grn.)
 DA3 . . . . .149 FU103
Speed Highwalk, EC2
 off Beech St 84 DQ71
Speed Ho, EC2 . . . . . . .197 K6
Speedwell Ct, Grays RM17 .110 GE80
Speedwell St, SE8 . . . . .103 EA80
Speedy Pl, WC1 . . . . . .195 P3
Speer Rd, T.Ditt. KT7 . . .137 CF99
Speirs Cl, N.Mal. KT3 . . .139 CT100
Spekehill, SE9 . . . . . . .125 EM90
Speke Ho, SE5 . . . . . . .102 DQ80
Speke Rd, Th.Hth. CR7 . . .142 DR96
Speldhurst Cl, Brom. BR2 .144 EF99
Speldhurst Rd, E9 . . . . . .85 DX66
 W4 . . . . .98 CR76
Spellbrook Wk, N1
 off Basire St 84 DQ67
Spelman St, E1 . . . . . . .84 DU71
Spelthorne Gro, Sun. TW16 .115 BT94

Spelthorne La, Ashf. TW15 .135 BQ95
★ Spelthorne Mus, Stai.
 TW18 . . . . .113 BE92
Spence Av, W.Byf. (Byfleet)
 KT14 . . . . .152 BL114
Spence Cl, SE16 . . . . . .203 M5
Spencer Av, N13 . . . . . .45 DM51
 Hayes UB4 . . . . .77 BU71
 Waltham Cross (Chsht.) EN7 .14 DS26
Spencer Cl, N3 . . . . . . .43 CZ54
 NW10 . . . . .80 CM69
 Epsom KT18 . . . . . . .172 CS119
 Orpington BR6 . . . . . .145 ES103
 Uxbridge UB8 . . . . . .76 BJ69
 Woking GU21 . . . . . .151 BC113
 Woodford Green IG8 . . .48 EJ50
H Spencer Close Mental Hosp,
 Epp. CM16 . . . . .18 EV29
Spencer Ct, NW8
 off Marlborough Pl 82 DC68
Spencer Dr, N2 . . . . . . .64 DC58
Spencer Gdns, SE9 . . . .125 EM85
 SW14 . . . . .118 CQ85
 Egham (Eng.Grn.) TW20 .112 AX92
Spencer Hill, SW19 . . . .119 CY93
Spencer Hill Rd, SW19 . .119 CY94
★ Spencer Ho, SW1 . . . .199 K3
Spencer Ms, SW8
 off Lansdowne Way 101 DM81
 W6 off Greyhound Rd . . .99 CY79
Spencer Pk, SW18 . . . .120 DD85
Spencer Pas, E2
 off Pritchard's Rd 84 DV68
Spencer Pl, N1
 off Canonbury La 83 DP66
 Croydon CR0
 off Gloucester Rd 142 DR101
Spencer Ri, NW5 . . . . . .65 DH63
Spencer Rd, E6 . . . . . . .86 EK67
 E17 . . . . .47 EC53
 N8 . . . . .65 DM57
 N11 . . . . .45 DH49
 N17 . . . . .46 DU53
 SW18 . . . . .100 DD84
 SW20 . . . . .139 CV95
 W3 . . . . .80 CQ74
 W4 . . . . .98 CQ80
 Bromley BR1 . . . . . . .124 EE94
 Caterham CR3 . . . . . .176 DR121
 Cobham KT11 . . . . . .169 BV115
 East Molesey KT8 . . . .136 CC99
 Harrow HA3 . . . . . . .41 CE54
 Ilford IG3 . . . . .69 ET60
 Isleworth TW7 . . . . . .97 CD81
 Mitcham CR4 . . . . . . .140 DG97
 Mitcham (Bedd.Cor.) CR4 .140 DG101
 Rainham RM13 . . . . . .89 FD69
 Slough SL3 . . . . .93 AZ76
 South Croydon CR2 . . .160 DS106
 Twickenham TW2 . . . .117 CE90
 Wembley HA0 . . . . . .61 CJ61
Spencer St, EC1 . . . . . .196 F3
 Gravesend DA11 . . . . .131 GG87
 Southall UB2 . . . . . . .96 BX75
Spencer Wk, NW3
 off Hampstead High St . .64 DC63
 SW15 . . . . .99 CX84
 Rickmansworth WD3 . . .22 BJ43
 Tilbury RM18 . . . . . . .111 GG82
Spencer Yd, SE3
 off Blackheath Village . .104 EF82
Spenser Av, Wey. KT13 . .152 BN108
Spenser Cres, Upmin. RM14 .72 FQ59
Spenser Gro, N16 . . . . . .66 DS63
Spenser Ms, SE21
 off Croxted Rd 122 DR88
Spenser Rd, SE24 . . . . .121 DN85
Spenser St, SW1 . . . . . .199 L6
Spensley Wk, N16
 off Clissold Rd 66 DR62
Speranza St, SE18 . . . .105 ET78
Sperling Rd, N17 . . . . . .46 DS54
Spert St, E14 . . . . .85 DY73
Speyhawk Pl, Pot.B. EN6 . .12 DB30
Speyside, N14 . . . . .29 DJ44
Spey St, E14 . . . . .85 EC71
Spey Way, Rom. RM1 . . . .51 FE52
Spezia Rd, NW10 . . . . . .81 CU68
Spice Quay Hts, SE1 . . . .202 A3
Spicer Cl, SW9 . . . . . . .101 DP82
 Walton-on-Thames KT12 .136 BW100
Spicers Fld, Lthd. (Oxshott)
 KT22 . . . . .155 CD113
Spicersfield, Wal.Cr. (Chsht.)
 EN7 . . . . .14 DU27
Spice's Yd, Croy. CR0 . . .160 DQ105
Spielman Rd, Dart. DA1 . .108 FM84
Spigurnell Rd, N17 . . . . .46 DR53
Spikes Br Rd, Sthl. UB1 . .78 BY72
Spilsby Cl, NW9
 off Kenley Av 42 CS54
Spilsby Rd, Rom. RM3 . . .52 FK52
Spindle Cl, SE18 . . . . . .104 EL76
Spindles, Til. RM18 . . . .111 GG80
Spindlewood Gdns, Croy.
 CR0 . . . . .160 DS105
Spindlewoods, Tad. KT20 .173 CV122
Spindrift Av, E14 . . . . . .204 B8
Spinel Cl, SE18 . . . . . . .105 ET78
Spingate Cl, Horn. RM12 . .72 FK64
Spinnaker Cl, Bark. IG11 . .88 EV69
Spinnells Rd, Har. HA2 . . .60 BZ60
Spinney, The, N21 . . . . . .45 DN45
 SW16 . . . . .121 DK90
 Barnet EN5 . . . . .28 DB40
 Brentwood (Hutton) CM13 .55 GC44
 Epsom KT18 . . . . . . .173 CV119
 Leatherhead (Bkhm.) KT23 .170 CB124
 Leatherhead (Oxshott) KT22 .154 CC112
 Potters Bar EN6 . . . . .12 DD11
 Purley CR8 . . . . .159 DP111
 Sidcup DA14 . . . . . . .126 EY92
 Stanmore HA7 . . . . . .42 CL49
 Sunbury-on-Thames TW16 .135 BU95
 Sutton SM3 . . . . .157 CW105
 Swanley BR8 . . . . . . .147 FE96
 Watford WD17 . . . . . .23 BU39

Spinney, The, Wem. HA0 . . .61 CG62
Spinney Cl, Beck. BR3 . . .143 EB98
 Cobham KT11 . . . . . . .154 CA111
 New Malden KT3 . . . . .138 CS99
 Rainham RM13 . . . . . .89 FE68
 West Drayton UB7
 off Yew Av 76 BL73
Spinneycroft, Lthd. KT22 .171 CD115
Spinney Dr, Felt. TW14 . .115 BQ87
Spinney Gdns, SE19 . . . .122 DT92
 Dagenham RM9 . . . . . .70 EY64
Spinney Hill, Add. KT15 . .151 BE106
Spinney Oak, Brom. BR1 . .144 EL96
 Chertsey (Ott.) KT16 . . .151 BD107
Spinneys, The, Brom. BR1 .145 EM96
Spinney Way, Sev. (Cudham)
 TN14 . . . . .163 ER111
Spire, The, Grav. DA12 . .131 GH88
Spires, The, Dart. DA1 . . .128 FK89
Spires Shop Cen, The, Barn.
 EN5 . . . . .27 CY41
Spirit Quay, E1 . . . . . . .202 C2
★ Spitalfields Comm Fm, E1 .84 DU70
Spital La, Brwd. CM14 . . .54 FT48
Spital Sq, E1 . . . . .197 N6
Spital St, E1 . . . . .84 DU70
 Dartford DA1 . . . . . . .128 FK86
Spital Yd, E1 . . . . .197 N6
Spitfire Est, Houns. TW5 . .96 BW78
Spitfire Rd, Wall. SM6
 off Lancastrian Rd 159 DM108
Spitfire Way, Houns. TW5 . .96 BW78
Spode Wk, NW6
 off Lymington Rd 82 DB65
Spondon Rd, N15 . . . . . .66 DU56
Spoonbill Way, Hayes UB4 . .78 BX71
Spooners Dr, St.Alb. (Park St.)
 AL2 . . . . .8 CC27
Spooners Ms, W3
 off Churchfield Rd 80 CR74
Spooner Wk, Wall. SM6 . .159 DK106
Sporle Ct, SW11 . . . . . .100 DD83
Sportsbank St, SE6 . . . .123 EC87
Spotted Dog Path, E7
 off Upton La 86 EG65
Spottons Gro, N17
 off Gospatrick Rd 46 DQ53
Spout Hill, Croy. CR0 . . .161 EA106
Spout La, Eden. (Crock.H.)
 TN8 . . . . .189 EQ134
 Staines TW19 . . . . . . .114 BG85
Spout La N, Stai. TW19 . . .94 BH84
Spratt Hall Rd, E11 . . . . .68 EG58
Spratts All, Cher. (Ott.) KT16 .151 BE107
Spratts La, Cher. (Ott.) KT16 .151 BE107
Spray La, Twick. TW2 . . .117 CE86
Spray St, SE18 . . . . . . .105 EP77
Spreighton Rd, W.Mol. KT8 .136 CB98
Spriggs Oak, Epp. CM16
 off Palmers Hill 18 EU29
Sprimont Pl, SW3 . . . . .198 D10
Springall St, SE15 . . . . .102 DV80
Springate Fld, Slou. SL3 . .92 AY75
Spring Av, Egh. TW20 . . .112 AY93
Springbank, N21 . . . . . .29 DM44
Springbank Av, Horn. RM12 .72 FJ64
Springbank Rd, SE13 . . .123 ED86
Springbank Wk, NW1
 off St. Paul's Cres 83 DK66
Spring Bottom La, Red. RH1 .185 DN127
Springbourne Ct, Beck. BR3 .143 EC95
Spring Br Ms, W5
 off Spring Br Rd 79 CK73
Spring Br Rd, W5 . . . . . .79 CK73
Spring Cl, Barn. EN5 . . . .27 CX43
 Borehamwood WD6 . . . .26 CN39
 Chesham (Latimer) HP5 . .20 AX36
 Dagenham RM8 . . . . . .70 EX60
 Uxbridge (Hare.) UB9 . . .38 BK53
Springclose La, Sutt. SM3 .157 CY107
Spring Cotts, Surb. KT6
 off St. Leonard's Rd . . .137 CK99
Spring Ct, Sid. DA15
 off Station Rd 126 EU90
Spring Ct Rd, Enf. EN2 . . .29 DN38
Springcroft Av, N2 . . . . .64 DF56
Springdale Ms, N16
 off Springdale Rd 66 DR63
Springdale Rd, N16 . . . . .66 DR63
Spring Dr, Pnr. HA5
 off Eastcote Rd 59 BU58
Spring Fm Cl, Rain. RM13 . .90 FK69
Springfield, E5 . . . . .66 DV60
 Bushey (Bushey Hth.) WD23 .41 CD46
 Epping CM16 . . . . . . .17 ET32
 Oxted RH8 . . . . .187 ED130
Springfield Av, N10 . . . . .65 DJ55
 SW20 . . . . .139 CZ97
 Brentwood CM13 . . . . .55 GE45
 Hampton TW12 . . . . . .116 CB93
 Swanley BR8 . . . . . . .147 FF98
Springfield Cl, N12 . . . . .44 DB50
 Potters Bar EN6 . . . . .12 DD11
 Rickmansworth (Crox.Grn.)
 WD3 . . . . .23 BP43
 Stanmore HA7 . . . . . .41 CG48
 Woking (Knap.) GU21 . .166 AS118
Springfield Ct, Wall. SM6
 off Springfield Rd 159 DH106
Springfield Dr, Ilf. IG2 . . .69 EQ58
 Leatherhead KT22 . . . .171 CE119
Springfield Gdns, E5 . . . .66 DV60
 NW9 . . . . .62 CR57
 Bromley BR1 . . . . . . .145 EM98
 Ruislip HA4 . . . . .59 BV60
 Upminster RM14 . . . . .72 FQ62
 West Wickham BR4 . . .143 EB103
 Woodford Green IG8 . . .48 EJ52
Springfield Gro, SE7 . . . .104 EJ79
 Sunbury-on-Thames
 TW16 . . . . .135 BT95
H Springfield Hosp (London),
 SW17 . . . . .120 DE89
Springfield La, NW6 . . . . .82 DB67
 Weybridge KT13 . . . . .153 BP105

Springfield Meadows, Wey.
 KT13 . . . . .153 BP105
Springfield Mt, NW9 . . . .62 CS57
Springfield Pl, N.Mal. KT3 .138 CQ98
Springfield Ri, SE26 . . . .122 DV90
Springfield Rd, E4 . . . . . .48 EE46
 E6 . . . . .87 EM66
 E15 . . . . .86 EE69
 E17 . . . . .67 DZ58
 N11 . . . . .45 DH50
 N15 . . . . .66 DU56
 NW8 . . . . .82 DC67
 SE26 . . . . .122 DV92
 SW19 . . . . .119 CZ92
 W7 . . . . .79 CE74
 Ashford TW15 . . . . . .114 BM92
 Bexleyheath DA7 . . . . .107 FB83
 Bromley BR1 . . . . . . .145 EM98
 Epsom KT17 . . . . . . .157 CW110
 Grays RM16 . . . . . . .110 GD75
 Harrow HA1 . . . . . . .61 CE58
 Hayes UB4 . . . . .78 BW74
 Kingston upon Thames KT1 .138 CL97
 Slough SL3 . . . . .93 BB80
 Teddington TW11 . . . .117 CG92
 Thornton Heath CR7 . . .142 DQ95
 Twickenham TW2 . . . .116 CA88
 Wallington SM6 . . . . .159 DH106
 Waltham Cross (Chsht.) EN8 .15 DY32
 Watford WD25
 off Haines Way 7 BV33
 Welling DA16 . . . . . .106 EV83
Springfields, Wal.Abb. EN9 .16 EE34
Springfields Cl, Cher. KT16 .134 BH102
Springfield Wk, NW6 . . . .82 DB67
 Orpington BR6
 off Place Fm Av 145 ER102
Spring Gdns, N5 . . . . . .66 DQ64
 SE11 . . . . .200 B10
 SW1 . . . . .199 N2
 Hornchurch RM12 . . . .71 FH63
 Orpington BR6 . . . . . .164 EV107
 Romford RM7 . . . . . .71 FC57
 Wallington SM6 . . . . .159 DJ106
 Watford WD25 . . . . . .24 BW35
 West Molesey KT8 . . . .136 CC99
 Westerham (Bigg.H.) TN16 .178 EJ118
 Woodford Green IG8 . . .48 EJ52
Spring Gdns Ind Est, Rom.
 RM7 . . . . .71 FC57
SPRING GROVE, Islw. 97 CF81
Spring Gro, SE19 off Alma Pl .122 DT94
 W4 . . . . .98 CN78
 Gravesend DA12 . . . . .131 GH88
 Hampton TW12
 off Plevna Rd 136 CB95
 Leatherhead (Fetch.) KT22 .170 CB123
 Loughton IG10 . . . . . .32 EK44
 Mitcham CR4 . . . . . . .140 DG97
Spring Gro Cres, Houns. TW3 .96 CC81
Spring Gro Rd, Houns. TW3 .96 CB81
 Isleworth TW7 . . . . . .96 CB81
 Richmond TW10 . . . . .118 CM85
Springhead Enterprise Pk, Grav.
 DA11 . . . . .130 GC88
Springhead Rd, Erith DA8 .107 FF79
 Gravesend (Nthflt.) DA11 .130 GC87
Spring Hill, E5 . . . . .66 DU59
 SE26 . . . . .122 DW91
Springhill Cl, SE5 . . . . .102 DR83
Springholm Cl, West. (Bigg.H.)
 TN16 . . . . .178 EJ118
Springhurst Cl, Croy. CR0 .161 DZ105
Spring Lake, Stan. HA7 . . .41 CH49
Spring La, E5 . . . . .66 DV60
 N10 . . . . .64 DG55
 SE25 . . . . .142 DV100
 Oxted RH8 . . . . .187 ED131
Spring Ms, W1 . . . . . . .194 E6
 Epsom KT17
 off Old Schools La 157 CT109
 Richmond TW9
 off Rosedale Rd 98 CL84
Spring Pk Av, Croy. CR0 .143 DX103
Spring Pk Dr, N4 . . . . . .66 DQ60
Springpark Dr, Beck. BR3 .143 EC97
Spring Pk Rd, Croy. CR0 .143 DX103
Spring Pas, SW15
 off Embankment 99 CX83
Spring Path, NW3 . . . . . .64 DD64
Spring Pl, N3
 off Windermere Av 44 DA54
 NW5 . . . . .65 DH64
Springpond Rd, Dag. RM9 .70 EY64
Springrice Rd, SE13 . . . .123 EC86
Spring Ri, Egh. TW20 . . .112 AY93
Spring Rd, Felt. TW13 . . .115 BT90
Springs, The, Brox. EN10 . .15 DY25
Springshaw Cl, Sev. TN13 .190 FD123
Spring Shaw Rd, Orp. BR5 .146 EU95
Spring St, W2 . . . . .82 DD72
 Epsom KT17 . . . . . . .157 CT109
Spring Ter, Rich. TW9 . . .118 CL85
Spring Vale, Bexh. DA7 . .107 FB84
 Greenhithe DA9 . . . . .129 FW86
Springvale Av, Brent. TW8 .97 CK78
Springvale Cl, Swan. BR8 .147 FF95
Springvale Est, W14
 off Blythe Rd 99 CY76
Springvale N, Dart. DA1 . .128 FK87
Springvale Retail Pk, Orp.
 BR5 . . . . .146 EW97
Springvale S, Dart. DA1 . .128 FK87
Springvale Ter, W14 . . . .99 CX76
Springvale Way, Orp. BR5 .146 EW97
Spring Vil Rd, Edg. HA8 . . .42 CN52
Spring Wk, E1
 off Old Montague St 84 DU71
Springwater Cl, SE18 . . .105 EN81
Springway, Har. HA1 . . . .61 CD59
Springwell Av, NW10 . . . .81 CT67
 Rickmansworth (Mill End)
 WD3 . . . . .38 BG47
Springwell Cl, SW16
 off Etherstone Rd 121 DN91
Springwell Ct, Houns. TW4 .96 BX82

Springwell Hill, Uxb. (Hare.)
 UB9 . . . . .38 BH51
Springwell La, Rick. WD3 . .38 BG49
 Uxbridge (Hare.) UB9 . . .38 BG49
Springwell Rd, SW16 . . .121 DN91
 Hounslow TW4, TW5 . . .96 BX81
Springwood, Wal.Cr. (Chsht.)
 EN7 . . . . .14 DU26
Springwood Cl, Uxb. (Hare.)
 UB9 . . . . .38 BK53
Springwood Cres, Edg. HA8 .42 CP47
Spring Wds, Vir.W. GU25 .132 AV98
Springwood Way, Rom. RM1 .71 FG57
Sprowston Ms, E7 . . . . . .86 EG65
Sprowston Rd, E7 . . . . . .68 EG64
Spruce Cl, Red. RH1 . . . .184 DF133
Spruce Ct, W5
 off Elderberry Rd 98 CL76
Sprucedale Cl, Swan. BR8 .147 FE96
Sprucedale Gdns, Croy. CR0 .161 DX105
 Wallington SM6 . . . . .159 DK109
Spruce Hills Rd, E17 . . . .47 EC54
Spruce Pk, Brom. BR2
 off Cumberland Rd 144 EF98
Spruce Rd, West. (Bigg.H.)
 TN16 . . . . .178 EK116
Spruce Way, St.Alb. (Park St.)
 AL2 . . . . .8 CB27
Sprules Rd, SE4 . . . . . .103 DY82
Spur, The, Wal.Cr. (Chsht.) EN8
 off Welsummer Way . . .15 DX28
Spur Cl, Abb.L. WD5 . . . . .7 BR33
 Romford (Abridge) RM4 . .34 EV41
Spurfield, W.Mol. KT8 . . .136 CB97
Spurgate, Brwd. CM13 . . .55 GA47
Spurgeon Av, SE19 . . . .142 DR95
Spurgeon Rd, SE19 . . . .142 DR95
Spurgeon St, SE1 . . . . .201 K7
Spurling Rd, SE22 . . . . .102 DT84
 Dagenham RM9 . . . . . .88 EZ65
Spurrell Av, Bex. DA5 . . .127 FD91
Spur Rd, N15 off Philip La . .66 DR56
 SE1 . . . . .200 D4
 SW1 . . . . .199 K5
 Barking IG11 . . . . . . .87 EQ69
 Edgware HA8 . . . . . . .42 CL49
 Feltham TW14 . . . . . .115 BV85
 Isleworth TW7 . . . . . .97 CH80
 Orpington BR6 . . . . . .146 EU103
Spur Rd Est, Edg. HA8 . . .42 CM49
Spurstowe Rd, E8
 off Marcon Pl 84 DV65
Spurstowe Ter, E8 . . . . .66 DV64
Squadrons App, Horn. RM12 .90 FJ65
Square, The, W6 . . . . . .99 CW78
 Carshalton SM5 . . . . .158 DG106
 Hayes UB3 . . . . .77 BR74
 Ilford IG1 . . . . .69 EN59
 Richmond TW9 . . . . . .117 CK85
 Sevenoaks TN13
 off Amherst Hill 190 FE122
 Swanley BR8 . . . . . . .147 FD97
 Watford WD24
 off The Harebreaks . . .23 BV37
 West Drayton UB7 . . . .94 BH81
 Westerham (Tats.) TN16 .178 EJ120
 Weybridge KT13 . . . . .153 BQ105
 Woking (Wisley) GU23 . .168 BL116
 Woodford Green IG8 . . .48 EG50
Square Rigger Row, SW11
 off York Pl 100 DC83
Squarey St, SW17 . . . . .120 DC90
★ Squerryes Ct, West. TN16 .189 EQ128
Squerryes Mede, West. TN16 .189 EQ127
Squire Gdns, NW8
 off St. John's Wd Rd . . .82 DD69
Squires, The, Rom. RM7 . .71 FC58
Squires Br Rd, Shep. TW17 .134 BM98
Squires Ct, SW19 . . . . .120 DA91
 Chertsey KT16
 off Springfields Cl 134 BH102
Squires La, N3 . . . . .44 DB54
Squires Mt, NW3
 off East Heath Rd 64 DD62
Squires Rd, Shep. TW17 .134 BM98
Squires Wk, Ashf. TW15
 off Napier Rd 115 BR94
Squires Way, Dart. DA2 . .127 FD91
Squires Wd Dr, Chis. BR7 .124 EL94
Squirrel Cl, Houns. TW4 . .96 BW82
Squirrel Keep, W.Byf. KT14 .152 BH112
Squirrel Ms, W13 . . . . . .79 CG73
Squirrels, The, SE13 . . . .103 ED83
 Bushey WD23 . . . . . .25 CD44
 Pinner HA5 . . . . .60 BZ55
Squirrels Chase, Grays (Orsett)
 RM16 off Hornsby La . . .111 GG75
Squirrels Cl, N12
 off Woodside Av 44 DC49
 Uxbridge UB10 . . . . . .76 BN69
Squirrels Grn, Lthd. (Bkhm.)
 KT23 . . . . .170 CA123
 Worcester Park KT4 . . .139 CT102
Squirrels Heath Av, Rom. RM2 .71 FH55
Squirrels Heath La, Horn.
 RM11 . . . . .72 FJ56
 Romford RM2 . . . . . .72 FJ56
Squirrels Heath Rd, Rom. RM3 .72 FL55
Squirrels La, Buck.H. IG9 . .48 EK48
Squirrels Trd Est, The, Hayes
 UB3 . . . . .95 BU76
Squirrels Way, Epsom KT18 .172 CR115
Squirrel Wd, W.Byf. KT14 .152 BH112
Stable Cl, Nthlt. UB5 . . . .78 CA68
Stables, The, Buck.H. IG9 . .48 EJ45
 Cobham KT11 . . . . . . .154 BZ114
 Swanley BR8 . . . . . . .147 FH95
Stables End, Orp. BR6 . . .145 EQ104
Stables Ms, SE27 . . . . .122 DQ92
Stables Way, SE11 . . . . .200 D10
Stable Wk, N2 off Old Fm Rd .44 DD53
Stable Way, W10
 off Latimer Rd 81 CW72
Stable Yd, SW1 . . . . . . .199 K4

Stable Yd, SW9
 off Broomgrove Rd 101 DM82
SW15 off Danemere St . .99 CW83
Stable Yd Rd, SW1 . . . . . .199 K3
Stacey Av, N18 . . . . .46 DW49
Stacey Cl, E10 off Halford Rd .67 ED57
Gravesend DA12 . . . . . .131 GL92
Stacey St, N7 . . . . .65 DN62
WC2 . . . . .195 N9
Stackhouse St, SW3 . . . . . .198 D6
Stack Rd, Dart. (Hort.Kir.) DA4 .149 FR97
Stacy Path, SE5 off Harris St .102 DS80
Stadium Business Cen, Wem.
 HA9 . . . . .62 CP62
Stadium Retail Pk, Wem. HA9
 off Wembley Pk Dr 62 CN62
Stadium Rd, NW2 . . . . .63 CW59
SE18 . . . . .104 EL80
Stadium St, SW10 . . . . . . .100 DC80
Stadium Way, Dart. DA1 . . .127 FE85
Wembley HA9 . . . . .62 CM63
Staffa Rd, E10 . . . . .67 DY60
Stafford Av, Horn. RM11 . . .72 FK55
Stafford Cl, E17 . . . . .67 DZ58
N14 . . . . .29 DJ43
NW6 . . . . .82 DA69
Caterham CR3 . . . . . . .176 DT123
Grays (Chaff.Hun.) RM16 .109 FW77
Greenhithe DA9 . . . . . .129 FT85
Sutton SM3 . . . . .157 CY107
Waltham Cross (Chsht.) EN8 .14 DV29
Stafford Ct, W8 . . . . .100 DA76
Stafford Cross, Croy. CR0 . .159 DM106
Stafford Gdns, Croy. CR0 . .159 DM106
Stafford Pl, SW1 . . . . .199 K6
Richmond TW10 . . . . . .118 CM87
Stafford Rd, E3 . . . . .85 DZ68
E7 . . . . .86 EJ66
NW6 . . . . .82 DA69
Caterham CR3 . . . . . . .176 DT122
Croydon CR0 . . . . .159 DN105
Harrow HA3 . . . . .40 CC52
New Malden KT3 . . . . . .138 CQ97
Ruislip HA4 . . . . .59 BT63
Sidcup DA14 . . . . .125 ES91
Wallington SM6 . . . . . .159 DJ107
Staffordshire St, SE15 . . . .102 DU81
Stafford Sq, Wey. KT13
 off Rosslyn Pk 153 BR105
Stafford St, W1 . . . . .199 K2
Stafford Ter, W8 . . . . .100 DA76
Stafford Way, Sev. TN13 . . .191 FJ127
Staff St, EC1 . . . . .197 L3
Stagbury Av, Couls. CR5 . . .174 DE118
Stagbury Cl, Couls. CR5 . . .174 DE119
Stag Cl, Edg. HA8 . . . . .42 CP54
Staggart Grn, Chig. IG7 . . . .49 ET51
Stagg Hill, Barn. EN4 . . . . . .28 DD35
Potters Bar EN6 . . . . . . .28 DD35
Stag La, NW9 . . . . .62 CQ55
SW15 . . . . .119 CT89
Buckhurst Hill IG9 . . . . . .48 EH47
Edgware HA8 . . . . .42 CP54
Rickmansworth (Chorl.) WD3 .21 BC44
Stag Leys, Ashtd. KT21 . . . .172 CL120
Stag Leys Cl, Bans. SM7 . . .174 DD115
Stag Pl, SW1 . . . . .199 K6
Stag Ride, SW19 . . . . .119 CT90
Stags Way, Islw. TW7 . . . . .97 CF79
Stainash Cres, Stai. TW18 . .114 BH92
Stainash Par, Stai. TW18
 off Kingston Rd 114 BH92
Stainbank Rd, Mitch. CR4 . .141 DH98
Stainby Cl, West Dr. UB7 . . .94 BL76
Stainby Rd, N15 . . . . .66 DT56
Stainer Ho, SE3 off Ryan Cl .104 EJ84
Stainer Rd, Borwd. WD6 . . . .25 CK39
Stainer St, SE1 . . . . .201 L3
STAINES 114 BG91
⇌ Staines 114 BG92
Staines Av, Sutt. SM3 . . . . .139 CX103
Staines Br, Stai. TW18 . . . .113 BE92
Staines Bypass, Ashf. TW15 .114 BH91
 Staines TW18, TW19 . . .114 BH91
Staines La, Cher. KT16 . . . .133 BF99
Staines La Cl, Cher. KT16 . .133 BF100
Staines Rd, Cher. KT16 . . . .133 BF97
Feltham TW14 . . . . . . .115 BR87
Hounslow TW3, TW4 . . . .96 CB83
Ilford IG1 . . . . .69 EQ63
Staines TW18 . . . . .114 BH92
Staines (Wrays.) TW19 . .112 AY87
Twickenham TW2 . . . . . .116 CA90
Staines Rd E, Sun. TW16 . . .115 BU94
Staines Rd W, Ashf. TW15 . .115 BP93
Sunbury-on-Thames TW16 .115 BP93
Staines Wk, Sid. DA14
 off Evry Rd 126 EW93
Stainford Cl, Ashf. TW15 . . .115 BR92
Stainforth Rd, E17 . . . . . . .67 EA56
Ilford IG2 . . . . .69 ER59
Staining La, EC2 . . . . .197 J8
Stainmore Cl, Chis. BR7 . . .145 ER95
Stainsbury St, E2
 off Royston St 84 DW68
Stainsby Pl, E14 . . . . .85 EA72
 off Stainsby Rd
Stainsby Rd, E14 . . . . .85 EA72
Stains Cl, Wal.Cr. (Chsht.) EN8 .15 DY28
Stainton Rd, SE6 . . . . .123 ED86
Enfield EN3 . . . . .30 DW39
Stainton Wk, Wok. GU21
 off Inglewood 166 AW118
Stairfoot La, Sev. (Chipstead)
 TN13 . . . . .190 FC122
Staithes Way, Tad. KT20 . . .173 CV120
Stalbridge St, NW1 . . . . . .194 C6
Stalham St, SE16 . . . . .202 E7
Stalisfield Pl, Orp. BR6
 off Mill La 163 EN110
Stambourne Way, SE19 . . . .122 DS94
West Wickham BR4 . . . .143 EC104
Ⓗ Stamford, The, W6 . . . . .99 CU77
⊖ Stamford Brook 99 CT77
Stamford Brook Av, W6 . . . .99 CT76
Stamford Brook Rd, W6 . . . .99 CT76
Stamford Cl, N15 . . . . .66 DU56

Stamford Cl, NW3
 off Heath St 64 DC63
Harrow HA3 . . . . .41 CE52
Potters Bar EN6 . . . . . . .12 DD32
Southall UB1 . . . . .78 CA73
Stamford Cotts, SW10
 off Billing St 100 DB80
Stamford Ct, W6
 off Goldhawk Rd 99 CT77
Stamford Dr, Brom. BR2 . . .144 EF98
Stamford Gdns, Dag. RM9 . .88 EW66
Stamford Grn Rd, Epsom
 KT18 . . . . .156 CP113
Stamford Gro E, N16
 off Oldhill St 66 DU60
Stamford Gro W, N16
 off Oldhill St 66 DU60
STAMFORD HILL, N16 . . . . .66 DS60
⇌ Stamford Hill 66 DS59
Stamford Hill, N16 . . . . . . .66 DT61
Stamford Hill Est, N16 . . . . .66 DT60
Stamford Rd, E6 . . . . .86 EL67
N1 . . . . .66 DS66
N15 . . . . .66 DU57
Dagenham RM9 . . . . . . .88 EV67
Walton-on-Thames KT12
 off Kenilworth Dr 136 BX104
Watford WD17 . . . . .23 BV40
Stamford St, SE1 . . . . .200 D3
Stamp Pl, E2 . . . . .197 P2
Stanard Cl, N16 . . . . .66 DS59
Stanborough Av, Borwd. WD6 .26 CN37
Stanborough Cl, Borwd. WD6 .26 CN38
Hampton TW12 . . . . . . .116 BZ93
Stanborough Pk, Wat. WD25 .23 BV35
Stanborough Pas, E8
 off Abbot St 84 DT65
Stanborough Rd, Houns. TW3 .97 CD83
Stanbridge Pl, N21 . . . . . . .45 DP47
Stanbridge Rd, SW15 . . . . .99 CW83
Stanbrook Rd, SE2 . . . . . .106 EV75
Gravesend DA11 . . . . . .131 GF88
Stanbury Av, Wat. WD17 . . . .23 BS37
Stanbury Rd, SE15 . . . . . .102 DV81
Stancroft, NW9 . . . . .62 CS56
Standale Gro, Ruis. HA4 . . . .59 BQ57
Standard Ind Est, E16 . . . . .105 EM75
Standard Pl, EC2 . . . . .197 N3
Standard Rd, NW10 . . . . . . .80 CQ70
Belvedere DA17 . . . . . .106 FA78
Bexleyheath DA6 . . . . . .106 EY84
Enfield EN3 . . . . .31 DY38
Hounslow TW4 . . . . .96 BY83
Orpington BR6 . . . . . . .163 EN110
Standen Av, Horn. RM12 . . . .72 FK62
Standen Rd, SW18 . . . . . . .119 CZ87
Standfield Gdns, Dag. RM10
 off Standfield Rd 88 FA65
Standfield Rd, Dag. RM10 . . .70 FA64
Standish Ho, SE3 off Elford Cl .104 EJ84
Standish Rd, W6 . . . . .99 CU77
Standlake Pt, SE23 . . . . . . .123 DX90
Stane Cl, SW19
 off Hayward Cl 140 DB95
Stane St, Lthd. KT22 . . . . . .182 CL126
Stane Way, SE18 . . . . .104 EL80
Epsom KT17 . . . . .157 CU110
Stanfield Rd, E3 . . . . .85 DY68
Stanford Cl, Hmptn. TW12 . .116 BZ93
Romford RM7 . . . . .71 FB58
Ruislip HA4 . . . . .59 BQ58
Woodford Green IG8 . . . .48 EL50
Stanford Ct, SW6
 off Bagley's La 100 DB81
Waltham Abbey EN9 . . . .16 EG33
Stanford Gdns, S.Ock. (Aveley)
 RM15 . . . . .91 FR74
Stanford Ho, Bark. IG11 . . . .88 EV68
Stanford Pl, SE17 . . . . .201 M9
Stanford Rd, N11 . . . . .44 DF50
SW16 . . . . .141 DK96
W8 . . . . .100 DB76
Grays RM16 . . . . .110 GD76
Stanford St, SW1 . . . . .199 M9
Stanford Way, SW16 . . . . . .141 DK96
Stangate Cres, Borwd. WD6 .26 CS43
Stangate Gdns, Stan. HA7 . . .41 CH49
Stanger Rd, SE25 . . . . .142 DU98
Stanham Pl, Dart. DA1
 off Crayford Way 107 FG84
Stanham Rd, Dart. DA1 . . . .128 FJ85
Stanhope Cl, N3 . . . . .25 CZ55
Bromley BR2 . . . . .144 EF102
Harrow HA3 . . . . .41 CD53
Stanhope Cl, SE16 . . . . . . .203 J4
Stanhope Gdns, N4 . . . . . . .65 DP58
N6 . . . . .65 DH58
NW7 . . . . .43 CT50
SW7 . . . . .100 DC77
Dagenham RM8 . . . . . . .70 EZ62
Ilford IG1 . . . . .69 EM60
Stanhope Gate, W1 . . . . . . .198 G2
Stanhope Gro, Beck. BR3 . .143 DZ99
Stanhope Heath, Stai. (Stanw.)
 TW19 . . . . .114 BJ86
Stanhope Ms E, SW7 . . . . .100 DC77
Stanhope Ms S, SW7
 off Gloucester Rd 100 DC77
Stanhope Ms W, SW7 . . . . .100 DC77
Stanhope Par, NW1 . . . . . . .195 K2
Stanhope Pl, W2 . . . . .194 D9
Stanhope Rd, E17 . . . . .67 EB57
N6 . . . . .65 DJ58
N12 . . . . .44 DC50
Barnet EN5 . . . . .27 CW44
Bexleyheath DA7 . . . . . .106 EY82
Carshalton SM5 . . . . . .158 DG108
Croydon CR0 . . . . .142 DS104
Dagenham RM8 . . . . . . .70 EZ61
Greenford UB6 . . . . .78 CC71
Rainham RM13 . . . . .89 FG68
Sidcup DA15 . . . . .126 EU91
Swanscombe DA10 . . . .130 FZ85
Waltham Cross EN8 . . . . .15 DY33
Stanhope Row, W1 . . . . . . .199 H3

Stanhopes, Oxt. RH8 . . . . . .188 EH128
Stanhope St, NW1 . . . . . . .195 K3
Stanhope Ter, W2 . . . . .194 A10
Stanhope Way, Sev. TN13 . .190 FD122
Staines (Stanw.) TW19 . .114 BJ86
Stanier Cl, W14 off Aisgill Av .99 CZ78
Staniland Dr, Wey. KT13 . . .152 BM110
Stanlake Ms, W12 . . . . .81 CW74
Stanlake Rd, W12 . . . . .81 CV74
Stanlake Vil, W12 . . . . .81 CV74
Stanley Av, Bark. IG11 . . . . .87 ET68
Beckenham BR3 . . . . . .143 EC96
Dagenham RM8 . . . . . . .70 EZ60
Greenford UB6 . . . . .78 CC67
New Malden KT3 . . . . . .139 CU99
Romford RM2 . . . . .71 FG56
St. Albans AL2 . . . . .8 CA25
Wembley HA0 . . . . .80 CL66
Stanley Cl, SW8 . . . . .101 DM79
Coulsdon CR5 . . . . .175 DM117
Greenhithe DA9 . . . . . .129 FS85
Hornchurch RM12
 off Stanley Rd 72 FJ61
Romford RM2 . . . . .71 FG56
Uxbridge UB8 . . . . .76 BK67
Wembley HA0 . . . . .80 CL66
Stanley Cotts, Slou. SL2 . . . .74 AT74
Stanley Ct, Cars. SM5
 off Stanley Pk Rd 158 DG108
Stanley Cres, W11 . . . . .81 CZ73
Gravesend DA12 . . . . . .131 GK92
Stanleycroft Cl, Islw. TW7 . . .97 CE81
Stanley Gdns, NW2 . . . . . . .63 CW64
W3 . . . . .80 CS74
W11 . . . . .81 CZ73
Borehamwood WD6 . . . . .26 CL39
Mitcham CR4
 off Ashbourne Rd 120 DG93
South Croydon CR2 . . . .160 DU112
Wallington SM6 . . . . . . .159 DJ107
Walton-on-Thames KT12 .154 BW107
Stanley Gdns Ms, W11
 off Stanley Cres 81 CZ73
Stanley Gdns Rd, Tedd. TW11 .117 CE92
Stanley Grn E, Slou. SL3 . . . .93 AZ77
Stanley Grn W, Slou. SL3 . . .93 AZ77
Stanley Gro, SW8 . . . . .100 DG82
Croydon CR0 . . . . .141 DN100
Stanley Pk Dr, Wem. HA0 . . .80 CM66
Stanley Pk Rd, Cars. SM5 . .158 DF108
Wallington SM6 . . . . . . .159 DH107
Stanley Pas, NW1 . . . . .195 P1
Stanley Rd, E4 . . . . .47 ED46
E10 . . . . .67 EB58
E12 . . . . .68 EL64
E15 . . . . .85 ED67
E18 . . . . .48 EF53
N2 . . . . .64 DD55
N9 . . . . .46 DT46
N10 . . . . .45 DH52
N11 . . . . .45 DK51
N15 . . . . .65 DP56
NW9 off West Hendon Bdy .63 CU59
SW14 . . . . .98 CP84
SW19 . . . . .120 DA94
W3 . . . . .98 CQ76
Ashford TW15 . . . . .114 BL91
Bromley BR2 . . . . .144 EH98
Carshalton SM5 . . . . . .158 DG108
Croydon CR0 . . . . .141 DN101
Enfield EN1 . . . . .30 DS41
Gravesend (Nthflt.) DA11 .130 GE88
Grays RM17 . . . . .110 GB78
Harrow HA2 . . . . .60 CC61
Hornchurch RM12 . . . . . .72 FJ61
Hounslow TW3 . . . . .96 CC84
Ilford IG1 . . . . .69 ER61
Mitcham CR4 . . . . .120 DG94
Morden SM4 . . . . .140 DA98
Northwood HA6 . . . . .39 BU53
Orpington BR6 . . . . . . .146 EU102
Sidcup DA14 . . . . .126 EU91
Southall UB1 . . . . .78 BY73
Sutton SM2 . . . . .158 DB107
Swanscombe DA10 . . . .130 FZ86
Teddington TW11 . . . . . .117 CE91
Twickenham TW2 . . . . . .117 CD90
Watford WD17 . . . . .24 BW41
Wembley HA9 . . . . .80 CM65
Woking GU21 . . . . .167 AZ116
Stanley Rd N, Rain. RM13 . . .89 FE67
Stanley Rd S, Rain. RM13 . . .89 FF68
Stanley Sq, Cars. SM5 . . . .158 DF109
Stanley St, SE8 . . . . .103 DZ80
Caterham CR3
 off Coulsdon Rd 176 DQ122
Stanley Ter, N19 . . . . .65 DL61
Stanley Way, Orp. BR5 . . . .146 EV99
Stanmer St, SW11 . . . . .100 DE81
STANMORE 41 CG50
⊖ Stanmore 41 CK50
Stanmore Gdns, Rich. TW9 . .98 CM83
Sutton SM1 . . . . .140 DC104
Stanmore Hall, Stan. HA7 . . .41 CH48
Stanmore Hill, Stan. HA7 . . . .41 CG48
Stanmore Pk, Stan. HA7 . . . .41 CH50
Stanmore Pl, NW1
 off Arlington Rd 83 DH67
Stanmore Rd, E11 . . . . .68 EF60
N15 . . . . .65 DP56
Belvedere DA17 . . . . . .107 FC77
Richmond TW9 . . . . .98 CM83
Watford WD24 . . . . .23 BV39
Stanmore St, N1
 off Caledonian Rd 83 DM67
Stanmore Ter, Beck. BR3 . . .143 EA96
Stanmore Way, Loug. IG10 . .33 EN39
Stanmount Rd, St.Alb. AL2 . . .8 CA25
Stannard Ms, E8 . . . . .84 DU65
Stannard Rd, E8 . . . . .84 DU65
Stannary Pl, SE11 . . . . .101 DN78
Stannary St, SE11 . . . . .101 DN79
Stannet Way, Wall. SM6 . . . .159 DJ105
Stannington Path, Borwd.
 WD6 . . . . .26 CN39
Stansfeld Rd, E6 . . . . .86 EK71
Stansfield Rd, SW9 . . . . . . .101 DM83

Stansfield Rd, Houns. TW4 . .95 BV82
Stansgate Rd, Dag. RM10 . . .70 FA61
Stanstead Cl, Brom. BR2 . . .144 EF99
Stanstead Gro, SE6
 off Catford Hill 123 DZ88
Stanstead Manor, Sutt. SM1 .158 DA107
Stanstead Rd, E11 . . . . .68 EH57
SE6 . . . . .123 DX88
SE23 . . . . .123 DX88
Caterham CR3 . . . . . . .186 DR125
Hounslow (Hthrw.Air.) TW6 .114 BM86
Stansted Cl, Horn. RM12 . . . .89 FH65
Stansted Cres, Bex. DA5 . . .126 EX86
Stanswood Gdns, SE5
 off Sedgmoor Pl 102 DS80
Stanthorpe Cl, SW16 . . . . . .121 DL92
Stanthorpe Rd, SW16 . . . . .121 DL92
Stanton Av, Tedd. TW11 . . . .117 CE92
Stanton Cl, Epsom KT19 . . .156 CP106
Orpington BR5 . . . . . . .146 EW101
Worcester Park KT4 . . . .139 CX102
Stanton Ho, SE16 . . . . .203 M4
Stanton Rd, SE26
 off Stanton Way 123 DZ91
SW13 . . . . .99 CT82
SW20 . . . . .139 CX96
Croydon CR0 . . . . .142 DQ101
Stanton Sq, SE26
 off Stanton Way 123 DZ91
Stanton Way, SE26 . . . . . . .123 DZ91
Slough SL3 . . . . .92 AY77
Stanway Cl, Chig. IG7 . . . . . .49 ES50
Stanway Ct, N1 . . . . .197 N1
Stanway Gdns, W3 . . . . .80 CN74
Edgware HA8 . . . . .42 CQ50
Stanway Rd, Wal.Abb. EN9 . .16 EG33
Stanway St, N1 . . . . .84 DS68
STANWELL, Stai. 114 BL87
Stanwell Cl, Stai. (Stanw.)
 TW19 . . . . .114 BK87
Stanwell Gdns, Stai. (Stanw.)
 TW19 . . . . .114 BK86
STANWELL MOOR, Stai. . . .114 BG85
Stanwell Moor Rd, Stai.TW19 .114 BH85
West Drayton UB7 . . . . . .94 BH81
Stanwell New Rd, Stai. TW18 114 BH90
Stanwell Rd, Ashf. TW15 . . .114 BL87
Feltham TW14 . . . . .115 BQ87
Slough (Horton) SL3 . . . .93 BA83
Stanwick Rd, W14 . . . . .99 CZ77
Stanworth St, SE1 . . . . . . .201 P5
Stanwyck Dr, Chig. IG7 . . . . .49 EQ50
Stanwyck Gdns, Rom. RM3 . .52 FH50
Stapenhill Rd, Wem. HA0 . . .61 CH62
Staple Cl, Bex. DA5 . . . . . .127 FD90
Staplefield Cl, SW2 . . . . . . .121 DL86
Pinner HA5 . . . . .40 BY52
STAPLEFORD ABBOTTS, Rom. 35 FC43
★ Stapleford Airfield, Rom.
 RM4 . . . . .34 FA42
Stapleford Av, Ilf. IG2 . . . . . .69 ES57
Stapleford Cl, E4 . . . . .47 EC48
SW19 . . . . .119 CY87
Kingston upon Thames KT1 .138 CN96
Stapleford Ct, Sev. TN13 . . .190 FF123
Stapleford Gdns, Rom. RM5 . .50 FA51
Stapleford Rd, Rom. RM4 . . .35 FB42
Wembley HA0 . . . . .79 CK66
STAPLEFORD TAWNEY, Ong. CM5 .19 FC37
Stapleford Way, Bark. IG11 . .88 EV69
Staple Hall Rd, Wok. (Chob.Com.)
 GU24 . . . . .150 AS105
Staplehurst Rd, SE13 . . . . .124 EE85
Carshalton SM5 . . . . . .158 DE108
Staple Inn, WC1 . . . . .196 D7
Staple Inn Bldgs, WC1 . . . .196 D7
Staples Cl, SE16 . . . . .203 K2
Staples Cor, NW2 . . . . .63 CV60
Staples Cor Business Pk, NW2 .63 CV60
Staples Rd, Loug. IG10 . . . . .32 EL41
Staple St, SE1 . . . . .201 L5
Stapleton Cl, Pot.B. EN6 . . . .12 DD31
Stapleton Cres, Rain. RM13 . .89 FG65
Stapleton Gdns, Croy. CR0 . .159 DN106
Stapleton Hall Rd, N4 . . . . . .65 DM59
Stapleton Rd, SW17 . . . . . .120 DG90
Bexleyheath DA7 . . . . . .106 EZ80
Borehamwood WD6 . . . . .26 CN38
Orpington BR6 . . . . . . .145 ET104
Stapley Rd, Belv. DA17 . . . .106 FA78
Staplyton Rd, Barn. EN5 . . . .27 CY41
Star All, EC3 . . . . .197 N10
Star & Garter Hill, Rich. TW10 .118 CL88
Starboard Av, Green. DA9 . .129 FV86
Starboard Way, E14 . . . . . . .204 A6
Starch Ho La, Ilf. IG6 . . . . . .49 ER54
Starcross St, NW1 . . . . .195 L3
Starfield Rd, W12 . . . . .99 CU75
Star Hill, Dart. DA1 . . . . . . .127 FE85
Woking GU22 . . . . .166 AW119
Star Hill Rd, Sev. (Dunt.Grn.)
 TN14 . . . . .180 EZ116
Starkey Cl, Wal.Cr. (Chsht.) EN7
 off Shambrook Rd 14 DQ25
Star La, E16 . . . . .86 EE70
Coulsdon CR5 . . . . .174 DG122
Epping CM16 . . . . .18 EU30
Orpington BR5 . . . . . . .146 EW98
Starling Cl, Buck.H. IG9 . . . . .48 EG46
Pinner HA5 . . . . .60 BW55
Starling La, Pot.B. (Cuffley)
 EN6 . . . . .13 DM28
Starling Ms, SE28 . . . .
 off Whinchat Rd 105 ER75
Starlings, The, Lthd. (Oxshott)
 KT22 . . . . .154 CC113
Starling Wk, Hmptn. TW12
 off Oak Av 116 BY93
Starmans Cl, Dag. RM9 . . . .88 EY67
Star Path, Nthlt. UB5
 off Brabazon Rd 78 CA68
Star Pl, E1 . . . . .202 A1
Star Rd, W14 . . . . .99 CZ79
Isleworth TW7 . . . . .97 CD82
Uxbridge UB10 . . . . .77 BQ70

Starrock La, Couls. (Chipstead)
 CR5 . . . . .174 DF120
Starrock Rd, Couls. CR5 . . .175 DH119
Star St, E16 . . . . .86 EF71
W2 . . . . .194 A8
Starts Cl, Orp. BR6 . . . . . . .145 EN104
Starts Hill Av, Orp. BR6 . . . .163 EP105
Starts Hill Rd, Orp. BR6 . . . .145 EN104
Starveall Cl, West Dr. UB7 . . .94 BM76
Starwood Cl, W.Byf. KT14 . .152 BJ111
Starwood Ct, Slou. SL3
 off London Rd 92 AW76
Star Yd, WC2 . . . . .196 D8
State Fm Av, Orp. BR6 . . . .163 EP105
Staten Gdns, Twick. TW1 . . .117 CF88
Statham Gro, N16
 off Green Las 66 DQ63
N18 . . . . .46 DS50
Station App, E4 (Highams Pk.)
 off The Avenue 47 ED51
E7 off Woodford Rd 68 EH63
E11 (Snaresbrook)
 off High St 68 EG57
N11 off Friern Barnet Rd . .45 DH50
N12 (Woodside Pk.) 44 DB49
N16 (Stoke Newington)
 off Stamford Hill 66 DT61
NW10 off Station Rd 81 CT69
SE1 . . . . .200 C5
SE3 off Kidbrooke Pk Rd .104 EH83
SE9 (Mottingham) 125 EM88
SE26 (Lwr.Sydenham)
 off Worsley Br Rd 123 DZ92
SE26 (Sydenham)
 off Sydenham Rd 122 DW91
SW6 . . . . .99 CY83
SW16 . . . . .121 DK92
W7 . . . . .79 CE74
 Amersham (Lt.Chal.) HP7
Ashford TW15 . . . . .114 BL91
Barnet EN5 . . . . .28 DC42
Bexley DA5
 off Bexley High St 126 FA87
Bexleyheath DA7 . . . . . .106 EY82
Bexleyheath (Barne.) DA7 .107 FC82
Bromley (Hayes) BR2 . . .144 EG102
Buckhurst Hill IG9
 off Cherry Tree Ri 48 EK49
Chislehurst BR7 . . . . . .145 EN95
Chislehurst (Elm.Wds.) BR7 .124 EL93
Coulsdon CR5 . . . . .175 DK116
Coulsdon (Chipstead) CR5 .174 DF118
Dartford DA1 . . . . .128 FL86
Dartford (Cray.) DA1 . . . .127 FF86
Epping (They.B.) CM16
 off Coppice Row 33 ES36
Epsom KT18 . . . . .156 CR113
Epsom (Ewell E.) KT17 . .157 CV110
Epsom (Ewell W.) KT19
 off Chessington Rd 157 CT109
Epsom (Stoneleigh) KT19 .157 CU106
Esher (Hinch.Wd.) KT10 . .137 CF104
Gerrards Cross SL9 . . . . .56 AY57
Grays RM17 . . . . .110 GA79
Greenford UB6 . . . . .79 CD66
Hampton TW12
 off Milton Rd 136 CA95
Harrow HA1 . . . . .61 CE59
Hayes UB3 . . . . .95 BT75
Kenley CR8 off Hayes La .160 DQ114
Kingston upon Thames KT1 .138 CN95
Leatherhead KT22 . . . . .171 CG121
Leatherhead (Oxshott) KT22 .154 CC113
Loughton IG10 . . . . .32 EL43
Loughton (Debden) IG10 . .33 EQ42
Northwood HA6 . . . . .39 BS52
Orpington BR6 . . . . . . .145 ET103
Orpington (Chels.) BR6 . .145 EV106
Orpington (St.M.Cray) BR5 .146 EV98
Oxted RH8 . . . . .188 EE128
Pinner HA5 . . . . .60 BY55
Pinner (Hatch End) HA5
 off Uxbridge Rd 40 CA52
Purley CR8
 off Whytecliffe Rd S . . .159 DN111
Radlett WD7
 off Shenley Hill 25 CG35
Richmond TW9 . . . . .98 CN81
Rickmansworth (Chorl.) WD3 .21 BC42
Ruislip (S.Ruis.) HA4 . . . .59 BV64
Shepperton TW17 . . . . .135 BQ100
South Croydon CR2
 off Sanderstead Rd 160 DR109
Staines TW18 . . . . .114 BG92
Sunbury-on-Thames TW16 .135 BU95
Sutton (Belmont) SM2
 off Brighton Rd 158 DB110
Sutton (Cheam) SM2 . . .157 CY108
Swanley BR8 . . . . .147 FE98
Upminster RM14 . . . . . . .72 FQ61
Uxbridge (Denh.) UB9
 off Middle Rd 57 BD59
Virginia Water GU25 . . . .132 AX98
Waltham Cross EN8 . . . . .15 DY34
Waltham Cross (Chsht.)
 EN8 . . . . .15 DZ30
Watford WD18
 off Cassiobury Pk Av 23 BT41
Watford (Carp.Pk.) WD19
 off Prestwick Rd 40 BX48
Welling DA16 . . . . .105 ET82
Wembley HA0 . . . . .79 CH65
West Byfleet KT14 . . . . .152 BG112
West Drayton UB7 . . . . . .76 BL74
Weybridge KT13 . . . . . .152 BN107
Whyteleafe CR3 . . . . . .176 DU117
Woking GU22 . . . . .167 AZ117
Station App N, Sid. DA15 . . .126 EU89
Station App Rd, W4 . . . . . . .98 CQ80
Coulsdon CR5 . . . . .175 DK115
Tadworth KT20 . . . . . . .173 CW122
Tilbury RM18 . . . . .111 GG84

Sta - Sto

Station Av, SW9
off Coldharbour La **101** DP83
Caterham CR3 ....**176** DU124
Epsom KT19 ....**156** CS109
New Malden KT3 ....**138** CS97
Richmond TW9 ....**98** CN81
Walton-on-Thames KT12 .**153** BU105
Station Cl, N3 ....**44** DA53
N12 (Woodside Pk.) **44** DA49
Hampton TW12 ....**136** CB95
Hatfield AL9 off Station Rd .**11** CY26
Potters Bar EN6 ....**11** CZ31
Station Cres, N15 ....**66** DR56
SE3 ....**104** EG78
Ashford TW15 ....**114** BK90
Wembley HA0 ....**79** CH65
Stationers Hall Ct, EC4
off Ludgate Hill **83** DP72
Station Est, Beck. BR3
off Elmers End Rd **143** DX98
Station Est Rd, Felt. TW14 .**115** BV88
Station Footpath, Kings L.
WD4 ....**7** BP31
Station Garage Ms, SW16
off Estreham Rd **121** DK93
Station Gdns, W4 ....**98** CQ78
Station Gro, Wem. HA0 ....**80** CL65
Station Hill, Brom. BR2 ...**144** EG63
Station Ho Ms, N9 off Fore St .**46** DU49
Station Par, E11 ....**68** EG57
N14 off High St **45** DK46
NW2 ....**81** CW65
SW12 off Balham High Rd .**120** DG88
W3 ....**80** CN72
Ashford TW15
off Woodthorpe Rd **114** BM91
Barking IG11 ....**87** EQ66
Feltham TW14 ....**115** BV87
Hornchurch RM12
off Rosewood Av **71** FH63
Richmond TW9 ....**98** CN81
Sevenoaks TN13
off London Rd **190** FG124
Uxbridge (Denh.) UB9 ...**58** BG59
Virginia Water GU25 ...**132** AX98
Station Pas, E18
off Maybank Rd **48** EH54
Station Path, E8
off Amhurst Rd **84** DV65
Staines TW18 ....**113** BF91
Station Pl, N4
off Seven Sisters Rd **65** DN61
Station Ri, SE27
off Norwood Rd **121** DP89
Station Rd, E4 (Chingford) ..**47** ED46
E7 ....**68** EG63
E12 ....**68** EK63
E17 ....**67** DY58
N3 ....**44** DA53
N11 ....**45** DH50
N17 ....**66** DU55
N19 ....**65** DJ62
N21 ....**45** DP46
N22 ....**45** DM54
NW4 ....**63** CU58
NW7 ....**42** CS50
NW10 ....**81** CT68
SE13 ....**103** EC83
SE20 ....**122** DW93
SE25 (Norwood Junct.) .**142** DT98
SW13 ....**99** CU83
SW19 ....**140** DC95
W5 ....**80** CM72
W7 (Hanwell) **79** CE74
Addlestone KT15 ......**152** BJ105
Ashford TW15 ....**114** BM91
Barnet EN5 ....**28** DB43
Belvedere DA17 ....**106** FA76
Betchworth RH3 ....**182** CS131
Bexleyheath DA7 ......**106** EY83
Borehamwood WD6 .....**26** CN42
Brentford TW8 ....**97** CJ79
Bromley BR1 ....**144** EG95
Bromley (Short.) BR2 ...**144** EE96
Carshalton SM5 ....**158** DF105
Caterham CR3 ....**177** DZ123
Chertsey KT16 ....**133** BF102
Chessington KT9 ......**156** CL106
Chigwell IG7 ....**49** EP48
Cobham (Stoke D'Ab.) KT11 .**170** BY117
Croydon (E.Croy.) CR0 .**142** DR103
Croydon (W.Croy.) CR0 .**142** DQ102
Dartford (Cray.) DA1 ...**127** FF86
Dartford (Eyns.) DA4 ...**148** FK104
Dartford (S.Darenth) DA4 .**148** FK107
Edgware HA8 ....**42** CN51
Egham TW20 ....**113** BA92
Epping CM16 ....**18** EU31
Epping (N.Wld.Bas.) CM16 .**19** FB27
Esher KT10 ....**137** CD103
Esher (Clay.) KT10 ....**155** CD106
Gerrards Cross SL9 .....**56** AY57
Gravesend (Betsham) DA13 .**130** GA91
Gravesend (Nthflt.) DA11 .**130** GB86
Greenhithe DA9 ....**129** FU85
Hampton TW12 ....**136** CA95
Harrow HA1 ....**61** CF59
Harrow (N.Har.) HA2 ...**60** CB57
Hatfield (Brook.Pk.) AL9 ..**11** CY13
Hayes UB3 ....**95** BT76
Hounslow TW3 ....**96** CB84
Ilford IG1 ....**69** EP62
Ilford (Barkingside) IG6 ..**69** ER55
Kenley CR8 ....**160** DQ114
Kings Langley WD4 .....**7** BP29
Kingston upon Thames KT2 .**138** CM95
Kingston upon Thames
(Hmptn.W.) KT1 ......**137** CJ95
Leatherhead KT22 .....**171** CG121
Loughton IG10 ....**32** EL42
New Malden (Mots.Pk.) KT3 .**139** CV99
Orpington BR6 ....**145** ET103
Orpington (St.P.Cray) BR5 .**146** EW98

Station Rd, Pot.B. (Cuffley)
EN6 ....**13** DM29
Radlett WD7 ....**25** CG35
Redhill RH1 ....**184** DG133
Redhill (Merst.) RH1 ...**185** DJ128
Rickmansworth WD3 ....**38** BK45
Romford (Chad.Hth.) RM6 .**70** EX59
Romford (Gidea Pk.) RM2 .**71** FH56
Romford (Harold Wd.) RM3 .**52** FM53
St. Albans (Brick.Wd.) AL2 ..**8** CA31
Sevenoaks (Dunt.Grn.)TN13 .**181** FE120
Sevenoaks (Halst.) TN14 .**164** EZ111
Sevenoaks (Otford) TN14 .**181** FH116
Sevenoaks (Shore.) TN14 .**165** FG111
Shepperton TW17 .....**135** BQ99
Sidcup DA15 ....**126** EU91
Slough (Langley) SL3 ...**93** BA76
Staines (Wrays.) TW19 ..**112** AZ86
Sunbury-on-Thames TW16 .**115** BU94
Sutton (Belmont) SM2 ..**158** DA110
Swanley BR8 ....**147** FE98
Teddington TW11 ......**117** CF92
Thames Ditton KT7 ....**137** CF101
Twickenham TW1 ......**117** CF88
Upminster RM14 ....**72** FQ61
Uxbridge UB8 ....**76** BJ70
Waltham Cross EN8 ....**15** EA34
Watford WD17 ....**23** BV40
West Byfleet KT14 ....**152** BG112
West Drayton UB7 .....**76** BK74
West Wickham BR4 ....**143** EC102
Westerham (Brasted) TN16 .**180** EV123
Whyteleafe CR3 ......**176** DT118
Woking (Chobham) GU24 .**150** AT111
Station Rd E, Oxt. RH8 ...**188** EE128
Station Rd N, Belv. DA17 ..**107** FB76
Egham TW20 ....**113** BA92
Redhill (Merst.) RH1 ...**185** DJ128
Station Rd S, Red. (Merst.)
RH1 ....**185** DJ128
Station Rd W, Oxt. RH8 ...**188** EE129
Station Sq, Orp. (Petts Wd)
BR5 ....**145** EQ99
Romford RM2 ....**71** FH56
Station St, E15 ....**85** ED66
E16 ....**87** EP74
Station Ter, NW10 ....**81** CX68
SE5 ....**102** DQ81
St. Albans (Park St.) AL2
off Park St **9** CD26
Station Vw, Grnf. UB6 .....**79** CD67
Station Way, Buck.H. (Rod.Val.)
IG9 ....**48** EJ49
Epsom (Epsom) KT19 ..**156** CR113
Esher (Clay.) KT10 ....**155** CE107
Sutton (Cheam) SM3 ...**157** CY107
Station Yd, Twick. TW1 ...**117** CG87
Staunton Rd, Kings.T. KT2 .**118** CL93
Staunton St, SE8 ....**103** DZ79
★ **Stave Hill Ecological Pk,**
SE16 ....**103** DY75
Staveley Cl, E9
off Churchill Wk **66** DW64
N7 off Penn Rd **65** DL63
SE15 off Asylum Rd ...**102** DV81
Staveley Gdns, W4 ....**98** CR81
Staveley Rd, W4 ....**98** CR80
Ashford TW15 ....**115** BR93
Staveley Way, Wok. (Knap.)
GU21 ....**166** AS117
Staverton Rd, NW2 ....**81** CW66
Hornchurch RM11 ......**72** FK58
Stave Yd Rd, SE16 ....**203** K3
Stavordale Rd, N5 ....**65** DP63
Carshalton SM5 ....**140** DC101
Stayne End, Vir.W. GU25 ..**132** AU98
Stayner's Rd, E1 ....**85** DX70
Stayton Rd, Sutt. SM1 ...**140** DA104
Steadfast Rd, Kings.T. KT1 .**137** CK95
Stead St, SE17 ....**201** K9
Stean St, E8 ....**84** DT67
Stebbing Ho, W11 ....**81** CX74
Stebbing Way, Bark. IG11 ..**88** EU68
Stebondale St, E14 ....**204** E9
Stedham Pl, WC1 ....**195** P8
Stedman Cl, Bex. DA5 ....**127** FE90
Uxbridge UB10 ....**58** BN62
Steed Cl, Horn. RM11 .....**71** FH61
Steedman St, SE17 ......**201** H9
Steeds Rd, N10 ....**44** DF53
Steeds Way, Loug. IG10 ....**32** EL41
Steele Av, Green. DA9 ....**129** FT85
Steele Rd, E11 ....**68** EE63
N17 ....**66** DS55
NW10 ....**80** CQ68
W4 ....**98** CQ76
Isleworth TW7 ....**97** CG84
Steeles Ms N, NW3
off Steeles Rd **82** DF65
Steeles Ms S, NW3
off Steeles Rd **82** DF65
Steeles Rd, NW3 ....**82** DF65
Steele Wk, Erith DA8 ....**107** FB79
Steel's La, Lthd. (Oxshott)
KT22 ....**154** CB114
Steelyard Pas, EC4
off Upper Thames St ...**84** DR73
Steen Way, SE22
off East Dulwich Gro ..**122** DS85
Steep Cl, Orp. BR6 ....**163** ET107
Steep Hill, SW16 ....**121** DK90
Croydon CR0 ....**160** DS105
Steeplands, Bushey WD23 ..**40** CB45
Steeple Cl, SW6 ....**99** CY82
SW19 ....**119** CY92
Steeple Ct, E1 off Coventry Rd .**84** DV70
Steeple Gdns, Add. KT15
off Weatherall Cl **152** BH106
Steeple Hts Dr, West. (Bigg.H.)
TN16 ....**178** EK117
Steeplestone Cl, N18 ......**46** DQ50
Steeple Wk, N1 off Basire St .**84** DQ67
Steerforth St, SW18 ......**120** DB89
Steers Mead, Mitch. CR4 ..**140** DF95
Steers Way, SE16 ....**203** L5

Stellar Ho, N17 ....**46** DT51
Stella Rd, SW17 ....**120** DF93
Stelling Rd, Erith DA8 ....**107** FD80
Stellman Cl, E5 ....**66** DU62
Stembridge Rd, SE20 .....**142** DV96
Sten Cl, Enf. EN3
off Government Row **31** EA38
Stents La, Cob. KT11 ....**170** BZ120
Stepbridge Path, Wok. GU21
off Goldsworth Rd ...**166** AX117
Stepgates, Cher. KT16 ...**134** BH101
Stepgates Cl, Cher. KT16 .**134** BH101
Stephan Cl, E8 ....**84** DU67
Stephen Av, Rain. RM13 ..**89** FG65
Stephen Cl, Egh. TW20 ...**113** BC93
Orpington BR6 ....**145** ET104
Stephendale Rd, SW6 ....**100** DB82
Stephen Ms, W1 ....**195** M7
Stephen Pl, SW4
off Rectory Gro **101** DJ83
Stephen Rd, Bexh. DA7 ..**107** FC83
Stephens Cl, Rom. RM3 ...**52** FJ50
Stephenson Av, Til. RM18 .**111** GG81
Stephenson Rd, E17 ....**67** DY57
W7 ....**79** CF72
Twickenham TW2 .....**116** CA87
Stephenson St, E16 ....**86** EE70
NW10 ....**80** CS69
Stephenson Way, NW1 ...**195** L4
Watford WD24 ....**24** BX41
Stephen's Rd, E15 ....**86** EE67
Stephen St, W1 ....**195** M7
Stephens Wf, Hem.H. HP3
off Belswains La **6** BM25
STEPNEY, E1 ....**84** DW71
Stepney Causeway, E1 ....**85** DX72
🇭 **Stepney Day Hosp, E1** ...**84** DW72
⊖ **Stepney Green** **85** DX70
Stepney Grn, E1 ....**84** DW71
Stepney High St, E1 ......**85** DX71
Stepney Way, E1 ....**84** DV71
Sterling Av, Edg. HA8 .....**42** CM49
Pinner HA5 ....**60** BY59
Waltham Cross EN8 ....**15** DX34
Sterling Cl, NW10 ....**81** CU65
Pinner HA5 ....**60** BX60
Sterling Gdns, SE14 .....**103** DY79
Sterling Ho, SE3
off Cambert Way **104** EH84
Sterling Ind Est, Dag. RM10 .**71** FB63
Sterling Pl, W5 ....**98** CL77
Sterling Rd, Enf. EN2 ......**30** DR38
Sterling St, SW7 ....**198** C6
Sterling Way, N18 ....**46** DR50
★ **Sternberg Cen,**
N3 (Finchley) **44** DB54
Stern Cl, Bark. IG11 ....**88** EW68
Sterndale Rd, W14 ....**99** CX76
Dartford DA1 ....**128** FM87
Sterne St, W12 ....**99** CX75
Sternhall La, SE15 ....**102** DU83
Sternhold Av, SW2 ......**121** DK89
Sterry Cres, Dag. RM10
off Alibon Rd **70** FA64
Sterry Dr, Epsom KT19 ...**156** CS105
Thames Ditton KT7 ...**137** CE100
Sterry Gdns, Dag. RM10 ..**88** FA65
Sterry Rd, Bark. IG11 ......**87** ET67
Dagenham RM10 ......**70** FA63
Sterry St, SE1 ....**201** K5
Steucers La, SE23 ....**123** DY87
Steve Biko La, SE6 ....**123** EA91
Steve Biko Rd, N7 ....**65** DN62
Steve Biko Way, Houns. TW3 .**96** CA83
Stevedale Rd, Well. DA16 ..**106** EW83
Stevedore St, E1 ....**202** D2
Stevenage Cres, Borwd. WD6 .**26** CL39
Stevenage Rd, E6 ....**87** EN65
SW6 ....**99** CX80
Stevens Av, E9 ....**84** DW65
Stevens Cl, Beck. BR3 ...**123** EA93
Bexley DA5 ....**127** FD91
Steven's Cl, Dart. (Lane End)
DA2 ....**129** FS92
Stevens Cl, Epsom KT17
off Upper High St **156** CS113
Hampton TW12 ....**116** BY93
Pinner HA5
off Bridle Rd **60** BW57
Stevens Grn, Bushey
(Bushey Hth.) WD23 ..**40** CC46
Stevens La, Esher (Clay.)
KT10 ....**155** CG108
Stevenson Cl, Barn. EN5 ..**28** DD44
Erith DA8 ....**107** FH80
Stevenson Cres, SE16 ....**202** C10
Stevens Pl, Pur. CR8 .....**159** DP113
Stevens Rd, Dag. RM8 ....**70** EV62
Stevens St, SE1 ....**201** N6
Steven's Wk, Croy. CR0 ..**161** DY111
Stevens Way, Chig. IG7 ....**49** ES49
Steventon Rd, W12 ....**81** CT73
Steward Cl, Wal.Cr. (Chsht.)
EN8 ....**15** DY30
Stewards Cl, Epp. CM16 ...**18** EU33
Stewards Grn La, Epp. CM16 .**18** EU33
Stewards Grn Rd, Epp. CM16 .**18** EU33
Stewards Holte Wk, N11
off Coppies Gro **45** DH49
Steward St, E1 ....**197** N7
Stewards Wk, Rom. RM1 ...**71** FE57
Stewart, Tad. KT20 ......**173** CX121
Stewart Av, Shep. TW17 ..**134** BN98
Slough SL1 ....**74** AT71
Upminster RM14 ....**72** FQ62
Stewart Cl, NW9 ....**62** CQ58
Abbots Langley WD5 ...**7** BT32
Chislehurst BR7 ......**125** EP92
Hampton TW12 ....**116** BY92
Woking GU21
off Nethercote Av ...**166** AT117
Stewart Rainbird Ho, E12 ..**69** EN64
Stewart Rd, E15 ....**67** EC63
Stewartsby Cl, N18 ....**46** DQ50
Stewart's Gro, SW3 ......**198** A10
Stewart's Rd, SW8 ....**101** DJ80
Stewart St, E14 ....**204** E5

Stew La, EC4 ....**197** H10
Steyne Rd, W3 ....**80** CQ74
Steyning Cl, Ken. CR8 ...**175** DP116
Steyning Gro, SE9 ....**125** EM91
Steynings Way, N12 ....**44** DA50
Steynton Av, Bex. DA5 ...**126** EX89
Stickland Rd, Belv. DA17
off Picardy Rd **106** FA77
Stickleton Cl, Grnf. UB6 ...**78** CB69
Stifford Hill, Grays (N.Stfd.)
RM16 ....**91** FX74
South Ockendon RM15 .**91** FW73
Stifford Rd, S.Ock. RM15 ..**91** FR74
Stilecroft Gdns, Wem. HA0 .**61** CH62
Stile Hall Gdns, W4 ....**98** CN76
Stile Hall Par, W4
off Chiswick High Rd ..**98** CN78
Stile Path, Sun. TW16 ...**135** BU98
Stile Rd, Slou. SL3 ....**92** AX76
Stiles Cl, Brom. BR2 .....**145** EM100
Erith DA8 off Riverdale Rd .**107** FB78
Stillingfleet Rd, SW13 ....**99** CU79
Stillington St, SW1 ......**199** L8
Stillness Rd, SE23 ....**123** DY86
Stilton Cres, NW10 ....**80** CQ66
Stilton Path, Borwd. WD6 ..**26** CN38
Stilwell Dr, Uxb. UB8 .....**76** BM70
Stilwell Roundabout, Uxb.
UB8 ....**76** BN73
Stipularis Dr, Hayes UB4 ..**78** BX70
Stirling Cl, SW16 ....**141** DJ95
Banstead SM7 ....**173** CZ117
Rainham RM13 ....**89** FH69
Uxbridge UB8
off Ferndale Cres **76** BJ69
Stirling Cor, Barn. EN5 ....**26** CR44
Borehamwood WD6 .....**26** CR44
Stirling Dr, Orp. BR6 .....**164** EV106
Stirling Gro, Houns. TW3 ...**96** CC82
Stirling Rd, E13 ....**86** EH68
E17 ....**67** DY55
N17 ....**46** DU53
N22 ....**45** DP53
SW9 ....**101** DL82
W3 ....**98** CP55
Harrow HA3 ....**61** CF55
Hayes UB3 ....**77** BV73
Hounslow (Hthrw.Air.) TW6 .**116** BM86
Twickenham TW2 .....**116** CA87
Stirling Rd Path, E17 ......**67** DY55
Stirling Wk, N.Mal. KT3 ..**138** CQ99
Surbiton KT5 ....**138** CP100
Stirling Way, Abb.L. WD5 ...**7** BU32
Borehamwood WD6 .....**26** CR44
Croydon CR0 ....**141** DL101
Stites Hill Rd, Couls. CR5 .**175** DP116
Stiven Cres, Har. HA2 .....**60** BZ62
Stoats Nest Rd, Couls. CR5 .**159** DL114
Stoats Nest Village, Couls.
CR5 ....**175** DL115
Stockbury Rd, Croy. CR0 .**142** DW100
Stockdale Rd, Dag. RM8 ...**70** EZ61
Stockdove Way, Grnf. UB6 ..**79** CF69
Stocker Gdns, Dag. RM9 ...**88** EW66
Stockers Fm Rd, Rick. WD3 .**38** BK48
Stockers La, Wok. GU22 .**167** AZ120
★ **Stock Exchange, EC2** ...**197** L9
Stockfield Rd, SW16 .....**121** DM94
Esher (Clay.) KT10 ....**155** CE106
Stockham's Cl, S.Croy. CR2 .**160** DR111
Stock Hill, West. (Bigg.H.)
TN16 ....**178** EK116
Stockholm Ho, E1 ....**84** DU73
Stockholm Rd, SE16 .....**102** DW78
Stockholm Way, E1 ......**202** B2
Stockhurst Cl, SW15 ......**99** CW82
Stockingswater La, Enf. EN3 .**31** DY41
Stockland Rd, Rom. RM7 ...**71** FC58
Stock La, Dart. DA2 ....**128** FJ91
Stockley Cl, West Dr. UB7 ..**95** BP75
Stockley Fm Rd, West Dr. UB7
off Stockley Rd **95** BP76
Stockley Pk, Uxb. UB11 ....**77** BP74
Stockley Pk Roundabout, Uxb.
UB11 ....**77** BP74
Stockley Rd, Uxb. UB8 .....**77** BP73
West Drayton UB7 .....**95** BP77
Stock Orchard Cres, N7 ....**65** DM64
Stock Orchard St, N7 ......**65** DM64
Stockport Rd, SW16 .....**141** DK95
Rickmansworth (Herons.)
WD3 ....**37** BC45
Stocksfield Rd, E17 ....**67** EC55
Stocks Pl, E14 off Grenade St .**85** DZ73
Stock St, E13 ....**86** EG68
Stockton Cl, Barn. EN5 ....**28** DC42
Stockton Gdns, N17
off Stockton Rd **46** DQ52
NW7 ....**42** CS48
Stockton Rd, N17 ....**46** DQ52
N18 ....**46** DU51
STOCKWELL, SW9 ....**101** DK83
⊖ **Stockwell** **101** DL81
Stockwell Av, SW9 ......**101** DM83
Stockwell Cl, Brom. BR1 ..**144** EH96
Waltham Cross (Chsht.) EN7 .**14** DU28
Stockwell Gdns, SW9 ....**101** DM82
Stockwell Gdns Est, SW9 .**101** DL82
Stockwell Grn, SW9 ......**101** DM82
Stockwell La, SW9 ......**101** DM82
Waltham Cross (Chsht.)
EN7 ....**14** DU28
Stockwell Ms, SW9
off Stockwell Rd **101** DM82
Stockwell Pk Cres, SW9 ..**101** DM81
Stockwell Pk Est, SW9 ...**101** DM82
Stockwell Pk Rd, SW9 ...**101** DM81
Stockwell Pk Wk, SW9 ...**101** DM82
Stockwell Rd, SW9 ......**101** DM82
Stockwell St, SE10 ......**103** EC79
Stockwell Ter, SW9 ......**101** DM81
Stodart Rd, SE20 ....**142** DW95
Stofield Gdns, SE9
off Aldersgrove Av ...**124** EK90
Stoford Cl, SW19 ....**119** CY87
Stoke Av, Ilf. IG6 ....**50** EU51

Stoke Cl, Cob. (Stoke D'Ab.)
KT11 ....**170** BZ116
Stoke Common Rd, Slou.
(Fulmer) SL3 ....**56** AU63
Stoke Ct Dr, Slou. (Stoke P.)
SL2 ....**74** AS67
STOKE D'ABERNON, Cob. .**170** BZ116
Stoke Gdns, Slou. SL1 .....**74** AS74
STOKE GREEN, Slou. **74** AU70
Stoke Grn, Slou. (Stoke P.) SL2 .**74** AU70
Stokenchurch St, SW6 ...**100** DB81
⊖ **Stoke Newington** **66** DT62
STOKE NEWINGTON, N16 .**66** DS61
Stoke Newington Ch St, N16 .**66** DR62
Stoke Newington Common,
N16 ....**66** DT62
Stoke Newington High St,
N16 ....**66** DT62
Stoke Newington Rd, N16 .**66** DT64
Stoke Pl, NW10 ....**81** CT69
STOKE POGES, Slou. **74** AT66
Stoke Poges La, Slou.
SL1, SL2 ....**74** AS72
Stoke Rd, Cob. KT11 .....**170** BW115
Kingston upon Thames KT2 .**118** CQ94
Rainham RM13 ....**90** FK68
Slough SL2 ....**74** AT71
Walton-on-Thames KT12 .**136** BW104
Stokesay, Slou. SL2 ....**74** AT73
Stokesby Rd, Chess. KT9 .**156** CM107
Stokesheath Rd, Lthd. (Oxshott)
KT22 ....**154** CC111
Stokesley St, W12 ....**81** CT72
Stokes Ridings, Tad. KT20 .**173** CX123
Stokes Rd, E6 ....**86** EL70
Croydon CR0 ....**143** DX100
Stoke Wd, Slou. (Stoke P.) SL2 .**56** AT63
Stoll Cl, NW2 ....**63** CW62
Stompond La, Walt. KT12 .**135** BU103
Stonard Rd, N13 ....**45** DN48
Dagenham RM8 ....**70** EV64
Stonards Hill, Epp. CM16 ..**18** EW31
Loughton IG10 ....**33** EM44
Stondon Pk, SE23 ....**123** DY87
Stondon Wk, E6 ....**86** EK68
STONE, Green. **129** FT85
Stonebanks, Walt. KT12 ..**135** BU101
STONEBRIDGE, NW10 .....**80** CP67
Stonebridge Common, E8
off Mayfield Rd **84** DT66
⊖ **Stonebridge Park** **80** CN66
Stonebridge Park **80** CN66
Stonebridge Pk, NW10 ....**80** CP66
Stonebridge Rd, N15 ......**66** DS57
Gravesend (Nthflt.) DA11 .**130** GA85
Stonebridge Way, Wem. HA9 .**62** CP65
Stone Bldgs, WC2 ....**196** C7
Stonechat Sq, E6
off Peridot St **86** EL71
Stone Cl, SW4 off Larkhall Ri .**101** DJ82
Dagenham RM8 ....**70** EZ61
West Drayton UB7 .....**76** BM74
Stonecot Cl, Sutt. SM3 ...**139** CY102
Stonecot Hill, Sutt. SM3 .**139** CY102
Stone Cres, Felt. TW14 ..**115** BT87
Stonecroft Av, Iver SL0 ....**75** BE72
Stonecroft Cl, Barn. EN5 ...**27** CV42
Stonecroft Rd, Erith DA8 ..**107** FC80
Stonecroft Way, Croy. CR0 .**141** DL101
Stonecrop Cl, NW9 ....**62** CR55
⊜ **Stone Crossing** **129** FS85
Stonecutter Ct, EC4
off Stonecutter St **83** DP72
Stonecutter St, EC4 .....**196** F8
Stonefield Cl, Bexh. DA7 .**106** FA83
Ruislip HA4 ....**60** BY64
Stonefield St, N1 ....**83** DN67
Stonefield Way, SE7
off Greenbay Rd **104** EK80
Ruislip HA4 ....**60** BY63
Stonegate Cl, Orp. BR5
off Main Rd **146** EW97
Stonegrove, Edg. HA8 .....**42** CL49
Stonegrove Est, Edg. HA8 ..**42** CM49
Stonegrove Gdns, Edg. HA8 .**42** CM50
Stonehall Av, Ilf. IG2 ......**68** EL58
Stone Hall Gdns, W8
off St. Mary's Gate ...**100** DB76
Stone Hall Pl, W8
off St. Mary's Gate ...**100** DB76
Stone Hall Rd, N21 ....**45** DM45
Stoneham Rd, N11 ....**45** DJ51
STONEHILL, Cher. **150** AY107
Stonehill Cl, SW14 ......**118** CR85
Stonehill Cres, Cher. (Ott.)
KT16 ....**150** AY107
Stonehill Grn, Dart. DA2 ..**127** FC94
Stonehill Rd, SW14
off Wellesley Rd **98** CN78
Chertsey (Ott.) KT16 ..**151** BA105
Woking (Chobham) GU24 .**150** AW108
Stonehills Ct, SE21 ....**122** DS90
Stonehorse Rd, Enf. EN3 ..**30** DW43
Stonehouse Gdns, Cat. CR3 .**186** DS125
Stonehouse Hosp, Dart.
DA2 ....**128** FQ86
Stonehouse La, Purf. RM19 .**109** FS79
Sevenoaks (Halst.) TN14 .**164** EX109
Stonehouse Rd, Sev. (Halst.)
TN14 ....**164** EW110
Stoneings La, Sev. (Knock.)
TN14 ....**179** ET118
Stone Lake Retail Pk, SE7 .**104** EH77
STONELEIGH, Epsom **157** CU106
⊜ **Stoneleigh** **157** CU106
Stoneleigh Av, Enf. EN1 ...**30** DV39
Worcester Park KT4 ..**157** CU105
Stoneleigh Bdy, Epsom KT17 .**157** CU106
Stoneleigh Cl, Wal.Cr. EN8 .**15** DX33
Stoneleigh Cres, Epsom KT19 .**157** CT106
Stoneleigh Pk, Wey. KT13 .**153** BQ106
Stoneleigh Pk Av, Croy. CR0 .**143** DX100
Stoneleigh Pk Rd, Epsom
KT19 ....**157** CT107
Stoneleigh Pl, W11 ....**81** CX73

★ Place of interest ⊜ Railway station ⊖ London Underground station 🄳🄻🅁 Docklands Light Railway station ◇ Tramlink station 🄷 Hospital

Stoneleigh Rd, N17 66	DT55	
Carshalton SM5 140	DE101	
Ilford IG5 68	EL55	
Oxted RH8 188	EL130	
Stoneleigh St, W11 81	CX73	
Stoneleigh Ter, N19 65	DH61	
Stonells Rd, SW11		
off Chatham Rd 120	DF85	
Stonemasons Ct, N15 66	DR56	
Stone Ness Rd, Grays RM20 .109	FV79	
Stonenest St, N4 65	DM60	
Stone Pk Av, Beck. BR3 143	EA98	
Stone Pl, Wor.Pk. KT4 139	CU103	
Stone Pl Rd, Green. DA9 129	FS85	
Stone Rd, Brom. BR2 144	EF99	
Stones All, Wat. WD18 23	BV42	
Stones Cross Rd, Swan. BR8 .147	FC99	
Stones End St, SE1 201	H5	
Stones La, Epsom KT17 156	CS112	
Stone St, Croy. CR0 159	DN106	
Gravesend DA11 131	GH86	
Stoneswood Rd, Oxt. RH8 . . .188	EH130	
Stonewall, E6 87	EN71	
Stonewood, Dart. (Bean) DA2 .129	FW90	
Stonewood Rd, Erith DA8 . . .107	FE78	
Stoney All, SE18 105	EN82	
Stoneyard La, E14 204	B1	
Stoney Cft, Couls. CR5 175	DJ122	
Stoneycroft Cl, SE12 124	EF87	
Stoneycroft Rd, Wdf.Grn. IG8 .48	EL51	
Stoneydeep, Tedd. TW11		
off Twickenham Rd 117	CG91	
Stoneydown, E17 67	DY56	
Stoneydown Av, E17 67	DY56	
Stoneyfield Rd, Couls. CR5 . .175	DM117	
Stoneyfields Gdns, Edg. HA8 . .42	CQ49	
Stoneyfields La, Edg. HA8 42	CQ50	
Stoneylands Ct, Egh. TW20 . .113	AZ92	
Stoneylands Rd, Egh. TW20 . .113	AZ92	
Stoney La, E1 197	N8	
SE19 off Church Rd 122	DT93	
Hemel Hempstead (Bov.) HP3 .5	BB27	
Kings Langley (Chipper.) WD4 .5	BE30	
Stoney St, SE1 201	K2	
Stonhouse St, SW4 101	DK83	
Stonny Ct, Ashtd. KT21 172	CM117	
Stonor Rd, W14 99	CZ77	
Stonycroft Cl, Enf. EN3		
off Brimsdown Av 31	DY40	
Stony La, Amer. HP6 20	AY38	
Stony Path, Loug. IG10 33	EM40	
Stonyshotts, Wal.Abb. EN9 . . .16	EE34	
Stoop Ct, W.Byf. KT14 152	BH112	
Stopes St, SE15 102	DT80	
Stopford Rd, E13 86	EG67	
SE17 101	DP78	
Store Rd, E16 105	EN75	
Storers Quay, E14 204	F9	
Store St, E15 67	ED64	
WC1 195	M7	
Storey Rd, E17 67	DZ56	
N6 64	DF58	
Storey St, E16 87	EN74	
Storey's Gate, SW1 199	N5	
Stories Ms, SE5 102	DS82	
Stories Rd, SE5 102	DS83	
Stork Rd, E7 86	EF65	
Storksmead Rd, Edg. HA8 42	CS52	
Storks Rd, SE16 202	C7	
Stormont Rd, N6 64	DF59	
SW11 100	DG83	
Stormont Way, Chess. KT9 . .155	CJ106	
Stormount Dr, Hayes UB3 95	BQ75	
Stornaway Strand, Grav.		
DA12 131	GM91	
Storr Gdns, Brwd. CM13 55	GE44	
Storrington Rd, Croy. CR0 . . .142	DT102	
Story St, N1 off Carnoustie Dr .83	DM66	
Stothard Pl, EC2		
off Bishopsgate 84	DS71	
Stothard St, E1 off Colebert Av .84	DW70	
Stott Cl, SW18 120	DD86	
Stoughton Av, Sutt. SM3 157	CX106	
Stoughton Cl, SE11 200	C9	
SW15 off Bessborough Rd .119	CU88	
Stour Av, Sthl. UB2 96	CA76	
Stourcliffe St, W1 194	D9	
Stour Cl, Kes. BR2 162	EJ105	
Stourhead Cl, SW19		
off Castlecombe Dr 119	CX87	
Stourhead Gdns, SW20 139	CU97	
Stour Rd, E3 85	EA66	
Dagenham RM10 70	FA61	
Dartford DA1 107	FG83	
Grays RM16 111	GG78	
Stourton Av, Felt. TW13 116	BZ91	
Stour Way, Upmin. RM14 73	FS58	
Stowage, SE8 103	EA79	
Stow Cres, E17 47	DY52	
Stowe Ct, Dart. DA2 128	FQ87	
Stowe Cres, Ruis. HA4 59	BP58	
Stowe Gdns, N9 46	DT46	
Stowell Av, Croy. (New Adgtn.)		
CR0 161	ED110	
Stowe Pl, N15 66	DS56	
Stowe Rd, W12 99	CV75	
Orpington BR6 164	EU105	
Stowting Rd, Orp. BR6 163	ES105	
Stox Mead, Har. HA3 41	CD53	
Stracey Rd, E7 68	EG63	
NW10 80	CR67	
Strachan Pl, SW19		
off Woodhayes Rd 119	CW93	
Stradbroke Dr, Chig. IG7 49	EN51	
Stradbroke Gro, Buck.H. IG9 . .48	EK46	
Ilford IG5 68	EL55	
Stradbroke Pk, Chig. IG7 49	EP51	
Stradbroke Rd, N5 66	DQ63	
Stradbrook Cl, Har. HA2		
off Stiven Cres 60	BZ62	
Stradella Rd, SE24 122	DQ86	
Strafford Av, Ilf. IG5 49	EN54	
Strafford Cl, Pot.B. EN6		
off Strafford Gate 12	DA32	
Strafford Gate, Pot.B. EN6 . . .12	DA32	
Strafford Rd, W3 98	CQ75	

Strafford Rd, Bar. EN5 27	CY41	
Hounslow TW3 96	BZ83	
Twickenham TW1 117	CG87	
Strafford St, E14 203	P4	
Strahan Rd, E3 85	DY69	
Straight, The, Sthl. UB1 96	BX75	
Straight Rd, Rom. RM3 52	FJ52	
Windsor (Old Wind.) SL4 . .112	AU85	
Straightsmouth, SE10 103	EC80	
Strait Rd, E6 86	EL73	
Straker's Rd, SE22 102	DV84	
STRAND, WC2 195	P10	
Strand, WC2 199	P1	
Strand Cl, Epsom KT18 172	CR119	
Strand Ct, SE18		
off Strandfield Cl 105	ES78	
Strandfield Cl, SE18 105	ES78	
Strand La, WC2 196	C10	
Strand on the Grn, W4 98	CN79	
Strand Pl, N18 46	DR49	
Strand Sch App, W4		
off Thames Rd 98	CN79	
Strangeways, Wat. WD17 23	BS36	
Strangways Ter, W14		
off Melbury Rd 99	CZ76	
Stranraer Gdns, Slou. SL1 . . .74	AS74	
Stranraer Rd, Houns. (Hthrw.Air.)		
TW6 114	BL86	
Stranraer Way, N1 83	DL66	
Strasburg Rd, SW11 101	DH81	
Stratfield Pk Cl, N21 45	DP45	
Stratfield Rd, Borwd. WD6 26	CN41	
Slough SL1 92	AU75	
STRATFORD, E15 85	EC65	
≷ Stratford 85	EC65	
⊖ Stratford 85	EC66	
DLR Stratford 85	EC66	
Stratford Av, W8		
off Stratford Rd 100	DA76	
Uxbridge UB10 76	BM68	
Stratford Cen, The, E15 85	ED66	
Stratford Cl, Bark. IG11 88	EU66	
Dagenham RM10 89	FC66	
Stratford Ct, N.Mal. KT3		
off Kingston Rd 138	CR98	
Stratford Gro, SW15 99	CX84	
Stratford Ho Av, Brom. BR1 . .144	EL97	
Stratford Pl, W1 195	H9	
Stratford Rd, E13 86	EF67	
NW4 63	CX56	
W8 100	DA76	
Hayes UB4 77	BV70	
Hounslow (Hthrw.Air.)TW6 .115	BP86	
Southall UB2 96	BY77	
Thornton Heath CR7 141	DN98	
Watford WD17 23	BU40	
Stratford Vil, NW1 83	DJ66	
Stratford Way, St.Alb. (Brick.Wd.)		
AL2 8	BZ29	
Watford WD17 23	BT40	
Strathan Cl, SW18 119	CY86	
Strathaven Rd, SE12 124	EH86	
Strathblaine Rd, SW11 100	DD84	
Strathbrook Rd, SW16 121	DM94	
Strathcona Rd, Wem. HA9 61	CK61	
Strathdale, SW16 121	DM92	
Strathdon Dr, SW17 120	DD90	
Strathearn Av, Hayes UB3 95	BT80	
Twickenham TW2 116	CB88	
Strathearn Pl, W2 194	A10	
Strathearn Rd, SW19 120	DA92	
Sutton SM1 158	DA106	
Stratheden Par, SE3		
off Stratheden Rd 104	EG80	
Stratheden Rd, SE3 104	EG81	
Strathfield Gdns, Bark. IG11 . .87	ER65	
Strathleven Rd, SW2 121	DL85	
Strathmore Cl, Cat. CR3 176	DS121	
Strathmore Gdns, N3 44	DB53	
W8 off Palace Gdns Ter 82	DA74	
Edgware HA8 42	CP54	
Hornchurch RM12 71	FF60	
Strathmore Rd, SW19 120	DA90	
Croydon CR0 142	DQ101	
Teddington TW11 117	CE91	
Strathnairn St, SE1 202	C9	
Strathray Gdns, NW3 82	DE65	
Strath Ter, SW11 100	DE84	
Strathville Rd, SW18 120	DB89	
Strathyre Av, SW16 141	DN97	
Stratton Av, Enf. EN2 30	DR37	
Wallington SM6 159	DK109	
Stratton Chase Dr, Ch.St.G.		
HP8 36	AU47	
Stratton Cl, SW19 140	DA96	
Bexleyheath DA7 106	EY83	
Edgware HA8 42	CM51	
Hounslow TW3 96	BZ81	
Walton-on-Thames KT12		
off St. Johns Dr 136	BW102	
Strattondale St, E14 204	D6	
Stratton Dr, Bark. IG11 69	ET64	
Stratton Gdns, Sthl. UB1 78	BZ72	
Stratton Rd, SW19 140	DA96	
Bexleyheath DA7 106	EY83	
Romford RM3 52	FN50	
Sunbury-on-Thames TW16 .135	BT96	
Stratton St, W1 199	J2	
Stratton Ter, West. TN16		
off High St 189	EQ127	
Stratton Wk, Rom. RM3 52	FN50	
Strauss Rd, W4 98	CR75	
Strawberry Hill, Swan. BR8 . .147	FE95	
STRAWBERRY HILL, Twick. . .117	CE90	
≷ Strawberry Hill 117	CE90	
Strawberry Hill, Twick. TW1 . .117	CF90	
Strawberry Hill Cl, Twick. TW1 .117	CF90	
Strawberry Hill Rd, Twick.		
TW1 117	CF90	
Strawberry La, Cars. SM5 . . .140	DF104	
Strawberry Vale, N2 44	DD53	
Twickenham TW1 117	CG90	
Straw Cl, Cat. CR3 176	DQ123	
Strayfield Rd, Enf. EN2 29	DP37	
Streakes Fld Rd, NW2 63	CU61	
Stream Cl, W.Byf. (Byfleet)		
KT14 152	BK112	

Streamdale, SE2 106	EU79	
Stream La, Edg. HA8 42	CP50	
Streamside Cl, N9 46	DT46	
Bromley BR2 144	EG98	
Streamway, Belv. DA17 106	FA79	
Streatfield Av, E6 87	EM67	
Streatfield Rd, Har. HA3 61	CK55	
STREATHAM, SW16 121	DL91	
≷ Streatham 121	DL92	
Streatham Cl, SW16 121	DL89	
Streatham Common N,		
SW16 121	DL92	
Streatham Common S,		
SW16 121	DL93	
Streatham Ct, SW16 121	DL90	
Streatham High Rd, SW16 . . .121	DL92	
STREATHAM HILL, SW2 121	DM87	
≷ Streatham Hill 121	DL89	
Streatham Hill, SW2 121	DL87	
STREATHAM PARK, SW16 . . .121	DJ91	
Streatham Pl, SW2 121	DL87	
Streatham Rd, SW16 140	DG95	
Mitcham CR4 140	DG95	
Streatham St, WC1 195	N8	
STREATHAM VALE, SW16 . . .121	DK94	
Streatham Vale, SW16 121	DK94	
Streathbourne Rd, SW17 120	DG89	
Streatley Pl, NW3		
off New End Sq 64	DC63	
Streatley Rd, NW6 81	CZ66	
Street, The, Ashtd. KT21 172	CL119	
Betchworth RH3 182	CS134	
Dartford (Hort.Kir.) DA4 . . .148	FP98	
Kings Langley (Chipper.)WD4 .6	BG31	
Leatherhead (Fetch.) KT22 .171	CD122	
Streeters La, Wall. SM6 141	DK104	
Streetfield Ms, SE3 104	EG83	
Streimer Rd, E15 85	EC68	
Strelley Way, W3 80	CS73	
Stretton Pl, Amer. HP6 20	AT38	
Stretton Rd, Croy. CR0 142	DS101	
Richmond TW10 117	CJ89	
Stretton Way, Borwd. WD6 26	CL38	
Strickland Av, Dart. DA1 108	FL83	
Strickland Row, SW18 120	DD87	
Strickland St, SE8 103	EA82	
Strickland Way, Orp. BR6 163	ET105	
Stride Rd, E13 86	EF68	
Strides Ct, Cher. KT16		
off Brox Rd 151	BC107	
Stringham Copse, Wok. (Ripley)		
GU23 167	BF124	
Stripling Way, Wat. WD18 23	BU44	
Strode Cl, N10		
off Pembroke Rd 44	DG52	
Strode Rd, E7 68	EG63	
N17 46	DS54	
NW10 81	CU65	
SW6 99	CX80	
Strodes Coll La, Egh. TW20 . .113	AZ92	
Strodes Cres, Stai. TW18 114	BJ92	
Strode St, Egh. TW20 113	BA91	
Strone Rd, E7 86	EJ65	
E12 86	EK65	
Strone Way, Hayes UB4 78	BY70	
Strongbow Cres, SE9 125	EM85	
Strongbow Rd, SE9 125	EM85	
Strongbridge Cl, Har. HA2 60	CA60	
Stronsa Rd, W12 99	CT75	
Strood Av, Rom. RM7 71	FD60	
Stroud Cres, SW15 119	CU90	
STROUDE, Vir.W. 133	AZ96	
Stroude Rd, Egh. TW20 113	BA93	
Virginia Water GU25 132	AY98	
Stroudes Cl, Wor.Pk. KT4 138	CS101	
Stroud Fld, Nthlt. UB5 78	BY65	
Stroud Gate, Har. HA2 60	CB63	
STROUD GREEN, N4 65	DM58	
Stroud Grn Gdns, Croy. CR0 .142	DW101	
Stroud Grn Rd, N4 65	DM60	
Stroud Grn Way, Croy. CR0 . .142	DV101	
Stroud Rd, SE25 142	DU100	
SW19 120	DA90	
Strouds Cl, Rom. (Chad.Hth.)		
RM6 70	EV57	
Stroudwater Pk, Wey. KT13 . .153	BP107	
Stroud Way, Ashf. TW15		
off Courtfield Rd 115	BP93	
Strouts Pl, E2 197	P2	
Struan Gdns, Wok. GU21 166	AY115	
Strutton Grd, SW1 199	M6	
Struttons Av, Grav. (Nthflt.)		
DA11 131	GF89	
Strype St, E1 197	P7	
Stuart Av, NW9 63	CU59	
W5 80	CM74	
Bromley BR2 144	EG102	
Harrow HA2 60	BZ62	
Walton-on-Thames KT12 . .135	BV102	
Stuart Cl, Brwd. CM15 54	FV43	
Swanley BR8 127	FF94	
Uxbridge UB10 77	BP69	
Stuart Ct, Borwd. (Elstree) WD6		
off High St 25	CK44	
Stuart Cres, N22 45	DM53	
Croydon CR0 143	DZ104	
Hayes UB3 77	BQ72	
Stuart Evans Cl, Well. DA16 . .106	EW83	
Stuart Gro, Tedd. TW11 117	CE92	
Stuart Mantle Way, Erith DA8 .107	FD80	
Stuart Pl, Mitch. CR4 140	DF95	
Stuart Rd, NW6 82	DA69	
SE15 102	DW84	
SW19 120	DA90	
W3 80	CQ74	
Barking IG11 87	ET66	
Barnet EN4 44	DE45	
Gravesend DA11 131	GG88	
Grays RM17 110	GB78	
Harrow HA3 41	CF54	
Richmond TW10 117	CH89	
Thornton Heath CR7 142	DQ98	
Warlingham CR6 176	DV120	
Welling DA16 106	EV81	
Stuart Twr, W9 82	DC69	

Stuart Way, Stai. TW18 114	BH93	
Virginia Water GU25 132	AU97	
Waltham Cross (Chsht.)		
EN7 14	DV31	
Stubbers La, Upmin. RM14 . . .91	FR65	
Stubbins Hall La, Wal.Abb.		
EN9 15	EB28	
Stubbs Cl, NW9 62	CQ57	
Stubbs Dr, SE16 202	F10	
Stubbs End Cl, Amer. HP6 20	AS37	
Stubbs Hill, Sev. (Knock.)		
TN14 164	EW113	
Stubbs La, Tad. (Lwr.Kgswd.)		
KT20 183	CZ128	
Stubbs Ms, Dag. RM8		
off Marlborough Rd 70	EV63	
Stubbs Pt, E13 86	EH70	
Stubbs Way, SW19		
off Brangwyn Cres 140	DD95	
Stucley Pl, NW1		
off Hawley Cres 83	DH66	
Stucley Rd, Houns. TW5 96	CC80	
Studdridge St, SW6 100	DA82	
Studd St, N1 83	DP67	
Studholme Ct, NW3 64	DA63	
Studholme St, SE15 102	DV80	
Studio Pl, SW1 198	E5	
Studios, The, Bushey WD23 . . .24	CA44	
Studios Rd, Shep. TW17 134	BM97	
Studio Way, Borwd. WD6 26	CQ40	
Studland, SE17 201	K10	
Studland Cl, Sid. DA15 125	ET90	
Studland Rd, SE26 123	DX92	
W7 79	CD72	
Kingston upon Thames KT2 .118	CL93	
West Byfleet (Byfleet) KT14 .152	BM113	
Studland St, W6 99	CV77	
Studley Av, E4 47	ED52	
Studley Cl, E5 67	DY64	
Studley Ct, Sid. DA14 126	EV92	
Studley Dr, Ilf. IG4 68	EK58	
Studley Est, SW4 101	DL81	
Studley Gra Rd, W7 97	CE75	
Studley Rd, E7 86	EH65	
SW4 101	DL81	
Dagenham RM9 88	EX66	
Stukeley Rd, E7 86	EH66	
Stukeley St, WC2 196	A8	
Stump Rd, Epp. CM16 18	EW27	
Stumps Hill La, Beck. BR3 . . .123	EA93	
Stumps La, Whyt. CR3 176	DS117	
Sturdy Rd, SE15 102	DV82	
Sturge Av, E17 47	EB54	
Sturgeon Rd, SE17 102	DQ78	
Sturges Fld, Chis. BR7 125	ER93	
Sturgess Av, NW4 63	CV59	
Sturge St, SE1 201	H4	
Sturlas Way, Wal.Cr. EN8 15	DX33	
Sturmer Way, N7 65	DM64	
Sturminster Cl, Hayes UB4 78	BW72	
Sturrock Cl, N15 66	DR56	
Sturry St, E14 85	EB72	
Sturts La, Tad. KT20 183	CT127	
Sturt St, N1 197	J1	
Stutfield St, E1 84	DU72	
Stychens Cl, Red. (Bletch.)		
RH1 186	DQ133	
Stychens La, Red. (Bletch.)		
RH1 186	DQ132	
Stylecroft Rd, Ch.St.G. HP8 . . .36	AX47	
Styles Gdns, SW9 101	DP83	
Styles Way, Beck. BR3 143	EC98	
Styventon Pl, Cher. KT16 133	BF101	
Subrosa Dr, Red. RH1 185	DH130	
Succombs Hill, Warl. CR6 . . .176	DV120	
Whyteleafe CR3 176	DV120	
Succombs Pl, Warl. CR6 176	DV120	
Sudbourne Rd, SW2 121	DL85	
Sudbrooke Rd, SW12 120	DF86	
Sudbrook Gdns, Rich. TW10 . .117	CK90	
Sudbrook La, Rich. TW10 118	CL88	
SUDBURY, Wem. 61	CG64	
Sudbury, E6 off Newark Knok .87	EN72	
≷ Sudbury & Harrow Road . .61	CH64	
Sudbury Av, Wem. HA0 61	CK62	
Sudbury Ct, E5 67	DY63	
Sudbury Ct Dr, Har. HA1 61	CF62	
Sudbury Ct Rd, Har. HA1 61	CF62	
Sudbury Cres, Brom. BR1 124	EG93	
Wembley HA0 61	CH64	
Sudbury Gdns, Croy. CR0		
off Langton Way 160	DS105	
⊖ Sudbury Hill 61	CE63	
Sudbury Hill, Har. HA1 61	CE61	
Sudbury Hill Cl, Wem. HA0 . . .61	CE63	
≷ Sudbury Hill Harrow 61	CE63	
Sudbury Rd, Bark. IG11 69	ET64	
Sudbury Town 79	CH65	
Sudeley St, N1 196	G1	
Sudicamps Ct, Wal.Abb. EN9 . .16	EG33	
Sudlow Rd, SW18 100	DA84	
Sudrey St, SE1 201	H5	
Suez Av, Grnf. UB6 79	CF68	
Suez Rd, Enf. EN3 31	DY42	
Suffield Cl, S.Croy. CR2 161	DX112	
Suffield Rd, E4 47	EB48	
N15 66	DT57	
SE20 142	DW96	
Suffolk Cl, Borwd. WD6		
off Clydesdale Cl 26	CR43	
St. Albans (Lon.Col.) AL2 9	CJ26	
Suffolk Ct, E10 67	EA59	
Ilford IG3 69	ES58	
Suffolk La, EC4 197	K10	
Suffolk Pk Rd, E17 67	DY56	
Suffolk Pl, SW1 199	N2	
Suffolk Rd, E13 86	EF69	
N15 66	DR58	
NW10 80	CS66	
SE25 142	DT98	
SW13 99	CT80	
Barking IG11 87	ER66	
Dagenham RM10 71	FC64	

Suffolk Rd, Dart. DA1 128	FL86	
Enfield EN3 30	DV43	
Gravesend DA12 131	GK86	
Harrow HA2 60	BZ58	
Ilford IG3 69	ES58	
Potters Bar EN6 11	CY32	
Sidcup DA14 126	EW93	
Worcester Park KT4 139	CT103	
Suffolk St, E7 68	EG64	
SW1 199	N2	
Suffolk Way, Horn. RM11 72	FN56	
Sevenoaks TN13 191	FJ125	
Sugar Bakers Ct, EC3		
off Creechurch La 84	DS72	
Sugar Ho La, E15 85	EC68	
Sugar Loaf Wk, E2		
off Victoria Pk Sq 84	DW69	
Sugar Quay Wk, EC3 201	N1	
Sugden Rd, SW11 100	DG83	
Thames Ditton KT7 137	CH102	
Sugden Way, Bark. IG11 87	ET68	
Sulgrave Gdns, W6		
off Sulgrave Rd 99	CW75	
Sulgrave Rd, W6 99	CW75	
Sulina Rd, SW2 121	DL87	
Sulivan Ct, SW6 100	DA83	
Sulivan Rd, SW6 100	DA83	
Sullivan Av, E16 86	EK71	
Sullivan Cl, SW11 100	DE83	
Dartford DA1 127	FH86	
Hayes UB4 78	BW71	
West Molesey KT8		
off Victoria Av 136	CA97	
Sullivan Cres, Uxb. (Hare.)		
UB9 38	BK54	
Sullivan Rd, SE11 200	E8	
Tilbury RM18 111	GG81	
Sullivans Reach, Walt. KT12 . .135	BT101	
Sullivan Way, Borwd. (Elstree)		
WD6 25	CJ44	
Sultan Rd, E11 68	EH56	
Sultan St, SE5 102	DQ80	
Beckenham BR3 143	DX96	
Sumatra Rd, NW6 64	DA64	
Sumburgh Rd, SW12 120	DG86	
Sumburgh Way, Slou. SL1 74	AS71	
Summer Av, E.Mol. KT8 137	CE99	
Summercourt Rd, E1 84	DW72	
Summerene Cl, SW16 121	DJ94	
Summerfield, Ashtd. KT21 . . .171	CK119	
Summerfield Av, NW6 81	CY68	
Summerfield Cl, Add. KT15		
off Spinney Hill 151	BF106	
St. Albans (Lon.Col.) AL2 9	CJ26	
Summerfield La, Surb. KT6 . .137	CK103	
Summerfield Pl, Cher. (Ott.) KT16		
off Crawshaw Rd 151	BD107	
Summerfield Rd, W5 79	CH70	
Loughton IG10 32	EK44	
Watford WD25 23	BU35	
Summerfields Av, N12 44	DE51	
Summerfield St, SE12 124	EF87	
Summer Gdns, E.Mol. KT8 . . .137	CE99	
Summer Gro, Borwd. (Elstree)		
WD6 25	CK44	
Summerhayes Cl, Wok. GU21 .150	AY114	
Summerhays, Cob. KT11 154	BX113	
Summer Hill, Borwd. (Elstree)		
WD6 26	CN43	
Chislehurst BR7 145	EN96	
Summerhill Cl, Orp. BR6 145	ES104	
Summerhill Gro, Enf. EN1 30	DS44	
Summerhill Rd, N15 66	DR56	
Dartford DA1 128	FK87	
Summer Hill Vil, Chis. BR7 . . .145	EN95	
Summerhill Way, Mitch. CR4 .140	DG95	
Summerhouse Av, Houns.		
TW5 96	BY81	
Summerhouse Dr, Bex. DA5 . .127	FD91	
Dartford DA2 127	FD91	
Summerhouse La, Uxb. (Hare.)		
UB9 38	BG52	
Watford WD25 24	CC40	
West Drayton UB7 94	BK79	
Summerhouse Rd, N16 66	DS61	
Summerhouse Way, Abb.L.		
WD5 7	BT30	
Summerland Gdns, N10 65	DH55	
Summerlands Av, W3 80	CQ73	
Summerlay Cl, Tad. KT20 173	CY120	
Summerlee Av, N2 64	DF56	
Summerlee Gdns, N2 64	DF56	
Summerley St, SW18 120	DB89	
Summerly Av, Reig. RH2		
off Burnham Dr 184	DA133	
Summer Rd, E.Mol. KT8 137	CE99	
Thames Ditton KT7 137	CF99	
Summersby Rd, N6 65	DH58	
Summers Cl, Sutt. SM2		
off Overton Rd 158	DA108	
Wembley HA9 62	CP60	
Weybridge KT13 152	BN111	
Summers La, N12 44	DD52	
Summers Row, N12 44	DE51	
SUMMERSTOWN, SW17 120	DB90	
Summerstown, SW17 120	DC90	
Summer St, EC1 196	D5	
Summerswood Cl, Ken. CR8		
off Longwood Rd 176	DR116	
Summerswood La, Borwd.		
WD6 10	CS34	
Summerton Way, SE28 88	EX72	
Summer Trees, Sun. TW16		
off The Avenue 135	BV95	
Summerville Gdns, Sutt. SM1 .157	CZ107	
Summerwood Rd, Islw. TW7 .117	CF85	
Summit, The, Loug. IG10 33	EM39	
Summit Av, NW9 62	CR57	
Summit Cl, N14 45	DJ47	
NW9 62	CR56	
Edgware HA8 42	CN52	
Summit Ct, NW2 63	CY64	
Summit Dr, Wdf.Grn. IG8 48	EK54	
Summit Est, N16 66	DU59	

Summit Pl, Wey. KT13
  off Caenshill Rd 152 BN108
Summit Rd, E17 . . . . .67 EB56
  Northolt UB5 . . . . .78 CA66
  Potters Bar EN6 . . . . .11 CY30
Summit Way, N14 . . . . .45 DH47
  SE19 . . . . .122 DS94
Sumner Av, SE15
  off Sumner Rd 102 DT81
Sumner Cl, Lthd. (Fetch.)
  KT22 . . . . .171 CD124
  Orpington BR6 . . . . .163 EQ105
Sumner Est, SE15 . . . . .102 DT80
Sumner Gdns, Croy. CR0 . . .141 DN102
Sumner Pl, SW7 . . . . .198 A9
  Addlestone KT15 . . . . .152 BG106
Sumner Pl Ms, SW7 . . . . . . .198 A9
Sumner Rd, SE15 . . . . .102 DT80
  Croydon CR0 . . . . .141 DN102
  Harrow HA1 . . . . .60 CC59
Sumner Rd S, Croy. CR0 . . . .141 DN102
Sumner St, SE1 . . . . .200 G2
Sumpter Cl, NW3 . . . . .82 DC65
Sun All, Rich. TW9 off Kew Rd .98 CL84
Sunbeam Cres, W10 . . . . . . .81 CW70
Sunbeam Rd, NW10 . . . . . . .80 CQ70
SUNBURY, Sun. 153 BV107
  Sunbury 135 BT95
Sunbury Av, NW7 . . . . .42 CR50
  SW14 . . . . .98 CR84
Sunbury Ct, Sun. TW16 . . . . .136 BX96
Sunbury Ct Island, Sun.
  TW16 . . . . .136 BX97
Sunbury Ct Ms, Sun. TW16
  off Lower Hampton Rd 136 BX96
Sunbury Ct Rd, Sun. TW16 . . .136 BW96
Sunbury Cres, Felt. TW13
  off Ryland Cl 115 BT91
Sunbury Cross Cen, Sun.
  TW16 . . . . .115 BT94
Sunbury Gdns, NW7 . . . . . . .42 CR50
Sunbury La, SW11 . . . . .100 DD81
  Walton-on-Thames KT12 . . .135 BU100
Sunbury Lock Ait, Walt. KT12 .135 BV98
Sunbury Rd, Felt. TW13 . . . .115 BT90
  Sutton SM3 . . . . .139 CX104
Sunbury Way, Felt. TW13 . . . .116 BW92
Sun Ct, EC3 . . . . .197 L9
  Erith DA8 . . . . .107 FF82
Suncroft Pl, SE26 . . . . .122 DW90
Sundale Av, S.Croy. CR2 . . . .160 DW110
Sunderland Ct, SE22 . . . . . .122 DU87
Sunderland Gro, Wat. WD25
  off Ashfields 7 BT34
Sunderland Mt, SE23
  off Sunderland Rd 123 DX88
Sunderland Rd, SE23 . . . . . .123 DX88
  W5 . . . . .97 CK76
Sunderland Ter, W2 . . . . .82 DB72
Sunderland Way, E12 . . . . . . .68 EK61
Sundew Av, W12 . . . . .81 CU73
Sundew Ct, Grays RM17
  off Salix Rd 110 GD79
Sundial Av, SE25 . . . . .142 DT97
Sundon Cres, Vir.W. GU25 . . .132 AV99
Sundorne Rd, SE7 . . . . .104 EH78
Sundown Av, S.Croy. CR2 . . .160 DT111
Sundown Rd, Ashf. TW15 . . . .115 BQ92
Sundra Wk, E1
  off Beaumont Gro 85 DX70
SUNDRIDGE, Brom. 124 EJ93
SUNDRIDGE, Sev. 180 EZ124
Sundridge Av, Brom. BR1 . . .144 EK95
  Chislehurst BR7 . . . . .124 EK94
  Welling DA16 . . . . .105 ER82
Sundridge Cl, Dart. DA1 . . . .128 FN86
Sundridge Ho, Brom. BR1
  off Burnt Ash La 124 EH92
Sundridge La, Sev. (Knock.)
  TN14 . . . . .180 EV117
  Sundridge Park 124 EH94
Sundridge Pl, Croy. CR0
  off Inglis Rd 142 DU102
Sundridge Rd, Croy. CR0 . . . .142 DT101
  Sevenoaks (Dunt.Grn.)
  TN14 . . . . .180 FA120
  Woking GU22 . . . . .167 BA119
Sunfields Pl, SE3 . . . . .104 EH80
Sunflower Way, Rom. RM3 . . .52 FK53
Sun Hill, Long. (Fawk.Grn.)
  DA3 . . . . .149 FU104
  Woking GU22 . . . . .166 AU121
Sunken Rd, Croy. CR0
  off Coombe La 160 DW106
Sunkist Way, Wall. SM6 . . . . .159 DL109
Sunland Av, Bexh. DA6 . . . . .106 EY84
Sun La, SE3 . . . . .104 EH80
  Gravesend DA12 . . . . .131 GJ89
Sunleigh Rd, Wem. HA0 . . . . .80 CL67
Sunley Gdns, Grnf. UB6 . . . . .79 CG67
Sunlight Cl, SW19 . . . . .120 DC93
Sunlight Sq, E2 . . . . .84 DV69
Sunmead Cl, Lthd. (Fetch.)
  KT22 . . . . .171 CF122
Sunmead Rd, Sun. TW16 . . . .135 BU97
Sunna Gdns, Sun. TW16 . . . .135 BV96
Sunningdale, N14
  off Wilmer Way 45 DK50
Sunningdale Av, W3 . . . . .80 CS73
  Barking IG11 . . . . .87 ER67
  Feltham TW13 . . . . .116 BY89
  Rainham RM13 . . . . .89 FH70
  Ruislip HA4 . . . . .60 BW60
Sunningdale Cl, E6 . . . . .87 EM69
  SE16 off Ryder Dr 102 DV78
  SE28 . . . . .88 EX72
  Stanmore HA7 . . . . .41 CG52
  Surbiton KT6
  off Culsac Rd 138 CL103
Sunningdale Gdns, NW9 . . . .62 CQ57
  W8 off Lexham Ms 100 DA76
Sunningdale Rd, Brom. BR1 . .144 EL98
  Rainham RM13 . . . . .89 FG66

Sunningdale Rd, Sutt. SM1 . .157 CZ105
Sunningfields Cres, NW4 . . . .43 CV54
Sunningfields Rd, NW4 . . . . .43 CV54
Sunning Hill, Grav. (Nthflt.)
  DA11 . . . . .130 GE89
Sunninghill Rd, SE13 . . . . . .103 EB82
Sunnings La, Upmin. RM14 . . .90 FQ65
Sunningvale Av, West. (Bigg.H.)
  TN16 . . . . .178 EJ115
Sunningvale Cl, West. (Bigg.H.)
  TN16 . . . . .178 EK116
Sunny Bk, SE25 . . . . .142 DU97
Sunnybank, Epsom KT18 . . . .172 CQ116
Sunny Bk, Warl. CR6 . . . . . .177 DY117
Sunnybank Rd, Pot.B. EN6 . . .12 DA33
Sunnybank Vil, Red. RH1 . . . .186 DT132
Sunny Cres, NW10 . . . . .80 CQ66
Sunnycroft Gdns, Upmin.
  RM14 . . . . .73 FT59
Sunnycroft Rd, SE25 . . . . . . .142 DU97
  Hounslow TW3 . . . . .96 CB82
  Southall UB1 . . . . .78 CA71
Sunnydale, Orp. BR6 . . . . . .145 EN103
Sunnydale Gdns, NW7 . . . . . .42 CR51
Sunnydale Rd, SE12 . . . . . . .124 EH85
Sunnydell, St.Alb. AL2 . . . . . . .8 CB26
Sunnydene Av, E4 . . . . .47 ED50
  Ruislip HA4 . . . . .59 BU61
Sunnydene Cl, Rom. RM3 . . . .52 FM52
Sunnydene Gdns, Wem. HA0 . .79 CJ65
Sunnydene Rd, Pur. CR8 . . . .159 DP113
Sunnydene St, SE26 . . . . . . .123 DY91
Sunnyfield, NW7 . . . . .43 CT49
Sunnyfield Rd, Chis. BR7 . . . .146 EU97
Sunny Gdns Par, NW4
  off Great N Way 43 CW54
Sunny Gdns Rd, NW4 . . . . . .43 CV54
Sunny Hill, NW4 . . . . .63 CV55
Sunnyhill Cl, E5 . . . . .67 DY63
Sunnyhill Rd, SW16 . . . . . . .121 DL91
  Rickmansworth (Map.Cr.)
  WD3 . . . . .37 BD75
Sunnyhurst Cl, Sutt. SM1 . . . .140 DA104
Sunnymead Av, Mitch. CR4 . . .141 DJ97
Sunnymead Rd, NW9 . . . . . . .62 CR59
  SW15 . . . . .119 CV85
SUNNYMEADS, Stai. 92 AY84
  Sunnymeads 92 AY83
Sunnymede, Chig. IG7 . . . . . .50 EV48
Sunnymede Av, Cars. SM5 . . .158 DD111
  Chesham HP5 . . . . .4 AS28
  Epsom KT19 . . . . .156 CS109
Sunnymede Dr, Ilf. IG6 . . . . . .69 EP56
Sunny Nook Gdns, S.Croy. CR2
  off Selsdon Rd 160 DR107
Sunny Ri, Cat. CR3 . . . . .176 DR124
Sunny Rd, The, Enf. EN3 . . . .31 DX39
Sunnyside, NW2 . . . . .63 CZ62
  SW19 . . . . .119 CY93
  Walton-on-Thames KT12 . . .136 BW99
Sunnyside Cotts, Chesh. HP5 . .4 AU26
Sunnyside Dr, E4 . . . . .47 EC45
Sunnyside Gdns, Upmin.
  RM14 . . . . .72 FQ61
Sunnyside Pas, SW19 . . . . . .119 CY93
Sunnyside Pl, SW19
  off Sunnyside 119 CY93
Sunnyside Rd, E10 . . . . .67 EA60
  N19 . . . . .65 DK59
  W5 . . . . .79 CK74
  Epping CM16 . . . . .17 ET32
  Ilford IG1 . . . . .69 EQ62
  Teddington TW11 . . . . . . .117 CD91
Sunnyside Rd E, N9 . . . . .46 DU48
Sunnyside Rd N, N9 . . . . .46 DT48
Sunnyside Rd S, N9 . . . . .46 DT48
Sunnyside Ter, NW9
  off Edgware Rd 62 CR55
Sunny Vw, NW9 . . . . .62 CR57
Sunny Way, N12 . . . . .44 DE52
Sunray Av, SE24 . . . . .102 DR84
  Brentwood CM13 . . . . .55 GE44
  Bromley BR2 . . . . .144 EL100
  Surbiton KT5 . . . . .138 CP103
  West Drayton UB7 . . . . . . .94 BK75
Sunrise Av, Horn. RM12 . . . . .72 FJ62
Sunrise Cl, Felt. TW13
  off Exeter Rd 116 BZ90
  Swanscombe DA10 . . . . . .130 FZ86
Sunset Av, E4 . . . . .47 EB46
  Woodford Green IG8 . . . . . .48 EF49
Sunset Cl, Erith DA8 . . . . . . .107 FH81
Sunset Ct, Wdf.Grn. IG8
  off Navestock Cres 48 EJ52
Sunset Dr, Rom. (Hav.at.Bow.)
  RM4 . . . . .51 FH50
Sunset Gdns, SE25 . . . . .142 DT96
Sunset Rd, SE5 . . . . .102 DQ84
  SE28 . . . . .106 EU75
Sunset Vw, Barn. EN5 . . . . . .27 CY40
Sunshine Way, Mitch. CR4 . . .140 DF96
Sunstone Gro, Red. RH1 . . . .185 DL129
Sun St, EC2 . . . . .197 M7
  Waltham Abbey EN9 . . . . . .15 EC33
Sun St Pas, EC2 . . . . .197 M7
Sun Wk, E1 . . . . .202 B1
Sunwell Cl, SE15
  off Cossall Wk 102 DV81
Superior Dr, Orp. BR6 . . . . . .163 ET107
SURBITON, Surb. 138 CM101
  Surbiton 138 CK100
Surbiton Ct, Surb. KT6 . . . . .137 CJ100
Surbiton Cres, Kings.T. KT1 . .138 CL98
Surbiton Hall Cl, Kings.T.
  KT6 . . . . .138 CL100
Surbiton Hill Pk, Surb. KT5 . .138 CN99
Surbiton Hill Rd, Surb. KT6 . .138 CL98
Surbiton Par, Surb. KT6
  off St. Mark's Hill 138 CL100
Surbiton Rd, Kings.T. KT1 . . .138 CL98
Surlingham Cl, SE28 . . . . . . .88 EX73
Surma Cl, E1 . . . . .84 DV70
Surman Cres, Brwd. CM13 . . .55 GC45

Surmans Cl, Dag. RM9
  off Goresbrook Rd 88 EV67
Surrendale Pl, W9 . . . . .82 DA70
Surrey Canal Rd, SE14 . . . . .102 DW79
  SE15 . . . . .102 DW79
Surrey Cres, W4 . . . . .98 CN78
  Surrey Docks Fm, SE16 . .203 M5
Surrey Dr, Horn. RM11 . . . . . .72 FN56
Surrey Gdns, N4
  off Finsbury Pk Av 66 DQ58
  Leatherhead (Eff.Junct.)
  KT24 . . . . .169 BT123
Surrey Gro, SE17
  off Surrey Sq 102 DS78
  Sutton SM1 . . . . .140 DD104
Surrey Hills, Tad. KT20 . . . . .182 CP130
Surrey Hills Av, Tad. KT20 . . .182 CQ130
Surrey La, SW11 . . . . .100 DE81
Surrey La Est, SW11 . . . . . . .100 DE81
Surrey Lo, SE1 . . . . .200 D7
Surrey Ms, SE27
  off Hamilton Rd 122 DS91
Surrey Mt, SE23 . . . . .122 DV88
  Surrey Quays 203 H8
Surrey Quays Retail Cen,
  SE16 . . . . .103 DX76
Surrey Quays Rd, SE16 . . . . .202 G6
Surrey Rd, SE15 . . . . .123 DX85
  Barking IG11 . . . . .87 ES67
  Dagenham RM10 . . . . .71 FB64
  Harrow HA1 . . . . .60 CC57
  West Wickham BR4 . . . . . .143 EB102
Surrey Row, SE1 . . . . .200 F4
Surrey Sq, SE17 . . . . .201 M10
Surrey St, E13 . . . . .86 EH69
  WC2 . . . . .196 C10
  Croydon CR0 . . . . .142 DQ104
Surrey Ter, SE17 . . . . .201 N10
Surrey Twr, SE20 . . . . .122 DW94
Surrey Twrs, Add. KT15
  off Garfield Rd 152 BJ106
Surrey Water Rd, SE16 . . . . .203 J3
Surridge Cl, Rain. RM13 . . . . .90 FJ69
Surridge Gdns, SE19
  off Hancock Rd 122 DR93
Surr St, N7 . . . . .65 DL64
Susan Cl, Rom. RM7 . . . . . . .71 FC55
Susannah St, E14 . . . . .85 EB72
Susan Rd, SE3 . . . . .104 EH82
Susan Wd, Chis. BR7 . . . . . .145 EN95
Sussex Av, Islw. TW7 . . . . . . .97 CE83
  Romford RM3 . . . . .52 FM52
Sussex Cl, N19
  off Cornwallis Rd 65 DL61
  Chalfont St. Giles HP8 . . . .36 AV47
  Ilford IG4 . . . . .69 EM58
  New Malden KT3 . . . . .138 CS98
  Slough SL1 . . . . .92 AV75
  Twickenham TW1
  off Westmorland Cl 117 CH86
Sussex Cres, Nthlt. UB5 . . . . .78 CA65
Sussex Gdns, N4 . . . . .66 DQ57
  N6 off Great N Rd 64 DF57
  W2 . . . . .82 DD72
  Chessington KT9 . . . . .155 CK107
Sussex Keep, Slou. SL1
  off Sussex Cl 92 AV75
Sussex Ms, SE6
  off Ravensbourne Pk 123 EA87
Sussex Ms E, W2 . . . . .194 A9
Sussex Ms W, W2 . . . . .194 A10
Sussex Pl, NW1 . . . . .194 D3
  W2 . . . . .194 A9
  W6 . . . . .99 CW78
  Erith DA8 . . . . .107 FF80
  New Malden KT3 . . . . .138 CS98
  Slough SL1 . . . . .92 AV75
Sussex Ring, N12 . . . . .44 DA50
Sussex Rd, E6 . . . . .87 EN67
  Brentwood CM14 . . . . .54 FW49
  Carshalton SM5 . . . . .158 DF107
  Dartford DA1 . . . . .128 FN87
  Erith DA8 . . . . .107 FF80
  Harrow HA1 . . . . .60 CC57
  Mitcham CR4 off Lincoln Rd .141 DL99
  New Malden KT3 . . . . .138 CS98
  Orpington BR5 . . . . .146 EW100
  Sidcup DA14 . . . . .126 EV92
  South Croydon CR2 . . . . . .160 DR107
  Southall UB2 . . . . .96 BX76
  Uxbridge UB10 . . . . .59 BQ63
  Watford WD24 . . . . .23 BU38
  West Wickham BR4 . . . . . .143 EB102
Sussex Sq, W2 . . . . .194 A10
Sussex St, E13 . . . . .86 EH69
  SW1 . . . . .101 DH78
Sussex Wk, SW9 . . . . .101 DP84
Sussex Way, N7 . . . . .65 DL61
  N19 . . . . .65 DL60
  Barnet EN4 . . . . .28 DG43
  Uxbridge (Denh.) UB9 . . . .57 BF57
Sutcliffe Cl, NW11 . . . . .64 DB57
  Bushey WD23 . . . . .24 CC42
Sutcliffe Ho, Hayes UB3 . . . . .77 BU72
Sutcliffe Rd, SE18 . . . . .105 ES79
  Welling DA16 . . . . .106 EW82
Sutherland Av, W9 . . . . .82 DC69
  W13 . . . . .79 CH72
  Hayes UB3 . . . . .95 BU77
  Orpington BR5 . . . . .145 ET100
  Potters Bar (Cuffley) EN6 . .13 DK28
  Sunbury-on-Thames TW16 . .135 BT96
  Welling DA16 . . . . .105 ES84
  Westerham (Bigg.H.) TN16 .178 EK117
Sutherland Ct, Barn. EN5 . . . .27 CY42
  Greenhithe DA9 . . . . .129 FT85
Sutherland Gdns, SW14 . . . . .98 CS83
  Sunbury-on-Thames TW16
  off Sutherland Av 135 BT96
  Worcester Park KT4 . . . . . .139 CV102
Sutherland Gro, SW18 . . . . . .119 CY86
  Teddington TW11 . . . . . . .117 CE92
Sutherland Pl, W2 . . . . .82 DA72
Sutherland Rd, E17 . . . . .47 DX54
  N9 . . . . .46 DU46

Sutherland Rd, N17 . . . . .46 DU52
  W4 . . . . .98 CS79
  W13 . . . . .79 CG72
  Belvedere DA17 . . . . .106 FA76
  Croydon CR0 . . . . .141 DN101
  Enfield EN3 . . . . .31 DX43
  Southall UB1 . . . . .78 BZ72
Sutherland Rd Path, E17 . . . . .67 DX55
Sutherland Row, SW1 . . . . . .199 J10
Sutherland Sq, SE17 . . . . . . .102 DQ78
Sutherland St, SW1 . . . . .199 H10
Sutherland Wk, SE17 . . . . . . .102 DQ78
Sutherland Way, Pot.B. (Cuffley)
  EN6 . . . . .13 DK28
Sutlej Rd, SE7 . . . . .104 EJ80
Sutterton St, N7 . . . . .83 DM65
SUTTON 158 DB107
  Sutton 158 DC106
SUTTON AT HONE, Dart. 148 FN95
Sutton Av, Slou. SL3 . . . . . . .92 AW75
  Woking GU21 . . . . .166 AS119
Sutton Cl, Beck. BR3
  off Albemarle Rd 143 EB95
  Loughton IG10 . . . . .48 EL45
  Pinner HA5 . . . . .59 BU57
  Sutton Common 140 DB103
Sutton Common Rd, Sutt.
  SM1, SM3 . . . . .139 CZ101
Sutton Ct, W4 . . . . .98 CQ79
Sutton Ct Rd, E13 . . . . .86 EJ69
  W4 . . . . .98 CQ80
  Sutton SM1 . . . . .158 DC107
  Uxbridge UB10 . . . . .77 BP67
Sutton Cres, Barn. EN5 . . . . .27 CX43
Sutton Dene, Houns. TW3 . . . .96 CB81
Sutton Est, SW3 . . . . .198 C10
  W10 . . . . .81 CW71
Sutton Est, The, N1 . . . . .83 DP66
Sutton Gdns, Bark. IG11
  off Sutton Rd 87 ES67
  Croydon CR0 . . . . .142 DT99
  Redhill RH1 . . . . .185 DK129
Sutton Grn, Bark. IG11
  off Sutton Rd 87 ES67
Sutton Gro, Sutt. SM1 . . . . . .158 DD105
Sutton Hall Rd, Houns. TW5 . .96 CA80
Sutton Heritage Cen, Cars.
  SM5 . . . . .158 DF105
Sutton Hosp, Sutt. SM2 . . . .158 DB110
  Sutton Ho, E9 . . . . .66 DW64
Sutton La, Bans. SM7 . . . . . .174 DB115
  Hounslow TW3 . . . . .96 BZ83
  Slough SL3 . . . . .93 BC78
  Sutton SM2 . . . . .158 DB111
Sutton La N, W4 . . . . .98 CQ78
Sutton La S, W4 . . . . .98 CQ79
Sutton Par, NW4
  off Church Rd 63 CW56
Sutton Pk Rd, Sutt. SM1 . . . .158 DB107
Sutton Path, Borwd. WD6
  off Stratfield Rd 26 CN40
Sutton Pl, E9 . . . . .66 DW64
  Dartford DA4 . . . . .128 FP92
  Slough SL3 . . . . .93 BB79
Sutton Rd, E13 . . . . .86 EF70
  E17 . . . . .47 DX53
  N10 . . . . .44 DG54
  Barking IG11 . . . . .87 ES68
  Hounslow TW5 . . . . .96 CA81
  Watford WD17 . . . . .24 BW41
Sutton Row, W1 . . . . .195 N8
Suttons Av, Horn. RM12 . . . . .72 FJ62
Suttons Gdns, Horn. RM12 . . .72 FK62
Suttons La, Horn. RM12 . . . . .72 FK64
Sutton Sq, E9 off Urswick Rd .66 DW64
  Hounslow TW5 . . . . .96 BZ81
Sutton St, E1 . . . . .84 DW72
Sutton's Way, EC1 . . . . .197 J5
Sutton Wk, SE1 off York Rd . .83 DM74
Sutton Way, W10 . . . . .81 CW71
  Hounslow TW5 . . . . .96 BZ81
Swaby Rd, Slou. SL3 . . . . . . .93 BA77
Swaby Rd, SW18 . . . . .120 DC88
Swaffham Way, N22
  off White Hart La 45 DP52
Swaffield Rd, SW18 . . . . . . .120 DB87
  Sevenoaks TN13 . . . . .191 FJ122
Swain Cl, SW16 . . . . .121 DH93
Swain Rd, Th.Hth. CR7 . . . . .142 DQ99
Swains Cl, West Dr. UB7 . . . . .94 BL75
Swains La, N6 . . . . .64 DG62
Swainson Rd, W3 . . . . .99 CT75
Swains Rd, SW17 . . . . .120 DF94
Swain St, NW8 . . . . .194 B4
Swaisland Dr, Dart. (Cray.)
  DA1 . . . . .127 FF85
Swaisland Rd, Dart. DA1 . . . .127 FH85
Swakeleys Dr, Uxb. UB10 . . . .58 BM63
Swakeleys Rd, Uxb. (Ickhm.)
  UB10 . . . . .58 BM62
Swale Cl, S.Ock. (Aveley) RM15 .90 FQ72
Swaledale Cl, N11
  off Ribblesdale Av 44 DG51
Swaledale Rd, Dart. DA2 . . . .128 FQ88
Swale Rd, Dart. DA1 . . . . . . .107 FG83
Swallands Rd, SE6 . . . . .123 EA90
Swallow Cl, SE14 . . . . .102 DW81
  Bushey WD23 . . . . .40 CC46
  Erith DA8 . . . . .107 FE81
  Grays (Chaff.Hun.) RM16 . .109 FW77
  Greenhithe DA9 . . . . .129 FT85
  Rickmansworth WD3 . . . . .38 BJ45
  Staines TW18 . . . . .113 BF91
Swallow Dr, NW10
  off Kingfisher Way 80 CR65
  Northolt UB5 . . . . .78 CA68
Swallowfield, Egh. (Eng.Grn.)
  TW20 off Heronfield 112 AV93
Swallowfield Rd, SE7 . . . . . .104 EH78
Swallowfields, Grav. (Nthflt.)
  DA11 off Hillary Av 130 GE90
Swallowfield Way, Hayes UB3 .95 BR75
Swallow Gdns, SW16 . . . . . .121 DK92
Swallow Oaks, Abb.L. WD5 . . .7 BT31
Swallow Pas, W1 . . . . .195 J9

Swallow Pl, W1 . . . . .195 J9
Swallow St, E6 . . . . .86 EL71
  W1 . . . . .199 L1
  Iver SL0 . . . . .75 BD69
Swallowtail Cl, Orp. BR5 . . . .146 EX98
Swanage Rd, E4 . . . . .47 EC52
  SW18 . . . . .120 DC86
Swanage Waye, Hayes UB4 . . .78 BW72
Swan & Pike Rd, Enf. EN3 . . .31 EA38
Swan App, E6 . . . . .86 EL71
Swan Av, Upmin. RM14 . . . . . .73 FT60
Swanbourne Dr, Horn. RM12 . .72 FJ64
Swanbridge Rd, Bexh. DA7 . .106 FA81
Swan Business Pk, Dart. DA1 .108 FK84
Swan Cl, E17 . . . . .47 DY53
  Croydon CR0 . . . . .142 DS101
  Feltham TW13 . . . . .116 BY91
  Orpington BR5 . . . . .146 EU97
  Rickmansworth WD3
  off Parsonage Rd 38 BK45
Swan Ct, SW3
  off Flood St 100 DE78
Swandon Way, SW18 . . . . . .100 DB84
Swan Dr, NW9 . . . . .42 CS54
Swanfield Rd, Wal.Cr. EN8 . . .15 DY33
Swanfield St, E2 . . . . .197 P3
Swanland Rd, Hat. AL9 . . . . . .11 CV31
  Potters Bar EN6 . . . . .11 CV33
Swan La, EC4 . . . . .201 K1
  N20 . . . . .44 DC48
  Dartford DA1 . . . . .127 FF87
  Loughton IG10 . . . . .48 EJ45
SWANLEY 147 FE98
  Swanley 147 FD98
Swanley Bar La, Pot.B. EN6 . .12 DB28
Swanley Bypass, Sid. DA14 . .147 FC97
  Swanley BR8 . . . . .147 FC97
Swanley Cen, Swan. BR8 . . . .147 FE97
Swanley Cres, Pot.B. EN6 . . . .12 DB29
Swanley La, Swan. BR8 . . . . .147 FF97
Swanley Rd, Well. DA16 . . . . .106 EW81
SWANLEY VILLAGE, Swan. . .148 FJ95
Swanley Village Rd, Swan.
  BR8 . . . . .147 FH95
Swan Mead, SE1 . . . . .201 M7
  Hemel Hempstead HP3
  off Belswains La 6 BM25
Swan Pas, E1 off Cartwright St .84 DT73
Swan Path, E10 off Jesse Rd . .67 EC60
Swan Pl, SW13 . . . . .99 CT82
Swan Rd, SE16 . . . . .202 G4
  SE18 . . . . .104 EK76
  Feltham TW13 . . . . .116 BY92
  Iver SL0 . . . . .75 BF72
  Southall UB1 . . . . .78 CB72
  West Drayton UB7 . . . . . . .94 BK75
SWANSCOMBE 130 FZ86
  Swanscombe 130 FZ85
Swanscombe Ho, W11
  off St. Anns Rd 81 CX74
Swanscombe Rd, W4 . . . . . . .98 CS78
  W11 . . . . .81 CX74
Swanscombe St, Swans.
  DA10 . . . . .130 FY87
Swansea Ct, E16
  off Fishguard Way 87 EP74
Swansea Rd, Enf. EN3 . . . . . .30 DW42
  Hounslow (Hthrw.Air.) TW6
  off Southern Perimeter Rd .115 BQ86
Swanshope, Loug. IG10 . . . . .33 EP40
Swansland Gdns, E17
  off McEntee Av 47 DY53
Swanston Path, Wat. WD19 . . .40 BW48
Swan St, SE1 . . . . .201 J6
  Isleworth TW7 . . . . .97 CH83
Swanton Gdns, SW19 . . . . . .119 CX88
Swanton Rd, Erith DA8 . . . . .107 FB80
Swan Wk, SW3 . . . . .100 DF79
  Romford RM1 . . . . .71 FE57
  Shepperton TW17 . . . . . . .135 BS101
Swan Way, Enf. EN3 . . . . .31 DX40
Swanwick Cl, SW15 . . . . . . .119 CT87
Swan Yd, N1
  off Highbury Sta Rd 83 DP65
Sward Rd, Orp. BR5 . . . . . . .146 EU100
Swaton Rd, E3 . . . . .85 EA70
Swaylands Rd, Belv. DA17 . . .106 FA79
Swaynesland Rd, Eden. (Crock.H.)
  TN8 . . . . .189 EM134
Swaythling Cl, N18 . . . . .46 DV49
Swaythling Ho, SW15
  off Tunworth Cres 119 CT86
Swedenborg Gdns, E1 . . . . . .84 DU73
Sweden Gate, SE16 . . . . . . .203 K7
Sweeney Cres, SE1 . . . . .202 A5
Sweeps Ditch Cl, Stai. TW18 .134 BG95
Sweeps La, Egh. TW20 . . . . .113 AZ92
  Orpington BR5 . . . . .146 EX99
Sweet Briar Grn, N9 . . . . .46 DT48
Sweet Briar Gro, N9 . . . . .46 DT48
Sweet Briar La, Epsom KT18 .156 CR114
Sweet Briar Wk, N18 . . . . . . .46 DT49
Sweetcroft La, Uxb. UB10 . . . .76 BN66
Sweetmans Av, Pnr. HA5 . . . .60 BX55
Sweets Way, N20 . . . . .44 DD47
Swetenham Wk, SE18
  off Sandbach Pl 105 EQ78
Swete St, E13 . . . . .86 EG68
Sweyne Rd, Swans. DA10 . . .130 FY86
Sweyn Pl, SE3 . . . . .104 EG82
Swievelands Rd, West. (Bigg.H.)
  TN16 . . . . .178 EH119
Swift Cl, E17 . . . . .47 DY52
  Harrow HA2 . . . . .60 CB61
  Hayes UB3
  off Church Rd 77 BT72
  Upminster RM14 . . . . .73 FS60
Swift Rd, Felt. TW13 . . . . . . .116 BY90
  Southall UB2 . . . . .96 BZ76
Swiftsden Way, Brom. BR1 . . .124 EE93
Swift St, SW6 . . . . .99 CZ81
Swiftsure Rd, Grays (Chaff.Hun.)
  RM16 . . . . .109 FW77
SWILLET, THE, Rick. 21 BB44
Swinbrook Rd, W10 . . . . .81 CY71

Swi - Tay

Swinburne Ct, SE5
  off Basingdon Way **102** DR84
Swinburne Cres, Croy. CR0 .**142** DW100
Swinburne Gdns, Til. RM18 .**111** GH82
Swinburne Rd, SW15 .....**99** CU84
Swinderby Rd, Wem. HA0 ..**80** CL65
Swindon Cl, Ilf. IG3
  off Salisbury Rd **69** ES61
  Romford RM3 ....**52** FM50
Swindon Gdns, Rom. RM3 .**52** FM50
Swindon La, Rom. RM3 ....**52** FM50
Swindon Rd, Houns. (Hthrw.Air.)
  TW6 ....**115** BQ85
Swindon St, W12 ....**81** CV74
Swinfield Cl, Felt. TW13 ..**116** BY91
Swinford Gdns, SW9 .....**101** DP83
Swingate La, SE18 ....**105** ES79
Swinnerton St, E9 ....**85** DY64
Swinton Cl, Wem. HA9 ....**62** CP60
Swinton Pl, WC1 ....**196** B2
Swinton St, WC1 ....**196** B2
Swires Shaw, Kes. BR2 ..**162** EK105
Swiss Av, Wat. WD18 ....**23** BS42
Swiss Cl, Wat. WD18 .....**23** BS41
⊖ **Swiss Cottage** **82** DD66
Swiss Ct, W1 ....**199** N1
Swiss Ter, NW6 ....**82** DD66
Swithland Gdns, SE9 ....**125** EN91
Swyncombe Av, W5 ....**97** CH77
Swynford Gdns, NW4
  off Handowe Cl **63** CU56
Sybil Ms, N4 *off Lothair Rd N* .**65** DP58
Sybil Phoenix Cl, SE8 ....**203** J10
Sybil Thorndike Ho, N1
  off Clephane Rd **84** DQ65
Sybourn St, E17 ....**67** DZ59
Sycamore App, Rick. (Crox.Grn.)
  WD3 ....**23** BQ43
Sycamore Av, E3 ....**85** DZ67
  W5 ....**97** CK76
  Hayes UB3 ....**77** BS73
  Sidcup DA15 ....**125** ET86
  Upminster RM14 ....**72** FN62
Sycamore Cl, E16
  off Clarence Rd **86** EE70
  N9 *off Pycroft Way* **46** DU49
  SE9 ....**124** EL89
  W3 *off Bromyard Av* **80** CS74
  Barnet EN4 ....**28** DD44
  Bushey WD23 ....**24** BY40
  Carshalton SM5 ......**158** DF105
  Chalfont St. Giles HP8 ..**36** AU48
  Edgware HA8 *off Ash Cl* ..**42** CQ49
  Feltham TW13 ....**115** BU90
  Gravesend DA12 ......**131** GK87
  Leatherhead (Fetch.) KT22 .**171** CE123
  Loughton IG10 *off Cedar Dr* .**33** EP40
  Northolt UB5 ....**78** BY67
  Waltham Cross EN7 ....**14** DT27
  Watford WD25 ....**23** BV35
  West Drayton UB7
  off Whitethorn Av **76** BM73
Sycamore Ct, Surb. KT6
  off Penners Gdns **138** CL101
Sycamore Dr, Brwd. CM14
  off Copperfield Gdns ...**54** FW46
  St. Albans (Park St.) AL2 ...**9** CD27
  Swanley BR8 ....**147** FE97
Sycamore Gdns, W6 ......**99** CV75
  Mitcham CR4 ....**140** DD96
Sycamore Gro, NW9 ......**62** CQ59
  SE6 ....**123** EC86
  SE20 ....**122** DU94
  New Malden KT3 ......**138** CR97
Sycamore Hill, N11 ....**44** DG51
Sycamore Ms, SW4 ......**101** DJ83
Sycamore Ri, Bans. SM7 .**157** CX114
  Chalfont St. Giles HP8 ...**36** AU48
Sycamore Rd, SW19 .....**119** CW93
  Chalfont St. Giles HP8 ...**36** AU48
  Dartford DA1 ....**128** FK88
  Rickmansworth (Crox.Grn.)
  WD3 ....**23** BQ43
Sycamores, The, Rad. WD7
  off The Avenue **9** CH34
  South Ockendon (Aveley) RM15
  off Dacre Av **91** FR74
Sycamore St, EC1 ....**197** H5
Sycamore Wk, W10 *off Fifth Av* .**81** CY70
  Egham (Eng.Grn.) TW20 ..**112** AV93
  Ilford IG6 *off Civic Way* ..**69** EQ56
  Slough (Geo.Grn.) SL3 ...**74** AY72
Sycamore Way, S.Ock. RM15 .**91** FX70
  Teddington TW11 ....**117** CJ93
  Thornton Heath CR7 ...**141** DN99
SYDENHAM, SE26 ....**122** DW92
⇌ **Sydenham** **122** DW91
Sydenham Av, N21
  off Chadwick Av **29** DM43
  SE26 ....**122** DV92
Sydenham Cl, Rom. RM1 ..**71** FF56
Sydenham Cotts, SE12 ..**124** EJ89
⇌ **Sydenham Hill** **122** DT90
Sydenham Hill, SE23 ....**122** DV88
  SE26 ....**122** DV90
Sydenham Hill Est, SE26 .**122** DU90
Sydenham Pk, SE26 .....**122** DW90
Sydenham Pk Rd, SE26 ..**122** DW90
Sydenham Ri, SE23 .....**122** DV89
Sydenham Rd, SE26 .....**122** DW92
  Croydon CR0 ....**142** DR101
Sydmons Ct, SE23 ......**122** DW87
Sydner Ms, N16 *off Sydner Rd* .**66** DT63
Sydner Rd, N16 ....**66** DT63
Sydney Av, Pur. CR8 ....**159** DM112
Sydney Cl, SW3 ....**198** A9
Sydney Cres, Ashf. TW15 .**115** BP93
Sydney Gro, NW4 ....**63** CW57
Sydney Ms, SW3 ....**198** A9
Sydney Pl, SW7 ....**198** A9
Sydney Rd, E11
  off Mansfield Rd **68** EH58
  N8 ....**65** DN56
  N10 ....**44** DG53
  SE2 ....**106** EW76
  SW20 ....**139** CX96
  W13 ....**79** CG74
Sydney Rd, Bex. DA6 ....**106** EX84
  Enfield EN2 ....**30** DR42
  Feltham TW14 ....**115** BU88
  Ilford IG6 ....**49** EQ54
  Richmond TW9 ....**98** CL84
  Sidcup DA14 ....**125** ES91
  Sutton SM1 ....**158** DA106
  Teddington TW11 .....**117** CF92
  Tilbury RM18 ....**111** GG82
  Watford WD18 ....**23** BS43
  Woodford Green IG8 ...**48** EG49
Sydney St, SW3 ....**198** B10
Syke Cluan, Iver SL0 ....**93** BE75
Syke Ings, Iver SL0 .....**93** BE76
Sykes Dr, Stai. TW18 ....**114** BH92
Sylvana Cl, Uxb. UB10 ...**76** BM67
Sylvan Av, N3 ....**44** DA54
  N22 ....**45** DM52
  NW7 ....**43** CT51
  Hornchurch RM11 .....**72** FL58
  Romford RM6 ....**70** EZ58
Sylvan Cl, Grays (Chaff.Hun.)
  RM16 *off Warren La* ...**110** FY77
  Oxted RH8 ....**188** EH129
  South Croydon CR2 ...**160** DV110
  Woking GU22 ....**167** BB117
Sylvan Ct, N12 *off Holden Rd* .**44** DB49
Sylvan Est, SE19 ....**142** DT95
Sylvan Gdns, Surb. KT6 .**137** CK101
Sylvan Gro, NW2 ....**63** CX63
  SE15 ....**102** DV80
Sylvan Hill, SE19 ....**142** DS95
Sylvan Rd, E7 ....**86** EG65
  E11 ....**68** EG57
  E17 ....**67** EA57
  SE19 ....**142** DT95
  Ilford IG1 *off Hainault St* ..**69** EQ61
Sylvan Wk, Brom. BR1 ...**145** EM97
Sylvan Way, Chig. IG7 ....**50** EV48
  Dagenham RM8 ....**70** EV62
  West Wickham BR4 ...**162** EE105
Sylverdale Rd, Croy. CR0 .**141** DP104
  Purley CR8 ....**159** DP113
Sylvester Av, Chis. BR7 ..**125** EM93
Sylvester Gdns, Ilf. IG6 ...**50** EV50
Sylvester Path, E8
  off Sylvester Rd **84** DV65
Sylvester Rd, E8 ....**84** DV65
  E17 ....**67** DZ59
  N2 ....**44** DC54
  Wembley HA0 ....**61** CJ64
Sylvestres, Sev. (Rvrhd.) TN13 .**190** FD121
Sylvestrus Cl, Kings.T. KT1 .**138** CN95
Sylvia Av, Brwd. CM13 ...**55** GC47
  Pinner HA5 ....**40** BZ51
Sylvia Ter, Wem. HA9
  off Harrow Rd **80** CP66
Sylvia Gdns, Wem. HA9 ...**80** CP66
Symes Ms, NW1
  off Camden High St **83** DJ68
Symonds Ct, Wal.Cr. (Chsht.) EN8
  off High St **15** DX28
Symons St, SW3 ....**198** E9
Symphony Ms, W10
  off Third Av **81** CY69
Syon Gate Way, Brent. TW8 .**97** CG80
★ **Syon Ho & Pk**, Brent. TW8 .**97** CJ81
⇌ **Syon Lane** **97** CG80
Syon La, Islw. TW7 ......**97** CH80
Syon Pk Gdns, Islw. TW7 .**97** CF80
Syon Vista, Rich. TW9 ....**97** CK81
Syracuse Av, Rain. RM13 ..**90** FL69
Syringa Ct, Grays RM17 ..**110** GD80
Sythwood, Wok. GU21 ...**166** AV117

T

Tabard Cen, SE1
  off Prioress St **102** DR76
Tabard Gdn Est, SE1 ....**201** L5
Tabard St, SE1 ....**201** K5
Tabarin Way, Epsom KT17 .**173** CW116
Tabernacle Av, E13
  off Barking Rd **86** EG70
Tabernacle St, EC2 .....**197** L5
Tableer Av, SW4 ....**121** DK85
Tabley Rd, N7 ....**65** DL63
Tabor Gdns, Sutt. SM3 ..**157** CZ107
Tabor Gro, SW19 ....**119** CY94
Tabor Rd, W6 ....**99** CV76
Tabors Ct, Brwd. (Shenf.) CM15
  off Shenfield Rd **55** FZ45
Tabrums Way, Upmin. RM14 .**73** FS59
Tachbrook Est, SW1 .....**101** DK78
Tachbrook Ms, SW1 .....**199** K8
Tachbrook Rd, Felt. TW14 .**115** BT87
  Southall UB2 ....**96** BX77
  Uxbridge UB8 ....**76** BJ68
Tachbrook St, SW1 .....**199** L9
Tack Ms, SE4 ....**84** EA83
Tadema Rd, SW10 ......**100** DC80
Tadlows Cl, Upmin. RM14 ..**72** FP64
Tadmor Cl, Sun. TW16 ...**135** BT98
Tadmor St, W12 ....**81** CX74
Tadorne Rd, Tad. KT20 ..**173** CW121
TADWORTH **173** CV121
⇌ **Tadworth** **173** CW122
Tadworth Av, N.Mal. KT3 ..**139** CT99
Tadworth Cl, Tad. KT20 ..**173** CX122
Tadworth Par, Horn. RM12
  off Maylands Av **71** FH63
Tadworth Rd, NW2 ......**63** CU61
Tadworth St, Tad. KT20 ..**173** CW123
Taeping St, E14 ....**204** B8
Taffy's How, Mitch. CR4 ..**140** DE97
Taft Way, E3
  off St. Leonards St **85** EB69
Tagalie Pl, Rad. (Shenley) WD7
  off Porters Pk Dr **10** CL32
Tagg's Island, Hmptn. TW12 .**137** CD96
Tailworth St, E1
  off Chicksand St **84** DU71
Tait Rd, Croy. CR0 .....**142** DS101
Takeley Cl, Rom. RM5 ....**51** FD54
Takeley Cl, Wal.Abb. EN9 ...**15** ED33
Takhar Ms, SW11
  off Cabul Rd **100** DE82
Talacre Rd, NW5 ....**82** DG65
Talbot Av, N2 ....**64** DD55
  Slough SL3 ....**93** AZ76
  Watford WD19 ....**40** BY45
Talbot Cl, N15 ....**66** DT56
Talbot Ct, EC3 ....**197** L10
Talbot Cres, NW4 ....**63** CU57
Talbot Gdns, Ilf. IG3 .....**70** EU61
Talbot Ho, E14 *off Giraud St* .**85** EB72
  N7 *off Harvist Est* **65** DN62
Talbot Pl, SE3 ....**104** EE82
  Slough (Datchet) SL3 ...**92** AW81
Talbot Rd, E6 ....**87** EN68
  E7 ....**68** EG63
  N6 ....**64** DG58
  N15 ....**66** DT56
  N22 ....**45** DJ54
  SE22 ....**102** DS84
  W2 ....**81** CZ72
  W11 ....**81** CZ72
  W13 ....**79** CG73
  Ashford TW15 ....**114** BK90
  Bromley BR2
  off Masons Hill **144** EH98
  Carshalton SM5 ......**158** DG106
  Dagenham RM9 ....**88** EZ65
  Harrow HA3 ....**41** CF54
  Isleworth TW7 ....**97** CG84
  Rickmansworth WD3 ...**38** BL46
  Southall UB2 ....**96** BY77
  Thornton Heath CR7 ...**142** DR98
  Twickenham TW2 .....**117** CE88
  Wembley HA0 ....**62** CK64
Talbot Roundabout, Epp. (N.Wld.)
  CM16 ....**19** FD25
Talbot Sq, W2 ....**194** A9
Talbot Wk, NW10 *off Garnet Rd* .**80** CS65
  W11 ....**81** CY72
Talbot Yd, SE1 ....**201** K3
Talbrook, Brwd. CM14 ....**54** FT48
Taleworth Cl, Ashtd. KT21 .**171** CK120
Taleworth Pk, Ashtd. KT21 .**171** CK120
Taleworth Rd, Ashtd. KT21 .**171** CK119
Talfourd Pl, SE15 ......**102** DT81
Talfourd Rd, SE15 ......**102** DT81
Talgarth Rd, W6 ....**99** CY78
  W14 ....**99** CY78
Talgarth Wk, NW9 ....**62** CS57
Talisman Cl, Ilf. IG3 .....**70** EV60
Talisman Sq, SE26 ......**122** DU91
Talisman Way, Epsom KT17 .**173** CW116
  Wembley HA9 ....**62** CM62
Tallack Cl, Har. HA3
  off College Hill Rd **41** CE52
Tallack Rd, E10 ....**67** DZ60
Tall Elms Cl, Brom. BR2 ..**144** EF99
Tallents Cl, Dart. (Sutt.H.) DA4 .**128** FP95
Tallis Cl, E16 ....**86** EH72
Tallis Gro, SE7 ....**104** EH79
Tallis St, EC4 ....**196** E10
Tallis Vw, NW10 ....**80** CR65
Tallis Way, Borwd. WD6 ...**25** CK39
Tallon Rd, Brwd. CM13 ...**55** GE43
Tall Trees, SW16 ....**141** DM97
  Slough (Colnbr.) SL3 ...**93** BE81
Tall Trees Cl, Horn. RM11 ..**72** FK58
Tally Ho Cor, N12 ....**44** DC50
Tally Rd, Oxt. RH8 ......**188** EL131
Talma Gdns, Twick. TW2 ..**117** CE86
Talmage Cl, SE23
  off Tyson Rd **122** DW87
Talman Gro, Stan. HA7 ...**41** CK51
Talma Rd, SW2 ....**101** DN84
Talus Cl, Purf. RM19
  off Brimfield Rd **109** FR77
Talwin St, E3 ....**85** EB69
Tamar Cl, E3
  off Lefevre Wk **85** DZ67
  Upminster RM14 ....**73** FS58
Tamar Dr, S.Ock. (Aveley)
  RM15 ....**90** FQ72
Tamarind Yd, E1 ....**202** C2
Tamarisk Rd, S.Ock. RM15 ..**91** FW70
Tamarisk Sq, W12 ....**81** CT73
Tamar Sq, Wdf.Grn. IG8 ...**48** EH51
Tamar St, SE7
  off Woolwich Rd **104** EL76
Tamar Way, N17 ....**66** DU55
  Slough SL3 ....**93** BB78
Tamerton Sq, Wok. GU22 .**166** AY119
Tamesis Gdns, Wor.Pk. KT4 .**138** CS102
Tamesis Strand, Grav. DA12 .**131** GL92
Tamian Way, Houns. TW4 ..**96** BW84
Tamworth Av, Wdf.Grn. IG8 .**48** EE51
Tamworth La, Mitch. CR4 .**141** DH96
Tamworth Pk, Mitch. CR4 .**141** DH98
Tamworth Pl, Croy. CR0 ..**142** DQ103
Tamworth Rd, Croy. CR0 ..**141** DP103
Tamworth St, SW6 ......**100** DA79
Tancred Rd, N4 ....**65** DP58
Tandem Cen, SW19
  off Prince George's Rd .**140** DD95
Tandem Way, SW19 .....**140** DD95
TANDRIDGE, Oxt. **187** EA133
Tandridge Ct, Cat. CR3 ..**176** DU122
Tandridge Dr, Orp. BR6 ..**145** ER102
Tandridge Gdns, S.Croy. CR2 .**160** DT113
Tandridge La, Oxt. (Tand.)
  RH8 ....**187** EA131
Tandridge Pl, Orp. BR6
  off Tandridge Dr **145** ER101
Tandridge Rd, Warl. CR6 ..**177** DX119
Tanfield Av, NW2 ....**63** CT63
Tanfield Cl, Wal.Cr. EN7 ...**14** DU27
Tanfield Rd, Croy. CR0 ..**160** DQ105
Tangent Link, Rom. (Harold Hill)
  RM3 ....**52** FK53
Tangent Rd, Rom. RM3
  off Ashton Rd **52** FK53
Tangier Rd, Rich. TW10 ...**98** CP83
Tangier Way, Tad. KT20 ..**173** CY117
Tangier Wd, Tad. KT20 ..**173** CY118
Tanglebury Cl, Brom. BR1 .**145** EM98
Tangle Tree Cl, N3 ....**44** DB54
Tanglewood Cl, Cher. (Longcr.)
  KT16 ....**132** AV104
  Croydon CR0 ....**142** DW104
  Stanmore HA7 ....**41** CE47
  Uxbridge UB10 ....**76** BN69
  Woking GU22 ....**167** BD116
Tanglewood Way, Felt. TW13 .**115** BV90
Tangley Gro, SW15 ......**119** CT86
Tangley Pk Rd, Hmptn. TW12 .**116** BZ93
Tanglyn Av, Shep. TW17 .**135** BP99
Tangmere Cres, Horn. RM12 .**89** FH65
Tangmere Gdns, Nthlt. UB5 .**78** BW68
Tangmere Gro, Kings.T. KT2 .**117** CK92
Tangmere Way, NW9 .....**42** CS54
Tanhouse Rd, Oxt. RH8 ..**187** ED132
Tanhurst Wk, SE2
  off Alsike Rd **106** EX76
Tankerton Rd, Surb. KT6 .**138** CM103
Tankerton St, WC1 .....**196** A3
Tankerville Rd, SW16 ...**121** DK93
Tank Hill Rd, Purf. RM19 .**108** FN78
Tank La, Purf. RM19 ....**108** FN77
Tankridge Rd, NW2 ......**63** CV61
Tanner Pt, E13 *off Pelly Rd* ..**86** EG67
Tanners Cl, Walt. KT12 ..**135** BV100
Tanners Dean, Lthd. KT22 .**171** CJ122
Tanners End La, N18 .....**46** DS49
Tanners Hill, SE8 ....**103** DZ81
  Abbots Langley WD5 ....**7** BT31
Tanners La, Ilf. IG6 ....**69** EQ55
Tanner St, SE1 ....**201** N5
  Barking IG11 ....**87** EQ65
Tanners Wd Cl, Abb.L. WD5
  off Tanners Wd La **7** BS32
Tanners Wd La, Abb.L. WD5 ...**7** BS32
Tannery, The, Red. RH1
  off Oakdene Rd **184** DE134
Tannery Cl, Beck. BR3 ..**143** DX99
  Dagenham RM10 ....**71** FB62
Tannery La, Wok. (Send)
  GU23 ....**167** BF122
Tannington Ter, N5 ......**65** DN62
Tannsfeld Rd, SE26 .....**123** DX92
Tansley Cl, N7 *off Hilldrop Rd* .**65** DK64
Tanswell Est, SE1 ......**200** E5
Tanswell St, SE1 ....**200** D5
Tansy Cl, E6 ....**87** EN72
  Romford RM3 ....**52** FL51
Tantallon Rd, SW12 ....**120** DG88
Tant Av, E16 ....**86** EF72
Tantony Gro, Rom. RM6 ..**70** EX55
Tanworth Cl, Nthwd. HA6 .**39** BQ51
Tanworth Gdns, Pnr. HA5 .**39** BV54
Tanyard La, Bex. DA5
  off Bexley High St **126** FA87
Tanza Rd, NW3 ....**64** DF63
Tapestry Cl, Sutt. SM2 ..**158** DB108
Taplow, NW3 ....**82** DD66
  SE17 *off Thurlow St* ...**102** DS78
Taplow Rd, N13 ....**46** DQ49
Taplow St, N1 ....**197** J1
Tappesfield Rd, SE15 ..**102** DW83
Tapp St, E1 ....**84** DV70
Tapster St, Barn. EN5 ....**27** CZ42
Tara Ms, N8 *off Edison Rd* ..**65** DK58
Taransay Wk, N1
  off Marquess Rd **84** DR65
Tarbert Rd, SE22 ....**122** DS85
Tarbert Wk, E1 *off Juniper St* .**84** DW73
Tarbock Rd, Felt. TW14 ..**115** BS86
Tariff Cres, SE8 ....**203** M8
Tariff Rd, N17 ....**46** DU51
Tarleton Gdns, SE23 ....**122** DV88
Tarling Cl, Sid. DA14 ...**126** EV90
Tarling Rd, E16 ....**86** EF72
  N2 ....**44** DC54
Tarling St, E1 ....**84** DV72
Tarling St Est, E1 ....**84** DW72
Tarmac Way, West Dr. UB7 ..**94** BH80
Tarnbank, Enf. EN2 ......**29** DL43
Tarn St, SE1 ....**201** H7
Tarnwood Pk, SE9 ......**125** EM88
Tarnworth Rd, Rom. RM3 ..**52** FN50
Tarpan Way, Brox. EN10 ..**15** DZ26
Tarquin Ho, SE26 ....**122** DU91
Tarragon Cl, SE14 ......**103** DY80
Tarragon Gro, SE26 .....**123** DX93
Tarrant Pl, W1 ....**194** D7
Tarrington Cl, SW16 ....**121** DK90
Tarry La, SE8 ....**203** K9
Tartar Rd, Cob. KT11 ...**154** BW113
Tarver Rd, SE17 ....**101** DP78
Tarves Way, SE10 ......**103** EB80
Tash Pl, N11 *off Woodland Rd* .**45** DH50
Tasker Cl, Hayes UB3 ....**95** BQ80
Tasker Ho, Bark. IG11
  off Dovehouse Mead ...**87** ER68
Tasker Rd, NW3 ....**64** DF64
  Grays RM16 ....**111** GH76
Tasman Ct, E14
  off Westferry Rd **86** EB77
  Sunbury-on-Thames TW16 .**115** BS94
Tasmania Ho, Til. RM18
  off Hobart Rd **111** GG81
Tasmania Ter, N18 ......**46** DQ51
Tasman Rd, SW9 ....**101** DL83
Tasman Wk, E16 *off Royal Rd* .**86** EK72
Tasso Rd, W6 ....**99** CY79
Tatam Rd, NW10 ....**80** CQ66
Tatchbury Ho, SW15
  off Tunworth Cres **119** CT86
Tate & Lyle Jetty, E16 ...**104** EL75
★ **Tate Britain**, SW1 ....**199** P9
★ **Tate Modern**, SE1 ....**200** G2
Tate Rd, E16 *off Newland St* .**87** EM74
  Gerrards Cross (Chal.St.P.)
  SL9 ....**37** AZ50
  Sutton SM1 ....**158** DA106
TATLING END, Ger.Cr. ...**57** BB61
Tatnell Rd, SE23 ....**123** DY86
TATSFIELD, West. **178** EL120
Tatsfield App Rd, West. (Tats.)
  TN16 ....**178** EH123
Tatsfield La, West. (Tats.)
  TN16 ....**179** EM121

TATTENHAM CORNER,
  Epsom **173** CV118
⇌ **Tattenham Corner** ...**173** CV118
Tattenham Cor Rd, Epsom
  KT18 ....**173** CT117
Tattenham Cres, Epsom KT18 .**173** CU118
Tattenham Gro, Epsom KT18 .**173** CU118
Tattenham Way, Tad. KT20 .**173** CX118
Tattersall Cl, SE9 ......**124** EL85
Tatton Cres, N16
  off Clapton Common ...**66** DT59
Tatum St, SE17 ....**201** L9
Tauber Cl, Borwd. (Elstree)
  WD6 ....**26** CM42
Tauheed Cl, N4 ....**66** DQ61
Taunton Av, SW20 ......**139** CV96
  Caterham CR3 ....**176** DT123
  Hounslow TW3 ....**96** CC82
Taunton Cl, Bexh. DA7 ..**107** FD82
  Ilford IG6 ....**49** ET51
  Sutton SM3 ....**140** DA102
Taunton Dr, N2 ....**44** DC54
  Enfield EN2 ....**29** DN41
Taunton La, Couls. CR5 ..**175** DN119
Taunton Ms, NW1 ....**194** D5
Taunton Pl, NW1 ....**194** D4
Taunton Rd, SE12 ......**124** EE85
  Gravesend (Nthflt.) DA11 .**130** GA85
  Greenford UB6 ....**78** CB67
  Romford RM3 ....**52** FJ49
Taunton Vale, Grav. DA12 .**131** GK90
Taunton Way, Stan. HA7 ..**62** CL55
Tavern Cl, Cars. SM5 ...**140** DE101
Taverners Cl, W11
  off Addison Av **81** CY74
Taverner Sq, N5
  off Highbury Gra **66** DQ63
Taverners Way, E4
  off Douglas Rd **48** EE46
Tavern La, SW9 ....**101** DN82
Tavistock Av, E17 ....**67** DY55
  NW7 *off Bittacy Hill* ...**43** CY52
  Greenford UB6 ....**79** CG68
Tavistock Cl, N16 *off Crossway* .**66** DS64
  Potters Bar EN6 ....**12** DD31
  Romford RM3 ....**52** FK53
  Staines TW18 ....**114** BK94
Tavistock Ct, WC2
  off Tavistock St **83** DL73
Tavistock Cres, W11 .....**81** CZ71
  Mitcham CR4 ....**141** DL98
Tavistock Gdns, Ilf. IG3 ..**69** ES63
Tavistock Gate, Croy. CR0 .**142** DR102
Tavistock Gro, Croy. CR0 .**142** DR101
Tavistock Ms, E18
  off Avon Way **68** EG56
  W11 *off Lancaster Rd* ...**81** CZ72
Tavistock Pl, E18 *off Avon Way* .**68** EG55
  N14 *off Chase Side* **45** DH45
  WC1 ....**195** N4
Tavistock Rd, E7 ....**68** EF63
  E15 ....**86** EF65
  E18 ....**68** EG55
  N4 ....**46** DR58
  NW10 ....**81** CT68
  W11 ....**81** CZ72
  Bromley BR2 ....**144** EF98
  Carshalton SM5 ......**140** DD100
  Croydon CR0 ....**142** DR102
  Edgware HA8 ....**42** CN53
  Uxbridge UB10 ....**59** BQ64
  Watford WD24 ....**24** BX39
  Welling DA16 ....**106** EW81
  West Drayton UB7 .....**76** BK74
Tavistock Sq, WC1 .....**195** N4
Tavistock St, WC2 .....**196** A10
Tavistock Ter, N19 ......**65** DK62
Tavistock Twr, SE16 ....**203** K7
Tavistock Wk, Cars. SM5
  off Tavistock Rd **140** DD102
Taviton St, WC1 ....**195** M4
Tavy Cl, SE11 ....**200** E10
Tawney Common, Epp. CM16 .**18** FA32
Tawney Rd, SE28 ....**88** EV73
Tawny Cl, W13 ....**79** CH74
  Feltham TW13 *off Chervil Cl* .**115** BU90
Tawny Way, SE16 ......**203** J8
Tayben Av, Twick. TW2 ..**117** CE86
Taybridge Rd, SW11 ...**100** DG83
Tayburn Cl, E14 ....**85** EC72
Tayfield Cl, Uxb. UB10 ...**59** BQ62
Tayler Cotts, Pot.B. EN6
  off Crossoaks La **11** CT34
Tayles Hill, Epsom KT17
  off Tayles Hill Dr **157** CT110
Tayles Hill Dr, Epsom KT17 .**157** CT110
Taylor Av, Rich. TW9 ....**98** CP82
Taylor Cl, N17 ....**46** DU52
  SE8 ....**103** DZ79
  Epsom KT19
  off Williams Evans Rd .**156** CN111
  Hampton (Hmptn.H.) TW12 .**116** CC92
  Hounslow TW3 ....**96** CC81
  Orpington BR6 ....**163** ET105
  Romford RM5 ....**50** FA52
  Uxbridge (Hare.) UB9
  off High St **38** BJ53
Taylor Ct, E15 *off Clays La* .**67** EC64
Taylor Rd, Ashtd. KT21 ..**171** CK117
  Mitcham CR4 ....**120** DE94
  Wallington SM6 ......**159** DH106
Taylor Row, Dart. DA2 ..**128** FJ90
  Romford (Noak Hill) RM3
  off Cummings Hall La ..**52** FJ48
Taylors Bldgs, SE18
  off Spray St **105** EP77
Taylors Cl, Sid. DA14 ..**125** ET91
Taylors Grn, W3 *off Long Dr* .**80** CS72
Taylors La, NW10 ....**80** CS66
  SE26 ....**122** DV91
  Barnet EN5 ....**27** CZ39
Taymount Ri, SE23 .....**122** DW89
Taynton Dr, Red. RH1 ...**185** DK129

★ Place of interest   ⇌ Railway station   ⊖ London Underground station   **DLR** Docklands Light Railway station   Tramlink station   H Hospital

Tay - Thi

Tayport Cl, N1 . . . . .83 DL66
Tayside Dr, Edg. HA8 . . . . . .42 CP48
Tay Way, Rom. RM1 . . . . . . .51 FF53
Taywood Rd, Nthlt. UB5 . . . .78 BZ69
Teak Cl, SE16 . . . . .203 L3
Teal Av, Orp. BR5 . . . . .146 EX98
Teal Cl, E16 off Fulmer Rd . .86 EK71
  South Croydon CR2 . . . . .161 DX111
Teal Ct, Wall. SM6
  off Carew Rd 159 DJ107
Teal Dr, Nthwd. HA6 . . . . . . .39 BQ52
Teale St, E2 . . . . .84 DU68
Tealing Dr, Epsom KT19 . . . .156 CR105
Teal Pl, Sutt. SM1
  off Sandpiper Rd 157 CZ103
Teal St, SE10 . . . . .205 L6
Teal Way, Hem.H. HP3
  off Belswains La 6 BM25
Teardrop Ind Est, Swan. BR8 .147 FH99
Teasel Cl, Croy. CR0 . . . . . .143 DX102
Teasel Way, E15 . . . . .86 EE69
Teazle Meade, Epp. (Thnwd.) CM16
  off Carpenters Arms La 18 EV25
Teazle Wd Hill, Lthd. KT22 . .171 CE117
Teazlewood Pk, Lthd. KT22 . .171 CG117
Tebworth Rd, N17 . . . . .46 DT52
Teck Cl, Islw. TW7 . . . . .97 CG82
Tedder Cl, Chess. KT9 . . . . .155 CJ106
  Ruislip HA4 off West End Rd .59 BQ63
  Uxbridge UB10 . . . . .76 BM66
Tedder Rd, S.Croy. CR2 . . . .160 DW108
TEDDINGTON 117 CG93
  ⇌ Teddington 117 CG93
Teddington Cl, Epsom KT19 .156 CR110
Teddington Lock, Tedd. TW11 .117 CH91
H Teddington Mem Hosp, Tedd.
  TW11 . . . . .117 CE93
Teddington Pk, Tedd. TW11 . .117 CF92
Teddington Pk Rd, Tedd. TW11 .117 CF91
Tedworth Gdns, SW3
  off Tedworth Sq 100 DF78
Tedworth Sq, SW3 . . . . .100 DF78
Tee, The, W3 . . . . .80 CS72
Tees Av, Grnf. UB6 . . . . .79 CE68
Tees Cl, Upmin. RM14 . . . . . .73 FR59
Teesdale Cl, E2 . . . . .84 DU68
Teesdale Gdns, SE25 . . . . . .142 DS96
  Isleworth TW7 . . . . .97 CG81
Teesdale Rd, E11 . . . . .68 EF58
  Dartford DA2 . . . . .128 FQ88
Teesdale St, E2 . . . . .84 DV68
Teesdale Yd, E2 off Teesdale St .84 DU68
Tees Dr, Rom. RM3 . . . . .52 FK48
Teeswater Ct, Erith DA18
  off Middle Way 106 EX76
Teevan Cl, Croy. CR0 . . . . . .142 DU101
Teevan Rd, Croy. CR0 . . . . . .142 DU101
Teggs La, Wok. GU22 . . . . . .167 BF116
Teignmouth Cl, SW4 . . . . . .101 DK84
  Edgware HA8 . . . . .42 CM54
Teignmouth Gdns, Grnf. UB6 .79 CF68
Teignmouth Rd, NW2 . . . . . . .63 CX64
  Welling DA16 . . . . .106 EW82
Telcote Way, Ruis. HA4
  off Woodlands Av 60 BW59
★ Telecom Twr, W1 . . . . . . .195 K6
Telegraph Hill, NW3 . . . . . . .64 DB62
Telegraph La, Esher (Clay.)
  KT10 . . . . .155 CF107
Telegraph Ms, Ilf. IG3 . . . . . .70 EU60
Telegraph Path, Chis. BR7 . .125 EP92
Telegraph Pl, E14 . . . . .204 B8
Telegraph Rd, SW15 . . . . . .119 CV87
Telegraph St, EC2 . . . . .197 K8
Telegraph Track, Cars. SM5 .158 DG110
Telemann Sq, SE3 . . . . .104 EH83
Telephone Pl, SW6
  off Lillie Rd 99 CZ79
Telfer Cl, W3 off Church Rd . .98 CQ75
Telferscot Rd, SW12 . . . . . .121 DK88
Telford Av, SW2 . . . . .121 DL88
Telford Cl, E17 . . . . .67 DY59
  SE19 off St. Aubyn's Rd . . .122 DT93
  Watford WD25 . . . . .24 BX35
Telford Dr, Walt. KT12 . . . . .136 BW101
Telford Rd, N11 . . . . .45 DJ51
  NW9 off West Hendon Bdy . .63 CU58
  SE9 . . . . .125 ER89
  W10 . . . . .81 CY71
  St. Albans (Lon.Col.) AL2 . . .9 CJ27
  Southall UB1 . . . . .78 CB73
  Twickenham TW2 . . . . . . .116 CA87
Telfords Yd, E1 . . . . .202 C1
Telford Ter, SW1 . . . . .101 DJ79
Telford Way, W3 . . . . .80 CS71
  Hayes UB4 . . . . .78 BY71
Telham Rd, E6 . . . . .87 EN68
Tell Gro, SE22 . . . . .102 DT84
Tellisford, Esher KT10 . . . . .154 CB105
Tellson Av, SE18 . . . . .104 EL81
Telscombe Cl, Orp. BR6 . . . .145 ES103
Telston La, Sev. (Otford) TN14 .181 FF117
Temeraire St, SE16 . . . . . . .202 G5
Temperley Rd, SW12 . . . . . .120 DG87
Tempest Av, Pot.B. EN6 . . . . .12 DC32
Tempest Mead, Epp. (N.Wld.Bas.)
  CM16 . . . . .19 FB27
Tempest Rd, Egh. TW20 . . . .113 BC93
Tempest Way, Rain. RM13 . . .89 FG65
Templar Dr, SE28 . . . . .88 EX72
  Gravesend DA11 . . . . .131 GG92
Templar Ho, NW2
  off Shoot Up Hill 81 CZ65
  Rainham RM13
  off Chantry Way 89 FD68
Templar Pl, Hmptn. TW12 . . .116 CA94
Templars Av, NW11 . . . . .63 CZ58
Templars Cres, N3 . . . . .44 DA54
Templars Dr, Har. HA3 . . . . . .41 CD51
Templar St, SE5 . . . . .101 DP82
★ Temple, The, EC4 . . . . . .196 D10
⊖ Temple 196 C10
Temple, EC4 . . . . .83 DN73

Temple Av, EC4 . . . . .196 E10
  N20 . . . . .44 DD45
  Croydon CR0 . . . . .143 DZ103
  Dagenham RM8 . . . . .70 FA60
★ Temple Bar, EC4 . . . . . . .196 E9
Temple Bar Rd, Wok. GU21 . .166 AT119
Temple Cl, E11 off Wadley Rd .68 EE60
  N3 off Cyprus Rd 43 CZ54
  SE28 . . . . .105 EQ76
  Epsom KT19 . . . . .156 CR112
  Waltham Cross (Chsht.)
  EN7 . . . . .14 DU31
  Watford WD17 . . . . .23 BT40
Templecombe Ms, Wok. GU22
  off Dorchester Ct 167 BA116
Templecombe Rd, E9 . . . . . . .84 DW67
Templecombe Way, Mord.
  SM4 . . . . .139 CY98
Temple Ct, E1 off Rectory Sq .85 DX71
  Potters Bar EN6 . . . . .11 CY31
Templecroft, Ashf. TW15 . . . .115 BR93
Templedene Av, Stai. TW18 . .114 BH94
Templefield Cl, Add. KT15 . . .152 BH105
Temple Fortune Hill, NW11 . . .64 DA57
Temple Fortune La, NW11 . . . .64 DA58
Temple Fortune Par, NW11
  off Finchley Rd 63 CZ57
Temple Gdns, N21
  off Barrowell Grn 45 DP47
  NW11 . . . . .63 CZ58
  Dagenham RM8 . . . . .70 EX62
  Rickmansworth WD3 . . . . . .38 BP49
  Staines TW18 . . . . .133 BF95
Temple Gro, NW11 . . . . .64 DA58
  Enfield EN2 . . . . .29 DP41
Temple Hill, Dart. DA1 . . . . .128 FM86
Temple Hill Sq, Dart. DA1 . . .128 FM85
Templehof Av, NW2 . . . . .63 CW59
Temple La, EC4 . . . . .196 E9
Templeman Cl, Pur. CR8
  off Croftleigh Av 175 DP116
Templeman Rd, W7 . . . . .79 CF71
Templemead Cl, W3 . . . . .80 CS72
Temple Mead Cl, Stan. HA7 . .41 CH51
Templemere, Wey. KT13 . . . .135 BR104
Temple Mill La, E15 . . . . .67 EB63
★ Temple of Mithras, EC4
  off Queen Victoria St 197 J9
Templepan La, Rick. WD3 . . . .22 BL37
Temple Pk, Uxb. UB8 . . . . . . .76 BN69
Temple Pl, WC2 . . . . .196 C10
Templer Av, Grays RM16 . . . .111 GG77
Temple Rd, E6 . . . . .86 EL67
  N8 . . . . .65 DM56
  NW2 . . . . .63 CW63
  W4 . . . . .98 CQ76
  W5 . . . . .97 CK76
  Croydon CR0 . . . . .160 DR105
  Epsom KT19 . . . . .156 CR112
  Hounslow TW3 . . . . .96 CB84
  Richmond TW9 . . . . .98 CM83
  Westerham (Bigg.H.) TN16 .178 EK117
Temple Sheen, SW14 . . . . . .118 CQ85
Temple Sheen Rd, SW14 . . . .98 CP84
Temple St, E2 . . . . .84 DV68
Templeton Av, E4 . . . . .47 EA49
Templeton Cl, N16
  off Truman's Rd 66 DS64
  SE19 . . . . .142 DR95
Templeton Ct, NW7
  off Bittacy Hill 43 CY52
Templeton Pl, SW5 . . . . .100 DA77
Templeton Rd, N15 . . . . .66 DR58
Temple Way, Sutt. SM1 . . . . .140 DD104
Templewood, W13 . . . . .79 CH71
Templewood Av, NW3 . . . . . . .64 DB62
Templewood Gdns, NW3 . . . . .64 DB62
Templewood La, Slou. SL2 . . .56 AS63
Templewood Pk, Slou. SL2 . . .56 AT63
Templewood Pt, NW2
  off Granville Rd 63 CZ61
Tempsford Av, Borwd. WD6 . .26 CR42
Tempsford Cl, Enf. EN2
  off Gladbeck Way 30 DQ41
Temsford Cl, Har. HA2 . . . . . .40 CC54
Ten Acre, Wok. GU21
  off Abercorn Way 166 AU118
Ten Acre La, Egh. TW20 . . . .133 BC96
Ten Acres, Lthd. (Fetch.) KT22 .171 CD124
Ten Acres Cl, Lthd. (Fetch.)
  KT22 . . . . .171 CD124
Tenbury Cl, E7
  off Romford Rd 68 EK64
Tenbury Ct, SW2 . . . . .121 DK88
Tenby Av, Har. HA3 . . . . .41 CH54
Tenby Cl, N15
  off Hanover Rd 66 DT56
  Romford RM6 . . . . .70 EY58
Tenby Gdns, Nthlt. UB5 . . . . .78 CA65
Tenby Rd, E17 . . . . .67 DY57
  Edgware HA8 . . . . .42 CM53
  Enfield EN3 . . . . .30 DW41
  Romford RM6 . . . . .70 EY58
  Welling DA16 . . . . .106 EX81
Tenchleys La, Oxt. RH8 . . . .188 EK131
Tench St, E1 . . . . .202 D3
Tenda Rd, SE16 . . . . .202 D9
Tendring Way, Rom. RM6 . . . .70 EW57
Tenham Av, SW2 . . . . .121 DK88
Tenison Ct, W1 . . . . .195 K10
Tenison Way, SE1 . . . . .200 D3
Tennand Cl, Wal.Cr. (Chsht.)
  EN7 . . . . .14 DT26
Tenniel Cl, W2
  off Porchester Gdns 82 DC72
Tennis Ct La, E.Mol. KT8
  off Hampton Ct Way 137 CF97
Tennison Av, Borwd. WD6 . . .26 CP43
Tennison Cl, Couls. CR5 . . . .175 DP120
Tennison Rd, SE25 . . . . .142 DT98
Tennis St, SE1 . . . . .201 K4
Tenniswood Rd, Enf. EN1 . . . .30 DT39
Tennyson Av, E11 . . . . .68 EG59
  E12 . . . . .86 EL66
  NW9 . . . . .62 CQ55

Tennyson Av, Grays RM17 . . .110 GB76
  New Malden KT3 . . . . .139 CV99
  Twickenham TW1 . . . . .117 CF88
  Waltham Abbey EN9 . . . . . .16 EE34
Tennyson Cl, Enf. EN3 . . . . . .31 DX43
  Feltham TW14 . . . . .115 BT86
  Welling DA16 . . . . .105 ES81
Tennyson Rd, E10 . . . . .67 EB61
  E15 . . . . .86 EE66
  E17 . . . . .67 DZ58
  NW6 . . . . .81 CZ67
  NW7 . . . . .43 CU50
  SE20 . . . . .123 DX94
  SW19 . . . . .120 DC93
  W7 . . . . .79 CF73
  Addlestone KT15 . . . . .152 BL105
  Ashford TW15 . . . . .114 BL92
  Brentwood CM13 . . . . .55 GC45
  Dartford DA1 . . . . .128 FN85
  Hounslow TW3 . . . . .96 CC82
  Romford RM3 . . . . .52 FJ52
  St. Albans AL2 . . . . .8 CA26
Tennyson St, SW8 . . . . .101 DH82
Tennyson Wk, Grav. (Nthflt.)
  DA11 . . . . .130 GD90
  Tilbury RM18 . . . . .111 GH82
Tennyson Way, Horn. RM12 . .71 FF61
Tensing Av, Grav. (Nthflt.)
  DA11 . . . . .130 GE90
Tensing Rd, Sthl. UB2 . . . . . .96 CA76
Tentelow La, Sthl. UB2 . . . . . .96 CA78
Tenterden Cl, NW4 . . . . .63 CX55
  SE9 . . . . .125 EM91
Tenterden Dr, NW4 . . . . .63 CX55
Tenterden Gdns, NW4 . . . . . .63 CX55
  Croydon CR0 . . . . .142 DU101
Tenterden Gro, NW4 . . . . . . .63 CX56
Tenterden Rd, N17 . . . . .46 DT52
  Croydon CR0 . . . . .142 DU101
  Dagenham RM8 . . . . .70 EZ61
Tenterden St, W1 . . . . .195 J9
Tenter Grd, E1 . . . . .197 P7
Tenter Pas, E1 off Mansell St .84 DT72
Tent Peg La, Orp. BR5 . . . . .145 EQ99
Tent St, E1 . . . . .84 DV70
Terborch Way, SE22
  off East Dulwich Gro 122 DS85
Tercel Path, Chig. IG7 . . . . . .50 EV49
Teredo St, SE16 . . . . .203 J7
Terence Cl, Grav. DA12 . . . . .131 GM88
Terence Ct, Belv. DA17
  off Nuxley Rd 106 EZ79
Teresa Gdns, Wal.Cr. EN8 . . .14 DW34
Teresa Ms, E17 . . . . .67 EA56
Teresa Wk, N10
  off Connaught Gdns 65 DH57
Terling Cl, E11 . . . . .68 EF62
Terling Rd, Dag. RM8 . . . . . . .70 FA61
Terlings, The, Brwd. CM14 . . .54 FU48
Terling Wk, N1
  off Britannia Row 84 DQ67
Terminus Pl, SW1 . . . . .199 J7
Tern Gdns, Upmin. RM14 . . . .73 FS60
Tern Way, Brwd. CM14 . . . . . .54 FS49
Terrace, The, E4
  off Chingford Rd 48 EE48
  N3 off Hendon La 43 CZ54
  NW6 . . . . .82 DA67
  SW13 . . . . .98 CS82
  Addlestone KT15 . . . . .152 BL106
  Gravesend DA12 . . . . .131 GH86
  Sevenoaks TN13 . . . . .190 FD122
  Woodford Green IG8
  off Broadmead Rd 48 EG51
Terrace Gdns, SW13 . . . . . . .99 CT82
  Watford WD17 . . . . .23 BV40
Terrace La, Rich. TW10 . . . . .118 CL86
Terrace Rd, E9 . . . . .84 DW66
  E13 . . . . .86 EG67
  Walton-on-Thames KT12 . . .135 BU101
Terraces, The, Dart. DA2 . . . .128 FQ87
Terrace St, Grav. DA12 . . . . .131 GH86
Terrace Wk, Dag. RM9 . . . . . .70 EY64
Terrapin Rd, SW17 . . . . .121 DH90
Terretts Pl, N1 off Upper St . .83 DP66
Terrick Rd, N22 . . . . .45 DL53
Terrick St, W12 . . . . .81 CV72
Terrilands, Pnr. HA5 . . . . .60 BZ55
Terront Rd, N15 . . . . .66 DQ57
Tersha St, Rich. TW9 . . . . . . .98 CM84
Tessa Sanderson Pl, SW8 . . .101 DH83
Tessa Sanderson Way, Grnf. UB6
  off Lilian Board Way 61 CD64
Testers Cl, Oxt. RH8 . . . . . .188 EH131
Testerton Wk, W11 . . . . .81 CX73
Tetbury Pl, N1 off Upper St . .83 DP67
Tetcott Rd, SW10 . . . . .100 DC80
Tetherdown, N10 . . . . .64 DG55
Tetty Way, Brom. BR2 . . . . . .144 EG96
Teversham La, SW8 . . . . . . .101 DL81
Teviot Av, S.Ock. (Aveley)
  RM15 . . . . .90 FQ72
Teviot Cl, Well. DA16 . . . . . .106 EV81
Teviot St, E14 . . . . .85 EC71
Tewkesbury Av, SE23 . . . . . .122 DV88
  Pinner HA5 . . . . .60 BY57
Tewkesbury Cl, N15
  off Tewkesbury Rd 66 DR58
  Loughton IG10 . . . . .33 GC43
  West Byfleet (Byfleet) KT14 .152 BK111
Tewkesbury Gdns, NW9 . . . . .62 CP55
Tewkesbury Rd, N15 . . . . . . .66 DR58
  W13 . . . . .79 CG73
  Carshalton SM5 . . . . .140 DD102
Tewkesbury Ter, N11 . . . . . . .45 DJ51
Tewson Rd, SE18 . . . . .105 ES78
Teynham Av, Enf. EN1 . . . . . .30 DR44
Teynham Grn, Brom. BR2 . . .144 EG99
Teynton Ter, N17 . . . . .46 DQ53
Thackeray Av, N17 . . . . .46 DU54
  Tilbury RM18 . . . . .111 GH81
Thackeray Cl, SW19 . . . . . . .119 CX94
  Harrow HA2 . . . . .60 CA60
  Isleworth TW7 . . . . .97 CG82
  Uxbridge UB8
  off Dickens Av 77 BP72
Thackeray Dr, Rom. RM6 . . . .70 EU59

Thackeray Rd, E6 . . . . .86 EK68
  SW8 . . . . .101 DH82
Thackeray St, W8 . . . . .100 DB75
Thakeham Cl, SE26 . . . . . . .122 DV92
Thalia Cl, SE10 . . . . .103 ED79
Thalmassing Cl, Brwd. CM13 .55 GB47
Thame Rd, SE16 . . . . .203 J4
Thames Av, SW10 . . . . .100 DC81
  Chertsey KT16 . . . . .134 BG97
  Dagenham RM9 . . . . .89 FB70
  Greenford UB6 . . . . .79 CF68
Thamesbank Pl, SE28 . . . . . .88 EW72
Thames Bk, SW14 . . . . .98 CQ82
Thames Circle, E14 . . . . . . .204 A8
⇌ Thames Ditton 137 CF101
Thames Ditton Island, T.Ditt. .137 CG99
Thames Dr, Grays RM16 . . . .111 GG78
  Ruislip HA4 . . . . .59 BQ58
Thames Europort, Dart. DA2 .109 FR83
Thamesfield Ct, Shep. TW17 .135 BQ101
★ Thames Flood Barrier &
  Visitors Cen, SE18 . . . . . .104 EK76
Thames Gate, Dart. DA1
  off St. Edmunds Rd 108 FN84
Thamesgate Cl, Rich. TW10
  off Locksmeade Rd 117 CH91
Thames Gateway, Dag. RM9 . .88 EZ68
  Rainham RM13 . . . . .89 FG72
  South Ockendon RM15 . . . .108 FQ75
Thameshill Av, Rom. RM5 . . . .51 FC54
★ Thames Ho, SW1 . . . . . . .199 P8
Thameside, Tedd. TW11 . . . .117 CK94
Thameside Ind Est, E16 . . . .104 EL75
Thameside Wk, SE28 . . . . . . .87 ET72
THAMESMEAD, SE28 . . . . . .87 ES74
THAMESMEAD NORTH, SE28 .88 EW72
Thames Meadow, Shep.
  TW17 . . . . .135 BR102
  West Molesey KT8 . . . . . . .136 CA96
Thamesmead Spine Rd, Belv.
  DA17 . . . . .107 FB75
THAMESMEAD WEST, SE18 .105 EQ76
Thamesmere Dr, SE28 . . . . . .88 EU73
Thames Path, SE1 . . . . .200 E1
  SE7 . . . . .205 N7
  SE10 . . . . .205 N7
  W6 . . . . .99 CW79
Thames Pl, SW15 . . . . .99 CX83
Thames Quay, SW10
  off Harbour Av 100 DC81
Thames Rd, E16 . . . . .86 EK74
  W4 . . . . .98 CN79
  Barking IG11 . . . . .87 ET69
  Dartford DA1 . . . . .107 FF82
  Grays RM17 . . . . .110 GB80
  Slough SL3 . . . . .93 BA77
Thames Side, Cher. KT16 . . .134 BJ100
  Kingston upon Thames KT1 .137 CK96
  Staines TW18 . . . . .134 BH96
Thames St, SE10 . . . . .103 EB79
  Hampton TW12 . . . . .136 CB95
  Kingston upon Thames KT1 .137 CK96
  Staines TW18 . . . . .113 BE91
  Sunbury-on-Thames
  TW16 . . . . .135 BV98
  Walton-on-Thames KT12 . . .135 BT101
  Weybridge KT13 . . . . .135 BP103
Thamesvale Cl, Houns. TW3 . .96 CA83
H Thames Valley Nuffield
  Hosp, Slou. SL2 . . . . .74 AW67
Thames Vw, Grays RM16 . . . .111 GG78
Thames Village, W4 . . . . .98 CQ81
Thames Way, Grav. DA11 . . . .130 GD88
Thames Wf, E16 . . . . .205 K2
Thamley, Purf. RM19 . . . . . . .108 FN77
Thanescroft Gdns, Croy. CR0 .142 DS104
Thanet Dr, Kes. BR2
  off Phoenix Dr 144 EK104
Thanet Pl, Croy. CR0 . . . . . .160 DQ105
Thanet Rd, Bex. DA5 . . . . . . .126 FA87
  Erith DA8 . . . . .107 FE80
Thanet St, WC1 . . . . .195 P3
Thane Vil, N7 . . . . .65 DM62
Thane Wks, N7 . . . . .65 DM62
Thanington Ct, SE9 . . . . . . .125 ES86
Thant Cl, E10 . . . . .67 EB62
Tharp Rd, Wall. SM6 . . . . . . .159 DK106
Thatcham Gdns, N20 . . . . . . .44 DC45
Thatcher Cl, West Dr. UB7
  off Classon Cl 94 BL75
Thatcher Ct, Dart. DA1
  off Heath St 128 FK87
Thatchers Cl, Loug. IG10 . . . .33 EQ40
Thatchers Way, Islw. TW7 . . .117 CD85
Thatches Gro, Rom. RM6 . . . .70 EY56
Thavies Inn, EC1 . . . . .196 E8
Thaxted Ct, N1 . . . . .197 K1
Thaxted Grn, Brwd. CM13 . . .55 GC43
Thaxted Ho, Dag. RM10 . . . . .89 FB66
Thaxted Pl, SW20 . . . . .119 CX94
Thaxted Rd, SE9 . . . . .125 EQ89
  Buckhurst Hill IG9 . . . . .48 EL45
Thaxted Wk, Rain. RM13
  off Ongar Way 89 FF67
Thaxted Way, Wal.Abb. EN9 . .15 ED33
Thaxton Rd, W14 . . . . .99 CZ79
Thayers Fm Rd, Beck. BR3 . .143 DY95
Thayer St, W1 . . . . .194 G7
★ Theatre Royal, WC2 . . . . .196 A9
Theatre Sq, E15
  off Great Eastern Rd 85 ED65
Theatre St, SW11 . . . . .100 DF83
Theberton St, N1 . . . . .83 DN67
Theed St, SE1 . . . . .200 D3
Thellusson Way, Rick. WD3 . . .37 BF45

Thelma Cl, Grav. DA12 . . . . .131 GM92
Thelma Gdns, SE3 . . . . .104 EK81
  Feltham TW13 . . . . .116 BY90
Thelma Gro, Tedd. TW11 . . . .117 CG93
Theobald Cres, Har. HA3 . . . .40 CB53
Theobald Rd, E17 . . . . .67 DZ59
  Croydon CR0 . . . . .141 DP103
Theobalds Av, N12 . . . . .44 DC49
  Grays RM17 . . . . .110 GC78
Theobalds Cl, Pot.B. (Cuffley)
  EN6 . . . . .13 DM30
Theobalds Ct, N4
  off Queens Dr 66 DQ61
⇌ Theobalds Grove 15 DX32
Theobalds La, Wal.Cr. (Chsht.)
  EN8 . . . . .14 DV32
Theobalds Pk Rd, Enf. EN2 . . .29 DP35
Theobald's Rd, WC1 . . . . . . .196 B6
Theobalds Rd, Pot.B. (Cuffley)
  EN6 . . . . .13 DL30
Theobald St, SE1 . . . . .201 K7
  Borehamwood WD6 . . . . . . .26 CM40
  Radlett WD7 . . . . .25 CH36
Theodora Way, Pnr. HA5 . . . .59 BT55
Theodore Rd, SE13 . . . . . . .123 EC86
◆ Therapia Lane 141 DL101
Therapia La, Croy. CR0 . . . . .141 DL100
Therapia Rd, SE22 . . . . .122 DW86
Theresa Rd, W6 . . . . .99 CU77
Theresas Wk, S.Croy. CR2
  off Sanderstead Rd 160 DR110
Therfield Ct, N4
  off Brownswood Rd 66 DQ61
Thermopylae Gate, E14 . . . .204 C9
Theseus Wk, N1 . . . . .196 G1
Thesiger Rd, SE20 . . . . .123 DX94
Thessaly Rd, SW8 . . . . .101 DJ80
Thetford Cl, N13 . . . . .45 DP51
Thetford Gdns, Dag. RM9 . . . .88 EX66
Thetford Rd, Ashf. TW15 . . . .114 BL91
  Dagenham RM9 . . . . .88 EX67
  New Malden KT3 . . . . .138 CR100
Thetis Ter, Rich. TW9
  off Kew Grn 98 CN79
THEYDON BOIS, Epp. 33 ET37
  ◆ Theydon Bois 33 ET36
Theydon Bower, Epp. 18 EU31
Theydon Ct, Wal.Abb. EN9 . . .16 EG33
Theydon Gdns, Rain. RM13 . . .89 FE66
THEYDON GARNON, Epp. 34 EW35
Theydon Gate, Epp. (They.B.)
  CM16 off Coppice Row 33 ES37
Theydon Gro, Epp. CM16 . . . .18 EU30
  Woodford Green IG8 . . . . . . .48 EJ51
THEYDON MOUNT, Epp. 18 FA34
Theydon Pk Rd, Epp. (They.B.)
  CM16 . . . . .18 ES39
Theydon Pl, Epp. CM16 . . . . .18 ET31
Theydon Rd, E5 . . . . .66 DW61
  Epping CM16 . . . . .17 ER34
Theydon St, E17 . . . . .67 DZ59
Thicket, The, West Dr. UB7 . . .76 BL72
Thicket Cres, Sutt. SM1 . . . .158 DC105
Thicket Gro, SE20 . . . . .122 DU94
  Dagenham RM9 . . . . .88 EW65
Thicket Rd, SE20 . . . . .122 DU94
  Sutton SM1 . . . . .158 DC105
Thicketts, Sev. TN13 . . . . . .191 FJ123
Thickthorne La, Stai. TW18 . .114 BJ94
Third Av, E12 . . . . .68 EL63
  E13 . . . . .86 EG69
  E17 . . . . .67 EA57
  W3 . . . . .81 CT74
  W10 . . . . .81 CY69
  Dagenham RM10 . . . . .89 FB67
  Enfield EN1 . . . . .30 DT43
  Grays RM20 . . . . .109 FU79
  Hayes UB3 . . . . .77 BT74
  Romford RM6 . . . . .70 EW58
  Waltham Abbey EN9 off Breach
  Barn Mobile Home Pk 16 EH30
  Watford WD25 . . . . .24 BX35
  Wembley HA9 . . . . .61 CK61
Third Cl, W.Mol. KT8 . . . . . .136 CB98
Third Cross Rd, Twick. TW2 . .117 CD89
Third Way, Wem. HA9 . . . . . .62 CP63
Thirleby Rd, SW1 . . . . .199 L7
  Edgware HA8 . . . . .42 CR53
Thirlmere Av, Grnf. UB6 . . . .79 CJ69
Thirlmere Cl, Egh. TW20
  off Keswick Rd 113 BB94
Thirlmere Gdns, Nthwd. HA6 .39 BQ51
  Wembley HA9 . . . . .61 CJ60
Thirlmere Ho, Islw. TW7
  off Summerwood Rd 117 CF85
Thirlmere Ri, Brom. BR1 . . . .124 EF93
Thirlmere Rd, N10 . . . . .45 DH53
  SW16 . . . . .121 DK91
  Bexleyheath DA7 . . . . .107 FC82
Thirsk Cl, Nthlt. UB5 . . . . . . .78 CA65
Thirsk Rd, SE25 . . . . .142 DR98
  SW11 . . . . .100 DG83
  Borehamwood WD6 . . . . . . .26 CN37
  Mitcham CR4 . . . . .120 DG94
Thirston Path, Borwd. WD6 . .26 CN40
Thirza Rd, Dart. DA1 . . . . . .128 FM86
Thistlebrook, SE2 . . . . .106 EW76
Thistlebrook Ind Est, SE2 . . .106 EW75
Thistlecroft Gdns, Stan. HA7 .41 CK53
Thistlecroft Rd, Walt. KT12 . .154 BW105
Thistledene, T.Ditt. KT7 . . . .137 CE100
  West Byfleet KT14 . . . . . . .151 BF113
Thistledene Av, Har. HA2 . . . .60 BY62
  Romford RM5 . . . . .51 FB50
Thistledown, Grav. DA12 . . . .131 GK93
Thistle Gro, SW10 . . . . .100 DC78
Thistlemead, Chis. BR7 . . . .145 EP96
Thistle Mead, Loug. IG10 . . . .33 EN41
Thistle Rd, Grav. DA12 . . . . .131 GL87
Thistlewaite Rd, E5 . . . . .66 DV62
Thistlewood Cl, N7 . . . . .65 DM61
Thistlewood Cres, Croy.
  (New Adgtn.) CR0 . . . . . .161 ED112
Thistleworth Cl, Islw. TW7 . . .97 CD80
Thistley Cl, N12
  off Summerfields Av 44 DE51

Thomas a'Beckett Cl, Wem.
  HA0 . . . . .61 CF63
Thomas Av, Cat. CR3 . . . . . .176 DQ121
Thomas Baines Rd, SW11 . . .100 DD83
Thomas Cl, Brwd. CM15 . . . . .54 FY48
Thomas Cribb Ms, E6 . . . . . . .87 EM72
Thomas Darby Ct, W11 . . . . . .81 CY72
Thomas Dean Rd, SE26
  off Kangley Br Rd 123 DZ91
Thomas Dinwiddy Rd, SE12 .124 EH89
Thomas Doyle St, SE1 . . . . .200 F6
Thomas Dr, Grav. DA12 . . . .131 GK89
Thomas Hardy Ho, N22 . . . . .45 DM52
Thomas La, SE6 . . . . .123 EA87
Thomas Pl, W8
  off St. Mary's Pl 100 DB76
Thomas Rd, E14 . . . . .85 DZ72
Thomas Rochford Way, Wal.Cr.
  EN8 . . . . .15 DZ27
Thomas Sims Ct, Horn. RM12 .71 FH64
Thomas St, SE18 . . . . .105 EP77
Thomas Wall Cl, Sutt. SM1
  off Clarence Rd 158 DB106
Thompson Av, Rich. TW9 . . . .98 CN83
Thompson Cl, Ilf. IG1
  off High Rd 69 EQ61
  Slough SL3 . . . . .93 BA77
  Sutton SM3
  off Barrington Rd 140 DA102
Thompson Rd, SE22 . . . . . . .122 DT86
  Dagenham RM9 . . . . .70 EZ62
  Hounslow TW3 . . . . .96 CB84
  Uxbridge UB10 . . . . .76 BL66
Thompson's Av, SE5 . . . . . .102 DQ80
Thompsons Cl, Wal.Cr. EN7 . .14 DT29
Thompson's La, Loug. (High
  Beach) IG10 . . . . .32 EF39
Thompson Way, Rick. WD3 . .38 BG45
Thomson Cres, Croy. CR0 . . .141 DN102
Thomson Rd, Har. HA3 . . . . .61 CE55
Thong La, Grav. DA12 . . . . .131 GM90
Thorburn Sq, SE1 . . . . .202 B9
Thorburn Way, SW19 . . . . . .140 DC95
Thoresby St, N1 . . . . .197 J2
Thorkhill Gdns, T.Ditt. KT7 . .137 CG102
Thorkhill Rd, T.Ditt. KT7 . . . .137 CH101
Thorley Cl, W.Byf. KT14 . . . .152 BG114
Thorley Gdns, Wok. GU22 . . .152 BG114
Thornaby Gdns, N18 . . . . . . .46 DU51
Thornash Cl, Wok. GU21 . . . .166 AW115
Thornash Rd, Wok. GU21 . . . .166 AW115
Thornash Way, Wok. GU21 . . .166 AW115
Thorn Av, Bushey (Bushey Hth.)
  WD23 . . . . .40 CC46
Thornbank Cl, Stai. TW19 . . .114 BG85
Thornbridge Rd, Iver SL0 . . . .75 BC67
Thornbrook, Epp. (Thnwd.)
  CM16 . . . . .18 EX25
Thornbury Av, Islw. TW7 . . . .97 CD80
Thornbury Cl, N16
  off Truman's Rd 66 DS64
  NW7 off Bittacy Hill 43 CY52
Thornbury Gdns, Borwd.
  WD6 . . . . .26 CQ42
Thornbury Rd, SW2 . . . . . . .121 DL86
  Isleworth TW7 . . . . .97 CD81
Thornbury Sq, N6 . . . . .65 DJ60
Thornby Rd, E5 . . . . .66 DW62
Thorncliffe Rd, SW2 . . . . . . .121 DL86
  Southall UB2 . . . . .96 BZ78
Thorn Cl, Brom. BR2 . . . . . .145 EN100
  Northolt UB5 . . . . .78 BZ69
Thorncombe Rd, SE22 . . . . .122 DS85
Thorncroft, Egh. (Eng.Grn.)
  TW20 . . . . .112 AW94
  Hornchurch RM11 . . . . . . .71 FH58
Thorncroft Cl, Couls. CR5
  off Waddington Av 175 DN120
Thorncroft Dr, Lthd. KT22 . . .171 CH123
Thorncroft Rd, Sutt. SM1 . . .158 DB105
Thorncroft St, SW8 . . . . . . .101 DL80
Thorndales, Brwd. CM14 . . . .54 FX49
Thorndean St, SW18 . . . . . .120 DC88
Thorndene Av, N11 . . . . .44 DG46
Thorndike Av, Nthlt. UB5 . . . .78 BX67
Thorndike Cl, SW10 . . . . . . .100 DC80
Thorndike St, SW1 . . . . . . .199 M10
Thorndon Cl, Orp. BR5 . . . . .145 ET96
Thorndon Ct, Brwd. CM13 . . .53 FW51
Thorndon Gdns, Epsom
  KT19 . . . . .156 CS105
Thorndon Gate, Brwd. CM13 .53 GC50
Thorndon Rd, Orp. BR5 . . . .145 ET96
Thorn Dr, Slou. (Geo.Grn.)
  SL3 . . . . .74 AY72
Thorndyke Ct, Pnr. HA5
  off Westfield Pk 40 BZ52
Thorne Cl, E11 . . . . .68 EE63
  E16 . . . . .86 EG72
  Ashford TW15 . . . . .115 BQ94
  Erith DA8 . . . . .107 FC79
Thorneloe Gdns, Croy. CR0 . .159 DN106
Thorne Pas, SW13 . . . . .98 CS82
Thorne Rd, SW8 . . . . .101 DL80
Thorne St, E16 . . . . .86 EF72
  SW13 . . . . .98 CS83
Thornet Wd Rd, Brom. BR1 . .145 EN97
THORNEY, Iver 94 BH76
Thorney Cres, SW11 . . . . . . .100 DD80
Thorneycroft Cl, Walt. KT12 .136 BW100
Thorneycroft Dr, Enf. EN3
  off Government Row 31 EA38
Thorney Hedge Rd, W4 . . . . .98 CP77
Thorney La N, Iver SL0 . . . . .75 BF76
Thorney La S, Iver SL0 . . . . .93 BF75
Thorney Mill Rd, Iver SL0 . . .94 BG76
  West Drayton UB7 . . . . . .94 BG76
Thorney St, SW1 . . . . .199 P8
Thornfield Av, NW7 . . . . .43 CY53
Thornfield Rd, W12 . . . . .99 CV75
  Banstead SM7 . . . . .174 DA117
Thornford Rd, SE13 . . . . . . .123 EC85

Thorngate Rd, W9 . . . . .82 DA70
Thorngrove Rd, E13 . . . . .86 EH67
Thornham Gro, E15 . . . . .67 ED64
Thornham St, SE10 . . . . . . .103 EB79
Thornhaugh Ms, WC1 . . . . . .195 N5
Thornhaugh St, WC1 . . . . . .195 N6
Thornhill Av, SE18 . . . . .105 ES80
  Surbiton KT6 . . . . .138 CL103
Thornhill Br Wf, N1
  off Caledonian Rd 83 DM67
Thornhill Cres, N1 . . . . .83 DM67
Thornhill Gdns, E10 . . . . .67 EB61
  Barking IG11 . . . . .87 ES66
Thornhill Gro, N1
  off Lofting Rd 83 DM66
Thornhill Rd, E10 . . . . .67 EB61
  N1 . . . . .83 DN66
  Croydon CR0 . . . . .142 DQ101
  Northwood HA6 . . . . .39 BQ49
  Surbiton KT6 . . . . .138 CL103
  Uxbridge UB10 . . . . .58 BM63
Thornhill Sq, N1 . . . . .83 DM66
Thornhill Way, Shep. TW17 . .134 BN99
Thorn Ho, Beck. BR3 . . . . . .143 DY95
Thorn La, Rain. RM13 . . . . . .90 FK68
Thornlaw Rd, SE27 . . . . . . .121 DN91
Thornley Cl, N17 . . . . .46 DU52
Thornley Dr, Har. HA2 . . . . . .60 CB61
Thornley Pl, SE10
  off Caradoc St 104 EE78
Thornridge, Brwd. CM14 . . . .54 FV45
Thornsbeach Rd, SE6 . . . . . .123 EC88
Thornsett Pl, SE20 . . . . .142 DV96
Thornsett Rd, SE20 . . . . . . .142 DV96
  SW18 . . . . .120 DB89
Thornside, Edg. HA8
  off High St 42 CN51
Thorns Meadow, West. (Brasted)
  TN16 . . . . .180 EW123
Thorn Ter, SE15
  off Nunhead Gro 102 DW83
Thornton Av, SW2 . . . . .121 DK88
  W4 . . . . .98 CS77
  Croydon CR0 . . . . .141 DM100
  West Drayton UB7 . . . . . .94 BM76
Thornton Cl, West Dr. UB7 . . .94 BM76
Thornton Ct, SW20 . . . . . . .139 CX99
Thornton Cres, Couls. CR5 . .175 DN119
Thornton Dene, Beck. BR3 . .143 EA96
Thornton Gdns, SW12 . . . . .121 DK88
Thornton Gro, Pnr. HA5 . . . . .40 CA51
THORNTON HEATH 141 DP98
  Thornton Heath 142 DQ98
Thornton Hill, SW19 . . . . . . .119 CY94
Thornton Pl, W1 . . . . .194 E6
Thornton Rd, E11 . . . . .67 ED61
  N18 . . . . .46 DW48
  SW12 . . . . .121 DK87
  SW14 . . . . .98 CR83
  SW19 . . . . .119 CX93
  Barnet EN5 . . . . .27 CY41
  Belvedere DA17 . . . . . . .107 FB77
  Bromley BR1 . . . . .124 EG92
  Carshalton SM5 . . . . . . .140 DD102
  Croydon CR0 . . . . .141 DM101
  Ilford IG1 . . . . .69 EP63
  Potters Bar EN6 . . . . .12 DC30
  Thornton Heath CR7 . . . .141 DM101
Thornton Rd E, SW19
  off Thornton Rd 119 CX93
Thornton Rd Retail Pk, Croy.
  CR0 . . . . .141 DM100
Thornton Row, Th.Hth. CR7
  off London Rd 141 DN99
Thorntons Fm Av, Rom. RM7 .71 FD60
Thornton St, SW9 . . . . .101 DN82
Thornton Way, NW11 . . . . . .64 DB57
Thorntree Rd, SE7 . . . . .104 EK78
Thornville Gro, Mitch. CR4 . .140 DC96
Thornville St, SE8 . . . . .103 EA81
THORNWOOD, Epp. 18 EW25
Thornwood Cl, E18 . . . . .48 EH54
Thornwood Rd, SE13 . . . . . .124 EE85
  Epping CM16 . . . . .18 EV29
Thorogood Gdns, E15 . . . . . .68 EE64
Thorogood Way, Rain. RM13 . .89 FE67
Thorold Cl, S.Croy. CR2 . . . .161 DX110
Thorold Rd, N22 . . . . .45 DL52
  Ilford IG1 . . . . .69 EP61
Thoroughfare, The, Tad. KT20 .183 CU125
Thorparch Rd, SW8 . . . . . . .101 DK81
THORPE, Egh. 133 BC97
Thorpebank Rd, W12 . . . . . . .81 CU74
Thorpe Bypass, Egh. TW20 . .133 BB96
Thorpe Cl, W10
  off Cambridge Gdns 81 CY72
  Croydon (New Adgtn.) CR0 .161 EC110
  Orpington BR6 . . . . .145 ES103
🅷 Thorpe Coombe Hosp,
  E17 . . . . .67 EC55
Thorpe Cres, E17 . . . . .47 DZ54
  Watford WD19 . . . . .40 BW45
Thorpedale Gdns, Ilf. IG2, IG6 .69 EN56
Thorpedale Rd, N4 . . . . .65 DL60
THORPE GREEN, Egh. 133 BA98
Thorpe Hall Rd, E17 . . . . . . .47 EC53
Thorpe Ind Est, Egh. TW20 . .133 BC96
THORPE LEA, Egh. 113 BB93
Thorpe Lea Rd, Egh. TW20 . .113 BB93
Thorpe Lo, Horn. RM11 . . . . .72 FL59
Thorpe Rd, E6 . . . . .87 EM67
  E7 . . . . .68 EF63
  E17 . . . . .47 EC54
  N15 . . . . .66 DS58
  Barking IG11 . . . . .87 ER66
  Chertsey KT16 . . . . .133 BE98
  Kingston upon Thames KT2 .118 CL94
  Staines TW18 . . . . .113 BD93
Thorpeside Cl, Stai. TW18 . .133 BE96
Thorpewood Av, SE26 . . . . .122 DV89
Thorpland Av, Uxb. UB10 . . . .59 BQ62
Thorsden Cl, Wok. GU22 . . . .166 AY118
Thorsden Ct, Wok. GU22
  off Guildford Rd 166 AY118

Thorsden Way, SE19
  off Oaks La 122 DS91
Thorverton Rd, NW2 . . . . . . .63 CY62
Thoydon Rd, E3 . . . . .85 DY68
Thrale Rd, SW16 . . . . .121 DJ92
Thrale St, SE1 . . . . .201 J3
Thrasher Cl, E8 off Stean St . .84 DT67
Thrawl St, E1 . . . . .84 DT71
Threadneedle St, EC2 . . . . . .197 L9
Three Barrels Wk, EC4 . . . . .197 J10
Three Colts Cor, E2
  off Weaver St 84 DU70
Three Colts La, E2 . . . . .84 DV70
Three Colt St, E14 . . . . .85 DZ73
Three Cors, Bexh. DA7 . . . . .107 FB82
Three Cups Yd, WC1 . . . . . . .196 C7
Three Forests Way, Chig. IG7 .50 EW48
  Loughton IG10
  off The Clay Rd 32 EK38
  Romford RM4 . . . . .50 EW48
  Waltham Abbey EN9 . . . . .32 EK36
Three Gates Rd, Long.
  (Fawk.Grn.) DA3 . . . . . .149 FU102
Three Households, Ch.St.G.
  HP8 . . . . .36 AT49
Three Kings Rd, Mitch. CR4 . .140 DG97
Three Kings Yd, W1 . . . . . . .195 H10
Three Mill La, E3 . . . . .85 EC69
Three Oak La, SE1 . . . . .201 P4
Three Oaks Cl, Uxb. UB10 . . .58 BM62
Three Quays Wk, EC3 . . . . . .201 N1
Threshers Pl, W11 . . . . .81 CY73
Thriffwood, SE26 . . . . .122 DW90
Thrift, The, Dart. (Bean) DA2 .129 FW90
Thrift Fm La, Borwd. WD6 . . .26 CP40
Thrift Grn, Brwd. CM13
  off Knight's Way 55 GA48
Thrift La, Sev. (Cudham) TN14 .179 ER117
Thrifts Hall Fm Ms, Epp. (They.B.)
  CM16 off Abridge Rd 33 ET37
Thrifts Mead, Epp. (They.B.)
  CM16 . . . . .33 ES37
Thrigby Rd, Chess. KT9 . . . .156 CM107
Throckmorten Rd, E16 . . . . . .86 EH72
Throgmorton Av, EC2 . . . . . .197 L8
Throgmorton St, EC2 . . . . . .197 L8
Throwley Cl, SE2 . . . . .106 EW76
Throwley Rd, Sutt. SM1 . . . .158 DB106
Throwley Way, Sutt. SM1 . . .158 DB105
Thrums, The, Wat. WD24 . . . .23 BV37
Thrupp Cl, Mitch. CR4 . . . . .141 DH96
Thrupps Av, Walt. KT12 . . . .154 BX106
Thrupps La, Walt. KT12 . . . .154 BX106
Thrush Grn, Har. HA2 . . . . . .60 CA56
  Rickmansworth WD3 . . . . .38 BJ45
Thrush La, Pot.B. (Cuffley)
  EN6 . . . . .13 DL28
Thrush St, SE17 . . . . .201 H10
Thruxton Way, SE15
  off Daniel Gdns 102 DT80
Thunderer Rd, Dag. RM9 . . . .88 EY70
Thurbarn Rd, SE6 . . . . .123 EB92
Thurland Rd, SE16 . . . . .202 B6
Thurlby Cl, Har. HA1
  off Gayton Rd 61 CG58
  Woodford Green IG8 . . . . .49 EM50
Thurlby Rd, SE27 . . . . .121 DN91
  Wembley HA0 . . . . .79 CK65
Thurleigh Av, SW12 . . . . . . .120 DG86
Thurleigh Rd, SW12 . . . . . . .120 DG86
Thurleston Av, Mord. SM4 . .139 CY99
Thurlestone Av, N12 . . . . . . .44 DF51
  Ilford IG3 . . . . .69 ET63
Thurlestone Cl, Shep. TW17 .135 BQ100
Thurlestone Rd, SE27 . . . . . .121 DN90
Thurloe Cl, SW7 . . . . .198 B8
Thurloe Gdns, Rom. RM1 . . . .71 FF58
Thurloe Pl, SW7 . . . . .198 A8
Thurloe Pl Ms, SW7 . . . . . . .198 A8
Thurloe Sq, SW7 . . . . .198 B8
Thurloe St, SW7 . . . . .198 A8
Thurlow Cl, E4
  off Higham Sta Av 47 EB51
Thurlow Gdns, Ilf. IG6 . . . . . .49 ER51
  Wembley HA0 . . . . .61 CK64
Thurlow Hill, SE21 . . . . .122 DQ88
Thurlow Pk Rd, SE21 . . . . . .121 DP88
Thurlow Rd, NW3 . . . . .64 DD64
  W7 . . . . .97 CG75
Thurlow St, SE17 . . . . .201 L10
Thurlow Ter, NW5 . . . . .64 DG64
Thurlston Rd, Ruis. HA4 . . . . .59 BU62
Thurlton Ct, Wok. GU21
  off Chobham Rd 166 AY116
Thurnby Ct, Twick. TW2 . . . .117 CE90
Thurnham Way, Tad. KT20 . .173 CW120
Thurrock Lakeside, Grays
  RM20 . . . . .109 FV77
★ Thurrock Local History
  Mus, Grays RM17 . . . . . .110 GB78
Thurrock Pk Way, Til. RM18 .110 GD80
Thursby Rd, Wok. GU21 . . . .166 AU118
Thursland Rd, Sid. DA14 . . . .126 EY92
Thursley Cres, Croy. (New Adgtn.)
  CR0 . . . . .161 ED108
Thursley Gdns, SW19 . . . . . .119 CX89
Thursley Rd, SE9 . . . . .125 EM90
Thurso Cl, Rom. RM3 . . . . . . .52 FP51
Thurso St, SW17 . . . . .120 DD91
Thurstan Rd, SW20 . . . . . . .119 CV94
Thurston Rd, SE13 . . . . .103 EB82
  Slough SL1 . . . . .74 AS72
  Southall UB1 . . . . .78 BZ72
Thurston Rd Ind Est, SE13
  off Jerrard St 103 EB83
Thurtle Rd, E2 . . . . .84 DT67
Thwaite Cl, Erith DA8 . . . . . .107 FC79
Thyer Cl, Orp. BR6
  off Isabella Dr 163 EQ105
Thyra Gro, N12 . . . . .44 DB51
Tibbatts Rd, E3 . . . . .85 EB70
Tibbenham Wk, E13 . . . . .86 EF68
Tibberton Sq, N1
  off Popham Rd 84 DQ66
Tibbets Cl, SW19 . . . . .119 CX88
Tibbet's Cor, SW15 . . . . . . .119 CX87

Tibbet's Cor Underpass, SW15
  . . . . .119 CX87
Tibbet's Ride, SW15 . . . . . . .119 CX87
Tibbles Cl, Wat. WD25 . . . . . .24 BY35
Tibbs Hill Rd, Abb.L. WD5 . . . .7 BT30
Tiber Gdns, N1 off Treaty St . .83 DM67
Ticehurst Cl, Orp. BR5
  off Grovelands Rd 126 EU94
Ticehurst Rd, SE23 . . . . .123 DY89
Tichborne, Rick. (Map.Cr.) WD3 .37 BD50
Tichborne Rd, Epsom KT19 . .156 CQ110
Tickford Cl, SE2
  off Ampleforth Rd 106 EW75
Tidal Basin Rd, E16 . . . . . . .205 L1
Tidenham Gdns, Croy. CR0 . .142 DS104
Tideswell Rd, SW15 . . . . . . .119 CW85
  Croydon CR0 . . . . .143 EA104
Tideway Cl, Rich. TW10
  off Locksmeade Rd 117 CH91
Tidey St, E3 . . . . .85 EA71
Tidford Rd, Well. DA16 . . . . .105 ET82
Tidworth Rd, E3 . . . . .85 EA70
Tidy's La, Epp. CM16 . . . . . . .18 EV29
Tiepigs La, Brom. BR2 . . . . .144 EE103
  West Wickham BR4 . . . . .144 EE103
Tierney Rd, SW2 . . . . .121 DL88
Tiger La, Brom. BR2 . . . . . . .144 EH98
Tiger Way, E5 . . . . .66 DV63
Tilbrook Rd, SE3 . . . . .104 EJ83
TILBURY 111 GG81
Tilbury Cl, SE15
  off Willowbrook Rd 102 DT80
  Orpington BR5 . . . . .146 EV96
Tilbury Docks, Til. RM18 . . . .110 GE84
★ Tilbury Energy & Environmental
  Cen, Til. RM18 . . . . .111 GK83
★ Tilbury Fort, Til. RM18 . . . .111 GJ84
Tilbury Gdns, Til. RM18 . . . .111 GG84
Tilbury Hotel Rd, Til. RM18 . .111 GG84
Tilbury Rd, E6 . . . . .87 EM68
  E10 . . . . .67 EC59
≢ Tilbury Town 110 GE82
Tilbury Wk, Slou. SL3 . . . . . . .93 BB76
Tildesley Rd, SW15 . . . . . . .119 CW86
Tile Fm Rd, Orp. BR6 . . . . . .145 ER104
Tilehouse Cl, Borwd. WD6 . . .26 CM41
Tilehouse La, Ger.Cr. SL9 . . . .37 BE53
  Rickmansworth (Map.Cr.)
  WD3 . . . . .37 BE53
  Uxbridge (Denh.) UB9 . . . .57 BE58
Tilehouse Way, Uxb. (Denh.)
  UB9 . . . . .57 BF59
Tilehurst Pt, SE2
  off Yarnton Way 106 EW75
Tilehurst Rd, SW18 . . . . . . .120 DD88
  Sutton SM3 . . . . .157 CY106
Tilekiln Cl, Wal.Cr. EN7 . . . . .14 DT29
Tile Kiln La, N6
  off Winchester Rd 65 DH60
  N13 . . . . .46 DQ50
  Bexley DA5 . . . . .127 FC89
  Uxbridge (Hare.) UB9 . . . .58 BP59
Tile Yd, E14 off Commercial Rd .85 DZ72
Tileyard Rd, N7 . . . . .83 DL66
Tilford Av, Croy. (New Adgtn.)
  CR0 . . . . .161 EC109
Tilford Gdns, SW19 . . . . . . .119 CX89
Tilia Cl, Sutt. SM1 . . . . .157 CZ106
Tilia Rd, E5 off Clarence Rd . .66 DV63
Tilia Wk, SW9
  off Moorland Rd 101 DP84
Till Av, Dart. (Fnghm.) DA4 . .148 FM102
Tiller Rd, E14 . . . . .203 P6
Tillett Cl, NW10 . . . . .80 CQ65
Tillett Sq, SE16 . . . . .203 L5
Tillett Way, E2
  off Gosset St 84 DU69
Tilley La, Epsom (Headley)
  KT18 . . . . .172 CQ123
Tillgate Common, Red. RH1 . .186 DQ133
Tillingbourne Gdns, N3 . . . . .63 CZ55
Tillingbourne Grn, Orp. BR5 .146 EU98
Tillingbourne Way, N3
  off Tillingbourne Gdns . . .63 CZ55
Tillingdown Hill, Cat. CR3 . . .176 DU122
Tillingdown La, Cat. CR3 . . . .176 DV124
Tillingham Ct, Wal.Abb. EN9 . .16 EG33
Tillingham Way, N12 . . . . . . .44 DA49
Tilling Rd, NW2 . . . . .63 CW60
Tilling Way, Wem. HA9 . . . . . .61 CK61
Tillman St, E1 off Bigland St . .84 DV72
Tilloch St, N1
  off Carnoustie Dr 83 DM66
Tillotson Rd, N9 . . . . .46 DT47
  Harrow HA3 . . . . .40 CB52
  Ilford IG1 . . . . .69 EN59
Tilly's La, Stai. TW18 . . . . . .113 BF91
Tilmans Mead, Dart. (Fnghm.)
  DA4 . . . . .148 FM101
Tilney Ct, EC1 . . . . .197 J4
Tilney Dr, Buck.H. IG9 . . . . . .48 EG47
Tilney Gdns, N1 . . . . .84 DR65
Tilney Rd, Dag. RM9 . . . . . . .88 EZ65
  Southall UB2 . . . . .96 BW77
Tilney St, W1 . . . . .198 G2
Tilson Gdns, SW2 . . . . .121 DL87
Tilson Ho, SW2
  off Tilson Gdns 121 DL87
Tilson Rd, N17 . . . . .46 DU53
Tilston Cl, E11 off Matcham Rd .68 EF62
Tilt Cl, Cob. KT11 . . . . .170 BY116
Tilt Meadow, Cob. KT11 . . . .170 BY116
Tilton St, SW6 . . . . .99 CY79
Tilt Rd, Cob. KT11 . . . . .170 BW115
Tiltwood, The, W3 . . . . .80 CQ73
Tilt Yd App, SE9 . . . . .125 EM86
Timber Cl, Chis. BR7 . . . . . . .145 EN96
  Woking GU22
  off Hacketts La 151 BF114
Timber Ct, Grays RM17
  off Columbia Wf Rd 110 GA79
Timbercroft, Epsom KT19 . . .156 CS105
Timbercroft La, SE18 . . . . . .105 ES79
Timberdene, NW4 . . . . .43 CX54

Timberdene Av, Ilf. IG6 . . . . . .49 EP53
Timberhill, Ashtd. KT21
  off Ottways La 172 CL119
Timber Hill Cl, Cher. KT16 . . .151 BC108
Timber Hill Rd, Cat. CR3 . . . .176 DU124
Timberland Rd, E1 . . . . .84 DV72
Timber La, Cat. CR3
  off Timber Hill Rd 176 DU124
Timberling Gdns, S.Croy. CR2
  off Sanderstead Rd 160 DR109
Timber Mill Way, SW4 . . . . . .101 DK83
Timber Pond Rd, SE16 . . . . .203 J3
Timber Ridge, Rick. (Loud.)
  WD3 . . . . .22 BK42
Timberslip Dr, Wall. SM6 . . .159 DK109
Timber St, EC1 . . . . .197 H4
Timbertop Rd, West. (Bigg.H.)
  TN16 . . . . .178 EJ118
Timberwharf Rd, N16 . . . . . . .66 DU58
Timbrell Pl, SE16 . . . . .203 M3
Time Sq, E8 . . . . .66 DT64
Times Sq, Sutt. SM1 . . . . . . .158 DB106
Timothy Cl, SW4 off Elms Rd .121 DJ85
  Bexleyheath DA6 . . . . . .126 EY85
Timothy Ho, Erith DA18
  off Kale Rd 106 EY75
Timothy Rd, E3 . . . . .85 DZ71
Timperley Gdns, Red. RH1 . .184 DE132
Timsbury Wk, SW15 . . . . . . .119 CU88
Timsway, Stai. TW18 . . . . . .113 BF92
Tindale Cl, S.Croy. CR2 . . . .160 DR111
Tindall Cl, Rom. RM3 . . . . . . .52 FM54
Tindal St, SW9 . . . . .101 DP81
Tinderbox All, SW14 . . . . . . .98 CR83
Tine Rd, Chig. IG7 . . . . .49 ES50
Tingeys Top La, Enf. EN2 . . . .29 DN36
Tinniswood Cl, N5
  off Drayton Pk 65 DN64
Tinsey Cl, Egh. TW20 . . . . . .113 BB92
Tinsley Rd, E1 . . . . .84 DW71
Tintagel Cl, Epsom KT17 . . . .157 CT114
Tintagel Cres, SE22 . . . . . . .102 DT84
Tintagel Dr, Stan. HA7 . . . . . .41 CK49
Tintagel Gdns, SE22
  off Oxonian St 102 DT84
Tintagel Ho, N9
  off Salisbury Rd 46 DU48
Tintagel Rd, Orp. BR5 . . . . . .146 EW103
Tintagel Way, Wok. GU22 . . .167 BA116
Tintern Av, NW9 . . . . .62 CP55
Tintern Cl, SW15 . . . . .119 CY85
  SW19 . . . . .120 DC94
Tintern Gdns, N14 . . . . .45 DL45
Tintern Path, NW9
  off Ruthin Cl 62 CS58
Tintern Rd, N22 . . . . .46 DQ53
  Carshalton SM5 . . . . . . .140 DD102
Tintern St, SW4 . . . . .101 DL84
Tintern Way, Har. HA2 . . . . . .60 CB60
Tinto Rd, E16 . . . . .86 EG70
Tinwell Ms, Borwd. WD6
  off Cranes Way 26 CQ43
Tippendell La, St.Alb. (Park St.)
  AL2 . . . . .8 CB26
Tippetts Cl, Enf. EN2 . . . . . . .30 DQ39
Tipthorpe Rd, SW11 . . . . . . .100 DG83
Tipton Cotts, Add. KT15
  off Oliver Cl 152 BG105
Tipton Dr, Croy. CR0 . . . . . . .160 DS105
Tiptree Cl, E4 off Mapleton Rd .47 EC48
  Hornchurch RM11 . . . . . . .72 FN60
Tiptree Cres, Ilf. IG5 . . . . . . .69 EN55
Tiptree Dr, Enf. EN2 . . . . .30 DR42
Tiptree Est, Ilf. IG5 . . . . .69 EN55
Tiptree Rd, Ruis. HA4 . . . . . . .59 BV63
Tirlemont Rd, S.Croy. CR2 . .160 DQ108
Tirrell Rd, Croy. CR0 . . . . . . .142 DQ100
Tisbury Ct, W1 off Rupert St . .83 DK73
Tisbury Rd, SW16 . . . . .141 DL96
Tisdall Pl, SE17 . . . . .201 L9
Titan Rd, Grays RM17 . . . . . .110 GA78
Titchborne Row, W2 . . . . . . .194 C9
Titchfield Rd, NW8 . . . . .82 DF67
  Carshalton SM5 . . . . . . .140 DD102
  Enfield EN3 . . . . .31 DY37
Titchfield Wk, Cars. SM5
  off Titchfield Rd 140 DD101
Titchwell Rd, SW18 . . . . . . .120 DD87
Tite Hill, Egh. TW20 . . . . . . .112 AX92
Tite St, SW3 . . . . .100 DF78
★ Tithe Barn Agricultural & Folk
  Mus, The, Upmin. RM14 . .73 FR59
Tithe Barn Cl, Kings.T. KT2 . .138 CM95
Tithe Barn Ct, Abb.L. WD5
  off Dairy Way 7 BT29
Tithe Barn Way, Nthlt. UB5 . . .77 BV69
Tithe Cl, NW7 . . . . .43 CU53
  Hayes UB4
  off Gledwood Dr 77 BT71
  Virginia Water GU25 . . . .132 AX100
  Walton-on-Thames KT12 . .135 BV100
Tithe Ct, Slou. SL3 . . . . .93 BA77
Tithe Fm Av, Har. HA2 . . . . . .60 CA62
Tithe Fm Cl, Har. HA2 . . . . . .60 CA62
Tithe La, Stai. (Wrays.) TW19 .113 BA86
Tithe Meadow, Wat. WD18 . . .23 BR44
Tithe Meadows, Vir.W. GU25 .132 AX100
Tithepit Shaw La, Warl. CR6 .176 DV115
Tithe Wk, NW7 . . . . .43 CU53
Titian Av, Bushey (Bushey Hth.)
  WD23 . . . . .41 CE45
Titley Cl, E4 . . . . .47 EA50
Titmus Cl, Uxb. UB8 . . . . .77 BQ72
Titmuss Av, SE28 . . . . .88 EV73
Titmuss St, W12
  off Goldhawk Rd 99 CW75
TITSEY, Oxt. 188 EH125
Titsey Hill, Oxt. (Titsey) RH8 .178 EF123
Titsey Rd, Oxt. RH8 . . . . . . .188 EH125
Tiverton Av, Ilf. IG5 . . . . .69 EN55
Tiverton Dr, SE9 . . . . .125 EQ88
Tiverton Gro, Rom. RM3 . . . . .52 FN50
Tiverton Ho, Enf. EN3 . . . . . .31 DX41

Tiv - Tre

Tiverton Rd, N15 ....66 DR58
  N18 ....46 DS50
  NW10 ....81 CX67
  Edgware HA8 ....42 CM54
  Hounslow TW3 ....96 CC82
  Potters Bar EN6 ....12 DD31
  Ruislip HA4 ....59 BU62
  Thornton Heath CR7
   off Willett Rd 141 DN99
  Wembley HA0 ....80 CL68
Tiverton St, SE1 ....201 H7
Tiverton Way, NW7
  off Bittacy Hill 43 CY52
  Chessington KT9 ....155 CJ106
Tivoli Ct, SE16 ....203 M4
Tivoli Gdns, SE18 ....104 EL77
Tivoli Rd, N8 ....65 DK57
  SE27 ....122 DQ92
  Hounslow TW4 ....96 BY84
Toad La, Houns. TW4 ....96 BZ84
Tobacco Dock, E1 ....202 D1
Tobacco Quay, E1 ....202 D1
Tobago St, E14 ....203 P4
Tobin Cl, NW3 ....82 DE66
Toby La, E1 ....85 DY70
Toby Way, Surb. KT5 ....138 CP103
Todd Cl, Rain. RM13 ....90 FK70
Todds Wk, N7 off Andover Rd 65 DM61
Toft Av, Grays RM17 ....110 GD77
Tokenhouse Yd, EC2 ....197 K8
Token Yd, SW15
  off Montserrat Rd 99 CY84
TOKYNGTON, Wem. 80 CP65
Tokyngton Av, Wem. HA9 ....80 CN65
Toland Sq, SW15 ....119 CU85
Tolcarne Dr, Pnr. HA5 ....59 BV55
Toldene Ct, Couls. CR5 ....175 DM102
Toley Av, Wem. HA9 ....62 CL59
Toll Bar Ct, Sutt. SM2 ....158 DB109
Tollbridge Cl, W10
  off Kensal Rd 81 CY70
Tolldene Cl, Wok. (Knap.) GU21
  off Robin Hood Rd 166 AS117
Tollers La, Couls. CR5 ....175 DM119
Tollet St, E1 ....85 DX70
Tollgate Cl, Rick. (Chorl.) WD3 ....21 BF41
Tollgate Dr, SE21 ....122 DS88
  Hayes UB4 ....78 BX73
Tollgate Gdns, NW6 ....82 DB68
Tollgate Rd, E6 ....86 EK71
  E16 ....86 EJ71
  Dartford DA2 ....129 FR87
  Waltham Cross EN8 ....31 DX35
Tollhouse La, Wall. SM6 ....159 DJ109
Tollhouse Way, N19 ....65 DJ61
Tollington Pk, N4 ....65 DM61
Tollington Pl, N4 ....65 DM61
Tollington Rd, N7 ....65 DM63
Tollington Way, N7 ....65 DL62
Tolmers Av, Pot.B. (Cuffley) EN6 ....13 DL28
Tolmers Gdns, Pot.B. (Cuffley) EN6 ....13 DL29
Tolmers Ms, Hert. (Newgate St.) SG13 ....13 DL25
Tolmers Pk, Hert. (Newgate St.) SG13 ....13 DL25
Tolmers Rd, Pot.B. (Cuffley) EN6 ....13 DL27
Tolmers Sq, NW1 ....195 L4
Tolpits Cl, Wat. WD18 ....23 BT43
Tolpits La, Wat. WD18 ....23 BT44
Tolpuddle Av, E13
  off Rochester Av 86 EJ67
Tolpuddle St, N1 ....83 DN68
Tolsford Rd, E5 ....66 DV64
Tolson Rd, Islw. TW7 ....97 CG83
Tolvaddon, Wok. GU21
  off Cardingham 166 AU117
Tolverne Rd, SW20 ....139 CW95
TOLWORTH, Surb. 138 CN103
≷ Tolworth 138 CP103
Tolworth Cl, Surb. KT6 ....138 CP102
Tolworth Gdns, Rom. RM6 ....70 EX57
H Tolworth Hosp. Surb. KT6 ....138 CN103
Tolworth Pk Rd, Surb. KT6 ....138 CM103
Tolworth Ri N, Surb. KT5
  off Elmbridge Av 138 CQ101
Tolworth Ri S, Surb. KT5
  off Warren Dr S 138 CQ102
Tolworth Rd, Surb. KT6 ....138 CL103
Tolworth Twr, Surb. KT6 ....138 CP103
Tomahawk Gdns, Nthlt. UB5
  off Javelin Way 78 BX69
Tom Coombs Cl, SE9
  off Well Hall Rd 104 EL84
Tom Cribb Rd, SE28 ....105 EQ76
Tom Gros Cl, E15
  off Maryland St 67 ED64
Tom Hood Cl, E15
  off Maryland St 67 ED64
Tom Jenkinson Rd, E16 ....205 N2
Tomkins Cl, Borwd. WD6
  off Tallis Way 26 CL39
Tomkyns La, Upmin. RM14 ....73 FR56
Tomlin Cl, Epsom KT19 ....156 CR111
Tomlins Gro, E3 ....85 EA69
Tomlinson Cl, E2 ....84 DT69
  W4 off Oxford Rd N 98 CP78
Tomlins Orchard, Bark. IG11 ....87 EQ67
Tomlins Ter, E14
  off Rhodeswell Rd 85 DZ71
Tomlins Wk, N7 off Briset Way 65 DM61
Tomlyns Cl, Brwd. CM13 ....55 GE44
Tom Mann Cl, Bark. IG11 ....87 ES67
Tom Nolan Cl, E15 ....86 EE68
Tomo Ind Est, Uxb. UB8 ....76 BJ72
Tompion St, EC1 ....196 F3
Toms Hill, Kings L. WD4
  off Bucks Hill 6 BJ33
  Rickmansworth WD3 ....22 BL36
Toms La, Abb.L. (Bedmond) WD5 ....7 BR28

Toms La, Kings L. WD4 ....7 BP29
Tom Smith Cl, SE10
  off Maze Hill 104 EE79
Tomswood Ct, Ilf. IG6 ....49 EQ53
Tomswood Hill, Ilf. IG6 ....49 EP52
Tomswood Rd, Chig. IG7 ....49 EN51
Tom Thumbs Arch, E3
  off Malmesbury Rd 85 EA68
Tom Williams Ho, SW6
  off Clem Attlee Ct 99 CZ79
Tonbridge Cl, Bans. SM7 ....158 DF114
Tonbridge Cres, Har. HA3 ....62 CL56
Tonbridge Ho, SE25 ....142 DU97
Tonbridge Rd, Rom. RM3 ....52 FK52
  Sevenoaks TN13 ....191 FJ127
  West Molesey KT8 ....136 BY98
Tonbridge St, WC1 ....195 P2
Tonbridge Wk, WC1
  off Tonbridge St 83 DL69
Tonfield Rd, Sutt. SM3 ....139 CZ102
Tonge Cl, Beck. BR3 ....143 EA99
Tonsley Hill, SW18 ....120 DB85
Tonsley Pl, SW18 ....120 DB85
Tonsley Rd, SW18 ....120 DB85
Tonsley St, SW18 ....120 DB85
Tonstall Rd, Epsom KT19 ....156 CR110
  Mitcham CR4 ....140 DG96
Tony Cannell Ms, E3
  off Maplin St 85 DZ69
Tooke Cl, Pnr. HA5 ....40 BY53
Tookey Cl, Har. HA3 ....62 CM59
Took's Ct, EC4 ....196 D8
Tooley St, SE1 ....201 L2
  Gravesend (Nthflt.) DA11 ....130 GD87
Toorack Rd, Har. HA3 ....41 CD54
Toot Hill Rd, Ong. CM5 ....19 FF29
TOOTING, ...120 DG93
⊖ Tooting Bec 120 DF90
Tooting Bec Rd, SW16 ....121 DK91
  SW17 ....120 DG90
⊖ Tooting Broadway 120 DE92
TOOTING GRAVENEY, SW17 ....120 DE93
Tooting Gro, SW17 ....120 DE92
Tooting High St, SW17 ....120 DE93
Tootswood Rd, Brom. BR2 ....144 EE99
Tooveys Mill Cl, Kings L. WD4 ....6 BN28
Topaz Wk, NW2 off Marble Dr 63 CX59
Topcliffe Dr, Orp. BR6 ....163 ER105
Top Dartford Rd, Dart. DA2 ....127 FF94
  Swanley BR8 ....127 FF94
Topham Sq, N17 ....46 DQ53
Topham St, EC1 ....196 D4
Top Ho Ri, E4 off Parkhill Rd 47 EC45
Topiary, The, Ashtd. KT21 ....172 CL120
Topiary Sq, Rich. TW9 ....98 CM83
Topland Rd, Ger.Cr. (Chal.St.P.) SL9 ....36 AX52
Toplands Av, S.Ock. (Aveley) RM15 ....90 FP74
Topley St, SE9 ....104 EK84
Topmast Pt, E14 ....203 P5
Top Pk, Beck. BR3 ....144 EE99
Topping La, Uxb. UB8 ....76 BK69
Topp Wk, NW2 ....63 CW61
Topsfield Cl, N8
  off Wolseley Rd 65 DK57
Topsfield Par, N8
  off Tottenham La 65 DL57
Topsfield Rd, N8 ....65 DL57
Topsham Rd, SW17 ....120 DF90
Torbay Rd, NW6 ....81 CZ66
  Harrow HA2 ....60 BY61
Torbay St, NW1 off Hawley Rd 83 DH66
Torbitt Way, Ilf. IG2 ....69 ET57
Torbridge Cl, Edg. HA8 ....42 CL52
Torbrook Cl, Bex. DA5 ....126 EY86
Torcross Dr, SE23 ....122 DW89
Torcross Rd, Ruis. HA4 ....59 BV62
Tor Gdns, W8 ....100 DA75
Torin Ct, Egh. (Eng.Grn.) TW20 ....112 AW92
Torland Dr, Lthd. (Oxshott) KT22 ....155 CD114
Tor La, Wey. KT13 ....153 BQ111
Tormead Cl, Sutt. SM1 ....158 DA107
Tormount Rd, SE18 ....105 ES79
Toronto Av, E12 ....69 EM63
Toronto Rd, E11 ....67 ED63
  Ilford IG1 ....69 EP60
  Tilbury RM18 ....111 GG82
Torquay Gdns, Ilf. IG4 ....68 EK56
Torquay St, W2 off Harrow Rd 82 DB71
Torrance Cl, SE7 ....104 EK79
  Hornchurch RM11 ....71 FH60
Torrens Rd, E15 ....86 EF65
  SW2 ....121 DM85
Torrens Sq, E15 ....86 EE65
Torrens St, EC1 ....196 E1
Torrens Wk, Grav. DA12 ....131 GL92
Torres Sq, E14
  off Maritime Quay 103 EA78
Torre Wk, Cars. SM5 ....140 DE102
Torriano Av, NW5 ....65 DK64
Torriano Cotts, NW5
  off Torriano Av 65 DJ64
Torriano Ms, NW5
  off Torriano Av 65 DK64
Torridge Gdns, SE15 ....102 DW84
Torridge Rd, Slou. SL3 ....93 BB79
  Thornton Heath CR7 ....141 DP99
Torridon Cl, Wok. GU21 ....166 AV117
Torridon Rd, SE6 ....123 ED88
  SE13 ....123 ED87
Torrington Av, N12 ....44 DD50
Torrington Cl, N12 ....44 DD50
  Esher (Clay.) KT10 ....155 CE107
Torrington Dr, Har. HA2 ....60 CB63
  Loughton IG10 ....33 EQ42
  Potters Bar EN6 ....12 DD32
Torrington Gdns, N11 ....45 DJ51
  Greenford UB6 ....79 CJ66
  Loughton IG10 ....33 EQ42
Torrington Gro, N12 ....44 DE50
Torrington Pk, N12 ....44 DC50
Torrington Pl, E1 ....202 C2

Torrington Pl, WC1 ....195 L6
Torrington Rd, E18 ....68 EG55
  Dagenham RM8 ....70 EZ60
  Esher (Clay.) KT10 ....155 CE107
  Greenford UB6 ....79 CJ67
  Ruislip HA4 ....59 BT62
Torrington Sq, WC1 ....195 N5
  Croydon CR0
   off Tavistock Gro 142 DR101
Torrington Way, Mord. SM4 ....140 DA100
Tor Rd, Well. DA16 ....106 EW81
Torr Rd, SE20 ....123 DX94
Torver Rd, Har. HA1 ....61 CE56
Torver Way, Orp. BR6 ....145 ER104
Torwood La, Whyt. CR3 ....176 DT120
Torwood Rd, SW15 ....119 CU85
Torworth Rd, Borwd. WD6 ....26 CM39
Tothill St, SW1 ....199 M5
Totnes Rd, Well. DA16 ....106 EV80
Totnes Wk, N2 ....64 DD56
Tottan Ter, E1 ....85 DX72
Tottenhall Rd, N13 ....45 DN51
TOTTENHAM, N17 ....46 DS53
⊖ Tottenham Court Road 195 M8
Tottenham Ct Rd, W1 ....195 L5
Tottenham Grn E, N15 ....66 DT56
TOTTENHAM HALE, N17 ....66 DV55
≷ Tottenham Hale 66 DV55
⊖ Tottenham Hale 66 DV55
★ Tottenham Hotspur FC, N17 ....46 DT52
Tottenham La, N8 ....65 DL57
Tottenham Ms, W1 ....195 L6
Tottenham Rd, N1 ....84 DS65
Tottenham St, W1 ....195 L7
Totterdown St, SW17 ....120 DF91
TOTTERIDGE, N20 ....43 CY46
⊖ Totteridge & Whetstone 44 DB47
Totteridge Common, N20 ....43 CU47
Totteridge Grn, N20 ....44 DA47
Totteridge Ho, SW11 ....100 DD82
Totteridge La, N20 ....44 DA47
Totteridge Rd, Enf. EN3 ....31 DX37
Totteridge Village, N20 ....43 CY46
Totternhoe Cl, Har. HA3 ....61 CJ57
Totton Rd, Th.Hth. CR7 ....141 DN97
Toulmin St, SE1 ....201 H5
Toulon St, SE5 ....102 DQ80
Tournay Rd, SW6 ....99 CZ80
Tours Pas, SW11 ....100 DC84
Toussaint Wk, SE16 ....202 C6
Tovey Cl, St.Alb. (Lon.Col.) AL2 ....9 CK26
Tovil Cl, SE20 ....142 DU96
Towcester Rd, E3 ....85 EB70
Tower, The, Couls. CR5 ....175 DK122
★ Tower 42, EC2 ....84 DS72
Tower 42, EC2 ....197 M8
Tower Br, E1 ....201 P3
  SE1 ....201 P3
Tower Br App, E1 ....201 P2
★ Tower Bridge Experience, SE1 ....201 P3
Tower Br Piazza, SE1 ....201 P3
Tower Br Rd, SE1 ....201 M7
Tower Br Wf, E1 ....202 B3
Tower Cl, NW3
  off Lyndhurst Rd 64 DD64
  SE20 ....122 DV94
  Gravesend DA12 ....131 GL92
  Ilford IG6 ....49 EP51
  Orpington BR6 ....145 ET103
  Woking GU21 ....166 AX117
Tower Ct, WC2 ....195 P9
  Brentwood CM14 ....54 FV47
Tower Cft, Dart. (Eyns.) DA4
  off High St 148 FL103
Tower Gdns, Esher (Clay.) KT10 ....155 CG108
Tower Gdns Rd, N17 ....46 DQ53
★ Tower Gateway 84 DT73
Tower Gro, Wey. KT13 ....135 BS103
Tower Hamlets Rd, E7 ....68 EF63
  E17 ....67 EA55
⊖ Tower Hill 197 P10
Tower Hill, EC3 ....201 N1
  Brentwood CM14 ....54 FW47
  Kings Langley (Chipper.) WD4 ....5 BE29
Tower Hill Ter, EC3
  off Tower Hill 84 DS73
Tower La, Wem. HA9
  off Main Dr 61 CK62
Tower Ms, E17 ....67 EA56
Tower Mill Rd, SE15
  off Wells Way 102 DS79
★ Tower of London, EC3 ....201 P1
Tower Pk Rd, Dart. DA1 ....127 FF85
★ Tower Pier, EC3 ....201 N2
Tower Pier, EC3 ....201 N2
Tower Pl, Warl. CR6 ....177 EA115
Tower Pt, Enf. EN2 ....30 DR42
Tower Retail Pk, Dart. DA1 ....127 FF85
Tower Ri, Rich. TW9
  off Jocelyn Rd 98 CL83
Tower Rd, NW10 ....81 CU66
  Belvedere DA17 ....107 FC77
  Bexleyheath DA7 ....107 FB84
  Dartford DA1 ....128 FJ86
  Epping CM16 ....17 ES30
  Orpington BR6 ....145 ET103
  Tadworth KT20 ....173 CW123
  Twickenham TW1 ....117 CF90
Tower Royal, EC4 ....197 J10
Towers, The, Ken. CR8 ....176 DQ115
Towers Av, Uxb. (Hlgdn.) UB10 ....77 BQ69
Towers Pl, Rich. TW9
  off Eton St 118 CL85
Towers Rd, Grays RM17 ....110 GC78
  Pinner HA5 ....40 BY53
  Southall UB1 ....78 CA70
Tower St, WC2 ....195 N9
Towers Wk, Wey. KT13 ....153 BP107
Towers Wd, Dart. (S.Darenth) DA4 ....149 FR95
Tower Ter, N22 off Mayes Rd 45 DM54
Tower Vw, Croy. CR0 ....143 DX101
Towfield Rd, Felt. TW13 ....116 BZ89

Towing Path Wk, N1
  off York Way 83 DL67
Towncourt Cres, Orp. BR5 ....145 EQ99
Towncourt La, Orp. BR5 ....145 ER100
Town Ct Path, N4 ....66 DQ60
Town End, Cat. CR3 ....176 DS122
Town End Cl, Cat. CR3 ....176 DS122
Towney Mead, Nthlt. UB5 ....78 BZ68
Towney Mead Ct, Nthlt. UB5
  off Towney Mead 78 BZ68
Town Fm Way, Stai. (Stanw.)
  TW19 off Town La 114 BK87
Townfield, Rick. WD3 ....38 BJ45
Townfield Cor, Grav. DA12 ....131 GJ88
Town Fld La, Ch.St.G. HP8 ....36 AW48
Townfield Rd, Hayes UB3 ....77 BT74
Townfield Sq, Hayes UB3 ....77 BT74
Town Fld Way, Islw. TW7 ....97 CG82
Towngate, Cob. KT11 ....170 BY115
Town Hall App, N16
  off Milton Gro 66 DS63
Town Hall App Rd, N15 ....66 DT56
Town Hall Av, W4 ....98 CR78
Town Hall Rd, SW11 ....100 DF83
Townholm Cres, W7 ....97 CF76
Town La, Stai. (Stanw.) TW19 ....114 BK86
Townley Ct, E15 ....86 EF65
Townley Rd, SE22 ....122 DS85
  Bexleyheath DA6 ....126 EZ85
Townley St, SE17 ....201 K10
Townmead, Red. RH1 ....186 DR133
Town Meadow, Brent. TW8 ....97 CK80
Townmead Rd, SW6 ....100 DC82
  Richmond TW9 ....98 CP82
  Waltham Abbey EN9 ....15 EC34
Town Pier, Grav. DA11
  off West St 131 GH86
Town Quay, Bark. IG11 ....87 EP67
Town Rd, N9 ....46 DV47
Townsend Av, N14 ....45 DK49
Townsend Ind Est, NW10 ....80 CR68
Townsend La, NW9 ....62 CR59
  Woking GU22
   off St. Peters Rd 167 BB121
Townsend Rd, N15 ....66 DT57
  Ashford TW15 ....114 BL92
  Southall UB1 ....78 BY74
Townsend St, SE17 ....201 L9
Townsend Way, Nthwd. HA6 ....39 BT52
Townsend Yd, N6 ....65 DH60
Townshend Cl, Sid. DA14 ....126 EV93
Townshend Est, NW8 ....82 DE68
Townshend Rd, NW8 ....82 DE67
  Chislehurst BR7 ....125 EP92
  Richmond TW9 ....98 CM84
Townshend Ter, Rich. TW9 ....98 CM84
Townslow La, Wok. (Wisley) GU23 ....168 BJ116
Townson Av, Nthlt. UB5 ....77 BU69
Townson Way, Nthlt. UB5
  off Townson Av 77 BU68
Town Sq, Erith DA8
  off Pier Rd 107 FE79
  Woking GU21
   off Church St E 167 AZ117
Town Sq Cres, Green. (Bluewater) DA9 ....129 FT87
Town Tree Rd, Ashf. TW15 ....114 BN92
Towpath, Shep. TW17 ....134 BM103
Towpath Wk, E9 ....67 DZ64
Towpath Way, Croy. CR0 ....142 DT100
Towton Rd, SE27 ....122 DQ89
Toynbec Cl, Chis. BR7
  off Beechwood Ri 125 EP91
★ Toynbee Hall, E1 ....84 DT71
Toynbee Rd, SW20 ....139 CY95
Toynbee St, E1 ....197 P7
Toyne Way, N6
  off Gaskell Rd 64 DF58
Tracery, The, Bans. SM7 ....174 DB115
Tracey Av, NW2 ....63 CW64
Tracious Cl, Wok. GU21
  off Sythwood 166 AV116
Tracious La, Wok. GU21 ....166 AV116
Tracy Ct, Stan. HA7 ....41 CJ52
Trade Cl, N13 ....45 DN49
Trader Rd, E6 ....87 EP72
Tradescant Rd, SW8 ....101 DL80
Trading Est Rd, NW10 ....80 CQ70
Trafalgar Av, N17 ....46 DS51
  SE15 ....102 DT78
  Worcester Park KT4 ....139 CX102
Trafalgar Business Cen, Bark.
  IG11 ....87 ET70
Trafalgar Cl, SE16 ....203 K8
Trafalgar Ct, E1 ....202 G1
  Cobham KT11 ....153 BU113
Trafalgar Dr, Walt. KT12 ....135 BU104
Trafalgar Gdns, E1 ....85 DX71
  W8 off South End Row 100 DB76
Trafalgar Gro, SE10 ....103 ED79
Trafalgar Pl, E11 ....68 EG56
  N18 ....46 DU50
Trafalgar Rd, SE10 ....103 ED79
  SW19 ....120 DB94
  Dartford DA1 ....128 FJ86
  Gravesend DA11 ....131 GG87
  Rainham RM13 ....89 FF68
  Twickenham TW2 ....117 CD89
Trafalgar Sq, SW1 ....199 N2
  WC2 ....199 N2
Trafalgar St, SE17 ....201 K10
Trafalgar Ter, Har. HA1
  off Nelson Rd 61 CE60
Trafalgar Way, E14 ....204 D2
  Croydon CR0 ....141 DM103
Trafford Cl, E15 ....67 EB64
  Ilford IG6 ....49 ET51
  Radlett (Shenley) WD7 ....10 CL32
Trafford Rd, Th.Hth. CR7 ....141 DM99
Tralee Ct, SE16 ....202 E10
Tramshed Ind Est, Croy. CR0
  off Coomber Way 141 DK101
Tramway Av, E15 ....86 EE66
  N9 ....46 DV45

Tramway Cl, SE20
  off Oak Gro Rd 142 DW96
Tramway Path, Mitch. CR4 ....140 DF99
Tranby Pl, E9
  off Homerton High St 67 DX64
Tranley Ms, NW3
  off Fleet Rd 64 DE64
Tranmere Rd, N9 ....46 DT45
  SW18 ....120 DC89
  Twickenham TW2 ....116 CB87
Tranquil Dale, Bet. (Buckland)
  RH3 ....183 CT132
Tranquil Pas, SE3
  off Tranquil Vale 104 EF82
Tranquil Ri, Erith DA8
  off West St 107 FE78
Tranquil Vale, SE3 ....104 EE82
Transay Wk, N1
  off Marquess Rd 84 DR65
Transept St, NW1 ....194 B7
Transmere Cl, Orp. BR5 ....145 EQ100
Transmere Rd, Orp. BR5 ....145 EQ100
Transom Cl, SE16 ....203 L8
Transom Sq, E14 ....204 B9
Transport Av, Brent. TW8 ....97 CG78
Tranton Rd, SE16 ....202 C6
Traps Hill, Loug. IG10 ....33 EM41
Traps La, N.Mal. KT3 ....138 CS95
Travellers Way, Houns. TW4 ....96 BW82
Travers Cl, E17 ....47 DX53
Travers Rd, N7 ....65 DN62
Treacy Cl, Bushey (Bushey Hth.)
  WD23 ....40 CC47
Treadgold St, W11 ....81 CX73
Treadway St, E2 ....84 DV68
Treadwell Rd, Epsom KT18 ....172 CS115
Treaty Cen, Houns. TW3 ....96 CB83
Treaty Rd, Houns. TW3
  off Hanworth Rd 96 CB83
Treaty St, N1 ....83 DM67
Trebble Rd, Swans. DA10 ....130 FY86
Trebeck St, W1 ....199 H2
Trebovir Rd, SW5 ....100 DA78
Treby St, E3 ....85 DZ70
Trecastle Way, N7
  off Carleton Rd 65 DK63
Tredegar Ms, E3
  off Tredegar Ter 85 DZ69
Tredegar Rd, E3 ....85 DZ68
  N11 ....45 DK52
  Dartford DA2 ....127 FG89
Tredegar Sq, E3 ....85 DZ69
Tredegar Ter, E3 ....85 DZ69
Trederwen Rd, E8 ....84 DU67
Tredown Rd, SE26 ....122 DW92
Tredwell Cl, SW2
  off Hillside Rd 121 DM89
  Bromley BR2 ....144 EL98
Tredwell Rd, SE27 ....121 DP91
Treebourne Rd, West. (Bigg.H.)
  TN16 ....178 EJ117
Tree Cl, Rich. TW10 ....117 CK88
Treen Av, SW13 ....99 CT83
Tree Rd, E16 ....86 EJ72
Treeside Cl, West Dr. UB7 ....94 BK77
Tree Tops, Brwd. CM15 ....54 FW46
Treetops, Grav. DA12 ....131 GH92
  Whyteleafe CR3 ....176 DU118
Treetops Cl, SE2 ....106 EY78
  Northwood HA6 ....39 BR50
Treetops Vw, Loug. IG10 ....48 EK45
Treeview Cl, SE19 ....142 DS95
Treewall Gdns, Brom. BR1 ....124 EH91
Tree Way, Reig. RH2 ....184 DB131
Trefgarne Rd, Dag. RM10 ....70 FA61
Trefil Wk, N7 ....65 DL63
Trefoil Ho, Erith DA18
  off Kale Rd 106 EY75
Trefoil Rd, SW18 ....120 DC85
Trefusis Wk, Wat. WD17 ....23 BS39
Tregaron Av, N8 ....65 DL58
Tregaron Gdns, N.Mal. KT3
  off Avenue Rd 138 CS98
Tregarthen Pl, Lthd. KT22 ....171 CJ121
Tregarth Pl, Wok. GU21 ....166 AT117
Tregarvon Rd, SW11 ....100 DG84
Tregenna Av, Har. HA2 ....60 BZ63
Tregenna Cl, N14 ....29 DJ43
Tregenna Ct, Har. HA2 ....60 CA63
Tregony Rd, Orp. BR6 ....163 ET105
Trego Rd, E9 ....85 EA66
Tregothnan Rd, SW9 ....101 DL83
Tregunter Rd, SW10 ....100 DC79
Treheam Rd, Ilf. IG6 ....49 ER52
Treherne Ct, SW9
  off Eythorne Rd 101 DN81
  SW17 ....120 DG91
Trehern Rd, SW14 ....98 CR83
Trehurst St, E5 ....67 DY64
Trelawn Cl, Cher. (Ott.) KT16 ....151 BC108
Trelawney Av, Slou. SL3 ....92 AX76
Trelawney Cl, E17
  off Orford Rd 67 EB56
Trelawney Est, E9 ....84 DW65
Trelawney Gro, Wey. KT13 ....152 BN107
Trelawney Rd, Ilf. IG6 ....49 ER52
Trelawn Rd, E10 ....67 EC62
  SW2 ....121 DN85
Trellick Twr, W10 ....81 CZ70
Trellis Sq, E3
  off Malmesbury Rd 85 DZ69
Treloar Gdns, SE19 ....122 DR93
Tremaine Cl, SE4 ....103 EA82
Tremaine Rd, SE20 ....142 DV96
Trematon Pl, Tedd. TW11 ....117 CJ94
Tremlett Gro, N19 ....65 DJ62
Tremlett Ms, N19 ....65 DJ62
Trenance, Wok. GU21
  off Cardingham 166 AU117
Trenance Gdns, Ilf. IG3 ....70 EU62
Trenchard Av, Ruis. HA4 ....59 BV63
Trenchard Cl, NW9
  off Fulbeck Dr 42 CS53
  Stanmore HA7 ....41 CG51
  Walton-on-Thames KT12 ....154 BW106

Trenchard Ct, Mord. SM4
   off Green La **140** DB100
Trenchard St, SE10 . . . .**103** ED78
Trenches La, Slou. SL3 . . . . .**75** BA73
Trenchold St, SW8 . . . .**101** DL79
Trench Yd Ct, Mord. SM4
   off Green La **140** DB100
Trenear Cl, Orp. BR6 . . . . . .**164** EU101
Trenham Dr, Warl. CR6 . . . .**176** DW116
Trenholme Cl, SE20 . . . .**122** DV94
Trenholme Ct, Cat. CR3 . . . .**176** DU122
Trenholme Rd, SE20 . . . .**122** DV94
Trenholme Ter, SE20 . . . .**122** DV94
Trenmar Gdns, NW10 . . . .**81** CV69
Trent Av, W5 . . . .**97** CJ76
   Upminster RM14 . . . .**73** FR58
Trentbridge Cl, Ilf. IG6 . . . . .**49** ET51
Trent Cl, Rad. (Shenley) WD7
   off Edgbaston Dr **10** CL32
Trent Gdns, N14 . . . .**29** DH44
Trentham Cres, Wok. GU22 . .**167** BA121
Trentham Dr, Orp. BR5 . . . .**146** EU98
Trentham St, SW18 . . . .**120** DA88
★ Trent Park Country Pk, Barn.
   EN4 . . . .**29** DH40
Trent Rd, SW2 . . . .**121** DM85
   Buckhurst Hill IG9 . . . . . .**48** EH46
   Slough SL3 . . . .**93** BB79
Trent Way, Hayes UB4 . . . . . .**77** BS68
   Worcester Park KT4 . . . .**139** CW104
Trentwood Side, Enf. EN2 . . .**29** DM41
Treport St, SW18 . . . .**120** DB87
Tresco Cl, Brom. BR1 . . . . .**124** EE93
Trescoe Gdns, Har. HA2 . . . . .**60** BY59
   Romford RM5 . . . .**51** FC50
Tresco Gdns, Ilf. IG3 . . . .**70** EU61
Tresco Rd, SE15 . . . .**102** DV84
Tresham Cres, NW8 . . . .**194** B4
Tresham Rd, Bark. IG11 . . . . .**87** ET66
Tresham Wk, E9
   off Churchill Wk **66** DW64
Tresilian Av, N21 . . . .**29** DM43
Tresillian Way, Wok. GU21 . .**166** AU116
Tressell Cl, N1 off Sebbon St . .**83** DP66
Tressillian Cres, SE4 . . . . . .**103** EA83
Tressillian Rd, SE4 . . . .**103** DZ84
Tresta Wk, Wok. GU21 . . . . .**166** AU115
Trestis Cl, Hayes UB4
   off Jollys La **78** BY71
Treston Ct, Stai. TW18 . . . . .**113** BF92
Treswell Rd, Dag. RM9 . . . . .**88** EY67
Tretawn Gdns, NW7 . . . .**42** CS49
Tretawn Pk, NW7 . . . .**42** CS49
Trevanion Rd, W14 . . . .**99** CY78
Treve Av, Har. HA1 . . . .**60** CC59
Trevellance Way, Wat. WD25 . .**8** BW33
Trevelyan Av, E12 . . . .**69** EM63
Trevelyan Cl, Dart. DA1 . . . .**108** FM84
Trevelyan Cres, Har. HA3 . . . .**61** CK59
Trevelyan Gdns, NW10 . . . . .**81** CW67
Trevelyan Rd, E15 . . . .**68** EF63
   SW17 . . . .**120** DE92
Trevera Ct, Wal.Cr. EN8
   off Eleanor Rd **15** DY33
Trevereux Hill, Oxt. RH8 . . .**189** EM131
Treveris St, SE1 . . . .**200** F3
Treverton St, W10 . . . .**81** CX70
Treves Cl, N21 . . . .**29** DM43
Treville St, SW15 . . . .**119** CV87
Treviso Rd, SE23
   off Farren Rd **123** DX89
Trevithick Cl, Felt. TW14 . . .**115** BT88
Trevithick Dr, Dart. DA1 . . . .**108** FM84
Trevithick St, SE8 . . . .**103** EA78
Trevone Gdns, Pnr. HA5 . . . . .**60** BY58
Trevor Cl, Barn. EN4 . . . .**28** DD43
   Bromley BR2 . . . .**144** EF101
   Harrow HA3 off Kenton Rd . .**41** CF52
   Isleworth TW7 . . . .**117** CF85
   Northolt UB5 . . . .**78** BW68
Trevor Cres, Ruis. HA4 . . . . .**59** BT63
Trevor Gdns, Edg. HA8 . . . . .**42** CR53
   Northolt UB5 . . . .**78** BW68
   Ruislip HA4 off Clyfford Rd .**59** BU63
Trevor Pl, SW7 . . . .**198** C5
Trevor Rd, SW19 . . . .**119** CY94
   Edgware HA8 . . . .**42** CR53
   Hayes UB3 . . . .**95** BS76
   Woodford Green IG8 . . . . .**48** EG52
Trevor Sq, SW7 . . . .**198** D5
Trevor St, SW7 . . . .**198** C5
Trevor Wk, SW7
   off Trevor Sq **100** DF75
Trevose Av, W.Byf. KT14 . . .**151** BF114
Trevose Rd, E17 . . . .**47** ED53
Trevose Way, Wat. WD19 . . . .**40** BW48
Trewarden Av, Iver SL0 . . . . .**75** BD68
Trewenna Dr, Chess. KT9 . . .**155** CK106
   Potters Bar EN6 . . . .**12** DD32
Trewince Rd, SW20 . . . .**139** CW95
Trewint St, SW18 . . . .**120** DC89
Trewsbury Ho, SE2
   off Hartslock Dr **106** EX75
Trewsbury Rd, SE26 . . . . . .**123** DX92
Triandra Way, Hayes UB4 . . . .**78** BX71
Triangle, The, EC1
   off Goswell Rd **83** DP70
   N13 off Lodge Dr **45** DN49
   Barking IG11 off Tanner St . .**87** EQ55
   Hampton TW12 off High St .**136** CC95
   Kingston upon Thames KT1
   off Kenley Rd **138** CQ96
   Woking GU21 . . . .**166** AW118
Triangle Business Cen, NW10
   off Enterprise Way **81** CU69
Triangle Ct, E16 off Tollgate Rd .**86** EK71
Triangle Est, SE11
   off Kennington La **101** DM78
Triangle Pas, Barn. EN4
   off Station App **28** DC42
Triangle Pl, SW4 . . . .**101** DK84
Triangle Rd, E8 . . . .**84** DV67
Trident Cen, Wat. WD24 . . . . .**24** BW39
Trident Gdns, Nthlt. UB5
   off Jetstar Way **78** BX69
Trident Ind Est, Slou. (Colnbr.)
   SL3 . . . .**93** BE83

Trident Rd, Wat. WD25 . . . . . .**7** BT34
Trident St, SE16 . . . .**203** J8
Trident Way, Sthl. UB2 . . . . . .**95** BV76
Trigg's Cl, Wok. GU22 . . . . .**166** AX119
Trigg's La, Wok. GU21, GU22 **166** AW118
Trig La, EC4 . . . .**197** H10
Trigo Ct, Epsom KT19
   off Blakeney Cl **156** CR111
Trigon Rd, SW8 . . . .**101** DM80
Trilby Rd, SE23 . . . .**123** DX89
Trimmer Wk, Brent. TW8 . . . .**98** CL79
Trim St, SE14 . . . .**103** DZ79
Trinder Gdns, N19
   off Trinder Rd **65** DL60
Trinder Rd, N19 . . . .**65** DL60
   Barnet EN5 . . . .**27** CW43
Tring Av, W5 . . . .**80** CM74
   Southall UB1 . . . .**78** BZ72
   Wembley HA9 . . . .**80** CN65
Tring Cl, Ilf. IG2 . . . .**69** EQ57
   Romford RM3 . . . .**52** FL49
Tring Gdns, Rom. RM3 . . . . . .**52** FL49
Tringham Cl, Cher. (Ott.) KT16 **151** BC107
Tring Wk, Rom. RM3
   off Tring Gdns **52** FL49
Trinidad Gdns, Dag. RM10 . . .**89** FD66
Trinidad St, E14 . . . .**85** DZ73
Trinity Av, N2 . . . .**64** DD55
   Enfield EN1 . . . .**30** DT44
Trinity Buoy Wf, E14 . . . . . .**205** K1
Trinity Ch Pas, SW13 . . . .**99** CV79
Trinity Ch Rd, SW13 . . . .**99** CV79
Trinity Ch Sq, SE1 . . . .**201** J6
Trinity Cl, E8 . . . .**84** DT65
   E11 . . . .**68** EE61
   NW3 off Hampstead High St .**64** DD63
   SE13 off Wisteria Rd **103** ED84
   SW4 off The Pavement . . .**101** DJ84
   Bromley BR2 . . . .**144** EL102
   Hounslow TW4 . . . .**96** BY84
   Northwood HA6 . . . .**39** BS51
   South Croydon CR2 . . . .**160** DS109
   Staines (Stanw.) TW19 . . .**114** BJ86
Trinity Cotts, Rich. TW9
   off Trinity Rd **98** CM83
Trinity Ct, N1 off Downham Rd .**84** DS66
   NW2 off Anson Rd **63** CW64
   SE7 off Charlton La **104** EK77
Trinity Cres, SW17 . . . .**120** DF89
Trinity Gdns, E16 off Cliff Wk . .**86** EF70
   SW9 . . . .**101** DM84
   Dartford DA1
   off Summerhill Rd **128** FK86
Trinity Gro, SE10 . . . .**103** EC81
Trinity Hall Cl, Wat. WD24 . . .**24** BW41
★ Trinity Ho, EC3 . . . .**197** N10
Trinity La, Wal.Cr. EN8 . . . . .**15** DY34
Trinity Ms, SE20 . . . .**142** DV95
   W10 off Cambridge Gdns . .**81** CX72
Trinity Path, SE26 . . . .**122** DW90
Trinity Pl, Bexh. DA6 . . . . . .**106** EZ84
Trinity Ri, SW2 . . . .**121** DN88
Trinity Rd, N2 . . . .**64** DD55
   N22 . . . .**45** DL53
   SW17 . . . .**120** DF89
   SW18 . . . .**120** DD85
   SW19 . . . .**120** DA93
   Gravesend DA12 . . . .**131** GJ87
   Ilford IG6 . . . .**69** EQ55
   Richmond TW9 . . . .**98** CM83
   Southall UB1 . . . .**78** BY74
Trinity Sq, EC3 . . . .**201** N1
Trinity St, E16 off Vincent St . .**86** EG71
   SE1 . . . .**201** J5
   Enfield EN2 . . . .**30** DQ40
Trinity Wk, NW3 . . . .**82** DC65
Trinity Way, E4 . . . .**47** DZ51
   W3 . . . .**80** CS73
Trio Pl, SE1 . . . .**201** J5
Tripps Hill, Ch.St.G. HP8 . . . .**36** AU48
Tripps Hill Cl, Ch.St.G. HP8 . .**36** AU48
Tristan Sq, SE3 . . . .**104** EE83
Tristram Cl, E17 . . . .**67** ED55
Tristram Rd, Brom. BR1 . . . .**124** EF91
Triton Sq, NW1 . . . .**195** K4
Tritton Av, Croy. CR0 . . . . . .**159** DL105
Tritton Rd, SE21 . . . .**122** DR90
Trittons, Tad. KT20 . . . .**173** CW121
Triumph Cl, Grays (Chaff.Hun.)
   RM16 . . . .**109** FW77
   Hayes UB3 . . . .**95** BQ80
Triumph Ho, Bark. IG11 . . . . .**88** EV69
Triumph Rd, E6 . . . .**87** EM72
Trivett Cl, Green. DA9 . . . . .**129** FU85
★ Trocadero Cen, W1 . . . . . .**199** M1
Trocadero Shop Cen, W1 . . . .**83** DK73
Trojan Ct, NW6
   off Willesden La **81** CY66
Trojan Way, Croy. CR0 . . . . .**141** DM104
Trolling Down Hill, Dart. DA2 .**128** FP89
Troon Cl, SE16
   off Fairway Dr **88** EX72
   SE28 off Fairway Dr **88** EX72
Troon St, E1 . . . .**85** DY72
Troopers Dr, Rom. RM3 . . . . .**52** FK49
Trosley Av, Grav. DA11 . . . . .**131** GH89
Trosley Rd, Belv. DA17 . . . . .**106** FA79
Trossachs Rd, SE22 . . . . . .**122** DS85
Trothy Rd, SE1 . . . .**202** C8
Trotsworth Av, Vir.W. GU25 . .**132** AX98
Trotsworth Ct, Vir.W. GU25 . .**132** AX98
Trotters Bottom, Barn. EN5 . .**27** CU37
Trotters La, Wok. (Mimbr.)
   GU24 . . . .**150** AV112
Trotter Way, Epsom KT19
   off Abbots Av **156** CN112
Trott Rd, N10 . . . .**44** DF52
Trotts La, West. TN16 . . . . .**189** EQ127
Trott St, SW11 . . . .**100** DE81
Trotwood, Chig. IG7 . . . .**49** ER51
Trotwood, Brwd. CM15
   off Middleton Rd **54** FY46
Troughton Rd, SE7 . . . .**205** P10
Troutbeck Cl, Slou. SL2 . . . . .**74** AU73
Troutbeck Rd, SE14 . . . .**103** DY81
Trout La, West Dr. UB7 . . . . .**76** BJ73
Trout Ri, Rick. (Loud.) WD3 . . .**22** BH41

Trout Rd, West Dr. UB7 . . . . .**76** BK74
Troutstream Way, Rick. (Loud.)
   WD3 . . . .**22** BH42
Trouville Rd, SW4 . . . .**121** DJ86
Trowbridge Est, E9
   off Osborne Rd **85** DZ65
Trowbridge Rd, E9 . . . .**85** DZ65
   Romford RM3 . . . .**52** FK51
Trowers Way, Red. RH1 . . . .**185** DH131
Trowley Ri, Abb.L. WD5 . . . . . .**7** BS31
Trowlock Av, Tedd. TW11 . . . .**117** CJ93
Trowlock Island, Tedd. TW11 .**117** CK92
Trowlock Way, Tedd. TW11 . .**117** CK93
Troy Cl, Tad. KT20 . . . .**173** CV120
Troy Ct, SE18 . . . .**105** EP77
Troy Rd, SE19 . . . .**122** DR93
Troy Town, SE15 . . . .**102** DU83
Trubshaw Rd, Sthl. UB2
   off Havelock Rd **96** CB76
Truesdale Dr, Uxb. (Hare.)
   UB9 . . . .**58** BJ57
Truesdale Rd, E6 . . . .**87** EM72
Trulock Ct, N17 . . . .**46** DU52
Trulock Rd, N17 . . . .**46** DU52
Truman Cl, Edg. HA8
   off Pavilion Way **42** CP52
Truman's Rd, N16 . . . .**66** DS64
Trumpers Way, W7 . . . .**97** CE76
Trumper Way, Uxb. UB8 . . . . .**76** BJ67
Trumpington Rd, E7 . . . .**68** EF63
Trumps Grn Av, Vir.W. GU25 .**132** AX100
Trumps Grn Cl, Vir.W. GU25
   off Trumps Grn Rd **132** AY99
Trumps Grn Rd, Vir.W. GU25 .**132** AX100
Trumps Mill La, Vir.W. GU25 .**133** AZ100
Trump St, EC2 . . . .**197** J9
Trundlers Way, Bushey
   (Bushey Hth.) WD23 . . . . .**41** CE46
Trundle St, SE1 . . . .**201** H4
Trundleys Rd, SE8 . . . .**203** J10
Trundleys Ter, SE8 . . . .**203** J9
Trunks All, Swan. BR8 . . . . .**147** FB96
Truro Gdns, Ilf. IG1 . . . .**68** EL59
Truro Rd, E17 . . . .**67** DZ56
   N22 . . . .**45** DL52
   Gravesend DA12 . . . .**131** GK90
Truro St, NW5 . . . .**82** DG65
Truro Wk, Rom. RM3
   off Saddleworth Rd **52** FJ51
Truro Way, Hayes UB4
   off Portland Rd **77** BS69
Truslove Rd, SE27 . . . .**121** DN92
Trussley Rd, W6 . . . .**99** CW76
Trustees Way, Uxb. (Denh.)
   UB9 . . . .**57** BF57
Trustons Gdns, Horn. RM11 . .**71** FG59
Trust Rd, Wal.Cr. EN8 . . . . . .**15** DY34
Trust Wk, SE21
   off Peabody Hill **121** DP88
Tryfan Cl, Ilf. IG4 . . . .**68** EK57
Tryon Cres, E9 . . . .**84** DW67
Tryon St, SW3 . . . .**198** D10
Trys Hill, Cher. (Lyne) KT16 . .**133** AZ103
Trystings Cl, Esher (Clay.)
   KT10 . . . .**155** CG107
Tuam Rd, SE18 . . . .**105** ER79
Tubbenden Cl, Orp. BR6 . . . .**145** ES103
Tubbenden Dr, Orp. BR6 . . . .**163** ER105
Tubbenden La, Orp. BR6 . . . .**163** ER105
Tubbenden La S, Orp. BR6 . . .**163** ER104
Tubbs Rd, NW10 . . . .**81** CT68
Tubs Hill Par, Sev. TN13 . . . .**190** FG124
Tubwell Rd, Slou. (Stoke P.)
   SL2 . . . .**74** AV67
Tucker Rd, Cher. (Ott.) KT16 .**151** BD107
Tucker St, Wat. WD18 . . . . . .**24** BW43
Tuckey Gro, Wok. (Ripley)
   GU23 . . . .**167** BF124
Tuck Rd, Rain. RM13 . . . .**89** FG65
Tudor Av, Hmptn. TW12 . . . .**116** CA93
   Romford RM2 . . . .**71** FG55
   Waltham Cross (Chsht.) EN7 .**14** DU31
   Watford WD24 . . . .**24** BX38
   Worcester Park KT4 . . . .**139** CV104
Tudor Cl, N6 . . . .**65** DJ59
   NW3 . . . .**64** DE64
   NW7 . . . .**43** CU51
   NW9 . . . .**62** CQ61
   SW2 off Elm Pk **121** DM86
   Ashford TW15 . . . .**114** BL91
   Banstead SM7 . . . .**173** CY115
   Brentwood CM15 . . . .**55** FZ44
   Chessington KT9 . . . .**156** CL106
   Chigwell IG7 . . . .**49** EN49
   Chislehurst BR7 . . . .**145** EM95
   Cobham KT11 . . . .**154** BZ113
   Coulsdon CR5 . . . .**175** DN118
   Dartford DA1 . . . .**127** FH86
   Epsom KT17 . . . .**157** CT110
   Gravesend (Nthflt.) DA11 . .**130** GE88
   Leatherhead (Bkhm.) KT23 .**170** CA124
   Pinner HA5 . . . .**59** BU57
   South Croydon CR2 . . . .**176** DV115
   Sutton SM3 . . . .**157** CX106
   Wallington SM6 . . . .**159** DJ108
   Waltham Cross (Chsht.) EN7 .**14** DV31
   Woking GU22 . . . .**167** BA117
   Woodford Green IG8 . . . . .**48** EH50
Tudor Ct, E17 . . . .**67** DY59
   Borehamwood WD6 . . . . .**26** CL40
   Feltham TW13 . . . .**116** BW91
   Swanley BR8 . . . .**147** FC101
Tudor Ct N, Wem. HA9 . . . . . .**62** CN64
Tudor Ct S, Wem. HA9 . . . . . .**62** CN64
Tudor Cres, Enf. EN2 . . . .**29** DP39
   Ilford IG6 . . . .**49** EP51
Tudor Dr, Kings.T. KT2 . . . . .**118** CL92
   Morden SM4 . . . .**139** CX100
   Romford RM2 . . . .**71** FG56
   Walton-on-Thames KT12 . .**136** BX102
   Watford WD24 . . . .**24** BX38
Tudor Est, NW10 . . . .**80** CP68
Tudor Gdns, NW9 . . . .**62** CQ61
   SW13 off Treen Av **98** CS83
   W3 . . . .**80** CN72
   Harrow HA3 off Tudor Rd . . .**41** CD54
   Romford RM2 . . . .**71** FG56

Tudor Gdns, Twick. TW1 . . . .**117** CF88
   Upminster RM14 . . . .**72** FQ61
   West Wickham BR4 . . . . .**143** EC104
Tudor Gro, E9 . . . .**84** DW66
   N20 off Church Cres **44** DE48
Tudor Ho, Surb. KT6
   off Lenelby Rd **138** CN102
Tudor La, Wind. (Old Wind.)
   SL4 . . . .**112** AW87
Tudor Manor Gdns, Wat.
   WD25 . . . .**8** BX32
Tudor Ms, Rom. RM1
   off Eastern Rd **71** FF57
Tudor Par, Rick. WD3
   off Berry La **38** BG45
Tudor Pl, W1 . . . .**195** M8
   Mitcham CR4 . . . .**120** DE94
Tudor Rd, E4 . . . .**47** EB51
   E6 . . . .**86** EJ67
   E9 . . . .**84** DV67
   N9 . . . .**46** DV45
   SE19 . . . .**122** DT94
   SE25 . . . .**142** DV99
   Ashford TW15 . . . .**115** BR93
   Barking IG11 . . . .**87** ET67
   Beckenham BR3 . . . .**143** EB97
   Barnet EN5 . . . .**28** DA41
   Hampton TW12 . . . .**116** CA94
   Harrow HA3 . . . .**41** CD54
   Hayes UB3 . . . .**77** BR72
   Hounslow TW3 . . . .**97** CD84
   Kingston upon Thames KT2 .**118** CN94
   Pinner HA5 . . . .**40** BW54
   Southall UB1 . . . .**78** BY73
Tudor Sq, Hayes UB3 . . . .**77** BR71
Tudor St, EC4 . . . .**196** E10
Tudor Wk, Bex. DA5 . . . .**126** EX86
Tudorwalk, Grays RM17
   off Thurloe Wk **110** GA76
Tudor Way, N14 . . . .**45** DK46
   W3 . . . .**98** CN75
   Orpington BR5 . . . .**145** ER100
   Rickmansworth (Mill End)
   WD3 . . . .**38** BG46
   Uxbridge UB10 . . . .**76** BN65
   Waltham Abbey EN9 . . . . .**15** ED33
Tudor Well Cl, Stan. HA7 . . . .**41** CH50
Tudway Rd, SE3 . . . .**104** EH83
Tufnail Rd, Dart. DA1 . . . . . .**128** FM86
TUFNELL PARK, N7 . . . .**65** DK63
◉ Tufnell Park **65** DJ63
Tufnell Pk Rd, N7 . . . .**65** DJ63
   N19 . . . .**65** DJ63
Tufter Rd, Chig. IG7 . . . .**49** ET50
Tufton Gdns, W.Mol. KT8 . . .**136** CB96
Tufton Rd, E4 . . . .**47** EA49
Tufton St, SW1 . . . .**199** N6
Tugboat St, SE28 . . . .**105** ES75
Tugela Rd, Croy. CR0 . . . . . .**142** DR100
Tugela St, SE6 . . . .**123** DZ89
Tugmutton Cl, Orp. BR6
   off Acorn Way **163** EP105
Tuilerie St, E2 . . . .**84** DU68
Tulip Cl, E6
   off Bradley Stone Rd **87** EM71
   Brentwood CM15
   off Poppy Cl **54** FV43
   Croydon CR0 . . . .**143** DX102
   Hampton TW12
   off Partridge Rd **116** BZ93
   Romford RM3
   off Cloudberry Rd **52** FK51
   Southall UB2 off Chevy Rd . .**96** CC75
Tulip Ct, Pnr. HA5 . . . .**60** BW55
Tulip Gdns, Ilf. IG1 . . . .**87** EP65
Tulip Tree Ct, Sutt. SM2
   off The Crescent **158** DA111
Tulip Way, West Dr. UB7 . . . . .**94** BK77
Tull St, Mitch. CR4 . . . .**140** DF101
Tulse Cl, Beck. BR3 . . . .**143** EC97
TULSE HILL, SE21 . . . .**122** DQ88
⇌ Tulse Hill **121** DP89
Tulse Hill, SW2 . . . .**121** DN86
Tulse Hill Est, SW2 . . . .**121** DN86
Tulsemere Rd, SE27 . . . .**122** DQ89
Tulyar Cl, Tad. KT20 . . . .**173** CV120
Tumber St, Epsom (Headley)
   KT18 . . . .**182** CQ125
Tumblewood Rd, Bans. SM7 .**173** CY116
Tumbling Bay, Walt. KT12 . . .**135** BU100
Tummons Gdns, SE25 . . . . .**142** DS96
Tuncombe Rd, N18 . . . .**46** DS49
Tunis Rd, W12 . . . .**81** CV74
Tunley Grn, E14 off Burdett Rd .**85** DZ71
Tunley Rd, NW10 . . . .**80** CS67
   SW17 . . . .**120** DG88
Tunmarsh La, E13 . . . .**86** EJ69
Tunmers End, Ger.Cr. (Chal.St.P.)
   SL9 . . . .**36** AW53
Tunnan Leys, E6 . . . .**87** EN72
Tunnel Av, SE10 . . . .**204** G4
Tunnel Est, Grays RM20 . . . .**109** FT77
Tunnel Gdns, N11 . . . .**45** DJ52
Tunnel Rd, SE16 . . . .**202** F4
   Reigate RH2 off Church St .**184** DA133
Tunnel Wd Cl, Wat. WD17 . . .**23** BT37
Tunnel Wd Rd, Wat. WD17 . . .**23** BT37
Tunstall Av, Ilf. IG6 . . . .**50** EU51
Tunstall Cl, Orp. BR6 . . . . . .**163** ES105
Tunstall Rd, SW9 . . . .**101** DM84
   Croydon CR0 . . . .**142** DS102
Tunstall Wk, Brent. TW8 . . . .**98** CL79
Tunstock Way, Belv. DA17 . . .**106** EY76
Tunworth Cl, NW9 . . . .**62** CQ58
Tunworth Cres, SW15 . . . . .**119** CT86
Tun Yd, SW8 off Peardon St . .**101** DH82
Tupelo Rd, E10 . . . .**67** EB61
Tupwood Ct, Cat. CR3 . . . . .**186** DU125
Tupwood La, Cat. CR3 . . . . .**186** DU125
Tupwood Scrubbs Rd, Cat.
   CR3 . . . .**186** DU128
Turenne Cl, SW18 . . . .**100** DC84

Turfhouse La, Wok. (Chobham)
   GU24 . . . .**150** AS109
Turin Rd, N9 . . . .**46** DW45
Turin St, E2 . . . .**84** DU69
Turkey Oak Cl, SE19 . . . . . .**142** DS95
⇌ Turkey Street **30** DW37
Turkey St, Enf. EN1, EN3 . . . .**30** DV37
Turks Cl, Uxb. UB8
   off Harlington Rd **76** BN69
Turk's Head Yd, EC1 . . . . . .**196** F6
Turks Row, SW3 . . . .**198** F10
Turle Rd, N4 . . . .**65** DM60
   SW16 . . . .**141** DL96
Turlewray Cl, N4 . . . .**65** DM60
Turley Cl, E15 . . . .**86** EE67
Turnagain La, EC4 . . . .**196** F8
   Dartford DA2 . . . .**127** FG90
Turnage Rd, Dag. RM8 . . . . . .**70** EY60
Turnberry Cl, NW4 . . . .**43** CX54
   SE16 off Ryder Dr **102** DV78
Turnberry Ct, Wat. WD19 . . . .**40** BW48
Turnberry Dr, St.Alb. (Brick.Wd.)
   AL2 . . . .**8** BY30
Turnberry Quay, E14 . . . . . .**204** C6
Turnberry Way, Orp. BR6 . . .**145** ER102
Turnbull Cl, Green. DA9 . . . .**129** FS87
Turnbury Cl, SE28 . . . .**88** EX72
Turnchapel Ms, SW4
   off Cedars Rd **101** DH83
Turner Av, N15 . . . .**66** DS56
   Mitcham CR4 . . . .**140** DF95
   Twickenham TW2 . . . . . .**116** CC90
Turner Cl, NW11 . . . .**64** DB58
   SW9 . . . .**101** DP81
   Hayes UB4 off Charville La .**77** BQ68
   Hornchurch RM12
   off Upper Rainham Rd **71** FF61
   Wembley HA0 . . . .**61** CK64
Turner Ct, Dart. DA1 . . . . . .**128** FJ85
Turner Dr, NW11 . . . .**64** DB58
Turner Pl, SW11 off Cairns Rd .**120** DE85
Turner Rd, E17 . . . .**67** EC55
   Bushey WD23 . . . .**24** CC42
   Dartford (Bean) DA2 . . . .**129** FV90
   Edgware HA8 . . . .**62** CM55
   New Malden KT3 . . . . . .**138** CR101
   Slough SL3 . . . .**92** AW75
   Westerham (Bigg.H.) TN16 .**162** EJ112
Turners Cl, Stai. TW18 . . . . .**114** BH92
Turners Ct, Rom. (Abridge) RM4
   off Ongar Rd **34** EV41
Turners Gdns, Sev. TN13 . . .**191** FJ128
Turners Hill, Wal.Cr. (Chsht.)
   EN8 . . . .**15** DX30
Turners La, Walt. KT12 . . . . .**153** BV107
Turners Meadow Way, Beck.
   BR3 . . . .**143** DZ95
Turners Rd, E3 . . . .**85** DZ71
Turner St, E1 . . . .**84** DV71
   E16 . . . .**86** EF72
Turners Way, Croy. CR0 . . . .**141** DN103
Turners Wd, NW11 . . . .**64** DC59
Turners Wd Dr, Ch.St.G. HP8 .**36** AX48
Turneville Rd, W14 . . . .**99** CZ79
Turney Grn, E14 . . . .**85** DZ71
Turney Rd, SE21 . . . .**122** DR87
Turneys Orchard, Rick. (Chorl.)
   WD3 . . . .**21** BD43
TURNFORD, Brox. **15** DZ26
◉ Turnham Green **98** CS77
Turnham Grn Ter, W4 . . . .**98** CS77
Turnham Grn Ter Ms, W4
   off Turnham Grn Ter **98** CS77
Turnham Rd, SE4 . . . .**123** DY85
Turnmill St, EC1 . . . .**196** E5
Turnoak Av, Wok. GU22 . . . .**166** AY120
Turnoak La, Wok. GU22
   off Wych Hill La **166** AY119
Turnpike Cl, SE8 . . . .**103** DZ80
   off Amersham Vale **103** DZ80
Turnpike Dr, Orp. BR6 . . . . .**164** EW109
Turnpike Ho, EC1 . . . .**196** G3
◉ Turnpike Lane **65** DN55
Turnpike La, N8 . . . .**65** DN56
   Sutton SM1 . . . .**158** DC106
   Tilbury (W.Til.) RM18 . . . .**111** GK78
   Uxbridge UB10 . . . .**76** BL69
Turnpike Link, Croy. CR0 . . .**142** DS103
Turnpike Way, Islw. TW7 . . . .**97** CG81
Turnpin La, SE10 . . . .**103** EC79
Turnstone Cl, E13 . . . .**86** EG69
   NW9 off Kestrel Cl **42** CS54
   South Croydon CR2 . . . .**161** DY110
   Uxbridge (Ickhm.) UB10 . . .**59** BP64
Turnstones, The, Grav. DA12 .**131** GK89
   Watford WD25 . . . .**24** BY36
Turp Av, Grays RM16 . . . . . .**110** GC75
Turpentine La, SW1 . . . .**199** J10
Turpin Av, Rom. RM5 . . . .**50** FA52
Turpin Cl, Enf. EN3
   off Government Row **31** EA38
Turpington Cl, Brom. BR2 . . .**144** EL100
Turpington La, Brom. BR2 . . .**144** EL101
Turpin La, Erith DA8 . . . . . .**107** FG80
Turpin Rd, Felt. TW14
   off Staines Rd **115** BT86
Turpins La, Wdf.Grn. IG8 . . . .**49** EM50
Turpin Way, N19 . . . .
   off Elthorne Rd **65** DK61
   Wallington SM6 . . . .**159** DH108
Turquand St, SE17 . . . .**201** J9
Turret Gro, SW4 . . . .**101** DJ83
Turton Rd, Wem. HA0 . . . . . .**62** CL64
Turville St, E2 . . . .**197** P4
Tuscan Rd, SE18 . . . .**105** ER78
Tuskar St, SE10 . . . .**104** EE78
Tustin Est, SE15 . . . .**102** DW79
Tuttlebee La, Buck.H. IG9 . . . .**48** EG47
Tuxford Cl, Borwd. WD6 . . . . .**26** CL38
Twankhams All, Epp. CM16
   off Hemnall St **18** EU30
Tweedale Ct, E15 . . . .**67** EC64
Tweedale Gro, Uxb. UB10 . . .**59** BQ62

Twe - Uve

Tweeddale Rd, Cars. SM5 . . . .**140** DD102
Tweed Glen, Rom. RM1 . . . .**51** FD52
Tweed Grn, Rom. RM1 . . . .**51** FE52
Tweedmouth Rd, E13 . . . .**86** EH68
Tweed Rd, Slou. SL3 . . . .**93** BA79
Tweed Way, Rom. RM1 . . . .**51** FD52
Tweedy CI, Enf. EN1 . . . .**30** DT43
Tweedy Rd, Brom. BR1 . . . . . .**144** EF95
Tweezer's All, WC2 . . . .**196** D10
Twelve Acre CI, Lthd. (Bkhm.)
 KT23 . . . .**170** BZ124
Twelvetrees Cres, E3 . . . .**85** EC70
Twentyman CI, Wdf.Grn. IG8 . .**48** EG50
TWICKENHAM **117** CG89
≷ **Twickenham** **117** CF87
 Twickenham TW1 . . . .**117** CG85
Twickenham Br, Rich. TW9 . . .**117** CJ85
 Twickenham TW1 . . . .**117** CJ85
Twickenham CI, Croy. CR0 . . .**141** DM104
Twickenham Gdns, Grnf. UB6 .**61** CE52
 Harrow HA3 . . . .**41** CE52
Twickenham Rd, E11 . . . .**67** ED61
 Feltham TW13 . . . .**116** BZ90
 Isleworth TW7 . . . .**97** CG83
 Richmond TW9 . . . .**97** CJ84
 Teddington TW11 . . . .**117** CG92
Twickenham Trd Est, Twick.
 TW1 . . . .**117** CF86
Twig Folly CI, E2
 off Roman Rd **85** DX68
Twigg CI, Erith DA8 . . . .**107** FE80
Twilley St, SW18 . . . .**120** DB87
Twine CI, Bark. IG11
 off Thames Rd **88** EV69
Twine Ct, E1 . . . .**84** DW73
Twineham Grn, N12 . . . .**44** DA49
Twine Ter, E3 off Ropery St . .**85** DZ70
Twining Av, Twick. TW2 . . . . .**116** CC90
Twinn Rd, NW7 . . . .**43** CY51
Twinoaks, Cob. KT11 . . . .**154** CA113
Twin Tumps Way, SE28 . . . . . .**88** EU73
Twisden Rd, NW5 . . . .**65** DH63
Twisleton Ct, Dart. DA1
 off Priory Hill **128** FK86
Twitchells La, Beac. (Jordans)
 HP9 . . . .**36** AT51
TWITTON, Sev. **181** FF116
Twitton La, Sev. (Otford)TN14 .**181** FD115
Twitton Meadows, Sev. (Otford)
 TN14 . . . .**181** FE116
Two Rivers Retail Pk, Stai.
 TW18 . . . .**113** BE91
Twybridge Way, NW10 . . . . . .**80** CQ66
Twycross Ms, SE10 . . . .**205** J9
Twyford Abbey Rd, NW10 . . . .**80** CM69
Twyford Av, N2 . . . .**64** DF55
 W3 . . . .**80** CN73
Twyford Cres, W3 . . . .**80** CN74
Twyford Ho, N15
 off Chisley Rd **66** DS58
Twyford PI, WC2 . . . .**196** B8
Twyford Rd, Cars. SM5 . . . . .**140** DD102
 Harrow HA2 . . . .**60** CB60
 Ilford IG1 . . . .**69** EQ64
Twyford St, N1 . . . .**83** DM67
Tyas Rd, E16 . . . .**86** EF70
Tybenham Rd, SW19 . . . .**140** DA97
Tyberry Rd, Enf. EN3 . . . .**30** DV41
Tyburn La, Har. HA1 . . . .**61** CE59
Tyburns, The, Brwd. CM13 . . .**55** GC47
Tyburn Way, W1 . . . .**194** E10
Tycehurst Hill, Loug. IG10 . . . .**33** EM42
Tydcombe Rd, Warl. CR6 . . . .**176** DW119
Tye La, Epsom KT18 . . . .**182** CR127
 Orpington BR6 . . . .**163** EQ106
 Tadworth KT20
 off Dorking Rd **183** CT128
Tyers Est, SE1 . . . .**201** M4
Tyers Gate, SE1 . . . .**201** M4
Tyers St, SE11 . . . .**200** B10
Tyers Ter, SE11 . . . .**101** DM78
Tyeshurst CI, SE2 . . . .**106** EY78
Tyfield CI, Wal.Cr. (Chsht.) EN8 .**14** DW30
Tykeswater La, Borwd. (Elstree)
 WD6 . . . .**25** CJ39
Tylecroft Rd, SW16 . . . .**141** DL96
Tyle Grn, Horn. RM11 . . . .**72** FL56
Tylehurst Gdns, Ilf. IG1 . . . . . .**69** EQ64
Tyle PI, Wind. (Old Wind.) SL4 .**112** AU85
Tyler CI, E2 . . . .**84** DT68
Tyler Gdns, Add. KT15 . . . . . .**152** BJ105
Tyler Gro, Dart. DA1
 off Spielman Rd **108** FM84
Tyler Rd, Sthl. UB2
 off McNair Rd **96** CB76
Tylers CI, Gdse. RH9 . . . .**186** DV130
 Kings Langley WD4 . . . .**6** BL28
 Loughton IG10 . . . .**48** EL45
Tyler's Ct, W1 . . . .**195** M9
Tylers Cres, Horn. RM12 . . . . .**72** FJ64
Tylersfield, Abb.L. WD5 . . . .**7** BT31
Tylers Gate, Har. HA3 . . . .**62** CL58
TYLER'S GREEN, Gdse. **186** DU132
Tylers Grn Rd, Swan. BR8 . . .**147** FC100
Tylers Hill Rd, Chesh. HP5 . . . . .**4** AT30
Tylers Path, Cars. SM5
 off Rochester Rd **158** DF105
Tyler St, SE10 . . . .**104** EE78
Tylers Way, Wat. WD25 . . . . . .**25** CD42
Tyler Way, Brwd. CM14 . . . . . .**54** FV46
Tylney Av, SE19 . . . .**122** DT92
Tylney Rd, E7 . . . .**68** EJ63
 Bromley BR1 . . . .**144** EK96
Tymperley Ct, SW19
 off Windlesham Gro **119** CY88
Tynan CI, Felt. TW14
 off Sandycombe Rd **115** BU88
Tyndale Ct, E14 . . . .**204** B10
Tyndale La, N1 off Upper St .**83** DP66
Tyndale Ter, N1
 off Canonbury La **83** DP66
Tyndall Rd, E10 . . . .**67** EC61
 Welling DA16 . . . .**105** ET83
Tyne CI, Upmin. RM14 . . . .**73** FR58

Tynedale, St.Alb. (Lon.Col.) AL2
 off Thamesdale **10** CM27
Tynedale CI, Dart. DA2 . . . . . .**129** FR88
Tyne Gdns, S.Ock. (Aveley)
 RM15 . . . .**90** FQ73
Tyneham CI, SW11
 off Shirley Gro **100** DG83
Tyneham Rd, SW11 . . . .**100** DG82
Tynemouth CI, E6
 off Covelees Wall **87** EP72
Tynemouth Dr, Enf. EN1 . . . . . .**30** DU38
Tynemouth Rd, N15 . . . .**66** DT56
 SE18 . . . .**105** ET78
 Mitcham CR4 . . . .**120** DG94
Tynemouth St, SW6 . . . .**100** DC82
Tyne St, E1 off Old Castle St . .**84** DT72
Tynwald Ho, SW6 . . . .**100** DB81
Type St, E2 . . . .**85** DX68
Tyrawley Rd, SW6 . . . .**100** DB81
Tyre La, NW9
 off Sheaveshill Av **62** CS56
Tyrell CI, Har. HA1 . . . .**61** CE63
Tyrell Ct, Cars. SM5 . . . .**158** DF105
Tyrell Ri, Brwd. CM14 . . . .**54** FW50
Tyrells CI, Upmin. RM14 . . . . . .**72** FN61
Tyrols Rd, SE23
 off Wastdale Rd **123** DX88
Tyrone Rd, E6 . . . .**87** EM68
Tyron Way, Sid. DA14 . . . .**125** ES91
Tyrrell Av, Well. DA16 . . . .**126** EU85
Tyrrell Rd, SE22 . . . .**102** DU84
Tyrrells Hall CI, Grays RM17 . .**110** GD79
Tyrrell Sq, Mitch. CR4 . . . . . .**140** DE95
TYRRELL'S WOOD, Lthd. **172** CM123
Tyrrel Way, NW9 . . . .**63** CT59
Tyrwhitt Rd, SE4 . . . .**103** EA82
Tysea Hill, Rom. (Stap.Abb.)
 RM4 . . . .**51** FF45
Tysoe Av, Enf. EN3 . . . .**31** DZ36
Tysoe St, EC1 . . . .**196** D3
Tyson Rd, SE23 . . . .**122** DW87
Tyssen Pas, E8 . . . .**84** DT65
Tyssen PI, S.Ock. RM15 . . . . . .**91** FW69
Tyssen Rd, N16 . . . .**66** DT62
Tyssen St, E8 . . . .**84** DT65
 N1 off Hoxton St **84** DS68
Tytherton Rd, N19 . . . .**65** DK62

U

Uamvar St, E14 . . . .**85** EB71
Uckfield Gro, Mitch. CR4 . . . .**140** DG95
Uckfield Rd, Enf. EN3 . . . .**31** DX37
Udall Gdns, Rom. RM5 . . . .**50** FA51
Udall St, SW1 . . . .**199** L9
Udney Pk Rd, Tedd. TW11 . . .**117** CG92
Uffington Rd, NW10 . . . .**81** CU67
 SE27 . . . .**121** DN91
Ufford CI, Har. HA3
 off Ufford Rd **40** CB52
Ufford Rd, Har. HA3 . . . .**40** CB52
Ufford St, SE1 . . . .**200** E4
Ufton Gro, N1 . . . .**84** DR66
Ufton Rd, N1 . . . .**84** DR66
Uhura Sq, N16 . . . .**66** DS62
Ujima Ct, SW16
 off Sunnyhill Rd **121** DL91
Ullathorne Rd, SW16 . . . .**121** DJ91
Ulleswater Rd, N14 . . . .**45** DL49
Ullin St, E14
 off St. Leonards Rd **85** EC71
Ullswater Business Pk, Couls.
 CR5 . . . .**175** DL116
Ullswater CI, SW15 . . . .**118** CR91
 Bromley BR1 . . . .**124** EE93
 Hayes UB4 . . . .**77** BS68
Ullswater Ct, Har. HA2
 off Oakington Av **60** CA59
Ullswater Cres, SW15 . . . . . .**118** CR91
 Coulsdon CR5 . . . .**175** DL116
Ullswater Rd, SE27 . . . .**121** DP89
 SW13 . . . .**99** CU80
Ullswater Way, Horn. RM12 . . .**71** FG64
Ulstan CI, Cat. (Wold.) CR3 . . .**177** EA123
Ulster Gdns, N13 . . . .**46** DQ49
Ulster PI, NW1 . . . .**195** H4
Ulster Ter, NW1 . . . .**195** H4
Ulundi Rd, SE3 . . . .**104** EE79
Ulva Rd, SW15
 off Ravenna Rd **119** CX85
Ulverscroft Rd, SE22 . . . .**122** DT85
Ulverstone Rd, SE27 . . . .**121** DP89
Ulverston Rd, E17 . . . .**47** ED54
Ulwin Av, W.Byf. (Byfleet)
 KT14 . . . .**152** BL113
Ulysses Rd, NW6 . . . .**63** CZ64
Umberston St, E1
 off Hessel St **84** DV72
Umbria St, SW15 . . . .**119** CU86
Umfreville Rd, N4 . . . .**65** DP58
Undercliff Rd, SE13 . . . .**103** EA83
UNDERHILL, Barn. **28** DA43
Underhill, Barn. EN5 . . . .**28** DA43
Underhill Pk Rd, Reig. RH2 . . .**184** DA131
Underhill Pas, NW1
 off Camden High St **83** DH67
Underhill Rd, SE22 . . . .**122** DV86
Underhill St, NW1
 off Camden High St **83** DH67
Underne Av, N14 . . . .**45** DH47
UNDERRIVER, Sev. **191** FN130
Underriver Ho Rd, Sev. (Undrvr.)
 TN15 . . . .**191** FP130
Undershaft, EC3 . . . .**197** M9
Undershaw Rd, Brom. BR1 . . .**124** EE90
Underwood, Croy. (New Adgtn.)
 CR0 . . . .**161** EC106
Underwood, The, SE9 . . . .**125** EM89
Underwood Rd, E1 . . . .**84** DU70
 E4 . . . .**47** EB50
 Caterham CR3 . . . .**186** DS126
 Woodford Green IG8 . . . . . .**48** EK52
Underwood Row, N1 . . . .**197** J2
Underwood St, N1 . . . .**197** J2
Undine Rd, E14 . . . .**204** C8

Undine St, SW17 . . . .**120** DF92
Uneeda Dr, Grnf. UB6 . . . .**79** CD67
Unicorn Ho, Brom. BR1
 off Elmfield Rd **144** EG97
Unicorn Wk, Green. DA9 . . . .**129** FT85
Union CI, E11 . . . .**67** ED63
Union Cotts, E15
 off Welfare Rd **86** EE66
Union Ct, EC2 . . . .**197** M8
 Richmond TW9 off Eton St .**118** CL85
Union Dr, E1 off Canal CI **85** DY70
Union Gro, SW8 . . . .**101** DK82
Union Rd, N11 . . . .**45** DK51
 SW4 . . . .**101** DK82
 SW8 . . . .**101** DK82
 Bromley BR2 . . . .**144** EK99
 Croydon CR0 . . . .**142** DQ101
 Northolt UB5 . . . .**78** CA68
 Wembley HA0 . . . .**80** CL65
Union Sq, N1 . . . .**84** DQ67
Union St, E15 . . . .**85** EC67
 SE1 . . . .**200** G3
 Barnet EN5 . . . .**27** CY42
 Kingston upon Thames
 KT1 . . . .**137** CK96
Union Wk, E2 . . . .**197** N2
🏥 **United Elizabeth Garrett**
 Anderson Hosp & Soho
 Hosp for Women, NW1 .**195** N3
Unity CI, NW10 . . . .**81** CU65
 SE19 off Crown Dale **122** DQ98
 Croydon (New Adgtn.) CR0 .**161** EB109
Unity Rd, Enf. EN3 . . . .**30** DW37
Unity Trd Est, Wdf.Grn. IG8 . . .**68** EK55
Unity Way, SE18 . . . .**104** EK76
Unity Wf, SE1 . . . .**202** A4
University CI, NW7 . . . .**43** CT52
 Bushey WD23 . . . .**24** CA42
★ **University Coll London**,
 WC1 . . . .**195** M4
University Gdns, Bex. DA5 . . .**126** EZ87
🏥 **University Hosp Lewisham**,
 SE13 . . . .**123** EB85
★ **University of London**,
 WC1 . . . .**195** N5
★ **University of London - Royal**
 Holloway Coll, Egh. TW20 .**112** AX93
🏥 **University of London - UCL -**
 Uni Coll Hosp, WC1 . . . . .**195** L5
University PI, Erith DA8
 off Belmont Rd **107** FB80
University Rd, SW19 . . . .**120** DD93
University St, WC1 . . . .**195** L5
University Way, E16 . . . .**87** EN73
 Dartford DA1 . . . .**108** FJ84
Unwin Av, Felt. TW14 . . . .**115** BS85
Unwin CI, SE15 . . . .**102** DU79
Unwin Rd, SW7 . . . .**198** A6
 Isleworth TW7 . . . .**97** CE83
Upbrook Ms, W2
 off Chilworth St **82** DC72
Upcerne Rd, SW10 . . . .**100** DC80
Upchurch CI, SE20 . . . .**122** DV94
Up Cor, Ch.St.G. HP8 . . . .**36** AW47
Up Cor CI, Ch.St.G. HP8 . . . . . .**36** AV47
Upcroft Av, Edg. HA8 . . . .**42** CQ50
Updale CI, Pot.B. EN6 . . . .**11** CY33
Updale Rd, Sid. DA14 . . . .**125** ET91
Upfield, Croy. CR0 . . . .**142** DV103
Upfield Rd, W7 . . . .**79** CF70
Upgrove Manor Way, SW2
 off Trinity Ri **121** DN87
Uphall Rd, Ilf. IG1 . . . .**69** EP64
Upham Pk Rd, W4 . . . .**98** CS77
Uphill Dr, NW7 . . . .**42** CS50
 NW9 . . . .**62** CQ57
Uphill Gro, NW7 . . . .**42** CS49
Uphill Rd, NW7 . . . .**42** CS49
Upland Ct Rd, Rom. RM3 . . . . .**52** FM54
Upland Dr, Hat. AL9 . . . .**12** DB25
Upland Ms, SE22
 off Upland Rd **122** DU85
Upland Rd, E13 off Sutton Rd .**86** EF70
 SE22 . . . .**122** DU85
 Bexleyheath DA7 . . . .**106** EZ83
 Caterham CR3 . . . .**177** EB121
 Epping CM16 . . . .**17** ET25
 South Croydon CR2 . . . . . .**160** DR106
 Sutton SM2 . . . .**158** DD108
Uplands, The, Ger.Cr. SL9 . . . .**56** AY60
 Loughton IG10 . . . .**33** EM41
 Ruislip HA4 . . . .**59** BU60
 St. Albans (Brick.Wd.) AL2 . . .**8** BY30
Uplands Av, E17
 off Blackhorse La **47** DX54
Uplands Business Pk, E17 . . . .**47** DX54
Uplands CI, SW14
 off Monroe Dr **118** CP85
 Gerrards Cross SL9 . . . .**56** AY60
 Sevenoaks TN13 . . . .**190** FF123
Uplands Dr, Lthd. (Oxshott)
 KT22 . . . .**155** CD113
Uplands End, Wdf.Grn. IG8 . . .**48** EL52
Uplands Pk Rd, Enf. EN2 . . . . .**29** DN41
Uplands Rd, N8 . . . .**65** DM57
 Barnet EN4 . . . .**44** DG46
 Bromley BR1 . . . .**144** EH98
 Kenley CR8 . . . .**176** DQ116
 Orpington BR6 . . . .**146** EV102
 Romford RM6 . . . .**70** EX55
 Woodford Green IG8 . . . . . .**48** EL52
Uplands Way, N21 . . . .**29** DN43
 Sevenoaks TN13 . . . .**190** FF123
Upland Way, Epsom KT18 . . .**173** CW118
UPMINSTER **72** FQ62
≷ **Upminster** **72** FQ61
⊖ **Upminster** **72** FQ61
⊖ **Upminster Bridge** **72** FN61
Upminster Rd, Horn.
 RM11, RM12 . . . .**72** FM61
 Upminster RM14 . . . .**72** FM61
Upminster Rd N, Rain. RM13 .**90** FJ69
Upminster Rd S, Rain. RM13 . .**89** FG70

Upminster Trd Pk, Upmin.
 RM14 . . . .**73** FX59
⊖ **Upney**, Horn. RM12 . . . .**87** ET66
Upney CI, Horn. RM12
 off Tylers Cres **72** FJ64
Upney La, Bark. IG11 . . . .**87** ES65
Upnor Way, SE17 . . . .**201** N10
Uppark Dr, Ilf. IG2 . . . .**69** EQ58
Upper Abbey Rd, Belv. DA17 .**106** EZ77
Upper Addison Gdns, W14 . . . .**99** CY75
Upper Bk St, E14 . . . .**204** B3
Upper Bardsey Wk, N1
 off Clephane Rd **84** DQ65
Upper Belgrave St, SW1 . . . .**198** G6
Upper Berkeley St, W1 . . . . . .**194** D9
Upper Beulah Hill, SE19 . . . .**142** DS95
Upper Bourne End La, Hem.H.
 HP1 . . . .**5** BA25
Upper Brentwood Rd, Rom.
 RM2 . . . .**72** FJ56
Upper Br Rd, Red. RH1 . . . . .**184** DE134
Upper Brighton Rd, Surb. KT6 .**137** CK100
Upper Brockley Rd, SE4 . . . .**103** DZ82
Upper Brook St, W1 . . . .**198** F1
Upper Butts, Brent. TW8 . . . . .**97** CJ79
Upper Caldy Wk, N1
 off Clephane Rd **84** DQ65
Upper Camelford Wk, W11
 off Lancaster Rd **81** CY72
Upper Cavendish Av, N3 . . . . .**64** DA55
Upper Cheyne Row, SW3 . . . .**100** DE79
Upper Ch Hill, Green. DA9 . . .**129** FS85
Upper Clapton Rd, E5 . . . .**66** DV60
UPPER CLAPTON, E5 . . . .**66** DV60
Upper Clarendon Wk, W11
 off Lancaster Rd **81** CY72
Upper Cornsland, Brwd. CM14 .**54** FX48
Upper Ct Rd, Cat. (Wold.) CR3 .**177** EA123
 Epsom KT19 . . . .**156** CQ111
Upper Dengie Wk, N1
 off Popham Rd **84** DQ67
Upper Dr, West. (Bigg.H.) **178** EJ118
Upper Dunnymans, Bans. SM7
 off Basing Rd **157** CZ114
UPPER EDMONTON, N18 . . . .**46** DU51
UPPER ELMERS END, Beck. .**143** DZ100
Upper Elmers End Rd, Beck.
 BR3 . . . .**143** DY98
Upper Fairfield Rd, Lthd.
 KT22 . . . .**171** CH121
Upper Fm Rd, W.Mol. KT8 . . .**136** BZ98
Upper Fosters, NW4
 off New Brent St **63** CW57
Upper Grn E, Mitch. CR4 . . . .**140** DF97
Upper Grn W, Mitch. CR4
 off London Rd **140** DF97
Upper Grenfell Wk, W11
 off Whitchurch Rd **81** CX73
Upper Grosvenor St, W1 . . . .**198** F1
Upper Grotto Rd, Twick. TW1 .**117** CF89
Upper Grd, SE1 . . . .**200** D2
Upper Gro, SE25 . . . .**142** DS98
Upper Gro Rd, Belv. DA17 . . .**106** EZ79
Upper Guild Hall, Green.
 (Bluewater) DA9
 off Bluewater Parkway . . .**129** FU88
Upper Gulland Wk, N1
 off Clephane Rd **84** DQ65
UPPER HALLIFORD, Shep. . . .**135** BS97
≷ **Upper Halliford** **135** BS96
Upper Halliford Bypass, Shep.
 TW17 . . . .**135** BS99
Upper Halliford Grn, Shep. TW17 .**135** BS98
Upper Halliford Rd, Shep.
 TW17 . . . .**135** BS96
Upper Ham Rd, Kings.T. KT2 .**117** CK91
 Richmond TW10 . . . .**117** CK91
Upper Handa Wk, N1
 off Clephane Rd **84** DR65
Upper Hawkwell Wk, N1
 off Popham Rd **84** DQ67
Upper High St, Epsom KT17 .**156** CS113
Upper Highway, Abb.L. WD5 . .**7** BR33
 Kings Langley WD4 . . . .**7** BR33
Upper Hill Ri, Rick. WD3 . . . . .**22** BH44
Upper Hitch, Wat. WD19 . . . . .**40** BY44
UPPER HOLLOWAY, N19 . . . .**65** DJ62
≷ **Upper Holloway** **65** DK61
Upper Holly Hill Rd, Belv.
 DA17 . . . .**107** FB78
Upper James St, W1 . . . .**195** L10
Upper John St, W1 . . . .**195** L10
Upper Lismore Wk, N1
 off Clephane Rd **84** DQ65
Upper Mall, W6 . . . .**99** CU78
Upper Marsh, SE1 . . . .**200** C6
Upper Montagu St, W1 . . . . . .**194** D6
Upper Mulgrave Rd, Sutt.
 SM2 . . . .**157** CY108
Upper N St, E14 . . . .**85** EA71
UPPER NORWOOD, SE19 . . .**122** DP94
Upper Paddock Rd, Wat. WD19 .**24** BY44
Upper Palace Rd, E.Mol. KT8 .**136** CC97
Upper Pk, Loug. IG10 . . . .**32** EK42
Upper Pk Rd, N11 . . . .**45** DH50
 NW3 . . . .**64** DF64
 Belvedere DA17 . . . .**107** FB77
 Bromley BR1 . . . .**144** EH95
 Kingston upon Thames KT2 .**118** CN93
Upper Phillimore Gdns, W8 . .**100** DA75
Upper Pillory Down, Cars.
 SM5 . . . .**158** DG113
Upper Pines, Bans. SM7 . . . .**174** DF117
Upper Rainham Rd, Horn.
 RM12 . . . .**71** FF63
Upper Ramsey Wk, N1
 off Clephane Rd **84** DR65
Upper Rawreth Wk, N1
 off Popham Rd **84** DQ67
Upper Richmond Rd, SW15 . . .**99** CY84
Upper Richmond Rd W, SW14 .**98** CP84
 Richmond TW10 . . . .**98** CP84
Upper Rd, E13 . . . .**86** EG69
 Uxbridge (Denh.) UB9 . . . . .**58** BD59
 Wallington SM6 . . . .**159** DK106

Upper Rose Gallery, Green.
 (Bluewater) DA9
 off Bluewater Parkway . . .**129** FU88
Upper Ryle, Brwd. CM14 . . . . .**54** FV45
Upper St. Martin's La, WC2 . .**195** P10
Upper Sawley Wd, Bans.
 SM7 . . . .**157** CZ114
Upper Selsdon Rd, S.Croy.
 CR2 . . . .**160** DT108
Upper Sheppey Wk, N1
 off Clephane Rd **84** DQ66
Upper Sheridan Rd, Belv. DA17
 off Coleman Rd **106** FA77
Upper Shirley Rd, Croy. CR0 .**142** DW103
Upper Shott, Wal.Cr. (Chsht.)
 EN7 . . . .**14** DT26
Upper Sq, Islw. TW7 . . . .**97** CG83
Upper Sta Rd, Rad. WD7 . . . . .**25** CG35
Upper St, N1 . . . .**83** DN68
Upper Sunbury Rd, Hmptn.
 TW12 . . . .**136** BY95
Upper Sutton La, Houns. TW5 .**96** CA80
Upper Swaines, Epp. CM16 . . .**17** ET30
UPPER SYDENHAM, SE26 . . .**122** DU91
Upper Tachbrook St, SW1 . . .**199** K8
Upper Tail, Wat. WD19 . . . .**40** BY48
Upper Talbot Wk, W11
 off Lancaster Rd **81** CY72
Upper Teddington Rd, Kings.T.
 KT1 . . . .**137** CG93
Upper Ter, NW3 . . . .**64** DC62
Upper Thames St, EC4 . . . . . .**196** G10
Upper Thames Wk, Green.
 (Bluewater) DA9
 off Bluewater Parkway . . .**129** FU88
Upper Tollington Pk, N4 . . . . . .**65** DN60
Upperton Rd, Sid. DA14 . . . . .**125** ET92
Upperton Rd E, E13
 off Inniskilling Rd **86** EJ69
Upperton Rd W, E13 . . . .**86** EJ69
UPPER TOOTING, SW17 . . . .**120** DE90
Upper Tooting Pk, SW17 . . . .**120** DF89
Upper Tooting Rd, SW17 . . . .**120** DF91
Upper Town Rd, Grnf. UB6 . . . .**78** CB70
Upper Tulse Hill, SW2 . . . . . .**121** DM87
Upper Vernon Rd, Sutt. SM1 .**158** DD106
UPPER WALTHAMSTOW, E17 .**67** EB56
Upper Walthamstow Rd, E17 . .**67** ED56
≷ **Upper Warlingham** **176** DU118
Upper W St, Reig. RH2 . . . . . .**183** CZ134
Upper Wickham La, Well.
 DA16 . . . .**106** EV80
Upper Wimpole St, W1 . . . . . .**195** H6
Upper Woburn PI, WC1 . . . . . .**195** N3
Upper Woodcote Village, Pur.
 CR8 . . . .**159** DK112
Uppingham Av, Stan. HA7 . . . .**41** CH53
Upsdell Av, N13 . . . .**45** DN51
UPSHIRE, Wal.Abb. **16** EJ32
Upshirebury Grn, Wal.Abb. EN9
 off Horseshoe Hill **16** EK33
Upshire Rd, Wal.Abb. EN9 . . . .**16** EF32
Upshott La, Wok. GU22 . . . . . .**167** BF117
Upstall St, SE5 . . . .**101** DP81
UPTON, E7 . . . .**86** EH66
UPTON, Slou. **92** AU76
Upton, Wok. GU21 . . . .**166** AV117
Upton Av, E7 . . . .**86** EG66
Upton CI, NW2
 off Somerton Rd **63** CY62
 Bexley DA5 . . . .**126** EZ86
 St. Albans (Park St.) AL2 . . . .**9** CD25
 Slough SL1 . . . .**92** AT76
Upton Ct, SE20
 off Blean Gro **122** DW94
Upton Ct Rd, Slou. SL3 . . . . . .**92** AU76
Upton Dene, Sutt. SM2 . . . . . .**158** DB108
Upton Gdns, Har. HA3 . . . .**61** CH57
🏥 **Upton Hosp**, Slou. SL1 . . . . .**92** AT76
Upton La, E7 . . . .**86** EG66
Upton Lo CI, Bushey WD23 . . .**40** CC45
UPTON PARK, E6 . . . .**86** EJ67
UPTON PARK, Slou. **92** AT76
⊖ **Upton Park** **86** EH67
Upton Pk, Slou. SL1 . . . .**92** AT76
Upton Pk Rd, E7 . . . .**86** EH66
Upton Rd, N18 . . . .**46** DU50
 SE18 . . . .**105** EQ79
 Bexley DA5 . . . .**126** EZ86
 Bexleyheath DA6 . . . .**106** EY84
 Hounslow TW3 . . . .**96** CA83
 Slough SL1 . . . .**92** AU76
 Thornton Heath CR7 . . . . .**142** DR96
 Watford WD18 . . . .**23** BV42
Upton Rd S, Bex. DA5 . . . . . .**126** EZ86
Upway, N12 . . . .**44** DE52
 Gerrards Cross (Chal.St.P.)
 SL9 . . . .**37** AZ53
Upwood Rd, SE12 . . . .**124** EG86
 SW16 . . . .**141** DL95
Urban Av, Horn. RM12 . . . .**72** FJ62
Urlwin St, SE5 . . . .**102** DQ79
Urlwin Wk, SW9 . . . .**101** DN82
Urmston Dr, SW19 . . . .**119** CY88
Ursula Ms, N4 off Portland Ri .**66** DQ60
Ursula St, SW11 . . . .**100** DE81
Urswick Gdns, Dag. RM9
 off Urswick Rd **88** EY66
Urswick Rd, E9 . . . .**66** DW64
 Dagenham RM9 . . . .**88** EX66
Usborne Ms, SW8 . . . .**101** DM80
Usher Rd, E3 . . . .**85** DZ68
Usherwood CI, Tad. KT20 . . . .**182** CP131
Usk Rd, SW11 . . . .**100** DC84
 South Ockendon (Aveley)
 RM15 . . . .**90** FQ72
Usk St, E2 . . . .**85** DX69
Utopia Village, NW1
 off Chalcot Rd **82** DG67
Uvedale CI, Croy. (New Adgtn.)
 CR0 off Uvedale Cres **161** ED111
Uvedale Cres, Croy. (New Adgtn.)
 CR0 . . . .**161** ED111
Uvedale Rd, Dag. RM10 . . . . . .**70** FA62
 Enfield EN2 . . . .**30** DR43
 Oxted RH8 . . . .**188** EF129

Uverdale Rd, SW10 . . . . .100 DC80
UXBRIDGE 76 BK66
✈ Uxbridge 76 BK66
Uxbridge Gdns, Felt. TW13
 off Marlborough Rd 116 BX89
UXBRIDGE MOOR, Iver 76 BG67
UXBRIDGE MOOR, Uxb. 76 BG67
Uxbridge Rd, W3 . . . . .80 CL73
 W5 . . . . .80 CL73
 W7 . . . . .79 CF74
 W12 . . . . .81 CU74
 W13 . . . . .79 CF74
 Feltham TW13 . . . . .116 BW89
 Hampton (Hmptn.H.) TW12 .116 CA91
 Harrow HA3 . . . . .40 CC52
 Hayes UB4 . . . . .78 BW73
 Iver SL0 . . . . .74 AY71
 Kingston upon Thames KT1 .137 CK98
 Pinner HA5 . . . . .40 CB52
 Rickmansworth WD3 . . . . . .37 BF47
 Slough SL1, SL2, SL3 . . . . . .92 AU75
 Southall UB1 . . . . .78 CA74
 Stanmore HA7 . . . . .41 CF51
 Uxbridge UB10 . . . . .76 BN69
Uxbridge St, W8 . . . . .82 DA74
Uxendon Cres, Wem. HA9 . . . .62 CL60
Uxendon Hill, Wem. HA9 . . . .62 CM60

V

Vache La, Ch.St.G. HP8 . . . . .36 AW47
Vache Ms, Ch.St.G. HP8 . . . . .36 AW47
Vaillant Rd, Wey. KT13 . . . . .153 BQ105
Valance Av, E4 . . . . .48 EF46
Valan Leas, Brom. BR2 . . . . .144 EE97
Vale, The, N10 . . . . .44 DG53
 N14 . . . . .45 DK45
 NW11 . . . . .63 CX62
 SW3 . . . . .100 DD79
 W3 . . . . .80 CR74
 Brentwood CM14 . . . . .54 FW46
 Coulsdon CR5 . . . . .159 DK114
 Croydon CR0 . . . . .143 DX103
 Feltham TW14 . . . . .115 BV86
 Gerrards Cross (Chal.St.P.)
   SL9 . . . . .36 AX53
 Hounslow TW5 . . . . .96 BY79
 Ruislip HA4 . . . . .60 BW63
 Sunbury-on-Thames TW16
   off Ashridge Way 115 BU93
 Woodford Green IG8 . . . . . .48 EG52
Vale Av, Borwd. WD6 . . . . . . .26 CP43
Vale Border, Croy. CR0 . . . . .161 DX111
Vale Cl, N2 off Church Vale . . .64 DF55
 W9 off Maida Vale 82 DC69
 Brentwood CM15 . . . . .54 FT43
 Gerrards Cross (Chal.St.P.)
   SL9 . . . . .36 AX53
 Orpington BR6 . . . . .163 EN105
 Weybridge KT13 . . . . .135 BR104
 Woking GU21 . . . . .166 AY116
Vale Cotts, SW15
 off Kingston Vale 118 CR91
Vale Ct, W9 off Maida Vale . . .82 DC69
 Weybridge KT13 . . . . .135 BR104
Vale Cres, SW15 . . . . .118 CS90
Vale Cft, Esher (Clay.) KT10 . .155 CE108
 Pinner HA5 . . . . .60 BY57
Vale Dr, Barn. EN5 . . . . .27 CZ42
Vale End, SE22 off Grove Vale .102 DS84
Vale Gro, N4 . . . . .66 DQ59
 W3 off The Vale 80 CR74
 Slough SL1 . . . . .92 AS76
Vale Ind Est, Wat. WD18 . . . .39 BQ46
Vale La, W3 . . . . .80 CN71
Valence Av, Dag. RM8 . . . . . .70 EX62
Valence Circ, Dag. RM8 . . . . .70 EX62
Valence Dr, Wal.Cr. (Chsht.)
 EN7 . . . . .14 DU28
★ Valence Ho Mus, Dag.
 RM8 . . . . .70 EY61
Valence Rd, Erith DA8 . . . . . .107 FD80
Valence Wd Rd, Dag. RM8 . . .70 EX62
Valencia Rd, Stan. HA7 . . . . . .41 CJ49
Valency Cl, Nthwd. HA6 . . . . .39 BT49
Valentia Pl, SW9
 off Brixton Sta Rd 101 DN84
Valentine Av, Bex. DA5 . . . . .126 EY89
Valentine Ct, SE23 . . . . .123 DX89
Valentine Pl, SE1 . . . . .200 F4
Valentine Rd, E9 . . . . .85 DX65
 Harrow HA2 . . . . .60 CC62
Valentine Row, SE1 . . . . .200 F5
Valentines Rd, Ilf. IG1 . . . . . .69 EP60
Valentines Way, Rom. RM7 . . .71 FE61
Valentine Way, Ch.St.G. HP8 . .36 AX48
Valentyne Cl, Croy. (New Adgtn.)
 CR0 . . . . .162 EE111
Vale of Health, NW3
 off East Heath Rd 64 DD62
Vale Par, SW15
 off Kingston Vale 118 CR91
Valerian Way, E15 . . . . .86 EE69
Valerie Ct, Bushey WD23 . . . .40 CC45
 Sutton SM2 off Stanley Rd .158 DB108
Vale Ri, NW11 . . . . .63 CZ60
Vale Rd, E7 . . . . .86 EH65
 N4 . . . . .66 DQ59
 Bromley BR1 . . . . .145 EN96
 Bushey WD23 . . . . .24 BY43
 Dartford DA1 . . . . .127 FH88
 Epsom KT19 . . . . .157 CT105
 Esher (Clay.) KT10 . . . . . . .155 CE109
 Gravesend (Nthflt.) DA11 . .130 GD87
 Mitcham CR4 . . . . .141 DK97
 Sutton SM1 . . . . .158 DB105
 Weybridge KT13 . . . . .135 BR104
 Worcester Park KT4 . . . . . .157 CU105
Vale Rd N, Surb. KT6 . . . . . . .138 CL103
Vale Rd S, Surb. KT6 . . . . . . .138 CL103
Vale Row, N5 off Gillespie Rd .65 DP62
Vale Royal, N7 . . . . .83 DL66
Vale St, SE27 . . . . .122 DR90

Valeswood Rd, Brom. BR1 . .124 EF92
Vale Ter, N4 . . . . .66 DQ58
Valetta Gro, E13 . . . . .86 EG68
Valetta Rd, W3 . . . . .98 CS75
Valette St, E9 . . . . .84 DV65
Valiant Cl, Nthlt. UB5
 off Ruislip Rd 78 BX69
 Romford RM7 . . . . .50 FA54
Valiant Ho, SE7 . . . . .104 EJ78
Valiant Path, NW9
 off Blundell Rd 42 CS52
Valiant Way, E6 . . . . .87 EM71
Vallance Rd, E1 . . . . .84 DU70
 E2 . . . . .84 DU69
 N22 . . . . .45 DJ54
Vallentin Rd, E17 . . . . .67 EC56
Valley Av, N12 . . . . .44 DD49
Valley Cl, Dart. DA1 . . . . . . .127 FF86
 Loughton IG10 . . . . .33 EM44
 Pinner HA5 off Alandale Dr .39 BV54
 Waltham Abbey EN9 . . . . . . .15 EC32
Valley Ct, Cat. CR3
 off Beechwood Gdns 176 DU122
 Kenley CR8 off Hayes La . .160 DQ114
Valley Dr, NW9 . . . . .62 CN58
 Gravesend DA12 . . . . .131 GK91
 Sevenoaks TN13 . . . . .191 FH125
Valleyfield Rd, SW16 . . . . . .121 DM92
Valley Flds Cres, Enf. EN2 . . .29 DN40
★ Valley Gdns, The, Egh.
 TW20 . . . . .132 AS96
Valley Gdns, SW19 . . . . .120 DD94
 Wembley HA0 . . . . .80 CM66
Valley Gro, SE7 . . . . .104 EJ78
Valley Hill, Loug. IG10 . . . . . .48 EL45
Valley Link Ind Est, Enf. EN3 . .31 DY44
Valley Ms, Twick. TW1
 off Cross Deep 117 CG89
Valley Ri, Wat. WD25 . . . . .7 BV33
Valley Rd, SW16 . . . . .121 DM91
 Belvedere DA17 . . . . .107 FB77
 Bromley BR2 . . . . .144 EE96
 Dartford DA1 . . . . .127 FF86
 Erith DA8 . . . . .107 FD77
 Kenley CR8 . . . . .176 DR115
 Longfield (Fawk.Grn.) DA3 .149 FV100
 Orpington BR5 . . . . .146 EV95
 Rickmansworth WD3 . . . . . .22 BG43
 Uxbridge UB10 . . . . .76 BL68
Valley Side, E4 . . . . .47 EA47
Valley Side Par, E4
 off Valley Side 47 EA47
Valley Vw, Barn. EN5 . . . . . . .27 CY44
 Greenhithe DA9 . . . . .129 FV86
 Waltham Cross (Chsht.) EN7 .14 DQ26
 Westerham (Bigg.H.) TN16 .178 EJ118
Valley Vw Gdns, Ken. CR8
 off Godstone Rd 176 DS115
Valley Wk, Croy. CR0 . . . . . .142 DW103
 Rickmansworth (Crox.Grn.)
 WD3 . . . . .23 BQ43
Valley Way, Ger.Cr. SL9 . . . . .56 AW58
Valliere Rd, NW10 . . . . .81 CV69
Valliers Wd Rd, Sid. DA15 . . .125 ER88
Vallis Way, W13 . . . . .79 CG71
 Chessington KT9 . . . . .155 CK105
Valmar Rd, SE5 . . . . .102 DQ81
Val McKenzie Av, N7
 off Parkside Cres 65 DN62
Valnay St, SW17 . . . . .120 DF92
Valognes Av, E17 . . . . .47 DY53
Valonia Gdns, SW18 . . . . . . .119 CZ86
Vambery Rd, SE18 . . . . .105 EQ79
Vanbrough Cres, Nthlt. UB5 . .78 BW67
Vanbrugh Cl, E16
 off Fulmer Rd 86 EK71
Vanbrugh Dr, Walt. KT12 . . . .136 BW101
Vanbrugh Flds, SE3 . . . . . . .104 EF80
Vanbrugh Hill, SE3 . . . . .104 EF78
 SE10 . . . . .104 EF78
Vanbrugh Pk, SE3 . . . . .104 EF80
Vanbrugh Pk Rd, SE3 . . . . . .104 EF80
Vanbrugh Pk Rd W, SE3 . . . .104 EF80
Vanbrugh Rd, W4 . . . . .98 CR76
Vanbrugh Ter, SE3 . . . . .104 EF81
Vanburgh Cl, Orp. BR6 . . . . .145 ES102
Vancouver Cl, Epsom KT19 . .156 CQ111
 Orpington BR6 . . . . .163 ET105
Vancouver Rd, SE23 . . . . . . .123 DY89
 Edgware HA8 . . . . .42 CP53
 Hayes UB4 . . . . .78 BV70
 Richmond TW10 . . . . .117 CJ91
Vanderbilt Rd, SW18 . . . . . . .120 DC88
Vanderville Gdns, N2
 off Tarling Rd 44 DC54
Vandome Cl, E16 . . . . .86 EH72
Vandon Pas, SW1 . . . . .199 L6
Vandon St, SW1 . . . . .199 L6
Van Dyck Av, N.Mal. KT3 . . .138 CR101
Vandyke Cl, SW15 . . . . .119 CX87
 Redhill RH1 . . . . .184 DF131
Vandyke Cross, SE9 . . . . . . .124 EL85
Vandy St, EC2 . . . . .197 M5
Vane Cl, NW3 . . . . .64 DD63
 Harrow HA3 . . . . .62 CM58
Vanessa Cl, Belv. DA17 . . . . .106 FA78
Vanessa Wk, Grav. DA12 . . . .131 GM92
Vanessa Way, Bex. DA5 . . . . .127 FD90
Vane St, SW1 . . . . .199 L8
Vanguard Cl, E16 . . . . .86 EG71
 Croydon CR0 . . . . .141 DP102
 Romford RM7 . . . . .51 FB54
Vanguard St, SE8 . . . . .103 EA81
Vanguard Way, Cat. CR3
 off Slines Oak Rd 177 EB121
 Wallington SM6 . . . . .159 DL108
 Warlingham CR6 . . . . .177 EB121
Vanneck Sq, SW15 . . . . .119 CU85
Vanner Pt, E9 off Wick Rd 85 DX65
Vanners Par, W.Byf. (Byfleet)
 KT14 off Brewery La 152 BL113
Vanoc Gdns, Brom. BR1 . . . .124 EG90
Vanquisher Wk, Grav. DA12 .131 GM90
Vansittart Rd, E7 . . . . .68 EF63
Vansittart St, SE14 . . . . .103 DY80
Vanston Pl, SW6 . . . . .100 DA80
Vantage Ms, E14 . . . . .204 E3

Vantage Pl, W8
 off Abingdon Rd 100 DA76
Vant Rd, SW17 . . . . .120 DF92
Varcoe Rd, SE16 . . . . .102 DV78
Varden Cl, W3 . . . . .80 CR72
Varden St, E1 . . . . .84 DV72
Vardens Rd, SW11 . . . . .100 DD84
Varley Par, NW9 . . . . .62 CS56
Varley Rd, E16 . . . . .86 EH72
Varley Way, Mitch. CR4 . . . . .140 DD96
Varna Rd, SW6 . . . . .99 CY80
 Hampton TW12 . . . . .136 CB95
Varndell St, NW1 . . . . .195 K2
Varney Cl, Wal.Cr. (Chsht.) EN7 .14 DU27
Varsity Dr, Twick. TW1 . . . . . .117 CE85
Varsity Row, SW14
 off William's La 98 CQ82
Vartry Rd, N15 . . . . .66 DR58
Vassall Rd, SW9 . . . . .101 DN80
Vauban Est, SE16 . . . . .202 A7
Vauban St, SE16 . . . . .202 A7
Vaughan Av, NW4 . . . . .63 CU57
 W6 . . . . .99 CT77
 Hornchurch RM12 . . . . .72 FK63
Vaughan Cl, Hmptn. TW12
 off Oak Av 116 BY93
Vaughan Gdns, Ilf. IG1 . . . . . .69 EM59
Vaughan Rd, E15 . . . . .86 EF65
 SE5 . . . . .102 DQ83
 Harrow HA1 . . . . .60 CC59
 Thames Ditton KT7 . . . . . . .137 CH101
 Welling DA16 . . . . .105 ET82
Vaughan St, SE16 . . . . .203 M5
Vaughan Way, E1 . . . . .202 B1
Vaughan Williams Cl, SE8
 off Watson's St 103 EA80
Vaux Cres, Walt. KT12 . . . . . .153 BV107
VAUXHALL, SE11 . . . . .101 DL78
≷ Vauxhall 101 DL79
⊖ Vauxhall 101 DL78
Vauxhall Br, SE1 . . . . .101 DL78
 SW1 . . . . .101 DL78
Vauxhall Br Rd, SW1 . . . . . . .199 L8
Vauxhall Gdns, S.Croy. CR2 . .160 DQ107
Vauxhall Gdns Est, SE11 . . . .101 DM78
Vauxhall Gro, SW8 . . . . .101 DL79
Vauxhall Pl, Dart. DA1 . . . . . .128 FL87
Vauxhall St, SE11 . . . . .101 DM78
Vauxhall Wk, SE11 . . . . .200 B10
Vawdrey Cl, E1 . . . . .84 DW70
Veals Mead, Mitch. CR4 . . . .140 DE95
Vectis Gdns, SW17
 off Vectis Rd 121 DH93
Vectis Rd, SW17 . . . . .121 DH93
Veda Rd, SE13 . . . . .103 EA84
Vega Cres, Nthwd. HA6 . . . . .39 BT50
Vegal Cres, Egh. (Eng.Grn.)
 TW20 . . . . .112 AW92
Vega Rd, Bushey WD23 . . . . .40 CC45
Veldene Way, Har. HA2 . . . . . .60 BZ62
Velde Way, SE22
 off East Dulwich Gro 122 DS85
Velletri Ho, E2 . . . . .85 DX68
Vellum Dr, Cars. SM5 . . . . . .140 DG104
Venables Cl, Dag. RM10 . . . . .71 FB63
Venables St, NW8 . . . . .194 A6
Vencourt Pl, W6 . . . . .99 CU76
Venetian Rd, SE5 . . . . .102 DQ82
Venetia Rd, N4 . . . . .65 DP58
 W5 . . . . .97 CK75
Venette Cl, Rain. RM13 . . . . . .89 FH71
Venner Rd, SE26 . . . . .122 DW93
Venners Cl, Bexh. DA7 . . . . .107 FE82
Venn St, SW4 . . . . .101 DJ84
Ventnor Av, Stan. HA7 . . . . . .41 CH53
Ventnor Dr, N20 . . . . .44 DB48
Ventnor Gdns, Bark. IG11 . . . .87 ES65
Ventnor Rd, SE14 . . . . .103 DX80
 Sutton SM2 . . . . .158 DB108
Venton Cl, Wok. GU21 . . . . . .166 AV117
Ventura Pk, St.Alb. AL2 . . . . . .9 CF29
Venture Cl, Bex. DA5 . . . . . . .126 EY87
Venue St, E14 . . . . .85 EC71
Venus Hill, Hem.H. (Bov.) HP3 . .5 BA28
Venus Rd, SE18 . . . . .105 EM76
Veny Cres, Horn. RM12 . . . . .72 FK64
Vera Av, N21 . . . . .29 DN43
Vera Ct, Wat. WD19 . . . . .40 BX45
Vera Lynn Cl, E7
 off Dames Rd 68 EG63
Vera Rd, SW6 . . . . .99 CY81
Verbena Cl, E16
 off Pretoria Rd 86 EF70
 South Ockendon RM15 . . . . .91 FW72
 West Drayton UB7
   off Magnolia St 94 BK78
Verbena Gdns, W6 . . . . .99 CU78
Verdant La, SE6 . . . . .124 EE88
Verdayne Av, Croy. CR0 . . . . .143 DX102
Verdayne Gdns, Warl. CR6 . .176 DW116
Verderers Rd, Chig. IG7 . . . . .50 EU50
Verdun Rd, SE18 . . . . .106 AU79
 SW13 . . . . .99 CU79
Verdure Cl, Wat. WD25 . . . . . .8 BY32
Vereker Dr, Sun. TW16 . . . . .135 BU97
Vereker Rd, W14 . . . . .99 CY78
Vere Rd, Loug. IG10 . . . . .33 EQ42
Vere St, W1 . . . . .195 H9
Verity Cl, W11 . . . . .81 CY72
Vermeer Gdns, SE15
 off Elland Rd 102 DW84
Vermont Cl, Enf. EN2 . . . . . . .29 DP42
Vermont Rd, SE19 . . . . .122 DR93
 SW18 . . . . .120 DB86
 Sutton SM1 . . . . .140 DB104
Verney Gdns, Dag. RM9 . . . . .70 EY63
Verney Rd, SE16 . . . . .102 DU79
 Dagenham RM9 . . . . .70 EY64
 Slough SL3 . . . . .93 BA77
Verney St, NW10 . . . . .62 CR62
Verney Way, SE16 . . . . .102 DV78
Vernham Rd, SE18 . . . . .105 EQ79
Vernon Av, E12 . . . . .69 EM63
 SW20 . . . . .139 CX96
 Enfield EN3 . . . . .31 DY36

Vernon Av, Wdf.Grn IG8 . . . . .48 EH52
Vernon Cl, Cher. (Ott.) KT16 .151 BD107
 Epsom KT19 . . . . .156 CQ107
 Orpington BR5 . . . . .146 EV97
Vernon Ct, Stan. HA7
 off Vernon Dr 41 CH53
Vernon Cres, Barn. EN4 . . . . .28 DG44
 Brentwood CM13 . . . . .55 GA48
Vernon Dr, Cat. CR3 . . . . . . .176 DQ122
 Stanmore HA7 . . . . .41 CG53
 Uxbridge (Hare.) UB9 . . . . . .38 BJ53
Vernon Ms, E17 off Vernon Rd .67 DZ56
 W14 off Vernon St 99 CY77
Vernon Pl, WC1 . . . . .196 A7
Vernon Ri, WC1 . . . . .196 C2
 Greenford UB6 . . . . .61 CD64
Vernon Rd, E3 . . . . .85 DZ68
 E11 . . . . .68 EE60
 E15 . . . . .86 EE66
 E17 . . . . .67 DZ57
 N8 . . . . .65 DN55
 SW14 . . . . .98 CR83
 Bushey WD23 . . . . .24 BY43
 Feltham TW13 . . . . .115 BT89
 Ilford IG3 . . . . .69 ET60
 Romford RM5 . . . . .51 FC50
 Sutton SM1 . . . . .158 DC106
 Swanscombe DA10 . . . . . . .130 FZ86
Vernon Sq, WC1 . . . . .196 C2
Vernon St, W14 . . . . .99 CY77
Vernon Wk, Tad. KT20 . . . . . .173 CX120
Vernon Yd, W11
 off Portobello Rd 81 CZ73
Veroan Rd, Bexh. DA7 . . . . . .106 EY82
Verona Cl, Uxb. UB8 . . . . .76 BJ72
Verona Dr, Surb. KT6 . . . . . . .138 CL103
Verona Rd, E7 off Upton La . . .86 EG66
Veronica Gdns, SW16 . . . . . .141 DJ95
Veronica Rd, SW17 . . . . .121 DH90
Veronique Gdns, Ilf. IG6 . . . . .69 EP57
Verralls, Wok. GU22 . . . . . . .167 BB117
Verran Rd, SW12
 off Balham Gro 121 DH87
Versailles Rd, SE20 . . . . .122 DU94
Verulam Av, E17 . . . . .67 DZ58
 Purley CR8 . . . . .159 DJ112
Verulam Bldgs, WC1 . . . . . . .196 C6
Verulam Pas, Wat. WD17 . . . .23 BV40
Verulam Rd, Grnf. UB6 . . . . . .78 CA70
Verulam St, WC1 . . . . .196 D6
Verwood Dr, Barn. EN4 . . . . . .28 DF41
Verwood Rd, Har. HA2 . . . . . .40 CC54
Veryan, Wok. GU21 . . . . .166 AU117
Veryan Cl, Orp. BR5 . . . . . . .146 EW98
Vesey Path, E14
 off East India Dock Rd 85 EB72
Vespan Rd, W12 . . . . .99 CU75
Vesta Rd, SE4 . . . . .103 DY82
Vestris Rd, SE23 . . . . .123 DX89
Vestry Ms, SE5 . . . . .102 DS81
Vestry Rd, E17 . . . . .67 EB56
 SE5 . . . . .102 DS81
Vestry St, N1 . . . . .197 K2
Vetch Cl, Felt. TW14 . . . . . . .115 BT88
Vevey St, SE6 . . . . .123 DZ89
Vexil Cl, Purf. RM19 . . . . .109 FR77
Veysey Gdns, Dag. RM10 . . . .70 FA62
Viaduct Pl, E2 off Viaduct St . .84 DV69
Viaduct St, E2 . . . . .84 DV69
Vian Av, Enf. EN3 . . . . .31 DY35
Vian St, SE13 . . . . .103 EB83
Vibart Gdns, SW2 . . . . .121 DM87
Vibart Wk, N1 off Outram Pl . .83 DL67
Vicarage Av, SE3 . . . . .104 EG81
 Egham TW20 . . . . .113 BB93
Vicarage Cl, Brwd. CM14 . . . .54 FS49
 Erith DA8 . . . . .107 FC79
 Northolt UB5 . . . . .78 BZ66
 Potters Bar EN6 . . . . .12 DF30
 Ruislip HA4 . . . . .59 BR59
 Tadworth KT20 . . . . .173 CY124
 Worcester Park KT4 . . . . . .138 CS102
Vicarage Ct, W8
 off Vicarage Gate 100 DB75
 Egham TW20 . . . . .113 BB93
 Feltham TW14 . . . . .115 BQ87
Vicarage Cres, SW11 . . . . . .100 DD81
 Egham TW20 . . . . .113 BB92
Vicarage Dr, SW14 . . . . .118 CR85
 Barking IG11 . . . . .87 EQ66
 Beckenham BR3 . . . . .143 EA95
 Gravesend (Nthflt.) DA11 . .130 GC86
Vicarage Fm Rd, Houns.
 TW3, TW5 . . . . .96 BY82
Vicarage Flds, Walt. KT12 . . .136 BW100
Vicarage Fld Shop Cen, Bark.
 IG11 . . . . .87 EQ66
Vicarage Gdns, SW14
 off Vicarage Rd 118 CQ85
 W8 . . . . .82 DA74
 Mitcham CR4 . . . . .140 DE97
Vicarage Gate, W8 . . . . .82 DB75
Vicarage Gate Ms, Tad. KT20 .173 CY124
Vicarage Gro, SE5 . . . . .102 DR81
Vicarage Hill, West. TN16 . . .189 ER126
Vicarage La, E6 . . . . .87 EM69
 E15 . . . . .86 EE66
 Chigwell IG7 . . . . .49 EQ47
 Epsom KT17 . . . . .157 CU109
 Hemel Hempstead (Bov.) HP3 . .5 BB26
 Ilford IG1 . . . . .69 ER60
 Kings Langley WD4 . . . . .6 BM29
 Leatherhead KT22 . . . . . . .171 CH122
 Sevenoaks (Dunt.Grn.) TN13
   off London Rd 181 FD119
 Staines (Laleham) TW18 . .134 BH97
 Staines (Wrays.) TW19 . . . .112 AY88
Vicarage Path, N8 . . . . .65 DL59
Vicarage Pl, Slou. SL1 . . . . . . .92 AU76
Vicarage Rd, E10 . . . . .67 EB60
 E15 . . . . .86 EF66
 N17 . . . . .46 DU52
 NW4 . . . . .63 CU58
 SE18 . . . . .105 EQ78

Vicarage Rd, SW14 . . . . .118 CQ85
 Bexley DA5 . . . . .127 FB88
 Croydon CR0 . . . . .141 DN104
 Dagenham RM10 . . . . .89 FB65
 Egham TW20 . . . . .113 BB93
 Epping CM16 . . . . .18 EW29
 Hornchurch RM12 . . . . .71 FG60
 Kingston upon Thames KT1 .137 CK96
 Kingston upon Thames
   (Hmptn.W.) KT1 . . . . .137 CJ95
 Staines TW18 . . . . .113 BE91
 Sunbury-on-Thames TW16 .115 BT92
 Sutton SM1 . . . . .158 DB105
 Teddington TW11 . . . . .117 CG92
 Twickenham TW2 . . . . .117 CE89
 Twickenham (Whitton) TW2 .116 CC86
 Watford WD18 . . . . .23 BU44
 Woking GU22 . . . . .167 AZ121
 Woodford Green IG8 . . . . . .48 EL52
Vicarage Sq, Grays RM17 . . .110 GA79
Vicarage Wk, Reig. RH2
 off Chartway 184 DB134
Vicarage Way, NW10 . . . . . . .62 CR62
 Gerrards Cross SL9 . . . . . . .57 AZ58
 Harrow HA2 . . . . .60 CA59
 Slough (Colnbr.) SL3 . . . . . .93 BC80
Vicars Br Cl, Wem. HA0 . . . . .80 CL68
Vicars Cl, E9 off Northiam St . .84 DW67
 E15 . . . . .86 EG67
 Enfield EN1 . . . . .30 DS40
Vicars Hill, SE13 . . . . .103 EB84
Vicars Moor La, N21 . . . . .45 DN45
Vicars Oak Rd, SE19 . . . . . . .122 DS93
Vicars Rd, NW5 . . . . .64 DG64
Vicars Wk, Dag. RM8 . . . . . . .70 EV62
Viceroy Cl, N2 off Market Pl . . .64 DE56
Viceroy Ct, NW8
 off Prince Albert Rd 82 DE68
Viceroy Par, N2 off High Rd . . .64 DE55
Viceroy Rd, SW8 . . . . .101 DL81
Vickers Cl, Wall. SM6
 off Hurricane Rd 159 DM108
Vickers Dr N, Wey. KT13 . . . .152 BL110
Vickers Dr S, Wey. KT13 . . . .152 BL111
Vickers Rd, Erith DA8 . . . . . .107 FD78
Vickers Way, Houns. TW4 . . .116 BY85
Victor App, Horn. RM12
 off Abbs Cross Gdns 72 FK60
Victor Cl, Horn. RM12 . . . . . .72 FK60
Victor Ct, Horn. RM12 . . . . . .72 FK60
 Rainham RM13
   off Askwith Rd 89 FD68
Victor Gdns, Horn. RM12 . . . .72 FK60
Victor Gro, Wem. HA0 . . . . . .80 CL66
≷ Victoria 199 J8
⊖ Victoria 199 J7
★ Victoria & Albert Mus,
 SW7 . . . . .198 A7
Victoria Arc, SW1
 off Terminus Pl 101 DH76
Victoria Av, E6 . . . . .86 EK67
 EC2 . . . . .197 N7
 N3 .43 CZ53
 Barnet EN4 . . . . .28 DD42
 Gravesend DA12
   off Sheppy Pl 131 GH87
 Grays RM16 . . . . .110 GC75
 Hounslow TW3 . . . . .116 BZ85
 Romford RM5 . . . . .51 FB51
 South Croydon CR2 . . . . . .160 DQ110
 Surbiton KT6 . . . . .137 CK101
 Uxbridge UB10 . . . . .77 BP66
 Wallington SM6 . . . . .140 DG104
 Wembley HA9 . . . . .80 CP65
 West Molesey KT8 . . . . . . .136 CA97
Victoria Cl, Barn. EN4 . . . . . . .28 DD42
 Grays RM16 . . . . .110 GC75
 Hayes UB3
   off Commonwealth Av 77 BR72
 Rickmansworth WD3
   off Nightingale Rd 38 BK45
 Waltham Cross EN8 . . . . . . .15 DX30
 West Molesey KT8
   off Victoria Av 136 CA97
 Weybridge KT13 . . . . .135 BR104
★ Victoria Coach Sta, SW1 . .199 H9
Victoria Cotts, Rich. TW9 . . . .98 CM81
Victoria Ct, Wem. HA9 . . . . . .80 CN65
Victoria Cres, N15 . . . . .66 DS57
 SE19 . . . . .122 DS93
 SW19 . . . . .119 CZ94
 Iver SL0 . . . . .75 BG73
Victoria Dock Rd, E16 . . . . . .86 EE72
Victoria Dr, SW19 . . . . .119 CX87
 Dartford (S.Darenth) DA4 . .149 FR96
Victoria Embk, EC4 . . . . .200 B1
 SW1 . . . . .200 A4
 WC2 . . . . .200 B1
★ Victoria Embankment Gdns,
 WC2 . . . . .200 A1
Victoria Gdns, W11 . . . . .82 DA74
 Hounslow TW5 . . . . .96 BY81
 Westerham (Bigg.H.) TN16 .178 EJ115
Victoria Gro, N12 . . . . .44 DD51
 W8 . . . . .100 DC76
Victoria Gro Ms, W2
 off Ossington St 82 DB73
Victoria Hill Rd, Swan. BR8 . .147 FF95
H Victoria Hosp, Rom. RM1 . .71 FF56
Victoria Ind Est, NW10 . . . . . .80 CS69
Victoria Ind Pk, Dart. DA1 . . .128 FL85
Victoria La, Barn. EN5 . . . . . .27 CZ42
 Hayes UB3 . . . . .95 BQ78
Victoria Ms, NW6 . . . . .82 DA67
 SW4 off Victoria Ri 101 DH84
 SW18 . . . . .120 DC88
Victorian Gro, N16 . . . . .66 DS62
Victorian Rd, N16 . . . . .66 DS62
★ Victoria Park, E9 . . . . .85 DY66
Victoria Pk, E9 . . . . .85 DY66
Victoria Pk Rd, E9 . . . . .84 DW67
Victoria Pk Sq, E2 . . . . .84 DW69
Victoria Pas, NW8
 off Cunningham Pl 82 DD70

Victoria Pas, Wat. WD18 .....23 BV42
Victoria Pl, SW1 ....199 J8
 Epsom KT17 ....156 CS112
 Richmond TW9 ....117 CK85
Victoria Pt, E13
 off Victoria Rd 86 EG68
Victoria Retail Pk, Ruis. HA4 .60 BY64
Victoria Ri, SW4 ....101 DH83
Victoria Rd, E4 ....48 EE46
 E11 ....68 EE63
 E13 ....86 EG68
 E17 ....47 EC54
 E18 ....48 EH54
 N4 ....65 DM59
 N9 ....46 DT49
 N15 ....66 DU56
 N18 ....46 DT49
 N22 ....45 DJ53
 NW4 ....63 CW56
 NW6 ....81 CZ67
 NW7 ....43 CT50
 NW10 ....80 CR71
 SW14 ....98 CR83
 W3 ....80 CR71
 W5 ....79 CH71
 W8 ....100 DC76
 Addlestone KT15 ....152 BK105
 Barking IG11 ....87 EP65
 Barnet EN4 ....28 DD42
 Bexleyheath DA6 ....106 FA84
 Brentwood CM14 ....54 FW49
 Bromley BR2 ....144 EK99
 Buckhurst Hill IG9 ....48 EK47
 Bushey WD23 ....40 CB46
 Chislehurst BR7 ....125 EN92
 Coulsdon CR5 ....175 DK115
 Dagenham RM10 ....71 FB66
 Dartford DA1 ....128 FK85
 Erith DA8 ....107 FE79
 Feltham TW13 ....115 BV88
 Gravesend (Nthflt.) DA11 .131 GF88
 Kingston upon Thames KT1 .138 CM96
 Mitcham CR4 ....120 DE94
 Romford RM1 ....71 FE58
 Ruislip HA4 ....60 BW64
 Sevenoaks TN13 ....191 FH125
 Sidcup DA15 ....125 ET90
 Slough SL2 ....74 AV74
 Southall UB2 ....96 BZ76
 Staines TW18 ....113 BE90
 Surbiton KT6 ....137 CK100
 Sutton SM1 ....158 DD106
 Teddington TW11 ....117 CG93
 Twickenham TW1 ....117 CG87
 Uxbridge UB8
 off New Windsor St 76 BJ66
 Waltham Abbey EN9 .....15 EC34
 Watford WD24 ....23 BV38
 Weybridge KT13 ....135 BR104
 Woking GU22 ....166 AY117
Victoria Scott Ct, Dart. DA1 .177 FE83
Victoria Sq, SW1 ....199 J6
Victoria Sta, SW1 ....199 J8
 off Kew Br Rd 98 CM79
Victoria St, E15 ....86 EE66
 SW1 ....199 K7
 Belvedere DA17 ....106 EZ78
 Egham (Eng.Grn.) TW20 ...112 AW93
 Slough SL1 ....92 AT75
Victoria Ter, N4 ....65 DN60
 NW10 off Old Oak La ...80 CS69
 Harrow HA1 ....61 CE60
★ Victoria Twr, SW1 ....199 P6
Victoria Vil, Rich. TW9 ....98 CM83
Victoria Way, SE7 ....205 P10
 Weybridge KT13 ....135 BR104
 Woking GU21 ....166 AY117
Victoria Wf, E14 ....203 L1
Victoria Yd, E1
 off Fairclough St 84 DU72
Victor Rd, NW10 ....81 CV69
 SE20 ....123 DX94
 Harrow HA2 ....60 CC55
 Teddington TW11 ....117 CE91
Victors Cres, Brwd. CM13 ...55 GB47
Victors Dr, Hmptn. TW12 ..116 BY93
Victor Smith Ct, St.Alb. AL2 ...8 CA31
Victors Way, Barn. EN5 ....27 CZ41
Victor Vil, N9 ....46 DR48
Victor Wk, NW9 ....42 CS53
 Hornchurch RM12
 off Abbs Cross Gdns 72 FK60
Victory Av, Mord. SM4 ....140 DC99
Victory Business Cen, Islw.
 TW7 ....97 CF83
Victory Cl, Grays (Chaff.Hun.)
 RM16 ....109 FW77
Victory Pk Rd, Add. KT15 ..152 BJ105
Victory Pl, E14 off Northey St .85 DY73
 SE17 ....201 J8
 SE19 off Westow St 122 DS93
Victory Rd, E11 ....68 EH56
 SW19 ....120 DC94
 Chertsey KT16 ....134 BG102
 Rainham RM13 ....89 FG68
Victory Rd Ms, SW19
 off Victory Rd 120 DC94
Victory Wk, SE8 off Ship St .103 EA81
Victory Way, SE16 ....203 L5
 Dartford DA2 ....108 FQ84
 Hounslow TW5 ....96 BW78
 Romford RM7 ....51 FB54
Vidler Cl, Chess. KT9
 off Merritt Gdns 155 CJ107
Vienna Cl, Ilf. IG5 ....68 EK55
View, The, SE2 ....106 EY78
View Cl, N6 ....64 DF59
 Chigwell IG7 ....49 ER50
 Harrow HA1 ....61 CD56
 Westerham (Bigg.H.) TN16 .178 EJ116
Viewfield Cl, Har. HA3 ....62 CL59
Viewfield Rd, SW18 ....119 CZ86
 Bexley DA5 ....126 EW88

Viewland Rd, SE18 ....105 ET78
Viewlands Av, West. TN16 ...179 ES120
View Rd, N6 ....64 DF59
 Potters Bar EN6 ....12 DC32
Viga St, N21 ....29 DN44
Vigerons Way, Grays RM16 ..111 GH77
Viggory La, Wok. GU21 ....166 AW115
Vigilant Cl, SE26 ....122 DU91
Vigilant Way, Grav. DA12 ..131 GL92
Vignoles Rd, Rom. RM7 ....70 FA59
Vigo St, W1 ....199 K1
Viking Cl, E3 off Selwyn Rd ..85 DY68
Viking Ct, SW6 ....100 DA79
Viking Gdns, E6
 off Jack Dash Way 86 EL70
Viking Pl, E10 ....67 DZ60
Viking Rd, Grav. (Nthflt.)
 DA11 ....130 GC90
 Southall UB1 ....78 BY73
Viking Way, Brwd. CM15 ...54 FV45
 Erith DA8 ....107 FC76
 Rainham RM13 ....89 FG70
Villa Ct, Dart. DA1
 off Greenbanks 128 FL89
Villacourt Rd, SE18 ....106 EU80
Village, The, SE7 ....104 EJ79
 Greenhithe (Bluewater)
 DA9 ....129 FT87
Village Arc, E4 off Station Rd .47 ED46
Village Cl, E4 ....47 EC50
 NW3 off Ornan Rd 64 DE64
 Weybridge KT13
 off Oatlands Dr 135 BR104
Village Ct, E17
 off Eden Rd 67 EB57
Village Gdns, Epsom KT17 .157 CT110
Village Grn Av, West. (Bigg.H.)
 TN16 ....178 EL117
Village Grn Rd, Dart. DA1 ..107 FG84
Village Grn Way, West. (Bigg.H.)
 TN16 off Main Rd 178 EL117
Village Hts, Wdf.Grn. IG8 ...48 EF50
Village Ms, NW9 ....62 CR61
Village Pk Cl, Enf. EN1 ....30 DS44
Village Rd, N3 ....43 CY53
 Egham TW20 ....133 BC97
 Enfield EN1 ....30 DS44
 Uxbridge (Denh.) UB9 ....57 BF61
Village Row, Sutt. SM2 ....158 DA108
Village Way, NW10 ....62 CR63
 SE21 ....122 DR86
 Amersham HP7 ....20 AX40
 Ashford TW15 ....114 BM91
 Beckenham BR3 ....143 EA96
 Pinner HA5 ....60 BY59
 South Croydon CR2 ....160 DU113
Village Way E, Har. HA2 ....60 BZ59
Villa Rd, SW9 ....101 DN83
Villas Rd, SE18 ....105 EQ77
Villa St, SE17 ....102 DR78
Villier Ct, Uxb. UB8
 off Villier St 76 BK68
Villiers, The, Wey. KT13 ...153 BR107
Villiers Av, Surb. KT5 ....138 CM99
 Twickenham TW2 ....116 BZ88
Villiers Cl, E10 ....67 EA61
 Surbiton KT5 ....138 CM98
Villiers Ct, N20
 off Buckingham Av 44 DC45
Villiers Gro, Sutt. SM2 ....157 CX109
Villiers Path, Surb. KT5 ...138 CL99
Villiers Rd, NW2 ....81 CU65
 Beckenham BR3 ....143 DX96
 Isleworth TW7 ....97 CE82
 Kingston upon Thames KT1 .138 CM97
 Southall UB1 ....78 BZ74
 Watford WD19 ....24 BY44
Villiers St, WC2 ....199 P1
Villier St, Uxb. UB8 ....76 BK68
Vincam Cl, Twick. TW2 ....116 CA87
Vincent Av, Cars. SM5 ....158 DD111
 Croydon CR0 ....161 DY111
 Surbiton KT5 ....138 CP102
Vincent Cl, SE16 ....203 K5
 Barnet EN5 ....28 DA41
 Bromley BR2 ....144 EH98
 Chertsey KT16 ....133 BE101
 Esher KT10 ....136 CB104
 Ilford IG6 ....49 EQ51
 Leatherhead (Fetch.) KT22 .170 CB123
 Sidcup DA15 ....125 ES88
 Waltham Cross (Chsht.) EN8 .15 DY28
 West Drayton UB7 ....94 BN79
Vincent Dr, Shep. TW17 ...135 BS97
 Uxbridge UB10
 off Birch Cres 76 BM67
Vincent Gdns, NW2 ....63 CT62
Vincent Gm, Couls. CR5
 off High Rd 174 DF120
Vincent Ms, E3 ....85 EA68
Vincent Rd, E4 ....47 ED51
 N15 ....66 DQ56
 N22 ....45 DN54
 SE18 ....105 EP77
 W3 ....98 CQ76
 Chertsey KT16 ....133 BE101
 Cobham (Stoke D'Ab.) KT11 .170 BY116
 Coulsdon CR5 ....175 DJ116
 Croydon CR0 ....142 DS101
 Dagenham RM9 ....88 EY66
 Hounslow TW4 ....96 BX82
 Isleworth TW7 ....97 CD81
 Kingston upon Thames KT1 .138 CN97
 Rainham RM13 ....90 FJ70
 Wembley HA0 ....80 CM66
Vincent Row, Hmptn. (Hmptn.H.)
 TW12 ....116 CC93
Vincent's Cl, Couls. CR5 ..174 DF120
Vincents Path, Nthlt. UB5
 off Arnold Rd 78 BY65
Vincent Sq, SW1 ....199 L8
 Westerham (Bigg.H.) TN16 .162 EJ113
Vincent St, E16 ....86 EF71
 SW1 ....199 M8
Vincent Ter, N1 ....83 DP68
Vince St, EC1 ....197 L3
Vine, The, Sev. TN13 ....191 FH124

Vine Av, Sev. TN13 ....191 FH124
Vine Cl, Stai. TW19 ....114 BG85
 Surbiton KT5 ....138 CM100
 Sutton SM1 ....140 DC104
 West Drayton UB7 ....94 BN77
Vine Ct, E1
 off Whitechapel Rd 84 DU71
 Harrow HA3 ....62 CL58
Vine Ct Rd, Sev. TN13 .....191 FJ124
Vine Gdns, Ilf. IG1 ....69 EQ64
Vinegar All, E17 ....67 EB56
Vinegar St, E1 ....202 D2
Vinegar Yd, SE1 ....201 M4
Vine Gro, Uxb. UB10 ....76 BN66
Vine Hill, EC1 ....196 D5
Vine La, SE1 ....201 N3
 Uxbridge UB10 ....76 BM67
Vine Pl, W5 off The Common .80 CL72
 Hounslow TW3 ....96 CB84
Viner Cl, Walt. KT12 ....136 BW100
Vineries, The, N14 ....29 DJ43
 Enfield EN1 ....30 DS41
Vineries Bk, NW7 ....43 CV50
Vineries Cl, Dag. RM9
 off Heathway 88 FA65
 West Drayton UB7 ....94 BN79
Vine Rd, E15 ....86 EF66
 SW13 ....99 CT83
 East Molesey KT8 ....136 CC98
 Orpington BR6 ....163 ET107
 Slough (Stoke P.) SL2 ....74 AT65
Vines Av, N3 ....44 DB53
Vine Sq, W14 ....99 CZ78
Vine St, EC3 ....197 P10
 W1 ....199 L1
 Romford RM7 ....71 FC57
 Uxbridge UB8 ....76 BK67
Vine St Br, EC1 ....196 E5
Vine Way, Brwd. CM14 ....54 FW46
Vine Yd, SE1 ....201 J4
Vineyard, The, Rich. TW10 .118 CL85
Vineyard Av, NW7 ....43 CY52
Vineyard Cl, SE6 ....123 EA80
 Kingston upon Thames
 KT1 ....138 CM97
Vineyard Gro, N3 ....44 DB53
Vineyard Hill, Pot.B. (Northaw)
 EN6 ....12 DG29
Vineyard Hill Rd, SW19 ...120 DA91
Vineyard Pas, Rich. TW9
 off Paradise Rd 118 CL85
Vineyard Path, SW14 ....98 CR83
Vineyard Rd, Felt. TW13 ...115 BU90
Vineyard Row, Kings.T. KT1 .137 CJ95
Vineyards Rd, Pot.B. EN6 ...12 DF30
Vineyard Wk, EC1 ....196 D4
Viney Bk, Croy. CR0 ....161 DZ109
Viney Rd, SE13 ....103 EB83
Vining St, SW9 ....101 DN84
Vinlake Av, Uxb. UB10 ....58 BM62
Vinson Cl, Orp. BR6 ....146 EU102
Vintners Pl, EC4
 off Upper Thames St 84 DQ73
Vintry Ms, E17
 off Cleveland Pk Cres ...67 EA56
Viola Av, SE2 ....106 EV77
 Feltham TW14 ....116 BW86
 Staines TW19 ....114 BK88
Viola Cl, S.Ock. RM15 ....91 FW69
Viola Sq, W12 ....81 CT73
Violet Av, Enf. EN2 ....30 DR38
 Uxbridge UB8 ....76 BM71
Violet Cl, E16 ....86 EE70
 SE8 off Dorking Cl 103 DZ79
 Wallington SM6 ....141 DH102
Violet Gdns, Croy. CR0 ...159 DP106
Violet Hill, NW8 ....82 DC68
Violet La, Croy. CR0 ......159 DP106
Violet Rd, E3 ....85 EB70
 E17 ....67 EA58
 E18 ....48 EH54
Violet St, E2
 off Three Colts La 84 DV70
Violet Way, Rick. (Loud.) WD3 .22 BJ42
Virgil Pl, W1 ....194 D7
Virgil St, SE1 ....200 C6
Virginia Av, Vir.W. GU25 ..132 AW99
Virginia Beeches, Vir.W.
 GU25 ....132 AW97
Virginia Cl, Ashtd. KT21
 off Skinners La 171 CK118
 New Malden KT3
 off Willow Rd 138 CQ98
 Romford RM5 ....51 FC52
 Staines TW18
 off Blacksmiths La 134 BJ97
 Weybridge KT13 ....153 BQ107
Virginia Dr, Vir.W. GU25 ..132 AW99
Virginia Gdns, Ilf. IG6 ....49 EQ54
Virginia Pl, Cob. KT11 ....153 BU114
Virginia Rd, E2 ....197 P3
 Thornton Heath CR7 ....141 DP95
Virginia St, E1 ....202 C1
Virginia Wk, SW2 ....121 DM86
 Gravesend DA12 ....131 GK63
VIRGINIA WATER 132 AX99
⚏ Virginia Water 132 AY99
Viscount Cl, N11 ....45 DH50
Viscount Dr, E6 ....87 EM71
Viscount Gdns, W.Byf. KT14 .152 BL112
Viscount Gro, Nthlt. UB5
 off Wayfarer Rd 78 BX69
Viscount Rd, Stai. (Stanw.)
 TW19 ....114 BK88
Viscount St, EC1 ....197 H5
Viscount Way, Houns. (Hthrw.Air.)
 TW6 ....95 BS84
Vista, The, SE9 ....124 EK86
 Sidcup DA14
 off Langdon Shaw 125 ET92
Vista Av, Enf. EN3 ....31 DX40
Vista Dr, Ilf. IG4 ....68 EK57
Vista Way, Har. HA3 ....62 CL58
Viveash Cl, Hayes UB3 ....95 BT76
Vivian Av, NW4 ....63 CV57
 Wembley HA9 ....62 CN64

Vivian Cl, Wat. WD19 .....39 BU46
Vivian Comma Cl, N4
 off Blackstock Rd 65 DP62
Vivian Gdns, Wat. WD19 ..39 BU46
 Wembley HA9 ....62 CN64
Vivian Rd, E3 ....85 DY68
Vivian Sq, SE15
 off Scylla Rd 102 DV83
Vivian Way, N2 ....64 DD57
Vivien Cl, Chess. KT9 ....156 CL108
Vivienne Cl, Twick. TW1 ..117 CJ86
Voce Rd, SE18 ....105 ER80
Voewood Cl, N.Mal. KT3 ..139 CT100
Voltaire Rd, SW4 ....101 DK83
Voltaire Way, Hayes UB3
 off Judge Heath La 77 BS73
Volt Av, NW10 ....80 CR69
Volta Way, Croy. CR0 ....141 DM102
Voluntary Pl, E11 ....68 EG58
Vorley Rd, N19 ....65 DJ61
Voss Ct, SW16 ....121 DL93
Voss St, E2 ....84 DU69
Voyagers Cl, SE28 ....88 EW72
Voysey Cl, N3 ....63 CY55
Vulcan Cl, E6 ....87 EN72
 Wallington SM6
 off De Havilland Rd ...159 DM108
Vulcan Gate, Enf. EN2 ....29 DN40
Vulcan Rd, SE4 ....103 DZ82
Vulcan Sq, E14 ....204 A9
Vulcan Ter, SE4 ....103 DZ82
Vulcan Way, N7 ....83 DM65
 Croydon (New Adgtn.)
 CR0 ....162 EE110
Vyne, The, Bexh. DA7 ....107 FB83
Vyner Rd, W3 ....80 CR73
Vyner St, E2 ....84 DV67
Vyners Way, Uxb. UB10 ...58 BN64
Vyse Cl, Barn. EN5 ....27 CW42

W

Wacketts, Wal.Cr. (Chsht.) EN7
 off Spicersfield 14 DU27
Wadbrook St, Kings.T. KT1 .137 CK96
Wadding St, SE17 ....201 K9
Waddington Av, Couls. CR5 .175 DN120
Waddington Cl, Couls. CR5 .175 DP119
 Enfield EN1 ....30 DS42
Waddington Rd, E15 ....67 ED64
Waddington St, E15 ....85 ED65
Waddington Way, SE19 ...122 DQ94
WADDON, Croy. 141 DN103
⚏ Waddon 159 DN105
Waddon Cl, Croy. CR0 ....141 DN104
Waddon Ct Rd, Croy. CR0 .159 DN105
⟁ Waddon Marsh 141 DM102
Waddon Marsh Way, Croy.
 CR0 ....141 DM102
Waddon New Rd, Croy. CR0 .141 DP104
Waddon Pk Av, Croy. CR0 .159 DN105
Waddon Rd, Croy. CR0 ....141 DN105
Waddon Way, Croy. CR0 ..159 DP107
Wade Av, Orp. BR5 ....146 EX101
Wades Gro, N21 ....45 DN45
Wades Hill, N21 ....29 DN44
Wades La, Tedd. TW11
 off High St 117 CG92
Wades Ms, N21 off Wades Hill .45 DN45
Wadeson St, E2 ....84 DV68
Wades Pl, E14 ....85 EB73
Wadeville Av, Rom. RM6 ...70 EZ59
Wadeville Cl, Belv. DA17 ..106 FA79
Wadham Av, E17 ....47 EB53
Wadham Cl, Shep. TW17 ..135 BQ101
Wadham Gdns, NW3 ....82 DE67
 Greenford UB6 ....79 CD65
Wadham Rd, E17 ....47 EB53
 SW15 ....99 CY84
 Abbots Langley WD5 .....7 BT31
Wadhurst Cl, SE20 ....142 DV96
Wadhurst Rd, SW8 ....101 DJ81
 W4 ....98 CR76
Wadley Rd, E11 ....68 EE59
Wadsworth Business Cen, Grnf.
 UB6 ....79 CJ68
Wadsworth Cl, Enf. EN3 ...31 DX43
 Greenford UB6 ....79 CJ68
Wadsworth Rd, Grnf. UB6 ..79 CH68
Waggon Ms, N14
 off Chase Side 45 DJ46
Waggon Rd, Barn. EN4 ....28 DC37
Waghorn Rd, E13 ....86 EJ67
 Harrow HA3 ....61 CK55
Waghorn St, SE15 ....102 DU83
Wagner St, SE15 ....102 DW80
Wagon Rd, Barn. EN4 ....28 DB36
Wagon Way, Rick. (Loud.)
 WD3 ....22 BJ41
Wagstaff Gdns, Dag. RM9 ..88 EW66
Wagtail Cl, NW9
 off Swan Dr 42 CS54
Wagtail Gdns, S.Croy. CR2 .161 DY110
Wagtail Wk, Beck. BR3 ....143 EC99
Wagtail Way, Orp. BR5 ...146 EX98
Waid Cl, Dart. DA1 ....128 FM86
Waights Ct, Kings.T. KT2 ..138 CL95
Wain Cl, Pot.B. EN6 ....12 DB29
Wainfleet Av, Rom. RM5 ...51 FC54
Wainford Cl, SW19
 off Windlesham Gro ...119 CX88
Wainwright Av, Brwd. CM13 .55 GD44
Wainwright Gro, Islw. TW7 ..97 CD81
Waite Davies Rd, SE12 ....124 EF87
Waite St, SE15 ....102 DT79
Waithman St, EC4 ....196 F9

Wakefield Rd, N11 ....45 DK50
 N15 ....66 DT57
 Greenhithe DA9 ....129 FW85
 Richmond TW10 ....117 CK85
Wakefield St, E6 ....86 EK67
 N18 ....46 DU50
 WC1 ....196 A4
Wakefield Wk, Wal.Cr. (Chsht.)
 EN8 ....15 DY31
Wakehams Hill, Pnr. HA5 ...60 BZ55
Wakeham St, N1 ....84 DR65
Wakehurst Path, Wok. GU21 .151 BC114
Wakehurst Rd, SW11 ....120 DE85
Wakeling Rd, W7 ....79 CF71
Wakeling St, E14 ....85 DY72
Wakelin Rd, E15 ....86 EE68
Wakely Cl, West. (Bigg.H.)
 TN16 ....178 EJ118
Wakeman Rd, NW10 ....81 CW69
Wakemans Hill Av, NW9 ...62 CR57
Wakerfield Cl, Horn. RM11 ..72 FM57
Wakering Rd, Bark. IG11 ...87 EQ65
Wakerley Cl, E6
 off Truesdale Rd 87 EM72
Wake Rd, Loug. (High Beach)
 IG10 ....32 EJ38
Wakley St, EC1 ....196 F2
Walberswick St, SW8 ....101 DL80
Walbrook, EC4 ....197 K10
Walbrook Ho, N9 ....46 DW46
Walbrook Wf, EC4
 off Upper Thames St ...84 DQ73
Walburgh St, E1
 off Bigland St 84 DV72
Walburton Rd, Pur. CR8 ..159 DJ113
Walcorde Av, SE17 ....201 J9
Walcot Rd, Enf. EN3 ....31 DZ40
Walcot Sq, SE11 ....200 E8
Walcott St, SW1 ....199 L8
Waldair Ct, E16
 off Barge Ho Rd 105 EP75
Waldair Wf, E16 ....105 EP75
Waldeck Gro, SE27 ....121 DP90
Waldeck Rd, N15 ....65 DP56
 SW14
 off Lower Richmond Rd .98 CQ83
 W4 ....98 CN79
 W13 ....79 CH72
 Dartford DA1 ....128 FM86
Waldeck Ter, SW14
 off Lower Richmond Rd .98 CQ83
Waldegrave Av, Tedd. TW11
 off Waldegrave Rd 117 CF92
Waldegrave Ct, Upmin. RM14 .72 FP60
Waldegrave Gdns, Twick. TW1 .117 CF89
 Upminster RM14 ....72 FP60
Waldegrave Pk, Twick. TW1 .117 CF91
Waldegrave Rd, N8 ....65 DN55
 SE19 ....122 DT94
 W5 ....80 CM72
 Bromley BR1 ....144 EL98
 Dagenham RM8 ....70 EW61
 Teddington TW11 ....117 CF91
 Twickenham TW1 ....117 CF91
Waldegrove, Croy. CR0 ...142 DT104
Waldemar Av, SW6 ....99 CY81
 W13 ....79 CJ74
Waldemar Rd, SW19 ....120 DA92
Walden Av, N13 ....46 DQ49
 Chislehurst BR7 ....125 EM91
 Rainham RM13 ....89 FD68
Walden Cl, Belv. DA17 ....106 EZ78
Walden Gdns, Th.Hth. CR7 .141 DM97
Waldenhurst Rd, Orp. BR5 .146 EX101
Walden Par, Chis. BR7
 off Walden Rd 125 EM93
Walden Rd, N17 ....46 DR53
 Chislehurst BR7 ....125 EM93
 Hornchurch RM11 ....72 FK58
Waldens Cl, Orp. BR5 ....146 EX101
Waldenshaw Rd, SE23 ....122 DW88
Waldens Pk Rd, Wok. GU21 .166 AW116
Waldens Rd, Orp. BR5 ....146 EY101
 Woking GU21 ....166 AX117
Walden St, E1 ....84 DV72
Walden Way, NW7 ....43 CX51
 Hornchurch RM11 ....72 FK58
 Ilford IG6 ....49 ES52
Waldo Cl, SW4 ....121 DJ85
Waldo Pl, Mitch. CR4 ....120 DE94
Waldorf Cl, S.Croy. CR2 ..159 DP109
Waldo Rd, NW10 ....81 CU69
 Bromley BR1 ....144 EK97
Waldram Cres, SE23 .....122 DW88
Waldram Pk Rd, SE23 ....123 DX88
Waldram Pl, SE23
 off Waldram Cres 122 DW88
Waldrist Way, Erith DA18 .106 EZ75
Waldron Gdns, Brom. BR2 .143 ED97
Waldronhyrst, S.Croy. CR2 .159 DP105
Waldron Ms, SW3
 off Old Ch St 100 DD79
Waldron Rd, SW18 ....120 DC90
 Harrow HA1, HA2 ....61 CE60
Waldrons, The, Croy. CR0 .159 DP105
 Oxted RH8 ....188 EF131
Waldrons Path, S.Croy. CR2 .160 DQ105
Waldstock Rd, SE28 ....88 EU73
Waleran Cl, Stan. HA7
 off Chenduit Way 41 CF51
Walerand Rd, SE13 ....103 EC82
Waleran Flats, SE1
 off Old Kent Rd 102 DS77
Wales Av, Cars. SM5 .....158 DF106
Wales Cl, SE15 ....102 DV80
Wales Fm Rd, W3 ....80 CR71
Waleton Acres, Wall. SM6 .159 DJ107
Waley St, E1 ....85 DX71
Walfield Av, N20 ....44 DB45
Walford Rd, N16 ....66 DS63
 Uxbridge UB8 ....76 BJ68
Walfrey Gdns, Dag. RM9 ...88 EY66
WALHAM GREEN, SW6 ....100 DB80
Walham Grn Ct, SW6
 off Waterford Rd 100 DB80
Walham Gro, SW6 ....100 DA80
Walham Ri, SW19 ....119 CY93

Walham Yd, SW6
  off Walham Gro **100** DA80
Walk, The, Horn. RM11 . . . . . . **72** FM61
  Oxted (Tand.) RH8 . . . .**187** EA133
  Potters Bar EN6 . . . .**12** DA32
  Sunbury-on-Thames TW16 .**115** BR94
Walkden Rd, Chis. BR7 . . . . .**125** EN92
Walker Cl, N11 . . . .**45** DJ49
  SE18 . . . .**105** EQ77
  W7 . . . .**79** CE74
  Dartford DA1 . . . .**107** FF83
  Feltham TW14
  off Westmacott Dr **115** BT87
  Hampton TW12
  off Fearnley Cres **116** BZ93
Walker Ms, SW2 off Effra Rd .**121** DN85
Walkers Ct, E8 off Wilton Way .**84** DU65
  W1 . . . .**195** M10
Walkerscroft Mead, SE21 . . .**122** DQ88
Walkers Pl, SW15
  off Felsham Rd **99** CY83
Walkfield Dr, Epsom KT18 . . .**173** CV117
Walkford Way, SE15
  off Daniel Gdns **102** DT80
Walkley Rd, Dart. DA1 . . . . . .**127** FH85
Walks, The, N2 . . . .**64** DD55
Walkynscroft, SE15
  off Firbank Rd **102** DV82
Wallace Cl, SE28
  off Haldane Rd **88** EX73
  Shepperton TW17 . . . .**135** BR98
  Uxbridge UB10
  off Grays Rd **76** BL68
★ **Wallace Collection**, W1 .**194** F8
Wallace Cres, Cars. SM5 . . . .**158** DF106
Wallace Flds, Epsom KT17 . .**157** CT112
Wallace Gdns, Swans. DA10
  off Milton St **130** FY86
Wallace Rd, N1 . . . .**84** DQ65
  Grays RM17 . . . .**110** GA76
Wallace Sq, Couls. CR5
  off Cayton Rd **175** DK122
Wallace Wk, Add. KT15 . . . . .**152** BJ105
Wallace Way, N19
  off Giesbach Rd **65** DK61
Wallasey Cres, Uxb. UB10 . . .**58** BN62
Wallcote Av, NW2 . . . .**63** CX60
Walled Gdn, The, Tad. KT20
  off Heathcote **173** CX122
Wall End Rd, E6 . . . .**87** EN66
Wallenger Av, Rom. RM2 . . . .**71** FH55
Waller Dr, Nthwd. HA6 . . . . . .**39** BU54
Waller La, Cat. CR3 . . . .**176** DT123
Waller Rd, SE14 . . . .**103** DX81
Wallers Cl, Dag. RM9 . . . .**87** EY67
  Woodford Green IG8 . . . . . .**49** EM51
Wallers Hoppit, Loug. IG10 . .**32** EL40
Waller Way, SE10
  off Greenwich High Rd . . .**103** EB80
Wallflower St, W12 . . . .**81** CT73
Wallgrave Rd, SW5 . . . .**100** DB77
Wallhouse Rd, Erith DA8 . . . .**107** FH80
Wallingford Av, W10 . . . .**81** CX71
Wallingford Rd, Uxb. UB8 . . .**76** BH68
WALLINGTON **159** DJ106
≷ **Wallington** **159** DH107
Wallington Cl, Ruis. HA4 . . . . .**59** BQ58
Wallington Cor, Wall. SM6
  off Manor Rd N **159** DH105
Wallington Rd, Ilf. IG3 . . . . . .**69** ET59
Wallington Sq, Wall. SM6
  off Woodcote Rd **159** DH107
Wallis All, SE1 . . . .**201** J4
Wallis Cl, SW11 . . . .**100** DD83
  Dartford DA2 . . . .**127** FF90
  Hornchurch RM11 . . . .**71** FH60
Wallis Ct, Slou. SL1
  off Nixey Cl **92** AU76
Wallis Ms, N22
  off Brampton Pk Rd **65** DN55
  Leatherhead (Fetch.) KT22 .**171** CG122
Wallis Pk, Grav. (Nthflt.) DA11 .**130** GB85
Wallis Rd, E9 . . . .**85** DZ65
  Southall UB1 . . . .**78** CB72
Wallis's Cotts, SW2 . . . .**121** DL87
Wallman Pl, N22
  off Bounds Grn Rd **45** DM53
Wallorton Gdns, SW14 . . . . . .**98** CR84
Wallside, EC2 . . . .**197** J7
Wall St, N1 . . . .**84** DR65
Wallwood Rd, E11 . . . .**67** ED60
Wallwood St, E14 . . . .**85** DZ71
Walmar Cl, Barn. EN4 . . . .**28** DD39
Walmer Cl, E4 . . . .**47** EB47
  Orpington BR6
  off Tubbenden La S **163** ER105
  Romford RM7 . . . .**51** FB54
Walmer Gdns, W13 . . . .**97** CG75
Walmer Ho, N9 . . . .**46** DT45
Walmer Pl, W1 . . . .**194** D6
Walmer Rd, W10
  off Latimer Rd **81** CW72
  W11 . . . .**81** CY73
Walmer St, W1 . . . .**194** D6
Walmer Ter, SE18 . . . .**105** EQ77
Walmgate Rd, Grnf. UB6 . . . . .**79** CH67
Walmington Fold, N12 . . . .**44** DA51
Walm La, NW2 . . . .**63** CX64
Walmsley Ho, SW16
  off Colson Way **121** DJ91
Walney Wk, N1
  off St. Paul's Rd **84** DQ65
Walnut Av, West Dr. UB7 . . . . .**94** BN76
Walnut Cl, SE8 off Clyde St .**103** DZ79
  Carshalton SM5 . . . .**158** DF106
  Dartford (Eyns.) DA4 . . . . .**148** FK104
  Epsom KT18 . . . .**173** CT115
  Hayes UB3 . . . .**77** BS73
  Ilford IG6 off Civic Way . . .**69** EQ56
  St. Albans (Park St.) AL2 . . .**8** CC27
Walnut Ct, W5 . . . .**98** CL75
Walnut Dr, Tad. (Kgswd.) KT20
Walnut Flds, Epsom KT17 . . .**157** CT109
Walnut Gdns, E15
  off Burgess Rd **68** EE63

Walnut Grn, Bushey WD23 . . .**24** BZ40
  Enfield EN1 . . . .**30** DR43
Walnut Ms, Sutt. SM2 . . . . . .**158** DC108
Walnut Rd, E10 . . . .**67** EA61
Walnuts, The, Orp. BR6
  off High St **146** EU102
Walnut Shop Cen, Orp. BR6 .**146** EU102
Walnuts Rd, Orp. BR6 . . . . . .**146** EU102
Walnut Tree Av, Dart. DA1 . . .**128** FL89
  Mitcham CR4
  off De'Arn Gdns **140** DE97
Walnut Tree Cl, SW13 . . . .**99** CT81
  Banstead SM7 . . . .**157** CY112
  Chislehurst BR7 . . . .**145** EQ95
  Waltham Cross (Chsht.)
  EN8 . . . .**15** DX31
Walnut Tree Cotts, SW19
  off Church Rd **119** CY91
Walnut Tree La, W.Byf. (Byfleet)
  KT14 . . . .**152** BK112
Walnut Tree Rd, SE10 . . . . . .**104** EE78
  Brentford TW8 . . . .**98** CL79
  Dagenham RM8 . . . .**70** EX61
  Erith DA8 . . . .**107** FE78
  Hounslow TW5 . . . .**96** BZ79
  Shepperton TW17 . . . .**135** BQ96
Walnut Tree Wk, SE11 . . . . . .**200** D8
Walnut Way, Buck.H. IG9 . . . .**48** EK48
  Ruislip HA4 . . . .**78** BW65
  Swanley BR8 . . . .**147** FD96
Walpole Av, Couls. CR5 . . . . .**174** DF118
  Richmond TW9 . . . .**98** CM82
Walpole Cl, W13 . . . .**97** CJ75
  Grays RM17
  off Palmers Dr **110** GC77
  Pinner HA5 . . . .**40** CA51
Walpole Cres, Tedd. TW11 . . .**117** CF92
  Twickenham TW2 . . . .**117** CE89
Walpole Gdns, W4 . . . .**98** CQ78
  Twickenham TW2 . . . .**117** CE89
Walpole Ms, NW8
  off Queen's Gro **82** DD67
  SW19 off Walpole Rd **120** DD93
Walpole Pk, W5 . . . .**79** CJ74
  Weybridge KT13 . . . .**152** BN108
Walpole Pl, SE18
  off Anglesea Rd **105** EP77
  Teddington TW11 . . . .**117** CF92
Walpole Rd, E6 . . . .**86** EJ66
  E17 . . . .**67** DY56
  E18 . . . .**48** EF53
  N17 (Downhills Way) **66** DQ55
  N17 (Lordship La) **46** DQ54
  SW19 . . . .**120** DD93
  Bromley BR2 . . . .**144** EK99
  Croydon CR0 . . . .**142** DR103
  Surbiton KT6 . . . .**138** CL100
  Teddington TW11 . . . .**117** CF92
  Twickenham TW2 . . . .**117** CE89
  Windsor (Old Wind.) SL4 . .**112** AV87
Walpole St, SW3 . . . .**198** D10
Walrond Av, Wem. HA9 . . . . . .**62** CL64
Walsham Cl, N16
  off Braydon Rd **66** DU59
  SE28 . . . .**88** EX73
Walsham Rd, SE14 . . . .**103** DX82
  Feltham TW14 . . . .**115** BV87
Walsh Cres, Croy. (New Adgtn.)
  CR0 . . . .**162** EE112
Walshford Way, Borwd. WD6 . .**26** CN38
Walsingham Gdns, Epsom
  KT19 . . . .**156** CS105
Walsingham Pk, Chis. BR7 . . .**145** ER96
Walsingham Pl, SW4 off Clapham
  Common W Side **100** DF84
  SW11 . . . .**120** DG86
Walsingham Rd, E5 . . . .**66** DU62
  W13 . . . .**79** CG74
  Croydon (New Adgtn.) CR0 .**161** EC110
  Enfield EN2 . . . .**30** DR42
  Mitcham CR4 . . . .**140** DF99
  Orpington BR5 . . . .**146** EV95
Walsingham Wk, Belv. DA17 .**106** FA79
Walsingham Way, St.Alb.
  (Lon.Col.) AL2 . . . .**9** CJ27
Walter Rodney Cl, E6
  off Stevenage Rd **87** EM65
Walters Cl, Wal.Cr. (Chsht.)
  EN7 . . . .**13** DP25
Walters Ho, SE17 off Otto St .**101** DP79
Walters Mead, Ashtd. KT21 . .**172** CL117
Walters Rd, SE25 . . . .**142** DS98
  Enfield EN3 . . . .**30** DW43
Walter St, E2 . . . .**85** DX69
  Kingston upon Thames KT2
  off Sopwith Way **138** CL95
Walters Way, SE23 . . . .**123** DX66
Walters Yd, Brom. BR1 . . . . .**144** EG96
Walter Ter, E1 . . . .**85** DX72
Walterton Rd, W9 . . . .**81** CZ70
Walter Wk, Edg. HA8 . . . .**42** CQ51
★ **WALTHAM ABBEY** **32** EF35
★ **Waltham Abbey (ruins)**,
  Wal.Abb. EN9 . . . .**15** EC33
Waltham Av, NW9 . . . .**62** CN58
  Hayes UB3 . . . .**95** BQ76
Waltham Cl, Brwd. (Hutton)
  CM13 off Bannister Dr **55** GC44
  Dartford DA1 . . . .**127** FG86
  Orpington BR5 . . . .**146** EX102
★ **WALTHAM CROSS** **15** DZ33
≷ **Waltham Cross** **15** DY34
Waltham Dr, Edg. HA8 . . . .**42** CN54
Waltham Gdns, Enf. EN3 . . . . .**30** DW36
Waltham Gate, Wal.Cr. EN8 . .**15** DZ26
Waltham Pk Way, E17 . . . .**47** EA53
Waltham Rd, Cars. SM5 . . . . .**140** DD101
  Caterham CR3 . . . .**176** DV122
  Southall UB2 . . . .**96** BY76
  Waltham Abbey EN9 . . . . . .**16** EF26
  Woodford Green IG8 . . . . . .**48** EL51
★ **WALTHAMSTOW**, E17 . . . . .**67** EB54
Walthamstow Av, E4 . . . .**47** EA52
Walthamstow Business Cen,
  E17 . . . .**47** EC54
≷ **Walthamstow Central** **67** EA56
⊖ **Walthamstow Central** **67** EA56

≷ **Walthamstow Queens**
  Road **67** DZ57
Waltham Way, E4 . . . .**47** DZ49
Waltheof Av, N17 . . . .**46** DR53
Waltheof Gdns, N17 . . . .**46** DR53
Walton Av, Har. HA2 . . . .**60** BZ64
  New Malden KT3 . . . .**139** CT98
  Sutton SM3 . . . .**139** CZ104
  Wembley HA9 . . . .**62** CP62
Walton Br, Shep. TW17 . . . . .**135** BS101
  Walton-on-Thames KT12
  off Bridge St **135** BS101
Walton Br Rd, Shep. TW17 . . .**135** BS101
Walton Cl, E5
  off Orient Way **67** DX62
  NW2 . . . .**63** CV61
  SW8 . . . .**101** DL80
  Harrow HA1 . . . .**61** CD56
Walton Comm Hosp, Walt.
  KT12 . . . .**135** BV103
Walton Ct, Wok. GU21 . . . . . .**167** BA116
Walton Cres, Har. HA2 . . . . . .**60** BZ63
Walton Dr, NW10
  off Mitchellbrook Way **80** CR65
  Harrow HA1 . . . .**61** CD56
Walton Gdns, W3 . . . .**80** CP71
  Brentwood CM13 . . . .**55** GC43
  Feltham TW13 . . . .**115** BT91
  Waltham Abbey EN9 . . . . . .**15** EB33
  Wembley HA9 . . . .**62** CL61
Walton Grn, Croy. (New Adgtn.)
  CR0 . . . .**161** EC108
Walton La, Shep. TW17 . . . . .**135** BQ101
  Walton-on-Thames KT12 . .**135** BQ102
  Weybridge KT13 . . . .**135** BP103
Walton Pk, Walt. KT12 . . . . . .**136** BX103
Walton Pk La, Walt. KT12 . . . .**136** BX103
Walton Pl, SW3 . . . .**198** D6
Walton Rd, E12 . . . .**69** EN63
  E13 . . . .**86** EJ68
  N15 . . . .**66** DT57
  Bushey WD23 . . . .**24** BX42
  East Molesey KT8 . . . .**136** CA98
  Epsom (Epsom Downs)
  KT18 . . . .**173** CT117
  Epsom (Headley) KT18 . . . .**172** CQ121
  Harrow HA1 . . . .**61** CD56
  Romford RM5 . . . .**50** EZ52
  Sidcup DA14 . . . .**126** EW89
  Walton-on-Thames KT12 . .**136** BW99
  West Molesey KT8 . . . .**136** BY99
  Woking GU21 . . . .**167** AZ116
Walton St, SW3 . . . .**198** C8
  Enfield EN2 . . . .**30** DR39
  Tadworth KT20 . . . .**173** CU124
Walton Ter, Wok. GU21 . . . . .**167** BB115
Walton Way, W3 . . . .**80** CP71
  Mitcham CR4 . . . .**141** DJ98
Walt Whitman Cl, SE24
  off Shakespeare Rd **101** DP84
Walverns Cl, Wat. WD19 . . . . .**24** BW44
★ **WALWORTH**, SE17 . . . .**201** H10
★ **Walworth Garden Fm -
  Horticultural Training Cen**,
  SE17 . . . .**101** DP78
Walworth Pl, SE17 . . . .**102** DQ78
Walworth Rd, SE1 . . . .**201** H8
  SE17 . . . .**201** H8
Walwyn Av, Brom. BR1 . . . . .**144** EK97
Wambrook Cl, Brwd. CM13 . . .**55** GC46
Wanborough Dr, SW15 . . . . . .**119** CV88
Wanderer Dr, Bark. IG11 . . . . .**88** EV69
Wandle Bk, SW19 . . . .**120** DD93
  Croydon CR0 . . . .**141** DL104
Wandle Ct, Epsom KT19 . . . .**156** CQ105
Wandle Ct Gdns, Croy. CR0 . .**159** DL105
⊖ **Wandle Park** **141** DN103
Wandle Rd, SW17 . . . .**120** DE89
  Croydon CR0 . . . .**142** DQ104
  Croydon (Waddon) CR0 . . .**141** DL104
  Morden SM4 . . . .**140** DC99
  Wallington SM6 . . . .**141** DH103
Wandle Side, Croy. CR0 . . . .**141** DM104
  Wallington SM6 . . . .**141** DH104
Wandle Technology Pk, Mitch.
  CR4 off Goat Rd **140** DF101
Wandle Trd Est, Mitch. CR4
  off Budge La **140** DF101
Wandle Way, SW18 . . . .**120** DB88
  Mitcham CR4 . . . .**140** DF99
Wandon Rd, SW6 . . . .**100** DB80
★ **WANDSWORTH**, SW18 . . .**119** CZ85
≷ **Wandsworth Br**, SW6 . . . .**100** DB83
  SW18 . . . .**100** DB83
Wandsworth Br Rd, SW6 . . . .**100** DB81
≷ **Wandsworth Common** . . .**120** DF88
Wandsworth Common,
  SW12 . . . .**120** DE86
Wandsworth Common W Side,
  SW18 . . . .**120** DC85
Wandsworth High St, SW18 .**120** DA85
★ **Wandsworth Mus**, SW18 . .**120** DB85
  off Garratt La **120** DB85
Wandsworth Plain, SW18 . . .**120** DB85
≷ **Wandsworth Road** **101** DJ82
≷ **Wandsworth Rd**, SW8 . . . .**101** DK80
Wandsworth Shop Cen,
  SW18 . . . .**120** DB86
≷ **Wandsworth Town** **100** DB84
Wangey Rd, Rom. RM6 . . . . . .**70** EX59
Wang Ho, Brent. TW8 . . . .**97** CJ78
Wanless Rd, SE24 . . . .**102** DQ83
Wanley Rd, SE5 . . . .**102** DR84
Wanlip Rd, E13 . . . .**86** EH70
Wanmer Ct, Reig. RH2
  off Birkheads Rd **184** DA133
Wannions Cl, Chesh. HP5 . . . . .**4** AU30
Wansbeck Rd, E9 . . . .**85** DZ66
Wansbury Way, Swan. BR8 . .**147** FG99
Wansdown Pl, SW6
  off Fulham Rd **100** DB80
Wansey St, SE17 . . . .**201** H9
Wansford Cl, Brwd. CM14 . . . .**54** FT48

Wansford Grn, Wok. GU21
  off Kenton Way **166** AT117
Wansford Pk, Borwd. WD6 . . .**26** CS42
Wansford Rd, Wdf.Grn. IG8 . . .**48** EJ53
★ **WANSTEAD**, E11 . . . .**68** EH59
⊖ **Wanstead** **68** EH58
Wanstead Cl, Brom. BR1 . . . .**144** EJ96
Wanstead La, Ilf. IG1 . . . .**68** EK58
≷ **Wanstead Park** **68** EH63
Wanstead Pk, E11 . . . .**68** EH59
Wanstead Pk Av, E12 . . . .**68** EK61
Wanstead Pk Rd, Ilf. IG1 . . . .**68** EM60
Wanstead Pl, E11 . . . .**68** EG58
Wanstead Rd, Brom. BR1 . . .**144** EJ96
Wansunt Rd, Bex. DA5 . . . . . .**127** FC88
Wantage Rd, SE12 . . . .**124** EF85
Wantz La, Rain. RM13 . . . .**89** FH70
Wantz Rd, Dag. RM10 . . . .**71** FB63
Waplings, The, Tad. KT20 . . .**173** CV124
★ **WAPPING**, E1 . . . .**202** C2
⊖ **Wapping** **202** F3
Wapping Dock St, E1 . . . .**202** E3
Wapping High St, E1 . . . .**202** B3
Wapping La, E1 . . . .**202** E1
Wapping Wall, E1 . . . .**202** F2
Wapseys La, Slou. (Hedg.)
  SL2 . . . .**56** AS58
Wapshott Rd, Stai. TW18 . . . .**113** BE93
Warbank Cl, Croy. (New Adgtn.)
  CR0 . . . .**162** EE111
Warbank Cres, Croy. (New Adgtn.)
  CR0 . . . .**162** EE110
Warbank La, Kings.T. KT2 . . . .**119** CT98
Warbeck Rd, W12 . . . .**81** CV74
Warberry Rd, N22 . . . .**45** DM54
Warblers Grn, Cob. KT11 . . . .**154** BZ114
Warboys App, Kings.T. KT2 . . .**118** CP93
Warboys Cres, E4 . . . .**47** EC50
Warboys Rd, Kings.T. KT2 . . . .**118** CP93
Warburton Cl, N1
  off Culford Rd **84** DS65
  Harrow HA3 . . . .**41** CD51
Warburton Rd, E8 . . . .**84** DV66
  Twickenham TW2 . . . .**116** CB88
Warburton St, E8
  off Warburton Rd **84** DV67
Warburton Ter, E17 . . . .**47** EB54
War Coppice Rd, Cat. CR3 . .**186** DR127
Wardalls Gro, SE14 . . . .**102** DW80
Ward Av, Grays RM17 . . . . . .**110** GA77
Ward Cl, Erith DA8 . . . .**107** FD79
  Iver SL0 . . . .**75** BF72
  South Croydon CR2 . . . . . .**160** DS106
  Waltham Cross (Chsht.) EN7
  off Spicersfield **14** DU27
Wardell Cl, NW7 . . . .**42** CS52
Wardell Fld, NW9 . . . .**42** CS53
Warden Av, Har. HA2 . . . .**60** BZ60
  Romford RM5 . . . .**51** FC50
Warden Rd, NW5 . . . .**82** DG65
Wardens Fld Cl, Orp. BR6 . . .**163** ES107
Wardens Gro, SE1 . . . .**201** H3
Ward Gdns, Rom. (Harold Wd.)
  RM3 off Whitmore Av **52** FK54
Ward La, Warl. CR6 . . . .**176** DW116
Wardle St, E9 . . . .**67** DX64
Wardley St, SW18
  off Garratt La **120** DB87
Wardo Av, SW6 . . . .**99** CY81
Wardour Ms, W1 . . . .**195** L9
Wardour St, W1 . . . .**195** M10
Ward Rd, E15 . . . .**85** ED67
  N19 . . . .**65** DJ62
Wardrobe Pl, EC4 . . . .**196** G10
Wardrobe Ter, EC4 . . . .**196** G10
Wards La, Borwd. (Elstree)
  WD6 . . . .**25** CG40
Ward's Pl, Egh. TW20 . . . .**113** BC93
Wards Rd, Ilf. IG2 . . . .**69** ER59
Wareham Cl, Houns. TW3 . . . .**96** CB84
Waremead Rd, Ilf. IG2 . . . .**69** EP57
Warenford Way, Borwd. WD6 . .**26** CN39
Warenne Rd, Lthd. (Fetch.)
  KT22 . . . .**170** CC122
Ware Pt Dr, SE28 . . . .**105** ER75
Warescot Cl, Brwd. CM15 . . . .**54** FV45
Warescot Rd, Brwd. CM15 . . . .**54** FV45
Warfield Rd, NW10 . . . .**81** CX69
  Feltham TW14 . . . .**115** BS87
  Hampton TW12 . . . .**136** CB95
Warfield Yd, NW10
  off Warfield Rd **81** CX69
Wargrave Av, N15 . . . .**66** DT58
Wargrave Rd, Har. HA2 . . . . . .**60** CC62
Warham Rd, N4 . . . .**65** DN57
  Harrow HA3 . . . .**41** CF54
  Sevenoaks (Otford) TN14 . .**181** FH116
  South Croydon CR2 . . . . . .**160** DQ106
Warham St, SE5 . . . .**101** DP80
Waring Cl, Orp. BR6 . . . .**163** ET107
Waring Dr, Orp. BR6 . . . .**163** ET107
Waring Rd, Sid. DA14 . . . .**126** EW93
Waring St, SE27 . . . .**122** DQ91
Warkworth Gdns, Islw. TW7 . .**97** CG80
Warkworth Rd, N17 . . . .**46** DR52
Warland Rd, SE18 . . . .**105** ER80
★ **WARLEY**, Brwd. **54** FV50
Warley Av, Dag. RM8 . . . .**70** EZ59
  Hayes UB4 . . . .**77** BU71
Warley Cl, E10 off Millicent Rd .**67** DZ60
Warley Gap, Brwd. CM13 . . . .**53** FV52
Warley Hill, Brwd. CM13,
  CM14 . . . .**53** FV51
H Warley Hosp, Brwd. CM14 .**54** FV50
Warley Mt, Brwd. CM14 . . . . . .**54** FV49
Warley Rd, N9 . . . .**46** DW47
  Brentwood CM13 . . . .**53** FT54
  Hayes UB4 . . . .**77** BU72
  Ilford IG5 . . . .**49** EN54
  Upminster RM14 . . . .**52** FQ54
  Woodford Green IG8 . . . . . .**48** EH52
Warley St, E2 . . . .**85** DX69
  Brentwood CM13 . . . .**73** FW58
  Upminster RM14 . . . .**73** FW58
Warley St Flyover, Brwd.
  CM13 . . . .**73** FX57
Warley Wds Cres, Brwd. CM14 .**54** FV49

WARLINGHAM **177** DX118
Warlingham Rd, Th.Hth. CR7 .**141** DP98
Warlock Rd, W9 . . . .**82** DA70
Warlow Cl, Enf. EN3
  off Government Row **31** EA37
Warlters Cl, N7
  off Warlters Rd **65** DL63
Warlters Rd, N7 . . . .**65** DL63
Warltersville Rd, N19 . . . .**65** DL59
Warmington Cl, E5
  off Orient Way **67** DX62
Warmington Rd, SE24 . . . . . .**122** DQ86
Warmington St, E13
  off Barking Rd **86** EG70
Warminster Gdns, SE25 . . . .**142** DU96
Warminster Rd, SE25 . . . . . .**142** DT96
Warminster Sq, SE25 . . . . . .**142** DU96
Warminster Way, Mitch. CR4 .**141** DH95
Warndon St, SE16 . . . .**202** G9
Warneford Pl, Wat. WD19 . . . .**24** BY44
Warneford Rd, Har. HA3 . . . . .**61** CK55
Warneford St, E9 . . . .**84** DV67
Warne Pl, Sid. DA15
  off Westerham Dr **126** EV86
Warner Av, Sutt. SM3 . . . . . .**139** CY103
Warner Cl, E15 . . . .**68** EE64
  NW9 . . . .**63** CT59
  Hampton TW12
  off Tangley Pk Rd **116** BZ92
  Hayes UB3 . . . .**95** BR80
Warner Ho, SE13
  off Conington Rd **103** EB82
Warner Par, Hayes UB3 . . . . .**95** BR80
Warner Pl, E2 . . . .**84** DU68
Warner Rd, E17 . . . .**67** DY56
  N8 . . . .**65** DK56
  SE5 . . . .**102** DQ81
  Bromley BR1 . . . .**124** EF94
Warners Cl, Wdf.Grn. IG8 . . . .**48** EG50
Warners La, Kings.T. KT2 . . . .**117** CK91
Warners Path, Wdf.Grn. IG8 . .**48** EG50
Warner St, EC1 . . . .**196** D5
Warner Ter, E14 . . . .**85** EA71
Warner Yd, EC1 . . . .**196** D5
Warnford Ho, SW15
  off Tunworth Cres **119** CT86
Warnford Ind Est, Hayes UB3 .**95** BS75
Warnford Rd, Orp. BR6 . . . . .**163** ET106
Warnham Ct Rd, Cars. SM5 . .**158** DF108
Warnham Rd, N12 . . . .**44** DE50
Warple Ms, W3
  off Warple Way **98** CS75
Warple Way, W3 . . . .**80** CS74
Warren, The, E12 . . . .**68** EL63
  Ashtead KT21 . . . .**172** CL119
  Carshalton SM5 . . . .**158** DD109
  Gerrards Cross (Chal.St.P.)
  SL9 . . . .**37** AZ52
  Gravesend DA12 . . . .**131** GK91
  Hayes UB4 . . . .**77** BU72
  Hounslow TW5 . . . .**96** BZ80
  Leatherhead (Oxshott) KT22 .**154** CC112
  Radlett WD7
  Tadworth (Kgswd.) KT20 . .**173** CY123
  Worcester Park KT4 . . . . .**156** CR105
Warren Av, E10 . . . .**67** EC62
  Bromley BR1 . . . .**124** EE94
  Orpington BR6 . . . .**163** ET106
  Richmond TW10 . . . .**98** CP84
  South Croydon CR2 . . . . . .**161** DX108
  Sutton SM2 . . . .**157** CZ110
Warren Cl, N9 . . . .**47** DX45
  SE21 off Lairdale Cl **122** DQ87
  Bexleyheath DA6 . . . .**126** FA85
  Esher KT10 . . . .**154** CB105
  Hayes UB4 . . . .**78** BW71
  Slough SL3 . . . .**92** AY76
  Wembley HA9 . . . .**61** CK61
Warren Ct, Chig. IG7 . . . .**49** ER49
  Sevenoaks TN13 . . . .**191** FJ125
  Weybridge KT13 . . . .**152** BN106
Warren Cres, N9 . . . .**46** DT46
Warren Cutting, Kings.T. KT2 .**118** CR94
Warrender Rd, N19 . . . .**65** DJ62
  Chesham HP5 . . . .**4** AS29
Warrender Way, Ruis. HA4 . . .**59** BU59
Warren Dr, Grnf. UB6 . . . .**78** CB70
  Hornchurch RM12 . . . .**71** FG62
  Orpington BR6 . . . .**164** EV106
  Ruislip HA4 . . . .**60** BX59
  Tadworth (Kgswd.) KT20 . .**173** CZ122
Warren Dr, The, E11 . . . .**68** EJ59
Warren Dr N, Surb. KT5 . . . . .**138** CP102
Warren Dr S, Surb. KT5 . . . . .**138** CQ102
Warreners La, Wey. KT13 . . . .**153** BR109
Warren Fld, Epp. CM16 . . . . . .**18** EU32
  Iver SL0 . . . .**75** BC68
Warrenfield Cl, Wal.Cr. (Chsht.)
  EN7 off Portland Dr **14** DU31
Warren Flds, Stan. HA7
  off Valencia Rd **41** CJ49
Warren Footpath, Twick. TW1 .**117** CJ88
Warren Gdns, E15
  off Ashton Rd **67** ED64
  Orpington BR6 . . . .**164** EU106
Warrengate La, Pot.B. EN6 . . .**11** CW31
Warrengate Rd, Hat. AL9 . . . . .**11** CW28
Warren Gro, Borwd. WD6 . . . .**26** CR42
Warren Hastings Ct, Grav. DA11
  off Pier Rd **131** GF86
Warren Hts, Grays (Chaff.Hun.)
  RM16 . . . .**110** FY77
  Loughton IG10
  off Warren Hill **32** EJ43
Warren Hill, Epsom KT18 . . . .**172** CR116
  Loughton IG10 . . . .**32** EJ44
Warren Ho, E3
  off Bromley High St **85** EB69
Warren La, SE18 . . . .**105** EP76
  Grays RM16 . . . .**109** FU77
  Leatherhead (Oxshott) KT22 .**154** CC111
  Oxted RH8 . . . .**188** EF134
  Stanmore HA7 . . . .**41** CF48

War - Wea

Warren La, Wok. GU22 . . . . . .168 BH118
Warren Lo Dr, Tad. (Kgswd.)
  KT20 . . . . .173 CY124
Warren Mead, Bans. SM7 . .173 CW115
Warren Ms, W1 . . . . .195 K5
Warrenne Way, Reig. RH2 . .184 DA134
Warren Pk, Kings.T. KT2 . . . .118 CQ93
  Tadworth KT20 . . . . .182 CQ131
  Warlingham CR6 . . . . .177 DX118
Warren Pk Rd, Sutt. SM1 . . .158 DD107
Warren Pl, E1
  off Pitsea St 85 DX72
Warren Pond Rd, E4 . . . . .48 EF46
Warren Ri, N.Mal. KT3 . . . . .138 CR95
Warren Rd, E4 . . . . .47 EC47
  E10 . . . . .67 EC62
  E11 . . . . .68 EJ60
  NW2 . . . . .63 CT61
  SW19 . . . . .120 DE93
  Addlestone (New Haw)
    KT15 . . . . .152 BG110
  Ashford TW15 . . . . .115 BS94
  Banstead SM7 . . . . .157 CW114
  Bexleyheath DA6 . . . . . . .126 FA85
  Bromley BR2 . . . . .144 EG103
  Bushey (Bushey Hth.) WD23 . .40 CC46
  Croydon CR0 . . . . .142 DS102
  Dartford DA1 . . . . .128 FK90
  Gravesend (Sthflt.) DA13 . .130 GB92
  Ilford IG6 . . . . .69 ER57
  Kingston upon Thames KT2 .118 CQ93
  Orpington BR6 . . . . .163 ET106
  Purley CR8 . . . . .159 DP112
  Reigate RH2 . . . . .184 DB133
  Sidcup DA14 . . . . .126 EW90
  Twickenham TW2 . . . . . . .116 CC86
  Uxbridge UB10 . . . . .58 BL63
Warrens Shawe La, Edg. HA8 . .42 CP46
⊖ Warren Street, W1 . . . . . . .195 L4
Warren St, W1 . . . . .195 J5
Warren Ter, Grays RM16
  off Arterial Rd W Thurrock .109 FX75
  Romford RM6 . . . . .70 EX56
Warren Wk, SE7 . . . . .104 EJ79
Warren Way, NW7 . . . . .43 CY51
  Weybridge KT13 . . . . .153 BQ106
Warren Wd Cl, Brom. BR2 . .144 EF103
Warriner Av, Horn. RM12 . . . .72 FK61
Warriner Dr, N9 . . . . .46 DU48
Warriner Gdns, SW11 . . . . . .100 DF81
Warrington Cres, W9 . . . . .82 DC70
Warrington Gdns, W9
  off Warrington Av 82 DC70
  Hornchurch RM11 . . . . .72 FJ58
Warrington Pl, E14 . . . . .204 E2
Warrington Rd, Croy. CR0 . .141 DP104
  Dagenham RM8 . . . . .70 EX61
  Harrow HA1 . . . . .61 CE57
  Richmond TW10 . . . . .117 CK85
Warrington Spur, Wind.
  (Old Wind.) SL4 . . . . .12 AV87
Warrington Sq, Dag. RM8 . . . .70 EX61
Warrior Av, Grav. DA12 . . . .131 GJ91
Warrior Sq, E12 . . . . .69 EN63
Warsaw Cl, Ruis. HA4
  off Glebe Av 77 BV65
Warsdale Dr, NW9
  off Mardale Dr 62 CR57
Warspite Rd, SE18 . . . . .104 EL76
Warton Rd, E15 . . . . .85 EC66
Warwall, E6 . . . . .87 EP72
⊖ Warwick Avenue, W9 . . . . . .82 DC70
Warwick Av, W2 . . . . .82 DC70
  W9 . . . . .82 DC70
  Edgware HA8 . . . . .42 CP48
  Egham TW20 . . . . .133 BC95
  Harrow HA2 . . . . .60 BZ60
  Potters Bar (Cuffley) EN6 . .13 DK27
  Staines TW18 . . . . .114 BJ93
Warwick Cl, Barn. EN4 . . . . . .28 DD43
  Bexley DA5 . . . . .126 EZ87
  Bushey (Bushey Hth.) WD23
    off Magnaville Rd 41 CE45
  Hampton TW12 . . . . .116 CC94
  Orpington BR6 . . . . .146 EU104
  Potters Bar (Cuffley) EN6 . .13 DK27
Warwick Ct, SE15 . . . . .102 DU82
  WC1 . . . . .196 C7
  Rickmansworth (Chorl.) WD3 .21 BF41
  Surbiton KT6 off Hook Rd . .138 CL103
Warwick Cres, W2 . . . . .82 DC71
  Hayes UB4 . . . . .77 BT70
Warwick Deeping, Cher. (Ott.)
  KT16 . . . . .151 BC106
Warwick Dene, W5 . . . . .80 CL74
Warwick Dr, SW15 . . . . .99 CV83
  Waltham Cross (Chsht.)
    EN8 . . . . .15 DX28
Warwick Est, W2 . . . . .82 DB71
Warwick Gdns, N4 . . . . .66 DQ57
  W14 . . . . .99 CZ76
  Ashtead KT21 . . . . .171 CJ117
  Barnet EN5 off Great N Rd . .27 CZ38
  Ilford IG1 . . . . .69 EP60
  Romford RM2 . . . . .72 FJ55
  Thames Ditton KT7 . . . . . .137 CF99
Warwick Gro, E5 . . . . .66 DV60
  Surbiton KT5 . . . . .138 CM101
Warwick Ho St, SW1 . . . . . .199 N2
Warwick La, EC4 . . . . .196 G9
  Rainham RM13 . . . . .90 FM68
  Upminster RM14 . . . . .90 FN68
  Woking GU21 . . . . .166 AU119
Warwick Pas, EC4 . . . . .196 G8
Warwick Pl, W5 off Warwick Rd .97 CK75
  W9 . . . . .82 DC71
  Gravesend (Nthflt.) DA11 . .130 GB85
  Uxbridge UB8 . . . . .76 BJ66
Warwick Pl N, SW1 . . . . . . .199 K9
Warwick Quad Shop Mall, Red.
  RH1 off London Rd 184 DG134
Warwick Rd, E4 . . . . .47 EA50
  E11 . . . . .68 EH57
  E12 . . . . .68 EL64

Warwick Rd, E15 . . . . .86 EF65
  E17 . . . . .47 DZ53
  N11 . . . . .45 DK51
  N18 . . . . .46 DS49
  SE20 . . . . .142 DV97
  SW5 . . . . .99 CZ77
  W5 . . . . .97 CK75
  W14 . . . . .99 CZ77
  Ashford TW15 . . . . .114 BL92
  Barnet EN5 . . . . .28 DB42
  Borehamwood WD6 . . . . . .26 CR41
  Coulsdon CR5 . . . . .159 DJ114
  Enfield EN3 . . . . .31 DZ37
  Hounslow TW4 . . . . .95 BV83
  Kingston upon Thames KT1 .137 CJ95
  New Malden KT3 . . . . .138 CQ97
  Rainham RM13 . . . . .90 FJ70
  Redhill RH1 . . . . .184 DF133
  Sidcup DA14 . . . . .126 EV92
  Southall UB2 . . . . .96 BZ76
  Sutton SM1 . . . . .158 DC105
  Thames Ditton KT7 . . . . . .137 CF99
  Thornton Heath CR7 . . . . .141 DN97
  Twickenham TW2 . . . . . . .117 CE88
  Welling DA16 . . . . .106 EW83
  West Drayton UB7 . . . . . . .94 BL75
Warwick Row, SW1 . . . . . . .199 J6
Warwickshire Path, SE8 . . . .103 DZ80
Warwick Sq, EC4 . . . . .196 G8
  SW1 . . . . .199 K10
Warwick Sq Ms, SW1 . . . . . .199 K9
Warwick Ter, SE18 . . . . .105 ER79
Warwick Way, SW1 . . . . . . .199 K9
  Rickmansworth (Crox.Grn.)
    WD3 . . . . .23 BQ42
WARWICK WOLD, Red. 185 DN129
Warwick Wold Rd, Red. RH1 .185 DN128
Warwick Yd, EC1 . . . . .197 J5
Washington Av, E12 . . . . .68 EL63
Washington Cl, Reig. RH2 . . .184 DA131
Washington Rd, E6
  off St. Stephens Rd 86 EJ66
  E18 . . . . .48 EF54
  SW13 . . . . .99 CU80
  Kingston upon Thames KT1 .138 CN96
  Worcester Park KT4 . . . . . .139 CV103
Wash La, Pot.B. EN6 . . . . . . .11 CV33
Washneys Rd, Orp. BR6 . . . .164 EV113
Washpond La, Warl. CR6 . . . .177 EC118
Wash Rd, Brwd. CM13 . . . . . .55 GD44
Wastdale Rd, SE23 . . . . .123 DX88
Watchfield Ct, W4 . . . . .98 CQ78
Watchgate, Dart. (Lane End)
  DA2 . . . . .129 FR91
Watcombe Cotts, Rich. TW9 . .98 CN79
Watcombe Pl, SE25
  off Albert Rd 142 DV99
Watcombe Rd, SE25 . . . . . . .142 DV99
Waterbank Rd, SE6 . . . . .123 EB89
Waterbeach Rd, Dag. RM9 . . .88 EW65
Waterbrook La, NW4 . . . . . . .63 CW57
Water Circ, Green. (Bluewater)
  DA9 . . . . .129 FT88
Watercress Pl, N1
  off Hertford Rd 84 DS66
Watercress Rd, Wal.Cr. (Chsht.)
  EN7 . . . . .14 DR26
Watercress Way, Wok. GU21 .166 AV117
Watercroft Rd, Sev. (Halst.)
  TN14 . . . . .164 EZ110
Waterdale Rd, SE2 . . . . .106 EU79
Waterdales, Grav. (Nthflt.)
  DA11 . . . . .130 GD88
Waterdell Pl, Rick. WD3
  off Uxbridge Rd 38 BG47
Waterden Rd, E15 . . . . .67 EA64
WATER END, Hat. 11 CV26
Waterer Gdns, Tad. KT20 . . .173 CX118
Waterer Ri, Wall. SM6 . . . . . .159 DK107
Waterfall Cl, N14 . . . . .45 DJ48
  Virginia Water GU25 . . . . .132 AU97
Waterfall Cotts, SW19 . . . . . .120 DD93
Waterfall Rd, N11 . . . . .45 DH49
  N14 . . . . .45 DJ48
  SW19 . . . . .120 DD93
Waterfall Ter, SW17 . . . . . . .120 DE93
Waterfield, Rick. (Herons.)
  WD3 . . . . .37 BC45
  Tadworth KT20 . . . . .173 CV119
Waterfield Cl, SE28 . . . . .88 EV74
  Belvedere DA17 . . . . .106 FA76
Waterfield Gdns, SE25 . . . . .142 DS99
Waterfield Grn, Tad. KT20 . . .173 CW120
Waterfields, Lthd. KT22 . . . . .171 CH119
Waterfields Way, Wat. WD17 .24 BX42
Waterford Cl, Cob. KT11 . . . .154 BY111
Waterford Rd, SW6 . . . . .100 DB81
Water Gdns, Stan. HA7 . . . . . .41 CH51
Water Gdns, The, W2 . . . . . .194 C8
Watergardens, The, Kings.T.
  KT2 . . . . .118 CQ93
Watergate, EC4 . . . . .196 F10
Watergate, The, Wat. WD19 . .40 BX47
Watergate St, SE8 . . . . .103 EA79
Watergate Wk, WC2 . . . . . . .200 A2
Wateridge Ind Pk, Grays
  RM20 . . . . .109 FT78
Waterhall Av, E4 . . . . .48 EE49
Waterhall Cl, E17 . . . . .47 DX53
Waterhead Cl, Erith DA8 . . . .107 FE80
Waterhouse Cl, E16 . . . . .86 EK71
  NW3 off Lyndhurst Rd 64 DD64
  W6 off Great Ch La 99 CX77
Waterhouse La, Ken. CR8 . . .236 DQ119
  Redhill (Bletch.) RH1 . . . . .186 DT132
  Tadworth (Kgswd.) KT20 . .173 CY121
Waterhouse Sq, EC1 . . . . . . .196 D7
Wateridge Cl, E14 . . . . .203 P7
Wateringbury Cl, Orp. BR5 . .146 EV97
Water La, E15 . . . . .86 EE65
  EC3 . . . . .201 M1
  N9 . . . . .46 DV46
  NW1 off Kentish Town Rd . .83 DH66
  SE14 . . . . .102 DW80
  Cobham KT11 . . . . .170 BY115

Water La, Hem.H. (Bov.) HP3 . .5 BA29
  Ilford IG3 . . . . .69 ES62
  Kings Langley WD4 . . . . . . .7 BP29
  Kingston upon Thames KT1 .137 CK95
  Oxted (Titsey) RH8 . . . . . .188 EG126
  Purfleet RM19 . . . . .108 FN77
  Redhill RH1 . . . . .185 DP130
  Richmond TW9 . . . . .117 CK85
  Sevenoaks (Shore.) TN14 . .165 FF112
  Sidcup DA14 . . . . .126 EZ89
  Twickenham TW1
    off The Embankment 117 CG88
  Watford WD17 . . . . .24 BW42
  Westerham TN16 . . . . .189 ER127
Water Lily Cl, Sthl. UB2
  off Navigator Dr 96 CC75
⊖ Waterloo 200 D4
⊕ Waterloo 200 D4
Waterloo Br, SE1 . . . . .200 B1
  WC2 . . . . .200 B1
Waterloo Cl, E9
  off Churchill Wk 66 DW64
  Feltham TW14 . . . . .115 BT88
⊕ Waterloo East 200 D3
Waterloo Est, E2 . . . . .84 DW68
Waterloo Gdns, E2 . . . . .84 DW68
  N1 off Barnsbury St 83 DP66
  Romford RM7 . . . . .71 FD58
⊕ Waterloo International 200 C4
Waterloo Pas, NW6 . . . . .81 CZ66
Waterloo Pl, SW1 . . . . .199 M2
  Richmond TW9
    off Sheen Rd 118 CL85
  Richmond (Kew) TW9 . . . . .98 CN79
Waterloo Rd, E6 . . . . .86 EJ66
  E7 off Wellington Rd 68 EF64
  E10 . . . . .67 EA59
  NW2 . . . . .63 CU60
  SE1 . . . . .200 D4
  Brentwood CM14 . . . . .54 FW46
  Epsom KT19 . . . . .156 CR112
  Ilford IG6 . . . . .49 EQ54
  Romford RM7 . . . . .71 FE57
  Sutton SM1 . . . . .158 DD106
  Uxbridge UB8 . . . . .76 BJ67
Waterloo St, Grav. DA12 . . . .131 GJ87
Waterloo Ter, N1 . . . . .83 DP66
Waterlow Ct, NW11
  off Heath Cl 64 DB59
Waterlow Rd, N19 . . . . .65 DJ60
  Redhill RH1 . . . . .185 DH134
Waterman St, SW15 . . . . .99 CX83
Watermans Wk, SE16 . . . . . .203 K6
Watermans Way, Epp.
  (N.Wld.Bas.) CM16 . . . . . .18 FA27
Waterman Way, E1 . . . . .202 D2
Watermead, Felt. TW14 . . . . .115 BS88
  Tadworth KT20 . . . . .173 CV120
  Woking GU21 . . . . .166 AT116
Watermead La, Cars. SM5
  off Middleton Rd 140 DF101
Watermeadow Cl, Erith DA8 . .107 FH81
Watermead La, SW6 . . . . . . .100 DC82
Watermead Rd, SE6 . . . . .123 EC91
Watermead Twr, SW6 . . . . . .100 DC81
Watermead Way, N17 . . . . . . .66 DV55
Watermen's Sq, SE20 . . . . . .122 DW94
Water Ms, SE15 . . . . .102 DW84
Watermill Cl, Rich. TW10 . . . .117 CJ90
Watermill La, N18 . . . . .46 DS50
Watermill Way, SW19 . . . . . .140 DC95
Water Mill Way, Dart. (S.Darenth)
  DA4 . . . . .148 FP96
Watermint Cl, Orp. BR5
  off Wagtail Way 146 EX98
Watermint Quay, N16 . . . . . . .66 DU59
Waterperry La, Wok. (Chobham)
  GU24 . . . . .150 AT110
Water Rd, Wem. HA0 . . . . . . .80 CM67
Watersedge, Epsom KT19 . . .156 CQ105
Watersfield Way, Edg. HA8 . . .41 CK52
Waters Gdns, Dag. RM10 . . . .70 FA64
Waterside, Beck. BR3
  off Rectory Rd 143 EA95
  Dartford DA1 . . . . .127 FE85
Water Side, Kings L. WD4 . . . .6 BN29
Waterside, Rad. WD7 . . . . . . .9 CH34
  St. Albans (Lon.Col.) AL2 . .10 CL27
  Uxbridge UB8 . . . . .76 BJ71
Waterside Cl, E3 . . . . .85 DZ67
  SE16 . . . . .202 C5
  Barking IG11 . . . . .70 EU63
  Northolt UB5 . . . . .78 BZ69
  Romford (Harold Wd.) RM3 .52 FN52
  Surbiton KT6
    off Culsac Rd 138 CL103
Waterside Dr, Slou. (Langley)
  SL3 . . . . .93 AZ75
  Walton-on-Thames KT12 . .135 BU99
Waterside Pl, NW1
  off Princess Rd 82 DG67
Waterside Pt, SW11 . . . . .100 DE80
Waterside Rd, Sthl. UB2 . . . . .96 CA76
Waterside Trd Cen, W7 . . . . . .97 CE76
Waterside Way, SW17 . . . . . .120 DC91
  Woking GU21
    off Winnington Way 166 AV118
Watersmeet Way, SE28 . . . . . .88 EW73
Waterson Rd, Grays RM16 . . .111 GH77
Waterson St, E2 . . . . .197 N2
Watersplash Cl, Kings.T. KT1 .138 CL96
Watersplash La, Hayes UB3 . .95 BU77
  Hounslow TW5 . . . . .95 BV78
Watersplash Rd, Shep. TW17 .134 BN98

Waters Rd, SE6 . . . . .124 EE90
  Kingston upon Thames KT1 .138 CP96
Waters Sq, Kings.T. KT1 . . . .138 CP97
Water St, WC2 . . . . .196 C10
Waterton Av, Grav. DA12 . . . .131 GL87
Water Twr Cl, Uxb. UB8 . . . . .58 BL64
Water Twr Hill, Croy. CR0 . . .160 DR105
Water Twr Pl, N1
  off Old Royal Free Sq 83 DN67
Waterview Ho, E14 . . . . .85 DY71
Waterway Rd, Lthd. KT22 . . .171 CG122
Waterworks La, E5 . . . . .67 DX61
Waterworks Rd, SW2 . . . . . . .121 DM86
Waterworks Yd, Croy. CR0
  off Surrey St 142 DQ104
Watery La, SW20 . . . . .139 CZ96
  Chertsey (Lyne) KT16 . . . . .133 BD102
  Northolt UB5 . . . . .78 BW68
  St. Albans (Flam.) AL3 . . . . .9 CK28
  Sidcup DA14 . . . . .126 EV93
Wates Way, Brwd. CM15 . . . .54 FX46
  Mitcham CR4 . . . . .140 DF100
Wates Way Ind Est, Mitch. CR4
  off Wates Way 140 DF100
Wateville Rd, N17 . . . . .46 DQ53
WATFORD 23 BT41
⊕ Watford 23 BT41
Watford Arches Retail Pk, Wat.
  WD17 off Lower High St . . .24 BX43
⊕ Watford Business Pk, Wat.
  WD18 . . . . .23 BS44
Watford Bypass, Borwd. WD6 .41 CG45
Watford Cl, SW11
  off Petworth St 100 DE81
Watford Fld Rd, Wat. WD18 . .24 BW43
★ Watford FC, Wat. WD18 . . .23 BV43
Ⓗ Watford Gen Hosp, Wat.
  WD18 . . . . .23 BV43
WATFORD HEATH, Wat. 40 BY46
Watford Heath, Wat. WD19 . . .40 BX45
⊕ Watford High Street 24 BW42
⊕ Watford Junction 24 BW40
★ Watford Mus, Wat. WD17 . .24 BW43
⊕ Watford North 24 BW37
Watford Rd, E16 . . . . .86 EG71
  Borehamwood (Elstree)
    WD6 . . . . .25 CJ44
  Harrow HA1 . . . . .61 CG61
  Kings Langley WD4 . . . . . . .7 BP32
  Northwood HA6 . . . . .39 BT52
  Radlett WD7 . . . . .9 CH34
  Rickmansworth (Crox.Grn.)
    WD3 . . . . .23 BQ43
  St. Albans AL2 . . . . .8 CA27
  Wembley HA0 . . . . .61 CG61
⊕ Watford Stadium Halt
  (closed) 23 BU44
Watford Way, NW4 . . . . .63 CU56
  NW7 . . . . .63 CU56
⊕ Watford West (closed) 23 BT43
Watkin Rd, Wem. HA9 . . . . . . .62 CP62
Watkins Ri, Pot.B. EN6
  off The Walk 12 DB32
Watling Av, Edg. HA8 . . . . . . .42 CR52
Watling Ct, EC4 . . . . .197 J9
  Borehamwood WD6 . . . . . .25 CK44
Watling Fm Cl, Stan. HA7 . . . .41 CJ46
Watling Gdns, NW2 . . . . .81 CY65
Watling Knoll, Rad. WD7 . . . . .9 CF33
Watlings Cl, Croy. CR0 . . . . .143 DY100
Watling St, EC4 . . . . .197 H9
  SE15 off Dragon Rd 102 DS79
  Bexleyheath DA6 . . . . .107 FB84
  Borehamwood (Elstree)
    WD6 . . . . .25 CJ40
  Dartford DA1, DA2 . . . . . . .128 FP87
  Gravesend DA11,
    DA12, DA13 . . . . .130 GC90
  Radlett WD7 . . . . .9 CF32
  St. Albans AL2 . . . . .8 CC25
Watling St Caravan Site
  (Travellers), St.Alb. AL2 . . .8 CC25
Watlington Gro, SE26 . . . . . .123 DY92
Watney Mkt, E1
  off Commercial Rd 84 DV72
Watney Rd, SW14 . . . . .98 CQ83
Watneys Rd, Mitch. CR4 . . . .141 DK99
Watney St, E1 . . . . .84 DV72
Watson Av, E6 . . . . .87 EN66
  Sutton SM3 . . . . .139 CY103
Watson Cl, N16
  off Matthias Rd 66 DR64
  SW19 . . . . .120 DE93
  Grays RM20 . . . . .109 FU81
Watson Gdns, Rom. (Harold Wd.)
  RM3 . . . . .52 FK54
Watson's Ms, W1 . . . . .194 C7
Watsons Rd, N22 . . . . .45 DM53
Watson's St, SE8 . . . . .103 EA80
Watson St, E13 . . . . .86 EH68
Watsons Yd, NW2
  off North Circular Rd 63 CT61
Wattendon Rd, Ken. CR8 . . . .175 DP115
Wattisfield Rd, E5 . . . . .66 DW62
Watts Cl, N15 off Seaford Rd . .66 DS57
  Tadworth KT20 . . . . .173 CX122
Watts Fm Par, Wok. (Chobham)
  GU24 off Barnmead 150 AT110
Watts Gro, E3 . . . . .85 EB71
Watts La, Chis. BR7 . . . . .145 EP95
  Tadworth KT20 . . . . .173 CX122
  Teddington TW11 . . . . . . .117 CG92
Watts Mead, Tad. KT20 . . . . .173 CX122
Watts Pt, E13 off Brooks Rd . .86 EG67
Watts Rd, T.Ditt. KT7 . . . . . .137 CG101
Watts St, E1 . . . . .202 E2
  SE15 . . . . .102 DT81
Watts Way, SW7 . . . . .198 A6
Wat Tyler Rd, SE3 . . . . .103 EC82
  SE10 . . . . .103 EC82
Wauthier Cl, N13 . . . . .45 DP50
Wavell Cl, Wal.Cr. (Chsht.)
  EN8 . . . . .15 DY27
Wavell Dr, Sid. DA15 . . . . . . .125 ES86
Wavel Ms, N8 . . . . .65 DK56

Wavel Ms, NW6 off Acol Rd . .82 DB66
Wavel Pl, SE26
  off Sydenham Hill 122 DT91
Wavendene Av, Egh. TW20 . .113 BB94
Wavendon Av, W4 . . . . .98 CR78
Waveney Av, SE15 . . . . .102 DW84
Waveney Cl, E1 . . . . .202 C2
Waverley Av, E4 . . . . .47 DZ49
  E17 . . . . .67 ED55
  Kenley CR8 . . . . .176 DS116
  Surbiton KT5 . . . . .138 CP100
  Sutton SM1 . . . . .140 DB103
  Twickenham TW2 . . . . . . .116 CA87
  Wembley HA9 . . . . .62 CM64
Waverley Cl, E18 . . . . .48 EJ53
  Bromley BR2 . . . . .144 EK99
  Hayes UB3 . . . . .95 BR77
  West Molesey KT8 . . . . . . .136 CA99
Waverley Ct, Wok. GU22 . . . .166 AY118
Waverley Cres, SE18 . . . . . . .105 ER78
  Romford RM3 . . . . .52 FJ52
Waverley Dr, Cher. KT16 . . . .133 BD104
  Virginia Water GU25 . . . . .132 AU97
Waverley Gdns, E6
  off Oliver Gdns 86 EL71
  NW10 . . . . .80 CM69
  Barking IG11 . . . . .87 ES68
  Grays RM16 . . . . .110 GA75
  Ilford IG6 . . . . .49 EQ54
  Northwood HA6 . . . . .39 BU53
Waverley Gro, N3 . . . . .63 CY55
Waverley Ind Est, Har. HA1 . . .61 CD55
Waverley Pl, N4
  off Adolphus Rd 65 DP61
  NW8 . . . . .82 DD68
Waverley Rd, E17
  off Church Rd 171 CH122
Waverley Rd, E17 . . . . .67 EC55
  E18 . . . . .48 EJ53
  N8 . . . . .65 DK58
  N17 . . . . .46 DV52
  SE18 . . . . .105 EQ78
  SE25 . . . . .142 DV98
  Cobham (Stoke D'Ab.) KT11 .154 CB114
  Enfield EN2 . . . . .29 DP42
  Epsom KT17 . . . . .157 CV106
  Harrow HA2 . . . . .60 BZ60
  Leatherhead (Oxshott) KT22 .154 CB114
  Rainham RM13 . . . . .89 FH69
  Southall UB1 . . . . .78 CA73
  Weybridge KT13 . . . . .152 BN106
Waverley Vil, N17 . . . . .46 DT54
Waverley Wk, W2 . . . . .82 DA71
Waverley Way, Cars. SM5 . . .158 DE107
Waverton Ho, E3 . . . . .85 DZ67
Waverton Rd, SW18 . . . . . . .120 DC87
Waverton St, W1 . . . . .198 G2
Wavertree Ct, SW2
  off Streatham Hill 121 DM88
Wavertree Rd, E18 . . . . .48 EG54
  SW2 . . . . .121 DL88
Waxlow Cres, Sthl. UB1 . . . . .78 CA72
Waxlow Rd, NW10 . . . . .80 CQ68
Waxwell Cl, Pnr. HA5 . . . . . . .40 BX54
Waxwell La, Pnr. HA5 . . . . . . .40 BX54
Waxwell Ter, SE1 . . . . .200 C5
Way, The, Reig. RH2 . . . . . . .184 DD133
Wayborne Gro, Ruis. HA4 . . . .59 BQ58
Waycross Rd, Upmin. RM14 . .73 FS58
Waye Av, Houns. TW5 . . . . . . .95 BU81
Wayfarer Rd, Nthlt. UB5 . . . . .78 BX70
Wayfaring Grn, Grays (Bad.Dene)
  RM17 off Curling La 110 FZ78
Wayfield Link, SE9 . . . . .125 ER86
Wayford St, SW11 . . . . .100 DE82
Wayland Av, E8 . . . . .66 DU64
Waylands, Hayes UB3 . . . . . . .77 BR71
  Staines (Wrays.) TW19 . . .112 AY86
  Swanley BR8 . . . . .147 FF98
Waylands Cl, Sev. (Knock.)
  TN14 . . . . .180 EY115
Waylands Mead, Beck. BR3 . .143 EB95
Wayleave, The, SE28 . . . . . . .88 EV73
Waylett Pl, SE27 . . . . .121 DP90
  Wembley HA0 . . . . .61 CK63
Wayman Ct, E8 . . . . .84 DV65
Wayne Cl, Orp. BR6 . . . . . . .145 ET104
Waynflete Twr Av, Esher
  KT10 . . . . .136 CA104
Waynflete Av, Croy. CR0 . . . .141 DP104
Waynflete Sq, W10 . . . . .81 CX73
Waynflete St, SW18 . . . . . . .120 DC89
Wayside, NW11 . . . . .63 CY60
  SW14 . . . . .118 CQ85
  Croydon CR0 off Field Way .161 EB107
  Kings Langley (Chipper.)
    WD4 . . . . .6 BH30
  Potters Bar EN6 . . . . .12 DD33
  Radlett (Shenley) WD7 . . . . .9 CK33
Wayside Av, Bushey WD23 . . .25 CD44
  Hornchurch RM12 . . . . .72 FK61
Wayside Cl, N14 . . . . .29 DJ44
  Romford RM1 . . . . .71 FF55
Wayside Commercial Est, Bark.
  IG11 . . . . .88 EU67
Wayside Ct, Twick. TW1 . . . . .117 CJ86
  Wembley HA9
    off Oakington Av 62 CN62
  Woking GU21
    off Langmans Way 166 AS116
Wayside Gdns, SE9
  off Wayside Gro 125 EM91
  Dagenham RM10 . . . . .70 FA64
  Gerrards Cross SL9 . . . . . . .56 AX59
Wayside Gro, SE9 . . . . .125 EM91
Wayside Ms, Ilf. IG2
  off Gaysham Av 69 EN57
Wayville Rd, Dart. DA1 . . . . .128 FP87
Way Volante, Grav. DA12 . . .131 GL91
Weald, The, Chis. BR7 . . . . . .144 EM93
Weald Cl, SE16 . . . . .202 D10
  Brentwood CM14 . . . . .54 FU48
  Bromley BR2 . . . . .144 EL103
  Gravesend (Istead Rise)
    DA13 . . . . .130 GE94
★ Weald Country Pk, Brwd.
  CM14 . . . . .54 FS45

Weald Hall La, Epp. (Thnwd.)
CM16 . . . . .18 EW25
Weald La, Har. HA3 . . . . .41 CD54
Weald Pk Way, Brwd. CM14 . .54 FS48
Weald Ri, Har. HA3 . . . . . . .41 CF52
Weald Rd, Brwd. CM14 . . . . .53 FR46
Sevenoaks TN13 . . . . . .191 FH129
Uxbridge UB10 . . . . . . .76 BN68
Weald Sq, E5
off Rossington St 66 DV61
WEALDSTONE, Har. 61 CF55
Wealdstone Rd, Sutt. SM3 . .139 CZ103
Weald Way, Cat. CR3 . . . .186 DS128
Wealdway, Grav. DA13 . . . .131 GH93
Weald Way, Hayes UB4 . . . .77 BS69
Romford RM7 . . . . .71 FB58
Wealdwood Gdns, Pnr. HA5
off Highbanks Rd 40 CB51
Weale Rd, E4 . . . . .47 ED48
Weall Cl, Pur. CR8 . . . . . .159 DM112
Weall Grn, Wat. WD25 . . . . . .7 BV32
Weardale Av, Dart. DA2 . . . .128 FQ89
Weardale Gdns, Enf. EN2 . . . .30 DR39
Weardale Rd, SE13 . . . . . .103 ED84
Wear Pl, E2 . . . . .84 DV69
Wearside Rd, SE13 . . . . . .103 EB84
Weasdale Ct, Wok. GU21
off Roundthorn Way 166 AT116
Weatherall Cl, Add. KT15 . . .152 BH106
Weatherley Cl, E3 . . . . . . .85 DZ71
Weaver Cl, E6 off Trader Rd . .87 EP73
Croydon CR0 . . . . .160 DT105
Weavers Cl, Grav. DA11 . . . .131 GG88
Isleworth TW7 . . . . . . .97 CE84
Weavers La, Sev. TN14 . . . .191 FJ121
Weavers Orchard, Grav. (Sthflt.)
DA13 . . . . .130 GA93
Weavers Ter, SW6 . . . . . . .100 DA79
Weaver St, E1 . . . . .84 DU70
Weavers Way, NW1 . . . . . .83 DK67
Weaver Wk, SE27 . . . . . . .121 DP91
Webb Cl, W10 . . . . .81 CW70
Slough SL3 . . . . .92 AX77
Webber Cl, Borwd. (Elstree)
WD6 off Rodgers Cl 25 CK44
Erith DA8 . . . . .107 FH80
Webber Row, SE1 . . . . . . .200 E6
Webber St, SE1 . . . . .200 E4
Webb Est, E5 . . . . .66 DU59
Webb Gdns, E13
off Kelland Rd 86 EG70
Webb Pl, NW10
off Old Oak La 81 CT69
Webb Rd, SE3 . . . . .104 EF79
Webb's All, Sev. TN13, TN15 . .191 FH121
Webbscroft Rd, Dag. RM10 . .71 FB63
Webbs Rd, SW11 . . . . . . .120 DF85
Hayes UB4 . . . . .77 BV69
Webb St, SE1 . . . . .201 M7
Webster Cl, Horn. RM12 . . . .72 FK62
Leatherhead (Oxshott)
KT22 . . . . .154 CB114
Waltham Abbey EN9 . . . . .16 EG33
Webster Gdns, W5 . . . . . .79 CK74
Webster Rd, E11 . . . . .67 EC62
SE16 . . . . .202 C7
Websters Cl, Wok. GU22 . . .166 AU120
Wedderburn Rd, NW3 . . . . .64 DD64
Barking IG11 . . . . .87 ER67
Wedgewood Cl, Epp. CM16
off Theydon Gro 18 EU30
Northwood HA6 . . . . . . .39 BQ51
Wedgewoods, West. (Tats.) TN16
off Westmore Rd 178 EJ121
Wedgewood Wk, NW6
off Lymington Rd 64 DB64
Wedgwood Ms, W1 . . . . . .195 N9
Wedgwood Pl, Cob. KT11
off Portsmouth Rd 153 BU114
Wedgwood Way, SE19 . . . .122 DQ94
Wedlake Cl, Horn. RM11 . . . .72 FL60
Wedlake St, W10
off Kensal Rd 81 CY70
Wedmore Av, Ilf. IG5 . . . . . .49 EN53
Wedmore Gdns, N19 . . . . . .65 DK61
Wedmore Ms, N19
off Wedmore St 65 DK62
Wedmore Rd, Grnf. UB6 . . . .79 CD69
Wedmore St, N19 . . . . .65 DK62
Wednesbury Gdns, Rom. RM3 . .52 FM52
Wednesbury Grn, Rom. RM3
off Wednesbury Gdns 52 FM52
Wednesbury Rd, Rom. RM3 . . .52 FM52
Weech Rd, NW6 . . . . .64 DA63
Weedington Rd, NW5 . . . . . .64 DG64
Weedon Cl, Ger.Cr. (Chal.St.P.)
SL9 . . . . .36 AV53
Weekley Sq, SW11
off Thomas Baines Rd . . .100 DD80
Weigall Rd, SE12 . . . . . . .104 EG84
Weighhouse St, W1 . . . . . .194 G9
Weighton Rd, SE20 . . . . . .142 DV96
Harrow HA3 . . . . .41 CD53
Weihurst Gdns, Sutt. SM1 . . .158 DD106
Weimar St, SW15 . . . . .99 CY83
Weind, The, Epp. (They.B.)
CM16 . . . . .33 ES36
Weirdale Av, N20 . . . . .44 DF47
Weir Est, SW12 . . . . .121 DJ87
Weir Hall Av, N18 . . . . .46 DR51
Weir Hall Gdns, N18 . . . . . .46 DR50
Weir Hall Rd, N17 . . . . .46 DR50
N18 . . . . .46 DR50
Weir Pl, Stai. TW18 . . . . . .133 BE95
Weir Rd, SW12 . . . . .121 DJ87
SW19 . . . . .120 DB90
Bexley DA5 . . . . .127 FB87
Chertsey KT16 . . . . . . .134 BH101
Walton-on-Thames KT12 . .135 BU100
Weirside Gdns, West Dr. UB7 . .76 BK74
Weir's Pas, NW1 . . . . .195 N2
Weiss Rd, SW15 . . . . .99 CX83
Welbeck Av, Brom. BR1 . . . .124 EG91
Hayes UB4 . . . . .77 BV70
Sidcup DA15 . . . . .126 EU88
Welbeck Cl, N12
off Torrington Pk 44 DD50

Welbeck Cl, Borwd. WD6 . . . .26 CN41
Epsom KT17 . . . . .157 CU108
New Malden KT3 . . . . . .139 CT99
Welbeck Rd, E6 . . . . .86 EK69
Barnet EN4 . . . . .28 DD44
Carshalton SM5 . . . . . .140 DE102
Harrow HA2 . . . . .60 CB60
Sutton SM1 . . . . .140 DD103
Welbeck St, W1 . . . . .195 H8
Welbeck Wk, Cars. SM5
off Welbeck Rd 140 DE102
Welbeck Way, W1 . . . . . . .195 H8
Welby St, SE5 . . . . .101 DP81
Welch Ho, Enf. EN3
off Beaconsfield Rd 31 DX37
Welch Pl, Pnr. HA5 . . . . . . .40 BW53
Welcomes Rd, Ken. CR8 . . .176 DQ116
Welcote Dr, Nthwd. HA6 . . . .39 BR51
Welden, Slou. SL2 . . . . . . .74 AW72
Welders La, Beac. (Jordans)
HP9 . . . . .36 AT52
Gerrards Cross (Chal.St.P.)
SL9 . . . . .36 AT52
Weldon Cl, Ruis. HA4 . . . . . .77 BV65
Weldon Dr, W.Mol. KT8 . . . .136 BZ98
Weldon Way, Red. RH1 . . . .185 DK129
Weld Pl, N11 . . . . .45 DH50
Welfare Rd, E15 . . . . .86 EE66
Welford Cl, E5 off Denton Way . .67 DX62
Welford Pl, SW19 . . . . . . .119 CY91
Welham Rd, SW16 . . . . . .120 DG92
SW17 . . . . .120 DG92
Welhouse Rd, Cars. SM5 . . .140 DE102
Wellacre Rd, Har. HA3 . . . . .61 CH58
Wellan Cl, Sid. DA15 . . . . .126 EV85
Welland Cl, Slou. SL3 . . . . .93 BA79
Welland Gdns, Grnf. UB6 . . . .79 CF68
Welland Ms, E1 . . . . .202 C2
Wellands Cl, Brom. BR1 . . . .145 EM96
Welland St, SE10 . . . . . . .103 EC79
Wellbrook Rd, Orp. BR6 . . . .163 EN105
Well Cl, SW16 . . . . .121 DM91
Ruislip HA4
off Parkfield Cres 60 BY62
Woking GU21 . . . . . . .166 AW117
Wellclose Sq, E1 . . . . .84 DU73
Wellclose St, E1 . . . . .202 C1
Wellcome Av, Dart. DA1 . . . .108 FM84
★ Wellcome Trust, NW1 . . . . .83 DK70
Well Cottage Cl, E11 . . . . . .68 EJ59
Well Ct, EC4 . . . . .197 J9
SW16 . . . . .121 DM91
Welldon Cres, Har. HA1 . . . . .61 CE58
WELL END, Borwd. 26 CR38
Well End Rd, Borwd. WD6 . . .26 CQ37
Weller Cl, Amer. HP6 . . . . . .20 AS37
Weller Dr, Amer. HP6 . . . . . .20 AS37
Wellers Cl, West. TN16 . . . .189 EQ127
Weller's Ct, NW1 . . . . . . .195 P1
Wellers Gro, Wal.Cr. (Chsht.)
EN7 . . . . .14 DU28
Weller St, SE1 . . . . .201 H4
Wellesford Cl, Bans. SM7 . . .173 CZ117
Wellesley Av, W6 . . . . .99 CV76
Iver SL0 . . . . .93 BF76
Northwood HA6 . . . . . . .39 BT50
Wellesley Ct, W9
off Maida Vale 82 DC69
Wellesley Ct Rd, Croy. CR0 . .142 DR103
Wellesley Cres, Pot.B. EN6 . . .11 CY33
Twickenham TW2 . . . . . .117 CE89
Wellesley Gro, Croy. CR0 . . .142 DR103
Wellesley Pk Ms, Enf. EN2 . . .29 DP40
Wellesley Pas, Croy. CR0
off Wellesley Rd 142 DQ103
Wellesley Path, Slou. SL1
off Wellesley Rd 92 AU75
Wellesley Pl, NW1 . . . . . . .195 M3
➤ Wellesley Road 142 DQ103
Wellesley Rd, E11 . . . . . . .68 EG57
E17 . . . . .67 EA58
N22 . . . . .45 DN54
NW5 . . . . .64 DG64
W4 . . . . .98 CN78
Brentwood CM14 . . . . . .54 FW46
Croydon CR0 . . . . .142 DQ102
Harrow HA1 . . . . .61 CE57
Ilford IG1 . . . . .69 EP61
Slough SL1 . . . . .92 AU75
Sutton SM2 . . . . .158 DC107
Twickenham TW2 . . . . . .117 CD90
Wellesley St, E1 . . . . .85 DX71
Wellesley Ter, N1 . . . . . . .197 J2
Welley Av, Stai. (Wrays.) TW19 .92 AY84
Welley Rd, Slou. (Horton) SL3 .92 AY84
Staines (Wrays.) TW19 . . . .92 AY84
Wellfield Av, N10 . . . . .65 DH55
Wellfield Gdns, Cars. SM5 . . .158 DE109
Wellfield Rd, SW16 . . . . . .121 DL91
Wellfields, Loug. IG10 . . . . . .33 EN41
Wellfield Wk, SW16 . . . . . .121 DM92
Wellfit St, SE24 off Hinton Rd .101 DP83
Wellgarth, Grnf. UB6 . . . . . .79 CH65
Wellgarth Rd, NW11 . . . . . .64 DB60
Well Gro, N20 . . . . .44 DC45
Well Hall Par, SE9
off Well Hall Rd 105 EM84
Well Hall Rd, SE9 . . . . . . .105 EM83
WELL HILL, Orp. 165 FB107
Well Hill, Orp. BR6 . . . . . . .165 FB107
Well Hill La, Orp. BR6 . . . . .165 FB108
Well Hill Rd, Sev. TN14 . . . .165 FC107
Wellhouse La, Barn. EN5 . . . .27 CW42
Wellhouse Rd, Beck. BR3 . . .143 DZ98
WELLING 106 EU83
➤ Welling 106 EU82
Welling High St, Well. DA16 . .106 EV83
Wellings Ho, Hayes UB3 . . . .77 BV74
★ Wellington Arch, W1 . . . . .198 G4
Wellington Av, E4 . . . . .47 EA47
N9 . . . . .46 DV48
N15 . . . . .66 DT58
Hounslow TW3 . . . . . . .116 CA85
Pinner HA5 . . . . .40 BZ53
Sidcup DA15 . . . . .126 EU86

Wellington Av, Vir.W. GU25 . .132 AV99
Worcester Park KT4 . . . .157 CW105
Wellington Bldgs, SW1
off Ebury Br Rd 101 DH78
Wellington Cl, SE14
off Rutts Ter 103 DX81
W11 off Ledbury Rd 82 DA72
Dagenham RM10 . . . . . . .89 FC66
Walton-on-Thames KT12
off Hepworth Way 135 BT102
Watford WD19
off Highfield 40 BZ48
Wellington Ct, NW8
off Wellington Rd 82 DD68
Ashford TW15
off Wellington Rd 114 BL92
Staines TW19 off Clare Rd .114 BL87
Wellington Cres, N.Mal. KT3 . .138 CQ97
Purley CR8 . . . . .159 DM110
Wellington Dr, Dag. RM10 . . .89 FC66
Wellington Gdns, SE7 . . . . .104 EJ79
Twickenham TW2 . . . . . .117 CD91
Wellington Gro, SE10
off Crooms Hill 103 ED80
Wellington Hill, Loug.
(High Beach) IG10 . . . . . .32 EG37
Ⓗ Wellington Hosp North,
NW8 . . . . .194 A1
Ⓗ Wellington Hosp South,
NW8 . . . . .194 A1
Wellingtonia Av, Rom.
(Hav.at.Bow.) RM4 . . . . . .51 FE48
Wellington Ms, SE7 . . . . . .104 EJ79
SE22 off Peckham Rye . . .102 DU84
SW16 off Woodbourne Av .120 DK90
Wellington Pk Est, NW2 . . . .63 CU61
Wellington Pas, E11
off Wellington Rd 68 EG57
Wellington Pl, N2
off Great N Rd 64 DE57
NW8 . . . . .194 A2
Brentwood CM14 . . . . . .54 FW50
Cobham KT11 . . . . . . .154 BZ112
Wellington Rd, E6 . . . . .87 EM68
E7 . . . . .68 EF63
E10 . . . . .67 DY60
E11 . . . . .68 EG57
E17 . . . . .67 DY55
NW8 . . . . .82 DD68
NW10 . . . . .81 CX69
SW19 . . . . .120 DA89
W5 . . . . .97 CJ76
Ashford TW15 . . . . . . .114 BL92
Belvedere DA17 . . . . . .106 EZ78
Bexley DA5 . . . . .126 EX85
Bromley BR2 . . . . .144 EJ98
Caterham CR3 . . . . . . .176 DQ122
Croydon CR0 . . . . .141 DP101
Dartford DA1 . . . . .128 FJ86
Enfield EN1 . . . . .30 DS42
Epping (N.Wld.Bas.) CM16 . .18 FA27
Feltham TW14 . . . . . . .115 BS85
Hampton TW12 . . . . . . .117 CD92
Harrow HA3 . . . . .61 CE55
Orpington BR5 . . . . . . .146 EV100
Pinner HA5 . . . . .40 BW55
St. Albans (Lon.Col.) AL2 . . .9 CK26
Tilbury RM18 . . . . .111 GG83
Twickenham TW2 . . . . . .117 CD92
Uxbridge UB8 . . . . .76 BJ67
Watford WD17 . . . . .24 BW40
Wellington Rd N, Houns. TW4 .96 BZ83
Wellington Rd S, Houns. TW4 .96 BZ84
Wellington Row, E2 . . . . . . .84 DT69
Wellington Sq, SW3 . . . . . .198 D10
SW1 . . . . .196 A10
Wellington St, SE18 . . . . . .105 EN77
WC2 . . . . .196 A10
Barking IG11 off Axe St . . .87 EQ67
Gravesend DA12 . . . . . .131 GJ87
Slough SL1 . . . . .92 AT75
Wellington Ter, E1 . . . . . . .202 D2
W2 off Notting Hill Gate . . .82 DB73
Harrow HA1 off West St . . .61 CD60
Woking (Knap.) GU21
off Victoria Rd 166 AS118
Wellington Way, E3 . . . . . . .85 EA69
Weybridge KT13 . . . . . .152 BN110
Welling Way, SE9 . . . . . . .105 ER83
Welling DA16 . . . . .105 ER83
Well La, SW14 . . . . .118 CQ85
Brentwood CM15 . . . . . .54 FT41
Woking GU21 . . . . . . .166 AW117
Wellmeade Dr, Sev. TN13 . . .191 FH127
Wellmeadow Rd, SE6 . . . . .124 EE87
SE13 . . . . .124 EE86
W7 . . . . .97 CG77
Wellow Wk, Cars. SM5 . . . .140 DD102
Well Pas, NW3 . . . . .64 DD62
Well Path, Wok. GU21
off Well La 166 AW117
Well Rd, NW3 . . . . .64 DD62
Barnet EN5 . . . . .27 CW43
Potters Bar EN6 . . . . . . .12 DE28
Wells, The, N14 . . . . .45 DK45
Wells Cl, Lthd. KT23 . . . . . .170 CB124
Northolt UB5 off Yeading La .78 BW69
South Croydon CR2 . . . .160 DS106
Waltham Cross (Chsht.) EN7
off Bloomfield Rd 14 DQ25
Wells Dr, NW9 . . . . .62 CR60
Wells Gdns, Dag. RM10 . . . .71 FB64
Ilford IG1 . . . . .68 EL59
Rainham RM13 . . . . . . .89 FF65
Wells Ho Rd, NW10 . . . . . . .80 CS71
Wellside Cl, Barn. EN5 . . . . .27 CW42
Wellside Gdns, SW14
off Well La 118 CQ85
Wells Ms, W1 . . . . .195 L7
Wellsmoor Gdns, Brom. BR1 .145 EN97
Wells Pk Rd, SE26 . . . . . . .122 DU90
Wells Pl, Red. RH1 . . . . . . .185 DH130
Wells Ri, NW8 . . . . .82 DF67
Wells Rd, W12 . . . . .99 CW75
Bromley BR1 . . . . .145 EM96
Epsom KT18 . . . . .156 CN114
Wells Sq, WC1 . . . . .196 B3

Wellstead Av, N9 . . . . .46 DW45
Wellstead Rd, E6 . . . . .87 EN68
Wells St, W1 . . . . .195 K7
Wells Ter, N4 . . . . .65 DN61
Wellstones, Wat. WD17 . . . . .23 BV41
Wellstones Yd, Wat. WD17
off Wellstones 23 BV41
Well St, E9 . . . . .84 DV66
E15 . . . . .86 EE65
Wells Way, SE5 . . . . .102 DS79
SW7 . . . . .100 DD76
Wells Yd S, N7 off George's Rd .65 DN64
Well Wk, NW3 . . . . .64 DD63
Well Way, Epsom KT18 . . . .172 CN115
Wellwood Cl, Couls. CR5
off The Vale 159 DL114
Wellwood Rd, Ilf. IG3 . . . . . .70 EU60
Welsford St, SE1 . . . . .202 B10
Welsh Cl, E13 . . . . .86 EG69
Welshpool Ho, E8
off Benjamin Cl 84 DU67
Welshpool St, E8
off Broadway Mkt 84 DV67
Welshside Wk, NW9
off Fryent Gro 62 CS58
Welstead Way, W4 . . . . .99 CT77
Welsummer Way, Wal.Cr. EN8 .15 DX27
Weltje Rd, W6 . . . . .99 CU78
Welton Rd, SE18 . . . . .105 ES80
Welwyn Av, Felt. TW14 . . . .115 BT86
Welwyn St, E2 off Globe Rd . . .84 DW69
Welwyn Way, Hayes UB4 . . . .77 BS70
WEMBLEY 62 CL64
➤ Wembley Central 62 CL64
➤ Wembley Central 62 CL64
Wembley Commercial Cen,
Wem. HA9 . . . . .61 CK61
★ Wembley Conf Cen, Wem.
HA9 . . . . .62 CM63
Wembley Hill Rd, Wem. HA9 . .62 CM64
WEMBLEY PARK, Wem. 62 CM61
➤ Wembley Park 62 CN62
Wembley Pk Business Cen,
Wem. HA9 . . . . .62 CP62
Wembley Pk Dr, Wem. HA9 . . .62 CM62
Wembley Pt, Wem. HA9 . . . . .80 CP66
Wembley Rd, Hmptn. TW12 . .116 CA94
★ Wembley Stadium
(under redevelopment),
Wem. HA9 . . . . .62 CN63
➤ Wembley Stadium 62 CN63
Wembley Way, Wem. HA9 . . .80 CP65
Wemborough Rd, Stan. HA7 . .41 CJ52
Wembury Ms, N6
off Wembury Rd 65 DH59
Wembury Rd, N6 . . . . .65 DH59
Wemyss Rd, SE3 . . . . . . .104 EF82
Wend, The, Couls. CR5 . . . .159 DK114
Croydon CR0 . . . . .161 DZ111
Wendela Cl, Wok. GU22 . . . .167 AZ118
Wendela Ct, Har. HA1 . . . . . .61 CE62
Wendell Rd, W12 . . . . .99 CT75
Wendle Ct, SW8 . . . . .101 DL79
Wendley Dr, Add. (New Haw)
KT15 . . . . .151 BF110
Wendling Rd, Sutt. SM1 . . . .140 DD102
Wendon St, E3 . . . . .85 DZ67
Wendover, SE17 . . . . .102 DS78
Wendover Cl, Hayes UB4
off Kingsash Dr 78 BY70
Wendover Dr, N.Mal. KT3 . . .139 CT100
Wendover Gdns, Brwd. CM13 .55 GB47
Wendover Pl, Stai. TW18 . . .113 BD92
Wendover Rd, NW10 . . . . . .81 CT68
SE9 . . . . .104 EK83
Bromley BR2 . . . . .144 EH97
Staines TW18 . . . . .113 BC92
Wendover Way, Bushey WD23 .24 CC44
Hornchurch RM12 . . . . . .72 FJ64
Orpington BR6
off Glendower Cres 146 EU100
Welling DA16 . . . . .126 EU85
Wendron Cl, Wok. GU21
off Shilburn Way 166 AU118
Wendy Cl, Enf. EN1 . . . . . . .30 DT44
Wendy Way, Wem. HA0 . . . . .80 CL67
Wenham Gdns, Brwd. CM13
off Bannister Dr 55 GC44
Wenlack Cl, Uxb. (Denh.) UB9
off Lindsey Rd 58 BG62
Wenlock Cl, N1 . . . . .197 L1
Wenlock Gdns, NW4
off Rickard Cl 63 CU56
Wenlock Rd, N1 . . . . .197 H1
Edgware HA8 . . . . .42 CP52
Wenlock St, N1 . . . . .197 J1
WENNINGTON, Rain. 90 FK73
Wennington Rd, E3 . . . . . . .85 DX68
Rainham RM13 . . . . . . .89 FG70
Wensley Av, Wdf.Grn. IG8 . . .48 EF52
Wensley Cl, N11
off Pickering Gdns 44 DG51
SE9 . . . . .125 EM86
Romford RM5 . . . . .50 FA50
Wensleydale Av, Ilf. IG5 . . . . .48 EL54
Wensleydale Gdns, Hmptn.
TW12 . . . . .116 CB94
Wensleydale Pas, Hmptn.
TW12 . . . . .136 CA95
Wensleydale Rd, Hmptn.
TW12 . . . . .116 CA93
Wensley Rd, N18 . . . . .46 DV51
Wensum Way, Rick. WD3 . . . .38 BK46
Wentbridge Path, Borwd. WD6 .26 CN38
Wentland Cl, SE6 . . . . . . .123 ED89
Wentland Rd, SE6 . . . . . . .123 ED89
WENTWORTH, Vir.W. 132 AS100
Wentworth Av, N3 . . . . .44 DA52
Borehamwood (Elstree) WD6 .26 CM44
Wentworth Cl, N3 . . . . .44 DB52
SE28 . . . . .88 EX72
Ashford TW15
off Reedsfield Rd 115 BP91
Bromley BR2
off Hillside La 144 EG103
Gravesend DA11 . . . . . .131 GG92
Morden SM4 . . . . .140 DA101

Wentworth Cl, Orp. BR6 . . . .163 ES106
Potters Bar EN6
off Strafford Gate 12 DA31
Surbiton KT6 . . . . .137 CK103
Watford WD17 . . . . .23 BT38
Woking (Ripley) GU23 . . .168 BH121
Wentworth Dr, Dart. DA1 . . .127 FG86
Pinner HA5 . . . . .59 BU57
Virginia Water GU25 . . . .132 AT98
Wentworth Gdns, N13 . . . . .45 DP49
★ Wentworth Golf Course,
Vir.W. GU25 . . . . .132 AT100
Wentworth Hill, Wem. HA9 . . .62 CM60
Wentworth Ms, E3
off Eric St 85 DZ70
Wentworth Pk, N3 . . . . .44 DA52
Wentworth Pl, Grays RM16 . .110 GD76
Stanmore HA7
off Greenacres Dr 41 CH51
Wentworth Rd, E12 . . . . . . .68 EK63
NW11 . . . . .63 CZ58
Barnet EN5 . . . . .27 CX41
Croydon CR0 . . . . .141 DN101
Southall UB2 . . . . .96 BW77
Wentworth St, E1 . . . . . . .197 P8
Wentworth Way, Pnr. HA5 . . .60 BX56
Rainham RM13 . . . . . . .89 FH69
South Croydon CR2 . . . .160 DU114
Wenvoe Av, Bexh. DA7 . . . .107 FB82
Wernbrook St, SE18 . . . . . .105 EQ79
Werndee Rd, SE25 . . . . . . .142 DU98
Werneth Hall Rd, Ilf. IG5 . . . .69 EM55
Werrington St, NW1 . . . . . .195 L1
Werter Rd, SW15 . . . . .99 CY84
Wescott Way, Uxb. UB8 . . . .76 BJ68
Wesleyan Pl, NW5
off Gordon Ho Rd 65 DH63
Wesley Av, E16 . . . . .205 P2
NW10 . . . . .80 CR69
Hounslow TW3 . . . . . . .96 BY82
Wesley Cl, N7 . . . . .65 DM61
SE17 . . . . .200 G9
Harrow HA2 . . . . .60 CC61
Orpington BR5 . . . . . . .146 EW98
Waltham Cross (Chsht.) EN7 .14 DQ28
Wesley Dr, Egh. TW20 . . . . .113 BA93
Wesley Rd, E10 . . . . .67 EC59
NW10 . . . . .80 CQ67
Hayes UB3 . . . . .77 BU73
★ Wesley's Ho, EC1 . . . . . .197 L4
Wesley Sq, W11 off Bartle Rd .81 CY72
Wesley St, W1 . . . . .194 G7
Wessels, Tad. KT20 . . . . . .173 CX121
Wessex Av, SW19 . . . . . . .140 DA96
Wessex Cl, Ilf. IG3 . . . . . . .69 ES58
Kingston upon Thames KT1
off Gloucester Rd 138 CP95
Thames Ditton KT7 . . . . .137 CF103
Wessex Ct, Erith DA8 . . . . .107 FE81
Pinner HA5 . . . . .40 BY52
Wessex Dr, Erith DA8 . . . . .107 FE81
Pinner HA5 . . . . .40 BY52
Wessex Gdns, NW11 . . . . . .63 CY60
Wessex La, Grnf. UB6 . . . . . .79 CD68
Wessex Rd, Houns. (Hthrw.Air.)
TW6 . . . . .94 BK82
Wessex St, E2 . . . . .84 DW69
Wessex Way, NW11 . . . . . .63 CY60
West 12 Shop Cen, W12
off Shepherds Bush Grn . . .99 CX75
Westacott, Hayes UB4 . . . . .77 BS71
Westacott Cl, N19 . . . . .65 DK60
Westacres, Esher KT10 . . . .154 BZ108
WEST ACTON, W3 . . . . .80 CN72
➤ West Acton 80 CN72
Westall Rd, Loug. IG10 . . . . .33 EP41
West App, Orp. BR5 . . . . . .145 EQ99
West Arbour St, E1 . . . . . . .85 DX72
West Av, E17 . . . . .67 EB56
N3 . . . . .44 DA51
NW4 . . . . .63 CX57
Hayes UB3 . . . . .77 BT73
Pinner HA5 . . . . .60 BZ58
St. Albans AL2 . . . . .8 CB25
Southall UB1 . . . . .78 BZ73
Wallington SM6 . . . . . .159 DL106
Walton-on-Thames KT12 . .153 BS109
West Av Rd, E17 . . . . .67 EA56
West Bk, N16 . . . . .66 DS59
Barking IG11
off Highbridge Rd 87 EP67
Enfield EN2 . . . . .30 DQ40
Westbank Rd, Hmptn. (Hmptn.H.)
TW12 . . . . .116 CC93
WEST BARNES, N.Mal. 139 CU99
West Barnes La, SW20 . . . .139 CV97
New Malden KT3 . . . . . .139 CV97
Westbeech Rd, N22 . . . . . . .65 DN55
Westbere Dr, Stan. HA7 . . . .41 CK49
Westbere Rd, NW2 . . . . . . .63 CY63
Westbourne Av, W3 . . . . . . .80 CR72
Sutton SM3 . . . . .139 CY103
Westbourne Br, W2 . . . . . . .82 DC71
Westbourne Cl, Hayes UB4 . . .77 BV70
Westbourne Cres, W2 . . . . . .82 DD73
Westbourne Cres Ms, W2
off Westbourne Cres 82 DD73
Westbourne Dr, SE23 . . . . .123 DX89
Brentwood CM14 . . . . . .54 FT49
Westbourne Gdns, W2 . . . . .82 DB72
WESTBOURNE GREEN, W2 . .82 DA71
Westbourne Gro, W2 . . . . . .82 DA72
W11 . . . . .81 CZ73
Westbourne Gro Ms, W11
off Westbourne Gro 82 DA72
Westbourne Gro Ter, W2 . . . .82 DB72
➤ Westbourne Park 81 CZ71
Westbourne Pk Ms, W2
off Westbourne Gdns 82 DB72
Westbourne Pk Pas, W2 . . . .82 DA71
off Westbourne Pk Vil 82 DA71
Westbourne Pk Rd, W2 . . . . .82 DA71

Wes - Wes

Westbourne Pk Rd, W11 ....81 CY72
Westbourne Pk Vil, W2 ....82 DA71
Westbourne Pl, N9
  off Eastbournia Av 46 DV48
Westbourne Rd, N7 ....83 DN65
  SE26 ....123 DX93
  Bexleyheath DA7 ....106 EY80
  Croydon CR0 ....142 DT100
  Feltham TW13 ....115 BT90
  Staines TW18 ....114 BH94
  Uxbridge UB8 ....77 BP70
Westbourne St, W2 ....82 DD73
Westbourne Ter, SE23 ....123 DX89
  W2 ....82 DD72
Westbourne Ter Ms, W2 ....82 DC72
Westbourne Ter Rd, W2 ....82 DC71
Westbridge Rd, SW11 ....100 DD81
WEST BROMPTON, SW10 ....100 DB79
≋ West Brompton 100 DA78
⊖ West Brompton 100 DA78
Westbrook Av, Hmptn. TW12 .116 BZ94
Westbrook Cl, Barn. EN4 ....28 DD41
Westbrook Cres, Barn. EN4 ..28 DD41
Westbrook Dr, Orp. BR5 ....146 EW102
Westbrooke Cres, Well. DA16 .106 EW83
Westbrooke Rd, Sid. DA15 ..125 ER89
  Welling DA16 ....106 EV83
Westbrook Rd, SE3 ....104 EH81
  Hounslow TW5 ....96 BZ80
  Staines TW18 off South St .114 BF92
  Thornton Heath CR7 ....142 DP95
Westbrook Sq, Barn. EN4
  off Westbrook Cres 28 DD41
Westbury Av, N22 ....65 DP55
  Esher (Clay.) KT10 ....155 CF107
  Southall UB1 ....78 CA70
  Wembley HA0 ....80 CL66
Westbury Cl, Ruis. HA4 ....59 BU59
  Shepperton TW17
  off Burchetts Way 135 BP100
  Whyteleafe CR3
  off Beverley Way 176 DS116
Westbury Dr, Brwd. CM14 ....54 FV47
Westbury Gro, N12 ....44 DA51
Westbury La, Buck.H. IG9 ....48 EJ47
Westbury Lo Cl, Pnr. HA5 ....60 BX55
Westbury Par, SW12
  off Balham Hill 121 DH86
Westbury Pl, Brent. TW8 ....97 CK79
Westbury Rd, E7 ....68 EH64
  E17 ....67 EA56
  N11 ....45 DL51
  N12 ....44 DA51
  SE20 ....143 DX95
  W5 ....80 CL72
  Barking IG11 ....87 ER67
  Beckenham BR3 ....143 DY97
  Brentwood CM14 ....54 FW47
  Bromley BR1 ....144 EK95
  Buckhurst Hill IG9 ....48 EJ47
  Croydon CR0 ....142 DR100
  Feltham TW13 ....116 BX88
  Ilford IG1 ....69 EM61
  New Malden KT3 ....138 CR98
  Northwood HA6 ....39 BS49
  Waltham Cross (Chsht.) EN8
  off Turners Hill 15 DX30
  Watford WD18 ....23 BV43
  Wembley HA0 ....80 CL66
Westbury St, SW8 ....101 DJ82
Westbury Ter, E7 ....86 EH65
  Upminster RM14 ....73 FS61
  Westerham TN16 ....189 EQ127
WEST BYFLEET 152 BH114
≋ West Byfleet 152 BG112
Westcar La, Walt. KT12 ....153 BV107
West Cen St, WC1 ....195 P8
West Cen Av, W10
  off Harrow Rd 81 CV69
West Chantry, Har. HA3
  off Chantry Rd 40 CB53
Westchester Dr, NW4 ....63 CX55
West Cl, N9 ....46 DT48
  Ashford TW15 ....114 BL91
  Barnet EN5 ....27 CV43
  Barnet (Cockfos.) EN4 ....28 DG42
  Greenford UB6 ....78 CC68
  Hampton TW12
  off Oak Av 116 BY93
  Rainham RM13 ....89 FH70
  Wembley HA9 ....62 CM60
Westcombe Av, Croy. CR0 ..141 DL100
Westcombe Ct, SE3
  off Westcombe Pk Rd 104 EF80
Westcombe Dr, Barn. EN5 ....28 DA43
Westcombe Hill, SE3 ....104 EG78
  SE10 ....104 EG78
Westcombe Lo Dr, Hayes
  UB4 ....77 BR71
≋ Westcombe Park 104 EG78
Westcombe Pk Rd, SE3 ....104 EE79
West Common, Ger.Cr. SL9 ..56 AX57
West Common Cl, Ger.Cr.
  SL9 ....56 AY57
West Common Rd, Brom.
  BR2 ....144 EG103
  Keston BR2 ....162 EH105
  Uxbridge UB8 ....58 BK64
Westcoombe Av, SW20 ....139 CT95
Westcote Ri, Ruis. HA4 ....59 BQ59
Westcote Rd, SW16 ....121 DJ92
West Cotts, NW6 ....64 DA64
Westcott Av, Grav. (Nthflt.)
  DA11 ....131 GG90
Westcott Cl, N15
  off Ermine Rd 66 DT58
  Bromley BR1
  off Ringmer Way 144 EL99
  Croydon (New Adgtn.) CR0
  off Castle Hill Av 161 EB109
Westcott Cres, W7 ....79 CE72
Westcott Rd, SE17 ....101 DP79

Westcott Way, Sutt. SM2 ....157 CW110
WESTCOURT, Grav. 131 GL89
West Ct, SE18
  off Prince Imperial Rd 105 EM81
Westcourt, Sun. TW16 ....135 BV96
West Ct, Wem. HA0 ....61 CJ61
West Cres Rd, Grav. DA12 ..131 GH86
Westcroft Cl, NW2 ....63 CY63
  Enfield EN3 ....30 DW38
Westcroft Gdns, Mord. SM4 .139 CZ97
Westcroft Rd, Cars. SM5 ....158 DG105
  Wallington SM6 ....158 DG105
Westcroft Sq, W6 ....99 CU77
Westcroft Way, NW2 ....63 CY63
West Cromwell Rd, SW5 ....99 CZ77
  W14 ....99 CZ77
West Cross Cen, Brent. TW8 .97 CG79
West Cross Route, W10 ....81 CX73
  W11 ....81 CX73
West Cross Way, Brent. TW8 .97 CG79
≋ West Croydon 142 DQ102
⊖ West Croydon 142 DQ102
Westdale Pas, SE18 ....105 EP79
Westdale Rd, SE18 ....105 EP79
Westdean Av, SE12 ....124 EH88
Westdean Cl, SW18 ....120 DB86
West Dene, Sutt. SM3
  off Park La 157 CY107
West Dene Dr, Rom. RM3 ....52 FK50
Westdene Way, Wey. KT13 ..135 BS104
Westdown Rd, E15 ....67 EC63
  SE6 ....123 EA87
WEST DRAYTON 94 BK76
≋ West Drayton 76 BL74
West Drayton Pk Av, West Dr.
  UB7 ....94 BL76
West Drayton Rd, Uxb. UB8 ..77 BP71
West Dr, SW16 ....121 DJ91
  Carshalton SM5 ....158 DD110
  Harrow HA3 ....41 CD51
  Sutton (Cheam) SM2 ....157 CX109
  Tadworth KT20 ....173 CX118
  Virginia Water GU25 ....132 AT101
  Watford WD25 ....23 BV36
West Dr Gdns, Har. HA3 ....41 CD51
WEST DULWICH, SE21 ....122 DR90
≋ West Dulwich 122 DR88
⊖ West Ealing 79 CH73
West Eaton Pl, SW1 ....198 F8
West Eaton Pl Ms, SW1 ....198 F8
Wested La, Swan. BR8 ....147 FG101
West Ella Rd, NW10 ....80 CS66
WEST END, Esher 154 BZ107
West End Av, E10 ....67 EC57
  Pinner HA5 ....60 BX56
West End Cl, NW10 ....80 CQ66
West End Ct, Pnr. HA5 ....60 BX56
  Slough (Stoke P.) SL2 ....74 AT67
West End Gdns, Esher KT10 .154 BZ106
  Northolt UB5 off Edward Ct .78 BW68
West End La, NW6 ....82 DA67
  Barnet EN5 ....27 CX42
  Esher KT10 ....154 BZ107
  Hayes UB3 ....95 BQ80
  Pinner HA5 ....60 BX55
  Slough (Stoke P.) SL2 ....74 AS67
West End Rd, Nthlt. UB5 ....78 BW66
  Ruislip HA4 ....59 BV64
  Southall UB1 ....78 BY74
Westerdale Rd, SE10 ....104 EG78
Westerfield Rd, N15 ....66 DT57
Westerfolds Cl, Wok. GU22 .167 BC116
Westergate Rd, SE2 ....106 EY78
WESTERHAM 189 EQ126
Westerham Av, N9 ....46 DR48
Westerham Cl, Add. KT15 ..152 BJ107
  Sutton SM2 ....158 DA110
Westerham Dr, Sid. DA15 ..126 EV86
Westerham Hill, West. TN16 .179 EN121
Westerham Rd, E10 ....67 EB59
  Keston BR2 ....162 EK107
  Oxted RH8 ....188 EF129
  Sevenoaks TN13 ....190 FC123
  Westerham TN16 ....189 EM128
  Westerham (Brasted)
  TN16 ....189 ET125
Westerley Cres, SE26 ....123 DZ92
Westerley Ware, Rich. TW9
  off Kew Grn 98 CN79
Westermain, Add. (New Haw)
  KT15 ....152 BJ110
Western Av, NW11 ....63 CX58
  W3 ....80 CR71
  W5 ....80 CM70
  Brentwood CM14 ....54 FW46
  Chertsey KT16 ....134 BG97
  Dagenham RM10 ....89 FC65
  Egham TW20 ....133 BB97
  Epping CM16 ....17 ET32
  Grays RM20 ....109 FT78
  Greenford UB6 ....79 CK69
  Northolt UB5 ....78 BZ67
  Romford RM2 ....52 FJ54
  Ruislip HA4 ....77 BP65
  Uxbridge (Denh.) UB9 ....58 BJ63
  Uxbridge (Ickhm.) UB10 ....77 BP65
Western Av Business Pk, W3
  off Mansfield Rd 80 CP70
Western Av Underpass, W5
  off Western Av 80 CM69
Western Beach Apartments,
  E16 ....205 M2
Western Cl, Cher. KT16
  off Western Av 134 BG97
Western Ct, N3 off Huntley Dr .44 DA51
Western Cross Cl, Green. DA9
  off Johnsons Way 129 FW86
Western Dr, Shep. TW17 ....135 BR100
Western Gdns, W5 ....80 CN73
  Brentwood CM14 ....54 FW47
Western La, SW12 ....120 DG87
Western Ms, W9
  off Great Western Rd 81 CZ70
Western Par, Barn. EN5
  off Great N Rd 28 DA43
Western Pathway, Horn.
  RM12 ....90 FJ65

Western Perimeter Rd, Houns.
  (Hthrw.Air.) TW6 ....94 BH83
Western Pl, SE16 ....202 G4
Western Rd, E13 ....86 EJ67
  E17 ....67 EC57
  N2 ....64 DF56
  N22 ....64 DM54
  NW10 ....80 CQ70
  SW9 ....101 DN83
  SW19 ....140 DD95
  W5 ....79 CK73
  Brentwood CM14 ....54 FW47
  Epping CM16 ....17 ET32
  Mitcham CR4 ....140 DD95
  Romford RM1 ....71 FE57
  Southall UB2 ....96 BX76
  Sutton SM1 ....158 DA106
Western Ter, W6
  off Chiswick Mall 99 CU78
Western Trd Est, NW10 ....80 CQ70
Western Vw, Hayes UB3 ....95 BT75
Westernville Gdns, Ilf. IG2 ..69 EQ59
Western Way, SE28 ....105 ER76
  Barnet EN5 ....28 DA44
WEST EWELL, Epsom 156 CS108
West Fm Av, Ashtd. KT21 ..171 CJ118
West Fm Cl, Ashtd. KT21 ..171 CJ119
West Fm Dr, Ashtd. KT21 ..171 CK119
Westferry 85 EA73
Westferry Circ, E14 ....203 P2
Westferry Rd, E14 ....203 N2
WESTFIELD, Wok. 167 AZ122
Westfield, Ashtd. KT21 ....172 CM118
  Loughton IG10 ....32 EJ43
  Reigate RH2 ....184 DB131
  Sevenoaks TN13 ....191 FJ122
Westfield Av, S.Croy. CR2 ..160 DR113
  Watford WD24 ....24 BW37
  Woking GU22 ....166 AY121
Westfield Cl, NW9 ....62 CQ55
  SW10 ....100 DC80
  Enfield EN3 ....31 DY41
  Gravesend DA12 ....131 GJ93
  Sutton SM1 ....157 CZ105
  Waltham Cross EN8 ....15 DZ31
Westfield Common, Wok.
  GU22 ....166 AY122
Westfield Dr, Har. HA3 ....61 CK57
  Leatherhead (Bkhm.)
  KT23 ....170 CA122
Westfield Gdns, Har. HA3 ....61 CK56
Westfield Gro, Wok. GU22 ..167 AZ120
Westfield La, Har. HA3 ....61 CK56
  Slough (Geo.Grn.) SL3 ....74 AX73
Westfield Par, Add. (New Haw)
  KT15 ....152 BK110
Westfield Pk, Pnr. HA5 ....40 BZ52
Westfield Pk Dr, Wdf.Grn. IG8 .48 EL51
Westfield Rd, NW7 ....42 CR48
  W13 ....79 CG74
  Beckenham BR3 ....143 DZ96
  Bexleyheath DA7 ....107 FC82
  Croydon CR0 ....141 DP103
  Dagenham RM9 ....70 EY63
  Mitcham CR4 ....140 DF96
  Surbiton KT6 ....137 CK99
  Sutton SM1 ....157 CZ105
  Walton-on-Thames KT12 .136 BY101
  Woking GU22 ....166 AX122
Westfields, SW13 ....99 CT83
Westfields Av, SW13 ....98 CS83
Westfields Rd, W3 ....80 CP71
Westfield St, SE18 ....104 EK76
Westfield Wk, Wal.Cr. EN8
  off Westfield Cl 15 DZ31
Westfield Way, E1 ....85 DY69
  Ruislip HA4 ....59 BS62
  Woking GU22 ....166 AY122
⊖ West Finchley 44 DB51
West Gdn Pl, W2 ....194 C9
West Gdns, E1 ....202 F1
  SW17 ....120 DE93
  Epsom KT17 ....156 CS110
West Gate, W5 ....80 CL69
Westgate Cl, Epsom KT18
  off Chalk La 172 CR115
Westgate Ct, Wal.Cr. EN8
  off Holmesdale 31 DX35
Westgate Ho, Brent. TW8 ....97 CK78
Westgate Rd, SE25 ....142 DV98
  Beckenham BR3 ....143 DB96
  Dartford DA1 ....128 FK86
Westgate St, E8 ....84 DV67
Westgate Ter, SW10 ....100 DB78
Westglade Ct, Har. HA3 ....61 CK57
West Gorse, Croy. CR0 ....161 DY112
WEST GREEN, N15 ....66 DQ55
West Grn Pl, Grnf. UB6
  off Uneeda Dr 79 CD67
West Grn Rd, N15 ....65 DP56
West Gro, SE10 ....103 EC81
  Walton-on-Thames KT12 .153 BV105
  Woodford Green IG8 ....48 EJ51
Westgrove La, SE10 ....103 EC81
West Halkin St, SW1 ....198 F6
West Hallowes, SE9 ....124 EK88
Westhall Rd, Warl. CR6 ....176 DW119
West Hall Rd, Rich. TW9 ....98 CR81
WEST HAM, E15 ....86 EF66
≋ West Ham 86 EE69
⊖ West Ham 86 EE69
West Ham La, E15 ....86 EE66
West Ham Pk, E7 ....86 EG66
WEST HAMPSTEAD, NW6 ....64 DB64
≋ West Hampstead 82 DA65
⊖ West Hampstead 82 DA65
West Hampstead Ms, NW6 ..82 DB65
≋ West Hampstead
  (Thameslink) 82 DA65
★ West Ham United FC, E13 .86 EJ68
West Harding St, EC4 ....196 E8
West Harold, Swan. BR8 ....147 FD97
WEST HARROW, Har. 60 CC59
⊖ West Harrow 60 CC58
West Hatch Manor, Ruis. HA4 .59 BT60
Westhay Gdns, SW14 ....118 CP85

WEST HEATH, SE2 ....106 EX79
West Heath, Oxt. RH8 ....188 EG130
West Heath Av, NW11 ....64 DA60
West Heath Cl, NW3 ....64 DA62
  Dartford DA1
  off West Heath Rd 127 FF86
West Heath Dr, NW11 ....64 DA60
West Heath Gdns, NW3 ....64 DA60
West Heath La, Sev. TN13 ..191 FH128
West Heath Rd, NW3 ....64 DA61
  SE2 ....106 EX79
  Dartford DA1 ....127 FF86
WEST HENDON, NW9 ....62 CS59
West Hendon Bdy, NW9 ....63 CT58
West Hill, SW15 ....119 CX87
  SW18 ....120 DA85
  Dartford DA1 ....128 FK86
  Epsom KT19 ....156 CQ113
  Harrow HA2 ....61 CE61
  Orpington BR6 ....163 EM112
  Oxted RH8 ....187 ED130
  South Croydon CR2 ....160 DS110
  Wembley HA9 ....62 CM60
West Hill Av, Epsom KT19 ..156 CQ112
West Hill Bk, Oxt. RH8 ....187 ED130
West Hill Dr, Dart. DA1 ....128 FK86
West Hill Pk, N6 ....64 DF61
  off Merton La 64 DF61
West Hill Ri, Dart. DA1 ....128 FK86
West Hill Rd, SW18 ....120 DA86
  Woking GU22 ....166 AX119
West Hill Way, N20 ....44 DB46
Westholm, NW11 ....64 DB56
West Holme, Erith DA8 ....107 FC81
Westholme, Orp. BR6 ....145 ES101
Westholme Gdns, Ruis. HA4 .59 BU60
Westhorne Av, SE9 ....124 EJ86
  SE12 ....124 EG87
Westhorpe Gdns, NW4 ....63 CW55
Westhorpe Rd, SW15 ....99 CW83
West Ho Cl, SW19 ....119 CY88
Westhurst Dr, Chis. BR7 ....125 EP92
West Hyde La, Ger.Cr. (Chal.St.P.)
  SL9 ....37 AZ52
West India Av, E14 ....203 P2
West India Dock Rd, E14 ....85 DZ72
West India Quay 204 B1
⊖ West India Quay 204 B1
⊖ West Kensington 99 CZ78
West Kent Av, Grav. (Nthflt.)
  DA11 ....130 GC86
West Kent Cold Storage, Sev.
  (Dunt.Grn.) TN14 ....181 FF120
West Kentish Town Est, NW5 .64 DG64
WEST KILBURN, W9 ....81 CZ69
  Hayes UB4 off Lochan Cl ..78 BY70
Westlake Rd, Wem. HA9 ....61 CK61
Westland Av, Horn. RM11 ....72 FL60
Westland Cl, Stai. (Stanw.)
  TW19 ....114 BL86
  Watford WD25 off Ashfields .7 BT34
Westland Dr, Brom. BR2 ....144 EF103
  Hatfield AL9 ....11 CY27
Westland Ho, E16
  off Rymill St 87 EN74
Westland Pl, N1 ....197 K2
Westlands Cl, Hayes UB3
  off Granville Rd 95 BU77
Westlands Ct, Epsom KT18 .172 CQ115
Westlands Ter, SW12
  off Gaskarth Rd 121 DJ86
Westlands Way, Oxt. RH8 ..187 ED127
West La, SE16 ....202 D5
Westlea Av, Wat. WD25 ....24 BY37
Westlea Rd, W7 ....97 CG76
Westleigh Av, SW15 ....119 CV85
  Coulsdon CR5 ....174 DG116
Westleigh Dr, Brom. BR1 ..144 EL95
Westleigh Gdns, Edg. HA8 ..42 CN53
Westlinks, Wem. HA0
  off Alperton La 79 CK69
Westlinton Cl, NW7 ....43 CY51
West Lo Av, W3 ....80 CN74
Westlyn Cl, Rain. RM13 ....90 FJ69
Westmacott Dr, Felt. TW14 .115 BT88
West Mall, W8
  off Palace Gdns Ter 82 DA74
West Malling Way, Horn.
  RM12 ....72 FJ64
Westmark Pt, SW15
  off Norley Vale 119 CV88
Westmead, SW15 ....119 CV86
West Mead, Epsom KT19 ..156 CS107
  Ruislip HA4 ....60 BW63
Westmead, Wok. GU21 ....166 AV117
Westmead Cor, Cars. SM5
  off Colston Av 158 DE105
Westmead Rd, Sutt. SM1 ..158 DD105
Westmeade Cl, Wal.Cr. (Chsht.)
  EN7 ....14 DV29
Westmede, Chig. IG7 ....49 EQ51
Westmere Dr, NW7 ....42 CR48
West Mersea Cl, E16 ....205 P3
West Ms, N17 ....46 DV51
  SW1 ....199 J9
H West Middlesex Uni Hosp,
  Islw. TW7 ....97 CG82
West Mill, Grav. DA11 ....131 GF86
Westmill, N4
  off Brownswood Rd 66 DQ61
WESTMINSTER, SW1 ....199 K6
⊖ Westminster 200 A5
★ Westminster Abbey,
  SW1 ....199 P6
★ Westminster Abbey Mus,
  SW1 ....199 P6
Westminster Av, Th.Hth.
  CR7 ....141 DP96
Westminster Br, SE1 ....200 A5
  SW1 ....199 P5
Westminster Br Rd, SE1 ....200 C5
★ Westminster Cathedral,
  SW1 ....199 K7

★ Westminster City Hall,
  SW1 ....199 L6
Westminster Cl, Felt. TW14 .115 BU88
  Ilford IG6 ....49 ER54
  Teddington TW11 ....117 CG92
Westminster Dr, N13 ....45 DL50
Westminster Gdns, E4 ....48 EE46
  SW1 ....199 P8
  Barking IG11 ....87 ES68
  Ilford IG6 ....49 EQ54
★ Westminster Pier, SW1 ..200 A4
Westminster Rd, N9 ....46 DV46
  W7 ....79 CE74
  Sutton SM1 ....140 DD103
Westmoat Cl, Beck. BR3 ....123 EC94
WEST MOLESEY 136 BZ99
Westmont Rd, Esher KT10 ..137 CE103
Westmoor Gdns, Enf. EN3 ..31 DX40
Westmoor Rd, Enf. EN3 ....31 DX40
Westmoor St, SE7 ....104 EJ76
Westmore Grn, West. (Tats.)
  TN16 ....178 EJ121
Westmoreland Av, Horn.
  RM11 ....72 FJ57
  Welling DA16 ....105 ES83
Westmoreland Bldgs, EC1
  off Bartholomew Cl 84 DQ71
Westmoreland Dr, Sutt. SM2 .158 DB109
Westmoreland Pl, SW1 ....101 DH78
  W5 off Mount Av 79 CK71
  Bromley BR1 ....144 EG97
Westmoreland Rd, NW9 ....62 CN56
  SE17 ....102 DQ79
  SW13 ....99 CT81
  Bromley BR1, BR2 ....144 EE99
Westmoreland St, W1 ....194 G7
Westmoreland Ter, SW1 ....101 DH78
Westmoreland Wk, SE17 ..102 DR79
Westmore Rd, West. (Tats.)
  TN16 ....178 EJ121
Westmorland Cl, E12 ....68 EK61
  Epsom KT19 ....156 CS110
  Twickenham TW1 ....117 CH86
Westmorland Rd, E17 ....67 EA58
  Harrow HA1 ....60 CB57
Westmorland Sq, Mitch. CR4
  off Westmorland Way 141 DL99
Westmorland Ter, SE20 ....122 DV94
Westmorland Way, Mitch.
  CR4 ....141 DK98
Westmount Rd, SE9 ....105 EM82
WEST NORWOOD, SE27 ..122 DQ90
≋ West Norwood 121 DP90
West Oak, Beck. BR3 ....143 ED95
Westoe Rd, N9 ....46 DV47
Weston Av, Add. KT15 ....152 BG105
  Grays RM20 ....109 FT77
  Thames Ditton KT7 ....137 CE101
  West Molesey KT8 ....136 BY97
Weston Cl, Brwd. CM13 ....55 GC45
  Coulsdon CR5 ....175 DM120
  Potters Bar EN6 ....11 CZ32
Weston Ct, N4 off Queens Dr .66 DQ62
  N20 off Farnham Cl 44 DC45
Weston Dr, Cat. CR3
  off Coulsdon Rd 176 DQ122
  Stanmore HA7 ....41 CH53
West One Shop Cen, W1
  off Oxford St 83 DH72
Weston Gdns, Islw. TW7 ....97 CD81
  Woking GU22 ....167 BE116
WESTON GREEN, T.Ditt. ..137 CF102
Weston Grn, Dag. RM9 ....70 EZ63
  Thames Ditton KT7 ....137 CE102
Weston Grn Rd, Esher KT10 .137 CD102
  Thames Ditton KT7 ....137 CE102
Weston Gro, Brom. BR1 ....144 EF95
Weston Pk, N8 ....65 DL58
  Kingston upon Thames KT1
  off Fairfield W 138 CL96
  Thames Ditton KT7 ....137 CE102
Weston Pk Cl, T.Ditt. KT7
  off Weston Pk 137 CE102
Weston Ri, WC1 ....196 C1
Weston Rd, W4 ....98 CQ76
  Bromley BR1 ....124 EF94
  Dagenham RM9 ....70 EY63
  Enfield EN2 ....30 DR39
  Epsom KT17 ....156 CS111
  Thames Ditton KT7 ....137 CE102
Weston St, SE1 ....201 L6
Weston Wk, E8 off Mare St ..84 DV66
Weston Way, Wok. GU22 ..167 BE116
Westover Cl, Sutt. SM2 ....158 DB109
Westover Hill, NW3 ....64 DA61
Westover Rd, SW18 ....120 DC86
Westow Hill, SE19 ....122 DS93
Westow St, SE19 ....122 DS93
West Palace Gdns, Wey.
  KT13 ....135 BP104
West Pk, SE9 ....124 EL89
West Pk Av, Rich. TW9 ....98 CN81
West Pk Cl, Houns. TW5
  off Heston Gra La 96 BZ79
  Romford RM6 ....70 EX57
H West Park Hosp, Epsom
  KT19 ....156 CM112
West Pk Rd, Epsom KT19 ..156 CM112
  Richmond TW9 ....98 CN81
  Southall UB2 ....78 CC74
West Parkside, SE10 ....205 L7
  Warlingham CR6 ....177 EA115
West Pier, E1 ....202 D3
West Pl, SW19 ....119 CW92
Westpoint Trd Est, W3 ....80 CP71
Westpole Av, Barn. EN4 ....28 DG42
Westport Rd, E13 ....86 EH70
Westport St, E1 ....85 DX72
West Poultry Av, EC1 ....196 F7
West Quarters, W12 ....81 CU72
West Quay Dr, Hayes UB4 ..78 BY71
West Ramp, Houns. (Hthrw.Air.)
  TW6 ....94 BN81
West Ridge Gdns, Grnf. UB6 .78 CC68
West Riding, St.Alb. (Brick.Wd.)
  AL2 ....8 BZ30

★ Place of interest   ≋ Railway station   ⊖ London Underground station   DLR Docklands Light Railway station   ⊕ Tramlink station   H Hospital

West Rd, E15 . . . . .86 EF67
N17 . . . . .46 DV51
SW3 . . . . .100 DF79
SW4 . . . . .121 DK85
W5 . . . . .80 CL71
Barnet EN4 . . . . .44 DG46
Chessington KT9 . . . . .155 CJ112
Feltham TW14 . . . . .115 BR86
Kingston upon Thames KT2 .138 CQ95
Romford (Chad.Hth.) RM6 .70 EX58
Romford (Rush Grn.) RM7 .71 FD59
South Ockendon RM15 .91 FV69
West Drayton UB7 . . . . .94 BM76
Weybridge KT13 . . . . .153 BP109
Westrow, SW15 . . . . .119 CW85
West Row, W10 . . . . .81 CY70
Westrow Dr, Bark. IG11 .87 ET65
Westrow Gdns, Ilf. IG3 .69 ET61
⇌ West Ruislip 59 BQ61
⊖ West Ruislip 59 BQ61
West Shaw, Long. DA3 .149 FX96
West Sheen Vale, Rich. TW9 .98 CM84
Westside, NW4 . . . . .43 CV54
West Side, Brox. EN10
  off High Rd Turnford 15 DY25
West Side Common, SW19 .119 CW92
West Smithfield, EC1 . . . . .196 F7
West Spur Rd, Uxb. UB8 .76 BK69
West Sq, SE11 . . . . .200 F7
  Iver SL0 off High St 75 BF72
West St, E2 . . . . .84 DV68
  E11 . . . . .68 EE62
  E17 off Grove Rd 67 EB57
  WC2 . . . . .195 N9
  Bexleyheath DA7 . . . . .106 EZ84
  Brentford TW8 . . . . .97 CJ79
  Bromley BR1 . . . . .144 EG95
  Carshalton SM5 . . . . .140 DF104
  Croydon CR0 . . . . .160 DQ105
  Epsom KT18 . . . . .156 CR113
  Epsom (Ewell) KT17 .156 CS110
  Erith DA8 . . . . .107 FD77
  Gravesend DA11 . . . . .131 GG86
  Grays RM17 . . . . .110 GA79
  Harrow HA1 . . . . .61 CD60
  Reigate RH2 . . . . .183 CY133
  Sutton SM1 . . . . .158 DB106
  Watford WD17 . . . . .23 BV40
  Woking GU21
    off Church St E 167 AZ117
West St La, Cars. SM5 .158 DF105
⇌ West Sutton 158 DA105
West Temple Sheen, SW14 .98 CP84
West Tenter St, E1 . . . . .84 DT72
West Thamesmead Business Pk,
  SE28 . . . . .105 ET76
WEST THURROCK, Grays .109 FU78
West Thurrock Way, Grays
  RM20 . . . . .109 FT77
WEST TILBURY, Til. .111 GL79
West Twrs, Pnr. HA5 . . . . .60 BX58
Westvale Ms, W3 . . . . .80 CS74
West Valley Rd, Hem.H. HP3 .6 BJ25
West Vw, NW4 . . . . .63 CW56
  Feltham TW14 . . . . .115 BQ87
  Loughton IG10 . . . . .33 EM41
West Vw Av, Whyt. CR3
  off Station Rd 176 DU118
Westview Cl, NW10 . . . . .63 CT64
  W7 . . . . .79 CE72
  W10 . . . . .81 CW72
  Rainham RM13 . . . . .90 FJ69
West Vw Ct, Borwd. (Elstree)
  WD6 off High St 25 CK44
Westview Cres, N9 . . . . .46 DS45
Westview Dr, Wdf.Grn. IG8 ..48 EK54
West Vw Gdns, Borwd. (Elstree)
  WD6 off High St 25 CK44
West Vw Rd, Dart. DA1 .128 FM86
  Swanley BR8 . . . . .147 FG98
  Swanley (Crock.) BR8 .147 FD100
Westview Rd, Warl. CR6 .176 DV119
Westville Rd, W12 . . . . .99 CU75
  Thames Ditton KT7 .137 CG102
West Wk, W5 . . . . .80 CL71
  Barnet EN4 . . . . .44 DG45
  Hayes UB3 . . . . .77 BU74
West Walkway, The, Sutt. SM1
  off Cheam Rd 158 DB106
Westward Rd, E4 . . . . .47 DZ50
Westward Way, Har. HA3 ..62 CL58
West Warwick Pl, SW1 .199 J9
WEST WATFORD, Wat. .23 BU42
West Way, N18 . . . . .46 DR49
  NW10 . . . . .62 CR62
Westway, SW20 . . . . .139 CV97
  W2 . . . . .82 DA71
  W9 . . . . .82 DA71
  W10 . . . . .81 CY72
  W12 . . . . .81 CU73
West Way, Brwd. CM14 .54 FU48
  Carshalton SM5 . . . . .158 DD110
Westway, Cat. CR3 .176 DR122
West Way, Croy. CR0 .143 DY103
  Edgware HA8 . . . . .42 CP51
  Hounslow TW5 . . . . .96 BZ81
Westway, Orp. BR5 .145 ER99
West Way, Pnr. HA5 . . . . .60 BX56
  Rickmansworth WD3 ..38 BH46
  Ruislip HA4 . . . . .59 BT60
  Shepperton TW17 . . . . .135 BR100
  West Wickham BR4 .143 ED100
Westway Cl, SW20 .139 CV97
Westway Cross Shop Pk, Grnf.
  UB6 . . . . .79 CE67
West Way Gdns, Croy. CR0 .143 DX103
Westway Gdns, Red. RH1 .184 DG131
Westways, Epsom KT19 .157 CT105
  Westerham TN16 . . . . .189 EQ126
Westwell Cl, Orp. BR5 .146 EX102
Westwell Rd, SW16 . . . . .121 DL93
Westwell Rd App, SW16
  off Westwell Rd 121 DL93
Westwick Gdns, W14 .99 CX75
  Hounslow TW4 . . . . .95 BV82
WEST WICKHAM .143 EC103
⇌ West Wickham 143 EC101

Westwick Pl, Wat. WD25 . . . . .8 BW34
Westwood Av, SE19 .142 DQ95
  Addlestone (Woodham)
    KT15 . . . . .151 BF112
  Brentwood CM14 . . . . .54 FU49
  Harrow HA2 . . . . .60 CB63
Westwood Cl, Amer. HP6 ..20 AX39
  Bromley BR1 . . . . .144 EK97
  Esher KT10 . . . . .136 CC104
  Potters Bar EN6 . . . . .12 DA30
  Ruislip HA4 . . . . .59 BP58
Westwood Dr, Amer. HP6 ..20 AX39
Westwood Gdns, SW13 .99 CT83
Westwood Hill, SE26 .122 DU92
Westwood La, Sid. DA15 .126 EU85
  Welling DA16 . . . . .105 ET83
Westwood Pk, SE23 .122 DV87
Westwood Rd, SE26 .122 DU91
Westwood Rd, E16 .205 P3
  SW13 . . . . .99 CT83
  Coulsdon CR5 . . . . .175 DK118
  Gravesend (Sthflt.) DA13 .130 FY93
  Ilford IG3 . . . . .69 ET60
West Woodside, Bex. DA5 .126 EY87
West World, W5 . . . . .80 CL69
West Yoke, Sev. (Ash) TN15 .149 FX103
Wetheral Dr, Stan. HA7 .41 CH53
Wetherby Cl, Nthlt. UB5 .78 CB65
Wetherby Gdns, SW5 .100 DC77
Wetherby Ms, SW5
  off Bolton Gdns 100 DB78
Wetherby Pl, SW7 . . . . .100 DC77
Wetherby Rd, Borwd. WD6 ..26 CL39
  Enfield EN2 . . . . .30 DQ39
Wetherby Way, Chess. KT9 .156 CL108
Wetherden St, E17 . . . . .67 DZ59
Wetherell Rd, E9 . . . . .85 DX67
Wetherill Rd, N10 . . . . .44 DG53
★ Wetlands Cen, The, SW13 .99 CV80
Wettern Cl, S.Croy. CR2
  off Purley Oaks Rd 160 DS110
Wetton Pl, Egh. TW20 .113 AZ92
Wexfenne Gdns, Wok. GU22 .168 BH116
Wexford Rd, SW12 .120 DF87
⊞ Wexham Park Hosp, Slou.
  SL2 . . . . .74 AW70
Wexham Pk La, Slou. (Wexham)
  SL3 . . . . .74 AX70
Wexham Pl, Slou. (Wexham)
  SL2 . . . . .74 AX65
Wexham Rd, Slou. SL1, SL2 .74 AV71
WEXHAM STREET, Slou. .74 AW67
Wexham St, Slou. (Wexham)
  SL2, SL3 . . . . .74 AW70
Wexham Wds, Slou. (Wexham)
  SL3 . . . . .74 AW71
Wey Av, Cher. KT16 .134 BG97
Weybank, Wok. (Wisley)
  GU23 . . . . .168 BL116
Wey Barton, W.Byf. (Byfleet)
  KT14 . . . . .152 BM113
Weybourne Pl, S.Croy. CR2 .160 DR110
Weybourne St, SW18 .120 DC89
WEYBRIDGE .152 BN105
⇌ Weybridge 152 BN107
Weybridge Business Pk, Add.
  KT15 . . . . .152 BL105
Weybridge Ct, SE16
  off Argyle Way 102 DU78
⊞ Weybridge Hosp, Wey.
  KT13 . . . . .152 BN105
Weybridge Pk, Wey. KT13 .153 BP106
Weybridge Pt, SW11 .100 DG82
Weybridge Rd, Add. KT15 .134 BK104
  Thornton Heath CR7 .141 DN98
  Weybridge KT13 . . . . .134 BL104
Weybridge Trd Est, Add.
  KT15 . . . . .152 BL105
Wey Cl, W.Byf. KT14
  off Broadoaks Cres 152 BH113
Wey Ct, Add. (New Haw)
  KT15 . . . . .152 BK109
  Epsom KT19 . . . . .156 CQ105
Weydown Cl, SW19 .119 CY88
Weyhill Rd, E1
  off Commercial Rd 84 DU72
Weylands Cl, Walt. KT12 .136 BZ102
Weylands Pk, Wey. KT13 .153 BR107
Weylond Rd, Dag. RM8 .70 EZ62
Wey Manor Rd, Add. (New Haw)
  KT15 . . . . .152 BK109
Weyman Rd, SE3 . . . . .104 EJ81
Weymead Cl, Cher. KT16 .134 BJ102
Wey Meadows, Wey. KT13 .152 BL106
Weymede, W.Byf. (Byfleet)
  KT14 . . . . .152 BM112
Weymouth Av, NW7 .42 CS50
  W5 . . . . .97 CJ76
Weymouth Cl, E6
  off Coolees Wall 87 EP72
Weymouth Ct, Sutt. SM2 .158 DA108
Weymouth Ms, W1 . . . . .195 H6
Weymouth Rd, Hayes UB4 ..77 BS69
Weymouth St, W1 . . . . .194 G7
Weymouth Ter, E2 . . . . .84 DT68
Weymouth Wk, Stan. HA7 ..41 CG51
Wey Rd, Wey. KT13 . . . . .134 BM104
Weyside Cl, W.Byf. (Byfleet)
  KT14 . . . . .152 BM112
Weystone Rd, Add. KT15
  off Weybridge Rd 152 BM105
Whadcote St, N4
  off Seven Sisters Rd 65 DN61
Whalebone Av, Rom. RM6 ..70 EZ58
Whalebone Ct, EC2 . . . . .197 L8
Whalebone Gro, Rom. RM6 ..70 EZ58
Whalebone La, E15
  off West Ham La 86 EE66
Whalebone La N, Rom. RM6 ..70 EY57
Whalebone La S, Dag. RM8 ..70 EZ59
  Romford RM6 . . . . .70 EZ59
Whaley Rd, Pot.B. EN6 .12 DC33
Wharfdale Cl, N11
  off Ribblesdale Av 44 DG51
Wharfdale Rd, E5
  off Rushmore Rd 67 DX63

Wharfdale Rd, N1 . . . . .83 DL68
Wharfdale Gdns, Th.Hth.
  CR7 . . . . .141 DM98
Wharfedale Rd, Dart. DA2 .128 FQ88
Wharfedale St, SW10 .100 DB78
Wharf La, Rick. WD3 . . . . .38 BL46
  Twickenham TW1 . . . . .117 CG88
  Woking (Ripley) GU23 .168 BJ118
  Woking (Send) GU23 .167 BC123
Wharf Pl, E2 . . . . .84 DU67
Wharf Rd, E15 . . . . .85 ED67
  N1 . . . . .84 DQ68
  Brentwood CM14 . . . . .54 FW48
  Enfield EN3 . . . . .31 DY44
  Gravesend DA12 . . . . .131 GL86
  Grays RM17 . . . . .110 FZ79
  Staines (Wrays.) TW19 .112 AW87
Wharf Rd S, Grays RM17 .110 FZ79
Wharfside Rd, E16 . . . . .86 EE71
Wharf St, E16 . . . . .86 EE71
Wharncliffe Dr, Sthl. UB1 ..79 CD74
Wharncliffe Gdns, SE25 .142 DS96
Wharncliffe Rd, SE25 .142 DS96
Wharton Cl, NW10 . . . . .80 CS65
Wharton Cotts, WC1
  off Wharton St 83 DM69
Wharton Rd, Brom. BR1 .144 EH95
Wharton St, WC1 . . . . .196 C3
Whateley Rd, SE20 .123 DX94
  SE22 . . . . .122 DT85
Whatley Av, SW20 .139 CY97
Whatman Rd, SE23 .123 DX87
Whatmore Cl, Stai. TW19 .114 BG86
Wheatash Rd, Add. KT15 .134 BH103
Wheatcroft, Wal.Cr. (Chsht.)
  EN7 . . . . .14 DV28
Wheatfields, E6 off Oxleas .87 EP72
  Enfield EN3 . . . . .31 DY40
Wheatfield Way, Kings.T.
  KT1 . . . . .138 CL96
Wheathill Rd, SE20 .142 DV97
Wheat Knoll, Ken. CR8 .176 DQ116
Wheatlands, Houns. TW5 ..96 CA79
Wheatlands Rd, SW17
  off Stapleton Rd 120 DG90
  Slough SL3 . . . . .92 AW76
Wheatley Cl, NW4 . . . . .43 CU54
  Greenhithe DA9
    off Steele Av 129 FU85
  Hornchurch RM11 . . . . .72 FK57
Wheatley Cres, Hayes UB3 ..77 BU73
Wheatley Ho, SW15
  off Tangley Gro 119 CU87
Wheatley Rd, Islw. TW7 .97 CF83
Wheatley's Ait, Sun. TW16 .135 BU99
Wheatley St, W1 . . . . .194 G7
Wheatley Ter Rd, Erith DA8 .107 FF79
Wheatley Way, Ger.Cr. (Chal.St.P.)
  SL9 . . . . .36 AY51
Wheat Sheaf Cl, E14 .204 B8
Wheatsheaf Cl, Cher. (Ott.)
  KT16 . . . . .151 BD107
  Northolt UB5 . . . . .60 BY64
  Woking GU21 . . . . .166 AY116
Wheatsheaf Hill, Sev. (Halst.)
  TN14 . . . . .164 EZ109
Wheatsheaf La, SW6 .99 CW80
  SW8 . . . . .101 DL80
  Staines TW18 . . . . .113 BF94
Wheatsheaf Rd, Rom. RM1 .71 FF58
Wheatsheaf Ter, SW6 .99 CZ80
Wheatstone Cl, Mitch. CR4 .140 DE95
Wheatstone Rd, W10 . . . . .81 CY71
Wheeler Av, Oxt. RH8 .187 ED129
Wheeler Cl, Wdf.Grn. IG8
  off Chigwell Rd 49 EM50
Wheeler Gdns, N1
  off Outram Pl 83 DL67
Wheelers, Epp. CM16 .17 ET29
Wheelers Cross, Bark. IG11 ..87 ER68
Wheelers Dr, Ruis. HA4
  off Wallington Cl 59 BQ58
Wheelers Fm Gdns, Epp.
  (N.Wld.Bas.) CM16 . . . . . . .19 FB26
Wheelers La, Epsom KT18 .156 CP113
Wheelers Orchard, Ger.Cr.
  (Chal.St.P.) SL9 . . . . .36 AY51
Wheel Fm Dr, Dag. RM10 ..71 FC62
Wheelock Cl, Erith DA8 . . . . .107 FB80
Wheelwright Cl, Bushey WD23
  off Ashfield Av 24 CB44
Wheelwright St, N7 . . . . .83 DM66
Whelan Way, Wall. SM6 .141 DK104
Wheler St, E1 . . . . .197 P5
Whellock Rd, W4 . . . . .98 CS76
WHELPLEY HILL, Chesh. 4 AX26
Whelpley Hill Pk, Chesh.
  (Whel.Hill) HP5 . . . . .4 AX26
Whenman Av, Bex. DA5 .127 FC89
Wherside Cl, SE28 . . . . .88 EW73
WHETSTONE, N20 . . . . .44 DB47
Whetstone Cl, N20
  off Oakleigh Rd N 44 DD47
Whetstone Pk, WC2 .196 B8
Whetstone Rd, SE3 . . . . .104 EJ82
Whewell Rd, N19 . . . . .65 DL61
Whichcote St, SE1 . . . . .200 D3
Whidborne Cl, SE8
  off Cliff Ter 103 EA82
Whidborne St, WC1 .196 A3
Whiffins Orchard, Epp. CM16 .18 EX29
Whimbrel Cl, SE28 . . . . .88 EW73
  South Croydon CR2 .160 DR111
Whimbrel Way, Hayes UB4 ..78 BX72
Whinchat Rd, SE28 .105 ER76
Whinfell Cl, SW16 .121 DK92
Whinfell Way, Grav. DA12 .131 GM91
Whinyates Rd, SE9 .104 EL83
Whippendell Cl, Orp. BR5 .146 EV95
Whippendell Hill, Kings.L.
  WD4 . . . . .6 BJ30
Whippendell Rd, Wat. WD18 .23 BU43
Whippendell Way, Orp. BR5 .146 EV95
⊞ Whipps Cross Hosp, E11 ..67 ED58
Whipps Cross Rd, E11 .67 ED57
Whiskin St, EC1 . . . . .196 F3

Whisperwood, Rick. (Loud.)
  WD3 . . . . .22 BH41
Whisperwood Cl, Har. HA3 ..41 CE52
Whistler Gdns, Edg. HA8 ..42 CM54
Whistler Ms, SE15
  off Commercial Way 102 DT80
  Dagenham RM8
    off Fitzstephen Rd 70 EV64
Whistlers Av, SW11 .100 DD80
Whistler St, N5 . . . . .65 DP63
Whistler Wk, SW10
  off World's End Est 100 DD80
Whiston Rd, E2 . . . . .84 DT68
Whitakers Way, Loug. IG10 ..33 EM39
Whitbread Cl, N17 . . . . .46 DU53
Whitbread Rd, SE4 . . . . .103 DY84
★ Whitbread Shire Horse Stables,
  EC1 off Garrett St 197 J4
Whitburn Rd, SE13 . . . . .103 EB84
Whitby Av, NW10 . . . . .80 CP69
  Westerham (Bigg.H.) TN16 .178 EH119
Whitby Cl, Green. DA9 .129 FU85
Whitby Gdns, NW9 . . . . .62 CN55
  Sutton SM1 . . . . .140 DD103
Whitby Rd, SE18 . . . . .105 EM77
  Harrow HA2 . . . . .60 CC62
  Ruislip HA4 . . . . .59 BV62
  Sutton SM1 . . . . .140 DD103
Whitby St, E1 . . . . .197 P4
Whitcher Cl, SE14 . . . . .103 DY79
Whitcher Pl, NW1
  off Rochester Rd 83 DJ66
Whitchurch Av, Edg. HA8 ..42 CM52
Whitchurch Cl, Edg. HA8 ..42 CM51
Whitchurch Gdns, Edg. HA8 ..42 CM51
Whitchurch La, Edg. HA8 ..41 CK52
Whitchurch Rd, W11 . . . . .81 CX73
  Romford RM3 . . . . .52 FK49
Whitcomb Ct, WC2
  off Whitcomb St 83 DK73
Whitcombe Ms, Rich. TW9 ..98 CP81
Whitcomb St, WC2 .199 N1
White Acre, NW9 . . . . .42 CS54
Whiteadder Way, E14 .204 C8
Whitear Wk, E15 . . . . .85 ED65
White Av, Grav. (Nthflt.)
  DA11 . . . . .131 GF90
Whitebarn La, Dag. RM10 ..88 FA67
Whitebeam Av, Brom. BR2 .145 EN10
Whitebeam Cl, SW9
  off Clapham Rd 101 DM80
  Radlett (Shenley) WD7
    off Mulberry Gdns 10 CM33
  Waltham Cross EN7
    off The Laurels 14 DS26
Whitebeam Dr, S.Ock. RM15 ..91 FW69
White Beams, St.Alb. (Park St.)
  AL2 . . . . .8 CC28
Whitebeam Twr, E17
  off Hillyfield 67 DY55
White Beam Way, Tad. KT20 .173 CU121
White Bear Pl, NW3
  off New End Sq 64 DD63
White Br Av, Mitch. CR4 .140 DD98
Whitebridge Cl, Felt. TW14 .115 BT86
White Butts Rd, Ruis. HA4 ..60 BX62
WHITECHAPEL, E1 . . . . .84 DU72
⊖ Whitechapel 84 DV71
★ Whitechapel Art Gall, E1 ..84 DT72
Whitechapel High St, E1 ..84 DT72
Whitechapel Rd, E1 . . . . .84 DU72
White Ch La, E1 . . . . .84 DU72
White Ch Pas, E1
  off White Ch La 84 DU72
⊖ White City 81 CW73
White City Cl, W12 . . . . .81 CW73
White City Est, W12 . . . . .81 CV73
White City Rd, W12 . . . . .81 CV73
White Conduit St, N1
  off Chapel Mkt 83 DN68
Whitecote Rd, Sthl. UB1 .78 CB72
White Craig Cl, Pnr. HA5 ..40 CA50
Whitecroft, Swan. BR8 .147 FE96
Whitecroft Cl, Beck. BR3 .143 ED98
Whitecroft Way, Beck. BR3 .143 EC99
Whitecross Pl, EC2 .197 L6
Whitecross St, EC1 .197 J4
Whitefield Av, NW2 . . . . .63 CW59
  Purley CR8 . . . . .175 DN116
Whitefield Cl, SW15 .119 CY86
  Orpington BR5 . . . . .146 EW97
Whitefields Rd, Wal.Cr. (Chsht.)
  EN8 . . . . .14 DW28
Whitefoot La, Brom. BR1 .123 EC91
Whitefoot Ter, Brom. BR1 .123 EC90
Whiteford Rd, Slou. SL2 .74 AS71
White Friars, Sev. TN13 .190 FG127
Whitefriars Av, Har. HA3 ..41 CE54
Whitefriars Dr, Har. HA3 ..41 CD54
Whitefriars St, EC4 .196 E9
White Gdns, Dag. RM10 ..88 FA65
Whitegate Gdns, Har. HA3 ..41 CF52
White Gates, Horn. RM12 ..72 FJ61
Whitegates, Whyt. CR3
  off Court Bushes Rd 176 DU119
Whitegate Way, Tad. KT20 .173 CV120
Whitehall, SW1 . . . . .199 P2
White Hall, Rom. (Abridge) RM4
  off Market Pl 34 EV41
Whitehall Cl, Chig. IG7 .50 EU48
  Uxbridge UB8 . . . . .76 BJ67
Whitehall Ct, SW1 . . . . .199 P3
Whitehall Cres, Chess. KT9 .155 CK106
Whitehall Fm La, Vir.W.
  GU25 . . . . .132 AY96
Whitehall Gdns, E4 . . . . .48 EE46
  SW1 . . . . .199 P3
  W3 . . . . .80 CN74
  W4 . . . . .98 CP79
Whitehall La, Buck.H. IG9 ..48 EG47
  Egham TW20 . . . . .113 AZ94
  Erith DA8 . . . . .107 FF82
  Grays RM17 . . . . .110 GC78
  Staines (Wrays.) TW19 .113 BA86

Whitehall Pk, N19 . . . . .65 DJ60
Whitehall Pk Rd, W4 . . . . .98 CP79
Whitehall Pl, E off Station Rd .68 EG64
  SW1 . . . . .199 P3
  Wallington SM6
    off Bernard Rd 159 DH105
Whitehall Rd, E4 . . . . .48 EE47
  W7 . . . . .97 CG75
  Bromley BR2 . . . . .144 EK99
  Grays RM17 . . . . .110 GC77
  Harrow HA1 . . . . .61 CE59
  Thornton Heath CR7 .141 DN99
  Uxbridge UB8 . . . . .76 BK67
  Woodford Green IG8 ..48 EE47
Whitehall St, N17 . . . . .46 DT52
White Hart Cl, Ch.St.G. HP8 ..36 AU48
  Sevenoaks TN13 . . . . .191 FJ128
White Hart Ct, EC2
  off Bishopsgate 84 DS72
  Woking (Ripley) GU23 .168 BJ121
⇌ White Hart Lane 46 DT52
White Hart La, N17 . . . . .46 DT52
  N22 . . . . .45 DN53
  NW10 off Church Rd 81 CT65
  SW13 . . . . .98 CS83
  Romford RM7 . . . . .50 FA53
White Hart Meadows, Wok.
  (Ripley) GU23 . . . . .168 BJ121
White Hart Rd, SE18 .105 ES77
  Orpington BR6 . . . . .146 EU101
White Hart Row, Cher. KT16
  off Heriot Rd 134 BG101
White Hart Slip, Brom. BR1
  off Market Sq 144 EG96
White Hart St, SE11 .200 E10
White Hart Wd, Sev. TN13 .191 FJ129
White Hart Yd, SE1 . . . . .201 K3
Whitehaven, Slou. SL1 .74 AT73
Whitehaven Cl, Brom. BR2 .144 EG98
Whitehaven St, NW8 .194 B5
Whitehead Cl, N18 . . . . .46 DR50
  SW18 . . . . .120 DC87
  Dartford DA2 . . . . .128 FJ90
Whitehead's Gro, SW3 .198 C10
Whiteheart Av, Uxb. UB8 ..77 BQ71
Whiteheath Av, Ruis. HA4 ..59 BQ59
White Heron Ms, Tedd. TW11 .117 CF93
White Hill, Couls. (Chipstead)
  CR5 . . . . .174 DC124
  Northwood HA6 . . . . .38 BN51
  Rickmansworth WD3 ..38 BN51
  South Croydon CR2
    off St. Mary's Rd 160 DR109
Whitehill La, Grav. DA12 .131 GK90
  Redhill RH1 . . . . .186 DR121
  Woking GU23 . . . . .169 BQ123
Whitehill Par, Grav. DA12 .131 GJ90
Whitehill Pl, Vir.W. GU25 .132 AY99
White Hill Rd, Chesh. HP5 . . . .4 AX26
Whitehill Rd, Dart. DA1 .127 FG85
  Gravesend DA12 . . . . .131 GJ89
  Gravesend (Hook Grn.)
    DA13 . . . . .149 FX96
  Longfield DA3 . . . . .149 FX96
Whitehills Rd, Loug. IG10 ..33 EN41
White Horse All, EC1
  off Cowcross St 83 DP71
White Horse Dr, Epsom
  KT18 . . . . .156 CQ114
Whitehorse Hill, Chis. BR7 .125 EN91
White Horse La, E1 . . . . .85 DX70
Whitehorse La, SE25 .142 DR98
White Horse La, St.Alb. (Lon.Col.)
  AL2 . . . . .10 CL25
  Woking (Ripley) GU23 .168 BJ121
White Horse Ms, SE1 .200 E6
White Horse Rd, E1 . . . . .85 DY72
  E6 . . . . .87 EM69
Whitehorse Rd, Croy. CR0 .142 DR100
  Thornton Heath CR7 .142 DR100
White Horse St, W1 .199 H3
White Horse Yd, EC2 .197 K8
Whitehouse Av, Borwd. WD6 .26 CP41
White Ho Cl, Ger.Cr. (Chal.St.P.)
  SL9 . . . . .36 AY52
White Ho Dr, Stan. HA7 .41 CJ49
Whitehouse La, Abb.L.
  (Bedmond) WD5 . . . . .7 BV26
  Enfield EN2
    off Brigadier Hill 30 DQ39
White Ho La, Sev. TN14 .190 FF130
White Ho Rd, Sev. TN14 .190 FF130
Whitehouse Way, N14 . . . . .45 DH47
  Iver SL0 . . . . .75 BD69
  Slough SL3 . . . . .92 AW76
White Kennett St, E1 .197 N8
White Knights Rd, Wey.
  KT13 . . . . .153 BQ108
White Knobs Way, Cat. CR3 .186 DU125
Whitelands Av, Rick. (Chorl.)
  WD3 . . . . .21 BC42
Whitelands Way, Rom. RM3 ..52 FK54
White La, Oxt. RH8 .178 EH123
  Warlingham CR6 . . . . .178 EH123
Whiteledges, W13 . . . . .79 CJ72
Whitelegg Rd, E13 . . . . .86 EF68
Whiteley Rd, SE19 .122 DR92
Whiteleys Cotts, W14 .99 CZ77
Whiteleys Shop Cen, W2 ..82 DB72
Whiteleys Way, Felt. TW13 .116 CA90
WHITELEY VILLAGE, Walt. .153 BS110
White Lion Ct, EC3 .197 M9
White Lion Ct, Amer. HP7 ..20 AU39
  SE15 . . . . .102 DV80
White Lion Hill, EC4 .196 G10
White Lion Rd, Amer. HP7 ..20 AT38
White Lion St, N1 .196 D1
White Lo, SE19 . . . . .121 DP94
White Lo Cl, N2 . . . . .64 DD58
  Sevenoaks TN13 . . . . .191 FH124
  Sutton SM2 . . . . .158 DC108
White Lyon Ct, EC2
  off Fann St 84 DQ70
White Lyons Rd, Brwd.
  CM14 . . . . .54 FW47

A B C D E F G H I J K L M N O P Q R S T U V W X Y Z

Whi - Wil

White Oak Business Pk, Swan.
  BR8 off London Rd 147 FE97
White Oak Dr, Beck. BR3 . . . . 143 EC96
White Oak Gdns, Sid. DA15 . 125 ET87
Whiteoaks, Bans. SM7 . . . . . . 158 DB113
Whiteoaks La, Grnf. UB6 . . . . 79 CD68
White Orchards, N20 . . . . . . 43 CZ45
  Stanmore HA7 . . . . 41 CG50
White Post Hill, Dart. (Fnghm.)
  DA4 . . . . 148 FN101
Whitepost Hill, Red. RH1 . . 184 DG134
White Post La, E9 . . . . 85 DZ66
  SE13 . . . . 103 EA83
White Post St, SE15 . . . . . . 102 DW80
White Rd, E15 . . . . 86 EE66
  Betchworth RH3 . . . . 182 CN133
  Tadworth KT20 . . . . 182 CN133
White Rose La, Wok. GU22 . 167 AZ117
Whites Av, Ilf. IG2 . . . . 69 ES58
Whites Cl, Green. DA9 . . . . 129 FW86
Whites Grds, SE1 . . . . 201 N5
Whites Grds Est, SE1 . . . . . 201 N4
White Shack La, Rick. WD3 . 22 BM37
Whites La, Slou. (Datchet)
  SL3 . . . . 92 AV79
White's Row, E1 . . . . 197 P7
White's Sq, SW4
  off Nelson's Row 101 DK84
Whitestile Rd, Brent. TW8 . . 97 CJ78
Whitestone La, NW3
  off Heath St 64 DC62
Whitestone Wk, NW3
  off North End Way 64 DC62
White St, Sthl. UB1 . . . . 96 BX75
White Swan Ms, W4
  off Bennett St 98 CS79
Whitethorn Av, Couls. CR5 . 174 DG115
  West Drayton UB7 . . . . . . 76 BL73
Whitethorn Gdns, Croy. CR0 142 DV103
  Enfield EN2 . . . . 30 DR43
  Hornchurch RM11 . . . . . . 72 FJ58
Whitethorn Pl, West Dr. UB7
  off Whitethorn Av 76 BM74
Whitethorn St, E3 . . . . 85 EA70
Whiteways Ct, Stai. TW18
  off Pavilion Gdns 114 BH94
Whitewebbs La, Enf. EN2 . . 30 DS35
Whitewebbs Pk, Enf. EN2 . . 30 DQ35
Whitewebbs Rd, Enf. EN2 . . 30 DM35
Whitewebbs Way, Orp. BR5 . 145 ET95
Whitewood Cotts, West. (Tats.)
  TN16 . . . . 178 EJ120
Whitfield Pl, W1 . . . . 195 K5
Whitfield Rd, E6 . . . . 86 EJ66
  SE3 . . . . 103 ED81
  Bexleyheath DA7 . . . . 106 EZ80
Whitfield St, W1 . . . . 195 M7
Whitfield Way, Rick. (Mill End)
  WD3 . . . . 37 BF46
Whitford Gdns, Mitch. CR4 . 140 DF97
Whitgift Av, S.Croy. CR2 . . 160 DQ106
Whitgift Cen, Croy. CR0 . . 142 DQ103
Whitgift St, SE11 . . . . 200 B8
  Croydon CR0 . . . . 142 DQ104
Whit Hern Ct, Wal.Cr. EN8
  off College Rd 14 DW30
Whiting Av, Bark. IG11 . . . . 87 EP66
Whitings, Ilf. IG2 . . . . 69 ER57
Whitings Rd, Barn. EN5 . . . 27 CW43
Whitings Way, E6 . . . . 87 EN71
Whitland Rd, Cars. SM5 . . . 140 DD102
Whitlars Dr, Kings L. WD4 . . 6 BM28
Whitley Cl, Abb.L. WD5 . . . . 7 BU32
  Staines (Stanw.) TW19 . . . 114 BL86
Whitley Rd, N17 . . . . 46 DS54
Whitlock Dr, SW19 . . . . 119 CY87
Whitman Rd, E3
  off Mile End Rd 85 DY70
Whitmead Cl, S.Croy. CR2 . 160 DS107
Whitmore Av, Rom. (Harold Wd.)
  RM3 . . . . 52 FL54
Whitmore Cl, N11 . . . . 45 DH50
Whitmore Est, N1 . . . . 84 DS67
Whitmore Gdns, NW10 . . . . 81 CW68
Whitmore Rd, N1 . . . . 84 DS67
  Beckenham BR3 . . . . 143 DZ97
  Harrow HA1 . . . . 60 CC59
Whitmores Cl, Epsom KT18 172 CQ115
Whitnell Way, SW15 . . . . . . 119 CX85
Whitney Av, Ilf. IG4 . . . . 68 EK56
Whitney Rd, E10 . . . . 67 EB59
Whitney Wk, Sid. DA14 . . . . 126 EY93
Whitstable Cl, Beck. BR3 . . 143 DZ95
  Ruislip HA4
  off Chichester Av 59 BS61
Whitstable Ho, W10 . . . . . . 81 CX72
Whitstable Pl, Croy. CR0 . . 160 DQ105
Whittaker Av, Rich. TW9
  off Hill St 117 CK85
Whittaker Rd, E6 . . . . 86 EJ66
  Sutton SM3 . . . . 139 CZ104
Whittaker St, SW1 . . . . 198 F9
Whittaker Way, SE1 . . . . . . 202 C9
Whitta Rd, E12 . . . . 68 EK63
Whittell Gdns, SE26 . . . . . . 122 DW90
Whittenham Cl, Slou. SL2 . . 74 AU74
Whittingstall Rd, SW6 . . . . . 99 CZ81
Whittington Av, EC3 . . . . . . 197 M9
  Hayes UB4 . . . . 77 BT71
Whittington Ct, N2 . . . . 64 DF57
[H] Whittington Hosp, N19 . . . 65 DJ61
Whittington Ms, N12
  off Fredericks Pl 44 DC49
Whittington Rd, N22 . . . . . . 45 DL52
  Brentwood CM13 . . . . . . 55 GC44
Whittington Way, Pnr. HA5 . 60 BY57
Whittlebury Cl, Cars. SM5 . 158 DF108
Whittle Cl, E17 . . . . 67 DY58
  Southall UB1 . . . . 78 CB72
Whittle Rd, Houns. TW5 . . . 96 BW80
  Southall UB2 off Post Rd . . 96 CB75
Whittlesea Cl, Har. HA3 . . . 40 CC52
Whittlesea Path, Har. HA3 . 40 CC53
Whittlesea Rd, Har. HA3 . . 40 CC53

Whittlesey St, SE1 . . . . 200 D3
WHITTON, Twick. 116 CB87
⇌ Whitton 116 CC87
Whitton Av E, Grnf. UB6 . . . 61 CE64
Whitton Av W, Grnf. UB6 . . 60 CC64
  Northolt UB5 . . . . 60 CC64
Whitton Cl, Grnf. UB6 . . . . . 79 CH65
Whitton Dene, Houns. TW3 . 116 CB85
  Isleworth TW7 . . . . 117 CD85
Whitton Dr, Grnf. UB6 . . . . . 79 CG67
Whitton Manor Rd, Islw.
  TW7 . . . . 116 CC85
Whitton Rd, Houns. TW3 . . . 96 CB84
  Twickenham TW1,TW2 . . . 117 BX88
Whitton Wk, E3 . . . . 85 EA68
Whitton Waye, Houns. TW3 . 116 CA86
Whitwell Rd, E13 . . . . 86 EG69
  Watford WD25 . . . . 24 BX35
Whitworth Pl, SE18 . . . . 105 EP77
Whitworth Rd, SE18 . . . . . . 105 EN80
  SE25 . . . . 142 DS97
Whitworth St, SE10 . . . . . . 205 J10
Whopshott Av, Wok. GU21 . 166 AW116
Whopshott Cl, Wok. GU21 . 166 AW116
Whopshott Dr, Wok. GU21 . 166 AW116
Whorlton Rd, SE15 . . . . 102 DV83
Whybridge Cl, Rain. RM13 . 89 FE67
Whychcote Pt, NW2
  off Claremont Rd 63 CW59
Whymark Av, N22 . . . . 65 DN55
Whytebeam Vw, Whyt. CR3 . 176 DT118
Whytecliffe Rd N, Pur. CR8 . 159 DP111
Whytecliffe Rd S, Pur. CR8 . 159 DN111
Whytecroft, Houns. TW5 . . . 96 BX80
WHYTELEAFE, Cat. 176 DS118
⇌ Whyteleafe 176 DT117
Whyteleafe Business Village, Whyt.
  CR3 off Whyteleafe Hill . 176 DT118
Whyteleafe Hill, Whyt. CR3 . 176 DT118
Whyteleafe Rd, Cat. CR3 . . 176 DS120
⇌ Whyteleafe South 176 DU119
Whyteville Rd, E7 . . . . 86 EH65
Wichling Cl, Orp. BR5 . . . . . 146 EX102
Wickenden Rd, Sev. TN13 . 191 FJ122
Wicken's Meadow, Sev.
  (Dunt.Grn.) TN14 . . . . . . 181 FF119
Wickersley Rd, SW11 . . . . . 100 DG82
Wickers Oake, SE19 . . . . . . 122 DT91
Wicker St, E1 off Burslem St . 84 DV72
Wicket, The, Croy. CR0 . . . 161 EA106
Wicket Rd, Grnf. UB6 . . . . . 79 CG69
Wickets, The, Ashf. TW15 . . 114 BL91
Wickets End, Rad. (Shenley)
  WD7 . . . . 10 CL33
Wickets Way, Ilf. IG6 . . . . . . 49 ET51
Wickford Cl, Rom. RM3
  off Wickford Dr 52 FM50
Wickford Dr, Rom. RM3 . . . . 52 FM50
Wickford St, E1 . . . . 84 DW70
Wickford Way, E17 . . . . 67 DX56
Wickham Av, Croy. CR0 . . . 143 DY103
  Sutton SM3 . . . . 157 CW106
Wickham Chase, W.Wick.
  BR4 . . . . 143 ED101
Wickham Cl, E1 . . . . 84 DW71
  Enfield EN3 . . . . 30 DV41
  New Malden KT3 . . . . 139 CT99
  Uxbridge (Hare.) UB9 . . . 38 BK53
Wickham Ct Rd, W.Wick.
  BR4 . . . . 143 EC103
Wickham Cres, W.Wick. BR4 143 EC103
Wickham Fld, Sev. (Otford)
  TN14 . . . . 181 FF116
Wickham Gdns, SE4 . . . . . . 103 DZ83
Wickham La, SE2 . . . . 106 EU78
  Egham TW20 . . . . 113 BA94
  Welling DA16 . . . . 106 EU78
Wickham Ms, SE4 . . . . 103 DZ82
Wickham Rd, E4 . . . . 47 EC52
  SE4 . . . . 103 DZ84
  Beckenham BR3 . . . . 143 EB96
  Croydon CR0 . . . . 143 DX103
  Grays RM16 . . . . 111 GJ75
  Harrow HA3 . . . . 41 CD54
Wickham St, SE11 . . . . 200 B10
  Welling DA16 . . . . 105 ES82
Wickham Way, Beck. BR3 . . 143 EC98
Wick La, E3 . . . . 85 EA68
  Egham (Eng.Grn.) TW20 . 112 AT92
Wickliffe Av, N3 . . . . 43 CY54
Wickliffe Gdns, Wem. HA9 . 62 CP61
Wicklow St, WC1 . . . . 196 B2
Wick Rd, E9 . . . . 85 DX65
  Egham (Eng.Grn.) TW20 . 112 AV94
  Teddington TW11 . . . . . . 117 CH94
Wicks Cl, SE9 . . . . 124 EK91
Wick Sq, E9 off Eastway . . . 85 DZ65
Wicksteed Cl, Bex. DA5 . . . 127 FD90
Wicksteed Ho, Brent. TW8
  off Green Dragon La 98 CM78
Wickwood St, SE5 . . . . 101 DP82
Wid Cl, Brwd. CM13 . . . . . . 55 GD43
Widdecombe Av, Har. HA2 . 60 BY61
Widdenham Rd, N7 . . . . 65 DM63
Widdin St, E15 . . . . 86 ED66
Widecombe Cl, Rom. RM3 . 52 FK53
Widecombe Gdns, Ilf. IG4 . 68 EL56
Widecombe Rd, SE9 . . . . . . 124 EL90
Widecombe Way, N2 . . . . . . 64 DD57
Widecroft Rd, Iver SL0 . . . . 75 BE72
Widegate St, E1 . . . . 197 N7
Widenham Cl, Pnr. HA5
  off Bridle Rd 60 BW57
Wide Way, Mitch. CR4 . . . . 141 DK97
Widewing Cl, Tedd. TW11 . 117 CH94
Widgeon Cl, E16
  off Maplin Rd 86 EH72
Widgeon Rd, Erith DA8 . . . . 107 FH80
Widgeon Way, Wat. WD25 . 24 BY36
Widley Rd, W9 . . . . 82 DA69
WIDMORE, Brom. 144 EH97
WIDMORE GREEN, Brom. . 144 EJ95
Widmore Lo Rd, Brom. BR1 144 EK96
Widmore Rd, Brom. BR1 . . 144 EG96
  Uxbridge UB8 . . . . 77 BP70
Widworthy Hayes, Brwd.
  CM13 . . . . 55 GB46

Wieland Rd, Nthwd. HA6 . . . 39 BU52
Wigan Ho, E5 off Warwick Gro . 66 DV60
Wigeon Path, SE28 . . . . 105 ER76
Wigeon Way, Hayes UB4 . . 78 BX72
Wiggenhall Rd, Wat. WD18 . 23 BV42
Wiggie La, Red. RH1 . . . . . 184 DG132
Wiggins La, Rich. TW10 . . . 117 CJ89
Wiggins Mead, NW9 . . . . . . 43 CT52
Wigginton Av, Wem. HA9 . . 80 CP65
Wigham Ho, Bark. IG11 . . . . 87 EQ66
Wightman Rd, N4 . . . . 65 DN57
  N8 . . . . 65 DN56
Wigley Bush La, Brwd. CM14 54 FS47
Wigley Rd, Felt. TW13 . . . . 116 BX88
Wigmore Pl, W1 . . . . 195 H8
Wigmore Rd, Cars. SM5 . . . 140 DD103
Wigmore St, W1 . . . . 194 F9
Wigmore Wk, Cars. SM5 . . 140 DD103
Wigram Rd, E11 . . . . 68 EJ58
Wigram Sq, E17 . . . . 47 EC54
Wigston Cl, N18 . . . . 46 DS50
Wigston Rd, E13 . . . . 86 EH70
Wigton Gdns, Stan. HA7 . . . 42 CL53
Wigton Pl, SE11
  off Milverton St 101 DN78
Wigton Rd, E17 . . . . 47 DZ53
  Romford RM3 . . . . 52 FL49
Wigton Way, Rom. RM3 . . . 52 FL49
Wilberforce Rd, N4 . . . . 65 DP61
  NW9 . . . . 63 CU58
Wilberforce Way, SW19 . . . 119 CX93
  Gravesend DA12 . . . . 131 GK92
Wilbraham Pl, SW1 . . . . . . 198 E8
Wilbury Av, Sutt. SM2 . . . . 157 CZ110
Wilbury Rd, Wok. GU21 . . . 166 AX117
Wilbury Way, N18 . . . . 46 DR50
Wilby Ms, W11 . . . . 81 CZ74
Wilcon Way, Wat. WD25 . . . 8 BX34
Wilcot Av, Wat. WD19 . . . . . 40 BY45
Wilcot Cl, Wat. WD19
  off Wilcot Av 40 BY45
Wilcox Cl, SW8 . . . . 101 DL80
  Borehamwood WD6 . . . . . 26 CQ39
Wilcox Gdns, Shep. TW17 . 134 BM97
Wilcox Pl, SW1 . . . . 199 L7
Wilcox Rd, SW8 . . . . 101 DL80
  Sutton SM1 . . . . 158 DB105
  Teddington TW11 . . . . . . 117 CD91
Wildacres, Nthwd. HA6 . . . . 39 BT49
  West Byfleet KT14 . . . . . . 152 BJ111
Wildbank Ct, Wok. GU22
  off White Rose La 167 AZ118
Wild Ct, WC2 . . . . 196 B8
Wildcroft Gdns, Edg. HA8 . 41 CK51
Wildcroft Rd, SW15 . . . . . . 119 CW87
Wilde Cl, E8 . . . . 84 DU67
  Tilbury RM18
  off Coleridge Rd 111 GJ82
Wilde Pl, N13
  off Medesenge Way 45 DP51
  SW18 off Heathfield Rd . . 120 DD87
Wilder Cl, Ruis. HA4 . . . . . . 59 BV60
Wilderness, The, E.Mol. KT8 136 CC99
  Hampton (Hmptn.H.) TW12
  off Park Rd 116 CB91
WILDERNESSE, Sev. 191 FL122
Wildernesse Av, Sev. (Seal)
  TN15 . . . . 191 FL122
Wildernesse Mt, Sev. TN13 191 FK122
Wilderness Rd, Chis. BR7 . 125 EP94
  Oxted RH8 . . . . 188 EG130
Wilde Rd, Erith DA8 . . . . . . 107 FB80
Wilders Cl, Wok. GU21 . . . . 166 AW118
Wilderton Rd, N16 . . . . 66 DS59
Wildfell Rd, SE6 . . . . 123 EB87
Wild Goose Dr, SE14 . . . . . 102 DW81
Wild Grn N, Slou. SL3
  off Verney Rd 93 BA77
Wild Grn S, Slou. SL3
  off Swabey Rd 93 BA77
Wild Hatch, NW11 . . . . 64 DA58
Wild Oaks Cl, Nthwd. HA6 . 39 BT51
Wild's Rents, SE1 . . . . 201 M6
Wild St, WC2 . . . . 196 A9
Wildwood, Nthwd. HA6 . . . . 39 BR51
Wildwood Av, St.Alb. (Brick.Wd.)
  AL2 . . . . 8 BZ30
Wildwood Cl, SE12 . . . . 124 EF87
  Woking GU22 . . . . 167 BF115
Wildwood Ct, Ken. CR8 . . . 176 DR115
Wildwood Gro, NW3
  off North End Way 64 DC60
Wildwood Ri, NW11 . . . . . . 64 DC60
Wildwood Rd, NW11 . . . . . . 64 DC59
Wildwood Ter, NW3 . . . . . . 64 DC60
Wilford Cl, Enf. EN2 . . . . . . 30 DR41
  Northwood HA6 . . . . 39 BR52
Wilford Rd, Slou. SL3 . . . . . 93 AZ77
Wilfred Av, Rain. RM13 . . . . 89 FG71
Wilfred Owen Cl, SW19
  off Tennyson Rd 120 DC93
Wilfred St, SW1 . . . . 199 K6
  Gravesend DA12 . . . . 131 GH86
  Woking GU21 . . . . 166 AX118
Wilfred Turney Est, W6
  off Hammersmith Gro . . . 99 CW76
Wilfrid Gdns, W3 . . . . 80 CQ71
Wilhelmina Av, Couls. CR5 . 175 DJ119
Wilkes Rd, Brent. TW8 . . . . 98 CL79
  Brentwood CM13 . . . . . . 55 GD43
Wilkes St, E1 . . . . 84 DT71
Wilkie Way, SE22
  off Lordship La 122 DU88
Wilkins Cl, Hayes UB3 . . . . 95 BT78
  Mitcham CR4 . . . . 140 DE95
Wilkinson Cl, Dart. DA1 . . . 108 FM84
  Uxbridge UB10 . . . . 77 BP67
  Waltham Cross (Chsht.)
  EN7 . . . . 14 DQ26
Wilkinson Rd, E16 . . . . 86 EJ72
Wilkinson St, SW8 . . . . 101 DM80
Wilkinson Way, W4 . . . . 98 CR75
Wilkin St, NW5 . . . . 83 DH65
Wilkin St Ms, NW5
  off Wilkin St 83 DH65
Wilkins Way, West. (Brasted)
  TN16 . . . . 180 EV124

Wilks Av, Dart. DA1 . . . . . . 128 FM89
Wilks Gdns, Croy. CR0 . . . 143 DY102
Wilks Pl, N1 . . . . 197 N1
Willan Rd, N17 . . . . 46 DR54
Willan Wall, E16
  off Victoria Dock Rd 86 EF73
Willard St, SW8 . . . . 101 DH83
Willats Cl, Cher. KT16
  off Alwyns La 133 BF100
Willcocks Cl, Chess. KT9 . 138 CL104
Willcott Rd, W3 . . . . 80 CP74
Will Crooks Gdns, SE9 . . . 104 EJ84
Willen Fld Rd, NW10 . . . . . . 80 CQ68
Willenhall Av, Barn. EN5 . . 28 DC44
Willenhall Dr, Hayes UB3 . . 77 BS73
Willenhall Rd, SE18 . . . . . . 105 EP78
WILLESDEN, NW10 . . . . . . 81 CT65
[H] Willesden Comm Hosp,
  NW10 . . . . 81 CU66
WILLESDEN GREEN, NW10 . 81 CV66
◯ Willesden Green 81 CW65
⇌ Willesden Junction 81 CT69
◯ Willesden Junction 81 CT69
Willesden La, NW2 . . . . 81 CX65
  NW6 . . . . 81 CX65
Willes Rd, NW5 . . . . 83 DH65
Willett Cl, Nthlt. UB5
  off Broomcroft Av 78 BW69
  Orpington BR5 . . . . 145 ES100
Willett Pl, Th.Hth. CR7
  off Willett Rd 141 DN99
Willett Rd, Th.Hth. CR7 . . . 141 DN99
Willetts La, Uxb. (Denh.) UB9 57 BF63
Willett Way, Orp. BR5 . . . . 145 ER99
Willey Broom La, Cat. CR3 . 185 DN125
Willey Fm La, Cat. CR3 . . . 186 DQ126
Willey La, Cat. CR3 . . . . . . 186 DR125
William Barefoot Dr, SE9 . . 125 EN91
William Bonney Est, SW4 . . 101 DK84
William Booth Rd, SE20 . . . 142 DU95
William Carey Way, Har. HA1 61 CE59
William Cl, N2 off King St . . 64 DD55
  Romford RM5 . . . . 51 FC53
  Southall UB2
  off Windmill Av 96 CC75
William Cory Prom, Erith
  DA8 . . . . 107 FE78
William Covell Cl, Enf. EN2 . 29 DM38
William Dunbar Ho, NW6 . . 81 CZ68
William Dyce Ms, SW16
  off Babington Rd 121 DK91
William Ellis Cl, Wind. (Old Wind.)
  SL4 . . . . 112 AU85
William Ellis Way, SE16 . . . 202 C7
William IV St, WC2 . . . . 199 P1
William Gdns, SW15 . . . . . 119 CV85
William Guy Gdns, E3
  off Talwin St 85 EB69
William Harvey Ho, SW19
  off Whitlock Dr 119 CY88
William Margrie Cl, SE15 . . 102 DU82
William Morley Cl, E6 . . . . . 86 EK67
William Morris Cl, E17 . . . . 67 DZ55
William Morris Way, SW6 . . 100 DC83
★ William Morris Gall, Lloyd Pk,
  E17 . . . . 67 EA55
William Nash Ct, Orp. BR5
  off Brantwood Way 146 EW97
William Pl, E3 off Roman Rd . 85 DZ68
William Rd, NW1 . . . . 195 J3
  SW19 . . . . 119 CY94
  Caterham CR3 . . . . 176 DR122
  Sutton SM1 . . . . 158 DC106
William Russell Ct, Wok. GU21
  off Raglan Rd 166 AS118
Williams Av, E17 . . . . 47 DZ53
Williams Bldgs, E2 . . . . 84 DW70
Williams Cl, N8
  off Coolhurst Rd 65 DK58
  Addlestone KT15
  off Monks Cres 152 BH106
Williams Evans Rd, Epsom
  KT19 . . . . 156 CN111
Williams Gro, N22 . . . . 45 DN53
  Surbiton KT6 . . . . 137 CJ100
William's La, SW14 . . . . 98 CQ83
Williams La, Mord. SM4 . . . 140 DC99
Williamson Cl, SE10 . . . . . . 205 K10
Williamson Rd, N4 . . . . 65 DP58
Williamson St, N7 . . . . 65 DL63
Williamson Way, NW7 . . . . 43 CY51
  Rickmansworth WD3 . . . . 38 BG46
William Sq, SE16 . . . . 203 L1
Williams Rd, W13 . . . . 79 CG73
  Southall UB2 . . . . 96 BY77
Williams Ter, Croy. CR0 . . . 159 DN107
Williams Ter, E10 . . . . 67 EB58
  N17 . . . . 46 DT52
  SW1 . . . . 198 E5
  Barking IG11 . . . . 87 EQ66
  Bushey WD23 . . . . 24 BX41
  Carshalton SM5 . . . . 140 DE104
  Gravesend DA12 . . . . 131 GH87
  Grays RM17 . . . . 110 GB79
  Slough SL1 . . . . 74 AT74
Williams Way, Rad. WD7 . . 25 CJ35
Willifield Way, NW11 . . . . . 63 CZ56
Willingale Cl, Brwd. CM13
  off Fairview Av 55 GE44
  Loughton IG10
  off Willingale Rd 33 EQ40
  Woodford Green IG8 . . . . 48 EK51
Willingale Rd, Loug. IG10 . 33 EQ41
Willingdon Rd, N22 . . . . . . 45 DP54
Willinghall Cl, Wal.Abb. EN9 15 ED32
Willingham Cl, NW5
  off Leighton Rd 65 DJ64
Willingham Ter, NW5
  off Leighton Rd 65 DJ64
Willingham Way, Kings.T.
  KT1 . . . . 138 CN97

Willington Ct, E5
  off Mandeville St 67 DY62
Willington Rd, SW9 . . . . . . 101 DL83
Willis Av, Sutt. SM2 . . . . . . 158 DE107
Willis Cl, Epsom KT18 . . . . 156 CP113
Willis Rd, E15 . . . . 86 EF67
  Croydon CR0 . . . . 142 DQ101
  Erith DA8 . . . . 107 FC77
Willmore End, SW19 . . . . . 140 DB95
Willoughby Av, Croy. CR0 . 159 DM105
Willoughby Ct, St.Alb. (Lon.Col.)
  AL2 . . . . J CK26
Willoughby Dr, Rain. RM13 . 89 FE66
Willoughby Gro, N17 . . . . . 46 DV52
Willoughby Ho, EC2
  off The Barbican 84 DQ71
Willoughby La, N17 . . . . . . 46 DV52
Willoughby Ms, SW4
  off Wixs La 101 DH84
Willoughby Pk Rd, N17 . . . 46 DV52
Willoughby Pas, E14 . . . . . 203 P2
Willoughby Rd, N8 . . . . 65 DN55
  NW3 . . . . 64 DD63
  Kingston upon Thames KT2 138 CM95
  Slough SL3 . . . . 93 BA76
  Twickenham TW1 . . . . . . 117 CK86
Willoughbys, The, SW14
  off Upper Richmond Rd W . 98 CS84
Willoughby St, WC1 . . . . . . 195 P7
Willoughby Way, SE7 . . . . . 205 P8
Willow Av, SW13 . . . . 99 CT82
  Sidcup DA15 . . . . 126 EU86
  Swanley BR8 . . . . 147 FF97
  Uxbridge (Denh.) UB9 . . . 58 BJ64
  West Drayton UB7 . . . . . . 76 BM73
Willow Bk, SW6 . . . . 99 CY83
  Richmond TW10 . . . . 117 CH90
  Woking GU22 . . . . 166 AY122
Willowbank Gdns, Tad. KT20 173 CV122
Willowbank Pl, Pur. CR8
  off Kingsdown Av 159 DP109
Willow Br Rd, N1 . . . . 84 DQ65
Willowbrook Est, SE15
  off Sumner Rd 102 DT80
Willowbrook Rd, SE15 . . . . 102 DT79
  Southall UB2 . . . . 96 CA76
  Staines TW19 . . . . 114 BL89
Willow Business Cen, Mitch. CR4
  off Willow La 140 DF99
Willow Cl, Add. (Woodham)
  KT15 . . . . 151 BF111
  Bexley DA5 . . . . 126 EZ86
  Brentford TW8 . . . . 97 CJ79
  Brentwood CM13 . . . . . . 55 GB44
  Bromley BR2 . . . . 145 EM99
  Buckhurst Hill IG9 . . . . . . 48 EK48
  Erith DA8 off Willow Rd . . 107 FG81
  Hornchurch RM12 . . . . . . 71 FH62
  Orpington BR5 . . . . 146 EV101
  Slough (Colnbr.) SL3 . . . . 93 BC80
  Thornton Heath CR7 . . . . 141 DP100
  Waltham Cross (Chsht.)
  EN7 . . . . 14 DS26
Willow Cotts, Mitch. CR4 . . 141 DJ97
  Richmond TW9
  off Kew Grn 98 CN79
Willow Ct, EC2 . . . . 197 M4
  Edgware HA8 . . . . 42 CL49
Willowcourt Av, Har. HA3 . . 61 CH57
Willow Cres E, Uxb. (Denh.)
  UB9 . . . . 58 BJ64
Willow Cres W, Uxb. (Denh.)
  UB9 . . . . 58 BJ64
Willowdene, N6
  off Denewood Rd 64 DF59
  Brentwood CM15 . . . . . . 54 FT43
Willow Dene, Bushey
  (Bushey Hth.) WD23 . . . . 41 CE45
  Pinner HA5 . . . . 40 BX54
Willowdene, Wal.Cr. EN8 . . 15 DY27
Willowdene Cl, Twick. TW2 . 116 CC87
Willowdene Ct, Brwd. CM14 54 FW49
Willow Dr, Barn. EN5 . . . . . 27 CY42
  Woking (Ripley) GU23 . . . 168 BG124
Willow Edge, Kings L. WD4 . 6 BN29
Willow End, N20 . . . . 44 DA47
  Northwood HA6 . . . . 39 BU51
  Surbiton KT6 . . . . 138 CL102
Willow Fm La, SW15
  off Queens Ride 99 CV83
Willowfield Cl, SE18 . . . . . . 105 ES78
Willow Gdns, Houns. TW3 . 96 CA81
  Ruislip HA4 . . . . 59 BT61
Willow Grn, NW9
  off Clayton Fld 42 CS53
  Borehamwood WD6 . . . . . 26 CR43
Willow Gro, E13
  off Libra Rd 86 EG68
  Chislehurst BR7 . . . . 125 EN93
  Ruislip HA4 . . . . 59 BT61
Willowhayne Dr, Walt. KT12 135 BV101
Willowhayne Gdns, Wor.Pk.
  KT4 . . . . 139 CW104
Willowherb Wk, Rom. RM3
  off Clematis Cl 52 FJ52
Willow La, SE18 . . . . 105 EM77
  Amersham HP7 . . . . 20 AT41
  Mitcham CR4 . . . . 140 DF99
  Watford WD18 . . . . 23 BU43
Willow Mead, Chig. IG7 . . . 50 EU48
Willowmead, Stai. TW18
  off Northfield Rd 134 BH95
Willowmead Cl, W5 . . . . . . 79 CK71
  Woking GU21 . . . . 166 AU116
Willowmere, Esher KT10 . . 154 CC105
Willow Mt, Croy. CR0
  off Langton Way 142 DS104
Willow Pk, Sev. (Otford)
  TN14 . . . . 181 FF117
  Slough (Stoke P.) SL2 . . . 74 AU66
Willow Path, Wal.Abb. EN9 . 16 EE34
Willow Pl, SW1 . . . . 199 L8
Willow Rd, NW3 . . . . 64 DD63
  W5 . . . . 98 CL75
  Dartford DA1 . . . . 128 FJ88
  Enfield EN1 . . . . 30 DS41

Wil- Win

Willow Rd, Erith DA8 . . . . .107 FG81
New Malden KT3 . . . . . .138 CQ98
Romford RM6 . . . . . . .70 EY58
Slough (Colnbr.) SL3 . . . .93 BE82
Wallington SM6 . . . . . .159 DH108
Willows, The, Buck.H. IG9 . .48 EK48
Esher (Clay.) KT10
off Albany Cres 155 CE107
Grays RM17 . . . . . . .110 GE79
Rickmansworth (Mill End) WD3
off Uxbridge Rd 38 BG47
Watford WD19
off Brookside Rd 39 BV45
West Byfleet (Byfleet)
KT14 . . . . .152 BL113
Weybridge KT13 . . . . .134 BN104
Willows Av, Mord. SM4 . . .140 DB99
Willows CI, Pnr. HA5 . . . .40 BW54
Willowside, St.Alb. (Lon.Col.)
AL2 . . . . .10 CL27
Willows Path, Epsom KT18 .156 CP114
Willow St, E4 . . . . . . .47 ED45
EC2 . . . . .197 M4
Romford RM7 . . . . . .71 FC56
Willow Tree CI, E3
off Birdsfield La 85 DZ67
SW18 off Cargill Rd 120 DB88
Hayes UB4 . . . . . . .78 BW70
Romford (Abridge) RM4 . . .34 EV41
Uxbridge UB10 . . . . . .59 BQ62
Willow Tree La, Hayes UB4 . .78 BW70
Willowtree Marina, Hayes
UB4 . . . . .78 BY72
Willow Tree Wk, Brom. BR1 .144 EH95
Willowtree Way, Th.Hth. CR7
off Kensington Av 141 DN95
Willow Vale, W12 . . . . . .81 CU74
Chislehurst BR7 . . . . .125 EP93
Leatherhead (Fetch.) KT22 .170 CB123
Willow Vw, SW19 . . . . . .140 DD95
Willow Wk, E17 . . . . . .67 DZ57
N2 . . . . .44 DD54
N15 . . . . .65 DP56
N21 . . . . .29 DM44
SE1 . . . . .201 N8
Chertsey KT16 . . . . . .134 BG101
Dartford DA1 . . . . . .128 FJ85
Egham (Eng.Grn.) TW20 . . .111 AW92
Orpington BR6 . . . . . .145 EP104
Sutton SM3 . . . . . . .139 CZ104
Tadworth KT20 off Oak La .182 CQ130
Upminster RM14 . . . . . .73 FS60
Willow Way, N3 . . . . . . .44 DB52
SE26 . . . . .122 DV90
W11 off Freston Rd 81 CX74
Epsom KT19 . . . . . . .156 CR107
Godstone RH9 . . . . . .186 DV132
Potters Bar EN6 . . . . . .12 DB33
Radlett WD7 . . . . . . .25 CE36
Romford RM3 . . . . . . .52 FP51
St. Albans AL2 . . . . . . .8 CA27
Sunbury-on-Thames
TW16 . . . . .135 BU98
Tadworth KT20 off Oak Dr .182 CP130
Twickenham TW2 . . . . .116 CB89
Wembley HA0 . . . . . . .61 CG62
West Byfleet KT14 . . . . .152 BJ111
Woking GU22 . . . . . .166 AX121
Willow Wd Cres, SE25 . . . .142 DS100
Willrose Cres, SE2 . . . . .106 EW78
Wills Cres, Houns. TW3 . . .116 CB86
Wills Gro, NW7 . . . . . . .43 CU50
Willson Rd, Egh. (Eng.Grn.)
TW20 . . . . .112 AV92
Wilman Gro, E8 . . . . . .84 DU66
Wilmar CI, Hayes UB4 . . . .77 BR70
Uxbridge UB8 . . . . . .76 BK66
Wilmar Gdns, W.Wick. BR4 .143 EB102
Wilmcote Ho, W2 . . . . . .82 DB71
Wilmer CI, Kings.T. KT2 . . .118 CM92
Wilmer Cres, Kings.T. KT2 .118 CM92
Wilmer Gdns, N1 . . . . . .84 DS67
Wilmerhatch La, Epsom
KT18 . . . . .172 CP118
Wilmer Lea CI, E15 . . . . .85 EC66
Wilmer PI, N16 off Stoke
Newington Ch St 66 DT61
Wilmer Way, N14 . . . . . .45 DK50
WILMINGTON, Dart. 128 FK91
Wilmington Av, W4 . . . . . .98 CR80
Orpington BR6 . . . . . .146 EW103
Wilmington Ct Rd, Dart.
DA2 . . . . .127 FG90
Wilmington Gdns, Bark. IG11 .87 ER65
Wilmington Sq, WC1 . . . .196 D3
Wilmington St, WC1 . . . .196 D3
Wilmot CI, N2 . . . . . . .44 DC54
SE15 . . . . .102 DU80
Wilmot Grn, Brwd. CM13 . . .53 FW51
Wilmot PI, NW1 . . . . . .83 DJ66
W7 off Boston Rd 79 CE74
Wilmot Rd, E10 . . . . . .67 EB61
N17 . . . . .66 DR55
Carshalton SM5 . . . . .158 DF106
Dartford DA1 . . . . . .127 FH85
Purley CR8 . . . . . . .159 DN112
Wilmots CI, Reig. RH2 . . . .184 DC133
Wilmot St, E2 . . . . . . .84 DV70
Wilmot Way, Bans. SM7 . . .158 DA114
Wilmount St, SE18 . . . . .105 EP77
Wilna Rd, SW18 . . . . . .120 DC87
Wilsham St, W11 . . . . . .81 CX74
Wilshaw CI, NW4 . . . . . .63 CU55
Wilshaw St, SE14 . . . . .103 EA81
Wilsman Rd, S.Ock. RM15 . .91 FW68
Wilsmere Dr, Har. HA3 . . . .41 CF52
Northolt UB5 . . . . . . .78 BY65
Wilson Av, Mitch. CR4 . . . .120 DE94
Wilson CI, S.Croy. CR2
off Bartlett St 160 DR106
Wembley HA9 . . . . . . .62 CM59
Wilson Dr, Cher. (Ott.) KT16 .151 BB106
Wembley HA9 . . . . . . .62 CM59
Wilson Gdns, Har. HA1 . . . .60 CC59
Wilson Gro, SE16 . . . . .202 D5
Wilson La, Dart. DA4 . . . .149 FT96
Wilson Rd, E6 . . . . . . .86 EK69

Wilson Rd, SE5 . . . . . .102 DS81
Chessington KT9 . . . . .156 CM107
Ilford IG1 . . . . .69 EM59
Wilsons, Tad. KT20 . . . . .173 CX121
Wilsons PI, E14 off Salmon La .85 DZ72
Wilsons Rd, W6 . . . . . .99 CX78
Wilson St, E17 . . . . . . .67 EC57
EC2 . . . . .197 L6
N21 . . . . .45 DN45
Wilson Way, Wok. GU21 . . .166 AX116
Wilstone CI, Hayes UB4
off Kingsash Dr 78 BY70
Wilthorne Gdns, Dag. RM10
off Acre Rd 89 FB66
Wilton Av, W4 . . . . . . .98 CS78
Wilton CI, West Dr. UB7 . . .94 BK79
Wilton Cres, SW1 . . . . .198 F5
SW19 . . . . .139 CZ95
Wilton Dr, Rom. RM5 . . . .51 FC52
Wilton Gdns, Walt. KT12 . . .136 BX102
West Molesey KT8 . . . .136 CA97
Wilton Gro, SW19 . . . . .139 CZ95
New Malden KT3 . . . . .139 CT100
Wilton Ms, SW1 . . . . . .198 G6
Wilton Par, Felt. TW13
off Highfield Rd 115 BU89
Wilton Pk Ct, SE18
off Prince Imperial Rd . . .105 EN81
Wilton PI, SW1 . . . . . .198 F5
Addlestone (New Haw)
KT15 . . . . .152 BK109
Wilton Rd, N10 . . . . . . .44 DG54
SE2 . . . . .106 EW76
SW1 . . . . .199 J7
SW19 . . . . .120 DE94
Barnet (Cockfos.) EN4 . . . .28 DF42
Hounslow TW4 . . . . . .96 BX83
Ilford IG1 off Ilford La 69 EP62
Wilton Row, SW1 . . . . . .198 F5
Wilton Sq, N1 . . . . . . .84 DR67
Wilton St, SW1 . . . . . .199 H6
Wilton Ter, SW1 . . . . . .198 F6
Wilton Vil, N1 . . . . . . .84 DR67
Wilton Way, E8 . . . . . . .84 DU65
Wiltshire Av, Horn. RM11 . . .72 FM56
Wiltshire CI, NW7 . . . . . .43 CT50
SW3 . . . . .198 D8
Dartford DA2 . . . . . .129 FR87
Wiltshire Gdns, N4 . . . . . .66 DQ58
Twickenham TW2 . . . . .116 CC88
Wiltshire La, Pnr. HA5 . . . .59 BT55
Wiltshire Rd, SW9 . . . . .101 DN83
Orpington BR6 . . . . . .146 EU101
Thornton Heath CR7 . . . .141 DN97
Wiltshire Row, N1 . . . . . .84 DR67
Wilverley Cres, N.Mal. KT3 . .138 CS100
Wimbart Rd, SW2 . . . . .121 DM87
WIMBLEDON, SW19 . . . . .119 CY93
⇌ Wimbledon 119 CZ93
⊖ Wimbledon 119 CZ93
⊖ Wimbledon 119 CZ93
★ Wimbledon (All England Tennis
& Croquet Club), SW19 .119 CY91
Wimbledon Br, SW19 . . . .119 CZ93
★ Wimbledon Chase 139 CY96
⇌ Wimbledon Common,
SW19 . . . . .119 CT91
Wimbledon Common, SW19 .119 CU91
★ Wimbledon FC (share
Selhurst Pk with Crystal
Palace FC), SE25 . . . . .142 DS98
Wimbledon Hill Rd, SW19 . .119 CY93
WIMBLEDON PARK, SW19 . .119 CZ90
⊖ Wimbledon Park 120 DA90
Wimbledon Pk, SW19 . . . .119 CZ89
Wimbledon Pk Est, SW19 . .119 CY88
Wimbledon Pk Rd, SW18 . .119 CZ87
SW19 . . . . .119 CZ88
Wimbledon Pk Side, SW19 .119 CX89
Wimbledon Rd, SW17 . . . .120 DC91
Wimbledon Sta, SW19 . . . .119 CZ93
★ Wimbledon Windmill Mus,
SW19 . . . . .119 CV89
Wimbolt St, E2 . . . . . . .84 DU69
Wimborne Av, Hayes UB4 . . .77 BV72
Southall UB2 . . . . . . .96 CA77
Wimborne CI, SE12 . . . . .124 EF85
Buckhurst Hill IG9 . . . . .48 EH47
Epsom KT17 . . . . . . .156 CS113
Worcester Park KT4 . . . .139 CW102
Wimborne Dr, NW9 . . . . .62 CN55
Pinner HA5 . . . . . . .60 BX59
Wimborne Gdns, W13 . . . .79 CH72
Wimborne Gro, Wat. WD17 . .23 BS37
Wimborne Rd, N9 . . . . . .46 DU47
N17 . . . . .46 DS54
Wimborne Way, Beck. BR3 .143 DX97
Wimbourne Av, Chis. BR7 . .145 ET98
Orpington BR5 . . . . . .145 ET98
Wimbourne Ct, N1
off Wimbourne St 84 DR68
Wimbourne St, N1 . . . . . .84 DR68
Wimpole CI, Brom. BR2 . . .144 EJ98
Kingston upon Thames
KT1 . . . . .138 CM96
Wimpole Ms, W1 . . . . . .195 H6
Wimpole Rd, West Dr. UB7 . .76 BK74
Wimpole St, W1 . . . . . .195 H8
Wimshurst CI, Croy. CR0 . . .141 DL102
Winans Wk, SW9 . . . . . .101 DN82
Wincanton Cres, Nthlt. UB5 . .60 CA64
Wincanton Gdns, Ilf. IG6 . . .69 EP55
Wincanton Rd, SW18 . . . .119 CZ87
Romford RM3 . . . . . . .52 FK48
Winchcombe Rd, Cars. SM5 .140 DD101
Winchcomb Gdns, SE9 . . .104 EK83
Winchelsea Av, Bexh. DA7 . .106 EZ80
Winchelsea CI, SW15 . . . .119 CX85
Winchelsea Rd, E7 . . . . .68 EG62
N17 . . . . .66 DS55
NW10 . . . . .80 CR67
Winchelsey Ri, S.Croy. CR2 .160 DT107
Winchendon Rd, SW6 . . . .99 CZ80
Teddington TW11 . . . . .117 CD91
Winchester Av, NW6 . . . .81 CY67
NW9 . . . . .62 CN55

Winchester Av, Houns. TW5 . .96 BZ79
Upminster RM14 . . . . . .73 FT60
Winchester CI, E6
off Boultwood Rd 86 EL72
SE17 . . . . .200 G9
Amersham HP7 . . . . . .20 AS39
Bromley BR2 . . . . . .144 EF97
Enfield EN1 . . . . . . .30 DS43
Esher KT10 . . . . . . .154 CA105
Kingston upon Thames
KT2 . . . . .118 CP94
Slough (Colnbr.) SL3 . . . .93 BE81
Winchester Ct, E17
off Billet Rd 47 DY53
Winchester Cres, Grav.
DA12 . . . . .131 GK90
Winchester Dr, Pnr. HA5 . . .60 BX57
Winchester Gro, Sev. TN13 .191 FH123
Winchester Ho, SE18
off Shooter's Hill Rd 104 EK80
Winchester Ms, NW3
off Winchester Rd 82 DD66
Winchester Pk, Brom. BR2 . .144 EF97
Winchester PI, E8
off Kingsland High St . . .66 DT64
N6 . . . . .65 DH60
W3 off Avenue Rd 98 CQ75
Winchester Rd, E4 . . . . . .47 EC52
N6 . . . . .65 DH59
N9 . . . . .46 DU46
NW3 . . . . .82 DD66
Bexleyheath DA7 . . . . .106 EX82
Bromley BR2 . . . . . .144 EF97
Feltham TW13 . . . . . .116 BZ90
Harrow HA3 . . . . . . .62 CL56
Hayes UB3 . . . . .95 BS80
Ilford IG1 . . . . .69 ER62
Northwood HA6 . . . . . .59 BT55
Orpington BR6 . . . . . .164 EW105
Twickenham TW1 . . . . .117 CH86
Walton-on-Thames KT12 . .135 BU102
Winchester Sq, SE1 . . . . .201 K2
Winchester St, SW1 . . . . .199 J10
W3 . . . . .80 CQ74
Winchester Wk, SE1 . . . . .201 K2
Winchester Way, Rick. (Crox.Grn.)
WD3 . . . . .23 BP43
Winchet Wk, Croy. CR0 . . .142 DW100
Winchfield CI, Har. HA3 . . . .61 CJ58
Winchfield Ho, SW15
off Highcliffe Dr 119 CT86
Winchfield Rd, SE26 . . . .123 DY92
Winchfield Way, Rick. WD3 . .38 BJ45
Winchilsea Cres, W.Mol. KT8 .136 CC96
WINCHMORE HILL, N21 . . .45 DM45
⇌ Winchmore Hill 45 DN46
Winchmore Hill Rd, N14 . . .45 DK46
N21 . . . . .45 DK46
Winchstone CI, Shep. TW17 .134 BM98
Winckley CI, Har. HA3 . . . .62 CM57
Wincott St, SE11 . . . . . .200 E8
Wincrofts Dr, SE9 . . . . .105 ER84
Windall CI, SE19 . . . . . .142 DU95
Windborough Rd, Cars. SM5 .158 DG108
Windermere Av, N3 . . . . .64 DA55
NW6 . . . . .81 CY67
SW19 . . . . .140 DB97
Harrow HA3 . . . . . . .61 CJ59
Hornchurch RM12 . . . . .71 FG64
Ruislip HA4 . . . . . . .60 BW59
Wembley HA9 . . . . . . .61 CJ59
Windermere CI, Dart. DA1 . .127 FH88
Egham TW20
off Derwent Rd 113 BB94
Feltham TW14 . . . . . .115 BT88
Orpington BR6 . . . . . .145 EP104
Rickmansworth (Chorl.)
WD3 . . . . .21 BC43
Staines TW19 off Viola Av .114 BL88
Windermere Ct, SW13 . . . .99 CT79
Kenley CR8 . . . . . . .175 DP115
Wembley HA9
off Windermere Av 61 CJ59
Windermere Gdns, Ilf. IG4 . .68 EL57
Windermere Gro, Wem. HA9
off Windermere Av 61 CJ60
Windermere Ho, Islw. TW7
off Summerwood Rd . . .117 CF85
Windermere Pt, SE15
off Ilderton Rd 102 DW80
Windermere Rd, N10 . . . .45 DH53
N19 off Holloway Rd 65 DJ61
SW15 . . . . .118 CS91
SW16 . . . . .141 DJ95
W5 . . . . .97 CJ76
Bexleyheath DA7 . . . . .107 FC82
Coulsdon CR5 . . . . . .175 DL115
Croydon CR0 . . . . . .142 DT102
Southall UB1 . . . . . . .78 BZ71
West Wickham BR4 . . . .144 EE103
Windermere Way, Reig. RH2 .184 DD133
West Drayton UB7
off Providence Rd 76 BM74
Winders Rd, SW11 . . . . .100 DE82
Windfield, Lthd. KT22 . . . .171 CH121
Windfield CI, SE26 . . . . .123 DX91
Windham Av, Croy. (New Adgtn.)
CR0 . . . . .161 ED110
Windham Rd, Rich. TW9 . . .98 CM83
Windhover Way, Grav. DA12 .131 GL91
Windings, The, S.Croy. CR2 .160 DT111
Winding Way, Dag. RM8 . . .70 EW62
Harrow HA1 . . . . . . .61 CE63
Windlass PI, SE8 . . . . . .203 L9
Windlesham Gro, SW19 . . .119 CX88
Windley CI, SE23 . . . . . .122 DW89
Windmill All, W4
off Windmill Rd 98 CS77
Windmill Av, Epsom KT17 . .157 CT111
Southall UB2 . . . . . . .96 CC75
Windmill Br Ho, Croy. CR0 . .142 DS102
Windmill CI, SE1 . . . . . .202 C8
SE13 . . . . .103 EC82
Caterham CR3 . . . . . .176 DQ121
Epsom KT17 . . . . . . .157 CT112
Sunbury-on-Thames TW16 .115 BS94
Surbiton KT6 . . . . . .137 CH102

Windmill CI, Upmin. RM14 . .72 FN61
Waltham Abbey EN9 . . . .16 EE34
Windmill Ct, NW2 . . . . . .81 CY65
Windmill Dr, NW2 . . . . . .63 CY62
SW4 . . . . .121 DJ85
Keston BR2 . . . . . . .162 EJ105
Leatherhead KT22 . . . .171 CJ123
Reigate RH2 . . . . . . .184 DD132
Rickmansworth (Crox.Grn.)
WD3 . . . . .22 BM44
Windmill End, Epsom KT17 .157 CT112
Windmill Gdns, Enf. EN2 . . .29 DN41
Windmill Grn, Shep. TW17 . .135 BS101
Windmill Gro, Croy. CR0 . . .142 DQ101
WINDMILL HILL, Grav. 131 GG88
Windmill Hill, NW3 . . . . .64 DC62
Enfield EN2 . . . . . . .29 DP41
Kings Langley WD4 . . . . .5 BF32
Ruislip HA4 . . . . . . .59 BT59
Windmill Ho, E14 . . . . . .203 P8
Windmill La, E15 . . . . . .85 ED65
Barnet EN5 . . . . . . .27 CT44
Bushey (Bushey Hth.)
WD23 . . . . .41 CE46
Epsom KT17 . . . . . . .157 CT112
Greenford UB6 . . . . . .78 CC71
Isleworth TW7 . . . . . .97 CE77
Southall UB2 . . . . . . .96 CC76
Surbiton KT6 . . . . . .137 CH100
Waltham Cross (Chsht.)
EN8 . . . . .15 DX30
Windmill Ms, W4
off Windmill Rd 98 CS77
Windmill Pas, W4 . . . . . .98 CS77
Windmill Ri, Kings.T. KT2 . . .118 CP94
Windmill Rd, N18 . . . . . .46 DR49
SW18 . . . . .120 DD86
SW19 . . . . .119 CV88
W4 . . . . .98 CS77
W5 . . . . .97 CJ77
Brentford TW8 . . . . . .97 CK78
Croydon CR0 . . . . . .142 DQ101
Gerrards Cross (Chal.St.P.)
SL9 . . . . .36 AX52
Hampton (Hmptn.H.) TW12 .116 CB92
Mitcham CR4 . . . . . .141 DJ99
Sevenoaks TN13 . . . . .191 FH130
Slough (Fulmer) SL3 . . . .56 AX64
Sunbury-on-Thames TW16 .135 BS95
Windmill Rd W, Sun. TW16 .135 BS96
Windmill Row, SE11 . . . . .101 DN78
Windmill Shott, Egh. TW20
off Rusham Rd 113 AZ93
Windmill St, W1 . . . . . .195 M7
Bushey (Bushey Hth.) WD23 .41 CE46
Gravesend DA12 . . . . .131 GH86
Windmill Wk, SE1 . . . . . .200 E3
Windmill Way, Reig. RH2 . .184 DD132
Ruislip HA4 . . . . . . .59 BT60
Windmore Av, Pot.B. EN6 . .11 CW31
Windover Av, NW9 . . . . .62 CR56
Windrose CI, SE16 . . . . .203 H4
Windrush, N.Mal. KT3 . . . .138 CP98
Windrush Av, Slou. SL3 . . .93 BB77
Windrush CI, SW11
off Maysoule Rd 100 DD84
W4 . . . . .98 CQ81
Uxbridge UB10 . . . . . .58 BM63
Windrush La, SE23 . . . . .123 DX90
Windrush Rd, NW10 . . . . .80 CR67
off Milton Av
Windrush Sq, SW2
off Rushcroft Rd 101 DN84
Windsock CI, SE16 . . . . .203 M8
WINDSOR 92 AS82
Windsor Av, E17 . . . . . .47 DY54
SW19 . . . . .140 DC95
Edgware HA8 . . . . . . .42 CP49
Grays RM16 . . . . . . .110 GB75
New Malden KT3 . . . . .138 CQ99
Sutton SM3 . . . . . . .139 CY104
Uxbridge UB10 . . . . . .77 BP67
West Molesey KT8 . . . .136 CA97
★ Windsor Castle, Wind.
SL4 . . . . .92 AS81
Windsor Castle, Wind. SL4 . .92 AS80
Windsor Cen, The, SE27
off Advance Rd 122 DQ91
Windsor CI, N3 . . . . . . .43 CY54
SE27 . . . . .122 DQ91
Borehamwood WD6 . . . .26 CN39
Brentford TW8 . . . . . .97 CH79
Chislehurst BR7 . . . . .125 EP92
Harrow HA2 . . . . . . .60 CA62
Hemel Hempstead (Bov.)
HP3 . . . . .5 BA28
Northwood HA6 . . . . . .39 BU54
Waltham Cross (Chsht.) EN7 .14 DU30
Windsor Ct, N14 . . . . . .45 DJ45
Sunbury-on-Thames TW16
off Windsor Rd 115 BU93
Windsor Ct Rd, Wok. (Chobham)
GU24 . . . . .150 AS109
Windsor Cres, Har. HA2 . . .60 CA63
Wembley HA9 . . . . . . .62 CP62
Barnet EN4 . . . . . . .28 DF44
Dartford DA1 . . . . . .127 FG86
Orpington BR6 . . . . . .164 EU107
Windsor Gdns, W9 . . . . . .82 DA71
Croydon CR0
off Richmond Rd 141 DL104
Hayes UB3 . . . . .95 BR76
★ Windsor Great Pk,
Egh. & Wind. 112 AS93
Windsor Gro, SE27 . . . . .122 DQ91
Windsor PI, SW1 . . . . . .199 L7
Chertsey KT16
off Windsor St 134 BG100
Windsor Rd, E4 off Chivers Rd .47 EB49
E7 . . . . .68 EH64
E10 . . . . .67 EB61
E11 . . . . .68 EG60
N3 . . . . .43 CY54
N7 . . . . .65 DL62
N13 . . . . .45 DN48

Windsor Rd, N17 . . . . . .46 DU54
NW2 . . . . .81 CV65
W5 . . . . .80 CL73
Barnet EN5 . . . . . . .27 CY44
Bexleyheath DA6 . . . . .106 EY84
Brentwood (Pilg.Hat.) CM15 .54 FV44
Dagenham RM8 . . . . . .70 EY62
Egham (Eng.Grn.) TW20 . .113 AZ90
Enfield EN3 . . . . . . .31 DX36
Gerrards Cross SL9 . . . .56 AW60
Gravesend DA12 . . . . .131 GH90
Harrow HA3 . . . . . . .41 CD53
Hornchurch RM11 . . . . .72 FJ59
Hounslow TW4 . . . . . .95 BV82
Ilford IG1 . . . . .69 EP63
Kingston upon Thames KT2 .118 CL94
Richmond TW9 . . . . . .98 CM82
Slough SL1 . . . . .92 AS76
Slough (Datchet) SL3 . . . .92 AT80
Slough (Stoke P.) SL2 . . . .56 AU63
Southall UB2 . . . . . . .96 BZ76
Staines (Wrays.) TW19 . . .112 AY86
Sunbury-on-Thames TW16 .135 BU93
Teddington TW11 . . . . .117 CD92
Thornton Heath CR7 . . . .141 DP96
Watford WD24 . . . . . .24 BW38
Woking (Chobham) GU24 . .150 AS109
Worcester Park KT4 . . . .139 CU103
Windsors, The, Buck.H. IG9 . .48 EL47
Windsor St, N1 . . . . . . .83 DP67
Chertsey KT16 . . . . . .134 BG100
Uxbridge UB8 . . . . . . .76 BJ66
Windsor Ter, N1 . . . . . .197 J2
Windsor Wk, SE5 . . . . . .102 DR82
Walton-on-Thames KT12
off King George Av 136 BX102
Weybridge KT13 . . . . .153 BP106
Windsor Way, W14 . . . . . .99 CX77
Rickmansworth WD3 . . . .38 BG46
Woking GU22 . . . . . .167 BC116
Windsor Wf, E9 . . . . . . .67 DZ64
Windsor Wd, Wal.Abb. EN9
off Monkswood Av 16 EE33
Windspoint Dr, SE15
off Ethnard Rd 102 DV79
Windus Rd, N16 . . . . . .66 DT60
Windus Wk, N16 . . . . . .66 DT60
Windward CI, Enf. EN3
off Bullsmoor La 31 DX35
Windycroft CI, Pur. CR8 . . .159 DK113
Windy Hill, Brwd. CM13 . . .53 GC46
Windy Ridge, Brom. BR1 . . .144 EL95
Windyridge CI, SW19 . . . .119 CX92
Wine CI, E1 . . . . .202 F1
Wine Office Ct, EC4 . . . . .196 E8
Winern Glebe, W.Byf. (Byfleet)
KT14 . . . . .152 BK113
Winery La, Kings.T. KT1 . . .138 CM97
Winey CI, Chess. KT9
off Nigel Fisher Way 155 CJ108
Winfield Mobile Home Pk, Wat.
WD25 . . . . .24 CB39
Winford Ho, E3 . . . . . . .85 DZ66
Winford Par, Sthl. UB1
off Telford Rd 78 CB72
Winforton St, SE10 . . . . .103 EC81
Winfrith Rd, SW18 . . . . .120 DC87
Wingate Cres, Croy. CR0 . .141 DK100
Wingate Rd, W6 . . . . . .99 CV76
Ilford IG1 . . . . .69 EP64
Sidcup DA14 . . . . . .126 EW92
Wingate Trd Est, N17 . . . .46 DU52
Wing CI, Epp. (N.Wld.Bas.) CM16
off Epping Rd 18 FA72
Wingfield, Grays (Bad.Dene)
RM17 . . . . .110 FZ78
Wingfield Bk, Grav. (Nthflt.)
DA11 . . . . .130 GC89
Wingfield CI, Add. (New Haw)
KT15 . . . . .152 BH110
Brentwood CM13
off Pondfield La 55 GA48
Wingfield Gdns, Upmin. RM14 .73 FT58
Wingfield Ms, SE15
off Wingfield St 102 DU83
Wingfield Rd, E15 . . . . . .68 EE64
E17 . . . . .67 EB57
Gravesend DA12 . . . . .131 GH87
Kingston upon Thames KT2 .118 CN93
Wingfield St, SE15 . . . . .102 DU83
Wingford Rd, SW2 . . . . .121 DL86
Wingletye La, Horn. RM11 . .72 FM60
Wingmore Rd, SE24 . . . .102 DQ83
Wingrave Cres, Brwd. CM14 .54 FS49
Wingrave Rd, W6 . . . . . .99 CW79
Wingrove Dr, Purf. RM19 . .108 FP78
Wingrove Rd, SE6 . . . . .124 EE89
Wings CI, Sutt. SM1 . . . . .158 DA105
Wing Way, Brwd. CM14
off Geary Dr 54 FW46
Winifred Av, Horn. RM12 . . .72 FK63
Winifred Gro, SW11 . . . .100 DF84
Winifred PI, N12 off High Rd . .44 DC50
Winifred Rd, SW19 . . . . .140 DA95
Coulsdon CR5 . . . . . .174 DG116
Dagenham RM8 . . . . . .70 EY61
Dartford DA1 . . . . . .127 FH85
Erith DA8 . . . . .107 FE78
Hampton (Hmptn.H.) TW12 .116 CA91
Winifred St, E16 . . . . . .87 EM74
Winifred Ter, E13
off Victoria Rd 86 EG68
Enfield EN1
off Great Cambridge Rd . .46 DT45
Winkers CI, Ger.Cr. (Chal.St.P.)
SL9 . . . . .37 AZ53
Winkers La, Ger.Cr. (Chal.St.P.)
SL9 . . . . .37 AZ53
Winkfield Rd, E13 . . . . . .86 EH68
N22 . . . . .45 DN54
Winkley St, E2 . . . . . . .84 DV68
Winkworth PI, Bans. SM7
off Bolters La 157 CZ114

Win - Woo

Winkworth Rd, Bans. SM7 ..157 CZ114
Winlaton Rd, Brom. BR1 ..123 ED91
Winmill Rd, Dag. RM8 ....70 EZ62
Winnards, Wok. GU21
  off Abercorn Way 166 AV118
Winn Common Rd, SE18 ..105 ES79
Winnett St, W1 ....195 M10
Winningales Ct, Ilf. IG5
  off Vienna Cl 68 EL55
Winnings Wk, Nthlt. UB5
  off Arnold Rd 78 BY65
Winnington Cl, N2 ....64 DD58
Winnington Rd, N2 ....64 DD59
  Enfield EN3 ....30 DW38
Winnington Way, Wok. GU21 ..166 AV118
Winnipeg Dr, Orp. BR6 ..163 ET107
Winnock Rd, West Dr. UB7 ..76 BK74
Winn Rd, SE12 ....124 EG88
Winns Av, E17 ....67 DY55
Winns Ms, N15
  off Grove Pk Rd 66 DS56
Winns Ter, E17 ....47 EA54
Winsbeach, E17 ....67 ED55
Winscombe Cres, W5 ......79 CK70
Winscombe St, N19 ....65 DH61
Winscombe Way, Stan. HA7 ..41 CG50
Winsford Rd, SE6 ....123 DZ90
Winsford Ter, N18 ....46 DR50
Winsham Gro, SW11 ....120 DG85
Winslade Rd, SW2 ....121 DL85
Winslade Way, SE6
  off Rushey Grn 123 EB87
Winsland Ms, W2
  off London St 82 DD72
Winsland St, W2 ....82 DD72
Winsley St, W1 ....195 K8
Winslow, SE17 ....102 DS78
Winslow Cl, NW10
  off Neasden La N 62 CS62
  Pinner HA5 ....59 BV58
Winslow Gro, E4 ....48 EE47
Winslow Rd, W6 ....99 CW79
Winslow Way, Felt. TW13 ..116 BX90
  Walton-on-Thames KT12 ..136 BW104
Winsor Ter, E6 ....87 EN71
Winsor Ter Roundabout, E6
  off Royal Docks Way ...87 EP71
Winstanley Rd, Cob. KT11 ..153 BV114
Winstanley Est, SW11 ...100 DD83
Winstanley Rd, SW11 ....100 DD83
Winstanley Wk, Cob. KT11
  off Winstanley Cl 153 BU114
Winstead Gdns, Dag. RM10 ..71 FC64
Winston Av, NW9 ....62 CS59
Winston Cl, Green. DA9 ..129 FT85
  Harrow HA3 ....41 CF51
  Romford RM7 ....71 FB56
Winston Ct, Har. HA3 ....40 CB52
Winston Dr, Cob. (Stoke D'Ab.)
  KT11 ....170 BY116
Winston Rd, N16 ....66 DR63
Winston Wk, W4
  off Beaconsfield Rd ...98 CR77
Winston Way, Ilf. IG1 ...69 EP62
  Potters Bar EN6 ....12 DA34
  Woking (Old Wok.) GU22 ..167 BB120
Winstre Rd, Borwd. WD6 ..26 CN39
Winter Av, E6 ....86 EL67
Winterborne Av, Orp. BR6 ..145 ER104
Winterbourne Gro, Wey.
  KT13 ....153 BQ107
Winterbourne Rd, SE6 ...123 DZ88
  Dagenham RM8 ....70 EW61
  Thornton Heath CR7 ...141 DN97
Winter Box Wk, Rich. TW10 ..98 CM84
Winterbrook Rd, SE24 ...122 DQ86
Winterburn Cl, N11 ......44 DG51
Winterdown Gdns, Esher
  KT10 ....154 BZ107
Winterdown Rd, Esher KT10 ..154 BZ107
Winterfold Cl, SW19 ....119 CY89
Wintergarden, Green. (Bluewater)
  DA9 off Bluewater Parkway ..129 FU88
Winter Gdn Cres, Green.
  (Bluewater) DA9 ......129 FU87
Wintergreen Cl, E6
  off Yarrow Cres 86 EL71
Winters Cft, Grav. DA12 ..131 GK93
Wintersells Rd, W.Byf. (Byfleet)
  KT14 ....152 BK110
Winters Rd, T.Ditt. KT7 ..137 CH101
Winterstoke Gdns, NW7 ..43 CU50
Winterstoke Rd, SE6 ....123 DZ88
Winters Way, Wal.Abb. EN9 ..16 EG33
Winterton Ho, E14 ....84 DV72
Winterton Pl, SW10
  off Park Wk 100 DC79
Winterwell Rd, SW2 .....121 DL85
Winthorpe Rd, SW15 .....99 CY84
Winthrop St, E1 ....84 DV71
Winthrop Wk, Wem. HA9
  off Everard Way 62 CL62
Winton App, Rick. (Crox.Grn.)
  WD3 ....23 BQ43
Winton Av, N11 ....45 DJ52
Winton Cl, N9 ....47 DX45
Winton Cres, Rick. (Crox.Grn.)
  WD3 ....23 BP43
Winton Dr, Rick. (Crox.Grn.)
  WD3 ....23 BP44
  Waltham Cross (Chsht.)
  EN8 ....15 DY29
Winton Gdns, Edg. HA8 ..42 CM52
Winton Rd, Orp. BR6 ....163 EP105
Winton Way, SW16 ....121 DN92
Winvale, Slou. SL1 ......92 AS76
Winwood, Slou. SL2 .....74 AW72
Wireless Rd, West. (Bigg.H.)
  TN16 ....178 EK115
Wisbeach Rd, Croy. CR0 ..142 DR99
Wisborough Rd, Croy. CR2 ..160 DT109
Wisdons Cl, Dag. RM10 ..71 FB60
Wise La, NW7 ....43 CV51
  West Drayton UB7 .....94 BK77

Wiseman Ct, SE19 ....122 DS92
Wiseman Rd, E10 ....67 EA61
Wise Rd, E15 ....85 ED67
Wise's La, Hat. AL9 .....11 CW27
Wisham Rd, SW17 ....120 DE88
Wishart Rd, SE3 ....104 EK81
Wishbone Way, Wok. GU21 ..166 AT116
Wishford Ct, Ashtd. KT21
  off The Marld 172 CM118
WISLEY, Wok. 168 BL116
Wisley Common Rd, Wok. GU23 ..168 BN117
Wisley Ct, S.Croy. CR2
  off Sanderstead Rd ...160 DS110
Wisley La, Wok. (Wisley)
  GU23 ....168 BL116
Wisley Rd, SW11 ....120 DG85
  Orpington BR5 ....126 EU94
Wistaria Cl, Brwd. CM15 ..54 FW45
Wisteria Cl, NW7 ....43 CT51
  Ilford IG1 ....69 EP64
  Orpington BR6 ....145 EP103
Wisteria Gdns, Swan. BR8 ..147 FD96
Wisteria Rd, SE13 ......103 ED84
Witan St, E2 ....84 DV69
Witches La, Sev. TN13 ..190 FD122
Witham Cl, Loug. IG10 ..32 EL44
Witham Rd, SE20 ....142 DW97
  Dagenham RM10 ....70 FA64
  Isleworth TW7 ....97 CD81
  Romford RM2 ....71 FH57
Withens Cl, Orp. BR5 ...146 EW98
Witherby Cl, Croy. CR0 ..160 DS106
Witherings, The, Horn. RM11 ..72 FL57
Witherington Rd, N5 ....65 DN64
Withers Cl, Chess. KT9
  off Coppard Gdns 155 CJ107
Withers Mead, NW9 ......43 CT53
Witherston Way, SE9 ...125 EN89
Witheygate Av, Stai. TW18 ..114 BH93
Withies, The, Lthd. KT22 ..171 CH120
  Woking (Knap.) GU21 ..166 AS117
Withybed Cor, Tad. KT20 ..173 CV123
Withycombe Rd, SW19 ...119 CX87
Withycroft, Slou. (Geo.Grn.)
  SL3 ....74 AY72
Withy La, Ruis. HA4 .....59 BQ57
Withy Mead, E4 ....47 ED48
Witley Cres, Croy. (New Adgtn.)
  CR0 ....161 EC107
Witley Gdns, Sthl. UB2 ..96 BZ77
Witley Pt, SW15
  off Wanborough Dr ...119 CV88
Witley Rd, N19
  off Holloway Rd 65 DJ61
Witney Cl, Pnr. HA5 ....40 BZ51
  Uxbridge UB10 ....58 BM63
Witney Path, SE23 ......123 DX90
Wittenham Way, E4 .....47 ED48
Wittering Cl, Kings.T. KT2 ..117 CK92
Wittering Wk, Horn. RM12 ..90 FJ65
Wittersham Rd, Brom. BR1 ..124 EF92
Wivenhoe Cl, SE15 ......102 DW83
Wivenhoe Ct, Houns. TW3 ..96 BZ84
Wivenhoe Rd, Bark. IG11 ..88 EU68
Wiverton Rd, SE26 .....122 DW93
Wixom Ho, SE3
  off Romero Sq 104 EJ84
Wix Rd, Dag. RM9 ....88 EX67
Wixs La, SW4 ....101 DH84
Woburn Av, Epp. (They.B.)
  CM16 ....33 ES37
  Hornchurch RM12 ......71 FG63
  Purley CR8 off High St ..159 DN111
Woburn Cl, SE28
  off Summerton Way 88 EX72
  SW19 off Tintern Cl ..120 DC93
  Bushey WD23 ....24 CC43
Woburn Ct, SE16
  off Masters Dr 102 DV78
Woburn Hill, Add. KT15 ..134 BJ103
Woburn Pl, WC1 ....195 N4
Woburn Rd, Cars. SM5 ..140 DE102
  Croydon CR0 ....142 DQ102
Woburn Sq, WC1 ....195 N5
Woburn Wk, WC1 ....195 N3
Wodehouse Av, SE5 .....102 DT81
Wodehouse Rd, Dart. DA1 ..108 FN84
Woffington Cl, Kings.T. KT1 ..137 CJ95
Wokindon Rd, Grays RM16 ..111 GH76
WOKING 167 AZ118
⇌ Woking 167 AZ118
Woking Business Pk, Wok.
  GU21 ....167 BB115
Woking Cl, SW15 ....99 CT84
Ⓗ Woking Comm Hosp, Wok.
  GU22 ....167 AZ118
Ⓗ Woking Nuffield Hosp, Wok.
  GU21 ....150 AY114
Wold, The, Cat. (Wold.) CR3 ..177 EA122
Woldham Pl, Brom. BR2 ..144 EJ98
Woldham Rd, Brom. BR2 ..144 EJ98
WOLDINGHAM, Cat. 177 EB122
⇌ Woldingham 177 DX122
WOLDINGHAM GARDEN
  VILLAGE, Cat. 177 DY121
Woldingham Rd, Cat. (Wold.)
  CR3 ....176 DV120
Wolds Dr, Orp. BR6 ....163 EN105
Wolfe Cl, Brom. BR2 ...144 EG100
  Hayes UB4 off Ayles Rd ..77 BV69
Wolfe Cres, SE7 ....104 EK78
  SE16 ....203 H5
Wolferton Rd, E12 ......69 EM63
Wolffe Gdns, E15 ....86 EF65
Wolfram Cl, SE13 .....124 EE85
Wolfington Rd, SE27 ...121 DP91
Wollaston Cl, SE1 .....201 H8
Wolmer Cl, Edg. HA8 ....42 CP49
Wolmer Gdns, Edg. HA8 ..42 CN48

Wolseley Av, SW19 .....120 DA89
Wolseley Gdns, W4 ......98 CP79
Wolseley Rd, E7 ....86 EH66
  N8 ....65 DK58
  N22 ....45 DM53
  W4 ....98 CQ77
  Harrow HA3 ....61 CE55
  Mitcham CR4 ....140 DG101
  Romford RM7 ....71 FD59
Wolseley St, SE1 ....202 A5
Wolsey Av, E6 ....87 EN69
  E17 ....67 DZ55
  Thames Ditton KT7 ...137 CF99
  Waltham Cross (Chsht.)
  EN7 ....14 DT29
Wolsey Business Pk, Wat.
  WD18 ....39 BR45
Wolsey Cl, SW20 ....119 CV94
  Hounslow TW3 ....96 CC84
  Kingston upon Thames KT2 ..138 CP95
  Southall UB2 ....96 CC76
  Worcester Park KT4 ..157 CU105
Wolsey Cres, Croy. (New Adgtn.)
  CR0 ....161 EC109
  Morden SM4 ....139 CY101
Wolsey Dr, Kings.T. KT2 ..118 CL92
  Walton-on-Thames KT12 ..136 BX102
Wolsey Gdns, Ilf. IG6 ...49 EQ51
Wolsey Gro, Edg. HA8 ...42 CR52
  Esher KT10 ....154 CB105
Wolsey Ms, NW5 ....83 DJ65
  Orpington BR6
  off Osgood Av 163 ET106
Wolsey Pl Shop Cen, Wok. GU21
  off Commercial Way ..166 AY117
Wolsey Rd, N1 ....66 DR64
  Ashford TW15 ....114 BL91
  East Molesey KT8 ....137 CD98
  Enfield EN1 ....30 DV40
  Esher KT10 ....154 CB105
  Hampton (Hmptn.H.) TW12 ..116 CB93
  Northwood HA6 ....39 BQ47
  Sunbury-on-Thames TW16 ..115 BT94
Wolsey St, E1
  off Sidney St 84 DW71
Wolsey Wk, Wok. GU21 ..166 AY117
Wolsey Way, Chess. KT9 ..156 CN106
Wolsley Cl, Dart. DA1 ..127 FE85
Wolstan Cl, Uxb. (Denh.) UB9
  off Lindsey Rd 58 BG62
Wolstonbury, N12 ....44 DA50
Wolvercote Rd, SE2 ....106 EX75
Wolverley St, E2
  off Bethnal Grn Rd ...84 DV69
Wolverton, SE17 ....201 L10
Wolverton Av, Kings.T. KT2 ..138 CN95
Wolverton Gdns, W5 .....80 CM73
  W6 ....99 CX77
Wolverton Rd, Stan. HA7 ..41 CH51
Wolverton Way, N14 .....29 DJ43
Wolves La, N13 ....45 DN52
  N22 ....45 DN52
Wombell Gdns, Grav. (Nthflt.)
  DA11 ....130 GE89
WOMBWELL PARK, Grav. ..130 GD89
Womersley Rd, N8 ....65 DM58
Wonersh Way, Sutt. SM2 ..157 CX109
Wonford Cl, Kings.T. KT2 ..138 CS95
  Tadworth KT20 ....183 CU126
Wontford Rd, Pur. CR8 ..175 DN115
Wontner Cl, N1
  off Greenman St 84 DQ66
Wontner Rd, SW17 ......120 DF89
Wooburn Cl, Uxb. UB8
  off Aldenham Dr 77 BP70
Woodall Cl, E14
  off Lawless St 85 EB73
Woodall Rd, Enf. EN3 ....31 DX44
Wood Av, Purf. RM19 ...108 FQ77
Woodbank, Rick. WD3 ....22 BJ44
Woodbank Av, Ger.Cr. SL9 ..56 AX58
Woodbank Dr, Ch.St.G. HP8 ..36 AX48
Woodbank Rd, Brom. BR1 ..124 EF90
Woodbastwick Rd, SE26 ..123 DX92
Woodberry Av, N21 ......45 DN47
  Harrow HA2 ....60 CB56
Woodberry Cl, NW7
  off Bittacy Hill 43 CY52
  Sunbury-on-Thames TW16
  off Ashridge Way 115 BU93
Woodberry Cres, N10 ....65 DH55
Woodberry Down, N4 ....66 DQ59
  Epping CM16 ....18 EU29
Woodberry Down Est, N4 ..66 DQ59
Woodberry Gdns, N12 ....44 DC51
Woodberry Gro, N4 ......66 DQ59
  N12 ....44 DC51
  Bexley DA5 ....127 FD90
Woodberry Way, E4 ......47 EC46
  N12 ....44 DC51
Woodbine Cl, Twick. TW2 ..117 CD88
  Waltham Abbey EN9 ....32 EJ35
Woodbine Gro, SE20 ....122 DV94
  Enfield EN2 ....30 DR38
Woodbine La, Wor.Pk. KT4 ..139 CW104
Woodbine Pl, E11 ....68 EG58
Woodbine Rd, Sid. DA15 ..125 ES88
Woodbines Av, Kings.T. KT1 ..137 CK97
Woodbine Ter, E9
  off Morning La 84 DW65
Woodborough Rd, SW15 ..99 CV84
Woodbourne Av, SW16 ..121 DK90
Woodbourne Cl, SW16
  off Woodbourne Av ...121 DL90
Woodbourne Dr, Esher (Clay.)
  KT10 ....155 CF107
Woodbourne Gdns, Wall.
  SM6 ....159 DH108
Woodbridge Av, Lthd. KT22 ..171 CG118
Woodbridge Cl, N7 ......65 DM61
  NW2 ....62 CU62
  Romford RM3 ....52 FK49
Woodbridge Ct, Wdf.Grn. IG8 ..48 EL52
Woodbridge Gro, Lthd. KT22 ..171 CG118
Woodbridge Rd, Bark. IG11 ..69 ET64
Woodbridge St, EC1 ....196 F4

Woodbrook Gdns, Wal.Abb.
  EN9 ....16 EE33
Woodbrook Rd, SE2 .....106 EU79
Woodburn Cl, NW4 ....63 CX57
Woodbury Cl, E11 ....68 EH56
  Croydon CR0 ....142 DT103
  Westerham (Bigg.H.) TN16 ..179 EM118
Woodbury Dr, Sutt. SM2 ..158 DC110
Woodbury Hill, Loug. IG10 ..32 EL41
Woodbury Hollow, Loug. IG10 ..32 EL40
Woodbury Pk Rd, W13 ...79 CH70
Woodbury Rd, E17 ......67 EB56
  Westerham (Bigg.H.) TN16 ..179 EM118
Woodbury St, SW17 .....120 DE92
Woodchester Sq, W2 .....82 DB71
Woodchurch Cl, Sid. DA14 ..125 ER90
Woodchurch Dr, Brom. BR1 ..124 EK94
Woodchurch Rd, NW6 ....82 DA66
Wood Cl, E2 ....84 DU70
  NW9 ....62 CR59
  Bexley DA5 ....127 FE90
  Harrow HA1 ....61 CD59
Woodclyffe Dr, Chis. BR7 ..145 EN96
Woodcock Ct, Har. HA3 ..62 CL59
Woodcock Dell Av, Har. HA3 ..61 CK59
Woodcock Hill, Har. HA3 ..61 CK59
  Rickmansworth WD3 ....38 BL50
Woodcocks, E16 ....86 EJ71
Woodcombe Cres, SE23 ..122 DW88
WOODCOTE, Epsom 172 CQ116
WOODCOTE, Pur. 159 DK111
Woodcote Av, NW7 ....43 CW51
  Hornchurch RM12 ......71 FG63
  Thornton Heath CR7 ..141 DP98
  Wallington SM6 ......159 DH108
Woodcote Cl, Enf. EN3 ..30 DW44
  Epsom KT18 ....156 CR114
  Kingston upon Thames KT2 ..118 CM92
  Waltham Cross (Chsht.) EN8 ..14 DW30
Woodcote Dr, Orp. BR6 ..159 ER102
  Purley CR8 ....159 DK110
Woodcote End, Epsom KT18 ..172 CR115
Woodcote Grn, Wall. SM6 ..159 DJ109
Woodcote Grn Rd, Epsom
  KT18 ....172 CQ116
Woodcote Gro, Couls. CR5 ..159 DH112
Woodcote Gro Rd, Couls.
  CR5 ....175 DK115
Woodcote Hurst, Epsom
  KT18 ....172 CQ116
Woodcote La, Pur. CR8 ..159 DK111
Woodcote Ms, Loug. IG10 ..48 EK45
  Wallington SM6 ......159 DH107
Woodcote Pk Av, Pur. CR8 ..159 DJ112
Woodcote Pk Rd, Epsom
  KT18 ....172 CQ116
Woodcote Pl, SE27 .....121 DP91
Woodcote Rd, E11 ....68 EG59
  Epsom KT18 ....156 CR114
  Purley CR8 ....159 DJ109
  Wallington SM6 ......159 DH107
Woodcote Side, Epsom KT18 ..172 CP115
Woodcote Valley Rd, Pur.
  CR8 ....159 DK113
Woodcott Ho, SW15
  off Ellisfield Dr 119 CU87
Woodcrest Rd, Pur. CR8 ..159 DL113
Woodcrest Wk, Reig. RH2 ..184 DE132
Woodcroft, N21 ....45 DM46
  SE9 ....125 EM90
  Greenford UB6 ....79 CG65
Woodcroft Av, NW7 ......42 CS52
  Stanmore HA7 ....41 CF53
Woodcroft Cres, Uxb. UB10 ..77 BP67
Woodcroft Ms, SE8 .....203 K9
Woodcroft Rd, Th.Hth. CR7 ..141 DP99
Woodcutters Av, Grays RM16 ..110 GC75
Wood Dr, Chis. BR7 ....124 EL93
  Sevenoaks TN13 ......190 FF124
Woodedge Cl, E4 ....48 EF46
Woodend, SE19 ....122 DQ93
  Esher KT10 ....136 CC103
Wood End, Hayes UB3 ...77 BS72
  St. Albans (Park St.) AL2 ..8 CC28
Woodend, Sutt. SM1 ....140 DC103
Wood End, The, Wall. SM6 ..159 DH109
Wood End Av, Har. HA2 ..60 CB63
Wood End Cl, Nthlt. UB5 ..61 CD64
  Woking GU21 ....166 AU119
Woodend Gdns, Enf. EN2 ..29 DL42
Wood End Gdns, Nthlt. UB5 ..60 CC64
Wood End Grn Rd, Hayes UB3 ..77 BR71
Wood End La, Nthlt. UB5 ..78 CB65
Woodend Pk, Cob. KT11 ..170 BX115
Woodend Rd, E17 ....47 EC54
Wood End Rd, Har. HA1 ..61 CG63
Wood End Way, Nthlt. UB5 ..60 CC64
Wooder Gdns, E7 ....68 EF63
Wooderson Cl, SE25 ....142 DS98
Woodfall Av, Barn. EN5 ..27 CZ43
Woodfall Dr, Dart. DA1 ..107 FE84
Woodfall Rd, N4 ....65 DN60
Woodfall St, SW3 ......100 DF78
Woodfarrs, SE5 ....102 DR84
Woodfield, Ashtd. KT21 ..171 CK117
Woodfield Av, NW9 ......62 CS56
  SW16 ....121 DK90
  W5 ....79 CJ70
  Carshalton SM5 .....158 DG107
  Gravesend DA11 .....131 GH88
  Northwood HA6 ....39 BS49
  Wembley HA0 ....61 CJ62
Woodfield Cl, SE19 ....122 DQ94
  Ashtead KT21 ....171 CK117
  Coulsdon CR5 ....175 DJ119
  Enfield EN1 ....30 DS42
  Redhill RH1 ....184 DG131
Woodfield Cres, W5 .....79 CJ70
Woodfield Dr, Barn. EN4 ..44 DG46
  Romford RM2 ....71 FG56
Woodfield Gdns, W9
  off Woodfield Rd 81 CZ71
  New Malden KT3 .....139 CT99
Woodfield Gro, SW16 ...121 DK90
Woodfield Hill, Couls. CR5 ..175 DH119
Woodfield La, SW16 ....121 DK90
  Ashtead KT21 ....172 CL116

Woodfield Pl, W9 ....81 CZ70
Woodfield Ri, Bushey WD23 ..41 CD45
Woodfield Rd, W5 ....79 CJ70
  W9 ....81 CZ71
  Ashtead KT21 ....171 CK117
  Hounslow TW4 ....95 BV82
  Radlett WD7 ....25 CG36
  Thames Ditton KT7 ..137 CF103
Woodfields, Sev. TN13 ..190 FD122
Woodfields, The, S.Croy. CR2 ..160 DT111
Woodfield Ter, Epp. (Thnwd.)
  CM16 off High Rd 18 EW25
  Uxbridge (Hare.) UB9 ..38 BH54
Woodfield Way, N11 ....45 DK52
  Hornchurch RM12 ......72 FK60
  Redhill RH1 ....184 DE132
Woodfines, The, Horn. RM11 ..72 FL58
WOODFORD, Wdf.Grn. 48 EH51
  ⊖ Woodford 48 EH51
Woodford Av, Ilf. IG2, IG4 ..69 EM57
  Woodford Green IG8 ...68 EK55
WOODFORD BRIDGE, Wdf.Grn. ..49 EM52
Woodford Br Rd, Ilf. IG4 ..68 EK55
Woodford Ct, W12
  off Shepherds Bush Grn ..99 CX75
  Waltham Abbey EN9 ....16 EG33
Woodford Cres, Pnr. HA5 ..39 BV54
WOODFORD GREEN 48 EF49
Woodford New Rd, E17 ..68 EE56
  E18 ....48 EE53
  Woodford Green IG8 ...48 EE53
Woodford Pl, Wem. HA9 ..62 CL60
Woodford Rd, E7 ....68 EH63
  E18 ....68 EG56
  Watford WD17 ....23 BV40
WOODFORD WELLS, Wdf.Grn. ..48 EH49
Woodgate, Wat. WD25 ....7 BV33
Woodgate Av, Chess. KT9 ..155 CK106
  Potters Bar EN6 ......13 DH33
Woodgate Cres, Nthwd. HA6 ..39 BU51
Woodgate Dr, SW16 ....121 DK94
Woodgavil, Bans. SM7 ..173 CZ116
Woodger Rd, W12
  off Goldhawk Rd 99 CW75
Woodget Cl, E6
  off Remington Rd 86 EL72
Woodgrange Av, N12 ....44 DD51
  W5 ....80 CN74
  Enfield EN1 ....30 DU44
  Harrow HA3 ....61 CJ57
Woodgrange Cl, Har. HA3 ..61 CK57
Woodgrange Gdns, Enf. EN1 ..30 DU44
  ⇌ Woodgrange Park ...68 EK64
Woodgrange Rd, E7 ......68 EH63
Woodgrange Ter, Enf. EN1
  off Great Cambridge Rd ..30 DU44
WOOD GREEN, N22 ....45 DL53
  ⊖ Wood Green 45 DN54
Woodgreen Rd, Wal.Abb. EN9 ..32 EJ35
Wood Grn Shop City, N22
  off High Rd 45 DN54
Wood Grn Way, Wal.Cr. (Chsht.)
  EN8 ....15 DY31
Woodhall Av, SE21 .....122 DT90
  Pinner HA5 ....40 BY54
Woodhall Cl, Chess. KT9
  off Ashlyns Way 155 CK107
  Uxbridge UB8 ....58 BK64
Woodhall Dr, SE21 .....122 DT90
  Pinner HA5 ....40 BX53
Woodhall Gate, Pnr. HA5 ..40 BX52
Woodhall Ho, SW18
  off Fitzhugh Gro 120 DD86
Woodhall La, Rad. (Shenley)
  WD7 ....26 CL35
  Watford WD19 ....40 BX49
Woodhall Rd, Pnr. HA5 ..40 BX52
WOODHAM, Add. 151 BF111
Woodham Ct, E18 ....68 EF56
Woodham La, Add. (New Haw)
  KT15 ....152 BG110
  Woking GU21 ....151 BB114
Woodham Pk Rd, Add.
  (Woodham) KT15 .....151 BF109
Woodham Pk Way, Add.
  (Woodham) KT15 .....151 BF111
Woodham Ri, Wok. GU21 ..151 AZ114
Woodham Rd, SE6 ......123 EC90
  Woking GU21 ....166 AY115
Woodham Waye, Wok. GU21 ..151 BB113
Woodhatch Cl, E6
  off Remington Rd 86 EL72
Woodhatch Spinney, Couls.
  CR5 ....175 DL116
Woodhaven Gdns, Ilf. IG6
  off Brandville Gdns ..69 EQ55
Woodhaw, Egh. TW20 ...113 BB91
Woodhayes Av, SW19 ...119 CW94
Woodhead Dr, Orp. BR6
  off Sherlies Av 145 ES103
Woodheyes Rd, NW10 ...62 CR64
Woodhill, SE18 ....104 EL77
Woodhill Av, Ger.Cr. SL9 ..57 BA58
Woodhill Cres, Har. HA3 ..61 CK58
Wood Ho, SW17 off Laurel Cl ..120 DE92
Woodhouse Av, Grnf. UB6 ..79 CF68
Woodhouse Cl, Grnf. UB6 ..79 CF68
  Hayes UB3 ....95 BS76
Woodhouse Eaves, Nthwd.
  HA6 ....39 BU50
Woodhouse Gro, E12 ....86 EL65
Woodhouse Rd, E11 .....68 EF62
  N12 ....44 DD51
Woodhurst Av, Orp. BR5 ..145 EQ100
  Watford WD25 ....24 BX35
Woodhurst Dr, Uxb. (Denh.)
  UB9 ....57 BF57
Woodhurst La, Oxt. RH8 ..188 EE130
Woodhurst Pk, Oxt. RH8 ..188 EE130
Woodhurst Rd, SE2 .....106 EU78
  W3 ....80 CQ73
Woodhyrst Gdns, Ken. CR8
  off Firs Rd 175 DP115
Woodington Cl, SE9 ....125 EN86
Woodknoll Dr, Chis. BR7 ..145 EM95

Woodland App, Grnf. UB6 ....79 CG65
Woodland Av, Brwd. CM13 ..55 GC43
Woodland Cl, NW9 ....62 CQ58
SE19
off Woodland Hill 122 DS93
Brentwood CM13 ....55 GC43
Epsom KT19 ....156 CS107
Uxbridge (Ickhm.) UB10 ..59 BP61
Weybridge KT13
off Woodland Gro 153 BR105
Woodford Green IG8 ....48 EH48
Woodland Ct, Oxt. RH8 ...187 ED128
Woodland Cres, SE10 ....104 EE79
SE16 ....203 H5
Woodland Dr, Wat. WD17 ..23 BT39
Woodland Gdns, N10 .....65 DH57
Epsom KT18 ....173 CW117
Isleworth TW7 ....97 CE82
South Croydon CR2 ....160 DW111
Woodland Gro, SE10 ....104 EE79
Epping CM16 ....18 EU31
Weybridge KT13 ....153 BR105
Woodland Hill, SE19 ....122 DS93
Woodland La, Rick. (Chorl.)
WD3 ....21 BD41
Woodland Pl, Rick. (Chorl.)
WD3 ....21 BF42
Woodland Ri, N10 ....65 DH56
Greenford UB6 ....79 CG65
Oxted RH8 ....188 EE130
Sevenoaks TN15 ......191 FL123
Woodland Rd, E4 ....47 EC46
N11 ....45 DH50
SE19 ....122 DS92
Loughton IG10 ....32 EL41
Rickmansworth (Map.Cr.)
WD3 ....21 BD50
Thornton Heath CR7 ...141 DN98
WOODLANDS, Islw. 97 CE82
Woodlands, NW11 ....63 CY58
SW20 ....139 CW98
Gerrards Cross SL9 ....57 AZ57
Harrow HA2 ....60 CA56
Hatfield AL9 ....12 DB26
Radlett WD7 ....9 CG34
St. Albans (Park St.) AL2 ..8 CC27
Woking GU22
off Constitution Hill ...166 AY118
Woodlands, The, N14 ....45 DH46
SE13 ....123 ED87
SE19 ....122 DQ94
Beckenham BR3 ....143 EC95
Esher KT10 ....136 CC103
Isleworth TW7 ....97 CF82
Orpington BR6 ....164 EV107
Wallington SM6 ....159 DH109
Woodlands Av, E11 .....68 EH60
N3 ....44 DC52
W3 ....80 CP74
Hornchurch RM11 ......72 FK57
New Malden KT3 ......138 CQ95
Romford RM6 ....70 EY58
Ruislip HA4 ....60 BW60
Sidcup DA15 ....125 ES88
West Byfleet KT14 .....151 BF113
Worcester Park KT4 ....139 CT103
Woodlands Cl, NW11 ....63 CY57
Borehamwood WD6 ....26 CP42
Bromley BR1 ....145 EM96
Chertsey (Ott.) KT16 ...151 BB110
Esher (Clay.) KT10 ....155 CF108
Gerrards Cross SL9 ....57 AZ58
Grays RM16 ....110 GE76
Swanley BR8 ....147 FF97
Woodlands Copse, Ashtd.
KT21 ....171 CK116
Woodlands Ct, Wok. GU22
off Constitution Hill ...166 AY119
Woodlands Dr, Kings L. WD4 ..7 BQ28
Stanmore HA7 ....41 CF51
Sunbury-on-Thames TW16 .136 BW96
Woodlands Gro, Couls. CR5 .174 DG117
Isleworth TW7 ....97 CE82
Woodlands La, Cob. (Stoke D'Ab.)
KT11 ....170 CA117
Woodlands Par, Ashf. TW15 ..115 BQ93
Woodlands Pk, Add. KT15 ..151 BF106
Bexley DA5 ....127 FC91
Tadworth KT20 ....182 CP131
Woking GU21
off Blackmore Cres 151 BC114
Woodlands Pk Rd, N15 ...65 DP57
SE10 ....104 EE79
Woodlands Ri, Swan. BR8 ..147 FF96
Woodlands Rd, E11 .....68 EE61
E17 ....67 EC55
N9 ....46 DW46
SW13 ....99 CT83
Bexleyheath DA7 ......106 EY83
Bromley BR1 ....144 EL96
Bushey WD23 ....24 BY43
Enfield EN2 ....30 DR39
Epsom KT18 ....172 CN115
Harrow HA1 ....61 CF57
Hemel Hempstead HP3 ..6 BN27
Ilford IG1 ....69 EQ62
Isleworth TW7 ....97 CE82
Leatherhead KT22 .....171 CD117
Orpington BR6 ....164 EU107
Romford RM1 ....71 FF57
Romford (Harold Wd.) RM3 .52 FN53
Southall UB1 ....78 BX74
Surbiton KT6 ....137 CK101
Virginia Water GU25 ...132 AW98
West Byfleet KT14 .....151 BF114
Woodlands Rd E, Vir.W.
GU25 ....132 AW98
Woodlands Rd W, Vir.W.
GU25 ....132 AW97
Woodlands St, SE13 ....123 ED87
Woodland St, E8
off Dalston La 84 DT65
Woodlands Vw, Sev. (Bad.Mt.)
TN14 ....164 FA110
Woodlands Way, SW15
off Oakhill La 119 CZ85
Ashtead KT21 ....172 CN116

Woodlands Way, Tad. KT20 ..182 CQ130
Woodland Ter, SE7 ....104 EL77
Woodland Wk, NW3 ....64 DE64
SE10 off Woodland Gro ..104 EE78
Bromley BR1 ....124 EE91
Woodland Way, N21 .....45 DN47
NW7 ....42 CS51
SE2 ....106 EX77
Abbots Langley (Bedmond)
WD5 ....7 BT27
Caterham CR3 ....186 DS128
Croydon CR0 ....142 DY102
Epping (They.B.) CM16 ..33 ER35
Greenhithe DA9 ....109 FU84
Mitcham CR4 ....120 DG94
Morden SM4 ....139 CZ98
Orpington BR5 ....145 EQ98
Purley CR8 ....159 DN113
Surbiton KT5 ....138 CP103
Tadworth KT20 ....173 CY122
Waltham Cross (Chsht.)
EN7 ....13 DP28
West Wickham BR4 ....161 EB105
Weybridge KT13 ....153 BR106
Woodford Green IG8 ....48 EH48
Wood La, N6 ....65 DH58
NW9 ....62 CS59
W12 ....81 CW72
Caterham CR3 ....176 DR124
Dagenham RM8, RM9,
RM10 ....70 EW63
Dartford (Lane End) DA2 .129 FR91
Hornchurch RM12 .....71 FG64
Isleworth TW7 ....97 CF80
Iver SL0 ....75 BC71
Ruislip HA4 ....60 BR60
Stanmore HA7 ....41 CG48
Tadworth KT20 ....173 CZ116
Weybridge KT13 ....153 BQ109
Woodford Green IG8 ....48 EF50
Wood La Cl, Iver SL0 ....75 BB69
Woodlawn Cl, SW15 .....119 CZ85
Woodlawn Cres, Twick. TW2 ..116 CB89
Woodlawn Dr, Felt. TW13 ..116 BX89
Woodlawn Gro, Wok. GU21 ..167 AZ115
Woodlawn Rd, SW6 .....99 CX80
Woodlea Dr, Brom. BR2 ..144 EE99
Woodlea Gro, Nthwd. HA6 ..39 BQ51
Woodlea Rd, N16 ....66 DS62
Woodlee Cl, Vir.W. GU25 ..132 AW96
Woodleigh, E18
off Churchfields 48 EG53
Woodleigh Av, N12 ......44 DE51
Woodleigh Gdns, SW16 ..121 DL90
Woodley Cl, SW17
off Arnold Rd 120 DF94
Woodley La, Cars. SM5 ...140 DD104
Woodley Rd, Orp. BR6 ...146 EW103
Wood Lo Gdns, Brom. BR1 ..124 EL94
Wood Lo La, W.Wick. BR4 ..143 EC104
Woodmancote Gdns, W.Byf.
KT14 ....152 BG113
Woodman La, E4 ....32 EE43
Woodman Path, Ilf. IG6 ...49 ES51
Woodman Rd, Brwd. CM14 ..54 FW50
Coulsdon CR5 ....175 DJ115
Woodmans Gro, NW10 ...63 CT64
Woodmans Ms, W12 .....81 CV71
WOODMANSTERNE, Bans. ..174 DD115
Woodmansterne 175 DH116
Woodmansterne La, Bans.
SM7 ....174 DB115
Carshalton SM5 ....158 DF112*
Wallington SM6 ....159 DH111
Woodmansterne Rd, SW16 ..141 DK95
Carshalton SM5 ....158 DE109
Coulsdon CR5 ....175 DJ115
Woodmansterne St, Bans.
SM7 ....174 DE115
Woodman St, E16 ......87 EN74
Wood Meads, Epp. CM16 ..18 EU29
Woodmere, SE9 ....125 EM88
Woodmere Av, Croy. CR0 ..143 DX101
Watford WD24 ....24 BX38
Woodmere Cl, SW11
off Lavender Hill 100 DG83
Croydon CR0 ....143 DX101
Woodmere Gdns, Croy. CR0 ..143 DX101
Woodmere Way, Beck. BR3 ..143 ED99
Woodmount, Swan. BR8 ..147 FC101
Woodnook Rd, SW16 ....121 DH92
Woodpecker Cl, N9 ......30 DV44
Bushey WD23 ....40 CC46
Cobham KT11 ....154 BY112
Harrow HA3 ....41 CF53
Woodpecker Mt, Croy. CR0 ..161 DY109
Woodpecker Rd, SE14 ...103 DY79
SE28 ....88 EW73
Woodpecker Way, Wok.
GU22 ....166 AX123
Woodplace Cl, Couls. CR5 ..175 DJ119
Woodplace La, Couls. CR5 ..175 DJ118
Wood Pt, E16 off Fife Rd ..86 EG71
Woodquest Av, SE24 ....122 DQ85
Woodredon Fm La, Wal.Abb.
EN9 ....32 EK35
Wood Retreat, SE18 ....105 ER80
Woodridden Hill, Wal.Abb.
EN9 ....32 EK35
Wood Ride, Barn. EN4 ...28 DD39
Orpington BR5 ....145 ER98
Woodridge Cl, Enf. EN2 ..29 DN39
Woodridge Way, Nthwd. HA6 ..39 BS51
Wood Riding, Wok. GU22
off Pyrford Wds Rd 167 BF115
Woodridings Av, Pnr. HA5 ..40 BZ53
Woodridings Cl, Pnr. HA5 ..40 BY52
Woodriffe Rd, E11 ......67 ED59
Wood Rd, Pnr. HA5 .....59 BU57
Wood Rd, NW10
off Fawood Av 80 CQ66
Shepperton TW17 ......134 BN98
Westerham (Bigg.H.)
TN16 ....178 EJ118
Woodrow, SE18 ....105 EM77
Woodrow Av, Hayes UB4 ..77 BT71
Woodrow Cl, Grnf. UB6 ...79 CH66

Woodrow Ct, N17
off Heybourne Rd 46 DV52
Woodrush Cl, SE14
off Southerngate Way ..103 DY80
Woodrush Way, Rom. RM6 ..70 EX56
Woods, The, Nthwd. HA6 ..39 BU50
Radlett WD7 ....9 CH34
Uxbridge UB10 ....59 BP63
Wood's Bldgs, E1
off Whitechapel Rd 84 DV71
Woodseer St, E1 ....84 DT71
Woodsford, SE17
off Portland St 102 DR78
Woodsford Sq, W14 .....99 CY75
Woodshire Rd, Dag. RM10 ..71 FB62
Woodshore Cl, Vir.W. GU25 ..132 AV100
Wood Street 67 EC56
WOODSIDE, Croy. 142 DU100
WOODSIDE, Wat. 7 BU33
Woodside, NW11 ....64 DA57
SW19 ....119 CZ93
Borehamwood (Elstree)
WD6 ....26 CM42
Buckhurst Hill IG9 .....48 EJ47
Epping (Thnwd.) CM16 ..18 EX27
Leatherhead (Fetch.) KT22 .170 CB122
Orpington BR6 ....164 EU106
Tadworth (Lwr.Kgswd.)
KT20 ....183 CZ128
Waltham Cross (Chsht.)
EN7 ....14 DU31
Walton-on-Thames KT12
off Ashley Rd 135 BU102
Watford WD24 ....23 BU36
Woodside Av, N6 ....64 DF57
N10 ....64 DF57
N12 ....44 DC49
SE25 ....142 DV100
Chislehurst BR7 ....125 EQ92
Esher KT10 ....137 CE101
Walton-on-Thames KT12 .153 BV105
Wembley HA0 ....80 CL67
Woodside Cl, Bexh. DA7 ..107 FD84
Brentwood CM13 ......55 GD43
Caterham CR3 ....176 DS124
Gerrards Cross (Chal.St.P.)
SL9 ....36 AY54
Rainham RM13 ....90 FJ70
Stanmore HA7 ....41 CH50
Surbiton KT5 ....138 CQ101
Wembley HA0 ....80 CL67
Woodside Commercial Est,
Epp. (Thnwd.) CM16 ...18 EX26
Woodside Ct, N12
off Woodside Av 44 DC49
Woodside Ct Rd, Croy. CR0 ..142 DU101
Woodside Cres, Sid. DA15 ..125 ES90
Woodside Dr, Dart. DA2 ..127 FE91
Woodside End, Wem. HA0 ..80 CL67
Woodside Gdns, E4 .....47 EB50
N17 ....46 DS54
Woodside Gra Rd, N12 ..44 DB49
Woodside Grn, SE25 ....142 DV100
Woodside Gro, N12 .....44 DC48
Woodside Hill, Ger.Cr. (Chal.St.P.)
SL9 ....36 AY54
Woodside La, N12 ......44 DB48
Bexley DA5 ....126 EX86
Woodside Ms, SE22
off Heber Rd 122 DT86
Woodside Park 44 DA98
Woodside Pk, SE25 ....142 DU99
Woodside Pk Av, E17 ...67 ED56
Woodside Pk Rd, N12 ...44 DB49
Woodside Pl, Wem. HA0 ..80 CL67
Woodside Rd, E13 ......86 EJ70
N22 ....45 DM52
SE25 ....142 DV100
Abbots Langley WD5 ...7 BU31
Bexleyheath DA7 ......107 FD84
Bromley BR1 ....144 EL99
Cobham KT11 ....154 CA113
Kingston upon Thames KT2 .118 CL94
New Malden KT3 ......138 CR96
Northwood HA6 ....39 BT52
Purley CR8 ....159 DK113
St. Albans (Brick.Wd.) AL2 ..8 BZ30
Sevenoaks TN13 ......190 FG123
Sevenoaks (Sund.) TN14 .180 EX124
Sidcup DA15 ....125 ES90
Sutton SM1 ....140 DC104
Watford WD25 ....7 BV31
Woodford Green IG8 ....48 EG49
Woodside Way, Croy. CR0 ..142 DV100
Mitcham CR4 ....141 DH95
Virginia Water GU25 ...132 AV97
Woods Ms, W1 ....194 G10
Woodsome Lo, Wey. KT13 ..153 BQ107
Woodsome Rd, NW5 ....64 DG62
Woods Pl, SE1 ....201 N7
Woodspring Rd, SW19 ..119 CY89
Woods Rd, SE15 ....102 DV81
Woodstead Gro, Edg. HA8 ..42 CL51
Woodstock Av, NW11 ...63 CY59
W13 ....97 CG76
Isleworth TW7 ....117 CG85
Romford RM3 ....52 FP50
Slough SL3 ....92 AX77
Southall UB1 ....78 BZ69
Sutton SM3 ....139 CZ101
Woodstock Cl, Bex. DA5 ..126 EZ88
Stanmore HA7 ....42 CL54
Woking GU21 ....166 AY116
Woodstock Ct, SE12 ....124 EG86
SE11 ....200 D10
Woodstock Cres, N9 ....30 DV44
Woodstock Dr, Uxb. UB10 ..58 BL63
Woodstock Gdns, Beck. BR3 ..143 EB95
Hayes UB4 ....77 BT71
Ilford IG3 ....70 EU61
Woodstock Gro, W12 ....99 CX75
Woodstock La N, Surb. KT6 ..137 CJ103
Woodstock La S, Chess. KT9 ..155 CJ105
Esher (Clay.) KT10 ....155 CH106
Woodstock Ms, W1 .....194 G7
Woodstock Ri, Sutt. SM3 ..139 CZ101
Woodstock Rd, E7 .....86 EJ66
E17 ....47 ED54

Woodstock Rd, N4 ....65 DN60
NW11 ....63 CZ59
W4 ....98 CS78
Bushey (Bushey Hth.) WD23 .41 CE45
Carshalton SM5 ....158 DG106
Coulsdon CR5
off Chipstead Valley Rd .175 DH116
Croydon CR0 ....142 DR104
Wembley HA0 ....80 CM66
Woodstock St, E16
off Victoria Dock Rd ...86 EE72
W1 ....195 H9
Woodstock Ter, E14 ....85 EB73
Woodstock Way, Mitch. CR4 .141 DH96
Woodstone Av, Epsom KT17 .157 CU106
Wood Street 67 EC56
Wood St, E17 ....67 EC55
EC2 ....197 J9
W4 ....98 CS78
Barnet EN5 ....27 CW42
Grays RM17 ....110 GC79
Kingston upon Thames KT1 .137 CK95
Mitcham CR4 ....140 DG101
Redhill RH1 ....185 DJ129
Swanley BR8 ....148 FJ96
Woodsway, Lthd. (Oxshott)
KT22 ....155 CE114
Woodsyre, SE26 ....122 DT91
Woodthorpe Rd, SW15 ..99 CV84
Ashford TW15 ....114 BL91
Woodtree Cl, NW4
off Ashley La 43 CW54
Wood Vale, N10 ....65 DJ57
SE23 ....122 DV88
Woodvale Av, SE25 ....142 DT97
Wood Vale Est, SE23 ...122 DW86
Woodvale Wk, SE27
off Elder Rd 122 DQ92
Woodvale Way, NW11
off The Vale 63 CX62
Woodview, Chess. KT9 ..155 CJ111
Grays RM16, RM17 ....110 GE50
Woodview Av, E4 ......47 EC49
Woodview Cl, N4 ......65 DP59
SW15 ....118 CR91
Orpington BR6
off Crofton Rd 145 EQ103
South Croydon CR2 ...160 DV114
Woodview Rd, Swan. BR8 ..147 FC96
Woodville, SE3 ....104 EH81
Woodville Cl, SE12 ....124 EG85
Teddington TW11 .....117 CG91
Woodville Ct, Wat. WD17 ..23 BU40
Woodville Gdns, NW11 ..63 CX59
W5 ....80 CL72
Ilford IG6 ....69 EP55
Ruislip HA4 ....59 BQ58
Woodville Gro, Well. DA16 ..106 EU83
Woodville Pl, Cat. CR3 ..176 DQ121
Woodville Rd, E11 .....68 EF60
E17 ....67 DY56
E18 ....48 EH54
N16 ....66 DS64
NW6 ....81 CZ68
NW11 ....63 CX59
W5 ....79 CK72
Barnet EN5 ....28 DB41
Leatherhead KT22 .....171 CH120
Morden SM4 ....140 DA98
Richmond TW10 ....117 CH90
Thornton Heath CR7 ...142 DQ98
Woodville St, SE18
off Woodhill 104 EL77
Wood Wk, Rick. (Chorl.) WD3 .21 BE40
Woodward Av, NW4 ....63 CU57
Woodward Cl, Esher (Clay.)
KT10 ....155 CF107
Grays RM17 ....110 GB77
Woodwarde Rd, SE22 ...122 DS86
Woodward Gdns, Dag. RM9
off Woodward Rd 88 EW66
Stanmore HA7 ....41 CF52
Woodward Hts, Grays RM17 .110 GB77
Woodward Rd, Dag. RM9 ..88 EV66
Woodward Ter, Green. DA9 ..129 FS86
Woodway, Brwd. CM13,
CM15 ....55 GA46
Wood Way, Orp. BR6 ...145 EN103
Woodway Cres, Har. HA1 ..61 CG58
Woodwaye, Wat. WD19 ..40 BW45
Woodwell St, SW18
off Huguenot Pl 120 DC85
Wood Wf, SE10 ....103 EB79
Woodwicks, Rick. (Map.Cr.)
WD3 ....37 BD50
Woodyard, The, Epp. CM16 ..18 EW28
Woodyard Cl, NW5 ....64 DG63
Woodyard La, SE21 ....122 DS87
Woodyates Rd, SE12 ...124 EG86
Woolacombe Rd, SE3 ...104 EJ81
Woolacombe Way, Hayes UB3 .95 BS77
Woolbrook Rd, Dart. DA1
off Lower Sta Rd 127 FE86
Wooler St, SE17 ....102 DR78
Woolf Cl, SE28 ....88 EV74
Woolf Ms, WC1 off Burton St .83 DK70
Woolf Wk, Til. RM18
off Coleridge Rd 111 GJ82
Woolhampton Way, Chig. IG7 .50 EV48
Woolhams, Cat. CR3 ....186 DT126
Woollard St, Wal.Abb. EN9 ..15 EC34
Woollaston Rd, N4 .....65 DP58
Woollett Cl, Dart. (Cray.) DA1 .107 FG84
Woolmead Av, NW9 ....63 CU59
Woolmer Cl, Borwd. WD6 ..26 CN38
Woolmerdine Ct, Bushey
WD23 ....24 BX41
Woolmer Gdns, N18 ....46 DU50
Woolmer Rd, N18 ......46 DU50
Woolmore St, E14 .....85 EC73
Woolneigh St, SW6 ....100 DB83
Woolpack Ho, Enf. EN3
off Hertford Rd 31 DX37
Wool Rd, SW20 ....119 CV93

Woolston Cl, E17
off Riverhead Cl 47 DX54
Woolstone Rd, SE23 ...123 DY89
WOOLWICH 105 EN78
Woolwich Arsenal 105 EP77
Woolwich Ch St, SE18 ..104 EL76
★ Woolwich Common,
SE18 ....105 EM80
Woolwich Common, SE18 ..105 EN79
Woolwich Dockyard 105 EM77
Woolwich Ferry Pier, E16 ..105 EN75
Woolwich Foot Tunnel, E16 ..105 EN75
SE18 ....105 EN75
Woolwich Garrison, SE18 ..105 EM79
Woolwich High St, SE18 ..105 EN76
Woolwich Ind Est, SE28
off Hadden Rd 105 ES76
Woolwich Manor Way, E6 ..87 EM70
E16 ....105 EP75
Woolwich Mkt, SE18 ...105 EP77
Woolwich New Rd, SE18 ..105 EN78
Woolwich Rd, SE2 .....106 EX79
SE7 ....104 EG78
SE10 ....205 K10
Belvedere DA17 ......106 EX79
Bexleyheath DA7 .....106 FA84
Wooster Gdns, E14 ....85 ED72
Wooster Ms, Har. HA2
off Fairfield Dr 60 CC55
Wooster Pl, SE1 ....201 L8
Wootton Cl, Epsom KT18 ..173 CT115
Hornchurch RM11 .....72 FK57
Wootton Gro, N3 ......44 DA53
Wootton St, SE1 ......200 E4
Worbeck Rd, SE20 ....142 DV96
Worcester Av, N17 ....46 DU52
Upminster RM14 ......73 FT61
Worcester Cl, NW2
off Newfield Ri 63 CV62
Croydon CR0 ....143 DZ103
Gravesend (Istead Rise)
DA13 ....131 GF94
Greenhithe DA9 ......109 FV84
Mitcham CR4 ....141 DH97
Worcester Ct, Walt. KT12
off Rodney Rd 136 BW102
Worcester Cres, NW7 ..42 CS48
Woodford Green IG8 ...48 EH50
Worcester Dr, W4 .....98 CS75
Ashford TW15 ....115 BP93
Worcester Gdns, SW11
off Grandison Rd 120 DF85
Greenford UB6 ....78 CC65
Ilford IG1 ....68 EL59
Worcester Park KT4 ...138 CS104
Worcester Ms, NW6
off Lymington Rd 82 DB65
WORCESTER PARK 139 CT103
Worcester Park 139 CU102
Worcester Pk Rd, Wor.Pk.
KT4 ....138 CQ104
Worcester Rd, E12 ....69 EM63
E17 ....47 DX54
SW19 ....119 CZ92
Reigate RH2 ....184 DA133
Sutton SM2 ....158 DB107
Uxbridge UB8 ....76 BJ71
Worcesters Av, Enf. EN1 ..30 DU38
Wordsworth Av, E6 ....86 EL65
E18 ....68 EF55
Greenford UB6 ....79 CD68
Kenley CR8 off Valley Rd .176 DR115
Wordsworth Cl, Rom. RM3 ..52 FJ53
Tilbury RM18 ....111 GJ82
Wordsworth Dr, Sutt. SM3 .157 CW105
Wordsworth Mead, Red. RH1 .184 DG132
Wordsworth Rd, N16 ...66 DS63
SE1 ....201 P9
SE20 ....123 DX94
Addlestone KT15 .....152 BK105
Hampton TW12 ......116 BZ91
Wallington SM6 ......159 DJ107
Welling DA16 ....105 ES81
Wordsworth Wk, NW11 ..64 DA56
Wordsworth Way, Dart. DA1 .108 FN84
West Drayton UB7 ....94 BL77
Worfield St, SW11 ....100 DE80
Worgan St, SE11 ......200 B10
SE16 ....203 J7
World's End, Enf. 29 DN41
World's End, Cob. KT11 ..153 BU114
World's End Est, SW10 ..100 DD80
Worlds End La, N21 ....29 DM43
Enfield EN2 ....29 DM43
Orpington BR6 ....163 ET107
World's End Pas, SW10
off Riley Rd 100 DD80
World's End Pl, SW10
off King's Rd 100 DC80
Worlidge St, W6 ......99 CW78
Worlingham Rd, SE22 ..102 DT84
Wormholt Rd, W12 ....81 CU73
Wormley Ct, Wal.Abb. EN9
off Winters Way 16 EG33
Wormwood St, EC2 ....197 M8
Wormyngford Ct, Wal.Abb. EN9
off Ninefields 16 EG33
Wornington Rd, W10 ...81 CY71
Woronzow Rd, NW8 ....82 DD79
Worple, The, Stai. (Wrays.)
TW19 ....113 AZ86
Worple Av, SW19 .....119 CX94
Isleworth TW7 ....117 CG85
Staines TW18 ....114 BH93
Worple Cl, Har. HA2 ...60 BZ60
Worple Rd, SW19 .....119 CY94
SW20 ....139 CW96
Epsom KT18 ....156 CS114
Isleworth TW7 ....97 CG84
Leatherhead KT22 ....171 CH123
Staines TW18 ....114 BH94
Worple Rd Ms, SW19 ..119 CZ93
Worplesdon 166 AV124

Wor - Zof

Worple St, SW14 . . . . .98 CR83
Worple Way, Har. HA2 . . . . .60 BZ60
Richmond TW10 . . . . .118 CL85
Worrin Cl, Brwd. CM15 . . . . . .55 FZ46
Worrin Rd, Brwd. CM15 . . . . . .55 FZ47
Worsfold Cl, Wok. (Send)
GU23 . . . . .167 BB123
Worships Hill, Sev. TN13 . . . . .190 FE123
Worship St, EC2 . . . . .197 L5
Worslade Rd, SW17 . . . . . . .120 DD91
Worsley Br Rd, SE26 . . . . . . .123 DZ91
Beckenham BR3 . . . . .123 DZ92
Worsley Gro, E5 . . . . .66 DU63
Worsley Rd, E11 . . . . .68 EE63
Worsopp Dr, SW4 . . . . .121 DJ85
Worsted Grn, Red. RH1 . . . . .185 DJ129
Worth Cl, Orp. BR6 . . . . . . .163 ES105
Worthfield Cl, Epsom KT19 . .156 CR108
Worth Gro, SE17
off Merrow St 102 DR78
Worthing Cl, E15 off Mitre Rd . .86 EE68
Grays RM20 . . . . .110 FY79
Worthing Rd, Houns. TW5 . . . .96 BZ79
Worthington Cl, Mitch. CR4 . .141 DH97
Worthington Rd, Surb. KT6 . .138 CM102
Worthy Down Ct, SE18
off Prince Imperial Rd 105 EN81
Wortley Rd, E6 . . . . .86 EK66
Croydon CR0 . . . . .141 DN101
Worton Gdns, Islw. TW7 . . . . .97 CD82
Worton Hall Ind Est, Islw. TW7 .97 CE84
Worton Rd, Islw. TW7 . . . . . . .97 CE83
Worton Way, Houns. TW3 . . . .97 CD82
Isleworth TW7 . . . . .96 CC81
Wotton Grn, Orp. BR5 . . . . . .146 EX98
Wotton Rd, NW2 . . . . .63 CW63
SE8 . . . . .103 DZ79
Wotton Way, Sutt. SM2 . . . . .157 CW110
Wouldham Rd, E16 . . . . .86 EF72
Grays RM20 . . . . .110 FY79
Wrabness Way, Stai. TW18 . .134 BH95
Wragby Rd, E11 . . . . .68 EE62
Wrampling Pl, N9 . . . . .46 DU46
Wrangley Ct, Wal.Abb. EN9 . . .16 EG33
Wrangthorn Wk, Croy. CR0
off Epsom Rd 159 DN105
Wray Av, Ilf. IG5 . . . . .69 EN55
Wray Cl, Horn. RM11 . . . . . . .72 FJ59
Wray Common, Reig. RH2 . . .184 DD132
Wray Common Rd, Reig.
RH2 . . . . .184 DC133
Wray Cres, N4 . . . . .65 DL61
Wrayfield Av, Reig. RH2 . . . .184 DC133
Wrayfield Rd, Sutt. SM3 . . . .139 CX104
Wraylands Dr, Reig. RH2 . . . .184 DD132
Wray La, Reig. RH2 . . . . . . .184 DC132
Wray Mill Pk, Reig. RH2 . . . .184 DD132
Wray Pk Rd, Reig. RH2 . . . . .184 DB133
Wray Rd, Sutt. SM2 . . . . . . .157 CZ109
WRAYSBURY, Stai. 113 AZ86
⇌ Wraysbury 113 BA86
Wraysbury Cl, Houns. TW4
off Dorney Way 116 BY85
Wraysbury Gdns, Stai. TW19 .113 BE91
Wraysbury Rd, Stai. TW18,
TW19 . . . . .113 BC90
Wrays Way, Hayes UB4
off Balmoral Dr 77 BS70
Wrekin Rd, SE18 . . . . .105 EQ80
Wren Av, NW2 . . . . .63 CW64
Southall UB2 . . . . .96 BZ77
Wren Cl, E16 off Ibbotson Av . .86 EF72
N9 off Chaffinch Cl 47 DX46
Orpington BR5 . . . . .146 EX97
South Croydon CR2 . . . . . .161 DX109
Wren Ct, Slou. SL3
off New Rd 93 BA76
Wren Cres, Add. KT15 . . . . .152 BK106
Bushey WD23 . . . . .40 CC46
Wren Dr, Wal.Abb. EN9 . . . . .16 EG34
West Drayton UB7 . . . . .94 BK76
Wren Gdns, Dag. RM9 . . . . . .70 EX64
Hornchurch RM12 . . . . . . .71 FF60
Wren Landing, E14 . . . . .204 A2
Wren Ms, SE13
off Lee High Rd 104 EE84
Wren Path, SE28 . . . . .105 ER76
Wren Pl, Brwd. CM14 . . . . . . .54 FX48
Wren Rd, SE5 . . . . .102 DR81
Dagenham RM9 . . . . .70 EX64
Sidcup DA14 . . . . .126 EW91
Wrens Av, Ashf. TW15 . . . . . .115 BQ92
Wrens Cft, Grav. (Nthflt.)
DA11 . . . . .130 GE91
Wrens Hill, Lthd. (Oxshott)
KT22 . . . . .170 CC115
Wren St, WC1 . . . . .196 C4
Wren Ter, Ilf. IG5
off Tiptree Cres 69 EN55
Wrentham Av, NW10 . . . . . . .81 CX68
Wrenthorpe Rd, Brom. BR1 . .124 EE91
Wren Wk, Til. RM18 . . . . . . .111 GH80
Wrenwood Way, Pnr. HA5 . . . .59 BV56
Wrestlers Ct, EC3
off Camomile St 84 DS72
Wrexham Rd, E3 . . . . .85 EA68
Romford RM3 . . . . .52 FK48
Wricklemarsh Rd, SE3 . . . . .104 EH81
Wrigglesworth St, SE14 . . . .103 DX80
Wright Cl, Swans. DA10
off Milton St 129 FX86
Wright Gdns, Shep. TW17
off Laleham Rd 134 BN99
Wright Rd, N1 off Burder Cl . . .84 DS65
Hounslow TW5 . . . . .96 BW80
Wrights All, SW19 . . . . .119 CW93
Wrightsbridge Rd, Brwd.
CM14 . . . . .52 FN46
Wrights Cl, SE13
off Wisteria Rd 103 ED84
Dagenham RM10 . . . . .71 FB62
Wrights Grn, SW4
off Nelson's Row 101 DK84
Wrights La, W8 . . . . .100 DB75

Wrights Pl, NW10
off Mitchell Way 80 CQ65
Wrights Rd, E3 . . . . .85 DZ68
SE25 . . . . .142 DS97
Wrights Row, Wall. SM6 . . . .159 DH105
Wrights Wk, SW14 . . . . .98 CR83
Wrigley Cl, E4 . . . . .47 ED50
Wriotsley Way, Add. KT15
off Coombelands La 152 BG107
Writtle Wk, Rain. RM13 . . . . . .89 FF67
Wrotham Pk, Barn. EN5 . . . . .27 CZ34
★ Wrotham Park, Barn. EN5 . .27 CZ36
Wrotham Rd, NW1
off Agar Pl 83 DJ66
W13 off Mattock La 79 CH74
Barnet EN5 . . . . .27 CY40
Gravesend DA11, DA13 . . .131 GG88
Welling DA16 . . . . .106 EW81
Wroths Path, Loug. IG10 . . . . .33 EM39
Wrottesley Rd, NW10 . . . . . . .81 CU68
SE18 . . . . .105 EQ79
Wroughton Rd, SW11 . . . . . .120 DF86
Wroughton Ter, NW4 . . . . . . .63 CW56
Wroxall Rd, Dag. RM9 . . . . . .88 EW65
Wroxham Gdns, N11 . . . . . . .45 DJ52
Enfield EN2 . . . . .29 DN35
Potters Bar EN6 . . . . .11 CX31
Wroxham Rd, SE28 . . . . .88 EX73
Wroxton Rd, SE15 . . . . .102 DV82
WRYTHE, THE, Cars. 140 DE103
Wrythe Grn, Cars. SM5
off Wrythe Grn Rd 140 DF104
Wrythe Grn Rd, Cars. SM5 . .140 DF104
Wrythe La, Cars. SM5 . . . . . .140 DC102
Wulfstan St, W12 . . . . .81 CT72
Wulstan Pk, Pot.B. EN6
off Tempest Av 12 DD32
Wyatt Cl, SE16 . . . . .203 M5
Bushey (Bushey Hth.)
WD23 . . . . .41 CE45
Feltham TW13 . . . . .116 BW88
Hayes UB4 . . . . .77 BU71
Wyatt Dr, SW13 . . . . .99 CW80
Wyatt Pk Rd, SW2 . . . . .121 DL89
Wyatt Rd, E7 . . . . .86 EG65
N5 . . . . .66 DQ62
Dartford DA1 . . . . .107 FF83
Staines TW18 . . . . .114 BG92
Wyatts Cl, Rick. (Chorl.) WD3 . .22 BG41
Wyatt's Covert Caravan Site, Uxb.
(Denh.) UB9 . . . . .57 BF56
Wyatts La, E17 . . . . .67 EC55
Wyatts Rd, Rick. (Chorl.) WD3 . .21 BF42
Wybert St, NW1 . . . . .195 J4
Wyborne Way, NW10 . . . . . . .80 CQ66
Wyburn Av, Barn. EN5 . . . . . .27 CZ41
Wyche Gro, S.Croy. CR2 . . . .160 DQ108
Wych Elm Cl, Horn. RM11 . . . .72 FN59
Wych Elm Dr, Brom. BR1
off London La 124 EF94
Wych Elm Pas, Kings.T. KT2 .118 CM94
Wych Elm Rd, Horn. RM11 . . .72 FN58
Wych Elms, St.Alb. (Park St.)
AL2 . . . . .8 CB28
Wycherley Cl, SE3 . . . . .104 EF80
Wycherley Cres, Barn. EN5 . . .28 DB44
Wych Hill, Wok. GU22 . . . . . .166 AW119
Wych Hill La, Wok. GU22 . . . .166 AY119
Wych Hill Pk, Wok. GU22 . . . .166 AX119
Wych Hill Ri, Wok. GU22 . . . .166 AW119
Wych Hill Way, Wok. GU22 . . .166 AX119
Wychwood Av, Edg. HA8 . . . . .41 CK51
Thornton Heath CR7 . . . . .142 DQ97
Wychwood Cl, Edg. HA8 . . . . .41 CK51
Sunbury-on-Thames TW16 .115 BU93
Wychwood End, N6 . . . . .65 DJ59
Wychwood Gdns, Ilf. IG5 . . . . .69 EM56
Wychwood Way, SE19
off Roman Ri 122 DR93
Northwood HA6 . . . . .39 BT52
Wycliffe Cl, Well. DA16 . . . . .105 ET81
Wycliffe Ct, Abb.L. WD5 . . . . . .7 BS32
Wycliffe Rd, SW11 . . . . .100 DG82
SW19 . . . . .120 DB93
Wycliffe Row, Grav. (Nthflt.)
DA11 . . . . .131 GF88
Wyclif St, EC1 . . . . .196 F3
Wycombe Gdns, NW11 . . . . . .64 DA61
Wycombe Pl, SW18 . . . . . . .120 DC86
Wycombe Rd, N17 . . . . .46 DU53
Ilford IG2 . . . . .69 EM57
Wembley HA0 . . . . .80 CN67
Wydehurst Rd, Croy. CR0 . . .142 DU101
Wydell Cl, Mord. SM4 . . . . . .139 CW100
Wydeville Manor Rd, SE12 . .124 EH91
Wye Cl, Ashf. TW15 . . . . . . .115 BP91
Orpington BR6 . . . . .145 ET101
Ruislip HA4 . . . . .59 BQ58
Wyedale, St.Alb. (Lon.Col.)
AL2 . . . . .10 CM27
Wyemead Cres, E4 . . . . .48 EE47
Wye Rd, Grav. DA12 . . . . . . .131 GK89
Wye St, SW11 . . . . .100 DD82
Wyeth's Ms, Epsom KT17 . . .157 CT113
Wyeths Rd, Epsom KT17 . . . .157 CT113
Wyevale Cl, Pnr. HA5 . . . . . . .59 BU55
Wyfields, Ilf. IG5
off Ravensbourne Gdns . . .49 EP53
Wyfold Ho, SE2
off Wolvercote Rd 106 EX75
Wyfold Rd, SW6 . . . . .99 CY80
Wyhill Wk, Dag. RM10 . . . . . .89 FC65
Wyke Cl, Islw. TW7 . . . . .97 CF79
Wyke Gdns, W7 . . . . .97 CG76
Wykeham Av, Dag. RM9 . . . . .88 EW65
Hornchurch RM11 . . . . . . .72 FK58
Wykeham Cl, Grav. DA12 . . . .131 GL93
West Drayton UB7 . . . . . . .94 BN78
Wykeham Grn, Dag. RM9 . . . .88 EW65
Wykeham Hill, Wem. HA9 . . . .62 CM60
Wykeham Pl, Dart. DA1 . . . . .128 FK86
Wykeham Ri, N20 . . . . .43 CY46
Wykeham Rd, NW4 . . . . .63 CW57
Harrow HA3 . . . . .61 CH56
Wyke Rd, E3 . . . . .85 EA66
SW20 . . . . .139 CW96
Wylands Rd, Slou. SL3 . . . . . .93 BA77

Wylchin Cl, Pnr. HA5 . . . . . . .59 BT56
Wyldes Cl, NW11
off Wildwood Rd 64 DC60
Wyldfield Gdns, N9 . . . . .46 DT47
Wyld Way, Wem. HA9 . . . . . . .80 CP65
Wyleu St, SE23 . . . . .123 DY87
Wylie Rd, Sthl. UB2 . . . . .96 CA76
Wyllen Cl, E1 . . . . .84 DW70
Wyllyotts Cl, Pot.B. EN6 . . . . .11 CZ32
Wyllyotts La, Pot.B. EN6 . . . . .11 CZ32
Wyllyotts Pl, Pot.B. EN6 . . . . .11 CZ32
Wylo Dr, Barn. EN5 . . . . .27 CU44
Wymering Rd, W9 . . . . .82 DA69
Wymond St, SW15 . . . . .99 CW83
Wynan Rd, E14 . . . . .204 B10
Wynash Gdns, Cars. SM5 . . .158 DE106
Wynaud Ct, N22
off Palmerston Rd 45 DM51
Wyncham Av, Sid. DA15 . . . .125 ES88
Wynchgate, N14 . . . . .45 DK46
N21 . . . . .45 DL46
Harrow HA3 . . . . .41 CE52
Wyncote Way, S.Croy. CR2 . .161 DX109
Wyncroft Cl, Brom. BR1 . . . .145 EM97
Wyndale Av, NW9 . . . . .62 CN58
Wyndcliff Rd, SE7 . . . . .104 EH79
Wyndcroft Cl, Enf. EN2 . . . . . .29 DP41
Wyndham Av, Cob. KT11 . . . .153 BU113
Wyndham Cl, Orp. BR6 . . . . .145 EQ102
Sutton SM2 . . . . .158 DA108
Wyndham Cres, N19 . . . . . . .65 DJ62
Hounslow TW4 . . . . .116 CA86
Wyndham Est, SE5 . . . . .102 DQ80
Wyndham Ms, W1 . . . . .194 D7
Wyndham Pl, W1 . . . . .194 D7
Wyndham Rd, E6 . . . . .86 EK66
SE5 . . . . .101 DP80
W13 . . . . .97 CH76
Barnet EN4 . . . . .44 DF46
Kingston upon Thames KT2 .118 CM94
Woking GU21 . . . . .166 AV118
Wyndham St, W1 . . . . .194 D6
Wyndham Yd, W1 . . . . .194 D7
Wyneham Rd, SE24 . . . . . . .122 DR85
Wynell Rd, SE23 . . . . .123 DX90
Wynford Gro, Orp. BR5 . . . . .146 EV97
Wynford Pl, Belv. DA17 . . . . .106 FA79
Wynford Rd, N1 . . . . .83 DM68
Wynford Way, SE9 . . . . .125 EM90
Wynlie Gdns, Pnr. HA5 . . . . . .39 BV54
Wynn Br Cl, Wdf.Grn. IG8
off Chigwell Rd 48 EJ53
Wynndale Rd, E18 . . . . .48 EH53
Wynne Rd, SW9 . . . . .101 DN82
Wynns Av, Sid. DA15 . . . . . .126 EU85
Wynnstay Gdns, W8 . . . . . . .100 DA76
Wynnstow Pk, Oxt. RH8 . . . .188 EF131
Wynter St, SW11 . . . . .100 DC84
Wynton Gdns, SE25 . . . . . . .142 DT99
Wynton Gro, Walt. KT12 . . . .135 BU104
Wynton Pl, W3 . . . . .80 CP72
Wynyard Cl, Rick. (Sarratt)
WD3 . . . . .22 BG36
Wynyard Ter, SE11 . . . . .200 C10
Wynyatt St, EC1 . . . . .196 F3
Wyre Gro, Edg. HA8 . . . . .42 CP48
Hayes UB3 . . . . .95 BU77
Wyresdale Cres, Grnf. UB6 . . .79 CF69
Wyteleaf Cl, Ruis. HA4 . . . . . .59 BQ58
Wythburn Pl, W1 . . . . .194 D9
Wythenshawe Rd, Dag. RM10 .70 FA62
Wythens Wk, SE9 . . . . .125 EP86
Wythes Cl, Brom. BR1 . . . . . .145 EM96
Wythes Rd, E16 . . . . .86 EL74
Wythfield Rd, SE9 . . . . .125 EM86
Wyvenhoe Rd, Har. HA2 . . . . .60 CC62
Wyvern Cl, Dart. DA1 . . . . . .128 FJ87
Orpington BR6 . . . . .146 EV104
Wyvern Est, N.Mal. KT3 . . . .139 CU98
Wyvern Gro, Hayes UB3 . . . . .95 BP80
Wyvern Pl, Add. KT15
off Green La 152 BH105
Wyvern Rd, Pur. CR8 . . . . . .159 DP110
Wyvern Way, Uxb. UB8 . . . . .76 BH66
Wyvil Est, SW8
off Luscombe Way 101 DL80
Wyvil Rd, SW8 . . . . .101 DL79
Wyvis St, E14 . . . . .85 EB71

Y

Yabsley St, E14 . . . . .204 E2
Yaffle Rd, Wey. KT13 . . . . . .153 BQ110
Yalding Cl, Orp. BR5 . . . . . . .146 EX98
Yalding Rd, SE16 . . . . .202 B7
Yale Cl, Houns. TW4
off Bramley Way 116 BZ85
Yale Way, Horn. RM12 . . . . . .71 FG63
Yaohan Plaza, NW9 . . . . .62 CR55
Yarborough Rd, SW19 . . . . . .120 DD95
Yarbridge Cl, Sutt. SM2 . . . .158 DB110
Yardley Cl, E4 . . . . .31 EB43
Reigate RH2 . . . . .184 DB132
Yardley Ct, Sutt. SM3
off Hemingford Rd 157 CW105
Yardley La, E4 . . . . .31 EB43
Yardley St, WC1 . . . . .196 D3
Yard Mead, Egh. TW20 . . . . .113 BA90
Yarm Cl, Lthd. KT22 . . . . . . .171 CJ123
Yarm Ct Rd, Lthd. KT22 . . . .171 CJ123
Yarmouth Cres, N17 . . . . .66 DV57
Yarmouth Pl, W1 . . . . .199 H3
Yarmouth Rd, Wat. WD24 . . . .24 BW38
Yarm Way, Lthd. KT22 . . . . .171 CJ123
Yarnfield Sq, SE15 . . . . .102 DU81
Yarnton Way, SE2 . . . . .106 EX75
Erith DA18 . . . . .106 EZ76
Yarrow Cres, E6 . . . . .86 EL71
Yarrowfield, Wok. GU22 . . . .166 AX123
Yarrowside, Amer. HP7 . . . . . .20 AV41
Yateley Cl, St.Alb. SE18 . . . .104 EK76
Yates Ct, NW2 . . . . .81 CX65
YEADING, Hayes 77 BV69

Yeading Av, Har. HA2 . . . . . . .60 BY61
Yeading Fork, Hayes UB4 . . . .78 BW71
Yeading Gdns, Hayes UB4 . . . .77 BW71
Yeading La, Hayes UB4 . . . . . .77 BW72
Northolt UB5 . . . . .78 BW69
Yeames Cl, W13 . . . . .79 CG72
Yeate St, N1 . . . . .84 DR66
Yeatman Rd, N6 . . . . .64 DF58
Yeats Cl, NW10 . . . . .80 CS65
SE13 off Eliot Pk 103 ED82
Yeats Cl, N15
off Tynemouth Rd 66 DT56
Ye Cor, Wat. WD19 . . . . .24 BY44
Yeend Cl, W.Mol. KT8 . . . . . .136 CA98
Yeldham Rd, W6 . . . . .99 CX78
Yellow Hammer Ct, NW9
off Eagle Dr 42 CS54
Yellowpine Way, Chig. IG7 . . .50 EV49
Yelverton Cl, Rom. RM3 . . . . .52 FK53
Yelverton Rd, SW11 . . . . . . .100 DD82
Yenston Cl, Mord. SM4 . . . . .140 DA100
Yeoman Cl, E6 off Ferndale St .87 EP73
SE27 . . . . .121 DP90
Yeoman Rd, Nthlt. UB5 . . . . . .78 BY66
Yeomanry Cl, Epsom KT17
off Dirdene Gdns 157 CT112
Yeomans Acre, Ruis. HA4 . . . .59 BU58
Yeomans Keep, Rick. (Chorl.) WD3
off Rickmansworth Rd 21 BF41
Yeomans Meadow, Sev.
TN13 . . . . .190 FG126
Yeoman's Ms, Islw. TW7
off Queensbridge Pk 117 CE78
Yeoman's Row, SW3 . . . . . . .198 C7
Yeoman St, SE8 . . . . .203 K8
Yeomans Way, Enf. EN3 . . . . .30 DW40
Yeomans Yd, E1
off Chamber St 84 DT73
Yeomen Way, Ilf. IG6 . . . . . . .49 EQ51
Yeo St, E3 . . . . .85 EB71
Yeoveney Cl, Stai. TW19 . . . .113 BD89
Yeovil Cl, Orp. BR6 . . . . .145 ES103
Yeovilton Pl, Kings.T. KT2 . . .117 CJ92
Yerbury Rd, N19 . . . . .65 DK62
Yester Dr, Chis. BR7 . . . . . . .124 EL94
Yester Pk, Chis. BR7 . . . . . . .125 EM94
Yester Rd, Chis. BR7 . . . . . . .125 EM94
Yevele Way, Horn. RM11 . . . . .72 FL59
Yew Av, West Dr. UB7 . . . . . . .76 BL73
Yewbank Cl, Ken. CR8 . . . . . .176 DR115
Yew Cl, Buck.H. IG9 . . . . .48 EK47
Waltham Cross EN7 . . . . . .14 DS27
Yewdale Cl, Brom. BR1 . . . . .124 EE93
Yewdells Cl, Bet. (Buckland)
RH3 . . . . .183 CU133
Yewfield Rd, NW10 . . . . .81 CT66
Yew Gro, NW2 . . . . .63 CX63
Yewlands Cl, Bans. SM7 . . . .174 DC115
Yew Pl, Wey. KT13 . . . . .135 BT104
Yews, The, Ashf. TW15 . . . . .115 BP91
Gravesend DA12 . . . . .131 GK88
Yews Av, Enf. EN1 . . . . .30 DV36
Yew Tree Bottom Rd, Epsom
KT17, KT18 . . . . .173 CV116
Yew Tree Cl, N21 . . . . .45 DN45
Welling DA16 . . . . .106 EU81
Worcester Park KT4 . . . . .138 CS102
Yew Tree Ct, Borwd. (Elstree)
WD6 off Barnet La 25 CK44
Yew Tree Dr, Cat. CR3 . . . . .186 DT125
Hemel Hempstead (Bov.)
HP3 . . . . .5 BB28
Yewtree End, St.Alb. (Park St.)
AL2 . . . . .8 CB27
Yew Tree Gdns, Epsom KT18 .172 CP115
Romford RM7 . . . . .71 FD57
Romford (Chad.Hth.) RM6 . .70 EY57
Yew Tree La, Reig. RH2 . . . .184 DB131
Yew Tree Rd, W12 . . . . .81 CT73
Yewtree Rd, Beck. BR3 . . . . .143 DZ97
Yew Tree Rd, Slou. SL1 . . . . .92 AU76
Uxbridge UB10 . . . . .76 BM67
Yew Trees, Egh. TW20 . . . . .133 BC97
Shepperton TW17
off Laleham Rd 134 BM98
Yew Tree Wk, Houns. TW4 . . .116 BZ85
Purley CR8 . . . . .160 DQ110
Yew Tree Way, Croy. CR0 . . .161 DY110
Yew Wk, Har. HA1 . . . . .61 CE60
YIEWSLEY, West Dr. 76 BL74
Yoakley Rd, N16 . . . . .66 DS61
Yoke Cl, N7 off Ewe Cl 83 DL65
Yolande Gdns, SE9 . . . . .124 EL85
Yonge Pk, N4 . . . . .65 DN62
York Av, SW14 . . . . .118 CQ85
W7 . . . . .79 CE74
Hayes UB3 . . . . .77 BQ71
Sidcup DA15 . . . . .125 ES89
Stanmore HA7 . . . . .41 CH53
York Br, NW1 . . . . .194 F4
York Bldgs, WC2 . . . . .200 A1
York Cl, E6 off Boultwood Rd . .87 EM72
W7 off York Av 79 CE74
Amersham HP7 . . . . .20 AT39
Brentwood CM15 . . . . .55 FZ45
Kings Langley WD4 . . . . . . .6 BN29
Morden SM4 . . . . .140 DB98
West Byfleet (Byfleet)
KT14 . . . . .152 BL112
York Cres, Borwd. WD6 . . . . .26 CR40
Loughton IG10 . . . . .32 EL41
Yorke Gdns, Reig. RH2 . . . . .184 DA133
Yorke Gate Rd, Cat. CR3 . . . .176 DR122
Yorke Rd, Reig. RH2 . . . . . . .183 CZ133
Rickmansworth (Crox.Grn.)
WD3 . . . . .22 BN44
York Gdns, Walt. KT12 . . . . .136 BX103
York Gate, N14 . . . . .45 DL48
NW1 . . . . .194 F5
York Gro, SE15 . . . . .102 DW81

Yeading Av, Har. HA2 . . . . . . .60 BY61
York Hill, SE27 . . . . .121 DP90
Loughton IG10 . . . . .32 EL41
York Hill Est, SE27 . . . . .121 DP90
York Ho, Wem. HA9 . . . . .62 CM63
York Ho Pl, W8 . . . . .100 DB75
Yorkland Av, Well. DA16 . . . .105 ET83
York Ms, NW5
off Kentish Town Rd 65 DH64
Ilford IG1
off York Rd 69 EN62
York Par, Brent. TW8 . . . . . . .97 CK78
York Pl, SW11 . . . . .100 DD83
WC2 . . . . .200 A1
Dagenham RM10 . . . . .89 FC65
Grays RM17 . . . . .110 GA79
Ilford IG1
off York Rd 69 EN61
York Ri, NW5 . . . . .65 DH62
Orpington BR6 . . . . .145 ES102
York Rd, E4 . . . . .47 EA50
E7 . . . . .86 EG65
E10 . . . . .67 EC62
E17 . . . . .67 DX57
N11 . . . . .45 DK51
N18 . . . . .46 DV51
N21 . . . . .46 DR45
SE1 . . . . .200 C4
SW11 . . . . .100 DC83
SW18 . . . . .100 DC83
SW19 . . . . .120 DC93
W3 . . . . .80 CQ72
W5 . . . . .97 CJ76
Barnet EN5 . . . . .28 DA43
Brentford TW8 . . . . .97 CK78
Brentwood CM15 . . . . .55 FZ45
Croydon CR0 . . . . .141 DN101
Dartford DA1 . . . . .128 FM87
Epping (N.Wld.Bas.) CM16 . .18 FA27
Gravesend DA12 . . . . .131 GJ90
Gravesend (Nthflt.) DA11 . .130 GD87
Hounslow TW3 . . . . .96 CB83
Ilford IG1 . . . . .69 EN62
Kingston upon Thames KT2 .118 CM94
Northwood HA6 . . . . .39 BU54
Rainham RM13 . . . . .89 FD66
Richmond TW10
off Albert Rd 118 CM85
South Croydon CR2 . . . . . .161 DX110
Sutton SM2 . . . . .158 DA107
Teddington TW11 . . . . . . .117 CE91
Uxbridge UB8 . . . . .76 BK66
Waltham Cross EN8 . . . . . .15 DY34
Watford WD18 . . . . .24 BW42
West Byfleet (Byfleet) KT14 .152 BK112
Westerham (Bigg.H.) TN16 .178 EK116
Weybridge KT13 . . . . .153 BQ105
Woking GU22 . . . . .166 AY118
Yorkshire Cl, N16 . . . . .66 DS62
Yorkshire Gdns, N18 . . . . . . .46 DV50
Yorkshire Grey Pl, NW3
off Heath St 64 DC63
Yorkshire Grey Yd, WC1 . . . .196 B7
Yorkshire Rd, E14 . . . . .85 DY72
Mitcham CR4 . . . . .141 DL99
York Sq, E14 . . . . .85 DY72
York St, W1 . . . . .194 E6
Barking IG11 off Abbey Rd . .87 EQ67
Mitcham CR4 . . . . .140 DG101
Twickenham TW1 . . . . . . .117 CG88
York Ter, Enf. EN2 . . . . .30 DQ38
Erith DA8 . . . . .107 FC81
York Ter E, NW1 . . . . .194 G5
York Ter W, NW1 . . . . .194 F5
Yorkton St, E2 . . . . .84 DU68
York Way, N1 . . . . .83 DL67
N7 . . . . .83 DK65
N20 . . . . .44 DF48
Borehamwood WD6 . . . . . .26 CR40
Chessington KT9 . . . . . . .156 CL108
Feltham TW13 . . . . .116 BZ90
Watford WD25 . . . . .24 BX36
York Way Ct, N1 . . . . .83 DL67
York Way Est, N7 off York Way .83 DL65
Youngmans Cl, Enf. EN2 . . . . .30 DQ39
Young Rd, E16 . . . . .86 EJ72
Young's Bldgs, EC1 . . . . .197 J4
★ Young's Ram Brewery,
SW18 . . . . .120 DB85
Youngs Rd, Ilf. IG2 . . . . .69 ER57
Young St, W8 . . . . .100 DB75
Youngstroat La, Wok. GU21,
GU24 . . . . .150 AY110
Yoxley App, Ilf. IG2 . . . . .69 EQ58
Yoxley Dr, Ilf. IG2 . . . . .69 EQ58
Yukon Rd, SW12 . . . . .121 DH87
Yule Cl, St.Alb. (Brick.Wd.)
AL2 . . . . .8 BZ30
Yuletide Cl, NW10 . . . . .80 CS66
Yunus Khan Cl, E17 . . . . .67 EA57

Z

Zampa Rd, SE16 . . . . .102 DW78
Zander Ct, E2
off St. Peter's Cl 84 DU68
Zangwill Rd, SE3 . . . . .104 EK81
Zealand Av, West Dr. UB7 . . . .94 BK80
Zealand Rd, E3 . . . . .85 DY68
Zelah Rd, Orp. BR5 . . . . .146 EV101
Zeland Cl, NW2 . . . . .63 CW60
Zennor Rd, SW12 . . . . .121 DJ88
Zenoria St, SE22 . . . . .102 DT84
Zermatt Rd, Th.Hth. CR7 . . . .142 DQ98
Zetland St, E14 . . . . .85 EB71
Zig Zag Rd, Ken. CR8 . . . . . .176 DQ116
Zion Pl, Grav. DA12 . . . . .131 GH87
Thornton Heath CR7 . . . . .142 DR98
Zion Rd, Th.Hth. CR7 . . . . . .142 DR98
Zion St, Sev. (Seal) TN15
off Church Rd 191 FM121
Zoar St, SE1 . . . . .201 H2
Zoffany St, N19 . . . . .65 DK61

★ Place of interest   ⇌ Railway station   ● London Underground station   DLR Docklands Light Railway station   ◆ Tramlink station   H Hospital